Introducing New York Math A

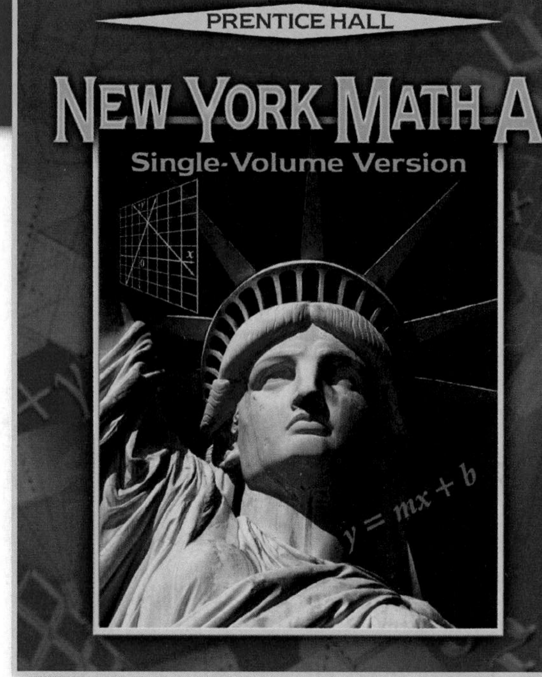

Contents

Test-Taking Strategies for the Math A Exam

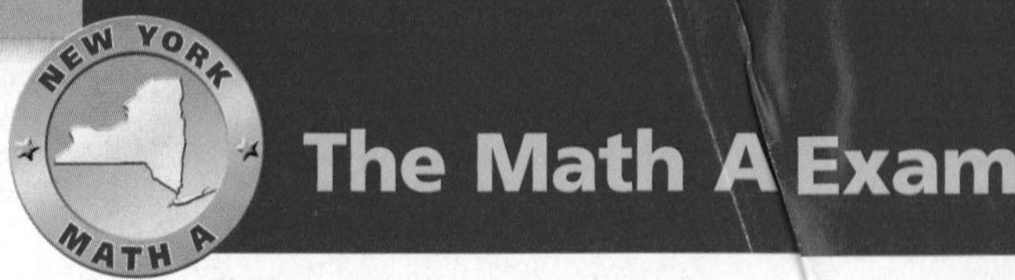

The Math A Exam

Introduction

The Regents High School Examination for Mathematics A is developed by the Board of Regents of the University of the State of New York. The examination covers concepts and skills in a curriculum designed to raise standards in high school mathematics. The key ideas and performance indicators for this curriculum are outlined on the next two pages.

A specified minimum score on one of the Regents exams in mathematics is necessary for a high school diploma in New York State.

Math A and the Prentice Hall Math Course

This book, New York Math A consists of two volumes. Volume 1 has a focus on Algebra and Volume 2 has a focus on Geomtery. Taken together, the two volumes cover all of the content assessed on the Mathematics A exam. Geometry, statistics, probability, and trigonometry are woven through the chapters in Volume 1 to provide an integrated approach. In Volume 2 algebraic topics and content from the other strands are integrated throughout.

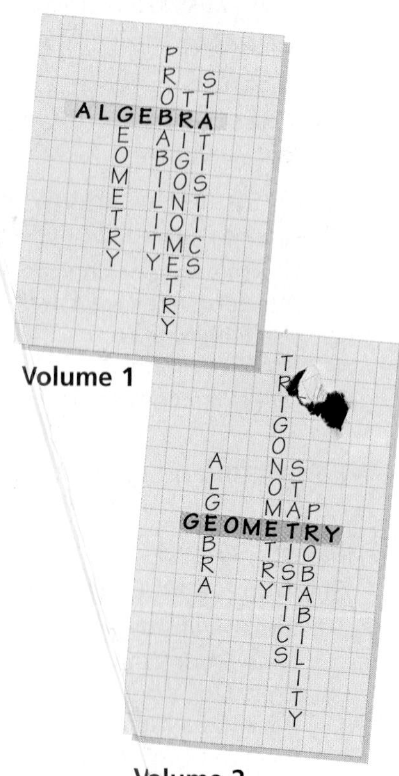

As you can see from the lesson and page references on the next two pages, you will have studied most of the Math A curriculum when you have completed Volume 1, which usually takes at least two semesters. The rest of Math A is covered in Volume 2.

Most students will take the exam after three or four semesters of Math A. Some students will wait until they have completed five or six semesters. Your mathematics teachers or counselors will be the best guides as to when you should take the Math A exam.

Options for Taking the Math A Exam

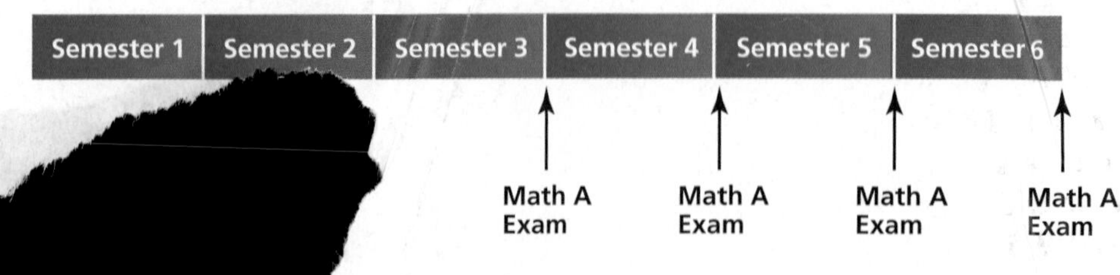

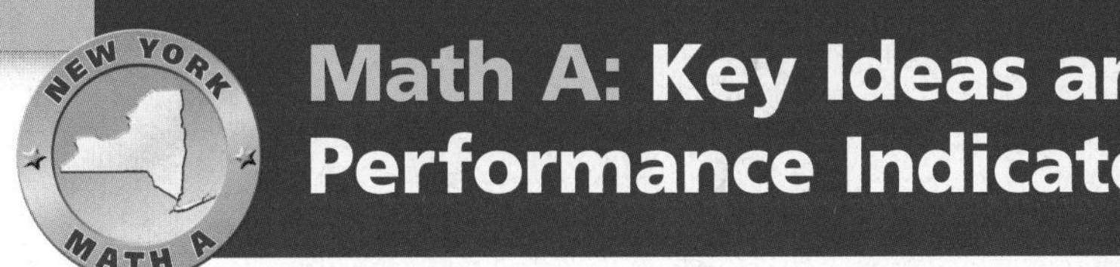

Math A: Key Ideas and Performance Indicators

The learning objectives for Mathematics A are organized under seven Key Ideas. Each Key Idea includes Performance Indicators that describe skills, concepts, and procedures in mathematics.

Following each performance indicator is a list of the lessons that cover all or part of the indicator.

Correlation of Prentice Hall *New York Math A: Single-Volume Version* to New York Core Curriculum

Key Idea 1

Mathematical Reasoning

1A Construct valid arguments.
Volume 1, Page 201; New York 1
Volume 2, Lessons 1-5, 1-7, 4-1, 4-3, 4-5, New York 13

1B Follow and judge the validity of arguments.
Volume 1, Page 133
Volume 2, Lessons 4-1, 4-3, 4-5

Key Idea 2

Number and Numeration

2A Understand and use rational and irrational numbers.
Volume 1, Lessons 1-6, 3-5, 3-7, 3-8, 7-4, 9-4, 9-5
Volume 2, Lessons 5-3, 5-4, 5-6, 5-7, 5-8

2B Recognize the order of real numbers.
Volume 1, Lessons 1-4, 1-6, 4-3, 4-5, 4-6, 4-7, 4-8, 4-9, 7-4

2C Apply the properties of real numbers to various subsets of numbers.
Volume 1, Lessons 1-6, 3-4, 7-4, 9-5
Volume 2, Lessons 1-7 New York 12

Key Idea 3

Operations

3A Use addition, subtraction, multiplication, division, and exponentiation with real numbers and algebraic expressions.
Volume 1, Lessons 1-2, 1-3, 1-4, 1-5, 1-6, 3-4, 4-4, 8-1, 8-4, 8-6, 8-7, 8-8

3B Use integral exponents on integers and algebraic expressions.
Volume 1, Lessons 8-1, 8-4, 8-5, 8-6, 8-7, 8-8

3C Recognize and identify symmetry and transformations on figures.
Volume 1, Lessons 2-4, 2-5, 2-6, 2-7, 4-4, 5-4, 5-7
Volume 2, Lessons 3-2, 3-3, 3-4

3D Use field properties to justify mathematical procedures.
Volume 1, Page 35; Lessons 3-2, 3-4, 4-2, 10-2, 10-6
Volume 2, Lesson 1-7

Key Idea 4

Modeling/Multiple Representation

4A Represent problem situations symbolically by using algebraic expressions, sequences, tree diagrams, geometric figures, and graphs.
Volume 1, Lessons 1-1, 1-2, 1-8, 1-9, 2-1, 2-2, 2-3, 2-8, 3-1, 3-2, 5-1, 5-4, 5-5, 5-6, 7-2, 7-3, 9-1, 9-2, 10-6, 10-7, 11-6
Volume 2, Lessons 1-1, 1-4, 2-1, 2-2, 2-3, 2-4, 4-6, 5-3, 6-1, New York 2

4B Justify the procedures for basic geometric constructions.
Volume 2, Lessons 1-6, New York 3

4C Use transformations in the coordinate plane.
Volume 1, Lessons 2-7, 7-2
Volume 2, Lessons 3-1, 3-2, 3-3, 3-4, 3-5, 3-7

4D Develop and apply the concept of basic loci to compound loci.
Volume 2, Lessons 4-7, 5-7

4E Model real-world problems with systems of equations and inequalities.
Volume 1, Lessons 6-1, 6-2, 6-3, 6-4, 6-5, 6-6, 6-7, 6-8
Volume 2, Lesson 1-2

Key Idea 5

Measurement

5A Apply formulas to find measures such as length, area, volume, weight, time, and angle in real-world contexts.
Volume 1, Lessons 4-1, 5-3, 8-5, 10-2
Volume 2, Lessons 1-4, 5-1, 5-2, 5-3, 5-4, 5-5, 5-6, 5-7, 5-8, 6-2, 6-3, 6-4, 6-5, 6-6

5B Choose and apply appropriate units and tools in measurement situations.
Volume 1, Lessons 4-1, 9-1, 9-2, 9-3
Volume 2, Lessons 1-4, 1-6, 2-2, 4-4

5C Use dimensional analysis techniques.
Volume 1, Page 219
Volume 2, Page 869

5D Use statistical methods including the measures of central tendency to describe and compare data.
Volume 1, Lessons 1-1, 2-1, 5-6; New York 9
Volume 2, Lesson 2-5

5E Use trigonometry as a method to measure indirectly.
Volume 1, Lesson 9-3
New York 6, New York 7, New York 8

5F Apply proportions to scale drawings and direct variation.
Volume 1, Lessons 4-1, 5-2, 5-3
Volume 2, Lesson 2-6

5G Relate absolute value, distance between two points, and the slope of a line to the coordinate plane.
Volume 1, Lessons 4-3, 5-1, 5-4, 5-5, 5-8, 9-2
Volume 2, Lessons 1-5, 1-8, 2-3, 4-4, 5-3

5H Explain the role of error in measurement and its consequence on subsequent calculations.
New York 11

5I Use geometric relationships in relevant measurement problems involving geometric concepts.
Volume 1, Lessons 9-1, 9-2, 9-3
Volume 2, Lessons 2-6, 4-4, 5-3, New York 4, New York 5

Key Idea 6

Uncertainty

6A Judge the reasonableness of results obtained from applications in algebra, geometry, trigonometry, probability, and statistics.
Volume 1, Lessons 1-7, 2-1, 2-8, 4-9, 9-3, 11-6, 11-7
Volume 2, Lessons 1-1, 1-7, 2-4, 4-1, 4-5, 6-8

6B Use experimental and theoretical probability to represent and solve problems involving uncertainty.
Volume 1, Lessons 1-7, 2-8, 3-6
Volume 2, Lesson 6-8

6C Use the concept of random variable in computing probabilities.
Volume 1, Lessons 2-8, 3-6; New York 10

6D Determine probabilities, using permutations and combinations.
Volume 1, Lessons 11-6, 11-7

Key Idea 7

Patterns/Functions

7A Represent and analyze functions, using verbal descriptions, tables, equations, and graphs.
Volume 1, Lessons 2-4, 2-5, 2-6, 2-7, 2-8, 5-2, 5-4, 5-7, 6-8, 7-1, 7-2, 7-3

7B Apply linear and quadratic functions in the solution of problems.
Volume 1, Lessons 5-5, 5-8, 5-9, 7-5, 7-6, 7-7

7C Translate among the verbal descriptions, tables, equations, and graphic forms of functions.
Volume 1, Lessons 2-4, 2-5, 2-6, 2-7, 2-8, 5-2, 5-4, 5-7, 7-1, 7-2, 7-3

7D Model real-world situations with the appropriate function.
Volume 1, Lessons 2-4, 2-6, 2-7, 5-5, 7-1, 7-5, 7-7, 8-1, 8-2, 8-3, 9-7, 11-1, 11-2, 11-3

7E Apply axiomatic structure to algebra.
Volume 1, Lessons 3-1, 3-2, 3-3, 3-5, 3-7, 4-1, 4-2, 4-3, 4-5, 4-6, 4-7, 4-8, 6-1, 6-2, 6-3, 6-4, 6-5, 6-6, 6-8, 10-6

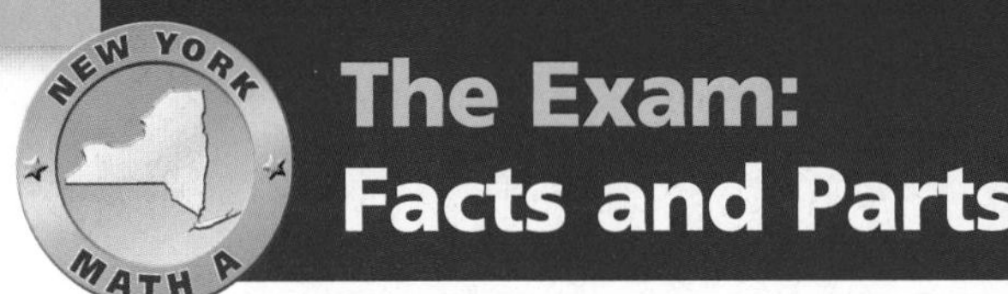

The Exam: Facts and Parts

Facts About the Math A Exam

The Regents High School Examination for Mathematics A covers the skills and concepts in the Math A curriculum. The Performance Indicators on the previous two pages give you an idea of the kinds of topics the exam will cover. Here are some important facts about the Math A exam.

- It is a 3-hour exam.
- You can answer the problems in any order you like. For example, you could answer Part IV first if you wished.
- Scrap paper is not permitted. Work must be done on the pages of the test booklet. One piece of scrap graph paper is provided, although you may request more graph paper.
- Scientific calculators, straightedges, compasses, and extra graph paper will be provided. The use of a graphing calculator is optional.
- Graphs and drawings must be done in pencil. All other work must be done in ink. Bring several pencils, several pens, and a good eraser.
- If you skip a question, you receive 0 points, but no points are subtracted for wrong answers. You should answer all the questions.
- Copies of previous Math A exams can be downloaded from the Web site of the New York State Education Department at **www.nysed.gov**.

The Parts of the Math A Exam

The Regents High School Examination for Mathematics A has four parts. The questions in Part I are in multiple-choice form. The questions in Parts II, III, and IV are not in multiple-choice form.

- There are a total of 85 possible credits. The four parts do not contribute equally to the total number of credits.

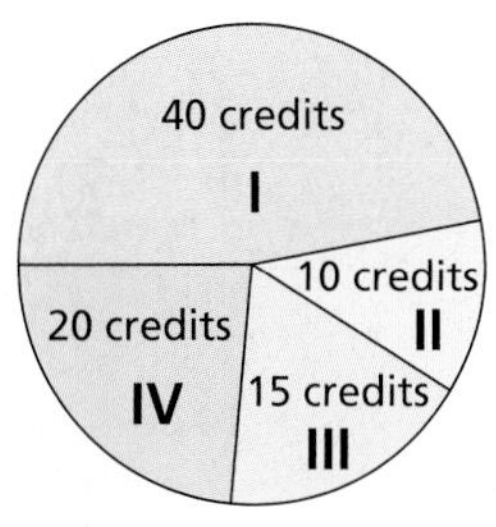

Part I	Part II	Part III	Part IV
20 questions	5 questions	5 questions	5 questions
2 credits each	2 credits each	3 credits each	4 credits each
40 credits possible	10 credits possible	15 credits possible	20 credits possible
47.1% of total	11.8% of total	17.6% of total	23.5% of total

- Answers for Part I are written on a separate answer sheet. Answers for Parts II, III, and IV are written in the test booklet.
- For Parts II, III, and IV, you MUST show your work. A correct answer without any work shown will receive only 1 credit.
- For Parts II, III, and IV, partial credit will be awarded according to the Exam's Scoring Key.

Part I: Strategies and Examples

General Strategies

- Bring a watch so you can keep track of the time. Be sure to leave enough time for Parts II, III, and IV.
- Write the Part I answers on the separate answer sheet. Use a pen to mark the answer sheet.
- Any marks or answers on the test pages do not count for your score. Do your computation in pencil on the test pages. If you need more space, you can erase previous work.
- Mark any questions you might want to re-check later.
- You can do the test problems in any order you like. Some students find multiple-choice questions to be difficult. If you wish, you can do Parts II, III, and IV before you do Part I, but make sure you allow plenty of time for Part I. The most credits can be earned from Part I.
- Answer ALL the Part I multiple-choice questions. There is no advantage in leaving an answer space blank. If you are not sure of the answer, use the strategies on the next few pages to make an educated guess.

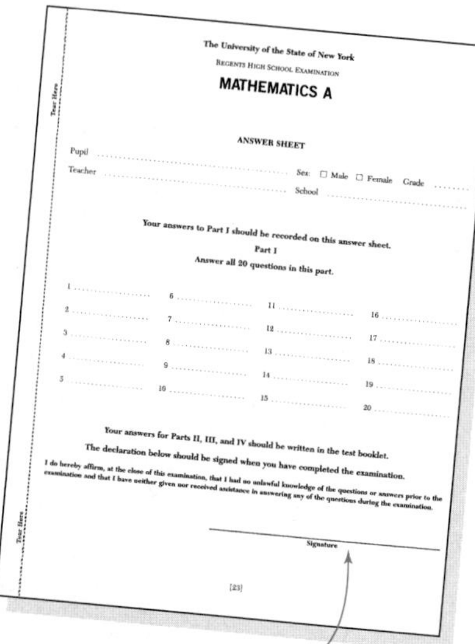
The University of the State of New York
REGENTS HIGH SCHOOL EXAMINATION
MATHEMATICS A

ANSWER SHEET

Pupil .... Sex: ☐ Male ☐ Female Grade ......
Teacher .... School ....

Your answers to Part I should be recorded on this answer sheet.
Part I
Answer all 20 questions in this part.

1	6	11	16 ......
2	7	12	17 ......
3	8	13	18 ......
4	9	14	19 ......
5	10	15	20 ......

Your answers for Parts II, III, and IV should be written in the test booklet.
The declaration below should be signed when you have completed the examination.
I do hereby affirm, at the close of this examination, that I had no unlawful knowledge of the questions or answers prior to the examination and that I have neither given nor received assistance in answering any of the questions during the examination.

Signature

[23]

Tear Here

Tear Here

Remember to sign the statement at the bottom of the answer sheet when you are finished.

This section includes some test-taking strategies for Part I. (Since the questions for Parts II, III, and IV are not in multiple-choice form, different strategies are appropriate for those parts of the test.) Each strategy that follows has an example and a practice problem for you to try. The examples come from actual questions on past Math A exams.

Use the Answer Choices

For any multiple-choice math question, read the question and all the answer choices before you begin. The answers may give you some valuable information, or hints as to how to approach the problem.

Example

The expression $\frac{y}{x} - \frac{1}{2}$ is equivalent to ■.

(1) $\frac{2y - x}{2x}$ (3) $\frac{1 - y}{2x}$

(2) $\frac{x - 2y}{2x}$ (4) $\frac{y - 1}{x - 2}$

Strategy Three of the four answer choices have the denominator $2x$. This may remind you that you must use a common denominator when subtracting fractions. It also allows you to eliminate choice (4).

THINK AND DISCUSS

Which expression is equivalent to 6.02×10^{23}?

(1) 0.602×10^{21} (3) 602×10^{21}
(2) 60.2×10^{21} (4) 6020×10^{21}

1. What is the second factor in all four answer choices? Describe a strategy suggested by this fact.
2. Use answer choice (4). Divide the first factor by 100. Multiply the second factor by 100. What happens? What strategy does this suggest?
3. The Think and Discuss question deals with scientific notation. Use the Index at the back of your book to find a lesson that covers this topic.

Answer Every Question

Answer ALL the Part I multiple-choice questions. There is no advantage in leaving an answer space blank.

Example

Which equation is an illustration of the additive identity property?

(1) $x \cdot 1 = x$ (3) $x - x = 0$

(2) $x + 0 = x$ (4) $x \cdot \frac{1}{x} = 1$

Strategy Assume that you do not know what the *additive identity property* is. Therefore, you will have to guess. Look over the answer choices. Notice that only one has a plus sign. Since *additive* might have something to do with addition, you could guess choice (2).

THINK AND DISCUSS

When the point $(2, -5)$ is reflected in the x-axis, what are the coordinates of its image?

(1) $(-5, 2)$ (3) $(2, 5)$
(2) $(-2, 5)$ (4) $(5, 2)$

1. Assume that you do not know what *reflected in the x-axis* means. You will have to guess. You sketch a graph, plot $(2, -5)$, and decide the answer should be above the x-axis. What should you do now?
2. If you had to guess an answer, which choice would you pick and why?
3. The Think and Discuss question deals with graphing ordered pairs. Use the Index at the back of your book to find a lesson that reviews this topic.

Use Elimination

If you do not know how to work a problem, you may be able to eliminate one or more possible answers before you make an educated guess. Cross out the answers you eliminate in the test booklet. Remember, only the answer sheet for Part I is scored.

Example

Which number has the greatest value?

(1) $1\frac{2}{3}$ (3) $\frac{\pi}{2}$

(2) $\sqrt{2}$ (4) 1.5

Strategy Assume you are not certain of the values for $\sqrt{2}$ and $\frac{\pi}{2}$. You can, however, still compare choices (1) and (4). Choice (4) is less than choice (1), so you can eliminate choice (4). You might then guess among the remaining three choices.

THINK AND DISCUSS

The formula $C = \frac{5}{9}(F - 32)$ can be used to find the Celsius temperature (C) for a given Fahrenheit temperature (F). What Celsius temperature is equal to a Fahrenheit temperature of 77°?

(1) 8° (3) 45°
(2) 25° (4) 171°

1. A student subtracts 32 from 77 to get 45. Even before multiplying $\frac{5}{9}$ times 45, the student eliminates choices (3) and (4). Explain the student's reasoning.
2. A student happens to remember that water boils at 100° C. What answer choice does this eliminate?
3. A student uses choice (4) and substitutes to get $171 = \frac{5}{9}(77 - 32)$. Without computing, tell why 171 is not a reasonable answer.
4. The Think and Discuss question deals with substituting numbers to evaluate algebraic expressions. Use the Index at the back of your book to find a lesson that covers evaluating expressions.

Use Estimation

Using estimation may help you find the answer, check the answer, or eliminate one or more answer choices.

Example

The expression $\sqrt{50}$ can be simplified to ■.

(1) $5\sqrt{2}$ (3) $2\sqrt{25}$

(2) $5\sqrt{10}$ (4) $25\sqrt{2}$

Strategy Assume that you do not know how to simplify $\sqrt{50}$. However, you do know that $\sqrt{49} = 7$. So, $\sqrt{50}$ is a little more than 7. Since choice (2) is greater than 15, choice (3) equals 10, and choice (4) is greater than 25, the answer must be choice (1).

THINK AND DISCUSS

During a recent winter, the ratio of deer to foxes was 7 to 3 in one county of New York State. If there were 210 foxes in the county, what was the number of deer in the county?

(1) 90 (3) 280
(2) 147 (4) 490

1. A student makes this chart.

deer	foxes
7	3
	210

Why does the chart help eliminate choices (1) and (2)?

2. Since 7 is more than twice as large as 3, the number of deer must be more than twice the number of foxes. Why does this eliminate choice (3)?

3. The Think and Discuss question deals with solving a proportion for a missing term. Use the Index at the back of your book to find a lesson that covers solving proportions.

Make Sketches or Drawings

Making a sketch can sometimes help you estimate an answer to a problem, particularly if the problem is geometrical. You can request another sheet of graph paper to use for making sketches.

Example

A plot of land is in the shape of rhombus *ABCD* as shown below.

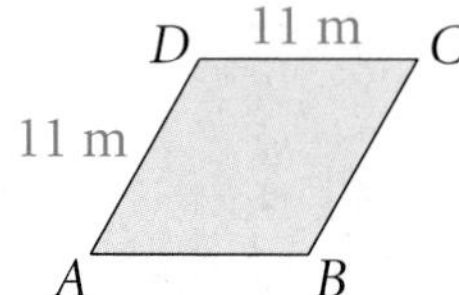

Which can *not* be the length of diagonal *AC*?

(1) 24 m
(2) 16 m
(3) 11 m
(4) 14 m

Strategy You know that all four sides of the rhombus are 11 m long. You make some sketches like the ones below showing points *D* and *B* getting closer and closer together. When point *D* coincides with point *B*, the diagonal *AC* will be 22 m, the sum of the two 11-m sides. So the diagonal (the shortest distance between points *A* and *C*) must be less than 22 m. Since 24 m is greater than 22 m, you know that (1) 24 m cannot be the length of the diagonal.

THINK AND DISCUSS

What is the perimeter of an equilateral triangle whose height is $2\sqrt{3}$?

(1) 6
(2) 12
(3) $6\sqrt{3}$
(4) $12\sqrt{3}$

1. Sketch the triangle. Explain how your sketch helps you solve the problem.
2. Using the square root key on a calculator, you will find that $2\sqrt{3}$ is about 3.5. How does knowing this eliminate choice (1)?
3. The Think and Discuss question involves simplifying radicals. Use the Index at the back of your book to find the lesson that covers simplifying radicals.

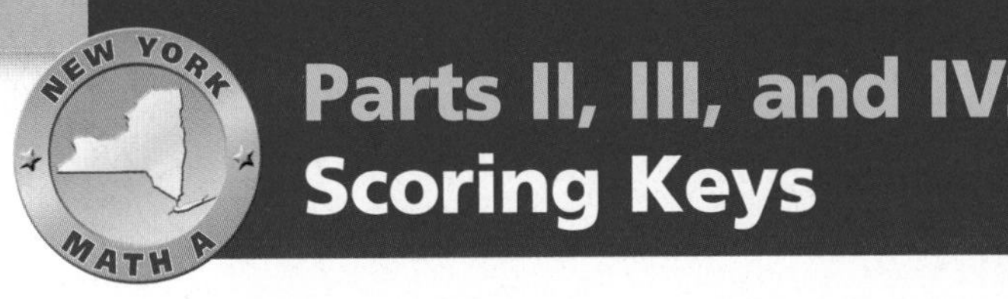

Parts II, III, and IV: Scoring Keys

The Math A Regents Exam is scored by committees of teachers. For Parts II, III, and IV of the exam, the teachers are given scoring keys. Each key describes how many credits should be awarded for different types of answers.

Example (2-credit question)

The graph shows the hair colors of all the students in a class. What is the probability that a student chosen at random from this class has black hair?

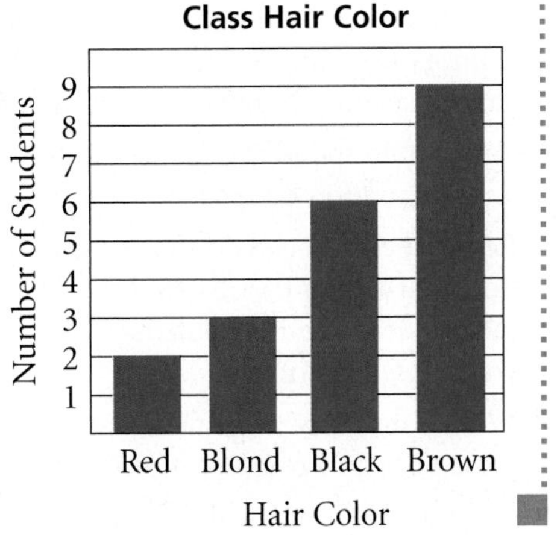

Scoring Key

[2] $\frac{6}{20}$ and appropriate work is shown.

[1] $\frac{6}{20}$ and no work is shown *or* a fraction with correct numerator or denominator and some work is shown.

[0] The response is completely incorrect, irrelevant, or incoherent *or* is a correct response arrived at using an obviously incorrect procedure.

A student can get 0, 1, or 2 credits for this question. Notice particularly the first 1-credit answer above. It includes the phrase *and no work is shown.* If you write only a correct answer and show no work, you can get only 1 credit—even for a 4-credit question. Compare these three responses and then answer the questions below.

0 credits	1 credit	2 credits
6 students have black hair.	total students = $9+8+7+6+5+4+3+2+1=45$ 6 students have black hair. $\frac{6}{45}=\frac{2}{15}$	total students = $2+3+6+9=20$ 6 students have black hair. $\frac{6}{20}$

THINK AND DISCUSS

1. Compare the 1-credit response with the 2-credit response. What is the difference?
2. Why is the 0-credit response completely wrong?

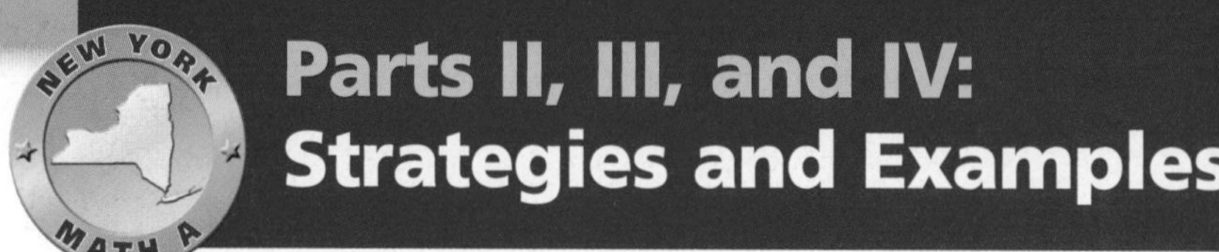

Parts II, III, and IV: Strategies and Examples

General Strategies

Parts II, III, and IV each have five questions that are not in multiple-choice format. A Part II question is worth a maximum of 2 credits, a Part III question is worth a maximum of 3 credits, and a Part IV question is worth a maximum of 4 credits.

- Watch your time. Remember, each Part II question is worth the same number of points as one of the multiple-choice questions in Part I. It is easy to spend too much time on the Part II questions.
- You should spend about 20 minutes on Part II, 30 minutes on Part III, and 40 minutes on Part IV.
- Remember, you can do the test questions in any order. You may want to do Part IV, then Part III, and then Part II. If you are a good reader, quickly read the 15 problems in these sections of the test. Do the ones you are certain of first.
- Write your answer in ink on the same page as the test question. Be sure to cross out any wrong solutions so they do not affect your score.
- The test directions will tell you: Use ink for answers and computation. Use pencil for graphs and drawings.
- You will be given one sheet of scrap graph paper, but you can ask for more. Any work on this graph paper does NOT count towards your score.
- It's sometimes good to skip a question. If you skip a question, there is no penalty. If you know nothing about a question, it may be better to skip it than to take too much time trying to answer it. Come back to the question after you have finished the other questions.
- You must show your work to get maximum credit. Even if your answer is correct, you will get only 1 credit if you do not show your work.
- If you skip a question, you will get 0 credits for it. There is no other penalty.
- Some questions will have more than one part. Even if you can't answer part (a), you may be able to answer part (b) or part (c). Each part is probably worth at least 1 credit.
- You may lose a credit if you forget to label an answer with the unit of measure. Even if a question asks something like, "How many square feet are in the area?" it is still a good idea to label your answer with "square feet."
- In general, the Part IV questions are the most difficult. However, it depends on what you know. If you know a topic for a Part IV question well, that question will be easier for you than a Part II question about which you know little.

The next section describes test-taking strategies that will help you with Parts II, III, and IV.

Show Your Work

Even if an answer is obvious to you, you must show your work to get the maximum number of credits.

Example

Paloma has 3 jackets, 6 scarves, and 4 hats. Determine the number of different outfits consisting of a jacket, a scarf, and a hat that Paloma can wear.

Strategy This is a Part II question, so it is worth a maximum of 2 credits. You might use mental math to multiply the three numbers and get the correct answer, 72. However, writing "72" gives you only 1 credit. You must show work or describe a method to get the full 2 credits.

0 credits	1 credit	2 credits
$3+6+4=13$	72 outfits	$3 \times 6 \times 4 = 72$ 72 possible outfits I used the Multiplication Counting Principle to find the number of possible outcomes.

THINK AND DISCUSS

Which number below is irrational?

$\sqrt{\frac{4}{9}}$, $\sqrt{20}$, $\sqrt{121}$

Why is the number you chose an irrational number?

1. The correct answer is $\sqrt{20}$. How many credits would a student get if he or she circled $\sqrt{20}$?
2. A student wrote, "The square root of $\frac{4}{9}$ is $\frac{2}{3}$, and the square root of 121 is 11. So, the answer must be the square root of 20." Does this response completely answer the question? Explain.
3. Would guessing help you on this question? Explain.
4. The Think and Discuss question requires the definition of an irrational number. Where in this book can you find that definition?

Cross Out Wrong Answers

If you write two solutions for the same question, one completely correct and one completely wrong, you will not score the maximum credits possible. Be sure to cross out an incorrect solution.

Example

Judy needs a mean (average) score of 86 on four tests to earn a midterm grade of B. If the mean of her scores for the first three tests was 83, what is the *lowest* score on a 100-point scale that she can receive on the fourth test to have a midterm grade of B?

Strategy This is a Part III question, so it is worth a maximum of 3 credits. One way to do this problem is to multiply 86 by 4, then multiply 83 by 3, and then subtract the products. This correct method is shown in the chart under the 3-credit response. Notice that the 1-credit response has both the correct approach and an earlier, incorrect response.

1 credit	2 credits	3 credits
$86 + 83 = 169$ $169 \div 2 = 84.5$ $86 \times 4 = 344$ $83 \times 3 = 249$ $344 - 249 = 95$	$86 \times 4 = 344$ $83 \times 3 = 249$ $344 - 249 = 105$	~~$86 + 83 = 169$~~ ~~$169 \div 2 = 84.5$~~ $86 \times 4 = 344$ $83 \times 3 = 249$ $344 - 249 = 95$

THINK AND DISCUSS

1. Why must you cross out wrong trials rather than erasing them?
2. What is the difference between the 2-credit response and the 3-credit response?
3. The Example question deals with a type of average called a mean. Use the Index at the back of your book to find the lesson that covers finding the mean.

Describe a Method

You may be able to get 1 credit for describing a correct method—even if you do not completely finish the problem and get a correct answer.

Example

The midpoint M of line segment $\overline{AB}$ has coordinates $(-3, 4)$. If point A is the origin, $(0, 0)$, what are the coordinates of point B?

Strategy This is a Part II question, so it is worth a maximum of 2 credits. Assume you are not completely sure how to solve this problem. You could write, "I will use the midpoint formula for segment AB and substitute the given coordinates to solve the problem." You might get 1 point just for writing this much. You have nothing to lose by trying!

One correct approach is to double the coordinates to get the solution $(-6, 8)$. Compare these different responses.

0 credits	1 credit	2 credits
I divided each coordinate in half like this: $-3 \div 2 = -1.5$ $4 \div 2 = 2$ $(-1.5, 2)$	$(-6, 8)$	Doubling the coordinates will give the correct answer. $(-3, \; 4)$ $\times 2 \quad \times 2$ $(-6, \; 8)$

THINK AND DISCUSS

1. Why does the response on the left earn 0 credits?
2. Why does the middle response earn only 1 credit?
3. Suggest another approach to solving the problem.
4. This example deals with the midpoint of a line segment. Use the Index at the back of your book to find the lesson that explains the midpoint formula.

Include Units of Measure

You may lose a credit if you forget to label an answer with the unit of measure. Even if a question asks something like, "How many square feet are in the area?" it is still a good idea to label your answer with "square feet."

Example

The cross section of an attic is in the shape of an isosceles trapezoid as shown in the accompanying figure. If the height of the attic is 9 feet, $BC = 12$ feet, and $AD = 28$ feet, find the length of $\overline{AB}$ to the *nearest foot.*

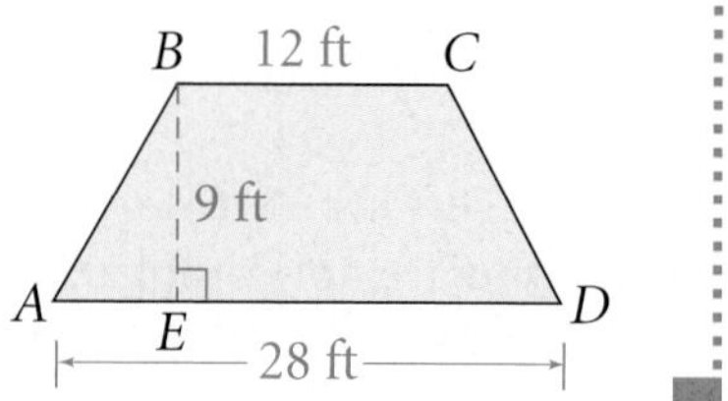

Strategy This is a Part IV question, so it is worth a maximum of 4 credits. Read the 4-credit response below. Notice the student starts by describing the method to be used. This is a good idea because you might get credit for the method even if you do not carry the solution out to a correct answer.

2 credits	3 credits	4 credits
To find the length of $\overline{AB}$, I need to find the length of $\overline{AE}$. $28 - 12 = 16$ $16 \div 2 = 8$ $AE = 8$ $AB^2 = 9^2 + 8^2$ $AB^2 = 81 + 64$ $AB^2 = 145$ $AB = 145$ feet	To find the length of $\overline{AB}$, I need to find the length of $\overline{AE}$. $28 - 12 = 16$ $16 \div 2 = 8$ $AE = 8$ $AB^2 = 9^2 + 8^2$ $AB^2 = 81 + 64$ $AB^2 = 145$ $AB = \sqrt{145}$ $\sqrt{145} =$ about 12 $AB = 12$	To find the length of $\overline{AB}$, I need to find the length of $\overline{AE}$. $28 - 12 = 16$ $16 \div 2 = 8$ $AE = 8$ $AB^2 = 9^2 + 8^2$ $AB^2 = 81 + 64$ $AB^2 = 145$ $AB \sqrt{145}$ $\sqrt{145} =$ about 12 $AB = 12$ feet

THINK AND DISCUSS

1. Compare the 3-credit response and the 4-credit response. How are they different?
2. Read the 2-credit response. What mistake did this student make?
3. The example question involves the Pythagorean theorem. Use the Index at the back of your book to find the lesson that covers the Pythagorean theorem.

PRENTICE HALL

NEW YORK MATH A

Single-Volume Version

Contents

NEW YORK MATH A

Volume 1 — Focus on Algebra

Contents

PRENTICE HALL

NEW YORK MATH A

Single-Volume Version

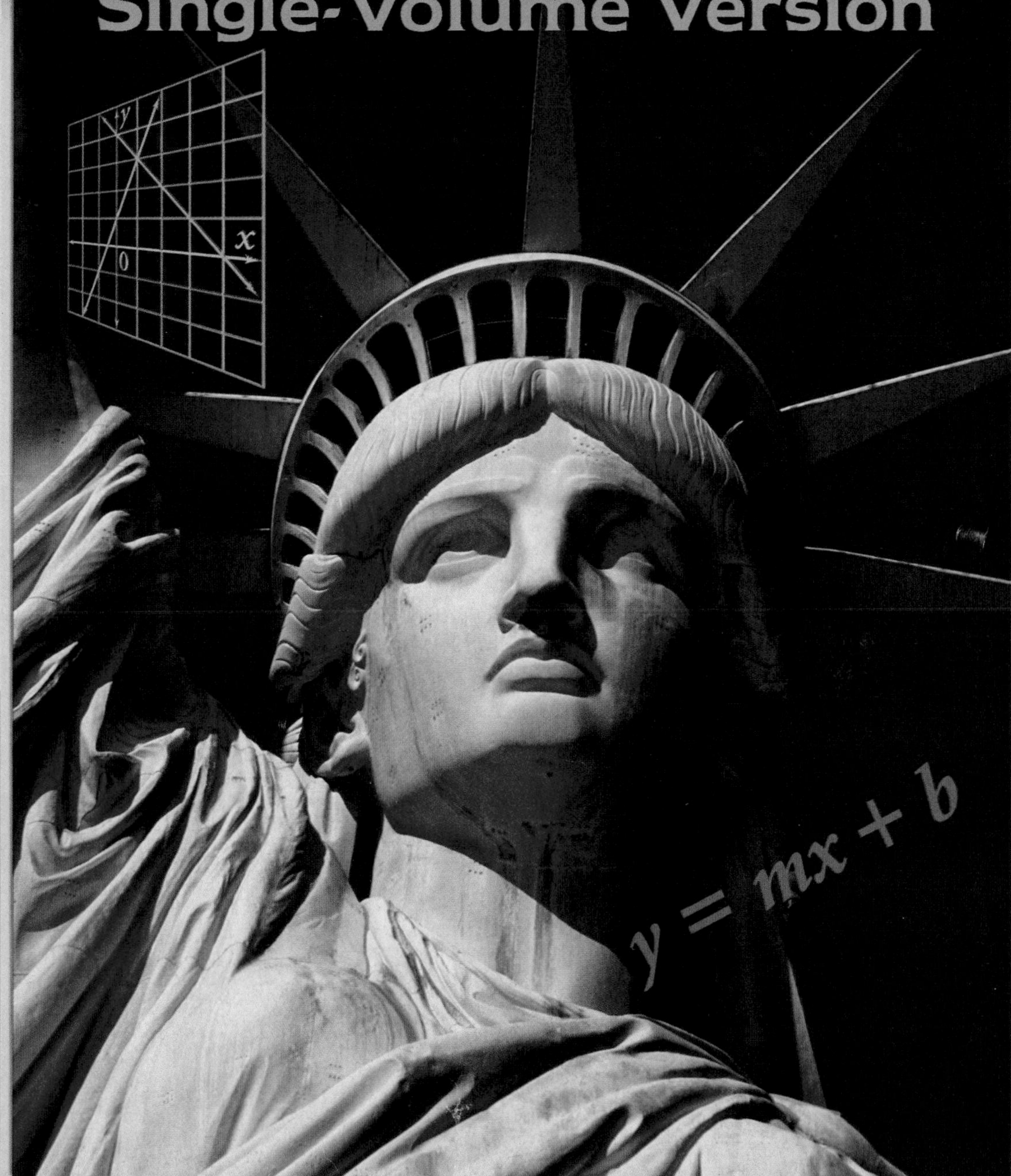

Volume 1

Authors, Algebra & Advanced Algebra

Allan Bellman
Blake High School
Silver Spring, Maryland

Sadie Chavis Bragg, Ed.D.
Borough of Manhattan
Community College
The City University of New York
New York, New York

Suzanne H. Chapin, Ed.D.
Boston University
Boston, Massachusetts

Theodore J. Gardella
Formerly, Bloomfield Hills
Public Schools
Bloomfield Hills, Michigan

Bettye C. Hall
Mathematics Consultant
Houston, Texas

William G. Handlin, Sr.
Spring Woods High School
Houston, Texas

Edward Manfre
Mathematics Consultant
Albuquerque, New Mexico

Authors, Geometry

Laurie E. Bass
The Fieldston School
Riverdale, New York

Basia Rinesmith Hall
East District
Houston Independent School District
Houston, Texas

Art Johnson, Ed.D.
Nashua High School
Nashua, New Hampshire

Dorothy F. Wood
Formerly, Kern High School District
Bakersfield, California

Contributing Author
Simone W. Bess, Ed.D.
University of Cincinnati
College of Education
Cincinnati, Ohio

ISBN: 0-13-122377-1

2 3 4 5 6 7 8 9 10 07 06 05 04 03

REVIEWERS

New York Math A

A. Rose Primiani, Ed.D., Program Consultant/Planner for Prentice Hall Math A

Howard Brenner, Assistant Principal, Mathematics, Fort Hamilton High School, Brooklyn, New York

William Caroscio, Elmira City School District, Elmira Southside High School, Elmira, New York

Raymond Ruby, Mathematics Curriculum Coordinator, Averill Park Central School District, Averill Park, New York

Joseph G. Ryan, Cardinal Hayes High School, Bronx, New York

Series Reviewers

James Gates, Ed.D.
Executive Director Emeritus, National Council of Teachers of Mathematics, Reston, Virginia

Vinetta Jones, Ph.D.
National Director, EQUITY 2000, The College Board, New York, New York

Algebra

John J. Brady III
Hume-Fogg High School
Nashville, Tennessee

Elias P. Rodriguez
Leander Junior High School
Leander, Texas

Dorothy S. Strong, Ed.D.
Chicago Public Schools
Chicago, Illinois

Art W. Wilson, Ed.D.
Abraham Lincoln High School
Denver, Colorado

Advanced Algebra

Eleanor Boehner
Methacton High School
Norristown, Pennsylvania

Laura Price Cobb
Dallas Public Schools
Dallas, Texas

William Earl, Ed.D.
Formerly Mathematics Education Specialist
Utah State Office of Education
Salt Lake City, Utah

Geometry

Sandra Argüelles Daire
Miami Senior High School
Miami, Florida

Priscilla P. Donkle
South Central High School
Union Mills, Indiana

Tom Muchlinski, Ph.D.
Wayzata High School
Plymouth, Minnesota

Bonnie Walker
Texas ASCD
Houston, Texas

Karen Doyle Walton, Ed.D.
Allentown College of
Saint Francis de Sales
Center Valley, Pennsylvania

CHAPTER

1 Tools of Algebra

CHAPTER 2

Functions and Their Graphs

Connections and Applications

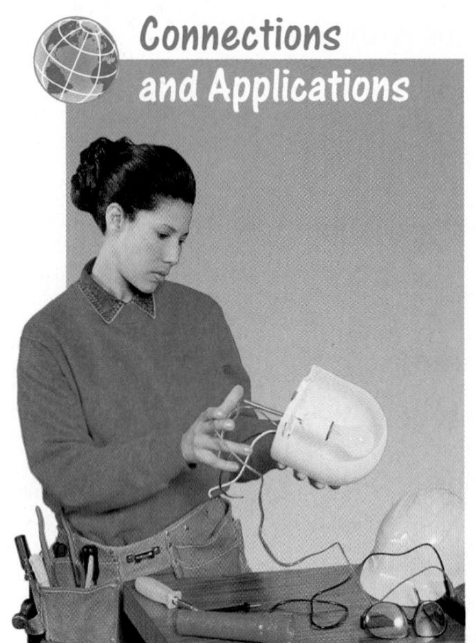

CHAPTER 3

Algebraic Concepts and Simple Equations

Connections and Applications

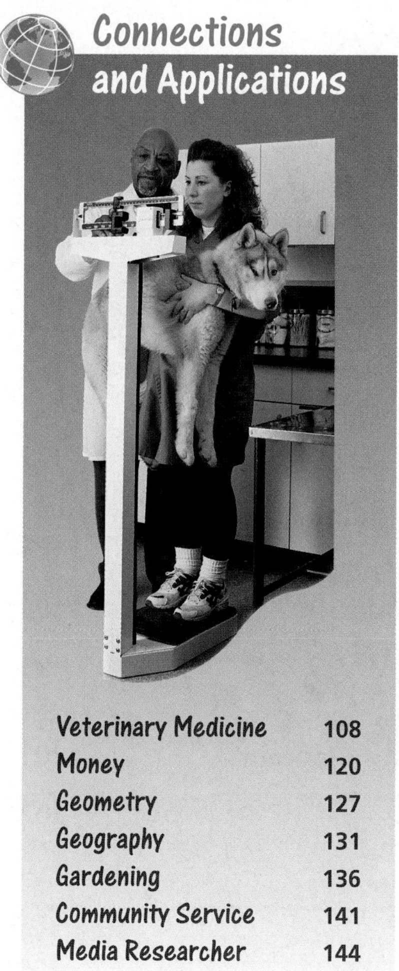

CHAPTER 4

Equations and Inequalities

Connections and Applications

CHAPTER 5

Graphing and Writing Linear Equations

Connections and Applications

CHAPTER 6

Systems of Equations and Inequalities

Connections and Applications

Chapter Project *Let's Dance!* *Planning a Dance*

CHAPTER

7 Quadratic Equations and Functions

Connections and Applications

CHAPTER 8

Exponents and Exponential Functions

Connections and Applications

CHAPTER 9

Right Triangles and Radical Expressions

Connections and Applications

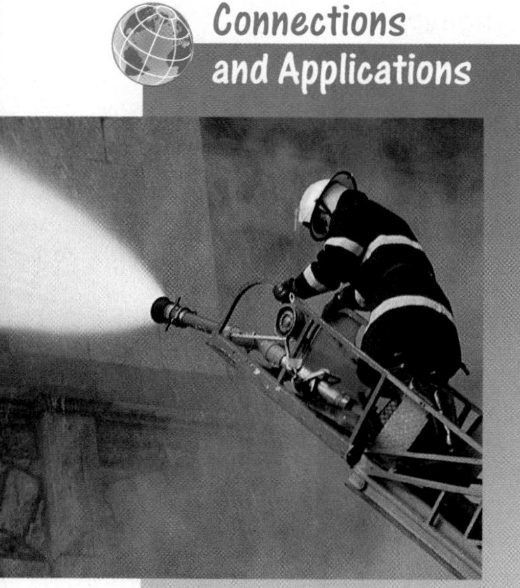

CHAPTER 10

Polynomials

Connections and Applications

CHAPTER 11

Rational Expressions and Functions

Connections and Applications

CHAPTER 1 Tools of Algebra

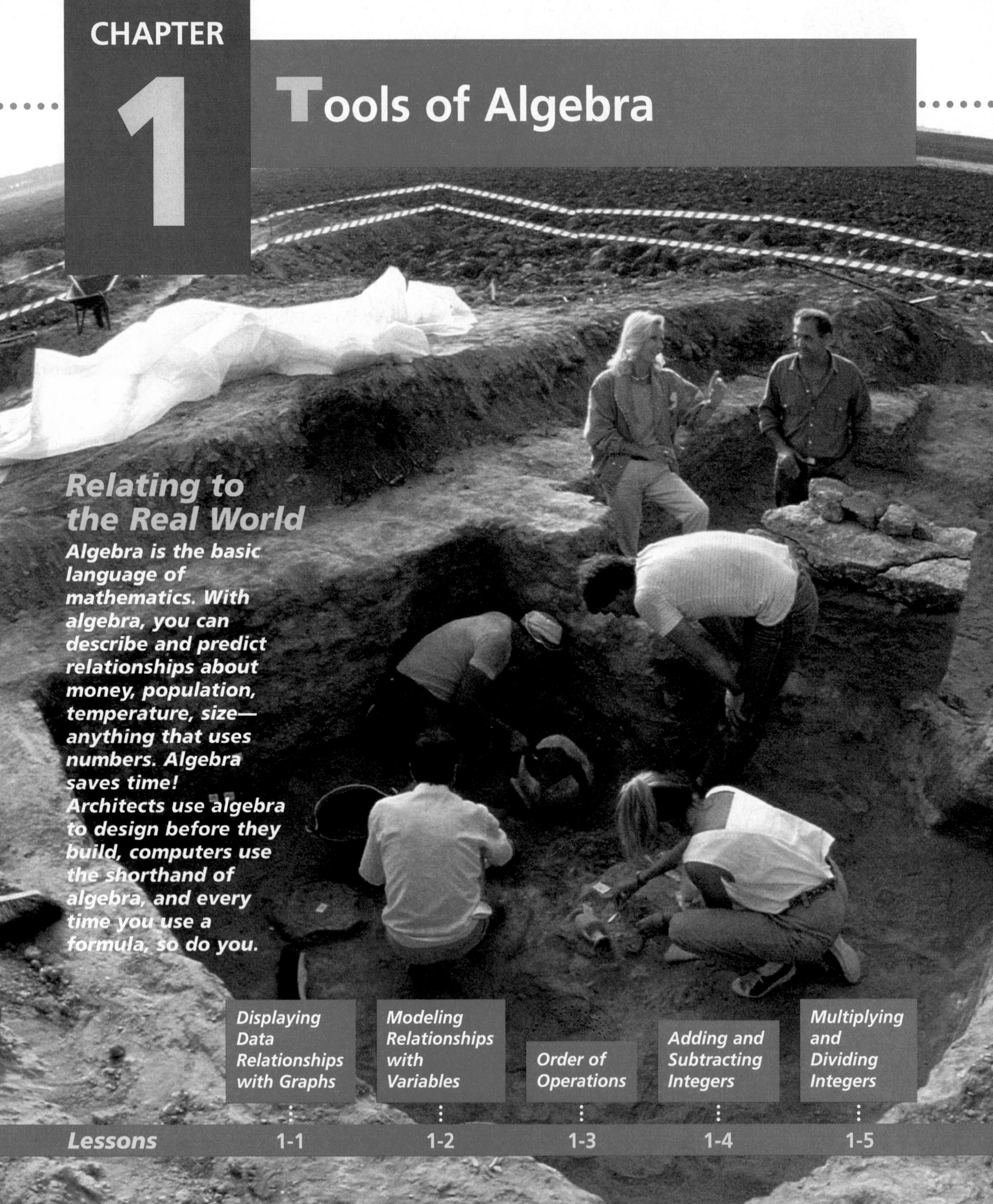

Relating to the Real World

Algebra is the basic language of mathematics. With algebra, you can describe and predict relationships about money, population, temperature, size—anything that uses numbers. Algebra saves time! Architects use algebra to design before they build, computers use the shorthand of algebra, and every time you use a formula, so do you.

CHAPTER PROJECT

The BIG DIG!

humerus
radius
tibia

Your bones tell a lot about your body. Archaeologists and forensic scientists study bones to estimate a person's height, build, and age. These data are helpful in learning about ancient people and in solving crimes. The lengths of major bones such as the humerus, radius, or tibia can be substituted into formulas to find a person's height.

As you work through the chapter, you will collect data about bones from your classmates and from adults. You will use formulas to analyze the data and predict heights. Then you will decide how to organize and display your results in graphs and spreadsheets.

To help you complete the project:

- **p. 9** *Find Out by Graphing*
- **p. 29** *Find Out by Calculating*
- **p. 39** *Find Out by Analyzing*
- **p. 49** *Find Out by Creating*
- **p. 50** *Finishing the Project*

1-6	1-7	1-8	1-9
Real Numbers and Rational Numbers	*Experimental Probability and Simulations*	*Organizing Data in Matrices*	*Variables and Formulas in Spreadsheets*

Connections Jobs . . . and more

What You'll Learn

- Finding the mean, median, and mode of sets of data
- Drawing and interpreting graphs

...And Why

To analyze real-world data, such as age and employment statistics

1-1 Displaying Data Relationships with Graphs

WORK TOGETHER

Work in groups.

Line plots are simple graphs that help you see the relationship between data items. At the right is the start of a line plot for data collected on birth months of a group of students. Each × represents one student.

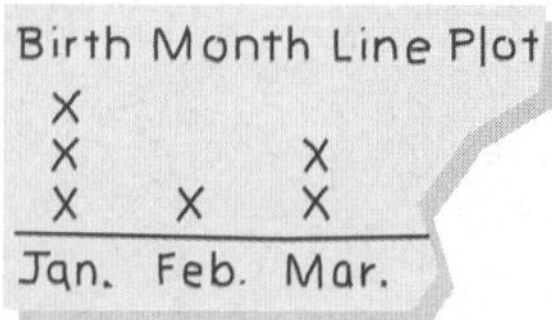

1. What do you think a line plot for the birth months of the students in your class would look like?

2. **a.** Data Collection Find the birth month of each student in your group. Share this information with other groups.
b. Draw a line plot of your class data.
c. Does the line plot of your class data look similar to what you expected? Explain.

THINK AND DISCUSS

Finding Mean, Median, and Mode

You can use a line plot or *histogram* to show the frequency, or number of times, a data item occurs. The data item with the greatest frequency is the **mode.**

Birth Months of Presidents of the United States

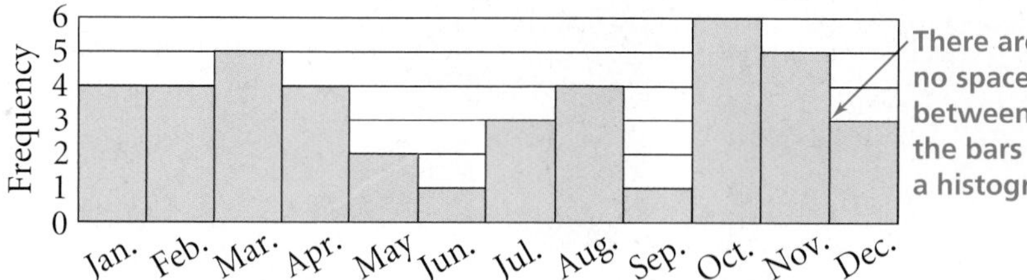

Mount Rushmore in South Dakota has carvings of four Presidents: Washington, Jefferson, T. Roosevelt, and Lincoln. Washington's head is as tall as a five-story building.

3. What is the mode of the data in the histogram above?

4. In which months were the fewest Presidents born?

5. **a.** Draw a histogram of the data you collected in the Work Together.
b. Can you predict birth-month patterns for all the people in the United States based on your class data? Why or why not?

6. What is the mode (or modes) of your class data?

Age When Elected

First Presidents	Recent Presidents
Washington—57	Ford—61
J. Adams—61	Carter—52
Jefferson—57	Reagan—69
Madison—57	Bush—64
Monroe—58	Clinton—46

Do you think that the ages of the Presidents have changed a lot since the beginning of the United States in 1776? One way to find out is to compare the mean ages of the first Presidents with those of recent Presidents. Use this ratio to find the mean.

$$\textbf{Mean} = \frac{\text{sum of the data items}}{\text{total number of data items}}$$

7. **a.** Find the mean of each group of ages.
   b. Has there been much change in the mean age of the Presidents? Explain.

8. Would the mode be as useful as the mean in comparing the ages of the first Presidents to recent Presidents? Explain.

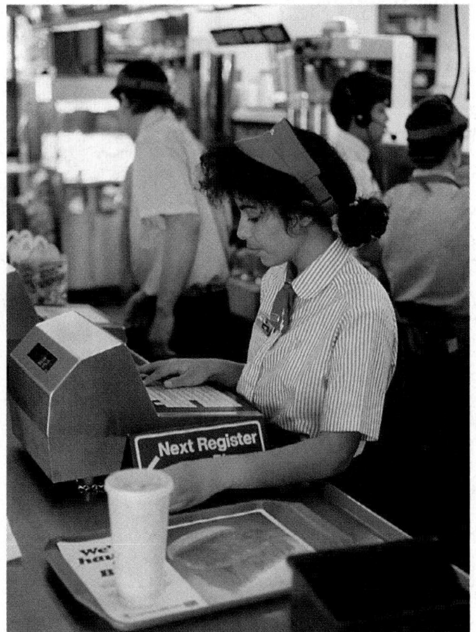

A third type of measure is the median. The **median** is the middle value in an ordered set of numbers. The mean, median, and mode may give a different picture of data—sometimes slightly different, sometimes very different.

Example 1 *Relating to the Real World* 

Jobs Find the mean, median, and mode of the data below.

What Employees Earn at a Local Fast Food Restaurant

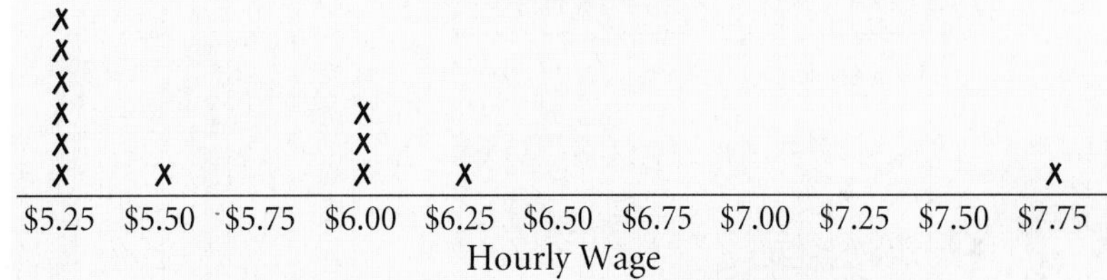

QUICK REVIEW

You can indicate multiplication of two numbers in any of these ways:

6(5.25) (6)(5.25)
6 · 5.25 6 × 5.25

You can multiply 6 times 5.25 as a shortcut for adding 5.25 + 5.25 + 5.25 + 5.25 + 5.25 + 5.25.

Mean: $\frac{6(5.25) + 5.50 + 3(6.00) + 6.25 + 7.75}{12} = 5.75$

12 ← total number of employees

Median: 5.25 5.25 5.25 5.25 5.25 5.25 5.50 6.00 6.00 6.00 6.25 7.75

For an even number of data items, find the mean of the middle terms. → $\frac{5.25 + 5.50}{2} \approx 5.38$

Mode: 5.25 ← the data item that occurs most often

The mean is \$5.75/h. The median is about \$5.38/h.

The mode is \$5.25/h.

9. **Try This** Suppose the worker earning $7.75/h resigns. Her replacement earns $5.75/h. How does this change affect the mode? the median? the mean?

10. **Critical Thinking** Does the mean, median, or mode best describe the set of wages in the line plot? **Justify** your answer.

Drawing and Interpreting Graphs

Bar graphs are useful when you wish to compare amounts. Whenever you make a graph to display data, you must choose an appropriate scale so that the graph is neither too big for your paper nor too small to read.

Example 2 **Relating to the Real World** 

Social Studies Draw a multiple bar graph for the median income data.

Median Household Income

	1987	1989	1991	1993
Calif.	$37,231	$37,348	$34,677	$33,083
Conn.	$40,586	$47,884	$43,423	$38,369
Ind.	$27,812	$29,302	$27,904	$28,618
Tex.	$30,531	$29,289	$28,568	$27,892
Utah	$32,764	$34,755	$28,859	$34,746

Source: *U. S. Bureau of the Census*

The highest projected income is $47,884. So a reasonable range for the vertical scale is from 0 to $50,000 with every $5000 labeled on the axis.

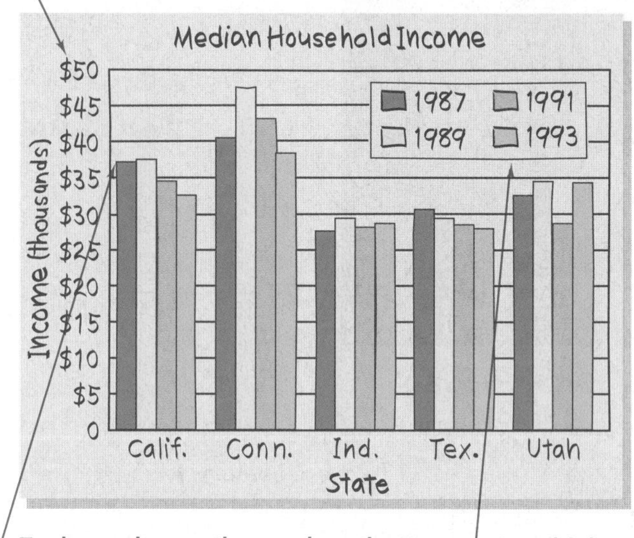

To draw a bar on the graph, estimate its placement based on the vertical scale. The value $37,231 is a little less than $\frac{1}{2}$ the distance from $35,000 to $40,000.

A multiple bar graph must include a key.

11. **Try This** Suppose you were drawing a graph of the data. How would you estimate where to put the top of the bar showing the median income for Texas in 1991?

12. Why is the key necessary for the graph above?

13. **a.** Which states decreased in median income for each of the last two years shown on the graph?
    b. Did you use the table or the graph to answer part (a)? Why?

14. *Critical Thinking* The United States had an economic recession in the late 1980s and early 1990s. Which states seemed to be least affected by the recession? Explain.

Line graphs allow you to see how a set of data changes over time. You can use line graphs to look for trends in data.

Example 3 **Relating to the Real World**

Aluminum Soft Drink Cans (in billions)		
Year	**Manufactured**	**Recycled**
1989	45.7	27.8
1990	49.2	31.3
1991	53.0	33.0
1992	54.9	37.3
1993	58.0	36.6

Source: *Can Manufacturing Institute*

Recycling Make a double line graph of the table at the left.

The least and greatest numbers in the chart are 27.8 and 58.0. A reasonable vertical scale is from 20 to 60 with every 10 units labeled on the axis.

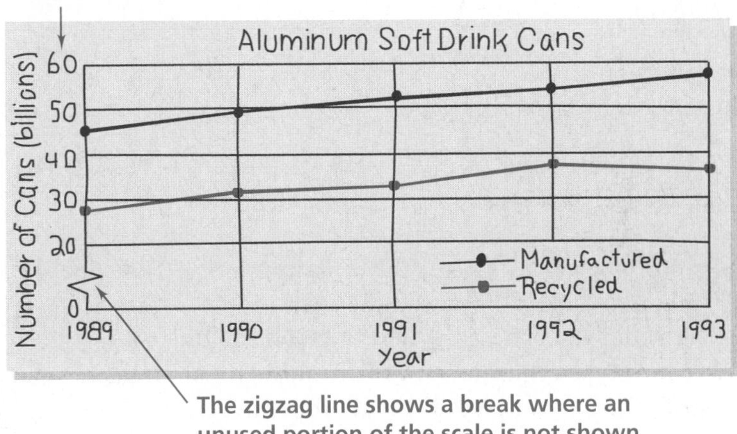

The zigzag line shows a break where an unused portion of the scale is not shown.

15. a. Describe the trend for the number of cans manufactured.
    b. Describe the trend for the number of cans recycled.

16. a. *Critical Thinking* Suppose you draw the graph without a break in the vertical scale. How would this affect the way the graph looks?
    b. Would drawing the graph without a break in the scale improve the graph? Why or why not?

17. *Critical Thinking* From 1989–1993, did the amount of waste from soft drink cans increase, decrease, or stay the same? Explain.

Exercises ON YOUR OWN

1. An interviewer asked 25 people, "How many children live in your home?" Here are their responses.
   2, 1, 3, 0, 4, 2, 2, 1, 0, 3, 2, 6, 4,
   3, 3, 2, 1, 1, 3, 0, 0, 2, 1, 1, 2
   a. Draw a line plot for the data. Include a title for the line plot.
   b. Find the mean, median, and mode of the data.

2. a. Entertainment Use the data about television viewing to draw a double line graph.
   b. What trend do you see in the total number of households viewing the top-rated program?
   c. What trend do you see in the number of households with TV?
   d. Critical Thinking What could explain the differing trends you see in your graph?

3. Standardized Test Prep Suppose your mean on four literature tests is 78. Which score would raise the mean to 80?
   A. 95 B. 80 C. 100 D. 88 E. not possible

TV Viewing 1970–1990 (in millions)

Year	Total Viewing Top-Rated Program	Households with TV
1970	28.0	60.1
1975	30.3	71.5
1980	41.5	77.8
1985	39.4	84.9
1990	39.0	92.1

Source: *Nielsen Media Research*

Find the mean, median, and mode of each set of data. Round to the nearest tenth.

4. 2, 6, 3, 2, 4
5. 10, 10, 20, 0
6. 80, 90, 85, 80, 90, 90, 40, 85
7. 25, 25, 25, 25
8. 22, 23, 28, 33, 24, 27, 24, 26, 23, 26, 25, 29, 21, 30
9. 35.2, 42.6, 41.0, 37.2, 34.5, 35.0, 36.8, 41.0, 37.9, 42.1, 41.5

10. a. Recording Industry Use a triple bar graph or a triple line graph to display the data at the right.
    b. Why did you choose the type of graph you did?
    c. Which type of music showed the most growth in sales over the six-year period? **Justify** your answer.

Recording Industry Sales (in millions of dollars)

Year	Rock	Country	Jazz
1989	$2823	$447	$375
1990	$2722	$724	$362
1991	$2726	$1003	$298
1992	$2852	$1570	$313
1993	$3034	$1879	$311
1994	$4236	$1967	$362

Source: *Recording Industry Association of America*

11. a. Sports The median height of the 21 players on a girls' soccer team is 5 ft 7 in. What is the greatest possible number of girls who are less than 5 ft 7 in. tall?
    b. Critical Thinking Suppose three girls are 5 ft 7 in. tall. How would this change your answer to part (a)? Explain.

12. a. Agriculture What trend do you see in the graph showing the number of farms in the United States?
    b. What trend do you see in the graph showing the average size of farms in the United States?
    c. Writing Do you think the two trends are related? Explain.

United States Farms

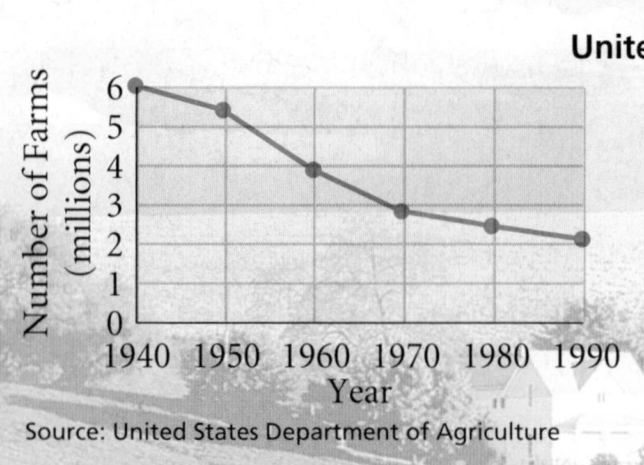

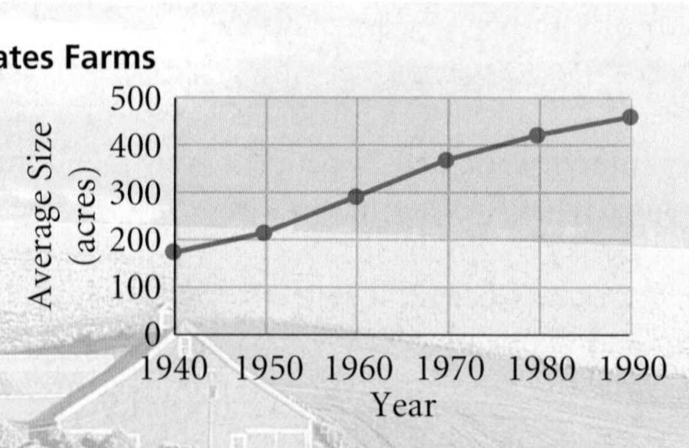

Source: United States Department of Agriculture

13. *Languages* Do Spanish words have more letters than English words? Compare the word lengths in the following excerpt from the Preamble to the United Nations Charter.

We the peoples of the United Nations determined to save succeeding generations from the scourge of war, which twice in our lifetime has brought untold sorrow to mankind, and

To reaffirm faith in fundamental human rights, in the dignity and worth of the human person, in the equal rights of men and women and of nations large and small . . . have resolved to combine our efforts to accomplish these aims.

Nosotros los pueblos de las Naciones Unidas resueltos a preservar a las generaciones venideras del flagelo de la guerra que dos veces durante nuestra vida ha infligido a la Humanidad sufrimientos indecibles,

a reafirmar la fe en los derechos fundamentales del hombre, en la dignidad y el valor de la persona humana, en la igualdad de derechos de hombres y mujeres y de las naciones grandes y pequeñas . . . hemos decidido aunar nuestros esfuerzos para realizar estos designios.

a. For each version, draw a line plot of word lengths.
b. Find the mean, median, and mode of the data in each line plot.
c. *Writing* Which language do you think has the longer word length? **Justify** your answer.

Chapter Project — Find Out by Graphing

- Measure the length of your radius bone to the nearest half inch.
- Collect the data for the class, and display the data in a graph.
- Find the mean, median, and mode for the data you collected. Write a description of the data.

Open-ended **Create a set of data for the given mean, median, and mode.**

14. mean = 10, median = 10, mode = 10

15. mean = 100, median = 80, mode = 70

16. mean = 3, median = 2, no mode

17. mean = 5, median = 5, mode = 8 and 3

Exercises MIXED REVIEW

Write as a decimal, a fraction or mixed number, and a percent.

18. $\frac{5}{8}$ 19. 40% 20. 0.75 21. 25% 22. 4.6 23. $1\frac{4}{5}$

24. *Open-ended* Suppose a pair of shoes costs $25, a shirt costs $15, and a pair of pants costs $30. You have a budget of $100 and the sales tax is 6%. How many of each item would you buy? Explain.

Getting Ready for Lesson 1-2

Write the next three numbers in each pattern.

25. 1, 3, 5, ■, ■, ■ 26. 28, 25, 22, ■, ■, ■ 27. 4, 12, 36, ■, ■, ■

Math ToolboX — Skills Review

Stem-and-Leaf Plots

After Lesson 1-1

For a class project, a student gathered data from her classmates. She made this request: "Tomorrow morning, find out how many minutes it takes you to get ready—from the time you get up until the time you leave your house for school." Here are the responses:

47 28 78 47 58 93 34 76 35 72 45 53 23

43 75 27 23 87 33 43 25 35 49 35 48 37 28

You can use a *stem-and-leaf plot* to give you a better picture of this information. A stem-and-leaf plot displays the data items in order. The digit (or digits) to the left is the *stem*. The digit farthest to the right is the *leaf*.

58
stem ↗ ↖ leaf

For Exercises 1–4, use the stem-and-leaf plot at the right.

Time to Get Ready

Stem	Leaves
2	3 3 5 7 8 8
3	3 4 5 5 5 7
4	3 3 5 7 7 8 9
5	3 8
6	
7	2 5 6 8
8	7
9	3

key: 2|3 means 23 min

1. How many students responded?
2. What does the stem 2 and leaf 8 represent?
3. How many students took more than 50 min to get ready in the morning?
4. a. Explain how you would use the stem-and-leaf plot to find the median and the mode of the data.
   b. What is the median? the mode?
5. Consider the data on notebook prices.
   a. What would be the stems for the notebook data?
   b. What would be the key?
   c. Make a stem-and-leaf plot for this set of data.
   d. Find the median and mode of this set of data.

Notebook Prices

$2.00	$2.50	$2.25	$2.50
$2.29	$1.97	$2.16	$2.49
$2.21	$2.36	$2.09	$1.95
$2.05	$2.57	$2.40	$1.99

6. **Writing** The two graphs below display the information on the time it takes to get ready in the morning. Compare the graphs with the stem-and-leaf plot. Describe the advantages and disadvantages of using each to display the data.

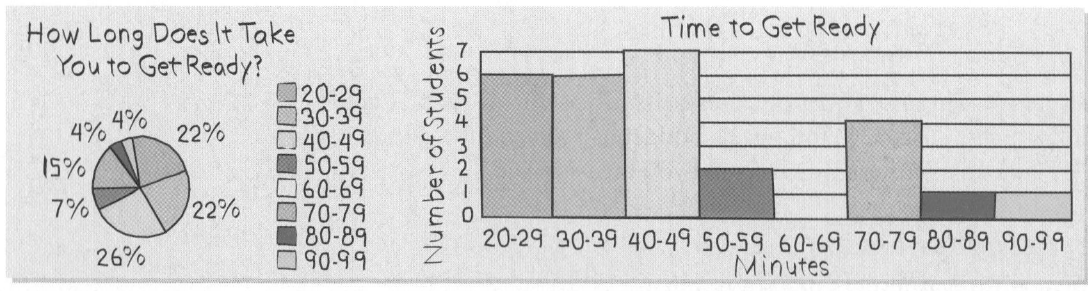

What You'll Learn

- Describing relationships between sets of data
- Using variables as a shorthand way to express relationships

...And Why

To model relationships in areas such as geometry, music, and sales

1-2 Modeling Relationships with Variables

THINK AND DISCUSS

Geometry The band Numerica is designing a stage to use in its new music video. Their set designer made the sketches shown below.

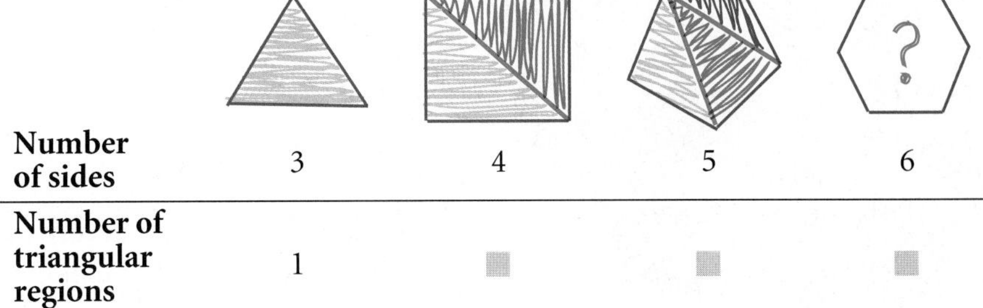

Number of sides	3	4	5	6
Number of triangular regions	1	■	■	■

1. Use the sketches to help you complete the table.
2. **Analyze** the data in the table. What relationship do you see between the number of sides a stage has and the number of triangular regions created by the line segments?
3. Numerica plans to use a 12-sided stage. How many triangular regions can the designer form with the segments starting at one corner?

You could use the letter s to represent the number of sides of the stage. Since s can change in value, it is a **variable.** A **variable expression** is a mathematical phrase that contains at least one variable. The variable expression $s - 2$ is a short way to represent the number of triangular regions created by the segments.

4. Could you use a letter other than s to represent the number of sides of the stage? Explain.

terms

$$7a^2 + \frac{1}{2}b - 5$$

QUICK REVIEW

$7a$ is a short way to write $7 \times a$ or $7 \cdot a$.

Variable expressions are made up of one or more terms. A **term** is a number, a variable, or the product of numbers and variables.

5. How many terms does the expression $7a^2 + \frac{1}{2}b - 5$ have?
6. How many terms does the expression $s - 2$ have?

You can use variable expressions to write an equation. The **equation** $t = s - 2$ indicates that the two expressions t and $s - 2$ are equal.

Example 1 Relating to the Real World 

Music Each CD at Track One Records costs \$12. Write an equation you can use to find the total cost when you know the number of CDs bought.

The plan below shows how you can go from a word problem to a short statement of the problem using variables.

Relate The total cost is 12 times the number of CDs bought.

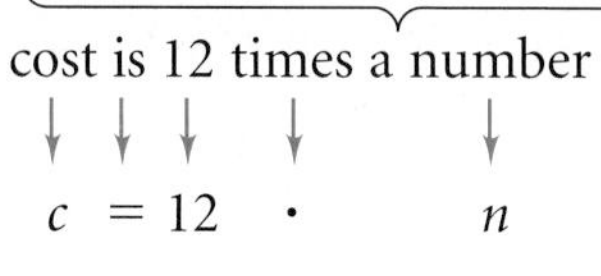

cost is 12 times a number

↓ ↓ ↓ ↓ ↓

Write $c = 12 \cdot n$

$c = 12n$

7. What do the variables c and n represent in Example 1?
8. A worker at Track One Records says that 5 CDs cost \$125 because $c = 12n$ and $n = 5$. Explain the worker's error.
9. **Try This** Suppose the manager at Track One Records raises the price of CDs to \$15. Write an equation to find the cost of n CDs.
10. Suppose the manager at Track One Records uses the equation $c = 10.99n$. What does this mean?

Before writing an equation for data in a table, it is helpful to write a short sentence describing the relationship between the data. Then translate the sentence to an equation. Be sure to tell what each variable represents.

Example 2 Relating to the Real World 

Sales Write an equation for the data in the table.

Change from a \$20 Bill

Cost of Items Purchased	Amount of Change
\$20.00	\$0
\$19.00	\$1.00
\$17.50	\$2.50
\$11.59	\$8.41

Define $c =$ cost of items purchased
$a =$ amount of change

Relate Amount of change equals \$20.00 minus cost of items purchased.

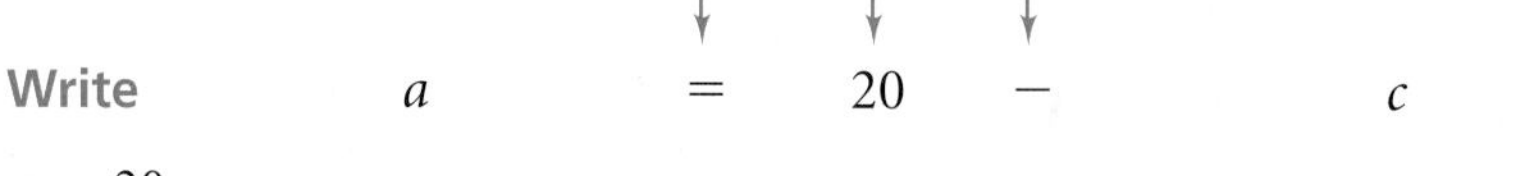

↓ ↓ ↓

Write $a = 20 - c$

$a = 20 - c$

11. Could you define the variables after writing the sentence describing the relationship between the data? Explain.
12. In Example 2, could the letter c represent the cost and also represent the change? Why or why not?
13. Suppose you wrote "The cost of items plus the amount of change equals \$20" for the relationship between the data in the table. Model this statement with an equation.

Exercises ON YOUR OWN

State the number of terms in each expression.

1. $3x + 5y - 12$
2. $9x^3 + 2x^2 + 5x + 7$
3. $\frac{2}{5}y - 4$
4. 15
5. **Open-ended** Write an expression that has four terms.
6. **Writing** Use an example to explain the meaning of *variable.*

Use an equation to model each situation.

7. Total cost equals number of cans times $.70.
8. The perimeter of a square equals four times a side.
9. The total amount of rope, in feet, used to put up scout tents is 60 times the number of tents.
10. What is the number of slices of pizza left from an 8-slice pizza after you have eaten some slices?

Use an equation to model the relationship in each table.

11.

Hours	Distance
1	50 mi
2	100 mi
3	150 mi
4	200 mi

12.

Hours	Pay
4	$24
6	$36
8	$48
10	$60

13.

Days	Growth
1	0.165 in.
2	0.330 in.
3	0.495 in.
4	0.660 in.

14.

Tapes	Cost
1	$8.50
2	$17.00
3	$25.50
4	$34.00

15.

Workers	Radios
1	13
2	26
3	39
4	52

16.

Earned	Saved
$15	$7.50
$20	$10.00
$25	$12.50
$30	$15.00

17.

Number of Sales	Total Earnings
5	$2.00
10	$4.00
15	$6.00
20	$8.00

18.

Time (months)	Length (inches)
1	4.1
2	8.2
3	12.3
4	16.4

19. **Open-ended** Choose one table from Exercises 11–18. Describe a situation for which the data is reasonable.

20. Does each statement fit the data at the right? Explain.
    a. hours worked = lawns mowed · 2
    b. hours worked = lawns mowed + 3

Lawns Mowed	Hours
1	
2	
3	6

21. a. Which statement in Exercise 20 better describes the relationship between hours worked and lawns mowed? Explain.
    b. Use your answer to part (a). Copy and complete the table. How many hours would it take to mow 5 lawns?

Use the table at the right for Exercises 22 and 23. The table shows the result when a ball is dropped from different heights.

22. a. Write an equation to describe the relationship between the height of the first bounce and the drop height.

b. Suppose you drop the ball from a window 20 ft above the ground. **Predict** how high the ball will bounce.

23. Suppose the second bounce is $\frac{1}{4}$ of the original drop height. Write an equation to represent the height of the second bounce.

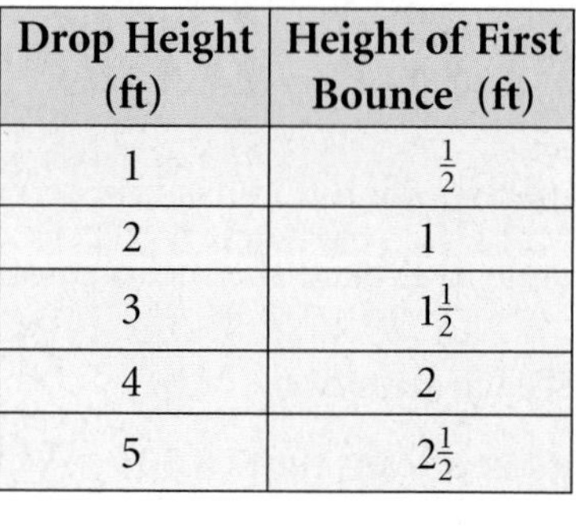

Drop Height (ft)	Height of First Bounce (ft)
1	$\frac{1}{2}$
2	1
3	$1\frac{1}{2}$
4	2
5	$2\frac{1}{2}$

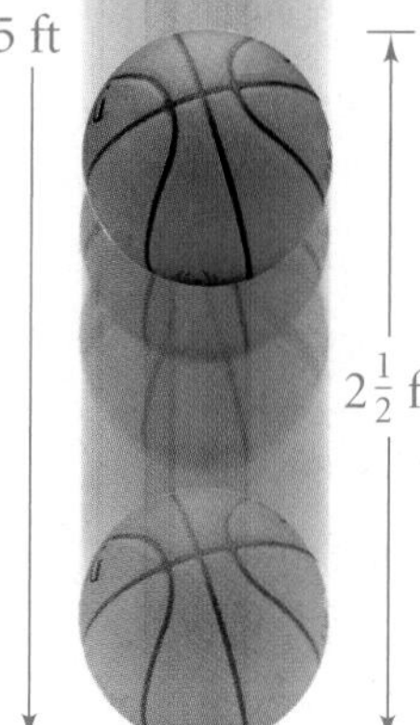

24. *Standardized Test Prep* Compare the quantities in Column A and Column B.

Column A	Column B
the total cost of items bought by a customer	the change the customer receives when paying with a $10 bill

A. The quantity in Column A is greater.
B. The quantity in Column B is greater.
C. The quantities are equal.
D. The relationship cannot be determined from the information given.

25. a. Write an equation to show how the amount of money in a bag of quarters relates to the number of quarters in the bag.

b. The bag contains 13 quarters. How much money is this?

Exercises MIXED REVIEW

26. For a project, a student asked 25 classmates the number of television news programs they watched in a week. She recorded these results:

3 5 1 4 2 0 4 5 3 6 5 5
2 0 0 1 2 5 3 1 1 4 6 3 1

a. Make a histogram of the data.

b. Find the mean, median, and mode(s) of the data.

27. List four prime numbers between 20 and 50.

28. Write the prime factorization of 105.

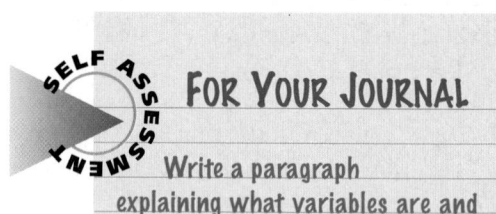

SELF ASSESSMENT

FOR YOUR JOURNAL

Write a paragraph explaining what variables are and how you use them to model the relationship between sets of data.

Getting Ready for Lesson 1-3

Find the value of each expression.

29. $3 + 12 - 7$ **30.** $4 \cdot 3 - 5$ **31.** $15 \div 3 + 2$ **32.** $6 \cdot 1 \div 2$ **33.** $4 - 2 + 9$

1-3 Order of Operations

What You'll Learn

- Using the order of operations
- Evaluating variable expressions

...And Why

To find the total cost of items with tax

What You'll Need

- calculator

Astronaut Ellen Ochoa served on space flights in 1993 and 1994. She studied the solar corona and the effect of solar changes on Earth's environment.

WORK TOGETHER

Work with a partner.

Geometry Two formulas for the perimeter of a rectangle are $P = 2l + 2w$ and $P = 2(l + w)$.

1. Let $l = 12$ and $w = 8$. Find the perimeter of the rectangle using each formula.
2. When you used the formula $P = 2l + 2w$, did you add first or did you multiply first?
3. When you used the formula $P = 2(l + w)$, did you add first or did you multiply first?
4. Which formula do you prefer to use? Why?

THINK AND DISCUSS

Evaluating Expressions

In the Work Together activity, you used your past experience to simplify the expressions to find the perimeter. Look at this new expression and the two ways that it has been simplified.

$3 + 5 - 6 \div 2$	$3 + 5 - 6 \div 2$
$8 - 6 \div 2$	$3 + 5 - 3$
$2 \div 2$	$8 - 3$
1 ⟵ Different results! ⟶	5 ⟵ This one is correct.

To avoid having two results for the same problem, mathematicians have agreed on an order for doing the operations when simplifying.

Order of Operations

1. Perform any operation(s) inside grouping symbols.
2. Simplify any term with exponents.
3. Multiply and divide in order from left to right.
4. Add and subtract in order from left to right.

QUICK REVIEW

An ***exponent*** indicates repeated multiplication.

base ⟶ $3^4 = 3 \cdot 3 \cdot 3 \cdot 3$ (exponent: 4)

The base 3 is used as a factor four times.

You read 3^4 as "three to the fourth power."

5. Which operation should you do first to simplify each expression?
   a. $3 + 6 \cdot 4 \div 2$ **b.** $3 \cdot 6 - 4^2$ **c.** $3 \cdot (6 - 4) \div 2$

You **evaluate** an expression with variables by substituting a number for each variable. Then simplify the expression using the order of operations.

Example 1 **Relating to the Real World** 

Sales Find the total cost of the sneakers shown in the ad. Use the expression at the right.

$p + r \cdot p$ — p: original price; r: sales tax rate; $r \cdot p$: sales tax

$p + r \cdot p = 59 + (0.06)59$ ← Substitute 59 for p. Change 6% to 0.06 and substitute 0.06 for r.
$= 59 + 3.54$ ← Multiply first.
$= 62.54$ ← Then add.

The total cost of the sneakers is $62.54.

6. **Calculator** Some calculators have the order of operations programmed into them. To check your calculator, use the key sequence below. Does your calculator use the order of operations? Explain.

59 [+] .06 [×] 59 [=]

Keep in mind that the base for an exponent is the number, variable, or expression directly to the left of the exponent.

Example 2

Evaluate $3a^2 - 12 \div b$ for $a = 7$ and $b = 4$.

$3a^2 - 12 \div b = 3 \cdot 7^2 - 12 \div 4$ ← Substitute 7 for a and 4 for b.
$= 3 \cdot 49 - 12 \div 4$ ← Simplify 7^2.
$= 147 - 3$ ← Multiply and divide from left to right.
$= 144$ ← Subtract.

7. A student evaluated the expression above for $a = 8$ and $b = 6$. Her result is 94. Is her answer correct? If not, what error did she make?

8. **Try This** Evaluate $25 \div p + 2q^2$ for $p = 5$ and $q = 7$.

Example 3

Evaluate each expression for $c = 15$ and $d = 12$.

a. cd^2

$cd^2 = 15(12)^2$
$= 15(144)$
$= 2160$

b. $(cd)^2$

$(cd)^2 = (15 \cdot 12)^2$
$= (180)^2$
$= 32{,}400$

CALCULATOR HINT

In part (b), you can use two different key sequences to find 180^2:

180 [x^2] [ENTER] or
180 [^] 2 [ENTER].

9. Write an expression for each phrase. Then simplify your expression.
a. four times three, squared **b.** the square of three, times four

Evaluating Expressions With Grouping Symbols

When you evaluate expressions work within the parentheses first. A fraction bar is also a grouping symbol. Do any calculations above or below a fraction bar before simplifying the fraction.

Example 4 **Relating to the Real World** 

Community Students participating in a neighborhood clean-up project are cleaning a vacant lot, which has the shape of a trapezoid. They plan to turn the vacant lot into a park. Use the expression $h\left(\frac{b_1 + b_2}{2}\right)$ to find the lot's area.

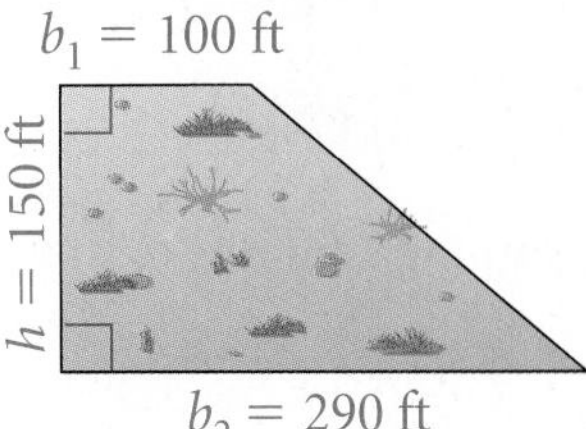

$$
\begin{aligned}
h\left(\frac{b_1 + b_2}{2}\right) &= 150\left(\frac{100 + 290}{2}\right) && \leftarrow \text{Substitute 150 for } h\text{, 100 for } b_1\text{, and 290 for } b_2. \\
&= 150\left(\frac{390}{2}\right) && \leftarrow \text{Simplify the numerator.} \\
&= 150(195) && \leftarrow \text{Simplify the fraction.} \\
&= 29{,}250
\end{aligned}
$$

The area of the lot is 29,250 ft^2.

PROBLEM SOLVING

Look Back You can also use the expression $\frac{1}{2}h(b_1 + b_2)$ to find the area of a trapezoid. Explain why $h\left(\frac{b_1 + b_2}{2}\right)$ is equivalent to $\frac{1}{2}h(b_1 + b_2)$.

10. Would the result be the same if you substituted 290 for b_1 and 100 for b_2? Why or why not?

11. Describe the steps you would use to simplify $\frac{12 + 18}{3 + 9}$.

12. Explain the difference in the meaning of the expressions $5\frac{1}{6}$ and $5\left(\frac{1}{6}\right)$.

You can also use brackets [ ] as grouping symbols. When an expression has several grouping symbols, simplify the innermost expression first.

13. **Try This** Simplify each expression.

a. $5[4^2 + 3(2 + 1)]$ **b.** $12 + 3[18 + 5(16 - 3^2)]$

Exercises ON YOUR OWN

Simplify each numerical expression.

1. $18 + 20 \div 4$ **2.** $(2.4 - 1.6) \div 0.4$ **3.** $\frac{6 \cdot 2 - 1}{9 + 2}$ **4.** $(5^2 - 3)6$

5. $(10 - 2)^2$ **6.** $6\left(\frac{4 + 10}{2}\right)$ **7.** $24.6 \div 2 \cdot 4.1$ **8.** $25 - [2(3 + 7)]$

9. $3 \cdot 5^2$ **10.** $(3 \cdot 5)^2$ **11.** $(5^2 + 3) \div 2$ **12.** $\frac{(2 + 3)^2}{2}$

13. **Open-ended** Write an expression that includes addition, subtraction, multiplication, and parentheses. Simplify your expression.

14. a. **Geometry** What is the volume of the juice can at the right? The formula for the volume of a cylinder is $V = \pi r^2 h$.
    b. About how many cubic inches does an ounce of juice fill?

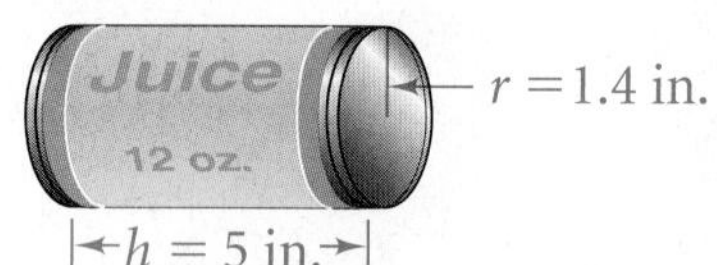

Evaluate each expression.

15. $a - 7 \cdot 2$ for $a = 15$
16. $\frac{q}{q + 8}$ for $q = 4$
17. $r + 2s$ for $r = 5.2$ and $s = 3.8$
18. $5a^2 - 4$ for $a = 3$
19. $2b^2 + 4b$ for $b = 6.3$
20. $(5x)^2$ for $x = 3$
21. $2\left(\frac{5d - 6}{3}\right)$ for $d = 9$
22. $[(5.2 + a) + 4]10$ for $a = 3.5$
23. $\frac{m^2}{m + 9}$ for $m = 6$

Use grouping symbols to make each equation true.

24. $10 + 6 \div 2 - 3 = 5$
25. $14 - 2 + 5 - 3 = 4$
26. $8 + 4 \div 3 - 1 = 10$

27. **Critical Thinking** Use the problem solving strategy *Guess and Test* to find two values of n that make the equation $2n = n^2$ true.

28. a. **Entertainment** You can use the expression $2.4t + 0.779$ to model the number of subscribers, in millions, to cable television. Copy and complete the table.
    b. **Statistics** Use your table to draw a line graph.

Cable TV Subscribers (in millions)

Year	Subscribers
1970 ($t = 0$)	■
1980 ($t = 10$)	■
1990 ($t = 20$)	■
2000 ($t = 30$)	■

Writing **Tell if each equation is *true* or *false*. If false, use the order of operations to explain why.**

29. $3(2^3) = 6^3$
30. $2^4 = (1 + 1)^4$
31. $(4 + 5)^2 = 4^2 + 5^2$

32. **Calculator** Which key sequence could you use to simplify $\frac{3 + 8^2}{5}$? Explain why your choice works and the other choices do not.

A. (3 + 8) ^ 2 ÷ 5 ENTER
B. 3 + 8 ^ 2 ÷ 5 ENTER
C. (3 + 8 ^ 2) ÷ 5 ENTER
D. (3 + 8 ÷ 5 ^ 2) ENTER

Exercises MIXED REVIEW

Write each fraction as a fraction or mixed number in simplest form.

33. $\frac{4}{6}$
34. $\frac{15}{10}$
35. $\frac{27}{6}$
36. $\frac{9}{12}$
37. $\frac{12}{15}$

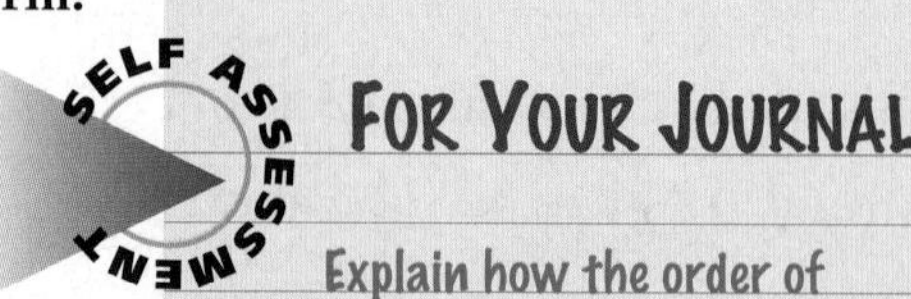

FOR YOUR JOURNAL

Explain how the order of operations prevents confusion when you are simplifying an expression.

Getting Ready for Lesson 1-4

Use the number line at the right.

38. What number corresponds to point A on the number line?
39. How far is B from zero?
40. How far is D from zero?
41. How far is C from zero?
42. How far is A from D?

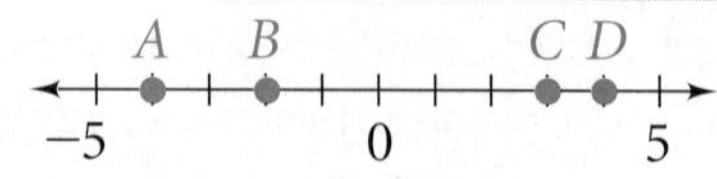

1-4 Adding and Subtracting Integers

What You'll Learn

- Adding and subtracting with integers and decimals
- Finding absolute value
- Evaluating expressions

...And Why

To calculate with data that include negative numbers

WORK TOGETHER

Science Work with a partner. Falling snow has chemical traces of the environmental events that occur each year. In 1994, scientists in Antarctica drilled a core of ice 7000 ft deep. The diagram shows some of what scientists found.

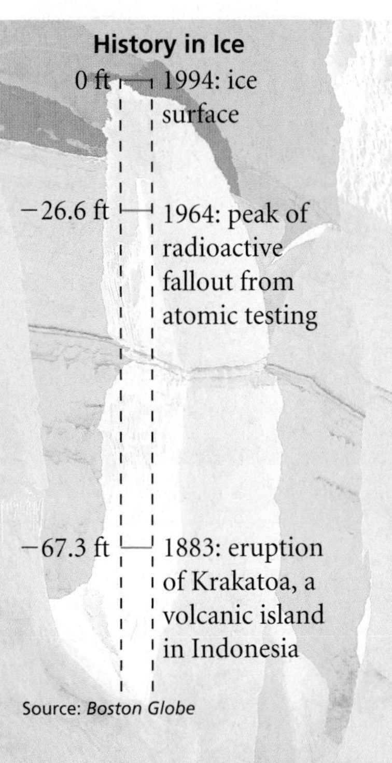

1. Draw a diagram. Place the events listed below where you think they would appear in the core of ice.
   - **a.** 1906: San Francisco earthquake
   - **b.** 1923: Tokyo earthquake and fires
   - **c.** 1935–36: "Dust Bowl" of the U.S.
   - **d.** 1986: nuclear accident at Chernobyl, in the former U.S.S.R.

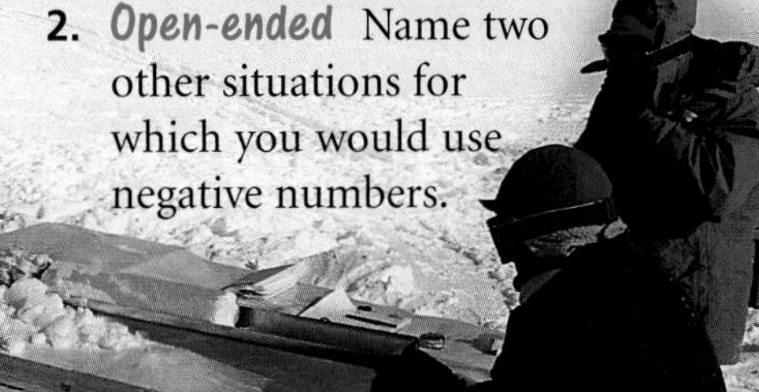

2. **Open-ended** Name two other situations for which you would use negative numbers.

THINK AND DISCUSS

Adding Integers and Decimals

A number line can help you see the relationship between numbers.

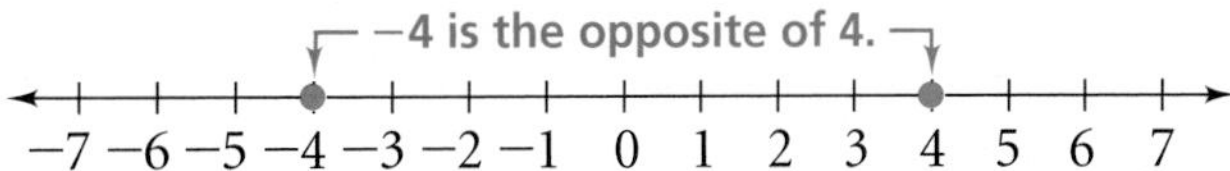

Two numbers are **opposites** if they are the same distance from zero on the number line. Since −4 and 4 are both a distance of 4 units from 0, they are opposites. **Integers** are whole numbers and their opposites.

QUICK REVIEW

Whole numbers are 0, 1, 2, 3 . . . .

3. **Try This** What is the opposite of 3? −5? −100? 0?
4. **Try This** Name the two integers that are a distance of 7 units from 0 on the number line.

Tiles to Represent Integers

■ 1 ■ −1

PROBLEM SOLVING

Look Back Which do you find more helpful when adding: using tiles or using a number line? Explain.

The sum of a number and its opposite, or *additive inverse,* is zero.

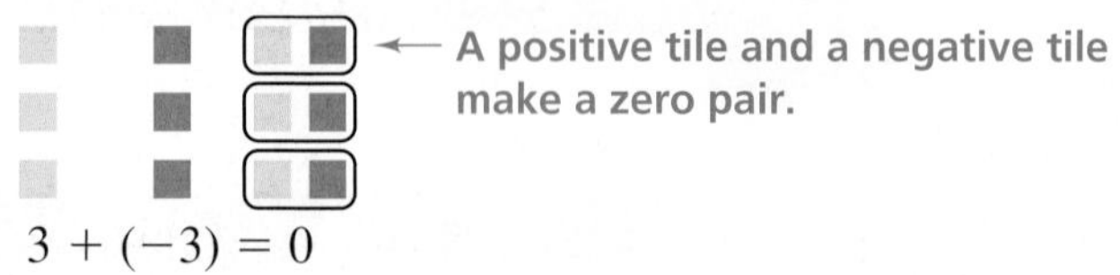
A positive tile and a negative tile make a zero pair.

$3 + (-3) = 0$

Example 1 **Relating to the Real World** 

Sports On two plays a football team gains 2 yd and then loses 7 yd. What is the result of the two plays? You need to find $2 + (-7)$.

Method 1: Use a number line.

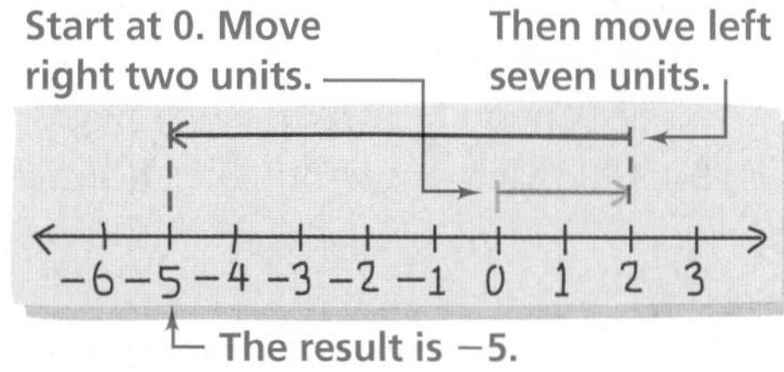
Start at 0. Move right two units.
Then move left seven units.
−6 −5 −4 −3 −2 −1 0 1 2 3
The result is −5.

$2 + (-7) = -5$

Method 2: Use tiles.

Start with 2 positive tiles and 7 negative tiles.

Make zero pairs.

There are 5 negative tiles left.

$2 + (-7) = -5$

The result of the two plays is a loss of 5 yd.

5. **Try This** Use a model to find each sum.
   a. $-6 + 4$ **b.** $4 + (-6)$ **c.** $-3 + (-8)$ **d.** $9 + (-3)$

To understand the rules for addition, you need to be familiar with absolute value. The **absolute value** of a number is its distance from zero on a number line. Using symbols, you write "the absolute value of −6" as $|-6|$.

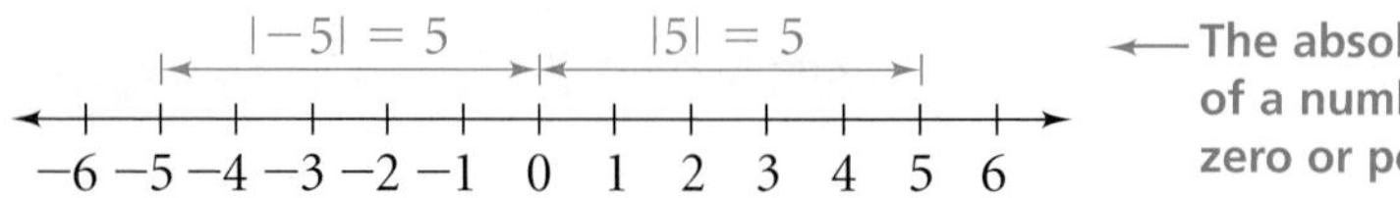
|−5| = 5
|5| = 5
−6 −5 −4 −3 −2 −1 0 1 2 3 4 5 6

The absolute value of a number is either zero or positive.

Absolute value symbols are also grouping symbols. Simplify expressions within absolute value symbols before finding the absolute value.

6. **Try This** Find the value of each expression.
   a. $|-12|$ **b.** $|2.5|$ **c.** $|-5 + 3|$ **d.** $|5 + (-5)|$

7. What is the sign of each sum?
   a. $6 + 4$ **b.** $4 + 6$ **c.** $-6 + (-4)$ **d.** $-4 + (-6)$

8. Use your answers to Question 7. When adding two numbers that have the same sign, how can you **predict** the sign of their sum?

9. For each expression below, which number has the greater absolute value? What is the sign of each sum?
   a. $6 + (-4)$ **b.** $-4 + 6$ **c.** $-6 + 4$ **d.** $4 + (-6)$

10. Use your answers to Question 9. When adding two numbers that have different signs, how can you **predict** the sign of their sum?

Addition Rules

To add two numbers with the same sign, *add* their absolute values. The sum has the same sign as the numbers.

Example: $3 + 5 = 8$ $\quad -3 + (-5) = -8$

To add two numbers with different signs, find the *difference* between their absolute values. The sum has the same sign as the number with the greater absolute value.

Example: $-3 + 5 = 2$ $\quad 3 + (-5) = -2$

CALCULATOR HINT

To find $-12.5 + 4.8$, use this sequence:

(-) 12.5 + 4.8 ENTER

11. Try This Find each sum.

a. $-12 + 4$ **b.** $26 + (-8)$ **c.** $-12.5 + 4.8$ **d.** $14.7 + (-8.3)$

12. Try This Evaluate each expression for $n = 3.5$.

a. $5.2 + n$ **b.** $-5.2 + n$ **c.** $-n + 5.2$ **d.** $-n + (-5.2)$

Subtracting Integers and Decimals

Example 2

Find each difference.

a. $4 - 7$

← Start with 4 positive tiles.

← Add zero pairs until there are 7 positive tiles.

← Remove 7 positive tiles.

There are 3 negative tiles left.

$4 - 7 = -3$

b. $3 - (-5)$

← Start with 3 positive tiles.

← Add zero pairs until there are 5 negative tiles.

← Remove 5 negative tiles.

There are 8 positive tiles left.

$3 - (-5) = 8$

Math A Test Prep

1 Which expression has a value of 16?
(1) $20 \div 5 + 4 \cdot 2$
(2) $4^2 \cdot 3 - 2$
(3) $21 \div 3 + (4 - 1)^2$
(4) $(7^2 - 11) \cdot 3$

2 Use an equation to model this situation: The total cost of a refrigerator is the cost of the item and the $39 delivery charge.

13. Use tiles to find each difference and sum.
a. $2 - 6$, $2 + (-6)$ **b.** $5 - (-9)$, $5 + 9$ **c.** $-3 - 8$, $-3 + (-8)$ **d.** $7 - 2$, $7 + (-2)$

14. Use your answers to Question 13. What do you notice about each pair of sums and differences?

The relationship you found between subtraction and addition is summarized in a rule for subtraction.

Subtraction Rule

To subtract a number, add its opposite.

Example: $3 - 5 = 3 + (-5)$
$= -2$

15. **Try This** Find each difference.
a. $-6 - 2$ **b.** $8 - (-4)$ **c.** $7.1 - (-5.4)$ **d.** $11.5 - 15.6$

The expression $-n$ means the opposite of n. The expression $-n$ can represent a negative number, zero, or a positive number.

16. **a.** What is the value of $-n$ when $n = -4$?
b. What is the value of $-n$ when $n = 4$?
c. For what values of n will $-n$ be positive? negative?

Example 3

Evaluate $-a - b$ for $a = -3$ and $b = -5$.

$-a - b = -(-3) - (-5)$ ← Substitute –3 for a and –5 for b.
$= 3 - (-5)$ ← The opposite of –3 is 3.
$= 3 + 5$ ← To subtract –5, add its opposite, 5.
$= 8$

17. ***Open-ended*** Choose negative values for a and b other than -3 and -5. Evaluate the expression in Example 3 using the values you chose.

Exercises ON YOUR OWN

1. ***Critical Thinking*** Which is greater, the sum of -227 and 319 or the sum of 227 and -319? Explain.

2. ***Open-ended*** Use a number line or tiles to show why the sum of a number and its opposite is zero.

Write *positive* or *negative* to indicate the sign of the sum or difference.

3. $-6 + 13$ **4.** $6 - 13$ **5.** $-6 + (-13)$ **6.** $6 - (-13)$ **7.** $|-6 - 13|$

Evaluate each expression for $p = 4$ and $q = -3$.

8. $3 - q$ **9.** $3p - q$ **10.** $q - 7p$ **11.** $|p - 9|$ **12.** $|-12 + q|$

Choose **Use a calculator, paper and pencil, or mental math to add or subtract.**

13. $-21 + (-14)$ **14.** $13 + (-9)$ **15.** $6 - (-5)$ **16.** $-12 + 12$

17. $-16 - 12$ **18.** $|-16 - 12|$ **19.** $|-16| - |12|$ **20.** $15 - 19$

21. $-18.6 - 25.3$ **22.** $14.4 - 19.7$ **23.** $|43.7 + (-45.2)|$ **24.** $-25.7 - (-18.3)$

25. $62.5 - 89.4$ **26.** $-54.1 + 99.4$ **27.** $|-28.2| + 17.5$ **28.** $-65.7 - 98.9$

Critical Thinking **Use the number line for Exercises 29 – 31.**

29. If P is the opposite of T, what is the value of S?

30. If Q is the opposite of T, is R positive or negative? Why?

31. If R is the opposite of T, which of the labeled points has the greatest absolute value? Why?

32. **Critical Thinking** Explain what is wrong with the reasoning in the statement: *Since 20 is the opposite of −20, then 20∞F must be very hot, because −20∞F is very cold.*

33. **Critical Thinking** Is $|a - b|$ always equal to $|b - a|$? Use examples to illustrate your answer.

34. **Physics** Superconductors allow for very efficient passage of electric currents. For practical use, a superconductor must work above −196°C (the boiling point of nitrogen). In 1987, Paul Chu discovered a new class of materials that conduct electricity at −178°C.

a. At how many degrees above the boiling point of nitrogen did the new materials conduct electricity?

b. In 1990, researchers created a miniature transistor that conducts electricity at a temperature that is 48°C above the boiling point of nitrogen. What temperature is this?

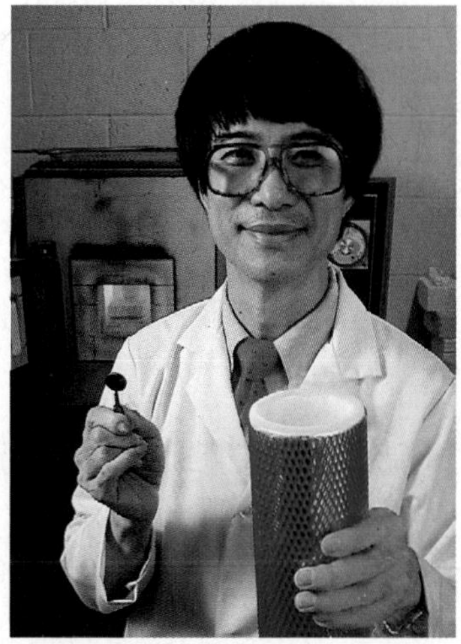

Paul Ching-Wu Chu (b. 1941) is a physicist who heads a research group at the University of Houston.

35. **Critical Thinking** In the cartoon below, does the total "12 27" make sense? Explain.

Frank & Ernest

36. *Geography* Suppose you travel from Park Headquarters to the floor of Death Valley.
   a. What is your change in elevation?
   b. Why does it make sense to write your change in elevation with a negative number?

Telescope Peak to Death Valley

Site	Elevation
Telescope Peak	11,049 ft
Park Headquarters	−190 ft
Floor of Death Valley	−282 ft

37. Find the change in elevation from Telescope Peak to Death Valley.

38. *Writing* Suppose a friend missed class today. Write an explanation for adding two numbers with different signs.

Evaluate each expression for $a = -2$, $b = 3$, and $c = -4$.

39. $6 - a$
40. $a - b + c$
41. $c - b + a$
42. $|-a + 2|$
43. $-|a|$
44. $|a| + |b|$
45. $|a + b|$
46. $-|3 + a|$
47. $a - b$
48. $b - a$
49. $4b - a$
50. $4b - |a|$
51. $a + 3b$
52. $|a| + |3b|$
53. $c + a + 5$
54. $|c + a + 5|$

55. *Standardized Test Prep* Evaluate $(a - b) - (c - d)$ for $a = -15$, $b = -8$, $c = 6$, and $d = 9$.
   A. −20 B. −4 C. −10 D. −26 E. none of these

56. *Chemistry* A charged particle of magnesium has 12 protons and 10 electrons. Each proton has a charge of $^{+}1$ and each electron a charge of $^{-}1$. What is the total charge of the particle?

Exercises MIXED REVIEW

57. a. *Statistics* Draw a graph of the data in the table to show change in tuition from 1990 to 1993.
   b. Why did you choose the graph you drew?
   c. *Open-ended* **Predict** what the tuition will be for a 2-year public college and a 4-year public college the year you graduate from high school. Explain.

Yearly College Tuition 1990–1993

Year	Public 2-Year Colleges	Public 4-Year Colleges
1990	$ 756	$2035
1991	$ 824	$2159
1992	$ 937	$2410
1993	$1018	$2610

Evaluate each expression.

58. $5t + 6$ for $t = 2$
59. $18 - 7m$ for $m = 2$

Simplify.

60. $\frac{3 + 5}{6 + 10}$
61. $\frac{7 - 2}{12 + 8}$
62. $\frac{1 + 4}{21 - 6}$
63. $\frac{8 - 5}{16 - 7}$

Getting Ready for Lesson 1-5

Patterns **Write the next three numbers in each pattern.**

64. −5, −1, 3, ■, ■, ■
65. 9, 6, 3, 0, ■, ■, ■
66. −15, −10, −5, ■, ■, ■
67. 6, 4, 2, ■, ■, ■

What You'll Learn

- Multiplying and dividing with integers and decimals
- Simplifying expressions with exponents
- Evaluating expressions

...And Why

To compute with real-world data, like temperatures, that are negative as well as positive

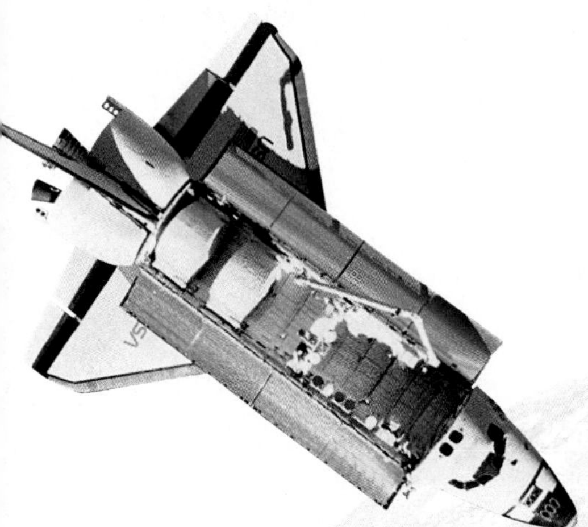

1-5 Multiplying and Dividing Integers

WORK TOGETHER

Work with a partner.

Space Flight When the space shuttle is in the first stage of its return to Earth, it descends about 3.5 mi/min. You can write the rate as -3.5 mi/min.

To find how far the shuttle descends in 10 min, you need to find $(-3.5)(10)$. You know that $(3.5)(10) = 35$.

1. Did the shuttle's altitude *increase* or *decrease* during the 10 min?
2. Which phrase better describes descending 35 mi? Why?
   A. a change in altitude of 35 mi **B.** a change in altitude of –35 mi
3. Is the product (–3.5)(10) equal to 35 or –35? Why?
4. Tell which result makes more sense and explain why.

	Situation	Expression	Result
a.	in football, the total of 2 penalties of 5 yd each	$2(-5)$	10 or -10?
b.	the average hourly decrease in temperature when it falls 20°F in a 4-h period	$\frac{-20}{4}$	5 or -5?
c.	the monthly income of a company with losses of $48,000 for one year	$\frac{-48{,}000}{12}$	4000 or -4000?

5. **a. Generalize:** Is the product of a positive and a negative number *positive* or *negative*?
   b. Generalize: Is the quotient of a positive and a negative number *positive* or *negative*?
6. **Patterns** Use your knowledge of patterns to complete each column.

a.	b.
$3 \cdot (-4) = ■$	$15 \div (-5) = ■$
$2 \cdot (-4) = ■$	$10 \div (-5) = ■$
$1 \cdot (-4) = ■$	$5 \div (-5) = ■$
$0 \cdot (-4) = ■$	$0 \div (-5) = ■$
$-1 \cdot (-4) = ■$	$-5 \div (-5) = ■$
$-2 \cdot (-4) = ■$	$-10 \div (-5) = ■$
$-3 \cdot (-4) = ■$	$-15 \div (-5) = ■$

7. Use the patterns you developed in Question 6. Is the product or quotient of two negative numbers positive or negative?
8. Compare your results with another pair of students. If you do not have the same results, explain your reasoning to each other.

THINK AND DISCUSS

Multiplying and Dividing

The multiplication and division rules summarize what you discovered in the Work Together activity.

QUICK REVIEW

You can indicate division using a fraction bar. $\frac{15}{5}$ means $15 \div 5$. Remember that division by 0 is undefined.

MULTIPLICATION AND DIVISION RULES

The product or quotient of two positive numbers is positive. The product or quotient of two negative numbers is positive.

Examples: $3 \cdot 5 = 15$ $\quad -3 \cdot (-5) = 15$

$\frac{15}{5} = 3$ $\quad \frac{-15}{-5} = 3$

The product or quotient of a positive number and a negative number is negative.

Examples: $-3 \cdot 5 = -15$ $\quad 3 \cdot (-5) = -15$

$\frac{-15}{5} = -3$ $\quad \frac{15}{-5} = -3$

Example 1

Evaluate $\frac{-x}{-4} + 2yz$ for $x = -20$, $y = 6$, and $z = -1$.

$\frac{-x}{-4} + 2yz = \frac{-(-20)}{-4} + 2(6)(-1)$ ← Substitute –20 for *x*, 6 for *y*, and –1 for *z*.

$= \frac{20}{-4} + 2(6)(-1)$ ← The opposite of –20 is 20.

$= -5 + (-12)$ ← Divide and multiply.

$= -17$ ← Add.

9. **Try This** Evaluate the expression in Example 1 for $x = 8$, $y = -7$, and $z = -3$.

When you divide, sometimes you need to round your result. The number line shows that -5.8 is closer to -6 than to -5. So, you round -5.8 to -6.

−5.8
−6 −5

21 The Weekly Herald

Fairbanks, Alaska One Week in January

	High	Low
Sunday	−17°	−38°
Monday	−18°	−38°
Tuesday	−9°	−32°
Wednesday	−7°	−33°
Thursday	−6°	−31°
Friday	4°	−33°
Saturday	1°	−34°

Temperatures in Fahrenheit

Example 2 Relating to the Real World

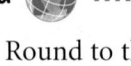

Math in the Media Find the mean high temperature. Round to the nearest degree.

$$\text{mean high temperature} = \frac{-17 + (-18) + (-9) + (-7) + (-6) + 4 + 1}{7}$$

$$= \frac{-52}{7}$$

$$\approx -7.428571429$$

The mean high temperature is about –7°F.

10. Try This Find the mean low temperature to the nearest degree.

11. a. Suppose the temperature at 6 P.M. is $-8°$. Write an equation to find the temperature if the temperature falls 2°/h. Let n represent the number of hours since 6 P.M.
    b. Find the temperature at 10 P.M.

12. Try This **Predict** whether the product of each expression is *positive* or *negative.* Then multiply.
    a. $(-1)(-2)$
    b. $(-1)(-2)(-3)$
    c. $(-1)(-2)(-3)(-4)$
    d. $(-1)(-2)(-3)(-4)(-5)$

13. Use your results in Question 12 to complete each statement.
    a. For an even number of negative factors, the product will be __?__.
    b. For an odd number of negative factors, the product will be __?__.
    c. For a product that includes negative and positive factors, do the positive factors affect the sign of the product?

Simplifying Expressions with Exponents

A term like -3^4 means the opposite of 3^4. Keep this in mind as you simplify expressions that have exponents and negatives.

QUICK REVIEW

1. Perform operations inside grouping symbols.
2. Simplify any terms with exponents.
3. Multiply and divide in order from left to right.
4. Add and subtract in order from left to right.

Example 3

Use the order of operations to simplify each expression.

a. -3^4

$$-3^4 = -(3 \cdot 3 \cdot 3 \cdot 3) = -81$$

b. $(-3)^4$

$$(-3)^4 = (-3)(-3)(-3)(-3) = 81$$

14. Evaluate each expression for $b = -2$.

    Sample: $b^2 = (-2)^2 = 4$

    a. b^3 b. b^4 c. b^5 d. b^6

15. Critical Thinking How can you use the exponent to predict whether an expression like $(-2)^{76}$ is positive or negative?

Exercises ON YOUR OWN

Simplify.

1. $10(-12)$
2. $(-8)(-5)$
3. -9^2
4. $(-9)^2$
5. $18 \div (-3)$
6. $-18 \div (-3)$
7. $\frac{-36}{9}$
8. $(-20)(-5)$
9. $(-1)^{23}$
10. $-(-2)^3$
11. $(-2)(5)(-3)$
12. $3(-4)^3$
13. $|4 + 8(-6)|$
14. $13 - 3(6)$
15. $\frac{(3 - 14)}{-2}$
16. $(-5)(-1)^4$

17. Suppose a and b are integers.
  a. When is the product ab positive?
  b. When is the product ab negative?

18. a. A parachutist opens her parachute at an altitude of 5000 feet. Her change in altitude is -25 ft/s. Write an equation to find her altitude at time t after she opens her parachute.
  b. How far has she descended in 12.5 s?
  c. What is her altitude 12.5 s after she opens her parachute?

Evaluate each expression for $m = -4$, $n = 3$, and $p = -1$.

19. mn
20. mnp
21. $3m - n$
22. $-5p^2$
23. $2m$
24. $7p - 2n$
25. m^3
26. $\frac{m}{p} - n$
27. $\frac{m}{n}$
28. $8p \div (-2n)$
29. $4n^3 \div m$
30. $m \div n + (-n)$

31. **Writing** In your own words, write the rules for adding, subtracting, multiplying, and dividing a positive number and a negative number. Write an example for each rule.

32. **Critical Thinking** Does $|ab|$ always equal $|a| \cdot |b|$? Explain.

Is the value of each expression *positive* or *negative*? Explain.

33. $(-3)^4$
34. $(-4)^3$
35. $(-3)^{103}$
36. $(10)^5$
37. $-(-3)^2$
38. $(-7)^2$
39. -5^{10}
40. -5^{11}

Open-ended **Use $a = -3$, $b = 2$, and $c = -5$ to write an expression that has each value.**

41. 17
42. 0
43. -1
44. 1
45. 7

46. **Oceanography** To map the features of the ocean floor, scientists take several sonar readings. Find the mean of these readings: $-14{,}235$ ft; $-14{,}246$ ft; and $-14{,}230$ ft.

47. Complete each statement:
  a. $(-7)^n < 0$ if n is __?__.
  b. $(-7)^n > 0$ if n is __?__.

48. **Entertainment** You can find the approximate height, in feet, above the ground of a roller-coaster car plunging down the hill of the roller coaster at the right. Use the formula $h = 155 - 16t^2$ where t is the number of seconds since the start of the descent.
  a. How far is a rider from the bottom of the hill after 1 s? 2 s?
  b. **Critical Thinking** Does it take more than or less than 4 s to reach the bottom? Explain.
  c. Use your calculator and the problem solving strategy *Guess and Test* to find the time the roller coaster descends to the nearest tenth of a second.

Chapter Project — *Find Out by Calculating*

Scientists use these formulas to approximate a person's height H, in inches, when they know the length of the tibia t, the humerus h, or the radius r.

- Use your tibia, humerus, and radius bone lengths to calculate your height. Are the calculated heights close to your actual height? Explain.
- An archaeologist found an 18-in. tibia on the site of an American colonial farm. Do you think it belonged to a man or a woman? Why?
- Choose one radius measurement from the data you collected for the Find Out question on page 9. Calculate the person's height. Can you tell whose height you have found? Explain.

Male
$H = 32.2 + 2.4t$
$H = 29.0 + 3.0h$
$H = 31.7 + 3.7r$
Female
$H = 28.6 + 2.5t$
$H = 25.6 + 3.1h$
$H = 28.9 + 3.9r$

Exercises MIXED REVIEW

Statistics **Use the line plot at the right.**

49. How many people watched more than three hours of television?

50. What other kind of graph could you use for the data? Explain.

51. a. Find the mean, median, and mode of the data.
b. Is the *mean*, *median*, or *mode* the most useful to describe people's viewing habits? Why?

Hours Spent Watching TV Each Day

```
X
X   X       X
X   X   X   X
X   X   X   X   X   X
1   2   3   4   5   6
```

Getting Ready for Lesson 1-6

Find each sum or difference.

52. $\frac{3}{8} + \frac{1}{4}$ **53.** $\frac{7}{12} - \frac{1}{3}$ **54.** $\frac{5}{6} + \frac{2}{3}$ **55.** $\frac{1}{2} - \frac{1}{6}$ **56.** $\frac{7}{8} - \frac{3}{5}$

Exercises CHECKPOINT

Simplify.

1. $8 + 4 \cdot 3$ **2.** $(-3)^2 + (-5)$ **3.** $\frac{7+5}{7-5}$ **4.** $(9^2 - 60) \div 3$

Evaluate each expression for $a = -7$ and $b = 4$.

5. $-a$ **6.** a^2 **7.** $a + b$ **8.** $|a - b|$ **9.** $2b^2 + 3a$

10. **Writing** Is -5^2 positive or negative? Explain.

11. Find the mean, median, and mode. Round to the nearest tenth.
$-12, 15, 8, -4, -6, 7, -4, 8, -5, -12, 0, -2, 5, -4$

12. Write an equation to describe the relationship shown at the right.

boxes	tissues
1	175
2	350
3	525

1-6 Real Numbers and Rational Numbers

What You'll Learn

- Comparing and ordering rational numbers
- Evaluating expressions with rational numbers

...And Why

To solve real-world problems, such as converting temperatures

What You'll Need

- calculator

THINK AND DISCUSS

Comparing Rational Numbers

The Venn diagram shows the relationship of sets of numbers.

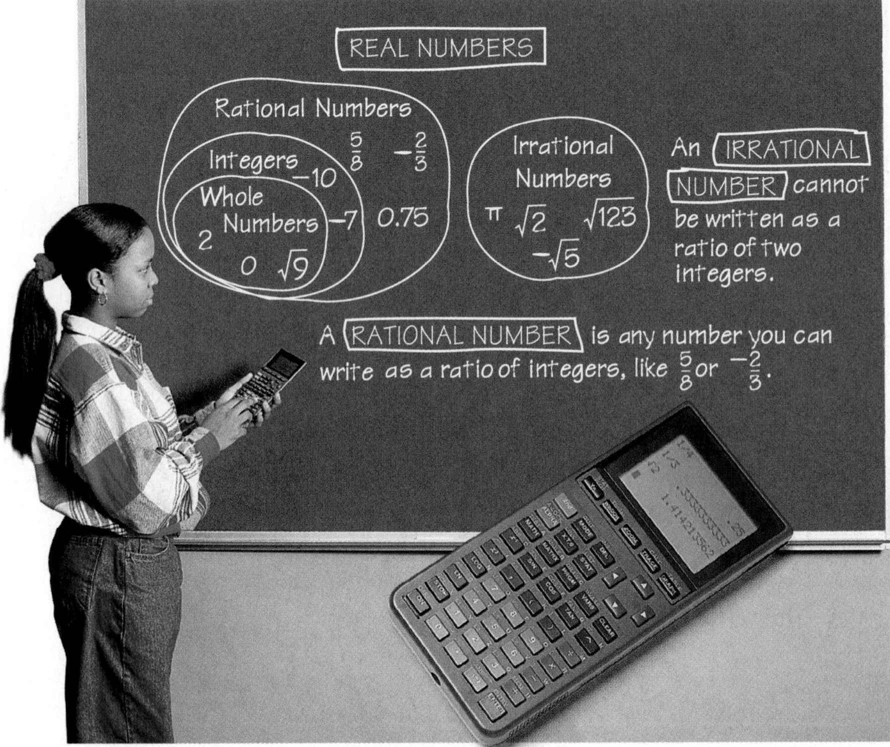

QUICK REVIEW

$\frac{1}{4} = 0.25$, which is a terminating decimal.

$\frac{1}{3} = 0.\overline{3}$, which is a repeating decimal.

Integers are rational numbers because you can write them as ratios using 1 as the denominator: $7 = \frac{7}{1}$. Rational and irrational numbers make up the set of **real numbers.**

1. Write three numbers that are rational numbers but not integers. Choose numbers different from the ones in the diagram above.
2. Show that 0.75 is a rational number by writing it as a ratio.
3. ***Open-ended*** Where have you used irrational numbers?
4. ***Calculator*** Use a calculator to find the square root of the numbers 1 through 10. Which do you think are rational? irrational?

An irrational number expressed in decimal form is a nonterminating and nonrepeating decimal. If you use a calculator to express an irrational number as a decimal, the calculator gives you a decimal approximation.

Math A Test Prep

1 What is the value of $|a - b|$ when $a = -2$ and $b = 6$?
(1) 4
(2) 8
(3) −4
(4) −8

2 The average temperature for one day is the mean of the day's high temperature and the day's low temperature. One January day, the high was 8°F and the low was −12°F. What was the average temperature for that day?

When you compare two real numbers, only one of these can be true:

$a < b$	or	$a = b$	or	$a > b$
less than		**equal to**		**greater than**

Example 1

Use a number line to compare $-\frac{1}{8}$ and $-\frac{1}{2}$.

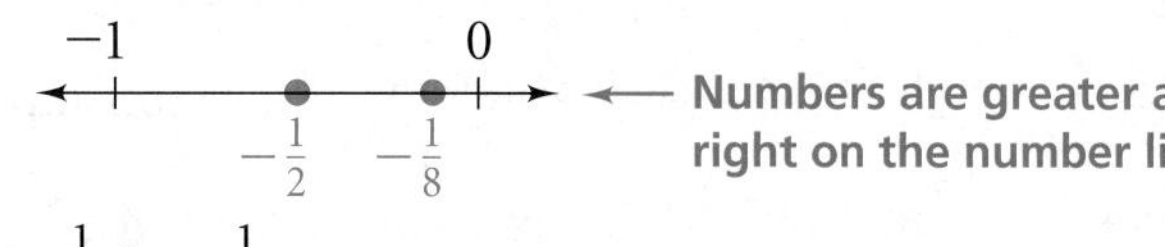

−1
0
$-\frac{1}{2}$
$-\frac{1}{8}$
Numbers are greater as you move to the right on the number line.

$-\frac{1}{8} > -\frac{1}{2}$

5. Rewrite the answer to Example 1 using the symbol for *less than*.

6. **Critical Thinking** Suppose you are comparing $-25\frac{1}{2}$ and $-25\frac{1}{8}$. Do you need a different number line from the one in Example 1 to determine which mixed number is greater? Explain.

Many ratios are not easy to compare using a number line. Another method is to write the ratios as decimals and then compare.

Example 2

Write $-\frac{3}{8}$, $-\frac{1}{2}$, and $-\frac{5}{12}$ in order from least to greatest.

Use a calculator to write the rational numbers as decimals.

$-\frac{3}{8}$	(−) 3 ÷ 8 ENTER	−.375
$-\frac{1}{2}$	(−) 1 ÷ 2 ENTER	−.5
$-\frac{5}{12}$	(−) 5 ÷ 12 ENTER	−.4166666667

$-0.5 < -0.41\overline{6} < -0.375$

From least to greatest the ratios are $-\frac{1}{2}$, $-\frac{5}{12}$, and $-\frac{3}{8}$.

7. **Try This** Write $\frac{1}{12}$, $-\frac{2}{3}$, and $-\frac{5}{8}$ in order from least to greatest.

Evaluating Expressions

You evaluate expressions using rational numbers by substituting and performing the indicated operations.

Example 3

Evaluate $a + 2b$ where $a = \frac{2}{3}$ and $b = -\frac{5}{8}$.

$a + 2b = \frac{2}{3} + 2\left(-\frac{5}{8}\right)$ ← Substitute the values for *a* and *b*.

$= \frac{2}{3} - \frac{5}{4}$

$= -\frac{7}{12}$

CALCULATOR HINT

You can use this key sequence:

(2 ÷ 3) − (5 ÷ 4) ENTER

Example 4 Relating to the Real World 

Weather Use the expression $\frac{5}{9}(F - 32)$ to change from the Fahrenheit scale to the Celsius scale. What is 10°F in Celsius?

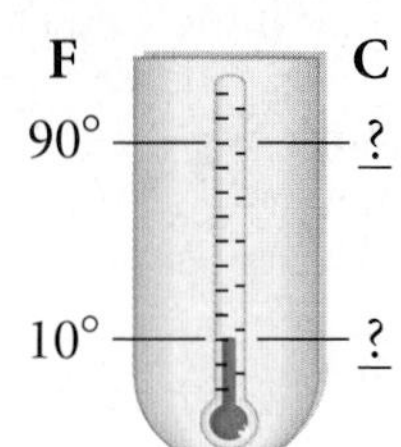

$$\frac{5}{9}(F - 32) = \frac{5}{9}(10 - 32) \quad \leftarrow \text{Substitute 10 for } F.$$
$$= \frac{5}{9}(-22)$$
$$\approx -12$$

The temperature is about -12°C.

8. Find the Celsius temperature when the Fahrenheit temperature is 90°.

The **reciprocal,** or *multiplicative inverse,* of a nonzero number $\frac{a}{b}$ is $\frac{b}{a}$. Zero does not have a reciprocal because division by zero is undefined.

9. a. **Patterns** Complete the chart.

b. What is the product of a number and its reciprocal?

10. Is a number's reciprocal the same as its opposite? Explain.

Number	Reciprocal	Product
3	$\frac{1}{3}$	$3 \cdot \frac{1}{3} =$ ■
$\frac{1}{5}$	$\frac{5}{1}$ or 5	$\frac{1}{5} \cdot 5 =$ ■
$-\frac{2}{3}$	$-\frac{3}{2}$	$-\frac{2}{3} \cdot \left(-\frac{3}{2}\right) =$ ■

You know $12 \div 3 = 12 \cdot \frac{1}{3}$. This means that dividing by a nonzero number is the same as multiplying by its reciprocal.

$$a \div \frac{b}{c} = a \cdot \frac{c}{b} \text{ for } b \neq 0 \text{ and } c \neq 0$$

Example 5

Evaluate $\frac{x}{y}$ for $x = -\frac{3}{4}$ and $y = -\frac{5}{2}$.

$$\frac{x}{y} = x \div y$$
$$= -\frac{3}{4} \div \left(-\frac{5}{2}\right)$$
$$= -\frac{3}{4} \cdot \left(-\frac{2}{5}\right) \quad \leftarrow \text{Multiply by } -\tfrac{2}{5}\text{, the reciprocal of } -\tfrac{5}{2}.$$
$$= \frac{3}{10}$$

11. **Try This** Evaluate the expression in Example 5 for $x = 8$ and $y = -\frac{4}{5}$.

Exercises ON YOUR OWN

Use <, =, or > to compare.

1. $1\frac{2}{3}$ ■ $1\frac{1}{6}$

2. $-1\frac{2}{3}$ ■ $-1\frac{1}{6}$

3. $\frac{15}{8}$ ■ $1\frac{6}{8}$

4. $\frac{3}{5}$ ■ 0.6

5. $\frac{1}{2}$ ■ $\frac{1}{4}$

6. 0.14 ■ $\frac{1}{7}$

7. $-17\frac{1}{5}$ ■ $-17\frac{1}{4}$

8. -3.02 ■ -3.002

Complete with a rational number that makes each statement true.

9. $\frac{3}{5} \cdot ■ = 1$

10. $-4 \cdot ■ = 1$

11. $■ \cdot \frac{7}{8} = 1$

12. $■ \cdot \left(-\frac{8}{3}\right) = 1$

Evaluate.

13. $x - \frac{3}{4}$ for $x = -1\frac{1}{4}$

14. $a - b$ for $a = -\frac{1}{2}, b = \frac{1}{5}$

15. rs for $r = \frac{2}{15}, s = 5$

16. $-p + t$ for $p = 1\frac{3}{8}, t = \frac{5}{8}$

17. $2xy$ for $x = -\frac{2}{3}, y = -\frac{3}{4}$

18. $\frac{v}{w}$ for $v = -\frac{5}{8}, w = -\frac{5}{6}$

19. ab for $a = 2\frac{1}{4}, b = -3$

20. $\frac{m}{n}$ for $m = -\frac{1}{2}, n = 5$

21. $\frac{1}{2}(q - p)$ for $q = 4, p = -\frac{1}{3}$

22. $4rs$ for $r = -3\frac{1}{4}, s = -\frac{1}{5}$

23. $b + c$ for $b = -2\frac{1}{3}, c = \frac{1}{4}$

24. $\frac{1}{5}z - y$ for $z = 1.5, y = 0.3$

Write each group of numbers in order from least to greatest.

25. $-\frac{1}{2}, -\frac{2}{3}, \frac{1}{4}$

26. $-1.5, -\frac{4}{3}, -1\frac{1}{4}$

27. $-9.7, -9\frac{7}{12}, -9\frac{3}{4}$

28. $-4.12, -4.22, -4.05$

29. **Science** Air temperature drops as altitude increases. In the formula $t = (-5.5)\left(\frac{a}{1000}\right)$, t is the approximate change in Fahrenheit temperature, and a is the increase in altitude in feet.

a. Find the change in temperature for the balloon.

b. Suppose the temperature is 40°F at ground level. What is the approximate temperature at the balloon?

c. **Research** Find the height of a mountain that is near you or that you are interested in. Suppose the temperature at the base of the mountain is 80°F. What is the approximate temperature at the top of the mountain?

30. **Weather** In the formula $w = -39 + \frac{3}{2}t$, w is the approximate windchill temperature when the wind speed is 20 mi/h, and t is the actual air temperature. Find the approximate windchill temperature when the actual air temperature is 10°F and the wind speed is 20 mi/h.

Rewrite each expression using the symbol ÷, then find each quotient.

Sample $\frac{-\frac{7}{12}}{4} = -\frac{7}{12} \div 4$ ← Rewrite as $-\frac{7}{12} \div 4$.

$= -\frac{7}{12} \cdot \left(\frac{1}{4}\right)$ ← Multiply by $\frac{1}{4}$, the reciprocal of 4.

$= -\frac{7}{48}$

31. $\frac{\frac{3}{8}}{-\frac{2}{3}}$

32. $\frac{5}{\frac{4}{9}}$

33. $\frac{-\frac{5}{6}}{8}$

34. $\frac{-\frac{2}{5}}{-\frac{4}{5}}$

35. **a.** **Open-ended** Name a point between -2 and -3 on a number line.

b. Name a point between -2.8 and -2.9.

c. Name a point between $-2\frac{1}{16}$ and $-2\frac{3}{8}$.

d. On a number line, is it possible to find a point between any two given points? Explain.

Evaluate.

36. $x + y$ for $x = \frac{13}{4}, y = -\frac{5}{2}$

37. $\frac{1}{5}(r - t)$ for $r = 6, t = -7$

38. $\frac{3}{4}w - 7$ for $w = 1\frac{1}{3}$

39. $\frac{x}{2y}$ for $x = 3.6, y = -0.4$

40. $\frac{3a}{b} + c$ for $a = -2, b = -5, c = -1$

41. $\frac{n}{m}$ for $n = -\frac{4}{5}, m = 8$

Writing **Decide if each statement is *true* or *false*. Justify your answer.**

42. All integers are rational numbers.

43. All negative numbers are integers.

44. All rational numbers are integers.

45. Some real numbers are integers.

Exercises MIXED REVIEW

For Exercises 46–48, write an equation to model each situation.

46. the cost of several movie tickets that are $6.26 each

47. the change from a $10 bill after a purchase

48. the total cost of an item with a shipping fee of $3.98.

49. **Real Estate** Boulder City, Nevada, bought 107,500 acres of land in Nevada's Eldorado Valley from the United States government. The price was $12/acre. How much did the city pay for the land?

Getting Ready for Lesson 1-7

50. **Probability** How much of the spinner is red? yellow? blue?

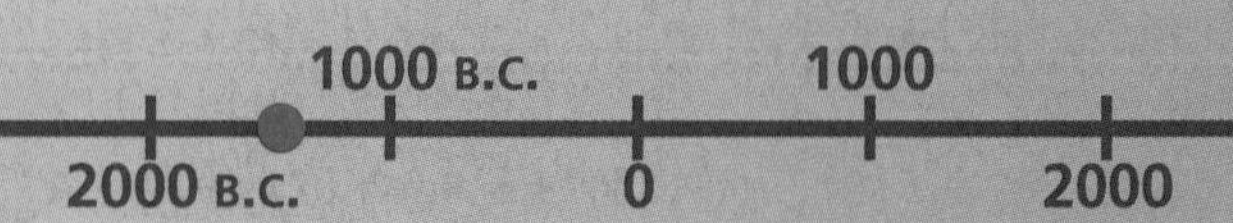

The Rhind Papyrus

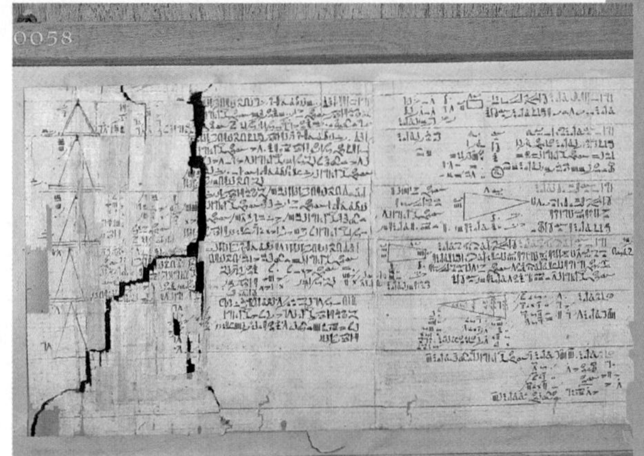

A scroll discovered in Egypt shows that Egyptians were using symbols for plus, minus, equals, and an unknown quantity over 3500 years ago. Named for the British Egyptologist A. Henry Rhind, the papyrus is 18 ft long and 1 ft wide. It is a practical handbook containing 85 problems including work with rational numbers. In the Rhind Papyrus, rational numbers are written as unit fractions. A unit fraction has 1 as its numerator. Here are some examples.

$\frac{3}{4} = \frac{1}{2} + \frac{1}{4}$ $\quad \frac{3}{8} = \frac{1}{4} + \frac{1}{8}$ $\quad \frac{21}{30} = \frac{1}{6} + \frac{1}{5} + \frac{1}{3}$

Math ToolboX

Skills Review

Using Properties

After Lesson 1-6

These properties of mathematics help you to perform arithmetic and algebraic operations.

Commutative Properties of Addition and Multiplication

For all real numbers a and b:

$a + b = b + a$ $\quad$ $a \cdot b = b \cdot a$

Examples: $2 + 3 = 3 + 2$ $\quad$ $4 \cdot 5 = 5 \cdot 4$

Associative Properties of Addition and Multiplication

For all real numbers a, b, and c:

$(a + b) + c = a + (b + c)$ $\quad$ $(a \cdot b) \cdot c = a \cdot (b \cdot c)$

Examples: $(5 + 6) + 7 = 5 + (6 + 7)$ $\quad$ $(2 \cdot 3) \cdot 4 = 2 \cdot (3 \cdot 4)$

Identity Properties of Addition and Multiplication

For every real number a:

$a + 0 = a$ and $0 + a = a$ $\quad$ $a \cdot 1 = a$ and $1 \cdot a = a$

Examples: $5 + 0 = 5$ and $0 + 5 = 5$ $\quad$ $7 \cdot 1 = 7$ and $1 \cdot 7 = 7$

Name the property that each exercise illustrates.

1. $1m = m$

2. $(-3 + 4) + 5 = -3 + (4 + 5)$

3. $3(8 \cdot 0) = (3 \cdot 8)0$

4. $2 + 0 = 2$

5. $np = pn$

6. $f + g = g + f$

Use the properties to simplify each expression.

7. $(5 \cdot 83) \cdot 2$

8. $47 + 39 + 3 + 11$

9. $25 \cdot 74 \cdot 2 \cdot 2$

10. $-5(7y)$

11. $8 + 9m + 7$

12. $4.75 + 2.95 + 1.25 + 6$

13. $6\frac{1}{2} + 4\frac{1}{3} + 1\frac{1}{2} + \frac{2}{3}$

14. $25 \cdot 1.7 \cdot 4$

15. $(3p)(4q)(6r)$

16. *Writing* Justify your answers to these questions: Is subtraction commutative? Is subtraction associative? Is division commutative? Is division associative?

Connections Medical Technician . . . and more

1-7 Experimental Probability and Simulations

What You'll Learn

- Finding experimental probability
- Using simulations to find experimental probability

...And Why

To solve problems in business and sports

What You'll Need

- two number cubes

WORK TOGETHER

Work with a partner.

1. Suppose you roll two number cubes many times. Do you think that all of the sums will occur about the same number of times, or will some sums occur more often than others? Explain.
2. **Data Collection** Roll two number cubes sixty times. On a line plot numbered from 2 to 12, mark the sum of the cubes each time you roll.
3. How well do your results of rolling the number cubes match your **prediction** in Question 1? Explain.

THINK AND DISCUSS

Finding Experimental Probability

Probability measures how likely something, usually called an **event,** is to happen. For **experimental probability** you gather data through observations or experiments. Use this ratio to find experimental probability.

You read *P* (event) as "the probability of an event."

$$P(\text{event}) = \frac{\text{number of times an event happens}}{\text{number of times experiment is done}}$$

Suppose that in the Work Together activity, the sum 3 occurred five times. Then, $P(3) = \frac{5}{60}$, or $\frac{1}{12}$. Each time you repeat an experiment, the experimental probability of an event may vary. The more data you collect, the more reliable your results will be.

4. a. Use your Work Together data to find $P(2)$, $P(7)$, and $P(12)$.
   b. Which sum in part (a) has the greatest probability? Do you think this will be true if you repeat the experiment? Explain.

You can conduct an experiment by choosing items *at random.* This means that each item has an equal chance of being picked.

Example 1 Relating to the Real World 

Business After receiving complaints, a retailer checked 100 light bulbs at random. Eighty of the bulbs worked. What is *P*(bulb works)?

$$P(\text{bulb works}) = \frac{\text{number of times an event happens}}{\text{number of times the experiment is done}}$$

$$= \frac{80}{100} \quad \leftarrow \text{The light bulbs worked 80 times.}$$

$$= \frac{4}{5} = 0.8 = 80\%$$

The probability that a light bulb works is 80%.

QUICK REVIEW

You can write $\frac{4}{5}$ as a fraction, decimal, or percent:

$\frac{4}{5} = 0.8 = 80\%$

5. There are 500 light bulbs in stock. **Predict** how many of the light bulbs will work. (*Hint*: Multiply the probability found in Example 1 by the number of light bulbs in the shipment.)

Conducting a Simulation

A **simulation** is a model of a real-life situation. One way to do a simulation is to use a table of numbers that a computer has picked at random.

GRAPHING CALCULATOR HINT

You can generate random numbers using a graphing calculator or computer software.

Example 2 **Relating to the Real World** 

Medical Technician According to the American Red Cross, 40% of the people in the United States have type A blood. What is the probability that the next two people who donate blood have type A blood?

Define how the simulation will be done.

Use a random number table.

Random Number Table

23948 71470 12573 05954
65628 22310 09311 94864
41261 09943 34078 79481
34831 94510 71490 93312

Let the numbers 0–3 in the random number table represent having type A blood. Let 4–9 represent not having type A blood. Since the simulation is for two people, list the numbers in pairs. Look at twenty pairs.

← 40% of the numbers must represent having type A blood.

Conduct the simulation.

23 94 87 14 70 12 57 30 59 54 65 62 82 23 10 09 31 19 48 64
↑ ↑ ↑ ↑ ↑ ↑

The arrows point to pairs in which both "people" have type A blood.

Interpret the simulation.

Six pairs represent "both people have type A blood" because these pairs contain only the numbers 0–3.

$$P(\text{both have type A blood}) = \frac{\text{number of times an event happens}}{\text{number of times the experiment is done}}$$
$$= \frac{6}{20}$$
$$= \frac{3}{10} = 0.3 = 30\%$$

The probability that both of the next two people have type A blood is 30%. ■

6. For the simulation in Example 2, could you use any four numbers from 0–9 to represent having type A blood? Explain.

7. **Try This** In the United States, about 50% of the people have type O blood. Use the random number table above to find the probability that the next two donors have type O blood.

Exercises ON YOUR OWN

1. a. *Group Activity* What do you expect the probability is for getting heads when you toss a coin?
   b. Have each member in your group toss a coin 20 times, one person at a time. Use a table like the one below to record your data. After each person's turn, find the P(head) based on the total number of heads and the total number of tosses for your group.

Team Member	Number of Heads	Number of Tosses	Total Number of Heads	Total Number of Tosses	P(head)
1	■	20	■	20	■
2	■	20	■	40	■

   c. As the total number of coin tosses increases, does the probability get closer to what you expect? Explain.

A driver collects data on the color of a certain traffic light. When she arrives at the light, it is green 16 times, yellow 5 times, and red 9 times. Find each probability.

2. P(red)
3. P(green)
4. P(yellow)
5. P(not green)

6. Suppose you bought a box of marbles. You select twelve marbles at random and record the color. The results are at the right.
   a. Find P(red), P(green), P(blue), and P(yellow).
   b. Suppose the box contains 160 marbles. About how many blue marbles do you expect?
   c. Do you think there will be exactly 80 red marbles? Explain.

Suppose you grab a handful of coins from your change jar, and these coins are a random sample of the coins in your jar. You have 13 pennies, 3 quarters, 2 nickels, and 6 dimes. Find the probability that each is the next coin you select. Write each probability as a percent.

7. P(nickel)
8. P(penny)
9. P(coin worth less than 10¢)

10. a. A softball player is at bat 25 times. She gets a hit 7 times. What is the probability that she gets a hit the next time she comes to bat?
    b. *Writing* Suppose the player gets a hit the 26th time at bat. Explain how getting a hit changes the experimental probability.

11. *Health* The table shows the results of the 1954 trials for the Salk polio vaccine. To test the vaccine, researchers gave a test group shots with vaccine and a control group shots without vaccine. Compare the probability of developing polio in the test group and in the control group.

Results of Polio Vaccine Trials

Group	Number of Children	Number of Cases of Polio
Test	200,745	82
Control	201,229	162

Use the data in the line plot to find each probability.

12. P(Sunday) 13. P(Tuesday) 14. P(Wednesday)

15. P(weekend day) 16. P(weekday) 17. P(*not* Friday)

Students' Birthdays

Su	M	Tu	W	Th	F	Sa
X					X	
X	X				X	X
X	X	X		X	X	X
X	X	X		X	X	X

18. Suppose you guess the answers to a two-question true/false test. Your probability of getting one answer correct is 50%. Do a simulation of this test by flipping a coin for each question. Let "heads" represent a correct answer and "tails" represent an incorrect answer. Simulate the test ten times and record the results. Find P(both answers are correct).

19. Suppose there are three stoplights on your way to school. Each one has a 30% chance of stopping you. Use the random number table on page 37 to do a simulation. Record your data and find P(stopped by all three lights). Write your probability as a decimal rounded to the nearest hundredth. Then write it as a percent. (*Hint*: Let the numbers 0–2 represent being stopped and 3–9 represent not being stopped.)

20. **Critical Thinking** Suppose you are taking a poll for student council elections. Which is the best method for choosing students at random? Explain your choice.
    - **A.** You choose every 20th student on a list of all students.
    - **B.** You choose students as they leave a band concert.
    - **C.** You choose students in line at lunch.

21. **Open-ended** Conduct a simulation to find the experimental probability that exactly two children in a family of five children will be girls. Record the results of your simulation.

22. a. **Data Collection** Roll a number cube and record how often each of the numbers 1 through 6 occurs. Roll the cube 50 times.
    b. Find the experimental probability for each number.
    c. Are the probabilities for each number the same? Explain.

Chapter Project ***Find Out by Analyzing***

When predicting height, scientists use different formulas for men and women.

- Review the data collected for the Find Out by Question on page 9. Separate the data by male and female.
- Organize and display the data to see if there are differences between the sexes.

Exercises MIXED REVIEW

Simplify each expression.

23. $13 + 16(-2)$ 24. $36 \div (-4) - 2(-15)$

25. -7^2 26. $(-7)^2$

Getting Ready for Lesson 1-8

27. What number is in the first row, second column?

28. What number is in the second row, first column?

17	53.6	42
32	52.5	−7
4	98	5.6

SELF ASSESSMENT **FOR YOUR JOURNAL**

Explain why the experimental probability of an event can vary each time you perform the same experiment.

What You'll Learn

- Adding and subtracting matrices

...And Why

To investigate real-world data, such as school enrollment and employee wages

1992 School Enrollment in the United States (in millions)

Level	Public	Private
Elementary	27.1	3.1
High School	12.3	1.0
College	11.1	3.0

Source: *Statistical Abstract of the United States*

1-8 Organizing Data in Matrices

THINK AND DISCUSS

A **matrix** is a rectangular arrangement of numbers. The numbers are arranged in rows and columns and are usually written inside brackets. The matrix below displays the school enrollment data at the left.

$$\begin{array}{l} \\ \text{Elementary} \\ \text{High School} \\ \text{College} \end{array} \begin{array}{c} \text{Public} \quad \text{Private} \\ \begin{bmatrix} 27.1 & 3.1 \\ 12.3 & 1.0 \\ 11.1 & 3.0 \end{bmatrix} \end{array}$$

(row: the second row is highlighted; column: the first column is highlighted)

You identify the size of a matrix by the number of rows and the number of columns. This matrix has 3 rows and 2 columns, so it is a 3×2 matrix. Each item in a matrix is an **entry.**

1. What entry is in row 1, column 2? in row 2, column 1?
2. **Open-ended** Make a 2×3 matrix.

Two matrices are equal if corresponding entries are equal.

corresponding entries

$$\begin{bmatrix} 0.5 & \frac{3}{8} \\ \frac{1}{4} & 0.4 \end{bmatrix} \quad \begin{bmatrix} \frac{1}{2} & 0.375 \\ 0.25 & \frac{2}{5} \end{bmatrix}$$

3. Are the two matrices equal? Explain.

You can add or subtract matrices if they are the same size. You do this by adding or subtracting corresponding entries.

Example 1

Subtract the two matrices. $\begin{bmatrix} 7 & -4 & 11 \\ 6 & 5 & -1 \end{bmatrix} - \begin{bmatrix} 5 & 9 & 7 \\ 8 & -7 & -3 \end{bmatrix}$

$$\begin{bmatrix} 7 & -4 & 11 \\ 6 & 5 & -1 \end{bmatrix} - \begin{bmatrix} 5 & 9 & 7 \\ 8 & -7 & -3 \end{bmatrix} = \begin{bmatrix} 7-5 & -4-9 & 11-7 \\ 6-8 & 5-(-7) & -1-(-3) \end{bmatrix}$$

$$= \begin{bmatrix} 2 & -13 & 4 \\ -2 & 12 & 2 \end{bmatrix}$$

4. What size are the matrices in Example 1?
5. **Try This** Add the two matrices that were subtracted in Example 1.

Matrices are a handy way to organize real-world data so that you can add or subtract the data.

Example 2 ***Relating to the Real World*** 

Environment Write each table as a matrix. Then add the matrices to find the total of endangered and threatened species.

Endangered Species

Species	United States Only	Both United States and Foreign	Foreign Only	Total
Mammals	36	20	251	307
Birds	57	16	153	226
Reptiles	8	8	63	79
Amphibians	6	0	8	14
Fishes	60	3	11	74

Threatened Species

Species	United States Only	Both United States and Foreign	Foreign Only	Total
Mammals	5	4	22	31
Birds	8	9	0	17
Reptiles	15	4	14	33
Amphibians	4	1	0	5
Fishes	32	6	0	38

$$\begin{bmatrix} 36 & 20 & 251 & 307 \\ 57 & 16 & 153 & 226 \\ 8 & 8 & 63 & 79 \\ 6 & 0 & 8 & 14 \\ 60 & 3 & 11 & 74 \end{bmatrix} + \begin{bmatrix} 5 & 4 & 22 & 31 \\ 8 & 9 & 0 & 17 \\ 15 & 4 & 14 & 33 \\ 4 & 1 & 0 & 5 \\ 32 & 6 & 0 & 38 \end{bmatrix} = \begin{bmatrix} 41 & 24 & 273 & 338 \\ 65 & 25 & 153 & 243 \\ 23 & 12 & 77 & 112 \\ 10 & 1 & 8 & 19 \\ 92 & 9 & 11 & 112 \end{bmatrix}$$

What? The Endangered Species Act of 1973 protects plant and animal species. *Endangered* species are close to extinction. The survival of *threatened* species is of great concern.

6. How many species of mammals are endangered or threatened?

7. ***Critical Thinking*** The grizzly bear is threatened in the United States but endangered in Mexico. So it is counted twice in the totals. There is a total of four mammal species counted twice. What is the actual total of endangered or threatened mammals?

Exercises ON YOUR OWN

What is the size of each matrix?

1. $\begin{bmatrix} 5 & 4 & 7 \\ 6 & 9 & 8 \end{bmatrix}$

2. $\begin{bmatrix} 4 & 1 \end{bmatrix}$

3. $\begin{bmatrix} 1 & 2 \\ 3 & 4 \\ 5 & 6 \end{bmatrix}$

4. $\begin{bmatrix} -8 \end{bmatrix}$

5. $\begin{bmatrix} 16 & -22 & 24 & 35 \\ 17 & -35 & 19 & 41 \\ 28 & -10 & 15 & 50 \end{bmatrix}$

Mental Math **Find each sum or difference.**

6. $\begin{bmatrix} 1 & 2 \\ 5 & 3 \\ -1 & -4 \end{bmatrix} + \begin{bmatrix} 2 & 0 \\ 9 & 1 \\ 3 & -8 \end{bmatrix}$

7. $\begin{bmatrix} 4 & 2 \\ 1 & -3 \end{bmatrix} + \begin{bmatrix} -4 & -2 \\ -1 & 3 \end{bmatrix}$

8. $\begin{bmatrix} -6 & -1 & 7 \\ 3 & -2 & -5 \end{bmatrix} - \begin{bmatrix} -8 & 6 & -2 \\ 14 & -3 & 1 \end{bmatrix}$

9. What is the value of m, n, and p in the matrices?

$$\begin{bmatrix} 5 & -1 \\ m & 0 \end{bmatrix} = \begin{bmatrix} n & -1 \\ -6 & p \end{bmatrix}$$

Add each pair of matrices. Then subtract the second matrix from the first matrix in each pair.

10. $\begin{bmatrix} 16 & 11 & -20 \\ 22 & 8 & -10 \end{bmatrix}, \begin{bmatrix} 9 & 10 & 14 \\ -15 & -10 & 5 \end{bmatrix}$

11. $\begin{bmatrix} 42 & -36 \\ -10 & 54 \end{bmatrix}, \begin{bmatrix} 39 & 4 \\ 37 & 46 \end{bmatrix}$

12. $\begin{bmatrix} 3 & 2 & 1 \\ 4 & 2 & 0 \\ 0 & -2 & 5 \end{bmatrix}, \begin{bmatrix} 1 & -2 & 3 \\ -4 & 5 & -6 \\ 7 & -8 & 9 \end{bmatrix}$

13. $\begin{bmatrix} 3.4 & 2.1 \\ -6.4 & 5.7 \\ 8.8 & -9.3 \end{bmatrix}, \begin{bmatrix} 4.9 & -7.9 \\ 3.8 & -2.8 \\ 4.2 & 1.5 \end{bmatrix}$

14. $\begin{bmatrix} 5.0 & -1.7 \\ 1.2 & -3.8 \\ 1.5 & 2.4 \end{bmatrix}, \begin{bmatrix} 5.7 & 6.8 \\ -4.0 & -1.2 \\ 6.2 & 8.1 \end{bmatrix}$

15. $\begin{bmatrix} \frac{2}{3} & \frac{4}{5} \\ \frac{1}{8} & \frac{1}{6} \end{bmatrix}, \begin{bmatrix} \frac{1}{2} & \frac{2}{5} \\ \frac{3}{4} & 1 \end{bmatrix}$

16. $\begin{bmatrix} 356 & -190 & 171 \\ -256 & 321 & -150 \end{bmatrix}, \begin{bmatrix} 1 & 6 & -4 \\ -17 & -3 & 5 \end{bmatrix}$

17. $\begin{bmatrix} 3.5 & -0.2 \\ 0 & -7 \end{bmatrix}, \begin{bmatrix} -1 & 0.5 \\ -8.1 & 9.7 \end{bmatrix}$

18. a. **Sports** Write each table of data as a matrix.
   b. Make a matrix that shows the change in participation from 1987 to 1992.
   c. Did any categories lose participants? Which ones?
   d. In which category did the number of participants increase the most?
   e. **Writing** Suppose you have money to invest in sports equipment. In which sport would you invest? Use entries from your matrix to explain your choice.

19. **Critical Thinking** Suppose two matrices are equal. What will the matrix for their difference look like?

20. a. **Open-ended** Make two 3 × 5 matrices.
   b. Add your two matrices.
   c. Subtract your two matrices.

Participation in Sports Activities (in millions)

	Sport	7–11 yr	12–17 yr	18–24 yr
1987	Basketball	3.7	8.3	5.1
	Tennis	1.0	3.4	3.9
	Soccer	3.6	4.1	0.9
	Volleyball	2.0	6.6	4.7

	Sport	7–11 yr	12–17 yr	18–24 yr
1992	Basketball	5.5	8.2	4.9
	Tennis	1.4	3.2	3.9
	Soccer	4.2	3.8	1.3
	Volleyball	1.6	5.2	5.1

Simplify each entry in the matrix.

21. $\begin{bmatrix} \frac{5}{6} \div \frac{2}{3} & -4 - 2\frac{1}{2} \\ \left(3\frac{1}{3}\right)\left(\frac{3}{4}\right) & \frac{1}{2} - \left(\frac{2}{5}\right)\left(\frac{5}{4}\right) \end{bmatrix}$

22. $\begin{bmatrix} 8 + 2 \div 4 & 2^5 & -12 - 15 \\ 45 + 5(-13) & \frac{10 + 16}{4} & 4 - 2^2 \end{bmatrix}$

23. a. ***Jobs*** Create a matrix to find the total number of workers in each pay category for each work shift.

b. How many weekend employees on the evening shift earn \$5.50/h?

c. ***Critical Thinking*** Suppose all employees work 8-h shifts both Saturday and Sunday. How could you use the matrix to find the total wages of the weekend employees?

Number of Employees

Saturday Schedule

Shift	Hourly Wage \$5.25	\$5.50	\$6.00	\$6.50
Day	8	3	5	1
Evening	10	2	2	1
Night	4	1	0	1

Sunday Schedule

Shift	Hourly Wage \$5.25	\$5.50	\$6.00	\$6.50
Day	5	2	1	1
Evening	8	2	0	1
Night	2	1	0	1

Multiply each matrix by the given value.

Sample $2\begin{bmatrix} 2 & -3 \\ 1 & 5 \end{bmatrix} = \begin{bmatrix} 2(2) & 2(-3) \\ 2(1) & 2(5) \end{bmatrix}$ ← Multiply each entry by the factor outside the matrix.

$= \begin{bmatrix} 4 & -6 \\ 2 & 10 \end{bmatrix}$

24. $3\begin{bmatrix} -9 & 2 \\ 6 & -12 \end{bmatrix}$ **25.** $-5\begin{bmatrix} 70 & 30 & -10 \\ 80 & 20 & -50 \end{bmatrix}$ **26.** $0\begin{bmatrix} -15 & 12 \\ 17 & 21 \end{bmatrix}$

Exercises MIXED REVIEW

Evaluate each expression for $a = -5$, $b = 2.4$, $c = -0.5$, and $d = 3.7$.

27. $a + (-b) +$ **28.** $2b + (-d) + ac$ **29.** $a \div c + 2d$ **30.** $a^2 + bc$

Getting Ready for Lesson 1-9

Geometry **Use the formula $A = \frac{1}{2}bh$ to find the area of each triangle.**

31. $b = 12$ in. $h = 4$ in. **32.** $b = 15$ cm $h = 7$ cm **33.** $b = 9.2$ m $h = 14.8$ m

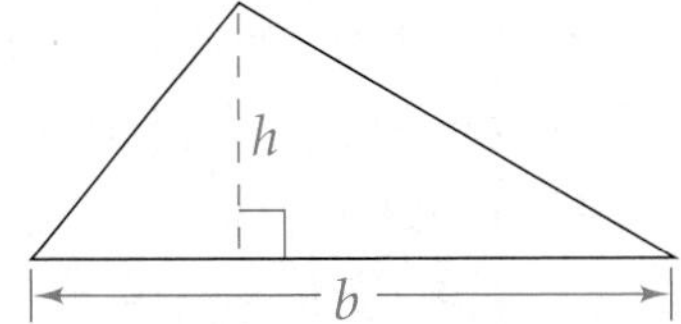

Exercises CHECKPOINT

Evaluate each expression.

1. $2a - b$ for $a = \frac{3}{4}, b = \frac{7}{8}$ **2.** $3m - 2n$ for $m = 3.5, n = -0.8$ **3.** $p \div q$ for $p = -\frac{5}{8}, q = -\frac{4}{5}$

Simplify.

4. $\begin{bmatrix} 3 & 5 \\ -4 & 2 \end{bmatrix} + \begin{bmatrix} \frac{1}{2} & -6 \\ 8 & -11 \end{bmatrix}$ **5.** $\begin{bmatrix} 3.3 & 0.4 & 3.0 \\ -1.7 & 9.6 & -6.5 \end{bmatrix} - \begin{bmatrix} -2.3 & 7.2 & -8.5 \\ 4.1 & 6.3 & 9.2 \end{bmatrix}$

6. ***Open-ended*** Write a problem you could solve by using a simulation. Describe how the simulation would be done.

Math ToolboX

Technology

Matrices

After Lesson 1-8

You can use your graphing calculator to add or subtract matrices. In the calculator, a matrix is named using a variable. Some calculators will put brackets, [ ], around a variable to indicate a matrix. Before entering the values for a matrix, you must enter the size of the matrix.

$[A] = \begin{bmatrix} 1 & 2 & 3 \\ 4 & 5 & 6 \end{bmatrix}$ $[B] = \begin{bmatrix} 6 & 9 & 2 \\ -1 & 4 & -7 \end{bmatrix}$ ← Remember that $[A]$ and $[B]$ can be added or subtracted because they are the same size, 2×3.

The key sequences below are for entering and adding two matrices. Do all the steps for matrix A, then for matrix B.

	Matrix A	Matrix B
To edit a matrix:	MATRX ▶ ▶ 1	MATRX ▶ ▶ 2
To enter matrix size:	2 ENTER 3 ENTER	2 ENTER 3 ENTER
To enter values for row 1:	1 ENTER 2 ENTER 3 ENTER	6 ENTER 9 ENTER 2 ENTER
To enter values for row 2:	4 ENTER 5 ENTER 6 ENTER	(–) 1 ENTER 4 ENTER (–) 7 ENTER
To go to the Home screen:	2nd QUIT	2nd QUIT

To add $[A]$ and $[B]$: MATRX 1 + MATRX 2 ENTER

Your calculator screen will display the sum.

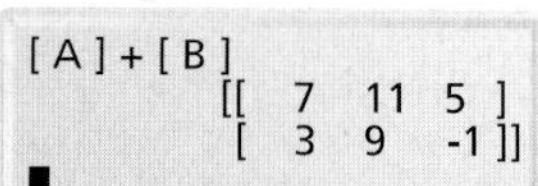

Use a graphing calculator. Find $[A] + [B]$ and $[A] - [B]$.

1. $[A] = \begin{bmatrix} 3.8 & 2.1 \\ 1.5 & -0.8 \\ -1.4 & 1.9 \end{bmatrix}, [B] = \begin{bmatrix} 1.1 & -1.4 \\ 0.6 & 1.5 \\ -1.7 & 0.8 \end{bmatrix}$

2. $[A] = \begin{bmatrix} 123 & 87 \\ 112 & 63 \end{bmatrix}, [B] = \begin{bmatrix} 112 & 64 \\ 92 & 50 \end{bmatrix}$

3. $[A] = \begin{bmatrix} 5 & -4 & 7 & -13 \\ 4 & -9 & -10 & 5 \\ 6 & -7 & -6 & 12 \end{bmatrix}, [B] = \begin{bmatrix} -5 & 8 & 13 & -12 \\ 4 & 11 & 7 & 10 \\ -15 & 6 & -8 & -3 \end{bmatrix}$

4. $[A] = \begin{bmatrix} 122 & 48 & -63 \\ 95 & 167 & 78 \\ -110 & 59 & 45 \\ -87 & 114 & 132 \end{bmatrix}, [B] = \begin{bmatrix} -89 & 67 & -101 \\ 42 & -53 & 77 \\ -81 & 103 & 96 \\ 59 & 88 & -107 \end{bmatrix}$

5. a. Use the matrices in Exercise 1 to find $[B] + [A]$ and $[B] - [A]$.

b. *Writing* Does changing the order of the matrices affect the result when you add matrices? subtract matrices? Explain.

What You'll Learn

- Using variables and formulas in spreadsheets

...And Why

To investigate real-world situations, such as television viewership

1-9 Variables and Formulas in Spreadsheets

THINK AND DISCUSS

How much time do you spend watching television? Is it about average for a teenager? You can use the spreadsheet below to find out.

Like a matrix, a **spreadsheet** organizes data in rows and columns. A **cell** is a box where a row and column meet.

Hours of Weekly TV Viewing

	A	B	C	D
1	Viewing Group	Nov. 91	Nov. 93	Change
2	Children 2–5	26.4	21.5	–4.9
3	Children 6–11	21.2	20.0	–1.2
4	Female Teens	22.2	20.8	–1.4
5	Male Teens	22.7	21.2	–1.5
6	Women 18–24	28.9	25.7	–3.2
7	Men 18–24	23.0	22.5	–0.5
8	Women 25–54	32.8	30.6	–2.2
9	Men 25–54	28.1	28.1	0
10	Women 55 and over	43.5	44.2	0.7
11	Men 55 and over	39.8	38.5	–1.3

column
cell B4
row

Math A Test Prep

1 Of the first 20 customers at a music store, 7 bought tapes, 10 bought CDs, and 3 bought neither. If this trend continues, what is the probability that the next customer will buy a tape or CD?

(1) $\frac{17}{20}$ (3) $\frac{3}{20}$

(2) $\frac{17}{3}$ (4) $\frac{7}{10}$

2 A report said that five salespeople earned bonuses of $300, $250, $325, $375, and $250. An error was found in the report. The fifth salesperson had actually earned a bonus of $350. How does the corrected amount affect the mean, median, and mode?

1. a. *Estimate* About how many hours do you watch TV in a week?

b. Compare your weekly TV viewing hours with the November 1993 average for your group.

You can use spreadsheet formulas to calculate the values in column D. The spreadsheet you see on a computer screen shows the value in the cell. The formula used to calculate the value is not shown in the spreadsheet.

Cell	Formula in Cell	Value Shown in Cell
D2	C2 − B2	−4.9
D3	C3 − B3	−1.2
D4	C4 − B4	−1.4
⋮	⋮	⋮

You can save time by using expressions to write formulas in cells. Suppose you change the value in cell B4. The computer will automatically evaluate the formula C4 − B4 and change the value in cell D4.

TECHNOLOGY HINT

A spreadsheet program allows you to put a formula in one cell and copy its format in other cells.

A computer spreadsheet program uses these operation symbols:

- To multiply: 3 * 5 means $3 \cdot 5$.
- To divide: 3/5 means $3 \div 5$.
- To raise to a power: 3^5 means 3^5.

	A	B	C	D	E
1	x	x^3	x − 3	3x	▪
2	−4	▪	▪	▪	▪
3	−1	▪	▪	▪	▪

Example 1

Cell A2 contains a value for the variable x. Write a spreadsheet formula for cell B2 to evaluate the expression in cell B1.

Expression	Cell	Formula in Cell	Value Shown in Cell
x^3	B2	A2^3	−64

2. What formulas would the computer use to find the values in cells C2 and D2?

3. Write the formulas and find the values for cells B3, C3, and D3.

4. Suppose you use column E to evaluate $2x^3 - 5$. What spreadsheet formula would you use in cell E2?

Example 2 *Relating to the Real World* 

Package Delivery Both the United States Postal Service (USPS) and the United Parcel Service (UPS) add the girth of a package to its length to find its delivery size. Both USPS and UPS measure dimensions in inches.

Write a formula for cell D2 that will find the delivery size of a package. Then find the delivery size of the package in row 2.

	A	B	C	D
1	width	height	length	delivery size
2	5	10	20	▪
3	16	28	30	▪
4	18.5	20.5	26	▪

formula for cell D2: girth + length

$= 2w + 2h + l$

$= 2 * A2 + 2 * B2 + C2$

delivery size: $2 \cdot 5 + 2 \cdot 10 + 20$

$= 50$

The delivery size of the package in row 2 is 50 in.

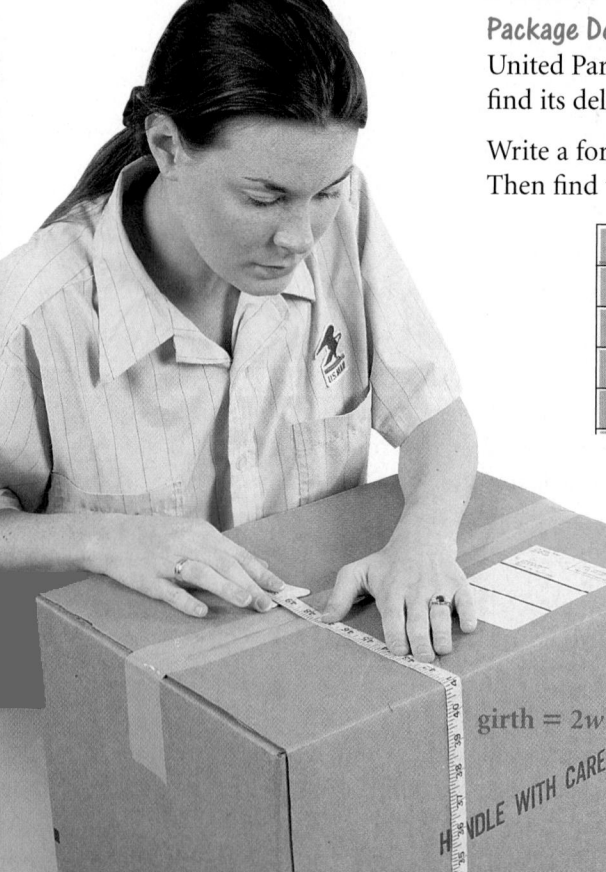

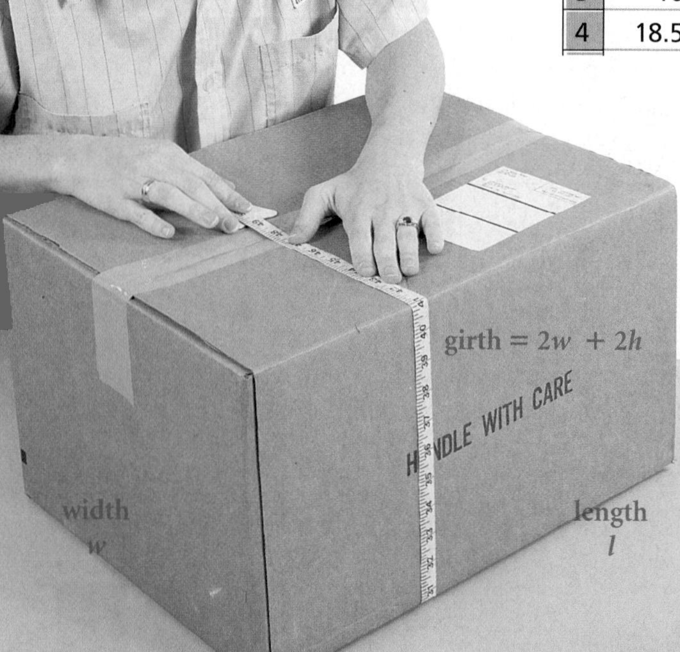

The length of a package is its longest dimension.

5. The maximum delivery size for packages sent by USPS is 108 in. For UPS the maximum delivery size is 130 in. Find the values in cells D3 and D4. Which package or packages qualify for UPS delivery but not for USPS delivery?

6. **Critical Thinking** Suppose for the package in row 4 you used 26 in. as the height and 20.5 in. as the length. Is this helpful to the person mailing the package? Explain.

Exercises ON YOUR OWN

1. **Critical Thinking** How are spreadsheet formulas similar to other kinds of formulas you have used? How are they different?

2. Suppose you are an employer. You must find your employees' wages, taxes, and income after taxes. Can a spreadsheet program save you time? Explain.

Use the spreadsheet.

	A	B	C	D	E
1	x	4x^2	2x – 5	3x + 7	■
2	7	■	■	■	■
3	-2	■	■	■	■

3. Write the formulas you would use in cells B2, C2, and D2 to evaluate the expressions in cells B1, C1, and D1.

4. Find the values for cells B2, C2, and D2.

5. Find the values for cells B3, C3, and D3.

6. **Open-ended** Write an expression of your own for cell E1. Then write the formula for cell E2 that you would use to evaluate your expression.

Evaluate each spreadsheet expression.

7. mean of three numbers: (A2 + B2 + C2)/3
   a. for A2 = −3, B2 = − 9, C2 = 3
   b. for A2 = −10.8, B2 = 4.5, C2 = 0.6

8. total of hourly wage minus deductions: A4 * B4 − C4
   a. for A4 = 6, B4 = 10, C4 = 20
   b. for A4 = 11.70, B4 = 40, C4 = 135

	A	B	C	D
1	length	width	height	volume
2	20	12	8	■
3	14.8	9.8	5	■
4	30	25.4	7	■

9. **Geometry** The formula for the volume of a rectangular prism is $V = lwh$. The spreadsheet gives the dimensions in feet for three rectangular prisms.
   a. Write a formula for cell D2 to find the volume of the rectangular prism in row 2.
   b. Find the volume of each rectangular prism.

10. **Writing** You can find the volume of a cube using the formula $V = s^3$, where s is the length of a side. Explain how to set up a spreadsheet to find the volumes of cubes with sides 4, 12, 3.8, and 6.25.

11. a. **Business** Write a formula for cell D2 in the spreadsheet for Milo Construction Company.
b. Find the values for cells D2, D3, D4, and D5.
c. Suppose a worker earned the mean yearly wage in 1995. She worked 40 h each week and 50 weeks in a year. What was her hourly wage?

Milo Construction Company

	A	B	C	D
1	Year	Number of Workers	Total Wages Paid to All Workers	Mean Yearly Wage
2	1980	13	$241,400	■
3	1985	20	$485,190	■
4	1990	35	$969,570	■
5	1995	39	$1,203,580	■

Geometry **Evaluate each spreadsheet expression.**

12. area of a parallelogram: B2 * C2
a. for B2 = 9, C2 = 12
b. for B2 = 15.3, C2 = 8.9

13. surface area of a sphere: 4/3 * 3.14 * A2^3
a. for A2 $= \frac{3}{4}$
b. for A2 = 7.2

14. volume of a cylinder: 3.14 * B3^2 * C3
a. for B3 = 5, C3 = 8
b. for B3 = 3.5, C3 = 4.2

15. surface area of a rectangular prism:
2 * B2 * C2 + 2 * B2 * D2 + 2 * C2 * D2
a. for B2 = 2, C2 = 3, D2 = 4
b. for B2 = 3.5, C2 = 5.8, D2 = 4.2

16. a. How are the values in column G below related to values in columns A and D?
b. Write formulas to find the values of the cells in columns G and H.
c. **Critical Thinking** How does this spreadsheet model adding matrices?

	A	B	C	D	E	F	G	H
1	−3	4		−2	−4		−5	0
2	0	5		−1	7		−1	12
3	3	−2		4	−6		7	−8

17. **Computer** Eva Arturo owns Shine On, a small shop in the mall. She buys earrings for $6.75 and sells them for $8.95. The store sold 127 pairs of earrings in January, 174 in February, and 156 in March. Create a spreadsheet to calculate each amount.
a. the monthly earring sales
b. the monthly profit from earring sales

18. **Critical Thinking** In Exercise 17, what computer formula could you use to find the total profit for all three months?

Population of Four Cities in the United States

	A	B	C	D	E	F
1	City	1950 Population	1990 Population	Population change (1950 to 1990)	Area (mi^2)	1990 Density (people/mi^2)
2	Fort Wayne, IN	133,607	172,971	■	62.7	■
3	Albuquerque, NM	96,815	384,619	■	132.2	■
4	Houston, TX	596,163	1,629,902	■	539.9	■
5	Norfolk, VA	213,513	261,229	■	53.8	■

Source: *The World Almanac* and *The Statistical Abstract of the United States*

19. *Standardized Test Prep* For the spreadsheet, which statements are correct?

I. The formula for cell D2 is C2 − B2.

II. In column D, negative entries indicate a population loss.

III. The formula for cell F5 is B5/E5.

A. I and III **B.** II and III **C.** I and II **D.** I, II, and III

Chapter Project *Find Out by Creating*

- Measure the tibia, humerus, and radius bones and the height of several adults to the nearest half-inch.
- Create a spreadsheet. Organize the measurements. Use the formulas from the Find Out question on page 29 in your spreadsheet to predict the heights of the adults.
- Compare the predicted heights with the measured heights. Does one of the formulas predict heights better than the other formulas? Explain.

Exercises MIXED REVIEW

Simplify each expression.

20. $8 - 14 \div 2$

21. $(8 - 14) \div 2$

22. $|8 - 32 \div 4| + 1$

23. $(20 - 12) \div (3 + 1)$

24. $9(3 + 5) + 6 \div 3$

25. $[9(3 + 5) + 6] \div 3$

26. $\frac{6 - 18}{2}$

27. $\frac{-5 - 4^2}{-7}$

28. $6 + 3^2 - 2 \cdot 5$

29. $10 - 4 \cdot 8 - 7^2$

30. **a.** A notebook costs $1.95. Write an equation to find the cost of any number of notebooks.

b. What is the cost of three notebooks?

PORTFOLIO

Select one or two items from your work for this chapter. Consider:
- corrected work
- diagrams, graphs, or charts
- a journal entry

Explain why you have included each selection that you make.

CHAPTER PROJECT

Finishing the Chapter Project

The BIG DIG!

Questions on pages 9, 29, 39, and 49 should help you to complete your project. Assemble all the parts of your project in a notebook. Add a summary of what you have learned about using the height formulas. What difficulties did you have? Are there ways to avoid these problems? What advice would you give to an archaeologist or forensic scientist about predicting heights from bone lengths?

Reflect and Revise

Ask a classmate to review your project notebook with you. Together, check that your graphs are clearly labeled and accurate. Check that you have used formulas correctly and that your calculations are accurate. Is your spreadsheet well organized and easy to follow? Make any revisions necessary to improve your work.

Follow Up

Archaeologists and forensic scientists use many other formulas about the human body. Research these by contacting your local police department or by using one of the resources listed below.

For More Information

Avi-Yonah, Michael. *Dig This! How Archaeologists Uncover Our Past.* Minneapolis, Minnesota: Runestone, 1993.

Stones and Bones! How Archaeologists Trace Human Origins. Prepared by the Geography Department, Runestone Press. Minneapolis, Minnesota: Runestone, 1994.

"It's a Boy." *Scholastic Math Magazine* (April 1993):12–13.

"The Arm Bone's Connected to Math." *Scholastic Math Magazine* (October 1992): 8–9.

CHAPTER 1

Wrap Up

Key Terms

absolute value (p. 20)
bar graph (p. 6)
base (p. 15)
cell (p. 45)
entry (p. 40)
equation (p. 11)
evaluate (p. 16)
event (p. 36)
experimental probability (p. 36)
exponent (p. 15)
integers (p. 19)
irrational numbers (p. 30)
line graph (p. 7)
line plot (p. 4)
matrix (p. 40)
mean (p. 5)
median (p. 5)
mode (p. 4)
opposite (p. 19)
order of operations (p. 15)
rational numbers (p. 30)
real numbers (p. 30)
reciprocal (p. 32)
simulation (p. 37)
spreadsheet (p. 45)
term (p. 11)
variable (p. 11)
variable expression (p. 11)

How am I doing?

SELF ASSESSMENT

- State three ideas from this chapter that you think are important. Explain your choices.
- Describe the rules for the order of operations that you must use to simplify expressions.

Displaying Data Relationships with Graphs 1-1

You can use a **line plot** or **histogram** to show frequency, or the number of times a data item occurs. A **bar graph** compares amounts. A **line graph** shows how a set of values changes over time. **Mean**, **median**, and **mode** are three measures of central tendency.

Find the mean, median, and mode for each set of data.

1. 24, 45, 33, 27, 24
2. 80, 87, 81, 92, 87, 80, 83
3. 2.4, 2.3, 2.1, 2.5, 2.3, 2.2

Use the bar graph.

4. Find the difference between the 1996 and the 1997 sales for March.
5. Which month had the most sales in 1996?
6. Find the average number of video recorders sold during the first three months for each year.

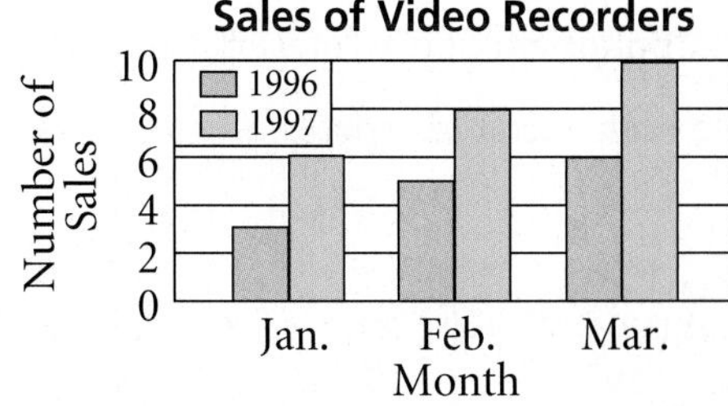

Variables, Order of Operations, Evaluating Expressions 1-2, 1-3

A **variable** represents changing values. To **evaluate** a variable expression, you substitute a given number for each variable. Then you simplify the expression using the **order of operations**.

Evaluate each expression for $a = 3, b = 2,$ and $c = 1$.

7. $4a - b^2$
8. $9(a + 2b) + c$
9. $\frac{2a + b}{2}$
10. $2a^2 - (4b + c)$

11. ***Open-ended*** Use 3, –, 6, x, 5, and + to write a variable expression: Simplify your expression.

12. A data entry operator can input 140 records into a computer each day. The table shows the relationship between the number of days worked and the number of records entered.
    a. Write an equation to describe this relationship.
    b. How many records will be entered after 21 days? after 30 days?

Days	Records Entered
1	140
2	280
3	420
4	560

Adding and Subtracting Integers 1-4

Two numbers are **opposites** if they are the same distance from zero on the number line. Whole numbers and their opposites are **integers.** The **absolute value** of a number is its distance from zero on a number line.

To add two numbers with the same sign, *add* their absolute values. The sum has the same sign as the addends. To add two numbers with different signs, find the *difference* of their absolute values. The sum has the same sign as the number with the greater absolute value. To subtract a number, add its opposite.

Add or subtract.

13. $(-13) + (-4)$ **14.** $5 - 17$ **15.** $-12.4 + 22.3$ **16.** $|54.3 - 29.4|$ **17.** $-12 - (-7)$

Evaluate each expression for $a = -5$, $b = 8$, and $c = -7$.

18. $a + c$ **19.** $b - c$ **20.** $-a + b$ **21.** $|c - a|$ **22.** $-|b| + |c|$

Multiplying and Dividing Integers 1-5

The product or quotient of two integers with the same sign is *positive.* The product or quotient of two integers with different signs is *negative.*

Evaluate each variable expression for $x = 4$, $y = -2$, and $z = -3$.

23. $-3^2 + z^2$ **24.** $y + (-4)x$ **25.** $5xy$ **26.** $\frac{x}{-2} + 2z$ **27.** $\frac{x - y}{3}$

28. Evaluate $a^2 - 2b^3$ for $a = -5$ and $b = -3$. Choose the correct answer.
A. -29 **B.** 79 **C.** 43 **D.** 241 **E.** -181

Real Numbers and Rational Numbers 1-6

A **rational number,** such as $\frac{5}{8}$ or $\frac{2}{3}$, is a ratio of two integers. An **irrational number** like π or $\sqrt{2}$, cannot be written as a ratio of integers. The product of a nonzero number and its **reciprocal** is 1.

Evaluate each expression for $a = \frac{5}{6}$ and $b = -\frac{2}{3}$.

29. $a - 3b$ **30.** $3a - 4b$ **31.** $6ab$ **32.** $a \div b$ **33.** $a + b^2$

Experimental Probability and Simulations 1-7

Experimental probability is based on data gathered through observations. The probability of an event, *P*(event), equals the number of times an event happens divided by the number of times the experiment is done.

34. The results of a blind taste test of fruit juices are at the right. Find each probability.

a. *P* (preferred Brand A) **b.** *P* (preferred Brand B)
c. *P* (preferred Brand C) **d.** *P* (did *not* prefer Brand C)

Brand A	Brand B	Brand C
卌 |	卌 卌	卌 卌 ||

Organizing Data in Matrices 1-8

A **matrix** is a rectangular arrangement of numbers in rows and columns. You can add or subtract matrices if they are the same size. You add and subtract matrices by adding or subtracting corresponding entries.

Find the sum of each pair of matrices. Then find the difference of each pair of matrices by subtracting the second matrix from the first matrix.

35. $\begin{bmatrix} 2 & -3 \\ 9 & -1 \end{bmatrix}, \begin{bmatrix} 5 & 10 \\ -11 & -9 \end{bmatrix}$ **36.** $\begin{bmatrix} 1.2 & -1.1 \\ 2.7 & 2.9 \\ -3.2 & -1.1 \end{bmatrix}, \begin{bmatrix} 3.1 & 1.7 \\ -1.7 & -3.2 \\ 1.5 & 2.3 \end{bmatrix}$ **37.** $\begin{bmatrix} -\frac{1}{2} \\ \frac{2}{5} \end{bmatrix}, \begin{bmatrix} \frac{5}{8} \\ -\frac{3}{4} \end{bmatrix}$

Variables and Formulas in Spreadsheets 1-9

You can use a **spreadsheet** to analyze data. A spreadsheet organizes data in rows and columns. A **cell** is a box where a row and column meet. Spreadsheets use formulas to calculate values.

38. **Writing** A. Jones earns \$5.85/h, and M. Vasquez earns \$6.30/h. Explain how you could use a spreadsheet to find each person's total wage.

Employee	M	T	W	TH	F
A. Jones	7.8	7.3	7.9	7.2	7.3
M. Vasquez	7.5	7.6	7.4	7.8	7.8

Getting Ready for.......... CHAPTER 2

Evaluate each expression.

39. $3n + 2$ for $n = 1.2$ **40.** $8(g + 1) - 3$ for $g = -2$ **41.** $5.4b + 2.6b$ for $b = 10$

Complete the spreadsheet at the right for each value of *x*.

		A	B	C	D	E
	1	x	x + 2	2x	x^2	x^3
42.	2	−2	■	■	■	■
43.	3	0	■	■	■	■
44.	4	4	■	■	■	■

CHAPTER 1

Assessment

Use an equation to model the relationship in each table.

1.

Number	Cost
1	\$2.30
2	\$4.60
3	\$6.90

2.

Payment	Change
\$1	\$9
\$2	\$8
\$3	\$7

Simplify each expression.

3. $3 + 5 - 4$
4. $8 - 2^4 \div 2$
5. $\frac{2 \cdot 3 - 1}{3^2}$
6. $36 - (4 + 5 \cdot 4)$

Evaluate each expression for $x = 3, y = -1$, and $z = 2$.

7. $2x + 3y + z$
8. $-xyz$
9. $-3x - 2z - 7$
10. $-z^3 - 2z + z$
11. $\frac{xy - 3z}{-5}$
12. $x^2 + (-x)^2$

Find the sum or difference.

13. $\begin{bmatrix} 3 & 2 \\ -1 & 5 \end{bmatrix} + \begin{bmatrix} 8 & -5 \\ 3 & 0 \end{bmatrix}$

14. $\begin{bmatrix} 1 & 9 & -4 \\ 5 & 2 & -1 \\ -6 & -2 & -1 \end{bmatrix} - \begin{bmatrix} 2 & -6 & 7 \\ -8 & 3 & -3 \\ 4 & -7 & 9 \end{bmatrix}$

Explain why each statement is true or false.

15. All rational numbers are integers.

16. The absolute value of a number is always positive.

17. A random survey of 60 students showed that 36 students used calculators for computation. What is the probability that a student chosen at random uses a calculator for computation?

18. Complete the following: $3^2 \cdot ▒ = 1$

A. $\frac{1}{9}$ B. -3^2 C. 0 D. 2^3 E. $-\frac{1}{3}$

19. **Writing** Tell if each of the subtraction sentences would *always*, *sometimes*, or *never* be true. Support your answer with two examples.
a. $(+) - (+) = (+)$ **b.** $(+) - (-) = (-)$
c. $(-) - (-) = (-)$ **d.** $(-) - (+) = (+)$

20. **Open-ended** Write four rational numbers. Then use a number line to order them from least to greatest.

Evaluate each spreadsheet expression.

21. (A3 + B1 + C2)/4
for A3 = −5.3, B1 = 7.5, C2 = 6.48

22. A1 − B1 * C2
for A1 = 16.09, B1 = 9.16, C2 = −5

23. A softball player made a hit 54 times in the last 171 times at bat. Find the probability that the softball player will get a hit the next time at bat.

24. The double line graph shows the quarterly profit for a software company.

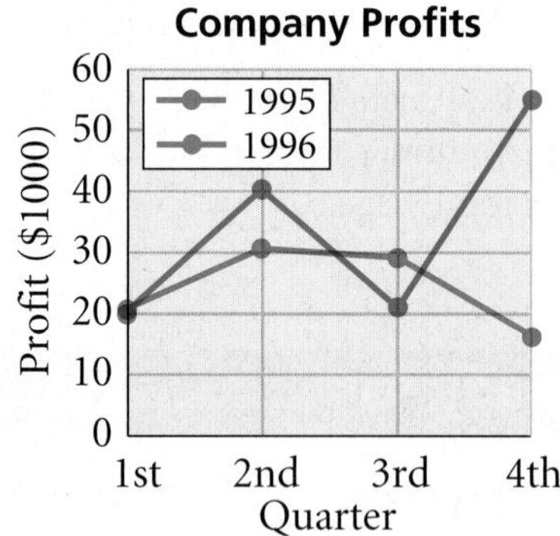

a. In which quarter did the company have its lowest quarterly profit?

b. Estimate the company's profit for each quarter. Then find the mean quarterly profit for each year.

25. **Writing** Explain why the equation below is not always true.

$$\left|\frac{a}{b}\right| = \frac{a}{b}$$

CHAPTER 1

Preparing for the Math A Exam

Part I

1 Tamara's teacher allows students to decide whether to use the mean, median, or mode for their test averages. Tamara will receive the highest average if she uses the mean. Which set of test scores could be Tamara's?

(1) 95, 82, 76, 95, 96 (3) 65, 84, 75, 74, 65
(2) 79, 80, 91, 83, 80 (4) 100, 87, 94, 94, 81

2 Which equation models the relationship in the table?

Speed *s* (mi/h)	Distance *d* (mi)
30	90
40	120
50	150
60	180

(1) $d = s + 60$ (3) $d = 3s$
(2) $d = \frac{1}{3}s$ (4) $d = s - 60$

3 The expression $2(5 - 3)^2 + 4 \div 2$ can be simplified to ■.
(1) 6 (3) 10
(2) 8 (4) 18

4 Which is the greatest sum or difference?
(1) $19.8 - (-2.4)$ (3) $37 + (-15)$
(2) $-17 - 31$ (4) $-18.3 + 4.7$

5 What is the value of $\frac{3x - (-4)}{7}$ when $x = -6$?
(1) 2 (3) -3
(2) 3 (4) -2

6 Which of the following does *not* equal 27 when $x = -3$?
(1) $-x^3$ (3) $-(-x)^3$
(2) $-9x$ (4) $3x^2$

7 The Fuller Book Company inspects a sample of 860 books and finds that 172 books have defective bindings. What is the probability that a book has a defective binding?
(1) $\frac{1}{4}$ (2) $\frac{1}{3}$ (3) $\frac{1}{2}$ (4) $\frac{1}{5}$

8 Which equation illustrates the identity property of addition?
(1) $x + 0 = 0$ (3) $1 + x = x$
(2) $0 + x = x$ (4) $x + 1 = 1$

Part II

9 Write the negation of the sentence: $30 \div 5 \geq 6$. Determine the truth value of the original sentence and its negation.

10 Simplify: $\frac{3^2 + 3^2 + 3^2}{4^2 + 4^2 + 4^2}$.

11 Evaluate $\frac{s}{t}$ for $s = \frac{3}{8}$ and $t = \frac{5}{16}$.

Part III

12 Write a formula for cells C2 and C3 in the spreadsheet. Then calculate the values for cells C2 and C3 using the formula.

Areas of Triangles

	A	B	C
1	base	height	Area
2	4	6	■
3	5	9	■

13 Write in order from least to greatest: $\frac{5}{6}, -\frac{6}{7}, 0.4, -0.75$.

Part IV

14 The table below shows the number of questions the students in Ms. Lee's class answered correctly on the quiz.

Correct Answers on Quiz

Number Correct	1	2	3	4	5
Frequency	1	5	6	7	3

a Draw a histogram of the data.
b What is the mode of the data?
c What is the median of the data?

CHAPTER 2

Functions and Their Graphs

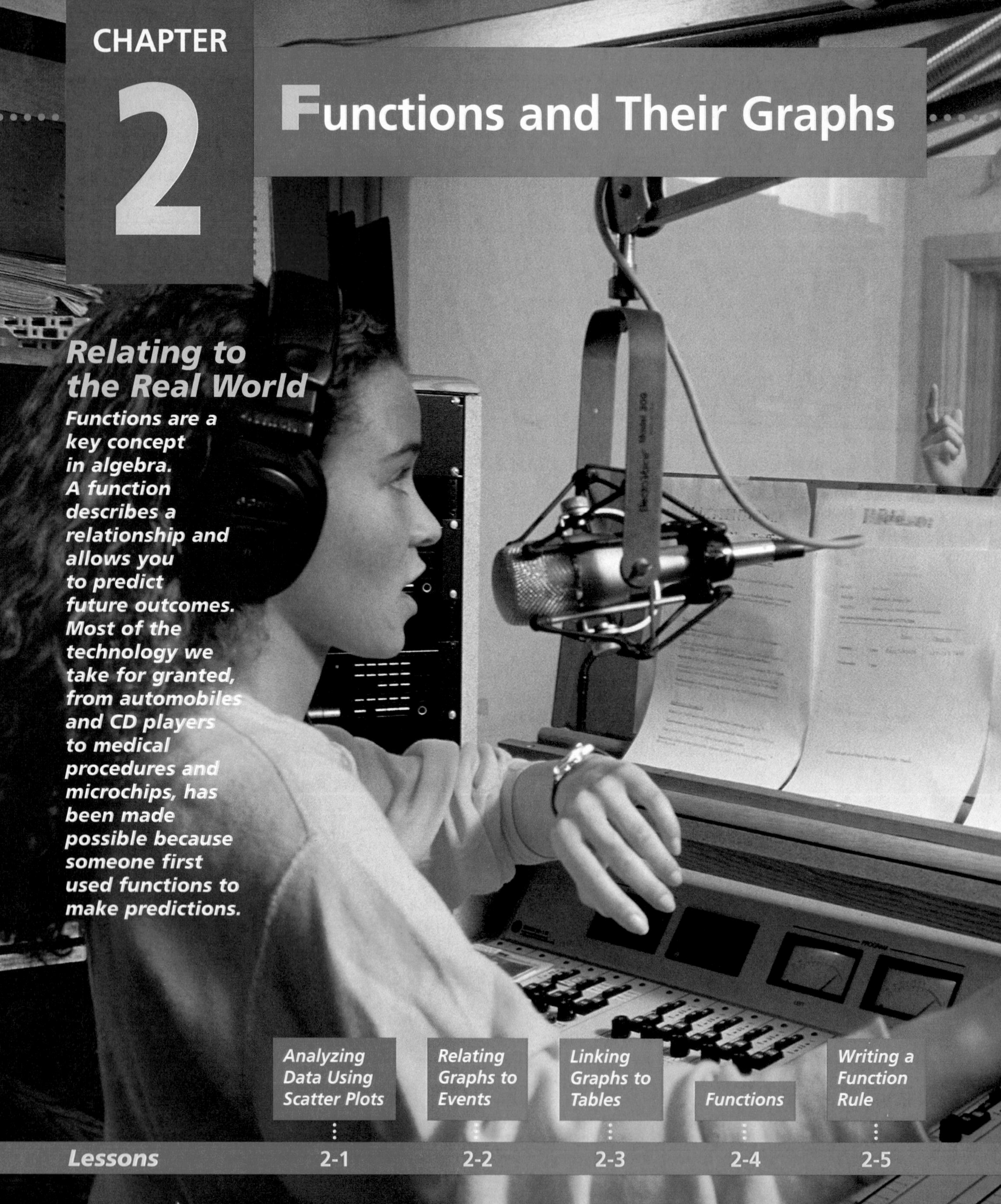

Relating to the Real World

Functions are a key concept in algebra. A function describes a relationship and allows you to predict future outcomes. Most of the technology we take for granted, from automobiles and CD players to medical procedures and microchips, has been made possible because someone first used functions to make predictions.

Lessons	2-1	2-2	2-3	2-4	2-5
	Analyzing Data Using Scatter Plots	*Relating Graphs to Events*	*Linking Graphs to Tables*	*Functions*	*Writing a Function Rule*

The Three Views of a Function — 2-6

Families of Functions — 2-7

The Probability Formula — 2-8

CHAPTER PROJECT

FAST TALKER

Radio announcers have to time their speech so that commericals and news updates are the correct length. Do you know how fast you talk? How about your friends? Try saying these tongue twisters: "The sunshade sheltered Sarah from the sunshine." — "Lavonne lingered, looking longingly for her lost laptop."

As you work through the chapter, you will time people as they say tongue twisters. You will use scatter plots and graphs to help investigate and display relationships in the data you collect. Then, using functions, you will summarize your findings and make predictions.

To help you complete the project:

- p. 63 *Find Out by Doing*
- p. 72 *Find Out by Graphing*
- p. 83 *Find Out by Writing*
- p. 94 *Find Out by Analyzing*
- p. 100 *Finishing the Project*

Skills Review

The Coordinate Plane

Before Lesson 2-1

The **coordinate plane** is formed when two number lines intersect at right angles. The horizontal axis is the ***x*-axis** and the vertical axis is the ***y*-axis.** The axes intersect at the **origin** and divide the coordinate plane into four sections called **quadrants.**

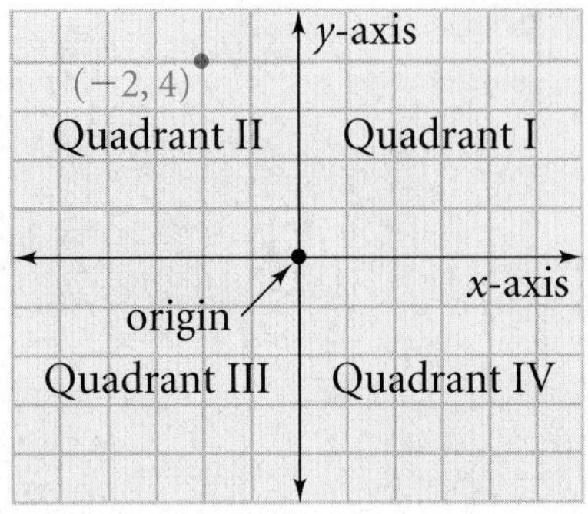

An **ordered pair** of numbers identifies the location of a point. These numbers are the **coordinates** of the point.

(−2, 4)

***x*-coordinate** ***y*-coordinate**

Name the point with the given coordinates in the graph at the right.

1. (2, 3) **2.** (−5, −3)

3. (−3, 2) **4.** (0, −5)

Name the coordinates of each point in the graph at the right.

5. *A* **6.** *F*

7. *D* **8.** *I*

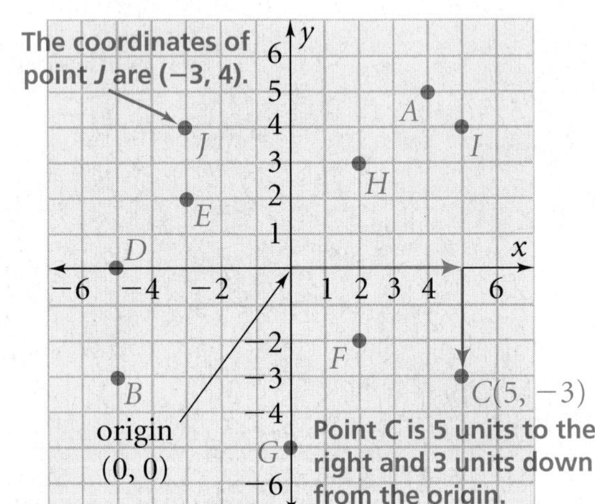

Graph each point on a coordinate plane.

9. (3, 0) **10.** (−1, 8)

11. (−2, −3) **12.** (7, −7)

In which quadrant or on which axis would you find each point?

13. (−10, 6) **14.** (−12, 0) **15.** (8, −18) **16.** (0, 30)

17. **a.** Graph each point on a coordinate plane.
(−4, 0), (0, 1), (1, 5), (2, 1), (6, 0), (2, −1), (1, −5),(0, −1), (−4, 0)
b. Connect the points in order and describe the figure formed.

18. **Writing** Write a sentence describing the *x*- and *y*-coordinates of all points in Quadrant IV.

2-1 Analyzing Data Using Scatter Plots

What You'll Learn

- Drawing and interpreting scatter plots
- Analyzing trends in scatter plots

...And Why

To predict trends related to television and transportation

What You'll Need

- graph paper
- tape measure

WORK TOGETHER

Work in groups.

1. a. **Data Collection** Measure the heights and arm spans for each member of your group.
   b. Write the measurements as ordered pairs (height, arm span).
   c. Graph the ordered pairs for your data. Label the graph as shown.

2. a. **Data Collection** Share your data with all other groups in your class.
   b. Graph the data for your entire class.

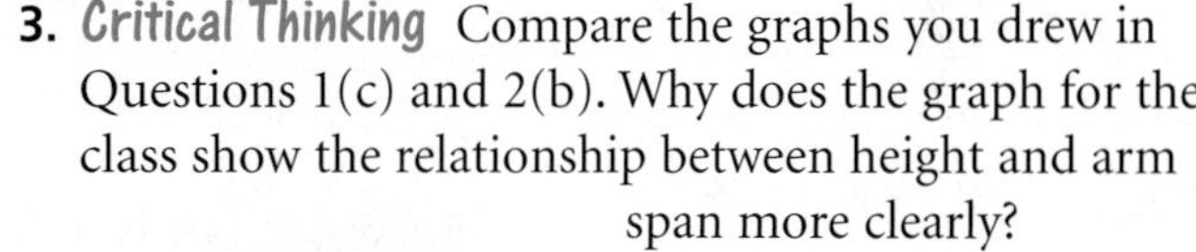

3. **Critical Thinking** Compare the graphs you drew in Questions 1(c) and 2(b). Why does the graph for the class show the relationship between height and arm span more clearly?
4. **Discussion** Describe the relationship between height and arm span.

TECHNOLOGY HINT

You can use spreadsheet software or a graphing calculator to make a scatter plot.

THINK AND DISCUSS

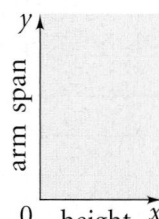

Drawing and Interpreting Scatter Plots

A **scatter plot** is a graph that relates data from two different sets. To make a scatter plot, the two sets of data are plotted as ordered pairs.

Example 1 **Relating to the Real World** 

Television A group of students set out to see if the hours of television they watched yesterday relates to their scores on today's test. They polled each student in the group. Draw a scatter plot of the data.

A Test of Television

Hours Watched	Test Score	Hours Watched	Test Score
0	92	2	80
0	100	2.5	65
0.5	89	2.5	70
1	82	3	68
1	90	3.5	60
1	95	4	65
1.5	85	4.5	55
2	70	5	60

Plot as: (2, 80)

The highest test score is 100. So, a reasonable scale on the vertical axis is from 0 to 100 with every ten points labeled.

A Test of Television

Test Score: 0, 10, 20, 30, 40, 50, 60, 70, 80, 90, 100

Hours Spent Watching Television: 0, 1, 2, 3, 4, 5

5. Two students in the sample watched 2 hours of television. What does the graph tell you about the students' test scores?

6. a. A student in the sample scores 85 on the test. How many hours of television did this student watch?
   b. How can you tell by looking at the scatter plot?

7. **Try This** Each ordered pair represents (unit price, quantity sold) of various items for sale in a store. Draw a scatter plot of the data. (\$5.00, 56), (\$9.99, 4), (\$8.49, 21), (\$1.09, 71), (\$.35, 92), (\$5.00, 32)

Analyzing Trends in Data

You use scatter plots to investigate trends relating two sets of data. These trends show positive, negative, or no correlation.

A **trend line** on a scatter plot shows a correlation more clearly.

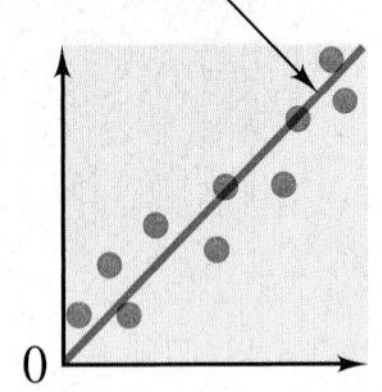

Positive correlation
In general, both sets of data increase together.

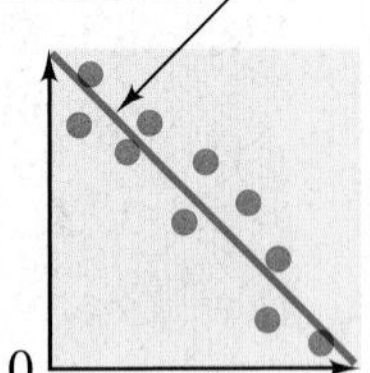

Negative correlation
In general, one set of data decreases as the other set increases.

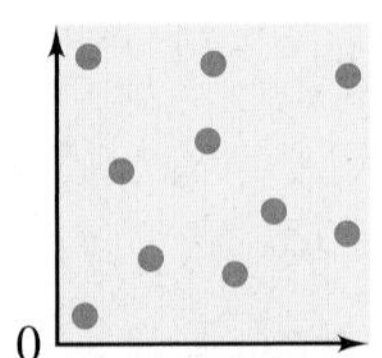

No correlation
Sometimes data sets are not related.

Example 2 **Relating to the Real World** 

Cars The scatter plot below shows information from newspaper advertisements for a particular car model. Is there a *positive correlation,* a *negative correlation,* or *no correlation* between the ages and asking prices of these cars? Explain.

Advertised Prices of a Car Model

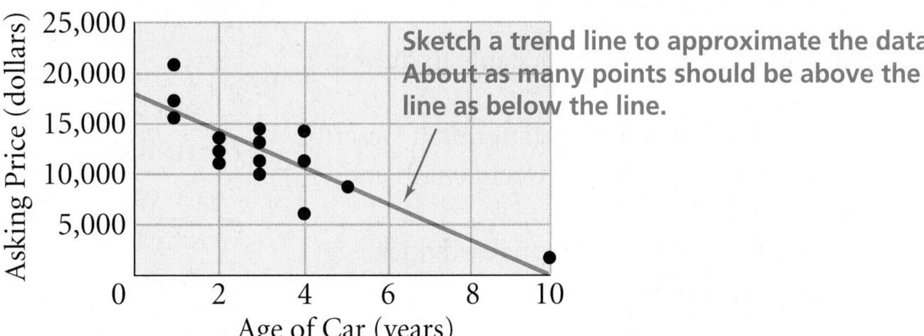

GRAPHING CALCULATOR HINT

You can use a graphing calculator to draw a trend line.

This trend line slants downward, so there is a negative correlation. As the age of the car increases, the price of the car decreases.

8. **Critical Thinking** What does each data point in Example 2 represent? Think of your answer in terms of (*x*–coordinate, *y*–coordinate).
9. **Predict** the asking price of a 7-year old car of the same model.

Exercises ON YOUR OWN

Critical Thinking **Would you expect a *positive correlation,* a *negative correlation,* or *no correlation* between the two data sets? Why?**

1. Amount of Free Time vs. Number of Classes Taken
2. Air Pollution Levels vs. Number of Cars on the Road
3. Snow Shovel Sales vs. Amount of Snowfall
4. Length at Birth vs. Month of Birth
5. the Number of Gallons of Heating Oil Consumed vs. Average Daily Temperature
6. Number of Cavities vs. Number of Times you Floss Your Teeth
7. Cost of a Pair of Sneakers vs. Sneaker Size
8. Number of Calories Burned vs. Time Exercising
9. a. **Math in the Media** Think about the weather and its effect on voters. What correlation would you expect between inches of precipitation and voter turnout? Explain.
   b. Should candidates in the election be concerned about the weather forecast? Why or why not?

See special election-day supplement with complete guide to ballot questions.

The Daily Tribune

RAIN, HEAVY AT TIMES
CHANCE OF SNOW
HIGH: 38 LOW: 30
FULL REPORT ON PAGE 20

4, 1997

10. During one month at a local deli, the number of pounds of ham sold decreased as the number of pounds of turkey sold increased.
   a. Is this an example of a *positive correlation, negative correlation,* or *no correlation?*
   b. **Critical Thinking** Does this mean that fewer pounds of ham were sold *because* the deli sold more pounds of turkey? Could there be another reason? Explain.

11. a. **Nature** Use the data in the table to draw a scatter plot.
   b. Draw a trend line on the scatter plot. Describe the correlation, if any, between length and mass of a bird egg.
   c. Measure the length of the mallard duck egg at the right. **Predict** its mass.

How Big Is a Bird Egg?

Type of Bird Egg	Length (cm)	Mass (g)
Swallow	1.9	2
Swift	2.5	3.6
Turtledove	3.1	9
Partridge	3.6	14
Barn owl	3.9	20.7
Arctic tern	4.0	19
Louisiana egret	4.5	27.5
Grey heron	6.0	60
Chicken (small)	5.3	42.5
Chicken (extra large)	6.3	63.8

Is there a *positive correlation,* a *negative correlation,* or *no correlation* between the two data sets in each scatter plot?

12.

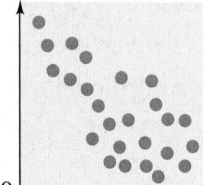

13. 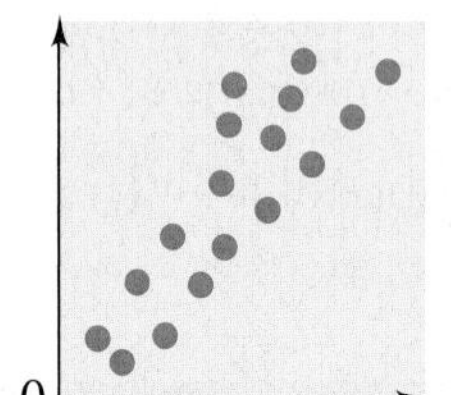

14. 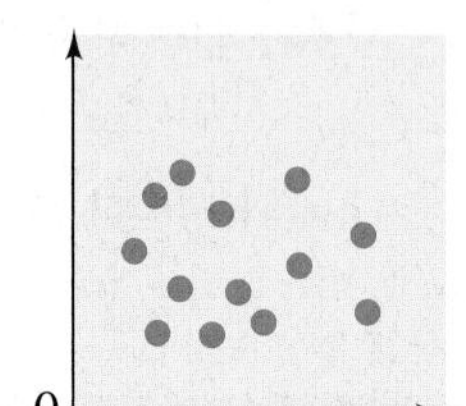

15. 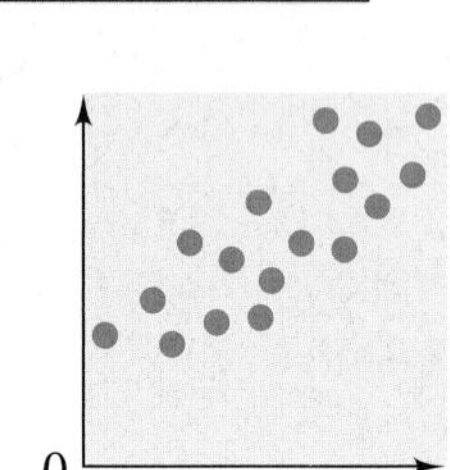

16. **Open-ended** Describe three different situations: one that shows a positive correlation, one that shows a negative correlation, and one that shows no correlation.

Nutrition **Use the table below for Exercises 17–18.**

Calories and Fat in Some Common Foods

	Milk	Eggs	Chicken	Ham	Ice Cream	Corn	Ground Beef	Broccoli	Cheese
Grams of Fat*	8	6	4	19	14	1	10	1	9
Number of Calories*	150	80	90	245	270	70	185	45	115

*per serving

Source: *Home and Garden Bulletin No. 72*

17. a. Draw a scatter plot. Label the x-axis as Fat (g) and the y-axis as Number of Calories.
   b. Is there a *positive correlation, negative correlation,* or *no correlation* between calories and grams of fat?

18. a. **Writing** Write a statement to **generalize** the relationship between calories and grams of fat.
   b. **Critical Thinking** Do you think this statement is always true? **Justify** your answer with an example.

Toll Charges for 12 Vehicles on the Indiana Toll Road

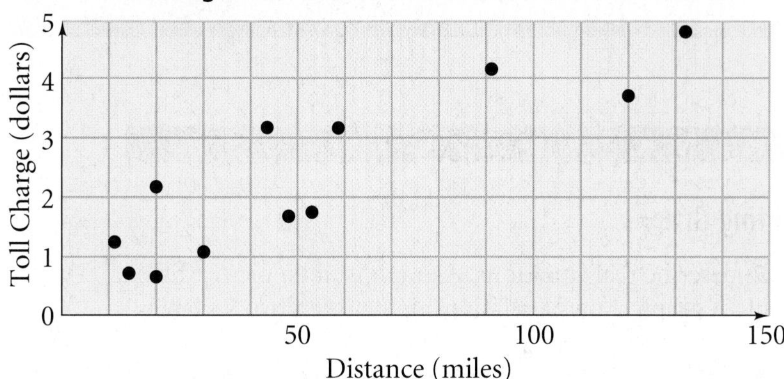

Source: *Indiana Department of Highways*

Transportation **Use the scatter plot above.**

19. What does each data point in the scatter plot represent? Think of your answer in terms of (x-coordinate, y-coordinate).

20. How can you tell which vehicles traveled the same distance?

21. a. How can you tell which vehicles paid the same toll charge?

b. **Open-ended** Why might two vehicles that travel different distances pay the same toll charge?

22. Is there a correlation between distance traveled and toll charges? Explain your reasoning.

Chapter Project **Find Out by Doing**

Work in a group. Choose a tongue twister from p. 57.

- Time one person saying the tongue twister. Record the time to the nearest tenth of a second.
- Time two people saying the tongue twister. Be sure they speak one after the other.
- Add more people. Make a table for the data you collect.
- Collect data from other groups.
- Draw a scatter plot for all the data. Describe any correlation you see.

Exercises MIXED REVIEW

Evaluate each expression for $x = -3, y = 5$, and $z = 1$.

23. $3x + 2y - z$

24. $x^3 - 3z + y$

25. $\dfrac{y^2 + 2z}{x}$

26. $6x^2 - 4z^2$

27. $\dfrac{x + 6z}{2y}$

28. $z(y - 8)$

29. $x^2 + y^2 - z$

30. $z^3 - x^2$

31. **Critical Thinking** Is it easiest to find the mean, median, or mode of data in a line plot? Explain.

Getting Ready for Lesson 2-2

Use the graph at the right.

32. Describe the trend in minimum wage earnings.

33. Over which years did the minimum wage remain the same?

34. Over which years did the greatest increase in minimum wage occur? How do you know?

Minimum Wages

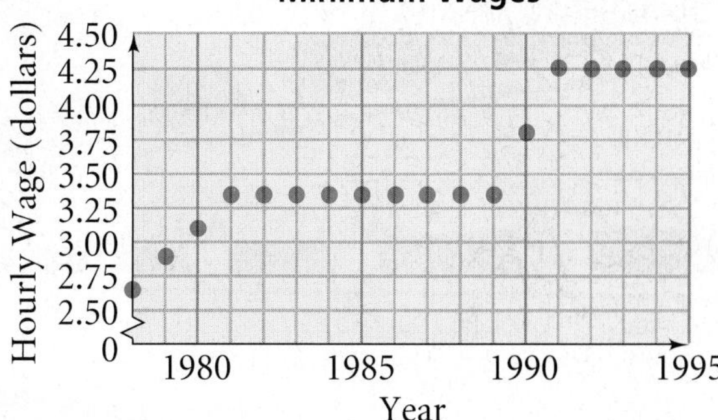

Source: *Statistical Abstract*

What You'll Learn

- Interpreting and sketching graphs from stories
- Classifying data as discrete or continuous

...And Why

To solve problems relating to travel and transportation

2-2 Relating Graphs to Events

THINK AND DISCUSS

Interpreting Graphs

Graphs can describe real situations. A graph is not a picture like a photograph. A graph shows a relationship between two variables.

PROBLEM SOLVING

Look Back Another way to solve Example 1 is by writing a description. Write a short paragraph to describe the graph.

Example 1 **Relating to the Real World**

Transportation A commute home from school combines walking with taking the subway. The graph describes the trip by relating the variables time and total distance. Describe what the graph shows.

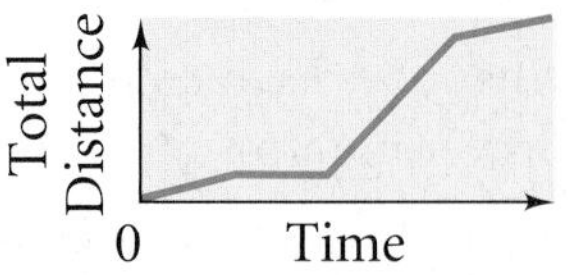

A Commute Home

Total Distance

0 Time

To describe a graph, you can label each part.

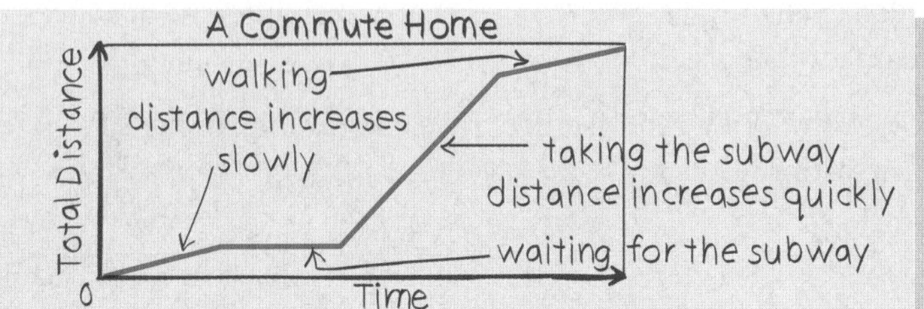

1. **Critical Thinking** Explain why the section of the graph showing the person waiting for the subway is flat.

2. Why is the subway section steeper than the walking sections?

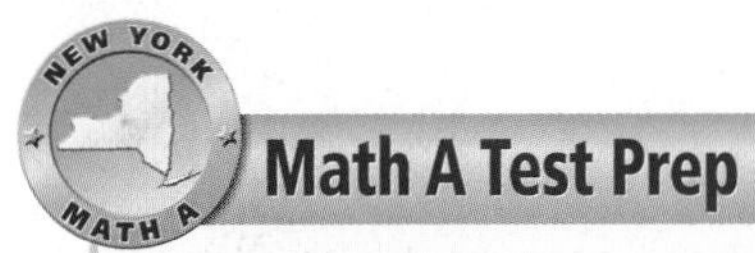

1 Between which two data sets would you expect a negative correlation?
(1) Annual Income vs. Years of Education
(2) Number of Vehicles Passing through Intersection vs. Inches of Snowfall
(3) Math Test Scores vs. Day of Birth
(4) Number of People at Beach vs. Temperature

2 This graph shows Dave's morning run. Compare and contrast the intervals between times 10 and 15 and times 15 and 20.

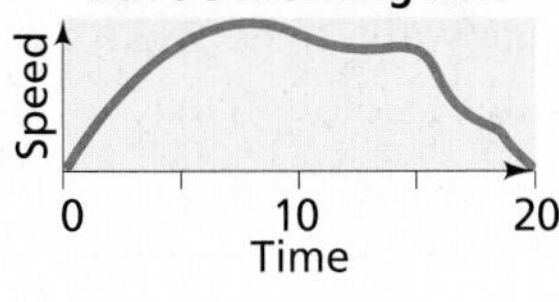

This graph shows the relationship between time and speed on a bike ride.

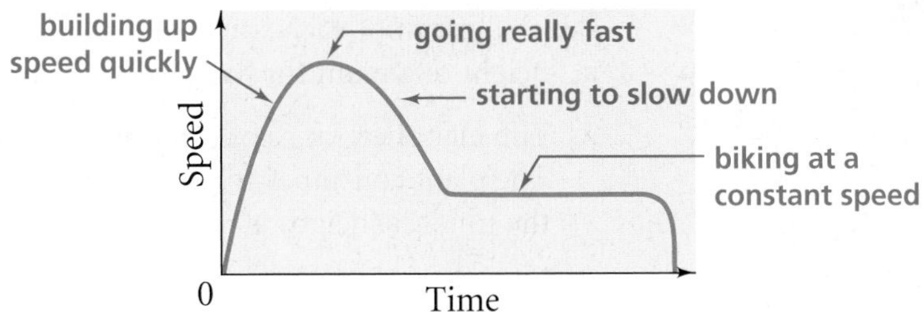

3. A friend mistakenly states that this graph describes a person bicycling up and then down a hill. What would you say to this friend to help clear up the misconception?

Sketching Graphs

When you draw a graph without actual data, the graph is called a *sketch.* A sketch is useful when you want to get an idea of what a graph looks like.

Example 2 Relating to the Real World

Travel The Shermans are visiting friends several miles from home. On the way, they stop to buy juice drinks. After a few hours, they return home. Sketch a graph to describe the trip. Label the sections.

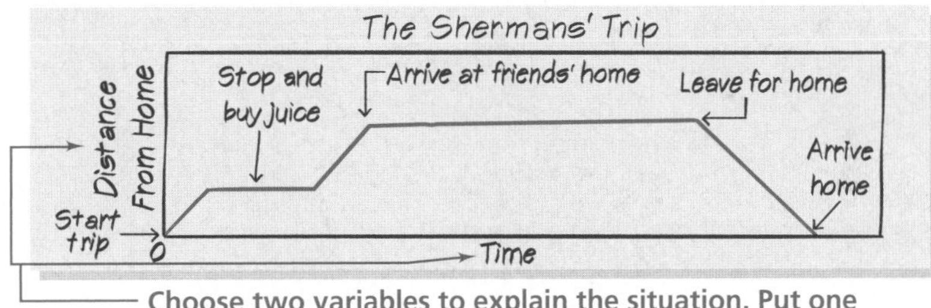

Choose two variables to explain the situation. Put one on the horizontal axis and the other on the vertical axis.

4. How is an increase in distance from home shown on the graph? a decrease?

5. **Try This** Sketch a graph to describe your height from the ground on a roller coaster ride. Explain the activity in each section of the graph.

Classifying Data

In this lesson you have worked with variables such as time and distance. Variables represent data values that are *discrete* or *continuous.* **Continuous data** usually involve a measurement, such as temperature, length, or weight. **Discrete data** involve a count, such as a number of people or objects.

Who? In 1926, a Japanese plant pathologist named E. Kurosawa found a way to increase plant growth. He used a plant hormone called *gibberellin* to increase the growth rate of rice and corn stems.

Source: *Encyclopedia of Science and Technology*

Example 3

Classify the data as *continuous* or *discrete*. Explain your reasoning and sketch a graph of each situation.

a. height of a plant for five days **b.** class attendance for five days

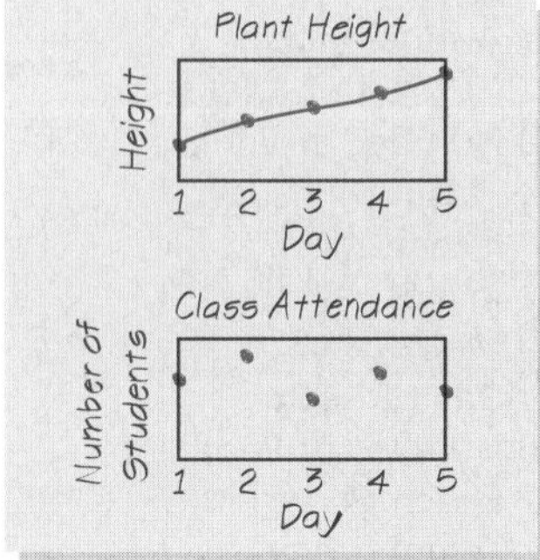

a. The plant height is continuous. The plant continues to grow between the times its height is measured.

b. The attendance is discrete. Each day's count is distinct. For example, there is no meaning for values between Monday's and Tuesday's counts.

6. **a. Generalize** how graphs of continuous and discrete data differ.
   b. *Open-ended* Give another example of each type of data.

WORK TOGETHER

Students get to school in a variety of ways. They may walk, drive, take a bus or subway, or ride a bike. The graph shows one student's daily trip.

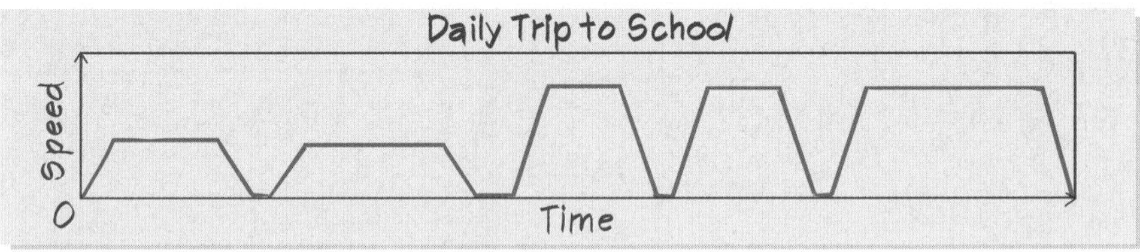

Work with a partner.

7. Write a story describing how this student traveled to school and the events that took place during the trip.
8. Draw two new graphs to represent your daily trip and your partner's. Present your graphs to the class.

Exercises ON YOUR OWN

Sketch a graph to describe each situation. Explain the activity in each section of the graph.

1. your distance from the ground as you jump rope
2. your energy level during one gym class
3. your pulse rate as you watch a scary movie
4. your speed as you skateboard downhill

5. **Critical Thinking** What is wrong with the graph at the right? Explain how you would fix this graph.

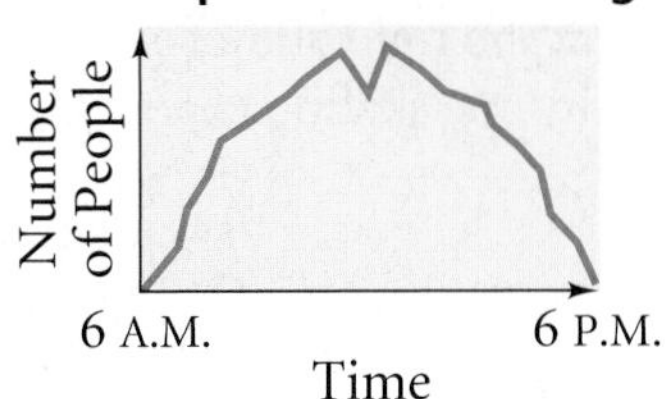

6. **Meteorology** The graph shows barometric pressure in Pittsburgh, Pennsylvania, during the blizzard of 1993. Describe what happened to pressure during the storm.

Source: *Purdue Weather Processor*

Classify the data as *discrete* or *continuous*. Explain your reasoning and sketch a graph of each situation.

7. your weight from birth to age 14
8. your algebra test grades for one term
9. the time you get up each morning for one week
10. temperatures throughout one week
11. number of books you bring home each day for a week
12. length of your hair between haircuts
13. your walking speed from this class to your locker
14. time you spend reading each day for a week

15. The graph at the right shows the weight of a baby and the weight of a puppy for their first two years.
    a. Which curve represents the puppy's weight? the baby's?
    b. Describe the growth patterns of the baby and the puppy.

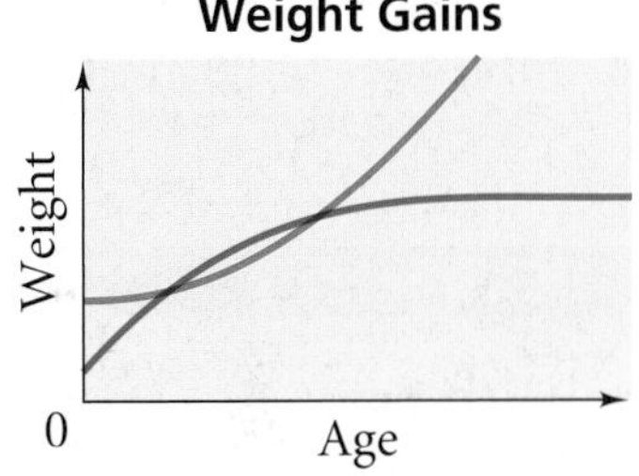

16. **Open-ended** Give an example of discrete data changing over time. Explain your reasoning and sketch a graph of the situation.

17. **Cars** On a highway, a driver sets a car's cruise control for a constant speed of 55 mi/h. Which graph shows the distance the car travels? Which graph shows the speed of the car? Explain your reasoning.

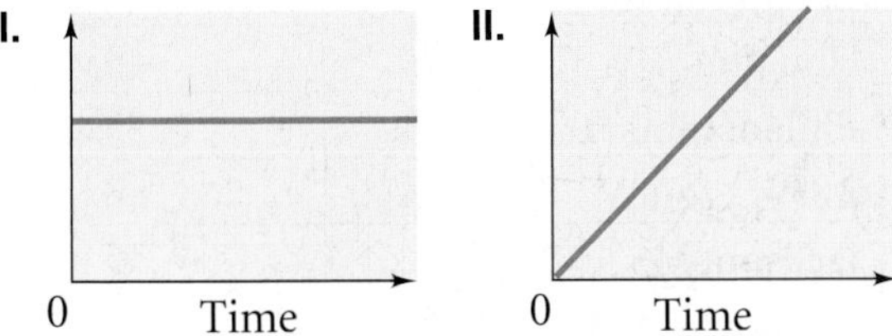

18. Use the cartoon at the right.
    a. What do you think the labels of the axes are?
    b. What is the presenter trying to imply with his graph?
    c. Why is his presentation misleading?
    d. Why might he want to do this?

"As you can see, our profit picture is steady."

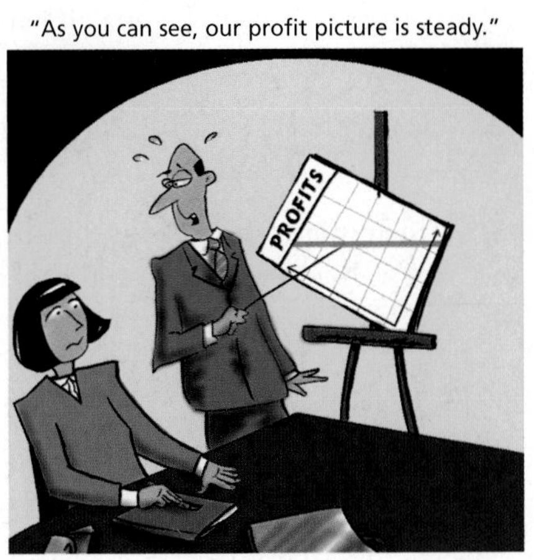

19. **Writing** Describe what the graph at the right shows about a student's in-line skating experience.

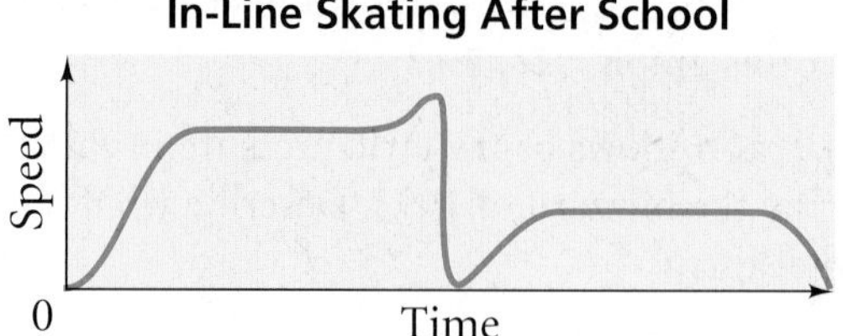

Exercises MIXED REVIEW

In Exercises 20–22, add or subtract.

20. $\begin{bmatrix} 2 & -3 \\ 0 & 8 \end{bmatrix} + \begin{bmatrix} -5 & 9 \\ 7 & -6 \end{bmatrix}$

21. $\begin{bmatrix} 18 & 26 \\ 37 & 12 \end{bmatrix} - \begin{bmatrix} 32 & 15 \\ 39 & 63 \end{bmatrix}$

22. $\begin{bmatrix} 2.3 & 7.5 \\ 0.9 & 8.1 \end{bmatrix} - \begin{bmatrix} 6.8 & 9.2 \\ 1.3 & 0.9 \end{bmatrix}$

23. a. **Cooking** A hotel kitchen uses 200 lb more vegetables than fruit each day. Write an expression for how many pounds of vegetables the kitchen uses.
    b. Suppose the kitchen uses 1000 lb of fruit daily. How many pounds of fruit and vegetables does the kitchen use each week?

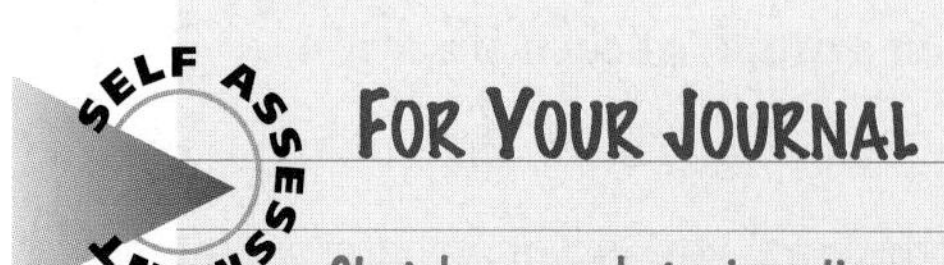

FOR YOUR JOURNAL

Sketch a graph to describe a situation that happened to you. Explain the activity in each section of the graph.

Getting Ready for Lesson 2-3

Graph each ordered pair on a coordinate plane.

24. (0, 4) 25. (−9, 3) 26. (−3, −2) 27. (2.4, −6)

Exercises CHECKPOINT

1. a. **Statistics** Use the data to draw a scatter plot.
   b. Draw a trend line on the scatter plot. Describe the correlation, if any, between latitude and average low temperature.
   c. What would you expect the average low temperature to be in a city at 20° north latitude?

City	Latitude (°N)	Average Daily Low Temperature in January (°F)
Miami, FL	26	59
Honolulu, HI	21	66
Houston, TX	30	40
Philadelphia, PA	40	23
Burlington, VT	44	8
Jackson, MS	32	33
Cheyenne, WY	41	15
San Diego, CA	33	49

Source: *Statistical Abstract of the United States*

2. **Open-ended** Describe a situation that shows a positive correlation.

3. Which graph shows your distance from home as you walk to the library and back? Explain.

A. Distance / 0 / Time

B. 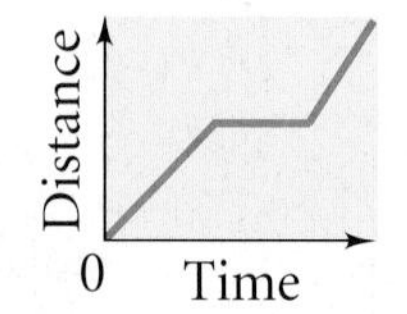

C. 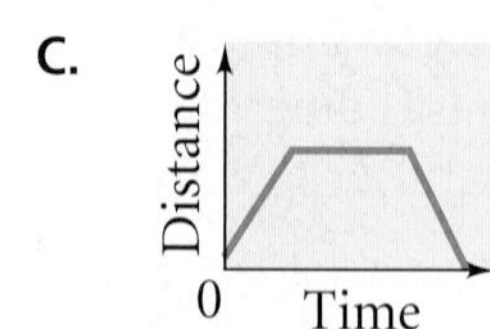

D. 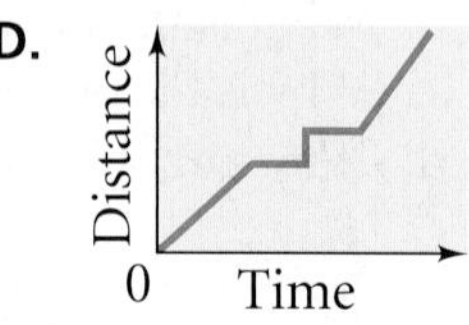

2-3 Linking Graphs to Tables

What You'll Learn

- Choosing a scale and graphing data in tables
- Identifying independent and dependent variables

...And Why

To solve problems that involve health and weather

What You'll Need

- blocks or tiles

WORK TOGETHER

Patterns Work with a partner to construct or sketch stairs out of blocks.

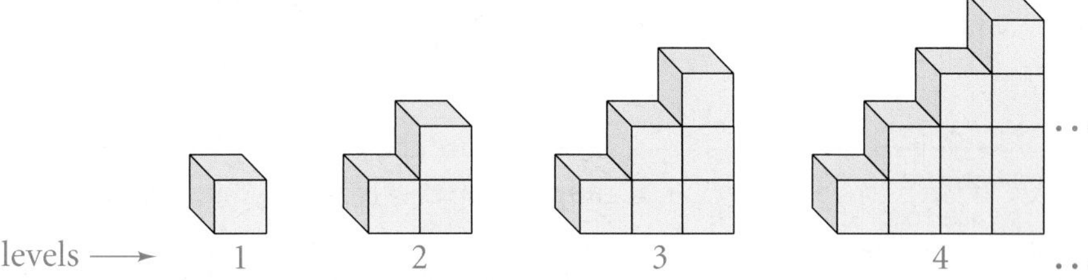

Number of Levels	Number of Blocks
1	1
2	3
3	■
4	■
5	■
6	■

1. Copy and complete the table at the left.
2. a. Graph the data in the table. Plot the points as the ordered pairs (number of levels, number of blocks).
   b. Should the points be connected? Why or why not?
   c. Describe any trends you see between the number of levels and the number of blocks.

THINK AND DISCUSS

Health You use tables to organize data. Sometimes a graph shows patterns or trends in data better than a table does.

Target Heart Rates

Age in Years	Beats per Minute
15	143.5
20	140.0
25	136.5
30	133.0
35	129.5
40	126.0
45	122.5

Source: *World Almanac and Book of Facts*

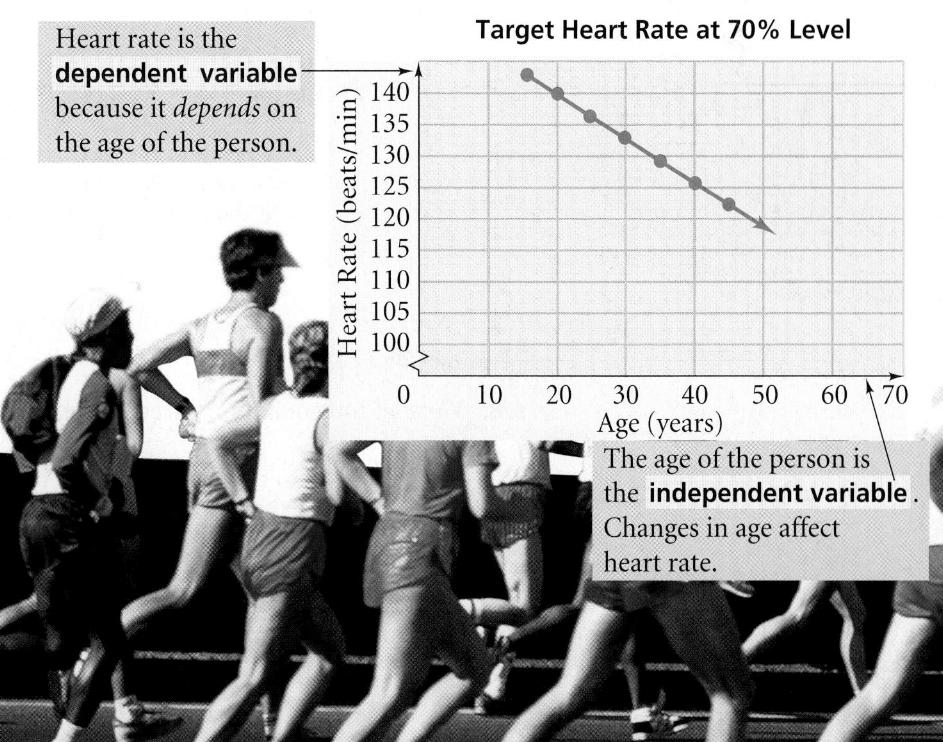

3. **Health** What is the target heart rate for a 70-year-old? Explain how you got your answer.

4. **Critical Thinking** Describe the relationship between the age of a person and the target heart rate.

5. Which axis relates to the independent variable? the dependent variable? Write a statement to **generalize** this.

6. **Try This** Identify the independent and dependent variables in the Work Together activity.

TECHNOLOGY HINT

You can use spreadsheet software to graph data in tables. You can improve the look of your graph by changing the scales on the *x*-axis and *y*-axis.

You can use data in tables to make graphs. You need to choose an appropriate scale so the data are easy to graph and understand.

Example **Relating to the Real World** 

Weather Graph the data in the table on a coordinate plane.

To draw a graph, first identify the least and greatest values for each set of data. Then, select a scale that includes these values and can easily be divided into equal sections.

How Altitude Affects Temperature

Altitude (meters)	Temperature (°C)
0	13.0
144	12.0
794	11.4
1501	11.4
3100	5.6
5781	−9.7
7461	−22.5
9511	−36.3
10,761	−44.9

Source: The University of Illinois at Urbana-Champaign's Web site *Weather World*

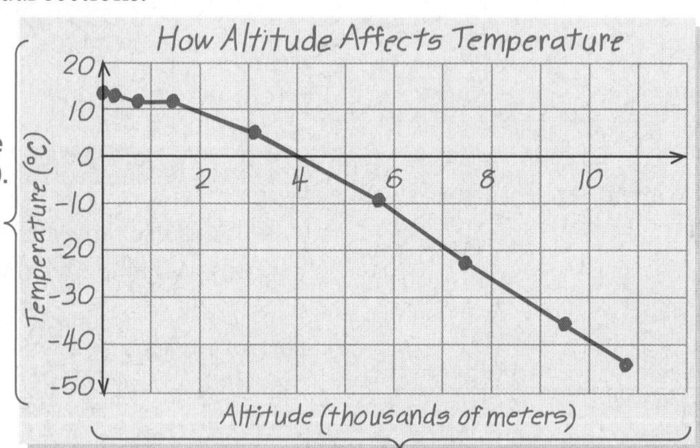

The *y*-values range from −44.9 to 13.0. So, choose a scale from −50 to 20 and label intervals of 10.

The *x*-values range from 0 to 10,761. So, choose a scale from 0 to 12,000 and label intervals of 2000. The *x*-axis is in thousands of meters to make graphing easier.

7. **Try This** Which variable is the dependent variable? the independent variable? Explain.

8. Were all four quadrants needed to graph the data? Why or why not?

9. Describe what happens to the temperature as the altitude increases.

10. a. **Open-ended** Write a question that might be of interest to a meteorologist and can be answered using the table or graph.
    b. Answer the question you wrote in part (a).

Exercises ON YOUR OWN

1. a. *Science* What scales do you need to graph the data in the table?
   b. Draw the graph.
   c. How can you use the graph to approximate your own weight on the moon?

Weight on Earth (lb)	143	94	127	171
Weight on Moon (lb)	23.6	15.5	21	28.2

Identify the independent and dependent variables.

2. hours worked, amount paid
3. area of a square, length of a side
4. weight of book, number of pages
5. weight of apples, cost of apples
6. For Exercises 2–5, write a statement using the word *depends*.

Match each table of data to its graph.

7.

x	y
−1	−1
0	0
1	−1
2	−4

8.

x	y
−2	$\frac{1}{4}$
−1	$\frac{1}{2}$
1	2
2	4

9.

x	y
−2	3
−1	1
0	−1
1	−3

A.
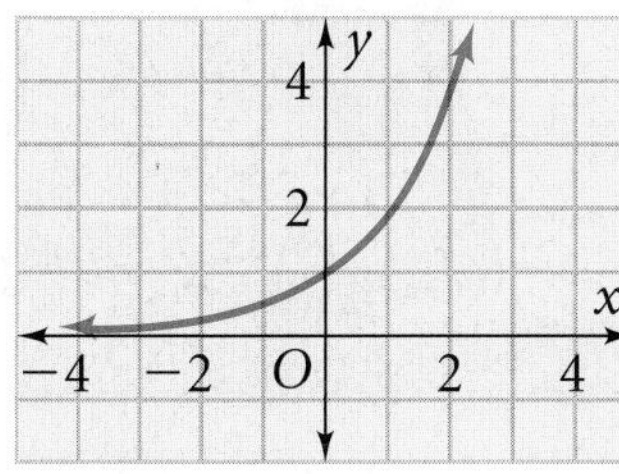

B.
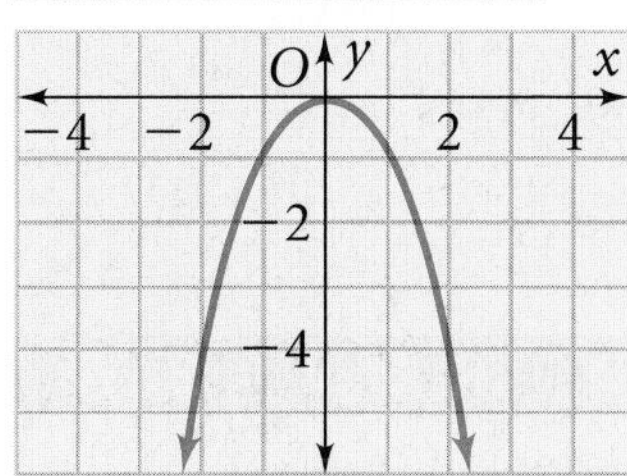

C.
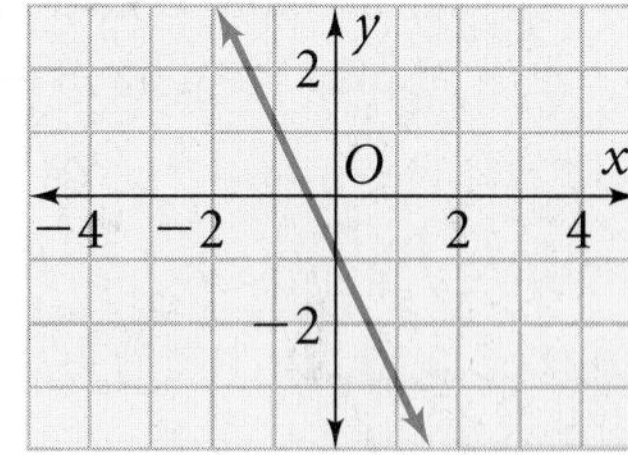

10. *Banking* Many people borrow money when they buy a car. The length of the loan might be anywhere from 2 to 6 years. The table shows the monthly payments on a loan of $10,000 at 9% interest.

Length of Loan (yr)	2	3	4	5	6
Monthly Payment ($)	456.95	318.08	248.92	207.64	180.31

   a. *Critical Thinking* What can you tell about the relationship between the length of the loan and the monthly payments?
   b. Identify the independent and dependent variables.
   c. Graph the data.
   d. Is it easier to see the relationship on a graph or in a table? **Justify** your answer.

11. a. Graph the data in the table at the right.
    b. What scales did you use and why?

High School Dance

Minutes Dancing	Admission
43	$5
12	$5
16	$5
111	$5
90	$5

12. **Physics** *Charles's Law* relates the volume of a gas to its temperature.
   a. What quadrant(s) do you need to draw to graph the data?
   b. Identify the dependent and independent variables.
   c. What happens to the volume of a gas as temperature increases?
   d. Graph the data.

Charles's Law

Temperature (°C)	Volume (m^3)
−100	173
−50	223
0	273
50	323
100	373

13. **Writing** Define *dependent variable* and *independent variable* in your own words. Provide an example to illustrate your definitions.

14. **Baseball** In 1919, Babe Ruth broke the record for the longest home run.
   a. Graph the data in the table to approximate the path of the ball.
   b. Use the graph to estimate how far Babe Ruth hit the ball.
   c. In 1960, Mickey Mantle of the New York Yankees hit a home run 643 ft. Did he break Babe Ruth's record?
   d. **Research** How far would a home run need to be hit to clear the baseball stadium nearest you?

Babe Ruth's Record Home Run

Distance	Height
0	3
100	83
200	132
300	147
400	128
500	75
575	13

BABE RUTH
LIFETIME BATTING STATISTICS
1925

Chapter Project ***Find Out by Graphing***

Sopchoppy, Florida, is the home of the Sopchoppy Shoe Shop. Time the tongue twister "The Sopchoppy Shoe Shop sells shoes" with a group of at least ten people. Use the same method you used in the Find Out question on page 63.

- Identify the dependent and independent variables.
- Record your data in a table.
- Display the data in an appropriate graph.

Exercises MIXED REVIEW

Sketch a graph to describe each situation. Explain the activity in each section of the graph.

15. your speed as you march in a parade

16. the money you spend each day for a week

17. a. **Statistics** Make a line plot for the data: 33, 36, 32, 33, 35, 33, 36.
   b. What is the mode of the data?
   c. **Open-ended** What situation could the data represent?

Getting Ready for Lesson 2-4

Evaluate each expression.

18. $3a - 2$ for $a = -5$

19. $\frac{x + 3}{-6}$ for $x = 3$

20. $8p - p$ for $p = -11$

21. $3x^2$ for $x = 6$

22. $\frac{x + 5}{-2}$ for $x = 9$

23. $b^3 - 4b$ for $b = -1$

24. $7 - a$ for $a = -3$

25. $\frac{3b}{4}$ for $b = 12$

SELF ASSESSMENT
FOR YOUR JOURNAL
Record an example of anything you found difficult in today's lesson.

What You'll Learn

- Defining relations, functions, domain, and range
- Evaluating functions
- Analyzing graphs

...And Why

To solve problems involving money and exercise

2-4 Functions

THINK AND DISCUSS

Identifying Relations and Functions

Suppose your summer job pays $4.25 an hour. Your pay *depends* on the number of hours you work. The number of hours is the independent variable and pay is the dependent variable. So, you can say that pay *is a function of* the number of hours you work.

1. Identify the independent and dependent variables for each situation.
   a. number of magazines sold and the profit made selling magazines
   b. amount of money in the yearbook committee treasury and the number of days the committee can afford to rent camera equipment

2. Write each situation in Question 1 using the words *is a function of*.

Your Summer Job

Hours Worked	Pay
0	$0
1	$4.25
2	$8.50
3	$12.75

You can write the data in the table as a set of ordered pairs {(0, 0),(1, 4.25), (2, 8.50), (3, 12.75)}. Any set of ordered pairs is called a **relation.**

A **function** is a relation that assigns exactly one value of the dependent variable to each value of the independent variable. So, if x is the independent variable and y is the dependent variable, there can be only one y-value for each x-value.

PROBLEM SOLVING

Look Back Graph$(-2, -1)$ and $(-2, 1)$ on a coordinate plane. How are these points alike? How are they different?

Example 1

Determine if each relation is a function.

a.

x	y	
11	−2	→ (11, −2)
12	−1	→ (12, −1)
13	0	→ (13, 0)
20	7	→ (20, 7)

The relation is a function because exactly one y-value is assigned to each x-value.

b.

x	y	
−2	−1	→ (−2, −1)
−3	0	→ (−3, 0)
6	3	→ (6, 3)
−2	1	→ (−2, 1)

The relation is not a function because two y-values, −1 and 1, are assigned to one x-value, −2.

3. a. ***Open-ended*** Create a data table or set of ordered pairs that is a relation but *not* a function.

b. ***Open-ended*** Create a data table or set of ordered pairs that is a function.

Evaluating Functions

QUICK REVIEW

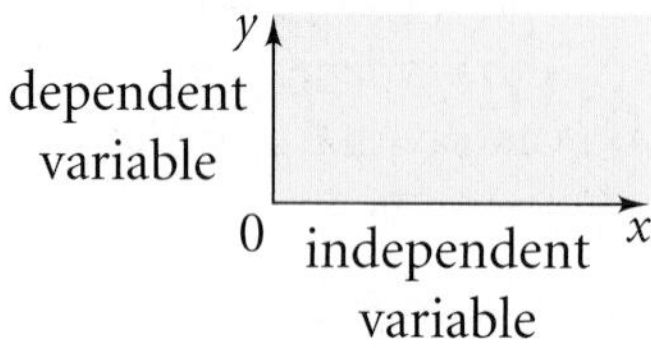

A **function rule** is an equation that describes a function. If you know the input values, you can use a function rule to find the output values.

$$y = 3x + 4$$

The rule shows you that y is a function of x.

output values dependent variable (points to y)

input values independent variable (points to x)

Example 2

Evaluate the function rule $y = 2x^2 - 7$ for $x = -4$.

$y = 2x^2 - 7$

$y = 2(-4)^2 - 7$ ← Substitute –4 for x.

$y = 2(16) - 7$ ← Find $(-4)^2$ first.

$y = 32 - 7$ ← Then multiply.

$y = 25$

When the x-value is –4, the y-value is 25.

QUICK REVIEW

Follow the Order of Operations.

1. Perform any operation(s) inside grouping symbols.
2. Simplify any terms with exponents.
3. Multiply and divide in order from left to right.
4. Add and subtract in order from left to right.

4. a. Evaluate the function rule in Example 2 for $x = 4$.

b. ***Critical Thinking*** Explain why $y = 2x^2 - 7$ is a function.

5. **Try This** Evaluate each function rule for $x = 6$.

a. $y = x - 11$

b. $y = -3x^2 + 1$

c. $y = \frac{1}{2}x^2$

d. $y = 1.5 + 2x$

Names Used with a Function

independent variable	dependent variable
input	output
domain	range
x-values	y-values

The **domain** of a function is the set of all possible input values. The **range** of a function is the set of all possible output values. You can write both the domain and the range using braces, {}. The summary box at the left shows some common names for the input and output values of a function.

Example 3

Find the domain and range of the function $\{(-2, 4), (-1, 1), (0, 0), (1, 1), (2, 4)\}$.

The domain is the set of all input values $\{-2, -1, 0, 1, 2\}$.

The range is the set of all output values $\{0, 1, 4\}$.

Example 4 Relating to the Real World 

Bicycling The distance a wheel moves forward is a function of the number of rotations. The function rule $d = 7n$ describes the relationship between the distance d the wheel in the photo moves in feet and the number of rotations n. Find the range when the domain is {0, 2.5, 8}.

Substitute 0 for *n*.	Substitute 2.5 for *n*.	Substitute 8 for *n*.
$d = 7n$	$d = 7n$	$d = 7n$
$d = 7(0)$	$d = 7(2.5)$	$d = 7(8)$
$d = 0$	$d = 17.5$	$d = 56$

The range of the function is {0, 17.5, 56}.

6. Describe what the domain and the range represent in Example 3.

Analyzing Graphs

The domain and range values can be written as ordered pairs (x, y). These ordered pairs are points on the graph of a function. You can tell if a relation is a function by analyzing its graph. One way is to use the **vertical-line test.** If a vertical line passes through a graph more than once, the graph is not the graph of a function.

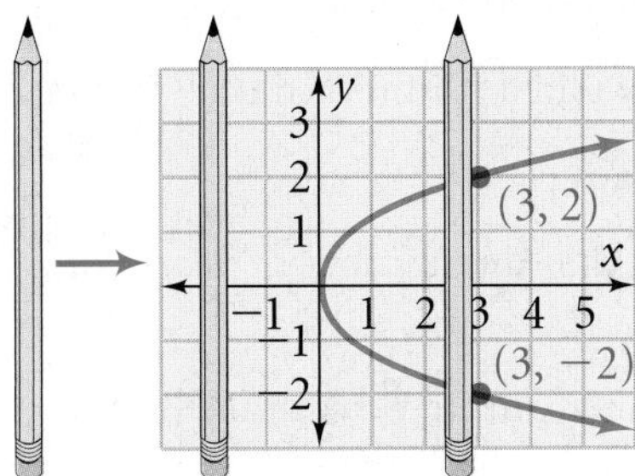

Pass a pencil across the graph as shown. Keep your pencil straight to represent a vertical line.

The pencil goes through more than one point on the graph. This graph is not the graph of a function because there are two y-values for the same x-value.

7. Why does the vertical-line test work? (*Hint*: How does the vertical-line test relate to the definition of a function?)

WORK TOGETHER

Work with a partner.

8. Use the vertical-line test to determine if the graphs are graphs of functions. Explain why or why not.

a. 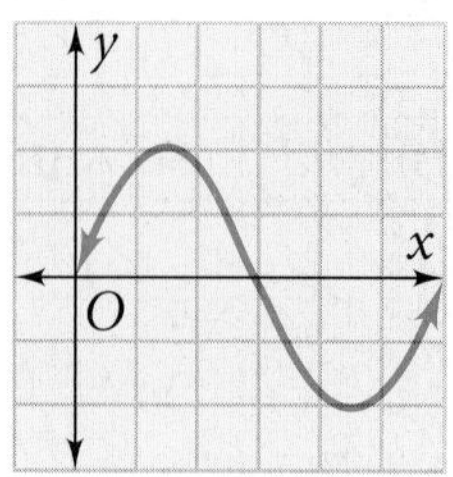

b. 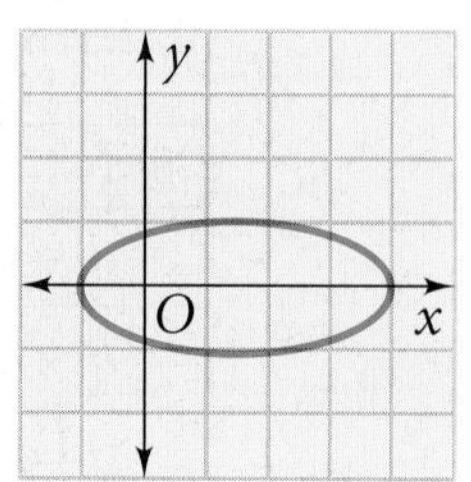

c. 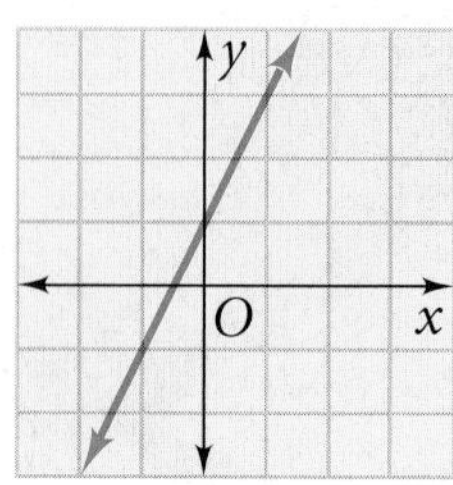

9. Can the graph of a function be a horizontal line? a vertical line? Why or why not?

Exercises ON YOUR OWN

Evaluate each function rule for $x = -3$.

1. $y = x + 7$
2. $y = 11x - 1$
3. $y = x^2$
4. $y = -4x$
5. $y = 15 - x$
6. $y = 3x^2 + 2$
7. $y = \frac{1}{4}x$
8. $y = -x + 2$

Does each graph represent a function? Why or why not?

9. 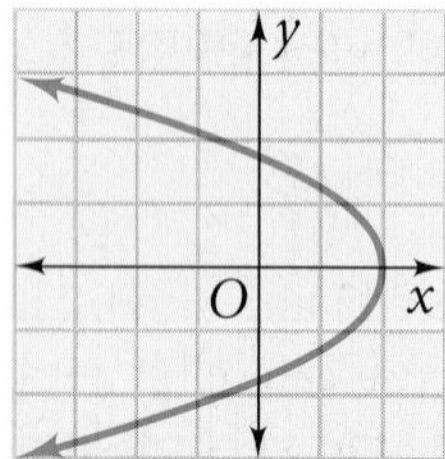

10. 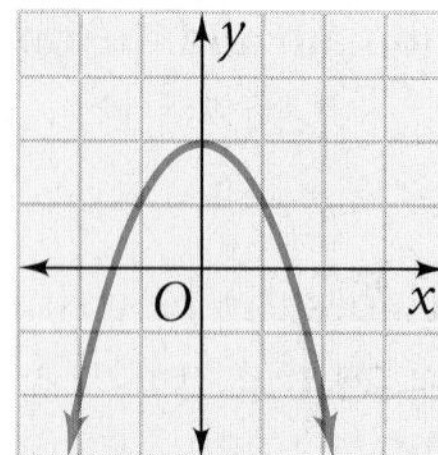

11. 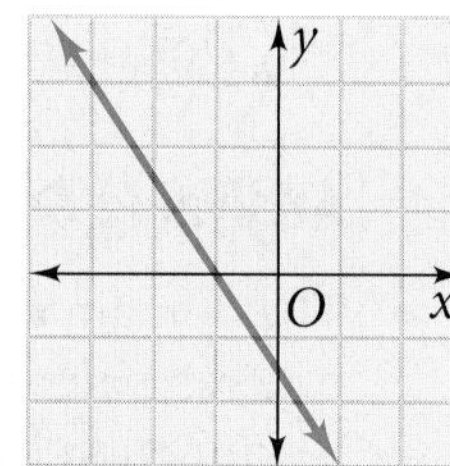

12. 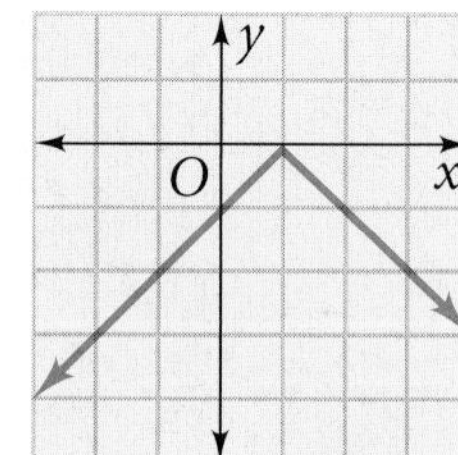

Which relations in Exercises 13–17 are functions? If the relation is a function, identify the dependent and independent variables.

13. number of tickets sold for a benefit play and amount of money made
14. students' heights and grade point averages
15. amount of your monthly loan payment and the number of years you pay back the loan
16. cost of electricity to run an air conditioner during peak usage hours and the number of hours it runs
17. time it takes to travel 50 miles and the speed of the vehicle

Determine whether each relation is a function. If the relation is a function, state the domain and the range.

18.

x	y
1	−3
6	−2
9	−1
10	0
1	3

19.

x	y
0	2
0	−2
3	1
3	−1
5	3

20.

x	y
2	12
1	5
0	0
−1	−3
−4	0

21.

x	y
−4	−4
−1	−4
0	−4
2	−4
3	−4

22. **Communications** The cost of a telephone call c is a function of the time spent talking t in minutes. The rule $c = 0.22t$ describes this function. At the right, a student calculates how much a 2-h phone call will cost.

c = 0.22 × 2
= 0.44
$.44 for 2 hours

a. **Mental Math** Why does the student's answer seem unreasonable?
b. What mistake(s) did the student make?
c. How much does it cost to make a 2-h phone call?

23. **a.** **Open-ended** Sketch a graph of a relation that is not a function.
b. **Writing** Explain why the graph you drew is not a function graph.

24. **a.** **Business** A store bought disposable cameras for \$300. The store's profit p is a function of the number of cameras sold c. Find the range of $p = 6c - 300$ when the domain is {0, 15, 50, 62}.
b. In this situation, what do the domain and range represent?

Find the range of each function when the domain is {–1, 0, 6}.

25. $g = 5 + r$ **26.** $b = \frac{1}{2}a + 110$ **27.** $w = \frac{11(h - 40)}{2}$ **28.** $y = x^2 + 1$

29. $q = 4p - 7$ **30.** $p = 2.4h$ **31.** $t = 6s^2$ **32.** $d = 60r$

33. $y = -x^3 + 6$ **34.** $d = 5t$ **35.** $y = x^2 - x$ **36.** $y = -\frac{x}{14}$

37. **a.** **Language Arts** Copy and complete the analogy:
"Input value is to output value as independent variable is to _?_.
b. Write an analogy using *input, output, domain,* and *range.*

38. **Music** There are 52 white keys on a piano. The frequency of each key is the number of vibrations per second the key's string makes.
a. Is this relation a function? Explain your reasoning.
b. **Writing** Describe the patterns in the table.

Key Position	1	8	15	22	29	36	43
Frequency	27.5	55	110	220	440	880	1760

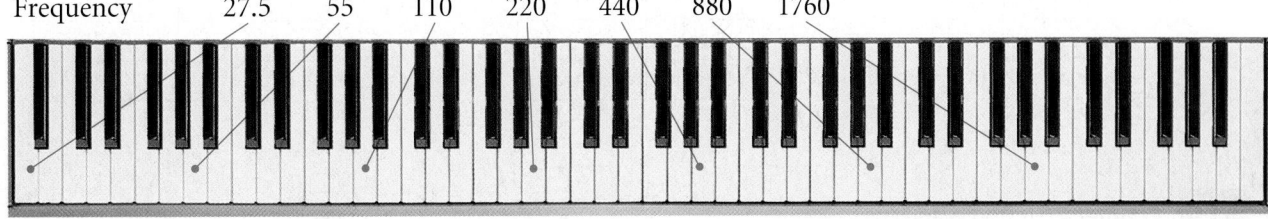

Evaluate each function rule for $x = 0.6$.

39. $y = x + 1.53$ **40.** $y = 3x^2$ **41.** $y = \frac{1}{3}x - 4.5$ **42.** $y = -4x$

43. $y = \frac{x^2}{9}$ **44.** $y = 34 - x$ **45.** $y = -x^2 + 2x$ **46.** $y = \frac{4x - 2}{7}$

Find the range of the function rule $y = x^2$ for each domain.

47. $\{0.5, 11\}$ **48.** $\{-1.2, 0, 4\}$ **49.** $\{-5, -1, 0, 2, 10\}$ **50.** $\left\{-\frac{1}{2}, \frac{1}{4}, \frac{2}{5}\right\}$

51. *Critical Thinking* Suppose a classmate looks at the graph at the right and says, "This graph is not a function because both 2 and –2 have a y-value of 4." Explain what is wrong with this student's statement.

(–2, 4) (2, 4) 4 2 y x –4 –2 O 2 4 –2

52. *Science* Light travels at a speed of approximately 186,000 miles per second. The function rule $d = 186{,}000t$ describes the relationship between distance d in miles and time t in seconds.

a. How far does light travel in 20 seconds?

b. How far does light travel in 1 minute?

c. Make a table of values for this function rule.

53. *Standardized Test Prep* What is the range of the function $y = x^2 - 3$ when the domain is $\{2, 4, 6\}$?

A. $\{-1, 1, 3\}$ **B.** $\{1, 5, 9\}$ **C.** $\{1, 1, 9\}$ **D.** $\{1, 13, 33\}$ **E.** $\{6, 10, 14\}$

Exercises MIXED REVIEW

54. a. Which variable is the independent variable? the dependent variable?

b. Graph the data in the table.

c. Use your graph to **predict** the retail price of an item with a \$30 wholesale price.

Wholesale Price (\$)	10.00	15.00	20.00	25.00
Retail Price (\$)	17.50	26.25	35.00	43.75

Simplify each expression.

55. $72 \div (8 + 4)$ **56.** $5^2 + 9.5$ **57.** $86 - 18 \div 3$ **58.** $\frac{6 + 2}{4}$ **59.** $\frac{2}{5} - \frac{1}{2}$

Getting Ready for Lesson 2-5

Use an equation to model the relationship in each table.

60.

Number of People	Total Bill
1	\$3.00
2	\$6.00
3	\$9.00
4	\$12.00

61.

Amount Earned	Amount Spent
\$15	\$5
\$30	\$10
\$45	\$15
\$60	\$20

62.

Number of Days	Supplies Remaining
0	12 lb
2	10 lb
4	8 lb
6	6 lb

What You'll Learn

- Writing rules for functions from tables and words

...And Why

To solve problems related to computers and jobs

2-5 Writing a Function Rule

THINK AND DISCUSS

Understanding Function Notation

In the last lesson, you learned that a function rule is an equation that describes a function. Sometimes the equation is written using function notation. To write a rule in **function notation,** you use the symbol $f(x)$ in place of y. You read $f(x)$ as "f of x."

QUICK REVIEW

You can also write a function rule using "$y =$." For example, $f(x) = 2x + 5$ is equivalent to $y = 2x + 5$.

$$f(x) = 2x - 5$$

output values dependent variable ($f(x)$); input values independent variable (x)

The rule shows you that $f(x)$ is a function of x.

Function notation allows you to see the input value. Suppose the input value above is -2. Here is how to find $f(-2)$.

$$f(-2) = 2x - 5$$
$$f(-2) = 2(-2) - 5$$
$$f(-2) = -9$$

Be careful: $f(x)$ does not mean "f times x"!

When the input value is -2, the output value is -9.

1. **Try This** Find $f(7)$ and $f(0)$.
2. **a.** Write an equation equivalent to $y = 7x + 6$ using function notation.
   b. Find the range of the function when the domain is $\{-1, 0, 5\}$.

QUICK REVIEW

domain = input values
range = output values

Using a Table of Values

You can write a rule for a function by analyzing a table of values.

Example 1

Patterns Write a function rule for each table.

a.

x	$f(x)$
1	5
2	6
3	7
4	8

Look for a pattern relating x and $f(x)$.

Ask yourself, "What can I do to 1 to get 5, 2 to get 6, . . . ?"

Relate $f(x)$ equals x plus four
Write $f(x) = x + 4$

b.

x	$f(x)$
0	0
3	9
6	36
9	81

Ask yourself, "What can I do to 3 to get 9, 6 to get 36, . . . ?"

$f(x)$ equals x times itself
$f(x) = x^2$

Price	Tax
\$5.00	\$.25
\$3.00	\$.15
\$2.00	\$.10
\$.60	\$.03

3. **a.** Find $f(7)$ for parts (a) and (b) in Example 1.
b. Did you use the function rule or the table in each case? Why?

4. **a.** Identify the independent variable and the dependent variable for the table at the left.
b. **Try This** Let the independent variable be x and the dependent variable be $f(x)$. Write a function rule for the table.

Using Words to Write a Rule

You can also write a rule from a description of a situation. When you define variables, you may wish to use letters other than x and $f(x)$.

Example 2 **Relating to the Real World** 

Computers The Computer Museum in Boston, Massachusetts, features an exhibit called The Walk-Through Computer™ 2000. You can walk on and through this giant computer and experience it firsthand. The exhibit is about 20 times larger than a normal-sized desktop computer. Write a function rule to describe this relationship.

Define	$n =$ normal size				
	$L(n)$ = larger size shown in museum exhibit				
Relate	larger size	is	20	times	normal size
Write	$L(n)$	$=$	20	$\cdot$	n

The rule $L(n) = 20n$ describes the relationship.

5. The space bar in the normal-sized computer measures $4\frac{3}{8}$ in. $\times$ $\frac{5}{8}$ in. Approximate the dimensions of the space bar in the museum exhibit.

6. **Critical Thinking** The keyboard in the exhibit is 20 ft long and 10 ft wide. Find the approximate dimensions in inches of the normal-sized keyboard.

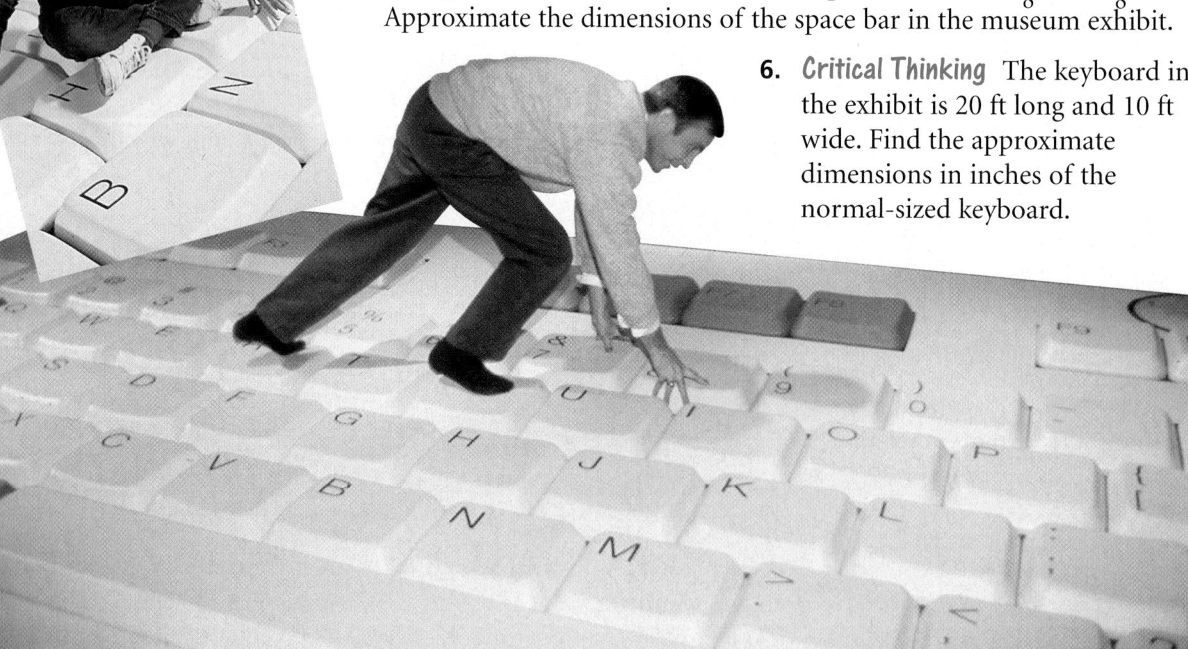

Writing a rule from words may involve more than one operation.

Example 3 ***Relating to the Real World*** 

Jobs Suppose you borrow money from a relative to buy a lawn mower that costs \$245. You charge \$18 to mow an average-size yard. Write a rule to describe your profit as a function of the number of lawns mowed.

Define l = number of lawns mowed
$P(l)$ = total profit

Relate	total profit	is	\$18	times	lawns mowed	minus	cost of mower
Write	$P(l)$	$=$	18	$\cdot$	l	$-$	245

The function rule $P(l) = 18l - 245$ describes your profit.

7. ***Critical Thinking*** Find $P(9)$.What does $P(9)$ mean?

8. How many lawns would you need to mow to pay for the lawn mower?

Exercises ON YOUR OWN

Find $f(-4)$ for each function.

1. $f(x) = x^2$ **2.** $f(x) = 5 - x$ **3.** $f(x) = 7(x + 2)^2$ **4.** $f(x) = -x^3$

5. $f(x) = -x - 2$ **6.** $f(x) = x^3 + 6$ **7.** $f(x) = x + 25$ **8.** $f(x) = 6x$

9. ***Laundry*** Use the function in the table at the right.
   a. Identify the dependent and independent variables.
   b. Write a rule to describe the function.
   c. How many gallons of water will you use for 7 loads of laundry?
   d. ***Critical Thinking*** In one month, you used 546 gal of water. How many loads did you wash? How did you find your answer?

Number of Loads	Gallons of Water Used
1	42
2	84
3	126
4	168

10. ***Food*** At a supermarket salad bar, the price of a salad depends on its weight. Salad costs \$.19 per ounce.
   a. Write a rule to describe the function. **b.** How much will an 8-ounce salad cost?

11. ***Writing*** What advantage(s) can you see of having a function rule instead of a table of values for a function?

Match each table of values with a rule at the right.

12.

x	$f(x)$
-2	-4
-1	-3
0	-2
1	-1

13.

x	$f(x)$
-1	-2
-2	-4
-3	-6
-4	-8

14.

x	$f(x)$
-1	-3
0	-4
1	-5
2	-6

A. $f(x) = 2x$
B. $f(x) = x - 2$
C. $f(x) = -4 - x$

Math in the Media **Use the advertisement for Exercises 15–17.**

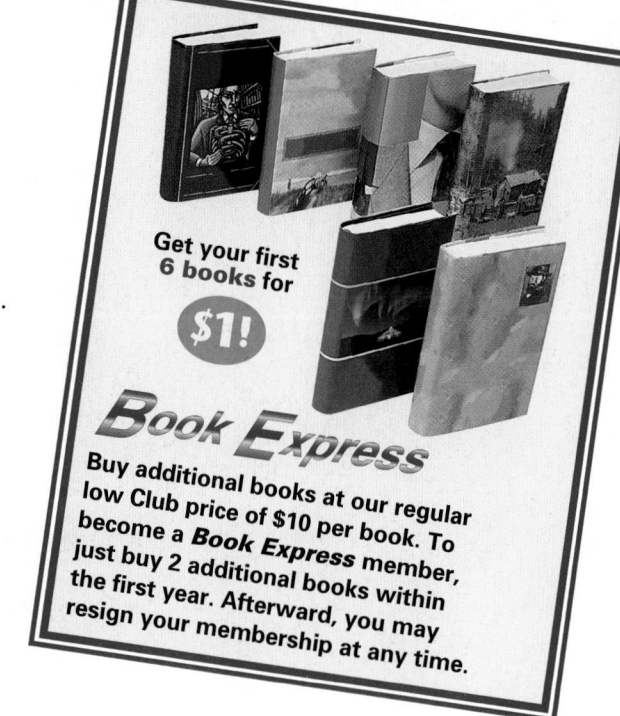

Get your first 6 books for $1!

Book Express

Buy additional books at our regular low Club price of $10 per book. To become a *Book Express* member, just buy 2 additional books within the first year. Afterward, you may resign your membership at any time.

15. a. Write a rule to find the total cost $T(a)$ for all the books a person buys through Book Express. Let a represent the additional books bought (after the first 6 books).
    b. Suppose a person buys 9 books in all. Find the total cost.

16. A bookstore sells the same books for an average price of $6 each.
    a. Suppose you plan to buy 12 books. What is the average cost per book as a member of Book Express?
    b. Is it less expensive to buy 12 books at the club or at a bookstore? **Justify** your answer.

17. a. **Research** Find an ad for another book club in a magazine.
    b. Select 9 books you would be interested in buying. Compare the cost of the 9 books you selected to the cost at Book Express.

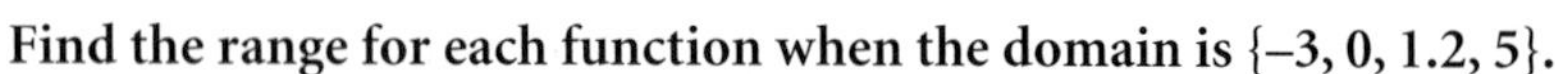

Find the range for each function when the domain is {–3, 0, 1.2, 5}.

18. $f(x) = x^3$
19. $C(g) = 15 - g$
20. $y = 1.3x$
21. $R(s) = -s^2$
22. $y = -4x$
23. $f(g) = g^2 + 1$
24. $G(n) = (n - 5)^2$
25. $f(x) = 6x - 4$

Patterns **Write a function rule for each table.**

26.

x	$f(x)$
1	0.5
2	1
3	1.5
4	2

27.

x	y
−2	−8
−1	−4
0	0
1	4

28.

x	y
3	9
6	18
9	27
12	36

29.

x	$f(x)$
1	1
2	8
3	27
4	64

30. Write another equivalent equation for each table in Exercises 26–29.

31. **Food** Kathy and Rheta share an 8-slice pizza. The number of slices Rheta can eat depends on how many slices Kathy eats. Write a function rule to describe this relationship. What are the domain and range?

For Exercises 32–33, write a function rule to describe each statement.

32. change from a one-dollar bill when buying pencils that cost 20¢ each

33. a worker's earnings when the worker is paid $4.25/h

34. **Standardized Test Prep** Compare the quantities in Column A and Column B.
    A. The quantity in Column A is greater.
    B. The quantity in Column B is greater.
    C. The quantities are equal.
    D. The relationship cannot be determined from the information given.

Column A	Column B
$f(3)$ when $f(x) = 4x - 12$	$f(0)$ when $f(x) = x + 1$

Chapter Project

Find Out by Writing

The function $t(n) = 4.3n$ predicts the time t (in seconds) it takes n people in a row to say the tongue twister "A cricket critic cricked his neck at a critical cricket match."

- Find $t(5)$. Explain what it represents.
- What does $t(0) = 0$ mean?
- Suppose the output is 34.4 s. How can you find the input? What does the input represent?
- Make a table of values for the function and graph it.

Exercises MIXED REVIEW

Evaluate each expression for $t = -2$, $m = 5$, and $s = 1.3$.

35. $m^2 + t$ **36.** $|s| - |t|$ **37.** $-mt$ **38.** $s^2 + t^2$ **39.** $\frac{m}{t}$

Getting Ready for Lesson 2-6

Graph the data in each table.

40.

x	y
−3	−7
−1	−1
0	2
2	8

41.

x	y
−3	4
−2	0
0	−2
2	4

42.

x	y
−4	−3
0	−2
2	−1.5
4	−1

43.

x	y
−2	0.5
1	2
4	3.5
7	5

Exercises CHECKPOINT

1. a. The table at the right shows the number of words read within certain times. Identify the independent and dependent variables.

b. Graph the data. What scales did you use and why?

Number of Minutes	Number of Words Read
4	1100
8	2200
12	3300
16	4400

2. **Writing** Define *relation* and *function* in your own words.

3. Explain how you would find $f(3)$ for $f(x) = 4x - 12$.

Write a function rule to describe each statement.

4. the price of rolls if they cost $.30 each

5. the cost of your dinner if you leave a 15% tip

Find the range of each function when the domain is {–7, 0, 1, 3}.

6. $y = 12(x - 3)$ **7.** $v = 9 - u^2$ **8.** $y = 4x + 2.5$ **9.** $t = s + 4$

Connections — Electrician . . . and more

2-6 The Three Views of a Function

What You'll Learn

- Graphing a function
- Creating a table of values from a rule and a graph

...And Why

To solve problems involving electrician costs

THINK AND DISCUSS

You can model functions using rules, tables, and graphs. Suppose a car gets 30 mi/gal. Then the distance $d(g)$ that the car travels is a function of the number of gallons g.

Rule

$d(g) = 30g$

A function rule shows how the variables are related.

Table of Values

Gallons	Miles
g	$d(g)$
0	0
1	30
2	60
3	90

A table identifies specific values that satisfy the function.

Graph

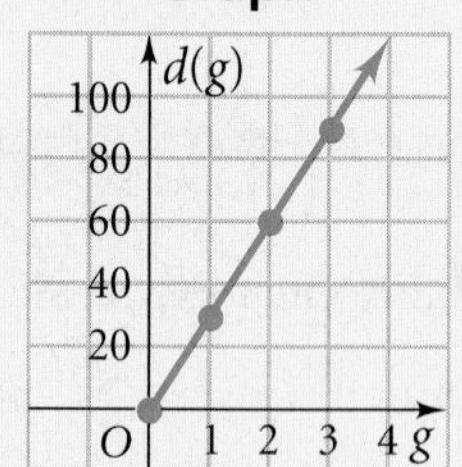

A graph gives a visual picture of the function.

1. a. Suppose the car used 14 gal of gasoline. How far did the car travel?
   b. How did you find your answer to part (a)?
   c. Describe another method of solving the problem.

You can use a rule to model a function with a table of values and a graph.

Example 1 — Relating to the Real World

Electrician Suppose you hire an electrician to install an electrical outlet in a wall. The electrician charges \$68 for materials plus \$40 an hour for service. The total cost $C(h)$ is a function of the number of hours it takes to do the job. Use the rule $C(h) = 68 + 40h$ to make a table of values and then a graph.

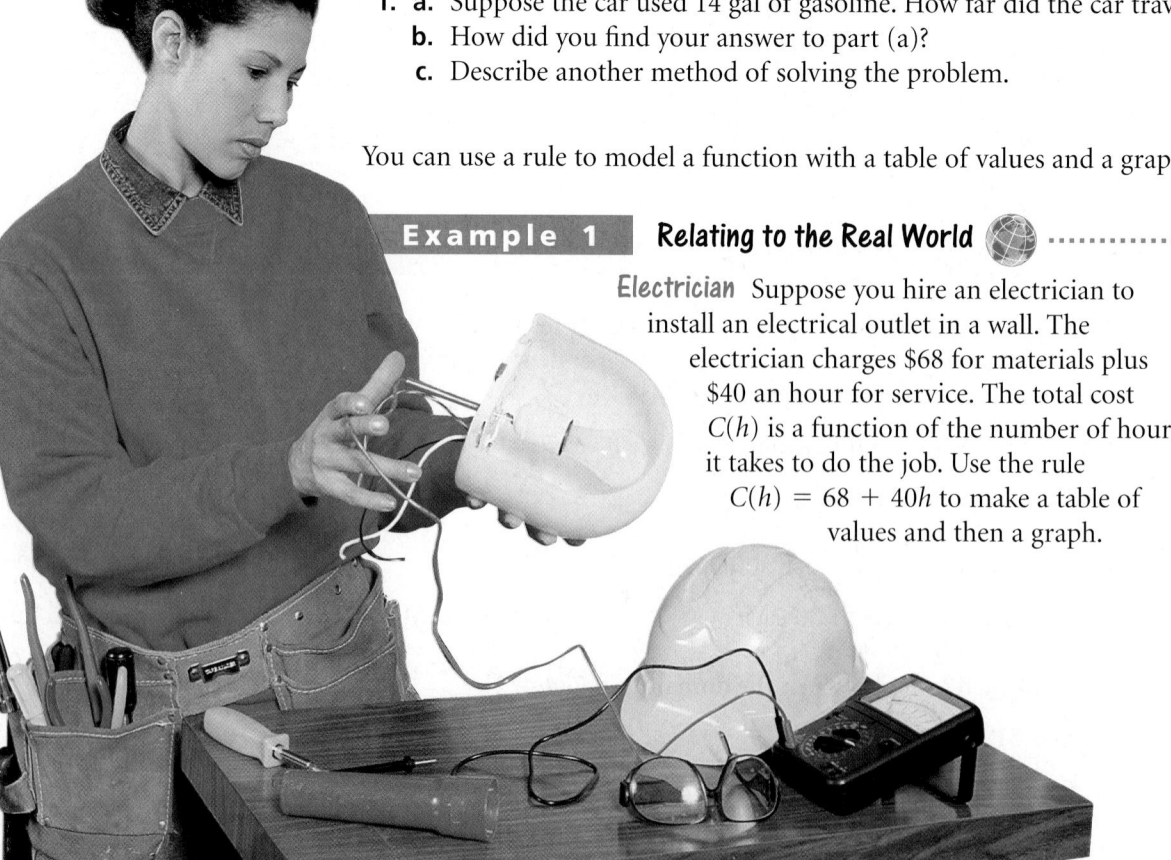

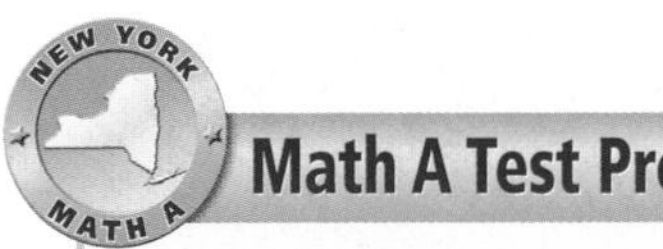

Math A Test Prep

1 Which function is graphed below?

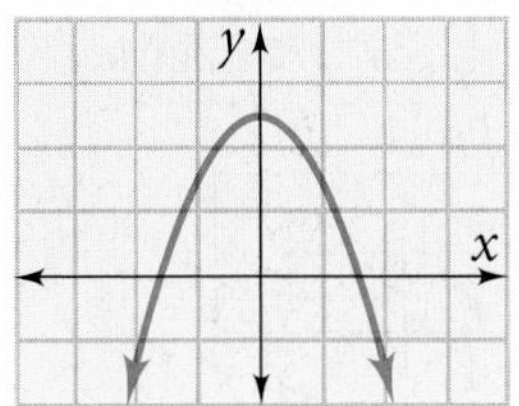

(1) $y = x + 1.5$
(2) $y = -1.625x^2 + 2.5$
(3) $y = 2x + 2.5$
(4) $y = -x^2 + 2.5$

2 A car ad costs \$5.00 plus \$.40 per word.
  a Write a function rule for the cost of an ad.
  b What is the cost of an ad that has 30 words?

STEP 1: Choose values for h that seem reasonable, such as 1, 2.5, 4, and 7.

STEP 2: Input the values for h. Evaluate to find $C(h)$.

h	$C(h) = 68 + 40h$	$(h, C(h))$
1	$68 + 40(1) = 108$	$(1, 108)$
2.5	$68 + 40(2.5) = 168$	$(2.5, 168)$
4	$68 + 40(4) = 228$	$(4, 228)$
7	$68 + 40(7) = 348$	$(7, 348)$

STEP 3: Plot the ordered pairs.

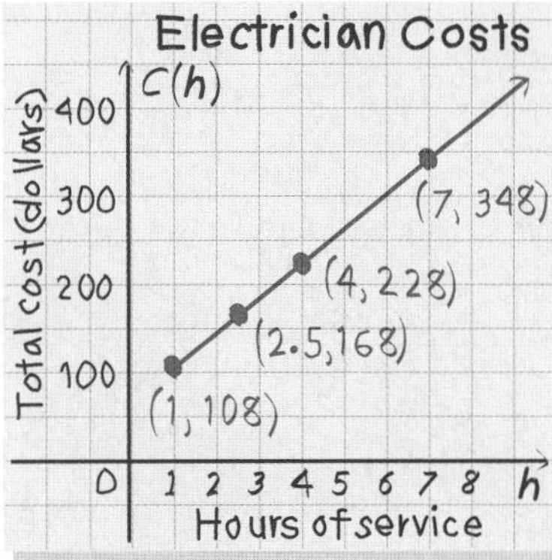

2. a. What is the total cost of the job if it takes $5\frac{1}{2}$ hours?
   b. Did you use the rule, the table, or the graph to answer part (a)?
3. Why are the points on the graph connected by a line?
4. Are negative values for h reasonable? Explain.
5. **Electrician** Suppose this electrician tells you the job will take 2 to 6 hours to complete. What is the range of your costs?
6. **Try This** Model each rule with a table of values and a graph.
   a. $f(x) = -3x + 5$ b. $f(x) = \frac{1}{2}x$

Quick Review

You can also write a function rule using "$y =$ " form. For example, $f(x) = x^2 - x - 6$ is equivalent to $y = x^2 - x - 6$.

Some functions have graphs that are not straight lines. You can graph a function as long as you know its rule.

Example 2

Graph the function $y = x^2 - x - 6$.

First, make a table of values.

x	$y = x^2 - x - 6$	(x, y)
-2	$(-2)^2 - (-2) - 6 = 0$	$(-2, 0)$
-1	$(-1)^2 - (-1) - 6 = -4$	$(-1, -4)$
0	$(0)^2 - (0) - 6 = -6$	$(0, -6)$
1	$(1)^2 - (1) - 6 = -6$	$(1, -6)$
2	$(2)^2 - (2) - 6 = -4$	$(2, -4)$
3	$(3)^2 - (3) - 6 = 0$	$(3, 0)$

Then graph the data.

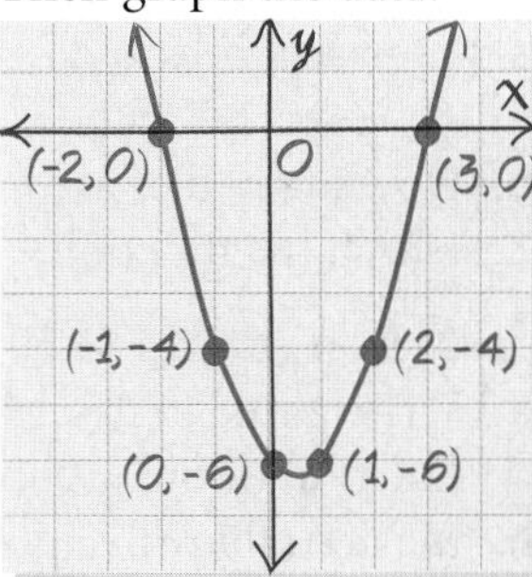

7. What advantage(s) does a rule have in describing a function?
8. **Try This** Graph each function.
   a. $y = -3x^2 + 1$ b. $f(x) = x^2 - 4x - 5$

You can create a table of values from a graph.

Example 3

Make a table of values for the graph below.

Use the scale of the graph to find ordered pairs.

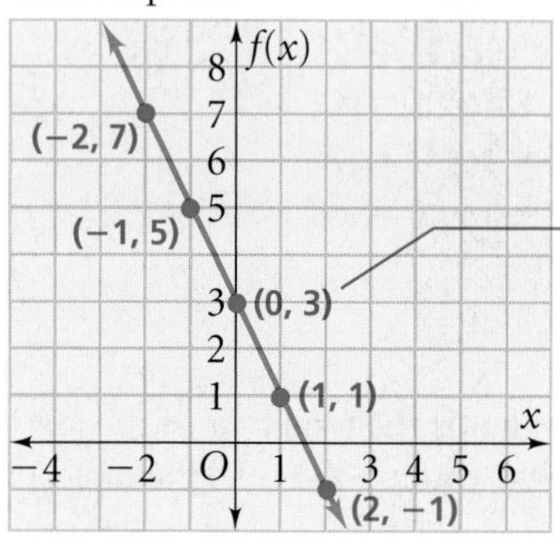

Put the ordered pairs in a table.

x	$f(x)$
−2	7
−1	5
0	3
1	1
2	−1

Exercises ON YOUR OWN

Model each rule with a table of values and a graph.

1. $y = -3x$ **2.** $y = x^2 - 4x + 4$ **3.** $f(x) = 2x - 7$ **4.** $y = 6x^2$

5. $f(x) = \frac{1}{3}x$ **6.** $f(x) = 8 - x$ **7.** $f(x) = x^2 - 2$ **8.** $y = 5 + 4x$

9. **Patterns** The table of values below describes the perimeter of each figure in the pattern of blue tiles at the right. The perimeter P is a function of the number of tiles t.

Number of Tiles (t)	1	2	3	4
Perimeter (P)	4	6	8	10

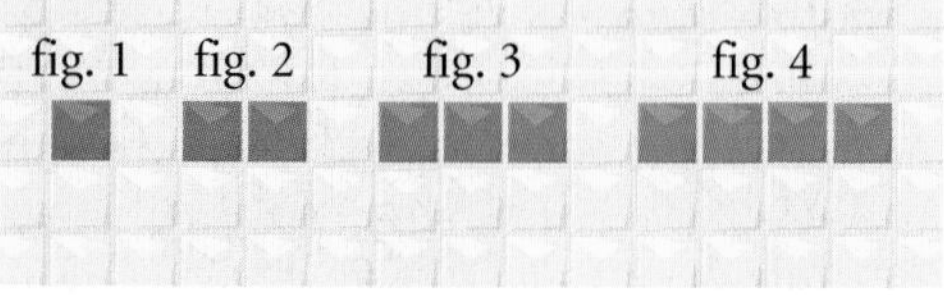

a. Choose a rule to describe the function in the table.

A. $P = t + 3$ **B.** $P = 4t$ **C.** $P = 2t + 2$ **D.** $P = 6t - 2$

b. How many tiles are in the figure if the perimeter is 20?

c. Graph the function.

10. **Jobs** Juan charges \$3.50 per hour for baby-sitting.

a. Write a rule to describe how the amount of money M earned is a function of the number of hours h spent baby-sitting.

b. Make a table of values.

c. Graph the function.

d. **Estimation** Use the graph to estimate how long it will take Juan to earn \$30.

e. **Critical Thinking** Do you think of baby-sitting data as discrete or continuous? Explain your reasoning.

QUICK REVIEW

Continuous data are usually measurements, such as temperatures and lengths. *Discrete data* are distinct counts, such as numbers of people or objects.

11. **Conservation** Use the data at the right.

a. Write a function rule for a standard shower head.

b. Write a function rule for a water-saving shower head.

c. Suppose you take a 6-min shower as recommended and use a water-saving head. How much water do you save compared to an average shower with a standard head?

d. Graph both functions on the same coordinate plane. What does the graph show you?

e. **Open-ended** How much water did you use during your last shower? How did you find your answer?

How Long Does Your Shower Last?

• average shower: 12.2 min

• recommended shower: 6 min

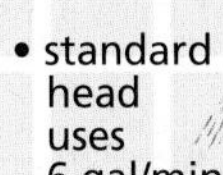

• standard head uses 6 gal/min

• water-saving head cuts water flow in half

Source: *Opinion Research Corp.*

Graph each function.

12. $f(x) = x - 2$
13. $y = -10x$
14. $y = \frac{3}{4}x + 7$
15. $f(x) = x^2$
16. $y = x^2 - 3x + 2$
17. $f(x) = x$
18. $f(x) = x^2 - 9$
19. $y = 7 - 5x$
20. $f(x) = 6x + 1$
21. $f(x) = x - 3$
22. $y = x + \frac{1}{2}$
23. $y = 3.5x$
24. $f(x) = 4x$
25. $y = 1 - x^2$
26. $f(x) = 12 - x$
27. $f(x) = -5x^2$

Make a table of values for each graph.

28.

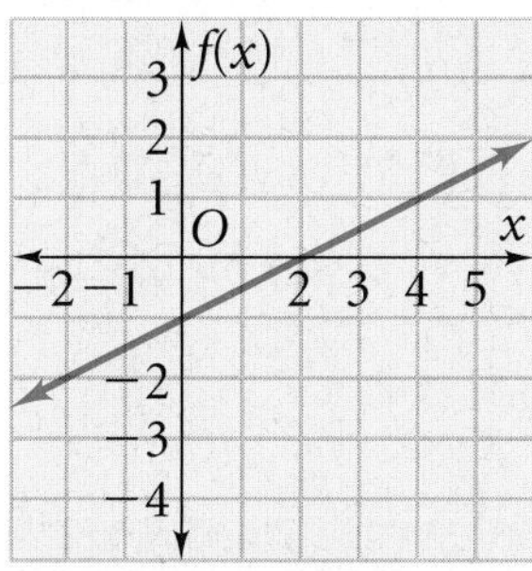

29.

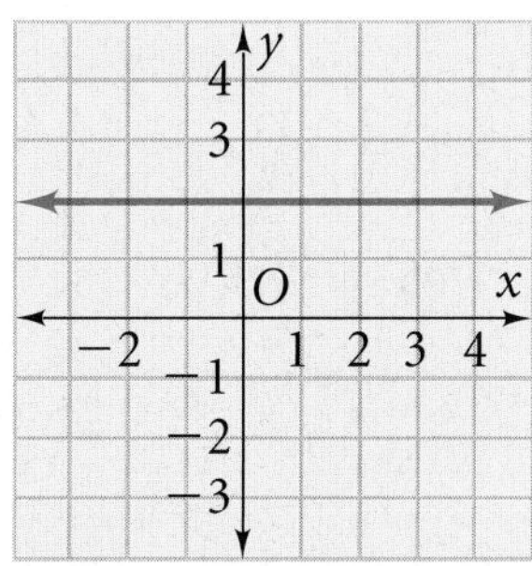

30.

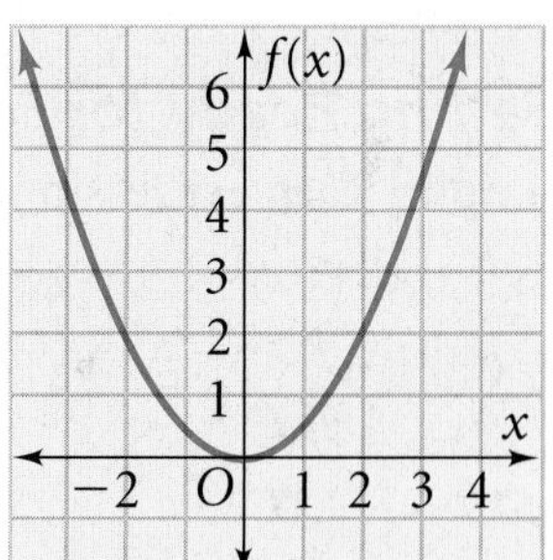

31. **Communications** The cost $C(a)$ of a call from Boston to Worcester, Massachusetts, is a function of the number of additional minutes a. The rule $C(a) = 0.27 + 0.11a$ closely models the cost.

a. How much will a 5-min call cost? (*Hint:* The number of additional minutes is one minute less than the length of the call.)

b. **Calculator** Make a table of values and graph the function.

c. **Critical Thinking** Suppose you don't want to spend any more than \$1.50 on this phone call. How many minutes can you talk?

32. a. **Research** Find the rate for weekday telephone calls in your area.

b. Write a rule to describe the cost of the call. Be sure to define your variables.

c. **Calculator** Make a table of values and graph the function.

33. **Standardized Test Prep** Which function is modeled by the table?

A. $f(x) = x - 2$
B. $f(x) = 2x + 1$
C. $f(x) = 2x$
D. $f(x) = -x + 1$
E. $f(x) = \frac{1}{2}x - 1$

x	$f(x)$
−3	−5
0	1
2	5
5	11

34. **Geometry** The function $A(l) = \frac{1}{2}l^2$ describes the area of an isosceles right triangle with leg l.

   a. Make a table of values for $l = 1, 2, 3, 4$.

   b. Graph the function.

35. **Writing** Suppose a student was not in class today. Describe to the student how to graph a function rule.

Exercises MIXED REVIEW

Use the scatter plot at the right.

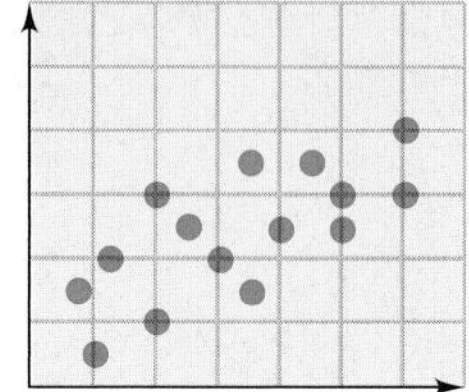

36. What kind of correlation does the scatter plot show?

37. a. **Open-ended** Describe a situation the scatter plot might represent.

    b. What would you label your axes?

Find the range of each function when the domain is {–2, 0, 1, 4}.

38. $f(x) = x - 1$ 39. $f(c) = 2c + 7$ 40. $f(z) = \frac{1}{4}z$ 41. $f(w) = -w + 2$ 42. $f(t) = -2t$

Getting Ready for Lesson 2-7

Simplify each expression.

43. $-4|5|$ 44. $|-5| + |-3.5|$ 45. $|-8 + 4|$ 46. $|-9.6|$ 47. $3 - |-4|$

A Point in Time

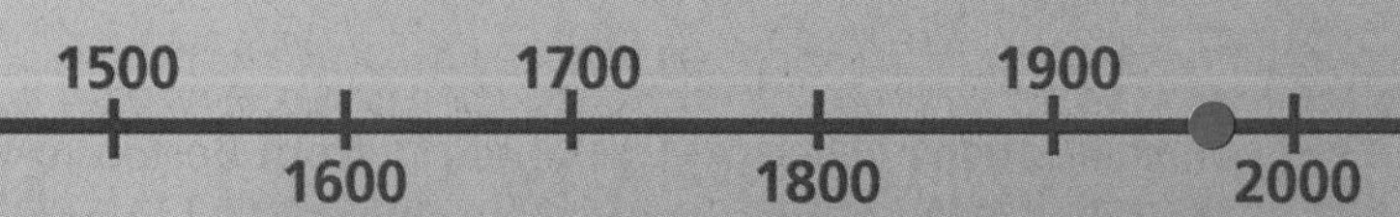

Romana Acosta Bañuelos

In 1971, Romana Acosta Bañuelos became the first Mexican American woman to hold the office of United States Treasurer. Before her appointment to this post by President Nixon, she founded and managed her own multimillion-dollar food enterprise and established the Pan American National Bank of East Los Angeles. As a highly successful businesswoman, she had to work on a daily basis with interest rates, balance sheets, investments, and other functions used in the corporate world.

Math ToolboX Technology

Graphing Functions

After Lesson 2-6

You can use a graphing calculator to graph a function. You can sketch a graph to record information about the function.

Example

Graph the function $y = x^2 - 9$. Use the standard setting for the range. Then sketch the graph on your paper.

STEP 1: Press ZOOM 6 to set the range at the **standard setting.** Press WINDOW to display the standard setting on the window screen.

STEP 2: Press Y= to go to the equation screen. Press CLEAR to get rid of any equation already in the calculator. Then press X,T,θ x^2 − 9 to enter the equation.

STEP 3: Press GRAPH to view the graph.

WINDOW FORMAT
Xmin = −10
Xmax = 10
Xscl = 1
Ymin = −10
Ymax = 10
Xscl = 1

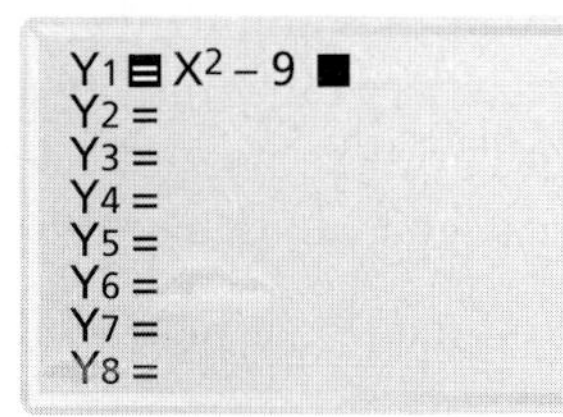

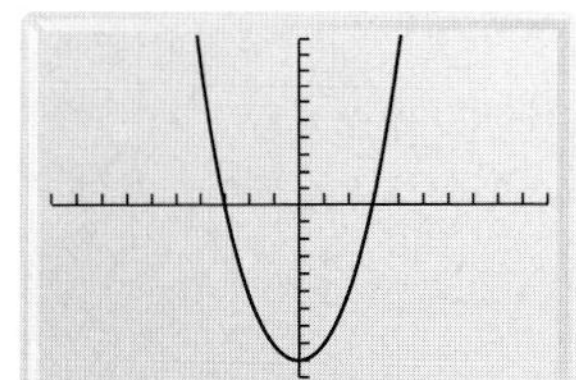

STEP 4: To sketch a graph that you see on your calculator screen, use the coordinates of at least three points. Plot these points on your paper and use them to make your sketch.

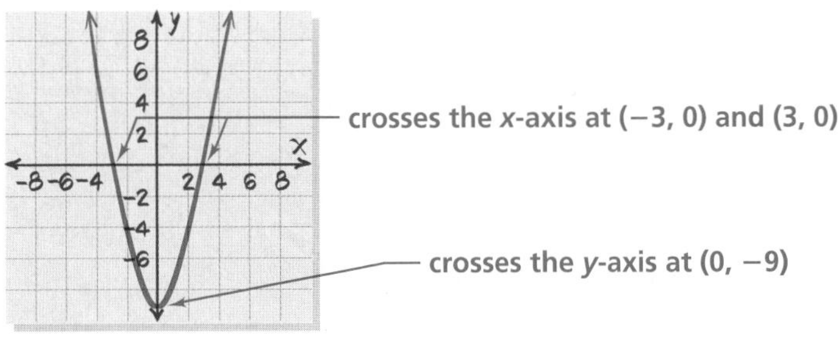

Graph each function on your graphing calculator. Use the standard setting for the range. Then sketch each graph.

1. $y = -2x + 4$

2. $y = \frac{1}{2}x - 2$

3. $y = x^2 + 2$

4. $y = x^3 - 1$

5. $y = 3x - 6$

6. $y = \frac{1}{3}x$

7. $y = 4 - x^2$

8. $y = 3x^2 - 7$

9. *Writing* Examine the Window screen and the Graph screen in the Example. Explain what the values Xmin, Xmax, Ymin, and Ymax represent on the graph.

Connections Medicine . . . and more

What You'll Learn

- Identifying families of functions for equations and graphs

...And Why

To predict what the graph of an equation will look like

What You'll Need

- graphing calculator
- note cards

GRAPHING CALCULATOR HINT

Use the ABS key and the ( ) keys to enter the absolute value.

2-7 Families of Functions

WORK TOGETHER

Work with a partner.

1. **Graphing Calculator** Graph each equation using the standard range setting. To help you keep track, sketch each graph on a note card. Label it with the correct equation.

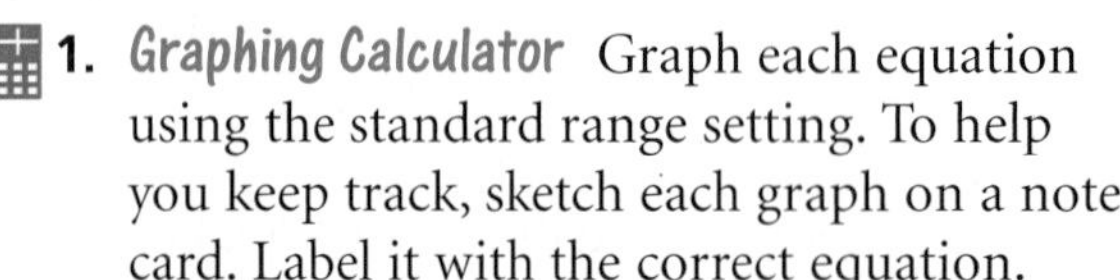

$y = x^2 - 6$	$y = x + 2$
$y = \|x\| - 4$	$y = 7x$
$y = \|x - 3\|$	$y = x^2 + 1$
$y = 3x^2$	$y = -3x$

2. a. Sort the cards into three categories by grouping graphs that look alike.
   b. What similarities among the graphs in each category do you see?
   c. What similarities among the equations in each category do you see?

The categories you made can help you make predictions.

3. What does the graph of $y = 2x^2$ look like?

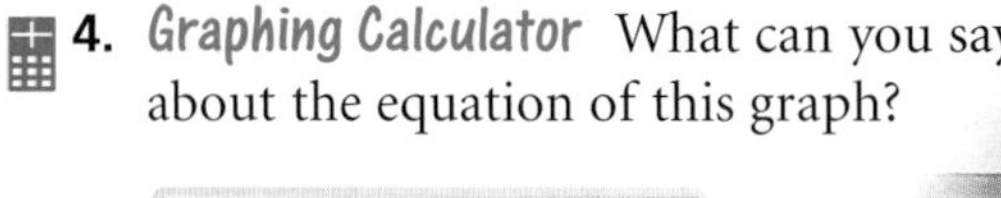

4. **Graphing Calculator** What can you say about the equation of this graph?

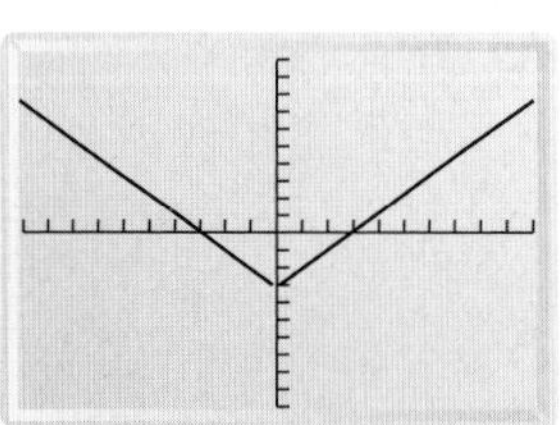

THINK AND DISCUSS

Identifying the Family of an Equation

You've already seen how grouping functions that are alike can help you make predictions. These groups are called *families of functions.* You can identify what family a function belongs to by looking at its equation.

QUICK REVIEW

Remember that $x = x^1$. So, the power of x is 1.

Example 1

To what family of functions does each equation belong? Explain.

a. $y = 2x - 6$

Its highest power of x is 1. So, $y = 2x - 6$ is a *linear function.*

b. $y = -8x^2$

Its highest power of x is 2. So, $y = -8x^2$ is a *quadratic function.*

5. The equation $y = |x + 7|$ is an *absolute value function.* What characteristic of the equation tells you this?

6. **Try This** To what family of functions does each equation belong? Explain.

a. $y = 6x^2 + 1$

b. $y = 3|x|$

c. $y = x^2 + 3x + 2$

7. **Open-ended** Create three equations that belong to the quadratic family of functions.

Identifying the Family of a Graph

You can identify what family a function belongs to by looking at its graph.

Example 2

Graphing Calculator To what family of functions does each graph belong? Explain.

a.

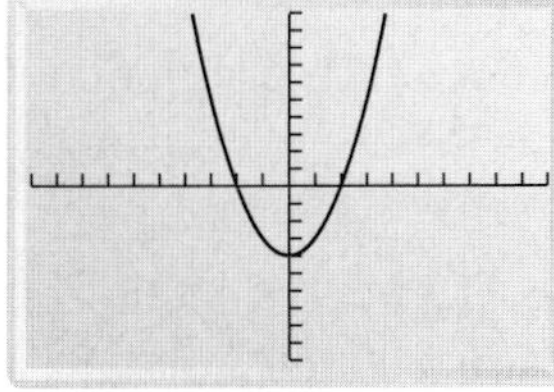

The graph is U-shaped. So, it is a *quadratic function.*

b.

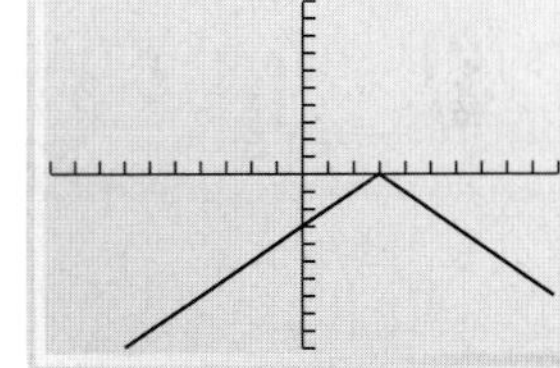

The graph forms a "V." So, it is an *absolute value function.*

8. **a.** The equation $y = -5x$ belongs to what family of functions? How do you know?

b. **Graphing Calculator** Graph $y = -5x$.

c. Look at your graph and **generalize.** What characteristic of a graph tells you it belongs to the *linear family of functions?*

9. **Open-ended** Sketch three graphs that belong to the absolute value family of functions.

The equations and graphs of functions that are in the same family are alike. Here are three families of functions.

Families of Functions

Linear Functions

$y = 2x - 1$

The highest power of x is 1.

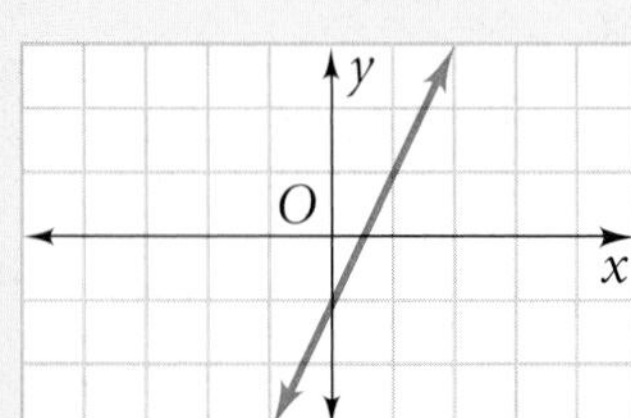

The graph forms a straight line.

Quadratic Functions

$y = -3x^2 - x + 1$

The highest power of x is 2.

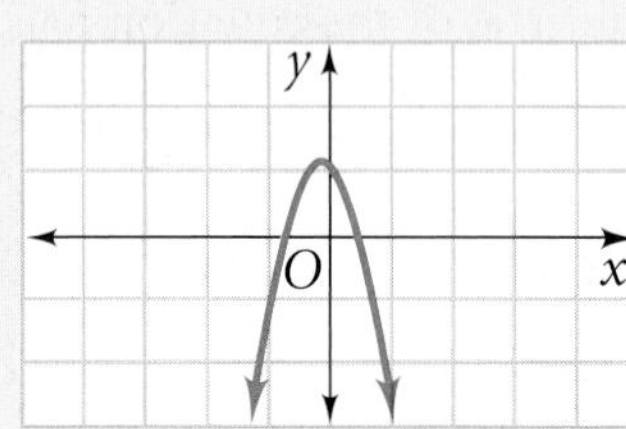

The graph is a U-shaped curve that opens up or down.

Absolute Value Functions

$y = |x + 2|$

There is an absolute value symbol around a variable expression.

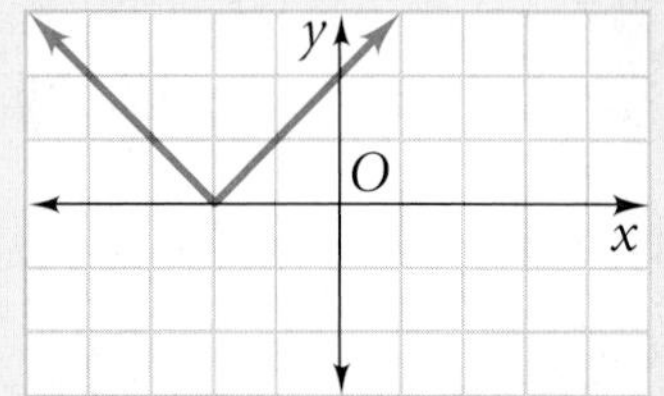

The graph forms a "V" that opens up or down.

Exercises ON YOUR OWN

To what family of functions does each equation belong? Explain.

1. $y = \frac{4}{7}x + 7$

2. $y = 49 - x^2$

3. $y = |2 + 3x|$

4. $y = -x^2 + 11$

5. $y = -6x^2 + 13x - 5$

6. $y = \frac{1}{4}x$

7. $y = 0.5x^2$

8. $y = -2|x|$

9. $y = |x - 2|$

Graphing Calculator **To what family of functions does each graph belong? Explain your reasoning.**

10. 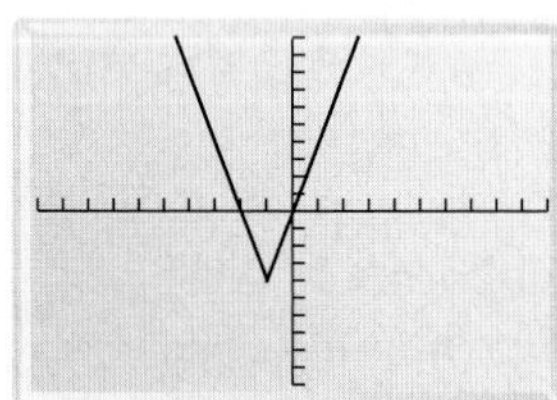

11. 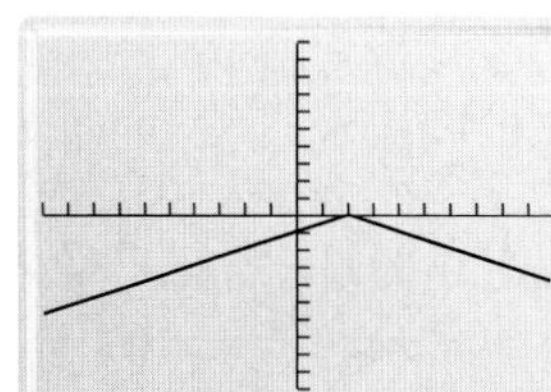

12. 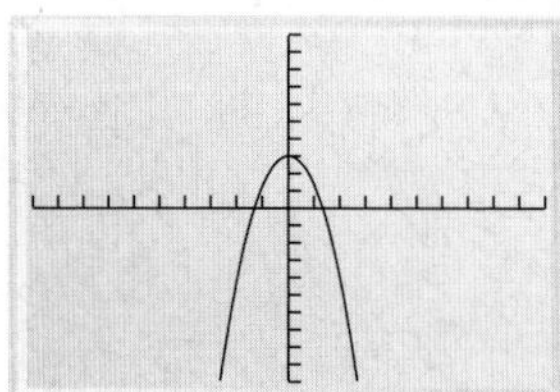

13. *Medicine* The recommended dosage D in milligrams of a certain medicine depends on a person's body weight w in kilograms. To what family of function does the formula $D = 0.1w^2 + 5w$ belong? Explain.

14. *Writing* How are linear functions and absolute value functions alike? How are they different?

15. Define a *family of functions* in your own words.

16. *Critical Thinking* Why are these graphs *not* quadratic or absolute value functions?

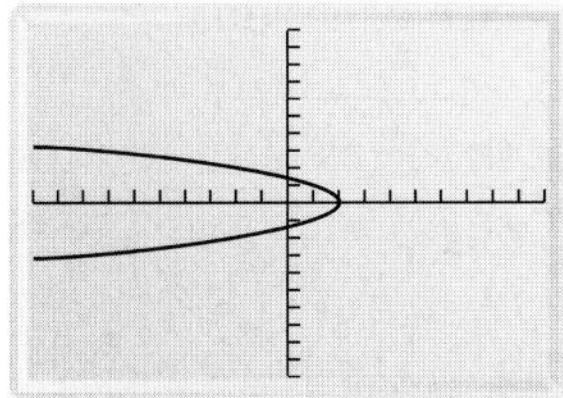

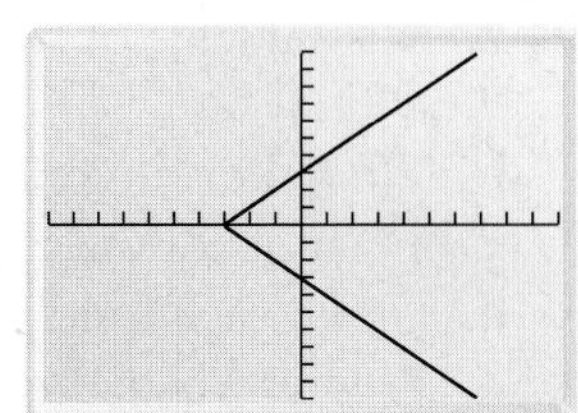

17. *Critical Thinking* Is a vertical line the graph of a linear function? Why or why not?

18. *Open-ended* Write two linear, two quadratic, and two absolute value equations.

What characteristic do you look for to identify the family of each?

19. graph of a quadratic function
20. equation of a linear function
21. graph of an absolute value function
22. equation of a quadratic function

Critical Thinking **Determine to which family of functions each graph belongs. Then sketch a graph to model each situation.**

23. Income is a function of of hours worked.
24. Height of a fly ball is a function of time.

Graphing Calculator **Predict the shape of the graph. Be as specific as you can. Graph each equation to verify your prediction.**

25. $y = 7 - x$
26. $y = -4x^2$
27. $y = |1 - x|$
28. $y = 2x + 1$
29. $y = -|x| + 6$
30. $y = 2x^2 - 6$
31. $y = x^2 + 3$
32. $y = -x + 10$
33. $y = |-x| + 3$

To what family of functions does the function suggested by each picture belong? Explain your reasoning.

34.

35.

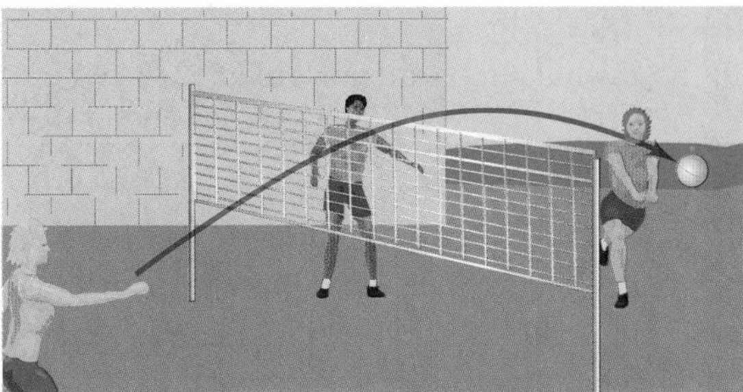

36.

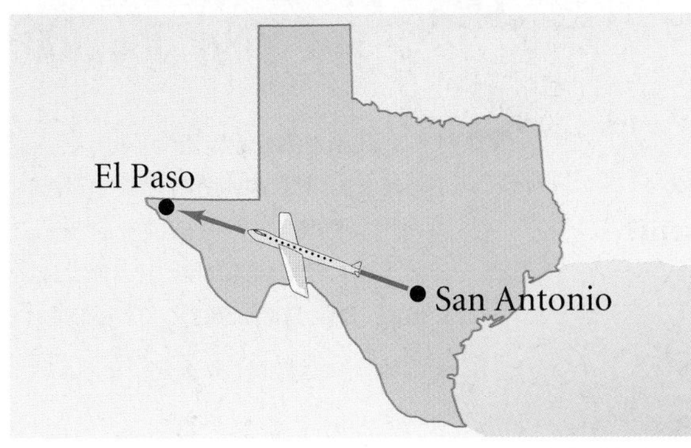

37.

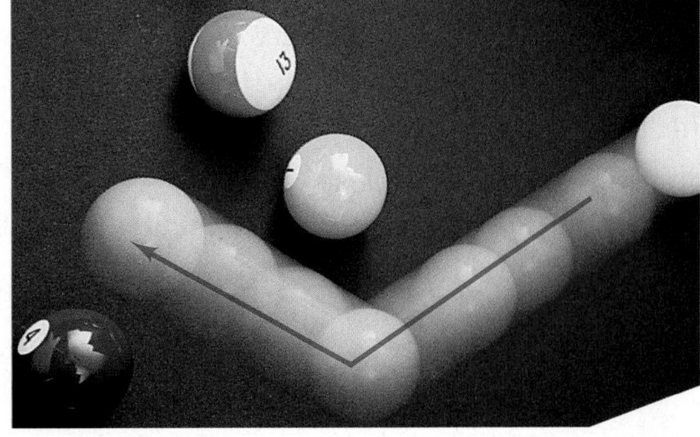

38. **a.** Make a table of values for each equation.
  I. $y = |x|$ **II.** $y = -x^2$
b. What do you notice about the signs of the y-values?
c. What quadrant(s) do you expect each graph to be in?
d. Graph each function.
e. **Predict** whether each graph will open up or down. Graph each function to test your prediction.
  I. $y = -|x|$ **II.** $y = x^2$

39. **a.** **Predict** the shape and opening of the graph $y = |x - 2|$.
b. *Graphing Calculator* Test your prediction.

40. *Standardized Test Prep* Which equation is shown in the graph?

A. $y = x + 2$
B. $y = -|x| + 2$
C. $y = -x^2 + 2$
D. $y = x^2 + 2$
E. None of these

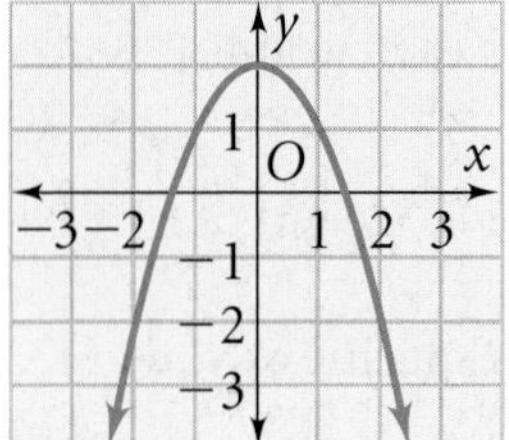

Chapter Project ***Find Out by Analyzing***

Think of a tongue twister not yet used in this chapter. (You may know one in a language other than English.)

- Use a group of at least ten people. Use the same method to record times as you did for the Find Out question on page 63.
- Graph the data.
- Do your data points form a line? Explain.
- Write a function rule that you could use to predict the time for n people to say your tongue twister.

Exercises MIXED REVIEW

Graph each function.

41. $f(x) = 5x - 1$
42. $f(x) = -3x^2$
43. $f(w) = 3w + 4.5$
44. $q(p) = 3p - 1$
45. $f(x) = x^2 + 7$
46. $f(t) = t + 2.5$
47. $d(t) = 55t$
48. $f(x) = \frac{1}{2}x + \frac{3}{2}$

49. **a.** Evaluate the function rule $f(x) = -2x^2 + 12$ for $x = -8$.
b. Write the steps you used to evaluate the function.

50. *Probability* Use the random number table.
a. *Open-ended* A sock drawer has an equal number of white and blue socks. Simulate choosing a sock without looking in the drawer. Which numbers will represent white? blue?
b. Conduct the simulation. What is the experimental probability of drawing a blue sock?

Random Number Table

23948	71477	12573	05954
65628	22310	09311	94864
41261	09943	34078	70481

Getting Ready for Lesson 2-8

A bag of fruit has 5 apples, 6 bananas, 4 oranges, and one pomegranate. What fraction of the fruit does each represent?

51. apples
52. oranges
53. not pomegranates
54. bananas
55. not apples
56. bananas and apples

SELF ASSESSMENT **FOR YOUR JOURNAL**

Summarize what you understand about functions. Give examples of how to write them and how to use them. Be specific about how they relate to graphs.

2-8 The Probability Formula

What You'll Learn

- Finding theoretical probability
- Using a tree diagram and a sample space to find probability

...And Why

To make predictions about real-world situations such as mall promotions and game shows

THINK AND DISCUSS

Finding Theoretical Probability

To promote the new Westside Mall, the mall manager gives away a store gift certificate. The winning shopper chooses the store by picking a piece of paper from a box. The box contains the names of 170 stores.

1. What type of store is the winner most likely to pick? Explain.

In Chapter 1, you found experimental probability by conducting experiments. The possible results of an experiment are called **outcomes.** An event is any group of outcomes.

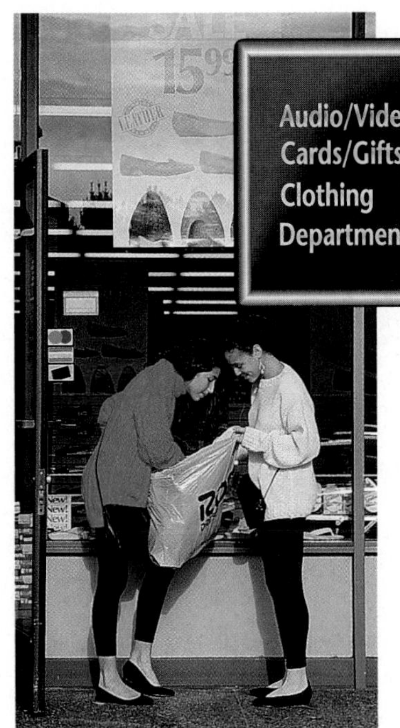

Stores at the Westside Mall

Audio/Video/Electronics	8	Food	25	Health/Beauty	9
Cards/Gifts/Books	11	Footwear	16	Specialty Shops	10
Clothing	47	Home Furnishings	7	Toys/Hobby/Sport	9
Department Store	4	Jewelry	14	Other	10

Total Number of Stores: 170

In the shopping mall giveaway, each store represents an outcome. If you want to pick a food store, the 25 food stores are *favorable outcomes.* If each outcome has an equal chance of happening, you can find **theoretical probability** using this formula.

$$P(\text{event}) = \frac{\text{number of favorable outcomes}}{\text{number of possible outcomes}}$$

Example 1 Relating to the Real World 

Shopping What is the probability of the winning shopper choosing a footwear store? Express your answer as a percent.

$$P(\text{footwear store}) = \frac{\text{number of favorable outcomes}}{\text{number of possible outcomes}}$$

$$= \frac{16}{170}$$ ← There are 16 footwear stores in the mall and 170 stores in all.

$$\approx 0.09 = 9\%$$

The probability of choosing a footwear store is about 0.09, or 9%.

2. *Calculator* Suppose you are the winning shopper. What is the probability you get a gift certificate to a jewelry store?

All probabilities range from 0 to 1.

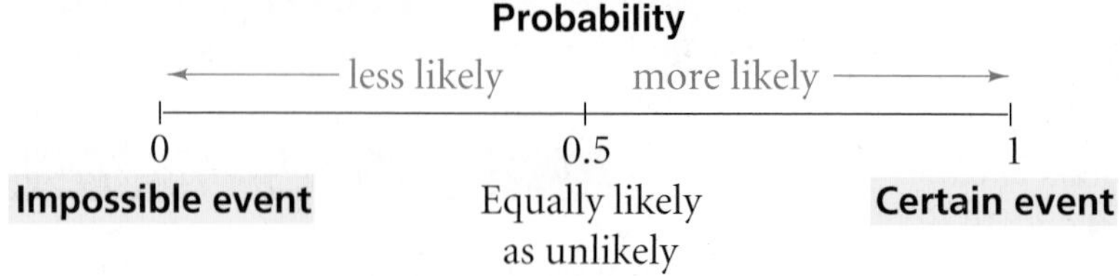

When you roll a number cube marked with numbers from 1 to 6, rolling a 7 is an impossible event. Rolling a number less than 7 is a certain event.

3. **Try This** Find each probability when rolling a number cube.
   a. $P(\text{even})$ b. $P(0)$ c. $P(5)$

4. **Open-ended** Suppose you chose a letter tile from a bag containing the letter tiles A, A, A, E, I, O, O, and U.
   a. Name a certain event.
   b. Name an impossible event.
   c. Name an event that is more likely than choosing the letter I.

The **complement of an event** consists of all possible outcomes not in the event. For example, when you roll a number cube, the complement of "rolling a 4 or less" is "rolling a 5 or 6." The sum of the probabilities of an event and its complement is 1. You can use this formula to find the probability of the complement of an event.

$$P(\text{complement of event}) = 1 - P(\text{event})$$

You can write $P(\text{complement of event})$ as $P(\text{not event})$.

Example 2 **Relating to the Real World** 

Games On a popular television game show, the winning contestant must choose from five envelopes. Each envelope contains a grand prize, such as a car or a trip.

a. What is the probability of choosing a particular grand prize?
b. What is the probability of not choosing that grand prize?

a. $P(\text{grand prize}) = \frac{\text{number of favorable outcomes}}{\text{number of possible outcomes}} = \frac{1}{5}$

The probability the contestant chooses a specific grand prize is $\frac{1}{5}$.

b. $P(\text{not grand prize}) = 1 - P(\text{grand prize})$

$$= 1 - \frac{1}{5}$$

$$= \frac{4}{5}$$

The probability the contestant does not choose that grand prize is $\frac{4}{5}$.

PROBLEM SOLVING

Look Back Describe another method you could use to find *P*(not grand prize).

5. Suppose you choose from three colored envelopes: red, orange, blue.
   a. What is $P(\text{blue})$? b. What is $P(\text{not blue})$?

Math A Test Prep

1 A nickel is flipped and a regular six-sided number cube is rolled. On the first flip and roll, what is the probability of rolling 1 and flipping heads?

(1) $\frac{2}{3}$ (3) $\frac{1}{6}$

(2) $\frac{1}{2}$ (4) $\frac{1}{12}$

2 Which value(s) of x *cannot* fill in the blank below, if the relation is a function?

x	y
2	4
6	11
■	9
3	0
8	6

Using a Tree Diagram to Find a Sample Space

The set of all possible outcomes is the **sample space.** Displaying the sample space with a *tree diagram* can help you find the probability of an event.

Example 3 **Relating to the Real World** 

Genetics What is the probability that there are at least two girls in a family of three children?

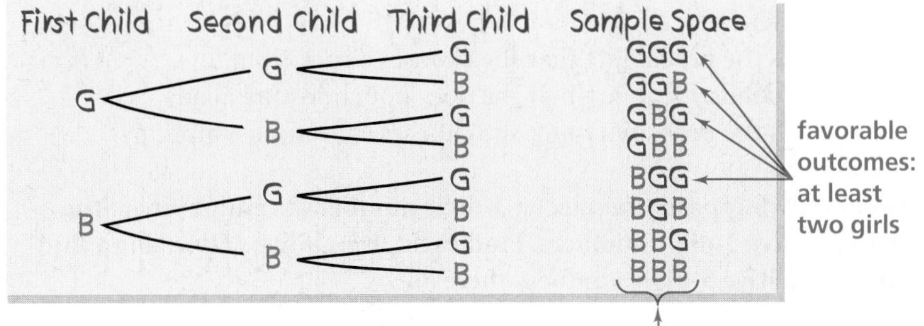

$$P(\text{at least two girls}) = \frac{\text{number of favorable outcomes}}{\text{total number of possible outcomes}} = \frac{4}{8} = \frac{1}{2}$$

The probability that there are at least two girls is $\frac{1}{2}$ or 50%.

6. **Try This** What is the probability that there are exactly two girls in a family of three children?

Exercises ON YOUR OWN

For Exercises 1–9, use the spinner at the right. Find each probability.

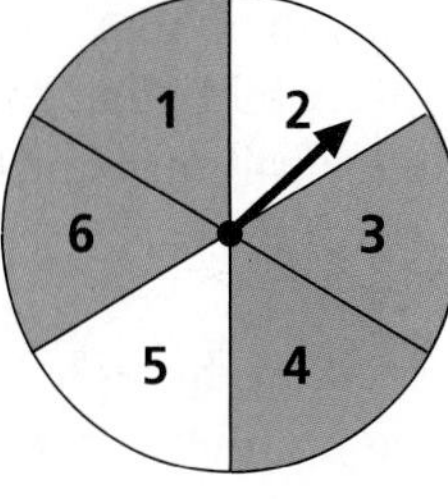

1. P(red)
2. P(white)
3. P(5)
4. P(even)
5. P(red or blue)
6. P(not 2)
7. P(number < 4)
8. P(not blue)
9. P(8)

10. **Open-ended** Suppose your teacher chooses a student at random from your algebra class.
    a. What is the probability that you are selected?
    b. What is the probability that a boy is not selected?
    c. How did you find P(not boy) in part (b)? Describe another way.

11. **Critical Thinking** What is the difference between theoretical probability and experimental probability?

12. Suppose you have a 20% chance of being picked for a committee at school. What is the probability that you will not be picked? Express your answer as a percent.

13. **a.** Suppose you roll a number cube and toss a coin at the same time. Copy and complete the tree diagram to list the possible outcomes in the sample space.
b. What is *P*(4 and heads)?
c. What is *P*(tails)?
d. What is *P*(even number and tails)?

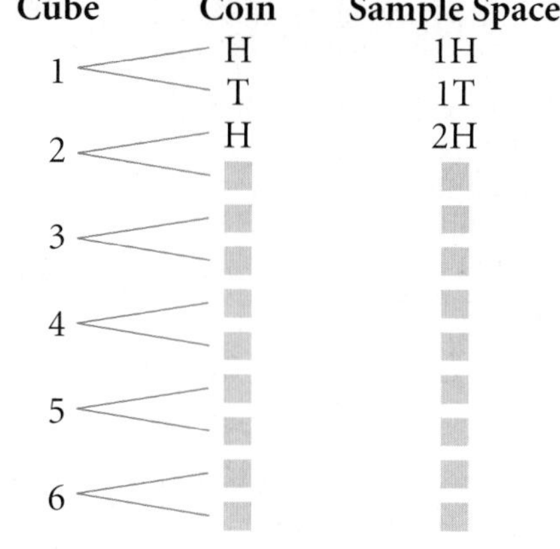

14. **Music** A disc jockey makes music selections for a radio program. For her first selection, she can choose from eight rock songs, three jazz pieces, five country-western ballads, and four rhythm and blues songs. Assume each selection has an equal chance of being chosen.
a. What is the probability that she chooses a rock song?
b. What is the probability that she does not choose a ballad?
c. What is the probability that she chooses a classical symphony?

Discrete Math **Suppose you select a 3-digit number at random from the set of all positive 3-digit numbers. Find each probability. (*Hint:* First find how many positive 3-digit numbers there are.)**

15. *P*(an odd number)
16. *P*(number > 900)
17. *P*(number < 100)
18. *P*(number is a multiple of 30)
19. *P*(number < 500)
20. *P*(number = 243 or 244)

21. On Cap Day each person who attends the baseball game receives a free cap. You have an equal chance of receiving any of the combinations at the right.
a. Use a tree diagram to show the sample space.
b. Find *P*(yellow cap, green visor, team mascot).
c. Find *P*(red cap, blue or green visor, team logo)

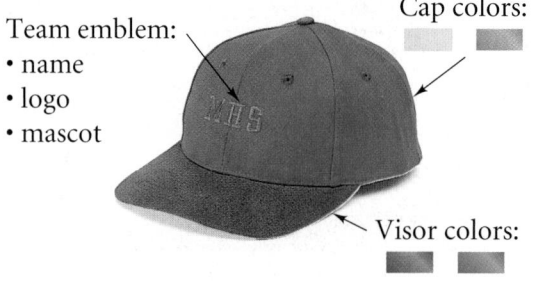

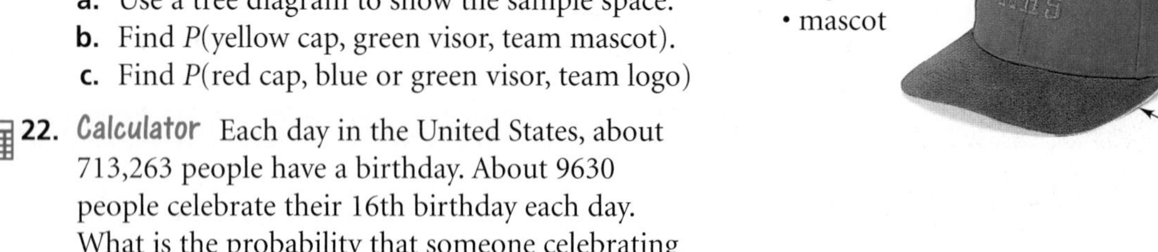

22. **Calculator** Each day in the United States, about 713,263 people have a birthday. About 9630 people celebrate their 16th birthday each day. What is the probability that someone celebrating a birthday today will turn 16? Express your answer as a percent.

Use the sample space at the right. Find each probability for the sum of two number cubes.

23. *P*(7)
24. *P*(2)
25. *P*(not 11)
26. *P*(11 or 12)
27. *P*(a multiple of 3)
28. *P*(9)
29. *P*(15)
30. *P*(even number)

Sample Space for Two Number Cubes

(1, 1)	(1, 2)	(1, 3)	(1, 4)	(1, 5)	(1, 6)
(2, 1)	(2, 2)	(2, 3)	(2, 4)	(2, 5)	(2, 6)
(3, 1)	(3, 2)	(3, 3)	(3, 4)	(3, 5)	(3, 6)
(4, 1)	(4, 2)	(4, 3)	(4, 4)	(4, 5)	(4, 6)
(5, 1)	(5, 2)	(5, 3)	(5, 4)	(5, 5)	(5, 6)
(6, 1)	(6, 2)	(6, 3)	(6, 4)	(6, 5)	(6, 6)

The outcome (2, 5) has a sum of 7.

Make a tree diagram to show the sample space for four tosses of a coin. Use the sample space to find each probability.

31. P(exactly 2 tails) **32.** P(exactly 3 heads) **33.** P(at least 2 heads) **34.** P(4 tails)

35. P(exactly 1 tail) **36.** P(no tails) **37.** P(5 tails) **38.** P(1 or 2 heads)

39. **Standardized Test Prep** You are going to roll a number cube once. Which has the same probability as P(not rolling a 4 or a 5)?
 A. P(rolling an even number) **B.** P(rolling a factor of 6) **C.** P(rolling a number less than 3)
 D. P(rolling a 1 or a 2) **E.** P(not rolling an odd number)

40. **Cars** A car dealer has an equal chance of receiving any of the colors or styles in the diagram. What is the probability that the next car the dealer receives is a red or black convertible with a gray interior?

Car Colors	Interior Colors	Style

Use the formula below to find the *odds in favor* of an event.

$$\text{Odds} = \frac{\text{number of favorable outcomes}}{\text{number of unfavorable outcomes}}$$

Sample Find the odds in favor of the spinner stopping on red.

$$\text{odds in favor of red} = \frac{\text{number of favorable outcomes}}{\text{number of unfavorable outcomes}} = \frac{3}{5}$$

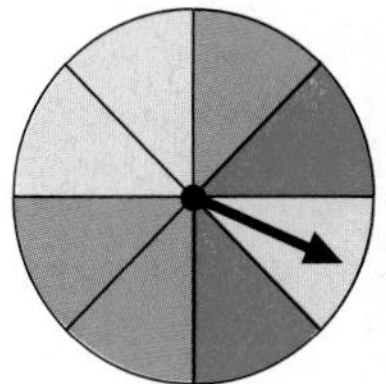

41. Find the odds in favor of the spinner stopping on blue.

42. Find the odds in favor of the spinner not stopping on yellow.

43. **Writing** Explain how you can use odds to find probability. Include an example.

Exercises MIXED REVIEW

Simplify each expression.

44. $|-8 - 3| \times 3$

45. $(7^2 - 4) \div 9$

46. $-3\frac{1}{2} - 5\frac{1}{6}$

47. $5.6 \div 7 - 0.2$

48. $-9^2 + 5$

49. $-\frac{2}{3} \div 6$

50. **a.** Suppose you want a garden consisting of 8 tomato plants. Each plant costs \$1.50. How much will you spend on tomato plants?
 b. A gardening "rule of thumb" is that for every dollar you spend on plants, you will spend three dollars on supplies. How much should you budget for supplies?
 c. Estimate the total cost of your tomato garden.

PORTFOLIO

For your portfolio, select one or two items from your work for this chapter. Here are some possibilities.
- corrected work
- most improved work

Explain why you have included each selection.

CHAPTER PROJECT

Finishing the Chapter Project

Questions on pages 63, 72, 83, and 94 should help you complete your project. Present your project as a poster or other visual display. For each tongue twister, show a scatter plot, a table and graph, or a function rule and graph. Your presentation should discuss correlation, input and output values, and how a function rule can be used to predict the time it will take n people to repeat a tongue twister consecutively.

Reflect and Revise

Show your project to an adult and review your work together. Are your graphs, tables, and other work easy to follow? Have you included all the required information? How can you modify your work to answer any questions that arise? Consider adding artwork or illustrations to your project. Make any revisions necessary to improve your work.

Follow Up

Most people cannot sustain speech at more than 300 words/min. Experiment with your own rate of speech. How will you measure it? You might compare familiar memorized speech, reading aloud, and saying tongue twisters. How can you express these rates as functions?

For More Information

Brandreth, Gyles. *The Biggest Tongue Twister Book in the World.* New York, New York: Sterling, 1978.

Schwartz, Alvin. *A Twister of Twists, a Tangler of Tongues.* Philadelphia, Pennsylvania: J. P. Lippincott, 1972.

CHAPTER 2

Wrap Up

Key Terms

absolute value function (p. 92)
certain event (p. 96)
complement of an event (p. 96)
continuous data (p. 65)
dependent variable (p. 69)
discrete data (p. 65)
domain (p. 74)
family of functions (p. 90)
function (p. 73)
function notation (p. 79)
function rule (p. 74)
impossible event (p. 96)
independent variable (p. 69)
linear function (p. 92)
negative correlation (p. 60)
no correlation (p. 60)
outcomes (p. 95)
positive correlation (p. 60)
quadratic function (p. 92)
range (p. 74)
relation (p. 73)
sample space (p. 97)
scatter plot (p. 59)
theoretical probability (p. 95)
tree diagram (p. 97)
trend line (p. 60)
vertical-line test (p. 75)

How am I doing?

- State three ideas from this chapter that you think are important. Explain your choices.
- Describe the different ways you can model a function.

Analyzing Data Using Scatter Plots 2-1

You use **scatter plots** to find trends in data. Two data sets that increase together show a **positive correlation.** There is a **negative correlation** when one data set increases as another decreases. If there is no trend, there is **no correlation.**

Would you expect a *positive correlation, negative correlation,* or *no correlation* between the two data sets. Why?

1. daily temperature vs. the sales of juice drinks

2. hours a swimmer trains each day vs. the time it takes to swim 100 m

3. *Open-ended* Describe two data sets that show a negative correlation.

Relating Graphs to Events 2-2

Graphs show a relationship between two variables. **Continuous data** usually involve measurements, such as temperatures, lengths, and weights. **Discrete data** involve a count, such as a number of people or objects.

Write a story to describe each graph.

4.
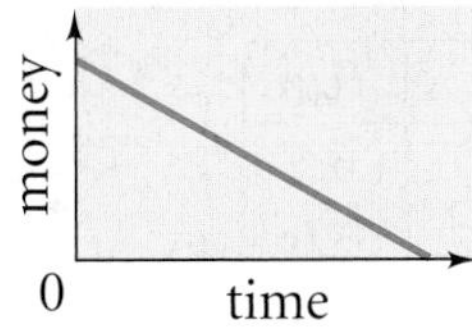

5.
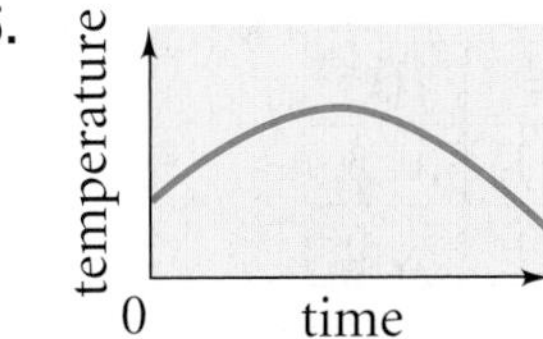

6.
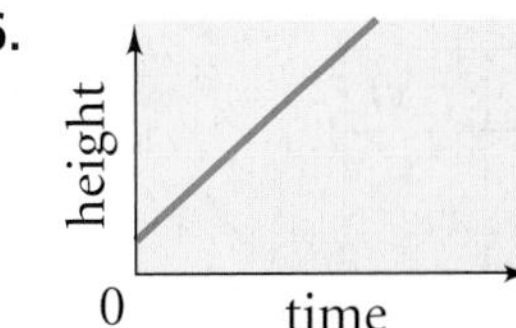

Sketch a graph to describe each situation. Explain the activity in each section of the graph.

7. the height of a sunflower over a summer

8. the number of people in a restaurant each hour

Linking Graphs to Tables **2-3**

When you graph data from a table, put the **independent variable** on the horizontal axis and the **dependent variable** on the vertical axis. The dependent variable *depends* on the independent variable.

Cost of a Median Priced House

Year	1985	1986	1987	1988	1989	1990	1991	1992	1993	1994
Price	$75,500	$80,300	$85,600	$90,600	$93,100	$97,500	$99,700	$100,900	$106,100	$107,600

9. a. Which variable in the table is independent? dependent?

b. Graph the data.

c. What scales did you use for your axes? Explain why.

Functions **2-4**

A set of ordered pairs is a **relation.** A **function** is a relation that has exactly one y-value for each x-value. A **function rule** is an equation that describes a function. The **domain** of a function is the set of all possible input values. The **range** of a function is the set of all possible output values. You can tell when a relation is a function by using the **vertical-line test.**

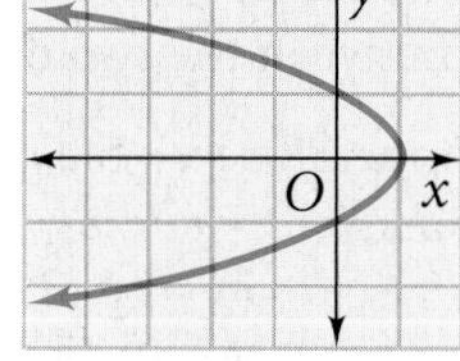

Find the range of each function when the domain is {–4, 0, 1, 5}.

10. $y = 4x - 7$

11. $m = 0.5n + 3$

12. $p = q^2 + 1$

13. Use the vertical-line test to determine if the graph is a function.

14. **Writing** Explain when a relation is also a function.

Writing a Function Rule **2-5**

A rule written using **function notation** allows you to see the input value. You can write a rule using a table of values or a description of a situation.

Write a function rule for each table of values.

15.

x	$f(x)$
2	3
4	5
6	7
8	9

16.

x	$f(x)$
−3	3
0	0
3	−3
6	−6

17.

x	$f(x)$
3.0	6.5
3.5	7.0
4.0	7.5
4.5	8.0

The Three Views of a Function, Families of Functions 2-6, 2-7

You can model functions using rules, tables, and graphs. Functions that are alike can be arranged into groups called *families of functions.* Some families are *quadratic, linear,* and *absolute value* functions.

Model each rule with a table of values and a graph.

18. $f(x) = 4x^2 - 3$ **19.** $f(x) = |x + 5|$ **20.** $f(x) = 2x + 1$ **21.** $f(x) = |x| - 7$

22. For Exercises 18–21, determine whether each equation is a quadratic function, a linear function, or an absolute value function. Explain.

The Probability Formula 2-8

You can find the **theoretical probability** of an event using this formula.

$$P(\text{event}) = \frac{\text{number of favorable outcomes}}{\text{number of possible outcomes}}$$

An **impossible event** has a probability of 0. A **certain event** has a probability of 1. The **complement** of an event consists of all outcomes not in the event. The set of all possible outcomes is the **sample space.**

Find each probability for one roll of a number cube.

23. $P(3)$ **24.** $P(\text{not } 5)$ **25.** $P(2 \text{ or } 6)$ **26.** $P(\text{number} \geq 7)$

27. Suppose you toss a coin 4 times.
- **a.** What is the probability that you toss exactly 3 heads?
- **b.** Explain what $P(\text{not 3 heads})$ means in your own words.

28. An astronomer calculates that the probability in favor of a visible meteor shower occurring in May is $\frac{3}{14}$. What is the probability that a visible meteor shower does not occur in May?

A. 0 **B.** 1 **C.** $\frac{3}{14}$ **D.** $\frac{3}{17}$ **E.** $\frac{11}{14}$

Getting Ready for... CHAPTER 3

Simplify each expression.

29. $\frac{7 + 9}{2}$ **30.** $3(2 + 1) - 4(2 + 1)$ **31.** $\frac{3}{4}(3 + 5)$

32. $\frac{7 - 4}{6}$ **33.** $5(\frac{6 + 1}{3 + 4})$ **34.** $(4 - 4^2) \div 10$

Evaluate each expression for $m = 2, t = -3,$ and $w = 1.5$.

35. $t + 2$ **36.** $4m - 1$ **37.** $w(m + 1)$ **38.** $\frac{3}{2}w - t$

CHAPTER 2

Assessment

Is there a *positive correlation,* a *negative correlation,* or *no correlation* for the data sets in each scatter plot?

1. 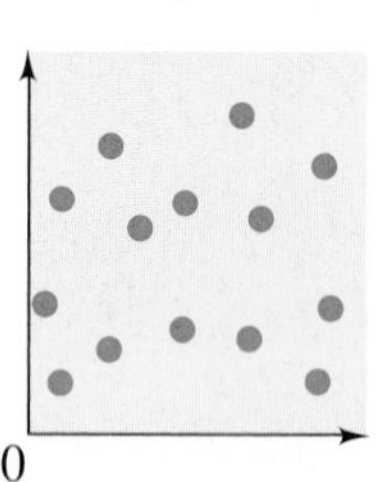

2. 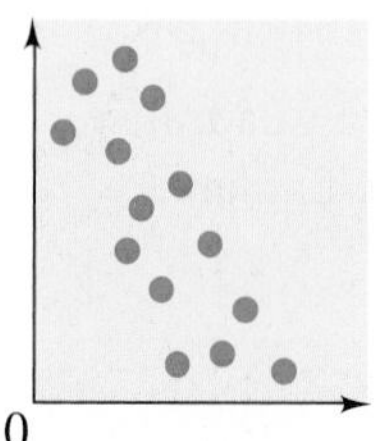

3. 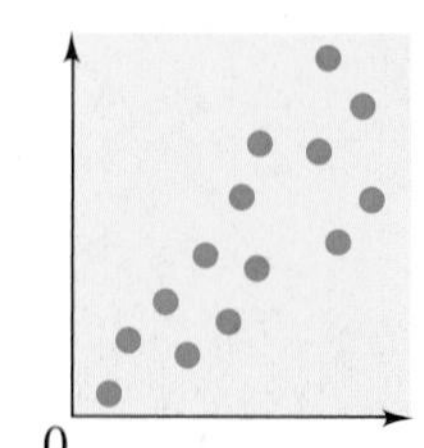

4. 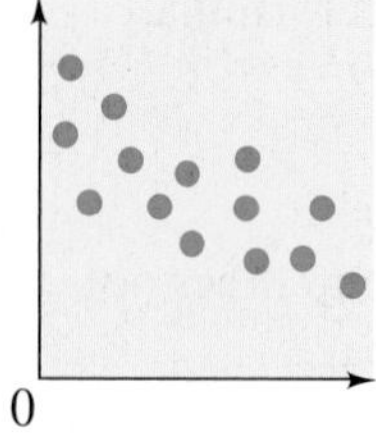

5. Which scatter plot above could be titled "Amount of Rain vs. Umbrella Sales"?

Classify the data as *discrete* or *continuous.*

6. your height from age 3 to age 14
7. the amount of money in a store's cash register during one day

Sketch a graph to describe each situation. Explain the activity in each section of the graph.

8. the speed of a bicycle during an afternoon ride
9. the amount of milk in your container over one lunch period

Determine if each relation is a function.

10.

x	y
−2	5
8	6
3	1.2
5	6

11.

x	y
9	6
3	8
4	9.5
9	2

12. **Writing** Explain how to use the vertical-line test to determine if a graph is a function graph.

Find the range of each function when the domain is {−3, −1.5, 0, 1, 4}.

13. $r = 4t^2 + 5$

14. $m = -3n - 2$

Write a function rule to describe each statement.

15. the cost of printing dollar bills when it costs 3.8¢ to make a dollar bill
16. the amount of money you earn mowing lawns at $15 per lawn
17. For Exercises 15 and 16, identify the independent and dependent variables.

Model each rule with a table of values and a graph.

18. $f(x) = 1.5x - 3$

19. $f(x) = -x^2 + 4$

20. **Open-ended** Describe a situation that could be modeled by the equation $y = 5x$.

21. Which graph is the graph of $y = -x + 2$?

A. 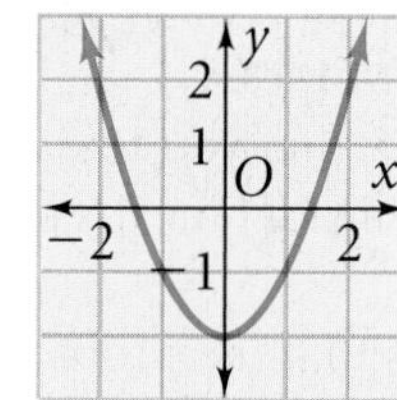

B. 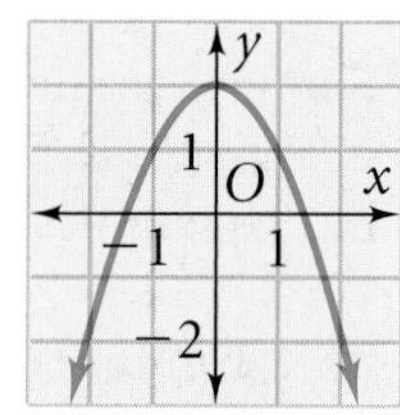

C. 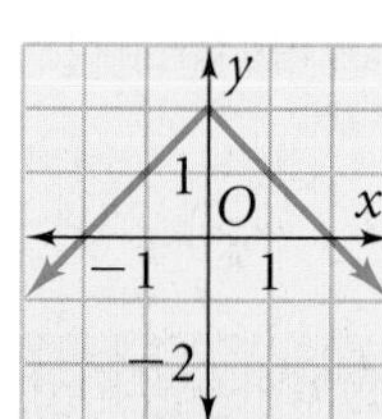

D. 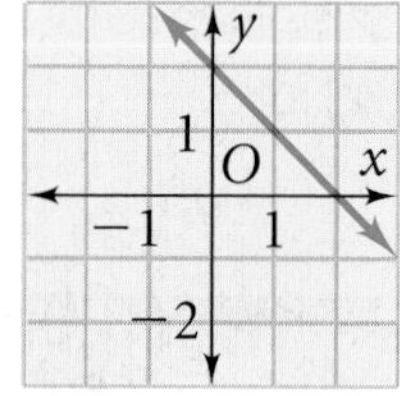

22. A vendor sells T-shirts in sizes small, medium, and large. The available colors are green, blue, red, purple, and black. All combinations of sizes and colors are equally likely.
    a. Draw a tree diagram showing all the possible combinations of sizes and colors.
    b. Find the probability of randomly selecting a black T-shirt that is size large.

Preparing for the Math A Exam

Part I

1 Which title would be most appropriate for this scatter plot?

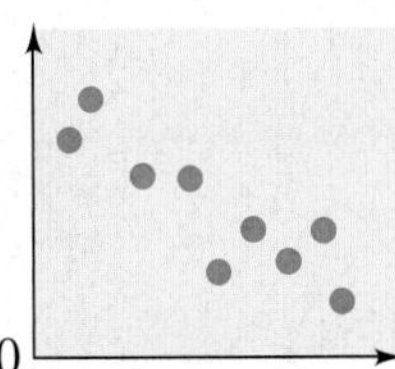

(1) Swimsuits Sold vs. Temperature
(2) Hourly Earnings vs. Teen's Age
(3) Coats Sold vs. Temperature
(4) Temperature vs. People Visiting the Beach

2 Which points lie on the graph shown?

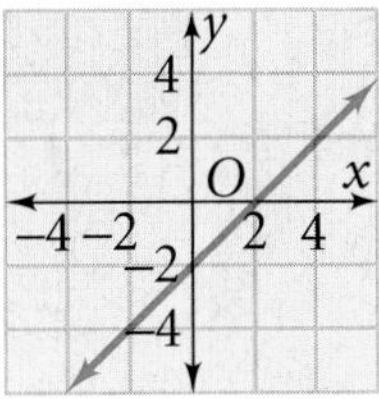

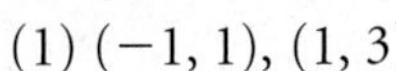

(1) $(-1, 1), (1, 3)$
(2) $(0, -2), (0, 2)$
(3) $(-1, 2), (1, 1)$
(4) $(-1, -3), (1, -1)$

3 Which graph does *not* represent a function?

(1)

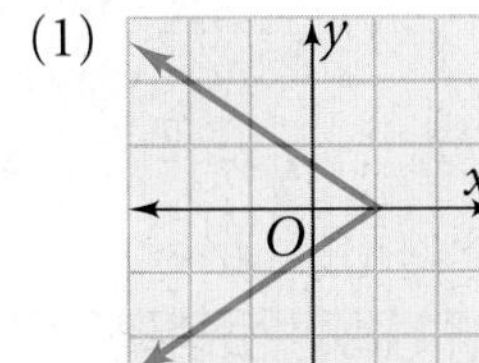

(3)

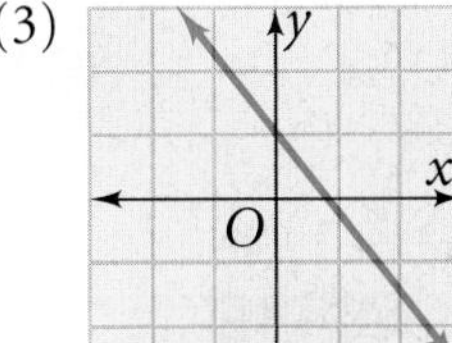

(2)

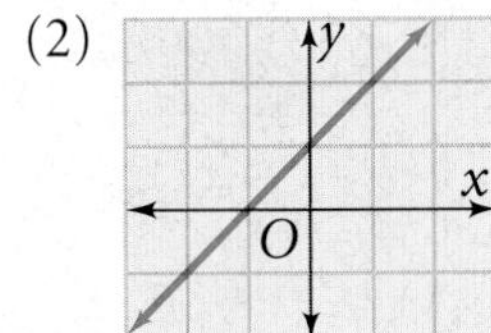

(4)

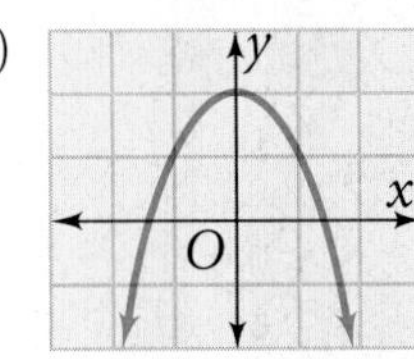

4 When $f(x) = -3x^2 + 4x$, $f(-2)$ is ■.

(1) 4 (3) -12
(2) -20 (4) 26

5 Find the range of $f(x) = |2x - 3|$ when the domain is $\{-5, -2, -1\}$.

(1) all integers (3) $\{5, 7, 13\}$
(2) $\{-13, -7, -5\}$ (4) $\{1, 4, 7\}$

Part II

6 A vendor sells sweatshirts with the features described below. No sweatshirt is favored over any other sweatshirt by the customer.

Colors: white, blue, yellow
Emblem colors: black, red
Emblem designs: team name, team mascot

a What is the probability that the vendor sells a blue sweatshirt with a red team mascot?
b What is the probability that the vendor sells a sweatshirt with the team name in black?

Part III

7 Suppose your scores on four math tests were 95, 90, 88, and 90.
a Find the mean of your scores.
b Suppose your score on the fifth test was 88. Find the new mean.
c What score would you need on your sixth math test to raise the mean to 91?

8 The numbers in the box are the numbers of times some people in a survey said they ate dinner out last month.

7	2	11	25	3	16	14	16	3	11	8	17	6	12	21
21	6	12	10	12	30	7	15	9	19	5	11	10	14	20

a Make a cumulative frequency table for the data using intervals of 5 times.
b Make a cumulative frequency histogram.
c What percent ate dinner out more than 20 times last month?

Part IV

9 A pizza costs \$8.00. Each topping costs an additional \$.50.
a Identify the independent and dependent variables.
b Write a function rule for the cost of a pizza.
c Graph the function.

CHAPTER

3

Algebraic Concepts and Simple Equations

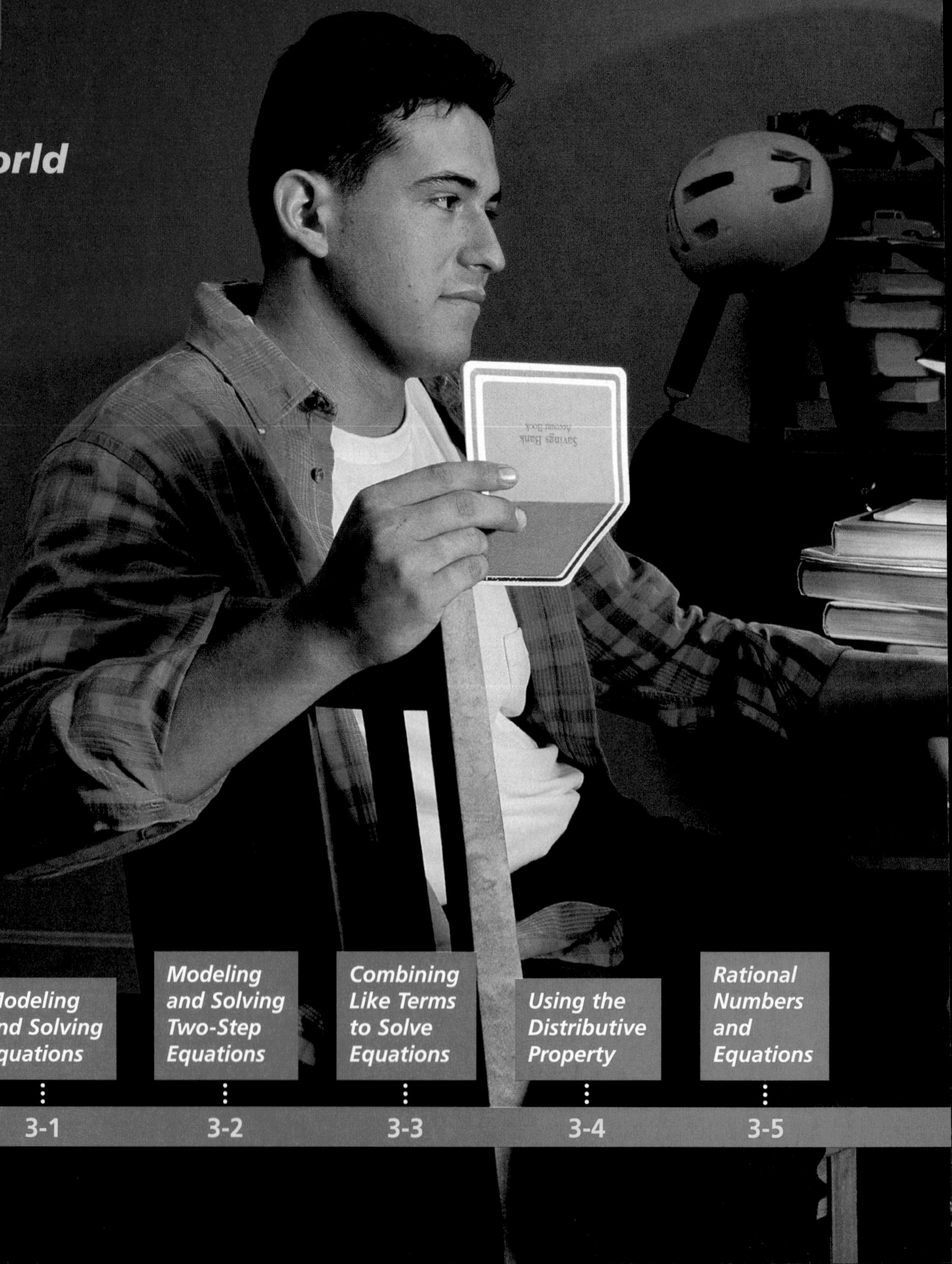

Relating to the Real World

How do you solve a problem? Do you first decide what the problem really is, and then take a series of steps to improve the situation? In algebra, that's exactly what happens. To solve problems, many people, including pharmacists, marine biologists, and money managers, all use simple equations and step-by-step methods.

CHAPTER PROJECT

checks and balances

Sale!
$99.99
Personal CD Playe
with Headphones
• Rich, full sound
• 16-program mem
Take it anywhere!
(runs on 2 AA ba

When there is something you really want to buy, do you already have money saved for it? Or, do you put money aside each week until you can afford it? Maybe you just dream about it! A budget for your money can help you change dreams to reality.

As you work through the chapter, you will use equations to help model your personal finances. You will develop spreadsheets to analyze your weekly budget, including regular savings. You will use percents to create graphs. Then you will display and present your budget plan using the graphs and spreadsheets.

To help you complete the project:

- p. 113 *Find Out by Researching*
- p. 118 *Find Out by Modeling*
- p. 123 *Find Out by Organizing*
- p. 143 *Find Out by Graphing*
- p. 150 *Finishing the Project*

3-1 Modeling and Solving Equations

What You'll Learn

- Solving one-step equations
- Using equations to solve real-world problems

...And Why

To organize your thoughts and your work

THINK AND DISCUSS

Solving Addition and Subtraction Equations

An equation is like a balance scale because it shows that two quantities are equal.

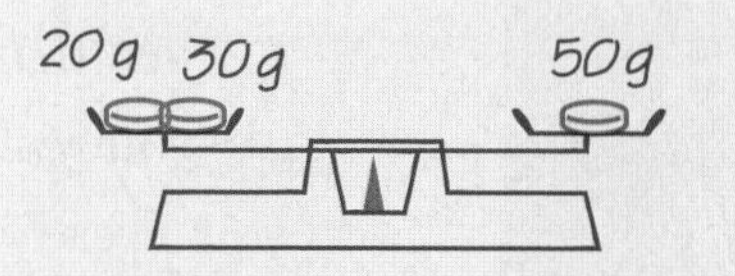

Equation: $20 + 30 = 50$

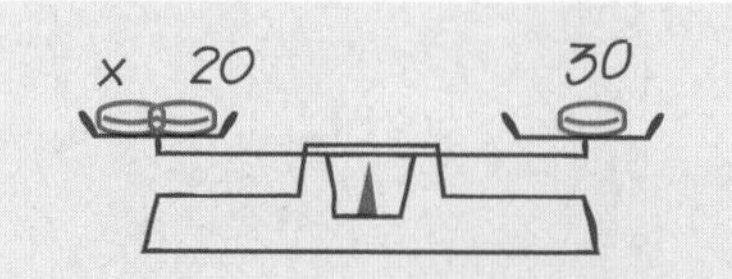

Equation: $x + 20 = 30$

To solve an equation containing a variable, you find the value (or values) of the variable that make the equation true. These values are called **solutions.**

1. **Mental Math** Solve each equation.

a. $x + 5 = 6$ **b.** $y - 10 = 2$

c. $-4 = -2 + b$

One way to solve an equation is to get the variable alone on one side of the equal sign. You can do this by using **inverse operations,** which are operations that undo one another.

Example 1 Relating to the Real World

Veterinary Medicine A veterinary assistant holds a dog and steps on a scale. The scale reads 193.7 lb. Alone, the assistant weighs 135 lb. To find the weight of the dog, solve the equation $x + 135 = 193.7$.

$$x + 135 = 193.7$$
$$x + 135 - 135 = 193.7 - 135$$
$$x = 58.7$$

← The inverse operation for addition is subtraction. Subtract 135 from each side.

The dog weighs 58.7 lb.

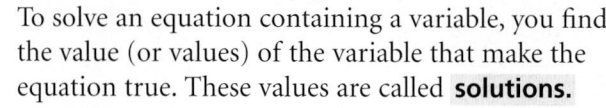

Check $x + 135 = 193.7$

$58.7 + 135 \stackrel{?}{=} 193.7$ ← Substitute 58.7 for *x*.

$193.7 = 193.7$ ✓

QUICK REVIEW

The expression $-a$ means the opposite of a.

2. **Try This** What is the inverse operation for subtraction? Use this operation to solve $a - 14 = -26$.

3. **Mental Math** Solve each equation by finding opposites.
   a. $-x = 7$ b. $-y = -2$ c. $5 = -z$

Equivalent equations are equations that have the same solution. You can add or subtract the same number from each side of an equation to form an equivalent equation.

Addition Property of Equality

For any numbers a, b, and c, if $a = b$, then $a + c = b + c$.

Example: Since $\frac{8}{2} = 4$, then $\frac{8}{2} + 3 = 4 + 3$.

Subtraction Property of Equality

For any numbers a, b, and c, if $a = b$, then $a - c = b - c$.

Example: Since $\frac{15}{3} = 5$, then $\frac{15}{3} - 2 = 5 - 2$.

Solving Multiplication and Division Equations

For simple multiplication and division equations, you can use mental math to find the solutions.

4. **Mental Math** Solve each equation.
   a. $4a = 12$ b. $20 = -2x$ c. $\frac{n}{6} = 5$

5. **Mental Math** Is -16 a solution to the equation $-3x = -48$? Explain.

Multiplication and division are inverse operations. You use multiplication to undo division and division to undo multiplication.

PROBLEM SOLVING

Look Back Show how you would check the solution.

Example 2

Solve $-\frac{r}{4} = -10.4$.

$-\frac{r}{4} = -10.4$ ← The operation is division. Multiply to undo.

$-4(-\frac{r}{4}) = -4(-10.4)$ ← Multiply each side of the equation by –4.

$r = 41.6$

The solution is 41.6.

Math A Test Prep

1 Which equation is equivalent to $-3x = -6$?
(1) $\frac{x}{-9} = -2$
(2) $4x = 12$
(3) $5 + x = 3$
(4) $x - (-7) = 9$

2 It took Lana 9 hours to drive 522 miles. What was Lana's average speed? Write an equation to model this problem. Then solve it.

6. a. *Calculator* Using his calculator to solve Example 2, Li got the answer 416. What error did he make?
   b. *Estimation* How could Li use estimation to catch his error?

You can use multiplication and division to form equivalent equations.

Multiplication Property of Equality

For any numbers a, b, and c, if , then .
Example: Since , then .

Division Property of Equality

For any numbers a, b, and c, with $c \neq 0$, if , then .
Example: Since $3 + 1 = 4$, then $\frac{3+1}{2} = \frac{4}{2}$.

7. **Try This** Solve each equation.
   a. $3.2m = 5.44$ b. $\frac{b}{4} = -18$ c. $100.8 = -16y$

8. *Critical Thinking* When you divide both sides of an equation by the same number, you cannot use the number zero. Explain what would result from the equation $3 \cdot 0 = 4 \cdot 0$ if you could divide both sides of the equation by zero.

Modeling by Writing Equations

A good strategy for solving a real-world problem is to model the problem with an equation. It organizes your thoughts and, of course, your work.

Example 3 *Relating to the Real World* 

Weather The average annual precipitation of Houston, Texas, is about 5.2 times that of El Paso, Texas. What is the average annual precipitation of El Paso?

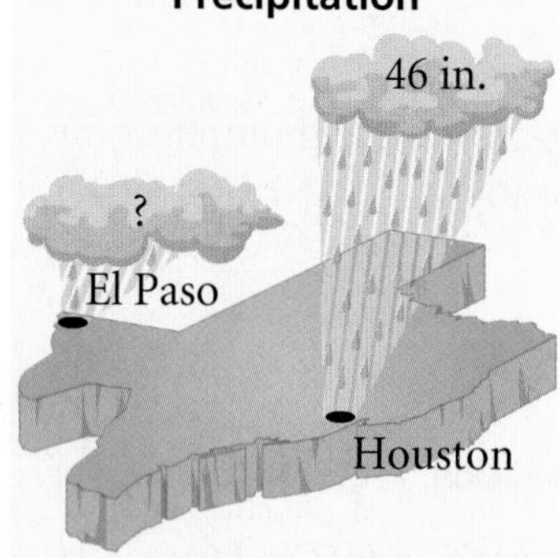

Define p = El Paso's precipitation
Relate Houston's precipitation is 5.2 times El Paso's precipitation
Write $46 = 5.2 \times p$

$$46 = 5.2p$$
$$\frac{46}{5.2} = \frac{5.2p}{5.2} \quad \leftarrow \text{Divide each side by 5.2.}$$
$$8.8 \approx p$$

The average annual precipitation of El Paso is about 8.8 in.

9. a. Calculator What does your calculator display for 46 ÷ 5.2 ENTER ?
   b. Critical Thinking Akira thinks that 8.846153846 more accurately describes El Paso's precipitation than 8.8 does. Abdul thinks that because of the phrase "about 5.2 times greater," 8.8 is a better answer. Do you agree with Akira or Abdul? Explain.

Exercises ON YOUR OWN

1. Critical Thinking To solve $c - 3 = 12$, Kendra added 3 to each side of the equation. Ted subtracted 12 from each side, then added 15. Which method is better? Why?

2. Which property of equality do the balance scales model?

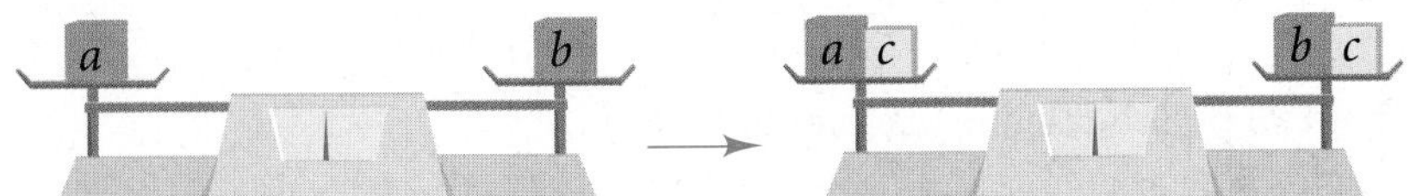

Mental Math Solve each equation mentally.

3. $4a = 24$
4. $-6 + y = -11$
5. $z - 8 = 0$
6. $\frac{x}{7} = -3$
7. $5 = -9 + v$
8. $36 = -4x$
9. $\frac{y}{5} = 100$
10. $-5 = n - 2$

11. Which equation is not equivalent to the others?
   A. $m + 7 = -4$
   B. $7 + m = -4$
   C. $-4 = m - 7$
   D. $-4 = 7 + m$

12. Estimation Use estimation to check whether 96.26 is a reasonable solution for the equation $m - 62.74 = 159$. Explain your method.

Write an equation to model. Then solve each problem.

13. Geometry Suppose $\angle A$ and $\angle B$ are supplementary angles, and the measure of $\angle A$ is 109°. What is the measure of $\angle B$?

14. Wages Suppose you work as a carpenter's apprentice. You earn $93.50 for working 17 h. What is your hourly wage?

15. Physician's Assistant You measure a child and find that his height is $41\frac{1}{2}$ in. At his last visit, he was $38\frac{3}{4}$ in. tall. How much did he grow?

QUICK REVIEW

Two angles are *supplementary* if the sum of their measures is 180°.

Solve and check.

16. $5p = -75$
17. $2 = -2x$
18. $y - \frac{2}{3} = \frac{1}{3}$
19. $-8j = 12.56$
20. $-7 + a = 28$
21. $-\frac{p}{7} = 28$
22. $-7n = 28$
23. $y + 18 = 13.5$
24. $-3.4 + x = 9.5$
25. $10 = \frac{m}{-2}$
26. $\frac{t}{2} = 98$
27. $-5\frac{1}{3} = x + \frac{1}{2}$
28. $z - 0.35 = 1.65$
29. $a + 3\frac{1}{4} = 7\frac{1}{2}$
30. $6n = -120$
31. $-\frac{y}{7} = 35$

Use the cartoon for Exercises 32 and 33.

32. **Writing** Explain what the student does *not* understand about using letters in algebra.

33. What property of equality did the teacher use to solve the equation?

"Just a minute! Yesterday you said X equals two!"

34. **Standardized Test Prep** Which equations are equivalent?

A. II and III	I. $x - 5 = 10$
B. II and IV	II. $4x = 20$
C. I and V	III. $-\frac{x}{8} = -40$
D. II, III, and IV	IV. $8 + x = 13$
E. I, II, and IV	V. $-30 = 2x$

Open-ended Describe a situation that can be modeled by each equation.

35. $\frac{m}{3} = 6$
36. $p - 0.5 = 19.5$
37. $14 + t = 16.1$
38. $0.25q = 10$

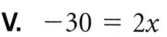

Choose Use a calculator, paper and pencil, or mental math to solve each equation. Check your solutions.

39. $z - 18 = 13.5$
40. $\frac{x}{18} = 13.5$
41. $-196 = m - 97$
42. $9\frac{2}{3} = a + 19$
43. $0.9x = 11.7$
44. $-6 = -3n$
45. $q - 28\frac{1}{2} = -12$
46. $-\frac{r}{3} = -101$
47. $-1\frac{3}{4} = p - \frac{1}{2}$
48. $\frac{m}{4} = -80$
49. $15x = 172.5$
50. $15.9 = r + 27.3$

Write an equation to model. Then solve each problem.

51. **Parking** In Los Angeles, the fine for illegally parking in a zone reserved for people with disabilities is \$330. This is \$280 higher than the fine in New York City. How much is the fine in New York City?

52. **Recreation** The federal government spends \$25.2 million each year to operate parks and historic sites in Washington, D.C. This is \$7.8 million more than it spends to run Yellowstone National Park. How much does it cost to run Yellowstone National Park?

53. **Car Repair** Your bill for a car repair is \$166.50.
   a. One third of the bill is for labor. How much is the charge for labor?
   b. The mechanic worked on your car for 1.5 h. What is the hourly charge for labor?

54. **Sports** The total distance around a baseball diamond is 360 ft. What is the distance from third base to home plate?

Baseball Diamond

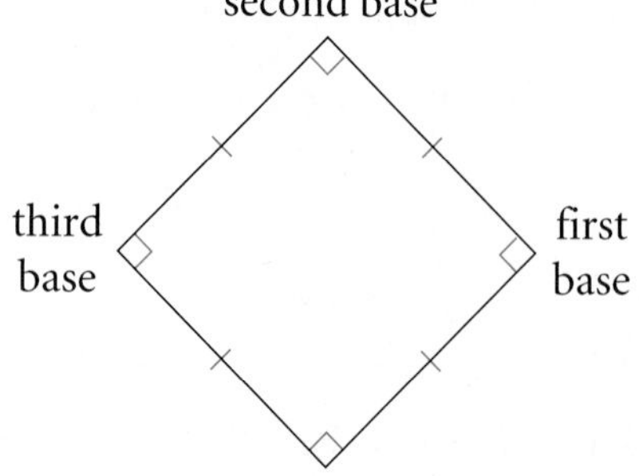

Solve each equation.

55. $5 + v = -13$ **56.** $\frac{x}{6} = -10$ **57.** $8y = -64$ **58.** $m - 1.2 = -2.5$

59. $p + \frac{1}{4} = -3\frac{1}{2}$ **60.** $-\frac{a}{7} = 2.5$ **61.** $314 = n + 576$ **62.** $-1\frac{1}{3} = b - 5\frac{1}{2}$

63. $-3.2x = 14.4$ **64.** $32 = -0.8m$ **65.** $b + 6\frac{1}{8} = 5\frac{3}{4}$ **66.** $-\frac{p}{4} = 55$

67. $-1.05 = t - 6.17$ **68.** $-\frac{b}{3} = 107$ **69.** $6x = -\frac{1}{4}$ **70.** $-4.87 = x + 0.025$

Write an equation to model. Then solve each problem.

71. *Geometry* The Pentagon is the headquarters of the United States Department of Defense. Its shape is a regular pentagon, and its perimeter is about 1.6 km. How long is one side of the Pentagon?

QUICK REVIEW

A *regular pentagon* has five sides of equal length.

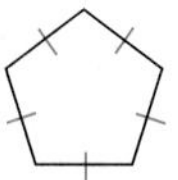

72. *Sports* In 1994, German Silva of Mexico won the New York Marathon with a time of 2 h 11 min 21 s. In the same year, Cosmas N'Deti of Kenya won the Boston Marathon with a time that was 4 min 6 s faster than Silva's time in New York. How long did it take N'Deti to run the Boston Marathon?

Chapter Project ***Find Out by Researching***

Think of several items you would like to buy for less than $150, such as a CD player, sports equipment, or some clothes.

- Price these items using ads or by visiting several stores.
- What factors other than price should you consider? Explain.
- After completing your research, choose one item as a goal to buy. Explain your decision.

Exercises MIXED REVIEW

73. Find $f(2)$ when $f(x) = 3x + 2$.

74. Find the range of $f(x) = x^2 - 1$ when the domain is $\{-2, 1, 3\}$.

75. *Cities* The population of New York City is about 15 times the population of New Orleans, Louisiana. The population of New York City is about 7,300,000. What is the population of New Orleans?

SELF ASSESSMENT — FOR YOUR JOURNAL

Describe some ways you can solve simple equations. Give a sample equation and solution for each method listed.

Getting Ready for Lesson 3-2

Evaluate each expression.

76. $3n + 5$ for $n = -6$ **77.** $2.8 + 5x$ for $x = 7.9$

78. $3x - 7$ for $x = -12$ **79.** $-4w - 17$ for $w = -12$

80. $\frac{k}{5} + 3.8$ for $k = 14$ **81.** $8 - \frac{x}{2}$ for $x = -40$

3-2 Modeling and Solving Two-Step Equations

What You'll Learn

- Solving two-step equations
- Using two-step equations to solve real-world problems

...And Why

To solve problems involving money

What You'll Need

- tiles

QUICK REVIEW

▢ represents 1.
▪ represents -1.

▢ ▪ is a zero pair.

WORK TOGETHER

Work in pairs. To model equations, use the ▮ tile to represent x.

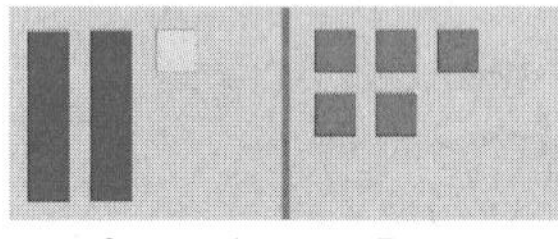

$2x + 1 = -5$

3x − 2 is the same as 3x + (−2).

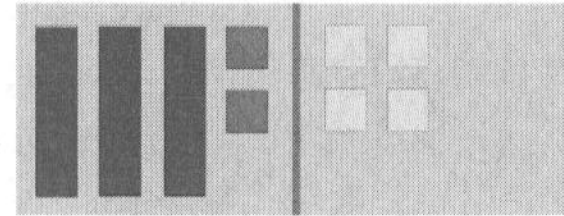

$3x - 2 = 4$

1. Write an equation for each model.
   a. 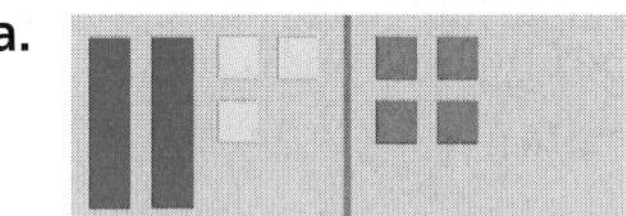
   b.  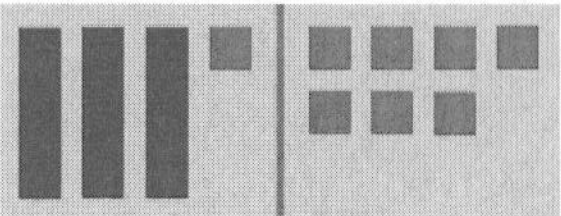

2. Use tiles to create a model for each equation.
   a. $2x = 8$ b. $x + 5 = -7$ c. $4x + 3 = -5$

THINK AND DISCUSS

Using Tiles

A **two-step equation** is an equation that has two operations. You can use tiles to model and solve a two-step equation.

Example 1 Relating to the Real World 

Jobs Suppose you earn \$4/h baby-sitting and pay \$1 in bus fare each way. You want to buy a T-shirt that costs \$10. To find the number of hours you must work to buy the T-shirt, solve the equation $4x - 2 = 10$.

Model the equation with tiles.

$4x - 2 = 10$

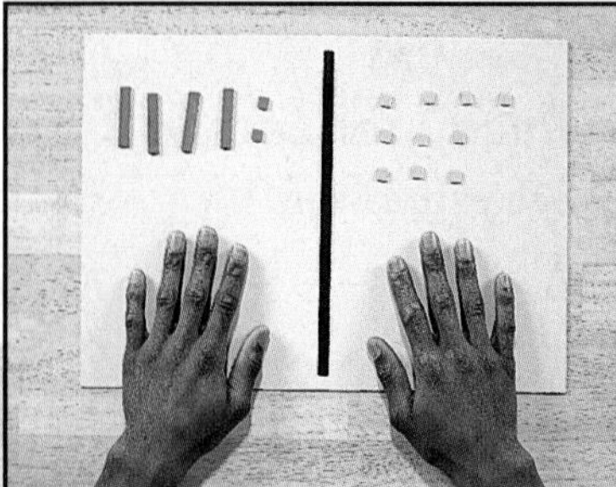

1 Add 2 to each side of the equation. $4x - 2 + 2 = 10 + 2$

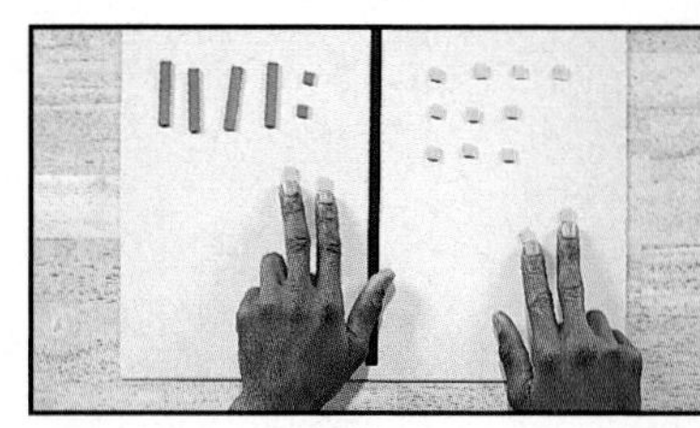

2 Simplify by removing zero pairs. $4x = 12$

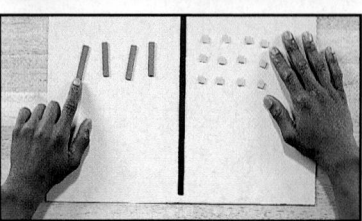

3 Divide each side into four identical groups. $\frac{4x}{4} = \frac{12}{4}$

4 Solve for $1x$.

$1x = 3$

$x = 3$

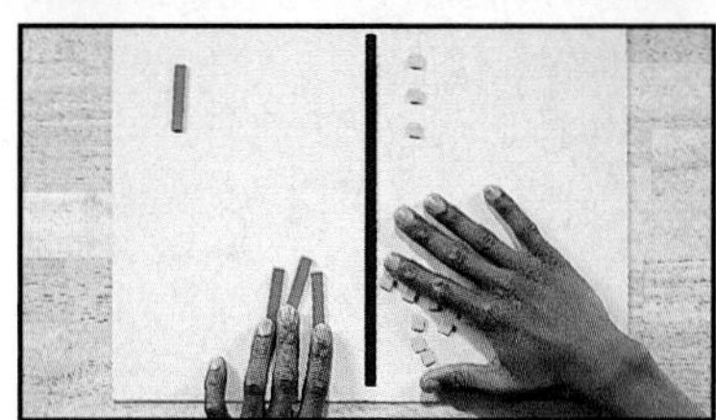

The solution is 3. You must baby-sit for 3 h to buy the T-shirt.

Check $4x - 2 = 10$

$4(3) - 2 \stackrel{?}{=} 10$ ← **Replace x with 3.**

$12 - 2 \stackrel{?}{=} 10$

$10 = 10$ ✓

3. Which two operations were used to solve the equation? Why?

4. **Try This** Use tiles to model and solve each equation.

a. $2y - 3 = 7$ **b.** $5 = 4m + 1$ **c.** $3z - 2 = -8$

Using Properties

To help you solve equations, you can write them in different ways. The variable x means $1x$. Similarly, $-x$ means $-1x$. Subtracting a variable is the same as adding its opposite. So, you can rewrite $4 - x$ as $4 + (-x)$.

5. It takes two operations to solve the equation $-x + 7 = 12$.

a. Subtract 7 from each side of the equation.

b. Multiply each side of the equation by -1. What is the solution?

6. Solve each equation.

a. $-11 = -b + 6$ **b.** $-9 - m = -2$ **c.** $15 = 3 - x$

Example 2

Solve the equation $1 = -\frac{k}{12} + 5$.

$$1 = -\frac{k}{12} + 5$$

$$1 - 5 = -\frac{k}{12} + 5 - 5 \quad \leftarrow \text{Subtract 5 from each side.}$$

$$-4 = -\frac{k}{12}$$

$$-12(-4) = -12\left(-\frac{k}{12}\right) \quad \leftarrow \text{Multiply each side by } -12.$$

$$48 = k$$

The solution is 48.

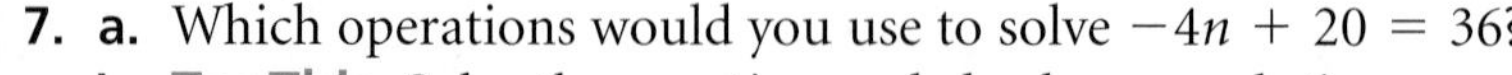

7. **a.** Which operations would you use to solve $-4n + 20 = 36$?
   b. **Try This** Solve the equation and check your solution.

Example 3 Relating to the Real World 

Money Suppose you have \$18.75 to spend at Paradise Park. Admission is \$5.50. How many ride tickets can you buy?

Define r = number of ride tickets you can buy

Relate	entrance fee	plus	cost of ride tickets	equals	total cost
Write	5.5	+	1.5r	=	18.75

$$5.5 + 1.5r = 18.75$$

$$5.5 + 1.5r - 5.5 = 18.75 - 5.5 \quad \leftarrow \text{Subtract 5.5 from each side.}$$

$$1.5r = 13.25$$

$$\frac{1.5r}{1.5} = \frac{13.25}{1.5} \quad \leftarrow \text{Divide each side by 1.5.}$$

$$r \approx 8.8$$

You can buy 8 ride tickets.

CALCULATOR HINT

You can use a calculator to solve this equation. Write it in **calculator-ready form:** $x = (18.75 - 5.5) \div 1.5$. Use the sequence: (18.75 − 5.5) ÷ 1.5 ENTER.

8. Why should 8.8 be rounded to 8 in this situation?

9. If you buy 8 ride tickets, how much money do you have left?

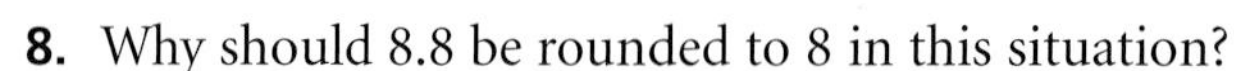

Exercises ON YOUR OWN

Write an equation for each model.

1. 

2. 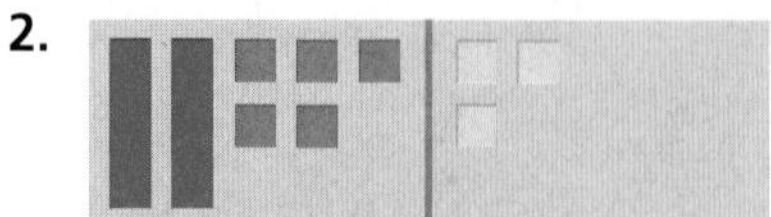

3. 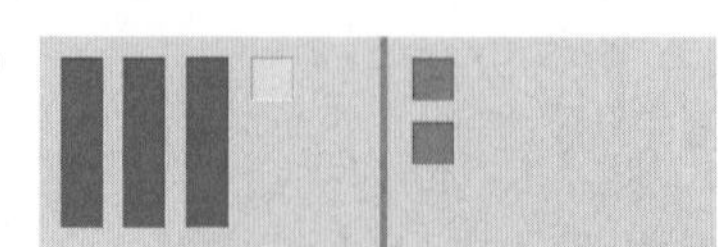

Use tiles to solve each equation.

4. $2n - 5 = 7$
5. $3 + 4x = -1$
6. $3b + 7 = -2$
7. $-10 = -6 + 2y$
8. $5y - 2 = -2$
9. $0 = 3x - 3$
10. $2z + 4 = -6$
11. $4x + 9 = 1$

Solve each equation. Check your solutions.

12. $3x + 2 = 20$
13. $-b + 5 = -16$
14. $\frac{y}{2} + 5 = -12$
15. $7 - 3k = -14$
16. $1 + \frac{m}{4} = -1$
17. $41 = 5 - 6h$
18. $1.3n - 4 = 2.5$
19. $\frac{x}{3} - 9 = 0$
20. $-t - 4 = -3$
21. $3.5 + 10m = 7.32$
22. $7 = -2x + 7$
23. $14 + \frac{h}{5} = 2$

Use an equation to model and solve each problem.

24. **Farming** An orange grower ships oranges in boxes that weigh 2 kg. Each orange weighs 0.2 kg. The total weight of a box filled with oranges is 10 kg. How many oranges are packed in each box?

25. **Food Preparation** Suppose you are helping to prepare a large meal. You can peel 2 carrots/min. You need 60 peeled carrots. How long will it take you to finish if you have already peeled 18 carrots?

26. You can find the value of each variable in the matrices at the right by writing and solving equations. For example, solving the equation $2a + 1 = 11$, you get $a = 5$. Find the values of x, y, and k.

$$\begin{bmatrix} 2a + 1 & -6 \\ -7 & -3k \end{bmatrix} = \begin{bmatrix} 11 & x - 5 \\ 5 - 2y & 27 \end{bmatrix}$$

Choose **Use a calculator, paper and pencil, or mental math to solve each equation. Check your solutions.**

27. $-y + 7 = 13$
28. $5 - b = 2$
29. $10 = 2n + 1$
30. $6 - 2p = 14$
31. $3x - 15 = 33$
32. $\frac{m}{3} - 9 = -21$
33. $14 - \frac{y}{2} = -1$
34. $\frac{x}{10} + 1.5 = 3.8$
35. $-7 = 11 + 3b$
36. $-6 + 6z = 0$
37. $\frac{a}{5} + 15 = 30$
38. $34 = 14 - 4p$
39. $4 = 4 - \frac{a}{9}$
40. $3x - 1 = 8$
41. $-8 - c = 11$
42. $\frac{m}{3} - 18 = 7$
43. $3x - 2.1 = 4.5$
44. $2 = -1 - \frac{k}{12}$
45. $\frac{m}{2} - 1.002 = 0.93$
46. $3 - 0.5c = 1.2$

47. **Math in the Media** You rent a car for one day. Your total bill is \$60.
    a. **Estimation** You estimate your mileage to be about 100 mi. Does the bill seem reasonable? Explain.
    b. Exactly how many miles did you drive?

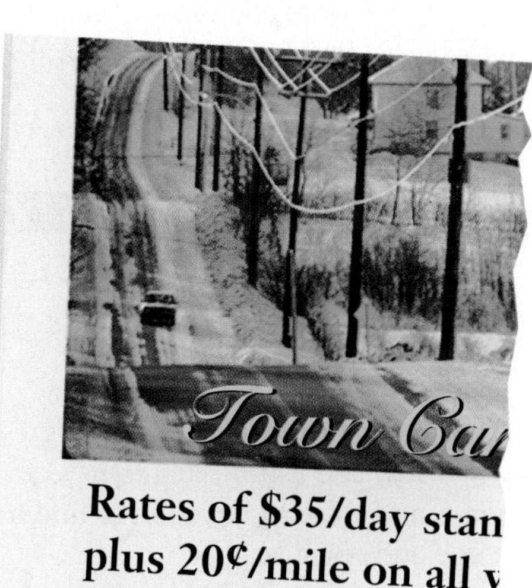

48. **Insurance** One insurance policy pays people for claims by multiplying the claim amount by 0.8 and then subtracting \$500. If a person receives a check for \$4650, how much was the claim amount?

49. **Gardening** Tulip bulbs cost \$.75 each plus \$3.00 for shipping an entire order. You have \$14.00. How many bulbs can you order?

50. **Open-ended** Write a problem that you can model with a two-step equation. Define the variable and show the solution to the problem.

51. **Critical Thinking** If you multiply each side of the equation $0.24r + 5.25 = -7.23$ by 100, the result is an equivalent equation. Explain why it might be helpful to do this.

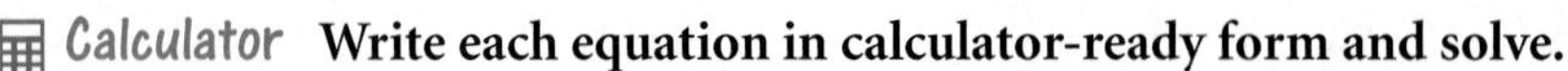

Calculator **Write each equation in calculator-ready form and solve.**

52. $1.2x + 0.6 = 32.4$ **53.** $2.8 = 1.34 + \frac{r}{2}$ **54.** $\frac{y}{4.5} - 9 = 3.5$ **55.** $0.05n - 0.5 = 8$

56. $9.007 - b = 8.32$ **57.** $5.3 - 0.8n = 7$ **58.** $0.3z + 0.91 = -0.08$ **59.** $3 - \frac{t}{2.5} = -7.06$

60. *Temperature* The formula for converting a temperature from Celsius, C, to Fahrenheit, F, is $F = 1.8C + 32$.

a. Copy and complete the table. Round to the nearest degree.

b. *Mental Math* To convert from Celsius to Fahrenheit, you can get an estimate by using this rule: multiply the Celsius temperature by 2, then add 30. Use this strategy to convert 4°C, 15°C, and 50°C.

Fahrenheit	Celsius	Description of Temperature
212°	■	boiling point of water
■	37°	human body temperature
68°	■	room temperature
■	7°	average January high in Baltimore
■	0°	freezing point of water
19°	■	average January low in Chicago

61. *Writing* Describe a situation that you can model with the equation $185 - 15n = 110$. Explain what the variable represents.

Chapter Project — *Find Out by Modeling*

To make a successful budget, you need to think about savings.

- Geraldo has already saved \$40 and wants to buy a CD player for \$129 in about four months. To find how much he should save each week, he wrote $40 + 16x = 129$. Explain his equation.
- On page 113, you chose one item as the goal for your project. How much does it cost? When do you want to buy this item?
- Write and solve an equation to find how much you should save per week.

Exercises MIXED REVIEW

Solve each equation.

62. $4s = 18$ **63.** $x - 3 = 9$ **64.** $\frac{m}{5} = 3$ **65.** $-7 = n + 2$

66. In 1995, the Library of Congress had 110 million books and other items. It is projected to have about 117.2 million items in 1999. Write and solve an equation to find how many items the Library of Congress adds each year.

Getting Ready for Lesson 3-3

Simplify.

67. $8 - (-1)$ **68.** $9 - 11$ **69.** $-15 + (-5)$ **70.** $5 + (-12)$ **71.** $-6 - (-9)$

What You'll Learn

- Combining like terms
- Solving equations by combining like terms

...And Why

To find the price of an item by using the total bill

What You'll Need

- tiles

3-3 Combining Like Terms to Solve Equations

WORK TOGETHER

Work with a partner. When you use tiles to model an expression, you can combine variable tiles and integer tiles to create a simpler expression. You can use the ▮ tile to represent $-x$.

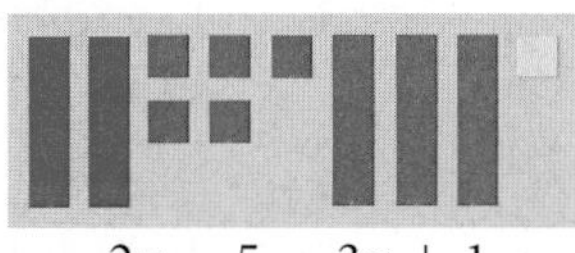

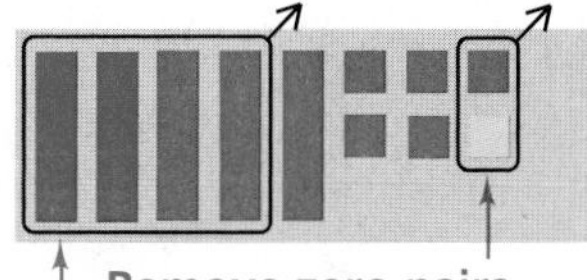

Remove zero pairs. → $-x - 4$

QUICK REVIEW

▯ ▮ represents zero.

1. Model each expression. If possible, combine tiles and write a simpler expression.

a. $4x - 2x$	**b.** $5 + 2x - 1$	**c.** $3x - 6x + 4$
d. $8 + 3x - x - 6$	**e.** $6 + 6x$	**f.** $3x + 3x - x$
g. $2x - 1$	**h.** $-5 - x + 4x - 4$	**i.** $x + x + 1 + x$

2. Which expressions in Question 1 could not be simplified? Explain.

THINK AND DISCUSS

Combining Like Terms

QUICK REVIEW

A *term* is a number or a variable or the product of numbers and variables.

If a term has a variable, the numerical factor is called the **coefficient.** To identify the coefficients of each term in the expression $-x + 5y + 17$, you can write the expression as $-1x + 5y + 17$.

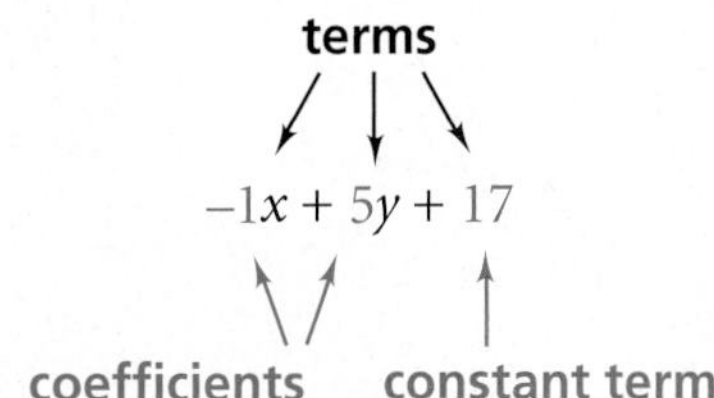

Terms are **like terms** if they have exactly the same variable factors. Terms like $5y$ and $2y^2$ are not like terms because their variable factors have different exponents. In the Work Together activity, you combined like terms using tiles. You can also combine like terms by adding coefficients.

Example 1

Simplify the expression $-2 + 6x + z - 2x + 8 - 4z$.

terms with x	terms with z	constant terms	←Group like terms.
$6x - 2x$	$1z - 4z$	$-2 + 8$	←Then add or subtract.
$4x$	$-3z$	6	

The simplified expression is $4x - 3z + 6$.

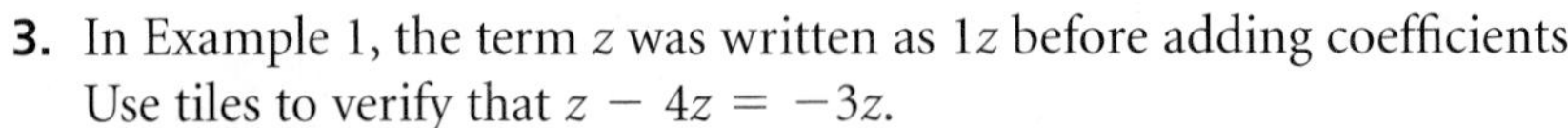

3. In Example 1, the term z was written as $1z$ before adding coefficients. Use tiles to verify that $z - 4z = -3z$.

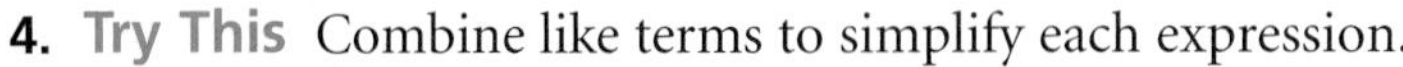

4. **Try This** Combine like terms to simplify each expression.

a. $9a + 10 - a + 3x - 5$ **b.** $-4 + y - 9m - m + 2y$

Solving Equations

You can combine like terms to solve equations.

Example 2 **Relating to the Real World**

Money Each used book at the library sale sold for the same amount. Suppose you bought 6 mysteries and 8 science-fiction books. Then you bought a poster for \$2.40. You spent a total of \$8.70. Solve the equation $6n + 8n + 2.40 = 8.70$ to find the cost of each book.

$$6n + 8n + 2.40 = 8.70$$

$$14n + 2.40 = 8.70 \quad \leftarrow \text{Combine like terms.}$$

$$14n + 2.40 - 2.40 = 8.70 - 2.40 \quad \leftarrow \text{Subtract 2.40 from each side.}$$

$$14n = 6.30$$

$$\frac{14n}{14} = \frac{6.30}{14} \quad \leftarrow \text{Divide each side by 14.}$$

$$n = 0.45$$

Each book costs \$.45.

5. **Try This** Solve each equation.

a. $b + 5b = 42$

b. $3x - 4x + 6 = -2$

c. $7 = 4m - 2m + 1$

Example 3 Relating to the Real World 

What? The largest rock concert that has yet taken place was held on July 21, 1990, in Berlin, Germany, to celebrate German reunification.

Source: *The Guinness Book of Records*

Entertainment As a gift for your brother, you order two concert tickets. Two days before the concert a friend asks to join you. When you order the third ticket, there is a \$12 charge for express delivery to be sure the ticket arrives on time. The total bill is \$78. How much does each person owe?

Define c = charge for each of the original tickets
$c + 12$ = total charge for the late ticket

Relate	charge for the original tickets	plus	total charge for the late ticket	is	78
Write	$2c$	$+$	$c + 12$	$=$	78

$$2c + c + 12 = 78$$
$$3c + 12 = 78 \quad \leftarrow \text{Combine like terms.}$$
$$3c + 12 - 12 = 78 - 12 \quad \leftarrow \text{Subtract 12 from both sides.}$$
$$3c = 66$$
$$\frac{3c}{3} = \frac{66}{3} \quad \leftarrow \text{Divide each side by 3.}$$
$$c = 22$$

You owe 2(\$22), or \$44. Your friend owes \$22 + \$12, or \$34.

Check \$44 + \$34 = \$78 ✔

6. ***Shopping*** Suppose you buy 1.35 lb of apples and 3.55 lb of oranges. After you use a 50¢-off coupon, the total cost is \$4.89. If apples and oranges sell for the same price, find their cost per pound.

Exercises ON YOUR OWN

1. Use tiles to simplify $-y + 5 + 3y - 4$.

2. ***Critical Thinking*** Suppose you want to solve the equation $-3m + 4 + 5m = -6$. As a first step, would you combine $-3m$ and $5m$ or subtract 4 from each side of the equation? Why?

Simplify each expression.

3. $2n - 3n$ **4.** $28 - a + 4a$ **5.** $-4 + 3b + 2 + 5b$ **6.** $x + 1.3 + 7x$

7. $-x + 7n - 3x + n$ **8.** $4 + 5z + z - 6\frac{1}{2}$ **9.** $8 + x - 7x + m$ **10.** $2k - 5b - b - k$

Write and solve each equation modeled by tiles.

11. 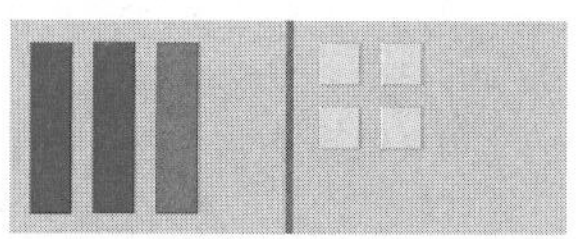

12. 

13. 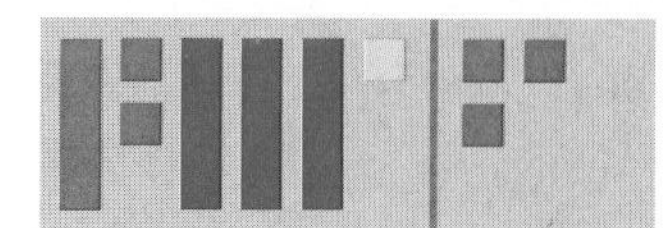

Solve and check each equation.

14. $7x - 3x - 6 = 6$ **15.** $y + y + 2 = 18$ **16.** $-13 = 2b - b - 10$ **17.** $5 - t - t = -1$

18. $9 = -3 + n + 2n$ **19.** $13 = 5 - 13 + 3x$ **20.** $1.6y + 3.2y = 96$ **21.** $0.5t - 3t + 5 = 0$

Use an equation to solve each problem.

22. **Geometry** A rectangle has perimeter 42 cm. The length is 3 cm greater than the width. Find the width and length of the rectangle.

23. **Entertainment** Movie tickets for an adult and three children cost \$20. An adult's ticket costs \$2 more than a child's ticket. Find the cost of an adult's ticket.

24. **Writing** Three students simplify the expression $3p - 4p$. They get -1, $-p$, and $-1p$. State which answers are correct and explain why.

25. **Open-ended** Write an expression with four terms that can be simplified to an expression with two terms.

Choose **Use a calculator, paper and pencil, or mental math to solve each equation. Check your answers.**

26. $4y - 2y = 18$ **27.** $-2b + 7b = 30$ **28.** $x + 3x - 7 = 29$ **29.** $6 - a + 4a = -6$

30. $1 - 6t - 4t = 1$ **31.** $s + s - 6\frac{2}{3} = 4\frac{1}{3}$ **32.** $72 + 4 - 14r = 36$ **33.** $a + 6a - 9 = 30$

34. $2 + 3n - n = -7$ **35.** $4x + 3.6 + x = 1.2$ **36.** $0 = -7n + 4 - 5n$ **37.** $3m + 4.5m = 18$

38. $x + x + 1 + x + 2 = -3.75$ **39.** $x + x + 2 + 3x - 6 = 31$

Use an equation to solve each problem.

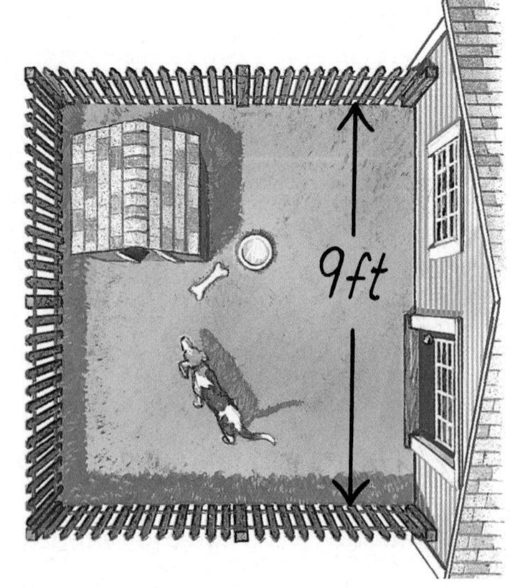

40. Suppose you are fencing a rectangular puppy kennel with 25 ft of fence. The side of the kennel next to your house does not need a fence. This side is 9 ft long. Find the dimensions of the kennel.

41. **Art** An art gallery owner wants to frame a 30 in.-wide portrait of poet Maya Angelou. He wants the width of the framed poster to be $38\frac{1}{2}$ in. How wide should each section of the frame be?

Solve each consecutive integer problem.

Sample Find three consecutive integers with sum 219.

Consecutive integers are integers that differ by one.
Let the integers equal n, $n + 1$, and $n + 2$. Then solve this equation. $n + n + 1 + n + 2 = 219$

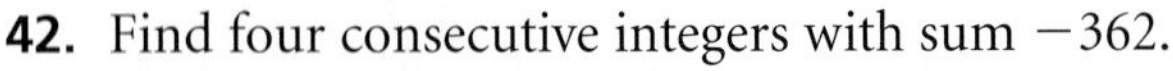

42. Find four consecutive integers with sum -362.

43. Three friends were born in consecutive years. The sum of their birth years is 5961. Find the year in which each person was born.

44. The sum of four consecutive even integers is 308. Find the integers.

Geometry **Use equations to find the value of each variable.**

45.

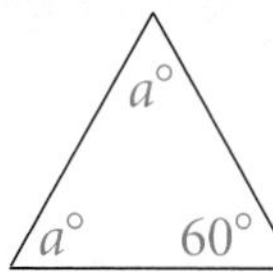

46.

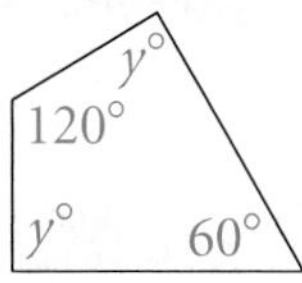

47.

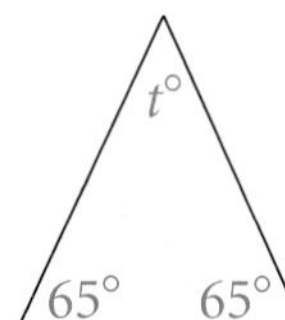

48.

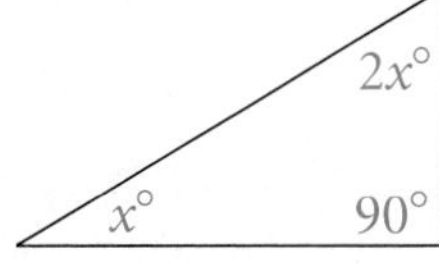

49. $n°$ 130° 130° $n°$

QUICK REVIEW

The sum of the measures of the angles of a triangle is 180°. The sum of the measures of the angles of a quadrilateral is 360°.

Chapter Project — *Find Out by Organizing*

A spreadsheet can help you organize your information.

- Begin your budget by recording the amount of money you earn, the amount of money you save, and the amount of money you spend for two weeks.
- Analyze your expenses to plan how much you can spend each week, while still meeting your savings goal.
- Design a spreadsheet to show all the important categories in your budget plan. Include a column or row to show the total you will have saved after each week.
- Will you reach your savings goal when you hope to? Enter dollar amounts into your spreadsheet and verify that your budget works.

what I earn (chores, job)
what I save
what I spend each week (lunch, bus)
what I spend occasionally (movie, magazine)

Exercises MIXED REVIEW

Write a function rule for each table.

50.

x	y
3	7.5
4	10.0
5	12.5

51.

x	y
2	−4
4	−8
6	−12

52.

x	y
27	−3
28	−2
29	−1

53. Sketch a graph that shows your speed as you traveled to school today. Explain the activity in each section of the graph.

Getting Ready for Lesson 3-4

Simplify.

54. $2(3 + 7)$ **55.** $3(2 - 5)$ **56.** $-2(4 + 8)$ **57.** $-4(21 - 9)$

What You'll Learn

- Using the distributive property
- Solving equations that involve the distributive property

...And Why

To solve problems involving electricity

3-4 Using the Distributive Property

WORK TOGETHER

Sports A high school basketball court is 84 ft long by 50 ft wide. A college basketball court is 10 ft longer than a high school basketball court.

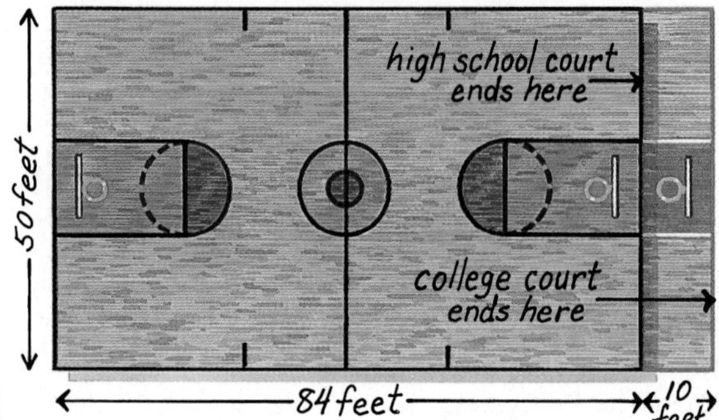

1. Work with a partner to evaluate each expression.
   a. $50(84 + 10)$ **b.** $50(84) + 50(10)$
2. Explain how each of the expressions in Question 1 represents the area of a college basketball court.

THINK AND DISCUSS

Simplifying Variable Expressions

Using two methods to find area illustrates the *distributive property*.

Distributive Property

For all real numbers a, b, and c:

$a(b + c) = ab + ac \quad (b + c)a = ba + ca$

$a(b - c) = ab - ac \quad (b - c)a = ba - ca$

Examples:

$5(20 + 6) = 5(20) + 5(6) \quad (20 + 6)5 = 20(5) + 6(5)$

$9(30 - 2) = 9(30) - 9(2) \quad (30 - 2)9 = 30(9) - 2(9)$

You can use the distributive property to simplify expressions.

$$2(5x + 3) = 2(5x) + 2(3) = 10x + 6$$

$$(3b - 2)\tfrac{1}{3} = 3b(\tfrac{1}{3}) - 2(\tfrac{1}{3}) = b - \tfrac{2}{3}$$

To simplify an expression like $-(6x + 4)$, first rewrite it as $-1(6x + 4)$.

$$\begin{aligned} -(6x + 4) &= -1(6x + 4) \\ &= -1(6x) + (-1)(4) \\ &= -6x - 4 \end{aligned} \qquad \begin{aligned} -(-2 - 9m) &= -1(-2 - 9m) \\ &= -1(-2) - (-1)(9m) \\ &= 2 + 9m \end{aligned}$$

3. **Critical Thinking** A student rewrote $4(3x + 10)$ as $12x + 10$. Explain the student's error.

4. **Try This** Use the distributive property to simplify each expression.
   a. $-3(2x - 1)$ **b.** $-(7 - 5b)$ **c.** $(3 - 8a)\frac{1}{4}$

Solving and Modeling Equations

Example 1 **Relating to the Real World** 

Shopping Posters of astronaut Sally Ride were on sale for \$3 off the regular price. Suppose you bought two posters and paid a total of \$8. Solve the equation $2(x - 3) = 8$ to find the regular price of each poster.

Model the equation with tiles.

You represent $2(x - 3)$ as two groups of tiles each containing $x - 3$. →

$2(x - 3) = 8$

Rearrange tiles and use the distributive property.

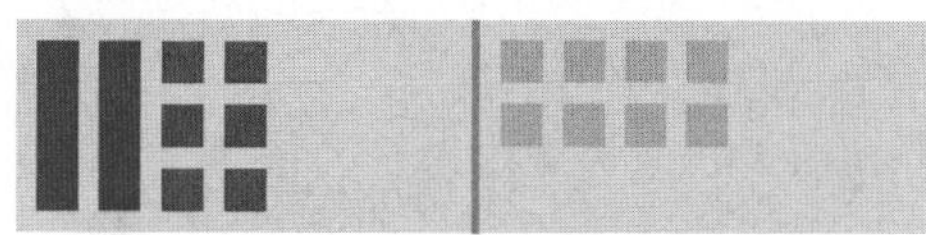

$2(x - 3) = 8$

$2x - 6 = 8$

Add six to each side.

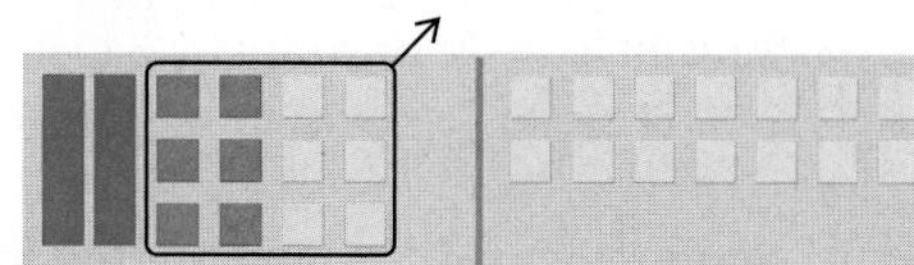

$2x - 6 + 6 = 8 + 6$

$2x = 14$

Divide each side into two identical groups.

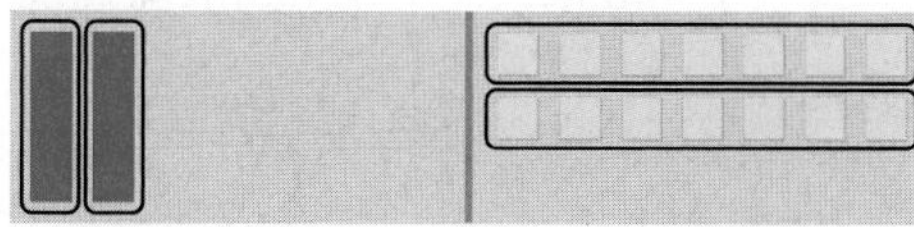

$\frac{2x}{2} = \frac{14}{2}$

Solve for x.

$x = 7$

Each poster regularly costs \$7.

Who? Lewis Latimer (1848–1928) was an inventor who in 1882 received a patent for his method of making a light bulb filament. He was the author of the first book on electrical lighting.

Source: *Black Achievers in Science*

You can use the distributive property to justify steps in combining like terms. For example :

$3x - 5x = (3 - 5)x$ ← distributive property

$= -2x$ ← arithmetic

You can use the distributive property to solve real-world problems.

Example 2 Relating to the Real World 

Electricity Several 6- and 12-volt batteries are wired so that the sum of their voltages produces a power supply of 84 volts. The total number of batteries is ten. How many of each type of battery are used?

Define $x =$ number of 6-volt batteries

$10 - x =$ number of 12-volt batteries

Relate voltage from 6-volt batteries plus voltage from 12-volt batteries equals total voltage

Write $6x \quad + \quad 12(10 - x) \quad = \quad 84$

$$6x + 12(10 - x) = 84$$

$$6x + 120 - 12x = 84 \quad \leftarrow \text{Use the distributive property.}$$

$$-6x + 120 = 84 \quad \leftarrow \text{Combine like terms.}$$

$$-6x + 120 - 120 = 84 - 120 \quad \leftarrow \text{Subtract 120 from each side.}$$

$$-6x = -36$$

$$\frac{-6x}{6} = \frac{-36}{-6} \quad \leftarrow \text{Divide each side by } -6.$$

$$x = 6$$

There are six 6-volt batteries.

$10 - x = 10 - 6 = 4$; there are four 12-volt batteries.

Check 6(6 volts) + 4(12 volts) $\stackrel{?}{=}$ 84 volts

36 volts + 48 volts = 84 volts ✔

5. **a.** Suppose you let x represent the number of 12-volt batteries. Write and solve a new equation that models the problem in Example 2.
   b. Do you get a different answer to the problem? Explain.

Exercises ON YOUR OWN

Write and solve each equation modeled by tiles.

1. 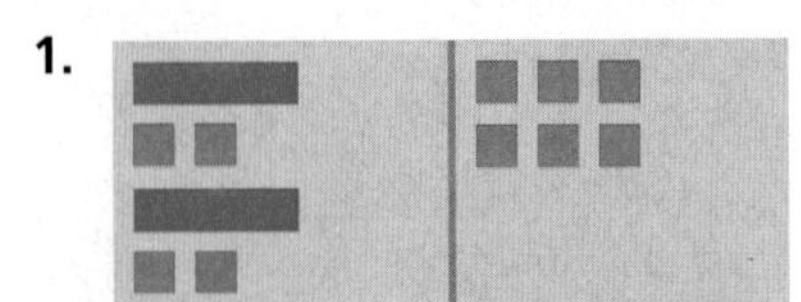

2. 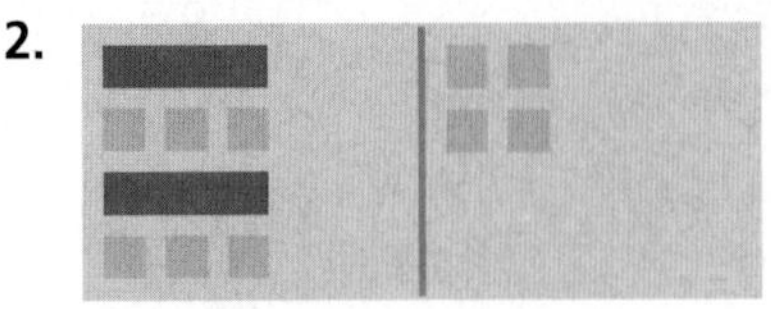

3. 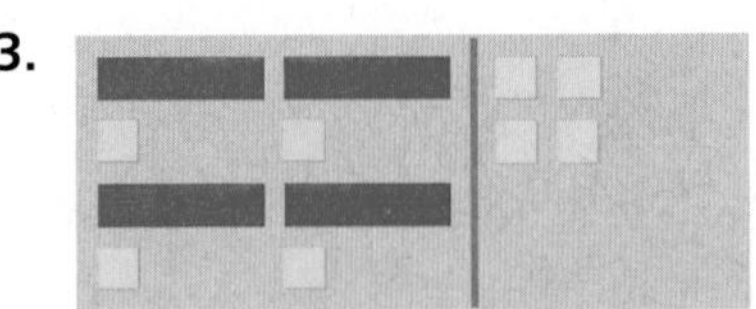

4. **Writing** In your own words, explain what the word *distribute* means.

5. **Critical Thinking** Does $2ab = 2a \cdot 2b$? Explain your answer.

Use the distributive property to simplify each expression.

6. $7(t - 4)$
7. $-2(n - 6)$
8. $-(7x - 2)$
9. $(5b - 4)\frac{2}{5}$
10. $-2(x + 3)$
11. $\frac{2}{3}(6y + 9)$
12. $(4 - z)(-1)$
13. $(3n - 7)(6)$
14. $6x - x$
15. $-4b + 3b$
16. $4.8w - 2.5w$
17. $-8n - 3n$

Geometry **If a polygon has *n* sides, the sum of the measures of its interior angles is $(n - 2)180°$. Use this for Exercises 18–20.**

18. The sum of the measures of the interior angles of a pentagon is 540°. What is the value of x in the figure to the right?

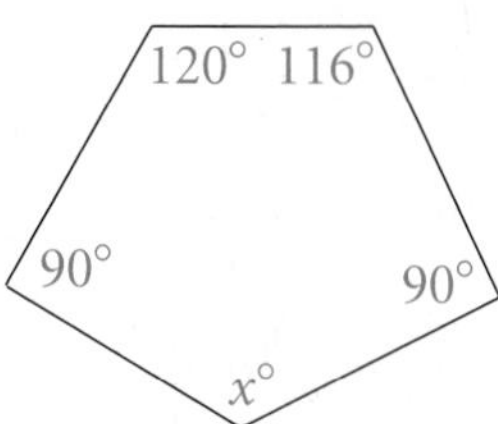

19. A polygon has seven sides. What is the sum of the measures of its interior angles?

20. The sum of the measures of the interior angles of a polygon is 1440°. Use an equation to find the number of sides of the polygon.

Solve and check each equation.

21. $2(8 + w) = 22$
22. $m + 5(m - 1) = 11$
23. $-(z + 5) = -14$
24. $0.5(x - 12) = 4$
25. $8y - (2y - 3) = 9$
26. $\frac{1}{4}(m - 16) = 7$
27. $15 = -3(x - 1) + 9$
28. $\frac{3}{4}(8n - 4) = -2$
29. $5(a - 1) = 35$
30. $6(x + 4) - 2x = -8$
31. $-3(2t - 1) = 15$
32. $-8 = -(3 + y)$
33. $0 = \frac{1}{3}(6b + 9) + b$
34. $2(1.5c + 4) = -1$
35. $n - (3n + 4) = -6$
36. $-\frac{1}{5}(10d - 5) = 9$

In Exercises 37–40, use an equation to model and solve each problem.

37. **Geography** The shape of Colorado is nearly a rectangle. The length is 100 miles more than the width. The perimeter is about 1320 mi. Find the length and width of Colorado.

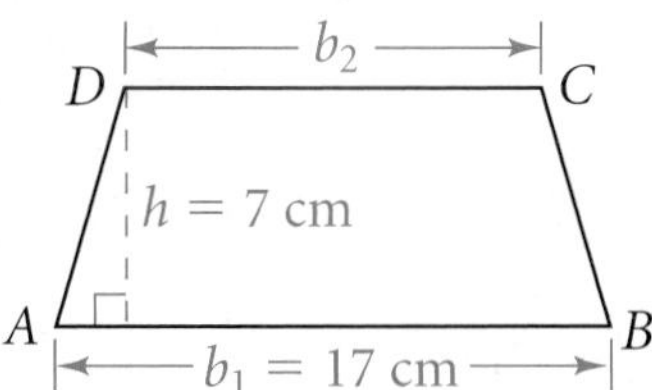

38. **Geometry** The formula for the area of a trapezoid is $A = \frac{1}{2}h(b_1 + b_2)$. The area of $ABCD$ is 98 cm^2. Find the value of b_2.

39. **Sports** A baseball team buys 15 bats for \$405. Aluminum bats cost \$25 and wooden bats cost \$30. How many of each type did they buy?

40. **Business** A company buys a copier for \$10,000. The Internal Revenue Service values the copier at $\$10{,}000(1 - \frac{n}{20})$ after n years. After how many years will the copier be valued at \$6500?

41. **Open-ended** Describe a situation where you would use the distributive property to solve a real-life problem.

42. **Standardized Test Prep** If $y = 3x - 10$, what is the value of $\frac{y}{3}$?

    A. $-x + 10$ **B.** $x + \frac{10}{3}$ **C.** $x - \frac{10}{3}$ **D.** $-x + \frac{10}{3}$ **E.** $x - 10$

Mental Math **You can use mental math and the distributive property to find prices quickly. Find each price.**

43. 4($.99)

44. 6($1.97)

45. 5($5.91)

46. 7($29.93)

47. 3 computer games at $32.99 each

48. 4 cans of fruit punch at $.69 each

$4(2.89) = 4(3.00 - 0.11)$
$= 4(3.00) - 4(0.11)$
$= 12 - 0.44$
$= 11.56$

$11.56

Exercises MIXED REVIEW

Solve and check.

49. $m - 4m = 2$

50. $9 = -4y + 6y - 5$

51. $2t - 8t + 1 = 43$

52. $3.5 = 12s - 5s$

53. **Technology** Use the spreadsheet at the right.

a. Write a formula for cell C2 if there are 250 million people in the United States.

b. Use your formula to find the missing values in the spreadsheet to one decimal place.

c. Suppose a gallon of cranberry juice costs about $4. How much do people in the United States spend on cranberry juice in one year?

Annual U.S. Fruit Juice Sales

	A	B	C
1	juice	gal (millions)	gal/person
2	orange	734	
3	apple	213	
4	cranberry	126	

Source: *Florida Dept. of Citrus*

Getting Ready for Lesson 3-5

Evaluate each expression.

54. $\frac{2}{3}n + 4$ for $n = -6$

55. $\frac{k}{5} + \frac{2k}{7}$ for $k = -35$

56. $\frac{3a + 1}{4}$ for $a = 7$

Exercises CHECKPOINT

Solve and check.

1. $x - 7 = -6$

2. $\frac{w}{3} = 11$

3. $15 = 0.75v$

4. $2t - 1 = 4$

5. $\frac{b}{3} - 20 = 20$

6. $-12 - 4x + 3 = -1$

7. $10 = -5m - m - 2$

8. $3n + n - 8 = 32$

9. $-(z - 5) = -13\frac{1}{3}$

10. $-0.8 - y = 1.9$

11. $9(n + 7) = -81$

12. $x + 2(3 - x) = 4$

13. **Sewing** Suppose you are sewing a braid border on the edges of a quilt. The quilt is 20 in. longer than it is wide. You need 292 in. of braid to cover the edges of the quilt. What are the dimensions of the quilt?

14. Which equation has the greatest solution?

A. $\frac{m}{4} = -12$ **B.** $10 = 0.5(z + 3)$ **C.** $4w - 5w + 9 = 8.4$ **D.** $2c - 7 = 4$

3-5 Rational Numbers and Equations

What You'll Learn

- Solving equations involving rational numbers

...And Why

To solve nutrition and transportation problems

THINK AND DISCUSS

Multiplying by a Reciprocal

In Chapter 1 you learned that a rational number can be represented as a ratio of two numbers. You can use reciprocals to solve equations involving rational numbers.

MILK
The Calcium Winner
One ounce of cheddar cheese has only two-thirds the calcium of one cup of skim milk.

Example 1 **Relating to the Real World** 

Nutrition There are about 200 mg of calcium in 1 oz of cheddar cheese. How many milligrams of calcium are in 1 c of skim milk?

Define m = calcium (mg) in 1 c skim milk

Relate	two-thirds calcium in 1 c skim milk	equals	calcium in 1 oz cheddar cheese
Write	$\frac{2}{3}m$	$=$	200

$$\frac{2}{3}m = 200$$

$$\frac{3}{2}\left(\frac{2}{3}m\right) = \frac{3}{2}(200) \quad \leftarrow \text{Multiply each side by } \tfrac{3}{2}\text{, the reciprocal of } \tfrac{2}{3}.$$

$$m = 300$$

There are about 300 mg of calcium in 1 c of skim milk.

Check Two-thirds of the calcium in 1 c skim milk is 200.

$\frac{2}{3} \cdot 300 = 200$ ✔

1. Solve the equation in Example 1 by multiplying each side by 3 and then dividing each side by 2. Which method do you prefer? Explain.

You can also use reciprocals to solve equations like $\frac{x}{5} = -7$. Write $\frac{x}{5}$ as $\frac{1}{5}x$ and multiply each side of the equation by 5, which is the reciprocal of $\frac{1}{5}$.

2. **Try This** Solve each equation.
   a. $\frac{2}{5}y = 1$ **b.** $-\frac{b}{8} = 2$ **c.** $-\frac{3}{4}x = 6$ **d.** $-2 = \frac{4c}{9}$
3. To solve $-\frac{1}{2}(3x - 5) = 7$, you can use the distributive property or you can multiply each side of the equation by –2, the reciprocal of $-\frac{1}{2}$. Explain why the second method is easier. Then solve the equation.

QUICK REVIEW

A *common denominator* of an equation is a multiple of all the denominators in the equation.

Multiplying by a Common Denominator

To simplify an equation containing a fraction, you can multiply each side by the denominator of the fraction. The resulting equation is easier to solve.

Example 2 Relating to the Real World 

Score	Grade
90–100	A
80–89	B
70–79	C
60–69	D

School Your test scores are 92 and 75. Without extra credit, can you raise your test average to an A with your next test? Explain.

Define x = your next test score

Relate average of the scores equals lowest score for an A

Write $\frac{92 + 75 + x}{3} = 90$

$$\frac{92 + 75 + x}{3} = 90$$

$$3\left(\frac{92 + 75 + x}{3}\right) = 3(90) \quad \longleftarrow \text{Multiply each side by 3.}$$

$$92 + 75 + x = 270$$

$$167 + x = 270 \quad \longleftarrow \text{Simplify each side.}$$

$$167 + x - 167 = 270 - 167 \quad \longleftarrow \text{Subtract 167 from each side.}$$

$$x = 103$$

Without extra credit the next test cannot bring your average to an A.

CALCULATOR HINT

You can write the solution to this equation in calculator-ready form as $x = 3(90) - 92 - 75$. To calculate, use the sequence 3 × 90 − 92 − 75 ENTER.

4. **Critical Thinking** How is multiplying by the denominator in Example 2 similar to multiplying by a reciprocal?

To solve an equation that has two or more fractions, multiply both sides of the equation by a common denominator.

Example 3 Relating to the Real World 

Cars You fill your car's gas tank when it is about $\frac{1}{2}$ empty. Later you fill the tank when it is about $\frac{3}{4}$ empty. You bought a total of $18\frac{1}{2}$ gal of gas on those two days. About how many gallons does the tank hold?

Define x = amount of gas (gal) the tank holds

Relate gallons from first fill plus gallons from second fill equals total bought

Write $\frac{1}{2} \cdot x + \frac{3}{4} \cdot x = 18\frac{1}{2}$

$$\frac{1}{2}x + \frac{3}{4}x = 18\frac{1}{2}$$

$$4\left(\frac{1}{2}x + \frac{3}{4}x\right) = 4\left(18\frac{1}{2}\right) \quad \longleftarrow \text{Multiply each side by 4.}$$

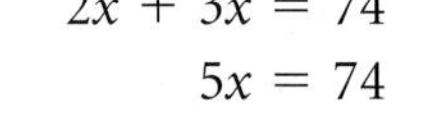

$$4\left(\frac{1}{2}x\right) + 4\left(\frac{3}{4}x\right) = 74 \quad \longleftarrow \text{Use the distributive property.}$$

$$2x + 3x = 74 \quad \longleftarrow \text{Simplify each term.}$$

$$5x = 74 \quad \longleftarrow \text{Combine like terms.}$$

$$\frac{5x}{5} = \frac{74}{5} \quad \longleftarrow \text{Divide each side by 5.}$$

$$x = 14.8$$

The gas tank holds about 14.8 gallons of gas.

5. What other common denominator could have been used in Example 3?

6. *Open-ended* Name a common denominator that you would use to solve each equation.

a. $\frac{2}{3}x - \frac{5}{8}x = 26$ b. $\frac{y}{8} + \frac{y}{12} = -4$ c. $\frac{1}{2} = \frac{2}{3}b + \frac{1}{6}b$

Exercises ON YOUR OWN

Mental Math **Solve each equation mentally.**

1. $\frac{3}{4}y = 9$
2. $-\frac{2}{3}x = 6$
3. $-4 = \frac{2}{5}a$
4. $\frac{b}{10} = 5$
5. $\frac{-7x}{8} = \frac{7}{8}$
6. $\frac{3}{7}y = 0$
7. $-\frac{n}{8} = 6$
8. $\frac{2}{3}c = -18$

9. *Critical Thinking* Explain the error in the student's work shown at the right.

$$\frac{3}{8}x - 1 = 4$$
$$3x - 1 = 32$$
$$3x = 33$$
$$x = 11$$

10. *Jobs* Suppose you apply for a nurse's aide job that pays a \$12.90/h overtime wage. The overtime wage is $1\frac{1}{2}$ times the regular wage. What is the regular wage for the job?

11. Suppose you buy $1\frac{1}{4}$ lb of roast beef for \$5. If p = price of the roast beef per pound, which equation models this situation?

A. $1\frac{1}{4}p = 5$ B. $p = 5 \cdot 1\frac{1}{4}$ C. $5p = 1\frac{1}{4}$ D. $p = 1\frac{1}{4} \div 5$

12. *Geography* The area of Kentucky is about 40,000 mi^2. This is about $\frac{5}{7}$ the area of Wisconsin. What is the area of Wisconsin?

13. *Sewing* Suppose you buy $\frac{5}{8}$ of a yard of fabric for \$2.50. What is the price of the fabric per yard?

Choose **Use a calculator, paper and pencil, or mental math to solve each equation. Check your answers.**

14. $\frac{7}{8}x = 14$
15. $-\frac{2}{9}y = 10$
16. $\frac{x}{4} + \frac{3x}{5} = 17$
17. $\frac{z}{3} = -1$
18. $\frac{5a - 1}{8} = -5\frac{1}{4}$
19. $5 = -\frac{x}{6} + \frac{x}{2}$
20. $5 = \frac{a}{6}$
21. $\frac{y + 4}{3} = -1$
22. $12 = \frac{7}{5}y$
23. $5 = -\frac{1}{3}y + \frac{2}{7}$
24. $10 = -\frac{4}{3}d$
25. $\frac{-1 - 5x}{7} = 7$
26. $\frac{2x - 1}{5} = 3$
27. $-\frac{3x}{8} = -12$
28. $\frac{6a + 4}{3} = -14$
29. $2y - \frac{3}{8}y = \frac{3}{4}$
30. $\frac{3}{4} = \frac{3 - b + 4b}{12}$
31. $-\frac{n}{2} = 30$
32. $\frac{2x}{3} + \frac{x}{2} = 7$
33. $\frac{1}{3}x + \frac{1}{6}x = 27$

Travel **Solve each problem using the formula $d = r \cdot t$.**

34. If you drive 65 mi/h for 3 h, how far do you drive?

35. If you drive 200 mi in $3\frac{1}{4}$ h, how fast do you drive?

36. If you drive 210 mi at 60 mi/h, how long do you drive?

37. **Work** What would the average number of hours per week have to be in the 1990s, to make the average for the three decades be 35 h/wk?

Average Work Week for Production Workers

Decade	Hours Per Week
1970s	36.4
1980s	34.9
1990s	■

38. **Writing** Explain how you can use common denominators to solve equations involving rational numbers. Give an example.

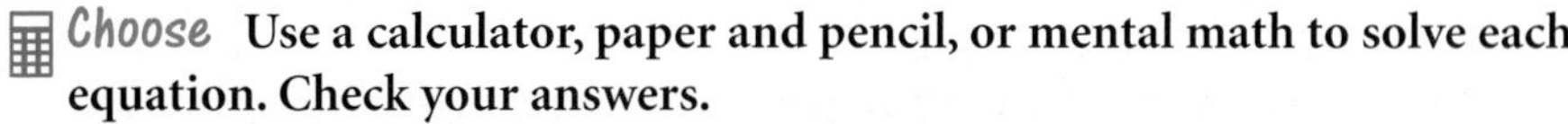

Choose **Use a calculator, paper and pencil, or mental math to solve each equation. Check your answers.**

39. $\frac{2x}{7} + \frac{x}{3} = -13$ **40.** $-\frac{1}{5}(3x + 4) = 1$ **41.** $\frac{2c - 1}{3} = 3$ **42.** $1 = \frac{a}{7} - \frac{a}{3}$

43. $-\frac{8}{11}b = 24$ **44.** $\frac{1}{2}(5d + 4) = 6$ **45.** $-1 = \frac{2x - 1}{3}$ **46.** $x - \frac{5x}{6} = -\frac{2}{3}$

47. $\frac{3}{8}y + \frac{2}{3}y = \frac{5}{8}$ **48.** $\frac{n}{60} + \frac{n}{15} = -1$ **49.** $\frac{7x}{3} = -21$ **50.** $\frac{3t}{2} - \frac{3t}{4} = \frac{3}{2}$

51. $\frac{3}{4}(2n - 5) = -1$ **52.** $\frac{5c - 8}{18} = \frac{2}{3}$ **53.** $\frac{b}{5} + \frac{5b}{3} = 2$ **54.** $-\frac{3t}{8} = \frac{3}{2}$

55. **Entertainment** As of 1994, the rental income for the movie *Back to the Future* was about \$105.5 million. This was about three fourths the rental income for *Home Alone.* Find the rental income for *Home Alone.*

56. **Family Budget** A family allows $\frac{1}{3}$ of its monthly income for housing and $\frac{1}{4}$ of its monthly income for food. It budgets a total of \$1050 a month for housing and food. What is the family's monthly income?

57. **School** Suppose that on an average day, you spend $\frac{1}{5}$ of your homework time on math and $\frac{1}{2}$ of your homework time on literature. The time for these subjects totals $1\frac{3}{4}$ h. How much time do you spend on your homework?

Exercises MIXED REVIEW

Solve and check each equation.

58. $8h - 3 + 2h = 7$ **59.** $-x + 6x = -35$ **60.** $5k + 6 = -14$ **61.** $m - 7m + 3 = 0$

62. $y + 15 + 2y = 0$ **63.** $c - (5c - 1) = -47$ **64.** $9(w - 1) = -27$ **65.** $2j - 6j + 5 = 1$

66. **Transportation** On Atlanta's rapid rail system, the MARTA, trains leave Airport Station every 8 min from 7:11 A.M. to 6:31 P.M.

a. You get to Airport Station at 7:55 A.M. How long will you have to wait for a train?

b. The ride to Doraville Station takes 41 min. When will you arrive?

Getting Ready for Lesson 3-6

Probability **You have five quarters in your pocket. Their mint dates are 1987, 1991, 1989, 1994, and 1991. You pick one. Find each probability.**

67. *P*(mint date 1987) **68.** *P*(a quarter) **69.** *P*(mint date 1991) **70.** *P*(a dime)

Math ToolboX

Problem Solving

Using Logical Reasoning

Before Lesson 3-6

You can use the strategy *Logical Reasoning* to solve problems. Organize what you know in a table. Use an X to eliminate an answer, and then draw conclusions.

Example

Space Exploration Astronauts Mae Carol Jemison, Ellen Ochoa, and Sidney M. Gutierrez flew separate space shuttle missions on the *Columbia*, the *Discovery*, and the *Endeavour*. Ellen Ochoa's mission occurred after the *Columbia's* mission. No crew member's initials were the same as the initial of his or her shuttle. On which shuttle did each person travel?

	M.C. Jemison	E. Ochoa	S.M. Gutierrez
Columbia	X	X	
Discovery			
Endeavour		X	

Ellen Ochoa's mission occurred after the *Columbia*'s, so she was not on the *Columbia*.
Eliminate possibilities with matching initials.

In both the first row and the second column, only one possibility remains. Put a check in each box.

	M.C. Jemison	E. Ochoa	S.M. Gutierrez
Columbia	X	X	✓
Discovery		✓	
Endeavour	✓	X	

Sidney M. Gutierrez was on the *Columbia*.
Ellen Ochoa was on the *Discovery*.
Mae Carol Jemison was on the *Endeavour*.

Use the strategy *Logical Reasoning* to solve. Show your work.

1. The 1992 Olympic gold, silver, and bronze medals for soccer went to Ghana, Poland, and Spain, but not necessarily in that order. No country's medal began with the same letter as the country. If Ghana did not win the silver medal, what medal did each country win?

2. Latisha, Ken, and Ervin live on different floors of the same three-story building. The person on the third floor is the uncle of the person on the second floor. If Latisha lives on a higher floor than Ervin, where does each person live?

3. Coretta, David, Nando, and Helen live in Chicago, Dallas, New York, and Houston, but not necessarily in that order. No person's city begins with the same letter as his or her name. Coretta and Helen do not live in Texas. Where does each person live?

4. **Writing** You could have solved the space shuttle problem by using the problem solving strategy *Guess and Test* instead of *Logical Reasoning*. Which method do you prefer? Explain your reasons.

3-6 Using Probability

What You'll Learn

- Finding the probability of independent and dependent events
- Using equations to solve probability problems

...And Why

To find probability in games of chance

What You'll Need

- colored cubes or chips
- bag

WORK TOGETHER

Work with a partner.

Play the game "Double Yellows." Put three yellow cubes and one red cube in a bag.

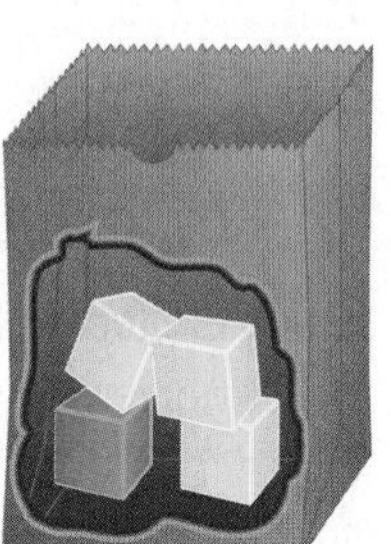

Partner *X*: Pick a cube. Put it back into the bag. Then pick again.

Partner *Y*: Pick a cube. Do not put it back into the bag. Then pick again.

Each partner takes turns choosing two cubes as described above. If a partner picks two yellow cubes, he or she scores a point.

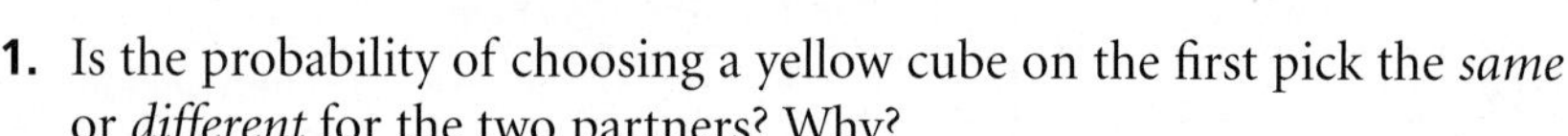

1. Is the probability of choosing a yellow cube on the first pick the *same* or *different* for the two partners? Why?
2. Is the probability of choosing a yellow cube on the second pick the *same* or *different* for the two partners? Why?
3. **Predict** which partner is more likely to score points in "Double Yellows." Explain why.
4. Play the game with your partner. Have each partner take ten turns. How do your results compare with the prediction you made in Question 1?

THINK AND DISCUSS

Finding the Probability of Independent Events

In the game "Double Yellows" above, the two draws for Partner X are **independent events** because the result of the first draw does not affect the result of the second draw.

> **Probability of Two Independent Events**
>
> If A and B are independent events, you multiply the probabilities of the events to find the probability of both events occurring.
>
> $P(A \text{ and } B) = P(A) \cdot P(B)$

Example 1 Relating to the Real World 

Games In a word game, you choose a tile from a bag containing the letter tiles shown. You *replace* the first tile in the bag and then choose again. What is the probability of choosing an *A* and then choosing an *E*?

Since you replace the first tile, the events are independent.

$P(A) = \frac{4}{15}$ ← There are 4 *A*'s in the 15 tiles.

$P(E) = \frac{3}{15}$ ← There are 3 *E*'s in the 15 tiles.

$$P(A \text{ and } E) = P(A) \cdot P(E) = \frac{4}{15} \cdot \frac{3}{15} = \frac{4}{75}$$

The probability of choosing an *A*, then an *E* is $\frac{4}{75}$.

5. Write the answer to Example 1 as a decimal rounded to the nearest hundredth. Then write the decimal as a percent.

Finding the Probability of Dependent Events

When the outcome of one event affects the outcome of a second event, the events are **dependent events.** In the game "Double Yellows," if you choose a second cube without replacing the first cube, the events are dependent.

Probability of Two Dependent Events

If *A* and *B* are dependent events, then

$P(A \text{ and } B) = P(A) \cdot P(B \text{ after } A)$.

Example 2 Relating to the Real World 

Games Suppose you play the word game again. This time you *do not replace* the first tile before you choose the second tile. What is the probability of choosing an *A* and then choosing an *E*?

The events are dependent.

$P(A) = \frac{4}{15}$ ← There are 4 *A*'s in the 15 tiles.

$P(E \text{ after } A) = \frac{3}{14}$ ← There are 3 *E*'s in the 14 tiles left.

$$P(A \text{ and } E) = P(A) \cdot P(E \text{ after } A) = \frac{4}{15} \cdot \frac{3}{14} = \frac{2}{35}$$

The probability of choosing an *A* and then an *E* is $\frac{2}{35}$.

Math A Test Prep

1 Michael said, "I solved this equation by adding 2 to 10 and dividing by 4." Which equation did Michael solve?

(1) $\frac{x}{4} - 2 = 10$

(2) $4x + 2 = 10$

(3) $\frac{x}{4} + 2 = 10$

(4) $4x - 2 = 10$

2 A basketball team buys 12 uniforms for $612. Each shirt costs $28. How much does each pair of shorts cost? Write an equation to model this problem. Then solve it.

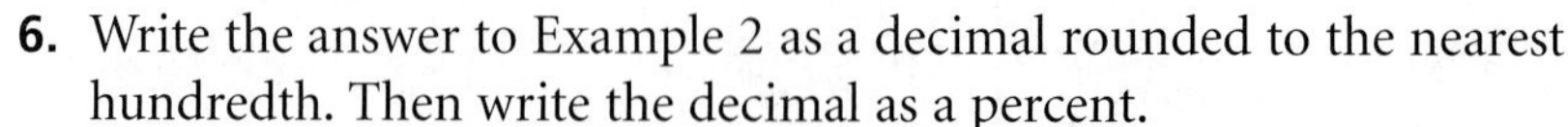

6. Write the answer to Example 2 as a decimal rounded to the nearest hundredth. Then write the decimal as a percent.

7. **Try This** What is the probability of choosing two *I*'s if you pick a tile, do not replace it, and pick again?

Finding Probability Using an Equation

You can write an equation to solve some probability problems. When you are given two probabilities, solve the equation for the missing probability.

Example 3

Kevin is colorblind, so he buys only white socks and black socks. The probability that he picks out a pair of white socks is $\frac{1}{3}$. The probability that he reaches in and grabs one white sock is $\frac{3}{5}$. What is the probability that he chooses the second white sock?

Define $n = P(\text{white after choosing white})$

Relate $P(\text{two white}) = P(\text{white}) \cdot P(\text{white after choosing white})$

Write $\frac{1}{3} = \frac{3}{5} \cdot n$

$$\frac{1}{3} = \frac{3}{5}n$$

$$\frac{5}{3}\left(\frac{1}{3}\right) = \frac{5}{3}\left(\frac{3}{5}n\right) \quad \leftarrow \text{Multiply each side by } \frac{5}{3}.$$

$$\frac{5}{9} = n$$

The probability that Kevin will get the second white sock after choosing a white sock is $\frac{5}{9}$.

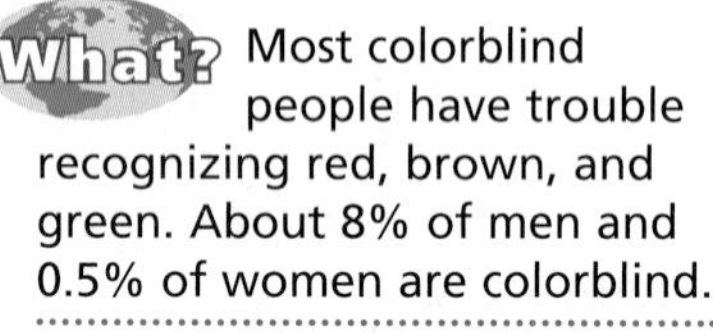

What? Most colorblind people have trouble recognizing red, brown, and green. About 8% of men and 0.5% of women are colorblind.

Source: *World Book Encyclopedia*

8. The probability of Kevin choosing a white sock on his first try is $\frac{3}{5}$.

a. What does this tell you about the number of white socks he has?

b. **Critical Thinking** If Kevin has 10 socks altogether, how many of them are white?

Exercises ON YOUR OWN

Are the two events *dependent* or *independent*? Explain.

1. Toss a coin twice.

2. Pick a vowel at random. Then pick a different vowel.

3. Pick a ball from a basket of both yellow and pink balls. Pick again.

4. **Gardening** A gardener's flat contains two plants with pink flowers, two with purple flowers, and two with white flowers. The plants have not yet flowered. You choose two plants from the flat. What is the probability that they both will have pink flowers?

You have three $1 bills, two $5 bills, and a $20 bill in your pocket. You choose two bills. Find each probability.

5. $P(\$5 \text{ and } \$1)$ with replacing
6. $P(\$1 \text{ and } \$20)$ without replacing
7. $P(\$20 \text{ and } \$1)$ with replacing
8. $P(\$1 \text{ and } \$1)$ without replacing
9. A and B are independent. $P(A \text{ and } B) = \frac{1}{4}$ and $P(B) = \frac{3}{5}$. Find $P(A)$.

10. **Writing** Use your own words to explain the difference between independent and dependent events. Give an original example of each.

You pick two marbles from the bag at the right. You replace the first one before you choose the second one. Find each probability.

11. P(red and green)
12. P(two greens)
13. P(blue and red)
14. P(two yellows)
15. P(blue and green)
16. P(two reds)

You pick two marbles from the bag at the right. You pick the second one without replacing the first one. Find each probability.

17. P(red and blue)
18. P(two blues)
19. P(blue and green)
20. P(two reds)
21. P(green and yellow)
22. P(two greens)

23. **School** Suppose you guess all the answers on a three-question "true or false" quiz. What is the probability you will guess them all correctly?
    A. $\frac{1}{2}$ B. $\frac{3}{2}$ C. $\frac{3}{8}$ D. $\frac{1}{8}$ E. $\frac{1}{3}$

24. A bag contains red cubes and blue cubes. You pick two cubes without replacing the first one. The probability of drawing two red cubes is $\frac{1}{15}$. The probability that your second cube is red if your first cube is red is $\frac{2}{9}$. Find the probability that the first cube you pick is red.

25. **Open-ended** Make up a game like "Double Yellows." Give rules for playing the game. Explain the probability of winning and the independence or dependence of the events in your game.

Government **Use the data at the right.**

26. An acre of land in Idaho is chosen at random. What is the probability that the land is owned by the federal government?

27. An acre of land is chosen at random from each of the three states listed. What is the probability that all three acres of land are owned by the federal government?

28. **Research** How many acres of land in your state are federally owned? What percent of the total land in your state is this?

State	Percent of Land Federally Owned
Idaho	62%
New Mexico	32%
Virginia	6%

29. **Quality Control** The probability that a spark plug is defective is 0.06. You need two new spark plugs for a motorcycle. What is the probability that both spark plugs you buy are defective?

A and B are independent events. Find the missing probability.

30. $P(A) = \frac{5}{8}$, $P(A \text{ and } B) = \frac{1}{4}$. Find $P(B)$.

31. $P(A) = \frac{1}{3}$, $P(B) = \frac{3}{5}$. Find $P(A \text{ and } B)$.

32. $P(A) = \frac{3}{20}$, $P(B) = \frac{5}{6}$. Find $P(A \text{ and } B)$.

33. $P(A) = \frac{1}{4}$, $P(A \text{ and } B) = \frac{3}{20}$. Find $P(B)$.

34. $P(A) = \frac{12}{35}$, $P(B) = \frac{7}{8}$. Find $P(A \text{ and } B)$.

35. $P(A) = \frac{2}{3}$, $P(A \text{ and } B) = \frac{8}{15}$. Find $P(B)$.

36. $P(A) = \frac{1}{20}$, $P(A \text{ and } B) = \frac{1}{50}$. Find $P(B)$.

37. $P(A) = \frac{7}{9}$, $P(A \text{ and } B) = \frac{21}{36}$. Find $P(B)$.

38. **School** A hat contains all the names of the students in a class that has 12 girls and 10 boys. To select representatives of the class, the teacher draws two names from the hat without replacing the first name.
    a. Find P(two girls).
    b. Find P(two boys).
    c. Find P(boy, then girl).
    d. Find P(girl, then boy).
    e. **Predict** the sum of the probabilities in parts (a)–(d). Check to see that the sum agrees with your prediction.

39. **Standardized Test Prep** You pick two balls from a bag containing balls of different colors. The bag contains at least two green balls. Compare the quantities in Column A and Column B.

Column A	Column B
P(two greens) with replacement	P(two greens) without replacement

A. The quantity in Column A is greater.
B. The quantity in Column B is greater.
C. The quantities are equal.
D. The relationship cannot be determined from the given information.

Exercises MIXED REVIEW

Solve each equation.

40. $3.2(m + 5) = 16$

41. $\frac{s}{5} - \frac{s}{3} = 8$

42. $w - 13w = 3$

43. $\frac{2c + 1}{7} = 3$

44. a. **Communications** Of the 99 million households in the United States in 1995, 35 million were not listed in phone books. Six million of these households did not have phones. How many households had phones, but did not list their numbers?
    b. Of the 35 million households not listed, $\frac{3}{7}$ had recently moved. How many households does this represent?

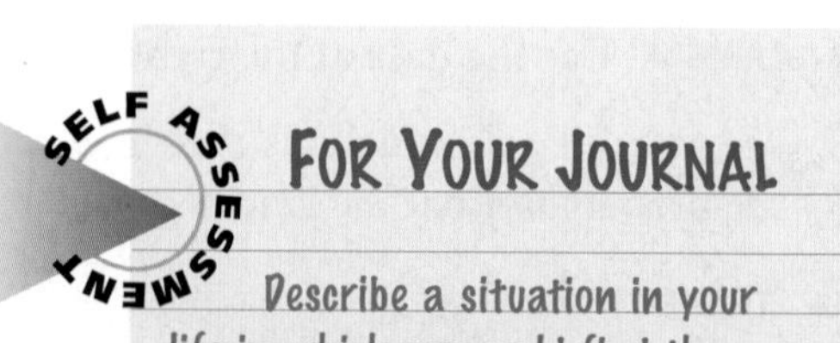

SELF ASSESSMENT
FOR YOUR JOURNAL
Describe a situation in your life in which you could find the probability of independent and dependent events.

Getting Ready for Lesson 3-7

Write each number as a percent.

45. 0.45

46. $\frac{3}{4}$

47. 0.328

48. 1.2

49. $\frac{5}{5}$

50. 0.005

3-7 Percent Equations

What You'll Learn

- Using equations to solve problems involving percents
- Finding simple interest

...And Why

To solve problems involving commission, interest, and circle graphs

What You'll Need

- protractor
- compass

QUICK REVIEW

A *percent* is a ratio that compares a number to 100. You can write a percent with the percent symbol or as a fraction or decimal. For example, you can write 40% as $\frac{40}{100}$ or as 0.40.

THINK AND DISCUSS

Solving Percent Equations

To model a percent problem with an equation, express each percent as a decimal. Three types of percent problems are modeled and solved below.

What is 40% of 8?	16 is 25% of what?	What percent of 40 is 5?
$n = 0.4 \times 8$	$16 = 0.25 \times n$	$n \times 40 = 5$
$n = 3.2$	$\frac{16}{0.25} = \frac{0.25n}{0.25}$	$\frac{40n}{40} = \frac{5}{40}$
	$64 = n$	$n = 0.125$
		$n = 12.5\%$

1. In the equations above, what symbol represents each of these words?
 a. is **b.** of **c.** what

2. Match each problem with the equation that models it.
 A. 15 is what percent of 12? **I.** $n = 0.15 \times 12$
 B. What is 15% of 12? **II.** $12 = 0.15n$
 C. 12 is 15% of what? **III.** $15 = n \times 12$

3. Write an equation to model each question. Solve each equation.
 a. What is 25% of 80? **b.** 3 is 75% of what?
 c. What percent of 44 is 11? **d.** 16% of what is 200?

Writing Equations to Solve Percent Problems

Example 1 Relating to the Real World

Sales Suppose you work at a computer store. You earn 5% commission on everything you sell. How much do you earn on a computer you sell for $1900?

Define n = amount of your commission

Relate Your commission is 5% of $1900.

Write

$$n = 0.05 \times 1900$$
$$n = 0.05(1900)$$
$$n = 95$$

You earn $95 commission.

4. Tupi sells cars. He earns $145/wk in salary plus 8% commission. In one week he sells $36,000 worth of cars. How much does he earn?

You can use a circle graph to find data expressed in percents.

Example 2 **Relating to the Real World** 

What Do You Think Is the Number One Problem in the World Today ?

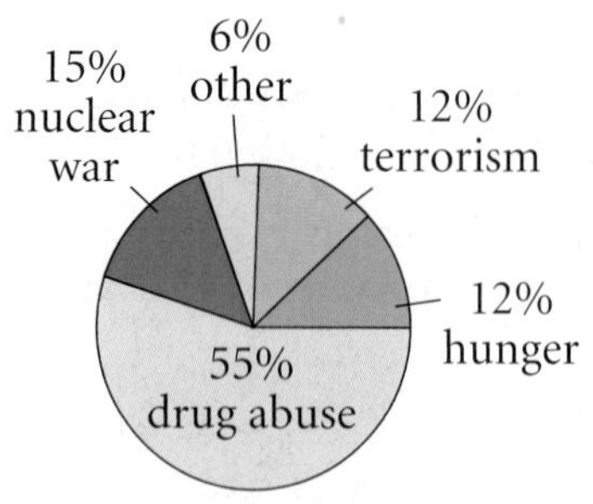

Source: *The Second Kids' World Almanac*

Surveys In a survey by *The Second Kids' World Almanac,* 1650 students said that drug abuse is the number one problem in the world today. How many students were surveyed?

Define n = the number of students surveyed

Relate 55% of the students surveyed is 1650.

Write $0.55 \times \quad n \quad = 1650$

$$0.55n = 1650$$

$$\frac{0.55n}{0.55} = \frac{1650}{0.55} \quad \leftarrow \text{Divide each side by 0.55.}$$

$$n = 3000$$

There were 3000 students surveyed.

Check 0.55 [×] 3000 [ENTER]

1650 ✓

5. How many students chose hunger as the number one problem?

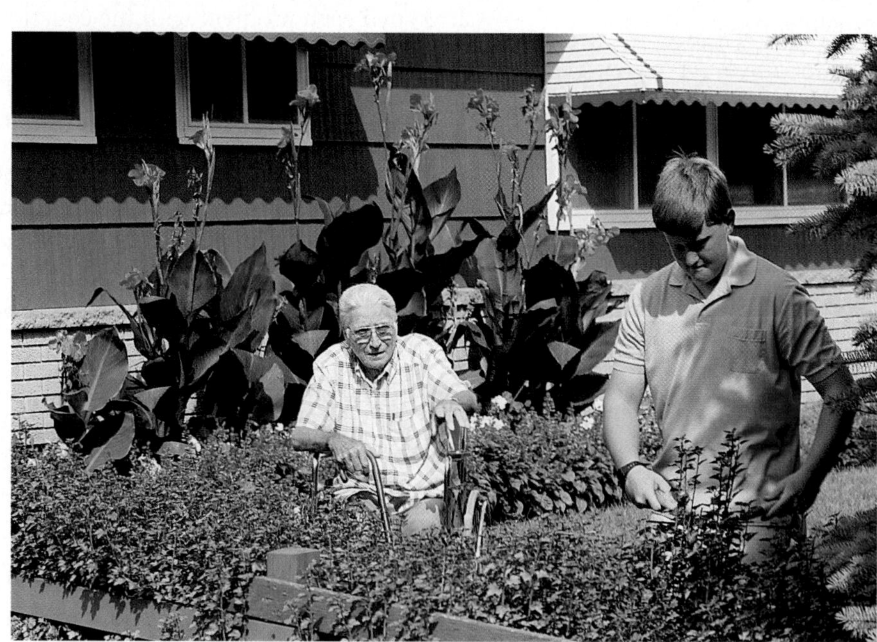

Percents can be numbers greater than 100. Suppose you agree to do some yardwork with your grandfather for $20. You do such a good job that he pays you $30. A payment of $20 is 100% of what you expect. The payment of $30 is more than 100% of what you expect.

6. ***Open-ended*** Think of two more situations in which you would use a percent greater than 100%.

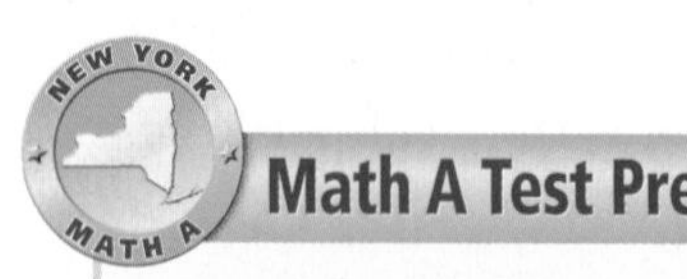

1 A bag of marbles contains 3 red, 8 green, 3 yellow, 6 purple, and 4 black marbles. Find the probability of drawing a purple marble, and then another purple marble, without replacing the first.

(1) $\frac{5}{92}$ (3) $\frac{3}{46}$

(2) $\frac{1}{16}$ (4) $\frac{1}{12}$

2 Suppose you plan to tip 15% on a restaurant bill of $35.45. What is the total you will pay?

Example 3 Relating to the Real World 

Community Service Suppose your school requires 36 hours of community service. You spent 56 hours volunteering at a hospital. What percent of the requirement have you fulfilled?

Define n = the percent of the requirement you have fulfilled

Relate 56 is what percent of 36?

Write $56 = n \times 36$

$56 = 36n$

$\frac{56}{36} = \frac{36n}{36}$ ← Divide each side by 36.

$n = 1.555555555$

$n \approx 1.56$

You have fulfilled about 156% of the community-service requirement.

7. **Mental Math** How many hours would fulfill 200% of the requirement?

Simple Interest

$I = prt$
I is the interest.
p is the principal.
r is the interest rate per year.
t is the time in years.

Today banks use *compound interest,* which you will study in Chapter 8. Compound interest is based on **simple interest.** Its formula is $I = prt$.

Example 4 Relating to the Real World 

Finance Suppose you invested $900 for two years. You earned $67.50 in simple interest. What was the annual rate of interest?

$I = prt$ ← Use the formula $I = prt$.

$67.50 = 900 \cdot r \cdot 2$ ← Substitute 67.50 for I, 900 for p, and 2 for t.

$\frac{67.50}{1800} = \frac{1800r}{1800}$ ← Divide each side by 1800.

$r = 0.0375$, or 3.75%

The annual rate of interest was 3.75%.

8. **Try This** Find the simple interest on $550 at 4.5% for one year.

QUICK REVIEW

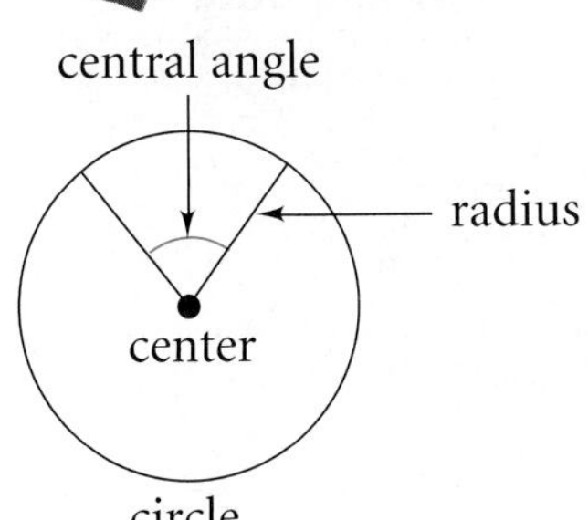

WORK TOGETHER

Data Collection Work with a partner. Ask at least 10 people "How many pets do you have?" Complete these steps to construct a circle graph.

9. **a.** Find the percent of your data in each of these categories: no pets, one pet, two pets, three or more pets.
   b. Express each percent as a decimal and multiply by 360°. This gives the number of degrees in the central angle for each category.
   c. Draw a circle and use a protractor to draw each central angle.

Exercises ON YOUR OWN

Write an equation for each question. Do not solve the equation.

1. What is 4% of 150?
2. 32 is what percent of 40?
3. 24 is 150% of what?

Model with an equation. Then answer each question.

4. What percent of 51 is 17?
5. 10% of what is 8?
6. $7\frac{1}{2}$% of \$200 is what?
7. 6% of what is 36?
8. 9% of 315 is what?
9. What percent of 45 is 18?

Number of Telephones in U.S. Households in 1994

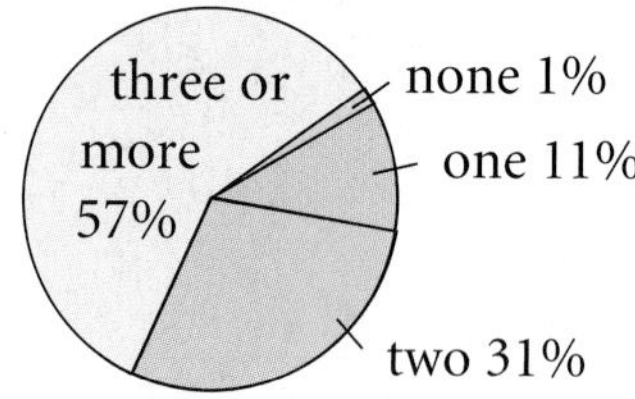

10. **Communications** There were 96 million households in the United States in 1994. How many households had two telephones?
11. **Finance** A bank pays $3\frac{1}{4}$ % simple interest annually. How much interest does \$640 earn in three years?
12. **Estimation** Estimate a 15% tip for a restaurant bill of \$7.25.
13. **Open-ended** What percent of your time do you spend sleeping? Describe the method you used to find this percent.
14. Choose the equation you would use to answer the question: What percent of 60 is 15?
    A. $15n = 60$ B. $60(15) = n$ C. $60n = 15$ D. $n = \frac{60}{15}$

Choose **Use a calculator, paper and pencil, or mental math to answer each question.**

15. What is 25% of \$80?
16. 1% of what is 7?
17. 5 is what percent of 10?
18. What percent of 27.7 is 1.8?
19. 80% of 49 is what?
20. 120% of what is 60?
21. 9 is what percent of 200?
22. 225% of 40 is what?
23. What is 55% of 600?
24. What percent of 150 is $7\frac{1}{2}$?
25. 5.4 is what percent of 9?
26. 95% of what is 83.125?
27. **Sales Tax** In Louisiana the state sales tax is 4%. If you buy a \$2100 computer in Louisiana, how much tax will you pay?
28. **Geography** Alaska is the largest state in the United States, with an area of 570,374 mi^2. It accounts for about 15% of the country's area. Estimate the area of the United States.
29. **Finance** You received \$41.60 in interest for a two-year investment at 6.5% simple interest. How much money did you invest?
30. **Geography** The information in the table gives the length of each of the four coastlines of the United States.
    a. How long is the coastline of the United States?
    b. Find the percent of the coastline of the United States that each coast represents. Round to the nearest hundredth of a percent.
    c. Draw and label a circle graph that represents the data.

U.S. Coastline Data

Coast	Miles
Arctic	1060
Atlantic	2069
Gulf	1631
Pacific	7623

Math in the Media **Use the news article.**

31. What percent of residents of the United States are 65 or older?

32. About how many elderly residents live below the poverty level?

33. What percent of elderly residents' income is from Social Security?

34. **Estimation** The population of Florida is about 13,000,000. Estimate the number of Florida residents who are 65 or older.

35. **Writing** Explain how to use facts from the article to estimate the population of the United States in the year 2050.

34 Million U.S. Residents are 65 or Older

Nearly 34 million of the 270 million residents of the United States have passed their 65th birthday. By the year 2050, roughly 20%, or 80 million people, will be 65 or older.

One of eight elderly residents lives below the poverty level. Two of every five dollars older residents earn are from Social Security.

Florida has the highest percent of elderly, with 18.4%. Alaska has the smallest share at 4.6%.

Finance **Use the formula for simple interest, $I = prt$. Find each missing value.**

36. $I = \blacksquare$, $p = \$340$, $r = 6\%$, $t = 3$ yr

37. $I = \$312.50$, $p = \blacksquare$, $r = 5\%$, $t = 5$ yr

38. $I = \$392$, $p = \$1400$, $r = \blacksquare$, $t = 4$ yr

39. $I = \$1540$, $p = \$22{,}000$, $r = 3.5\%$, $t = \blacksquare$

Chapter Project ***Find Out by Graphing***

Make a circle graph for the personal budget you created in the Find Out question on page 123. In a table, show the dollar amounts, percents, and angle degrees you used to create the graph.

Exercises MIXED REVIEW

Make a table, then graph each function.

40. $f(x) = 3x + 2$

41. $f(x) = 1.5x - 2$

42. $f(x) = \frac{4}{5}x - 0.5$

43. $f(x) = 4x + 1$

44. According to *USA TODAY*, children smile an average of 400 times a day. About how many times does a child smile in a week? in the month of October?

45. Find the range of the function $f(x) = |x| - 3$ when the domain is $\{-2, -1, 0, 1, 2\}$.

Getting Ready for Lesson 3-8

Simplify. Leave each answer in decimal form rounded to the nearest hundredth.

46. $\frac{45 - 35}{45}$

47. $\frac{100 - 25}{100}$

48. $\frac{80 - 21}{80}$

49. $\frac{32 - 4}{32}$

Exercises CHECKPOINT

Solve.

1. $\frac{5w + 2}{3} = -4$
2. $\frac{3}{4}m = 7.2$
3. $\frac{t}{8} + \frac{t}{7} = 1$
4. $-\frac{4}{5}x - 2 = 7$
5. $6 = -\frac{1}{2}(3 - 5z)$

Suppose you have marbles in your pocket. One is red, three are blue, two are green, and three are yellow. You pick two marbles. Find each probability.

6. P(two yellow) with replacing
7. P(red and blue) without replacing
8. P(red and blue) with replacing
9. P(two green) without replacing
10. **Writing** Explain how P(yellow and blue) changes if you switch from replacing to not replacing.
11. **Government** A majority is any number greater than 50% of the total. When the 435 voting members of the House of Representatives use majority rule, how many members are needed to make a majority?
12. **Open-ended** Give an example of a situation in which you would use percents.

Algebra at Work

Media Researcher

Nielsen Media Research estimates the number of people who watch each network television show. The company polls a random sample of viewers. For national surveys, Nielsen polls about 10,000 viewers. For local surveys, they poll about 300 to 500 viewers. The results are then applied to the larger population. Nielsen Media Research estimates a 2–4% possible error for its local surveys, but only 1–2% for national polls. As you can see, the estimated error decreases as the sampling size increases.

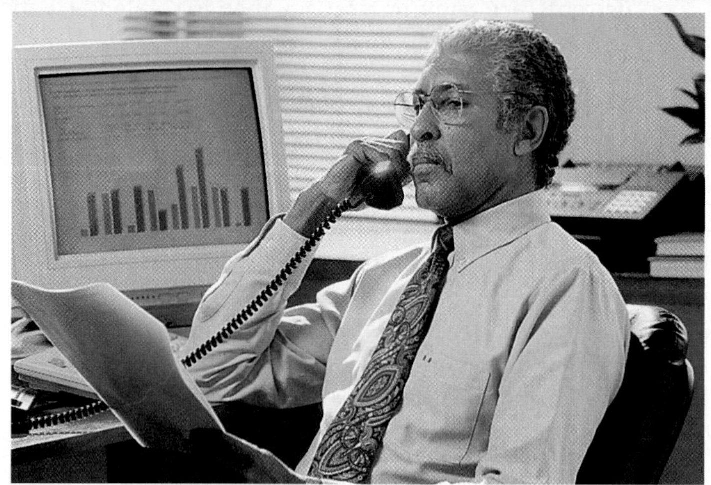

Mini Project: Describe how you would choose and contact a sample of 100 people to represent the entire population of your city.

Using a Graphing Program

After Lesson 3-7

In Chapter 1 you worked with graphs. In the last lesson you drew circle graphs. Computers can make graphing easier. To use a graphing program, you enter data in a spreadsheet. Then you choose the type of graph you want to draw. You must choose the type carefully because the computer will create the graph even if it is not appropriate for your data.

Instruments Played by Amateurs

	A	B
1	Instrument	People (millions)
2	Piano	24
3	Guitar	10
4	Flute	4
5	Drum	3

Source: *USA TODAY*

Instruments Played by Amateurs

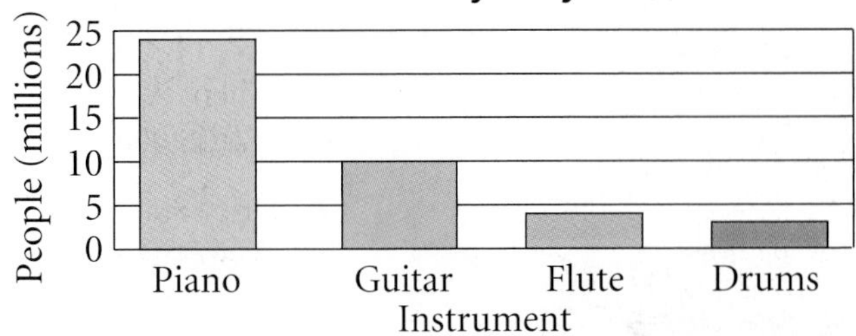

A bar graph is a good choice for this set of data. You can use a bar graph to compare amounts.

Instruments Played by Amateurs

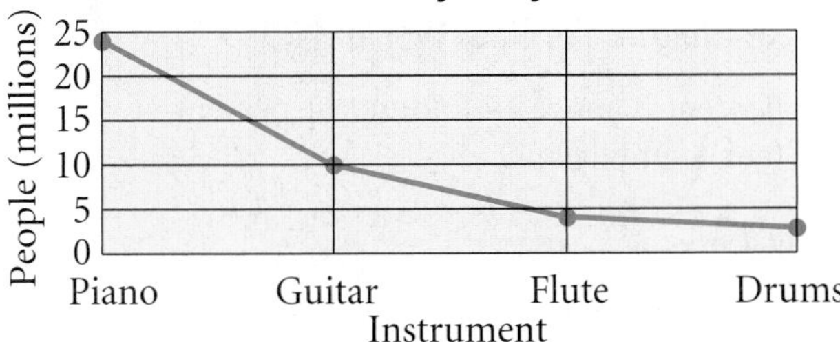

A line graph is *not* a good choice for this set of data. A line graph shows a trend between two sets of data.

Instruments Played by Amateurs

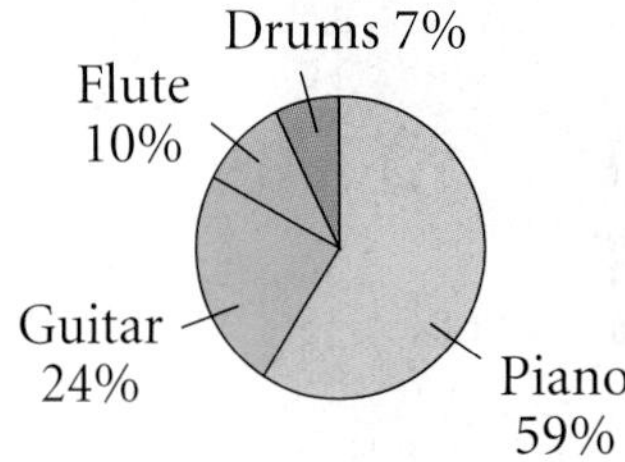

A circle graph is *not* a good choice for this set of data. A circle graph displays parts of a whole.

Use a graphing program to make an appropriate graph for the data.

1. **Who Buys Take-Out Food?**

Age	18–29	30–44	45–59	60 plus
Percent	73%	64%	57%	39%

2. **People Who Telecommute (use a computer or a phone to work at home)**

Year	1990	1991	1992	1993
People (millions)	4.0	5.5	6.6	7.6

3. "How often do you lose your television remote control each week?" Here is how people answered. Never: 44%, 1–5 times: 38%, Over 5 times: 17%, Don't know: 1%. Make a graph of this set of data.

4. *Writing* For Exercises 1–3, explain why you chose each type of graph.

What You'll Learn

- Finding percent of change
- Solving problems involving percent of change

...And Why

To solve problems involving careers in medicine and agriculture

3-8 Percent of Change

THINK AND DISCUSS

News reporters often use statistics to present information. Here are two different ways a reporter related this fact: The number of female physicians in the United States increased from 25,400 in 1970 to 104,200 in 1990.

A: From 1970 to 1990, the number of female physicians more than quadrupled.

B: From 1970 to 1990, the number of female physicians increased about 310%.

Statement A is easy to verify by estimating: 104,200 is about 4 times 25,400, since $4(25{,}000) = 100{,}000$.

To verify Statement B, you need to look at the percent of change in the data. The **percent of change** is the percent an amount changes from its original amount. The amount of change is the difference between these two values.

$$\text{percent of change} = \frac{\text{amount of change}}{\text{original amount}}$$

When a value increases from its original amount, you call the percent of change the **percent of increase.**

Who? Dr. Graciela Solis Alarcón is a professor of medicine. Dr. Alarcón has won numerous awards for her research in rheumatology, which is the study of diseases of the muscles and joints.

Example 1 Relating to the Real World 

Medical Careers Verify statement B above by finding the percent of increase in the number of female physicians.

$$\begin{aligned}\text{percent of change} &= \frac{\text{amount of change}}{\text{original amount}}\\ &= \frac{104{,}200 - 25{,}400}{25{,}400} && \leftarrow \text{Substitute.}\\ &= \frac{78{,}800}{25{,}400} && \leftarrow \text{Simplify the numerator.}\\ &\approx 3.10, \text{ or } 310\% && \leftarrow \text{Divide.}\end{aligned}$$

The percent of increase is about 310%.

1. **a.** Explain why stating that an amount quadrupled is the same as stating that it increased 300%.
   b. What would an increase of 100% mean?
2. When you find the percent of change, why is it important to know which amount is the original amount?
3. **Try This** From 1970 to 1990, the total number of physicians in the United States increased from 334,000 to 615,400.
   a. Find the amount of change.
   b. Find the percent of increase.

When a value decreases from its original amount, you call the percent of change the **percent of decrease.**

Example 2 Relating to the Real World 

Agriculture Changes in the economy have affected the location and number of farms in the United States. Find the percent of decrease in the number of farms from 1940 to 1990.

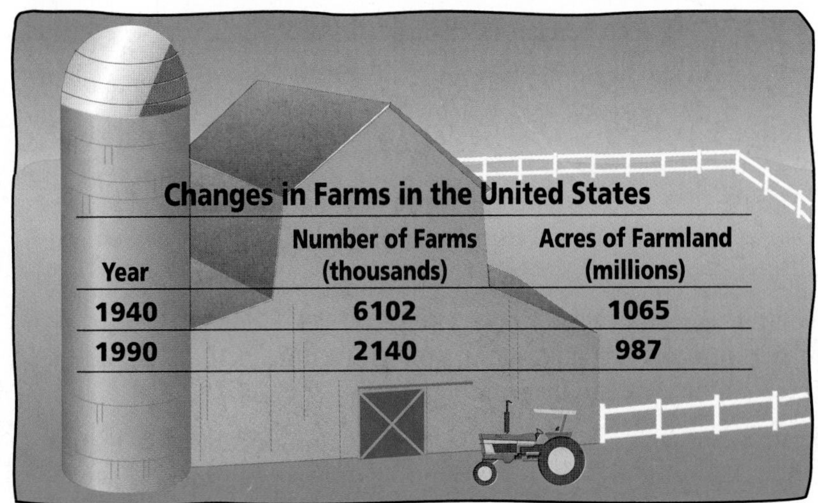

Changes in Farms in the United States

Year	Number of Farms (thousands)	Acres of Farmland (millions)
1940	6102	1065
1990	2140	987

Computer technology is used to vary the rate and type of fertilizer applied to a field.

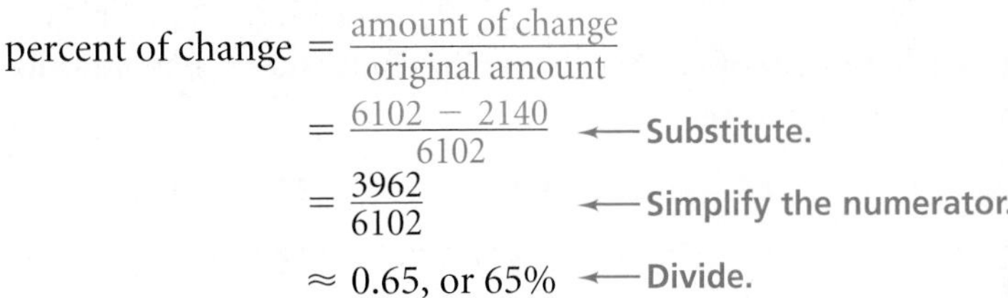

$$\text{percent of change} = \frac{\text{amount of change}}{\text{original amount}}$$

$$= \frac{6102 - 2140}{6102} \quad \longleftarrow \text{Substitute.}$$

$$= \frac{3962}{6102} \quad \longleftarrow \text{Simplify the numerator.}$$

$$\approx 0.65, \text{ or } 65\% \quad \longleftarrow \text{Divide.}$$

The percent of decrease in the number of farms is about 65%.

4. a. Find the percent of decrease in the number of acres of farmland from 1940 to 1990.

b. ***Critical Thinking*** While the number of farms decreased by 65%, the number of acres of farmland decreased by a much smaller percent. What can you conclude about the size of the average farm?

Exercises ON YOUR OWN

Choose **Use a calculator, pencil and paper, or mental math to find each percent of change. Describe the percent of change as a percent of increase or decrease. Round to the nearest percent.**

1. \$12 to \$9 **2.** 19 in. to 25 in. **3.** $5\frac{1}{2}$ ft to $5\frac{3}{4}$ ft **4.** 180 lb to 150 lb

5. 18 to $17\frac{1}{2}$ **6.** 15,000 to 12,000 **7.** \$1.75 to \$1.25 **8.** \$6/h to \$6.50/h

9. **Physical Therapy** Physical therapists measure strength on a dynamometer, which uses units called foot-pounds. Suppose you increase the strength in your elbow from 90 foot-pounds to 125 foot-pounds. Find the percent of increase.

10. **Environment** From 1987 to 1993, the number of days of unhealthy air quality in Atlanta dropped from 15 to 4. Find the percent of decrease in the number of days of unhealthy air.

Mental Math **Find each percent of change.**

11. 5 cm to 10 cm	12. \$3.00 to \$1.50	13. \$10 to \$4	14. 12 in. to 6 in.
15. 3 ft to 4 ft	16. \$20,000 to \$25,000	17. 2 m to 6 m	18. \$15 to \$5

19. **Open-ended** Choose an item that you buy that has changed in price. Give its original price and its new price. Find the percent of change.

20. **Sports** In the 1960 Olympics, Wilma Rudolph of the United States won the women's 100-m run in 11.0 s. In 1988, Florence Griffith-Joyner, also of the United States, won with a time of 10.54 s. Find the percent of decrease in the winning time.

21. **Writing** Suppose you increase the price of a product by 20%, then reduce the price by 20%. Is the resulting price greater than, less than, or equal to the price you started with? Explain your answer.

Calculator **Find each percent of change. Describe the percent of change as a percent of increase or decrease.**

22. \$26 to \$20	23. \$8/h to \$8.45/h	24. 21 in. to 54 in.	25. \$4.95 to \$3.87
26. 132 lb to 120 lb	27. \$24,000 to \$25,000	28. \$8.99 to \$3.99	29. 25 mi/h to 55 mi/h
30. \$42.69 to \$49.95	31. 2.3 cm to 2.8 cm	32. 10.5 km to 4.2 km	33. \$3.99/lb to \$2.89/lb

34. **Transportation** The number of cars in China increased from 1986 to 1993. Use the data at the right to find the percent of increase.

35. **Sales** Suppose that you are selling sweatshirts for a class fund-raiser. The wholesaler charges you \$8 for each sweatshirt.
    a. You charge \$16 for each sweatshirt. Find the percent of increase.
    b. **Generalize** your answer to part (a). Doubling a price is the same as a __?__ percent increase.
    c. After the fund-raiser is over, you reduce the price on the remaining sweatshirts to \$8. Find the percent of decrease.
    d. **Generalize** your answer to part (c). Cutting a price in half is the same as a __?__ percent decrease.
    e. A few of the sale sweatshirts do not sell, so you give them away free to charity. Find the percent of decrease from the sale price.
    f. **Generalize** your answer to part (e). Reducing a price to zero is the same as a __?__ percent decrease.

Passenger Cars in China

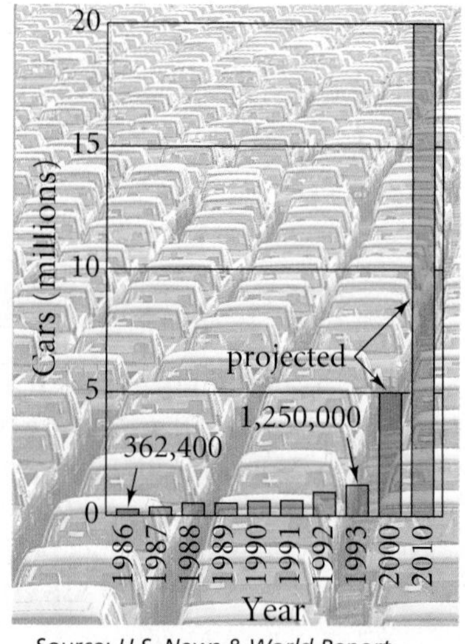

Source: *U.S. News & World Report*

36. **Math in the Media** Use the news article at the right.
   a. How does the information in the second sentence verify the "more than 40%" claim in the first sentence?
   b. In 1994, what percent of the people employed in the United States worked for businesses owned by women?

37. **Standardized Test Prep** All of the following are equal *except:*
   A. \$100 increased by 50%   B. \$150   C. 50% of \$100
   D. 150% of \$100   E. \$100 increased by half

38. **Animal Studies** In 10 years, the African elephant population in Kenya decreased from 150,000 to 30,000.
   a. Find the percent of decrease.
   b. On average, how many fewer elephants were there each year?

Women-Owned Businesses on the Rise

The number of businesses owned by women grew more than 40% in the three years from 1991 to 1994. The National Foundation for Women Business Owners reported that 7.7 million companies were owned by women in 1994, up from 5.4 million in 1991. In 1994, these businesses employed about 15.5 million of the 131 million people employed in the United States.

Find the percent of change in each price.

39. \$15 marked up to \$24
40. \$750 discounted to \$600
41. \$3500 marked up to \$4000
42. \$1.80 marked up to \$2.20
43. \$39.99 discounted to \$19.99
44. \$24 marked up to \$36

45. a. Find the percent of change from 20 min to 25 min.
   b. Find the percent of change from 25 min to 30 min.
   c. **Writing** Explain why the percent of change is different for parts (a) and (b) even though the amount of change is the same.

Exercises MIXED REVIEW

Solve each equation.

46. $2 = \frac{c}{15}$
47. $8w = 12$
48. $z - 17 = -10$
49. $m - 4 = 9$

50. **Health** About 55 million Americans have foot problems. About 4.6 million of them have flat feet or fallen arches. What percent of people with foot problems have flat feet or fallen arches?

51. **Probability** You pick a colored chip from a bag, note its color, and replace it. You do this 20 times and get 7 red chips, 5 blue chips, and 8 green chips. What is the experimental probability that the next chip you choose will *not* be green?

52. Match each scatter plot correlation with the line that describes it.
   A. no correlation   I. downward slanted line (\)
   B. positive correlation   II. no line
   C. negative correlation   III. upward slanted line (/)

SELF ASSESSMENT

PORTFOLIO

For your portfolio, choose one or two items from your work for this chapter. Here are some possibilities:
- a journal entry
- corrected work
- a Find Out question

Explain why you include each selection you make.

CHAPTER PROJECT

Finishing the Chapter Project

checks and balances

Questions on pages 113, 118, 123, and 143 should help you to complete your project. Assemble all the parts of your project—the research on what you would like to buy, your expense record, your spreadsheet, and your circle graph. Are the expenses you recorded for two weeks typical for you? Does your budget support your purchase goal? Summarize what you think are the strengths and weaknesses of your budget.

Reflect and Revise

Present your budget and your purchase goal to a small group of classmates. Compare your decisions with theirs. Demonstrate to the group two equations of your own from the project. Check each other's work (including the circle graph) for reasonableness and accuracy. Use the comments and suggestions of your group to revise and improve your project.

Follow Up

Stick to your budget for several weeks. Are your savings on track? If not, what expenses can you reduce? Can you increase your income? Some of the resources listed below may give you ideas for a money-making project.

For More Information

Drew, Bonnie and Noel. *Fast Cash for Kids.* Hawthorne, New Jersey: Career Press, 1995.

Lamancusa, Joe. Kid Cash: *Creative Money-Making Ideas.* Blue Ridge Summit, Pennsylvania: TAB Books, 1993.

Spiselman, David. *A Teenager's Guide to Money, Banking, and Finance.* New York: J. Messner, 1987.

"The *Zillions* Allowance Survey." *Zillions* (April/May 1995): 14–17.

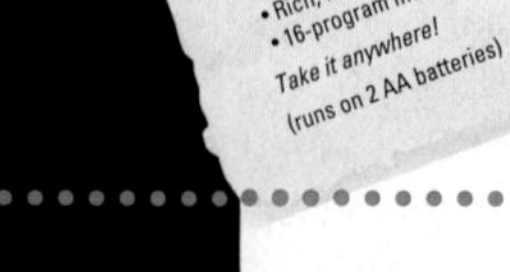

Sale!
$99.99
Personal CD Player with Headphones
• Rich, full sound
• 16-program memory
Take it anywhere!
(runs on 2 AA batteries)

CHAPTER 3

Wrap Up

Key Terms

coefficient (p. 119)
constant term (p. 119)
dependent events (p. 135)
distributive property (p. 124)
equivalent equations (p. 109)
independent events (p. 134)
inverse operations (p. 108)
like terms (p. 119)
percent of change (p. 146)
percent of increase (p. 146)
percent of decrease (p. 147)
properties of equality (p. 109, 110)
simple interest (p. 141)
solutions (p. 108)

How am I doing?

SELF ASSESSMENT

- State three ideas from this chapter that you think are important. Explain your choices.
  - Describe several important rules that you must apply in order to solve equations.

Modeling and Solving Equations 3-1

The value (or values) of a variable that make an equation true are called **solutions.** To solve an equation you can use **inverse operations,** which are operations that undo one another. To solve an addition or subtraction equation, subtract or add the same value to each side of the equation. To solve a multiplication or division equation, divide or multiply each side of the equation by the same nonzero value.

Solve and check.

1. $y - 7 = 9$
2. $\frac{x}{12} = -3$
3. $w + 23 = 54$
4. $5d = 120$
5. $-9 + t = 35$
6. $c + 0.25 = 4.5$
7. $7b = 84$
8. $\frac{z}{4} = \frac{1}{2}$

Modeling and Solving Two-Step Equations 3-2

A **two-step equation** is an equation that has two operations. You can use tiles to model and solve a two-step equation. To solve a two-step equation, first add or subtract. Then multiply or divide.

Write and solve each equation modeled by tiles.

9. 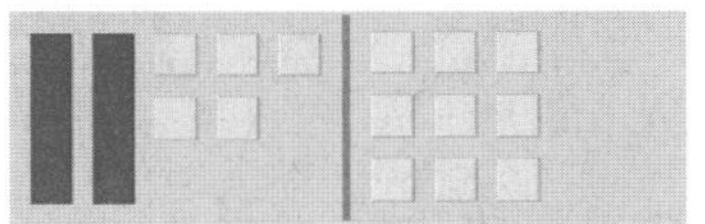

10. 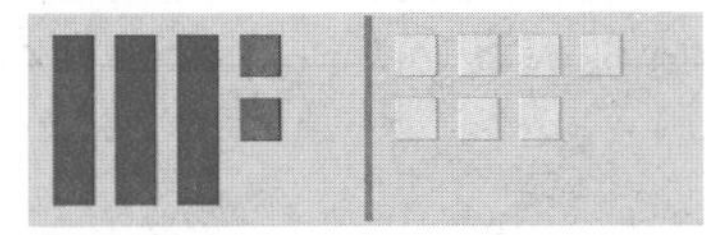

11. 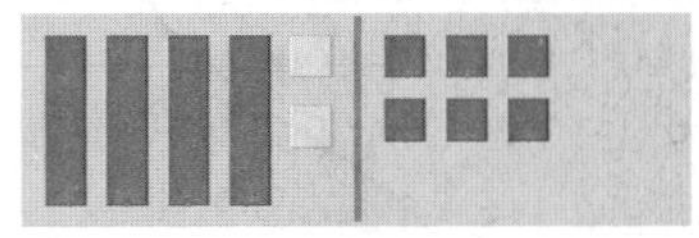

For Exercises 12–19, solve and check each equation.

12. $8u + 2 = 6$
13. $7t - 3 = 18$
14. $-2q - 5 = -11$
15. $11y + 9 = 130$
16. $-z + 11 = -7$
17. $5x - 8 = 12$
18. $3m + 8 = 2$
19. $10h - 4 = -94$

20. **Writing** Describe a situation that you can model with $6m + 3 = 27$. Explain what the variable represents and solve the equation.

Combining Like Terms and Using the Distributive Property 3-3, 3-4

Terms with exactly the same variable factors are **like terms.** You can combine like terms and use the distributive property to simplify expressions and solve equations.

Simplify each expression.

21. $9m - 5m + 3$ **22.** $2b + 8 - b + 2$ **23.** $-5(w - 4)$ **24.** $9(4 - 3j)$

Solve and check each equation.

25. $6b + 4b = -90$ **26.** $-x + 7x = 24$ **27.** $2(t + 5) = 9$ **28.** $-2(r - \frac{1}{2}) = -2$

29. $2b + 5(b + 1) = -9$ **30.** $-(3 - 10y) = 12$ **31.** $x - (4 - x) = 0$ **32.** $1 = z + 3(z - 1)$

33. **Geometry** The width of a rectangle is 6 cm less then the length. The perimeter is 72 cm. Write and solve an equation to find the dimensions of the rectangle.

Rational Numbers and Equations 3-5

You can simplify an equation that has fractional coefficients by multiplying each side of the equation by a reciprocal or by a common denominator.

34. Which operation will solve the equation $\frac{3}{4}w = \frac{9}{8}$?

A. Divide each side by $\frac{4}{3}$. **B.** Subtract $\frac{4}{3}$ from each side.

C. Multiply each side by $\frac{4}{3}$. **D.** Add $\frac{4}{3}$ to each side.

Solve and check each equation.

35. $-\frac{2}{5}x = 18$ **36.** $\frac{2y}{3} + \frac{y}{4} = 22$ **37.** $\frac{3n - 2}{5} = -7$ **38.** $-\frac{1}{3}(4b + 1) = 5$

39. Suppose you spend $\frac{3}{5}$ of your monthly budget on food and $\frac{1}{4}$ on bus fare. Food and bus fare total \$34/mo. What is your monthly budget?

Using Probability 3-6

Independent events do not affect one another. When the outcome of one event affects the outcome of a second event, the events are **dependent events.**

For independent events A and B: $P(A \text{ and } B) = P(A) \cdot P(B)$

For dependent events A and B: $P(A \text{ and } B) = P(A) \cdot P(B \text{ after } A)$

For Exercises 40 and 41, you choose two numbers from a box containing tiles numbered 1–10. State whether the two events are *independent* or *dependent* and then find each probability.

40. P(6 and an even number) without replacing **41.** P(1 and an odd number) with replacing

42. **Writing** Compare what the words *independent* and *dependent* mean in mathematics with what they mean in social studies.

Percent Equations 3-7

You can use an equation to solve a percent problem.

The formula to calculate **simple interest** is $I = p \cdot r \cdot t$, where I is the interest, p is the principal, r is the annual interest rate, and t is the time in years.

Write and solve an equation to answer each question. Check your answer.

43. What is 15% of 86? **44.** What percent of 5 is 40? **45.** 1.8 is 72% of what?

46. In one high school, 30 of the school's 800 students work on the school paper. What percent of the students work on the paper?

47. *Finance* You invest $2000 in a bank account paying 5.5% simple interest annually. How much interest will you receive after 2 yr?

Percent of Change 3-8

The **percent of change** $= \frac{\text{amount of change}}{\text{original amount}}$. If a value increases from its original amount, the percent of change is called the percent of increase. If a value decreases from its original amount, the percent of change is called the **percent of decrease.**

For Exercises 48–50, find each percent of change. Describe the percent of change as a percent of increase or decrease.

48. $75,000 to $85,000 **49.** 20 ft to 15 ft **50.** 60 h to 40 h

51. In Irvine, California, parents donated 220,624 h of service to the schools in the 1993–1994 school year. This increased by about 60,000 hours the next year. Find the percent of increase of donated hours.

52. *Open-ended* Describe a situation that involves a percent of increase that is more than 100%.

Getting Ready for CHAPTER 4

Evaluate each expression.

53. $|-6| - |y|$ for $y = 8$ **54.** $|t - 7|$ for $t = 5.6$ **55.** $|c| + 9$ for $c = -10$

56. $|x| + 3$ for $x = -4$ **57.** $3z - 4.5$ for $z = 3$ **58.** $13 - 5y$ for $y = -1$

Solve and check.

59. $\frac{2}{3}k = \frac{1}{6}$ **60.** $\frac{1}{2}b = \frac{4}{7}$ **61.** $\frac{1}{3} = \frac{1}{9}d$ **62.** $\frac{3}{2}l = \frac{2}{3}$

63. $5t + 4 = -16$ **64.** $7 - m = 2$ **65.** $2(w - 7) = 90$ **66.** $3y + 8 = -1$

CHAPTER 3

Assessment

Solve and check each equation.

1. $5n = -20$
2. $t + 7 = 4$
3. $\frac{r}{3} = 21$
4. $u - 8 = -15$
5. $3q - 2 = 10$
6. $-2z + 1 = -9$

Write and solve each equation modeled by tiles.

7.  

8.  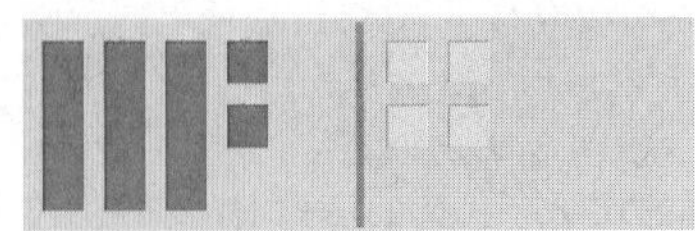

Solve and check each equation.

9. $3w + 2 - w = -4$
10. $-9.5b + 4.5b = 25$
11. $\frac{1}{4}(k - 1) = 10$
12. $6(y + 3) = 24$
13. $\frac{5n + 1}{8} = \frac{1}{2}$

14. **Open-ended** Describe a situation that you can model with the equation $\frac{m}{5} = 4$.

15. If $2t + 3 = -9$, what is the value of $-3t - 7$?
    A. –6 B. 11
    C. –3 D. 2
    E. –9

16. Which equation is *not* equivalent to the equation $2x - 4 = -7$?
    A. $4 = -7 - 2x$ B. $-4 = -7 - 2x$
    C. $4 = 2x + 7$ D. $2x = -3$
    E. $-2x + 4 = 7$

Solve an equation to answer each question.

17. What is 16% of 250?
18. 8 is what percent of 12.5?
19. 19 is 95% of what?

20. **Finance** You invest \$500 for three years and receive \$60 in simple interest. What is the annual interest rate?

21. Suppose a person contributes 6% of her salary to her retirement account. She works 20 h/wk at \$5.50/h. Find her weekly contribution.

Calculate the percent of change. Describe each as a percent of increase or a percent of decrease.

22. \$4.50/h to \$5/h
23. 60 km/h to 45 km/h
24. 150 lb to 135 lb
25. \$18 to \$24

26. The game Monopoly™ was introduced in 1935. The table shows how much some amounts in the game should have increased to have kept up with inflation.

	1935	1995
Total money in game	\$15,140	\$184,794
Amount each player starts the game with	1500	18,308
Park Place rent with no houses	35	428
Money collected when passing GO	200	2441

Source: Parker Brothers

   a. Estimate the percent of inflation from 1935 to 1995 by finding the percent of increase in any one of the dollar amounts.
   b. **Writing** Describe the steps you used to calculate your answer to part (a).
   c. Explain another way to get the same result.

27. You have 8 red checkers and 8 black checkers in a bag. You choose two checkers. Find each probability.
   a. P(red and red) with replacing
   b. P(red and black) without replacing
   c. P(black and red) with replacing

28. **Open-ended** Write and solve a probability problem involving dependent events.

CHAPTER 3

Preparing for the Math A Exam

Part I

1 The table shows values for a linear function. Which equation describes the function?

x	1	2	3	4	5	6	7
$f(x)$	−2	−1	0	1	2	3	4

(1) $f(x) = -2x$ (3) $f(x) = x - 3$
(2) $f(x) = 2x$ (4) $f(x) = x + 3$

2 Which equation is equivalent to $s + 6 = 3$?
(1) $\frac{s}{2} = -3$ (3) $12 = 4s$
(2) $-7 = s - 4$ (4) $s + 5 = -2$

3 What is the solution of $-16 + \frac{n}{2} = -20$?
(1) $n = -4$ (3) $n = 2$
(2) $n = -2$ (4) $n = -8$

4 The expression $9a + 3b - 3 - 4a + 7 - 8b$ can be simplified to ■.
(1) $5a - 5b + 4$ (3) $6a - 12b + 4$
(2) $5a + 11b - 10$ (4) $5a - 5b$

5 What is the solution of $4(z - 3) = -4$?
(1) $z = -13$ (3) $z = -4$
(2) $z = -1$ (4) $z = 2$

6 Which equation models "16 is 25% of what?"
(1) $16 = 0.25n$ (3) $n = 0.25(16)$
(2) $16 = \frac{n}{0.25}$ (4) $16 = 25n$

7 The graph shows the results of a survey of 2400 high school students. How many students worked 11–16 hours per week?

Hours Worked Weekly

(1) 672 (2) 520
(3) 46 (4) 1248

8 What is the greatest possible percent of error for a measurement of 17.0 cm?
(1) 2.9% (2) 50% (3) 0.3% (4) 0.6%

9 A bicycle is priced at \$100. Then the price is raised by 10%. Then, during a sale, the price is lowered by 10%. The final price is ■.
(1) \$98 (3) \$100
(2) \$99 (4) \$101

Part II

10 Suppose you can buy a pound of grapes for \$1.36. How much would you pay for $1\frac{3}{4}$ pounds of grapes?

11 Suppose you received \$67.50 for a 3-year investment at $4\frac{1}{2}$% simple interest. How much money had you invested?

Part III

12 The cost to mail a first-class letter in the U.S. in 1999 was \$.33 for the first ounce, and \$.22 for each additional ounce. If the cost to mail a letter was \$.99, how much did the letter weigh? Write an equation to model this problem. Solve it.

13 Three coins are tossed.
a Make a probability distribution table showing the probabilities of tossing 0, 1, 2, and 3 tails.
b Make a histogram for the probability distribution.

Part IV

14 Three uncles were born in the same month in three consecutive years. The sum of their ages is 171. What are their ages? Write an equation to model this problem. Then solve it.

15 You have three red marbles, two blue marbles, and four green marbles in your pocket.
a You pick one marble, replace it, and pick another marble. What is the probability that you pick a blue marble and a green marble?
b You pick a marble, do *not* replace it, and pick again. What is the probability that you pick two green marbles?

CHAPTER

4 Equations and Inequalities

Relating to the Real World

You can use equations and formulas to model a variety of real-world problems. Business and industry, science, sports, travel, architecture, banking—these are some of the areas that rely on equations and inequalities to find solutions to problems, often by making comparisons and analyzing results.

Lessons	4-1	4-2	4-3	4-4	4-5
	Using Proportions	*Equations with Variables on Both Sides*	*Solving Absolute Value Equations*	*Transforming Formulas*	*Solving Inequalities Using Addition and Subtraction*

CHAPTER PROJECT

NO SWEAT!

Your good health and physical fitness will enhance your quality of life for years to come. As you grow older, your needs will change. How much exercise should you get? What should your blood pressure be? You can use formulas and inequalities to describe many aspects of good health.

As you work through the chapter, you will use formulas for physical fitness and health. You will work with equations and inequalities that allow for differences in weight, height, and age. Finally, you will design an exercise plan for yourself.

To help you complete the project:

- **p. 162** *Find Out by Calculating*
- **p. 178** *Find Out by Solving*
- **p. 194** *Find Out by Researching*
- **p. 200** *Find Out by Writing*
- **p. 205** *Find Out by Interviewing*
- **p. 206** *Finishing the Project*

What You'll Learn

- Solving proportions
- Using proportions to solve real-world problems

...And Why

To solve problems by comparing and evaluating quantities

What You'll Need

- centimeter ruler
- calculator

4-1 Using Proportions

WORK TOGETHER

A **ratio** is a comparison of two numbers by division. For example, $\frac{3}{4}$ and 5 : 2 are ratios. The **scale** of a blueprint is the ratio of a length on the blueprint to the actual length it represents.

1. a. Work with a partner. Measure the length and width of the two rooms in the apartment blueprint in centimeters.
   b. For the two rooms, record the measurements in a table like the one below. Complete the table by finding the ratios of the blueprint measurements to the actual measurements.

Length	Blueprint ■ cm	Actual ■ m	Blueprint : Actual (cm : m) ■ : ■
Width	Blueprint ■ cm	Actual ■ m	Blueprint : Actual (cm : m) ■ : ■

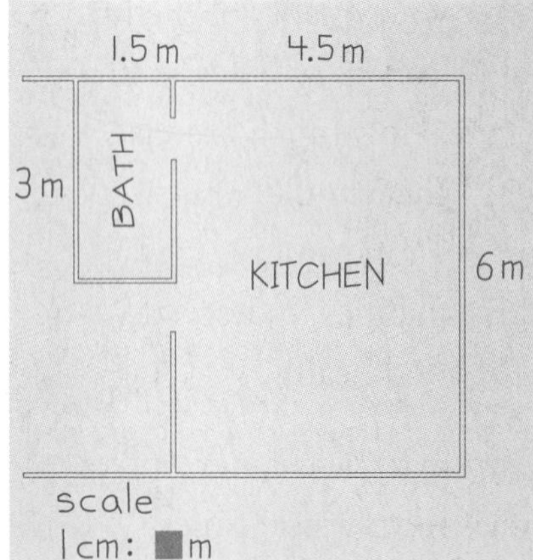

2. Use the ratios in your table to complete the blueprint scale.

THINK AND DISCUSS

Using Properties of Equality

A **proportion** is a statement that two ratios are equal. Another way to write the sample at the right is 3 : 4 = 12 : 16. Read this "3 is to 4 as 12 is to 16."

$$\frac{3}{4} = \frac{12}{16}$$

To solve a proportion with a variable, you can use the multiplication property of equality.

Example 1

Solve $\frac{t}{9} = \frac{5}{6}$.

$\frac{t}{9} \cdot 54 = \frac{5}{6} \cdot 54$ ← Multiply each side by a common denominator such as 54.

$6t = 45$

$\frac{6t}{6} = \frac{45}{6}$ ← Divide each side by 6.

$t = 7.5$

The solution is 7.5. The ratios $\frac{7.5}{9}$ and $\frac{5}{6}$ are equal. ■

QUICK REVIEW

Multiplication Property of Equality

For any numbers a, b, and c, if $a = b$, then $ac = bc$.

3. Instead of 54, would another number have worked in Example 1? What number is the best choice? Why?

Using Cross Products

The numerators and denominators of the ratios that form a proportion have a special relationship. The **cross products** of a proportion are equal.

$\frac{3}{4} = \frac{12}{16}$ 3 · 16 and 4 · 12 are cross products.
3 · 16 = 48 and 4 · 12 = 48

Cross Products of a Proportion

In a proportion, where $b \neq 0$ and $d \neq 0$; if $\frac{a}{b} = \frac{c}{d}$ then $ad = bc$.
Example: $\frac{2}{3} = \frac{8}{12}$ so $2 \cdot 12 = 3 \cdot 8$.

4. Use cross products to **justify** each statement.
a. $\frac{8}{3}$ and $\frac{4}{1.5}$ form a proportion. **b.** $\frac{5}{8}$ and $\frac{7}{10}$ do not form a proportion.

Another way to solve a proportion with a variable is to use cross products.

PROBLEM SOLVING

Look Back What steps would you take to solve this proportion using the multiplication property of equality?

Example 2

Solve $\frac{y}{2.5} = -\frac{3}{4}$.

$y(4) = (2.5)(-3)$ ← Use cross products.

$\frac{4y}{4} = \frac{-7.5}{4}$ ← Divide each side by 4.

$y = -1.875$ ← Simplify.

The solution is -1.875.

5. a. Is $-4 = \frac{x}{16}$ a proportion? Why or why not?
b. Explain how to solve for x. Find x.

Similar figures are figures that have the same shape but not necessarily the same size. The corresponding angles of similar figures are equal and the corresponding sides are in proportion.

Example 3

Geometry In the figure, $\triangle ABC$ is similar to $\triangle DFE$. Find length DE.

C, 21, 18, A, 15, B, E, x, D, 10, F

Define x = unknown length DE

Relate $\frac{\text{length } AB}{\text{length } DF} = \frac{\text{length } AC}{\text{length } DE}$

Write $\frac{15}{10} = \frac{21}{x}$ ← Write a proportion comparing the lengths of corresponding sides.

$15x = 10(21)$ ← Use cross products.

$\frac{15x}{15} = \frac{210}{15}$ ← Divide each side by 15.

$x = 14$

The length $DE = 14$. ← Simplify.

QUICK REVIEW

The *perimeter* is the sum of the lengths of the sides of a figure.

6. a. Try This Find length EF in the figure shown in Example 3.
   b. What is the perimeter of $\triangle DFE$?
   c. Write a ratio comparing the perimeters of $\triangle DFE$ and $\triangle ABC$.
   d. How does the ratio of the perimeters in part (c) compare with the ratio of length DE to length AC?

Solving Percent Problems Using Proportions

QUICK REVIEW

$n\% = \frac{n}{100}$ ← part ← whole

In Chapter 3 you used equations to solve problems involving percents. Recall that percent is a ratio that compares a number to 100. You can use proportions to solve word problems that involve percent.

Example 4 **Relating to the Real World** 

Aquaculture In 1994, U.S. trout farms produced 52,100,000 lb of trout. Suppose a trout farmer raised 858,000 lb of trout. What percent of the 1994 U.S. trout production did the farmer raise? Round your answer to the nearest tenth of a percent.

Define n = the farmer's part of the trout production

Relate 858,000 is what percent of 52,100,000?

Write

$\frac{858{,}000}{52{,}100{,}000} = \frac{n}{100}$ ← part ← whole

$858{,}000(100) = 52{,}100{,}000n$ ← Use cross products.

$\frac{858{,}000(100)}{52{,}100{,}000} = \frac{52{,}100{,}000n}{52{,}100{,}000}$ ← Divide each side by 52,100,000.

$\frac{858{,}000(100)}{52{,}100{,}000} = n$ ← Write in a calculator-ready form.

$1.6468330134 = n$ ← Use a calculator.

$1.6 \approx n$ ← Round to the nearest tenth.

The farmer raised about 1.6% of the 1994 U.S. trout production.

7. a. A trout farm can produce 8800 lb/acre each year. At that rate, how many acres were needed to raise the 1994 U.S. trout production?
   b. How many acres did the farmer in Example 4 need?

8. Critical Thinking How are these three questions and their answers different from each other?
   - 10 is what percent of 25?
   - What number is 10% of 25?
   - 10% of what number is 25?

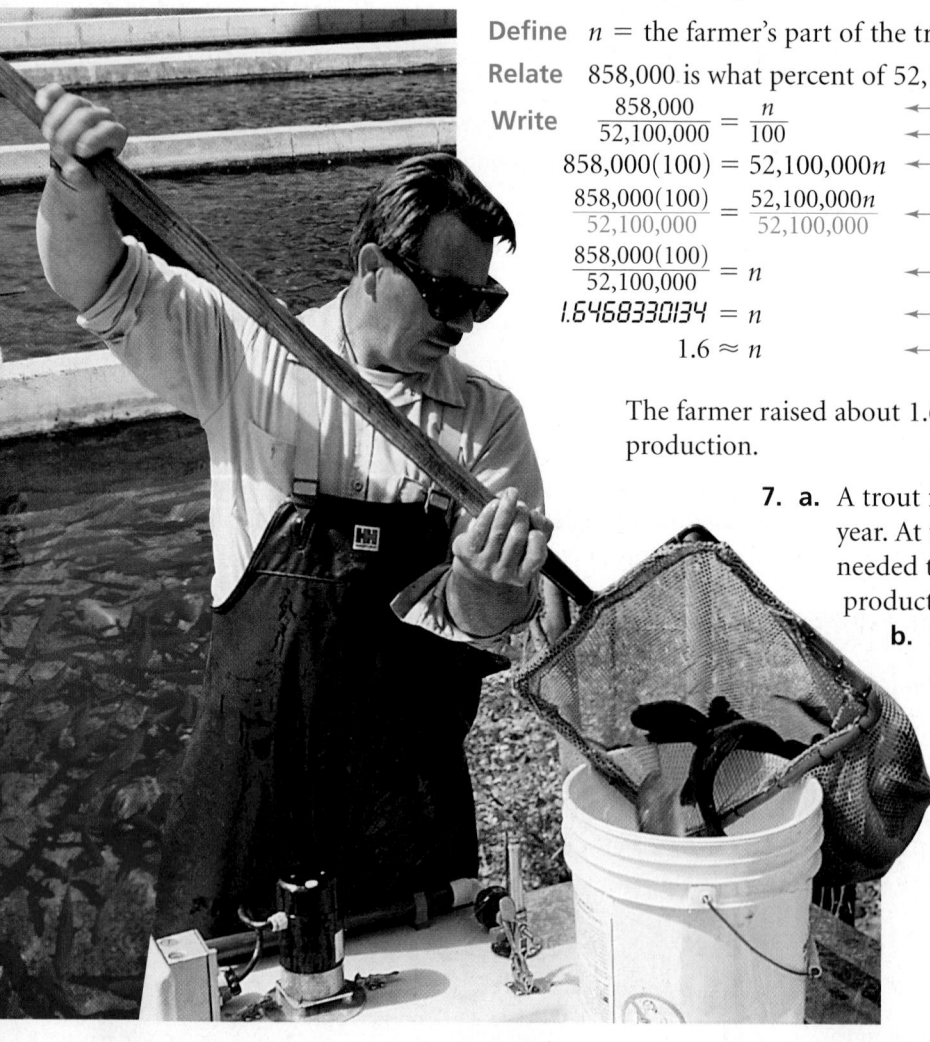

Exercises ON YOUR OWN

Which pairs of ratios could form a proportion? Justify each answer.

1. $\frac{6}{8}, \frac{15}{20}$ **2.** $\frac{9}{12}, \frac{4}{5}$ **3.** $-\frac{0.12}{0.15}, -\frac{0.4}{0.5}$ **4.** $\frac{5}{6}, \frac{20}{24}$ **5.** $-\frac{3}{100}, -\frac{1}{25}$ **6.** $\frac{51}{3}, \frac{17}{1}$

7. A canary's heart beats 130 times in 12 s. Use a proportion to find how many times its heart beats in 40 s.

8. *Open-ended* Write a problem that you can solve using the proportion $\frac{2}{5} = \frac{x}{9}$. Then show the solution to your problem.

Use a proportion to answer Exercises 9–20. Round your answer to the nearest tenth or to the nearest tenth of a percent.

9. Find 45% of \$120. **10.** What percent of 200 is 25? **11.** 17 is what percent of 85?

12. 12.5 is 75% of what number? **13.** What is $33\frac{1}{3}$% of 150? **14.** 22 is 80% of what number?

15. What percent of 87 is 24? **16.** 15 is 35% of what number? **17.** Find 89% of 345.

18. What number is 75% of 250? **19.** 12.5 is 80% of what number? **20.** What is 23% of 27?

21. *Architecture* A blueprint scale is 1.5 in. : 6 ft. On the plan, the den measures 2.5 in. by 3 in. What are the actual dimensions of the den?

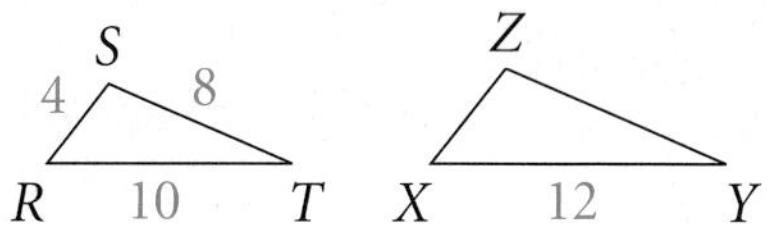

22. *Geometry* In the figure, $\triangle RST$ is similar to $\triangle XZY$. Find length ZY.

23. *Standardized Test Prep* Which equation does not have the same solution as $\frac{12}{x} = \frac{45}{60}$?

A. $12 \cdot 60 = 45x$ **B.** $\frac{12}{45} = \frac{x}{60}$ **C.** $\frac{x}{12} = \frac{60}{45}$ **D.** $\frac{x}{60} = \frac{12}{45}$ **E.** $\frac{60}{x} = \frac{12}{45}$

Mental Math **Solve each proportion mentally.**

24. $\frac{x}{6} = \frac{12}{18}$ **25.** $-\frac{12}{20} = -\frac{3}{y}$ **26.** $\frac{8}{d} = \frac{40}{30}$ **27.** $\frac{1}{2} = \frac{z}{25}$

Choose **Use a calculator, paper and pencil, or mental math. Solve each proportion.**

28. $\frac{c}{6} = \frac{12}{15}$ **29.** $\frac{21}{12} = \frac{7}{y}$ **30.** $-\frac{37}{24} = \frac{k}{6}$ **31.** $\frac{15}{n} = \frac{39}{13}$

32. $\frac{17}{51} = \frac{n}{1}$ **33.** $-\frac{4.5}{x} = -\frac{1.8}{5}$ **34.** $\frac{q}{56} = \frac{15}{14}$ **35.** $\frac{2.5}{1.8} = -\frac{1.2}{r}$

36. a. *Geometry* Rectangle $ABCD$ is 6 in. wide and 16 in. long. It is similar to rectangle $KLMN$, whose length is 24 in. What is the width of rectangle $KLMN$?

b. Are the areas of the two rectangles proportional to the lengths of their corresponding sides? Explain.

37. a. Do the two phrases in the picture offer the same discount? Explain.

b. *Open-ended* What would you expect to pay at the store's sale for a jacket regularly priced at \$67? Explain.

38. a. **Travel** Use a ruler and the map at the right. Find the distance from each town to the others.

b. A student lives halfway between Lincoln and San Paulo and goes by the shortest route to school in Duncanville. How far does the student travel each day to and from school?

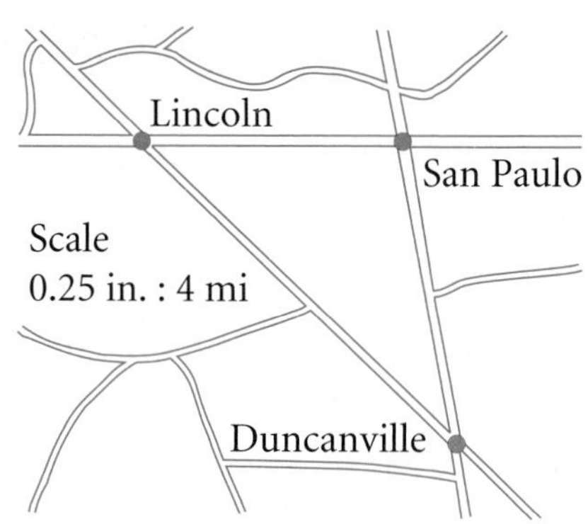

39. Suppose $\frac{12}{72} = \frac{x}{24}$ and $\frac{x}{36} = \frac{y}{81}$. Find y.

40. **Writing** Write an explanation telling an absent classmate how to use cross products to solve a proportion. Include an example.

41. **Hobbies** Some model trains are built to $\frac{1}{87}$ of actual size. Suppose an actual boxcar is 40 ft long. How many *inches* long is the model?

42. **Statistics** In the southern United States, 68.6% of the population, or 58,656,000 people, live in urban areas. What is the total population of the southern United States?

43. In 1992, there were 255,082,000 people living in the United States. Of these, 18,100,000 were 10–14 years old. What percent of the population was this? Round your answer to the nearest tenth of a percent.

Chapter Project *Find Out by Calculating*

When you exercise, the number of calories you burn is roughly proportional to your weight.

- Write and solve a proportion to find how many calories you would burn if you performed one activity in the table for 60 min.
- Write and solve a proportion to find how many calories you would burn if you did the activity for 60 min three times in a week.

Calories Burned During Exercise
(150-lb person exercising for 60 min)

Exercise	Calories
Dancing	250
Biking, walking (3–5 mph)	300
Soccer, jogging (4–5 mph)	400
Swimming, skiing	500
Running (5–7 mph)	650

Exercises MIXED REVIEW

Add or subtract.

44. $\begin{bmatrix} 11 & -2 & 4 \\ 3.5 & 6.9 & 12.2 \end{bmatrix} + \begin{bmatrix} -5.4 & 3.2 & -8 \\ 7.6 & 2.3 & -9.7 \end{bmatrix}$

45. $\begin{bmatrix} -4.3 & 7.9 \\ 2.1 & -0.8 \end{bmatrix} - \begin{bmatrix} -3.1 & -6.7 \\ 3.5 & 4.9 \end{bmatrix}$

Find the value of each function when $x = 3$.

46. $f(x) = 4x - 1$

47. $f(x) = -1.5x - 7$

48. $f(x) = 8x + 2$

49. You have one foot of space left on a bookshelf, and your paperbacks are $\frac{3}{4}$ in. thick. How many more paperbacks can you fit on the shelf?

Getting Ready for Lesson 4-2

Solve and check each equation.

50. $7x + 4 - 15x = 36$

51. $w + (w + 2) = -27$

52. $6(7 - 2y) = 30$

4-2 Equations with Variables on Both Sides

What You'll Learn

- Solving equations with variables on both sides
- Identifying equations that have no solution or are identities

...And Why

To solve equations that model real-world situations, such as distance problems

What You'll Need

- tiles
- calculator

WORK TOGETHER

In Chapter 3 you used tiles and solved equations. Model each equation with tiles. Then solve.

1. $x - 4 = -9$ **2.** $-10 = 5y$ **3.** $3a + 8 = 2$ **4.** $-12 = 8 + 4b$

Now look at an equation with variables on both sides: $6x + 3 = 4x + 9$.

5. Model this equation with tiles.

6. Discuss how you might use tiles to solve the equation.

7. Use the problem solving strategy *Guess and Test* to solve the equation.

THINK AND DISCUSS

Using Tiles to Solve Equations

Some equations cannot be solved easily using the strategy *Guess and Test.* In this lesson you will learn how to solve equations with variables on both sides. First you will use tiles to help you understand the process.

Example 1

Solve the equation

$$5x - 3 = 2x + 12.$$

Model the equation with tiles.

$$5x - 3 = 2x + 12$$

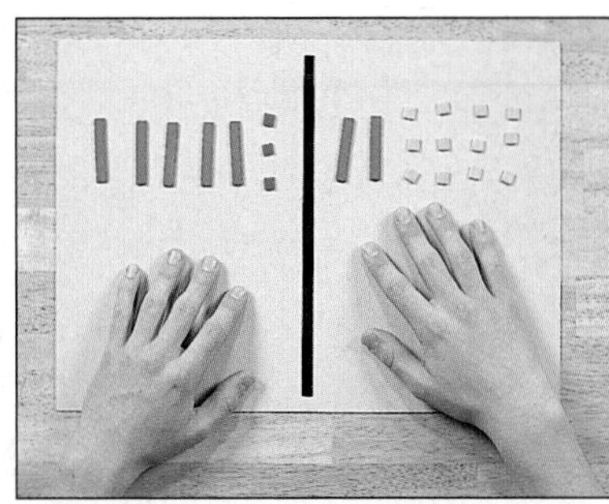

Add $-2x$ to each side, and simplify by removing zero pairs.

$$5x - 3 - 2x = 2x + 12 - 2x$$
$$3x - 3 = 12$$

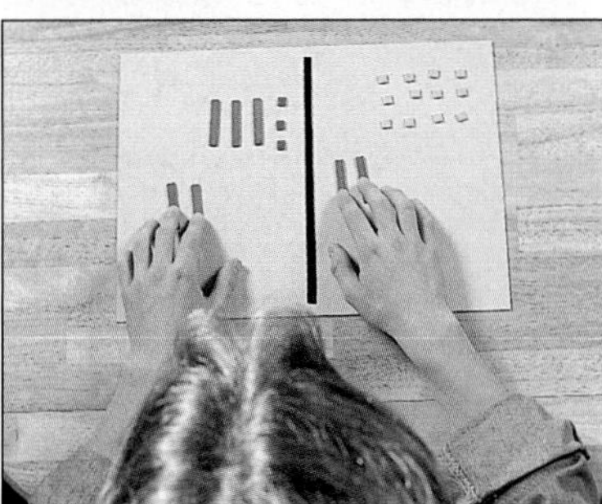

QUICK REVIEW

represents 0.

Math A Test Prep

1 A scale drawing is made of a rectangular room whose dimensions are 18 ft by 24 ft. The scale is 3 ft = 1 in. What is the perimeter of the room in the scale drawing?
(1) 84 in. (3) 28 in.
(2) 42 in. (4) 14 in.

2 Beth said the equation $5v - 9 = 3(v - 3) + 2v$ is an identity. Explain what she meant by this. Show how she could reach this conclusion.

Add 3 to each side and simplify by removing zero pairs.

$$3x - 3 + 3 = 12 + 3$$
$$3x = 15$$

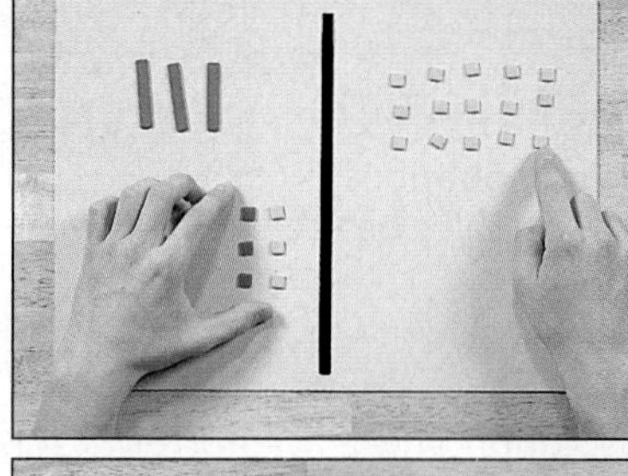

Divide each side into three identical groups.

$$\frac{3x}{3} = \frac{15}{3}$$

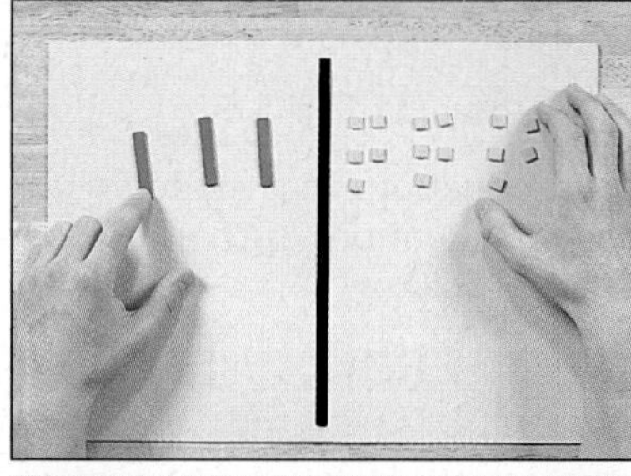

Solve for x.

$$x = 5$$

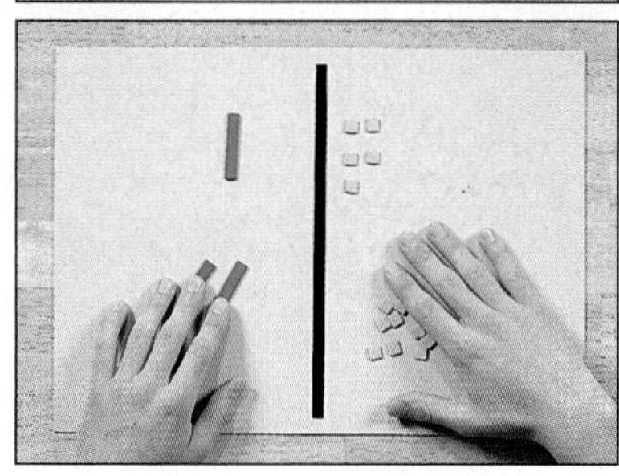

The solution is 5.

Check $5x - 3 = 2x + 12$

$5(5) - 3 \stackrel{?}{=} 2(5) + 12$ ← Substitute 5 for x.

$22 = 22$ ✓

8. Try This Use tiles to model and solve each equation.

a. $6x - 2 = x + 13$ **b.** $4(x + 1) = 2x - 2$

c. Summarize the steps you used to solve the equations.

Using Properties of Equality

You can use the properties of equality to get terms with variables on the same side of the equation.

Example 2

Solve $5t - 8 = 9t - 10$.

$5t - 8 + 10 = 9t - 10 + 10$ ← Add 10 to each side.

$5t + 2 = 9t$ ← Simplify each side.

$5t + 2 - 5t = 9t - 5t$ ← Subtract $5t$ from each side.

$2 = 4t$ ← Combine like terms.

$\frac{2}{4} = \frac{4t}{4}$ ← Divide each side by 4.

$\frac{1}{2} = t$ ← Simplify each side.

The solution is $\frac{1}{2}$.

GRAPHING CALCULATOR HINT

You can check your solution to Example 2 by using the TEST feature to see if $\frac{1}{2}$ is the solution of the equation.

9. **Verify** the solution of Example 2.

10. **a.** Suppose you began solving the equation in Example 2 by subtracting $9t$ from each side of the equation. Write the steps you would use to solve the equation.

b. Compare your solution to the solution in Example 2. Does it matter that the variables are on different sides of the equal sign? Explain.

QUICK REVIEW

A formula for distance is distance = rate · time, or $d = rt$.

Equations are helpful when you solve distance problems.

Example 3 Relating to the Real World 

Transportation Mary and Jocelyn are sisters. They left school at 3:00 P.M. and bicycled home along the same bike path. Mary bicycled at a speed of 12 mi/h. Jocelyn bicycled at 9 mi/h. Mary got home 15 min before Jocelyn. How long did it take Mary to get home?

PROBLEM SOLVING HINT

Draw a diagram to help you visualize the conditions of the problem in Example 3.

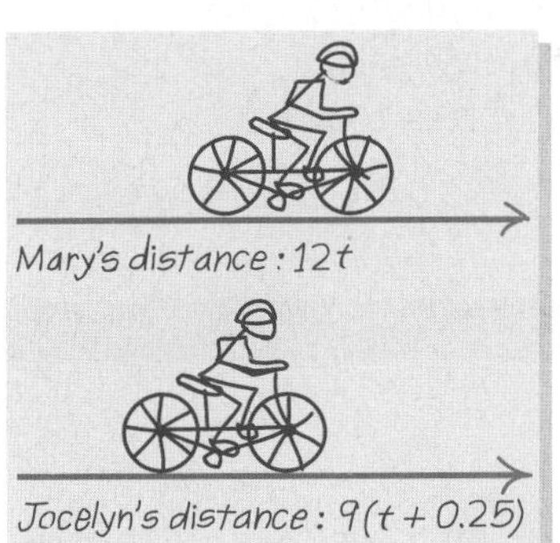

Define t = Mary's time in hours

$t + 0.25$ = Jocelyn's time in hours

Relate Mary's distance (rate · time) equals Jocelyn's distance (rate · time)

Write $12t$ = $9(t + 0.25)$

$12t = 9(t + 0.25)$

$12t = 9t + 2.25$ ← Use the distributive property.

$12t - 9t = 9t + 2.25 - 9t$ ← Subtract $9t$ from each side.

$3t = 2.25$ ← Combine like terms.

$\frac{3t}{3} = \frac{2.25}{3}$ ← Divide each side by 3.

$t = 0.75$ ← Use a calculator.

It took Mary 0.75 h, or 45 min, to get home.

11. **Critical Thinking** To solve the problem in Example 3, Ben wrote the equation $12t = 9(t + 15)$. What mistake did he make?

Solving Special Types of Equations

An equation has **no solution** if no value makes the equation true.

Example 4

Solve $6m - 5 = 7m + 7 - m$.

$6m - 5 = 7m + 7 - m$

$6m - 5 = 6m + 7$ ← Combine like terms.

$6m - 5 - 6m = 6m + 7 - 6m$ ← Subtract $6m$ from each side.

$-5 = 7$ Not true for any m!

This equation has no solution.

12. Is an equation that has 0 for a solution the same as an equation with no solution? Explain.

An equation that is true for every value of the variable is an **identity.**

Example 5

Solve $10 - 8a = 2(5 - 4a)$.

$$10 - 8a = 2(5 - 4a)$$
$$10 - 8a = 10 - 8a \quad \leftarrow \text{Use the distributive property.}$$
$$10 - 8a + 8a = 10 - 8a + 8a \quad \leftarrow \text{Add } 8a \text{ to each side.}$$
$$10 = 10 \quad \text{Always true!}$$

This equation is true for any value of a, so the equation is an identity.

13. Could you have stopped solving the equation when you saw that $10 - 8a = 10 - 8a$? Explain.

14. **Mental Math** Without writing the steps of a solution, tell whether the equation has *one solution*, *no solution*, or is an *identity*.
 a. $9 + 5a = 5a - 1$
 b. $5a + 9 = 2a$
 c. $9 + 5a = 2a + 9$
 d. $9 + 5a = 5a + 9$

Exercises ON YOUR OWN

Write an equation for each model and solve.

1. 

2. 

3. 

4. 

Model each equation with tiles. Then solve.

5. $4x - 3 = 3x + 4$
6. $5x + 3 = 3x + 9$
7. $8 - x = 2x - 1$

Solve and check. If the equation is an identity or if it has no solution, write *identity* or *no solution*.

8. $3(x - 4) = 2x + 6$
9. $4x - 7 = x + 3(4 + x)$
10. $5x = 3(x - 1) + (3 + 2x)$
11. $0.5y + 2 = 0.8y - 0.3y$
12. $6 + 3m = -m - 6$
13. $3t + 8 = 5t + 8 - 2t$

Critical Thinking **Find the mistake in the solution of each equation. Explain the mistake and solve the equation correctly.**

14.
$$\begin{aligned} 2x &= 11x + 45 \\ 2x - 11x &= 11x - 11x + 45 \\ 9x &= 45 \\ \frac{9x}{9} &= \frac{45}{9} \\ x &= 5 \end{aligned}$$

15.
$$\begin{aligned} 4.5 - y &= 2(y - 5.7) \\ 4.5 - y &= 2y - 11.4 \\ 4.5 - y - y &= 2y - y - 11.4 \\ 4.5 &= y - 11.4 \\ 4.5 + 11.4 &= y - 11.4 + 11.4 \\ 15.9 &= y \end{aligned}$$

Mental Math **Solve and check each equation.**

16. $5y = y - 40$

17. $7w = -7w$

18. $r + 1 = 4r + 1$

19. $6t + 1 = 6t - 8$

20. $2q + 4 = 4 - 2q$

21. $3a + 1 = 9 - a$

Choose **Use tiles, paper and pencil, calculator, or mental math to solve each equation. If appropriate, write *identity* or *no solution*.**

22. $t + 1 = 3t - 5$

23. $7y - 8 = 7y + 9$

24. $0.5k + 3.6 = 4.2 - 1.5k$

25. $2r + 16 = r - 25$

26. $\frac{3}{4}x = \frac{1}{2} + \frac{2}{3}x$

27. $\frac{1}{3}(x - 7) = 5x$

28. $0.7m = 0.9m + 2.4 - 0.2m$

29. $14 - (2q + 5) = -2q + 9$

30. $0.3t + 1.4 = 4.2 - 0.1t$

31. Find the value of each variable in the matrices. $\begin{bmatrix} 2x + 1 & a - 1 \\ w - 4 & 9y \end{bmatrix} = \begin{bmatrix} -5x - 6 & 5a \\ 3w + 4 & -3y \end{bmatrix}$

32. **Business** A toy company spends \$1500 each day on plant costs plus \$8 per toy for labor and materials. The toys sell for \$12 each. How many toys must the company sell in one day to equal its daily costs?

33. **Writing** Describe the two situations you learned about in this lesson that cannot occur when you are solving an equation with the variable on only one side of the equal sign. Give examples.

34. **Transportation** A truck traveling 45 mi/h and a train traveling 60 mi/h cover the same distance. The truck travels 2 h longer than the train. How many hours did each travel?

35. **Recreation** You can buy used in-line skates from your cousin for \$40, or you can rent them from the park. Either way you must rent safety equipment. How many hours must you skate at the park to justify buying your cousin's skates?

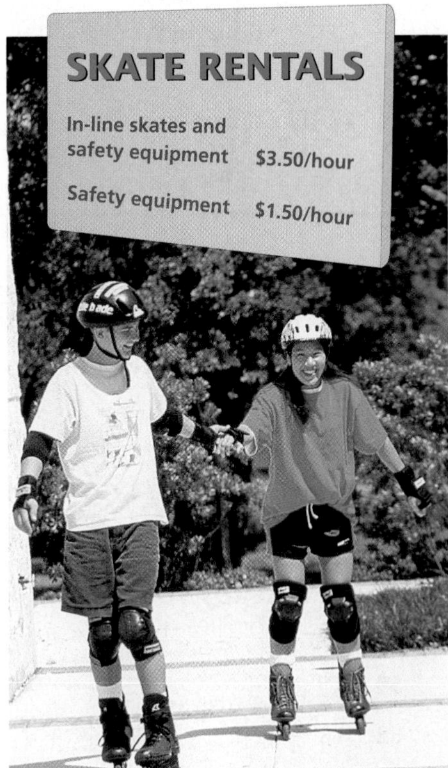

SKATE RENTALS
In-line skates and safety equipment $3.50/hour
Safety equipment $1.50/hour

Open-ended **Write an equation with variables on both sides for each of the following solutions.**

36. $x = 0$

37. x is a positive number.

38. x is a negative number.

39. All values of x are solutions.

40. $x = 1$

41. No values of x are solutions.

42. a. **Technology** Write formulas for cells B2 and C2 to evaluate the expressions at the top of Columns B and C.
b. Enter the integers from –5 to 5 in Column A. Evaluate the expressions in Columns B and C using the values in Column A.
c. What is the value in Column A when the numbers in Columns B and C are equal?
d. What equation have you solved?
e. Use a spreadsheet to solve $5.2n - 9 = 11.2n + 3$.

	A	B	C
1	x	5(x – 3)	4 – 3(x + 1)
2	–5	–40	16
3	–4	–35	13
4	–3	▒	▒

43. **Geometry** $\triangle ABC$ is congruent to $\triangle DEF$. Find the lengths of the sides of $\triangle DEF$.

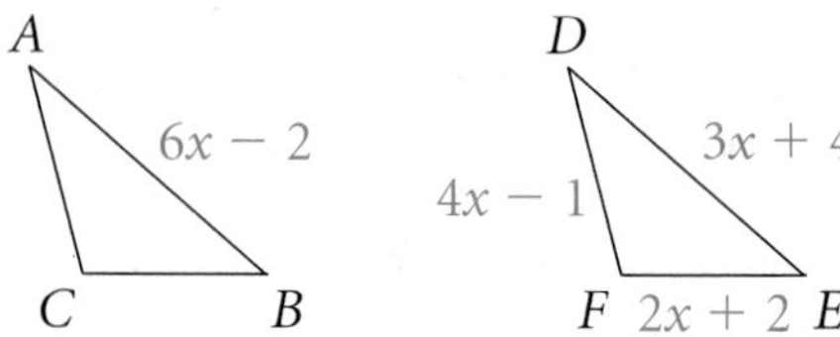

Solve each equation. Check your answers.

44. $2n - 5 = 8n + 7$
45. $3x + 4 = x + 18$
46. $3b + 5 - b = 4b$
47. $5a - 14 = -5 + 8a$
48. $4 - 6d = d + 4$
49. $-10t + 6.25 = t + 11.75$
50. $4x - 10 = x + 3x - 2x$
51. $6x = 4(x + 5)$
52. $\frac{3}{2}z - 2 = -\frac{5}{4}z - 4$

53. **Standardized Test Prep** Compare the quantities in Column A and Column B. Which statement is true for all values of x?

Column A	Column B
$5(x - 3)$	$7x - 12 - (2x + 3)$

A. The quantity in Column A is greater.
B. The quantity in Column B is greater.
C. The quantities are equal.
D. The relationship cannot be determined from the given information.

Exercises MIXED REVIEW

Solve and check each equation.

54. $-\frac{12}{14} = \frac{-9}{m}$
55. $\frac{1}{3}(h - 5) = -11$
56. $2x = 7x + 10$
57. $\frac{w}{7} = \frac{11}{10}$

58. **Money** The sales tax in Austin, Texas, is 8%. How much would you pay for three \$12 books and two \$15 books in Austin?

Getting Ready for Lesson 4-3

Simplify.

59. $|15|$
60. $|-12|$
61. $|-34|$
62. $|18 - 12|$
63. $|9 + 2|$
64. $|-12 - (-12)|$
65. $-|-19|$
66. $-|32|$
67. $-|-10 + 8|$

SELF ASSESSMENT
FOR YOUR JOURNAL
Summarize what you know about solving equations with variables on both sides by writing a list of steps for solving this type of equation.

Math ToolboX

Technology

Using Graphs to Solve or Check Equations

After Lesson 4-2

You can use a graphing calculator to solve equations with variables on both sides. When you graph each side of an equation separately, the x-coordinate of the point where the graphs meet gives the solution to the equation.

Example

Find the solution of $-\frac{1}{2}c = \frac{1}{2}c + 5$ using a graphing calculator.

STEP 1: Press [Y=] to go to the equation screen. Press [CLEAR] to clear the first equation. Then press [(-)] [.] [5] [X,T,θ] to enter the left-hand side of the equation.

STEP 2: Press the down arrow once. Press [CLEAR]. Then press [.] [5] [X,T,θ] [+] [5] to enter the right-hand side of the equation.

STEP 3: Press [GRAPH] to view the graphs of the equations.

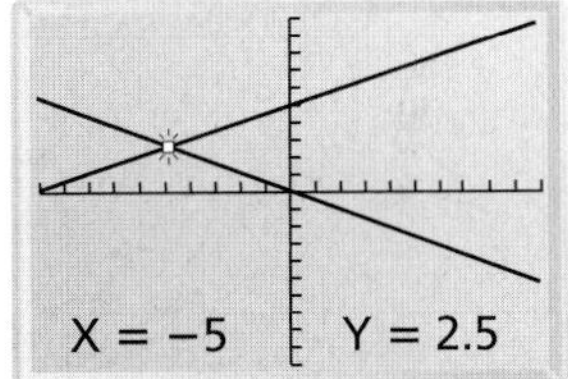

STEP 4: Press [2nd] [CALC] [5]. Move the cursor near the point of intersection. Press [ENTER] three times to find the coordinates of the intersection point.

The x-coordinate of the point of intersection is -5. The solution of the equation $-\frac{1}{2}c = \frac{1}{2}c + 5$ is -5.

1. The graphing calculator screen at the right shows the solution of $2x - 1 = x + 1$.
   a. What two equations were graphed?
   b. What is the x-coordinate of the point where the graphs intersect?
   c. What is the solution of the equation?

2. David solved $3(a + 1) = 5a + 4$. His solution was $-\frac{3}{2}$. Graph $y = 3(x + 1)$ and $y = 5x + 4$. Use the [CALC] feature to find the x-coordinate of the intersection of the two lines. Is David's solution correct? Explain.

Use your graphing calculator to solve each equation.

3. $3d - 9 = 0$ **4.** $2n - 5 = 8n + 7$ **5.** $2x - 15 = 3(x - 15)$ **6.** $4 - 7q = -3$

Use your graphing calculator to check each solution.

7. $5(n + 1) = n + 2; \frac{1}{4}$ **8.** $2x - 9 = -3(x - 6); 5\frac{2}{5}$ **9.** $b - 0 = -2(b + 1); 3\frac{2}{3}$

10. **Writing** Explain the significance of the y-value of the point of intersection. (*Hint:* Use a pencil and paper to solve an equation and check the solution.)

4-3 Solving Absolute Value Equations

What You'll Learn

- Solving equations that involve absolute value
- Using absolute value equations to model real-world problems

...And Why

To solve problems involving opinion polls and quality control

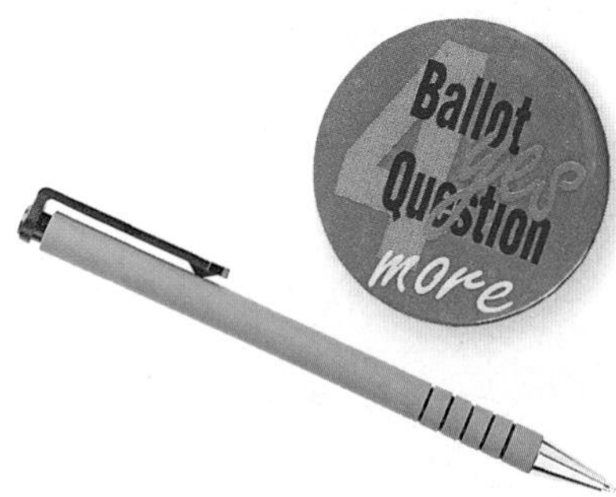

WORK TOGETHER

Math in the Media Work with a partner to answer these questions.

1. The actual results could vary from the poll results by –3% to +3%.
   a. What is the greatest percent of voters who might vote for Blake?
   b. What is the least percent of voters who might vote for Cortez?
2. According to this poll, can Cortez get a majority of the votes? Explain.
3. **Open-ended** Write a short news article that includes numbers and a range around the numbers. (The article does not have to include percents and should not be about elections.)

Poll Shows Cortez Leading

A telephone poll of likely voters in the senate race was conducted by this newspaper and radio station KLRW. The poll shows that Maria Cortez has 49% of the vote, James Blake has 42%, and 9% of those polled are undecided. The results are accurate to within 3%.

THINK AND DISCUSS

Solving Absolute Value Equations

Situations involving a range of numbers can often be represented by absolute value equations. You can use a number line and the definition of absolute value to solve these equations.

QUICK REVIEW

The *absolute value* of a number is its distance from 0 on a number line. The symbol for the absolute value of *a* is $|a|$.

An absolute value is either zero or a positive number.

Example 1

Use a number line to solve $|m| = 2.5$.

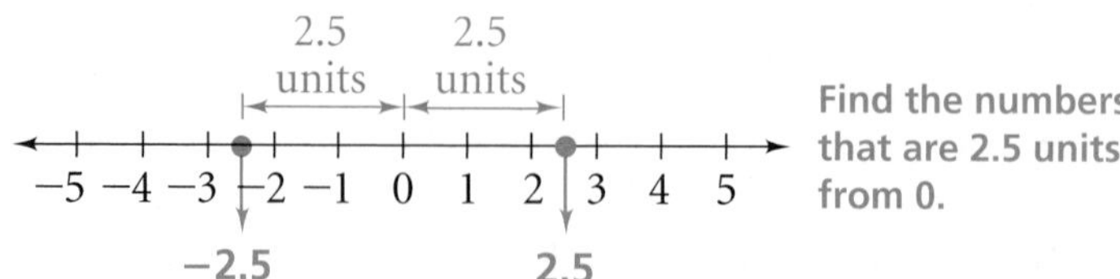

The solution is -2.5 or 2.5.

4. **Try This** Use a number line to solve each equation.
   a. $|b| = 2$ b. $4 = |y|$ c. $|w| = 4.5$
5. Explain how the equations $|x| = 5$ and $x = |5|$ are different.

6. **Critical Thinking** Is there a solution for $|m| = -3$? Explain.

7. For what value of a does the equation $|x| = a$ have just one solution?

You can use the properties of equality to solve an absolute value equation. Remember that you must get the absolute value by itself on one side of the equation.

Example 2

Solve $|x| + 5 = 11$.

$$|x| + 5 = 11$$
$$|x| + 5 - 5 = 11 - 5 \quad \leftarrow \text{Subtract 5 from each side.}$$
$$|x| = 6$$
$$x = 6 \text{ or } x = -6 \quad \leftarrow \text{The value of } x \text{ is either 6 or } -6.$$

The solution is 6 or -6.

Check both solutions.

$$|x| + 5 = 11$$
$$|-6| + 5 \stackrel{?}{=} 11 \quad \text{or} \quad |6| + 5 \stackrel{?}{=} 11 \quad \leftarrow \text{Substitute 6 and } -6 \text{ for } x.$$
$$6 + 5 = 11 \checkmark \qquad 6 + 5 = 11 \checkmark$$

8. What happens when you try to solve $|x| + 11 = 5$? Explain.

9. **Try This** Solve each equation.
   a. $3 = |w| - 4$ **b.** $4|n| = 32$ **c.** $-6 = \frac{|x|}{-2}$ **d.** $|x| - 5 = -9$

Sometimes the absolute value expression has more than one term. You can use what you know about absolute value to write and solve two equations. The solutions of both equations are solutions of the absolute value equation.

Example 3

Read the article from the Work Together again. The equation $|p - 9| = 3$ represents the maximum and minimum percent of people in the election poll who are undecided. Solve the equation.

$$|p - 9| = 3 \quad \leftarrow \text{The value of the expression } p - 9 \text{ is 3 or } -3.$$
$$p - 9 = 3 \quad \text{or} \quad p - 9 = -3 \quad \leftarrow \text{Write two equations.}$$
$$p - 9 + 9 = 3 + 9 \qquad p - 9 + 9 = -3 + 9$$
$$p = 12 \qquad p = 6$$

Anywhere from 6% to 12% of the voters polled are undecided.

Check both solutions.

$$|p - 9| = 3$$
$$|12 - 9| \stackrel{?}{=} 3 \quad \text{or} \quad |6 - 9| \stackrel{?}{=} 3 \quad \leftarrow \text{Substitute 12 and 6 for } p.$$
$$|3| = 3 \checkmark \qquad |-3| = 3 \checkmark$$

10. Try This Solve and check. If there is no solution, explain why.

a. $|c - 2| = 6$ **b.** $-5.5 = |t + 2|$ **c.** $|x + 8| = 5$

d. $|7d| = 14$ **e.** $12.9 = |3b|$ **f.** $-6 = |x - 1|$

Modeling by Writing Equations

To maintain quality, a manufacturer sets limits for how much an item can vary from its specifications. You can use an absolute value equation to model a quality-control situation.

Example 4 **Relating to the Real World** 

Manufacturing The ideal diameter of a cylindrical machine part is 12.000 mm. At the factory that makes the parts, the quality control inspector is told that the actual diameter can vary from the ideal by at most 0.017 mm. Find the maximum and minimum diameters of the part.

Define d = actual diameter in mm of the cylindrical part

Relate greatest difference between actual and ideal is 0.017 mm

Write $|d - 12.000| = 0.017$

$|d - 12.000| = 0.017$ ← The value of the expression $d - 12.000$ is 0.017 or −0.017.

$d - 12.000 = 0.017$ or $d - 12.000 = -0.017$ ← Write two equations.

$d = 12.017$ or $d = 11.983$

The maximum diameter is 12.017 mm and the minimum is 11.983 mm.

PROBLEM SOLVING

Look Back Show how you could find the maximum and minimum diameters by sketching the situation.

11. a. Critical Thinking To solve the problem in Example 4, Mei wrote the equation $|d - 0.017| = 12.000$ and got the solution $d = 12.017$ or $d = -11.983$. Why is this solution not reasonable?

b. How would you explain why her original equation was incorrect?

Exercises ON YOUR OWN

Evaluate each expression.

1. $|x + 4|$ for $x = -1$ **2.** $|x - 7|$ for $x = -4$ **3.** $|8 - 2x|$ for $x = 3$ **4.** $|x| + 4$ for $x = 1$

5. $2|x|$ for $x = -3$ **6.** $|-3x|$ for $x = 2$ **7.** $6 - |x|$ for $x = -10$ **8.** $-|x|$ for $x = 7$

9. Open-ended Use each of the symbols $|\ |$, x, 5, 3, −12, +, and = to write an absolute value equation. Then solve your equation.

10. a. Graphing Calculator Graph $y = 3|x| - 2$ and $y = 8$.

b. Use the CALC feature of the calculator to identify the x-coordinates of the points where the graphs intersect.

c. What absolute value equation have you solved?

Solve and check each equation. If there is no solution, explain.

11. $|n| - 8 = -2$
12. $\frac{|v|}{-3} = -4.2$
13. $|a + \frac{1}{2}| = 3\frac{1}{2}$
14. $3 = |u| + 9$
15. $|r - 8| = 5$
16. $|t| + 7 = 4.5$
17. $9 = |c + 7|$
18. $|n - 4| = 0$
19. $|m + 2| - 4 = 3$
20. $21 = |2d| + 3$
21. $|5p| = 3.6$
22. $3|v - 5| = 12$

Write an absolute value equation for each solution graphed below.

23. −4 −2 0 2 4

24. −1 0 1

25. 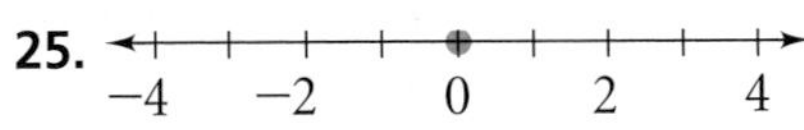

26. **Polling** One poll reported that 53% of county residents favored building a recreation center. The polling service stated that this poll was accurate to within 4.5%. Use an absolute value equation to find the minimum and maximum percents of county residents who are in favor of building a recreation center.

27. **Writing** Describe how solving $3|c| - 4 = 9$ is similar to solving $3c - 4 = 9$ and how it is different.

28. **Critical Thinking** For what values of a and b will the equation $|x - a| = b$ have exactly one solution?

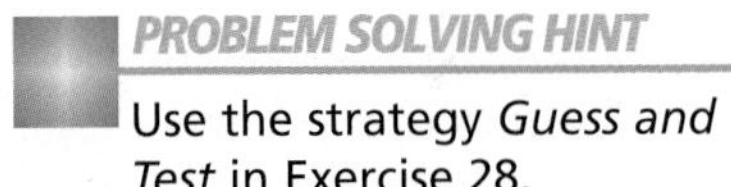

PROBLEM SOLVING HINT

Use the strategy *Guess and Test* in Exercise 28.

Write *true* or *false* for each statement. Justify your response.

29. If $|q + 4| = -1$, there is no solution.
30. If $|h| + 9 = 4$, then $h = 5$ or $h = -5$.
31. If $|3 + z| = 3$, then $z = -3$ or $z = 0$.
32. If $|6 - s| = 0$, then $s = 0$.

Mental Math **Solve each equation. If there is no solution, explain.**

33. $|b| = 12$
34. $|x| = 8$
35. $|m + 48| = 0$
36. $-2 = |b|$
37. $|n| - 3 = 7$
38. $|z| + 5 = 1$
39. $|2m| = 18$
40. $|b| - 10 = -1$

41. **Meteorology** A meteorologist reported that the previous day's temperatures varied 14°F from the normal temperature of 25°F. What were the maximum and minimum temperatures on the previous day?

42. **Manufacturing** A box of crackers should weigh 454 g. The quality control inspector weighs every twentieth box. The inspector sends back any box that is not within 5 g of the ideal weight.
    a. Write an absolute value equation for this situation.
    b. What are the minimum and maximum weights allowed?

43. a. **Banking** To check that there are 40 nickels in a roll, a bank weighs the roll and allows for an error of 0.015 oz in the total weight. What are the maximum and minimum acceptable weights if the wrapper weighs 0.05 oz?
    b. **Critical Thinking** If the roll weighs exactly 7.25 oz, can you be certain that all the coins are acceptable? Explain.

44. *Standardized Test Prep* Compare the quantities in Column A and Column B. Which statement is true for all numbers t?

Column A	Column B
$\|t - 4\|$	$\|4 - t\|$

A. The quantity in Column A is greater.
B. The quantity in Column B is greater.
C. The two quantities are equal.
D. The relationship cannot be determined from the information given.

Exercises MIXED REVIEW

Solve and check each equation.

45. $-3c + 7 = 25$ **46.** $\frac{1}{2}y = y - 6$ **47.** $9d + 3.5 = 2d$

48. $4x - 5 = \frac{2}{3}(6x + 3)$ **49.** $9.2t = 6.3t - 7.25$ **50.** $5.6m + 3.8 = 0.3$

51. Elio earns \$2 per hour more than Ted. They each worked for 5 h. Together they earned a total of \$65. What is each person's pay rate?

Getting Ready for Lesson 4-4

52. *Geometry* Explain how you can use the formula $C = \pi d$ to find the diameter of a tree without cutting down the tree.

53. *Geometry* The formula for the area of a rectangle is $A = lw$. A rectangular room is 28 ft long and its area is 672 ft^2. What is its width?

Algebra at Work

Cartographer

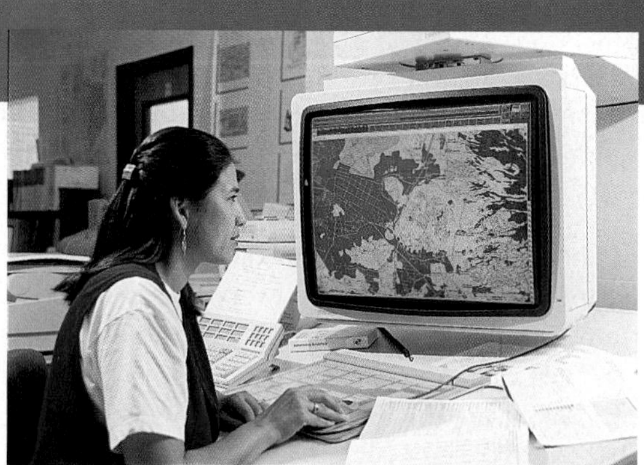

A cartographer, or map maker, makes exact measurements of the area being mapped. The cartographer uses these dimensions to create the scale of the map, showing the ratio of map distance to actual distance. Knowing the scale of a map means that you can use a proportion to calculate any distance on the map.

Mini Project: Find two maps of the same area that use different scales. Choose several points that are on both maps. Calculate the actual distance between each pair of points on both maps. Are the distances the same? What could account for any differences you find? Write a paragraph detailing your conclusions. Include the maps and your calculations.

What You'll Learn

- Using formulas to solve real-world problems
- Solving a literal equation for one of its variables

...And Why

To transform formulas for real-world situations, such as sports, wage, and temperature problems

4-4 Transforming Formulas

THINK AND DISCUSS

A formula shows the relationship between two or more variables. You can transform a formula to describe one quantity in terms of the others.

Example 1 Relating to the Real World 

Sports Suppose a track coach wants to calculate the average speed of each track team member for an event. Transform the formula $d = rt$ to find a formula for the average speed r in terms of distance and time.

$$d = rt$$

$$\frac{d}{t} = \frac{rt}{t} \quad \leftarrow \text{Divide each side by } t,\ t \neq 0.$$

$$\frac{d}{t} = r \quad \leftarrow \text{Simplify.}$$

The formula for average speed is $r = \frac{d}{t}$.

PROBLEM SOLVING

Look Back What property of equality was used to transform $d = rt$ into $r = \frac{d}{t}$?

1. In 1994, Sevetheda Fynes took first place at the New England Track and Field Championships. Shown at the right, she ran 200 m in 23.10 s. Find her average speed.

Example 2 Relating to the Real World 

Science The formula $C = \frac{5}{9}(F - 32)$ gives the Celsius temperature C in terms of the Fahrenheit temperature F. Transform the formula to find Fahrenheit temperature in terms of Celsius temperature.

$$C = \frac{5}{9}(F - 32)$$

$$\frac{9}{5} \cdot C = \frac{9}{5} \cdot \frac{5}{9}(F - 32) \quad \leftarrow \text{Multiply each side by } \tfrac{9}{5}.$$

$$\frac{9}{5}C = F - 32 \quad \leftarrow \text{Simplify.}$$

$$\frac{9}{5}C + 32 = F - 32 + 32 \quad \leftarrow \text{Add 32 to each side.}$$

$$\frac{9}{5}C + 32 = F \quad \leftarrow \text{Simplify.}$$

The formula for Fahrenheit temperature is $F = \frac{9}{5}C + 32$.

PROBLEM SOLVING

Look Back Show how you can solve $C = \frac{5}{9}(F - 32)$ for F if you start by applying the distributive property to the right side of the formula.

2. The highest temperature ever recorded in the state of Oklahoma occurred in Tishomingo on July 26, 1943, when the temperature reached 49°C. Find the equivalent Fahrenheit temperature.

Example 3 Relating to the Real World 

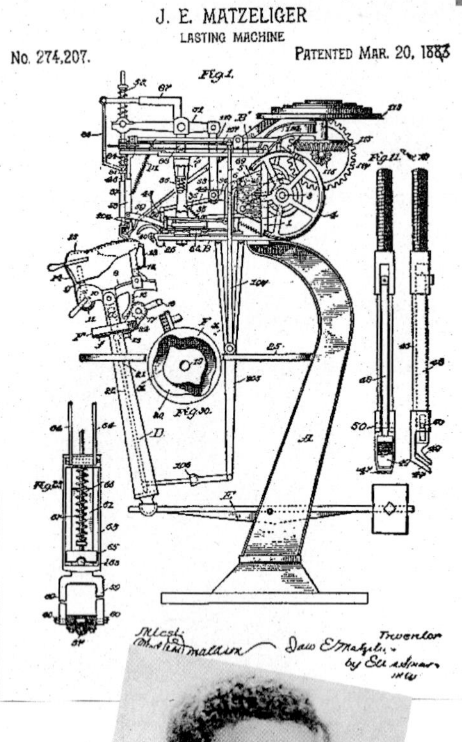

J. E. MATZELIGER
LASTING MACHINE
No. 274,207.
PATENTED MAR. 20, 1883

History In 1883, Jan Matzeliger invented the shoe-lasting machine to attach the upper part of a shoe to its sole. Before that, each shoe was assembled and sewn by hand. Wages were calculated using this formula.

hourly wage in \$ ⟶ $w = (0.34)(\frac{p}{t})$ ⟵ price in \$ of a pair of shoes; ⟵ time in minutes to assemble

Transform the formula to find the price of a pair of shoes in terms of the worker's hourly wage and the time needed to assemble the shoe.

$$w = (0.34)(\tfrac{p}{t})$$

$$w \cdot t = (0.34)(\tfrac{p}{t}) \cdot t$$ ⟵ Multiply each side by t.

$$wt = 0.34p$$ ⟵ Simplify.

$$\frac{wt}{0.34} = \frac{0.34p}{0.34}$$ ⟵ Divide each side by 0.34.

$$\frac{wt}{0.34} = p$$ ⟵ Simplify.

You can use the formula $p = \frac{wt}{0.34}$ to find the price of a pair of shoes.

3. **Try This** Transform the formula $w = (0.34)\frac{p}{t}$ to find a formula for time in terms of hourly wage and price.

4. In 1891 a worker who used the shoe-lasting machine could assemble one pair of shoes in two minutes and earned \$.16/h. What was the price of a pair of shoes in 1891?

Who? Jan Matzeliger (1852–1889) immigrated to the United States and worked in a shoe factory in Lynn, Massachusetts.

A **literal equation** is an equation involving two or more variables. Formulas are special types of literal equations. You solve for one variable in terms of the others when you transform a literal equation.

Example 4

Solve $ax + b = c$ for x in terms of a, b, and c.

$$ax + b = c$$

$$ax + b - b = c - b$$ ⟵ Subtract b from each side.

$$ax = c - b$$ ⟵ Simplify.

$$\frac{ax}{a} = \frac{c - b}{a}$$ ⟵ Divide each side by a, $a \neq 0$.

$$x = \frac{c - b}{a}$$ ⟵ Simplify.

5. **Critical Thinking** Describe the approach you would use to solve each equation for m.
   a. $2n = 7(3 - m)$ b. $\frac{m - 5}{6} = -3x$ c. $\frac{2}{3}(2m + 4) = 9y$

6. Explain why you did or did not use the distributive property in each equation in Question 5.

Exercises ON YOUR OWN

Solve each equation for the given variable.

1. $3r + 4 = s; r$
2. $c = \frac{d}{g}; g$
3. $\frac{m}{n} = \frac{p}{q}; p$
4. $ax + by = c; y$
5. $C = 2\pi r; r$
6. $5x - 2y = -6; y$
7. $3m = 2(4 + t); t$
8. $y = 3(t - s); s$

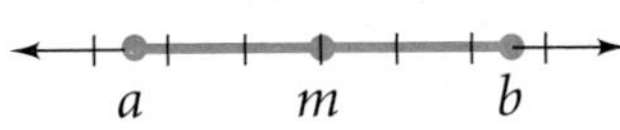

9. **Geometry** Suppose a and b are the coordinates of the endpoints of a line segment. To find the midpoint of the segment, you can use the formula $m = \frac{a + b}{2}$.
   a. Find the midpoint of a segment with endpoints 8.2 and 3.5.
   b. Transform the formula to find b in terms of a and m.
   c. Find the missing endpoint of a segment starting at –1.7 that has midpoint 2.1. Use the transformed formula from part (b).

Solve each equation for the given variable.

10. $x + y = 20; y$
11. $4m - n = 6; n$
12. $2(t + r) = 5; t$
13. $z - a = y; z$
14. $\pi = \frac{C}{d}; d$
15. $\frac{a}{2} = \frac{b}{7}; b$
16. $\frac{a + b}{c} = \frac{d}{4}; a$
17. $A = \frac{1}{2}bh; b$
18. $dx = c; x$
19. $V = lwh; h$
20. $V = \frac{1}{3}\pi r^2 h; h$
21. $|ap - b| = r; p$

22. a. **Travel** Manuel plans to drive to an amusement park. He will travel 121 mi on the highway at an average speed of 55 mi/h. Transform the formula $d = rt$ to find a formula for time.
    b. How much time does Manuel need for this part of his trip?

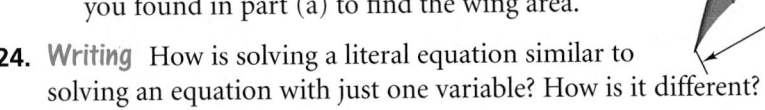

23. a. **Recreation** The aspect ratio of a hang glider measures its ability to glide and soar. The formula $R = \frac{s^2}{A}$ gives the aspect ratio R for a glider with wingspan s and wing area A. Solve this formula for A.
    b. Suppose you want to design a glider with a 9-ft wingspan and an aspect ratio of 3. Use the formula you found in part (a) to find the wing area.

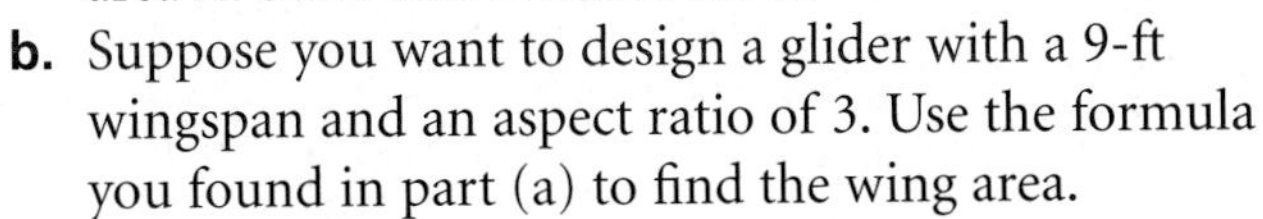

24. **Writing** How is solving a literal equation similar to solving an equation with just one variable? How is it different?

25. **Open-ended** Write an equation using more than one variable. Solve the equation for each variable. Show all your steps.

26. a. **Banking** The formula $I = prt$ gives the amount of simple interest I earned by principal p at an annual interest rate r over t years. Solve this formula for p.
    b. Find p if $r = 0.035$, $t = 4$, and $I = \$420$. Write a sentence to explain the meaning of your answer.

27. a. Solve $2y + x = 4$ for y.
    b. **Graphing Calculator** Graph the equation you found in part (a).
    c. Use your graph and the TABLE feature of the calculator to find y when $x = 3$, $x = 4$, and $x = 5$.

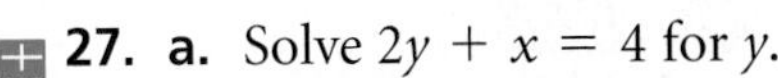

Chapter Project

Find Out by Solving

The volume of air an adult's lungs can hold decreases with age. The formula $V = 0.104h - 0.018a - 2.69$ estimates air volume V (in liters) of a person's lungs for someone of height h inches and age a years.

- Estimate your own lung volume. Then find 90% of your lung volume.
- Solve the formula for age a. Estimate how old you will be when your air volume is 90% of its current value. (Use your current height.)
- Substitute your current height for h in the original formula. Then graph the function to show how air volume changes as age increases.

Exercises MIXED REVIEW

28. 2.8 is what percent of 3.5? **29.** 70 is $12\frac{1}{2}$% of what number? **30.** What is 17% of 123?

31. a. Earnings Suppose you earn \$5.75/h and you work 12 h during one week. What are your earnings for the week?

b. Write an equation that a worker paid hourly can use to find his or her earnings. Explain what each variable represents.

Getting Ready for Lesson 4-5

Complete each statement with <, =, or >.

32. $-3 \blacksquare -5$ **33.** $4.8 \blacksquare 4.29$ **34.** $-1 - 2 \blacksquare 6 - 9$ **35.** $-\frac{3}{4} \blacksquare -\frac{4}{5}$ **36.** $\frac{1}{2} + \frac{1}{2} \blacksquare \frac{1}{3} + \frac{1}{3}$

Exercises CHECKPOINT

Solve for the given variable.

1. $s = n - 90; n$ **2.** $y = mx + b; b$ **3.** $L = \frac{2b^2}{a}; a$ **4.** $W = fd; f$

Solve and check each equation. If there is no solution, explain.

5. $\frac{6}{30} = \frac{m}{84}$ **6.** $-4(t + 1) = 4 - 4t$ **7.** $|x| = -7$ **8.** $8w = 6w$

9. $|n| + 2 = 10$ **10.** $y + 21 = 4y - 8$ **11.** $5(2w - 4) = 6w$ **12.** $|y - 4.5| = 3$

13. Maps The scale on a map is 3 cm : 10 km. On the map, the distance between two cities is 5.2 cm. What is the actual distance?

14. Geometry $P = 2l + 2w$ gives the perimeter P of a rectangle of length l and width w. Suppose a rectangle has perimeter 14.48 cm and length 4.16 cm. Which key sequence could you use to find the width?

A. 2 [×] 14.48 [+] 2 [×] 4.16 [ENTER]
B. 14.48 [−] 2 [×] 4.16 [÷] 2 [ENTER]
C. [(] 14.48 [−] 2 [×] 4.16 [)] [÷] 2 [ENTER]
D. [(] 2 [×] 4.16 [−] 14.48 [)] [÷] 2 [ENTER]

What You'll Learn

- Using addition and subtraction to solve one-step inequalities
- Using inequalities to model real-world problems

...And Why

To solve inequalities that model real-world situations such as checking accounts

QUICK REVIEW

$<$ is less than
$\leq$ is less than or equal to
$>$ is greater than
$\geq$ is greater than or equal to
$\neq$ is not equal to

4-5 Solving Inequalities Using Addition and Subtraction

WORK TOGETHER

Work with a partner.

1. Define a variable and write an inequality for each sign.

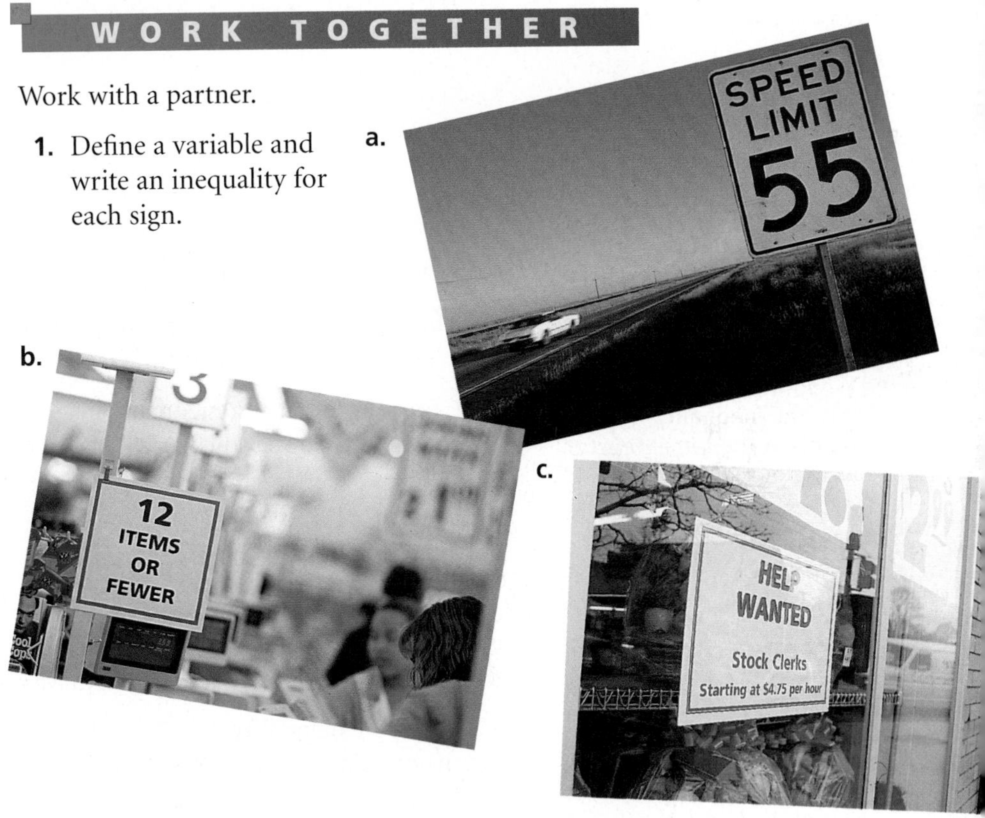

2. Define a variable and write an inequality for each situation.
   a. Persons under 17 are not admitted.
   b. Visibility at the airport is less than two miles.
   c. You must be more than 36 in. tall to ride an amusement park ride.
3. *Open-ended* Describe three other situations that involve inequalities. Write an inequality for each situation.

THINK AND DISCUSS

Graphing and Writing Inequalities

Some inequalities contain a variable. Any value of the variable that makes the inequality true is called a **solution of the inequality.** The solutions of the inequality $x < 3$ are all the numbers less than 3.

4. Tell whether each number is a solution of $x < 3$.
   a. 1 b. -7.3 c. 9.004 d. 0 e. 3

The number lines show the solutions of $x < 3$ along with the graphs of three other inequalities comparing x and 3.

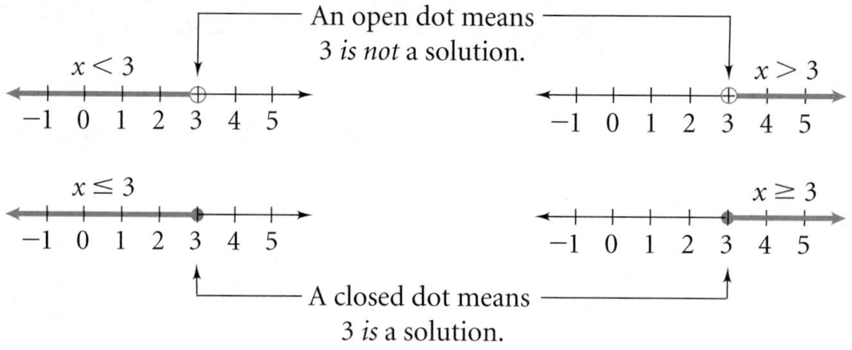

An open dot means
3 *is not* a solution.
x < 3
x > 3
−1 0 1 2 3 4 5
x ≤ 3
x ≥ 3
−1 0 1 2 3 4 5
A closed dot means
3 *is* a solution.

5. Explain how the inequality $x < 3$ is different from the equation $x = 3$.

6. *Critical Thinking* Describe how you can display the solutions of the inequality $x \neq 3$ on a number line.

PROBLEM SOLVING HINT

When the variable is on the left, the inequality symbol points in the same direction as the graph.

7. You can rewrite an inequality like $4 > n$ as $n < 4$. Rewrite each inequality so that the variable is on the left, then graph the solutions.

a. $2 < x$ **b.** $-5 \geq b$ **c.** $0 \leq r$

Using Addition to Solve Inequalities

The solutions of an inequality like $x < 3$ are easy to recognize. To solve some other inequalities, you may need to find a simpler, equivalent inequality. **Equivalent inequalities** have the same set of solutions.

Consider the inequality $-4 < 1$. The number line shows what happens when you add 2 to each side of the inequality.

$$-4 < 1$$
$$-4 + 2 < 1 + 2$$
$$-2 < 3$$

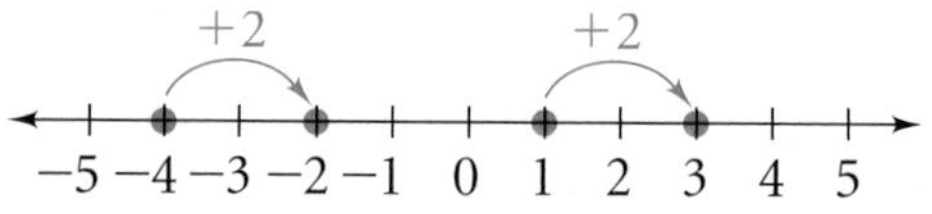

+2
+2
−5 −4 −3 −2 −1 0 1 2 3 4 5

Notice that addition does not change the relationship between the numbers or the direction of the inequality symbol.

Addition Property of Inequality

For all real numbers a, b, and c, if $a > b$, then $a + c > b + c$.

Example: $5 > -1$, so $5 + 2 > -1 + 2$

For all real numbers a, b, and c, if $a < b$, then $a + c < b + c$.

Example: $-4 < 1$, so $-4 + 2 < 1 + 2$

8. What number would you add to both sides of each inequality to get a simpler, equivalent inequality?

a. $x + 3 > -2$ **b.** $0 < -\frac{4}{3} + g$ **c.** $1.6 \geq z - 4.3$

You can use the Addition Property of Inequality to solve inequalities.

Example 1

Solve $x - 3 < 5$. Graph the solutions on a number line.

$$x - 3 < 5$$
$$x - 3 + 3 < 5 + 3 \quad \leftarrow \text{Add 3 to each side.}$$
$$x < 8 \quad \leftarrow \text{Combine like terms.}$$

The solutions are all numbers less than 8.

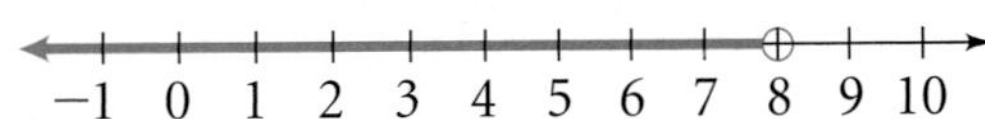

9. a. Substitute a number greater than 8 for x in the inequality $x - 3 < 5$. Is your result true?
   b. Substitute 8 for x in the inequality $x - 3 < 5$. Is your result true?
   c. Substitute a number less than 8 for x in the inequality $x - 3 < 5$. Is your result true?
   d. Parts (a), (b), and (c) can serve as a check for Example 1. **Generalize** the steps you can use to check the solutions of an inequality.

10. a. **Try This** Solve the inequality $f - 2 > -4$. Graph the solutions on a number line.
    b. Use the steps from Question 9, part (d), to check your work.

Using Subtraction to Solve Inequalities

Just as you can add the same number to each side of an inequality, you can subtract the same number from each side. The order, or direction, of the inequality is not changed.

Subtraction Property of Inequality

For all real numbers a, b, and c, if $a > b$, then $a - c > b - c$.

Example: $3 > -1$, so $3 - 2 > -1 - 2$

For all real numbers a, b, and c, if $a < b$, then $a - c < b - c$.

Example: $-5 < 4$, so $-5 - 2 < 4 - 2$

11. Solve and check the inequality $y + 2 < -6$. Graph the solutions on a number line.

12. What number would you subtract from both sides of each inequality to get a simpler, equivalent inequality?

    a. $w + 2 > -1$ b. $8 < \frac{5}{3} + r$ c. $5.7 \geq k - 3.1$

You can use inequalities to model real-world problems.

Example 2 ***Relating to the Real World*** 

Banking The First National Bank offers free checking for accounts with a balance of at least \$500. Suppose you have a balance of \$516.46 and you write the check at the left. How much must you deposit to avoid being charged a service fee?

Define d = the amount you must deposit

Relate	current balance	minus ↓	amount of check	plus ↓	amount of deposit	is at least	\$500 ↓
Write	516.46	−	31.50	+	d	≥	500

$516.46 - 31.50 + d \geq 500$

$484.96 + d \geq 500$ ← Combine like terms.

$484.96 + d - 484.96 \geq 500 - 484.96$ ← Subtract 484.96 from each side.

$d \geq 15.04$ ← Simplify.

You must deposit at least \$15.04 in your account.

13. **a.** Check the answer to Example 2 by choosing three values and checking the values in the original inequality.
b. ***Critical Thinking*** Explain why checking the values in the inequality does not guarantee that your solution is correct.

14. Explain how the phrases "at least" and "at most" affect the inequality you write when you model a real-world problem.

Exercises ON YOUR OWN

Define a variable and write an inequality to model each situation.

1. A bus can seat 48 students or fewer.

2. There are over 20 species of crocodiles.

3. In many states, you must be at least 16 years old to obtain a driver's license.

4. At least 350 students attended the dance Friday night.

5. You may not use a light bulb of more than 60 watts in this light fixture.

6. The Navy's flying team, the Blue Angels, makes more than 75 appearances each year.

7. **a.** ***Group Activity*** Write an inequality for the tiles shown.
b. Add four positive tiles to each side. Write an inequality for the tiles.
c. Use the original set of tiles. Subtract seven positive tiles from each side. Write an inequality to represent the tiles.
d. Show how to use tiles to **verify** the inequality $-5 + 3 > -7 + 3$.
e. ***Open-ended*** Write an inequality you can solve with tiles. Solve the inequality. Show all the steps.

Write four numbers that are solutions of each inequality.

8. $v \geq -5$
9. $0.5 > c$
10. $2 + q < -7$
11. $f - 10 \leq 16$
12. $5 > 4 - z$

Tell what you must do to the first inequality in order to get the second.

13. $36 \leq -4 + y$; $40 \leq y$
14. $9 + b > 24$; $b > 15$
15. $m - \frac{1}{2} < \frac{3}{8}$; $m < \frac{7}{8}$

Write each inequality in words.

16. $n < 5$
17. $b > 0$
18. $x \leq 7$
19. $m \leq -1$
20. $g - 2 < 7$
21. $z \geq -4$

22. **Writing** How is solving an addition or subtraction inequality similar to solving an addition or subtraction equation? How is it different?

23. To earn an A in Ms. Orlando's math class, students must score a total of at least 135 points on the three tests. On the first two tests, Amy's scores were 47 and 48. What is the minimum score she must get on the third test in order to meet the requirement?

24. **Banking** Suppose you must maintain a balance of at least \$750 in your checking account in order to have free checking. The balance in your account is \$814.22 before you write a check for \$25. How much cash can you withdraw from the account and still have free checking?

Solve each inequality. Graph the solutions on a number line.

25. $x - 1 > 10$
26. $w + 4 \leq 9$
27. $h + \frac{3}{4} \geq \frac{1}{2}$
28. $-5 > b - 1$
29. $0 \leq x + 1.7$
30. $n - 2\frac{1}{2} > \frac{1}{3}$
31. $3.5 < m - 2$
32. $\frac{3}{2} + k \geq -45$
33. $y - 0.3 < 2.8$
34. $2 < s - 8$
35. $9.4 \leq t - 3.5$
36. $h - \frac{1}{2} \geq -1$
37. $-6 > n - \frac{1}{5}$
38. $8 + b < 1$
39. $-7.7 \neq x - 2$
40. $a + 3 \geq 2.7$
41. $c + \frac{1}{2} \neq 3\frac{2}{7}$
42. $f - 2.3 \leq -1.21$
43. $\frac{3}{2} + g \leq \frac{1}{3}$
44. $0 > k - 2\frac{3}{5}$
45. $7.5 + y < 13$
46. $-1.4 + s + 2.1 > 11$
47. $-7\frac{3}{4} + m + \frac{1}{2} \leq -2\frac{1}{4}$
48. $\frac{2}{3} + t - \frac{5}{6} \neq 0$

49. a. **Open-ended** Use the inequality symbols $<$, $\leq$, $>$, and $\geq$ to write four addition or subtraction inequalities.
    b. Solve each of the inequalities in part (a) and graph the solutions on separate number lines.

50. **Critical Thinking** Sam says that he can solve $z - 8.6 \leq 5.2$ by replacing z with 13, 14, and 15. When $z = 13$, the inequality is false. When $z = 14$ and $z = 15$, the inequality is true. So Sam says that the solution is $z \geq 14$ Is his reasoning correct? **Justify** your answer.

51. **Standardized Test Prep** If $x - y > 0$, which expression(s) must equal $|x - y|$? Choose A, B, C, D, or E.
    I. $x - y$ II. $-(x - y)$ III. $|y - x|$
    A. I and II only B. II and III only C. III only D. I, II, and III E. I and III only

Statistics **Use the bar graph about education.**

52. Let w represent the average yearly income for women. For what education levels is $w > 22{,}000$ a true statement?

53. Write a single inequality that describes the average income for a man who does not graduate from high school.

54. On average, how much more do men who have at least a bachelor's degree earn than those who have a high school diploma?

55. On average, how much more do women earn per year if they graduate from high school instead of dropping out before 9th grade?

56. At what education level does a woman's average income exceed the average income for a man with no high school education?

57. **Research** Find the average salaries for men and women in a job of your choice. What level of education is necessary to get that job? Write inequalities to compare those salaries with the average salaries for that education level.

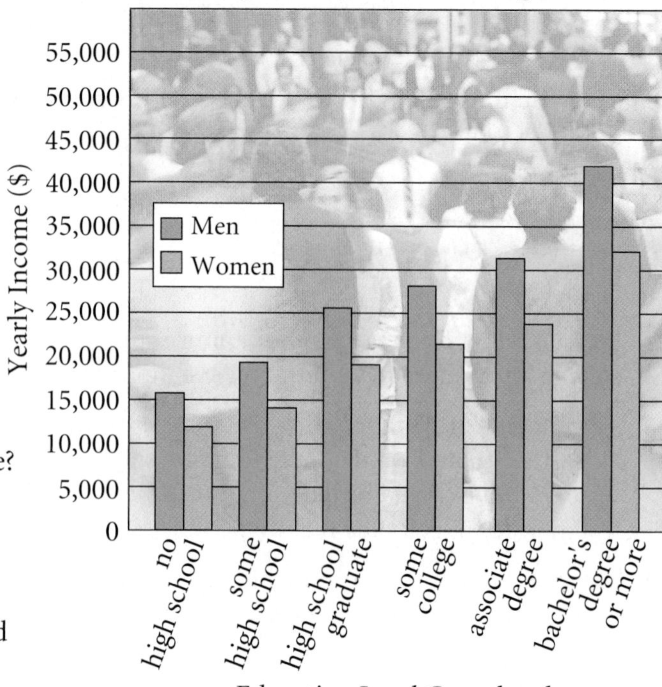

Exercises MIXED REVIEW

Find the sum or difference.

58. $\begin{bmatrix} 2 & 9 & 3 \\ 11 & 5 & 7 \end{bmatrix} + \begin{bmatrix} 18 & 0 & 15 \\ 6 & 12 & 4 \end{bmatrix}$

59. $\begin{bmatrix} -4 & 13 \\ 8 & 1 \end{bmatrix} - \begin{bmatrix} 4 & -5 \\ 10 & -14 \end{bmatrix}$

Solve.

60. $\frac{x}{3} = \frac{8}{24}$

61. $|m + 6| = 5$

62. $\frac{3}{4}k = 15$

63. $|p| - 2 = 10$

64. **Law Enforcement** In 1995, the 108-year-old California State Police became part of the California Highway Patrol. In what year was the California State Police founded?

Getting Ready for Lesson 4-6

65. State the multiplication property of equality and the division property of equality in your own words.

Solve and check each equation.

66. $8 = \frac{1}{2}t$

67. $14 = -21x$

68. $\frac{x}{6} = -1$

69. $5d = 32$

70. $0.5w = 4.5$

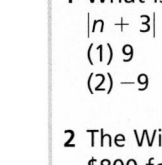

What You'll Learn

- Using multiplication and division to solve one-step inequalities
- Using inequalities to model real-world problems

...And Why

To solve inequalities that model real-world situations such as fundraising

What You'll Need

- calculator

4-6 Solving Inequalities Using Multiplication and Division

WORK TOGETHER

Work with a partner to explore what happens to an inequality when you multiply each side by the same number. Consider the inequality $4 > 1$.

1. Complete each statement by replacing each ■ with $<, >$, or $=$.
2. What happens to the inequality when you multiply it by a positive number? by zero? by a negative number?

$4 \cdot 3$ ■ $1 \cdot 3$
$4 \cdot 2$ ■ $1 \cdot 2$
$4 \cdot 1$ ■ $1 \cdot 1$
$4 \cdot 0$ ■ $1 \cdot 0$
$4 \cdot -1$ ■ $1 \cdot -1$
$4 \cdot -2$ ■ $1 \cdot -2$
$4 \cdot -3$ ■ $1 \cdot -3$

THINK AND DISCUSS

Solving Inequalities Using Multiplication

You can find an equivalent inequality by multiplying or dividing each side of an inequality by the same number. If the number is positive, the order remains the same. If the number is negative, you *reverse* the order.

Multiplication Property of Inequality

For all real numbers a and b, and for $c > 0$:

If $a > b$, then $ac > bc$. If $a < b$, then $ac < bc$.

Examples: $4 > -1$, so $4(5) > -1(5)$
$-6 < 3$, so $-6(5) < 3(5)$

For all real numbers a and b, and for $c < 0$:

If $a > b$, then $ac < bc$. If $a < b$, then $ac > bc$.

Examples: $4 > -1$, so $4(-2) < -1(-2)$
$-6 < 3$, so $-6(-2) > 3(-2)$

3. Consider the inequality $-2 \geq -5$.
   a. What inequality do you get when you multiply each side by 3?
   b. What inequality do you get when you multiply each side by -3?
   c. Explain why the Multiplication Property of Inequality applies to inequalities involving $\geq$ and $\leq$.

NEW YORK MATH A — Math A Test Prep

1 What is the solution of $|n + 3| - 5 = 7$?
(1) 9 (3) -15, 9
(2) -9 (4) -9, 9

2 The Wilson family has \$800 for gas, motel, and food while on vacation. They estimate that they will spend \$200 for gas and \$250 for the motel. Write and solve an inequality to show what they can spend for food.

You can use the Multiplication Property of Inequality to write a simpler, equivalent inequality.

Example 1

Solve $\frac{x}{2} < -1$. Graph the solutions on a number line.

$$\frac{x}{2} < -1$$

$$2\left(\frac{x}{2}\right) < 2(-1) \quad \leftarrow \text{Multiply each side by 2.}$$

$$x < -2 \quad \leftarrow \text{Simplify each side.}$$

The solutions are all numbers less than –2.

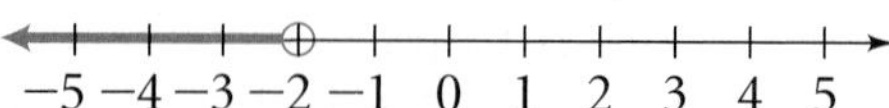

4. Describe the solutions for the inequality $\frac{x}{2} \leq -1$.

5. Jamal solved the inequality $-2 > \frac{y}{3}$ and got $-6 > y$. Erica solved the same inequality and got $y < -6$. Are they both correct? Explain.

Example 2

Solve $-\frac{2}{3}x \geq 2$. Graph the solutions on a number line.

$$-\frac{2}{3}x \geq 2$$

$$\left(-\frac{3}{2}\right)\left(-\frac{2}{3}x\right) \leq \left(-\frac{3}{2}\right)(2) \quad \leftarrow \text{Multiply each side by } -\tfrac{3}{2}\text{. Reverse the order of the inequality.}$$

$$x \leq -3 \quad \leftarrow \text{Simplify each side.}$$

The solutions are all numbers less than or equal to –3.

−6 −5 −4 −3 −2 −1 0 1 2 3 4

PROBLEM SOLVING

Look Back How would the solution be different if the inequality were $\frac{2}{3}x \geq -2$?

6. How can you use substitution to explain to a classmate why the solution to Example 2 cannot be $x \geq -3$?

7. a. **Try This** Solve the inequality $-t < \frac{1}{2}$.
   b. Graph the solution on a number line.
   c. Name four integers that are solutions of the inequality.

Solving Inequalities Using Division

You can use division to simplify and solve inequalities.

8. Consider the inequality $12 > 6$. Make a table to show what happens when you divide each side by the same number.

9. What happens when an inequality is divided by a positive number? by a negative number?

The pattern you see in your table can help you understand the Division Property of Inequality.

Division Property of Inequality

For all real numbers a and b, and for $c > 0$:

If $a > b$, then $\frac{a}{c} > \frac{b}{c}$. If $a < b$, then $\frac{a}{c} < \frac{b}{c}$.

Examples: $6 > -4$, so $\frac{6}{2} > \frac{-4}{2}$ $-2 < 8$, so $\frac{-2}{2} < \frac{8}{2}$

For all real numbers a and b, and for $c < 0$:

If $a > b$, then $\frac{a}{c} < \frac{b}{c}$. If $a < b$, then $\frac{a}{c} > \frac{b}{c}$.

Examples: $6 > -4$, so $\frac{6}{-2} < \frac{-4}{-2}$ $-2 < 8$, so $\frac{-2}{-2} > \frac{8}{-2}$

10. *Critical Thinking* Why can't $c = 0$ in the Multiplication and Division Properties of Inequality?

Example 3 Relating to the Real World 

Community Service The student council is sponsoring a recycling drive to raise money to buy food for a food bank. A case of 12 jars of spaghetti sauce costs $13.50. What is the greatest number of cases of sauce the student council can buy if they collect $216?

Define $c =$ the number of cases of spaghetti sauce

Relate	13.5 ↓	times ↓	the number of cases	is less than or equal to	216 ↓
Write	13.5	$\cdot$	c	$\leq$	216

$$13.5c \leq 216$$

$$\frac{13.5c}{13.5} \leq \frac{216}{13.5} \quad \leftarrow \text{Divide each side by 13.5.}$$

$$c \leq 16 \quad \leftarrow \text{Use a calculator.}$$

The council can buy at most 16 cases of sauce for the food bank.

11. Explain why you use the symbol $\leq$ in the inequality in Example 3.

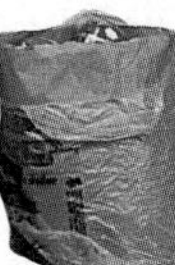

Exercises ON YOUR OWN

1. a. By what number can you divide each side of the inequality $-t \leq 7$ to get $t \geq -7$?
   b. By what number can you multiply each side of the inequality $-m > -3$ to get $m < 3$?

Tell what you must do to the first inequality in order to get the second.

2. $5z > -25; z > -5$
3. $-b \geq 3.4; b \leq -3.4$
4. $-\frac{7}{8}m > \frac{3}{4}; m < -\frac{6}{7}$

Write four numbers that are solutions of each inequality.

5. $v \geq -5$
6. $0.5 > \frac{1}{2}c$
7. $2q < -7$
8. $-3f \leq 16$
9. $\frac{r}{3} \geq -4$
10. $-3.5 < -m$

Replace each ■ with the number that makes the inequalities equivalent.

11. ■$s > 14; s < -7$
12. $x +$ ■ $\geq 25; x \geq -12$
13. $8u \leq$ ■$; u \leq \frac{1}{2}$
14. ■ $> -17 + a; a < -9$
15. $36 <$ ■ $r; r < -3.6$
16. $-k \leq$ ■$; k \geq -7.5$

Solve each inequality. Check your solutions. Graph the solutions on a number line.

17. $-4x \leq -16$
18. $6 < -9g$
19. $\frac{5}{6}x > -5$
20. $-1 \geq \frac{t}{3}$
21. $-1.5d < -8$
22. $-\frac{5}{3}u > 1$

23. **Jobs** Suppose you earn \$5.85 per hour working part time at a dry cleaner. You need to earn at least \$100. How many full hours must you work to earn the money?

24. **Fund-raising** The science club is sponsoring a car wash. At \$2.50 per car, how many cars do they have to wash to earn at least \$300?

25. **Standardized Test Prep** The number line shows the graph of all the solutions of an inequality. Which could *not* be that inequality?

−5 −4 −3 −2 −1 0 1 2

A. $-2x > 4$
B. $-4 > 2x$
C. $-x < 2$
D. $8 < -4x$
E. $-2 > x$

Estimation **Estimate the solution of each inequality.**

26. $-2.099r < 4$
27. $3.87j > -24$
28. $20.95 \geq \frac{1}{2}p$
29. $\frac{20}{39}s \leq -14$

30. **Construction** Swivel desks that each need 20 in. of space are being installed side by side in a new lecture hall. Each row of desks can be no longer than 25 ft. Find the maximum number of desks that will fit in each row.

31. a. Kia solved $-15q \leq 135$ by adding 15 to each side of the inequality. What mistake did she make?
b. **Critical Thinking** Kia's solution was $q \leq 150$. She checked her work by substituting 150 for q in the original problem. Why didn't her check let her know she'd made a mistake?
c. What substitution would have let her know she'd made a mistake? **Justify** your answer.

Solve each inequality. Graph the solutions on a number line.

32. $4d \leq -28$
33. $\frac{u}{7} > 5$
34. $2 < -8s$
35. $\frac{3}{2}k \geq -45$
36. $0.3y < 2.7$
37. $9.4 \leq -4t$
38. $-h \geq 4$
39. $24 < -3x$
40. $\frac{5}{2}x > 5$
41. $0 < -7b$
42. $\frac{5}{6} > -\frac{1}{3}p$
43. $-0.2m \geq 9.4$

44. **Writing** Write a paragraph explaining the Multiplication and Division Properties of Inequality to a classmate.

45. **Remodeling** The Sumaris' den floor measures 18 ft by 15 ft. They want to cover the floor with tiles that cover $\frac{9}{16}$ ft^2.
a. What is the least number of tiles they need to cover the floor?
b. Why might they need more tiles than the answer to part (a)?

46. **Open-ended** Write four different inequalities that you can solve using multiplication or division. Choose your inequalities so that the solution of each inequality is all numbers greater than 3.

Exercises MIXED REVIEW

Solve for y in terms of x.

47. $2x + 3y = 6$
48. $5x - y + 8 = 4$
49. $-5y + 4x = 15$
50. $2x + 3y = -20$

51. a. **Biology** There are approximately 20 million bats in Bracken Cave, Texas. They eat about 250 tons of insects every night. How many tons do they eat in a week?
b. About how much does a single bat eat each night?

Getting Ready for Lesson 4-7

Solve and check each equation.

52. $3(c + 4) = 5$
53. $2x - 7 + 3x + 4 = -25$
54. $5p + 9 = 2p - 1$
55. $7x + 2(8 - x) = 4$
56. $\frac{1}{2}k - \frac{2}{3} + k = \frac{7}{6}$
57. $2t - 32 = \frac{15}{4}t + 1$

4-7 Solving Multi-Step Inequalities

What You'll Learn

- Solving multi-step inequalities and graphing the solutions on a number line
- Using multi-step inequalities to model and solve real-world problems

...And Why

To solve inequalities that model real-world situations such as designing

THINK AND DISCUSS

Solving with Variables on One Side

When you solve equations, sometimes you need to use more than one step. The same is true when you solve inequalities.

Example 1 Relating to the Real World

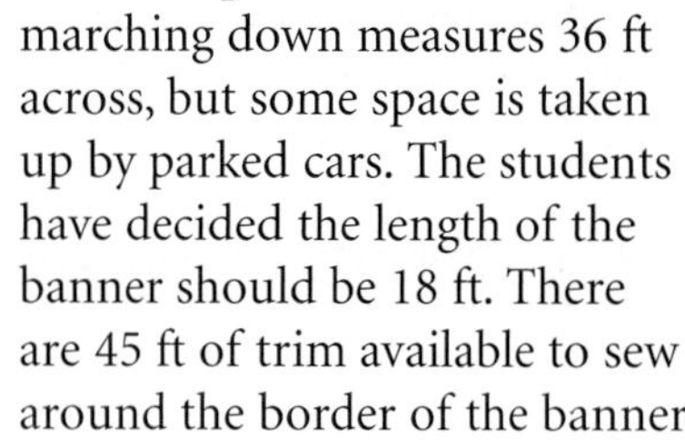

Design A school group needs a banner to carry in a parade. The narrowest street the parade is marching down measures 36 ft across, but some space is taken up by parked cars. The students have decided the length of the banner should be 18 ft. There are 45 ft of trim available to sew around the border of the banner. What is the greatest possible width for the banner?

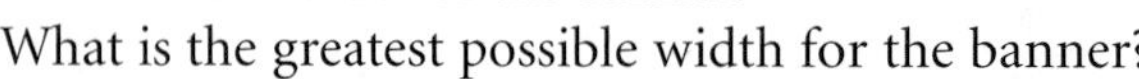

PROBLEM SOLVING HINT

Draw a diagram.

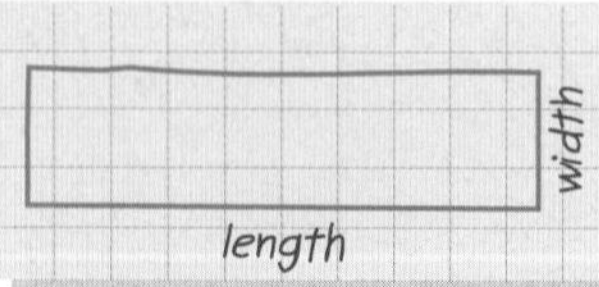

Define w = width of the banner

Relate Since the border goes around the edges of the banner, you can use the perimeter formula: $P = 2l + 2w$.

	twice the length	plus	twice the width	can be no more than	the border
Write	$2(18)$	$+$	$2w$	$\leq$	45

$$2(18) + 2w \leq 45$$
$$36 + 2w \leq 45 \quad \leftarrow \text{Simplify the left side.}$$
$$36 + 2w - 36 \leq 45 - 36 \quad \leftarrow \text{Subtract 36 from each side.}$$
$$2w \leq 9$$
$$\frac{2w}{2} \leq \frac{9}{2} \quad \leftarrow \text{Divide each side by 2.}$$
$$w \leq 4.5$$

The greatest possible width for the banner is 4.5 ft.

1. What could the model $2l + 2w > 45$ mean in the situation described in Example 1?

Sometimes solving an inequality involves the distributive property.

Example 2

Solve $2(w + 2) - 3w \geq -1$. Graph the solutions on a number line.

$$
\begin{aligned}
2(w + 2) - 3w &\geq -1 \\
2w + 4 - 3w &\geq -1 && \leftarrow \text{Use the distributive property.} \\
-1w + 4 &\geq -1 && \leftarrow \text{Combine like terms.} \\
-1w + 4 - 4 &\geq -1 - 4 && \leftarrow \text{Subtract 4 from each side.} \\
-w &\geq -5 && \leftarrow \text{Simplify.} \\
\frac{-w}{-1} &\leq \frac{-5}{-1} && \leftarrow \text{Divide each side by } -1\text{. Reverse the order of the inequality.} \\
w &\leq 5
\end{aligned}
$$

All numbers less than or equal to 5 are solutions.

−1 0 1 2 3 4 5 6 7 8 9

PROBLEM SOLVING

Look Back What happens if you multiply each side of $-1w \geq -5$ by -1?

2. You can check the solutions to Example 2 by substituting values into the inequality $2(w + 2) - 3w \geq -1$.
   a. Use the values 4, 5, and 6. Which values make the inequality true?
   b. Explain how part (a) serves as a check on Example 2.

Solving with Variables on Both Sides

Example 3

Solve $8z - 6 < 3z + 12$. Graph the solutions on a number line.

$$
\begin{aligned}
8z - 6 &< 3z + 12 \\
8z - 6 - 3z &< 3z + 12 - 3z && \leftarrow \text{Subtract } 3z \text{ from each side.} \\
5z - 6 &< 12 && \leftarrow \text{Combine like terms.} \\
5z - 6 + 6 &< 12 + 6 && \leftarrow \text{Add 6 to each side.} \\
5z &< 18 \\
\frac{5z}{5} &< \frac{18}{5} && \leftarrow \text{Divide each side by 5.} \\
z &< 3.6
\end{aligned}
$$

All numbers less than 3.6 are solutions.

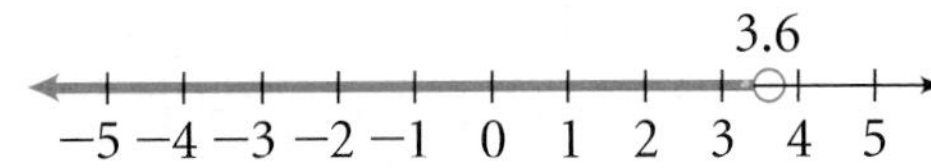

GRAPHING CALCULATOR HINT

You can check your solutions to Example 3 by using the TEST feature.

3. What happens when you replace z with 3.6 in $8z - 6 < 3z + 12$?

4. **a.** **Try This** Solve $3b + 12 > 21 - 2b$.
   b. Graph the solutions on a number line.

QUICK REVIEW

Equations such as $1 + 3a = 3a + 1$ are *identities*. Equations such as $2 + a = a - 2$ have *no solution.*

Like equations, some inequalities are true for all values of the variable, and some inequalities are false for all values of the variable. When an inequality is false for all values of the variable, it has no solution.

5. **Critical Thinking** Without writing the steps of a solution, tell whether the inequality is *true* or *false* for all values of the variable. **Justify** your response.

a. $4s - 5 < 4s - 7$ **b.** $4s - 5 < 3 + 4s$
c. $4s + 6 \ge 6 + 4s$ **d.** $4s + 6 > 6 + 4s$
e. $4s - 9 < 4s$ **f.** $4s \le 4s$

Exercises ON YOUR OWN

Tell what you must do to the first inequality in order to get the second. Be sure to list *all* the steps.

1. $4j + 5 \ge 23; j \ge 4.5$ **2.** $2(q - 3) < 8; q < 7$ **3.** $8 - 4s > 16; -4s > 8$
4. $-8 > \frac{z}{-5} - 2; 30 < z$ **5.** $2y - 5 > 9 + y; y > 14$ **6.** $\frac{2}{3}g + 7 \ge 9; \frac{2}{3}g \ge 2$
7. $6 < 12 - s; s < 6$ **8.** $3 + 5t \ge 6(t - 1) - t; 3 \ge -6$ **9.** $6.2 < -r; -6.2 > r$

Match each inequality with its graph below.

10. $2x - 2 > 4$ **11.** $2 - 2x > 4$ **12.** $2x + 2 > 4$
13. $2x + 2 > 4x$ **14.** $-2x - 2 > 4$ **15.** $-2(x - 2) > 4$

A.

B.

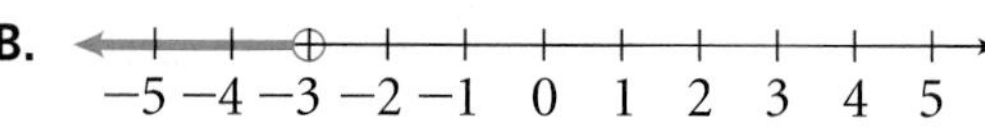

C.

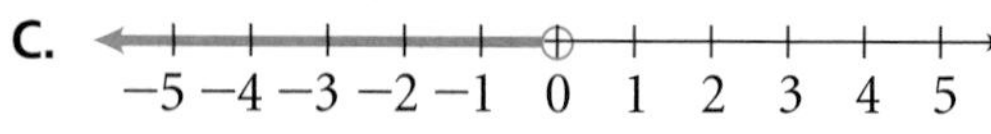

D.

E.

F.

16. **Recreation** The sophomore class is planning a picnic. The cost of a permit to use the park is \$250. To pay for the permit, there is a fee of \$.75 for each sophomore and \$1.25 for each guest who is not a sophomore. Two hundred sophomores plan to attend. How many guests must attend in order to pay for the permit?

Solve each inequality. Graph the solutions on a number line.

17. $5 \le 11 + 3h$ **18.** $3(y - 5) > 6$ **19.** $-4x - 2 < 8$
20. $r + 6 + 3r \ge 15 - 2r$ **21.** $5 - 2n \le 3 - n$ **22.** $3(2v - 4) \le 2(3v - 6)$
23. $2(m - 8) - 3m < -8$ **24.** $-(6b - 2) > 0$ **25.** $7a - (9a + 1) > 5$

26. **Writing** Suppose a friend is having difficulty solving the inequality $2.5(p - 4) > 3(p + 2)$. Explain how to solve the inequality, showing all necessary steps and identifying the properties you would use.

27. **Freight Handling** The freight elevator of a building can safely carry a load of at most 4000 lb. A worker needs to move supplies in 50-lb boxes from the loading dock to the fourth floor of the building. The worker weighs 160 lb. The cart she uses weighs 95 lb.
   a. What is the greatest number of boxes she can move in one trip?
   b. The worker must deliver 310 boxes to the fourth floor. How many trips must she make?

28. **Critical Thinking** Find a value of a such that the number line below shows all the solutions of $ax + 4 \leq -12$.

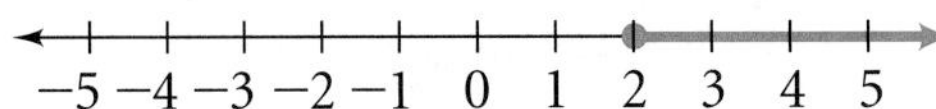

Choose **Use a calculator or paper and pencil. Solve and check each inequality.**

29. $2 - 3k < 4 + 5k$
30. $\frac{1}{2}n - \frac{1}{8} \geq \frac{3}{4} + \frac{5}{6}n$
31. $-3(v - 3) \geq 5 - 3v$
32. $8 \leq 5 - m + 1$
33. $0.5(3 - 8t) > 20(1 - 0.2t)$
34. $\frac{2}{3}d - 4 > d + \frac{1}{8} - \frac{1}{3}d$
35. $38 - k \leq 5 - 2k$
36. $\frac{4}{3}r - 3 < r + \frac{2}{3} - \frac{1}{3}r$
37. $-2(0.5 - 4s) \geq -3(4 + 3.5s)$

38. **Standardized Test Prep** Which value of n is a solution of both $2(n + 5) \geq 4$ and $3(n - 1) < 3$?
   A. -7 B. -3 C. 2
   D. 4 E. none of these

39. **Open-ended** Write two different inequalities that you can solve by adding 5 and multiplying by -3. Show how to solve each inequality.

40. a. **Generalize** Solve $ax + b > c$ for x, where a is positive.
   b. Solve $ax + b > c$ for x, where a is negative.

41. **Jobs** JoLeen is a sales associate in a clothing store. Each week she earns \$250 plus a commission equal to 3% of her sales. This week she would like to earn no less than \$460. What dollar amount of clothes must she sell?

42. **Geometry** Artists often use the *golden rectangle* because it is considered to be pleasing to the eye. The length of a golden rectangle is about 1.62 times its width. Suppose you are making a picture frame in the shape of a golden rectangle. You have a 46-in. piece of wood. What are the length and width of the largest frame you can make? (Round your answers to the nearest tenth of an inch.)

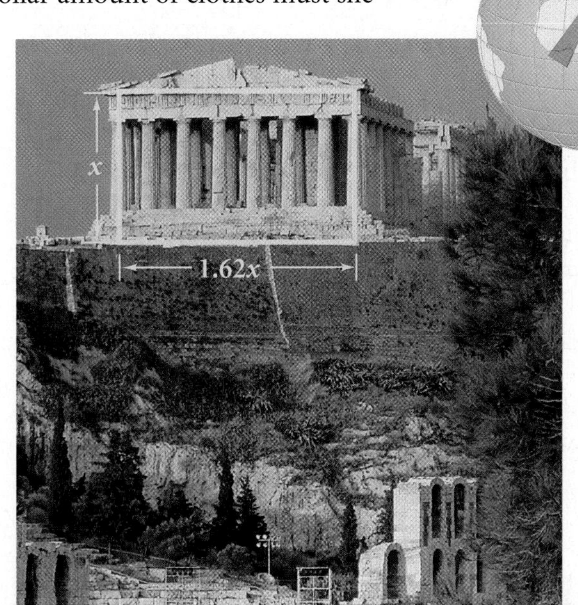

The Parthenon, an ancient Greek temple, was designed so that its dimensions form a golden rectangle.

43. *Business* Carlos plans to start a part-time word processing business out of his home. He is thinking of charging his customers $15 per hour. The table shows his expected monthly business expenses. Write an inequality to find the least number of hours he must work in a month to make a profit of at least $1200.

Monthly Expenses

Expense	Cost
Equipment Rental	$490
Materials	$45
Business Phone	$65

Chapter Project

Find Out by Researching

Systolic blood pressure, the higher number in a blood pressure reading, is measured as your heart muscle contracts. The formula $P \leq \frac{1}{2}a + 110$ gives the normal systolic blood pressure P based on age a.

- Find your normal systolic blood pressure.
- At age 20, does 120 represent a maximum or a minimum systolic pressure? Explain.
- A blood pressure reading higher than the normal value indicates a possible need for a change in lifestyle or for special medication. Research some lifestyle changes that can help reduce high blood pressure.

Exercises MIXED REVIEW

Write an inequality to model each situation.

44. An octopus can be up to 10 ft long.

45. A hummingbird migrates more than 1850 mi.

To which family of functions does each graph belong? Explain your reasoning.

46. $y = x^2 - 3x$

47. $y = |x| - 2$

48. $y = 5x + 1$

49. $y = 9 - x^2$

50. It takes 4.5 million jasmine petals to make 450 g of jasmine oil. How many petals are needed to make 1 kg of jasmine oil?

51. *Recycling* Each year, 9.5 million vehicles are recycled.
  a. About 75% of each vehicle's mass is reused. The average vehicle weighs 1.5 tons. About how many tons of materials can be reused from one vehicle?
  b. How many tons of materials can be reused from all the recycled vehicles each year?

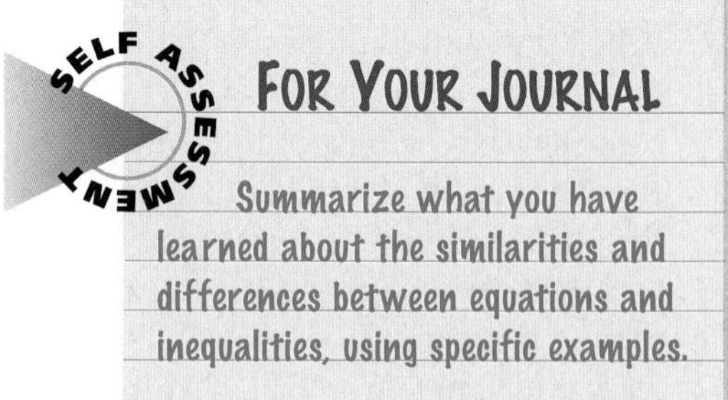

SELF ASSESSMENT
FOR YOUR JOURNAL
Summarize what you have learned about the similarities and differences between equations and inequalities, using specific examples.

Getting Ready for Lesson 4-8

Graph each pair of inequalities on one number line.

52. $c < 8; c \geq 10$

53. $t \geq -2; t \leq -5$

54. $m \leq 7; m > 12$

55. $h > 1; h < 0$

What You'll Learn

- Solving compound inequalities and graphing the solutions on a number line
- Solving absolute value inequalities and graphing the solutions on a number line

...And Why

To solve problems involving the chemistry of a swimming pool

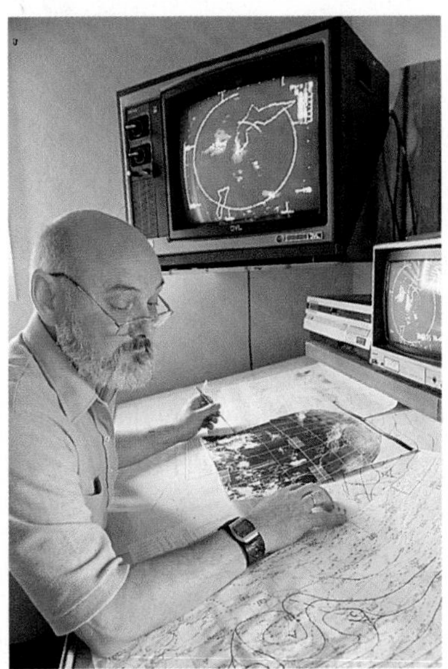

Meterologists use a variety of equipment to predict temperatures.

4-8 Compound Inequalities

THINK AND DISCUSS

Solving Compound Inequalities Containing "And"

Today's temperatures will be above 32°F, but not as high as 40°F.

You can write this prediction as $32 < t$ and $t < 40$. Then you can combine the two inequalities into one, which you can read in two ways.

$$32 < t < 40$$

t is greater than 32, and less than 40. *t is between 32 and 40.*

The graph of $32 < t < 40$ is an *interval* on a number line.

30 31 32 33 34 35 36 37 38 39 40 41 42

In the same way, you can write an inequality with $>$, $\leq$, or $\geq$.

$$32 \leq t \leq 40$$

t is greater than or equal to 32, and less than or equal to 40. *t is between 32 and 40 inclusive.*

1. Graph $32 \leq t \leq 40$ on a number line.

Two inequalities that are joined by the word *and* or the word *or* form a **compound inequality.** A solution of a compound inequality joined by *and* is any number that makes both inequalities true.

Example 1

Solve $-4 < r - 5 \leq -1$. Graph the solutions on a number line.

Write the compound inequality as two inequalities joined by *and.*

$-4 < r - 5$	and	$r - 5 \leq -1$	
$-4 + 5 < r - 5 + 5$	|	$r - 5 + 5 \leq -1 + 5$	← Add 5.
$1 < r$	and	$r \leq 4$	← Simplify.

The solutions are all numbers greater than 1 *and* less than or equal to 4.

−5 −4 −3 −2 −1 0 1 2 3 4 5

What? You can search the Internet for more than one topic at once. If you join two topics with *or,* you get all the references for either topic. If you join the topics with *and,* you get only those that relate to both topics.

Source: America Online

2. In Example 1, why is there an open circle at 1 and a closed circle at 4?

3. To check the solution to Example 1, choose a value in the interval shown in the graph. Substitute your value in the original inequality to **verify** that the statement is true.

A second way to solve a compound inequality involving *and* is to work on all three parts of the inequality at the same time. You work to get the variable alone between the inequality symbols.

Example 2 **Relating to the Real World** 

Chemistry The acidity of the water in a pool is considered normal if the average of three pH readings is between 7.2 and 7.8, inclusive. The first two readings for a pool are 7.4 and 7.9. What possible values for the third reading will make the pH normal?

Define p = value of third reading

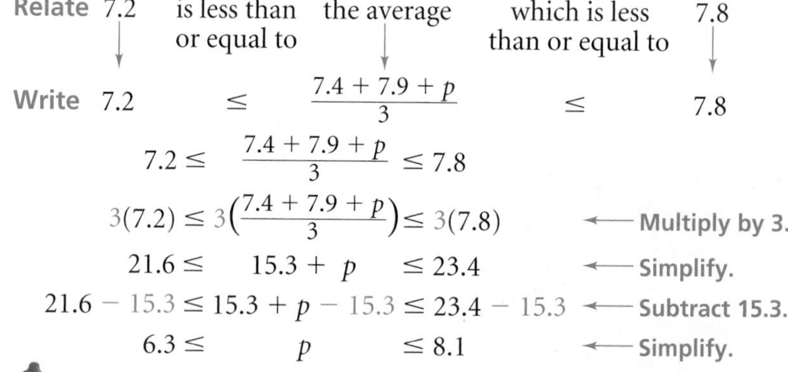

Relate	7.2	is less than or equal to	the average	which is less than or equal to	7.8
Write	7.2	$\leq$	$\frac{7.4 + 7.9 + p}{3}$	$\leq$	7.8

$$7.2 \leq \frac{7.4 + 7.9 + p}{3} \leq 7.8$$

$$3(7.2) \leq 3\left(\frac{7.4 + 7.9 + p}{3}\right) \leq 3(7.8) \quad \leftarrow \text{Multiply by 3.}$$

$$21.6 \leq 15.3 + p \leq 23.4 \quad \leftarrow \text{Simplify.}$$

$$21.6 - 15.3 \leq 15.3 + p - 15.3 \leq 23.4 - 15.3 \quad \leftarrow \text{Subtract 15.3.}$$

$$6.3 \leq p \leq 8.1 \quad \leftarrow \text{Simplify.}$$

The value for the third reading must be between 6.3 and 8.1, inclusive.

4. Check the solution to Example 2 to **verify** that the solution gives an average pH in the normal range.

Solving Compound Inequalities Containing "Or"

A solution of a compound inequality containing *or* is any number that makes *either* inequality true.

Example 3

Solve $4v + 3 < -5$ or $-2v + 7 < 1$. Graph the solutions.

$4v + 3 < -5$	or	$-2v + 7 < 1$
$4v + 3 - 3 < -5 - 3$		$-2v + 7 - 7 < 1 - 7$
$4v < -8$		$-2v < -6$
$\frac{1}{4}(4v) < \frac{1}{4}(-8)$		$-\frac{1}{2}(-2v) > -\frac{1}{2}(-6)$
$v < -2$	or	$v > 3$

The solutions are all numbers that are less than -2 *or* are greater than 3.

−5 −4 −3 −2 −1 0 1 2 3 4 5

5. **Try This** Graph each compound inequality on a separate line.
   a. $r < -1$ or $r > 3$ b. $r > -1$ and $r < 3$

6. Compare and contrast your graphs in Question 5.

Solving Absolute Value Inequalities

$|n| < 3$

$|n| > 3$

You can express the absolute value inequality $|n| < 3$ as the compound inequality $-3 < n < 3$. In a similar way, you can express the absolute value inequality $|n| > 3$ as the compound inequality $n > 3$ or $n < -3$. The graphs are at the left.

QUICK REVIEW

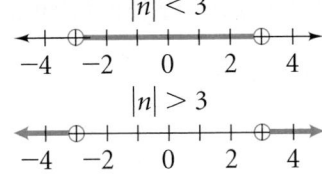

$|x| = 6$ means $x = 6$ or $x = -6$

7. Complete each statement with *less than* or *greater than.*
   a. For $|n| < 3$, the graph includes all points whose distance from zero is __?__ 3 units.
   b. For $|n| > 3$, the graph includes all points whose distance from zero is __?__ 3 units.

8. Write an absolute value inequality to describe each graph.

   a.

   b. 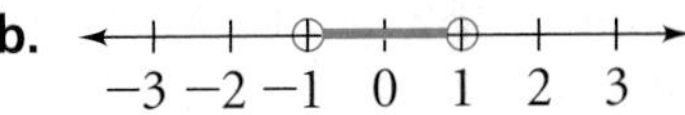

You can use absolute value inequalities to describe distances from numbers other than zero. The inequality $|n - 1| < 3$ represents all numbers whose distance from 1 is less than three units.

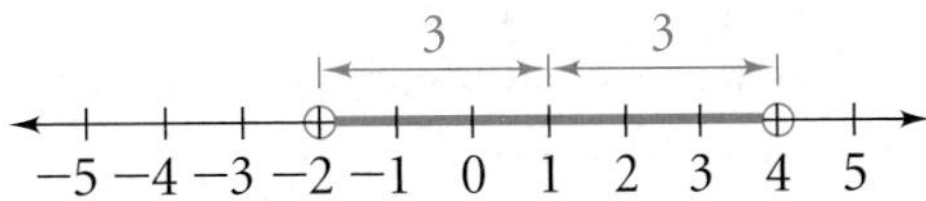

9. What does the inequality $|n - 1| > 3$ represent?

You can also solve an absolute value inequality by first writing it as a compound inequality.

Example 4

Solve $|v - 3| \geq 4$. Graph the solutions on a number line.

Write $|v - 3| \geq 4$ as two inequalities joined by *or.*

$$v - 3 \leq -4 \quad \text{or} \quad v - 3 \geq 4$$
$$v - 3 + 3 \leq -4 + 3 \quad | \quad v - 3 + 3 \geq 4 + 3 \quad \leftarrow \textbf{Add 3.}$$
$$v \leq -1 \quad \text{or} \quad v \geq 7$$

The solutions are all numbers less than or equal to –1 *or* greater than or equal to 7.

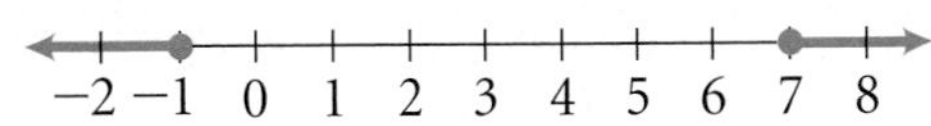

PROBLEM SOLVING

Look Back How would the solution be different if the inequality were $|v - 3| > 4$?

10. How could you solve $|v - 3| \geq 4$ using only a graph?

11. a. Try This Solve $|v - 3| \leq 4$. Graph the solutions on a number line.
    b. Compare your solutions with the solutions in Example 4.

Exercises ON YOUR OWN

For each situation, define a variable and write a compound inequality.

1. The highest elevation in North America is 20,320 ft above sea level, at Mount McKinley, Alaska. The lowest elevation is 282 ft below sea level at Death Valley, California.

2. Wind speeds of a *tropical storm* are at least 40 mi/h but no more than 74 mi/h.

Write a compound inequality that each graph could represent.

3. −4 −3 −2 −1 0 1 2 3 4

4. −4 −3 −2 −1 0 1 2 3 4

5. −4 −3 −2 −1 0 1 2 3 4

6. −4 −3 −2 −1 0 1 2 3 4

7. −4 −3 −2 −1 0 1 2 3 4

8. −4 −3 −2 −1 0 1 2 3 4

Choose a variable and write an absolute value inequality that represents each set of numbers on a number line.

9. all numbers less than 3 units from 0

10. all numbers no less than 7.5 units from 0

11. all numbers more than 2 units from 6

12. all numbers at least 3 units from –1

Solve each inequality and graph the solutions.

13. $-3 < j + 2 < 7$

14. $12 > -3q$ and $-2q > -12$

15. $4 + k > 3$ or $6k < -30$

16. $x - 5 \leq 0$ or $x + 1 > -2$

17. $3 \geq 4r - 5 \geq -1$

18. $-1 \leq 3t - 2$ and $\frac{1}{2}t < -3$

19. $-2.8 \geq 2r + 0.2 > -3.8$

20. $6 - a < 1$ or $3a \leq 12$

21. $6.5 > w + 3 > 1.5$

22. $3a > -6$ and $7a < 14$

23. $0.25t \leq 3.5$ and $t \geq 4$

24. $25g < 400$ or $100 < 4g$

25. Open-ended Describe a real-life situation that you could represent with the inequality $-2 < x < 8$.

26. Sports A *welterweight* wrestler weighs at least 74 kg but no more than 82 kg. You can use the formula $k = 0.45p$ to find pounds p or kilograms k when one of the quantities is known. Write a compound inequality to describe the weight of a welterweight in pounds.

27. Manufacturing An electronics manufacturer needs a conveyer belt for its assembly plant. The completed conveyer belt may be 15 cm longer or shorter than shown. Find the possible lengths of the conveyer belt.

28. Writing Suppose a friend is having difficulty solving absolute value inequalities. Write an explanation of the process, with examples.

Express each absolute value inequality as a compound inequality. Solve and graph the solutions on a number line.

29. $|f| > 2.5$
30. $|x + 3| < 5$
31. $|n + 8| \geq 5$
32. $|2y - 3| \geq 7$
33. $|w| > 2$
34. $|n| \leq 5$
35. $|6.5x| < 39$
36. $|3d| \geq 6$
37. $|y - 2| \geq 1$
38. $|2c - 3| < 9$
39. $|5t - 4| \geq 16$
40. $|p - 3| < 5$
41. $|3t + 1| > 8$
42. $|\frac{3}{4}x| - 3 < -5$
43. $4.5 + |3m - 2| > 2$
44. $0 \leq |3d - 1|$

Geometry The sum of the lengths of any two sides of a triangle must be greater than the third side. The lengths of two sides of a triangle are given. Find the range of values for the possible lengths of the third side.

Sample 3 cm, 7 cm

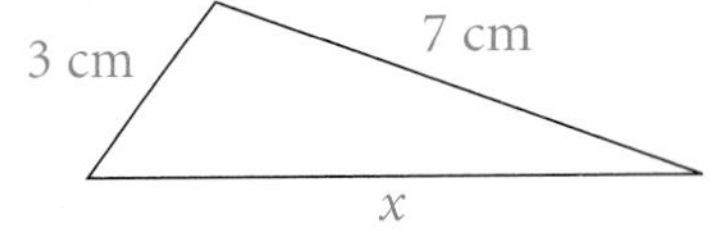

$x + 3 > 7$ and $x + 7 > 3$ and $3 + 7 > x$ ← Write inequalities.
$x > 4$ and $x > -4$ and $10 > x$ ← Solve each inequality.
$4 < x < 10$ ← Express as a compound inequality.

The length of the third side is greater than 4 cm and less than 10 cm.

45. 2.5 cm, 5 cm
46. 1 in., 4 in.
47. 28 mm, 21 mm
48. 12 ft, 18 ft

Meteorology The *high–low graph* shows the average monthly high and low temperatures for Detroit, Michigan, and Charlotte, North Carolina.

49. Write a compound inequality to represent the average temperature in Charlotte in June.

50. Write a compound inequality to represent the average temperature in Detroit in January.

51. Use a compound inequality to describe the yearly temperature range for each city.

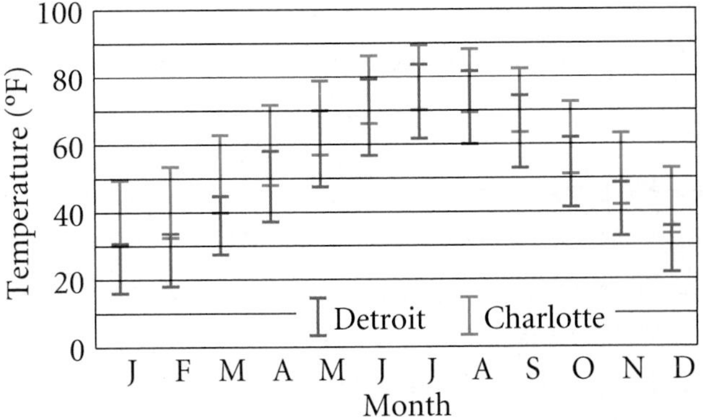

Source: *Statistical Abstract of the United States*

Chapter Project

Find Out by Writing

When you exercise, your pulse rate rises. Recommended pulse rates vary with age and physical condition. For vigorous exercise, such as jogging, the inequality $0.7(220 - a) \le R \le 0.85(220 - a)$ gives a target range for pulse rate R (in beats per minute), based on age a (in years).

- In what range should your pulse rate be when you are jogging?
- What is the target range for a person 25 years old?
- Why should you see a doctor before starting an exercise program?

Exercises MIXED REVIEW

Solve and check. State if the equation is an *identity* or has *no solution*.

52. $3y + 1 = 2.5$ **53.** $-6m - 1 = 2m$ **54.** $4(w + 8) = 10$ **55.** $-2 = 7c - 5c$

56. $8p - 4 = 4(2p - 1)$ **57.** $3.8 = |4x| + 0.2$ **58.** $-5k + 5 = 5(-1 - k)$ **59.** $|t - \frac{1}{2}| = \frac{3}{4}$

60. **Biology** Plasma makes up 55% of blood by volume. A 155-lb man has about 1.3 gal of blood. How much plasma does his blood contain?

Getting Ready for Lesson 4-9

Which of –3, –2, –1, 0, 1, 2, 3 are solutions of each inequality?

61. $m + 2 \le 3$ **62.** $-4q > 0$ **63.** $\frac{1}{2}z - 1 \le 0$ **64.** $3t + 5 < -4$

Exercises CHECKPOINT

Solve each inequality. Graph the solutions.

1. $8 < c + 2$ **2.** $3x \le -24$ **3.** $-9m \ge 36$ **4.** $7 - c \le 12$

5. $5 < 6b + 3$ **6.** $12n \le 3n + 27$ **7.** $2 + 4r \ge 5(r - 1)$ **8.** $8w + 3w \le -22$

9. $6 + h \ge 2$ **10.** $0 \le 2t - 10t \le 4$ **11.** $\frac{x}{-3} > 9$ *or* $3x > 12$ **12.** $|g - 3| > 2$

Solve each absolute value inequality. Graph the solutions.

13. $|5d| \ge 15$ **14.** $|x + 3| < 7$ **15.** $|2x - 3| < 5$ **16.** $|4y - 2| \ge 18$ **17.** $\frac{4}{5} \ge |\frac{1}{2}x - 2|$

18. **Medicine** Normal body temperature is within 0.6°C of 36.6°C. Write a compound inequality for the range of normal body temperature.

19. **Open-ended** Write a compound inequality to **predict** the temperature range for tomorrow.

20. **Writing** Explain the difference between the words *and* and *or* in a compound inequality.

Math ToolboX — Problem Solving

Using a Venn Diagram

After Lesson 4-8

You can use a Venn diagram to illustrate relationships between sets and solve problems. First draw overlapping circles to represent the sets. Then draw a box around the circles to include any other information. Finally, fill in the diagram with information from the problem.

Example

An English teacher surveyed 48 ninth-grade students and found that 18 had read *Treasure Island*, 20 had read *Anne of Green Gables*, and 11 had read both books. How many students had not read either book?

After completing Steps 1 through 5, you can see that 21 students had not read either *Treasure Island* or *Anne of Green Gables.*

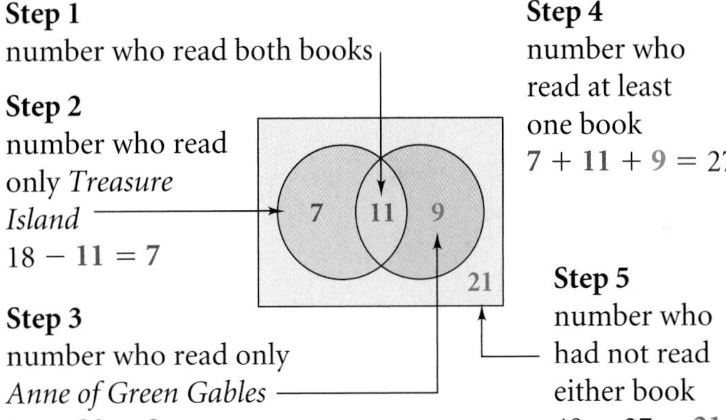

Use a Venn diagram to illustrate and solve each problem.

PROBLEM SOLVING HINT

For each exercise, first decide how many circles you need to draw.

1. Between 1933 and 1995 there were 11 presidents of the United States and 14 vice presidents. If 9 of the vice presidents were never president, how many of the presidents were never vice president?
2. Recently there were 118,519 female physicians in the United States. Of these, 16,573 were pediatricians, 40,431 were under the age of 35, and 6761 of the pediatricians were under the age of 35.
   a. How many female pediatricians were age 35 or older?
   b. How many female physicians were 35 or older and not pediatricians?
3. In the 1994 Winter Olympics, 67 countries participated. The table shows how many countries won each possible medal.
   a. How many countries won gold, but not silver or bronze?
   b. How many countries won gold and silver, but not bronze?
   c. How many countries did not win any medals?
4. **Writing** Write a problem that you could solve using a Venn diagram. Then give your solution to the problem.

1994 Winter Olympics
14 won gold.
12 won gold and silver.
11 won gold and bronze.
17 won silver.
14 won bronze and silver.
18 won bronze.
10 won gold, silver, and bronze.

Source: *The Guinness Book of Records*

What You'll Learn

- Solving inequalities given a specific replacement set
- Checking the reasonableness of solutions

...And Why

To model real-world situations, like car inspection problems

What You'll Need

- calculator

4-9 Interpreting Solutions

THINK AND DISCUSS

Solving Inequalities Given a Replacement Set

When you solve inequalities, the set of possible values for the variable, or **replacement set,** often is any real number, There are times, however, when the replacement set is limited to the set of integers or some other set. Your solution depends on the replacement set for the variable.

Example 1

Solve $-4 < 2k \leq 5$. Then graph the solutions on a separate number line for each replacement set.

a. the real numbers **b.** the integers **c.** $\{-5, -3, -2, 0, 3\}$

$$-4 < 2k \leq 5$$

$$\tfrac{1}{2}(-4) < \tfrac{1}{2}(2k) \leq \tfrac{1}{2}(5) \quad \longleftarrow \text{Multiply by } \tfrac{1}{2}.$$

$$-2 < k \leq 2\tfrac{1}{2} \quad \longleftarrow \text{Simplify.}$$

a. All real numbers greater than –2 and less than or equal to $2\frac{1}{2}$ satisfy the inequality.

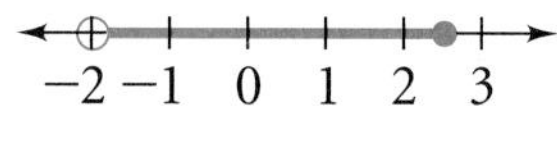

b. The integers that satisfy the inequality are –1, 0, 1, and 2.

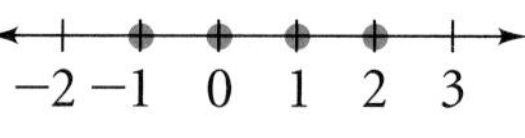

c. The value from {–5, –3, –2, 0, 3} that satisfies the inequality is 0.

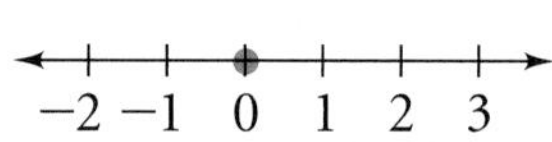

1. Try This Match each replacement set with its graph of $|y| < 4$.

A. the real numbers **I.**

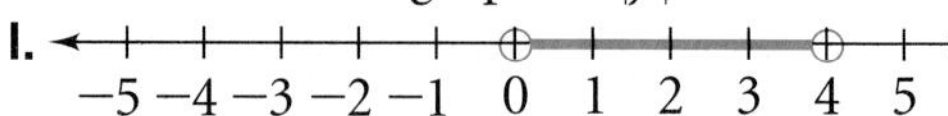

B. the integers **II.**

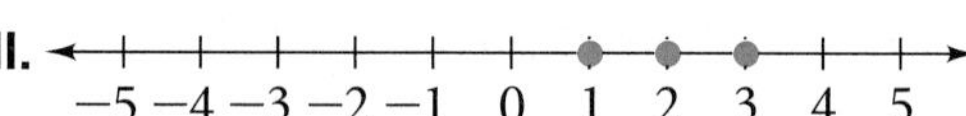

C. the positive integers **III.**

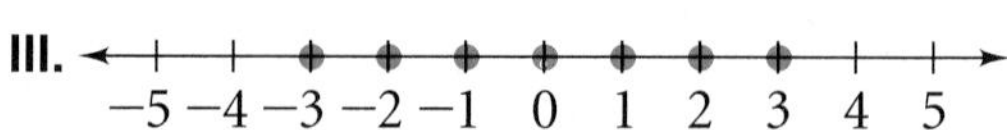

D. the positive real numbers **IV.**

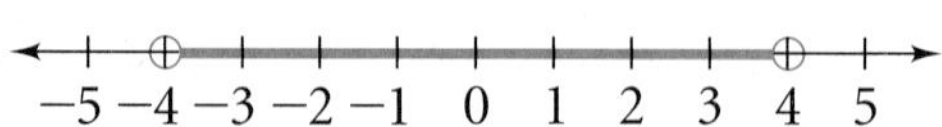

2. *Open-ended* Write an inequality whose solutions are graphed on the number line below. Identify the replacement set for the variable.

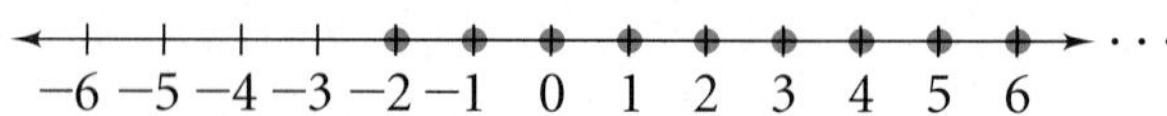

QUICK REVIEW

Three dots (• • •) indicate that a pattern continues.

Math A Test Prep

1 Choose the inequality whose solutions are shown on the number line.

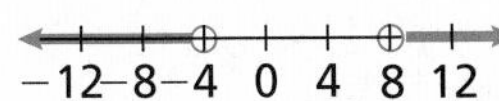

(1) $|w - 2| > 6$
(2) $|w - 2| \leq -6$
(3) $|w - 2| \geq 6$
(4) $|w - 2| < 6$

2 When Jamie exercises, her heart rate goal is at least 160 beats per minute.
  a Write an inequality to show the number of beats Jamie should count in 10 seconds.
  b What is the replacement set for the variable in the inequality?
  c What is the minimum number of beats Jamie should count in 10 seconds?

Determining a Reasonable Answer

In many problems, you are given restrictions that indicate the replacement set for the variable. Other restrictions arise from common sense.

Example 2 **Relating to the Real World** 

Car Service Felix Ramiro's Garage has just purchased special equipment for the state emission inspection. The equipment cost \$1500. Each inspection costs the garage \$2.60 for labor and supplies. The garage gets to keep \$8.20 of each vehicle's inspection fee. How many inspections must the garage perform in order to make a profit?

Define	x = number of inspections				
Relate	income from inspections	is greater than	cost of equipment	plus	expense of inspections
Write	$8.2x$	$>$	1500	$+$	$2.6x$

$$8.2x > 1500 + 2.6x$$
$$8.2x - 2.6x > 1500 + 2.6x - 2.6x \quad \text{← Subtract } 2.6x \text{ from each side.}$$
$$5.6x > 1500$$
$$\frac{5.6x}{5.6} > \frac{1500}{5.6} \quad \text{← Divide each side by 5.6.}$$
$$x > 267.8571429$$

Since x represents the number of inspections, it makes sense to consider integer values only. So, the solutions are $x \geq 268$, where x is an integer. The garage must perform at least 268 inspections to make a profit.

266 267 268 269 270 271 . . .

3. Show how you would check Example 2. Be sure you check the words of the original problem, not simply the math of the inequality.

4. a. **Car Service** Felix's garage is open six days a week. It has enough mechanics to do 11 inspections a day. What is the minimum number of weeks it will take to make a profit on inspections? Explain.
   b. What is the maximum number of weeks it will take to make a profit on inspections? Explain.

QUICK REVIEW

A set of data that involves measurements, such as length, weight, or temperature, is usually *continuous*.

A set of data that involves a count, such as numbers of people or objects, is *discrete*.

It is important to consider replacement sets when you use an inequality to model a real-world situation. For instance, consider this situation:

The temperature t ranges from 25°F to 35°F, inclusive.

A set of temperatures is a continuous set of data. You graph $25 \leq t \leq 35$ as an interval, with the real numbers as the replacement set for t.

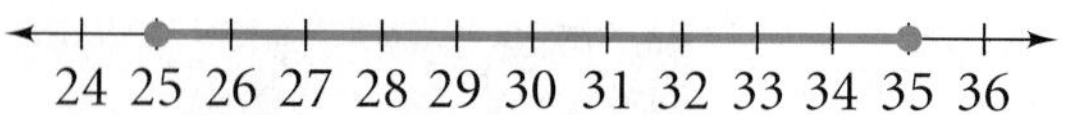

Now suppose you want to model this situation:

The number n of students in a homeroom is between 25 and 35, inclusive.

The numbers of students is a discrete set of data. You graph $25 \leq n \leq 35$ as a set of points, with the positive integers as the replacement set for n.

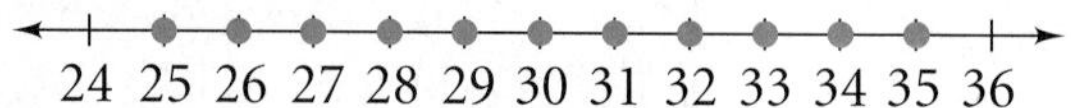

Exercises ON YOUR OWN

Graph each inequality on a number line. Use the positive integers as a replacement set. If there are no solutions, write *no solutions*.

1. $p \leq 6$ **2.** $|c - 2| > 3$ **3.** $w \leq 0$ **4.** $-g > -8$

5. $-3 \leq a < 1$ **6.** $r < 3$ or $r \geq 5$ **7.** $-4 < k + 1 < 7$ **8.** $3(d + 2) < 6$

9. $-y < -4.2$ **10.** $|3 - r| > 2$ **11.** $2 > u$ or $u \geq 3$ **12.** $w \geq 0$

13. $-4 \leq q < 2.25$ **14.** $3(d - 1) \leq 4.5$ **15.** $4 < 2 - 2m \leq 8$ **16.** $|2a + 1| < 9$

Write an inequality that represents each situation. Graph the solutions on a number line.

17. If you are 12 to 64 years old, you pay full price for admission to the Science Museum.

18. A market researcher surveyed women who were at least 19 but less than 25 years old.

19. The circumference of a baseball is between 23 cm and 23.5 cm.

20. A box can hold from 15 to 20 books, inclusive.

21. **Nursing** In nursing school, students learn temperature ranges for bath water. Tepid water is approximately 80°F to 93°F, warm water is approximately 94°F to 98°F, and hot water is approximately 110°F to 115°F. Model these ranges on one number line. Label each interval.

22. **Open-ended** Create a problem for which the solution is any number between two positive numbers a and b.

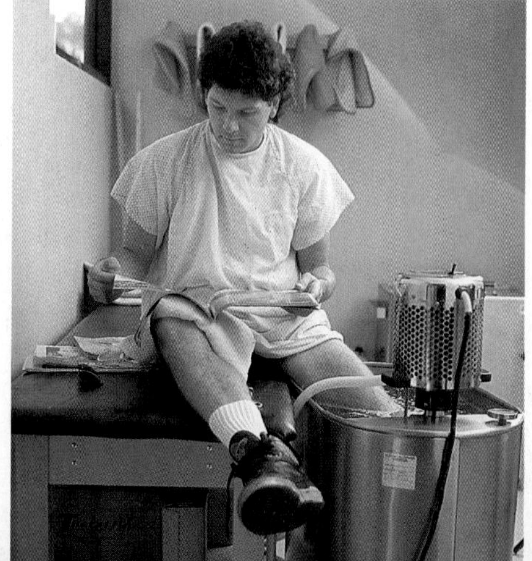

23. a. *Jobs* A summer employee at a store can work at most 8 h/day. How many hours must Nadine work on Friday to meet her goal of earning at least $175 for the week?
b. **Summarize** the steps you would use to find the number of hours each employee must work on Friday in order to meet that goal.

Employee	Hourly Wage	Mon.	Tues.	Wed.	Thurs.
Radam	$5.25	7	7	8	8
Nadine	$5.30	8	6	7	7

24. *Veterinary Science* The table lists respiratory rates for certain birds.
a. Model the respiratory rate for a parrot on a number line.
b. Draw two other number lines and align the 0 marks on them with the 0 mark on the number line in part (a). Model the respiratory rates for canaries and cockatiels on the number lines.

At-Rest Respiratory Rates

Bird	Breaths/min
Canary	60–100
Cockatiel	100–125
Parrot	25–40

25. *Writing* Explain what a replacement set is and why you need to think about it when you are using an inequality to solve a problem.

Graph each inequality for the given replacement set.

26. $-8 < 2(c + 5) < 14$, for the set of negative integers
27. $-3 \leq 9v + 6 \leq 24$, for $\{-4, -2, 0, 2, 4\}$
28. $12 \geq |6y - 3|$, for the set of positive real numbers
29. $|2n + 6| < 12$, for the set of integers

Chapter Project — Find Out by Interviewing

How much exercise is enough? What kind of exercise is best for you?

- Interview a coach, a trainer, or a health professional to find out what type and amount of exercise they recommend for a teenager like you.
- Design your own exercise plan. Consider goals (muscle tone, heart workout) and amount and type of exercise.

Exercises MIXED REVIEW

Find each statistic for the data 1, 3, 4, 4, 5, 5, 7, 9, 9, 9, 13.

30. mean
31. median
32. mode

Find the percent of change.

33. $24 to $36
34. 20 lb to 15 lb
35. 300 to 750

36. Write an equation and solve.
a. *Weather* In August 1995, a storm in Stillwater, Oklahoma, dropped 5 in. of rain in 3 h. What was the hourly rate?
b. Suppose it rained all day at this rate. How many inches of rain would fall in a 24-h period?

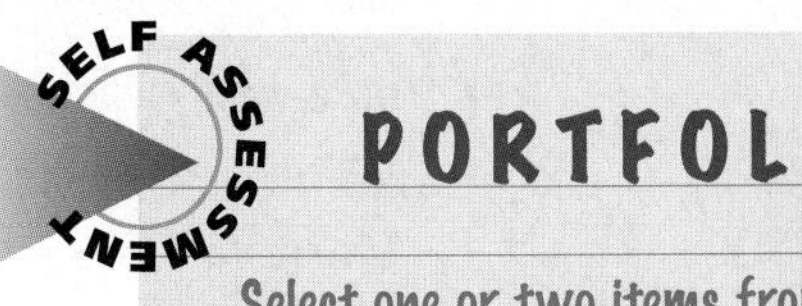

PORTFOLIO

Select one or two items from your work for this chapter. Consider
- corrected work
- work based on manipulatives
- open-ended questions

Explain why you have included each selection you make.

CHAPTER PROJECT

Finishing the Chapter Project

NO SWEAT!

Questions on pages 162, 178, 194, 200, and 205 should help you to complete your project. Present all your information for the project in a notebook. Is your exercise plan realistic for your available time and resources? How close is it to what you already do? (If it is very different, you should begin only with an adult's guidance.) Be sure to include what you have learned about blood pressure and about personal exercise.

Reflect and Revise

Organize your notebook around your use of equations and inequalities (one section for each). Share your notebook with an adult. Check your work for accuracy and look for any items that are not clear. Make any changes necessary in your work.

Follow Up

Find out about cross-training techniques or the training programs used in an Olympic sport.

For More Information

Kettelkamp, Larry. *Modern Sport Science.* New York: William Morrow, 1986.

"Physical Fitness." *Marshall Cavendish Encyclopedia of Health* (Vol. 10: 568–574). North Bellmore, New York: Marshall Cavendish, 1991.

Schwarzenegger, Arnold. *Arnold's Fitness for Kids Ages 11–14.* New York: Doubleday, 1993.

Virtue, Doreen. "What's Your Fitness Personality? Find an Exercise Plan that Really Fits." *Vegetarian Times* (January 1995): 55.

CHAPTER 4

Wrap Up

Key Terms

compound inequalities (p. 195)
cross products (p. 159)
equivalent inequalities (p. 180)
identity (p. 166)
no solution (p. 165)
literal equation (p. 176)
proportion (p. 158)
ratio (p. 158)
replacement set (p. 202)
scale (p. 158)
similar figures (p. 159)
solution of the inequality (p. 179)

How am I doing?

- State three ideas from this chapter that you think are important. Explain your choices.
- Describe several important rules that you must apply in order to solve inequalities.

Using Proportions 4-1

A **ratio** is a comparison of two numbers by division. A **proportion** is a statement that two ratios are equal. You can solve a proportion with a variable by using the **cross products.**

Solve each proportion.

1. $\frac{4}{12} = \frac{c}{6}$ **2.** $\frac{t}{5} = \frac{23}{50}$ **3.** $-\frac{9}{m} = \frac{3}{2}$ **4.** $\frac{5}{4} = \frac{12.5}{z}$ **5.** $\frac{x}{4} = -\frac{1}{10}$ **6.** $\frac{8}{b} = \frac{16}{3}$

7. *Hobbies* A model airplane can be built to $\frac{1}{48}$ of actual size. Suppose a wing of the model airplane is $\frac{3}{4}$ ft long. How long is the wing of the full-size airplane?

Equations with Variables on Both Sides 4-2

You can use the properties of equality to solve an equation. An equation has no solution if no value of the variable makes the equation true. An equation is an **identity** if every value of the variable makes the equation true.

Write an equation for each model and solve.

8. 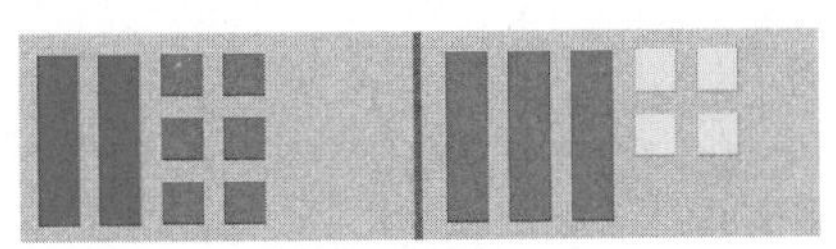

9. 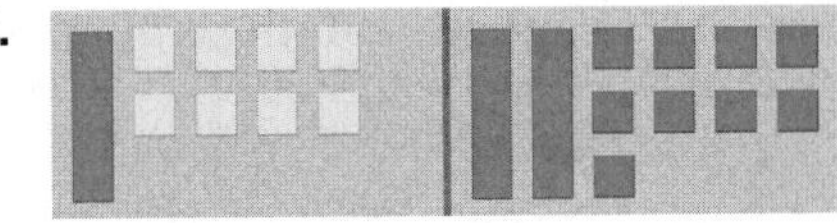

Solve and check. If the equation is an identity or if it has no solution, write *identity* or *no solution*.

10. $5w = 6w + 11$ **11.** $3(2t - 6) = 2(3t - 9)$ **12.** $4n - 6n = 2n$ **13.** $9c + 4 = 3c - 8$

Solving Absolute Value Equations 4-3

You can solve an **absolute value equation** by getting the absolute value by itself on one side of the equation. When the expression within the absolute value symbol contains more than one term, you must write and solve two equations.

Solve and check each equation. If there is no solution, explain.

14. $|y| = 5$
15. $|p + 3| = 9.5$
16. $|6 - b| = -1$
17. $|k - 8| = 0$

18. **Open-ended** Write an absolute value equation that has no solution and another that has one solution. Solve the one that has one solution.

Transforming Formulas 4-4

A formula shows the relationship between two or more variables. When you express one variable in terms of the others, you are solving the equation for that variable.

Solve each equation for the given variable.

19. $m = \frac{a + b + c}{3}; c$
20. $C = \pi d; d$
21. $y = mx + b; x$
22. $A = \frac{1}{2}bh; h$

23. **Science** Ohm's Law states that in an electrical circuit $E = IR$, where E represents the potential (in volts), I represents the current (in amperes), and R represents the resistance (in ohms).
    a. Solve this formula for I.
    b. Find I if $E = 6$ volts and $R = 0.15$ ohms of resistance.

Solving Inequalities 4-5, 4-6, 4-7

You can add or subtract a number from both sides of an inequality to find a simpler **equivalent inequality.** You can multiply or divide both sides of an inequality by the same number to find a simpler equivalent inequality. If you multiply or divide by a positive number, the order of the inequality stays the same. If the number is negative, the order is *reversed*.

Solve each inequality. Graph the solutions on a number line.

24. $h + 3 > 2$
25. $4k - 1 \leq -3$
26. $\frac{5}{8}b < 25$
27. $-\frac{2}{7}y - 6 \geq 42$
28. $6(c - 1) \leq -18$
29. $3m > 5m + 12$
30. $t - 4 < -9$
31. $5x - 2 \geq 4x + 7$

32. **Critical Thinking** Without writing the steps of the solution, describe the solutions of the inequality $-2x + \frac{3}{4} \leq -2x + \frac{1}{4}$. **Justify** your answer.

Compound Inequalities 4-8

Compound inequalities are two inequalities that are joined by the word *and* or the word *or*. A solution of a compound inequality joined by *and* makes *both* inequalities true. A solution of a compound inequality joined by *or* makes *either* inequality true.

Solve each inequality and graph the solutions.

33. $|n + 2| \geq 4$ **34.** $-3 \leq z - 1 < 6$ **35.** $7t \geq 49$ or $2t \leq -4$ **36.** $0 < -8b \leq 12$

37. $-2 \leq 3a - 8 < 4$ **38.** $-6 < d + \frac{1}{2} < 4\frac{1}{2}$ **39.** $-1 \leq a - 3 < 2$ **40.** $|3x + 5| > -2$

41. *Standardized Test Prep* Which number is *not* a solution of the compound inequality $5w - 2 > 8$ or $-3w + 1 \geq 10$?
A. –3 **B.** 5 **C.** 2 **D.** 3 **E.** –5

Interpreting Solutions 4-9

When you solve an inequality, the set of possible values for the variable is called the **replacement set.**

Graph each inequality on a number line. Use all integers as the replacement set. If there are no solutions, write *no solution.*

42. $|4h - 1| \geq 7$ **43.** $3t \leq 10$ **44.** $2 < y + 1 < 3$ **45.** $-3 \leq m < 0$ **46.** $-2q > -q$

Write and graph an inequality for each statement.

47. *Meteorology* Cumulus clouds form $\frac{1}{4}$ mi to 4 mi above the Earth's surface.

48. *Languages* There are more than 1000 different languages spoken on the continent of Africa.

49. *Writing* Suppose you use an inequality to model a real-world situation. Explain why you may need to specify a replacement set.

Getting Ready for CHAPTER 5

Graph each set of points on a coordinate plane.

50. (1, 2), (0, 1), (–2, –1), (4, 5) **51.** (4, –2), (2, 1), (–6, 3), (2, –1) **52.** (3, 1), (3, 4), (3, –2), (3, 3)

Write a function rule for each table.

53.

x	$f(x)$
0	−5
1	−4
2	−3
3	−2

54.

x	$f(x)$
−2	7
5	14
12	21
19	28

55.

x	$f(x)$
4	2
10	5
16	8
22	11

56.

x	$f(x)$
−2	−6
1	3
4	12
7	21

CHAPTER 4

Assessment

Solve. If the equation is an identity or if it has no solution, write *identity* or *no solution*.

1. $\frac{3}{4} = \frac{c}{20}$

2. $\frac{8}{15} = \frac{4}{w}$

3. $\frac{w}{6} = \frac{6}{15}$

4. $\frac{5}{t} = \frac{21}{100}$

5. $9j + 3 = 3(3j + 1)$

6. $8n = 5 + 3n$

7. $4v - 9 = 6v + 7$

8. $|8b - 3| = -21$

9. $|t - 6| = 4$

10. $|m + 1| = 11$

11. Find the value of each variable in the matrices.

$$\begin{bmatrix} w + 5 & 3x - 1 \\ 2y & z + 6 \end{bmatrix} = \begin{bmatrix} 2w - 6 & 8x \\ 2 - 4y & 12 \end{bmatrix}$$

12. The ratio of the length of a side of one square to that of another square is 3 : 4. A side of the smaller square is 9 cm. Find the length of a side of the larger square.

13. **Writing** Are $|x + 4| = 7$ and $|x| + 4 = 7$ equivalent equations? Explain.

14. Suppose you score 9.1, 9.6, 9.7, 9.3, and 9.4 in a diving competition. The diver who is in first place has a final score of 56.4. What is the lowest score you can get on your last dive to win the competition?

15. A taxicab company charges a flat fee of \$1.85 plus an additional \$.40 per quarter-mile.

a. Write a formula to find the total cost for each fare.

b. Use this formula to find the total cost for traveling 8 mi.

Solve each equation for the given variable.

16. $t = \frac{v + m}{3}$; m

17. $8b - 5c = 2$; c

18. $A = \frac{1}{2}bh$; b

19. $V = 2\pi r^2 h$; h

20. **Standardized Test Prep** If $6m + 3t = 8w$, then $m = \blacksquare$.

A. $\frac{4}{3}w - 3t$ **B.** $\frac{8w - 3t}{6}$ **C.** $(8 - 3t) \div 6$

D. $\frac{8w + 3t}{6}$ **E.** $\frac{1}{2}t + 8w$

21. **Open-ended** Write two different inequalities that you can solve by first subtracting 7, then multiplying by –6. Solve each inequality.

Define a variable and write an inequality to model each situation.

22. A student can take at most 7 classes.

23. The school needs at least 5 runners.

24. Elephants can drink up to 40 gal at a time.

25. The paper route has more than 32 homes.

Write a compound inequality that each graph could represent.

26.

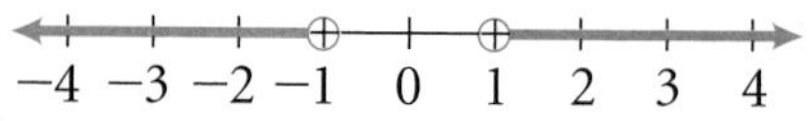

27.

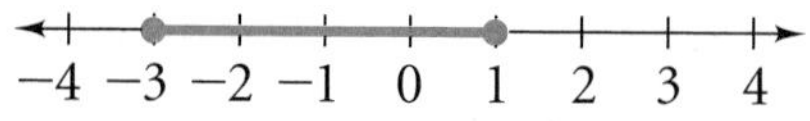

Solve each inequality. Graph the solutions on a number line.

28. $8 + u > 4$

29. $-5 + 4t \leq 3$

30. $5w \geq -6w + 11$

31. $-\frac{7}{2}m < 13$

32. $|x - 5| \geq 10$

33. $|2h + 1| < 5$

34. $9 \leq 6 - b < 12$

35. $-10 < 4q < 12$

36. $4 + 3n \geq 1$ or $-5n > 25$

37. $10k < 75$ and $4 - k \geq 0$

38. **Jobs** A clerk at the Radio Barn makes \$300 a week plus 4% commission. How much does she have to sell to make at least \$500 this week?

39. Solve $-13 \leq 5g + 7 < 20$ for each replacement set.

a. positive integers **b.** all integers

40. Solve the equation modeled by tiles.

CHAPTER 4

Preparing for the Math A Exam

Part I

1 Which equation does not have the same solution as $\frac{7}{y} = \frac{31}{36}$?

(1) $\frac{7}{31} = \frac{y}{36}$ (3) $\frac{36}{31} = \frac{7}{y}$

(2) $\frac{y}{36} = \frac{7}{31}$ (4) $\frac{y}{7} = \frac{36}{31}$

2 A blueprint scale is 0.5 in. : 4 ft. On the plan, a living room measures 2.25 in. by 2.5 in. What are the actual dimensions of the living room?

(1) 18 ft by 20 ft (3) 9 ft by 10 ft

(2) 11.25 ft by 12.5 ft (4) 16 ft by 20 ft

3 Which equation is an example of an identity?

(1) $8x + 5 = -2(4x - 1) + 3$

(2) $8x - 5 = 2(4x - 1) - 3$

(3) $8x + 5 = 2(4x - 3) - 1$

(4) $8x - 5 = -3 - 2(4x + 1)$

4 What is the solution of $|a - 5| = 12$?

(1) 18 (3) −7

(2) 17, −7 (4) −17, 17

5 Which inequality is equivalent to $-6x > 12$?

(1) $x > -2$ (3) $3x < -6$

(2) $-2x < -4$ (4) $x < 2$

6 What is the solution of the inequality $4x + 2 < x - 5$?

(1) $x \leq -\frac{1}{7}$ (3) $x \geq -\frac{7}{3}$

(2) $x > \frac{7}{3}$ (4) $x < -\frac{7}{3}$

7 Which inequality is represented by this graph?

−4 −3 −2 −1 0 1 2 3 4

(1) $|s| \leq 3$ (3) $|s| \geq 3$

(2) $|s| > 3$ (4) $|s| < 3$

8 A spinner numbered from 1 to 6 is spun. Each outcome is equally likely. What is the probability of getting an odd number?

(1) $\frac{1}{6}$ (2) 0.16 (3) $\frac{2}{3}$ (4) 50%

Part II

9 Solve $w + 6 < -2$. Graph the solutions on a number line.

10 Suppose you want to save at least \$200 for new speakers. You save \$15 each week from your part-time job. How many full weeks of saving will it take you? Write an inequality to model this problem. Then solve it.

11 The number of subscribers to a magazine fell from 210,000 to 190,000. To the nearest whole number, find the percent of decrease this drop represents.

Part III

12 The formula $P = 2\ell + 2w$ gives the perimeter P of a rectangle with length ℓ and width w.

a Solve this formula for ℓ.

b Suppose you have 80 ft of fencing to enclose a garden. If you make the enclosure 25 ft long, how wide can you make it?

13 Graph the solutions of the inequality $-5 < 4(k + 6) \leq 28$ for the set of negative integers.

Part IV

14 A car traveling for 6 hours covers the same distance as a truck traveling for 7.2 hours. The car is traveling 10 mi/h faster than the truck.

a Write an equation to model this problem.

b What is the car's speed?

c What is the truck's speed?

15 A pair of jeans that normally costs \$36 are on sale for \$24.99.

a To the nearest whole percent, how much are the jeans discounted?

b What is the percent of decrease in price, to the nearest whole percent?

c How are the two percents you have found related?

5 Graphing and Writing Linear Equations

Relating to the Real World

Algebra provides a shorthand way to look at a whole class of relationships. Many cause-and-effect relationships in everyday life, especially those involving time and money, use linear equations and graphs as models. By understanding properties of linear models, both economists and home budget makers can plan wisely.

Lessons	5-1	5-2	5-3	5-4	5-5
	Slope	*Rates of Change*	*Direct Variation*	*Slope-Intercept Form*	*Writing the Equation of a Line*

Taking THE PLUNGE

Do you have a job? If not, what will your first job be? What expenses will you have? How much money will you actually earn? How can you compare earnings between two jobs? Linear equations can help to answer all these questions.

As you work through the chapter, you will make graphs and write equations that model different jobs. You will use these models to predict income. After interviewing someone about their first job, you will choose a job that you might like to have and explain why.

To help you complete the project:

- p. 224 *Find Out by Graphing*
- p. 239 *Find Out by Modeling*
- p. 255 *Find Out by Interviewing*
- p. 260 *Finishing the Project*

Connections Airplanes . . . and more

What You'll Learn

- Calculating the slope of a line
- Drawing a line through a point with a given slope

...And Why

To find slope in real-world situations, such as the landing of an airplane, and interpret its meaning

What You'll Need

- graph paper

5-1 Slope

WORK TOGETHER

Carpentry Carpenters use the terms rise and run to describe the steepness of a stairway or a roof line. You can use rise and run to describe the steepness of a hill.

rise

run

$$\text{steepness} = \frac{\text{rise}}{\text{run}}$$

1. Which hill appears to be steeper in the photos?

A.

B.

2. a. Find a ratio for the steepness of each hill.

b. For which hill is the ratio greater?

THINK AND DISCUSS

Counting Units to Find Slope

The mathematical term to describe steepness is slope.

$$\textbf{slope} = \frac{\text{vertical change (rise)}}{\text{hortizontal change (run)}}$$

Example 1

Find the slope of each line.

a.

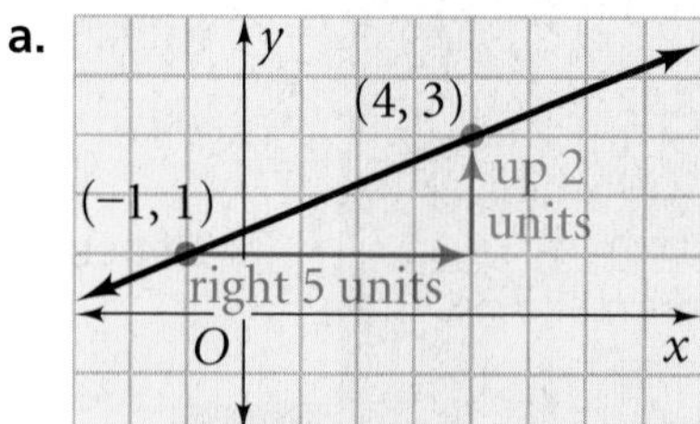

$$\text{slope} = \frac{\text{vertical change}}{\text{horizontal change}}$$
$$= \frac{2}{5}$$

The slope of the line is $\frac{2}{5}$.

b.

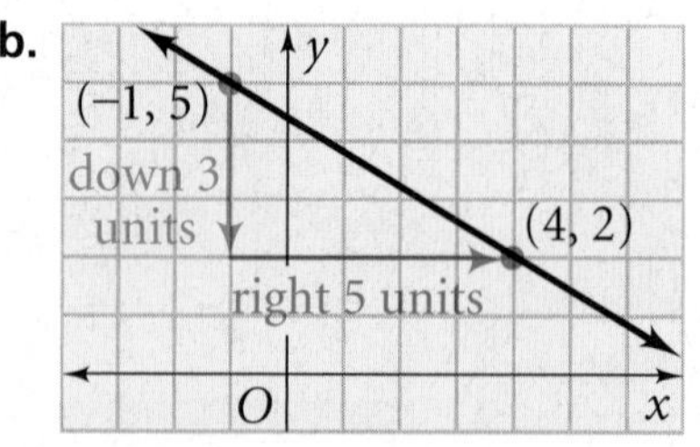

$$\text{slope} = \frac{\text{vertical change}}{\text{horizontal change}}$$
$$= -\frac{3}{5}$$

The slope of the line is $-\frac{3}{5}$.

Math A Test Prep

NEW YORK MATH A

1 A line that passes through which pair of points will have the steepest slope?
(1) (2, 5) and (−3, 7)
(2) (−3, 0) and (0, 4)
(3) (4, −1) and (−6, −6)
(4) (5, 5) and (−4, 6)

2 Graph a line that passes through the point (−1, 4) and has a slope of $-\frac{2}{3}$.

3. Complete each statement with *upward* or *downward*.
   a. A line with positive slope goes ■ from left to right.
   b. A line with negative slope goes ■ from left to right.

You use the units associated with the axes to explain the meaning of the slope in a real-world situation.

Example 2 **Relating to the Real World** 

Airplanes The graph models the altitude of an airplane from the time the wheels are lowered (time = 0 s) to when the plane lands. Find the slope of the line. Explain what the slope means in this situation.

Find any two points on the graph. Use the points to find the slope.

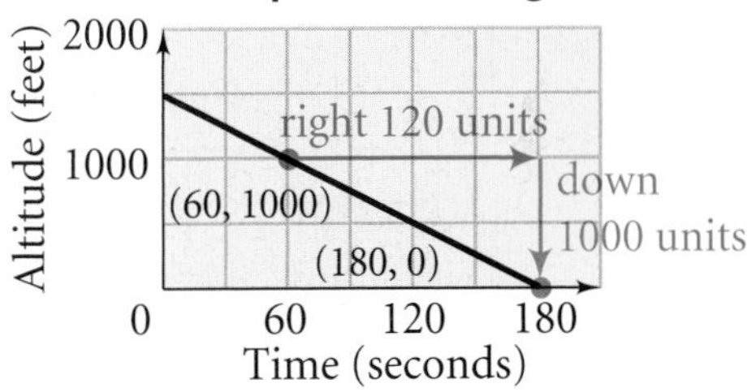

$$\text{slope} = \frac{\text{vertical change}}{\text{horizontal change}} = \frac{-1000}{120} = -8\tfrac{1}{3}$$

The slope of the line is $-8\frac{1}{3}$. The plane is descending $8\frac{1}{3}$ ft/s.

4. **Critical Thinking** Suppose a graph of a line with slope 12 indicates the relationship between altitude and time for another airplane. What would the slope mean in this situation?

Using Coordinates to Find Slope

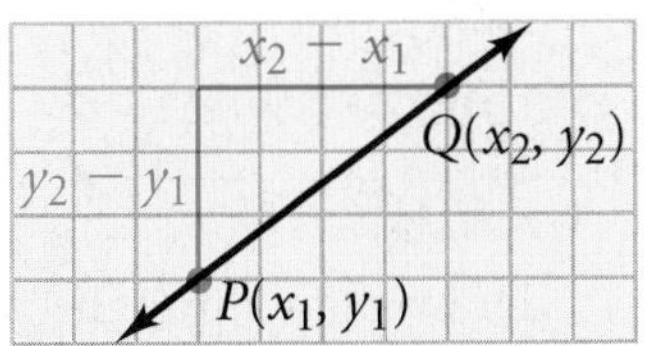

You read the coordinates (x_1, y_1) as "x sub 1, y sub 1."

You can use any two points on a line to find its slope. To find the slope of a line PQ (written $\overleftrightarrow{PQ}$), you can use this formula:

$$\text{slope} = \frac{\text{vertical change}}{\text{horizontal change}} = \frac{y_2 - y_1}{x_2 - x_1}, \text{ where } x_2 - x_1 \neq 0$$

5. **Critical Thinking** Why does the formula for the slope include the statement "where $x_2 - x_1 \neq 0$"?

Example 3

Find the slope of a line through $A(-2, 1)$ and $B(5, 7)$.

$$\text{slope} = \frac{y_2 - y_1}{x_2 - x_1}$$

$$= \frac{7 - 1}{5 - (-2)} \quad \leftarrow \text{Substitute } (5, 7) \text{ for } (x_2, y_2) \text{ and } (-2, 1) \text{ for } (x_1, y_1).$$

$$= \frac{6}{7}$$

The slope of $\overleftrightarrow{AB}$ is $\frac{6}{7}$.

6. Try This Find the slope of the line through $C(4, 0)$ and $D(-1, 5)$.

Example 4

Using the points shown, find the slope and equation of each line.

a.

$$\text{slope} = \frac{y_2 - y_1}{x_2 - x_1} = \frac{2 - 2}{4 - 1} = \frac{0}{3} = 0$$

The slope of a horizontal line is 0. All points on the graph have a y-coordinate of 2. The equation of the line is $y = 2$.

b.

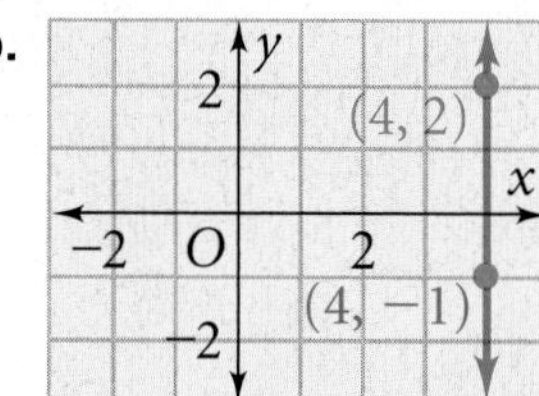

$$\text{slope} = \frac{y_2 - y_1}{x_2 - x_1} = \frac{2 - (-1)}{4 - 4} = \frac{3}{0}, \text{ undefined}$$

The slope of a vertical line is undefined. All points on the graph have an x-coordinate of 4. The equation of the line is $x = 4$.

7. Try This Describe the graph of $x = -5$ and the graph of $y = \frac{1}{2}$.

Graphing a Line Given Its Slope and a Point

Example 5

Draw a line through the point $(1, 2)$ with the slope $-\frac{3}{2}$.

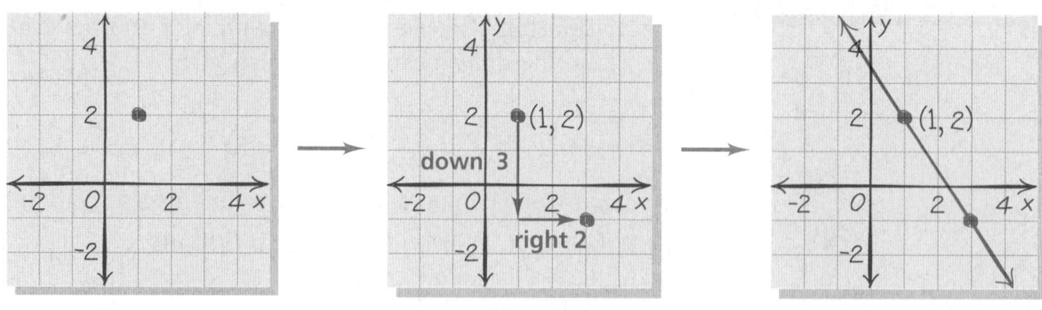

Plot $(1, 2)$. → Find another point using the slope $-\frac{3}{2}$. → Draw a line through the points.

8. Try This Graph the line through the point $(2, -3)$ with slope $\frac{5}{4}$.

Slope of Lines

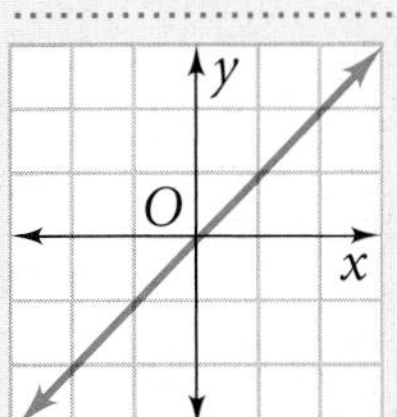

A line with positive slope goes upward from left to right.

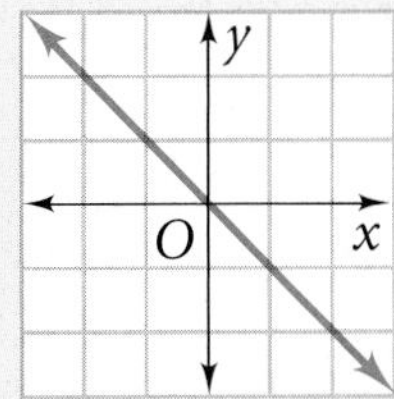

A line with negative slope goes downward from left to right.

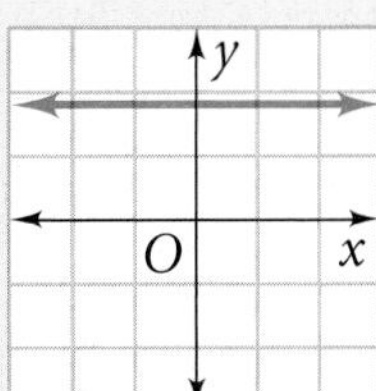

The slope of a horizontal line is 0. The equation of this line is $y = 1.8$.

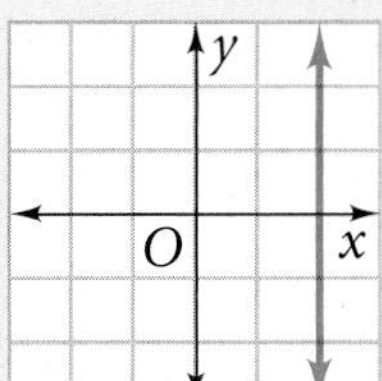

The slope of a vertical line is undefined. The equation of this line is $x = 2$.

Exercises ON YOUR OWN

Use the diagram at the right for Exercises 1 and 2.

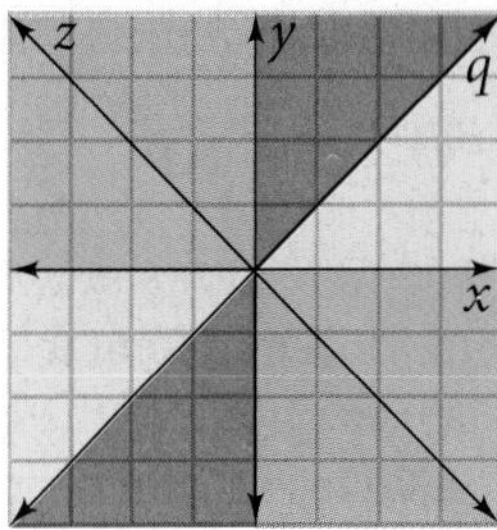

1. What is the slope of line q? of line z?
2. Open-ended What is the slope of a line through the origin that is in the red region? the yellow region? the green region? the blue region?

Find the slope of the line passing through each pair of points.

3. $(-8, 0), (1, 5)$
4. $(8, 3), (-4, 3)$
5. $(-4, -5), (-9, 1)$
6. $(\frac{1}{2}, 8), (1, -2)$
7. $(4, -1), (4, 7)$
8. $(9, -2), (3, 4)$

Through the given point, graph a line with the given slope.

9. $(3, 4)$; slope $= \frac{1}{2}$
10. $(-2, 1)$; slope $= -2$
11. $(0, 3)$; slope $= 0$
12. $(-5, -2)$; slope $= \frac{3}{4}$
13. $(1, -3)$; slope $= -\frac{2}{3}$
14. $(2, 5)$; slope $= -\frac{4}{3}$
15. $(-1, 5)$; undefined slope
16. $(-2, 3)$; slope $= -\frac{5}{3}$
17. Write equations for the lines described in Excercises 4, 7, 11, and 15.

Critical Thinking **Tell whether each statement is *true* or *false*. Explain.**

18. All horizontal lines have the same slope.
19. A line with slope 1 passes through the origin.
20. Two lines may have the same slope.
21. The slope of a line in Quadrant III must be negative.

Carpentry **Tell whether the slope would *increase, decrease,* or *remain the same.***

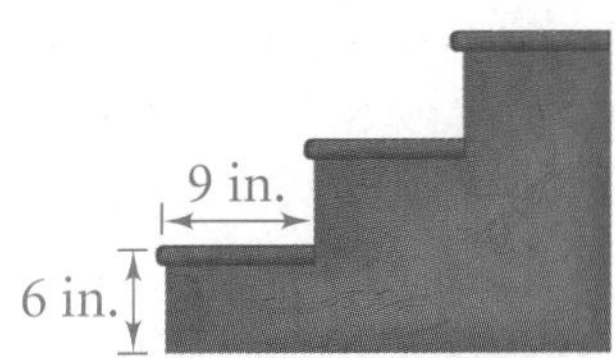

22. The rise of each step *increases* 1 in.
23. The run of each step *decreases* 1 in.
24. The rise and run both *increase* 1 in.

Geometry **Find the slope of the sides of each figure.**

25.
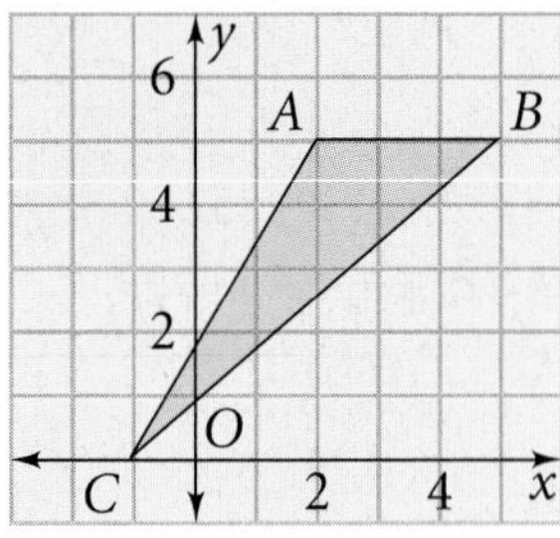

26.
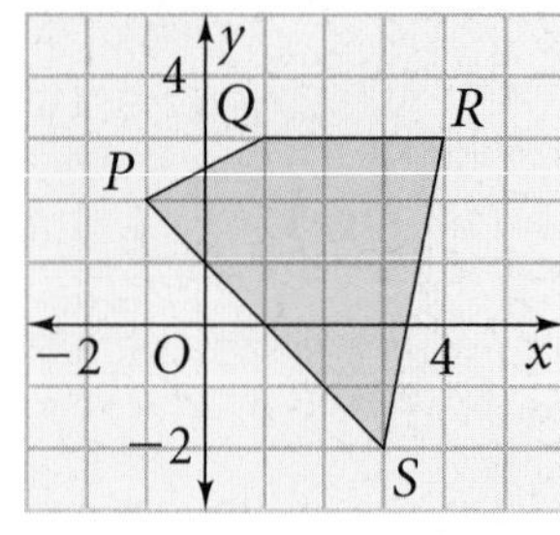

27.
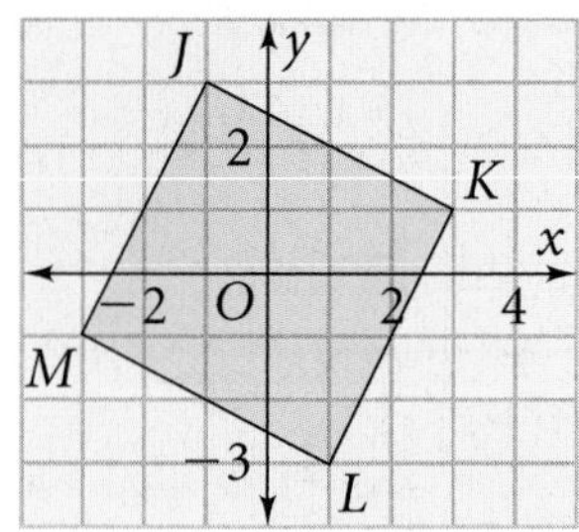

Do the points lie on the same line?

Sample $A(1, 3), B(4, 2), C(-2, 4)$

slope of $\overleftrightarrow{AB} = \frac{2-3}{4-1} = -\frac{1}{3}$ slope of $\overleftrightarrow{BC} = \frac{4-2}{-2-4} = \frac{2}{-6} = -\frac{1}{3}$

$\overleftrightarrow{AB}$ and $\overleftrightarrow{BC}$ have the same slope. So the points lie on the same line.

28. $A(3, 5), B(-1, 3), C(7, 7)$ **29.** $P(4, 1), Q(-1, 5), R(1, 2)$ **30.** $L(6, 4), M(3, 2), N(0, 0)$

31. **Fairs** The graph shows how much it costs to rent carousel equipment for a fair. Rental includes the cost of an operator.
- **a.** Estimate the slope of the line. What does that number mean?
- **b.** Customers pay \$2 for a ride. What is the number of customers needed per hour to cover the rental cost?

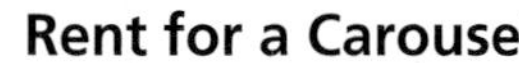

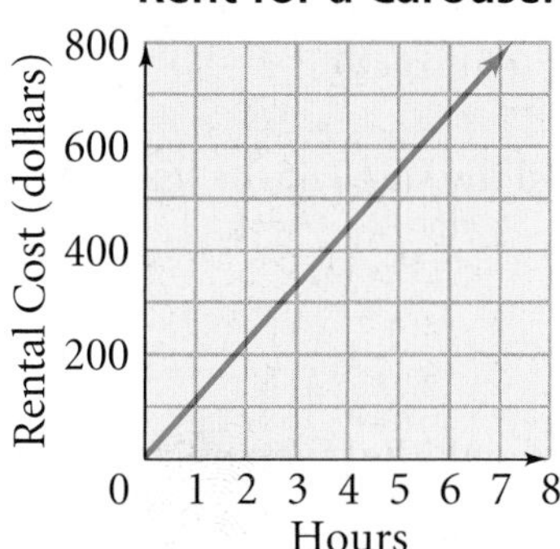

32. **Writing** A friend says the slope of the line passing through (1, 7) and (3, 9) is equal to the ratio $\frac{1-9}{7-3}$. Is this correct? Explain.

33. **Standardized Test Prep** A line has a slope of $\frac{4}{3}$. Through which two points could this line pass?

A. $(-4, 10), (8, 19)$ **B.** $(8, 10), (0, 16)$ **C.** $(-8, 10), (-2, 2)$
D. $(4, -4), (10, 2)$ **E.** none of the above

Exercises MIXED REVIEW

Find each probability based on one roll of a number cube.

34. $P(1)$ **35.** $P(\text{even number})$ **36.** $P(3 \text{ or } 5)$ **37.** $P(\text{integer})$ **38.** $P(10)$

39. **Environment** In 1994, biologists released 200,000 salmon into Alaska's Ninilchik River. In 1995, they released only 50,000 because the native salmon population had grown. Find the percent of change.

Getting Ready for Lesson 5-2

Identify the independent and dependent variable for each function.

40. distance an airplane flies and the time a flight takes

41. the amount of home heating fuel used and the outside temperature

Math ToolboX

Skills Review

Dimensional Analysis

Before Lesson 5-2

You can use conversion factors to change from one unit of measure to another. The process of analyzing units to decide which conversion factors to use is called **dimensional analysis.**

Since 60 min = 1 h, $\frac{60\text{ min}}{1\text{ h}}$ equals 1. You can use $\frac{60\text{ min}}{1\text{ h}}$ to convert hours to minutes.

$7\ \cancel{\text{h}} \cdot \frac{60\text{ min}}{1\ \cancel{\text{h}}} = 420\text{ min}$

The hour units cancel, and the result is minutes.

Sometimes you need to use more than one conversion factor.

Example

Animals A cheetah ran 300 ft in 2.92 s. What was the cheetah's speed in miles per hour?

You need to convert feet to miles and seconds to hours.

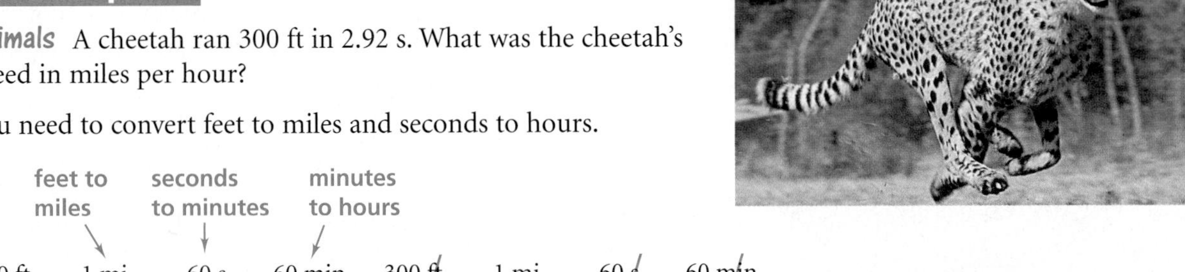

feet to miles — seconds to minutes — minutes to hours

$$\frac{300\text{ ft}}{2.92\text{ s}} \cdot \frac{1\text{ mi}}{5280\text{ ft}} \cdot \frac{60\text{ s}}{1\text{ min}} \cdot \frac{60\text{ min}}{1\text{ h}} = \frac{300\ \cancel{\text{ft}}}{2.92\ \cancel{\text{s}}} \cdot \frac{1\text{ mi}}{5280\ \cancel{\text{ft}}} \cdot \frac{60\ \cancel{\text{s}}}{1\ \cancel{\text{min}}} \cdot \frac{60\ \cancel{\text{min}}}{1\text{ h}}$$

← The feet, seconds, and minutes cancel. The result is miles per hour.

$$= \frac{(300 \cdot 1 \cdot 60 \cdot 60)\text{mi}}{(2.92 \cdot 5280 \cdot 1 \cdot 1)\text{h}}$$

← Use a calculator.

$$\approx 70\text{ mi/h}$$

The cheetah's speed was about 70 mi/h.

Choose A or B for the correct conversion factor for changing the units.

1. quarts to gallons
A. $\frac{1\text{ gal}}{4\text{ qt}}$ **B.** $\frac{4\text{ qt}}{1\text{ gal}}$

2. ounces to pounds
A. $\frac{1\text{ lb}}{16\text{ oz}}$ **B.** $\frac{16\text{ oz}}{1\text{ lb}}$

3. inches to yards
A. $\frac{36\text{ in.}}{1\text{ yd}}$ **B.** $\frac{1\text{ yd}}{36\text{ in.}}$

Write each in the given unit or units.

4. 8 h = ■ s

5. 120 in. = ■ yd

6. \$1.85/3.25 lb = ■ ¢/oz

7. 18 qt/s = ■ gal/min

Express each in miles per hour.

8. 300 yd in 10.9 min

9. 1 mi in 3.79 min

10. 120 ft in 30 s

11. 250 mi in 45 sec

12. *Writing* Explain how you determine which conversion factors to use when changing 3 in./s to feet per minute.

What You'll Learn

- Finding rates of change from tables and graphs

...And Why

To find rates of change in real-world situations, such as the rate of descent for a parachute or the cost of renting a computer

What You'll Need

- graph paper

5-2 Rates of Change

QUICK REVIEW

A *rate* is a ratio that compares two quantities measured in different units.

THINK AND DISCUSS

Finding Rate of Change

Suppose you type 140 words in 4 minutes. What is your typing rate?

$$\frac{140 \text{ words}}{4 \text{ min}} \text{ or } \frac{35 \text{ words}}{1 \text{ min}} \begin{array}{l} \leftarrow \text{dependent variable} \\ \leftarrow \text{independent variable} \end{array}$$

The number of words depends on the number of minutes you type. So, the number of words is the dependent variable.

1. Write each as a rate.
  a. You buy 5 yards of fabric for $19.95.
  b. You travel 268.8 mi on 12 gal of gasoline.

You use a rate to find the amount of one quantity per one unit of another, such as typing 35 words in 1 min. The **rate of change** allows you to see the relationship between two quantities that are changing.

$$\text{rate of change} = \frac{\text{change in the dependent variable}}{\text{change in the independent variable}}$$

On a graph, you show the dependent variable on the vertical axis and the independent variable on the horizontal axis. The slope of a line is the rate of change relating the variables.

$$\text{slope} = \frac{\text{vertical change}}{\text{horizontal change}} = \frac{\text{change in the dependent variable}}{\text{change in the independent variable}}$$

Example 1 Relating to the Real World 

Parachuting Find the rate of change for data graphed on the line. Then explain what the rate of change means in this situation.

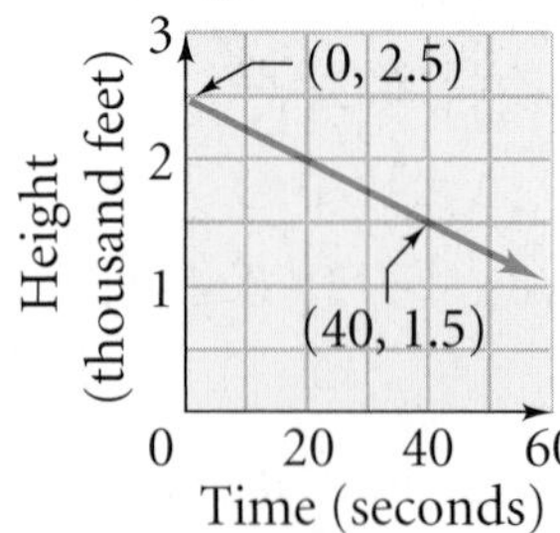

Find two points on the graph. Use the points to find the slope, which is also the rate of change.

$$\text{slope} = \frac{\text{vertical change}}{\text{horizontal change}} = \frac{1.5 - 2.5}{40 - 0} = -\frac{1}{40}$$

The rate of change is $-\frac{1}{40}$, which means that the parachute descends 1000 ft every 40 seconds.

2. In Example 1, why is height the dependent variable?

3. How many feet does the parachute descend in a second?

Using a Table

Example 2 **Relating to the Real World** 

Cost of Renting a Computer

Number of Days	Hraibe's Rental Company
1	$60
2	$75
3	$90
4	$105
5	$120

Rental Business You can rent a computer from Hraibe's Rental Company. The first day's rent is $60. Find the rate of change for renting a computer after the first day.

$$\text{rate of change} = \frac{\text{change in the dependent variable}}{\text{change in the independent variable}}$$

$$= \frac{\text{change in cost}}{\text{change in number of days}}$$ ← Cost depends on the number of days.

$$= \frac{105 - 60}{4 - 1}$$ ← Use any two pairs of data.

$$= \frac{45}{3}$$

$$= \frac{15}{1}$$

The rate of change is $\frac{15}{1}$, which means that it costs $15 for each day a computer is rented after the first day.

4. Will the rate of change for the data in the table be the same for any pair of data items? Explain.

Linear Functions

The graph of a **linear function** is a line. You can also use a table to tell whether the relationship between sets of data is linear.

Graph

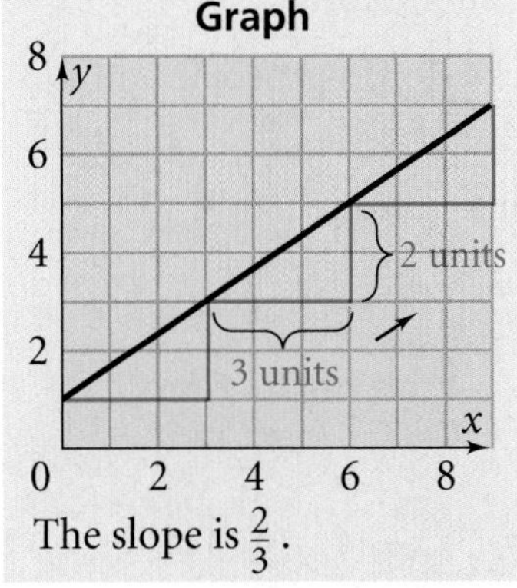

The slope is $\frac{2}{3}$.

Table

x	y
0	1
3	3
6	5
9	7

(x increases by 3 each step; y increases by 2 each step)

3 units → 2 units

Rate of Change

(0, 1) to (3, 3) $\frac{2}{3}$

(3, 3) to (6, 5) $\frac{2}{3}$

(6, 5) to (9, 7) $\frac{2}{3}$

As you can see from the table for the graph, the rate of change between consecutive pairs of data is constant. So, the relationship between the x-values and the y-values is linear.

Example 3 Relating to the Real World 

Science Tell whether the relationship shown by the data is linear.

Boiling Temperature of Water

Altitude	Temperature
0 ft	212° F
4,000 ft	204.6° F
8,000 ft	197.2° F
12,000 ft	189.8° F

(Altitude changes: 4000, 4000, 4000; temperature changes: −7.4, −7.4, −7.4)

Each rise of 4000 ft in altitude results in a 7.4° decline in the boiling temperature of water. So the relationship is linear.

5. **Critical Thinking** How much does the boiling temperature of water change for each 1000-ft rise in altitude?

6. **Critical Thinking** How could you find the boiling temperature of water in Denver, which has an altitude of 5300 ft?

7. **Try This** Is the relationship shown by the data linear?

x	0	1	3	5	7	9
y	0	1	4	9	16	25

Exercises ON YOUR OWN

Find the rate of change for each situation.

1. A baby is 18 in. long at birth and 27 in. at ten months.
2. The cost of group tickets for a museum is \$48 for four people and \$78 for ten people.
3. You drive 30 mi in one hour and 120 mi in four hours.

Find the rate of change.

4. 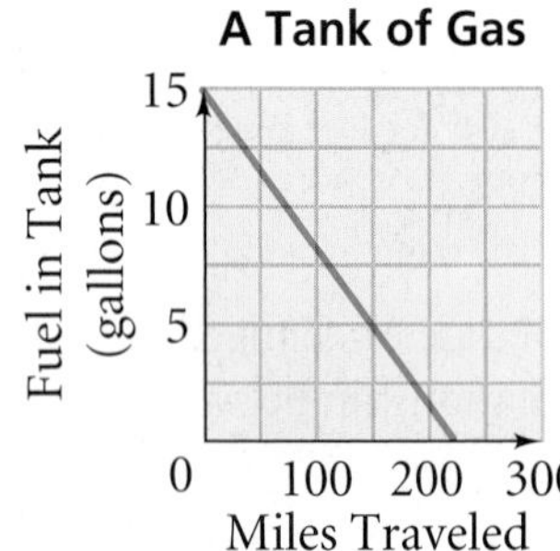

5. 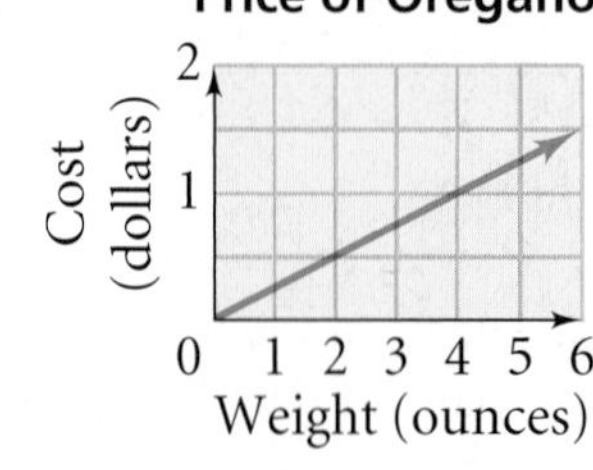

6. 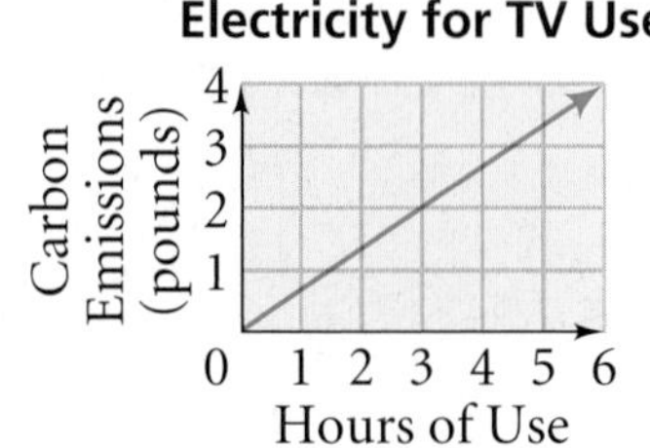

7. a. At colder temperatures, people burn more calories. Is the relationship between the two quantities linear? Explain.
   b. **Critical Thinking** How can you find the number of calories burned at 20°F?

Working Outdoors

Temperature	Calories Burned Per Day
68°F	3030
62°F	3130
56°F	3230
50°F	3330

Critical Thinking Tell whether each statement is *true* or *false*. If true, explain why. If false, give an example.

8. Rates of change are always constant.
9. The rate of change for a linear function is constant.
10. Two linear functions with positive slope are graphed on the same coordinate plane. The function with the greater rate of change will be steeper.
11. A rate of change must be either positive or zero.

Is the relationship shown by the data in each table linear?

12.

x	y
3	1
4	−2
5	−5
6	−8

13.

x	y
2	0
4	1
6	4
8	9

14.

x	y
0	3
1	6
2	9
3	12

15.

x	y
−3	5
−1	8
1	12
3	17

16.

x	y
1	0
8	1
15	2
22	3

17.

x	y
9	−4
5	1
1	6
−3	11

18. a. **Critical Thinking** Find the rate of change between consecutive pairs of data.

x	1	3	4	7
y	3	7	9	15

   b. Is the relationship shown by the data linear? Explain.

19. **Video Recording** The graph shows the lengths of videotape used in 30 min at three different settings of a VCR.
   a. At which setting does the tape move fastest? slowest? Explain.
   b. **Critical Thinking** At which setting can you record for the longest time? Explain.

Video Recording

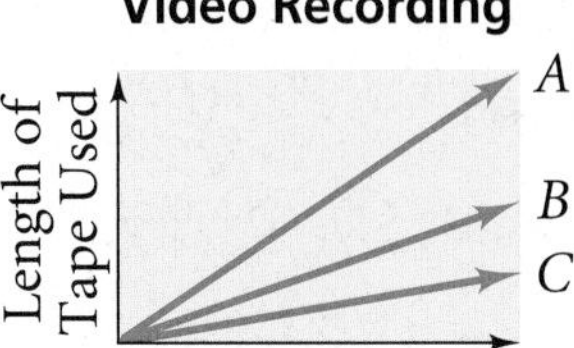

20. **Writing** How can you tell if the relationship between two sets of data is linear?

21. a. **Patterns** Draw the next two figures for the pattern at the right.
   b. Make a table for the relationship between the number of squares and the perimeter of each figure.
   c. Is the relationship between the number of squares and the perimeter linear? Explain.

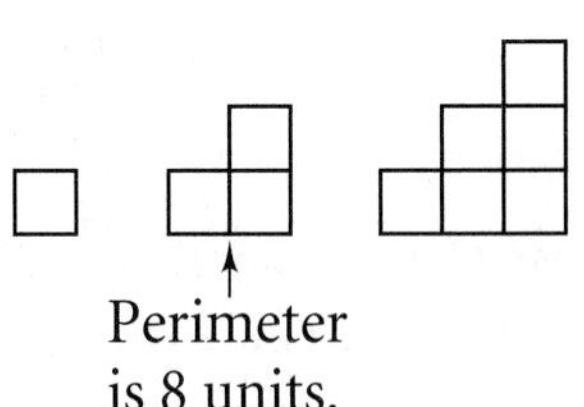

22. **a.** **Biology** Which line in the graph at the right is the steepest?
b. During the 5-week period, which plant had the greatest rate of change? the least rate of change? How do you know?

23. **Open-ended** Lanai is hiking up a mountain. She monitors and records her distance every half hour. Do you think the rates of change for every half hour are constant? Explain.

Plant Growth

Height (in.)

4
3
2
1
O 1 2 3 4 5

A
B
C

Time (weeks)

24. **a.** Find the rate of change for the line.

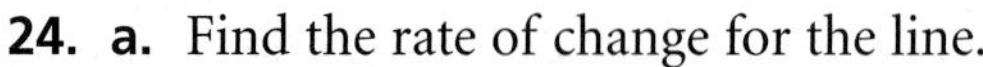

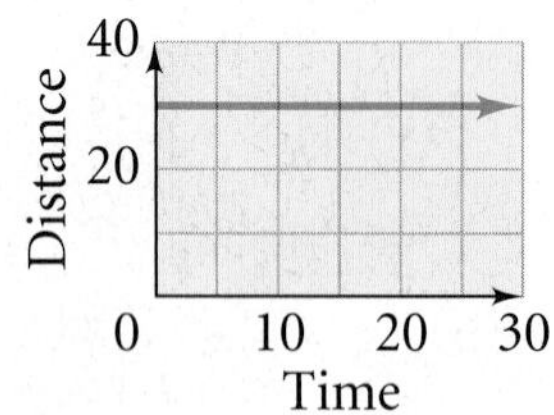

b. **Writing** What situation could be modeled by the graph?
c. **Critical Thinking** What do you think is true about the rate of change for a horizontal line? Explain.

Chapter Project

Find Out by Graphing

Find the starting hourly wage for two jobs that interest you.

- Make a graph that shows the income for each job. Show hours worked (0 to 10) on the horizontal axis and income on the vertical axis.
- Suppose you work eight hours. Explain how your graph shows the difference in income from the two jobs.

Exercises MIXED REVIEW

Solve.

25. $x + 3 = 2x - 1$

26. $3(2t + 5) = -9$

27. $2.8m - 1.3m = 4.5$

28. $\frac{6s + 4}{8} = \frac{1}{2}$

29. **Food** In the United States, people eat about 340 million pounds of cranberries per year. About 73 million pounds are eaten during Thanksgiving week alone. About what percent of the cranberries is consumed during the week of Thanksgiving?

Getting Ready for Lesson 5-3

Model each rule with a table of values and a graph.

30. $y = 3x$

31. $y = 0.8x$

32. $y = \frac{3}{4}x$

33. $y = 7.2x$

5-3 Direct Variation

What You'll Learn

- Relating slope to constant of variation
- Using constant of variation to solve problems

...And Why

To solve real-world problems, such as finding the force needed to lift a given weight

Movie projectors run at 24 frames/s. Video cameras project at 30 frames/s.

THINK AND DISCUSS

Direct Variation

Movies As you watch a movie, 24 individual pictures, or frames, flash on the screen each second. Here are three ways you can model the relationship between the number of frames and the number of seconds.

Table

x number of seconds	y number of frames
1	24
2	48
3	72
4	96
5	120

Graph

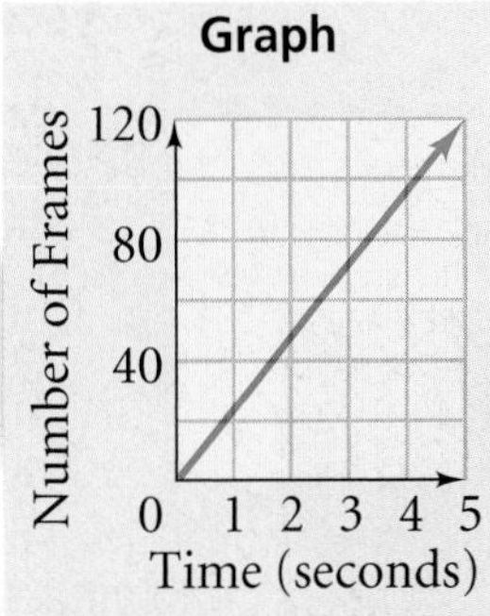

Function Rule

$y = 24x$

1. a. What is the rate of change for the data in the table?
   b. What is the slope of the line shown in the graph?
   c. What is the relationship between the rate of change, the slope, and the coefficient of x in the function rule?

The number of frames *varies directly* with the number of seconds the movie has been shown. This relationship is called a direct variation.

> **Direct Variation**
>
> A **direct variation** is a linear function that can be written in the form $y = kx$, where $k \neq 0$.
>
> ↑ constant of variation

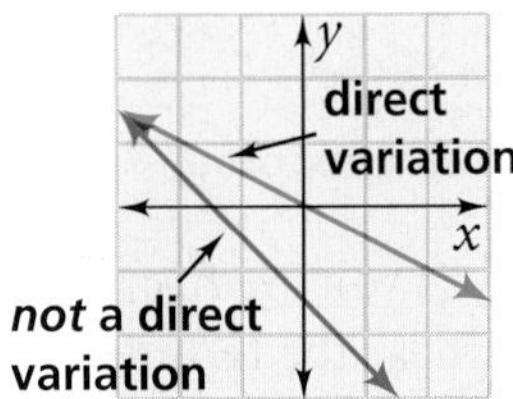

The function rule for a linear function is called a **linear equation.** Since a direct variation can be written as the linear equation $y = kx$, then when $x = 0$, $y = 0$. So the graph of a direct variation will pass through the origin, (0, 0).

You can write the linear equation $y = kx$ as $k = \frac{y}{x}$, where $x \neq 0$. The **constant of variation** k equals the rate of change for data that describe the variation. The value of k also equals the slope of the line that graphs the equation.

2. The direct variation graphed at the left includes the point $(2, -1)$. What is its constant of variation?

To tell if a linear equation is a direct variation, you can transform the equation by solving for y.

Example 1

Is each equation a direct variation? If it is, find the constant of variation.

a. $5x + 2y = 0$

$2y = -5x$ ← Solve for y. →

$y = -\frac{5}{2}x$

Yes, $y = -\frac{5}{2}x$ is in the form $y = kx$. The constant of variation is $-\frac{5}{2}$.

b. $5x + 2y = 9$

$2y = -5x + 9$

$y = -\frac{5}{2}x + \frac{9}{2}$

No, the equation is *not* in the form $y = kx$.

3. Critical Thinking Diane tries substituting (0, 0) for (x, y) to see if an equation is a direct variation. Does her method work? Explain.

4. Try This Is each equation a direct variation? If it is, find the constant of variation.

a. $7y = 2x$ **b.** $3y + 4x = 8$ **c.** $y - 7.5x = 0$

Using the Constant of Variation to Write Equations

Example 2 **Relating to the Real World** 

Weather The time it takes you to hear thunder varies directly with your distance from the lightning. If you are 2 mi from where lightning strikes, you will hear thunder about 10 s after you see the lightning. Write an equation for the relationship between time and distance.

Define x = your distance in miles from the lightning

y = the number of seconds between seeing lightning and hearing thunder

Relate The time varies directly with the distance. When $x = 2, y = 10$.

Write

$y = kx$ ← Use the general form of a direct variation.

$10 = k(2)$ ← Substitute 2 for x and 10 for y.

$\frac{10}{2} = \frac{2k}{2}$ ← Solve for k.

$5 = k$

$y = 5x$ ← Substitute 5 for k to write an equation.

The equation $y = 5x$ relates the distance x in miles you are from lightning to the time y in seconds it takes you to hear the thunder.

What? A bolt of lightning that you see during a thunderstorm has a speed that varies from 100 to 1000 mi/s.

Source: *The Guinness Book of Records*

5. Use the equation in Example 2 to find about how far you are from lightning if you hear thunder 7 s after you see lightning.

You can use the ratio $\frac{y}{x}$ to tell if two sets of data vary directly.

Example 3

For each table, tell whether y varies directly with x. If it does, write a function rule for the relationship shown by the data.

Find the ratio $\frac{y}{x}$ for each pair of data.

a.

x	y	$\frac{y}{x}$
-3	2.25	$\frac{2.25}{-3} = -0.75$
1	-0.75	$\frac{-0.75}{1} = -0.75$
4	-3	$\frac{-3}{4} = -0.75$

Yes, the constant of variation is -0.75. The function is $y = -0.75x$.

b.

x	y	$\frac{y}{x}$
2	-1	$\frac{-1}{2}$
4	1	$\frac{1}{4}$
6	3	$\frac{3}{6} = \frac{1}{2}$

No, the ratio $\frac{y}{x}$ is not the same for each pair of data.

6. **a.** Find the rate of change for the data in each table in Example 3.
   b. Is the relationship shown by the data in each table linear? Explain.
   c. **Critical Thinking** A direct variation is a linear function. Are all linear functions direct variations? Explain.

Using Proportions

In a direct variation, the ratio $\frac{y}{x}$ is the same for any pair of data where $x \neq 0$. So the proportion $\frac{y_1}{x_1} = \frac{y_2}{x_2}$ is true for the ordered pairs (x_1, y_1) and (x_2, y_2) where $x_1 \neq 0$ and $x_2 \neq 0$.

Example 4 **Relating to the Real World** 

Physics The force you must apply to lift an object varies directly with the object's weight. You need to apply 0.625 lb of force to the windlass to lift a 28-lb weight. How much force would you need to lift 100 lb?

Relate The force of 0.625 lb lifts 28 lb. The force of n lb lifts 100 lb.

Define $\text{force}_1 = 0.625$ lb $\text{force}_2 = n$
$\text{weight}_1 = 28$ lb $\text{weight}_2 = 100$ lb

Write

$$\frac{\text{force}_1}{\text{weight}_1} = \frac{\text{force}_2}{\text{weight}_2} \quad \leftarrow \text{Use a proportion.}$$

$$\frac{0.625}{28} = \frac{n}{100} \quad \leftarrow \text{Substitute.}$$

$$100(0.625) = 28n \quad \leftarrow \text{Cross-multiply.}$$

$$\frac{100(0.625)}{28} = n \quad \leftarrow \text{Divide each side by 28.}$$

$$n \approx 2.232142857 \quad \leftarrow \text{Use a calculator.}$$

You need about 2.2 lb of force to lift a 100-lb object.

7. Write an equation for the direct variation in Example 4.

8. a. Try This Use your equation in Question 7 or proportions to find how much weight you can lift with a force of 4.3 lb.

   b. Why did you choose the method you used for part (a)?

Exercises ON YOUR OWN

1. Which of the lines at the right are graphs of direct variations? Explain.

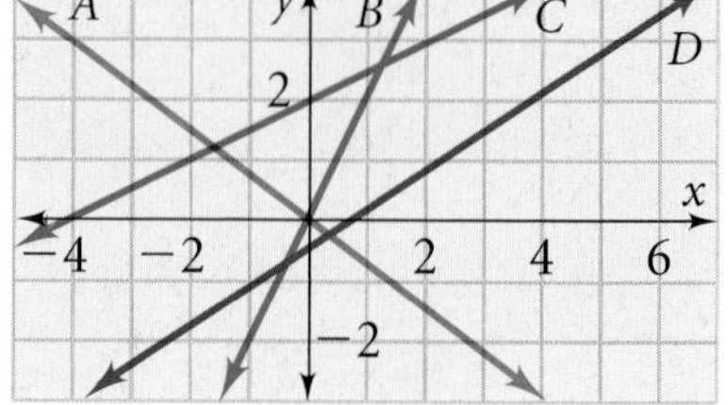

Is each equation a direct variation? If it is, what is the constant of variation?

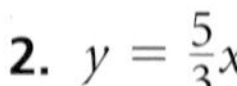

2. $y = \frac{5}{3}x$

3. $y = 2x + 4$

4. $y^2 = 2x$

5. $y = \frac{x}{4}$

6. $3y = 8x$

7. $x + 5y = 10$

8. Critical Thinking Can the points (2, 3) and (4, 6) be on the graph of the same direct variation? Explain.

For each table, tell whether y varies directly with x. If it does, write a function rule for the relationship shown by the data.

9.

x	y
3	5.4
7	12.6
12	21.6

10.

x	y
−2	1
3	6
8	11

11.

x	y
−6	9
1	−1.5
8	−12

12.

x	y
−5	−13
3	7.8
9	21.6

Draw the graph of a direct variation that includes the given point. Write an equation of the line.

13. (2, 5)

14. (−2, 5)

15. (2, −5)

16. (−2, −5)

17. Physics The maximum weight you can lift with the lever in the diagram varies directly with the amount of force you apply. What force do you need to lift a friend who weighs 130 lb?

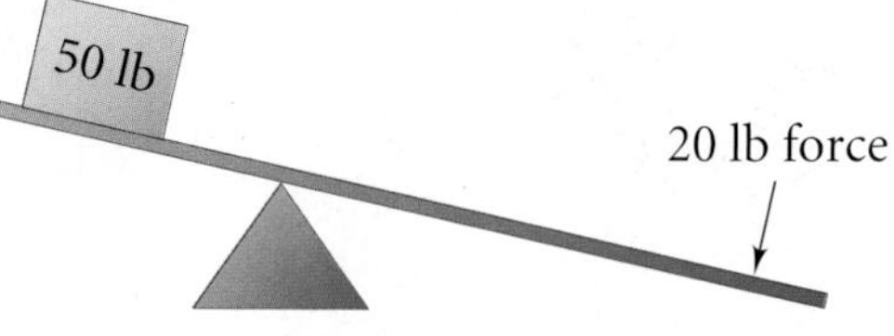

18. Critical Thinking For what value of c is $ax - by = c$ a direct variation?

Critical Thinking **Is each statement true? Explain.**

19. The graph of a direct variation may pass through (0, 3).

20. If you double an x-value of a direct variation, the y-value also doubles.

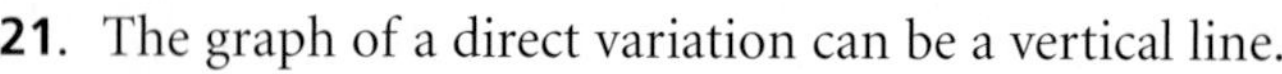

21. The graph of a direct variation can be a vertical line.

22. a. Writing How can you tell whether two sets of data vary directly?

    b. How can you tell if a line is the graph of a direct variation?

23. **Biology** The amount of blood in a person's body varies directly with body weight. Someone weighing 160 lb has about 5 qt of blood.

a. Find the constant of variation and write an equation relating quarts of blood to weight.

b. Graph your equation.

c. **Open-ended** Estimate the number of quarts of blood in your body.

24. **Bicycling** A bicyclist traveled at a constant speed during a timed practice period. Use an equation or proportions to find the distance the cyclist will travel in 30 min.

Bicyclist's Practice

Elapsed Time	Distance
10 min	3 mi
25 min	7.5 mi

Suppose the ordered pairs in each exercise are for the same direct variation. Find each missing value.

25. $(3, 4)$ and $(9, y)$ **26.** $(-1, 2)$ and $(4, y)$ **27.** $(-5, 3)$ and $(x, -4.8)$ **28.** $(1, y)$ and $(\frac{3}{2}, -9)$

29. $(2, 5)$ and $(x, 12.5)$ **30.** $(-2, 5)$ and $(x, -5)$ **31.** $(-6, -3)$ and $(-4, y)$ **32.** $(x, -4)$ and $(-9, -12)$

33. **a.** Write an equation relating the data in the cartoon.

b. How many dog years are 12 human years?

from the cartoon *Mother Goose and Grimm*

Exercises MIXED REVIEW

Solve each equation. Graph the solutions on a number line.

34. $4m + 3 < 2$ **35.** $9 > 5 - 3t$ **36.** $-z + 8 \geq 5$

37. Jeans are on sale at four different stores. The original price of the jeans at each store is \$35. Which of the following sales will give you the best price on the jeans?

A. 25% off the original price **B.** $\frac{1}{3}$ off the original price

C. pay 70% of the original price **D.** \$10 off the original price

SELF ASSESSMENT

FOR YOUR JOURNAL

Explain how rate of change, slope, and constant of variation are related.

Getting Ready for Lesson 5-4

Draw a line with the given slope that passes through the given point.

38. slope $= 3$, passes through $(0, -5)$ **39.** slope $= -\frac{7}{8}$, passes through $(0, 4)$

5-4 Slope-Intercept Form

What You'll Learn

- Using the slope and y-intercept to draw graphs and write equations

...And Why

To investigate flag designs and real-world situations, such as salary plus commission

What You'll Need

- graphing calculator

WORK TOGETHER

1. a. **Graphing Calculator** Graph these equations on the same screen.
   $y = \frac{1}{2}x$ $\quad y = x \quad$ $y = 5x$

   b. **Generalize** How does the coefficient of x affect the graph of an equation?

2. a. **Graphing Calculator** Many national flags include designs formed from straight lines. You can use equations to model these designs. Choose values for k in the equation $y = kx$ to create a display like the one for the flag of Jamaica. Use the standard settings.

Jamaica

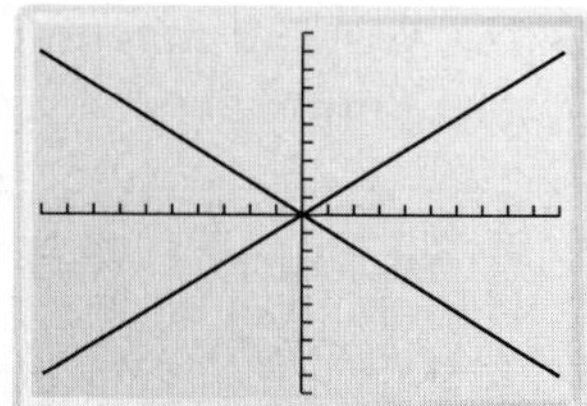

   b. What do you notice about the values of k for the lines you graphed?

3. a. **Graphing Calculator** Graph these equations on the same screen.
   $y = 2x$ $\quad y = 2x + 3 \quad$ $y = 2x - 4$

   b. Where does each line cross the y-axis?

Tanzania

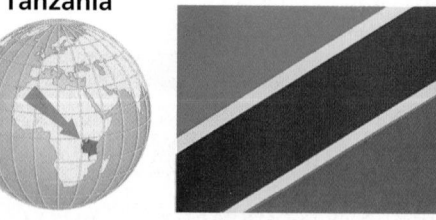

4. Choose values for b in the equation $y = 1.1x + b$. Create a display that resembles the Tanzanian flag. Write the equations you used for your display.

5. **Generalize** What effect does the value of b have on the graph of an equation?

6. **Open-ended** Make a flag design of your own. Write the equations you use for your design.

THINK AND DISCUSS

Defining Slope-Intercept Form

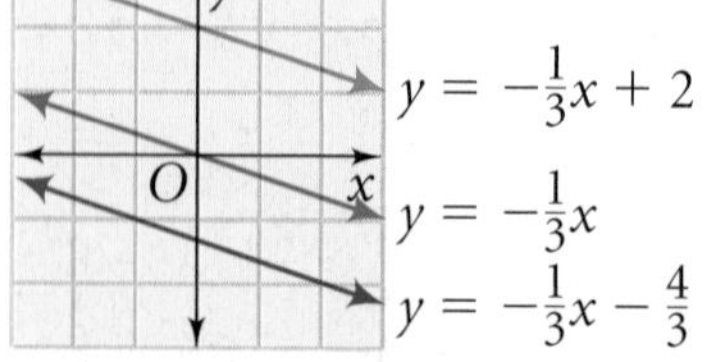

The point where a line crosses the y-axis is the **y-intercept.**

7. a. What is the y-intercept of each line at the left?

   b. **Generalize** What is the connection between a line's equation and its y-intercept?

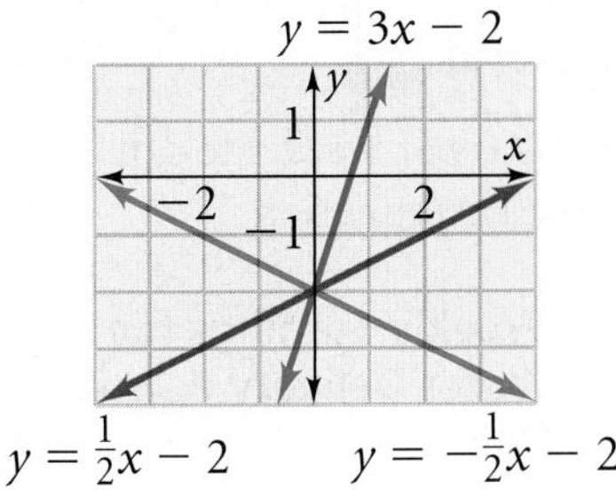

8. **a.** What is the slope of each line at the left?
   b. **Generalize** What is the connection between a line's equation and its slope?

In the last lesson you learned that the letter k indicates the constant of variation of a direct variation. For linear equations in general, the letter m indicates the slope and the letter b indicates the y-intercept.

Slope-Intercept Form of a Linear Equation

The **slope-intercept form** of a linear equation is $y = mx + b$.
(slope: m; y-intercept: b)

9. **Try This** What are the slope and y-intercept of the line for each equation?
   a. $y = 3x - 5$ **b.** $y = \frac{7}{6}x + \frac{3}{4}$ **c.** $y = -\frac{4}{5}x$

10. **Try This** Write an equation of a line with the given slope and y-intercept.
   a. $m = \frac{2}{3}, b = -5$ **b.** $m = -\frac{1}{2}, b = 0$ **c.** $m = 0, b = -2$

You can use the slope and y-intercept to graph an equation.

Example 1

Graph the equation $y = 3x - 1$.

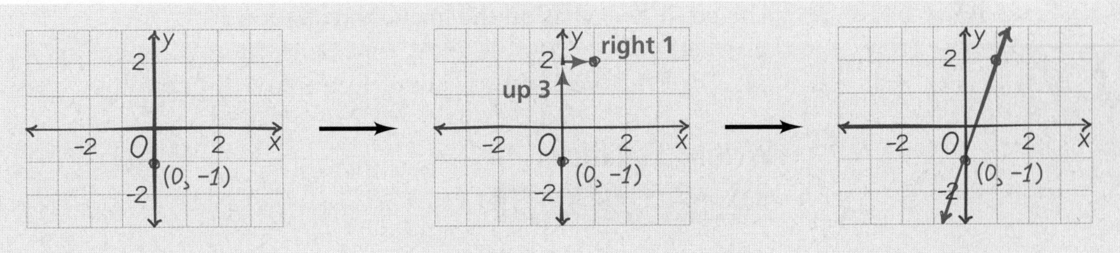

The y-intercept is -1, so plot a point at $(0, -1)$. The slope is 3, or $\frac{3}{1}$. Use the slope to plot a second point. Draw a line through the points.

11. **Critical Thinking** Could you find a second point by going down 3 and to the left 1? Explain.

12. **Try This** Graph $y = -\frac{3}{2}x + 2$.

You may need to rewrite a linear equation to express it in slope-intercept form.

Example 2 Relating to the Real World 

Jobs The base pay of a water delivery person is \$210 per week. He can also earn 20% commission on any sales he makes. The equation $t = 210 + 0.2s$ relates total earnings t to sales s. Rewrite the equation in slope-intercept form. Then graph the equation.

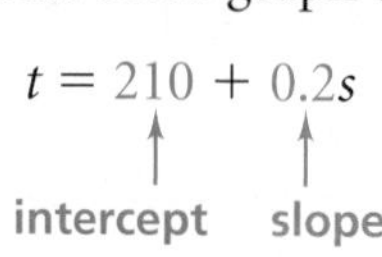

$t = 210 + 0.2s$

intercept ↑ slope ↑

$t = 0.2s + 210$ ← slope-intercept form

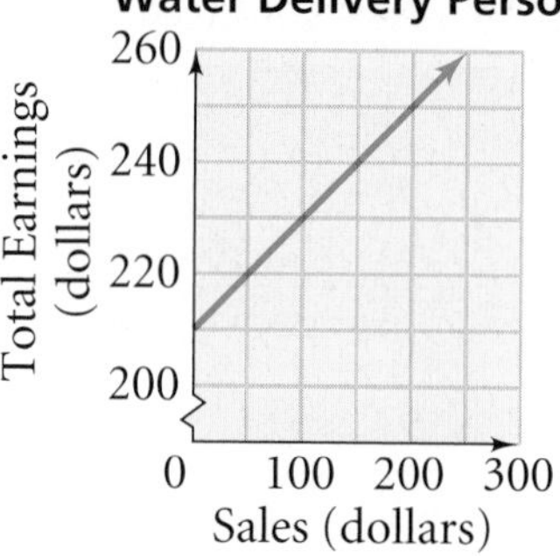

13. Try This Rewrite $y + 5 = 4x$ in slope-intercept form.

You can use the equation of a line to determine if a point lies on the line.

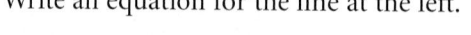

Example 3

Does the point (8, 4) lie on the line with equation $y = \frac{3}{4}x - 2$?
Test the coordinates of the point in the equation of the line.

$y = \frac{3}{4}x - 2$

$4 \stackrel{?}{=} \frac{3}{4}(8) - 2$ ← Substitute 8 for x and 4 for y.

$4 \stackrel{?}{=} 6 - 2$ ← Simplify.

$4 = 4$ ✔ ← The values of x and y satisfy the equation.

The point (8, 4) lies on the line with equation $y = \frac{3}{4}x - 2$.

14. Try This **Verify** the result of Example 3 by graphing.

Writing Equations

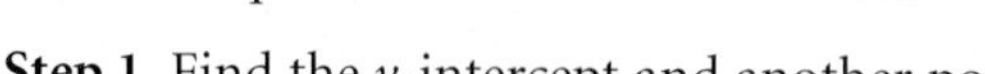

Example 4

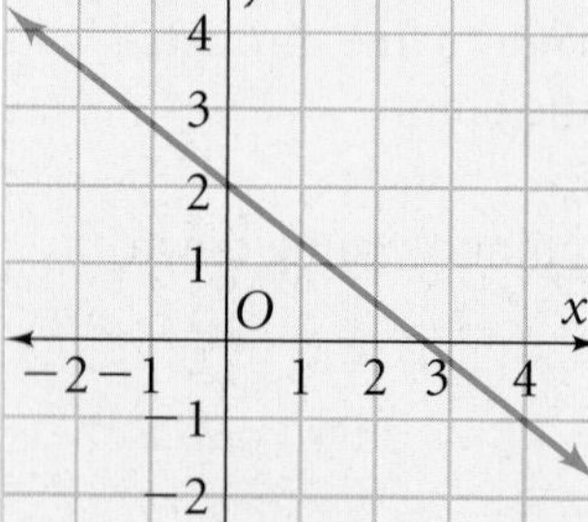

Write an equation for the line at the left.

Step 1 Find the y-intercept and another point.

The y-intercept is 2; (0, 2) and (4, −1) lie on the line.

Step 2 Find the slope.
Use (0, 2) and (4, −1).

$$\text{slope} = \frac{-1 - 2}{4 - 0}$$
$$= -\frac{3}{4}$$

Step 3 Write an equation in slope-intercept form.
Substitute $-\frac{3}{4}$ for m and 2 for b.

$$y = mx + b$$
$$y = -\frac{3}{4}x + 2$$

Exercises ON YOUR OWN

Find the slope and y-intercept of each equation.

1. $y = -\frac{3}{4}x - 5$ **2.** $y = \frac{1}{2}x$ **3.** $3x - 9 = y$ **4.** $2x = y + 7$ **5.** $y = 3$

6. *Standardized Test Prep* A music store sells CDs for \$12 each. Customers may use one coupon good for \$4 off the total purchase. Suppose a customer buys n number of CDs using a coupon. Which equation models the relationship between the total cost t and the number of CDs a customer buys?

A. $t = 12n - 4$ **B.** $t = 4n - 12$ **C.** $4t = 12n$ **D.** $t = 12 - 4n$ **E.** $t = 4 - 12n$

Match the graph with the correct equation.

7. $y = x + 5$ **8.** $y = -\frac{5}{2}x + 5$ **9.** $y = -\frac{1}{2}x + 5$

I.

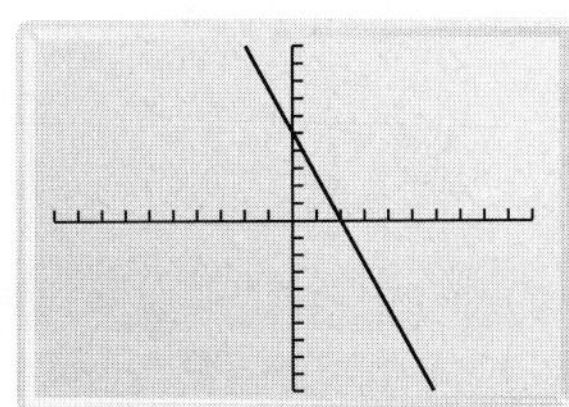

II.

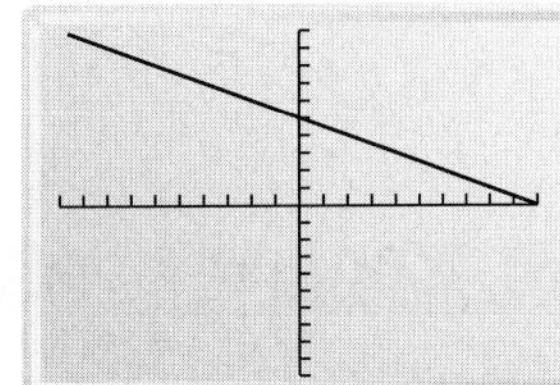

III.

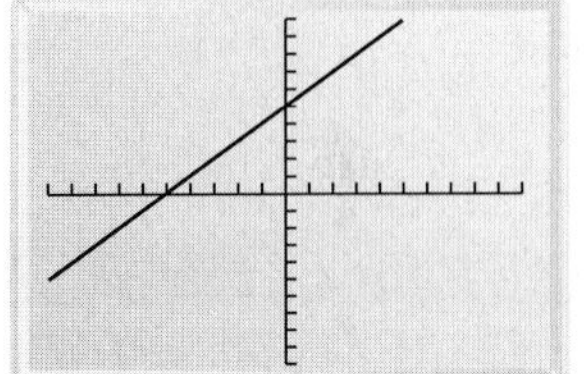

10. *Graphing Calculator* Suppose you want to graph the equation $y = \frac{5}{4}x - 3$. Enter each key sequence and display the graphs.

a. Y= 5 ÷ 4 X,T,θ − 3 **b.** Y= (5 ÷ 4) X,T,θ − 3

c. Which key sequence gives you the graph of $y = \frac{5}{4}x - 3$? Explain.

Graph each equation.

11. $y = -x + 3$ **12.** $y = 2x - 1$ **13.** $y = 5 + 2x$ **14.** $y - 4 = x$

15. $y + \frac{3}{4}x = 0$ **16.** $y = 7$ **17.** $y = -\frac{1}{2}x + \frac{3}{2}$ **18.** $y = -\frac{2}{3}x$

19. Does the point $(-3, 4)$ lie on the graph of $y = -2x + 1$? Explain.

20. Does the point $(2, 4)$ lie on the graph of $y = 3x - 2$? Explain.

Find the slope and y-intercept. Write an equation of each line.

21.

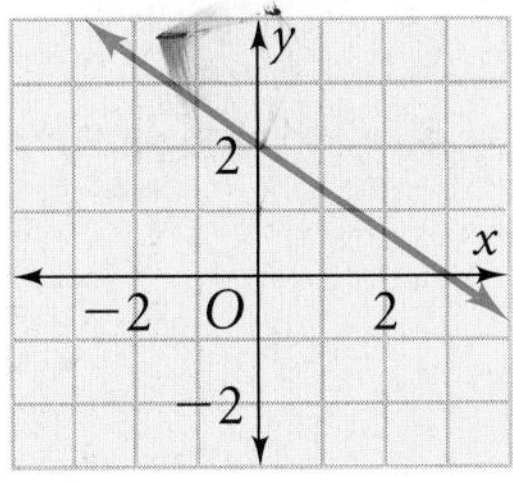

22.

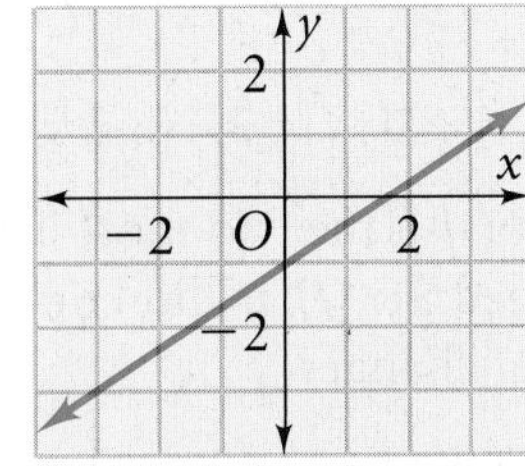

23.

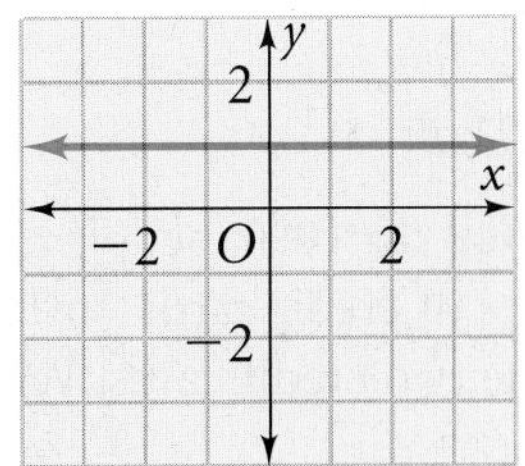

24. **Recreation** A group of mountain climbers begins an expedition with 265 lb of food. They plan to eat a total of 15 lb of food per day. The equation $r = 265 - 15d$ relates the remaining food supply r to the number of days d.
   a. Write the equation in slope-intercept form.
   b. Graph your equation.
   c. The group plans to eat the last of their food the day their expedition ends. Use your graph to find how many days the expedition will last.

25. **Open-Ended** Write an equation of your own. Identify the slope and y-intercept. Graph your equation.

26. **Writing** Explain how you would graph the line $y = \frac{3}{4}x + 5$.

Write an equation of a line with the given slope and y-intercept.

27. $m = \frac{2}{9}, b = 3$ 28. $m = 5, b = -\frac{2}{3}$ 29. $m = -\frac{5}{4}, b = 0$ 30. $m = 0, b = 1$

Exercises MIXED REVIEW

Find the slope of the line through each set of points.

31. $(-2, 8), (5, -1)$ 32. $(4, 6), (2, -1)$ 33. $(1, 2), (6, 1)$

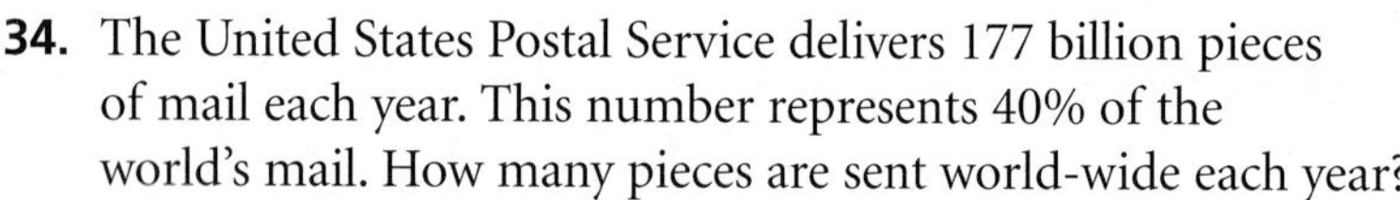
34. The United States Postal Service delivers 177 billion pieces of mail each year. This number represents 40% of the world's mail. How many pieces are sent world-wide each year?

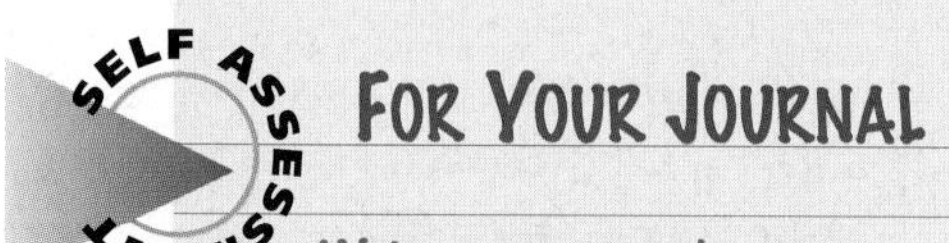

Write a paragraph explaining how to use the slope and y-intercept to write an equation and to draw a graph.

Getting Ready for Lesson 5-5

Through the given point, graph a line with the given slope. Then identify the y-intercept.

35. $(2, 0); m = -1$ 36. $(2, 3); m = \frac{3}{2}$ 37. $(3, 2); m = \frac{1}{3}$ 38. $(-2, 1); m = -\frac{5}{2}$

Exercises CHECKPOINT

Is a line through the given point with the given slope a direct variation? Explain.

1. $(4, 2); m = \frac{1}{2}$ 2. $(-2, -2); m = -1$ 3. $(6, 9)$; m is undefined 4. $(-3, 5); m = -\frac{5}{3}$

5. **Money** In 1990, people charged \$534 billion on the two most used types of credit cards. In 1994, people charged \$1.021 trillion on these same two credit cards. What was the rate of change?

6. **Writing** How are the graphs of $y = 3x + 5$, $y = \frac{2}{3}x + 5$, and $y = \frac{3}{5}x + 5$ alike? How are they different?

Math ToolboX

Technology

Exploring Range and Scale

After Lesson 5-4

The minimum and maximum values for an axis determine the range of values shown on that axis. Screens A and B show the graph of $y = 4x$.

Screen A

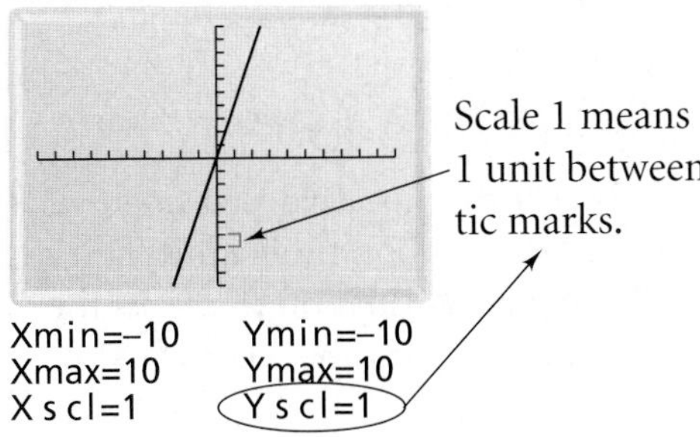

Scale 1 means 1 unit between tic marks.

Xmin=–10 Ymin=–10
Xmax=10 Ymax=10
Xscl=1 Yscl=1

Screen A shows standard settings for a graphing calculator screen.

Screen B

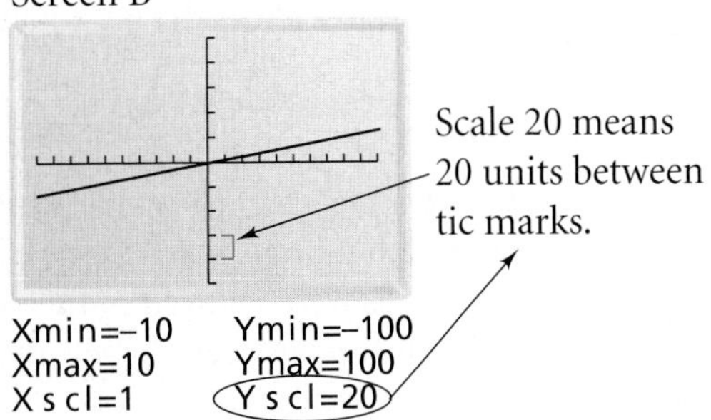

Scale 20 means 20 units between tic marks.

Xmin=–10 Ymin=–100
Xmax=10 Ymax=100
Xscl=1 Yscl=20

The range on the y-axis is 10 times greater for Screen B than Screen A. So the line in Screen B appears flatter than the line in Screen A.

1. a. Explain how you would find the Xscl and Yscl for the screen at the right.
b. Write an equation for the line shown on the screen.

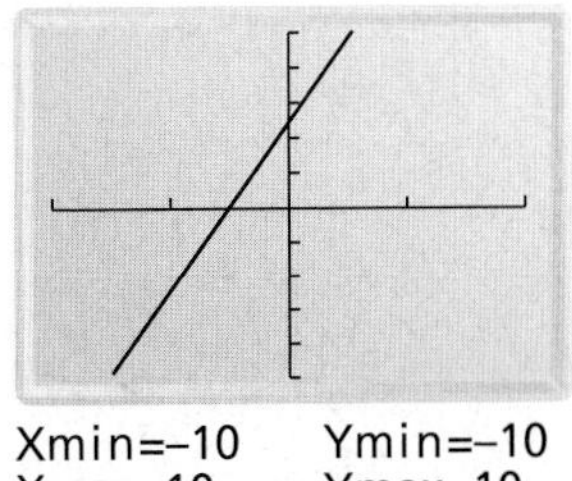

Xmin=–10 Ymin=–10
Xmax=10 Ymax=10
Xscl= Yscl=

To change the range, use the WINDOW feature. Then change the values of Xmin, Xmax, Ymin, or Ymax. For a negative number, use the (–) key. You can return to standard settings by pressing ZOOM 6.

2. a. *Open-ended* Graph the line $y = 2x + 30$ using standard settings. Then change the Ymin or Ymax value so that the y-intercept is on your screen. What Ymin or Ymax value did you choose?
b. *Open-ended* Change the Xmin or Xmax value until you see where the line crosses the x-axis. Sketch your graph. State the minimum and maximum values you used for each axis.

Find Xmin, Xmax, Ymin, and Ymax values that allow you to see where each line crosses both axes. Sketch the graph of each equation.

3. $y = 3x + 20$ **4.** $y = -x + 100$ **5** $y = \frac{1}{5}x - 30$ **6.** $y = -\frac{1}{50}x + \frac{1}{10}$

7. $y = \frac{2}{3}x + 1500$ **8.** $y = -0.3x - 60$ **9.** $y = 55x + 55$ **10.** $y = -25x - \frac{1}{25}$

11. *Writing* How does changing the range affect how a graph looks?

Connections Environment . . . and more

5-5 Writing the Equation of a Line

What You'll Learn

- Writing an equation given the slope and a point
- Writing an equation given two points from a graph or a table

...And Why

To write equations to investigate real-world situations, such as carbon monoxide emissions

THINK AND DISCUSS

In some real-world situations you can identify the rate of change, or slope, and an ordered pair. Then you can use the slope and ordered pair to model the situation with a linear equation.

Example 1 *Relating to the Real World* 

Environment World-wide carbon monoxide emissions are decreasing about 2.6 million metric tons each year. In 1991, carbon monoxide emissions were 79 million metric tons. Use a linear equation to model the relationship between carbon monoxide emissions and time. Let $x = 91$ correspond to 1991.

Step 1 Use the data to write the slope and an ordered pair.

slope: -2.6; ordered pair: $(91, 79)$

Step 2 Find the y-intercept using the slope and the ordered pair.

$$y = mx + b$$
$$79 = -2.6(91) + b$$ ← Substitute (91, 76) for (x, y) and -2.6 for m.
$$79 = -236.6 + b$$
$$315.6 = b$$

Step 3 Substitute values for m and b to write an equation.

$$y = mx + b$$
$$y = -2.6x + 315.6$$ ← Substitute -2.6 for m and 315.6 for b.

The equation $y = -2.6x + 315.6$ models the relationship between carbon monoxide emissions and time.

1. a. Using the equation in Example 1, estimate the emissions for 1990.
   b. According to this model, what will the emissions be for 2000?

2. **Try This** Write an equation of a line with slope $\frac{2}{5}$ through the point $(4, -3)$.

You can use two points on a line to find an equation for the line. First find the slope of the line through the points. Then use the slope and one point to find the y-intercept and to write an equation of the line.

Example 2

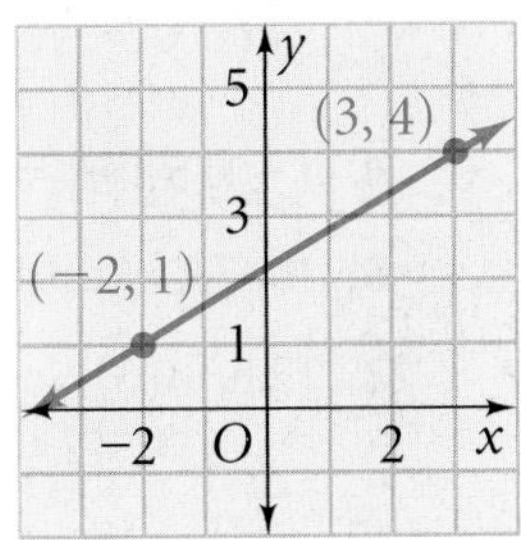

Find an equation of the line at the left.

Step 1 Use the coordinates of two points to find the slope of the line.

$$\text{slope} = \frac{y_2 - y_1}{x_2 - x_1}$$
$$= \frac{4 - 1}{3 - (-2)} \quad \leftarrow \text{Substitute (3, 4) for } (x_2, y_2) \text{ and } (-2, 1) \text{ for } (x_1, y_1).$$
$$= \frac{3}{5}$$

Step 2 Find the y-intercept.

$$y = mx + b$$
$$4 = \frac{3}{5}(3) + b \quad \leftarrow \text{Substitute (3, 4) for } (x, y) \text{ and } \frac{3}{5} \text{ for } m. \text{ Solve for } b.$$
$$4 = \frac{9}{5} + b$$
$$2\frac{1}{5} = b$$

Step 3 Substitute values in $y = mx + b$.

$$y = \frac{3}{5}x + 2\frac{1}{5} \quad \leftarrow \text{Substitute } \frac{3}{5} \text{ for } m \text{ and } 2\frac{1}{5} \text{ for } b.$$

3. Try This Find an equation of the line through (–5, 3) and (–2, –4).

You can also write a linear equation for data in tables. Two sets of data have a linear relationship if the rate of change between consecutive pairs of data is the same.

Example 3

x	y
−1	4
3	6
5	7
9	9

Is the relationship shown by the data linear? If it is, write an equation.

Step 1 Find the rate of change for consecutive ordered pairs.

(−1, 4) to (3, 6): $\frac{6-4}{3-(-1)} = \frac{2}{4} = \frac{1}{2}$

(3, 6) to (5, 7): $\frac{7-6}{5-3} = \frac{1}{2}$

(5, 7) to (9, 9): $\frac{9-7}{9-5} = \frac{2}{4} = \frac{1}{2}$

The relationship is linear. The rate of change equals the slope. The slope is $\frac{1}{2}$.

Step 2 Find the y-intercept and write an equation.

$$y = mx + b$$
$$4 = \frac{1}{2}(-1) + b \quad \leftarrow \text{Substitute } (-1, 4) \text{ for } (x, y) \text{ and } \frac{1}{2} \text{ for } m.$$
$$4 = -\frac{1}{2} + b$$
$$4\frac{1}{2} = b \quad \leftarrow \text{Add } \frac{1}{2} \text{ to each side of the equation.}$$
$$y = \frac{1}{2}x + 4\frac{1}{2} \quad \leftarrow \text{Substitute } \frac{1}{2} \text{ for } m \text{ and } 4\frac{1}{2} \text{ for } b \text{ in } y = mx + b.$$

PROBLEM SOLVING

Look Back Could you use a graph to find whether the relationship is linear? Explain.

4. Critical Thinking Is (−1, 4) the only ordered pair that you could use to find the y-intercept in Example 3? Explain.

Exercises ON YOUR OWN

Write an equation of a line through the given point with the given slope.

1. $(3, -5); m = 2$ **2.** $(1, 2); m = -3$ **3.** $(2, 6); m = \frac{4}{3}$ **4.** $(-1, 5); m = -\frac{3}{5}$

5. $(0, 3); m = 1$ **6.** $(3, 0); m = -1$ **7.** $(-5, 2); m = 0$ **8.** $(6, 7)$; m undefined

9. $(3, 3); m = -\frac{1}{4}$ **10.** $(5, -2); m = \frac{7}{2}$ **11.** $(-6, 1); m = -\frac{3}{4}$ **12.** $(2.8, 10.5); m = 0.25$

13. a. *Physics* Each gram of mass stretches the spring 0.025 cm. Use $m = 0.025$ and the ordered pair (50, 8.5) to write a linear equation that models the relationship between the length of the spring and the mass.

b. *Critical Thinking* What does the y-intercept mean in this situation?

c. What is the length of the spring for a mass of 70 g?

8.5 cm

50g

Write an equation of a line through the given points.

14. $(3, -3), (-3, 1)$ **15.** $(7, 3), (2, 2)$ **16.** $(3, 5), (5, 3)$

17. $(-8, 2), (1, 3)$ **18.** $(-0.5, 2), (-2, 1.5)$ **19.** $(25, 100), (15, 120)$

Write an equation of each line.

20.

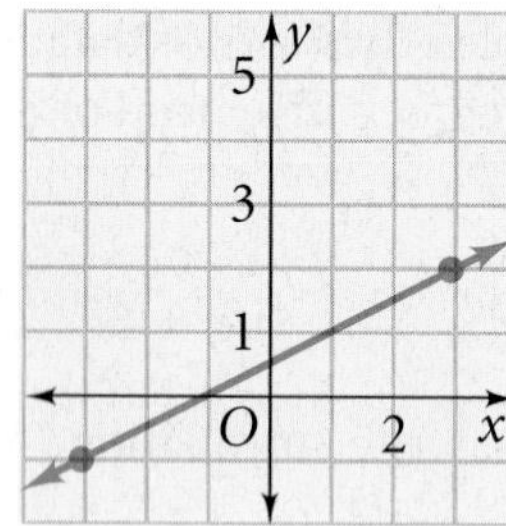

21.

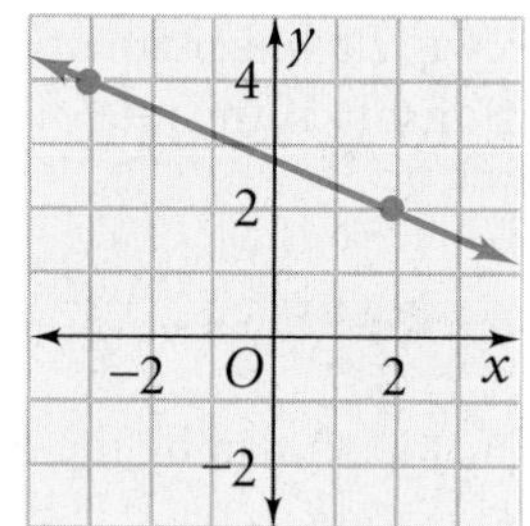

22.

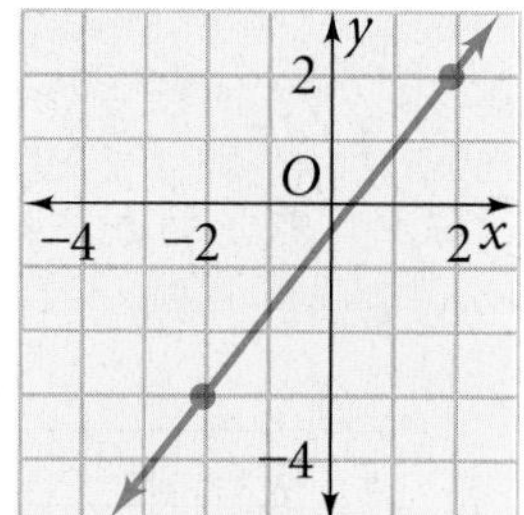

23. *Entertainment* Total receipts for motion picture theaters were \$3.9 billion in 1986. Receipts were \$6.9 billion in 1992.

a. Write an equation to model the relationship between receipts and time in years. Let 86 correspond to 1986.

b. Use your equation to **predict** motion picture theater receipts in the year 2010. (*Hint:* Think about the number you will use for 2010.)

Tell whether the relationship shown by the data is linear. If it is, write an equation for the relationship.

24.

x	y
−10	−7
0	−3
5	−1
20	5

25.

x	y
−4	9
2	−3
5	−9
9	−17

26.

x	y
1	7
2	8
3	10
4	13

27.

x	y
−10	−5
−2	19
5	40
11	58

28.

x	y
3	1
6	4
9	13
15	49

29. a. **Business** A taxicab ride that is 2 mi long costs \$7. One that is 9 mi long costs \$24.50. Write an equation relating cost to length of ride.
   b. What do the slope and y-intercept mean in this situation?

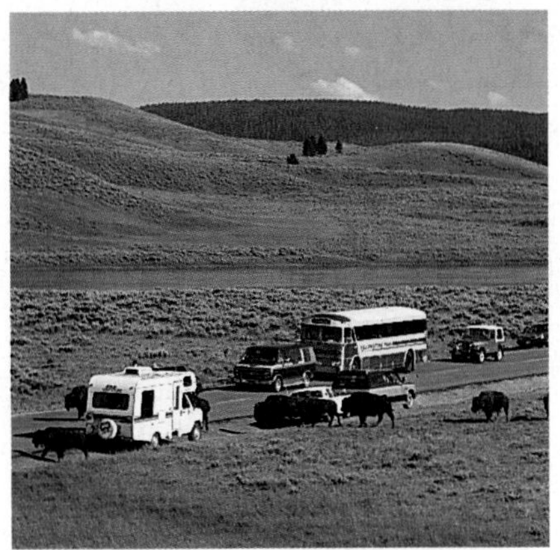

30. **National Parks** The number of recreational visits to National Parks in the United States increases by about 9.3 million visits each year. In 1990 there were about 263 million visits.
   a. Write an equation to model the relationship between the number of visits and time in years. Let 90 correspond to 1990.
   b. **Open-ended** Suppose the number of recreational visits to National Parks continues to increase at the same rate. How many visits will there be this year?

Chapter Project ***Find Out by Modeling***

Suppose you earn \$5.50/h at a bakery. From your first paycheck you discover that \$1.15/h is withheld for taxes and benefits. You work x hours during a five-day week and you spend \$3.75 each day for lunch.

- Write an equation for your earnings for a week after taxes and expenses.
- In this situation what does the slope represent? the y-intercept?
- How many hours must you work to earn \$120 after taxes and expenses?

Exercises MIXED REVIEW

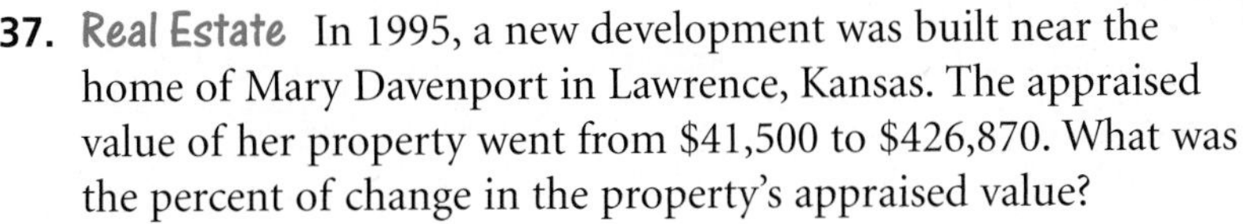

Solve.

31. $4c < 24 + c$
32. $\frac{t}{2} + \frac{t}{3} = 5$
33. $-4m \geq 7$
34. $|5c| < 16$
35. $4(3h + 2) = 5h - 3$
36. $|2n + 5| \geq 9$

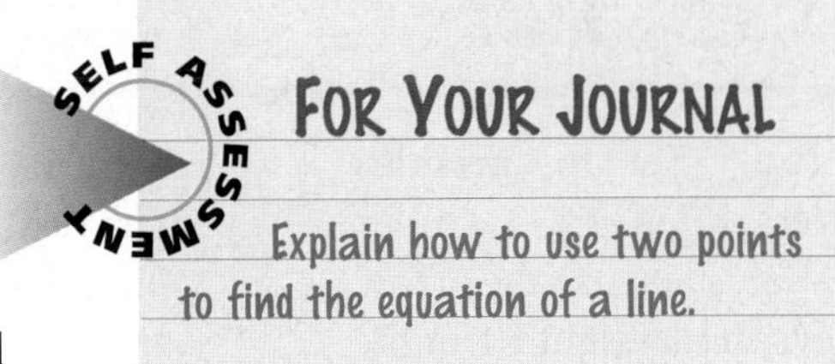

SELF ASSESSMENT
FOR YOUR JOURNAL
Explain how to use two points to find the equation of a line.

37. **Real Estate** In 1995, a new development was built near the home of Mary Davenport in Lawrence, Kansas. The appraised value of her property went from \$41,500 to \$426,870. What was the percent of change in the property's appraised value?

Getting Ready for Lesson 5-6

Determine whether each scatter plot shows *positive, negative,* or *no correlation.*

38. 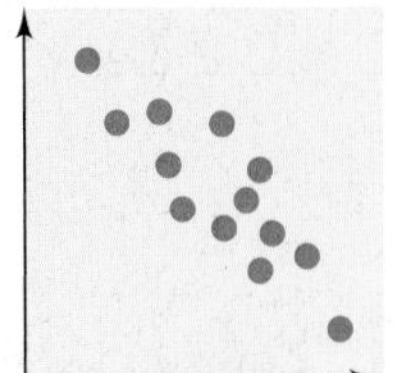

39. 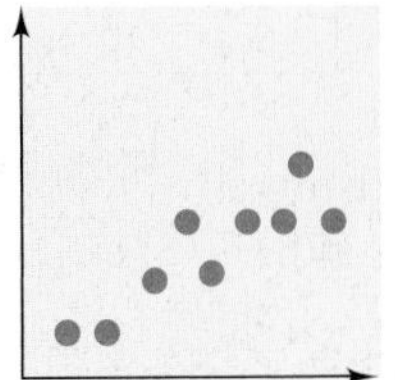

40. 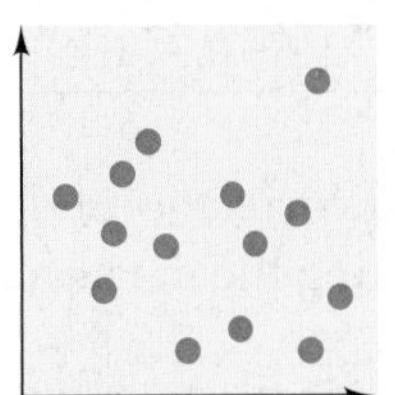

41. 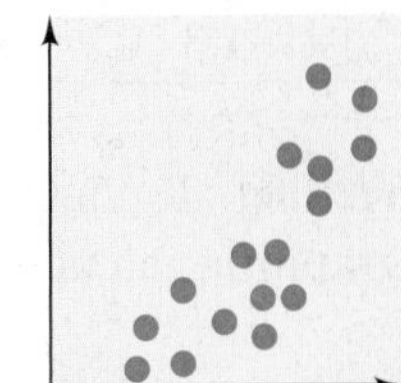

Math ToolboX

Technology

Displaying Data

Before Lesson 5-6

The data in the table are displayed on the two graphing calculator screens.

Data

Year	Profit (in thousands of dollars)
1990 ↔ 90	125
91	205
92	296
93	510
94	620
95	904
96	1040

List Display

L1	L2	L3
90	125	-----
91	205	
92	296	
93	510	
94	620	
95	904	
96	1040	

L2 (7)=1040

Scatter Plot Display

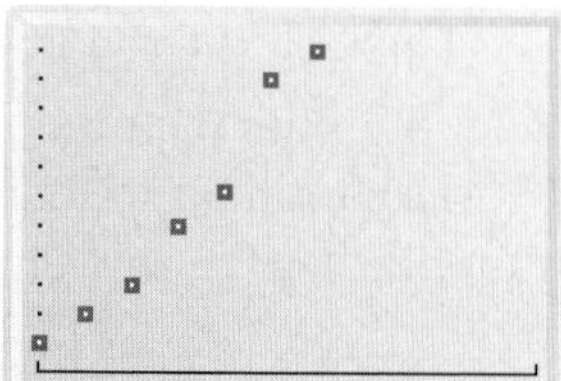

List Display To enter data into a list, press STAT 1. Clear old data in column L1, by pressing ▲ CLEAR ENTER. Enter the year data in the first list. After each data item press ENTER. Press ▶ to move to column L2. Then clear any old data. Enter the second set of data.

Scatter Plot Display You can make a scatter plot of data that are in lists.

SET UP CALCS
1–Var Stats
Xlist: L1 L2 L3 L4 L5 L6
Freq: 1 L1 L2 L3 L4 L5 L6
2–Var Stats
Xlist: L1 L2 L3 L4 L5 L6
Ylist: L1 L2 L3 L4 L5 L6
Freq: 1 L1 L2 L3 L4 L5 L6

Step 1 Set Up Variables Press STAT ▶ 3. Under 2-Var Stats, use the arrow keys to highlight L1 in the Xlist. Press ENTER. Highlight L2 in the Ylist.

WINDOW FORMAT
Xmin=90
Xmax=100
Xscl=10
Ymin=0
Ymax=1100
Yscl=100

Step 2 Choose Range The range for each variable should include the least and greatest number in the corresponding list.

Plot1
On Off
Type:
Xlist: L1 L2 L3 L4 L5 L6
Ylist: L1 L2 L3 L4 L5 L6
Mark: ▪ + ·

Step 3 Make Graph Press 2nd Y= 1 ENTER. Move the cursor and press ENTER to select the options shown. Then press GRAPH.

Display the data in a scatter plot. For each exercise, tell whether the data have a *positive correlation, negative correlation,* or *no correlation.*

1.

x	105	95	73	120	74	147	55	62
y	1.3	0.9	0.5	1.7	0.6	1.6	0.3	0.4

2.

x	10.1	10.6	11.1	12.3	9.3	13.1	10.6
y	47	35	64	22	55	27	9

3. **Writing** To view data to find correlations, do you prefer using a graphing calculator or graphing the data on graph paper? Why?

Connections Entertainment . . . and more

5-6 Scatter Plots and Equations of Lines

What You'll Learn

- Finding the equation of a trend line
- Using a calculator to find an equation for a line of best fit

...And Why

To analyze and make predictions based on real-world data

What You'll Need

- graphing calculator
- graph paper
- clock or watch with second hand

Ticket Sales for *Forrest Gump*	
Week	**Sales (in millions)**
1	\$39.9
2	\$39.2
3	\$35.3
4	\$28.6
5	\$22.9
6	\$21.5

Source: *Variety*

THINK AND DISCUSS

Trend Line

Sometimes you can describe data that show a positive or negative correlation with a trend line. Then you can use the trend line to make predictions.

Example 1 Relating to the Real World 

Entertainment A film usually makes the most money in ticket sales during the first few weeks after its release. Find the equation of a trend line for the data about ticket sales for *Forrest Gump.*

Step 1 Draw a scatter plot. Then use a straightedge to draw a trend line. There should be about the same number of points above and below the trend line. Estimate two points on your trend line.

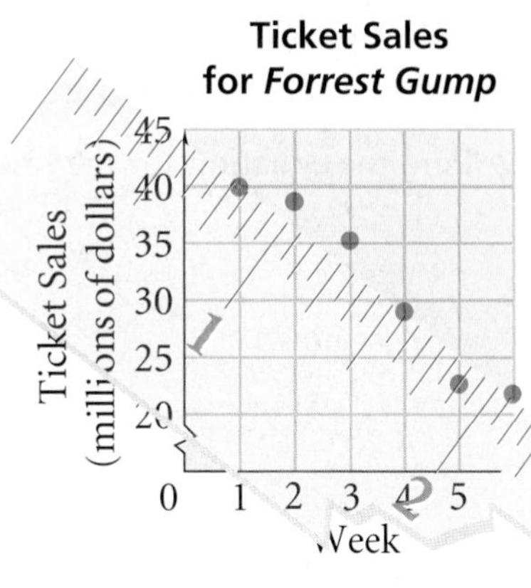

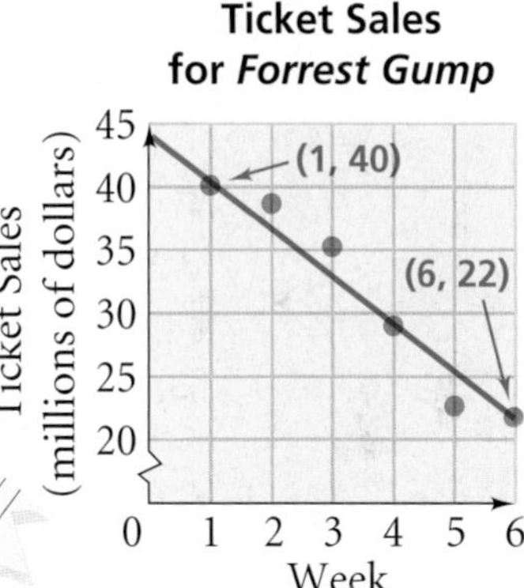

Step 2 Find the slope and y intercept.

$$\text{slope} = \frac{22-40}{6-1} \quad \longleftarrow \frac{y_2 - y_1}{x_2 - x_1}$$

$$= -\frac{18}{5} = -3.6$$

$y = mx + b$ ⟵ Use slope-intercept form to find the y-intercept.

$22 = -3.6(6) + b$ ⟵ Substitute –3.6 for m and (6, 22) for (x, y). Then solve for b.

$22 = -21.6 + b$

$43.6 = b$ ⟵ the y-intercept

Step 3 Write an equation of the line.

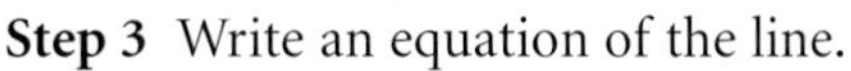

$y = -3.6x + 43.6$ ⟵ Substitute –3.6 for m and 43.6 for b.

The equation $y = -3.6x + 43.6$ models the ticket sales.

1. **Predict** the ticket sales in the tenth week after the film's release.

GRAPHING CALCULATOR HINT

The equation of the line of best fit will be in one of these forms:

$y = ax + b$ (a: slope, b: y-intercept)

$y = a + bx$ (a: y-intercept, b: slope)

Line of Best Fit

The most accurate trend line showing the relationship between two sets of data is called the **line of best fit.** A graphing calculator computes the equation of a line of best fit using a method called linear regression.

The graphing calculator also gives you the **correlation coefficient** r, which will tell you how closely the equation models the data.

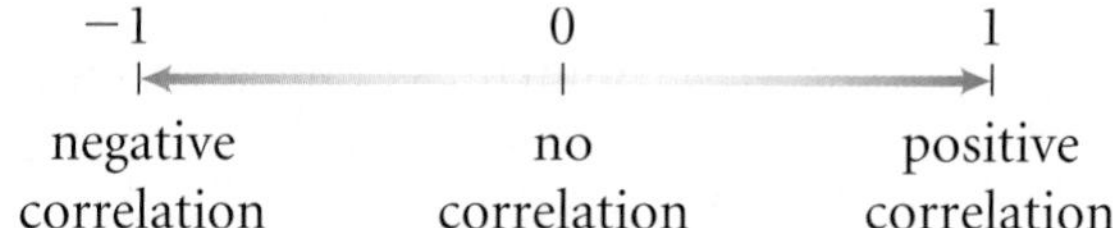

When the data points cluster around a line, there is a strong correlation between the line and the data. The nearer r is to -1 or 1, the more closely the data cluster around the line of best fit.

Example 2 *Relating to the Real World* 

Greeting Card Sales

Year	Sales (in billions)
1980	$2.05
1981	$2.30
1982	$2.45
1983	$2.70
1984	$3.20
1985	$3.45
1986	$3.65
1987	$3.75
1988	$3.90
1989	$4.20
1990	$4.60
1991	$5.00
1992	$5.35
1993	$5.60

Source: Greeting Card Association

Business Use a graphing calculator to find the equation of the line of best fit for the data at the left. Is there a strong correlation shown by the data?

Step 1 Let 80 correspond to 1980. Enter the data for years and then the data for sales in your graphing calculator.

Step 2 Find the equation for the line of best fit.

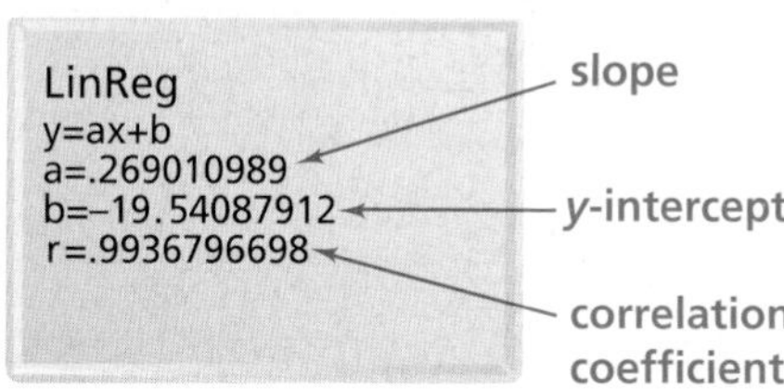

The equation for the line of best fit is $y = 0.269010989x - 19.54087912$. Since r is very close to 1, there is a strong correlation shown by the data.

2. *Critical Thinking* What is the meaning of the slope for the data in Example 2?

3. Use the equation in Example 2 to **predict** sales of greeting cards in the year 2010.

4. *Try This* Find the equation of the line of best fit. Tell whether there is a strong correlation between the data.

a.

x	1	2	3	4	5
y	2	−3	8	9	−25

b.

x	1	2	3	4	5
y	21	15	12	9	7

WORK TOGETHER

Music When you sing a song, your inner clock helps you keep the rhythm. Work with a partner or two to see if you keep a steady beat.

5. **Data Collection** Choose a song. While you hum your song to yourself, tap out the beats. Have someone in your group count the number of beats you tap in 10 s, 20 s, 30 s, and 40 s.
6. Graph the data and find the equation of a trend line or use a graphing calculator to find the equation of the line of best fit.
7. Repeat Questions 5 and 6 for each person in your group.
8. Which song had the fastest beat? the slowest? How do you know?
9. Which of you kept a steady beat the best? How do you know?

Exercises ON YOUR OWN

Decide if the data in each scatter plot follow a linear pattern. If they do, find the equation of a trend line.

1.

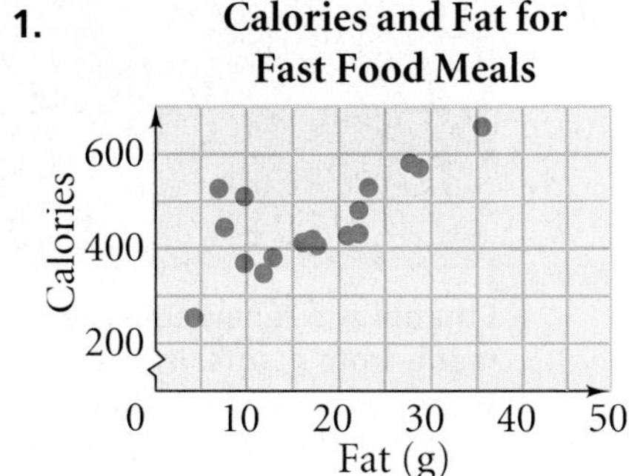

2.

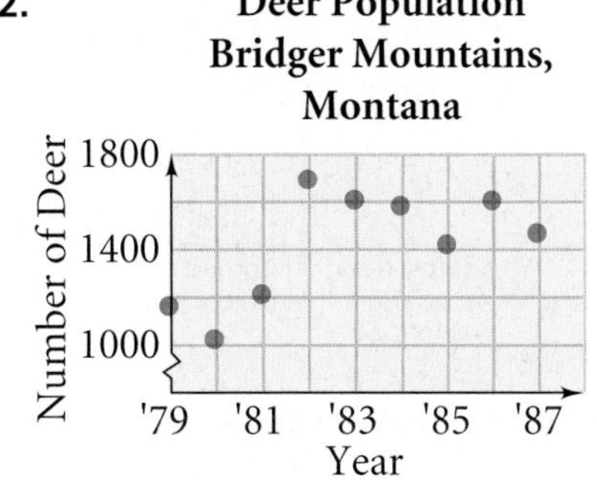

3.

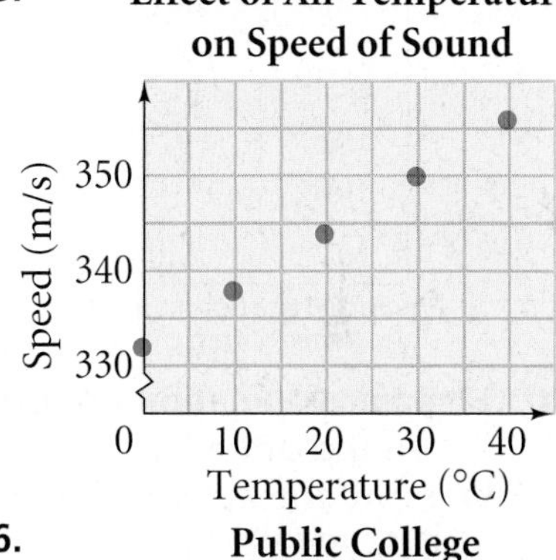

4.

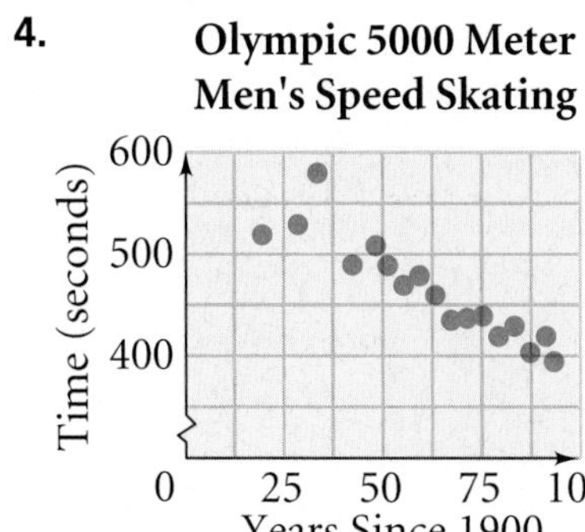

5.

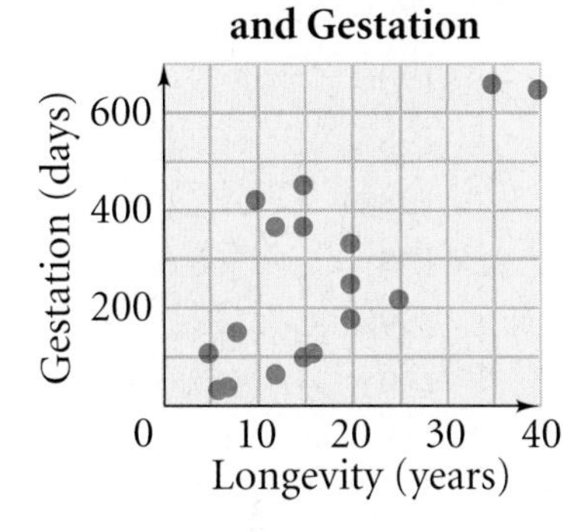

6.

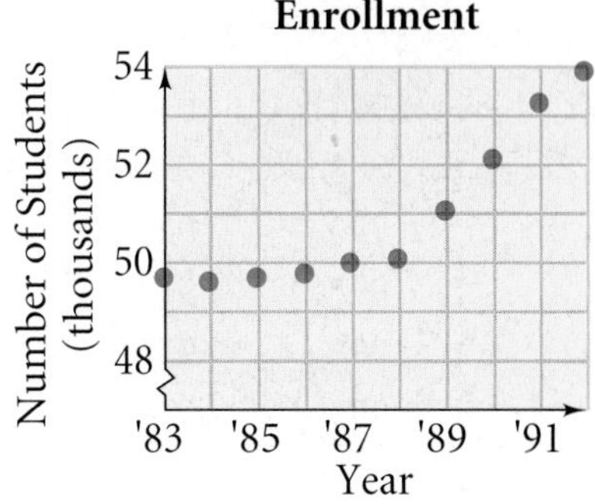

7. a. **Data Collection** Measure the wrist and neck sizes of five different people. Make a scatter plot with the data you collected.
   b. Write an equation for your data. Then **predict** the neck size of someone whose wrist measures 6.5 in.

Critical Thinking **Match each graph with its correlation coefficient.**

8. 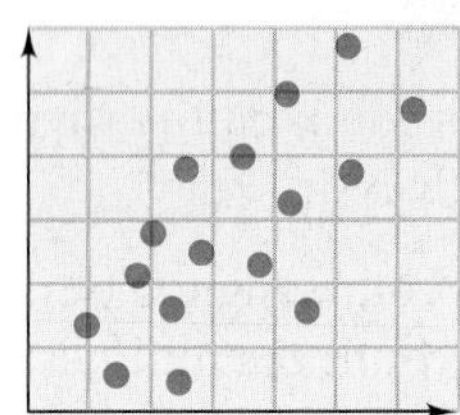

9. 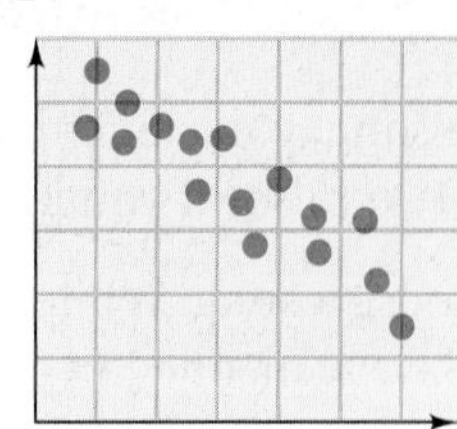

10.

A. $r = -0.95$

B. $r = 0.13$

C. $r = 0.77$

For Exercises 11–14, follow these instructions.

a. Make a scatter plot of the data.

b. *Choose* Use paper and pencil to find the equation of a trend line, or use a graphing calculator to find the equation of the line of best fit.

c. Use your equation to make a prediction for the year 2005.

11. **Households with Television sets (in millions)**

Year	Number
1986	158
1987	163
1988	168
1989	176
1990	193
1991	193
1992	192
1993	201

Source: *Statistical Abstract of the United States*

12. **Gallons of Ethanol Fuel Produced Annually (in millions)**

Year	Amount
1987	820
1988	830
1989	850
1990	900
1991	960
1992	1080
1993	1200

Source: National Corn Growers Association; Renewable Fuels Association

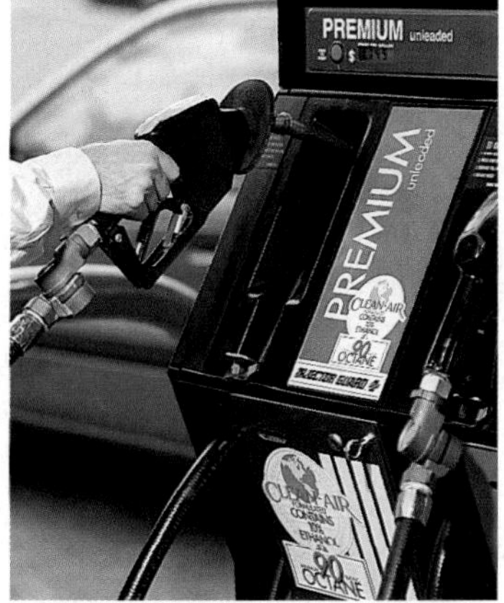

Ethanol is a renewable fuel made from plants. In the United States, it is usually made from corn. In Brazil, the largest producer of ethanol, it is made from sugar cane.

13. **Hispanic Population Growth in the United States (percent of total population)**

Year	Percent
1970	4.5
1980	6.4
1988	7.1
1990	9.0
1991	9.3
1992	9.5
1993	9.8

Source: United States Census Bureau

14. **Fast Food Sales (in billions)**

Year	Sales
1985	$46.4
1986	$49.4
1987	$57.6
1988	$65.0
1989	$68.3
1990	$74.2
1991	$77.0

Source: United States Department of Agriculture

15. a. *Open-ended* Make a table of data for a linear function. Use a graphing calculator to find the equation of the line of best fit.

b. What is the correlation coefficient for your linear data?

16. a. **Business** Make a scatter plot of the data at the right. Find the equation of a trend line, or use a graphing calculator to find the equation of the line of best fit.
b. Use your equation to **predict** the percent of refillable bottles used in 1950 and the percent that will be used in the year 2000.
c. Are your answers to part(b) reasonable in the real-world situation? Explain.

Refillable Soft-Drink Containers

Year	Percent of Total Sold
1960	96
1965	84
1970	65
1975	57
1980	34
1985	23
1990	7

17. **Writing** Decide whether the following statement is *true* or *false.* Then explain your answer: A trend line is a line that connects as many points in a set of data as possible.

18. a. **Research** Choose a topic below or one of your own. You can find data in an almanac or the *Statistical Abstract of the United States.*
• population density of a state and its crime rate
• population of a state and the number of physicians who practice there
b. Find the equation of a trend line or use a graphing calculator to find the line of best fit for the data.
c. Is there a strong correlation shown by the data? Explain.
d. If the correlation is strong, use your equation to make a prediction.

19. a. Make a scatter plot of the data in the table below.
b. Use a graphing calculator to find the equation of the line of best fit.
c. Does the data show a strong correlation? Explain.
d. **Critical Thinking** Do you think that the correlation would be similar for other school choruses? Why or why not?

Members of the School Chorus

Age (in years)	13	15	17	16	16	13	14	15	17	17	16	14	14
Height (in inches)	62	70	65	62	71	59	64	63	68	60	67	60	61

Exercises MIXED REVIEW

20. **Health** The spreadsheet shows the breathing rates for people of different ages.
a. Write a formula for cell D2.
b. Find the values of cells D2 through D7.

	A	B	C	D
1	Age	Breaths/min	Liters of oxygen/min	Liters of oxygen/breath
2	30–39	14.7	146.7	■
3	40–49	14.6	139.1	■
4	50–59	14.6	127.8	■
5	60–69	14.2	117.3	■
6	70–79	14.4	106.2	■
7	80–89	13.2	75.5	■

Source: *Prevention's Giant Book of Health Facts*

Solve each equation.

21. $3x + 4 = 73$
22. $-2.5 - 5z = -3z$
23. $\frac{4}{x} = \frac{2}{3 + x}$
24. $0.2t + 1.3 = -9.1$
25. $4(3y - 5) = 16$
26. $\frac{1}{2}x - \frac{3}{4} = \frac{3}{2} + x$

Getting Ready for Lesson 5-7

Find the value of x when $y = 0$.

27. $y = 3x + 8$
28. $4x - 5y = 7$
29. $y = \frac{1}{2}x - 10$
30. $y = 2x$

What You'll Learn

- Graphing equations using x- and y-intercepts
- Writing equations in $Ax + By = C$ form
- Modeling situations with equations in the form $Ax + By = C$

...And Why

To investigate real-world situations, such as burning calories when running and jogging

What You'll Need

- graph paper
- graphing calculator

5-7 $Ax + By = C$ Form

THINK AND DISCUSS

Graphing Equations

The slope-intercept form is just one form of a linear equation. Another form is $Ax + By = C$, which is useful in making quick graphs.

$Ax + By = C$ Form of a Linear Equation

$Ax + By = C$ is a linear equation, where A and B cannot both be zero.

$$\begin{array}{ccc} \downarrow & \downarrow & \downarrow \end{array}$$
$3x + 4y = 8$

To make a quick graph, you can use the x- and y-intercepts. The **x-intercept** is the x-coordinate of the point where a line crosses the x-axis.

Example 1

Graph $3x + 4y = 8$.

Step 1 To find the x-intercept, substitute 0 for y and solve for x.

$$3x + 4y = 8$$
$$3x + 4(0) = 8$$
$$3x = 8$$
$$x = \frac{8}{3}, \text{ or } 2\frac{2}{3}$$

The x-intercept is $2\frac{2}{3}$.

Step 2 To find the y-intercept, substitute 0 for x and solve for y.

$$3x + 4y = 8$$
$$3(0) + 4y = 8$$
$$4y = 8$$
$$y = 2$$

The y-intercept is 2.

Step 3 Plot $(2\frac{2}{3}, 0)$ and $(0, 2)$. Draw a line through the points.

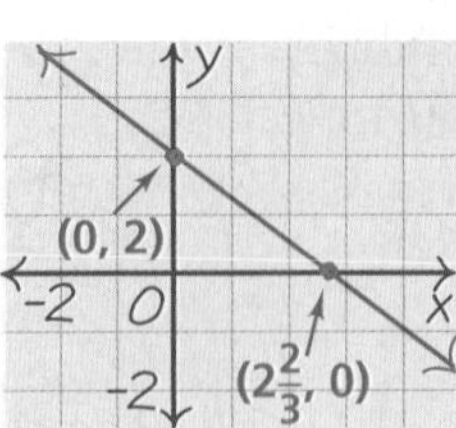

1. **Mental Math** Find the x- and y-intercept of each equation.
   a. $3x + 4y = 12$
   b. $5x + 2y = -10$
   c. $2x - y = 4$

To graph an equation on a graphing calculator, you must transform the equation to slope-intercept form. You can use the x- and y-intercepts to find an appropriate range for each axis.

Math A Test Prep

1 Which equation represents a direct variation?
(1) $y = 2x$
(2) $y = x + 2$
(3) $y = x^2$
(4) $x + 2y = 2$

2 The equation of a line is $x - 3y = 6$. Find the slope of the line and the y-intercept.

Example 2

Graphing Calculator Graph $5x - 3y = 120$.

Step 1 Write the equation in slope-intercept form.

$5x - 3y = 120$ ← Solve for y.

$-3y = -5x + 120$ ← Subtract $5x$ from each side.

$y = \frac{5}{3}x - 40$ ← Divide each side by -3.

Step 2 Find the x- and y-intercepts.

$5x - 3y = 120$

$5x - 3(0) = 120$

$5x = 120$

$x = 24$ ← x-intercept

From Step 1, the y-intercept is –40.

Step 3 Set the ranges to include the x- and y-axes and the intercepts. Then graph $y = \frac{5}{3}x - 40$.

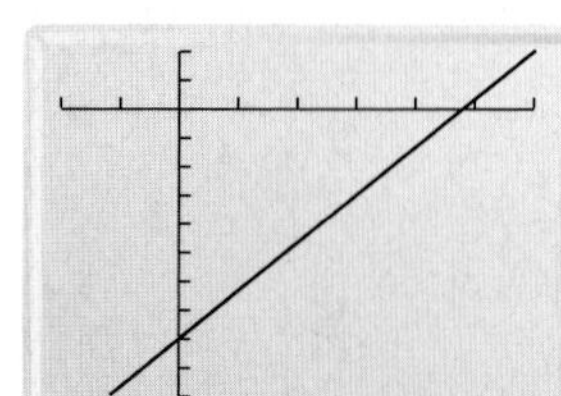

Xmin=–10 Ymin=–50
Xmax=30 Ymax=10
Xscl=5 Yscl=5

2. *Critical Thinking* What advantage is there in making Xmin less than 0 and Xmax greater than 24 for the graph on the calculator?

3. *Graphing Calculator* Graph $4x - 12y = 54$. Sketch your graph. Include Xmin, Xmax, Ymin, Ymax, and the x- and y-intercepts.

Writing Equations

You can write equations for real-world situations using the $Ax + By = C$ form.

Example 3 Relating to the Real World

Fitness When you jog, you burn 7.3 calories/min. When you run, you burn 11.3 calories/min. Write an equation to find the times you would need to run and jog in order to burn 500 calories.

Define x = minutes spent jogging y = minutes spent running

Relate 7.3 × minutes jogging + 11.3 × minutes running = 500

Write $7.3x + 11.3y = 500$

4. a. Use the intercepts to graph the equation in Example 3, or graph the equation on a graphing calculator.
   b. *Open-ended* Use your graph to estimate three different running and jogging times needed to burn 500 calories.

You can write an equation in $Ax + By = C$ form if you know the slope and one point. For a line with slope m through point (x_1, y_1), begin with the **point-slope form:**

$$\frac{y - y_1}{x - x_1} = m$$

Example 4

Write an equation of the line with slope $-\frac{1}{2}$ through the point $(-1, 7)$.

$\frac{y - y_1}{x - x_1} = m$ ← Use the point-slope form.

$\frac{y - 7}{x - (-1)} = -\frac{1}{2}$ ← Substitute (–1, 7) for (x_1, y_1) and $-\frac{1}{2}$ for m.

$2(y - 7) = -1(x + 1)$ ← Simplify $x - (-1)$ and cross multiply.

$2y - 14 = -x - 1$ ← Use the distributive property.

$x + 2y = 13$ ← Add x and 14 to each side in order to write $Ax + By = C$ form.

5. ***Critical Thinking*** How is $\frac{y - y_1}{x - x_1}$ related to the ratio for finding the slope of a line through two points?

Exercises ON YOUR OWN

Match the equation with its graph.

1. $2x + 5y = 10$

2. $2x - 5y = 10$

3. $-2x + 5y = 10$

A.

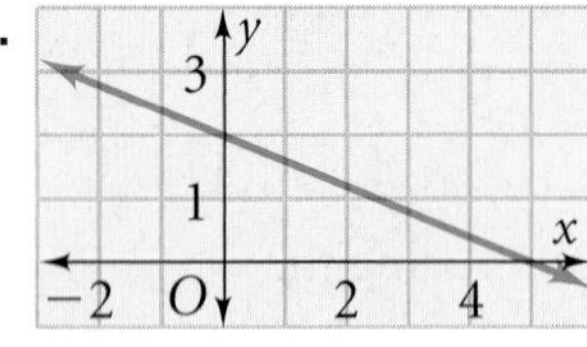

B.

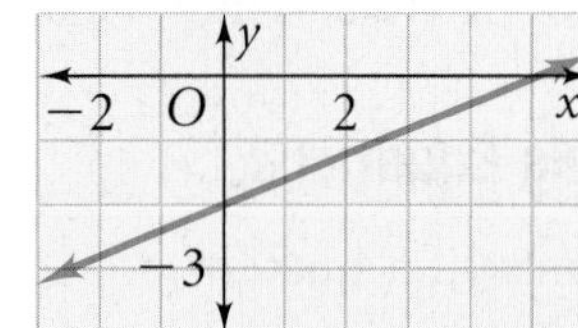

C.

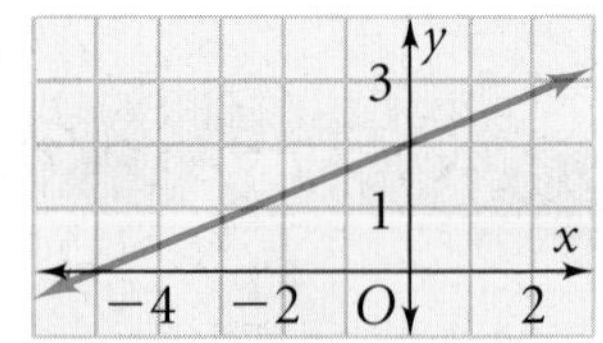

Graph each equation.

4. $x + y = 2$

5. $5x - 12y = 30$

6. $-3x + y = 6$

7. $x - y = -7$

8. $-4x + y = -6$

9. $2x + 5y = 10$

10. $2x - y = 8$

11. $-3x + 4y = 12$

12. a. ***Fund Raising*** Suppose your school is having a dinner to raise money for new music and art supplies. You estimate that 200 children and 150 adults will attend. Write an equation to find what ticket prices you should set to raise $900.

b. ***Open-ended*** Graph your equation. Choose three possible prices you could set for children's and adults' tickets. Explain which you think is the best choice.

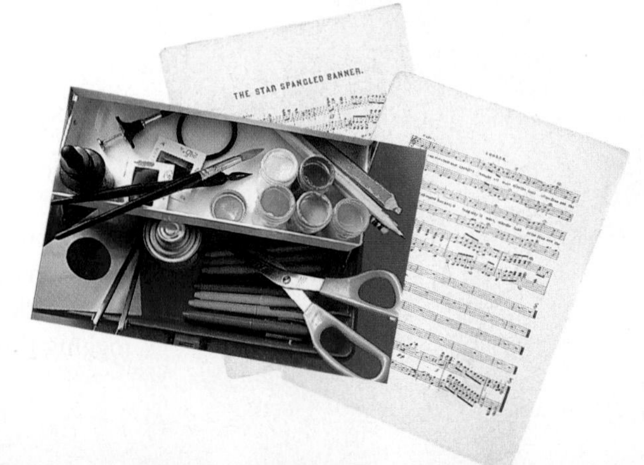

13. **Writing** Two forms of a linear equation are the slope-intercept form and the $Ax + By = C$ form. Explain when each is most useful.

14. An equation is in standard form when A, B, and C are integers for $Ax + By = C$. Write each equation in standard form.

Sample: $Ax + By = C$ Form → Standard Form

$3.5x + 7.2y = 12$ → $35x + 72y = 120$ ← **Multiply each side by 10.**

a. $3.8x + 7.2y = 5.4$ **b.** $0.5x - 0.75y = 1.25$ **c.** $\frac{2}{3}x + \frac{1}{6}y = 4$

Graphing Calculator **Graph each equation. Make a sketch of the graph. Include the x- and y-intercepts.**

15. $12x + 15y = -60$
16. $8x - 10y = 100$
17. $-5x + 11y = 120$
18. $4x - 9y = -72$
19. $-3x + 7y = -42$
20. $12x - 9y = 144$
21. $9x + 7y = 210$
22. $3x - 8y = 72$

23. **Standardized Test Prep**
    a. Write $Ax + By = C$ in slope-intercept form by solving for y.
    b. Which expression equals the slope m?
    A. $-\frac{B}{A}$ **B.** $\frac{C}{A}$ **C.** $-\frac{A}{B}$ **D.** A **E.** $\frac{C}{B}$
    c. Which expression equals the y-intercept b?
    A. $-\frac{B}{A}$ **B.** $\frac{C}{A}$ **C.** $-\frac{A}{B}$ **D.** A **E.** $\frac{C}{B}$

Write an equation in $Ax + By = C$ form for the line through the given point with the given slope.

24. $(3, -4)$; $m = 6$
25. $(4, 2)$; $m = -\frac{5}{3}$
26. $(0, 2)$; $m = \frac{4}{5}$
27. $(-2, -7)$; $m = -\frac{3}{2}$
28. $(4, 0)$; $m = 1$
29. $(5, -8)$; $m = -3$
30. $(-5, 2)$; $m = 0$
31. $(1, -8)$; $m = -\frac{1}{5}$

32. **Nutrition** Suppose you are preparing a snack mix. You want the total protein from peanuts and granola to equal 28 g.
    a. Write an equation for the protein content of your mix.
    b. Graph your equation. Use your graph to find how many ounces of granola you should use if you use one ounce of peanuts.

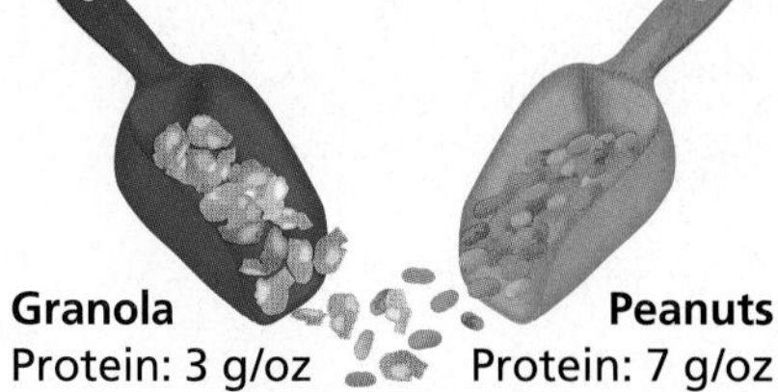

Exercises MIXED REVIEW

Probability **Find each probability.**

33. P(rolling a 2, then a 4 on a number cube)
34. P(getting heads on both coins when you toss two coins)

Getting Ready for Lesson 5-8

Graph each pair of lines on one set of axes.

35. $y = 4x + 1$
    $y = 4x - 3$
36. $y = 3x - 8$
    $y = -\frac{1}{3}x - 2$
37. $3y = 2x + 6$
    $y = \frac{2}{3}x + 4$
38. $4y = x - 8$
    $y = -4x - 1$

What You'll Learn

- Writing equations for parallel and perpendicular lines
- Using slope to determine if lines are parallel, perpendicular, or neither

...And Why

To investigate real-world situations, such as urban planning

5-8 Parallel and Perpendicular Lines

WORK TOGETHER

Work in pairs.

1. Match the story with its graph. Explain your choices.

a. Elena gives her younger sister Rosa a head start in a race. Elena runs faster than her sister.

b. Elena gives her younger sister Rosa a head start in a race. Elena is surprised that she and her sister run at the same rate.

A.

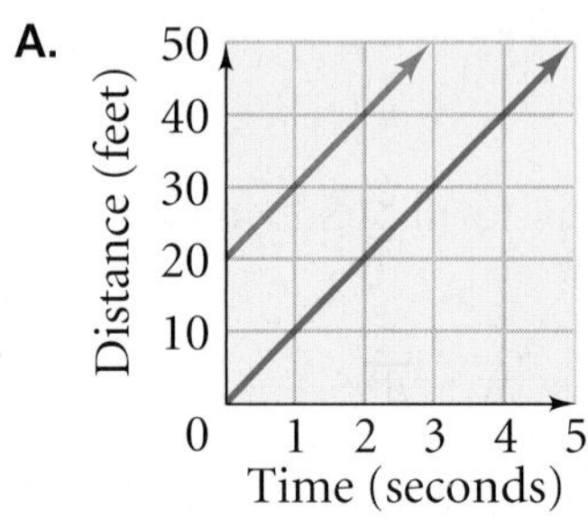

B.

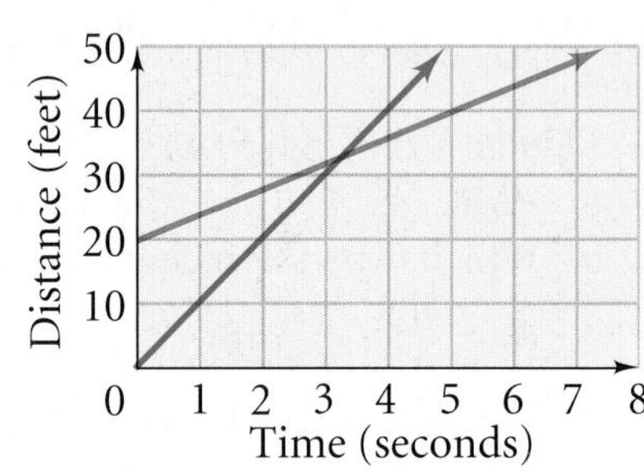

2. a. In graph A, how far apart are the two runners at 0 s? 1 s? 2 s? 3 s?

b. Suppose the race were longer and the pattern for the distance between runners remained the same as in part (a). Would the lines intersect? Explain.

3. What is the slope of each line in graph A?

THINK AND DISCUSS

Parallel Lines

In the Work Together activity, the lines in graph A are parallel. Two **parallel lines** are always the same distance apart. They do not intersect.

> **Slopes of Parallel Lines**
>
> Nonvertical lines are parallel if they have the same slope and different y-intercepts. Vertical lines are parallel.
>
> **Example** The slope of $y = 2x + 3$ and $y = 2x - 5$ is 2. The graphs of these two equations are parallel.

4. Are horizontal lines parallel? Explain.

5. Try This What is the slope of a line parallel to $y = \frac{3}{5}x - 4$?

You can use slope to write an equation of a line parallel to a given line.

Example 1

Write an equation for a line that contains $(-2, 3)$ and is parallel to the graph of $5x - 2y = 8$.

Find the slope of $5x - 2y = 8$.

$$5x - 2y = 8$$
$$-2y = -5x + 8$$
$$y = \frac{5}{2}x - 4 \quad \leftarrow \text{The slope is } \frac{5}{2}.$$

Use the slope-intercept form to find the y-intercept.

$$y = mx + b$$
$$3 = \frac{5}{2}(-2) + b \quad \leftarrow \text{Substitute the coordinates } (-2, 3) \text{ for } (x, y) \text{ and } \frac{5}{2} \text{ for } m.$$
$$3 = -5 + b$$
$$8 = b \quad \leftarrow \text{The } y\text{-intercept is 8.}$$

The equation is $y = \frac{5}{2}x + 8$.

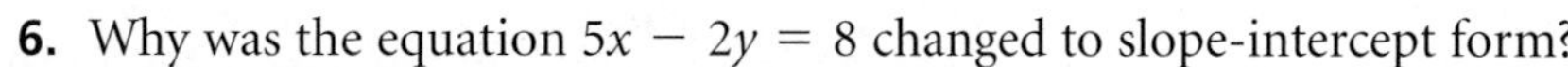

6. Why was the equation $5x - 2y = 8$ changed to slope-intercept form?

7. Graph $5x - 2y = 8$ and $y = \frac{5}{2}x + 8$. Do the lines appear parallel?

8. **Try This** Write an equation for the line that is parallel to $5x - 2y = 8$ and passes through the point $(4, 9)$.

9. ***Critical Thinking*** Is the line graphed by the equation $3x - 4y = 9$ parallel to the line graphed by the equation $y = -\frac{3}{4}x + 5$? Explain.

Perpendicular Lines

Perpendicular lines are lines that form right angles. The slopes of perpendicular lines also have a special relationship.

10. Find the slopes of the lines in each graph.

a.

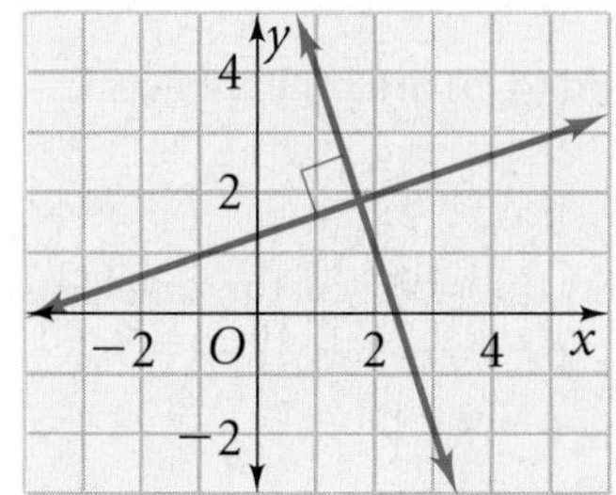

b.

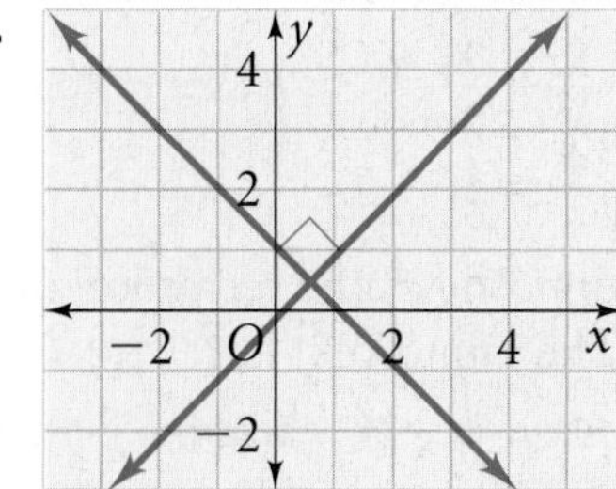

c.

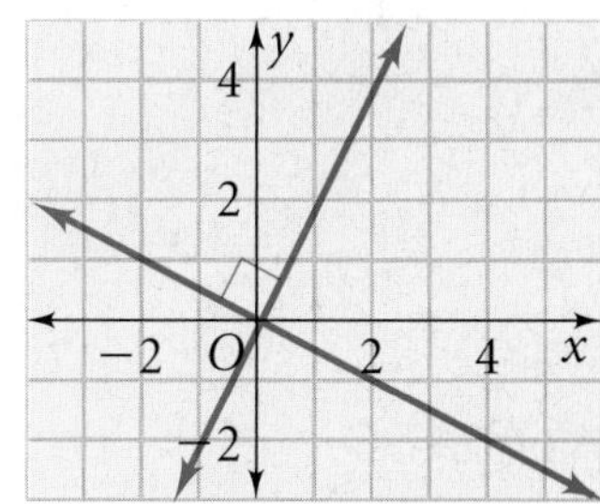

11. **a.** For each pair of lines, find the product of the slopes.
b. What do you notice about the products of the slopes of the perpendicular lines?

Slopes of Perpendicular Lines

Two lines are perpendicular if the product of their slopes is -1. A vertical and a horizontal line are perpendicular.

Example The slope of $y = -4x + 7$ is -4. The slope of $y = \frac{1}{4}x + 2$ is $\frac{1}{4}$. Since $-4 \cdot \frac{1}{4} = -1$, the graphs of the equations are perpendicular.

The product of two numbers is -1 if one number is the opposite of the reciprocal of the other. These numbers are called opposite reciprocals.

fraction: $-\frac{3}{5}$ reciprocal: $-\frac{5}{3}$ opposite reciprocal: $\frac{5}{3}$

12. Is $-\frac{2}{3}$ the opposite reciprocal of $\frac{3}{2}$? Explain.

13. **Try This** Find the slope of a line perpendicular to a line with this slope.

a. -2 **b.** $\frac{2}{7}$ **c.** $\frac{1}{5}$ **d.** 0

You can use slope to write an equation of a line perpendicular to a given line.

Example 2 Relating to the Real World

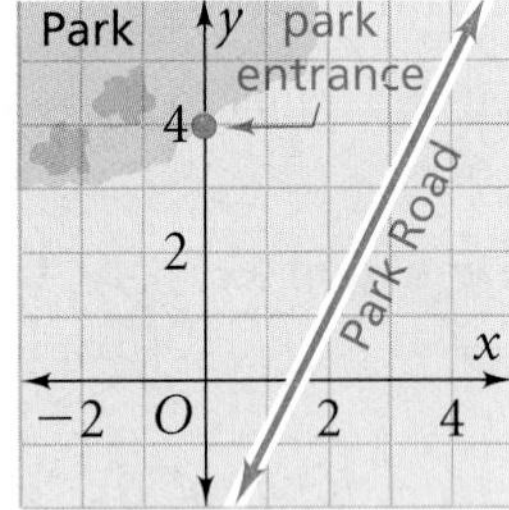

Urban Planning A bike path for a new city park will connect the park entrance to Park Road. The path will be perpendicular to Park Road. Write an equation for the line representing the bike path.

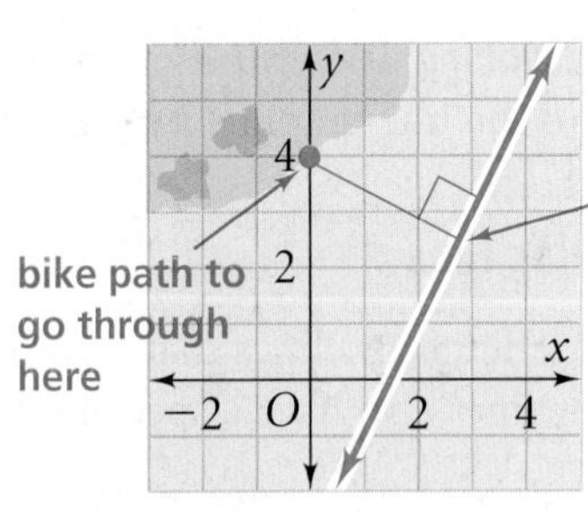

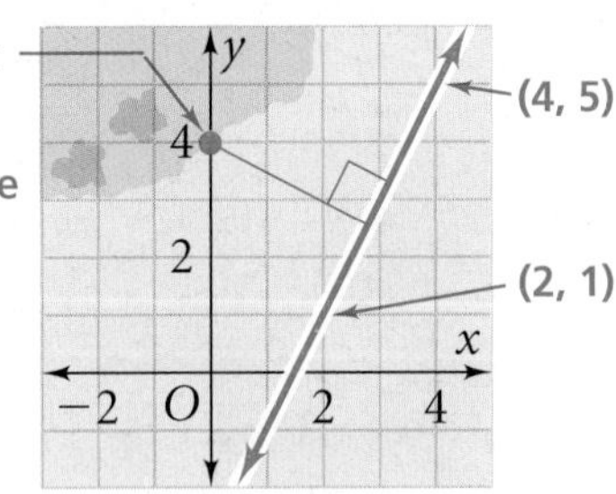

Find the slope m of Park Road.

$$m = \frac{y_2 - y_1}{x_2 - x_1} = \frac{5 - 1}{4 - 2}$$ ← Points (2, 1) and (4, 5) are on Park Road.

$$= \frac{4}{2} = 2$$

The opposite of the reciprocal of 2 is $-\frac{1}{2}$. So the slope of the bike path is $-\frac{1}{2}$. The y-intercept is 4.

$y = mx + b$ ← Use the y-intercept form.

$y = -\frac{1}{2}x + 4$ ← Substitute $-\frac{1}{2}$ for m and 4 for b.

The equation for the bike path is $y = -\frac{1}{2}x + 4$.

14. **Critical Thinking** How can you use slope to tell if two lines are parallel, perpendicular, or neither?

Exercises ON YOUR OWN

Find the slope of a line parallel to the graph of each equation.

1. $y = \frac{1}{2}x + 2.3$ **2.** $y = -\frac{2}{3}x - 1$ **3.** $3x + 4y = 12$ **4.** $2x - 3y = -2$

5. $y = 6$ **6.** $x = 5$ **7.** $2x - y = 0$ **8.** $x = 0$

9. $y = -3x + 2.3$ **10.** $7x + 2y = 12$ **11.** $15x - 12y = 7$ **12.** $y = 0.5x - 8$

Find the slope of a line perpendicular to the graph of each equation.

13. $y = 2x$ **14.** $y = -3x$ **15.** $y = \frac{7}{5}x - 2$ **16.** $y = x$

17. $2x + 3y = 5$ **18.** $y = \frac{x}{-5} - 7$ **19.** $y = -8$ **20.** $x = 3$

21. $4x - 2y = 9$ **22.** $3x + 5y = 7$ **23.** $y = \frac{9}{2}x + 5$ **24.** $y = 0.25x$

Tell whether the lines for the pair of equations are *parallel, perpendicular,* or *neither.*

25. $y = 4x + \frac{3}{4}, y = -\frac{1}{4}x + 4$ **26.** $y = \frac{x}{3} - 4, y = \frac{1}{3}x + 2$ **27.** $y = -x + 5, y = x + 5$

28. $5x + y = 3, -5x + y = 8$ **29.** $x = 2, y = 9$ **30.** $y = x, y = x + 2$

31. **Graphing Calculator** The graphs of $y = x$ and $y = -x$ are shown on the standard screen at the right. The product of the slopes is -1. Explain why the lines do not appear to be perpendicular.

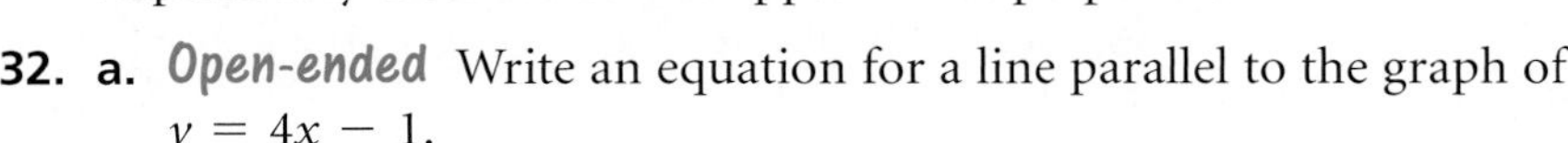

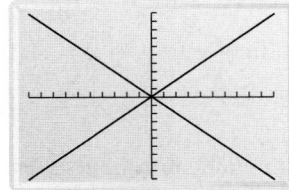

32. **a.** **Open-ended** Write an equation for a line parallel to the graph of $y = 4x - 1$.

b. Can you write more than one equation for part (a)? Explain.

33. **a.** Are the lines $3x + 5y = 6$ and $3x + 5y = 2$ parallel? Explain.

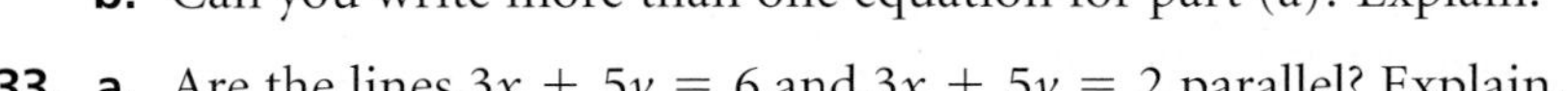

b. Explain how you can tell that the lines $7x - 3y = 5$ and $7x - 3y = 8$ are parallel without finding slopes.

34. **Writing** Suppose a friend missed class today. Explain what you would tell your friend about using slope to find each equation.

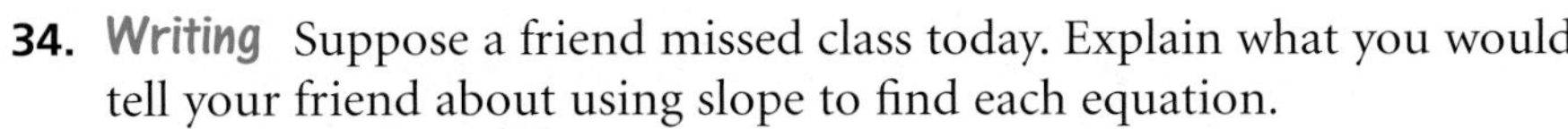

a. the equation of a line parallel to a given line

b. the equation of a line perpendicular to a given line

35. **Geometry** Are the points (3, 8), (5, 4) and $(-3, 3)$ the vertices of a right triangle? Explain.

36. **a.** **Maps** What is the slope of New Hampshire Avenue?

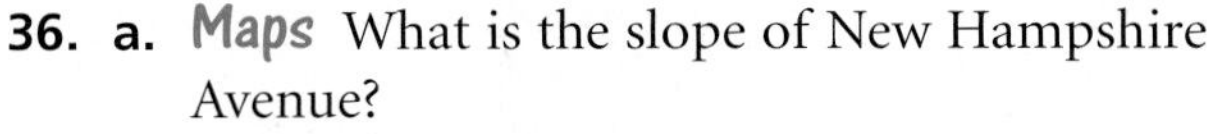

b. Show that parts of Pennsylvania Avenue and Massachusetts Avenue near New Hampshire Avenue are parallel.

c. Show that New Hampshire Avenue is not perpendicular to Pennsylvania Avenue.

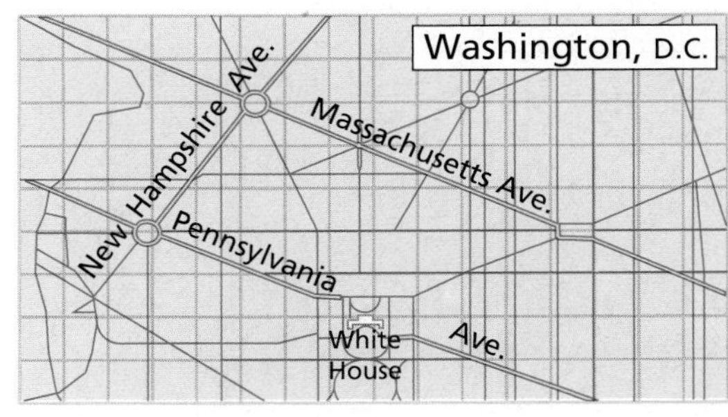

Geometry **A quadrilateral with both pairs of opposite sides parallel is a parallelogram. Use slopes to show if each figure is a parallelogram.**

37. 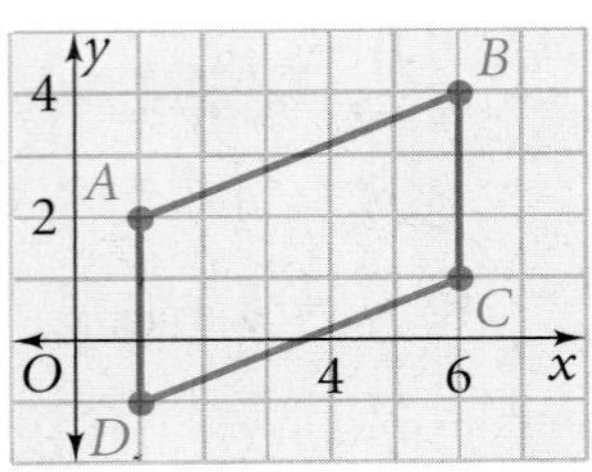

38. 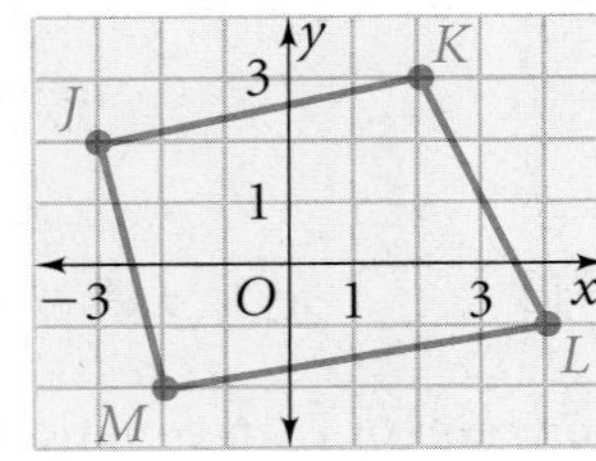

39. 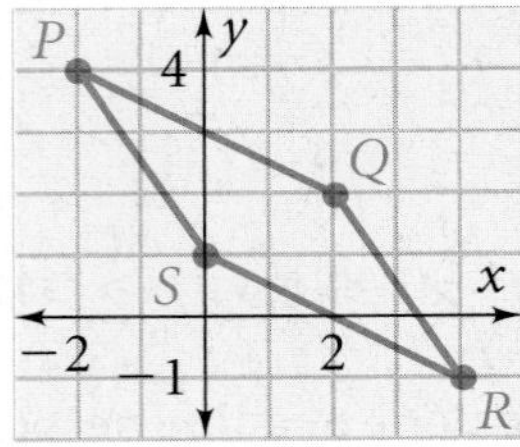

40. **Standardized Test Prep** Which of the following statements is true for the graphs of equations I and II?

I: $2x + y = 15$ **II:** $3y = -6x + 30$

A. The graphs of I and II are parallel.
B. The graphs of I and II are perpendicular.
C. The graphs of I and II are the same line.
D. The graphs of I and II are neither parallel nor perpendicular.
E. none of the above

Write an equation that satisfies the given conditions.

41. parallel to $y = 6x - 2$, through $(0, 0)$

42. perpendicular to $y = 2x + 7$, through $(0, 0)$

43. perpendicular to $y = x - 3$, through $(4, 6)$

44. parallel to $y = -3x$, through $(3, 0)$

45. parallel to $y = -\frac{2}{3}x + 12$, through $(5, -3)$

46. perpendicular to $y = -4x - \frac{5}{2}$, through $(1, 6)$

Tell whether each statement is *true* or *false*. Explain your choice.

47. In a coordinate plane, every horizontal line is perpendicular to every vertical line.

48. Two lines with positive slopes can be perpendicular.

49. Two lines with positive slopes must be parallel.

50. The graphs of two direct variations can be parallel.

Geometry **A quadrilateral with four right angles is a rectangle. Use slopes to show whether each figure is a rectangle.**

51. 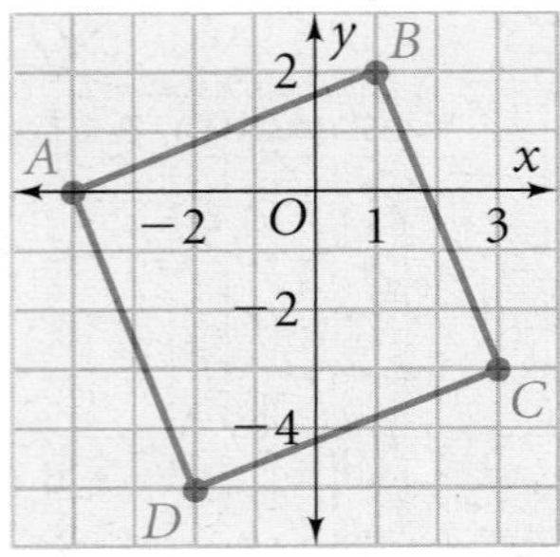

52. 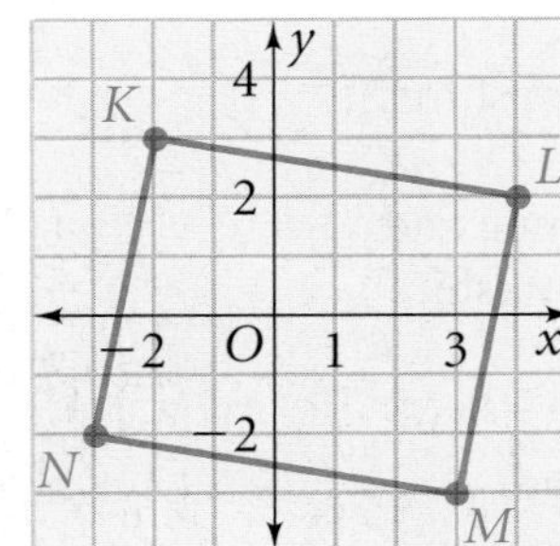

53. 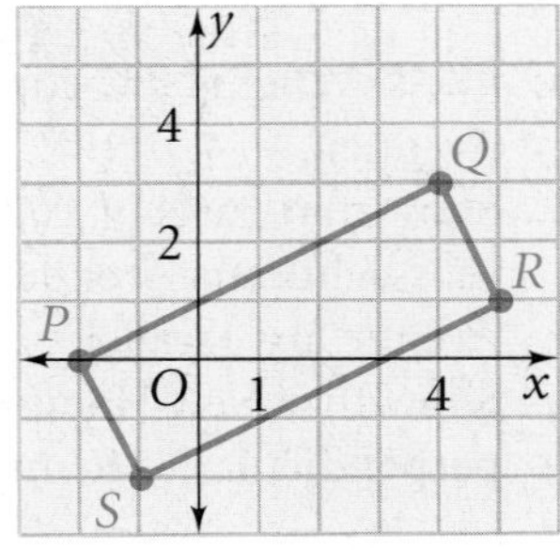

Chapter Project *Find Out by Interviewing*

Interview an adult about a job he or she had as a teenager. Ask about positive and negative aspects of the job, salary, and expenses. Set up an equation that describes the person's earnings after expenses for a week.

Exercises MIXED REVIEW

Solve.

54. $\frac{x}{2} + \frac{x}{3} = 6$
55. $3m - 4m > 2$
56. $-\frac{x}{4} > 3$
57. $9y - 3 > 5y + 1$
58. *Social Studies* There were 132,300 African Americans among the troops serving in the Gulf War, or 24.5% of the total. How many troops served in the Gulf War?

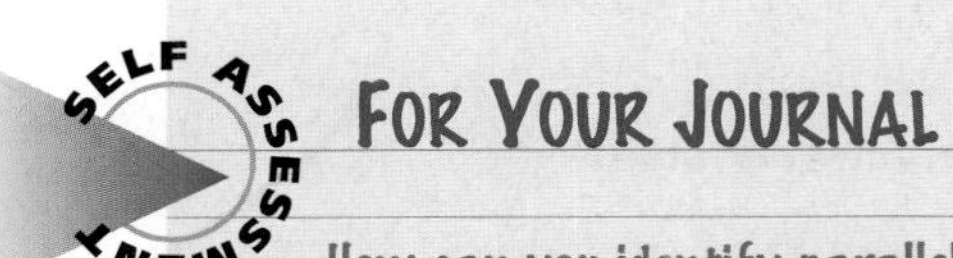

For Your Journal

How can you identify parallel and perpendicular lines from their slopes?

Getting Ready for Lesson 5-9

Find the value of x when $y = 0$.

59. $y = 3x + 8$
60. $4x - 5y = 7$
61. $y = \frac{1}{2}x - 10$
62. $2x + 3y = 6$

Exercises CHECKPOINT

Change each equation to $Ax + By = C$ form.

1. $3y = 2x + 6$
2. $y = 4x - 7$
3. $y = \frac{1}{3}x + 5$
4. $15y = 9x - 12$

Write an equation for a line that contains the given points.

5. $(3, 4)$ and $(-1, 5)$
6. $(0, -3)$ and $(\frac{1}{2}, 6)$
7. $(-7, -5)$ and $(7, 5)$
8. $(5, 9)$ and $(5, 10)$

Find the equation of a trend line or the line of best fit.

9.

x	1	2	3	4	5	6	7
y	7	12	19	20	28	33	40

10.

x	1	2	3	4	5	6	7
y	54	52	45	40	33	27	18

Open-ended **Write an equation of a line that is parallel to each line and an equation of a line that is perpendicular to each line.**

11. $y = 3x - 2$
12. $4x + 5y = 10$
13. $y = \frac{2}{3}x + \frac{1}{6}$
14. $y = 1.6x - 0.4$
15. *Standardized Test Prep* Which equation represents a line with the same y-intercept as $y = 4x - 3$?
    A. $y - 3 = x$ **B.** $y = 8x + 3$ **C.** $2y = 8x - 3$ **D.** $5x + 6y = -18$ **E.** $x = 3$

What You'll Learn

- Using the x-intercept of a linear equation to solve the related one-variable equation

...And Why

To use graphs to solve and check equations and to investigate business situations

What You'll Need

- graph paper
- graphing calculator

5-9 Using the x-intercept

WORK TOGETHER

Work with a partner.

1. Solve the equation $\frac{2}{3}x + 4 = 0$.
2. a. Graph the function $y = \frac{2}{3}x + 4$.
   b. What is the value of x when the line crosses the x-axis?
   c. What is the value of y when the line crosses the x-axis?
3. Compare the results of Questions 1 and 2. What do you notice?

THINK AND DISCUSS

QUICK REVIEW

The *x-intercept* is the x-coordinate of the point where a line crosses the x-axis.

There is a special relationship between a one-variable equation and the related linear function. The solution of a one-variable equation equals the x-intercept of the graph of the related linear function.

One-Variable Equation	Related Linear Function
$\frac{2}{3}x + 4 = 0$	$y = \frac{2}{3}x + 4$

Notice that one side of the one-variable equation is 0. You replace 0 with y to write the related linear function.

Math A Test Prep

1 A line parallel to $y = \frac{2}{3}x - 5$ passes through the point (6, 8). Which other point lies on the line?
(1) (15, 2) (3) (2, 14)
(2) (−3, 2) (4) (−3, 14)

2 You are setting ticket prices for the fair, estimating that 350 students and 200 adults will attend.
a Write an equation for ticket prices that result in sales of \$1300.
b Graph the equation.
c Choose two possible pairs of ticket prices that you could set. Explain.

Example 1

Solve $\frac{3}{4}x - 2 = -5$ by graphing.

Step 1 Write the equation so that one side is 0.

$\frac{3}{4}x - 2 = -5$

$\frac{3}{4}x + 3 = 0$ ← Add 5 to both sides.

Step 2 Replace 0 with y to write a function.

$y = \frac{3}{4}x + 3$

Step 3 Graph the function. Then find the x-intercept.

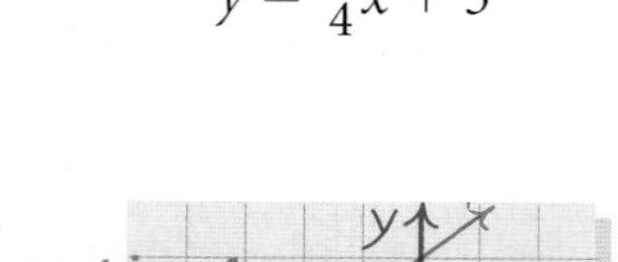
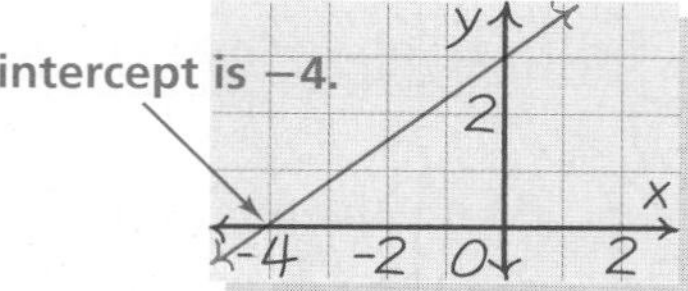

The solution of $\frac{3}{4}x - 2 = -5$ is -4.

Check

$\frac{3}{4}x - 2 = -5$

$\frac{3}{4}(-4) - 2 \stackrel{?}{=} -5$ ← Substitute −4 for x.

$-3 - 2 \stackrel{?}{=} -5$

$-5 = -5$ ✔

4. **Try This** Solve each equation by graphing. Check each solution.
   a. $2x + 4 = 0$ **b.** $6x + 7 = 10$ **c.** $\frac{1}{2}x - 3 = 0$

You can use a graphing calculator to solve a one-variable equation. Graph the related linear function. Next graph the equation for the x-axis, $y = 0$. To find the x-intercept, find the intersection point of the two lines.

Example 2

Graphing Calculator Find the solution of $5x - 12 = 0$.

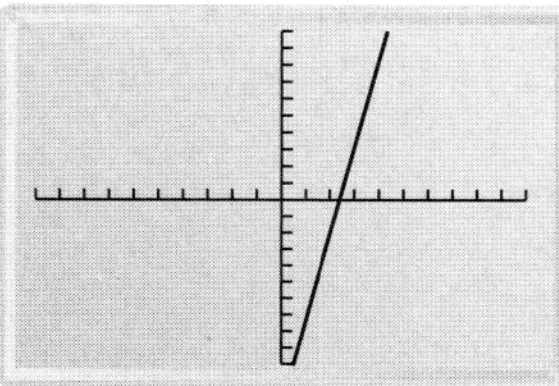

Graph $y = 5x - 12$ and $y = 0$.

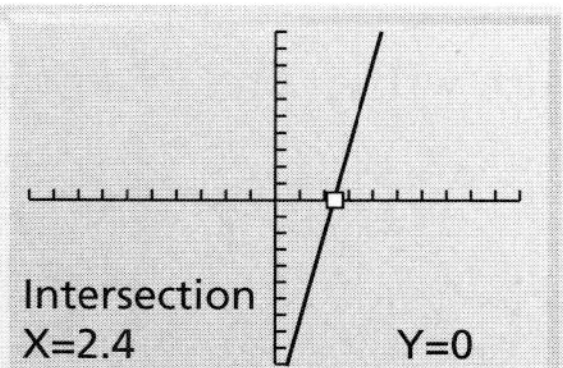

Use the CALC feature to find the coordinates of the intersection point.

The solution is 2.4.

PROBLEM SOLVING

Look Back Describe how to check the solution of Example 2. Then check that the solution is 2.4.

When starting a business, people want to know the **break-even point,** the point at which their income equals their expenses.

Example 3 Relating to the Real World

Business Suppose you invested \$140 to start a business selling painted T-shirts. You sell each shirt for \$7.50. Find the break-even point.

Relate income = expenses

Define x = the number of shirts you sell

Write $7.50x = 140$

Rewrite the equation as $7.50x - 140 = 0$. The related function is $y = 7.5x - 140$.

Select a range that includes the x-intercept.

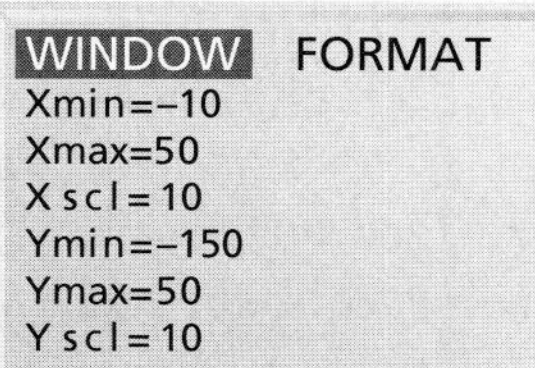

Graph $y = 7.5x - 140$ and $y = 0$. Find the intersection point of the lines.

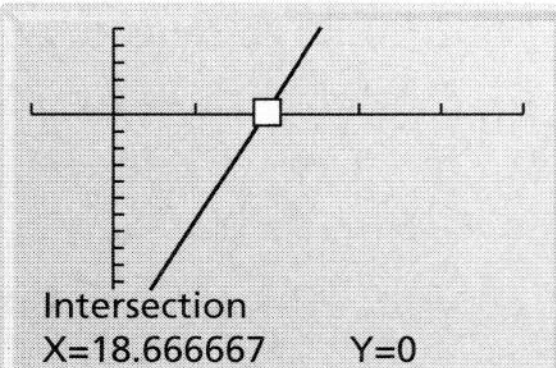

The break-even point is about 18.7. You must sell 19 shirts to make a profit.

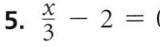

5. *Graphing Calculator* Use the TABLE feature on your calculator to find values for y close to 0 in Example 3. How can the TABLE feature help you choose range values for the x-axis?

Exercises ON YOUR OWN

Write the function you would graph to find the solution of each one-variable equation.

1. $3x - 8 = 0$
2. $7 = \frac{1}{2}x + 4$
3. $-x + 5 = 9$

Match each equation with its related graph.

4. $5 - 3x = 0$
5. $\frac{x}{3} - 2 = 0$
6. $x + 5 = 0$

A.
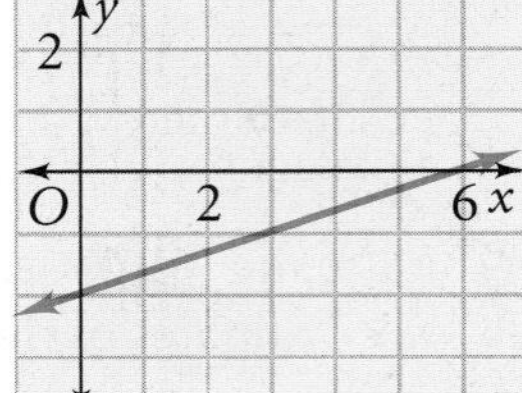

B.
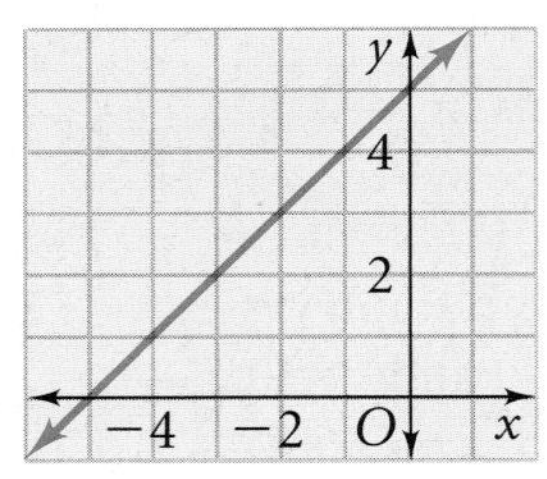

C.
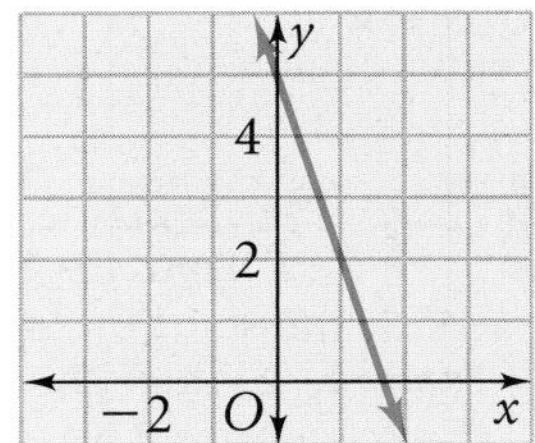

Solve each equation using a graph. Check each answer.

7. $0 = 2x + 3$
8. $3x + 4 = 13$
9. $4x - 3 = 9$
10. $-x + 7 = 13$

Choose **Solve each equation using a graphing calculator or with paper and pencil. Check each answer.**

11. $3x - 5 = 12$
12. $\frac{2x}{5} = -4$
13. $3x = 75$
14. $5(x + 2) = 18$
15. $27 = \frac{x}{3} + 15$
16. $\frac{3}{4}x + 6 = -20$
17. $4(x - 6) = 5$
18. $25x - 18 = 72$

19. *Money* Suppose you build birdhouses. An investment of \$100 allows you to build ten houses. You sell each house for \$15.
    a. Write an equation relating the income to the expenses.
    b. Graph a related linear function to find the break-even point.
    c. Suppose you sell all the houses. How much profit will you make?

20. *Physical Science* In 1787, the French scientist Jacques Charles discovered that as a gas cooled at a constant pressure, the relationship between volume and temperature was linear. Suppose that at 60°C the volume of the gas is 555 cm^3 and at 30°C the volume is 505 cm^3.
    a. Write a linear function relating volume of gas to temperature.
    b. Jacques Charles used a linear function to find *absolute zero*, the temperature at which a gas theoretically will have no volume. Graph your function to find absolute zero in degrees Celsius.

Jacques Charles

21. *Open-ended* Write a one-variable equation. Solve your equation using a graph.

22. **Writing** What advantages and disadvantages do you see in using a calculator to solve equations?

Graphing Calculator **Solve each equation using a graphing calculator.**

23. $\frac{2x}{7} + 5 = 0$

24. $2x + 10 = -15$

25. $-8(x - 6) = 18$

26. $\frac{4}{5}x - 18 = 15$

Critical Thinking **Is each statement *true* or *false*? Explain.**

27. A vertical line has no x-intercept.

28. The x-intercept of a direct variation is 0.

29. The x-intercept of $y = mx + b$ is the solution to $mx + b = 0$.

Exercises MIXED REVIEW

Evaluate each function for $x = -3.2$.

30. $f(x) = |5 - x|$

31. $f(x) = 3x - 2$

32. $f(x) = 4x^2 - 8$

33. $f(x) = (x + 1)^2$

34. **Zoology** In July 1995, three Siberian tigers were born in Garden City, Kansas. There were already about 100 Siberian tigers in the United States. By what percent did the population increase?

PORTFOLIO

For your portfolio, choose one or two items from your work for this chapter. Here are some possibilities:

- a journal entry
- corrected work

Explain why you include each selection that you make.

A Point in Time

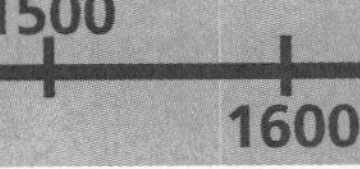

Judith A. Resnik

On August 30, 1984, Astronaut Judith A. Resnik became the second American woman to fly in space, on the shuttle *Discovery's* first voyage. Resnik was an electrical engineer with a Ph.D. from the University of Maryland. On the ground she helped to design and develop a remote manipulator system, a task that required skill in linear equations. Her job during *Discovery's* six-day voyage was to manipulate a robotic arm and to extend and retract the shuttle's solar power array. Resnik died tragically in the shuttle *Challenger* disaster in 1986.

CHAPTER PROJECT

Finishing the Chapter Project

Taking THE PLUNGE

Questions on pages 224, 239, and 255 should help you complete your project. Work with several classmates. Share what you have learned about jobs for a teenager. List positive and negative features about income and expenses for several jobs. On your own, assemble your graphs, equations, and job information in a notebook. Write a final paragraph that explains what job you would like and why.

Reflect and Revise

Your notebook should present job comparison information in a well-organized format. Are your graphs easy to understand? Have you explained clearly how your equations fit each job? Make any revisions necessary to improve your project.

Follow Up

Sometimes employers will hire only people with experience. You can get experience by creating your own job. Find out how to start your own business from the resources below.

For More Information

Bernstein, Daryl. *Better Than a Lemonade Stand: Small Business Ideas for Kids.* Hillsboro, Oregon: Beyond Words Publications, 1992.

Menzies, Linda. *A Teen's Guide to Business: The Secrets to a Successful Enterprise.* New York: MasterMedia, 1992.

CHAPTER 5

Wrap Up

Key Terms

$Ax + By = C$ form (p. 246)
break-even point (p. 257)
constant of variation (p. 225)
correlation coefficient (p. 242)
dimensional analysis (p. 219)
direct variation (p. 225)
linear equation (p. 225)
linear function (p. 221)
line of best fit (p. 242)
parallel lines (p. 250)
perpendicular lines (p. 251)
rate of change (p. 220)
slope (p. 214)
slope-intercept form (p. 231)
x-intercept (p. 246)
y-intercept (p. 230)

How am I doing?

SELF ASSESSMENT

- State three ideas from this chapter that you think are important. Explain your choices.
- Describe two ways that you can write an equation of a line.

Slope and Rates of Change 5-1, 5-2

Rate of change allows you to look at how two quantities change relative to each other. **Slope** is the ratio of the vertical change to the horizontal change. The rate of change is also called slope.

$$\text{slope} = \frac{\text{vertical change}}{\text{horizontal change}} = \frac{\text{rise}}{\text{run}} \qquad \text{rate of change} = \frac{\text{change in the dependent variable}}{\text{change in the independent variable}}$$

Find two points on each graph. Then find the slope.

1. Time (h) vs. Distance (mi); vertical axis 0, 1, 2; horizontal axis 0, 20, 40, 60

2.

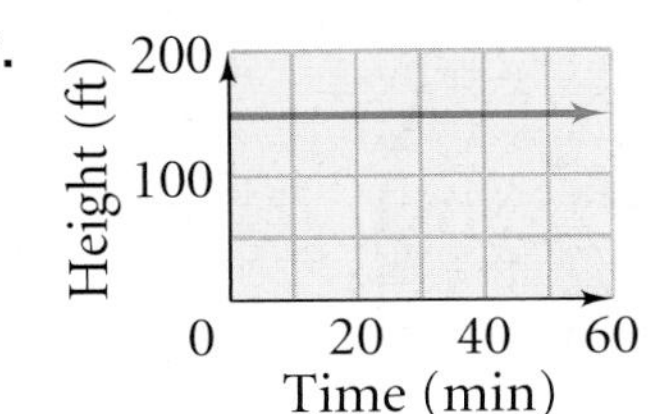

3.

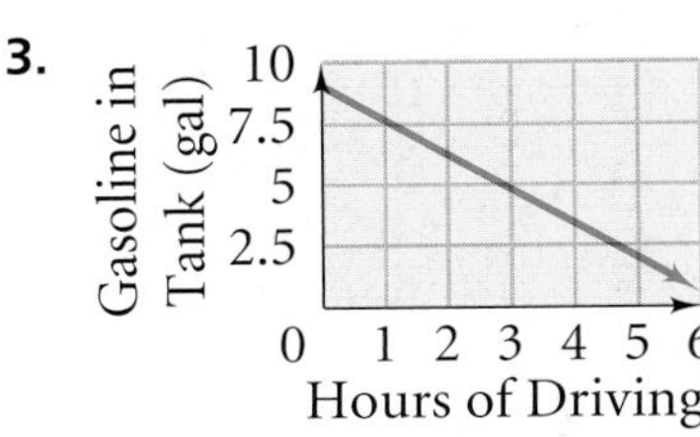

Find the rate of change for each situation.

4. reading 5 pages in 6 min and 22 pages in 40 min

5. walking 1.5 mi in 25 min and 4 mi in 80 min

6. scoring 3 goals in 5 games and 9 goals in 7 games

7. copying 4 pages in 1 min and 52 pages in 5 min

Direct Variation 5-3

A function is a **direct variation** if it has the form $y = kx$, where $k \neq 0$. The coefficient k is the **constant of variation**.

Each set of ordered pairs is for a direct variation. Find each missing value.

8. $(4, 8)$ and $(3, y)$

9. $(-3, 9)$ and $(x, -12)$

10. $(16, y)$ and $(4, -1)$

Slope-Intercept Form 5-4

The ***y*-intercept** of a line is the y-coordinate of the point where the line crosses the y-axis. The **slope-intercept form** of a linear equation is $y = mx + b$, where m is the slope and b is the y-intercept.

Write an equation of a line with the given slope and *y*-intercept. Then graph each equation.

11. $m = \frac{3}{4}, b = 8$

12. $m = -7, b = \frac{1}{2}$

13. $m = \frac{2}{5}, b = 0$

14. $m = 0, b = -3$

Writing the Equation of a Line 5-5

When you know the slope of a line and a point on it, solve for the y-intercept. Then use the slope and the y-intercept to write an equation.

When you know two points on a line, first find the slope of the line through the points. Then find the y-intercept and write an equation.

Write an equation of a line through the given points.

15. (4, 3), (–2, 1)

16. (5, –4), (0, 2)

17. (–1, 0), (–3, –1)

18. (2, 7), (–8, 4)

Write an equation for each line.

19.

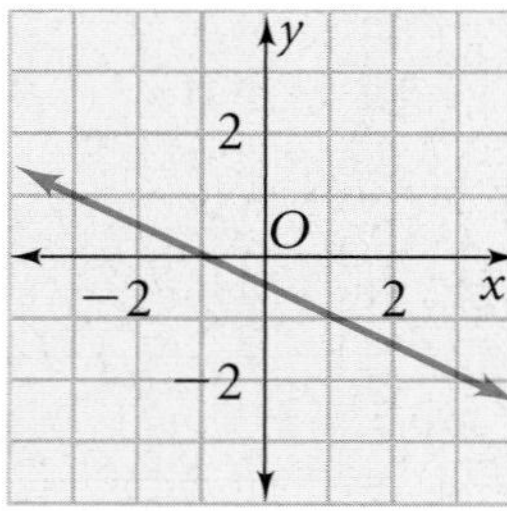

20.

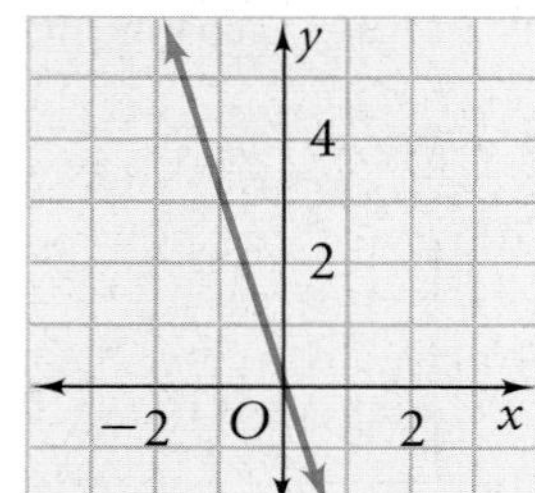

21.

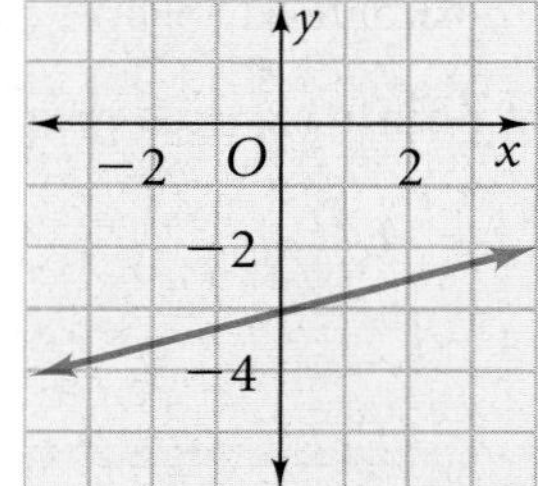

Scatter Plots and Equations of Lines 5-6

The **line of best fit** of a scatter plot is the most accurate trend line showing the relationship between the sets of data. You can find the equation of the line of best fit using a graphing calculator. The **correlation coefficient** tells how closely the equation models the data.

22. The table shows the average person's consumption of poultry from 1970 to 1993.

a. Find the equation of a trend line or use a graphing calculator to find the equation of the line of best fit.

b. Use your equation to **predict** how much poultry the average person will eat in 2005.

Average Poultry Consumption (pounds/person)

Year	Pounds
1970	33.8
1975	32.9
1980	40.6
1985	45.2
1990	56.0
1993	61.1

$Ax + By = C$ Form 5-7

The **x-intercept** of a line is the x-coordinate of the point where the line crosses the x-axis. When a line is in **$Ax + By = C$ form,** you can use the x- and y-intercepts to make a graph of the equation.

Find the x- and y- intercepts. Then graph each equation.

23. $5x + 2y = 10$ **24.** $6.5x - 4y = 52$ **25.** $-x + 3y = -15$ **26.** $8x - y = 104$

Parallel and Perpendicular Lines 5-8

Parallel lines have the same slope. Two lines are **perpendicular** if the product of their slopes is -1.

Write an equation that satisfies the given conditions.

27. parallel to $y = 5x - 2$, through $(2, -1)$

28. perpendicular to $y = -3x + 7$, through $(3, 5)$

29. parallel to $y = 9x$, through $(0, -5)$

30. perpendicular to $y = 8x - 1$, through $(4, 10)$

31. ***Open-ended*** Write the equations of four lines that form a rectangle.

Using the x-intercept 5-9

You can use a linear function to solve the related one-variable equation. Graph the linear function. The x-intercept is the solution of the related one-variable equation.

32. You start a lawn-mowing business. You buy a used power mower for \$175. You plan to charge \$30 per lawn.
  a. Write an equation relating your income to expenses.
  b. Graph the related linear function to find your break-even point.

33. ***Writing*** How is the break-even point related to profit?

34. ***Standardized Test Prep*** What is the x-intercept of $3x - 2y = 6$?
  A. -3 **B.** -2 **C.** 2 **D.** 3 **E.** -5

Getting Ready for... CHAPTER 6

Graph each pair of equations on the same set of axes.

35. $y = 3x - 6$
$y = -x + 2$

36. $y = -2x - 4$
$y = 0.5x + 9$

37. $y = 6x + 1$
$y = 6x - 4$

38. $y = x + 5$
$y = -3x + 5$

39. $y = x^2$
$y = 4x + 9$

40. $y = -4$
$y = 2x^2 + 1$

CHAPTER 5

Assessment

Tell if each statement is *true* or *false*. Explain.

1. A rate of change must be positive.
2. The rate of change for a vertical line is 0.

Find the slope of the line passing through each pair of points.

3. (4, 3), (3, 8)
4. (−2, 1), (6, −1)

Draw the graph of a direct variation that includes the given point.

5. (2, 2)
6. (−8, −4)
7. (3, −1)
8. (−5, 3)

Write each equation in $y = mx + b$ form.

9. $-7y = 8x - 3$
10. $x - 3y = -18$
11. $5x + 4y = 100$
12. $9x = 2y + 13$

Find the *x*- and *y*-intercepts of each line.

13. $3x + 4y = -24$
14. $2y = 3x - 8$
15. $y = 0.3x + 6$
16. $y = -x + 1$

17. **Writing** Explain why the *x*- and *y*-intercepts of a direct variation are always zero.

Write an equation of the line with the given slope that contains the given point.

18. slope = 3, (4, −8)
19. slope = $\frac{8}{3}$, (−2, −7)
20. slope = $-\frac{1}{2}$, (0, 3)
21. slope = −5, (9, 0)

Write an equation of the line that contains the given points.

22. (4, 9), (−2, −6)
23. (−1, 0), (3, 10)
24. (5, −8), (−9, −8)
25. (0, 7), (1, 5)

26. Which of the following lines is *not* perpendicular to $y = -2.5x + 13$?
    - A. $y = 0.4x - 7$
    - B. $-2x + 5y = 8$
    - C. $y = \frac{2}{5}x + 4$
    - D. $2y = 5x + 1.5$

Write an equation of a line that satisfies the given conditions.

27. parallel to $y = 5x$, through (2, −1)
28. perpendicular to $y = -2x$, through (4, 0)
29. parallel to $y = 5$, through (−3, 6)
30. perpendicular to $x = -7$, through (0, 2)

31. **Open-ended** Write the equation of a line parallel to $y = 0.5x - 10$.

32. You start a pet-washing service. You spend $30 on supplies. You charge $5 to wash each pet.
    a. Write an equation to relate your income *y* to the number of pets *x* you wash.
    b. Graph the equation. What are the *x*- and *y*-intercepts?
    c. How many pets do you need to wash to break even?

Use the data below for Exercises 33 and 34.

Local Governments in the United States (in thousands)

Year	Municipalities	School Districts
1962	18.0	34.7
1967	18.0	21.8
1972	18.5	15.8
1977	18.9	15.2
1982	19.1	14.9
1987	19.2	14.7
1992	19.3	14.6

33. a. **Graphing Calculator** Find the equation of a trend line or the line of best fit for the number of municipalities and the year.
    b. **Predict** the number of municipalities in 2005.

34. a. **Graphing Calculator** Find the equation of a trend line or the line of best fit for the number of school districts and the year.
    b. Do the data show a strong correlation? Explain.

CHAPTER 5

Preparing for the Math A Exam

Part I

1 A horizontal line passes through $(5, -2)$. Which other point does it also pass through?

(1) $(5, 2)$ (3) $(-5, 2)$
(2) $(-5, -2)$ (4) $(5, 0)$

2 During the 6-week period, which kitten's weight showed the greatest rate of change?

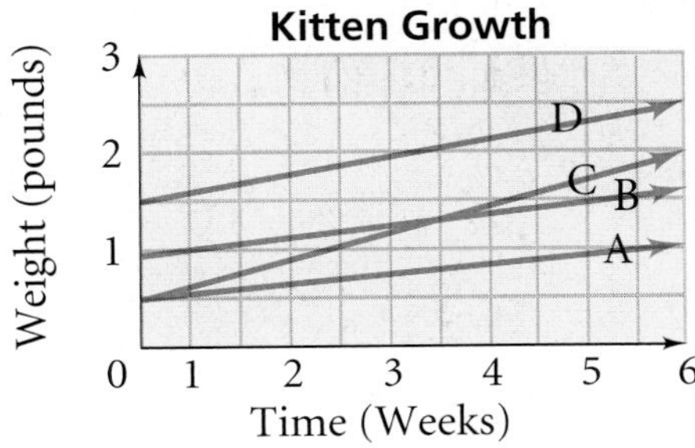

(1) Kitten A (3) Kitten C
(2) Kitten B (4) Kitten D

3 Which equation represents a direct variation?

(1) $5y = 2x$ (3) $x + 5y = 2$
(2) $y^2 = 5x$ (4) $y = \frac{2}{5}x + 2$

4 Which equation is represented by this graph?

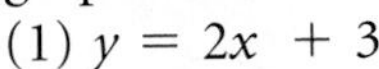

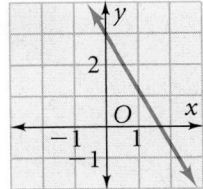

(1) $y = 2x + 3$
(2) $y = -2x + 3$
(3) $y = 2x - 3$
(4) $y = -2x - 3$

5 Which equation describes the line that passes through $(4, -8)$ and has a slope of $\frac{1}{4}$?

(1) $y = 4x - 8$ (3) $y = -\frac{1}{2}x + \frac{1}{4}$
(2) $y = \frac{1}{4}x + 6$ (4) $y = \frac{1}{4}x - 9$

6 A line perpendicular to $y = 3x - 2$ passes through the point $(0, 6)$. Which other point lies on the line?

(1) $(9, 3)$ (3) $(-9, -3)$
(2) $(-9, 3)$ (4) $(9, -3)$

7 Which inequality describes the numbers for which the following statement is true? The sum of a number and 15 is more than 27 but less than 32.

(1) $27 < n < 32$ (3) $n + 27 < 32$
(2) $n + 15 > 27$ (4) $12 < n < 17$

8 If $3x + 2 = 11$, then $5x + 1 = \blacksquare$.

(1) 3 (2) 21 (3) 16 (4) 15

Part II

9 Each gram of fat in a certain food contains 9 calories. Find the constant of variation and write an equation relating calories c to grams of fat g.

10 Write an equation for the line that passes through the points $(2, 3)$ and $(-4, 1)$.

Part III

11 Mariko runs 800 ft in one minute. What is the rate of change in her position, in miles per hour? Round to the nearest unit.

12 Find the x- and y- intercepts of the line described by the equation $5x + 3y = 15$. Then graph the line.

Part IV

13 Graph the data shown in the table. Draw a trend line and write its equation.

x	1	1	2	3	4	4	5	6
y	0	–1	1	6	8	7	12	15

14 The base charge for cab fare is \$1.20. There is an additional charge of \$.40 for each $\frac{1}{5}$ mile the cab travels.

a Write an equation in slope-intercept form that relates total cab fare to length of trip.
b Graph your equation.
c Use your graph to find the cost of taking a cab 1.8 miles from the train station to the museum.

CHAPTER

6 Systems of Equations and Inequalities

Relating to the Real World

Often real-world problems contain more than one unknown quantity and more than one simple relationship. By writing two or more equations and solving the system, environmental and industrial planners can find the best way of assigning and using resources.

Lessons

6-1	6-2	6-3	6-4	6-5
Solving Systems by Graphing	*Solving Systems Using Substitution*	*Solving Systems Using Elimination*	*Writing Systems*	*Linear Inequalities*

Let's Dance!

Suppose you are a member of the student council and must plan a dance. Plans include a band and refreshments. You want to keep the ticket price as low as possible to encourage students to attend.

As you work through the chapter, you will use systems of equations to analyze costs and make decisions. You will write a report detailing your choice of a band, the cost of a catering service, and what you would recommend as a ticket price.

To help you complete the project:

- **p. 274** *Find Out by Graphing*
- **p. 284** *Find Out by Calculating*
- **p. 293** *Find Out by Writing*
- **p. 299** *Find Out by Graphing*
- **p. 310** *Finishing the Project*

Systems of Linear Inequalities
6-6

Concepts of Linear Programming
6-7

Systems with Nonlinear Equations
6-8

Math ToolboX

Problem Solving

Guess and Test

Before Lesson 6-1

You can use the *Guess and Test* strategy to solve many types of problems. First, make a guess. Then test your guess against the conditions of the problem. Use the results from your first guess to make a more accurate guess. Continue to guess and test until you find the correct answer.

Example

The ratio of boys to girls in a ninth-grade class at a high school is about 3 to 2. There are about 600 ninth-graders. How many are boys? girls?

Guess the number of boys. → Number of Boys

Subtract your guess from 600. → Number of Girls

Write the ratio and compare. → $\frac{\text{boys}}{\text{girls}} \stackrel{?}{=} \frac{3}{2} = 1.5$

	Number of Boys	Number of Girls	$\frac{\text{boys}}{\text{girls}} \stackrel{?}{=} \frac{3}{2} = 1.5$	
First guess	400	$600 - 400 = 200$	$\frac{400}{200} = 2$	← too high, so try a lower number of boys
Second guess	350	$600 - 350 = 250$	$\frac{350}{250} = 1.4$	← too low, so try a number between 350 and 400
Third guess	375	$600 - 375 = 225$	$\frac{375}{225} = 1.\overline{6}$	← too high, so try a number between 350 and 375
Fourth guess	360	$600 - 360 = 240$	$\frac{360}{240} = 1.5$	← correct

There are about 360 ninth-grade boys and 240 ninth-grade girls.

Solve each problem.

1. Find a pair of integers with a product of 32 and a sum of 12.
2. Find a pair of integers with a sum of 114 and a difference of 2.
3. Livingston is 25 mi east of Bozeman, Montana. Lisa left Bozeman at 2:00 P.M., driving east on I-90 at 65 mi/h. Jerome left Livingston at 2:00 P.M., driving west on I-90 at 55 mi/h.
   a. At what time will Lisa pass Jerome?
   b. How far will Lisa be from Bozeman when she passes Jerome?
4. Shigechiyo Izumi of Japan lived to be one of the oldest people in the world. Carrie White was the oldest known person in the United States. Carrie lived 4 years fewer than Izumi. The sum of their ages is 236 years. How many years did each person live?
5. **Writing** Describe some advantages and disadvantages of using *Guess and Test* to solve a problem.

6-1 Solving Systems by Graphing

What You'll Learn

- Solving systems of linear equations by graphing

...And Why

To solve problems by comparing costs for services like television

What You'll Need

- graph paper
- graphing calculator

THINK AND DISCUSS

Solving Systems with One Solution

How can you show all the solutions of the linear equation $y = 2x - 3$? Graph the line, of course! Each point on the line is a solution.

Linear Equation
$y = 2x - 3$

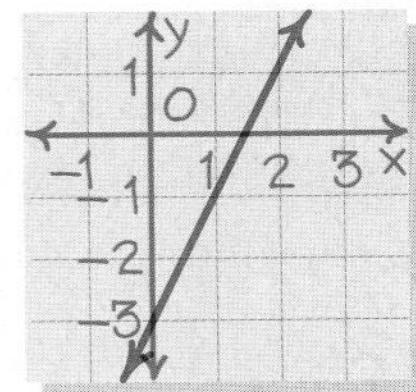

1. **Open-ended** Use the graph to write three different solutions of the equation $y = 2x - 3$. Then show that each ordered pair makes the equation true.

Two or more linear equations together form a **system of linear equations.** One way to solve a system of linear equations is by graphing. Any point common to all the lines is a **solution of the system.** So, any ordered pair that makes *all* the equations true is a solution of the system.

QUICK REVIEW

The slope-intercept form of a linear equation is $y = mx + b$, with m = slope and b = y-intercept.

Example 1

Solve the system of linear equations by graphing.

$$y = 2x - 3$$
$$y = x - 1$$

Graph both equations on the same coordinate grid.

$y = 2x - 3$: slope is 2, y-intercept is -3.
$y = x - 1$: slope is 1, y-intercept is -1.

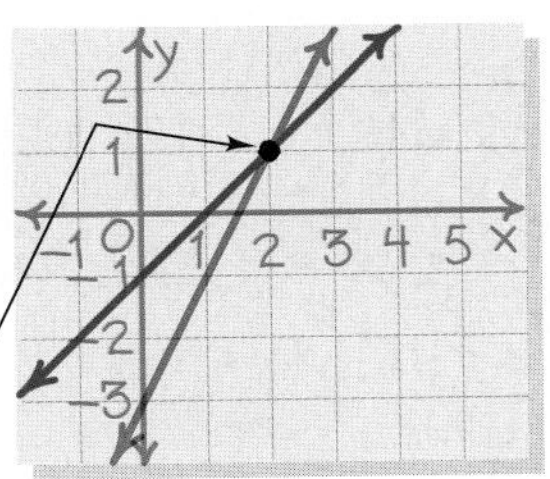

Find the point of intersection.

The lines intersect at (2, 1), so (2, 1) is the solution of the system.

Check See if (2, 1) makes both equations true.

Substitute (2, 1) for (x, y).

$y = 2x - 3$	$y = x - 1$
$1 \stackrel{?}{=} 2(2) - 3$	$1 \stackrel{?}{=} 2 - 1$
$1 \stackrel{?}{=} 4 - 3$	$1 = 1$ ✔
$1 = 1$ ✔	

It checks, so (2, 1) is the solution of the system of linear equations.

2. **Try This** Solve the system $y = x + 5$. Check your solution.
$y = -4x$

3. **Critical Thinking** Do you think a system of linear equations always has exactly one solution? Draw diagrams to support your answer.

You can use the graph of a system of linear equations to solve problems.

Example 2 **Relating to the Real World** 

Watch Pay-Per-View!
Great Rates for Members Only:
Pay only $24/year . . .
Watch all your favorites
for ONLY $4 each!
(Non-members pay $5.50!)

Entertainment A cable company offers a "pay-per-view" club. Let c = the annual cost and n = the number of movies you watch in a year. Graph the system of equations below to decide whether to join the club.

Members: $c = 4n + 24$
Non-members: $c = 5.50n$

Step 1: Set an appropriate range.

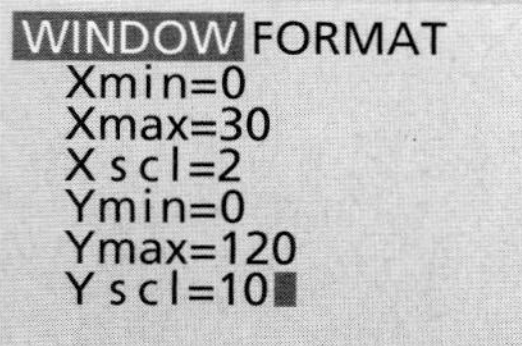

Step 2: Input the equations. Let $n = x$ and $c = y$.

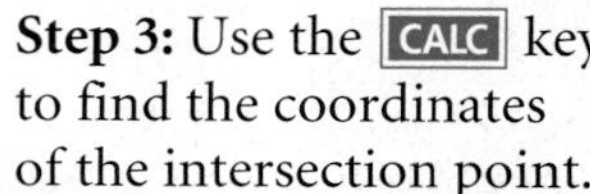
Step 3: Use the CALC key to find the coordinates of the intersection point.

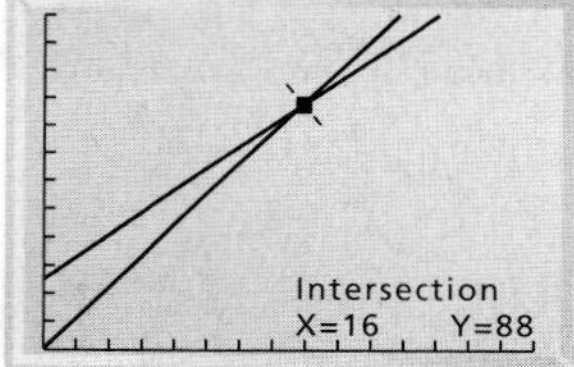

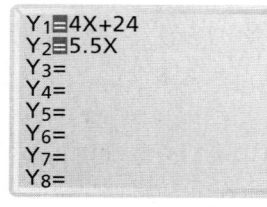

The solution of the system is (16, 88) where $(x, y) = (n, c)$.

Check See if (16, 88) makes both equations true.

$c = 4n + 24$
$88 \stackrel{?}{=} 4(16) + 24$
$88 \stackrel{?}{=} 64 + 24$
$88 = 88$ ✓

← Substitute 16 for n and 88 for c. →

$c = 5.50n$
$88 \stackrel{?}{=} 5.50(16)$
$88 = 88$ ✓

You find that 16 movies in a year cost $88 for both members and nonmembers. If you plan to watch more than 16 movies in a year, join the club. If you plan to watch fewer than 16, do not join the club.

GRAPHING CALCULATOR HINT

You can also use the TABLE feature to find the intersection point. The ZOOM and TRACE keys will only estimate the intersection point.

PROBLEM SOLVING HINT

For Question 4, you can use *Guess and Test* or *Draw a Graph.*

4. Suppose the annual fee is $15 instead of $24. What advice would you give a friend on whether or not to join the club?

Math A Test Prep

1 Find the solution of this system.

$x = -1$
$x - y = -2$

(1) $(-1, -1)$
(2) $(1, -1)$
(3) $(-1, 1)$
(4) $(1, 1)$

2 Corey said that if a point is not a solution of a system of two equations, then it is not a solution of either equation in the system. Is he correct? Explain.

Solving Special Types of Systems

A system of linear equations has **no solution** when the graphs of the equations are parallel. There are no points of intersection, so there is no solution.

$y = -x + 1$
$y = -x - 1$

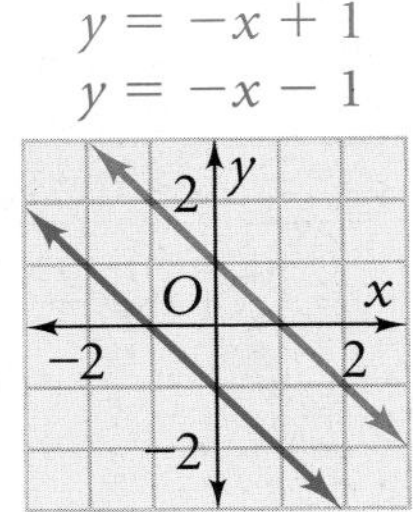

$y = 3x - 2$
$y = 3x$

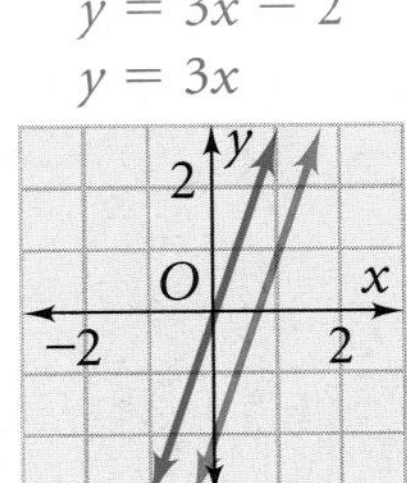

5. **Critical Thinking** Without graphing, how can you tell that a system has no solution? Give an example.

A system of linear equations has **infinitely many solutions** when the graphs of the equations are the same line. All points on the line are solutions of the system.

Example 3

Solve the system by graphing. $-4y = 4 + x$

$\frac{1}{4}x + y = -1$

First, write each equation in slope-intercept form.

$-4y = 4 + x$ $\quad\quad$ $\frac{1}{4}x + y = -1$

$y = -\frac{1}{4}x - 1$ $\quad\quad$ $y = -\frac{1}{4}x - 1$

Then graph each equation on the same coordinate plane.

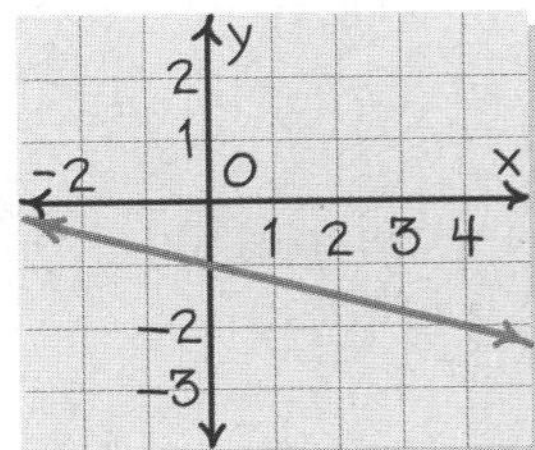

Since the graphs are the same line, the system has infinitely many solutions.

6. What do you notice about the slope-intercept form of each equation in Example 3? How could this help you solve a linear system?

7. **Try This** Solve each system by graphing.
   a. $y = x$
      $y = x + 6$
   b. $2x + 2y = 1$
      $y = -x + \frac{1}{2}$
   c. $x = 1$
      $x = -2$

GRAPHING CALCULATOR HINT

To enter an equation on a graphing calculator, you need to put it in slope-intercept form.

WORK TOGETHER

PROBLEM SOLVING HINT

Start with the known information and use the strategy *Work Backward* to write an appropriate system.

Work with a partner to copy and complete the table. Your goal is to create a system of equations that satisfies the conditions given.

	System of Equations	Description of Graph	One Solution of the System	Number of Solutions
8.	■	2 intersecting lines	$(1, -5)$	■
9.	■	2 non-intersecting lines	■	■
10.	■	■	■	infinitely many

Exercises ON YOUR OWN

Graphing Calculator **Solve each system of linear equations by graphing. Sketch the graph on your paper.**

1. $y = \frac{1}{3}x + 3$
$y = \frac{1}{3}x - 3$

2. $y = x$
$y = 5x$

3. $y = 1$
$y = x$

4. $2x + y = 3$
$x - 2y = 4$

5. $3x - y = 7$
$y = 3x - 7$

6. **Number Theory** You can represent the set of nonnegative even numbers by the expression $2n$, for $n = 0, 1, 2, \ldots$. You can represent the set of nonnegative odd numbers by $2n + 1$, for $n = 0, 1, 2, \ldots$.

a. Copy and complete the table at the right.

b. Graph the system. $y = 2n$ $\quad y = 2n + 1$

c. **Writing** Why does it makes sense that this system has no solution?

n	Even Numbers $2n$	Odd Numbers $2n + 1$
0	$2(0) = 0$	$2(0) + 1 = 1$
1	■	■
2	■	■
3	■	■
4	■	■
5	■	■

Is (–1, 5) a solution of each system? Verify your answer.

7. $x + y = 4$
$x = -1$

8. $y = -x + 4$
$y = -\frac{1}{5}x$

9. $y = 5$
$x = y - 6$

10. $y = 2x + 7$
$y = x + 6$

11. Below is a retelling of an Aesop fable. Use the story to answer the questions below.

One Day, the tortoise challenged the hare to a race. The hare laughed, while bragging about how fast a runner he was. On the day of the race, the hare was so confident that he took a nap during the race. When he awoke, he ran as hard as he could, but he could not beat the slow-but-sure tortoise across the finish line.

a. The graph shows the race of the tortoise and the hare. What labels should be on each axis?

b. Which color indicates the tortoise? Which indicates the hare?

c. What does the point of intersection mean?

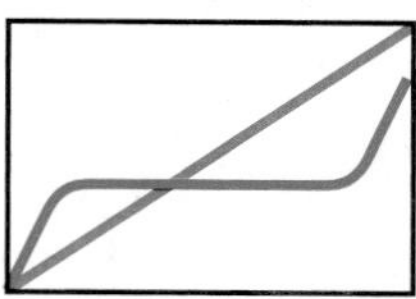

12. **Math in the Media** Suppose you see the two summer jobs advertised at the right. Let x = the amount of sales and y = money earned in a week.

Cellular Phone Sales:	$y = 150 + 0.2x$
Stereo Sales:	$y = 200 + 0.1x$

a. To earn the same amount of money at both jobs, how much will you need to sell in a week?

b. After talking with salespeople, you estimate weekly sales of about \$600 with either job. At which job will you earn more money?

Sales Position
Salesperson Wanted
Knowledge of Cellular Phones
On-Site Sales
\$150/week + 20% commission

CAREER OPPORTUNITY
Sell Stereo Equipment in
National Electronics Retail Chain!
\$200/week + 10% commission

Solve each system by graphing. Write *no solution* or *infinitely many solutions* where appropriate.

13. $y = -x + 4$; $y = 2x + 1$

14. $x = 10$; $y = -7$

15. $y = 3x$; $y = 5x$

16. $y = 3x + 4$; $4y = 12x + 16$

17. $3x + y = 5$; $x - y = 7$

18. $2x - 2y = 4$; $y - x = 6$

19. $x + y = -1$; $x + y = 1$

20. $y = 1$; $3y + x = 9$

21. $y = \frac{1}{2}x - 1$; $y = -\frac{1}{2}x - 1$

22. $x + 2y = 3$; $-x = 2y - 3$

23. $y = 4x - 3$; $y = 4x + 2$

24. $y = \frac{3}{4}x - 5$; $x = 4$

Critical Thinking **Is each statement *true* or *false*? Explain your reasoning.**

25. A system of linear equations can have one solution, no solution, or infinitely many solutions.

26. If a point is a solution of a system of linear equations, it is also a solution of each linear equation in the system.

27. If a point is a solution of a linear equation, it is also a solution of any system containing that linear equation.

28. If a system of linear equations has no solution, the graphs of the lines are parallel.

PROBLEM SOLVING HINT

For Exercises 25–28, you can *Draw a Graph.*

Without graphing, decide whether the lines in each system *intersect, are parallel,* or *are the same line.* Then write the number of solutions.

29. $y = 2x$; $y = 2x - 5$

30. $x + y = 4$; $2x + 2y = 8$

31. $y = -3x + 1$; $y = 3x + 7$

32. $3x - 5y = 0$; $y = \frac{3}{5}x$

33. $2y - 10x = 2$; $y = 5x + 1$

34. $y = -4x + 4$; $y = -4x + 8$

35. $y = x + 1$; $y = \frac{1}{2}x$

36. $y = 2x + 3$; $y - 2x = 5$

Open-ended **Write a system of two linear equations with the given characteristics.**

37. one solution; perpendicular lines

38. no solutions; one equation is $y = 2x + 5$

39. one solution; (0, –4)

40. infinitely many solutions; one equation is $y = 4x$

41. **Music** Suppose you and your friends form a band, and you want to record a demo tape. Studio A rents for \$100 plus \$50/h. Studio B rents for \$50 plus \$75/h. Let t = the number of hours and c = the cost.

Studio A:	$c = 100 + 50t$
Studio B:	$c = 50 + 75t$

a. Solve the system by graphing.
b. Explain what the solution of the system means in terms of your band renting a studio.

42. **Writing** When equivalent equations form a system, there are infinitely many solutions. Explain in your own words why this is true.

Chapter Project ***Find Out by Graphing***

Band A charges \$600 to play for the evening. Band B charges \$350 plus \$1.25 for each ticket sold. Write a linear equation for the cost of each band. Graph each equation and find the number of tickets for which the cost of the two bands will be equal.

Estimation **Estimate the solution of each system. Use the equations to test your estimate. Adjust your estimate until you find the exact solution.**

43. $y = 6.5$
$y = x + 2$

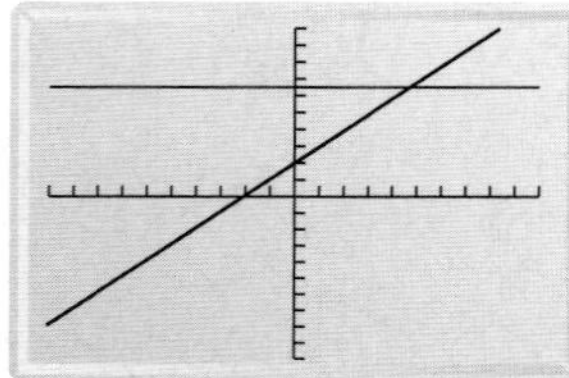

44. $y = -4x - 10$
$y = -6$

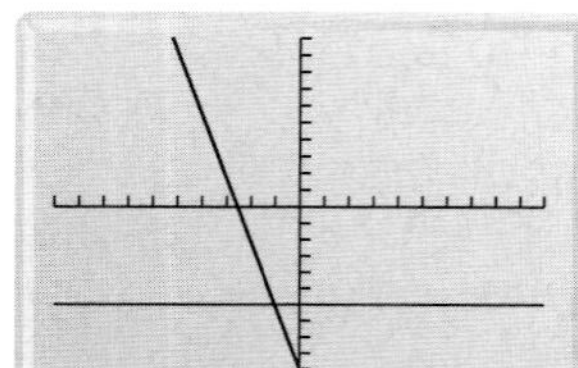

45. $y = -0.75x - 3$
$y = 0.25x - 7$

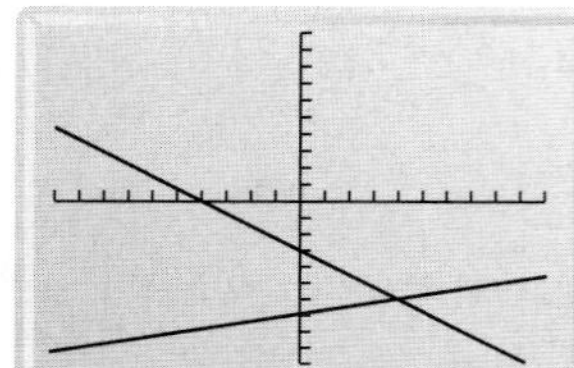

46. $y = -x - 1$
$y = x + 8$

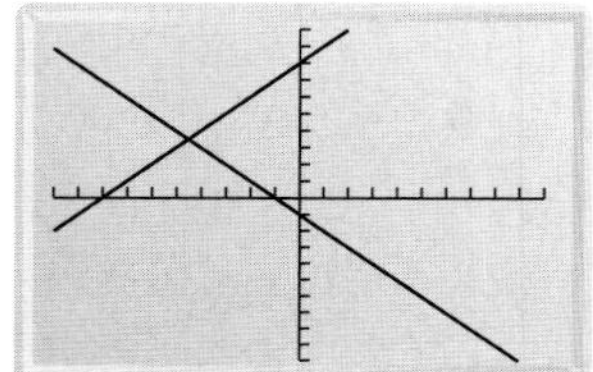

Exercises MIXED REVIEW

Probability **Find each probability for two rolls of a number cube.**

47. P(3, then 4)
48. P(1, then even)
49. P(two integers)
50. P(at least one 1)

Write an inequality to model each situation.

51. Polar bears can swim as fast as 6 mi/h.
52. Each eyelash is shed every 3 to 5 months.

53. a. **Geography** Cairo, Egypt, has about 18 million residents. The average population density is 130,000 people/mi^2. What is Cairo's area?
b. Cairo has $\frac{1}{4}$ of Egypt's population. What is the population of Egypt?

Getting Ready for Lesson 6-2

Solve each equation for the given variable.

54. $x - y = 3; y$
55. $\frac{1}{2}x = 4y; x$
56. $\frac{x}{2} = \frac{y}{4}; y$
57. $2x - 3y = 5; x$

6-2 Solving Systems Using Substitution

What You'll Learn

- Solving systems of linear equations by substitution

...And Why

To solve problems involving transportation

What You'll Need

- graph paper
- graphing calculator

System:
$y = x + 6.1$
$y = -2x - 1.4$

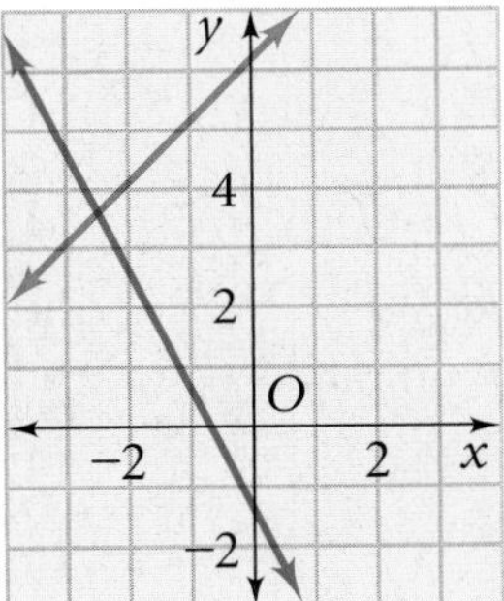

WORK TOGETHER

Work with a partner.

1. **Estimation** Use the graph at the left to estimate the solution of the system.
2. a. **Graphing Calculator** Graph the system at the left.
   b. Use the CALC or TABLE features to find the intersection point.
3. Compare your estimate to your answer in Question 2(b).
4. **Choose** Use paper and pencil or a calculator to solve each system.
   a. $y = 3x - 6$, $y = -6x$
   b. $y = x + 2.5$, $y = 2x - 0.5$
   c. $2y - x = 3$, $y = x - 2$
5. Explain why you chose the method(s) you used in Question 4.

THINK AND DISCUSS

Solving Systems with One Solution

Sometimes you won't have a graphing calculator to use. Another way to solve a system is to use substitution. **Substitution** allows you to create a one-variable equation.

Example 1

Solve the system $y = x + 6.1$ using substitution.
$y = -2x - 1.4$

$y = -2x - 1.4$ ← Start with one equation.
$x + 6.1 = -2x - 1.4$ ← Substitute $x + 6.1$ for y in that equation.
$3x = -7.5$ ← Solve for x.
$x = -2.5$

Substitute -2.5 for x in either equation and solve for y.

$y = (-2.5) + 6.1$
$y = 3.6$

Since $x = -2.5$ and $y = 3.6$, the solution is $(-2.5, 3.6)$.

Check See if $(-2.5, 3.6)$ satisfies the other equation.

$3.6 \stackrel{?}{=} -2(-2.5) - 1.4$
$3.6 \stackrel{?}{=} 5 - 1.4$
$3.6 = 3.6$ ✔

PROBLEM SOLVING

Look Back Does the solution agree with the graph of the system in the Work Together?

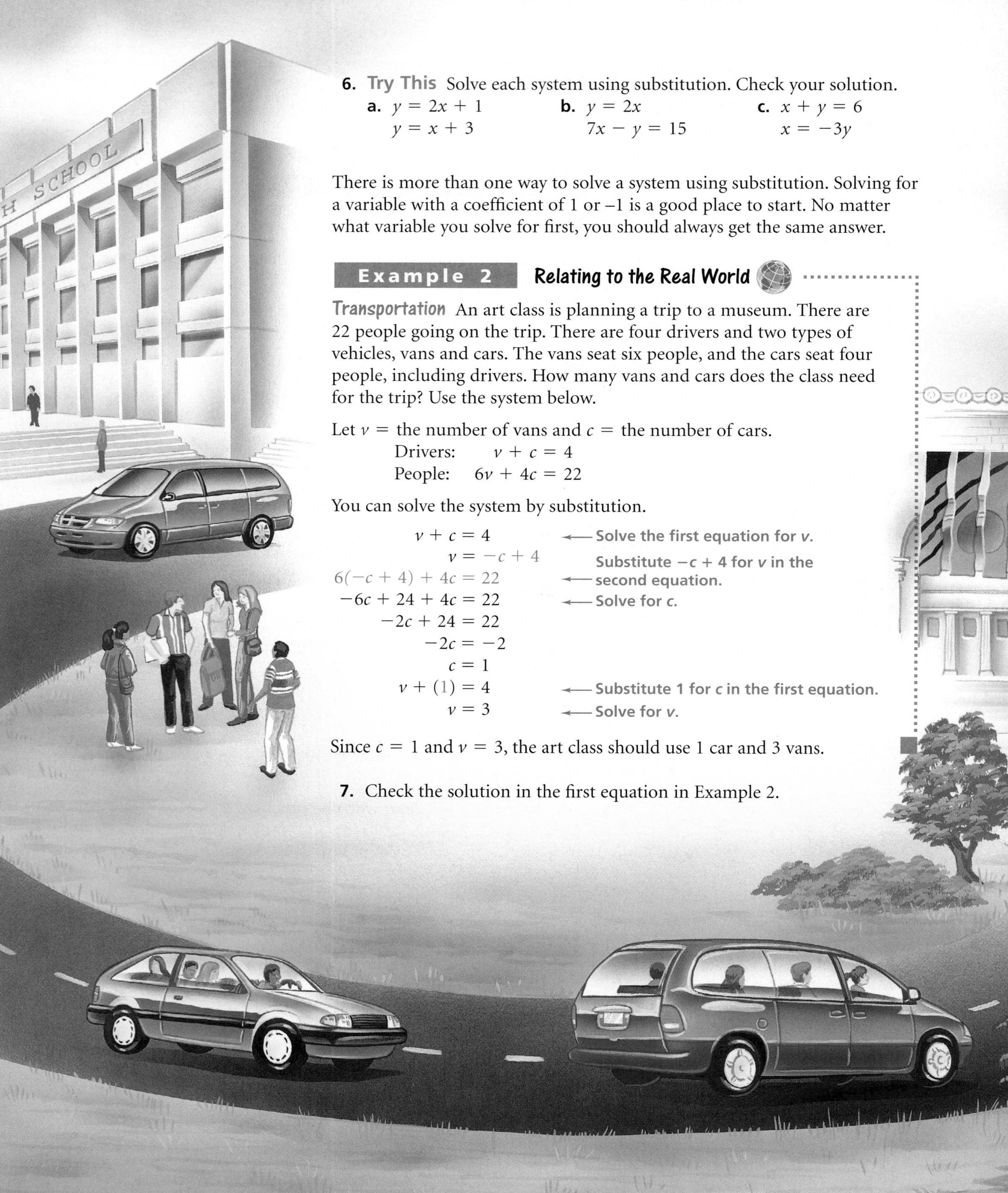

6. **Try This** Solve each system using substitution. Check your solution.

a. $y = 2x + 1$
$y = x + 3$

b. $y = 2x$
$7x - y = 15$

c. $x + y = 6$
$x = -3y$

There is more than one way to solve a system using substitution. Solving for a variable with a coefficient of 1 or –1 is a good place to start. No matter what variable you solve for first, you should always get the same answer.

Example 2 **Relating to the Real World**

Transportation An art class is planning a trip to a museum. There are 22 people going on the trip. There are four drivers and two types of vehicles, vans and cars. The vans seat six people, and the cars seat four people, including drivers. How many vans and cars does the class need for the trip? Use the system below.

Let v = the number of vans and c = the number of cars.

Drivers: $v + c = 4$

People: $6v + 4c = 22$

You can solve the system by substitution.

$v + c = 4$ ← Solve the first equation for v.

$v = -c + 4$

$6(-c + 4) + 4c = 22$ ← Substitute $-c + 4$ for v in the second equation.

$-6c + 24 + 4c = 22$ ← Solve for c.

$-2c + 24 = 22$

$-2c = -2$

$c = 1$

$v + (1) = 4$ ← Substitute 1 for c in the first equation.

$v = 3$ ← Solve for v.

Since $c = 1$ and $v = 3$, the art class should use 1 car and 3 vans.

7. Check the solution in the first equation in Example 2.

8. a. Solve the system in Example 2 again. This time, start by solving the second equation for c.
   b. **Critical Thinking** Why is this procedure more difficult?

9. Describe a possible first step for solving each system by substitution.

   a. $3x - y = 17$
      $2x + y = 8$

   b. $x + 3y = 5$
      $2x - 4y = -5$

   c. $y = -2x - 3$
      $y = x$

Solving Special Types of Systems

You can use substitution to learn that systems have *no solution* or *infinitely many solutions.*

Example 3

Solve the system using substitution. $x + y = 6$
$5x + 5y = 10$

$$x + y = 6 \quad \leftarrow \text{Solve the first equation for } x.$$
$$x = 6 - y \quad \text{Substitute } 6 - y \text{ for } x$$
$$5(6 - y) + 5y = 10 \quad \leftarrow \text{in the second equation.}$$
$$30 - 5y + 5y = 10 \quad \leftarrow \text{Solve for } y.$$
$$30 = 10 \quad \leftarrow \text{False!}$$

Since $30 = 10$ is a false statement, the system has no solution.

10. Describe the graph of the system in Example 3. Graph the system to **verify** your answer.

11. **Critical Thinking** How many solutions does a system of linear equations have if you get each result?
    a. a true statement, such as $2 = 2$
    b. a false statement, such as $10 = 1$
    c. a statement such as $x = 4$

12. Graphs of systems with no solution are parallel lines. What do you know about the equations of parallel lines?

13. Graphs of systems with infinitely many solutions are the same line. What do you know about the equations?

14. Without using substitution, decide whether each system has *no solution* or *infinitely many solutions.* (*Hint:* Write each equation in slope-intercept form and compare.)

    a. $3x - y = -2$
       $y = 3x + 2$

    b. $y = 4x$
       $2x - 0.5y = 0$

    c. $3x + y = 5$
       $6x + 2y = 1$

Exercises ON YOUR OWN

Critical Thinking **Suppose you try to solve a system of linear equations and get the following result. How many solutions does each system have?**

1. $x = 0$ **2.** $5 = 5$ **3.** $-3 = 2$ **4.** $n = 10$

5. $0 = 0$ **6.** $-8 = k$ **7.** $y = 6$ **8.** $0 = -9$

9. Geometry A rectangle is 4 times longer than it is wide ($l = 4w$). The perimeter of the rectangle is 30 cm ($2l + 2w = 30$). Find the dimensions of the rectangle.

10. Internet Suppose you want access to the Internet. With a subscription to *Access,* you pay \$7.95 per month plus \$2.95 per on-line hour. With a subscription to *Network,* you pay \$12.95 per month plus \$1.95 per on-line hour. The system below models this situation. Let c = the monthly cost and h = the number of on-line hours.

Access: $c = 7.95 + 2.95h$

Network: $c = 12.95 + 1.95h$

a. Use substitution to solve the system.

b. Explain how to decide which subscription to buy.

Solve each system using substitution. Write *no solution* or *infinitely many solutions* where appropriate.

E.

11. $y = 2x$
$6x - y = 8$

12. $2x + y = 5$
$2y = 10 - 4x$

13. $y = 3x + 1$
$x = 3y + 1$

14. $x - 3y = 14$
$x - 2 = 0$

15. $2x + 2y = 5$
$y = \frac{1}{4}x$

16. $y = -3x$
$y + 3x = 2$

17. $4x + y = -2$
$-2x - 3y = 1$

18. $3x + 5y = 2$
$x + 4y = -4$

19. $y = x + 2$
$y = 2x - 1$

20. $y = 3$
$y = \frac{4}{3}x + 2$

21. $x + 4y = -3$
$2x + 8y = -6$

22. $2y = 0.2x + 7$
$3y - 2x = 2$

Estimation **Graph each system to estimate the solution. Then use substitution to find the exact solution of the system.**

23. $y = 2x$
$y = -6x + 4$

24. $y = \frac{1}{2}x + 4$
$y = -4x - 5$

25. $x + y = 0$
$5x + 2y = -3$

26. $y = 0.7x + 3$
$y = -1.5x - 7$

27. $y = 3x + 1$
$y = 3x - 2.5$

28. Writing Describe the advantages of using substitution to solve a system. **Justify** your answer with an example.

29. Standardized Test Prep Which system has no solution?

A. $y = x + 3$
$y + 4x = -2$

B. $2x + 2y = 1$
$y = -x + \frac{1}{2}$

C. $y = \frac{1}{2}x + 1$
$6y - 3x = 6$

D. $y = x + 6$
$2y - 2x = 3$

$y = 2x - 1$
$y = -2x$

Mental Math **Match each system with its solution at the right.**

30. $y = x + 1$
$y = 2x - 1$

31. $2y - 8 = x$
$2y + 2x = 2$

32. $2y = x + 3$
$x = y$

33. $x - y = 1$
$x = \frac{1}{2}y + 2$

A. (3, 2)

B. (3, 3)

C. (−2, 3)

D. (2, 3)

How many solutions does each system have?

34. $3y + x = -1$
$x = -3y$

35. $2x + 4y = 0$
$y = -\frac{1}{2}x$

36. $y = 6x$
$y = 3x$

37. $5x - y = 1$
$5x - y = 7$

38. If two linear equations have the same slope and different y-intercepts, their graphs are __?__ lines. Such a system has __?__ solution(s).

39. **Agriculture** A farmer grows only soybeans and corn on his 240-acre farm ($s + c = 240$). This year he wants to plant 80 more acres of soybeans than of corn ($s = c + 80$). How many acres does the farmer need to plant of each crop?

40. **Open-ended** Write a system of linear equations with exactly one solution. Use substitution to solve your system.

Choose **Solve each system by graphing or using substitution.**

41. $y = -2x + 3$
$y = x - 6$

42. $y = \frac{1}{4}x$
$x + 2y = 12$

43. $y = 0$
$4x - y = 1$

44. $x - 3y = 1$
$2x - 6y = 2$

45. $x - y = 20$
$2x + 3y = 0$

46. $y = -x$
$x + y = 5$

47. $x = -2$
$3x - 2y = 4$

48. $0.4x + 0.5y = 1$
$x - y = 7$

Exercises MIXED REVIEW

Find the slope and y-intercept of each line.

49. $y = 7x - 4$

50. $3x + 8y = 16$

51. $y = 9x$

52. $5y = 6x - 25$

53. Write a linear function that passes through the points (2, 3) and (4, 6).

54. **Human Biology** The largest bone in the body is the femur. In a 5-ft tall woman, the femur is about 1.3 ft long. The smallest bone in the body, the stapes, is in the ear. It is only about 0.1 in. long. The femur is about how many times as long as the stapes?

stapes

femur

Getting Ready for Lesson 6-3

Simplify each expression.

55. $(x + 4) - 4(2x + 1)$

56. $5(2x - 3) + (7x + 15)$

57. $3(x - 2) + 6(2x + 1)$

Connections Sales . . . and more

6-3 Solving Systems Using Elimination

What You'll Learn

- Solving systems of linear equations using elimination

...And Why

To investigate real-world situations, such as sales

What You'll Need

- graph paper

THINK AND DISCUSS

Adding or Subtracting Equations

When both linear equations of a system are in the form $Ax + By = C$, you can solve the system using **elimination.** You can add or subtract the equations to eliminate a variable.

QUICK REVIEW

If $a = b$ and $c = d$, then $a + c = b + d$ and $a - c = b - d$.

Example 1

Solve the system using elimination. Check your solution.

$$5x - 6y = -32$$
$$3x + 6y = 48$$

First, eliminate one variable.

$$\begin{aligned} 5x - 6y &= -32 \\ 3x + 6y &= 48 \\ \hline 8x + 0 &= 16 \quad \leftarrow \text{Add the equations to eliminate } y. \\ x &= 2 \quad \leftarrow \text{Solve for } x. \end{aligned}$$

PROBLEM SOLVING

Look Back Why was y eliminated?

Then, find the value of the eliminated variable.

$$\begin{aligned} 3x + 6y &= 48 \quad \leftarrow \text{Pick one equation.} \\ 3(2) + 6y &= 48 \quad \leftarrow \text{Substitute 2 for } x. \\ 6 + 6y &= 48 \quad \leftarrow \text{Solve for } y. \\ 6y &= 42 \\ y &= 7 \end{aligned}$$

Since $x = 2$ and $y = 7$, the solution is $(2, 7)$.

Check See if $(2, 7)$ makes the other equation true.

$$\begin{aligned} 5(2) - 6(7) &\stackrel{?}{=} -32 \\ 10 - 42 &\stackrel{?}{=} -32 \\ -32 &= -32 \checkmark \end{aligned}$$

Example 2 Relating to the Real World 

Basketball Altogether 292 tickets were sold for a high school basketball game. An adult ticket costs \$3. A student ticket costs \$1. Ticket sales were \$470. Use the system to find the number of each type of ticket sold.

number of tickets sold: $a + s = 292$
money collected: $3a + s = 470$

First, eliminate one variable.

$$\begin{aligned} a + s &= 292 \\ 3a + s &= 470 \\ \hline -2a + 0 &= -178 \quad \leftarrow \text{Subtract the equations to eliminate } s. \\ a &= 89 \quad \leftarrow \text{Solve for } a. \end{aligned}$$

Then, find the value of the eliminated variable.

$89 + s = 292$ ← Substitute 89 for *a* in the first equation.

$s = 203$ ← Solve for *s*.

There were 89 adult tickets sold and 203 student tickets sold.

1. Check the solution to Example 2.

2. Would you *add* or *subtract* the equations to eliminate a variable?

a. $a - b = 8$
$a + 2b = 5$

b. $-3x + 2y = 1$
$4x - 2y = -3$

c. $m + t = 6$
$5m + t = 14$

3. **Try This** Use elimination to solve the system in Question 2(a).

Multiplying First

To eliminate a variable, you may need to multiply one or both equations in a system by a nonzero number. Then add or subtract the equations.

Example 3 **Relating to the Real World** 

Sales Suppose your class receives $1084 for selling 205 packages of greeting cards and gift wrap. Let w = the number of packages of gift wrap sold and c = the number of packages of greeting cards sold. Use the system to find the number of each type of package sold.

total number of packages: $w + c = 205$

total amount of sales: $4w + 10c = 1084$

In the first equation, the coefficient of w is 1. In the second equation, the coefficient of w is 4. So multiply the first equation by 4. Then subtract to eliminate w.

$w + c = 205$: $4w + 4c = 820$ ← Multiply each side of the first equation by 4.

$4w + 10c = 1084$

$-6c = -264$ ← Subtract the two equations.

$c = 44$ ← Solve for *c*.

Find w.

$w + c = 205$ ← Use the first equation.

$w + 44 = 205$ ← Substitute 44 for *c*.

$w = 161$ ← Solve for *w*.

The class sold 161 packages of gift wrap and 44 packages of greeting cards.

4. Could you have multiplied the first equation by 10 rather than 4 and then solved the system? Why or why not?

For systems with no solution or infinitely many solutions, look for the same results as you did when you used substitution.

When you solve systems using elimination, plan a strategy. A flowchart like this one may help you to decide how to eliminate a variable.

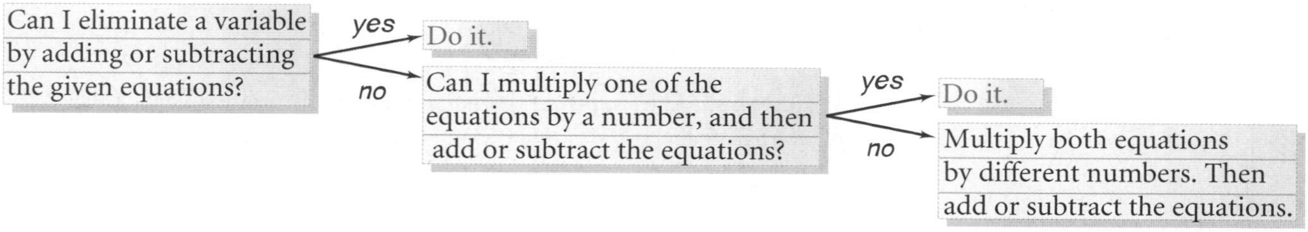

Can I eliminate a variable by adding or subtracting the given equations?
- *yes* → Do it.
- *no* → Can I multiply one of the equations by a number, and then add or subtract the equations?
  - *yes* → Do it.
  - *no* → Multiply both equations by different numbers. Then add or subtract the equations.

WORK TOGETHER

Work in groups.

5. Suppose you want to solve this system using elimination.
$3x - 2y = 6$
$5x + 7y = 41$
  a. What would you multiply each equation by to eliminate x?
  b. What would you multiply each equation by to eliminate y?
  c. Solve the system using elimination. Be sure to check your solution.

Decide which method makes solving each system easier: graphing, substitution, or elimination. Then solve the system and explain the method you chose.

6. $-5a + 14b = 13$
$9a = 72b$

7. $3p - 8q = 4$
$9p - 4q = 5$

8. $y = \frac{2}{3}x - 1$
$y = -x + 4$

9. Describe how to solve this system using elimination.
$x - 2y = 8$
$y = x + 4$

Exercises ON YOUR OWN

Describe a first step for solving each system using elimination. Then solve each system.

1. $3x - y = 21$
$2x + y = 4$

2. $3x + 4y = -10$
$5x - 2y = 18$

3. $2x - y = 6$
$-3x + 4y = 1$

4. $x - y = 12$
$x + y = 22$

5. $2r - 3n = 13$
$8r + 3n = 7$

6. $5a + 6b = 54$
$3a - 3b = 17$

7. $x + y = 6$
$x + 3y = 10$

8. $2p - 5q = 6$
$4p + 3q = -1$

9. *Business* A company orders two types of parts, brass b and steel s. One shipment contains 3 brass and 10 steel parts and costs \$48. A second shipment contains 7 brass and 4 steel parts and costs \$54. Solve the system to find the cost of each type of part.
$3b + 10s = 48$
$7b + 4s = 54$

Solve each system using elimination. Check your solution.

10. $x + y = 12$
$x - y = 2$

11. $-a + 2b = -1$
$a = 3b - 1$

12. $3u + 4w = 9$
$-3u - 2w = -3$

13. $3x + 2y = 9$
$-x + 3y = 8$

14. $r - 3p = 1$
$6r - p = 6$

15. $5x + 3y = 1.5$
$-8x - 2y = 20$

16. $-2z + y = 3$
$z + 4y = 3$

17. $m - n = 0$
$m + n = 28$

18. $2k - 3c = 6$
$6k - 9c = 9$

19. $3b + 4e = 6$
$-6b + e = 6$

20. $4x = -2y + 1$
$2x + y = 4$

21. $2p - 3t = 4$
$3p + 2t = 6$

22. $3x + y = 8$
$x - y = -12$

23. $x + 4y = 1$
$3x + 12y = 3$

24. $h = 2s - 1$
$2s - h = 1$

25. $4x - 2y = 3$
$5x - 3y = 2$

26. **Writing** Explain how to solve a system using elimination. Give examples of when you use addition, subtraction, and multiplication.

27. **Electricity** Two batteries produce a total voltage of 4.5 volts ($B_1 + B_2 = 4.5$). The difference in their voltages is 1.5 volts ($B_1 - B_2 = 1.5$). Determine the voltages of the two batteries.

Critical Thinking **Do you *agree* or *disagree* with each statement? Explain.**

28. A system of linear equations written in the form $Ax + By = C$ is solved most easily by elimination.

29. A system of linear equations written in slope-intercept form, $y = mx + b$, is solved most easily by substitution.

Choose **Choose any method to solve each system.**

30. $y = x + 5$
$x + y = 1$

31. $4x - 2y = 6$
$-2x + y = -3$

32. $y = 0.25x$
$y = -4$

33. $-5x + 2y = 14$
$-3x + y = -2$

34. $y = -2x + 7$
$y = 4x - 5$

35. $y = 4$
$3x - y = 5$

36. $2x - 3y = 4$
$2x + y = -4$

37. $5x + 3y = 6$
$2x - 4y = 5$

38. **Open-ended** Write a system of linear equations that you would solve using elimination. Solve the system.

39. **Vacation** A weekend at the Beach Bay Hotel in Florida includes two nights and four meals. A week includes seven nights and ten meals. The system of linear equations below models this situation. Let $n =$ the cost of one night and $m =$ the cost of one meal.

Weekend: $2n + 4m = 195$
Week: $7n + 10m = 650$

a. Use elimination to solve the system.
b. What does the solution mean in terms of the prices of the room and meals?

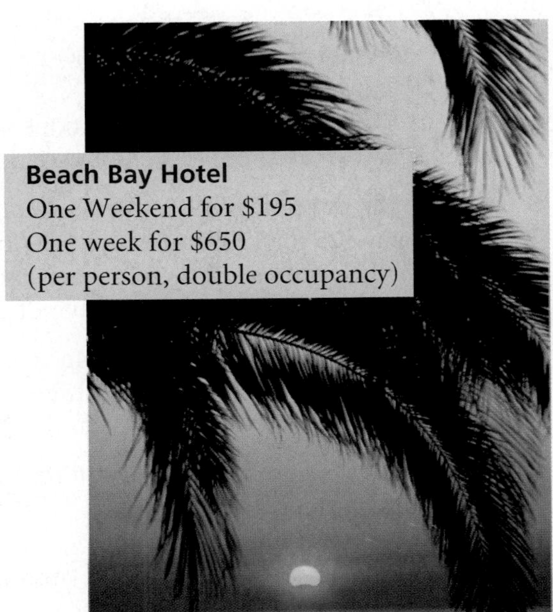

Beach Bay Hotel
One Weekend for $195
One week for $650
(per person, double occupancy)

Chapter Project ***Find Out by Calculating***

A caterer charges a fixed cost for preparing dinner plus a cost for each person served. You know that the cost for 100 people will be \$750 and the cost for 150 people will be \$1050. Find the caterer's fixed cost and the cost per person served.

Exercises MIXED REVIEW

Write an equation of the line passing through the given points.

40. $(3, -7)$ and $(-4, 1)$ **41.** $(0, 4)$ and $(0, -7)$ **42.** $(5, -8)$ and $(9, 0)$ **43.** $(10, 2)$ and $(10, -2)$

44. **Health** In 1980, there were 400,000 cases of polio reported worldwide. From 1980 to 1993, the number of cases declined 75%. How many cases of polio were reported in 1993?

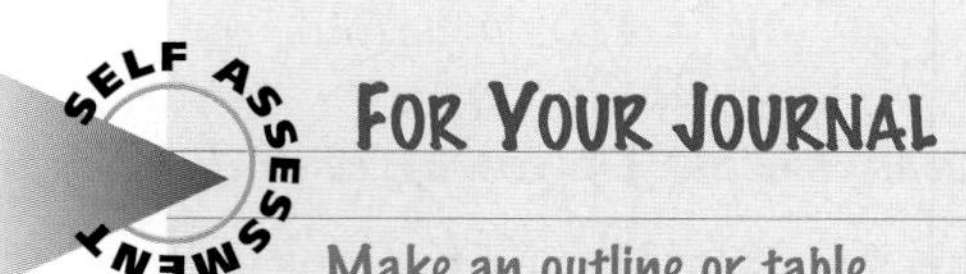

FOR YOUR JOURNAL

Make an outline or table titled "Methods for Solving Systems of Equations." Provide descriptions of procedures, helpful hints, and examples for each method.

Getting Ready for Lesson 6-4

Write an equation to model each situation.

45. Two sandwiches and a drink cost \$6.50.

46. A stack of ten paperbacks and three hardcover books is 18 in. high.

47. Five pieces of plywood and two bags of nails weigh 32 lb.

Exercises CHECKPOINT

Solve each system of equations.

1. $x + 2y = 5$
$-4x + y = 8$

2. $5x - 3y = 27$
$5x + 4y = -1$

3. $x + y = 19$
$10x - 7y = 20$

4. $6x - \frac{3}{4}y = 16$
$y = -\frac{8}{3}x$

5. **Open-ended** Write a system of equations where the solution is $x = 5$ and $y = 7$.

6. **Photography** A photographer offers two options for portraits. You can pay \$25 for 12 pictures and \$.40 for each extra print, or \$30 for 12 pictures and \$.15 for each extra print. Let $c =$ the total cost and $p =$ the number of extra prints.

first option: $c = 25 + 0.4p$
second option: $c = 30 + 0.15p$

a. Solve the system.
b. **Writing** Which option would you recommend to a friend? Explain.

6-4 Writing Systems

What You'll Learn

- Writing and solving systems of linear equations
- Using systems to find the break-even point

...And Why

To model real-world situations, such as publishing a newsletter

THINK AND DISCUSS

In the Math Toolbox before Lesson 6-1, the following problem was solved using the strategy *Guess and Test.*

The ratio of boys to girls in a ninth-grade class at a high school is about 3 to 2. There are about 600 ninth-graders. How many are boys? How many are girls?

You can also solve this problem using a system of linear equations.

Example 1 Relating to the Real World

Schools Use a system of linear equations to solve the problem stated above.

Define b = the number of boys
g = the number of girls

Relate	The total number of ninth-graders is 600.	The ratio of boys to girls is 3 to 2.
Write	$b + g = 600$	$\frac{b}{g} = \frac{3}{2}$

You can solve the system by substitution.

$\frac{b}{g} = \frac{3}{2}$ ← Solve the second equation for b.

$b = \frac{3}{2}g$

$b + g = 600$ ← Use the first equation.

$\frac{3}{2}g + g = 600$ ← Substitute $\frac{3}{2}g$ for b.

$\frac{5}{2}g = 600$ ← Combine like terms.

$g = 240$ ← Multiply both sides by $\frac{2}{5}$.

$\frac{b}{g} = \frac{3}{2}$ ← Use the second equation.

$\frac{b}{240} = \frac{3}{2}$ ← Substitute 240 for g.

$b = 360$ ← Multiply both sides by 240.

There are about 360 ninth-grade boys and 240 ninth-grade girls.

PROBLEM SOLVING

Look Back Which method would you prefer to solve the system: substitution, graphing, or elimination? Why?

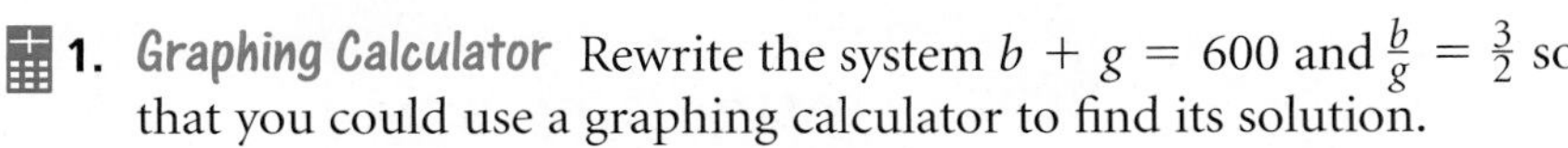

1. **Graphing Calculator** Rewrite the system $b + g = 600$ and $\frac{b}{g} = \frac{3}{2}$ so that you could use a graphing calculator to find its solution.

QUICK REVIEW

The *break-even point* is when income equals expenses.

In Chapter 5, you found the break-even point for a business using one equation and the x-intercept of its graph. The graph shows the break-even point of two equations.

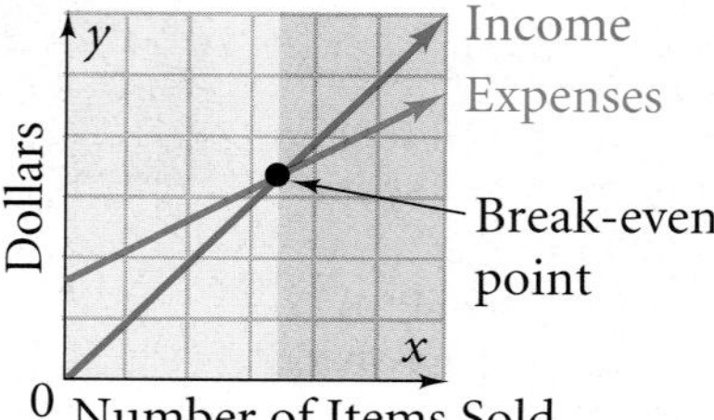

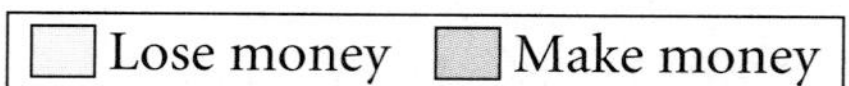

Example 2 Relating to the Real World 

Publishing Suppose a paper manufacturer publishes a newsletter. Expenses are \$.90 for printing and mailing each copy, plus \$600 for research and writing. The price of the newsletter is \$1.50 per copy. How many copies of the newsletter must the company sell to break even?

Define x = the number of copies
y = the money for expenses or income

Relate	Expenses \$.90 × copies printed + \$600	Income \$1.50 × copies sold
Write	$y = 0.9x + 600$	$y = 1.50x$

Choose a method to solve the system. Use substitution, since it is easy to substitute for y using these equations.

$$y = 0.9x + 600$$
$$y = 1.5x$$

$1.5x = 0.9x + 600$ ← Substitute $1.5x$ for y in the first equation.

$0.6x = 600$ ← Subtract $0.9x$ from each side.

$x = 1000$ ← Divide each side by 0.6.

To break even, the manufacturer must sell 1000 copies.

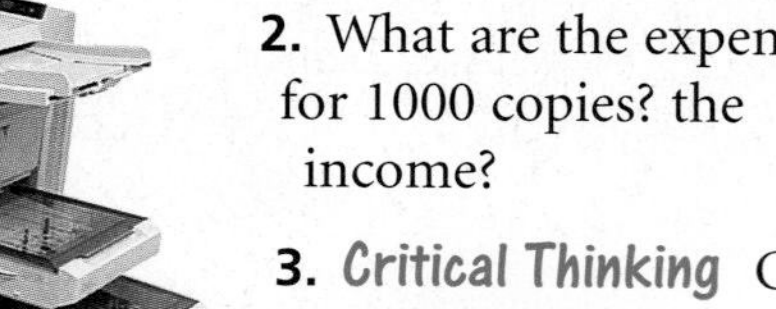

2. What are the expenses for 1000 copies? the income?

3. **Critical Thinking** Can the company print more than it sells, but still earn a profit? If so, give an example. If not, explain why not.

4. **Try This** Suppose printing and mailing expenses increase to \$1.00 for each copy. How many copies of the newsletter must the company sell at \$1.50 per copy to break even?

Exercises ON YOUR OWN

1. **Geometry** The difference of the measures of two supplementary angles is 35°. Find both angle measures.

2. Suppose you have just enough coins to pay for a loaf of bread priced at \$1.95. You have a total of 12 coins, with only quarters and dimes.
   a. Let q = the number of quarters and d = the number of dimes. Complete: ▪ + ▪ = 12
   b. Complete: 0.25▪ + 0.10▪ = ▪
   c. Use the equations you wrote for parts (a) and (b) to find how many of each coin you have.

3. Suppose you have 10 coins that total \$.85. Some coins are dimes and some are nickels. How many of each coin do you have?

4. **Open-ended** Write a problem for the total of two types of coins. Then give your problem to a classmate to solve.

QUICK REVIEW

The sum of the measures of supplementary angles is 180°.

Choose **Solve each linear system using any method. Tell why you chose the method you used.**

5. $y = x + 2$
   $y = -2x + 3$

6. $3x + 4y = -10$
   $5x = 2y + 18$

7. $5y = x$
   $2x - 3y = 7$

8. $3x - 2y = -12$
   $5x + 4y = 2$

9. $4x = 5y$
   $8x = 10y + 15$

10. $x = y - 3$
    $x + 2y = 3$

11. $y = 3x$
    $y = -\frac{1}{2}x$

12. $y = 2x$
    $7x - y = 35$

13. **School Musical** Suppose you are the treasurer of the drama club. The cost for scripts for the spring musical is \$254. The cost of props and costumes is \$400. You must also pay royalty charges of \$1.20 per ticket to the play's publisher. You charge \$4.00 per ticket and expect to make \$150 on refreshments.
    a. Write an equation for the expenses.
    b. Write an equation for the expected income.
    c. How many tickets must the drama club sell to break even?
    d. What method did you use to solve part (c)? Why?

14. **Pets** The ratio of cats to dogs at your local animal shelter is about 5 to 2. The shelter accepts 40 cats and dogs. From about how many dogs would you have to choose?

15. **Business** Suppose you invest \$10,000 in equipment to manufacture a new board game. Each game costs \$2.65 to manufacture and sells for \$20. How many games must you make and sell before your business breaks even?

16. **Writing** Explain to a friend how to decide whether to rent a car from Auto-Rent or from Cars, Inc.

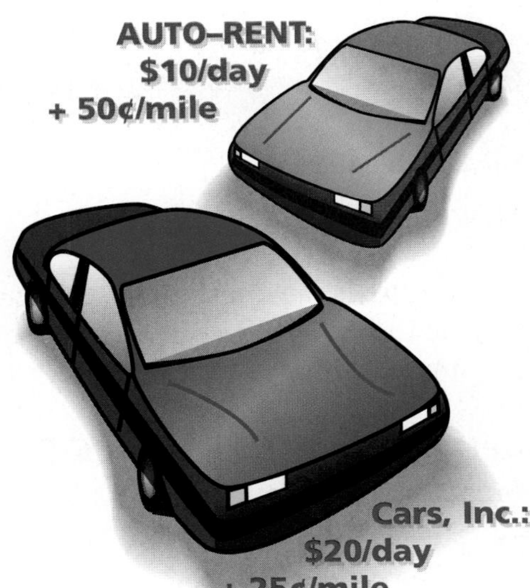

17. **Chemistry** A piece of glass with an initial temperature of 99°C is cooled at a rate of 3.5°C/min. At the same time, a piece of copper with an initial temperature of 0°C is heated at a rate of 2.5°C/min. Let m = the number of minutes and t = the temperature in °C. Which system models the given information?

A. $t = 99 + 3.5m$
$t = 0 + 2.5m$

B. $t = 99 - 3.5m$
$t = 0 - 2.5m$

C. $t = 99 - 3.5m$
$t = 0 + 2.5m$

D. $t = 99 + 3.5m$
$t = 0 - 2.5m$

18. Solve the system that models the situation in Exercise 17. Explain what the solution means in this situation.

Glass can be drawn into optical fibers 16 km long. One fiber can carry 20 times as many phone calls as 500 copper wires.

Without solving, what method would you choose to solve each system: *graphing, substitution,* or *elimination*? Explain your reasoning.

19. $4s - 3t = 8$
$t = -2s - 1$

20. $y = 3x - 1$
$y = 4x$

21. $3m - 4n = 1$
$3m - 2n = -1$

22. $y = -2x$
$y = -\frac{1}{2}x + 3$

23. $2x - y = 4$
$x + 3y = 16$

24. $u = 4v$
$3u - 2v = 7$

25. **Geometry** The perimeter of an isosceles triangle is 12 cm. The two sides s are each three times the length of the third side t.

a. Write an equation for the perimeter of the triangle.

b. Write an equation that describes the relationship between one side s and side t.

c. Find the length of each side.

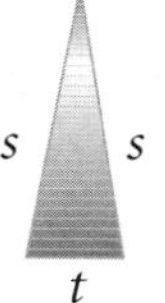

26. **Number Theory** Find two integers with a sum of 1244 and a difference of 90.

Exercises MIXED REVIEW

Solve each equation.

27. $7t + 4 = -10$

28. $j + 9 = -j - 1$

29. $|c - 4| = 21$

30. $m - 5 = -6$

31. In 1995, about $\frac{2}{3}$ of United States currency in circulation was outside the United States. There was \$390 billion in circulation. How much was in use within the United States?

Getting Ready for Lesson 6-5

Graph each equation.

32. $y = 2x + 1$

33. $y - 4 = 0$

34. $y = -\frac{2}{3}x + 1$

35. $y + 2x = -5$

6-5 Linear Inequalities

What You'll Learn

- Graphing linear inequalities

...And Why

To solve budget problems using linear inequalities

What You'll Need

- graph paper

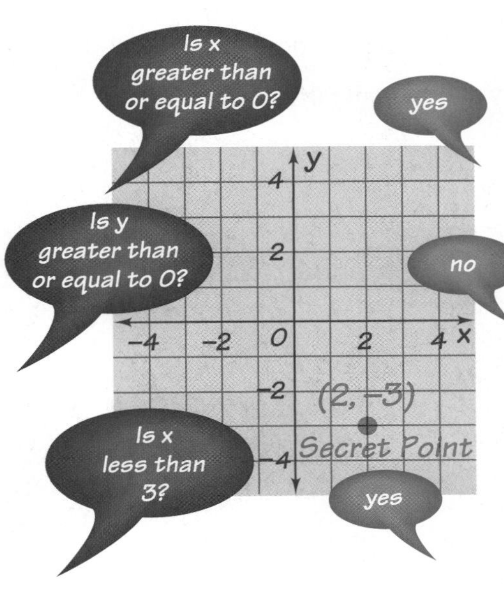

WORK TOGETHER

1. Play the game "What's the Point?" with a partner.

Object of the Game: To locate a secret point on the coordinate plane by asking as few questions as possible.

How to Play:

- Player A chooses a secret point on the coordinate plane. Each coordinate must be an integer from −10 to 10.
- Player B asks questions that contain the words *less than* or *greater than*. Player A answers each question with only *yes* or *no*. Count the number of questions asked until Player B names the secret point.
- The players switch roles to complete one round of the game.

How to Win: The player who names the point by asking fewer questions wins the round. The first player to win 3 rounds wins the game.

2. How many questions did you need to ask to locate the secret point?
3. If you were as lucky as possible, how many questions would you need to ask to locate the secret point? Explain with an example.
4. How do inequalities help you locate the secret point?
5. Describe a strategy for winning the game.

QUICK REVIEW

$<$ "less than"
$\leq$ "less than or equal to"
$>$ "greater than"
$\geq$ "greater than or equal to"

THINK AND DISCUSS

Just as you have used inequalities to describe graphs on a number line, you can use inequalities to describe regions of a coordinate plane.

Number line
$x < 1$

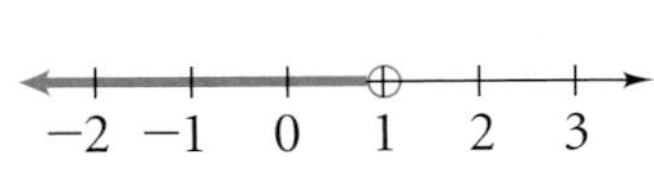

Coordinate plane
$x < 1$

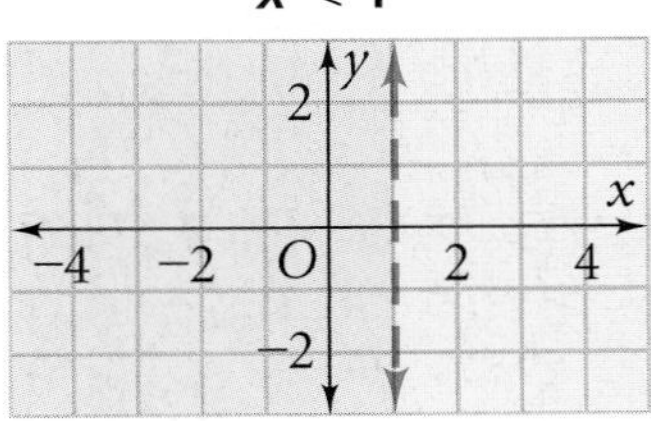

6. What do you think the graph of $y > 2$ looks like on a coordinate grid?

A **linear inequality** describes a region of the coordinate plane that has a boundary line. Every point in the region is a **solution of the inequality.**

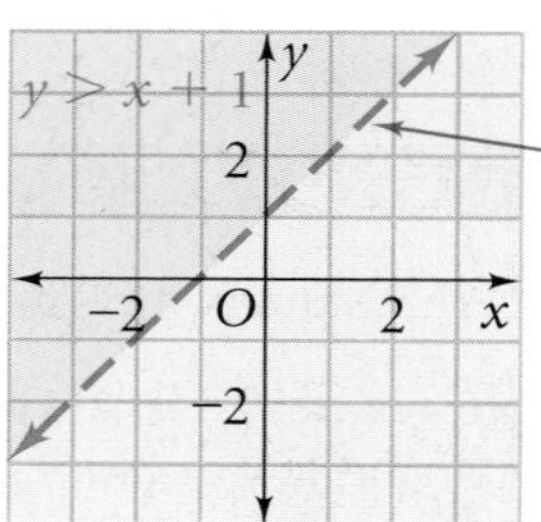

Each point on a *dashed* boundary line is not a solution.

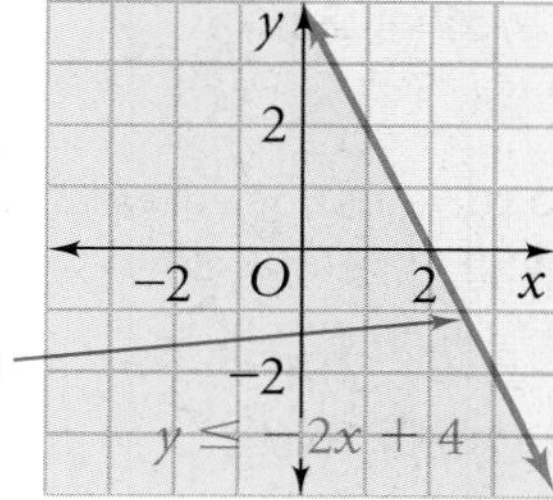

Each point on a *solid* boundary line is a solution.

7. Is (1, 2) a solution for either inequality shown above? Explain.

8. **Open-ended** For each inequality above, name three solutions.

Example 1

Graph $y < 2x + 3$.

First, graph the boundary line $y = 2x + 3$.

Points on the boundary line do *not* make the inequality true. Use a dashed line.

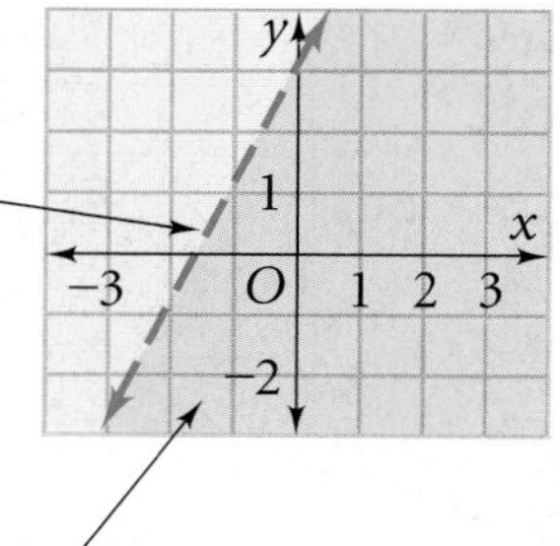

Next, test a point. Use (0, 0).

$y < 2x + 3$

$0 < 2(0) + 3$

$0 < 3$ **True**

The inequality is true for (0, 0). Shade the region containing (0, 0).

QUICK REVIEW

Use the slope m and the y-intercept b to graph an equation in the form $y = mx + b$.

PROBLEM SOLVING

Look Back Why did you test a point? Could you test the point (0, 3) to make your graph?

9. **Try This** Graph the inequality $y \geq 2x + 3$.

10. You can test any point on the graph. Why is (0, 0) a good choice?

Sometimes it helps to rewrite the inequality to find its solution.

Example 2

Graph $2x - 5y \leq 10$.

Write the inequality in slope-intercept form.

$2x - 5y \leq 10$

$-5y \leq -2x + 10$

$y \geq \frac{2}{5}x - 2$ ← Reverse the inequality symbol.

Graph $y = \frac{2}{5}x - 2$.

Test (0, 0) in $y \geq \frac{2}{5}x - 2$.

$0 \geq (0)x - 2$

$0 \geq -2$ **True**

Shade the region containing (0, 0).

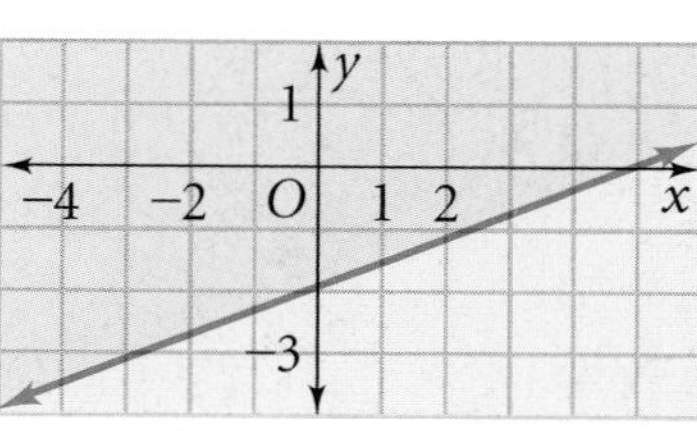

11. a. When you graphed $y \geq \frac{2}{5}x - 2$ in Example 2, did you shade *above* or *below* the line?
b. When you graphed $y < 2x + 3$ in Example 1, did you shade *above* or *below* the line?
c. **Critical Thinking** Both inequalities are in slope-intercept form. Make a **conjecture** about the inequality symbol and the region shaded.
d. Does your **conjecture** stay true for inequalities in $Ax + By < C$ form? Explain.

You can graph inequalities to solve real-world problems.

Example 3 Relating to the Real World 

Food Shopping Suppose you intend to spend no more than $12 on peanuts and cashews for a party. How many pounds of each can you buy?

Peanuts: $2/lb
Cashews: $4/lb

Define x = the number of pounds of peanuts
y = the number of pounds of cashews

Relate cost of peanuts + cost of cashews $\leq$ maximum total cost

Write $2x + 4y \leq 12$

QUICK REVIEW

Use the intercepts to graph an equation in the form $Ax + By = C$.

Graph the boundary line $2x + 4y = 12$ using a solid line. Use only Quadrant I, since you cannot buy a negative amount of nuts.

Test (0, 0): $2(0) + 4(0) \leq 12$
$0 \leq 12$

Shade the region containing (0, 0).

Party Snacks
y
4
3
2
1
x
0 1 2 3 4 5 6 7
Cashews (lb)
Peanuts (lb)

The graph shows all the possible solutions of the problem. For example, if you buy 2 lb of peanuts you can buy no more than 2 lb of cashews.

12. Which are solutions to Example 3?
A. 2 lb peanuts and 1 lb cashews
B. 6 lb peanuts and no cashews
C. 1 lb peanuts and 3 lb cashews
D. 1.5 lb peanuts and 2 lb cashews

Exercises ON YOUR OWN

Choose the linear inequality that describes each graph.

1. 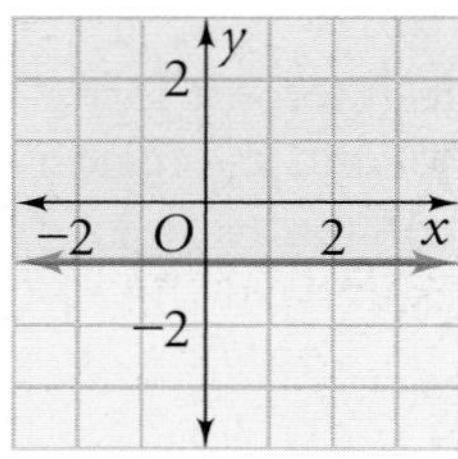

A. $y \geq -1$

B. $y \leq -1$

2. 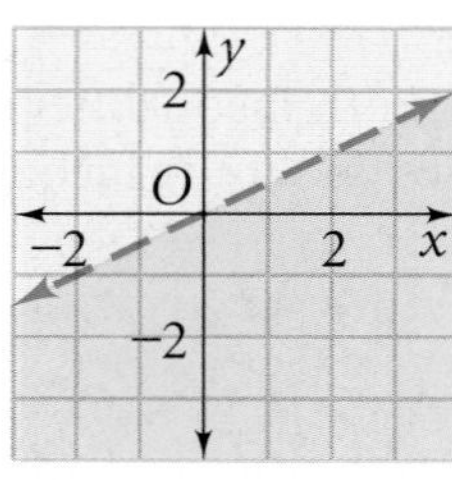

A. $y > \frac{1}{2}x$

B. $y < \frac{1}{2}x$

3. 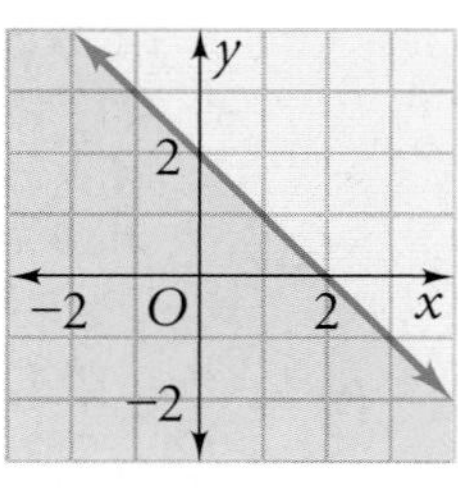

A. $x + y \geq 2$

B. $x + y \leq 2$

4. 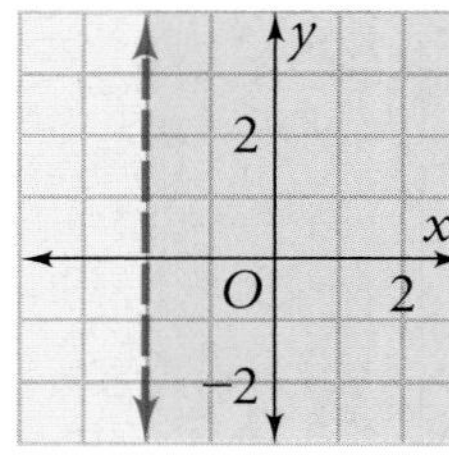

A. $x > -2$

B. $x < -2$

5. For which of the graphs in Exercises 1–4 is $(-2, -1)$ a solution?

6. **Manufacturing** A company makes backpacks. How many backpacks must the company sell to make a profit of more than \$250?

a. Write a linear inequality that describes the situation.
b. Graph the linear inequality.
c. Write three possible solutions to the problem.
d. Why is "10 nylon packs and 22 canvas packs" *not* a solution?

7. **Writing** Explain why a linear inequality is useful when there are many solutions to a problem.

Graph each linear inequality.

8. $x < -2$

9. $y \geq 1$

10. $y < \frac{1}{4}x - 1$

11. $6y - 4x > 0$

12. $y < 5x - 5$

13. $y \leq 4x - 1$

14. $y < -3x + 4$

15. $y > -3x$

16. $x + y \geq 2$

17. $x + 3y \leq 6$

18. $\frac{1}{2}x + \frac{3}{2}y \geq \frac{3}{4}$

19. $y \geq \frac{1}{2}x$

20. $4y > 6x + 2$

21. $2x + 3y \leq 6$

22. $4x - 4y \geq 8$

23. $y - 2x < 2$

24. **Standardized Test Prep** Which statement describes the graph?

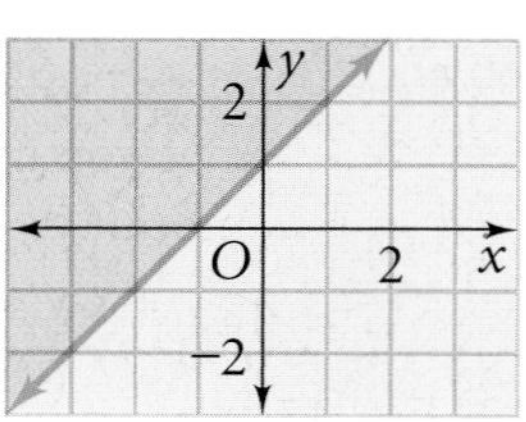

A. $y > x + 1$ **B.** $y < x + 1$ **C.** $y \leq x + 1$
D. $y \geq x + 1$ **E.** $y = x + 1$

25. Write an inequality that describes the part of the coordinate plane *not* included in the graph of $y \geq x + 2$.

26. **Probability** Suppose you play a carnival game. You toss a blue and a red number cube. If the number on the blue cube is greater than the number on the red cube, you win a prize. The graph shows all the possible outcomes for tossing the cubes.

Comparing Cubes

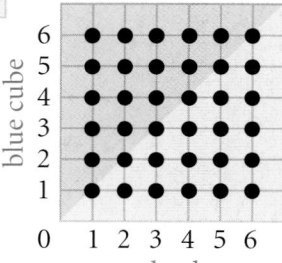

(graph: blue cube 0–6 vertical axis, red cube 1 2 3 4 5 6 horizontal axis)

a. Copy the graph and shade the region $b > r$.
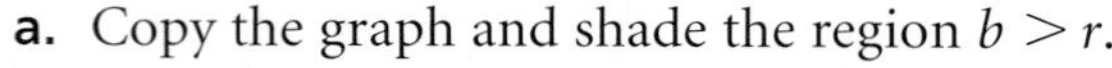
b. Does the shaded region include all of the winning outcomes?
c. What is the probability that you will win a prize?

Write the inequality shown in each graph.

27. 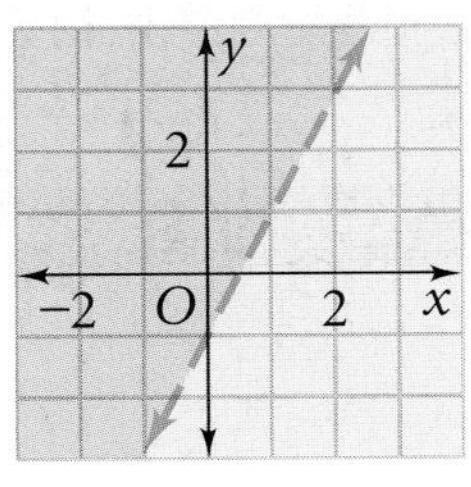

28. 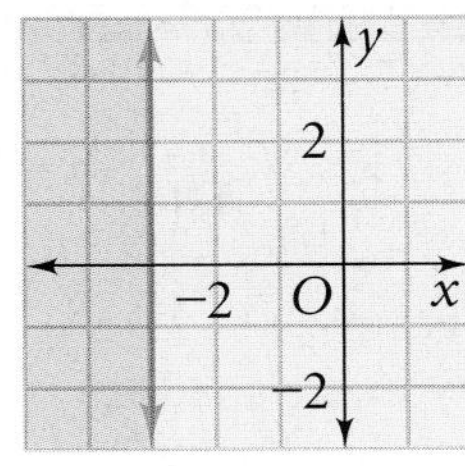

29. 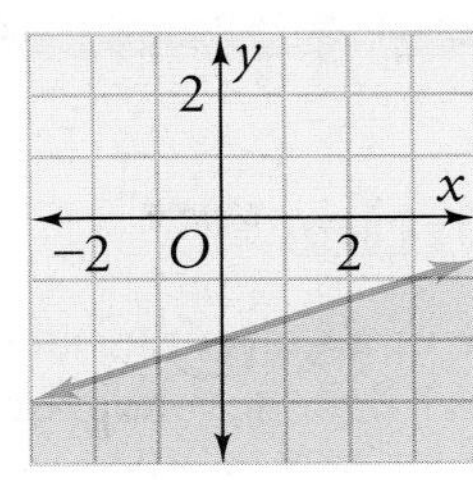

30. 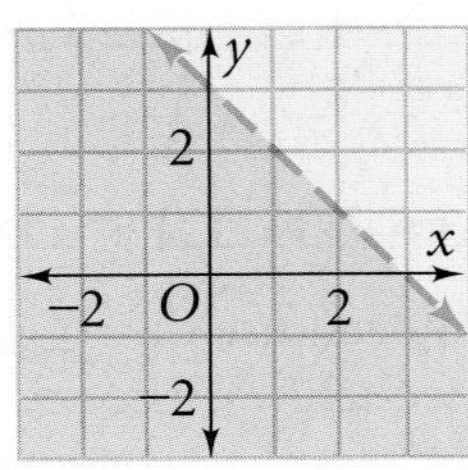

Write the linear inequality described. Then graph the inequality.

31. x is positive.
32. y is negative.
33. y is not negative.
34. x is less than y.

35. **Geometry** Suppose you have 50 ft of fencing. You want to fence a rectangular area of your yard for a garden.
    a. Use the formula for the perimeter of a rectangle to write a linear inequality that describes this situation.
    b. Graph the inequality.
    c. **Open-ended** Give two possible sizes for a square garden.
    d. Can you make the garden 12 ft by 15 ft? **Justify** your answer, using both your graph and the inequality you wrote in part (a).

Chapter Project **Find Out by Writing**

Use your information from the Find Out questions on pages 274 and 284. Assume that 200 people will come to the dance. Write a report listing which band you would choose and the cost per ticket that you need to charge to cover expenses. Then repeat the process assuming that 300 people will come.

Is point P a solution of the linear inequality?

36. $y \leq -2x + 1$; $P(2, 2)$
37. $x < 2$; $P(1, 0)$
38. $y \geq 3x - 2$; $P(0, 0)$
39. $y > x - 1$; $P(0, 1)$

40. **Consumer** Suppose you are shopping for crepe paper to decorate the gym for a school dance. Gold crepe paper costs \$5 per roll, and blue crepe paper costs \$3 per roll. You have at most \$48 to spend. How much gold and blue crepe paper can you buy? Explain your solution.

Exercises MIXED REVIEW

Find the slope of each line.

41. $y = 5x - 9$
42. $7x + 4y = 20$
43. $3y = 8x - 12$
44. $y = 8x + 1$

45. **Automobiles** The average car is parked 95% of the time. How many hours is the average car on the road each day?

Getting Ready for Lesson 6-6

Solve each system of equations.

46. $y = 2x - 3$, $y = -4x$
47. $4y = 3x + 11$, $y = 2x - 1$
48. $y = 5x + 2$, $y = 4x - 6$
49. $y = 8x$, $y = 2x + 28$

Graphing Inequalities

After Lesson 6-5

You can use the DRAW feature of a graphing calculator to graph inequalities. The order you enter data depends on whether you are shading above or below a line. When shading below Y_1, use Shade (Ymin, Y_1). When shading above Y_1, use Shade (Y_1, Ymax). You do not have to use a close parenthesis before pressing ENTER.

Example

Graph each inequality.

a. $y < 2x + 3$

Shade below Y_1 for *less than.*

b. $y > 0.5x - 1$

Shade above Y_1 for *greater than.*

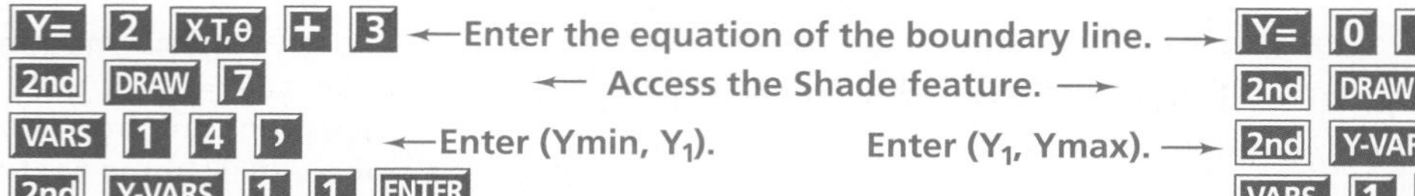

Y= 0 . 5 X,T,θ − 1
2nd DRAW 7
2nd Y-VARS 1 1 ,
VARS 1 5 ENTER

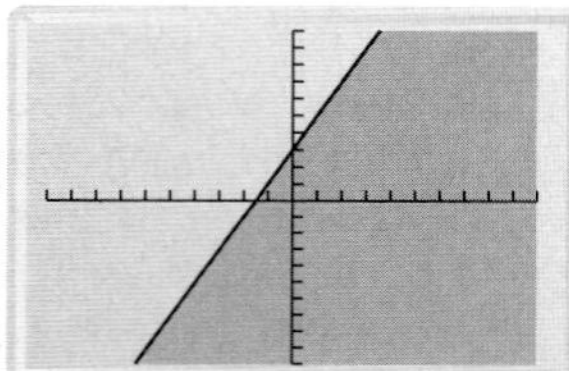

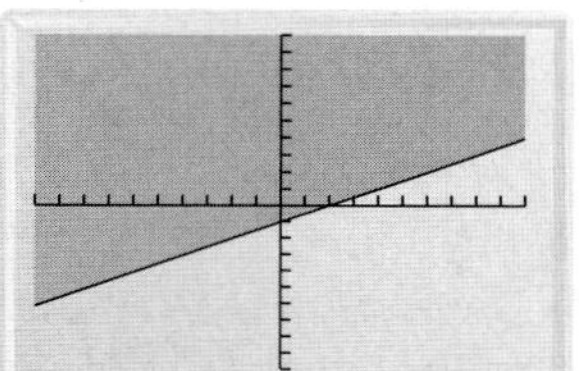

You can vary the darkness of the shading by entering an integer from 1 (dark) to 8 (light). Add a comma and the integer before pressing ENTER. The graph at the right has a darkness level of 2.

The graphing calculator does not make a distinction between a boundary line that is dotted (like *less than*) and a boundary line that is solid (like *less than or equal to*). You must decide if a boundary line should be solid or dotted when you sketch the inequality on your paper.

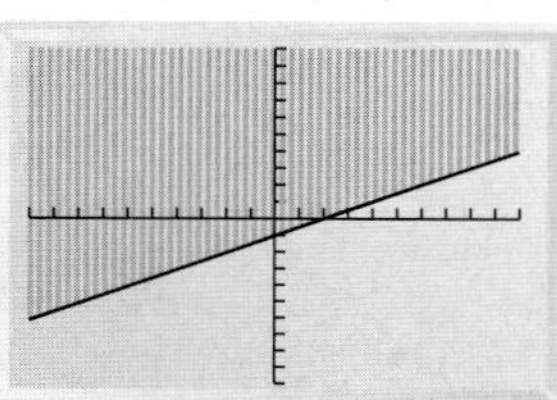

Shade(Y_1,Ymax,2)

Use a graphing calculator to graph each inequality. Sketch your graph.

1. $y < x$

2. $y > 2x + 1$

3. $y \geq -x + 3$

4. $y \leq 5$

5. $x - y \geq 4$

6. $2x + 3y \leq 12$

7. $6x - 30y < 45$

8. $x - 2y \geq 50$

9. **Writing** What instructions would you need to change in Example (b) to graph $y > 0.5x - 1$ using Y_2 instead of Y_1?

What You'll Learn

- Solving systems of linear inequalities by graphing

...And Why

To solve real-world problems that have many possible solutions, such as those in agriculture

What You'll Need

- graph paper
- graphing calculator

6-6 Systems of Linear Inequalities

WORK TOGETHER

Work in pairs. Explore what happens when you graph lines or linear inequalities on the same coordinate plane.

1. Can two lines be drawn with the given intersection? Support each answer with a diagram or an explanation.
   a. a point **b.** a line **c.** a region **d.** no intersection
2. Can the graphs of two linear inequalities be drawn with the given intersection? Support each answer with a diagram or an explanation.
   a. a point **b.** a line **c.** a region **d.** no intersection
3. **Summarize** your findings in Questions 1 and 2. Compare the possible intersections of two lines with the possible intersections of the graphs of two linear inequalities. What do you notice?
4. Find the possible intersections for more than two lines.
5. Find the possible intersections for the graphs of more than two linear inequalities.

THINK AND DISCUSS

Two or more linear inequalities together form a **system of linear inequalities.** Here is an example of a system that describes the shaded region of the graph. Notice that there are two boundary lines.

System of Linear Inequalities

$x \geq 2$

$y < -1$

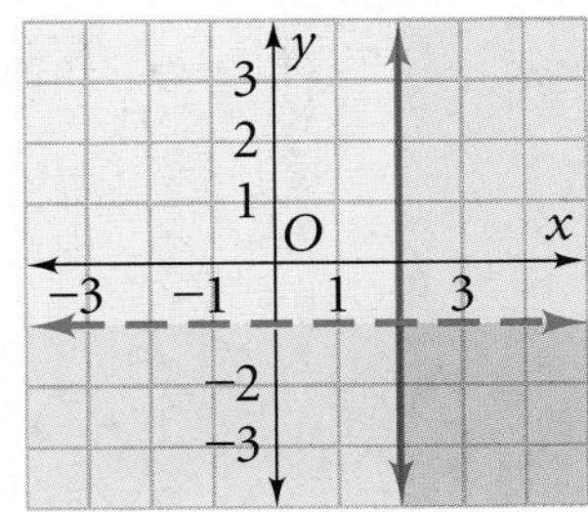

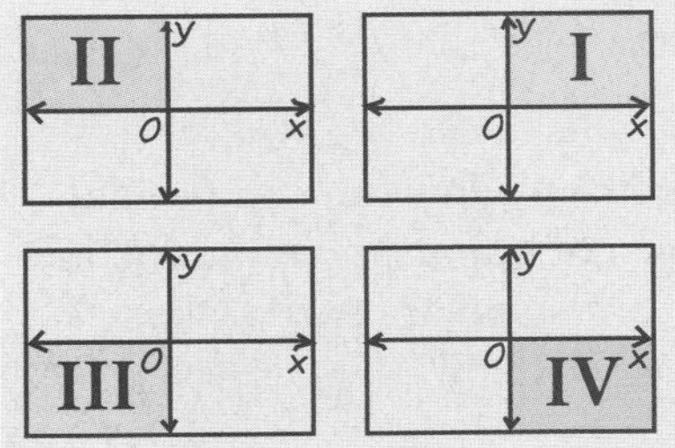

6. You can describe all the points of a quadrant with a system of linear inequalities. Match each system with a quadrant.

   A. $x > 0$, $y > 0$ **B.** $x > 0$, $y < 0$ **C.** $x < 0$, $y > 0$ **D.** $x < 0$, $y < 0$

A **solution of a system of linear inequalities** makes each inequality in the system true. The graph of a system shows all of its solutions.

Math A Test Prep

1 Which inequality is graphed below?

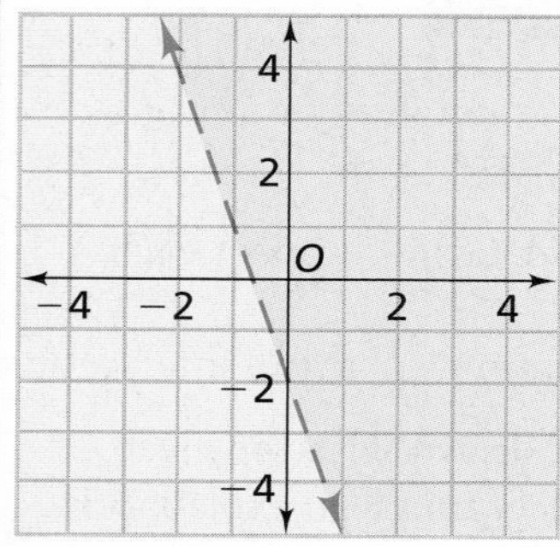

(1) $y \geq -3x - 2$
(2) $y = -3x - 2$
(3) $y \leq -3x - 2$
(4) $y > -3x - 2$

2 Solve this system.
$x + 2y = 6$
$2x - 3y = 5$

Example 1 Relating to the Real World 

Animal Studies A zoo keeper wants to fence a rectangular pen for goats. The length of the pen should be at least 80 ft, and the distance around it should be no more than 310 ft. What are the possible dimensions of the pen?

Define x = width of the pen
y = length of the pen

Relate	The length	is at least	80 ft.	The perimeter	is no more than	310 ft.
Write	y	$\geq$	80	$2x + 2y$	$\leq$	310

Use slope-intercept form to graph.

$y \geq 80$
$m = 0$
$b = 80$

Test (0, 1).
$y \geq 80$
$(1) \geq 80$ **False**

Shade above.

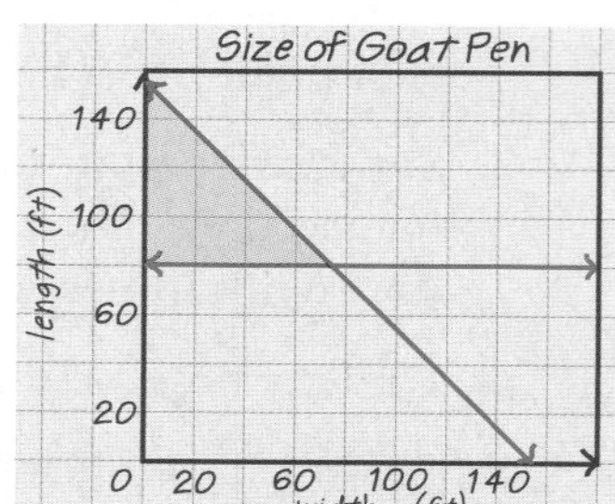

Use intercepts to graph.

$2x + 2y \leq 310$
(155, 0)
(0, 155)

Test (0, 0).
$2(0) + 2(0) \leq 310$
$0 \leq 310$ **True**

Shade below.

The solutions are all the points in the shaded region above $y = 80$ but below $2x + 2y \leq 310$.

7. Give three possible dimensions (length and width) for the pen. How many solutions does this system have?

8. Why is the solution region shown only in Quadrant I?

9. **Graphing Calculator** Use the *Shade* feature to graph the system of linear inequalities in Example 1.

10. **Try This** Solve each system by graphing.
    a. $y \leq 2x + 3$
       $y \geq x - 1$
    b. $y > x$
       $x \leq 3$
    c. $x + y > -2$
       $x - y > 2$

11. **Critical Thinking** How can you decide whether or not points on boundary lines of a solution region are part of the solution of a system?

Some systems of linear inequalities do not have a solution region. The graphs of the inequalities might intersect in a line or not at all.

Example 2

Solve the system by graphing. $4y \geq 6x$
$-3x + 2y \leq -6$

Use slope-intercept form to graph.

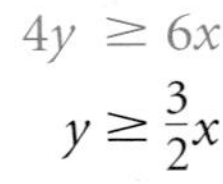

Test (0, 1).
Shade above.

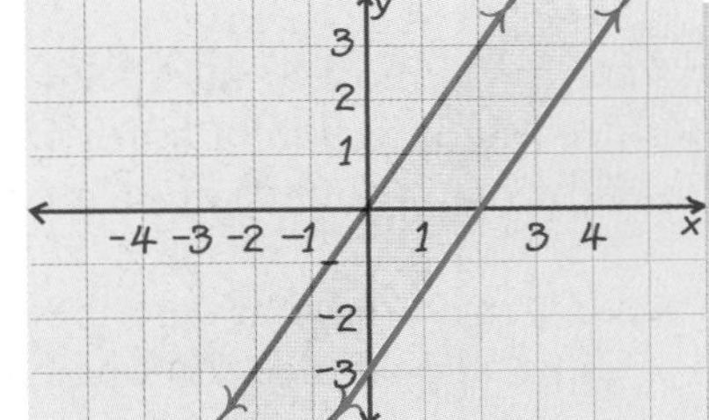

Use intercepts to graph.

$-3x + 2y \leq -6$
(0, −3)
(2, 0)

Test (0, 0).
Shade below.

Since the shaded regions do not overlap, the system has no solution.

12. Explain why (0, 0) was not tested when $4y \geq 6x$ was graphed.

13. How are the boundary lines in Example 2 related?

PROBLEM SOLVING HINT

For Questions 14 and 15, first draw a diagram. Then write the inequalities.

14. a. **Open-ended** Write another system of two linear inequalities that has no solution.

b. Must the boundary lines be parallel? Explain.

15. **Critical Thinking** Write a system of linear inequalities in which the solution is a line.

Exercises ON YOUR OWN

1. **Standardized Test Prep** Which of these points is a solution of the system $y \leq x + 5$ and $y + x > 3$?

A. (0, 0) **B.** (−1, 4) **C.** (3, 3) **D.** (−2, 6) **E.** (2, 0)

2. Which system is represented in the graph at the right?

A. $x + y \leq 3$, $y > x - 3$
B. $x + y > 3$, $y \leq x - 3$
C. $x + y \geq 3$, $y < x - 3$
D. $x + y < 3$, $y \geq x - 3$

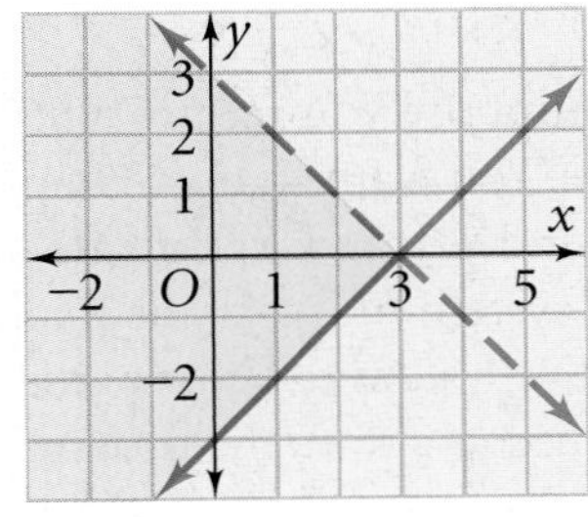

3. **Critical Thinking** Without graphing, explain why the point where the boundary lines intersect in the system $2x + y > 2$ and $x - y \geq 3$ is *not* a solution of the system.

4. **Writing** Write a problem that can be solved using the system of inequalities at the right.

$2l + 2w \leq 100$
$l \leq 30$

Solve each system of linear inequalities by graphing.

5. $x \geq 2$
   $y < 4$

6. $y > 3$
   $x < -1$

7. $y \leq x$
   $y \geq x + 1$

8. $y > 4x + 2$
   $y \leq 4$

9. $y \leq 2x + 2$
   $y < -x + 1$

10. $y \geq -2x + 1$
    $y < x + 2$

11. $x + y \leq 6$
    $x - y < 1$

12. $y - 3x < 6$
    $y > 3x + 9$

13. $x > y$
    $y > 0$

14. $x + y \leq 5$
    $x \geq 1$

15. $y < \frac{1}{2}x$
    $y > \frac{1}{2}x - 3$

16. $-x - y \leq 2$
    $y - 2x > 1$

17. *Construction* A contractor has at most \$33 to spend on nails for a project. The contractor needs at least 9 lb of finish nails and at least 12 lb of common nails. How many pounds of each type of nail should the contractor buy?
    a. Write a system of three inequalities that describes this situation.
    b. Graph the system to show all possible solutions.
    c. Name a point that is a solution of the system.
    d. Name a point that is *not* a solution of the system.

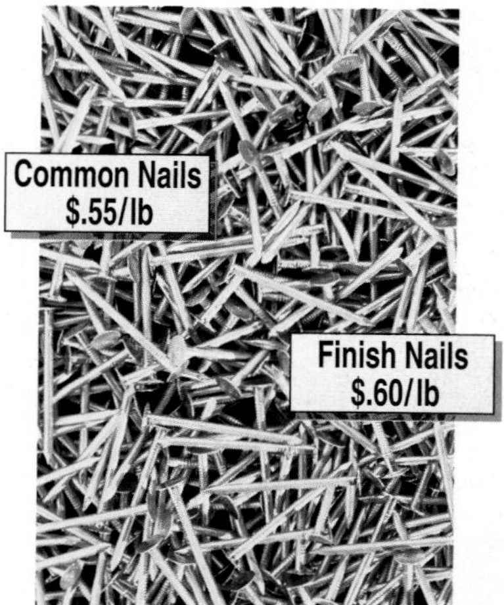

Open-ended **Write a system of linear inequalities with the given characteristics.**

18. (0, 0) is a solution.

19. Solutions are only in Quadrant II.

20. There is no solution.

21. The solution region is triangular.

22. a. Solve the system of three inequalities at the right by graphing.
    b. **Verify** your solution by testing a point from the overlapping region in all three inequalities.

$x \leq 4$
$y < x + 2$
$x + 2y \geq -2$

Geometry **For the solution region of each system of linear inequalities, (a) describe the shape, (b) find the vertices, and (c) find the area.**

23. $y \geq \frac{1}{2}x + 1$
    $y \leq 2$
    $x \geq -4$

24. $x \geq 1$
    $x \leq 5$
    $y \geq -1$
    $y \leq 3$

25. $x \geq 0$
    $x \leq 2$
    $y \geq -4$
    $y \leq -x + 2$

26. $x \geq 2$
    $y \geq -3$
    $x + y \leq 4$

27. *Shopping* Suppose you receive a \$50 gift certificate to the Music and Books store. You want to buy some books and at least one CD. How can you spend your gift certificate on x paperbacks and y CDs?
    a. Write a system of linear inequalities that describes this situation.
    b. Graph the system to show possible solutions to this problem.
    c. What purchase does the ordered pair (2, 6) represent? Is it a solution to your system? Explain.
    d. Find a solution in which you spend almost all of the gift certificate.
    e. What is the greatest number of paperbacks you can buy and still buy one CD?

Chapter Project *Find Out by Graphing*

In the Find Out question on page 293, you found two ticket prices. Each price covers the cost of the dance under certain conditions. Decide what the ticket price should be. Plan for between 200 and 300 people. Graph a system of linear inequalities to show the total amount received from tickets.

Exercises MIXED REVIEW

Solve each equation.

28. $5m + 4 = 8m - 2$ **29.** $5(t + 1) = 10$ **30.** $4x = 2x + 5$ **31.** $6h - 11 = 13$

32. $3p = -\frac{3}{4}p + 5$ **33.** $-k - 7 = -3k + 1$ **34.** $\frac{3c - 1}{4} = \frac{5}{2}$ **35.** $\frac{1}{2}(t - 8) = 7$

36. **a.** Identify the independent and dependent variables.
b. Graph the data.
c. What scales did you use and why?

Price	Sales Tax
$1.00	$.05
$3.00	$.15
$4.00	$.20
$7.00	$.35

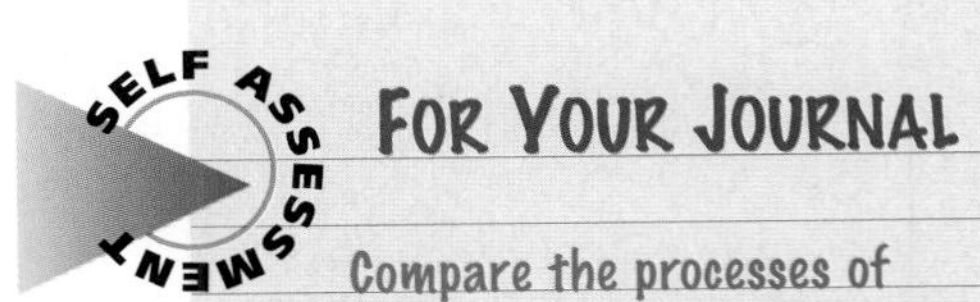

FOR YOUR JOURNAL

Compare the processes of graphing a system of linear inequalities and graphing a system of linear equations. How are they similar? How are they different?

Getting Ready for Lesson 6-7

Evaluate each formula for the given point.

37. $B = 2x + 5y$; (6, 10) **38.** $C = x + 6y$; (100, 550)

39. $P = 6x + 2y$; (200, 75) **40.** $P = 2l + 2w$; (30, 18)

Exercises CHECKPOINT

Solve each system of linear inequalities.

1. $y < -2x + 5$, $y > 3x - 1$

2. $y \geq 2x - 1$, $x \geq -5$

3. $y < 0.5x + 3$, $y \geq -x + 2.5$

4. $3x + 2y \leq 12$, $x - y < 10$

5. *Standardized Test Prep* Which of these points is a solution of the system $y \geq 4x - 1$ and $2x + 3y < 6$?
A. (3, 0) **B.** (0, 4) **C.** (4, 1) **D.** (−3, 1) **E.** (3, −4)

6. You are going out for pizza!
a. Write a system of equations for the cost of a large pizza at each restaurant.
b. Solve the system of equations. Interpret your solution.
c. *Open-ended* Where will you go for pizza? Explain your reasons.

What You'll Learn

- Solving linear programming problems

...And Why

To investigate real-world situations, such as time management

6-7 Concepts of Linear Programming

WORK TOGETHER

Suppose you are offered a part-time job. You wonder how much time you have available to work. You can use mathematics to help you organize your thoughts and make a good decision.

Work with a partner.

1. a. Write the different ways you spend your time during a week.
   b. Organize your list into no more than ten categories.
2. Make a personal calendar for the last week.
   a. Assign time to the categories from Question 1.
   b. How much time do you have available to work at a part-time job?
   c. Discuss what you could or could not give up in your schedule.

THINK AND DISCUSS

You can answer questions like those above by using a process called linear programming. **Linear programming** identifies conditions that make a quantity as large as or as small as possible. The variables used in the equation for the quantity have restrictions. The maximum and minimum values of the quantity occur at vertices of the graph of the restrictions.

Example 1

Use linear programming. Find the values of x and y that maximize the quantity.

Restrictions $\begin{cases} x + y \leq 8 \\ x \geq 0 \\ y \geq 3 \end{cases}$

Equation $Q = 3x + 2y$

Step 1
Graph the restrictions.

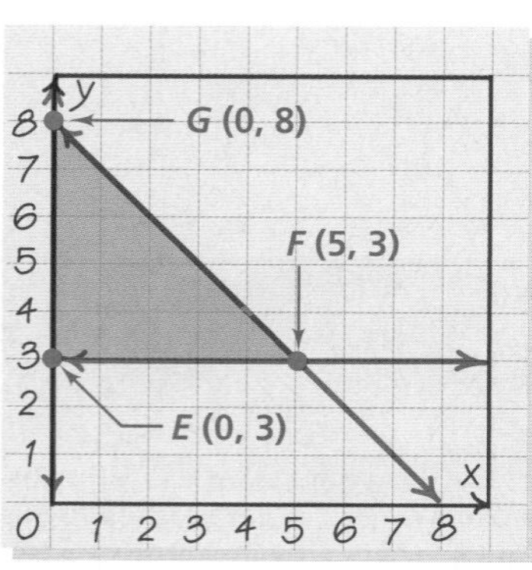

Step 2
Find coordinates of each vertex.

Step 3
Evaluate Q at each vertex.

Vertex	$Q = 3x + 2y$	
E (0, 3)	$Q = 3(0) + 2(3) = 6$	
F (5, 3)	$Q = 3(5) + 2(3) = 21$	← maximum value of Q
G (0, 8)	$Q = 3(0) + 2(8) = 16$	

The maximum value 21 occurs when $x = 5$ and $y = 3$.

3. Find the values of x and y that minimize the quantity in Example 1.

4. Find the value of the equation in Example 1 at each point.
a. $(1, 3)$ **b.** $(4, 3)$ **c.** $(4, 4)$ **d.** $(1, 7)$ **e.** $(3, 4)$

In the Work Together activity, you listed some restrictions you have on your time in relation to a part-time job. In the next example one student finds the best way to use her time.

Example 2 Relating to the Real World 

Time Management Marta plans to start a part-time job. Here are the restrictions she has found on her time for homework hours x and job hours y.

Restriction	Inequality
She has no more than 24 h/wk for homework and a job.	$x + y \leq 24$
The boss wants her to work at least 6 h/wk.	$y \geq 6$
She spends 10–15 h/wk on homework.	$x \geq 10$ $x \leq 15$

She decides that homework hours are twice as valuable as work hours. Find the best way B for Marta to split her time between homework and the job using the equation $B = 2x + y$.

Step 1
Graph the restrictions.

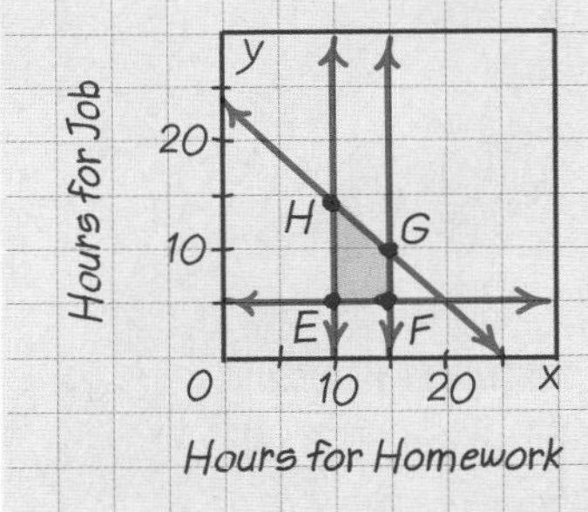

Step 2
Find the coordinates of each vertex.

Step 3
Evaluate B at each vertex.

Vertex	$\mathbf{B = 2x + y}$	
$E\,(10, 6)$	$B = 2(10) + 6 = 26$	
$F\,(15, 6)$	$B = 2(15) + 6 = 36$	
$G\,(15, 9)$	$B = 2(15) + 9 = 39$	← maximum value of B
$H\,(10, 14)$	$B = 2(10) + 14 = 34$	

The best way for Marta to split her time each week is to spend 15 h on homework and 9 h at her job.

5. What does the point $(10, 14)$ mean in terms of homework and job time?

6. **Critical Thinking** For each situation, would the best solution be a *maximum value* or a *minimum value?* Explain.
   a. You are selling tomatoes and beans from your garden. You want to determine how much of each to grow for the most profit.
   b. Suppose you manage a grocery store. You can buy tomatoes from two different farmers. You consider the price of the tomatoes and transportation costs. You must decide which supplier to use.

To solve linear programming problems, you must be able to write the inequalities for the restrictions and write the equation.

Example 3 Relating to the Real World 

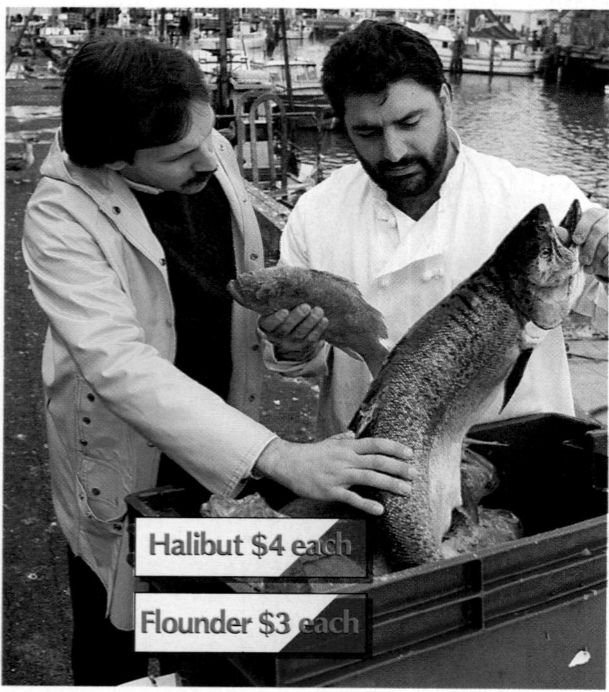

Business A seafood restaurant owner orders at least 50 fish. He cannot use more than 30 halibut or more than 35 flounder. How many of each fish should he use to minimize his cost?

Step 1 Write inequalities to describe the restrictions.

Define x = number of halibut used
y = number of flounder used

Relate	Write
He needs at least 50 fish.	$x + y \geq 50$
He cannot use more than 30 halibut.	$x \leq 30$
He cannot use more than 35 flounder.	$y \leq 35$

Step 2 Write the equation.

Define C = cost of fish

Relate cost is $4 for each halibut and $3 for each flounder

Write $C = 4x + 3y$

Step 3
Graph the restrictions.

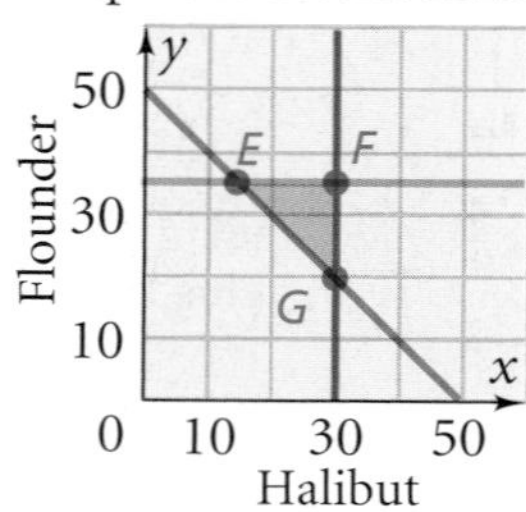

Step 4
Find the coordinates of each vertex.

Vertex
$E(15, 35)$
$F(30, 35)$
$G(30, 20)$

Step 5
Evaluate C at each vertex.

$\mathbf{C = 4x + 3y}$
$C = 4(15) + 3(35) = 165$ ← minimum value of C
$C = 4(30) + 3(35) = 225$
$C = 4(30) + 3(20) = 180$

The seafood restaurant owner should buy 15 halibut and 35 flounder to minimize his cost.

7. **Try This** Suppose the restaurant owner changes his order to at least 40 fish. How many of each kind should he use to minimize his cost?

Exercises ON YOUR OWN

Evaluate each equation at the points given. Which point gives the maximum value? the minimum value?

1. $Q = 3x + 5y$
   (8, 0), (4, 4), (3, 5), (0, 6)
2. $B = 40x + 20y$
   (0, 0), (0, 40), (15, 10), (25, 0)
3. $A = 35x + 10y$
   (0, 0),(0, 10), (0, 40), (20, 10)

Find the values of x and y that maximize or minimize each quantity for each graph.

4. Maximum for
   $P = x + y$

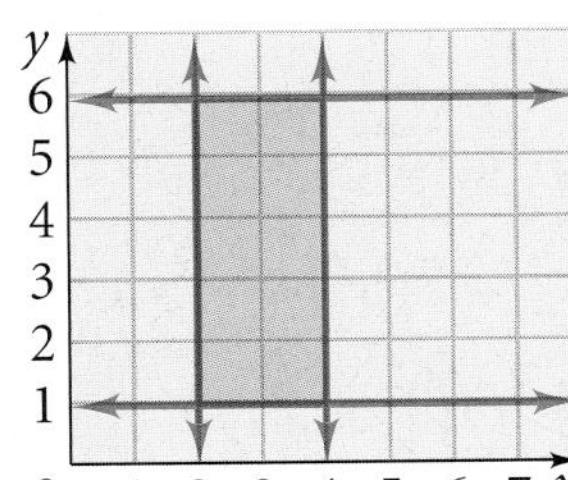

5. Maximum for
   $P = 3x + 2y$

6. Minimum for
   $C = 2x + 5y$

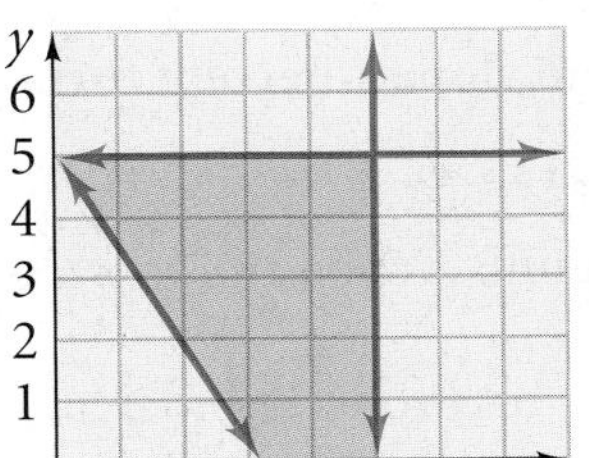

7. Minimum for
   $C = \frac{1}{2}x + y$

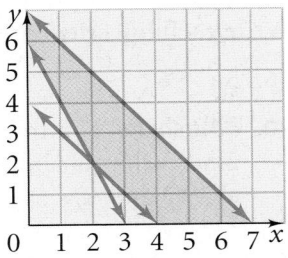

Evaluate the equation to find minimum and maximum values.

8. $x \geq 2$
   $x \leq 5$
   $y \geq 3$
   $y \leq 6$
   $A = 5x + 4y$
9. $x \geq 0$
   $y \geq 0$
   $x + y \leq 12$
   $D = 3x + y$
10. $y \geq -x + 4$
    $y \leq -2x + 10$
    $x \geq 0$
    $y \geq 0$
    $P = 2x + 3y$
11. $y \leq -x + 8$
    $y \geq 2x - 2$
    $x \geq 0$
    $y \geq 0$
    $Q = x + y$

12. **Open-ended** Write a system of restrictions that form a trapezoid.

13. **Environment** A town is trying to find the best mix of sand and salt for treating icy roads. One consideration is cost, which they want to minimize. Sand costs \$8 per ton, and salt costs \$20 per ton. Write the equation for minimizing cost.

14. **Manufacturing** A toy manufacturer wants to minimize her cost for producing two lines of toy airplanes. Because of the supply of materials, no more than 40 Flying Bats can be built each day, and no more than 60 Flying Falcons can be built each day. There are enough workers to build at least 70 toy airplanes each day.
    a. Write the inequalities for the restrictions.
    b. It costs \$12 to manufacture a Flying Bat and \$8 to build a Flying Falcon. Write an equation for the cost of manufacturing the toy airplanes.
    c. Use linear programming to find how many of each toy airplane should be produced each day to minimize cost.
    d. **Critical Thinking** What else should the manufacturer consider before deciding how many of each toy to manufacture each day?

15. **Business** A computer company has budgeted \$6000 to rent display space at two locations for a new line of computers. Each location requires a minimum of 100 ft^2.

Rental Locations

Location	Cost	Potential
A	\$10/ft^2	30 customers/ft^2
B	\$20/ft^2	40 customers/ft^2

a. **Writing** Explain what each inequality represents.
Restrictions: $10x + 20y \leq 6000$, $x \geq 100$, $y \geq 100$

b. Write an equation for the potential number of customers.

c. Use linear programming to find the amount of space to rent at each location to maximize the number of potential customers.

Exercises MIXED REVIEW

Write each linear equation in slope-intercept form.

16. $5y = 6x - 3$
17. $4x + 8y = 20$
18. $y = 3(x - 2)$
19. $9y = 24x$

20. **Probability** You roll a number cube and toss a coin at the same time. Find each probability.
a. $P(3 \text{ and } T)$
b. $P(\text{odd number and } H)$
c. $P(\text{prime and } T)$
d. $P(6)$

Getting Ready for Lesson 6-8

To which family of functions does each function belong?

21. $y = 3x^2 - x + 6$
22. $y = |5x - 2|$
23. $y = 4x - 9$
24. $y = -7x^2 - 1$

Algebra at Work

Businessperson

Some of the goals of a business are to minimize costs and maximize profits. People in business use linear programming to analyze data in order to achieve these goals. The illustration lists some of the variables involved in operating a small manufacturing company. To solve a problem, a businessperson must identify the variables and restrictions and then search for the best possible solutions.

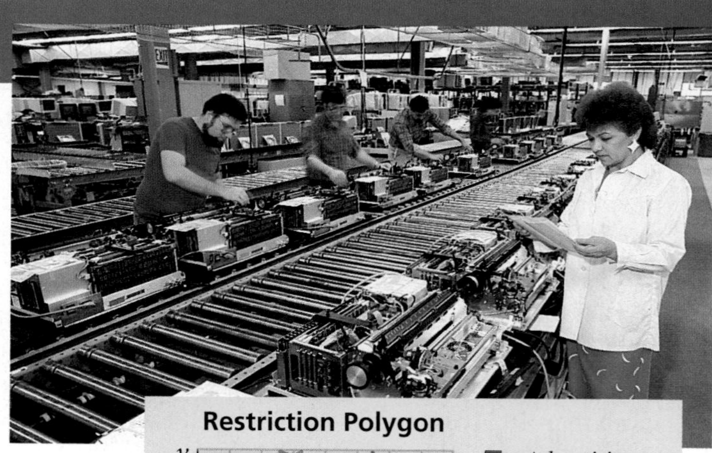

Restriction Polygon

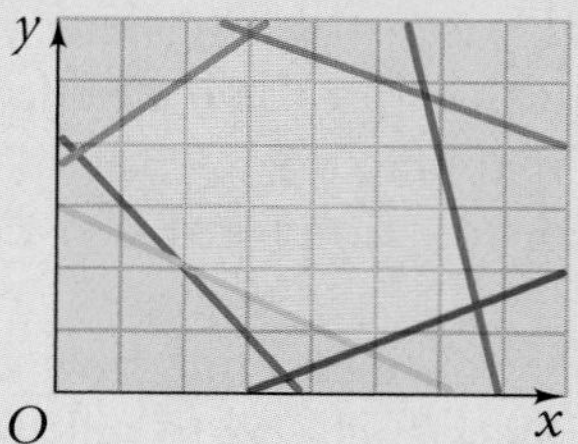

Mini Project: Work with a partner. Decide on a small business you could start. Identify the variables connected with your business and the restrictions on the variables.

Connections · Engineering . . . and more

What You'll Learn

- Solving systems with linear, quadratic, and absolute value equations by graphing

...And Why

To solve problems involving engineering and architecture

What You'll Need

- graphing calculator
- graph paper

6-8 Systems with Nonlinear Equations

THINK AND DISCUSS

A system of equations can include equations that are not linear. The system shown consists of a linear equation and a quadratic equation.

$$y = x + 2$$
$$y = -x^2 + 4$$

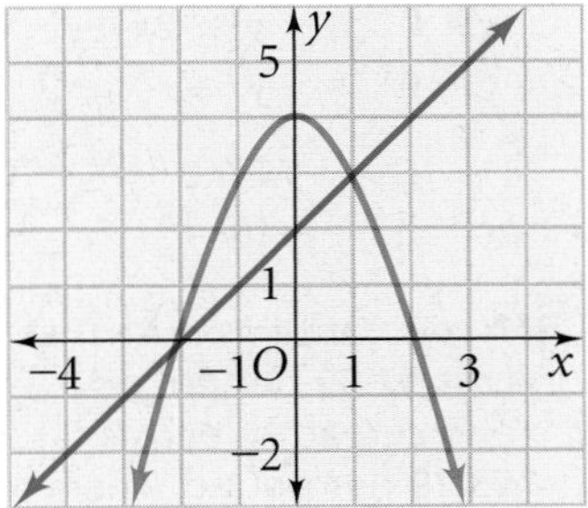

Notice that the graphs intersect at (–2, 0) and (1, 3). These two points are solutions of the system.

1. Check (–2, 0) and (1, 3) in both equations to **verify** that they are solutions of the system.

You can solve a system with a nonlinear equation by graphing.

Example 1

Solve the system of equations. $y = \frac{1}{2}x + 1$
$y = |x - 1|$

Graph each equation.

$y = \frac{1}{2}x + 1$

Use $y = mx + b$.

$m = \frac{1}{2}$

$b = 1$

$y = |x - 1|$

Make a table of values.

x	y
−2	3
−1	2
0	1
1	0
2	1
3	2

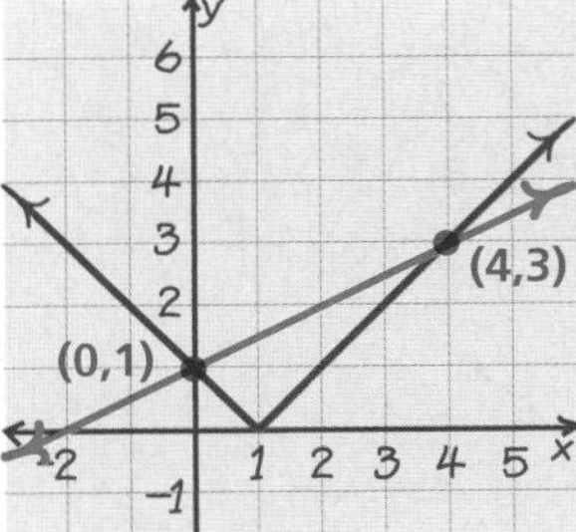

The graphs intersect at (0, 1) and (4, 3).

Check (0, 1):

$y = \frac{1}{2}x + 1$
$1 \stackrel{?}{=} \frac{1}{2}(0) + 1$
$1 \stackrel{?}{=} 0 + 1$
$1 = 1$ ✔

$y = |x - 1|$
$1 \stackrel{?}{=} |0 - 1|$
$1 \stackrel{?}{=} |-1|$
$1 = 1$ ✔

Check (4, 3):

$y = \frac{1}{2}x + 1$
$3 \stackrel{?}{=} \frac{1}{2}(4) + 1$
$3 \stackrel{?}{=} 2 + 1$
$3 = 3$ ✔

$y = |x - 1|$
$3 \stackrel{?}{=} |4 - 1|$
$3 \stackrel{?}{=} |3|$
$3 = 3$ ✔

Math A Test Prep

1 What is the maximum value for $R = 2x - y$ given the following restrictions?

$x \geq 0$ $\quad y \geq 2x + 1$

$y \geq 0$ $\quad y \leq -x + 7$

(1) -9 $\quad$ (3) 0

(2) -1 $\quad$ (4) 14

2 A mix contains nuts that cost $2.89 per pound and cereal that costs $3.79 per pound. There are at least 3 pounds of nuts, and the total cost is not more than $15.00.

a Write a system of linear inequalities that describes this situation.

b Name three possible combinations of nuts and cereal.

2. ***Critical Thinking*** Do systems made up of one linear equation and one absolute-value equation always have two solutions? If not, what are the other possibilities? Give examples.

Some systems of nonlinear equations have no solution.

Example 2

Solve the system of equations. $\quad y = x^2 + 3$
$\quad y = x$

Graph each equation.

$y = x^2 + 3$

Make a table of values.

x	y
−2	7
−1	4
0	3
1	4
2	7

$y = x$

Use $y = mx + b$.

$m = 1 \qquad b = 0$

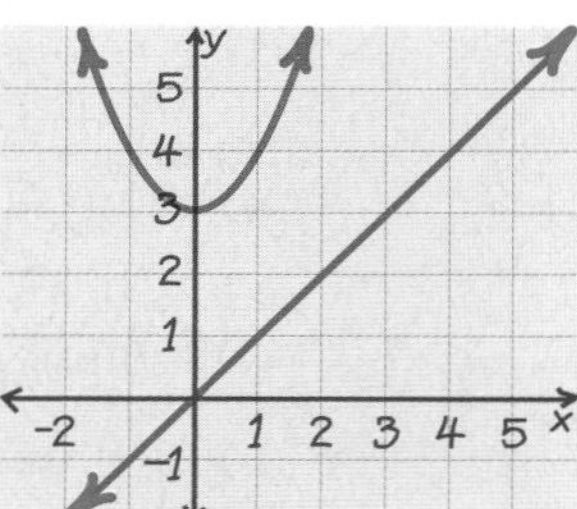

The graphs do not intersect, so the system has no solution.

3. **Try This** Solve each system.

a. $y = |x| + 2$
$y = 4x - 1$

b. $y = -x^2$
$y = x^2 - 8$

c. $y = |x - 2|$
$y = -\frac{1}{3}x + 2$

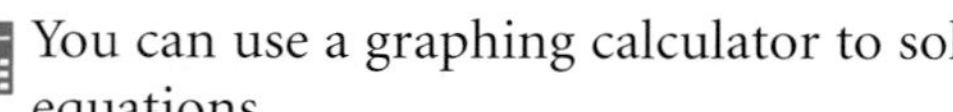

You can use a graphing calculator to solve systems with nonlinear equations.

Example 3 *Relating to the Real World*

Engineering Use the bridge diagram to find the coordinates of the points where the top arch intersects the road. Round answer to the nearest unit.

Arch $y = -\frac{1}{600}x^2 + 100$

Road $y = 40$

GRAPHING CALCULATOR HINT

You can use the TABLE feature or the ZOOM and TRACE keys to estimate the intersection points.

Set an appropriate range.

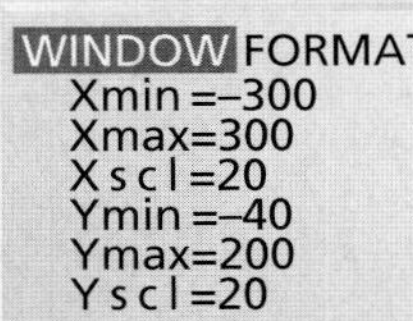

Input the equations.

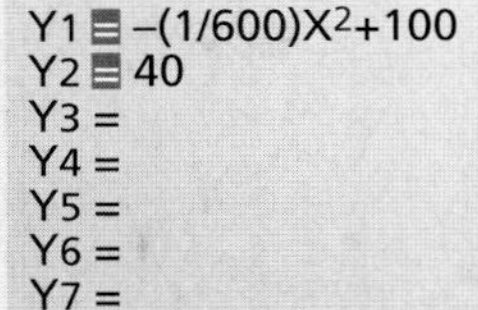

Use the CALC key to find the coordinates of the intersection points.

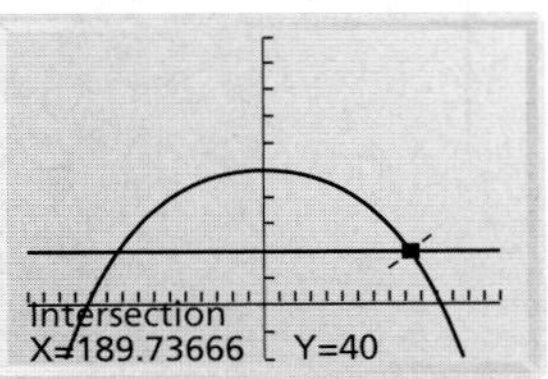

The solutions, rounded to the nearest unit, are (190, 40) and (–190, 40).

4. Each unit in Example 3 equals 1 ft. Find the length of the bridge.

Exercises ON YOUR OWN

Write the solution(s) of each system of equations. Check that each solution makes both equations of the system true.

1. $y = 2x$
$y = x^2$

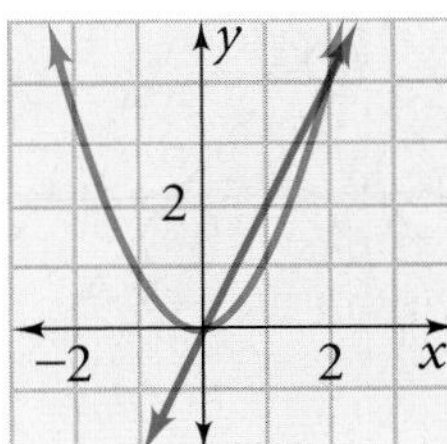

2. $y = 3$
$y = |x|$

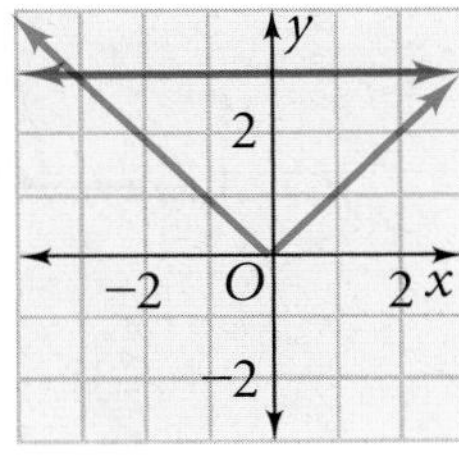

3. $y = -0.4x^2$
$y = -4x^2$

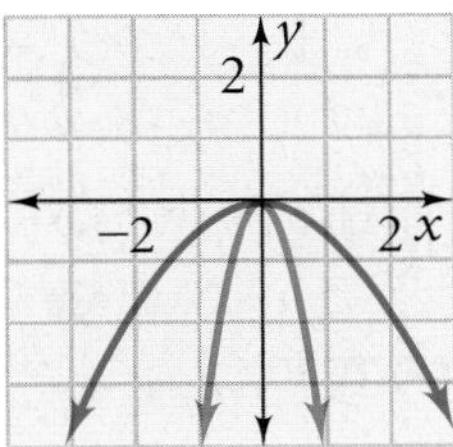

4. $y = |x|$
$y = -x + 5$

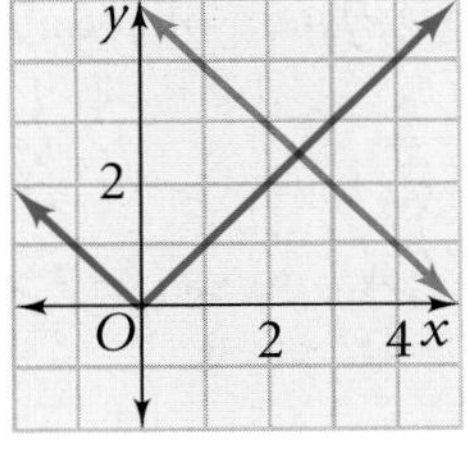

5. $y = -|x|$
$y = x^2 - 6$

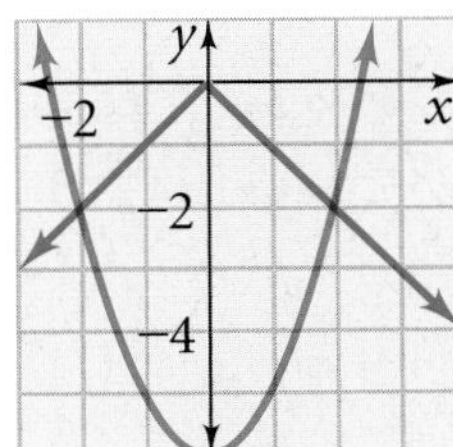

6. $y = x$
$y = -x^2$

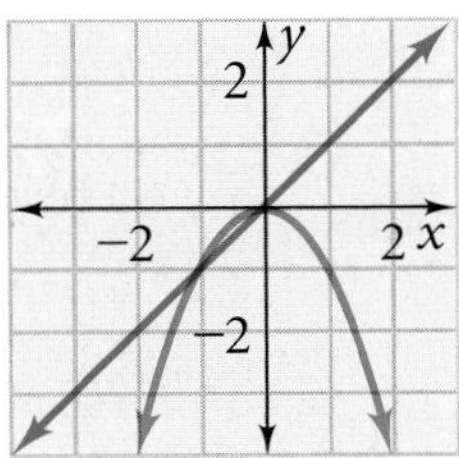

7. $y = |0.5x|$
$y = |3x| - 5$

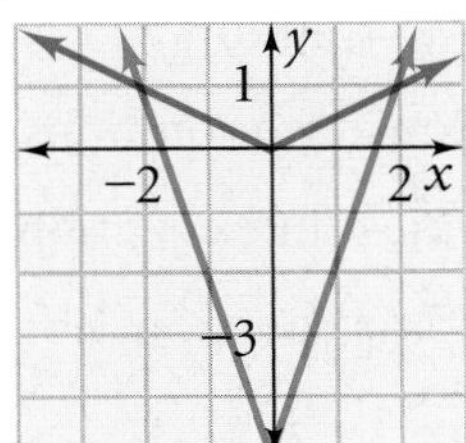

8. $y = x^2 + 2$
$y = -x^2 + 2$

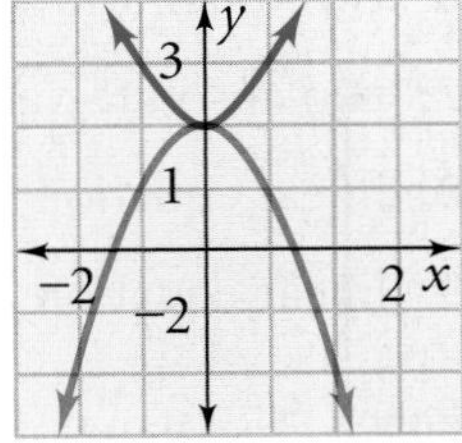

9. ***Communications*** Satellite dishes are used to receive television and radio signals. Use a graphing calculator to find the coordinates of S and T, the points at which the horn supports meet the dish. Round your answers to the nearest hundredth.

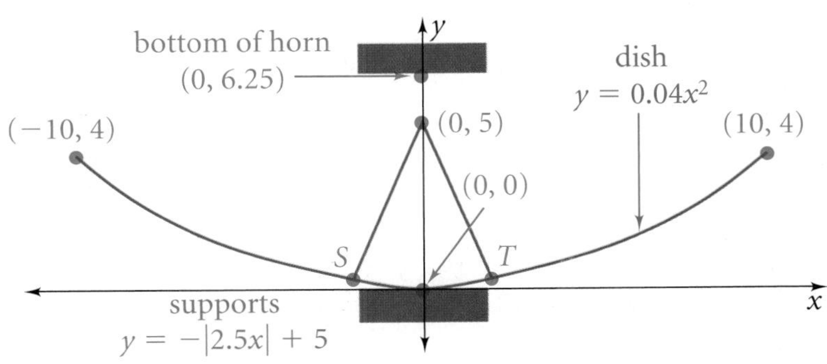

Match each system of equations with its graph. Write the solution(s) of the system.

10. $y = |x + 2|$
$y = |x - 2|$

11. $y = -2$
$y = x^2 - 3$

12. $y = 2.5x + 5$
$y = -|x - 2|$

13. $y = x^2 + 2$
$y = -\frac{1}{2}x^2$

A. 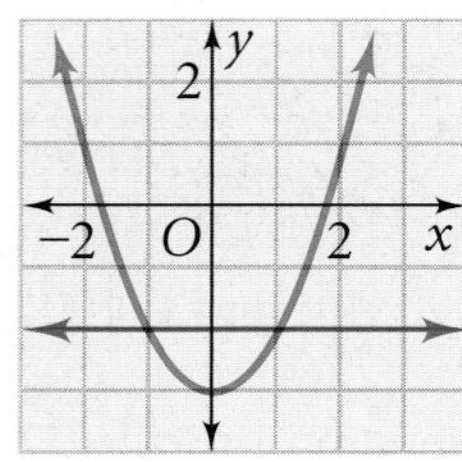

B. 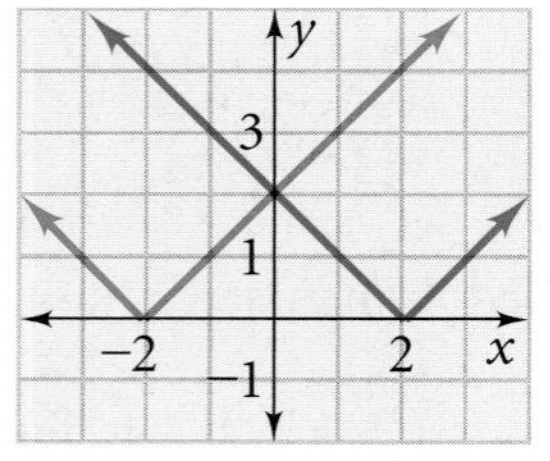

C. 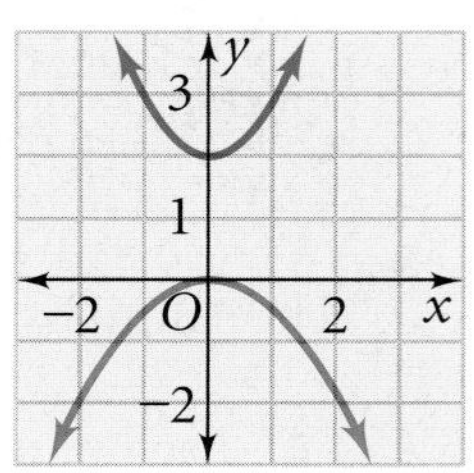

D. 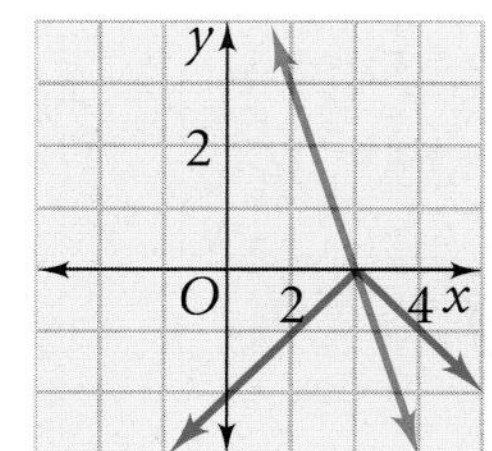

14. *Native American Art* This design was created by the Crow. The Crow are a people of the northern Great Plains of the United States. Patterns in the design can be described with a system of nonlinear equations. Find the coordinates of the points A and B.

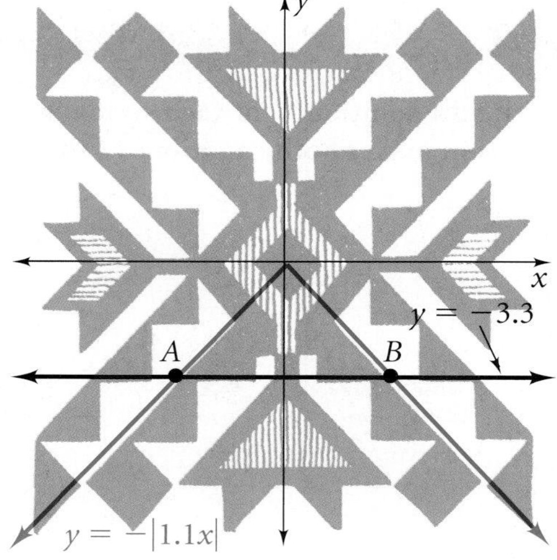

15. *Standardized Test Prep* How many solutions does this system of equations have?

$$y = \frac{1}{2}x^2$$
$$y = -|x + 3|$$

A. one **B.** two **C.** three
D. none **E.** infinitely many

Open-ended **Sketch the graph of a system of two equations with the given characteristics.**

16. two quadratic equations, no solution

17. two absolute-value equations, two solutions

18. linear equation and absolute-value equation, one solution

19. linear equation and quadratic equation, no solution

Choose **Use paper and pencil or a graphing calculator to solve each system of equations.**

20. $y = 3x - 4$
$y = -|x|$

21. $y = |x + 3|$
$y = \frac{1}{2}x$

22. $y = \frac{3}{2}x + 1$
$y = |x| + 1$

23. $y = x^2 - 1$
$y = -x + 1$

24. $y = |x|$
$y = -|x|$

25. $y = -x^2 + 2$
$y = x + 3$

26. $y = 2x$
$y = |x| + 3$

27. $y = -2x^2$
$y = |3x| - 5$

28. $y = -3$
$y = |x - 2|$

29. $y = x^2$
$y = x^2 - 2$

30. $y = |2x| - 3$
$y = |x|$

31. $y = \frac{1}{4}x^2$
$y = \frac{1}{2}x + 2$

32. a. **Architecture** The University of Illinois Assembly Hall in Urbana can be described by a system with nonlinear equations. Use a graphing calculator to find the coordinates of points S and E.

b. Find the length of $\overline{SE}$.

33. **Writing** How can you tell if a system with nonlinear equations has any solutions?

Exercises MIXED REVIEW

34. What is 15% of 96?

35. 34 is what percent of 32?

36. What percent of 40 is 27?

37. 6 is what percent of 92?

38. What percent of 6 is 2?

39. What is 85% of 108,000?

Find each sum or difference.

40. $\begin{bmatrix} -4 & a & 5 \\ 0 & b & 4c \end{bmatrix} + \begin{bmatrix} -12 & -a & 0 \\ d & 3b & -2c \end{bmatrix}$

41. $\begin{bmatrix} 7 & x \\ 0 & -2y \\ 4z & -x \end{bmatrix} - \begin{bmatrix} x & 5 \\ 3x & -y \\ -4z & -x \end{bmatrix}$

42. **Writing** Explain the difference between the solution of an equation and the solution of a system of two equations.

43. a. **Medicine** Write a formula for cell D2 in the spreadsheet.

b. Find the values in cells D2 and D3.

44. What is the rate of change in the total number of doctors from 1900 to 1995?

	A	B	C	D
1	Year	Number of Doctors	Population	Number of Doctors per Million People
2	1900	119,749	75,994,575	▒
3	1995	638,200	263,434,000	▒

PORTFOLIO

For your portfolio, choose one or two items from your work for this chapter. Here are some possibilities:

- a journal entry
- corrected work
- a Find Out question

Explain why you include each selection you make.

CHAPTER PROJECT

Finishing the Chapter Project

Questions on pages 274, 284, 293, and 299 should help you complete your project. Your report should include your analysis of the cost for refreshments and each band, depending on how many people buy tickets. Include your recommended ticket price and note any conditions under which this ticket price leads to a loss for the event. Illustrate your reasoning with graphs of linear equations and inequalities.

Client: Northwood High School

CHARGES

One-Time Fee
- set up
- transportation
- equipment
- staff
- clean up

Cost Per Person
- juice, soda, seltzer
- appetizers

Reflect and Revise

Present your analysis of this dance to a small group of classmates. After you have heard their analyses and presented your own, decide if your work is complete, clear, and convincing. If necessary, make changes to improve your presentation.

Follow Up

Are there other expenses you could expect to have in planning and holding this dance? Estimate them and change your recommended ticket price if necessary.

For More Information

Splaver, Bernard R. *Successful Catering*. New York: Van Nostrand Reinhold, 1991.

Watkins, Andrea and Patricia Clarkson. *Dancing Longer, Dancing Stronger: A Dancer's Guide to Improving Technique and Preventing Injury*. Princeton, New Jersey: Princeton Book Company, 1990.

CHAPTER 6

Wrap Up

Key Terms

elimination (p. 280)
infinitely many solutions (p. 271)
linear inequality (p. 290)
linear progamming (p. 300)
no solution (p. 271)
solution of a system of linear inequalities (p. 295)
solution of the inequality (p. 290)
solution of the system (p. 269)
substitution (p. 275)
system of linear equations (p. 269)
system of linear inequalities (p. 295)

How am I doing?

- State three ideas from this chapter that you think are important. Explain your choices.
- Describe the different ways you can solve systems of equations and inequalities.

Solving Systems by Graphing — 6-1

Two or more linear equations form a **system of linear equations.** You can solve a system of linear equations by graphing. Any point where all the lines intersect is the **solution of the system.**

For each graph, write the system of linear equations and its solution.

1. 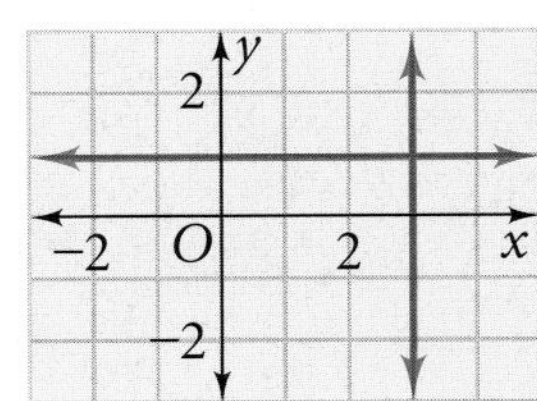

2. 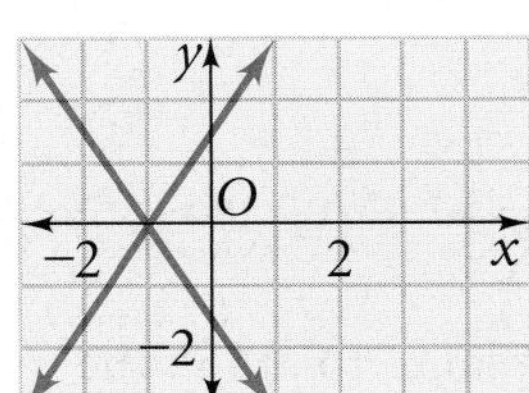

3. 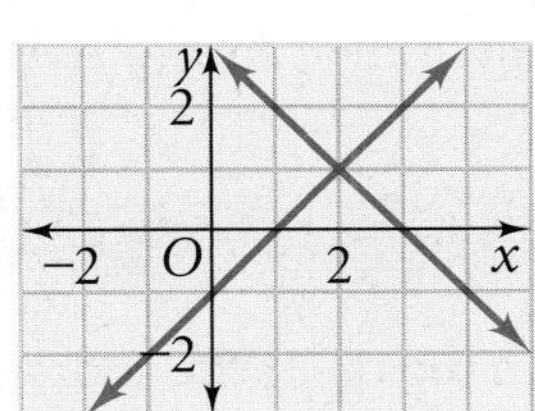

4. 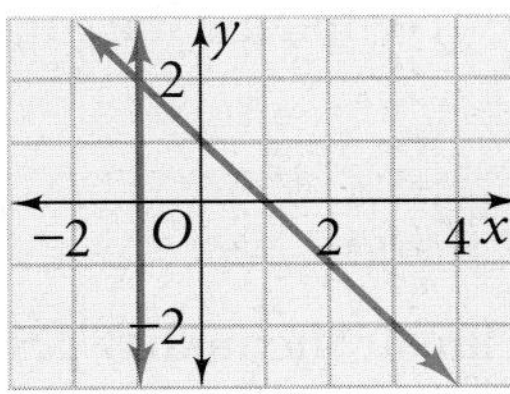

Solve each system by graphing.

5. $y = 3x - 1$
   $y = -x + 3$

6. $x - y = -3$
   $3x + y = -1$

7. $-x + 2y = -2$
   $y = \frac{1}{2}x + 3$

8. $y = -2x + 1$
   $y = 2x - 3$

Solving Systems Using Substitution — 6-2

You can also solve a system of linear equations using **substitution.** First, solve for one variable in terms of the other. Then substitute this result in either equation and solve.

Solve each system using substitution.

9. $y = 3x + 11$
   $y = -2x + 1$

10. $4x - y = -12$
    $-6x + 5y = -3$

11. $y = 5x - 8$
    $5y = 2x + 6$

12. $8x = -2y - 10$
    $2x = 4y$

13. *Writing* Explain how you determine if a system has no solution or infinitely many solutions when you solve a system using substitution.

Solving Systems Using Elimination 6-3

You can solve a system of linear equations using **elimination.** You add or subtract the equations to eliminate one variable. You can multiply one or both of the equations by a nonzero number before adding or subtracting.

Solve each system using elimination. Check your solution.

14. $y = -3x + 5$
$y = -4x - 1$

15. $2x - 3y = 5$
$x + 2y = -1$

16. $x + y = 10$
$x - y = 2$

17. $-x + 4y = 12$
$2x - 3y = 6$

Writing Systems 6-4

You can use systems of linear equations to solve word problems. First, define variables. Then model the situation with a system of linear equations.

Solve using any method. Check your solution.

18. A furniture finish consists of turpentine and linseed oil. It contains twice as much turpentine as linseed oil. If you need 16 fl oz of furniture finish, how much turpentine do you need?

19. **Geometry** The difference between the measures of two complementary angles is 36°. Find both angle measures. (*Hint:* Two angles are complementary if the sum of their measures is 90°.)

Linear Inequalities 6-5

A **linear inequality** describes a region of the coordinate plane. To graph the **solution of the inequality,** first graph the boundary line. Then test a point to shade the region that makes the inequality true.

Graph each linear inequality.

20. $y < -3x + 8$

21. $y \geq 2x - 1$

22. $y \leq 0.5x + 6$

23. $y > -\frac{1}{4}x - 2$

Systems of Linear Inequalities 6-6

Two or more linear inequalities form a **system of linear inequalities.** To find the **solution of a system of linear inequalities,** graph each linear inequality. The solution region is where all the inequalities are true.

Solve each system of linear inequalities by graphing.

24. $y \geq -4x + 1$
$y \leq 3x - 5$

25. $x - y < 10$
$x + y \leq 8$

26. $y \leq x - 3$
$y > x - 7$

27. $y < 5x$
$y \geq 0$

28. **Open-ended** Write a system of linear inequalities for which the solution region is a pentagon.

Concepts of Linear Programming 6-7

You can use **linear programming** to minimize or maximize quantities. The variables used in the equation for the quantity have restrictions. The maximum and minimum values of the equation occur at the vertices of the graph of the restrictions.

Evaluate the equation to find minimum and maximum values.

29. $x + y \leq 7$
$x + 2y \leq 8$
$x \geq 0$
$y \geq 0$
$P = 3x + y$

30. $x + 2y \leq 5$
$x \geq 0$
$y \geq 1$
$P = 2x + 3y$

31. $x + y \leq 6$
$2x + y \leq 10$
$x \geq 0$
$y \geq 0$
$P = 4x + y$

32. $x \geq 1$
$x \leq 4$
$y \geq 3$
$y \leq 6$
$P = x + 2y$

33. *Standardized Test Prep* Which point minimizes the equation $C = 5x + 2y$?

A. (4, 1) **B.** (5, 0) **C.** (2, 6) **D.** (3, 2) **E.** (1, 5)

Systems with Nonlinear Equations 6-8

You can solve systems that have linear, absolute value, and quadratic equations. Graph the equations on the same coordinate plane. Any point where the graphs intersect is a solution.

Solve each system of equations.

34. $y = x^2 - 4$
$y = -x + 2$

35. $y = |2x| - 3$
$y = x - 1$

36. $y = -x + 3$
$y = |2x - 3|$

37. $y = 2x + 6$
$y = x^2 + 3$

38. *Critical Thinking* How many solutions can a system with an absolute-value equation and a quadratic equation have? Explain.

Getting Ready for... CHAPTER 7

Find the square of each number.

39. 3 **40.** -7 **41.** 4.5 **42.** $\frac{1}{2}$ **43.** 11 **44.** -8.2

Make a table of values to graph each function.

45. $y = x^2 - 4x + 3$ **46.** $y = x^2 + x - 2$ **47.** $y = -x^2 + 4x + 5$

Evaluate the expression $b^2 - 4ac$ for the given values.

48. $a = 2, b = -5, c = 3$ **49.** $a = -7, b = 9, c = 1$ **50.** $a = 4.5, b = 8, c = 0$

51. $a = 1, b = 3, c = -2$ **52.** $a = 0.5, b = 4, c = 2.5$ **53.** $a = -8, b = -3.2, c = 5$

CHAPTER 6

Assessment

Solve each system of linear equations by graphing.

1. $y = 3x - 7$
   $y = -x + 1$

2. $4x + 3y = 12$
   $2x - 5y = -20$

Critical Thinking **Suppose you try to solve a system of linear equations using substitution and get this result. How many solutions does each system have?**

3. $x = 8$

4. $5 = y$

5. $-7 = 4$

6. $x = -1$

7. $2 = y$

8. $9 = 9$

Solve each system using substitution.

9. $y = 4x - 7$
   $y = 2x + 9$

10. $y = -2x - 1$
    $y = 3x - 16$

Solve each system using elimination.

11. $4x + y = 8$
    $-3x - y = 0$

12. $2x + 5y = 20$
    $3x - 10y = 37$

13. $x + y = 10$
    $-x - 2y = -14$

14. $3x + 2y = -19$
    $x - 12y = 19$

Write a system of equations to model each situation. Then use your system to solve.

15. **Cable Service** Your local cable television company offers two plans: basic service with one movie channel for \$35 per month, or basic service with two movie channels for \$45 per month. What is the charge for the basic service and the charge for each movie channel?

16. **Education** A writing workshop enrolls novelists and poets in a ratio of 5 to 3. There are 24 people at the workshop. How many novelists are there? How many poets?

17. You have 15 coins in your pocket that are either quarters or nickels. They total \$2.75. How many of each coin do you have?

18. **Writing** Compare solving a linear equation with solving a linear inequality. What are the similarities? What are the differences?

19. **Standardized Test Prep** Which point is *not* a solution of $y < 3x - 1$?
    A. (2, –4) B. (5, 7) C. (0, –1)
    D. (–3, –13) E. (4, –8)

Solve each system by graphing.

20. $y > 4x - 1$
    $y \leq -x + 4$

21. $y \geq 3x + 5$
    $y > x - 2$

22. $y = x^2 + x + 1$
    $y = -3x + 6$

23. $y = 4x - 5$
    $y = |3x + 1|$

Open-ended **Write a system of equations with the given characteristics.**

24. two linear equations with no solution

25. a linear equation and a quadratic equation with two solutions

26. three linear inequalities with a triangular solution region

27. **Fund Raising** You are making bread to sell at a holiday fair. A loaf of oatmeal bread takes 2 cups of flour and 2 eggs. A loaf of banana bread takes 3 cups of flour and 1 egg. You have 12 cups of flour and 8 eggs.

    x = number of loaves of oatmeal bread
    y = number of loaves of banana bread
    Restrictions: $2x + 3y \leq 12$
    $2x + y \leq 8$
    $x \geq 0, y \geq 0$

    a. Explain each restriction.
    b. You will make \$1 profit for each loaf of oatmeal bread and \$2 profit for each loaf of banana bread. Write the equation.
    c. Use linear programming to find how many loaves of each type you should make to maximize profits.

CHAPTER 6

Preparing for the Math A Exam

Part I

1 The graph of which of the following equations is a vertical line through $(-7, -4)$?

(1) $x = -7$ (3) $y = 7$
(2) $x = -4$ (4) $y = -4$

2 What is true of the graphs of $3y - 8 = -5x$ and $3x = 2y - 18$?

(1) no intersection (3) intersect at $(-2, 6)$
(2) intersect at $(2, -6)$ (4) are identical

3 Which system has no solutions?

(1) $y = 3x + 1$, $3y = x - 12$
(3) $2x - 5y = -15$, $y = \frac{2}{5}x + 3$
(2) $x + y = 4$, $y = x + 4$
(4) $y = 2x + 3$, $2x - y = 6$

4 Which inequality is shown in the graph?

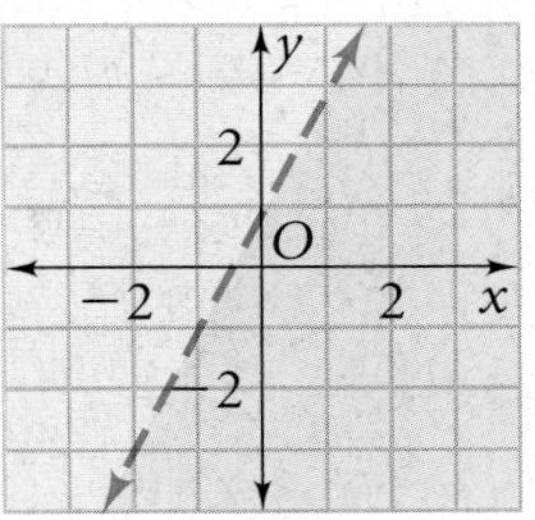

(1) $y \leq 2x + 1$
(2) $y \geq 2x + 1$
(3) $y < 2x + 1$
(4) $y > 2x + 1$

5 Which statement is true for every solution of the following system?

$2y > x + 4$
$3y + 3x > 13$

(1) $x \leq -3$ (3) $x > 4$
(2) $y > 2$ (4) $y < 5$

6 Which system of equations has only one solution?

(1) $y = |x + 3|$, $y = x^2$
(3) $y = x^2 + 3$, $y = 2x + 4$
(2) $y = |x - 3|$, $y = 3x - 4$
(4) $y = -3$, $y = 2x^2 - 4$

7 Which x and y values minimize the quantity $Q = 3x - 4y$?

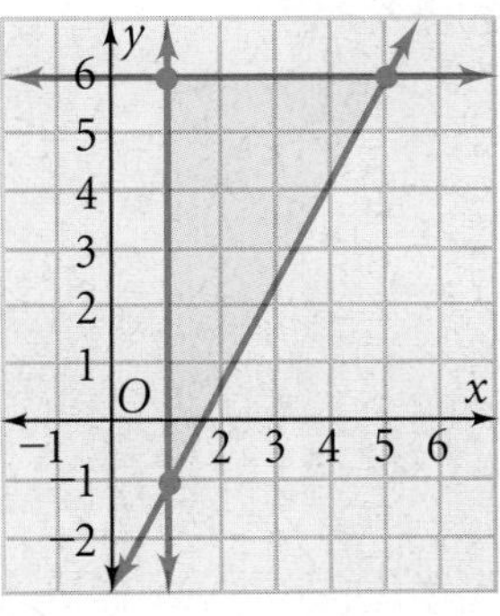

(1) $(1, -1)$
(3) $(5, 6)$
(2) $(3, 6)$
(4) $(1, 6)$

Part II

8 Solve this system using substitution.

$y = x + 10$
$y = 2x + 8$

9 Solve this system using elimination.

$5x - y = 5$
$3x + y = 11$

Part III

10 Plumber A charges \$40 for a house call plus \$30 per hour for labor. Plumber B charges \$20 for a house call plus \$35 per hour for labor. How long must a job take before plumber A is the less expensive choice for the homeowner?

11 The drama club sold 700 tickets to the school play and received \$3400. Adult tickets cost \$6 each, and student tickets cost \$4 each. How many of each type ticket did the club sell?

Part IV

12 Suppose you want to spend less than \$30 for the meat for subs at a party. Turkey costs \$4.00 per pound, and ham costs \$6.00 per pound. You want to buy at least 2 pounds of turkey as well as some ham.

a Write a system of linear inequalities that describes this situation.
b Graph the system of inequalities.
c Name three possible solutions.

CHAPTER 7

Quadratic Equations and Functions

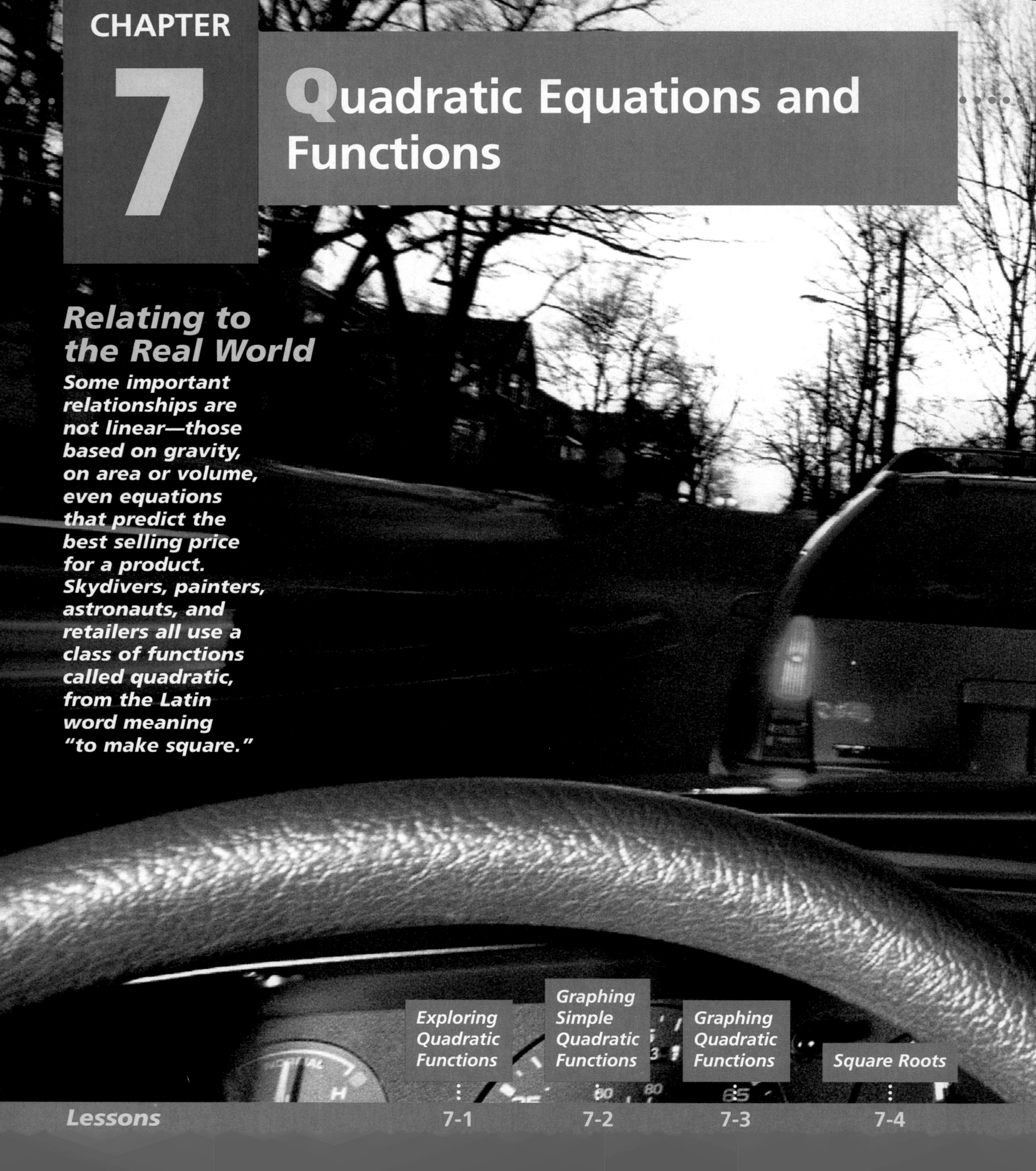

Relating to the Real World

Some important relationships are not linear—those based on gravity, on area or volume, even equations that predict the best selling price for a product. Skydivers, painters, astronauts, and retailers all use a class of functions called quadratic, from the Latin word meaning "to make square."

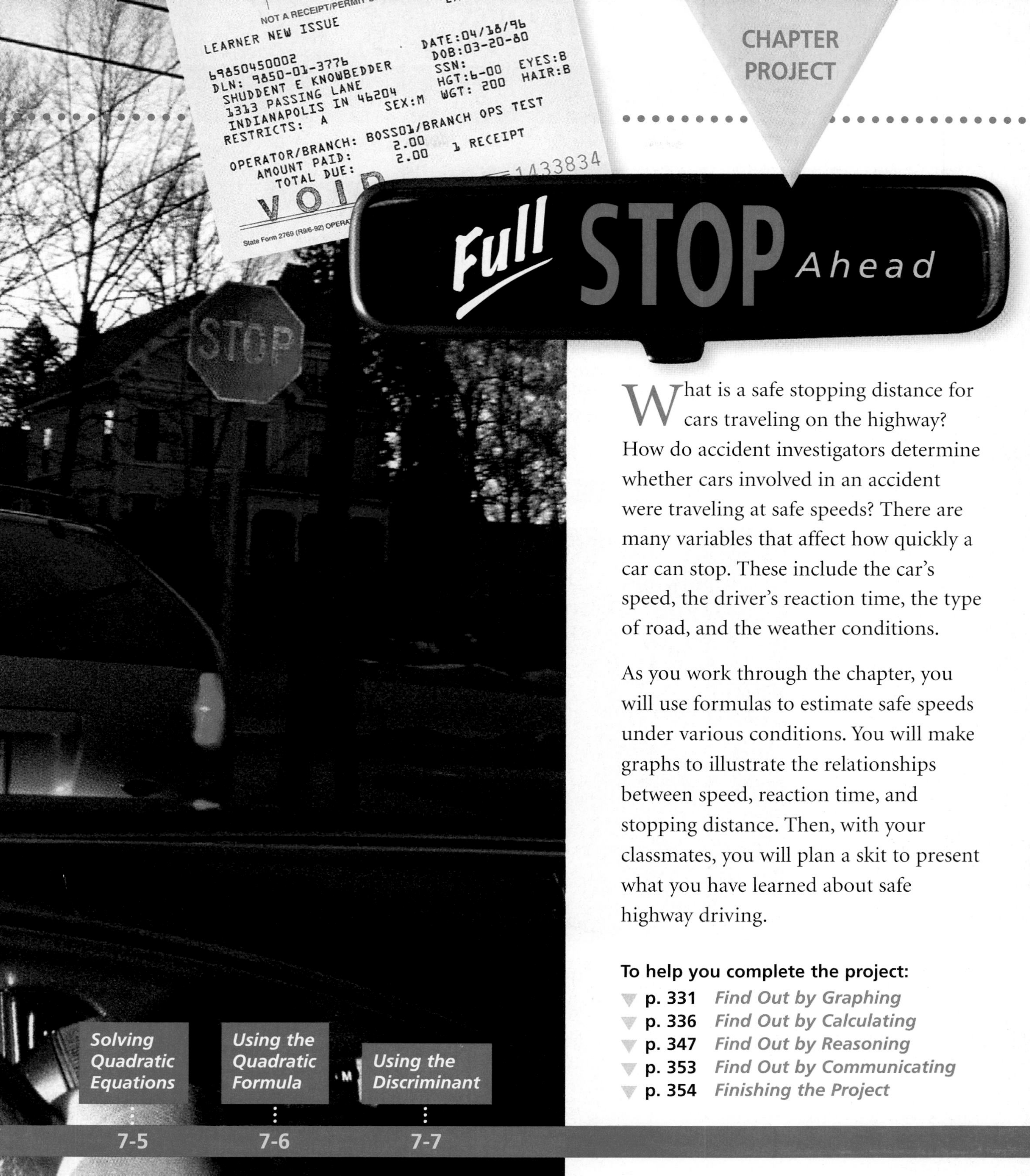

CHAPTER PROJECT

Full STOP *Ahead*

What is a safe stopping distance for cars traveling on the highway? How do accident investigators determine whether cars involved in an accident were traveling at safe speeds? There are many variables that affect how quickly a car can stop. These include the car's speed, the driver's reaction time, the type of road, and the weather conditions.

As you work through the chapter, you will use formulas to estimate safe speeds under various conditions. You will make graphs to illustrate the relationships between speed, reaction time, and stopping distance. Then, with your classmates, you will plan a skit to present what you have learned about safe highway driving.

To help you complete the project:

- **p. 331** *Find Out by Graphing*
- **p. 336** *Find Out by Calculating*
- **p. 347** *Find Out by Reasoning*
- **p. 353** *Find Out by Communicating*
- **p. 354** *Finishing the Project*

What You'll Learn

- Graphing quadratic functions of the form $y = ax^2$

...And Why

To understand how changing *a* affects the graph of a quadratic function

What You'll Need

- graphing calculator

7-1 Exploring Quadratic Functions

WORK TOGETHER

Work with a partner. Complete a table of values and plot points, or use a graphing calculator set at the standard scale.

x	y
−2	■
−1	■
0	■
1	■
2	■

1. **a.** Graph the equations $y = x^2$ and $y = 3x^2$.
   b. How are the graphs in part (a) alike? different?
2. **a.** Graph the equations $y = -x^2$ and $y = -3x^2$.
   b. How are the graphs in part (a) different from the graphs in Question 1? How are they like the graphs in Question 1?

THINK AND DISCUSS

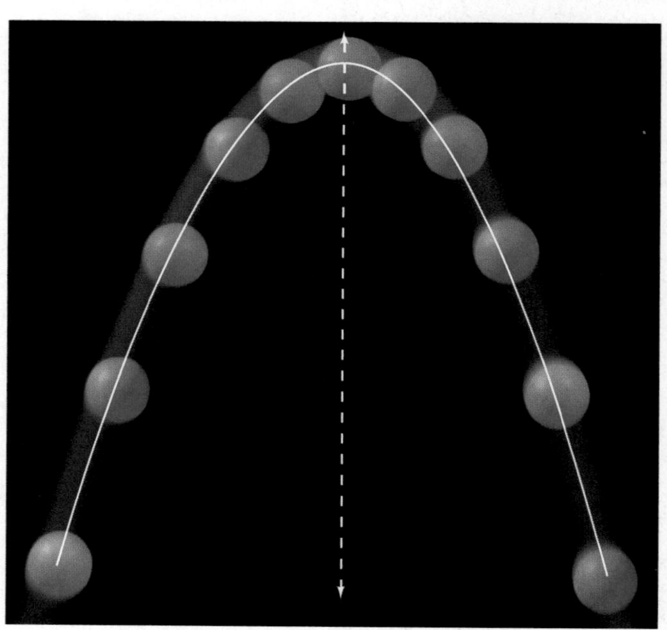

Quadratic Functions

The graphs you analyzed in the Work Together are all examples of **parabolas.** If you draw a parabola on a piece of paper, you can fold the paper down the middle of the parabola and the two sides will match exactly. The line down the middle of the parabola is the **axis of symmetry.**

3. **Try This** Trace each parabola on a sheet of paper and draw its axis of symmetry.

a.

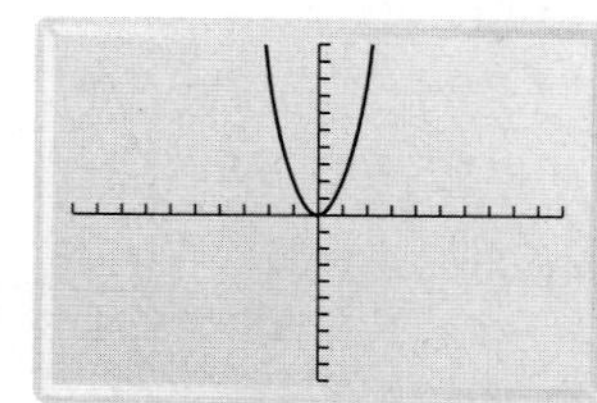

b.

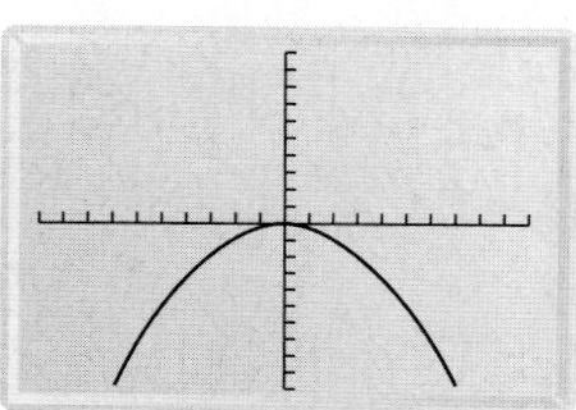

Math A Test Prep

1 How does the graph of $y = \frac{2}{3}x^2$ differ from the graph of $y = -\frac{2}{3}x^2$?

(1) $y = \frac{2}{3}x^2$ is wider.

(2) $y = \frac{2}{3}x^2$ is narrower.

(3) $y = \frac{2}{3}x^2$ opens upward rather than downward.

(4) $y = \frac{2}{3}x^2$ opens downward rather than upward.

2 Tonya said that the graph of $y = -2x^2$ is wider than the graph of $y = 3x^2$. Is she correct? How do you know?

Each parabola that you have seen is the graph of a *quadratic function.*

Quadratic Function

For $a \neq 0$, the function $y = ax^2 + bx + c$ is a **quadratic function.**

Examples: $y = 2x^2$, $y = x^2 + 2$, $y = -x^2 - x - 3$

When a quadratic function is written in the form $y = ax^2 + bx + c$, it is in **standard form.**

4. Name the values of a, b, and c for each quadratic function.
a. $y = 3x^2 - 2x + 5$ **b.** $y = 3x^2$ **c.** $y = -0.5x^2 + 2x$

5. Write each quadratic function in standard form.
a. $y = 7x + 9x^2 - 4$ **b.** $y = 3 - x^2$

The Role of "a"

When you graph a quadratic function, if the value of a is positive, the parabola opens upward. If the value of a is negative, the parabola opens downward.

Example 1

Make a table of values and graph the quadratic functions $y = 2x^2$ and $y = -2x^2$.

x	$y=2x^2$	$y=-2x^2$
−3	18	−18
−2	8	−8
−1	2	−2
0	0	0
1	2	−2
2	8	−8
3	18	−18

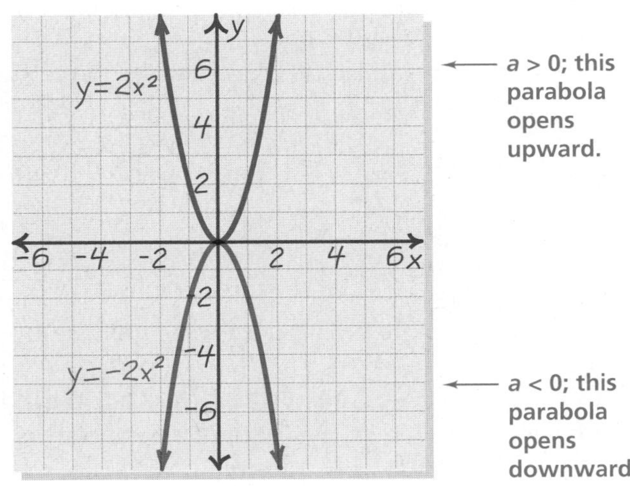

6. What is the axis of symmetry for the graphs in Example 1?

7. What would happen to the graph of $y = 2x^2$ if you could fold the graph over the x-axis? Explain.

The highest or lowest point on a parabola is called the **vertex** of the parabola.

When a parabola opens upward, the y-coordinate of the vertex is the **minimum value** of the function.

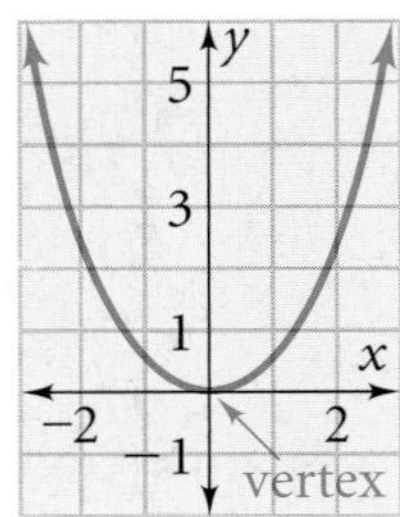

When a parabola opens downward, the y-coordinate of the vertex is the **maximum value** of the function.

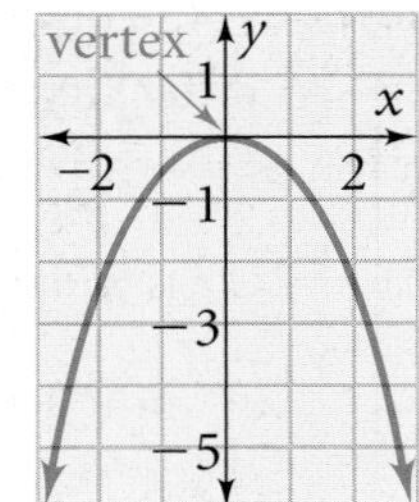

8. Answer these questions for $y = -3x^2$ and $y = 4x^2$.
   a. What is the value of a?
   b. In which direction does each graph open?
   c. Is the y-coordinate of the vertex a minimum or a maximum value of the function?

9. **Summarize** what you know so far about how the value of a affects the parabola.

The value of a also affects the width of a parabola.

Example 2

Graph $-4x^2$, $y = \frac{1}{4}x^2$, and $y = x^2$. Compare the widths of the graphs.

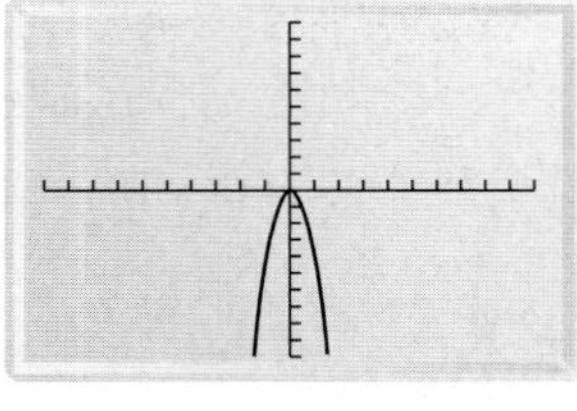

$y = -4x^2$

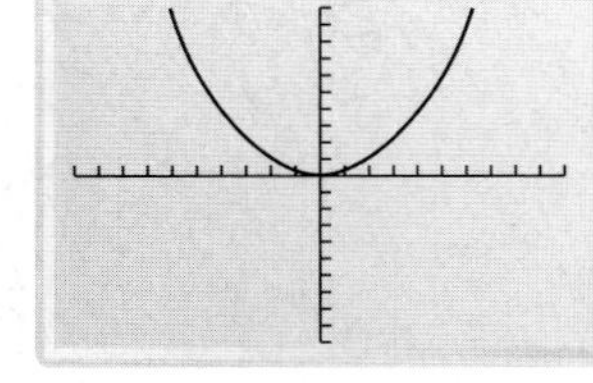

$y = \frac{1}{4}x^2$

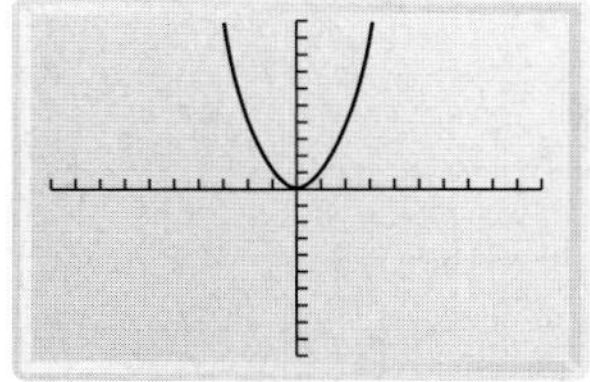

$y = x^2$

Of the three graphs, $y = \frac{1}{4}x^2$ is the widest, $y = x^2$ is narrower, and $y = -4x^2$ is the narrowest.

10. **Critical Thinking** What does the absolute value of a tell you about the width of a parabola? Use the graphs in Example 2 to explain your answer.

11. **Try This** Order each group of quadratic functions from widest to narrowest graph.
   a. $y = 2x^2, y = 3x^2, y = -5x^2$
   b. $y = \frac{3}{2}x^2, y = \frac{2}{3}x^2, y = \frac{1}{2}x^2$

Exercises ON YOUR OWN

Find the values of *a*, *b*, and *c* for each quadratic function.

1. $y = x^2 + 2x + 4$ **2.** $y = 2x^2$ **3.** $y = -x^2 - 3x - 9$ **4.** $y = -2x^2 + 5$

Tell whether each parabola opens *upward* or *downward* and whether the *y*-coordinate of the vertex is a *maximum* or a *minimum*.

5. $y = x^2$ **6.** $y = 9x^2$ **7.** $y = -\frac{2}{5}x^2$ **8.** $y = -6x^2$

Choose **Graph each quadratic function. Use either a table of values or a graphing calculator.**

9. $y = \frac{1}{2}x^2$ **10.** $y = 1.5x^2$ **11.** $y = -4x^2$ **12.** $y = -\frac{1}{3}x^2$

13. $y = 4x^2$ **14.** $y = \frac{1}{3}x^2$ **15.** $y = -1.5x^2$ **16.** $y = -\frac{1}{2}x^2$

Order each group of quadratic functions from widest to narrowest graph.

17. $y = 3x^2,\ y = x^2,\ y = 7x^2$ **18.** $y = 4x^2,\ y = \frac{1}{3}x^2,\ y = x^2$

19. $y = -2x^2,\ y = -\frac{2}{3}x^2,\ y = -4x^2$ **20.** $y = -\frac{1}{2}x^2,\ y = 5x^2,\ y = -\frac{1}{4}x^2$

Give the letter or letters of the graph(s) that make each statement true.

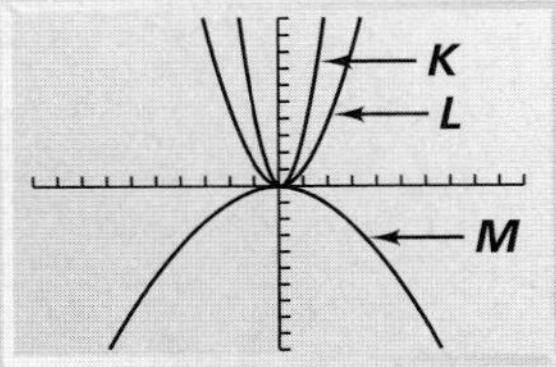

21. $a > 0$ **22.** $a < 0$

23. $|a|$ has the greatest value. **24.** $|a|$ has the least value.

Trace each parabola on a sheet of paper and draw its axis of symmetry.

25.

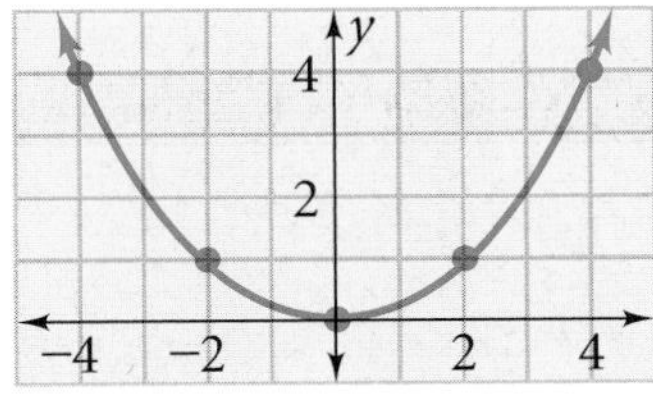

26.

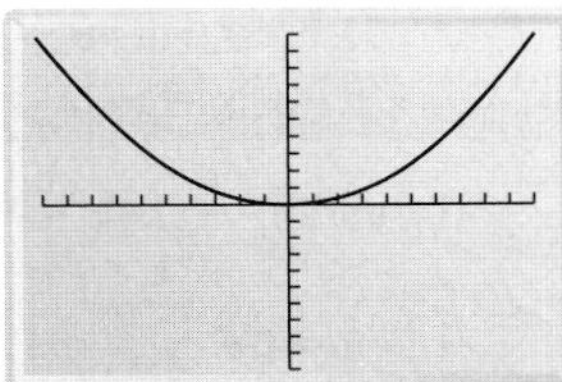

27.

28.

Writing **Without graphing, describe how each graph differs from the graph of $y = x^2$.**

29. $y = 2x^2$

30. $y = -x^2$

31. $y = 1.5x^2$

32. $y = \frac{1}{2}x^2$

33. **Open-ended** Give an example of a quadratic function for each description.
 a. Its graph opens upward.
 b. Its graph has the same shape as the graph in part (a), but the graph opens downward.
 c. Its graph is wider than the graph in part (b).

Match each function with its graph.

A. $y = x^2$ B. $y = -x^2$ C. $y = 3.5x^2$ D. $y = -3.5x^2$ E. $y = \frac{1}{4}x^2$ F. $y = -\frac{1}{4}x^2$

34.
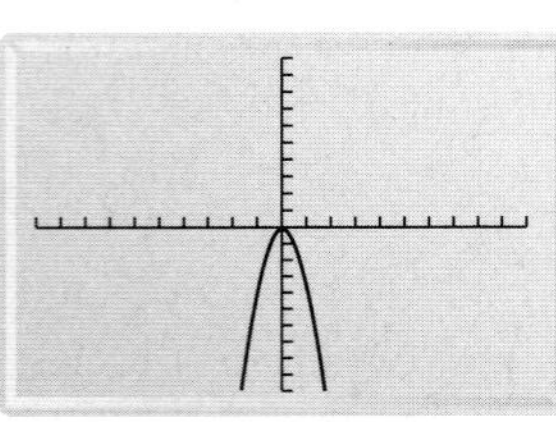

35.
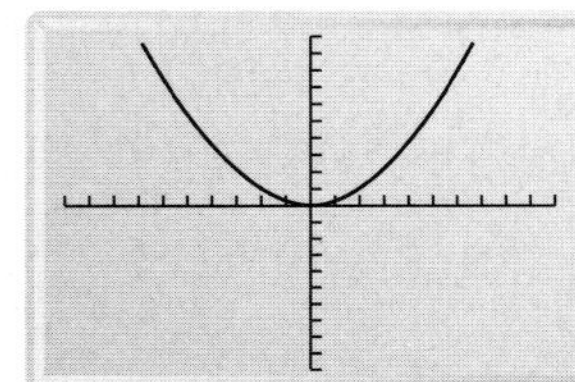

36.
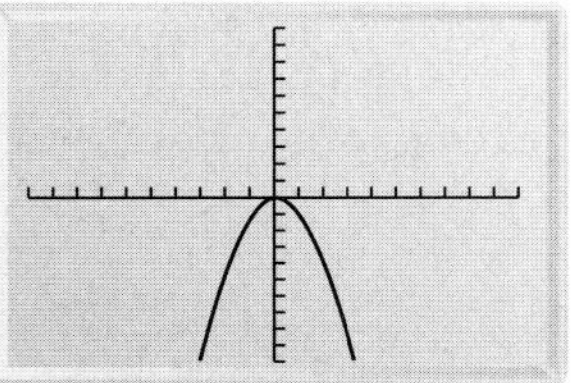

37.
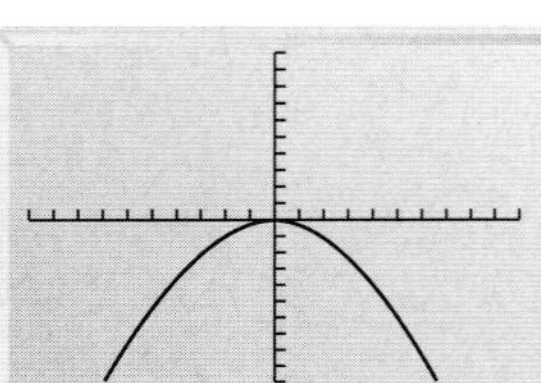

38.
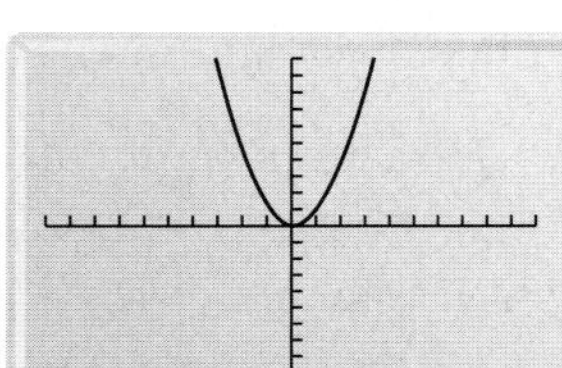

39.
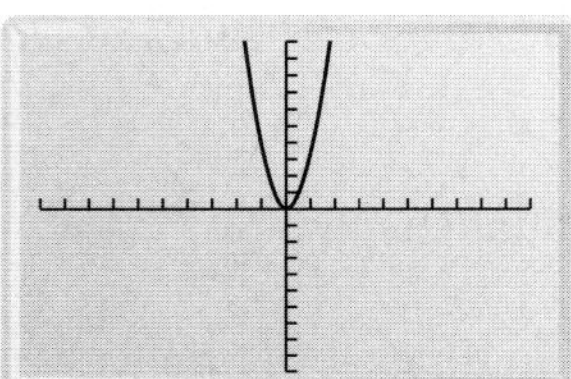

Exercises MIXED REVIEW

Find each percent of change.

40. 12 lb to 14 lb

41. 5 ft to 7 ft

42. \$4.50 to \$2.25

43. A type of spring toy begins as 80 ft of wire. In 50 years of production, 3,030,000 mi of wire weighing 50,000 tons have been used.
 a. How many of these toys have been made?
 b. How much does 1 mi of wire weigh?
 c. The 3,030,000 mi of wire could go around the equator 126 times. What is the length of the equator? What is the diameter of Earth?

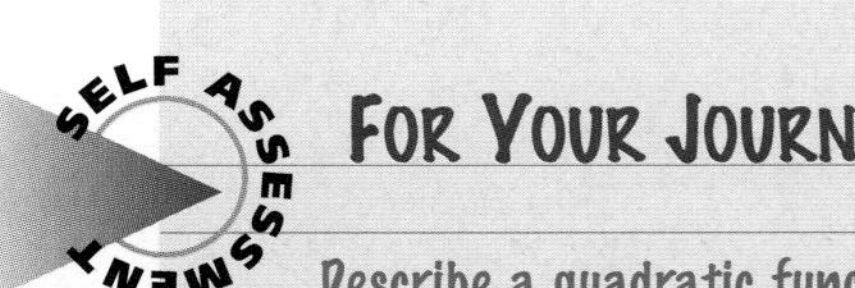

FOR YOUR JOURNAL

Describe a quadratic function and its graph. Explain how the value of "a" affects the graph. Give examples of quadratic functions to support your statements.

Getting Ready for Lesson 7-2

Graph each linear equation.

44. $y = 2x$

45. $y = 2x - 3$

46. $y = 2x + 1$

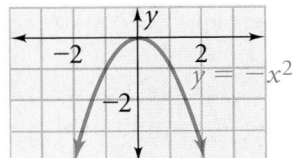

Connections Nature . . . and more

What You'll Learn

- Graphing quadratic functions of the form $y = ax^2 + c$
- Graphing quadratic functions that represent real-life situations

...And Why

To understand how changing c affects the graph of a quadratic function

What You'll Need

- graphing calculator

7-2 Graphing Simple Quadratic Functions

WORK TOGETHER

Work with a partner. Use a table of values or a graphing calculator set at the standard scale.

1. a. Graph the quadratic functions $y = x^2$, $y = x^2 - 5$, and $y = x^2 + 1$.

b. How are the graphs in part (a) alike? How are they different?

2. a. Graph the quadratic functions $y = -\frac{1}{2}x^2$, $y = -\frac{1}{2}x^2 + 4$, and $y = -\frac{1}{2}x^2 - 2$

b. How are the graphs in part (a) alike? How are they different?

THINK AND DISCUSS

You have seen that changing the value of a in the function $y = ax^2$ affects whether the parabola opens upward or downward and how wide or narrow the parabola is. Changing the value of c in the function $y = ax^2 + c$ changes the position of the parabola.

Example 1

Graph the quadratic functions $y = -x^2 + 3$ and $y = -x^2 - 1$. Compare them to the graph of $y = -x^2$ at the left.

Make a table of values.

x	$y=-x^2+3$	$y=-x^2-1$
-3	-6	-10
-2	-1	-5
-1	2	-2
0	3	-1
1	2	-2
2	-1	-5
3	-6	-10

Plot the points. Connect the points to form smooth curves.

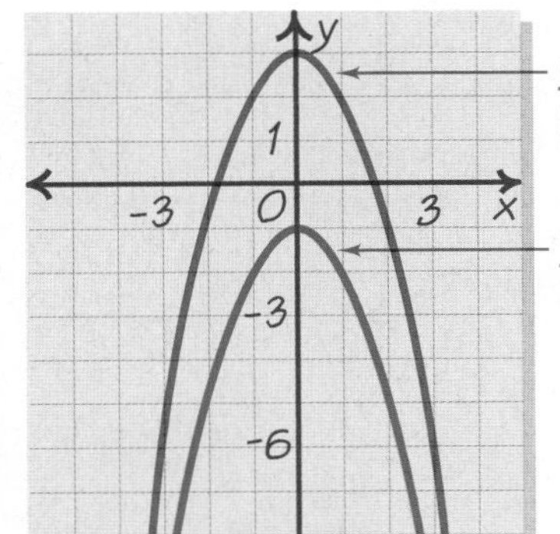

$y = -x^2 + 3$ shifts the parabola $y = -x^2$ *up* 3 units.

$y = -x^2 - 1$ shifts the parabola $y = -x^2$ *down* 1 unit.

3. **Try This** Graph $y = 2x^2$ and $y = 2x^2 - 4$. Compare the graphs.

4. **Summarize** how the graphs of $y = ax^2$ and $y = ax^2 + c$ are different and how they are alike.

5. Since the parabolas in Example 1 open downward, the y-coordinate of each vertex is a maximum value. Find the maximum value of each function.

When you graph a quadratic function that represents a real-life situation, you should limit the domain and range of your graph to x- and y-values that make sense in the situation.

Example 2 Relating to the Real World 

Nature Suppose you see an eagle flying over a canyon. The eagle is 30 ft above the level of the canyon's edge when it drops a stick from its claws. The function $d = -16t^2 + 30$ gives the height of the stick in feet after t seconds. Graph this quadratic function.

Graph t on the horizontal or x-axis. Graph d on the vertical or y-axis.

Choose nonnegative values of *t* that represent the first few seconds of the stick's fall.

Choose values for *d* that show the height of the stick as it falls.

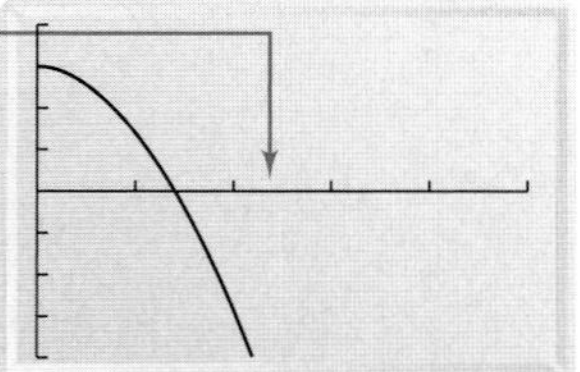

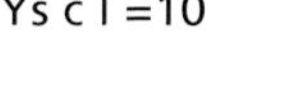

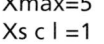

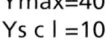

Xmin=0 Ymin=–40
Xmax=5 Ymax=40
Xscl=1 Yscl=10

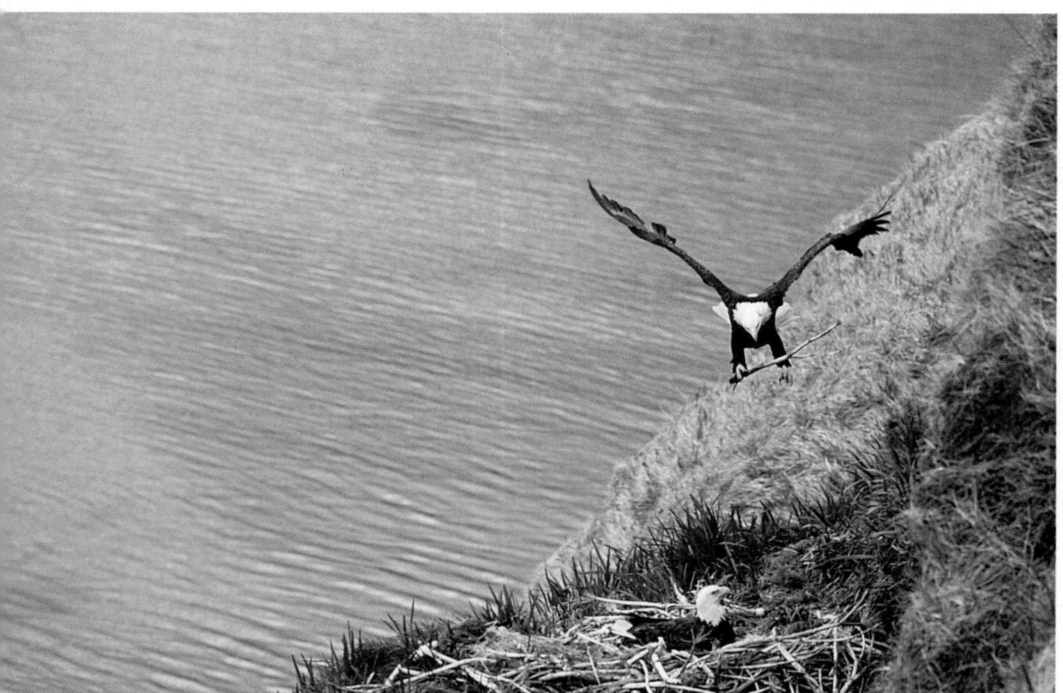

6. In Example 2, why is the domain limited to nonnegative values of t?

7. Explain why the range does not include any values greater than 30.

8. The height of the stick is represented by d. From what level is the height measured?

Exercises ON YOUR OWN

1. **Writing** Describe how the graphs of the functions $y = 5x^2$, $y = 5x^2 + 50$, and $y = 5x^2 - 90$ are alike and how they are different.

Describe whether each quadratic function has a *maximum* or *minimum*.

2. $y = x^2 - 2$
3. $y = -x^2 + 6$
4. $y = 3x^2 + 1$
5. $y = -\frac{1}{2}x^2 - 9$

Choose **Graph each quadratic function. Use either a table of values or a graphing calculator.**

6. $y = x^2 + 2$
7. $y = x^2 - 3$
8. $y = -x^2 + 4$
9. $y = -x^2 - 1$
10. $y = -2x^2 + 2$
11. $y = -2x^2 - 2$
12. $y = -\frac{1}{4}x^2$
13. $y = -\frac{1}{4}x^2 + 3$
14. $y = 4x^2$
15. $y = 4x^2 - 7$
16. $y = -1.5x^2 + 5$
17. $y = -1.5x^2 - 1$

Open-ended **Give an example of a quadratic function for each description.**

18. It opens upward and its vertex is below the origin.
19. It opens downward and its vertex is above the origin.

20. **Geometry** Suppose that a pizza must fit into a box with a base that is 12 in. long and 12 in. wide. You can use the quadratic function $A = \pi r^2$ to find the area of a pizza in terms of its radius.

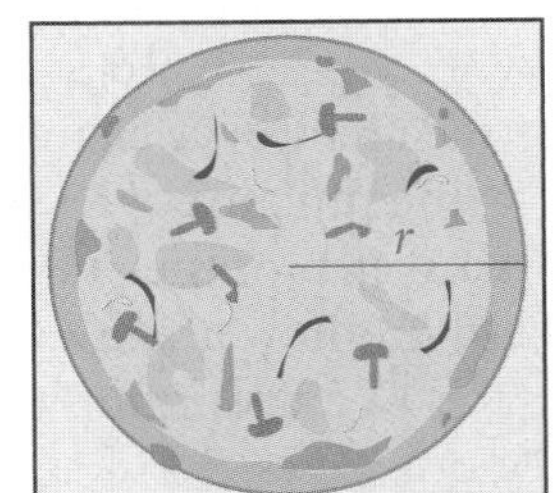

   a. What values of r make sense in the function?
   b. What values of A make sense in the function?
   c. Graph the function. Use $\pi \approx 3.14$.

Match each function with its graph.

A. $y = x^2 - 1$
B. $y = x^2 + 4$
C. $y = -x^2 + 2$
D. $y = 3x^2 - 5$
E. $y = -3x^2 + 8$
F. $y = -0.2x^2 + 5$

21. 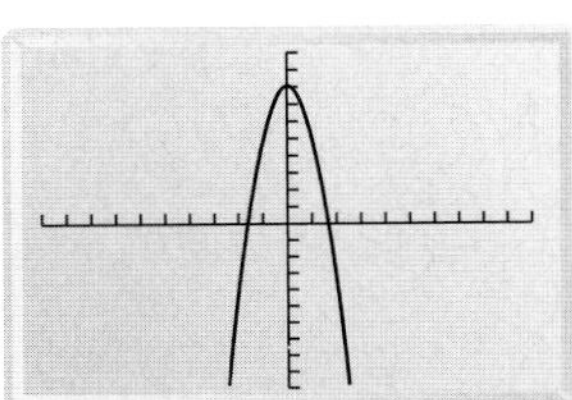

22. 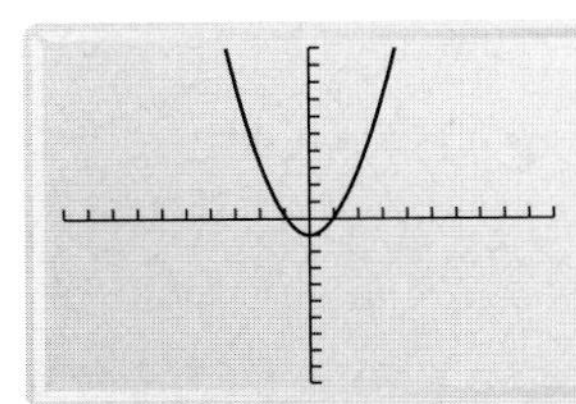

23. 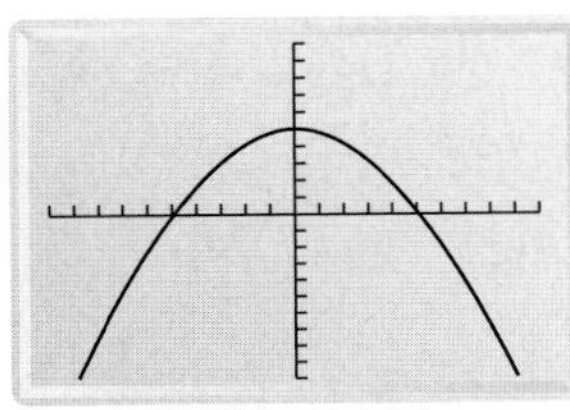

24. 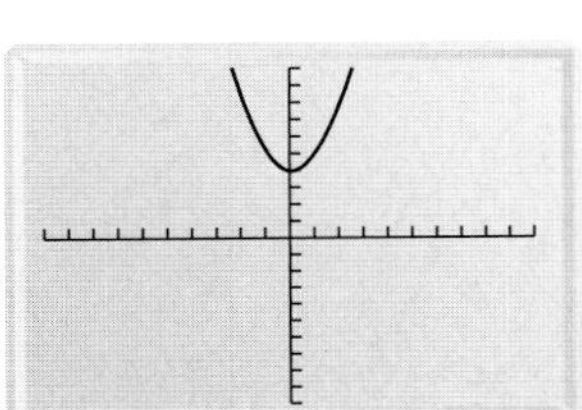

25. 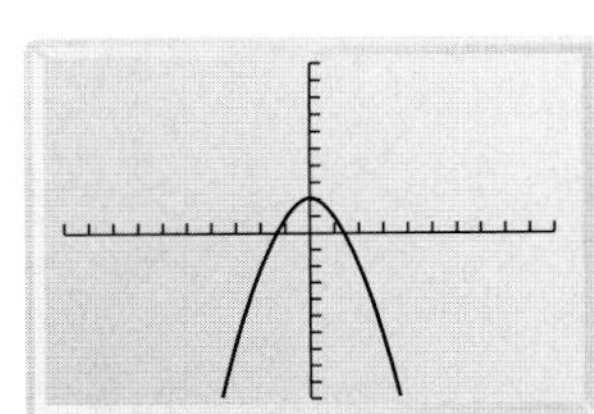

26. 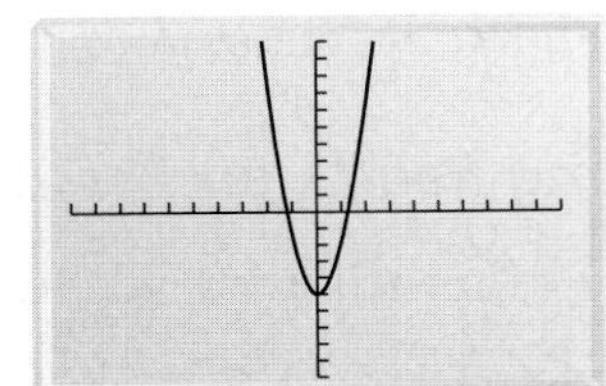

Give the letter of the parabola(s) that make each statement true.

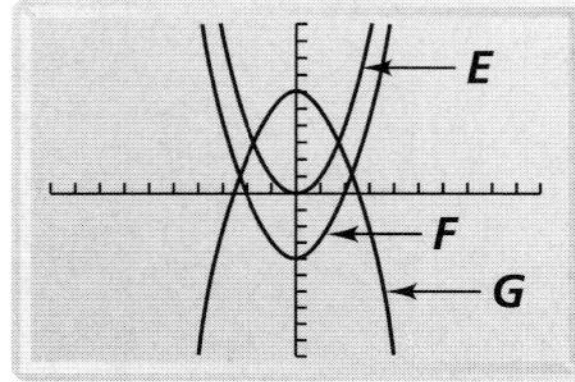

27. $c > 0$

28. $c < 0$

29. $a > 0$

30. $a < 0$

31. The function has a maximum.

32. The function has a minimum.

33. a. **Landscaping** The plan for a rectangular patio has a square garden centered in the patio with sides parallel to the sides of the patio. The patio is 20 ft long by 12 ft wide. If each side of the garden is x ft, the function $y = 240 - x^2$ gives the area of the patio in ft^2. Graph this function.
    b. What values make sense for the domain? Explain why.
    c. What is the range of the function? Explain why.

34. **Architecture** An architect wants to design an archway with these requirements.
    - The archway is 6 ft wide and has vertical sides 7 ft high.
    - The top of the archway is modeled by the function $y = -\frac{1}{3}x^2 + 10$.

    a. Sketch the architect's design by drawing vertical lines 7 units high at $x = -3$ and $x = 3$ and graphing the portion of the quadratic function that lies between $x = -3$ and $x = 3$.
    b. The plan for the archway is changed so that the top is modeled by the function $y = -0.5x^2 + 11.5$. Make a revised sketch of the archway.
    c. **Research** Find out how arches were used by the architects of ancient Rome or during the Middle Ages.

Exercises MIXED REVIEW

Write an equation of the line perpendicular to the given line through the given point.

35. $y = 5x - 2$; $(7, 0)$

36. $y = -2x + 9$; $(3, 5)$

37. $y = 0.5x$; $(-8, -2)$

38. $x + y = 6$; $(3, 1)$

39. $y - 4x = 2$; $(0, 3)$

40. $y = -6x - 2$; $(0, 0)$

41. **Real Estate** Fox Island is a 4.5-acre island in Rhode Island. It has an assessed value of \$290,400. Use a proportion to find out how much a similar 2-acre island nearby might be worth.

Getting Ready for Lesson 7-3

Find $\frac{-b}{2a}$ for each quadratic function.

42. $y = x^2 + 4x - 2$

43. $y = -8x^2 + x + 13$

44. $y = 6x^2 + x + 7$

7-3 Graphing Quadratic Functions

What You'll Learn

- Graphing quadratic functions of the form $y = ax^2 + bx + c$
- Finding the axis of symmetry and vertex
- Graphing quadratic inequalities

...And Why

To solve problems involving weather and road safety

What You'll Need

- graph paper

WORK TOGETHER

To find the reflection of the point $(-1, 2)$ over the line $x = 2$, fold your paper on the line. Then mark the image of the original point.

Work with a partner to find the image of each point.

1. Find the reflection over the line $x = -2$.
   a. $(-4, 5)$ b. $(-6, 1)$ c. $(2, -2)$ d. $(-1, 0)$ e. $(0, 4)$

THINK AND DISCUSS

Graphing $y = ax^2 + bx + c$

In the quadratic functions you have graphed so far, $b = 0$. When $b \neq 0$, the parabola shifts right or left. The axis of symmetry is no longer the y-axis.

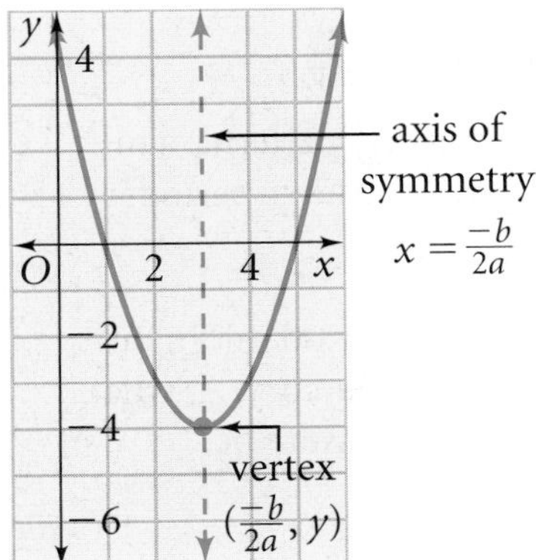

Graph of a Quadratic Function

The graph of $y = ax^2 + bx + c$, where $a \neq 0$, has the line $x = \frac{-b}{2a}$ as its axis of symmetry. The x-coordinate of the vertex is $\frac{-b}{2a}$.

The y-intercept of the graph of a quadratic function is c. This is because substituting $x = 0$ gives you the function value c. You can use the axis of symmetry and the y-intercept to help you graph the function.

Example 1

Graph the quadratic function $f(x) = 5 - 4x - x^2$.

Step 1 Find the y-intercept.

The value of c is 5, so the y-intercept of the graph is 5.

Step 2 Find the equation of the axis of symmetry and the coordinates of the vertex.

$f(x) = -x^2 - 4x + 5$ ← Write the function in standard form.

$x = -\frac{b}{2a} = -\frac{-4}{2(-1)} = -2$ ← Find the equation of the axis of symmetry.

The x-coordinate of the vertex is -2.

$f(x) = -(-2)^2 - 4(-2) + 5$ ← To find the y-coordinate of the vertex, substitute –2 for x.

$f(x) = 9$

The vertex is at $(-2, 9)$.

Step 3 Make a table of values and graph the function.

Pair each point on one side of the axis of symmetry with a point on the other side that will have the same $f(x)$ value.

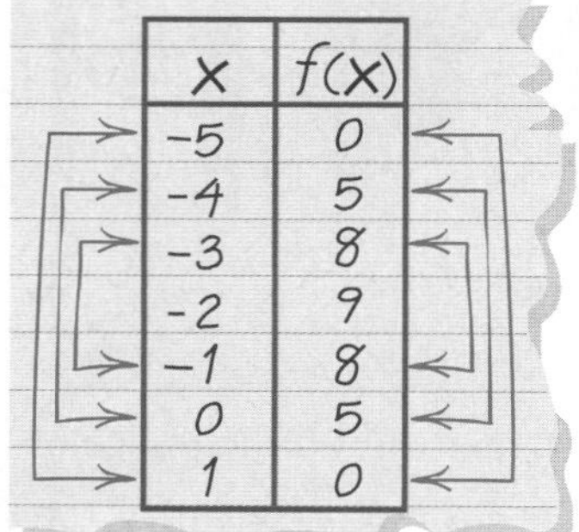

x	f(x)
-5	0
-4	5
-3	8
-2	9
-1	8
0	5
1	0

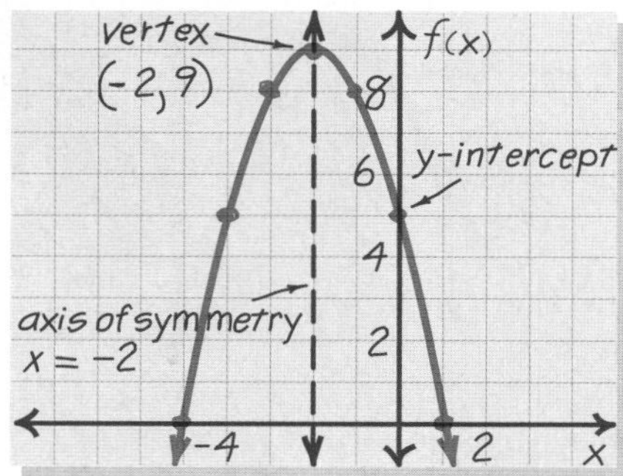

2. **Try This** Graph $y = x^2 - 6x + 9$. Find the equation of the axis of symmetry, the coordinates of the vertex, and the y-intercept.

You can use what you know about quadratic functions to find maximum or minimum values in real-world problems.

Example 2 Relating to the Real World 

Weather Meteorologists use equations to model weather patterns. This function predicts atmospheric pressure over a certain 24-hour period.

$$y = 0.005x^2 - 0.113x + 30.22$$

In the equation, x represents the number of hours after 12:00 midnight and y represents the atmospheric pressure in inches of mercury. At what time will the pressure be lowest? What will the lowest pressure be?

Weather balloons measure conditions in the atmosphere. About 1600 balloons a day are launched in the world.

PROBLEM SOLVING

Look Back Use the graph of the function to check your solution.

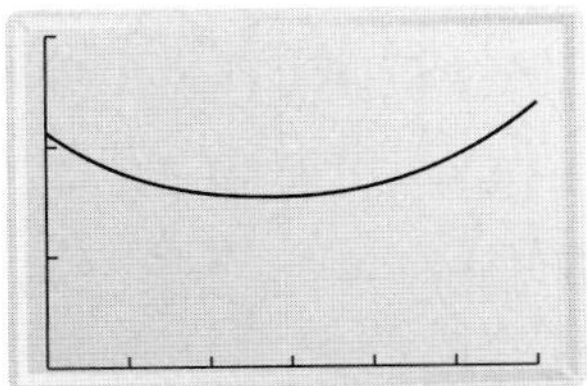

Xmin=0	Ymin=28
Xmax=24	Ymax=31
Xscl=4	Yscl=1

Since the coefficient of x^2 is positive, the curve opens upward and the y-coordinate of the vertex is a minimum.

$$-\frac{b}{2a} = -\frac{-0.113}{2(0.005)} = 11.3 \quad \leftarrow \text{Find the } x\text{-coordinate of the vertex.}$$

After 11.3 hours (at 11:18 A.M.), the pressure will be at its lowest.

$$y = 0.005(11.3)^2 - 0.113(11.3) + 30.22 \quad \leftarrow \text{Substitute 11.3 for } x.$$

$$y = 29.58$$

The minimum pressure will be 29.58 in. of mercury.

3. Why is it important to check the coefficient of the squared term when solving a real-world maximum or minimum problem?

Quadratic Inequalities

Graphing a quadratic inequality is similar to graphing a linear inequality. The curve is dashed if the inequality involves $<$ or $>$. The curve is solid if the inequality involves $\leq$ or $\geq$.

Example 3 Relating to the Real World 

Road Safety An archway over a road is cut out of rock. Its shape is modeled by the quadratic function $y = -0.1x^2 + 12$. Can a camper 6 ft wide and 7 ft high fit under the arch without crossing the median line?

The camper will fit if each point on it satisfies $y < -0.1x^2 + 12$. Graph the inequality $y < -0.1x^2 + 12$.

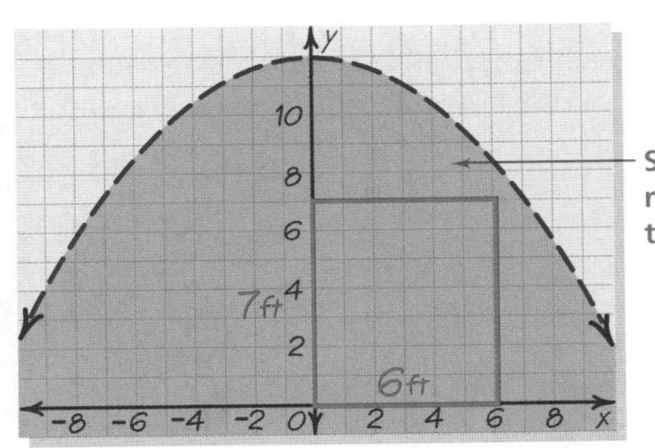

The camper should be able to fit since each point that represents the camper is in the shaded region.

4. Check the solution by showing that the values $x = 6$ and $y = 7$ satisfy the inequality $y < -0.1x^2 + 12$.

5. How does the graph of $y > -0.1x^2 + 12$ differ from the graph above?

6. **Try This** Graph $y \geq x^2 + 2x + 1$.

Exercises ON YOUR OWN

Find the equation of the axis of symmetry and the coordinates of the vertex of the graph of each function.

1. $y = 0.2x^2 + 4$

2. $y = x^2 - 8x - 9$

3. $y = 2x^2 + 4x - 5$

4. $y = 3x^2 - 9x + 5$

5. $f(x) = 4x^2 - 3$

6. $y = 3x^2 - 9$

7. $f(x) = x^2 + 4x + 3$

8. $y = 2x^2 - 6x$

9. $y = 12 + x^2$

Match each graph with its function.

A. $y = x^2 - 6x$
B. $y = x^2 + 6x$
C. $y = -x^2 - 6x$
D. $y = -x^2 + 6x$
E. $y = -x^2 + 6$
F. $y = x^2 - 6$

10.
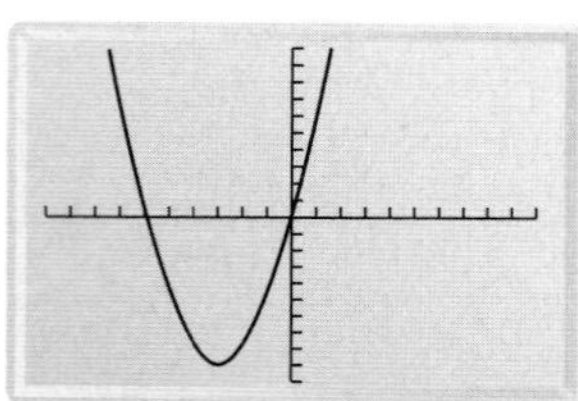

11.
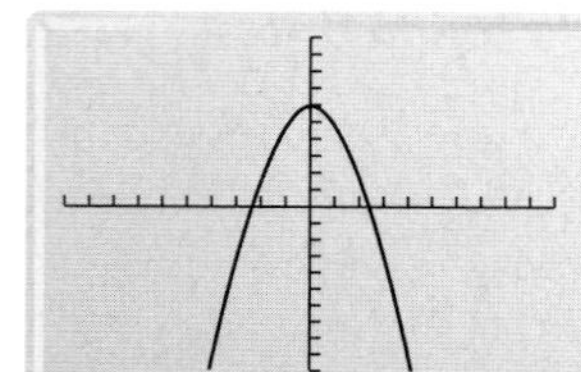

12.
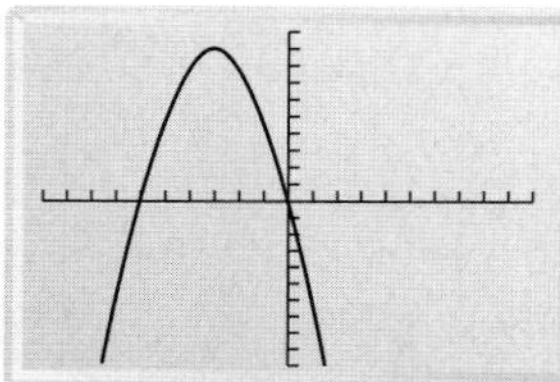

13.
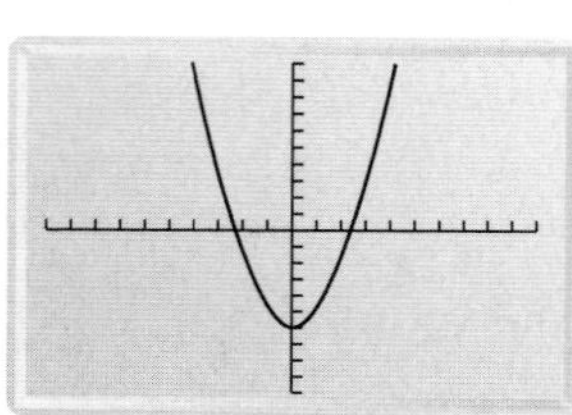

14.
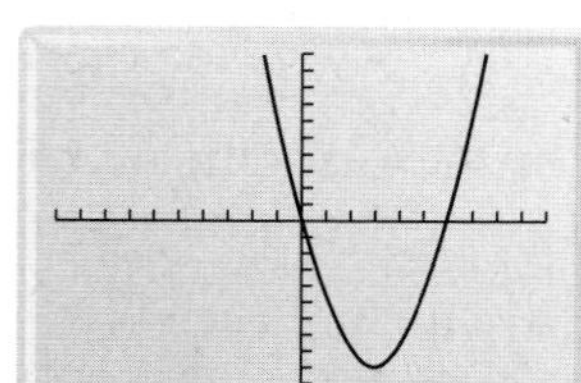

15.
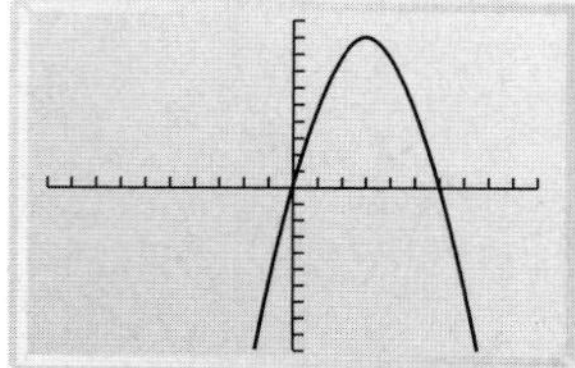

Choose **Graph each function. Use a graphing calculator or a table of values. Label the axis of symmetry, the vertex, and the *y*-intercept.**

16. $f(x) = x^2 - 6x + 8$

17. $y = -x^2 + 4x - 4$

18. $y = x^2 + 1$

19. $y = -x^2 + 4x$

20. $y = -2x^2 + 6$

21. $f(x) = 3x^2 + 6x$

22. $y = x^2 - 4x + 3$

23. $f(x) = -x^2 - 4x - 6$

24. $y = x^2 - 2x + 1$

25. $f(x) = 2x^2 + x - 3$

26. $y = x^2 + 3x + 2$

27. $y = -x^2 + 4x - 7$

28. ***Fireworks*** A skyrocket is shot into the air. Its altitude h in feet after t seconds is given by the function $h = -16t^2 + 128t$.

a. In how many seconds does the skyrocket reach maximum altitude?

b. What is the skyrocket's maximum altitude?

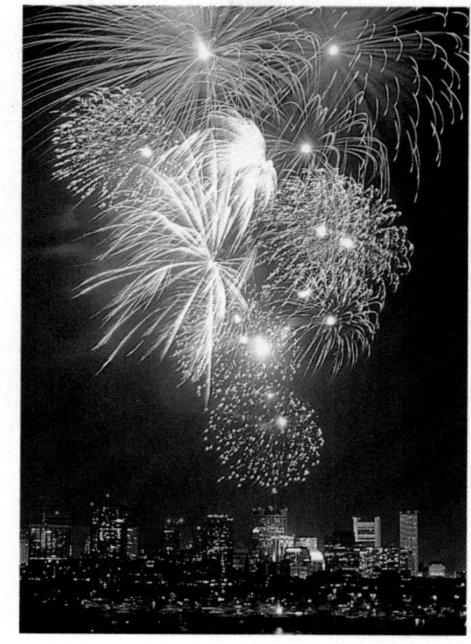

29. ***Gardening*** Suppose you have 80 ft of fence to enclose a rectangular garden. The function $A = 40x - x^2$ gives you the area of the garden in square feet where x is the width in feet. What width gives you the maximum gardening area? What is the maximum area?

30. **Writing** Explain how changing the values of a, b, and c in a quadratic function affects the graph of the function.

Graph each quadratic inequality.

31. $y > x^2$
32. $y < -x^2$
33. $y \leq x^2 + 3$
34. $y < -x^2 + 4$
35. $y \geq -2x^2 + 6$
36. $y > -x^2 + 4x - 4$
37. $y \leq x^2 + 5x + 6$
38. $y < x^2 - x - 6$
39. $y \geq 3x^2 + 6x$

Open-ended **Give a quadratic function for each description.**

40. Its axis of symmetry is to the right of the y-axis.
41. Its graph opens downward and has vertex at (0, 0).
42. Its graph lies entirely above the x-axis.

Chapter Project ***Find Out by Graphing***

To avoid skidding, you want to know what a safe stopping distance is. Assume you are traveling on a dry road and have an average reaction time. The formula $f(x) = 0.044x^2 + 1.1x$ gives you a safe stopping distance in feet, where x is your speed in miles per hour. Make a table of values for speeds of 10, 20, 30, 40, 50, and 60 mi/h. Then graph the function.

Exercises MIXED REVIEW

Find each probability for two rolls of a number cube.

43. P(even and odd)
44. P(7 and 5)
45. P(two odd numbers)
46. P(6 and 2)

47. a. **Rowing** The-Head-of-the-Charles Regatta is a 3 mi rowing race held annually in Cambridge, Massachusetts. In 1994, Xeno Muller won the men's singles title in 17 min, 47 s. What was his pace in mi/h? Round your answer to the nearest tenth.
    b. Muller rowed at 32 strokes/min. How many strokes did he row over the course of the race?

SELF ASSESSMENT **FOR YOUR JOURNAL**

Summarize what you have learned about graphing quadratic functions. Include examples to support your statements.

Getting Ready for Lesson 7-4

Evaluate for $a = -1$, $b = 2$, $c = 3$, and $d = -4$.

48. a^2
49. $-a^2$
50. $-b^2$
51. dc^2
52. $(dc)^2$

What You'll Learn

- Finding square roots
- Using square roots

...And Why

To use square roots in real-world situations, such as finding the distance from a satellite to the horizon

What You'll Need

- calculator

7-4 Square Roots

THINK AND DISCUSS

Finding Square Roots

The diagram shows the relationship between squares and square roots. Every positive number has *two* square roots.

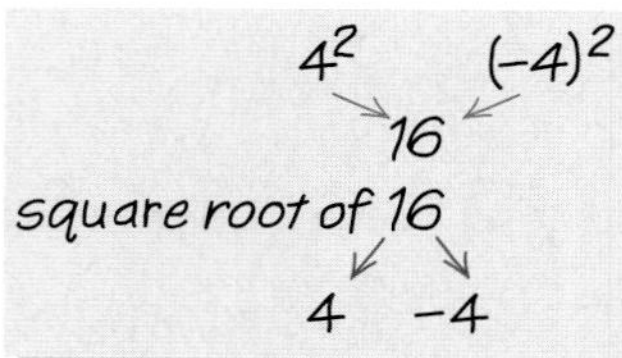

Square Root

If $a^2 = b$, then a is a **square root** of b.

Example: $4^2 = 16$ and $(-4)^2 = 16$, so 4 and -4 are square roots of 16.

A radical symbol $\sqrt{}$ indicates a square root. The expression $\sqrt{16}$ means the **principal** (or positive) **square root** of 16. The expression $-\sqrt{16}$ means the **negative square root** of 16. You can use the symbol ±, read "plus or minus," to indicate both square roots.

Example 1

Simplify each expression.

a. $\sqrt{64} = 8$ ← positive square root

b. $-\sqrt{100} = -10$ ← negative square root

c. $\pm\sqrt{\frac{9}{16}} = \pm\frac{3}{4}$ ← The square roots are $\frac{3}{4}$ and $-\frac{3}{4}$.

d. $\pm\sqrt{0} = 0$ ← There is only one square root of 0.

e. $\sqrt{-16}$ is undefined ← For real numbers, the square root of a negative number is undefined.

1. **Try This** Simplify each expression.
   a. $\sqrt{49}$ b. $\pm\sqrt{36}$ c. $-\sqrt{121}$ d. $\sqrt{\frac{1}{25}}$

QUICK REVIEW

Rational and irrational numbers make up the set of *real numbers.* In decimal form, *rational* numbers terminate or repeat. *Irrational* numbers continue without repeating number patterns.

Some square roots are rational numbers and some are irrational numbers.

Rational: $\pm\sqrt{81} = \pm 9$, $-\sqrt{1.44} = -1.2$, $\sqrt{\frac{4}{9}} = \frac{2}{3} = 0.\overline{6}$

Irrational: $-\sqrt{5} = -2.23606797\ldots$, $\sqrt{\frac{1}{3}} = 0.57735026\ldots$

2. **Try This** Classify each expression as *rational* or *irrational.*
   a. $\sqrt{8}$ b. $\pm\sqrt{225}$ c. $-\sqrt{75}$ d. $\sqrt{\frac{1}{4}}$

Math A Test Prep

1 $\sqrt{83}$ is between which pair of consecutive integers?
(1) 7 and 8
(2) 8 and 9
(3) 9 and 10
(4) 41 and 42

2 Describe the graph of the inequality $y > -4x^2 - 4x + 2$. Tell the direction it opens, the shape, and the location of any shading. Include its vertex and axis of symmetry.

Estimating and Using Square Roots

The squares of integers are called **perfect squares.**

consecutive integers:	1	2	3	4	5	6	7
	↓	↓	↓	↓	↓	↓	↓
consecutive perfect squares:	1	4	9	16	25	36	49

You can estimate square roots by using perfect squares and by using a calculator.

Example 2

Estimation Between what two consecutive integers is $\sqrt{14.52}$?

$\sqrt{9} < \sqrt{14.52} < \sqrt{16}$ ← **14.52 is between the two consecutive square numbers 9 and 16.**

$3 < \sqrt{14.52} < 4$

$\sqrt{14.52}$ is between 3 and 4.

3. Try This Between what two consecutive integers is $-\sqrt{105}$?

Example 3

Calculator Find $\sqrt{14.52}$ to the nearest hundredth.

[√] 14.52 [ENTER] 3.810511777 ← **Use a calculator.**

$\sqrt{14.52} \approx 3.81$

4. Critical Thinking How can you use consecutive perfect squares to mentally check calculator answers for square roots?

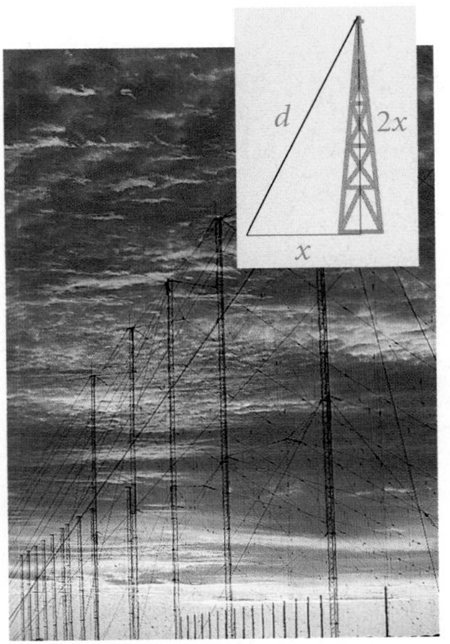

Example 4 Relating to the Real World 

Towers A tower is supported with a wire. The formula $d = \sqrt{x^2 + (2x)^2}$ gives the length d of the wire for the tower at the left. Find the length of the wire if $x = 12$ ft.

$d = \sqrt{x^2 + (2x)^2}$

$d = \sqrt{12^2 + (2 \cdot 12)^2}$ ← **Substitute 12 for x.**

$d = \sqrt{144 + 576}$ ← **Simplify.**

$d = \sqrt{720}$

$d = 26.83281573$ ← **Use a calculator.**

$d \approx 26.8$

The wire is about 26.8 ft long.

5. Try This Suppose the tower is 140 ft tall. How long is the supporting wire?

Exercises ON YOUR OWN

Find both the principal and negative square root of each number.

1. 169
2. 1.96
3. $\frac{1}{9}$
4. 900
5. 0.25
6. $\frac{36}{49}$
7. 1.21
8. 1681

Tell whether each expression is *rational* or *irrational*.

9. $\sqrt{37}$
10. $-\sqrt{0.04}$
11. $\pm\sqrt{\frac{1}{5}}$
12. $-\sqrt{\frac{16}{121}}$

Between what two consecutive integers is each square root?

13. $\sqrt{35}$
14. $\sqrt{27}$
15. $-\sqrt{245}$
16. $\sqrt{880}$

Calculator **Use a calculator to simplify each expression. Round to the nearest hundredth.**

17. $\sqrt{12}$
18. $-\sqrt{203}$
19. $\sqrt{11{,}550}$
20. $-\sqrt{150}$

21. **Sports** The elasticity coefficient e of a ball relates the height r of its rebound to the height h from which it is dropped. You can find the elasticity coefficient using the function $e = \sqrt{\frac{r}{h}}$.
    a. What is the elasticity coefficient for a tennis ball that rebounds 3 ft after it is dropped from a height of 3.5 ft?
    b. **Critical Thinking** Suppose that the elasticity coefficient of a basketball is 0.88. How high is its rebound if it is dropped 6 ft?

22. **Critical Thinking** What number other than 0 is its own square root?

Find the square roots of each number.

23. 0.36
24. 144
25. $\frac{25}{16}$
26. 0.01
27. 400
28. 0
29. 625
30. $\frac{9}{49}$
31. $\frac{1}{81}$
32. 1.69
33. 729
34. 2.25

35. a. **Space** Find the distance to the horizon from a satellite 4200 km above Earth. The formula $d = \sqrt{12{,}800h + h^2}$ tells you the distance d in kilometers to the horizon from a satellite h kilometers above Earth.
    b. Find the distance to the horizon from a satellite 3600 km above Earth.

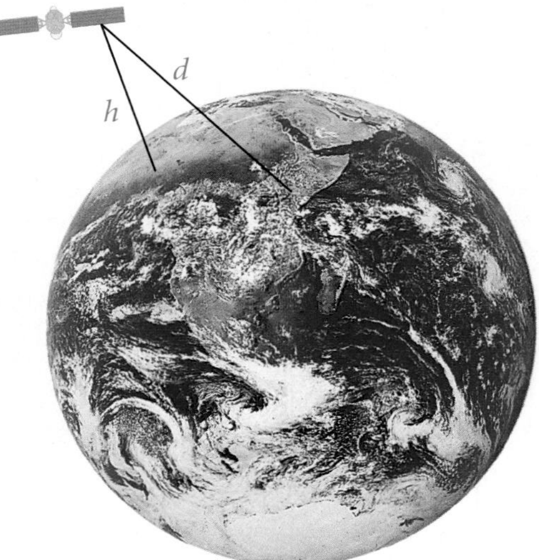

36. **Standardized Test Prep** If $x^2 = 16$ and $y^2 = 25$, choose the least possible value for the expression $y - x$.
    A. -1 B. 0 C. 1
    D. -9 E. -4

37. In the cartoon, to what number is the golfer referring?

from cartoon *Bound and Gagged*

Choose **Use a calculator, paper and pencil, or mental math. Find the value of each expression. If the value is irrational, round to the nearest hundredth.**

38. $\sqrt{441}$
39. $-\sqrt{\frac{4}{25}}$
40. $\sqrt{2}$
41. $\sqrt{\frac{1}{36}}$
42. $-\sqrt{1.6}$
43. $-\sqrt{157}$
44. $\sqrt{200}$
45. $-\sqrt{13}$
46. $\sqrt{30}$
47. $\sqrt{1089}$
48. $-\sqrt{0.64}$
49. $\sqrt{41}$

50. **Writing** Explain the difference between $-\sqrt{1}$ and $\sqrt{-1}$.

51. **Open-ended** Find two integers a and b, both between 1 and 25, such that $a^2 + b^2$ is a perfect square.

Tell whether each expression is *rational, irrational,* or *undefined.*

52. $-\sqrt{3600}$
53. $\sqrt{8}$
54. $\sqrt{-25}$
55. $\sqrt{6.25}$
56. $\sqrt{12.96}$
57. $\sqrt{129.6}$
58. $-\sqrt{12.96}$
59. $\sqrt{-12.96}$

60. **Physics** If you drop an object, the time t in seconds that it takes to fall d feet is given by $t = \sqrt{\frac{d}{16}}$.

a. Find the time it takes an object to fall 400 ft.
b. Find the time it takes an object to fall 1600 ft.
c. **Critical Thinking** In part (b), the object falls four times as far as in part (a). Does it take four times as long to fall? Explain.

Tell whether each statement is *true* or *false*. If the statement is false, rewrite it as a true statement.

61. $6 < \sqrt{38} < 7$
62. $-7 < -\sqrt{56} < -6$
63. $-4 < -\sqrt{17} < -5$
64. $3.3 \leq \sqrt{10.25} < 3.4$
65. $-16 < -\sqrt{280} < -15$
66. $21 < \sqrt{436} < 22$
67. $-38 < -\sqrt{1300} < -37$
68. $-9 \leq -\sqrt{72} < -8$
69. $0.1 < \sqrt{0.03} < 0.2$

Chapter Project: Find Out by Calculating

Suppose a car left a skid mark d feet long. The formulas shown will estimate the speed s in miles per hour at which the car was traveling when the brakes were applied. Use the formulas to complete the table of estimated speeds.

- Why do you think the estimates of speed do not double when the skid marks double in length?
- Based on these results, what conclusions can you make about safe following distances?

Traveling Speed		
Dry Road	$s = \sqrt{27d}$	
Wet Road	$s = \sqrt{13.5d}$	
Skid Mark Length (d)	**Estimated Speed (s)**	
	Dry Road	Wet Road
60 ft	■	■
120 ft	■	■

Exercises MIXED REVIEW

Solve each inequality. Graph the solution on a number line.

70. $2x > 8$ **71.** $14 < -7s$ **72.** $z - 1 \geq -1$ **73.** $-2 - b > 4$

74. $5b + 4 < -6$ **75.** $-2c \geq 5c - 1$ **76.** $8(m - 3) \leq 4$ **77.** $2 > 7 - 3t$

78. One in four residents of the United States has myopia, or nearsightedness. What is the probability that two people chosen at random are both nearsighted?

Getting Ready for Lesson 7-5

Solve each equation.

79. $3x - 14 = 27$ **80.** $4(y - 5) = 20$ **81.** $-6b + 12 = 12$ **82.** $3 - 9m = 0$

Exercises CHECKPOINT

Graph each quadratic function. Find the vertex of each parabola.

1. $y = 4x^2$ **2.** $y = 2x^2 + 7$ **3.** $y = -x^2 - 2x + 10$

Choose **Use a calculator, paper and pencil, or mental math to find the value of each square root. Round to the nearest hundredth.**

4. $\sqrt{7}$ **5.** $-\sqrt{100}$ **6.** $\sqrt{23}$ **7.** $\sqrt{144}$ **8.** $-\sqrt{150}$ **9.** $-\sqrt{\frac{1}{9}}$

10. *Writing* What does the rule for a quadratic function tell you about how the graph of the function will look?

11. *Open-ended* Give an example of a quadratic function for each of the following descriptions.

a. Its graph opens downward. **b.** Its graph is wider than the graph of $y = \frac{1}{2}x^2 - 3$.

What You'll Learn

- Solving quadratic equations in $ax^2 = c$ form
- Finding if a quadratic equation has two solutions, one solution, or no solution

...And Why

To solve real-world problems, such as finding the radius of a pond

What You'll Need

- calculator

7-5 Solving Quadratic Equations

WORK TOGETHER

1. Work with a partner. Find the x-intercepts of each graph.
   a. $y = 2x - 3$
   b. $y = -x^2 - 2x + 3$

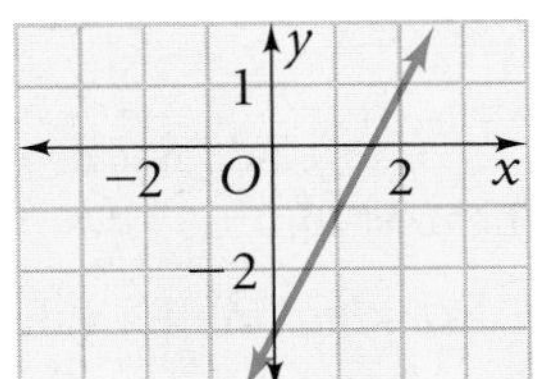

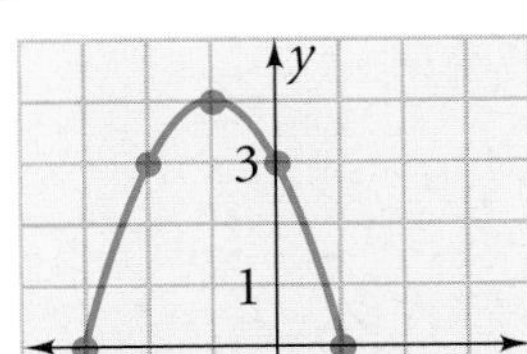

2. Use the graph in Question 1(a) to find the solution of $2x - 3 = 0$.
3. Are the x-intercepts that you found in Question 1(b) solutions of $-x^2 - 2x + 3 = 0$? Explain.
4. Graph $y = x^2 + x - 6 = 0$.
5. a. Where does the graph of $y = x^2 + x - 6$ cross the x-axis?
   b. Do the values you found in part (a) satisfy the equation $x^2 + x - 6 = 0$?

THINK AND DISCUSS

Using Square Roots to Solve Equations

In the Work Together, you investigated a quadratic equation and its related quadratic function. Any values that make the equation true are solutions.

Standard Form of a Quadratic Equation

A **quadratic equation** is an equation that can be written in **standard form**:

$$ax^2 + bx + c = 0, \text{ where } a \neq 0$$

6. Write $6x^2 = 5x - 12$ in standard form.
7. Is $5x - 3 = 0$ a quadratic equation? Why or why not?

There are two square roots for numbers greater than 0. So there are two solutions for an equation like $x^2 = 36$. You can solve equations in the form $x^2 = a$ by finding the square roots of each side.

$$x^2 = 36 \longrightarrow x = \pm 6$$

Example 1

Solve $2x^2 - 98 = 0$.

$$2x^2 - 98 = 0 + 98 \quad \longleftarrow \text{Add 98 to each side.}$$
$$2x^2 = 98$$
$$x^2 = 49 \quad \longleftarrow \text{Divide each side by 2.}$$
$$\sqrt{x^2} = \pm\sqrt{49} \quad \longleftarrow \text{Find the square roots.}$$
$$x = \pm 7$$

8. **Try This** Use a calculator to solve $x^2 - 7 = 0$. Round your solutions to the nearest tenth.

9. **Critical Thinking** Find a value for c so that the equation $x^2 - c = 0$ has 11 and -11 as solutions.

You can solve many geometric problems by finding square roots.

Example 2 Relating to the Real World 

City Planning A city is planning a circular duck pond for a new park. The depth of the pond will be 4 ft. Because of water resources, the maximum volume will be 20,000 ft^3. Find the radius of the pond. Use the equation $V = \pi r^2 h$, where V is the volume, r is the radius, and h is the depth.

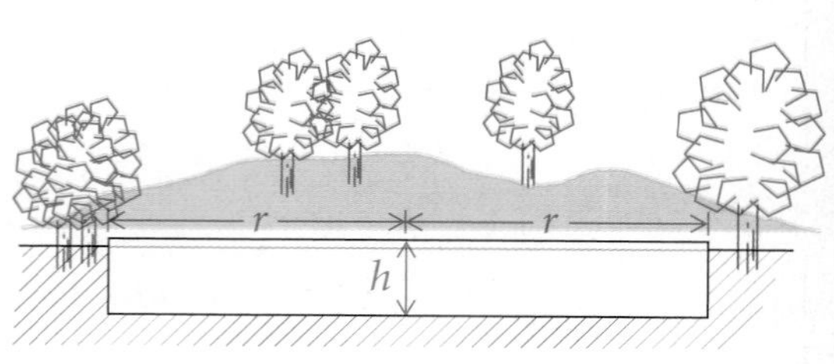

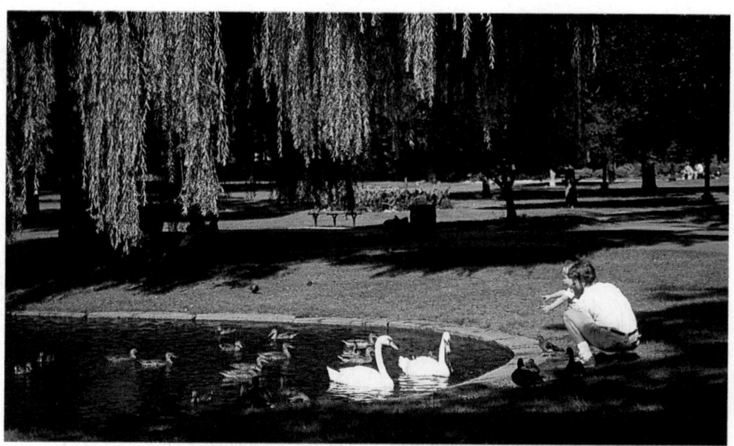

$$V = \pi r^2 h$$
$$20{,}000 = \pi r^2(4) \quad \longleftarrow \text{Substitute 20,000 for } V \text{ and 4 for } h.$$
$$\frac{20{,}000}{\pi(4)} = r^2 \quad \longleftarrow \text{Put in calculator-ready form.}$$
$$\sqrt{\frac{20{,}000}{\pi(4)}} = r \quad \longleftarrow \text{Find the principal square root.}$$
$$39.89422804 = r \quad \longleftarrow \text{Use a calculator.}$$

The pond will have a radius of about 39.9 ft.

10. **Critical Thinking** Why is the principal square root the only root that makes sense in Example 2?

11. **Justify** this step in Example 2:
If $20{,}000 = \pi r^2(4)$, then $\frac{20{,}000}{\pi(4)} = r^2$.

12. **Calculator** Which keystrokes can you use to find r in Example 2?
A. [√‾] [(] 20000 [÷] [(] [π] [×] 4 [)] [)] [ENTER]
B. [√‾] 20000 [÷] [π] [×] 4 [ENTER]

13. **a.** **Try This** Suppose the pond could have a volume of 40,000 ft^3. What will be the radius of the pond if the depth is not changed?
b. **Critical Thinking** Does the radius of the pond double when the volume doubles? Explain.

Finding the Number of Solutions

You have seen quadratic equations that have two real numbers as solutions. For real numbers, a quadratic equation can have two solutions, one solution, or no solution.

You can use a graph to find the solution(s) of a quadratic equation by finding the x-intercepts of the related quadratic function.

Example 3

Solve each equation by graphing the related function.

a. $x^2 - 4 = 0$ **b.** $x^2 = 0$ **c.** $x^2 + 4 = 0$

Graph $y = x^2 - 4$. Graph $y = x^2$. Graph $y = x^2 + 4$.

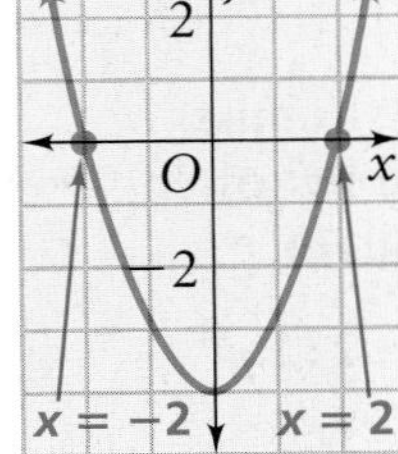

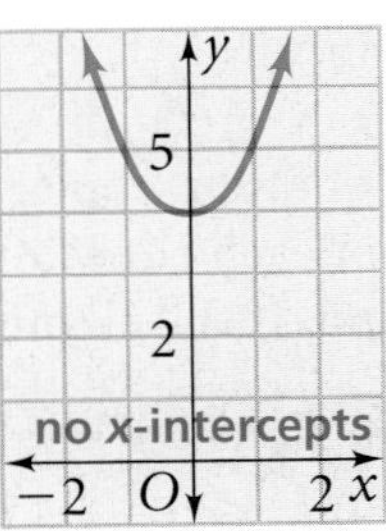

There are two solutions, $x = \pm 2$. There is one solution, $x = 0$. There is no solution.

14. **a.** **Critical Thinking** For what values of c will $x^2 = c$ have two solutions?
b. For what value of c will $x^2 = c$ have one solution?
c. For what values of c will $x^2 = c$ have no solution?

15. **Mental Math** Tell the number of solutions for each equation.
a. $x^2 = -36$ **b.** $x^2 - 12 = 6$ **c.** $x^2 - 15 = -15$

Exercises ON YOUR OWN

Choose **Solve each equation by graphing, using mental math, or using paper and pencil. If the equation has no solution, write *no solution*.**

1. $x^2 = 4$
2. $x^2 = 49$
3. $3x^2 + 27 = 0$
4. $x^2 + 25 = 25$
5. $3x^2 - 7 = -34$
6. $x^2 - 225 = 0$
7. $49x^2 - 16 = -7$
8. $x^2 - 9 = 16$
9. $4x^2 = 25$
10. $x^2 + 36 = 0$
11. $4x^2 - 100 = -100$
12. $x^2 - 63 = 81$

13. **Critical Thinking** Michael solved $x^2 + 25 = 0$ and found the solutions -5 and 5. Explain the mistake that Michael made.

Solve each equation. Round solutions to the nearest tenth.

14. $b^2 = 3$
15. $8x^2 = 64$
16. $n^2 - 5 = 16$
17. $3m^2 + 7 = 13$
18. $2x^2 - 179 = 0$
19. $b^2 - 1 = 20$

Model each problem with a quadratic equation. Then solve.

20. **Photography** Find the dimensions of the square picture that make the area of the picture equal to 75% of the total area enclosed by the frame.

21. **Geometry** Find the radius of a sphere with surface area 160 in.^{2}. Use the formula $A = 4\pi r^2$, where A is the surface area and r is the radius of the sphere. Round your answer to the nearest tenth of an inch.

x

12 in.

Susan La Flesche Picotte (1865–1915) was a physician and the leader of the Omaha people.

For each equation, you are given a statement about the number of solutions of each equation. If the claim is true, verify it by solving the equation. If the claim is false, write a correct statement.

22. $n^2 + 2 = 11$; there are two solutions.
23. $g^2 = -49$; there are two solutions.
24. $x^2 + 9 = 25$; there is one solution.
25. $4x^2 - 96 = 0$; there is one solution.
26. $-4r^2 = -64$; there are two solutions.
27. $4n^2 - 256 = 0$; there are two solutions.
28. $4b^2 + 9 = 9$; there are two solutions.
29. $-x^2 - 15 = 0$; there is no solution.

30. **Open-ended** Suppose you have 225 square tiles, all the same size. You can tile one surface using all the tiles. How could you tile more than one square surface using all the tiles? No surface can have only one tile.

31. **Painting** Suppose you have a can of paint that will cover 400 ft^2. Find the radius of the largest circle you can paint. Round your answer to the nearest tenth of a foot. (*Hint:* Use the formula $A = \pi r^2$.)

Physics **Use this information for Exercises 32–35.** The time t it takes a pendulum to make a complete swing back and forth depends on the length of the pendulum. This formula relates the length of a pendulum ℓ in meters to the time t in seconds.

$$\ell = \frac{2.45t^2}{\pi^2}$$

32. Find the length of the pendulum if $t = 1$ s. Round to the nearest tenth.

33. Find t if $\ell = 1.6$ m. Round to the nearest tenth.

34. Find t if $\ell = 2.2$ m. Round to the nearest tenth.

35. **Writing** You can adjust a clock with a pendulum by making the pendulum longer or shorter. If a clock is running slowly, would you lengthen or shorten the pendulum to make the clock run faster? Explain.

36. **Standardized Test Prep** Suppose that $2x^2 - 36 = x^2 - 49$. Which statement is correct?

A. The equation has two real solutions.
B. The equation has no real solutions.
C. The equation has exactly one real solution.
D. You cannot determine the number of real solutions.

Solve each equation. If the equation has no solution, write *no solution*.

37. $5x^2 + 9 = 40$

38. $2x^2 + 8x^2 + 16 = 16$

39. $8x^2 - 4 - 3x^2 + 6 = 30$

40. $x^2 + 3 - 2x^2 - 9 = 30$

41. $3x^2 - 10 + 5x^2 + 3 = 25$

42. $6x^2 + 22 + 2x^2 + 50 = 60$

Exercises MIXED REVIEW

Solve each system of equations.

43. $3x + 2y = 12$
$x - 2y = -4$

44. $-x + 4y = 18$
$3x + y = -2$

45. $0.4x - 1.2y = 24$
$1.6x + 0.6y = 15$

46. **a.** **Space** NASA astronauts must be between 4 ft $10\frac{1}{2}$ in. and 6 ft 4 in. tall. Russian cosmonauts must be between 5 ft $4\frac{1}{2}$ in. and 6 ft. Change these values to inches. Use a number line to graph an inequality that models each situation.

b. Use a number line to graph the heights that are acceptable for an astronaut but not acceptable for a cosmonaut.

Getting Ready for Lesson 7-6

Evaluate each expression. Round to the nearest hundredth, where necessary.

47. $\sqrt{5^2 - 15}$

48. $\sqrt{36 + 64}$

49. $\sqrt{(-4)^2 - (2)(-3)}$

50. $-3 - \sqrt{36}$

Math ToolboX

Technology

Finding Roots

After Lesson 7-5

The solutions of a quadratic equation are the x-intercepts of the related quadratic function. The solutions of a quadratic equation and the related x-intercepts are often called *roots of the equation* or *roots of the function.*

Example

Use a graphing calculator to solve $x^2 - 6x + 3 = 0$.

Step 1

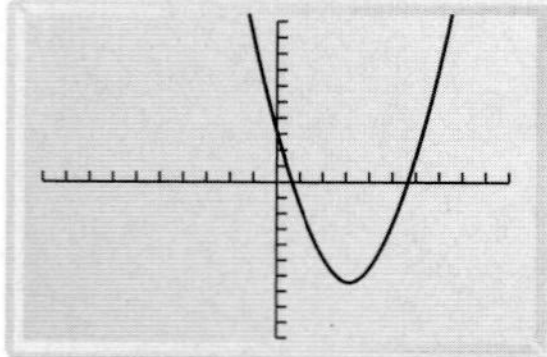

Enter $y = x^2 - 6x + 3$. Use the CALC feature. Select 2:ROOT. The calculator will plot the graph.

Step 2

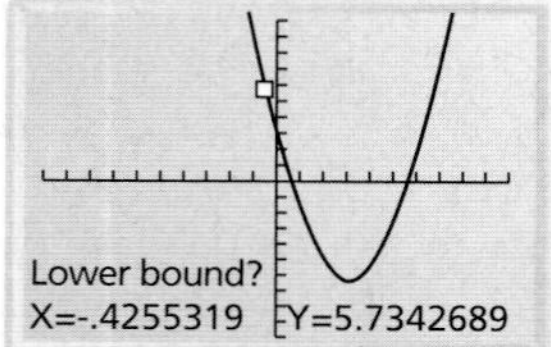

Move the cursor to the left of the first x-intercept. Press ENTER to set the lower bound.

Step 3

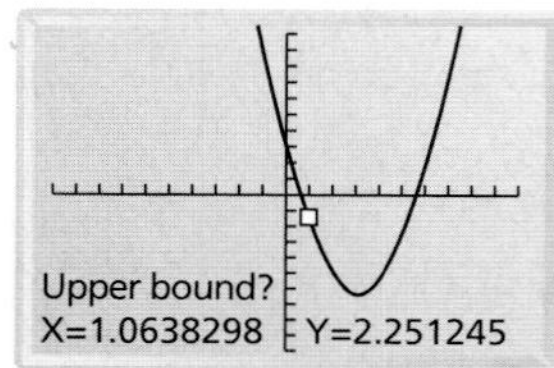

Move the cursor slightly to the right of the intercept. Press ENTER to set the upper bound.

Step 4

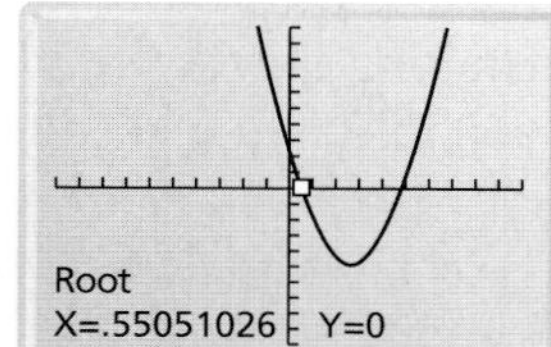

Press ENTER to display the first root, which is about 0.55.

Repeating the steps near the second intercept, you find the second root is about 5.45. So, the solutions are about 0.55 and 5.45.

Suppose you cannot see both of the x-intercepts on your graph. You can find the range for the x-axis by using the TABLE feature. The calculator screen at the right shows part of the table for $y = 2x^2 - 48x + 285$.

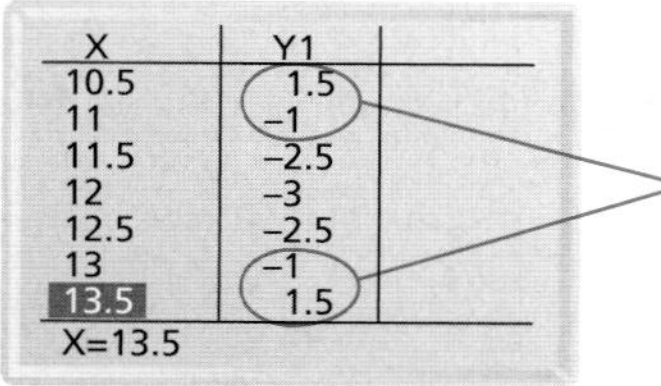

X	Y1
10.5	1.5
11	−1
11.5	−2.5
12	−3
12.5	−2.5
13	−1
13.5	1.5

X=13.5

The graph crosses the x-axis when the values for y change signs. So the range of values of x should include 10.5 and 13.5.

1. Find the x-intercepts of $y = 2x^2 - 48x + 285$.

Use a graph to solve each equation.

2. $x^2 - 6x - 16 = 0$
3. $2x^2 + x - 6 = 0$
4. $\frac{1}{3}x^2 + 8x - 3 = 0$
5. $x^2 - 18x + 5 = 0$
6. $0.25x^2 - 8x - 45 = 0$
7. $0.5x^2 + 3x - 36 = 0$
8. **Writing** Solve $3x^2 = 48$ using a calculator or paper and pencil. Explain why you chose the method you used.

What You'll Learn

- Using the quadratic formula to solve quadratic equations

...And Why

To investigate real-world situations, such as the vertical motion of model rockets

What You'll Need

- calculator

7-6 Using the Quadratic Formula

THINK AND DISCUSS

In Lesson 7-5, you solved some simple quadratic equations by finding square roots and by graphing. In this lesson, you will learn to solve any quadratic equation by using the **quadratic formula.** In Chapter 10 you will learn additional ways to solve a quadratic equation.

Quadratic Formula

If $ax^2 + bx + c = 0$ and $a \neq 0$, then $x = \dfrac{-b \pm \sqrt{b^2 - 4ac}}{2a}$.

Example 1

Solve $x^2 + 5x + 6 = 0$ by using the quadratic formula.

$$x = \frac{-b \pm \sqrt{b^2 - 4ac}}{2a}$$ ← Use the quadratic formula.

$$x = \frac{-(5) \pm \sqrt{5^2 - (4)(1)(6)}}{2(1)}$$ ← Substitute 1 for *a*, 5 for *b*, and 6 for *c*.

$$x = \frac{-5 \pm \sqrt{1}}{2}$$

$$x = \frac{-5 + 1}{2} \quad \text{or} \quad x = \frac{-5 - 1}{2}$$ ← Write two solutions.

$$x = -2 \quad \text{or} \quad x = -3$$

The solutions are -2 and -3.

Check for $x = -2$

$$(-2)^2 + 5(-2) + 6 \stackrel{?}{=} 0$$
$$4 - 10 + 6 \stackrel{?}{=} 0$$
$$0 = 0 \checkmark$$

for $x = -3$

$$(-3)^2 + 5(-3) + 6 \stackrel{?}{=} 0$$
$$9 - 15 + 6 \stackrel{?}{=} 0$$
$$0 = 0 \checkmark$$

PROBLEM SOLVING

Look Back Could you check the solutions by graphing? Explain.

1. **Try This** Use the quadratic formula to solve $x^2 - 2x - 8 = 0$.
2. What values would you use for *a*, *b*, and *c* in the quadratic formula to solve $2x^2 = 140$?
3. How many solutions does $9x^2 - 24x + 16 = 0$ have? Explain.

When the quantity under the radical sign in the quadratic formula is not a perfect square, you can use a calculator to approximate the solutions of an equation.

Example 2

Solve $2x^2 + 4x - 7 = 0$. Round the solutions to the nearest hundredth.

$$x = \frac{-b \pm \sqrt{b^2 - 4ac}}{2a}$$ ← Use the quadratic formula.

$$x = \frac{-4 \pm \sqrt{4^2 - (4)(2)(-7)}}{2(2)}$$ ← Substitute 2 for a, 4 for b, and −7 for c.

$$x = \frac{-4 \pm \sqrt{72}}{4}$$

$$x = \frac{-4 + \sqrt{72}}{4} \text{ or } x = \frac{-4 - \sqrt{72}}{4}$$ ← Write two solutions.

$$x \approx \frac{-4 + 8.485281374}{4} \text{ or } x \approx \frac{-4 - 8.485281374}{4}$$ ← Use a calculator.

$x \approx 1.12$ or $x \approx -3.12$

The solutions are approximately 1.12 and −3.12.

Check Graph the related function $y = 2x^2 + 4x - 7$. Use the ROOT option to find the x-intercept.

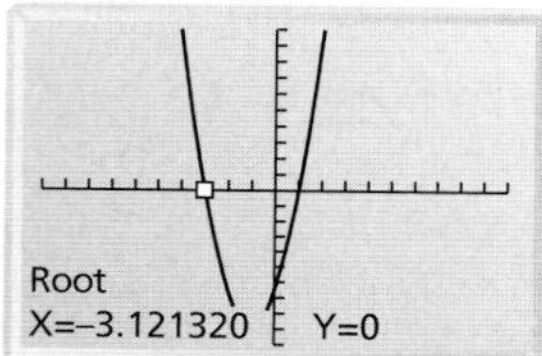

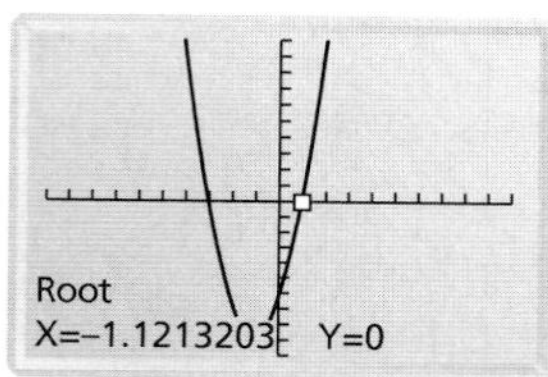

4. Do the graphing calculator screens indicate that the solutions in Example 2 check? Explain.

5. Try This Find the solutions of $-3x^2 + 5x - 2 = 0$. Round to the nearest hundredth.

The quadratic formula is important in physics when finding vertical motion. When an object is dropped, thrown, or launched either straight up or down, you can use the **vertical motion formula** to find the height of the object.

Vertical motion formula: $h = -16t^2 + vt + s$
h is the height of the object in feet.
t is the time it takes an object to rise or fall to a given height.
v is the starting velocity in feet per second.
s is the starting height in feet.

$s = 0$ because the rocket is launched from the ground.

Example 3 **Relating to the Real World** 

Model Rockets Members of the science club launch a model rocket from ground level with starting velocity of 96 ft/s. After how many seconds will the rocket have an altitude of 128 ft?

$h = -16t^2 + vt + s$ ← Use the vertical motion formula.

$128 = -16t^2 + 96t + 0$ ← Substitute 128 for h, 96 for v, and 0 for s.

$0 = -16t^2 + 96t - 128$ ← Subtract 128 from each side.

$x = \dfrac{-b \pm \sqrt{b^2 - 4ac}}{2a}$ ← Use the quadratic formula.

$t = \dfrac{-(96) \pm \sqrt{(96)^2 - (4)(-16)(-128)}}{2(-16)}$ ← Substitute −16 for a, 96 for b, and −128 for c.

$t = \dfrac{-96 \pm \sqrt{9216 - 8192}}{-32}$ ← Simplify.

$t = \dfrac{-96 \pm \sqrt{1024}}{-32}$

$t = \dfrac{-96 + 32}{-32}$ or $t = \dfrac{-96 - 32}{-32}$ ← Write two solutions and simplify.

$t = 2$ or $t = 4$

The rocket is 128 ft above the ground after 2 s and after 4 s.

6. **Critical Thinking** Use a diagram to explain how the rocket could have an altitude of 128 ft at two different times.

7. a. **Try This** In Example 3, after how many seconds of flight does the rocket have an altitude of 80 ft?
   b. **Critical Thinking** Estimate the number of seconds it will take the rocket to reach its maximum height. Explain how you made your estimate.

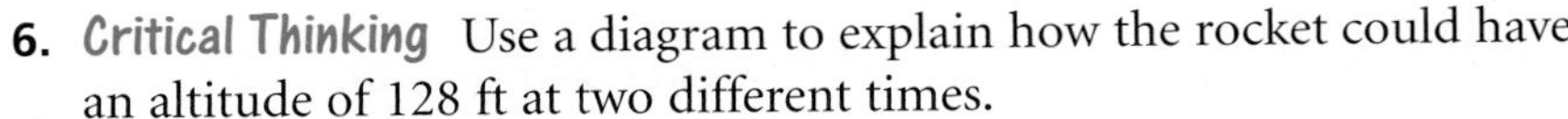

Exercises ON YOUR OWN

Write each equation in standard form.

1. $3x^2 - 10 = -13x$
2. $4x^2 = 144x$
3. $x^2 - 3x = 2x + 7$
4. $5x^2 = -7x - 8$
5. $-12x^2 + 25x = 84$
6. $-x^2 + 9x = 4x - 12$

Use the quadratic formula to solve each equation. Round solutions to the nearest hundredth when necessary.

7. $6x^2 + 7x - 5 = 0$
8. $3x^2 - 3x - 1 = 0$
9. $6x^2 - 130 = 0$
10. $x^2 + 6x + 8 = -1$
11. $5x^2 - 4x = 33$
12. $3x^2 = 6x + 4$
13. $9x^2 - 5x = 0$
14. $7x^2 = 13$
15. $2x^2 + 3x - 1 = 0$
16. $2x^2 - 12 = 11x$
17. $2x^2 + 5x + 3 = 0$
18. $4x^2 = 12x - 9$

19. **Population** The function below models the United States population P in millions since 1900, where t is the number of years after 1900.

$$P = 0.0089t^2 + 1.1149t + 78.4491$$

a. **Open-ended** Use the function to estimate the United States population the year you graduate from high school.
b. Estimate the United States population in 2025.
c. Use the function to **predict** the year in which the population reaches 300 million.

20. **Recreation** Suppose you throw a ball in the air with a starting velocity of 30 ft/s. The ball is 5 ft high when it leaves your hand. After how many seconds will it hit the ground? Use the vertical motion formula $h = -16t^2 + vt + s$.

Choose **Use any method you choose to solve each equation.**

21. $2t^2 = 72$
22. $3x^2 + 2x - 4 = 0$
23. $5b^2 - 10 = 0$
24. $3x^2 + 4x = 10$
25. $x^2 = -5x - 6$
26. $m^2 - 4m = -4$
27. $d^2 - d - 6 = 0$
28. $13n^2 - 117 = 0$
29. $3s^2 - 4s = 2$
30. $5b^2 - 2b - 7 = 0$
31. $15x^2 - 12x - 48 = 0$
32. $4t^2 = 81$

33. **Writing** Compare how you solve the linear equation $mx + b = 0$ with how you solve the quadratic equation $ax^2 + bx + c = 0$.

34. **Open-ended** Give an example of a quadratic equation that is easier to solve by finding the square roots of each side than by using the quadratic formula or by graphing. Explain your choice.

35. **Math in the Media** Use the data at the right. Suppose that a cleaner at the top of the Gateway Arch drops a cleaning brush. Use the vertical motion formula $h = -16t^2 + vt + s$.

a. What is the value of s, the starting height?
b. What is the value of h when the brush hits the ground?
c. The starting velocity is 0. Find how many seconds it takes the brush to hit the ground.

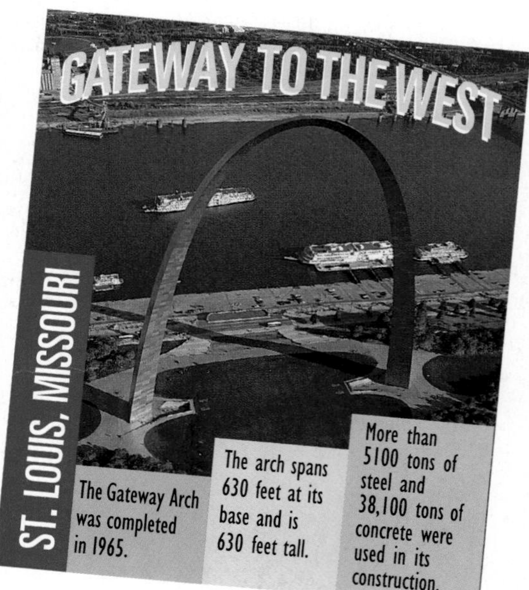

GATEWAY TO THE WEST
ST. LOUIS, MISSOURI
The Gateway Arch was completed in 1965.
The arch spans 630 feet at its base and is 630 feet tall.
More than 5100 tons of steel and 38,100 tons of concrete were used in its construction.

Chapter Project — Find Out by Reasoning

The formula $d = 0.044s^2 + 1.1s$ relates the maximum speed s in miles per hour that you should travel in order to be able to stop in d feet. Suppose you have 150 ft (about 10 car lengths) between your car and the car in front of you. Find the maximum speed you should travel.

Exercises MIXED REVIEW

Find each probability for two rolls of a number cube.

36. P(a 2 and a 6)

37. P(two odds)

38. P(two 5's)

39. P(two fractions)

40. a. Transportation A commuter train has a 150-ton locomotive and 70-ton double-decker passenger cars. Write a linear function for the weight of a train with c passenger cars.

b. How much does a train with 7 passenger cars weigh?

FOR YOUR JOURNAL

Write and answer three questions that review what you learned about quadratic equations in this chapter.

Getting Ready for Lesson 7-7

For each equation, find the value of $b^2 - 4ac$.

41. $2x^2 + 3x - 4 = 0$

42. $3x^2 + 2x + 1 = 0$

43. $x^2 + 2x - 5 = 0$

44. $3x^2 - 6x = 5$

45. $2x^2 - 5x = 3$

46. $2x^2 + 3 = 7x$

Exercises CHECKPOINT

Solve each equation.

1. $x^2 - 16 = 49$

2. $8x^2 + 1 = 33$

3. $x^2 - 120 = 1$

Use the quadratic formula to solve each equation.

4. $x^2 - 4x + 3 = 0$

5. $5x^2 + 3x - 2 = 0$

6. $4x^2 = 14x - 3$

7. Standardized Test Prep Which expression could you use to solve $2x^2 + 5 = 3x$?

A. $\dfrac{-5 \pm \sqrt{5^2 - (4)(2)(3)}}{4}$

B. $\dfrac{-3 \pm \sqrt{3^2 - (4)(2)(5)}}{4}$

C. $\dfrac{-(-3) \pm \sqrt{(-3)^2 - (4)(2)(-3)}}{4}$

D. $\dfrac{-(-3) \pm \sqrt{(-3)^2 - (4)(2)(5)}}{4}$

Math ToolboX

Problem Solving

Work Backward

After Lesson 7-6

Sometimes you can solve a problem by working backward. To write a quadratic function from its graph, you need to find the x- and y-intercepts.

Example

Work backward to write the equation of the quadratic function shown in the graph.

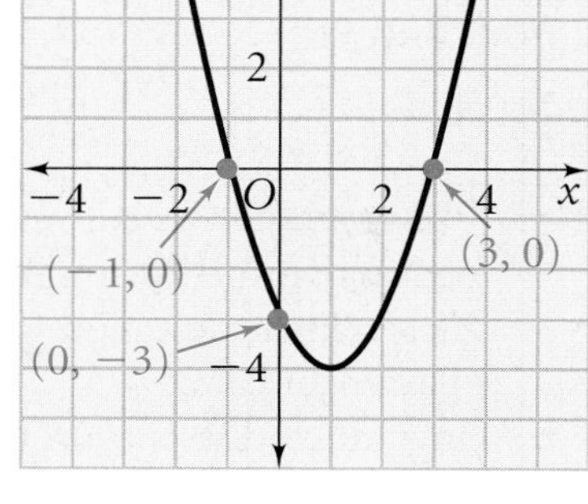

A quadratic function is in the form $y = ax^2 + bx + c$ $(a \neq 0)$. Since the y-intercept of the graph is -3, you know that $c = -3$. Notice that the graph has x-intercepts at -1 and 3. Substitute the points $(-1, 0)$ and $(3, 0)$ into $y = ax^2 + bx - 3$. The result is a system of equations.

$y = ax^2 + bx - 3$	$y = ax^2 + bx - 3$
$0 = a(-1)^2 + b(-1) - 3$	$0 = a(3)^2 + b(3) - 3$
$0 = a - b - 3$	$0 = 9a + 3b - 3$
$a - b = 3$	$9a + 3b = 3$
	$3a + b = 1$

When you solve the system of equations, you find that $a = 1$ and $b = -2$.

$$a - b = 3$$
$$3a + b = 1$$

The equation of the graph above is $y = x^2 - 2x - 3$.

Work backward to find the equation of each graph.

1.

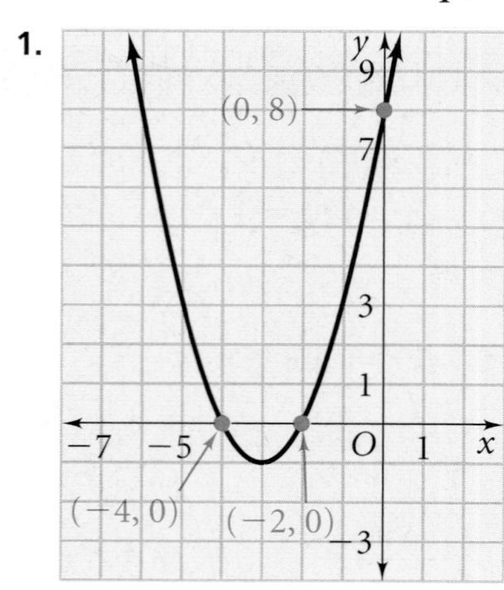

2.

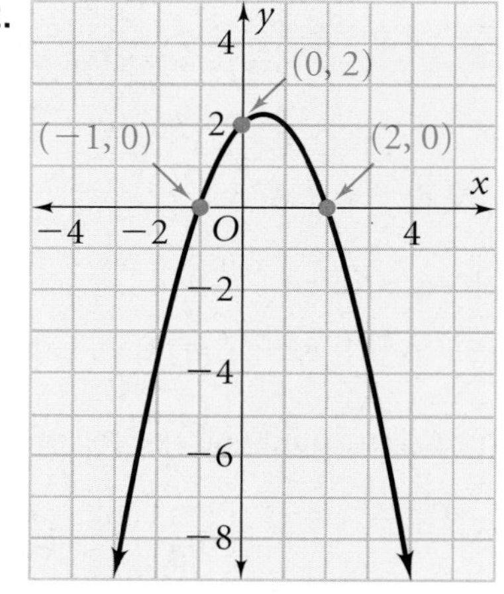

3.

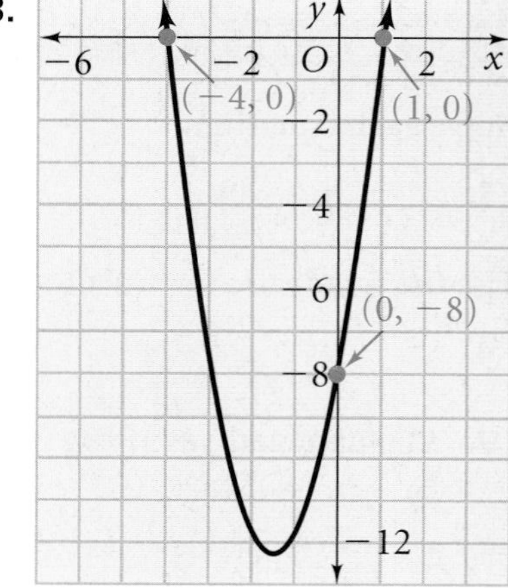

4. **Writing** Explain why this method would not be ideal for all graphs.

7-7 Using the Discriminant

What You'll Learn

- Using the discriminant to find the number of solutions of a quadratic equation

...And Why

To solve physics and home improvement problems

What You'll Need

- graphing calculator

WORK TOGETHER

Work with a partner.

1. Each equation is in the form of $ax^2 + bx + c = 0$. Find the value of the expression $b^2 - 4ac$ for each equation.
   a. $x^2 + 2x + 5 = 0$ b. $-3x^2 + 2x - 1 = 0$ c. $\frac{1}{2}x^2 + x + 4 = 0$

2. a. *Graphing Calculator* Graph the related function for each equation in Question 1.
   b. How many x-intercepts do these graphs have?
   c. How many solutions do the equations in Question 1 have?

3. **Generalize** Based on Questions 1 and 2, complete this statement: For an equation in which $b^2 - 4ac$ ■ 0, the equation has ■ solutions.

THINK AND DISCUSS

In the Work Together activity, you investigated the discriminant of three quadratic equations. The quantity $b^2 - 4ac$ is called the **discriminant** of a quadratic equation. The discriminant is part of the quadratic formula.

$$x = \frac{-b \pm \sqrt{b^2 - 4ac}}{2a} \quad \longleftarrow \text{the discriminant}$$

The graph of the related function of a quadratic equation gives you a picture of what happens when a discriminant is positive, 0, or negative.

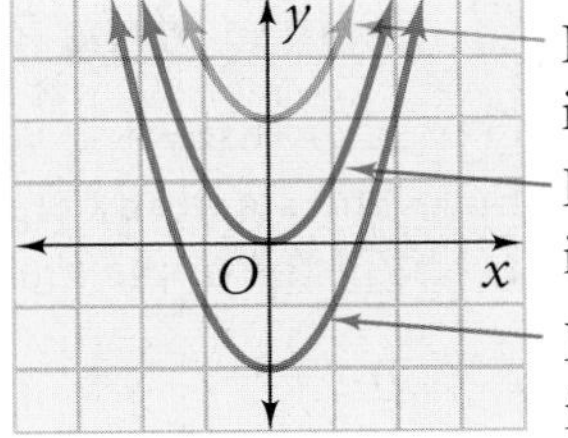

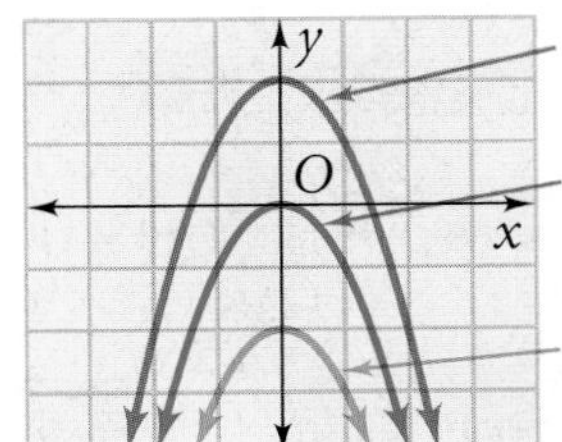

4. How many solutions will an equation have if the discriminant is positive? Explain.
5. How many solutions will an equation have if the discriminant is 0? Explain.
6. How many solutions will an equation have if the discriminant is negative? Explain.
7. Does the direction a graph opens affect the number of solutions found by using the discriminant?

Math A Test Prep

1 Which equation has exactly one solution?
(1) $2x^2 - 5x + 5 = 0$
(2) $2x^2 - 4x + 2 = 0$
(3) $2x^2 - 5x + 2 = 0$
(4) $2x^2 - 4x - 2 = 0$

2 A model rocket is launched from the ground. Its height h in feet after t seconds is given by the function $h = -16t^2 + 84t$. Solve each problem to the nearest tenth.
a In how many seconds will the rocket be at a height of 100 ft?
b In how many seconds will the rocket reach its maximum height?

Property of the Discriminant

For the quadratic equation $ax^2 + bx + c = 0$ where a $\neq 0$, the value of the discriminant tells you the number of solutions.

Discriminant	Number of Solutions
$b^2 - 4ac > 0$	two solutions
$b^2 - 4ac = 0$	one solution
$b^2 - 4ac < 0$	no solution

Example 1

Find the number of solutions of $3x^2 - 5x = 1$.

$3x^2 - 5x - 1 = 0$ ⟵ Write in standard form.

$$\begin{aligned} b^2 - 4ac &= (-5)^2 - (4)(3)(-1) \quad \longleftarrow \text{Substitute for } a, b, \text{ and } c. \\ &= 25 - (-12) \\ &= 37 \end{aligned}$$

Since $37 > 0$, the equation has two solutions.

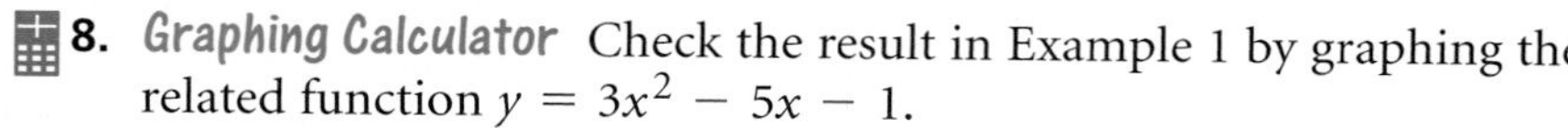

8. *Graphing Calculator* Check the result in Example 1 by graphing the related function $y = 3x^2 - 5x - 1$.

9. *Try This* Find the number of solutions of $x^2 = 2x - 3$.

10. *Critical Thinking* Kenji claimed that the discriminant of $2x^2 + 5x - 1 = 0$ had the value 17. What error did he make?

Example 2 **Relating to the Real World** 

Physics A construction worker throws an apple toward a fellow worker who is 25 ft above ground. The starting height of the apple is 5 ft. Its starting velocity is 30 ft/s. Will the apple reach the second worker?

$$h = -16t^2 + vt + s \quad \longleftarrow \text{Use the vertical motion formula.}$$

$$25 = -16t^2 + 30t + 5 \quad \longleftarrow \text{Substitute 25 for } h, \text{ 30 for } v, \text{ and 5 for } s.$$

$$0 = -16t^2 + 30t - 20 \quad \longleftarrow \text{Write in standard form.}$$

$$\begin{aligned} b^2 - 4ac &= (30)^2 - 4(-16)(-20) \quad \longleftarrow \text{Evaluate the discriminant.} \\ &= 900 - 1280 \\ &= -380 \end{aligned}$$

The discriminant is negative. The apple will not reach the second worker.

11. **Try This** Suppose the first construction worker in Example 2 goes up to the next floor. He then throws the apple at a starting height of 17 ft and starting velocity of 30 ft/s. Will the apple reach the second worker?

Exercises ON YOUR OWN

For which discriminant is each graph possible?

1. 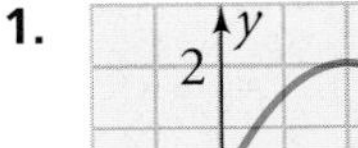
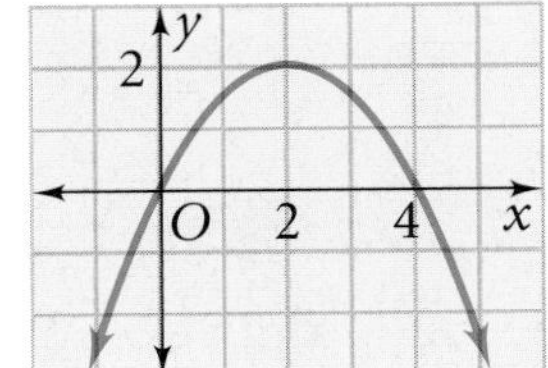

2. 
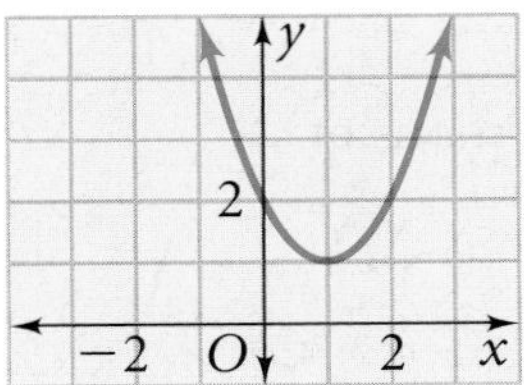

3. 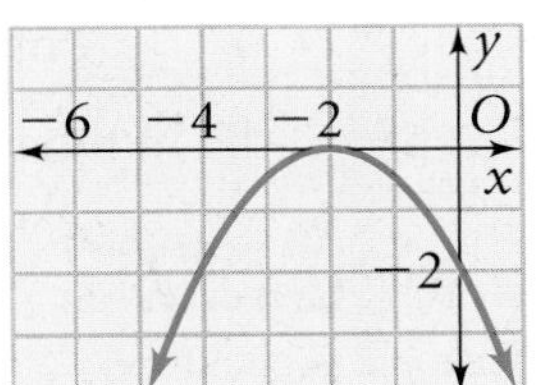

A. $b^2 - 4ac = 0$

B. $b^2 - 4ac = -2$

C. $b^2 - 4ac = 5$

Mental Math **Find the number of solutions of each equation.**

4. $x^2 - 3x + 4 = 0$
5. $x^2 - 6x + 9 = 0$
6. $x^2 + 4x - 2 = 0$
7. $x^2 - 1 = 0$
8. $x^2 - 2x - 3 = 0$
9. $x^2 + x = 0$
10. $2x^2 - 3x + 4 = 0$
11. $2x^2 + 4x = -15$
12. $x^2 - 7x + 6 = 0$
13. $x^2 + 2x + 1 = 0$
14. $4x^2 + 5x = -2$
15. $x^2 - 8x = -12$

16. **Open-ended** Write a quadratic equation that has no solution.

17. **Home Improvements** The Reeves family garden is 18 ft long and 15 ft wide. They want to modify it according to the diagram at the right. The new area is modeled by the equation $A = -x^2 + 3x + 270$.
    a. What value of x, if any, will give a new area of 280 ft^2?
    b. Is there any value of x for which the garden has an area of 266 ft^2? Explain.

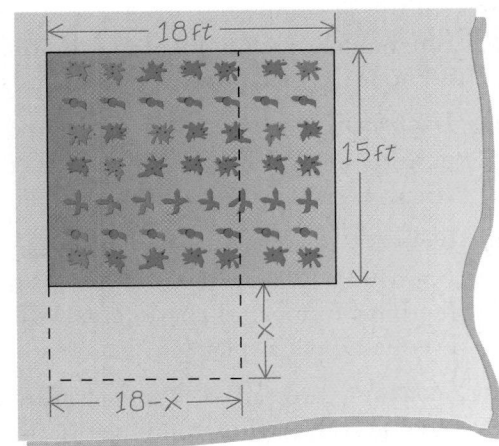

18 ft
15 ft
x
18 − x

18. **Writing** How can you use the discriminant to write a quadratic equation that has two solutions?

19. **Physics** Suppose the equation $h = -16t^2 + 35t$ models the altitude a football will reach t seconds after it is kicked. Which of the following altitudes are possible?
    A. $h = 16$ ft
    B. $h = 25$ ft
    C. $h = 30$ ft
    D. $h = 35$ ft

20. Find the value of the discriminant and the solutions of each equation.
    a. $x^2 - 6x + 5 = 0$
    b. $x^2 + x - 20 = 0$
    c. $2x^2 - 7x - 3 = 0$

21. **Critical Thinking** Use your results to Question 20. When the discriminant is a perfect square, are the solutions rational or irrational? Explain.

Find the number of x-intercepts of each function.

22. $y = x^2 - 6x + 5$

23. $y = 2x^2 + 4x - 3$

24. $y = x^2 + 2x + 9$

25. $y = -x^2 - 2x$

26. $y = x^2$

27. $y = 3x^2 - 2x + 5$

28. $y = 8x^2 - 2x - 45$

29. $y = -x^2 - 2$

30. $y = -x^2$

31. **Standardized Test Prep** Compare the quantities in Column A and Column B.

Column A	Column B
the number of solutions of $35 = 20x^2 - 15x + 47$	the number of solutions of $15x + 7 = 0$

A. The quantity in Column A is greater.
B. The quantity in Column B is greater.
C. The quantities are equal.
D. The relationship cannot be determined from the information given.

For each function, decide if its graph crosses the x-axis. For those that do, find the coordinates of the points at which they cross.

32. $y = x^2 - 2x + 5$

33. $y = 2x^2 - 4x + 3$

34. $y = 4x^2 + x - 5$

35. $y = -3x^2 - x + 2$

36. $y = x^2 - 5x + 7$

37. $y = 2x^2 - 3x - 5$

38. For the equation $x^2 + 4x + k = 0$, find all values of k such that the equation has each number of solutions.

a. none **b.** one **c.** two

39. **Electrical Engineering** The function $P = 3i^2 - 2i + 450$ models the power P in an electric circuit with a current i. Can the power in this circuit ever be zero? If so, at what value of i?

40. **Business** An apartment rental agency uses the formula $I = 5400 + 300n - 50n^2$ to find its monthly income I based on renting n number of apartments. Will the agency's monthly income ever be \$7000? Explain.

41. **Computer** You can use a spreadsheet like the one at the right to find the discriminant for each value of b shown in column A.

a. What spreadsheet formula would you use to find the value in cell B2? in cell C2?

b. Describe the integer values of b for which $x^2 + bx + 1 = 0$ has solutions.

c. Describe the integer values of b for which $x^2 + bx + 2 = 0$ has no solution.

	A	B	C
1	b	x^2 + bx + 1 = 0	x^2 + bx + 2 = 0
2	−3	■	■
3	−2	■	■
4	−1	■	■
5	0	■	■
6	1	■	■
7	2	■	■
8	3	■	■

Chapter Project — Find Out by Communicating

Work with a group of your classmates to plan a skit that will present what you have learned about safe distances in driving. Illustrate the relationships among reaction time, road conditions, speed, and stopping distances.

Exercises MIXED REVIEW

Solve each system by graphing.

42. $4x + y \leq 5$
$3x - 2y > 10$

43. $-6x - 3y \geq 8$
$y > -9$

44. $x < 7$
$-3x + 7y \geq 0$

45. $y = 3x - 2$
$y = -x + 6$

Evaluate each function for $x = 3$.

46. $f(x) = \frac{1}{2}x + 3$

47. $g(x) = \frac{x + 3}{2}$

48. $h(x) = 3 - x$

49. $f(x) = -x - 1$

50. *Geology* Mount Shishalding is a 9372-ft tall volcano on Unimak Island, Alaska. In 1995 it erupted and sent up a 35,000-ft plume of ash. How far above sea level did the ash reach?

PORTFOLIO

Select one or two items from your work for this chapter. Consider:
- cooperative work
- work you found challenging
- diagrams, graphs, or charts

Explain why you have included each selection that you make.

A Point in Time

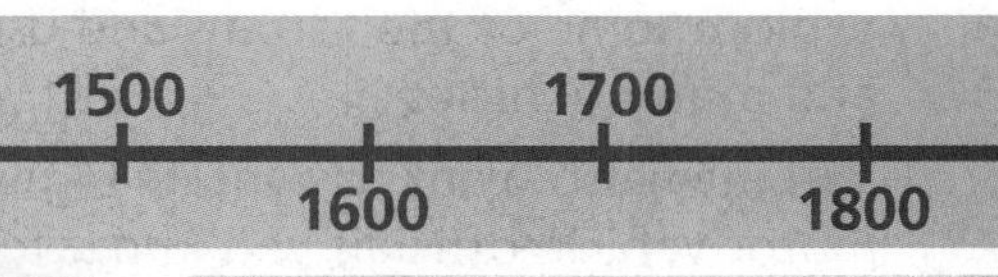

Juan de la Cierva

In 1923, Juan de la Cierva (1895–1936) designed the first successful autogyro, a rotor-based aircraft. The autogyro had rotating blades to give the aircraft lift, a propeller for forward thrust, and short, stubby wings for balance. Autogyros needed only short runways for takeoff and could descend almost vertically.

By hinging the rotor blades at the hub, de la Cierva allowed each blade to respond to aerodynamic forces. This was a significant contribution in the development of the modern helicopter.

De la Cierva's work on problems of lift and gravity, like the work of aeronautical engineers of today, involved quadratic functions.

CHAPTER PROJECT

Finishing the Chapter Project

Questions on pages 331, 336, 347, and 353 should help you to complete your project. Gather together all the data you compiled as you worked on the project. Include the equations you analyzed and your graphs. Discuss your conclusions about safe driving, stopping distance, road conditions, and so on with your classmates. Then, as a group, plan and rehearse your skit.

Reflect and Revise

Present your skit to a small group of classmates. After you have heard their comments, decide if your presentation is clear and convincing. If needed, make changes to improve your skit for the rest of the class.

Follow Up

If you have access to a commercial online service or the Internet, explore some of the forums and user groups that are related to driving and motor vehicles.

You may also want to contact highway patrol officers or registry of motor vehicle officials you know for information about the habits of drivers. Ask them what errors or violations are most common.

For More Information:

Highway Safety: Motorcycle helmet laws save lives and reduce costs to society. A Report to Congressional Requesters. Washington, D.C.: U.S. General Accounting Office, 1991.

Hewett, Joan. *Motorcycle on Patrol.* New York: Clarion Books, 1986.

Ross, Daniel Charles. "Ford F150." *Car and Driver* (January 1996): 134.

Saperstein, Robert. *Surviving an Auto Accident.* Ventura, California: Pathfinder Publishers, 1994.

CHAPTER 7

Wrap Up

Key Terms

axis of symmetry (p. 318)
discriminant (p. 349)
maximum value (p. 320)
minimum value (p. 320)
negative square root (p. 332)
parabola (p. 318)
perfect squares (p. 333)
principal square root (p. 332)
quadratic equation (p. 337)
quadratic formula (p. 343)
quadratic function (p. 319)
square root (p. 332)
standard form of a quadratic equation (p. 337)
standard form of a quadratic function (p. 319)
vertex (p. 320)
vertical motion formula (p. 344)

How am I doing?

- State three ideas from this chapter that you think are important. Explain your choices.
- Describe the different ways you can solve quadratic equations.

Exploring Quadratic Functions 7-1

A function of the form $y = ax^2 + bx + c$ is a **quadratic function.** The shape of its graph is a **parabola.** The **axis of symmetry** of a parabola divides the parabola into two congruent halves.

The **vertex** of a parabola is where the axis of symmetry intersects the parabola. When a parabola opens downward, the y-coordinate of the vertex is a **maximum value** of the function. When a parabola opens upward, the y-coordinate of the vertex is a **minimum value** of the function.

The value of a determines whether the parabola opens upward or downward and how wide or narrow it is.

Open-ended **Give an example of a quadratic function for each of the following descriptions.**

1. Its graph opens downward.

2. Its graph opens upward.

3. Its vertex is at the origin.

4. Its graph is wider than $y = x^2$.

Graphing Simple Quadratic Functions 7-2

Changing the value of c in a quadratic function $y = ax^2 + c$ shifts the parabola up or down. The value of c is the y-intercept of the graph.

Graph each quadratic equation.

5. $y = \frac{2}{3}x^2$

6. $y = -x^2 + 1$

7. $y = x^2 - 4$

8. $y = 5x^2 + 8$

State whether each function has a *maximum* or *minimum* value.

9. $y = 4x^2 + 1$

10. $y = -3x^2 - 7$

11. $y = \frac{1}{2}x^2 + 9$

12. $y = -x^2 + 6$

Graphing Quadratic Functions 7-3

The graph of $y = ax^2 + bx + c$, where $a \neq 0$, has the line $x = \frac{-b}{2a}$ as its axis of symmetry. The x-coordinate of the vertex is $\frac{-b}{2a}$.

Graph each function. Label the axis of symmetry and the vertex.

13. $y = -\frac{1}{2}x^2 + 4x + 1$ **14.** $y = -2x^2 - 3x + 10$ **15.** $y = x^2 + 6x - 2$

Graph each quadratic inequality.

16. $y \leq 3x^2 + x - 5$ **17.** $y > 2x^2 + 6x - 3$ **18.** $y \geq -x^2 - x - 8$

Square Roots 7-4

If $a^2 = b$, then a is a **square root** of b. The **principal** (or positive) **square root** of b is indicated by $\sqrt{b}$. The **negative square root** is indicated by $-\sqrt{b}$. The squares of integers are called **perfect squares.**

Tell whether each expression is *rational* or *irrational*.

19. $\sqrt{86}$ **20.** $-\sqrt{1.21}$ **21.** $\pm\sqrt{\frac{1}{2}}$ **22.** $\sqrt{64}$ **23.** $\sqrt{2.55}$ **24.** $-\sqrt{\frac{4}{25}}$

Find the value of each expression. If the value is irrational, round your answer to the nearest hundredth.

25. $\sqrt{9}$ **26.** $-\sqrt{47}$ **27.** $\sqrt{0.36}$ **28.** $\sqrt{140}$ **29.** $-\sqrt{1}$ **30.** $\sqrt{196}$

31. *Standardized Test Prep* What is the principal square root of 2.25?
A. 15 **B.** 1.5 **C.** −15 **D.** −1.5 **E.** 0.15

Solving Quadratic Equations 7-5

A **quadratic equation** can be written in the **standard form** $ax^2 + bx + c = 0$, where $a \neq 0$. Quadratic equations can have two, one, or no real solutions. You can solve some quadratic equations by taking the square root of each side, or by finding the x-intercepts of the related quadratic function.

If the statement is true, verify it by solving the equation. If it is false, write a true statement.

32. $x^2 - 10 = 3$; there is one solution. **33.** $3x^2 = 27$; there are two solutions.

Solve each equation. If the equation has no solution, write *no solution*.

34. $6(x^2 - 2) = 12$ **35.** $-5m^2 = -125$ **36.** $9(w^2 + 1) = 9$ **37.** $3r^2 + 27 = 0$

38. *Geometry* The area of a circle is given by the formula $A = \pi r^2$. Find the radius of a circle with area 16 in.^{2} to the nearest tenth of an inch.

Using the Quadratic Formula 7-6

You can solve a quadratic equation using the **quadratic formula.**

If $ax^2 + bx + c = 0$ and $a \neq 0$, then $x = \frac{-b \pm \sqrt{b^2 - 4ac}}{2a}$.

Use the quadratic formula to solve each equation. Round solutions to the nearest hundredth when necessary.

39. $4x^2 + 3x - 8 = 0$ **40.** $2x^2 - 7x = -3$ **41.** $-x^2 + 8x + 4 = 5$ **42.** $9x^2 - 270 = 0$

43. **Vertical Motion** Suppose you throw a ball in the air. The ball is 6 ft high when it leaves your hand. Use the equation $0 = -16t^2 + 20t + 6$ to find the number of seconds t that the ball is in the air.

Using the Discriminant 7-7

You can use the **discriminant** to find the number of real solutions of a quadratic equation. When a quadratic equation is in the form $ax^2 + bx + c = 0$ $(a \neq 0)$, the discriminant is $b^2 - 4ac$.

If $b^2 - 4ac > 0$, there are two solutions.
If $b^2 - 4ac = 0$, there is one solution.
If $b^2 - 4ac < 0$, there is no solution.

Evaluate the discriminant. Determine the number of real solutions of each equation.

44. $x^2 + 5x - 6 = 0$ **45.** $-3x^2 - 4x + 8 = 0$ **46.** $2x^2 + 7x + 11 = 0$

47. **Writing** Explain why a quadratic equation has one real solution if its discriminant equals zero.

Getting Ready for... CHAPTER 8

Use exponents to write each expression.

48. $3 \cdot 3 \cdot 5 \cdot 5 \cdot 5$ **49.** $8 \cdot 8 \cdot 8 \cdot x \cdot x \cdot x \cdot x$ **50.** $h \cdot h \cdot h \cdot h \cdot h \cdot w \cdot w$

Simplify each expression.

51. $5 \cdot 10^3$ **52.** $-4^3 - (-4)^3$ **53.** $8 \cdot 10^4$

54. $\frac{3^4}{3^2}$ **55.** $10(3^2 - 3^4)$ **56.** $7 \cdot 10^2 \div 10^3$

Evaluate each expression.

57. $d^2 \cdot g^2$ for $d = -2$ and $g = 3$ **58.** $7n^8 - 5n^3$ for $n = -1$ **59.** $\frac{m^3}{m^4}$ for $m = 3$

CHAPTER 7 Assessment

Match each function with its graph.

1. $y = 3x^2$
2. $y = -3x^2 + 1$
3. $y = -2x^2$
4. $y = x^2 - 3$

A. 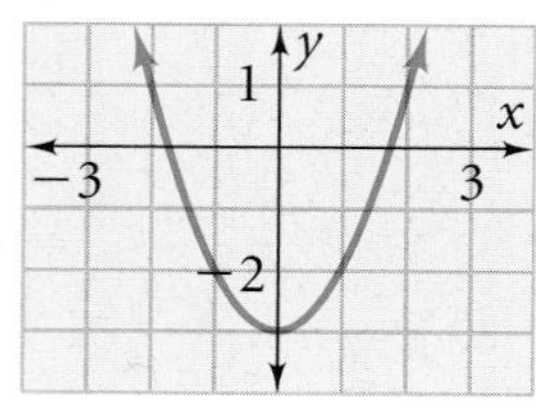

B. 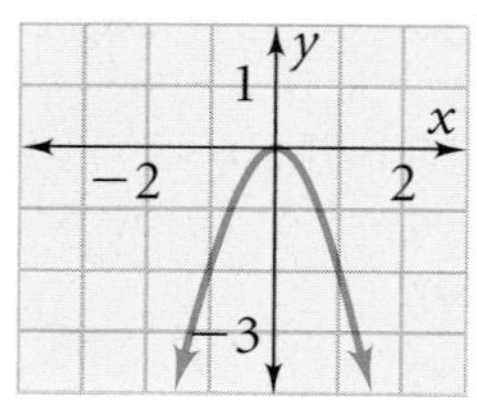

C. 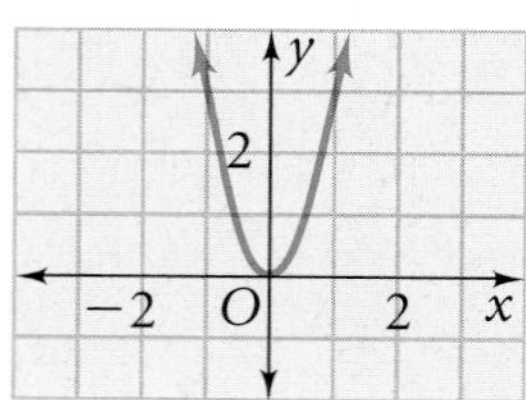

D. 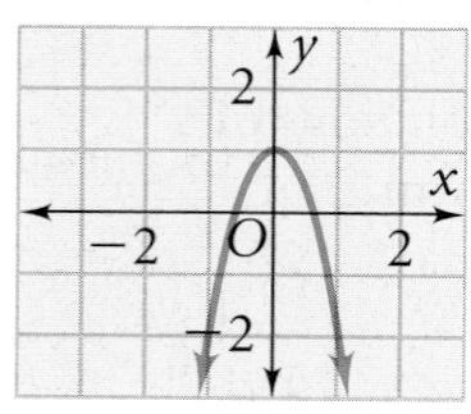

Find the coordinates of the vertex of the graph and an equation for the axis of symmetry.

5. $y = 3x^2 - 7$
6. $y = x^2 - 3x + 2$
7. $y = -2x^2 + 10x - 1$
8. $y = \frac{1}{2}x^2 + 6x$

Make a table of values and graph each function.

9. $y = x^2 - 4$
10. $y = -x^2 + 1$
11. $y = 5x^2$
12. $y = \frac{1}{2}x^2 - 2$
13. **Writing** Explain what you can determine about the shape of a parabola from its equation without graphing.

Find the number of x-intercepts of each function.

14. $y = 5x^2$
15. $y = 3x^2 + 10$
16. $y = -2x^2 + x + 7$
17. $y = x^2 - 4x$

Graph each quadratic function.

18. $y = -3x^2 - x + 10$
19. $y = \frac{1}{2}x^2 + 2x + 4$
20. $y = x^2 - 3x + 5$

Find both the principal and negative square roots of each number.

21. 1.44
22. 1600
23. $\frac{4}{9}$

Between what two consecutive integers is each square root?

24. $\sqrt{28}$
25. $\sqrt{136}$
26. $\sqrt{332}$

Use any method to solve each quadratic equation. Round solutions to the nearest hundredth.

27. $2x^2 = 50$
28. $-3x^2 + 7x = -10$
29. $x^2 + 6x + 9 = 25$
30. $-x^2 - x + 2 = 0$
31. **Open-ended** Write the equation of a parabola that has two x-intercepts and a maximum value. Include a graph of your parabola.

Model each problem with a quadratic equation. Then solve the problem.

32. **Geometry** The volume of a cylinder is given by the formula $V = \pi r^2 h$, where r is the radius of the cylinder and h is the height. A cylinder with height of 10 ft has volume 140 ft^3. What is the radius to the nearest tenth of a foot?
33. **Landscaping** The area of a rectangular patio is 800 ft^2. The length of the patio is twice the width. Find the dimensions of the patio. (*Hint*: use the formula $A = l \cdot w$.)

Evaluate the discriminant. Determine the number of real solutions of each equation.

34. $x^2 + 4x = 5$
35. $x^2 - 8 = 0$
36. $2x^2 + x = 0$
37. $3x^2 - 9x = -5$
38. **Standardized Test Prep** Find the value of k for which the equation $kx^2 - 10x + 25k = 0$ has one real root.
    A. −1 B. 2 C. 3 D. 5 E. 10

CHAPTER 7

Preparing for the Math A Exam

Part I

1 The graph of $y = -3x^2 + 1$
(1) opens upward.
(2) is narrower than the graph of $y = 4x^2$.
(3) has its vertex at the origin.
(4) is narrower than the graph of $y = -\frac{1}{3}x^2$.

2 What is the equation of the axis of symmetry of $y = 5x^2 - 2x + 3$?
(1) $x = -\frac{1}{5}$ (3) $x = \frac{1}{5}$
(2) $y = \frac{4}{5}$ (4) $y = -\frac{4}{5}$

3 What is the maximum value of y in $y = -3x^2 - 6x - 1$?
(1) 2 (3) -1
(2) -2 (4) 0

4 Between what two consecutive integers is $\sqrt{52}$?
(1) 5 and 6 (3) 7 and 8
(2) 6 and 7 (4) 8 and 9

5 How many solutions are there for the equation $2x^2 + 7 = 20$?
(1) 0 (3) 2
(2) 1 (4) 3

6 Which is the best approximation of the solutions of $3x^2 - 5x + 1 = 0$?
(1) 2 and -3 (3) 1.5 and 1.75
(2) 1.5 and 0.25 (4) 1.5 and -0.5

7 What is the value of the discriminant of $0 = 3x^2 - 4x - 3$?
(1) -20 (3) 25
(2) 52 (4) 4

8 How many solutions are there for the system $y = x^2$ and $6y - x = 24$?
(1) 0 (3) 2
(2) 1 (4) 3

9 What is the solution of the system $-2x - 3y = -15$ and $3x + 2y = 0$?
(1) $(-6, 9)$ (3) $(6, -9)$
(2) $(4, -6)$ (4) $(-6, 6)$

10 How many solutions are there for the system $x - y = -4$ and $x = -2$?
(1) one (3) infinitely many
(2) two (4) none

Part II

11 Graph $y = -\frac{1}{2}x^2 + 2$.

12 Find the vertex and the axis of symmetry of the graph of the equation $y = 4x^2 - 3x$.

13 Solve $x^2 - 6x + 8 = 0$.

Part III

14 Graph the inequality $y < 2x^2 - 8x + 1$.

15 A square photograph with sides of 15 in. must be reduced to an area 40% of its original size to fit in a book. Find the length of a side of the reduced photograph by modeling the problem with a quadratic equation and solving it.

Part IV

16 The plan for a square garden has a circular fountain centered in it. The garden has sides 20 ft long. If the radius of the fountain is x ft, the function $y = \pi x^2$ gives the area of the fountain in square feet.
a What values make sense for the domain?
b What values make sense for the range?

17 Suppose you throw a ball upward at 40 ft/sec. The ball is 4 ft high when it leaves your hand. Use the vertical motion formula

$$h = -16t^2 + vt + s.$$

a What is the height h when the ball hits the ground?
b What is the value of v, the starting velocity?
c What is the starting height s?
d How many seconds does it take the ball to hit the ground?

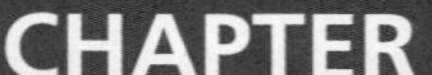

CHAPTER

8 Exponents and Exponential Functions

Relating to the Real World

Vhat do money in a savings ccount, the opulation of the world, and adioactive vaste all have in common? You an use xponential unctions to lescribe them and predict the future. Exponential elationships are videly used by cientists, business people, and even oliticians trying o predict budget surpluses and deficits.

Lessons	8-1	8-2	8-3	8-4	8-5
	Exploring Exponential Functions	Exponential Growth	Exponential Decay	Zero and Negative Exponents	Scientific Notation

CHAPTER PROJECT

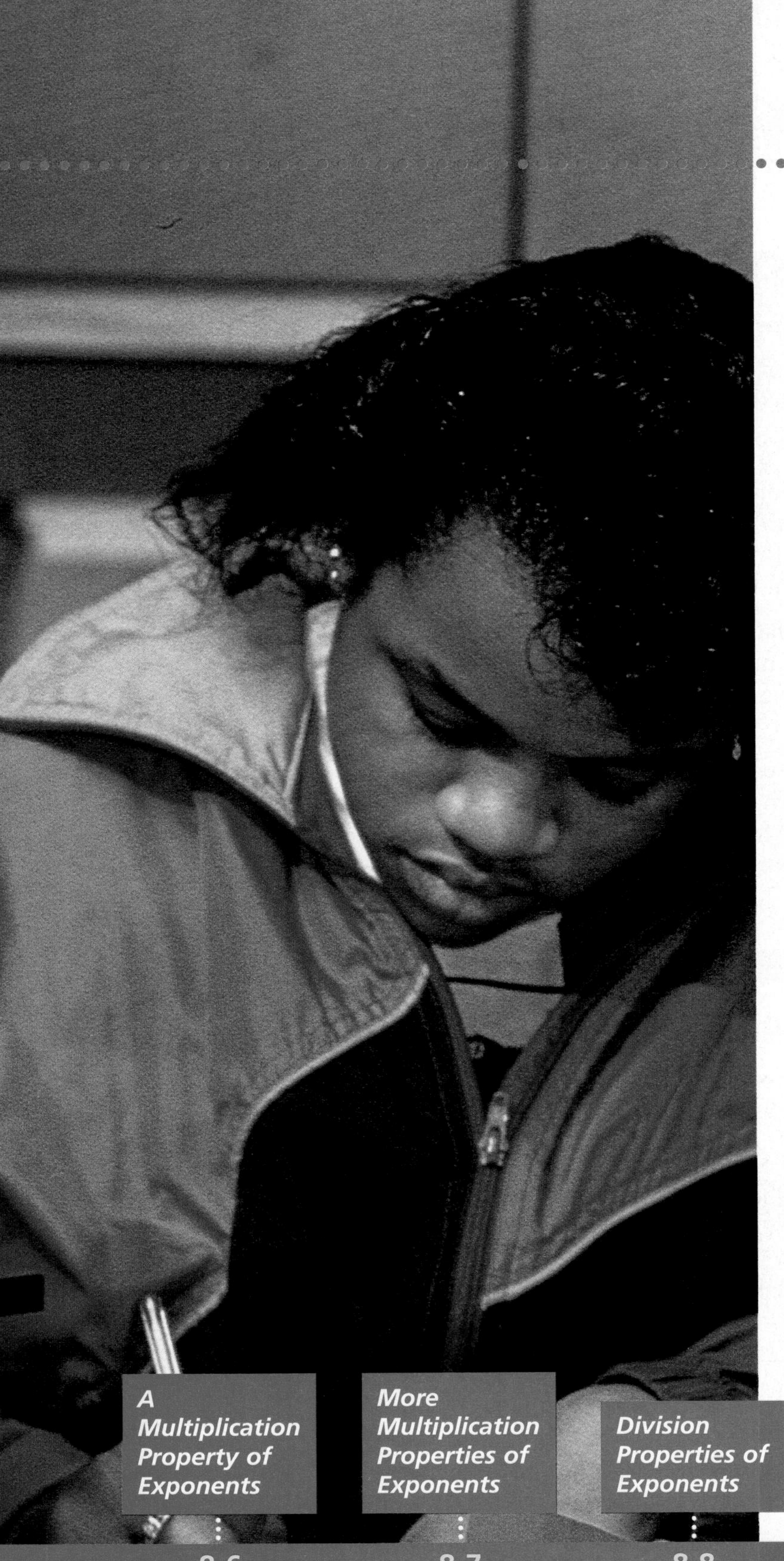

MOLDY OLDIES

You take a piece of bread from the bread bag and find that there is green mold on it. The bread was fine two days ago! You open the refrigerator to look for a snack only to see that the cheese is covered with a fuzzy white mold. So, just how fast does mold grow, anyway?

As you work through the chapter, you will grow your own mold. You will gather data, create graphs, and make predictions. As part of your research, you will plan and complete an experiment to monitor growth.

To help you complete the project:

- p. 366 *Find Out by Doing*
- p. 372 *Find Out by Recording*
- p. 389 *Find Out by Graphing*
- p. 395 *Find Out by Analyzing*
- p. 400 *Find Out by Interpreting*
- p. 406 *Finishing the Project*

What You'll Learn

- Examining patterns in exponential functions

...And Why

To model different patterns

What You'll Need

- notebook paper
- calculator

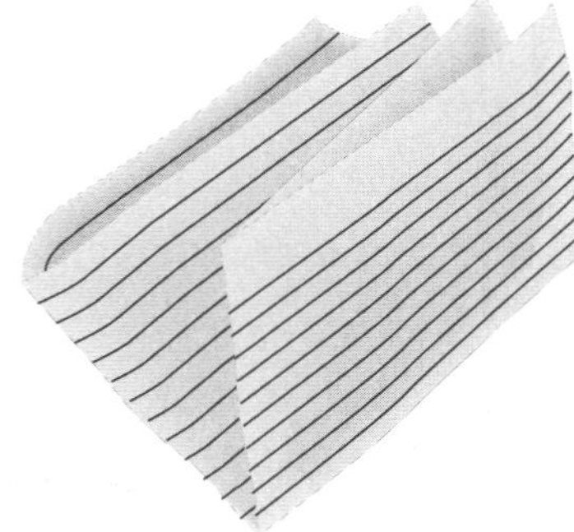

8-1 Exploring Exponential Functions

WORK TOGETHER

Work with a partner.

1. Fold a sheet of notebook paper in half. Notice that the fold line divides the paper into 2 rectangles.
2. Fold the paper in half again. Now how many rectangles are there?
3. Continue folding the paper in half until you cannot make another fold. Keep track of your results in a table like the one at the right.
4. *Patterns* What pattern do you notice in the number of rectangles as the number of folds increases? Explain.
5. Suppose you could continue to fold the paper. Extend your table to include 10 folds. How many rectangles would there be?

Number of Folds	Number of Rectangles
0	1
1	2
2	4
3	■
4	■
5	■

THINK AND DISCUSS

Exploring Exponential Patterns

The pattern that you explored in the Work Together involves repeated multiplication by 2. The table below uses exponents to show the pattern.

QUICK REVIEW

base → b^x ← exponent

Number of Folds	Number of Rectangles	Pattern	Written with Exponents
0	1		
1	2	$= 2$	$= 2^1$
2	4	$= 2 \cdot 2$	$= 2^2$
3	8	$= 2 \cdot 2 \cdot 2$	$= 2^3$
4	16	$= 2 \cdot 2 \cdot 2 \cdot 2$	$= 2^4$
5	32	$= 2 \cdot 2 \cdot 2 \cdot 2 \cdot 2$	$= 2^5$

6. Use an exponent to write each number.
   a. $3 \cdot 3 \cdot 3 \cdot 3$ **b.** $(-2)(-2)(-2)$ **c.** 125

Example 1 Relating to the Real World 

Biology Suppose there are 20 rabbits on an island and that the rabbit population can triple every half-year. How many rabbits would there be after 2 years?

Time	Number of Rabbits
Initial	20
$\frac{1}{2}$ year	$20 \cdot 3 = 60$
1 year	$60 \cdot 3 = 180$
$1\frac{1}{2}$ years	$180 \cdot 3 = 540$
2 years	$540 \cdot 3 = 1620$

Use the problem-solving strategy *Make a Table.*

To triple the amount, multiply the previous half-year's total by 3.

After two years, there would be 1620 rabbits.

Rabbits were brought from Europe to Australia around 1860. The number of rabbits increased exponentially, and by 1870 there were millions of rabbits.

Evaluating Exponential Functions

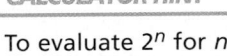

CALCULATOR HINT

To evaluate 2^n for $n = 10$, press 2 y^x 10 = or press 2 ^ 10 ENTER.

You can write the pattern you found in the Work Together as a function with a variable as an exponent. To find the number of rectangles r created by n folds, use the function $r = 2^n$. You read the expression 2^n as "2 to the nth power." The number of rectangles increases *exponentially* as the paper-folding continues.

7. a. Substitute 10 for n in the function $r = 2^n$. Use your calculator to find the value for r.

b. How does your answer compare to your answer to Question 5?

The function $r = 2^n$ is an *exponential function.*

Exponential Function

For all numbers a and for $b > 0$ and $b \neq 1$, the function $y = a \cdot b^x$ is an **exponential function.**

Examples: $y = 0.5 \cdot 2^x$; $f(x) = -2 \cdot 0.5^x$

QUICK REVIEW

The order of operations is parentheses, exponents, multiplication and division, addition and subtraction.

Example 2

Evaluate each exponential function.

a. $y = 5^x$ for $x = 2, 3, 4$

x	$y = 5^x$	y
2	$5^2 = 25$	25
3	$5^3 = 125$	125
4	$5^4 = 625$	625

b. $t(n) = 4(3^n)$ for the domain $\{3, 6\}$

n	$t(n) = 4(3^n)$	$t(n)$
3	$4 \cdot 3^3 = 4 \cdot 27 = 108$	108
6	$4 \cdot 3^6 = 4 \cdot 729 = 2916$	2916

8. **Try This** Evaluate the functions $y = 6^x$ and $y = 3(2^x)$ for $x = 1, 2,$ and 3. Which function increases more quickly? Why?

Graphing Exponential Functions

The graphs of many exponential functions look alike.

Example 3 Relating to the Real World

Technology Some photocopiers allow you to choose how large you want an image to be. The function $f(x) = 1.5^x$ models the increase in size of a picture being copied over and over at 150%. Graph the function.

Make a table of values.

x	$f(x) = 1.5^x$	$f(x)$
1	$1.5^1 = 1.5$	1.5
2	$1.5^2 = 2.25$	2.25
3	$1.5^3 = 3.375 \approx 3.4$	3.4
4	$1.5^4 = 5.0625 \approx 5.1$	5.1
5	$1.5^5 = 7.59375 \approx 7.6$	7.6

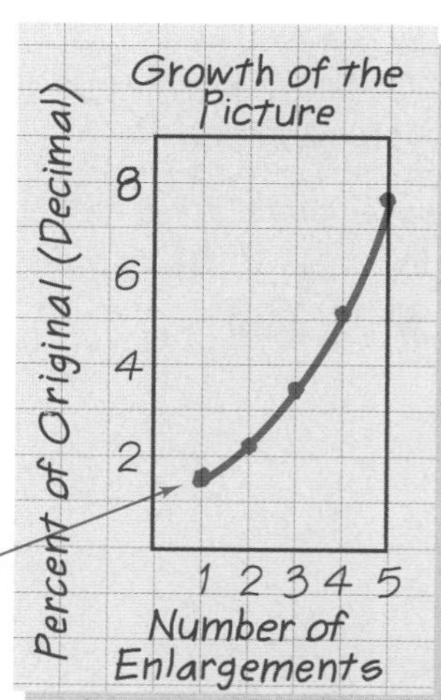

Plot the points. Connect the points with a smooth curve.

GRAPHING CALCULATOR HINT

These range values will give you a clear picture of $y = 2^x$.

Xmin = 0 Ymin = 0
Xmax = 10 Ymax = 100
Xscl = 1 Yscl = 10

9. a. **Graphing Calculator** Use your graphing calculator to graph the function $y = 2^x$.

b. How is the graph of $y = 2^x$ similar to the graph of $f(x) = 1.5^x$? How is it different?

Exercises ON YOUR OWN

1. **Patterns** Bacteria in a laboratory culture can double in number every 20 min. Suppose a culture starts with 75 cells. Copy, complete, and extend the table to find when there will be more than 30,000 bacteria cells.

Time	Number of 20-min Time Periods	Pattern	Number of Bacteria Cells
Initial	0	75	75
20 min	1	$75 \cdot 2$	$75 \cdot 2^{■} = 150$
40 min	■	$75 \cdot 2 \cdot 2$	$75 \cdot 2^{■} = 300$
■	■	■	$75 \cdot 2^{■} = 600$
■	■	■	$75 \cdot 2^{■} = $ ■

2. **Finance** An investment of \$10,000 doubles in value every 13 years. How much is the investment worth after 52 years? after 65 years?

Which function is greater at the given value?

3. $y = 5^x$ and $y = x^5$ at $x = 5$
4. $f = 10 \cdot 2^t$ and $f = 200 \cdot t^2$ at $t = 7$
5. $f(x) = 2^x$ and $f(x) = 100x^2$ at $x = 10$
6. $y = 3^x$ and $y = x^3$ at $x = 4$

Evaluate each function for the domain $\{1, 2, 3, 4, 5\}$. Is the function *increasing, decreasing,* or *neither?*

7. $f(x) = 4^x$
8. $c = a^3$
9. $h(x) = 1^x$
10. $f(x) = 5 \cdot 4^x$
11. $y = 0.5^x$
12. $y = \left(\frac{2}{3}\right)^x$
13. $g(x) = 4 \cdot 10^x$
14. $d = 100 \cdot 0.3^t$

15. **Standardized Test Prep** A population of 6000 doubles in size every 10 years. Which equation relates the size of the population y to the number of 10-year periods x?
 A. $y = 6000 \cdot 10^x$ **B.** $y = 6000 \cdot 2^x$ **C.** $y = 10 \cdot 2^x$ **D.** $y = 2 \cdot 10^x$ **E.** $y = 2 \cdot 6000^x$

16. **Graphing Calculator** Graph the functions $y = x^2$ and $y = 2^x$ on the same set of axes.
 a. What happens to the graphs between $x = 1$ and $x = 3$?
 b. **Critical Thinking** How do you think the graph of $y = 6^x$ would compare to the graphs of $y = x^2$ and $y = 2^x$?

17. **Writing** **Analyze** the range for the function $f(x) = 500 \cdot 1^x$ using the domain $\{1, 2, 3, 4, 5\}$. Explain why the restriction $b \neq 1$ is included in the definition of an exponential function.

18. **Ecology** In 50 days, a water hyacinth can generate 1000 offspring (the number of plants is multiplied by 1000). How many hyacinth plants could there be after 150 days?

Evaluate each expression.

19. $50 \cdot x^5$ for $x = 0.5$

20. $50{,}000 \cdot m^3$ for $m = 1.1$

21. $0.0125 \cdot c^4$ for $c = 2$

22. **Open-ended** Select one of the exponential functions from this lesson.

a. What number is multiplied repeatedly in your example?

b. As the exponent increases, tell whether the outputs of your function increase, decrease, or do neither.

23. Match each table with the function that models the data.

Table I

x	y
1	3
2	6
3	9
4	12

Table II

x	y
1	3
2	9
3	27
4	81

Table III

x	y
1	1
2	8
3	27
4	64

Functions:

A. $y = 3x$

B. $y = x^3$

C. $y = 3^x$

24. **Critical Thinking** Why don't two 150% enlargements on a photocopier produce the same size picture as one 300% enlargement?

25. **Patterns** The base in the function $y = (-2)^x$ is a negative number.

a. Make a table of values for the domain $\{1, 2, 3, 4, 5, 6\}$.

b. What pattern do you see in the outputs?

c. **Critical Thinking** Is $y = (-2)^x$ an exponential function? **Justify** your answer.

Graph each function.

26. $y = 3^x$

27. $y = 3\left(\frac{3}{2}\right)^x$

28. $y = 1.5^x$

29. $y = \frac{1}{4} \cdot 2^x$

30. $y = 0.1 \cdot 2^x$

31. $y = 10^x$

Chapter Project ***Find Out by Doing***

Gather the materials for your project: $\frac{1}{16}$ in. or 1 mm graph paper, a packet of unflavored gelatin, a flat dish or plate, a small piece of unprocessed cheese, and plastic wrap.

- Decide where you will keep your dish. A warm, humid place is best for growing mold.
- Cut the graph paper to cover the bottom of the dish. Follow the directions on the gelatin packet. Cover the graph paper with about $\frac{1}{8}$ in. of gelatin. Add the cheese to the gelatin. Leave the dish uncovered overnight; then cover tightly with the plastic wrap.

Exercises MIXED REVIEW

Solve each equation.

32. $5(g - 1) = \frac{1}{2}$

33. $t^2 + 3t - 4 = 0$

34. $|m - 7| = 9$

35. $x^2 - 5x + 6 = 0$

36. **Books** The smallest book in the Library of Congress is *Old King Cole.* Each square page has area $\frac{1}{25}$ in.^{2}. How wide is one page?

Getting Ready for Lesson 8-2

Find the range of each function for the domain $\{1, 2, 3, 4, 5\}$.

37. $y = 2^x$

38. $y = 4 \cdot 2^x$

39. $y = 0.5 \cdot 2^x$

40. $y = \frac{3}{2} \cdot 2^x$

41. $y = 3 \cdot 2^x$

42. How are the functions in Exercises 37–41 alike? How are they different?

8-2 Exponential Growth

What You'll Learn

- Modeling exponential growth
- Calculating compound interest

...And Why

To solve problems involving medical costs and finance

What You'll Need

- calculator

QUICK REVIEW

A 10% increase in an amount means you have 110% of the original amount. To find 110%, multiply by 1.1.

Time	Job A	Job B
Start	\$5.00	\$4.80
6 mo	■	■
1 yr	■	■

WORK TOGETHER

Jobs Suppose you are offered a choice of two jobs. Job A has a starting wage of \$5.00/h, with a \$.50 raise every 6 months. Job B starts at \$4.80/h, with a 10% raise every 6 months. Work with a partner.

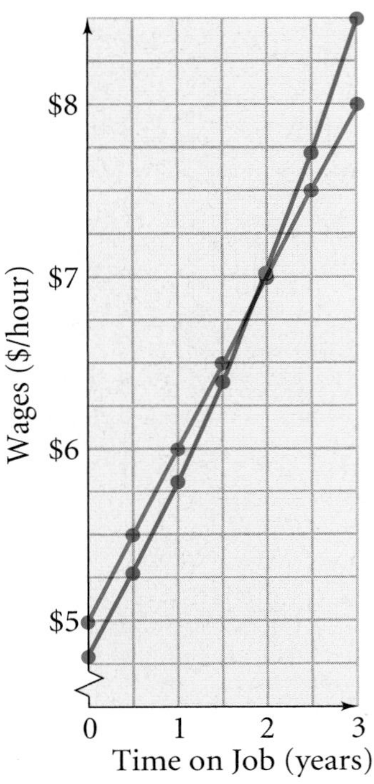

1. How do you find the new wage after each raise for Job A?
2. In Job B, each new wage is 110% of the previous wage. How do you find each new wage for Job B?
3. Organize the wages for each job in a table like the one at the left. Show wages from the start of the job through the raise at three years. Round each wage to the nearest cent.
4. **a.** *Patterns* Which wage pattern involves repeated multiplication?
   b. Which wage pattern results in a linear function?
5. Which graph represents the wages for Job A? for Job B?
6. When would you prefer to have Job A? Job B? Explain.

THINK AND DISCUSS

Modeling Exponential Growth

You can use an exponential function to show how the wages for Job B grow.

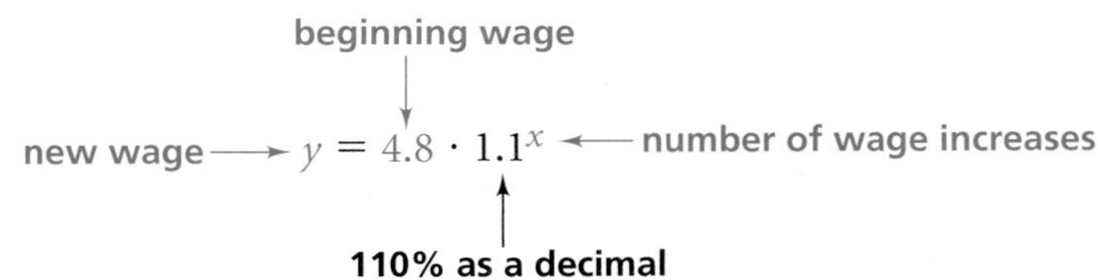

Because multiplying over and over by 1.1 causes the wage to increase, this kind of exponential function is an example of *exponential growth.*

Exponential Growth

For $a > 0$ and $b > 1$, the function $y = a \cdot b^x$ models **exponential growth.**

$$y = a \cdot b^x$$

- a: starting amount
- x: number of increases
- b: the base, called the **growth factor**

Example: $y = 1000 \cdot 2^x$

When you use exponential functions to model real-world situations, you must identify the initial amount a and the growth factor b. To show growth, b must be greater than 1.

7. Suppose the population of a city is 50,000 and is growing 3% each year.

a. The initial amount a is ■.

b. The growth factor b is 100% + 3%, which is 1 + ■ = ■.

c. To find the population after one year, you multiply ■ · 1.03.

d. Complete the equation to find the population after x years.

$$y = ■ \cdot ■^{■}$$

e. Use your equation to find the population after 25 years.

Example 1 — Relating to the Real World 

Medical Care Since 1985, the daily cost of patient care in community hospitals in the United States has increased about 8.6% per year. In 1985, hospital costs were an average of \$460 per day.

a. Write an equation to model the cost of hospital care.

b. Use your equation to find the approximate cost per day in 1995.

a. Use an exponential function to model repeated percent increases.

Relate $y = a \cdot b^x$

Define x = the number of years since 1985
y = the cost of hospital care at various times
b = 100% plus 8.6% of the cost = 108.6% = 1.086
a = initial cost in 1985 = \$460

Write $y = 460 \cdot 1.086^x$ ← Substitute values for the initial amount a and the growth factor b.

b. 1995 is 10 years after 1985, so solve the equation for $x = 10$.

$y = 460 \cdot 1.086^{10}$ ← Substitute.
$= 1049.677974$

The average cost per day in 1995 was about \$1050.

CALCULATOR HINT

To evaluate $460 \cdot 1.086^{10}$ press 460 [×] 1.086 [^] 10 [ENTER].

8. Try This **Predict** the cost per day for the year 2000.

PROBLEM SOLVING HINT

For Questions 9 and 10, use the *Guess and Test* strategy.

9. Find the first year in which the predicted cost per day will be greater than $2000.

10. The cost per day more than doubled between 1985 and 1995. Using the function from Example 1, about how long will it take to double the 1995 cost per day?

Finding Compound Interest

QUICK REVIEW

Principal is the amount of money you put in a bank account. *Interest* is the amount the bank pays you for letting it use your money.

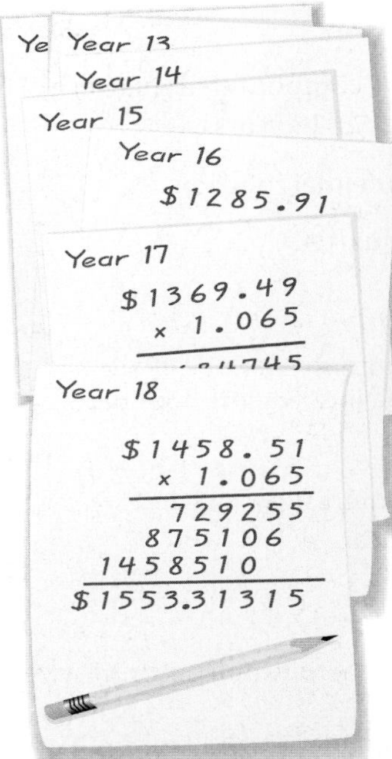

When a bank pays interest on both the principal *and* the interest an account has already earned, the bank is paying **compound interest.** An **interest period** is the length of time over which interest is calculated. Compound interest is an exponential growth situation.

Example 2 **Relating to the Real World** 

Savings Suppose your parents deposited $500 in an account paying 6.5% interest, compounded annually (once a year), when you were born. Find the account balance after 18 years.

Relate $y = a \cdot b^x$ ← Use an exponential function.

Define $x =$ the number of interest periods
$y =$ the balance at various times
$a = 500$ ← initial deposit
$b = 1.065$ ← 100% + 6.5% = 106.5% = 1.065

Write $y = 500 \cdot 1.065^x$
$= 500 \cdot 1.065^{18}$ ← Once a year for 18 years is 18 interest periods. Substitute 18 for *x*.
$= 1553.32719$

The balance after 18 years will be $1553.33.

11. **Try This** Suppose the interest rate on the account was 8%. How much would be in the account after 18 years?

Math A Test Prep

1 Which equation represents a population of 26,000 growing at a rate of 2% per year?
(1) $y = 26{,}000 \cdot 1.02^x$
(2) $y = 26{,}000 \cdot 0.02^x$
(3) $y = 0.02 \cdot 26{,}000^x$
(4) $y = 26{,}000 \cdot x^{1.02}$

2 Certain bacteria in a lab culture double in number every 15 minutes. If a culture originally contains 50 cells, how many cells will it contain at the end of 1 hour?

Banks sometimes pay compound interest more than once a year. When they use shorter interest periods, the interest rate for each period is also reduced.

Annual Interest Rate of 8%

Compounded	Periods per Year	Rate per Period
annually	1	8% every year
semi-annually	2	$\frac{8\%}{2} = 4\%$ every 6 months
quarterly	4	$\frac{8\%}{4} = 2\%$ every 3 months
monthly	12	$\frac{8\%}{12} = 0.\bar{6}\%$ every month

12. In an account that pays 6.5% interest, what is the interest rate if the interest is compounded quarterly? monthly?

Example 3

Suppose the account in Example 2 paid interest compounded quarterly instead of annually. Find the account balance after 18 years.

Relate $y = a \cdot b^x$ ← Use an exponential function.

Define $x =$ the number of interest periods (quarters)
$y =$ the balance at various times
$a = 500$ ← initial deposit
$b = 1 + \frac{0.065}{4}$ ← There are 4 interest periods in 1 year, so divide the interest into four parts.
$= 1.01625$

Write $y = 500 \cdot 1.01625^x$
$= 500 \cdot 1.01625^{72}$ ← $18 \cdot 4 = 72$ interest periods in 18 years
$= 1595.916716$ ← Use a calculator.

The balance after 18 years will be $1595.92.

13. a. How many interest periods per year are there for an account with interest compounded daily?

b. **Try This** Suppose the account above paid interest compounded daily. How much money would be in the account after 18 years?

Exercises ON YOUR OWN

Identify the initial amount *a* and the growth factor *b* in each exponential function.

1. $g(x) = 20 \cdot 2^x$ **2.** $y = 200 \cdot 1.0875^x$ **3.** $y = 10{,}000 \cdot 1.01^x$ **4.** $f(t) = 1.5^t$

What repeated percent of increase is modeled in each function?

5. $r = 70 \cdot 1.5^n$ **6.** $f(t) = 30 \cdot 1.095^t$ **7.** $y = 1000 \cdot 1.04^x$ **8.** $y = 2^x$

Write the growth factor used to model each percent of increase in an exponential function.

9. 4%

10. 5%

11. 3.7%

12. 8.75%

13. 0.5%

14. 15%

Write an exponential function to model each situation. Tell what each variable you use represents.

15. A population of 130,000 grows 1% per year

16. A price of $50 increases 6% each year

17. A deposit of $3000 earns 5% annual interest compounded monthly.

18. **Writing** Would you rather have $500 in an account paying 6% interest compounded quarterly or $750 in an account paying 5.5% compounded annually? **Summarize** your reasoning.

19. **Education** The function $y = 355 \cdot 1.08^x$ models the average annual cost y (in dollars) for tuition and fees at public two-year colleges. The variable x represents the number of years since 1980.

a. What was the average annual cost in 1980?

b. What is the average percent increase in the annual cost?

c. Find the average annual cost for 1990.

d. **Open-ended** **Predict** the average annual cost for the year you plan to graduate from high school.

20. **History** The Dutch bought Manhattan Island in 1626 for $24 worth of merchandise. Suppose the $24 had been invested in 1626 in an account paying 4.5% interest compounded annually. Find the balance today.

21. **Standardized Test Prep** An investment of $100 earns 5% interest compounded annually. Which expression represents the value of the investment after 10 years?

A. $10 \cdot 100^5$ **B.** $100 \cdot 0.05^{10}$ **C.** $100 \cdot 10^{0.05}$

D. $10 \cdot 100^{1.05}$ **E.** $100 \cdot 1.05^{10}$

22. **a.** **Math in the Media** Write an equation to model the sales of workstation computers since 1987.

b. Use your model to find the total sales in 1995.

Workstations Replace Supercomputers

Workstations–sophisticated computers that sit on a desktop–are replacing larger mainframe computers in industry. Since 1987, sales of workstation computers in industry have increased about 30% per year. In 1987, sales totaled about $3 billion.

Graph the function represented in each table. Then tell whether the table represents a *linear function* or an *exponential function*.

23.

x	y
1	20
2	40
3	60
4	80

24.

x	y
1	3
2	9
3	27
4	81

25.

x	y
1	6
2	12
3	24
4	48

26.

x	y
1	3
2	9
3	15
4	21

Tell whether each graph is a *linear function,* an *exponential function,* or *neither.* Justify your reasoning.

27. 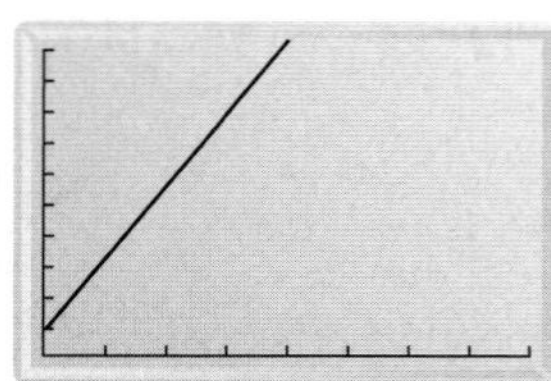

28. 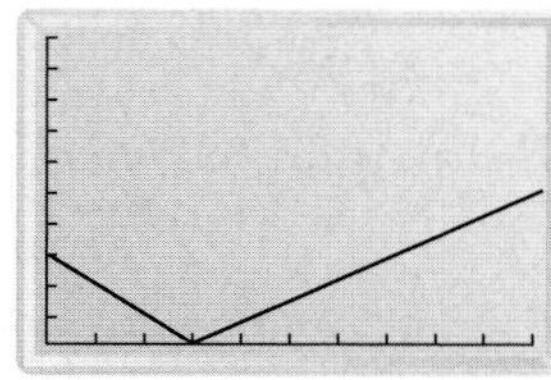

29. 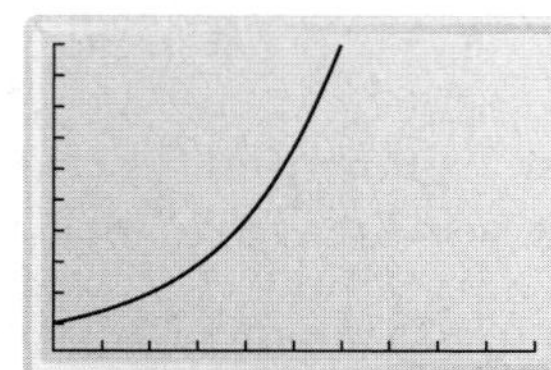

30. **Statistics** Since 1970, the population of Virginia has grown at an average annual rate of about 1.015%. In 1970, the population was about 4,651,000.

a. **Graphing Calculator** Write and graph a function to model population growth in Virginia since 1970.

b. Estimate the population of Virginia in 1980 and 1990.

c. **Predict** the population of Virginia in the years 2000 and 2025.

Chapter Project ***Find Out by Recording***

Count the number of graph paper squares covered by mold once a day for 10 days. Record the mold growth. (Don't worry if you don't see any mold for the first few days.)

Write an exponential function to model each situation. Find each amount after the specified time.

31. \$20,000 principal
3.5% compounded
quarterly10 years

32. \$30 principal
4.5% compounded daily
2 years

33. \$2400 principal
7% compounded annually
10 years

34. \$2400 principal
7% compounded monthly
10 years

Exercises MIXED REVIEW

Find the vertex of each parabola. Identify it as a *maximum* or a *minimum*.

35. $y = 3x^2 + 2x - 8$

36. $y = \frac{1}{2}x^2 - 5x + 1$

37. $y = 4x^2 - 11$

38. a. **History** The boardwalk in Atlantic City was 1 mi long and 12 ft wide when it was built in 1870. What was its area in square feet?

b. In 1995, the boardwalk was 4.5 mi long and up to 60 ft wide. What could be its maximum area in square feet?

c. About how many times larger was the boardwalk in 1995 than in 1870?

Getting Ready for Lesson 8-3

Simplify each expression.

39. $\left(\frac{1}{2}\right)^2$

40. 0.5^4

41. $\left(\frac{3}{4}\right)^1$

42. 0.9^3

43. 0.98^2

44. $\left(\frac{5}{6}\right)^2$

8-3 Exponential Decay

What You'll Learn

- Modeling exponential decay
- Using half-life models

...And Why

To solve problems involving population and radioactive decay

What You'll Need

- calculator

THINK AND DISCUSS

In Lesson 8-2 you used the exponential function $y = a \cdot b^x$ to model growth. You can also use it to model decay. The difference between growth and decay is the value of b, the base. With growth, b is greater than 1. With decay, b is between 0 and 1 and is called the **decay factor.**

Exponential Decay

For $a > 0$ and $0 < b < 1$, the function $y = a \cdot b^x$ models **exponential decay.**

Example: $y = 5 \cdot \left(\frac{1}{2}\right)^x$

Exponential Decay y-values decrease because of repeated multiplication by a number between 0 and 1.

$y = 5 \cdot 2^x$

$y = 5 \cdot \frac{1}{2}^x$

Xmin=0 Ymin=0
Xmax=4 Ymax=15
Xscl=0.5 Yscl=1

Exponential Growth y-values increase because of repeated multiplication by a number greater than 1.

You can use an exponential function to model the decay of a radioactive substance.

Who? Marie Curie (1867–1934) was born in Poland. She received Nobel Prizes in physics and chemistry for her pioneering work with radioactive elements. The *curie* is named for Marie Curie.

Example 1 Relating to the Real World 

Medicine To treat some forms of cancer, doctors use radioactive iodine. Use the graph to find how much iodine-131 is left in a patient eight days after the patient receives a dose of 20 mCi (millicuries).

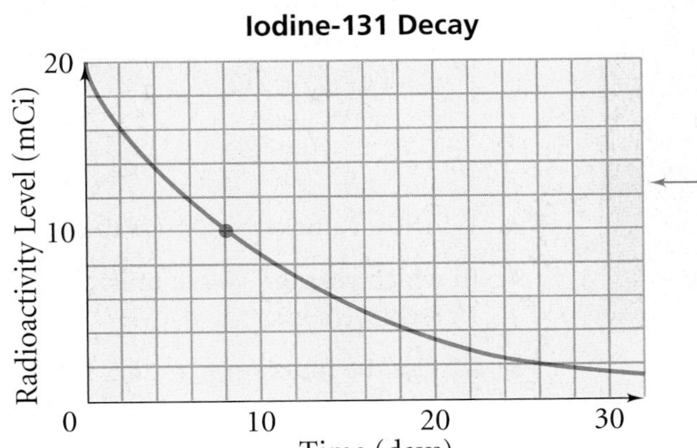

The x-value 8 represents eight days. The y-value 10 represents the amount of iodine-131 remaining.

After eight days, there are 10 mCi of iodine-131 left.

1. **Try This** Use the graph in Example 1 to find the amount of iodine-131 left after 24 days.

The *half-life* of a radioactive substance is the length of time it takes for one half of the substance to decay.

2. **a.** How long does it take for half of the 20 mCi dose in Example 1 to decay? How much is left?
   b. Use your answer to part (a). How long does it take for half of that amount to decay? How much is left?
   c. What is the half-life of iodine-131?
   d. How many half-lives of iodine-131 occur in 32 days?
   e. **Critical Thinking** Suppose you start with a 50 mCi sample of iodine-131. What is its half-life? How much iodine-131 is left after one half-life? after two half-lives?

You can use exponential decay to model other real-world situations.

Example 2 **Relating to the Real World** 

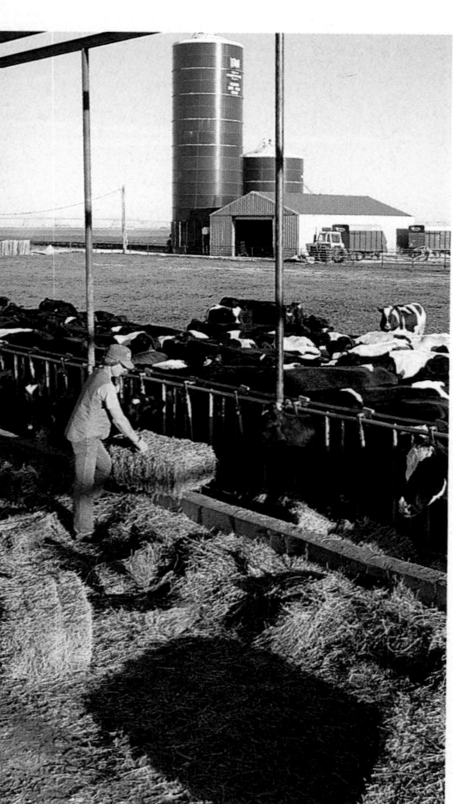

Consumer Trends An exponential function models the amount of whole milk each person in the United States drinks in a year. Graph the function $y = 21.5 \cdot 0.955^x$, where y is the number of gallons of whole milk and x is the number of years since 1975.

Make a table of values.

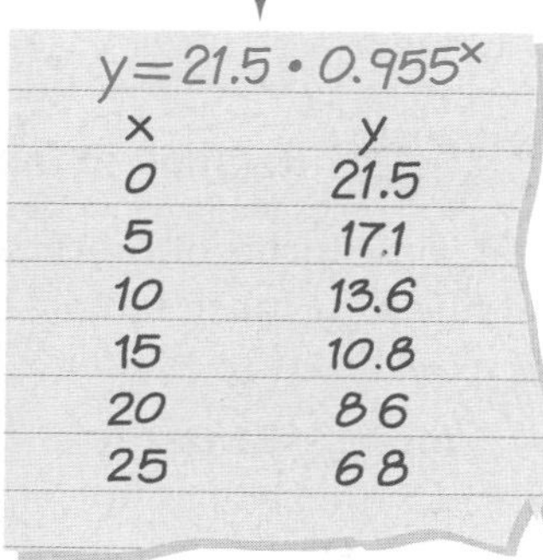

$y = 21.5 \cdot 0.955^x$

x	y
0	21.5
5	17.1
10	13.6
15	10.8
20	8.6
25	6.8

Graph the points. Draw a smooth curve through the points.

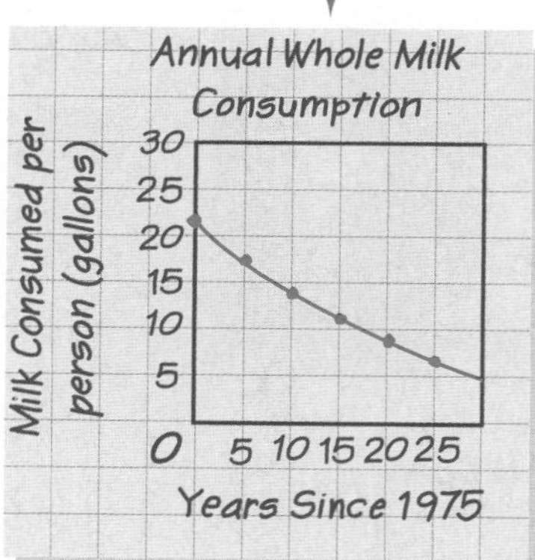

3. Which x-value corresponds to the year 1995?

4. In which year did whole milk consumption fall to about 10.8 gal/person?

5. **a.** Use the function $y = 21.5 \cdot 0.955^x$ and your calculator to **predict** whole milk consumption for the year 2010.
   b. **Open-ended** Use the function to **predict** whole milk consumption 10 years from now.

Example 3

Consumer Trends Use the equation $y = 21.5 \cdot 0.955^x$ to find the annual percent of decrease in whole milk consumption in the United States.

$0.955 = 95.5\%$ ← Change the decay factor to a percent.

$100\% - 95.5\% = 4.5\%$ ← Subtract.

Whole milk consumption is decreasing by 4.5% per year.

6. Try This What percent of decrease does each decay factor model?
a. 0.75 **b.** 0.4 **c.** 0.135 **d.** 0.0074

7. By what number would you multiply 15 to decrease it
a. by 6%? **b.** by 12%? **c.** by 3.5%? **d.** by 53.9%?

8. Suppose an initial population of 10,000 people decreases by 2.4% each year. Write an exponential function in the form $y = \blacksquare \cdot \blacksquare^x$ to model the population y after x years have passed.

Exercises ON YOUR OWN

Identify each function as *exponential growth* or *exponential decay*.

1. $y = 0.68 \cdot 2^x$ **2.** $y = 2 \cdot 0.68^x$ **3.** $y = 68 \cdot 2^x$ **4.** $y = 68 \cdot 0.2^x$

Identify the decay factor in each function.

5. $y = 5 \cdot 0.5^x$ **6.** $f(x) = 10 \cdot 0.1^x$ **7.** $g(x) = 100 \cdot \left(\frac{2}{3}\right)^x$ **8.** $y = 0.1 \cdot 0.9^x$

Find the percent of decrease for each function.

9. $r = 70 \cdot 0.9^n$ **10.** $f(t) = 45 \cdot 0.998^t$ **11.** $r = 50 \cdot \left(\frac{1}{2}\right)^n$ **12.** $y = 1000 \cdot 0.75^x$

Use the graph to estimate the half-life of each radioactive substance.

13.

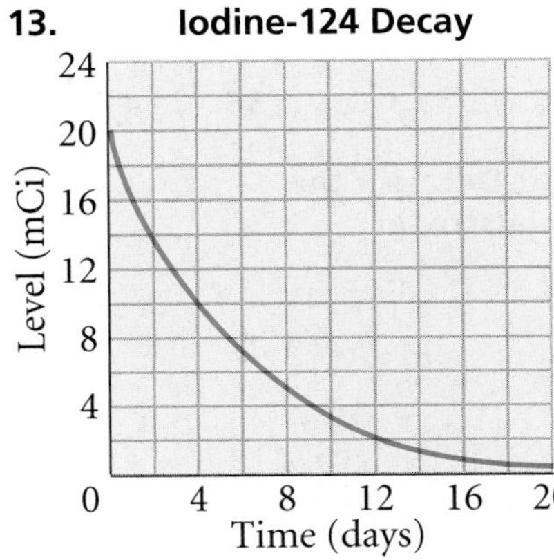

14.

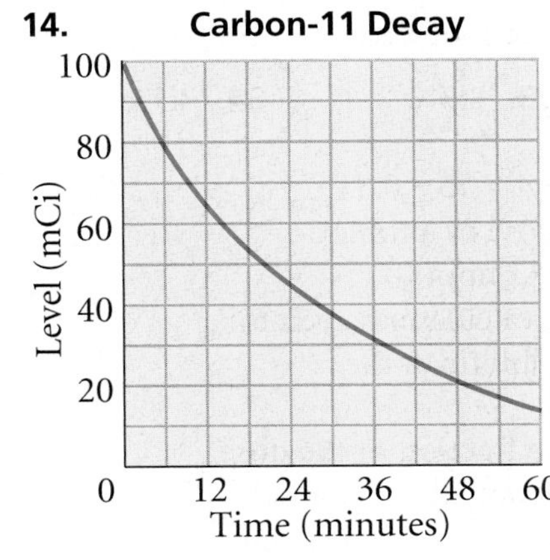

15.

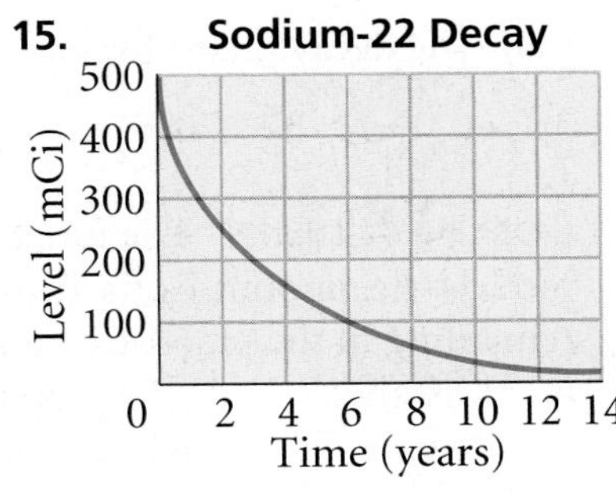

Choose **Use a graphing calculator or make a table of values to graph each function. Label each graph as *exponential growth* or *exponential decay*.**

16. $f(x) = 100 \cdot 0.9^x$

17. $s = 64 \cdot \left(\frac{1}{2}\right)^n$

18. $g = 8 \cdot 1.5^x$

19. $y = 3.5 \cdot 0.01^x$

20. $y = 2 \cdot 10^x$

21. $g(x) = \left(\frac{1}{10}\right) \cdot 0.1^x$

22. $f = 10 \cdot 0.1^x$

23. $y = \frac{2}{5} \cdot \left(\frac{1}{2}\right)^x$

24. $y = 0.5 \cdot 2^x$

25. **Writing** Describe a situation that can be modeled by the equation $y = 100 \cdot 0.9^x$.

Write an exponential function to model each situation. Find each amount after the specified time.

26. 3,000,000 initial population
1.5% annual decrease
10 years

27. \$900 purchase
20% loss in value each year
6 years

28. \$10,000 investment
12.5% loss each year
7 years

29. **Statistics** In 1980, the population of Warren, Michigan, was about 161,000. Since then the population has decreased about 1% per year.

a. Write an equation to model the population of Warren since 1980.

b. **Estimation** Estimate the population of Warren in 1990.

c. Suppose the current trend continues. **Predict** the population of Warren in 2010.

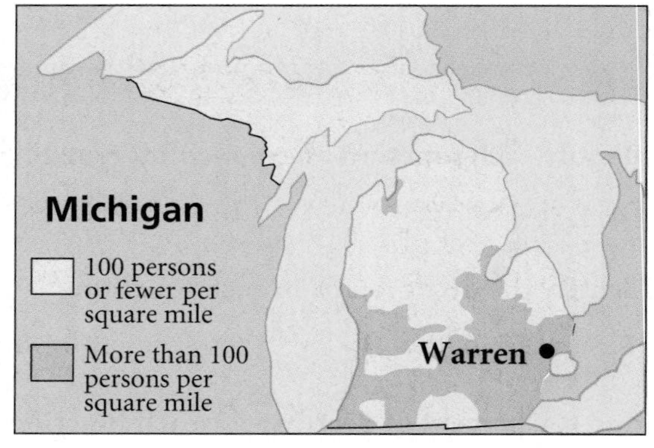

30. a. **Open-ended** Write two exponential decay functions, one with a base near 0 and one with a base near 1.

b. Find the range of each function using the domain {1, 2, 3, 4}.

c. Graph each function.

Calculate the decay factor for each percent of decrease.

31. 3%

32. 70%

33. 2.6%

34. 4.75%

35. 0.7%

36. 23.4%

37. **Graphing Calculator** The function $y = 15 \cdot 0.84^x$ models the amount y of a 15-mg dose of antibiotic remaining in the bloodstream after x hours.

a. **Estimation** Study the graphing calculator screen to estimate the half-life of this antibiotic in the bloodstream.

b. Use your estimate to **predict** the fraction of the dose that will remain in the bloodstream after 8 hours.

c. **Verify** your prediction by using the function to find the amount of antibiotic remaining after 8 hours.

Antibiotic Decay in the Bloodstream

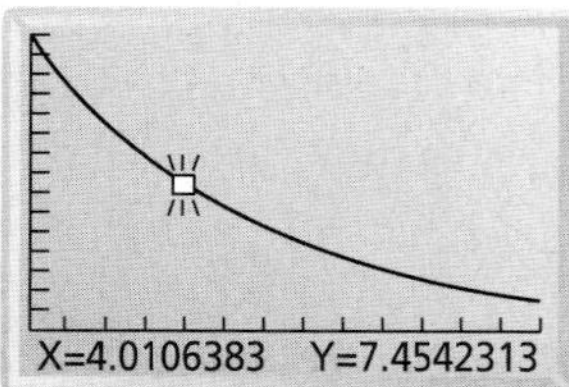

Xmin=0 Ymin=0
Xmax=13 Ymax=15

How many half-lives occur in each length of time?

38. 2 days (1 half-life = 8 h)

39. 300 years (1 half-life = 75 yr)

Exercises MIXED REVIEW

Solve.

40. $3 = |x - 7|$

41. $2 - x > 5$

42. $\frac{t}{3} - \frac{t}{6} = 15$

43. $j^2 + 3 = 12$

44. **Biology** A mouse's heart beats 600 times/min. The average mouse lives about 3 yr. About how many times does the average mouse's heart beat in its lifetime?

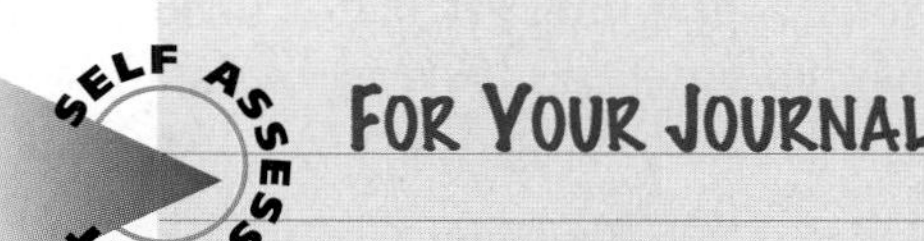

Explain the differences and similarities between exponential growth and exponential decay. Give an example of each.

Getting Ready for Lesson 8-4

Complete each expression.

45. $\frac{1}{2^2} = \frac{1}{■}$

46. $\frac{8}{27} = \frac{2^{■}}{3^{■}}$

47. $\frac{2^2}{4^2} = \frac{■}{■} = ■$

Exercises CHECKPOINT

Write an exponential function to model each situation. Find each amount after the specified time.

1. \$65,000 initial market value
3.2% annual increase
15 years

2. 200,000 initial population
5% loss each year
20 years

3. \$300 initial value
doubles every 10 years
50 years

4. **Standardized Test Prep** From 1790 to 1860, the population of the United States grew slowly but steadily from 4 million. Which exponential function is the most likely model for the population p in the years after 1790?

A. $p = 4 \cdot 2.6^x$ **B.** $p = 4 \cdot 1.03^x$ **C.** $p = 4 \cdot 0.98^x$ **D.** $p = 4 \cdot 3^x$ **E.** $p = 0.98 \cdot 4^x$

Graph each function. Label each graph as *exponential growth* or *exponential decay*.

5. $y = \left(\frac{9}{10}\right) \cdot 2^x$

6. $f(x) = 5 \cdot 0.5^x$

7. $y = 2 \cdot \left(\frac{3}{2}\right)^x$

8. **Open-ended** Suppose you have \$1000 to deposit into a savings account for your education. One account pays 6.7% compounded annually. Another account pays 5% compounded monthly.

a. Which account would you choose? Consider the length of time you would leave the money in the account. **Summarize** your reasoning.

b. Calculate how much will be in the account if you close it when you are 18.

Math ToolboX

Technology

Fitting Exponential Curves to Data

After Lesson 8-3

In Chapter 5, you learned how to find a line of best fit for a set of data. Some data sets are better modeled by exponential functions. A graphing calculator makes it easy to graph exponential functions for a set of data.

U.S. Sales of Compact Discs

Year	Millions of CDs
1987 ↔ 7	102.1
8	149.7
9	207.2
10	286.5
11	333.3
12	407.5
13	495.4
1994 ↔ 14	662.1

Example

Use a graphing calculator to graph the data and find the best-fitting exponential function $y = a \cdot b^x$.

Step 1: Use the STAT feature to enter the data. Let 1980 correspond to $x = 0$.

Step 2: Use the STAT PLOT feature to graph the data in a scatter plot.

Step 3: Find the equation for the best-fitting exponential function. Press STAT ▶ ALPHA A ENTER to get the ExpReg equation.

```
ExpReg
y=a*b^x
a=19.82510651
b=1.287856937
r=.9908425236
```

Step 4: Graph the function. Press Y= CLEAR VARS 5 ▶ ▶ 7 to enter the ExpReg results. Press GRAPH to display the data and the function together.

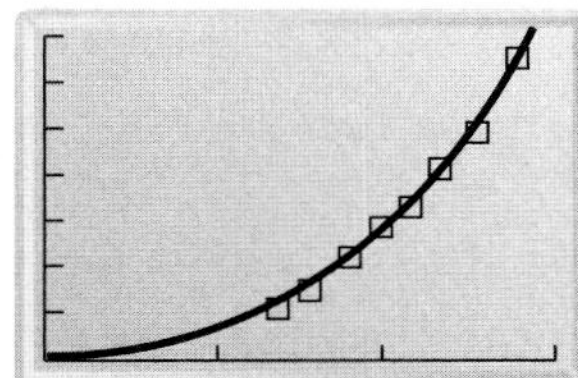

Xmin=0 Ymin=0
Xmax=15 Ymax=700
Xscl=5 Yscl=100

Use a graphing calculator to write the exponential function that fits each set of data. Sketch the graph of the function and show the data points.

1. **U.S. Movie Earnings.** Let 1980 correspond to $x = 0$.

Year	1986	1987	1988	1989	1990	1991	1992
Billions of Dollars	23.8	27.8	31.2	35.0	38.1	41.1	43.8

2. **U.S. Homes Heated by Coal.** Let 1950 correspond to $x = 0$.

Year	1950	1960	1970	1980	1991
Percent of Homes	33.8	12.2	2.9	0.4	0.3

Population of New Mexico (millions)

1970	1.017
1980	1.303
1985	1.438
1990	1.515
1994	1.654

3. a. The table gives the population of New Mexico at various times. Use the best-fitting exponential function to **predict** the population of New Mexico in 2010.
   b. *Writing* Explain how the r-value affects your answer to part (a).

What You'll Learn

- Evaluating and simplifying expressions in which zero and negative numbers are used as exponents

...And Why

To analyze exponential functions over a broader domain

What You'll Need

- graphing calculator

8-4 Zero and Negative Exponents

WORK TOGETHER

Work with a partner to copy and complete the table. Replace each box with a whole number or a fraction in lowest terms.

$y = 2^x$	$y = 5^x$	$y = 10^x$
$2^2 = 4$	$5^2 = 25$	$10^2 = 100$
$2^1 = 2$	$5^1 = 5$	$10^1 = 10$
$2^0 = ■$	$5^0 = ■$	$10^0 = ■$
$2^{-1} = ■$	$5^{-1} = ■$	$10^{-1} = ■$
$2^{-2} = ■$	$5^{-2} = ■$	$10^{-2} = ■$

1. You can describe what happens in the first column of the table as division by 2. What happens in the other columns of the table?

Xmin=–3
Xmax=3
Xscl =1
Ymin=0
Ymax=100
Yscl =10

2. a. Graph the three functions on your calculator. Use the range values at the left. Sketch the graphs.
   b. At what point do the three graphs intersect?
3. a. What pattern do you notice in the row containing 0 as an exponent?
   b. Use your calculator to calculate other numbers to the zero power. What do you notice?
4. Copy and complete each expression.
   a. $2^{-1} = \frac{1}{■} = \frac{1}{2^{■}}$ b. $2^{-2} = \frac{1}{■} = \frac{1}{2^{■}}$ c. $2^{-3} = \frac{1}{■} = \frac{1}{2^{■}}$
5. *Critical Thinking* Look for a pattern in your answers to Question 4. Does this pattern hold true for the other columns? Explain.

THINK AND DISCUSS

Using Zero and Negative Integers as Exponents

The pattern you saw in Question 3 is an important property of exponents.

Zero as an Exponent

For any nonzero number a, $a^0 = 1$.

Examples: $5^0 = 1$; $(-2)^0 = 1$; $\left(\frac{3}{8}\right)^0 = 1$; $1.02^0 = 1$

Notice that 0 is excluded as a base. The expression 0^0 is undefined, just as the expressions $\frac{2}{0}$ and $\frac{0}{0}$ are undefined.

Example 1 **Relating to the Real World** 

Population Growth The function $f(t) = 1000 \cdot 2^t$ models an initial population of 1000 insects that doubles every time period t. Evaluate the function for $t = 0$. Then describe what $f(0)$ represents in the situation.

$$\begin{aligned} f(0) &= 1000 \cdot 2^0 && \leftarrow \text{Substitute 0 for } t. \\ &= 1000 \cdot 1 && \leftarrow 2^0 = 1 \\ &= 1000 \end{aligned}$$

The value of $f(0)$ represents the initial population of insects. This makes sense because when $t = 0$, no time has passed.

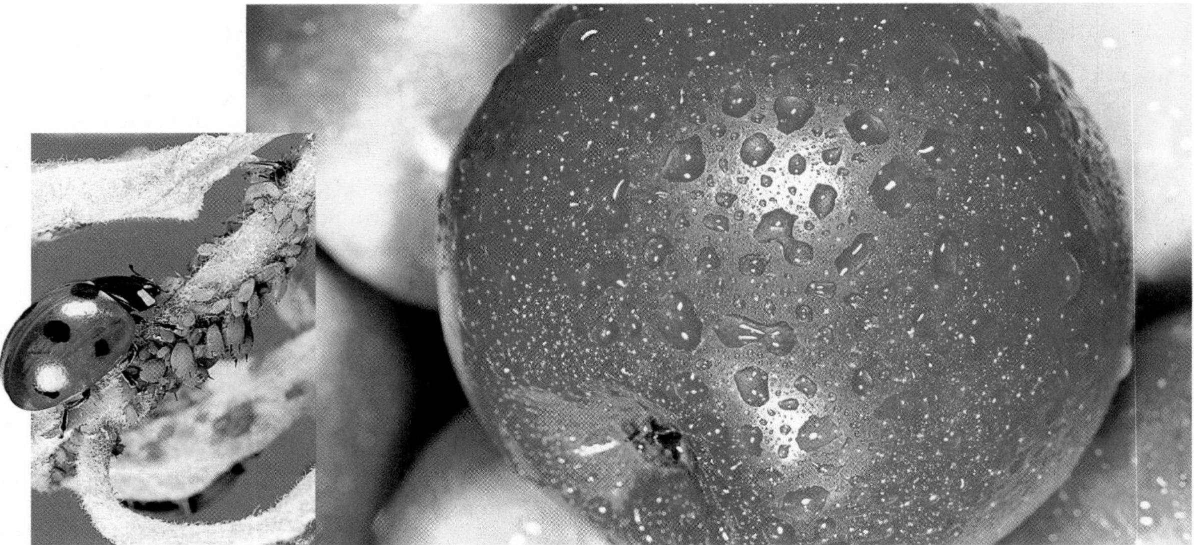

A large aphid population can destroy an apple orchard's produce. One way of controlling the aphids is to release ladybugs into the orchard, where they feed on the apple aphid colonies.

The pattern from Questions 4 and 5 illustrates another important property.

Negative Exponents

For any nonzero number a and any integer n, $a^{-n} = \frac{1}{a^n}$.

Examples: $6^{-4} = \frac{1}{6^4}$ and $7^{-1} = \frac{1}{7^1}$

Example 2

Write each expression as a simple fraction.

a. 4^{-3}

$4^{-3} = \frac{1}{4^3}$ ← definition of a negative exponent

$= \frac{1}{64}$

b. $(-3)^{-2}$

$(-3)^{-2} = \frac{1}{(-3)^2}$

$= \frac{1}{9}$

QUICK REVIEW

Unless grouping symbols are used, exponents operate on only one factor.

$-4^2 = -(4 \cdot 4) = -16$

$(-4)^2 = -4 \cdot -4 = 16$

$2x^3 = 2 \cdot x \cdot x \cdot x$

$(2x)^3 = 2x \cdot 2x \cdot 2x$

6. **Try This** Write each expression as a simple fraction.

a. 3^{-4} b. $(-7)^0$ c. $(-4)^{-3}$ d. 7^{-3} e. -3^{-2}

Math A Test Prep

1 Which expression does not equal $\frac{1}{27}$?

(1) $\frac{3^0}{3^3}$ (3) -3^3

(2) $\left(\frac{1}{3}\right)^3$ (4) 3^{-3}

2 Use x, y, 0.74, and 38 to write an exponential decay function. Explain what each value and variable in the function represents.

You can use what you know about rewriting the expression a^{-n} to see how the values of a^n and a^{-n} are related.

$$a^n \cdot a^{-n} = a^n \cdot \frac{1}{a^n}$$
$$= \frac{a^n}{1} \cdot \frac{1}{a^n} = 1$$

Therefore, a^n and a^{-n} are *reciprocals.*

7. **Verify** that a^n and a^{-n} are reciprocals by evaluating each product.
   a. $3^2 \cdot 3^{-2}$ b. $2^4 \cdot 2^{-4}$ c. $5^3 \cdot 5^{-3}$

8. Write the reciprocal of each number in two ways: as a simple fraction and using a negative exponent.
   a. 10^1 b. 10^2 c. 1000 d. 10,000

9. Write each expression as a decimal.
   a. 10^{-3} b. $3 \cdot 10^{-2}$ c. $-5 \cdot 10^{-4}$ d. 10^{-6}

Example 3

Rewrite each expression so that all exponents are positive.

a. $4yx^{-3} = 4y\left(\frac{1}{x^3}\right)$ ← definition of negative exponent

$= \frac{4y}{x^3}$

b. $\frac{1}{w^{-4}} = 1 \div w^{-4}$ ← rewrite using a division symbol

$= 1 \div \frac{1}{w^4}$

$= 1 \cdot w^4$ ← multiply by the reciprocal

$= w^4$

10. **Try This** Complete each expression using only positive exponents.
   a. $\frac{1}{x^{-3}} = x^{\blacksquare}$ b. $\frac{1}{v^{-2}} = v^{\blacksquare}$ c. $w^{-3} = \frac{1}{w^{\blacksquare}}$ d. $\frac{w^{-3}}{v^{-2}} = \frac{\blacksquare^{\blacksquare}}{\blacksquare^{\blacksquare}}$

Relating the Properties to Exponential Functions

Zero and negative integer exponents allow you to understand the graph of an exponential function more completely.

Example 4

Graphing Calculator Graph the functions $y = 2^x$ and $y = \left(\frac{1}{2}\right)^x$ on the same set of axes. Show the functions over the domain $\{-3 \le x \le 3\}$.

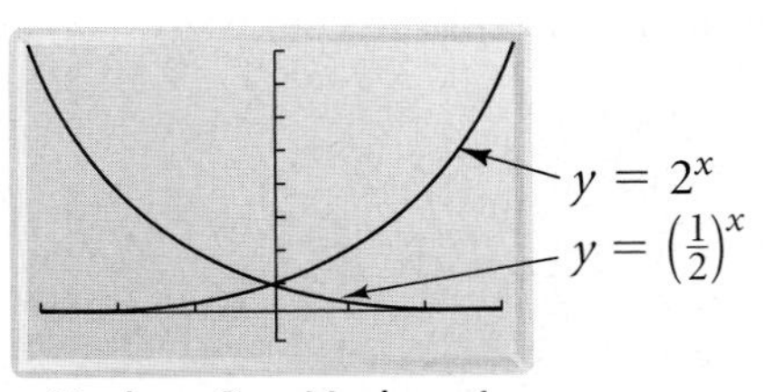

Xmin=–3 Ymin=–1
Xmax=3 Ymax=8

GRAPHING CALCULATOR HINT

You can generate values for a function with the TABLE key on some graphing calculators.

11. **a.** Is the value of 2^x always positive? Explain.

b. In what quadrants do the graphs of $y = 2^x$ and $y = \left(\frac{1}{2}\right)^x$ appear? Explain.

12. **Critical Thinking** The graph of $y = 2^{-x}$ is identical to one of the two graphs shown in Example 4. Use the definition of negative exponents to help decide which one. Explain.

Exercises ON YOUR OWN

Write each expression as an integer or simple fraction.

1. -2.57^0
2. 4^{-2}
3. $(-5)^{-1}$
4. $\left(\frac{2}{3}\right)^{-1}$
5. $\frac{1}{2^{-3}}$
6. 5^{-3}
7. $\left(\frac{1}{3}\right)^{-2}$
8. -3^{-4}
9. 2^{-6}
10. $(-12)^{-1}$
11. $45 \cdot (0.5)^0$
12. $\left(\frac{2}{5}\right)^{-2}$
13. $54 \cdot 3^{-2}$
14. $\left(-\frac{1}{4}\right)^{-3}$
15. $5 \cdot 10^{-2}$
16. $\frac{5^{-2}}{7^{-3}}$
17. $\frac{4^{-1}}{9^0}$
18. $\frac{(-3)^{-1}}{-2^{-1}}$

19. **a. Patterns** Complete the pattern.

$\frac{1}{5^2} = \blacksquare$ $\quad \frac{1}{5^1} = \blacksquare$ $\quad \frac{1}{5^0} = \blacksquare$ $\quad \frac{1}{5^{-1}} = \blacksquare$ $\quad \frac{1}{5^{-2}} = \blacksquare$

b. Write $\frac{1}{5^{-4}}$ using a positive exponent.

c. Generalize Rewrite $\frac{1}{a^{-n}}$ so that the power of a is in the numerator.

Write each expression so that it contains only positive exponents.

20. $\frac{1}{c^{-1}}$
21. $\frac{1}{x^{-7}}$
22. $3ab^0$
23. $(5x)^{-4}$
24. $\frac{5^{-2}}{p}$
25. $a^{-4}b^0$
26. $\frac{3x^{-2}}{y}$
27. $12xy^{-3}$
28. $\frac{7ab^{-2}}{3w}$
29. $5ac^{-5}$
30. $x^{-5}y^{-7}$
31. $\frac{8a^{-5}}{c^{-3}d^3}$
32. $x^{-5}y^7$
33. $\frac{7s^{-5}}{5t^{-3}}$
34. $\frac{6a^{-1}c^{-3}}{b^0}$
35. $\frac{1}{a^{-3}b^3}$
36. $\frac{c^4}{x^2y^{-1}}$
37. $\frac{mn^{-4}}{p^0q^{-2}}$

Evaluate each expression for $a = 3$, $b = 2$, and $c = -4$.

38. c^b
39. $a^{-b}b$
40. b^{-a}
41. b^c
42. $c^{-a}b^{ab}$
43. c^a

Graph each function over the domain $\{-3 \leq x \leq 3\}$.

44. $y = 2^x$
45. $f(x) = (2)^{-x}$
46. $g(x) = 0.5 \cdot 3^x$
47. $y = 1.5 \cdot (1.5)^{-x}$

Match each graphing calculator screen with the functions it displays.

48. 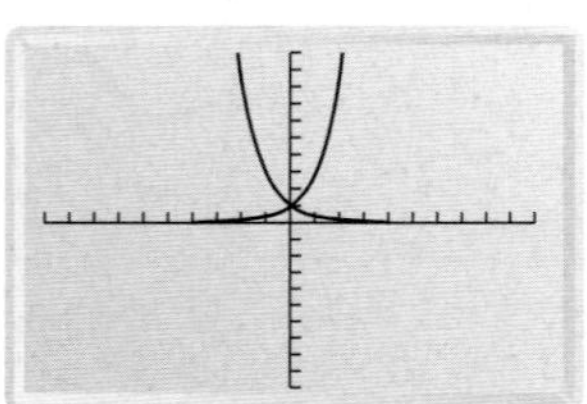

49. 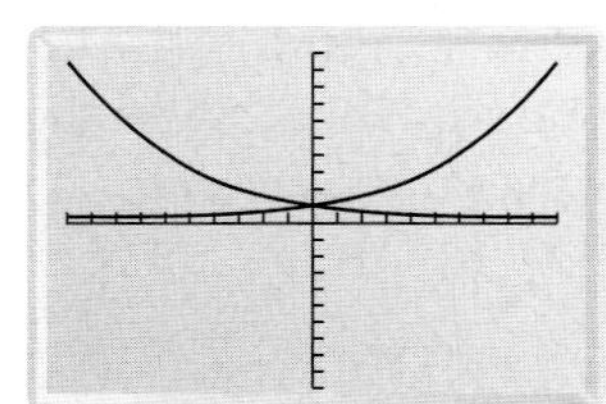

I. $y = \left(\frac{5}{4}\right)^x; y = \left(\frac{4}{5}\right)^x$

II. $y = 3^x; y = \left(\frac{1}{3}\right)^x$

III. $y = 15^x; y = \left(\frac{1}{15}\right)^x$

50. **Writing** Explain why the value of -3^0 is negative and the value of $(-3)^0$ is positive.

51. Copy and complete the table.

a	4	0.2	■	■	$\frac{7}{8}$	■
a^{-1}	■	■	3	$\frac{1}{6}$	■	0.5

Determine whether the value of each expression is *positive* or *negative*.

52. -2^2 53. $(-2)^2$ 54. 2^{-2} 55. $(-2)^3$ 56. $(-2)^{-3}$ 57. 4^{-1}

Copy and complete each equation.

58. $2^{\blacksquare} = 0.5$
59. $3xy^{\blacksquare} = \frac{3x}{y^3}$
60. $\frac{x^{\blacksquare}}{2y^{\blacksquare}} = \frac{1}{2x^{-3}y^4}$
61. $\frac{a^{\blacksquare}}{3b^{\blacksquare}} = \frac{b^3}{3}$
62. $(-5)^{\blacksquare} = -\frac{1}{125}$
63. $\frac{4n^{\blacksquare}}{m^{\blacksquare}} = \frac{4m^2}{n^3}$
64. $\frac{5x^{\blacksquare}}{y^{\blacksquare}} = \frac{5}{xy^2}$
65. $\frac{x^{\blacksquare}}{y^{\blacksquare}} = x^{-2}y^3$

66. **Standardized Test Prep** Compare the quantities in Column A and Column B.

Column A	Column B
3^x	3^{-x}

A. The quantity in Column A is greater.
B. The quantity in Column B is greater.
C. The quantities are equal.
D. The relationship cannot be determined from the information given.

67. Which expressions equal $\frac{1}{4}$?

A. 4^{-1} B. 2^{-2} C. -4^1
D. $\frac{1}{2^2}$ E. 1^4 F. -2^{-2}

68. **Open-ended** Choose a fraction to use as a value for the variable a. Find the values of a^{-1}, a^2, and a^{-2}.

69. **Research** Certain small units of length have special names. For each unit, give its length in the form $10^{\blacksquare}$ meters.

a. fermi b. micron c. angstrom

70. **Botany** A botanist studying plant life on a remote island in the Pacific Ocean discovers that the number of plants of a particular species is increasing at a high rate. Each month for the next eight months, she counts the number of these plants in an acre plot of land. She then fits an exponential function to the data.

a. By what percent is the number of plants increasing each month?
b. If $x = 0$ represents the time of her initial count of the plants, what does $x = -3$ represent?
c. **Graphing Calculator** Graph the function on a graphing calculator. Use the TRACE feature to estimate when the plant was first introduced to the island. (*Hint:* Find the value of x when $y = 1$.)

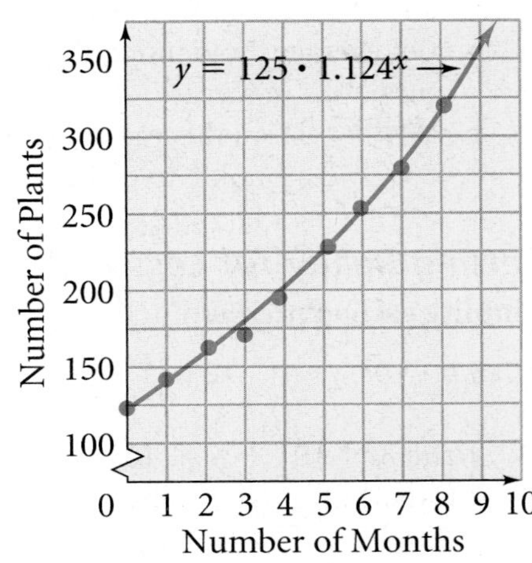

71. **Communications** Suppose you are the only person in your class who knows a story. After a minute you tell a classmate. Each minute after that, every student who knows the news tells another student (sometimes the person being told will already have heard it). In a class of 30 students, the formula $N = \frac{30}{1 + 29 \cdot 2^{-t}}$ predicts the number of people N who will have heard the news after t minutes. Find how many students will have heard your news after 2 minutes, 5 minutes, and 10 minutes.

72. **Critical Thinking** Are $3x^{-2}$ and $3x^2$ reciprocals? Explain.

Graph each pair of functions on the same set of axes over the domain $\{-3 \leq x \leq 3\}$.

73. $y = 10 \cdot 2^x; y = 20 \cdot 2^x$

74. $y = 1.2^x; y = 1.8^x$

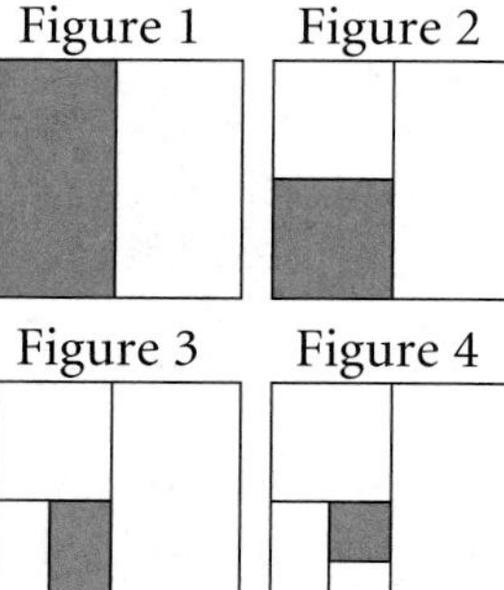

75. a. **Geometry** What fraction of each figure is shaded?
    b. Rewrite each fraction from part (a) in the form $2^{■}$.
    c. **Patterns** Look for a pattern in your answers to part (b). Write a function that relates the figure number n to the shaded rectangle r.
    d. What portion of the square would be shaded in Figure 10?

Exercises MIXED REVIEW

Solve each system.

76. $2x + 2y = 3$
$4x + 3y = 5$

77. $4x + y < 8$
$2x \geq 3$

78. $3y = \frac{1}{3}|x| - 2$
$|x| + 9y = 6$

79. Each person in Colorado spends an average of \$31.17/yr on books.
    a. Write a function to represent the amount b a group of p people spend on books in a year.
    b. On average, how much does a family of four living in Denver spend on books in a year?
    c. **Writing** Does this mean every person in Colorado spends exactly \$31.17 on books? Explain.

Getting Ready for Lesson 8-5

Simplify each expression.

80. $3.4 \cdot 10^1$

81. $7 \cdot 10^{-2}$

82. $8.2 \cdot 10^5$

83. $3 \cdot 10^{-3}$

84. $6 \cdot 10^4$

85. Write $3 \times 10^3 + 6 \times 10^1 + 7 \times 10^0 + 8 \times 10^{-1} + 5 \times 10^{-2}$ as a standard decimal number.

What You'll Learn

- Writing numbers in scientific notation
- Using scientific notation

...And Why

To calculate with very large or very small numbers

What You'll Need

- calculator

8-5 Scientific Notation

THINK AND DISCUSS

Writing Numbers in Scientific Notation

Jupiter has an average radius of 69,075 km. What is Jupiter's volume?

To answer this question, you probably want to find the formula for the volume of a sphere and use a calculator.

$V = \frac{4}{3}\pi r^3$ ← formula for the volume of a sphere

$= \frac{4}{3}\pi(69{,}075)^3$ ← Substitute 69,075 for r.

When you use a calculator to find the answer, the display looks something like 1.380547297E15.

The calculator displays the answer in this form, called *scientific notation*, because the answer contains more digits than the calculator can display. Scientific notation is a kind of shorthand for very large or very small numbers.

Scientific Notation

A number is in **scientific notation** if it is written in the form

$$a \times 10^n,$$

where n is an integer and $1 \leq |a| < 10$.

Examples: 3.4×10^6, 5.43×10^{13}, 9×10^{-10}

You can change a number from scientific notation into standard notation.

1.380547297E15

$\approx 1.38 \times 10^{15}$ ← scientific notation

$= 1.38 \times 1{,}000{,}000{,}000{,}000{,}000$ ← 10^{15} has 15 zeros.

$= 1{,}380{,}000{,}000{,}000{,}000$ ← standard notation

Jupiter has a volume slightly greater than 1 quintillion km^3.

1. a. **Try This** Evaluate the expression $\frac{4}{3}\pi(6000)^3$ on your calculator. What does your calculator display?
   b. Write the number in standard notation.

To write a number in scientific notation, you use a *power of 10*. A **power of 10** is an expression in the form $10^{\blacksquare}$.

2. **a.** Copy and complete the table.

Power of 10	$10^{\blacksquare}$	10^3	$10^{\blacksquare}$	$10^{\blacksquare}$	$10^{\blacksquare}$
Standard Notation	1,000,000	■	1	0.001	■
Unit Name	millions	■	ones	■	millionths

computer-generated image of the solar system

b. *Patterns* What pattern did you notice in part (a)?

3. **a.** Order the data in the table from least to greatest mass.

Masses of Planets (kg)

Jupiter	Saturn	Uranus	Neptune
1.9×10^{27}	5.7×10^{26}	8.7×10^{25}	1.0×10^{26}

b. **Summarize** the reasoning you used and the steps you took to order the data.

4. *Physical Science* Write each number in scientific notation.
   a. mass of Earth's atmosphere: 5,700,000,000,000,000 tons
   b. mass of the smallest insect, a parasitic wasp: 0.000 004 92 g

You can use what you know about place value and multiplication by 10 to convert from scientific notation to standard notation.

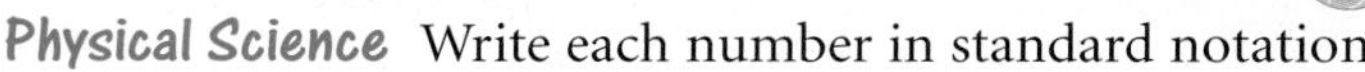

Example 1 *Relating to the Real World*

Physical Science Write each number in standard notation.

a. temperature at the Sun's core: 1.55×10^6 K

b. lowest temperature ever in a lab: 2×10^{-11} K

What? One kelvin (1 K) is equal to 1°C, but the kelvin temperature scale starts at absolute zero (–273.15°C). Because nothing can be colder than absolute zero, there are no negative temperatures on the kelvin scale.

a. $1.55 \times 10^6 = 1.550000.$ ← **A positive exponent indicates a large number. Move the decimal point 6 places to the right.**

$= 1{,}550{,}000$

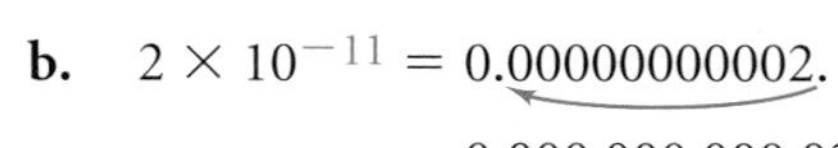

b. $2 \times 10^{-11} = 0.00000000002.$ ← **A negative exponent indicates a small number. Move the decimal point 11 places to the left.**

$= 0.000\ 000\ 000\ 02$

5. **Try This** Write each number in standard notation.
   a. distance light travels in one year (one light-year): 5.88×10^{12} mi
   b. highest elevation in Florida: 6.53×10^{-2} mi

6. Which numbers are *not* in scientific notation? Explain. Write each number in scientific notation.
   a. 11.24×10^4 **b.** 2.004×10^{-23} **c.** -12×10^{-2}

Standard Notation	Scientific Notation
0.0617	$6.17 \times 10^{■}$
0.617	$6.17 \times 10^{■}$
6.17	$6.17 \times 10^{■}$
61.7	$6.17 \times 10^{■}$
617	$6.17 \times 10^{■}$
6170	$6.17 \times 10^{■}$

Calculating with Scientific Notation

7. a. Copy and complete the table at the left.

b. *Patterns* Look for a pattern in the exponents as you scan down the table. As you multiply a number by 10 repeatedly, the exponent in the power of 10 __?__ by ■ repeatedly.

8. Write each expression as a single power of ten.

a. $10^{12} \times 10$ **b.** 10×10^{-8} **c.** $10^{-7} \times 10$

Example 2

Mental Math Simplify $7 \times (4 \times 10^5)$. Give your answer in scientific notation.

$7 \times (4 \times 10^5) = 28 \times 10^5$ ← Multiply whole numbers.

$= 2.8 \times 10 \times 10^5$ ← Write 28 as 2.8×10.

$= 2.8 \times 10^6$ ← Combine powers of 10.

9. *Try This* Simplify. Give each answer in scientific notation.

a. $2.5 \times (6 \times 10^3)$ **b.** $1.5 \times (3 \times 10^4)$ **c.** $9 \times (7 \times 10^{-9})$

10. *Mental Math* Double each number. Give your answers in scientific notation.

a. 4×10^5 **b.** \$6.3 million **c.** 1.2×10^{-3}

11. You express 1 billion as 10^9. Explain why you express 436 billion as 4.36×10^{11}.

Most calculators have a key labeled EE or EXP that allows you to enter a number in scientific notation.

Example 3 Relating to the Real World

Telecommunications In 1993, 436 billion telephone calls were placed by 130 million United States telephone subscribers. What was the average number of calls placed per subscriber?

$\frac{\text{436 billion calls}}{\text{130 million subscribers}} = \frac{4.36 \times 10^{11}}{1.3 \times 10^{8}}$ ← Write in scientific notation.

= 4.36 EE 11 ÷ 1.3 EE 8 ENTER

= 3353.846154

Each subscriber made an average of 3354 calls in 1993.

12. *Try This* The closest star to Earth (other than the sun) is Alpha Centauri, 4.35 light-years from Earth. How many miles from Earth is Alpha Centauri? (*Hint:* See Question 5(a).)

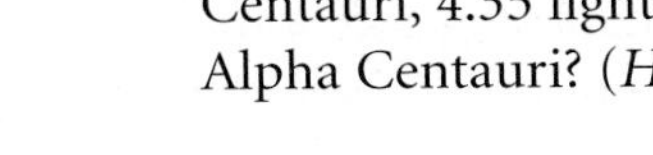

Exercises ON YOUR OWN

Order each set of numbers from least to greatest.

1. $10^5, 10^{-3}, 10^0, 10^{-1}, 10^1$
2. $6.2 \times 10^7, 5.1 \times 10^7, 8 \times 10^7, 1.02 \times 10^7$
3. $4.02 \times 10^5, 4.1 \times 10^4, 4.1 \times 10^5, 4 \times 10^5$
4. $5.1 \times 10^{-3}, 4.8 \times 10^{-1}, 5.2 \times 10^{-3}, 5.6 \times 10^{-2}$

Determine whether each number is in scientific notation. If it is not, write it in scientific notation.

5. 23×10^7
6. 385×10^{-6}
7. 0.0027×10^{-4}
8. 9.37×10^{-8}
9. 25.79×10^{-5}

Write each number in scientific notation.

10. 0.00325
11. 9,040,000,000
12. 13,030,000
13. 0.00092
14. 0.001 002
15. 370 billion
16. 9.3 million
17. 41.8 billion
18. 60.7×10^{22}
19. 62.9×10^{15}
20. 2 thousandths
21. 33 billionths
22. 950 millionths
23. 83.5×10^{-6}
24. 350×10^{-9}
25. lightest blue whale: 418,000 lb
26. thinnest glass: 0.00098 in.
27. lightest bird egg: 0.0128 oz
28. diameter of thinnest copper wire: 0.000 5 in.
29. diameter of smallest bacteria cells: 4 millionths in.
30. closest star (other than the Sun): 25.6 trillion mi

31. **Writing** Explain how to convert numbers like 350 billion, 7.2 trillion, or 48 millionths quickly to scientific notation.

Write each number in standard notation.

32. 7.042×10^9
33. 4.69×10^{-6}
34. 1.7×10^{-13}
35. 5×10^{10}
36. 1.097×10^8

Mental Math **Calculate each product or quotient. Give your answers in scientific notation.**

37. $8 \times (7 \times 10^{-3})$
38. $8 \times (3 \times 10^{14})$
39. $2 \times (3 \times 10^2)$
40. $(28 \times 10^5) \div 7$
41. $(8 \times 10^{-8}) \div 4$
42. $(8 \times 10^{12}) \div 4$

43. **Probability** In 1990, there were approximately 249 million residents of the United States. The census counted 37,306 centenarians (age 100 or greater). What is the probability that a randomly selected U.S. resident is a centenarian? Give your answer in scientific notation.

44. **Precious Metals** Earth's crust contains approximately 120 trillion metric tons of gold. One metric ton of gold is worth about \$11.5 million. What is the approximate value of the gold in Earth's crust?

45. **Astronomy** Light travels through space at a constant speed of about 3×10^5 km/s. Earth is about 1.5×10^8 km from the Sun. How long does it take for light from the sun to reach Earth?

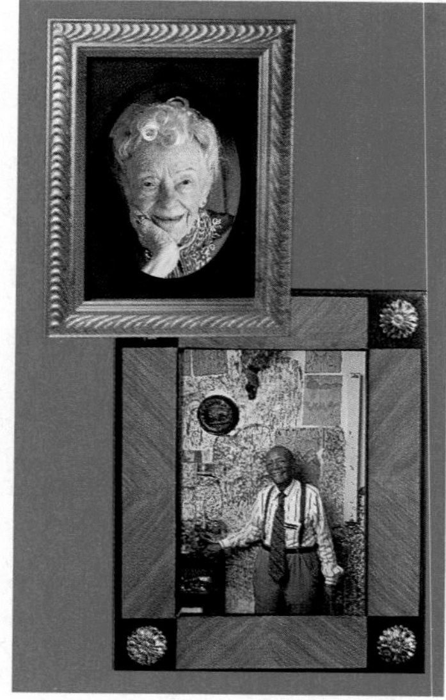

Marie Rinne, 101, is a retired teacher. Ezekiel Gibbs, 102, is a folk artist.

FOX TROT by Bill Amend

46. a. Write 500 trillion in scientific notation.

b. Since the 10-second length of the movie is off by a factor of 500 trillion, what time span does the movie actually represent?

c. *Open-ended* Find out the length of one of your favorite movies. Calculate how many frames it has, and express the number of frames in scientific notation.

Chapter Project — Find Out by Graphing

Make a scatter plot of the growth data. Compare your graph with graphs made by other students in your group. Do the data plots look exponential? Are there differences that seem to be related to where and how long the dish was exposed?

Mental Math **Double each number. Give your answers in scientific notation.**

47. 3.5×10^{-3} **48.** \$75 million **49.** 450×10^{-1}

50. 3550 **51.** 250×10^{5} **52.** 790

53. *Health Care* The total amount spent for health care in the United States in 1993 was \$884.2 billion. The U.S. population in 1993 was 258.1 million. What was the average amount spent per person on health care?

Exercises MIXED REVIEW

Find each sum or difference.

54. $\begin{bmatrix} 2 & 9 & 5 \\ 3 & 6 & 1 \end{bmatrix} + \begin{bmatrix} 5 & 2 & 9 \\ 3 & 4 & 7 \end{bmatrix}$ **55.** $\begin{bmatrix} 2.6 & 4 \\ 8.1 & 6.7 \end{bmatrix} - \begin{bmatrix} 5.8 & 1.6 \\ 4 & 7.9 \end{bmatrix}$

56. *Sports* In the hockey statistics, the FOR column tells the number of goals made by each team. The OPP column tells the number of goals made by a team's opponents. The DIF column reports the difference. Find the errors in the DIF column.

Hockey Standings Central Division

Goals	FOR	OPP	DIF
Detroit	356	275	+81
Toronto	280	243	−37
Dallas	286	265	+21
St. Louis	270	283	−13
Chicago	254	240	−14
Winnipeg	245	344	+99

Getting Ready for Lesson 8-6

Rewrite each expression using exponents.

57. $t \cdot t \cdot t \cdot t \cdot t \cdot t \cdot t$ **58.** $(6 - m)(6 - m)(6 - m)$ **59.** $5 \cdot 5 \cdot 5 \cdot s \cdot s \cdot s$

Math ToolboX

Skills Review

Significant Digits

After Lesson 8-5

Significant digits tell scientists how precise a measurement is. The more significant digits there are, the more precise the measurement is. Scientists consider all the significant digits in a measurement to be exact except for the final digit, which is considered to be rounded.

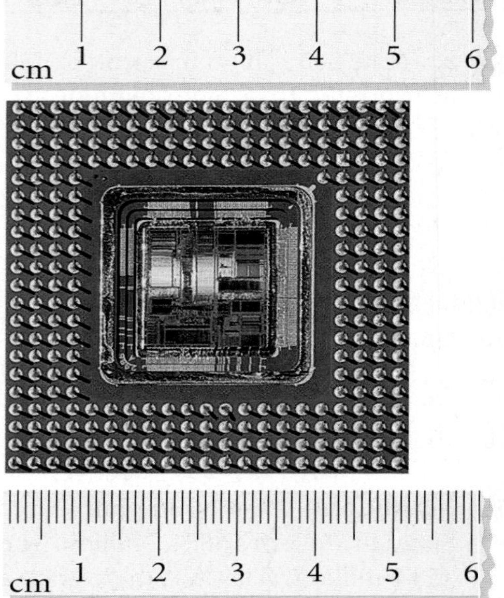

Example 1

Express the length of the computer chip in centimeters to (a) one significant digit and (b) two significant digits.

a. The length of the chip is 5 cm.
b. The length of the chip is 5.2 cm.

Example 2

The moon can come within 221,463 mi of Earth. Express this distance in scientific notation to three significant digits.

$221{,}463 = 2.21463 \times 10^5$ ← Write in scientific notation.

$\approx 2.21 \times 10^5$ ← Round 2.21463 to the hundredths' place.

To three significant digits, the distance is 2.21×10^5 mi.

Tell how many significant digits are in each measurement.

1. Mercury's period of revolution: 87.9686 da

2. largest known galaxy: 3.3×10^{19} mi in diameter

3. tallest sand castle: 19.5 ft high

Express each number in scientific notation to three significant digits.

4. the surface area of Earth: 196,949,970 mi^2

5. smallest diamond: 0.000 102 2 carat

6. thinnest commercial glass: 0.000 984 in.

7. the farthest the moon can be from Earth: 252,710 mi

8. average weight of the smallest bone in the inner ear: 0.010 853 75 oz

9. 1991 U.S. deaths from heart disease: 725,010

10. *Writing* When would it be important to measure something to three or more significant digits? Explain.

8-6 A Multiplication Property of Exponents

What You'll Learn

- Multiplying powers with the same base

...And Why

To solve problems that involve the multiplication of numbers in scientific notation

What You'll Need

- calculator

WORK TOGETHER

To evaluate $5^3 \cdot 5^5$, you could multiply the value of 5^3 by the value of 5^5. But is there a shortcut for finding the value of expressions like this? Work in your group to find one.

1. **Calculator** Find the value of each expression.
   a. $5^3 \cdot 5^5$ b. $5^6 \cdot 5^2$ c. $5^1 \cdot 5^7$ d. $5^4 \cdot 5^4$
2. **Patterns** What pattern do you notice in your answers to Question 1?
3. Write each expression from Question 1 in the form shown below.
   $$5^3 \cdot 5^5 = (5 \cdot 5 \cdot 5) \cdot (5 \cdot 5 \cdot 5 \cdot 5 \cdot 5) = 5^8$$
4. Look for a pattern in the expressions you wrote in Question 3. Write a shortcut for finding the value of expressions such as $5^3 \cdot 5^5$.
5. Use your shortcut to find the missing value in each expression. **Verify** your answers by using a calculator.
   a. $5^3 \cdot 5^4 = 5^{\blacksquare}$ b. $3^2 \cdot 3^5 = 3^{\blacksquare}$
   c. $1.2^3 \cdot 1.2^3 = 1.2^{\blacksquare}$ d. $7^3 \cdot 7^2 = 7^{\blacksquare}$

CALCULATOR HINT

Use the y^x or $\wedge$ key to evaluate expressions with exponents.

THINK AND DISCUSS

Multiplying Powers

Any expression in the form a^n, such as 5^4, is called a **power.** In the Work Together, you discovered a shortcut for multiplying powers with the same base. This shortcut works because the factors of a power such as 8^6 can be combined in different ways. Here are two examples:

$$8^6 = \underbrace{8 \cdot 8 \cdot 8 \cdot 8}_{8^4} \cdot \underbrace{8 \cdot 8}_{8^2} = 8^4 \cdot 8^2 \qquad 8^6 = \underbrace{8 \cdot 8 \cdot 8}_{8^3} \cdot \underbrace{8 \cdot 8 \cdot 8}_{8^3} = 8^3 \cdot 8^3$$

QUICK REVIEW

Read 5^4 as "5 to the 4th power."

Notice that $8^4 \cdot 8^2 = 8^3 \cdot 8^3 = 8^6$. When you multiply powers with the same base, you add the exponents.

Multiplying Powers with the Same Base

For any nonzero number a and any integers m and n, $a^m \cdot a^n = a^{m+n}$.

Example: $3^5 \cdot 3^4 = 3^{5+4} = 3^9$

6. Write 5^7 as a product of powers in three different ways.

7. Does $3^2 \cdot 3^5 \cdot 3^1 = 3^{2+5+1} = 3^8$? Explain.

8. Does $3^4 \cdot 2^2 = 6^{4+2}$? Explain.

QUICK REVIEW

The coefficient in is the numerical factor 3.

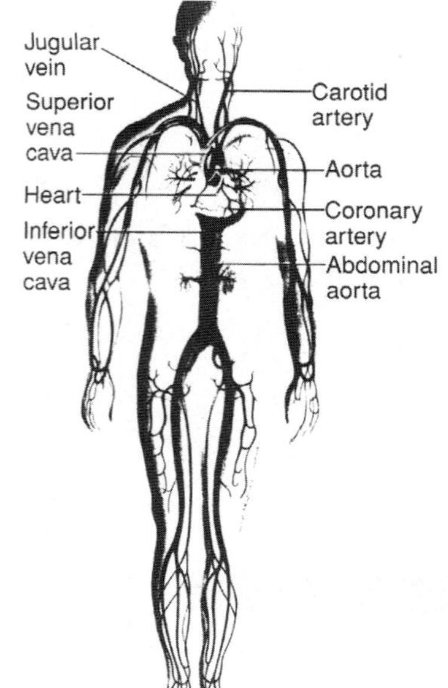

Example 1

Simplify each expression.

a. $c^4 \cdot d^3 \cdot c^2$

$= c^4 \cdot c^2 \cdot d^3$ ← Rearrange factors.

$= c^{4+2} \cdot d^3$ ← Add exponents of powers with the same base.

$= c^6 d^3$

b. $5x \cdot 2y^4 \cdot 3x^8$

Rearrange factors. → $= (5 \cdot 2 \cdot 3)(x \cdot x^8)(y^4)$

Multiply coefficients. → $= (30)(x^1 \cdot x^8)(y^4)$

Add exponents of powers with the same base. → $= (30)(x^{1+8})(y^4)$

$= 30x^9y^4$

9. **Try This** Simplify each expression.

a. $a \cdot b^2 \cdot a^5$

b. $6x^2 \cdot 3y^3 \cdot 2y^4$

c. $m^2 \cdot n^2 \cdot 7m$

Working with Scientific Notation

Example 2 **Relating to the Real World** 

Biology A human body contains about 3.2×10^4 μL (microliters) of blood for each pound of body weight. Each microliter of blood contains about 5×10^6 red blood cells. Find the approximate number of red blood cells in the body of a 125-lb person.

$\text{pounds} \cdot \frac{\text{microliters}}{\text{pound}} \cdot \frac{\text{cells}}{\text{microliter}} = \text{cells}$ ← Use dimensional analysis.

$125 \text{ lb} \cdot (3.2 \times 10^4)\frac{\mu\text{L}}{\text{lb}} \cdot (5 \times 10^6)\frac{\text{cells}}{\mu\text{L}}$

$= (125 \cdot 3.2 \cdot 5) \cdot (10^4 \cdot 10^6)$ ← Rearrange factors.

$= (125 \cdot 3.2 \cdot 5) \cdot 10^{10}$ ← Add exponents.

$= 2000 \cdot 10^{10}$ ← Simplify.

$= 2 \times 10^3 \cdot 10^{10}$ ← Write 2000 as 2×10^3.

$= 2 \times 10^{13}$ ← Use scientific notation.

There are about 2×10^{13} (20 trillion!) red blood cells in a 125-lb person.

10. **Try This** About how many red blood cells are in your body?

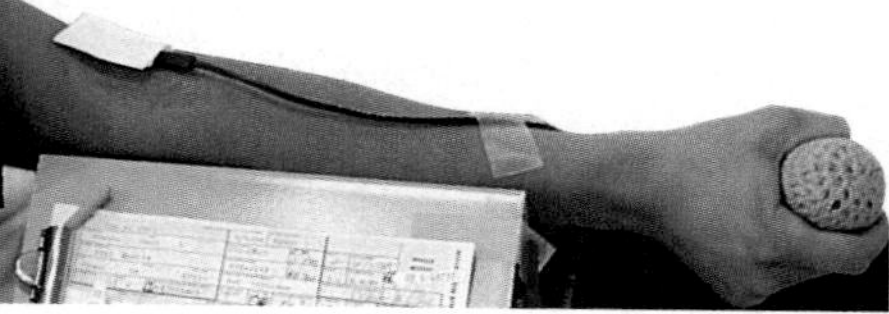

The average blood donation is 1 pint, which contains about 2.4×10^{12} red blood cells.

The property of multiplying powers with the same base works with negative exponents, also.

Example 3

Simplify $(0.2 \times 10^5)(4 \times 10^{-12})$. Give the answer in scientific notation.

$(0.2 \times 10^5)(4 \times 10^{-12})$

$= (0.2 \times 4)(10^5 \times 10^{-12})$ ← Rearrange factors.

$= 0.8 \times 10^{5+(-12)}$ ← Multiply.

$= 0.8 \times 10^{-7}$ ← Add exponents.

$= 8 \times 10^{-1} \times 10^{-7}$ ← Write 0.8 as 8×10^{-1}.

$= 8 \times 10^{-8}$ ← Add exponents.

11. **Try This** Simplify each expression. Give your answers in scientific notation.
    a. $(0.5 \times 10^{13})(0.3 \times 10^{-4})$
    b. $(0.7 \times 10^{-9})(0.03 \times 10^8)$

12. **Verify** that $2^5 \cdot 2^{-2} = 2^3$ by writing 2^5 as an integer and 2^{-2} as a fraction, then multiplying.

Exercises ON YOUR OWN

Write each expression as a product of powers, then simplify.

1. $(x \cdot x \cdot x \cdot x)(x \cdot x \cdot x)$
2. $(x \cdot x)\left(\frac{1}{x \cdot x \cdot x}\right)$
3. $\left(\frac{1}{x \cdot x}\right)\left(\frac{1}{x \cdot x \cdot x \cdot x \cdot x}\right)$

Complete each equation.

4. $5^2 \cdot 5^{■} = 5^{11}$
5. $5^7 \cdot 5^{■} = 5^3$
6. $a^{12} \cdot a^{■} = a^{12}$
7. $a \cdot a \cdot a^3 = a^{■}$
8. $2^{■} \cdot 2^4 = 2^1$
9. $a^{■} \cdot a^4 = 1$
10. $c^{-5} \cdot c^{■} = c^6$
11. $x^3y^{■} \cdot x^{■} = y^2$

Multiply. Give your answers in scientific notation.

12. $(9 \times 10^7)(3 \times 10^{-16})$
13. $(8 \times 10^{-3})(0.1 \times 10^9)$
14. $(0.7 \times 10^{-12})(0.3 \times 10^8)$
15. $(2 \times 10^6)(3 \times 10^3)$
16. $1 \times 10^3 \cdot 10^{-8}$
17. $(4 \times 10^6) \times 10^{-3}$

18. **Standardized Test Prep** Simplify $p^8 \cdot 9q^2 \cdot q^4 \cdot p^3 \cdot 2q$.
    A. $-11p^{11}q^7$ B. $11p^{14}q^8$ C. $18p^{11}q^6$ D. $18p^{11}q^7$ E. $18pq^{17}$

19. a. **Open-ended** Write y^8 in four different ways as the product of two powers with the same base. Use only positive exponents.
    b. Write y^8 in four different ways as the product of two powers with the same base, using negative or zero exponents in each.
    c. How many ways are there to write y^8 as the product of two powers? **Summarize** your reasoning.

Simplify each expression. Use only positive exponents.

20. $(0.99^2)(0.99^4)$
21. $(1.025)^3(1.025)^{-3}$
22. $c^{-2}c^7$
23. $3r \cdot r^4$
24. $5t^{-2} \cdot 2t^{-5}$
25. $(a^2b^3)(a^6)$
26. $(x^5y^2)(x^{-6}y)$
27. $3x^2 \cdot x^2$
28. $(1.03^8)(1.03^4)$
29. $-(0.99^3)(0.99^0)$
30. $a \cdot a^{-7}$
31. $b^{-2} \cdot b^4 \cdot b$
32. $10^{-13} \cdot 10^5$
33. $(-2m^3)(3.5m^{-3})$
34. $(7x^5)(8x)$
35. $(15a^3)(-3a)$
36. $(-2.4n^4)(2n^{-1})$
37. $bc^{-6} \cdot b$
38. $(5x^5)(3y^6)(3x^2)$
39. $(4c^4)(ac^3)(3a^5c)$
40. $x^6 \cdot y^2 \cdot x^4$
41. $a^6b^3 \cdot a^2b^{-2}$
42. $\frac{1}{x^2 \cdot x^{-5}}$
43. $\frac{1}{a^3 \cdot a^{-2}}$
44. $\frac{5}{c \cdot c^{-4}}$
45. $2a^2(3a + 5)$
46. $8m^3(m^2 + 7)$
47. $-4x^3(2x^2 - 9x)$

48. **Chemistry** The term *mole* is used in chemistry to refer to a specific number of atoms or molecules. One mole is equal to 6.02×10^{23}. The mass of a single hydrogen atom is approximately 1.67×10^{-24} gram. What is the mass of 1 mole of hydrogen atoms?

49. a. Jerome wrote $a^3b^2b^4 = (a \cdot a \cdot a)(b \cdot b)(b \cdot b \cdot b \cdot b)$. Jeremy wrote $a^3b^2b^4 = ab^9$. Whose work is correct? Explain.
    b. Use the correct work to simplify $a^3b^2b^4$.

50. **Writing** Explain why $x^3 \cdot y^5$ cannot be simplified.

Geometry **Find the area of each figure.**

51. 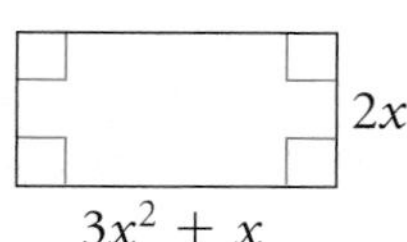

52. 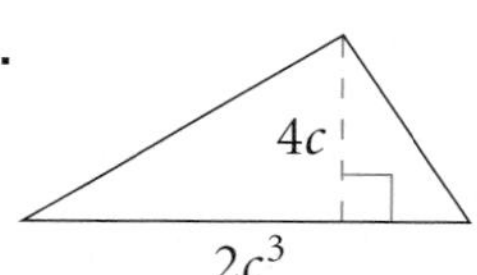

53. 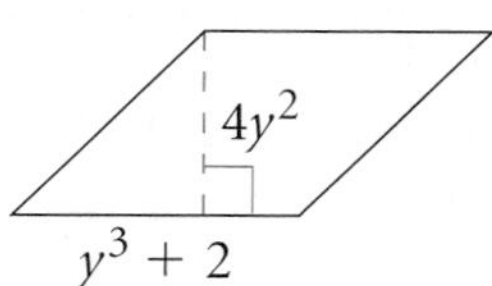

54. 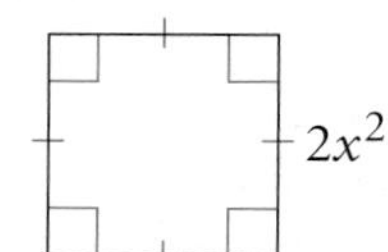

Critical Thinking **Find and correct the errors in Exercises 55–57.**

55. $(3x^2)(-2x^4) = 3(-2)x^{2 \cdot 4}$
$= -6x^8$

56. $4a^2 \cdot 3a^5 = (4 + 3)a^{2+5}$
$= 7a^7$

57. $x^6 \cdot x \cdot x^3 = x^{6+3}$
$= x^9$

58. **Technology** A CD-ROM stores about 600 megabytes (6×10^8 bytes) of information along a spiral track. Each byte uses about 9 micrometers (9×10^{-6} m) of space along the track. Find the length of the track.

59. **Medicine** Medical X-rays, with a wavelength of about 10^{-10} m, can penetrate the flesh (but not the bones) of your body.
    a. Ultraviolet rays, which cause sunburn by penetrating only the top layers of skin, have a wavelength about 1000 times as long as X-rays. Find the wavelength of ultraviolet rays.
    b. **Critical Thinking** The wavelengths of visible light are between 4×10^{-7}m and 7.5×10^{-7}m. Are these wavelengths longer or shorter than those of ultraviolet rays?

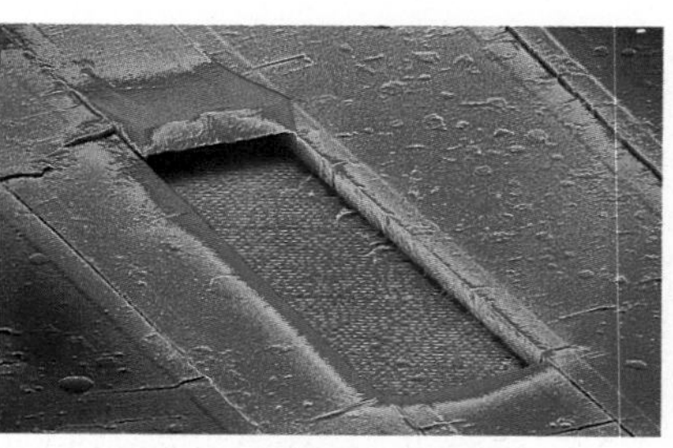

The music on a compact disc comes from a series of notches that can be read by a laser. The disc is enclosed in two layers of plastic. The plastic surface of this CD is cracked to show the notched layer underneath.

Chapter Project *Find Out by Analyzing*

- Starting with the first day you see at least one square of mold, find the percent of growth from each day to the next.
- Use the average of these percents as an estimate for the base of an exponential function.
- Write an exponential function to fit the data. Graph it on your data plot.

Exercises MIXED REVIEW

Identify each square root as *rational* or *irrational*. Simplify if possible.

60. $\sqrt{121}$ **61.** $\sqrt{67}$ **62.** $-\sqrt{49}$ **63.** $\sqrt{\frac{1}{4}}$ **64.** $-\sqrt{13}$ **65.** $\sqrt{\frac{9}{16}}$

66. **Sports** In 1989, United States sales of in-line skates were \$21 million. In 1994, sales were \$369 million. Find the percent of increase.

Getting Ready for Lesson 8-7

Rewrite each expression with one exponent.

67. $3^2 \cdot 3^2 \cdot 3^2$ **68.** $2^3 \cdot 2^3 \cdot 2^3 \cdot 2^3$ **69.** $5^7 \cdot 5^7 \cdot 5^7 \cdot 5^7$ **70.** $7 \cdot 7 \cdot 7$

Exercises CHECKPOINT

Write each expression as an integer or simple fraction.

1. $(-7.3)^0$ **2.** 3^{-2} **3.** -8^{-1} **4.** $\left(\frac{1}{5}\right)^{-3}$ **5.** -4^2 **6.** $(-2)^{-3}$

Simplify each expression. Use only positive exponents.

7. $s^{-2} \cdot s^4 \cdot s$ **8.** $a^7b^2 \cdot 21a^{-6}$ **9.** $(2a^3)(-3a^{-3})(\frac{1}{6}a^0)$ **10.** g^3h^{-4} **11.** $\frac{x^{-5}}{y^2y^{-8}}$

Mental Math **Simplify. Give your answers in scientific notation.**

12. $(5 \times 10^6) \times 3$ **13.** $0.4 \times (2 \times 10^{-7})$ **14.** $(9 \times 10^{11}) \div 3$ **15.** $6 \times (4 \times 10^3)$

16. a. **Biology** Georg Frey collected beetles. When he died, his collection contained 3 million beetles of 90,000 different species. Write each number in scientific notation.

b. About how many beetles fit into each of his 6500 packing cases?

17. **Writing** LaWanda wrote $a^5 + a^5 = 2a^5$. Amanda wrote $a^5 + a^5 = a^{10}$. Whose work is correct? Explain.

Graph each function over the domain $\{-3 \leq x \leq 3\}$.

18. $f(x) = 0.8 \cdot 2^x$ **19.** $y = 0.5 \cdot 1.5^x$ **20.** $g(x) = 2 \cdot 3^x$

Connections — Physical Science . . . and more

What You'll Learn

- Using two more multiplication properties of exponents

...And Why

To solve problems that involve raising numbers in scientific notation to a power

What You'll Need

- calculator

8-7 More Multiplication Properties of Exponents

THINK AND DISCUSS

Raising a Power to a Power

In Lesson 8-6, you used patterns to discover how to multiply powers with the same base. You can use what you discovered there to find a shortcut for simplifying expressions such as $(8^6)^3$.

1. Copy and complete each statement.

a. $(a^3)^2 = a^3 \cdot a^3 = a^{\blacksquare + \blacksquare} = a^{3 \cdot \blacksquare} = a^{\blacksquare}$

b. $(4^5)^3 = 4^5 \cdot 4^5 \cdot 4^5 = 4^{\blacksquare + \blacksquare + \blacksquare} = 4^{5 \cdot \blacksquare} = 4^{\blacksquare}$

c. $(2^7)^4 = 2^7 \cdot 2^7 \cdot 2^7 \cdot 2^7 = 2^{7 \cdot \blacksquare} = 2^{\blacksquare}$

d. $(8^6)^2 = 8^6 \cdot 8^6 = 8^{6 \cdot \blacksquare} = 8^{\blacksquare}$

e. $(g^4)^3 = g^4 \cdot g^4 \cdot g^4 = g^{4 \cdot \blacksquare} = g^{\blacksquare}$

2. *Patterns* Look for a pattern in your answers to Question 1. Write a shortcut for simplifying an expression such as $(8^6)^3$.

You can use the property below to simplify some exponential expressions.

> **Raising a Power to a Power**
>
> For any nonzero number a and any integers m and n, $(a^m)^n = a^{mn}$.
>
> **Example:** $(5^4)^2 = 5^{4 \cdot 2} = 5^8$

3. The work you did in Question 1 involves repeated multiplication. Simplify each expression below by using repeated multiplication. Then check your work by using the property.

a. $(2^3)^2$ **b.** $(h^2)^4$ **c.** $(3^3)^4$

4. Simplify each expression. What do you notice?

a. $(5^2)^4 = 25^4 = \blacksquare$ **b.** $(5^2)^4 = 5^8 = \blacksquare$

5. Use the property to find each missing value. Then use a calculator to evaluate each expression and verify your answers.

a. $(3^{\blacksquare})^4 = 9^4$ **b.** $(5^2)^{\blacksquare} = 5^8$ **c.** $(2^{\blacksquare})^{\blacksquare} = 4^2$

d. $(3^4)^2 = 3^{\blacksquare}$ **e.** $(1.1^5)^7 = 1.1^{\blacksquare}$ **f.** $(123^0)^{87} = 123^{\blacksquare}$

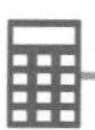

CALCULATOR HINT

When evaluating an expression such as $(3^4)^2$, you do not need to use parentheses because the calculator evaluates powers from left to right. Pressing 3 ^ 4 ^ 2 ENTER will give you 6561.

Example 1

Simplify each expression.

a. $(x^3)^6 = x^{3 \cdot 6}$ ← Multiply exponents when raising a power to a power.

$= x^{18}$ ← Simplify.

b. $c^5(c^3)^2 = c^5 \cdot c^{3 \cdot 2}$ ← Multiply exponents in $(c^3)^2$.
$= c^5 \cdot c^6$ ← Simplify.
$= c^{5+6}$ ← Add exponents when multiplying powers with the same base.
$= c^{11}$

6. **Try This** Simplify $(a^4)^2 \cdot (a^2)^5$.

Raising a Product to a Power

You can use repeated multiplication to simplify expressions like $(5y)^3$.

$$\begin{aligned}(5y)^3 &= 5y \cdot 5y \cdot 5y\\ &= 5 \cdot 5 \cdot 5 \cdot y \cdot y \cdot y\\ &= 5^3 \cdot y^3\\ &= 125y^3\end{aligned}$$

Notice from the steps above that $(5y)^3 = 5^3y^3$. This illustrates another property of exponents.

Raising a Product to a Power

For any nonzero numbers a and b and any integer n, $(ab)^n = a^nb^n$.

Example: $(3x)^4 = 3^4x^4 = 81x^4$

7. **Calculator** **Verify** each equation for two values of the variable (other than 0 and 1).
   a. $(5y)^3 = 125y^3$ **b.** $(3x)^4 = 3^4x^4$ **c.** $(7c)^2 = 49c^2$

Example 2

Simplify each expression.

a. $(2x^2)^4 = 2^4(x^2)^4$ ← Raise each factor to the 4th power.
$= 2^4x^8$ ← Multiply exponents.
$= 16x^8$ ← Simplify.

b. $(x^{-2})^2(3xy^2)^4 = (x^{-2})^2 \cdot 3^4x^4(y^2)^4$ ← Raise three factors to the 4th power.
$= x^{-4} \cdot 3^4x^4y^8$ ← Multiply exponents.
$= 3^4 \cdot x^{-4} \cdot x^4 \cdot y^8$ ← Rearrange factors.
$= 3^4x^0y^8$ ← Add exponents.
$= 81y^8$ ← Simplify.

8. **Try This** Simplify each expression.
   a. $(15z)^3$ **b.** $(4g^5)^2$ **c.** $(6mn)^3(5m^{-3})^4$

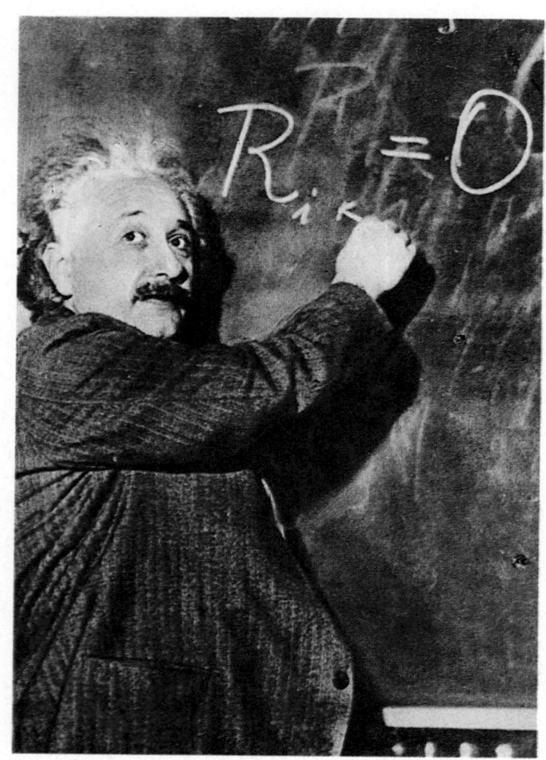

Who? Albert Einstein is famous for discovering the relationship $e = mc^2$, where e is energy (in joules), m is mass (in kg), and c is the speed of light (about 3×10^8 meters per second).

You can use the properties of exponents to solve real-world problems.

Example 3 **Relating to the Real World** 

Physical Science All objects, even resting ones, contain energy. The expression $10^{-3} \cdot (3 \times 10^8)^2$ describes the amount of resting energy a raisin contains, where 10^{-3} kg is the mass of the raisin. Simplify the expression.

$10^{-3} \cdot (3 \times 10^8)^2$

$= 10^{-3} \cdot 3^2 \cdot (10^8)^2$ ← Raise two factors to the 2nd power.

$= 10^{-3} \cdot 3^2 \cdot 10^{16}$ ← Multiply exponents.

$= 3^2 \cdot 10^{-3} \cdot 10^{16}$ ← Rearrange factors.

$= 3^2 \cdot 10^{-3+16}$ ← Add exponents.

$= 9 \times 10^{13}$ ← Simplify.

One raisin contains about 9×10^{13} joules of resting energy.

9. Multiply. Give your answers in scientific notation.
   a. $(4 \times 10^5)^2$
   b. $(2 \times 10^{-10})^3$
   c. $(10^3)^4(4.3 \times 10^{-8})$

10. **Energy** An hour of television use consumes 1.45×10^{-1} kWh of electricity. Each kilowatt-hour (kWh) of electric use is equivalent to 3.6×10^6 joules of energy.
   a. How many joules does a television use in 1 h? (Hint: Use a proportion.)
   b. Suppose you could release the resting energy in a raisin. About how many hours of television use could be powered by that energy?

Exercises ON YOUR OWN

Simplify each expression. Use positive exponents.

1. $(xy)^9$	2. $(c^5)^2$	3. $(a^2b^4)^3$	4. $(3m^3)^4$
5. $(g^{10})^{-4}$	6. $g^{10} \cdot g^{-4}$	7. $(x^3y)^4$	8. $(x^{-2})^3x^{-12}$
9. $(0.5^2)^{-2}$	10. $(2xy)^3x^2$	11. $(g \cdot g^4)^2$	12. $(c^2)^{-2}(c^3)^4$
13. $s^3(s^2)^4$	14. $(mg^4)^{-1}$	15. $m(g^4)^{-1}$	16. $(7cd^4)^2$
17. $(2p^6)^0$	18. $(5ac^3)^{-2}$	19. $(4a^2b)^3(ab)^3$	20. $(4xy^2)^4(2y)^{-3}$
21. $3^7 \cdot \left(\frac{1}{3}\right)^7$	22. $(5x)^2+5x^2$	23. $2^4 \cdot 5^4$	24. $(64.1^{-3})^0$
25. $(b^n)^3b^2$	26. $15^2 \cdot (0.2)^2$	27. $(4.1)^5 \cdot (4.1)^{-5}$	28. $3^2 \cdot (3x)^3$

29. a. **Geography** Earth has a radius of about 6.4×10^6 m. Approximate the surface area of Earth by using the formula for the surface area of a sphere, $S = 4\pi r^2$.

b. Earth's surface is about 70% water, almost all of it in oceans. About how many square meters of Earth's surface are covered with water?

c. The oceans have an average depth of 3795 m. What is the approximate volume of water on Earth?

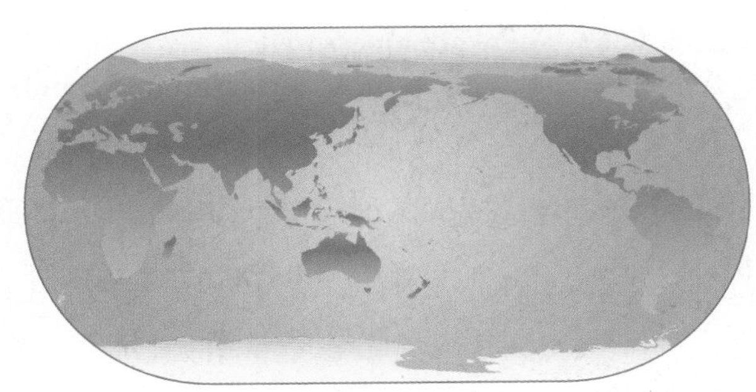

Multiply. Give your answers in scientific notation.

30. $(3 \times 10^5)^2$ **31.** $(2 \times 10^{-3})^3$ **32.** $(7 \times 10^4)^2$

33. $(6 \times 10^{12})^2$ **34.** $(3 \times 10^{-4})^3$ **35.** $(4 \times 10^8)^{-2}$

36. Which expression or expressions do *not* equal 64?
A. $2^5 \cdot 2$ **B.** 2^6 **C.** $2^2 \cdot 2^3$ **D.** $(2^3)^2$ **E.** $(2^2)(2^2)^2$

37. **Writing** Explain how the properties of exponents help you simplify algebraic expressions.

38. a. **Geometry** Write an expression for the surface area of each cube.

b. How many times greater than the surface area of the small cube is the surface area of the large cube?

c. Write an expression for the volume of each cube.

d. How many times greater than the volume of the small cube is the volume of the large cube?

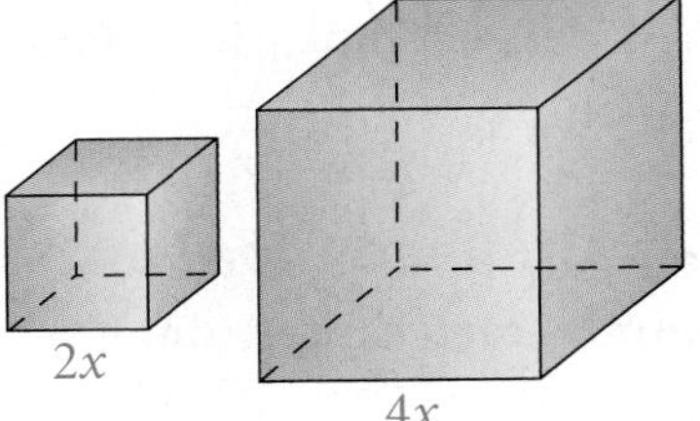

39. **Open-ended** Write a^{24} as a product of the form $(a^m)^n$ in four different ways. Use only positive exponents.

40. **Technology** In computer memory chips currently being developed, a square piece of chip is one thousandth of an inch (10^{-3} in.) on each side. It will hold 3000 bits of data. Find the area of the piece of chip.

Complete each equation.

41. $(x^2)^{■} = x^6$ **42.** $(x^{■})^3 = x^{-12}$ **43.** $(ab^2)^{■} = a^4b^8$

44. $(5x^{■})^2 = 25x^4$ **45.** $(3x^3y^{■})^3 = 27x^6$ **46.** $(m^2n^3)^{■} = \frac{1}{m^6n^9}$

Solve each equation. Use the sample below.

Sample:

$25^3 = 5^x$

$(5^2)^3 = 5^x$ ← **Write 25 as a power of 5.**

$5^6 = 5^x$ ← **Multiply exponents.**

$x = 6$

The solution is 6.

47. $8^2 = 2^x$ **48.** $3^x = 27^4$ **49.** $4^x = 2^6$ **50.** $5^6 = 25^x$

51. **Biology** There are an estimated 200 million insects for each person on Earth. The world population is about 5.5 billion. About how many insects are there on Earth?

Write each expression with only one exponent. Use parentheses.

52. $m^4 \cdot n^4$

53. $(a^5)(b^5)(a^0)$

54. $49x^2y^2z^2$

55. $\frac{12x^{-2}}{3y^2}$

Chapter Project ***Find Out by Interpreting***

Use your exponential function to predict the growth of your mold at two weeks. Compare your predictions to the actual growth of the mold. Discuss any factors that may influence the accuracy of your exponential model.

Exercises MIXED REVIEW

56. Solve $3x^2 - 5x - 2 = 0$.

57. Solve $x^2 + 2x + 1 = 0$.

58. **Textiles** To make felt, thin layers of cotton are built up $\frac{1}{32}$ in. at a time. How many layers does it take to make felt $\frac{1}{4}$ in. thick?

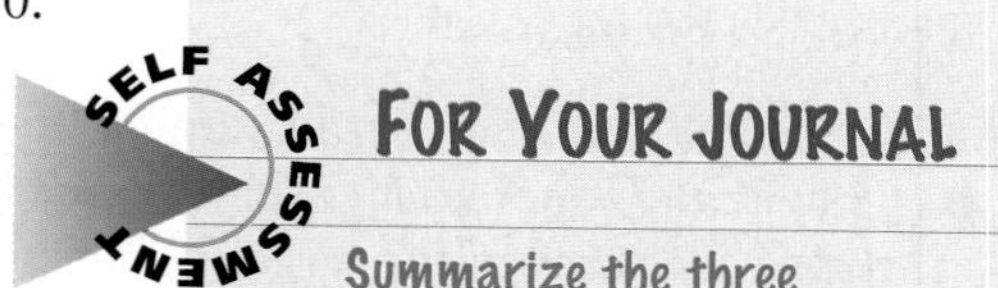

Summarize the three multiplication properties of exponents that you have learned in the last two lessons. Give an example of each.

Getting Ready for Lesson 8-8

Simplify each expression.

59. $x^2 \cdot x^{-3}$

60. $u^8 \cdot u^{-4}$

61. $t^{-6} \cdot t$

62. $h^{-3} \cdot h^0$

A Point in Time

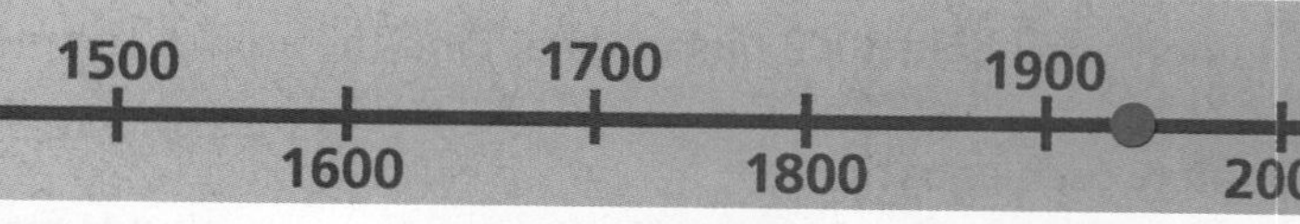

Dr. Jewel Plummer Cobb

Dr. Jewel Plummer Cobb was born in 1924 and obtained her master's and doctorate degrees in cell physiology from New York University. Dr. Cobb has concentrated on the study of normal and malignant skin cells and has published nearly fifty books, articles, and reports.

Because the number of cancer cells grows exponentially, cell biologists often write cancer cell data in scientific notation.

What You'll Learn

- Applying division properties of exponents

...And Why

To solve problems that involve dividing numbers in scientific notation

What You'll Need

- calculator

8-8 Division Properties of Exponents

THINK AND DISCUSS

Dividing Powers with the Same Base

In Lessons 8-6 and 8-7 you studied patterns that occur when you multiply powers with the same base. You can see a similar pattern when you divide powers with the same base.

You can use repeated multiplication to simplify fractions. Expand the numerator and denominator using repeated multiplication. Then cancel like terms.

$$\frac{5^6}{5^2} = \frac{\cancel{5} \cdot \cancel{5} \cdot 5 \cdot 5 \cdot 5 \cdot 5}{\cancel{5} \cdot \cancel{5}} = 5^4$$

1. Simplify each expression by expanding the numerator and the denominator and then canceling. Describe any patterns you see.

   a. $\frac{5^7}{5^3}$ b. $\frac{5^{12}}{5^8}$ c. $\frac{5^8}{5^4}$ d. $\frac{5^5}{5^1}$ e. $\frac{5^5}{5^8}$

Dividing Powers with the Same Base

For any nonzero number a and any integers m and n, $\frac{a^m}{a^n} = a^{m-n}$.

Example: $\frac{3^7}{3^2} = 3^{7-2} = 3^5$

2. **Calculator** Find each missing value. Use a calculator to check.

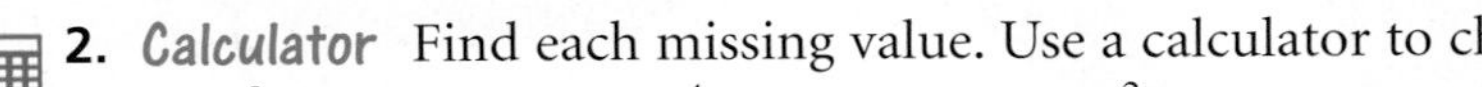

   a. $\frac{5^9}{5^2} = 5^{\blacksquare}$ b. $\frac{2^4}{2^3} = 2^{\blacksquare}$ c. $\frac{3^2}{3^5} = 3^{\blacksquare}$ d. $\frac{5^3}{5^2} = 5^{\blacksquare}$

Example 1

Simplify each expression. Use only positive exponents.

a. $\frac{a^6}{a^{14}} = a^{6-14}$ ← Subtract exponents when dividing powers with the same base.

$= a^{-8}$

$= \frac{1}{a^8}$ ← Rewrite using positive exponents.

b. $\frac{c^{-1}d^3}{c^5d^{-4}} = c^{-1-5} \cdot d^{3-(-4)}$ ← Subtract exponents.

$= c^{-6}d^7$

$= \frac{d^7}{c^6}$ ← Use positive exponents.

3. **Try This** Simplify each expression. Use positive exponents.

   a. $\frac{b^4}{b^9}$ b. $\frac{z^{10}}{z^5}$ c. $\frac{a^2b}{a^4b^3}$ d. $\frac{m^{-1}n^2}{m^3n}$ e. $\frac{x^2yz^4}{xy^4z^{-3}}$

Example 2 Relating to the Real World 

Environment In 1993 the total amount of waste paper and cardboard recycled in the United States was 77.8 million tons. The population in 1993 was 258.1 million. How much paper was recycled per person?

$$\frac{77.8 \text{ million tons}}{258.1 \text{ million people}} = \frac{77.8 \times 10^7 \text{ tons}}{2.581 \times 10^8 \text{ people}}$$ ← Write in scientific notation.

$$= \frac{7.78}{2.581} \times 10^{7-8}$$ ← Subtract exponents when dividing powers with the same base.

$$= \frac{7.78}{2.581} \times 10^{-1}$$

$$\approx 3.01 \times 10^{-1}$$ ← Simplify.

$$\approx 0.3$$

In 1993, 0.3 ton (600 lb!) of waste paper was recycled per person.

4. Only 34% of the waste paper generated in 1993 was recycled. How many pounds of waste paper were generated per person in 1993?

5. **Try This** Find each quotient. Give your answer in scientific notation.
   a. $\frac{2 \times 10^3}{8 \times 10^8}$ b. $\frac{7.5 \times 10^{12}}{2.5 \times 10^{-4}}$ c. $\frac{4.2 \times 10^5}{12.6 \times 10^2}$

Raising a Quotient to a Power

You can use repeated multiplication to simplify the expression $\left(\frac{x}{y}\right)^3$.

$$\left(\frac{x}{y}\right)^3 = \frac{x}{y} \cdot \frac{x}{y} \cdot \frac{x}{y}$$

$$= \frac{x \cdot x \cdot x}{y \cdot y \cdot y}$$

$$= \frac{x^3}{y^3}$$

6. **Calculator** **Verify** that $\left(\frac{x}{y}\right)^3 = \frac{x^3}{y^3}$ for three values of x and y.

Raising a Quotient to a Power

For any nonzero numbers a and b, and any integer n, $\left(\frac{a}{b}\right)^n = \frac{a^n}{b^n}$.

Example: $\left(\frac{4}{5}\right)^3 = \frac{4^3}{5^3} = \frac{64}{125}$

Math A Test Prep

1 What is the simplest form of $\left(\frac{3c^{-5}d}{c^{-3}}\right)^4$?

(1) $81c^{-8}d^4$
(2) $81cd^4$
(3) $\frac{12d^4}{c^4}$
(4) $\frac{81d^4}{c^8}$

2 A cubic inch is approximately 0.0000214 cubic yards.

a How is this measure expressed in scientific notation?

b The volume of a wooden puzzle cube is 9 cubic inches. Express the volume in cubic yards using scientific notation.

Example 3

Simplify each expression.

a. $\left(\frac{4}{x^2}\right)^3 = \frac{4^3}{(x^2)^3}$ ← Raise the numerator and denominator to the 3rd power.

$= \frac{4^3}{x^6}$ ← Multiply exponents.

$= \frac{64}{x^6}$ ← Simplify.

b. $\left(-\frac{3}{5}\right)^{-2} = \left(\frac{-3}{5}\right)^{-2}$ ← Write the fraction with a negative numerator.

$= \frac{(-3)^{-2}}{5^{-2}}$ ← Raise the numerator and denominator to the −2 power.

$= \frac{5^2}{(-3)^2}$ ← Apply the definition of negative exponents.

$= \frac{25}{9}$ ← Simplify.

7. In Example 3, part (b), the first step could have been to rewrite the fraction as $\left(\frac{3}{-5}\right)^{-2}$. Explain how this step would affect the rest of your work.

8. ***Open-ended*** Suppose you wanted to simplify $\left(\frac{5}{3}\right)^3$. What would be your first step?

When you have reduced an expression as far as possible, and when all your exponents are positive, the expression is in **simplest form.**

9. Is each expression in simplest form? If not, simplify it.

a. $\frac{(x^3)^2}{y^7}$ **b.** $x^{-3}y^2$ **c.** $\frac{a^5}{ab}$ **d.** $\frac{(2x)^2}{2x^2}$

Sometimes you can combine steps to shorten your work.

10. Copy and complete each statement.

a. $\left(\frac{4a^3}{b}\right)^2 = \frac{\blacksquare a^{\blacksquare}}{b^{\blacksquare}}$ ← Raising products, quotients, and powers to a power.

b. $\frac{x^{-3}x^8}{x^2} = x^{\blacksquare + \blacksquare - \blacksquare} = x^{\blacksquare}$ ← Multiplying and dividing powers with the same base.

11. **Try This** Simplify each expression.

a. $\left(\frac{2m^5}{m^2}\right)^4$ **b.** $\left(\frac{2n^3t}{t^2}\right)^2$ **c.** $\left(\frac{5x^7y^4}{x^{-2}}\right)^2$

Exercises ON YOUR OWN

Simplify each expression. Use only positive exponents.

1. $\frac{2^5}{2^7}$ **2.** $\left(\frac{2^2}{5}\right)^2$ **3.** $\left(\frac{3}{4}\right)^2$ **4.** $\left(\frac{2}{3}\right)^{-2}$ **5.** $\left(\frac{3^3}{3^4}\right)^2$ **6.** $\frac{c^{12}}{c^{15}}$

7. $\frac{x^{13}y^2}{x^{13}y}$ **8.** $\frac{m^{-2}}{m^{-5}}$ **9.** $\frac{(2a^7)(3a^2)}{6a^3}$ **10.** $\left(\frac{3b^2}{5}\right)^0$ **11.** $\left(\frac{-2}{3}\right)^{-3}$ **12.** $\frac{3^2 \cdot 5^0}{2^3}$

Explain why each expression is *not* in simplest form.

13. 5^3m^3　14. x^5y^{-2}　15. $(2c)^4$　16. $\frac{d^7}{d}$　17. x^0y　18. $(3z^2)^3$

Choose **Use a calculator, paper and pencil, or mental math to simplify each quotient. Give your answers in scientific notation.**

19. $\frac{6.5 \times 10^{15}}{1.3 \times 10^8}$　20. $\frac{2.7 \times 10^8}{0.9 \times 10^3}$　21. $\frac{2.7 \times 10^8}{3 \times 10^5}$　22. $\frac{8.4 \times 10^{-5}}{2 \times 10^{-8}}$　23. $\frac{4.7 \times 10^{-4}}{3.1 \times 10^2}$

24. a. **Writing** While simplifying the expression $\frac{c^4}{c^6}$, Kneale said, "I've found a property of exponents that's not in my algebra book!" Write an explanation of why Kneale's method works.
b. **Open-ended** Apply Kneale's method to an example you create.

Kneale

$$\frac{c^4}{c^6} = \frac{1}{c^{6-4}} = \frac{1}{c^2}$$

25. a. **Television** In 1999 people in the United States will watch television a total of 450 billion hours, according to industry projections. The population will be about 274 million people. Find the number of hours of TV viewing per person for 1999.
b. According to these projections, about how many hours per day will people watch television in 1999?

26. Lena and Jared used different methods to simplify $\left(\frac{b^7}{b^3}\right)^2$. Are both methods correct? Explain.

Lena

$$\left(\frac{b^7}{b^3}\right)^2 = \frac{b^{14}}{b^6} = b^8$$

Jared

$$\left(\frac{b^7}{b^3}\right)^2 = (b^4)^2 = b^8$$

Simplify each expression. Use only positive exponents.

27. $\frac{2^7}{2^5}$　28. $2^5 \cdot 2^{-7}$　29. $\left(\frac{3^5}{3^2}\right)^2$　30. $\frac{a^7}{a^9}$　31. $\frac{6c^7}{3c}$　32. $\frac{5x^5}{15x^3}$

33. $\frac{a^7b^3c^2}{a^2b^6c^2}$　34. $\frac{a^{-21}a^{15}}{a^3}$　35. $\frac{c^3d^7}{c^8d^{-1}}$　36. $\frac{p^7qr^{-1}}{pq^{-2}r^5}$　37. $\frac{5x^3}{(5x)^3}$　38. $\left(\frac{5x^3}{20x}\right)^3$

39. $\left(\frac{c^5}{c^9}\right)^3$　40. $\left(\frac{7a}{b^3}\right)^2$　41. $\left(\frac{3b^0}{5}\right)^2$　42. $\frac{(3a^3)^2}{10a^{-1}}$　43. $\left(\frac{5m^3n}{m^5}\right)^3$　44. $\left(\frac{x^4x}{x^{-2}}\right)^{-4}$

Write each expression with only one exponent. You may need to use parentheses.

45. $\frac{3^5}{5^5}$　46. $\frac{m^7}{n^7}$　47. $\frac{d^8}{d^5}$　48. $\frac{10^7 \cdot 10^0}{10^{-3}}$　49. $\frac{27x^3}{8y^3}$　50. $\frac{4m^2}{169m^4}$

51. a. **Finance** In 1980, the U.S. Government owed \$909 billion to its creditors. The population of the United States was 226.5 million people. How much did the government owe per person in 1980?
b. In 1994 the debt had grown to \$4.64 trillion, with a population of 260 million. How much did the government owe per person?
c. What was the percent of increase in the amount owed per person from 1980 to 1994?

PROBLEM SOLVING HINT

Use a proportion.

Which property(ies) of exponents would you use to simplify each expression?

52. 2^{-3} **53.** $\frac{2^2}{2^5}$ **54.** $\left(\frac{1}{2}\right)^3$ **55.** $\frac{1}{2^{-4} \cdot 2^7}$ **56.** $\frac{(2^4)^3}{2^{15}}$

57. *Astronomy* The ratio of a planet's maximum to minimum distance from the Sun is a measure of how circular its orbit is.

a. Copy and complete the table below.

b. Which planet has the least circular orbit? the most circular orbit? Explain your reasoning.

Distances from the Sun (km)

Planet	Maximum	Minimum	Maximum : Minimum
Mercury	6.97×10^7	4.59×10^7	■ : ■ $= \frac{6.97 \times 10^7}{4.59 \times 10^7} = \frac{6.97}{4.59} \approx 1.52$
Venus	1.089×10^8	1.075×10^8	1.089×10^8 : ■ ≈ ■
Earth	1.521×10^8	1.471×10^8	■ : 1.471×10^8 ≈ ■
Mars	2.491×10^8	2.067×10^8	■ : ■ ≈ ■
Jupiter	8.157×10^8	7.409×10^8	■ : ■ ≈ ■
Saturn	1.507×10^9	1.347×10^9	■ : ■ ≈ ■
Uranus	3.004×10^9	2.735×10^9	■ : ■ ≈ ■
Neptune	4.537×10^9	4.457×10^9	■ : ■ ≈ ■
Pluto	7.375×10^9	4.425×10^9	■ : ■ ≈ ■

min.

max.

58. *Medicine* If you donate blood regularly, the American Red Cross recommends a 56-day waiting period between donations. One pint of blood contains about 2.4×10^{12} red blood cells. Your body normally produces about 2×10^6 red blood cells per second.

a. At its normal rate, in how many seconds will your body replace the red blood cells lost by giving one pint of blood?

b. Convert your answer from part (a) to days.

Exercises MIXED REVIEW

Solve each equation.

59. $x^2 = 0.36$ **60.** $t^2 - 13 = 0$ **61.** $m + 4 = -2$

Graph each inequality.

62. $y \leq 3x - 4$ **63.** $y > -2x$ **64.** $y \geq -x + 1$

65. The Folsom Dam in California holds 1 million acre-feet of water in a reservoir. An acre-foot of water is the amount of water that covers an acre to the depth of one foot, or 326,000 gal. How many gallons are in the reservoir?

SELF ASSESSMENT

PORTFOLIO

For your portfolio, select one or two items from your work for this chapter. Here are some possibilities:
- best work
- work you found challenging
- part of your project

Explain why you have included each selection that you make.

CHAPTER PROJECT

Finishing the Chapter Project

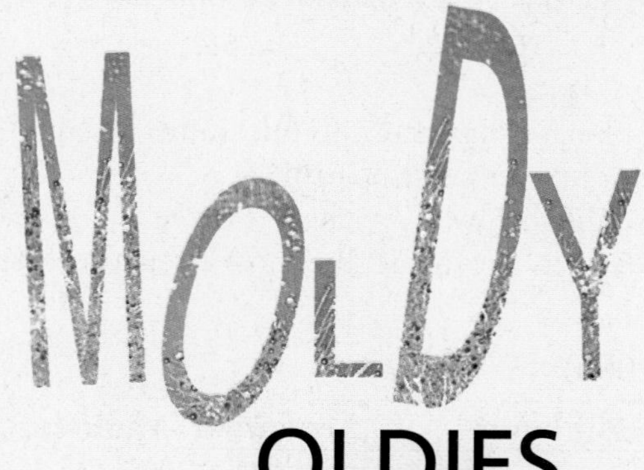

OLDIES

Questions on pages 366, 372, 389, 395, and 400 should help you to complete your project. Record all your information for the project in a notebook. Be sure to include your data and calculations. Include a picture or illustration of the mold as it appeared when it began to grow and at the end of your experiment. Add any additional information you feel is necessary.

Reflect and Revise

Share your notebook with others in your group. Check that your presentation is clear and accurate. Make any changes necessary in your work.

Follow Up

What difference in the rate of growth of the mold might have occurred if you had placed the cheese in a cooler environment? in a drier environment? Investigate other sources of mold and fungus in the natural environment.

For More Information

Dashevsky, H. Steve. *Microbiology: 49 Science Fair Projects.* Blue Ridge Summit, Pennsylvania: TAB Books, 1994.

Hershey, David R. *Plant Biology Science Projects.* New York: John Wiley & Sons, 1995.

VanCleave, Janice Pratt. *Janice VanCleave's A+ Projects in Biology: Winning Experiments for Science Fairs and Extra Credit.* New York: John Wiley & Sons, 1993.

CHAPTER 8

Wrap Up

Key Terms

compound interest (p. 369)
decay factor (p. 373)
exponential decay (p. 373)
exponential function (p. 363)
exponential growth (p. 368)
growth factor (p. 368)
interest period (p. 369)
power (p. 391)
power of ten (p. 386)
scientific notation (p. 385)
simplest form (p. 403)

How am I doing?

- State three ideas from this chapter that you think are important. Explain your choices.
- Describe several rules that you can use to simplify expressions with exponents.

Exploring Exponential Functions 8-1

You can use exponents to show repeated multiplication. An **exponential function** repeatedly multiplies an amount by the same positive number.

Evaluate each function for the given values.

1. $f(x) = 3 \cdot 2^x$ for the domain $\{1, 2, 3, 4\}$

2. $y = 10 \cdot (0.75)^x$ for the domain $\{1, 2, 3\}$

3. a. One kind of bacterium in a laboratory culture triples in number every 30 minutes. Suppose a culture is started with 30 bacteria cells. How many bacteria will there be after 2 hours?

b. After how many minutes will there be more than 20,000 bacteria?

Exponential Growth and Decay 8-2, 8-3

The general form of an exponential function is $y = a \cdot b^x$.

When $b > 1$, the function increases, and the function shows **exponential growth.** The base, b, of the exponent is called the **growth factor.** An example of exponential growth is **compound interest.**

When $0 < b < 1$, the function decreases, and the function shows **exponential decay.** Then b is called the **decay factor.** An example of exponential decay is half-life.

Identify each exponential function as *exponential growth* or *exponential decay.* Then identify the growth or decay factor.

4. $y = 5.2 \cdot 3^x$

5. $y = 0.15 \cdot \left(\frac{3}{2}\right)^x$

6. $y = 7 \cdot 0.32^x$

7. $y = 1.3 \cdot \left(\frac{1}{4}\right)^x$

Graph each function.

8. $f(x) = 2.5^x$

9. $y = 0.5 \cdot (0.5)^x$

10. $f(x) = \left(\frac{1}{2}\right) \cdot 3^x$

11. $y = 0.1^x$

What percent increase or decrease is modeled in each function?

12. $y = 100 \cdot 1.025^x$

13. $y = 32 \cdot 0.75^x$

14. $y = 0.4 \cdot 2^x$

15. $y = 1.01 \cdot 0.9^x$

16. The population of a city is 100,000 and is growing 7% each year.
   a. Write an equation to model the population of the city after any number of years.
   b. Use your equation to find the population after 25 years.

17. a. **Finance** Suppose you earned \$1200 last summer and you put it into a savings account that pays 5.5% interest compounded quarterly. Find the balance after 9 months and after 12 months.
   b. **Writing** Would you rather have an account that pays 5.5% interest compounded quarterly or 6% interest compounded annually? Explain.

18. **Chemistry** The half-life of radioactive carbon-11 is 20 min. You start an experiment with 160 mCi of carbon-11. After 2 h, how much radioactivity remains?

Zero and Negative Exponents — 8-4

You can use zero and negative numbers as exponents. For any nonzero number a, $a^0 = 1$. For any nonzero number a and any integer n, $a^{-n} = \frac{1}{a^n}$.

Write each expression so that all exponents are positive.

19. $b^{-4}c^0d^6$ 20. $\frac{x^{-2}}{y^{-8}}$ 21. $7k^{-8}h^3$ 22. $\frac{1}{p^2q^{-4}r^0}$ 23. $\left(\frac{2}{3}\right)^{-4}$

24. **Critical Thinking** Is $(-3b)^4 = -12b^4$? Why or why not?

25. **Standardized Test Prep** If $a = 4$, $b = -3$, and $c = 0$, which expression has the greatest value?
   A. a^b B. b^c C. $\frac{1}{b^{-a}}$ D. $\frac{a^c}{b^c}$ E. $\frac{c}{a^{-b}}$

Scientific Notation — 8-5

You can use **scientific notation** to express very large or very small numbers. A number is in scientific notation if it is in the form $a \times 10^n$, where $1 \leq |a| < 10$ and n is an integer.

Determine whether each number is in scientific notation. If it is not, write it in scientific notation.

26. 950×10^5 27. 72.35×10^8 28. 1.6×10^{-6} 29. 84×10^{-5} 30. 0.26×10^{-3}

Write each number in scientific notation.

31. The space probe *Voyager 2* traveled 2,793,000 miles.

32. There are 189 million passenger cars and trucks in use in the United States.

Double each number. Give your answers in scientific notation.

33. 8.03×10^7 34. 2.3×10^{-9} 35. 7.084×10^6 36. 5×10^{-13}

Multiplication Properties of Exponents 8-6, 8-7

To multiply powers with the same base, add the exponents.

$$a^m \cdot a^n = a^{m+n}$$

To raise a power to a power, multiply the exponents.

$$(a^m)^n = a^{mn}$$

To raise a product to a power, raise each factor in the product to the power.

$$(ab)^n = a^n b^n$$

Simplify each expression. Use only positive exponents.

37. $2d^2d^3$ **38.** $(q^3r)^4$ **39.** $(5c^{-4})(-4m^2c^8)$ **40.** $(1.34^2)^5(1.34)^{-8}$ **41.** $(12x^2y^{-2})^5(4xy^{-3})^{-8}$

42. **Estimation** Each square inch of your body has about 6.5×10^2 pores. The back of your hand has area about 0.12×10^2 in.^{2}. About how many pores are on the back of one hand?

43. **Open-ended** Write and solve a problem that involves multiplying exponents.

Division Properties of Exponents 8-8

To divide powers with the same base, subtract the exponents. $\frac{a^m}{a^n} = a^{m-n}$

To raise a quotient to a power, raise the dividend and the divisor to the power. $\left(\frac{a}{b}\right)^n = \frac{a^n}{b^n}$

Determine whether each expression is in simplest form. If it is not, simplify it.

44. $\frac{w^2}{w^5}$ **45.** $(8^3) \cdot 8^{-5}$ **46.** $\left(\frac{21x^3}{5y^2}\right)$ **47.** $\left(\frac{n^5}{v^3}\right)^7$ **48.** $\frac{e^{-6}c^3}{e^5}$ **49.** $\left(\frac{x^9}{s^{-3}}\right)^5$

Find each quotient. Give your answer in scientific notation.

50. $\frac{4.2 \times 10^8}{2.1 \times 10^{11}}$ **51.** $\frac{3.1 \times 10^4}{12.4 \times 10^2}$ **52.** $\frac{4.5 \times 10^3}{9 \times 10^7}$ **53.** $\frac{5.1 \times 10^5}{1.7 \times 10^2}$

54. **Writing** List the steps that you would follow to simplify $\left(\frac{5a^8}{10a^6}\right)^{-3}$.

Getting Ready for... CHAPTER 9

Find the distance between the numbers on a number line.

55. 5 and 3 **56.** –7 and 4 **57.** –5 and –11

Simplify each expression.

58. $7r(11 + 4x)$ **59.** $8m(3 - 2t)$ **60.** $b(8 + 2b)$

61. $8p + 6d - 3p$ **62.** $-5n - 4n + 10n$ **63.** $5^2 + 6^2$

64. $9^2 - 4^2$ **65.** $(3t)^2 + (2t)^2$ **66.** $20y^2 - (4y)^2$

Find the range and mean of each set of data.

67. \$40, \$58, \$44, \$47, \$39, \$58, \$56

68. 4 kg, 3 kg, 6 kg, 3 kg, 5 kg, 8 kg, 4 kg, 3 kg

69. 1.3 min, 1.4 min, 1.1 min, 1.0 min, 1.4 min

CHAPTER

8 Assessment

Evaluate each function for $x = 1, 2,$ and 3.

1. $y = 3 \cdot 5^x$
2. $f(x) = \frac{1}{2} \cdot 4^x$
3. $f(x) = 4 \cdot (0.95)^x$
4. $g(x) = 5 \cdot \left(\frac{3}{4}\right)^x$
5. The function $y = 10 \cdot 1.08^x$ models the cost of annual tuition (in thousands of dollars) at a local college in the years since 1987.
   a. Graph the function.
   b. What is the annual percent increase?
   c. How much was tuition in 1987? in 1992?
   d. How much will tuition be the year you plan to graduate from high school?
6. The function $y = 1.3 \cdot (1.07)^n$ models a city's annual electrical consumption for the n years since 1965, where y is billions of kilowatt-hours.
   a. Determine whether the function models exponential growth or decay, and find the growth or decay factor.
   b. What value of n should be substituted to find the value of y now? Use this value for n to find y.
   c. What will be the annual electrical usage in 10 years?
   d. What was the annual electrical usage 10 years ago?
7. **Open-ended** Write and solve a problem involving exponential decay.
8. **Writing** Explain when the function $y = a \cdot b^x$ shows exponential growth and when it shows exponential decay.
9. **Standardized Test Prep** If $a = -3$, which expression has the least value?
   A. a^2a^0 B. a^a C. a^8a^{-5}
   D. $-a^aa^{-4}$ E. $(a^3a^{-4})^2$

Graph each function.

10. $y = \frac{1}{2} \cdot 2^x$
11. $y = 2 \cdot \left(\frac{1}{2}\right)^x$
12. $f(x) = 3^x$

13. **Critical Thinking** Is there a solution to the equation $3^x = 5^x$? Explain.

Write each number in scientific notation.

14. There were 44,909,000 votes cast for Bill Clinton in the 1992 presidential election.
15. More than 450,000 households in the United States have reptiles as pets.

Determine whether each number is in scientific notation. If it is not, write it in scientific notation.

16. 76×10^{-9}
17. 7.3×10^5
18. $4.05 \times 10 \times 10^{-8}$
19. 32.5×10^{13}

Simplify each expression. Use positive exponents.

20. $\frac{r^3t^{-7}}{t^5}$
21. $\left(\frac{a^3}{m}\right)^{-4}$
22. $\frac{t^{-8}m^2}{m^{-3}}$
23. $c^3v^9c^{-1}c^0$
24. $h^2k^{-5}d^3k^2$
25. $9y^4j^2y^{-9}$
26. $(w^2k^0p^{-5})^{-7}$
27. $2y^{-9}h^2(2y^0h^{-4})^{-6}$
28. $(1.2)^5(1.2)^{-2}$
29. $(-3q^{-1})^3q^2$

30. a. **Astronomy** The speed of light in a vacuum is 186,300 mi/s. Use scientific notation to express how far light travels in one hour.
    b. How long does light take to travel to Saturn, about 2.3×10^9 mi away from Earth?
31. **Banking** A customer deposits \$1000 in a savings account that pays 4% interest compounded quarterly. How much money will the customer have in the account after 2 years? after 5 years?
32. **Automobiles** Suppose a new car is worth \$14,000. Its value decreases by one fifth each year. The function $y = 14{,}000(0.8)^x$ models the car's value after x years.
    a. Find the value of the car after one year.
    b. Find the value of the car after four years.

CHAPTER

8 Preparing for the Math A Exam

Part I

1 Which function models exponential decay?
(1) $y = 0.25 \cdot 5^x$
(2) $y = 5 \cdot 0.25^x$
(3) $y = 0.5 \cdot 2.5^x$
(4) $y = 2.5 \cdot 5^x$

2 What percent of increase or decrease is modeled in the function $y = 45 \cdot 1.6^x$?
(1) 40% decrease
(2) 160% increase
(3) 60% increase
(4) 60% decrease

3 Which expression is equivalent to $\frac{4m^{-2}}{xy^{-4}}$?
(1) $\frac{4xy^4}{m^2}$
(2) $\frac{xy^4}{4m^2}$
(3) $\frac{4y^4}{m^2x}$
(4) $\frac{4y^{-4}}{m^{-2}x}$

4 Which expression has the least value when $b = 3$ and $c = -2$?
(1) c^b
(2) b^c
(3) b^0c^0
(4) $(b^c)^b$

5 Which number is expressed in scientific notation as 4.278×10^{-6}?
(1) 0.0000004278
(2) 0.004278
(3) 0.427800
(4) 0.000004278

6 Which expression is in simplest form and equivalent to $(3s^3)(2t^2)(4s^4)$?
(1) $24st^9$
(2) $24s^{12}t^2$
(3) $24s^7t^2$
(4) $(12s^7)(2t^2)$

7 Which expression is equivalent to $\frac{a^2}{b^3}$?
(1) $\frac{a^6b^3}{a^3b^9}$
(2) $\frac{a^2a}{b^{-1}b^4}$
(3) $\frac{a^6b^2}{a^4b^5}$
(4) $\frac{a^8b^{-1}}{a^4b^{-2}}$

8 If a is positive and b is negative, which of the following is negative?
(1) $|ab|$
(2) $a + |b|$
(3) $a|b|$
(4) $|a|b$

9 You flip a coin and roll a number cube. Find the probability of getting a head and a multiple of 3.
(1) $\frac{1}{4}$
(2) $\frac{1}{6}$
(3) $\frac{1}{12}$
(4) $\frac{5}{6}$

Part II

10 An investment of $5000 doubles every 6 years. How much is this investment worth after 30 years?

11 Write an exponential function to model an initial population of 60,000 that has a steady annual loss of 1.75%.

12 Simplify: $(m^{-4})^2(4n)^3$. Use positive exponents.

Part III

13 Evaluate $f(x) = 0.8^x$ for the domain $\{1, 2, 3, 4\}$. Tell whether this function is increasing, decreasing, or neither.

14 Write a simplified binomial for the area of this parallelogram.

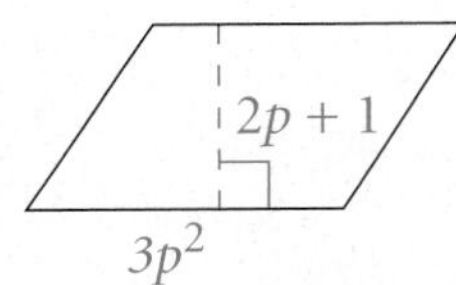

Part IV

15 Write a simplified binomial for the surface area of this rectangular prism.

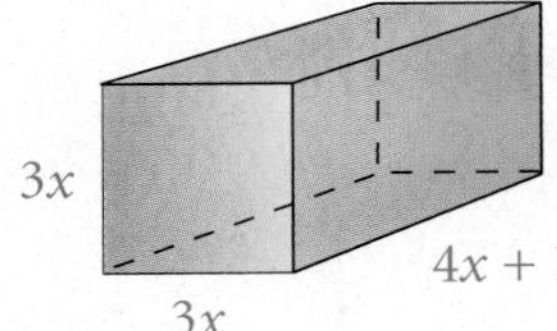

16 Light travels at 186,000 mi/sec. Sound travels at 1080 ft/sec. (5280 ft = 1 mi)
a Write the speed of light in ft/sec. Use scientific notation.
b Write the speed of sound in scientific notation.
c How much faster does light travel than sound?

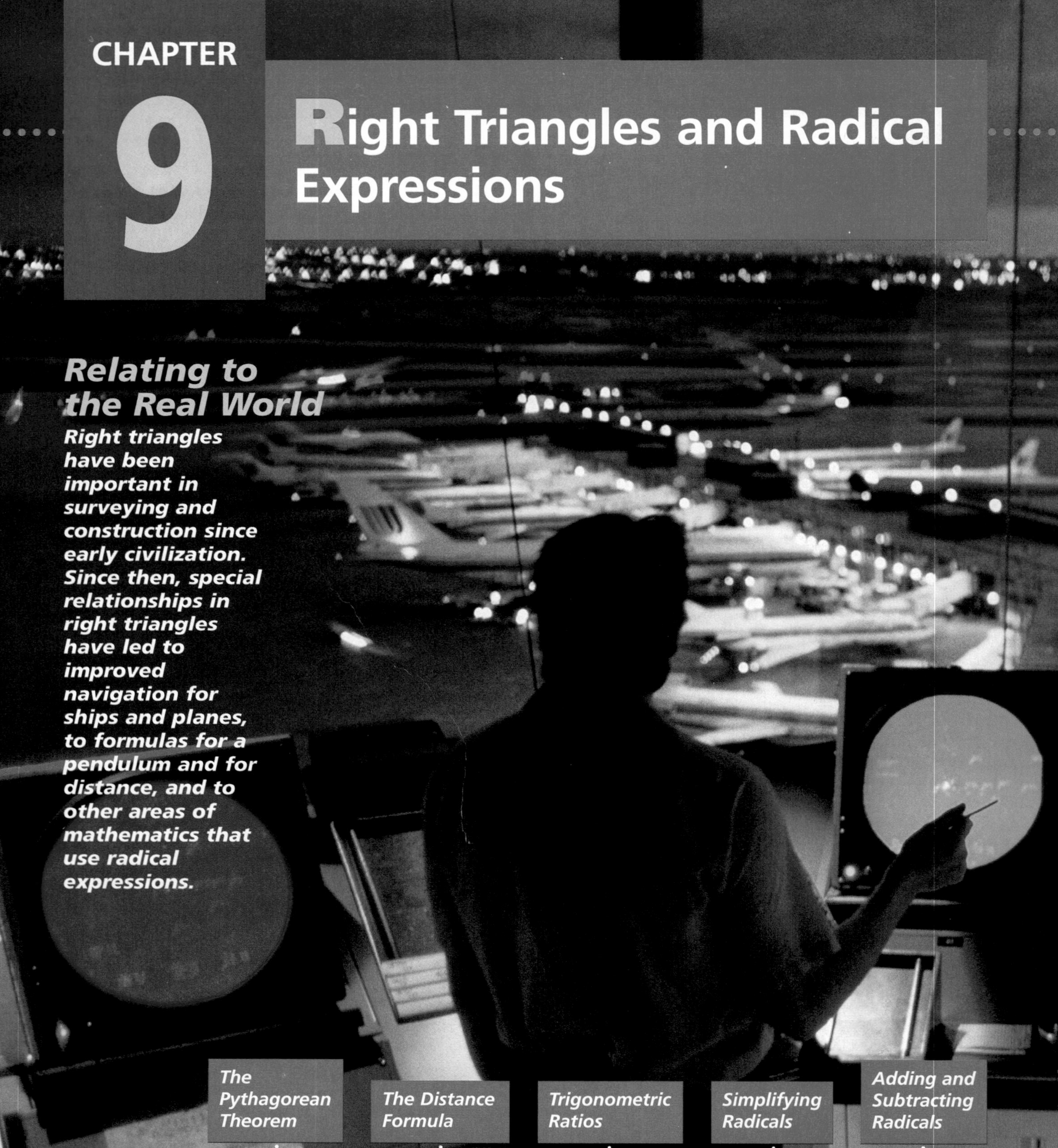

CHAPTER

9 Right Triangles and Radical Expressions

Relating to the Real World

Right triangles have been important in surveying and construction since early civilization. Since then, special relationships in right triangles have led to improved navigation for ships and planes, to formulas for a pendulum and for distance, and to other areas of mathematics that use radical expressions.

CHAPTER PROJECT

On a CLEAR Day...

Suppose it's a clear day and you have a view with no obstructions — maybe not as clear as from an air traffic control tower, but fairly clear. How far would you be able to see to the horizon? You can use the Pythagorean theorem and other concepts in this chapter to find this distance.

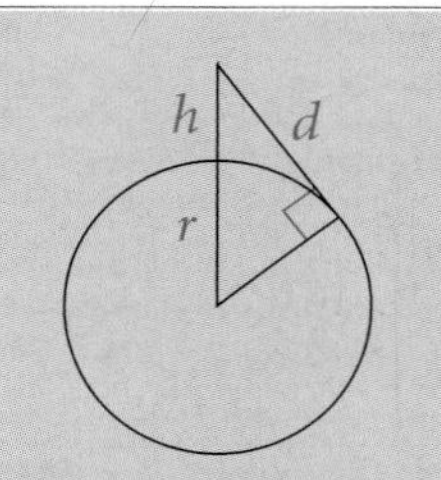

h = your height (ft)
r = radius of the planet (mi)
d = distance you can see (mi)

As you work through the chapter, you will determine and compare the distances you would be able to see to the horizon if you could stand on any planet, including Earth. Your project should include diagrams of the planets, formulas for the distances visible, and graphs of these formulas.

To help you complete the project:

- p. 418 *Find Out by Writing*
- p. 424 *Find Out by Calculating*
- p. 429 *Find Out by Researching*
- p. 444 *Find Out by Communicating*
- p. 449 *Find Out by Organizing*
- p. 456 *Finishing the Project*

Solving Radical Equations 9-6

Graphing Square Root Functions 9-7

Analyzing Data Using Standard Deviation 9-8

Connections Fire Rescue . . . and more

9-1 The Pythagorean Theorem

What You'll Learn

- Finding lengths of sides of a right triangle
- Deciding if a triangle is a right triangle

...And Why

To calculate distances that cannot be measured directly

What You'll Need

- rectangular objects
- ruler
- graph paper

WORK TOGETHER

Work with a partner.

1. Measure the length l and width w of the cover of your mathematics textbook. Be as precise in your measurements as you can.
2. Use a calculator to find the value of the expression $l^2 + w^2$.
3. Measure the length d of one of the diagonals of the cover of your book. Calculate the value of d^2.
4. What can you say about the values of $l^2 + w^2$ and d^2?
5. Choose rectangular objects or draw rectangles on graph paper. Repeat the same steps. What can you say about the length of a diagonal?

THINK AND DISCUSS

Solving Equations Using the Pythagorean Theorem

When you draw a diagonal of a rectangle, you separate the rectangle into two right triangles. In a right triangle, the side opposite the right angle is the longest. It is called the **hypotenuse.** The other two sides are called **legs.** There is a relationship among the lengths of the sides of a right triangle.

QUICK REVIEW

A *right triangle* is a triangle with one right angle.

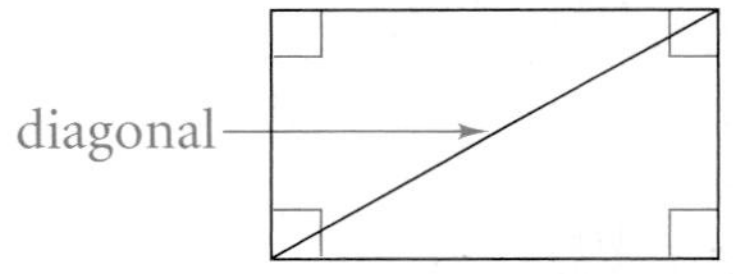

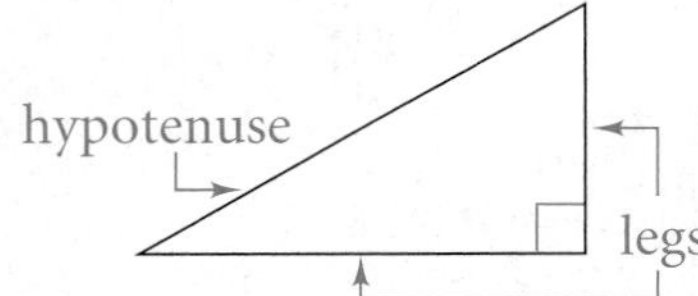

The Pythagorean Theorem

In a right triangle, the sum of the squares of the lengths of the legs is equal to the square of the length of the hypotenuse.

$$a^2 + b^2 = c^2$$

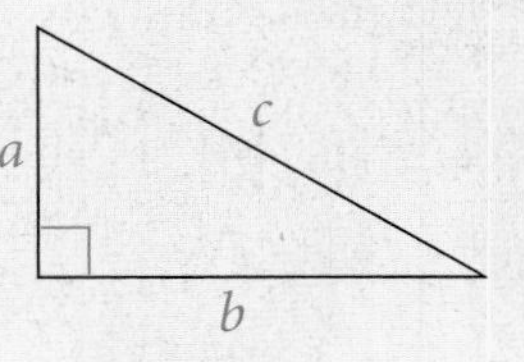

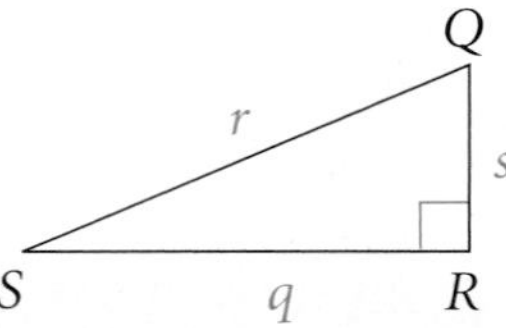

6. Restate the Pythagorean theorem for $\triangle QRS$ to the left.
7. A right triangle has legs of length 5 in. and 12 in. The length of the hypotenuse is 13 in. **Verify** that the Pythagorean theorem is true for this triangle.

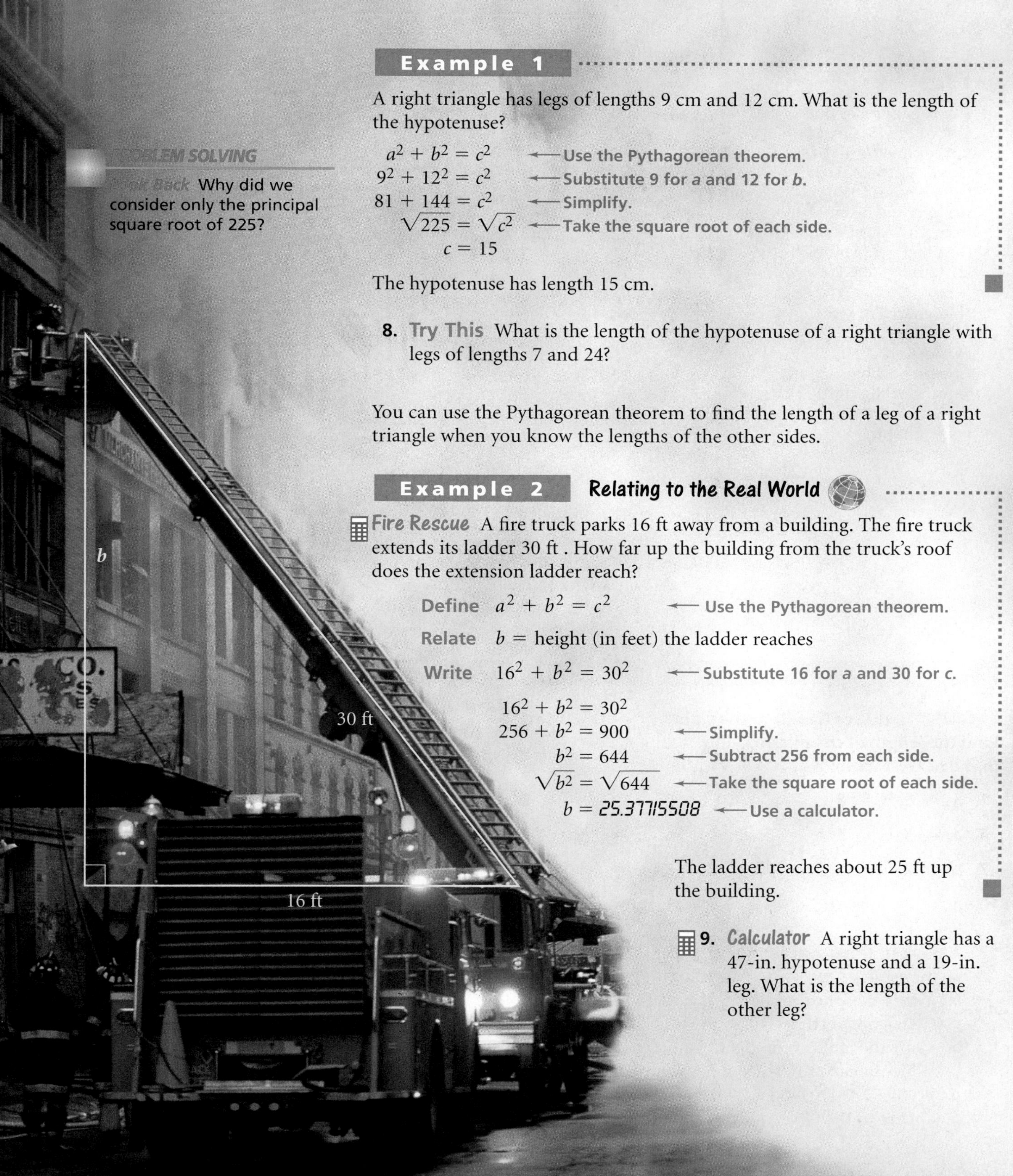

PROBLEM SOLVING

Look Back Why did we consider only the principal square root of 225?

Example 1

A right triangle has legs of lengths 9 cm and 12 cm. What is the length of the hypotenuse?

$$a^2 + b^2 = c^2 \quad \leftarrow \text{Use the Pythagorean theorem.}$$
$$9^2 + 12^2 = c^2 \quad \leftarrow \text{Substitute 9 for } a \text{ and 12 for } b.$$
$$81 + 144 = c^2 \quad \leftarrow \text{Simplify.}$$
$$\sqrt{225} = \sqrt{c^2} \quad \leftarrow \text{Take the square root of each side.}$$
$$c = 15$$

The hypotenuse has length 15 cm.

8. Try This What is the length of the hypotenuse of a right triangle with legs of lengths 7 and 24?

You can use the Pythagorean theorem to find the length of a leg of a right triangle when you know the lengths of the other sides.

Example 2 Relating to the Real World

Fire Rescue A fire truck parks 16 ft away from a building. The fire truck extends its ladder 30 ft . How far up the building from the truck's roof does the extension ladder reach?

Define $a^2 + b^2 = c^2$ ← Use the Pythagorean theorem.

Relate b = height (in feet) the ladder reaches

Write $16^2 + b^2 = 30^2$ ← Substitute 16 for a and 30 for c.

$$16^2 + b^2 = 30^2$$
$$256 + b^2 = 900 \quad \leftarrow \text{Simplify.}$$
$$b^2 = 644 \quad \leftarrow \text{Subtract 256 from each side.}$$
$$\sqrt{b^2} = \sqrt{644} \quad \leftarrow \text{Take the square root of each side.}$$
$$b = 25.37715508 \quad \leftarrow \text{Use a calculator.}$$

The ladder reaches about 25 ft up the building.

9. Calculator A right triangle has a 47-in. hypotenuse and a 19-in. leg. What is the length of the other leg?

Math A Test Prep

1 City A is 12 miles due east of City B. City C is 8 miles due north of City B. To the nearest mile, what is the straight-line distance from City A to City C?
(1) 20 mi (3) 14 mi
(2) 15 mi (4) 12 mi

2 The lengths of two sides of a right triangle are 4 and 6. Find all possible lengths of the third side. Round to the nearest tenth.

Using the Converse

You can find out whether a triangle is a right triangle by using the converse of the Pythagorean theorem.

The Converse of the Pythagorean Theorem

If a triangle has sides of lengths a, b, and c, and $a^2 + b^2 = c^2$, then the triangle is a right triangle with hypotenuse of length c.

Example 3

A triangle has sides of lengths 7, 9, and 12. Is it a right triangle?

Apply the converse of the Pythagorean theorem.

$a^2 + b^2 \stackrel{?}{=} c^2$

$7^2 + 9^2 \stackrel{?}{=} 12^2$ ← Substitute 12 for c, since 12 is the length of the longest side. Substitute 7 and 9 for a and b.

$49 + 81 \stackrel{?}{=} 144$

$130 \neq 144$

The triangle is not a right triangle.

10. Try This A triangle has sides of lengths 10, 24, and 26. Is the triangle a right triangle? Explain.

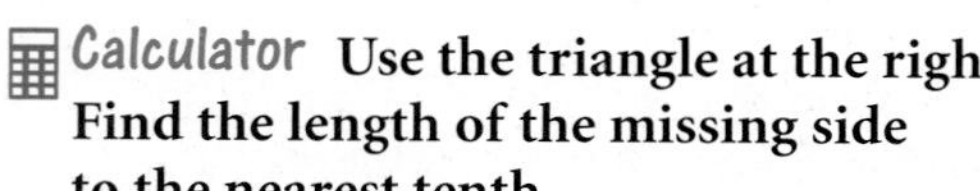

Exercises ON YOUR OWN

Calculator **Use the triangle at the right. Find the length of the missing side to the nearest tenth.**

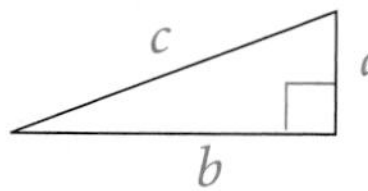

1. $a = 6, b = 8, c = ■$
2. $a = 8, b = 24, c = ■$
3. $a = 1, b = 2, c = ■$
4. $a = 3, b = ■, c = 5$
5. $a = ■, b = 7, c = 10$
6. $a = ■, b = 12, c = 13$
7. $a = 4, b = 4, c = ■$
8. $a = 13, b = 2, c = ■$
9. $a = 15, b = ■, c = 25$
10. $a = ■, b = 10, c = 15$
11. $a = 75, b = ■, c = 100$
12. $a = ■, b = 12, c = 18$

13. Any set of three positive integers that satisfies the relationship $a^2 + b^2 = c^2$ is called a *Pythagorean triple.*

a. Verify that the numbers 6, 8, and 10 form a Pythagorean triple.

b. Copy the table at the right. Complete the table so that the values in each row form a Pythagorean triple.

c. Group Activity Find a Pythagorean triple that does not appear in the table.

a	b	c
3	4	■
5	■	13
■	24	25
9	40	■

Find the missing length to the nearest tenth.

14. 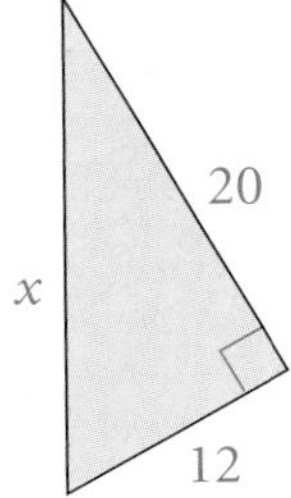

15. 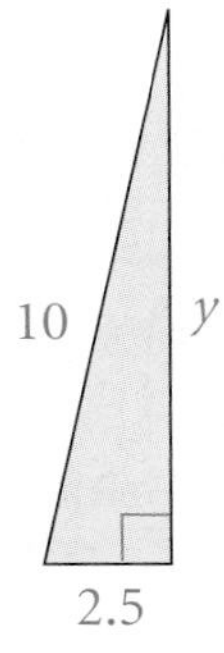

16. 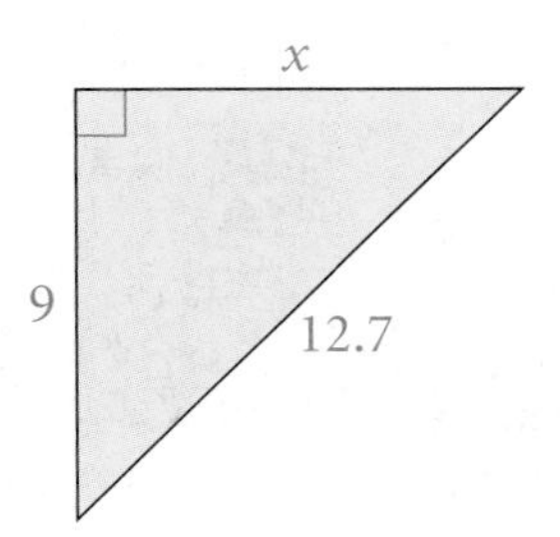

17. 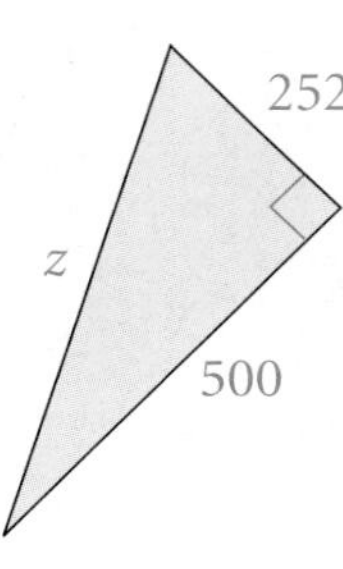

18. **Birds** A pigeon leaves its nest and flies 5 km due east. The pigeon then flies 3 km due north. How far is the pigeon from its nest?

19. You know that two sides of a right triangle measure 10 in. and 8 in.

a. **Writing** Why is this not enough information to be sure of finding the length of the third side?

b. Give two different possible values for the length of the third side. Explain how you found your answers.

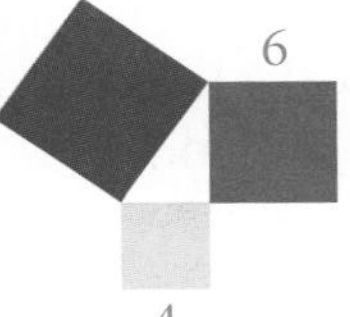

20. **Geometry** The yellow, green, and blue figures are squares. Use the Pythagorean theorem and your knowledge of lengths to find the length of one side of the blue square.

Can each set of three numbers represent the lengths of the sides of a right triangle? Explain your answers.

21. 9, 12, 15 **22.** 1, 2, 3 **23.** 2, 4, 5 **24.** 34, 16, 30

25. 4, 4, 8 **26.** 5000, 4000, 3000 **27.** 1.25, 3, 3.25 **28.** 19, 21, 23

29. 14, 48, 50 **30.** $\frac{1}{3}, \frac{1}{4}, \frac{1}{5}$ **31.** 2, 1.5, 1 **32.** 10, 24, 26

33. 4, 5, 6 **34.** 15, 20, 25 **35.** 18, 80, 82 **36.** $\frac{3}{4}, 1, 1\frac{1}{4}$

37. a. **Sightseeing** A gondola travels between two elevations along a cable. What is the distance the gondola travels from the bottom of the hill to the top?

b. The gondola travels from the bottom of the hill to the top of the hill in 20 min. What is the average speed of the gondola in feet per minute? in miles per hour?

upper elevation 7761 ft

lower elevation 6421 ft

3350 ft

38. **Solar Heating Technician** Find the length of the glass insert for the solar heating panel shown. Round your answer to the nearest inch.

39. What is the diameter of the smallest circular opening that the rectangular rod shown will fit through? Round your answer to the nearest tenth.

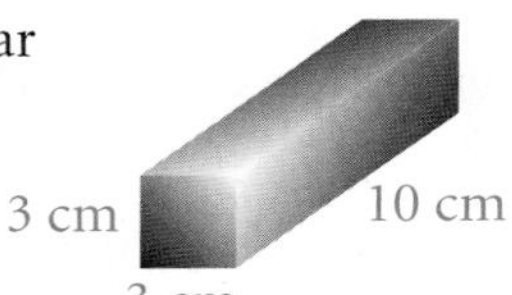

Chapter Project ***Find Out by Writing***

- How many feet are in a mile?
- How would you convert 15 ft into miles?
- How would you represent the quantity h feet in miles?
- In the diagram on page 413, replace h with the expression that represents h feet in miles. Use the Pythagorean theorem to write an equation relating r, d, and h. Do not simplify the equation.

Exercises MIXED REVIEW

Solve each system of equations by substitution.

40. $y = 3x + 5,\ x + y = 4$

41. $y = -3x + 2,\ x - y = 0$

42. **Architecture** A model of a house is $\frac{1}{25}$ of its actual size. One side of the model house is 48 in. long. How long is the corresponding side in the actual house?

Getting Ready for Lesson 9-2

Let $c = \sqrt{a^2 + b^2}$. For each set of values, calculate c to the nearest tenth.

43. $a = 3,\ b = 4$

44. $a = -2,\ b = 5$

45. $a = -3,\ b = 8$

46. $a = 7,\ b = -5$

Math ToolboX

Technology

Testing for a Right Triangle

After Lesson 9-1

With a graphing calculator, you can create a program and save it to use in the future. This program tests three numbers to see if they can be the lengths of the sides of a right triangle.

To input the program, choose PRGM, then NEW. To name the program, press 1, type PYTHAG, and then press ENTER.

To enter the program you will find commands in the PRGM feature under CTL and I/O. After each line press ENTER to go to the next line.

To type the variables *A*, *B*, and *C*, use ALPHA before typing each letter. You can use A-LOCK to type a string of letters such as the information in quotes. The equal sign is in the TEST feature.

After entering your program, press 2nd QUIT. To run your program, press PRGM, select PYTHAG, and choose EXEC.

```
PROGRAM:PYTHAG
:Prompt A,B,C
:If A²+B²=C²
:Goto 1
:Disp "NOT A RIGHT
TRIANGLE"
:Goto 2
:Lbl 1
:Disp "RIGHT TRIANGLE"
:Lbl 2
```

Use the program to tell if each set of numbers can represent the sides of a right triangle. Always input the longest side as *c*.

1. {3, 4, 5} **2.** {7, 9, 12} **3.** {9, 12, 15} **4.** {10, 11, 12}

5. {8, 15, 17} **6.** {17, 17, 17} **7.** {1.4, 4.8, 5} **8.** {6, 8, 10}

9. {3, 7, 8} **10.** {7, 24, 25 } **11.** {20, 21, 29} **12.** {12, 13, 20}

Use the program to see if each triangle is a right triangle.

13.

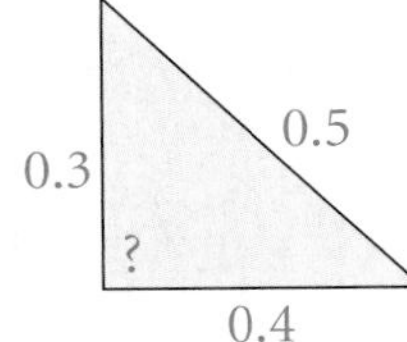

14.

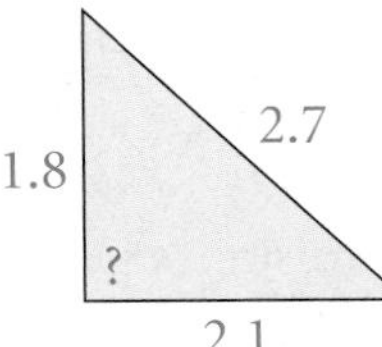

15.

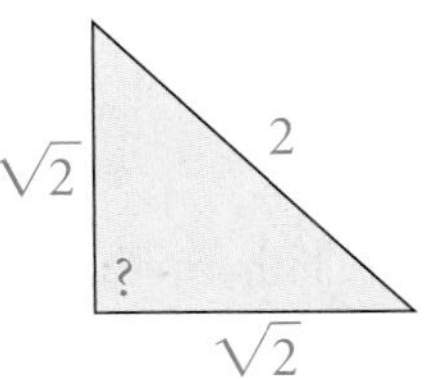

16. Any three integers a, b, and c form a Pythagorean triple if $a^2 + b^2 = c^2$. The following formulas generate Pythagorean triples using positive integers x and y where $x > y$.

$$a = x^2 - y^2$$
$$b = 2xy$$
$$c = x^2 + y^2$$

a. Find the Pythagorean triple that is generated by the values $x = 3$ and $y = 2$.

b. Find the values of x and y that generate the set {9, 40, 41}.

17. **Writing** The set {–3, –4, 5} could not represent the sides of a right triangle because the sides of triangles cannot have negative lengths. Explain why the calculator display indicates a right triangle when you input the values –3, –4, and 5.

```
prgmPYTHAG
A=?-3
B=?-4
C=?5
RIGHT TRIANGLE
                Done
```

9-2 The Distance Formula

What You'll Learn

- Finding the distance between two points in a coordinate plane
- Finding the coordinates of the midpoint of two points

...And Why

To find the distance between two groups of hikers

What You'll Need

- graph paper
- ruler

WORK TOGETHER

Work with a partner as you apply the Pythagorean theorem to find the distance between two points.

1. On graph paper, graph points $A(-3, 4)$, $B(1, 1)$, and $C(-3, 1)$. Then connect the points.
2. Find AC and BC.
3. $\triangle ABC$ is a right triangle. Use the Pythagorean theorem to write an equation relating AC, BC, and AB.
4. Substitute values for AC and BC in the equation you wrote in Question 3. Solve the equation to find AB.

QUICK REVIEW

AB is the distance between points A and B and the length of $\overline{AB}$.

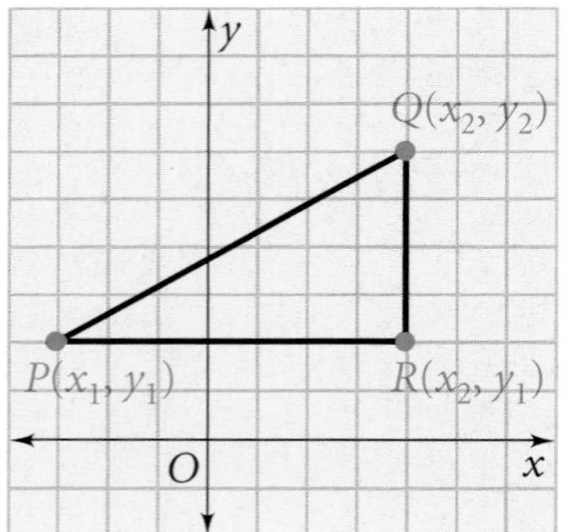

THINK AND DISCUSS

Finding the Distance

In the Work Together activity, you found the distance between two particular points. If you have any two points $P(x_1, y_1)$ and $Q(x_2, y_2)$, you can graph them and form a right triangle as shown in the diagram. You can then use the Pythagorean theorem to find the distance between the points.

$(PQ)^2 = (PR)^2 + (RQ)^2$ ← Use the Pythagorean theorem.

$(PQ)^2 = (x_2 - x_1)^2 + (y_2 - y_1)^2$ ← Substitute the lengths you know.

$PQ = \sqrt{(x_2 - x_1)^2 + (y_2 - y_1)^2}$ ← Take the principal square root of each side.

This method for finding the distance between two points is summarized in the *distance formula.*

The Distance Formula

The distance d between any two points (x_1, y_1) and (x_2, y_2) is
$d = \sqrt{(x_2 - x_1)^2 + (y_2 - y_1)^2}$.

Example 1 Relating to the Real World 

Hiking The Gato and Wilson families are staying at a campground. The Gatos leave camp and hike 2 km west and 5 km south. The Wilsons leave camp and hike 1 km east and 4 km north. How far apart are the families?

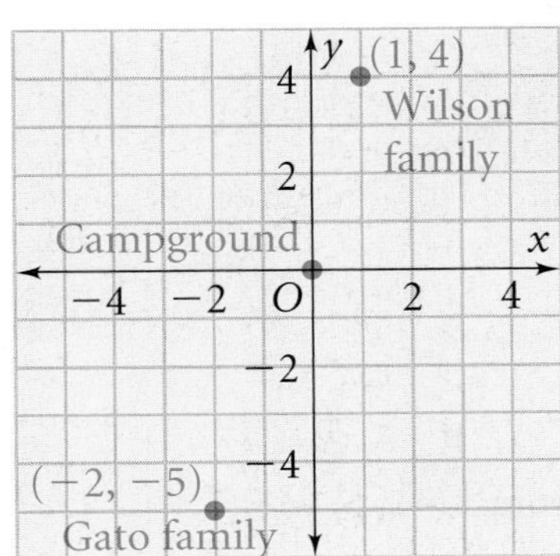

Let the campground be (0, 0). Then the Gato family's location is (−2, −5) and the Wilson family's location is (1, 4).

$d = \sqrt{(x_2 - x_1)^2 + (y_2 - y_1)^2}$ ← **Use the distance formula.**

$d = \sqrt{(1 - (-2))^2 + (4 - (-5))^2}$ ← **Substitute (1, 4) for (x_2, y_2) and (−2, −5) for (x_1, y_1).**

$d = \sqrt{3^2 + 9^2}$ ← **Simplify.**

$d = \sqrt{90}$

$d = 9.486832981$ ← **Use a calculator.**

The two families are about 9.5 km apart.

PROBLEM SOLVING

Look Back Would the result in Example 1 be different if you used (1, 4) for (x_1, y_1) and (−2, −5) for (x_2, y_2)? Explain your answer.

5. Try This One hiker is 4 mi west and 3 mi north of the campground. Another is 6 mi east and 3 mi south of the campground. How far apart are the hikers?

You can also use the distance formula to determine if lengths of opposite sides in a figure are equal.

Example 2

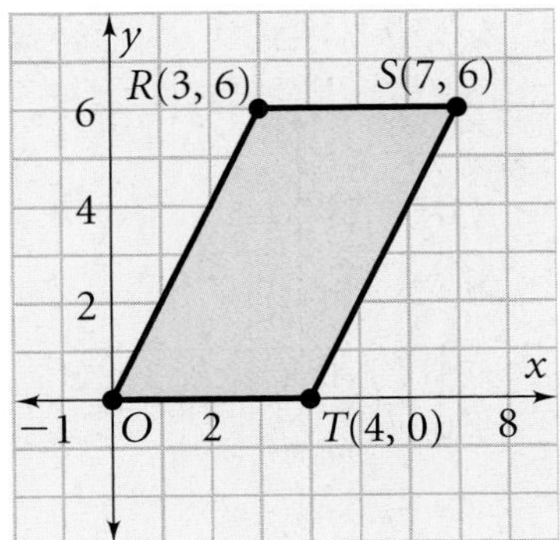

Geometry Quadrilateral *ORST* is shown here in a coordinate plane. Use the distance formula to show that $\overline{OR}$ and $\overline{ST}$ are equal in length.

$OR = \sqrt{(3 - 0)^2 + (6 - 0)^2}$ $\quad ST = \sqrt{(7 - 4)^2 + (6 - 0)^2}$

$OR = \sqrt{3^2 + 6^2}$ $\quad ST = \sqrt{3^2 + 6^2}$

$OR = \sqrt{45}$ $\quad ST = \sqrt{45}$

$OR = ST$. So, $\overline{OR}$ and $\overline{ST}$ are equal in length.

6. Use slopes to show that $\overline{OR}$ and $\overline{ST}$ are parallel.

7. **a.** **Try This** Quadrilateral *KLMN* has vertices with coordinates $K(-3, -2)$, $L(-5, 6)$, $M(2, 6)$, and $N(4, -2)$. Show that $LK = MN$.
   b. Use slopes to show that $\overline{LK}$ and $\overline{MN}$ are parallel.
   c. **Critical Thinking** Describe quadrilateral *KLMN* in as much detail as you can. **Justify** your descriptions and conclusions.

Using the Midpoint Formula

The **midpoint** of a segment $\overline{AB}$ is the point *M* halfway between *A* and *B* where $AM = MB$. The coordinates of the midpoint of a line segment are the averages of the coordinates of the endpoints.

The Midpoint Formula

The midpoint *M* of a line segment with endpoints $A(x_1, y_1)$ and $B(x_2, y_2)$ is $\left(\frac{x_1 + x_2}{2}, \frac{y_1 + y_2}{2}\right)$.

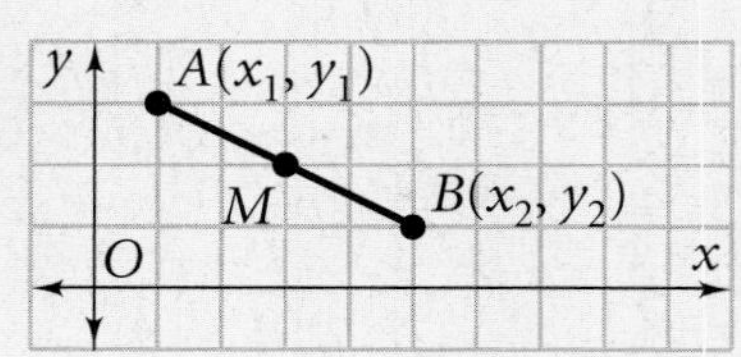

Example 3

Geometry Find the midpoint of the segment from $A(-1, 6)$ to $B(5, 0)$.

$$\left(\frac{x_1 + x_2}{2}, \frac{y_1 + y_2}{2}\right) = \left(\frac{-1 + 5}{2}, \frac{6 + 0}{2}\right)$$
$$= \left(\frac{4}{2}, \frac{6}{2}\right)$$
$$= (2, 3)$$

The midpoint of $\overline{AB}$ is $M(2, 3)$.

8. In Example 3, use the distance formula to **verify** that $AM = MB$.

9. **Try This** Find the coordinates of the midpoint of the line segment with endpoints $X(-7.2, 2)$ and $Y(4.5, 7.5)$.

Exercises ON YOUR OWN

Calculator **Approximate *AB* to the nearest tenth of a unit.**

1. 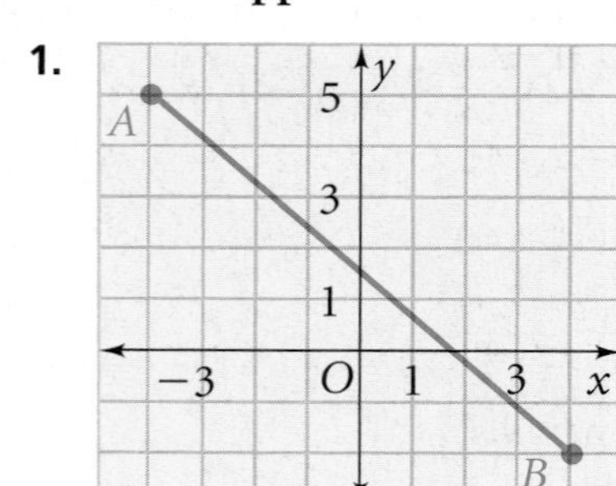

2. 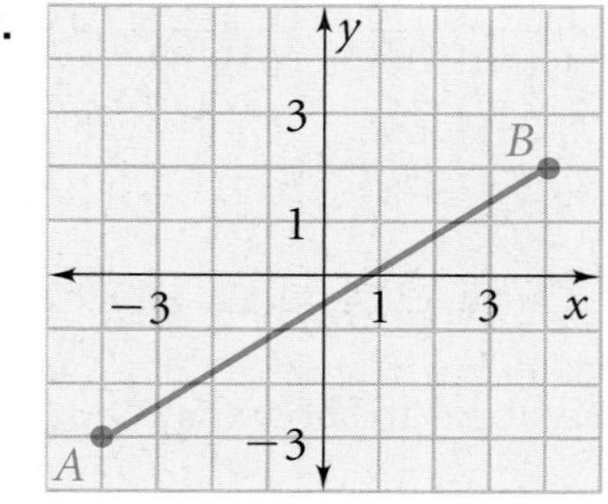

3. 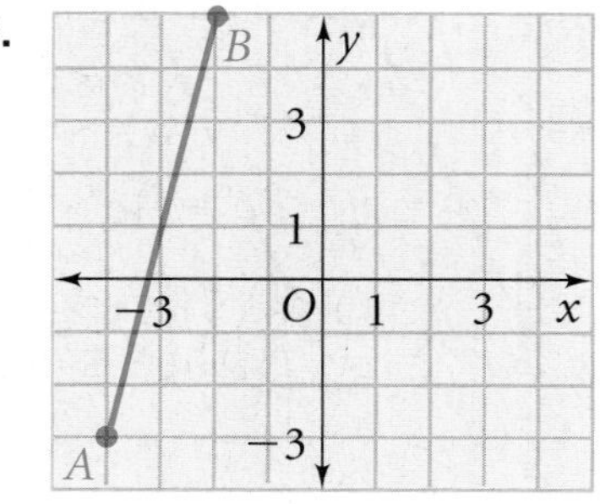

Find the distance between each pair of points to the nearest tenth.

4. $(3, -2), (-1, 5)$
5. $(-4, -4), (4, 4)$
6. $(0, 3), (13, -6)$
7. $(4, 0), (2, -1)$
8. $(7, -2), (-8, -2)$
9. $(5, 9), (10, -1)$
10. $(0, 0), (6, -9)$
11. $(-3, 7), (-11, 9)$
12. $(11, 0), (-3, -7)$
13. $(-2, 7), (-2, -7)$
14. $(9, 10), (11, 12)$
15. $(-3.5, 4.5), (-4.5, 5.5)$

16. a. **News Coverage** Two news helicopters are on their way to a political rally, flying at the same altitude. One helicopter is 20 mi due west of the rally. The other is 15 mi south and 15 mi east of the rally. How far apart are they?

b. How far from the rally are they?

c. Each helicopter is flying at 80 mi/h. How many minutes will it take each of them to arrive at the scene?

17. a. **Electrical Line Technician** Graph Mr. Tanaka's and Ms. Elisa's locations on a coordinate grid with the substation at the origin.

b. What are the coordinates of the point where they will meet?

c. Describe their meeting point in miles north/south and east/west of the substation.

I am 4 mi south and 3 mi west of the substation.
12

Ms. Elisa

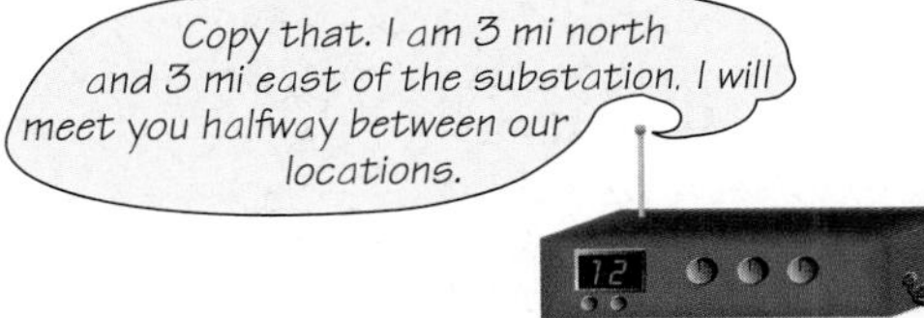

Copy that. I am 3 mi north and 3 mi east of the substation. I will meet you halfway between our locations.
12

Mr. Tanaka

Find the midpoint of $\overline{XY}$.

18. $X(2, 5)$ and $Y(0, 7)$
19. $X(-3, 14)$ and $Y(6, 1)$
20. $X(8, -5)$ and $Y(-4, 5.5)$
21. $X(4, 3)$ and $Y(-9, 3)$
22. $X(0, 6)$ and $Y(-5, -8)$
23. $X(-1, 8)$ and $Y(-7, 0)$
24. $X(4, 1)$ and $Y(1, 4)$
25. $X(5, -11)$ and $Y(12, -7)$
26. $X(2, 9)$ and $Y(-2, -9)$
27. $X(3, 11)$ and $Y(11, 3)$
28. $X\left(4\frac{1}{2}, -2\right)$ and $Y\left(-1\frac{1}{2}, 5\right)$
29. $X(9, 7)$ and $Y(-9, -7)$

30. a. **Transportation** On the map, each unit represents one mile. A van breaks down on its way to a factory. The driver calls a garage for a tow truck. There is a bridge halfway between the garage and the van. How far is the bridge from the van?

b. The van is towed to the factory and then to the garage. How many miles does the tow truck tow the van?

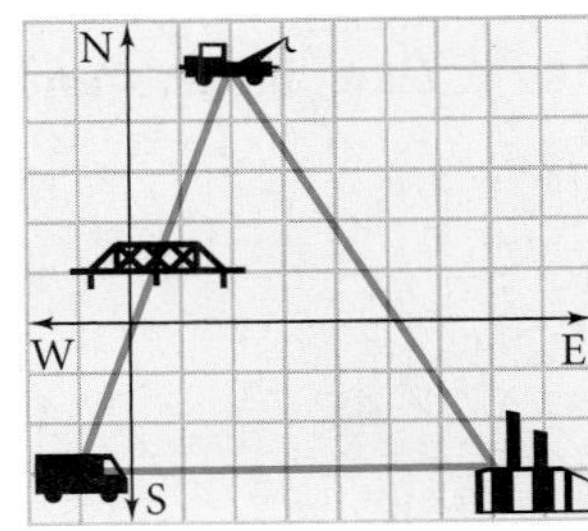

Geometry **Find the perimeter of each figure to the nearest tenth.**

31. 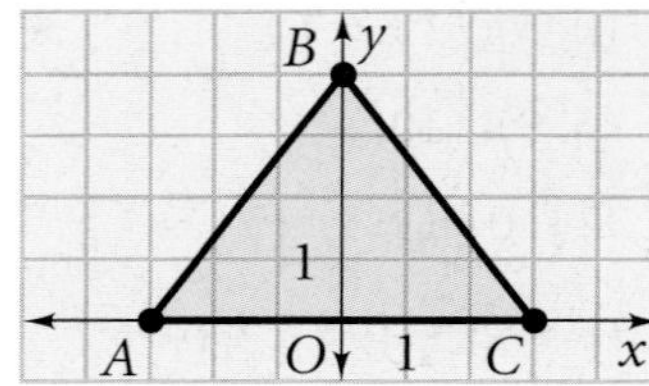

32. 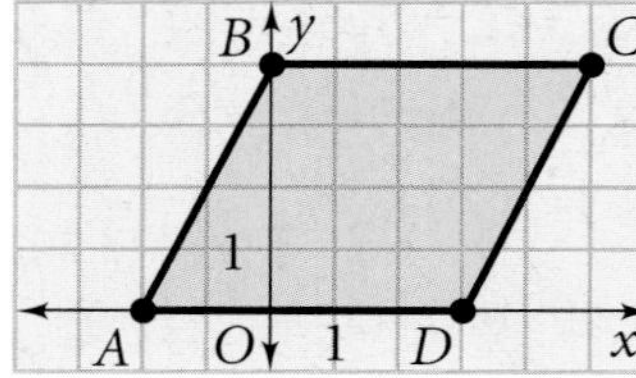

33. 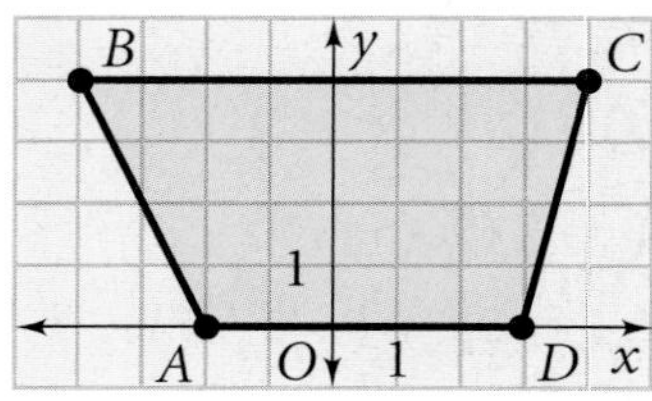

34. a. **Open-ended** Suppose the distance between two points on a coordinate plane is between 10 and 13 units. Identify two points A and B not directly above or across from one another that meet this requirement.

b. Plot your points on graph paper.

c. **Verify** that your points satisfy the requirement by finding AB.

35. **Critical Thinking** If the midpoint of a line segment is the origin, what must be true of the coordinates of the endpoints of the segment?

36. **Writing** **Summarize** the distance formula and the midpoint formula. Use examples of your own to show the use of each formula.

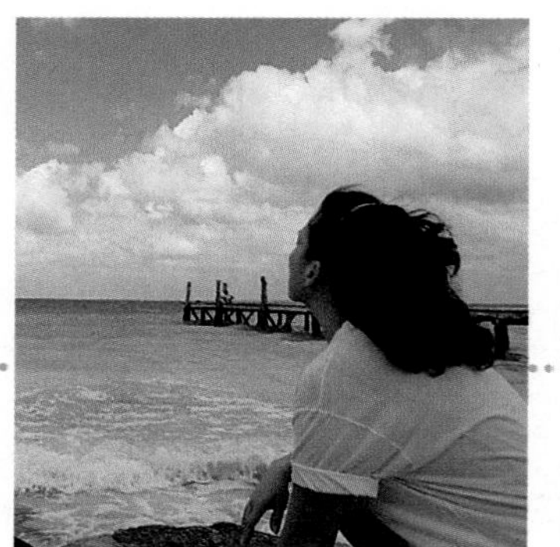

Chapter Project *Find Out by Calculating*

The radius of Earth is about 3960 mi. The formula for the distance you can see to the horizon on Earth is $d = 1.225\sqrt{h}$ where d is the distance visible in miles and h is your height in feet. How far can you see on a clear day with no obstructions?

Exercises MIXED REVIEW

Solve each equation for the given variable.

37. $2x + 7y = 4; x$ **38.** $3x - 5y = 7; y$ **39.** $V = \pi r^2 h; h$ **40.** $S = 2\pi rh; r$

41. **Finance** You deposit $3000 into a bank account paying 6% simple interest annually. How much interest will you receive after 4 years?

Getting Ready for Lesson 9-3

Let $c = \frac{A}{H}$, $s = \frac{O}{H}$, $t = \frac{O}{A}$. Calculate c, s, and t for each of the following.

42. $A = 3, O = 4, H = 5$ **43.** $A = 5, O = 12, H = 13$

Solve each equation.

44. $\frac{15}{x} = 0.75$ **45.** $\frac{x}{20} = 0.34$ **46.** $0.82x = 25$ **47.** $\frac{x}{0.52} = 14$

What You'll Learn

- Exploring and calculating trigonometric ratios
- Using sine, cosine, and tangent to solve problems

...And Why

To find distances indirectly

What You'll Need

- graph paper
- ruler

9-3 Trigonometric Ratios

WORK TOGETHER

Work with a partner.

1. On graph paper, draw a right triangle like the one at the left. Extend sides $\overline{AB}$ and $\overline{AC}$ to form a second triangle similar to the first triangle. One example is shown at the left.

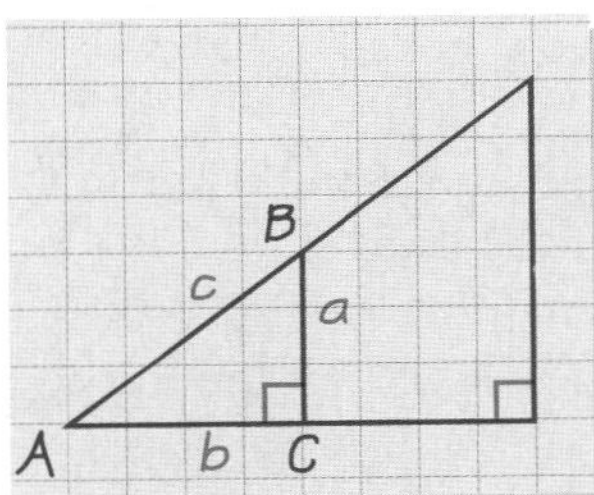

2. a. Copy the table below. Measure and record the lengths of the legs of each triangle.

Triangle	a	b	c	$\frac{a}{b}$	$\frac{a}{c}$	$\frac{b}{c}$
first	■	■	■	■	■	■
second	■	■	■	■	■	■

b. Calculate and record c, the length of each hypotenuse.

c. Calculate and record the ratios $\frac{a}{b}$, $\frac{a}{c}$, and $\frac{b}{c}$ for each triangle.

3. How do corresponding ratios in the two triangles compare?

THINK AND DISCUSS

Finding Trigonometric Ratios

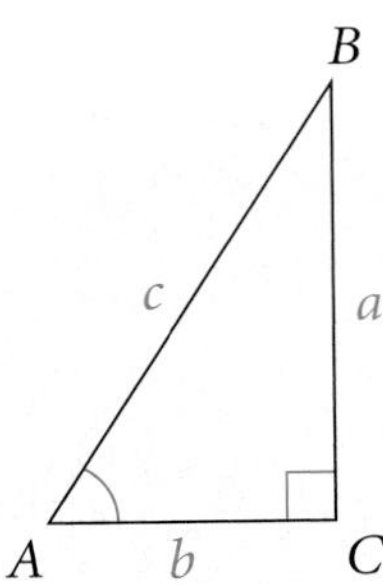

The ratios you explored in the Work Together are called **trigonometric ratios,** meaning triangle measurement ratios. In $\triangle ABC$, $\overline{BC}$ is the leg opposite $\angle A$ and $\overline{AC}$ is the leg adjacent to $\angle A$. The hypotenuse is $\overline{AB}$.

You can use these relationships to express trigonometric ratios.

sine of $\angle A = \dfrac{\text{length of leg opposite } \angle A}{\text{length of hypotenuse}}$ or $\textbf{sin } A = \dfrac{a}{c}$

cosine of $\angle A = \dfrac{\text{length of leg adjacent to } \angle A}{\text{length of hypotenuse}}$ or $\textbf{cos } A = \dfrac{b}{c}$

tangent of $\angle A = \dfrac{\text{length of leg opposite } \angle A}{\text{length of leg adjacent to } \angle A}$ or $\textbf{tan } A = \dfrac{a}{b}$

Example 1

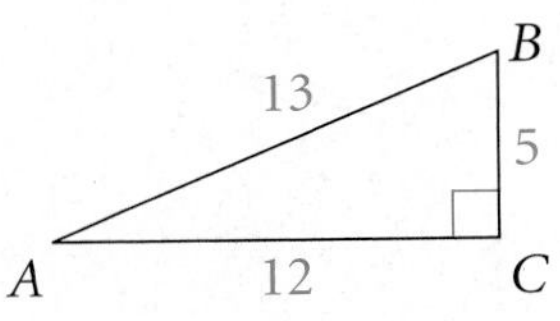

Use the diagram at the left. Find sin A, cos A, and tan A.

$\sin A = \frac{5}{13}$ $\quad\cos A = \frac{12}{13}$ $\quad\tan A = \frac{5}{12}$

4. Try This Use the diagram to find sin B, cos B, and tan B.

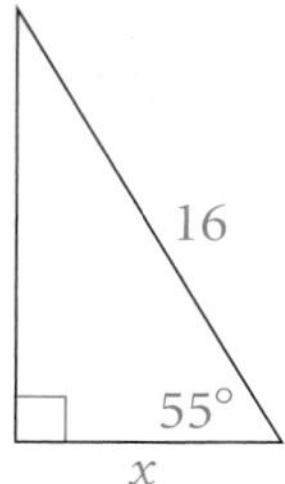

You can use trigonometry to find missing lengths in a triangle.

Example 2

Find the value of x in the triangle at the left.

First, decide which trigonometric ratio to use. You know the angle and hypotenuse and are trying to find the adjacent side. So use cosine.

$$\cos 55^\circ = \frac{\text{side adjacent}}{\text{hypotenuse}}$$ ← This is a short form of the definition.

$$\cos 55^\circ = \frac{x}{16}$$

$$0.573576436 = \frac{x}{16}$$ ← Use a calculator.

$$16(0.573576436) = x$$ ← Cross multiply.

$$9.177222982 = x$$ ← Use a calculator.

The value of x is about 9.2.

CALCULATOR HINT

Use degree mode when finding trigonometric ratios. Use the key sequence COS 55 ENTER.

5. You know the lengths of two sides of the triangle in Example 2. You can use different methods to find the length of the third side.

a. Use the Pythagorean theorem to find the length of the third side.

b. Use either the sine or tangent ratio to find the length of the third side.

c. Compare your answers to parts (a) and (b).

Solving Problems Using Trigonometric Ratios

You can use trigonometric ratios to measure distances indirectly when you know an angle of elevation. An **angle of elevation** is an angle from the horizontal up to a line of sight.

Example 3 Relating to the Real World

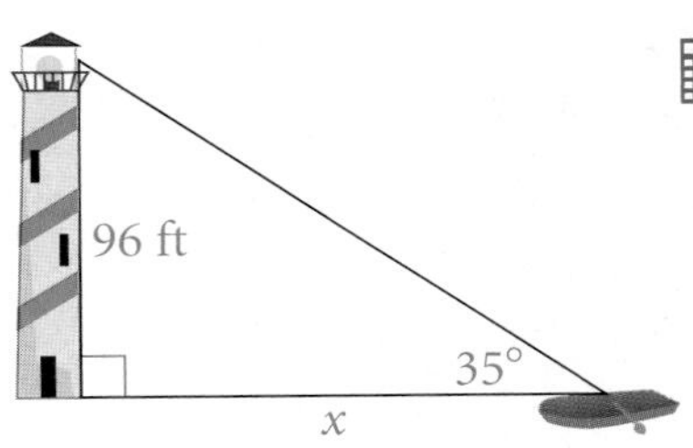

Navigation Suppose that an angle of elevation from a rowboat to a lighthouse is 35°. You know that the lighthouse is 96 ft tall. How far from the lighthouse is the rowboat?

Make a diagram.

Define $x =$ the distance from the lighthouse to the boat

Relate You know the angle and the opposite side and you are trying to find the adjacent side. So use tangent.

Write $\tan A = \frac{\text{side opposite}}{\text{side adjacent}}$

$\tan 35° = \frac{96}{x}$ ← Substitute for the angle and sides.

$x(\tan 35°) = 96$ ← Cross multiply.

$x = \frac{96}{\tan 35°}$ ← Divide to put in calculator-ready form.

$x = 137.1022086$ ← Use a calculator.

$x \approx 137$

The rowboat is about 137 ft from the lighthouse.

6. Could you use the sine or cosine to solve Example 3? Explain.

Exercises ON YOUR OWN

1. **Language Arts** Write a nonmathematical sentence using the word *adjacent.*

Use $\triangle RST$ to evaluate each expression.

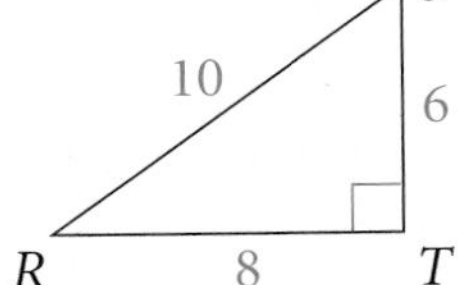

2. $\sin R$

3. $\cos R$

4. $\tan R$

5. $\sin S$

6. $\cos S$

7. $\tan S$

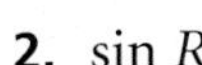

Calculator **Evaluate each expression. Round to four decimal places.**

8. $\sin 32°$

9. $\cos 40°$

10. $\tan 52°$

11. $\sin 85°$

12. $\tan 7°$

For each figure, find $\sin A$, $\cos A$, and $\tan A$.

13.

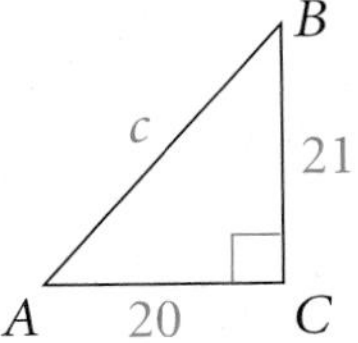

14.

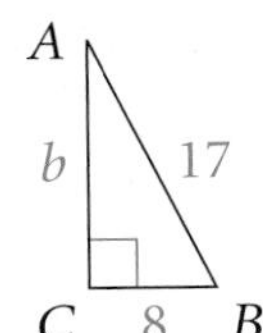

15.

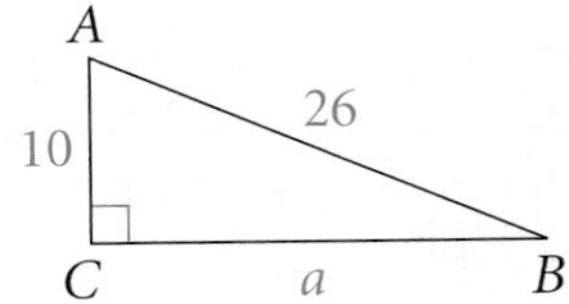

Find the value of x to the nearest tenth.

16. 

17. 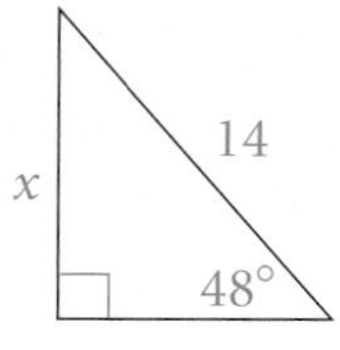

18. 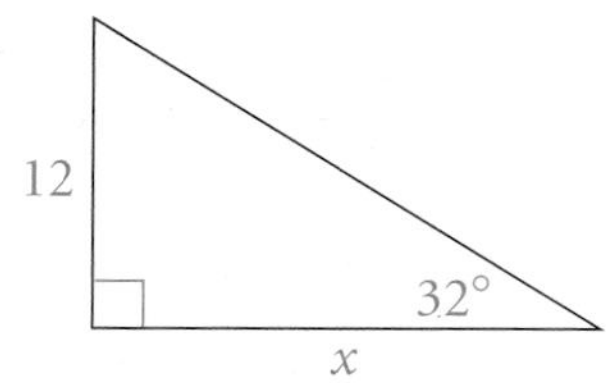

19. **Nature** Suppose you look up from a cabin on the floor of a canyon to a cliff at the top of a vertical wall of rock. The angle of elevation from your location to the cliff is 32°. The cabin is 400 ft from the base of the canyon wall. How high is the canyon wall?

20. **Recreation** A Ferris wheel is shown at the right. Find the distance x that the seat is above the horizontal line through the center of the wheel. Then find the seat's height above the ground.

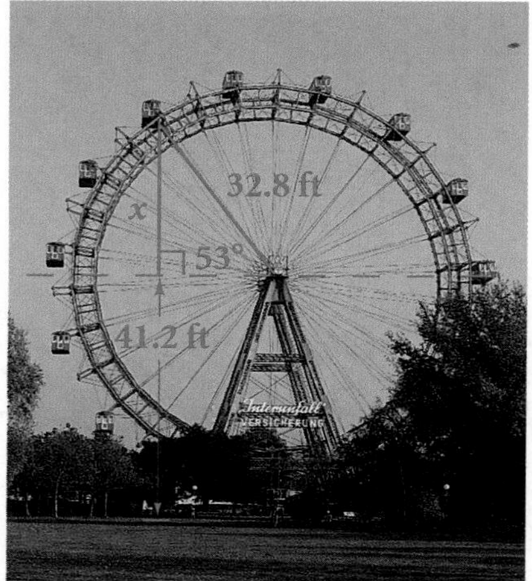

21. **Aviation** Suppose you live about 5 mi from a tower. From your home, you see a plane directly above the tower. Your angle of elevation to the plane is 21°. What is the plane's altitude?

22. **Writing** Suppose you know that a right triangle has a 30° angle and you know the length of the leg adjacent to the 30° angle. Describe how you would find the length of the leg opposite the 30° angle.

Find the indicated length to the nearest tenth.

23. 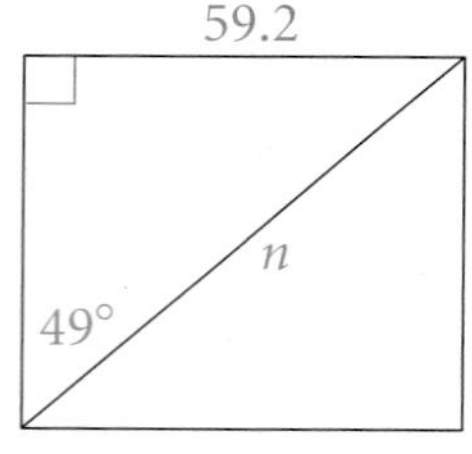

24. 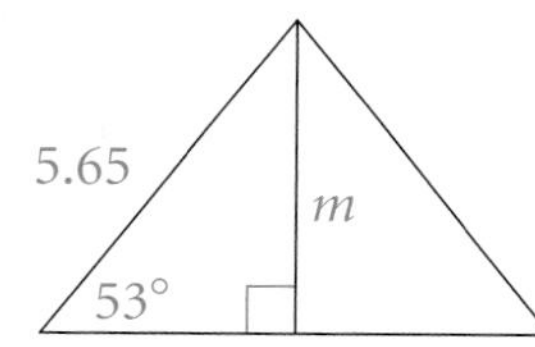

25. 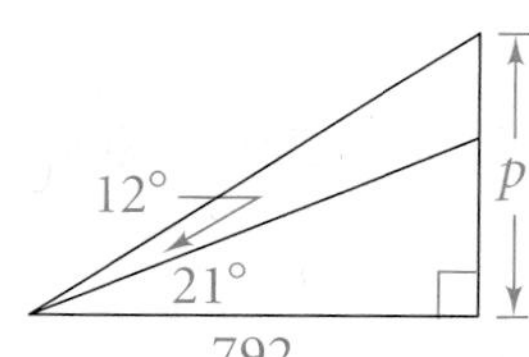

26. **Standardized Test Prep** $\triangle KLM$ is a right triangle with a right angle at M. Which of the following is false?

A. $\sin K = \frac{LM}{KL}$ **B.** $\cos K = \frac{KL}{KM}$ **C.** $\tan K = \frac{LM}{KM}$ **D.** $\cos L = \frac{LM}{KL}$ **E.** $\sin L = \frac{KM}{KL}$

27. **Open-ended** Name some ways you might use a trigonometric ratio to calculate a distance instead of measuring it directly.

28. **Nature** Suppose you are lying on the ground looking up at a California redwood tree. Your angle of elevation to the top of the tree is 42°. You are 280 ft from the base of the tree.

a. How tall is the tree?

b. How far would a bird have to fly to get from the top of the tree to your location?

Chapter Project — Find Out by Researching

Do research to find the radii of all the planets in our solar system. Express your answers in miles.

Exercises MIXED REVIEW

Graph each equation.

29. $y = x + 2$ **30.** $y = |x| + 2$

31. $y = x^2 + 2$ **32.** $y = 2^x$

33. **Transportation** A car is traveling at a constant speed. After 3 h, the car has gone 150 mi. How many miles will the car have gone after 5 h?

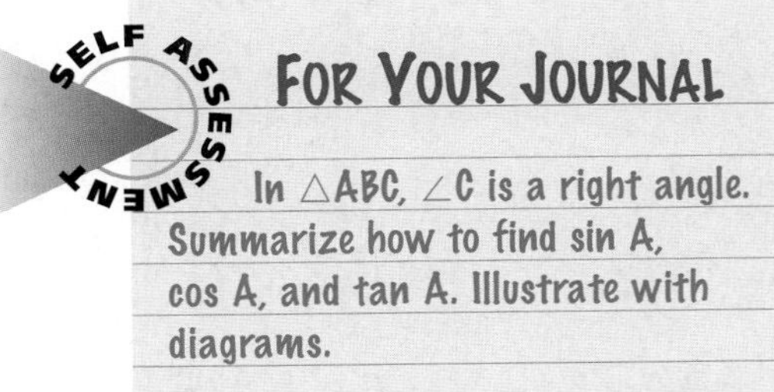

FOR YOUR JOURNAL

In $\triangle ABC$, $\angle C$ is a right angle. Summarize how to find sin A, cos A, and tan A. Illustrate with diagrams.

Getting Ready for Lesson 9-4

Find each value.

34. $\sqrt{4}$ **35.** $\sqrt{169}$ **36.** $3\sqrt{25}$ **37.** $-2\sqrt{9}$ **38.** $-3\sqrt{49}$

Exercises CHECKPOINT

A right triangle has legs of lengths *a* and *b* and hypotenuse of length *c*. Find the missing value.

1. $a = 2, b = 4$ **2.** $a = 3, b = 5$ **3.** $a = 1, b = 7$ **4.** $a = 4, b = 3$

5. $a = 10, c = 26$ **6.** $b = 3, c = 9$ **7.** $a = 8, c = 12$ **8.** $b = 20, c = 25$

9. **Writing** Describe how to find the distance between points (x_1, y_1) and (x_2, y_2). Include examples.

10. The angle of elevation from a point on the ground 300 ft from a tower is 42°. How tall is the tower?

Approximate *AB* to the nearest tenth.

11. $A(1, 4), B(2, 7)$ **12.** $A(-2, -1), B(4, 2)$ **13.** $A(-3, 5), B(6, 1)$ **14.** $A(2, 3), B(5, 4)$

15. **Open-ended** Write the coordinates of a pair of points *A* and *B*. Then find the midpoint of $\overline{AB}$.

In $\triangle ABC$, $\angle C$ is a right angle. Find the length of the indicated side.

16. $m\angle B = 43°, AB = 4, AC = ■$ **17.** $m\angle A = 33°, AC = 7, BC = ■$

What You'll Learn

- Simplifying radicals involving products and quotients
- Solving problems involving radicals

...And Why

To solve distance problems

9-4 Simplifying Radicals

THINK AND DISCUSS

Multiplication with Radicals

A radical expression is in **simplest form** when *all three* statements are true.

- The expression under the radical sign has no perfect square factors other than 1.
- The expression under the radical sign does not contain a fraction.
- The denominator does not contain a radical expression.

1. Explain why each expression *is* or *is not* in simplest form.
   a. $\sqrt{20}$ b. $4\sqrt{5}$ c. $\frac{1}{\sqrt{3}}$ d. $\sqrt{\frac{2}{5}}$

Multiplication Property of Square Roots

For any numbers $a \geq 0$ and $b \geq 0$, $\sqrt{ab} = \sqrt{a} \cdot \sqrt{b}$.

Example: $\sqrt{54} = \sqrt{9} \cdot \sqrt{6} = 3 \cdot \sqrt{6} = 3\sqrt{6}$

You can simplify radical expressions that contain numbers and variables. Assume that all variables under radicals represent positive numbers.

Example 1

Simplify each radical expression.

a. $\sqrt{192} = \sqrt{64 \cdot 3}$ ← 64 is a perfect square and a factor of 192.
$= \sqrt{64} \cdot \sqrt{3}$ ← Use the multiplication property.
$= 8\sqrt{3}$ ← Simplify $\sqrt{64}$.

b. $\sqrt{16a^3} = \sqrt{16} \cdot \sqrt{a^2} \cdot \sqrt{a}$ ← Use the multiplication property.
$= 4a\sqrt{a}$ ← Simplify.

Example 2

Simplify the radical expression $\sqrt{6} \cdot \sqrt{15}$.

$\sqrt{6} \cdot \sqrt{15} = \sqrt{90}$ ← Combine factors under one radical.
$= \sqrt{9 \cdot 10}$ ← 9 is a perfect square and a factor of 90.
$= \sqrt{9} \cdot \sqrt{10}$ ← Use the multiplication property.
$= 3\sqrt{10}$ ← Simplify $\sqrt{9}$.

2. **Try This** Simplify each expression.
   a. $5\sqrt{300}$ b. $\sqrt{13} \cdot \sqrt{52}$ c. $\sqrt{x^2y^5}$ d. $(3\sqrt{5})^2$

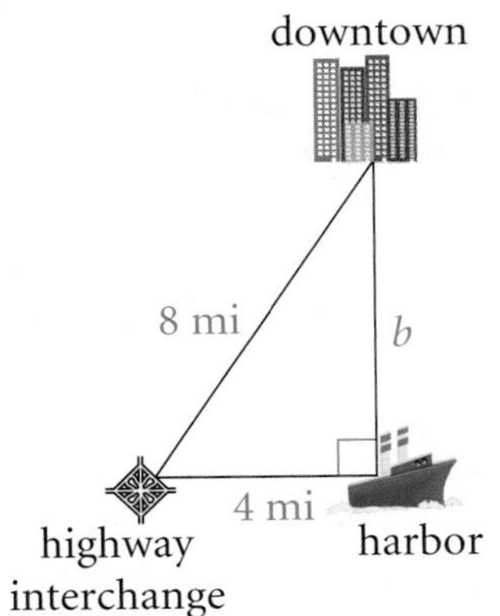

When you use radical expressions to solve real-world problems, you need to evaluate any radicals to get a numerical answer.

Example 3 **Relating to the Real World** 

Commuting Use the figure at the left. About how many miles is it from downtown to the harbor? Round to the nearest tenth of a mile.

$$a^2 + b^2 = c^2$$ ← Use the Pythagorean theorem.

$$4^2 + b^2 = 8^2$$ ← Substitute. Remember that the hypotenuse is the longest side.

$$b^2 = 8^2 - 4^2$$

$$b = \sqrt{8^2 - 4^2}$$ ← Solve for b.

$$= \sqrt{48}$$ ← Use a calculator.

$$= 6.92820323$$

It is about 6.9 miles from downtown to the harbor.

PROBLEM SOLVING

Look Back Explain how you can use $\sqrt{49}$ to check the reasonableness of the answer in Example 3.

3. **Calculator** Suppose a classmate did Example 3 and got the answer $4\sqrt{3}$. Use a calculator to check if this answer is correct.

Division with Radicals

You can use the division property of square roots to simplify expressions.

Division Property of Square Roots

For any numbers $a \geq 0$ and $b > 0$, $\sqrt{\frac{a}{b}} = \frac{\sqrt{a}}{\sqrt{b}}$.

Example: $\sqrt{\frac{4}{9}} = \frac{\sqrt{4}}{\sqrt{9}} = \frac{2}{3}$

4. Explain why there are the restrictions $a \geq 0$ and $b > 0$ in the properties of square roots.

Math A Test Prep

1 In right triangle ABC, $\overline{AB}$ is a shorter leg than $\overline{AC}$. Which of the following is the greatest?
(1) tan C (3) sin B
(2) tan B (4) cos B

2 Ella lives 2 miles west and 3 miles south of the high school. Maria lives 4 miles east and 6 miles north of the high school.
a What is the shortest distance between the homes of the girls?
b The girls plan to meet at a point halfway between their homes. Describe their meeting location in relation to Ella's home.

When you simplify a radical expression involving division, sometimes it is easier to simplify the numerator and denominator separately.

Example 4

Simplify each radical expression.

a. $\sqrt{\frac{11}{49}} = \frac{\sqrt{11}}{\sqrt{49}}$ ← Use the division property.

$= \frac{\sqrt{11}}{7}$ ← Simplify $\sqrt{49}$.

b. $\sqrt{\frac{25}{b^4}} = \frac{\sqrt{25}}{\sqrt{b^4}}$ ← Use the division property.

$= \frac{5}{b^2}$ ← Simplify $\sqrt{25}$ and $\sqrt{b^4}$.

When you simplify a radical expression involving division, sometimes it is easier to divide first and then simplify the radical expression.

Example 5

Simplify the radical expression $\frac{\sqrt{96}}{\sqrt{12}}$.

$\frac{\sqrt{96}}{\sqrt{12}} = \sqrt{\frac{96}{12}}$ ← Use the division property.

$= \sqrt{8}$ ← Divide.

$= \sqrt{4 \cdot 2}$ ← 4 is a perfect square and a factor of 8.

$= \sqrt{4} \cdot \sqrt{2}$ ← Use the multiplication property.

$= 2\sqrt{2}$ ← Simplify $\sqrt{4}$.

5. Try This Simplify each expression.

a. $\sqrt{\frac{144}{9}}$ **b.** $\frac{\sqrt{24}}{\sqrt{8}}$ **c.** $\sqrt{\frac{25c^3}{b^2}}$

When you have a square root in a denominator that is not a perfect square, you should **rationalize** the denominator. To do this, make the denominator a rational number without changing the value of the expression.

Example 6

Simplify $\frac{2}{\sqrt{5}}$.

$\frac{2}{\sqrt{5}} = \frac{2}{\sqrt{5}} \cdot \frac{\sqrt{5}}{\sqrt{5}}$ ← Multiply by $\frac{\sqrt{5}}{\sqrt{5}} = 1$.

$= \frac{2\sqrt{5}}{\sqrt{25}}$ ← Use the multiplication property.

$= \frac{2\sqrt{5}}{5}$ ← Simplify.

PROBLEM SOLVING

Look Back Why did you choose to multiply by $\frac{\sqrt{5}}{\sqrt{5}}$ to rationalize the expression?

6. Try This Simplify each expression by rationalizing the denominator.

a. $\frac{3}{\sqrt{3}}$ **b.** $\frac{14}{\sqrt{7}}$ **c.** $\frac{9}{\sqrt{10}}$

Exercises ON YOUR OWN

Tell whether each expression is in simplest form.

1. $\frac{13}{\sqrt{4}}$
2. $2\sqrt{12}$
3. $\frac{3}{\sqrt{13}}$
4. $5\sqrt{30}$
5. $\sqrt{\frac{2}{5}}$

Simplify each radical expression.

6. $\sqrt{25} \cdot \sqrt{100}$
7. $\sqrt{8} \cdot \sqrt{32}$
8. $3\sqrt{81} \cdot \sqrt{81}$
9. $\sqrt{10} \cdot \sqrt{40}$
10. $\sqrt{10^4}$
11. $\sqrt{200}$
12. $5\sqrt{320}$
13. $(5\sqrt{7})^3$
14. $\sqrt{96}$
15. $(2\sqrt{18})^2$
16. $\sqrt{12} \cdot \sqrt{75}$
17. $\sqrt{3} \cdot \sqrt{51}$
18. $\sqrt{26 \cdot 2}$
19. $2\sqrt{6 \cdot 4}$
20. $\sqrt{8} \cdot \sqrt{26}$

Use the Pythagorean theorem to find *s*. Express *s* as a radical in simplest form.

21. 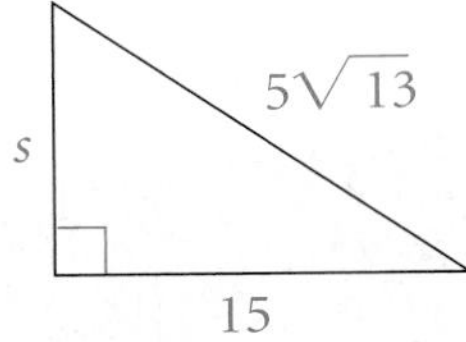

22. 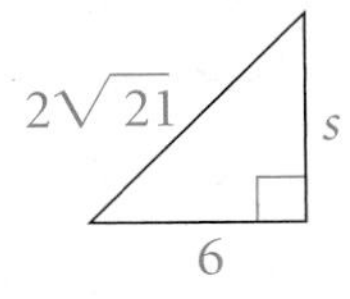

23. 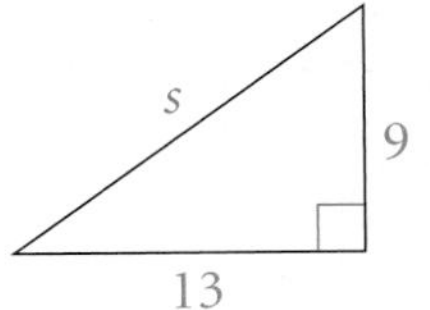

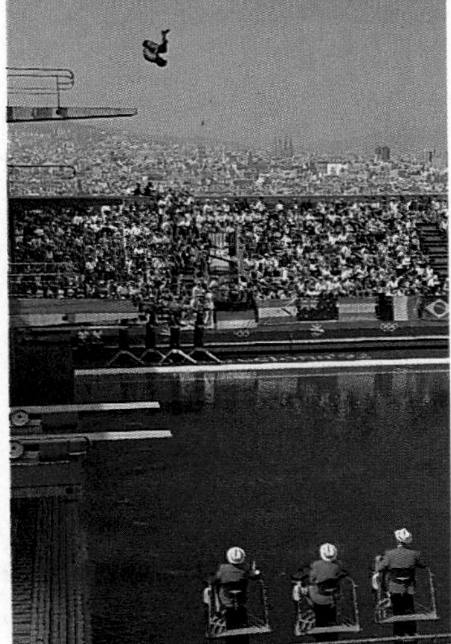

24. **Diving** Suppose you are standing at the top of a diving platform *h* feet tall. Looking down, you can see a raft on the water 8 feet from the bottom of the diving platform.
   a. Find the distance *d* from you to the raft if $h = 6$ ft.
   b. Find the distance *d* from you to the raft if $h = 12$ ft.
   c. Suppose you know the distance *d* from you to the raft is 16 ft. About how tall is the diving platform?
   d. **Critical Thinking** Could the distance *d* from you to the raft be 7 ft? Why or why not?

Simplify each radical expression.

25. $3\sqrt{\frac{1}{4}}$
26. $\sqrt{\frac{21}{49}}$
27. $\sqrt{\frac{625}{100}}$
28. $\frac{\sqrt{96}}{\sqrt{9}}$
29. $\sqrt{\frac{120}{121}}$
30. $\frac{\sqrt{15}}{\sqrt{5}}$
31. $\frac{\sqrt{72}}{\sqrt{64}}$
32. $\sqrt{\frac{48}{24}}$
33. $\frac{\sqrt{169}}{\sqrt{144}}$
34. $\frac{\sqrt{400}}{\sqrt{121}}$

35. **Packaging** Use the diagram at right. Find the width *w* that the box needs to be to fit the fishing rod.

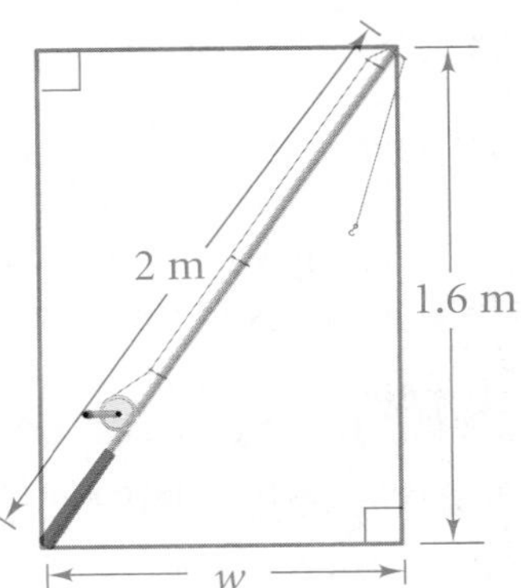

36. **Writing** How do you know when to rationalize a radical expression?

37. Suppose *a* and *b* are positive integers.
   a. **Verify** that if $a = 18$ and $b = 10$, then $\sqrt{a} \cdot \sqrt{b} = 6\sqrt{5}$.
   b. **Open-ended** Find several other pairs of positive integers *a* and *b* such that $\sqrt{a} \cdot \sqrt{b} = 6\sqrt{5}$.

38. *Sailing* The diagram at the right shows a sailboat.
   a. Use the Pythagorean theorem to find the height of the sail in simplest radical form.
   b. Use the result of part (a) and the formula for the area of a triangle to find the area of the sail. Round your answer to the nearest tenth.

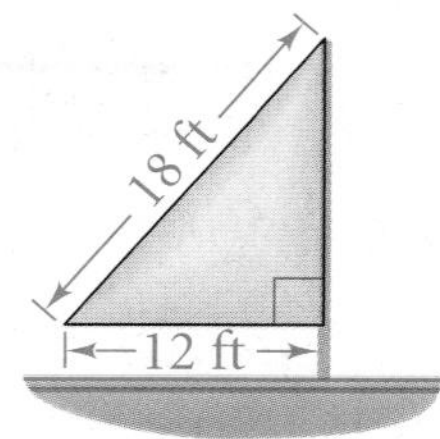

39. *Standardized Test Prep* Suppose that x and y are positive numbers. Which of the following is *not* equivalent to $\sqrt{24x^2y}$?
   A. $2x\sqrt{6y}$ B. $\sqrt{24x}\sqrt{xy}$ C. $\sqrt{4xy}\sqrt{6x}$
   D. $2x^2\sqrt{6y}$ E. $x\sqrt{24y}$

Simplify each radical expression. Assume that all variables represent positive numbers.

40. $\sqrt{v^6}$ 41. $\frac{2}{\sqrt{a^3}}$ 42. $\sqrt{20a^2b^3}$ 43. $\sqrt{a^3b^5c^3}$

44. $\sqrt{12x^3y^2}$ 45. $\sqrt{4y^4}$ 46. $\frac{\sqrt{x^2}}{\sqrt{y^3}}$ 47. $\sqrt{\frac{18x}{81}}$

Simplify each expression by rationalizing the denominator.

48. $\frac{3}{\sqrt{7}}$ 49. $\frac{12}{\sqrt{12}}$ 50. $\frac{2\sqrt{2}}{\sqrt{5}}$ 51. $\frac{9}{\sqrt{8}}$

52. $\frac{3\sqrt{2}}{\sqrt{6}}$ 53. $\frac{25}{\sqrt{5}}$ 54. $\frac{2\sqrt{5}}{\sqrt{12}}$ 55. $\frac{16}{\sqrt{6}}$

56. *Hobbies* Use the Pythagorean theorem to find the missing dimensions a, b, and c of each triangle in the quilt square.

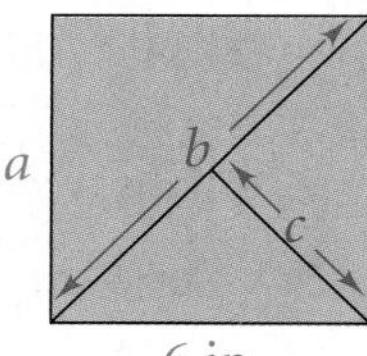

Exercises MIXED REVIEW

Find the x- and y-intercepts of each equation.

57. $2x + 3y = 6$ 58. $4x + 2y = 8$ 59. $-3x + 5y = 15$ 60. $-2x - 4y = 12$

61. *Consumer* You are shopping for food to serve for a lunch party. Crab sandwiches cost \$5 per serving and turkey sandwiches cost \$3 per serving. You have \$30.00 total to spend on sandwiches. Write an inequality to model the situation. How many of each kind can you buy?

Getting Ready for Lesson 9-5

Simplify each square root. Then add or subtract.

62. $\sqrt{16} + \sqrt{36}$ 63. $\sqrt{49} - \sqrt{64}$ 64. $\sqrt{121} + \sqrt{81}$ 65. $\sqrt{400} - \sqrt{100}$

9-5 Adding and Subtracting Radicals

What You'll Learn

- Simplifying radicals involving addition and subtraction
- Solving problems involving sums and differences of radicals

...And Why

To solve geometric problems involving art

WORK TOGETHER

Work in pairs.

1. Copy and complete the table.

a	b	$\sqrt{a}$	$\sqrt{b}$	$\sqrt{a}+\sqrt{b}$	$\sqrt{a+b}$	$\sqrt{a}-\sqrt{b}$	$\sqrt{a-b}$
9	16	■	■	■	■	■	■
25	100	■	■	■	■	■	■
64	36	■	■	■	■	■	■
4	121	■	■	■	■	■	■
49	1	■	■	■	■	■	■

2. **a.** Compare the values in the addition columns. What do you notice?
   b. In general, does $\sqrt{a} + \sqrt{b} = \sqrt{a + b}$? Explain.

3. **a.** Compare the values in the subtraction columns. What do you notice?
   b. Does $\sqrt{a} - \sqrt{b} = \sqrt{a - b}$? Explain.

4. Is there a rule for adding and subtracting radicals? **Justify** your reasoning.

THINK AND DISCUSS

Simplifying Sums and Differences

You can simplify radical expressions by combining like terms. Like terms have the same radical part.

like terms	unlike terms
$4\sqrt{7}$ and $-12\sqrt{7}$	$3\sqrt{11}$ and $2\sqrt{5}$

5. Identify each pair of expressions as like or unlike terms. **Justify** your answers.
   a. $\sqrt{8}$ and $2\sqrt{8}$ **b.** $2\sqrt{3}$ and $3\sqrt{2}$ **c.** $2\sqrt{7}$ and $-3\sqrt{7}$

Example 1

Simplify the expression $\sqrt{2} + 3\sqrt{2}$.

$\sqrt{2} + 3\sqrt{2} = 1\sqrt{2} + 3\sqrt{2}$ ← Both $1\sqrt{2}$ and $3\sqrt{2}$ have $\sqrt{2}$.

$= 4\sqrt{2}$ ← Combine like terms.

Example 2

Simplify the expression $4\sqrt{3} - \sqrt{12}$.

$$\begin{aligned} 4\sqrt{3} - \sqrt{12} &= 4\sqrt{3} - \sqrt{4 \cdot 3} && \leftarrow \text{4 is a perfect square and a factor of 12.} \\ &= 4\sqrt{3} - \sqrt{4} \cdot \sqrt{3} && \leftarrow \text{Use the multiplication property.} \\ &= 4\sqrt{3} - 2\sqrt{3} && \leftarrow \text{Simplify } \sqrt{4}. \\ &= 2\sqrt{3} && \leftarrow \text{Combine like terms.} \end{aligned}$$

6. **Try This** Simplify each expression.

a. $2\sqrt{5} + \sqrt{5}$ **b.** $3\sqrt{45} + 2\sqrt{5}$ **c.** $3\sqrt{3} - 2\sqrt{12}$

Simplifying Products, Sums, and Differences

QUICK REVIEW

The distributive property says *a(b + c) = ab + ac*.

Sometimes you need to use the distributive property and what you have learned in lessons 9-4 and 9-5 to simplify expressions.

Example 3 Relating to the Real World 

Art The ratio length : width of this painting by Mondrian is approximately equal to the *golden ratio* $(1 + \sqrt{5}) : 2$. The width of the painting is 50 in. Find the length of the painting. Express your answer in simplest radical form. Then estimate the length in inches.

Define 50 = width of painting
x = length of painting

Relate $(1 + \sqrt{5}) : 2$ = length : width

Write

$$\begin{aligned} \frac{1 + \sqrt{5}}{2} &= \frac{x}{50} \\ 50(1 + \sqrt{5}) &= 2x && \leftarrow \text{Cross multiply.} \\ \frac{50(1 + \sqrt{5})}{2} &= x && \leftarrow \text{Solve for } x. \\ 25(1 + \sqrt{5}) &= x \\ 25 + 25\sqrt{5} &= x && \leftarrow \text{Use the distributive property.} \\ 80.90169944 &= x && \leftarrow \text{Use a calculator.} \\ 81 &\approx x \end{aligned}$$

The length of Mondrian's painting is about 81 in.

7. a. **Calculator** Write the golden ratio as a decimal to the nearest hundredth.

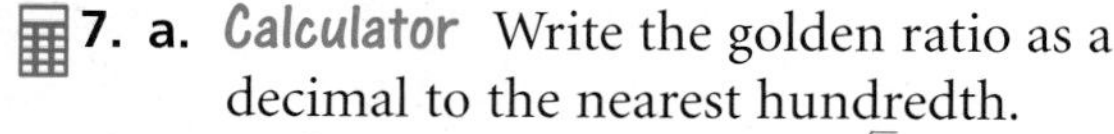

b. **Calculator** Write $\frac{25 + 25\sqrt{5}}{50}$ as a decimal to the nearest hundredth.

c. Compare your answers to parts (a) and (b). What do you notice about the two values?

Example 4

Simplify $\sqrt{2}(5 - \sqrt{8})$.

$$\begin{aligned} \sqrt{2}(5 - \sqrt{8}) &= \sqrt{2}(5) - \sqrt{2}(\sqrt{8}) && \leftarrow \text{Use the distributive property.} \\ &= 5\sqrt{2} - \sqrt{2 \cdot 8} && \leftarrow \text{Use the multiplication property.} \\ &= 5\sqrt{2} - \sqrt{16} && \leftarrow \text{Multiply.} \\ &= 5\sqrt{2} - 4 && \leftarrow \text{Simplify.} \end{aligned}$$

8. **Try This** Simplify each expression.
   a. $2(2 + \sqrt{3})$
   b. $\sqrt{2}(1 - 2\sqrt{10})$
   c. $\sqrt{3}(5\sqrt{2} - 2\sqrt{6})$
9. Simplify $3\sqrt{2}(\sqrt{24} + 2\sqrt{6})$ by first simplifying $\sqrt{24}$.

Exercises ON YOUR OWN

Simplify each expression.

1. $15\sqrt{9} - \sqrt{9}$
2. $3(\sqrt{27} + 1)$
3. $\sqrt{18} + \sqrt{3}$
4. $2\sqrt{12} - 7\sqrt{3}$
5. $2\sqrt{3}(\sqrt{3} - 1)$
6. $\sqrt{8} + 2\sqrt{2}$
7. $\sqrt{27} - \sqrt{18}$
8. $-3\sqrt{6} + 8\sqrt{6}$
9. $3\sqrt{7} - \sqrt{28}$
10. $16\sqrt{10} + 2\sqrt{10}$
11. $\sqrt{3}(\sqrt{15} + \sqrt{4})$
12. $\sqrt{5} - 3\sqrt{5}$
13. $\sqrt{12} + \sqrt{24} - \sqrt{36}$
14. $\sqrt{3}(\sqrt{2} + 2\sqrt{3})$
15. $\sqrt{2}(\sqrt{8} - 4)$

16. **Recreation** You can make a box kite in the shape of a rectangular solid. The opening at each end of the kite is a square.
    a. Suppose the sides of the square are 2 ft long. How long are the diagonal struts used for bracing?
    b. Suppose each side of the square has length *s*. Find the length of the diagonal struts in terms of *s*. Write your answer in simplest form.

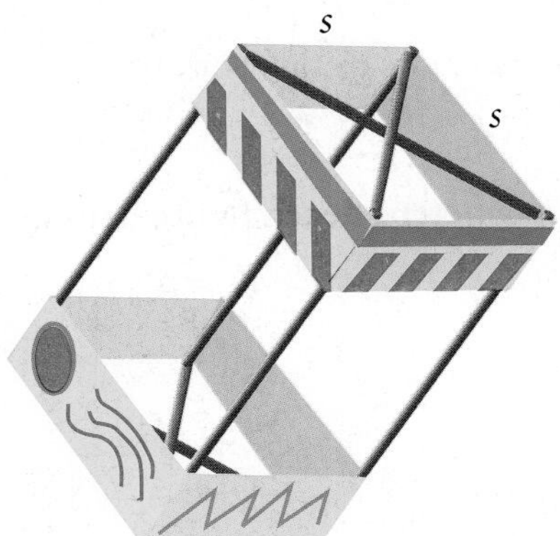

Calculator **Use a calculator to evaluate each expression. Round your answers to the nearest tenth.**

17. $\sqrt{2} + \sqrt{3}$
18. $4\sqrt{5} + \sqrt{10}$
19. $\sqrt{40} + \sqrt{90}$
20. $6\sqrt{8} - 8\sqrt{6}$
21. $\sqrt{3}(\sqrt{6} + 1)$
22. $\sqrt{18} + \sqrt{2}$
23. $5\sqrt{5} - \sqrt{7}$
24. $\sqrt{13} - 2\sqrt{2}$
25. $3\sqrt{2} - 3\sqrt{3}$

Simplify each expression.

26. $3\sqrt{3}(4\sqrt{27} - \sqrt{3})$
27. $\sqrt{12} + \sqrt{32}$
28. $\sqrt{5} + 2\sqrt{50}$
29. $2\sqrt{2}(-2\sqrt{32} + \sqrt{8})$
30. $3\sqrt{10}(\sqrt{10} + 4\sqrt{5})$
31. $3\sqrt{2}(2 + \sqrt{6})$
32. $\sqrt{18} - 2\sqrt{2}$
33. $\sqrt{68} + 17$
34. $-\sqrt{6}(\sqrt{6} - 5)$

35. **Open-ended** Make up three sums that are less than or equal to 50. Use the square roots of 2, 3, 5, or 7 and the whole numbers less than 10. For example, $8\sqrt{5} + 9\sqrt{7} \leq 50$.

36. **Choose** Use a calculator, paper and pencil, or estimation to find the value of the numerical expression in the cartoon.

from the cartoon *Bound & Gagged*

37. Bill wrote $\sqrt{24} + \sqrt{48} = 3\sqrt{24} = 6\sqrt{6}$.
    a. Simplify $\sqrt{24} + \sqrt{48}$.
    b. **Critical Thinking** What error did Bill make? Explain.

38. **Writing** Explain the errors in the work below.
    a. $\sqrt{5} + \sqrt{11} = \sqrt{16} = 4$
    b. $\sqrt{41} = \sqrt{16 + 25} = \sqrt{16} + \sqrt{25} = 9$

Geometry **Find the perimeter of each figure below.**

39.

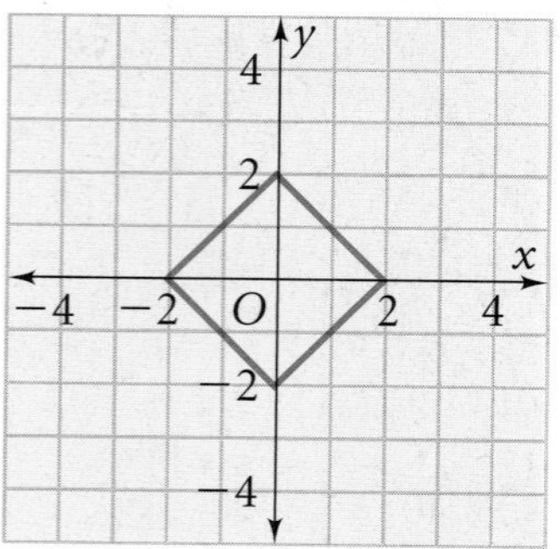

40.

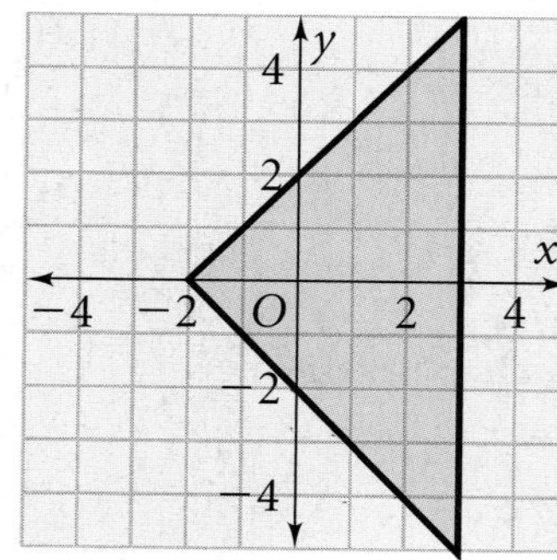

41.

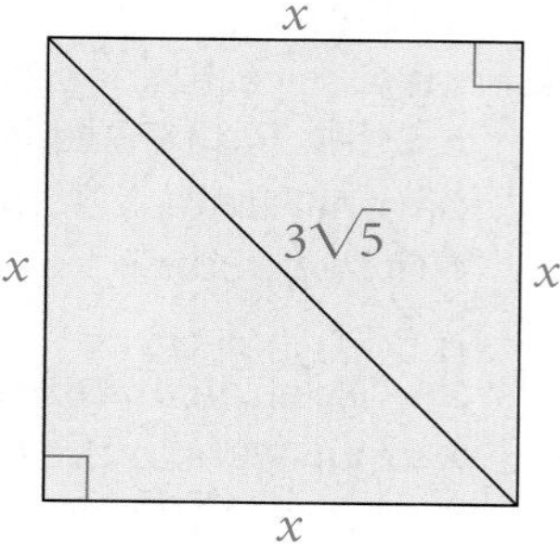

42. **Architecture** The ratio width : height of the front face of a building is equal to the *golden ratio* $(1 + \sqrt{5}) : 2$. The height of the front face of the building is 24 ft. Find the width of the building. Express your answer in simplest radical form. Then estimate in feet.

43. *Standardized Test Prep* Simplify $\frac{\sqrt{50} + \sqrt{32}}{\sqrt{2}}$.

A. $\sqrt{41}$ **B.** $5 + 4\sqrt{2}$ **C.** $4 + 5\sqrt{2}$ **D.** $9\sqrt{2}$ **E.** 9

Exercises MIXED REVIEW

44. a. *Travel* Aruba is changing $\frac{1}{4}$ of its 75 mi^2 into protected parkland. How many square miles will the protected area be?
    b. The island has 88,000 residents. What is its population density (people/mi^2) for the whole island?
    c. What is the population density excluding the protected parkland?

Aruba

Solve using the quadratic formula. Tell whether each solution is *rational* or *irrational*.

45. $x^2 - 2x - 15 = 0$

46. $x^2 + 6x + 2 = 0$

Getting Ready for Lesson 9-6

Evaluate each expression for the given value.

47. $\sqrt{x} - 3$ for $x = 16$

48. $\sqrt{x + 7}$ for $x = 9$

49. $2\sqrt{x + 3} - 4$ for $x = 1$

Algebra at Work

Auto Mechanic

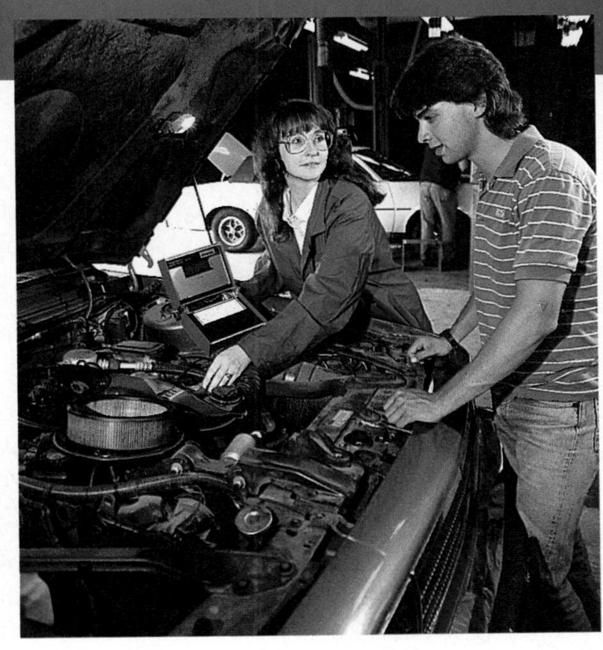

An auto mechanic's job is to see that car engines get the most out of every gallon of gas. Formulas used by mechanics often involve radicals. For example, a car gets its power when gas and air in each cylinder are compressed and ignited by a spark plug. An engine's efficiency (e) is given by the formula $e = \frac{c - \sqrt{c}}{c}$, where c is the compression ratio.

Because of the complexity of such formulas and of modern high-performance engines, today's auto mechanic must be a highly trained and educated professional who understands algebra, graph reading, and the operation of computerized equipment.

Mini Project: Evaluate the formula to find the engine efficiency for even-numbered compression ratios from 2 to 20.

What You'll Learn

- Solving equations that contain radicals
- Identifying extraneous solutions

...And Why

To design amusement park rides

9-6 Solving Radical Equations

THINK AND DISCUSS

Solving a Radical Equation

An equation that has a variable under a radical is a **radical equation.** You can often solve a radical equation by squaring both sides. To do this, first get the radical by itself on one side of the equation. Remember that the expression under the radical must be positive.

$$\text{When } x \geq 0, (\sqrt{x})^2 = x.$$

Example 1

Solve $\sqrt{x} - 3 = 4$. Check your solution.

$\sqrt{x} - 3 = 4$

$\sqrt{x} - 3 + 3 = 4 + 3$ ← Add 3 to both sides.

$\sqrt{x} = 7$ ← Simplify.

$(\sqrt{x})^2 = 7^2$ ← Square both sides.

$x = 49$

Check $\sqrt{x} - 3 = 4$

$\sqrt{49} - 3 \stackrel{?}{=} 4$ ← Substitute 49 for x.

$7 - 3 = 4$ ✓

The solution of $\sqrt{x} - 3 = 4$ is 49.

1. **a.** Find the values of $\sqrt{36} - 3$ and $\sqrt{64} - 3$.
   b. *Critical Thinking* Do the results in part (a) suggest that $x = 49$ is a reasonable solution to $\sqrt{x} - 3 = 4$? Explain.
   c. Explain how parts (a) and (b) are a form of estimation.
2. *Try This* Solve and check.
   a. $\sqrt{x} + 5 = 12$ **b.** $2\sqrt{x} + 7 = 19$ **c.** $\sqrt{x} + 3 = 5$
3. **a.** Solve $x^2 - 3 = 4$.
   b. Compare and contrast how you solved the equation in part (a) with how you solved $\sqrt{x} - 3 = 4$.

4. **a.** *Graphing Calculator* Graph $y = \sqrt{x} - 3$ and $y = 4$ together. Use the range shown on the screen at the left.
   b. How many intersection points are there?
   c. What are the coordinates of the intersection point(s)?
   d. *Critical Thinking* How does your answer to part (c) confirm the solution of $\sqrt{x} - 3 = 4$ in Example 1?

WINDOW FORMAT
Xmin=0
Xmax=64
Xscl=1
Ymin=−10
Ymax=10
Yscl=1

Example 2 Relating to the Real World 

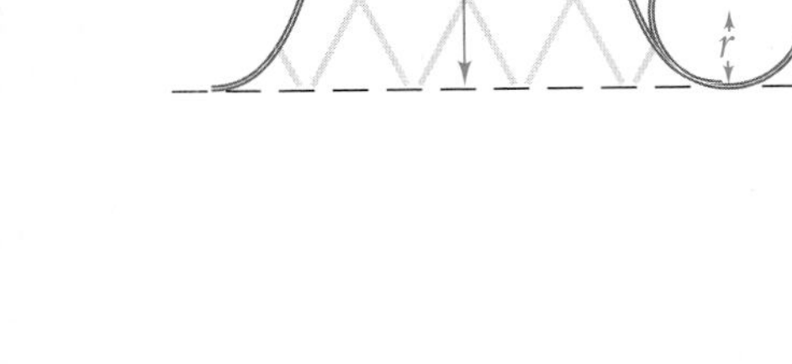

Amusement Parks On a roller coaster ride, your speed in a loop depends on the height of the hill you have just come down and the radius of the loop in feet. The equation $v = 8\sqrt{h - 2r}$ gives the velocity v in feet per second of a car at the top of the loop. Suppose the loop has a radius of 18 ft. You want the car to have a velocity of 30 ft/s at the top of the loop. How high should the hill be?

Solve $v = 8\sqrt{h - 2r}$ for $v = 30$ and $r = 18$.

$$30 = 8\sqrt{h - 2(18)} \quad \leftarrow \text{Substitute for } r \text{ and } v.$$
$$\frac{30}{8} = \sqrt{h - 2(18)} \quad \leftarrow \text{Divide each side by 8 to get the radical alone.}$$
$$3.75 = \sqrt{h - 36}$$
$$(3.75)^2 = (\sqrt{h - 36})^2 \quad \leftarrow \text{Square both sides.}$$
$$14.0625 = h - 36$$
$$50.0625 = h$$

The hill should be about 50 ft high.

5. **Try This** Find the height of the hill when the velocity at the top of the loop is 35 ft/s and radius of the loop is 24 ft.
6. **Try This** Find the radius of the loop when the hill is 150 ft high and the velocity of the car is 30 ft/s.
7. About how many miles per hour is 30 ft/s? (*Hint:* 1 mi = 5280 ft)
8. **Critical Thinking** Would you expect the velocity of the car to increase or decrease in each situation? Explain your reasoning.
   a. as the radius of the loop increases
   b. as the height of the hill decreases

Squaring both sides of an equation also works when each side of the equation is a radical expression.

Example 3

Solve $\sqrt{3x - 2} = \sqrt{x + 6}$.

$$(\sqrt{3x - 2})^2 = (\sqrt{x + 6})^2 \quad \longleftarrow \text{Square both sides.}$$
$$3x - 2 = x + 6$$
$$3x = x + 8$$
$$2x = 8$$
$$x = 4$$

The solution is 4.

PROBLEM SOLVING

Look Back Show how to check that 4 is the solution of $\sqrt{3x - 2} = \sqrt{x + 6}$.

9. ***Graphing Calculator*** Graph the equations $y = \sqrt{3x - 2}$ and $y = \sqrt{x + 6}$ together. How does the display confirm the solution of Example 3?

10. **Try This** Solve $\sqrt{5x - 6} = \sqrt{3x + 5}$. Check your solution.

Solving Equations with Extraneous Solutions

When you solve equations by squaring both sides, you sometimes find two possible solutions. You need to determine which solution actually satisfies the original equation.

Example 4

Solve $x = \sqrt{x + 6}$.

$$(x)^2 = (\sqrt{x + 6})^2 \quad \longleftarrow \text{Square both sides.}$$
$$x^2 = x + 6$$
$$x^2 - x - 6 = 0 \quad \longleftarrow \text{Subtract } x \text{ and 6 from both sides.}$$
$$x = \frac{-(-1) \pm \sqrt{(-1)^2 - 4(1)(-6)}}{2(1)} \quad \longleftarrow \text{Use the quadratic formula to solve for } x.$$
$$x = \frac{1 \pm \sqrt{1 - (-24)}}{2}$$
$$x = \frac{1 \pm \sqrt{25}}{2}$$
$$x = \frac{1 \pm 5}{2} \quad \longleftarrow \text{Simplify } \sqrt{25}.$$
$$x = \frac{1 + 5}{2} \text{ or } x = \frac{1 - 5}{2}$$
$$x = 3 \text{ or } x = -2$$

Check $x = \sqrt{x + 6}$

$3 \stackrel{?}{=} \sqrt{3 + 6}$ $\quad$ $-2 \stackrel{?}{=} \sqrt{-2 + 6}$ $\longleftarrow \sqrt{4} = 2$

$3 = 3$ ✔ $\quad$ $-2 \neq 2$

The only solution is 3.

QUICK REVIEW

The quadratic formula states that for an equation of the form $ax^2 + bx + c = 0$, if $a \neq 0$, then $x = \frac{-b \pm \sqrt{b^2 - 4ac}}{2a}$.

The value -2 is called an **extraneous solution** of Example 4. It is a solution of the derived equation ($x^2 = x + 6$), but not of the original equation ($x = \sqrt{x + 6}$).

11. How could you have determined that -2 was not a solution of $x = \sqrt{x + 6}$ without going through all the steps of the check?

Exercises ON YOUR OWN

Solve each radical equation. Check your solutions.

1. $\sqrt{5x + 10} = 5$

2. $7 = \sqrt{x + 5}$

3. $6 - \sqrt{3x} = -3$

4. $\sqrt{n} = \frac{7}{8}$

5. $20 = \sqrt{x} - 5$

6. $\sqrt{x} - 10 = 1$

7. **Geometry** In the right triangle $\triangle ABC$, the altitude $\overline{CD}$ is at a right angle to the hypotenuse. You can use $CD = \sqrt{(AD)(DB)}$ to find certain lengths.

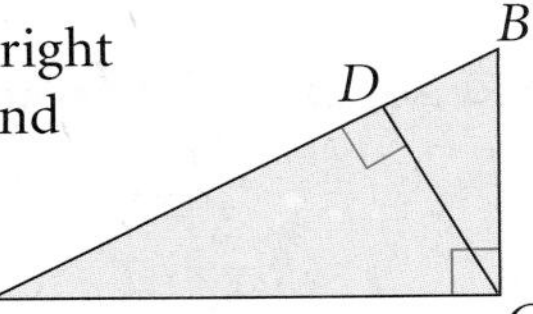

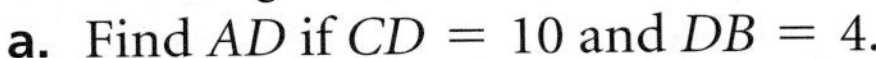

a. Find AD if $CD = 10$ and $DB = 4$.

b. Find DB if $AD = 20$ and $CD = 15$.

8. **Physics** The equation $T = \sqrt{\frac{2\pi^2 r}{F}}$ gives the time T in seconds it takes a body with mass 0.5 kg to complete one orbit of radius r meters. The force F in newtons pulls the body toward the center of the orbit.

a. It takes 2 s for an object to make one revolution with a force of 10 N (newtons). Find the radius of the orbit.

b. Find the radius of the orbit if the force is 160 N and $T = 2$.

Solve each radical equation. Check your solutions.

9. $\sqrt{3x + 1} = \sqrt{x}$

10. $\sqrt{x + 5} = \sqrt{3x + 6}$

11. $\sqrt{3x + 10} = \sqrt{9 - x}$

12. $\sqrt{7x + 5} = \sqrt{x - 3}$

13. $\frac{x}{2} = \sqrt{3x}$

14. $\sqrt{x + 12} = 3\sqrt{x}$

15. $\sqrt{5x - 4} = \sqrt{3x + 10}$

16. $\sqrt{2x} = \sqrt{9 - x}$

17. $x = \sqrt{2x + 3}$

18. **Standardized Test Prep** Which of the following radical equations has no *real* solution?

A. $-\sqrt{x} = -25x$

B. $\sqrt{2x + 1} = \sqrt{3x - 5}$

C. $-3\sqrt{3x} = -5$

D. $\sqrt{3x + 1} = -10$

E. $\frac{x}{2} = \sqrt{x - 1}$

19. **Packaging** The volume V in cubic units of a cylindrical can is given by the formula $V = \pi r^2 h$, where r is the radius of the can and h is its height. The radius of a can is 2.5 in. and the height of the can is 5 in. Find the can's volume in cubic inches.

20. **Writing** Tell how you would solve the equation $\sqrt{2x} + \sqrt{x + 2} = 0$.

Storage tanks in Knoxville, Tennessee

Solve each radical equation. Check your solutions.

21. $x = \sqrt{x + 2}$

22. $2x = \sqrt{10x + 6}$

23. $\frac{x}{3} = \sqrt{x - 2}$

24. $\sqrt{x + 5} = 2x$

25. $2x = 2\sqrt{x - 5}$

26. $\sqrt{2x - 15} = \frac{x}{4}$

27. $\sqrt{x + 12} = x$

28. $\sqrt{2x - 1} = \frac{x + 8}{2}$

29. $x = \sqrt{7x - 6}$

30. ***Writing*** Explain in your own words what an extraneous solution is.

31. The diagram shows a piece of cardboard that makes a box when sections of it are folded and taped. The ends of the box are x in. long and the box is 10 in. long.

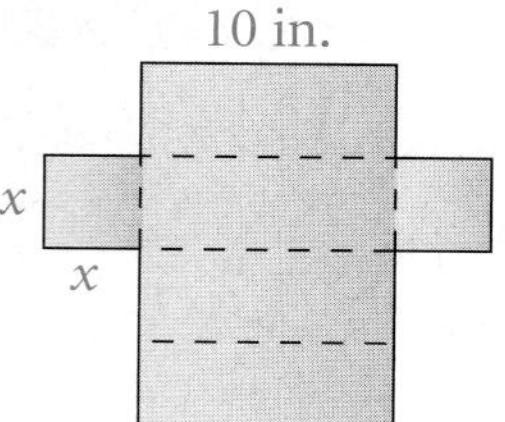

a. Write the formula for the volume V of the box.

b. Solve the equation in part (a) for x.

c. ***Open-ended*** Find some integer values of x that make the box have a volume between 40 in.^{3} and 490 in.^{3}.

Tell which solution(s), if any, are extraneous for the given equation.

32. $-x = \sqrt{-x + 6};\ x = -3, x = 2$

33. $\sqrt{12 - x} = x;\ x = -4, x = 3$

34. $x = \sqrt{2x};\ x = 0, x = 2$

35. $2x = \sqrt{4x + 3};\ x = \frac{3}{2}, x = -\frac{1}{2}$

36. $x = \sqrt{28 - 3x};\ x = 4, x = -7$

37. $-x = \sqrt{-6x - 5};\ x = -5, x = -1$

Chapter Project ***Find Out by Communicating***

- Solve the formula $d = 1.225\sqrt{h}$ for h where d is in miles and h is in feet. (*Hint:* See page 424.)
- How tall would a person on Earth have to be to see 7 mi to the horizon?
- Could a person possibly see such a distance? Why or why not?

Exercises MIXED REVIEW

Simplify each expression. Assume that no denominator is equal to zero.

38. $\frac{x^2y^7}{x^4y^5}$

39. $\frac{a^2b^5}{a^7b^{10}}$

40. $\frac{15x^4y^5}{45x^2y^3}$

41. $\frac{14x^2y^3}{7x^3y^5}$

42. ***Business*** A salesperson earns $750 per month plus 8% commission on the amount she sells. Write an equation to show how her monthly income relates to her sales in dollars.

Getting Ready for Lesson 9-7

Find the value of y for the given value of x.

43. $y = \sqrt{x + 7} - 3$ for $x = 2$

44. $y = 3\sqrt{x} + 2$ for $x = 9$

45. $y = -2\sqrt{x - 1} + 2$ for $x = 1$

Connections Firefighting . . . and more

9-7 Graphing Square Root Functions

What You'll Learn

- Graphing and exploring square root functions
- Solving real-world problems using square root functions

...And Why

To solve problems involving firefighting

What You'll Need

- graphing calculator

THINK AND DISCUSS

Firefighters When firefighters are trying to put out a fire, the rate at which they can spray water on the fire is very important to them. For a hose with a 2 in. nozzle diameter, the flow rate, f, in gal/min is given by this formula.

$$f = 120\sqrt{p}\text{, where } p \text{ is the nozzle pressure in lb/in.}^2$$

The flow-rate function is an example of a square root function. The simplest **square root function** is $y = \sqrt{x}$.

x	y
0	0
1	1
4	2
9	3
16	4

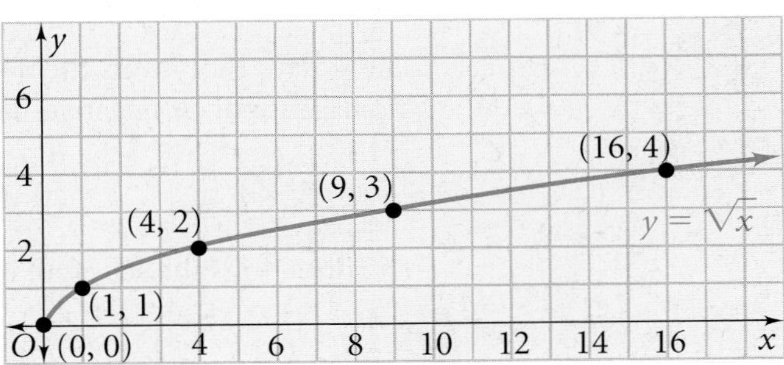

1. Why do you think the x-values in the table were chosen?
2. Find an approximate value of $\sqrt{3}$ and see if it seems to fit the graph.
3. Why is the graph not continued to the left of the y-axis?

Example 1

Compare the graph of $y = \sqrt{x} - 1$ to the graph of $y = \sqrt{x}$.

Method 1 Use a table.

x	$\sqrt{x}$	$\sqrt{x} - 1$
0	$\sqrt{0} = 0$	$\sqrt{0} - 1 = -1$
1	$\sqrt{1} = 1$	$\sqrt{1} - 1 = 0$
4	$\sqrt{4} = 2$	$\sqrt{4} - 1 = 1$
9	$\sqrt{9} = 3$	$\sqrt{9} - 1 = 2$
16	$\sqrt{16} = 4$	$\sqrt{16} - 1 = 3$

Method 2 Use a graphing calculator.

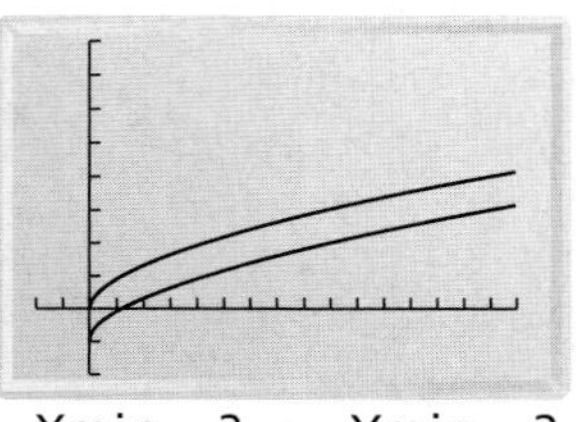

Xmin=–2 Ymin=–2
Xmax=16 Ymax=8
Xscl=1 Yscl=1

For each value of x, the value of $\sqrt{x} - 1$ is one less than the value of $\sqrt{x}$. The graph of $y = \sqrt{x} - 1$ is one unit lower than the graph of $y = \sqrt{x}$.

4. Try This **Analyze** the graph of $y = \sqrt{x} + 1$ by comparing it to the graph of $y = \sqrt{x}$.

5. a. Predict how the graph of $y = \sqrt{x} + k$ will compare to the graph of $y = \sqrt{x}$ when k is a negative number.

b. Graphing Calculator Confirm your prediction by graphing $y = \sqrt{x} - 3$ and $y = \sqrt{x}$.

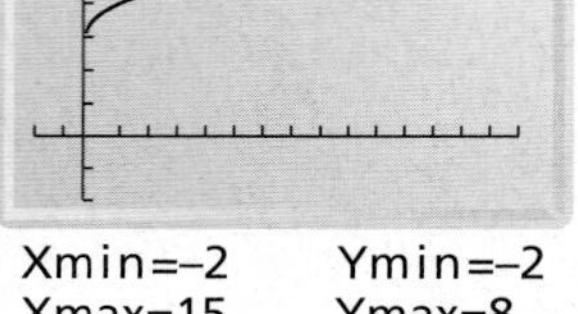

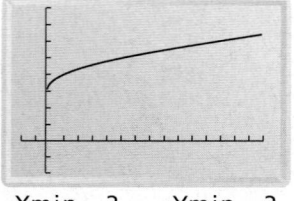

Xmin=–2 Ymin=–2
Xmax=15 Ymax=8
Xscl=1 Yscl=1

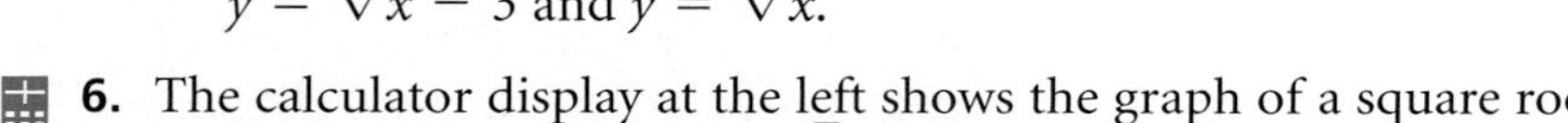

6. The calculator display at the left shows the graph of a square root function of the form $y = \sqrt{x} + k$. What is the value of k?

You can solve an inequality to find the domain of a square root function.

Example 2

Find the domain of $y = \sqrt{x + 3}$. Then graph the function.

The square root limits the domain because the expression under the radical cannot be negative. To find the domain, solve $x + 3 \geq 0$.

$$x + 3 \geq 0$$
$$x \geq -3$$

The domain is the set of all real numbers greater than or equal to –3.

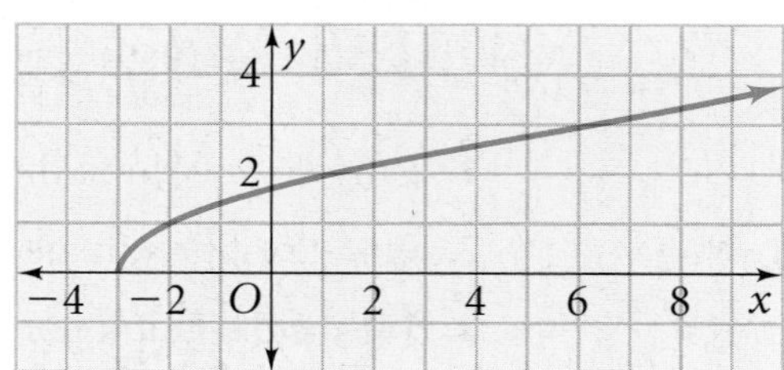

7. Compare the graph in Example 2 to the graph of $y = \sqrt{x}$.

8. **Try This** Find the domain of $y = \sqrt{x - 3}$. Then graph the function.

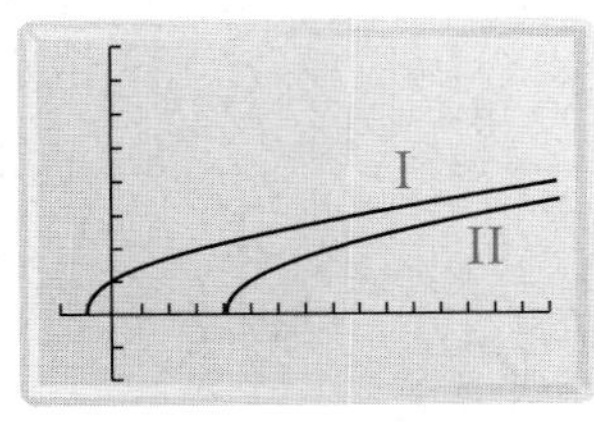

Xmin=–2 Ymin=–2
Xmax=16 Ymax=8
Xscl=1 Yscl=1

9. **a.** The diagram at the left shows the graphs of two functions of the form $y = \sqrt{x + k}$. Describe the domain of each function.
   b. Which graph is the graph of $y = \sqrt{x + 1}$? **Justify** your response.

10. **Summarize** how the graph of $y = \sqrt{x + k}$ compares to the graph of $y = \sqrt{x}$.

You can use square root functions to describe real-life situations.

Example 3 **Relating to the Real World** 

Firefighting Graph the flow-rate function $f = 120\sqrt{p}$ introduced on page 445. Evaluate the function when the nozzle pressure is 40 lb/in.^{2}.

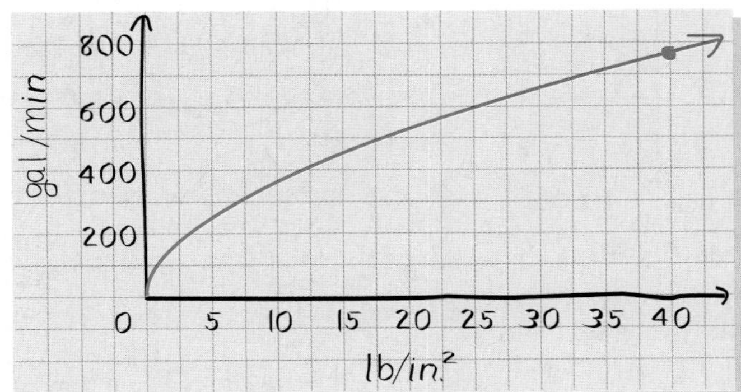

$f = 120\sqrt{40}$ ← Substitute 40 for p.
$= 758.9466384$ ← Use a calculator.

The flow rate is about 759 gal/min when the nozzle pressure is 40 lb/in.^{2}.

Math A Test Prep

1 What is the simplest form of the expression $\sqrt{12} \cdot \sqrt{48}$?
(1) $\sqrt{576}$ (3) 576
(2) $2\sqrt{36}$ (4) 24

2 Solve: $\sqrt{2x + 1} = \sqrt{3x - 5}$.

11. In Example 3, why are there different scales on the axes?

12. Compare the graph in Example 3 to the graph of $y = \sqrt{x}$.

13. **Summarize** how the graph of $y = k\sqrt{x}$ compares to the graph of $y = \sqrt{x}$.

Exercises ON YOUR OWN

Find the domain of each function.

1. $y = \sqrt{x - 2}$
2. $f(x) = \sqrt{4x + 3}$
3. $y = \sqrt{1.5x}$
4. $y = \sqrt{3x + 5}$
5. $y = \sqrt{7 + x}$
6. $f(x) = \sqrt{2 + x}$
7. $f(x) = \sqrt{3 + x}$
8. $y = \sqrt{x + 3} - 1$
9. $y = \sqrt{x - 5} + 1$

10. *Business* Last year a store had an advertising campaign. Sales figures for disposable cameras are shown. The function $n = 27\sqrt{5t} + 53$ models sales volume n of the cameras as a function of time t, the number of months after the start of the campaign.

   a. Evaluate the function to find how many disposable cameras the store sold in the seventh month.

   b. Solve an equation to find the month in which the number of disposable cameras sold was about 175.

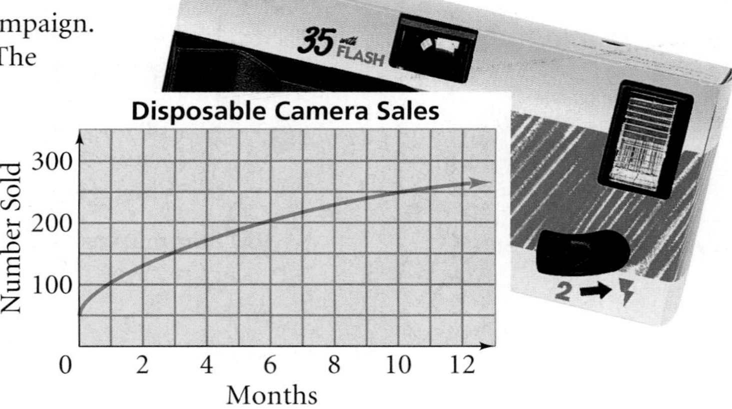

Match each function with its graph.

11. $y = \sqrt{x + 4}$

12. $y = \sqrt{x} - 2$

13. $y = 3\sqrt{x}$

A. 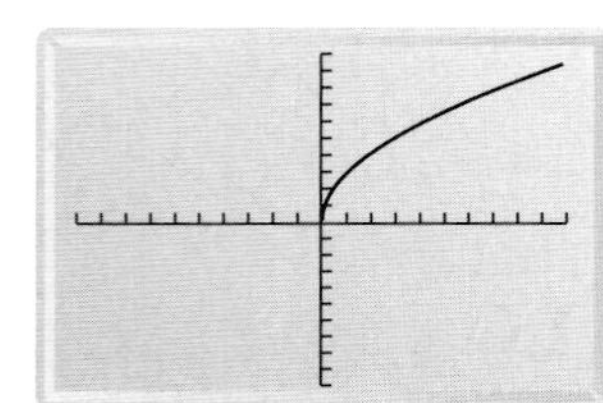

B. 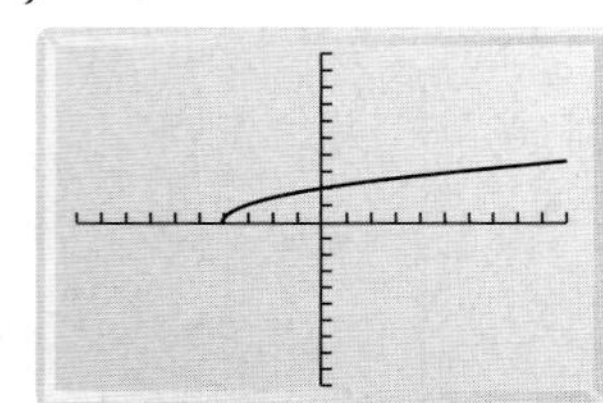

C. 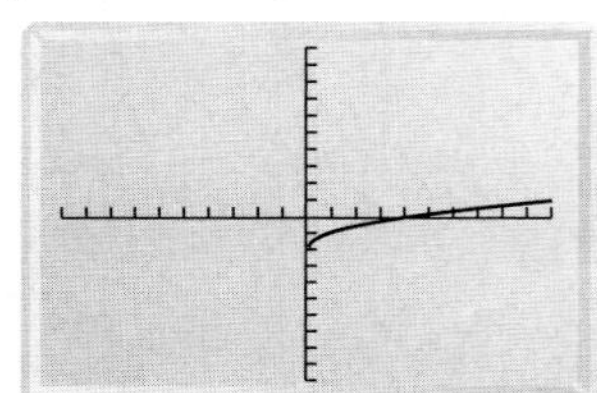

14. *Standardized Test Prep* In which of the following quadrants will your calculator display the graph of $y = \sqrt{x} + 7$?

   A. I, II, and III B. I and IV C. I D. IV E. I and II

Graph each function.

15. $y = \sqrt{x + 2}$
16. $y = \sqrt{x - 2.5}$
17. $f(x) = \sqrt{x} - 5$
18. $y = 4\sqrt{x}$
19. $f(x) = \sqrt{x} + 2$
20. $y = \sqrt{x + 3}$
21. $y = \sqrt{x - 6}$
22. $f(x) = 5\sqrt{x}$
23. $y = \sqrt{x - 2} + 3$
24. $f(x) = \sqrt{x - 3} - 1$
25. $y = \sqrt{x + 5} + 2$
26. $f(x) = \sqrt{x + 2} - 4$

Writing **Using words like "shift up," "shift down," "shift left," and "shift right," describe to a friend how to use the graph of $y = \sqrt{x}$ to obtain the graph of each function.**

27. $f(x) = \sqrt{x + 8}$
28. $y = \sqrt{x} - 10$
29. $y = \sqrt{x} + 12$
30. $f(x) = \sqrt{x - 9}$

31. a. *Open-ended* Give an example of a square root function in each form. Assume $k > 0$.

   $y = \sqrt{x} + k,$
   $y = \sqrt{x + k},$
   $y = k\sqrt{x}$

   b. Graph each function on the same coordinate grid.

Chapter Project — Find Out by Organizing

- The formula for the distance you can see on any planet is $d = \sqrt{\frac{rh}{2640}}$, where h is your height in feet and r is the radius of the planet in miles. Use the planet radii you researched on page 429 to write a separate formula for each planet.
- Graph each formula.

Exercises MIXED REVIEW

Solve each system of equations by graphing.

32. $x + y = 5$
$2x - 3y = -5$

33. $3x - y = 4$
$4x + 2y = 2$

34. **Finance** You deposit \$1000 into a bank account that pays 6% compounded annually. How much will be in the bank account at the end of 3 years?

SELF ASSESSMENT — FOR YOUR JOURNAL

Explain how to find the domain of a square root function. Include an example.

Getting Ready for Lesson 9-8

Find the mean of each set of data.

35. 4, 6, 8, 10, 11 **36.** 3, 4, 5, 7, 9 **37.** −8, −6, 0, 2, 3 **38.** −3, −2, 0, 2, 9

Exercises CHECKPOINT

Simplify each radical expression.

1. $\sqrt{3} \cdot \sqrt{27}$ **2.** $\sqrt{7 \cdot 28}$ **3.** $\sqrt{64b^5}$ **4.** $\sqrt{18} - \sqrt{8}$

5. $\sqrt{3}(\sqrt{3} + 4)$ **6.** $\frac{\sqrt{24}}{\sqrt{3}}$ **7.** $\sqrt{\frac{x^3}{4}}$ **8.** $\frac{6}{\sqrt{3}}$

Solve each radical equation. Check your solutions.

9. $8 = \sqrt{x - 4}$ **10.** $\sqrt{x} = \sqrt{3x - 12}$ **11.** $\sqrt{2x - 5} = \sqrt{11}$ **12.** $7 - \sqrt{2x} = 1$

Graph each function.

13. $y = \sqrt{x} + 4$ **14.** $f(x) = \sqrt{x - 5}$ **15.** $f(x) = 2\sqrt{x}$ **16.** $y = \sqrt{x} - 3$

17. **Writing** How is combining like terms with radicals similar to combining like terms with variables?

18. **Standardized Test Prep** What is the perimeter of the figure?

A. $2\sqrt{7} + \sqrt{5}$ **B.** $\sqrt{5} + \sqrt{7}$ **C.** $\sqrt{35}$
D. $2\sqrt{7} + 2\sqrt{5}$ **E.** none of the above

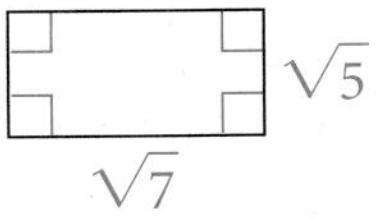

Math ToolboX

Skills Review

Box-and-Whisker Plots

Before Lesson 9-8

To show how data items are spread out, you can arrange a set of data in order from least to greatest. The maximum, minimum, and median give you some information about the data. You can better describe the data by dividing it into fourths. The **lower quartile** is the median of the lower half of the data. The **upper quartile** is the median of the upper half of the data.

The data below describes the highway gas mileage (mi/gal) for several brands of cars.

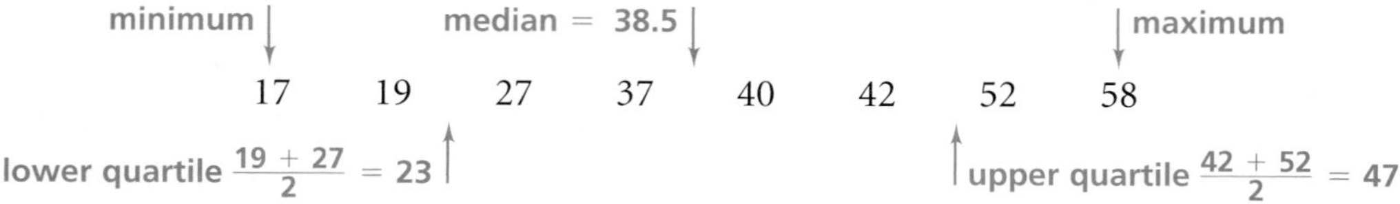

A **box-and-whisker plot** is a visual representation of data. The box-and-whisker plot at the right displays the gas mileage information. The box represents the data from the lower quartile to the upper quartile. The vertical line segment represents the median. Horizontal line segments called whiskers show the spread of the data to the minimum and to the maximum.

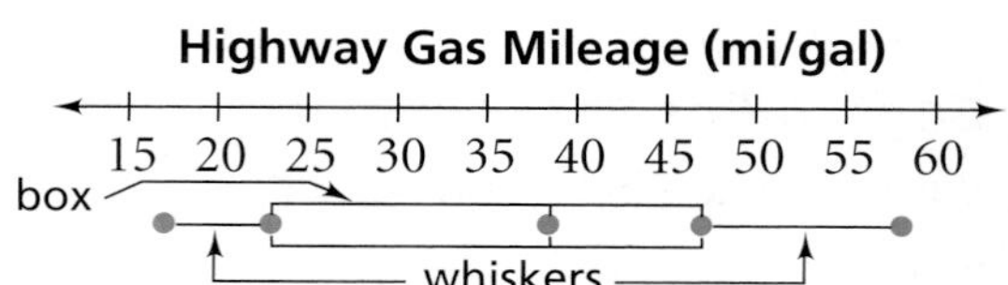

Create a box-and-whisker plot for each data set.

1. {3, 2, 3, 4, 6, 6, 7}
2. {1, 1.5, 1.7, 2, 6.1, 6.2, 7}
3. {1, 2, 5, 6, 9, 12, 7, 10}
4. {65, 66, 59, 61, 67, 70, 67, 66, 69, 70, 63}
5. {29, 32, 40, 31, 33, 39, 27, 42}
6. {3, 3, 5, 7, 1, 10, 10, 4, 4, 7, 9, 8, 6}
7. {1, 1.2, 1.3, 4, 4.1, 4.2, 7}
8. {1, 3.8, 3.9, 4, 4.3, 4.4, 7, 5}

9. *Jobs* Below are the number of hours a student worked each week at her summer job. When she applied for the job, she was told the typical work week was 29 hours.

   29, 23, 21, 20, 17, 16, 15, 33, 33, 32, 15

   a. Make a box-and-whisker plot for the data.
   b. How many weeks are above the upper quartile? What are the number of hours worked?
   c. What is the median number of hours she worked? What is the mean? Compare these to the typical work week.

10. *Writing* In what ways are histograms and box-and-whisker plots alike and in what ways are they different?

What You'll Learn

- Exploring standard deviation
- Calculating and using standard deviation

...And Why

To analyze job opportunities

9-8 Analyzing Data Using Standard Deviation

WORK TOGETHER

Jobs Work with a partner.

Four students had summer jobs at a camp last year. Four other students had jobs at a nursing home. Their weekly pay is listed below.

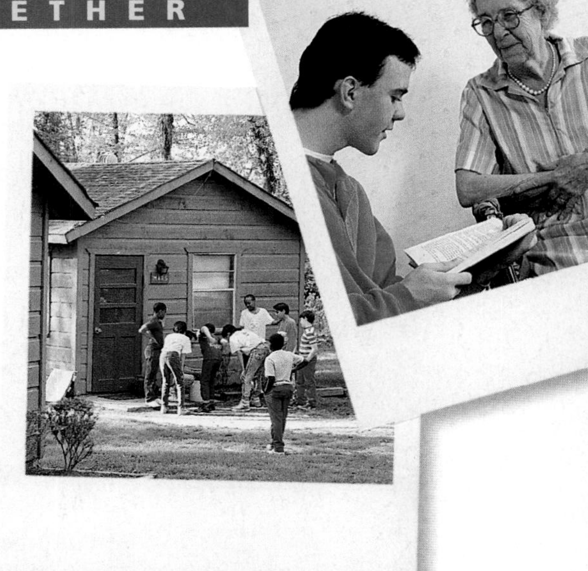

Salaries

Camp	Nursing Home
$150	$140
$160	$190
$220	$210
$270	$260

1. a. Calculate the mean for the pay in each location.
   b. What does the mean represent?

QUICK REVIEW

The *range* of a set of data is the difference between the greatest number and the least number in the set.

2. a What is the range of weekly pay for each location?
   b. Use the ranges to describe how the pay varies at the two locations.

3. Copy the table below.

Salary	Mean	Deviation from Mean	Square of Deviation
$150	$200	−50	2500
$160	$200	■	■
$220	$200	■	■
$270	$200	70	■
sum of the squares of the deviations →			■

4. You find deviation from the mean by subtracting the mean from each salary value. Fill in the missing values in column 3.
5. Complete column 4 by squaring each value in column 3.
6. Complete a table like the one above for the nursing home workers.
7. a. Compare the deviations from the mean at the two locations. At which location does the pay vary more from the mean?
   b. Compare the sum of the squares of the deviations for the two locations. How does this support your answer to part (a)?

THINK AND DISCUSS

A way to show how a set of data is spread out is the **standard deviation.** It reflects how all the data points in a set vary from the mean. The symbol for standard deviation is σ, pronounced "sigma."

small standard deviation ⟶ data cluster around the mean
large standard deviation ⟶ data spread out from the mean

You can calculate the standard deviation by following these six steps.

- Find the mean of the data set. The expression $\overline{x}$ represents the mean.
- Find the difference of each data value from the mean.
- Calculate the square of each difference.
- Find the sum of the squares of the differences.
- Divide the sum by the number of data values.
- Take the square root of the quotient just calculated.

Example 1

Find the standard deviation of the two data sets below.
a. Data Set 1 {83, 88, 75, 69, 70} **b.** Data Set 2 {69, 75, 76, 77, 88}

a. Find the mean.

mean

$= \frac{83 + 88 + 75 + 69 + 70}{5}$

$= \frac{385}{5}$

$= 77$

Calculate the standard deviation.

x	$\overline{x}$	$x - \overline{x}$	$(x - \overline{x})^2$
83	77	6	36
88	77	11	121
75	77	−2	4
70	77	−7	49
69	77	−8	64
		Sum:	274

sum of squares $= 274$

$\frac{\text{sum of squares}}{5} = \frac{274}{5}$

$= 54.8$

$\sqrt{54.8} =$ 7.402702209

The standard deviation is about 7.4.

b. Find the mean.

mean

$= \frac{69 + 75 + 76 + 77 + 88}{5}$

$= \frac{385}{5}$

$= 77$

Calculate the standard deviation.

x	$\overline{x}$	$x - \overline{x}$	$(x - \overline{x})^2$
69	77	−8	64
75	77	−2	4
76	77	−1	1
77	77	0	0
88	77	11	121
		Sum:	190

sum of squares $= 190$

$\frac{\text{sum of squares}}{5} = \frac{190}{5}$

$= 38$

$\sqrt{38} =$ 6.164414003

The standard deviation is about 6.2.

8. In which data set do the values cluster closer to the mean?

You can use a calculator to find the standard deviation of a set of data.

Example 2 **Relating to the Real World** 

Golf Three friends play golf. Their scores on six holes of golf are below. Calculate the mean and standard deviation for Player 1's scores.

Player 1	5	4	2	4	10	5
Player 2	5	5	5	5	5	5
Player 3	3	10	4	4	7	2

You can use a calculator to calculate the mean and standard deviation.

- Choose STAT and EDIT to enter your data.
- Choose STAT , CALC, and 1-VAR STATS to calculate.
- The screen displays information about your data including the mean, $\overline{x}$, the standard deviation, σx, and the number of entries, n.

The mean of Player 1's scores is 5. The standard deviation is about 2.4.

9. a. **Predict** whether the standard deviations of Player 2's and Player 3's scores will be greater or less than the standard deviation of Player 1's scores.
   b. Explain how you made your predictions in part (a).

10. a. **Try This** Use a calculator to find the mean and standard deviation for Player 2's and Player 3's golf scores.
    b. What does a standard deviation of zero mean?
    c. **Estimation** Suppose a friend got the answer 27.5 when using a calculator to find the standard deviation of Player 3's golf scores. How do you know that your friend made an error?

◀ **At age 20, Tiger Woods was a three-time United States Amateur champion.**

Exercises ON YOUR OWN

Calculator **Make a table like the one in Example 1 to find the standard deviation for each data set. Use a calculator to find the square root.**

1. $\{5, 3, 2, 5, 10\}$

2. $\{10, 9, 10, 12, 11, 14\}$

3. $\{3.5, 4.5, 6.0, 4.0, 2.5, 2.5, 5.0\}$

4. $\{11, 11, 17, 17, 10, 11, 12, 19\}$

5. Tell what you know about the following data sets.

a. Data Set 1: The mean is 25 and the standard deviation is 100.

b. Data Set 2: The mean is 25 and the standard deviation is 2.

6. The table at the right records the outdoor temperatures (°F) reported to a local meteorologist by twelve weather watchers near Denver, Colorado, in January. Find the standard deviation of the temperature data.

January Temperatures (°F)	
15.8°	16.3°
16.5°	17.0°
15.9°	16.1°
16.5°	16.2°
16.0°	16.4°
16.1°	16.6°

7. **Writing** Explain the effects of a very large or very small data value on the mean and standard deviation of a data set.

8. **Open-ended** Create data sets with at least 6 entries as follows.

a. The mean is 12 and the standard deviation is 0.

b. The mean is 7 and the range is 12.

9. **Jobs** When Lyman interviewed for a summer job, he asked about the average salary of summer employees. He was excited that the average weekly wage was \$400. When his employer offered him a job at \$265 a week, he was confused. His employer stated: "Of my 20 summer employees, 17 make \$265 per week."

a. During the job interview, what other statistics should Lyman have asked about in order to find out more information about salaries? Explain your choice(s).

b. The three highly-paid summer employees each earn the same amount. How much do they earn?

c. **Estimate** Do you expect the standard deviation for the company's summer salaries to be large or small? Why?

d. **Verify** your prediction by calculating the standard deviation.

10. The graph at the right shows the differences from the mean in a set of data containing eight data values.

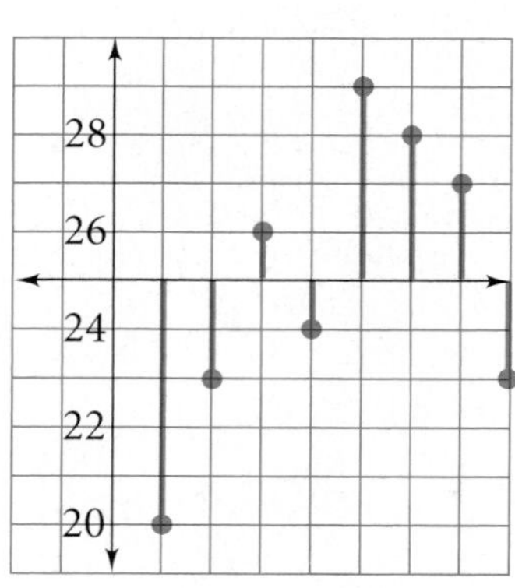

a. Find the square of each difference from the mean.

b. Find the sum of the squares calculated in part (a).

c. Use the result of part (b) to find the standard deviation of the data set.

Graphing Calculator **Use a calculator to find the standard deviation of each set of data.**

11. $\{11.4, 10.1, 9.5, 9.9, 10.1, 11.2, 12.0, 12.3\}$

12. $\{102.4, 100.8, 99.5, 103.4, 105.6, 111.5, 120.5\}$

13. $\{13, 19, 23, 50, 43, 44, 50, 52, 74, 83, 88, 90\}$

14. $\{-3.2, 0, 1.3, -2.0, -3.5, 0, 3.2, 2.3, 1.1, 0.3\}$

15. **Math in the Media** You are writing a magazine article on ski resorts in the Sierras. The information at the right is part of your research.
    a. What is the range for the price of a lift ticket?
    b. Find the standard deviation of the ticket prices.
    c. To give your readers a feel for the variability of ticket prices, you include the following sentence in your article. Fill in the blanks.

       Lift ticket prices vary about $ ■ around an average of $ ■ for an all-day adult ticket.

    d. **Writing** Explain why your sentence in part (c) is more helpful than simply telling your readers the range, as in "The prices vary from $26 to $46."

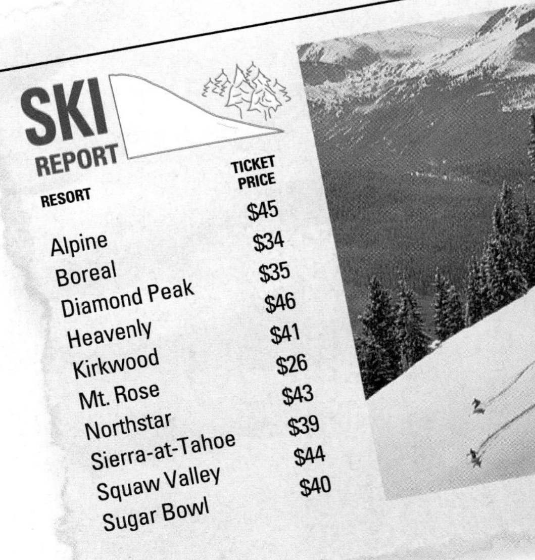

SKI
REPORT
RESORT
TICKET PRICE
Alpine $45
Boreal $34
Diamond Peak $35
Heavenly $46
Kirkwood $41
Mt. Rose $26
Northstar $43
Sierra-at-Tahoe $39
Squaw Valley $44
Sugar Bowl $40

16. **Research** Collect data on a topic of interest such as classmates' batting averages or students' curfew times. Gather at least 15 measurements and calculate the mean and standard deviation. Write a paragraph describing your data.

Exercises MIXED REVIEW

Write each number in scientific notation.

17. 0.00347

18. 3,112,200

19. 0.000825

20. 50,147,235

Solve each system of equations.

21. $3x + 2y = 7$
    $2x + 3y = 8$

22. $5x - 2y = 3$
    $4x + 2y = 6$

23. $x + y = 7$
    $2x - y = 8$

24. $3x - 4y = 5$
    $3x + 2y = 11$

Find the domain of each function.

25. $y = \sqrt{x - 5}$

26. $f(x) = 5 + \sqrt{6 + 3x}$

27. **Automobiles** A new car costs $20,000. It loses value at a rate of 7% per year. How much is the car worth in four years?

SELF ASSESSMENT

PORTFOLIO

For your portfolio, select one or two items from your work for this chapter. Here are possibilities:

- corrected work
- diagrams, graphs, or charts
- a journal entry

Explain why you have included each selection you make.

CHAPTER PROJECT

Finishing the Chapter Project

On a CLEAR Day...

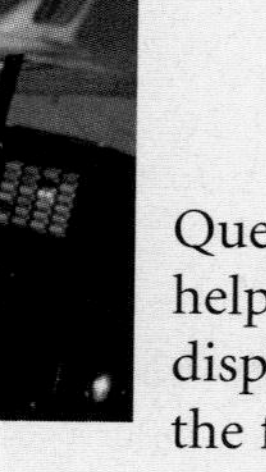

Questions on pages 418, 424, 429, 444, and 449 should help you to complete your project. Prepare a visual display and a report of your results. You should include the formula and graph for each planet and the formula for height on Earth when sight distance is known.

Reflect and Revise

Your notebook should present a comparison of sight distances and graphs for each planet. Check that your formulas and graphs are clearly labeled and easy to understand. Be sure that you have included a separate category with your display for Earth giving the formula for height on Earth when sight distance is known.

Follow Up

Suppose you were in an airplane at 30,000 ft above your town. How far could you see? Write a description of what you would see. Include any points of interest, cities or towns, and geological features like rivers or mountains.

For More Information

Adler, David. *Hyperspace! Facts and Fun from All Over the Universe.* New York: Viking Children's Books, 1982.

"Living and Working in Space: The Countdown Has Begun." PBS Video, 1320 Braddock Place, Alexandria, Virginia 22314. (800) 344-3337.

Free videotapes, slides, books, pamphlets: National Aeronautics and Space Administration, Education Programs Officer, NASA Headquarters, Code XEE, Washington, D.C. 20546. (202) 453-8396.

CHAPTER

9 rap Up

Key Terms

angle of elevation (p. 426)
box-and-whisker plot (p. 450)
converse of the Pythagorean theorem (p. 416)
cosine (p. 425)
distance formula (p. 420)
division property of square roots (p. 431)
extraneous solution (p. 443)
hypotenuse (p. 414)
legs (p. 414)
like terms (p. 435)
lower quartile (p. 450)
midpoint (p. 422)
midpoint formula (p. 422)
multiplication property of square roots (p. 430)
Pythagorean theorem (p. 414)
radical equation (p. 440)
rationalize (p. 432)
simplest form (p. 430)
sine (p. 425)
square root function (p. 445)
standard deviation (p. 452)
tangent (p. 425)
trigonometric ratios (p. 425)
unlike terms (p. 435)
upper quartile (p. 450)

How am I doing?

- State three ideas from this chapter that you think are important. Explain your choices.
- Describe the method for finding the distance between two points A and B.

The Pythagorean Theorem — 9-1

For a right triangle with **legs** a and b and **hypotenuse** c, the **Pythagorean theorem** states that $a^2 + b^2 = c^2$. The **converse of the Pythagorean theorem** states that if a triangle has sides of lengths a, b, and c, and if $a^2 + b^2 = c^2$, then it is a right triangle with hypotenuse of length c.

A rectangle has sides with lengths a and b. Find the length of the diagonal to the nearest hundredth.

1. $a = 3, b = 5$ **2.** $a = 11, b = 14$ **3.** $a = 7, b = 13$ **4.** $a = 4, b = 9$

5. **Writing** The hypotenuse of a right triangle is 26 cm. The length of one leg is 10 cm. Describe how to find the length of the other leg.

The Distance Formula — 9-2

The **distance formula** $d = \sqrt{(x_2 - x_1)^2 + (y_2 - y_1)^2}$ gives the distance between two points (x_1, y_1) and (x_2, y_2). The **midpoint formula** $M = \left(\frac{x_1 + x_2}{2}, \frac{y_1 + y_2}{2}\right)$ gives the coordinates of their midpoint.

Find the midpoint of $\overline{AB}$.

6. $A(3, 7), B(-2, 4)$ **7.** $A(5, -2), B(6, 14)$ **8.** $A(3, -9), B(14, 16)$ **9.** $A(12, 17), B(-7, 9)$

10. **Open-ended** Find two points with integer coordinates $\sqrt{74}$ units apart.

Trigonometric Ratios 9-3

Trigonometric ratios are triangle measurement ratios. For a right triangle of a given shape, they do not change no matter how large or small the triangle is. Three trigonometric ratios are **sine** (sin), **cosine** (cos), and **tangent** (tan), shown at the right.

$$\sin A = \frac{\text{length of side of opposite } \angle A}{\text{length of hypotenuse}}$$

$$\cos A = \frac{\text{length of side of adjacent to } \angle A}{\text{length of hypotenuse}}$$

$$\tan A = \frac{\text{length of side opposite } \angle A}{\text{length of side adjacent to } \angle A}$$

You can use trigonometric ratios to measure distances indirectly. You can use an **angle of elevation** to measure heights indirectly.

In $\triangle ABC$, $\angle C$ is a right angle. Find the lengths of the missing sides.

11. $AB = 12, m\angle A = 34°$ **12.** $BC = 9, m\angle B = 72°$ **13.** $AC = 8, m\angle B = 52°$

14. *Standardized Test Prep* In $\triangle ABC$, $\angle C$ is a right angle. Which of the following is (are) true?

I. $\cos B = \frac{AC}{AB}$ **II.** $\tan B = \frac{BC}{AC}$ **III.** $\sin A = \frac{BC}{AB}$

A. I only **B.** II only **C.** III only **D.** I and II **E.** II and III

Simplifying Radicals 9-4

You can simplify some radical expressions by using products or quotients. The **multiplication property of square roots** states that for any two nonnegative numbers $\sqrt{ab} = \sqrt{a} \cdot \sqrt{b}$. The **division property of square roots** is at the right.

$$\sqrt{\frac{a}{b}} = \frac{\sqrt{a}}{\sqrt{b}}$$

$a \geq 0, b > 0$
division property

Simplify each radical expression.

15. $\sqrt{32} \cdot \sqrt{144}$ **16.** $\frac{\sqrt{84}}{\sqrt{121}}$ **17.** $\sqrt{96} \cdot \sqrt{25}$ **18.** $\sqrt{\frac{100}{169}}$

19. A rectangle is 7 times as long as it is wide. Its area is 1400 cm^2. Find the dimensions of the rectangle in simplified form.

Adding and Subtracting Radicals 9-5

You can use the distributive property to simplify expressions with sums and differences of radicals. First, simplify the radicals to have like terms.

Simplify each radical expression.

20. $6\sqrt{7} - 2\sqrt{28}$ **21.** $5(\sqrt{20} + \sqrt{80})$ **22.** $\sqrt{54} - 2\sqrt{6}$ **23.** $\sqrt{125} - 3\sqrt{5}$

24. $\sqrt{10}(\sqrt{10} - \sqrt{20})$ **25.** $7\sqrt{90} + \sqrt{160}$ **26.** $\sqrt{72} + 3\sqrt{32}$ **27.** $\sqrt{28} + 5\sqrt{63}$

28. A box is 2 in. long, 3 in. wide, and 4 in. tall. What is the length of the longest distance between corners of the box? Express your answer in simplified form.

Solving Radical Equations 9-6

A **radical equation** has a variable under a radical. You can often solve a radical equation by solving for the square root, then squaring both sides of the equation. Squaring each side of an equation also works when both sides are square roots. When you square both sides of a radical equation, you may produce an **extraneous solution**. It is not a solution of the original equation.

Solve each radical equation.

29. $\sqrt{x + 7} = 3$ **30.** $\sqrt{x} + 3\sqrt{x} = 16$ **31.** $\sqrt{x + 7} = \sqrt{2x - 1}$ **32.** $\sqrt{x} - 5 = 4$

33. The volume V of a cylinder is given by $V = \pi r^2 h$, where r is the radius of the cylinder and h is its height. If the volume of a cylinder is 54 in.^{2}, and its height is 2 in., what is its radius to the nearest 0.01 in.?

Graphing Square Root Functions 9-7

The simplest **square root function** is $y = \sqrt{x}$. To find the domain of a square root function, solve the inequality where the expression under the radical is greater than or equal to zero.

Find the domain of each function. Then graph the function.

34. $y = \sqrt{x} + 5$ **35.** $y = \sqrt{x} - 2$ **36.** $y = \sqrt{x + 1}$ **37.** $y = 2\sqrt{x}$

Analyzing Data Using Standard Deviation 9-8

The **standard deviation** shows how spread out a set of data is from the mean. You can calculate the standard deviation by following these six steps. Find the mean, $\bar{x}$, of the data set. Find the difference of each data value from the mean. Square each difference. Find the sum of the squares of the differences. Divide the sum by the number of data values. The square root of the quotient just calculated is the standard deviation.

Find the standard deviation of each set of data.

38. 2, 7, 9, 15, 17 **39.** 5, 8, 11, 12, 19 **40.** 4, 10, 12, 13, 23 **41.** 7, 15, 20, 23, 29

Getting Ready for... CHAPTER 10

Use the quadratic formula to solve these equations to the nearest hundredth. If the equation has no real solution, write *no solution*.

42. $2x^2 + 5x - 4 = 0$ **43.** $3x^2 - 2x - 7 = 0$ **44.** $x^2 - 3x - 8 = 0$

45. $2x^2 - 5x + 15 = 0$ **46.** $5x^2 - 4x - 12 = 0$ **47.** $7x^2 + 2x - 18 = 0$

CHAPTER

9 Assessment

Find whether the following sets of numbers determine a right triangle.

1. 6, 8, 10
2. 6, 7, 9
3. 4, 5, 11
4. 10, 24, 26

Approximate AB to the nearest hundredth.

5. $A(1, -2), B(5, 7)$
6. $A(3, 5), B(7, 4)$
7. $A(4, 7), B(-11, -6)$
8. $A(0, -5), B(3, 2)$

Find the coordinates of the midpoint of $\overline{AB}$.

9. $A(4, 9), B(1, -5)$
10. $A(-2, -7), B(3, 0)$
11. $A(3, -10), B(-4, 6)$
12. $A(0, 8), B(-1, 1)$

Find the lengths to the nearest hundredth.

13. AB
14. AC

B
12
24°
A
C

15. The distance between consecutive bases in a baseball diamond is 90 ft. How far is it from first base to third base?

16. One house is 12 mi east of a school. Another house is 9 mi north of the school. How far apart from each other are the houses?

Simplify each radical expression.

17. $\sqrt{\frac{128}{64}}$
18. $\frac{\sqrt{27}}{\sqrt{75}}$
19. $\sqrt{48}$
20. $\sqrt{12} \cdot \sqrt{8}$
21. $3\sqrt{32} + 5\sqrt{2}$
22. $2\sqrt{27} + 5\sqrt{3}$
23. $7\sqrt{125} - 3\sqrt{175}$
24. $\sqrt{128} - \sqrt{192}$

25. **Standardized Test Prep** If x and y are positive, which expression(s) is (are) equivalent to $\sqrt{24x^2y^3}$?

I. $2xy\sqrt{12xy^2}$ II. $2xy\sqrt{6y}$ III. $xy\sqrt{24y}$

A. I only B. II only C. III only
D. I and II E. II and III

26. **Open-ended** Write a problem involving addition of two like terms with radical expressions. Simplify the sum.

Solve each radical equation.

27. $3\sqrt{x} + 2\sqrt{x} = 10$
28. $8 = \sqrt{5x - 1}$
29. $5\sqrt{x} = \sqrt{15x + 60}$
30. $\sqrt{x} = \sqrt{2x - 7}$
31. $3\sqrt{x + 3} = 2\sqrt{x + 9}$

32. A rectangle is 5 times as long as it is wide. The area of the rectangle is 100 ft^2. How wide is the rectangle? Express your answer in simplified form.

Find the domain of each function. Then graph the function.

33. $y = 3\sqrt{x}$
34. $y = \sqrt{x} + 4$
35. $y = \sqrt{x - 4}$
36. $y = \sqrt{x + 9}$

37. A cube has 3-in. sides. Find the longest distance between a pair of corners. Express your answer in simplified form.

Find the standard deviation of each set of data.

38. 5, 7, 9, 11, 12
39. 2, 4, 7, 11, 15
40. 4, 12, 13, 15, 17
41. 1, 2, 4, 6, 7

42. **Writing** Explain how these two data sets differ based on the following information.
Set A: mean 20; range 10; standard deviation 4
Set B: mean 20; range 20; standard deviation 2

43. **Geometry** The formula for the volume V of a cylinder of height h and radius r is $V = \pi r^2 h$. Solve the formula for r in terms of V and h.

44. From the ground you can see a satellite dish on the roof of a building 60 feet high. The angle of elevation is 62°. How far away is the building from you?

CHAPTER 9

Preparing for the Math A Exam

Part I

1 Which could be the lengths of the sides of a right triangle?

(1) 2, 5, 7　　(3) 36, 6, 8
(2) 24, 10, 26　　(4) 4, 7, 65

2 What is the midpoint of the segment from $C(-2, 10)$ to $D(8, 3)$?

(1) $(3, 6\frac{1}{2})$　　(3) $(4, 5\frac{1}{2})$
(2) $(5, 6\frac{1}{2})$　　(4) $(5, 5\frac{1}{2})$

3 The two shorter sides of right triangle PQR are $\overline{QP}$ and $\overline{QR}$. Which is true?

(1) $\sin P = \frac{QP}{PR}$　　(3) $\cos R = \frac{QR}{PR}$
(2) $\tan P = \frac{QR}{PR}$　　(4) $\tan R = \frac{QR}{QP}$

4 Which expression is in simplest form?

(1) $3\sqrt{20}$　　(3) $\frac{2}{\sqrt{6}}$
(2) $4\sqrt{35}$　　(4) $\sqrt{\frac{3}{10}}$

5 The simplest form of the sum of $\sqrt{3}$ and $2\sqrt{27}$ is ■.

(1) $3\sqrt{3}$　　(3) $6\sqrt{6}$
(2) $2\sqrt{30}$　　(4) $7\sqrt{3}$

6 What is the solution of $\sqrt{x - 8} = \sqrt{6x + 2}$?

(1) no solution　　(3) -2
(2) 2　　(4) $-1\frac{1}{5}$

7 In which set of data is the data spread farthest apart?

(1) The mean is 20; the standard deviation is 15.
(2) The mean is 70; the standard deviation is 10.
(3) The mean is 30; the standard deviation is 12.
(4) The mean is 10; the standard deviation is 9.

8 The sum of four consecutive integers is 190. What is the third integer?

(1) 45　　(3) 47
(2) 46　　(4) 48

Part II

9 Suppose you live at the base of a mountain. The angle of elevation from your home to the top of the mountain is 27°. The distance along this line of elevation is 3 miles. Find the height of the mountain to the nearest tenth of a mile.

10 Graph the function $y = \sqrt{x} - 4$.

Part III

11 Find the missing length. Express it as a radical in simplest form.

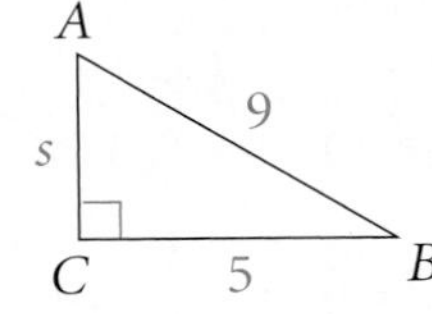

12 A square photo is placed in a frame 9 in. by 12 in. The area of the mat surrounding the photo is 65 in.^{2}. To the nearest tenth of an inch, what is the length of each side of the photo?

Part IV

13 The map shows the locations of Ms. Martin's house and the factory where she works. On the map, each unit represents one mile.

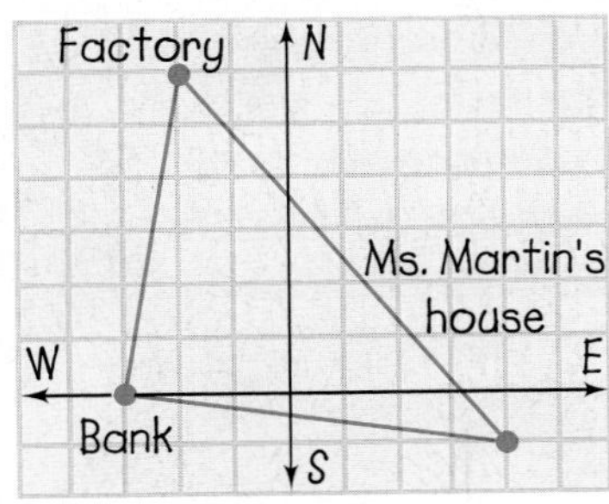

a What is the length of the shortest route from Ms. Martin's house to the factory?

b If Ms. Martin drives to work at an average speed of 40 mi/h, how long does it take her to drive the route found in (a)?

14 One city has five car rental agencies. The costs per day of renting an economy car with unlimited mileage in that city are: \$25, \$19, \$30, \$24, \$32.

a What is the range of the daily rates?

b What is the mean of the daily rates?

c Display the data in a box-and-whisker plot.

CHAPTER

10 Polynomials

Relating to the Real World

Algebra is useful because it provides tools for describing and solving problems. You can use polynomials and their properties to solve problems in engineering, communications, and economics. Properties of polynomials make it possible to find the most efficient use of time and materials.

CHAPTER PROJECT

Trees are us.

Rings indicate age.
Wood splits as it dries.
Scar shows fire damage.

Many schools celebrate Arbor Day by planting young trees to replenish our ecosystem. Trees use the carbon dioxide that humans and animals exhale to make oxygen. Trees anchor the soil and prevent erosion. They also produce fruit. Wood from trees is used for the construction of everything from pencils to houses.

As you work through the chapter, you will learn more about the uses of trees. You will use formulas to analyze data and predict the production of wood and fruit. Then you will decide how to organize and display your results.

To help you complete the project:

- **p. 474** *Find Out by Researching*
- **p. 479** *Find Out by Calculating*
- **p. 485** *Find Out by Calculating*
- **p. 495** *Find Out by Graphing*
- **p. 502** *Finishing the Project*

Connections Business . . . and more

10-1 Adding and Subtracting Polynomials

What You'll Learn

- Describing polynomials
- Adding and subtracting polynomials

...And Why

To use polynomials in real-world situations, such as working in a store

What You'll Need

- tiles

WORK TOGETHER

Business Work in groups. Suppose you work at a pet store. The spreadsheet shows the contents of several customers' orders.

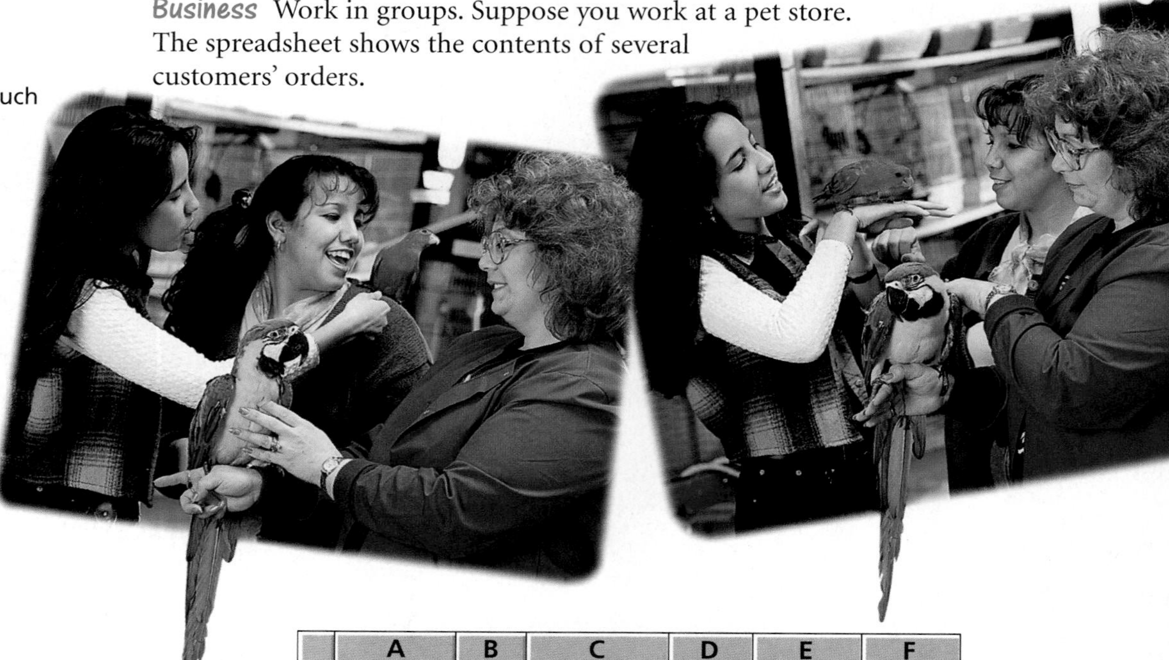

	A	B	C	D	E	F
1	Customer	Seed	Cuttlebone	Millet	G. Paper	Perches
2	Davis			✔		
3	Brooks	✔	✔			
4	Casic	✔		✔		
5	Martino	✔			✔	✔

ROCKY'S FRIENDS
Bird Supplies
• bird seed (5 lb) $3.99
• cuttlebone (2 ct) 2.00
• spray millet (5 lb) 24.00
• gravel paper (1 pkg) 2.29
• perches (2 ct) 1.89
Tidbits

The variables represent the number of each item ordered.
s = bags of birdseed m = bags of millet p = packages of perches
c = packages of cuttlebone g = packages of gravel paper

1. Which expression represents the cost of Casic's order?
   A. $27.99(s + m)$ **B.** $3.99s + 24m$ **C.** $27.99sm$
2. Write expressions to represent each of the other customers' orders.
3. Martino buys 10 bags of birdseed, 4 packages of gravel paper, and 2 packages of perches. What is the total cost of his order?
4. *Open-ended* Make up several orders and write expressions for these orders. Have other members of your group find the cost of your orders. Check each other's work.

THINK AND DISCUSS

QUICK REVIEW

A *term* is a number, a variable, or the product of numbers and variables.

Describing Polynomials

A **monomial** is a number, a variable, or a product of a number and one or more variables with nonnegative exponents. A **polynomial** is a monomial or a sum of monomials. A polynomial has no variables in a denominator. For a term that has only one variable, the **degree of a term** is the exponent of the variable.

$$x^3 - 4x + 5x^2 + 7$$

The degree of a constant is 0.

degree → 3 1 2 0

The **degree of a polynomial** is the same as the greatest degree of any of its terms.

QUICK REVIEW

$x = x^1$

Polynomial	Degree	Name Using Degree	Number of Terms	Name Using Number of Terms
$7x + 4$	1	linear	2	**binomial**
$3x^2 + 2x + 1$	2	quadratic	3	**trinomial**
$4x^3$	3	cubic	1	**monomial**

The polynomials in the chart are in **standard form,** which means the terms decrease in degree from left to right and no terms have the same degree.

Example 1

Write each polynomial in standard form. Then name each polynomial by its degree and the number of its terms.

a. $5 - 2x$
$-2x + 5$
linear binomial

b. $3x^4 - 4 + 2x^2$
$3x^4 + 2x^2 - 4$
fourth degree trinomial

c. $-2x + 5 - 4x^2 + x^3$
$x^3 - 4x^2 - 2x + 5$
cubic polynomial with four terms

5. **Try This** Write each polynomial in standard form. Then name each polynomial by its degree and the number of its terms.
a. $6x^2 + 7 - 9x^4$ **b.** $3y - 9 - y^3$ **c.** $9 + 7v$

Adding Polynomials

You can use tiles to add and subtract polynomials.

Opposite terms form zero pairs. →

x^2 $-x^2$ = 0 x $-x$ = 0 1 −1 = 0

6. What polynomial is shown using each set of tiles?

a. 

b. 

Example 2

Find $(2x^2 - 3x + 4) + (3x^2 + 2x - 3)$.

Method 1 Add using tiles.

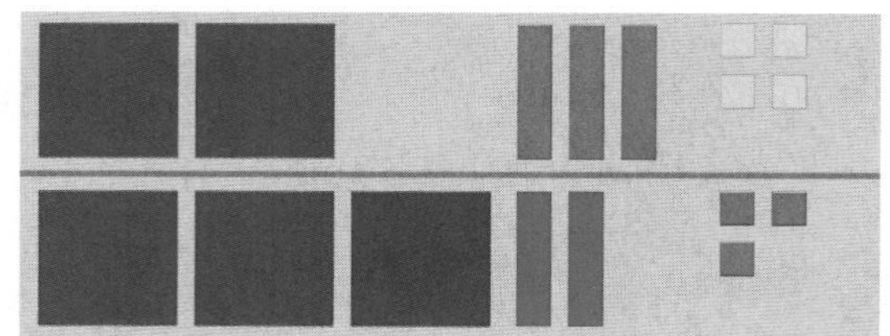

$2x^2 - 3x + 4$

$3x^2 + 2x - 3$

Group like tiles together. Remove zero pairs. Write an expression for the remaining tiles.

$5x^2 - x + 1$

QUICK REVIEW

Like terms are terms that have exactly the same variable factors.

Method 2 Add vertically.

Line up like terms.
Then add the coefficients.

$$\begin{array}{l} 2x^2 - 3x + 4 \\ \underline{3x^2 + 2x - 3} \\ 5x^2 - x + 1 \end{array}$$

The sum is $5x^2 - x + 1$.

Method 3 Add horizontally.

Group like terms. Then add the coefficients.

$$\begin{aligned} &(2x^2 - 3x + 4) + (3x^2 + 2x - 3) \\ &= (2x^2 + 3x^2) + (-3x + 2x) + (4 - 3) \\ &= 5x^2 - x + 1 \end{aligned}$$

7. a. Try This Find $(5x^2 + 4x - 7) + (-4x^2 + 8x - 1)$ using any method you choose.

b. Why did you choose the method you used?

Subtracting Polynomials

In Chapter 1, you learned that subtraction means to add the opposite. So when you subtract a polynomial, change each of its terms to the opposite. Then add the coefficients.

Math A Test Prep

1 Which statement about the expression $5x^4 - 3x^2 + 1$ is true?
(1) It is a binomial.
(2) It is a monomial.
(3) It is a third degree polynomial.
(4) It is a fourth degree polynomial.

2 The perimeter of the triangle is $13c + 3$. Write a polynomial expression in standard form for the missing side length.

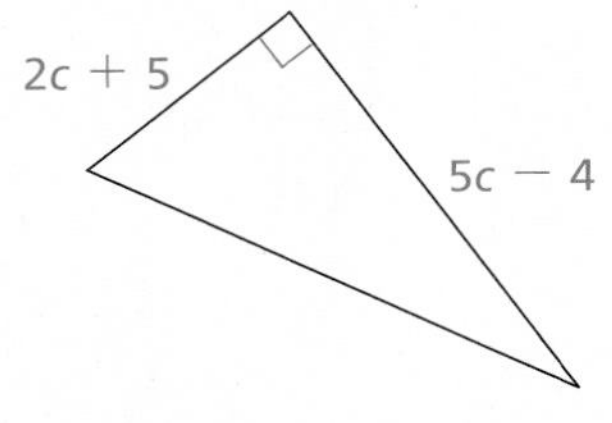

Example 3

Find $(7x^3 - 3x + 1) - (x^3 + 4x^2 - 2)$.

Method 1 Subtract vertically.

Line up like terms.

$$\begin{array}{rrrr} 7x^3 & & -\ 3x & +\ 1 \\ -(x^3 & +\ 4x^2 & & -\ 2) \\ \hline \end{array}$$

Add the opposite.

$$\begin{array}{rrrr} 7x^3 & & -\ 3x & +\ 1 \\ -x^3 & -\ 4x^2 & & +\ 2 \\ \hline 6x^3 & -\ 4x^2 & -\ 3x & +\ 3 \end{array}$$

Method 2 Subtract horizontally.

Write the opposite of each term in the polynomial being subtracted. Group like terms. Then add the coefficients of like terms.

$$(7x^3 - 3x + 1) - (x^3 + 4x^2 - 2)$$
$$= 7x^3 - 3x + 1 - x^3 - 4x^2 + 2$$
$$= (7x^3 - x^3) - 4x^2 - 3x + (1 + 2)$$
$$= 6x^3 - 4x^2 - 3x + 3$$

← The coefficients of $7x^3$ and $-x^3$ are 7 and −1. $7x^3 - 1x^3 = 6x^3$.

The difference is $6x^3 - 4x^2 - 3x + 3$.

Check Substitute a value for x to check. Here 2 is substituted for x.

$$(7x^3 - 3x + 1) - (x^3 + 4x^2 - 2) \stackrel{?}{=} 6x^3 - 4x^2 - 3x + 3$$
$$7(2^3) - 3(2) + 1 - [2^3 + 4(2^2) - 2] \stackrel{?}{=} 6(2^3) - 4(2^2) - 3(2) + 3$$
$$(56 - 6 + 1) - (8 + 16 - 2) \stackrel{?}{=} 48 - 16 - 6 + 3$$
$$51 - 22 \stackrel{?}{=} 29$$
$$29 = 29 \checkmark$$

8. **Try This** Subtract $(3x^2 + 4x - 1) - (x^2 - x - 2)$.
9. **Critical Thinking** How are subtracting vertically and subtracting horizontally alike?

Exercises ON YOUR OWN

Match each expression with its name.

1. $5x^2 - 2x + 3$
2. $\frac{3}{4}z + 5$
3. $7a^3 + 4a - 12$
4. $\frac{3}{x} + 5$
5. -15

A. constant monomial
B. *not* a polynomial
C. quadratic trinomial
D. linear binomial
E. cubic trinomial

Write each polynomial in standard form. Then name each polynomial by its degree and number of terms.

6. $4x - 3x^2$

7. $4x + 9$

8. $6 - 3x - 7x^2$

9. $9z^2 - 11z^3 + 5z - 5$

10. $y - 7y^3 + 15y^8$

11. $c^2 - 2 + 4c$

12. $7 + 5b^2$

13. $-10 + 4q^4 - 8q + 3q^2$

Find the sum of the two sets of tiles.

14.

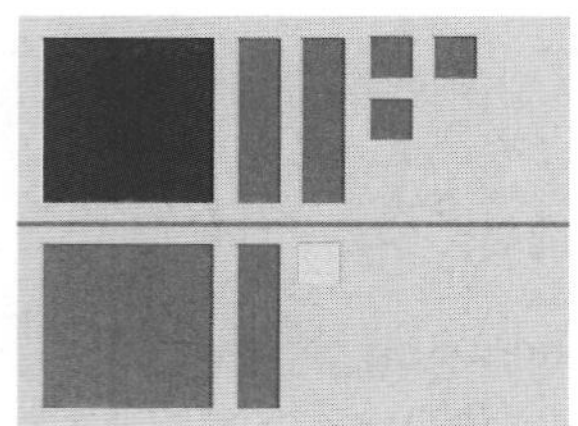

15.

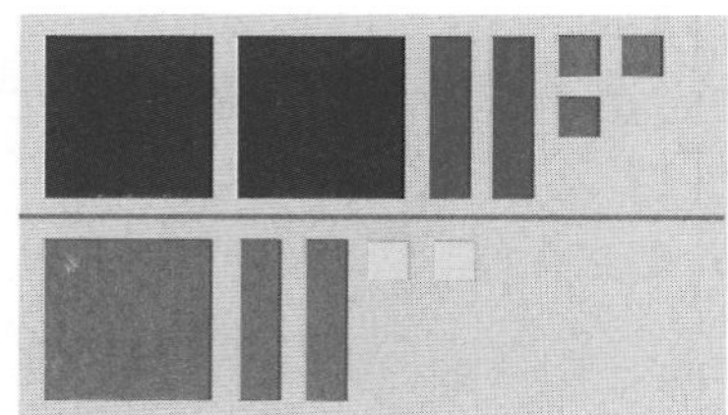

Find each sum or difference.

16. $(7y^2 - 3y + 4y) + (8y^2 + 3y^2 + 4y)$

17. $(2x^3 - 5x^2 + 3x - 1) - (8x^3 - 8x^2 + 4x + 3)$

18. $(-7z^3 + 3z - 1) - (-6z^2 + z + 4)$

19. $(7a^3 + 3a^2 - a + 2) + (8a^2 - 3a - 4)$

20. $(5y^3 + 7y) - (3y^3 + 9y^2) + (7y^3 + 2y)$

21. $(2x^2 - 4) + (3x^2 - 6) - (-x^2 + 2)$

22. **Critical Thinking** Kwan rewrote $(5x^2 - 3x + 1) - (2x^2 - 4x - 2)$ as $5x^2 - 3x + 1 - 2x^2 - 4x - 2$. What mistake did he make?

Language Arts **Use a dictionary if necessary.**

23. **Writing** Write the definition of each word.

a. monogram **b.** binocular **c.** tricuspid **d.** polyglot

24. **a.** **Open-ended** Find other words that begin with *mono*, *bi*, *tri*, or *poly*.

b. Do these prefixes have meanings similar to those in mathematics?

Geometry **Find the perimeter of each figure.**

25.

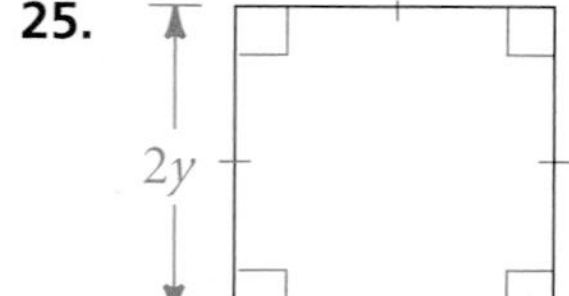

26.

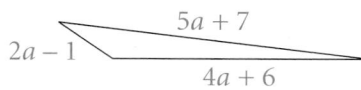

$5a + 7$

$2a - 1$

$4a + 6$

27.

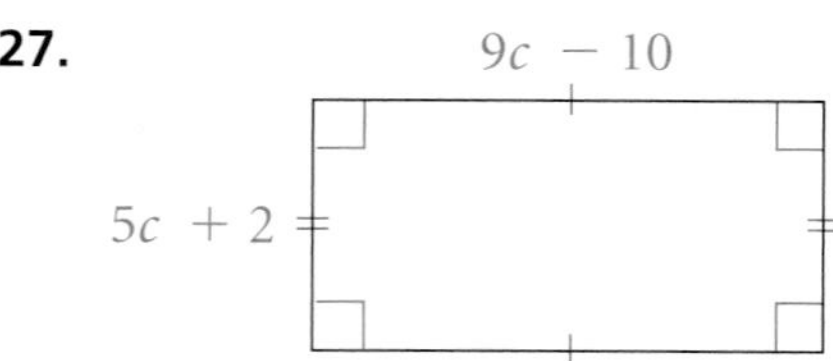

28.

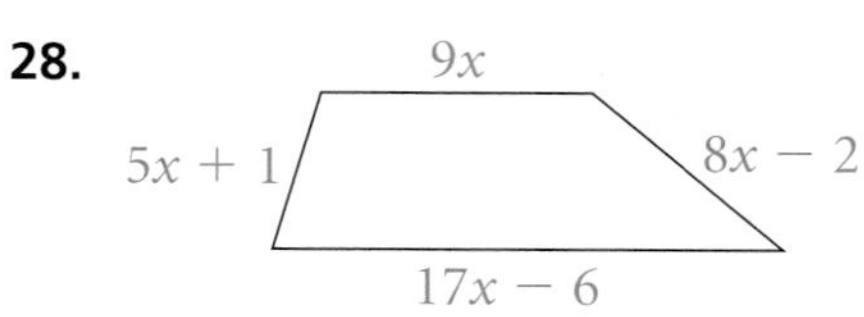

29. **Open-ended** In his will, Mr. McAdoo is leaving equal shares of the land shown at the right to his two brothers. Write a polynomial expression for the land that each brother should inherit.

30. **Critical Thinking** Is it possible to write a binomial with degree 0? Explain.

Geometry **Find each missing length.**

31. Perimeter $= 25x + 8$

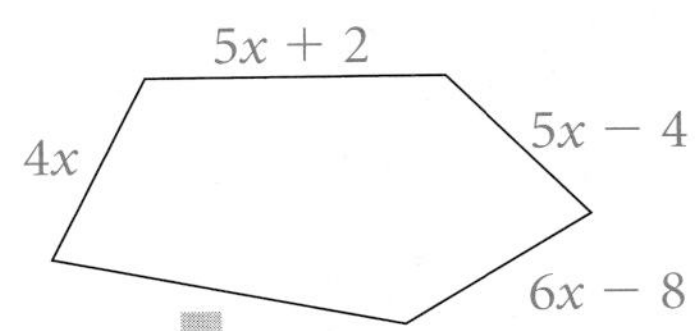

32. Perimeter $= 23a - 7$

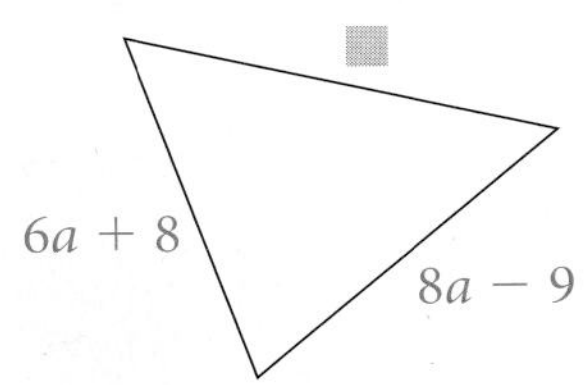

33. Perimeter $= 38y + 2$

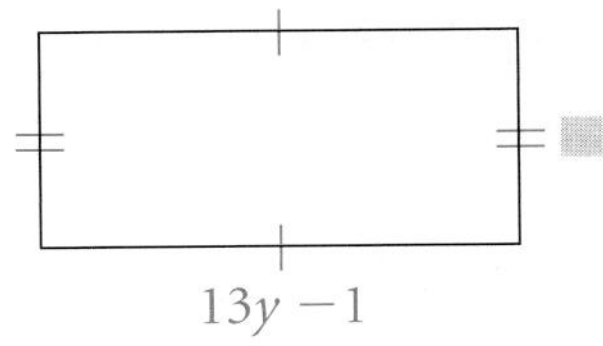

Simplify. Write each answer in standard form.

34. $(3 - 2x + 3x^2) + (7 + 6x - 2x^2)$
35. $(4x^3 - 2x^2 - 13) + (-4x^3 + 2 - 7x)$
36. $(3x^3 - 3x^2 - x - 1) - (3x^2 - 6x)$
37. $(-2r^2 + r - 6) - (1 + 2r - 4r^2)$
38. $(9c^3 - c + 8 + 6c^2) - (3c^3 + 3c - 4)$
39. $(b^4 - 6 + 5b) + (8b^4 + 2b - 3b^2)$

40. **Critical Thinking** Why is $3x^2$ a monomial and $3x^{-2}$ *not* a monomial?

Exercises MIXED REVIEW

Use exponential notation to write each expression.

41. $4 \cdot 4 \cdot 4 \cdot 4$
42. $(0.5)(0.5)(0.5)$
43. $\left(\frac{2}{3}\right)\left(\frac{2}{3}\right)\left(\frac{2}{3}\right)\left(\frac{2}{3}\right)$
44. $28 \cdot 28 \cdot 28$

Find the standard deviation of each set of numbers to the nearest tenth.

45. 10, 12, 16, 5, 2
46. 11, 7, 10, 12
47. 5, 3, 7, 8, 3, 4

48. **Science** The surface area of a sphere is found using the formula $S = 4\pi r^2$. The approximate radius of Jupiter is 4.4×10^4 mi. Find the approximate surface area of Jupiter.

Getting Ready for Lesson 10-2

Multiply.

49. $2(x - 3)$
50. $-6(3x - 2)$
51. $(-3)(-5a + 7)$
52. $(-7)(c^2 - 8c)$

What You'll Learn

- Multiplying a polynomial by a monomial
- Factoring a monomial from a polynomial

...And Why

To explore formulas for area

What You'll Need

- tiles

10-2 Multiplying and Factoring

THINK AND DISCUSS

Multiplying by a Monomial

You can use the distributive property to multiply polynomials. You can also use tiles to multiply polynomials.

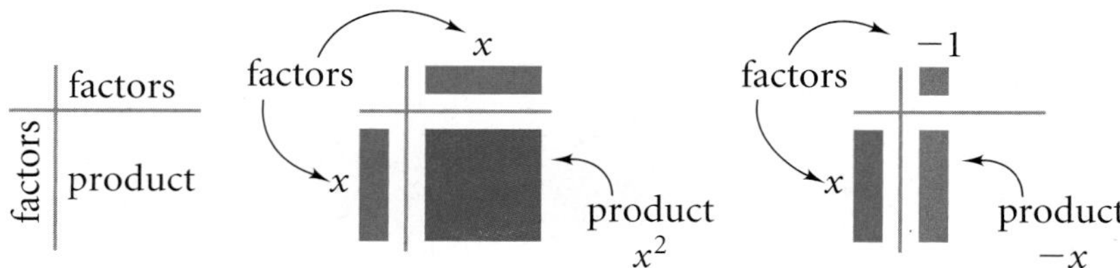

Example 1

Multiply $3x$ and $(2x + 1)$.

Method 1 Use tiles.

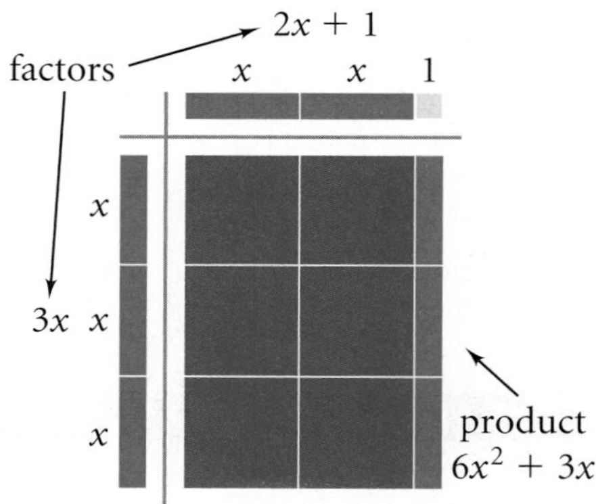

Method 2 Use the distributive property.

$$3x(2x + 1) = 3x(2x) + 3x(1)$$
$$= 6x^2 + 3x$$

1. **Try This** Use the distributive property to multiply $2x(x - 2)$. Then check your work by using tiles.
2. **a.** Use tiles to find each product: $2x(4x - 3)$ and $(4x - 3)(2x)$.
   b. Do both models represent the same area? Explain.
3. **a.** **Critical Thinking** Kevin said that $-2x(4x - 3) = -8x^2 - 6x$. Karla said that $-2x(4x - 3) = -8x^2 + 6x$. Who is correct?
   b. Explain the error that Kevin or Karla made.

Factoring Out a Monomial

Factoring a polynomial reverses the multiplication process. You can use tiles to make a rectangle to find the factors of a polynomial.

Example 2

Factor $2x^2 - 10x$.

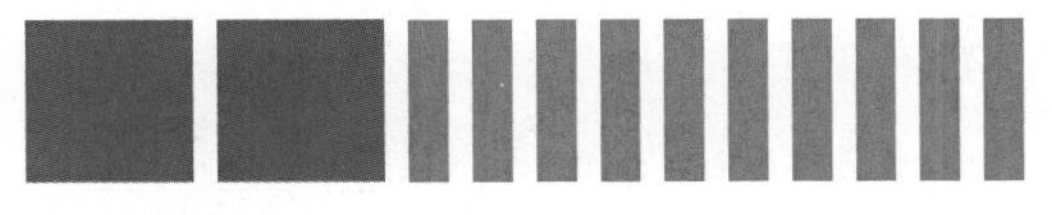

← Model using tiles.

← Make a rectangle that is as close to square as possible.

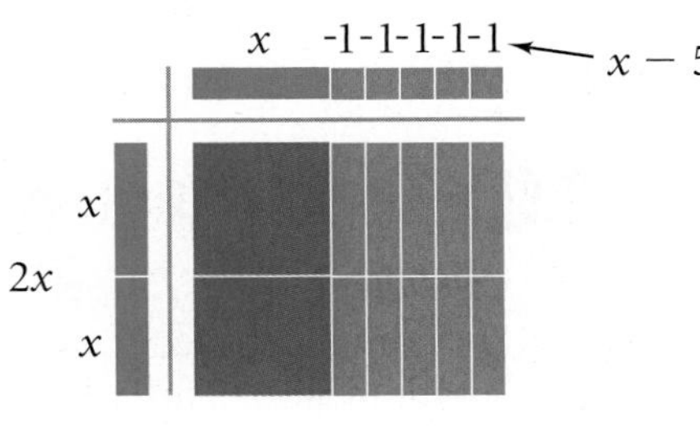

← Find the factors.

$2x^2 - 10x = 2x(x - 5)$

4. Try This Use tiles to factor each polynomial.

a. $x^2 + 8x$ **b.** $3x^2 - 12x$ **c.** $-3x^2 + 6x$

QUICK REVIEW

The *greatest common factor* (GCF) is the greatest factor that divides evenly into each term.

To factor out a monomial using the distributive property, it is helpful to find the greatest common factor (GCF).

Example 3

Find the GCF of the terms of the polynomial $4x^3 + 12x^2 - 8x$.

List the factors of each term. Identify the factors common to all terms.

$$4x^3 = 2 \cdot 2 \cdot x \cdot x \cdot x$$
$$12x^2 = 2 \cdot 2 \cdot 3 \cdot x \cdot x$$
$$8x = 2 \cdot 2 \cdot 2 \cdot x$$

The GCF is $2 \cdot 2 \cdot x$ or $4x$.

5. Try This Find the GCF of the terms of each polynomial.

a. $4x^3 - 2x^2 - 6x$ **b.** $5x^5 + 10x^3$ **c.** $3x^2 - 18$

Example 4

Factor $3x^3 - 9x^2 + 15x$.

Step 1 Find the GCF.

$$3x^3 = 3 \cdot x \cdot x \cdot x$$
$$9x^2 = 3 \cdot 3 \cdot x \cdot x$$
$$15x = 3 \cdot 5 \cdot x$$

The GCF is $3 \cdot x$ or $3x$.

Step 2 Factor out the GCF.

$$\begin{aligned} 3x^3 - 9x^2 + 15x &= 3x(x^2) - 3x(3x) + 3x(5) \\ &= 3x(x^2 - 3x + 5) \end{aligned}$$

6. Use the distributive property to check the factoring in Example 4.

7. **Try This** Use the GCF to factor each polynomial.

a. $8x^2 - 12x$ **b.** $5x^3 + 10x$ **c.** $6x^3 - 12x^2 - 24x$

Example 5

Relating to the Real World

Building Models Suppose you are building a model of the square castle shown. The moat of the model castle is made of silver paper. Find the area of the moat.

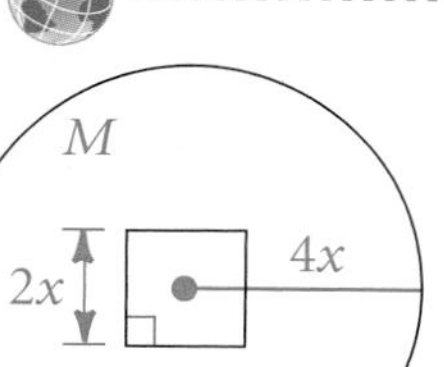

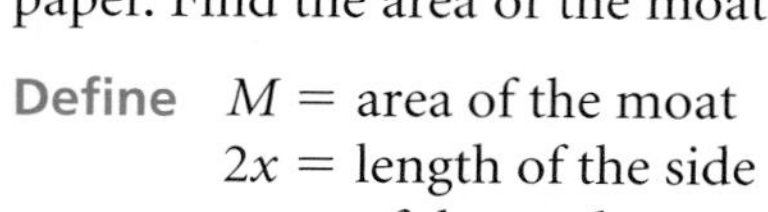

Define M = area of the moat
$2x$ = length of the side of the castle
$4x$ = radius of the moat
$A = \pi r^2$ ← formula for the area of a circle

Relate	area of moat	is	area of circle	minus	area of square
Write	M	$=$	$\pi(4x)^2$	$-$	$(2x)^2$

$$M = 16\pi x^2 - 4x^2$$ ← Simplify $(4x)^2$ and $(2x)^2$.
$$= 4x^2(4\pi - 1)$$ ← The GCF is $4x^2$.

The area of the moat is $4x^2(4\pi - 1)$.

8. **Try This** Use the GCF to factor each polynomial.

a. $2g^2 - 4$

b. $2x^3 - 4x^2 + 6x$

c. $6x^3 + 24x^2 + 6x$

Exercises ON YOUR OWN

Use tiles to find each product.

1. $3(x + 4)$
2. $x(x - 3)$
3. $2x(2x + 1)$
4. $4x(5x - 8)$
5. $4x(2x + 3)$

For each set of tiles, find the missing factors or product. Then write the factors and product as variable expressions.

6. 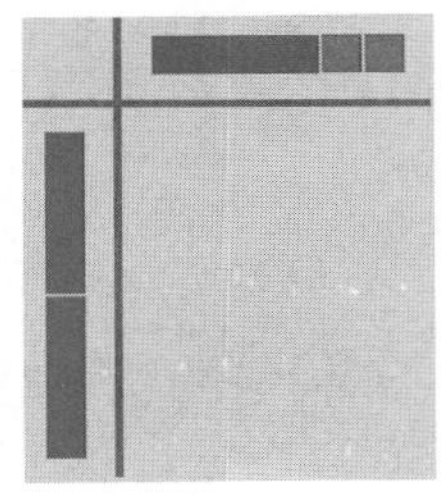

7. 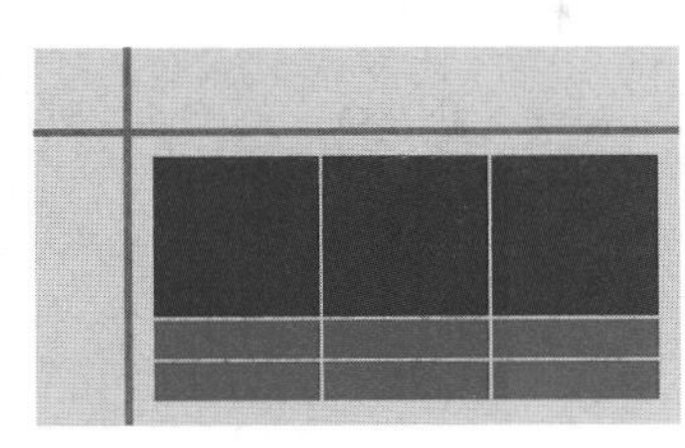

8. 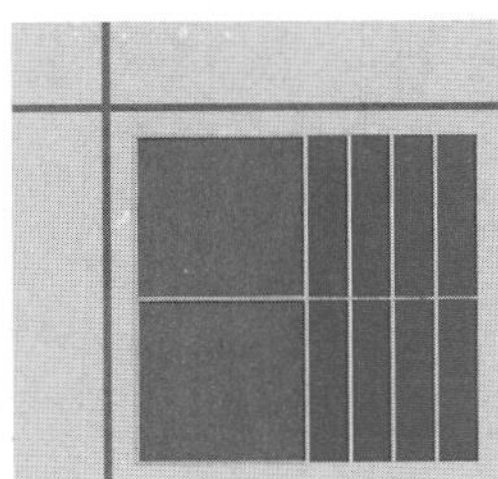

Find each product.

9. $4(2x + 7)$
10. $t(5t^2 + 6t)$
11. $6x(-9x^3 + 6x - 8)$
12. $2g^2(g^2 + 6g + 5)$
13. $-3a(4a^2 - 5a + 9)$
14. $7x^2(5x^2 - 3)$
15. $-3p^2(-2p^3 + 5p)$
16. $4n^2(2n^2 + 4n)$
17. $x(x + 3) - 5x(x - 2)$
18. $12c(-5c^2 + 3c - 4)$
19. $x^2(x + 1) - x(x^2 - 1)$
20. $-4j(3j^2 - 4j + 3)$

Find the greatest common factor (GCF) for each polynomial.

21. $15x + 21$
22. $6a^2 - 8a$
23. $36s + 24$
24. $x^3 + 7x^2 - 5x$
25. $5b^3 - 30$
26. $w^4 - 9w^2$
27. $9x^3 - 6x^2 + 12x$
28. $5r^5 - 3r^2 + 4r$
29. $25s^2 + 5s - 15s^3$
30. $8p^3 - 24p^2 + 16p$
31. $56x^4 - 32x^3 - 72x^2$
32. $2x + 3x^2$

33. a. **Open-ended** Draw two different tile diagrams to represent $6x^2 + 12x$ as a product. Place the x^2 tiles in the upper left area.
    b. Write the factored form of $6x^2 + 12x$ for each diagram in part (a).

34. a. Factor $n^2 - n$.
    b. **Writing** Suppose n is an integer. Is $n^2 - n$ *always, sometimes,* or *never* even? **Justify** your answer.

35. **Manufacturing** The diagram shows a solid block of metal with a cylinder cut out of it. The formula for the volume of a cylinder is $V = \pi r^2 h$, where r is the radius and h is the height.
    a. Write a formula for the volume of the cube in terms of s.
    b. Write a formula for the volume of the cylinder in terms of s.
    c. Write a formula in terms of s for the volume of the metal left after the cylinder has been removed.
    d. Factor your formula from part (c).
    e. What is the volume of the block of metal after the cylinder has been removed if $s = 15$ in?

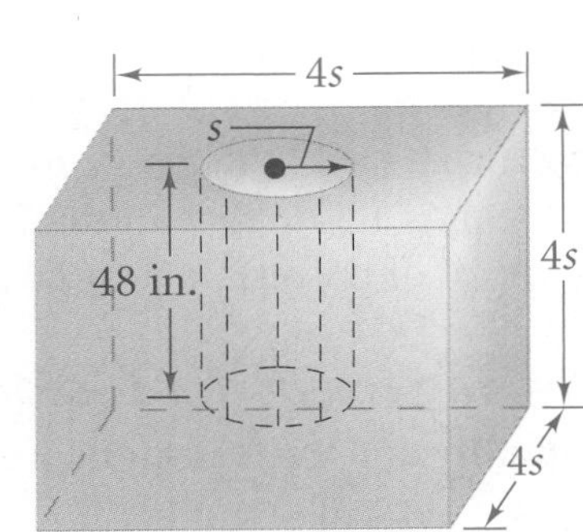

Factor each expression.

36. $6x - 4$
37. $s^4 + 4s^3 - 2s$
38. $10r^2 - 25r + 20$
39. $2x^2 - 4x^4$
40. $12p^3 + 4p^2 - 2p$
41. $7k^3 - 35k^2 + 70k$
42. $15n^3 + 3n^2 - 12n$
43. $9x + 12x^2$
44. $24n^3 - 12n^2 + 12n$
45. $6m^6 - 24m^4 + 6m^2$
46. $15k^3 + 3k^2 - 12k$
47. $5m^3 - 7m^2$

Factor by grouping like terms.

Sample $2x^3 + 2x + 3x^2 + 3$ ⟵ Group the terms with common factors together.

$2x(x^2 + 1) + 3(x^2 + 1)$ ⟵ Factor the GCF from each group.

$(2x + 3)(x^2 + 1)$ ⟵ Factor out the common polynomial.

48. $3v^3 + 18v^2 - 4v - 24$
49. $2x^3 + x^2 - 14x - 7$
50. $2x^3 + 3x^2 + 4x + 6$

51. a. *Geometry* How many sides does the polygon at the right have? How many diagonals does it have from one vertex?
    b. Suppose a polygon, like the one at the right, has n sides. How many diagonals will it have from one vertex?
    c. The number of diagonals that can be drawn from all the vertices is $\frac{n}{2}(n - 3)$. Multiply the two factors.

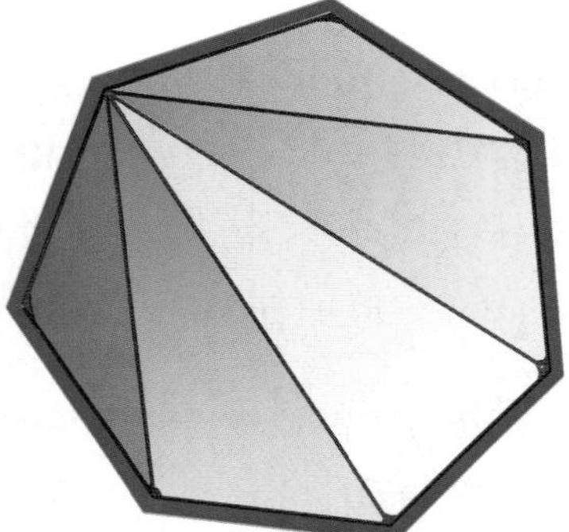

Chapter Project *Find Out by Researching*

A board foot is a linear measure of lumber equal to a square foot of wood 1 in. thick. What can you make from 10 board feet? 100 board feet? 1000 board feet? How is the size of a house related to the amount of wood used to build it? What different types of wood are needed for cabinets, floors, and roofs? What tools do carpenters use to make these items?

Exercises MIXED REVIEW

Use $\triangle ABC$ to find each trigonometric ratio.

52. $\sin A$
53. $\cos B$
54. $\tan A$
55. $\sin B$
56. $\cos A$
57. $\tan B$

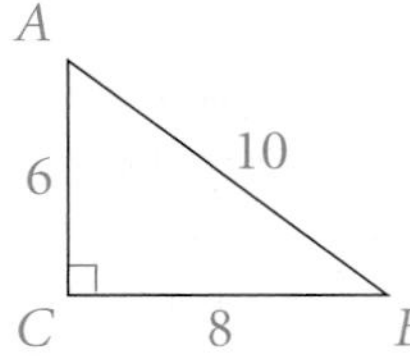

58. *Geography* Two buses are on their way to the same bus terminal. One bus is 1.5 mi due north of the terminal. The other bus is 2.0 mi due east of the terminal. How far from each other are the buses?

Getting Ready for Lesson 10-3

Simplify and write in standard form.

59. $(4x)(32) - (4x)(12x) + (4x)(7x^2)$
60. $(3y)(7) - (3y)(2y) + (3)(5y^2) - (7y)(6) - (7y)(8y)$

What You'll Learn

- Multiplying two binomials
- Multiplying a trinomial and a binomial

...And Why

To investigate real-world situations, such as savings accounts

What You'll Need

- tiles
- graphing calculator

10-3 Multiplying Polynomials

THINK AND DISCUSS

Multiplying Two Binomials

You can use tiles or the distributive property to multiply two binomials.

Example 1

Find the product $(2x + 1)(x - 5)$.

Method 1 Use tiles.

Step 1 Show the factors.

$(x - 5)$

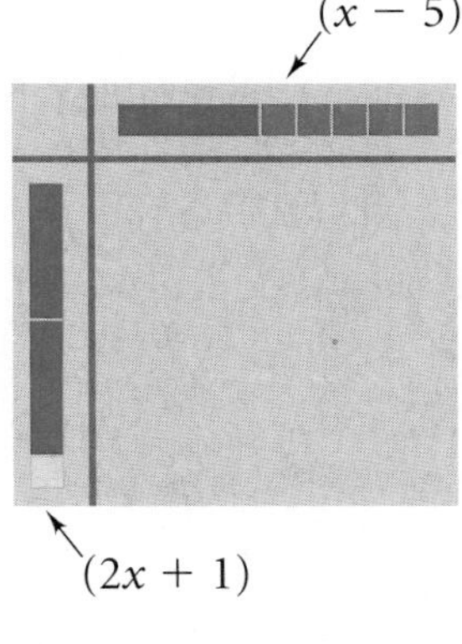

$(2x + 1)$

Step 2 Find the product.

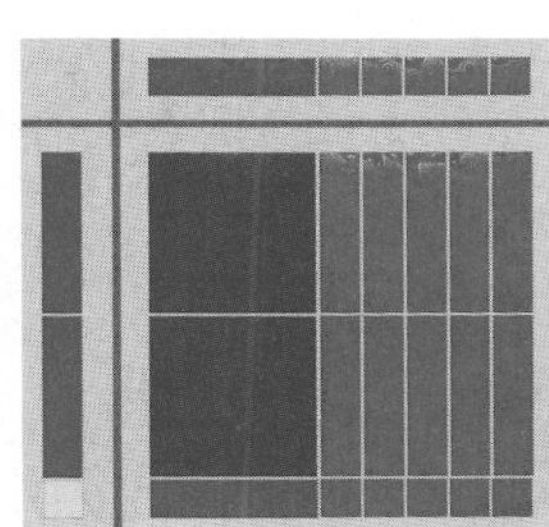

$2x^2 - 10x + x - 5$ ← Add coefficients of like terms.

$2x^2 - 9x - 5$

Method 2 Use the distributive property.

$$\begin{aligned}(2x + 1)(x - 5) &= 2x(x) + 2x(-5) + 1(x) + 1(-5)\\ &= 2x^2 - 10x + x - 5\\ &= 2x^2 - 9x - 5\end{aligned}$$

The product is $2x^2 - 9x - 5$.

1. Rework Example 1 using tiles. Put $2x + 1$ on the horizontal line and $x - 5$ on the vertical line. Do you get the same result as in Example 1?
2. **Try This** Find the product $(3x + 1)(2x + 3)$ using tiles.
3. **Try This** Find the product $(6x - 7)(3x + 5)$ using the distributive property.
4. a. **Graphing Calculator** Graph $y = (2x + 1)(x - 5)$ and $y = 2x^2 - 9x - 5$ on the same calculator screen. What appears to be true of the two graphs?
   b. Use graphs to check your answers to Questions 2 and 3.

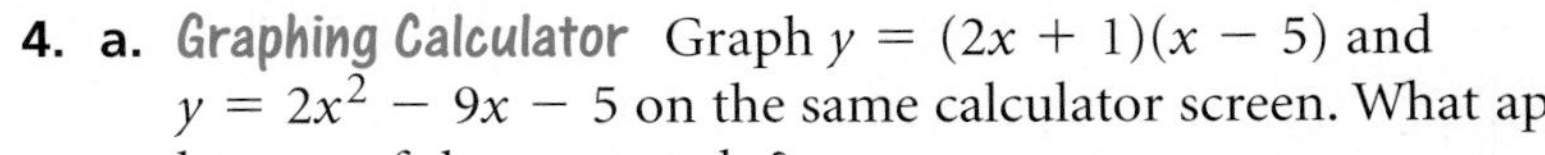

Multiplying Using FOIL

One way to organize how you multiply two binomials is to use *FOIL,* which stands for "First, Outer, Inner, Last." The term FOIL is a memory device for applying the distributive property.

Example 2

Find the product $(3x - 5)(2x + 7)$.

$$\begin{aligned}(3x - 5)(2x + 7) &= \overset{\text{First}}{(3x)(2x)} + \overset{\text{Outer}}{(3x)(7)} - \overset{\text{Inner}}{(5)(2x)} - \overset{\text{Last}}{(5)(7)} \\ &= 6x^2 + 21x - 10x - 35 \\ &= 6x^2 + 11x - 35\end{aligned}$$

First, Last, Inner, Outer — middle term: $11x$

The product is $6x^2 + 11x - 35$.

5. **Mental Math** What is the middle term of each product?
   a. $(2x + 3)(x + 1)$
   b. $(2x - 3)(x + 1)$
   c. $(2x + 3)(x - 1)$
   d. $(2x - 3)(x - 1)$
6. **Try This** Find each product.
   a. $(3x + 4)(2x + 5)$
   b. $(3x - 4)(2x + 5)$
   c. $(3x + 4)(2x - 5)$
   d. $(3x - 4)(2x - 5)$
7. **Graphing Calculator** Use a graphing calculator to check your answers in Question 6.

Example 3 **Relating to the Real World** 

Savings Many students and their families start saving money early to pay for college. Suppose you deposit \$500 at the beginning of each of two consecutive years. If your bank pays interest annually at the rate r, you can use the expression $(1 + r)(2 + r)500$ to find the amount in your account at the end of the two years. Write the expression in standard form.

$$\begin{aligned}&(1 + r)(2 + r)500 \\ &= (1 + r)(2 + r)500 &&\leftarrow \text{Use FOIL to simplify } (1 + r)(2 + r). \\ &= (2 + r + 2r + r^2)(500) \\ &= (2 + 3r + r^2)(500) &&\leftarrow \text{Add like terms.} \\ &= 1000 + 1500r + 500r^2 &&\leftarrow \text{Use the distributive property.} \\ &= 500r^2 + 1500r + 1000 &&\leftarrow \text{Write in standard form.}\end{aligned}$$

8. How much money is in your account if the interest rate in Example 3 is 4%? (*Hint*: Write the interest rate as a decimal.)

Math A Test Prep

1 The area of a rectangle is described by the expression $6x^4 - 12x^3 + 9x^2$. The GCF of the terms of the polynomial describe the width of the rectangle. What is the length?
(1) $2x - 4x + 9x$
(2) $3x^2$
(3) $3x^2 - 9x + 6$
(4) $2x^2 - 4x + 3$

2 Simplify: $(3x + 4)(2x - 1)$.

Multiplying a Trinomial and a Binomial

FOIL works when you multiply two binomials, but it is not helpful when multiplying a trinomial and a binomial. You can use the vertical method or the horizontal method to distribute each term in a factor.

Example 4

Find the product $(3x^2 + x - 6)(2x - 3)$.

Method 1 Multiply vertically.

$$\begin{array}{r} 3x^2 + x - 6 \\ 2x - 3 \\ \hline -9x^2 - 3x + 18 \\ 6x^3 + 2x^2 - 12x \\ \hline 6x^3 - 7x^2 - 15x + 18 \end{array}$$

← Multiply by −3.
← Multiply by 2x.
← Add like terms.

Method 2 Multiply horizontally.

$$(2x - 3)(3x^2 + x - 6)$$
$$= 2x(3x^2) + 2x(x) + 2x(-6) - 3(3x^2) - 3(x) - 3(-6)$$
$$= 6x^3 + 2x^2 - 12x - 9x^2 - 3x + 18$$
$$= 6x^3 - 7x^2 - 15x + 18$$ ← Add like terms.

The product is $6x^3 - 7x^2 - 15x + 18$.

9. a. Try This Find the product $(3a + 4)(5a^2 + 2a - 3)$ using both methods shown in Example 4.
b. Do you prefer the vertical or the horizontal method? Why?

Exercises ON YOUR OWN

What are the factors shown with the tiles? What will be the product?

1. 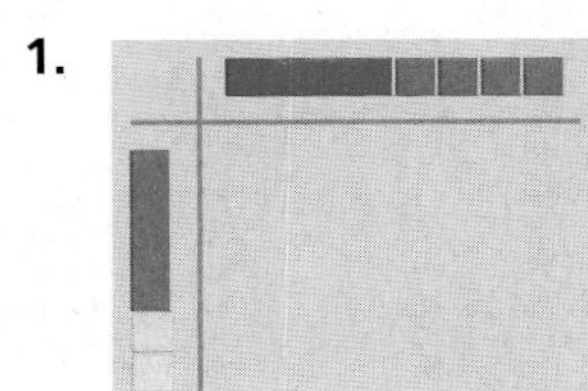

2. 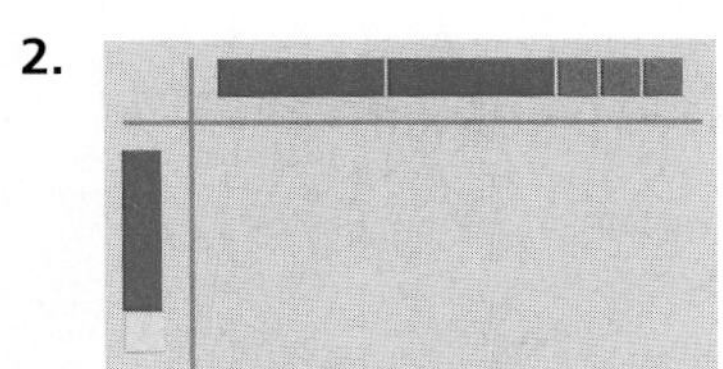

3. 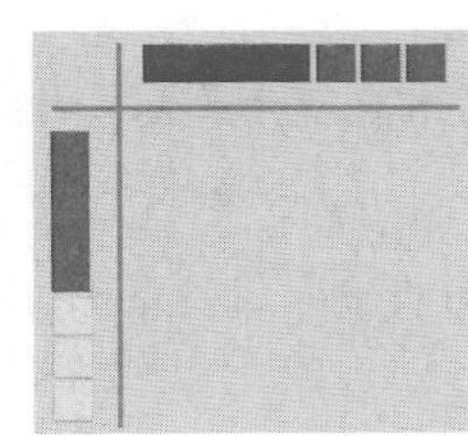

Use tiles to find each product.

4. $(x + 2)(x + 5)$

5. $(x - 5)(x + 4)$

6. $(2x - 1)(x + 2)$

Copy and fill in each blank.

7. $(5a + 2)(6a - 1) = \blacksquare a^2 + 7a - 2$

8. $(3c - 7)(2c - 5) = 6c^2 - 29c + \blacksquare$

9. $(z - 4)(2z + 1) = 2z^2 - \blacksquare z - 4$

10. $(2x + 9)(x + 2) = 2x^2 + \blacksquare x + 18$

Choose **Use any method you choose to find each product.**

11. $(x + 7)(x - 6)$

12. $(a - 8)(a - 9)$

13. $(2y + 5)(y - 3)$

14. $(r + 6)(r - 4)$

15. $(y + 4)(5y - 8)$

16. $(x + 9)(x^2 - 4x + 1)$

17. $(a - 4)(a^2 - 2a + 1)$

18. $(x - 3)(2x^2 + 3x + 3)$

19. $(2t^2 - 6t + 3)(2t - 5)$

20. **Geometry** Use the formula $V = lwh$ to write a polynomial in standard form for the volume of the box shown at the right.

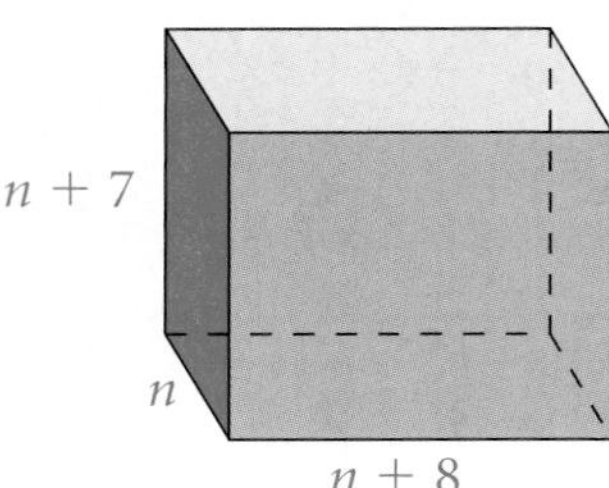

21. **Open-ended** Write a binomial and a trinomial. Find their product.

22. **Construction** You are planning a rectangular garden. Its length is 4 ft more than twice its width. You want a walkway 2 ft wide around the garden. Write an expression for the area of the garden and walk. (*Hint:* Draw a diagram.)

Find each product using FOIL.

23. $(x + 3)(x + 5)$

24. $(2y + 1)(3y + 4)$

25. $(a - 1)(a - 7)$

26. $(4x + 3)(4x - 3)$

27. $(5a - 2)(a + 3)$

28. $(6x + 1)(2x - 3)$

29. $(3y - 7)(-2y + 2)$

30. $(8 - 6x)(5 + 2x)$

31. **Writing** Which method do you prefer for multiplying two binomials? Why?

32. **Financial Planning** Suppose you deposit \$2000 in a savings account for college that has an annual interest rate r. At the end of three years, the value of your account will be $2000(1 + r)^3$ dollars.
    a. Simplify $2000(1 + r)^3$ by finding the product of $2000(1 + r)(1 + r)(1 + r)$. Write your answer in standard form.
    b. Find the amount of money in the account if the interest rate is 3%.

Lions and Tigers and Bears, oh My!
Tuition and Housing and Books, oh My!

Find each product. Is the product *rational* or *irrational?*

33. $(\sqrt{3} + \sqrt{2})(\sqrt{3} - \sqrt{2})$

34. $(\sqrt{3} + 2)^2(\sqrt{3} - 2)^2$

35. $(\sqrt{5} + 3)(\sqrt{5} + 7)$

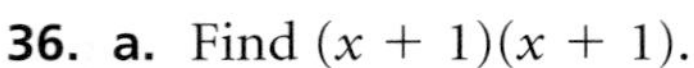

36. a. Find $(x + 1)(x + 1)$.
    b. Find $(x + 1)(x^2 + x + 1)$.
    c. Find $(x + 1)(x^3 + x^2 + x + 1)$.
    d. **Patterns** Use the pattern you see in parts (a) – (c) to **predict** the product of $(x + 1)(x^7 + x^6 + x^5 + x^4 + x^3 + x^2 + x + 1)$.

Chapter Project *Find Out by Calculating*

You can use the expression $0.0655\ell(1 - p)(d - s)^2$ to find the number of usable board feet in a log.

- Estimate the usable board feet in a 35-ft log if its diameter is 20 in. Assume the log loses 10% (0.10) of its volume from the saw cuts and a total of 2 in. is trimmed off the log.
- The diameter of a log is 25 in. A total of 2 in. will be trimmed off the log. The estimated volume loss due to saw cuts is 10%. How long must the log be to yield 600 board feet of lumber?

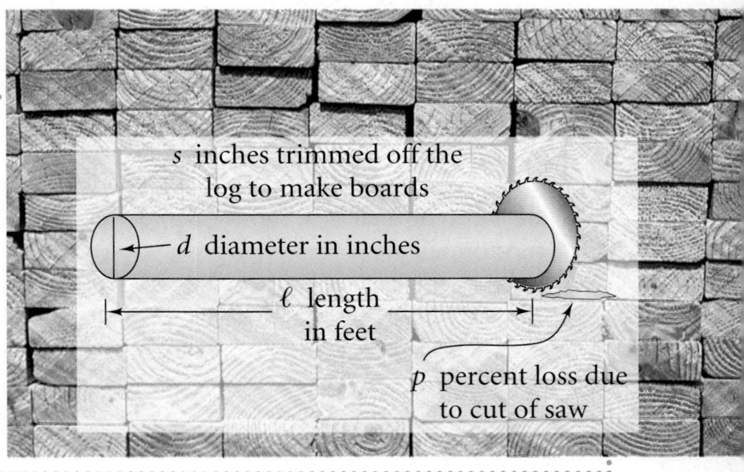

Exercises MIXED REVIEW

Solve each equation.

37. $6x^2 = 24$ **38.** $8x - 23 = 41$ **39.** $-x^2 + x + 2 = 0$

40. **Language** The *Oxford English Dictionary* defines 616,500 words. Write this number in scientific notation.

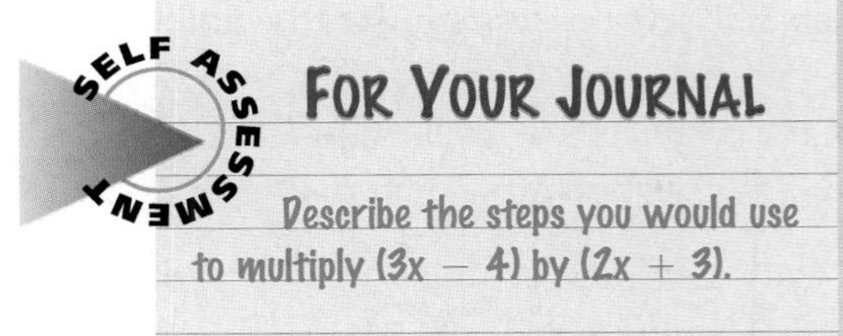

SELF ASSESSMENT
FOR YOUR JOURNAL
Describe the steps you would use to multiply (3x − 4) by (2x + 3).

Getting Ready for Lesson 10-4

Factor by grouping.

41. $2x(3x + 5) + 4(3x + 5)$ **42.** $5x(2x - 7) + 3(2x - 7)$ **43.** $-3x(4x + 1) + 5(4x + 1)$

Exercises CHECKPOINT

Simplify.

1. $(x^2 + x - 3) + (2x^2 + 4x - 1)$ **2.** $(3a^3 + 2a^2 - 5) - (a^3 + a^2 + 2)$

3. $(m^2 - m + 7) - (3m^2 + 4m - 1)$ **4.** $(6x^2 - 2x - 5) + (3x^2 + x - 3)$

Find each product.

5. $(-w + 3)(w + 3)$ **6.** $2t(-3t^2 - 2t + 6)$ **7.** $(m + 4)(m - 3)$ **8.** $(b - 6)(b - 3)$

Factor each expression.

9. $-3c^3 + 15c^2 - 3c$ **10.** $10a^3 + 5a^2 + 5a$ **11.** $8p^3 - 20p^2 - 24p$ **12.** $x^3 + 4x^2 + 7x$

13. **a.** **Open-ended** Write two binomials using the variable z.
b. Find the sum and product of the two binomials.

14. **Writing** How is distributing a number similar to distributing a term with a variable? Include examples.

Math ToolboX Exploration

Polynomial Division

After Lesson 10-3

To divide a polynomial by a monomial, divide each term of the polynomial by the monomial.

$$\begin{aligned}\frac{8x^4 + 4x^3 + 12x^2}{2x^2} &= \frac{8x^4}{2x^2} + \frac{4x^3}{2x^2} + \frac{12x^2}{2x^2}\\ &= 4x^2 + 2x^1 + 6x^0 \quad \leftarrow \text{Use the exponent rules for division.}\\ &= 4x^2 + 2x + 6\end{aligned}$$

To divide a polynomial by a binomial, use *polynomial long division.*

Example

Divide $x^3 + 3x^2 - 12$ by $x - 3$.

Step 1 Use a process similar to whole number long division.

$$\begin{array}{r} x^2 \\ x - 3 \overline{) x^3 + 3x^2 + 0x - 12} \\ \underline{x^3 - 3x^2} \\ 6x^2 + 0x \end{array}$$

Express the dividend in descending powers of the variable, with a 0 coefficient for any missing power.

← Divide: $\frac{x^3}{x} = x^2$

← Multiply: $x^2(x - 3) = x^3 - 3x^2$

← Subtract: $(x^3 + 3x^2) - (x^3 - 3x^2) = 6x^2$
Bring down $0x$.

Step 2 Repeat the process: divide, multiply, subtract, bring down.

$$\begin{array}{r} x^2 + 6x \\ x - 3 \overline{) x^3 + 3x^2 + 0x - 12} \\ \underline{x^3 - 3x^2} \\ 6x^2 + 0x \\ \underline{6x^2 - 18x} \\ 18x - 12 \end{array}$$

$$\begin{array}{r} x^2 + 6x + 18 \\ x - 3 \overline{) x^3 + 3x^2 + 0x - 12} \\ \underline{x^3 - 3x^2} \\ 6x^2 + 0x \\ \underline{6x^2 - 18x} \\ 18x - 12 \\ \underline{18x - 54} \\ 42 \end{array}$$

The remainder is 42. →

Therefore, $\frac{x^3 + 3x^2 - 12}{x - 3} = x^2 + 6x + 18 + \frac{42}{x - 3}$ ← $\frac{\text{dividend}}{\text{divisor}} = \text{quotient} + \frac{\text{remainder}}{\text{divisor}}$

Divide.

1. $(x^6 - x^5 + x^4) \div x^2$

2. $(12x^8 - 8x^5) \div 4x^4$

3. $(9x^4 + 6x^3 - 3x^2) \div 3x^2$

4. $(x^2 - 5x + 3) \div (x - 2)$

5. $(x^2 - 9) \div (x + 4)$

6. $(x^3 + x^2 - x + 2) \div (x + 2)$

7. The volume of a rectangular prism is $m^3 + 8m^2 + 19m + 12$. The height of the prism is $m + 3$. Find the area of the base of the prism.

10-4 Factoring Trinomials

What You'll Learn

- Factoring quadratic expressions
- Identifying quadratic expressions that cannot be factored

...And Why

To solve civil engineering and landscaping problems

What You'll Need

- tiles
- graph paper

WORK TOGETHER

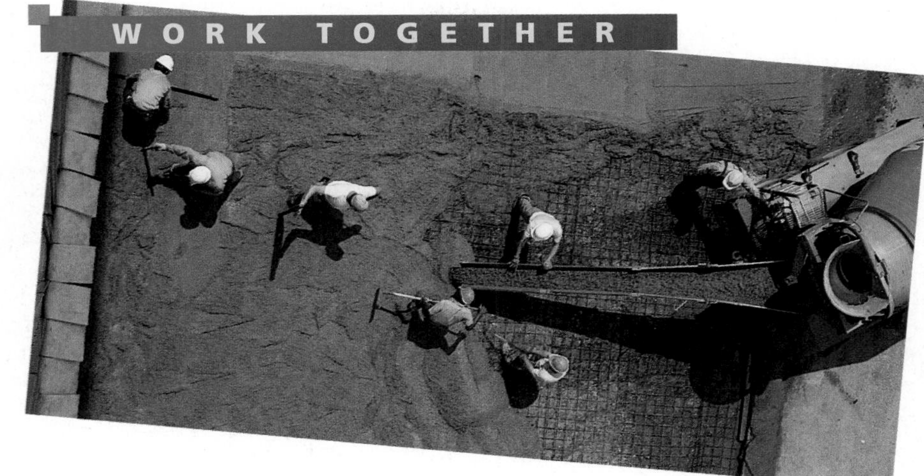

Construction A contractor has agreed to pour the concrete for the floor of a garage. He knows the area of the floor is 221 ft^2 but cannot remember its dimensions. He does remember that the dimensions are prime numbers.

Work with a partner to find the dimensions of the garage floor.

1. Explain how you know that 221 is not the product of two 1-digit numbers.
2. Explain how you could decide if 221 has a factor greater than 20 other than itself.
3. Use graph paper. Cut out several 10×10 squares, some 1×10 rectangles, and some 1×1 squares. Use these pieces to make a rectangle representing the garage floor. What are its dimensions?
4. Repeat this process to find a pair of prime numbers with each product.
   a. 133 **b.** 161 **c.** 209

THINK AND DISCUSS

Using Tiles

Some quadratic trinomials are the product of two **binomial factors.**

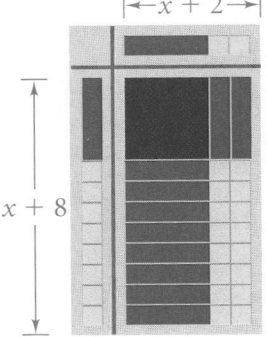

quadratic trinomial		binomial factors
$x^2 + 10x + 16$	$\longrightarrow$	$(x + 2)(x + 8)$

$x + 2$

$x + 8$

The diagram at the left shows how $x^2 + 10x + 16$ can be displayed as a rectangle with sides of length $x + 2$ and $x + 8$.

You can use tiles to factor quadratic trinomials.

Example 1

Use tiles to factor $x^2 + 7x + 12$.

Choose one x^2-tile, seven x-tiles and twelve 1-tiles. Use the strategy *Guess and Test* to form a rectangle using all the tiles.

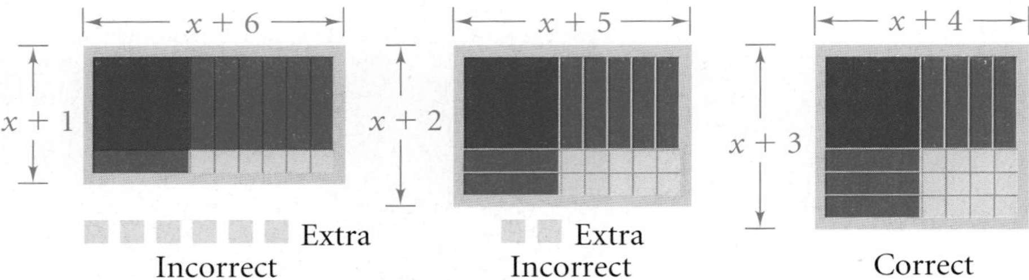

Extra
Incorrect

Extra
Incorrect

Correct

Write the correct factors as a product.

$x^2 + 7x + 12 = (x + 3)(x + 4)$

5. Try This Use tiles to factor these trinomials. **Verify** your answers using FOIL.

a. $x^2 + 6x + 8$ **b.** $x^2 + 11x + 10$

Testing Possible Factors

To factor trinomials of the form $x^2 + bx + c$, you can use FOIL with the strategy *Guess and Test.*

The sum of the numbers you use here must equal *b*.

$$x^2 + bx + c = (x + \square)(x + \square)$$

The product of the numbers you use here must equal *c*.

Example 2

Factor $x^2 - 9x + 20$.

Choose numbers that are factors of 20. Look for a pair with sum -9.

Factors of 20	Sum of Factors
-1 and -20	$-1 + (-20) = -21$
-2 and -10	$-2 + (-10) = -12$
-4 and -5	$-4 + (-5) = -9$

List only negative factors because you are looking for a sum of -9. Two positive numbers cannot have a negative sum.

The numbers -4 and -5 have a product of 20 and a sum of -9.
The correct factors are $(x - 4)$ and $(x - 5)$.
So, $x^2 - 9x + 20 = (x - 4)(x - 5)$.

Math A Test Prep

1 Which polynomial *cannot* be factored into two binomials?
(1) $x^2 + 5x - 3$
(2) $2x^2 - 7x + 6$
(3) $x^2 - 9x - 10$
(4) $3x^2 + 4x + 1$

2 Write a formula in factored form for the volume of the cylinder after the square hole has been drilled.

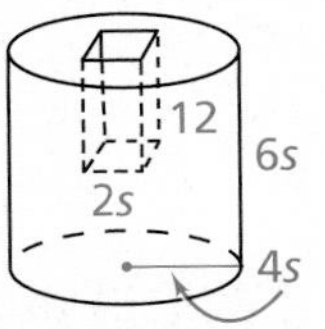

Check
$$x^2 - 9x + 20 \stackrel{?}{=} (x - 4)(x - 5)$$
$$x^2 - 9x + 20 \stackrel{?}{=} x^2 - 5x - 4x + 20$$
$$x^2 - 9x + 20 = x^2 - 9x + 20 \checkmark$$

← **Find the product of the right side.**

6. Critical Thinking Is $x^2 - 6x - 16 = (x - 8)(x + 2)$ factored correctly? Explain.

Example 3

Factor $x^2 - 2x - 8$.

Choose numbers that are factors of -8. Look for a pair with sum -2.

Factors of -8	Sum of Factors
-1 and 8	$-1 + 8 = 7$
-8 and 1	$-8 + 1 = -7$
-2 and 4	$-2 + 4 = 2$
-4 and 2	$-4 + 2 = -2$

← **-4 and 2 have a sum of -2.**

$x^2 - 2x - 8 = (x - 4)(x + 2)$

7. Try This Factor $x^2 - 4x - 12$.

Factoring $ax^2 + bx + c$

To factor quadratic trinomials where $a \neq 1$, list factors of a and c. Use these factors to write binomials. Test for the correct value for b.

Example 4

Factor $3x^2 - 7x - 6$.

List factors of 3: 1 and 3; -1 and -3.

List factors of -6: 1 and -6; -1 and 6; 2 and -3; -2 and 3.

Use the factors to write binomials. Look for -7 as the middle term.

$(\boxed{1}x + \boxed{1})(\boxed{3}x + \boxed{-6})$ $\quad -6x + 3x = -3x$

$(\boxed{1}x + \boxed{-6})(\boxed{3}x + \boxed{1})$ $\quad 1x - 18x = -17x$

$(\boxed{1}x + \boxed{-1})(\boxed{3}x + \boxed{6})$ $\quad 6x - 3x = 3x$

$(\boxed{1}x + \boxed{6})(\boxed{3}x + \boxed{-1})$ $\quad -1x + 18x = 17x$

$(\boxed{1}x + \boxed{2})(\boxed{3}x + \boxed{-3})$ $\quad -3x + 6x = 3x$

$(\boxed{1}x + \boxed{-3})(\boxed{3}x + \boxed{2})$ $\quad 2x - 9x = -7x$ **Correct!**

$3x^2 - 7x - 6 = (x - 3)(3x + 2)$.

8. Try This Factor $2x^2 - 3x - 5$.

Exercises ON YOUR OWN

Write the length and width of each rectangle as a binomial. Then write an expression for the area of each rectangle.

1. 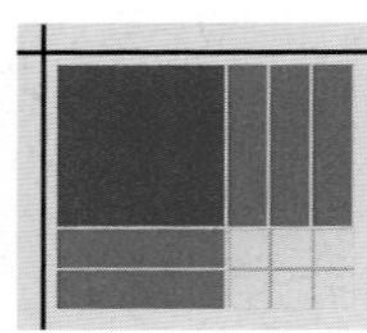

2. 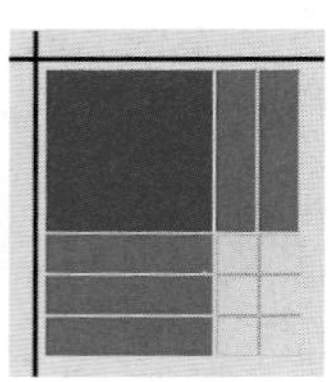

3. 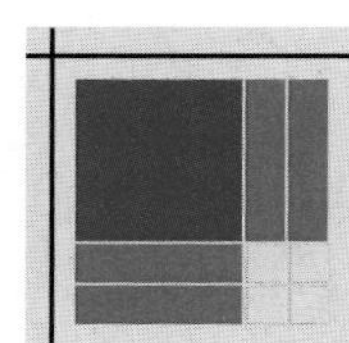

Can you form a rectangle using all the pieces in each set? Explain.

4. one x^2-tile, two x-tiles, and one 1-tile
5. one x^2-tile, five x-tiles, and eight 1-tiles
6. one x^2-tile, six x-tiles, and six 1-tiles
7. one x^2-tile, nine x-tiles, and eight 1-tiles

Use tiles or make drawings to represent each expression as a rectangle. Then write the area as the product of two binomials.

8. $x^2 + 4x + 3$
9. $x^2 - 3x + 2$
10. $x^2 + 3x - 4$
11. $x^2 - 2x - 8$
12. $x^2 + 5x + 6$
13. $x^2 - 3x - 4$
14. $x^2 + x - 6$
15. $x^2 - 2x + 1$

Complete.

16. $x^2 - 6x - 7 = (x + 1)(x + \blacksquare)$
17. $k^2 - 4k - 12 = (k - 6)(k + \blacksquare)$
18. $t^2 + 7t + 10 = (t + 2)(t + \blacksquare)$
19. $c^2 + c - 2 = (c + 2)(c + \blacksquare)$
20. $y^2 - 13y + 36 = (y - 4)(y + \blacksquare)$
21. $x^2 + 3x - 18 = (x + 6)(x + \blacksquare)$

22. **Writing** Suppose you can factor $x^2 + bx + c$ into the product of two binomials.
    a. Explain what you know about the factors if $c > 0$.
    b. Explain what you know about the factors if $c < 0$.

23. **Community Gardening** The diagram at the right shows 72 plots in a community garden.
    a. Write a quadratic expression that represents the area of the garden.
    b. Write the factors of the expression you wrote in part (a).

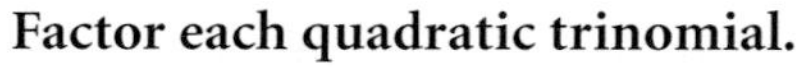

Factor each quadratic trinomial.

24. $x^2 + 6x + 8$
25. $a^2 - 5a + 6$
26. $d^2 - 7d + 12$
27. $k^2 + 9k + 8$
28. $y^2 - 4y - 45$
29. $r^2 - 10r - 11$
30. $c^2 + 2c + 1$
31. $x^2 + 2x - 15$
32. $t^2 + 7t - 18$
33. $x^2 + 12x + 35$
34. $y^2 - 10y + 16$
35. $a^2 - 9a + 14$
36. $r^2 + 6r - 16$
37. $y^2 + 13y - 48$
38. $x^2 + 10x + 25$
39. $w^2 - 2w - 24$

Open-ended **Find three different values to complete each expression so that it can be factored into the product of two binomials. Show each factorization.**

40. $x^2 - 3x - ■$ **41.** $x^2 + x - ■$ **42.** $x^2 + ■x + 12$

Factor each expression.

43. $2x^2 - 15x + 7$ **44.** $5x^2 - 2x - 7$ **45.** $2x^2 - x - 3$

46. $8x^2 - 14x + 3$ **47.** $2x^2 - 11x - 21$ **48.** $3x^2 + 13x - 10$

49. $2x^2 - 7x + 3$ **50.** $6t^2 + 13t - 5$ **51.** $7x^2 - 20x - 3$

52. $2x^2 + x - 3$ **53.** $3x^2 + 17x + 20$ **54.** $2x^2 + 3x - 20$

Chapter Project ***Find Out by Calculating***

20 ft

With aerial photography, you can study a forest of ponderosa pines without ever walking through it. To find the diameter in inches of trees in the forest, use this expression:

$3.76 + (1.35 \times 10^{-2})hv - (2.45 \times 10^{-6})hv^2 + (2.44 \times 10^{-10})hv^3$

The variable h is the height of the tree in feet, and v is the crown diameter visible in feet (from a photograph).

- Determine the diameter of 100-ft trees that have a visible crown diameter of 20 ft.

Exercises MIXED REVIEW

Find the distance between the given points.

55. $(3, 5); (6, 1)$ **56.** $(-2, 8); (4, -1)$

57. $(-7, -2); (-3, -9)$ **58.** $(8, 0); (-3, -4)$

Graph each inequality.

59. $y \leq 4x - 9$ **60.** $y > x^2 + 3x + 1$

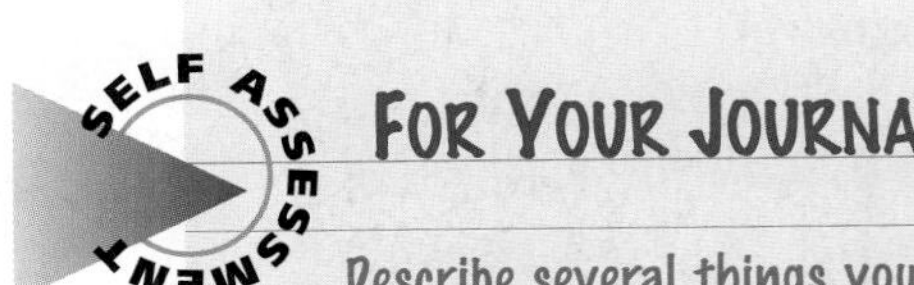

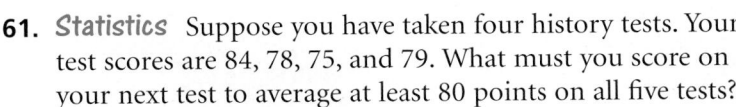

FOR YOUR JOURNAL

Describe several things you like and/or do not like about using tiles.

61. **Statistics** Suppose you have taken four history tests. Your test scores are 84, 78, 75, and 79. What must you score on your next test to average at least 80 points on all five tests?

Getting Ready for Lesson 10-5

Find each product.

62. $(x + 9)^2$ **63.** $(2x + 3)^2$ **64.** $(5x - 4)^2$ **65.** $(x + 8)(x - 8)$

66. $(x + 4)(x - 4)$ **67.** $(2x + 7)(2x - 7)$ **68.** $(3x + 5)(3x - 5)$ **69.** $(2x - 1)^2$

10-5 Factoring Special Cases

What You'll Learn

- Factoring the difference of two squares
- Factoring perfect square trinomials

...And Why

To solve problems related to geometry and construction

What You'll Need

- tiles
- graphing calculator

WORK TOGETHER

Work with a partner. Answer each question for Groups A, B, and C.

Group A	Group B	Group C
$(x + 7)(x - 7)$	$(x + 7)(x + 7)$	$(x - 7)(x - 7)$
$(k + 3)(k - 3)$	$(k + 3)(k + 3)$	$(k - 3)(k - 3)$
$(w + 5)(w - 5)$	$(w + 5)(w + 5)$	$(w - 5)(w - 5)$
$(3x + 1)(3x - 1)$	$(3x + 1)(3x + 1)$	$(3x - 1)(3x - 1)$

1. Describe the pattern in each of the pairs of factors.
2. Find each product.
3. How can you use mental math to quickly multiply binomials like those in each group? Explain using examples.

THINK AND DISCUSS

Factoring a Difference of Two Squares

As you saw in the Work Together activity, sometimes when you multiply two binomials, the *middle* term in the product is 0.

4. What polynomial is modeled by each set of tiles ? What are the factors of each polynomial?

a. 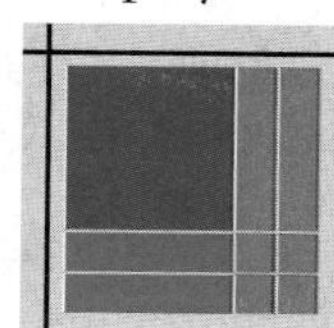

b. 

When you factor a difference of two squares, the result is two binomial factors that are the same except for the signs between the terms.

Difference of Two Squares

For all real numbers a and b, $a^2 - b^2 = (a + b)(a - b)$.

Example: $x^2 - 16 = (x + 4)(x - 4)$

Example 1

Factor $x^2 - 64$.

$x^2 - 64 = x^2 - 8^2$ ← Rewrite 64 as 8^2.

$= (x + 8)(x - 8)$ ← Factor.

Check Use FOIL to multiply.

$(x + 8)(x - 8)$

$x^2 - 8x + 8x - 64$

$x^2 - 64$ ✔

5. **Mental Math** Factor $x^2 - 36$.

Example 2

Factor $4x^2 - 121$.

$4x^2 - 121 = 4x^2 - 11^2$ ← Rewrite 121 as 11^2.

$= (2x)^2 - (11)^2$ ← Rewrite $4x^2$ as $(2x)^2$.

$= (2x + 11)(2x - 11)$ ← Factor.

QUICK REVIEW

For $a \neq 0$ and $b \neq 0$ and all integers n, $(ab)^n = a^n b^n$.

6. **Critical Thinking** Suppose a classmate factored $4x^2 - 121$ and got $(4x + 11)(4x - 11)$. What mistake did this classmate make?
7. **Mental Math** Factor $9x^2 - 25$.

Factoring a Perfect Square Trinomial

In the Work Together activity you multiplied a binomial by itself. This is called squaring a binomial. The result is a **perfect square trinomial.** When you factor a perfect square trinomial, the two binomial factors are the same.

Perfect Square Trinomial

For all real numbers a and b:

$$a^2 + 2ab + b^2 = (a + b)(a + b) = (a + b)^2$$
$$a^2 - 2ab + b^2 = (a - b)(a - b) = (a - b)^2$$

Examples:

$$x^2 + 10x + 25 = (x + 5)(x + 5) = (x + 5)^2$$
$$x^2 - 10x + 25 = (x - 5)(x - 5) = (x - 5)^2$$

Example 3

Factor $x^2 - 8x + 16$.

$x^2 - 8x + 16 = x^2 - 8x + 4^2$ ← Rewrite 16 as 4^2.

$= x^2 - 2(x)(4) + 4^2$ ← Does the middle term equal $2ab$? $8x = 2(x)(4)$ ✔

$= (x - 4)^2$ ← Factor as a squared binomial.

So, $x^2 - 8x + 16 = (x - 4)^2$.

8. a. *Graphing Calculator* Graph $y = x^2 - 8x + 16$.

b. Find the x-intercept(s) of the graph.

c. *Critical Thinking* What information about the factorization does the x-intercept(s) give you?

9. The expression $(3x + 4)^2$ equals $9x^2 + \blacksquare + 16$. What is the middle term?

Example 4

Factor $9x^2 + 12x + 4$

$9x^2 + 12x + 4$

$= (3x)^2 + 12x + 2^2$ ← Rewrite $9x^2$ as $(3x)^2$ and 4 as 2^2.

$= (3x)^2 + 2(3x)(2) + 2^2$ ← Does the middle term equal $2ab$? $12x = 2(3x)(2)$✔

$= (3x+ 2)^2$ ← Factor as a square binomial.

So, $9x^2 + 12x + 4 = (3x+ 2)^2$

PROBLEM SOLVING

Look Back Multiply the factors to check the factorization.

10. Try This Factor each trinomial.

a. $x^2 - 14x + 49$ **b.** $x^2 + 18x + 81$ **c.** $4x^2 - 12x + 9$

11. a. *Open-ended* Write a quadratic expression of your own that is a perfect square trinomial.

b. Explain how you know your trinomial is a perfect square trinomial.

Sometimes a quadratic expression looks like it can't be factored when actually it can. Take out any common factors. Then see if you can factor further.

Example 5

Factor $10x^2 - 40$.

$10x^2 - 40 = 10(x^2 - 4)$ ← Factor out the GCF: 10.

$= 10(x - 2)(x + 2)$ ← Factor $(x^2 - 4)$.

So, $10x^2 - 40 = 10(x - 2)(x + 2)$.

12. Try This Factor $8x^2 - 50$.

Exercises ON YOUR OWN

What polynomial is modeled by each set of tiles and what are the factors of each polynomial?

1. 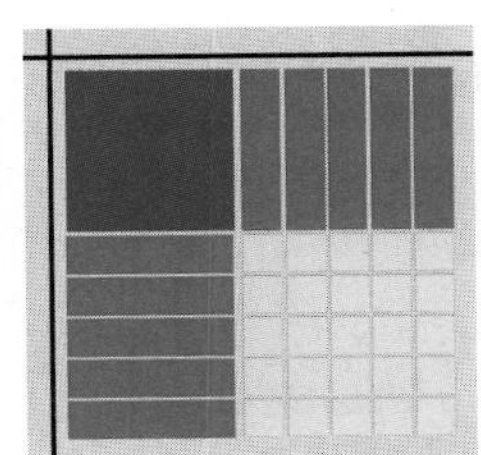

2. 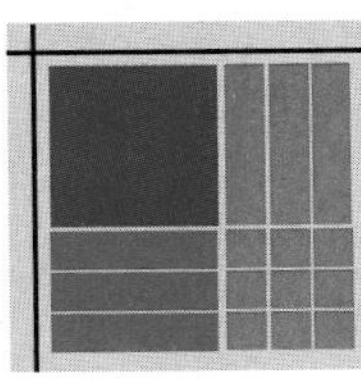

3. 

4. a. **Open-ended** Use a minimum of three x^2-tiles, one x-tile, and one 1-tile. Draw the model of the difference of two squares and a model of a perfect square trinomial.
   b. Represent each model from part (a) as a polynomial in both factored and unfactored form.

Factor each expression.

5. $x^2 + 2x + 1$
6. $t^2 - 144$
7. $x^2 - 18x + 81$
8. $15t^2 - 15$
9. $3x^2 - 6x + 3$
10. $9w^2 - 16$
11. $6x^2 - 150$
12. $k^2 - 6k + 9$
13. $x^2 - 49$
14. $a^2 + 12a + 36$
15. $4x^2 - 4x + 1$
16. $16n^2 - 56n + 49$
17. $9x^2 + 6x + 1$
18. $2g^2 + 24g + 72$
19. $x^2 - 400$
20. $2x^3 - 18x$

21. **Writing** **Summarize** the procedure for factoring a perfect square trinomial. Give at least two examples.

22. **Math in the Media** Use the brochure below.
   a. Show by factoring that this inequality is true.
   $(\pi d - \sqrt{15w})(\pi d + \sqrt{15w}) \geq 0$
   b. Show that $d \geq \dfrac{\sqrt{15w}}{\pi}$.
   c. **Calculator** Is a cable 3 in. in diameter sufficient to lift an object weighing 5 tons? **Justify** your response.

Load Requirements For Crane Operators

The weight of a load is limited by the diameter of the fiber cable. As the load gets heavier, the diameter of the cable must increase. To raise a load weighing w tons, a fiber cable having diameter d in inches must satisfy the inequality $(\pi d)^2 - (\sqrt{15w})^2 \geq 0$.

23. a. *Geometry* Write two expressions in terms of n and m for the area of the solid region at the right. One expression should be in factored form.

b. Use either form of your answer to part (a). Find the area of the solid region if $n = 10$ in. and $m = 3$ in.

24. *Standardized Test Prep* Which of the following expressions is the factorization of $100x^2 + 220x + 121$?

A. $(10x + 1)(10x - 1)$ B. $(10x - 11)(10x - 11)$
C. $(10x + 11)(10x + 11)$ D. $(10x - 10)(11x + 11)$

Mental Math **Find each product using the difference of two squares.**

Sample: $(17)(23) = (20 - 3)(20 + 3)$ ← Write the factors in the form $(a - b)(a + b)$.
$= 400 - 9$ ← Multiply.
$= 391$ ← Subtract.

25. $(27)(33)$ 26. $(19)(21)$ 27. $(43)(37)$ 28. $(29)(31)$

29. $(16)(24)$ 30. $(51)(49)$ 31. $(18)(22)$ 32. $(98)(102)$

Factor each expression using rational numbers in your factors.

33. $\frac{1}{4}m^2 - \frac{1}{9}$ 34. $\frac{1}{4}p^2 - 2p + 4$ 35. $\frac{1}{9}n^2 - \frac{1}{25}$ 36. $\frac{1}{25}k^2 + \frac{6}{5}k + 9$

37. a. *Critical Thinking* The expression $(t - 3)^2 - 16$ is a difference of two squares. Using the expression $a^2 - b^2$, identify a and b.

b. Factor $(t - 3)^2 - 16$.

38. a. *Graphing Calculator* Graph $y = 4x^2 - 12x + 9$.

b. Use the x-intercept(s) of the graph to write $4x^2 - 12x + 9$ in factored form.

Exercises MIXED REVIEW

Simplify each expression.

39. $\sqrt{25} + \sqrt{72}$ 40. $8^2 - (4 + \sqrt{8})$ 41. $\sqrt{5^2 + 4^2}$ 42. $\sqrt{100} - \sqrt{4}$

43. *Sales* Suppose you buy a watch for \$35 that regularly sells for \$50. Find the percent of decrease in the price of the watch.

Getting Ready for Lesson 10-6

Solve each equation.

44. $2x + 3 = 0$ 45. $-3x - 4 = 0$

46. $8x - 9 = 0$ 47. $-3x + 5 = 0$

10-6 Solving Equations by Factoring

What You'll Learn

- Solving quadratic equations by factoring

...And Why

To find the dimensions of a box that can be manufactured from a given amount of material

What You'll Need

- graphing calculator

THINK AND DISCUSS

When you solve a quadratic equation by factoring, you use the zero-product property.

Zero-Product Property

For all real numbers a and b, if $ab = 0$, then $a = 0$ or $b = 0$.

Example: If $(x + 3)(x + 2) = 0$, then $x + 3 = 0$ or $x + 2 = 0$.

Example 1

Solve $(x + 5)(x + 6) = 0$.

$(x + 5)(x + 6) = 0$
$x + 5 = 0$ or $x + 6 = 0$ ← Use the zero-product property.
$x = -5$ or $x = -6$ ← Solve for x.

The solutions are -5 and -6.

Check Substitute -5 for x.
$(-5 + 5)(-5 + 6) \stackrel{?}{=} 0$
$(0)(1) = 0$ ✔

Substitute -6 for x.
$(-6 + 5)(-6 + 6) \stackrel{?}{=} 0$
$(-1)(0) = 0$ ✔

PROBLEM SOLVING

Look Back How could you solve $(x + 5)(x + 6) = 0$ by graphing?

1. Try This Solve each equation.

a. $(x + 7)(x - 4) = 0$

b. $(3y - 5)(y - 2) = 0$

You can sometimes solve a quadratic equation by factoring. Write the equation in standard form. Factor the quadratic expression. Then use the zero-product property.

Example 2

Solve $2x^2 - 5x = 88$ by factoring.

$2x^2 - 5x = 88$
$2x^2 - 5x - 88 = 0$ ← Subtract 88 from each side.
$(2x + 11)(x - 8) = 0$ ← Factor $2x^2 - 5x - 88$.

$2x + 11 = 0$ or $x - 8 = 0$ ← Use the zero-product property.
$x = -5.5$ or $x = 8$ ← Solve for x.

The solutions are -5.5 and 8.

2. a. *Graphing Calculator* Graph $y = 2x^2 - 5x - 88$.
   b. In the  feature, use ROOT to find the x-intercepts of the graph.
   c. Explain how your answers to part (b) are related to the solutions found in Example 2.

3. a. Solve $x^2 - 12x + 36 = 0$ by factoring.
   b. *Critical Thinking* Why does the equation in part (a) have only one solution?

You can solve some real-world problems by factoring and using the zero-product property.

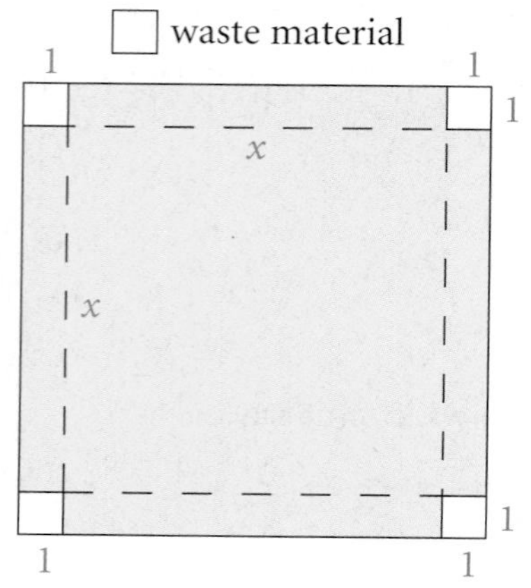

Example 3 Relating to the Real World 

Manufacturing The diagram shows a pattern for an open-top box. The total area of the sheet of material used to manufacture the box is 144 in.^{2}. The height of the box is 1 in. Therefore 1 in. $\times$ 1 in. squares are cut from each corner. Find the dimensions of the box.

Define width $= x + 1 + 1 = x + 2$
length $= x + 1 + 1 = x + 2$

Relate length $\times$ width $=$ area

Write $(x + 2)(x + 2) = 144$

$(x + 2)(x + 2) = 144$

$x^2 + 4x + 4 = 144$ ← Find the product $(x + 2)(x + 2)$.

$x^2 + 4x - 140 = 0$ ← Subtract 144 from each side.

$(x + 14)(x - 10) = 0$ ← Factor $x^2 + 4x - 140$.

$x + 14 = 0$ or $x - 10 = 0$ ← Use the zero-product property.

$x = -14$ or $x = 10$

Since the length must be positive, the solution is 10. The dimensions of the box are 10 in. $\times$ 10 in. $\times$ 1 in.

4. Suppose that a box with a square base has height 2 in. It is cut from a square sheet of material with area 121 in.^{2}. Find the dimensions of the box.

Exercises ON YOUR OWN

Mental Math **Use mental math to solve each equation.**

1. $(x - 3)(x - 7) = 0$
2. $(x + 4)(2x - 9) = 0$
3. $(7x + 2)(5x + 4) = 0$

Solve each equation by factoring.

4. $b^2 + 3b - 4 = 0$
5. $m^2 - 5m - 14 = 0$
6. $w^2 - 8w = 0$
7. $x^2 - 16x + 55 = 0$
8. $x^2 - 3x - 10 = 0$
9. $n^2 + n - 12 = 0$
10. $2x^2 - 7x + 5 = 0$
11. $x^2 - 10x = 0$
12. $4x^2 - 25 = 0$
13. $5q^2 + 18q = 8$
14. $z^2 - 5z = -6$
15. $10 = x^2 - 9x$

16. **Writing** **Summarize** the procedure for solving a quadratic equation by factoring. Include an example.

17. **Geometry** The sides of a square are each increased by 3 cm. The area of the new square is 64 cm^2. Find the length of a side of the original square.

Simplify each equation and write it in standard form. Then solve each equation.

18. $3a^2 + 4a = 2a^2 - 2a - 9$
19. $4x^2 + 20 = 10x + 3x^2 - 4$
20. $6y^2 + 12y + 13 = 2y^2 + 4$
21. $2q^2 + 22q = -60$
22. $3t^2 + 8t = t^2 - 3t - 12$
23. $4 = -5n + 6n^2$
24. $3x^2 = 9x + 30$
25. $20p^2 - 74 = 6$
26. $2x^2 + 5x^2 = 3x$
27. $7n^2 = 3n^2 + 100$
28. $12x^2 + 8x = -4x^2 + 8x$
29. $9c^2 = 36$

30. **Standardized Test Prep** If $a^2 + b^2 = 9$ and $ab = 6$, what does $(a + b)^2$ equal?
    A. 3 **B.** 15 **C.** 21 **D.** 30 **E.** 36

31. **Geometry** A rectangular box has volume 280 in.^{3}. Its dimensions are 4 in. × $(x + 2)$ in. × $(x + 5)$ in. Find x. Use the formula $V = lwh$.

32. **Baseball** Suppose you throw a baseball into the air from a starting height s. You toss the ball with an upward starting velocity of v ft/s. You can use the equation $h = -16t^2 + vt + s$ to find the ball's height h in feet t seconds after it is thrown.
    a. Suppose you toss a baseball directly upward with an starting velocity of 46 ft/s from a starting height of 6 ft. When will the ball hit the ground?
    b. **Graphing Calculator** Graph the related function for the equation you wrote in part (a). Use your graph to estimate how high the ball is tossed.

33. ***Sailing*** The height of a right-triangular sail on a boat is 2 ft greater than twice the base of the sail. Suppose the area of the sail is 110 ft^2.

a. Find the dimensions of the sail.

b. Find the approximate length of the hypotenuse of the sail. (*Hint:* Use the Pythagorean theorem $(c^2 = a^2 + b^2)$.)

34. ***Construction*** You are building a rectangular wading pool. You want the area of the bottom to be 90 ft^2. You want the length of the pool to be 3 ft longer than twice its width. What will be the dimensions of the pool?

Solve each cubic equation.

Sample: $x^3 + 7x^2 + 12x = 0$ ← The highest degree of a term is three. This is a cubic equation.

$x^3 + 7x^2 + 12x = 0$

$x(x^2 + 7x + 12) = 0$ ← Factor out the GCF.

$x(x + 3)(x + 4) = 0$ ← Factor the quadratic trinomial.

$x = 0,\ x + 3 = 0, \text{ or } x + 4 = 0$ ← Use the zero-product property.

$x = 0, \quad x = -3, \quad \text{or} \quad x = -4$ ← Solve for x.

The solutions are 0, −3, and −4.

35. $x^3 - 10x^2 + 24x = 0$

36. $x^3 - 5x^2 + 4x = 0$

37. $3x^3 - 9x^2 = 0$

38. $x^3 + 3x^2 - 70x = 0$

39. $3x^3 - 30x^2 + 27x = 0$

40. $2x^3 = -2x^2 + 40x$

In each diagram, you are given a right triangle that has special characteristics. Use the Pythagorean theorem ($c^2 = a^2 + b^2$) to find possible lengths of the sides of each right triangle.

41. three consecutive integers

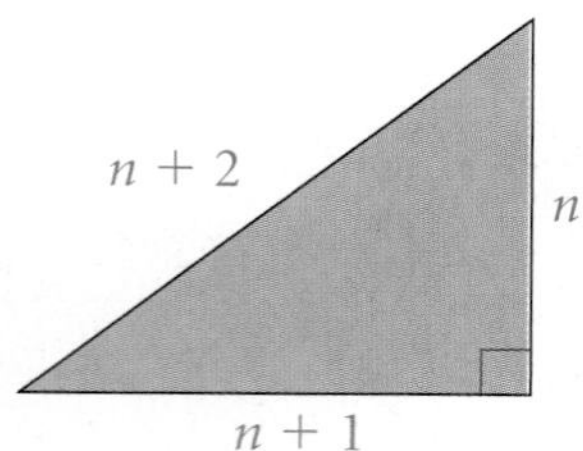

42. three consecutive even integers

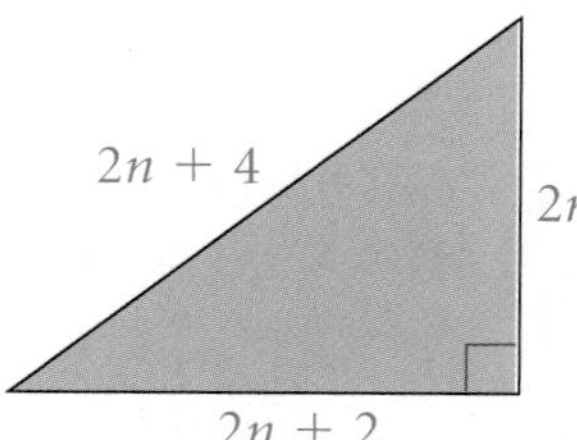

43. ***Critical Thinking*** A number plus its square equals zero. For which two numbers is this true?

44. ***Open-ended*** In the diagram at the right, x is a positive integer and a and b are integers. List several possible values for x, a, and b so that the large rectangle will have an area of 56 square units.

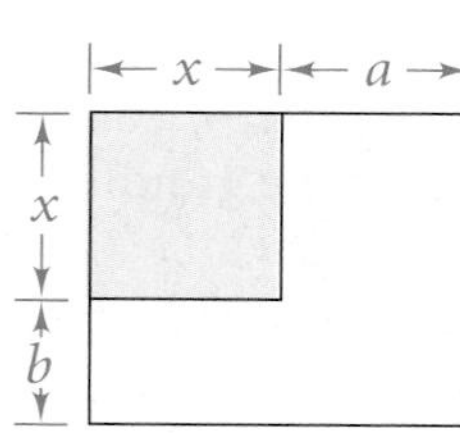

45. ***Manufacturing*** An open box with height 1 in. has a length that is 2 in. greater than its width. The box was made with minimum waste from an 80 $in.^2$ rectangular sheet of material. What were the dimensions of the sheet of material? (*Hint:* Draw a diagram.)

Chapter Project ***Find Out by Graphing***

You can use the function $b = -0.01t^2 + 0.8t$ to find the number of bushels b of walnuts produced on an acre of land. The variable t represents the number of trees per acre.

- Graph this function. What number of trees per acre gives the greatest yield?
- How many walnut trees would you advise a farmer to plant on 5 acres of land? Explain your reasoning.

Exercises MIXED REVIEW

Simplify.

46. $(x^2)^4$ **47.** $(3y^3)^{-1}$ **48.** $4(n^3)^0$ **49.** $(x^3)(x^{-3})$

Solve each equation.

50. $\sqrt{a} = 5$ **51.** $\sqrt{3a} = 5$ **52.** $3\sqrt{a} = \sqrt{a} + 18$

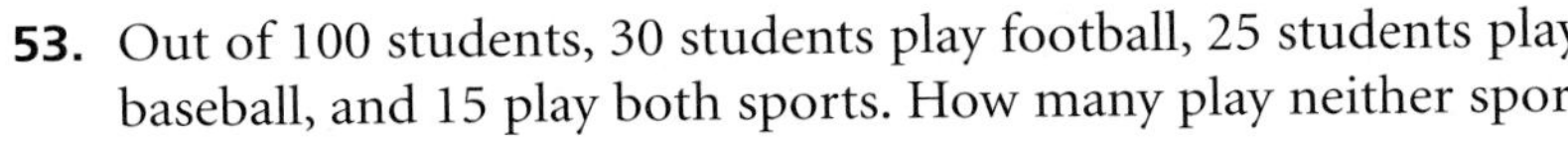

53. Out of 100 students, 30 students play football, 25 students play baseball, and 15 play both sports. How many play neither sport?

SELF ASSESSMENT **FOR YOUR JOURNAL**

Suppose you are to solve $2x^2 - 11x + 5 = 0$. Would you use the quadratic formula or factoring? Explain why.

Getting Ready for Lesson 10-7

Use the quadratic formula to solve each equation. If there is no real solution, write *no real solution*.

54. $x^2 + x - 12 = 0$ **55.** $10x^2 + 13x - 3 = 0$ **56.** $4x^2 + 4x + 3 = 0$

Exercises CHECKPOINT

Factor.

1. $x^2 - 5x + 6$ **2.** $n^2 - 6n + 9$ **3.** $g^2 - 8g - 20$ **4.** $9x^2 - 49$

Mental Math **Use mental math to solve each equation.**

5. $(a + 3)(3a - 2) = 0$ **6.** $(m - 6)(2m + 3) = 0$ **7.** $(x + 7)(x + 2) = 0$

Solve each equation.

8. $25x^2 - 100 = 0$ **9.** $9x^2 + 24x = -16$ **10.** $10x^2 - 11x - 6 = 0$

11. Standardized Test Prep If $x^2 + 4x = -4$, what is the value of x^3?
A. -8 **B.** 0 **C.** 8 **D.** 16
E. It cannot be determined from the information given.

Math ToolboX

Skills Review

Completing the Square

After Lesson 10-6

In Chapter 7, you solved quadratic equations by taking the square root of each side of an equation. In Lesson 10-5 you factored perfect square trinomials. Completing the square allows you to combine these skills to solve any quadratic equation that has real solutions.

What is the value of c needed to create a perfect square trinomial?

1. $y^2 + 4y + c$ **2.** $a^2 - 10a + c$ **3.** $n^2 + 14n + c$ **4.** $x^2 - 20x + c$

5. Explain the steps you used to find c in Questions 1–4.

To solve an equation using completing the square, you create a perfect square trinomial on one side of the equation so that you can take the square root of both sides.

Example

Solve by completing the square: $x^2 + 6x + 4 = 0$.

$x^2 + 6x + 4 = 0$

$x^2 + 6x = -4$ ⟵ Subtract 4 from each side.

$x^2 + 6x + 3^2 = -4 + 3^2$ ⟵ Find half of 6. Square it, and add the result to both sides.

$x^2 + 6x + 9 = 5$ ⟵ Simplify.

$(x + 3)^2 = 5$ ⟵ Write the left side in factored form.

$\sqrt{(x + 3)^2} = \pm\sqrt{5}$ ⟵ Take the square root of each side.

$x + 3 = \pm\sqrt{5}$ ⟵ Simplify.

$x = -3 + \sqrt{5}$ or $x = -3 - \sqrt{5}$ ⟵ Solve for x.

The solutions are $-3 \pm \sqrt{5}$.

Solve each equation by completing the square.

6. $x^2 - 2x - 3 = 0$ **7.** $x^2 + 8x + 12 = 0$ **8.** $x^2 + 2x = 8$ **9.** $x^2 + 6x = 16$

10. $x^2 + 10x = 16$ **11.** $x^2 + 4x = 12$ **12.** $x^2 - 4x = 3$ **13.** $x^2 - 4x - 45 = 0$

14. $x^2 - 12x = 4$ **15.** $x^2 + 10x = 10$ **16.** $x^2 - 6x = 10$ **17.** $x^2 + 8x + 3 = 0$

18. *Writing* Solve one of the equations in Exercises 6–17 using the quadratic formula. Which method do you prefer, completing the square or the quadratic formula? Why?

10-7 Choosing an Appropriate Method for Solving

What You'll Learn

- Choosing the best way to solve a quadratic equation

...And Why

To choose efficient ways to solve construction problems

What You'll Need

- graphing calculator

THINK AND DISCUSS

In this chapter and in Chapter 7, you learned many methods for solving quadratic equations. You can always use the quadratic formula to solve a quadratic equation, but sometimes another method may be easier. Other methods include graphing and factoring.

Methods for Solving Quadratic Equations

Example: $2x^2 - 4x - 6 = 0$

Graphing

Graph the related function.

$y = 2x^2 - 4x - 6$

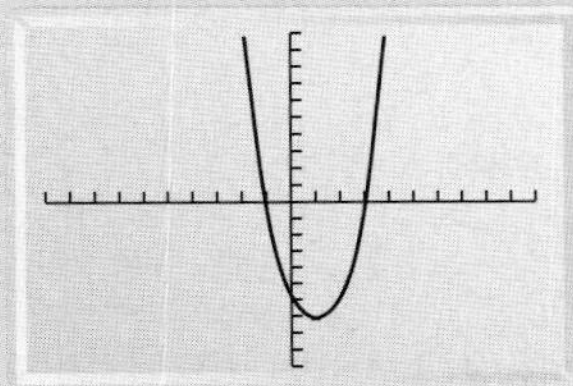

The x-intercepts are –1 and 3.

Quadratic Formula

If $ax^2 + bx + c = 0$ and $a \neq 0$,

$$x = \frac{-b \pm \sqrt{b^2 - 4ac}}{2a}.$$

$$x = \frac{-(-4) \pm \sqrt{(-4)^2 - (4)(2)(-6)}}{2(2)}$$

$$= \frac{4 \pm \sqrt{64}}{4}$$

$$= \frac{12}{4} \text{ or } \frac{-4}{4}$$

$$= 3 \text{ or } -1$$

Factoring

Factor the equation. Use the zero-product property.

$$2x^2 - 4x - 6 = 0$$

$$(2x - 6)(x + 1) = 0$$

$$2x - 6 = 0 \text{ or } x + 1 = 0$$

$$2x = 6$$

$$x = 3 \text{ or } x = -1$$

When you have an equation to solve, first write it in standard form. Then decide which method to use.

Method	When to Use
Graphing	Use if you have a graphing calculator handy.
Square Roots	Use if the equation has only an x^2 term and a constant term.
Factoring	Use if you can factor the equation easily.
Quadratic Formula	Use if you cannot factor the equation or if you are using a scientific calculator.

1. ***Open-ended*** Which method(s) would you choose to solve each equation? **Justify** your reasoning.
   - **a.** $2x^2 - 6 = 0$
   - **b.** $9x^2 + 24x + 16 = 0$
   - **c.** $25x^2 - 36 = 0$
   - **d.** $6x^2 + 5x - 6 = 0$
   - **e.** $2x^2 + 7x - 15 = 0$
   - **f.** $16t^2 - 96t + 135 = 0$

PROBLEM SOLVING HINT

Draw a diagram.

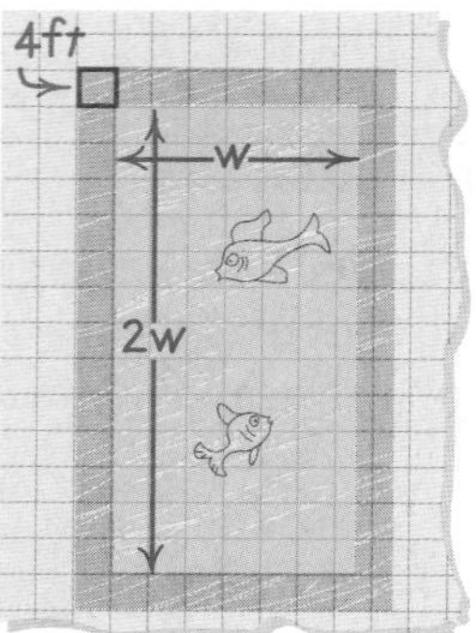

Example 1 Relating to the Real World 

City Parks A fountain has dimensions w and $2w$. The concrete walkway around it is 4 ft wide. Together, the fountain and walkway cover 1500 ft^2 of land. Find the dimensions of the fountain.

Define $w =$ width of fountain $\quad 2w =$ length of fountain

$w + 2(4) = w + 8 =$ width of fountain and walkway

$2w + 2(4) = 2w + 8 =$ length of fountain and walkway

Relate	width of fountain and walkway	times ↓	length of fountain and walkway	= ↓	area of fountain and walkway
Write	$(w + 8)$	$\cdot$	$(2w + 8)$	$=$	1500

$$(w + 8)(2w + 8) = 1500$$

$$2w^2 + 24w + 64 = 1500 \quad \leftarrow \text{Expand the product.}$$

$$2w^2 + 24w - 1436 = 0 \quad \leftarrow \text{Write in standard form.}$$

$$w = \frac{-24 \pm \sqrt{24^2 - 4(2)(-1436)}}{2(2)} \quad \leftarrow \text{Use the quadratic formula.}$$

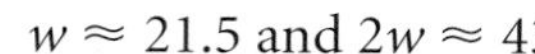

$$w = \frac{-24 + 109.8}{4} \quad \leftarrow \text{Take the positive square root.}$$

$$w \approx 21.5 \text{ and } 2w \approx 43$$

The fountain is about 21.5 ft wide and about 43 ft long.

2. **Critical Thinking** Why would using the negative square root have led to an unreasonable solution of Example 1?

3. Which of the methods for solving quadratic equations would *not* be appropriate for solving Example 1? Explain.

Example 2

Solve $7x^2 - 175 = 0$.

Because this equation has only an x^2 term and a constant, try taking the square root of both sides or factoring a difference of two squares.

Method 1 Square roots

$$7x^2 - 175 = 0$$
$$7x^2 = 175$$
$$x^2 = 25$$
$$x = \pm 5$$
$$x = 5 \text{ or } x = -5$$

Method 2 Factoring

$$7x^2 - 175 = 0$$
$$7(x^2 - 25) = 0$$
$$7(x - 5)(x + 5) = 0$$
$$x - 5 = 0 \text{ or } x + 5 = 0$$
$$x = 5 \text{ or } x = -5$$

Both methods give the same solutions.

QUICK REVIEW

Zero-Product Property

For all real numbers a and b, if $ab = 0$, then $a = 0$ or $b = 0$.

4. **Try This** Solve each equation.
   a. $4x^2 = 256$ **b.** $y^2 - 12 = 0$ **c.** $3t^2 - 192 = 0$

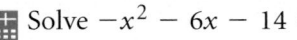

Example 3

Solve $-x^2 - 6x - 14 = 0$.

The equation cannot be easily factored, so you can use a graphing calculator.

Graph the related quadratic function $y = -x^2 - 6x - 14$. The related function has no x-intercepts. Therefore, the equation $-x^2 - 6x - 14 = 0$ has no real solutions.

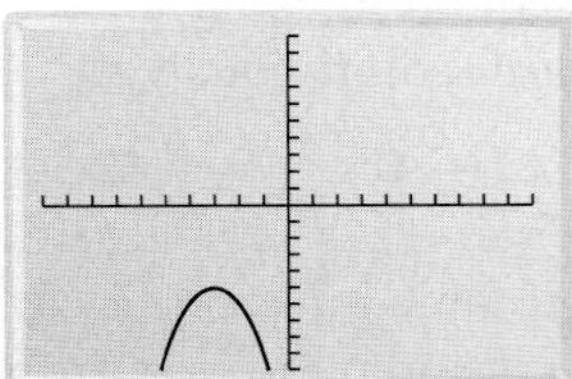

QUICK REVIEW

For a quadratic equation in standard form, the discriminant is $b^2 - 4ac$.

If $b^2 - 4ac < 0$, then there are no real number solutions.

5. Use the discriminant to show why the equation in Example 3 has no real number solutions.

6. **Try This** Solve each equation by graphing.
   a. $x^2 - 4x - 11 = 0$ **b.** $2x^2 + 7x - 15 = 0$

You can also use the discriminant to check if an equation can be factored. If the discriminant is a perfect square, then there are two rational solutions, and the equation can be factored.

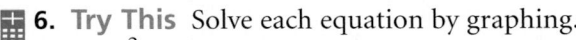

Example 4

Solve $2x^2 - 7x - 4 = 0$.

First, find the discriminant to determine if the equation can be factored.

$$\begin{aligned} b^2 - 4ac &= (-7)^2 - (4)(2)(-4) \\ &= 49 - (-32) \\ &= 81 \end{aligned}$$

Since the discriminant is a perfect square, you can factor.

$(x - 4)(2x + 1) = 0$ ← Use guess and test to factor.

$x - 4 = 0$ or $2x + 1 = 0$ ← Use the zero-product property.

$x = 4$ or $x = -0.5$ ← Solve for x.

PROBLEM SOLVING

Look Back Check the solutions of Example 4.

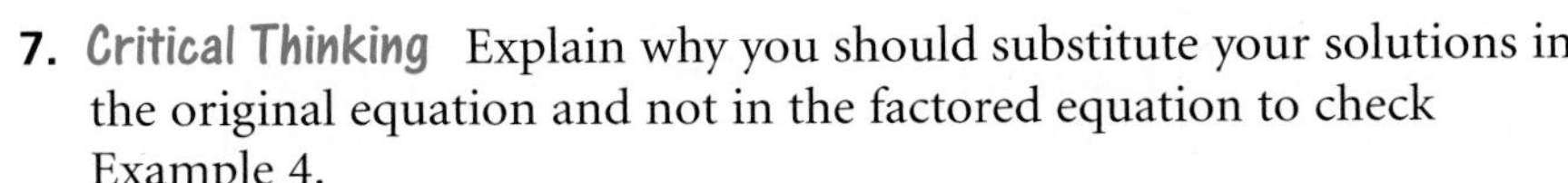
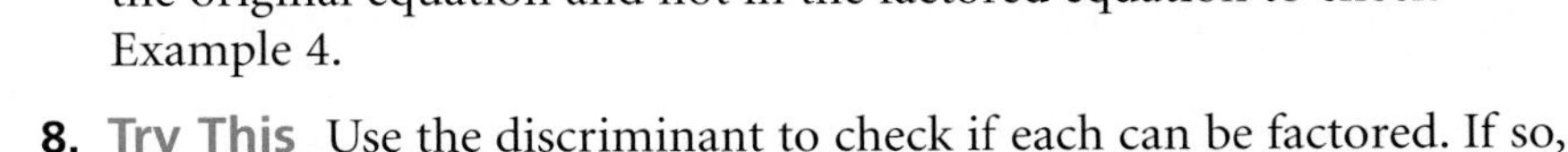

7. **Critical Thinking** Explain why you should substitute your solutions in the original equation and not in the factored equation to check Example 4.

8. **Try This** Use the discriminant to check if each can be factored. If so, solve each by factoring. Otherwise, use the quadratic formula.
   a. $5x^2 + 14x - 3 = 0$ **b.** $3c^2 - 6c + 1 = 0$
   c. $2d^2 - d + 1 = 0$ **d.** $6y^2 - 5y - 4 = 0$

Exercises ON YOUR OWN

Calculator **Use the quadratic formula to solve each equation. Round solutions to the nearest hundredth.**

1. $13x^2 + 170x + 13 = 0$
2. $2.5w^2 + 10w - 2 = 0$
3. $12n^2 + n = 20$
4. $49x^2 - 64x = 25$
5. $6x^2 - 2x + 4 = 0$
6. $-x^2 - 5x + 9 = 0$

Solve each equation using square roots and then using factoring. Compare your solutions.

7. $9d^2 - 81 = 0$
8. $36e^2 = 121$
9. $2n^2 - 8 = 0$
10. $98 = 128x^2$

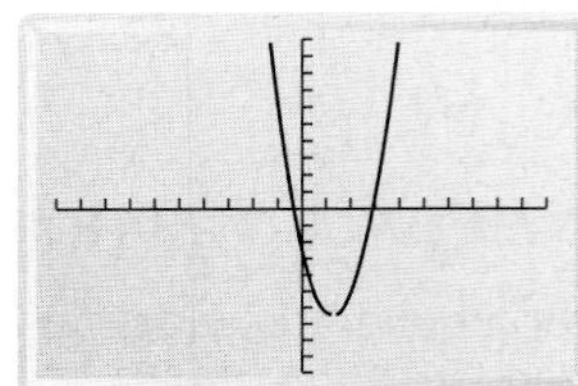

11. **a.** Find the x-intercepts of the parabola at the right.
    b. Use the graph to find the solutions of the equation $2x^2 - 5x - 3 = 0$.
    c. **Verify** your answer to part (b) by solving the equation using factoring.
12. **Writing** Explain how to solve $x^2 + 8 = 7x$ by graphing.

Graphing Calculator **Solve each quadratic equation by graphing the related quadratic function and finding the x-intercepts. If there are no real solutions, write *no real solutions*.**

13. $x^2 + 2x - 8 = 0$
14. $2x^2 + 3x = 6$
15. $x^2 - 2x + 5 = 0$
16. $8x^2 - 4x - 16 = 0$
17. $0.5x^2 + x = -2$
18. $x^2 = 2x$

Choose **Select a method to solve each quadratic equation. Explain why you chose each method. Then solve. If the equation has no real solutions, write *no real solutions*.**

19. $2k^2 = 16k - 32$
20. $4t^2 + 8t + 8 = 0$
21. $8n = 10n^2$
22. $-y^2 + y = -3$
23. $3k^2 - 9k - 27 = 0$
24. $36g^2 = 121$
25. $16k^2 - 56k + 49 = 0$
26. $1.5r^2 + 2r - 2.5 = 0$
27. $169 = 49b^2$
28. $5a^2 + 7a = 7a^2 + 5a - 2$
29. **Standardized Test Prep** Which quadratic equation has 2 and -7 as its solutions?
    A. $x^2 + 5x + 14 = 0$
    B. $x^2 + 5x - 14 = 0$
    C. $x^2 - 5x + 14 = 0$
    D. $x^2 - 5x - 14 = 0$
30. Show that the man in the cartoon is not a whiz at physics. Suppose he steps off the board. Use $0 = -16t^2 + 50$ to find the number of seconds before he hits the water. Use $v = -32t \cdot \frac{60}{88}$ to find his velocity in miles per hour when he hits the water.

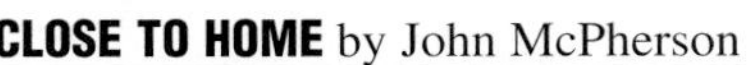

There are times when being a whiz at physics can be a definite drawback.

31. ***Surveying*** To find the distance across a marsh, a surveyor marked off a right triangle and measured two sides. Solve the equation $d^2 = 150^2 + 75^2$ to find this distance. Explain what solution method you used and why.

32. ***Geometry*** Find all values of x such that rectangle $ACDG$ at the right has an area of 70 square units *and* rectangle $ABEF$ has an area of 72 square units.

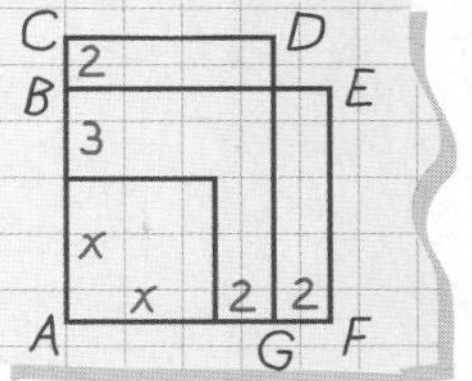

33. ***Open-ended*** Create an area situation and a question you can answer by solving a quadratic equation. Illustrate and solve your problem.

Exercises MIXED REVIEW

Find the minimum and maximum of each equation.

34. $x \geq 0, y \geq 0$
$x \leq 5$
$y \leq 4$
$C = x + 2y$

35. $x + y \leq 10$
$x \geq 2$
$y \geq 3$
$C = 2x + 3y$

36. $2x + y \leq 7$
$x \geq 0$
$y \geq 0$
$C = 4x + y$

37. Describe the graph of $y = x^2 - 4x + 3$. Where is the axis of symmetry? What is the y-intercept? What are the roots?

38. Find the product of $3x$ and $4x^2 - 2x + 5$.

PORTFOLIO

For your portfolio, select one or two items from your work for this chapter:

- corrected work
- diagrams, graphs, or charts
- a journal entry

Explain why you have included each selection that you make.

A Point in Time

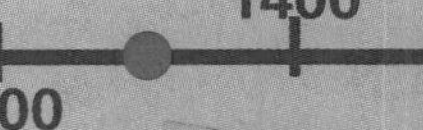

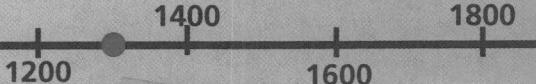

Chu Shih-Chieh

Very little is known about the life of Chu Shih-Chieh, the Chinese mathematician and teacher who had many pupils during the last two decades of the 1200s. In 1303 Chu wrote *Ssu-yüan-yü-chien*, "The Precious Mirror of the Four Elements." He described what is now known as Pascal's Triangle and how it could be used to solve polynomial equations. He also invented "the method of the celestial element" to write and solve polynomial equations and linear systems with up to four variables.

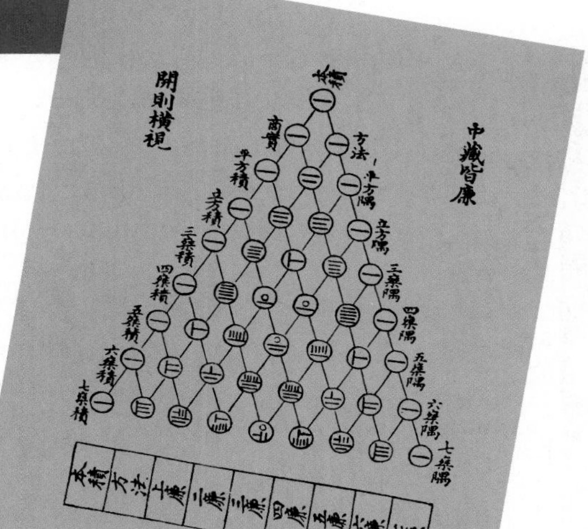

Finishing the Chapter Project

Trees are us.

Questions on pages 474, 479, 485, and 495 should help you to complete your project. Assemble all the parts of your project in a notebook. Add a summary telling what you have learned about the uses of trees.

Reflect and Revise

Ask a classmate to review your project notebook with you. Together, check that your graphs are clearly labeled and accurate. Check that you have used formulas correctly and that your calculations are accurate. Make any revisions necessary to improve your work.

Follow Up

Trees have many uses that you could investigate. You can do more research by contacting the United States Department of Agriculture Forest Service or a local, state, or national park. You can also get more information by using the Internet or one of the resources listed below.

For M Information

Hoadley, R. Bruce. *Identifying Wood: Accurate Results with Simple Tools.* Newtown, Connecticut: Taunton Press, 1990.

Miller, Cameron. *Woodlore.* New York: Ticknor & Fields Books for Young Readers, 1995.

The Encyclopedia of Wood. Alexandria, Virginia: Time-Life Books, 1993.

Warren, Jean. *Exploring Wood and the Forest.* Everett, Washington: Warren Publishing House, 1993.

CHAPTER

10 Wrap Up

Key Terms

binomial (p. 465)
binomial factors (p. 481)
degree of a polynomial (p. 465)
degree of a term (p. 465)
difference of two squares (p. 487)
monomial (p. 465)
perfect square trinomial (p. 487)
polynomial (p. 465)
standard form (p. 465)
trinomial (p. 465)
zero-product property (p. 491)

How am I doing?

- State three ideas from this chapter that you think are important. Explain your choices.
- Explain the different methods you can use to factor $2x^2 + 7x - 15$.

Adding and Subtracting Polynomials — 10-1

The **degree of a term** with one variable is the exponent of the variable. A **polynomial** is one term or the sum or difference of two or more terms. The **degree of a polynomial** is the same as the degree of the term with the highest degree. A polynomial can be named by its degree or by the number of its terms. You can simplify polynomials by adding the coefficients of like terms.

Find each sum or difference.

1. $(3x^3 + 8x^2 + 2x + 9) - (-4x^3 + 5x - 3)$

2. $(3g^4 + 5g^2 + 5) + (5g^4 - 10g^2 + 11g)$

3. $(-4b^5 + 3b^3 - b + 10) + (3b^5 - b^3 + b - 4)$

4. $(2t^3 - 4t^2 + 9t - 7) - (t^3 + t^2 - 3t + 1)$

5. ***Open-ended*** Write a polynomial using the variable z. What is the degree of your polynomial?

Multiplying and Factoring — 10-2

You can use the distributive property or tiles to multiply polynomials. You can factor a polynomial by finding the greatest common factor (GCF) of the terms of the polynomial, or by using tiles.

Find each product. Write it in standard form.

6. $8x(2 - 5x)$

7. $5g(3g + 7g^2 - 9)$

8. $8t^2(3t - 4 - 5t^2)$

9. $5m(3m + m^2)$

10. $-2w^2(4w - 10 + 3w^2)$

11. $b(10 + 5b - 3b^2)$

Find the greatest common factor (GCF) of the terms of each polynomial. Then factor the polynomial.

12. $9x^4 + 12x^3 + 6x$

13. $4t^5 - 12t^3 + 8t^2$

14. $40n^5 + 70n^4 - 30n^3$

Multiplying Polynomials 10-3

You can use tiles or the distributive property to multiply polynomials. You can use the FOIL method (First, Outer, Inner, Last) to multiply two binomials.

Find each product.

15. $(x + 3)(x + 5)$ **16.** $(5x + 2)(3x - 7)$ **17.** $(2x + 5)(3x - 2)$ **18.** $(x - 1)(-x + 4)$

19. $(x + 2)(x^2 + x + 1)$ **20.** $(4x - 1)(x - 5)$ **21.** $(x - 4)(x^2 - 5x - 2)$ **22.** $(3x + 4)(x + 2)$

23. **Geometry** A rectangle has dimensions $2x + 1$ and $x + 4$. Write an expression for the area of the rectangle as a product and as a polynomial in standard form.

Factoring Trinomials 10-4

Some quadratic trinomials are the product of two **binomial factors.** You can factor trinomials using tiles or by using FOIL with the strategy *Guess and Test.*

Factor each quadratic trinomial.

24. $x^2 + 3x + 2$ **25.** $y^2 - 9y + 14$ **26.** $x^2 - 2x - 15$ **27.** $2w^2 - w - 3$

28. $-b^2 + 7b - 12$ **29.** $2t^2 + 3t - 2$ **30.** $x^2 + 5x - 6$ **31.** $6x^2 + 10x + 4$

32. **Standardized Test Prep** What is $21x^2 - 22x - 8$ in factored form?

A. $(7x + 2)(3x - 4)$ **B.** $(21x + 8)(x - 1)$ **C.** $(3x + 2)(7x - 4)$

D. $(3x - 2)(7x + 4)$ **E.** $(x - 8)(21x + 1)$

Factoring Special Cases 10-5

When you factor a **difference of two squares,** the two binomial factors are the sum and difference of two terms.

$$a^2 - b^2 = (a + b)(a - b)$$

When you factor a **perfect square trinomial,** the two binomial factors are the same.

$$a^2 + 2ab + b^2 = (a + b)^2 \qquad a^2 - 2ab + b^2 = (a - b)^2$$

Factor each polynomial.

33. $q^2 + 2q + 1$ **34.** $b^2 - 16$ **35.** $x^2 - 4x + 4$ **36.** $4t^2 - 121$

37. $4d^2 - 20d + 25$ **38.** $9c^2 + 6c + 1$ **39.** $9k^2 - 25$ **40.** $x^2 + 6x + 9$

41. **Critical Thinking** Suppose you are using tiles to factor a quadratic trinomial. What do you know about the factors of the trinomial if the tiles form a square?

Solving Equations by Factoring 10-6

You can solve a quadratic equation by factoring and using the **zero-product property.** For all real numbers a and b, if $ab = 0$, then $a = 0$ or $b = 0$.

Simplify each equation if necessary. Then solve by factoring.

42. $x^2 + 7x + 12 = 0$

43. $5x^2 - 10x = 0$

44. $2x^2 - 9x = x^2 - 20$

45. $2x^2 + 5x = 3$

46. $3x^2 - 5x = -3x^2 + 6$

47. $x^2 - 5x + 4 = 0$

48. **Gardening** Alice is planting a garden. Its length is 3 feet less than twice its width. Its area is 170 ft^2. Find the dimensions of the garden.

Choosing an Appropriate Method for Solving 10-7

You can solve a quadratic equation four different ways. You can graph the related function and find the x-intercepts. For $x^2 = c$, you can take the square root of each side of the equation. You can factor the equation and use the zero-product property. You can use the quadratic formula.

If the discriminant is a perfect square, there are two rational solutions, and the equation can be factored.

Writing Solve each quadratic equation. Explain why you chose the method you used.

49. $5x^2 - 10 = x^2 + 90$

50. $9x^2 + 30x - 29 = 0$

51. $8x^2 - 6x = 4x^2 + 6x - 2$

52. A square pool has length p. The border of the pool is 1 ft wide. The combined area of the border and the pool is 400 ft^2. Find the area of the pool.

Getting Ready for... CHAPTER 11

Rewrite each decimal as an improper fraction.

53. 5.7 **54.** -8.25 **55.** 3.14 **56.** 10.4 **57.** -1.849 **58.** 7.67

Evaluate each expression.

59. $\frac{3}{2x + 1}$ for $x = 4$

60. $\frac{3x^2}{5x + 2}$ for $x = -2$

61. $\frac{-3}{y^2 + 3}$ for $y = 2$

62. $\frac{2x}{3x - 2}$ for $x = 5$

Solve each proportion.

63. $\frac{x}{3} = \frac{10}{4}$

64. $\frac{1}{y} = \frac{3}{7}$

65. $\frac{11}{3} = \frac{2r}{5}$

66. $\frac{6}{13} = \frac{12}{d}$

67. **Probability** Make a tree diagram to show all the possible outcomes of rolling two number cubes.

CHAPTER 10

Assessment

Simplify. Write each answer in standard form.

1. $(4x^2 + 2x + 5) + (7x^2 - 5x + 2)$
2. $(9a^2 - 4 - 5a) - (12a - 6a^2 + 3)$
3. $(-4m^2 + m - 10) + (3m + 12 - 7m^2)$
4. $(3c - 4c^2 + c^3) - (5c^2 + 8c^3 - 6c)$

5. **Open-ended** Write a trinomial with degree 6.

Write each product in standard form.

6. $8b(3b + 7 - b^2)$
7. $-t(5t^2 + t)$
8. $3q(4 - q + 3q^3)$
9. $2c(c^5 + 4c^3)$
10. $(x + 6)(x + 1)$
11. $(x + 4)(x - 3)$
12. $(2x - 1)(x - 4)$
13. $(2x + 5)(3x - 7)$
14. $(x + 2)(2x^2 - 5x + 4)$
15. $(x - 4)(6x^2 + 10x - 3)$

16. **Writing** Explain how to use the distributive property to multiply polynomials. Include an example.

Find the greatest common factor of the terms of each polynomial.

17. $21x^4 + 18x^2 + 36x^3$
18. $3t^2 - 5t - 2t^4$
19. $-3a^{10} + 9a^5 - 6a^{15}$
20. $9m^3 - 7m^4 + 8m^2$

Write an expression for each situation as a product and in standard form.

21. A plot of land has width x meters. The length of the plot of land is 5 m more than 3 times its width. What is the area of the land?

22. The height of a box is 2 in. less than its width w. The length of a box is 3 in. more than 4 times its width. What is the volume of the box in terms of w?

Factor each expression.

23. $x^2 - 5x - 14$
24. $x^2 + 10x + 25$
25. $9x^2 + 24x + 16$
26. $x^2 - 100$
27. $x^2 - 4x + 4$
28. $4x^2 - 49$

29. **Standardized Test Prep** Which of the following are perfect square trinomials?
    - I. $x^2 + 14x + 49$
    - II. $16x^2 + 25$
    - III. $9x^2 - 30x + 25$
    - IV. $4x^2 - 81$

    A. I only
    B. II only
    C. I and III
    D. I, III, and IV
    E. I, II, III, and IV

Write each equation in standard form. Then solve the equation.

30. $4x^2 - 5x = -2x^2 + 2x + 3$
31. $2x^2 + 3x = x^2 + 28$
32. $3x^2 - 4 = x^2 - 5x + 12$
33. $x^2 - 5 = -x^2 + 9x$

34. **Geometry** The base of a triangle is 8 ft more than twice its height. The area of the triangle is 45 ft^2. Find the dimensions of the triangle.

Use the quadratic formula to solve each equation to the nearest hundredth. If there are no real solutions, write *no real solutions*.

35. $4x^2 + 4x + 9 = 0$
36. $x^2 + 10x + 11 = 0$
37. $-2x^2 - x + 8 = 0$
38. $x^2 - 7x + 10 = 0$

39. **Writing** Explain when you would use the different methods of solving quadratic equations. Give examples.

CHAPTER

10 Preparing for the Math A Exam

Part I

1 Which of the following is a monomial?
(1) $5x^2$ (3) $\frac{1}{x}$
(2) $17x^{-2}$ (4) $x + 1$

2 The polynomial $3x^2 + 4x - 5$ is a
(1) constant monomial. (3) linear binomial.
(2) cubic trinomial. (4) quadratic trinomial.

3 The greatest common factor (GCF) of $18x^3 + 6x^2 - 4x$ is ■.
(1) $2x$ (3) $6x$
(2) x (4) 2

4 Find the product: $(3x - 1)(5x + 3)$.
(1) $15x^2 + 2x - 3$ (3) $15x^2 + 4x - 3$
(2) $15x^2 + 2x + 3$ (4) $15x^2 - 4x - 3$

5 Which of the following is a factor of $c^2 - 7c + 10$?
(1) $(c + 2)$ (3) $(c - 3)$
(2) $(c - 5)$ (4) $(c + 5)$

6 Which of the following equals the difference of two squares?
(1) $(x - 5)(x - 5)$ (3) $(x + 7)(x - 7)$
(2) $(x + 4) - (x + 4)$ (4) $(x + 6)(x + 6)$

7 Which relation(s) are functions?
(1) I (3) III
(2) II (4) II and III

I.

x	1	–1	2	1
y	3	4	5	7

II.

x	1	2	3	4
y	1	1	3	5

III.

x	0	1	2	3
y	0	1	3	2

8 A parachutist opens her parachute at 800 feet. Her rate of change in altitude is -30 ft/s. Which expression represents her altitude in feet t seconds after she opens her parachute?
(1) $30t$ (3) $800 - 30t$
(2) $-30t$ (4) $800 + 30t$

9 A and B are independent events. If $P(A) = \frac{5}{6}$ and $P(A \text{ and } B) = \frac{1}{8}$, what is $P(B)$?
(1) $\frac{1}{10}$ (3) $\frac{1}{5}$
(2) $\frac{3}{20}$ (4) $\frac{1}{4}$

10 One leg of a right isosceles triangle measures 8 cm. What is the length of the hypotenuse?
(1) 16 cm (3) $8\sqrt{3}$ cm
(2) $16\sqrt{2}$ cm (4) $8\sqrt{2}$ cm

Part II

11 Simplify: $(3x^2 - 4x + x^3 - 5) - (2x^2 + 6)$.

12 A rectangular prism is $3x + 1$ units long, x units wide, and 2 units high. Write the volume of the prism as a product and as a polynomial in standard form.

Part III

13 Solve: $x^2 - 7x - 18 = 0$.

14 The base of a triangle is $(2x + 2)$ units. Its height is $(x + 3)$ units, and its area is 24 square units. What is the value of x?

Part IV

15 Solve: $4x^2 + 4x - 15 = 0$.

16 The length of a rectangular swimming pool is 20 m longer than its width. The pool is surrounded by a walkway that is 2 m wide. Together, the pool and the walkway cover an area of 1836 m^2. Find the dimensions of the pool.

17 Suppose you are considering buying a season pass to the park pool for \$55. Without a pass, you must pay \$3 per visit to the pool. You decide to find the break-even point.
a Write an equation relating the cost of a pass to the cost of swimming without a pass.
b Graph the related linear function.
c How many times would you have to swim to pass the break-even point? Explain.

CHAPTER 11 Rational Expressions and Functions

Relating to the Real World

Sixty dollars will buy you six $10 pizzas or four $15 pizzas. This simple relationship leads to fractions with variables in the denominators, called rational expressions. Rational expressions give social scientists and others who use statistics flexibility in applying formulas to their work.

CHAPTER PROJECT

GOOD VIBRATIONS

Sounds are caused by vibrations—for example, a string vibrating on a violin. When the string is shortened it vibrates faster, and a higher pitch results. Pitch is also affected by tension (an example is your vocal cords).

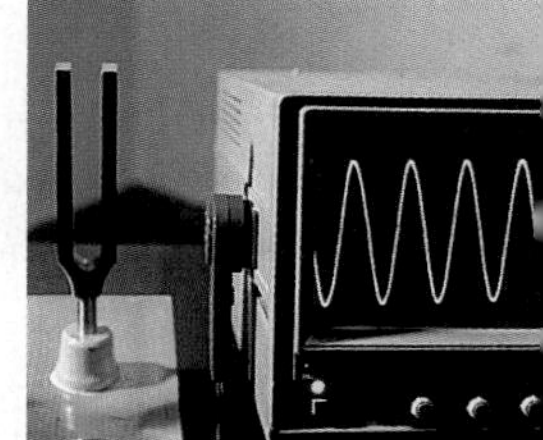

As you work through the chapter, you will investigate a variety of musical pitches. You will use inverse variation to find pitch. You will create simple musical instruments to compare ratios of lengths to different pitches. Finally, you will choose a musical instrument and explain how it produces sounds at different pitches.

To help you complete the project:

- **p. 514** *Find Out by Calculating*
- **p. 526** *Find Out by Analyzing*
- **p. 531** *Find Out by Creating*
- **p. 536** *Find Out by Interviewing*
- **p. 547** *Find Out by Communicating*
- **p. 548** *Finishing the Project*

Solving Rational Equations 11-5

Counting Outcomes and Permutations 11-6

Combinations 11-7

11-1 Inverse Variation

What You'll Learn

- Solving inverse variations
- Comparing direct and inverse variation

...And Why

To investigate real-world situations, such as those relating time and rate of work

WORK TOGETHER

Construction Suppose you are part of a volunteer crew constructing low-cost housing. Building a house requires a total of 160 workdays. For example, a crew of 20 people can complete a house in 8 days.

1. How long should it take a crew of 40 people?
2. Copy and complete the table.

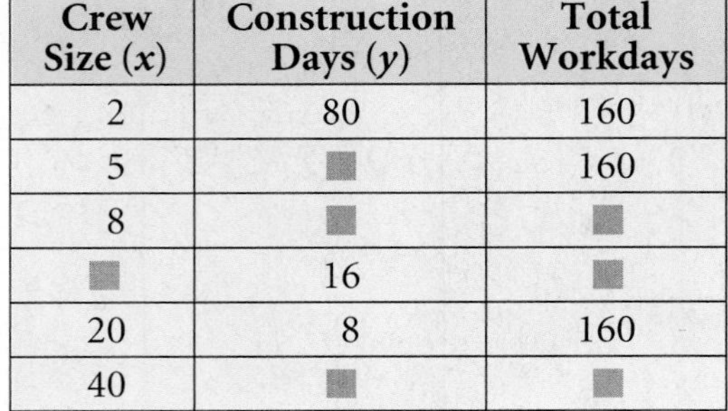

Crew Size (x)	Construction Days (y)	Total Workdays
2	80	160
5	■	160
8	■	■
■	16	■
20	8	160
40	■	■

3. Graph the (x, y) data from the table.
4. Describe what happens to construction time as the crew size increases.

Who? Using volunteers, Habitat for Humanity has helped build thousands of homes for low-income families around the world.

Source: Habitat for Humanity

THINK AND DISCUSS

Solving Inverse Variations

When the product of two quantities remains constant, they form an **inverse variation.** As one quantity increases, the other decreases. The product of the quantities is called the **constant of variation** k. An inverse variation can be written $xy = k$, or $y = \frac{k}{x}$.

5. a. In the Work Together, what two quantities vary?
   b. What is the constant of variation?
   c. Write an equation that models this variation.
6. a. Complete the table for the inverse variation $xy = 100$.

x	1	2	4	5	10	20	50	100
y	100	■	■	■	■	■	■	■

   b. Describe how the values of y change as the values of x increase.

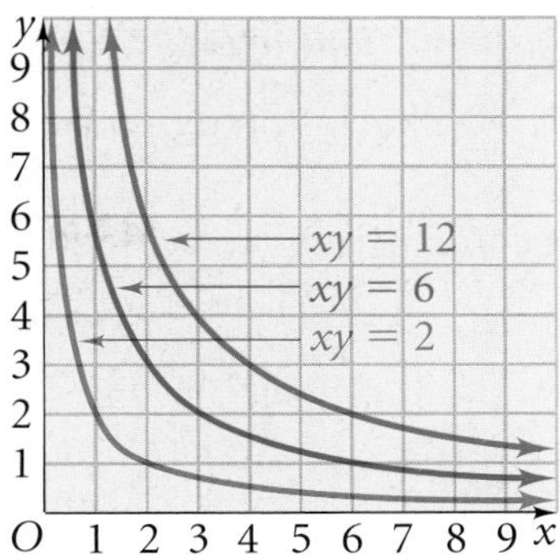

Inverse variations have graphs with the same general shape.

7. **a.** Name the constant of variation k for each graph shown above.
   b. ***Open-ended*** Name three points that lie on the graph of each inverse variation.

Suppose (x_1, y_1) and (x_2, y_2) are two ordered pairs in an inverse variation. Since each ordered pair has the same product, you can write the *product* equation $x_1 \cdot y_1 = x_2 \cdot y_2$. You can use this equation to solve problems involving inverse variation.

Example 1 ***Relating to the Real World*** 

Physics The weight needed to balance a lever varies inversely with the distance from the fulcrum to the weight. Where should Julio sit to balance the lever?

Relate A weight of 120 lb is 6 ft from the fulcrum.
A weight of 150 lb is x ft from the fulcrum.
Weight and distance vary inversely.

Define $\text{weight}_1 = 120$ lb
$\text{weight}_2 = 150$ lb
$\text{distance}_1 = 6$ ft
$\text{distance}_2 = x$ ft

Write $\text{weight}_1 \cdot \text{distance}_1 = \text{weight}_2 \cdot \text{distance}_2$ ← **Use a product equation.**

$$120 \cdot 6 = 150 \cdot x \quad \leftarrow \text{Substitute.}$$
$$720 = 150x$$
$$x = \frac{720}{150}$$
$$x = 4.8$$

Julio should sit 4.8 feet from the fulcrum to balance the lever.

8. **Try This** Solve each inverse variation.
   a. When $x = 75$, $y = 0.2$. Find x when $y = 3$.
   b. What weight placed on a lever 6 ft from the fulcrum will balance 80 lb placed 9 ft from the fulcrum?
   c. A trip takes 3 h at 50 mi/h. Find the time when the rate is 60 mi/h.

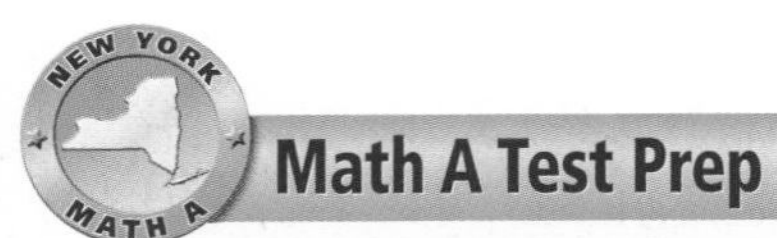

Math A Test Prep

1 Which situation is *not* a direct variation?
(1) total cost and number of an item purchased
(2) lengths and areas of rectangles with same width
(3) lengths and widths of rectangles with same area
(4) amount of sales tax and total amount

2 $\left(8, \frac{1}{2}\right)$ and $\left(\frac{1}{16}, y\right)$ are points on the graph of a direct variation. What is the value of y?

Comparing Direct and Inverse Variation

This summary will help you recognize and use direct and inverse variations.

Direct Variation	Inverse Variation
y varies directly with x.	y varies inversely with x.
y is directly proportional to x.	y is inversely proportional to x.
The ratio $\frac{y}{x}$ is constant.	The product xy is constant.

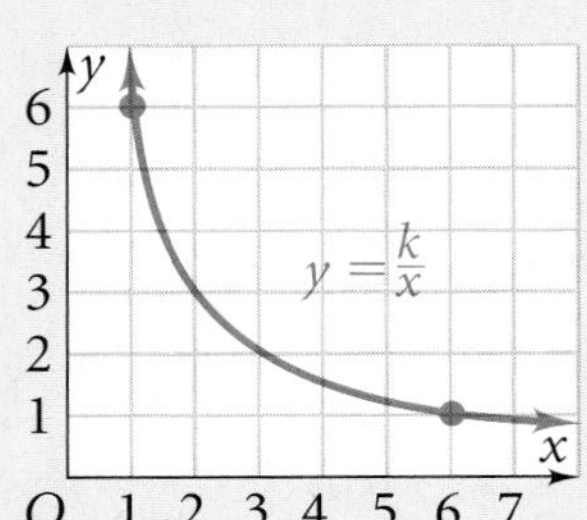

Example 2

Do the data in each table represent a *direct variation* or an *inverse variation?* For each table, write an equation to model the data.

a.

x	2	4	10
y	5	10	25

The values of y seem to vary directly with the values of x. Check the ratio $\frac{y}{x}$.

$\frac{y}{x} = \frac{5}{2} = 2.5$

$\frac{10}{4} = 2.5$

$\frac{25}{10} = 2.5$

The ratio $\frac{y}{x}$ is the same for each pair of data. So, this is a direct variation and $k = 2.5$. The equation is $y = 2.5x$.

b.

x	5	10	25
y	20	10	4

The values of y seem to vary inversely with the values of x. Check the product xy.

$xy = 5(20) = 100$

$10(10) = 100$

$25(4) = 100$

The product xy is the same for each pair of data. So, this is an inverse variation and $k = 100$. The equation is $xy = 100$.

9. Match each situation with the equation that models it. Is the relationship between the data *direct* or *inverse*?

a. The cost of \$20 worth of gasoline is split among several people.
b. You buy several markers for 20¢ each.
c. You walk 5 miles each day. Your pace (speed) and time vary from day to day.
d. Several people buy souvenirs for \$5 apiece.

I. $y = 5x$
II. $xy = 5$
III. $y = \frac{20}{x}$
IV. $y = 20x$

Exercises ON YOUR OWN

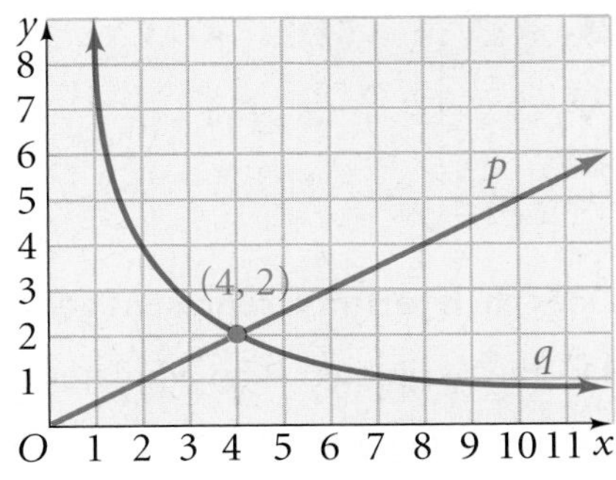

1. a. Suppose you want to earn \$80. How long will it take you if you are paid \$5/h; \$8/h; \$10/h; \$20/h?
   b. What are the two variable quantities in part (a)?
   c. Write an equation to represent this situation.

2. **Critical Thinking** The graphs p and q represent a direct variation and an inverse variation. Write the equation for each graph.

Each pair of points is from an inverse variation. Find the missing value.

3. $(6, 12)$ and $(9, y)$
4. $(3, 5)$ and $(1, n)$
5. $(x, 55)$ and $(5, 77)$
6. $(9.4, b)$ and $(6, 4.7)$
7. $(24, 1.6)$ and $(c, 0.4)$
8. $(\frac{1}{2}, 24)$ and $(6, y)$
9. $(x, \frac{1}{2})$ and $(\frac{1}{3}, \frac{1}{4})$
10. $(500, 25)$ and $(4, n)$
11. $(\frac{1}{2}, 5)$ and $(b, \frac{1}{8})$
12. $(x, 11)$ and $(1, 66)$
13. $(50, 13)$ and $(t, 5)$
14. $(4, 3.6)$ and $(1.2, g)$

15. **Standardized Test Prep** Which proportion represents an inverse variation?

   A. $\frac{x_2}{y_2} = \frac{y_1}{x_1}$ B. $\frac{x_1}{y_2} = \frac{y_1}{x_2}$ C. $\frac{x_2}{y_2} = \frac{x_1}{y_1}$ D. $\frac{x_1}{x_2} = \frac{y_2}{y_1}$ E. $\frac{x_1}{y_1} = \frac{x_2}{y_2}$

Find the constant of variation k for each inverse variation.

16. $y = 8$ when $x = 4$
17. $r = 3.3$ when $t = \frac{1}{3}$
18. $a = 25$ when $b = 0.04$
19. $x = \frac{1}{2}$ when $y = 5$
20. $p = 10.4$ when $q = 1.5$
21. $x = 5$ when $y = 75$

22. According to the First Law of Air Travel, will the distance to your gate be *greater* or *less* for this trip than for your last trip?
   a. You have more luggage.
   b. You have less time to make your flight.
   c. You have less luggage.

CLOSE TO HOME by John McPherson

The First Law of Air Travel: The distance to your connecting gate is directly proportional to the amount of luggage you are carrying and inversely proportional to the amount of time you have.

23. **Travel** The time to travel a certain distance is inversely proportional to your speed. Suppose it takes you $2\frac{1}{2}$ h to drive from your house to the lake at a rate of 48 mi/h.
   a. What is the constant of variation? What does it represent?
   b. How long will your return trip take at 40 mi/h?

Solve each inverse variation.

24. **Surveying** Two rectangular building lots are each one-quarter acre in size. One plot measures 99 ft by 110 ft. Find the length of the other plot if its width is 90 ft.

25. **Construction** If 4 people can paint a house working 3 days each, how long will it take a crew of 5 people?

Do the data in each table represent a *direct* or an *inverse* variation? Write an equation to model the data. Then complete the table.

26.

x	y
5	6
2	15
10	■

27.

x	y
0.4	28
1.2	84
■	63

28.

x	y
10	4
20	■
8	3.2

29.

x	y
1.6	30
4.8	10
■	96

30.

x	y
3	1
1	3
9	■

Does each formula represent a *direct* or an *inverse* variation? Explain.

31. the perimeter of an equilateral triangle: $P = 3s$

32. a rectangle with area 24 square units: $lw = 24$

33. the time t to travel 150 mi at r mi/h: $t = \frac{150}{r}$

34. the circumference of a circle with radius r: $C = 2\pi r$

35. Writing Explain how the variable y changes in each situation.
  a. y varies directly with x. The value of x is doubled.
  b. y varies inversely with x. The value of x is doubled.

36. Open-ended Write and graph a direct variation and an inverse variation that use the same constant of variation.

Chapter Project

Find Out by Calculating

Under equal tension, the frequency of a vibrating string varies inversely with the string length. Violins and guitars use this principle to produce the different pitches of a musical scale. Find the string lengths for a C-Major scale.

C-Major Scale

Pitch	C	D	E	F	G	A	B	C
Frequency (cycles/s)	523	587	659	698	784	880	988	1046
String length (mm)	420	■	■	■	■	■	■	■

Exercises MIXED REVIEW

Factor each polynomial.

37. $x^2 + 10x + 25$ **38.** $4t^2 - 9m^2$ **39.** $x^2 - 6x + 9$

40. Education The number of high school students taking advanced placement exams increased from 177,406 in 1984 to 459,000 in 1994. What percent increase is this?

Self Assessment

For Your Journal

Describe differences and similarities between direct variation and inverse variation. Include equations and graphs.

Getting Ready for Lesson 11-2

Find the reciprocal of each number.

41. 5 **42.** -4 **43.** $\frac{8}{3}$ **44.** $3\frac{1}{7}$ **45.** -1 **46.** $\frac{3}{4}$

Graphing Rational Functions

Before Lesson 11-2

When you use a graphing calculator to graph a rational function, sometimes false connections appear on the screen. When this happens, you need to make adjustments to see the true shape of the graph.

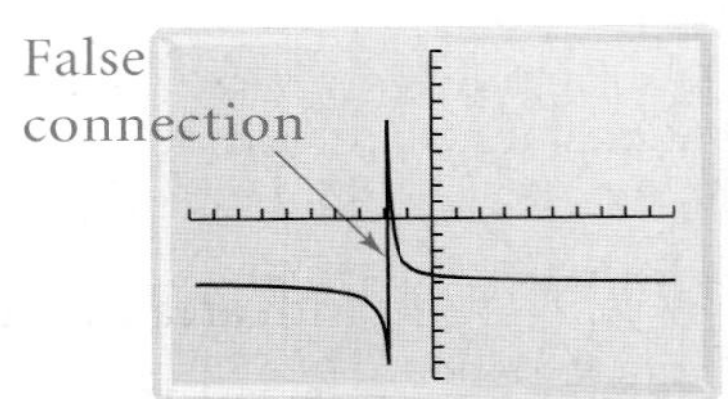

For example, on your graphing calculator the graph of the function $y = \frac{1}{x + 2} - 4$ may look like the graph at the right. The highest point and lowest point on the graph are not supposed to connect. If you trace the graph, no point on the graph lies on this connecting line. So, this is a false connection.

Here's how you can graph a rational function and avoid false connections.

First press the MODE key. Then scroll down and right to highlight the word "Dot." Then press ENTER.

Normal Sci Eng
Float 0123456789
Radian Degree
Func Par Pol Seq
Connected Dot
Sequential Simul
Full Screen Split

Graph again. Now the false connection is gone!

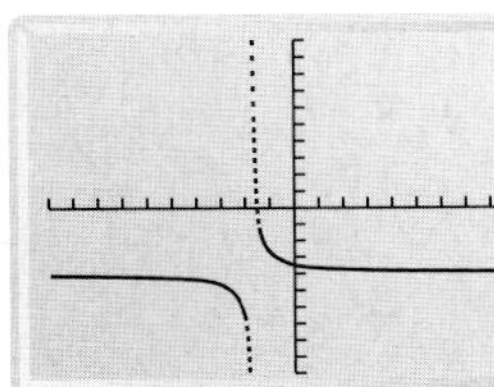

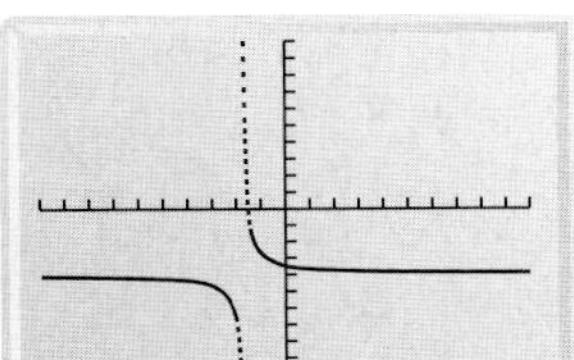

Use the TRACE key or TABLE key to find points on the graph. Sketch the graph.

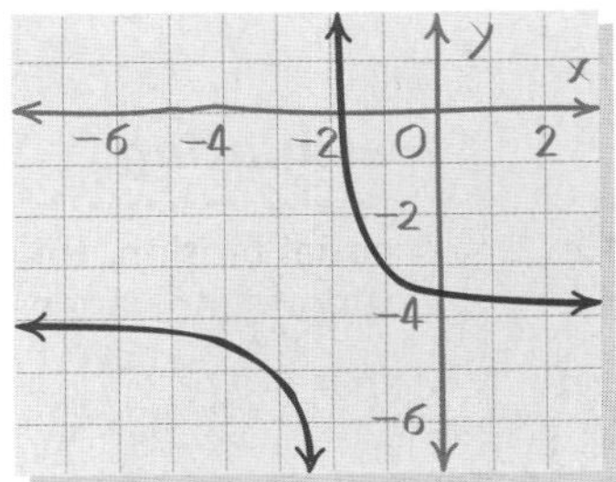

Graphing Calculator **Use a graphing calculator to graph each function. Then sketch the graph. (*Hint*: Use parentheses to enter binomials.)**

1. $y = \frac{1}{x - 3}$

2. $y = \frac{1}{x} + 3$

3. $y = \frac{5}{3x + 2}$

4. $y = \frac{4}{3x + 6}$

5. $y = \frac{x + 3}{x - 2}$

6. $y = \frac{1}{x - 2} + 1$

7. $y = \frac{6}{x^2 - x - 6}$

8. $y = \frac{1}{x - 4} + 2$

9. $y = \frac{8}{x}$

10. $y = \frac{4}{x + 1} - 3$

11. $y = \frac{3x}{x + 3}$

12. $y = \frac{2x + 1}{x - 4}$

13. **a.** **Graphing Calculator** Graph $y = \frac{1}{x}$, $y = \frac{1}{x - 3}$, and $y = \frac{1}{x + 4}$. What do you notice?

b. **Graphing Calculator** Graph $y = \frac{1}{x}$, $y = \frac{1}{x} - 3$, and $y = \frac{1}{x} + 4$. What do you notice?

14. **Writing** Graph $y = \frac{1}{x}$.

a. Examine both negative and positive values of x. Describe what happens to the y-values when x is near zero.

b. Describe what happens to the y-values as $|x|$ increases.

11-2 Rational Functions

What You'll Learn

- Evaluating rational functions
- Graphing rational functions

...And Why

To solve problems using rational functions, such as those involving light intensity

What You'll Need

- graph paper
- graphing calculator
- index cards

QUICK REVIEW

Two numbers are *reciprocals* of each other if their product is 1.

THINK AND DISCUSS

Exploring Rational Functions

Photography Automatic cameras calculate shutter speed based on the amount of available light. The relationship between shutter speed and the amount of light can be modeled with a rational function. A **rational function** is a function that can be written in the form $f(x) = \frac{\text{polynomial}}{\text{polynomial}}$.

1. Evaluate each rational function for $x = 3$.
   a. $f(x) = \frac{1}{x - 4}$ **b.** $y = \frac{2}{x^2}$ **c.** $g(x) = \frac{x^2 - 3x + 2}{x + 2}$

The function $y = \frac{1}{x}$ is an example of a rational function. You can use the graph of $y = \frac{1}{x}$ to show the relationship between reciprocals.

Table

Number (x)	-1	$-\frac{1}{3}$	1	1.5	3
Reciprocal (y)	-1	-3	1	$\frac{2}{3}$	$\frac{1}{3}$

Graph

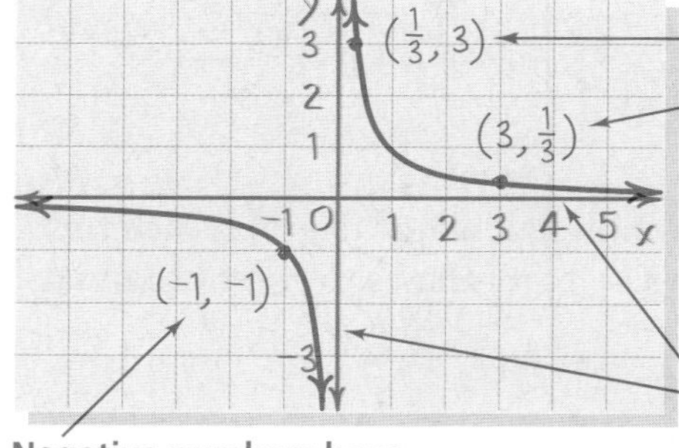

Since 3 and $\frac{1}{3}$ are reciprocals of each other, both $(3, \frac{1}{3})$ and $(\frac{1}{3}, 3)$ are on the graph.

For $x = 0$ and $y = 0$ the function is undefined. So the graph never intersects either axis.

Negative numbers have negative reciprocals.

2. Does each point lie on the graph of $y = \frac{1}{x}$? Why or why not?
   a. $(-100, -0.01)$ **b.** $(-5, 0.2)$ **c.** $(1{,}000{,}000, 0)$ **d.** $(0.04, 25)$

A line is an **asymptote** of a graph if the graph of the function gets closer and closer to the line, but does not cross it.

3. The y-axis is a vertical asymptote of the function $y = \frac{1}{x}$. Is there a horizontal asymptote of the graph? Explain.

Graphing Rational Functions

When you evaluate a rational function, some values of x may lead to division by zero. For the function $y = \frac{1}{x - 3}$, the denominator is zero for $x = 3$. So, the function is undefined when $x = 3$, and the vertical line $x = 3$ is an asymptote of the graph of $y = \frac{1}{x - 3}$.

Example 1

Graph $y = \frac{4}{x + 3}$.

Step 1 Find the vertical asymptote.

$$x + 3 = 0$$
$$x = -3 \leftarrow \text{vertical asymptote}$$

Step 2 Make a table using values of x near -3.

x	y
−6	$-\frac{4}{3}$
−5	−2
−4	−4
−2	4
−1	2
0	$\frac{4}{3}$

Step 3 Draw the graph.

Use a dashed line for the asymptote $x = -3$.

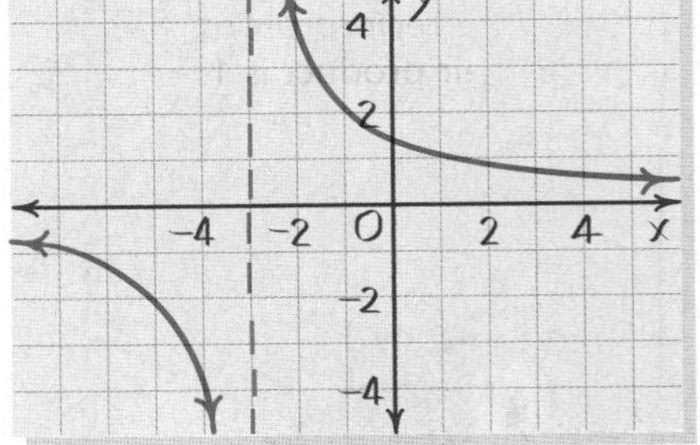

PROBLEM SOLVING

Look Back How does the graph of a rational function compare with the graph of an exponential function?

4. a. Copy the graph above and add the graph of the line $y = -x - 3$.

b. **Critical Thinking** Fold the graph along the line you drew. What is true about the two parts of the graph of $y = \frac{4}{x + 3}$?

5. a. Evaluate $y = \frac{4}{x + 3}$ for $x = 1000$ and $x = -1000$.

b. Is there a horizontal asymptote for the graph? Explain.

The graphs of many rational functions are related to each other.

$y = \frac{1}{x}$

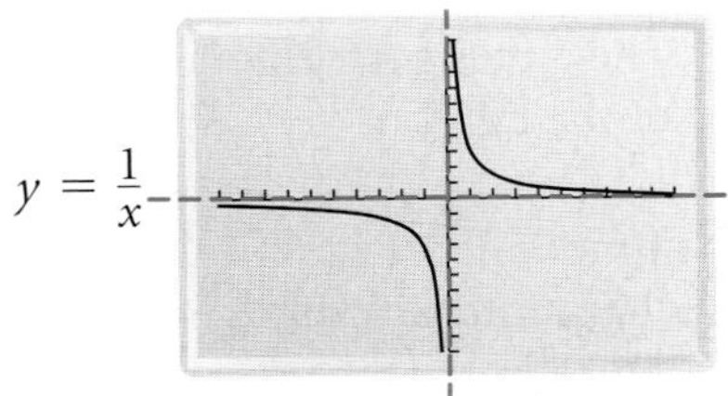

vertical asymptote when $x = 0$
horizontal asymptote along the x-axis

$y = \frac{1}{x - 2}$

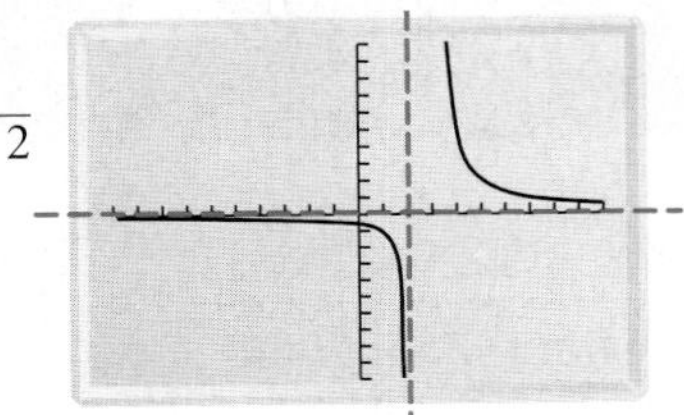

vertical asymptote when $x = 2$
horizontal asymptote along the x-axis

The graphs are identical in shape, but the second graph is shifted two units to the right.

6. Where is the vertical asymptote of the graph of each function?

a. $y = \frac{6}{x}$ b. $y = \frac{6}{x - 3}$ c. $y = \frac{6}{x + 1}$

7. **Try This** Graph each function in Question 6.

8. ***Critical Thinking*** Graph the functions $y = \frac{3}{x}$ and $y = \frac{3}{x} + 2$. Are the graphs identical in shape? What shift occurs?

You can use rational functions to describe relationships in the real world.

Example 2 Relating to the Real World 

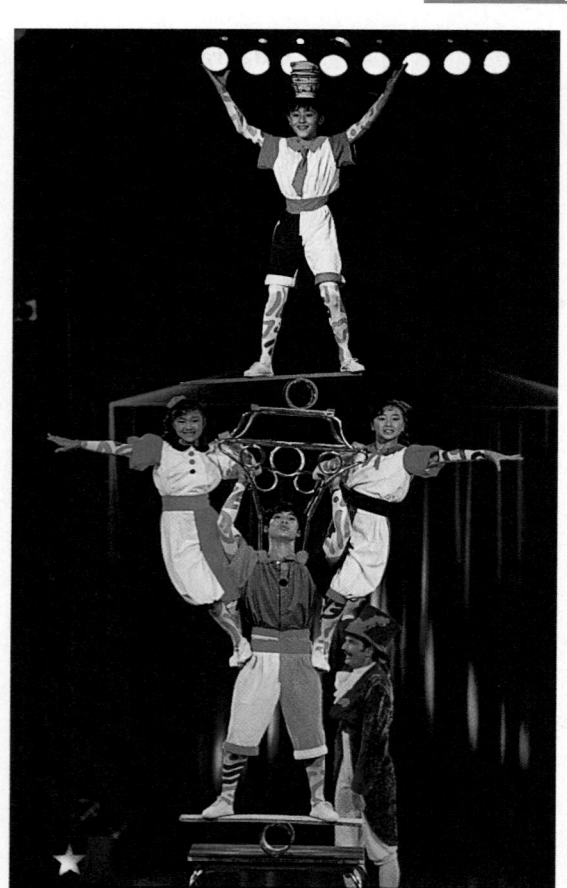

Photography The output from the photographer's lighting system is 72,000 lumens. To get a good photo, the intensity of light at the circus performers must be at least 600 lumens. The light intensity y is related to their distance x in feet from the light by the function $y = \frac{72{,}000}{x^2}$. How far can the circus performers be from the light?

Relate light intensity at performers is at least 600 lumens

Write $\frac{72{,}000}{x^2} \geq 600$

Use a graphing calculator. Enter $y = \frac{72{,}000}{x^2}$ and $y = 600$. Find the point of intersection.

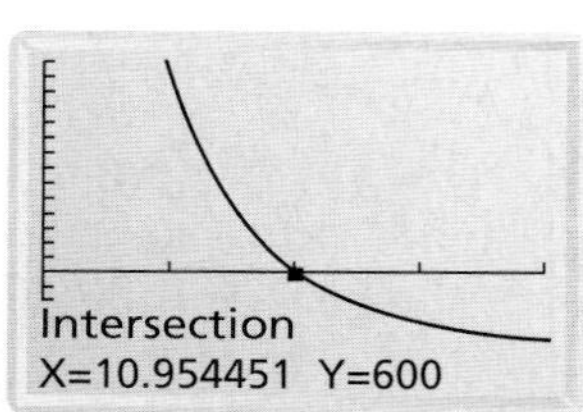

Xmin=0 Ymin=0
Xmax=20 Ymax=2000
Xscl=5 Yscl=100

The curved graph shows that the light intensity y decreases as the distance x increases.

The light intensity is about 600 lumens when $x \approx 11$. The circus performers should be within about 11 ft of the light.

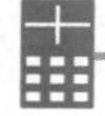

GRAPHING CALCULATOR HINT

Use a viewing window for Quadrant I, since distance and lumens are positive.

9. a. Use the function in Example 2 to find the light intensity at each distance in the table.

b. Describe how the light intensity changes when the distance doubles.

Distance (x)	Intensity (y)
3 ft	■
6 ft	■
12 ft	■

10. ***Graphing Calculator*** Graph $y = \frac{1}{x}$ and $y = \frac{1}{x^2}$.

a. What is the vertical asymptote of the graph of each function?

b. ***Critical Thinking*** What is the range of $y = \frac{1}{x}$? of $y = \frac{1}{x^2}$?

WORK TOGETHER

You have studied six families of functions this year. Their properties and graphs are shown in this summary.

Families of Functions

Linear function
$y = mx + b$

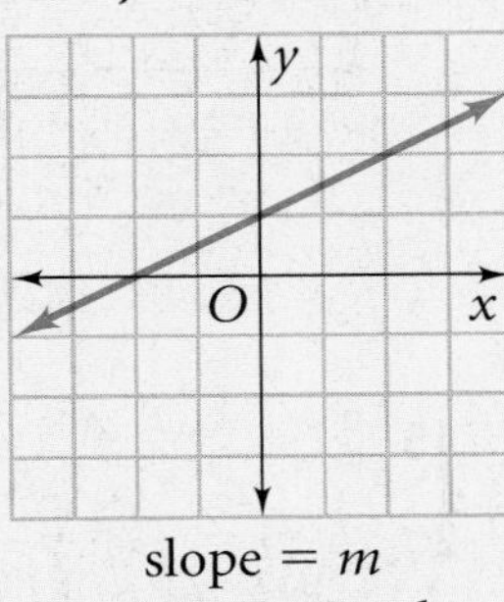

slope $= m$
y-intercept $= b$

Absolute value function
$y = |x - b|$

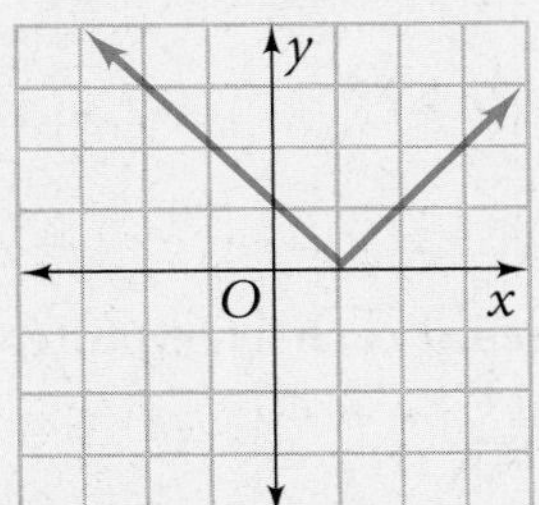

V-shape with vertex at $(b, 0)$

Quadratic function
$y = ax^2 + bx + c$

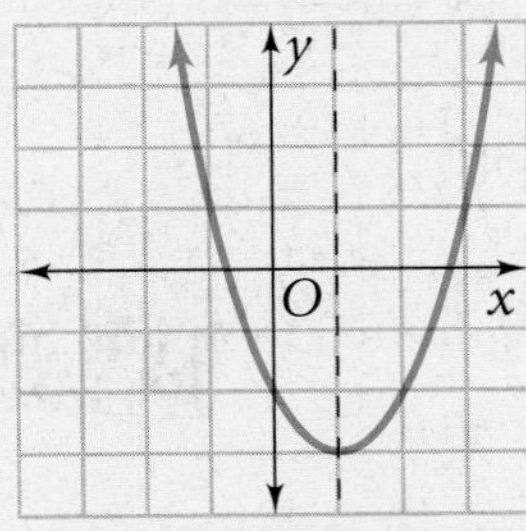

parabola with axis of symmetry at $x = -\frac{b}{2a}$

Exponential function
$y = ab^x$

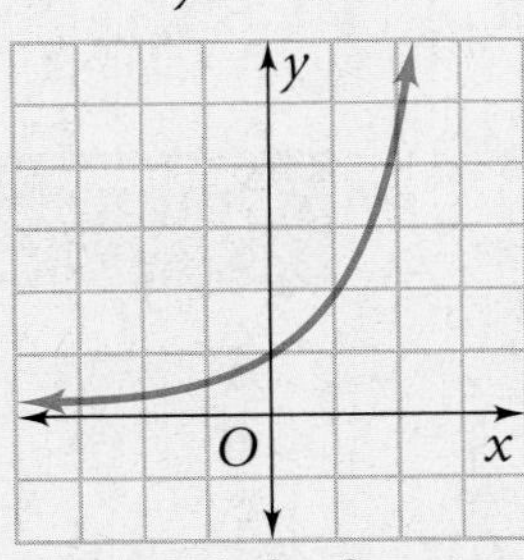

growth for $b > 1$
decay for $0 < b < 1$

Radical function
$y = \sqrt{x - b} + c$

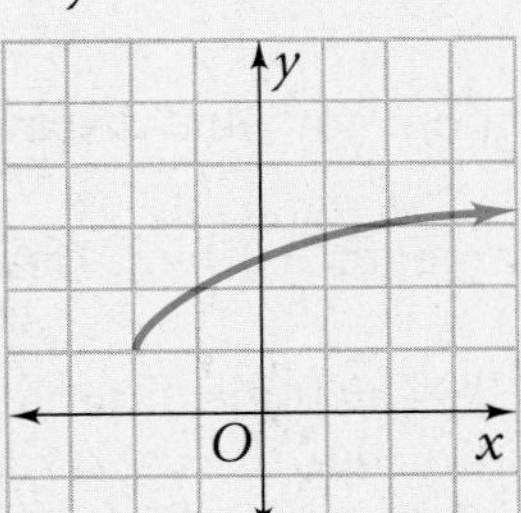

shift horizontally b units
shift vertically c units

Rational function
$y = \frac{k}{x - b} + c$

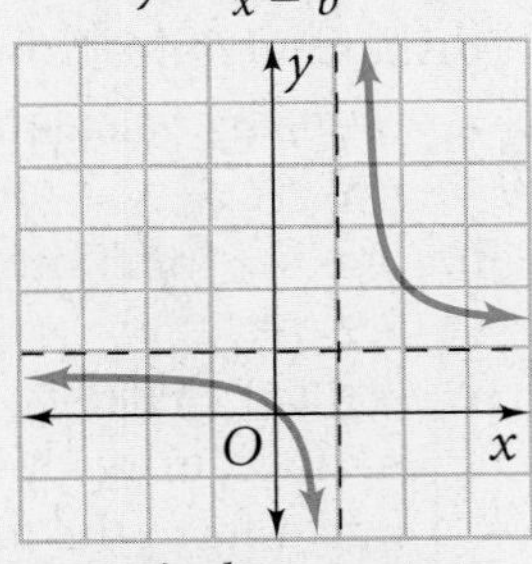

vertical asymptote at $x = b$

11. Work with a partner to prepare a note card for each family of functions. Include this information:

- one or more examples for that family
- a graph for each example
- notes about each function you have graphed (for instance, how to find the slope, the axis of symmetry, or an asymptote)

12. Make duplicate cards so that you and your partner each have a full set.

Exercises ON YOUR OWN

Evaluate each function for $x = -1, x = 2$, and $x = 4$.

1. $y = \frac{x - 2}{x}$
2. $f(x) = \frac{3}{x - 1}$
3. $y = \frac{2x}{x - 3}$
4. $g(x) = \frac{12}{x^2}$

What value of x makes the denominator of each function equal zero?

5. $f(x) = \frac{3}{x}$
6. $y = \frac{1}{x - 2}$
7. $y = \frac{x}{x + 2}$
8. $h(x) = \frac{3}{2x - 4}$

Describe the asymptotes in each graph.

9. 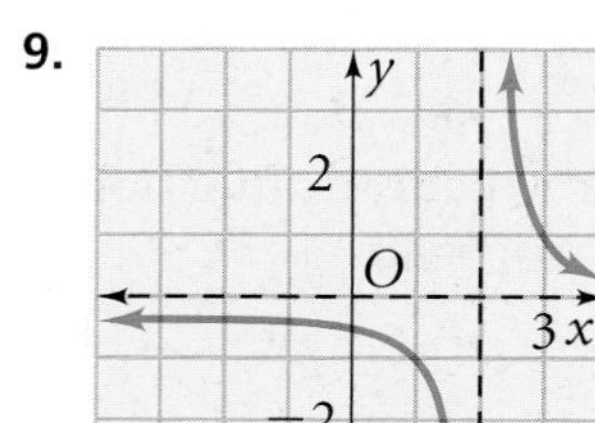

10. 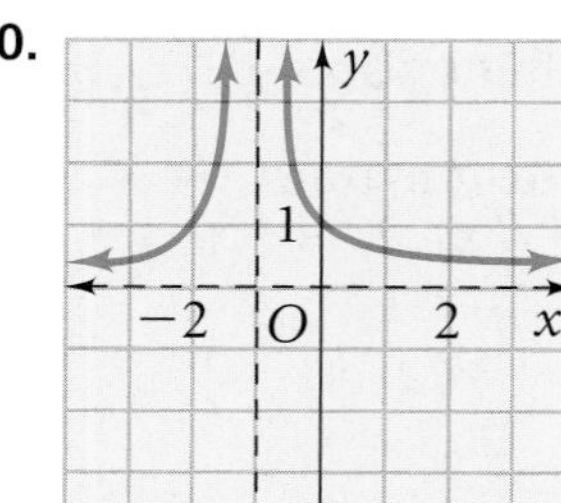

11. 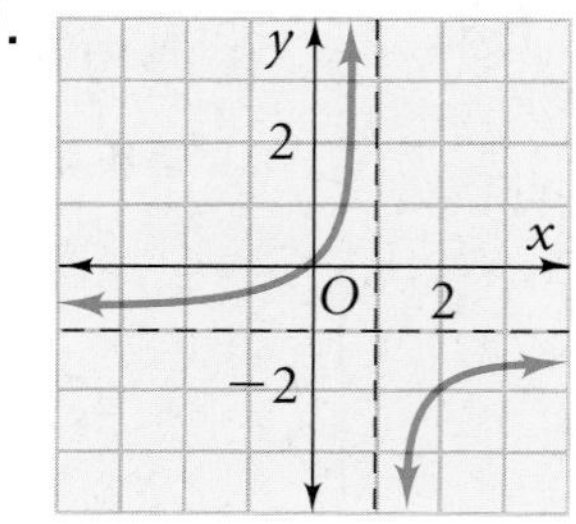

12. 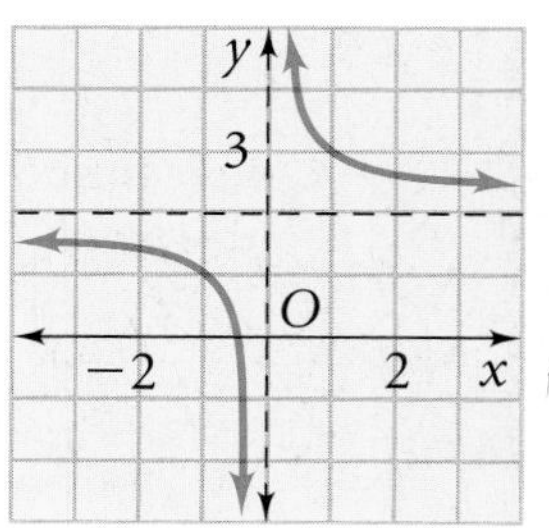

Graph each function. Include a dashed line for each asymptote.

13. $y = \frac{4}{x}$
14. $f(x) = \frac{4}{x - 5}$
15. $y = \frac{4}{x + 4}$
16. $g(x) = \frac{4}{x} + 2$
17. $g(x) = \frac{12}{x}$
18. $y = \frac{12}{x + 2}$
19. $f(x) = \frac{12}{x} - 3$
20. $h(x) = \frac{12}{x + 2} - 3$
21. $f(x) = \frac{-1}{x}$
22. $y = \frac{-4}{x}$
23. $g(x) = \frac{4}{x - 2} + 1$
24. $y = \frac{x + 2}{x - 2}$

25. 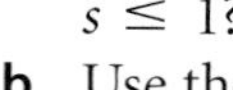 As radio signals move away from a transmitter, they become weaker. The function $s = \frac{1600}{d^2}$ relates the strength s of a signal at a distance d miles from the transmitter.

a. 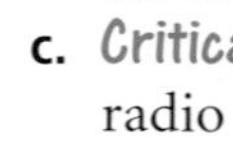 Graph the function. For what distances is $s \leq 1$?

b. Use the function to find the signal strength at 10 mi, 1 mi, and 0.1 mi.

c. **Critical Thinking** Suppose you drive by the transmitter for one radio station while your car radio is tuned to a second station. The signal from the first station can interfere and come through your radio. Use your results from part (b) to explain why.

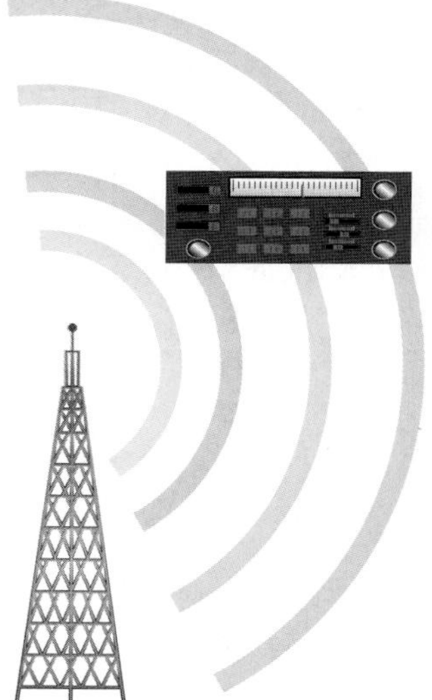

26. 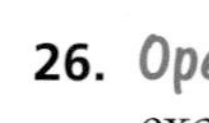 Write two rational functions whose graphs are identical except that one has been shifted vertically 3 units from the other.

27. 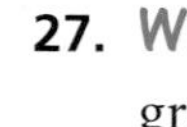 Suppose a friend missed class. How would you explain how to graph $y = \frac{5}{x - 1} + 2$?

28. In the formula $I = \frac{445}{x^2}$, I is the intensity of light at a distance x feet from the light bulb. What is the intensity of light 5 ft from the light bulb? 15 ft from the light bulb?

Graphing Calculator Graph each function on a graphing calculator. Then sketch the graph. Include a dashed line for each asymptote.

29. $y = \frac{x + 4}{x}$ **30.** $y = \frac{x + 1}{x + 3}$ **31.** $y = \frac{4}{x^2 - 1}$ **32.** $y = \frac{6}{x^2 - x - 2}$

Graph each function.

33. $y = x^2 + 3$ **34.** $y = \sqrt{x + 3}$ **35.** $y = x + 3$ **36.** $y = |x - 3|$

37. $y = 3x$ **38.** $y = 3^x$ **39.** $y = \frac{3}{x}$ **40.** $y = \frac{1}{x + 3} + 3$

41. $y = x^2 + 3x + 2$ **42.** $y = \left(\frac{1}{3}\right)^x$ **43.** $y = \frac{3}{x - 3}$ **44.** $y = \frac{3}{x} + 3$

Exercises MIXED REVIEW

Factor.

45. $g^2 - 12g + 35$ **46.** $9h^2 + 24h + 16$ **47.** $a^2 + 6a - 7$ **48.** $25x^2 - 4$

49. **Delivery Services** During the blizzard of 1996, a pizza delivery driver in Alexandria, Virginia, got tips that were 1000% of the usual $1 for each delivery. How much did the delivery driver receive in tips for a delivery during the blizzard?

Getting Ready for Lesson 11-3

Find the value(s) of x that makes each expression equal zero.

50. $10 - x$ **51.** $x^2 - 3x$ **52.** $x + 4$ **53.** $x^2 - 16$

Exercises CHECKPOINT

Each pair of points is from an inverse variation. Find the missing value.

1. (9, 2) and (x, 6) **2.** (8.2, 3) and (12.3, y) **3.** (0.5, 7.2) and (0.9, y)

Graph each function.

4. $y = \frac{5}{x}$ **5.** $y = \frac{8}{x - 4}$ **6.** $y = \frac{6}{x^2}$ **7.** $y = \frac{1}{x} + 4$

8. **Writing** Describe the similarities and differences between the graphs of $y = \frac{3}{x}$ and $y = \frac{-3}{x}$.

9. **Physics** What weight placed on a lever 9 ft from the fulcrum will balance 126 lb placed 6.5 ft from the fulcrum?

10. The graphs of a direct variation and an inverse variation both pass through the point (3, 5). Write an equation for each graph.

11-3 Rational Expressions

What You'll Learn

- Simplifying rational expressions
- Multiplying and dividing rational expressions

...And Why

To solve real-world problems that involve ratios of unknown quantities

WORK TOGETHER

Work in groups to review how to simplify, multiply, and divide rational numbers.

1. a. Simplify each expression.

$\frac{8}{2}$ $\qquad -\frac{15}{24}$ $\qquad \frac{25}{35}$

b. Consider the steps you took to simplify each expression in part (a). Write the steps you use to simplify rational numbers.

2. a. Express each product in simplest form.

$-\frac{8}{21} \cdot \frac{7}{4}$ $\qquad \frac{3}{5} \cdot \frac{2}{7}$ $\qquad -\frac{3}{4} \cdot (-2)$

b. Consider the steps you took to find each product in part (a). Write the steps you use to multiply rational numbers.

QUICK REVIEW

Rational numbers are numbers that can be represented as the ratio of two integers.

3. a. Express each quotient in simplest form.

$6 \div \frac{3}{8}$ $\qquad \frac{2}{3} \div \left(-\frac{4}{5}\right)$ $\qquad \frac{3}{4} \div 2$

b. Consider the steps you took to find each quotient in part (a). Write the steps you use to divide rational numbers.

THINK AND DISCUSS

Simplifying Rational Expressions

A **rational expression** is an expression that can be written in the form $\frac{\text{polynomial}}{\text{polynomial}}$, where a variable is in the denominator.

4. Evaluate each rational expression for $x = 2$. What do you notice?

a. $\frac{1}{x - 2}$ $\qquad$ **b.** $\frac{3}{x^2 - 4}$ $\qquad$ **c.** $\frac{2}{x^2 + x - 6}$

The **domain** of a rational expression is all real numbers excluding the values for which the denominator is zero. The values that are excluded are restricted from the domain. For the expression $\frac{1}{x - 2}$, 2 is restricted from the domain.

5. What other values are restricted from the domain in parts (b) and (c) of Question 4? (*Hint:* Solve an equation to find the values for which the denominator equals zero.)

A rational expression is in *simplest form* if the numerator and denominator have no common factors except 1.

Example 1

Simplify $\frac{6x + 12}{x + 2}$ and state any values restricted from the domain.

$x + 2 = 0, x = -2$ ← Find the values restricted from the domain.

$\frac{6x + 12}{x + 2} = \frac{6(x + 2)}{x + 2}$ ← Factor the numerator. The denominator cannot be factored.

$= \frac{6}{1} \cdot \frac{x + 2}{x + 2}$ ← Rewrite to show a fraction equal to 1.

$= 6$ ← Simplify.

The solution is 6. The domain does not include $x = -2$.

6. **Try This** Simplify each expression and state any restrictions on the domain of the variable.

a. $\frac{15b}{25b^2}$ **b.** $\frac{12c^2}{3c + 6}$ **c.** $\frac{x + 3}{x^2 - 9}$

Example 2 **Relating to the Real World**

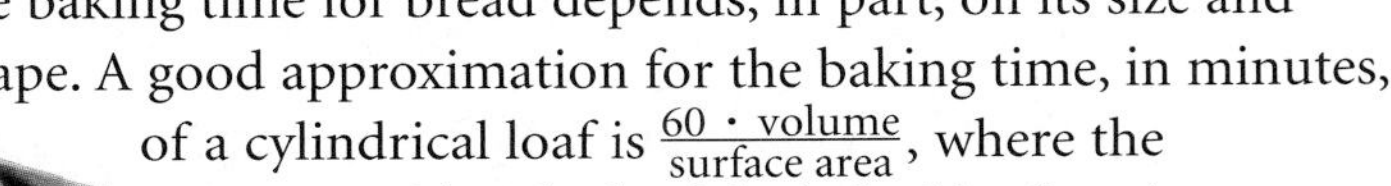

Baking The baking time for bread depends, in part, on its size and shape. A good approximation for the baking time, in minutes, of a cylindrical loaf is $\frac{60 \cdot \text{volume}}{\text{surface area}}$, where the radius r and height h of the baked loaf are in inches. Rewrite this expression in terms of r and h.

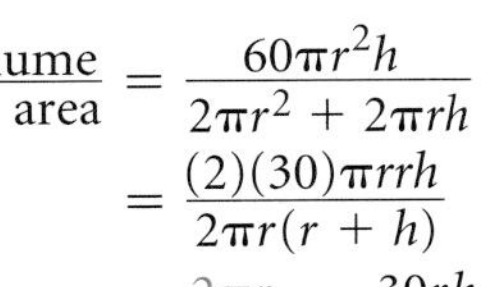

$\frac{60 \cdot \text{volume}}{\text{surface area}} = \frac{60\pi r^2 h}{2\pi r^2 + 2\pi rh}$ ← Use formulas for the volume and surface area of a cylinder.

$= \frac{(2)(30)\pi rrh}{2\pi r(r + h)}$ ← Factor the numerator and denominator.

$= \frac{2\pi r}{2\pi r} \cdot \frac{30rh}{r + h}$ ← Rewrite to show a fraction equal to 1.

$= \frac{30rh}{r + h}$ ← Simplify.

You can approximate the baking time using the expression $\frac{30rh}{r + h}$.

7. Check the answer to Example 2 by substituting values for r and h in both the original expression and the simplified expression.

8. **Critical Thinking** What values of r and h make sense in this situation? Would any values you would reasonably choose for r and h be restricted from the domain? Explain.

Multiplying and Dividing Rational Expressions

To multiply the rational expressions $\frac{a}{b}$ and $\frac{c}{d}$, where $b \neq 0$ and $d \neq 0$, you multiply the numerators and multiply the denominators. Then write the product in simplest form.

$$\frac{a}{b} \cdot \frac{c}{d} = \frac{ac}{bd}$$

Example 3

Multiply $\frac{2x+1}{3} \cdot \frac{6x}{4x^2-1}$.

$= \frac{2x+1}{3} \cdot \frac{6x}{(2x+1)(2x-1)}$ ← **Factor the denominator.**

$= \frac{\cancel{2x+1}^{\,1}}{\cancel{3}_{1}} \cdot \frac{\cancel{6x}^{\,2}}{\cancel{(2x+1)}_{1}(2x-1)}$ ← **Divide out the common factors 3 and (2x + 1).**

$= \frac{2x}{2x-1}$ ← **Simplify.**

9. What values are restricted from the domain in Example 3?

10. Check the solution to Example 3 by substituting a value for x in the original expression and the simplified expression.

11. Robin's first step in finding the product $\frac{2}{w} \cdot w^5$ was to rewrite the expression as $\frac{2}{w} \cdot \frac{w^5}{1}$. Why do you think Robin did this?

To divide the rational expression $\frac{a}{b}$ by $\frac{c}{d}$, where $b \neq 0$, $c \neq 0$, and $d \neq 0$, you multiply by the reciprocal of $\frac{c}{d}$.

$$\frac{a}{b} \div \frac{c}{d} = \frac{a}{b} \cdot \frac{d}{c}$$

12. Find the reciprocal of each expression.

a. $\frac{-6d^2}{5}$ **b.** $x^2 - 1$ **c.** $\frac{1}{s+4}$

Example 4

Divide $\frac{3x^3}{2}$ by $(-15x^5)$.

$\frac{3x^3}{2} \div (-15x^5) = \frac{3x^3}{2} \cdot \frac{1}{-15x^5}$ ← **Multiply by the reciprocal of $-15x^5$.**

$= \frac{\cancel{3x^3}^{\,1}}{2} \cdot \frac{1}{\cancel{-15x^5}_{-5x^2}}$ ← **Divide out the common factor $3x^3$.**

$= -\frac{1}{10x^2}$ ← **Simplify.**

13. Try This Find each product or quotient.

a. $\frac{8y^3}{3} \cdot \frac{9}{y^4}$ **b.** $\frac{m-2}{3m+9} \cdot (2m+6)$ **c.** $\frac{y+3}{y+2} \div (y+2)$

Exercises ON YOUR OWN

Simplify each expression and state any values restricted from the domain.

1. $\frac{5a^2}{20a}$
2. $\frac{3c}{12c^3}$
3. $\frac{4x - 8}{4x + 8}$
4. $\frac{24y + 18}{36}$
5. $\frac{6a + 9}{12}$
6. $\frac{5c - 15}{c - 3}$
7. $\frac{4x^3}{28x^4}$
8. $\frac{5 - 2m}{15 - 6m}$
9. $\frac{24 - 2p}{48 - 4p}$
10. $\frac{b - 4}{b^2 - 16}$
11. $\frac{2x^2 + 2x}{3x^2 + 3x}$
12. $\frac{2s^2 + s}{s^3}$
13. $\frac{3x^2 - 9x}{x - 3}$
14. $\frac{3x + 6}{3x^2}$
15. $\frac{w^2 + 7w}{w^2 - 49}$
16. $\frac{a^2 + 2a + 1}{a + 1}$

17. **Critical Thinking** Explain why $\frac{x^2 - 9}{x + 3}$ is not the same as $x - 3$.

18. **Baking** Use the expression $\frac{30rh}{r + h}$, where r is the radius and h is the height, to estimate the baking times in minutes for each type of bread shown.

a.

biscuit:
$r = 1$ in., $h = 0.75$ in.

b.

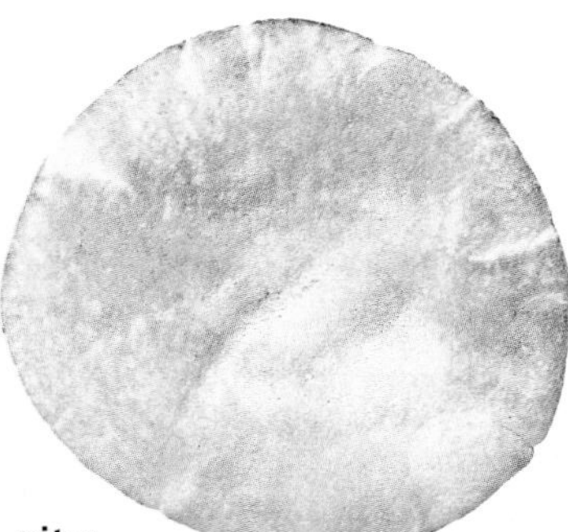

pita:
$r = 3.5$ in., $h = 0.5$ in.

c.

baguette:
$r = 1.25$ in., $h = 26$ in.

19. **Writing** Explain why the simplified form of $\frac{7 - x}{x - 7}$ is -1 when $x \neq 7$.

Find each product or quotient.

20. $\frac{7}{3} \cdot \frac{6}{21}$
21. $\frac{25}{4} \div \left(-\frac{4}{5}\right)$
22. $\frac{7b^2}{10} \div \frac{14b^3}{15}$
23. $\frac{6x^2}{5} \cdot \frac{10}{x^3}$
24. $15x^2 \div \frac{5x^4}{6}$
25. $\frac{-x^3}{8} \div \frac{-x^2}{16}$
26. $\frac{3}{a^2} \div 6a^4$
27. $\frac{5x^3}{x^2} \cdot \frac{3x^4}{10x}$
28. $\frac{x - 1}{x + 4} \div \frac{x + 3}{x + 4}$
29. $\frac{3t + 12}{5t} \div \frac{t + 4}{10t}$
30. $\frac{3x + 9}{x} \div (x + 3)$
31. $\frac{y - 4}{10} \div \frac{4 - y}{5}$
32. $\frac{4x + 1}{5x + 10} \cdot \frac{30x + 60}{2x - 2}$
33. $\frac{11k + 121}{7k - 15} \div (k + 11)$

34. **Open-ended** Write an expression that has 2 and -3 restricted from the domain.

35. **Geometry** Write and simplify the ratio for the $\frac{\text{volume of sphere}}{\text{surface area of sphere}}$. The formula for the volume of a sphere is $\frac{4}{3}\pi r^3$, and the formula for the surface area of a sphere is $4\pi r^2$, where r is the radius of the sphere.

36. *Standardized Test Prep* Compare the quantities in Column A and Column B. Assume $x \neq -1, 0$.

Column A	Column B
$\frac{-(5x+5)}{x+1}$	$-10x \cdot \frac{2x}{4x^2}$

A. The quantity in Column A is greater.
B. The quantity in Column B is greater.
C. The quantities are equal.
D. The relationship cannot be determined from the information given.

Geometry **Write an expression in simplest form for $\frac{\text{area of shaded figure}}{\text{area of larger figure}}$.**

37.

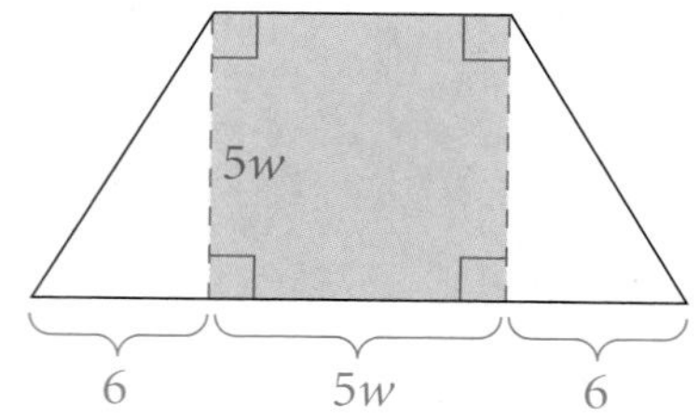

38.

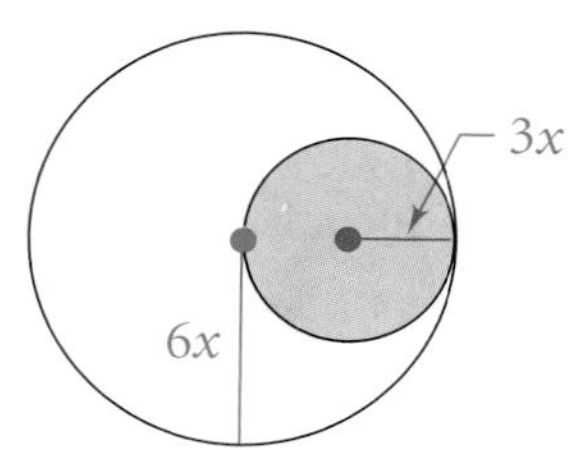

39.

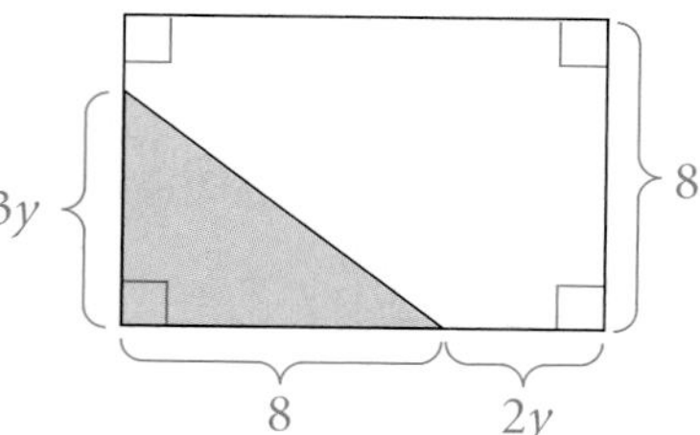

Chapter Project

Find Out by Analyzing

Pythagoras (540 B.C.) discovered that simple ratios of length produce pleasing combinations of musical pitches.

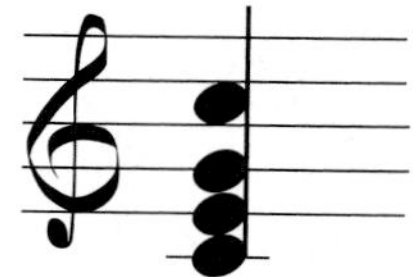

- Use the lengths you calculated in the Find Out question on page 514 to find pairs of pitches near each ratio.

  2 : 1 3 : 2 4 : 3 5 : 4 6 : 5

- A C-major chord consists of the pitches C, E, G, and C. What ratios are between the pitches of this chord?

Exercises MIXED REVIEW

Find each product.

40. $y^2(5 - y)$ **41.** $3^x \cdot 3^5$ **42.** $4x^7z^2 \cdot 9xz^{-6}$ **43.** $-6m(2m^3 + 3)$

44. *Writing* Explain why a vertical line cannot be the graph of a function.

Getting Ready for Lesson 11-4

Express each sum or difference in simplest form.

45. $\frac{1}{3} + \frac{1}{3}$ **46.** $\frac{1}{2} - \frac{2}{3}$ **47.** $\frac{4}{5} - \frac{1}{5}$ **48.** $\frac{4}{9} + \frac{1}{6}$

What You'll Learn

- Adding and subtracting rational expressions
- Finding the LCD of two rational expressions

...And Why

To investigate real-world situations, such as groundspeed for air travel

11-4 Operations with Rational Expressions

WORK TOGETHER

Work with a partner to complete the following.

1. Add.
   a. $\frac{4}{9} + \frac{2}{9}$ b. $\frac{4x}{9} + \frac{2x}{9}$ c. $\frac{4}{9x} + \frac{2}{9x}$
2. Subtract.
   a. $\frac{7}{12} - \frac{1}{12}$ b. $\frac{7x}{12} - \frac{x}{12}$ c. $\frac{7}{12x} - \frac{1}{12x}$
3. If $\frac{a}{b}$ and $\frac{c}{b}$ are rational expressions, where $b \neq 0$, write rules for adding and subtracting the two expressions.

THINK AND DISCUSS

In the Work Together activity, you added and subtracted rational expressions with the same monomial denominator. You use the same method when you have a denominator that is a polynomial.

Example 1

Simplify $\frac{2}{x+3} + \frac{5}{x+3}$.

$\frac{2}{x+3} + \frac{5}{x+3} = \frac{2+5}{x+3}$ ← **Add the numerators.**

$= \frac{7}{x+3}$ ← **Simplify the numerator.**

4. **Try This** Simplify each expression.
   a. $\frac{3}{x+2} - \frac{2}{x+2}$ b. $\frac{y}{y-5} + \frac{3y}{y-5}$ c. $\frac{2n+5}{n+1} - \frac{n-1}{n+1}$

To add or subtract rational expressions with different denominators, you must write the expressions with a common denominator. Your work will be simpler if you find the least common denominator (LCD), which is the least common multiple of the denominators.

5. Look at the table below. How is finding the LCD of $\frac{3}{4}$ and $\frac{1}{6}$ like finding the LCD of $\frac{3}{4x}$ and $\frac{1}{6x^2}$?

LCD of Numbers	*LCD of Variable Expressions*
$4 = 2 \cdot 2$	$4x = 2 \cdot 2 \cdot \quad x$
$6 = 2 \cdot \quad 3$	$6x^2 = 2 \cdot \quad 3 \cdot x \cdot x$
$\text{LCD} = 2 \cdot 2 \cdot 3 = 12$	$\text{LCD} = 2 \cdot 2 \cdot 3 \cdot x \cdot x = 12x^2$

Example 2

Simplify $\frac{2}{3x} + \frac{1}{6}$.

Step 1: Find the LCD of $\frac{2}{3x}$ and $\frac{1}{6}$.

$3x = 3 \cdot x$ and $6 = 2 \cdot 3$ ← **Factor each denominator.**

The LCD is $3 \cdot x \cdot 2$ or $6x$.

Step 2: Rewrite the original expression and add.

$\frac{2}{3x} = \frac{2 \cdot 2}{3x \cdot 2} = \frac{4}{6x}$ ← **Multiply numerator and denominator by 2.**

$\frac{1}{6} = \frac{1 \cdot x}{6 \cdot x} = \frac{x}{6x}$ ← **Multiply numerator and denominator by *x*.**

Step 3: Rewrite the original expression and add.

$\frac{2}{3x} + \frac{1}{6} = \frac{4}{6x} + \frac{x}{6x}$ ← **Replace each expression with its equivalent.**

$= \frac{4 + x}{6x}$ ← **Add the numerators.**

PROBLEM SOLVING

Look Back Why is multiplying both the numerator and the denominator of a fraction by $2x$ equivalent to multiplying the fraction by 1?

6. Try This Simplify.

a. $\frac{5}{12b} + \frac{1}{36b^2}$ **b.** $\frac{3}{7y^4} + \frac{2}{3y^2}$ **c.** $\frac{4}{25x} - \frac{49}{100}$

You can factor to find the LCD when the denominators are polynomials.

Example 3

Simplify $\frac{1}{y^2 + 5y + 4} - \frac{3}{5y + 5}$.

Step 1: Find the LCD.

$y^2 + 5y + 4 = (y + 1)(y + 4)$ and $5y + 5 = 5(y + 1)$ ← **Factor each denominator.**

The LCD is $5(y + 1)(y + 4)$.

Step 2: Write equivalent expressions with denominator $5(y + 1)(y + 4)$.

$\frac{1}{(y + 1)(y + 4)} = \frac{5}{5(y + 1)(y + 4)}$ ← **Multiply numerator and denominator by 5.**

$\frac{3}{5(y + 1)} = \frac{3(y + 4)}{5(y + 1)(y + 4)}$ ← **Multiply numerator and denominator by $(y + 4)$.**

Step 3: Subtract.

$$\frac{5}{5(y + 1)(y + 4)} - \frac{3(y + 4)}{5(y + 1)(y + 4)} = \frac{5 - 3(y + 4)}{5(y + 1)(y + 4)}$$

$$= \frac{5 - 3y - 12}{5(y + 1)(y + 4)}$$

$$= \frac{-7 - 3y}{5(y + 1)(y + 4)}$$

7. Explain why the LCD in Example 3 is not $5(y + 1)(y + 1)(y + 4)$.

NEW YORK MATH A

Math A Test Prep

1 Which is the axis of symmetry of the graph of $y = x^2 + 10x + 10$?
(1) $x = -5$ (3) $x = 3$
(2) $y = 4$ (4) $y = -4$

2 Find the quotient: $\frac{2m + 6}{m + 3} \div m$. State any values restricted from the domain.

You can combine rational expressions to investigate real-world situations.

Example 4 Relating to the Real World 

Air Travel The groundspeed for jet traffic from Los Angeles to New York City is about 15% faster than the groundspeed from New York City to Los Angeles. This difference is due to a strong westerly wind at high altitudes. If r is a jet's groundspeed from New York to Los Angeles, write an expression for the round-trip air time. The two cities are about 2500 mi apart.

NYC to LA time: $\frac{2500}{r}$ ← time = $\frac{\text{distance}}{\text{rate}}$

LA to NYC time: $\frac{2500}{1.15r}$ ← time = $\frac{\text{distance}}{\text{rate}}$

Write an expression for the total time.

$$\frac{2500}{r} + \frac{2500}{1.15r} = \frac{2875}{1.15r} + \frac{2500}{1.15r}$$ ← Rewrite using the LCD.

$$= \frac{5375}{1.15r}$$ ← Add.

$$\approx \frac{4674}{r}$$ ← Simplify.

The expression $\frac{4674}{r}$ approximates the total time for the trip, where r is the speed of the jet.

QUICK REVIEW

15% more than a number is 115% of the number. 115% = 1.15.

8. Suppose a jet flies from Los Angeles to New York City at 420 mi/h. How long will the round-trip take?

Exercises ON YOUR OWN

Simplify the following expressions.

1. $\frac{4}{5} + \frac{3}{5}$ **2.** $\frac{6}{x} + \frac{1}{x}$ **3.** $-\frac{2}{3b} - \frac{4}{3b}$ **4.** $\frac{5}{h} - \frac{3}{h}$

5. $\frac{7}{11g} - \frac{3}{11g}$ **6.** $\frac{3x}{7} + \frac{6x}{7}$ **7.** $\frac{5}{6d} + \frac{7}{6d}$ **8.** $\frac{5x}{9} - \frac{x}{9}$

9. $\frac{3n}{7} + \frac{2n}{7}$ **10.** $\frac{6}{17p} - \frac{9}{17p}$ **11.** $\frac{12r}{5} + \frac{14r}{5}$ **12.** $-\frac{8}{7k} - \frac{9}{7k}$

Find the LCD.

13. $\frac{1}{2x}; \frac{1}{4x^2}$ **14.** $\frac{b}{6}; \frac{2b}{9}$ **15.** $\frac{6}{2m^2}; \frac{1}{m}$ **16.** $\frac{1}{z}; \frac{3}{7z}$

17. $\frac{-5}{6t^5}; \frac{3}{2t^2}$ **18.** $\frac{3}{7s^5}; \frac{-4}{5s^2}$ **19.** $\frac{24}{23d^3}; \frac{25}{2d^4}$ **20.** $-\frac{3y^2}{15}; \frac{11y^5}{6}$

21. $\frac{6a}{5}; \frac{-5}{a}$ **22.** $\frac{7}{2k^4}; \frac{7}{9k^{11}}$ **23.** $\frac{8}{5b}; \frac{12}{7b^3}$ **24.** $\frac{6}{h^7}; \frac{1}{k^3}$

Simplify.

25. $\frac{7}{3a} + \frac{2}{5a^4}$ **26.** $\frac{4}{x} - \frac{2}{3x^5}$ **27** $\frac{6}{5x^8} + \frac{4}{3x^6}$ **28.** $\frac{12}{k} - \frac{5}{k^2}$

29. $\frac{3}{6b} - \frac{4}{2b^4}$ **30.** $\frac{2}{y} + \frac{3}{5y}$ **31.** $\frac{3}{8m^3} + \frac{1}{12m^2}$ **32.** $\frac{1}{5x^3} + \frac{3}{20x^2}$

33. $-\frac{5}{4k} - \frac{8}{9k}$ **34.** $\frac{27}{n^3} - \frac{9}{7n^2}$ **35.** $\frac{9}{4x^2} + \frac{9}{5}$ **36.** $\frac{5}{12m^3} + \frac{7}{6m^8}$

37. a. Exercise Suppose Jane walks one mile from her house to her grandparents' house. Then she returns home walking with her grandfather. Her return rate is 70% of her normal walking rate. Let r represent her normal walking rate. Write an expression for the amount of time Jane spends walking.

b. Suppose Jane's normal walking rate is 3 mi/h. How much time does she spend walking?

Simplify.

38. $\frac{10}{x - 1} - \frac{5}{x - 1}$ **39.** $\frac{7}{m + 1} + \frac{3}{m + 1}$ **40.** $\frac{4}{6m - 1} + \frac{3}{6m - 1}$

41. $\frac{m}{m + 3} + \frac{2}{m + 3}$ **42.** $\frac{3n + 2}{n + 4} - \frac{n - 6}{n + 4}$ **43.** $\frac{5}{t^2 + 1} - \frac{3}{t^2 + 1}$

44. $\frac{2y + 1}{y - 1} - \frac{y + 2}{y - 1}$ **45.** $\frac{s^2 + 3}{4s^2 + 2} + \frac{s^2 - 1}{4s^2 + 2}$ **46.** $\frac{1}{2 - b} - \frac{4}{2 - b}$

47. $\frac{1}{m + 2} + \frac{1}{m^2 + 3m + 2}$ **48.** $\frac{4}{x - 5} - \frac{3}{x + 5}$ **49.** $\frac{5}{y + 2} + \frac{4}{y^2 - y - 6}$

50. Writing When adding or subtracting rational expressions, will the answer be in simplest form if you use the LCD? Explain.

51. Open-ended Write two rational expressions with different denominators. Find the LCD and add the two expressions.

Chapter Project

Find Out by Creating

How does a flute or a pipe organ create different pitches? Get two cardboard tubes used to hold wrapping paper or to mail posters. Cut one tube into two lengths *A* and *B* whose ratio is 2:1. Hold your hand tightly over the longer piece (*A*) and blow over the open end until you get a pitch. Now try the shorter piece. What do you hear?

Cut two more pieces from the other tube by measuring them against piece *A*. Make one $\frac{2}{3}$ of *A* and the other $\frac{4}{5}$ of *A*. (You should have a small piece left over.) Get some friends together and play the first phrase of "The Star Spangled Banner."

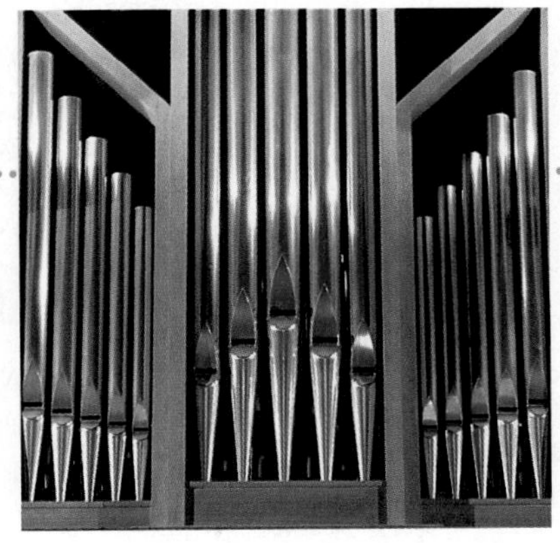

Exercises MIXED REVIEW

Find the hypotenuse of a right triangle with the given legs.

52. $a = 9, b = 12$ **53.** $a = 10, b = 7$ **54.** $a = 12, b = 5$ **55.** $a = 6, b = 9$

56. Population Surveys The 1990 census may have missed 4 million people out of about 250 million people living in the United States. What percent of the people may have been missed?

Getting Ready for Lesson 11-5

Mental Math **Find the value of each variable.**

57. $\frac{1}{2} + \frac{1}{m} = \frac{3}{4}$ **58.** $\frac{3}{x} + \frac{1}{x} = 1$ **59.** $\frac{2}{n} + \frac{1}{n} = \frac{1}{2}$ **60.** $\frac{4}{3} - \frac{2}{x} = \frac{2}{3}$

Algebra at Work

Electrician

More than half a million men and women make their livings as electricians. All are highly skilled technicians licensed by the states in which they work. Electricians use formulas containing rational expressions. For example, when a circuit connected "in parallel" contains two resistors with resistances r_1 and r_2 ohms, the total resistance R (in ohms) of the circuit can be found using the formula $\frac{1}{R} = \frac{1}{r_1} + \frac{1}{r_2}$.

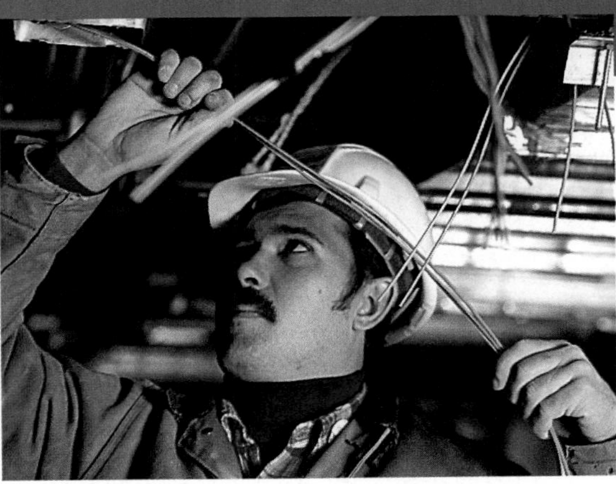

Mini Project: Research the difference between circuits connected *in parallel* and *in series*. Write a brief report of your findings. Include diagrams with your report.

What You'll Learn

- Solving equations involving rational expressions

...And Why

To solve real-world situations, such as those involving mail processors

11-5 Solving Rational Equations

THINK AND DISCUSS

A **rational equation** contains rational expressions. A method for solving rational equations is similar to the method you learned in Chapter 3 for solving equations with rational numbers.

Solving Equations with Rational Numbers

$$\frac{1}{2}x + \frac{3}{4} = \frac{1}{5}$$ ← The denominators are 2, 4, and 5. The LCD is 20.

$$20\left(\frac{1}{2}x + \frac{3}{4}\right) = 20\left(\frac{1}{5}\right)$$ ← Multiply each side by 20.

$$\overset{10}{\cancel{20}}\left(\frac{1}{\underset{1}{\cancel{2}}}x\right) + \overset{5}{\cancel{20}}\left(\frac{3}{\underset{1}{\cancel{4}}}\right) = \overset{4}{\cancel{20}}\left(\frac{1}{\underset{1}{\cancel{5}}}\right)$$ ← Use the distributive property.

$$10x + 15 = 4$$ ← No fractions! This equation is much easier to solve.

Solving Equations with Rational Expressions

$$\frac{1}{2x} + \frac{3}{4} = \frac{1}{5x}$$ ← The denominators are $2x$, 4, and $5x$. The LCD is $20x$.

$$20x\left(\frac{1}{2x} + \frac{3}{4}\right) = 20x\left(\frac{1}{5x}\right)$$ ← Multiply each side by $20x$.

$$\overset{10}{\cancel{20x}}\left(\frac{1}{\underset{1}{\cancel{2x}}}\right) + \overset{5}{\cancel{20}}x\left(\frac{3}{\underset{1}{\cancel{4}}}\right) = \overset{4}{\cancel{20x}}\left(\frac{1}{\underset{1}{\cancel{5x}}}\right)$$ ← Use the distributive property.

$$10 + 15x = 4$$ ← No rational expressions! Now you can solve.

1. Find the LCD of each equation.

a. $\frac{3}{4n} - \frac{1}{2} = \frac{2}{n}$ **b.** $\frac{1}{3x} + \frac{2}{5} = \frac{4}{3x}$ **c.** $\frac{1}{8y} = \frac{5}{6} - \frac{1}{y}$

There are often values that are excluded from the domain of a rational expression. When you solve rational equations, check your solutions to be sure that your answer satisfies the original equation.

Example 1

Solve $\frac{5}{x^2} = \frac{6}{x} - 1$.

$$x^2\left(\frac{5}{x^2}\right) = x^2\left(\frac{6}{x} - 1\right)$$ ← Multiply each side by the LCD, x^2.

$$\overset{1}{\cancel{x^2}}\left(\frac{5}{\underset{1}{\cancel{x^2}}}\right) = \overset{x}{\cancel{x^2}}\left(\frac{6}{\underset{1}{\cancel{x}}}\right) - x^2(1)$$ ← Use the distributive property.

$$5 = 6x - x^2$$ ← Simplify.

$$x^2 - 6x + 5 = 0$$ ← Collect terms on one side.

$$(x - 5)(x - 1) = 0$$ ← Factor the quadratic expression.

$(x - 5) = 0$ or $(x - 1) = 0$ ← Use the zero-product property.

$x = 5$ $\qquad x = 1$ ← Solve.

Check $\frac{5}{5^2} \stackrel{?}{=} \frac{6}{5} - 1 \qquad \frac{5}{1^2} \stackrel{?}{=} \frac{6}{1} - 1$

$\frac{1}{5} = \frac{1}{5}$ ✔ $\qquad 5 = 5$ ✔

Since 5 and 1 check in the original equation, they are the solutions.

Example 2 **Relating to the Real World** 

Business The Fresia Company owns two electronic mail processors. The newer machine works three times as fast as the older one. Together the two machines process 1000 pieces of mail in 25 min. How long does it take each machine, working alone, to process 1000 pieces of mail?

Define

	Time to process 1000 pieces (min)	Processing rate (pieces/min)
New machine	n	$\frac{1000}{n}$
Old machine	$3n$	$\frac{1000}{3n}$
Both machines	25	$\frac{1000}{25} = 40$

Relate Processing rate of new machine + Processing rate of old machine = Processing rate of both machines

Write $\frac{1000}{n} + \frac{1000}{3n} = 40$

$3n\left(\frac{1000}{n} + \frac{1000}{3n}\right) = 3n(40)$ ← Multiply each side by the LCD, $3n$.

$3n\left(\frac{1000}{n}\right) + 3n\left(\frac{1000}{3n}\right) = 3n(40)$ ← Use the distributive property.

$3000 + 1000 = 120n$ ← Simplify.

$4000 = 120n$

$33.3 \approx n$ ← Divide each side by 120.

The new machine can process 1000 pieces of mail in about 33 min. The old machine takes $3 \cdot 33.3$, or 100 min, to process 1000 pieces of mail.

Math A Test Prep

1 What is the LCD of $\frac{3}{2x + 1}$ and $\frac{6}{2x^2 - 5x - 3}$?
(1) $2x + 1$
(2) 3
(3) $2x^2 - 5x - 3$
(4) $x - 3$

2 Tom can rake all the leaves in his yard in half the time it takes his brother. Together it took the boys 4 hours to rake the yard. They filled 50 bags. How long would it have taken each brother working alone?

2. Try This Solve each equation.

a. $\frac{1}{3} + \frac{1}{3x} = \frac{1}{7}$ **b.** $\frac{2}{3x} = \frac{1}{5} - \frac{3}{x}$

The process of multiplying by the LCD can sometimes lead to a solution that does not check in the original equation.

Example 3

Solve $\frac{-1}{x - 2} = \frac{x - 4}{2(x - 2)} + \frac{1}{3}$.

The LCD is $6(x - 2)$. Multiply each side by the LCD, then solve.

$$6(x - 2)\left(\frac{-1}{x - 2}\right) = 6(x - 2)\left(\frac{x - 4}{2(x - 2)} + \frac{1}{3}\right)$$

$$6(x - 2)\left(\frac{-1}{x - 2}\right) = 6(x - 2)\left(\frac{x - 4}{2(x - 2)}\right) + 6(x - 2)\left(\frac{1}{3}\right)$$

$-6 = 3(x - 4) + 2(x - 2)$ ← Simplify.

$-6 = 3x - 12 + 2x - 4$ ← distributive property

$-6 = 5x - 16$ ← Combine like terms.

$10 = 5x$ ← Add 16 to each side.

$2 = x$ ← Divide each side by 5.

Check $\frac{-1}{2 - 2} \stackrel{?}{=} \frac{2 - 4}{2(2 - 2)} + \frac{1}{3}$

$\frac{-1}{0} = \frac{-2}{0} + \frac{1}{3}$ ← Undefined!

The equation has *no* solution because 2 makes a denominator equal 0.

3. Try This Solve each equation. Be sure to check your answers!

a. $\frac{2}{x} - \frac{8}{x^2} = -1$ **b.** $\frac{1}{w + 1} = 1 - \frac{1}{w(w + 1)}$

Exercises ON YOUR OWN

1. Carlos studied the problem at the right and said, "I'll start by finding the LCD." Ingrid studied the problem and said, "I'll start by cross-multiplying."

Solve $\frac{40}{x} = \frac{15}{x - 20}$.

a. Solve the equation using Carlos's method, and then using Ingrid's method.

b. **Writing** Which method do you prefer? Why?

c. **Critical Thinking** Will Ingrid's method work for all rational equations? Explain.

Solve each equation. Be sure to check your answers!

2. $\frac{1}{2} + \frac{2}{x} = \frac{1}{x}$ **3.** $\frac{1}{20} + \frac{1}{30} = \frac{1}{x}$ **4.** $5 + \frac{2}{p} = \frac{17}{p}$

5. $\frac{3}{a} - \frac{5}{a} = 2$ **6.** $\frac{5}{n} - \frac{1}{2} = 2$ **7.** $\frac{1}{x + 2} = \frac{1}{2x}$

8. $y - \frac{6}{y} = 5$

9. $\frac{30}{x + 3} = \frac{30}{x - 3}$

10. $\frac{4}{a + 1} = \frac{8}{2 - a}$

11. $\frac{5}{y} + \frac{3}{2} = \frac{1}{3y}$

12. $\frac{2}{3b} - \frac{3}{4} = \frac{1}{6b}$

13. $\frac{5}{2s} + \frac{3}{4} = \frac{9}{4s}$

14. **Business** The PRX Company owns one scanning machine that scans 10,000 documents in 25 min. The company then buys a newer scanner, and together, the two machines scan 10,000 documents in 10 min. How long would it take the newer machine, working alone, to scan 10,000 documents?

15. **Plumbing** You can fill a 30-gallon tub in 15 min with both faucets running. If the cold water faucet runs twice as fast as the hot water faucet, how long will it take to fill the tub with only cold water?

16. **Graphing Calculator** Write two functions using the expressions on each side of the equation $\frac{6}{x^2} + 1 = \frac{(x + 7)^2}{6}$. Graph the functions. Find the coordinates of the points of intersection. Are the x-values solutions to the equation? Explain.

Geometry **Find each value of x if the area of each shaded region is 64 square units. Assume that each quadrilateral shown is a rectangle.**

17.

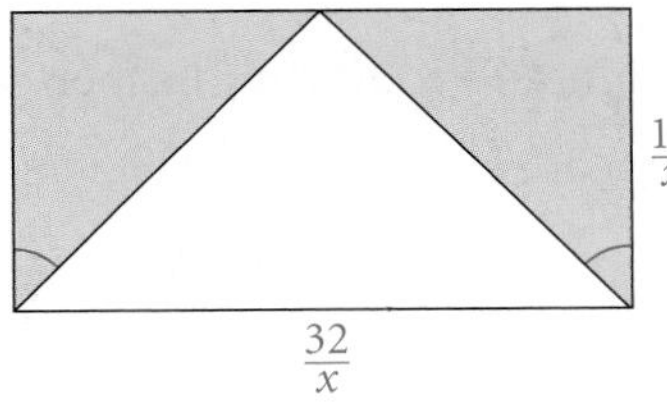

18.

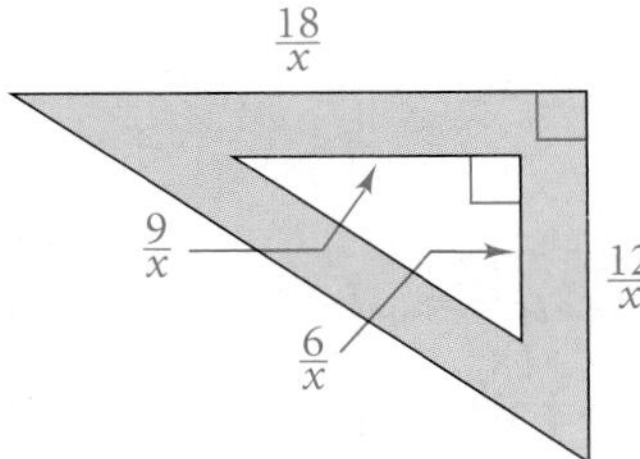

19.

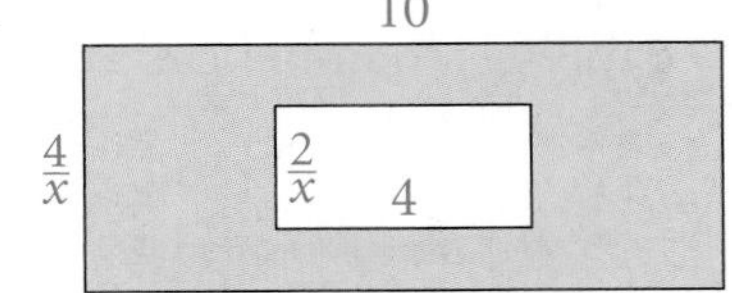

Solve each equation. Be sure to check your answers!

20. $\frac{1}{2} = -\frac{1}{3(x - 3)}$

21. $\frac{1}{t - 2} = \frac{t}{8}$

22. $\frac{x - 11}{3x} = \frac{x - 19}{5x}$

23. $\frac{4}{3(c + 4)} + 1 = \frac{2c}{c + 4}$

24. $\frac{8}{x + 3} = \frac{1}{x} + 1$

25. $\frac{x + 2}{x + 4} = \frac{x - 2}{x - 1}$

26. $\frac{2}{c - 2} = 2 - \frac{4}{c}$

27. $\frac{5}{3p} + \frac{2}{3} = \frac{5 + p}{2p}$

28. $\frac{3}{s - 1} + 1 = \frac{12}{s^2 - 1}$

29. **Standardized Test Prep** Which inequality contains both of the solutions of the equation $5x = \frac{7}{2} + \frac{6}{x}$?

A. $-1 < x < 3$

B. $0 < x < \frac{3}{2}$

C. $-2 \leq x < 0$

D. $-3 \leq x \leq -1$

E. none of the above

30. A plane flies 450 mi/h. It can travel 980 mi with a wind in the same amount of time as it travels 820 mi against the wind. Solve the equation $\frac{980}{450 + s} = \frac{820}{450 - s}$ to find the speed s of the wind.

31. Find the value of each variable. $\begin{bmatrix} \frac{5a}{3} & \frac{7}{3b} \\ \frac{2c - 15}{35c} & \frac{5}{2d} + \frac{3}{4} \end{bmatrix} = \begin{bmatrix} 2 + \frac{7a}{6} & 9 \\ \frac{1}{5c} & \frac{9}{4d} \end{bmatrix}$

Chapter Project ***Find Out by Interviewing***

The pitch produced by a vibrating string is affected by how tightly it is stretched, or its tension. Find out how a violin, guitar, or other stringed instrument is tuned by talking with someone who plays it.

Exercises MIXED REVIEW

Solve each equation. Round to the nearest hundredth, where necessary.

32. $x^2 = 3x + 8$ **33.** $x^2 - 4 = 0$ **34.** $2x^2 + 6 = 4x$ **35.** $7x = 5x - 11$

36. *Open-ended* Give an example of two quantities that vary inversely. Write an equation to go with your example.

Getting Ready for Lesson 11-6

List the possible outcomes of each action.

37. rolling a number cube once **38.** tossing a coin twice **39.** tossing a coin and rolling a number cube

Exercises CHECKPOINT

Simplify each expresssion and state any restrictions on the variable.

1. $\frac{8m^2}{2m^3}$ **2.** $\frac{6x^2 - 24}{x + 2}$ **3.** $\frac{3c + 9}{3c - 9}$ **4.** $\frac{3z^2 + 12z}{z^4}$

5. *Open-ended* Write an expression where the variable cannot equal 3.

Solve each equation.

6. $\frac{9}{t} + \frac{3}{2} = 12$ **7.** $\frac{10}{z + 4} = \frac{30}{2z + 3}$ **8.** $\frac{1}{m - 2} = \frac{5}{m}$ **9.** $c - \frac{8}{c} = 10$

Find each sum or difference.

10. $\frac{5}{c} + \frac{4}{c}$ **11.** $\frac{9}{x - 3} - \frac{4}{x - 3}$ **12.** $\frac{8}{m + 2} - \frac{6}{3 - m}$ **13.** $\frac{6}{t} + \frac{3}{t^2}$

14. *Standardized Test Prep* What is the LCD of $\frac{8}{n}$, $\frac{5}{3 - n}$, and $\frac{1}{n^2}$?

A. $n^2 + 3n$ **B.** $3n^2 - n^3$ **C.** $n^2 + 3$ **D.** $3n^3 - n^4$ **E.** $n^3 - 3n^2$

Problem Solving

Algebraic Reasoning

After Lesson 11-5

You can use the properties you have studied and the three below to prove algebraic relationships and to justify steps in the solution of an equation.

Properties of Equality

For all real numbers a, b, and c:

Reflexive Property: $a = a$ Example: $5x = 5x$

Symmetric Property: If $a = b$, then $b = a$. Example: If $15 = 3t$, then $3t = 15$.

Transitive Property: If $a = b$ and $b = c$, then $a = c$. Example: If $d = 3y$ and $3y = 6$, then $d = 6$.

Example 1

Prove that if $a = b$, then $ac = bc$.

Statements	Reasons
$a = b$ ⟵	Given
$ac = ac$ ⟵	Reflexive prop.
$ac = bc$ ⟵	Substitute b for a.

Example 2

Solve $-32 = 4(y - 3)$. Justify each step.

Steps	Reasons
$-32 = 4(y - 3)$ ⟵	Given
$-32 = 4y - 12$ ⟵	Distributive prop.
$-20 = 4y$ ⟵	Addition prop. of equality
$-5 = y$ ⟵	Division prop. of equality
$y = -5$ ⟵	Symmetric prop. of equality

Name the property that each exercise illustrates.

1. If $3.8 = z$, then $z = 3.8$.

2. If $x = \frac{1}{2}y$, and $\frac{1}{2}y = -2$, then $x = -2$.

3. $-4r = -4r$

Supply the missing reasons.

4. Solve $-5 = 1 + 3d$. Justify each step.

Steps	Reasons
$-5 = 1 + 3d$ ⟵	Given
$-6 = 3d$ ⟵	**a.** ?
$-2 = d$ ⟵	**b.** ?
$d = -2$ ⟵	**c.** ?

5. Prove that if $ax^2 + bx = 0$, then $x = 0$ or $-\frac{b}{a}$.

Statements	Reasons
$ax^2 + bx = 0$ ⟵	Given
$x^2 + \frac{b}{a}x = 0$ ⟵	**a.** ?
$x(x + \frac{b}{a}) = 0$ ⟵	**b.** ?
$x = 0$ or $x + \frac{b}{a} = 0$ ⟵	Zero-product prop.
$x = 0$ or $x = -\frac{b}{a}$ ⟵	**c.** ?

6. *Writing* If Cal is Mia's cousin, then Mia is Cal's cousin. This relationship is symmetric. Describe a relationship that is transitive.

What You'll Learn

- Using the multiplication counting principle to count outcomes
- Using permutations to count outcomes
- Finding probability

...And Why

To investigate the number of arrangements in situations such as the arrangement of players on a team

What You'll Need

- calculator

11-6 Counting Outcomes and Permutations

WORK TOGETHER

Entertainment Suppose you play the following CDs:

- *cracked rear view* by Hootie and the Blowfish
- *Design of a Decade* by Janet Jackson
- *Destiny* by Gloria Estefan

1. In how many different orders can you play the CDs?
2. Describe how you determined the number of different ways to order the CDs.
3. What is the probability that the CDs will be played in alphabetical order?

THINK AND DISCUSS

Using the Multiplication Counting Principle

One way you could find outcomes is to make an organized list or a tree diagram. Both help you to see if you have thought of all possibilities.

Suppose you have three shirts and two pair of pants that coordinate well together. You can use a tree diagram to find the number of possible outfits you have.

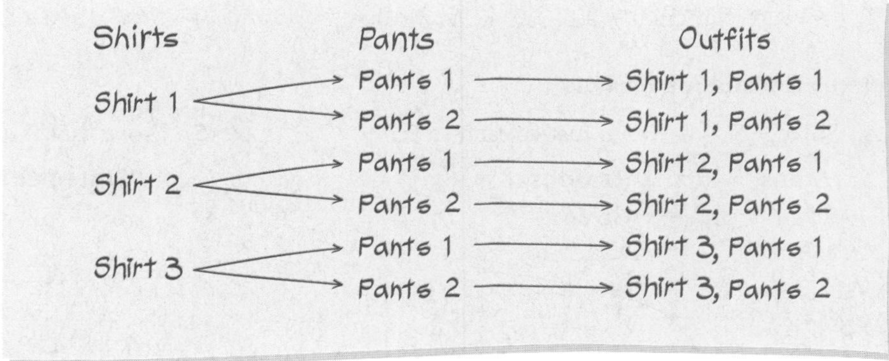

There are six possible outfits.

4. Would you want to use a tree diagram to find the number of outfits for five shirts and eight pairs of pants? Explain.

QUICK REVIEW

When one event does not affect the result of a second event, they are *independent events.*

When events are independent, you can find the number of outcomes by using the multiplication counting principle.

Multiplication Counting Principle

If there are m ways to make a first selection and n ways to make a second selection, there are $m \times n$ ways to make the two selections.

Example: For 3 shirts and 2 pairs of pants, the number of possible outfits is $3 \cdot 2 = 6$.

Example 1 Relating to the Real World 

Travel Suppose there are two routes you can choose to get from Austin, Texas, to Dallas, Texas, and four routes from Dallas to Tulsa, Oklahoma. How many routes are there from Austin to Tulsa through Dallas?

$2 \cdot 4 = 8$ ← routes from Austin to Tulsa through Dallas

(2: routes from Austin to Dallas; 4: routes from Dallas to Tulsa)

There are eight possible routes from Austin to Tulsa.

5. **Try This** At the neighborhood pizza shop, there are five vegetable toppings and three meat toppings for a pizza. How many possible pizzas can you order with one meat and one vegetable topping?

Finding Permutations

ABC	ACB
BAC	BCA
CAB	CBA

A common kind of counting problem is to find the number of arrangements of a set of objects. The list at the left shows the possible arrangements for the letters A, B, and C without repeating any letters in an arrangement.

Each of the arrangements is called a permutation. A **permutation** is an arrangement of some or all of a set of objects in a specific order.

Example 2 Relating to the Real World 

Sports In how many ways can nine baseball players be listed for batting order?

There are 9 choices for the first batter, 8 for the second, 7 for the third, and so on.

$9 \cdot 8 \cdot 7 \cdot 6 \cdot 5 \cdot 4 \cdot 3 \cdot 2 \cdot 1 = 362880$ ← Use a calculator.

There are 362,880 possible arrangements of the batters.

CALCULATOR HINT

The notation 9!, read as *nine factorial*, means the product of the integers from 9 to 1. Use this sequence to find 9!:

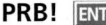

  PRB! ENTER

6. **Critical Thinking** Why are there only 8 choices for the second batter and 7 choices for the third batter?

CALCULATOR HINT

You can use the following calculator steps to find ${}_8P_3$:

8 MATH PRB ${}_NP_R$ 3 ENTER

In how many ways can you select a right, center, and left fielder from eight people? This means finding the number of permutations of 8 objects (players) arranged 3 at a time. You can use ${}_nP_r$ to express the number of permutations where n equals the number of objects and r equals the number of selections to make. Eight players arranged three at a time is ${}_8P_3$.

You can use the multiplication counting principle to evaluate permutations.

${}_8P_3 = 8 \cdot 7 \cdot 6$, or 336 arrangements of 8 players arranged 3 at a time.

${}_nP_r = n(n-1)(n-2)\ldots$ **Stop when you have r factors.**

first factor (n) **number of factors** (r)

7. **a.** Use ${}_nP_r$ to express the number of permutations of twelve players for five positions on a baseball team.
   b. ***Calculator*** Evaluate the number of permutations for part (a).

Example 3 **Relating to the Real World** 

Computers Suppose you use six different letters to make a computer password. Find the number of possible six-letter passwords.

There are 26 letters in the alphabet. You are finding the number of permutations of 26 letters arranged 6 at a time.

${}_{26}P_6 = 26 \cdot 25 \cdot 24 \cdot 23 \cdot 22 \cdot 21 = 165{,}765{,}600$ ← **Use a calculator.**

There are 165,765,600 six-letter passwords in which letters do not repeat.

8. What would ${}_{26}P_8$ mean if you were making a password?

9. **a.** ***Probability*** Lena wants a password that uses the four letters of her name. How many permutations are possible using each letter in her name only once?
   b. Suppose a four-letter password with no repeated letters is assigned randomly. What is the probability that it uses the letters L, E, N, and A?
   c. ***Critical Thinking*** Is creating a password based on your name a good idea? Explain.

Exercises ON YOUR OWN

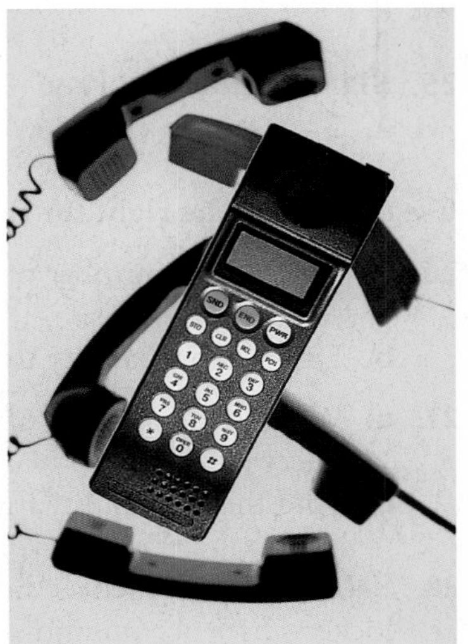

1. **Jobs** James must wear a shirt and tie for a job interview. He has two dress shirts and five ties. How many shirt-tie choices does he have?

2. **Telephones** A seven-digit telephone number can begin with any digit except 0 and 1.
   a. How many possible choices are there for the first digit? the second digit? the third digit? the seventh digit?
   b. How many different seven-digit telephone numbers are possible?

3. On a bookshelf there are five novels, two volumes of short stories, and three biographies. In how many ways can you select one of each?

4. A student council has 24 members. A 3-person committee is to arrange a car wash. Each person on the committee will have a task: One person will find a location, another will organize publicity, and the third will schedule workers. In how many different ways can three students be selected and assigned a job?

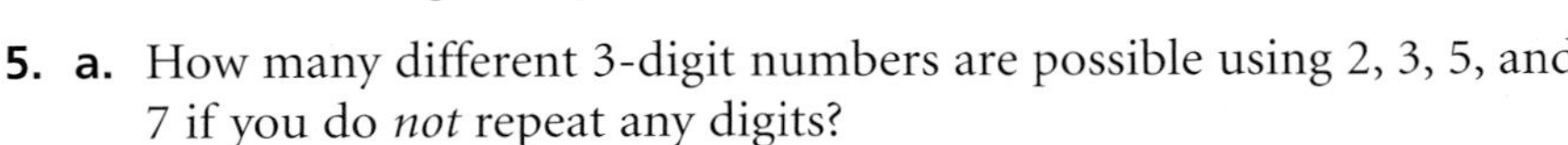

5. a. How many different 3-digit numbers are possible using 2, 3, 5, and 7 if you do *not* repeat any digits?
   b. **Critical Thinking** How many of the 3-digit numbers are even?
   c. **Writing** Explain how you found how many numbers are even in part (b).
   d. What is the probability that a number selected at random is even?

Calculator **Use a calculator to evaluate.**

6. ${}_8P_3$	7. ${}_7P_3$	8. ${}_6P_3$	9. ${}_5P_3$	10. ${}_4P_3$	11. ${}_3P_3$
12. ${}_7P_7$	13. ${}_7P_6$	14. ${}_7P_5$	15. ${}_7P_4$	16. ${}_7P_2$	17. ${}_7P_1$

18. **School Paper** For an article in the school newspaper, Cora took a poll in which she asked students to rank the top four basketball players on the high school team. There are fifteen members on the team. How many possible outcomes are there?

19. **Writing** Write a problem for which ${}_{24}P_3$ would be the solution.

20. a. **Open-ended** Use the letters of your last name. If any letters are repeated, use only one of them. For example, for the last name Bell, use the letters BEL. In how many ways can the resulting letters be arranged?
    b. In how many ways can two different letters be selected and arranged from your last name?

21. **Sports** In ice skating competitions, the order in which competitors skate is determined by a draw. If there are eight skaters in the finals, how many different orders are possible for the final program?

Calculator **Which is greater?**

22. ${}_8P_6$ or ${}_6P_2$

23. ${}_9P_7$ or ${}_9P_2$

24. ${}_{10}P_3$ or ${}_8P_4$

25. **Standardized Test Prep** For $r = 3$ and ${}_nP_r = 210$, find n.

A. 3 **B.** 6 **C.** 7 **D.** 8 **E.** 70

Use the tiles at the right for Exercises 26 and 27.

26. a. What is the number of possible arrangements in which you can select four letters?

b. Find the probability that you select C, A, R, and then E.

27. a. What is the number of possible arrangements in which you can select five letters?

b. Find the probability that you select B, R, A, I, and then N.

28. **Safety** A lock, such as the ones used on many bikes and school lockers, uses permutations. This is because the order of the numbers *is* important. Suppose you have a lock with the digits 0–9. A three-digit sequence opens the lock, and no numbers are repeated.

a. How many different sequences are possible?

b. How many sequences use a 7 as the first digit?

c. What is the probability that the sequence of numbers that opens your lock uses a 7 as the first digit?

d. **Critical Thinking** What is the probability that the sequence of numbers that opens your lock includes a 7?

Exercises MIXED REVIEW

Graph each function.

29. $y = 6x$

30. $y = \sqrt{x}$

31. $y = \frac{5}{x}$

32. $y = |x| + 3$

33. **Camping** Your family is planning a camping trip. The state park has two camping plans available. The first costs \$95 for four nights at a campsite with family trail passes for three days. The second costs \$70 for three nights at a campsite with family trail passes for two days. There is one daily charge for the campsite and one daily charge for the trail pass. Find each daily charge.

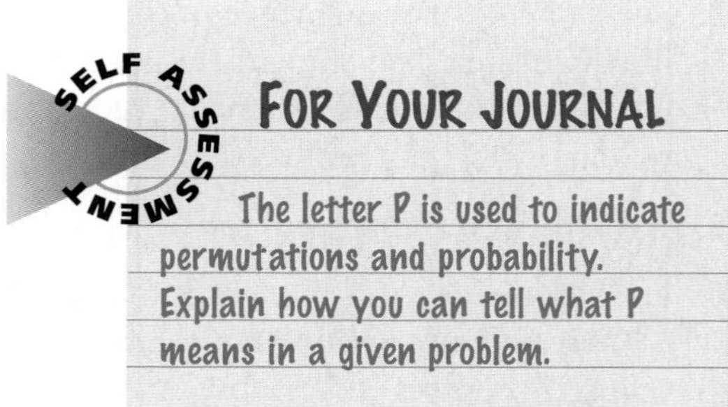

FOR YOUR JOURNAL

The letter P is used to indicate permutations and probability. Explain how you can tell what P means in a given problem.

Getting Ready for Lesson 11-7

***A* and *B* are independent events. Find *P*(*A* and *B*) for the given probabilities.**

34. $P(A) = \frac{1}{3}, P(B) = \frac{3}{4}$

35. $P(A) = \frac{1}{8}, P(B) = \frac{5}{9}$

36. $P(A) = \frac{9}{10}, P(B) = \frac{5}{6}$

11-7 Combinations

What You'll Learn

- Finding combinations
- Solving probability problems involving combinations

...And Why

To investigate situations like selecting a jury

What You'll Need

- calculator

THINK AND DISCUSS

Food Suppose you are making a sandwich with three of these ingredients: turkey, cheese, tomato, and lettuce. Below are the permutations of the four ingredients taken three at a time.

- turkey, cheese, tomato
- turkey, tomato, cheese
- cheese, tomato, turkey
- cheese, turkey, tomato
- tomato, turkey, cheese
- tomato, cheese, turkey

- turkey, cheese, lettuce
- turkey, lettuce, cheese
- cheese, lettuce, turkey
- cheese, turkey, lettuce
- lettuce, turkey, cheese
- lettuce, cheese, turkey

- turkey, tomato, lettuce
- turkey, lettuce, tomato
- tomato, lettuce, turkey
- tomato, turkey, lettuce
- lettuce, turkey, tomato
- lettuce, tomato, turkey

- cheese, tomato, lettuce
- cheese, lettuce, tomato
- tomato, lettuce, cheese
- tomato, cheese, lettuce
- lettuce, cheese, tomato
- lettuce, tomato, cheese

For sandwiches the *order* of the ingredients does not matter. So there are only four types of sandwiches. Each sandwich type is a **combination,** a collection of objects without regard to order.

The number of combinations of sandwiches equals the number of permutations divided by the number of times each type of sandwich is repeated.

$$\text{number of combinations} = \frac{\text{total number of permutations}}{\text{number of times the objects in each group are repeated}}$$

You can use the notation $_nC_r$ to write the number of combinations of n objects chosen r at time. The number of times each group of objects is repeated depends on r.

$$_4C_3 = \frac{_4P_3}{_3P_3} = \frac{4 \cdot 3 \cdot 2}{3 \cdot 2 \cdot 1}$$

$$_nC_r = \frac{_nP_r}{_rP_r} = \frac{n(n-1)(n-2)\ldots}{r(r-1)(r-2)\ldots} \quad \begin{array}{l}\leftarrow r \text{ factors starting with } n \\ \leftarrow r \text{ factors starting with } r\end{array}$$

CALCULATOR HINT

You can use the following calculator steps to find $_4C_3$:
4 MATH PRB $_NC_R$ 3 ENTER

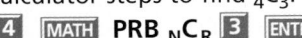

1. **Calculator** Evaluate each expression.
   a. $_4C_2$ b. $_8C_5$ c. $_7C_3$ d. $_{10}C_4$
2. a. **Try This** For your history report, you can choose to write about two of five Presidents of the United States. Use $_nC_r$ notation to write the number of combinations possible for your report.
   b. Calculate the number of combinations of presidents on whom you could report.

Example 1 Relating to the Real World 

Juries Twenty people report for jury duty. How many different twelve-person juries can be chosen?

The order in which jury members are listed does not distinguish one jury from another. You need the number of combinations of 20 objects chosen 12 at a time.

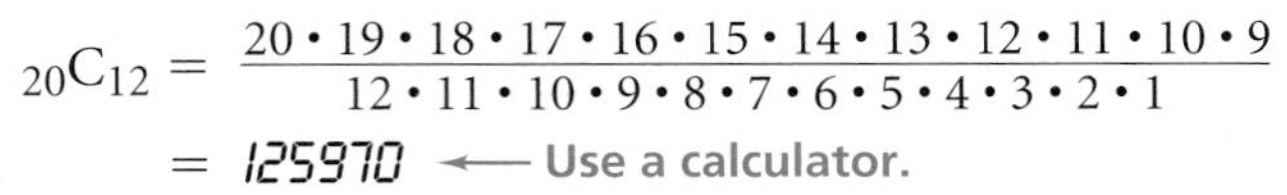

$$ {}_{20}C_{12} = \frac{20 \cdot 19 \cdot 18 \cdot 17 \cdot 16 \cdot 15 \cdot 14 \cdot 13 \cdot 12 \cdot 11 \cdot 10 \cdot 9}{12 \cdot 11 \cdot 10 \cdot 9 \cdot 8 \cdot 7 \cdot 6 \cdot 5 \cdot 4 \cdot 3 \cdot 2 \cdot 1} $$

$= 125970$ ← Use a calculator.

There are 125,970 different twelve-person juries possible.

3. For some civil cases, at least nine of twelve jurors must agree on a verdict. How many combinations of nine jurors are possible on a twelve-person jury?

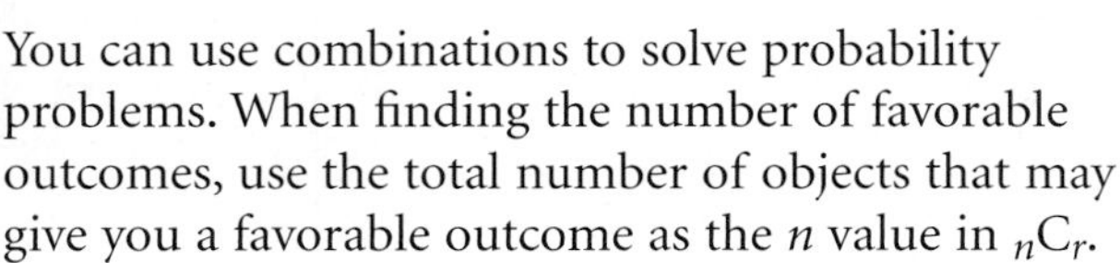

You can use combinations to solve probability problems. When finding the number of favorable outcomes, use the total number of objects that may give you a favorable outcome as the *n* value in ${}_nC_r$.

Example 2 Relating to the Real World 

Restaurants You and four friends visit a Thai restaurant. There are twelve different items on the menu. Seven are mild and the rest are spicy. You each order a different item at random. What is the probability that your group orders only mild items?

number of favorable outcomes $= {}_7C_5$ ← number of ways to choose 5 mild items from 7 mild items

number of possible outcomes $= {}_{12}C_5$ ← number of ways to choose 5 items from 12 items

$$ P(\text{5 mild menu items}) = \frac{\text{number of favorable outcomes}}{\text{total number of outcomes}} $$

$$ = \frac{{}_7C_5}{{}_{12}C_5} $$

$$ = \frac{7}{264} $$

The probability your group orders only mild items is $\frac{7}{264}$, or about 3%.

4. Suppose you and your friends like spicy food. What is the probability that you choose five different spicy items at random?

Exercises ON YOUR OWN

1. a. *Spelling Bee* Every spring the National Spelling Bee Championships are held in Washington, D.C. Prizes are awarded to the top three spellers. In 1995, 247 students competed. How many different arrangements of winners were possible?
   b. Many students in the competition hoped to make it to the final round of 10 students. How many combinations of 10 students were possible?

2. *Sports* A basketball team has 11 players. Five players are on the court at a time. Your little brother doesn't know much about basketball and randomly names 5 players on the team. What is the probability that your brother's line-up lists the same 5 players as the coach's line-up for the next game?

3. *Writing* Explain the difference between a permutation and a combination.

Calculator **Use a calculator to evaluate.**

4. ${}_6C_6$
5. ${}_6C_5$
6. ${}_6C_4$
7. ${}_6C_3$
8. ${}_6C_2$
9. ${}_6C_1$
10. ${}_{15}C_{11}$
11. ${}_{15}C_4$
12. ${}_8C_5$
13. ${}_8C_3$
14. ${}_7C_4$
15. ${}_7C_3$

16. a. Describe any patterns you see in the answers to Exercises 4–15.
    b. *Critical Thinking* Explain why the pattern you described is true.
    c. *Open-ended* Write two more combinations that have the pattern you described in part (a).

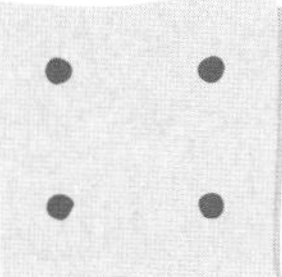

Figure 1

17. a. *Geometry* Draw four points on your paper like those in Figure 1. Draw line segments so that every point is joined with every other point.
    b. How many segments did you draw?
    c. Now find the number of segments you need for the drawing using combinations. You are joining four points, taking two at a time.
    d. How many segments would you need to join each point to all the others in Figure 2?

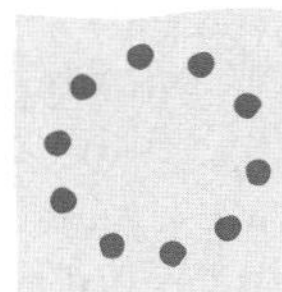

Figure 2

18. A famous problem, known as the Handshake Problem asks, "If ten people in a room shake hands with everyone else in the room, how many different handshakes occur?"
    a. Karen thinks that the Handshake Problem is a permutation problem while Tashia thinks it is a combination problem. What do you think? **Justify** your answer.
    b. Solve the problem.
    c. *Critical Thinking* Is the Handshake Problem similar to the problem in Exercise 17 (d)? Explain.

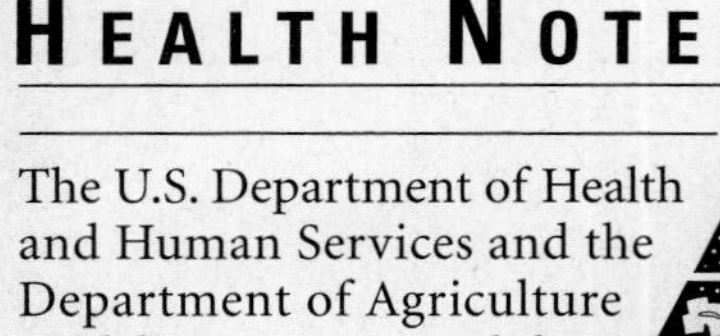

14

HEALTH NOTES

The U.S. Department of Health and Human Services and the Department of Agriculture guidelines recommend that daily food intake should include at least 3–5 servings of vegetables, at least 2–4 servings of fruit, 6–11 servings of grains, 2–3 servings of milk or cheese, and 2–3 servings of meat or poultry.

19. **Math in the Media** Suppose you want to have the highest number of recommended daily servings of fruit without repeating a fruit. Find how many different combinations of these products you can have.

One Serving of Fruit

apple	1
apple juice	1 cup
banana	1
cherries	10
grapefruit	$\frac{1}{2}$
orange	1
orange juice	1 cup
raisins	1 cup
strawberries	1 cup

Classify each of the following as a permutation or a combination problem. Explain your choice.

20. A locker contains eight books. You select three books at random. How many different sets of books could you select?

21. You rent three videos to watch during spring vacation. In how many different orders can you view the three videos?

22. The security guard at an auto plant must visit 10 different sections of the building each night. He varies his route each evening. How many different routes are possible?

23. A committee of four people needs to be formed from your homeroom of 25 students. How many four-person committees are possible?

24. **Standardized Test Prep** Compare the quantities in Columns A and B.

Column A	Column B
${}_{10}C_7$	${}_{7}P_4$

A. The quantity in Column A is greater.
B. The quantity in Column B is greater.
C. The quantities are equal.
D. The relationship cannot be determined from the given information.

Find the number of combinations of letters taken three at a time from each set of letters.

25. A B C D E

26. P Q R

27. E F G H I J K

28. M N O P

29. **Open-ended** Write and solve two problems: one that can be solved using permutations and one that can be solved using combinations.

30. For your birthday you received a gift certificate from a local music store for three CDs. There are eight that you would like to have. In how many different ways can you select your CDs?

31. **Manufacturing** Twelve computer screens are stored in a warehouse. The warehouse manager knows that three of the screens are defective, but the report telling him which ones are defective is missing. He selects five screens to begin testing.
   a. How many different choices of five screens does the manager have?
   b. In how many ways could he select five screens that include the defective ones?
   c. What is the probability that he finds the three defective screens when he tests the first five screens?

32. a. A committee of three people is to be selected from three boys and five girls. How many different committees are possible?
   b. How many committees could have all boys?
   c. What is the probability that a committee will have all boys?
   d. **Critical Thinking** What is the probability that the committee will have no boys?

33. The letters A, B, C, D, E, F, G, H, I, and J are written on slips of paper and placed in a hat. Two letters are drawn from the hat.
   a. What is the number of possible combinations of letters?
   b. How many combinations consist only of the vowels A, E, or I?
   c. What is the probability the letters chosen consist only of vowels?
   d. What is the probability the letters chosen consist only of B, C, D or F?

34. **Research** Find the number of members in your state legislature. Find how many ways a committee of ten people may be formed from the members of the legislature.

Find Out by Communicating

Every musical instrument has a part that vibrates to make different pitches. Choose an instrument and find out how it works. Make a poster that describes what vibrates and how different pitches are produced.

Exercises MIXED REVIEW

Evaluate.

35. $_4P_2$ 36. $_8P_3$ 37. $_7P_6$

38. $_8P_6$ 39. $_9P_1$ 40. $_7P_4$

PORTFOLIO

Select one or two items from your work for this chapter. Consider:
- corrected work
- diagrams, graphs, or charts
- a journal entry

Explain why you have included each selection you make.

Express each sum or difference in simplest form.

41. $\frac{4x^2}{3x} + \frac{5}{3x}$ 42. $\frac{5c}{8m} - \frac{7m}{c}$ 43. $\frac{9x}{x^2 - 4} + \frac{4}{x + 2}$

44. $\frac{9}{z} + \frac{10}{3z}$ 45. $\frac{12}{5n} - \frac{15}{4n}$ 46. $\frac{8w^2}{3 - w} - \frac{5w}{18 - 2w^2}$

47. a. **Weather** After a heavy snowfall, a homeowner had to clear about four tons of snow off a 20 ft by 20 ft driveway. A full shovel of snow weighs about 7 lb. How many times would the homeowner have to fill his shovel to clear the driveway?
   b. How many tons of snow would be on a 20 ft by 30 ft driveway?

CHAPTER PROJECT

Finishing the Chapter Project

GOOD VIBRATIONS

Questions on pages 514, 526, 531, 536, and 547 should help you to complete your project. Plan a presentation of what you have learned for your classmates. Include graphs, charts, illustrations, and demonstrations on homemade or professional instruments.

Reflect and Revise

Share your presentation with a small group of your classmates. Were your explanations clear and accurate? How does your musical instrument sound? Were you able to describe its pitch? If necessary, make any changes in your work.

Follow Up

In Western culture, C and C# are consecutive pitches in the chromatic scale. The ratio of their frequencies is about 1:1.06. Find out about the scales used in Asian cultures. How might their scales affect the design of their instruments?

For More Information

Haak, Sheila. "Using the Monochord: A Classroom Demonstration on the Mathematics of Musical Scales." *Applications of Secondary School Mathematics.* Reston, Virginia: National Council of Teachers of Mathematics, 1991.

Macaulay, David. *The Way Things Work*. Boston: Houghton Mifflin, 1988. Software Version: Dorling Kindersley Multimedia, 1994.

Wilkinson, Scott R. *Tuning In: Microtonality in Electronic Music: A Basic Guide to Alternate Scales, Temperaments, and Microtuning Using Synthesizers.* Milwaukee, Wisconsin: H. Leonard Books, 1988.

CHAPTER

11 Wrap Up

Key Terms

asymptote (p. 516)
combination (p. 543)
constant of variation (p. 510)
domain (p. 522)
inverse variation (p. 510)
multiplication counting principle (p. 539)
${}_nC_r$ (p. 543)
${}_nP_r$ (p. 540)
permutation (p. 539)
rational equation (p. 532)
rational expression (p. 522)
rational function (p. 516)

How am I doing?

- State three ideas from this chapter that you think are important. Explain your choices.
- Explain the importance of restrictions on the variable in rational expressions.

Inverse Variation 11-1

When two quantities are related so that their product is constant, they form an **inverse variation.** An inverse variation can be written $xy = k$, where k is the **constant of variation.**

Find the constant of variation for each inverse variation.

1. $m = 6$ when $n = 1$

2. $g = 90$ when $h = 0.1$

3. $s = 88$ when $t = 0.05$

For each table, tell whether it represents an inverse variation. If so, write an equation to model the data.

4.

x	1	1.4	3	7
y	4	5.6	12	28

5.

x	4	1	2	2.5
y	2.65	10.6	5.3	4.24

Rational Functions 11-2

A **rational function** can be written in the form $f(x) = \frac{\text{polynomial}}{\text{polynomial}}$. The graph of a rational function may have asymptotes. An **asymptote** is a line that a graph approaches, but does not cross.

Graph each function. Use a dashed line for each asymptote.

6. $y = \frac{8}{x}$

7. $y = \frac{20}{x}$

8. $y = \frac{6}{x - 5}$

9. $y = \frac{3}{x} + 2$

10. **Open-ended** Write the equation of a rational function with a graph that is in three quadrants only.

11. **Writing** Explain why the function $f(x) = \frac{5}{x + 3}$ has asymptotes.

Rational Expressions 11-3

A **rational expression** can be written in the form $\frac{\text{polynomial}}{\text{polynomial}}$ where a variable is in the denominator. The **domain** of a variable is all real numbers excluding the values for which the denominator is zero. A rational expression is in simplest form when the numerator and denominator have no common factors other than 1.

You can multiply and divide rational expressions.

$\frac{a}{b} \cdot \frac{c}{d} = \frac{ac}{bd}$, where b and d are nonzero

$\frac{a}{b} \div \frac{c}{d} = \frac{a}{b} \cdot \frac{d}{c}$, where b, c, and d are nonzero

Simplify each expression and state any restrictions on the variable.

12. $\frac{x^2 - 4}{x + 2}$ **13.** $\frac{5x}{20x + 15}$ **14.** $\frac{-3t}{t^3 - t^2}$ **15.** $\frac{z + 2}{2z^2 + z - 6}$

Find each product or quotient.

16. $\frac{8}{m - 3} \cdot \frac{3m}{m + 1}$ **17.** $\frac{2e + 1}{8e - 4} \div \frac{4e^2 + 4e + 1}{4e - 2}$ **18.** $\frac{5c + 3}{c^2 - 1} \cdot \frac{c + 1}{2c}$ **19.** $\frac{4n + 8}{3n} \div \frac{4}{9n}$

Operations with Rational Expressions 11-4

You can add and subtract rational expressions. Restate each expression with the LCD as the denominator, then add or subtract the numerators.

Add or subtract.

20. $\frac{5}{k} + \frac{3}{k}$ **21.** $\frac{8x}{x - 7} - \frac{4}{x - 7}$ **22.** $\frac{9}{3x - 1} + \frac{5x}{2x + 3}$ **23.** $\frac{7m}{(m + 1)(m - 1)} - \frac{10}{m + 1}$

24. *Standardized Test Prep* What is the LCD of $\frac{1}{4}$, $\frac{2}{x}$, $\frac{5x}{3x - 2}$, and $\frac{3}{8x}$?

A. $96x^3 - 64x^2$ **B.** $12x + 2$ **C.** $24x^2 - 16x$ **D.** $27x^2 - 6x - 8$ **E.** $6x + 2$

Solving Rational Equations 11-5

You can use the least common denominator (LCD) to solve **rational equations.** Check possible solutions in the original equation to make sure that they do not make the denominator equal to zero.

Solve each equation.

25. $\frac{1}{2} + \frac{3}{t} = \frac{5}{8}$ **26.** $\frac{3}{m - 4} + \frac{1}{3(m - 4)} = \frac{6}{m}$ **27.** $\frac{2c}{c - 4} - 2 = \frac{4}{c + 5}$

28. *Business* A new photocopier can make 72 copies in 2 min. When an older photocopier is working, the two photocopiers can make 72 copies in 1.5 min. How long does it take the older photocopier working alone to make 72 copies?

Counting Outcomes and Permutations 11-6

You can find a number of different outcomes using the **multiplication counting principle.** If there are m ways to make a first selection and n ways to make a second selection, there are $m \times n$ ways to make the two selections.

A **permutation** is an arrangement of objects in a definite order. To calculate ${}_nP_r$, the number of permutations of n objects taken r at a time, use the formula

$${}_nP_r = n(n - 1)(n - 2)\ldots \leftarrow r \text{ factors starting with } n$$

Evaluate.

29. ${}_5P_3$ **30.** ${}_8P_4$ **31.** ${}_6P_4$ **32.** ${}_5P_2$ **33.** ${}_9P_4$ **34.** ${}_7P_2$

35. a. Telephones Before 1995, three-digit area codes could begin with any number except 0 or 1. The middle number was either 0 or 1, and the last number could be any digit. How many possible area codes were there?

b. Beginning in 1995, area codes were not limited to having 0 or 1 as the middle number. How many new area codes became available?

Combinations 11-7

A **combination** is an arrangement of objects without regard to order. The

$$\text{number of combinations} = \frac{\text{number of permutations}}{\text{number of times the objects in each group are repeated}}.$$

To find ${}_nC_r$, the combinations of n objects taken r at a time, use the formula

$${}_nC_r = \frac{{}_nP_r}{{}_rP_r} = \frac{n(n-1)(n-2)\ldots}{r(r-1)(r-2)\ldots} \begin{array}{l}\leftarrow r \text{ factors starting with } n \\ \leftarrow r \text{ factors starting with } r\end{array}$$

Evaluate.

36. ${}_6C_5$ **37.** ${}_{10}C_4$ **38.** ${}_9C_2$ **39.** ${}_{11}C_3$ **40.** ${}_5C_4$ **41.** ${}_6C_4$

42. Nutrition You want to have three servings of dairy products without repeating a food. Milk, yogurt, cottage cheese, and cheddar cheese are in the refrigerator. How many different combinations can you have?

43. Ten friends go to an amusement park. A roller-coaster car holds eight people. Find how many different groups from the ten friends can ride in one car.

44. You subscribe to eight monthly magazines. Two are news magazines, three are on sports, two are on health and fitness, and one is about gardening. What is the probability that the next two magazines you receive in the mail are sports magazines?

CHAPTER 11

Assessment

Find the constant of variation for each inverse variation.

1. $y = 5$ when $x = 6$
2. $y = 2.4$ when $x = 10$
3. $y = 78$ when $x = 0.1$
4. $y = 5.3$ when $x = 9.1$

5. *Standardized Test Prep* Which point is *not* on the same graph of an inverse variation as the others?

   A. (3, 12)　B. (9, 4)　C. (6, 6)
   D. (16, 2)　E. (2, 18)

6. It took you 1.5 h to drive to a concert at 40 mi/h. How long will it take you to drive back driving at 50 mi/h?

Graph each function. Include a dashed line for each asymptote.

7. $y = \frac{6}{x}$
8. $y = \frac{15}{x}$
9. $y = \frac{1}{x} + 3$
10. $y = \frac{4}{x} + 3$

11. *Writing* Explain how direct variations and inverse variations are similar and different. Include an example of each.

Find each product or quotient.

12. $\frac{3}{x - 2} \cdot \frac{x^2 - 4}{12}$
13. $\frac{5x}{x^2 + 2x} \div \frac{30x^2}{x + 2}$
14. $\frac{4w}{3w - 5} \cdot \frac{7}{2w}$
15. $\frac{6c - 2}{c + 5} \div \frac{3c - 9}{c}$

16. *Open-ended* Write a rational expression for which 6 and 3 are restricted from the domain.

Solve each equation.

17. $\frac{v}{3} + \frac{v}{v + 5} = \frac{4}{v + 5}$
18. $\frac{16}{x + 10} = \frac{8}{2x - 1}$
19. $\frac{2}{3} + \frac{t + 6}{t - 3} = \frac{18}{2(t - 3)}$

20. If three people can clean an apartment working two hours each, how long will it take a crew of four people?

Simplify.

21. $\frac{5}{t} + \frac{t}{t + 1}$
22. $\frac{9}{n} - \frac{8}{n + 1}$
23. $\frac{2y}{y^2 - 9} - \frac{1}{y - 3}$
24. $\frac{4b - 2}{3b} + \frac{b}{b + 2}$

Classify each of the following as a combination or permutation problem. Explain your choice. Then solve the problem.

25. The 30-member debate club needs a president and treasurer. How many different pairs of officers are possible?

26. How many different ways can you choose two books from the six books on your shelf?

27. You have enough money for two extra pizza toppings. If there are six possible toppings, how many different pairs of toppings can you choose?

Find the number of combinations of letters taken four at a time from each set.

28. A E I O U Y
29. E Q U A T I O N
30. L E A R N

Evaluate.

31. ${}_4C_3$　32. ${}_8P_6$　33. ${}_{10}P_7$　34. ${}_5C_2$

35. You have 5 kinds of wrapping paper and 4 different colored bows. How many different combinations of paper and bows can you have?

36. There are 15 books on your summer reading list. Three of them are plays, one is poetry, and the rest are novels. What is the probability that you will choose three novels if you choose the books at random?

CHAPTER 11

Preparing for the Math A Exam

Part I

1 Suppose you buy two items that cost d dollars each. You give the cashier \$10. Which expression models the change you should receive?
(1) $10 - d$ (3) $10 + 2d$
(2) $10 - 2d$ (4) $d - 10$

2 Evaluate $2y + 7$ for $y = 4$.
(1) 31 (3) 13
(2) 11 (4) 15

3 Which of the following expressions has a value of 48?
(1) $[8 + (2 \cdot 4)] \cdot 3$ (3) $(8 + 2) \cdot 4 \cdot 3$
(2) $8 + 2 \cdot 4 \cdot 3$ (4) $(8 + 2) \cdot (4 \cdot 3)$

4 If $y - x > 0$, what does $|x - y|$ equal?
(1) $y - x$ and $|y - x|$
(2) $|y - x|$ and $x - y$
(3) $y - x$ and $x - y$
(4) $|y - x|$ only

5 A relation exists between an electronic store's profit and the number of computers it sells. In this relation, what is the dependent variable?
(1) store's profit
(2) price of each computer
(3) number of computers sold
(4) number of customers

6 Which equation is represented by the graph?
(1) $f(x) = |x| + 1$
(2) $f(x) = (x + 1)^2$
(3) $f(x) = x - 1$
(4) $f(x) = |x| - 1$

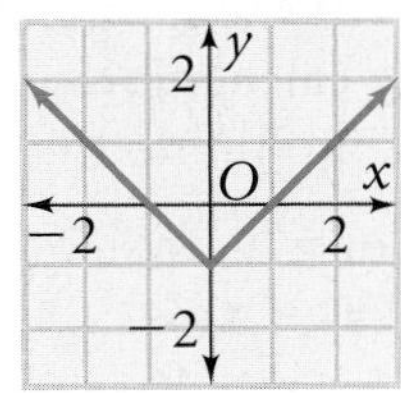

7 A baker can form two loaves of bread in 5 min. How many loaves can the baker form in an hour?
(1) 24 (3) 22
(2) 150 (4) 6

8 What is the solution of $|k + 2| = 13$?
(1) 11 only (3) -11 and 15
(2) -15 and 11 (4) no solution

9 Which is *not* a solution of $5x - 4 < 12$?
(1) 3 (3) 4
(2) 0 (4) -2

10 Which compound inequality represents the set of numbers shown on the number line?

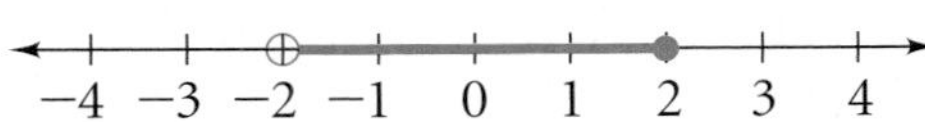

(1) $3 \le x < 2$ (3) $-2 < x \le 2$
(2) $3 \ge x$ and $x < 2$ (4) $-2 \le x \le 2$

11 Which of the following is an equation of a line passing through (5, 1) and (3, −3)?
(1) $y = \frac{3}{2}x - 2$ (3) $y = 2x - 9$
(2) $y = 2x - \frac{3}{2}$ (4) $y = 2x + 9$

12 A scatter plot shows a positive correlation. Which of the following could be an equation of the line of best fit?
(1) $y = -5x + 1$ (3) $2x + 3y = 6$
(2) $x = 16$ (4) $y = 2x - 1$

13 What is the minimum value of the function $f(x) = x^2 + x + 4$?
(1) $\frac{15}{4}$ (3) $\frac{17}{4}$
(2) 4 (4) -2

14 Which of the following points is *not* a solution of $y \le 2x^2 - 5x + 3$?
(1) (3, 6) (3) (−1, 4)
(2) (0, −2) (4) (2, 18)

15 If $x^2 = 36$ and $y^2 = 16$, what is the least possible value for $y - x$?
(1) 2 (3) 10
(2) -2 (4) -10

16 Suppose you deposit \$1000 in an account paying 5.5% interest, compounded annually. Which expression represents the value of the investment after 10 years?

(1) $1000 \cdot 1.55^{10}$ (3) $1000 \cdot 0.055^{10}$
(2) $1000 \cdot 1.055^{10}$ (4) $1000 \cdot 10^{1.055}$

17 Which expression is in simplest form and is equivalent to $-3a^8 \cdot cb^{-3} \cdot b^{12} \cdot 9c^5$?

(1) $-27a^8b^9c^6$ (3) $-27a^8b^9c^5$
(2) $6a^9b^5c^6$ (4) $-27a^8b^{15}c^6$

18 Which number has the least value?

(1) $2.8 \cdot 10^{-5}$ (3) $7.04 \cdot 10^{-8}$
(2) $8.3 \cdot 10^{-7}$ (4) $1.6 \cdot 10^{-8}$

19 A support wire from the top of a tower is 100 ft long. It is anchored at a spot 60 ft from the base of the tower. What is the height of the tower?

(1) 80 ft (3) 800 ft
(2) 40 ft (4) 160 ft

20 Which expression is equal to $8x^3 - 12x^2 + 4x$?

(1) $2x(4x^2 + 6x + 2)$
(2) $x(8x^3 - 12x + 4)$
(3) $4x(2x^2 - 3x + 1)$
(4) $4x(4x^2 - 3x + 1)$

21 The value of x varies inversely with y, and $x = 2$ when $y = 5$. What is x when $y = 10$?

(1) 4 (2) 5 (3) 7 (4) 1

22 What is the restriction on the variable in $\frac{x-8}{x-10}$?

(1) $x \neq 8$ (3) $x \neq 10$
(2) $x \neq 9$ (4) $x \neq 11$

23 What is the LCD of $\frac{1}{2}, \frac{3}{10x}, \frac{4x}{2x+3}$, and $\frac{5}{x}$?

(1) $40x^2 + 60x$ (3) $20x^2 + 30x$
(2) $10x + 6$ (4) $4x^2 + 6x$

24 What is the quotient $\frac{x-4}{x^2+2x} \div \frac{x^2-16}{x^2-x}$?

(1) $\frac{x-1}{x^2+6x+8}$ (3) $\frac{x^2-6^x+4}{x^2+x-4}$
(2) $\frac{1}{x^2+x-4}$ (4) $\frac{x^2+6x+8}{x^2-1}$

Part II

25 What is the solution set for $5h < 20$ if the replacement set is $\{1, 2, 3, 4, 5\}$?

26 Suppose your test scores are 88, 78, 81, 83, and 90. What score do you need on your next test to raise your median score to 85?

27 Suppose you toss three coins. What is the probability of getting 2 heads and 1 tail?

28 Translate the following mathematical sentence into an equation. Then solve the equation. Seventeen more than three times a number is 32.

29 A bag contains 10 red marbles and 20 white marbles. You draw a marble, keep it, and draw another. What is the probability of drawing two red marbles?

30 A bag contains 6 blue marbles and 4 yellow marbles. You draw a marble, replace it, and draw another marble. Make a probability distribution table showing the chances of getting 0, 1, or 2 blue marbles.

31 A new company employed 12 people. Two years later it employed a total of 20 people.

a What was the percent of increase?

b If one of the 20 people retires, what would be the percent of decrease?

32 The sides of a square are measured as $8\frac{1}{2}$ in. each.

a What is the greatest possible error in the calculation of the perimeter of the square?

b Write the greatest possible error in the calculation of the perimeter as a percent. Round to the nearest tenth of a percent.

33 Solve the system using elimination.

$x + y = 34$
$x - y = 16$

34 In triangle ABC, $\angle C$ is a right angle, $\overline{AB} = 7$ units, and $m\angle B = 28°$. What are the lengths of $\overline{BC}$ and $\overline{AC}$ to the nearest hundredth unit?

35 What is the simplest form of $\frac{3x-9}{x^2-6x+9}$?

Part III

36 What is the solution of $4x^2 - 4x - 3 \leq 0$?

37 Suppose you earn a commission of 6% on your first \$500 of sales and 10% on all sales above \$500. If you earn \$130 in commissions, what are your total sales?

38 Write an equation of the line that passes through $(2, -3)$ and is perpendicular to the graph of $y = \frac{2}{5}x - \frac{7}{8}$.

39 The slopes of four different lines are: $\frac{3}{5}$, $-\frac{10}{6}$, $-\frac{5}{3}$, and $\frac{9}{15}$. Fully describe the closed figure formed by these lines.

40 A manufacturing company spends \$1200 each day on plant costs plus \$7 per item for labor and materials. The items sell for \$23 each. How many items must the company sell in one day to equal its daily costs?

41 Find the x-intercepts of the function $y = 4x^2 - 9x + 2$. Then graph the function.

42 Find the x-intercept and the y-intercept of the graph of $y = \frac{5}{x - 2} + 1$.

43 Simplify: $\frac{3}{s - 1} + \frac{2}{s^2 + s - 2}$.

44 Suppose you have 12 coins that total \$1.95. Some coins are dimes and some are quarters. How many of each coin do you have?

Part IV

45 A truck traveling 45 mi/h and a car traveling 55 mi/h cover the same distance. The truck travels 4 h longer than the car. How far did they travel?

46 Workers at a local charity worked the following numbers of hours: 3, 5, 9, 5, 8, 4, 2, 10, 7, 3, 4, 6.

a Find the mean.

b Find the range of the data.

c Graph the data in a cumulative frequency histogram.

47 A box is 2 cm wide, 5 cm long, and 4 cm high. To the nearest tenth of a centimeter, what is the distance between the most distant pair of corners?

48 A rectangle was originally twice as long as it is wide. Its sides have each been increased by 10 cm. The area of the new rectangle is 252 cm^2. Find the dimensions of the original rectangle.

49 A group of people reported watching a certain television show. The table shows their ages, rounded to the nearest year.

a Compute the percentiles for each interval in the table. Round to the nearest tenth of a percent.

b Make a histogram for the data that shows percentiles on the vertical axis.

c What percent of the viewers are 20–39 years old?

Ages	Cumulative Frequency
0–9	27
10–19	79
20–29	165
30–39	235
40–49	300
50–59	364
60+	400

50 One baker can shape 24 bagels in 15 min. When the baker works with an apprentice, they can shape 24 bagels in 10 min. How long does it take the apprentice to shape 24 bagels working alone?

51 Solve: $\frac{-2}{x - 3} = \frac{x + 4}{2(x - 3)} + \frac{1}{4}$.

52 There are 20 people in the art club.

a The club needs a president, vice president, secretary, and treasurer. How many different groups of officers are possible?

b The club needs a publicity committee of four people. How many different ways can the committee be chosen?

NEW YORK MATH A

Volume 2 — Focus on Geometry

Contents

PRENTICE HALL

NEW YORK MATH A

Single-Volume Version

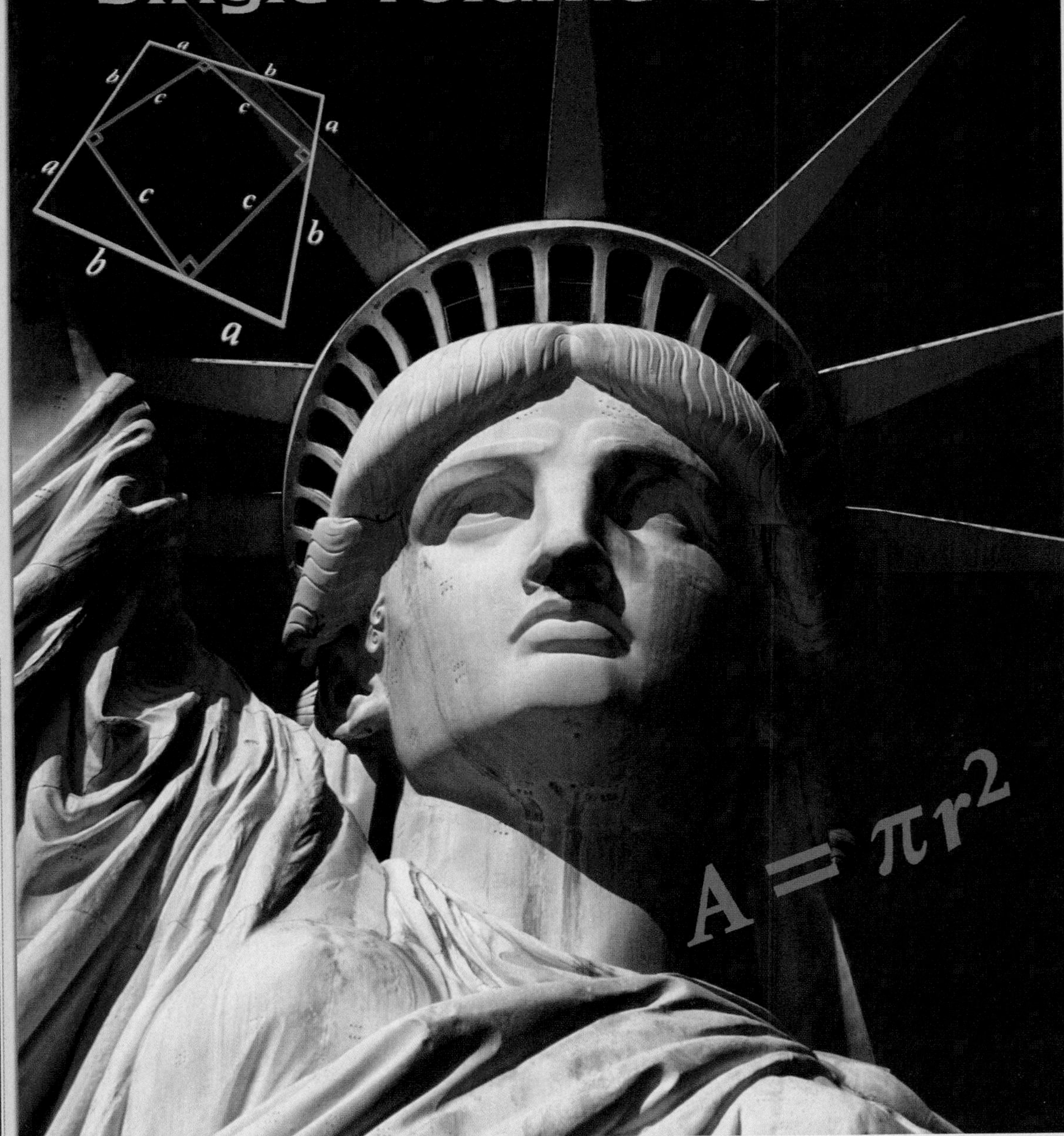

Volume 2

CHAPTER 1

Tools of Geometry

Connections and Applications

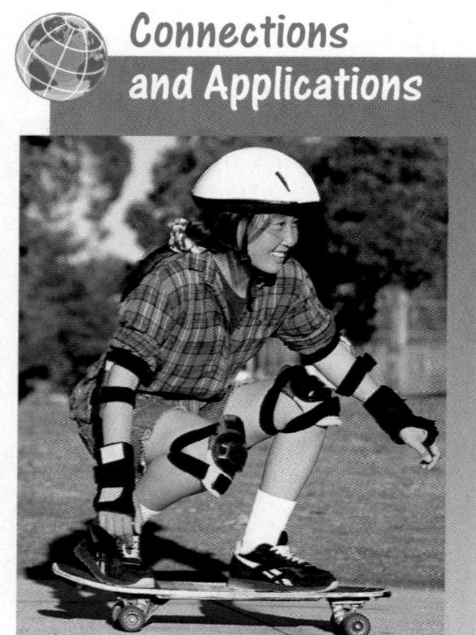

CHAPTER 2

Investigating Geometric Figures

Connections and Applications

CHAPTER 3

Transformations: Shapes in Motion

Connections and Applications

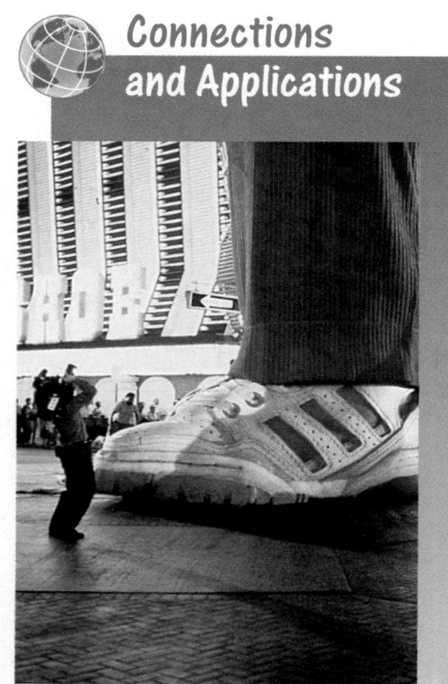

CHAPTER 4

Triangle Relationships

Connections and Applications

CHAPTER 5

Measuring in the Plane

Connections and Applications

CHAPTER 6

Measuring in Space

Connections and Applications

CHAPTER 1 Tools of Geometry

Relating to the Real World

Every day, you trust that people understand the meaning of the words you use. In this chapter, you'll learn some of the basic terms of geometry and become familiar with the tools you'll use.

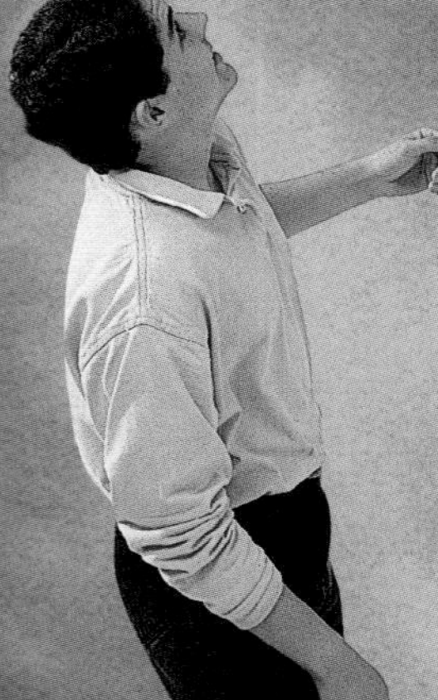

Lessons	1-1	1-2	1-3	1-4	1-5
	Using Patterns and Inductive Reasoning	*Points, Lines, and Planes*	*Segments, Rays, Parallel Lines and Planes*	*Measuring Angles and Segments*	*Good Definitions*

CHAPTER PROJECT

On Folded Wings

Some people look at a plain sheet of paper and see the hidden form of a swan or a seashell waiting to be revealed. Almost magically, with a few meticulous folds, an origami artist can produce startling replicas of

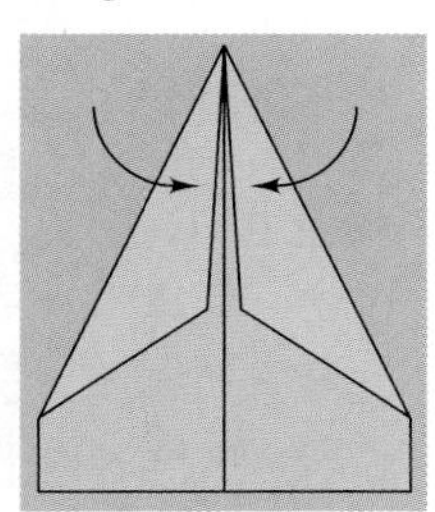

animals, flowers, buildings, vehicles, and even people. The ancient art of paper folding has come to us from Japan, where it has thrived since at least the twelfth century. As a child, every time you made a paper airplane or a paper hat, you were practicing the art of origami.

In this chapter project, you will use paper folding to explore geometric patterns. You will make origami models, and then use the language of geometry to tell others how to make them.

To help you complete the project:

- **p. 572** *Find Out by Doing*
- **p. 584** *Find Out by Creating*
- **p. 593** *Find Out by Researching*
- **p. 606** *Find Out by Writing*
- **p. 620** *Finishing the Project*

Basic Constructions 1-6

Using Deductive Reasoning 1-7

The Coordinate Plane 1-8

Connections Manufacturing . . . and more

1-1 Using Patterns and Inductive Reasoning

What You'll Learn

- Using inductive reasoning to make conjectures

...And Why

To sharpen your ability to reason inductively, a powerful tool used in mathematics and in making everyday decisions

WORK TOGETHER

The shortest path from the school to Longwood Avenue is six blocks long. One path is shown below in red.

PROBLEM SOLVING HINT

Copy the diagram. Find the number of ways to reach each intersection. Look for a number pattern.

1 1
1 2 1
? ? ? ?

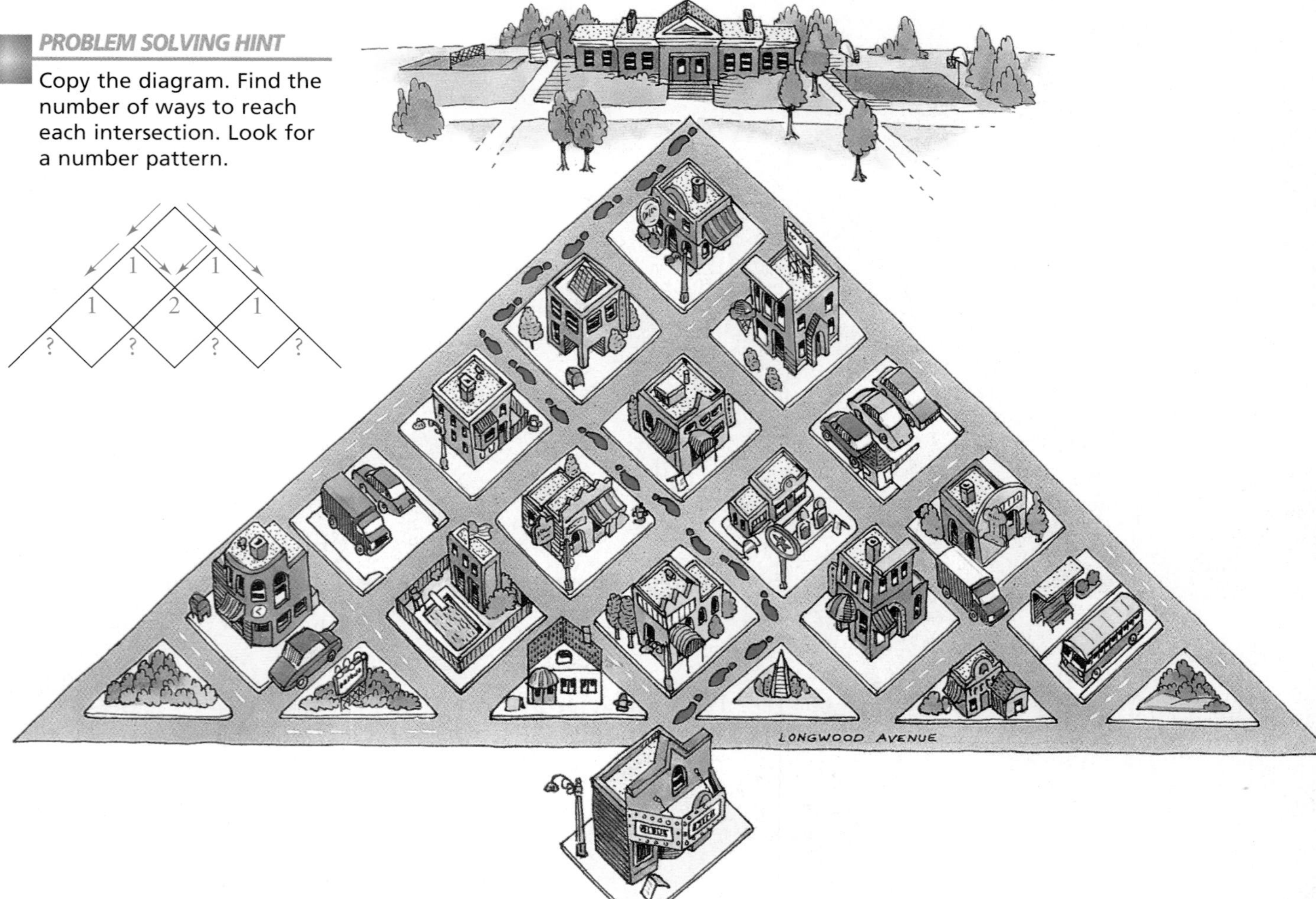

Who? The pattern of numbers you discovered in the Work Together is known as Pascal's Triangle, after the French mathematician Blaise Pascal (1623–1662).

Work with a group to answer the following questions.

1. How many different six-block paths can you take from the school to Longwood Avenue?
2. How many of these paths will end at the corner directly across from the movie theater?

THINK AND DISCUSS

To answer the questions in the Work Together, you used inductive reasoning. **Inductive reasoning** is a type of reasoning that allows you to reach conclusions based on a pattern of specific examples or past events. Mathematicians have made many discoveries using inductive reasoning.

3. a. Find the next two terms in this sequence: 2, 4, 6, 8, . . .
b. Describe the pattern you observed.

4. a. Find the next two terms in this sequence: 3, 6, 12, 24, . . .
b. Describe the pattern you observed.

5. a. Find the next two terms in this sequence: 1, 2, 4, 5, 10, 11, 22, . . .
b. Describe the pattern you observed.

A conclusion reached by using inductive reasoning is sometimes called a **conjecture.** For each sequence above, you found the next term by first finding a pattern, and then using the pattern to make a conjecture about the next term. Inductive reasoning from patterns is a powerful thinking process you will use throughout the year in geometry.

6. Try This Describe the next term in this sequence.

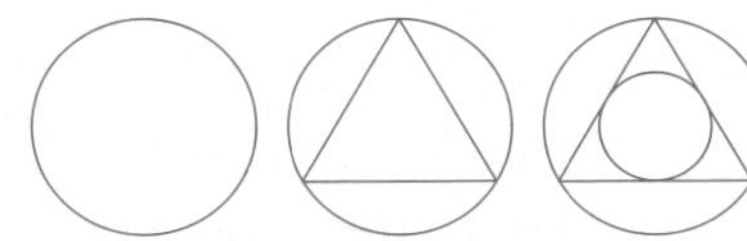

Example 1 Relating to the Real World 

Manufacturing A skateboard shop finds that for five consecutive months sales of skateboards with small wheels (39 mm to 48 mm in diameter) decreased.

January: 58 February: 55 March: 51 April: 48 May: 45

Use inductive reasoning to make a conjecture about the number of small-wheeled skateboards the shop will sell in June.

As the graph at the left shows, the number of small-wheeled skateboards is decreasing by about 3 skateboards each month. The skateboard shop can predict about 42 small-wheeled skateboards will be sold in June.

Not every conjecture or conclusion found by inductive reasoning is correct. The next problem illustrates the limitations of inductive reasoning.

Example 2

If six points on a circle are joined by as many segments as possible, how many nonoverlapping regions will the segments determine?

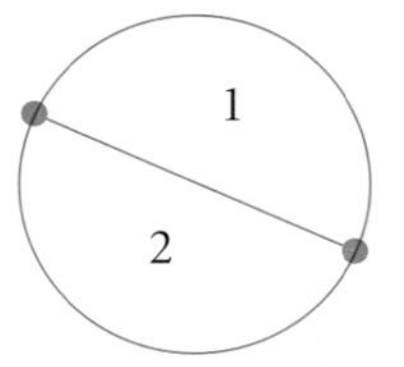
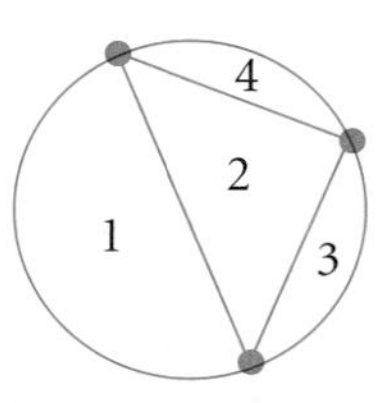
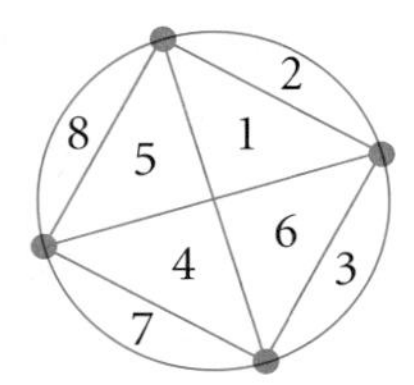
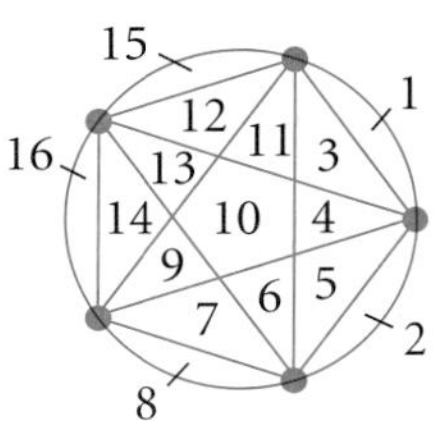

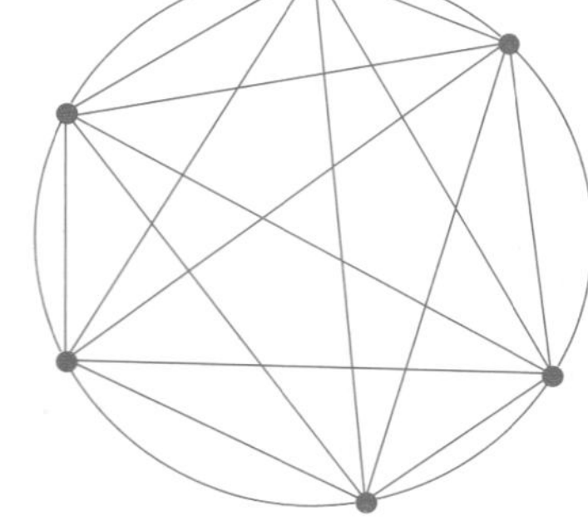

The table at the right shows the data for 2, 3, 4, and 5 points. The number of regions appears to double at each stage. Inductive reasoning would predict that there are 32 regions for 6 points on the circle. And yet, as the diagram at the left shows, there are only 31 regions formed. In this case, the conjecture is incorrect.

Points	Regions
2	2
3	4
4	8
5	16

Because the conjectures arrived at by inductive reasoning are not always true, you should verify them if possible.

7. **Try This** Candace examined five different examples and came up with this **conjecture:** "If any two positive numbers are multiplied, their product is always greater than either of the two numbers." Is her **conjecture** correct? Explain why or why not.

Sometimes you can use inductive reasoning to solve a problem that at first does not seem to have any pattern.

Example 3

Use inductive reasoning to find the sum of the first 20 odd numbers.

Find the first few sums. Notice that each sum is a perfect square.

$$1 = 1 = 1^2$$
$$1 + 3 = 4 = 2^2$$
$$1 + 3 + 5 = 9 = 3^2$$
$$1 + 3 + 5 + 7 = 16 = 4^2$$

Reasoning inductively, you would expect that the sum of the first 20 odd numbers would be 20^2, or 400.

8. **Try This** What is your **conjecture** for the sum of the first 30 odd numbers? Use your calculator to verify your **conjecture.**

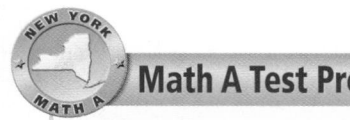

Math A Test Prep

1 What is the next number in the pattern 1, −4, 9, −16, . . .?
(1) −25 (3) 5
(2) −5 (4) 25

2 Study the sums of the first four even numbers.

$$2 = 2 = 1 \times 2$$
$$2 + 4 = 6 = 2 \times 3$$
$$2 + 4 + 6 = 12 = 3 \times 4$$
$$2 + 4 + 6 + 8 = 20 = 4 \times 5$$

a Describe the pattern.
b Use the pattern to find the sum of the first 30 even numbers.
c Write an algebraic expression for the value of the sum of the first *n* even numbers.

Exercises ON YOUR OWN

Find the next two terms in each sequence.

1. 5, 10, 20, 40, . . .
2. 3, 33, 333, 3333, . . .
3. 1, −1, 2, −2, 3, . . .
4. $1, \frac{1}{2}, \frac{1}{4}, \frac{1}{8}, \ldots$
5. 15, 12, 9, 6, . . .
6. 81, 27, 9, 3, . . .
7. O, T, T, F, F, S, S, E, . . .
8. J, F, M, A, M, . . .
9. 1, 2, 6, 24, 120, . . .
10. 1, 2, 4, 7, 11, 16, 22, . . .
11. $1, \frac{1}{4}, \frac{1}{9}, \frac{1}{16}, \frac{1}{25}, \ldots$
12. $1, \frac{1}{2}, \frac{1}{3}, \frac{1}{4}, \ldots$

13. **Writing** Choose two of the sequences in Exercises 9–12 and describe the pattern.

14. Deano has started working out regularly. When he first started exercising he could do 10 push-ups. After the first month he could do 14 push-ups. After the second month he could do 19, and after the third month he could do 25. How many push-ups would you **predict** he will be able to do after the fifth month of working out? Are you absolutely sure about your prediction? Why or why not?

15. Alexa rides a bus to school. On the first day the trip to school took 25 minutes. On the second day the trip took 24 minutes. On the third day the trip took 26 minutes. On the fourth day the trip took 25 minutes. What **conjecture** would you make?

16. **History** Leonardo of Pisa (c. 1175–c. 1258) was born in Italy and educated in North Africa. He was one of the the first Europeans to use modern numerals instead of Roman numerals. He is also known for the Fibonacci Sequence: 1, 1, 2, 3, 5, 8, 13, ... Find the next three terms.

Draw the next figure in each sequence.

17.
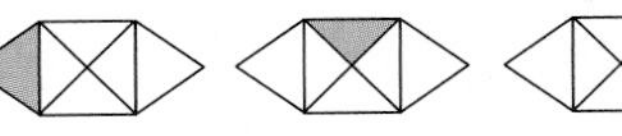

18.
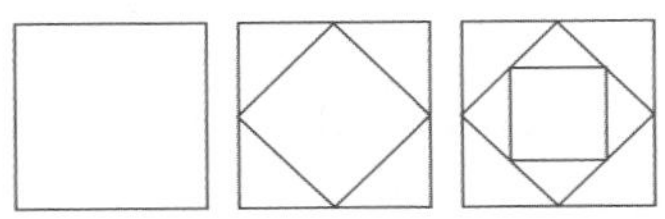

19.

20.
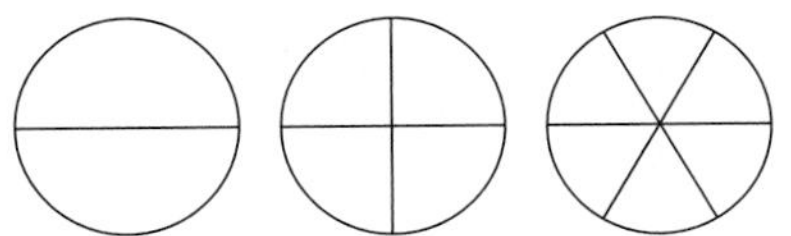

21.
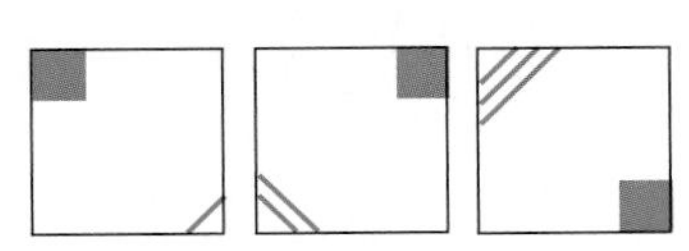

22.

23. Draw two parallel lines on your paper. Locate four points on the paper an equal distance from both lines. Describe the figure you would get if you continued to locate points an equal distance from both lines.

24. Draw a line on your paper. Locate four points on the paper that are each 1 in. from the line. Describe the figure you would get if you continued to locate points that are 1 in. from the line.

TECHNOLOGY HINT

Exercises 23 and 24 could be done using geometry software.

25. For the past four years Paulo has grown 2 in. every year. He is now 16 years old and is 5 ft 10 in. tall. He figures that when he is 22 years old he will be 6 ft 10 in. tall. What would you tell Paulo about his **conjecture**?

26. After testing her idea with eight different numbers, Jean stated the following **conjecture**: "The square of a number is always greater than the number you started with." What would you tell Jean about her **conjecture**?

Radio Stations

1950	2,773
1960	4,133
1970	6,760
1980	8,566
1990	10,819

27. a. **Communications** The number of radio stations in the United States is increasing. The table shows the number of radio stations for a 40-year period. Make a line graph of the data. Use the graph and inductive reasoning to make a **conjecture** about the number of radio stations in the United States by the year 2010.

b. How confident are you about your conjecture? Explain.

Find the next term in each sequence. Check your answer with a calculator.

28.
$12345679 \times 9 = 111111111$
$12345679 \times 18 = 222222222$
$12345679 \times 27 = 333333333$
$12345679 \times 36 = 444444444$
$12345679 \times 45 = ?$

29.
$1 \times 1 = 1$
$11 \times 11 = 121$
$111 \times 111 = 12321$
$1111 \times 1111 = 1234321$
$11111 \times 11111 = ?$

30. **Open-ended** Write two different sequences that begin with the same two numbers.

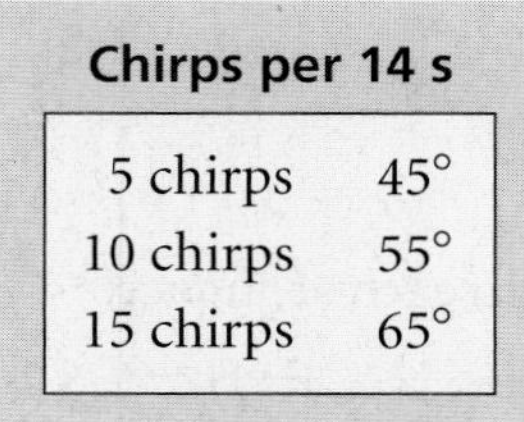

Chirps per 14 s

5 chirps	45°
10 chirps	55°
15 chirps	65°

31. **Weather** The temperature in degrees Fahrenheit determines how fast a cricket chirps. If you heard 20 cricket chirps in 14 seconds, what do you think the temperature would be?

32. a. A *triangular number* can be represented by a triangular arrangement of dots. The first two triangular numbers are 1 and 3. What are the next three triangular numbers?

b. What is the tenth triangular number?

c. **Algebra** Which of the following expressions represents the nth triangular number?

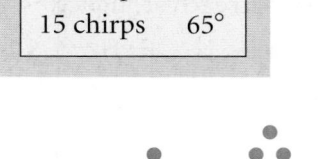

A. $n(n + 1)$ **B.** $n(n - 2)$ **C.** $\frac{n(n + 1)}{2}$ **D.** $\frac{n(n - 1)}{2}$

33. a. The first two *square numbers* are 1 and 4. Draw diagrams to represent the next two square numbers.

b. What is the twentieth square number? Describe the pattern.

c. **Algebra** Write an algebraic expression in terms of n for the nth square number.

34. **History** Nicomachus of Gerasa first described *pentagonal numbers* in *Introductio arithmetica* about A.D. 100. The first three pentagonal numbers are shown. Draw a diagram to represent the next pentagonal number.

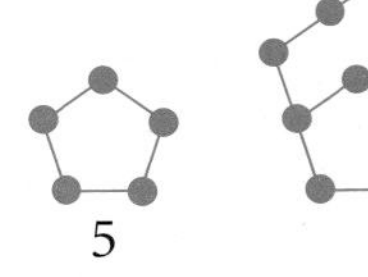
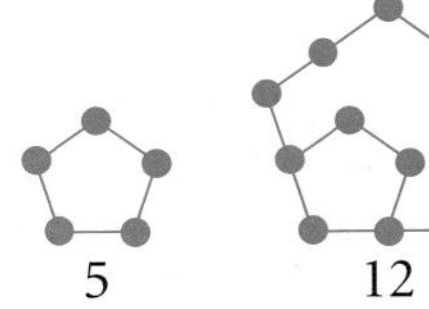

The Race to the Finish Line

Top female runners have been improving about twice as quickly as the fastest men, a new study says. If this pattern continues, women may soon outrun men in competition!

The study is based on world records collected at 10-year intervals, starting in 1905 for men. Reliable women's records were not kept until the 1920s. Women's marathon records date only from 1955.

If the trend continues, the top female and male runners in races ranging from 200 m to 1500 m might attain the same speeds sometime between 2015 and 2055. The rapid improvement in women's marathon records suggests that the marathon record for women will equal that of men even more quickly—perhaps by 2005.

Women's speeds may have improved so quickly because many more women started running competitively in recent decades, according to a professor of anatomy who studies locomotion and gait. This increase in the talent pool of female runners has improved the chance of finding better runners.

35. **a.** What conclusions were reached in the study mentioned in the newspaper clipping?
b. How was inductive reasoning used to reach the conclusions?
c. Explain why the conclusion that women may soon be outrunning men may be incorrect. For which race is the conclusion most suspect? For what reason?

36. **Standardized Test Prep** Which of the following can be a term in the sequence 1, 3, 7, 15, 31, . . . ?

A. 32 **B.** 47 **C.** 55 **D.** 127 **E.** 128

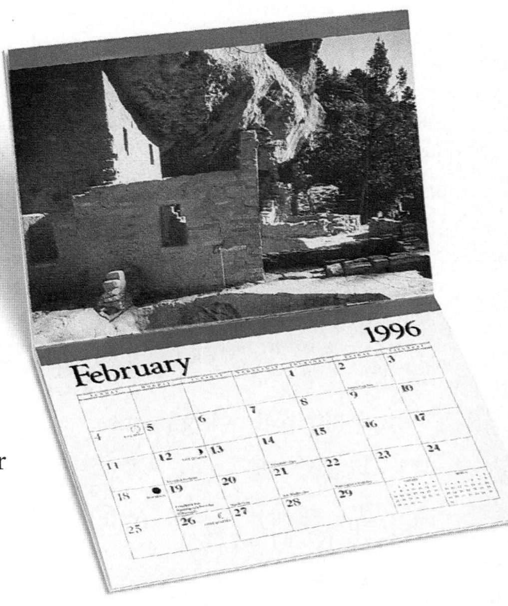

37. **a.** *Leap years* have 366 days. 1984, 1988, 1992, 1996, and 2000 are consecutive leap years. Make a **conjecture** about leap years.
b. Which of the following years do you think will be leap years?

2010, 2020, 2100, 2400

c. **Research** Find out if your **conjecture** for part (a) and your answer for part (b) are correct. How are leap years determined?

38. **a.** **Coordinate Geometry** Graph the following points:

$A(1, 5)$	$B(2, 2)$	$C(2, 8)$	$D(3, 1)$
$E(3, 9)$	$F(6, 0)$	$G(6, 10)$	$H(7, -1)$
$I(7, 11)$	$J(9, 1)$	$K(9, 9)$	$L(10, 2)$
$M(10, 8)$	$N(11, 5)$		

b. Which of the points do not fit the same pattern as the others?
c. Describe the figure you would get if you continued graphing points that fit the pattern.

QUICK REVIEW

The first coordinate is the *x*-coordinate. The second coordinate is the *y*-coordinate.

39. What is the last digit of 2^{85}? Make a table of values and use inductive reasoning.

$2^3 = 2 \times 2 \times 2$

40. **Patterns** How many different squares are there in this 5-by-5 grid?

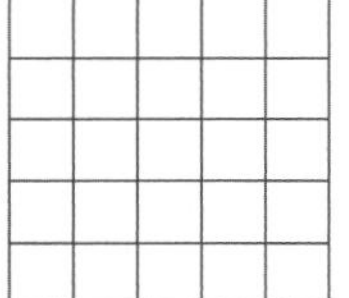

PROBLEM SOLVING HINT

Look at 1-by-1, 2-by-2, and 3-by-3 grids. Count squares and look for a pattern.

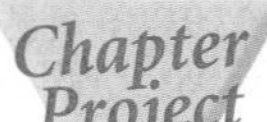

Chapter Project

Find Out by Doing

Most origami creations are made by folding square paper. You can create patterns while you practice paper folding.

- Carefully fold a square piece of paper four times as shown.

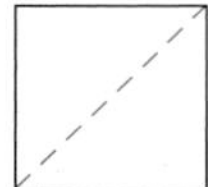 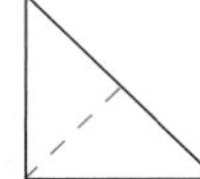   

- Unfold the paper after each fold. Count the number of non-overlapping triangles formed. Record your results in a table like the one below.

Fold	1st	2nd	3rd	4th
No. of $\triangle$s	2	■	■	■

- Make a fifth fold. How many triangles are formed? How many triangles do you think will be formed after a sixth fold? Extend the table and describe the number pattern.
- Keep this origami creation for use in upcoming project activities.

Exercises MIXED REVIEW

Graph the following points.

41. $Y(-5, -8)$ 42. $B(7, -10)$ 43. $M(9, 12)$ 44. $Q(-3, 2)$ 45. $G(-6, 0)$ 46. $F(-4, -5)$

47. $C(-7, 10)$ 48. $N(0, -5)$ 49. $R(4, 8)$ 50. $H(-4, -9)$ 51. $W(2, -5)$ 52. $T(0, 4)$

53. a. In Exercises 41–52, which points are in the fourth quadrant?
    b. Which points are on the y-axis?

Getting Ready for Lesson 1-2

54. Copy the diagram at the right. Draw as many different lines as you can to connect pairs of points.

A • •B C • •D

Math ToolboX

Algebra Review

Probability

Before Lesson 1-2

Probability ranges from 0, an impossible event, to 1, a certain event. You can find the probability of an event using this formula.

$$P(\text{event}) = \frac{\text{number of favorable outcomes}}{\text{number of possible outcomes}}$$

Example 1

What is the probability of answering correctly a four-option multiple choice question if you pick an answer at random?

There are 4 possible outcomes. One of them is correct. The probability of getting the correct answer is $\frac{1}{4}$.

Example 2

Find the probability that a point picked at random from the graph at the right is in the first quadrant.

Quadrant II, Quadrant I, Quadrant III, Quadrant IV

List the possible outcomes: *A, B, C, D, E, F, G, H, I, J*.
There are 10 outcomes.

List the favorable outcomes: *C* and *D*.
There are 2 favorable outcomes.

The probability of a point picked at random being in the first quadrant is $\frac{2}{10} = \frac{1}{5}$.

Use the graph from Example 2 to find each probability. Assume points are picked at random.

1. P(the point is in the fourth quadrant)
2. P(the point is on an axis)
3. P(the point is at the origin)
4. P(the point has a y-coordinate of 2)
5. P(the point has an x-coordinate less than 4)
6. P(the point is on the x-axis)
7. P(the point is to the right of the y-axis)
8. P(the point has an x-coordinate of 1)
9. P(the point is on the y-axis)
10. P(the point is below the x-axis)
11. P(the point has a y-coordinate greater than 1)
12. P(the point is in the third quadrant)

Use the spinner at the right. Find each probability.

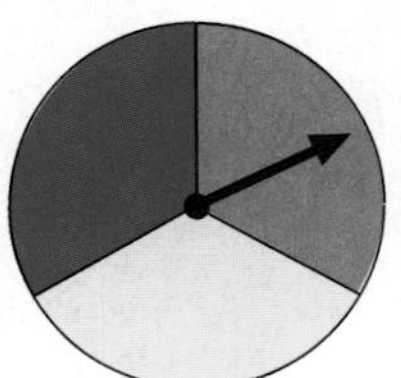

13. P(blue)
14. P(red)
15. P(yellow or red)
16. P(purple)
17. P(blue or red)
18. P(yellow or red or blue)

What You'll Learn

- Understanding basic terms of geometry
- Understanding basic postulates of geometry

...And Why

To lay the foundation for your study of geometry

What You'll Need

- ruler

1-2 Points, Lines, and Planes

WORK TOGETHER

Many constellations are named after animals and mythological figures. It takes some imagination to connect the points representing the stars so that the result is a recognizable figure such as Leo the Lion. There are many different ways to connect the points. How many different lines could be used to connect all ten points?

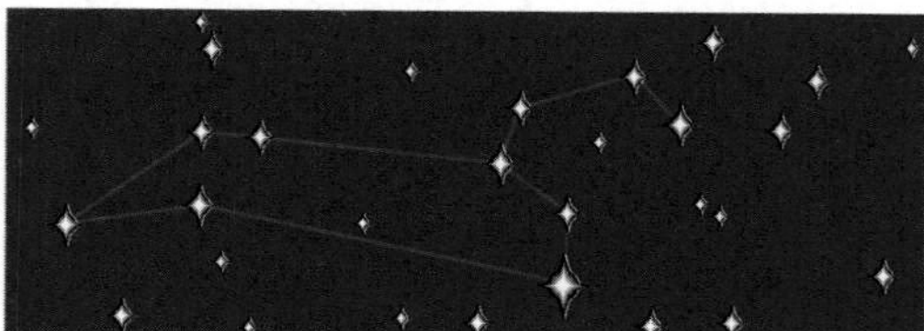

Ten major stars make up the constellation called Leo the Lion.

Work in groups of three. Make a table and look for a pattern to answer the following questions.

1. Put three points on a circle. Now connect the three points with as many lines as possible. How many lines do you need?
2. Put four points on another circle. How many lines can you draw connecting four points?
3. Repeat for five points on a circle and then for six points. How many lines can you draw to connect the points?
4. Use inductive reasoning to tell how many lines you could draw to connect the ten points of the constellation Leo the Lion.

THINK AND DISCUSS

Basic Terms

P•
point *P*

Since stars are so far away, they appear quite small to us. We think of them as points even though they are actually quite large. In geometry a **point** has no size. You can think of it as a location. A point is represented by a small dot and is named by a capital letter. All geometric figures are made up of points. **Space** is the set of all points.

5. ***Open-ended*** Name something in your classroom that is a physical representation of a point.

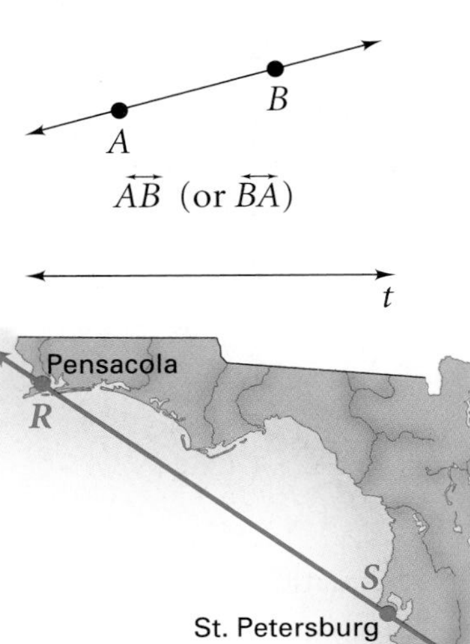

The points representing the three towns on this map are collinear.

You can think of a **line** as a series of points that extends in two opposite directions without end. You can name a line by two points on the line, such as $\overleftrightarrow{AB}$ (read "line *AB*"). Another way to name a line is with a single lowercase letter, such as line *t*.

6. **Open-ended** Describe some physical representations of lines in the real world.
7. **Critical Thinking** Why do you think arrowheads are used when drawing a line or naming a line such as $\overleftrightarrow{AB}$?
8. **Try This** Name the line at the left in as many ways as possible.

Points that lie on the same line are **collinear.**

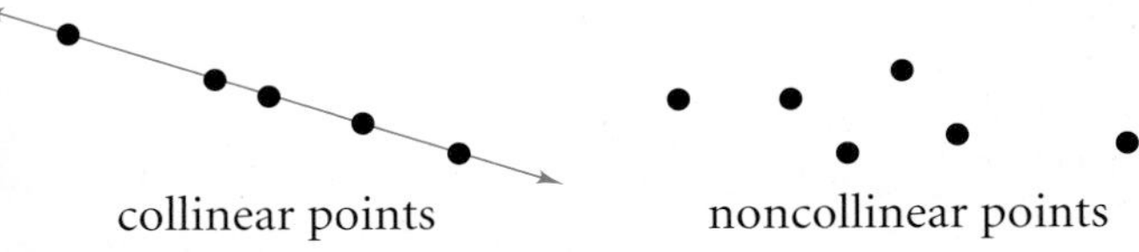

A **plane** is a flat surface that extends in all directions without end. It has no thickness.

9. **Open-ended** Name three objects in your classroom that represent planes.

You can name a plane either by a single capital letter or by naming at least three noncollinear points in the plane.

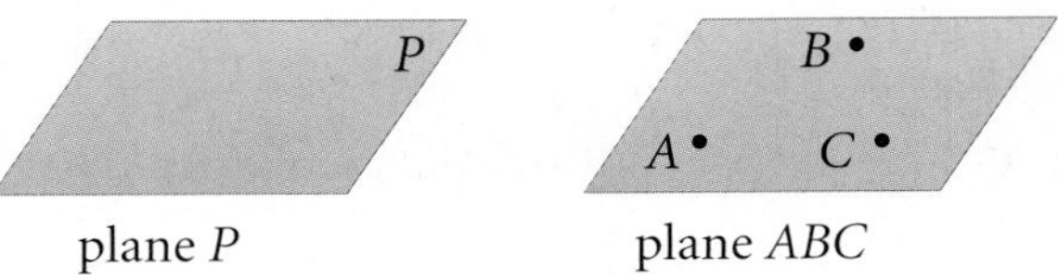

In the diagram, each surface of the ice cube is part of a plane.

10. How many planes are suggested by the surfaces of the ice cube?
11. **Try This** Name the plane represented by the front of the ice cube in several different ways.

Points and lines in the same plane are **coplanar.**

12. **Try This** Name a point that is coplanar with the given points.
    a. *E*, *F*, *G*
    b. *B*, *C*, *G*
    c. *A*, *D*, *E*
    d. *D*, *C*, *G*
13. **Try This** Name two lines that are coplanar with $\overleftrightarrow{AB}$ and $\overleftrightarrow{DC}$.

Basic Postulates

A **postulate** is an accepted statement of fact. You used some of the following geometry postulates in algebra. For example, when you graphed an equation such as $y = -2x + 8$, you began by plotting two points and then you drew the line through those two points.

Postulate 1-1 Through any two points there is exactly one line.

Line t is the only line that passes through points A and B.

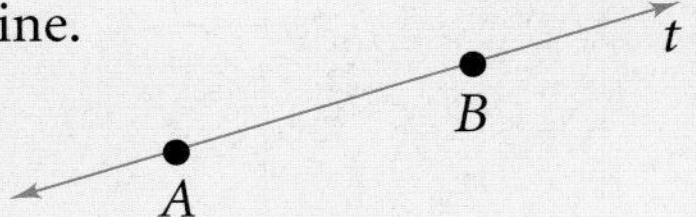

In algebra, one way to solve the following system of equations is to graph the two equations.

$$y = -2x + 8$$
$$y = 3x - 7$$

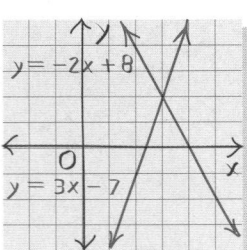

As the graph shows, the two lines intersect at a single point, (3, 2). The solution to the system of equations is $x = 3$, $y = 2$. This illustrates the following postulate.

Postulate 1-2 If two lines intersect, then they intersect in exactly one point.

14. ***Open-ended*** Describe two planes in your classroom that intersect. Also describe the intersection of the planes.

Postulate 1-3 If two planes intersect, then they intersect in a line.

Plane RST and plane STW intersect in $\overleftrightarrow{ST}$.

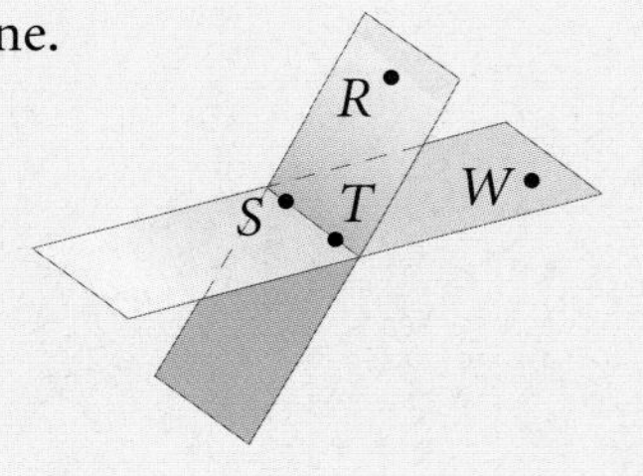

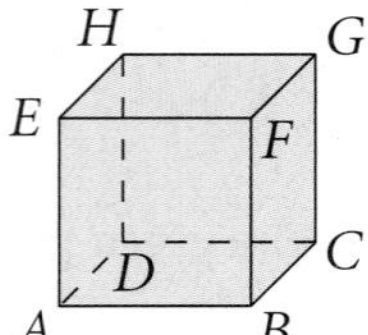

15. a. Try This What is the intersection of plane $HGFE$ and plane $BCGF$?

b. What is the intersection of plane AEF and plane BCG?

A three-legged stool will always be stable, as long as the feet of the stool don't lie on a line. This illustrates the following postulate.

Postulate 1-4 Through any three noncollinear points there is exactly one plane.

Example

Who? Euclid is known for compiling all the geometry of his time into postulates and theorems. His masterwork *The Elements* (about 300 B.C.) is the basis for geometry books today.

Are points *E, H, B,* and *C* coplanar?
Are points *E, H, F,* and *B* coplanar?

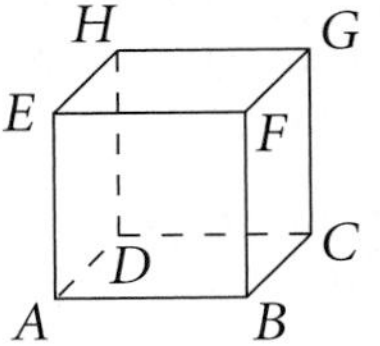

Yes, the plane that contains the three noncollinear points *E, H,* and *B* also contains *C.*

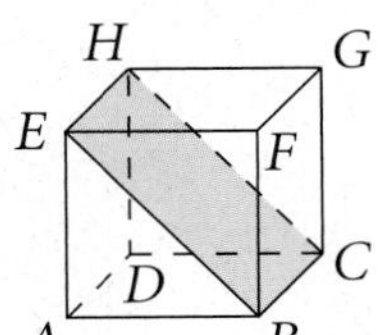

No, points *E, H,* and *F* lie in exactly one plane, which doesn't contain *B.*

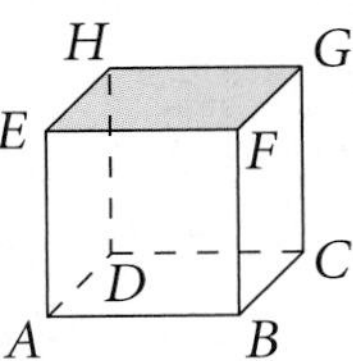

Exercises ON YOUR OWN

Are the points collinear?

1. *A, D, E* **2.** *B, C, D* **3.** *B, C, F* **4.** *A, E, C* **5.** *F, B, D*

Are the points coplanar?

6. *B, C, D, F* **7.** *A, C, D, F* **8.** *B, D, E, F* **9.** *A, C, E, F*

10. Name plane *M* in another way.

11. What is the intersection of plane *M* and $\overleftrightarrow{AE}$?

12. What is the intersection of $\overleftrightarrow{AE}$ and $\overleftrightarrow{BD}$?

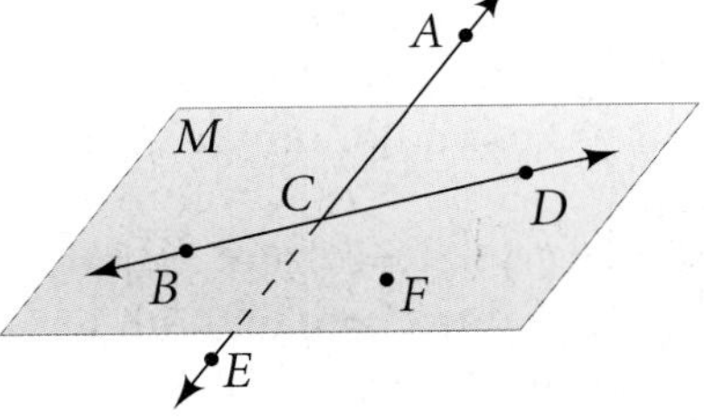

Exs. 1 – 12

Are the following coplanar?

13. *Q, V, R* **14.** *X, V, R* **15.** *U, V, W, S*

16. *W, V, Q, T* **17.** point *X*, $\overleftrightarrow{QT}$ **18.** $\overleftrightarrow{RS}$, point *X*

19. $\overleftrightarrow{XW}$, $\overleftrightarrow{UV}$ **20.** $\overleftrightarrow{UX}$, $\overleftrightarrow{WS}$ **21.** $\overleftrightarrow{UV}$, $\overleftrightarrow{WS}$

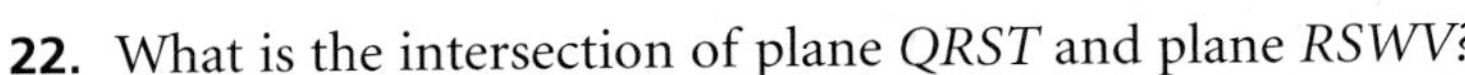

22. What is the intersection of plane *QRST* and plane *RSWV*?

23. What is the intersection of $\overleftrightarrow{UV}$ and plane *QTXU*?

24. Name three lines that intersect at point *S*.

25. Name two planes that intersect at $\overleftrightarrow{TS}$.

26. Name another point that is in the same plane as points *Q, T,* and *W*.

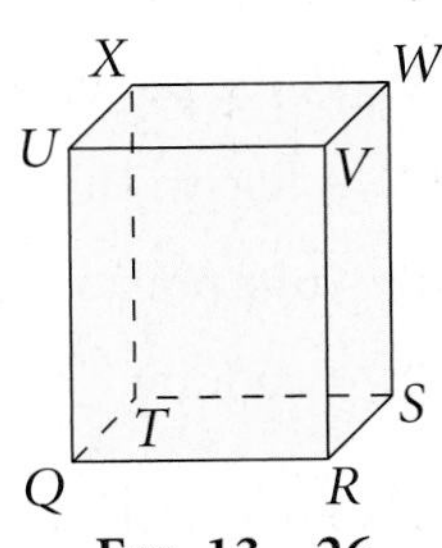

Exs. 13 – 26

27. *Writing* Surveyors and photographers use a *tripod,* or three-legged stand, for their instruments. Use one of the postulates to explain why.

28. *Research* Find out more about Euclid's book *The Elements.* What made it such a significant book? Where did Euclid get his information?

29. How many planes contain three collinear points? Explain.

30. Which postulate is sometimes stated as "Two points determine a line"?

31. *Standardized Test Prep* Which of the following is *not* an acceptable name for the plane shown?

A. plane *RSZ*
B. plane *RSWZ*
C. plane *WSZ*
D. plane *RSTW*
E. plane *STZ*

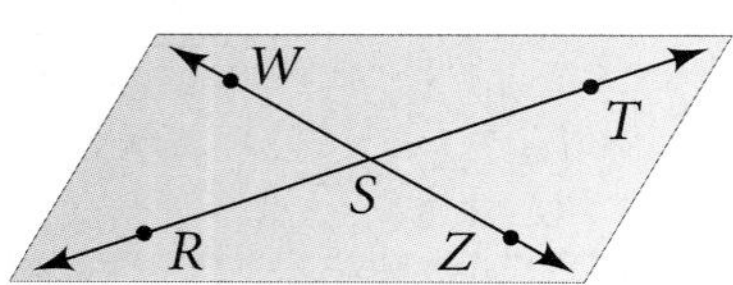

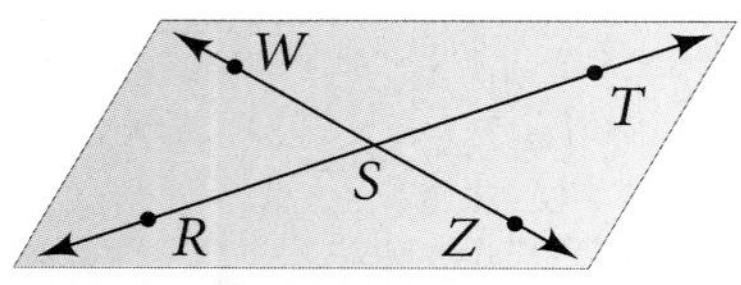

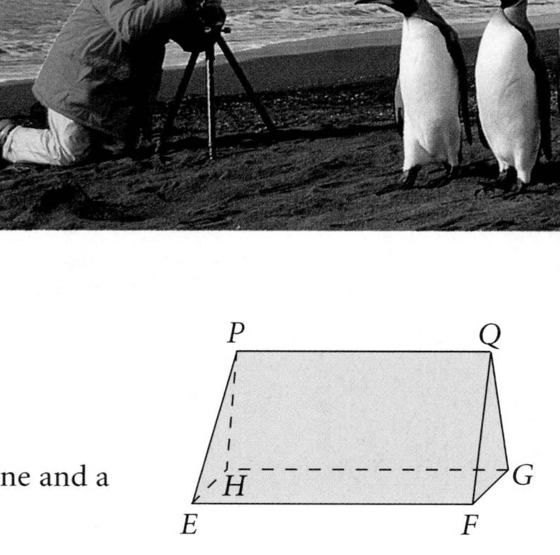

32. How many planes contain each line and point?

a. $\overleftrightarrow{EF}$ and point Q
b. $\overleftrightarrow{PH}$ and point E
c. $\overleftrightarrow{FG}$ and point P
d. $\overleftrightarrow{EP}$ and point G
e. Use inductive reasoning. What do you think is true of a line and a point not on the line?

33. *Logical Reasoning* Suppose two lines intersect. How many planes do you think contain both lines? Use the diagram at the right to explain your answer.

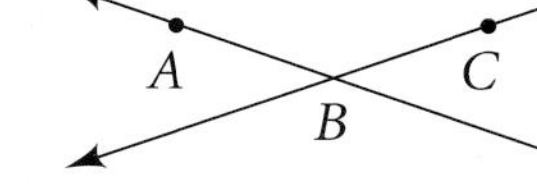

Complete with *always, sometimes,* or *never* to make a true statement.

34. Intersecting lines are __?__ coplanar.

35. Two planes __?__ intersect in exactly one point.

36. Three points are __?__ coplanar.

37. A line and a point not on the line are __?__ coplanar.

38. Four points are __?__ coplanar.

39. Two lines __?__ meet in more than one point.

Probability **Given points *A, B, C,* and *D* as shown, solve each problem.**

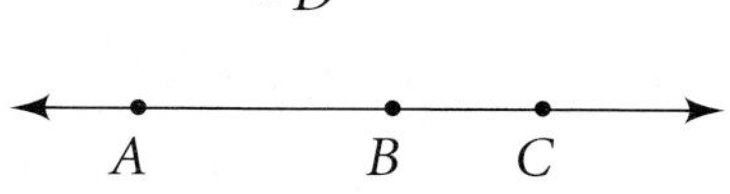

40. Two points are picked at random. Find P(they are collinear).

41. Three points are picked at random.

a. Find P(they are collinear).
b. Find P(they are coplanar).

42. **Navigation** Rescue teams use the principles in Postulates 1-1 and 1-2 to determine the location of a distress signal. In the diagram, a ship at point A receives a signal from the northeast. A ship at point B receives the same signal from due west. Trace the diagram and find the location of the distress signal. Explain how the two postulates help to find the location of the distress signal.

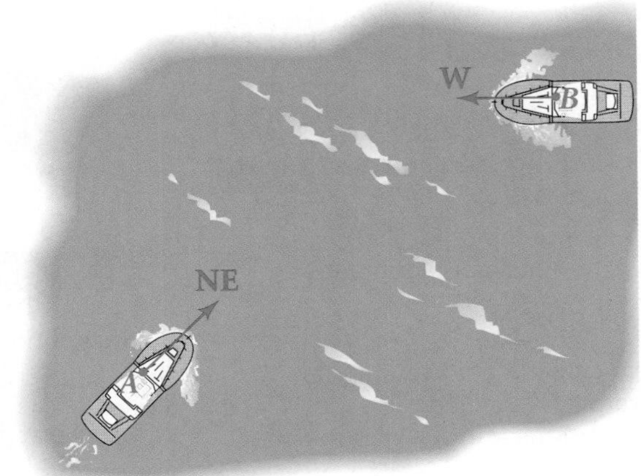

Coordinate Geometry **Are the points collinear? Graph them to find out.**

43. (1, 1), (4, 4), (−3, −3)
44. (2, 4), (4, 6), (0, 2)
45. (0, 0), (8, 10), (4, 6)
46. (0, 0), (0, 3), (0, −10)

47. **Open-ended** Give an example from your classroom or your home of three planes intersecting in one line.

48. **Optical Illusions** The diagram at the right is an optical illusion. Which points are collinear, A, B, C or A, B, D? Are you sure? Use a ruler to check your answer.

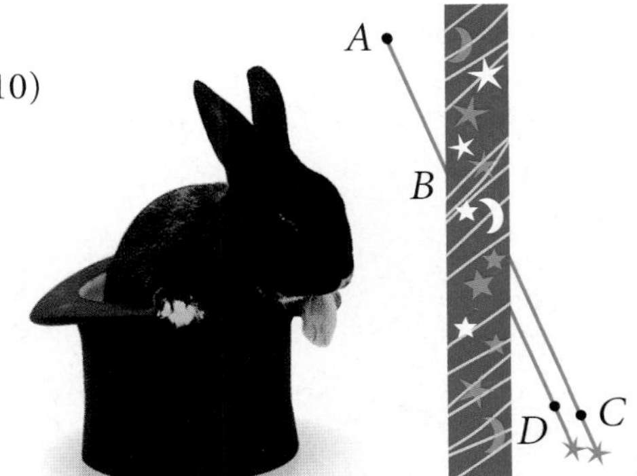

Exercises MIXED REVIEW

Algebra **Evaluate each expression for the given values.**

49. $a^2 + b^2$ for $a = 3$ and $b = -5$
50. $\frac{1}{2}bh$ for $b = 8$ and $h = 11$
51. $2\ell + 2w$ for $\ell = 3$ and $w = 7$
52. $b^2 - 4ac$ for $a = 2$, $b = 5$, and $c = 1$

53. **Patterns** What is the last digit of 3^{45}? Make a table and use inductive reasoning. Explain the pattern.

Getting Ready for Lesson 1-3

Will the lines intersect or not?

54.

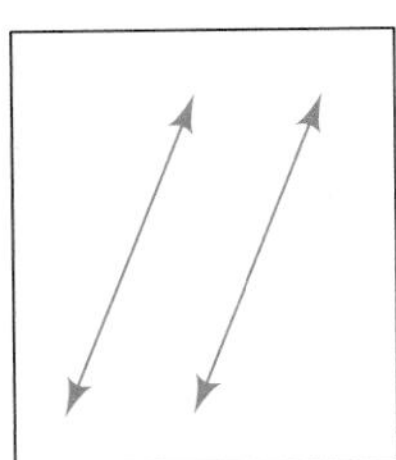

55.

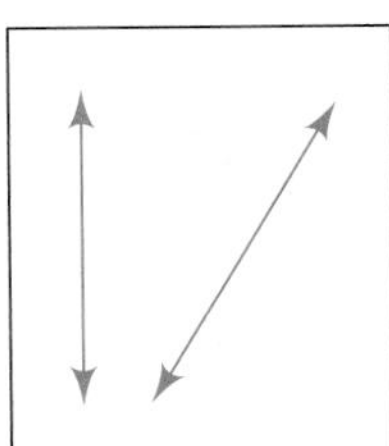

56.

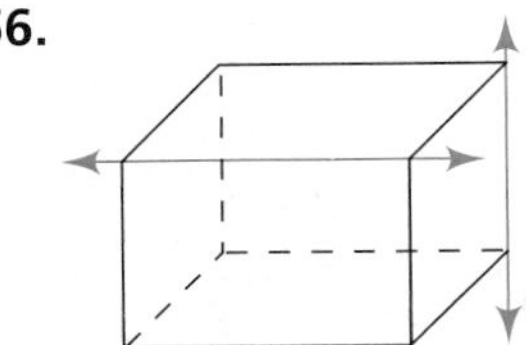

57.

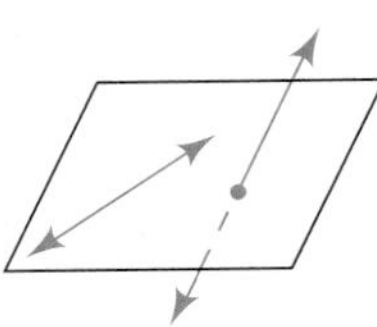

1-3 Segments, Rays, Parallel Lines and Planes

What You'll Learn

- Relating segments and rays to lines
- Recognizing parallel lines and parallel planes

...And Why

To provide a vocabulary of terms needed for communicating in geometry

What You'll Need

graph paper, colored pencils, tape

THINK AND DISCUSS

Many geometric figures, such as squares and angles, use only the parts of lines called segments and rays.

A **segment** is the part of a line consisting of two *endpoints* and all points between them.

segment *AB*

A B

endpoint $\overline{AB}$ endpoint

A **ray** is the part of a line consisting of one *endpoint* and all the points of the line on one side of the endpoint.

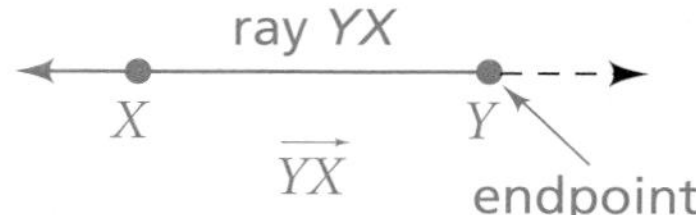

1. Is $\overline{AB}$ the same as $\overline{BA}$? Explain.
2. Is $\overrightarrow{YX}$ the same as $\overrightarrow{XY}$? Explain.
3. How is a ray like a line? How is a ray different from a line?

A ray in geometry is named after the rays of the sun.

Opposite rays are two collinear rays with the same endpoint. Opposite rays always form a line.

4. **a.** Name four different rays in the figure below.
   b. Name two opposite rays.

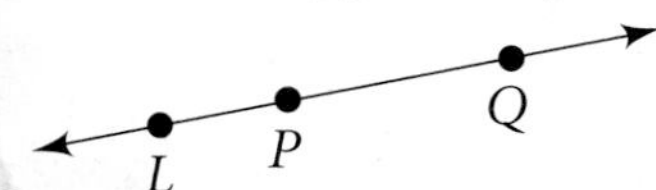

Lines that do not intersect may or may not be coplanar. **Parallel lines** are coplanar lines that do not intersect. Segments and rays are parallel if they lie in parallel lines.

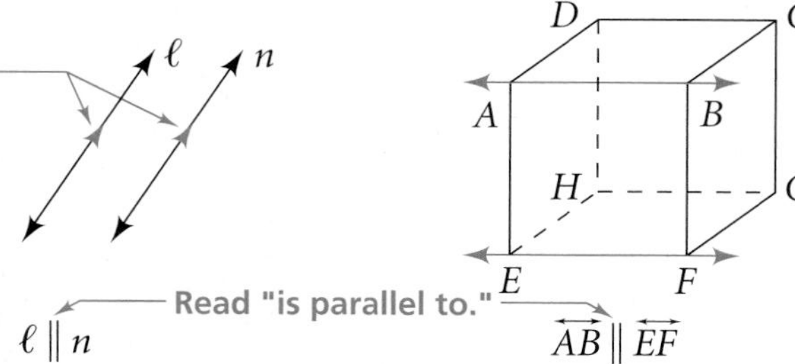

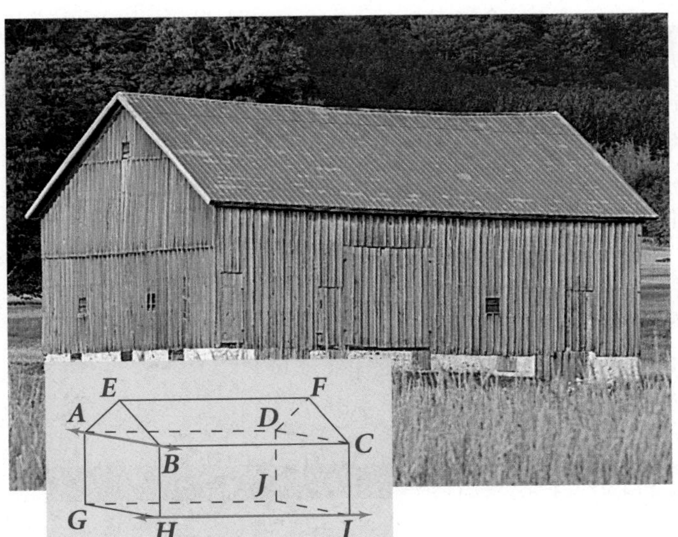

5. Name all the segments shown at the left that are parallel to:
a. $\overline{DC}$ **b.** $\overline{GJ}$ **c.** $\overline{AE}$

Skew lines do not lie in the same plane. They are neither parallel nor intersecting.

$\overleftrightarrow{AB}$ and $\overleftrightarrow{HI}$ are skew.

Parallel planes are planes that do not intersect.

plane $ABCD \parallel$ plane $GHIJ$

6. Name some other pairs of skew lines in the diagram at the left.
7. Name two more pairs of parallel planes.

A box diagram is a good way to represent parallel lines and segments, skew lines, and parallel planes. Some other ways to draw planes are shown below.

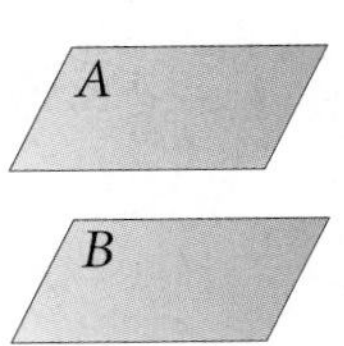

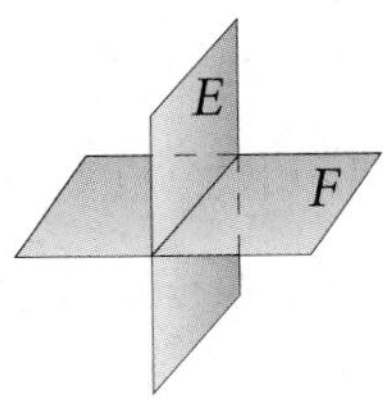

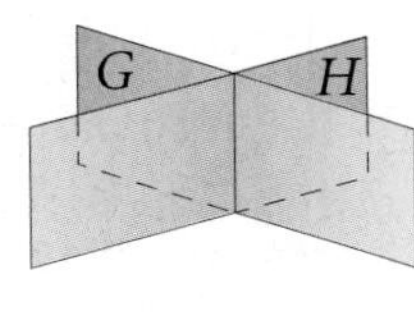

8. Which pairs of planes shown above are parallel? Which are intersecting?

Example

Draw planes A and B intersecting in $\overleftrightarrow{FG}$.

Using graph paper will help you draw parallel lines and representations of planes.

Step 1

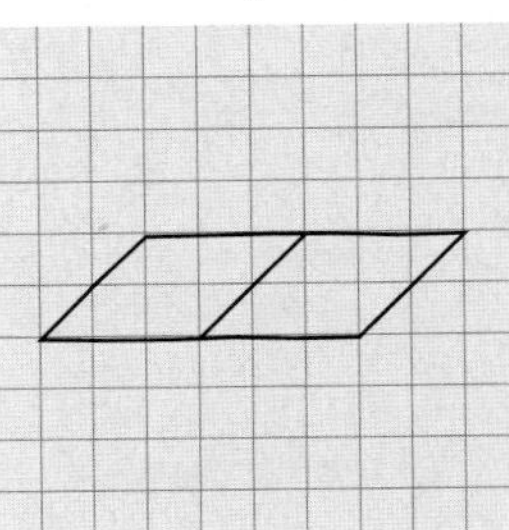

Step 2

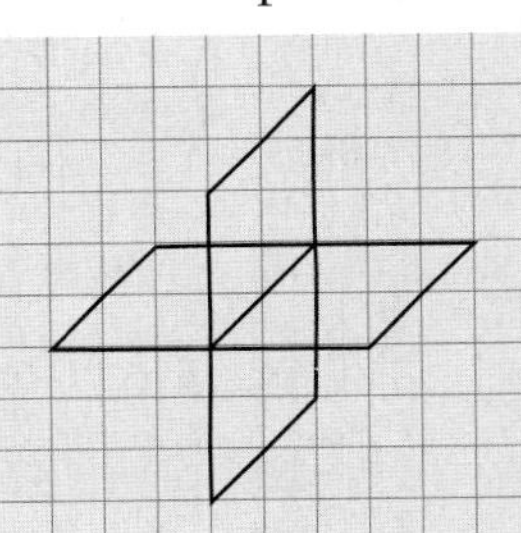

Step 3

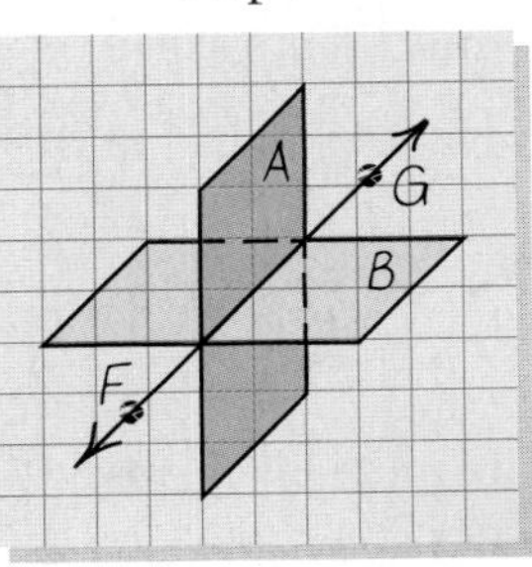

9. **Try This** Use graph paper and colored pencils to draw pairs of parallel and intersecting planes like those above Question 8.

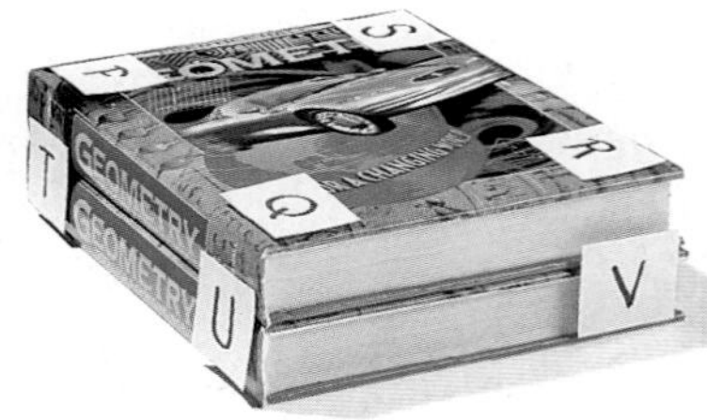

WORK TOGETHER

Work in pairs to answer these questions about the lines and planes determined by the surfaces of a rectangular solid.

Stack your geometry books to form a rectangular solid. Label the vertices *P, Q, R, S, T, U, V,* and *W*. Identify each of the following.

10. three pairs of parallel planes

11. all lines that are parallel to $\overleftrightarrow{PQ}$

12. all lines that are skew to $\overleftrightarrow{PQ}$

Exercises ON YOUR OWN

Name all the segments that are parallel to the given segment.

1. $\overline{AC}$ **2.** $\overline{EF}$ **3.** $\overline{AD}$

4. Name all the lines that form a pair of skew lines with $\overleftrightarrow{AD}$.

5. Name a pair of parallel planes.

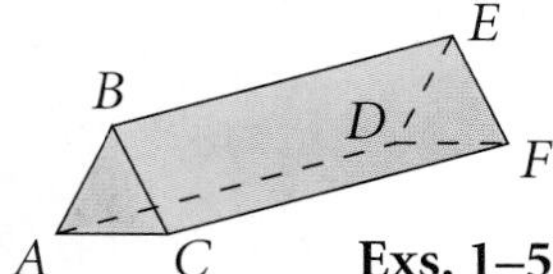

Exs. 1–5

Use the line at the right for Exercises 6–8.

6. a. Name a pair of opposite rays with point *T* as endpoint.
b. Name another pair of opposite rays.

7. Name all the segments shown.

8. Name $\overrightarrow{RT}$ two other ways.

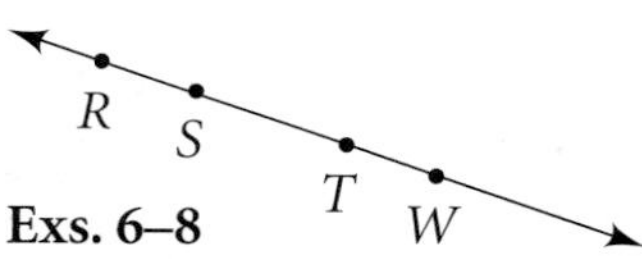

Exs. 6–8

Make a separate sketch for each of the following.

9. Draw three parallel lines *a, t,* and *q*.

10. Draw parallel planes *A* and *B*.

11. Draw $\overleftrightarrow{AB}$, $\overleftrightarrow{CD}$, and $\overleftrightarrow{EF}$ so that $\overleftrightarrow{AB} \parallel \overleftrightarrow{CD}$, $\overleftrightarrow{AB}$ and $\overleftrightarrow{EF}$ are skew, and $\overleftrightarrow{CD}$ and $\overleftrightarrow{EF}$ are skew.

12. Draw planes *C* and *D*, intersecting in $\overleftrightarrow{XY}$.

Write *true* or *false*.

13. $\overleftrightarrow{CB} \parallel \overleftrightarrow{GF}$

14. $\overleftrightarrow{ED} \parallel \overleftrightarrow{HG}$

15. plane *AED* $\parallel$ plane *FGH*

16. plane *ABH* $\parallel$ plane *CDF*

17. $\overleftrightarrow{AB}$ and $\overleftrightarrow{HG}$ are skew lines.

18. $\overleftrightarrow{AE}$ and $\overleftrightarrow{BC}$ are skew lines.

19. $\overleftrightarrow{CF}$ and $\overleftrightarrow{AI}$ are skew lines.

20. $\overleftrightarrow{CF}$ and $\overleftrightarrow{AJ}$ are skew lines.

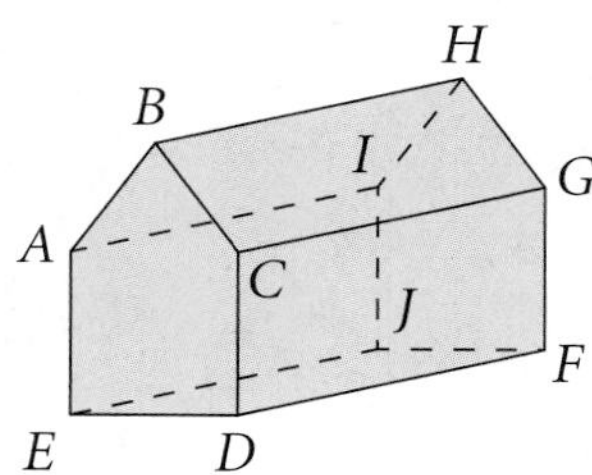

Complete with *always, sometimes,* or *never* to make a true statement.

21. $\overrightarrow{AB}$ and $\overrightarrow{BA}$ are __?__ the same ray.

22. $\overrightarrow{AB}$ and $\overrightarrow{AC}$ are __?__ the same ray.

23. $\overline{AX}$ and $\overline{XA}$ are __?__ the same segment.

24. $\overleftrightarrow{TQ}$ and $\overleftrightarrow{QT}$ are __?__ the same line.

25. Two parallel lines are __?__ coplanar.

26. Skew lines are __?__ coplanar.

27. Opposite rays __?__ form a line.

28. Two lines in the same plane are __?__ parallel.

29. Two planes that do not intersect are __?__ parallel.

30. Two lines that lie in parallel planes are __?__ parallel.

Directions are printed on a compass card, a circle divided into 32 equally-spaced compass points.

31. **Writing** **Summarize** the different ways that two lines may be related. Give examples from the real world that illustrate the relationships.

32. **Navigation** North and south are directions on a compass that are on opposite rays. Name two other pairs of compass directions that are on opposite rays.

33. **Coordinate Geometry** $\overrightarrow{AB}$ has endpoint $A(2, 3)$ and goes through $B(4, 6)$. Give some possible coordinates for point C so that $\overrightarrow{AB}$ and $\overrightarrow{AC}$ will be opposite rays. Graph your answer.

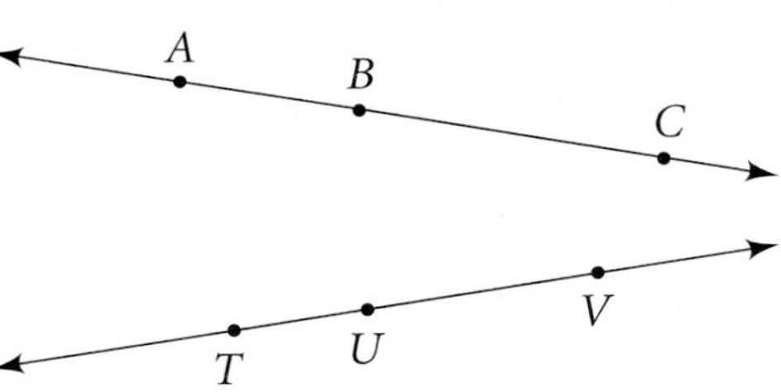

34. **Inductive Reasoning** Draw a diagram similar to the one shown.
Step 1: Draw $\overline{AU}$ and $\overline{BT}$. Label their intersection point as X.
Step 2: Draw $\overline{AV}$ and $\overline{CT}$. Label their intersection point as Y.
Step 3: Draw $\overline{BV}$ and $\overline{CU}$. Label their intersection point as Z.
Make a **conjecture** about points X, Y, and Z.

35. **Critical Thinking** Suppose two parallel planes A and B are each intersected by a third plane C. What do you think will be true of the intersection of planes A and C and the intersection of planes B and C? Give an example in your classroom.

36. **Research** In diamond, each carbon atom bonds to four other carbon atoms in a three-dimensional network. In graphite, each carbon atom bonds to three other carbon atoms in the same plane. The "sheets" or planes of graphite are parallel. Find out how these structures affect the properties of diamond and graphite.

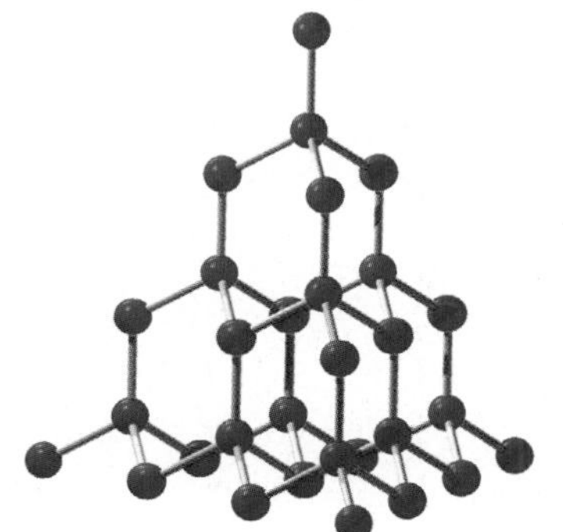

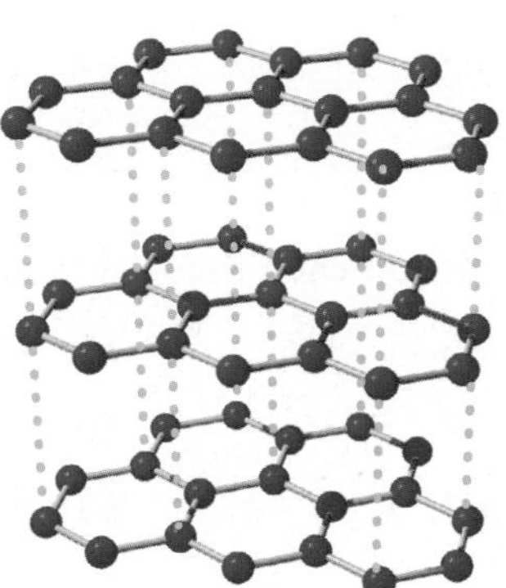

37. *Open-ended* List four pairs of parallel planes in your classroom.

38. *Writing* The term *skew* is from a Middle English word meaning "to escape." Explain why this might be an appropriate origin for the word that names skew lines.

39. *Standardized Test Prep* Which statement(s) can be true about three planes?
I. They intersect in a line. **II.** They intersect in a point. **III.** They have no points in common.
A. I only **B.** II only **C.** I and II only **D.** I and III only **E.** I, II, and III

Chapter Project

Find Out by Creating

Some artists create origami by experimenting. They fold and unfold a piece of paper until they see a resemblance to the real world. Take your folded square from the Find Out question on page 572 (or make a new one). Use the existing creases to construct the dog and the flower pictured at the right. Now try to create your own origami, starting with a fresh square of paper.

Exercises MIXED REVIEW

Find the next two terms in each sequence.

40. 0.1, 0.12, 0.123, 0.1234, . . .
41. $-1, -2, -4, -7, -11, -16, \ldots$
42. AB, BC, CD, DE, EF, . . .

State the ways you can name each geometric figure.

43. a line
44. a point
45. a plane

46. *Logical Reasoning* Raven made the following **conjecture**: "When you subtract a number from a given number, the answer is always smaller than the given number." Is her **conjecture** correct? Explain.

Getting Ready for Lesson 1-4

Simplify each expression.

47. $|-6|$
48. $|3.5|$
49. $|7 - 10|$
50. $|-4 - 2|$
51. $|8 - 5|$
52. $|4 + 1|$
53. $|-3 + 12|$
54. $|-21 + 6|$
55. $|-11 - (-2)|$

Graph each inequality on a number line.

56. $t > 6$
57. $9 \leq m$
58. $w < -4$
59. $5 > s$
60. $p \leq 7$
61. $-1.5 \geq b$
62. $x \geq -3$
63. $0 < q$
64. $-5 \leq v < -2$

SELF ASSESSMENT

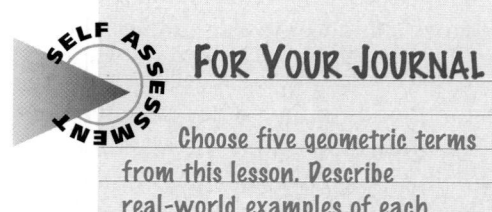

FOR YOUR JOURNAL

Choose five geometric terms from this lesson. Describe real-world examples of each.

Math ToolboX

Algebra Review

Solving Linear Equations

Before Lesson 1-4

Sometimes you need to combine like terms when you are solving linear equations.

Example 1

Solve $(5x + 8) - (2x - 9) = 38$.

$(5x + 8) + (-1)(2x - 9) = 38$	$-(2x - 9) = (-1)(2x - 9)$
$5x + 8 - 2x + 9 = 38$	Use the Distributive Property.
$3x + 17 = 38$	Simplify.
$3x = 21$	Subtract 17 from each side.
$x = 7$	Divide each side by 3.

When you are solving equations with variables on both sides, first get all the variables on the same side of the equation.

Example 2

Solve $4x - 9 = 7x - 15$.

$4x - 9 = 7x - 15$	
$-9 = 3x - 15$	Subtract $4x$ from each side.
$6 = 3x$	Add 15 to each side.
$2 = x$	Divide each side by 3.

Solve.

1. $5x + 10 - 6x + 3 = 6 - 2x - 2$

2. $(6a - 54) - (5a + 27) = 23$

3. $(2 + 4y) - (y + 9) = 26$

4. $7t - 8t + 4 = 5t - 2$

5. $(9k + 30) - (4k + 10) = 100$

6. $6x + 17 = 9x + 2$

7. $(3x + 10) - 5x = 6x - 50$

8. $(3y - 5) + (5y + 20) = 135$

9. $10n + 12 = 14n - 12$

10. $13c + 40 = 9c - 20 + c$

11. $(4w - 28) + (11w + 13) = 180$

12. $7f + 16 = 3f + 48$

13. $(7a + 3) + (-a - 5) = -16$

14. $3x - 35 = 9x - 59$

15. $7y + 44 = 12y + 11$

16. $(11x - 37) + (5x + 59) = 54$

17. $(7t - 21) + (t + 4) = 15$

18. $(5w + 24) + (2w + 13) = 156$

1-4 Measuring Angles and Segments

What You'll Learn

- Finding the length of a segment and the measure of an angle

...And Why

To understand the building blocks of many geometric figures

What You'll Need

protractor

WORK TOGETHER

Your family is traveling on Interstate 80 through Nebraska. You entered the highway at mileage marker 126. You decided to drive as far as you could before stopping for breakfast within $1\frac{1}{2}$ hours. Assume that on the highway you drive at an average speed of 60 mi/h. Work with a partner to answer these questions.

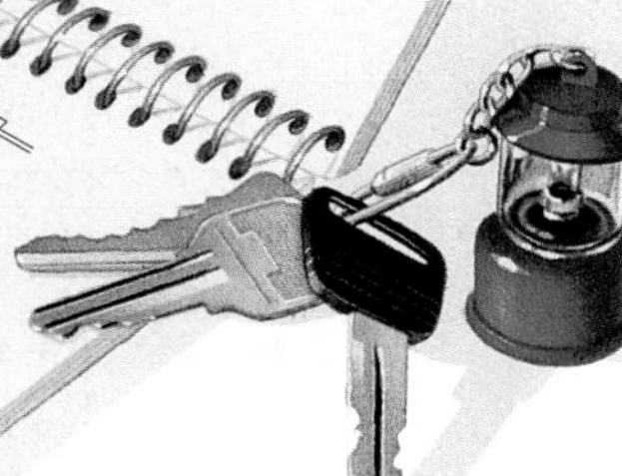

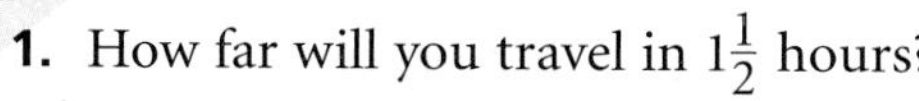

1. How far will you travel in $1\frac{1}{2}$ hours?
2. **a.** At what mileage marker will you exit to get breakfast?
   b. Is there another possible answer for the mileage marker?
3. Suppose you are traveling east on I-80, starting at mileage marker 126. Not counting side trips for sightseeing, you travel 111 mi on I-80 before you exit for a campground.
   a. Do mileage markers increase or decrease from west to east?
   b. What mileage marker is at your exit?
4. Does the *direction* you travel affect the *distance* you travel?

THINK AND DISCUSS

Measuring Segments

If you picture straightening out the map of Interstate 80, you will have a model for a number line. The mileage markers represent *coordinates.*

Postulate 1-5
Ruler Postulate

The points of a line can be put into a one-to-one correspondence with the real numbers so that the distance between any two points is the absolute value of the difference of the corresponding numbers.

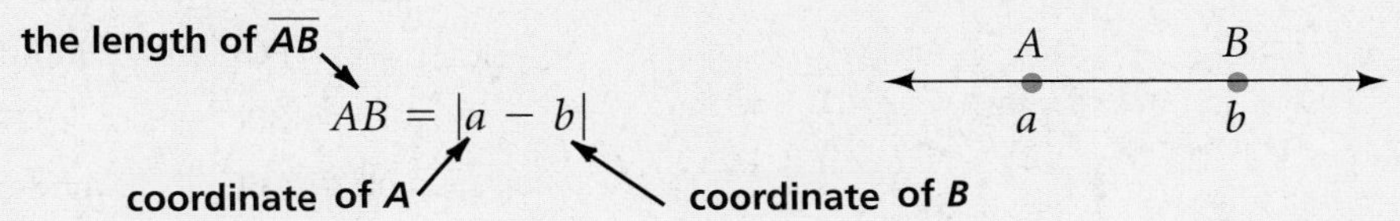

5. **Critical Thinking** Why do you think that absolute value is used to express the distance between two points?

Example 1

PROBLEM SOLVING HINT
Draw a diagram.

Find QS if the coordinate of Q is -3 and the coordinate of S is 21.

$QS = |-3 - 21| = |-24| = 24$

6. Suppose you subtracted -3 from 21 in Example 1. Would you get the same result? Why or why not?
7. **Try This** Find AB if the coordinate of point A is -8, and the coordinate of point B is 11.

Two segments with the same length are **congruent** ($\cong$). In other words, if $AB = CD$, then $\overline{AB} \cong \overline{CD}$. You can use these statements interchangeably. Segments can be marked alike to show that they are congruent.

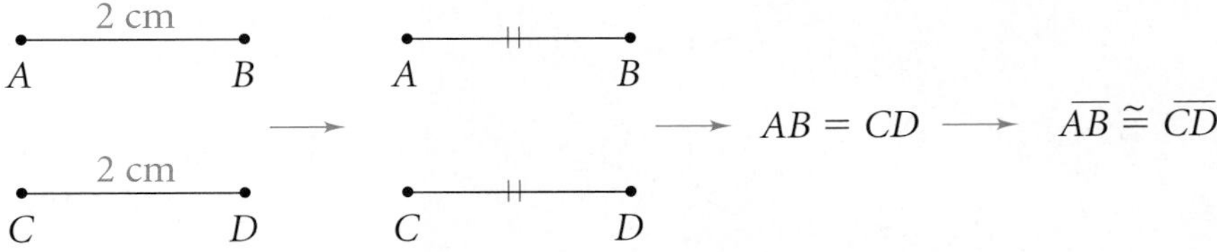

8. a. **Try This** Name two segments that are congruent.
   b. Name a second pair of congruent segments.

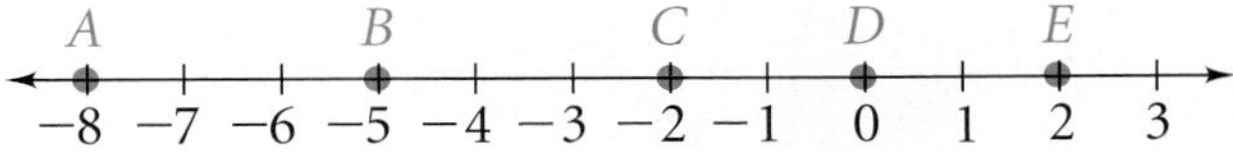

Postulate 1-6
Segment Addition Postulate

If three points A, B, and C are collinear and B is between A and C, then $AB + BC = AC$.

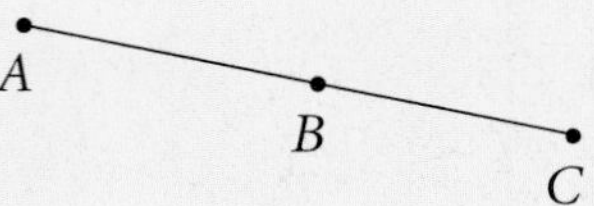

Example 2

Algebra If $DT = 60$, find the value of x. Then find DS and ST.

2x − 8 | 3x − 12
D S T

$$DS + ST = DT \quad \text{Segment Addition Postulate}$$
$$(2x - 8) + (3x - 12) = 60 \quad \text{Substitution}$$
$$5x - 20 = 60 \quad \text{Simplify.}$$
$$5x = 80 \quad \text{Add 20 to each side.}$$
$$x = 16 \quad \text{Divide each side by 5.}$$

$DS = 2x - 8 = 2(16) - 8 = 24$

$ST = 3x - 12 = 3(16) - 12 = 36$

9. Explain how to check the answers in Example 2.

4x − 20 | 2x + 30
E F G

10. a. **Try This** $EG = 100$. Find the value of x.
b. Find EF and FG.

Measuring Angles

An **angle** ($\angle$) is formed by two rays (called *sides* of the angle) with the same endpoint (called the *vertex* of the angle). You can name an angle several ways.

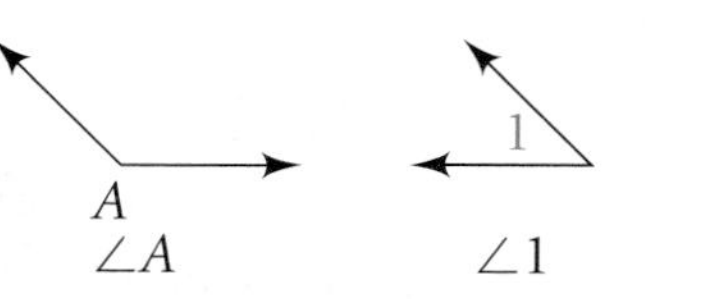

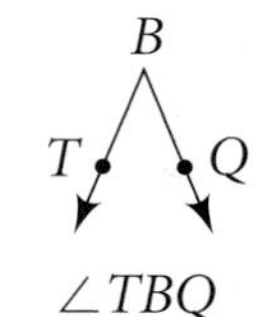

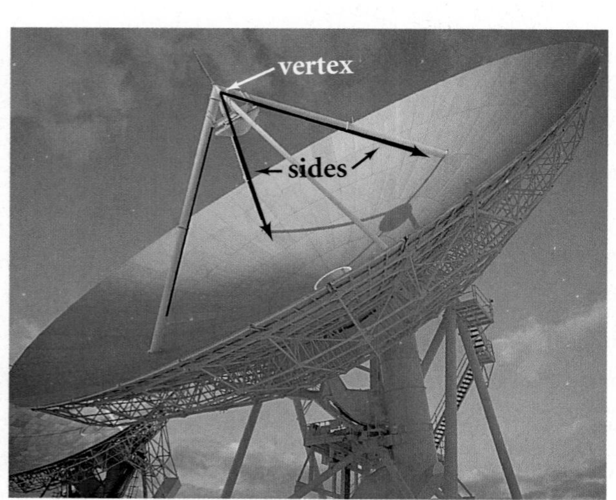

11. a. Name $\angle 1$ two other ways.
b. Name $\angle CED$ two other ways.
c. Would it be correct to refer to any of the angles at the right as $\angle E$? Why or why not?

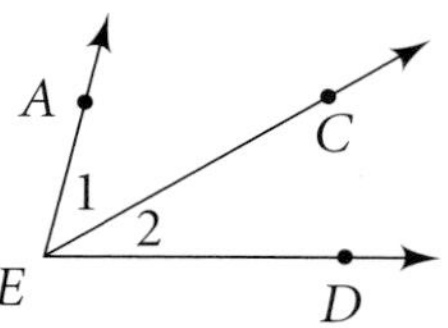

Angles are measured in *degrees*. The *measure* of $\angle A$ is written as $m\angle A$.

$m\angle A = 80$

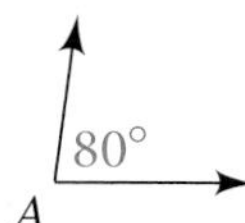

When you use a *protractor* to measure angles you are applying the following postulate.

Postulate 1-7
Protractor Postulate

Let $\overrightarrow{OA}$ and $\overrightarrow{OB}$ be opposite rays in a plane. $\overrightarrow{OA}$, $\overrightarrow{OB}$ and all the rays with endpoint O that can be drawn on one side of $\overleftrightarrow{AB}$ can be paired with the real numbers from 0 to 180 in such a way that:

a. $\overrightarrow{OA}$ is paired with 0 and $\overrightarrow{OB}$ is paired with 180.

b. If $\overrightarrow{OC}$ is paired with x and $\overrightarrow{OD}$ is paired with y, then $m\angle COD = |x - y|$.

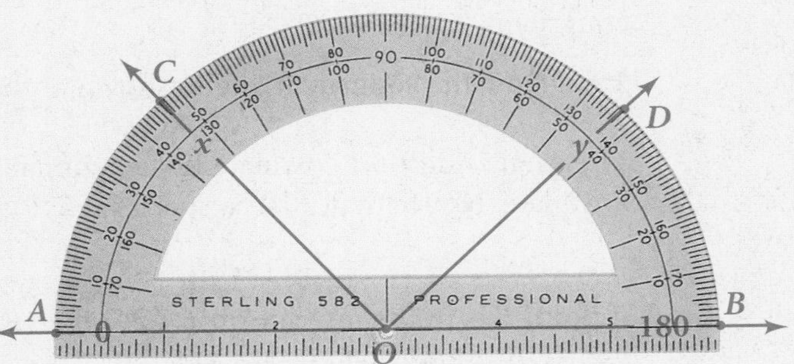

Math A Test Prep

1 The intersection of two planes is a
(1) point
(2) ray
(3) line segment
(4) line

2 At what hour(s) do the minute hand and hour hand of a clock form a 120° angle?

12. Try This Use a protractor to find the measure of each angle.
a. $m\angle AOC$ **b.** $m\angle EOB$ **c.** $m\angle DOF$ **d.** $m\angle COE$

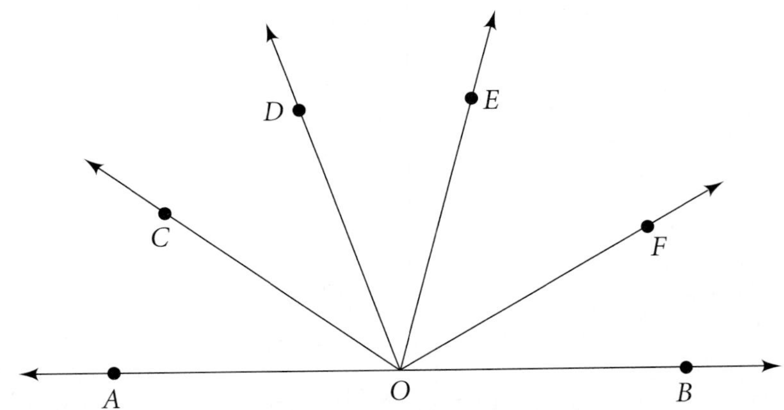

13. Try This Use a protractor to draw a 105° angle.

You can classify angles according to their measures.

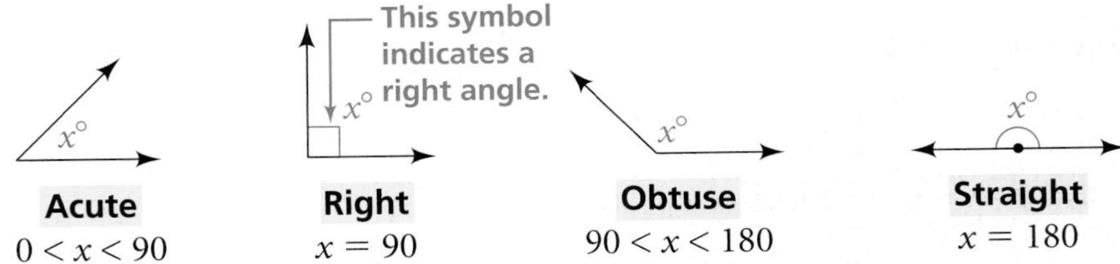

14. Estimate the measure of each angle. Then use a protractor to find the measure.

a. b. c.

15. Classify each angle in Exercise 14 as *acute, obtuse,* or *right.*

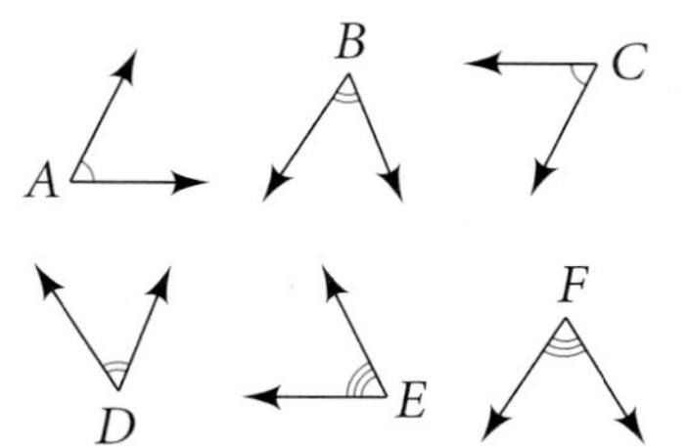

Angles with the same measure are **congruent.** In other words, if $m\angle 1 = m\angle 2$, then $\angle 1 \cong \angle 2$. You can use these statements interchangeably. Angles can be marked alike to show that they are congruent.

16. Name the congruent angles shown at the left.

The Angle Addition Postulate is very similar to the Segment Addition Postulate. Notice that it has a special case for straight angles.

Postulate 1-8
Angle Addition Postulate

If point B is in the interior of $\angle AOC$, then $m\angle AOB + m\angle BOC = m\angle AOC$.

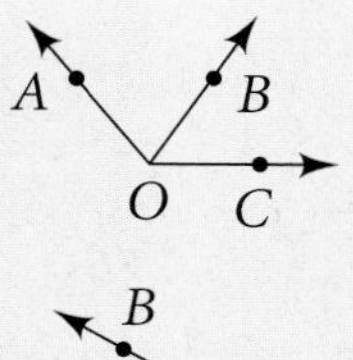

If $\angle AOC$ is a straight angle, then $m\angle AOB + m\angle BOC = 180$.

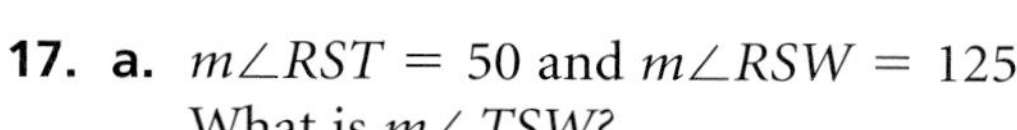

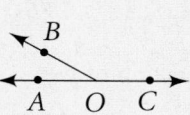

17. a. $m\angle RST = 50$ and $m\angle RSW = 125$. What is $m\angle TSW$?

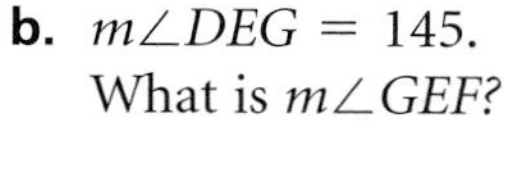

b. $m\angle DEG = 145$. What is $m\angle GEF$?

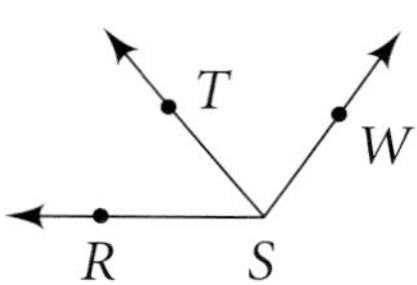

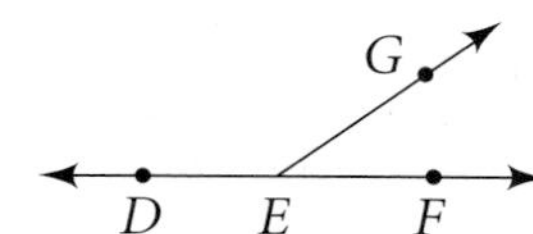

Exercises ON YOUR OWN

Complete each equation.

1. $AC = \blacksquare$ 2. $BD = \blacksquare$ 3. $AD = \blacksquare$ 4. $BE = \blacksquare$

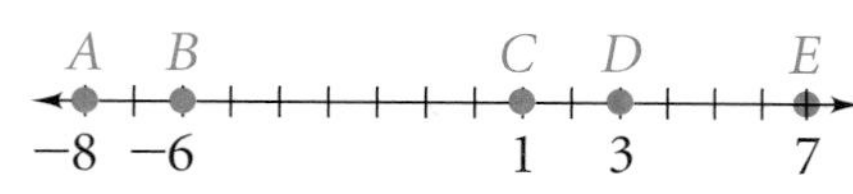

Exs. 1–10

Write *true* or *false*.

5. $\overline{AB} \cong \overline{ED}$ 6. $BD < CD$ 7. $AC + BD = AD$ 8. $AC + CD = AD$

9. Name two pairs of congruent segments.

10. $EG = 5$. Find the coordinate of point G. Is there another possibility?

Use the figure at the right for Exercises 11–14.

R S T

11. If $RS = 15$ and $ST = 9$, then $RT = \blacksquare$.

12. If $ST = 15$ and $RT = 40$, then $RS = \blacksquare$.

13. **Algebra** If $RS = 3x + 1$, $ST = 2x - 2$, and $RT = 64$, find the value of x. Then find RS and ST.

14. **Algebra** If $RS = 8y + 4$, $ST = 4y + 8$, and $RT = 15y - 9$, find the value of y. Then find RS and ST.

Use the figure at the right for Exercises 15–17.

15. If $m\angle MQV = 90$ and $m\angle VQP = 35$, what is $m\angle MQP$?

16. If $m\angle MVQ = 55$, what is $m\angle QVP$?

17. Judging by appearance, name each of the following.
- **a.** two acute angles
- **b.** two obtuse angles
- **c.** two right angles

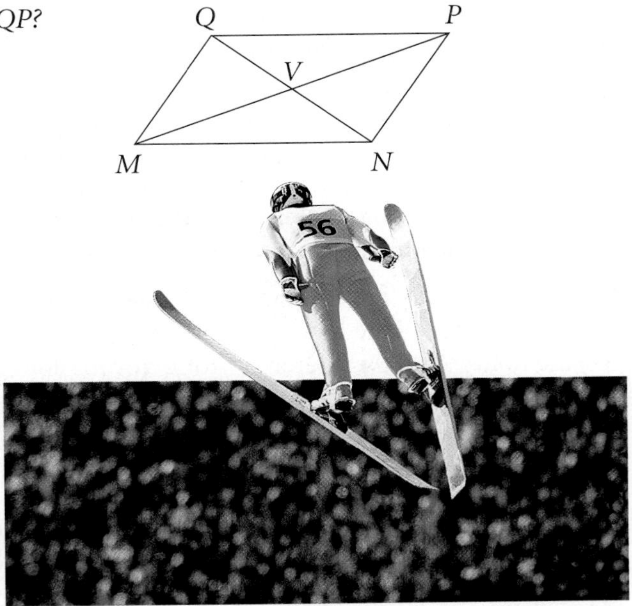

18. Without using your protractor, sketch angles with the following measures. Then use your protractor to see how close you are.
a. 30 **b.** 60 **c.** 120

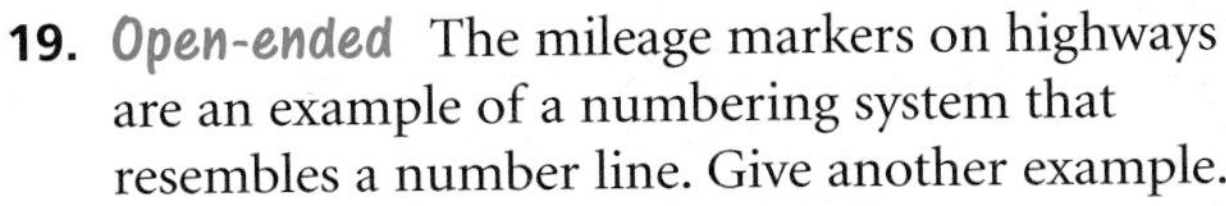

19. **Open-ended** The mileage markers on highways are an example of a numbering system that resembles a number line. Give another example.

20. **Ski Jumping** This ski jumper is using a new style of jumping. The skis are at an angle rather than parallel. Measure the angle formed by the two skis.

Estimation **Estimate the measure of each angle. Then use a protractor to measure it. Classify each angle.**

21. **22.** **23.**

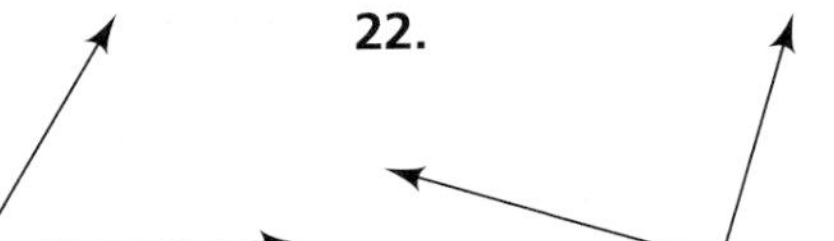

24. **Coordinate Geometry** $AB = 12$. Point A has coordinates $(3, 0)$. Give four possible locations for point B.

25. **Open-ended** Name two times when the hands of a clock
- **a.** form an acute angle.
- **b.** form a right angle.
- **c.** form an obtuse angle.
- **d.** form a straight angle.

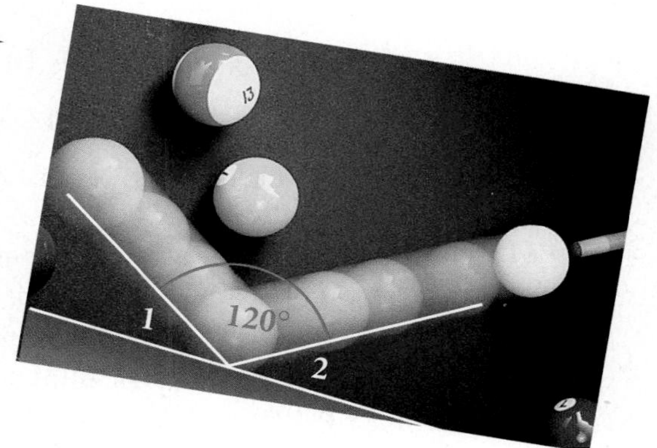

26. **Billiards** In billiards, the cue ball may bounce off a cushion on any shot. If there is no spin on the shot, $\angle 1$ and $\angle 2$ will be congruent. Find the measures of $\angle 1$ and $\angle 2$.

27. **Algebra** If $AD = 12$ and $AC = 4y - 36$, find the value of y.

28. **Algebra** If $ED = x + 4$ and $DB = 3x - 8$, find EB.

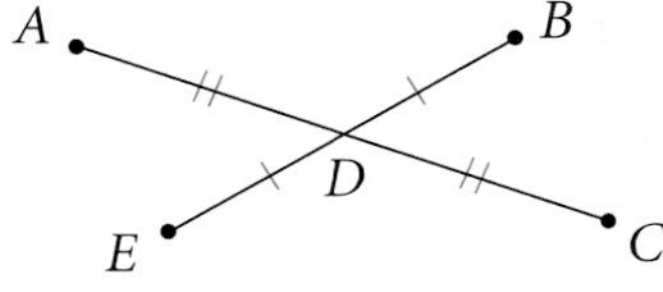

29. **Writing** The word "acute" can mean *sharp* in conversational English. Explain why this meaning describes an acute angle.

30. **Technology** Leon constructed an angle. Then he constructed a ray from the vertex of the angle to a point in the interior of the angle. He measured all the angles formed. Then he moved the interior ray.

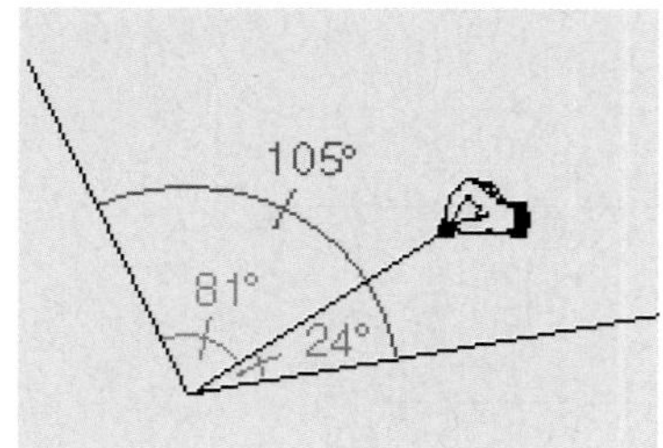

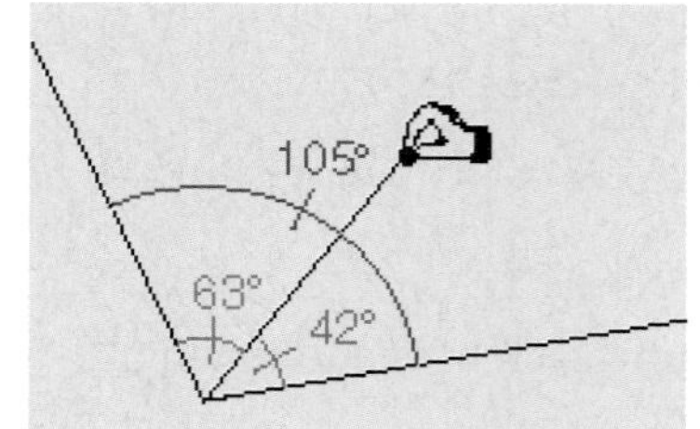

a. **Patterns** What patterns do you observe?

b. What postulate does this support?

31. **Golf Fun** Copy the diagram. (1) Estimate the distance in centimeters from the tee to the hole. Estimate the angle in degrees from the tee to the hole. (2) Use a ruler and protractor to plot your estimate. This is stroke 1. Add a penalty stroke if you land in the sand or the water. (3) Continue until you are at most 0.5 cm from the hole marked by the flag. What was your score?

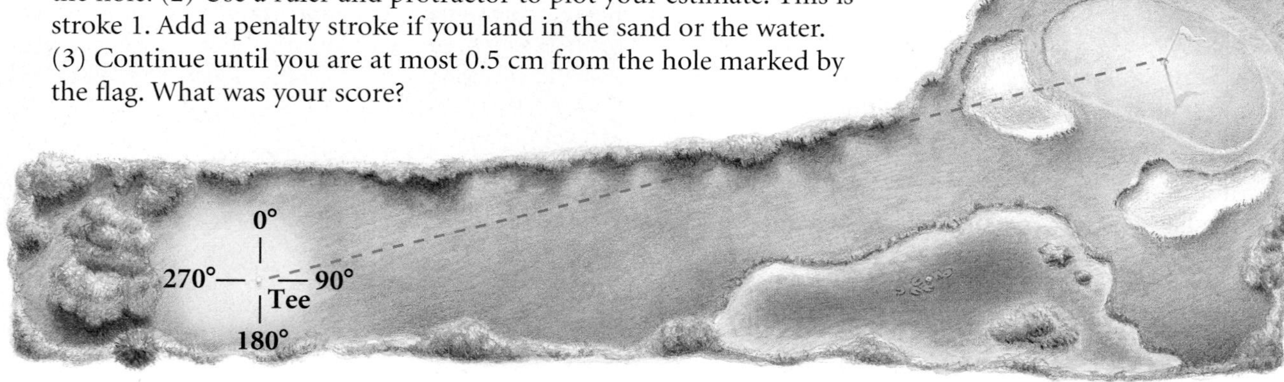

Algebra **Solve for x.**

32. $m\angle AOC = 7x - 2$, $m\angle AOB = 2x + 8$, $m\angle BOC = 3x + 14$

33. $m\angle AOB = 4x - 2$, $m\angle BOC = 5x + 10$, $m\angle COD = 2x + 14$

34. $m\angle AOB = 28$, $m\angle BOC = 3x - 2$, $m\angle AOD = 6x$

35. $m\angle AOB = 4x + 3$, $m\angle BOC = 7x$, $m\angle AOD = 16x - 1$

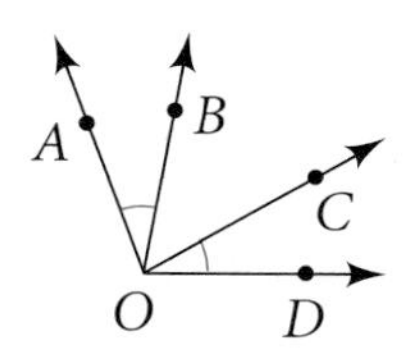

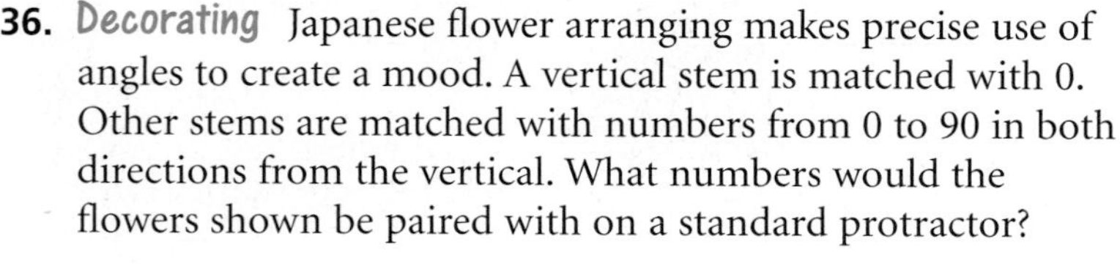

36. **Decorating** Japanese flower arranging makes precise use of angles to create a mood. A vertical stem is matched with 0. Other stems are matched with numbers from 0 to 90 in both directions from the vertical. What numbers would the flowers shown be paired with on a standard protractor?

Find Out by Researching

Choose one of the origami creations pictured on pages 564 and 565. Find a book that contains directions for making the figure, and follow the directions to make your favorite origami creation.

Exercises MIXED REVIEW

Find the next term in each sequence.

37. 5, 10, 15, 20, . . .

38. 5, 25, 125, 625, . . .

39. 14, 18, 22, 26, . . .

Complete each statement.

40. Three points are always __?__.

41. Intersecting lines are always __?__.

42. Two intersecting planes intersect in a __?__.

43. Two points are always __?__.

44. A 24-cm segment is divided into two segments. One segment is three times as long as the other. Find the lengths of both segments.

Getting Ready for Lesson 1-5

Sketch each figure.

45. $\overline{CD}$

46. $\overrightarrow{GH}$

47. $\overleftrightarrow{AB}$

48. line m

Exercises CHECKPOINT

Find the next two terms in each sequence.

1. 19, 21.5, 24, 26.5, . . .

2. 3.4, 3.45, 3.456, 3.4567, . . .

3. −2, 6, −18, 54, . . .

4. **Writing** Describe the pattern of the sequences in Exercises 1–3.

Are the following coplanar?

5. *A, E, F, B*

6. *F, C, B, H*

7. $\overleftrightarrow{DC}$, point *E*

8. *D, G, B*

9. $\overleftrightarrow{GC}$, $\overleftrightarrow{BC}$

10. What is the intersection of plane *EFGH* and $\overleftrightarrow{DH}$?

11. Name all the segments parallel to $\overline{HG}$.

12. Name two skew lines.

13. Name two parallel planes.

14. Name an acute, an obtuse, and a right angle.

15. **Algebra** If $AB = 4x + 5$ and $DC = 3x + 8$, find AB.

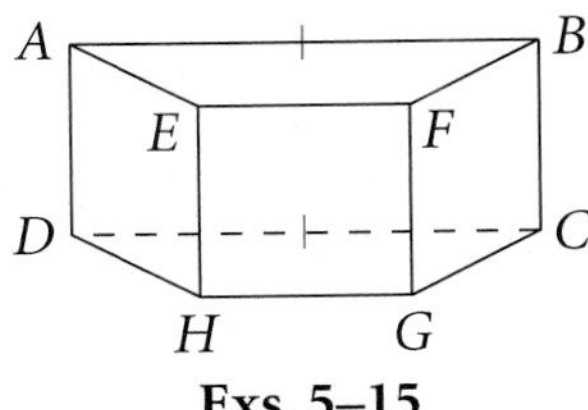

Exs. 5–15

Connections Language Arts . . . and more

1-5 Good Definitions

What You'll Learn

- Identifying a good definition
- Understanding the meaning of terms like *bisector* and *perpendicular*

...And Why

To sharpen a skill that is a key to communicating

WORK TOGETHER

Work with a partner to identify what makes a figure a *polyglob.*

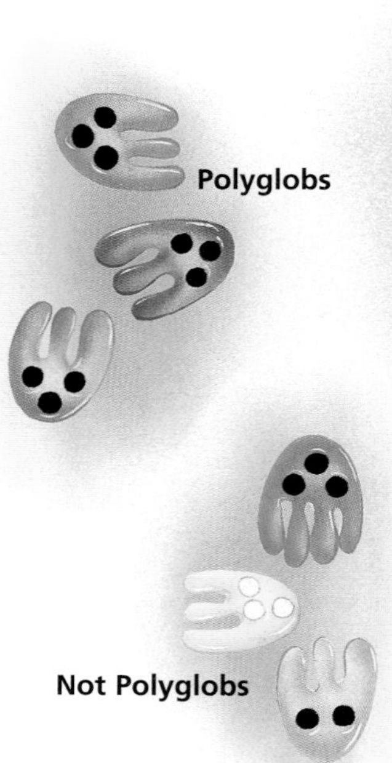

1. Which figures above are polyglobs?
2. Describe what a polyglob is.

THINK AND DISCUSS

Properties of Good Definitions

In geometry we start with undefined terms such as *point, line,* and *plane* whose meanings we understand intuitively. Then we use those terms to define other terms such as *collinear points.*

A good definition can help you identify or classify an object. A good definition has several important components.

✔ A good definition uses clearly understood terms. The terms should be commonly understood or previously defined.

✔ A good definition is precise. Good definitions avoid words such as *large, sort of,* and *some.*

✔ A good definition states what the term *is,* rather than what it is not. A poor definition of *big* is "Big is the opposite of small."

A **midpoint** of a segment is a point that divides a segment into two congruent segments.

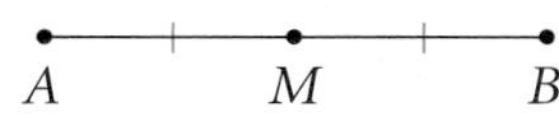

3. What previously defined terms are used in the definition of *midpoint?*

A good definition is *reversible.*

If $\overline{AM} \cong \overline{MB}$, then M is the midpoint of $\overline{AB}$.

If N is the midpoint of $\overline{CD}$, then $\overline{CN} \cong \overline{ND}$.

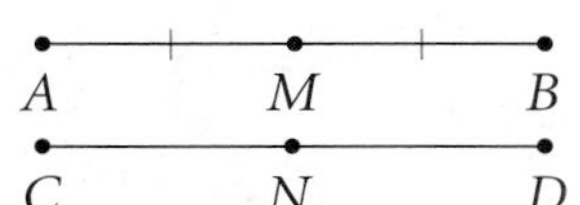

QUICK REVIEW

A right angle is an angle whose measure is 90.

4. a. If $\angle A$ is a right angle, what is the measure of $\angle A$?
b. If $m\angle B = 90$, classify $\angle B$.

Notice that you can use the definition of a right angle to justify your answer to each part of question 4.

One way to test a definition is to look for a *counterexample* that shows that the definition is wrong.

Relating to the Real World 

Language Arts Is the following an acceptable definition? Explain.

An airplane is a vehicle that flies.

The definition is not acceptable because a helicopter is also a vehicle that flies, and a helicopter is not an airplane.

5. Try This Is the following an acceptable definition? Explain.

A square is a figure with four right angles.

Bisectors

6. Study the diagrams below and write a definition of a *segment bisector.*

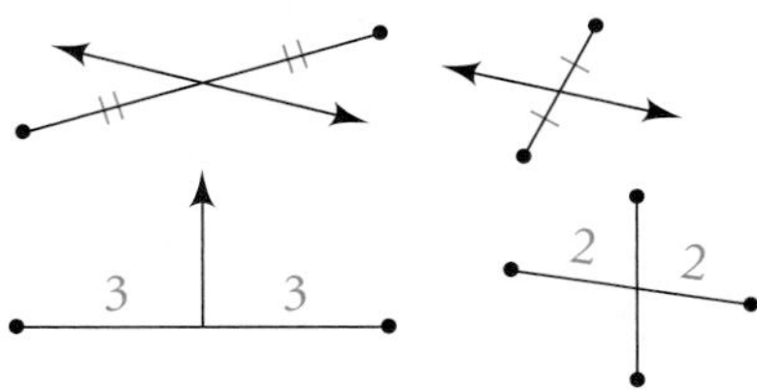

Segment bisectors

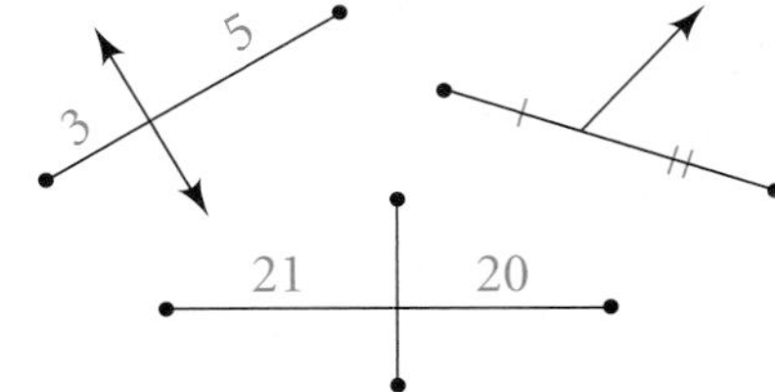

Not segment bisectors

Perpendicular lines are two lines that intersect to form right angles. The symbol $\perp$ is read as "is perpendicular to." In the diagram at the right, $\overleftrightarrow{AB} \perp \overleftrightarrow{CD}$.

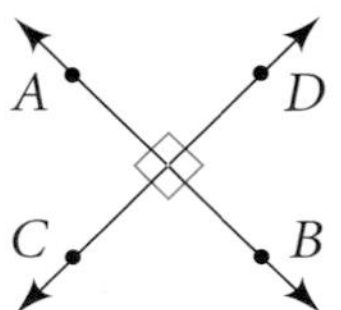

A $5 bill was folded in half. *How does the fold line meet the top step of the Lincoln Memorial?*

7. a. If $\overleftrightarrow{PQ} \perp \overleftrightarrow{RS}$, what is $m\angle PTR$? Explain.

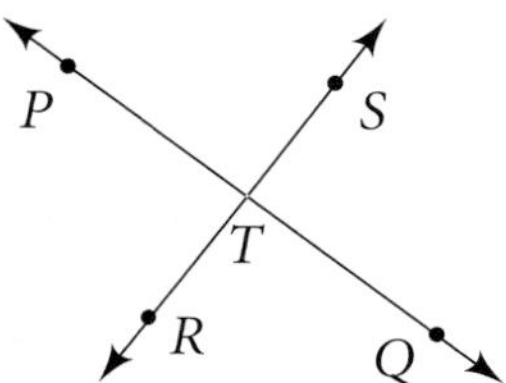

b. Which lines, if any, are perpendicular? Explain.

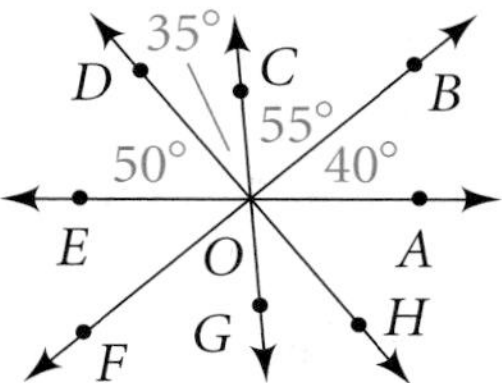

A **perpendicular bisector** of a segment is a line, segment, or ray that is perpendicular to a segment at its midpoint.

8. If you know that $\overleftrightarrow{JK}$ is the perpendicular bisector of $\overline{XY}$, what can you conclude about angles and segments in the diagram?

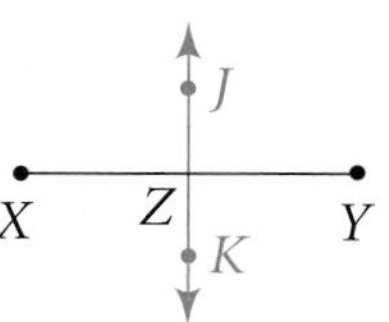

An **angle bisector** is a ray that divides an angle into two congruent angles.

9. a. Given: $\overrightarrow{CD}$ bisects $\angle ACB$. Name the congruent angles.

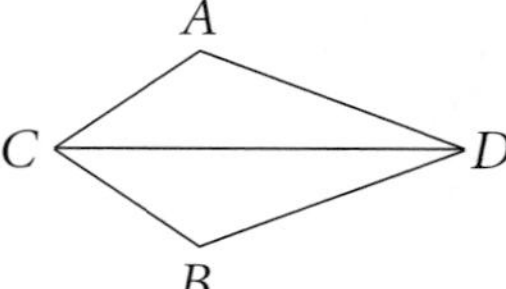

b. Given: $\angle RSW \cong \angle WST$ What can you conclude?

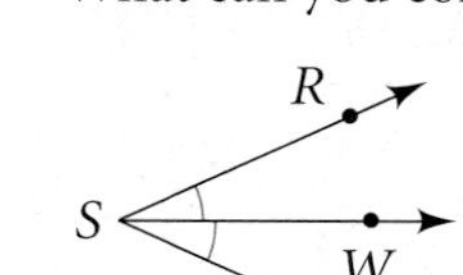

Example 2

$\overrightarrow{KN}$ bisects $\angle JKL$.
$m\angle JKN = 5x - 25$
$m\angle NKL = 3x + 5$
Solve for x and find $m\angle JKN$.

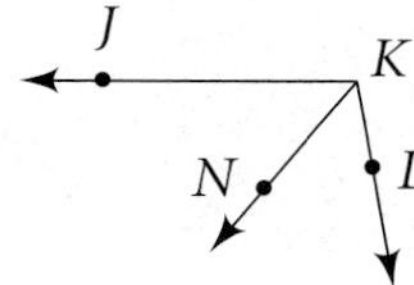

$\angle JKN \cong \angle NKL$, or $m\angle JKN = m\angle NKL$	**Def. of $\angle$ bisector**
$5x - 25 = 3x + 5$	**Substitution**
$5x - 25 + 25 = 3x + 5 + 25$	**Add 25 to each side.**
$5x = 3x + 30$	**Simplify.**
$5x - 3x = 3x - 3x + 30$	**Subtract 3*x* from each side.**
$2x = 30$	**Simplify.**
$x = 15$	**Divide each side by 2.**
$m\angle JKN = 5(15) - 25 = 50$	**Substitute 15 for *x*.**

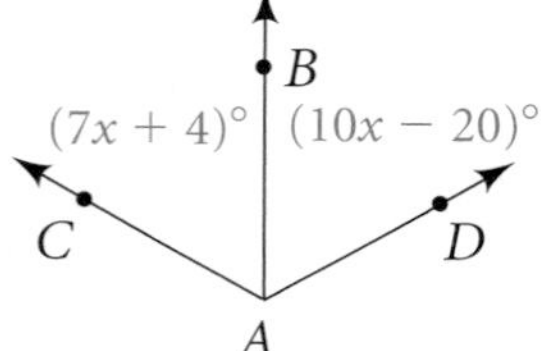

10. Try This In the diagram at the left, $\overrightarrow{AB}$ bisects $\angle CAD$. Solve for x and find $m\angle CAD$.

Exercises ON YOUR OWN

1. Which figures in the third group are *monopars*?

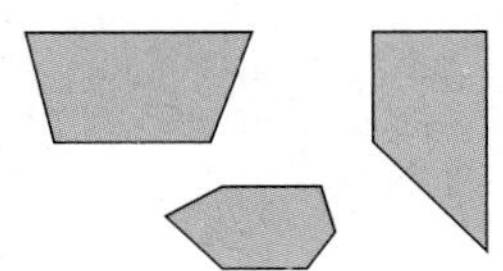

Monopars

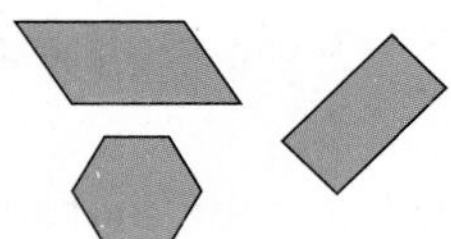

Not monopars

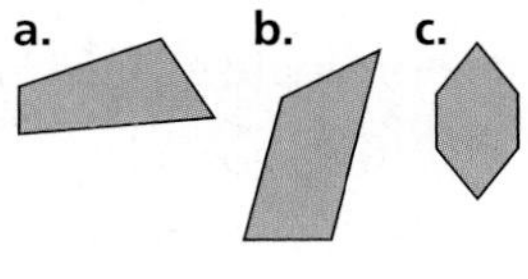

?????

Complete.

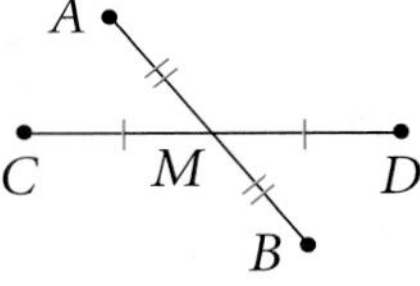

2. $DM = 8, MC = ▩$
3. $MB = 6, AM = ▩$
4. $MC = 9, DC = ▩$
5. $AB = 10, AM = ▩$
6. $2MA = ▩$
7. $\frac{1}{2}DC = ▩$
8. ▩ is the midpoint of ▩ and ▩.

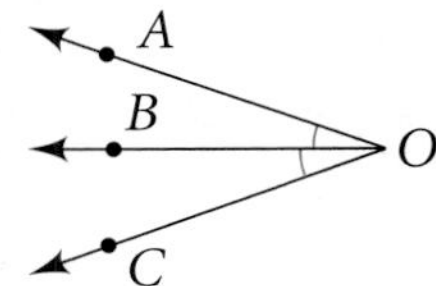

9. $m\angle AOB = 20, m\angle BOC = ▩, m\angle AOC = ▩$
10. $m\angle COA = 50, m\angle AOB = ▩$
11. $2m\angle AOB = m\angle ▩$
12. $\frac{1}{2}m\angle AOC = m\angle ▩$
13. ▩ is the angle bisector of ▩.

14. **Language Arts** Is the following an acceptable definition? Explain.

A cat is an animal with whiskers.

Write *true* or *false*.

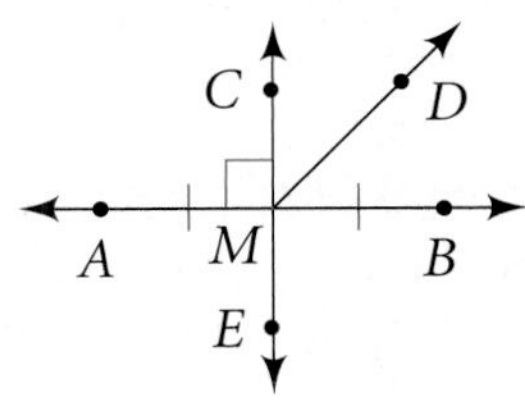

15. $\overline{AM} \cong \overline{MB}$
16. M is the midpoint of $\overline{AB}$.
17. $\angle AMC \cong \angle CMB$
18. $\overline{CM} \perp \overline{AB}$
19. $\overleftrightarrow{MC} \perp \overleftrightarrow{MD}$
20. $m\angle CMB = 90$
21. M is the midpoint of $\overleftrightarrow{CE}$.
22. $\frac{1}{2}AB = AM$

Draw a figure for each description.

23. $\overleftrightarrow{AB} \perp \overleftrightarrow{BD}$
24. $\overline{AY}$ bisects $\overline{CX}$ at point Q.
25. $\overrightarrow{BQ}$ is the bisector of $\angle RBT$.
26. $\overrightarrow{AC}$ bisects right $\angle DAF$.
27. $\overline{AB}$ and $\overline{CT}$ are perpendicular bisectors of each other.
28. $\overline{RS}$ is the perpendicular bisector of $\overline{XY}$, but $\overline{XY}$ is not the perpendicular bisector of $\overline{RS}$.

29. What is the midpoint of $\overline{AB}$?

30. What is the coordinate of the midpoint of $\overline{QB}$?

31. What is the coordinate of the midpoint of $\overline{WA}$?

32. The coordinate of the midpoint of $\overline{AR}$ is -5. What is the coordinate of point R?

33. The coordinate of the midpoint of $\overline{ST}$ is 7. What is the coordinate of point T?

34. Which figures in the third group are *vertical angles?*

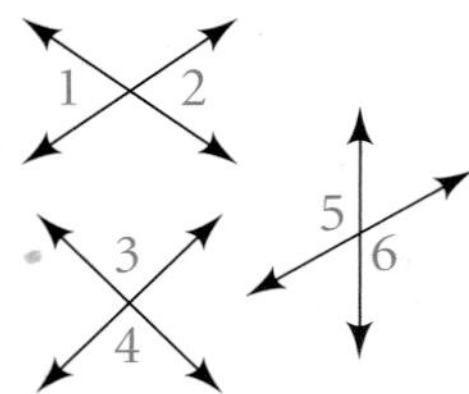

Vertical angles

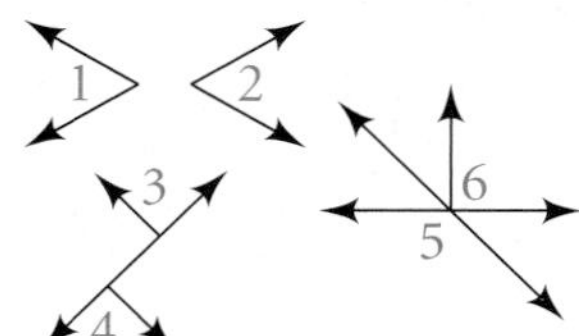

Not vertical angles

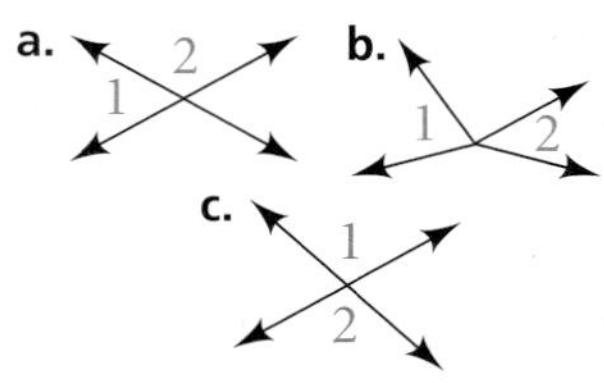

?????

Algebra **Solve for x.**

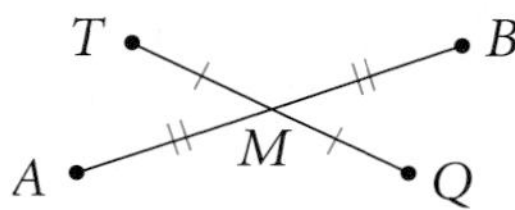

35. $AB = 24, MB = 2x + 4$

36. $TM = 3x + 5, MQ = x + 17$

37. $TQ = 4x + 16, TM = 20$

38. $MB = 8x + 7, AB = 126$

39. $TM = \frac{1}{2}x - 4, TQ = 12$

40. $AM = 5x - 1, AB = 38$

41. **a.** How many midpoints does a given segment have? How many bisectors does a given segment have?
b. Given a segment, consider any one plane that contains the segment. How many lines in that plane are perpendicular bisectors of the given segment?
c. **Geometry in 3 Dimensions** Given a segment, how many lines are there in space that are perpendicular bisectors of the given segment?

42. **Coordinate Geometry** Find the coordinates of the midpoint of $\overline{AB}$ with endpoints $A(0, 5)$ and $B(0, 13)$.

43. **a.** **Manipulatives** Cut out a strip of paper about 11 in. long and 1 in. wide. Twist it once and tape the ends together. You now have a *Möbius band.*
b. Cut the Möbius band along its center. Does cutting the band bisect it? Explain your answer.

44. **Writing** If point M is the midpoint of $\overline{AB}$, you know that $\overline{AM} \cong \overline{MB}$. How is AM related to AB? Write an equation about AM and AB and explain why your equation is correct.

45. **Open-ended** Describe some perpendicular lines in your home or classroom.

46. **Language Arts** Is the following an acceptable definition? Explain. An obtuse angle is an angle whose measure is greater than 90.

47. Which angles in the third group form a *linear pair?*

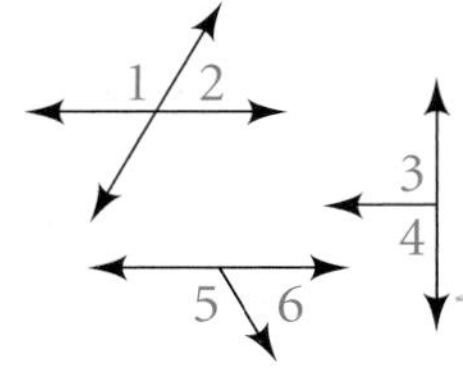

Linear pairs

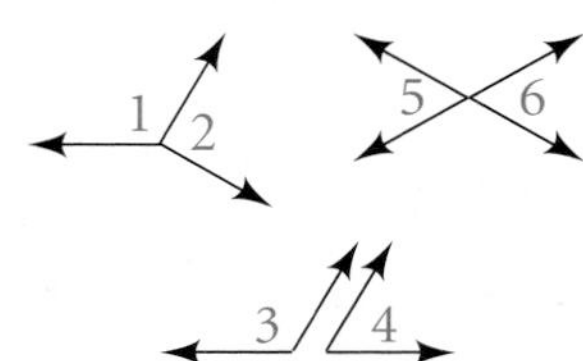

Not linear pairs

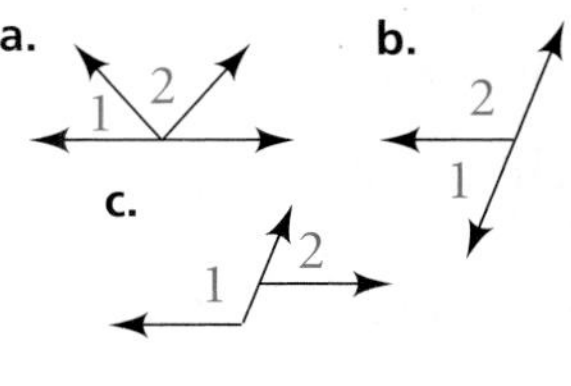

?????

Algebra $\overrightarrow{BX}$ **is the bisector of** $\angle ABC$**. Complete each equation.**

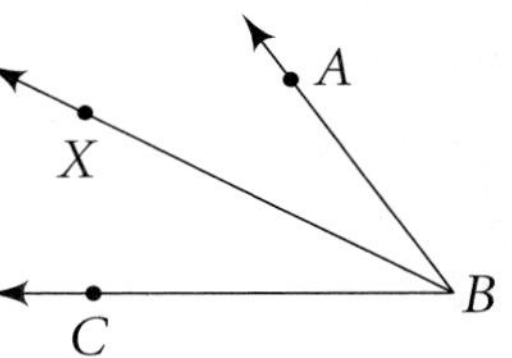

48. $m\angle ABX = 5x$, $m\angle XBC = 3x + 10$, $m\angle ABC =$ ■

49. $m\angle ABC = 4x - 12$, $m\angle ABX = 24$, $x =$ ■

50. $m\angle ABX = 4x - 16$, $m\angle CBX = 2x + 6$, $x =$ ■

51. $m\angle ABC = 5x + 18$, $m\angle CBX = 2x + 12$, $m\angle ABC =$ ■

52. **Critical Thinking** Lee knows that whenever $\angle ABC$ has $\overrightarrow{BX}$ as an angle bisector, $\angle ABX \cong \angle CBX$. Lee claims there is always a related equation, $m\angle ABX = \frac{1}{2}m\angle ABC$. Her friend Clarissa claims the related equation is $2m\angle ABX = m\angle ABC$. Which equation is correct? Explain. A diagram may be helpful.

53. **Standardized Test Prep** Point M is the midpoint of $\overline{PQ}$. Which of these is *not* true?
   A. $\overline{PM} \cong \overline{MQ}$ **B.** $PM + MQ = PQ$ **C.** $MQ = \frac{1}{2}PQ$
   D. $\overrightarrow{PM}$ and $\overrightarrow{PQ}$ are opposite rays. **E.** $PQ = 2PM$

54. **Writing** Write a definition of a line parallel to a plane.

55. Study the figures below. Complete the definition of a line perpendicular to a plane. A line is perpendicular to a plane if it is _?_ to every line in the plane that _?_.

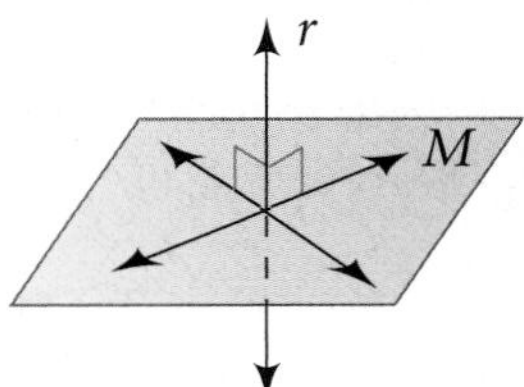

Line $r \perp$ plane M.

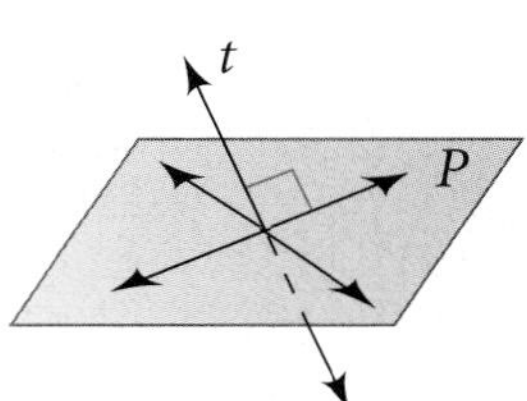

Line t is not $\perp$ plane P.

Exercises MIXED REVIEW

Use the diagram at the right for Exercises 56–60.

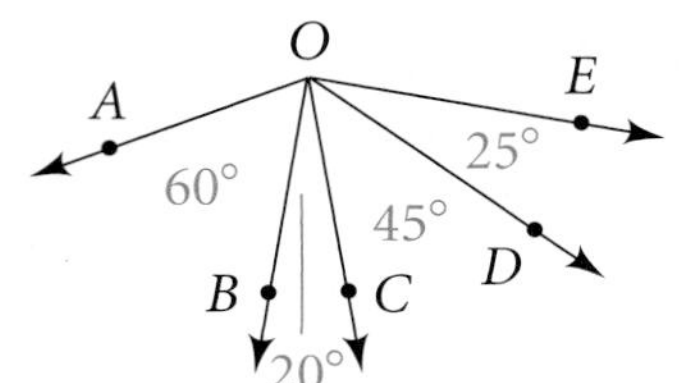

56. Find each measure.

a. $m\angle AOC$ **b.** $m\angle AOD$

c. $m\angle DOB$ **d.** $m\angle BOE$

57. Name an obtuse angle.

58. Name an acute angle.

59. Name a right angle.

60. Name all the rays.

61. Draw opposite rays $\overrightarrow{RS}$ and $\overrightarrow{RW}$. Find RS if $SW = 8$ and $RW = 5$.

Getting Ready For Lesson 1-6

62. $\overleftrightarrow{AX}$ is the perpendicular bisector of $\overline{QS}$ at point M. Name two congruent segments.

63. $\overrightarrow{PT}$ is the bisector of $\angle APR$. Name two congruent angles.

64. $\overrightarrow{OR}$ is the bisector of right $\angle TOS$. Find $m\angle TOR$.

Geometry at Work

Cabinetmaker

Cabinetmakers make not only cabinets but all types of wooden furniture. The artistry of cabinetmaking can be seen in the beauty and uniqueness of the finest doors, shelves, and tables. The craft of the profession is in knowing which types of wood and tools to use, and how to use them.

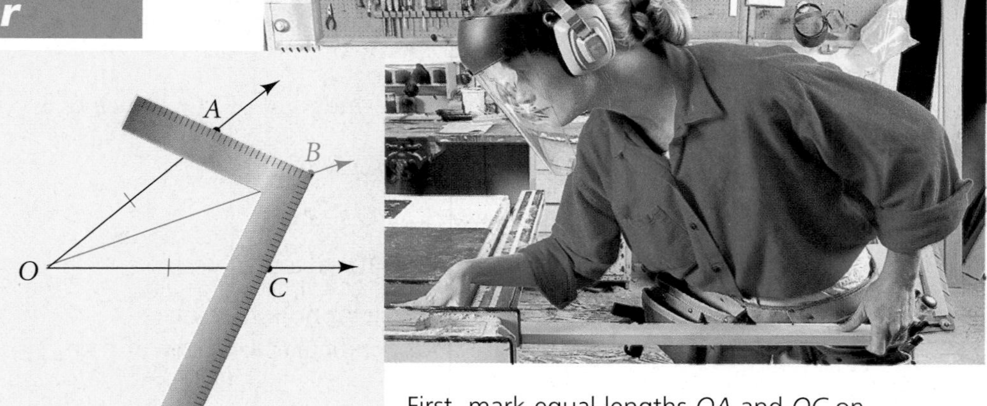

The carpenter's square is one of the most useful of the cabinetmaker's tools. It can be applied to a variety of measuring tasks. The figure shows how to use a carpenter's square to bisect $\angle O$.

First, mark equal lengths OA and OC on the sides of the angle. Then position the square so that $AB = BC$ to locate point B. Finally, draw $\overrightarrow{OB}$. $\overrightarrow{OB}$ bisects $\angle O$.

Mini Project: Make a carpenter's square out of cardboard. Mark the edges in equal intervals as shown in the figure. Draw a line segment. Then demonstrate how you can use the square to draw the perpendicular bisector of the segment.

What You'll Learn

- Using a compass and straightedge to construct congruent angles and congruent segments
- Using a compass and straightedge to bisect segments and angles

...And Why

To lay the foundation for more complex constructions you will use in later chapters

What You'll Need

ruler, compass, tracing paper

1-6 Basic Constructions

WORK TOGETHER

Use a ruler to draw a segment on tracing paper. Fold the paper so that one endpoint lies on the other endpoint. Unfold the paper and compare your result with a partner's.

1. What kinds of angles are formed by the segment and the fold line?
2. What is the relationship between the original segment and the segments determined by the fold line?
3. What geometric term best describes the fold line?

Draw an angle on tracing paper. Fold the paper so that one side of the angle lies on the other side and the fold line goes through the vertex of the angle.

4. What geometric term best describes the fold line?

THINK AND DISCUSS

Constructing Congruent Segments and Angles

Another method for creating the bisectors you made in the Work Together is by construction. A **construction** uses a straightedge and a compass to make geometric figures. A **straightedge** is a ruler with no markings on it. (You may use a ruler as a straightedge, but you have to ignore the markings.) A **compass** is a geometric tool used to draw circles and parts of circles called arcs.

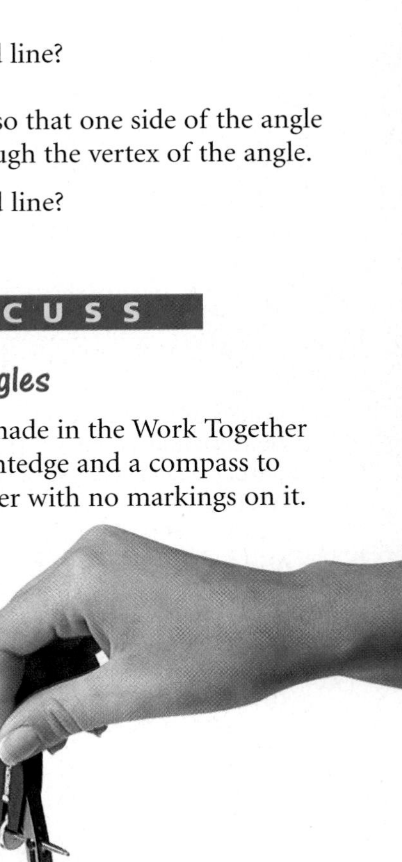

The four basic constructions involve constructing congruent segments and angles as well as constructing bisectors of segments and angles.

Construction 1
Congruent Segments

Construct a segment congruent to a given segment.

Given: $\overline{AB}$

A B

Step 1
Draw a ray with endpoint *C*.

Step 2
Open the compass to the length of $\overline{AB}$.

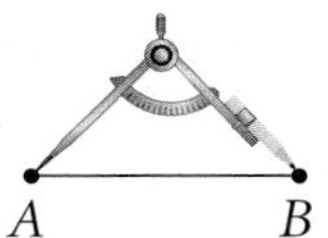

Step 3
With the same compass setting, put the compass point on *C*. Draw an arc that intersects the ray. Label the point of intersection *D*.
$\overline{CD} \cong \overline{AB}$

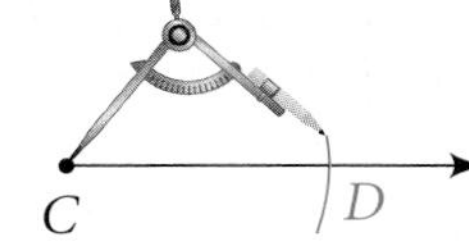

Construction 2
Congruent Angles

Construct an angle congruent to a given angle.

Given: $\angle A$

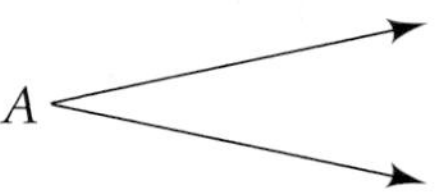

Step 1
Draw a ray with endpoint *S*.

Step 2
With the compass point on point *A*, draw an arc that intersects the sides of $\angle A$. Label the points of intersection *B* and *C*.

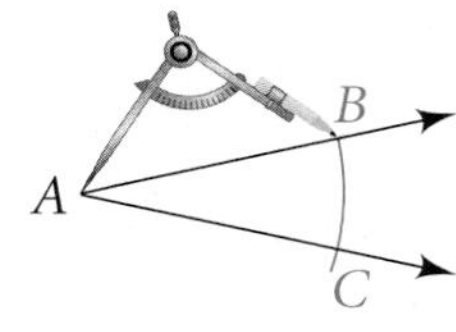

Step 3
With the same compass setting, put the compass point on point *S*. Draw an arc that intersects the ray at point *R*.

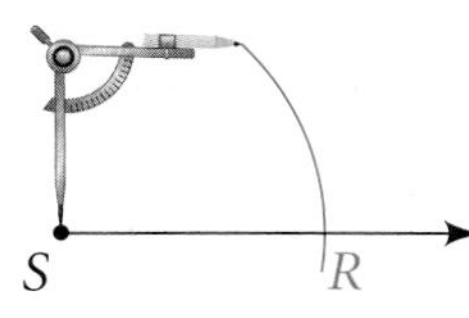

Step 4
Open the compass to the length of $\overline{BC}$. Keeping the same compass setting, put the compass point on *R*. Draw an arc to determine point *T*.

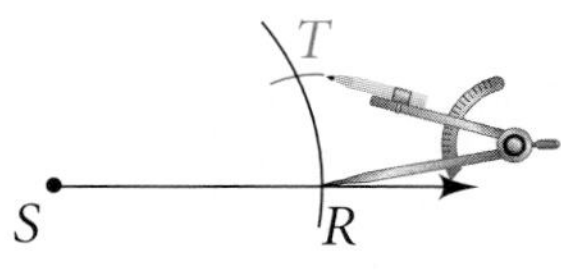

Step 5
Draw $\overrightarrow{ST}$.
$\angle S \cong \angle A$

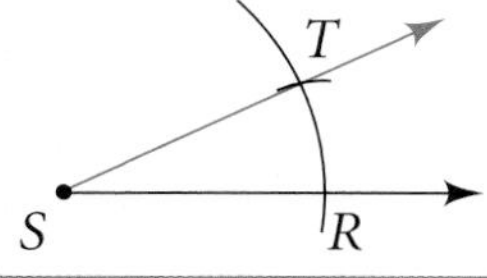

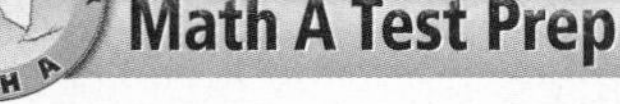

1 Which of the following points could be on a perpendicular bisector of $\overline{AB}$ with endpoints $A(-3, 3)$ and $B(5, 3)$?
(1) (2, 3) (3) (2, 6)
(2) (1, 6) (4) (4, 1)

2 $m\angle SPQ = 124°$, and $m\angle RPQ = 38°$. What is the value of *x*?

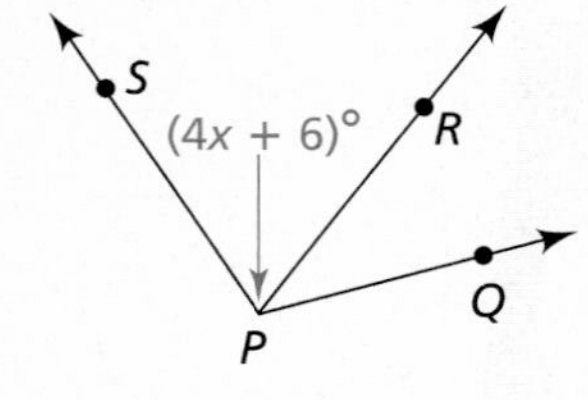

You can use these constructions to construct different geometric figures.

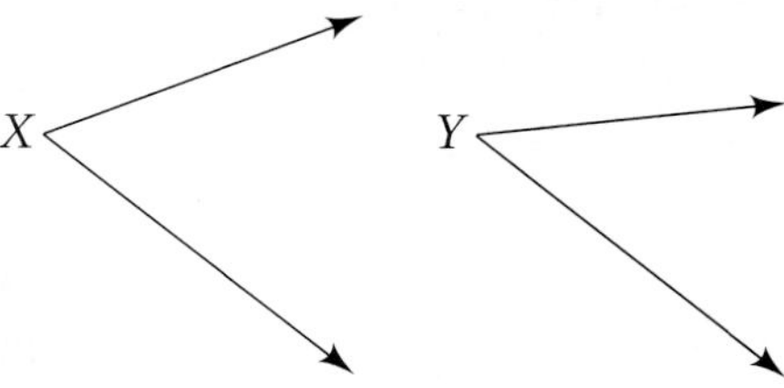

5. Try This Draw angles like $\angle X$ and $\angle Y$. Then construct $\angle Z$ so that $m\angle Z = m\angle X + m\angle Y$.

6. Describe how you would construct an angle, $\angle D$, so that $m\angle D = m\angle X - m\angle Y$.

To draw a circle or an arc with a SAFE-T-COMPASS®, use the center hole of the white dial as the center.

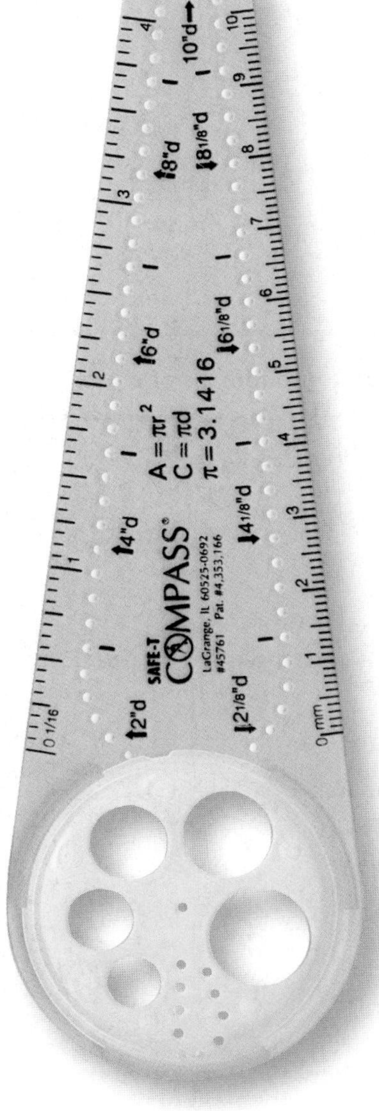

You can use a compass and straightedge to construct triangles with sides of specific lengths.

Example

Construct a triangle whose sides have the given lengths.

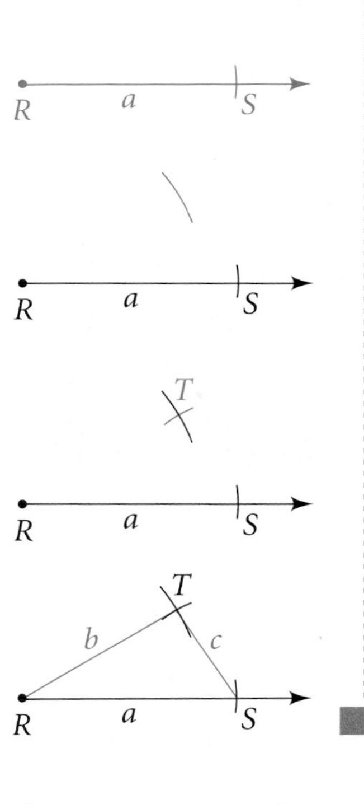

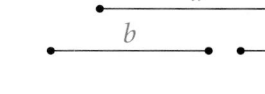

Step 1
Use Construction 1 to construct $\overline{RS}$ with length a.

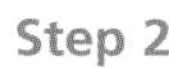
Step 2
Open the compass to the length b. Put the compass point on R and draw an arc.

Step 3
Open the compass to the length c. Put the compass point on S and draw an arc. Be sure the two arcs intersect. Label the intersection of the arcs as point T.

Step 4
Draw segments from point T to both R and S.

7. Try This Draw $\overline{XY}$. Then construct a triangle with three sides the length of $\overline{XY}$.

X Y

Constructing Perpendicular Bisectors and Angle Bisectors

The next two constructions will show you how to bisect segments and bisect angles. These constructions and Construction 2 are based on *congruent triangles*. You will see *why* the constructions work in future chapters.

Construction 3
Perpendicular Bisector

Construct the perpendicular bisector of a segment.

Given: $\overline{AB}$

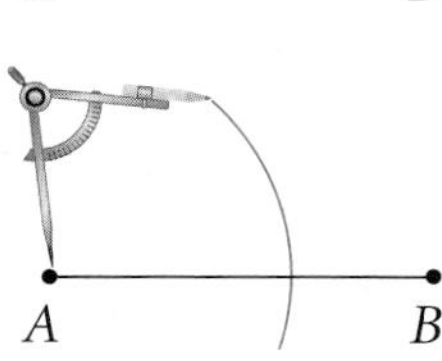

Step 1
Put the compass point on point A and draw an arc. Be sure the opening is greater than $\frac{1}{2}AB$. Keep the same compass setting for Step 2.

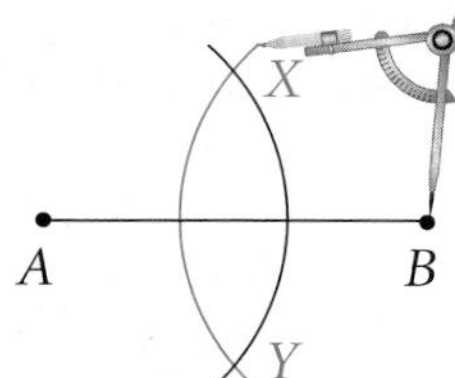

Step 2
Put the compass point on point B and draw an arc. Label the points where the two arcs intersect as X and Y.

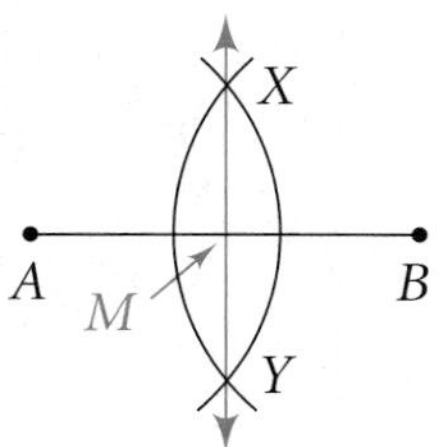

Step 3
Draw $\overleftrightarrow{XY}$. Label the intersection of $\overline{AB}$ and $\overleftrightarrow{XY}$ as point M.

$\overleftrightarrow{XY}$ is the perpendicular bisector of $\overline{AB}$. Point M is the midpoint of $\overline{AB}$.

Who? In 1672 Danish mathematician Georg Mohr showed that all constructions that use a compass and a straightedge can be done using only a compass.

You can use Construction 3 to divide any segment into fourths or eighths.

Construction 4
Angle Bisector

Construct the bisector of an angle.

Given: $\angle A$

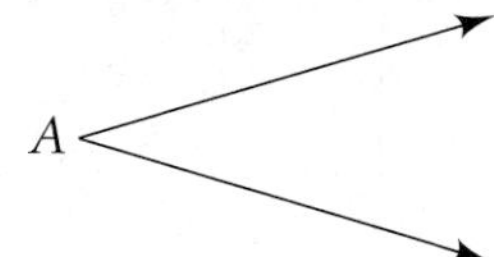

Step 1
Put the compass point on vertex A. Draw an arc that intersects the sides of $\angle A$. Label the points of intersection B and C.

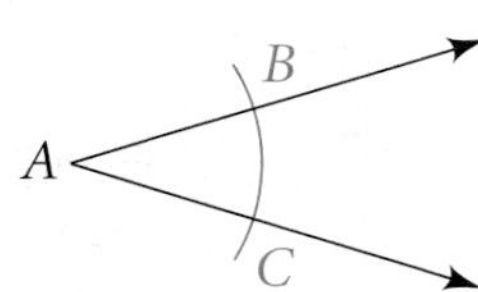

Step 2
Put the compass point on point C and draw an arc. Keep the same compass setting and repeat with point B. Be sure the arcs intersect. Label the point where the two arcs intersect as point X.

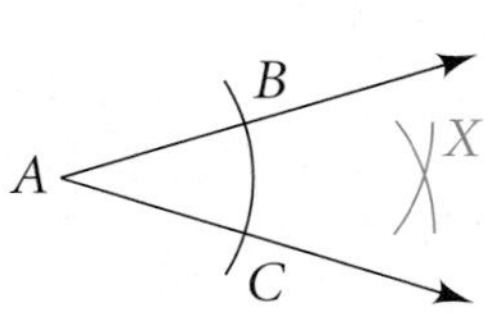

Step 3
Draw $\overrightarrow{AX}$.

$\overrightarrow{AX}$ is the angle bisector of $\angle CAB$.

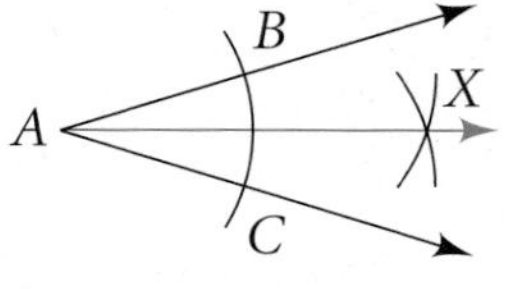

8. Describe how you could construct a 45° angle.

Exercises ON YOUR OWN

Draw a diagram similar to the given one. Then do the construction.

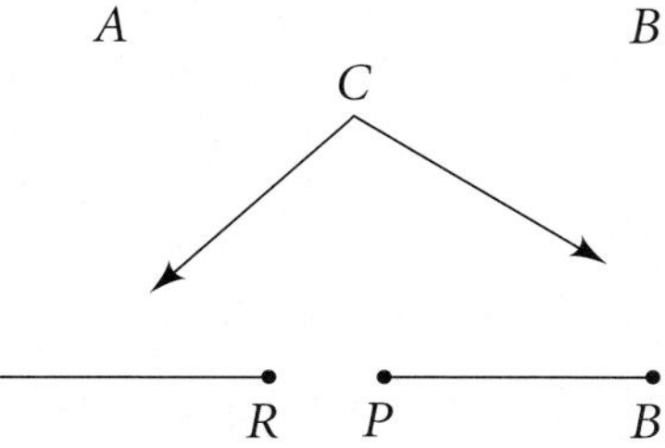

1. Construct $\overline{XY}$ congruent to $\overline{AB}$. Check your work with a ruler.
2. Construct the perpendicular bisector of $\overline{AB}$. Check your work with a ruler and a protractor.
3. Construct the angle bisector of $\angle C$. Check your work with a protractor.

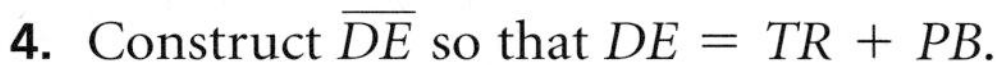

4. Construct $\overline{DE}$ so that $DE = TR + PB$.

T R P B

5. Construct $\overline{QS}$ so that $QS = TR - PB$.
6. Construct $\overline{XY}$ so that $XY = 2TR$.

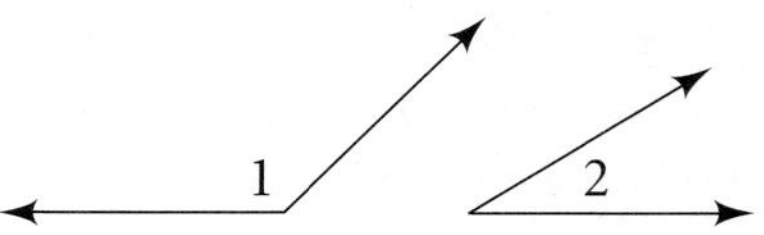

7. Construct $\angle B$ so that $m\angle B = m\angle 1 + m\angle 2$.
8. Construct $\angle C$ so that $m\angle C = m\angle 1 - m\angle 2$.
9. Construct $\angle D$ so that $m\angle D = 2m\angle 2$.

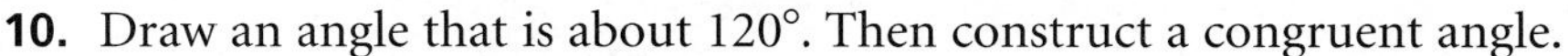

10. Draw an angle that is about 120°. Then construct a congruent angle.
11. Use a ruler to draw two segments that are 4 cm and 5 cm long. Then construct a triangle with sides 4 cm, 4 cm, and 5 cm long.
12. **a.** Construct a 45° angle.
    b. Construct a 135° angle.
13. **Writing** Describe how to construct the midpoint of a segment.
14. **Open-ended** Which method do you prefer for bisecting an angle—paper folding or construction with compass and straightedge? Why?
15. **Patterns** Draw a large triangle with three acute angles. Construct the angle bisectors of all three angles of the triangle. What is true about the intersection of the three angle bisectors? Repeat for another triangle that has an obtuse angle. Make a **conjecture** about the three angle bisectors of any triangle.
16. **Patterns** Draw a large triangle with three acute angles. Construct the perpendicular bisectors of all three sides. What is true about the intersection of the three perpendicular bisectors? Repeat for another triangle that has an obtuse angle. Make a **conjecture** about the three perpendicular bisectors of the sides of any triangle.
17. **a.** Draw a segment, $\overline{AB}$. Construct a triangle whose sides are all congruent to $\overline{AB}$.
    b. Measure the angles of the triangle.
    c. **Writing** Describe how to construct a 60° angle and a 30° angle.

18. **Art** You can create intricate designs using your compass. Follow these directions to design a *daisy wheel.*

a. Construct a circle. Keeping the same compass setting, put the compass point on the circle and construct an arc. The endpoints of the arc should be on the circle.

b. Keeping the same compass setting, put the compass point on each endpoint of the first arc and draw two new arcs.

c. Continue to make arcs around the circle from the new endpoints of arcs until you get a six-petal daisy wheel.

d. Personalize your daisy wheel by decorating it.

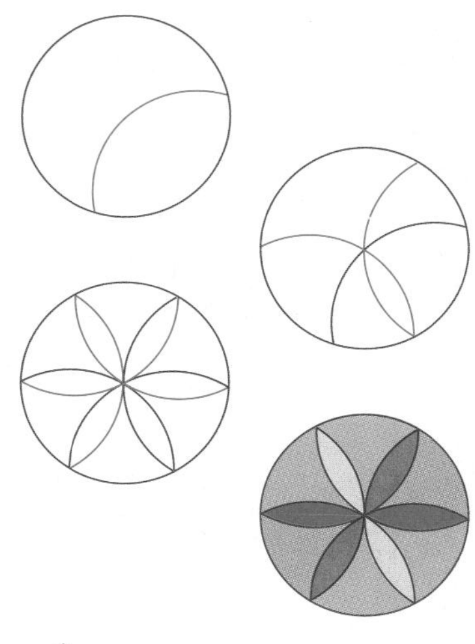

19. **a.** Use your compass to draw a circle. Locate three points A, B, and C on the circle.

b. Construct the perpendicular bisectors of $\overline{AB}$ and $\overline{BC}$.

c. **Critical Thinking** Label the intersection of the two perpendicular bisectors as point O. Describe point O.

Chapter Project

Find Out by Writing

Origami artists use a special notation to communicate how to construct their creations. To communicate your design, you can use the language of geometry instead. Use geometric terms and symbols along with sketches to write directions for the origami you created in the Find Out question on page 584. Test your directions by having a classmate construct your model following your directions.

Exercises MIXED REVIEW

Use the number line at the right to find the length of each segment.

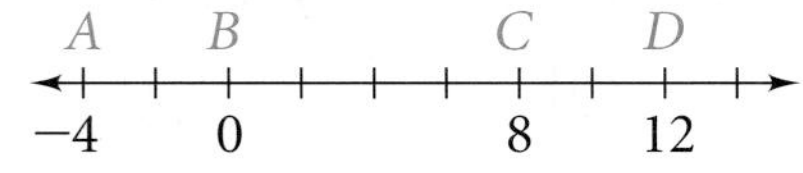

20. $\overline{AC}$ **21.** $\overline{AD}$ **22.** $\overline{CD}$ **23.** $\overline{BC}$

24. Make a sketch of three planes intersecting at one point.

Getting Ready For Lesson 1-7

25. Find the value of x.

130° x°

26. Find the value of y.

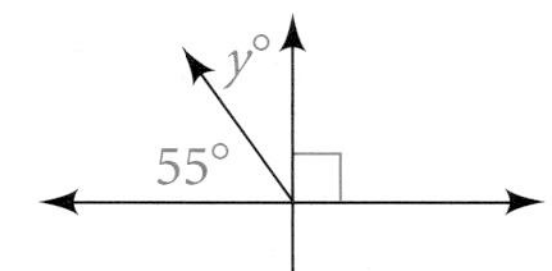

27. Find the value of z.

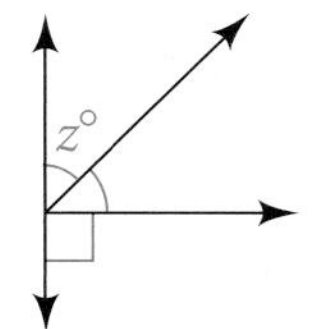

Math ToolboX

Technology

Exploring Constructions

After Lesson 1-6

Points, lines, and figures are created in geometry software using *draw* or *construct* tools. A figure created by *draw* has no constraints. When the figure is manipulated it moves or changes size freely. A figure created by *construct* is dependent upon an existing object. When you manipulate the existing object, the *construct* object moves or resizes similarly.

In this activity you will explore the difference between *draw* and *construct.* Before you begin, familiarize yourself with your software's tools.

Construct

- Draw $\overline{AB}$ and construct perpendicular bisector $\overleftrightarrow{DC}$.
- Draw $\overline{EF}$ and construct G, any point on $\overline{EF}$. Draw $\overleftrightarrow{HG}$. Find EG, GF, and $m\angle HGF$. Attempt to drag G so that $EG = GF$. Attempt to drag H so that $m\angle HGF = 90$. Were you able to draw the perpendicular bisector of $\overline{EF}$? Explain.

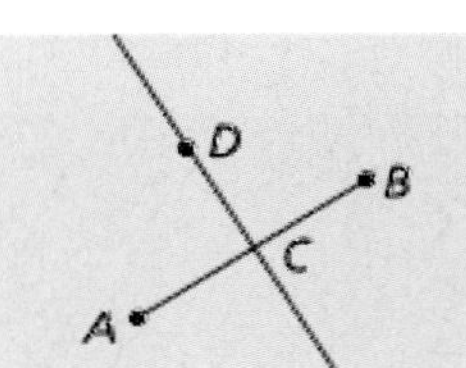

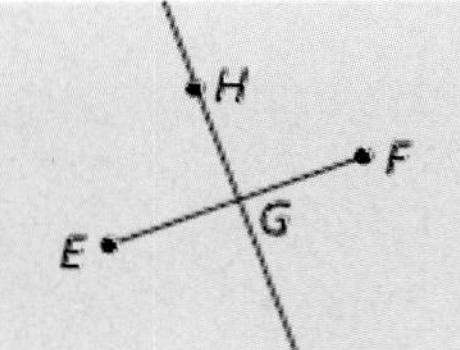

Investigate

- Drag A and B. Observe AC, CB, and $m\angle DCB$. Is $\overleftrightarrow{DC}$ always the perpendicular bisector of $\overline{AB}$ no matter how you manipulate the figure?
- Drag E and F. Observe EG, GF, and $m\angle HGF$. How is the relationship between $\overline{EF}$ and $\overleftrightarrow{HG}$ different from the relationship between $\overline{AB}$ and $\overleftrightarrow{DC}$?

Summarize

Write a description of the general difference between *draw* and *construct.* Use your description to explain why the relationship between $\overline{EF}$ and $\overleftrightarrow{HG}$ differs from the relationship between $\overline{AB}$ and $\overleftrightarrow{DC}$.

Extend

Draw $\angle JKL$ and construct its angle bisector, $\overrightarrow{KM}$. Draw $\angle NOP$. Draw $\overrightarrow{OQ}$ in the interior of $\angle NOP$. Drag Q until $m\angle NOQ = m\angle QOP$. Manipulate both figures and observe the different angle measures. Is $\overrightarrow{KM}$ always the angle bisector of $\angle JKL$? Is $\overrightarrow{OQ}$ always the angle bisector of $\angle NOP$?

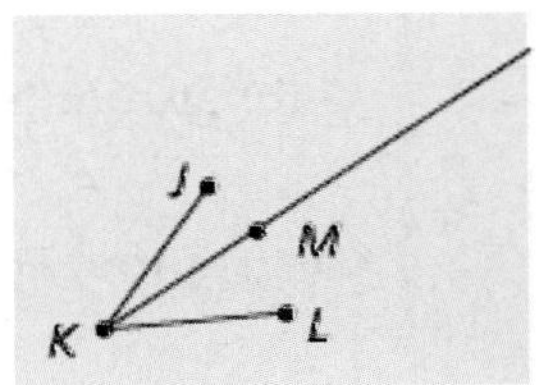

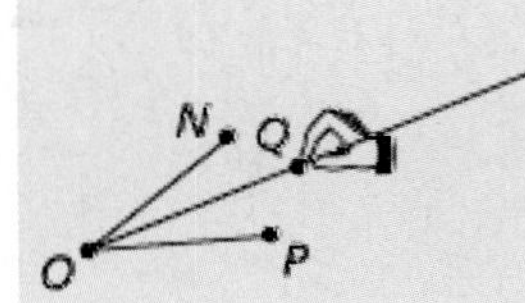

What You'll Learn

- Using deductive reasoning to solve problems and verify conjectures
- Understanding how certain angle pairs are related

...And Why

To reach valid conclusions in geometry and in life

What You'll Need

- tracing paper

1-7 Using Deductive Reasoning

THINK AND DISCUSS

Connecting Algebra and Geometry

Deductive reasoning is a process of reasoning logically from given facts to a conclusion. If the given facts are true, deductive reasoning always produces a valid conclusion. In geometry, we accept postulates and properties as true and use deductive reasoning to prove other statements.

1. **Try This** Maria's parents tell her she can go to the mall with her friends if she finishes her homework. Maria shows her parents her completed homework. What conclusion can you make?

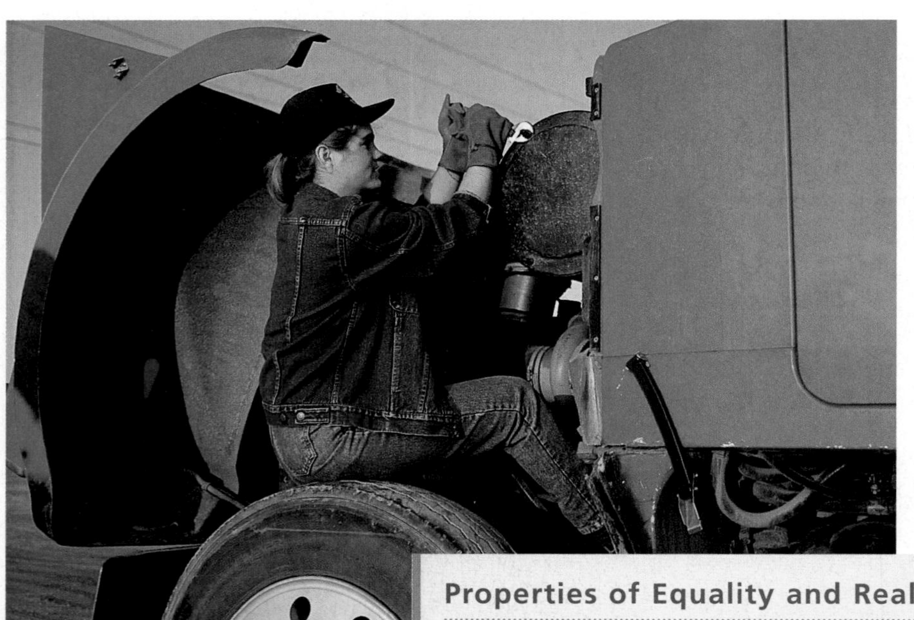

Many people use deductive reasoning in their jobs. A physician diagnosing a patient's illness uses deductive reasoning. A mechanic trying to determine what is wrong with a car uses deductive reasoning. A carpenter uses deductive reasoning to determine what materials are needed at a work site.

Do you remember these Properties of Equality and Real Numbers from algebra?

Properties of Equality and Real Numbers

Addition Property	If $a = b$, then $a + c = b + c$.
Subtraction Property	If $a = b$, then $a - c = b - c$.
Multiplication Property	If $a = b$, then $a \cdot c = b \cdot c$.
Division Property	If $a = b$, then $\frac{a}{c} = \frac{b}{c}$ $(c \neq 0)$.
Substitution Property	If $a = b$, then b can replace a in any expression.
Distributive Property	$a(b + c) = ab + ac$

You may not realize it, but you use deductive reasoning every time you solve an equation.

Example 1

Algebra $m\angle AOC = 140$. Solve for x and justify each step.

$m\angle AOB + m\angle BOC = m\angle AOC$	Angle Addition Postulate
$x + (2x + 20) = 140$	Substitution
$3x = 120$	Subtraction Property of Equality
$x = 40$	Division Property of Equality

These properties of congruence follow from the properties of equality.

QUICK REVIEW

Properties of Equality

Reflexive Property
$a = a$

Symmetric Property
If $a = b$, then $b = a$.

Transitive Property
If $a = b$ and $b = c$, then $a = c$.

Properties of Congruence

Reflexive Property	$\overline{AB} \cong \overline{AB}$
	$\angle A \cong \angle A$
Symmetric Property	If $\overline{AB} \cong \overline{CD}$, then $\overline{CD} \cong \overline{AB}$.
	If $\angle A \cong \angle B$, then $\angle B \cong \angle A$.
Transitive Property	If $\overline{AB} \cong \overline{CD}$ and $\overline{CD} \cong \overline{EF}$, then $\overline{AB} \cong \overline{EF}$.
	If $\angle A \cong \angle B$ and $\angle B \cong \angle C$, then $\angle A \cong \angle C$.

2. **Try This** Name the property of equality or congruence illustrated.
   a. $\angle K \cong \angle K$
   b. If $2x - 8 = 10$, then $2x = 18$.
   c. If $\overline{RS} \cong \overline{TW}$ and $\overline{TW} \cong \overline{PQ}$, then $\overline{RS} \cong \overline{PQ}$.
   d. If $m\angle A = m\angle B$, then $m\angle B = m\angle A$.

WORK TOGETHER

Draw two intersecting lines. Number the angles as shown.

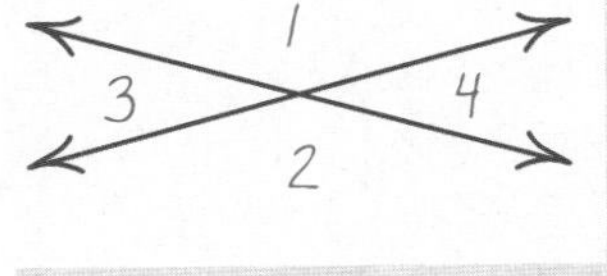

3. Fold the sides of $\angle 1$ onto $\angle 2$. What do you notice?

4. Fold the sides of $\angle 3$ onto $\angle 4$. What do you notice?

5. Compare your results with those of others in your group. Make a **conjecture** about the angles formed by two intersecting lines.

THINK AND DISCUSS

Angle Pairs

In the Work Together you made a conjecture about a pair of angles that has a special name, *vertical angles*. You will learn about several important angle pairs in this lesson.

vertical angles

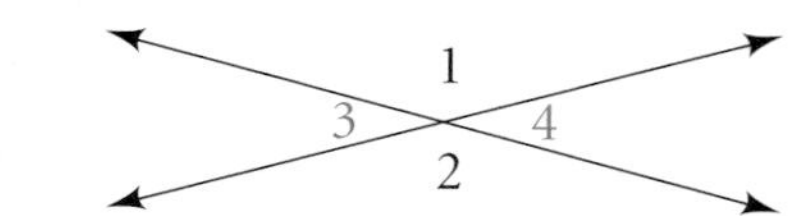

two angles whose sides are opposite rays

adjacent angles

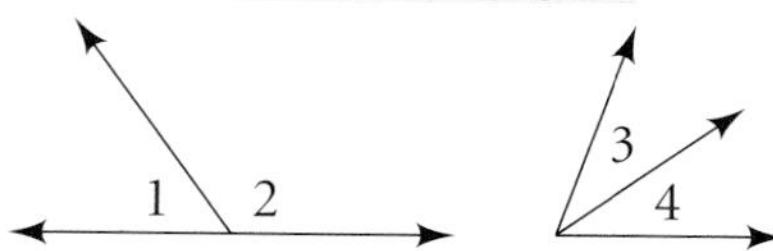

two coplanar angles with a common side, a common vertex, no common interior points

complementary angles

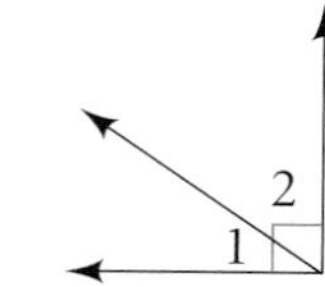

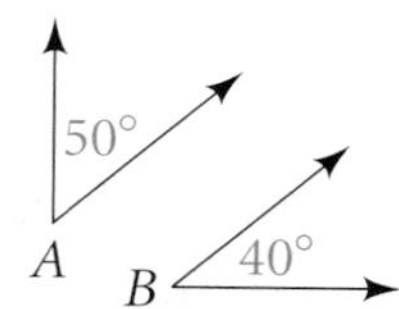

two angles, the sum of whose measures is 90

supplementary angles

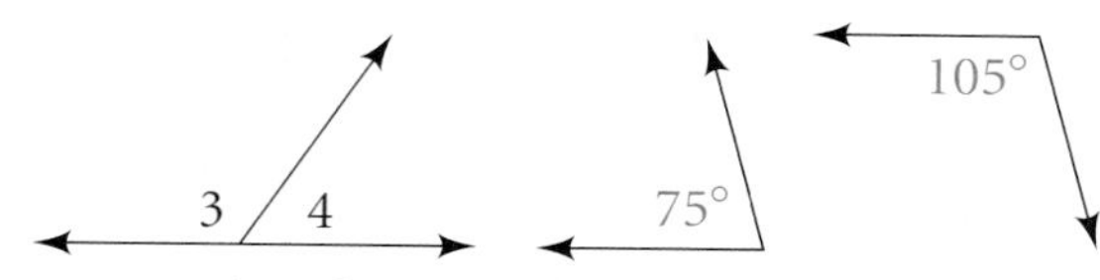

two angles, the sum of whose measures is 180

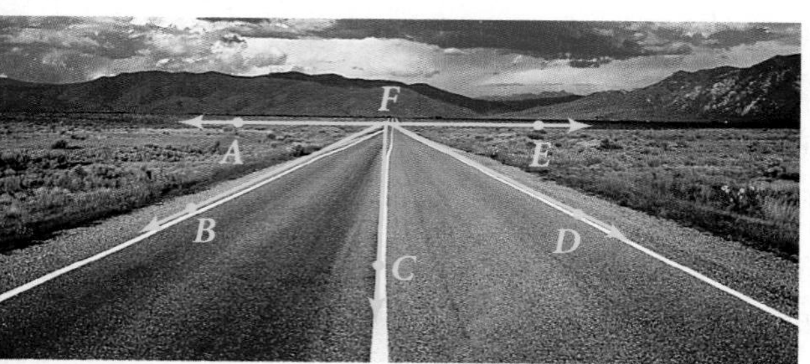

6. **a.** Name two pairs of adjacent angles in the photo at the left.
   b. Name two pairs of supplementary angles.

In the Work Together you used inductive reasoning to make a conjecture. Now, based on what you know, you can use deductive reasoning to show that your conjecture is always true.

Theorem 1-1
Vertical Angles Theorem

Vertical angles are congruent.

Example 2

Write a convincing argument that the Vertical Angles Theorem is true.

You are given that $\angle 1$ and $\angle 2$ are vertical angles. You must show that $\angle 1 \cong \angle 2$.

By the Angle Addition Postulate,
$m\angle 1 + m\angle 3 = 180$ and $m\angle 2 + m\angle 3 = 180$.
By substitution, $m\angle 1 + m\angle 3 = m\angle 2 + m\angle 3$. Subtract $m\angle 3$ from each side, and you get $m\angle 1 = m\angle 2$, or $\angle 1 \cong \angle 2$.

A convincing argument that uses deductive reasoning is also called a *proof*. A conjecture that is proven is a **theorem.** The Vertical Angles Theorem is actually a special case of the following theorem.

Theorem 1-2
Congruent Supplements Theorem

If two angles are supplements of congruent angles (or of the same angle), then the two angles are congruent.

Example 3

Write a convincing argument that supplements of the same angle are congruent.

Given: $\angle 1$ and $\angle 2$ are supplementary.
$\angle 3$ and $\angle 2$ are supplementary.

Prove: $\angle 1 \cong \angle 3$

Because $\angle 1$ and $\angle 2$ are supplementary, $m\angle 1 + m\angle 2 = 180$.
Because $\angle 3$ and $\angle 2$ are supplementary, $m\angle 3 + m\angle 2 = 180$.
So $m\angle 1 + m\angle 2 = m\angle 3 + m\angle 2$.
Therefore, $m\angle 1 = m\angle 3$, and $\angle 1 \cong \angle 3$.

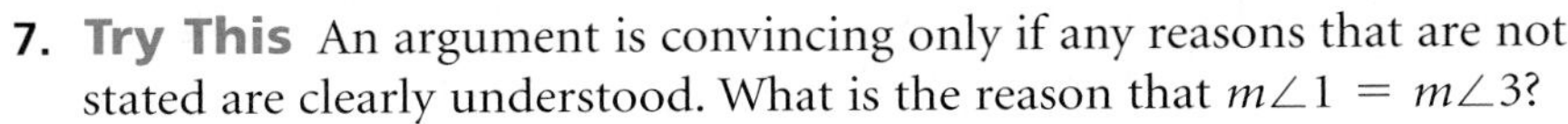

7. **Try This** An argument is convincing only if any reasons that are not stated are clearly understood. What is the reason that $m\angle 1 = m\angle 3$?

The next theorem is much like the Congruent Supplements Theorem.

Theorem 1-3
Congruent Complements Theorem

If two angles are complements of congruent angles (or of the same angle), then the two angles are congruent.

As you will see in Chapter 4, a proof may take many different forms. The format of a proof is not important. Logical use of deductive reasoning is.

You can draw certain conclusions directly from diagrams. You can conclude that angles are
- vertical angles
- adjacent angles
- adjacent supplementary angles.

Unless there are marks that give this information, you cannot assume that
- angles or segments are congruent
- an angle is a right angle
- lines are perpendicular or parallel.

8. What can you conclude? Explain.

a. 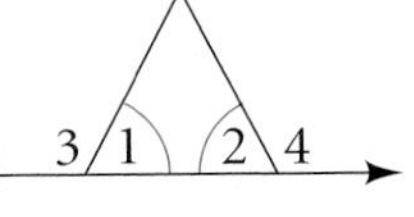

b. 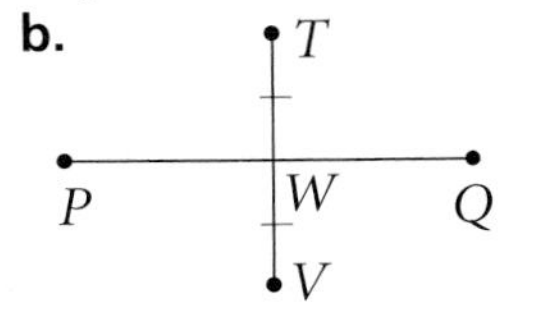

c. 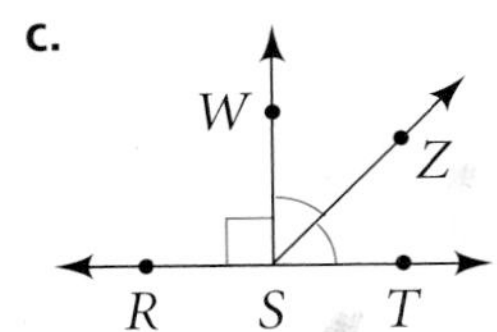

Exercises ON YOUR OWN

Name the property that justifies each statement.

1. $\angle Z \cong \angle Z$
2. If $12x = 84$, then $x = 7$.
3. If $\overline{ST} \cong \overline{QR}$, then $\overline{QR} \cong \overline{ST}$.
4. If $3x + 14 = 80$, then $3x = 66$.
5. If $2x + y = 5$ and $x = y$, then $2x + x = 5$.
6. If $AB - BC = 12$, then $AB = 12 + BC$.
7. If $m\angle A = 15$, then $3m\angle A = 45$.
8. $QR = QR$
9. If $\angle 1 \cong \angle 2$ and $\angle 2 \cong \angle 3$, then $\angle 1 \cong \angle 3$.
10. $2(3x + 5) = 6x + 10$

11. **Writing** How is a theorem different from a postulate?

12. **Open-ended** Give an example of vertical angles in your home.

Algebra **Find the values of the variables.**

13. 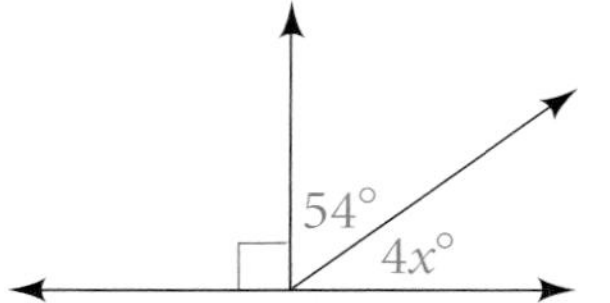

14. 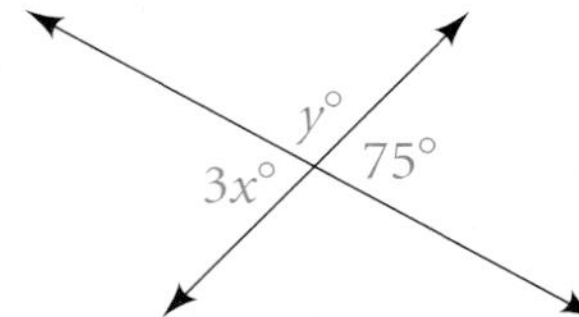

15. 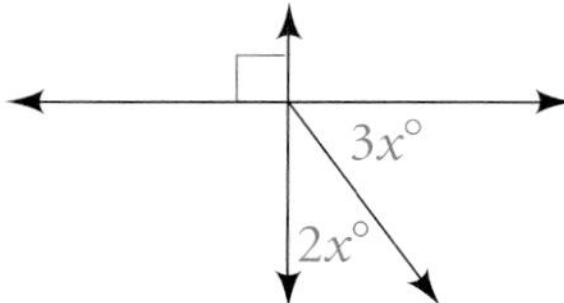

16. 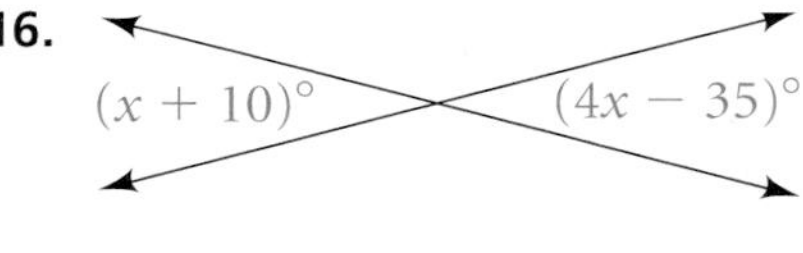

17. 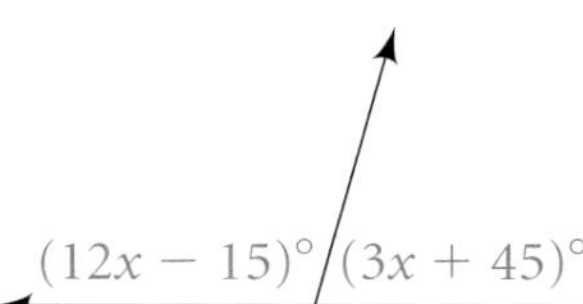

18. 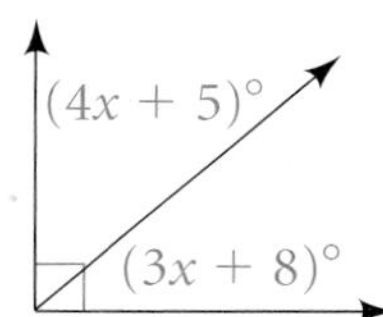

19. a. **Coordinate Geometry** $\angle AOX$ contains points $A(1, 3)$, $O(0, 0)$, and $X(4, 0)$. Find the coordinates of a point B so that $\angle BOA$ and $\angle AOX$ are adjacent complementary angles.
    b. Find the coordinates of a point C so that $\overrightarrow{OC}$ is a side of a different angle that is adjacent to and complementary to $\angle AOX$.
    c. $\angle DOE$ contains points $D(2, 3)$, $O(0, 0)$, and $E(5, 1)$. Find the coordinates of a point F so that $\overrightarrow{OF}$ is a side of an angle that is adjacent to and supplementary to $\angle DOE$.

20. **Algebra** $\angle A$ and $\angle B$ are supplementary angles. $m\angle A = 3x + 12$ and $m\angle B = 2x - 22$. Find the measures of both angles.

21. **Algebra** Solve for x and y.

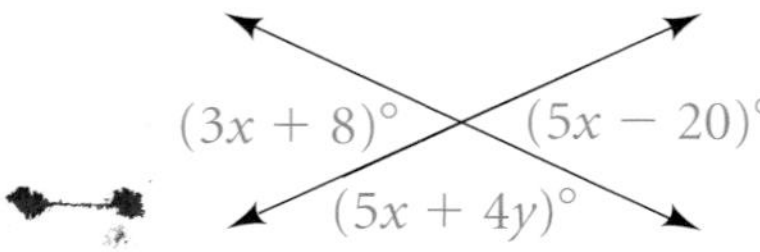

22. **Standardized Test Prep** In the diagrams at the right, which is greater, x or y?

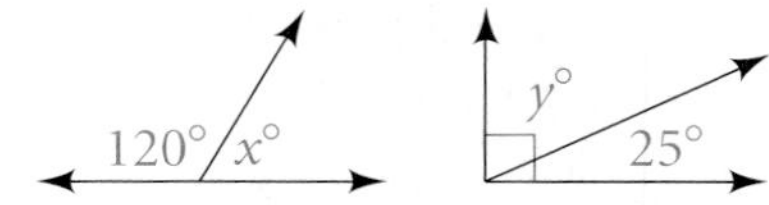

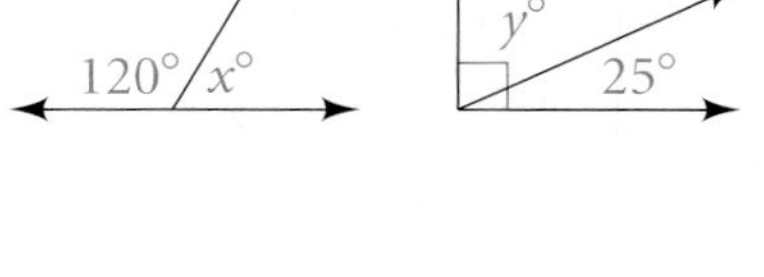

23. **Critical Thinking** If possible, find the measures of the angles described. If it is not possible, explain why.
    a. congruent adjacent supplementary angles
    b. congruent adjacent complementary angles
    c. congruent vertical angles

24. **Algebra** The measure of a supplement of $\angle 1$ is six times the measure of a complement of $\angle 1$. Find the measures of $\angle 1$, its supplement, and its complement.

PROBLEM SOLVING HINT

Let $x = m\angle 1$. Then $180 - x$ = measure of its supplement, and $90 - x$ = measure of its complement.

25. One angle is twice as large as its complement. Find the measures of both angles.

What can you conclude about the angles in each diagram? Justify your answers.

26.

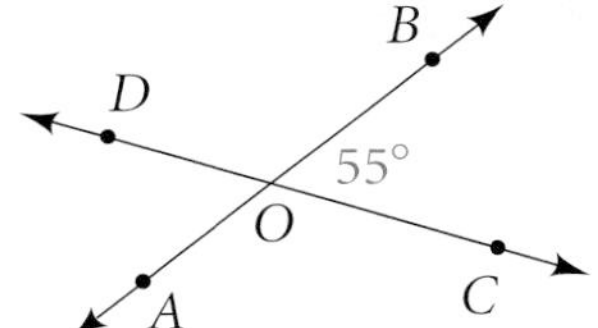

27.

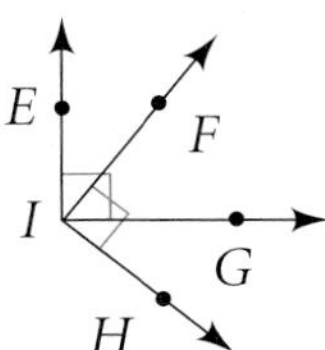

28.

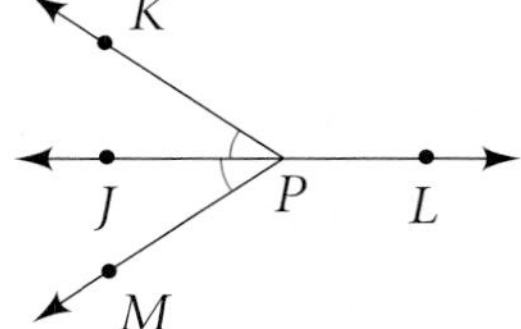

Give a reason for each step.

29.
$$3x - 15 = 105$$
$$3x = 120$$
$$x = 40$$

30.
$$12y + 24 = 96$$
$$12y = 72$$
$$y = 6$$

31.
$$\tfrac{1}{2}x - 5 = 10$$
$$2(\tfrac{1}{2}x - 5) = 20$$
$$x - 10 = 20$$
$$x = 30$$

32. **Preparing for Proof** Write a convincing argument that complements of the same angle are congruent.

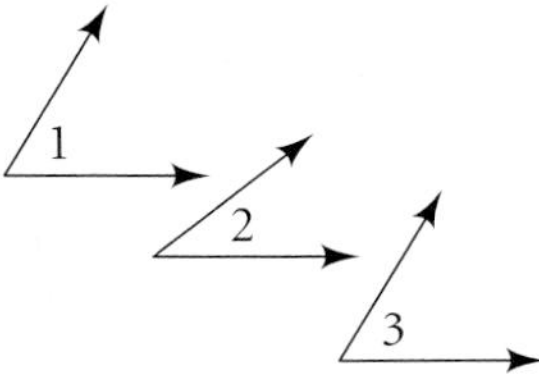

Given: $\angle 1$ and $\angle 2$ are complementary.
$\angle 3$ and $\angle 2$ are complementary.
Prove: $\angle 1 \cong \angle 3$

33. **Preparing for Proof** Write a convincing argument that supplements of congruent angles are congruent.

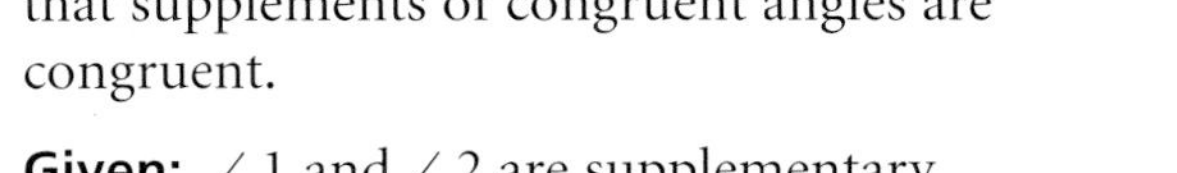

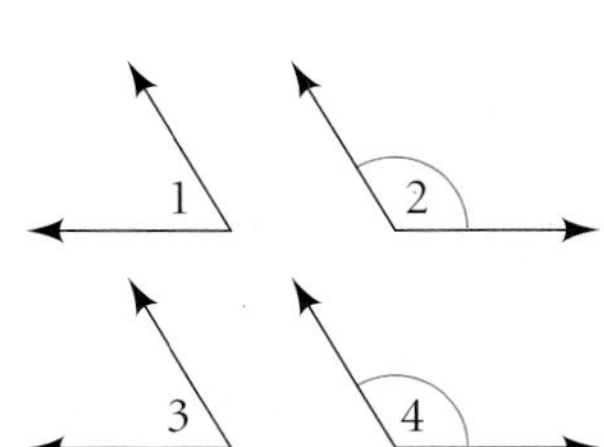

Given: $\angle 1$ and $\angle 2$ are supplementary.
$\angle 3$ and $\angle 4$ are supplementary.
$\angle 2 \cong \angle 4$
Prove: $\angle 1 \cong \angle 3$

Use the cartoon and deductive reasoning to answer *yes* or *no*. Explain any *no*.

34. Could a person with a red car park here on Tuesday at 10:00 A.M?

35. Could a man with a beard park here on Monday at 10:30 A.M.?

36. Could a woman with a wig park here on Saturday at 10:00 A.M.?

37. Could a person with a blue car park here on Tuesday at 9:05 A.M.?

38. Could a person with a convertible with leather seats park here on Sunday at 6:00 P.M.?

Exercises MIXED REVIEW

Sketch each of the following.

39. three collinear points **40.** two intersecting rays **41.** two perpendicular lines

42. Find the next three terms in the sequence: $1, 1, \frac{1}{2}, \frac{1}{3}, \frac{1}{5}, \frac{1}{8}, \ldots$

Getting Ready for Lesson 1-8

Calculator **Find the square root of each number to the nearest tenth.**

43. 25 **44.** 17 **45.** 123

46. 48 **47.** 96 **48.** 1023

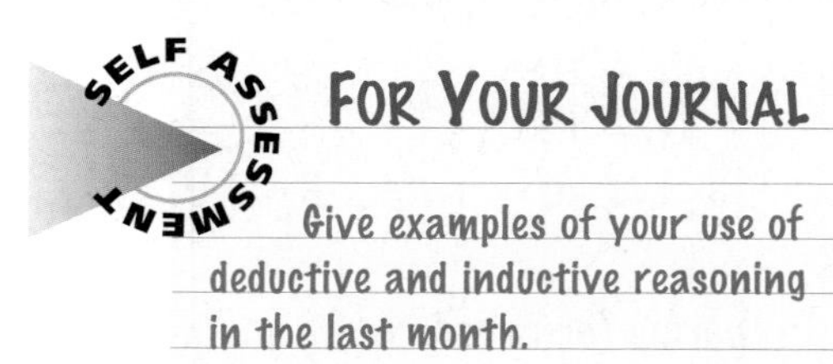

SELF ASSESSMENT
FOR YOUR JOURNAL
Give examples of your use of deductive and inductive reasoning in the last month.

Exercises CHECKPOINT

1. **Writing** What are the components of a good definition?

2. a. Use a protractor to draw $\angle R$ with measure 78.
b. Construct an angle whose measure is $2 \cdot m\angle R$.
c. Construct an angle whose measure is $\frac{1}{2} \cdot m\angle R$.

3. **Open-ended** Use a protractor to draw a pair of adjacent complementary angles. Then draw another pair of complementary angles that are *not* adjacent.

4. **Standardized Test Prep** If $-6 \leq x \leq 1$ is graphed on a number line, its graph is which of the following?
A. 7 points **B.** 8 points **C.** a segment **D.** a line **E.** a ray

What You'll Learn

- Finding the distance between two points in a coordinate plane
- Finding the coordinates of the midpoint of a segment in a coordinate plane

...And Why

To improve skills such as map reading

What You'll Need

tracing paper, ruler, graph paper

1-8 The Coordinate Plane

WORK TOGETHER

Much of New York City is laid out in a rectangular grid, as shown in this map. Most of the streets in the grid are either parallel or perpendicular.

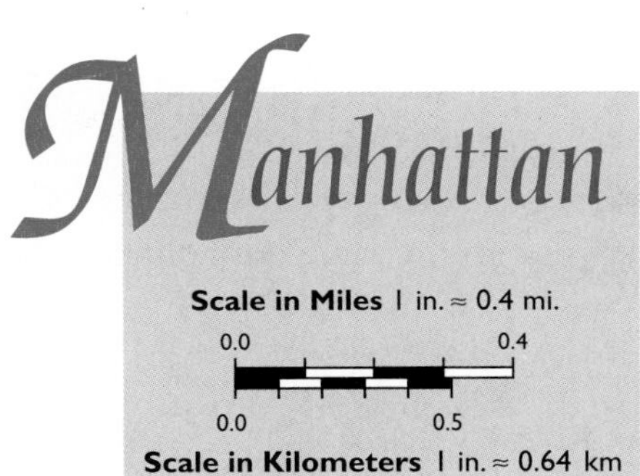

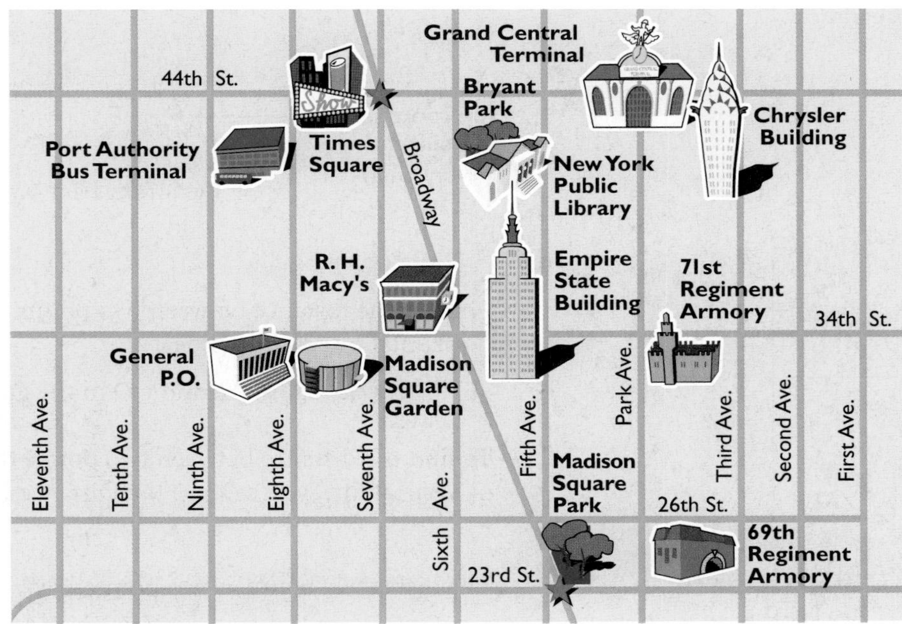

Yvonne's family is on the corner of 44th Street and 7th Avenue. They plan to walk to Madison Square Park at 23rd Street and 5th Avenue. There are several possible routes they can take.

Work with your group. Trace the routes on the map and answer the following questions.

1. Yvonne's father wants to walk east on 44th Street until they reach 5th Avenue. He then plans to walk south on 5th Avenue to Madison Square Park. About how long is his route?
2. Yvonne's mother wants to walk south on 7th Avenue until they reach 23rd Street. She then plans to walk east on 23rd Street to Madison Square Park. About how long is her route?
3. Yvonne notices on the map that Broadway cuts across the grid of streets and leads to Madison Square Park. She suggests walking all the way on Broadway. About how long is her route?
4. Whose route is the shortest? Why?
5. Whose route is the longest? Why?

THINK AND DISCUSS

You can think of a point as a dot, and a line as a series of points. In coordinate geometry you can describe a point with an ordered pair (x, y) and a line with an equation $y = mx + b$.

QUICK REVIEW

The x- and y-axes divide the coordinate plane into four quadrants.

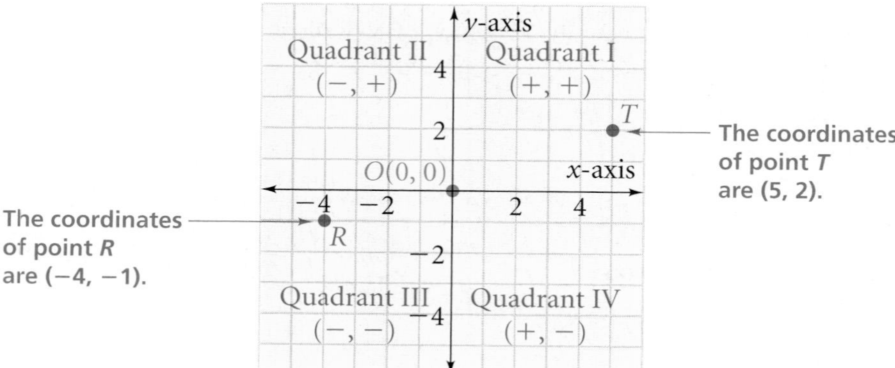

Finding the distance between two points is easy if the points lie on a horizontal or a vertical line.

6. Try This Find AB and CD in the graph at the left.

To find the distance between two points that are not on the same horizontal or vertical line, you can use the Distance Formula.

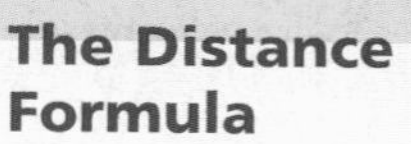

The Distance Formula

The distance d between two points $A(x_1, y_1)$ and $B(x_2, y_2)$ is

$$d = \sqrt{(x_2 - x_1)^2 + (y_2 - y_1)^2}.$$

Example 1 *Relating to the Real World* 

Transportation Luisa takes the subway from Oak Station to Jackson Station each morning. Oak Station is 1 mi west and 2 mi south of City Plaza. Jackson Station is 2 mi east and 4 mi north of City Plaza. How far does she travel by subway?

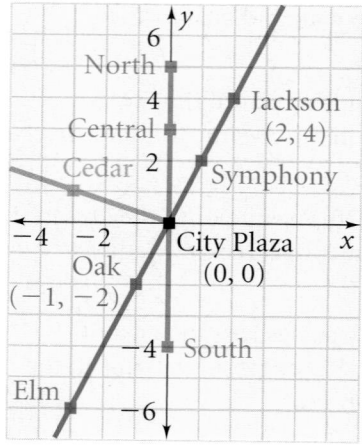

Let (x_1, y_1) and (x_2, y_2) represent Oak and Jackson, respectively. Then, $x_1 = -1, x_2 = 2, y_1 = -2,$ and $y_2 = 4$.

$d = \sqrt{(x_2 - x_1)^2 + (y_2 - y_1)^2}$ Use the Distance Formula.

$d = \sqrt{(2 - (-1))^2 + (4 - (-2))^2}$ Substitute.

$d = \sqrt{3^2 + 6^2}$ Simplify.

$d = \sqrt{9 + 36} = \sqrt{45}$

45 [√] 6.7082039 Use your calculator.

Luisa travels about 6.7 mi by subway.

The system of longitude and latitude lines on Earth is a type of coordinate system.

7. In Example 1 suppose you let (x_1, y_1) be (2, 4) and (x_2, y_2) be (−1, −2). Would you get the same result? Why or why not?

8. **Calculator** Find the length of $\overline{AB}$ with endpoints $A(1, -3)$ and $B(-4, 4)$ to the nearest tenth.

You know how to find the midpoint of a segment on a number line. Now you will use a similar process to find the midpoint of a segment in the coordinate plane.

Graph $\overline{TS}$ with endpoints $T(4, 3)$ and $S(8, 5)$. Let $\overline{TR}$ be a horizontal segment and $\overline{SR}$ be a vertical segment. Add the coordinates to your drawing as you answer these questions.

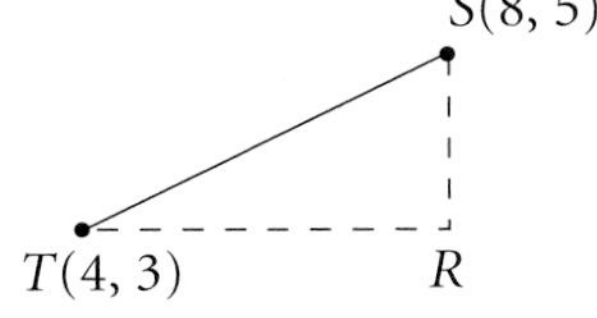

9. What are the coordinates of point R?

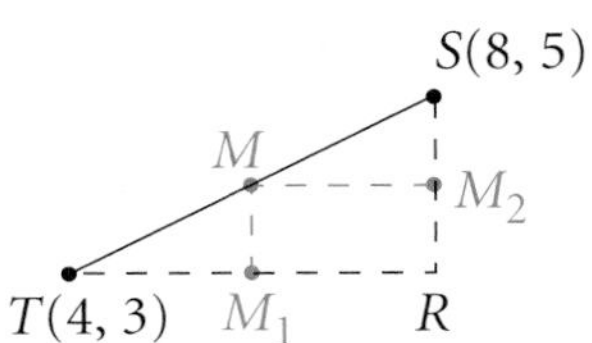

10. **a.** What are the coordinates of M_1, the midpoint of $\overline{TR}$?
    b. What are the coordinates of M_2, the midpoint of $\overline{SR}$?

11. What are the coordinates of M, the midpoint of $\overline{TS}$?

This specific case shows you how the Midpoint Formula was developed.

The Midpoint Formula

The coordinates of the midpoint M of $\overline{AB}$ with endpoints $A(x_1, y_1)$ and $B(x_2, y_2)$ are the following:

$$M = \left(\frac{x_1 + x_2}{2}, \frac{y_1 + y_2}{2}\right)$$

QUICK REVIEW

$\frac{x_1 + x_2}{2}$ is the *arithmetic mean* of x_1 and x_2. Another word for arithmetic mean is *average*.

Example 2

Find the coordinates of the midpoint M of $\overline{QS}$ with endpoints $Q(3, 5)$ and $S(7, -9)$.

Let $x_1 = 3, x_2 = 7, y_1 = 5$, and $y_2 = -9$.

$$x\text{-coordinate of } M = \frac{x_1 + x_2}{2} = \frac{3 + 7}{2} = \frac{10}{2} = 5$$

$$y\text{-coordinate of } M = \frac{y_1 + y_2}{2} = \frac{5 + (-9)}{2} = \frac{-4}{2} = -2$$

The coordinates of point M are (5, −2).

12. **Try This** Find the coordinates of the midpoint of $\overline{AB}$ with endpoints $A(2, -5)$ and $B(6, 13)$.

Exercises ON YOUR OWN

Graph each point in the same coordinate plane.

1. $A(5, -3)$
2. $B(-3, 0)$
3. $C(6, 2)$
4. $D(-6, 2)$
5. $E(-4, 3)$
6. $F(0, 5)$

Choose **Use mental math, pencil and paper, or a calculator to find the distance between the points to the nearest tenth.**

7. $J(2, -1), K(2, 5)$
8. $L(10, 14), M(-8, 14)$
9. $N(-11, -11), P(-11, -3)$
10. $A(0, 3), B(0, 12)$
11. $C(12, 6), D(-8, 18)$
12. $E(6, -2), F(-2, 4)$
13. $Q(12, -12), T(5, 12)$
14. $R(0, 5), S(12, 3)$
15. $X(-3, -4), Y(5, 5)$

Find the coordinates of the midpoint of $\overline{HX}$.

16. $H(0, 0), X(8, 4)$
17. $H(-1, 3), X(7, -1)$
18. $H(13, 8), X(-6, -6)$
19. $H(7, 10), X(5, -8)$
20. $H(-6.3, 5.2), X(1.8, -1)$
21. $H\left(5\frac{1}{2}, -4\frac{3}{4}\right), X\left(2\frac{1}{4}, -1\frac{1}{4}\right)$
22. The midpoint of $\overline{QS}$ is the origin. Point Q is located in Quadrant II. What quadrant contains point S?
23. $M(5, 12)$ is the midpoint of $\overline{AB}$. The coordinates of point A are $(2, 6)$. What are the coordinates of point B?
24. The midpoint of $\overline{QT}$ has coordinates $(3, -4)$. The coordinates of point Q are $(2, 3)$. What are the coordinates of point T?
25. The coordinates of A, B, C, and D are given at the right. Graph the points and draw the segments connecting them in order. Are the lengths of the sides of $ABCD$ the same? Explain.

    $A(-6, 2)$ $B(-3, 5)$
    $C(-6, 6)$ $D(-9, 5)$

26. **Open-ended** Graph $A(-2, 1)$ and $B(2, 3)$. Draw $\overleftrightarrow{AB}$. For each point described, give two sets of possible coordinates if they exist. Otherwise write "exactly one point" and give the coordinates.
    a. point D so that $\overleftrightarrow{CD}$ contains $C(-1, 4)$ and is parallel to $\overleftrightarrow{AB}$
    b. point E so that $\overleftrightarrow{AE}$ is parallel to $\overleftrightarrow{BC}$, $\overleftrightarrow{BC}$ contains $C(-1, 4)$, and $\overleftrightarrow{EC}$ is parallel to $\overleftrightarrow{AB}$
    c. point G so that $\overleftrightarrow{FG}$ contains $F(0, 2)$ and is perpendicular to $\overleftrightarrow{AB}$
    d. point H so that $\overleftrightarrow{HJ}$ contains $J(4, 2)$ and is perpendicular to $\overleftrightarrow{AB}$

27. **Writing** Why do you think that some cities are designed with a rectangular grid instead of a triangular grid or some other shape?
28. Graph the points $A(2, 1)$, $B(6, -1)$, $C(8, 7)$, and $D(4, 9)$. Draw quadrilateral $ABCD$. Use the Midpoint Formula to determine the midpoints of $\overline{AC}$ and $\overline{BD}$. What do you notice?

For each graph, find (a) the length of $\overline{AB}$ to the nearest tenth and (b) the coordinates of the midpoint of $\overline{AB}$.

29.

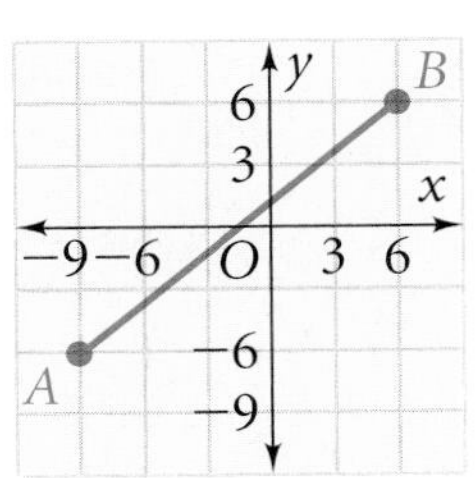

30.

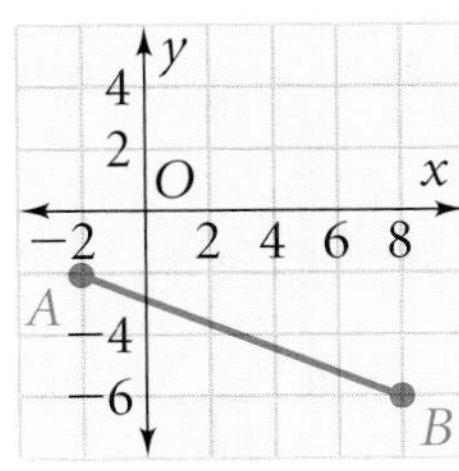

31.

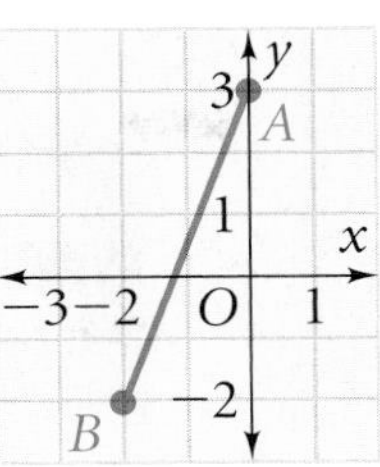

32. ***Communications*** Long-distance rates for telephone calls are determined mainly by the distance between the two ends of the call. To determine these distances, long-distance telephone companies have divided North America into a grid, with each unit equaling $\sqrt{0.1}$ mile. The distance between two customers is then determined by using the Distance Formula. The coordinates for certain customers in several cities are listed. Find the distance between customers in the following cities:

a. Boston and San Francisco
b. Houston and Chicago
c. Denver and New Orleans

San Francisco (8719, 8492)
Chicago (3439, 5985)
New Orleans (2637, 8482)
Denver (5899, 7501)
Los Angeles (7878, 9213)
Houston (3537, 8936)
Boston (1248, 4422)

33. ***Geometry in 3 Dimensions*** You can use three coordinates (x, y, z) to locate points in three dimensions. Point P has coordinates $(3, -3, 5)$.

a. Give the coordinates of points A, B, C, D, E, F, and G.
b. Draw three axes like those shown. Then graph $R(4, 5, 9)$.

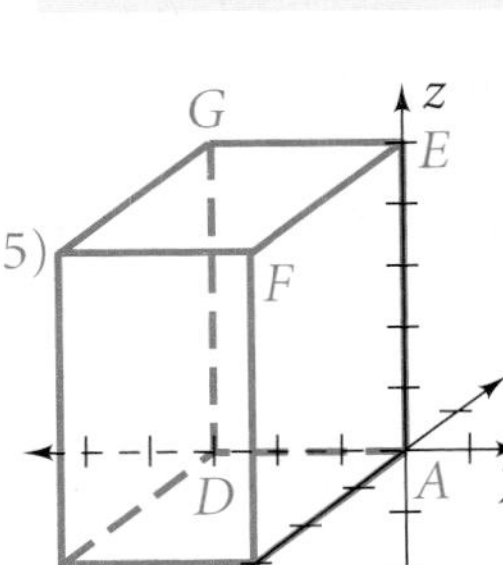

Exercises MIXED REVIEW

Find the measure of the complement and supplement of each angle, if possible.

34. $m\angle B = 56$ **35.** $m\angle R = 18$ **36.** $m\angle D = 179$

37. $m\angle P = 23.5$ **38.** $m\angle T = 108$ **39.** $m\angle E = 78$

40. The length of $\overline{AC}$ is 45. If $AB = x + 8$ and $BC = 3x - 3$, find the value of x.

SELF ASSESSMENT

PORTFOLIO

For your portfolio, select one or two items from your work for this chapter. Here are some possibilities.

- corrected work
- an origami creation
- a journal entry

Explain why you have included each selection you make.

Finishing the Chapter Project

On Folded Wings

Find Out questions on pages 572, 584, 593, and 606 should help you to complete your project. Prepare a *Geometry in Origami* display. Include the models you made, instructions for making them, and the geometric patterns you discovered. You may want to display origami creations in a hallway display case. Consider adding more origami creations or writing a short report on the history of origami. You can use the books listed below to find out more about origami.

Reflect and Revise

Ask a classmate to review your display with you. Together, check that your models are well constructed, your directions are clear and correct, and your explanations are sensible. Have you used geometric terms correctly? Is the display attractive as well as informative?

Follow Up

Use paper folding to illustrate some of the geometric terms, such as *midpoint, angle bisector,* and *perpendicular bisector*, that you learned in this chapter.

For More Information

Gray, Alice and Kunihiko Kasahara. *The Magic of Origami*. Tokyo: Japan Publications, Inc., 1977.

Jackson, Paul. *Step-By-Step Origami*. London: Anness Publishing, 1995.

Kenneway, Eric. *Complete Origami.* New York: St. Martin's Press, 1987.

Montroll, John. *Easy Origami*. New York: Dover Publications, 1992.

Weiss, Stephen. *Origami That Flies*. New York: St. Martin's Press, 1984.

CHAPTER 1

Wrap Up

Key Terms

acute angle (p. 589)
adjacent angles (p. 610)
angle (p. 588)
angle bisector (p. 596)
collinear (p. 575)
compass (p. 601)
complementary angles (p. 610)
congruent angles (p. 590)
congruent segments (p. 587)
conjecture (p. 567)
construction (p. 601)
coordinate (p. 587)
coplanar (p. 575)
deductive reasoning (p. 608)
inductive reasoning (p. 567)
line (p. 575)
measure of an angle (p. 588)
midpoint (p. 595)
obtuse angle (p. 589)
opposite rays (p. 580)
parallel lines (p. 580)
parallel planes (p. 581)
perpendicular bisector (p. 596)
perpendicular lines (p. 595)
plane (p. 575)
point (p. 574)
postulate (p. 576)
proof (p. 611)
quadrant (p. 616)
ray (p. 580)
right angle (p. 589)
segment (p. 580)
segment bisector (p. 595)
skew lines (p. 581)
space (p. 574)
straight angle (p. 589)
straightedge (p. 601)
supplementary angles (p. 610)
theorem (p. 611)
vertical angles (p. 610)

How am I doing?

- State three ideas from this chapter that you think are important. Explain your choices.
- Describe three types of mathematical statements.

Using Patterns and Inductive Reasoning

1-1

You use **inductive reasoning** when you make conclusions from specific examples or patterns. You can use inductive reasoning to make conjectures. A **conjecture** describes a conclusion reached from observations or inductive reasoning. Because conjectures are not always valid, you should verify them if possible.

Find the next two terms of each sequence and describe the pattern.

1. $1, 5, 9, 13, \dots$
2. $1, 3, 7, 15, 31, \dots$
3. $\frac{1}{2}, \frac{2}{3}, \frac{3}{4}, \frac{4}{5}, \dots$
4. $0, 1, -2, 3, -4, \dots$

5. Draw the next figure in the sequence.

6. a. Calculator Find the last two digits of 76^2, 76^4, 276^2, and 376^3.
   b. Make a **conjecture** about powers of numbers whose last two digits are 76.

Basic Concepts 1-2, 1-3

Points that lie on a line are **collinear**. Points and lines in the same plane are **coplanar**.

Two coplanar lines that do not intersect are **parallel**. Two lines in space that are not parallel and do not intersect are **skew**. Two planes that do not intersect are **parallel**.

Segments and **rays** are parts of lines.

7. ***Critical Thinking*** Explain why the postulate "Through any three noncollinear points there is exactly one plane" applies only to noncollinear points.

Use the figure to answer Exercises 8–13.

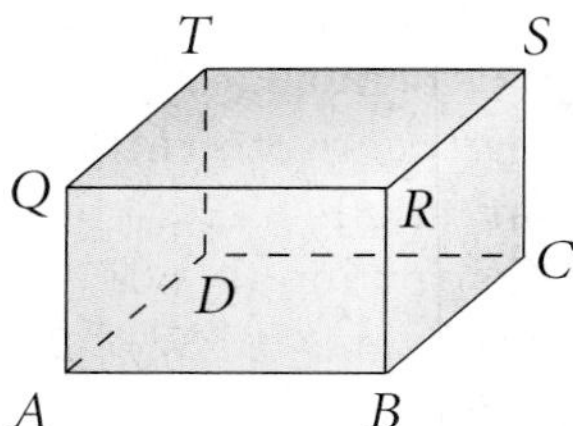

8. Name two intersecting lines.

9. Name a pair of skew lines.

10. Name three noncollinear points.

11. Name four noncoplanar points.

12. Name a pair of parallel planes.

13. Name three lines that intersect at *D*.

Complete with *always, sometimes,* or *never* to make a true statement

14. A line and a point are __?__ coplanar.

15. Two segments are __?__ coplanar.

16. Skew lines are __?__ coplanar.

17. Opposite rays __?__ have the same endpoint.

18. Two points are __?__ collinear.

19. Parallel lines are __?__ skew.

Angles, Segments, and Deductive Reasoning 1-4, 1-7

Segments with the same length are **congruent.** An **angle** is formed by two rays with the same endpoint. Angles are measured in degrees. Angles with the same measure are **congruent.**

Deductive reasoning is the process of reasoning logically from given facts to a conclusion. If the given facts are true, deductive reasoning always produces a valid conclusion.

Special relationships exist between certain angle pairs. For example, vertical angles are congruent. The sum of the measures of a pair of **complementary angles** is 90. The sum of the measures of a pair of **supplementary angles** is 180.

20. ***Open-ended*** Describe a real-world situation where you use deductive reasoning.

21. Find possible coordinates of point *Q* on the number line so that $PQ = 5$.

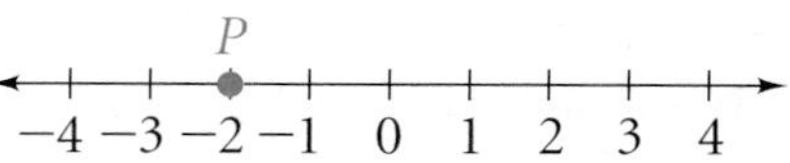

Algebra **Find the value of each variable in the diagrams below.**

22.

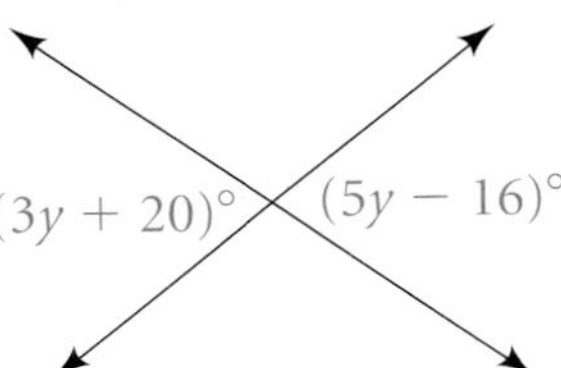

23.

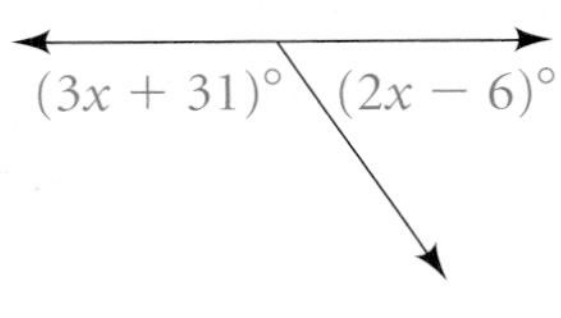

24.

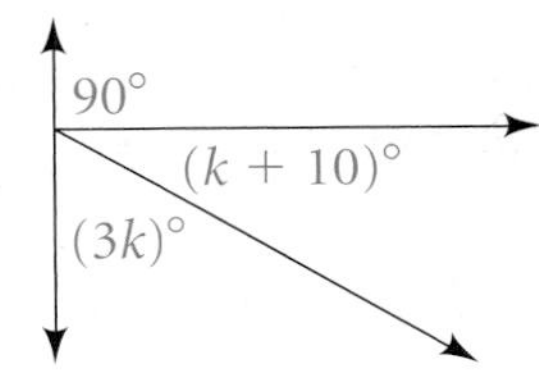

What can you conclude from each diagram? Justify your answers.

25.

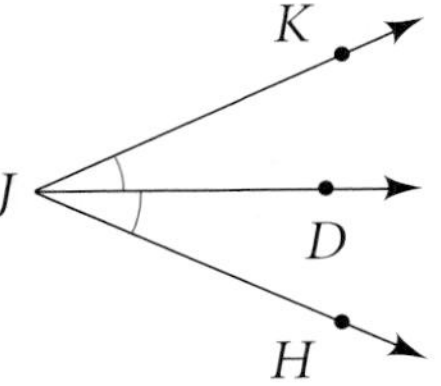

26.

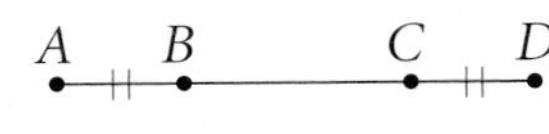

27.

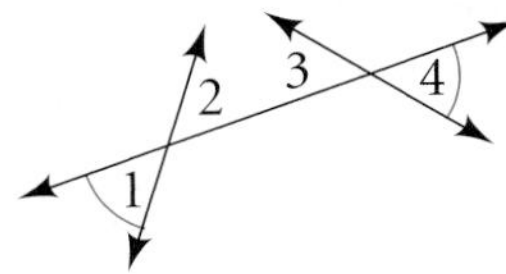

Good Definitions — 1-5

A good definition is precise. A good definition uses terms that have been previously defined or are commonly accepted.

The **midpoint** of a segment divides a segment into two congruent segments. **Perpendicular lines** intersect at right angles. A **perpendicular bisector** of a segment is perpendicular to a segment at its midpoint. An **angle bisector** divides an angle into two congruent angles.

28. **Writing** Rico defines a book as something you read. Explain what's wrong with this definition. Write a good definition for the word *book*.

29. **Critical Thinking** In the diagram at the right, $\overleftrightarrow{LJ}$ is the perpendicular bisector of $\overline{BK}$. Is $\overleftrightarrow{BK}$ necessarily the perpendicular bisector of $\overline{LJ}$? Explain.

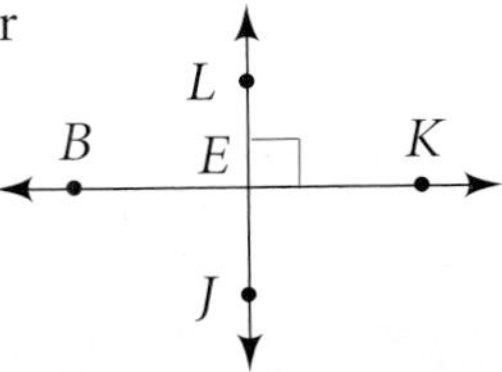

30. **Algebra** In the diagram at right, point E is the midpoint of $\overline{BK}$, $BE = 3y - 2$, and $EK = 2y + 1$. Find the value of y.

31. Find the coordinate of the midpoint of $\overline{GH}$.

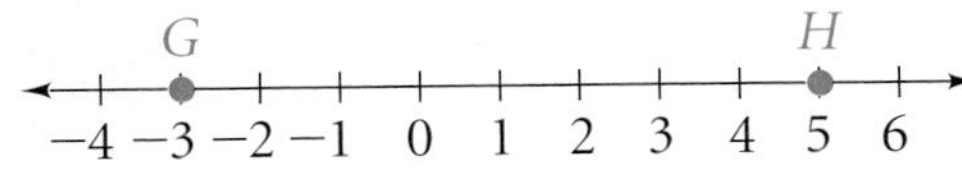

32. **Standardized Test Prep** In which figure is the $m\angle 1$ *not* equal to 60?

A.

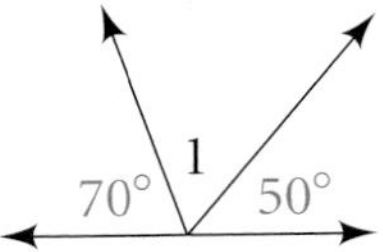

B.

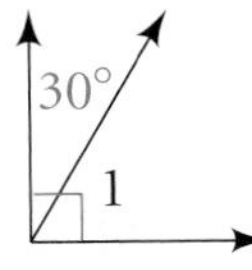

C.

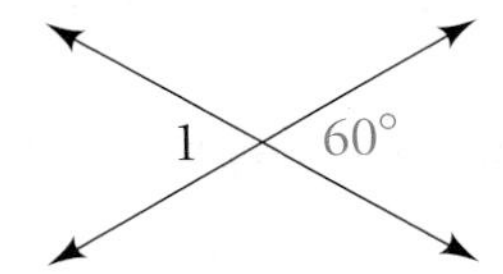

D.

E.

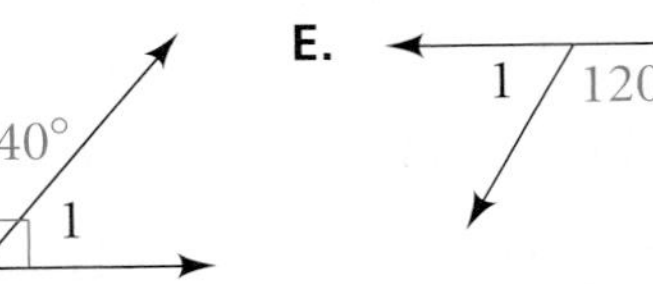

Basic Constructions 1-6

A **construction** is the process of making geometric figures using a **straightedge** and **compass**.

33. Use a protractor to draw a 72° angle. Then construct a congruent angle.

34. **a.** Construct $\overline{AB} \cong \overline{PQ}$.

b. Construct the perpendicular bisector of $\overline{AB}$.

P •———————• Q

35. *Writing* Describe how to construct a 45° angle.

The Coordinate Plane 1-8

The ***x*-axis** and the ***y*-axis** intersect at the **origin** (0, 0) and determine a **coordinate plane.** You can find the coordinates of the midpoint M of $\overline{AB}$ with endpoints $A(x_1, y_1)$ and $B(x_2, y_2)$ using the **Midpoint Formula.**

$$M = \left(\frac{x_1 + x_2}{2}, \frac{y_1 + y_2}{2}\right)$$

You can find the distance d between points $A(x_1, y_1)$ and $B(x_2, y_2)$ using the **Distance Formula.**

$$d = \sqrt{(x_2 - x_1)^2 + (y_2 - y_1)^2}$$

Graph each point in the same coordinate plane.

36. $A(-1, 5)$ **37.** $B(0, 4)$ **38.** $C(-1, -1)$ **39.** $D(6, 2)$ **40.** $E(-7, 0)$ **41.** $F(3, -4)$

42. $\overline{GH}$ has endpoints $G(-3, 2)$ and $H(3, -2)$. Find the coordinates of the midpoint of $\overline{GH}$.

43. *Calculator* Find the distance between points $B(4, -3)$ and $D(3, 0)$ to the nearest tenth.

Getting Ready for.... CHAPTER 2

44. **a.** Graph points $A(-1, 3)$, $B(-1, 6)$, and $C(4, 3)$ in the same coordinate plane and connect them to form a triangle.

b. *Choose* Use pencil and paper, mental math, or a calculator to find the lengths of the three sides of the triangle.

c. List the sides in order from longest to shortest.

Name a real-world object that has the given geometric shape.

45. triangle **46.** circle **47.** rhombus **48.** cylinder **49.** cube

CHAPTER 1 Assessment

Find the next two terms in each sequence.

1. 8, −4, 2, −1, . . .

2. 0, 2, 4, 6, 8, . . .

3. 

4. 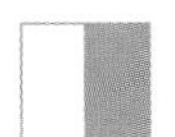 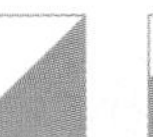 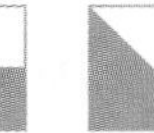 

5. **Open-ended** Write two different sequences whose first three terms are 1, 2, 4. Describe each pattern.

Use the figure to answer Exercises 6–10.

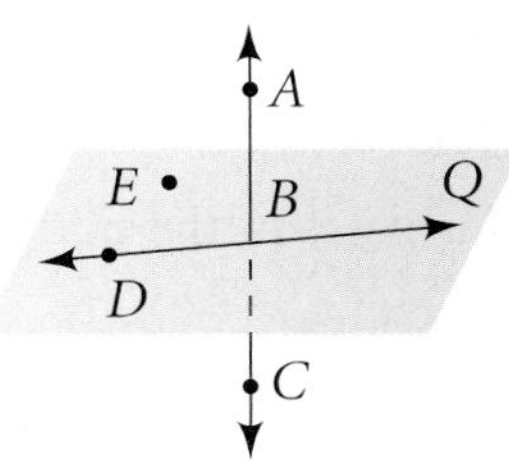

6. Name three collinear points.

7. Name four coplanar points.

8. Name four noncoplanar points.

9. What is the intersection of $\overleftrightarrow{AC}$ and plane Q?

10. How many planes contain each line and point?

a. $\overleftrightarrow{BD}$ and point A **b.** $\overleftrightarrow{AB}$ and point C
c. $\overleftrightarrow{BE}$ and point C **d.** $\overleftrightarrow{BD}$ and point E

Is the definition of the term in red acceptable? If not, write a good definition.

11. A pencil is a writing instrument.

12. Vertical angles are angles that are congruent.

13. Complementary angles are angles that form a right angle.

Complete with *always, sometimes,* or *never* to make each statement true.

14. $\overrightarrow{LJ}$ and $\overrightarrow{TJ}$ are __?__ opposite rays.

15. Four points are __?__ coplanar.

16. Skew lines are __?__ noncoplanar.

17. Two lines that lie in parallel planes are __?__ parallel.

18. The intersection of two planes is __?__ a point.

19. **Algebra** $JK = 48$. Find the value of x.

J H K
$4x - 15$ $2x + 3$

Algebra **Use the figure to find the values of the variables in Exercises 20 and 21.**

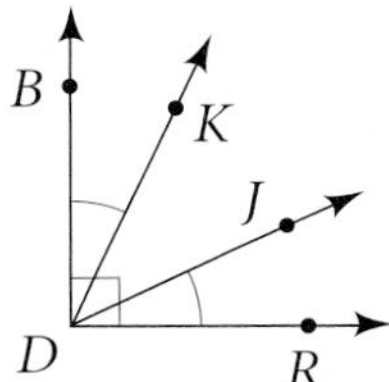

20. $m\angle BDK = 3x + 4$, $m\angle JDR = 5x - 10$

21. $m\angle BDJ = 7y + 2$, $m\angle JDR = 2y + 7$

22. **Writing** Why is it useful to have more than one way of naming an angle?

Name the property of equality or congruence that justifies each statement.

23. If $UV = KL$ and $KL = 6$, then $UV = 6$.

24. If $m\angle 1 + m\angle 2 = m\angle 4 + m\angle 2$, then $m\angle 1 = m\angle 4$.

25. $\angle ABC \cong \angle ABC$

26. If $\frac{1}{2}m\angle D = 45$, then $m\angle D = 90$.

27. If $\angle DEF \cong \angle HJK$, then $\angle HJK \cong \angle DEF$.

Use the figure to complete Exercises 28–32.

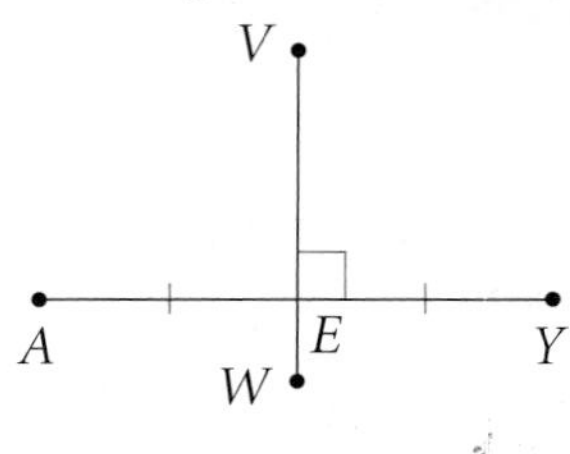

28. $\overline{VW}$ is the __?__ of $\overline{AY}$.

29. $EW + EV = \blacksquare$

30. If $EY = 3.5$, then $AY = \blacksquare$.

31. $\frac{1}{2}\blacksquare = AE$

32. $\blacksquare$ is the midpoint of $\blacksquare$.

33. Construct a triangle whose sides have the given lengths.

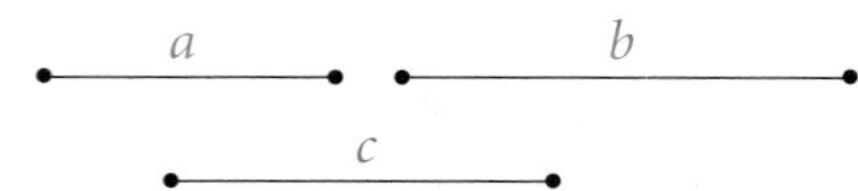

Algebra **Use the figure to complete Exercises 34 and 35. $\overrightarrow{AE}$ bisects $\angle DAC$. Find the values of the variables.**

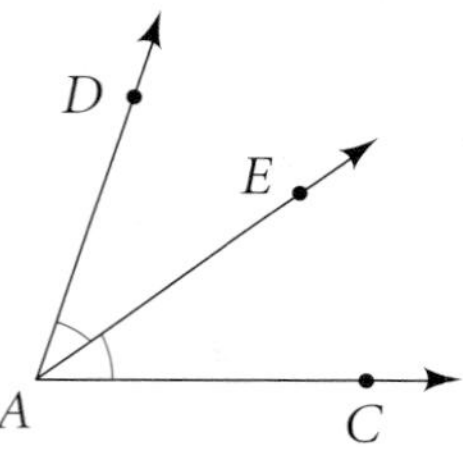

34. $m\angle DAE = 4y + 4$, $m\angle CAE = 6y - 12$

35. $m\angle CAE = 6c - 12$, $m\angle DAC = 72$

36. **Standardized Test Prep** The measure of an angle is $2z$. What is the measure of its supplement?

A. $90 - 2z$
B. 180
C. $2z$
D. $2z - 180$
E. $180 - 2z$

37. Find the measure of each angle.

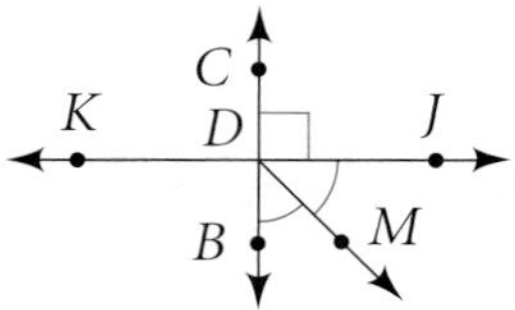

a. $\angle CDM$ **b.** $\angle KDM$
c. $\angle JDK$ **d.** $\angle JDM$
e. $\angle CDB$ **f.** $\angle CDK$

Use the graph to complete Exercises 38–41.

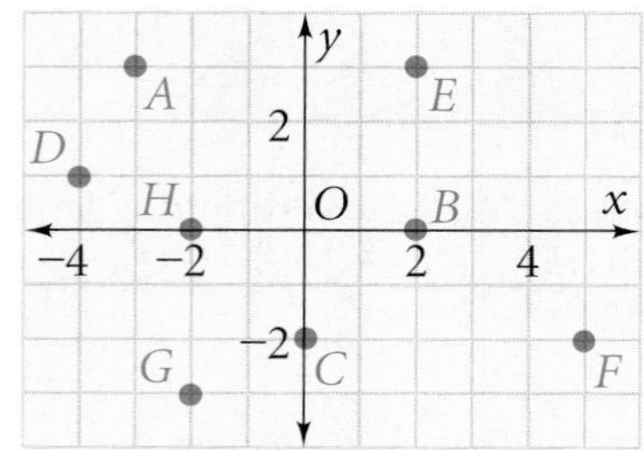

38. Find the coordinates of each labeled point.

39. Find the coordinates of the midpoint of $\overline{EH}$.

40. Find the coordinates of the midpoint of $\overline{AF}$.

41. Find the length of each segment to the nearest tenth.

a. $\overline{AC}$ **b.** $\overline{BH}$
c. $\overline{GB}$ **d.** $\overline{AF}$

What can you conclude from each diagram? Justify your answers.

42.

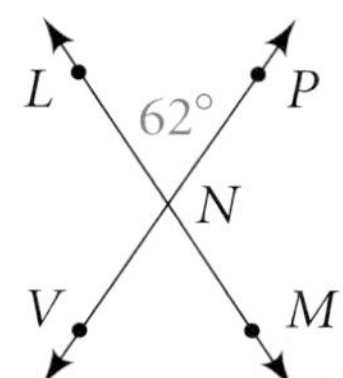

43.

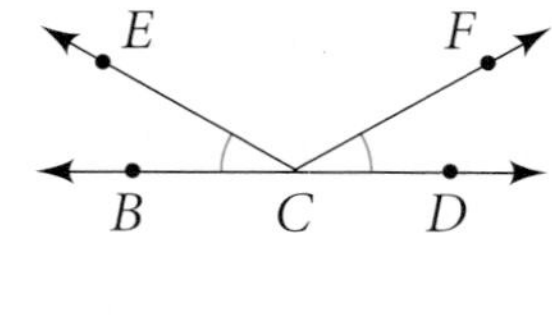

44. The coordinates of the midpoint of $\overline{RS}$ are $(-1, 1)$. The coordinates of R are $(3, 3)$. What are the coordinates of S?

45. Use a protractor to draw a 60° angle. Then construct its bisector.

CHAPTER 1

Preparing for the Math A Exam

Part I

1 Which must be coplanar?
(1) 2 lines (3) 4 points
(2) 3 points (4) 1 line and 2 points

2 Which lines appear to be parallel?
(1) $\overline{EF}$ and $\overline{FG}$
(2) $\overline{JH}$ and $\overline{JG}$
(3) $\overline{AE}$ and $\overline{DC}$
(4) $\overline{BC}$ and $\overline{IJ}$

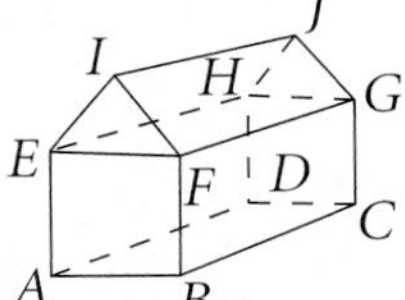

3 Which pair names the same ray?

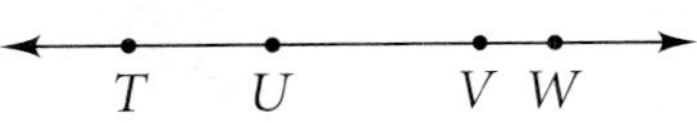

(1) $\overrightarrow{UW}$ and $\overrightarrow{UV}$ (3) $\overrightarrow{UV}$ and $\overrightarrow{VU}$
(2) $\overrightarrow{TV}$ and $\overrightarrow{UV}$ (4) $\overrightarrow{VT}$ and $\overrightarrow{UV}$

4 Which angle most likely measures 30°?
(1) $\angle JON$
(2) $\angle JOK$
(3) $\angle MON$
(4) $\angle NOL$

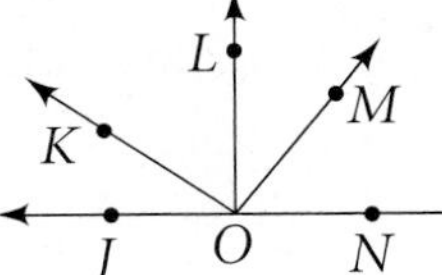

5 $\overline{MV}$ bisects $\overline{NW}$. Which statement can you *not* determine to be true based on the information given?
(1) $\angle MEN \cong \angle VEW$
(2) $\angle NEV \cong \angle WEM$
(3) $\overline{ME} \cong \overline{EV}$
(4) $\overline{EN} \cong \overline{EW}$

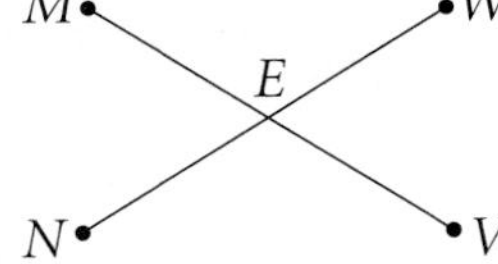

6 Two right angles *cannot* be
(1) supplementary. (3) adjacent.
(2) complementary. (4) vertical.

Part II

7 Draw the next figure in the sequence.

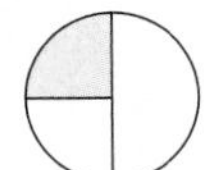 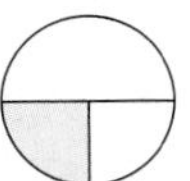 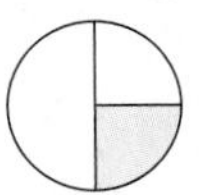 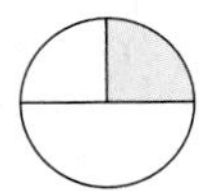

8 If $WY = 23$ cm and $XY = 9$ cm, what is the length of $\overline{WX}$?

9 Find the coordinates of the midpoint of $\overline{CD}$ with endpoints $C(5, 7)$ and $D(10, -3)$.

Part III

10 Anna said, "A line and a point are always coplanar." Explain why Anna's statement is true.

11 Construct an angle congruent to $\angle S$. Then construct its angle bisector.

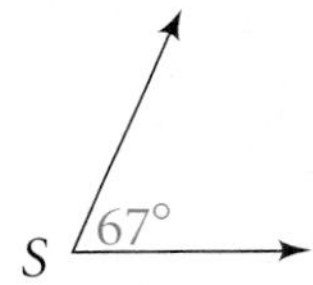

12 On the first day Marco opened his restaurant, he had 17 customers. On the following days he had 23, 31, and 41 customers.
a Predict how many customers he will have on the sixth day.
b Are you sure about your prediction? Explain.

Part IV

13 Find the values of x and y.

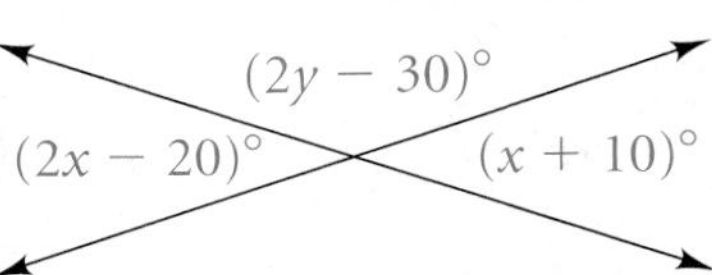

14 Jennifer's high school is 2 mi east and 3 mi south of the center of town. After school, Jennifer works at a grocery store 1 mi west and 5 mi north of the center of town.
a Use coordinates to describe the location of the school and the store. Use the center of town as the origin.
b Find the straight line distance between the school and the store.

CHAPTER 2

Investigating Geometric Figures

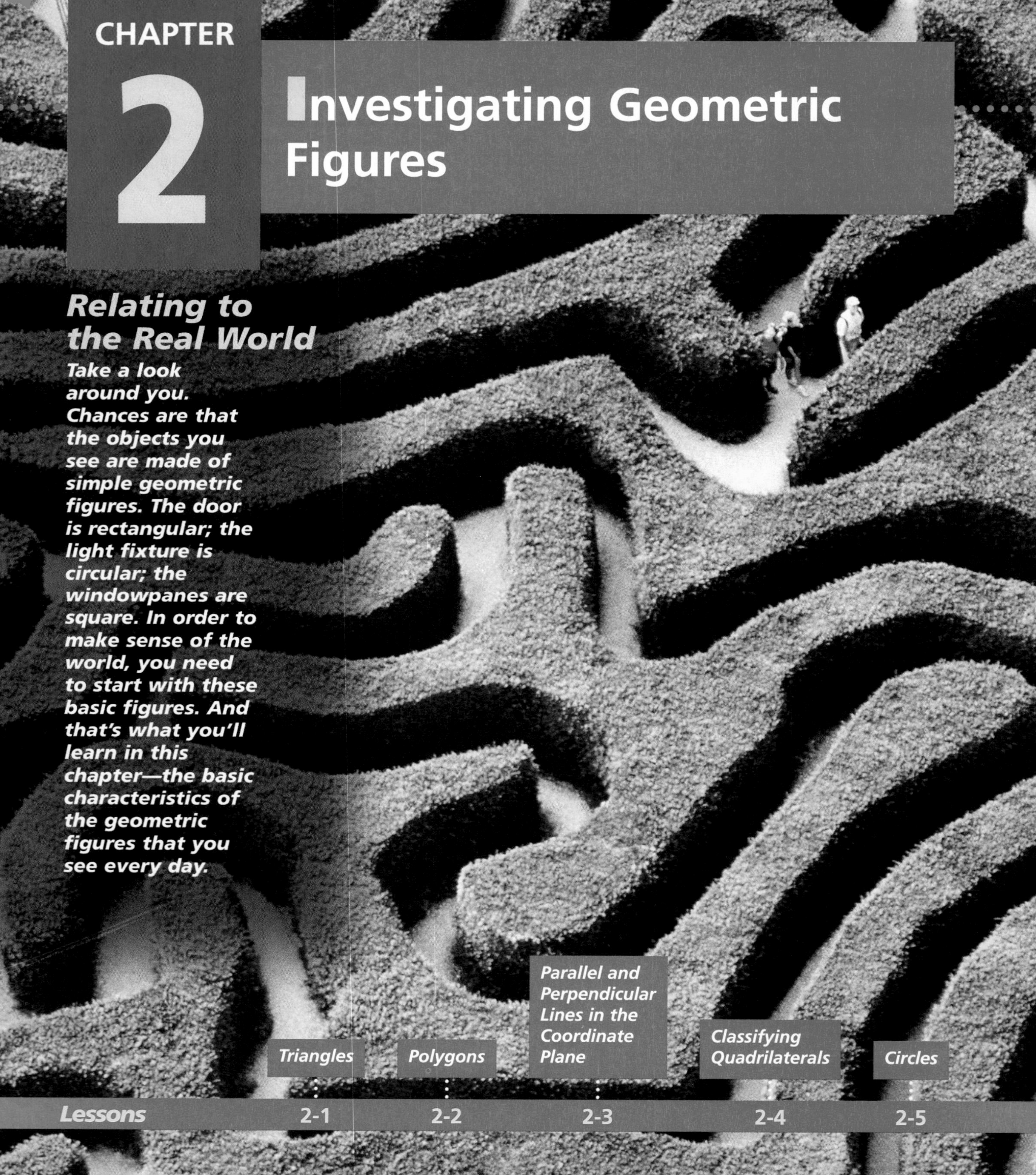

Relating to the Real World

Take a look around you. Chances are that the objects you see are made of simple geometric figures. The door is rectangular; the light fixture is circular; the windowpanes are square. In order to make sense of the world, you need to start with these basic figures. And that's what you'll learn in this chapter—the basic characteristics of the geometric figures that you see every day.

Lessons	2-1	2-2	2-3	2-4	2-5
	Triangles	*Polygons*	*Parallel and Perpendicular Lines in the Coordinate Plane*	*Classifying Quadrilaterals*	*Circles*

CHAPTER PROJECT

AMAZING SPACE

What is it about puzzles that makes them so popular? Is it that they always have a clear solution, in contrast to real-life problems? Or is it the way simple tasks can become complex and complex ones simple? Whatever the reasons, people have been solving puzzles since at least 2400 B.C. when magic squares were popular in China.

In this chapter project, you will explore shape puzzles, such as tangrams, which also originated in China. As you solve puzzles and create your own, you will see how simple shapes can mystify and enlighten—revealing secrets of how our world fits together.

To help you complete the project:

- **p. 636** *Find Out by Doing*
- **p. 643** *Find Out by Exploring*
- **p. 657** *Find Out by Analyzing*
- **p. 669** *Find Out by Investigating*
- **p. 677** *Find Out by Modeling*
- **p. 678** *Finishing the Project*

Congruent and Similar Figures 2-6

Isometric and Orthographic Drawings 2-7

2-1 Triangles

What You'll Learn

- Finding the measures of angles of a triangle
- Classifying triangles

...And Why

To increase your knowledge of triangles, the simplest polygons used in the design of furniture, buildings, and bridges

What You'll Need

- scissors
- protractor

TECHNOLOGY HINT

The Work Together could be done using geometry software.

WORK TOGETHER

Work in a group to explore the angle measures of triangles.

- Have each member of your group draw and cut out a large triangle.
- Number the angles and tear them off.
- Place the three angles adjacent to each other to form one angle.

1. Compare your results with group members. Describe your observations.
2. Make a **conjecture** about the sum of the measures of the angles of a triangle.

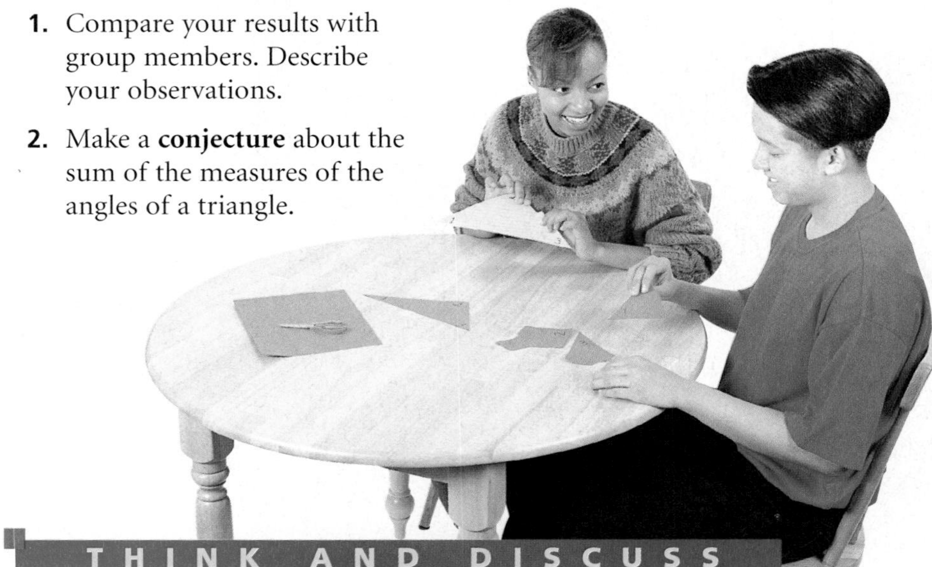

THINK AND DISCUSS

The Triangle Angle-Sum Theorem

The Work Together demonstrates the following theorem that you will prove in Chapter 7.

Theorem 2-1
Triangle Angle-Sum Theorem

The sum of the measures of the angles of a triangle is 180.

$m\angle A + m\angle B + m\angle C = 180$

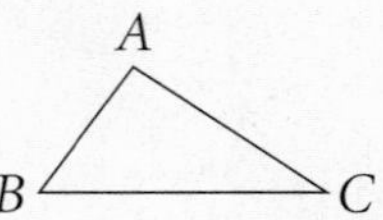

3. **Try This** Find the measure of each numbered angle.

a.
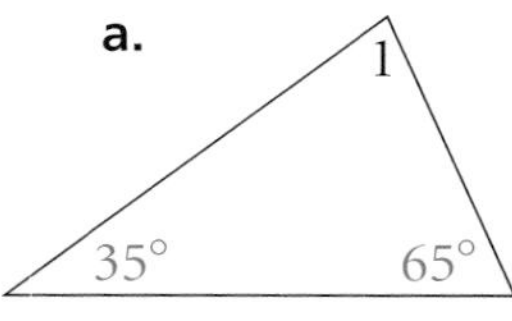

b.
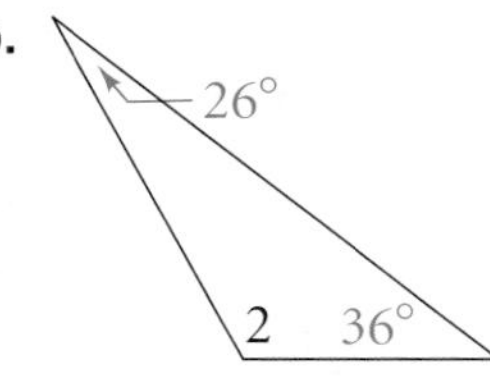

c.
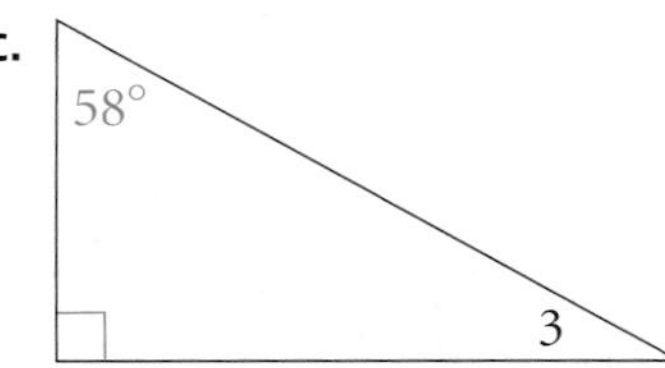

Example 1

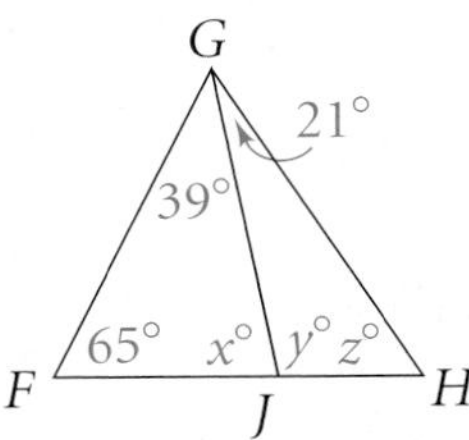

Find the values of x, y, and z.

To find the value of x, use $\triangle FJG$.

$65 + 39 + x = 180$	Triangle Angle-Sum Theorem
$104 + x = 180$	Simplify.
$x = 76$	Subtract 104 from each side.

To find the value of y, look at $\angle FJH$. It is a straight angle.

$m\angle GJF + m\angle GJH = 180$	Angle Addition Postulate
$76 + y = 180$	Substitution
$y = 104$	Subtract 76 from each side.

PROBLEM SOLVING

Look Back Check your answers by finding the sum of the measures of the angles in each triangle.

To find the value of z, use $\triangle GJH$.

$104 + 21 + z = 180$	Triangle Angle-Sum Theorem
$125 + z = 180$	Simplify the left side.
$z = 55$	Subtract 125 from each side.

4. **Critical Thinking** Describe how you could use $\triangle FGH$ instead of $\triangle GJH$ to find the value of z.
5. **Try This** Find the values of x and y.

a.

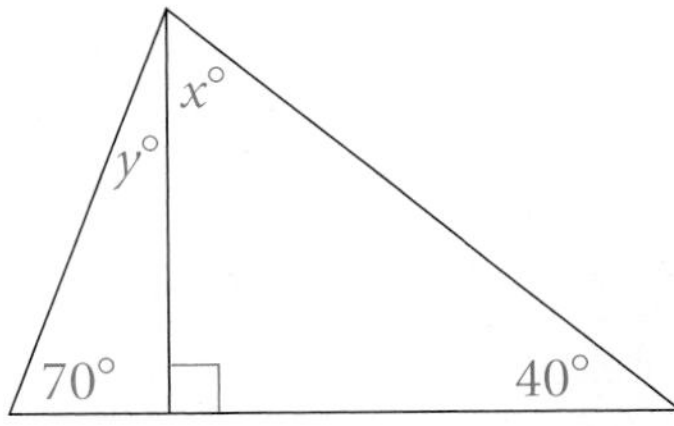

b.

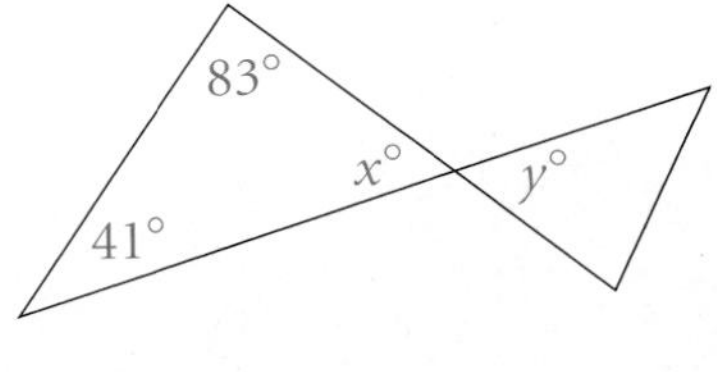

Exterior Angles of a Triangle

An **exterior angle** of a polygon is an angle formed by a side and an extension of a side. For each exterior angle of a triangle, the two non-adjacent interior angles are called its **remote interior angles.**

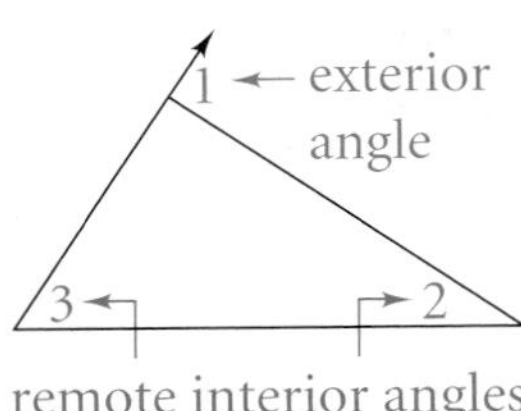

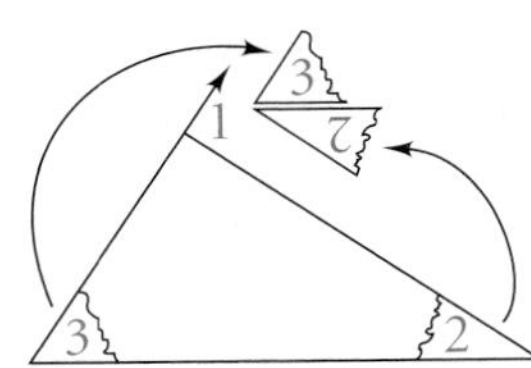

6. a. **Manipulatives** Draw and label a large triangle like the one shown at the left. Cut out the two remote interior angles and place them on the exterior angle as shown. What do you observe?
   b. Make a **conjecture** about the measure of an exterior angle of a triangle.

Your **conjecture** in Question 6 is the basis of the following theorem, which you will justify in Exercise 32.

Theorem 2-2
Exterior Angle Theorem

The measure of each exterior angle of a triangle equals the sum of the measures of its two remote interior angles.

$m\angle 1 = m\angle 2 + m\angle 3$

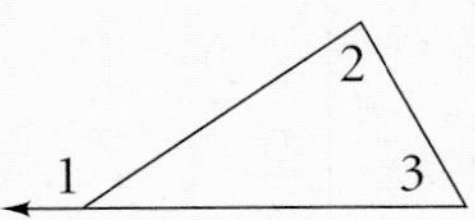

7. Try This Find the measure of each numbered exterior angle.

a. 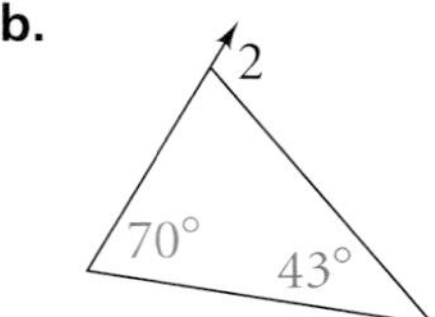

b. 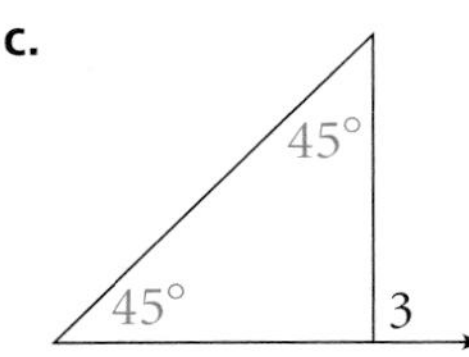

c.

A **corollary** is a statement that follows directly from a theorem. The following statement is a corollary to the Exterior Angle Theorem.

Corollary to Theorem 2-2

The measure of an exterior angle of a triangle is greater than the measure of either of its remote interior angles.

$m\angle 1 > m\angle 2$ and $m\angle 1 > m\angle 3$

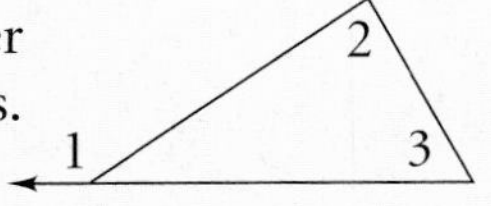

8. Use what you know from the Exterior Angle Theorem to explain why this corollary makes sense.

Example 2 **Relating to the Real World** 

Furniture Design The lounge chair has different settings that change the angle between the seat and the back. Find the angle at which the chair in the diagram at the left is reclining.

$m\angle 1 = m\angle LGN + m\angle GNL$	Exterior Angle Theorem
$m\angle 1 = 56 + 78$	Substitution
$m\angle 1 = 134$	Simplify.

The chair is reclining at a 134° angle.

9. Explain how you could have found $m\angle 1$ without using the Exterior Angle Theorem.

10. Try This You change the setting on the chair so that $m\angle NGL = 90$ and $m\angle GNL = 45$. Find the angle at which the chair is reclining.

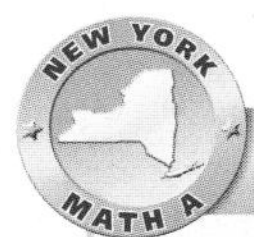

Math A Test Prep

1 Which angles could an obtuse triangle have?
(1) two right angles
(2) two obtuse angles
(3) two acute angles
(4) two vertical angles

2 Classify the triangle shown by its sides and angles. Then find the measure of each of the congruent angles.

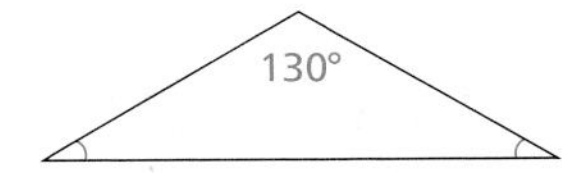

Classifying Triangles

In Chapter 1, you classified an angle by its measure. You can classify a triangle by its sides and by its angles.

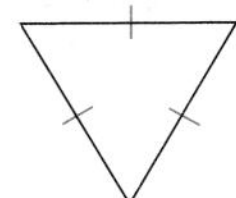

equilateral
all sides congruent

isosceles
at least two sides congruent

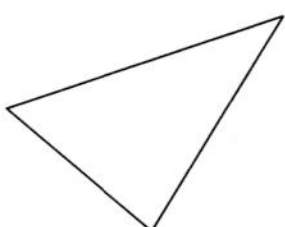

scalene
no sides congruent

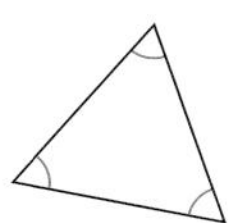

equiangular
all angles congruent

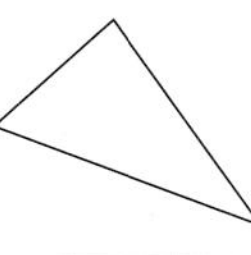

acute
all angles acute

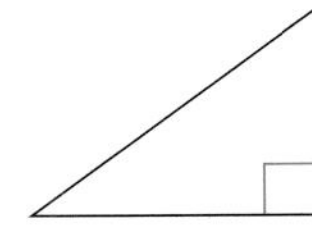

right
one right angle

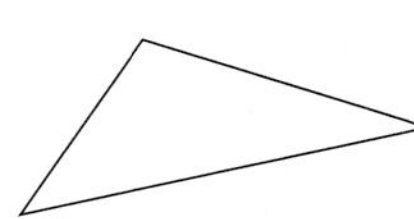

obtuse
one obtuse angle

11. Try This Draw and label a triangle to fit each description. If no triangle can be drawn, write *not possible* and explain.

a. acute scalene
b. right isosceles
c. obtuse equilateral
d. acute isosceles

Exercises ON YOUR OWN

Use a protractor and a centimenter ruler to measure the sides and angles of each triangle. Classify each triangle by its sides and angles.

1. 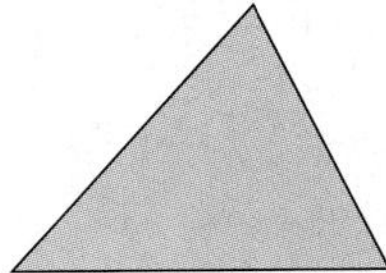

2. 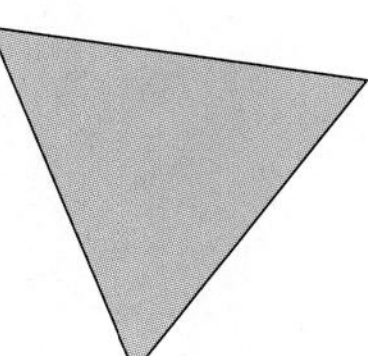

3. 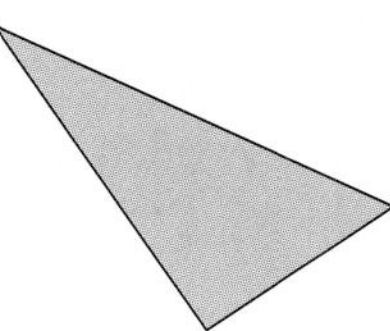

4. 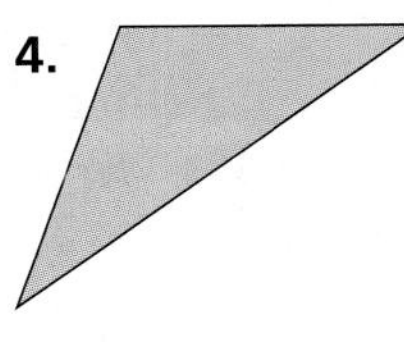

Sketch a triangle to fit each description. If no triangle can be drawn, write *not possible* and explain.

5. obtuse scalene
6. right equilateral
7. acute equilateral
8. obtuse isosceles

9. a. Logical Reasoning What is the measure of each angle of an equiangular triangle? **Justify** your reasoning.
b. What is the sum of the measures of the acute angles of a right triangle? **Justify** your reasoning.

Choose **Use paper and pencil, mental math, or a calculator to find the values of the variables.**

10.

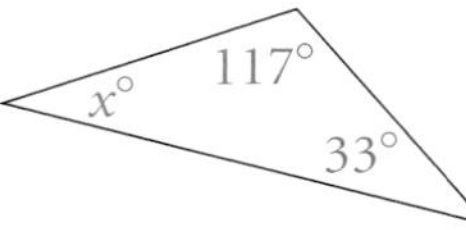

11.

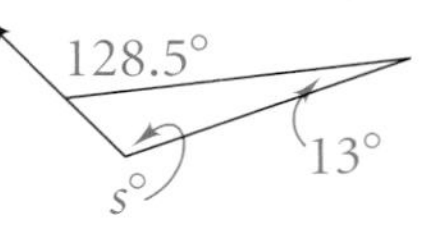

12.

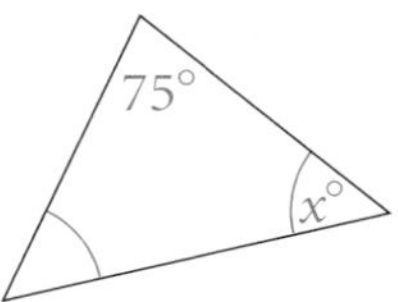

13.

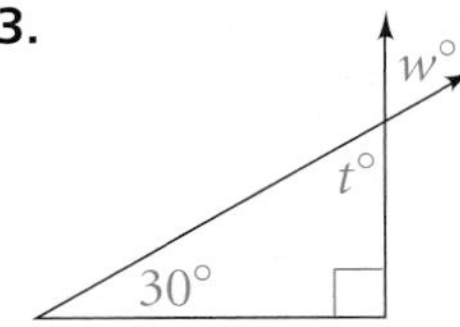

14.

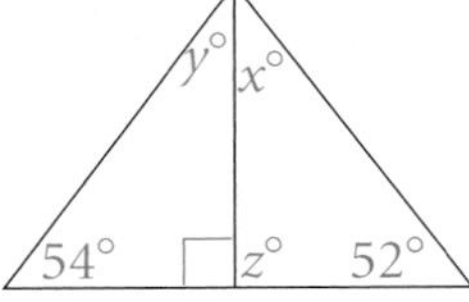

15.

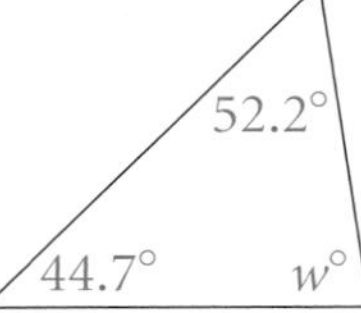

16.

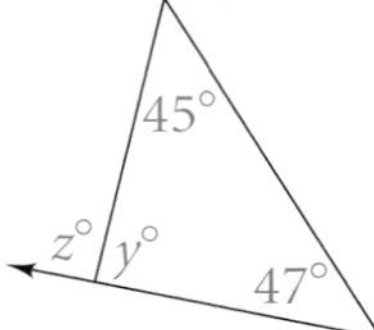

17.

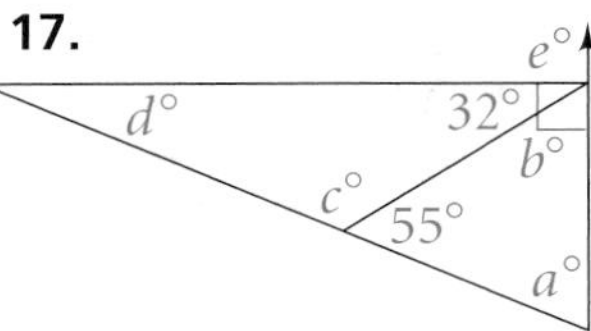

Use the figure at the right for Exercises 18–20.

18. Find $m\angle 3$ if $m\angle 5 = 130$ and $m\angle 4 = 70$.

19. Find $m\angle 1$ if $m\angle 5 = 142$ and $m\angle 4 = 65$.

20. Find $m\angle 2$ if $m\angle 3 = 125$ and $m\angle 4 = 23$.

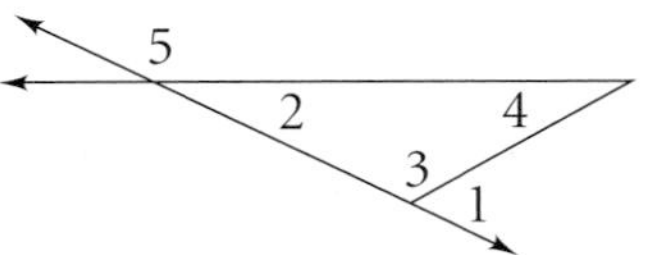

21. **Standardized Test Prep** The measures of the angles of a triangle are shown below. In which case is x *not* an integer?

A. $x, 2x, 3x$ **B.** $x, 3x, 5x$ **C.** $x, 3x, 4x$ **D.** $x, 4x, 7x$ **E.** $2x, 3x, 4x$

22. The measure of one angle of a triangle is 115. The other two angles are congruent. Find their measures.

23. **Writing** Is every equilateral triangle isosceles? Is every isosceles triangle equilateral? Explain.

24. **Algebra** A right triangle has acute angles whose measures are in the ratio 1 : 2. Find the measures of these angles. (*Hint:* Let x and $2x$ represent the angle measures.)

25. **Music** The top of a grand piano is held open by props of varying lengths, depending upon the desired volume of the music. The longest prop makes an angle of 57° with the piano. What is the angle of opening between the piano and its top?

26. **Critical Thinking** Rosa makes the following claim: The ratio of the lengths of the three sides of a triangle equals the ratio of the three angle measures. Give examples to support her claim or one counterexample to disprove it.

Algebra Find the measures of the angles of each triangle. Classify each triangle by its angles.

27. 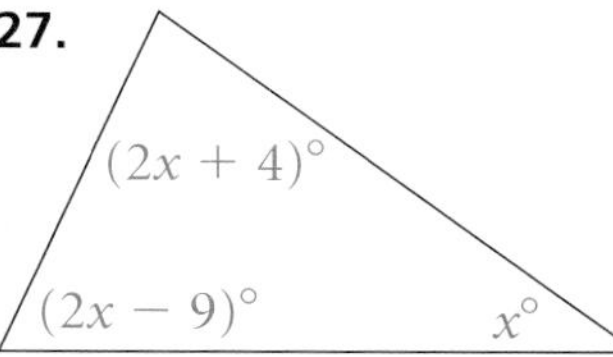

28. 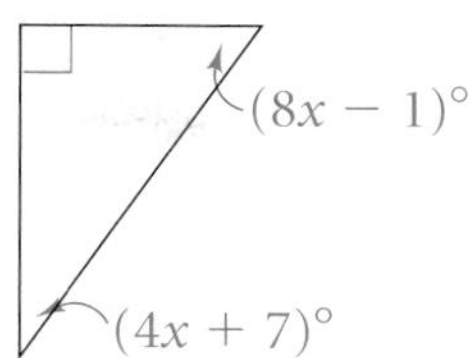

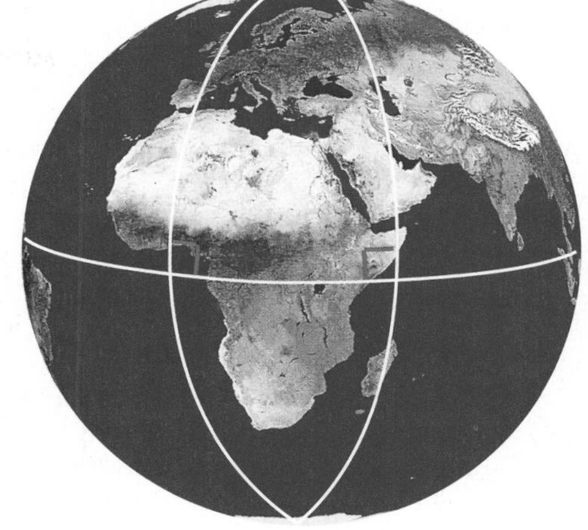

29. **Geometry on a Sphere** Suppose you were measuring the angles of a triangle on a globe. The meridians of longitude pass through both poles and are perpendicular to the equator. Will the sum of the measures of the angles of this triangle be equal to, greater than, or less than 180? Explain.

30. a. **Algebra** The ratio of the angle measures in $\triangle BCR$ is 2 : 3 : 4. Find the angle measures.
    b. What type of triangle is $\triangle BCR$?

31. a. **Probability** Find the probability that a triangle is equiangular if the measure of each of its angles is a multiple of 30.
    b. Find the probability that a triangle is equiangular if the measure of each of its angles is a multiple of 20.

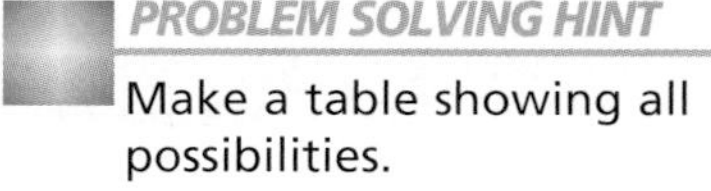

PROBLEM SOLVING HINT

Make a table showing all possibilities.

32. **Logical Reasoning** Complete the following statements to **justify** the Exterior Angle Theorem.
    a. By the Angle Addition Postulate, $m\angle 1 + m\angle 4 = ■$.
    b. By the Triangle Angle-Sum Theorem, $m\angle 2 + m\angle 3 + m\angle 4 = ■$.
    c. By the __?__ Property, $m\angle 1 + m\angle 4 = m\angle 2 + m\angle 3 + m\angle 4$.
    d. By the __?__ Property of Equality, $m\angle 1 = m\angle 2 + m\angle 3$.

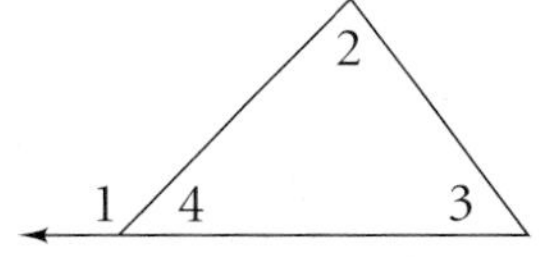

33. The measures of the angles of $\triangle RST$ are $\sqrt{x}$, $2\sqrt{x}$, and $3\sqrt{x}$.
    a. Find the value of x and the measures of the angles.
    b. What type of triangle is $\triangle RST$?

34. **Weaving** Patricia Tsinnie, a Navajo weaver, often uses isosceles triangles in her designs.
    a. Trace the design shown below. Then use a colored pencil to outline isosceles triangles used in the design.
    b. **Open-ended** Make a repeated design of your own that uses isosceles triangles.

Chapter Project

Find Out by Doing

The *tangram,* known in China as the *ch'i-ch'iao t'u,* meaning "ingenious seven-piece plan," is one of the oldest manipulative puzzles. You can use paper folding to make your own tangram.

- Fold a square sheet of paper in half four times and then unfold it. Draw the segments shown to form seven tangram pieces, called *tans.*

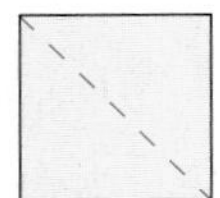 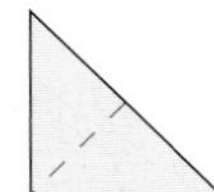   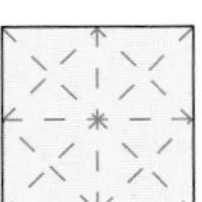 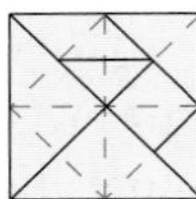

- Cut out the seven tans.

How many of the tans are triangles? Form other triangles by placing tans together. Make a sketch of each. Classify each triangle by its sides and angles. Can you make one triangle using all seven tans?

Exercises MIXED REVIEW

Draw the next figure in each sequence.

35.  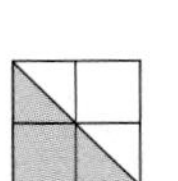 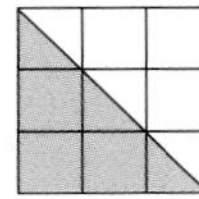

36. 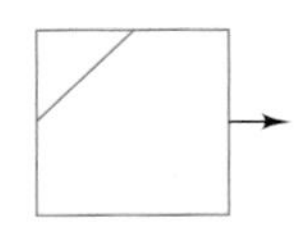 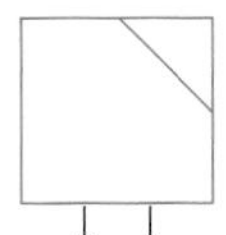 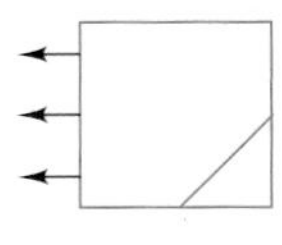

Find the length of $\overline{WZ}$ to the nearest tenth.

37. $W(8, -2)$ and $Z(2, 6)$

38. $W(-4.5, 1.2)$ and $Z(3.5, -2.8)$

39. In the figure, $m\angle AOB = 3x + 20$, $m\angle BOC = x + 32$, and $m\angle AOC = 80$. Find the value of x.

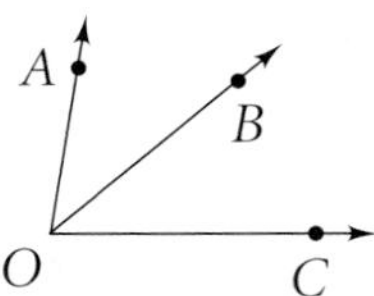

Getting Ready for Lesson 2-2

Find (a) the measure of each angle of quadrilateral *ABCD,* and (b) the sum of the measures of the angles of quadrilateral *ABCD.*

40. 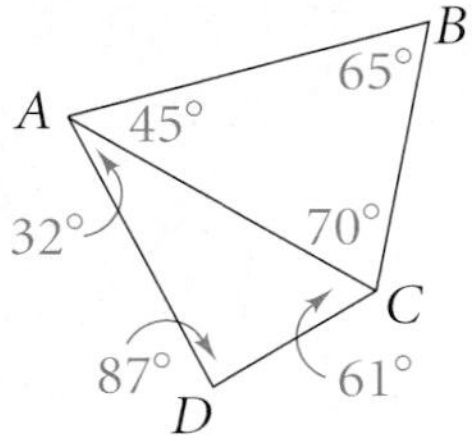

41. 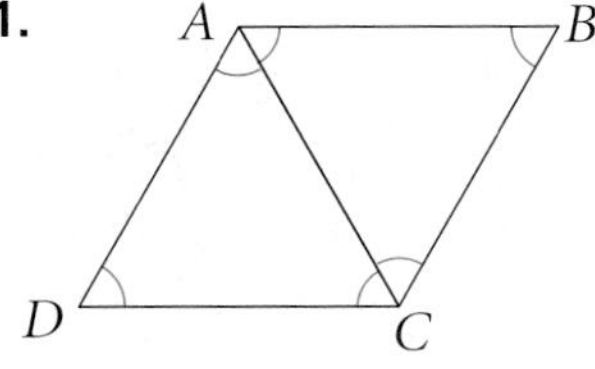

42. 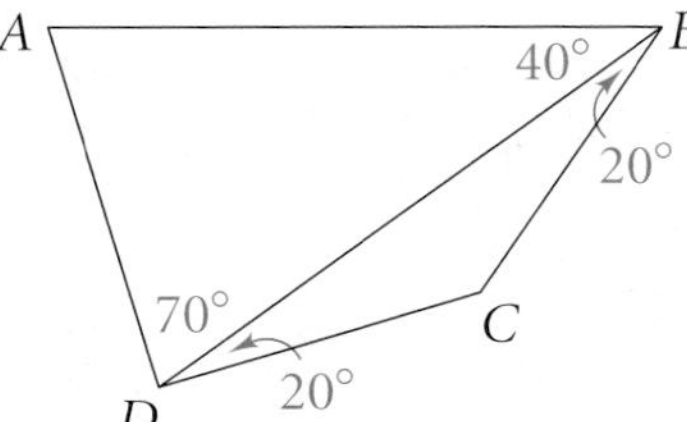

Technology

Exploring the Exterior Angles of a Polygon

With Lesson 2-2

Work in pairs or small groups.

Construct

Use geometry software. Construct a convex polygon. Extend each side as shown. To measure the exterior angles you will need to mark a point on each ray.

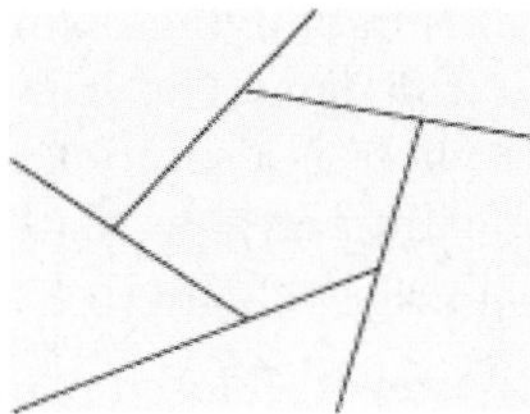

Investigate

- Measure each exterior angle.
- Calculate the sum of the measures of the exterior angles.
- Manipulate the polygon, making sure it remains convex. Observe the sum of the measures of the exterior angles.

Conjecture

- Write a conjecture about the sum of the measures of the exterior angles (one at each vertex) of a convex polygon.
- Test your conjecture with another polygon.

Extend

The figures below show a polygon that is decreasing in size until finally it "disappears." Describe how these figures could be used as a justification for your conjecture.

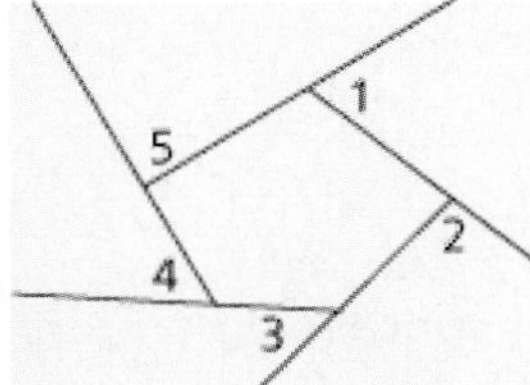

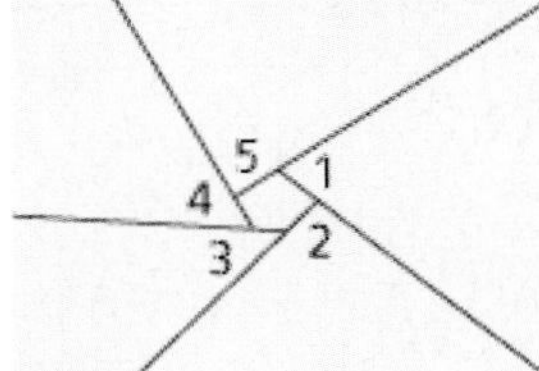

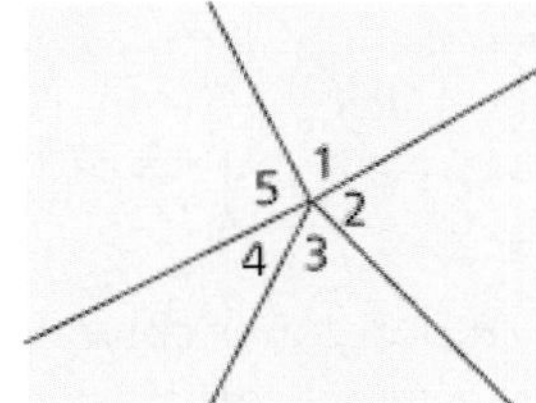

What You'll Learn

- Classifying polygons
- Finding the sum of the measures of the interior and exterior angles of polygons

...And Why

To increase your understanding of polygons, which are found in art and nature as well as in manufactured products

2-2 Polygons

THINK AND DISCUSS

Polygons and Interior Angles

Walking around a city, you can see polygons in buildings, windows, and traffic signs. The grillwork in the photo is a combination of different polygons that form a pleasing pattern.

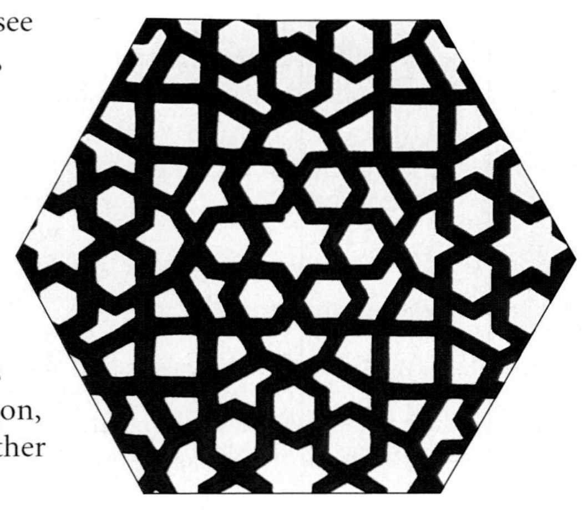

A **polygon** is a closed plane figure with at least three sides. The sides intersect only at their endpoints and no adjacent sides are collinear. To identify a polygon, start at any vertex and list the other vertices consecutively.

Polygon	Number of Sides
triangle	3
quadrilateral	4
pentagon	5
hexagon	6
heptagon	7
octagon	8
nonagon	9
decagon	10
dodecagon	12
n-gon	*n*

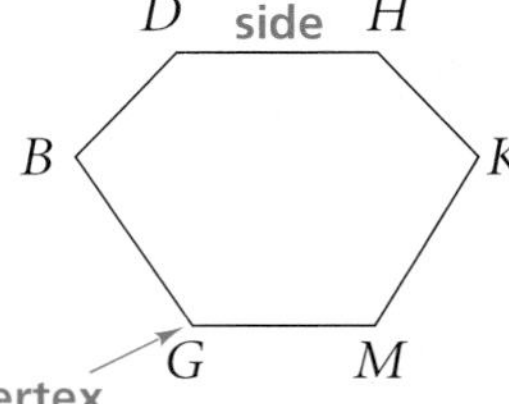

polygon $DHKMGB$

sides: $\overline{DH}, \overline{HK}, \overline{KM}, \overline{MG}, \overline{GB}, \overline{BD}$

vertices: D, H, K, M, G, B

angles: $\angle D, \angle H, \angle K, \angle M, \angle G, \angle B$

You can classify polygons by the number of sides. The most common polygons are listed at the left.

A polygon is **convex** if no diagonal contains points outside the polygon.

A polygon is **concave** if a diagonal contains points outside the polygon.

QUICK REVIEW

A diagonal of a polygon is a segment that connects two nonconsecutive vertices.

In this textbook, the term *polygon* refers to a convex polygon unless otherwise stated.

1. **Open-ended** Draw a convex and a concave octagon. Draw diagonals and explain why one octagon is convex and the other is concave.

WORK TOGETHER

You can use triangles and the Triangle Angle-Sum Theorem to find the measures of the interior angles of a polygon. Work with a partner. Record your data in a table like the one shown below.

- Sketch polygons with 4, 5, 6, 7, and 8 sides.
- Divide each polygon into triangles by drawing all the diagonals from one vertex.
- Multiply the number of triangles by 180 to find the sum of the measures of the interior angles of each polygon.

2. **Inductive Reasoning** Look for a pattern in the table. Write a rule for finding the sum of the measures of the interior angles of a polygon with n sides.

Polygon	Number of Sides	Number of Triangles Formed	Sum of the Interior Angle Measures
 ▱	4	▪	▪ • 180 = ▪

THINK AND DISCUSS

The results of the Work Together suggest the following theorem.

Theorem 2-3
Polygon Interior Angle-Sum Theorem

The sum of the measures of the interior angles of an n-gon is $(n - 2)180$.

3. **Try This** Find the sum of the measures of the interior angles of each polygon.
   a. 15-gon
   b. 20-gon
   c. decagon
   d. dodecagon

Example 1

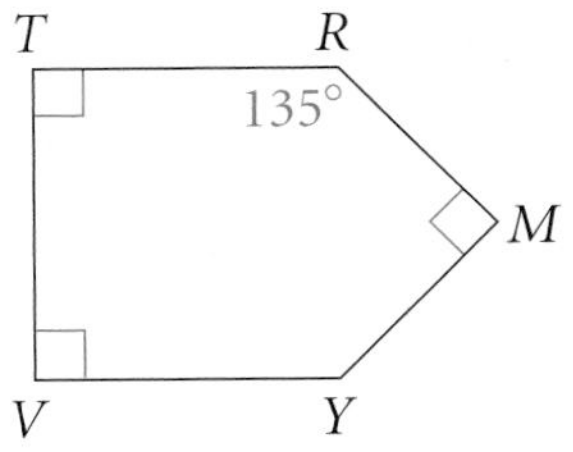

T R 135° M V Y

Find $m\angle Y$ in $TVYMR$.

Use the Polygon Interior Angle-Sum Theorem for $n = 5$.

$$m\angle T + m\angle V + m\angle Y + m\angle M + m\angle R = (5 - 2)180$$
$$90 + 90 + m\angle Y + 90 + 135 = 540$$
$$m\angle Y + 405 = 540$$
$$m\angle Y = 135$$

Math A Test Prep

1 Which of the following could be the measure of an interior angle of a regular polygon?
(1) 144° (3) 155°
(2) 110° (4) 121°

2 What is the value of k?

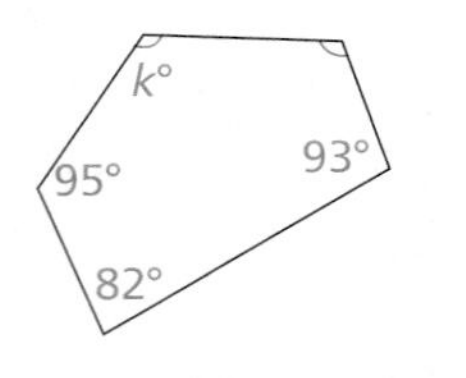

Exterior Angles

Technology The figures below show one exterior angle drawn at each vertex of each polygon.

4. a. Find the sum of the measures of the exterior angles (one at each vertex) of each polygon.

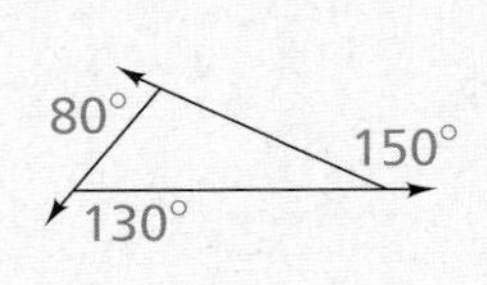

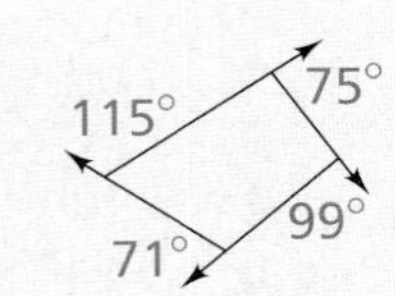

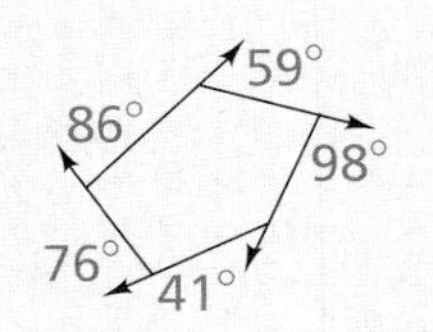

b. Make a conjecture about the sum of the measures of the exterior angles (one at each vertex) of a polygon.

This inductive reasoning leads to the following theorem.

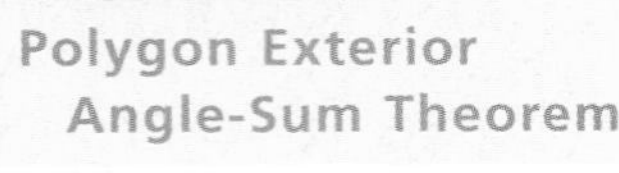

Theorem 2-4
Polygon Exterior Angle-Sum Theorem

The sum of the measures of the exterior angles of a polygon, one at each vertex, is 360.

An **equilateral polygon** has all sides congruent. An **equiangular polygon** has all angles congruent. A **regular polygon** is equilateral and equiangular.

Regular Octagon

Example 2

Find the measure of an interior angle and an exterior angle of a regular octagon.

Method 1: Find the measure of an interior angle first.

Sum of the measures of the interior angles = $(8 - 2)180 = 1080$

- Measure of one interior angle $= \frac{1080}{8} = 135$
- Measure of its adjacent exterior angle $= 180 - 135 = 45$

Method 2: Find the measure of an exterior angle first.

Sum of the measures of the exterior angles = 360

- Measure of one exterior angle $= \frac{360}{8} = 45$
- Measure of its adjacent interior angle = $180 - 45 = 135$

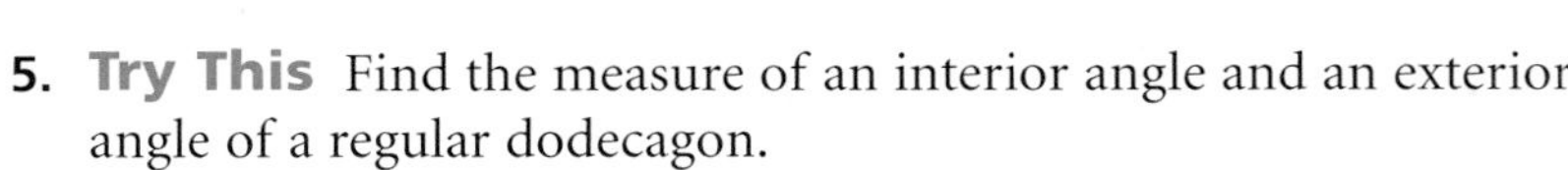

5. Try This Find the measure of an interior angle and an exterior angle of a regular dodecagon.

Example 3 Relating to the Real World 

Manufacturing Mindco, a toy manufacturer, is packaging a Chinese checkers game. The game consists of colored pegs and a regular hexagonal wooden board. Mindco is packaging the game in a rectangular box using four right triangles made of foam. Find the measures of the acute angles of each foam triangle.

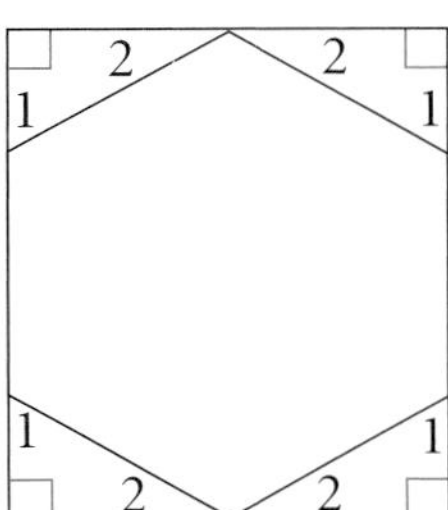

$\angle 1$ is an exterior angle of a regular hexagon.

Find $m\angle 1$ and then use the Triangle Angle-Sum Theorem to find $m\angle 2$.

$6 \cdot m\angle 1 = 360$	Sum of the measures of the exterior $\angle$s of a polygon = 360.
$m\angle 1 = 60$	Divide each side by 6.
$m\angle 1 + m\angle 2 + 90 = 180$	Triangle Angle-Sum Thm.
$60 + m\angle 2 + 90 = 180$	Substitution
$m\angle 2 + 150 = 180$	Simplify.
$m\angle 2 = 30$	Subtract 150 from each side.

The measures of the acute angles of each foam triangle are 60 and 30.

Exercises ON YOUR OWN

Classify each polygon by its number of sides. Identify which polygons are convex and which are concave.

1. 

2. 

3. 

4. 

Draw each regular polygon.

Sample: dodecagon

Draw a circle. Use a protractor to locate 12 points equidistant around a circle. (These points will be located every 30 degrees around a circle, since $360° \div 12 = 30°$.) Connect these points to form a regular dodecagon.

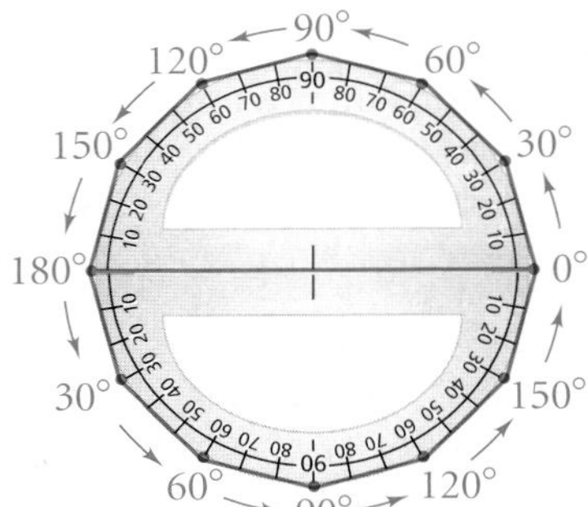

5. triangle

6. quadrilateral

7. pentagon

8. hexagon

9. **Design** A theater-in-the-round is constructed so that the audience surrounds the stage. Such theaters are not always circular in shape, however. Classify the theater-in-the-round shown in the diagram below the photo, by the number of sides. Find the measure of each numbered angle.

Find the measure of an interior angle and an exterior angle for each regular polygon.

10. pentagon 11. nonagon 12. 18-gon 13. y-gon

The measure of an exterior angle of a regular polygon is given. Find the number of sides.

14. 72 15. 36 16. 18 17. x

18. **Writing** Keach said that he drew a regular polygon and measured one of its interior angles. He got 130°. Explain to him why this is impossible.

Choose **Use pencil and paper, mental math, or a calculator to find the values of the variables.**

19.
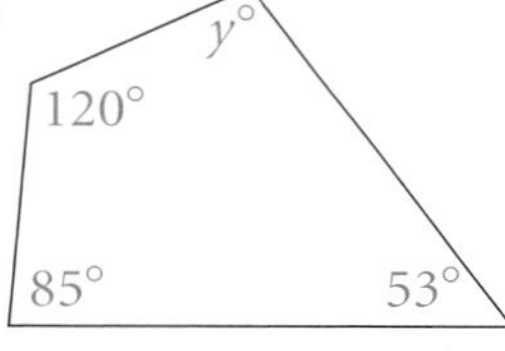

20.
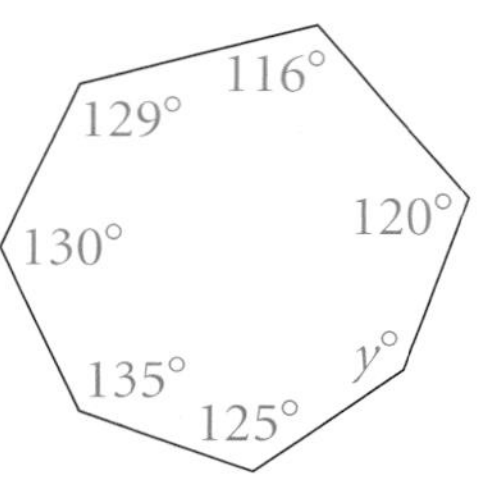

21.
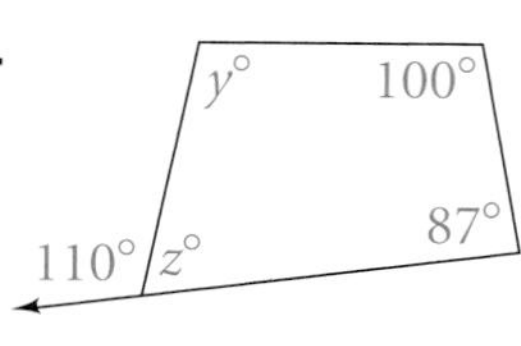

22.
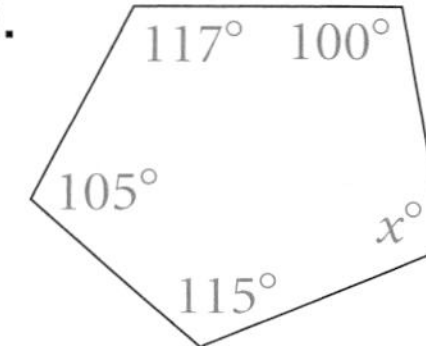

23.
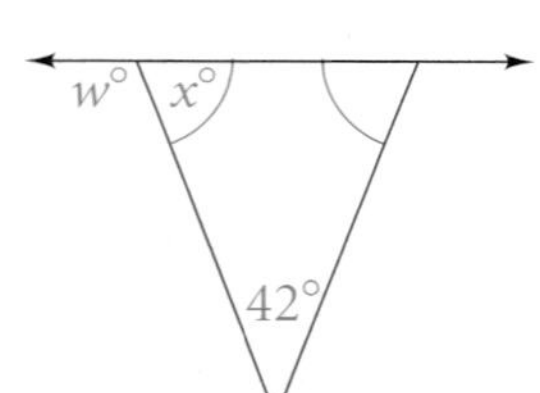

24.
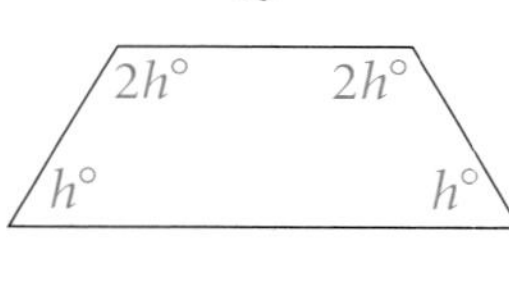

25.
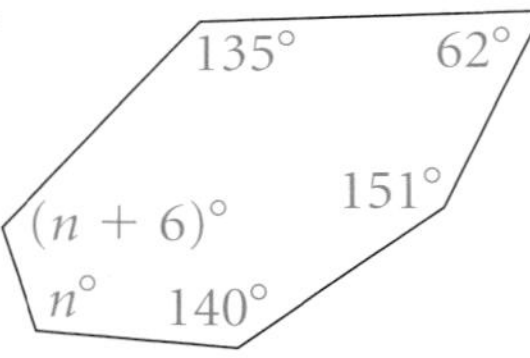

26.
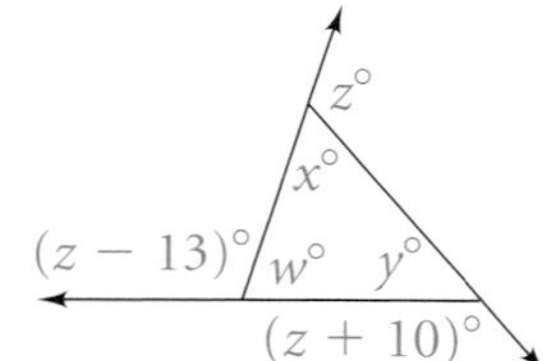

27. a. **Calculator** Find the measure of an interior angle of a regular n-gon for $n = 20, 40, 60, 80, \ldots 200$. Record your results as ordered pairs (n, measure of each interior angle).
b. Show your results on a graph like the one at the right.
c. **Data Analysis** What predictions would you make about the measure of an interior angle of a regular 1000-gon?
d. Is there a regular n-gon with an interior angle of 180°? Explain.

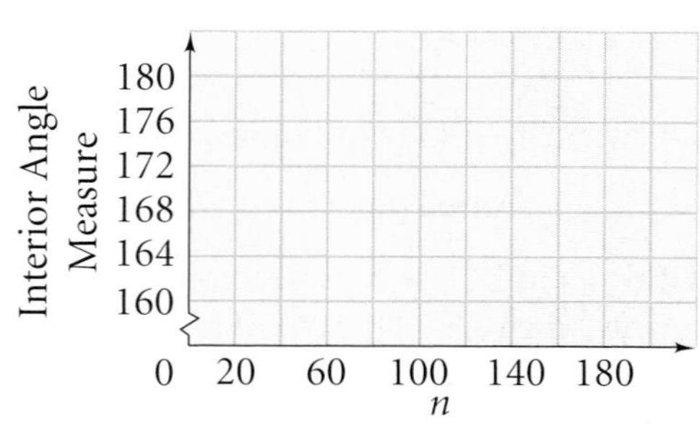

28. **Probability** Find the probability that the measure of an interior angle of a regular n-gon is a positive integer if n is an integer and $3 \leq n \leq 12$.

29. a. **Open-ended** Sketch a quadrilateral that is not equiangular.
    b. Sketch an equiangular quadrilateral that is not regular.

30. **Critical Thinking** Laura suggests another way to find the sum of the measures of the interior angles of an n-gon. She picks an interior point of the figure, draws segments to each vertex, counts the number of triangles, multiplies by 180, then subtracts 360. Does her method work? Explain.

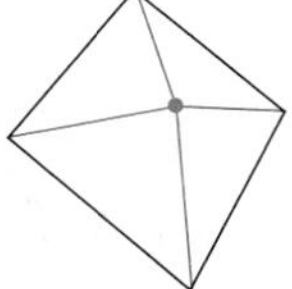

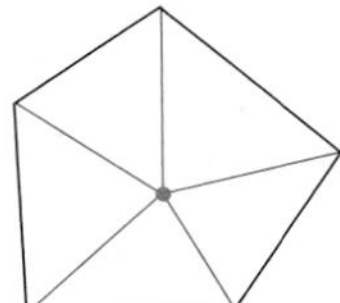

Chapter Project

Find Out by Exploring

In 1942, two mathematicians at the University of Chekiang in China proved that only 13 convex polygons could be formed by using all 7 tans. They were able to form 1 triangle, 6 quadrilaterals, 2 pentagons, and 4 hexagons. Try to make these using your set of tans. Make a sketch of each figure.

Exercises MIXED REVIEW

Identify the following.

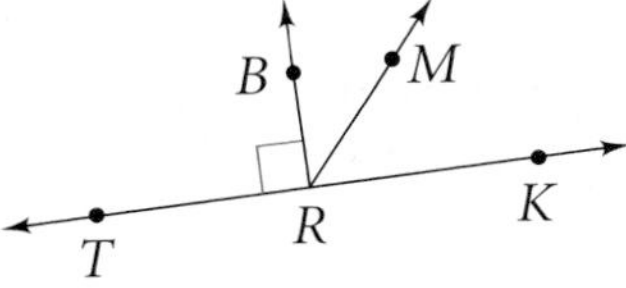

31. a pair of opposite rays
32. two right angles
33. a pair of supplementary angles
34. a pair of complementary angles

Choose **Use paper and pencil, mental math, or a calculator to find the values of the variables.**

35.
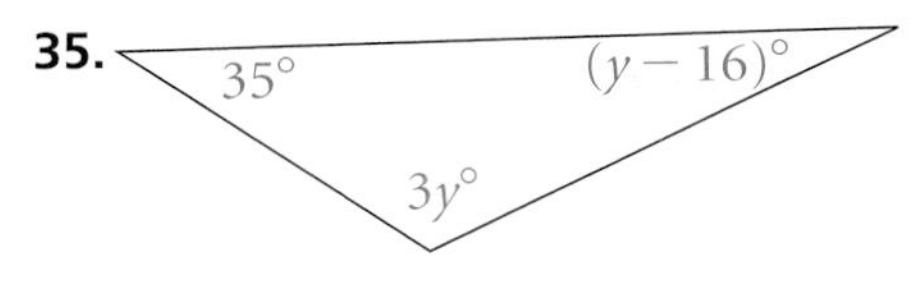

36.
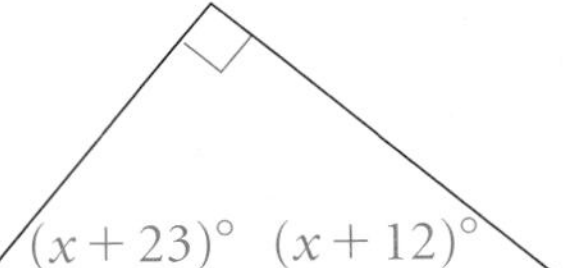

37.
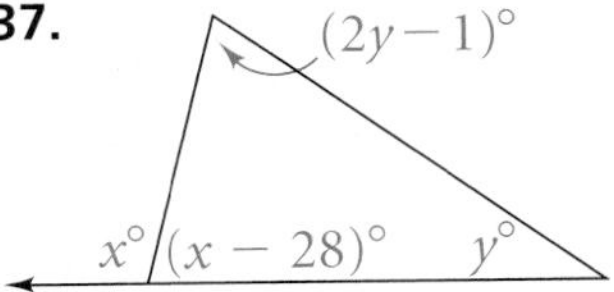

38. The measure of an angle is one-third the measure of its supplement. Find the measures of the angles.

39. The measure of an angle is four times the measure of its complement. Find the measures of the angles.

Getting Ready for Lesson 2-3

Find $\frac{y_2 - y_1}{x_2 - x_1}$.

40. $(x_1, y_1) = (3, 5)$ and $(x_2, y_2) = (1, 4)$
41. $(x_1, y_1) = (-2, 6)$ and $(x_2, y_2) = (3, 1)$
42. $(x_1, y_1) = (1, -8)$ and $(x_2, y_2) = (1, 2)$
43. $(x_1, y_1) = (-5, 3)$ and $(x_2, y_2) = (1, 3)$

Math ToolboX — Technology

Exploring Equations of Lines

With Lesson 2-3

Work in pairs or small groups. To make sure that the viewing grid on your graphing calculator screen is square, press ZOOM 5.

Investigate

- Use your graphing calculator to graph the lines $y = x$, $y = 2x$, and $y = 3x$. Experiment with other equations of lines in the form $y = mx$. Substitute fractions and negative numbers for m. How does the value of m affect the graph of a line?
- Graph the lines $y = x + 1$, $y = x + 2$, and $y = x + 3$. Experiment with other equations of lines in the form $y = x + b$. Substitute fractions and negative numbers for b. How does the value of b affect the graph of a line?

Conjecture

When you graph an equation in the form $y = mx + b$, how do the values of m and b affect the graph of the line? List all your **conjectures.**

Extend

- Graph the lines $y = -\frac{2}{3}x$, $y = -\frac{2}{3}x + 3$, and $y = -\frac{2}{3}x - 2$. What appears to be true of these lines? How are the values of m related? Make a **conjecture** about the graphs of equations of lines where the values of m are the same. Test your **conjecture** by graphing several equations of lines where the values of m are the same.
- Graph each pair of lines:

  a. $y = \frac{1}{2}x$, $y = -2x$

  b. $y = \frac{3}{4}x$, $y = -\frac{4}{3}x$

  c. $y = 5x$, $y = -\frac{1}{5}x$

  What appears to be true of these lines? For each pair, how are the values of m related? Make a **conjecture** about the graphs of equations of lines where the product of the values of m is -1. Test your **conjecture** by graphing several pairs of equations of lines where the product of the values of m is -1.

What You'll Learn

- Graphing lines in the coordinate plane
- Recognizing parallel and perpendicular lines by their slopes

...And Why

To familiarize yourself with parallel and perpendicular lines, which are essential to the construction of houses, furniture, and machinery

What You'll Need

graph paper, ruler

2-3 Parallel and Perpendicular Lines in the Coordinate Plane

THINK AND DISCUSS

Slope and Graphing Lines

In everyday life the word *slope* refers to the steepness of a mountain, the grade of a road, or the pitch of a roof. In algebra, the *slope* of a line is the ratio of the vertical change to the horizontal change between any two points on a line.

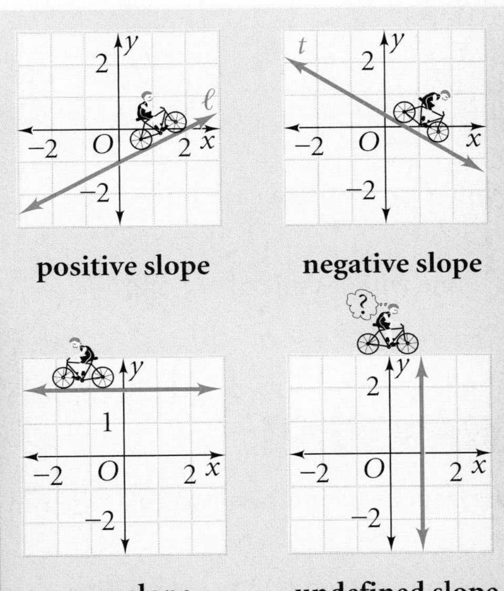

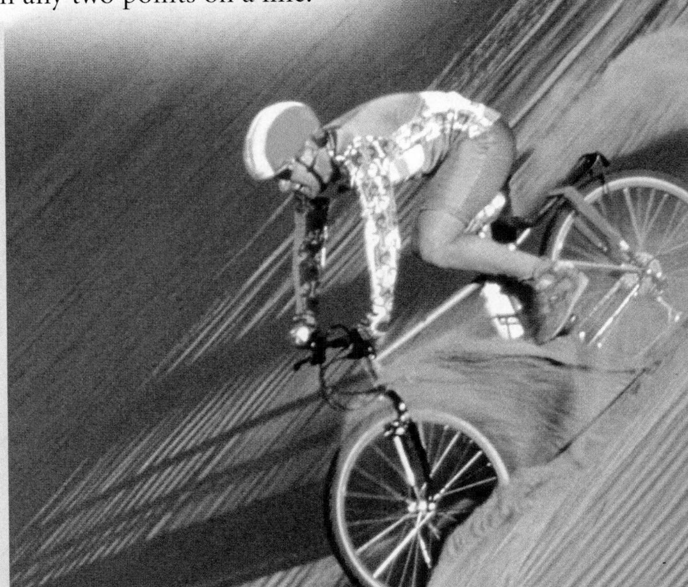

QUICK REVIEW

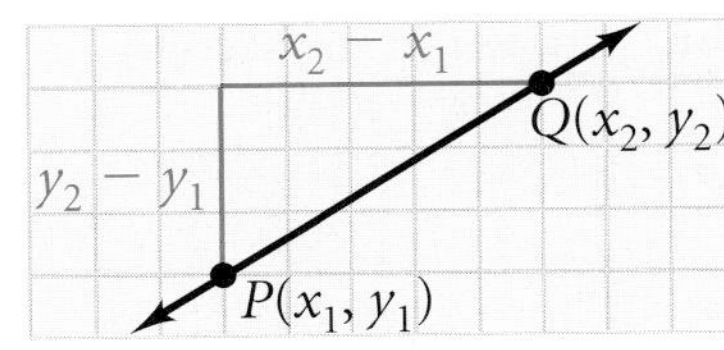

$$\text{Slope} = \frac{\text{vertical change (rise)}}{\text{horizontal change (run)}}$$

$$m = \frac{y_2 - y_1}{x_2 - x_1}$$

1. a. Use $\frac{\text{vertical change}}{\text{horizontal change}}$ to find the slopes of line ℓ and line t shown above.

b. Explain why the slope of a horizontal line is zero.

c. Explain why the slope of a vertical line is undefined.

2. Try This Use these pairs of points to answer parts (a)–(c).

$R(-3, -4), S(5, -4)$ $\quad$ $C(-2, 2), D(4, -2)$

$K(-3, 3), T(-3, 1)$ $\quad$ $P(3, 0), Y(0, -5)$

a. Graph and label a line that contains each pair of points.

b. Mental Math Decide whether the slope of each line is positive, negative, zero, or undefined.

c. Find the slope of each line.

You can graph a line by starting at a given point and using the slope of the line to plot another point.

Example 1

Graph the line $y = \frac{3}{4}x + 2$.

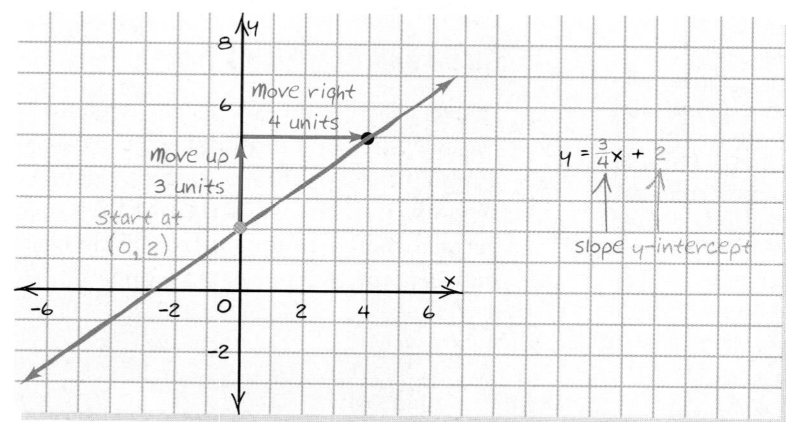

QUICK REVIEW

The slope-intercept form of a linear equation is

$y = mx + b$.

slope y-intercept

3. **Try This** Use the slope and y-intercept to graph each line.
   a. $y = 3x - 4$ b. $y = \frac{1}{2}x + 3$ c. $y = -2x - 1$.
4. Describe how you would graph a line with a slope of $-\frac{1}{2}$ and a y-intercept of 0.

WORK TOGETHER

Work in a group to explore the slopes of parallel and perpendicular lines in a coordinate plane.

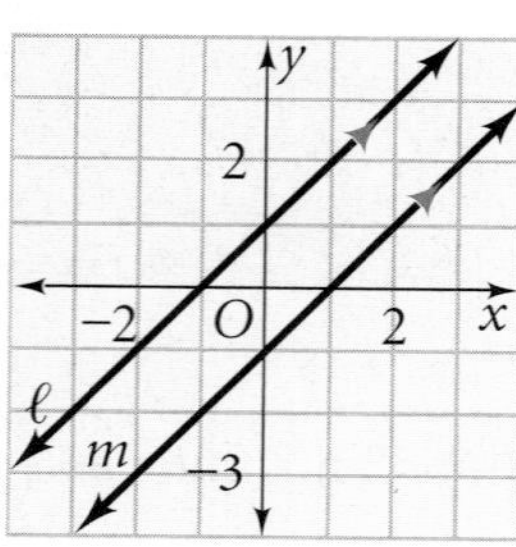

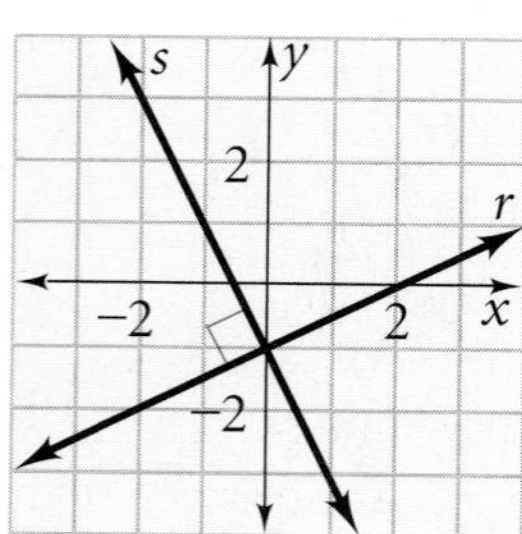

5. a. Find the slopes of both parallel lines shown in the first graph at the left.
   b. Have each member draw a pair of nonvertical parallel lines on graph paper and find the slopes of both lines.
   c. Compare your results with group members. Make a **conjecture** about the slopes of parallel lines.
6. a. Find the slopes of both perpendicular lines shown in the second graph at the left.
   b. Have each member draw a line on graph paper. (Do not use a vertical or horizontal line.) Then use a corner of the paper to draw a line perpendicular to it. Find the slopes of both lines. Find the product of the slopes.
   c. Compare your results with group members. Make a **conjecture** about the product of the slopes of two perpendicular lines.

THINK AND DISCUSS

Parallel and Perpendicular Lines

Your observations in the Work Together are summarized below.

Slopes of Parallel and Perpendicular Lines

The slopes of nonvertical parallel lines are equal. Two lines with the same slope are parallel. Vertical lines are parallel.

The product of the slopes of two perpendicular lines, neither of which is vertical, is -1. If the product of the slopes of the two lines is -1, then the lines are perpendicular. A horizontal and a vertical line are perpendicular.

7. **Try This** Which of these lines are parallel? Which are perpendicular?
   - **a.** $y = 2x + 1$
   - **b.** $y = -x$
   - **c.** $y = x - 4$
   - **d.** $y = \frac{1}{2}$
   - **e.** $y = -2x + 3$

8. **a.** Graph $y = 5$, $y = -1$, and $x = -4$.
   b. Which lines are parallel? Which are perpendicular?

Example 2

Find the slope of a line perpendicular to $y = -3x + 4$.

The slope of line $y = -3x + 4$ is -3.
Let m be the slope of the perpendicular line.

$-3 \cdot m = -1$ — The product of the slopes is -1.

$m = \frac{1}{3}$ — Divide each side by -3.

9. ***Open-ended*** Give an equation of a line parallel to $y = -3x + 4$.

Architecture There are parallel and perpendicular lines in the photo at the left.

10. If line $k \parallel$ line ℓ and line $r \parallel$ line ℓ, what is the relationship between lines k and r?

11. If line $t \perp$ line k and line $s \perp$ line k, what is the relationship between lines t and s?

Questions 10 and 11 demonstrate the following theorems.

Theorem 2-5 Two lines parallel to a third line are parallel to each other.

Theorem 2-6 In a plane, two lines perpendicular to a third line are parallel to each other.

Exercises ON YOUR OWN

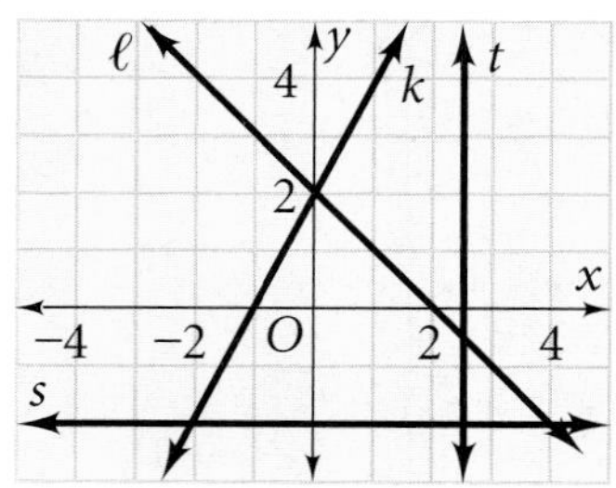

1. Identify the slope of each line in the graph as positive, negative, zero, or undefined.

2. a. What is the slope of the x-axis? Explain.
   b. What is the slope of the y-axis? Explain.

3. *Writing* A classmate claims that having no slope and having a slope of 0 are the same. Is your classmate right? Explain.

Choose Use pencil and paper, mental math, or a calculator to find the slopes of $\overleftrightarrow{AB}$ and $\overleftrightarrow{CD}$. Then determine if the lines are parallel, perpendicular, or neither.

4. $A(-1, \frac{1}{2})$, $B(-1, 2)$, $C(3, 7)$, $D(3, -1)$
5. $A(-2, 3)$, $B(-2, 5)$, $C(1, 4)$, $D(2, 4)$
6. $A(2, 4)$, $B(5, 4)$, $C(3, 2)$, $D(0, 8)$
7. $A(-3, 2)$, $B(5, 1)$, $C(2, 7)$, $D(1, -1)$
8. $A(1, -3)$, $B(3, 2)$, $C(4, 5)$, $D(2, 0)$
9. $A(4.5, 5)$, $B(2, 5)$, $C(1.5, -2)$, $D(3, -2)$

10. Use slope to show that the opposite sides of hexagon $RSTUVW$ are parallel.

11. Use slope to determine whether a triangle with vertices (3, 2), (8, 5), and (0, 10) is a right triangle. Explain.

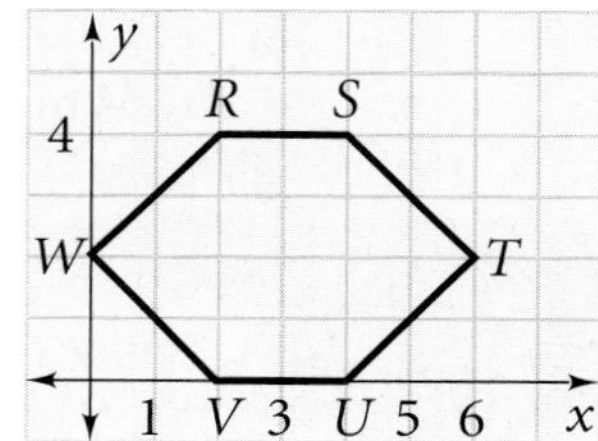

Sketch each pair of lines. Tell whether they are parallel, perpendicular, or neither.

12. $y = 5x - 4$
    $x = 2$
13. $y = \frac{1}{3}x - 1$
    $y = -3x + 5$
14. $x = -2$
    $x = 0$
15. $y = -4$
    $y = \frac{1}{4}$
16. $y = 2.5x + 1$
    $y = 2.5$
17. $y = x - \frac{1}{2}$
    $y = x + 1$
18. $y = \frac{3}{4}x - 2$
    $y = -2$
19. $y = -7$
    $x = -5$

20. *Standardized Test Prep* Which of the lines is *not* parallel to the line $y = -\frac{2}{3}x + 8$?
    A. $2x + 3y = 1$ **B.** $4x = 3 - 6y$ **C.** $x = -1.5y$ **D.** $24 = 2x - 3y$ **E.** $9y = -6x - 2$

21. a. Sketch vertical line t containing $(-5, 2)$.
    b. Write an equation for line t.
    c. On the same graph, sketch horizontal line s containing $(-5, 2)$.
    d. Write an equation for line s.
    e. What is the relationship between line t and line s? Explain.

22. a. Sketch line w perpendicular to $y = 5$, and containing $(1, 4)$.
    b. Write an equation for line w.
    c. On the same graph, sketch line r parallel to $y = 5$, and containing $(1, 4)$.
    d. Write an equation for line r.
    e. What is the relationship between line r and line w? Explain.

23. **Building** A law concerning wheelchair accessibility states that the slope of a ramp must be no greater than $\frac{1}{12}$. A local civic center plans to install a ramp. The height from the pavement to the main entrance is 3 ft and the distance from the sidewalk to the building is 10 ft. Is it possible for the center to design a ramp that complies with this law? Explain.

24. a. **Open-ended** Find the equations of two lines perpendicular to line $y = 3x - 2$.
    b. Find the equations of two lines parallel to line $y = 3x - 2$.

25. **Manipulatives** Use straws, toothpicks, or pencils.
    a. **Geometry in 3 Dimensions** Show how two lines that are each perpendicular to a third line can be perpendicular to each other.
    b. Show how two lines that are each perpendicular to a third line can be skew to each other.

26. a. Graph the points $A(1, 7)$, $B(2, 5)$, and $C(5, -1)$.
    b. What appears to be the relationship between these three points?
    c. Find the slopes of $\overleftrightarrow{AB}$, $\overleftrightarrow{BC}$, and $\overleftrightarrow{AC}$.
    d. **Logical Reasoning** Use part (c) to **justify** your answer to part (b).

27. **Geometry on a Sphere** Suppose you are investigating "lines" on a globe. The lines pass through both poles and are perpendicular to the equator. Are the lines of longitude "parallel" to each other? Explain.

28. a. Sketch line c with a slope -5 and line f with slope $\frac{1}{5}$.
    b. On the same graph, sketch line w perpendicular to line f.
    c. What is the relationship between line c and line w? Explain.

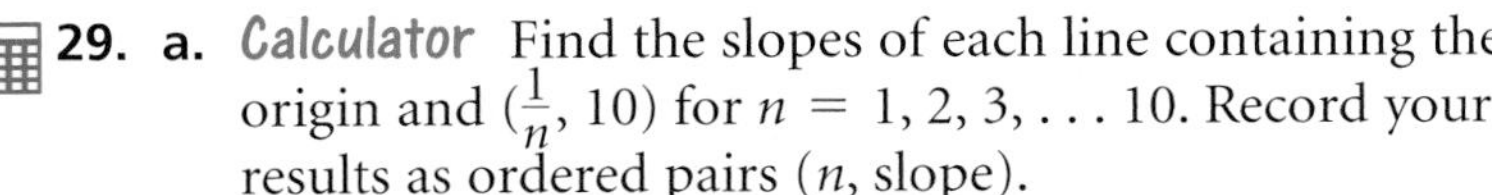

29. a. **Calculator** Find the slopes of each line containing the origin and $(\frac{1}{n}, 10)$ for $n = 1, 2, 3, \ldots 10$. Record your results as ordered pairs (n, slope).

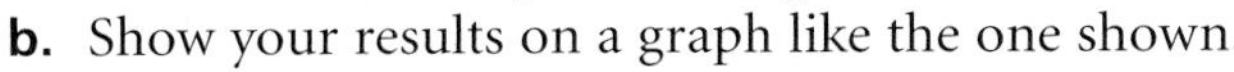

    b. Show your results on a graph like the one shown.
    c. **Data Analysis** What predictions can you make about the slope of the line when $n = 100$?
    d. **Critical Thinking** Do you think that the slope will get infinitely large? Explain your reasoning.

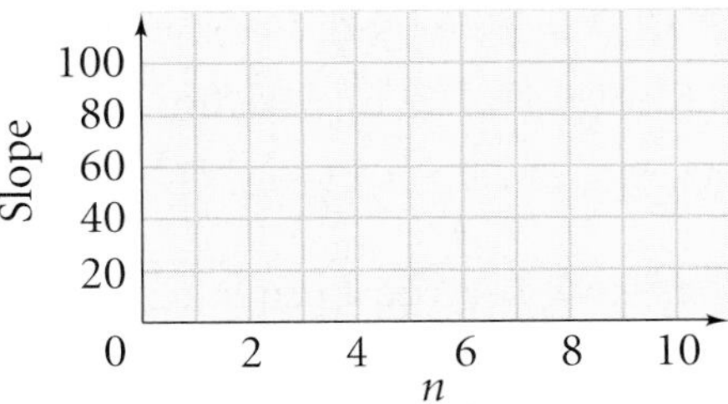

Exercises MIXED REVIEW

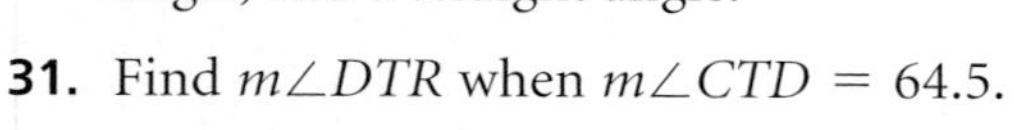

Use the diagram for the Exercises 30–32.

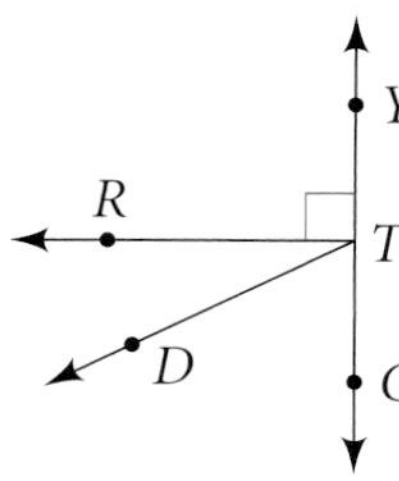

30. Name an acute angle, an obtuse angle, a right angle, and a straight angle.

31. Find $m\angle DTR$ when $m\angle CTD = 64.5$.

32. Find the value of x when $m\angle CTD = x + 32$ and $m\angle DTY = 3x + 20$. Then find the measures of both angles.

33. The measure of one acute angle of a right triangle is three times the measure of the other acute angle. Find the measures of the angles.

Getting Ready for Lesson 2-4

In each quadrilateral below, name any sides that appear to be parallel.

34.

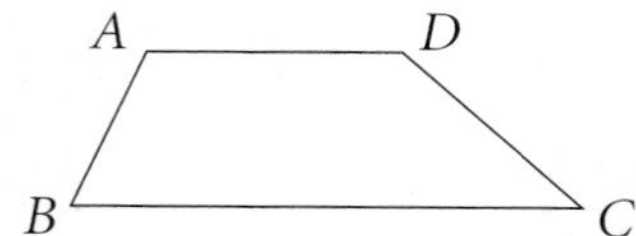

35.

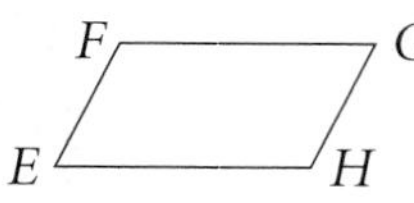

SELF ASSESSMENT — **FOR YOUR JOURNAL**

Describe real-world examples of parallel and perpendicular lines that you see on the way to school.

Exercises CHECKPOINT

Draw each figure. Mark congruent sides and angles.

1. equilateral triangle **2.** isosceles triangle **3.** right triangle **4.** acute triangle

5. obtuse triangle **6.** regular octagon **7.** concave decagon **8.** convex nonagon

9. **Writing** Describe two methods you can use to find the measure of each interior angle of a regular polygon.

Find the slope of lines $\overleftrightarrow{RS}$ and $\overleftrightarrow{TV}$. Then determine if $\overleftrightarrow{RS}$ and $\overleftrightarrow{TV}$ are *parallel, perpendicular,* or *neither*.

10. $R(-2, 6)$, $S(3, 4)$, $T(2, 5)$, $V(0, 0)$

11. $R(6, -1)$, $S(7, 0)$, $T(3, -4)$, $V(0, -1)$

12. $R(9, 1)$, $S(5, 6)$, $T(3, 8)$, $V(-2, 4)$

13. $R(5, -7)$, $S(-4, -9)$, $T(6, 2)$, $V(-3, 0)$

14. a. **Open-ended** Write an equation of a nonvertical line with a y-intercept of 2.

b. Write an equation of a line perpendicular to this line having the same y-intercept.

Math ToolboX

Algebra Review

Writing Linear Equations

After Lesson 2-3

When you know the slope of a line and a point on it, you can use the slope-intercept form of a line to write a linear equation.

Example 1

Write an equation of a line that has a slope of $\frac{1}{4}$ and contains the point $R(8, -3)$.

$y = mx + b$	Use the slope-intercept form.
$-3 = \frac{1}{4}(8) + b$	Substitute the slope and the *x*- and *y*-coordinates of the point.
$-3 = 2 + b$	Simplify.
$-5 = b$	Solve for *b*.

The equation of the line is $y = \frac{1}{4}x - 5$.

You can also use the slope-intercept form of a linear equation when you know the coordinates of two points on the line.

Example 2

Write an equation of a line containing $A(9, -2)$ and $B(3, 4)$.

$m = \frac{y_2 - y_1}{x_2 - x_1}$	Use the formula to find the slope.
$m = \frac{4 - (-2)}{3 - 9} = -1$	Substitute the coordinates of both points.
$y = -1x + b$	Substitute -1 for m in $y = mx + b$.
$4 = -1(3) + b$	Substitute the coordinates of one of the points and solve for *b*.
$7 = b$	

The equation of the line is $y = -1x + 7$ or $y = -x + 7$.

Write an equation of the line with the given slope, and containing point *T*.

1. $m = 3, T(0, 5)$
2. $m = \frac{2}{3}, T(-6, -1)$
3. $m = -\frac{1}{2}, T(4, -8)$
4. $m = 1, T(-1, 3)$
5. $m = -\frac{5}{4}, T(4, 3)$
6. $m = -1, T(-1, -8)$
7. $m = \frac{3}{2}, T(4, 4)$
8. $m = \frac{3}{4}, T(-12, -9)$

Write an equation of the line containing points *C* and *D*.

9. $C(9, -2), D(3, 4)$
10. $C(2, 1), D(-2, 3)$
11. $C(0, 3), D(-5, 0)$
12. $C(-5, 0), D(-2, 1)$
13. $C(2, 0), D(3, 5)$
14. $C(3, -1), D(2, -3)$
15. $C(0, 0), D(8, -2)$
16. $C(-8, 3), D(4, -6)$

What You'll Learn

- Defining and classifying special types of quadrilaterals

...And Why

To learn about the most commonly used polygons in buildings, architecture, and design

What You'll Need

- toothpicks

2-4 Classifying Quadrilaterals

WORK TOGETHER

Some quadrilaterals have special names.

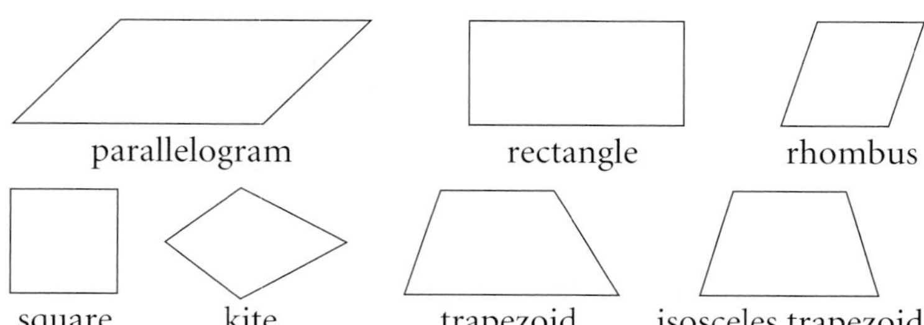

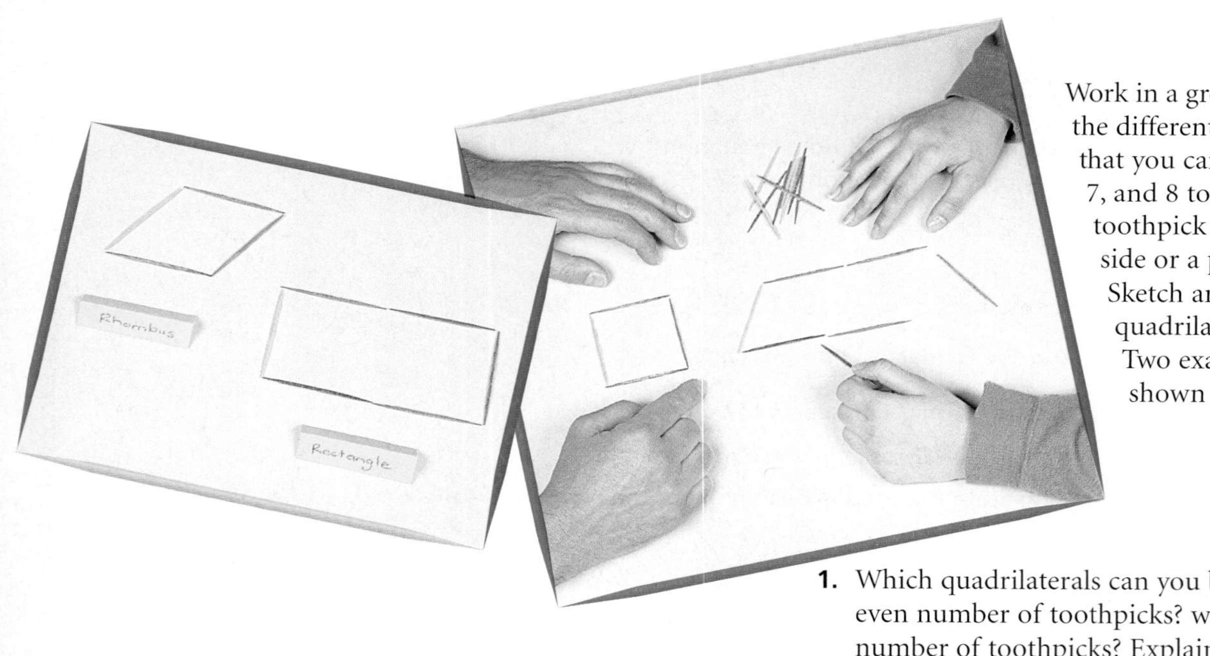

Work in a group to build all the different quadrilaterals that you can using 4, 5, 6, 7, and 8 toothpicks. Each toothpick represents a side or a part of a side. Sketch and name each quadrilateral you form. Two examples are shown at the left.

1. Which quadrilaterals can you build with an even number of toothpicks? with an odd number of toothpicks? Explain.

THINK AND DISCUSS

As you made quadrilaterals out of toothpicks, you probably noticed some of the properties of special quadrilaterals.

2. What appears to be true about the sides of the following quadrilaterals?
   a. rhombus **b.** trapezoid **c.** parallelogram **d.** kite
3. What appears to be true about the angles of a rectangle and a square?

Math A Test Prep

1 Which line is parallel to $y = 2x - 4$?
(1) $y = \frac{1}{2}x + 6$
(2) $y = 0.5x + 11$
(3) $y = 2x + 7$
(4) $y = -0.5x - 1$

2 Without graphing, tell what quadrilateral is formed by the intersection of these lines.
$y = -\frac{1}{2}x + 4$
$-x + y = 1$
$y = x - 7$
$x + 2y = -1$
Explain your thinking.

You can use characteristics of special quadrilaterals to define them.

Special Quadrilaterals

A **parallelogram** is a quadrilateral with both pairs of opposite sides parallel. In Chapter 9, you will prove that both pairs of opposite sides are also congruent. The symbol for a parallelogram is ▱.

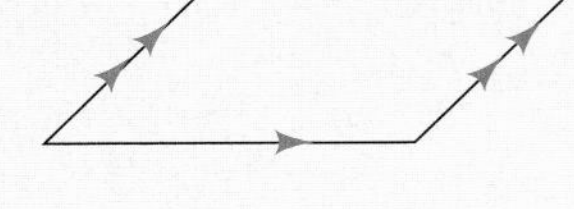

A **rhombus** is a parallelogram with four congruent sides.

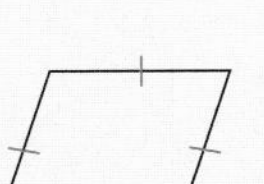

A **rectangle** is a parallelogram with four right angles.

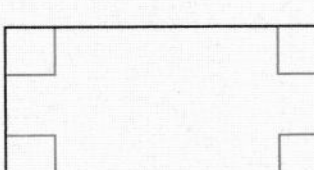

A **square** is a parallelogram with four congruent sides and four right angles.

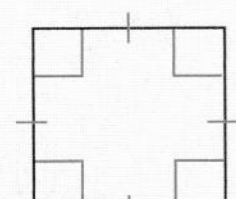

A **kite** is a quadrilateral with two pairs of adjacent sides congruent and no opposite sides congruent.

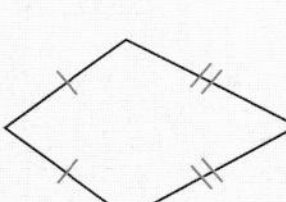

A **trapezoid** is a quadrilateral with exactly one pair of parallel sides.

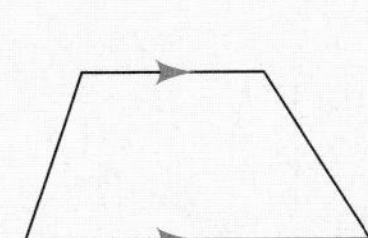

An **isosceles trapezoid** is a trapezoid whose nonparallel sides are congruent.

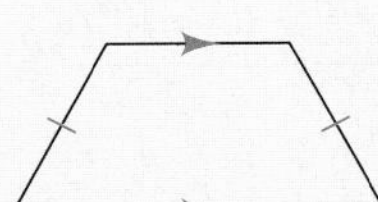

Example 1

D E G F

Judging by appearance, name *DEFG* in as many ways as possible.

It is a quadrilateral because it has four sides.

It is a parallelogram because both pairs of opposite sides are parallel.

It is a rectangle because it has four right angles.

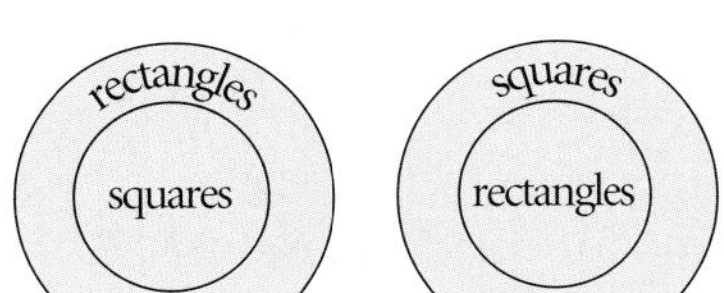

4. Which name do you think gives the most information about *DEFG*? Explain.

5. **Logical Reasoning** Which Venn diagram at the left shows the relationship between rectangles and squares? Explain.

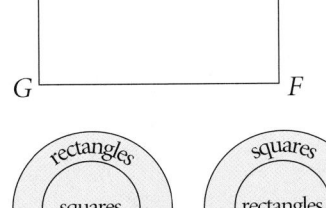

The diagram below shows the relationships among special quadrilaterals.

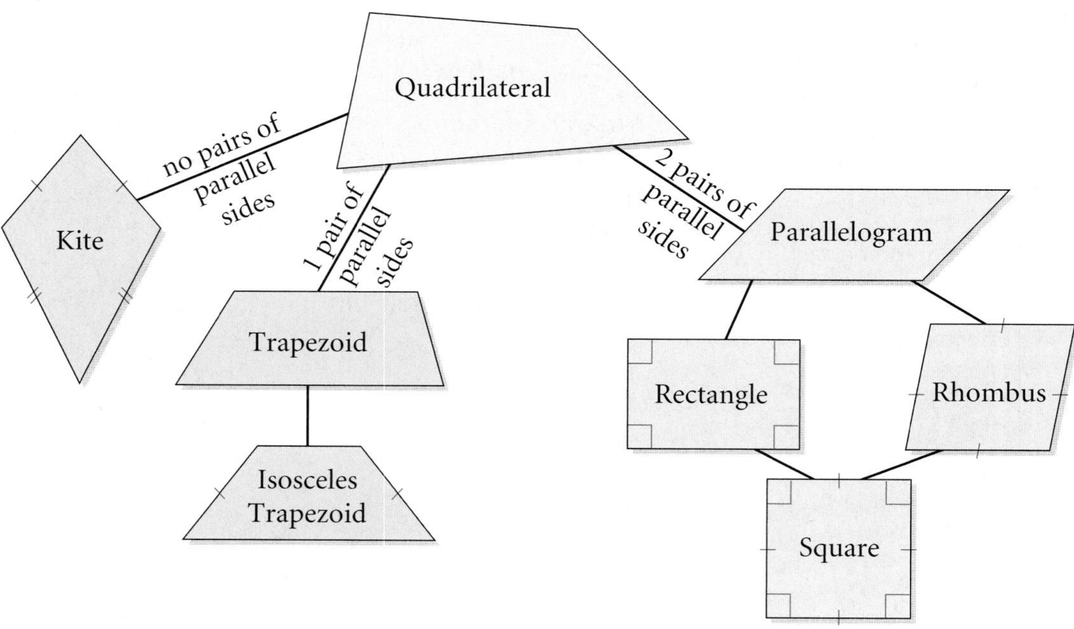

You can use the definitions of special quadrilaterals and what you know about slope and distance to classify a quadrilateral.

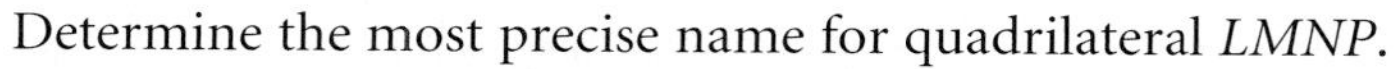

Example 2

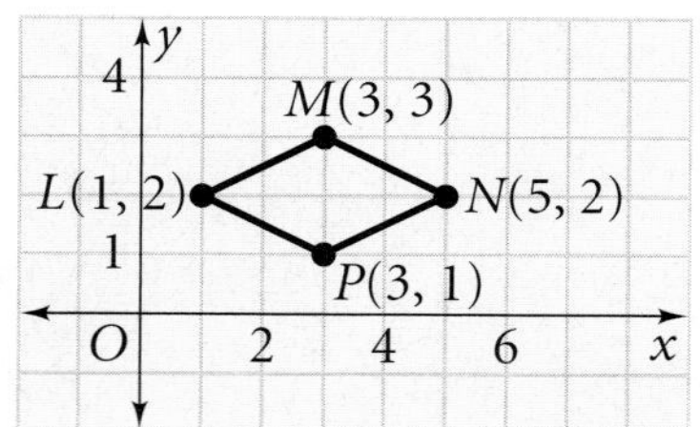

Determine the most precise name for quadrilateral *LMNP*.

Find the slope of each side.

slope of $\overline{LM} = \frac{3-2}{3-1} = \frac{1}{2}$ slope of $\overline{NP} = \frac{2-1}{5-3} = \frac{1}{2}$

slope of $\overline{MN} = \frac{3-2}{3-5} = -\frac{1}{2}$ slope of $\overline{LP} = \frac{2-1}{1-3} = -\frac{1}{2}$

Both pairs of opposite sides are parallel, so *LMNP* is a parallelogram.

Now use the Distance Formula to see if any of the sides are congruent.

$LM = \sqrt{(3-1)^2 + (3-2)^2} = \sqrt{5}$

$MN = \sqrt{(3-5)^2 + (3-2)^2} = \sqrt{5}$

$NP = \sqrt{(5-3)^2 + (2-1)^2} = \sqrt{5}$

$LP = \sqrt{(1-3)^2 + (2-1)^2} = \sqrt{5}$

All sides are congruent, so *LMNP* is a rhombus.

6. Explain how you know that *LMNP* is *not* a square.

7. Try This Determine the most precise name for quadrilateral *ABCD* with vertices $A(0, 4)$, $B(3, 0)$, $C(0, -4)$, $D(-3, 0)$.

You can use the definitions of special quadrilaterals to find lengths of sides of objects like kites.

Example 3

Find the values of the variables in the kite at the left.

$KB = JB$	Definition of kite
$3x - 5 = 2x + 4$	Substitution
$x - 5 = 4$	Subtract $2x$ from each side.
$x = 9$	Add 5 to each side.
$KT = x + 6$, $KT = 15$	Substitute 9 for x.
$KT = JT$	Definition of kite
$15 = 2y + 5$	Substitution
$10 = 2y$	Subtract 5 from each side.
$5 = y$	Divide each side by 2.

8. What are the lengths of the longer sides of the kite?

9. What types of triangles are formed when you draw diagonal $\overline{KJ}$?

10. What types of triangles are formed when you draw diagonal $\overline{BT}$?

Exercises ON YOUR OWN

Judging by appearance, name each quadrilateral in as many ways as possible.

1. 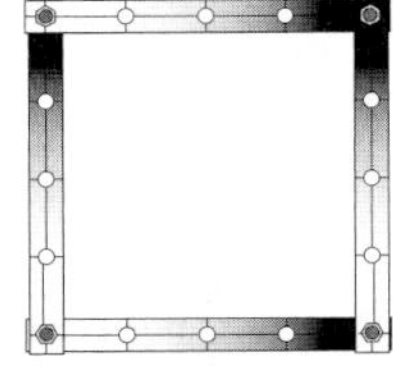

2. 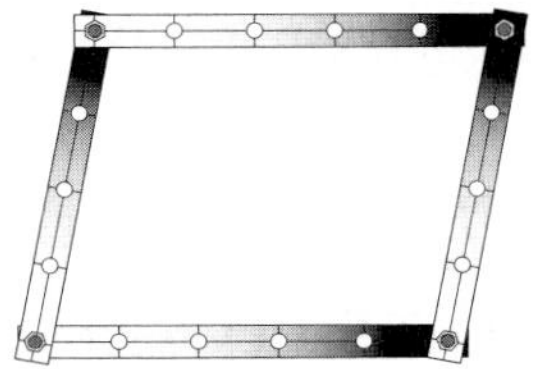

3. 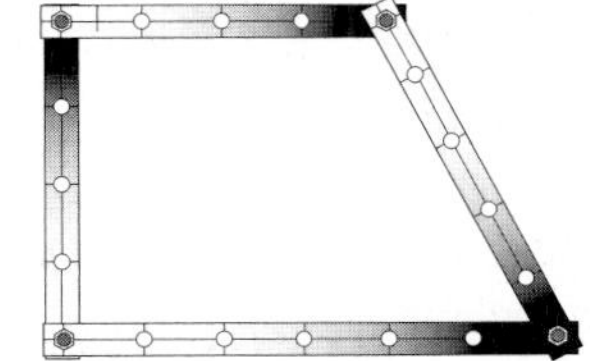

4. 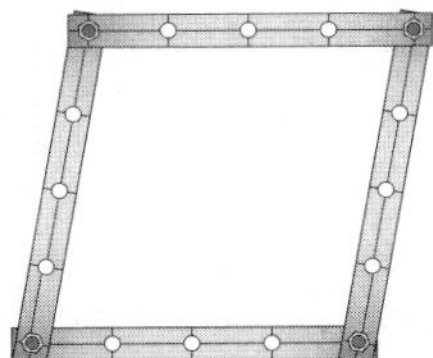

Copy the Venn diagram. Show the relationships of special quadrilaterals by adding the labels *Rectangles, Rhombuses,* and *Trapezoids.* Then use the diagram to decide whether each statement is true or false.

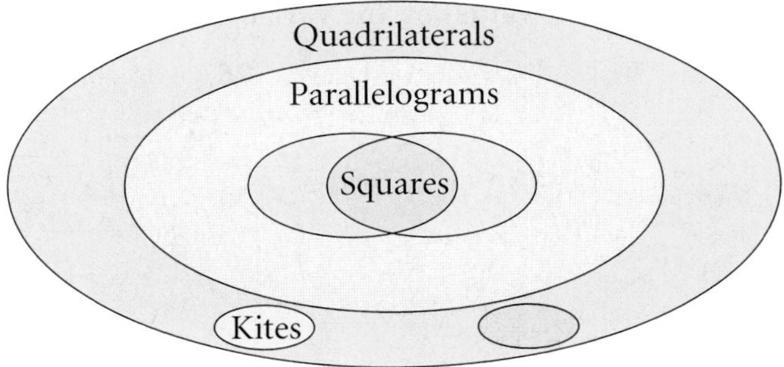

5. All squares are rectangles.

6. A trapezoid is a parallelogram.

7. A rhombus can be a kite.

8. Some parallelograms are squares.

9. A quadrilateral is a parallelogram.

10. **Art** Inspired by Cubists like Pablo Picasso, American artist Charles Demuth created *My Egypt*. Identify the geometric figures in this oil painting. List all the special quadrilaterals you see.

Draw each figure on graph paper.

11. parallelogram that is neither a rectangle nor a rhombus

12. trapezoid with a right angle

13. rhombus that is not a square

14. **Writing** Describe the difference between a rhombus and a kite.

15. a. **Open-ended** Graph and label points $K(-3, 0)$, $L(0, 2)$, and $M(3, 0)$. Find possible coordinates for point N so that $KLMN$ is a kite.

    b. Explain why there is more than one possible fourth vertex.

Coordinate Geometry **Graph and label each quadrilateral with the given vertices. Use slope and/or the Distance Formula to determine the most precise name for each figure.**

16. $A(3, 5)$, $B(7, 6)$, $C(6, 2)$, $D(2, 1)$

17. $W(-1, 1)$, $X(0, 2)$, $Y(1, 1)$, $Z(0, -2)$

18. $J(2, 1)$, $K(5, 4)$, $L(7, 2)$, $M(2, -3)$

19. $R(-2, -3)$, $S(4, 0)$, $T(3, 2)$, $V(-3, -1)$

20. **Paper Folding** Fold a rectangular piece of paper in half horizontally and then vertically. Draw and then cut along the line connecting the two corners containing a fold. What quadrilateral do you find when you unfold the paper? Explain.

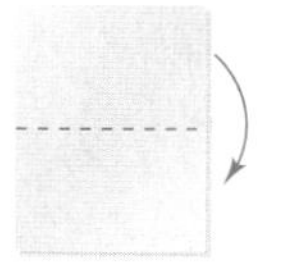

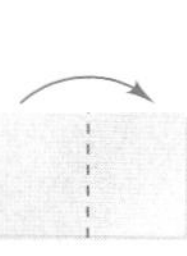

Name all special quadrilaterals that satisfy the given conditions. Make a sketch to support your answer.

21. exactly one pair of congruent sides

22. two pairs of parallel sides

23. four right angles

24. adjacent sides that are congruent

Algebra **Find the values of the variables and the lengths of the sides.**

25. kite $ABCD$

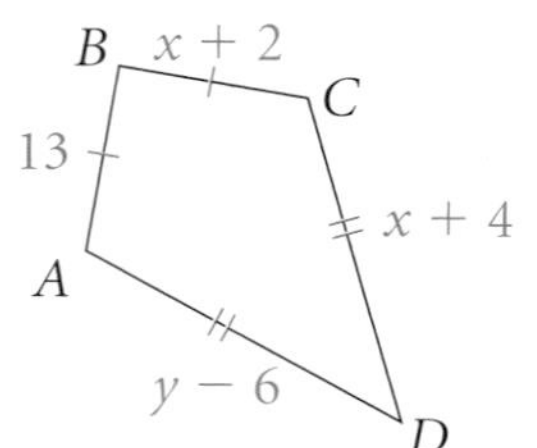

26. isosceles trapezoid $DEFG$

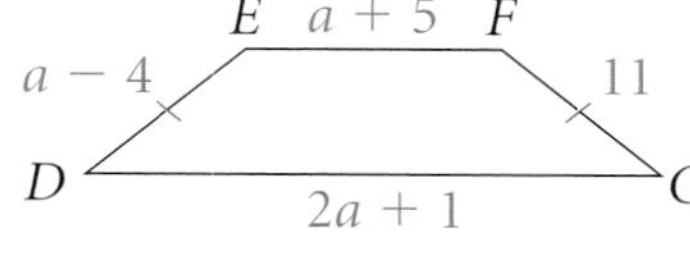

27. rhombus $HIJK$

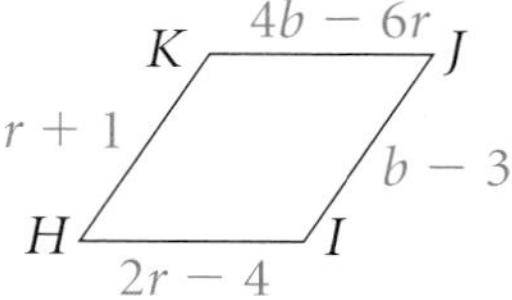

Part of each quadrilateral is covered. Name all special quadrilaterals that each could be. Explain each choice.

28. 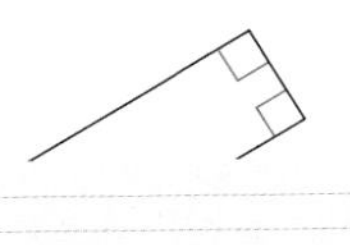

29. 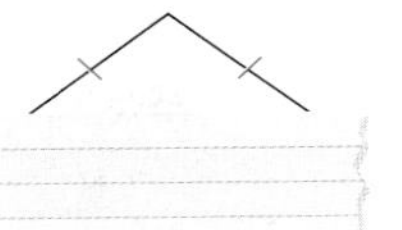

30. 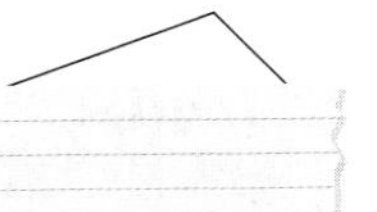

31. 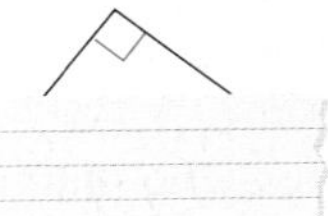

Chapter Project — *Find Out by Analyzing*

You can create another geometric puzzle, called *pentominoes,* by joining five unit squares. Each square shares a side with at least one other square.

These are pentominoes.

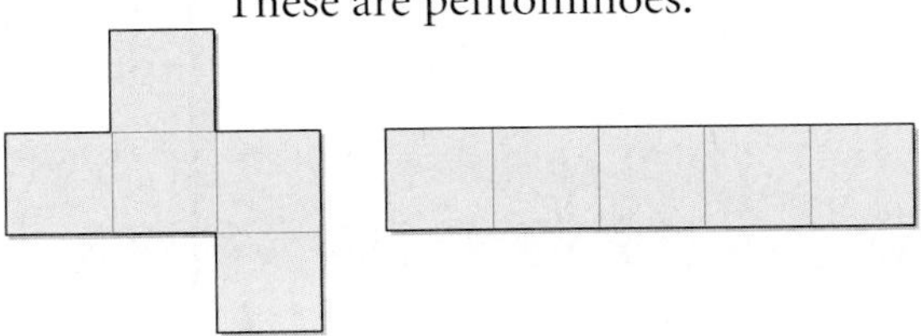

These are not pentominoes.

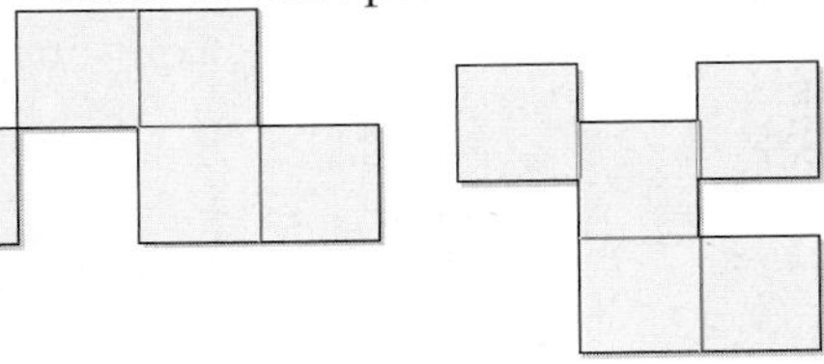

- There are twelve different pentominoes. Sketch the other ten pentominoes on graph paper.
- Make a set of pentominoes out of cardboard. Use any three pentominoes to form a 3 x 5 rectangle. Find and record as many solutions as you can.

Exercises MIXED REVIEW

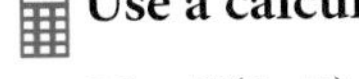

Use a calculator to find *TR* to the nearest tenth.

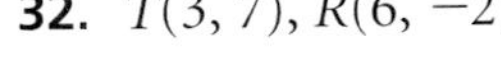

32. $T(3, 7), R(6, -2)$ **33.** $T(-8, 4), R(0, 2)$

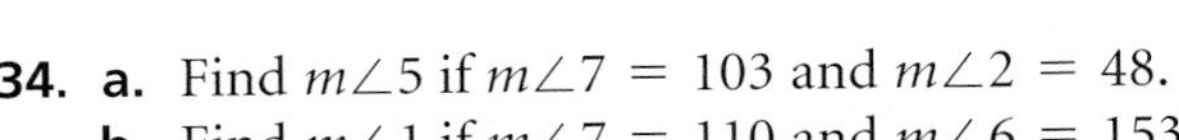

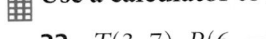

34. **a.** Find $m\angle 5$ if $m\angle 7 = 103$ and $m\angle 2 = 48$.
b. Find $m\angle 1$ if $m\angle 7 = 110$ and $m\angle 6 = 153$.
c. Find $m\angle 9$ if $m\angle 3 = 138$ and $m\angle 5 = 51$.

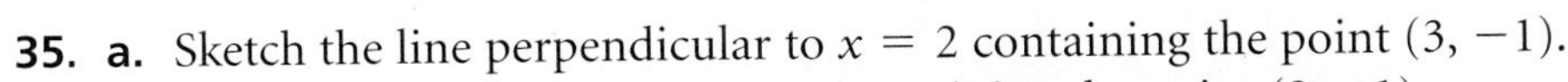

35. **a.** Sketch the line perpendicular to $x = 2$ containing the point $(3, -1)$.
b. Sketch the line parallel to $x = 2$ containing the point $(3, -1)$.

Getting Ready for Lesson 2-5

Estimate the percent of the circle that is shaded.

36. 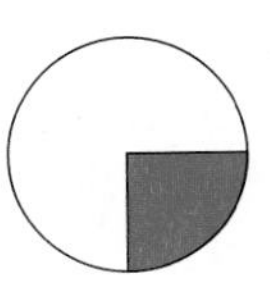

37. 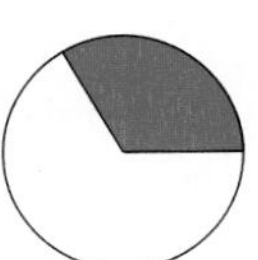

38. 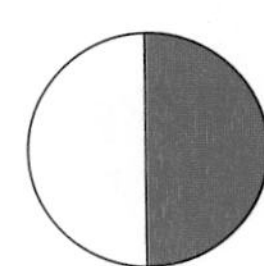

39. 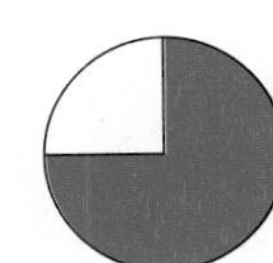

40. 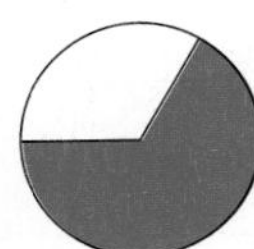

2-5 Circles

What You'll Learn

- Measuring central angles and arcs of circles.
- Displaying data in a circle graph.

...And Why

To learn about a geometric figure at the heart of the design of many things, including amusement park rides, satellite orbits, and circle graphs

What You'll Need

- compass
- protractor

WORK TOGETHER

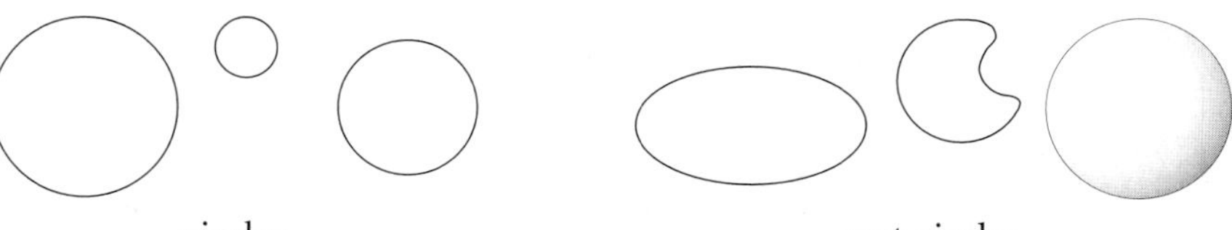

Have each person in your group write a definition of a circle. Exchange papers. Examine the definition you receive. Try to find a counterexample. Continue until your group has agreed on a definition of a circle.

THINK AND DISCUSS

Parts of a Circle

A **circle** is the set of all points in a plane *equidistant* from a given point, called the center. You name a circle by its center. Circle $P(\odot P)$ is shown.

A **radius** is a segment that has one endpoint at the center and the other endpoint on the circle. $\overline{PC}$ is a radius. $\overline{PA}$ and $\overline{PB}$ are also radii.

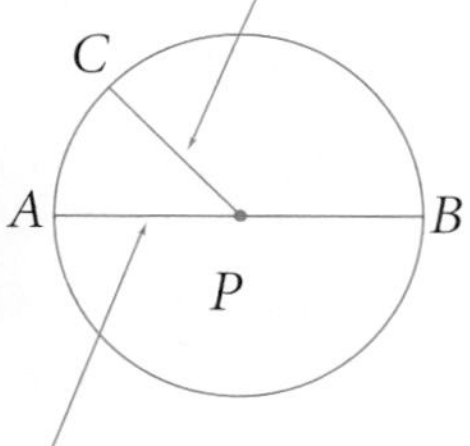

A **diameter** is a segment that contains the center of the circle and has both endpoints on the circle. $\overline{AB}$ is a diameter.

QUICK REVIEW

The length r of a radius is *the* radius of a circle. The length d of a diameter is *the* diameter of a circle. $d = 2r$

1. *Amusement Parks* The Scream Weaver amusement ride in North Carolina is a gondola ride with a diameter of 13.1 m. Find the length of each arm.
2. Complete: The center of a circle is the __?__ of a diameter.

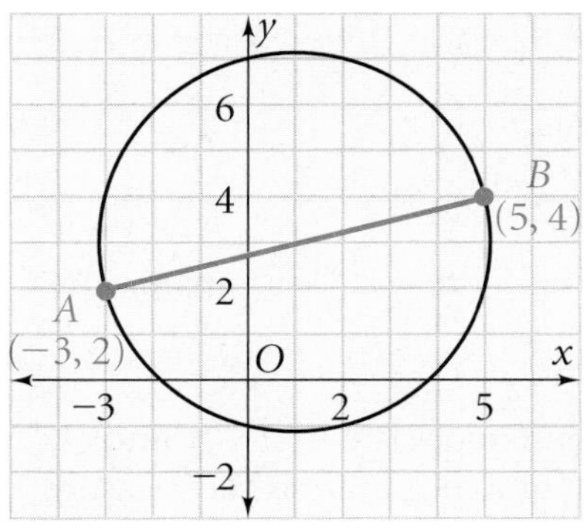

Example 1

Coordinate Geometry $\overline{AB}$ is a diameter of the circle. Find the coordinates of the center and the radius of the circle.

The center P of the circle is the midpoint of the diameter.

$$P = \left(\frac{-3 + 5}{2}, \frac{2 + 4}{2}\right) \quad \text{Use the Midpoint Formula.}$$

$$P = (1, 3) \quad \text{Simplify.}$$

The radius is the distance from the center to any point on the circle.

$$PB = \sqrt{(1 - 5)^2 + (3 - 4)^2} \quad \text{Use the Distance Formula.}$$

$$PB = \sqrt{(-4)^2 + (-1)^2} \quad \text{Simplify.}$$

$$PB = \sqrt{16 + 1} = \sqrt{17}$$

The center of the circle is $(1, 3)$. The radius is $\sqrt{17}$.

3. **Try This** Find the coordinates of the center and the radius of a circle with diameter $\overline{AB}$ whose endpoints are $A(1, 3)$ and $B(7, -5)$.

Central Angles and Arcs

You often see circle graphs in newspapers and magazines. When you make a circle graph you have to find the measure of each wedge, or central angle. A **central angle** is an angle whose vertex is the center of the circle.

Example 2 Relating to the Real World 

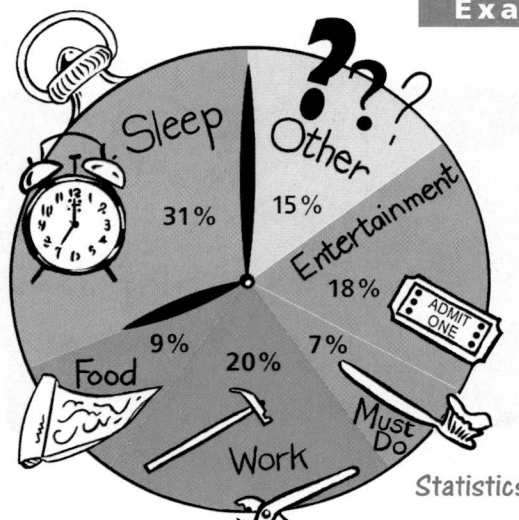

Source: *The New York Times*

How Do You Spend Your Day?

To learn how people really spend their time, a market research firm studied the hour-by-hour activities of more than 3,000 people. The participants were between 18 and 90 years old.

Each participant was sent a 24-h recording sheet every March for 3 years from 1992 to 1994. The study found that people spend most of their time sleeping, working, and watching television.

Statistics Find the measure of each central angle in the circle graph.

Since there are 360 degrees in a circle, multiply each percent by 360 to find the measure of each central angle in the circle graph.

Sleep: 31% of 360 = 111.6
Food: 9% of 360 = 32.4
Work: 20% of 360 = 72
Must Do: 7% of 360 = 25.2
Entertainment: 18% of 360 = 64.8
Other: 15% of 360 = 54

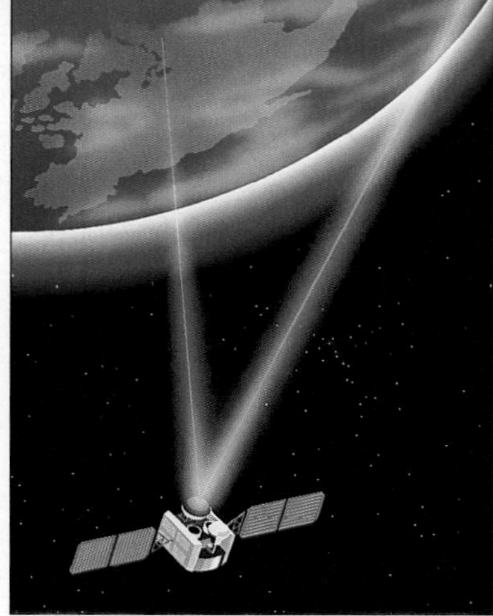

An *arc* is a part of a circle. There are three types of arcs: a *semicircle,* a *minor arc,* and a *major arc.*

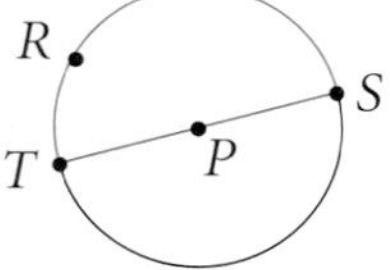

$\overset{\frown}{TRS}$ is a semicircle.
$m\overset{\frown}{TRS} = 180$

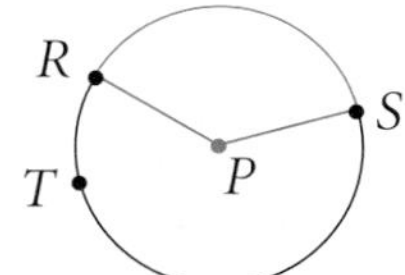

$\overset{\frown}{RS}$ is a minor arc.
$m\overset{\frown}{RS} = m\angle RPS$

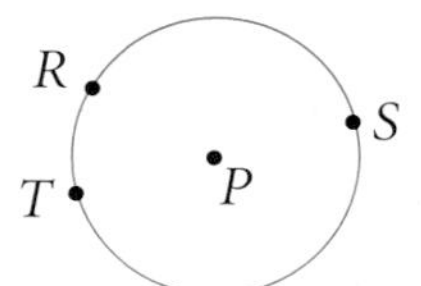

$\overset{\frown}{RTS}$ is a major arc.
$m\overset{\frown}{RTS} = 360 - m\overset{\frown}{RS}$

A **semicircle** is half a circle. The measure of a semicircle is 180. A **minor arc** is shorter than a semicircle. The measure of a minor arc is the measure of its corresponding central angle. A **major arc** is longer than a semicircle. The measure of a major arc is 360 minus the measure of its related minor arc.

What? Geosynchronous satellites stay above the same point on Earth's equator. They orbit Earth in a near-circular path every 24 hours at a distance 42,000 km from the Earth's center. The radius of Earth is about 6000 km. How far above Earth's surface are these satellites?

4. **Critical Thinking** What kind of arcs can you name with only two points? What kind of arcs must you name with three points? Why?

Adjacent arcs are two arcs in the same circle that have exactly one point in common. You can add the measures of adjacent arcs just as you can add the measures of adjacent angles.

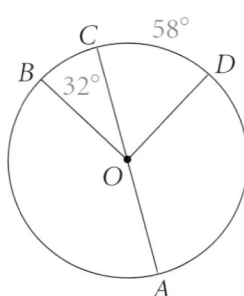

Arc Addition Postulate

The measure of the arc formed by two adjacent arcs is the sum of the measures of the two arcs.

$m\overset{\frown}{ABC} = m\overset{\frown}{AB} + m\overset{\frown}{BC}$

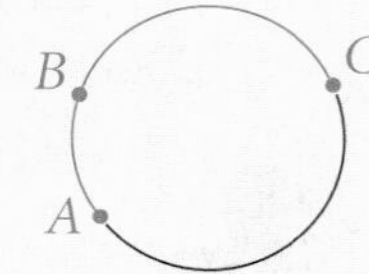

Example 3

Find the measure of each arc.

a. $\overset{\frown}{BC}$ **b.** $\overset{\frown}{BD}$ **c.** $\overset{\frown}{ABC}$ **d.** $\overset{\frown}{AB}$ **e.** $\overset{\frown}{BAD}$

a. $m\overset{\frown}{BC} = m\angle BOC = 32$

b. $m\overset{\frown}{BD} = 32 + 58 = 90$ — $m\overset{\frown}{BD} = m\overset{\frown}{BC} + m\overset{\frown}{CD}$

c. $m\overset{\frown}{ABC} = 180$ — $\overset{\frown}{ABC}$ is a semicircle.

d. $m\overset{\frown}{AB} = 180 - 32 = 148$

e. $m\overset{\frown}{BAD} = 360 - m\overset{\frown}{BD}$
$= 360 - 90 = 270$

5. **Try This** Find $m\angle COD$, $m\overset{\frown}{CDA}$, and $m\overset{\frown}{AD}$.

6. **a.** Use a compass to draw a circle. Then use a protractor to draw $\overset{\frown}{JK}$ with measure 75.
   b. Explain how to draw a longer arc that has a measure of 75.

Exercises ON YOUR OWN

Identify the following in $\odot O$.

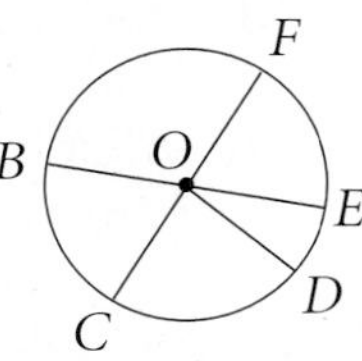

1. two minor arcs
2. two major arcs
3. two semicircles
4. three radii
5. two diameters
6. a pair of adjacent arcs
7. an acute central angle
8. an obtuse central angle
9. a pair of congruent angles

Find the diameter of a circle with the given radius.

10. 20 ft
11. 5 cm
12. $3\frac{1}{2}$ m
13. $6\sqrt{2}$ in.
14. r mi

Find the radius of a circle with the given diameter.

15. 13 cm
16. 10.5 m
17. $5\sqrt{3}$ in.
18. $\frac{1}{3}$ ft
19. d km

20. **Printing** Newspaper companies use offset presses to print. The paper passes between cylinders. The radius of each large cylinder is 7 in. Find PR in the diagram.

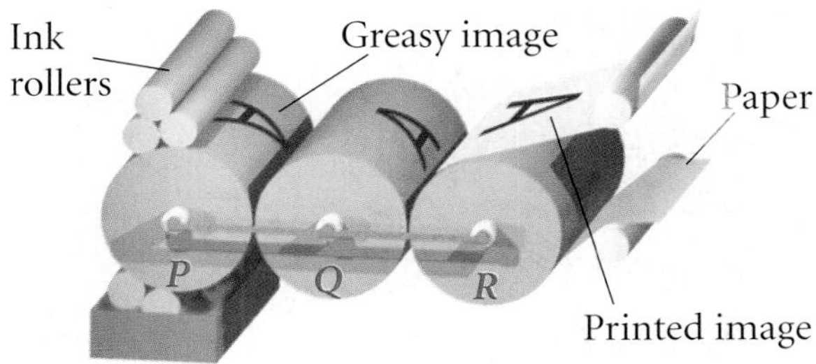

21. **Paper Folding** Use a compass to make a circle. Cut out the circle and use paper folding to form 90°, 45°, and 135° central angles.

Coordinate Geometry **Find the coordinates of the center and the radius of each circle with diameter $\overline{AB}$.**

22. $A(3, 4), B(-3, -4)$
23. $A(0, 4), B(-4, 6)$
24. $A(-2, -2), B(3, 10)$
25. $A(2, 3), B(-4, 5)$
26. $A(-6, -2), B(0, 6)$
27. $A(-1, -12), B(7, 3)$

Find the measure of each arc in $\odot P$.

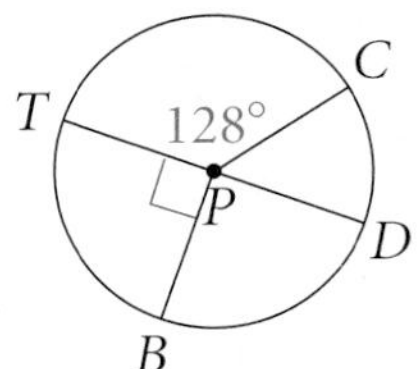

28. $\overset{\frown}{TC}$
29. $\overset{\frown}{TBD}$
30. $\overset{\frown}{BTC}$
31. $\overset{\frown}{CD}$
32. $\overset{\frown}{CBD}$
33. $\overset{\frown}{TCD}$
34. $\overset{\frown}{TDC}$
35. $\overset{\frown}{TB}$
36. $\overset{\frown}{BC}$

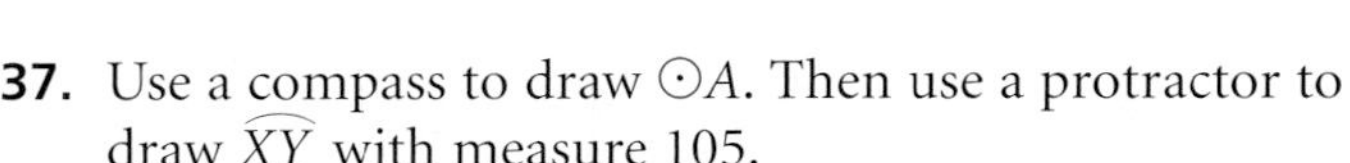

37. Use a compass to draw $\odot A$. Then use a protractor to draw $\overset{\frown}{XY}$ with measure 105.

38. **Statistics** Americans throw out more than 150 million tons of garbage each year. The circle graph shows the percent of different materials found in a typical city trash collection.
    a. Find the measure of the central angle for each category (rounded to the nearest whole number).
    b. Find the sum of the measures of these angles.
    c. **Writing** Explain why the sum might not equal 360.

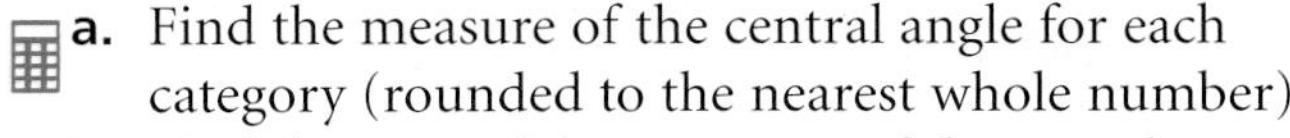

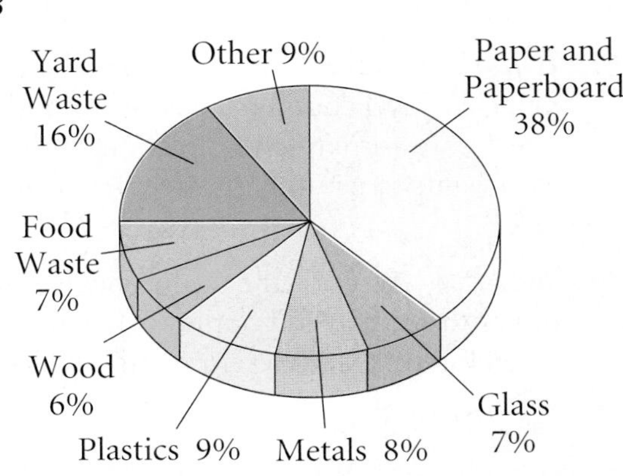

Source: *The American Almanac*

39. **a.** How many degrees does a minute hand move in 1 minute? in 5 minutes? in 20 minutes?
b. How many degrees does an hour hand move in 5 minutes? in 10 minutes? in 20 minutes?
c. What is the measure of the angle formed by the hands of the clock at 8:25?

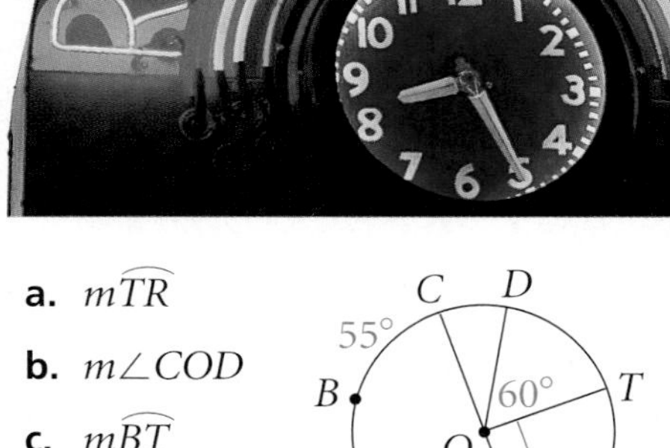

Find each indicated measure for $\odot O$.

40. **a.** $m\angle EOF$
b. $m\widehat{EJH}$
c. $m\widehat{FH}$
d. $m\angle FOG$
e. $m\widehat{JEG}$
f. $m\widehat{HFJ}$

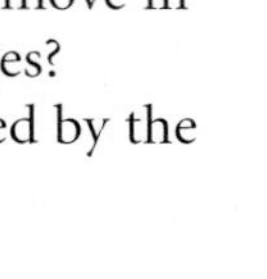

41. **a.** $m\widehat{TR}$
b. $m\angle COD$
c. $m\widehat{BT}$
d. $m\widehat{BR}$
e. $m\widehat{BTR}$
f. $m\widehat{TRB}$

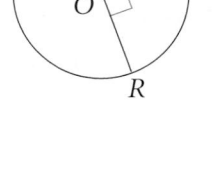

42. **a.** $m\angle LOM$
b. $m\widehat{QP}$
c. $m\widehat{PMQ}$
d. $m\angle QOL$
e. $m\widehat{QLP}$

43. **a.** $m\angle KOV$
b. $m\widehat{KZ}$
c. $m\angle SOW$
d. $m\widehat{YVK}$
e. $m\widehat{WSZ}$

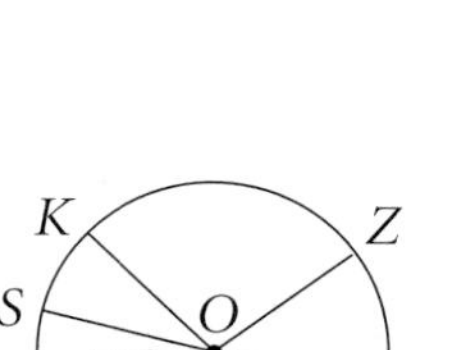

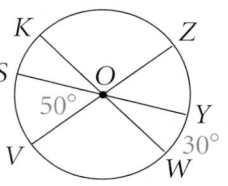

Algebra **Find $m\widehat{PQ}$ in $\odot A$.**

44.

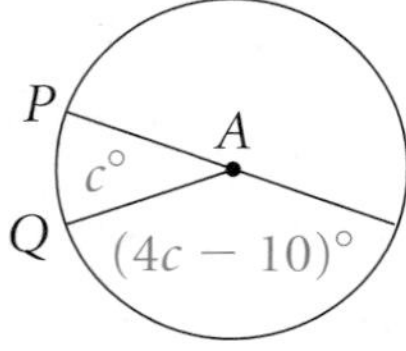

45.

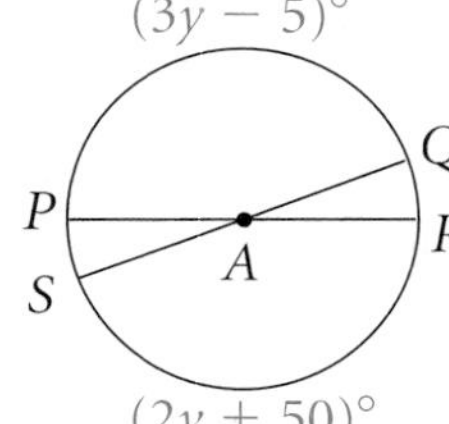

46.

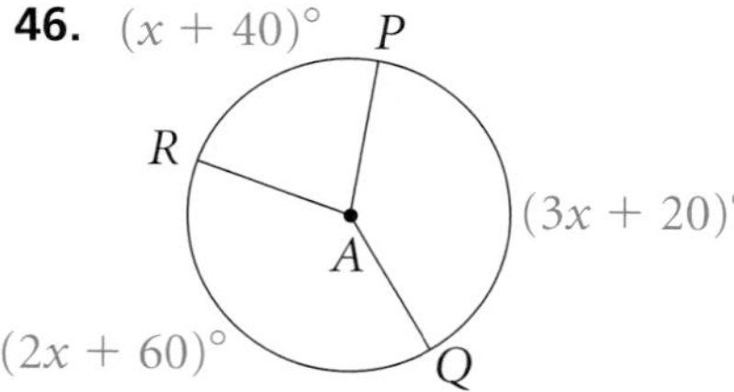

47. **Travel** Five streets come together at a traffic circle. Vehicles travel counterclockwise around the circle. Use arc measure to give directions to someone who wants to get to East Street from Neponset Street.

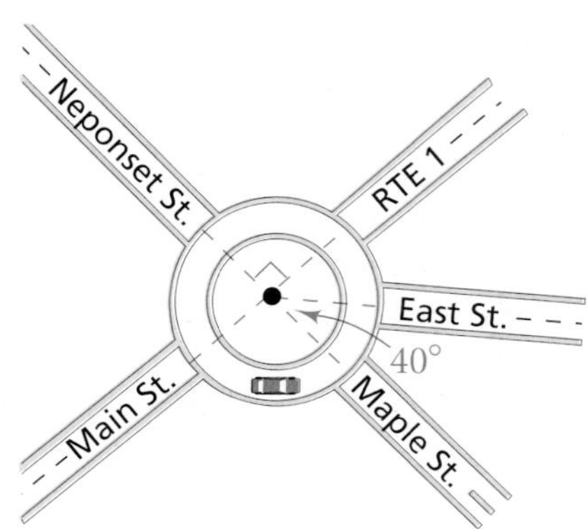

48. **Research** Describe the traditional life of the Zulus of South Africa. Find out how they use circles when building and designing their villages.

49. *Open-ended* Make a circle graph showing how you spend a 24-hour weekday.

50. *Statistics* In 1995, O'Reilly & Associates surveyed people 18 and older in the United States to find out "Who's Using the Internet?" The table shows Internet users by age groups. (Of those surveyed, 2% refused to answer.) Display the data in a circle graph.

Who's Using the Internet?

Age	% of Surveyed Internet Users	Age	% of Surveyed Internet Users
18–24 years	20%	35–44 years	25%
25–29 years	20%	44–54 years	15%
30–34 years	15%	55+ years	3%

Source: *U.S. News & World Report*

Exercises MIXED REVIEW

Find the values of the variables.

51. 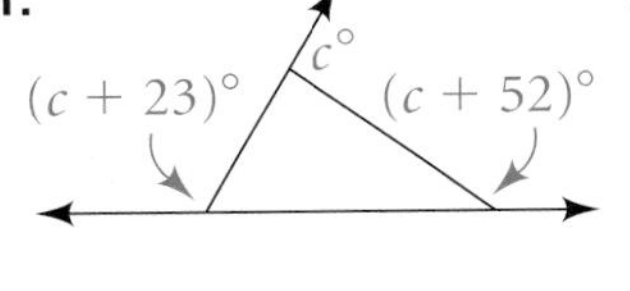

52. 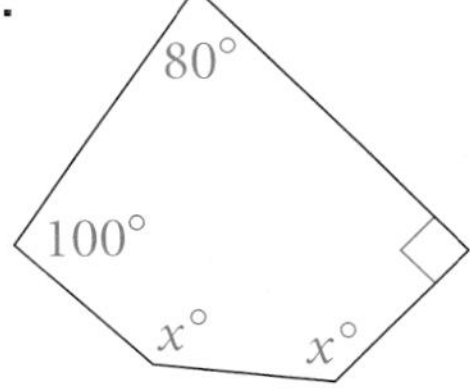

53. 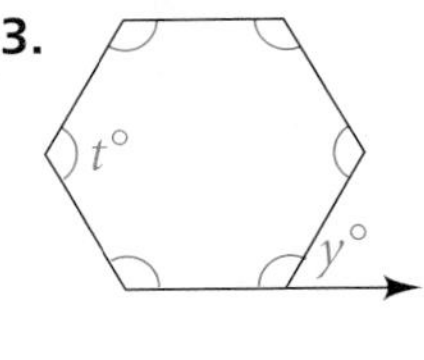

54. 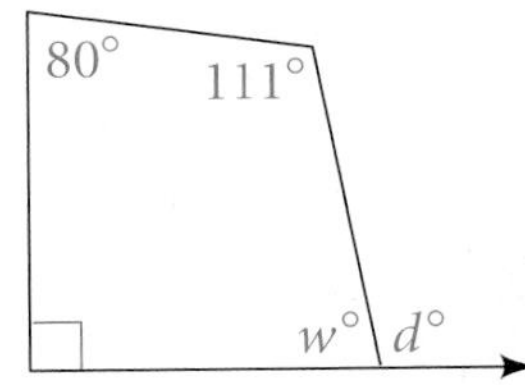

55. Find the measure of an angle that is 16° less than its complement.

Getting Ready for Lesson 2-6

56. The diagram below at the left shows a 4-by-4 square on graph paper. You can divide the square into two identical pieces by cutting along grid lines. One way to do this is to make a vertical or a horizontal line. Another way is shown below at the right. Find the four other ways of doing this.

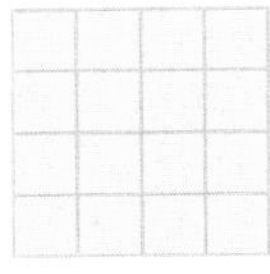

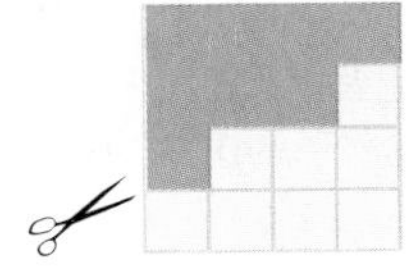

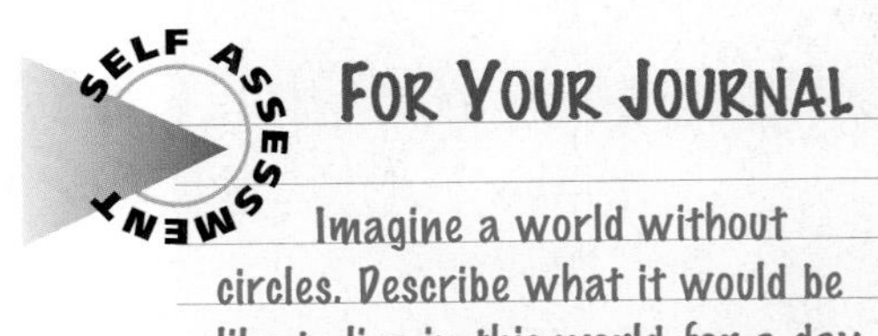

FOR YOUR JOURNAL

Imagine a world without circles. Describe what it would be like to live in this world for a day.

2-6 Congruent and Similar Figures

What You'll Learn

- Measuring congruent and similar figures
- Using properties of congruence and similarity

...And Why

To model real-world situations, such as mass production and photography

What You'll Need

- scissors
- protractor
- centimeter ruler

THINK AND DISCUSS

Congruent Figures

Congruent figures have exactly the same size and shape. When two figures are congruent you can slide, flip, or turn one so that it fits exactly on the other one.

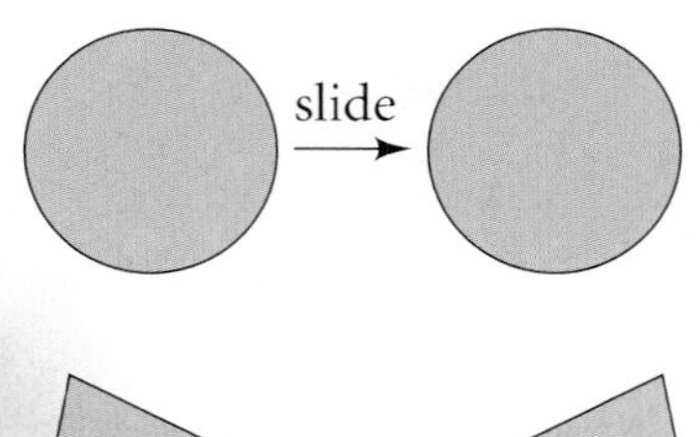

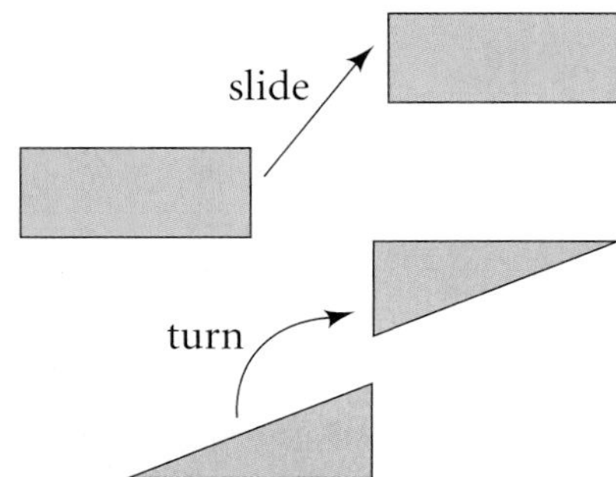

Congruent circles have congruent radii. **Congruent polygons** have congruent corresponding parts. The matching angles and sides of congruent polygons are called *corresponding parts.* Matching vertices are *corresponding vertices.* When you name congruent polygons, always list corresponding vertices in the same order.

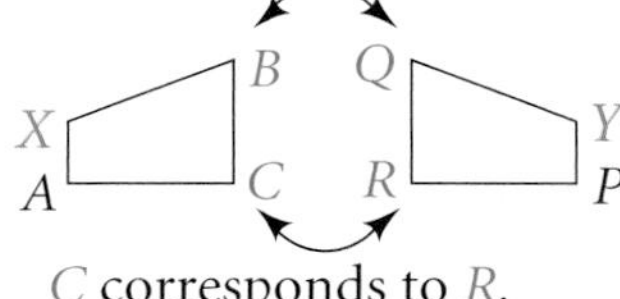

C corresponds to R.
$\angle B$ corresponds to $\angle Q$.
$\overline{AX}$ corresponds to $\overline{PY}$.
$ACBX \cong PRQY$

Example 1 Relating to the Real World 

Rocketry The fins of the rocket are congruent pentagons. Find $m\angle B$.

Because the fins are congruent, $\angle B \cong \angle E$. So you can find $m\angle B$ by first finding $m\angle E$.

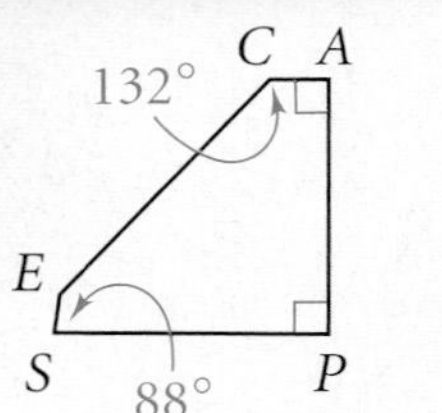

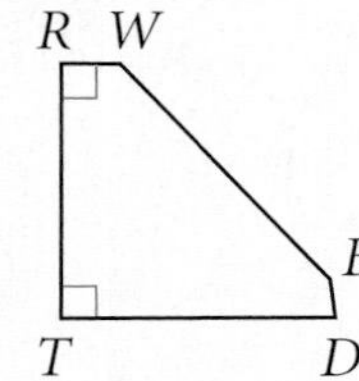

By the Polygon Interior Angle-Sum Theorem, you know that the sum of the measures of the interior angles of pentagon *SPACE* is $(5 - 2)180$, or 540.

$$\begin{aligned} m\angle S + m\angle P + m\angle A + m\angle C + m\angle E &= 540 \\ 88 + 90 + 90 + 132 + m\angle E &= 540 \\ 400 + m\angle E &= 540 \\ m\angle E &= 140 \end{aligned}$$

So $m\angle E = m\angle B = 140$.

Example 2

$\triangle TJD \cong \triangle RCF$. List congruent corresponding parts.

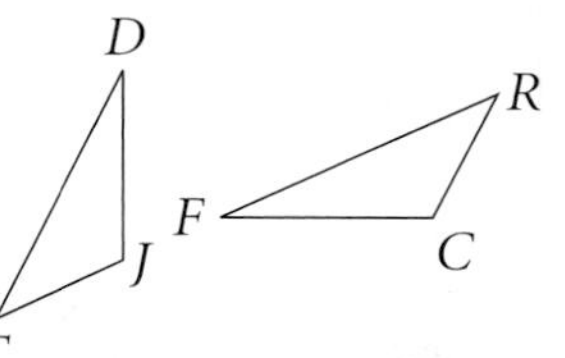

$\overline{TJ} \cong \overline{RC}$ $\overline{JD} \cong \overline{CF}$ $\overline{DT} \cong \overline{FR}$

$\angle T \cong \angle R$ $\angle J \cong \angle C$ $\angle D \cong \angle F$

1. **Try This** $\triangle WYS \cong \triangle MKV$. List congruent corresponding parts.

Similar Polygons

QUICK REVIEW

Corresponding sides are *proportional* if the ratios of their lengths are equal.

Two figures that have the same shape but not necessarily the same size are similar ($\sim$). Two polygons are **similar** if (1) corresponding angles are congruent and (2) corresponding sides are proportional. The ratio of the lengths of corresponding sides is the **similarity ratio.**

Example 3

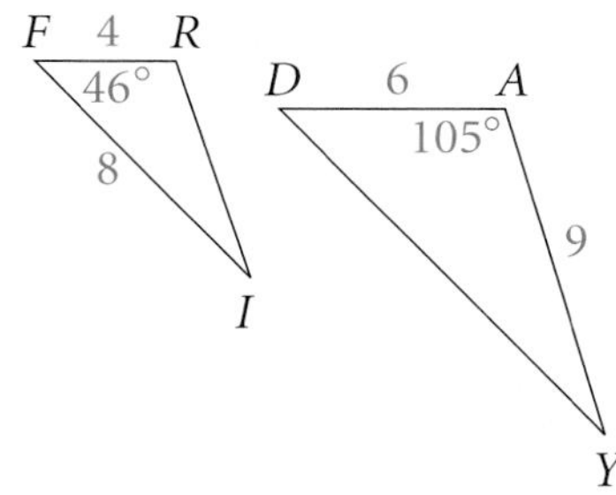

$\triangle FRI \sim \triangle DAY$. Find:

a. the similarity ratio **b.** $m\angle R$ **c.** RI

a. Since $\overline{FR}$ and $\overline{DA}$ are corresponding sides, the similarity ratio is $\frac{FR}{DA} = \frac{4}{6} = \frac{2}{3}$.

b. $\angle R$ corresponds to $\angle A$, so $m\angle R = m\angle A$.
$m\angle A = 105$, so $m\angle R = 105$.

c. Write a proportion to solve for RI.

$\frac{FR}{DA} = \frac{RI}{AY}$

$\frac{4}{6} = \frac{RI}{9}$ Substitution

$36 = 6 \cdot RI$ Use cross-products.

$6 = RI$ Divide each side by 6.

PROBLEM SOLVING

Look Back Describe how you could use the similarity ratio to solve for *RI*.

2. **Try This** Find DY and $m\angle D$.

3. **a.** Find the perimeter of $\triangle FRI$.
   b. Find the perimeter of $\triangle DAY$.
   c. What is the ratio of the perimeter of $\triangle FRI$ to the perimeter of $\triangle DAY$?
   d. Compare your answer to part (c) to the similarity ratio. Make a **conjecture** about the ratio of the perimeters of similar figures.
   e. Test your **conjecture** by drawing and measuring other pairs of similar polygons.

4. **Critical Thinking** What type of similar figures have a similarity ratio of 1?

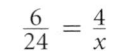

Example 4 Relating to the Real World 

Photography You want to enlarge a photo that is 4 in. tall and 6 in. wide into a poster. The poster will be 24 in. wide. How tall will it be?

$\frac{6}{24} = \frac{4}{x}$	Write a proportion.
$6 \cdot x = 24 \cdot 4$	Use cross-products.
$x = 16$	Divide each side by 6.

The poster will be 16 in. tall.

5. What is the similarity ratio of the photo to the poster?

6. **Critical Thinking** A school photo package comes with an 8 in.-by-10 in. photo and a 5 in.-by-7 in. photo. Are the photos similar? Explain.

WORK TOGETHER

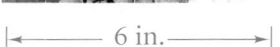

Trace the diagram and cut out the seven pieces. (Or use the tans you made in Lesson 2-1.)

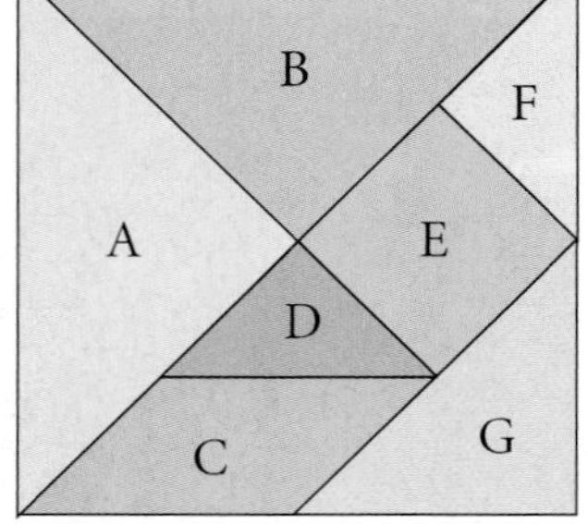

7. Which pieces are congruent?

8. Which pieces are similar? (Check that all pairs of corresponding angles are congruent and that corresponding sides are proportional.)

9. Find other congruent and similar pairs by placing pieces together. Record your answers.

Here are some examples:

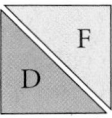

congruent

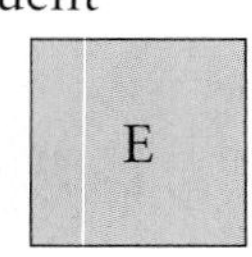

similar

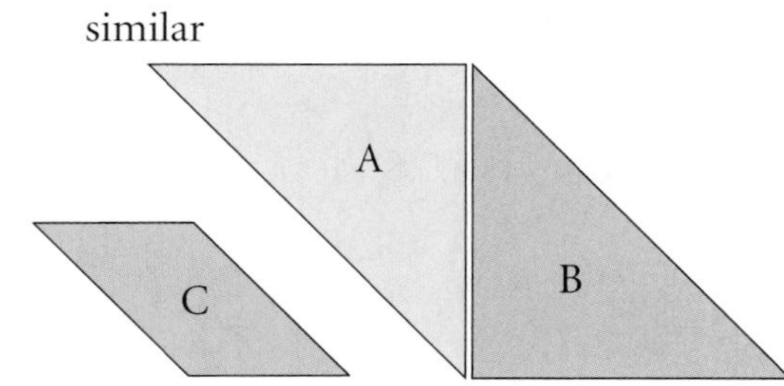

Exercises ON YOUR OWN

1. Identify the pairs of triangles that appear to be congruent.

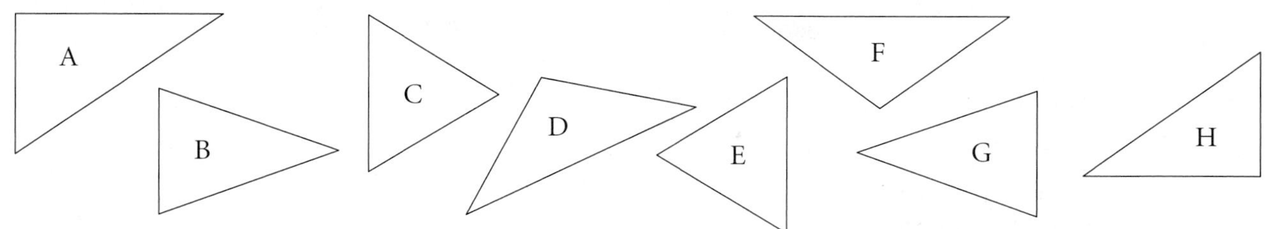

$\triangle LMC \cong \triangle BJK$. Complete the congruence statements.

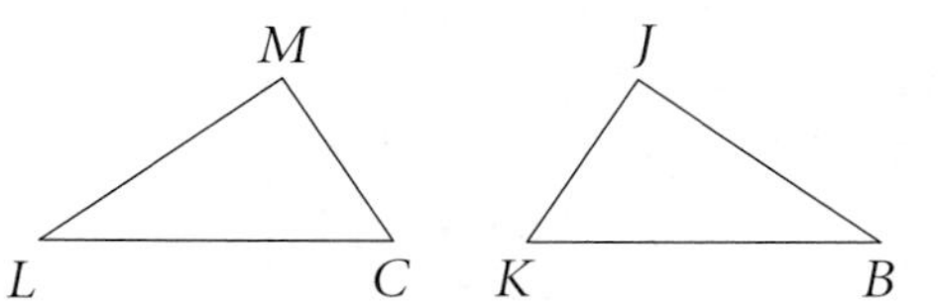

2. $\overline{LC} \cong$ ▒ 3. $\overline{KJ} \cong$ ▒ 4. $\overline{JB} \cong$ ▒

5. $\angle L \cong$ ▒ 6. $\angle K \cong$ ▒ 7. $\angle M \cong$ ▒

8. $\triangle CML \cong$ ▒ 9. $\triangle KBJ \cong$ ▒ 10. $\triangle MLC \cong$ ▒

$JDRT \sim JHYX$. Complete the proportions and congruence statements.

11. $\frac{JD}{JH} = \frac{DR}{▒}$ 12. $\frac{RT}{YX} = \frac{▒}{JX}$ 13. $\frac{▒}{DR} = \frac{YX}{RT}$

14. $\angle D \cong$ ▒ 15. $\angle Y \cong$ ▒ 16. $\angle T \cong$ ▒

$\triangle DFG \sim \triangle HKM$. Use the diagram to find the following.

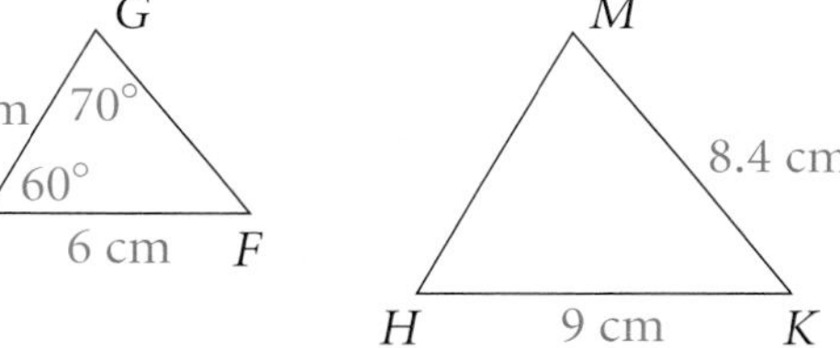

17. the similarity ratio of $\triangle DFG$ to $\triangle HKM$
18. the similarity ratio of $\triangle HKM$ to $\triangle DFG$

19. $m\angle F$ 20. $m\angle K$ 21. $m\angle M$

22. $\frac{DF}{HK}$ 23. HM 24. GF

In Exercises 25–27, $POLY \cong SIDE$.

25. List four pairs of congruent angles.
26. List four pairs of congruent sides.
27. Complete the congruence statements.
 a. $OLYP \cong$ ▒ b. $DESI \cong$ ▒

28. **Art** An art class is painting a mural for a spring festival. The students are working from a diagram that is 48 in. long and 36 in. high. Find the length of the mural if its height is to be 12 ft.

29. **Research** A *fractal* is a self-similar geometric pattern. It is made up of parts that are similar to the object itself. A good example of this is a fern frond. Break off any leaflet and the leaflet looks like a small fern frond. Investigate fractals and **summarize** your findings.

30. **a.** Draw two different-sized squares on graph paper. Find the ratio of each pair of corresponding sides.
    b. Are these squares similar? Explain.
    c. Draw two different-sized rectangles on graph paper. Find the ratio of each pair of corresponding sides.
    d. Are these rectangles similar? Explain.
    e. **Writing** Are all squares similar? Are all rectangles similar? Explain. Sketch pictures to support your conclusion.

31. **Critical Thinking** Kimi claims that all circles are similar. Is she right? Explain.

Write a congruence statement for each pair of triangles.

32.

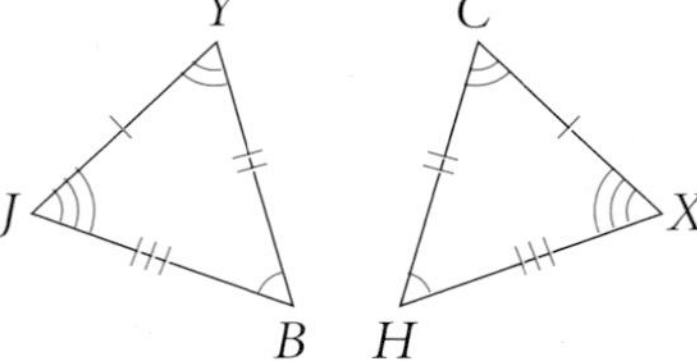

33.

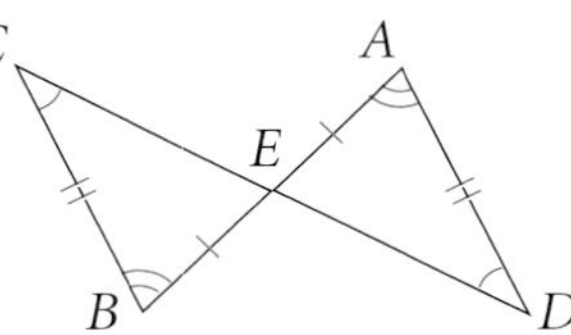

E is the midpoint of $\overline{CD}$.

34.

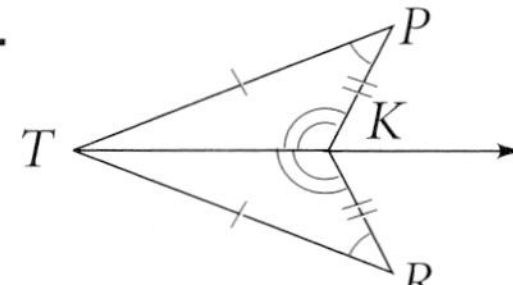

$\overrightarrow{TK}$ bisects $\angle PTR$.

Choose **Use pencil and paper, mental math, or a calculator to find the values of the variables.**

35.

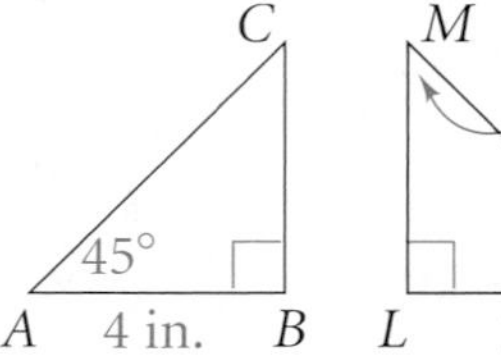

$\triangle ABC \cong \triangle KLM$

36.

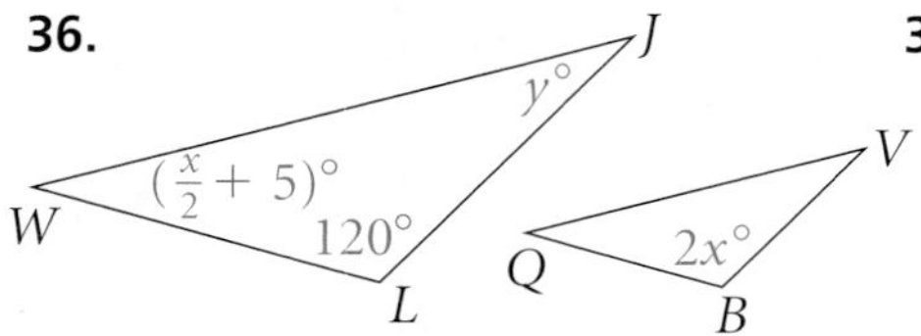

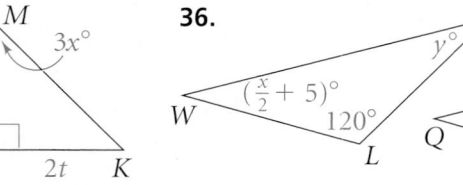

$\triangle WLJ \sim \triangle QBV$

37.

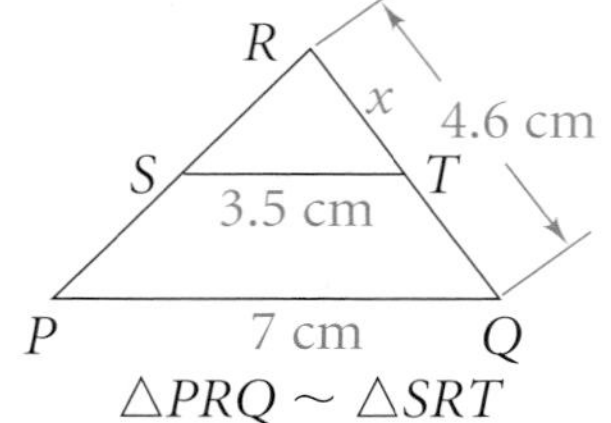

$\triangle PRQ \sim \triangle SRT$

38. **Standardized Test Prep** $\triangle KJH$ is congruent to the triangle shown. Which of these *cannot* be the coordinates of point H?

A. (5, 0) **B.** (5, 4) **C.** (6, 4)
D. (6, 0) **E.** (7, 0)

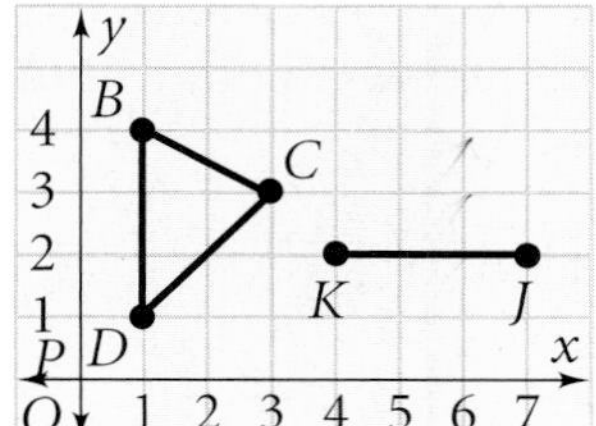

39. When you make an enlargement on a copy machine, the enlargement is similar to the original. You are making an enlargement of $\triangle ABC$. Suppose you choose the 120% enlargement setting. This means that the similarity ratio of the enlargement to the original is $\frac{120}{100}$, or $\frac{6}{5}$.

a. Find the lengths of the sides of the enlargement.

b. Find the measures of the angles of the enlargement.

c. Suppose you use the 150% setting. Find the lengths of the sides of the triangle.

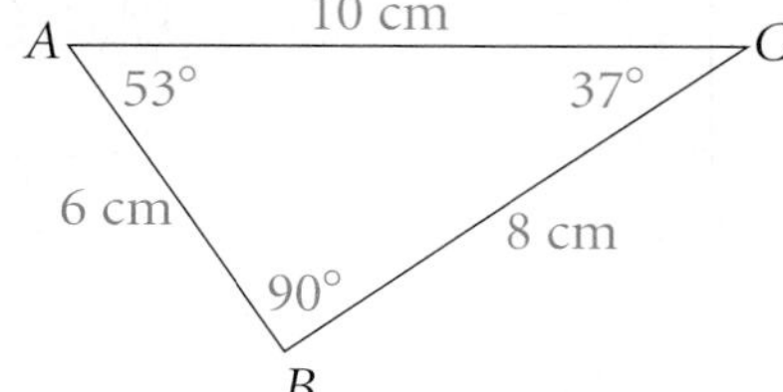

The triangles are similar. Find the similarity ratio of the first to the second.

40.

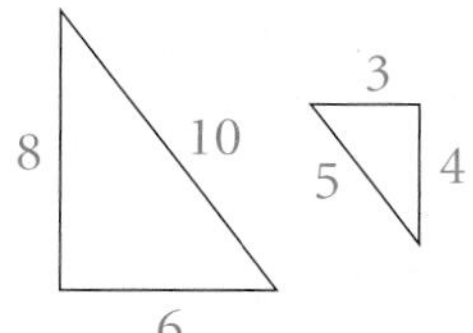

41.

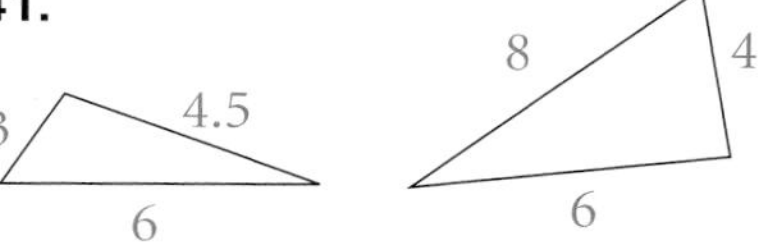

42.

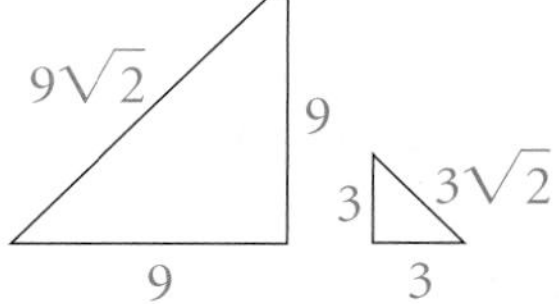

43. a. ***Photography*** Is an 8 in.-by-10 in. photograph similar to a 16 in.-by 20 in. photograph? Explain.

b. Is a 4 in.-by-5 in. photograph similar to a 5 in.-by-7 in. photograph? Explain.

44. ***Standardized Test Prep*** The circle shown is congruent to a circle with center $P(1, -4)$. Which of these *cannot* be the coordinates of a point on $\odot P$?

A. $(-1, -2)$ **B.** $(-1, -6)$ **C.** $(3, -2)$ **D.** $(3, -4)$ **E.** $(3, -6)$

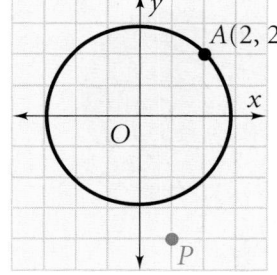

45. ***Open-ended*** Draw two quadrilaterals that have sides in the ratio 2 : 1 and yet are not similar.

Chapter Project ***Find Out by Investigating***

Use the pentominoes you made in the Find Out exercise on page 657 to investigate similarity.

- How many more pentominoes will it take to complete the 3-by-15 rectangle below? How do you know? Complete the rectangle and record your solution on graph paper.

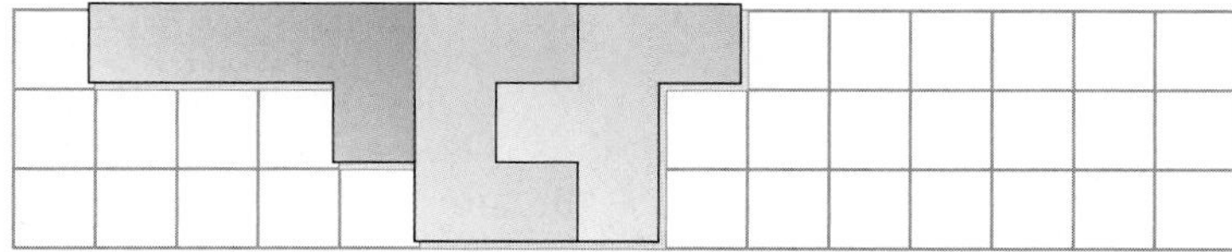

- Is this 3-by-15 rectangle *similar* to the rectangular pentomino piece? Explain. If it is, what is the similarity ratio?

Exercises MIXED REVIEW

46. **Constructions** Draw a 3-in. segment. Construct the perpendicular bisector of that segment. Check your work with a ruler and a protractor.

47. **Coordinate Geometry** Connect $A(3, 3)$, $B(5, 5)$, $T(9, 1)$, and $S(9, -3)$ in order. What type of quadrilateral is $ABTS$? Explain.

48. $M(-1, 0)$ is the midpoint of $\overline{AB}$. The coordinates of A are $(5, 1)$. Find the coordinates of B.

49. What is the measure of each interior angle of a regular 18-gon?

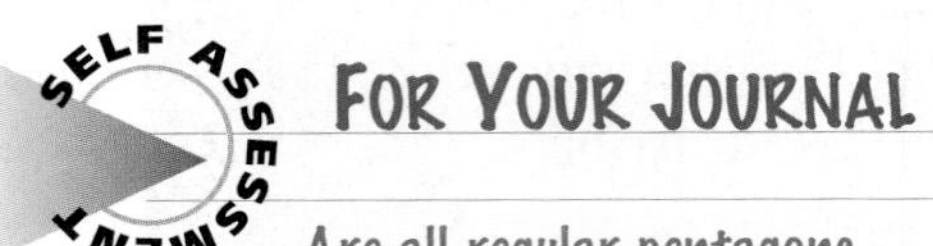

FOR YOUR JOURNAL

Are all regular pentagons similar? Are all regular hexagons similar? Make a conjecture about regular polygons and similarity. Justify your reasoning.

Getting Ready for Lesson 2-7

Imagine you are looking down at each of these figures from above. Describe the geometric figure you see.

50. 

51. 

52. 

Exercises CHECKPOINT

Find the center and radius of each circle with diameter $\overline{AB}$.

1. $A(4, 1), B(7, 5)$
2. $A(0, 8), B(3, 6)$
3. $A(-3, 9), B(4, -2)$
4. $A(-2, -5), B(-8, 4)$

Find the measure of each arc or angle in $\odot A$.

5. $\angle WAX$
6. $\overset{\frown}{RX}$
7. $\angle SAR$
8. $\overset{\frown}{TRW}$
9. $\angle TAW$
10. $\overset{\frown}{RT}$
11. $\overset{\frown}{SR}$
12. $\overset{\frown}{XST}$
13. $\overset{\frown}{STW}$

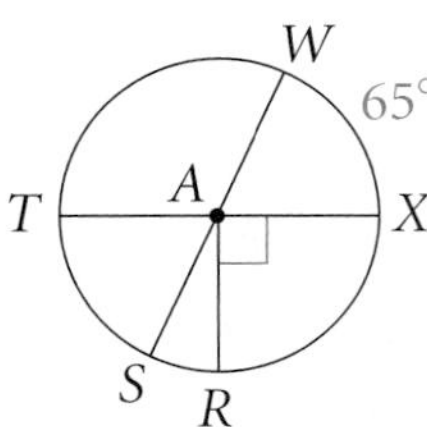

Draw a pair of figures to fit each description.

14. congruent right triangles
15. similar pentagons
16. similar rectangles

17. What is the most precise name for a quadrilateral with vertices at $(3, 5)$, $(-1, 4)$, $(7, 4)$, and $(3, -5)$?
A. kite **B.** rectangle **C.** parallelogram **D.** rhombus **E.** trapezoid

2-7 Isometric and Orthographic Drawings

What You'll Learn

- Drawing isometric and orthographic views of objects

...And Why

To practice a skill used in industries of all sorts

What You'll Need

- isometric dot paper
- graph paper
- straightedge
- cubes

THINK AND DISCUSS

Isometric Drawings

The figures that you've studied so far in this chapter have been two-dimensional. The *faces* of three-dimensional figures are two-dimensional. Many types of industries use two-dimensional drawings of three-dimensional objects. The makers of some animated cartoons for example, use computers to create *wire-frame models* of three-dimensional characters. These wire-frame images—basically complicated stick figures—are made up of polygons.

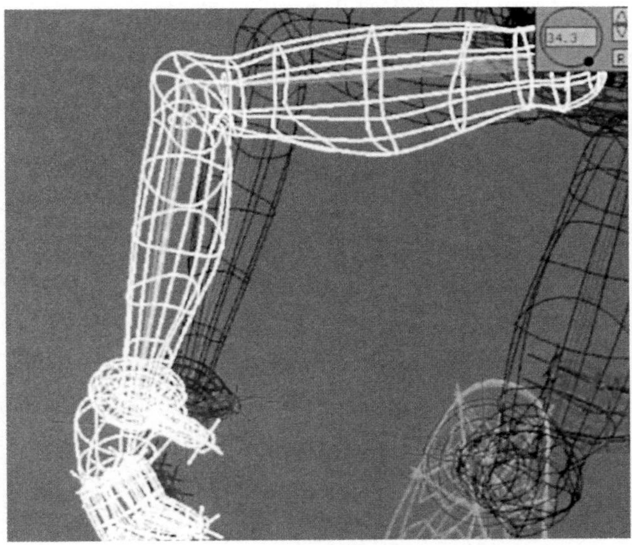

The wire frame model of the insect's leg is made up of polygons. Notice how they are joined to give the illusion of a curved surface.

The computer forms the final image by adding a "skin" to the wire-frame and then lighting the figure.

One way to show a three-dimensional object is with an isometric drawing. An **isometric drawing** shows a corner view. It shows three sides of an object in a single drawing. Here are two examples.

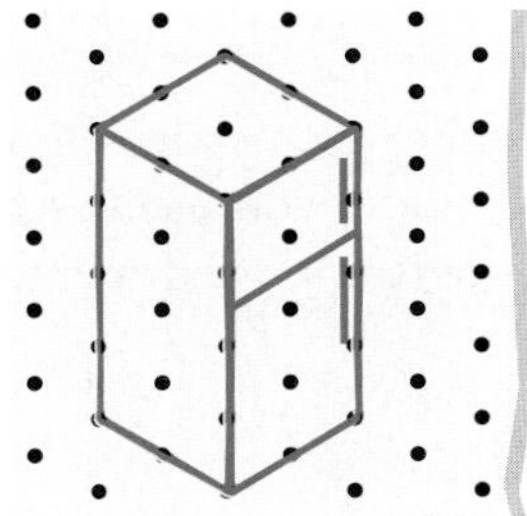

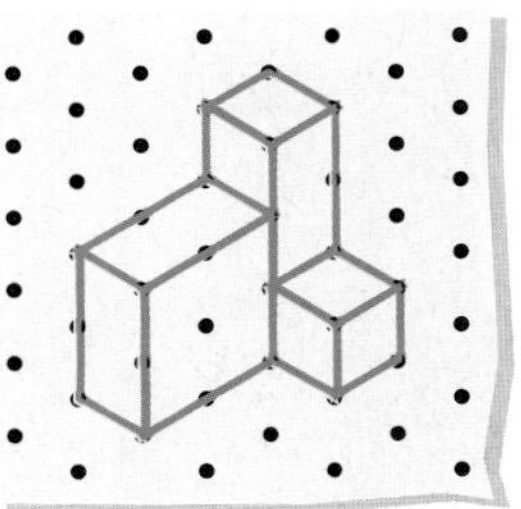

You can use isometric dot paper to draw cube structures.

Example 1

Create an isometric drawing of the cube structure at the left.

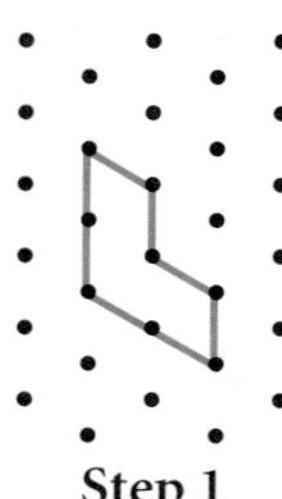

Step 1

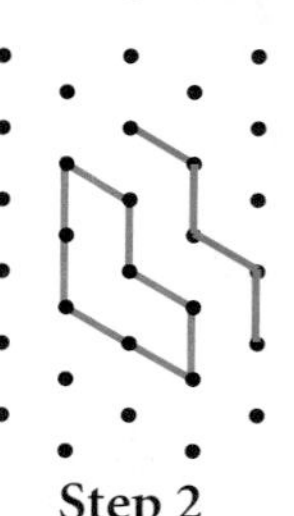

Step 2

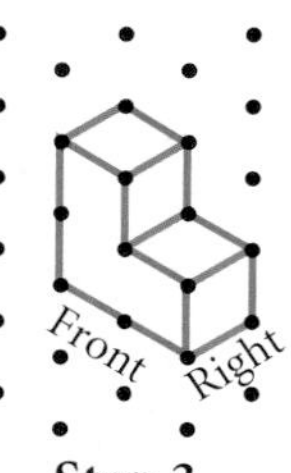

Step 3

1. **Try This** Build a structure using 4 cubes. Create an isometric drawing of your structure.

Another way to show some types of three-dimensional objects is with a foundation drawing. A **foundation drawing** shows the base of a structure and the height of each part. The diagram at the right is a foundation drawing of the Sears Tower in Chicago.

54	67	54
67	98	67
41	98	41

The Sears Tower is made up of nine sections. The numbers tell how many stories tall each section is.

Example 2

Create a foundation drawing for the isometric drawing below.

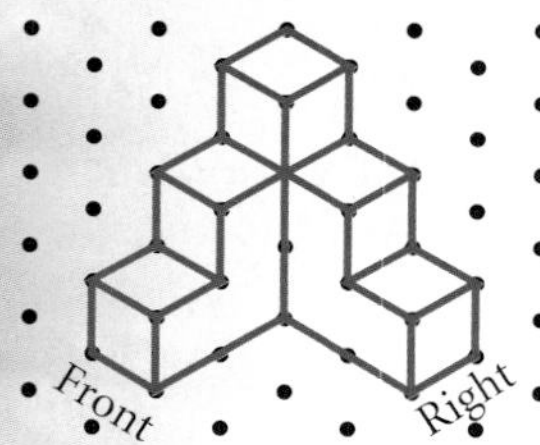

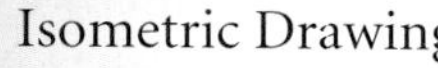

Isometric Drawing

3	2	1
2		
1		

Front

Right

Foundation Drawing

2. a. How many cubes are needed to make the structure in Example 2?
   b. Which drawing did you use to answer part (a), the foundation drawing or the isometric drawing? Why?

Orthographic Drawings

A third way to show three-dimensional figures is with an orthographic drawing. An **orthographic drawing** shows a top view, front view, and right-side view. Here is an example.

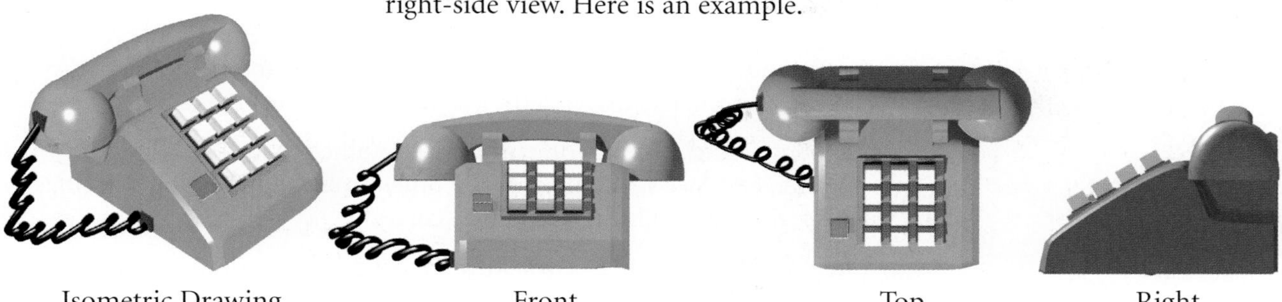
Isometric Drawing　　Front　　Top　　Right

Example 3

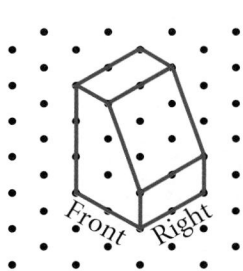

Create an orthographic drawing for each isometric drawing at the left.

Front　Right

Isometric Drawing

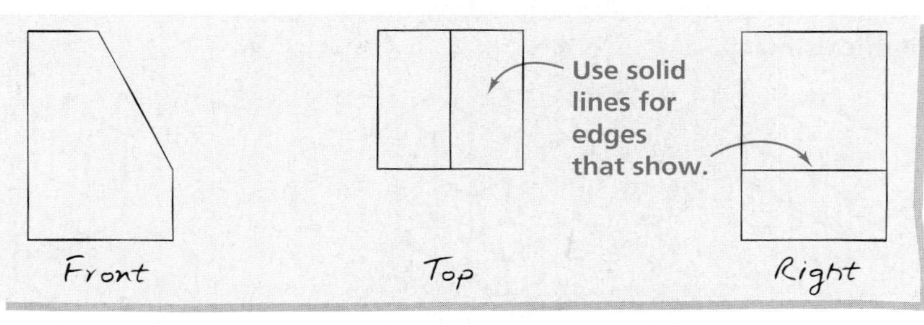

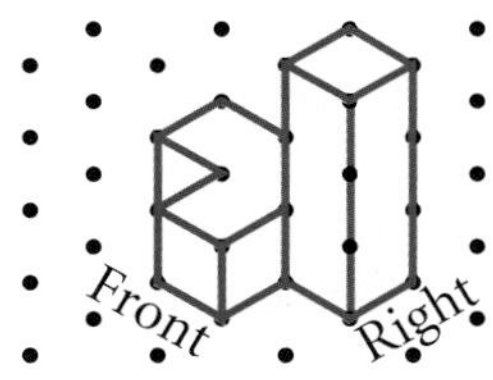

Isometric Drawing

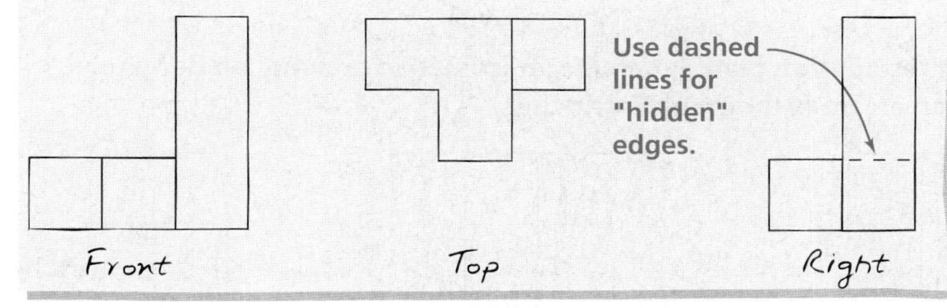

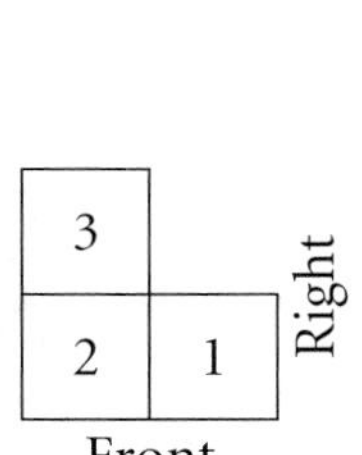

3. *Open-ended* Choose a simple object in your classroom. Make an orthographic drawing showing three views.

4. a. *Manipulatives* Build a cube structure for the foundation drawing at the left. Then create an isometric drawing for the structure.
   b. Create an orthographic drawing showing a top view, front view, and right-side view.

WORK TOGETHER

Step 1: Work in a group to build a structure using 12 cubes. Label the sides of the structure *Front, Back, Right,* and *Left.*

Step 2: Have each member of your group use graph paper to create a foundation drawing of the structure. Then use isometric dot paper to create an isometric drawing. In both drawings, label the sides.

Step 3: Trade isometric drawings with another group. Use their drawings to re-create their structure. Use the other group's foundation drawings to check that you built their structure correctly.

Step 4: Repeat Steps 1–3, substituting orthographic drawings for the isometric drawings in Steps 2 and 3.

Exercises ON YOUR OWN

For each figure, (a) create a foundation drawing, and (b) create an orthographic drawing.

1. 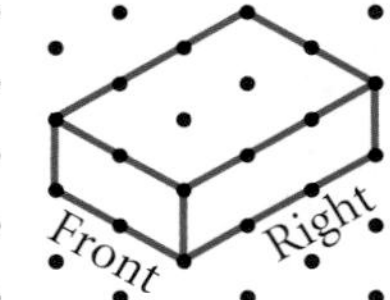

2. 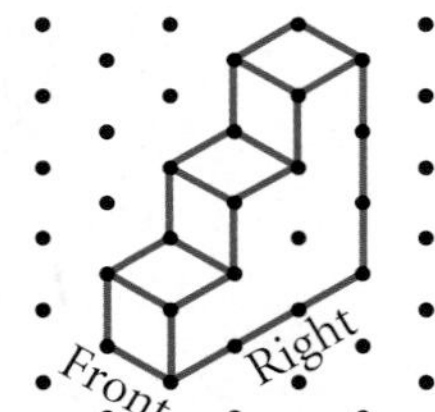

3. 

4. 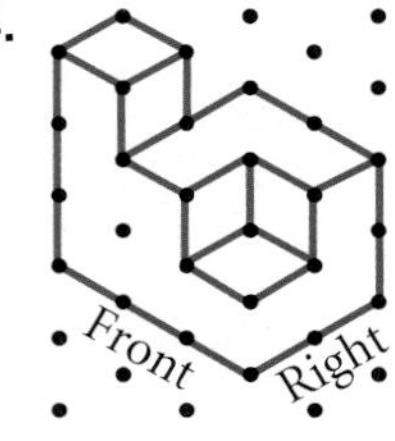

For each foundation plan, (a) create an isometric drawing on dot paper, and (b) create an orthographic drawing.

5.

3	3
2	1

Right
Front

6. 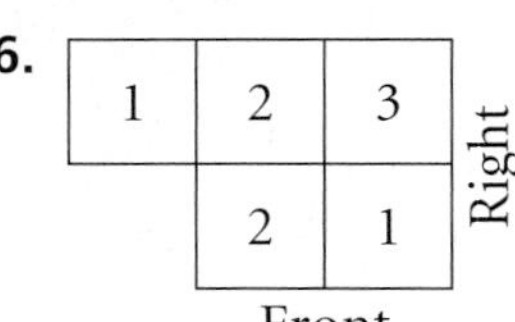

1	2	3
	2	1

Right
Front

7. 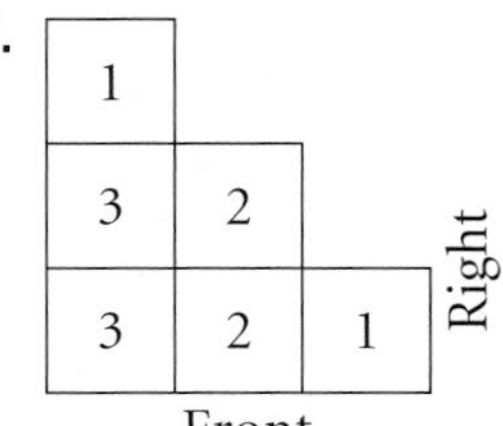

1		
3	2	
3	2	1

Right
Front

8.

4	3
2	
2	

Right
Front

9. a. **Open-ended** Create an isometric drawing of a figure that can be constructed using 8 cubes.
   b. Create an orthographic drawing of this structure.
   c. Create a foundation plan for the figure.

Read the comic strip and complete Exercises 10 and 11.

SHOE by Jeff MacNelly

10. What type of drawing that you've studied in this lesson is a "bird's-eye view"?

11. **Writing** Photographs of the Washington Monument are typically not taken from a bird's-eye view. Describe a situation in which you would want a photo showing a bird's-eye view.

Cross Sections **Imagine cutting straight through an orange. The *cross section* will always be a circle. Describe the cross section in each diagram.**

Sample:

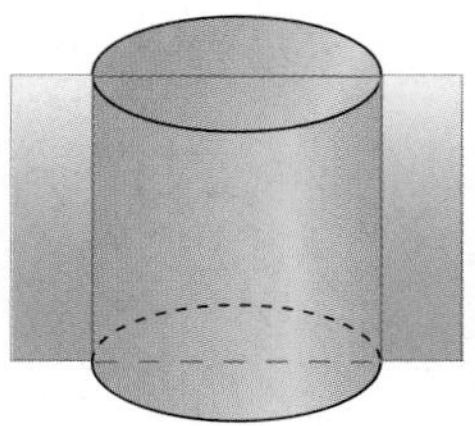

This cross section of a cylinder is a rectangle. The width of the rectangle is the diameter of the circular base of the cylinder. The length of the rectangle is the height of the cylinder.

12. 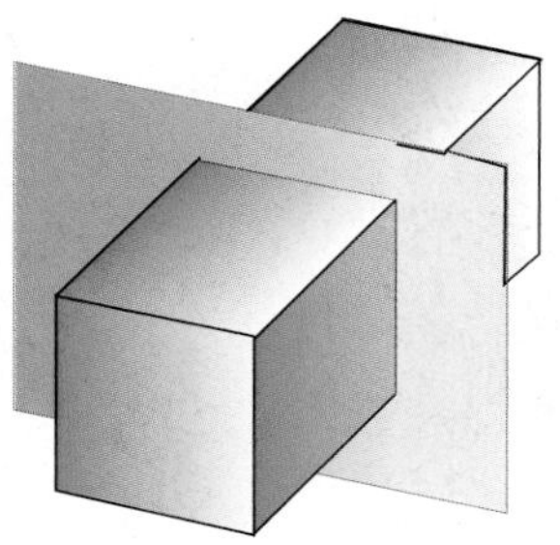

13. 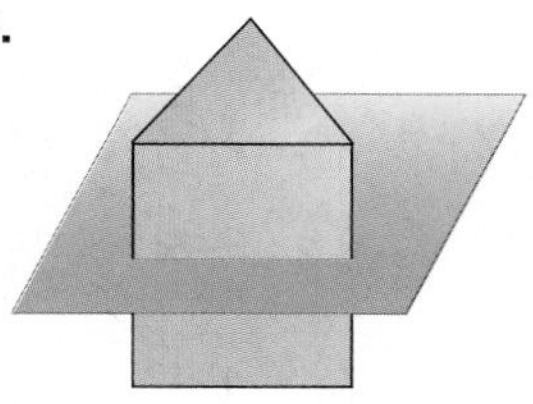

14. 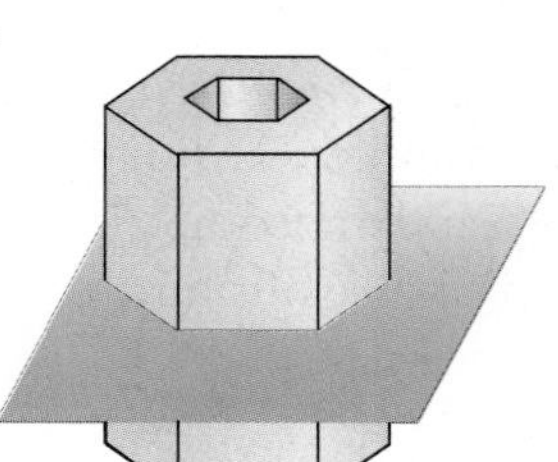

15. 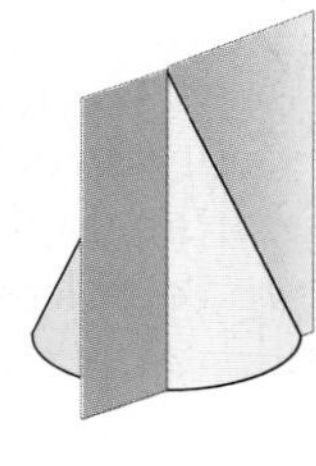

16. **Probability** Jake makes a structure using 27 wooden cubes. He paints four of the faces blue and leaves the top and bottom unpainted. Then he takes the structure apart and places the cubes in a bag. Leah closes her eyes, reaches into the bag, and pulls out a cube.
   a. What is the probability that the cube is unpainted?
   b. What is the probability that two of its faces are blue?
   c. What is the probability that only one of its faces is blue?

Match each isometric drawing with the correct orthographic drawing.

17. 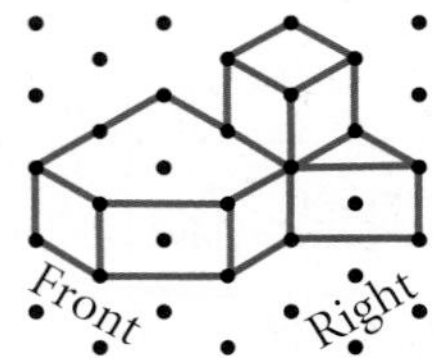

18. 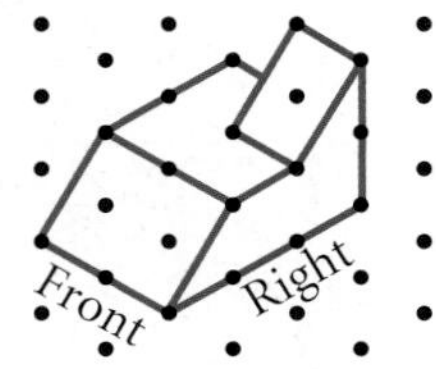

19. 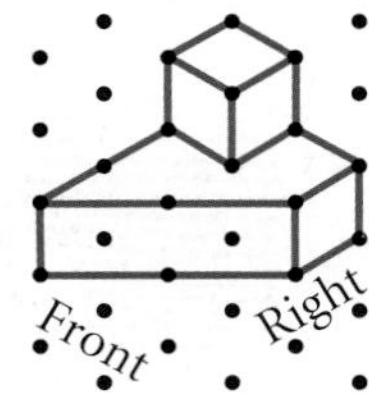

20. 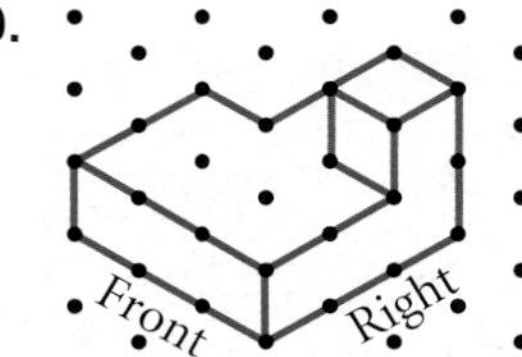

A. 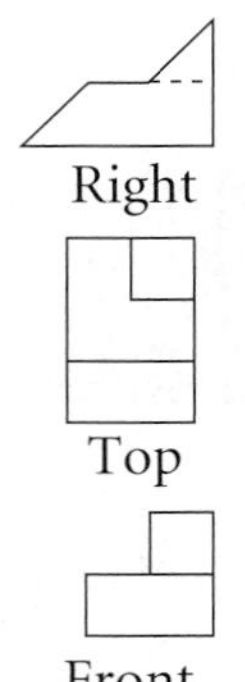

B.

Right

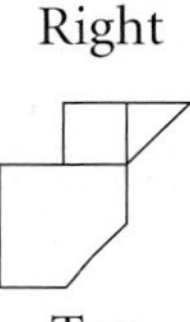

Top

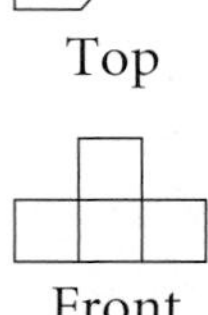

Front

C. 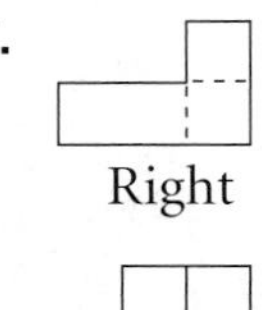

Right

Top

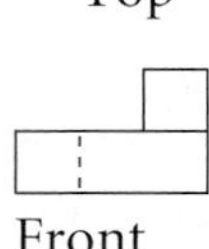

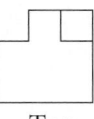

Front

D. 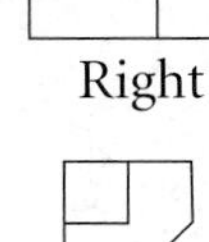

Right

Top

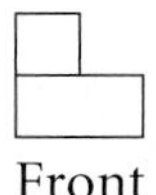

Front

Create an orthographic drawing for each isometric drawing.

21. 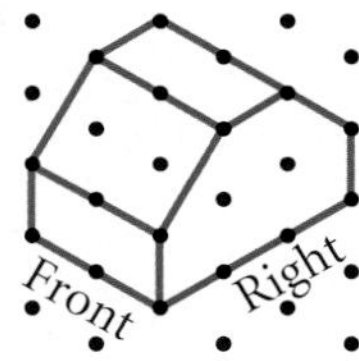

22. 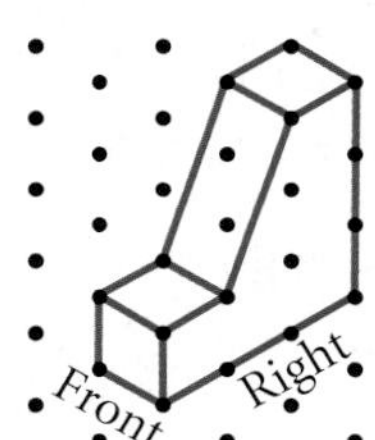

23. 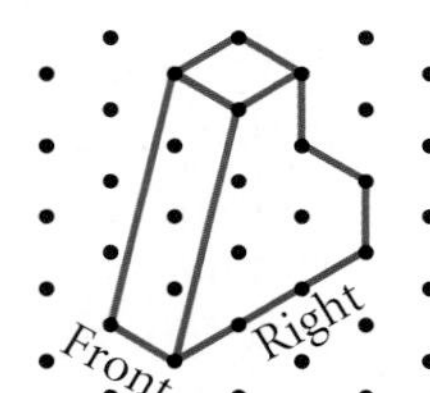

24. 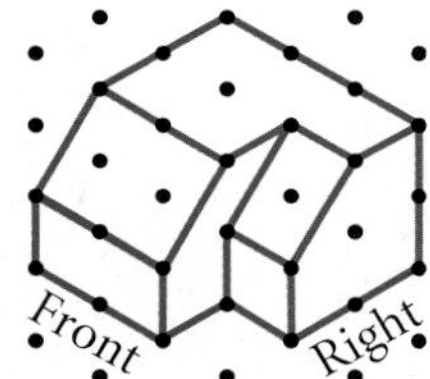

25. **Engineering** Engineers use an *engineering layout* to describe structures. A complete layout includes three orthographic views and an isometric view. Make a complete engineering layout for the foundation plan.

4	3	2
3	2	1
2	1	

Right

Front

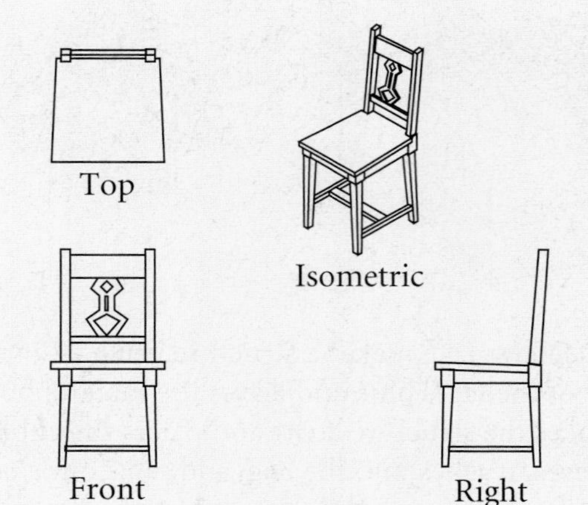

Engineering Layout

Chapter Project — Find Out by Modeling

Soma is a three-dimensional puzzle made of unit cubes. All Soma pieces consist of 3 or 4 unit cubes. Each cube shares a face with at least one other cube. Every Soma piece must contain at least two cubes, which meet to form a 90° dihedral angle. (A *dihedral angle* is an angle formed by two planes.) There are exactly seven Soma pieces, and all are different. The photograph shows two Soma pieces.

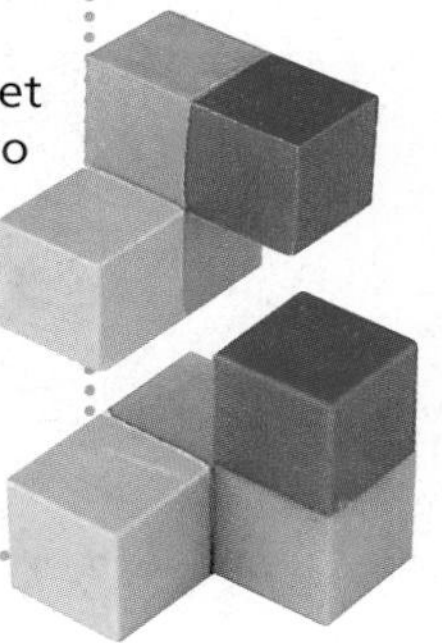

- Build a set of Soma pieces by gluing cubes together.
- Draw the other five Soma pieces on isometric dot paper.
- Use all seven Soma pieces to build a cube.

Exercises MIXED REVIEW

Find the length of each segment with the given endpoints. Then find the coordinates of the midpoint of each segment.

26. $A(4, 6)$ and $B(2, 9)$

27. $G(-3, -1)$ and $H(1, 2)$

28. Use slope to determine whether points $A(0, 1)$, $B(-3, -2)$, and $C(4, 5)$ are collinear.

Draw a diagram that illustrates each concept.

29. adjacent angles

30. perpendicular bisector

PORTFOLIO

For your portfolio, select one or two items from your work for this chapter. Here are some possibilities:
- most improved work
- a Journal entry

Explain why you have included each selection.

Geometry at Work

Industrial Designer

Industrial designers work on two-dimensional surfaces to develop products that have three-dimensional appeal to consumers. They use computer-aided design (CAD) software to create two-dimensional screen images and manipulate them for three-dimensional effects. Fashion designers use CAD to study their creations on electronic human forms from various angles and distances.

Mini Project: Design an athletic shoe. Use an engineering layout to display your design. Include three orthographic views and an isometric view.

CHAPTER PROJECT

Finishing the Chapter Project

AMAZING SPACE

Find Out exercises on pages 636, 643, 657, 669, and 677 should help you to complete your project. Prepare a *Geometric Diversions* display. Include the models you made, instructions for making them, and the geometric patterns you discovered.

Reflect and Revise

Ask a classmate to review your display with you. Together, check that your solutions are correct, your diagrams clear, and your explanations sensible. Have you used geometric terms correctly? Is the display organized, comprehensive, and visually appealing? Consider doing more research (using some of the books listed below) on other popular puzzles and writing a short report.

Follow Up

Now that you've had some experience exploring geometric puzzles, create your own puzzle. Start with any two- or three-dimensional figure and go from there. Challenge your classmates!

For More Information

Costello, Matthew J. *The Greatest Puzzles of All Time.* New York: Prentice Hall Press, 1988.

Gardner, Martin. *The Scientific American Mathematical Puzzles & Diversions.* New York: Simon & Schuster, 1959.

Gardner, Martin. *The 2nd Scientific American Book of Mathematical Puzzles & Diversions.* New York: University of Chicago Press, 1987.

Kenney, Margaret J., Stanley J. Bezuszka, and Joan D. Martin. *Informal Geometry Explorations.* Palo Alto, California: Dale Seymour Publications, 1992.

Reid, Ronald C. *Tangrams-330 Puzzles.* New York: Dover Publications, Inc., 1965.

CHAPTER 2

Wrap Up

Key Terms

acute triangle (p. 633)
adjacent arcs (p. 660)
circle (p. 658)
central angle (p. 659)
concave (p. 638)
congruent circles (p. 664)
congruent polygons (p. 664)
convex (p. 638)
corollary (p. 632)
diameter (p. 658)
equiangular polygon (p. 640)
equiangular triangle (p. 633)
equilateral polygon (p. 640)
equilateral triangle (p. 633)
exterior angle (p. 631)
foundation drawing (p. 672)
isometric drawing (p. 671)
isosceles trapezoid (p. 653)
isosceles triangle (p. 633)
kite (p. 653)
major arc (p. 660)
minor arc (p. 660)
obtuse triangle (p. 633)
orthographic drawing (p. 673)
parallelogram (p. 653)
polygon (p. 638)
radius (p. 658)
rectangle (p. 653)
regular polygon (p. 640)
remote interior angle (p. 631)
right triangle (p. 633)
scalene triangle (p. 633)
semicircle (p. 660)
similar polygons (p. 665)
similarity ratio (p. 665)
square (p. 653)
trapezoid (p. 653)

How am I doing?

- State three ideas from this chapter that you think are important. Explain your choices.
- Describe different ways of classifying triangles and quadrilaterals.

Triangles 2-1

The sum of the measures of the angles of a triangle is 180. The measure of each **exterior angle** of a triangle equals the sum of the measures of its two **remote interior angles,** and is therefore greater than the measure of either remote interior angle.

You can classify triangles according to their sides and angles.

Find the values of the variables. Then classify each triangle by its sides and angles.

1. 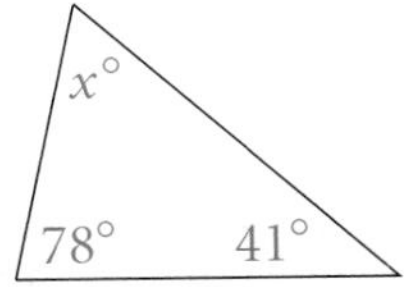

2. 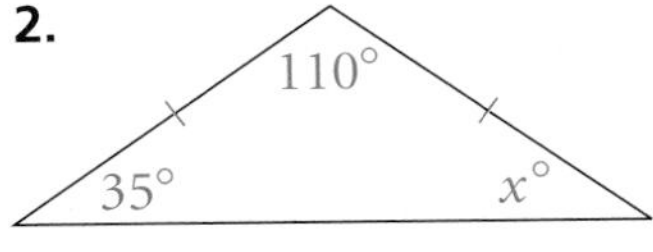

3. 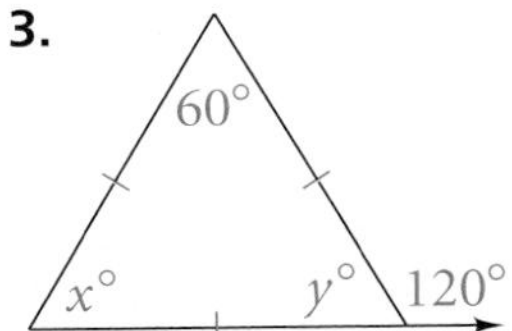

4. 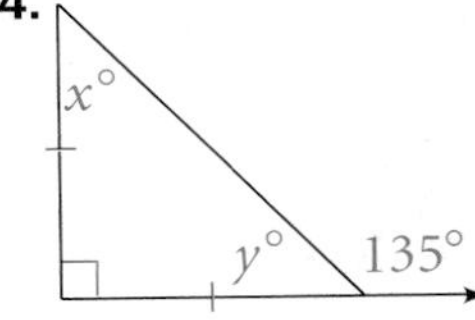

5. *Standardized Test Prep* The measures of the angles of different triangles are shown below. Which triangle is obtuse?
   A. $x + 10, x - 20, x + 25$
   B. $x, 2x, 3x$
   C. $20x + 10, 30x - 2, 7x + 1$
   D. $10x - 3, 14x - 20, x + 3$
   E. none of the above

Polygons and Classifying Quadrilaterals 2-2, 2-4

A **polygon** is a closed plane figure with at least three sides. A polygon is **convex** if no diagonal contains points outside the polygon. Otherwise, it is **concave**. A **regular polygon** is equilateral and equiangular.

The sum of the measures of the interior angles of an n-gon is $(n - 2)180$. The sum of the measures of the exterior angles (one at each vertex) of an n-gon is 360.

Quadrilaterals have four sides. Some quadrilaterals have special names.

Find the measure of each interior angle and exterior angle for each regular polygon.

6. a hexagon
7. an octagon
8. a decagon
9. a 24-gon

Algebra **Find the values of the variables and the lengths of the sides.**

10. isosceles trapezoid $ABCD$

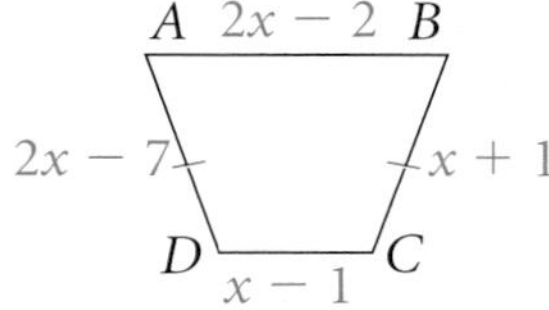

11. kite $KLMN$

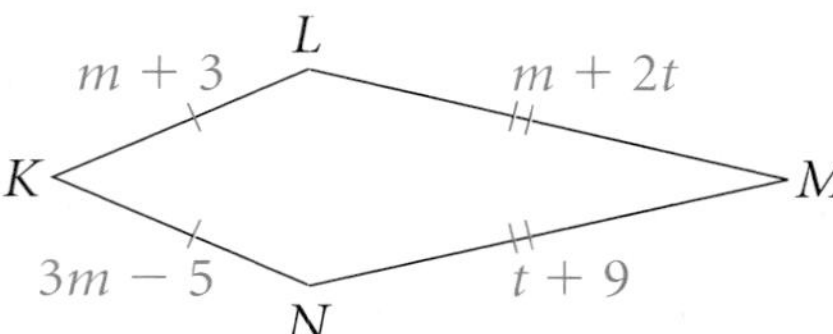

12. rhombus $PQRS$

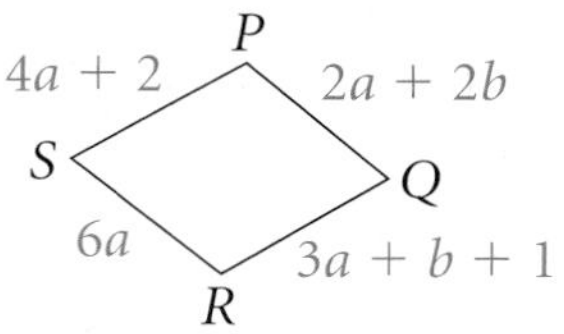

Parallel and Perpendicular Lines in the Coordinate Plane 2-3

The slopes of two nonvertical parallel lines are equal. Two lines parallel to a third line are parallel to each other.

The product of the slopes of two nonvertical perpendicular lines is -1. In a plane, two lines perpendicular to a third line are parallel to each other.

Find the slopes of $\overleftrightarrow{AB}$ and $\overleftrightarrow{CD}$. Then determine if the lines are parallel, perpendicular, or neither.

13. $A(-1, -4), B(2, 11), C(1, 1), D(4, 10)$
14. $A(2, 10), B(-1, -2), C(3, 7), D(0, -5)$
15. $A(-3, 3), B(0, 2), C(1, 3), D(-2, -6)$
16. $A(-1, 3), B(6, 10), C(-6, 0), D(4, 10)$

Circles 2-5

A **circle** is the set of all points in a plane equidistant from one point called the center. The measure of a minor arc is the measure of its corresponding central angle. The measure of a major arc is 360 minus the measure of its related minor arc. **Adjacent arcs** have exactly one point in common.

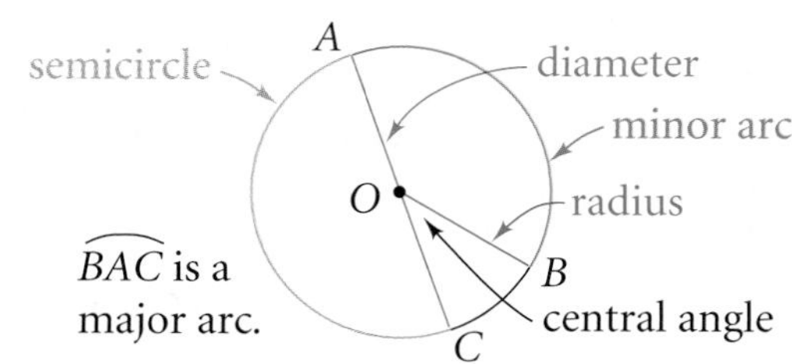

Find the coordinates of the center and the radius of each circle with diameter $\overline{AB}$.

17. $A(4, 0), B(4, 6)$ 18. $A(2, -3), B(0, 1)$ 19. $A(-4, -5), B(2, -1)$ 20. $A(7, 2), B(4, 8)$

Find each measure.

21. $m\angle APD$ 22. $m\widehat{AC}$

23. $m\widehat{ABD}$ 24. $m\angle CPA$

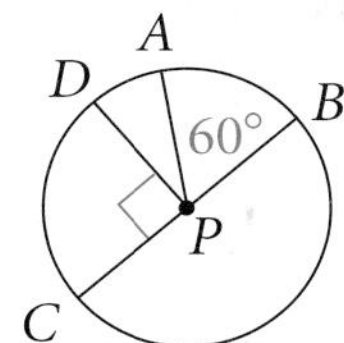

Congruent and Similar Figures 2-6

Congruent polygons have congruent corresponding parts. **Similar polygons** have congruent corresponding angles and proportional corresponding sides. The ratio of the lengths of corresponding sides is the **similarity ratio.**

***RSTUV* $\cong$ *KLMNO*. Complete each congruence statement.**

25. $\overline{TS} \cong$ ■ 26. $\angle N \cong$ ■ 27. $\overline{LM} \cong$ ■ 28. $VUTSR \cong$ ■

29. **Open-ended** Sketch a pair of similar hexagons.

Isometric and Orthographic Drawings 2-7

There are different ways to make two-dimensional drawings of three-dimensional objects. An **isometric drawing** shows three sides of an object in one drawing. A **foundation drawing** shows the bottom of a structure and the height of each part. An **orthographic drawing** shows the top, front, and right-side view of an object.

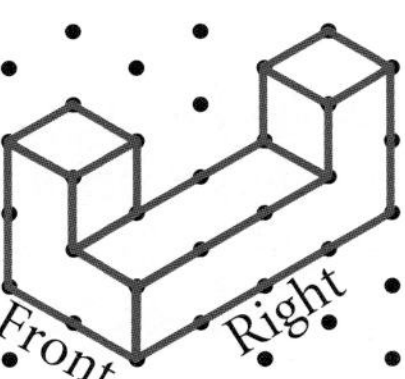

30. Use the isometric drawing at the right.
    a. Make an orthographic drawing.
    b. Make a foundation drawing.

31. **Writing** Describe a situation in which an orthographic drawing is useful.

Getting Ready for........ CHAPTER 3

Draw a pair of figures to fit each description.

32. similar acute triangles with similarity ratio $\frac{1}{2}$

33. similar quadrilaterals with similarity ratio $\frac{3}{4}$

Draw each figure. Then draw a line dividing the figure in half.

34. regular octagon 35. rectangle 36. isosceles trapezoid 37. kite

CHAPTER 2 Assessment

Use a protractor and a centimeter ruler to classify each triangle by its angles and sides.

1.

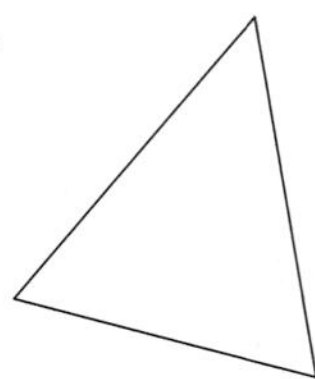

2.

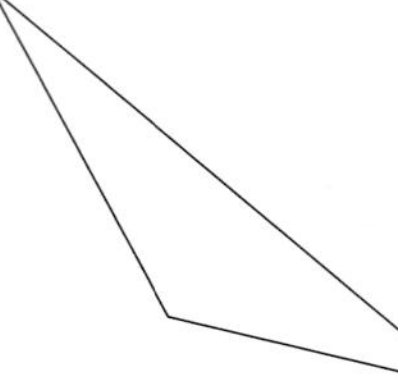

Algebra **Find the values of the variables.**

3.

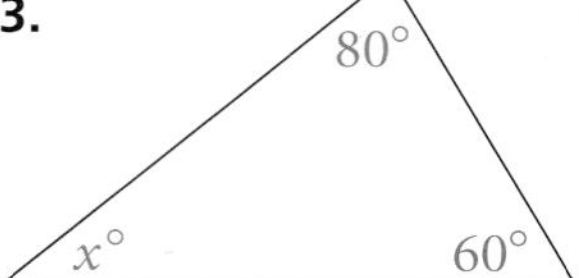

4.

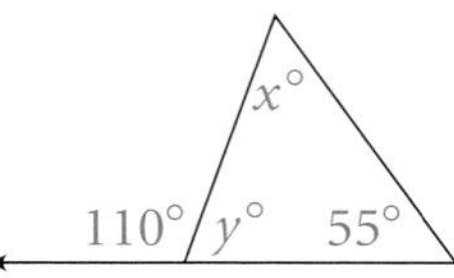

5.

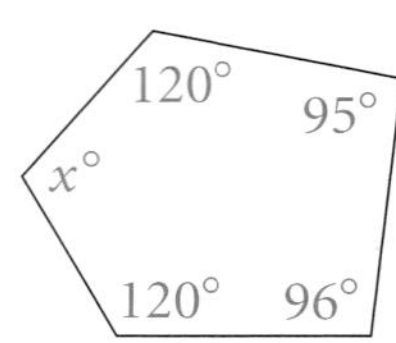

6.

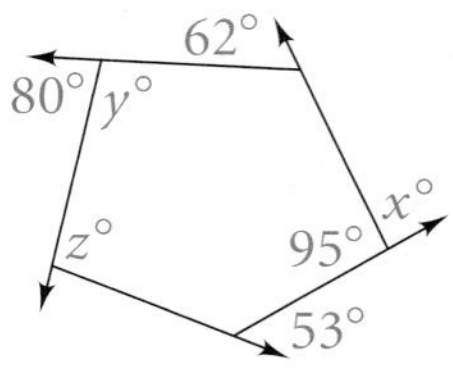

7. **Writing** Explain how you can determine if a polygon is concave or convex.

Sketch each pair of lines. Tell whether they are *parallel, perpendicular,* or *neither.*

8. $y = 4x + 7$
   $y = -\frac{1}{4}x - 3$

9. $y = 3x - 4$
   $y = 3x + 1$

10. $y = x + 5$
    $y = -5x - 1$

11. $y = x - 6$
    $y = -x + 2$

Coordinate Geometry **Graph quadrilateral *ABCD*. Then determine the most precise name for each figure.**

12. $A(1, 2), B(11, 2), C(7, 5), D(4, 5)$

13. $A(3, -2), B(5, 4), C(3, 6), D(1, 4)$

14. $A(1, -4), B(1, 1), C(-2, 2), D(-2, -3)$

15. **Open-ended** Write the coordinates of four points that determine each figure.
    a. square
    b. parallelogram
    c. rectangle
    d. trapezoid

Find the radius of a circle with the given diameter.

16. 6 ft

17. 5.1 m

18. $4\sqrt{5}$ in.

Find each measure for $\odot P$.

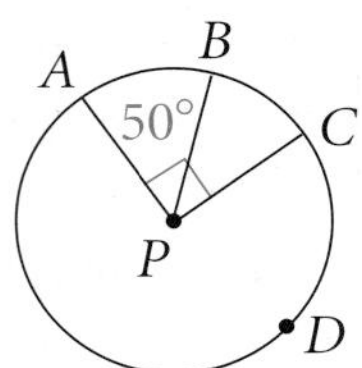

19. $m\angle BPC$

20. $m\widehat{AB}$

21. $m\widehat{ADC}$

22. $m\widehat{ADB}$

Find the values of the variables for each pair of similar figures.

23.

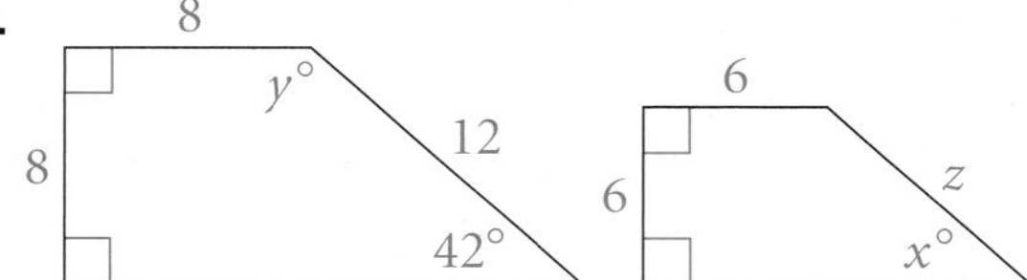

24.

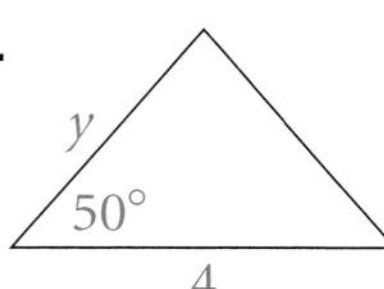

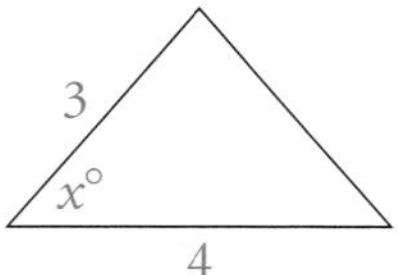

25. **Standardized Test Prep** What is the measure of each exterior angle of a regular 12-gon?

    A. 150 **B.** 30 **C.** 300 **D.** 210 **E.** 36

Use the figure below for Exercises 26 and 27.

26. Create an isometric drawing.

27. Create an orthographic drawing.

3	
1	1
2	1

Right

Front

CHAPTER 2 Preparing for the Math A Exam

Part I

1 $\triangle ABC$ is obtuse. Two vertices of the triangle are $A(3, 4)$ and $B(-1, 1)$. What could be the coordinates of point C?

(1) $(-1, -3)$ (3) $(3, 1)$
(2) $(0, 0)$ (4) $(-1, 4)$

2 An interior angle of a regular polygon measures 135°. What is the polygon?

(1) hexagon
(2) octagon
(3) decagon
(4) Not enough information is given to answer the question.

3 The graph of which equation is parallel to the graph of $y = 3x - 2$?

(1) $y = \frac{1}{3}x + 5$ (3) $y = -3x + 1$
(2) $y = 3x + 3$ (4) $y = -\frac{1}{3}x - 4$

4 Which names the quadrilateral in as many ways as possible?

(1) rectangle
(2) square and rhombus
(3) rectangle and rhombus
(4) rectangle and parallelogram

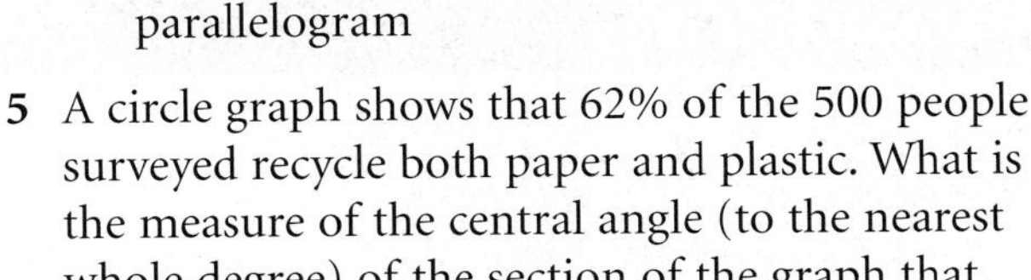

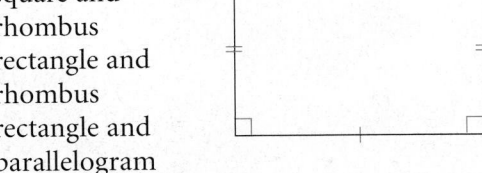

5 A circle graph shows that 62% of the 500 people surveyed recycle both paper and plastic. What is the measure of the central angle (to the nearest whole degree) of the section of the graph that shows this?

(1) 310° (3) 223°
(2) 62° (4) 112°

6 Which could be the dimensions of a rectangle similar to a rectangle 16 in. by 12 in. ?

(1) 4 in. by 3 in. (3) 30 in. by 24 in.
(2) 8 in. by 4 in. (4) 4 in. by 4 in.

Part II

7 Find the values of x and y. Then fully classify $\triangle ABC$.

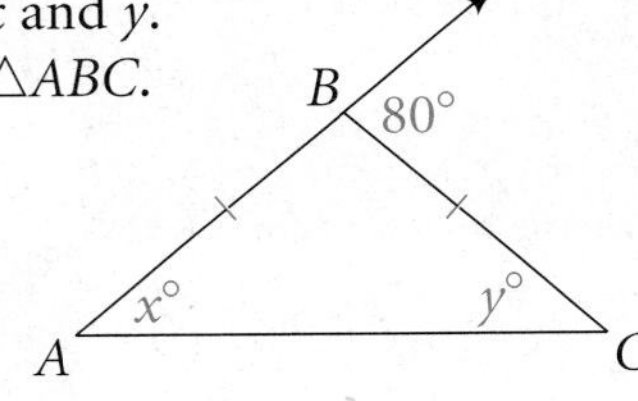

8 Write an equation of a line perpendicular to the graph of $y = 6x + 4$.

9 What is the diameter of a circle with radius $6\sqrt{5}$?

Part III

10 Solve the equation $-(b + 6) = 0$ and identify the properties you use.

11 Find the value of z.

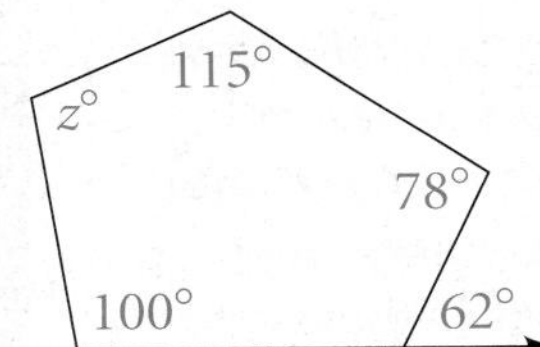

12 Find the lengths of all the sides of parallelogram $HIJK$.

H 3s + 1 I
t + 1
2s
K 3t − 2 J

13 A circle with diameter $\overline{CD}$ passes through $C(-4, -1)$ and $D(6, -3)$.

a What are the coordinates of the center of the circle?
b What is the radius of the circle?

Part IV

14 Find the values of the variables, given that the triangles are similar.

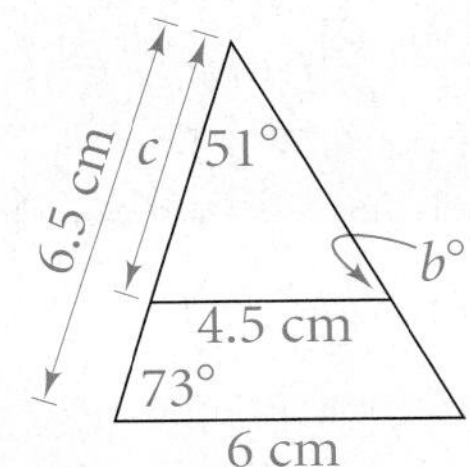

CHAPTER

3 Transformations: Shapes in Motion

Relating to the Real World

Many geometric figures in the real world do not sit still. They move; they change shape; they change size. You can describe these changes with transformational geometry. The principles you will study here have applications in many diverse fields—from science and architecture to music and history.

CHAPTER PROJECT

Ukrainian painted eggs, dollar bills, Native American pottery, Japanese kimonos, automobile tire treads, and African cloth are products of vastly diverse cultures, but these things all have something in common. They contain strips of repeating patterns, called *frieze patterns.*

In this chapter project, you will explore the underlying relationships among frieze patterns from around the world. You will also create your own designs. You will see how distinct civilizations—separated by oceans and centuries—are linked by their use of geometry to express themselves and to beautify their world.

To help you complete the project:

- **p. 699** *Find Out by Investigating*
- **p. 705** *Find Out by Modeling*
- **p. 712** *Find Out by Investigating*
- **p. 720** *Find Out by Classifying*
- **p. 733** *Find Out by Creating*
- **p. 735** *Finishing the Project*

Tessellations 3-6

Dilations 3-7

Connections Engineering . . . and more

What You'll Learn

- Identifying isometries
- Locating reflection images of figures

...And Why

To describe and explain the kinds of motions you encounter every day

What You'll Need

- straightedge
- protractor
- ruler
- graph paper
- MIRA™ (optional)

3-1 Reflections

THINK AND DISCUSS

An Introduction to Transformations

Have you ever put together a jigsaw puzzle? Think about opening the box and emptying all of the puzzle pieces onto a table.

1. Describe the kinds of motions you use to put the pieces together.

You probably didn't realize it, but you use transformations when you assemble a puzzle. A **transformation** is a change in position, shape, or size of a figure. The photos below illustrate four basic transformations that you will study. Each transformed figure is the **image** of the original figure. The original figure is called the **preimage.**

The figure flips.

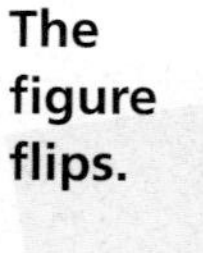

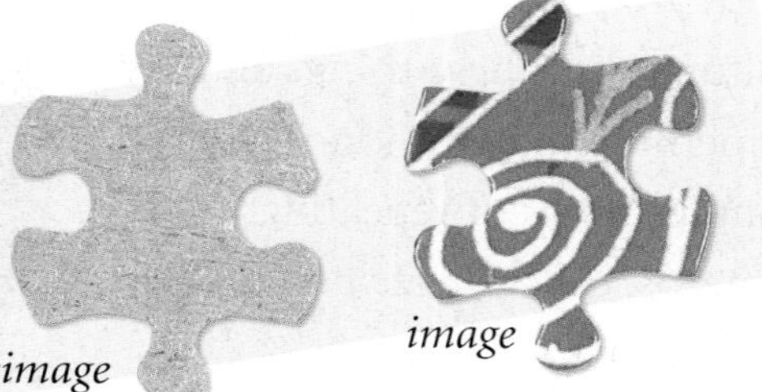

The figure slides.

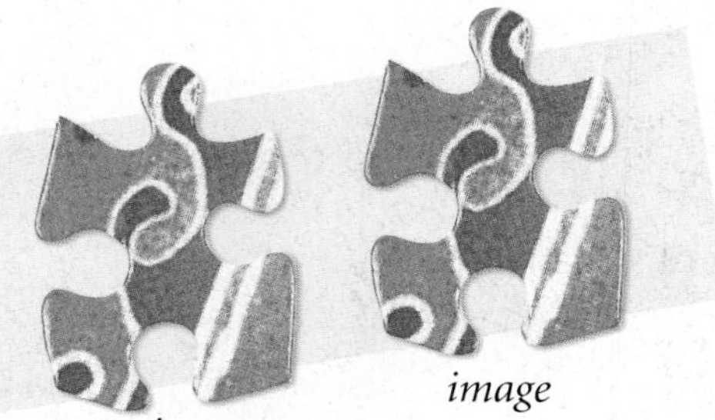

The figure turns.

The figure changes size.

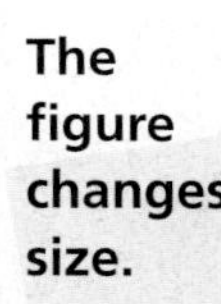

An **isometry** is a transformation in which the original figure and its image are congruent.

2. Which of the transformations shown above appear to be isometries?

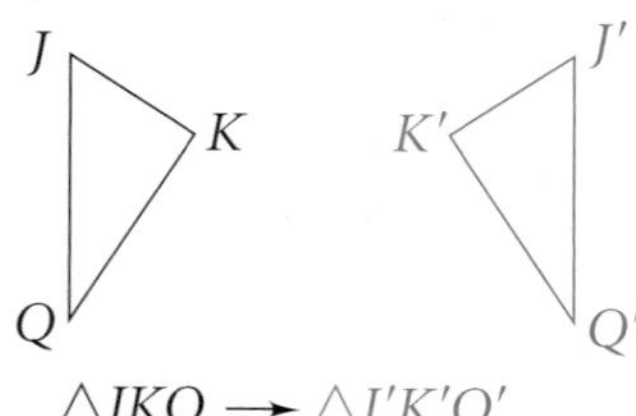

$\triangle JKQ \rightarrow \triangle J'K'Q'$
$\triangle JKQ$ maps to $\triangle J'K'Q'$.

A transformation **maps** a figure onto its image. An arrow ($\longrightarrow$) indicates a mapping. **Prime notation** is sometimes used to identify image points. In the diagram, K' (read "K prime") is the image of K. Notice that corresponding points of the original figure and its image are listed in the same order, just as corresponding points of congruent and similar figures are listed in the same order.

Math A Test Prep

1 What is the image of (3, −5) reflected in $x = -1$?
(1) (−5, −5)
(2) (2, −6)
(3) (3, 3)
(4) (−1, −5)

2 Given that $\triangle S'T'U'$ is the reflection of $\triangle STU$ in line *m*, list everything you know about the two figures and their relationship to line *m*.

Example 1

In the diagram, $E'F'G'H'$ is the image of $EFGH$.

a. Name the images of $\angle F$ and $\angle H$.

b. List all pairs of corresponding sides.

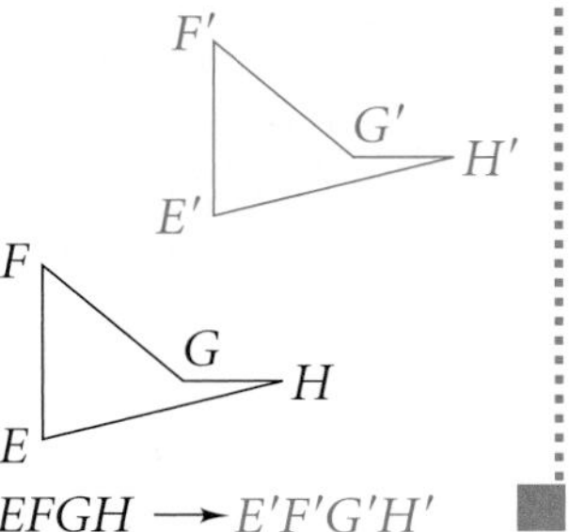

a. $\angle F'$ is the image of $\angle F$.
$\angle H'$ is the image of $\angle H$.

b. $\overline{EF}$ and $\overline{E'F'}$; $\overline{FG}$ and $\overline{F'G'}$;
$\overline{EH}$ and $\overline{E'H'}$; $\overline{GH}$ and $\overline{G'H'}$

3. Which of the four types of transformations shown on the previous page is illustrated in Example 1?

4. **Try This** List the corresponding segments and angles for the transformation $TORN \longrightarrow SAKE$.

Reflections

A flip is also known as a *reflection.* You see reflections almost every day. This morning, for example, you probably looked in the mirror before you headed out the door. In the following activity, you will investigate some properties of reflections.

WORK TOGETHER

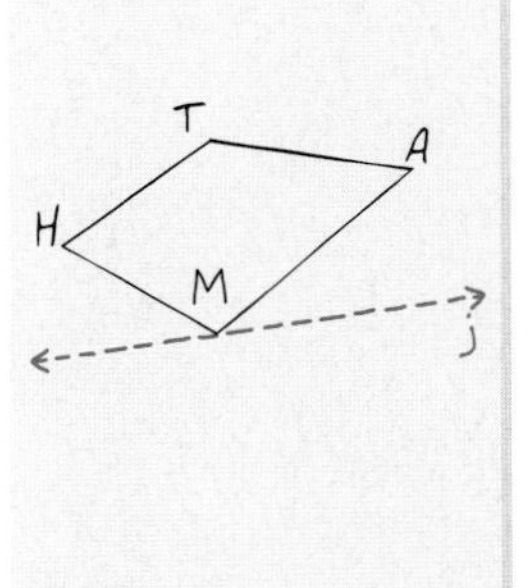

- Have each person in your group use a straightedge to draw a quadrilateral *MATH* on the top half of a sheet of paper. Draw a line *j* that intersects the quadrilateral at *M*.
- Fold the paper along line *j*, then use a straightedge to trace the reflection image of *MATH* onto the bottom portion of your paper. (You could also create the image by using a MIRA™.) Label the corresponding vertices of the image *M′*, *A′*, *T′*, and *H′*.

5. Measure corresponding angles and segments in *MATH* and *M′A′T′H′*. Is a reflection an isometry? Explain.

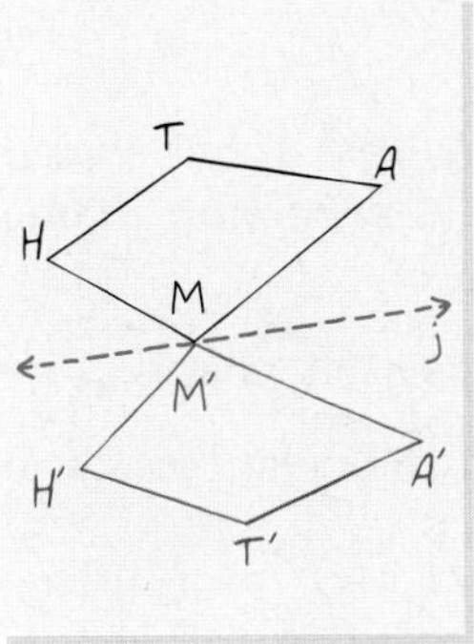

6. Make a **conjecture** about the image of a point that lies on the line of reflection. (*Hint:* Consider point *M* and its image.)

7. **a.** In your original figure, did you write the labels *M*, *A*, *T*, and *H* in clockwise or counterclockwise order around the quadrilateral?
   b. In the reflection image, do the labels *M′*, *A′*, *T′*, and *H′* appear in clockwise or counterclockwise order around the quadrilateral?
   c. What property of reflections do parts (a) and (b) suggest?

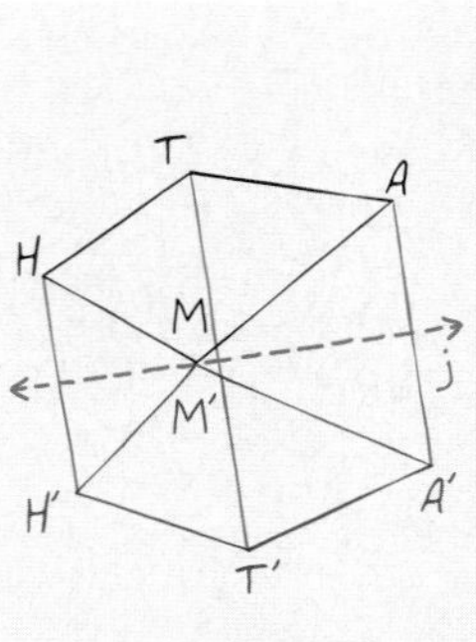

- Use a straightedge to draw segments $\overline{AA'}$, $\overline{TT'}$, and $\overline{HH'}$.

8. a. Line j divides each segment you drew into two parts. Compare the lengths of the two parts of each of the segments.
   b. Line j forms four angles with each segment you drew. Use a protractor to find the measures of each of the angles.
   c. Use your answers to parts (a) and (b) to complete the statement: Line j is the __?__ of the segment that connects a point and its image.

THINK AND DISCUSS

When you look at a word in a mirror, the image appears to be "backwards." The reflected word has the opposite **orientation** of the original word. Notice that the orientation of the word AMBULANCE in the photograph is reversed. The fronts of emergency vehicles often have mirror-image words on them so that drivers looking through rear-view mirrors can easily read them.

You discovered both of the following properties of reflections in the Work Together.

Properties of a Reflection

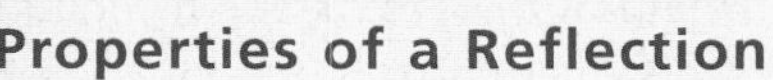

A reflection reverses orientation.

In the diagram, $\triangle BUG$ has *clockwise* orientation, so its image $\triangle B'U'G'$ has *counterclockwise* orientation.

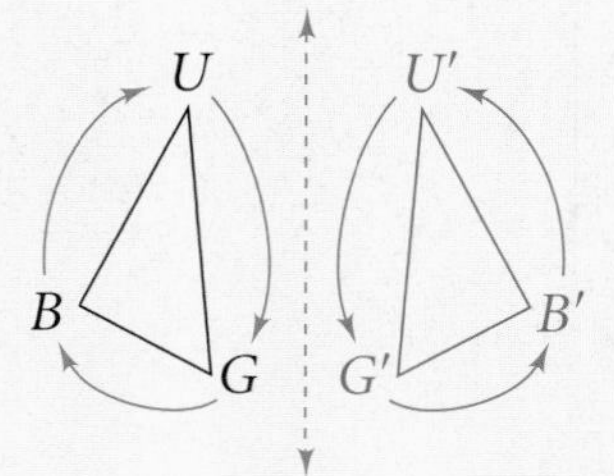

A reflection is an isometry.

In the diagram, $\triangle BUG \cong \triangle B'U'G'$.

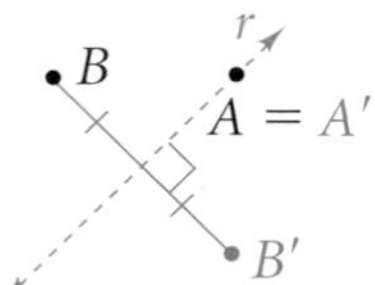

The other properties of reflections that you explored in the Work Together form the basis of the definition of a reflection. A **reflection** in line r is a transformation for which the following are true.

- If a point A is on line r, then the image of A is itself (that is, $A = A'$).
- If a point B is not on line r, then r is the perpendicular bisector of $\overline{BB'}$.

9. ***Critical Thinking*** Suppose you are given a point R and its reflection image R'. How could you find the line of reflection?

Example 2

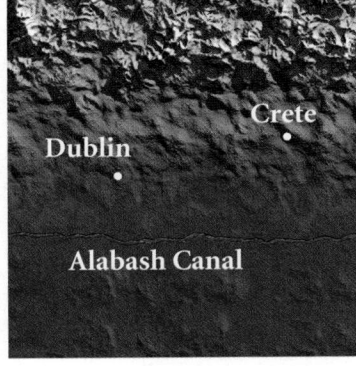

Coordinate Geometry Copy $\triangle ABC$ and draw its reflection image in each line.

a. the x-axis **b.** the y-axis

You can find A', B', and C' by paper folding or by locating points such that the line of reflection is the perpendicular bisector of $\overline{AA'}$, $\overline{BB'}$, and $\overline{CC'}$.

a.

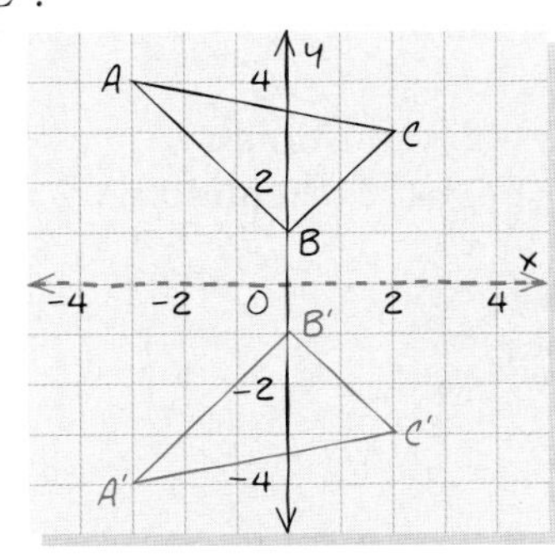

b.

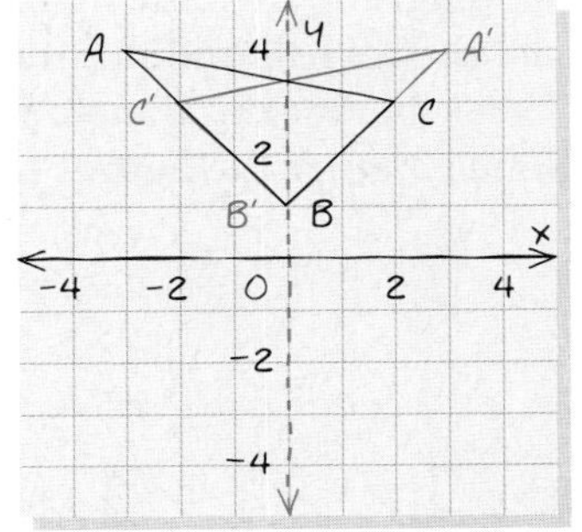

10. **Try This** Copy $\triangle ABC$ and draw its reflection image in $x = 3$.

Example 3 ***Relating to the Real World*** 

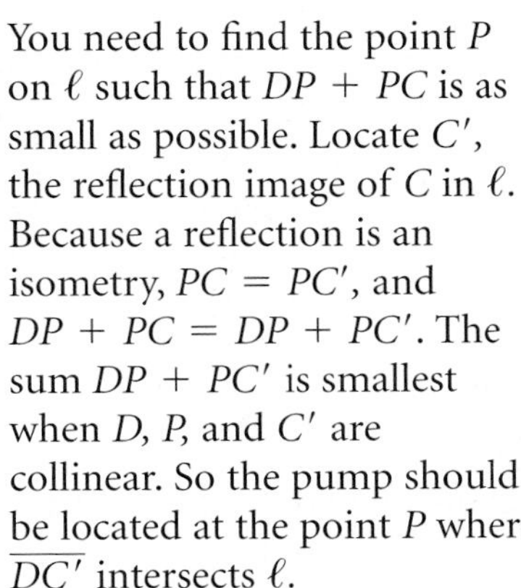

Engineering The state government wants to build a pumping station along the Alabash Canal to serve the towns of Crete and Dublin. Where along the canal should the pumping station be built to minimize the amount of pipe needed to connect the towns to the pump?

You need to find the point P on ℓ such that $DP + PC$ is as small as possible. Locate C', the reflection image of C in ℓ. Because a reflection is an isometry, $PC = PC'$, and $DP + PC = DP + PC'$. The sum $DP + PC'$ is smallest when D, P, and C' are collinear. So the pump should be located at the point P where $\overline{DC'}$ intersects ℓ.

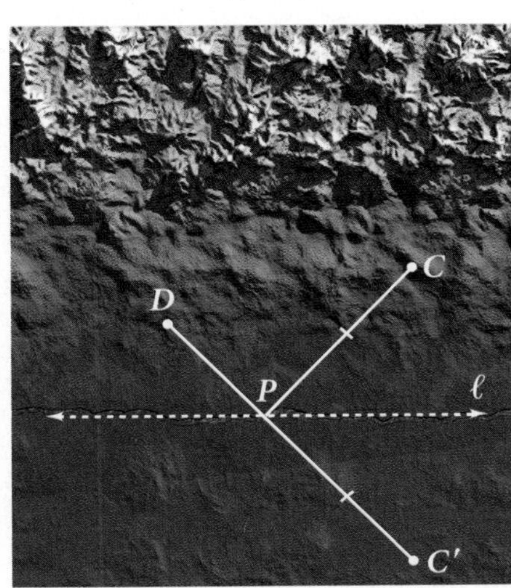

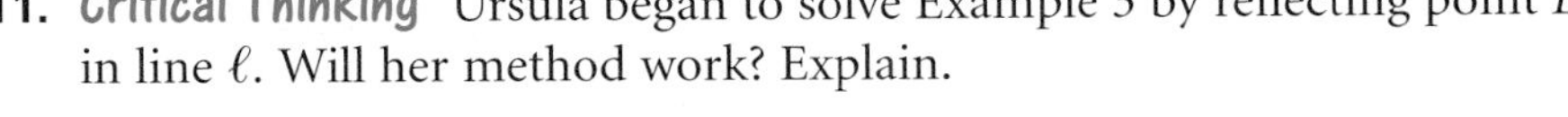

11. ***Critical Thinking*** Ursula began to solve Example 3 by reflecting point D in line ℓ. Will her method work? Explain.

Exercises ON YOUR OWN

Copy each diagram, then find the reflection image of the figure in line ℓ.

1.

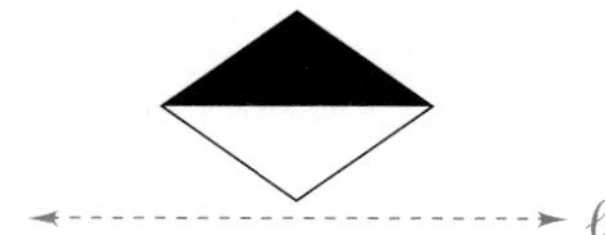

2.

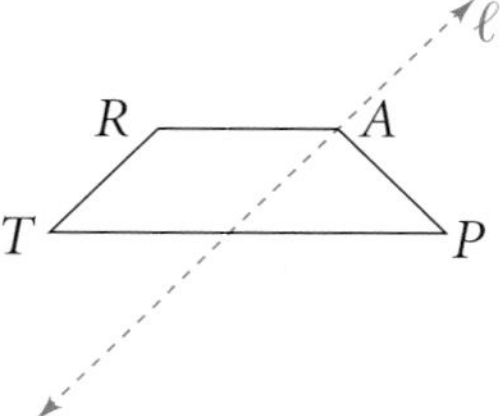

3.

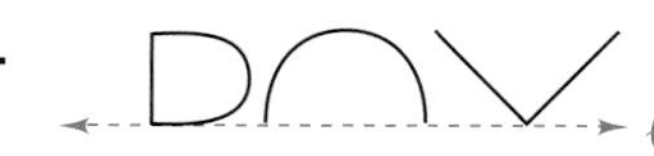

In each diagram, the blue figure is the image of the black figure.
(a) List the corresponding sides.
(b) State whether the transformation appears to be an isometry.
(c) State whether the figures have the *same* or *opposite* orientation.

4.

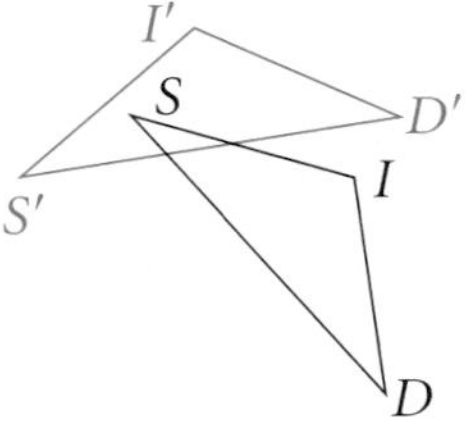

5.

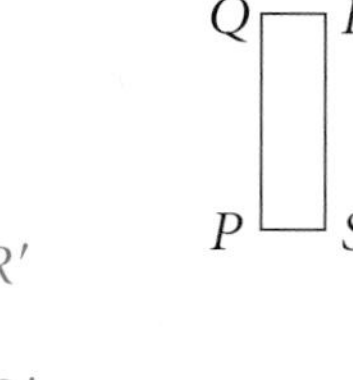

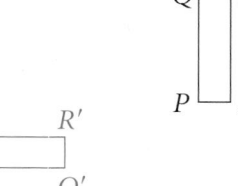

6.

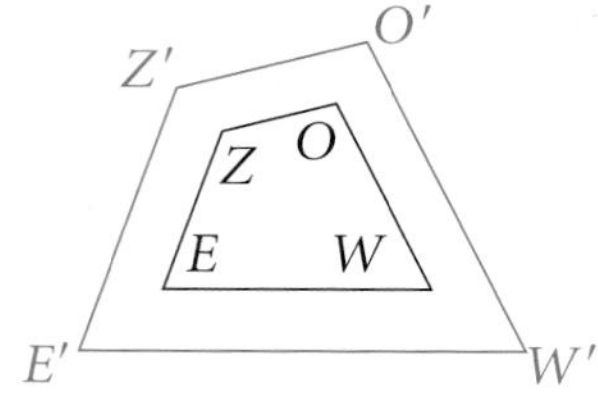

7.

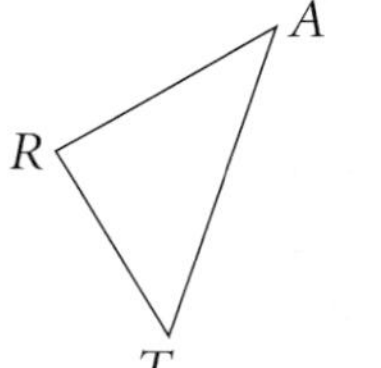

8.

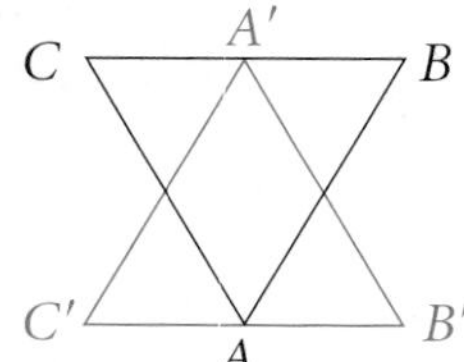

9.

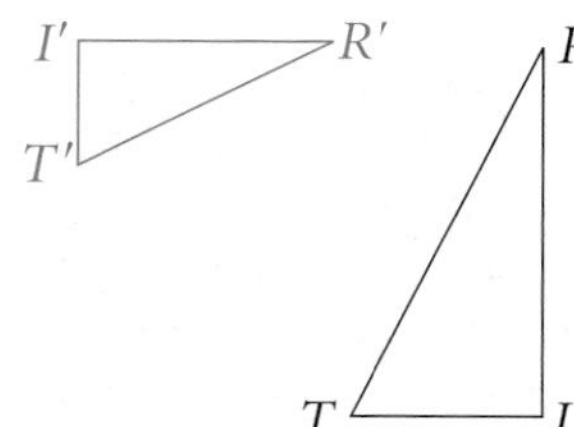

Coordinate Geometry **Given points $J(1, 4)$, $A(3, 5)$, and $R(2, 1)$, draw $\triangle JAR$ and its reflection image in the given line.**

10. the x-axis

11. $y = 2$

12. the y-axis

13. $x = -1$

14. $y = 5$

15. $x = 2$

16. $y = -x$

17. $y = x - 3$

18. **Critical Thinking** Given that the transformation $\triangle ABC \longrightarrow \triangle A'B'C'$ is an isometry, list everything you know about the two figures.

19. **Writing** Describe an example from everyday life of a flip, a slide, a turn, and a size change.

20. **Surveillance** SafeCo specializes in installing security cameras in department stores. Copy the diagram onto your paper. At what point on the mirrored wall should camera C be aimed in order to photograph door D?

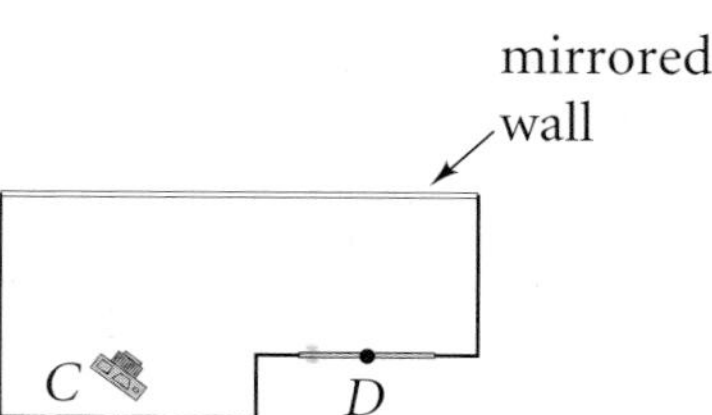

21. **History** An unusual characteristic of the work of 15th-century artist and scientist Leonardo da Vinci is his handwriting, which is a mirror image of normal handwriting.

   a. Explain why the fact that da Vinci was left-handed might have made it seem normal for him to write in this manner.

   b. Write the mirror image of this sentence. Use a mirror to check that your image is correct.

Copy each pair of figures, then find the line of reflection in which one figure is mapped onto the other.

22.

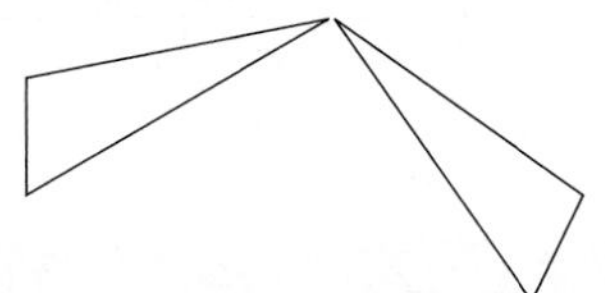
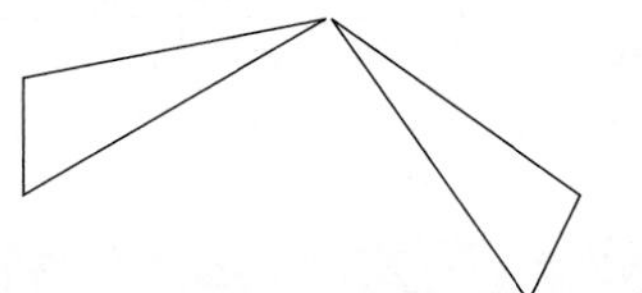

23.

24.

Some Drugs Aren't Ambidextrous

Your head aches. You take a pain reliever that cures this ache, but then your stomach starts to hurt. As you've no doubt noticed, many drugs have unwanted side-effects.

Most drugs are really made up of two versions of the same molecule—each a mirror image of the other. One version is known as an *R-isomer* and the other, an *S-isomer*. The isomers can have different healing properties.

Researchers have recently learned how to create pure batches of each isomer. They then run tests to determine which one produces the fewest side-effects. Drug companies can then produce drugs that contain only the "good" isomer.

For example, the R-isomer of the drug albuterol relieves asthma, while its twin has been shown to increase the chances of having future attacks.

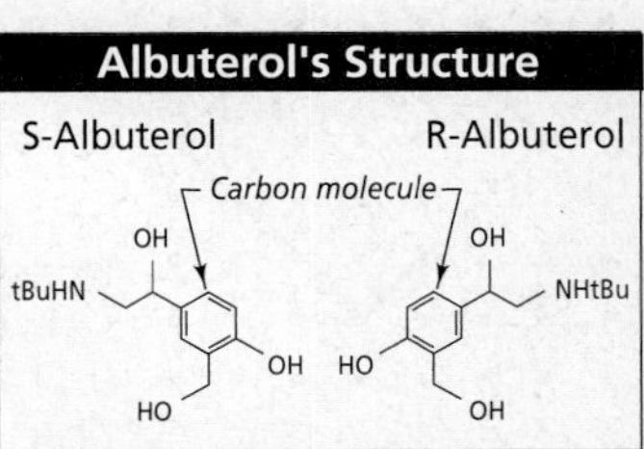

Source: *Wall Street Journal*

25. **Pharmacy** Consider the two "isomers" shown. In order for this drug to cure an illness, it needs to fit into the "receptor molecule" shown.

   a. Which isomer will cure the illness?

   b. **Open-ended** Give three examples from everyday life of objects that come in a left-handed version and a right-handed version.

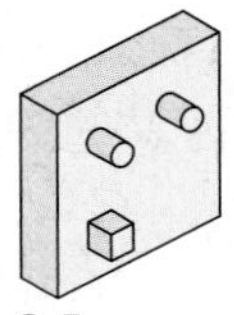
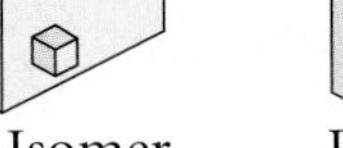

S-Isomer

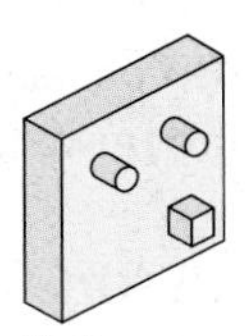

R-Isomer

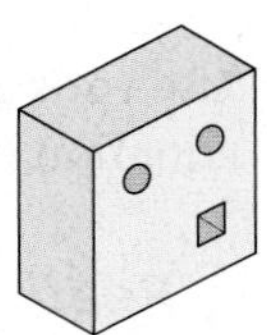

Receptor Molecule

26. **Standardized Test Prep** What is the image of $(-4, 5)$ under a reflection in the line $y = x$?

   A. $(5, -4)$ **B.** $(4, 5)$ **C.** $(-4, -5)$ **D.** $(4, -5)$ **E.** $(-5, 4)$

27. Which panels in the comic strip show the kind of reflection you studied in this lesson? Explain your answer.

Source: *K-Hito (Ricardo Garcia López). "Macaco."© K-Hito*

28. a. **Paper Folding** Plot the points $Y(-2, 5)$, $A(5, 0)$, and $K(-1, -2)$. Draw $\triangle YAK$, then use paper folding to find its image in $y = x$. Label the image $\triangle Y'A'K'$.
    b. **Patterns** Look for a pattern in the coordinates of $\triangle YAK$ and $\triangle Y'A'K'$. Write a general rule for finding the image of any point under a reflection in $y = x$.

29. **Critical Thinking** Under a reflection, do all points move the same distance? If not, which points move the farthest?

Exercises MIXED REVIEW

What type of quadrilateral is $ABB'A'$?

30. 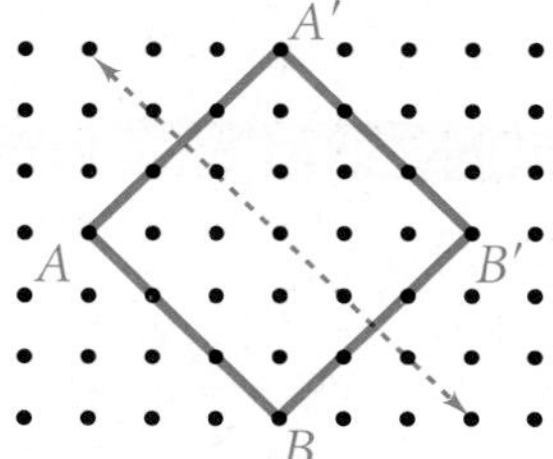

31. 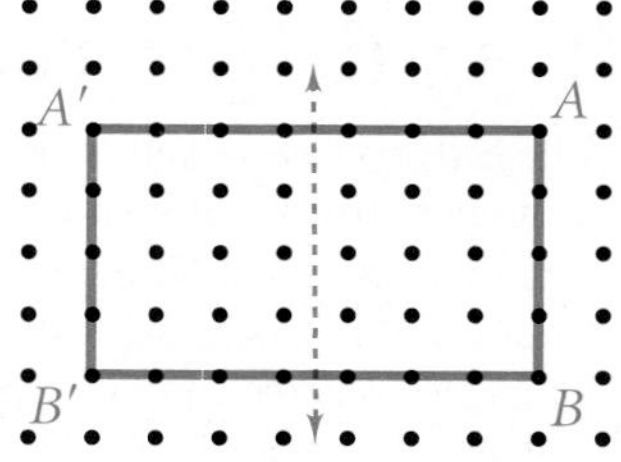

32. 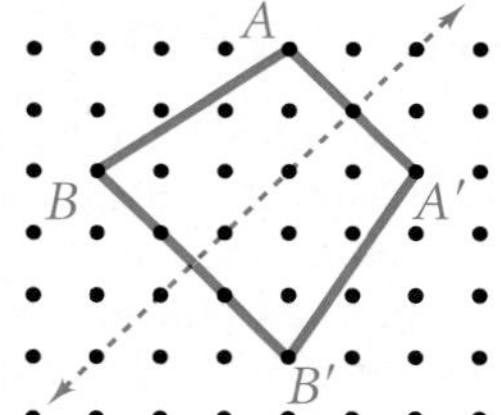

33. The points $P(2, 5)$ and $Q(-4, -7)$ are reflection images of one another.
    a. Find the coordinates of the midpoint of $\overline{PQ}$.
    b. Find the slope of $\overline{PQ}$.
    c. Find the slope of a line perpendicular to $\overline{PQ}$.
    d. Use your answers to parts (a) and (c) to write the equation of the line in which P is reflected to Q.

SELF ASSESSMENT

FOR YOUR JOURNAL

List the properties of reflections. Then draw a polygon, a line of reflection, and the reflection image of your polygon. Explain how the figures illustrate each property listed.

Getting Ready for Lesson 3-2

34. In the diagram, an isometry maps $\triangle HUB$ to $\triangle H'U'B'$.
    a. Is the transformation a flip, slide, or turn?
    b. Compare the slopes of $\overline{HH'}$, $\overline{UU'}$, and $\overline{BB'}$.
    c. Compare the lengths of $\overline{HH'}$, $\overline{UU'}$, and $\overline{BB'}$.

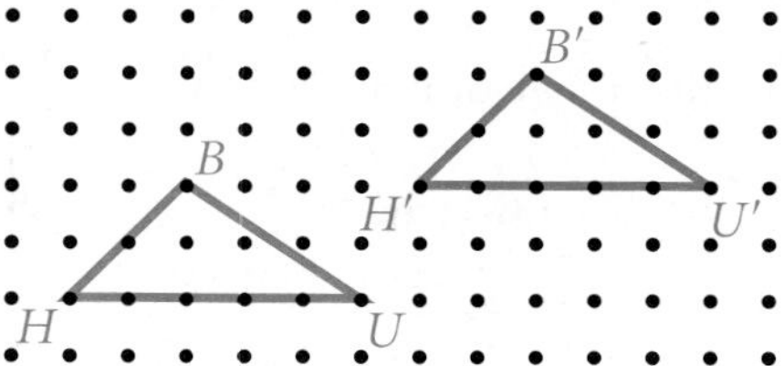

Math ToolboX — Algebra Review

Matrices

Before Lesson 3-2

A **matrix** is a rectangular arrangement of numbers. A matrix is usually written inside brackets. You identify the size of a matrix by the number of rows and columns. This matrix has two rows and three columns, so it is a 2 × 3 matrix. Each item in a matrix is called an **entry.**

$$\begin{bmatrix} -1 & 4 & 9 \\ -5 & 3 & 7 \end{bmatrix}$$

You can add or subtract matrices if they are the same size. You do this by adding or subtracting corresponding entries.

Example

Add $\begin{bmatrix} 6 & -5 \\ 0 & 3 \end{bmatrix} + \begin{bmatrix} 1 & 8 \\ -2 & 10 \end{bmatrix}$.

$$\begin{bmatrix} 6 & -5 \\ 0 & 3 \end{bmatrix} + \begin{bmatrix} 1 & 8 \\ -2 & 10 \end{bmatrix} = \begin{bmatrix} 6 + 1 & -5 + 8 \\ 0 + (-2) & 3 + 10 \end{bmatrix}$$ Add corresponding entries.

$$= \begin{bmatrix} 7 & 3 \\ -2 & 13 \end{bmatrix}$$

Add or subtract each pair of matrices.

1. $\begin{bmatrix} 3 & 8 \\ 1 & 5 \end{bmatrix} + \begin{bmatrix} 8 & 2 \\ 0 & 7 \end{bmatrix}$

2. $\begin{bmatrix} -6 & 3 \\ -8 & 1 \end{bmatrix} - \begin{bmatrix} -4 & -9 \\ 3 & 5 \end{bmatrix}$

3. $\begin{bmatrix} 1 & -6 \\ 2 & -7 \end{bmatrix} + \begin{bmatrix} \frac{1}{2} & -1 \\ \frac{2}{3} & -2 \end{bmatrix}$

4. $\begin{bmatrix} \frac{1}{3} & \frac{3}{4} \\ \frac{1}{2} & \frac{2}{5} \end{bmatrix} - \begin{bmatrix} -\frac{1}{6} & \frac{1}{4} \\ -\frac{3}{5} & \frac{2}{3} \end{bmatrix}$

5. $\begin{bmatrix} 2 & 9 \\ 6 & 7 \end{bmatrix} + \begin{bmatrix} 6 & 2.3 \\ 9 & 4.1 \end{bmatrix}$

6. $\begin{bmatrix} 3 & -7 & 4 \\ 0 & -4 & 9 \end{bmatrix} + \begin{bmatrix} -9 & 4 & 10 \\ 3 & -11 & 2 \end{bmatrix}$

7. $\begin{bmatrix} 5 & -3.5 \\ 10 & 14 \\ -5 & 4.7 \end{bmatrix} + \begin{bmatrix} -6.1 & 0.8 \\ 7 & -5 \\ 8.3 & 9 \end{bmatrix}$

8. $\begin{bmatrix} 4 & 2 & 9 \\ -11 & 20 & 5 \\ -18 & 21 & -2 \end{bmatrix} - \begin{bmatrix} 8 & 17 & 4 \\ -34 & 26 & -9 \\ 3 & 0 & 17 \end{bmatrix}$

9. Use the matrices to find the total number of students per grade involved in each activity.

Greenfield High School North

	Sports	Drama	Debate
9th	146	5	11
10th	201	15	4
11th	205	11	7
12th	176	19	13

Greenfield High School South

	Sports	Drama	Debate
9th	301	13	9
10th	345	8	6
11th	245	11	11
12th	220	11	9

What You'll Learn

- Finding translation images of figures
- Using vectors and matrix addition to represent translations

...And Why

To use translations in the arts, computer graphics, navigation, manufacturing, music, and other fields

What You'll Need

- centimeter ruler
- scissors
- graph paper

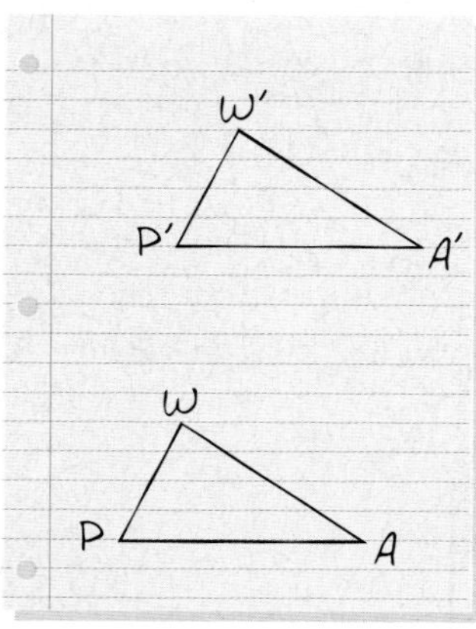

3-2 Translations

WORK TOGETHER

- Have each member of your group draw a triangle, cut it out, and label it $\triangle PAW$.
- Place your triangle on a sheet of lined paper so that $\overline{PA}$ lies on a horizontal line. Trace the triangle, and label it $\triangle PAW$.
- Slide the cutout to another location on your paper so that $\overline{PA}$ again lies on a horizontal line. Trace the triangle, and label it $\triangle P'A'W'$.

1. Does the transformation $\triangle PAW \longrightarrow \triangle P'A'W'$ appear to be an isometry? Explain.
2. Does the transformation $\triangle PAW \longrightarrow \triangle P'A'W'$ change the orientation of the triangle? Explain.

- Use a straightedge to draw $\overline{PP'}$, $\overline{AA'}$, and $\overline{WW'}$. Measure each segment with a ruler.

3. What do you notice about the lengths of the segments?
4. Notice the positions of $\overline{PP'}$, $\overline{AA'}$, and $\overline{WW'}$ in relation to one another. What appears to be true about them? Compare your answer with others in your group.

THINK AND DISCUSS

The sliding motion that maps $\triangle PAW$ to $\triangle P'A'W'$ in the Work Together is an example of a translation. A **translation** is a transformation that moves points the same distance and in the same direction. In the Work Together, you discovered the following properties of a translation.

Properties of a Translation

A translation is an isometry.

A translation does not change orientation.

5. Elevators, escalators, and people movers all suggest translations. Name some other examples of translations from the real world.

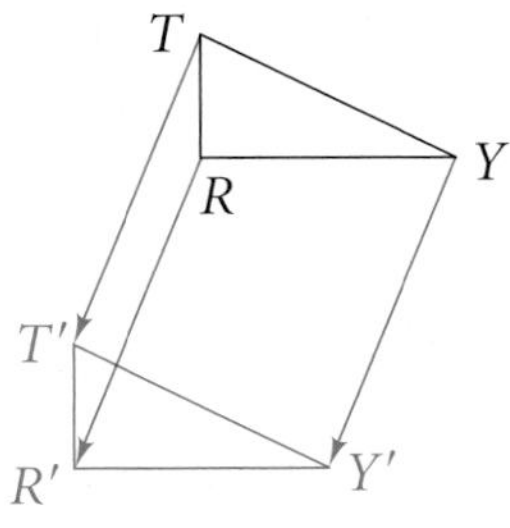

The distance and direction of a translation can be expressed as a vector. In the diagram, $\overrightarrow{TT'}$, $\overrightarrow{RR'}$, and $\overrightarrow{YY'}$ are vectors. Vectors have an *initial point* and a *terminal point*. *T*, *R*, and *Y* are initial points, and *T'*, *R'*, and *Y'* are terminal points. Note that although diagrams of vectors look identical to diagrams of rays, vectors do not go on forever in the indicated direction—they have a fixed length.

Example 1

Use the given vector and rectangle to create a sketch of a box.

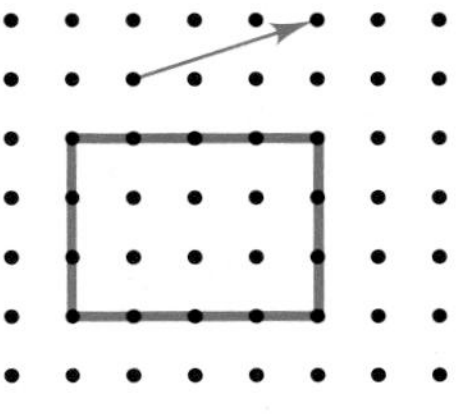

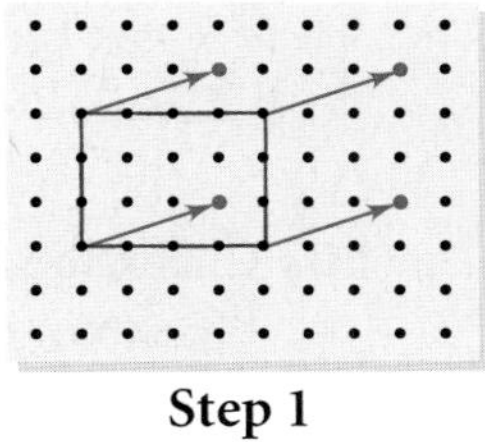

Step 1

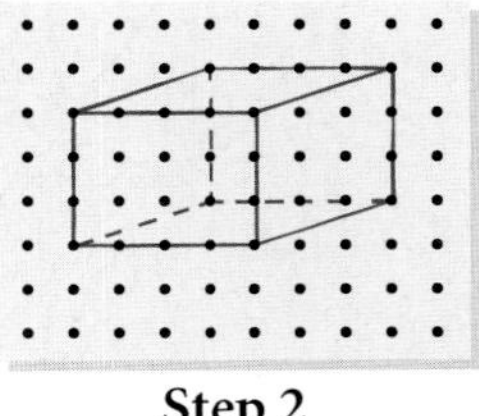

Step 2

Copy the rectangle, then translate each of its vertices 3 units to the right and 1 unit up. Next, connect points to form the box. Use dashed lines for parts of the figure that are hidden from view.

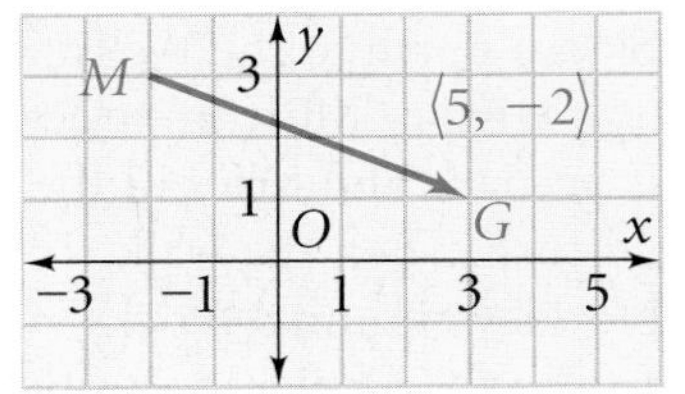

You can use *ordered pair notation*, ⟨*x*, *y*⟩, to represent a vector on the coordinate plane. In the notation, *x* represents horizontal change from the initial point to the terminal point and *y* represents vertical change from the initial point to the terminal point. The notation for vector $\overrightarrow{MG}$ is ⟨5, −2⟩.

6. **Try This** Describe the vector in Example 1 by using ordered pair notation.

7. Use vector notation to describe the vector with initial point (1, 3) and terminal point (6, 1).

Example 2

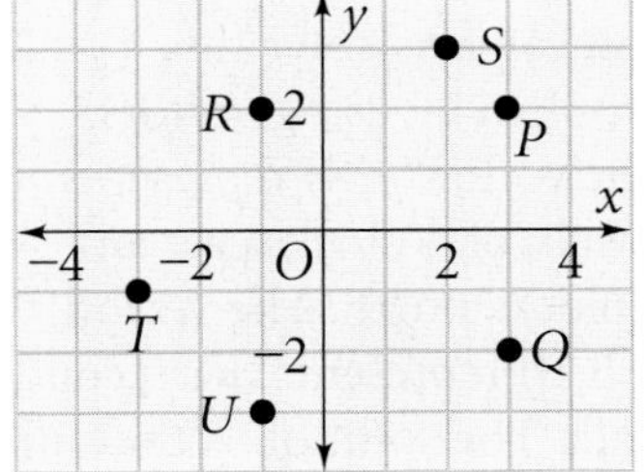

a. What is the image of *P* under the translation ⟨0, −4⟩?
b. What vector describes the translation *S* ⟶ *U*?

a. The vector ⟨0, −4⟩ represents a translation of 4 units down. The image of *P* is *Q*.
b. To get from *S* to *U*, you move 3 units left and 6 units down. The vector that describes this translation is ⟨−3, −6⟩.

8. **Try This** Refer to the diagram in Example 2.
   a. What is the image of *S* under the translation ⟨−3, −1⟩?
   b. What vector describes the translation *T* ⟶ *P*?

9. Describe in words the distance and direction of the translation represented by the vector ⟨18, 0⟩.

$$\begin{array}{r} \\ x\text{-coordinate} \\ y\text{-coordinate} \end{array} \begin{array}{c} \begin{matrix} \;S & \;\;U & \;\;D \end{matrix} \\ \begin{bmatrix} -1 & 2 & 3 \\ -1 & -5 & 2 \end{bmatrix} \end{array}$$

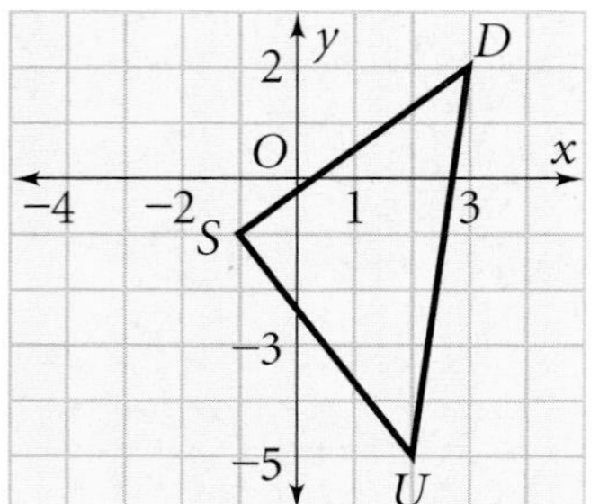

You can use matrices to help you translate figures in the coordinate plane. To do so, start by creating a matrix for the figure, as shown at the left.

Example 3

Use matrices to find the image of $\triangle SUD$ under the translation $\langle 4, -5 \rangle$.

To find the image of $\triangle SUD$, you add 4 to all of the x-coordinates and -5 to all of the y-coordinates.

Vertices of Preimage — Translation Matrix — Vertices of Image

$$\begin{array}{c} \begin{matrix} S & U & D \end{matrix} \\ \begin{bmatrix} -1 & 2 & 3 \\ -1 & -5 & 2 \end{bmatrix} \end{array} + \begin{bmatrix} 4 & 4 & 4 \\ -5 & -5 & -5 \end{bmatrix} = \begin{array}{c} \begin{matrix} S' & U' & D' \end{matrix} \\ \begin{bmatrix} 3 & 6 & 7 \\ -6 & -10 & -3 \end{bmatrix} \end{array}$$

10. Check the answer to Example 3 by sketching $\triangle SUD$ and $\triangle S'U'D'$ on the same set of axes.

Example 4 Relating to the Real World 

Travel Yolanda Pérez is visiting San Francisco. From her hotel near Union Square, she walked 4 blocks east and 4 blocks north to the Wells Fargo History Museum to see a stagecoach and relics of the gold rush. Then she walked 5 blocks west and 3 blocks north to the Cable Car Barn Museum. How many blocks from her hotel is she now?

As shown in the diagram, she is 1 block west and 7 blocks north of her hotel.

You can also solve this problem by using vectors. The vector $\langle 4, 4 \rangle$ represents a walk of 4 blocks east and 4 blocks north. The vector $\langle -5, 3 \rangle$ represents her second walk. The solution is the sum of the x- and y-coordinates of each vector: $\langle 4, 4 \rangle + \langle -5, 3 \rangle = \langle -1, 7 \rangle$.

Example 4 shows the composition of two translations. The term **composition** describes any two transformations in which the second transformation is performed on the image of the first transformation. As the solution to Example 4 suggests, a composition of translations can be rewritten as a single translation.

Exercises ON YOUR OWN

In each diagram, the blue figure is the image of the red figure. Use ordered pair notation to represent each translation.

1.

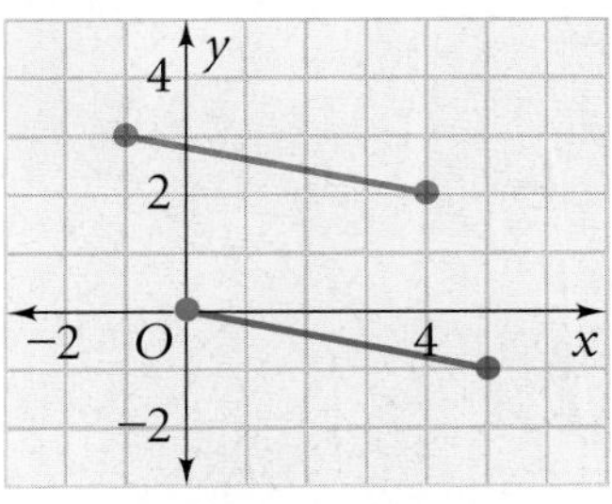

2.

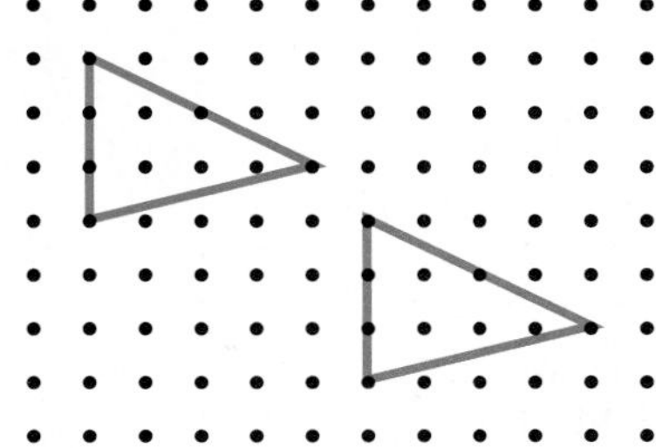

3.

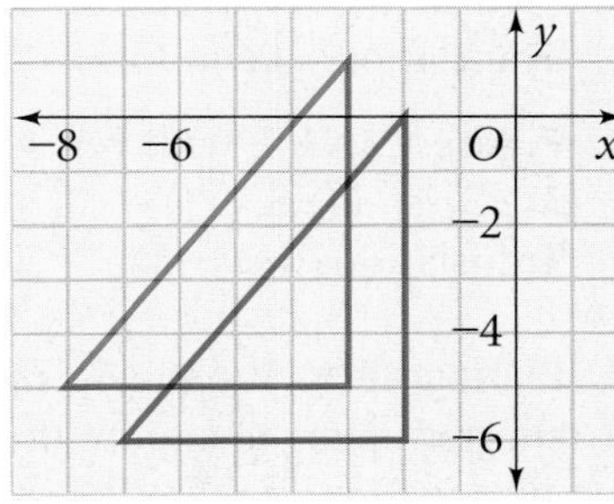

4.

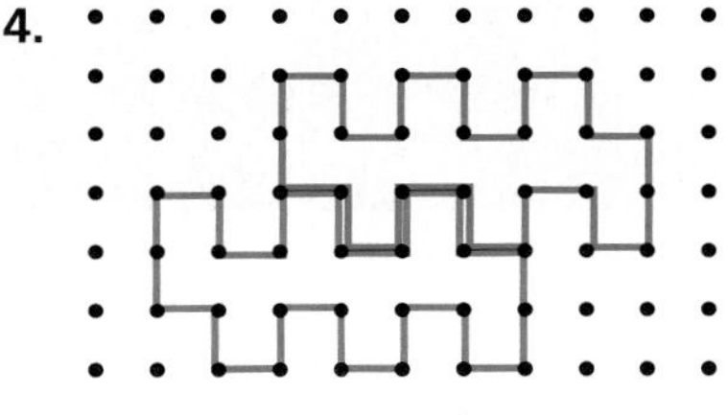

5.

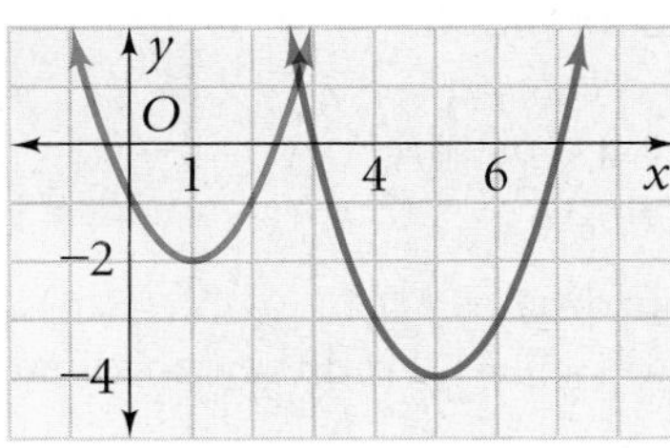

6.

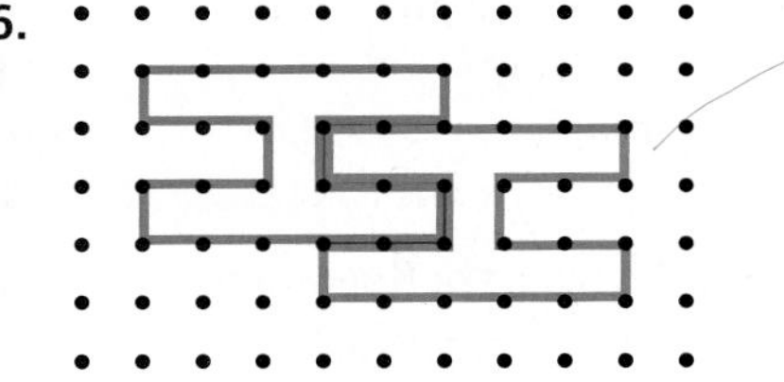

In Exercises 7–12, refer to the figure at the right.

7. What is the image of F under the translation $\langle -1, 4 \rangle$?

8. What vector describes the translation $G \longrightarrow H$?

9. What is the image of E under the translation $\langle 4, 1 \rangle$?

10. What vector describes the translation $B \longrightarrow E$?

11. What is the image of F under the translation $\langle 4, -1 \rangle$?

12. What vector describes the translation $I \longrightarrow C$?

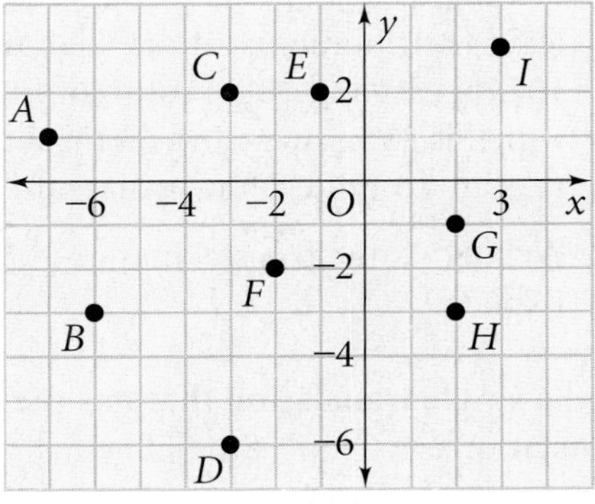

Use each figure and vector to sketch a three-dimensional figure.

13.

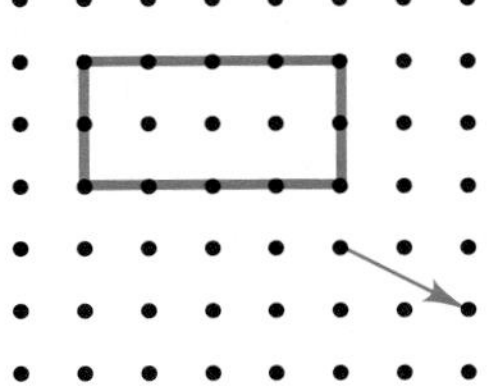

14.

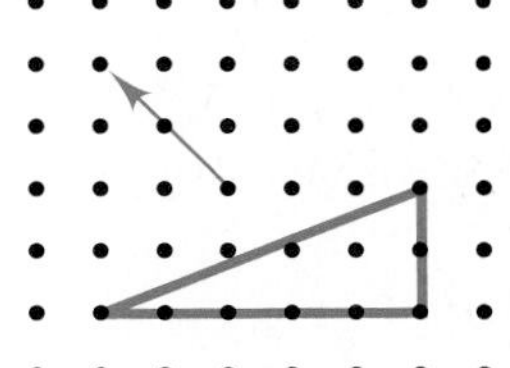

15.

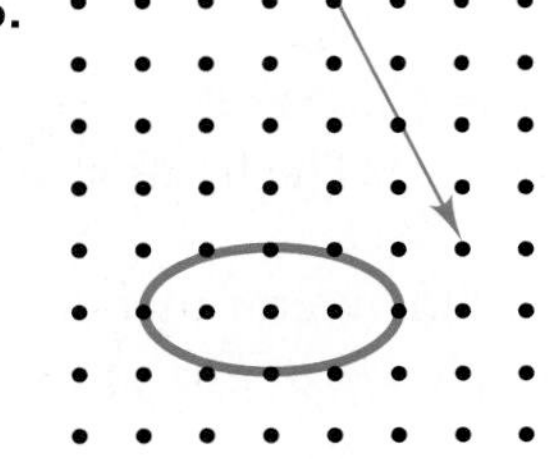

16. **Sailing** Emily left Galveston Bay at the east jetty and sailed 4 km north to an oil rig. She then sailed 5 km west to Redfish Island. Finally, she sailed 3 km southwest to the Spinnaker Restaurant. Draw vectors on graph paper that show her journey.

In Exercises 17–19, use matrix addition to find the image of each figure under the given translation.

17. Figure: $\triangle ACE$ with vertices $A(7, 2)$, $C(-8, 5)$, $E(0, -6)$
Translation: $\langle -9, 4 \rangle$

18. Figure: $\triangle PUN$ with vertices $P(1, 0)$, $U(4, 6)$, $N(-5, 8)$
Translation: $\langle 11, -13 \rangle$

19. Figure: $\square NILE$ with vertices $N(2, -5)$, $I(2, 2)$, $L(-3, 4)$, $E(-3, -3)$
Translation: $\langle -3, -4 \rangle$

20. **Photography** When you snap a photograph, a shutter opens to expose the film to light. The amount of time that the shutter remains open is known as the *shutter speed*. The photographer of the train used a long shutter speed to create an image that suggests a translation. Sketch a picture of your own that suggests a translation.

21. **Coordinate Geometry** $\triangle MUG$ has coordinates $M(2, -4)$, $U(6, 6)$ and $G(7, 2)$. A translation maps point M to $(-3, 6)$. Find the coordinates of U' and G' under this translation.

22. **Visiting Colleges** Nakesha and her parents are visiting colleges. They leave their home in Enid, Oklahoma, and head for Tulsa, which is 107 mi east and 18 mi south of Enid. From Tulsa, they head to Norman, which is 83 mi west and 63 mi south of Tulsa. Where is Norman in relation to Enid? Draw a diagram to show your solution.

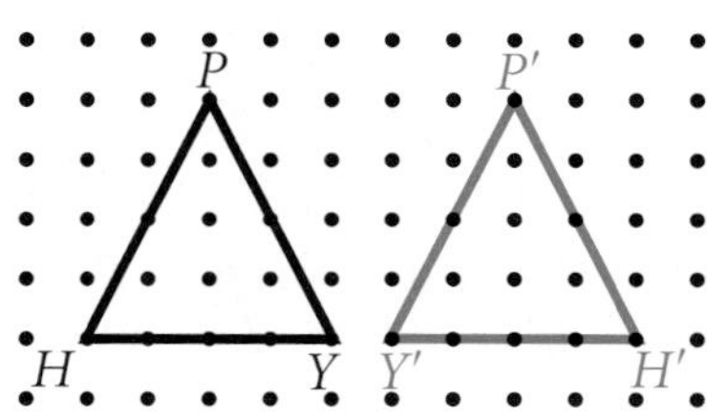

23. **Writing** Is the transformation $\triangle HYP \longrightarrow \triangle H'Y'P'$ a translation? Explain.

Find a single translation that has the same effect as each composition of translations.

24. $\langle 2, 5 \rangle$ followed by $\langle -4, 9 \rangle$

25. $\langle -3, 7 \rangle$ followed by $\langle 3, -7 \rangle$

26. $\langle 12, 0.5 \rangle$ followed by $\langle 1, -3 \rangle$

27. **Coordinate Geometry** $\square ABCD$ has vertices $A(3, 6)$, $B(5, 5)$, $C(4, 2)$, and $D(2, 3)$. The figure is translated so that the image of point C is the origin.
   a. Find the vector that describes the translation.
   b. Graph $\square ABCD$ and its image.

28. **Open-ended** You work for a company that specializes in creating unique, artistic designs for business stationery. One of your clients is Totter Toys. You have been assigned to create a design that forms a border at the top of their stationery. Create a design that involves translations to present to your client.

Totter Toys
4010 Tiptop Drive
Birchwood, TX 70988

Chapter Project

Find Out by Investigating

A **frieze pattern,** or **strip pattern,** is a design that repeats itself along a straight line. Every frieze pattern can be mapped onto itself by a translation. Some can also be mapped onto themselves by other transformations, such as reflections.

- Decide whether each frieze pattern can be mapped onto itself by a reflection in a horizontal line, a vertical line, or both.

a. Navaho Design

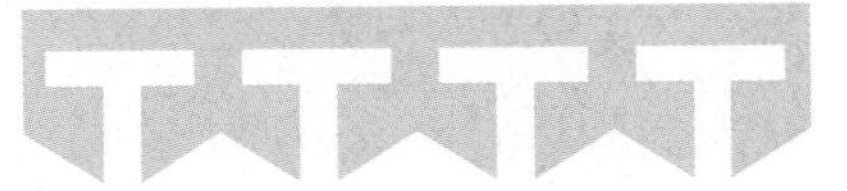

b. Design from Sandwich Islands

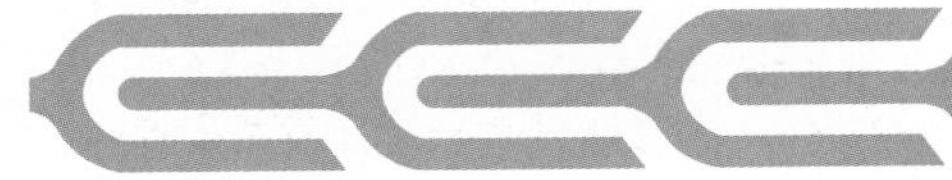

c. Medieval Ornament

d. Arabian Design

Exercises MIXED REVIEW

For Exercises 29 and 30, refer to the diagram.

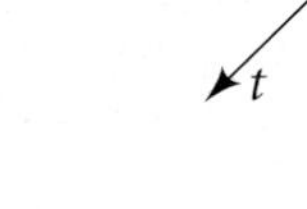

29. Line t is a _?_ of $\overline{AC}$.

30. $AB = 3x - 8$ and $BC = 5x - 36$. Find AC.

31. **a.** **Algebra** Graph $y = 2x - 3$, then draw its image under the translation $\langle 0, 5 \rangle$.
    b. Find the slope and y-intercept of the preimage and the image.
    c. How are the two lines related?

Getting Ready for Lesson 3-3

Cooking **What temperature will the oven be if the knob is turned the given number of degrees in a clockwise direction?**

32. 120° 33. 180° 34. 210° 35. 270°

3-3 Rotations

What You'll Learn

- Identifying and locating rotation images of figures

...And Why

To understand real-life objects that involve rotation, such as clocks, combination locks, and laser disc players

What You'll Need

- straightedge
- colored pencils (optional)
- protractor
- compass

WORK TOGETHER

Before beginning the activity, have each member of your group fold a piece of paper in half lengthwise and widthwise and then cut it into fourths.

Step 1: Place a piece of the paper over the figure below. Trace the six points on the circle, the center of the circle, and the triangle.

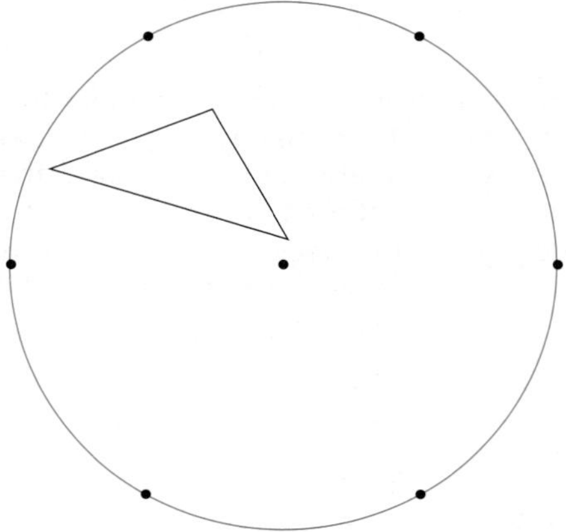

If you start with this in Step 4 . . .

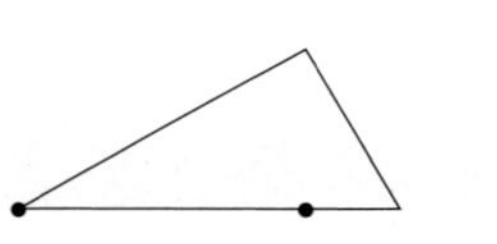

You could end up with this . . .

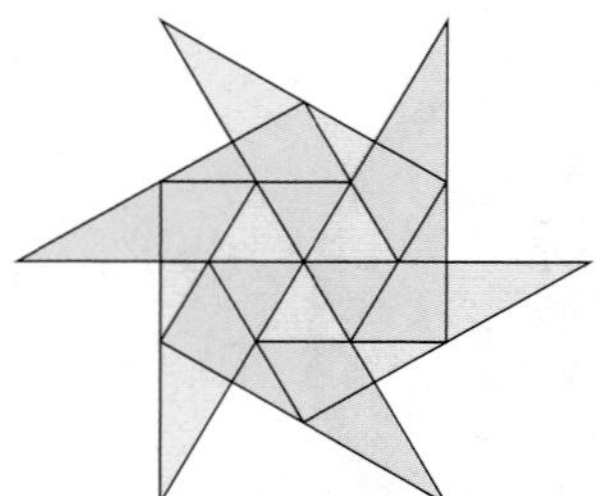

Step 2: Place the point of your pencil on the center of the circle and then rotate the paper until the six points again overlap. Trace the triangle in its new location.

Step 3: Repeat Step 2 until there are six triangles on your paper. Compare drawings within your group to be sure that your results look the same.

Step 4: Now it's your turn to be creative. Place a piece of paper over the figure above, trace the six points on the circle and the center of the circle, and then draw your own triangle on the paper.

Step 5: Place the paper from Step 4 on your desktop, and then use a blank piece of paper to repeat the process in Steps 1–3. Color your design, and then create a display of your group's designs.

THINK AND DISCUSS

In the Work Together, you used rotations to create a design. In order to describe a rotation, you need to know the center of rotation, the angle of rotation, and the direction of the rotation.

The direction of a rotation can be clockwise or counterclockwise. All rotations in this book will be in a *counterclockwise* direction.

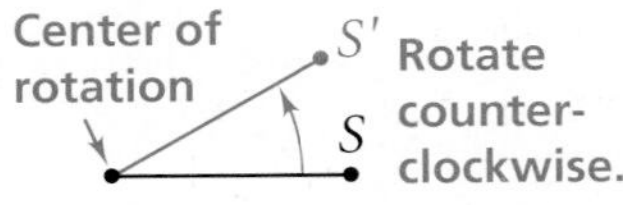

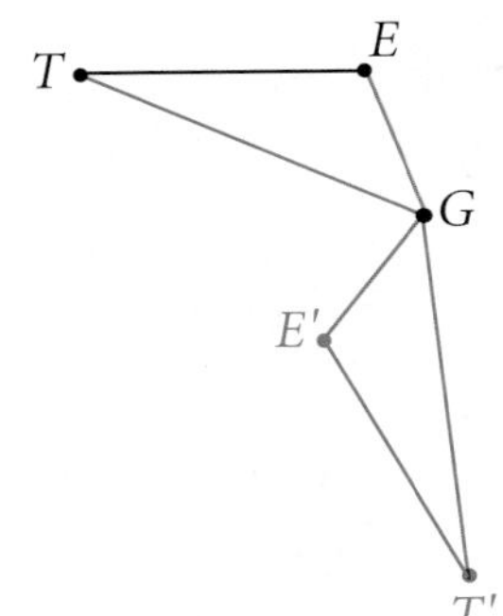

1. What was the angle of each rotation in the Work Together? (*Hint:* Each angle had the same measure.)
2. The diagram at the left shows $\overline{TE}$ rotated 120° about G.
   a. What appears to be true of EG and $E'G$? Of TG and $T'G$?
   b. What appears to be true of $m\angle TGT'$ and $m\angle EGE'$?

The properties of rotations that you noted in Question 2 form the basis of the definition of a rotation. A **rotation** of $x°$ about a point R is a transformation such that:

- For any point V, $RV' = RV$ and $m\angle VRV' = x$.
- The image of R is itself (that is, $R' = R$).

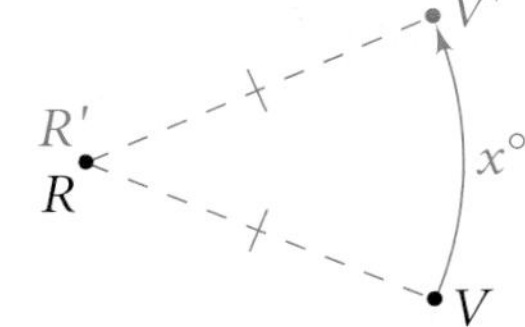

Example 1

Draw the image of $\triangle LOB$ under a 100° rotation about C.

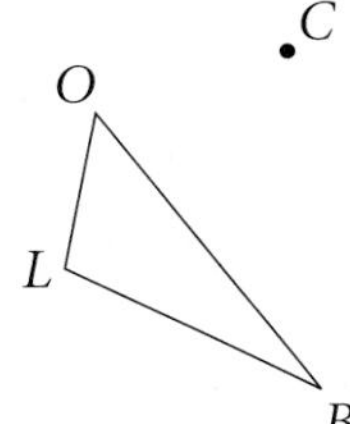

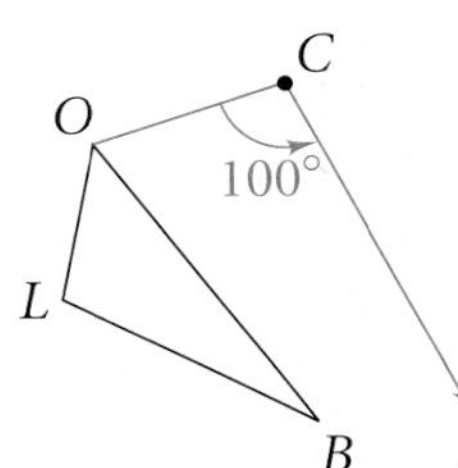

Step 1
Use a protractor to draw a 100° angle with side $\overrightarrow{OC}$.

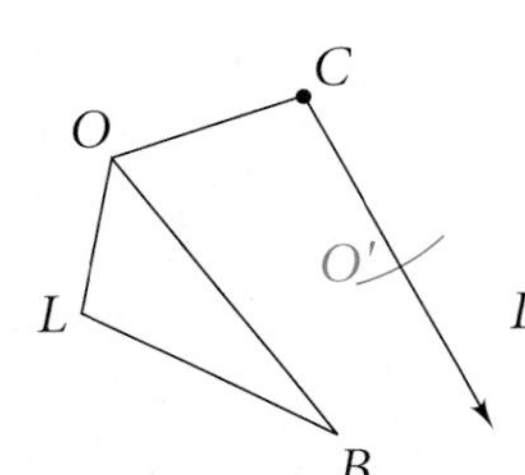

Step 2
Use a compass to construct $\overline{O'C} \cong \overline{OC}$.

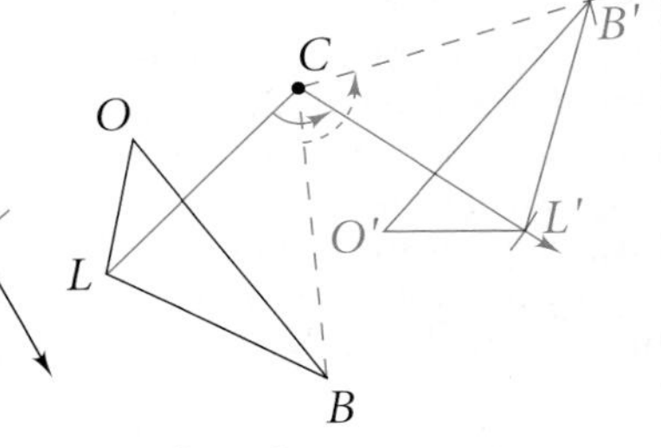

Step 3
Create B' and L' in a similar manner. Draw $\triangle L'O'B'$.

3. **Try This** Draw the image of $\triangle LOB$ under a 90° rotation about B.
4. **Critical Thinking** Under a rotation, does each point move the same distance? If not, which points move the farthest?

A comparison of $\triangle LOB$ and $\triangle L'O'B'$ in Example 1 reveals the following properties of a rotation.

Properties of a Rotation

A rotation is an isometry.

A rotation does not change orientation.

$360° \div 5 = 72°$

P, A, E, X, T, N

Example 2

Regular pentagon *PENTA* is divided into five congruent triangles.

a. Name the image of *E* under a 72° rotation about *X*.

b. Name the image of *P* under a 216° rotation about *X*.

a.

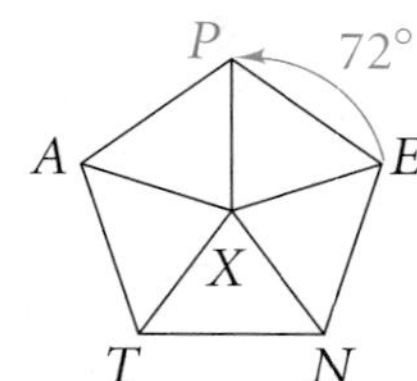

P is the image of *E*.

b.

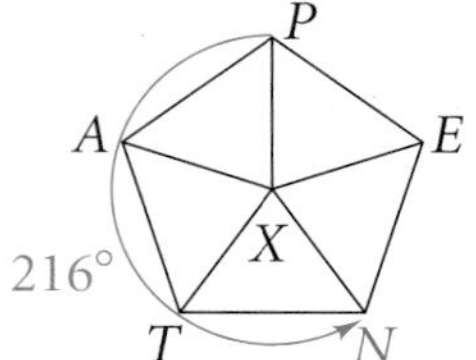

N is the image of *P*.

5. **Try This** Name the image of *T* under a 144° rotation about *X*.

6. In Example 2, $E \longrightarrow P$, then $P \longrightarrow N$. Describe a single rotation that maps *E* to *N*.

7. What is the image of any point under a 360° rotation?

What? Satellite photographs of the opposite side of the moon reveal that it is free of the large, dark regions that are visible from Earth. Early astronomers thought these regions looked like seas, so they named them *maria,* the Latin word for seas.

Example 3 Relating to the Real World

Astronomy The motion of the moon around Earth can be modeled by the type of rotation presented in this lesson. What effect does this have on our observations of the moon?

Earth

Moon

This portion of the moon is visible from Earth.

This portion is not.

This photo was taken in 1972 by astronauts aboard *Apollo 17,* the last flight in which humans explored the moon's surface.

When a figure is rotated, the point closest to the center of rotation remains closest to the center of rotation. In the case of the moon, the point on its surface closest to Earth remains closest to Earth as it moves. This means that from Earth, only one side of the moon is ever visible. Our knowledge of the moon was "one-sided" until 1966, when lunar probes transmitted pictures of the opposite side of the moon back to Earth.

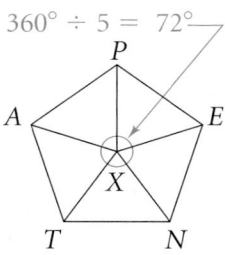

Exercises ON YOUR OWN

Copy each figure and point P. Rotate the figure the given number of degrees about P. Label the vertices of the image.

1. 60°

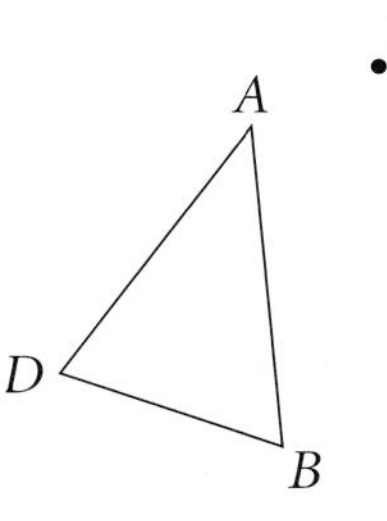

2. 90°

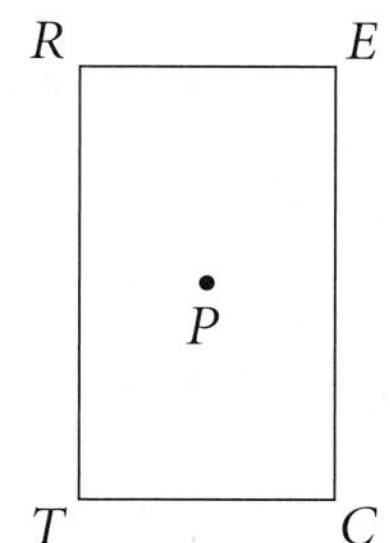

3. 180°

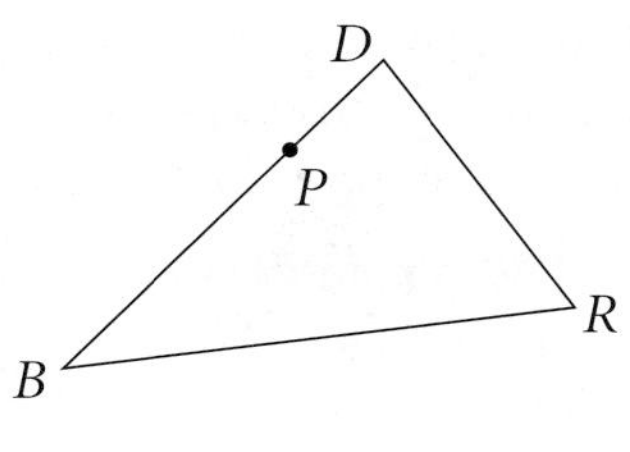

4. 140°

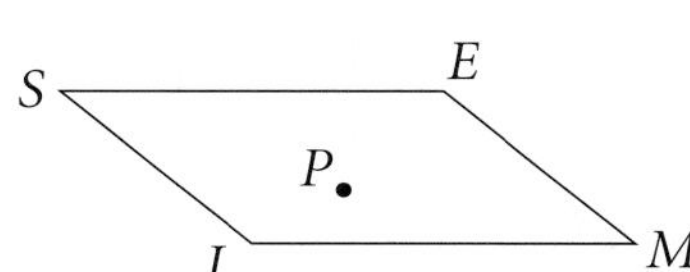

5. 90°

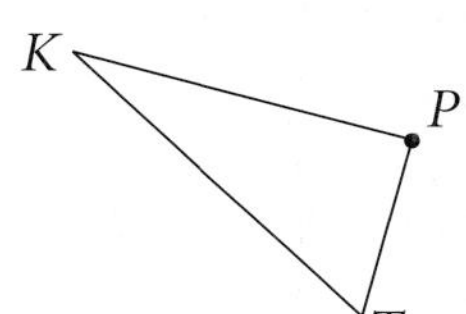

6. 45°

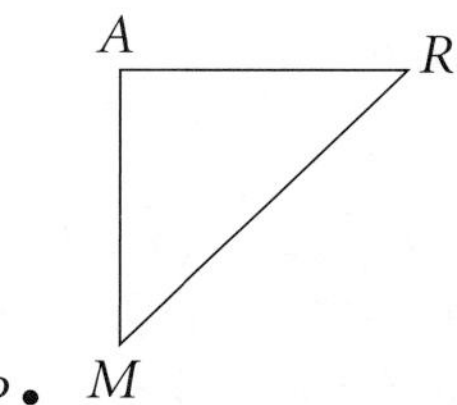

What is the measure of the rotation about C that maps the black figure onto the blue figure?

7.

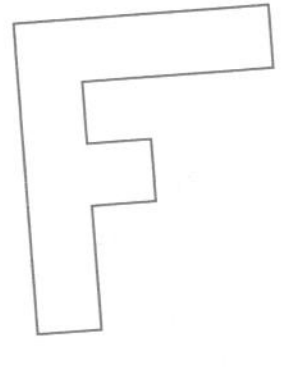

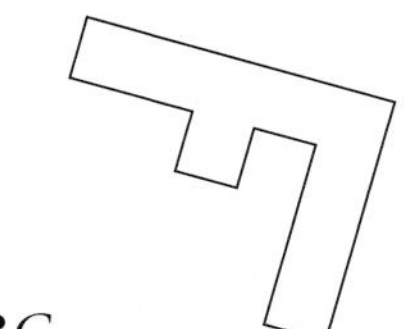

8.

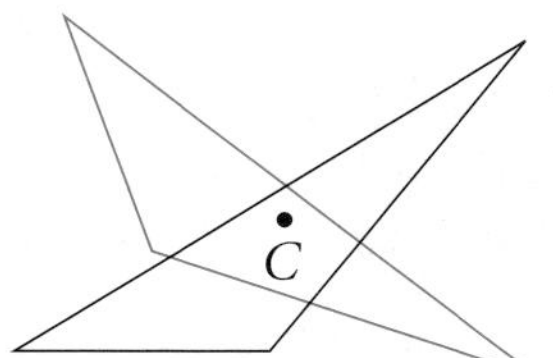

9.

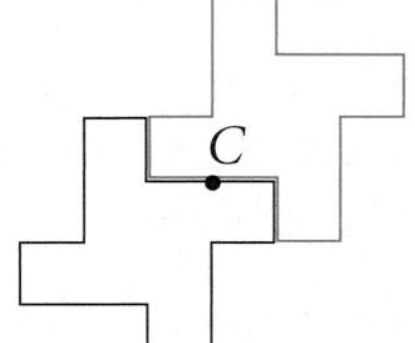

The green segments in the figure intersect to form 30° angles. The triangle, quadrilateral, and hexagon are all regular. Find the image of each point or segment.

10. 120° rotation of B about O

11. 270° rotation of L about O

12. 60° rotation of E about O

13. 300° rotation of $\overline{IB}$ about O

14. 120° rotation of $\overline{FE}$ about O

15. 120° rotation of F about H

16. 180° rotation of $\overline{JK}$ about O

17. 90° rotation of L about M

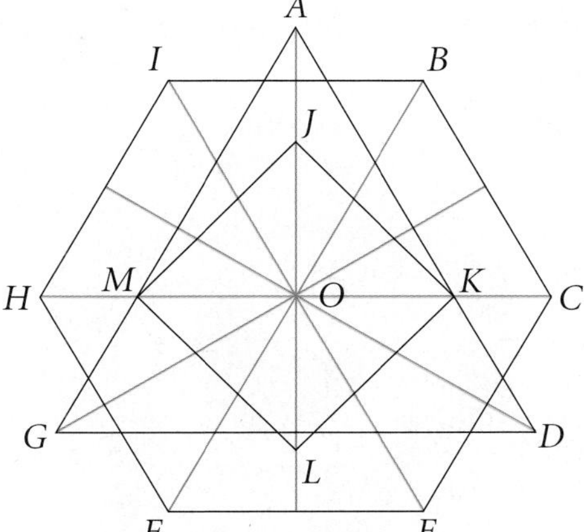

18. **Standardized Test Prep** Which figure is *not* the image of the figure at the left under a congruence transformation?

A. 

B. 

C. 

D. 

E. 

19. **Astronomy** Refer to Example 3. Suppose Earth's motion around the sun, like the moon's motion around Earth, could be described by the type of rotation in this lesson. How would life on Earth be different?

20. a. **Coordinate Geometry** Graph $A(5, 2)$, then graph B, the image of A under a 90° rotation about O (the origin). (*Hint:* Consider the slope of $\overline{OA}$.)
    b. Graph C, the image of A under a 180° rotation about O.
    c. Graph D, the image of A under a 270° rotation about O.
    d. What type of quadrilateral is $ABCD$? Explain.

21. $\overline{M'N'}$ is the rotation image of $\overline{MN}$ about point E. Name all the congruent angles and segments in the diagram.

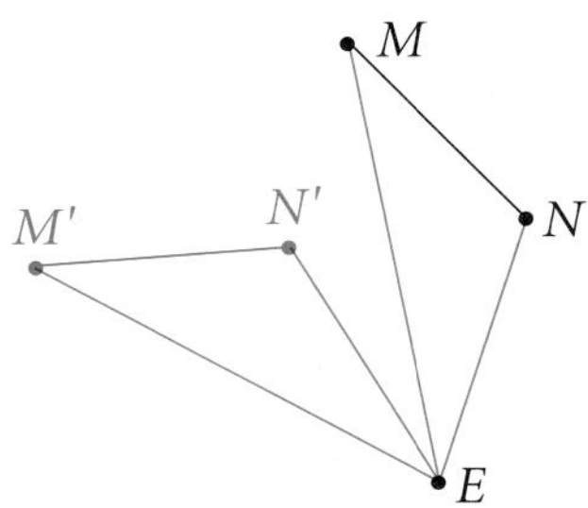

Copy each figure, then draw the image of $\overline{JK}$ under a 180° rotation about P.

22. 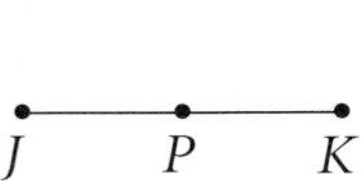

23. 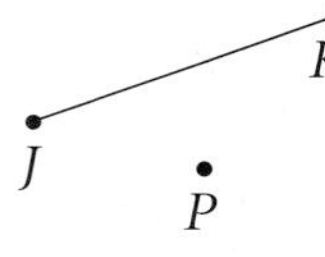

24. 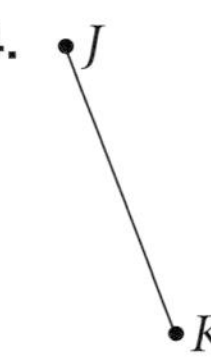

25. 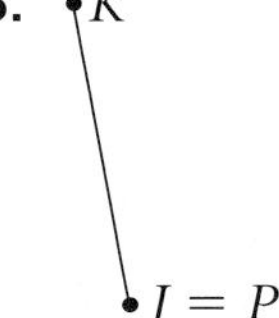

26. **Language Arts** The symbol ə is called a *schwa.* It is used in dictionaries to represent neutral vowel sounds such as *a* in *ago, i* in *sanity,* and *u* in *focus.* What transformation maps a ə to a lowercase e?

27. **Open-ended** Find a composition of rotations that has the same effect as a 360° rotation about a point X.

Native American Art **Find the measure of the rotation about C that maps Q to X.**

28. 

29. 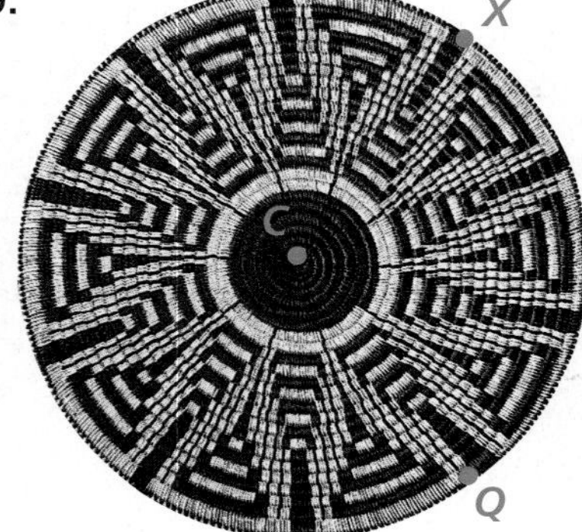

30. 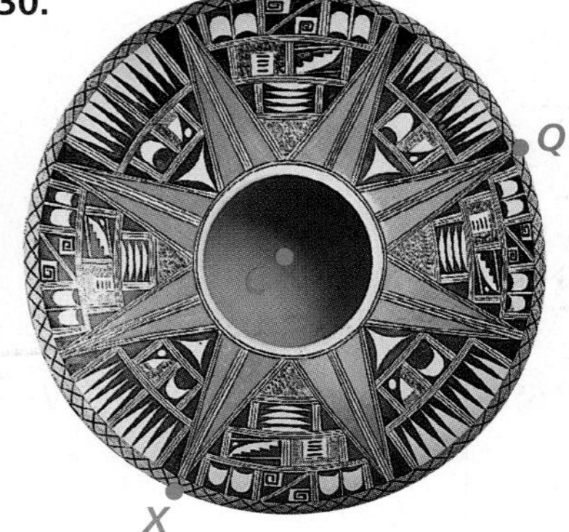

Chapter Project — *Find Out by Modeling*

Some frieze patterns can also be mapped onto themselves by a 180° rotation. Use tracing paper to make a copy of each pattern. Rotate your copy to help you determine whether the pattern can be mapped onto itself by a 180° rotation. Mark the centers of rotation on your copy.

a. Ancient Egyptian Ornament

b. Navaho Design

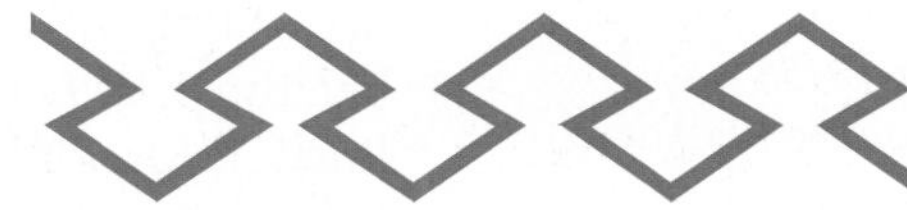

c. Oriental Design

d. Greek Vase Design

Exercises MIXED REVIEW

Create a separate sketch for each description.

31. skew lines
32. nonsimilar kites
33. parallel planes
34. similar trapezoids
35. perpendicular lines
36. nonsimilar rhombuses

37. **Writing** Determine whether a triangle with vertices (3, 2), (−1, 1), and (2, −1) is a right triangle. Explain how you know.

Getting Ready for Lesson 3-4

38. **Coordinate Geometry** Graph $H(5, 3)$ and J, its reflection image in the y-axis. Then graph K, the reflection image of J in the x-axis. Describe a rotation that maps H to K.

Exercises CHECKPOINT

Find the image of $T(3, 4)$ under each transformation.

1. reflection in the x-axis
2. rotation of 90° about (0, 0)
3. translation $\langle -2, 7\rangle$
4. rotation of 270° about (0, 0)
5. translation $\langle 1, -5\rangle$
6. reflection in the line $y = x$

7. **Writing** Explain how translations, reflections, and rotations affect the congruence and orientation of figures.

8. a. List the corresponding sides for the transformation shown.
b. Is the transformation an isometry? Explain.

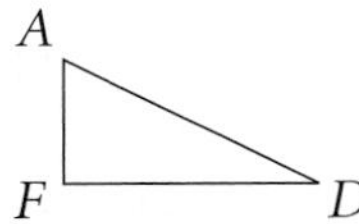

What You'll Learn

- Showing how reflections are related to the other isometries
- Identifying glide reflections

...And Why

To be able to describe how objects relate to one another

What You'll Need

- straightedge
- lined paper
- graph paper

3-4 Compositions of Reflections

WORK TOGETHER

- Have each member of your group use a straightedge to draw figures like those at the right on a piece of lined paper. Reflect the triangle in line ℓ_1; then reflect the image in line ℓ_2.

1. Compare results within your group. What transformation that you've studied has the same effect as the composition of two reflections in parallel lines?

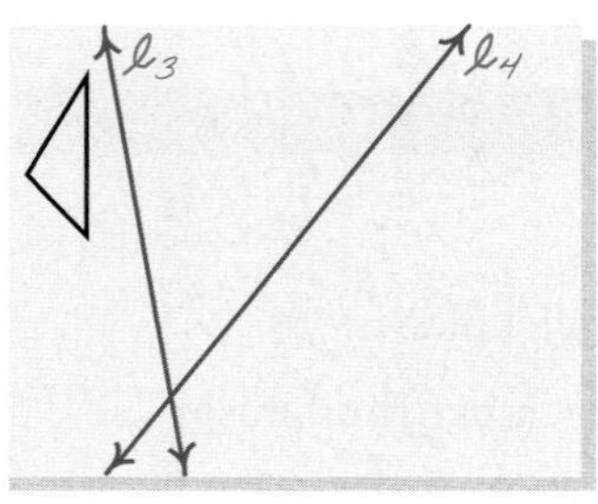

- Have each member of your group use a straightedge to draw figures like those at the left on a piece of paper. Reflect the triangle in line ℓ_3; then reflect the image in line ℓ_4.

2. Compare results within your group. What transformation that you've studied has the same effect as the composition of two reflections in intersecting lines?

THINK AND DISCUSS

Compositions of Two Reflections

The Work Together illustrates the two properties summarized in the theorems below.

Theorem 3-1 A composition of reflections in two parallel lines is a translation.

Theorem 3-2 A composition of reflections in two intersecting lines is a rotation.

The vibrant images of a kaleidoscope are produced by repeated reflections in intersecting mirrors.

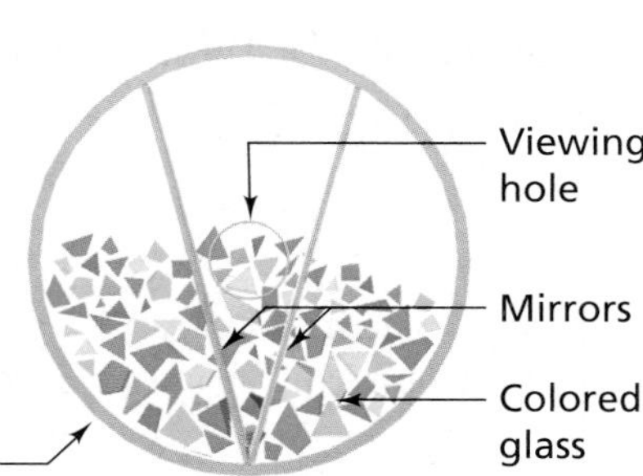

Cutaway view of a kaleidoscope

Example 1 **Relating to the Real World** 

Creative Art Determine the angle between the mirrors in this kaleidoscope image.

This wedge is repeated 6 times in 360°.

$360° \div 6 = 60°$

Suppose you are given two congruent figures in random positions in a plane. Could you use reflections to map one onto the other? If so, how many reflections would be needed? Example 2 shows that if the figures have the same orientation, only two reflections are needed.

Example 2

Paper folding The two P's at the right are congruent. Use two reflections to map one figure onto the other.

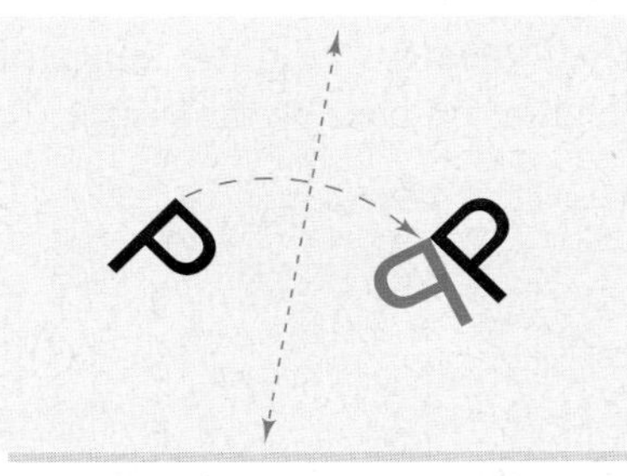

Reflection 1: Pick a point on one P, then fold it onto the corresponding point on the other P.

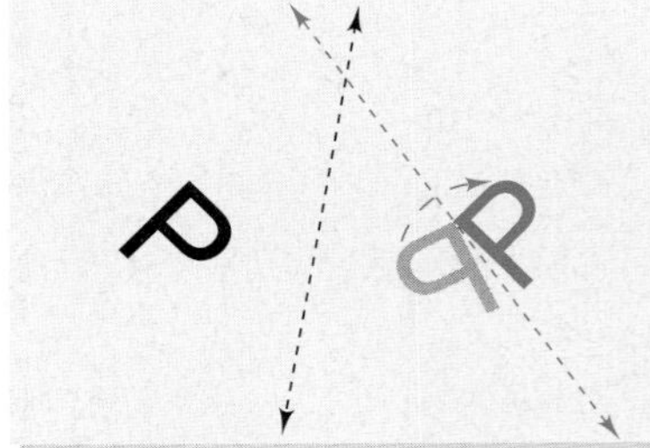

Reflection 2: Fold the two P's that share a point onto one another.

3. **Try This** Trace the two P's in Example 2 in different locations on your paper; then use paper folding to map one figure onto the other.
4. **Critical Thinking** What single isometry could be used to map one of the P's onto the other? Explain.

Compositions of Three Reflections

Example 2 shows that if two congruent figures have the *same* orientation, you can map one onto the other by exactly two reflections. If two congruent figures have *opposite* orientation, you may need to use three reflections.

Given: two figures with opposite orientation

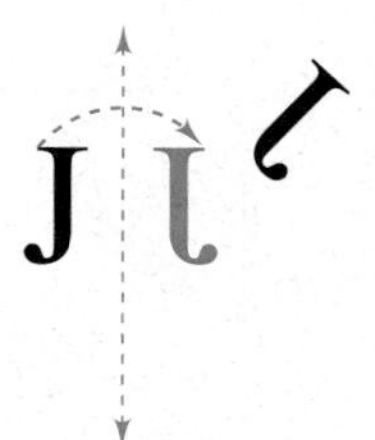

Reflect one figure in any line to change its orientation.

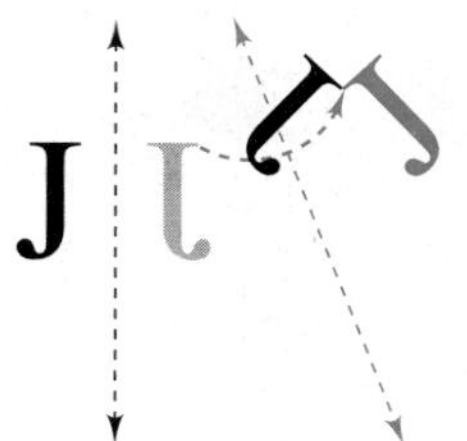

Then reflect the image twice, as shown in Example 2.

These paper-folding techniques illustrate the following theorem.

Theorem 3-3 In a plane, two congruent figures can be mapped onto one another by a composition of at most three reflections.

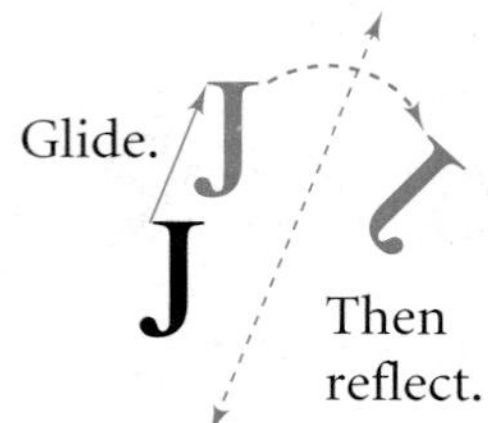

A composition of three reflections in lines that intersect in more than one point is called a **glide reflection.** It is called a glide reflection because any such composition of reflections can be rewritten as a translation (or glide) followed by a reflection in a line parallel to the translation vector.

5. ***Critical Thinking*** Explain why a glide reflection changes orientation.

Example 3

Coordinate Geometry Find the image of $\triangle TEX$ under a glide reflection where the glide is given by the vector $\langle 0, -5 \rangle$ and the reflection is in $x = 0$.

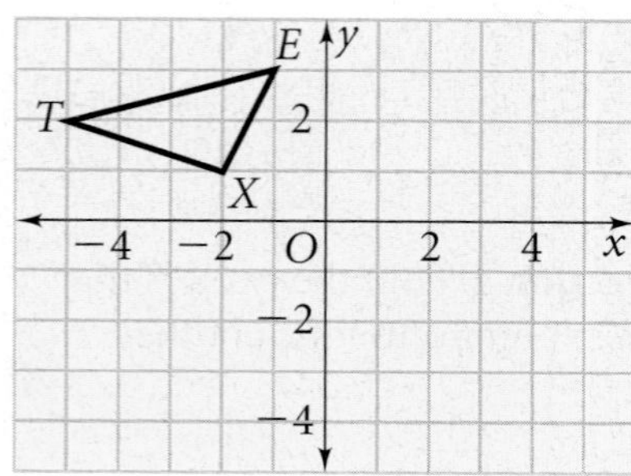

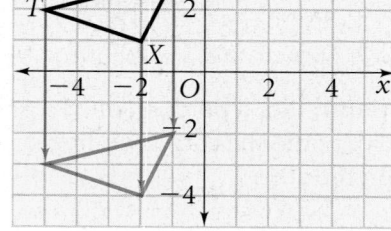

Translate $\triangle TEX$ by the vector $\langle 0, -5 \rangle$.

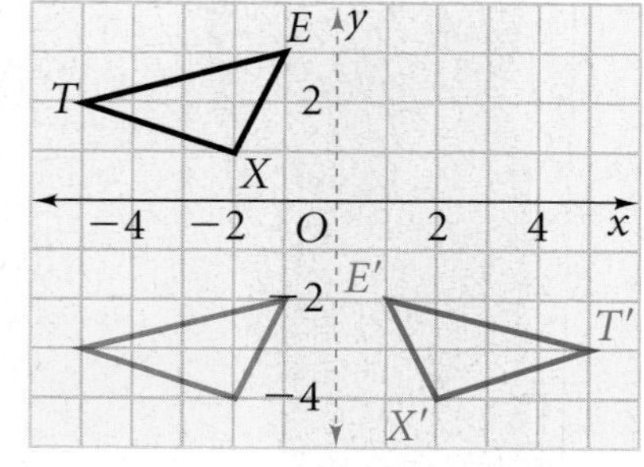

Reflect the image in $x = 0$.

6. Would the result of Example 3 be the same if you reflected $\triangle TEX$ first, then translated it?

7. **Try This** Find the image of $\triangle TEX$ under a glide reflection given by the vector $\langle 1, 0 \rangle$ and a reflection in $y = -2$.

You can map any two congruent figures onto one another by a single reflection, translation, rotation, or glide reflection. These four transformations are the only isometries.

Theorem 3-4
Isometry Classification Theorem

There are only four isometries. They are the following.

reflection	translation	rotation	glide reflection
R ⋮ Я	R → R	R rotated	R → R, reflected

Example 4

Each pair of figures is congruent. What isometry maps one to the other?

a. 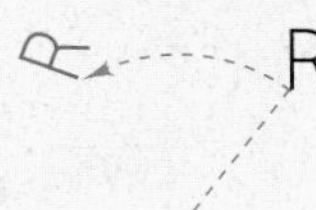

b. 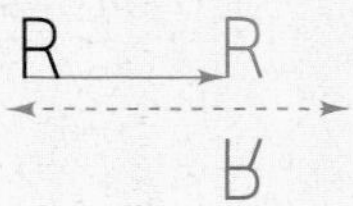

PROBLEM SOLVING HINT
Use Logical Reasoning.

a. These figures have the same orientation, so the transformation must be either a translation or a rotation. It's obviously not a translation, so it must be a rotation.

b. These figures have opposite orientation, so the transformation must be either a reflection or a glide reflection. Since it's not a reflection, it must be a glide reflection.

Exercises ON YOUR OWN

Creative Art **What is the angle between the mirrors for each kaleidoscope image?**

1. 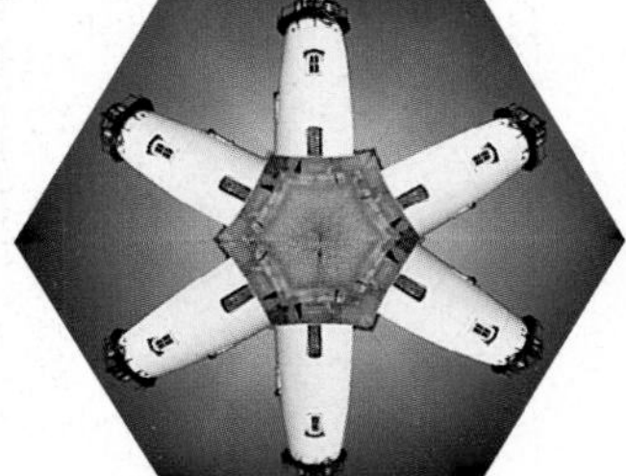

2. 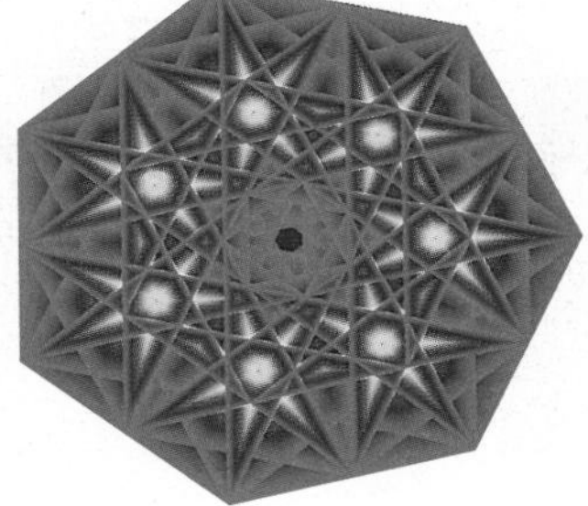

3. 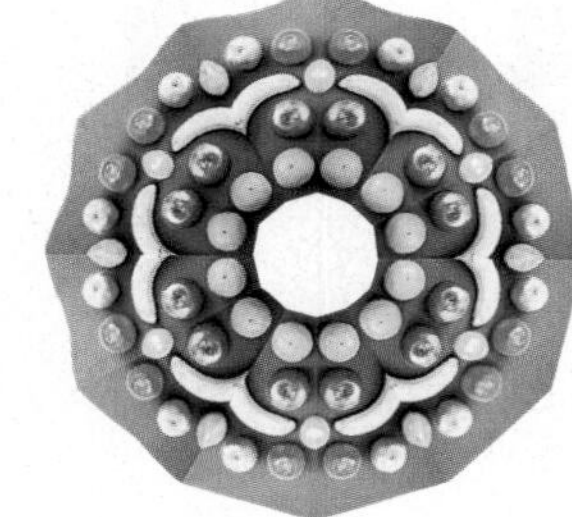

Match each image of the figure at the left with one of the following isometries: I. reflection II. rotation III. translation IV. glide reflection

4. 
a. 
b. 
c. 
d. 

5. 
a. 
b. 
c. 
d. 

6. 
a. 
b. 
c. 
d. 

Coordinate Geometry **Find the image of $\triangle PNB$ under each glide reflection.**

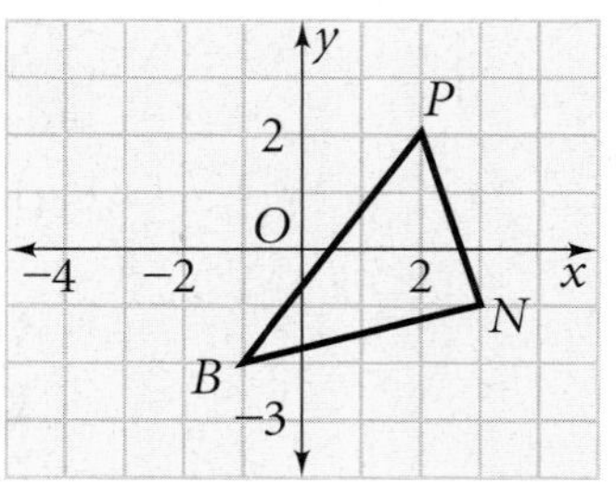

7. $\langle 2, 0\rangle$ and $y = 3$
8. $\langle 0, -3\rangle$ and $x = 0$
9. $\langle 0, 3\rangle$ and $x = -2$
10. $\langle -2, 0\rangle$ and $y = -1$
11. $\langle 2, 2\rangle$ and $y = x$
12. $\langle -1, 1\rangle$ and $y = -x$

Is the isometry that maps the black figure to the blue figure a translation, reflection, rotation, or glide reflection?

13. 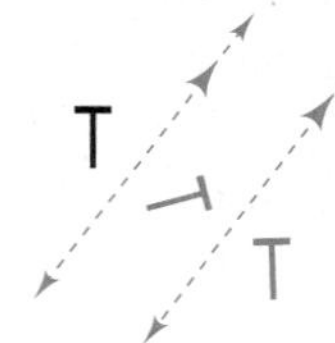
14. 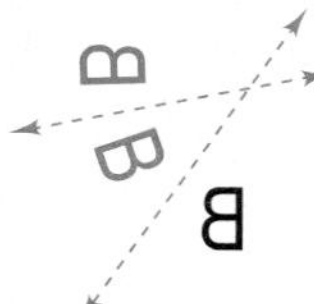
15. 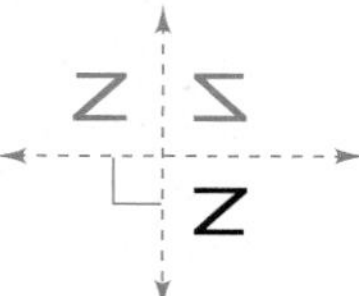
16. 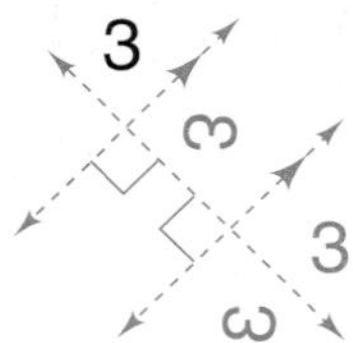

17. 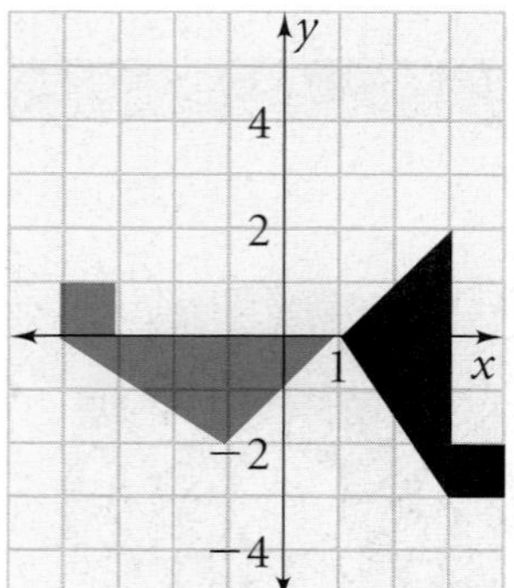

18. 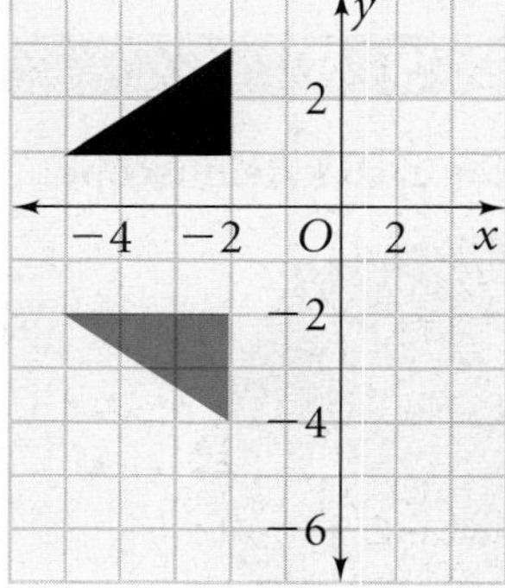

19. 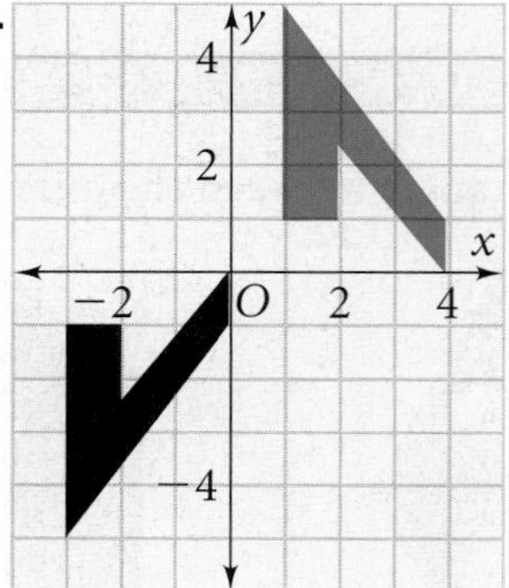

20. 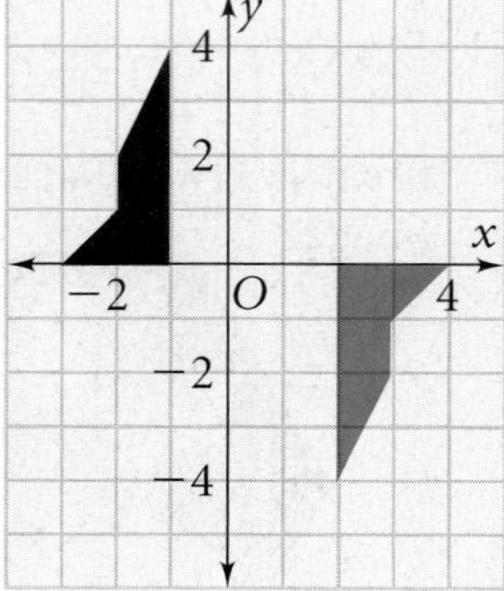

State whether each mapping is a reflection, rotation, translation, or glide reflection.

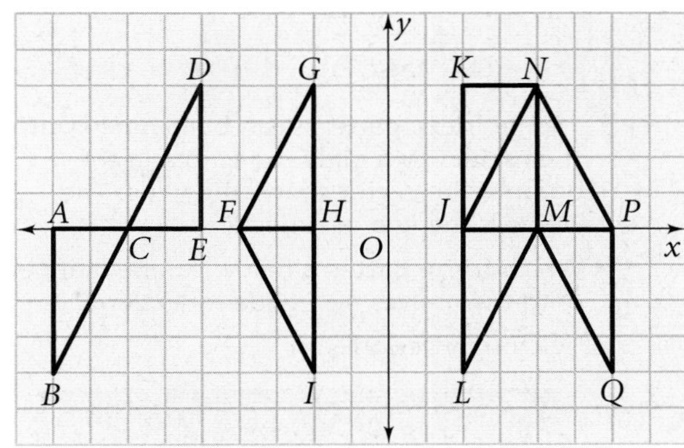

21. $\triangle ABC \longrightarrow \triangle EDC$
22. $\triangle EDC \longrightarrow \triangle PQM$
23. $\triangle MNJ \longrightarrow \triangle EDC$
24. $\triangle HIF \longrightarrow \triangle HGF$
25. $\triangle PQM \longrightarrow \triangle JLM$
26. $\triangle MNP \longrightarrow \triangle EDC$
27. $\triangle JLM \longrightarrow \triangle MNJ$
28. $\triangle PQM \longrightarrow \triangle KJN$

29. **Writing** Reflections and glide reflections are *odd isometries*, while translations and rotations are *even isometries*. Use what you learned in this lesson to explain why these categories make sense.

30. **Paper folding** Fold a rectangular piece of paper into sixths as shown. Then use scissors to cut a nonregular polygon into the folded paper. Unfold the paper and number each of the six figures represented by the holes. What isometries map Figure 1 onto Figures 2, 3, 4, 5, and 6?

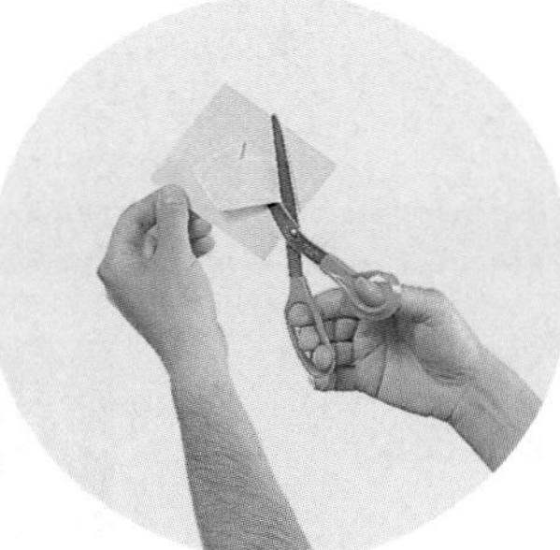
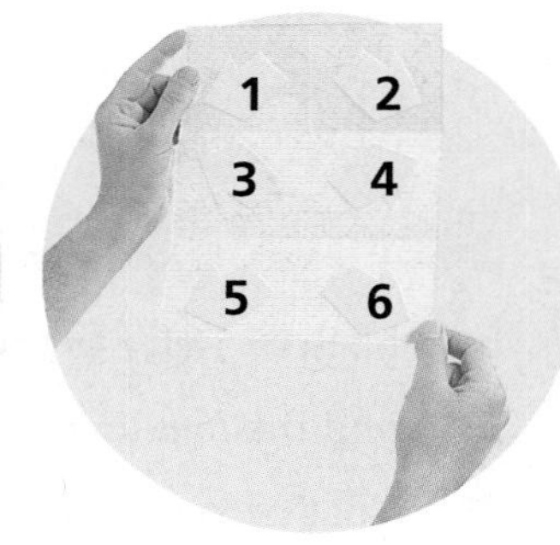

31. **Probability** Suppose you toss two cardboard cutouts of congruent figures into the air so that they land in random positions on the floor. Consider the isometry that maps one of the figures onto the other. Which of the four isometries, if any, are most likely to occur?

PROBLEM SOLVING HINT

Cut out two congruent figures and experiment. Look for a pattern.

32. **Architecture** These housing plans were created by the Swiss architect Le Corbusier for a development in Pessac, France. They illustrate each of the four isometries. Name the isometry illustrated by each design.

a.

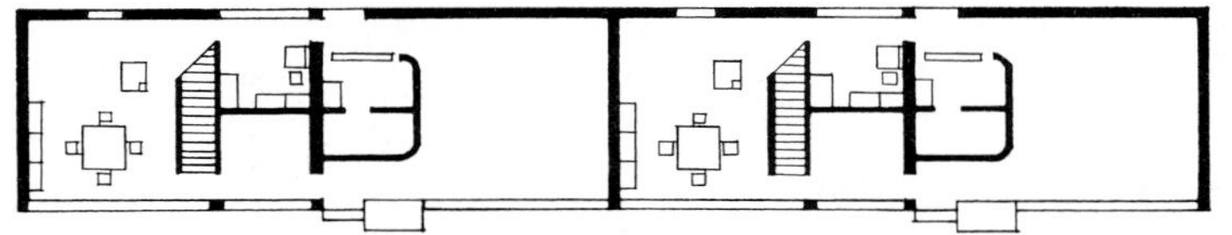

b.

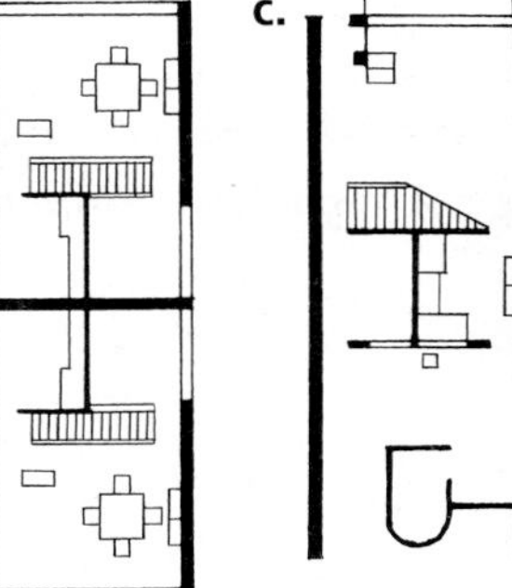

c.

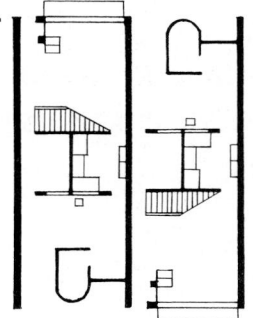

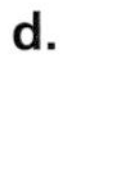

d.

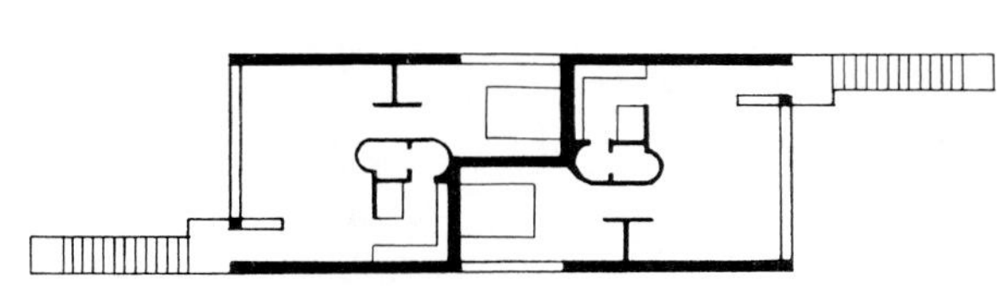

Chapter Project — Find Out by Investigating

Some frieze patterns can be mapped onto themselves by a glide reflection. In the diagrams, the vector shows the glide. The red line is the line of reflection.

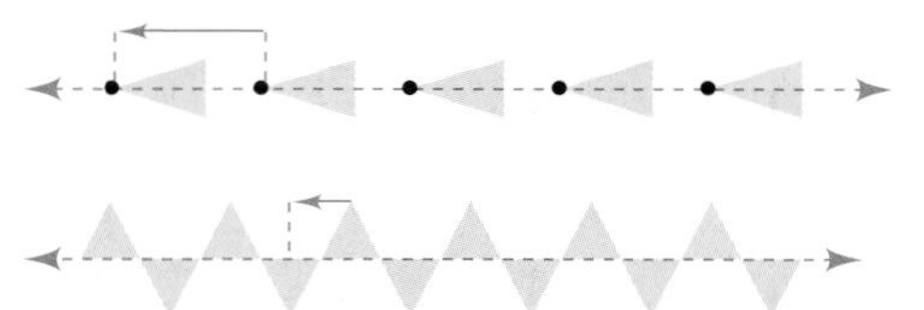

- Which frieze patterns below can be mapped onto themselves by a glide reflection?

a. Victorian Design

b. Chinese Design

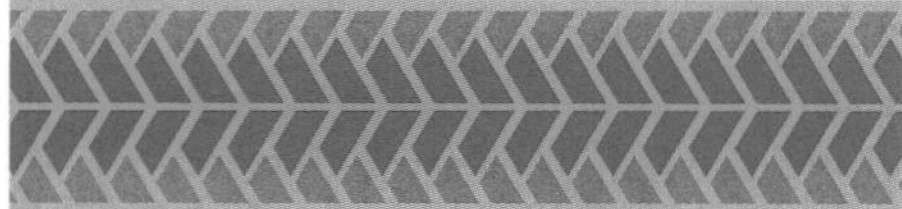

c. Nigerian Design

d. Turkish Design

Exercises MIXED REVIEW

Data Analysis Refer to the circle graph.

33. Find the measure of each central angle.

34. What percent of people use their ATM cards fewer than six times per month?

35. Which statements are true, based on the graph?

a. Most people use their ATM cards two or more times per month.

b. Most people have ATM cards.

c. At least 36% of people use their ATM cards one or more times per week.

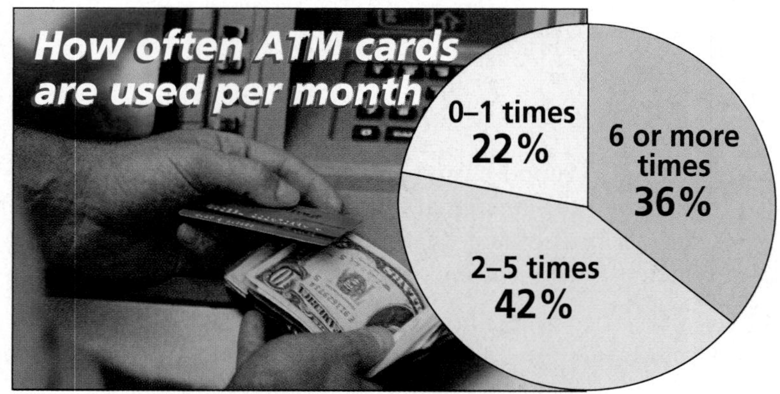

Source: *Research Partnership survey for Cirrus Systems*

Getting Ready for Lesson 3-5

Find the image of each figure under the given transformation.

36.

Rotation of 60° about O

37.

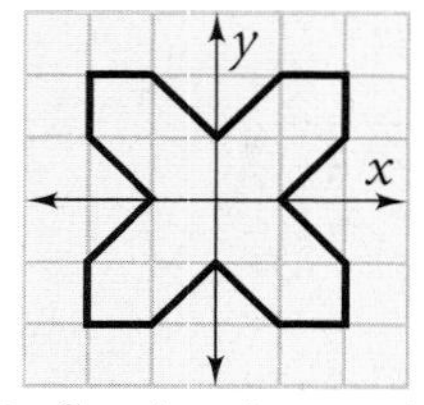

Reflection in y-axis

38.

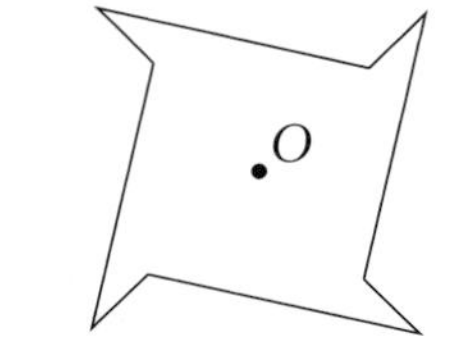

Rotation of 90° about O

Math ToolboX

Technology

Kaleidoscopes

Before Lesson 3-5

The mirrors in a kaleidoscope reflect objects to create a *symmetrical* design. Work in pairs or small groups to create your own kaleidoscope.

Construct

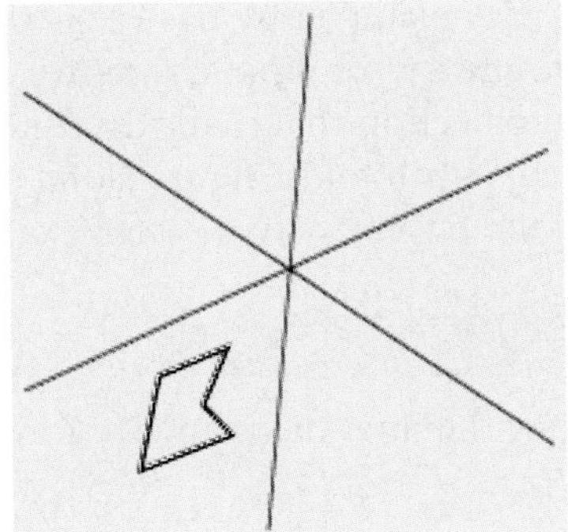

- Use geometry software. Draw a line and construct a point on the line. Rotate the line 60° about the point. Rotate the image 60° about the point.
- Construct a polygon in the interior of an angle, as shown. Reflect the polygon in the closest line in a clockwise direction. Reflect the image in the next closest line in a clockwise direction. Continue reflecting until the kaleidoscope is filled. Then hide the lines of reflection.

Investigate

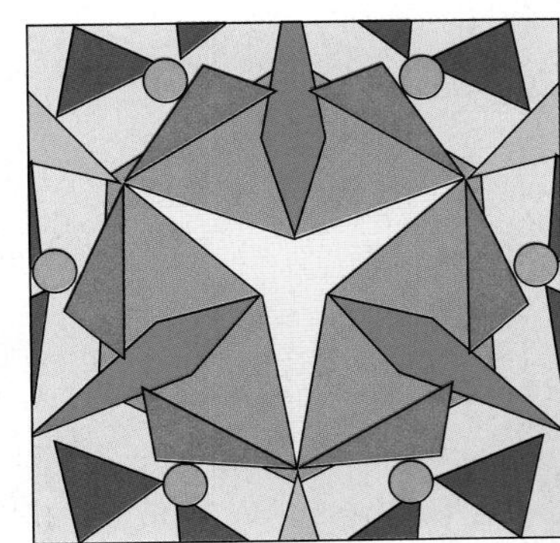

- Manipulate the original figure by dragging any of its vertices or selecting and moving it. As the figure is manipulated, what happens to the images? Does the design remain symmetrical? Continue manipulating the original figure until you are satisfied with your design. Print the design and color it.
- Now add other figures in addition to the original polygon. Reflect these figures to create a more interesting design, as shown at the right. (You may need to temporarily show the hidden lines of reflection.) Print your design and color it.

Extend

Create a kaleidoscope with four lines of reflection. Draw a line and construct a point on the line. Rotate the line 45° about the point and repeat until you have four lines. Add a figure to the interior of an angle and reflect it as described above.

Connections Advertising . . . and more

3-5 Symmetry

What You'll Learn

- Identifying types of symmetry in figures

...And Why

To understand a topic that influences art, dance, and poetry, and is an important tool of scientists

THINK AND DISCUSS

Reflectional Symmetry

A figure has **symmetry** if there is an isometry that maps the figure onto itself. A plane figure has **reflectional symmetry,** or **line symmetry,** if there is a reflection that maps the figure onto itself. If you fold a figure along a line of symmetry, the halves match exactly.

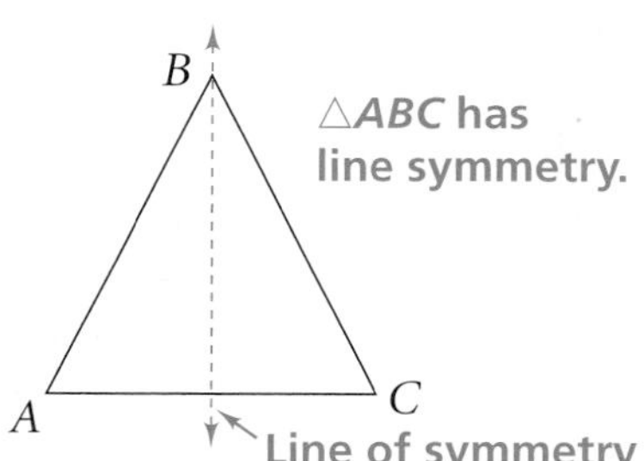

Example 1

Draw the lines of symmetry for each figure.

a. 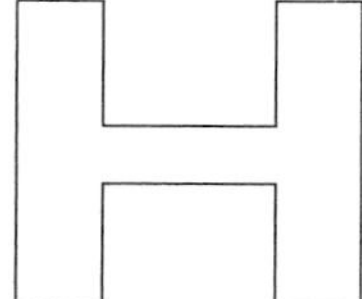

b. 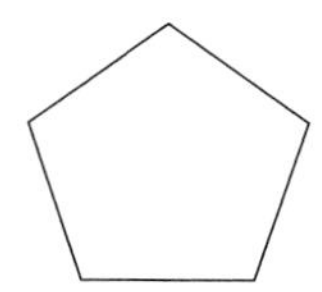

c. 

a. 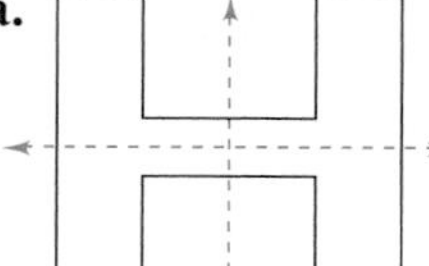

b. 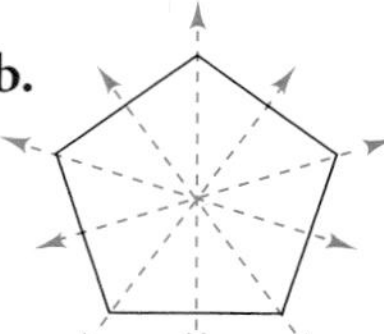

c. This figure has no lines of symmetry.

Symmetry is especially important to left-handers. Because about 95% of people are right-handed, right-handed versions of objects are easier to find (and often less expensive!) than left-handed versions of the same objects.

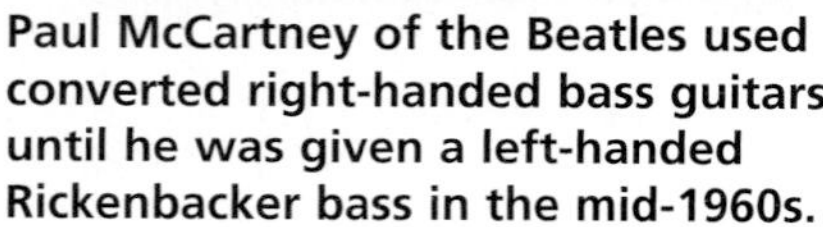

Paul McCartney of the Beatles used converted right-handed bass guitars until he was given a left-handed Rickenbacker bass in the mid-1960s.

Left-handed people appreciate reflectional symmetry because objects that have it can be used by both left-handers and right-handers.

Three-dimensional objects with reflectional symmetry can be divided into two congruent parts by a plane. You can sketch these symmetries in two dimensions by using orthographic views (top, front, or right side).

Example 2 **Relating to the Real World** 

Technical Drawing Show the reflectional symmetries of each object by sketching an orthographic view.

a.

b.

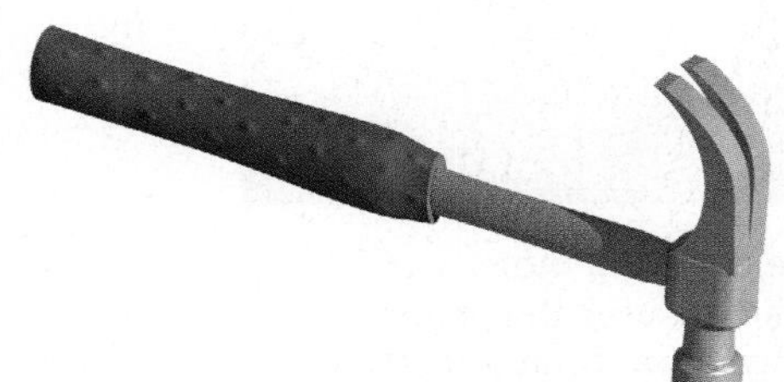

a.

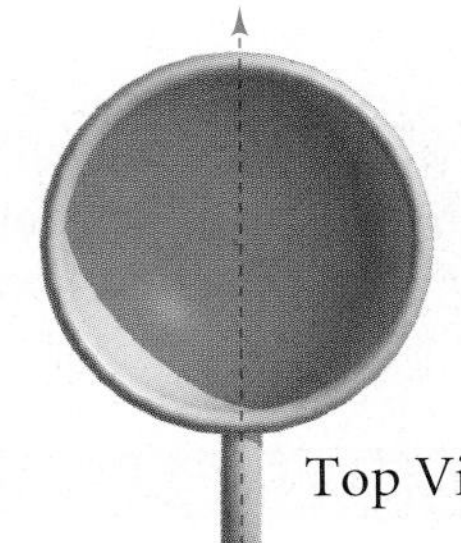

Top View

b.

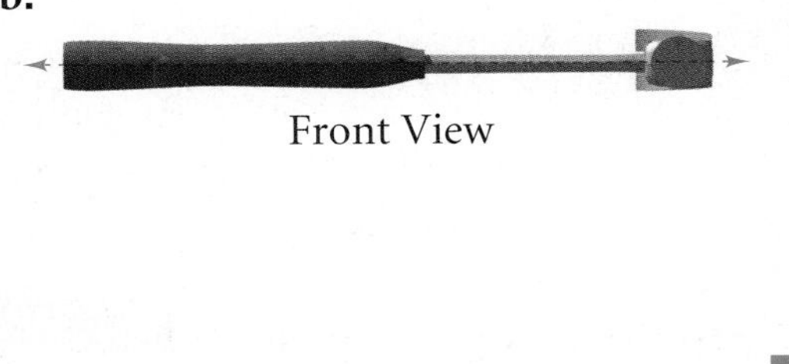

Front View

1. **Critical Thinking** Name an object that has more than one plane of symmetry.

Rotational Symmetry

A figure has **rotational symmetry** if there is a rotation of 180° or less that maps the figure onto itself.

The spinning motion of a lathe ensures that objects created on it have rotational symmetry.

Example 3

Which figures have rotational symmetry? For those that do, give the angle of rotation.

a. 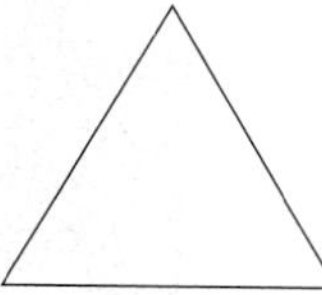

b. 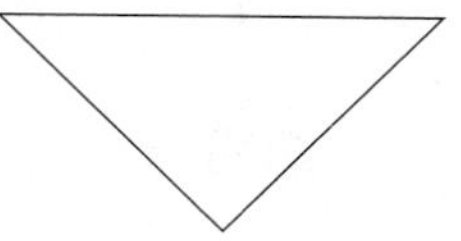

c. 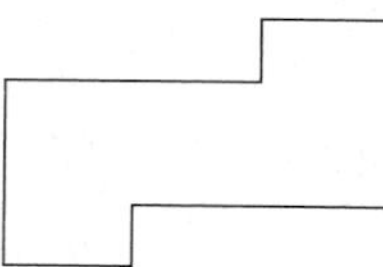

a. 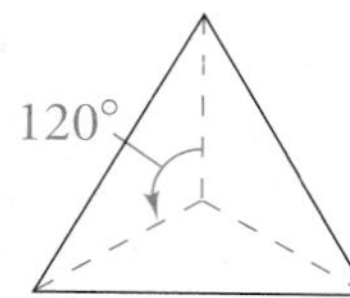

b. This figure does not have rotational symmetry.

c. 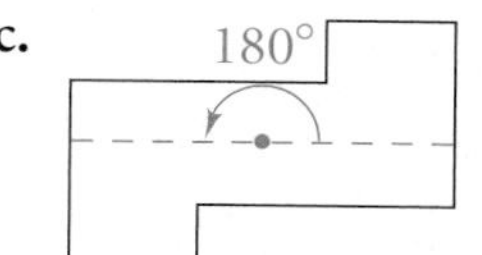

2. If a figure has rotational symmetry, must it also have line symmetry? Explain your answer.

A rotation of 180° is known as a **half-turn.** If a half-turn maps a plane figure onto itself, the figure has **point symmetry.**

3. Try This Which figures have point symmetry?

a. 

b. 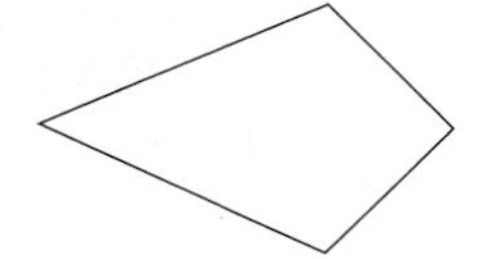

c. 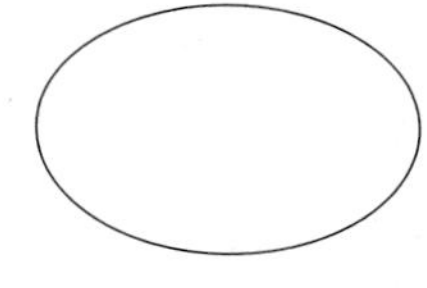

So far, you've looked at figures with reflectional and rotational symmetry. As you may have guessed, figures may also have *translational* or *glide reflectional symmetry*. You will discuss these symmetries in the next lesson.

WORK TOGETHER

- Work in groups to find examples of symmetrical objects in your classroom. For each object that you find, sketch an orthographic view and list its symmetries. You will have only ten minutes in which to search, so plan your time wisely!
- Determine your group's score by using the chart at the left.

Type of Symmetry	Points
Reflectional Symmetry	1
Rotational Symmetry of 180°	2
Rotational Symmetry other than 180°	3

Exercises ON YOUR OWN

What types of symmetry does each figure have? If it has reflectional symmetry, sketch the figure and the line(s) of symmetry. If it has rotational symmetry, state the angle of rotation.

1. 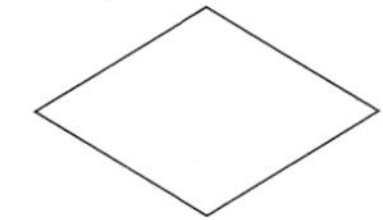

2. 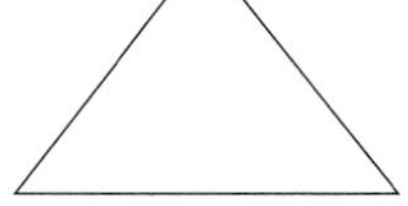

3. 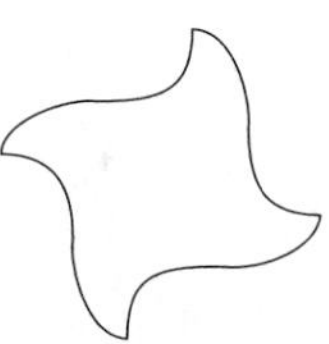

4. 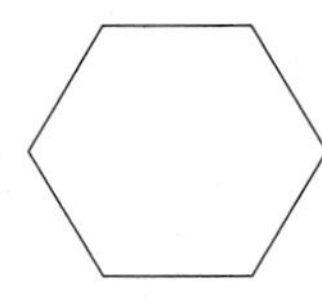

5. 

6. 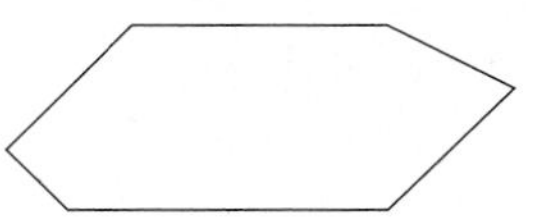

7. 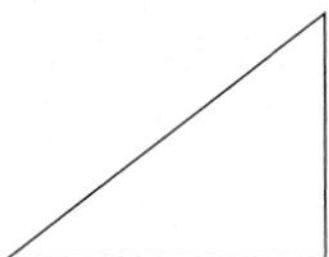

8. 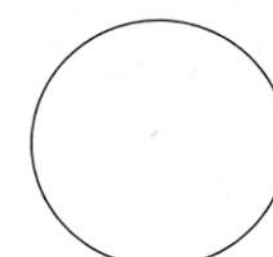

What types of symmetry are shown in each photograph?

9. 

10. 

11. 

12. 

13. Sketch a triangle that has reflectional symmetry but not rotational symmetry.

14. **a.** Copy the tree diagram of quadrilaterals on page 654. Then draw each figure's lines of symmetry.

b. **Patterns** How do the symmetries of the figures in the top portion of the tree diagram compare with the symmetries of those lower in the diagram?

Each diagram shows a shape folded along a red line of symmetry. Sketch the unfolded figure.

15.  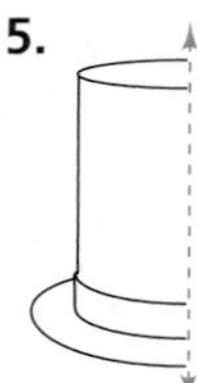

16. 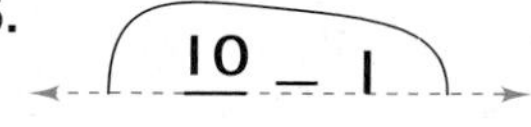

17. 

18. a. The word CODE has a horizontal line of symmetry through its center. Find three other words that have this type of symmetry.
    b. The word WAXY, when printed vertically, has a vertical line of symmetry. Find three other words that have this type of symmetry.

Advertising **Many automobile manufacturers have symmetrical logos. Describe the symmetry, if any, in each logo.**

19. 

20. 

21. 

22. 

23. 

24. 

25. 

26. 

27. 

28. 

29. *Research* Many company logos are symmetrical. Find three symmetrical logos in the Yellow Pages of your local phone book. Copy each logo, identify the name of the business, and describe the type(s) of symmetry illustrated.

Geometry in 3 Dimensions **Show the reflectional symmetries of each object by sketching an orthographic view.**

30. 

31. 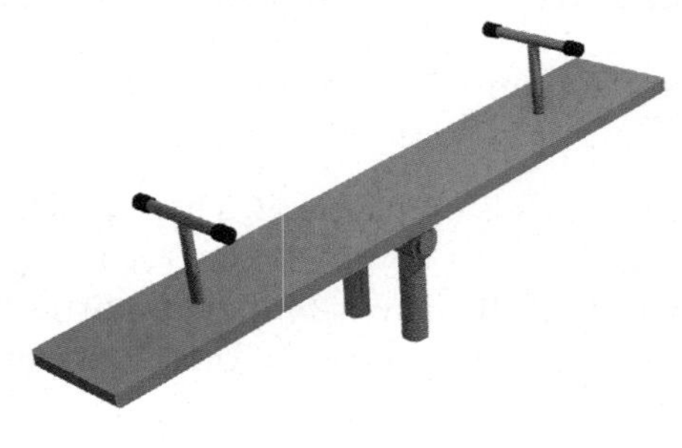

32. 

33. a. *Languages* Copy the chart at the right. Then use the alphabets below to list the letters in each category. Some letters will appear in more than one category.

b. Which alphabet is more symmetrical? Explain your reasoning.

A B C D E F G H I J K L M N O P Q R S T U V W X Y Z

Α Β Γ Δ Ε Ζ Η Θ Ι Κ Λ Μ Ν Ξ Ο Π Ρ Σ Τ Υ Φ Χ Ψ Ω

Type of Symmetry

Language	Horizontal Line	Vertical Line	Point
English			
Greek			

34. *Writing* Use what you learned in Lesson 3-4 to explain why a figure that has two or more lines of symmetry must also have rotational symmetry.

Algebra **Sketch the graph of each equation. Describe the symmetry of each graph.**

35. $y = x^2$ **36.** $y = (x - 2)^2$ **37.** $y = x^3$

38. *Open-ended* Copy the Venn diagram; then draw a figure in each of its six regions that shows that type of symmetry.

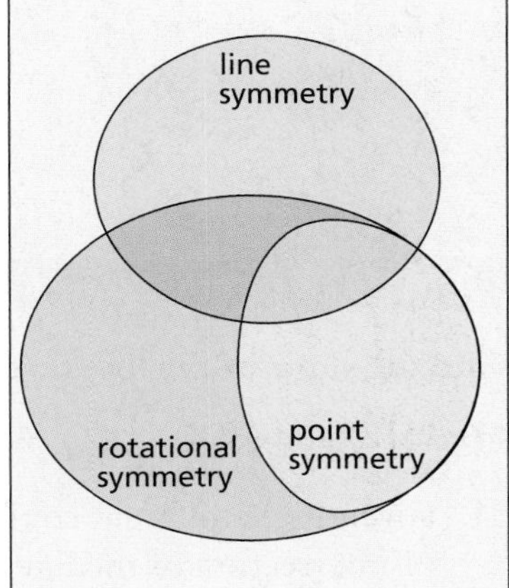

39. *Open-ended* The equation $\frac{10}{10} - 1 = 0 \div \frac{83}{83}$ is not only true, but also symmetrical. Write four other equations or inequalities that are both true and symmetrical.

40. a. Is the line that contains the bisector of an angle a line of symmetry of the angle? Explain.

b. Is a bisector of a segment a line of symmetry of the segment? Explain.

Each of the logos below is nearly symmetrical. For each logo, describe how you could alter it to make it symmetrical. Then, describe the symmetries of your altered logo.

41.

42.

43.

Coordinate Geometry **A figure has a vertex at (3, 4). If the figure has the given type of symmetry, state the coordinates of another vertex of the figure.**

44. line symmetry in the y-axis **45.** line symmetry in the x-axis **46.** point symmetry in the origin

Chapter Project

Find Out by Classifying

It may surprise you to find out that when you classify frieze patterns by their symmetries, there turn out to be only seven different types. Each pattern is identified by a different two-character code: 11, 1*g*, *m*1, 12, *mg*, 1*m*, or *mm*. Use the flow chart at the right to classify each frieze pattern below.

a. Caucasian Rug Design, Kazak

b. French, Empire Motif

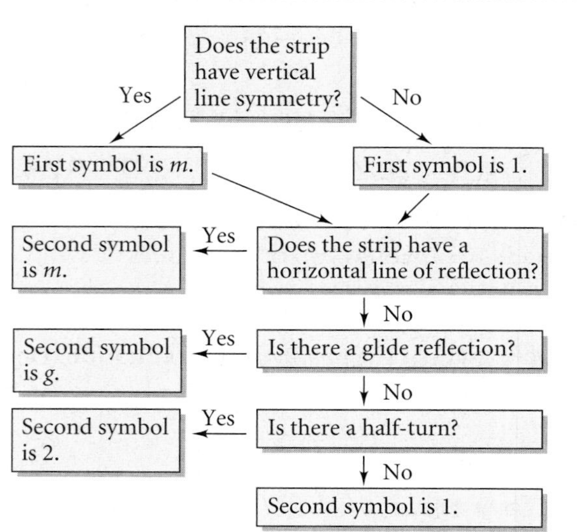

Exercises MIXED REVIEW

Find the slope of the line through the given points.

47. (5, 2) and (3, 0) **48.** (−2, 4) and (3, −7) **49.** (−5, −8) and (1, 6) **50.** (9, −1) and (−2, −7)

51. Given three different coplanar lines, what is the least number of points of intersection of the lines? the greatest number?

Getting Ready for Lesson 3-6

52. Refer to the figure. What is $m\angle 1 + m\angle 2 + m\angle 3 + m\angle 4$?

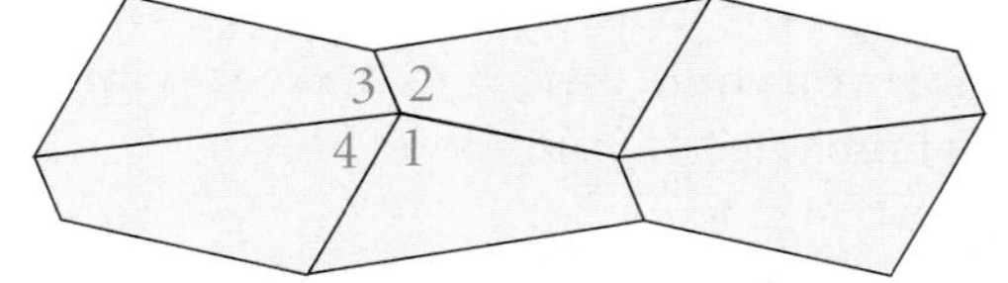

Exercises CHECKPOINT

What types of symmetry does each figure have?

1.

2.

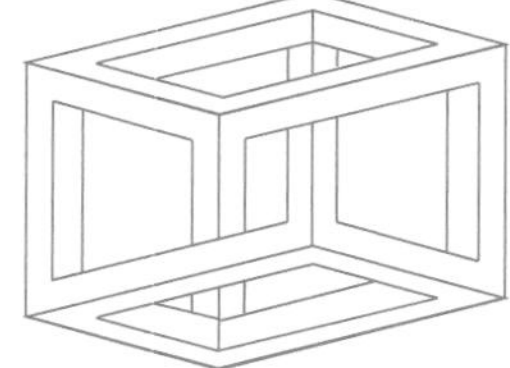

3.

4. $\triangle CAL$ has vertices $C(0, -1)$, $A(-3, 2)$, and $L(-1, -2)$. Find the image of $\triangle CAL$ under a glide reflection in $\langle 0, 4\rangle$ and $x = -2$.

5. *Open-ended* Sketch lines ℓ_1 and ℓ_2 so that the composition of reflections in the two lines is a translation.

3-6 Tessellations

What You'll Learn

- Identifying figures that tessellate
- Identifying symmetries of tessellations

...And Why

To recognize tessellations in nature, architecture, art, and other areas of life

What You'll Need

- scissors
- clear tape
- ruler

The Dutch artist Maurits Cornelis Escher (1898–1972) used transformational geometry in intriguing ways in his work. His work is very popular with the public, scientists, and mathematicians.

Source: © 1996 M. C. Escher Heirs/Cordon Art—Baam—Holland. All rights reserved.

THINK AND DISCUSS

Identifying Figures that Tessellate

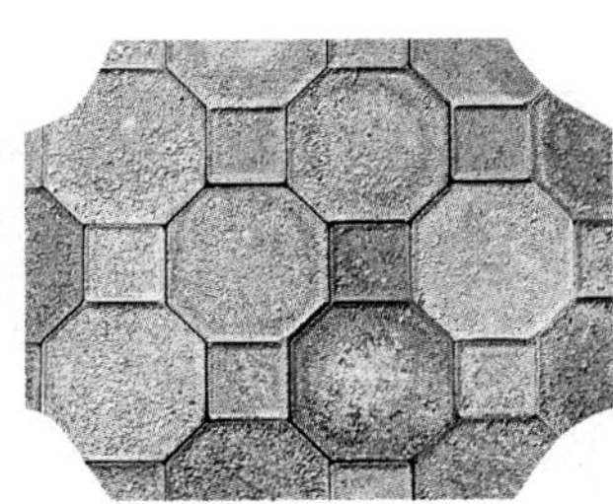

A **tessellation** is a repeating pattern of figures that completely covers a plane without gaps or overlaps. Tessellations are also called **tilings.** A set of figures that can be used to create a tessellation is said to *tessellate.* You can find tessellations in art, nature, and everyday life.

Example 1 Relating to the Real World 

Source: © 1996 M. C. Escher Heirs/ Cordon Art—Baam—Holland. All rights reserved.

Art Identify the repeating figures that make up this tessellation.

Repeating figures

1. **Try This** Identify the repeating figures that make up the tessellation of paving tiles at the top of this page.

Source: © 1996 M. C. Escher Heirs/ Cordon Art—Baam—Holland. All rights reserved.

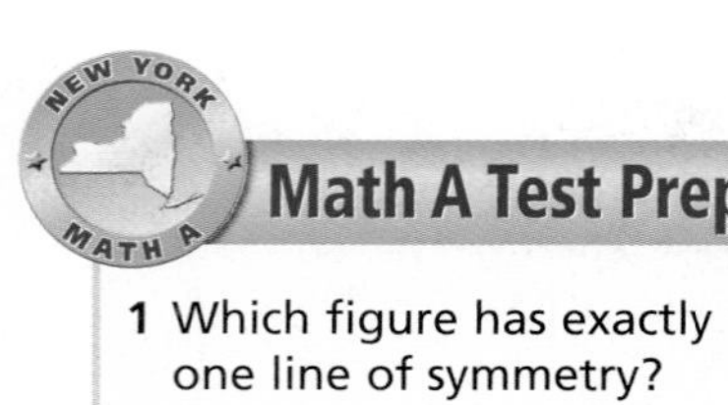

1 Which figure has exactly one line of symmetry?

(1) 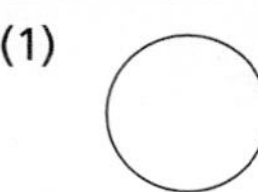

(2) 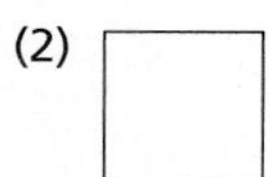

(3) 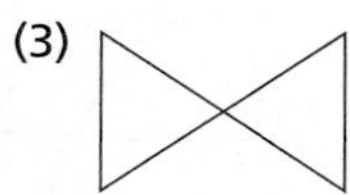

(4) 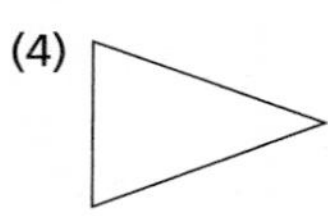

2 What is the image of (6, −9) under the translation ⟨5, −2⟩?

Because the figures in a tessellation do not overlap or leave gaps, the sum of the measures of the angles around any vertex must be 360.

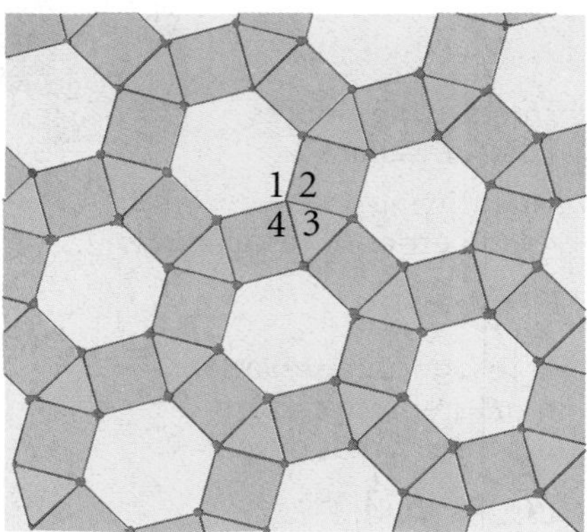

2. a. The tessellation shown consists of regular polygons. Find the measures of angles 1, 2, 3, and 4.

b. Check your answer to part (a) by making sure that the sum of the measures is 360.

A **pure tessellation** is a tessellation that consists of congruent copies of one figure. It may surprise you that there are only three pure tessellations made up of regular polygons. To see why this is the case, consider the following diagrams.

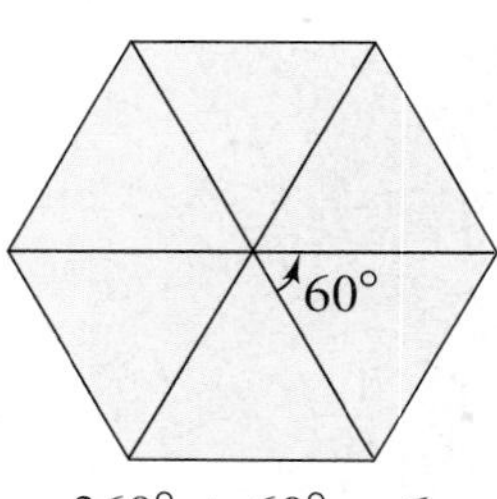

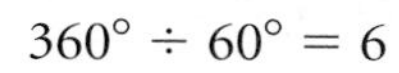
$360° \div 60° = 6$

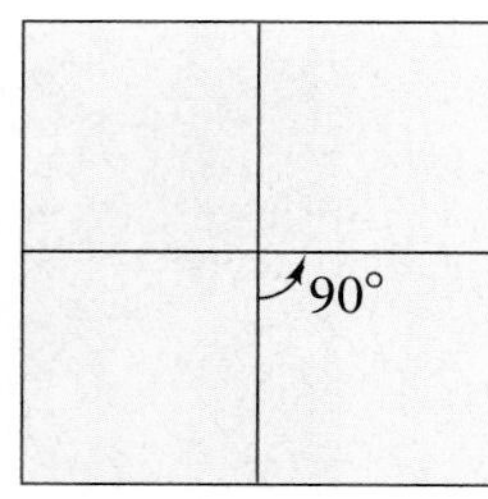

$360° \div 90° = 4$

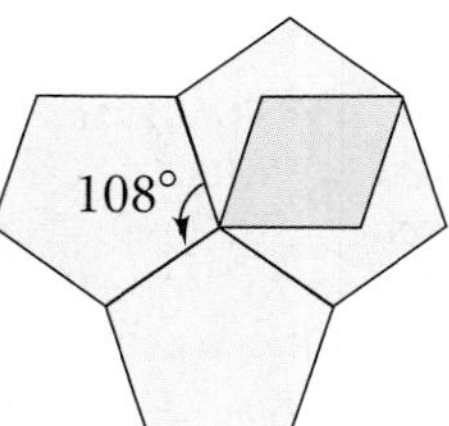

$360° \div 108° \approx 3.3$

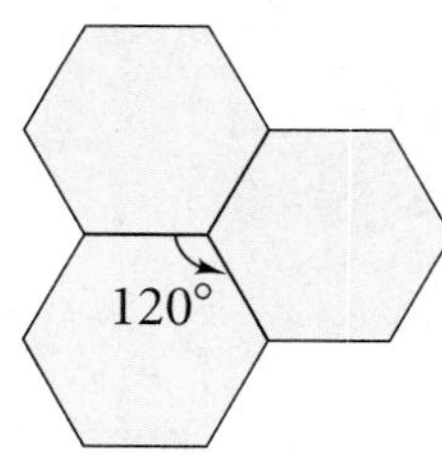

$360° \div 120° = 3$

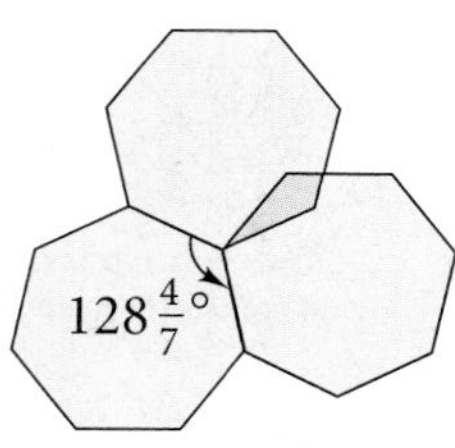

$360° \div 128\frac{4}{7}° \approx 2.8$

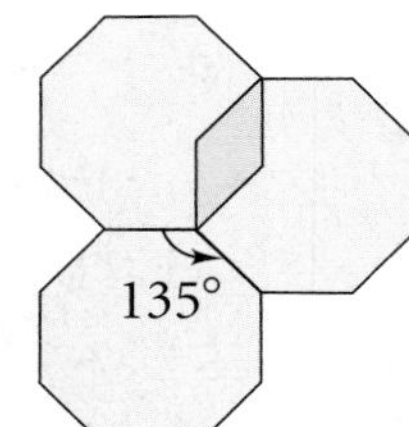

$360° \div 135° \approx 2.6$

3. ***Critical Thinking*** Explain why no regular polygons with more than six sides tessellate.

Regular triangles and quadrilaterals tessellate, but what about other triangles and quadrilaterals? Work in groups to explore this problem.

WORK TOGETHER

Step 1: Have each member of your group fold four pieces of paper into sixths, as shown in the photos.

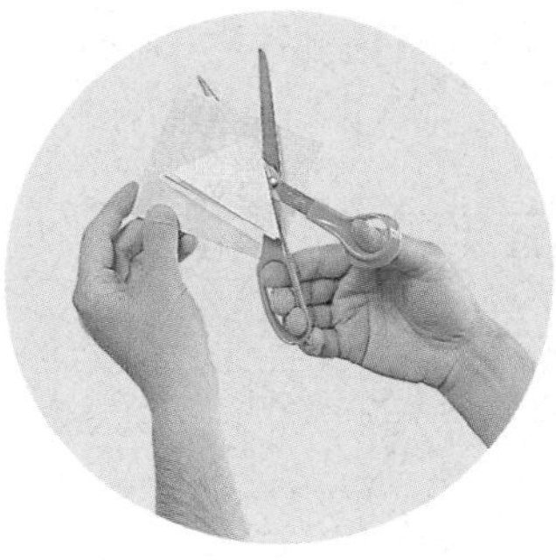

Step 2: Draw a triangle on one of the four folded pieces of paper; then cut through all six sheets of paper to create six congruent triangles. Create six more congruent triangles by tracing one of your cutouts onto another folded piece of paper and then cutting out six triangles.

4. a. Try to arrange your twelve congruent triangles into a tessellation. (*Hint:* Arrange vertices so that they meet.) Compare results within your group.

b. Use what you know about the sum of the measures of the angles of a triangle to explain your results from part (a).

Step 3: Set your triangles aside. Use the method in Step 2 to create twelve congruent quadrilaterals.

5. a. Try to arrange your twelve congruent quadrilaterals into a tessellation. Compare results within your group.

b. Use what you know about the sum of the measures of the angles of a quadrilateral to explain your results from part (a).

THINK AND DISCUSS

In the Work Together, you discovered the following properties of tessellations.

Theorem 3-5 Every triangle tessellates.

Theorem 3-6 Every quadrilateral tessellates.

Tessellations and Symmetry

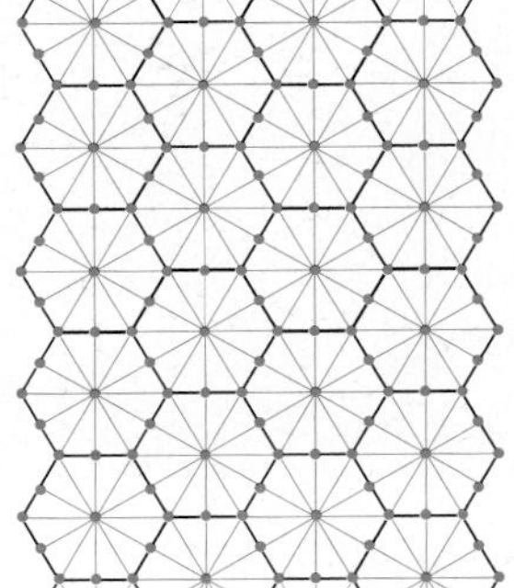

This pure tessellation of regular hexagons has reflectional symmetry in each of the blue lines. It has rotational symmetry centered at each of the red points. The tessellation also has two other types of symmetry—translational symmetry and glide reflectional symmetry.

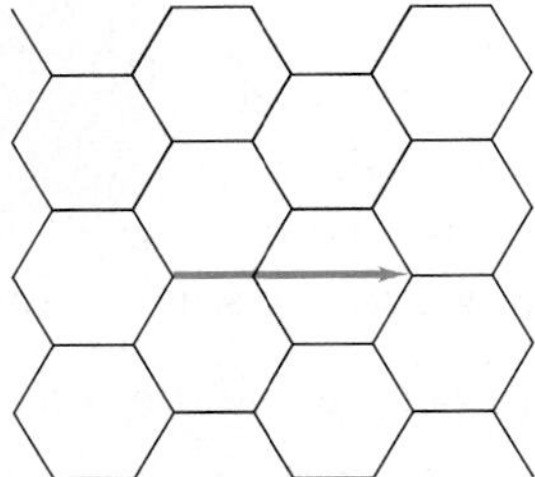

Translational Symmetry

A translation maps the tessellation onto itself.

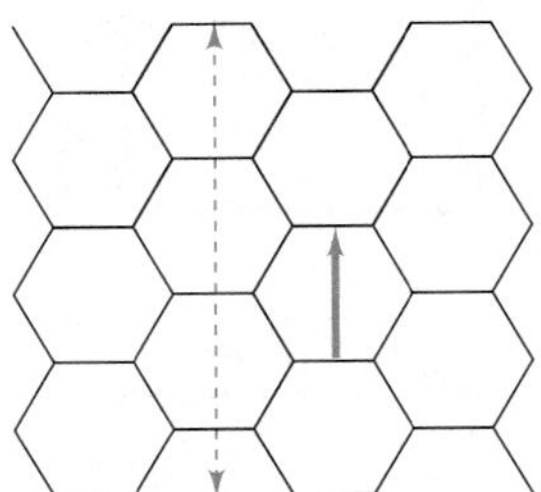

Glide Reflectional Symmetry

A glide reflection maps the tessellation onto itself.

Example 2

List the symmetries of each tessellation.

a.

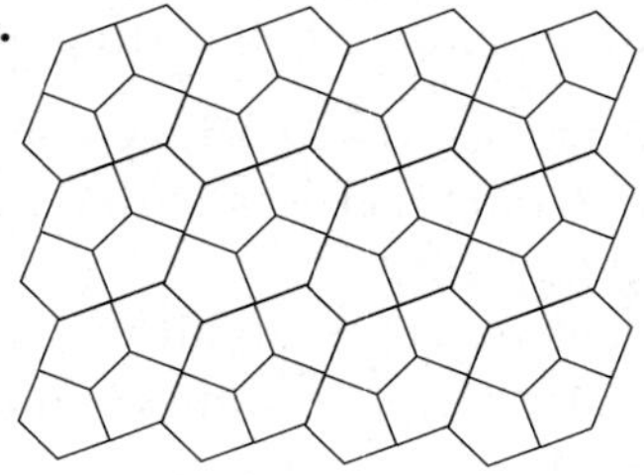

b.

a.

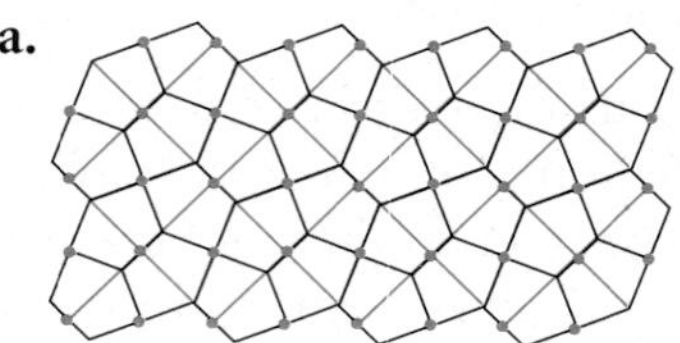

b.

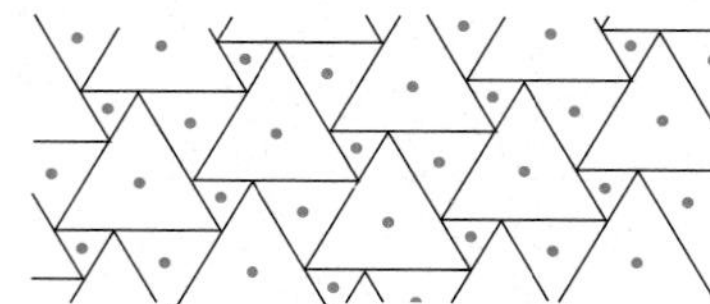

a.

- Line symmetry in the blue lines
- Rotational symmetry in the red points
- Translational symmetry
- Glide reflectional symmetry

b.

- Rotational symmetry in the red points
- Translational symmetry

WORK TOGETHER

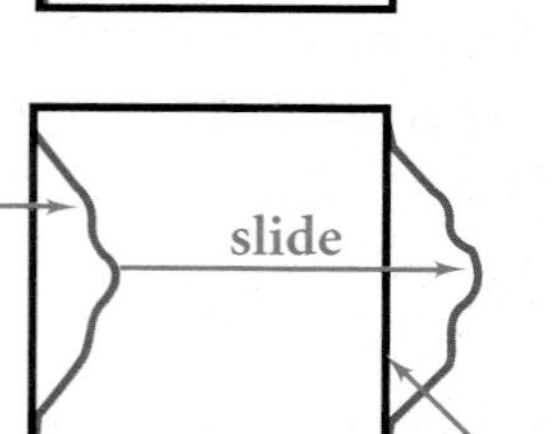

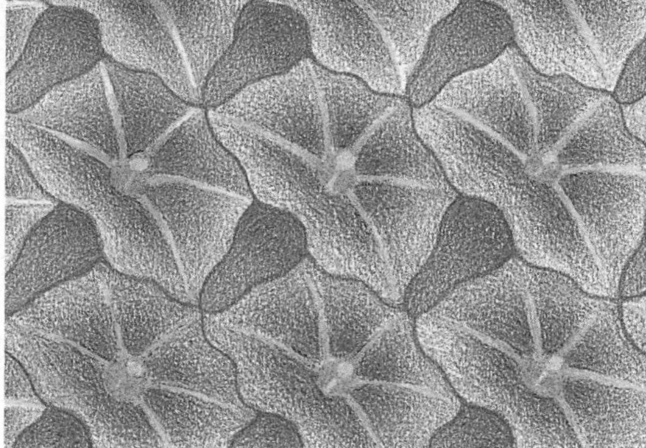

Create your own "Escher-like" tessellation! Start by having each member of your group draw a 1.5-inch square on a blank piece of paper and cut it out.

- Sketch a curve from one vertex to a consecutive vertex.
- Cut along the curve that you sketched and slide the resulting cutout to the opposite side of the square. Tape it in place using clear tape.

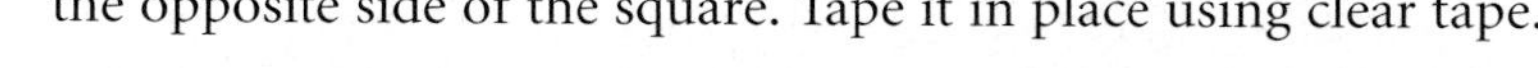

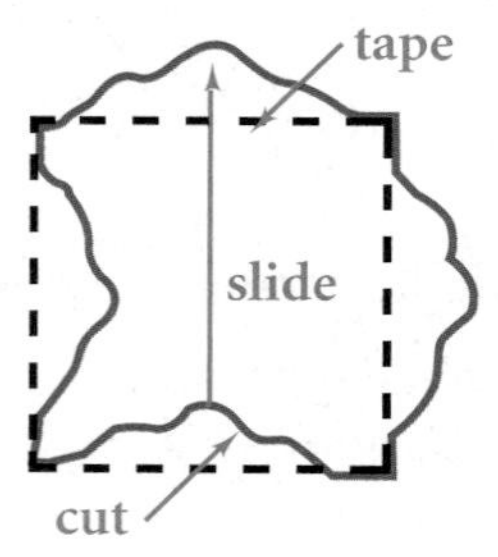

- Repeat this process using the remaining two sides of the square.
- Rotate the figure you end up with. What does it look like? A penguin with a hat on? A knight on horseback? A dog with floppy ears? Sketch whatever you come up with on your figure.
- Create a tessellation using your figure.

Exercises ON YOUR OWN

Identify the repeating figure or figures that make up each tessellation.

1. 

Fabric by *Fabric Traditions*

2. 

Arabian design

3. 

Honeycomb

Describe the symmetries of each tessellation. Copy a portion of the tessellation and draw any centers of rotational symmetry or lines of symmetry.

4. 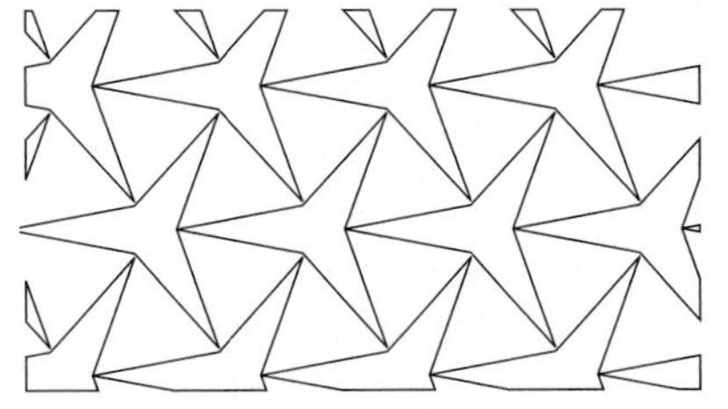

5. 

6. 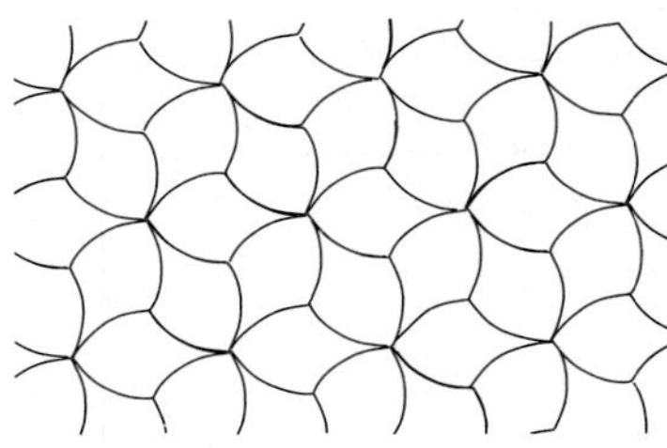

7. 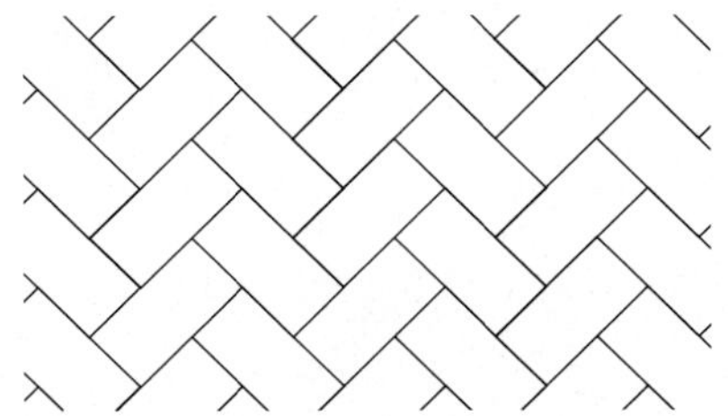

8. 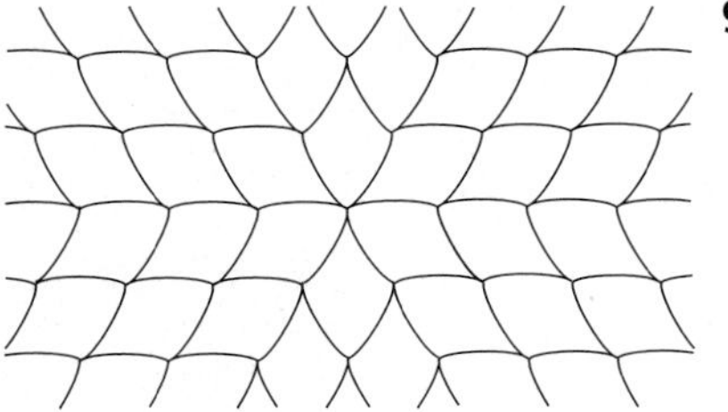

9. 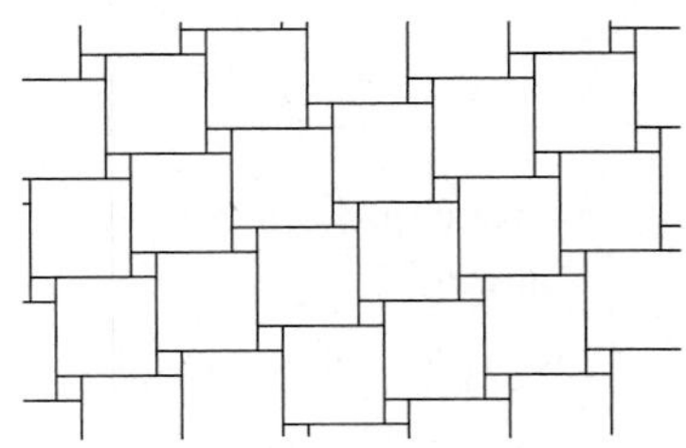

10. The figure shown at the right can be used to tile the plane in several different ways. Make copies of the figure and sketch two different tessellations.

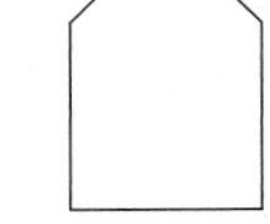

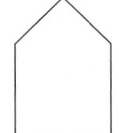

11. **Open-ended** Find and sketch two examples of tessellations found at home or at school.

12. **Writing** Is it possible to tile the plane with regular decagons? Explain why or why not.

Use each figure to create a tessellation on dot paper.

13.

14. 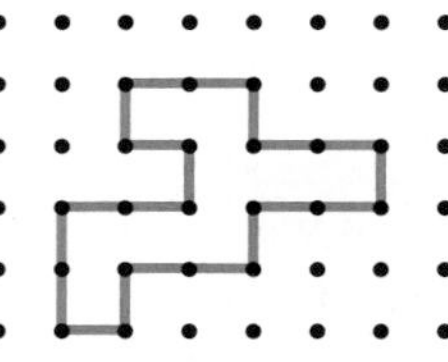

15. 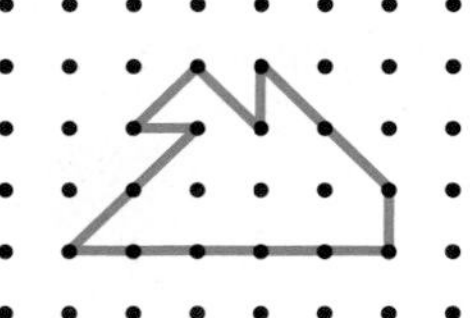

16. 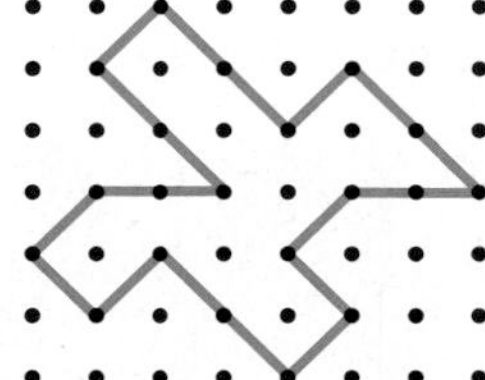

Identify the repeating figure or figures that make up each tessellation.

17. 

Mongolian design

18. 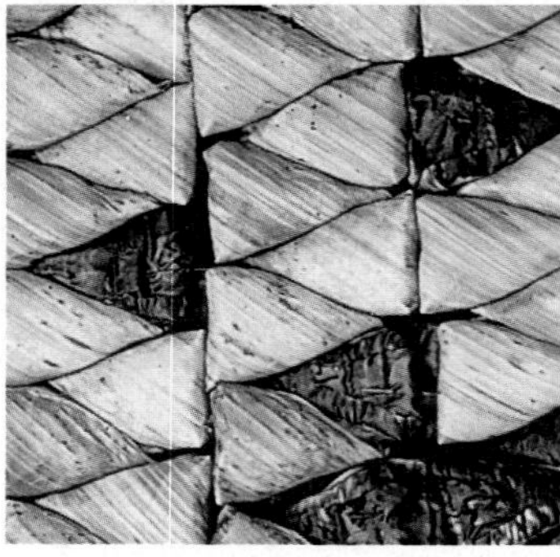

Rice wrapped in banana leaves

19. 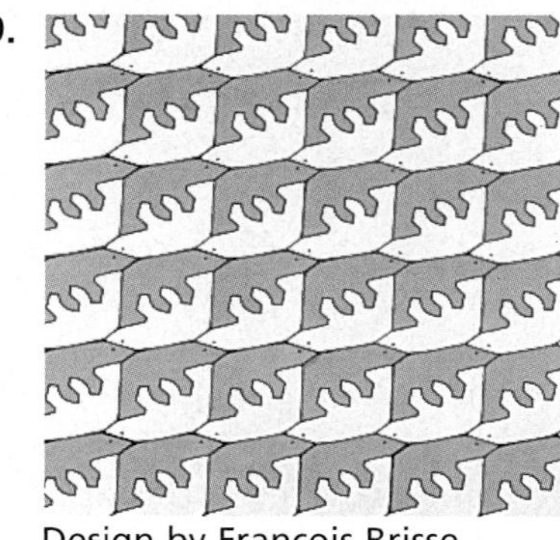

Design by François Brisse

20. Follow the steps below to create an "Escher-like" tessellation based on a regular hexagon.

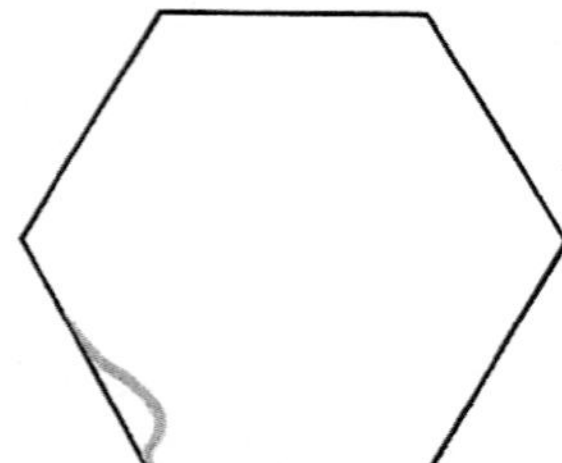

tape
slide
cut

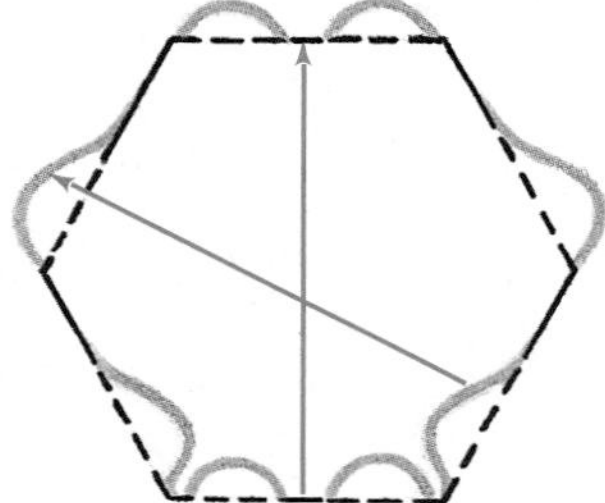

- Trace and cut out the regular hexagon above.
- Sketch a curve from one vertex to an adjacent vertex.
- Cut along the curve that you sketched. Slide the resulting cutout to the opposite side of the hexagon. Tape it in place using clear tape.
- Repeat this process on the remaining two pairs of opposite sides.
- Decorate the figure that you end up with and use it to make a tessellation.

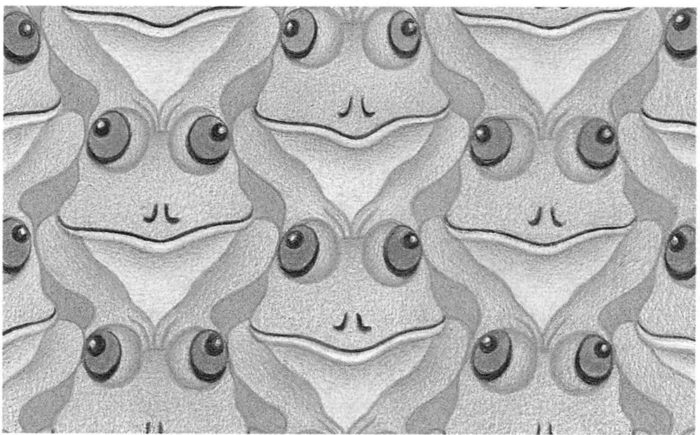

Exercises MIXED REVIEW

Classify each triangle by its sides and angles.

21. 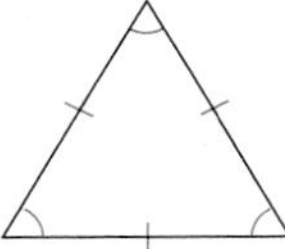

22. 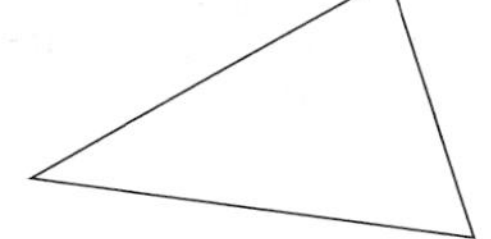

23. 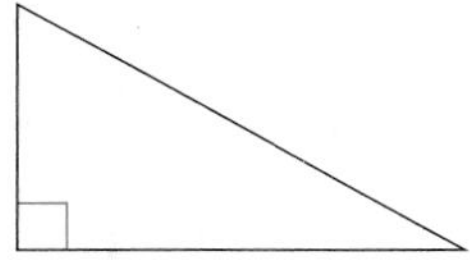

24. 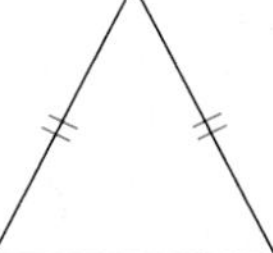

25. Given $\odot A$, identify each of the following.

a. a diameter **b.** a major arc
c. a minor arc **d.** a radius
e. a central angle **f.** a pair of adjacent arcs

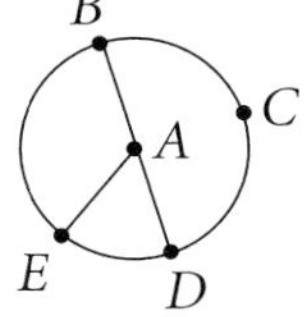

26. a. Find the measure of an interior angle of a regular 3-gon, 7-gon, and 42-gon.

b. Find the sum of the measures of the three angles from part (a).

SELF ASSESSMENT

FOR YOUR JOURNAL

Think about different products that you can buy at a grocery store. How is the idea of tessellation important in the design of containers for products?

Getting Ready for Lesson 3-7

27. In the diagram, $\triangle ABC \sim \triangle DEF$.

a. Find AB and EF.

b. Find the scale factor of the enlargement.

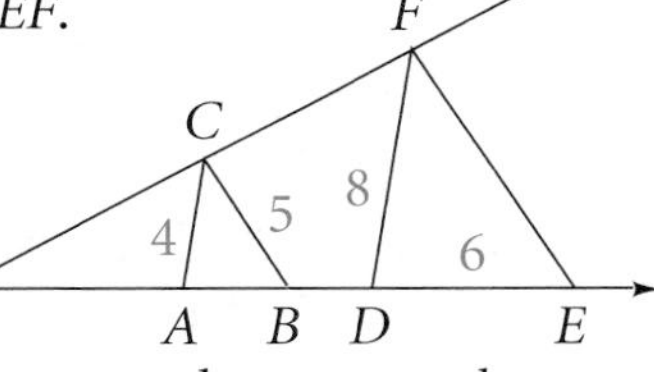

not drawn to scale

A Point in Time

1500 1600 2000

The Grand Mosaic of Mexico

A mosaic is a picture or decorative design made by setting tiny pieces of glass, stone, or other materials in clay or plaster. A mosaic may be a tessellation. Most mosaics, however, do not have a repeating pattern of figures. The art of constructing mosaics goes back at least 6,000 years to the Sumerians, who used tiles to both decorate and reinforce walls.

The Romans gave us the word *tessellate,* from the Latin *tessellare,* "to pave with tiles." During the second century A.D., Roman architects used 2 million tiles to create the magnificent mosaic of Dionysus in Germany. Large as it was, the Dionysus was less than a third the size of the work created in **1950** by the Mexican artist Juan O'Gorman. O'Gorman's mosaic, which depicts the cultural history of Mexico, is ten stories high and covers all four sides of the library of the National University of Mexico. Constructed of some 7.5 million stones, it is the largest mosaic in the world.

3-7 Dilations

What You'll Learn

- Locating dilation images of figures

...And Why

To recognize applications of dilations in maps, photographs, scale models, and architectural blueprints

What You'll Need

- centimeter ruler
- calculator
- graph paper

WORK TOGETHER

- Have each member of your group draw a triangle and a point outside the triangle. Draw your figures in roughly the same positions as shown in the diagram. Label the triangle $\triangle RST$ and the point C.

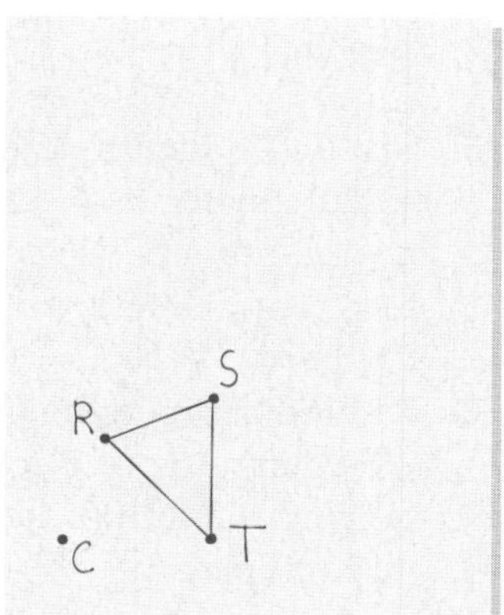

- Draw $\overrightarrow{CR}$, $\overrightarrow{CS}$, and $\overrightarrow{CT}$.
- Have each member of your group select a different number n from the set $\{\frac{1}{3}, \frac{1}{2}, 1\frac{1}{2}, 2, 3\}$.
- Measure $\overline{CR}$, $\overline{CS}$, and $\overline{CT}$ to the nearest millimeter. Then calculate $n \cdot CR$, $n \cdot CS$, and $n \cdot CT$.

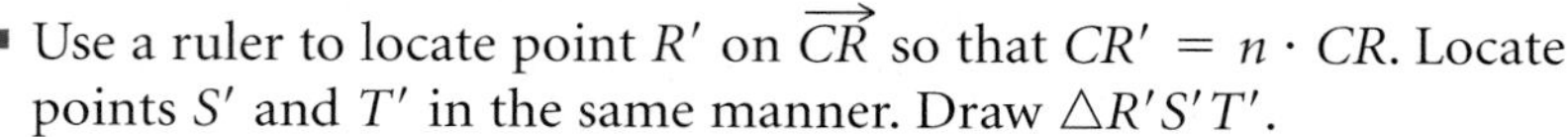

- Use a ruler to locate point R' on $\overrightarrow{CR}$ so that $CR' = n \cdot CR$. Locate points S' and T' in the same manner. Draw $\triangle R'S'T'$.

1. Compare corresponding angle measures in triangles $\triangle RST$ and $\triangle R'S'T'$. What do you notice? Compare results within your group.
2. Measure the lengths of the sides of $\triangle RST$ and $\triangle R'S'T'$ to the nearest millimeter. Then use a calculator to find the values of the ratios $\frac{R'S'}{RS}$, $\frac{S'T'}{ST}$, and $\frac{T'R'}{TR}$ to the nearest hundredth. What do you notice?
3. Use your results from Questions 1 and 2 to complete the statement: $\triangle RST$ is __?__ to $\triangle R'S'T'$.

Math A Test Prep

1 A dilation centered at the origin maps $(-3, 6)$ to $(-9, 18)$. Which of the following does *not* represent the same dilation?
(1) $(0, 5) \longrightarrow (0, 15)$
(2) $(1, -4) \longrightarrow (3, -12)$
(3) $(4, 3) \longrightarrow (9, 12)$
(4) $(6, 2) \longrightarrow (18, 6)$

2 $\triangle DEB$ has vertices $D(3, 7)$, $E(1, 4)$, and $B(-1, 5)$. In which quadrants is the image of $\triangle DEB$ under a 90° clockwise rotation about the origin?

THINK AND DISCUSS

The transformation that you performed in the Work Together is known as a *dilation.* Every dilation has a center and a scale factor. In the Work Together, the center of the dilation was C. The **scale factor** n described the size change from the original figure to the image. The dimensions of the image were n times that of the preimage. A **dilation** with center C and scale factor n, where $n > 0$, maps a point R to R' in such a way that R' is on $\overrightarrow{CR}$ and $CR' = n \cdot CR$. The center of dilation C is its own image (that is, $C' = C$).

$n \cdot CR$
R'
R
C

This is not a similarity transformation. Do you see why?

As you noticed in the Work Together, a dilation maps a figure to a similar figure. A dilation is a **similarity transformation.**

4. ***Critical Thinking*** Describe the dilation image of a figure when the scale factor is 1.

Example 1

Find the scale factor for the dilation that maps the red figure onto the blue figure.

a.

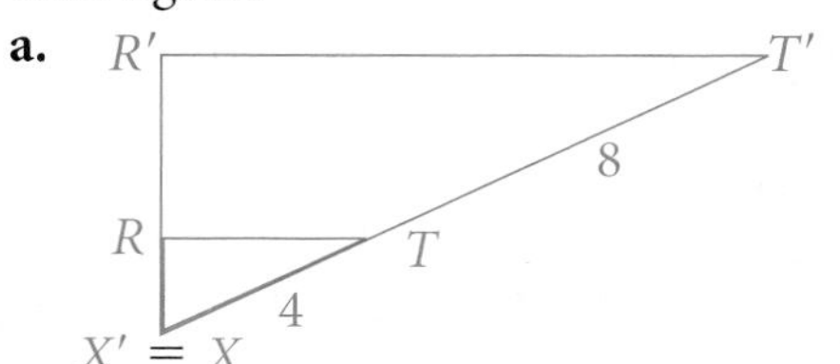

b.

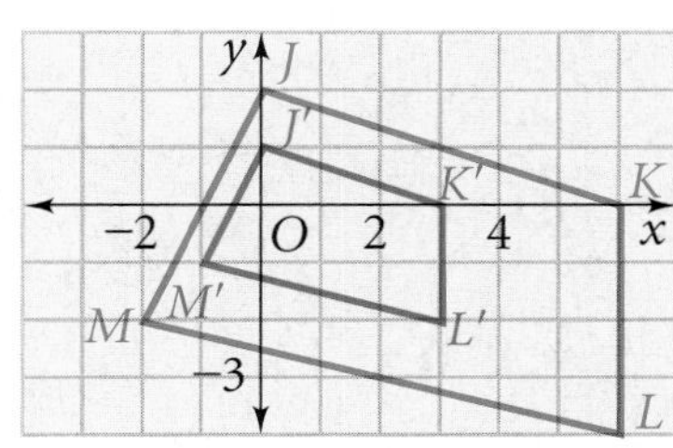

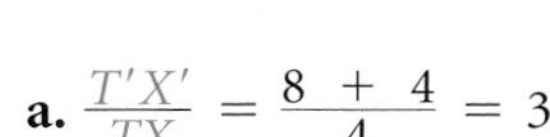

a. $\frac{T'X'}{TX} = \frac{8 + 4}{4} = 3$

b. $\frac{K'L'}{KL} = \frac{2}{4} = \frac{1}{2}$

There are two types of dilations. If the image is larger than the original figure, the dilation is an **enlargement.** If the image is smaller than the original figure, the dilation is a **reduction.**

5. What scale factors produce enlargements? reductions?

Example 2 *Relating to the Real World* 

6 ft

5 ft

4 ft

3 ft

2 ft

1 ft

Newborn 2 yr 6 yr 12 yr 20 yr

Human Development The diagram shows the growth of a human male from infancy through adulthood. Can human development be modeled by a dilation? Explain.

No. If human development could be modeled by a dilation, the red line would align with the chin in each figure. The 5 ft 9 in. adult figure shown would have a head about $1\frac{3}{4}$ ft long!

To find the image of a point on the coordinate plane under a dilation with center (0, 0), you multiply the x-coordinate and y-coordinate by the scale factor. Here are two examples.

Scale factor 4
$(x, y) \longrightarrow (4x, 4y)$

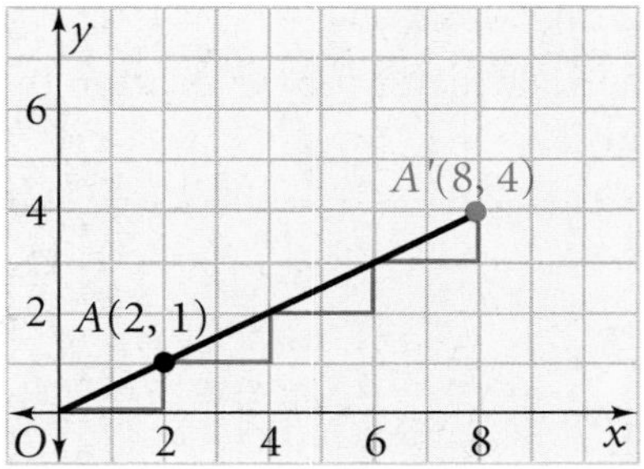

Scale factor $\frac{1}{3}$
$(x, y) \longrightarrow \left(\frac{1}{3}x, \frac{1}{3}y\right)$

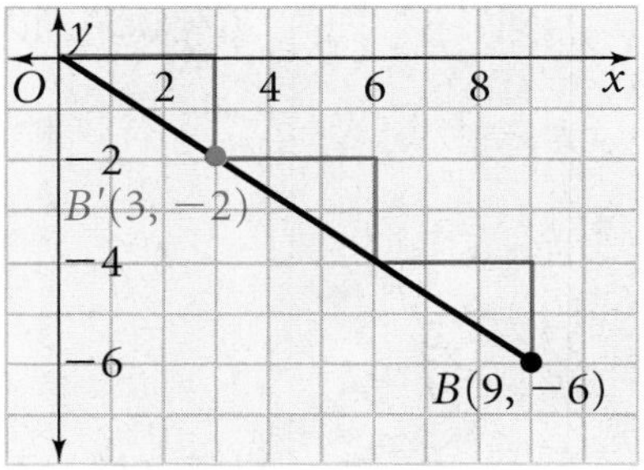

You can use matrices to perform dilations that are centered at the origin.

Example 3

Use matrices to find the image of $\triangle PZG$ under a dilation centered at the origin with scale factor 3.

$$\begin{array}{r} \\ x\text{-coordinate} \\ y\text{-coordinate} \end{array} \begin{array}{c} \begin{array}{ccc} P & Z & G \end{array} \\ \begin{bmatrix} 2 & -1 & 1 \\ 0 & \frac{1}{2} & -2 \end{bmatrix} \end{array}$$

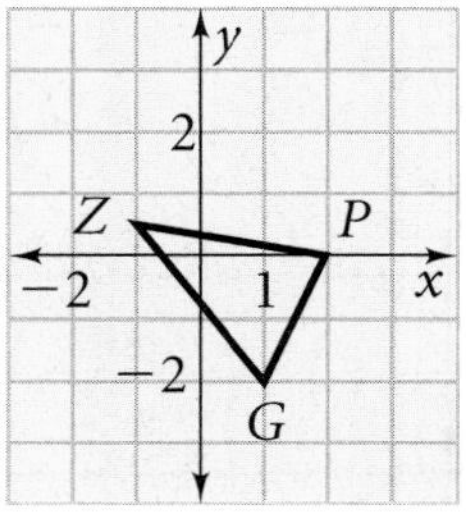

To find the dilation image of $\triangle PZG$, you multiply all the x-coordinates and y-coordinates by 3.

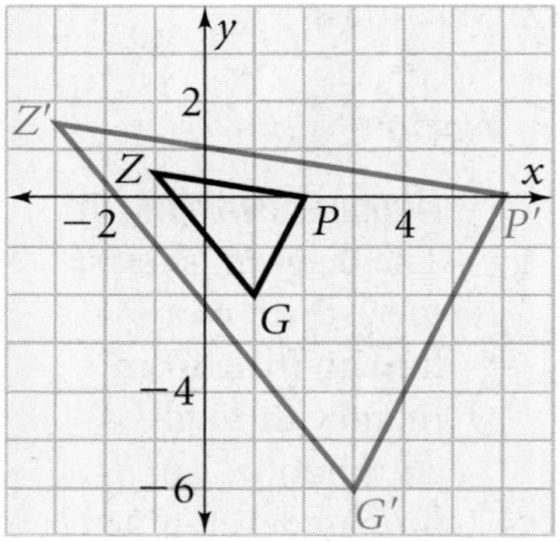

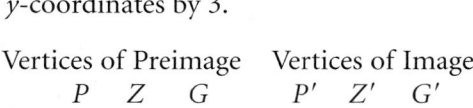

Vertices of Preimage $\qquad$ Vertices of Image

$$3 \cdot \overset{\begin{array}{ccc} P & Z & G \end{array}}{\begin{bmatrix} 2 & -1 & 1 \\ 0 & \frac{1}{2} & -2 \end{bmatrix}} = \overset{\begin{array}{ccc} P' & Z' & G' \end{array}}{\begin{bmatrix} 6 & -3 & 3 \\ 0 & \frac{3}{2} & -6 \end{bmatrix}}$$

6. **Try This** Use matrices to find the image of $\triangle PZG$ under a dilation centered at the origin with scale factor $\frac{1}{2}$.

The type of multiplication shown in Example 3, in which each entry of a matrix is multiplied by the same number, is called **scalar multiplication.**

Exercises ON YOUR OWN

Copy $\triangle TBA$ and point O. Draw $\triangle T'B'A'$ under the dilation with the given center and scale factor.

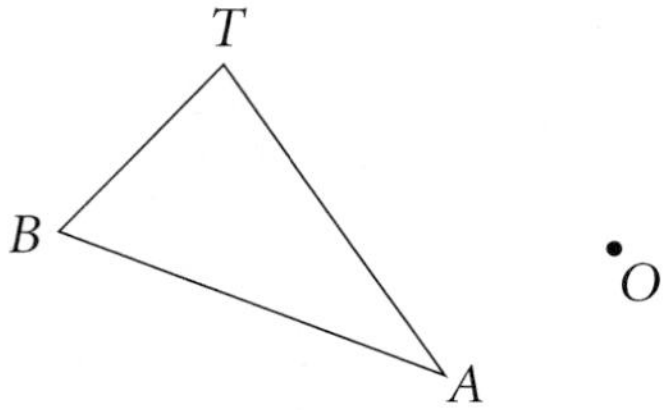

1. Center O, scale factor $\frac{1}{2}$
2. Center B, scale factor 3
3. Center T, scale factor $\frac{1}{3}$
4. Center O, scale factor 2

The blue figure is a dilation image of the red figure.
(a) Determine whether the dilation is a reduction or an enlargement.
(b) Find the scale factor.

5. 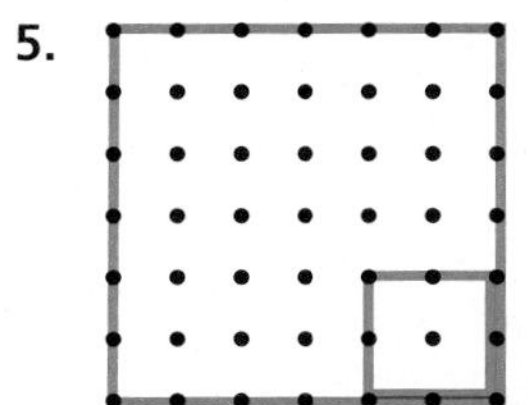

6. 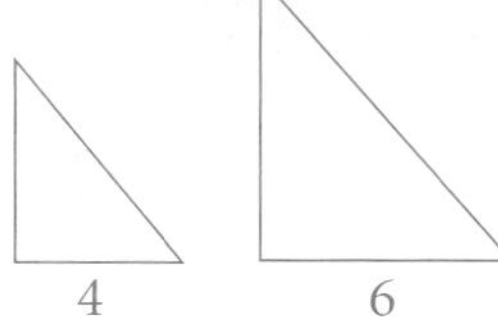

7. 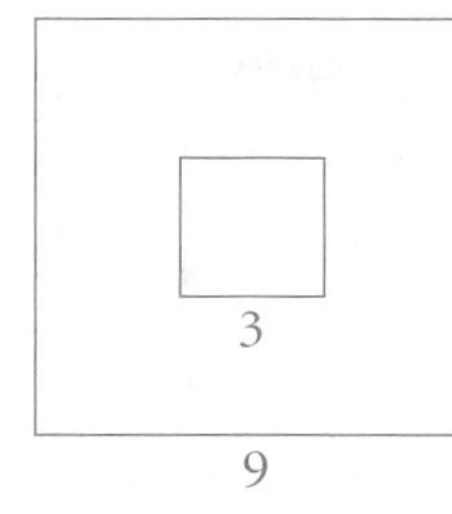

8. 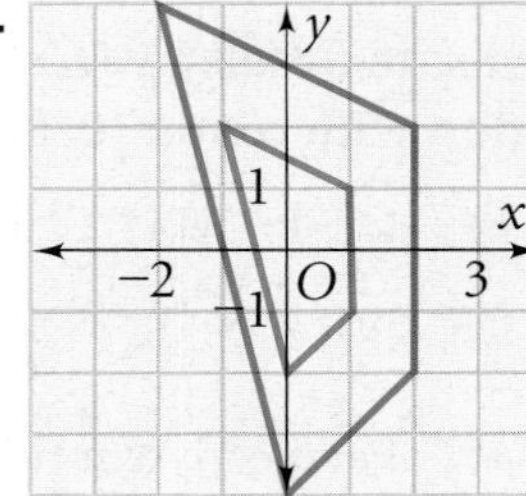

9. 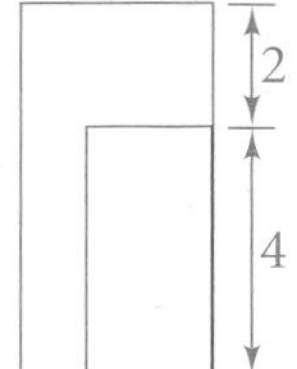

10. 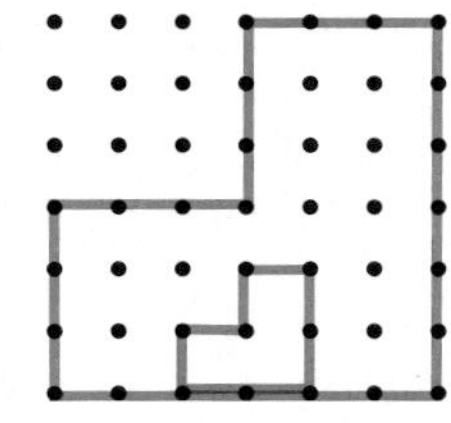

11. 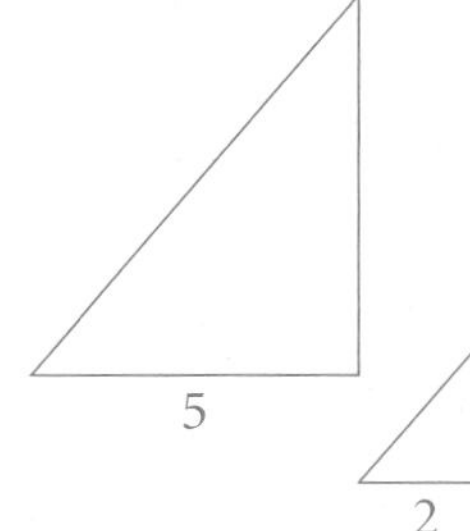

12. 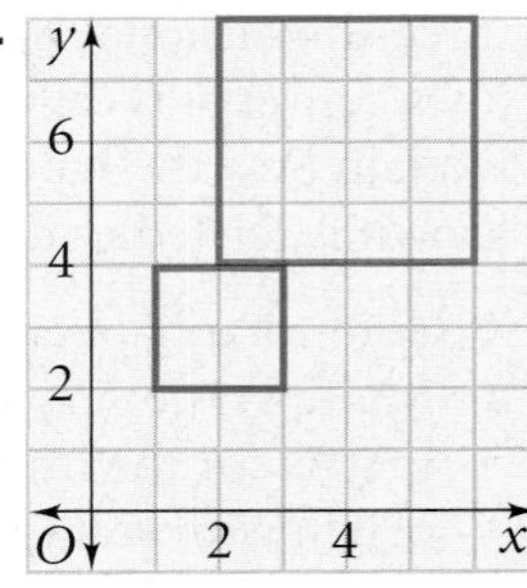

Use scalar multiplication to find the vertices of $\triangle A'B'C'$ under a dilation with center (0, 0) and the given scale factor.

13.
$$\begin{array}{l} \\ x\text{-coordinate} \\ y\text{-coordinate} \end{array} \begin{array}{c} \begin{array}{ccc} A & B & C \end{array} \\ \begin{bmatrix} 1 & 3 & 5 \\ 0 & 2 & 1 \end{bmatrix} \end{array}$$
scale factor 3

14.
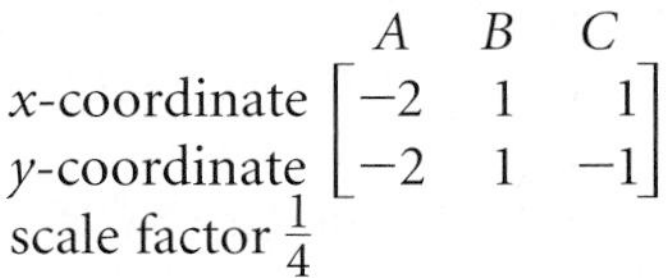
$$\begin{array}{l} \\ x\text{-coordinate} \\ y\text{-coordinate} \end{array} \begin{array}{c} \begin{array}{ccc} A & B & C \end{array} \\ \begin{bmatrix} -2 & 1 & 1 \\ -2 & 1 & -1 \end{bmatrix} \end{array}$$
scale factor $\frac{1}{4}$

15.
$$\begin{array}{l} \\ x\text{-coordinate} \\ y\text{-coordinate} \end{array} \begin{array}{c} \begin{array}{ccc} A & B & C \end{array} \\ \begin{bmatrix} -2 & -4 & -3 \\ 0 & -3 & 0 \end{bmatrix} \end{array}$$
scale factor 2

16. **Entertainment** In the film *Honey, I Blew Up the Kid*, a botched scientific experiment causes a two-year-old boy to grow to a height of 112 ft. If the average height of a two-year-old boy is 3 ft, what is the scale factor of this enlargement?

17. **Movies** The projection of a film onto a movie screen is an example of a dilation. Most movies are shot on film that is 35 mm wide. If the width of a movie screen is 12 m, what is the scale factor of this enlargement?

18. A regular triangle with 4-in. sides undergoes a dilation with scale factor 2.5.
a. What are the side lengths of the image?
b. What are the angle measures of the image?

A giant two-year-old walks through the streets of Las Vegas in a scene from *Honey, I Blew Up the Kid.*

19. **Constructions** Copy $\triangle GHI$ and point X onto your paper. Use a compass and straightedge to construct the image of $\triangle GHI$ under a dilation with center X and scale factor 2.

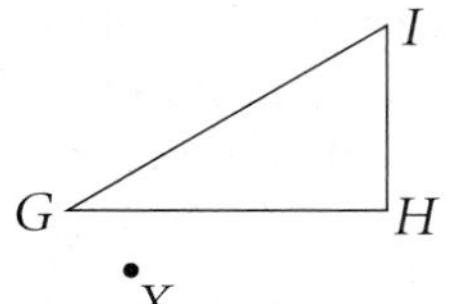

Coordinate Geometry Graph $MNPQ$ and its image $M'N'P'Q'$ under a dilation with center (0, 0) and the given scale factor.

20. $M(-1, -1)$, $N(1, -2)$, $P(1, 2)$, $Q(-1, 3)$; scale factor 2

21. $M(0, 0)$, $N(4, 0)$, $P(6, -2)$, $Q(-2, -2)$; scale factor $\frac{1}{2}$

22. **Art** Perspective drawing uses converging lines to give the illusion that an object is three-dimensional. The point at which the lines converge is called the vanishing point. Explain how the type of perspective drawing shown is related to dilations.

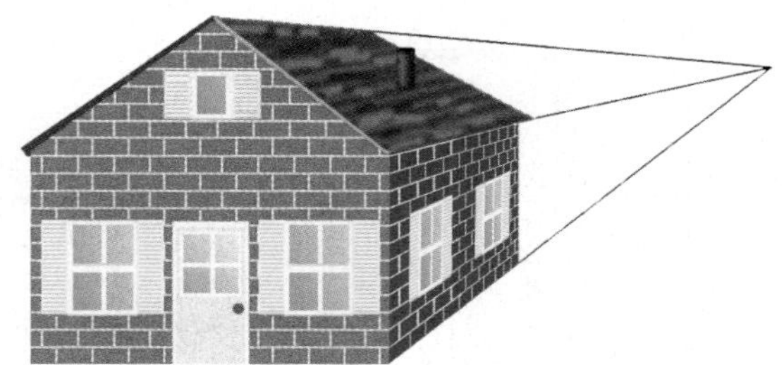

23. Explore what happens if you use a negative scale factor.
   a. Multiply the vertex matrix for $ABCD$ by -3. The result is a vertex matrix for the image of $ABCD$ under a dilation centered at the origin with scale factor -3.
   b. Graph $ABCD$ and $A'B'C'D'$ on the same set of axes.
   c. **Critical Thinking** Compare each point to its image. What conclusion can you draw about the effect of a negative scale factor?

$$\begin{matrix} A & B & C & D \end{matrix}$$
$$\begin{bmatrix} 2 & -2 & -2 & 2 \\ 2 & 2 & -2 & -2 \end{bmatrix}$$

24. **Critical Thinking** Given $\overline{AB}$ and its dilation image $\overline{A'B'}$, explain how to find the center of dilation. Assume $\overline{AB}$ and $\overline{A'B'}$ are not collinear.

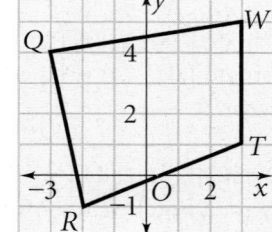

Use scalar multiplication to find the vertices of the image of $QRTW$ under a dilation with center (0, 0) and the given scale factor.

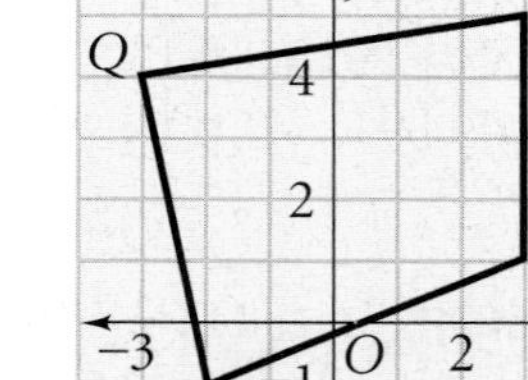

25. scale factor 3

26. scale factor $\frac{1}{2}$

27. scale factor 2

28. scale factor 0.9

Graphic Design The designs at the right were created by graphic artist Scott Kim. For each design, (a) describe the location of the center of dilation and (b) find the scale factor for the repeated reductions.

29.

30.

31. **Technology** Use geometry software or drawing software to create a design that involves repeated dilations. Print your design and color it. Feel free to use other transformations along with dilations.

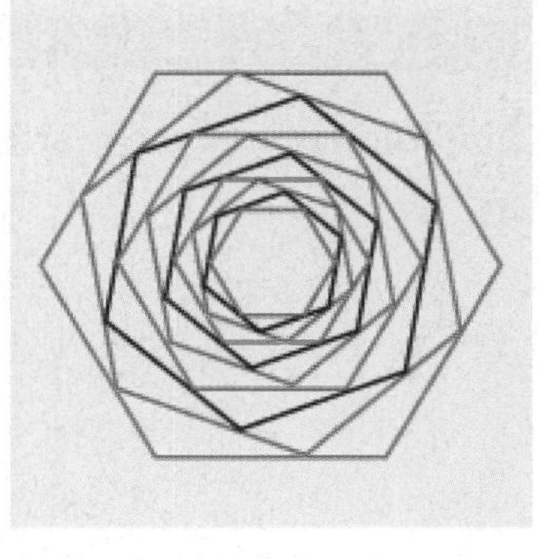

32. **Standardized Test Prep** $\triangle P'L'H'$ is the image of $\triangle PLH$ under a dilation with center X and scale factor 3. If P and L lie on $\overline{P'L'}$, what must be true of X?
    A. X is in the exterior of $\triangle PLH$. **B.** X is in the interior of $\triangle PLH$.
    C. X is on $\overline{L'H'}$. **D.** X is on $\overline{PL}$. **E.** $X = H$

A dilation maps $\triangle HIJ$ to $\triangle H'I'J'$. Find the missing values.

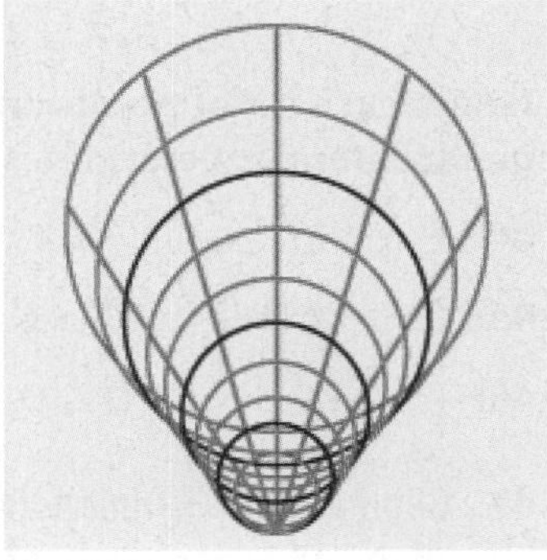

33.	**34.**	**35.**
$HI = 8$ in.	$HI = 7$ cm	$HI = \blacksquare$ ft
$IJ = 5$ in.	$IJ = 7$ cm	$IJ = 30$ ft
$HJ = 6$ in.	$HJ = \blacksquare$ cm	$HJ = 24$ ft
$H'I' = 16$ in.	$H'I' = 5.25$ cm	$H'I' = 8$ ft
$I'J' = \blacksquare$ in.	$I'J' = \blacksquare$ cm	$I'J' = \blacksquare$ ft
$H'J' = \blacksquare$ in.	$H'J' = 12$ cm	$H'J' = 6$ ft

Write *true* or *false*. Explain your answers.

36. A dilation with a scale factor greater than 1 is a reduction.
37. Under a dilation, corresponding angles of the image and preimage are congruent.
38. A dilation is an isometry.
39. A dilation changes orientation.
40. A dilation image cannot have any points in common with its preimage.

Chapter Project
Find Out by Creating

In previous Find Out questions, you investigated and classified frieze patterns from a variety of cultures. Now you can make your own. Use graph paper, dot paper, geometry or drawing software, or cutouts (such as your pentominoes from the Chapter 2 project). Make at least one frieze pattern for each of the seven types summarized below.

The Seven Types of Frieze Patterns

Type	Symmetries	Example
11	T	P P P P P P P
12	T, H	Z Z Z Z Z Z Z
*m*1	T, RV	Y Y Y Y Y Y Y
1g	T, G	D W D M D W D
1*m*	T, RH, G	D D D D D D D
mg	T, H, RV, G	M W M W M W M
mm	T, H, RV, RH, G	I I I I I I I

Key to Symmetries:
T = **T**ranslation
H = **H**alf-turn
RV = **R**eflection in **V**ertical Line
RH = **R**eflection in **H**orizontal Line
G = **G**lide reflection

Exercises MIXED REVIEW

Find the value of each variable.

41.

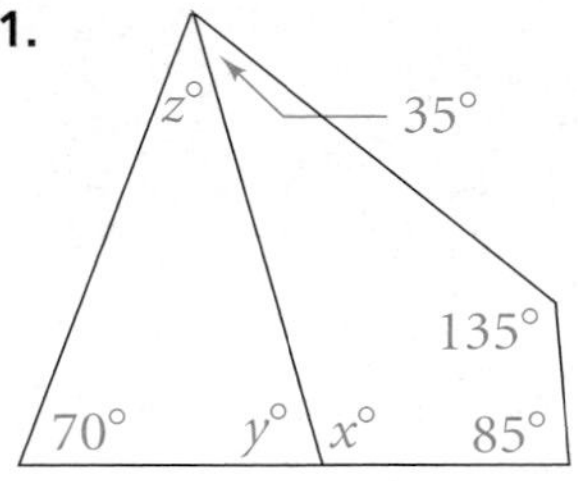

42.

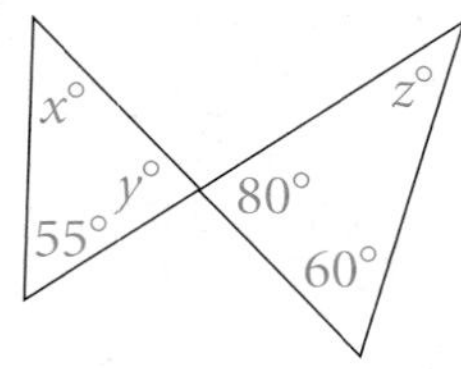

43.

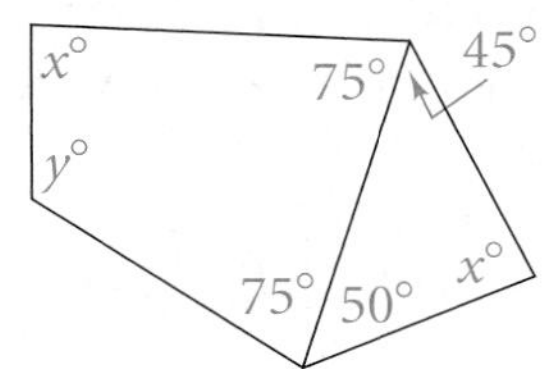

Graph each set of points and state which type of quadrilateral it determines.

44. $(-1, -2), (1, 4), (-3, 4), (3, -2)$

45. $(2, -1), (6, 2), (10, -1), (8, 2)$

46. $(-7, 1), (-5, 3), (-2, -4), (0, -2)$

47. *Geometry in 3 Dimensions* Planes T and G are parallel, and plane M is perpendicular to plane G. Sketch the three planes.

48. Find the coordinates of the midpoint of the segment with endpoints $A(4, 8)$ and $B(-3, -6)$.

PORTFOLIO

For your portfolio, select one or two items from your work for this chapter. Here are some possibilities:
- tessellations
- kaleidoscope patterns
- computer-generated designs involving transformations

Explain why you have included each selection.

Geometry at Work

Graphic Artist

Not too long ago, the graphic artist's main tools were the pen and paintbrush. Today, graphic artists are just as likely to have a computer mouse in hand as either of these. Computers have helped graphic artists produce effects that could only be imagined previously. Some of the "special effects" on the cover of this book, for instance, were produced using design software. Computers have also helped lower the cost of producing graphic art, because they allow the artist to work more quickly and to store and transport images easily.

You can find each of the transformations that you've studied in this chapter in software written for graphic artists. At the click of a mouse, the graphic artist rotates, reflects, translates, dilates, and creates!

Mini Project: Use a computer drawing program to create a new logo for your school's stationery. Try to use transformations in your logo.

Finishing the Chapter Project

Find Out questions and activities on pages 699, 705, 712, 720, and 733 will help you complete your project. Prepare a frieze pattern display. Include a brief explanation of frieze patterns as well as your original designs for each of the seven types of frieze patterns. Find more examples of frieze patterns from various cultures, as well as examples from buildings, clothing, and other places in your home, school, and community. Classify each example into one of the seven categories, and include them in your display.

Reflect and Revise

Ask a classmate to review your display with you. Together, check that your diagrams and explanations are clear and your information accurate. Have you used geometric terms correctly? Is the display attractive, organized, and complete? Have you included material that no one else has included? Revise your work as needed. Consider doing more research.

Follow Up

Use logical reasoning and what you've learned about transformations to explain why there are no more than seven different frieze patterns. List all other possible combinations of symmetries and show how each can be ruled out.

For More Information

Appleton, Le Roy H. *American Indian Design and Decoration.* New York: Dover, 1971.

Hargittai, István and Magdolna. *Symmetry: A Unifying Concept.* Berkeley, California: Ten Speed Press, 1994.

Schuman, Jo Miles. *Art from Many Hands: Multicultural Art Projects for Home and School.* Englewood Cliffs, New Jersey: Prentice Hall, 1981.

Stevens, Peter S. *Handbook of Regular Patterns: An Introduction to Symmetry in Two Dimensions.* Cambridge, Massachusetts: MIT, 1981.

CHAPTER 3 Wrap Up

Key Terms

composition (p. 697)
dilation (p. 728)
enlargement (p. 729)
entry (p. 693)
frieze pattern (p. 699)
glide reflection (p. 708)
glide reflectional symmetry (p. 723)
half-turn (p. 716)
image (p. 686)
isometry (p. 686)
line symmetry (p. 714)
map (p. 686)
matrix (p. 693)
orientation (p. 688)
point symmetry (p. 716)
preimage (p. 686)
prime notation (p. 686)
pure tessellation (p. 722)
reduction (p. 729)
reflection (p. 688)
reflectional symmetry (p. 714)
rotation (p. 701)
rotational symmetry (p. 716)
scalar multiplication (p. 730)
scale factor (p. 728)
similarity transformation (p. 729)
strip pattern (p. 699)
symmetry (p. 714)
tessellation (p. 721)
tiling (p. 721)
transformation (p. 686)
translation (p. 694)
translational symmetry (p. 723)

How am I doing?

- Describe the different transformations and their properties.
- State the different types of symmetry and draw examples of each.

Reflections 3-1

A **transformation** is a change made to the position, shape, or size of a figure. An **isometry** is a transformation in which the original figure and its image are congruent. The diagram shows a **reflection** of B to B' in line r. A reflection is an isometry that changes a figure's orientation.

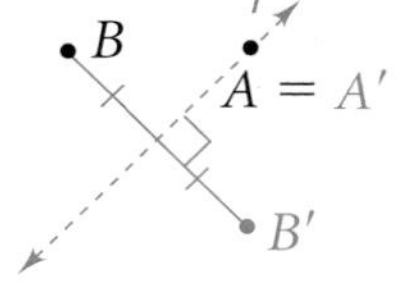

Coordinate Geometry **Given points $A(6, 4)$, $B(-2, 1)$, and $C(5, 0)$, draw $\triangle ABC$ and its reflection image in the given line.**

1. the x-axis
2. $x = 4$
3. $x = -3$
4. $y = x$

Trace each figure, then find its reflection image in line j.

5. 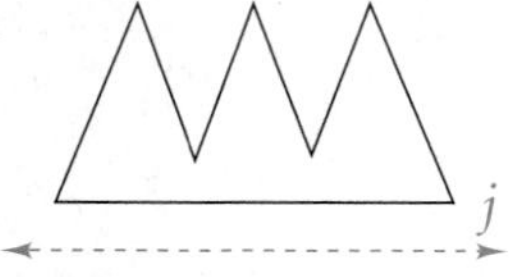

6. 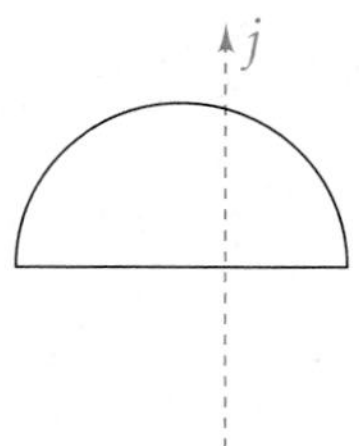

7. 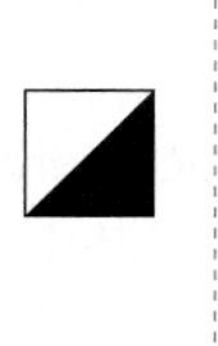

8. 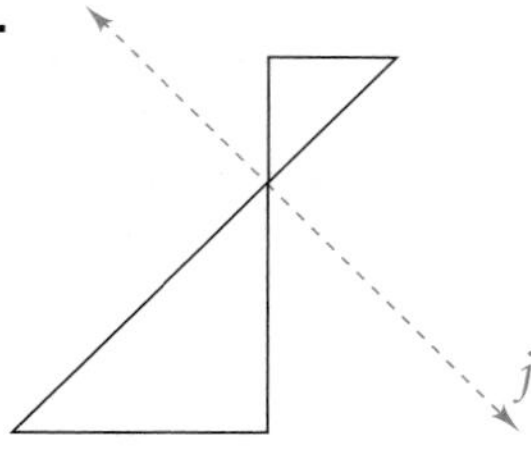

9. **Standardized Test Prep** What is the image of (5, 4) under a reflection in $y = 2$?
   A. $(-5, 4)$ **B.** $(5, -4)$ **C.** $(-1, 4)$ **D.** $(-5, -4)$ **E.** $(5, 0)$

Translations 3-2

A **translation** is a transformation that moves points the same distance and in the same direction. A translation is an isometry that does not change orientation. You can use vectors and matrices to describe a translation.

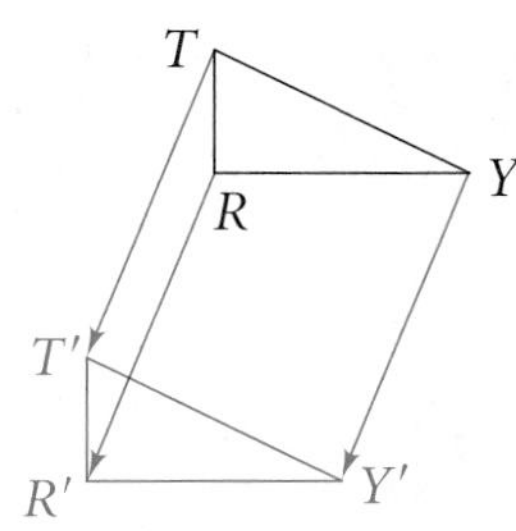

Under a **composition** of two transformations, the second transformation is performed on the image of the first.

10. *Open-ended* Draw a figure in the fourth quadrant. Draw a translation vector under which the figure would move to the second quadrant.

Use matrix addition to find the image of each figure under the given translation.

11. $\triangle ABC$ with vertices $A(5, 9)$, $B(4, 3)$, $C(1, 2)$
Translation: $\langle 2, 3 \rangle$

12. $\triangle RST$ with vertices $R(0, -4)$, $S(-2, -1)$, $T(-6, 1)$
Translation: $\langle -4, 7 \rangle$

Find a single translation that has the same effect as each composition of translations.

13. $\langle 4, 8 \rangle$ followed by $\langle -2, 0 \rangle$

14. $\langle -5, -7 \rangle$ followed by $\langle 3, 6 \rangle$

15. $\langle 10, -9 \rangle$ followed by $\langle 1, 5 \rangle$

Rotations 3-3

The diagram shows a **rotation** of point V about point R through $x°$. A rotation is an isometry that does not change orientation.

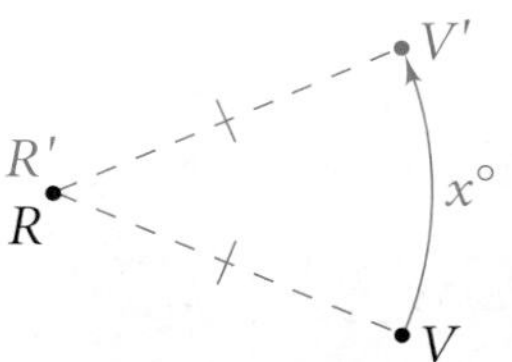

Copy each figure and point *P*. Rotate the figure the given number of degrees about *P*. Label the vertices of the image.

16. 180°

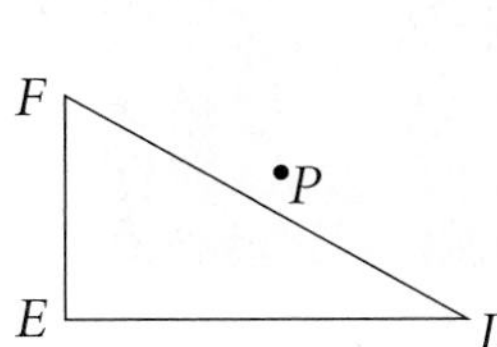

17. 135°

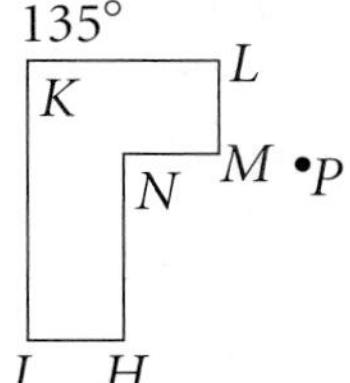

18. 60°

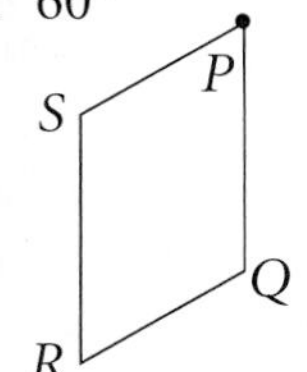

19. 90°

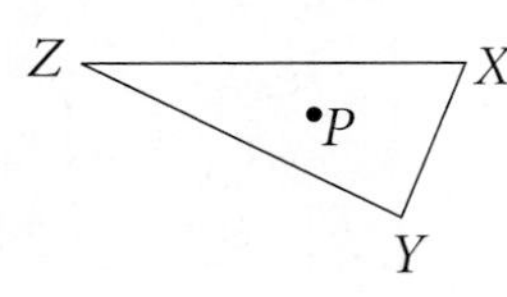

Find the image of each point under a 90° rotation about the origin.

20. $(5, 2)$

21. $(0, 3)$

22. $(-4, 1)$

23. $(7, 0)$

24. $(-2, -8)$

25. $(0, 0)$

Compositions of Reflections 3-4

A composition of reflections in two parallel lines is a translation. A composition of reflections in two intersecting lines is a rotation. The diagram shows a **glide reflection.** The only four isometries are reflection, translation, rotation, and glide reflection.

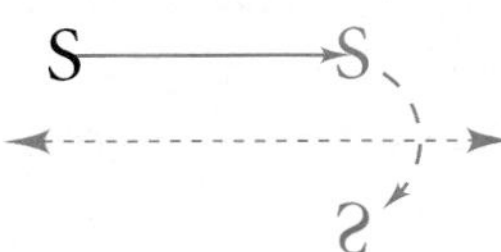

Match each image of the figure at the left with one of the following isometries. I. reflection II. rotation III. translation IV. glide reflection

26. 
a. 
b. 
c. 
d. 

27. 
a. 
b. 
c. 
d. 

28. $\triangle TAM$ has vertices $T(0, 5)$, $A(4, 1)$, and $M(3, 6)$. Find the image of $\triangle TAM$ under a glide reflection in $\langle -4, 0 \rangle$ and $y = -2$.

Symmetry 3-5

A figure has **symmetry** if there is an isometry that maps the figure onto itself. A plane figure has **reflectional symmetry,** or **line symmetry,** if there is a line in which the figure is reflected onto itself. A figure has **rotational symmetry** if there is a rotation of 180° or less that maps the figure onto itself. If a plane figure can be mapped onto itself by a rotation of 180° (a **half-turn**), it has **point symmetry.**

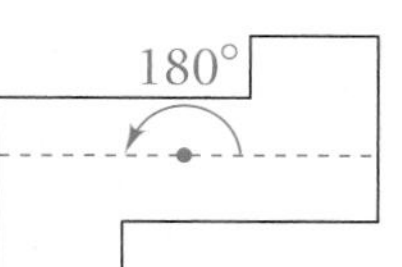

Point Symmetry

What type(s) of symmetry does each figure have? If it has rotational symmetry, state the angle of rotation.

29. 

30. 

31. 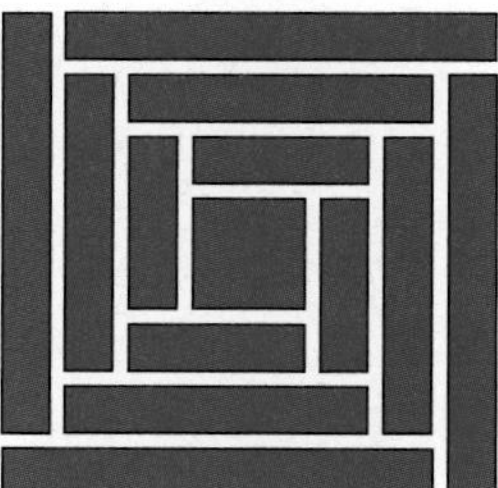

Tessellations 3-6

A **tessellation**, or **tiling**, is a repeating pattern of figures that completely covers a plane without gaps or overlaps. Every triangle and quadrilateral tessellates. Tessellations can have many kinds of symmetries, including **translational symmetry** and **glide reflectional symmetry.**

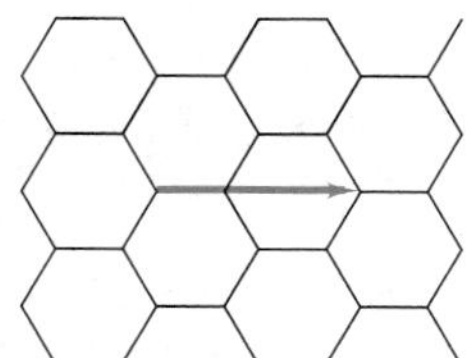
Translational Symmetry
A translation maps the tessellation onto itself.

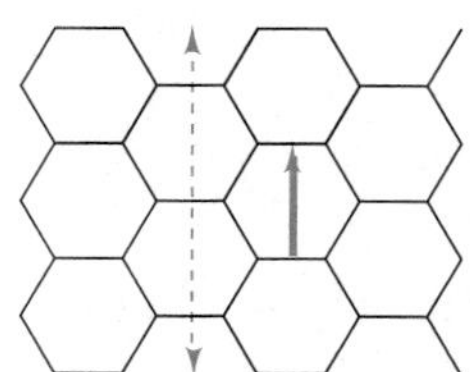
Glide Reflectional Symmetry
A glide reflection maps the tessellation onto itself.

In Exercises 32–34, (a) identify the repeating figure(s) that make up each tessellation, and (b) describe the symmetries of each tessellation.

32.

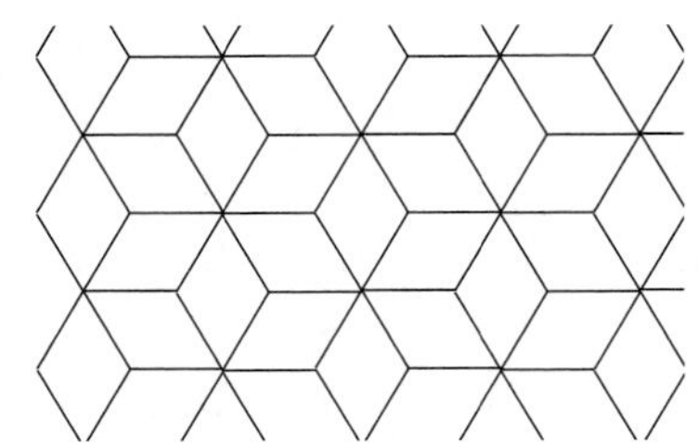

33.

34.

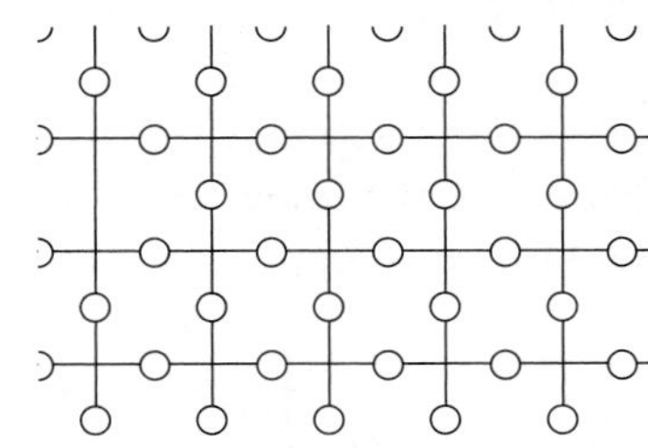

Dilations 3-7

The diagram shows a **dilation** with center C and **scale factor** n. A dilation is a **similarity transformation** because it maps figures to similar figures. When the scale factor is greater than 1, the dilation is an **enlargement.** When the scale factor is less than 1, the dilation is a **reduction.** In the coordinate plane, you can use **scalar multiplication** to find the image of a figure under a dilation centered at the origin.

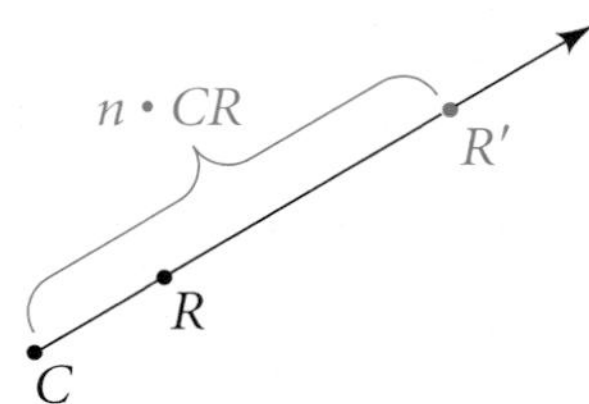

Use matrices to find the image of each set of points under a dilation centered at the origin with the given scale factor.

35. $M(-3, 4)$, $A(-6, -1)$, $T(0, 0)$, $H(3, 2)$; scale factor 5

36. $A(7, -1)$, $N(-4, -3)$, $D(0, 2)$; scale factor 2

37. $W(4, 5)$, $I(2, 6)$, $T(3, 8)$, $H(0, 7)$; scale factor 3

38. $F(-4, 0)$, $U(5, 0)$, $N(-2, -5)$; scale factor $\frac{1}{2}$

39. **Writing** Explain how each of the five transformations you studied in this chapter affects the orientation of a figure and its image.

Getting Ready for... CHAPTER 4

Find the coordinates of the midpoint of the segment with the given endpoints.

40. $C(3, 5)$ and $D(1, 11)$ **41.** $E(6, 7)$ and $F(-4, 7)$ **42.** $T(5, 8)$ and $W(5, 0)$

Classify each triangle by its sides and angles.

43.

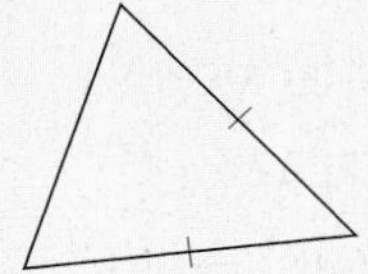

44.

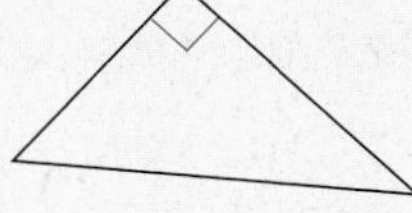

45.

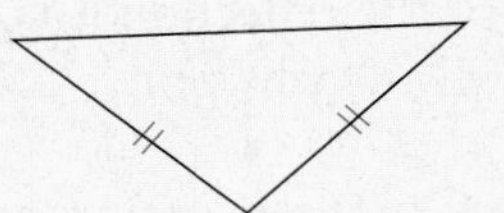

46.

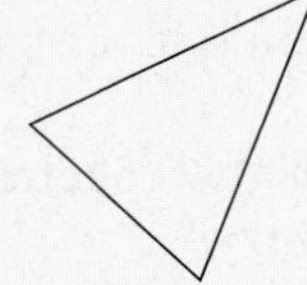

CHAPTER 3 Assessment

Coordinate Geometry **Find the coordinates of the vertices of the image of *ABCD* under each transformation.**

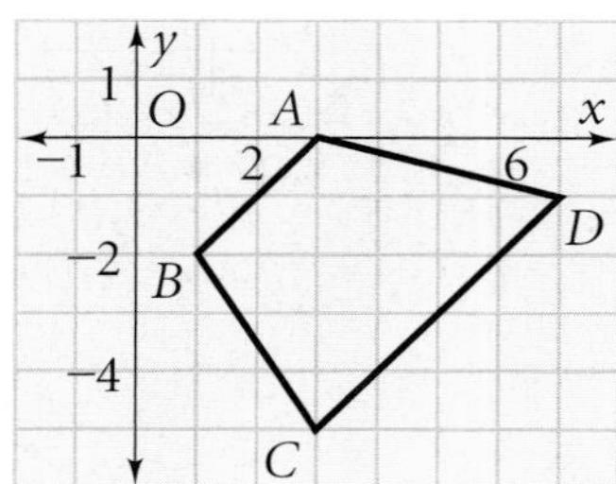

1. reflection in $x = -4$
2. translation $\langle -6, 8 \rangle$
3. rotation of 90° about the point (0, 0)
4. dilation with scale factor $\frac{2}{3}$ centered at the origin
5. glide reflection in $\langle 0, 3 \rangle$ and $x = 0$
6. reflection in $y = x$
7. rotation of 270° about the point (0, 0)
8. dilation with scale factor 5 centered at (0, 0)
9. glide reflection in $\langle -2, 0 \rangle$ and $y = 5$

What type of transformation has the same effect as each composition of transformations?

10. translation $\langle 4, 0 \rangle$ followed by reflection in $y = -4$
11. translation $\langle 4, 8 \rangle$ followed by $\langle -2, 9 \rangle$
12. reflection in $y = 7$, then in $y = 3$
13. reflection in $y = x$, then in $y = 2x + 5$

14. **Writing** Line m intersects $\overline{UH}$ at N, and $UN = NH$. Must H be the reflection image of U in line m? Explain why or why not.

Open-ended **Sketch a figure that has each type of symmetry.**

15. reflectional 16. rotational 17. point

18. Describe the symmetries of this tessellation. Copy a portion of the tessellation and draw any centers of rotational symmetry or lines of symmetry.

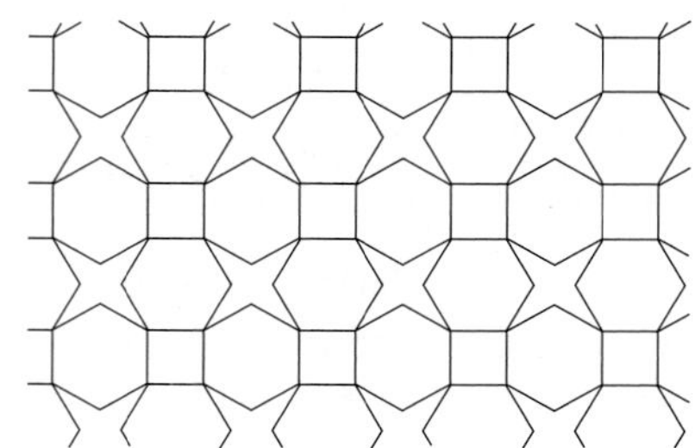

What type(s) of symmetry does each figure have?

19.

20.

21. **Standardized Test Prep** Which of the following letters does *not* tessellate?

A.  B. 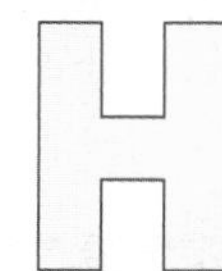 C. 

D. 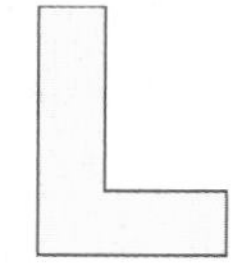 E. 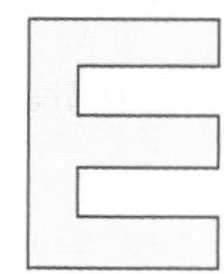

Find the image of $\triangle ABC$ under a dilation with center (0, 0) and the given scale factor.

22. $A(2, 4)$, $B(3, 7)$, $C(5, 1)$; scale factor 4
23. $A(0, 0)$, $B(-3, 2)$, $C(1, 7)$; scale factor $\frac{1}{2}$
24. $A(-2, 2)$, $B(2, -2)$, $C(3, 4)$; scale factor 3

CHAPTER 3 Preparing for the Math A Exam

Part I

1 What is the image of $(-3, 8)$ reflected in $y = 4$?
(1) $(-3, -8)$ (3) $(11, 8)$
(2) $(3, 8)$ (4) $(-3, 0)$

2 The image of $R(-2, -5)$ under a translation is $V(3, -1)$. What vector describes this?
(1) $\langle -1, -6 \rangle$ (3) $\langle 4, 5 \rangle$
(2) $\langle 5, 4 \rangle$ (4) $\langle -5, -4 \rangle$

3 The point $(2, 7)$ is reflected in the y-axis, then translated by $\langle 0, -7 \rangle$. Where is its image?
(1) x-axis (3) fourth quadrant
(2) third quadrant (4) origin

4 Identify the symmetries of this tessellation.
(1) translational symmetry
(2) glide reflectional symmetry
(3) translational and glide reflectional symmetry
(4) neither translational nor glide reflectional symmetry

5 Which names the symmetry of this figure in as many ways as possible?
(1) rotational, point
(2) reflectional, rotational
(3) reflectional, rotational, point
(4) reflectional, point

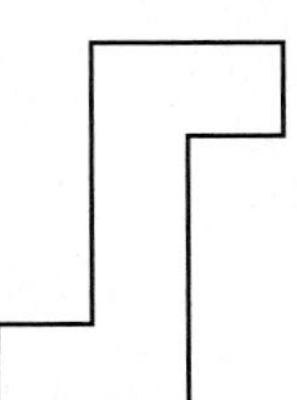

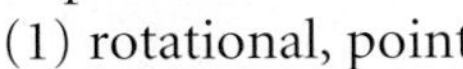

Part II

6 Trace the figure. Then draw its reflection image in line k.

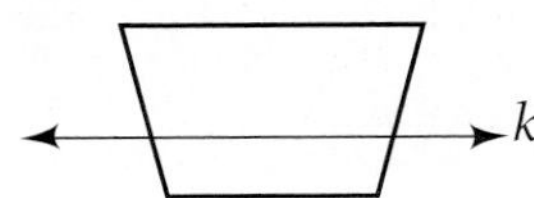

7 What is the image of $(4, 5)$ rotated $270°$ counterclockwise about the origin?

Part III

8 $\triangle CAT$ has vertices $C(4, 6)$, $A(3, -1)$, $T(-2, 2)$. Find the vertices of the image of $\triangle CAT$ under the translation $\langle -3, 2 \rangle$.

9 Trace the figure and point P. Then rotate the figure $180°$ about P. Label the vertices of the image.

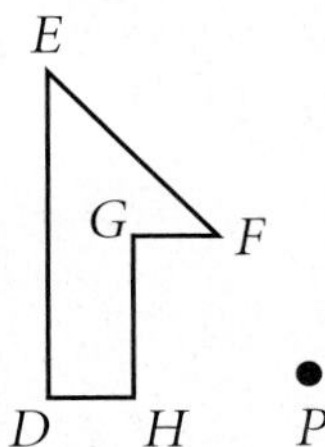

10 Figure $IJKL$ has vertices $I(-6, 6)$, $J(3, 0)$, $K(3, -6)$, and $L(-3, -9)$. Graph $IJKL$ and its image $I'J'K'L'$ under a dilation with center $(0, 0)$ and the scale factor $\frac{1}{3}$.

Part IV

11 $\triangle YES$ is transformed under a glide reflection given by the vector $\langle 0, -3 \rangle$ and a reflection in $x = -1$. Find the coordinates of the vertices of $\triangle Y'E'S'$.

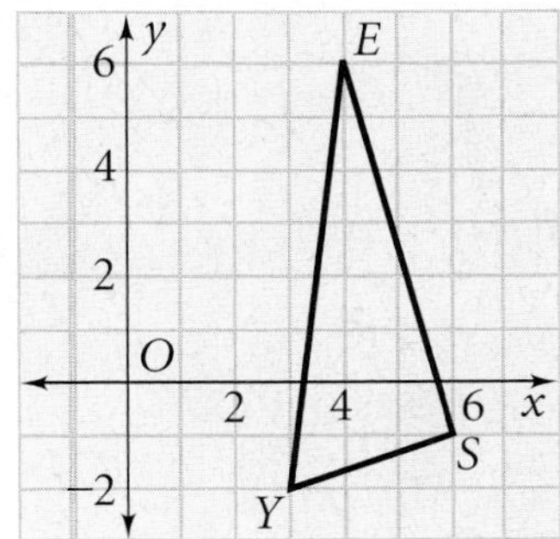

12 Two vertices of equilateral $\triangle ABC$ are $A(1, 7)$ and $B(5, 2)$. The triangle undergoes a dilation with scale factor 3.5. What is the perimeter of the image $A'B'C'$?

4 Triangle Relationships

Relating to the Real World

You are sitting in a meeting around a large table. An important decision needs to be made. Your boss turns to you and asks, "So, what do you think we should do?" Your response is clear and well-reasoned, and your co-workers nod in approval. The reasoning skills that you learn now will help you to succeed in life. In this chapter you will study the tools needed to become a better problem solver and logical thinker.

CHAPTER PROJECT

PUZZLING PIECES

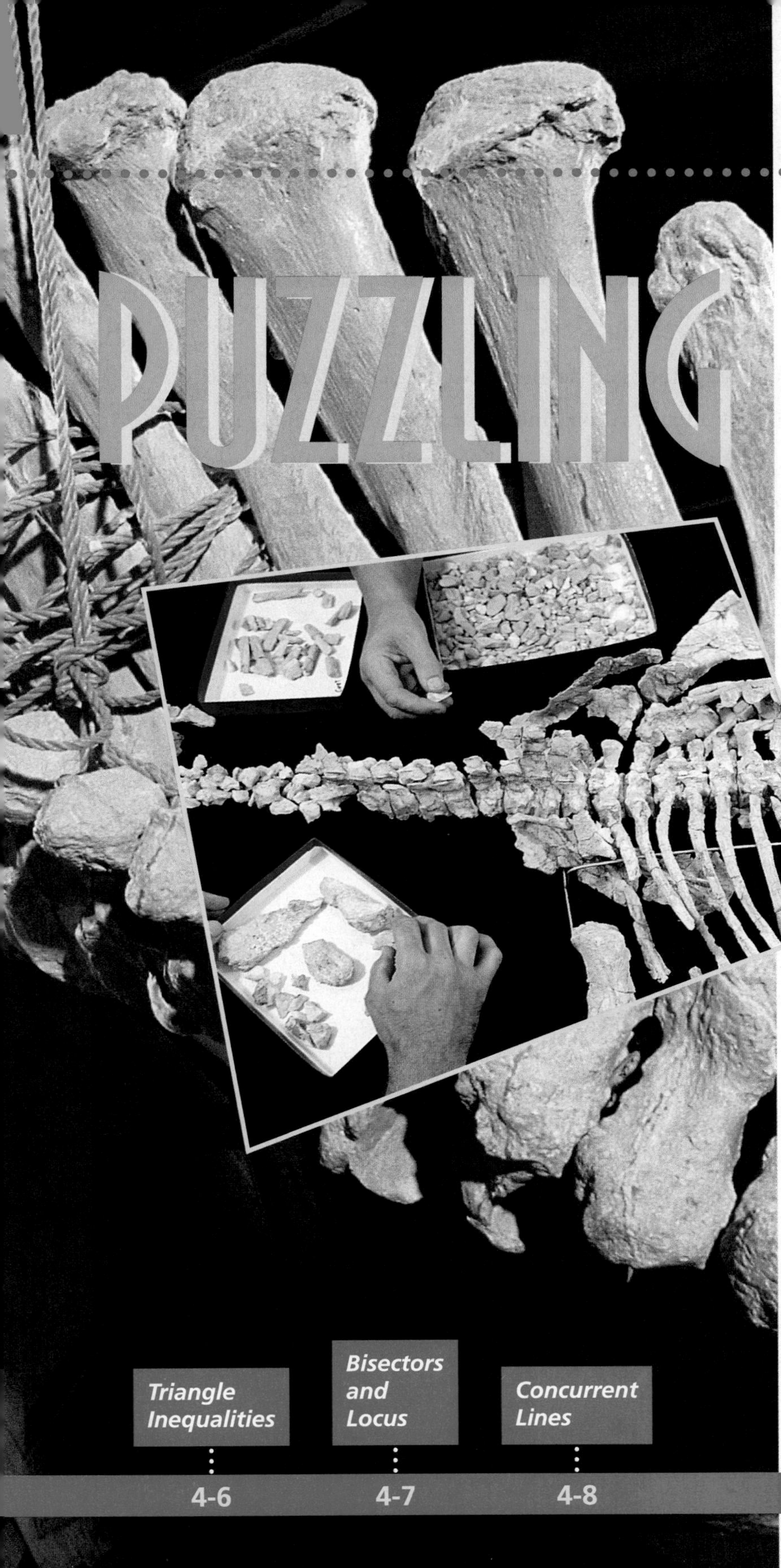

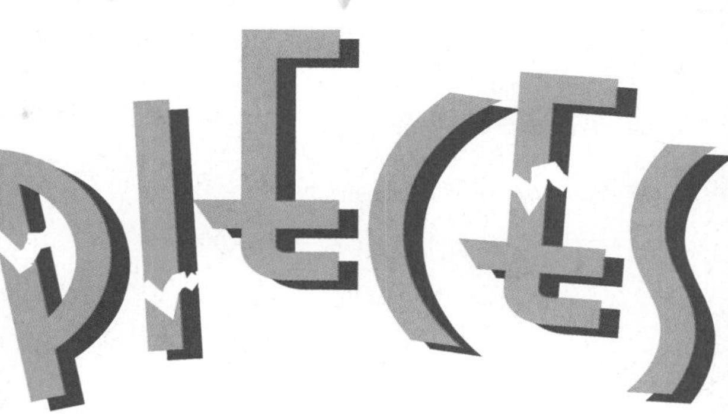

A paleontologist makes sense of the past by piecing together fossils. By using logical reasoning, she makes a few bones tell the story of an entire species. That feeling of discovery—that sense of "aha!"—has driven people throughout history to use logic to solve puzzles.

In your project for this chapter, you will explore ways of solving logic puzzles. You will also create your own puzzles. You will see how logic, though used for amusement, is the backbone of mathematics—a powerful tool for determining truth.

To help you complete the project:

- **p. 749** *Find Out by Listing*
- **p. 760** *Find Out by Organizing*
- **p. 767** *Find Out by Analyzing*
- **p. 787** *Find Out by Writing*
- **p. 795** *Finishing the Project*

Triangle Inequalities 4-6

Bisectors and Locus 4-7

Concurrent Lines 4-8

4-1 Using Logical Reasoning

What You'll Learn

- Writing and interpreting different types of conditional statements

...And Why

To help you analyze situations and become a better problem solver

THINK AND DISCUSS

Conditionals and Converses

- If Raúl's major is bagpipe, then he attends Carnegie-Mellon University.
- If a second goes by, then Earth has moved another $18\frac{1}{2}$ mi along its orbit.
- If a movie is scary, then the concession stands sell more popcorn.
- If you are not completely satisfied, then your money will be refunded.

1. You make and hear *if-then* statements like these many times each day. What are some *if-then* statements you have heard?

Another name for an *if-then statement* is a **conditional.** Every conditional has two parts. The part following *if* is the **hypothesis,** and the part following *then* is the **conclusion.**

Example 1

Identify the hypothesis and conclusion in this statement:

If it is February, then there are only 28 days in the month.

Hypothesis: It is February.
Conclusion: There are only 28 days in the month.

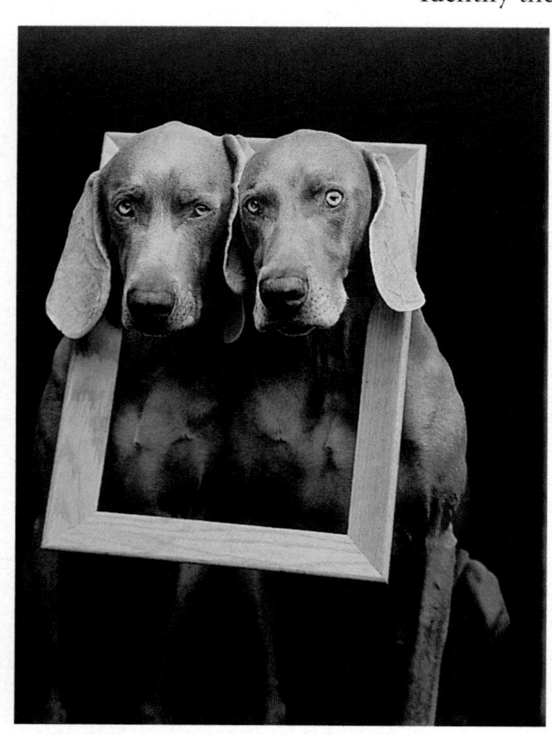

If you want double the love, then buy a pair.

2. Try This Identify the hypothesis and conclusion in the photo caption at the left.

When you determine whether a conditional is true or false, you determine its **truth value.** To show that a conditional is false, you need to find only one *counterexample* for which the hypothesis is true and the conclusion is false. The conditional in Example 1 is false because during a leap year February has 29 days.

3. Find a counterexample for this conditional: If the name of a state contains the word *New,* then the state borders an ocean.

Many sentences can be written as conditionals. For example, the sentence

Quadrilaterals have four sides.

can be rewritten in if-then form as

If a polygon is a quadrilateral, then it has four sides.

The **converse** of a conditional interchanges the hypothesis and conclusion.

Example 2

Write the converse of this statement: If a polygon is a quadrilateral, then it has four sides.

Conditional: If a polygon is a quadrilateral, then it has four sides.

Converse: If a polygon has four sides, then it is a quadrilateral. ■

Literature Notice that both statements in Example 2 have the same truth value. This is *not* true of all conditionals and their converses, as Alice discovers in this passage from Lewis Carroll's *Alice's Adventures in Wonderland.*

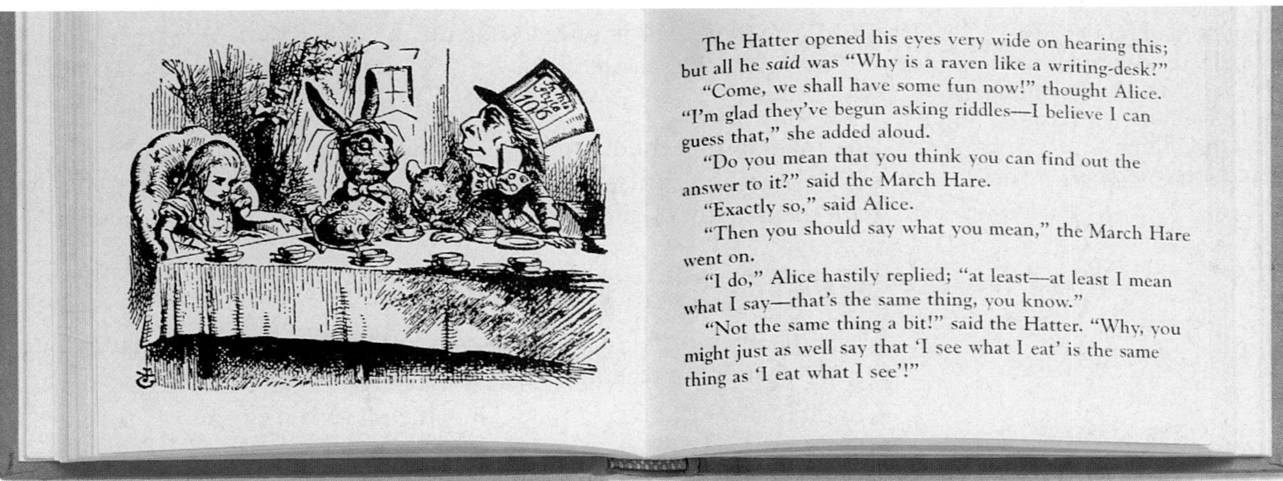

The Hatter opened his eyes very wide on hearing this; but all he *said* was "Why is a raven like a writing-desk?"

"Come, we shall have some fun now!" thought Alice. "I'm glad they've begun asking riddles—I believe I can guess that," she added aloud.

"Do you mean that you think you can find out the answer to it?" said the March Hare.

"Exactly so," said Alice.

"Then you should say what you mean," the March Hare went on.

"I do," Alice hastily replied; "at least—at least I mean what I say—that's the same thing, you know."

"Not the same thing a bit!" said the Hatter. "Why, you might just as well say that 'I see what I eat' is the same thing as 'I eat what I see'!"

The Hatter's statement "I see what I eat" can be rewritten in if-then form as "If I eat it, then I see it." The converse, "I eat what I see," can be rewritten as "If I see it, then I eat it."

4. Are the truth values for the Hatter's statement and its converse the same? Explain.

Biconditionals, Inverses, and Contrapositives

When a conditional and its converse are true, you can combine them as a **biconditional.** The conditionals from Example 2 can be combined as

If a polygon is a quadrilateral, then it has four sides, *and* if a polygon has four sides, then it is a quadrilateral.

This long sentence can be shortened by using the phrase *if and only if:*

A polygon is a quadrilateral *if and only if* it has four sides.

Math A Test Prep

1 What is the inverse of the statement "If you study, you will pass the test"?
(1) If you pass the test, you will study.
(2) If you do not study, you will not pass the test.
(3) If you do not pass the test, you will not study.
(4) You will study if and only if you pass the test.

2 Daniel said, "If a quadrilateral has two pairs of congruent sides, then it's a parallelogram." Is this statement true? If not, name a counterexample.

You learned in Chapter 1 that any good definition is "reversible." This means that any good definition can be written as a biconditional.

Example 3

Write the two statements that make up this definition: A right angle has measure 90. Then write the definition as a biconditional.

Conditional: If an angle is a right angle, then its measure is 90.

Converse: If the measure of an angle is 90, then it is a right angle.

Biconditional: An angle is a right angle if and only if its measure is 90.

The **negation** of a statement has the opposite meaning. For example, the negation of "An angle is acute" is "An angle is *not* acute."

5. Write the negation of each statement.
a. Two angles are vertical. **b.** Two lines are not parallel.

The **inverse** of a conditional negates both the hypothesis and the conclusion. The **contrapositive** of a conditional interchanges and negates both the hypothesis and the conclusion.

Example 4

Write the inverse and the contrapositive of this statement: If a figure is a square, then it is a rectangle.

Conditional: If a figure is a square, then it is a rectangle.

Negate both.

Inverse: If a figure is *not* a square, then it is *not* a rectangle.

Conditional: If a figure is a square, then it is a rectangle.

Negate both.

Contrapositive: If a figure is *not* a rectangle, then it is *not* a square.

6. Find the truth values of the three statements in Example 4.

7. Try This Write the inverse and contrapositive of this statement: If a quadrilateral is a parallelogram, then it has two pairs of parallel sides.

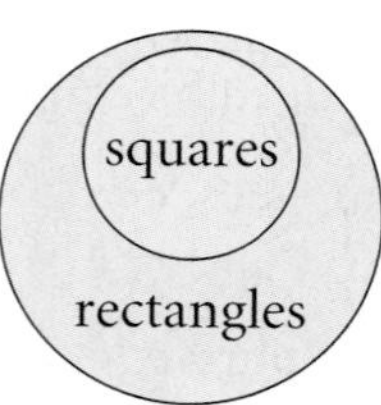

This Venn diagram shows the conditional "If a figure is a square, then it is a rectangle." It also shows its contrapositive "If a figure is *not* a rectangle, then it is *not* a square" because any point *not* in the larger circle is *not* in the smaller circle. Since the same diagram shows both statements, a conditional and its contrapositive always have the same truth value.

Summary of Conditionals

Statement	Form	Example
conditional	If ■, then ■.	If an angle is a straight angle, then its measure is 180.
converse	If ■, then ■.	If the measure of an angle is 180, then it is a straight angle.
inverse	If *not* ■, then *not* ■.	If an angle is *not* a straight angle, then its measure is *not* 180.
contrapositive	If *not* ■, then *not* ■.	If the measure of an angle is *not* 180, then it is *not* a straight angle.
biconditional	■ if and only if ■.	An angle is a straight angle if and only if its measure is 180.

Exercises ON YOUR OWN

1. Identify the hypothesis and conclusion in the cartoon.

FRANK AND ERNEST By BOB THAVES

For Exercises 2–5: (a) Rewrite each statement in if-then form. (b) Underline the hypothesis once and the conclusion twice.

2. Glass objects are fragile.

3. $3x - 7 = 14$ implies that $3x = 21$.

4. Numbers that have 2 as a factor are even.

5. An isosceles triangle has two congruent sides.

Find a counterexample for each statement.

6. If it is not a weekday, then it is Saturday.

7. Odd integers less than 10 are prime.

8. If you live in a country that borders the United States, then you live in Canada.

9. If you play a sport with a ball and bat, then you play baseball.

10. a. *Open-ended* Write a conditional with the same truth value as its converse.

b. Write a conditional whose converse has the opposite truth value.

For each statement, write (a) the converse, (b) the inverse, and (c) the contrapositive.

11. If you eat all of your vegetables, then you will grow.

12. *Transformations* If a figure has point symmetry, then it has rotational symmetry.

13. If a triangle is a right triangle, then it has a 90° angle.

14. If a quadrilateral has exactly two congruent sides, then it is not a rhombus.

15. If two segments are congruent, then they have the same length.

16. If you do not work, you will not get paid.

17. If a polygon is a pentagon, then the sum of the measures of its angles is 540.

18. If a conditional statement is false, then its contrapositive is false.

For Exercises 19–26: (a) Write the converse of each statement. (b) Determine the truth value of the statement and its converse. (c) If both statements are true, write a biconditional.

19. If you travel from the United States to Kenya, then you have a passport.

20. *Coordinate Geometry* If a point is in the first quadrant, then its coordinates are positive.

21. *Chemistry* If a substance is water, then its chemical formula is H_2O.

22. *Transformations* If a figure has two lines of symmetry, then it has rotational symmetry.

23. *Coordinate Geometry* If two nonvertical lines are parallel, then their slopes are equal.

24. If two angles are complementary, then the sum of their measures is 90.

25. If you are in Indiana, then you are in Indianapolis.

26. *Probability* If the probability that an event will occur is 1, then the event is certain to occur.

27. a. *Consumer Issues* Advertisements often suggest conditional statements. For example, an ad might imply that if you don't buy a product, you won't be popular. What conditional is implied in the ad at the right?
    b. *Research* Find magazine ads that use conditionals effectively. Make a poster to display these ads.

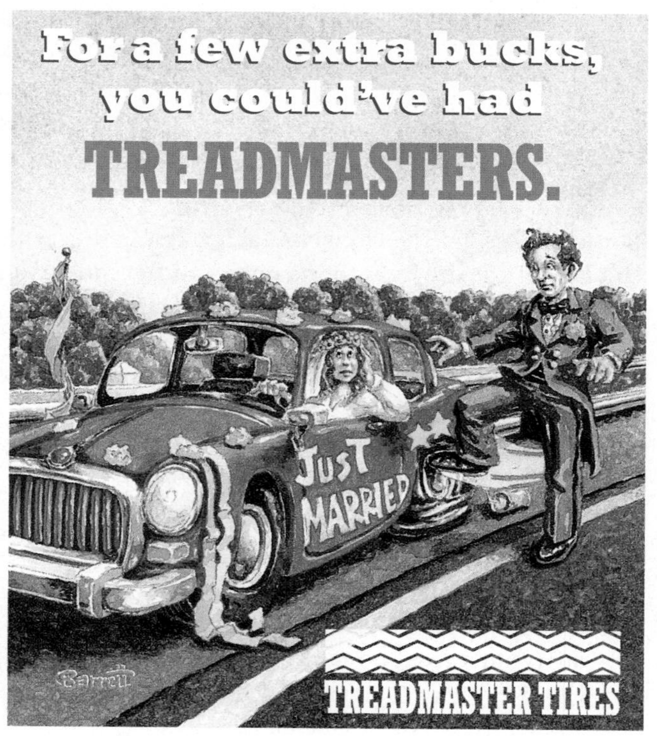

Write the two conditionals that make up each biconditional.

28. A swimmer wins a race if and only if she swims the fastest.

29. A number is divisible by 3 if and only if the sum of its digits is divisible by 3.

30. Two angles are congruent if and only if they have the same measure.

31. **Writing** Jynona knows that vertical angles are congruent. She thinks the converse is also true. Is she correct? Explain.

For each Venn diagram: (a) Write a conditional statement. (b) Write the contrapositive of the conditional.

32.
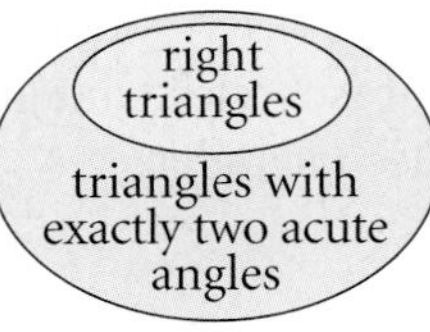

33.
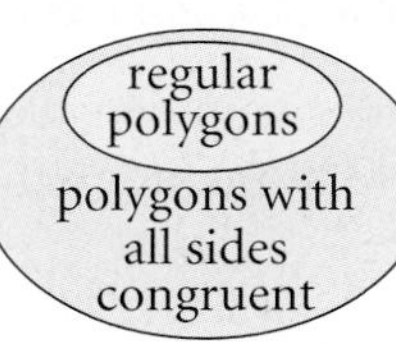

34.
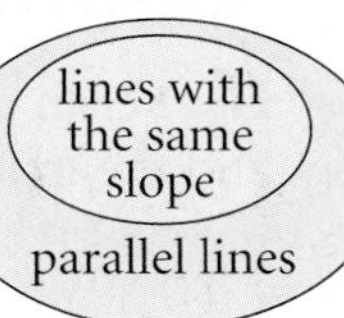

35.
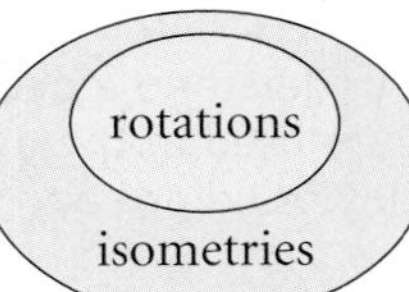

Chapter Project ***Find Out by Listing***

Three red hats and three blue hats are packed in three boxes, with two hats to a box. The boxes are all labeled incorrectly. To determine what each box actually contains, you may select one hat from one box, without looking at the contents of that box. Explain how this will allow you to determine the contents of each box. (*Hint:* List all possible solutions; then use logic to solve.)

Exercises MIXED REVIEW

Coordinate Geometry **Sketch a line with the given slope containing the given point.**

36. $m = \frac{1}{2}, (2, -6)$

37. $m = 1, (0, 5)$

38. $m = -2, (-3, 6)$

39. $m = \frac{1}{3}, (0, 0)$

40. An angle's measure is 10 more than its supplement. Find the measures of both angles.

41. **Transformational Geometry** Locate the coordinates of the image of $\triangle ABC$ with vertices $A(0, 3)$, $B(-4, -6)$, $C(6, 1)$ under a 180° rotation about the origin.

Getting Ready for Lesson 4-2

Find the value of *x*.

42.
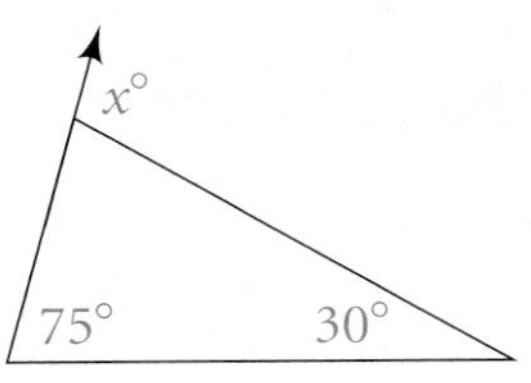

43.
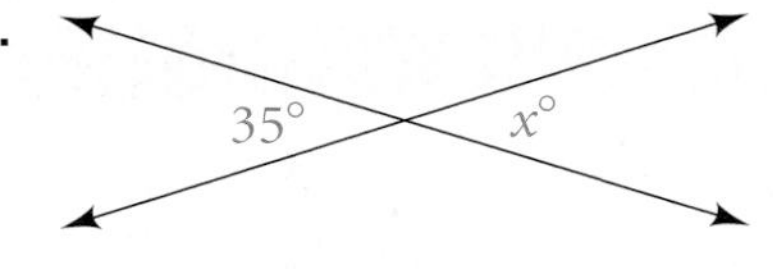

44.
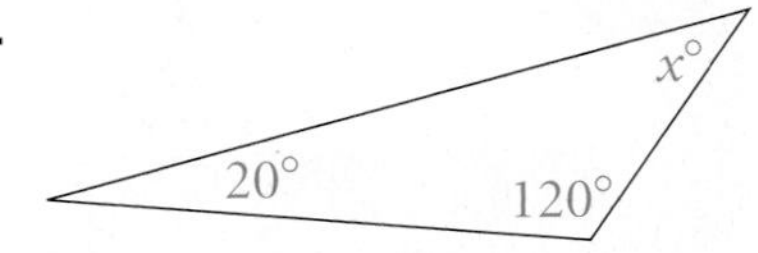

What You'll Learn

- Using and applying properties of isosceles triangles

...And Why

To understand a geometric figure used in the designs of many buildings and bridges

What You'll Need

- straightedge
- compass
- scissors

4-2 Isosceles Triangles

WORK TOGETHER

Have each member of your group construct a different isosceles triangle and then cut it out. Be sure to include acute and obtuse triangles.

- Label the triangle $\triangle ABC$, with A and B opposite the congruent sides.
- Bisect $\angle C$ by folding the triangle so that the congruent sides overlap. Label the intersection of the fold line and $\overline{AB}$ as point D.

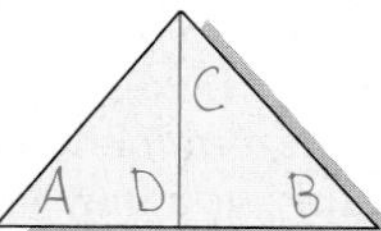

TECHNOLOGY HINT

The Work Together could be done using geometry software.

1. What do you notice about $\angle A$ and $\angle B$? Compare results within your group.
2. a. What types of angles do $\angle CDA$ and $\angle CDB$ appear to be?
   b. What do you notice about $\overline{AD}$ and $\overline{DB}$?
   c. Use your answers to parts (a) and (b) to complete the statement: $\overline{CD}$ is the __?__ of $\overline{AB}$.

- Construct a new triangle that has two congruent angles. Cut out the triangle and label it $\triangle EFG$, where $\angle E \cong \angle F$.

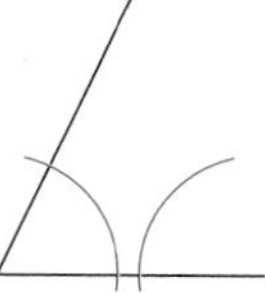
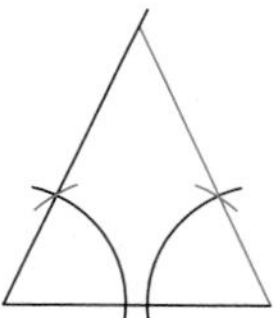

3. Fold the triangle so that the congruent angles overlap.
   a. What do you notice about $\overline{EG}$ and $\overline{FG}$? Compare results within your group.
   b. What type of triangle is $\triangle EFG$?

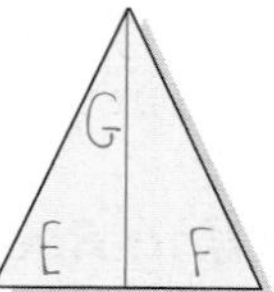

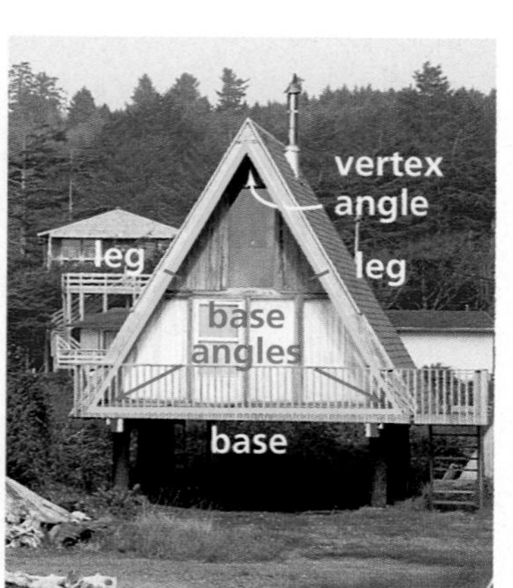

THINK AND DISCUSS

Isosceles triangles are common in the real world. You can find them in structures such as bridges and buildings. The congruent sides of an isosceles triangle are the **legs.** The third side is the **base.** The two congruent sides form the **vertex angle.** The other two angles are the **base angles.**

Your observations from the Work Together suggest the following theorems. The proofs of these theorems involve properties of congruent triangles that you will study in Chapter 8.

Theorem 4-1
Isosceles Triangle Theorem

If two sides of a triangle are congruent, then the angles opposite those sides are also congruent.

If $\overline{AC} \cong \overline{BC}$, then $\angle A \cong \angle B$.

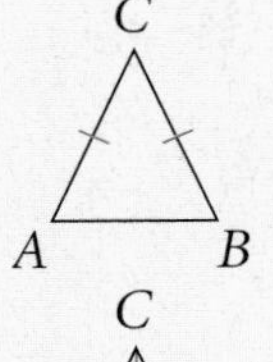

Theorem 4-2

The bisector of the vertex angle of an isosceles triangle is the perpendicular bisector of the base.

If $\overline{AC} \cong \overline{BC}$ and $\overline{CD}$ bisects $\angle ACB$,
then $\overline{CD} \perp \overline{AB}$ and $\overline{CD}$ bisects $\overline{AB}$.

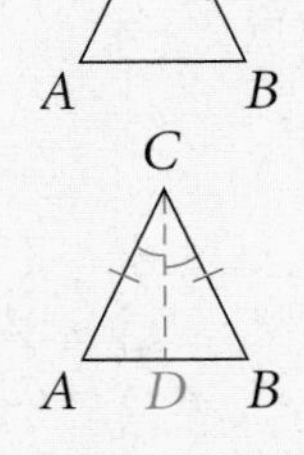

Theorem 4-3
Converse of Isosceles Triangle Theorem

If two angles of a triangle are congruent, then the sides opposite the angles are congruent.

If $\angle A \cong \angle B$, then $\overline{AC} \cong \overline{BC}$.

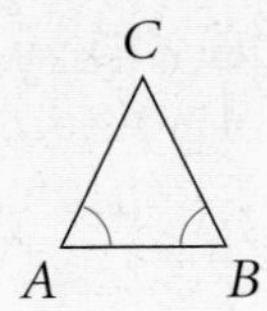

4. Write the Isosceles Triangle Theorem and its converse as a biconditional.

Example 1

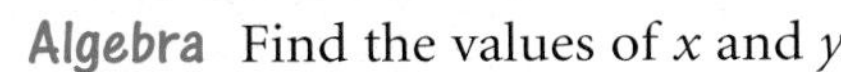

Algebra Find the values of x and y.

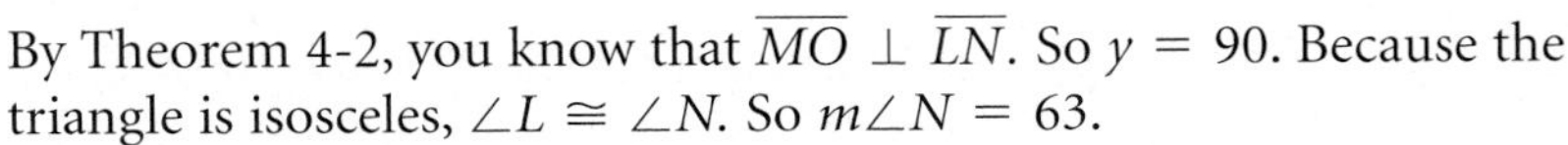

By Theorem 4-2, you know that $\overline{MO} \perp \overline{LN}$. So $y = 90$. Because the triangle is isosceles, $\angle L \cong \angle N$. So $m\angle N = 63$.

$m\angle N + x + y = 180$	Triangle Angle-Sum Theorem
$63 + x + 90 = 180$	Substitution
$x = 27$	Subtract 153 from each side.

So $x = 27$ and $y = 90$.

5. Try This Suppose $m\angle L = 43$. Find the values of x and y.

Example 2

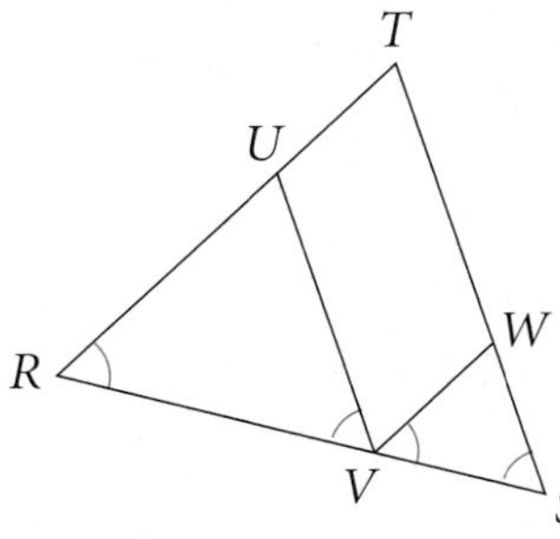

Complete each statement. Explain your answers.

a. $\overline{RT} \cong$ __?__ **b.** $\overline{RU} \cong$ __?__ **c.** $\overline{VW} \cong$ __?__

a. $\overline{RT} \cong \overline{ST}$ because $\angle R \cong \angle S$.

b. $\overline{RU} \cong \overline{VU}$ because $\angle R \cong \angle RVU$.

c. $\overline{VW} \cong \overline{SW}$ because $\angle WVS \cong \angle S$.

QUICK REVIEW

An equilateral triangle has three congruent sides. An equiangular triangle has three congruent angles.

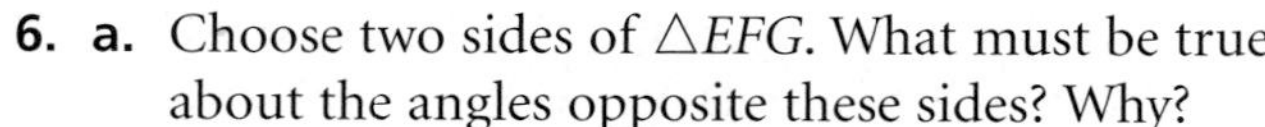

6. a. Choose two sides of $\triangle EFG$. What must be true about the angles opposite these sides? Why?

b. Repeat part (a) with a different pair of sides.

c. What is true about the angles of an equilateral triangle?

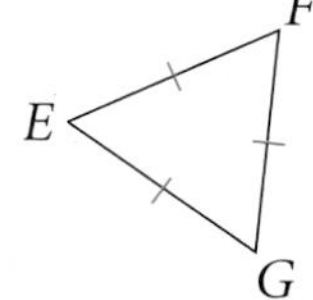

7. a. Choose two angles of $\triangle MNO$. What must be true about the sides opposite these angles? Why?

b. Repeat part (a) with a different pair of angles.

c. What is true about the sides of an equiangular triangle?

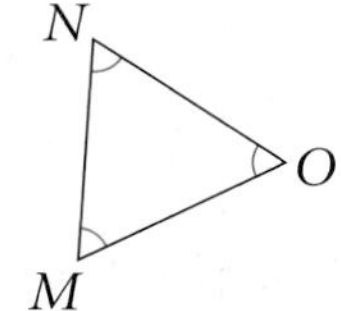

Your observations from Questions 6 and 7 are summarized below.

Corollary to Isosceles Triangle Theorem

If a triangle is equilateral, then it is equiangular.

If $\overline{XY} \cong \overline{YZ} \cong \overline{ZX}$, then $\angle X \cong \angle Y \cong \angle Z$.

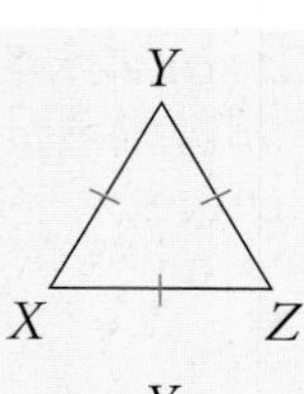

Corollary to Converse of Isosceles Triangle Theorem

If a triangle is equiangular, then it is equilateral.

If $\angle X \cong \angle Y \cong \angle Z$, then $\overline{XY} \cong \overline{YZ} \cong \overline{ZX}$.

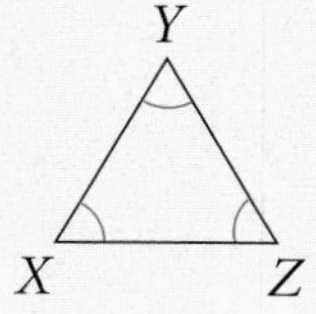

8. Use the corollaries above to write a biconditional.

Example 3

Relating to the Real World 

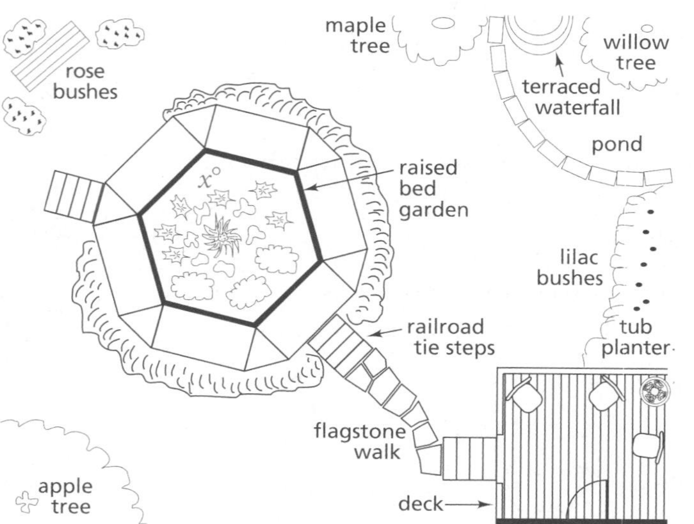

Landscaping A landscaper is building a raised bed garden to fit in the hexagonal space in the diagram. The path around the garden consists of rectangles and equilateral triangles. What is the measure of the angle marked x?

Each angle of a rectangle measures 90. Each angle of an equilateral triangle measures 60. (Why?)

$$x + 90 + 60 + 90 = 360$$

$$x = 120$$

The measure of the angle is 120.

Exercises ON YOUR OWN

Algebra Find the values of x and y.

1. 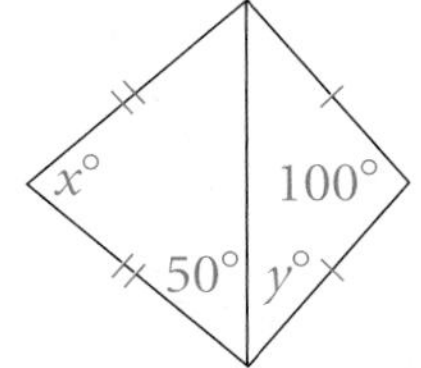

2. 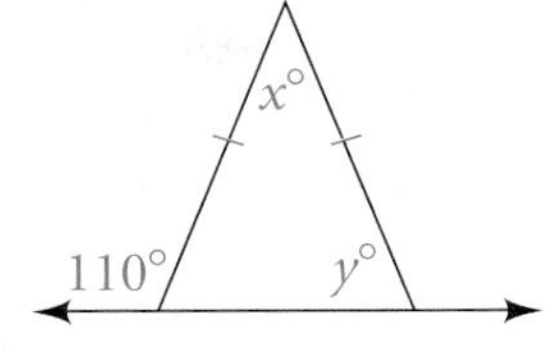

3. 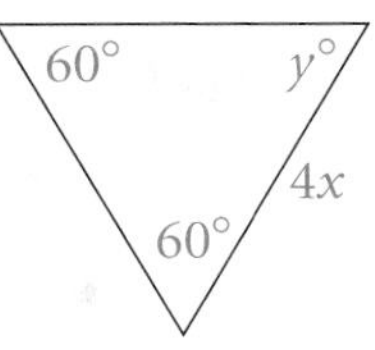

Perimeter is 54.

4. 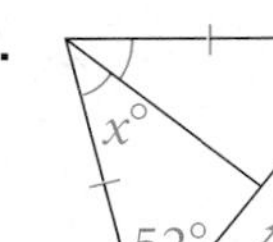
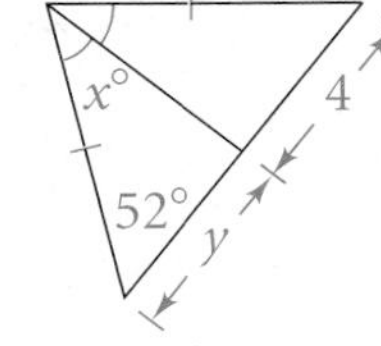

5. 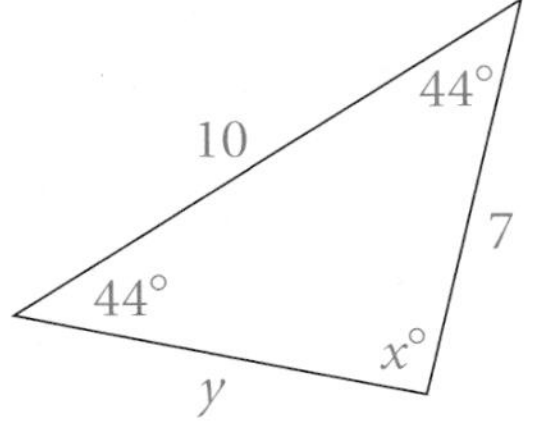

6. 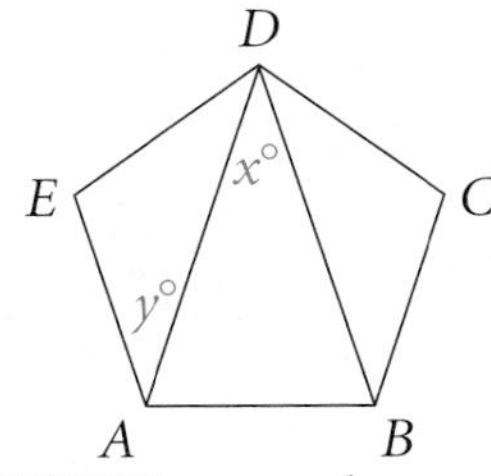

ABCDE is a regular pentagon.

7. 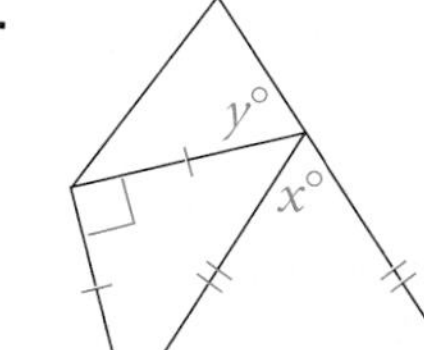

8. 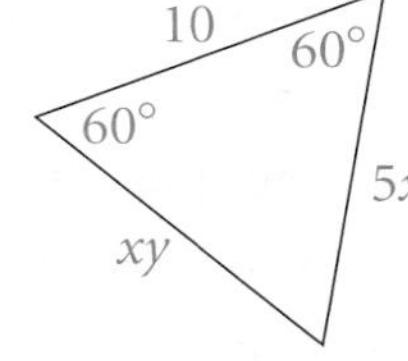

9. **Architecture** The Air Force Academy Cadet Chapel has 17 spires that point to the sky. Each spire is an isosceles triangle with a 40° vertex angle. Find the measures of the base angles.

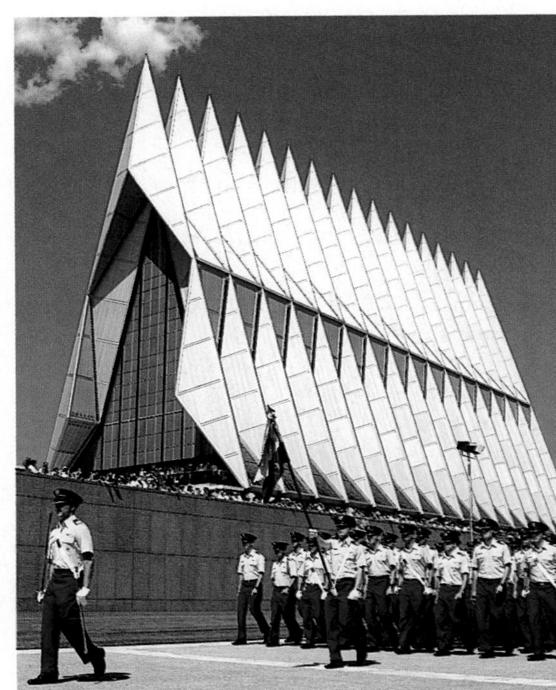

10. **Critical Thinking** What are the measures of the base angles of an isosceles right triangle? Explain.

11. **Coordinate Geometry** The vertices of the base angles of an isosceles triangle are at (0, 0) and (6, 0). Describe the possible locations of the third vertex.

Logical Reasoning Determine whether each statement is true or false. If it is false, provide a counterexample.

12. If a quadrilateral is equilateral, then it is equiangular.

13. If a quadrilateral is equiangular, then it is equilateral.

14. Every isosceles triangle has at least one line of symmetry.

15. Every equilateral triangle has exactly three lines of symmetry.

16. **Graphic Arts** The logo of the National Council of Teachers of Mathematics is shown at the right.
    a. Trace the logo onto your paper. Highlight an obtuse isosceles triangle in the design and then find its angle measures.
    b. **Open-ended** Repeat part (a) for each of the following figures: kite, pentagon, hexagon.

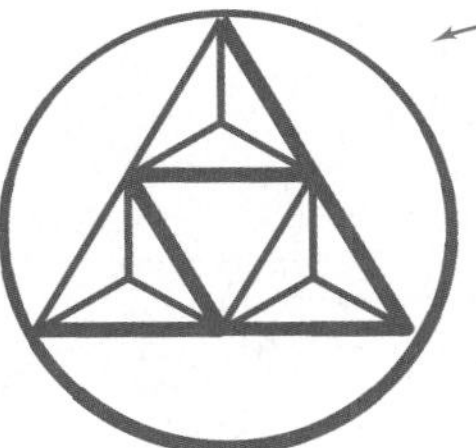

The triangles in the logo have these congruent sides and angles.

Coordinate Geometry **For each pair of points, there are six points that could be the third vertex of an isosceles right triangle. Find the coordinates of each point.**

17. (0, 0) and (5, 5)

18. (2, 3) and (5, 6)

19. **Algebra** A triangle has angle measures $x + 15$, $3x - 35$, and $4x$.
   a. Find the value of x.
   b. Find the measure of each angle.
   c. What type of triangle is it? Why?

20. **Writing** If a triangle is equiangular, is it also isosceles? Explain.

21. a. **Communications** In the diagram, what type of triangle is formed by the cable pairs and the ground?
   b. What are the two different base lengths of the triangles?
   c. How is the tower related to each of the triangles?

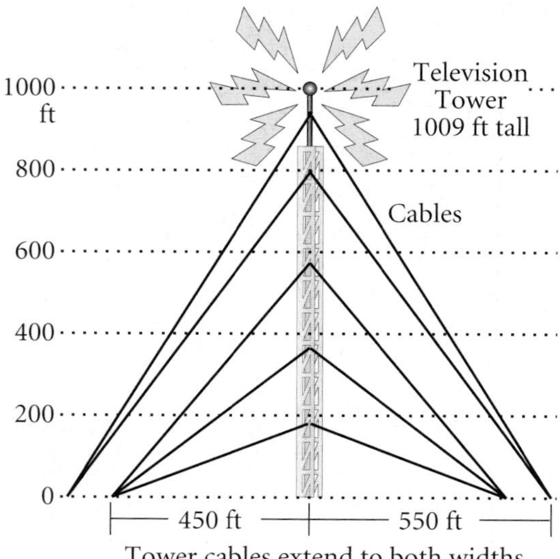

Tower cables extend to both widths.

Find each value.

22. If $m\angle L = 58$, then $m\angle LKJ =$ ■.

23. If $JL = 5$, then $ML =$ ■.

24. If $m\angle JKM = 48$, then $m\angle J =$ ■.

25. If $m\angle J = 55$, then $m\angle JKM =$ ■.

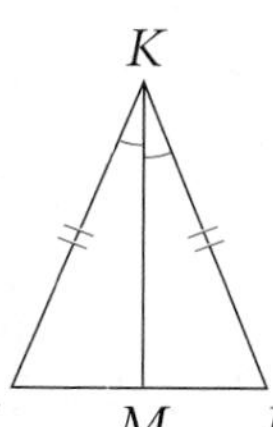

Choose **Use mental math, pencil and paper, or a calculator to find the values of the variables.**

26.

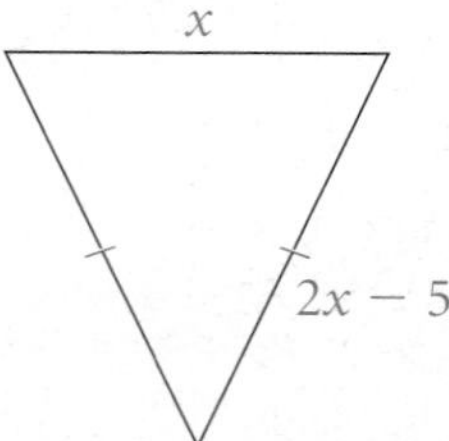

Perimeter is 20.

27.

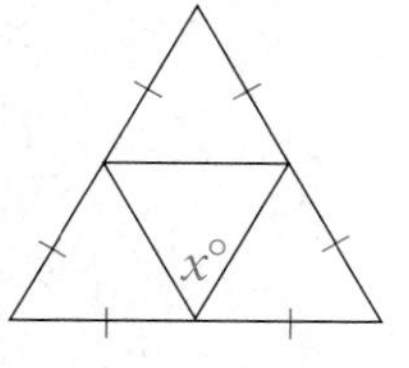

28.

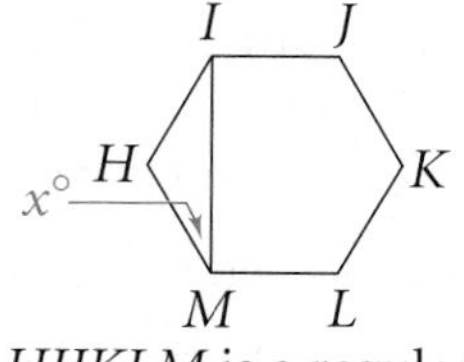

$HIJKLM$ is a regular hexagon.

29.

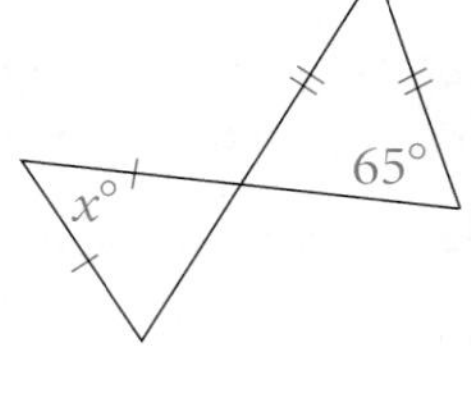

30.

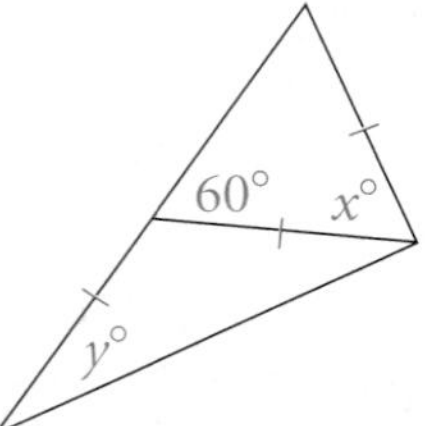

31.

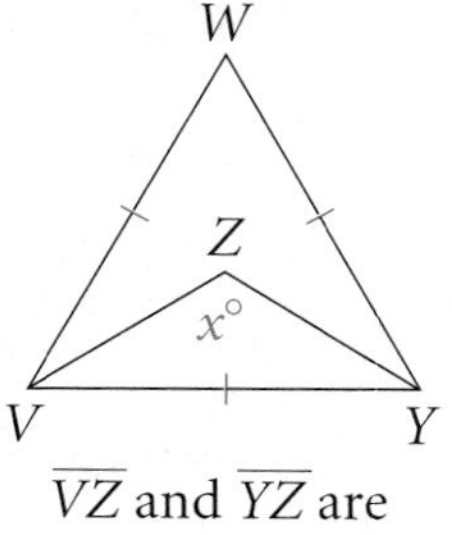

$\overline{VZ}$ and $\overline{YZ}$ are angle bisectors.

32.

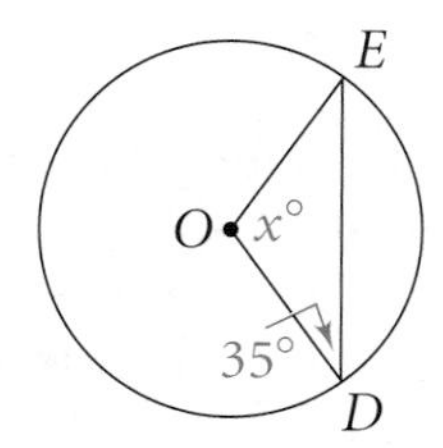

$\overline{OD}$ and $\overline{OE}$ are radii.

33.

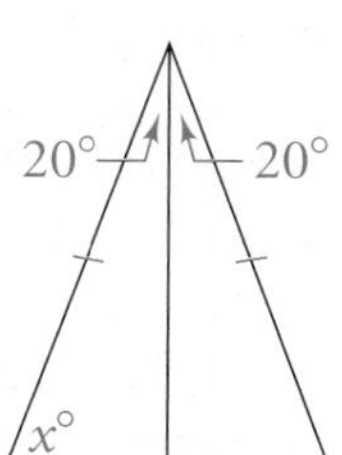

34. **Crafts** This design is used in Hmong crafts and in Islamic and Mexican tiles. To create it, the artist starts by drawing a circle and four equally spaced diameters.

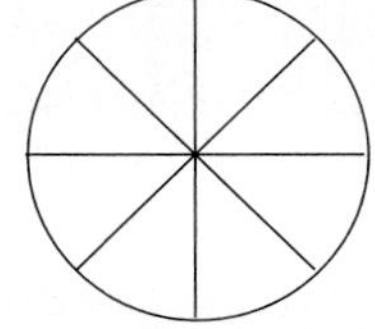

Step 1

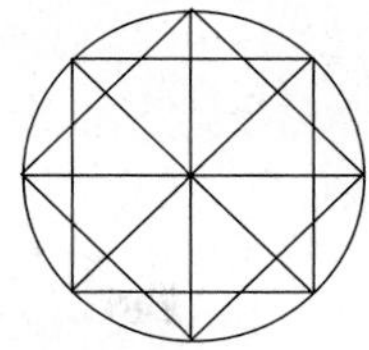

Step 2

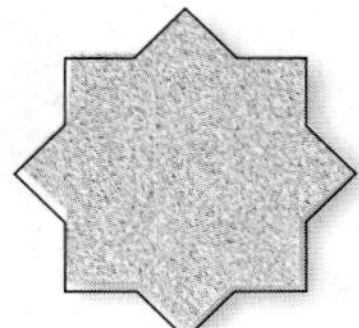

Step 3

a. How many different sizes of isosceles right triangles can you find in Step 2? Trace an example of each onto your paper.

b. For each size of triangle that you traced, count the number of times it appears in the diagram.

35. **Critical Thinking** Patrick defines the base of an isosceles triangle as "the bottom side of an isosceles triangle." Is his definition a good one? Explain why or why not.

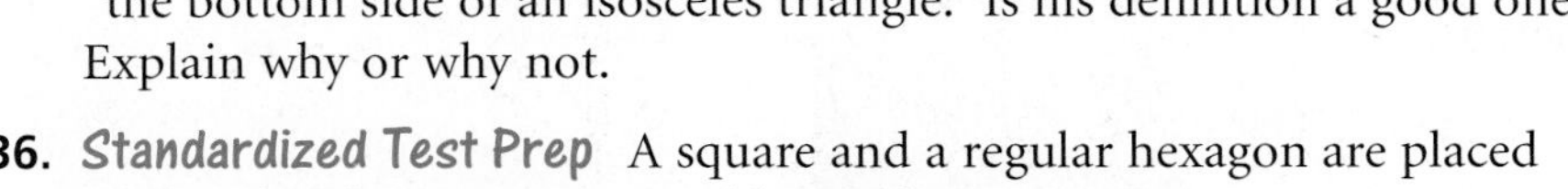

36. **Standardized Test Prep** A square and a regular hexagon are placed so that they have a common side. Find $m\angle HAS$.

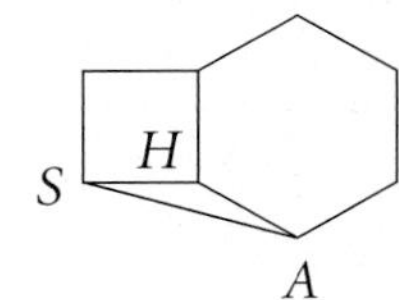

A. 9 **B.** 10 **C.** 15 **D.** 20 **E.** 30

Algebra **Find the values of m and n.**

37.

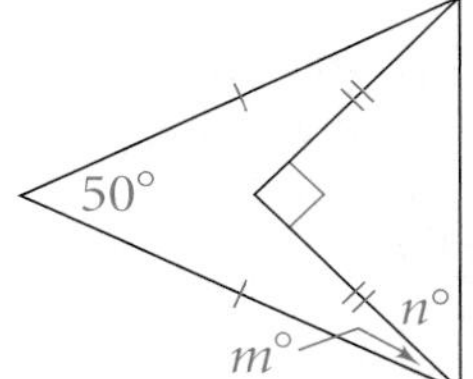

38.

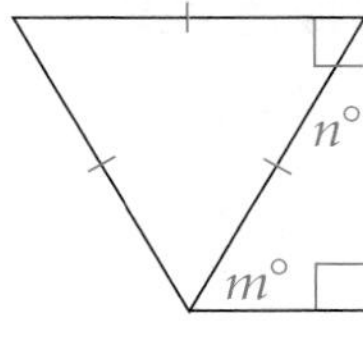

39.

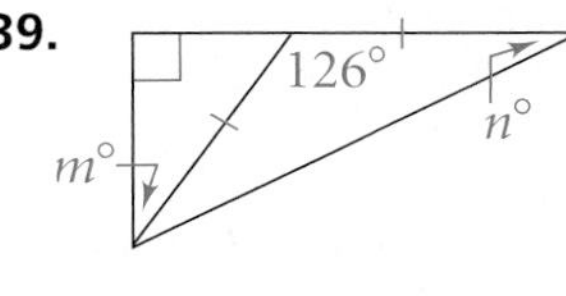

40.

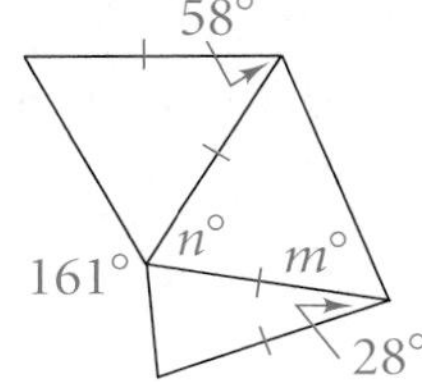

Exercises MIXED REVIEW

Coordinate Geometry **The endpoints of a diameter of a circle are given. Find the coordinates of the center and the length of a radius.**

41. (3, 8), (−1, 2) **42.** (−2, 5), (−5, 2) **43.** (3, 7), (−2, 6)

44. **Coordinate Geometry** Find the equation of the line that passes through (0, 4) and is parallel to $y = -3x - 5$.

45. Find the number of sides of a regular polygon whose exterior angles measure 15°.

Getting Ready for Lesson 4-3

What can you conclude from each diagram? Justify your answers.

46.

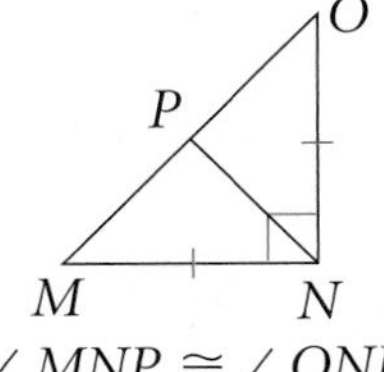

$\angle MNP \cong \angle ONP$

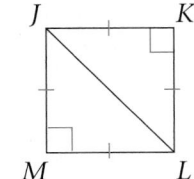

47.

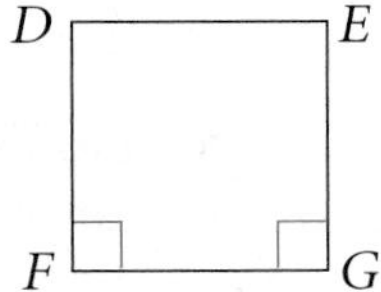

48. J K M L

Connections Logic Puzzles . . . and more

What You'll Learn

- Using different styles of proofs to write convincing arguments

...And Why

To help you think logically

4-3 Preparing for Proof

THINK AND DISCUSS

In everyday life, proof takes many forms.

A passport is proof of your citizenship when traveling in foreign countries.

PASSPORT
United States
of America

TIME RECORDER CO.

A punch clock record is proof of the number of hours you have worked.

A birth certificate is proof of the date and location of your birth.

1. Give some other examples of proof from everyday life.

Proofs in geometry can take several forms. Each form has these basic parts:

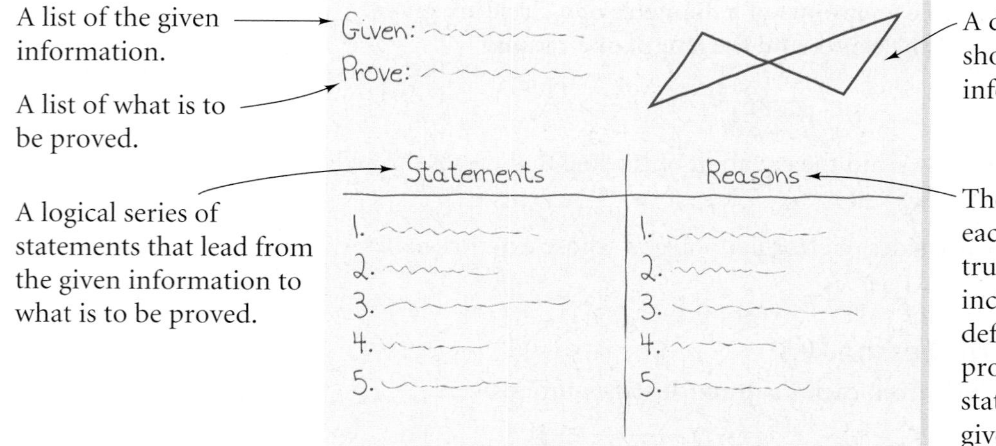

A list of the given information.
Given:
Prove:
A list of what is to be proved.
A diagram showing the given information.
Statements
Reasons
A logical series of statements that lead from the given information to what is to be proved.
The reasons why each statement is true. Reasons can include postulates, definitions, properties, previously stated theorems, or given facts.
1.
2.
3.
4.
5.

The diagram shows a **two-column proof.** In this style of proof, statements appear in one column and reasons in another.

In this lesson, you will study the proofs of the four theorems at the top of the next page.

Theorem 4-4	If a triangle is a right triangle, then the acute angles are complementary.
Theorem 4-5	If two angles of one triangle are congruent to two angles of another triangle, then the third angles are congruent.
Theorem 4-6	All right angles are congruent.
Theorem 4-7	If two angles are congruent and supplementary, then each is a right angle.

In a proof of a theorem, the *Given* information and the figure relate to the hypothesis of the theorem. You *Prove* the conclusion of the theorem.

Theorem 4-4
If a triangle is a right triangle, then the acute angles are complementary.

Hypothesis

Given: $\triangle EFG$ with right angle $\angle F$
Prove: $\angle E$ and $\angle G$ are complementary.

Conclusion

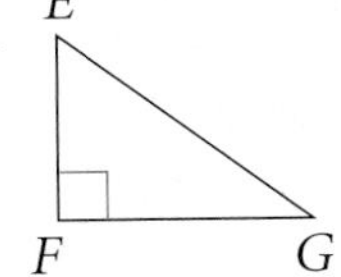

Two-Column Proof of Theorem 4-4

Statements	Reasons
1. $\angle F$ is a right angle.	**1.** Given
2. $m\angle F = 90$	**2.** Def. of right angle
3. $m\angle E + m\angle F + m\angle G = 180$	**3.** Triangle Angle-Sum Thm.
4. $m\angle E + 90 + m\angle G = 180$	**4.** Substitution
5. $m\angle E + m\angle G = 90$	**5.** Subtraction Prop. of Equality
6. $\angle E$ and $\angle G$ are complementary.	**6.** Def. of complementary angles

In a **paragraph proof,** the statements and reasons appear in sentences within a paragraph.

Example

Write a paragraph proof for Theorem 4-5.

Given: $\angle X \cong \angle Q$ and $\angle Y \cong \angle R$
Prove: $\angle Z \cong \angle S$

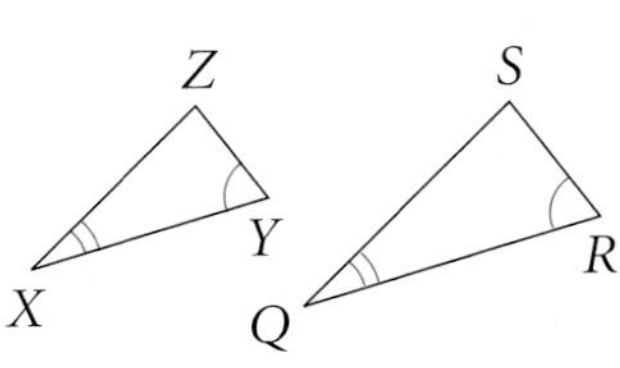

Paragraph Proof
By the Triangle Angle-Sum Theorem, $m\angle X + m\angle Y + m\angle Z = 180$ and $m\angle Q + m\angle R + m\angle S = 180$. By substitution, $m\angle X + m\angle Y + m\angle Z = m\angle Q + m\angle R + m\angle S$. We are given that $\angle X \cong \angle Q$ and $\angle Y \cong \angle R$ (or $m\angle X = m\angle Q$ and $m\angle Y = m\angle R$). Subtracting equal quantities from both sides of the equation leaves $m\angle Z = m\angle S$, so $\angle Z \cong \angle S$.

Math A Test Prep

1 An isosceles triangle has two angles measuring 49° and 82°. What is the measure of the third angle?
(1) 82° (3) 51°
(2) 49° (4) 8°

2 Find the values of x and y.

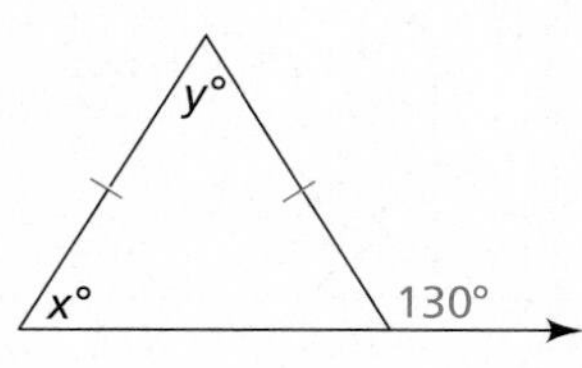

WORK TOGETHER

Work in pairs.

2. Rewrite this two-column proof of Theorem 4-6 as a paragraph proof.

Given: $\angle X$ and $\angle Y$ are right angles.

Prove: $\angle X \cong \angle Y$

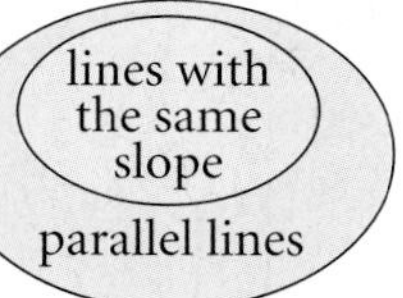

Two-Column Proof

Statements	Reasons
1. $\angle X$ and $\angle Y$ are right angles.	**1.** Given
2. $m\angle X = 90$, $m\angle Y = 90$	**2.** Def. of right angles
3. $m\angle X = m\angle Y$, or $\angle X \cong \angle Y$	**3.** Substitution

3. Rewrite this paragraph proof of Theorem 4-7 as a two-column proof.

Given: $\angle W$ and $\angle V$ are congruent and supplementary.

Prove: $\angle W$ and $\angle V$ are right angles.

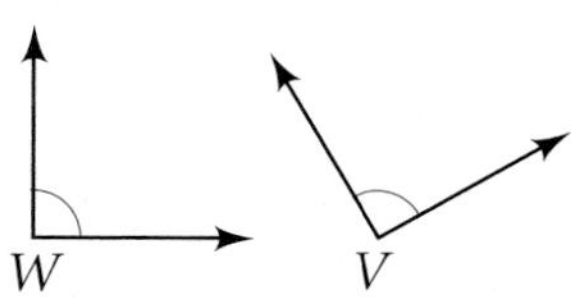

Paragraph Proof

$\angle W$ and $\angle V$ are congruent and supplementary, so $m\angle W = m\angle V$ and $m\angle W + m\angle V = 180$. Substituting $m\angle W$ for $m\angle V$ gives $m\angle W + m\angle W = 180$. Therefore, $m\angle W = 90$. Since $\angle W \cong \angle V$, $m\angle V = 90$, too. Thus both angles are right angles.

Exercises ON YOUR OWN

What can you conclude from each diagram? Justify your answers.

1.

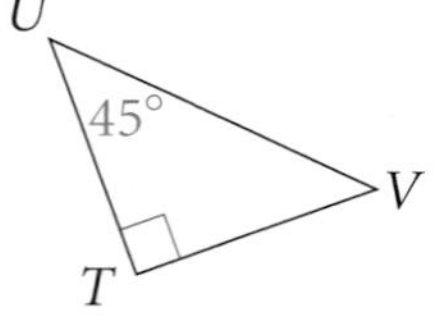

2.

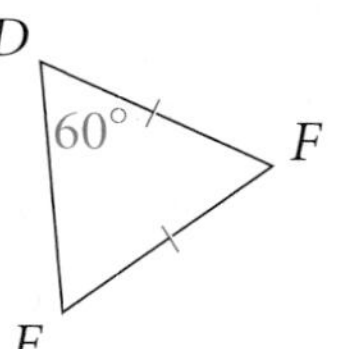

3.

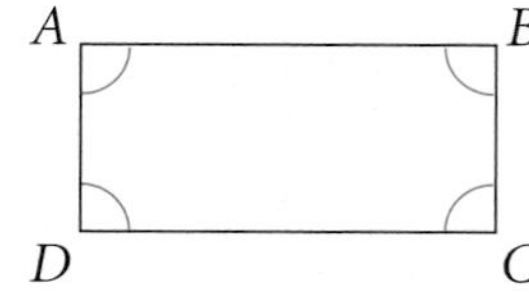

4.

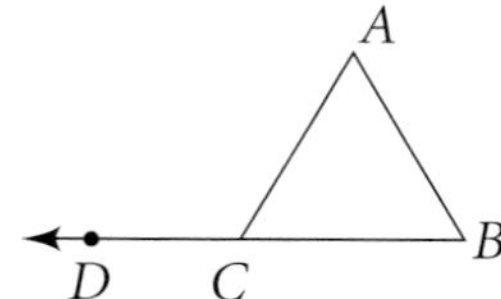

5.

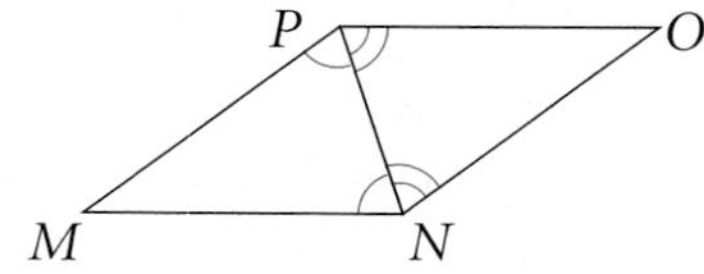

6.

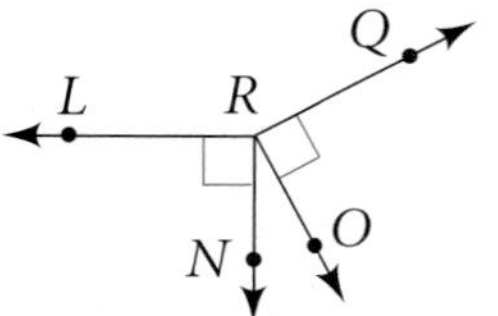

7. *Standardized Test Prep* Find the value of x in the figure.
A. 20 **B.** 30 **C.** 45 **D.** 60 **E.** none of these

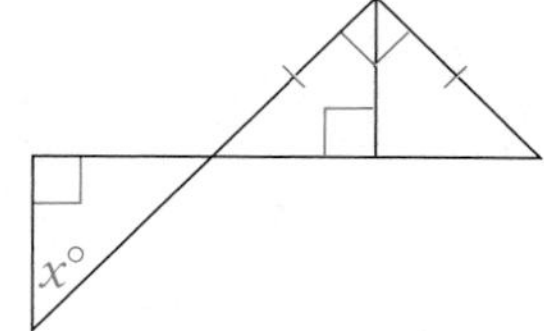

8. *Open-ended* Explain the similarities and differences between paragraph and two-column proofs. Which do you prefer? Why?

9. **Writing** Russell Black Elk found this multiple-choice question in a puzzle book. Solve the puzzle and explain your solution.

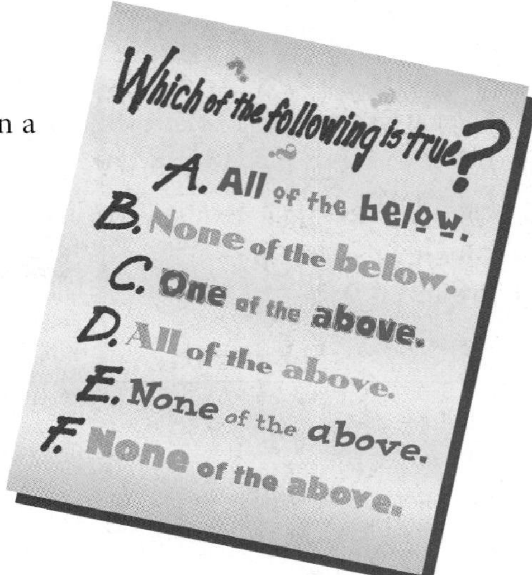

10. Rewrite this paragraph proof as a two-column proof.

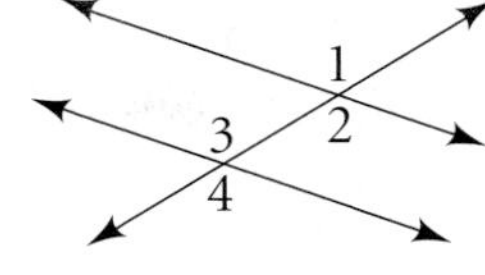

Given: $\angle 1 \cong \angle 4$

Prove: $\angle 2 \cong \angle 3$

$\angle 1$ and $\angle 2$ are vertical angles, as are $\angle 3$ and $\angle 4$. Vertical angles are congruent, so $\angle 1 \cong \angle 2$ and $\angle 3 \cong \angle 4$. We are given that $\angle 1 \cong \angle 4$. By the Transitive Property of Congruence, $\angle 2 \cong \angle 4$ and $\angle 2 \cong \angle 3$.

Refer to the diagrams to complete each statement.

11. a. $\angle OKN \cong$ ___?___
b. $\angle LKO \cong$ ___?___
c. $\angle LOK \cong$ ___?___

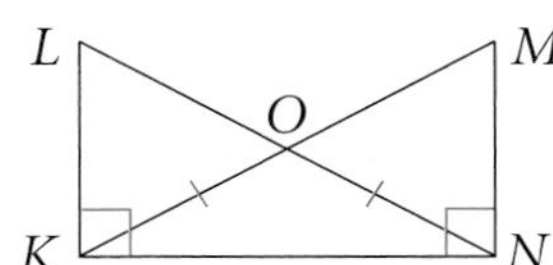

12. a. $m\angle USR =$ ___?___
b. $m\angle RUS =$ ___?___
c. $m\angle SUQ =$ ___?___
d. $m\angle USQ =$ ___?___
e. $m\angle QST =$ ___?___

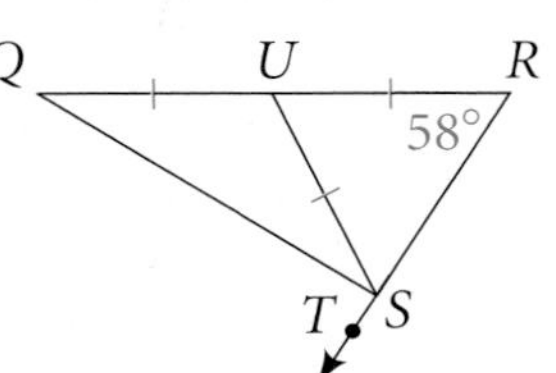

13. **Preparing for Proof** The reasons given in this proof are correct, but they are in the wrong order. List them in the correct order.

Given: $m\angle AOB = m\angle BOC$

Prove: $\overleftrightarrow{OA} \perp \overleftrightarrow{OB}$

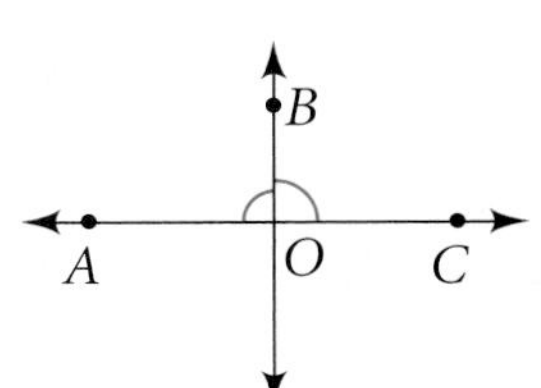

Statements	Reasons
1. $m\angle AOB = m\angle BOC$	a. Division Prop. of Equality
2. $m\angle AOB + m\angle BOC = 180$	b. Substitution
3. $m\angle AOB + m\angle AOB = 180$ or $2(m\angle AOB) = 180$	c. Def. of right angle
4. $m\angle AOB = 90$	d. Given
5. $\angle AOB$ is a right angle.	e. Def. of perpendicular lines
6. $\overleftrightarrow{OA} \perp \overleftrightarrow{OB}$	f. Angle Addition Postulate

14. **Preparing for Proof** Rewrite this proof as a paragraph proof.

Given: $\overline{XZ} \cong \overline{YZ}$ and $\overline{XW} \cong \overline{YW}$

Prove: $m\angle 1 = m\angle 2$

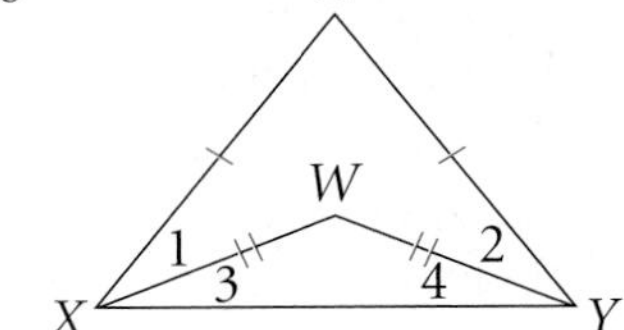

Statements	Reasons
1. $\overline{XZ} \cong \overline{YZ}$	1. Given
2. $\angle ZXY \cong \angle ZYX$ or $m\angle ZXY = m\angle ZYX$	2. Base $\measuredangle$s of an isosceles $\triangle$ are $\cong$.
3. $\overline{XW} \cong \overline{YW}$	3. Given
4. $\angle 3 \cong \angle 4$ or $m\angle 3 = m\angle 4$	4. Base $\measuredangle$s of an isosceles $\triangle$ are $\cong$.
5. $m\angle ZXY = m\angle 1 + m\angle 3$; $m\angle ZYX = m\angle 2 + m\angle 4$	5. Angle Addition Postulate
6. $m\angle 1 + m\angle 3 = m\angle 2 + m\angle 4$	6. Substitution
7. $m\angle 1 = m\angle 2$	7. Subtraction Prop. of Equality

15. **Logical Reasoning** Explain why this statement is true:
If $m\angle 1 + m\angle 2 = 180$ and $m\angle 2 + m\angle 3 = 180$, then $\angle 1 \cong \angle 3$.

16. **Logical Reasoning** Explain why this proof is invalid.

Given: $a = b$

Prove: $1 = 2$

Statements	Reasons
1. $a = b$	1. Given
2. $ab = b^2$	2. Multiplication Prop. of Equality
3. $ab - a^2 = b^2 - a^2$	3. Subtraction Prop. of Equality
4. $a(b - a) = (b + a)(b - a)$	4. Distributive Property
5. $a = b + a$	5. Division Prop. of Equality
6. $a = a + a$	6. Substitution
7. $a = 2a$	7. Distributive Property
8. $1 = 2$	8. Division Prop. of Equality

17. Supply the reasons to complete this proof of the Corollary to the Isosceles Triangle Theorem stated on page 190.

B

A

C

Given: $\triangle ABC$ with $\overline{AB} \cong \overline{BC} \cong \overline{CA}$

Prove: $\angle A \cong \angle B$, $\angle B \cong \angle C$, and $\angle A \cong \angle C$

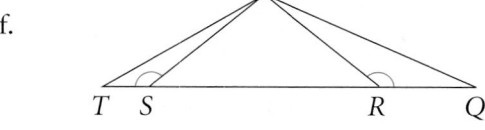

Statements	Reasons
1. $\overline{AB} \cong \overline{BC} \cong \overline{CA}$	a. _?_
2. $\angle A \cong \angle C$	b. _?_
3. $\angle C \cong \angle B$	c. _?_
4. $\angle A \cong \angle B$	d. _?_

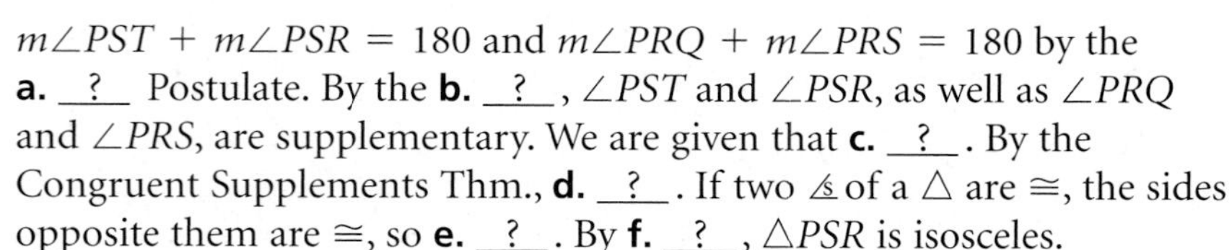

18. Complete this paragraph proof.

Given: $\angle PST \cong \angle PRQ$

Prove: $\triangle PSR$ is isosceles.

$m\angle PST + m\angle PSR = 180$ and $m\angle PRQ + m\angle PRS = 180$ by the **a.** _?_ Postulate. By the **b.** _?_, $\angle PST$ and $\angle PSR$, as well as $\angle PRQ$ and $\angle PRS$, are supplementary. We are given that **c.** _?_. By the Congruent Supplements Thm., **d.** _?_. If two ∠s of a △ are ≅, the sides opposite them are ≅, so **e.** _?_. By **f.** _?_, $\triangle PSR$ is isosceles.

Chapter Project

Find Out by Organizing

A drummer, guitarist, and keyboard player named Amy, Bob, and Carla are in a band. Use the clues to determine which instrument each plays.

Carla and the drummer wear different-colored shirts.
The keyboard player is older than Bob.
Amy, the youngest band member, lives next door to the guitarist.

You can solve this type of logic puzzle by eliminating possibilities. Make a grid. Put an X in a box once you eliminate it as a possibility.

Instrument	Amy	Bob	Carla
Drums			
Guitar			
Keyboard			

Exercises MIXED REVIEW

Statistics **For Exercises 19 and 20, refer to the circle graph.**

Source: *Louis Harris & Associates survey*

19. Find the measure of each central angle.

20. Are the statements *true* or *false?* Explain.
- **a.** Most adults want students who work to save or invest money.
- **b.** All of those surveyed are parents of high-school students.
- **c.** Most adults aren't in favor of allowing students who work to spend their earnings as they please.

21. **a.** **Transformational Geometry** Graph points $A(4, -8)$ and $A'(-6, 1)$. Sketch $\overrightarrow{AA'}$.
- **b.** Describe the translation of A to A' in words and using ordered pair notation.

Getting Ready for Lesson 4-4

22. **a.** **Coordinate Geometry** Find the slope of the line containing $A(-2,\ 3)$ and $B(3, 1)$.
- **b.** Find the coordinates of the midpoint of $\overline{AB}$.

A Point in Time

1500 1600 1700 1800 1900 2000

The Logic of Agatha Christie

Most people are not detectives, but as a young woman, the English writer Agatha Christie (1890–1976) correctly deduced that many people would *like* to be. In **1920** she published her first book, a detective novel entitled *The Mysterious Affair at Styles* in which she introduced the eccentric and ultra-logical Belgian detective Hercule Poirot. In this and in many subsequent novels, Poirot solved mysteries not with guns or car chases but with logical reasoning. He and Agatha Christie's other principal detective character, Jane Marple, always won in the end because they were more patient, more diligent, and, above all, more *clever* than the crooks. Readers made best-sellers of many of Christie's 78 detective novels. Many of her novels, including *Murder on the Orient Express* and *Death on the Nile,* have been adapted into popular films.

To date, her books have sold some 2 billion copies in 44 languages, making Agatha Christie by far the world's top-selling writer of fiction.

Investigating Midsegments

Before Lesson 4-4

Work in pairs or small groups.

Construct

Use geometry software to draw a triangle. Label it $\triangle ABC$. Construct the midpoints of $\overline{AB}$ and $\overline{AC}$, label them D and E, respectively, and then connect them with a *midsegment.*

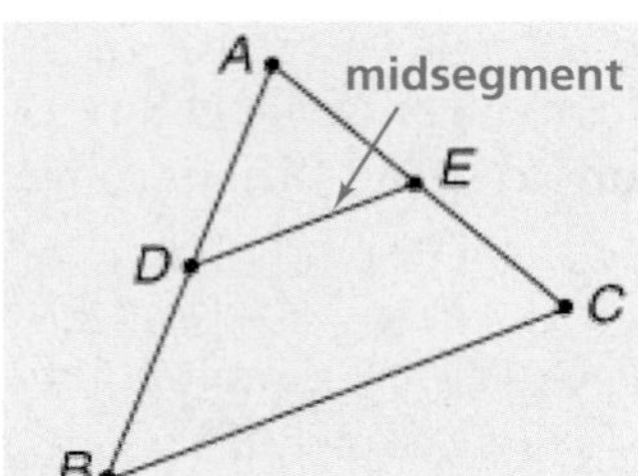

Investigate

- Measure the lengths of $\overline{DE}$ and $\overline{BC}$. Calculate $\frac{DE}{BC}$.
- Measure the slopes of $\overline{DE}$ and $\overline{BC}$.
- Manipulate the triangle and observe the lengths and slopes of the segments.

Conjecture

List all your **conjectures** about a midsegment.

Extend

- Construct the other two midsegments in $\triangle ABC$. Measure the angles of the four triangles determined by the three midsegments. How do they compare to the angles of the original triangle? Make **conjectures.**
- Measure the sides of the four triangles. Make a **conjecture** about the four triangles determined by the midsegments of a triangle. Make a **conjecture** about the relationship between the original triangle and the four triangles.
- Measure the areas of the four triangles formed by the midsegments of a triangle. Measure the area of the original triangle. Make a **conjecture** about the areas. Do the same for perimeter.

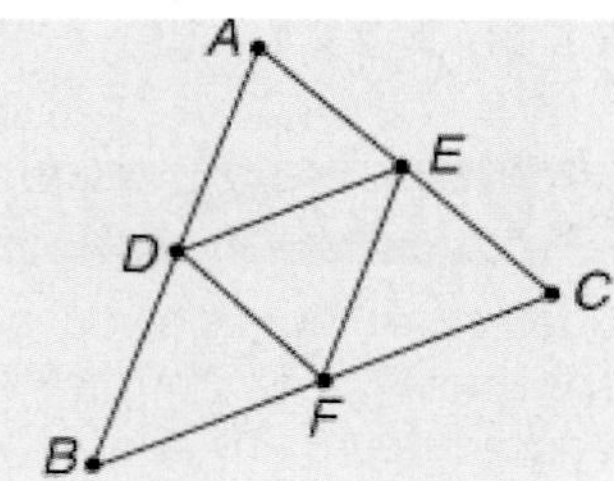

Connections Architecture . . . and more

What You'll Learn

- Using properties of midsegments to solve problems

...And Why

- To help you find lengths and distances indirectly

What You'll Need

- scissors
- straightedge

4-4 Midsegments of Triangles

WORK TOGETHER

Have each member of your group draw and cut out a large scalene triangle. Be sure to include right, acute, and obtuse triangles.

- Label the vertices of your triangle *A*, *B*, and *C*.

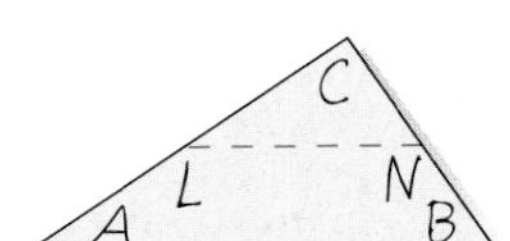

- Fold *A* onto *C* to find the midpoint of $\overline{AC}$. Do the same for $\overline{BC}$. Label the midpoints *L* and *N*, then draw $\overline{LN}$.

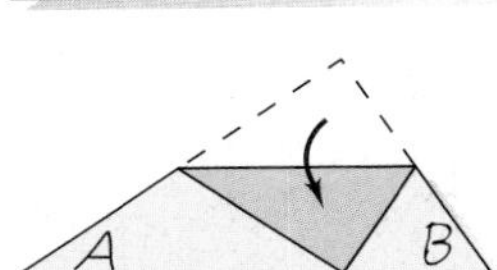

- Fold your triangle on $\overline{LN}$.

- Fold *A* to *C*. Do the same for *B*.

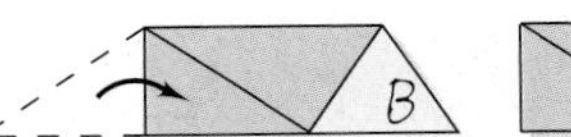

1. a. What type of quadrilateral does the folded triangle appear to form?
   b. What does this tell you about $\overline{LN}$ and $\overline{AB}$?
2. How does *LN* compare to *AB*? Explain.
3. Make a **conjecture** about how the segment joining the midpoints of two sides of a triangle is related to the third side of the triangle.

THINK AND DISCUSS

The segment you constructed in the Work Together is a midsegment. A **midsegment** of a triangle is a segment connecting the midpoints of two of its sides.

Theorem 4–8 Triangle Midsegment Theorem

If a segment joins the midpoints of two sides of a triangle, then the segment is parallel to the third side and half its length.

You can prove the Triangle Midsegment Theorem by using coordinate geometry and algebra. This style of proof is called a *coordinate proof*. You begin the proof by placing a triangle in a convenient spot on the coordinate plane. You then choose variables for the coordinates of the vertices.

Quick Review

Midpoint Formula:

$\left(\frac{x_1 + x_2}{2}, \frac{y_1 + y_2}{2}\right)$

Distance Formula:

$\sqrt{(x_2 - x_1)^2 + (y_2 - y_1)^2}$

Coordinate Proof of Theorem 4-8

Given: R is the midpoint of $\overline{OP}$.
S is the midpoint of $\overline{QP}$.

Prove: $\overline{RS} \parallel \overline{OQ}$ and $RS = \frac{1}{2}OQ$

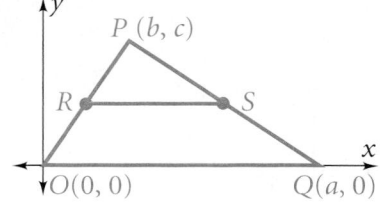

- Use the Midpoint Formula to find the coordinates of R and S.

R: $\left(\frac{0 + b}{2}, \frac{0 + c}{2}\right) = \left(\frac{b}{2}, \frac{c}{2}\right)$ $\quad$ S: $\left(\frac{a + b}{2}, \frac{0 + c}{2}\right) = \left(\frac{a + b}{2}, \frac{c}{2}\right)$

- To prove that $\overline{RS}$ and $\overline{OQ}$ are parallel, show that their slopes are equal. Because the y-coordinates of R and S are the same, the slope of $\overline{RS}$ is zero. The same is true for $\overline{OQ}$. Therefore, $\overline{RS} \parallel \overline{OQ}$.

- Use the Distance Formula to find RS and OQ.

$$RS = \sqrt{\left(\frac{a + b}{2} - \frac{b}{2}\right)^2 + \left(\frac{c}{2} - \frac{c}{2}\right)^2}$$

$$= \sqrt{\left(\frac{a}{2} + \frac{b}{2} - \frac{b}{2}\right)^2 + 0^2} = \sqrt{\left(\frac{a}{2}\right)^2} = \frac{a}{2} = \frac{1}{2}a$$

$$OQ = \sqrt{(a - 0)^2 + (0 - 0)^2}$$

$$= \sqrt{a^2 + 0^2} = a$$

Therefore, $RS = \frac{1}{2}OQ$.

4. Select numerical values for the coordinates of P and Q.
   a. Use the Midpoint Formula to find the coordinates of R and S.
   b. **Verify** that $RS = \frac{1}{2}OQ$ for the values you chose.
   c. **Verify** that $\overline{RS} \parallel \overline{OQ}$ for the values you chose.

Example 1

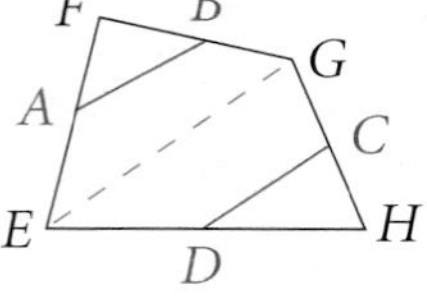

In quadrilateral $EFGH$, the points A, B, C, and D are midpoints and $EG = 18$ cm. Find AB and CD.

Consider $\triangle EFG$. By the Triangle Midsegment Theorem, $AB = \frac{1}{2}EG$. Using the same reasoning for $\triangle EHG$, you get $CD = \frac{1}{2}EG$. Because $EG = 18$ cm, $\frac{1}{2}EG = 9$ cm . Therefore, $AB = CD = 9$ cm.

5. **Critical Thinking** Is $\overline{AB} \parallel \overline{CD}$? **Justify** your answer.
6. **Try This** $FH = 25$ cm. Find BC and AD.
7. **Critical Thinking** What type of quadrilateral is $ABCD$? Explain.

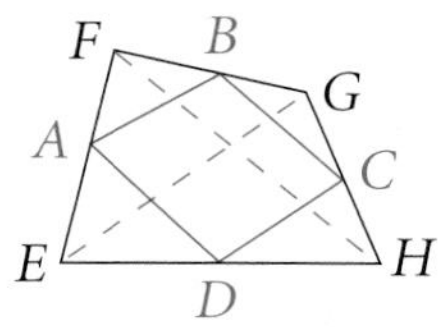

You can use the Triangle Midsegment Theorem to find lengths of segments that might otherwise be difficult to measure.

Example 2 Relating to the Real World 

Indirect Measurement DeAndre swims the length of a lake and wants to know the distance he swam. Here is what he does to find out.

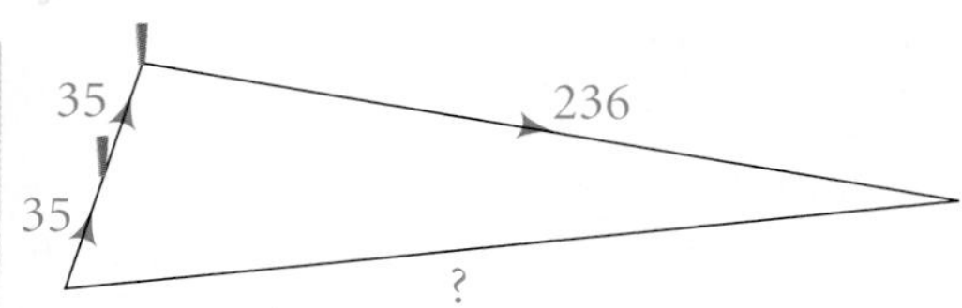

Step 1: From the edge of the lake, he paces 35 strides and sets a stake.

Step 2: He paces 35 more strides in the same direction and sets another stake.

Step 3: He paces to the other end of the lake, counting 236 strides.

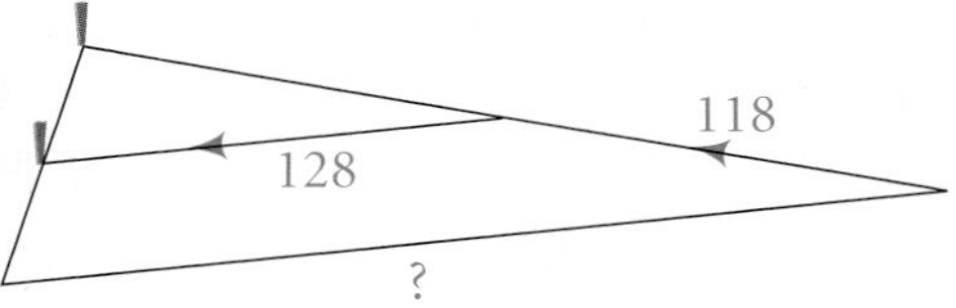

Step 4: He paces half the distance to the second stake (118 strides).

Step 5: He paces to the first stake, counting 128 strides.

If DeAndre's stride averages 3 ft, about how far did he swim?

2(128 strides) = 256 strides	Triangle Midsegment Theorem
256 ~~strides~~ $\times \frac{3 \text{ ft}}{1 \text{ stride}}$ = 768 ft	Convert strides to feet.

DeAndre swam approximately 768 ft.

Exercises ON YOUR OWN

Mental Math **Find the value of *x*.**

1. 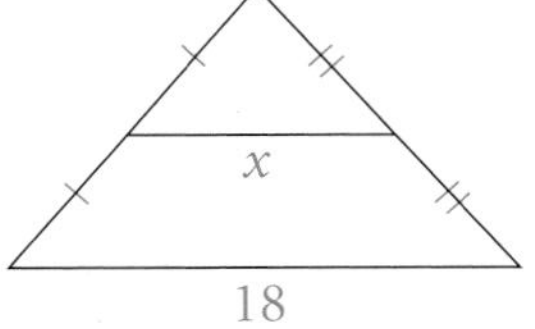

2. 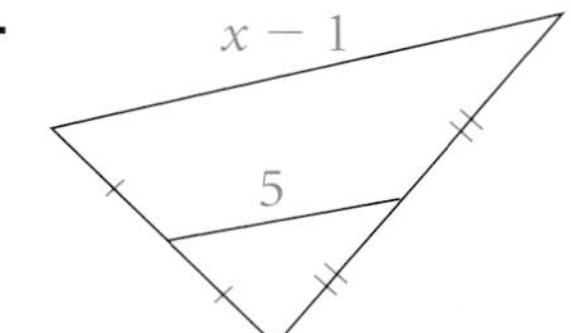

3. 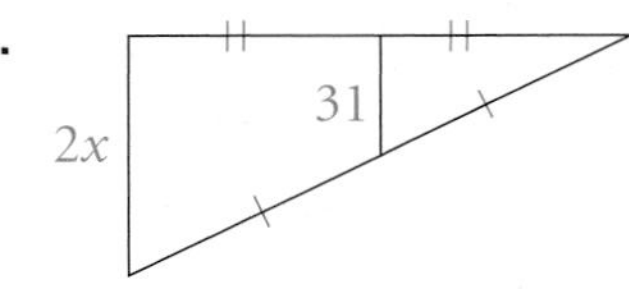

4. $\overline{IJ}$ is a midsegment of $\triangle FGH$.
   a. $IJ = 7$. Find FG.
   b. $FH = 13$ and $GH = 10$. Find the perimeter of $\triangle HIJ$.

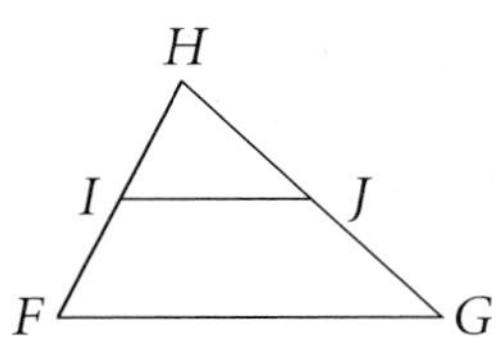

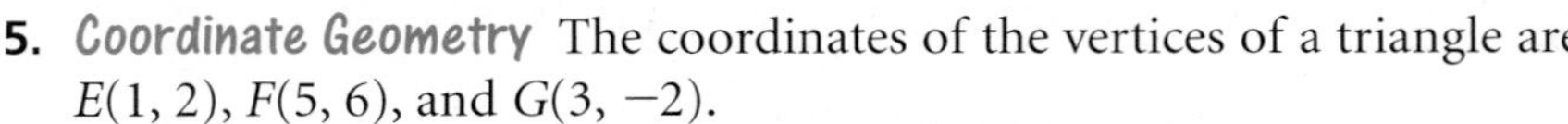

5. **Coordinate Geometry** The coordinates of the vertices of a triangle are $E(1, 2)$, $F(5, 6)$, and $G(3, -2)$.
   a. Find the coordinates of H, the midpoint of $\overline{EG}$, and J, the midpoint of $\overline{FG}$.
   b. **Verify** that $\overline{HJ} \parallel \overline{EF}$.
   c. **Verify** that $HJ = \frac{1}{2}EF$.

6. **Architecture** The triangular face of the Rock and Roll Hall of Fame in Cleveland, Ohio, is isosceles. The length of the base is 229 ft 6 in. The face consists of smaller triangles determined by the midsegments. What is the length of the base of the highlighted triangle?

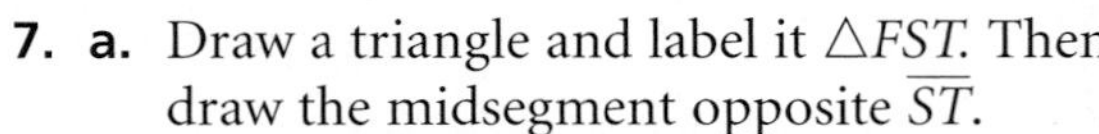

7. a. Draw a triangle and label it $\triangle FST$. Then draw the midsegment opposite $\overline{ST}$.
   b. **Transformational Geometry** Describe a transformation of $\triangle FST$ that produces the same diagram as in part (a).
   c. What does your answer to part (b) tell you about the triangles formed in part (a)?

8. **Open-ended** Draw a triangle and its three midsegments. Compare the four triangles determined by the midsegments. Repeat the experiment with a different triangle. Make a **conjecture** about your observations.

Choose Use mental math, pencil and paper, or a calculator to find the values of the variables.

9.

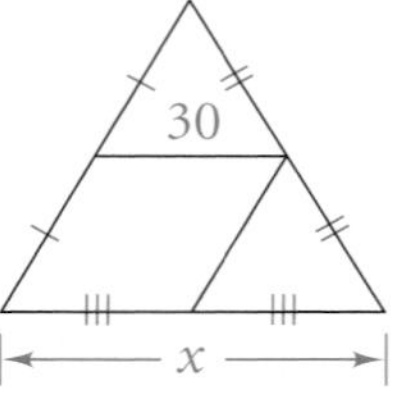

10.

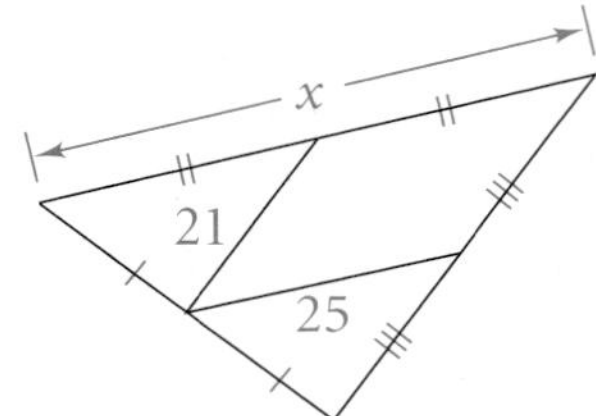

11.

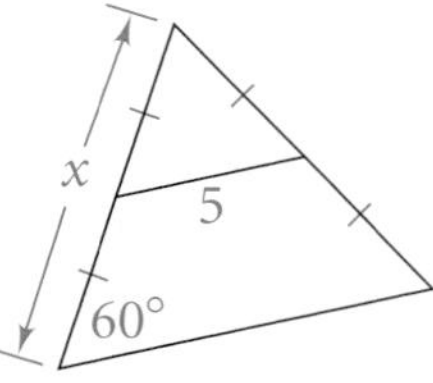

12.

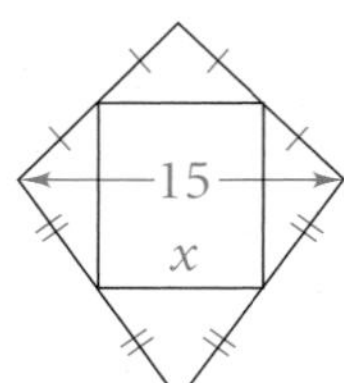

13.

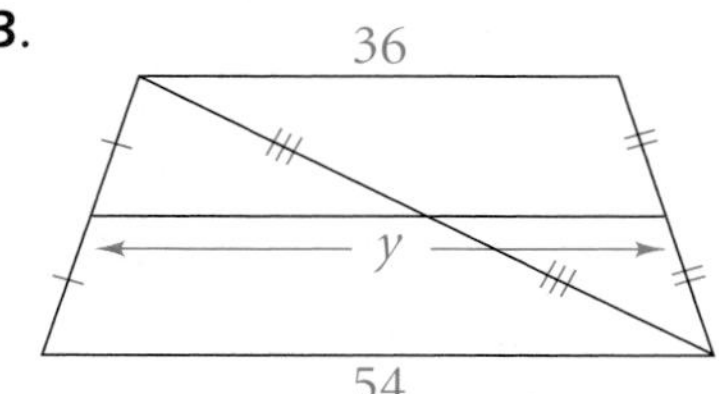

14.

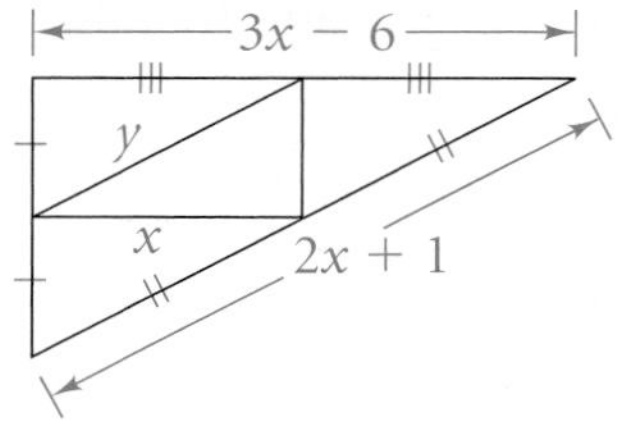

15. **Creative Arts** Marita is designing a kite for a competition. She plans to use a decorative ribbon to connect the midpoints of the sides of the kite. The diagonals of the kite measure 64 cm and 90 cm. Find the amount of ribbon she will need.

16. **Preparing for Proof** This is a proof that the midsegments of an equilateral triangle form an equilateral triangle. The reasons given in the proof are correct, but they are in the wrong order. List them in the correct order.

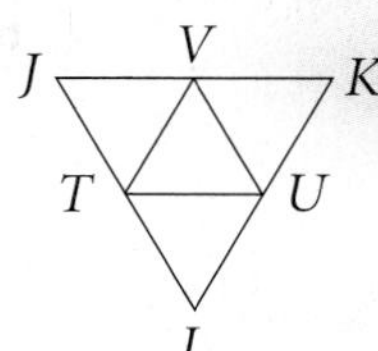

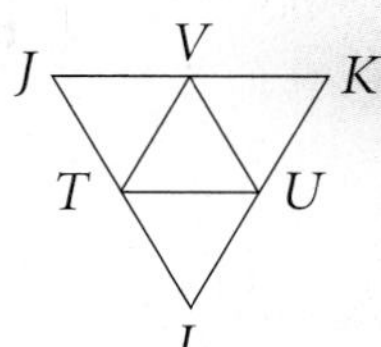

Given: Equilateral $\triangle JKL$ with midpoints T, U, and V

Prove: $\triangle TUV$ is equilateral.

Statements	Reasons
1. $\triangle JKL$ is equilateral.	**a.** Def. of equilateral triangle
2. $JK = KL = JL$	**b.** Multiplication Prop. of Equality
3. $\frac{1}{2}JK = \frac{1}{2}KL = \frac{1}{2}JL$	**c.** Substitution
4. T, U, and V are midpoints.	**d.** Def. of equilateral triangle
5. $TU = \frac{1}{2}JK$; $UV = \frac{1}{2}JL$; $TV = \frac{1}{2}KL$	**e.** Given
6. $TU = UV = TV$	**f.** Triangle Midsegment Thm.
7. $\triangle TUV$ is equilateral.	**g.** Given

17. **Patterns** The vertices of the smallest square are the midpoints of the sides of the larger square. The vertices of that square are the midpoints of the largest square. Find the length of the sides of the largest square. Write a sentence or two explaining the pattern.

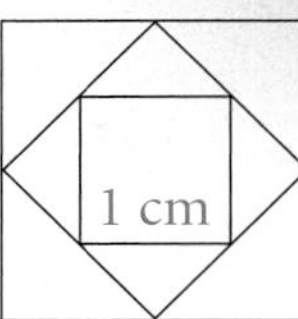

Chapter Project

Find Out by Analyzing

Try your powers of logic on this new version of an old puzzle.

Alan, Ben, and Cal are seated as shown with their eyes closed. Three hats are placed on their heads from a box they know contains 3 red and 2 blue hats. They open their eyes and look forward.

Alan says, "I cannot deduce what color hat I'm wearing."

Hearing that, Ben says, "I cannot deduce what color I'm wearing, either."

Cal then says, "I know what color I'm wearing!"

How does Cal know what color his hat is? (*Hint*: Use one of the strategies you used to solve the previous two puzzles on pages 749 and 760.)

Exercises MIXED REVIEW

Coordinate Geometry **Find the distance between the given points.**

18. $B(0, 9)$ and $E(4, 9)$

19. $V(8, -7)$ and $W(4, -4)$

20. $A(3, 2)$ and $N(-1, 0)$

21. **Transformational Geometry** State the coordinates of the point (6, 2) after a rotation of 90° about the origin.

22. **Standardized Test Prep** A circle and a square lie in a plane. What is the maximum number of points of intersection of the figures?

A. one **B.** two **C.** four **D.** six **E.** eight

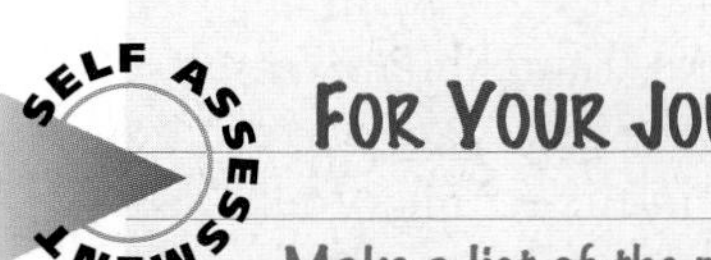

FOR YOUR JOURNAL

Make a list of the properties of triangles you've learned so far in this chapter. Include a diagram to illustrate each property. Add to your list as you continue with the chapter.

Getting Ready for Lesson 4-5

Write the negation of each statement.

23. Lines m and n intersect.

24. The integer x is odd.

25. $\triangle ABC$ is scalene.

26. $\overline{AB} \parallel \overline{KM}$

27. A given angle is neither acute, right, nor obtuse. What is its measure? Explain how you know.

Exercises CHECKPOINT

For Exercises 1 and 2: (a) Write the converse of each conditional. (b) Determine the truth value of the conditional and its converse. (c) If both statements are true, write a biconditional.

1. If a triangle is equilateral, then the measure of at least one of its angles is 60.

2. If a polygon is regular, then its angles are congruent.

3. **Writing** Explain the difference between a converse and a contrapositive.

4. **Standardized Test Prep** $\triangle ABC$ is isosceles, and $AC = 3x$, $AB = 2x + 30$, and $BC = 3x + 40$. Which of the following is true?

A. $\angle A \cong \angle B$ **B.** $\angle A \cong \angle C$ **C.** $\angle B \cong \angle C$

D. $\angle A \cong \angle B \cong \angle C$ **E.** none of the above

5. The measures of the angles of a triangle are $6x$, $7x - 9$, and $8x$.

a. **Algebra** Find the value of x.

b. What are the measures of the angles?

c. What type of triangle is this? Explain.

6. Determine whether this statement is true or false: If a triangle is obtuse, then it is not isosceles. **Justify** your answer.

7. M, N, O, and P are midpoints of the sides of trapezoid $ABCD$. $AC = BD = 18$. Find the perimeter of $MNOP$.

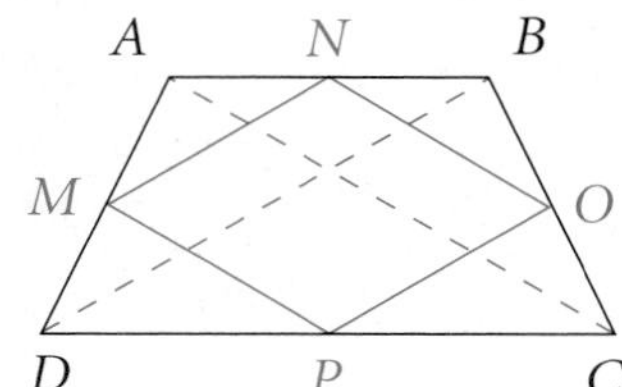

What You'll Learn

- Writing convincing arguments by using indirect reasoning

...And Why

To help you in real-life situations in which proving something directly isn't possible

4-5 Using Indirect Reasoning

THINK AND DISCUSS

Suppose that your brother tells you, "Susan called a few minutes ago." You have two friends named Susan, and you know that one of them is at play rehearsal. You deduce that the other Susan must be the caller.

This type of reasoning is called indirect reasoning. In **indirect reasoning,** all possibilities are considered and then all but one are proved false. The remaining possibility must be true. Mathematical proofs involving indirect reasoning usually follow the pattern in the following example.

Example 1 Relating to the Real World

Consumer Issues Use indirect reasoning to prove this statement: If Jaleen spends more than $50 to buy two items at a bicycle shop, then at least one of the items costs more than $25.

Given: The cost of two items is more than $50.
Prove: At least one of the items costs more than $25.

- Begin by assuming that the opposite of what you want to prove is true. That is, assume that neither item costs more than $25.
- This means that both items cost $25 or less. This, in turn, means that the two items together cost $50 or less. This contradicts the given information that the amount spent is more than $50. So, the assumption that neither item costs more than $25 must be incorrect.
- Therefore, at least one of the items costs more than $25. ■

The three parts of the proof in Example 1 are summarized below.

Writing an Indirect Proof

Step 1: Assume that the opposite of what you want to prove is true.

Step 2: Use logical reasoning to reach a contradiction of an earlier statement, such as the given information or a theorem. Then state that the assumption you made was false.

Step 3: State that what you wanted to prove must be true.

1. Write the first step of an indirect proof of each statement.
   a. Quadrilateral *TRWX* does not have four acute angles.
   b. An integer n is divisible by 5.
   c. The shoes cost no more than \$20.

2. Identify the pair of statements that form a contradiction.
   a. **I.** $\triangle ABC$ is acute.
   II. $\triangle ABC$ is scalene.
   III. $\triangle ABC$ is equiangular.
   b. **I.** $m\angle 1 + m\angle 2 = 180$
   II. $m\angle 1 - m\angle 2 = m\angle 2$
   III. $m\angle 1 \leq m\angle 2$
   c. **I.** Both items that Val bought cost more than \$10.
   II. Val spent \$34 for the two items.
   III. Neither of the two items that Val bought cost more than \$15.

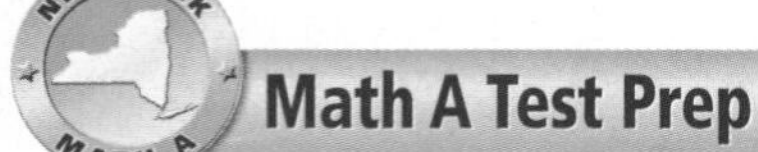

Math A Test Prep

1 What is the length of the trapezoid's midsegment?

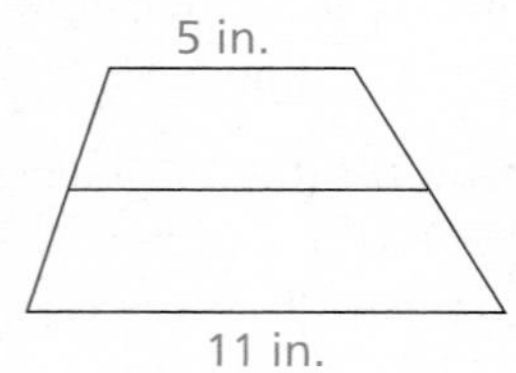

(1) 8 in. (3) 7 in.
(2) $5\frac{1}{2}$ in. (4) 6 in.

2 Vertex *K* of $\triangle KLM$ is at the origin. The midpoints of $\overline{KL}$ and $\overline{LM}$ are at (2, 3) and (8, 3), respectively. Use formulas to find the locations of *L* and *M*.

Example 2

Write an indirect proof.

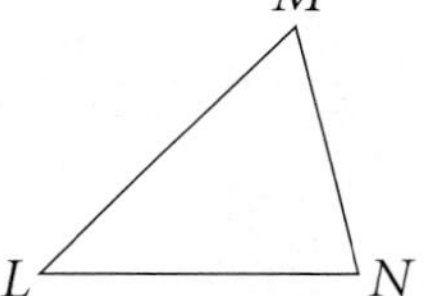

Given: $\triangle LMN$
Prove: $\triangle LMN$ has at most one right angle.

Indirect Proof

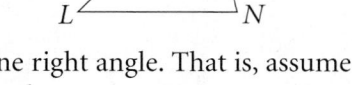

Step 1: Assume $\triangle LMN$ has more than one right angle. That is, assume that $\angle L$ and $\angle M$ are both right angles.

Step 2: If $\angle L$ and $\angle M$ are both right angles, then $m\angle L = m\angle M = 90$. According to the Triangle Angle-Sum Theorem, $m\angle L + m\angle M + m\angle N = 180$. Substitution gives $90 + 90 + m\angle N = 180$. Solving leaves $m\angle N = 0$. This means that there is no $\triangle LMN$, which contradicts the given statement. So the assumption that $\angle L$ and $\angle M$ are both right angles must be false.

Step 3: Therefore, $\triangle LMN$ has at most one right angle.

3. Try This Use indirect reasoning to show that a parallelogram with three right angles is a rectangle.

WORK TOGETHER

Play *What's My Number* in groups of three or four. Here's how to play.

- One member of the group chooses a number from 1 to 20.
- The remaining members ask yes-or-no questions about the number until they know what the number is.
- The person answering the questions records the number of questions required to guess the number.

Play the game at least three times, rotating roles with each game.

4. **Critical Thinking** Describe the best strategy for playing *What's My Number* to a friend who is just learning to play it.

Exercises ON YOUR OWN

Write the first step of an indirect proof of each statement.

1. It is raining outside.
2. $\angle J$ is not a right angle.
3. $\triangle PEN$ is isosceles.
4. At least one angle is obtuse.
5. $\overline{XY} \cong \overline{AB}$
6. $m\angle 2 > 90$

Identify the pair of statements that forms a contradiction.

7. I. $\triangle PQR$ is equilateral.
   II. $\triangle PQR$ is a right triangle.
   III. $\triangle PQR$ is isosceles.

8. I. $ABCD$ is a parallelogram.
   II. $ABCD$ is a trapezoid.
   III. $ABCD$ has two acute angles.

9. I. ℓ and m are skew.
   II. ℓ and m do not intersect.
   III. ℓ is parallel to m.

10. I. $\overline{FG} \parallel \overline{KL}$
    II. $\overline{FG} \perp \overline{KL}$
    III. $\overline{FG} \cong \overline{KL}$

What conclusion follows from each pair of statements?

11. There are three types of drawbridges: bascule, lift, and swing. This drawbridge does not swing or lift.

12. If this were the day of the party, our friends would be home. No one is home.

13. Every air traffic controller in the world speaks English on the job. Sumiko does not speak English.

14. If two nonvertical lines are perpendicular, then the product of their slopes is -1. The product of the slopes of nonvertical lines ℓ and n is not -1.

15. Given $\triangle ABC$ with $BC > AC$, use indirect reasoning to show that $\angle A \not\cong \angle B$.

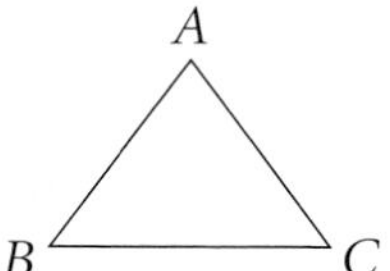

16. **Preparing for Proof** Complete this indirect proof that every quadrilateral contains at least one right or acute angle.

Assume that a quadrilateral does not contain **a.** __?__. That is, assume that the measure of each of the angles is greater than **b.** __?__. The sum of the measures of the four angles, then, is greater than **c.** __?__. By the **d.** __?__ Theorem, however, the sum of the measures of the interior angles of a quadrilateral is **e.** __?__. This contradicts **f.** __?__, so the assumption that **g.** __?__ is false. Therefore, **h.** __?__.

17. **Standardized Test Prep** Which of the following represents the measure of an interior angle of a regular polygon?

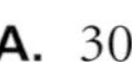

A. 30 **B.** 50 **C.** 70 **D.** 100 **E.** 140

PROBLEM SOLVING HINT

Use indirect reasoning. Eliminate all incorrect answer choices. The remaining choice must be correct.

18. Earlene lives near a noisy construction site at which work ends promptly at 5:00 each weekday. Earlene thinks, "Today is Tuesday. If it were before 5:00, I would hear construction noise, but I don't hear any. So it must be later than 5:00."
    - **a.** What does Earlene prove?
    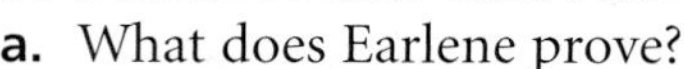
    - **b.** What assumption does she make?
    - **c.** What fact contradicts the assumption?

For Exercises 19–25, write a convincing argument that uses indirect reasoning.

19. Fresh skid marks appear behind a green car at the scene of an accident. Show that the driver of the green car applied the brakes.

20. Ice is forming on the sidewalk in front of Toni's house. Show that the temperature outside must be 32°F or less.

21. The sum of the measures of the interior angles of a polygon is 900. Show that the polygon is not a hexagon.

22. Show that a quadrilateral can have at most three acute angles.

23. An obtuse triangle cannot contain a right angle.

Given: $\triangle PQR$ with obtuse $\angle Q$

Prove: $m\angle P \neq 90$

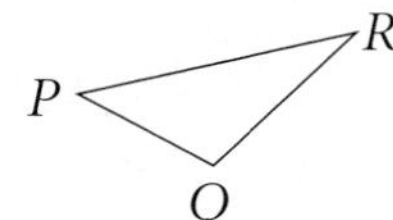

24. If a triangle is isosceles, then a base angle is not a right angle.

Given: $\overline{BC} \cong \overline{AC}$

Prove: $\angle B$ is not a right angle.

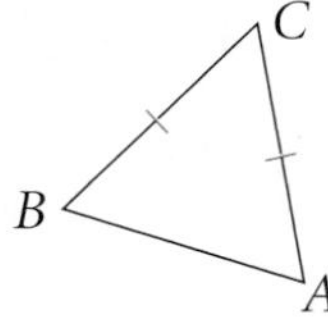

25. Mr. Pitt is a suspect in a robbery. Here are the facts:
    - A robbery occurred in Charlotte, North Carolina, at 1:00 A.M. on April 9.
    - A hotel clerk in Maine saw Mr. Pitt at 12:05 A.M. on April 9.
    - Mr. Pitt has an identical twin brother who was in Chicago during the time the robbery took place.
    - Mr. Pitt has receipts for purchases made in Maine on April 8.

    Show that Mr. Pitt was not the robber.

26. **Open-ended** Describe a real-life situation in which you used an indirect argument to convince someone of your point of view. Outline your argument.

27. **Mysteries** In Arthur Conan Doyle's story "The Sign of the Four," Sherlock Holmes talks to his sidekick Watson about how a culprit enters a room that has only four entrances: a door, a window, a chimney, and a hole in the roof.

> "You will not apply my precept," he said, shaking his head. "How often have I said to you that when you have eliminated the impossible, whatever remains, *however improbable*, must be the truth? We know that he did not come through the door, the window, or the chimney. We also know that he could not have been concealed in the room, as there is no concealment possible. Whence, then, did he come?"

How did the culprit enter the room? Explain.

Exercises MIXED REVIEW

Geometry in 3 Dimensions **Refer to the diagram for Exercises 28–31.**

28. Name two parallel planes.
29. Name two intersecting planes.
30. Name two skew lines.
31. Name four coplanar points.

32. a. Use the words *square, rhombus,* and *parallelogram* to write six conditionals in the form "If a figure is a __?__, then it is a __?__."
    b. **Probability** What is the probability that a conditional chosen at random from among the six is true?
    c. **Probability** What is the probability that the converse of a randomly chosen statement from part (a) is true?
    d. **Probability** What is the probability that the contrapositive of a randomly chosen statement from part (a) is true?

33. **Transformational Geometry** An isometry maps $LEFT \longrightarrow BURN$. Which statement is *not* necessarily true?
    A. $EF = UR$ B. $\angle TLE \cong \angle BUR$ C. $\angle F \cong \angle R$
    D. $LF = BR$ E. $FT = RN$

Getting Ready for Lesson 4-6

Coordinate Geometry **Graph the triangles whose vertices are given. List the sides in order from shortest to longest.**

34. $A(5, 0), B(0, 8), C(0, 0)$
35. $P(2, 4), Q(-5, 1), R(0, 0)$
36. $G(3, 0), H(4, 3), J(8, 0)$

Math ToolboX

Algebra Review

Solving Inequalities

Before Lesson 4-6

The solutions of an inequality are all the numbers that make the inequality true. Below is a review of the Properties of Inequality. To solve inequalities you will use the Addition and Multiplication Properties of Inequality.

Properties of Inequality

For all real numbers a, b, c, and d:

Addition If $a > b$ and $c \geq d$, then $a + c > b + d$.

Multiplication If $a > b$ and $c > 0$, then $ac > bc$.
If $a > b$ and $c < 0$, then $ac < bc$.

Transitive If $a > b$ and $b > c$, then $a > c$.

Comparison If $a = b + c$ and $c > 0$, then $a > b$.

Example

Solve $-6x + 7 > 25$.

$-6x + 7 - 7 > 25 - 7$ ← Add −7 to each side (or subtract 7 from each side).

$\frac{-6x}{-6} < \frac{18}{-6}$ ← Multiply each side by $-\frac{1}{6}$ (or divide each side by −6). Remember to reverse the order of the inequality.

$x < -3$ ← Simplify.

Solve each inequality.

1. $7x - 13 \leq -20$
2. $3z + 8 > 16$
3. $-2x + 5 < 16$
4. $8y + 2 \geq -14$
5. $5a + 1 \leq 91$
6. $-x - 2 > 17$
7. $-4z - 10 < -12$
8. $9x - 8 \geq 82$
9. $6n + 3 \leq -18$
10. $c + 13 > 34$
11. $3x - 5x + 2 < 12$
12. $x - 19 < -78$
13. $-n - 27 \leq 92$
14. $-9t + 47 < 101$
15. $8x - 4 + x > -76$
16. $2(y - 5) > -24$
17. $8b + 3 \geq 67$
18. $-3(4x - 1) \geq 15$
19. $r - 9 \leq -67$
20. $\frac{1}{2}(4x - 7) \geq 19$
21. $5x - 3x + 2x < -20$
22. $9x - 10x + 4 < 12$
23. $-3x - 7x \leq 97$
24. $8y - 33 > -1$
25. $4a + 17 \geq 13$
26. $-4(5z + 2) > 20$
27. $x + 78 \geq -284$

What You'll Learn

- Using inequalities involving triangle side lengths and angle measures to solve problems

...And Why

To use triangle inequalities in solving real-world problems when only some measures of a triangle are known

What You'll Need

scissors, straws, ruler, protractor

4-6 Triangle Inequalities

WORK TOGETHER

Work in groups of three. Have each member of your group cut straws into 2-, 3-, 4-, 5-, and 6-in. segments.

- Have each member pick three segments at random and test whether they form a triangle. Continue picking segments until you find three sets of segments that form a triangle and three that do not form a triangle. Record your results in a table like the one shown.

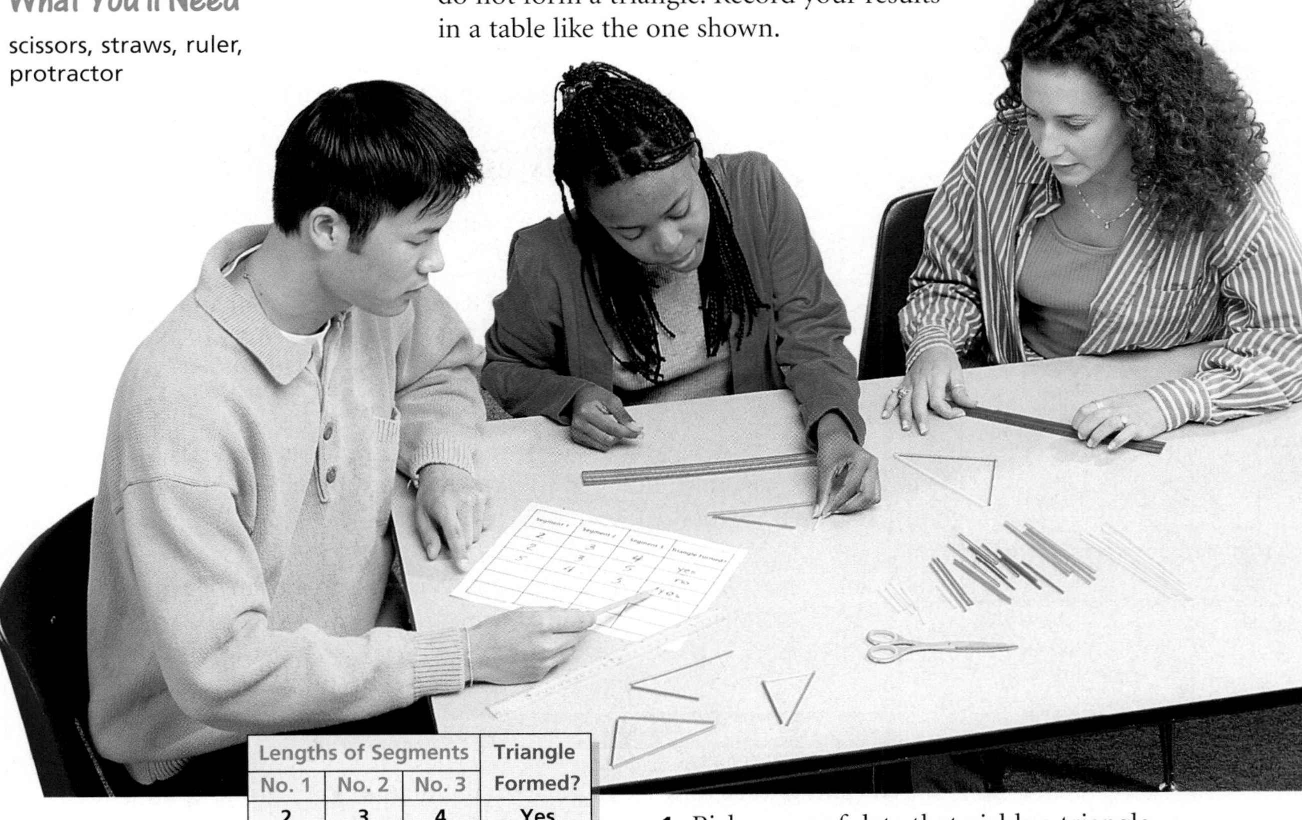

Lengths of Segments			Triangle
No. 1	No. 2	No. 3	Formed?
2	3	4	Yes
2	3	5	No
5	4	3	Yes

1. Pick a row of data that yields a triangle. Compare each quantity.
   a. Segment 1 + Segment 2 __?__ Segment 3
   b. Segment 1 + Segment 3 __?__ Segment 2
   c. Segment 2 + Segment 3 __?__ Segment 1

2. Pick a row of data that does *not* yield a triangle. Use it to complete parts (a)–(c) of Question 1.

3. **Patterns** Compare the results of Questions 1 and 2 within your group. Look for a pattern. Write a **conjecture** about the sum of the lengths of two sides of a triangle compared to the length of the third side.

THINK AND DISCUSS

Triangle Inequality Theorem

Your observations from the Work Together suggest the following theorem.

Theorem 4-9
Triangle Inequality Theorem

The sum of the lengths of any two sides of a triangle is greater than the length of the third side.

$XY + YZ > XZ$
$YZ + XZ > XY$
$XZ + XY > YZ$

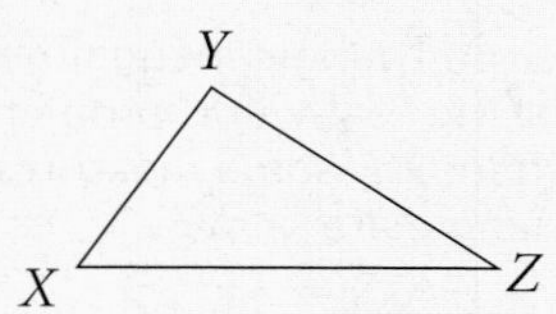

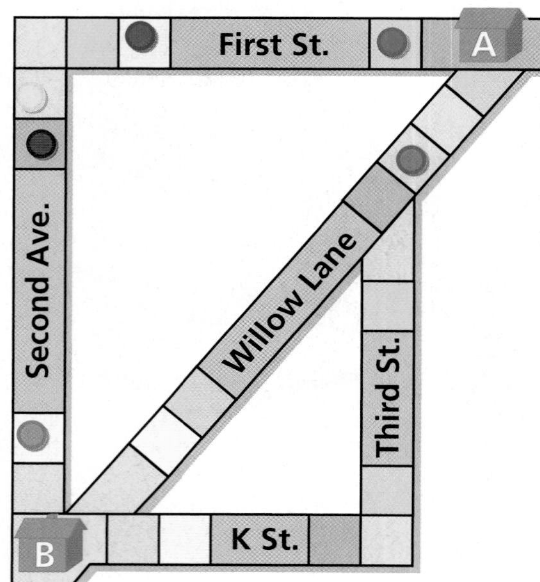

4. Use the Triangle Inequality Theorem to explain which route is the shortest distance from House *A* to House *B*.

Example 1

Is it possible for a triangle to have sides with the given lengths? Explain.

a. 3 cm, 7 cm, and 8 cm
$3 + 7 > 8$
$8 + 7 > 3$
$3 + 8 > 7$ **Yes**

b. 3 ft, 6 ft, and 10 ft
$3 + 6 \not> 10$ **No**

The sum of any two numbers in (a) is greater than the third number. In part (b), the sum of 3 and 6 is less than 10.

5. **Try This** Is it possible to form a triangle with side lengths 4 cm, 6 cm, and 10 cm? Explain.

WORK TOGETHER

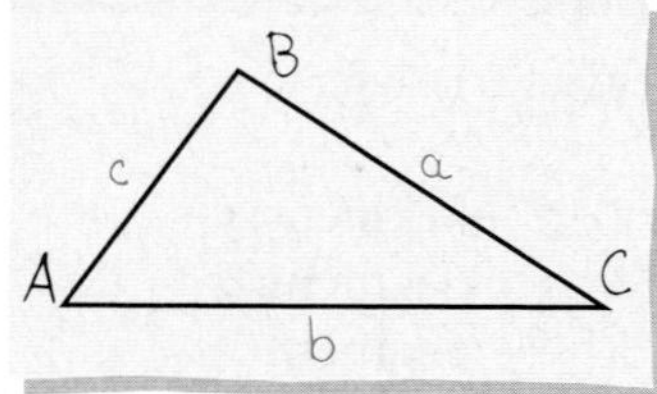

Work in groups of three. Have each member of your group draw a large scalene triangle. Label each triangle as shown. Include right, obtuse, and acute triangles.

- Measure the sides and angles of each triangle.

6. **a.** Use the letters *A*, *B*, and *C* to complete:
$m\angle\blacksquare < m\angle\blacksquare < m\angle\blacksquare$.
b. Use the letters *a*, *b*, and *c* to complete:
$\blacksquare < \blacksquare < \blacksquare$.

7. Compare your answer to Question 6 with others in your group. Make a **conjecture** about the longest side and the largest angle in a triangle.

THINK AND DISCUSS

Inequalities Relating Sides and Angles

Your observations in the Work Together lead to Theorems 4-10 and 4-11.

Theorem 4-10

If two sides of a triangle are not congruent, then the larger angle lies opposite the longer side.

If $XZ > XY$, then $m\angle Y > m\angle Z$.

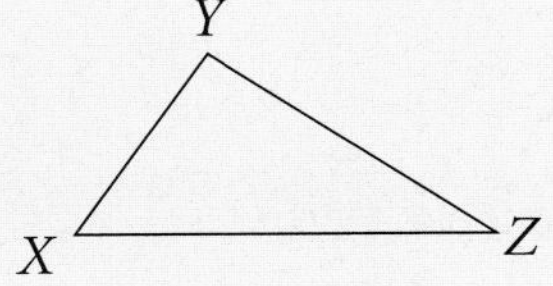

You will justify Theorem 4-10 in Exercise 35.

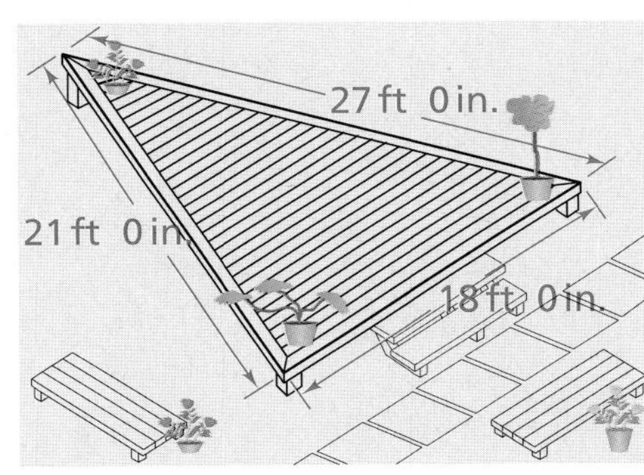

Example 2 **Relating to the Real World** 

Architecture A landscape architect is designing a triangular deck. She wants to place benches in the two largest corners. In which corners should she place the benches?

The two largest corners are opposite the two longest sides, 27 ft and 21 ft.

8. Try This The sides of a triangle are 14 in., 7 in., and 8 in. long. The smallest angle is opposite which side?

Theorem 4-11

If two angles of a triangle are not congruent, then the longer side lies opposite the larger angle.

Indirect Proof of Theorem 4-11

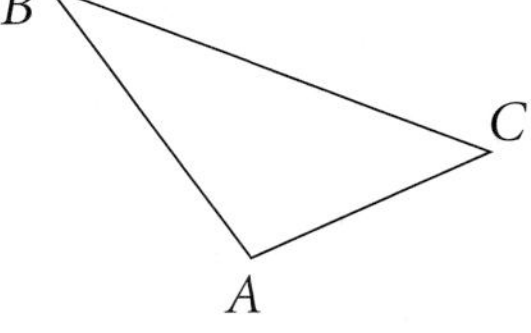

Given: $m\angle A > m\angle B$

Prove: $BC > AC$

Step 1: Assume $BC \not> AC$. That is, assume $BC < AC$ or $BC = AC$.

Step 2: If $BC < AC$, then $m\angle A < m\angle B$ (Theorem 4-10). That contradicts the given fact that $m\angle A > m\angle B$. Therefore, the assumption that $BC < AC$ must be false.

If $BC = AC$, then $m\angle A = m\angle B$ (Isosceles Triangle Theorem). This also contradicts the given fact that $m\angle A > m\angle B$. Therefore the assumption that $BC = AC$ must be false.

Step 3: Therefore, $BC > AC$ must be true.

Example 3

In $\triangle TUV$, which side is shortest?

By the Triangle Angle-Sum Theorem, $m\angle T = 60$. The smallest angle in $\triangle TUV$ is $\angle U$. Therefore, by Theorem 4-11, the shortest side is $\overline{TV}$.

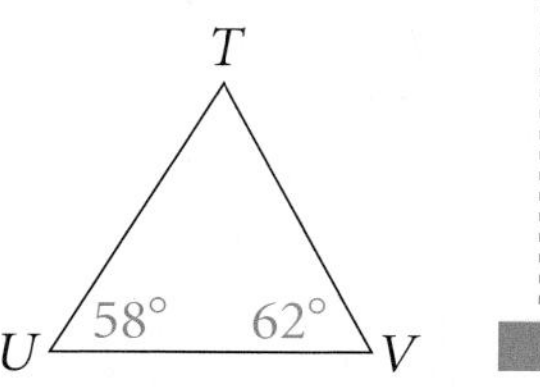

Exercises ON YOUR OWN

Is it possible for a triangle to have sides with the given lengths? Explain.

1. 2 in., 3 in., 6 in.
2. 11 cm, 12 cm, 15 cm
3. 6 ft, 10 ft, 13 ft
4. 8 m, 10 m, 19 m
5. 2 yd, 9 yd, 10 yd
6. 4 m, 7 m, 9 m
7. 5 in., 5 in., 5 in.
8. 1 cm, 15 cm, 15 cm

List the sides of each triangle in order from shortest to longest.

9.

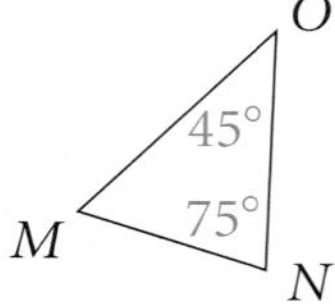

10.

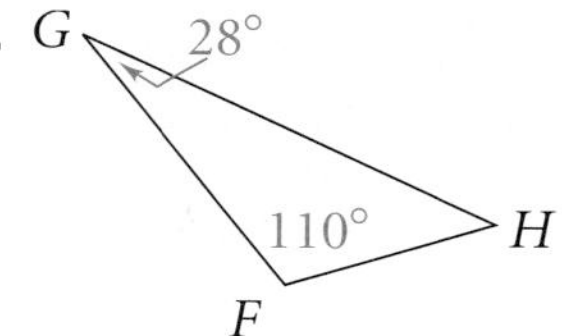

11.

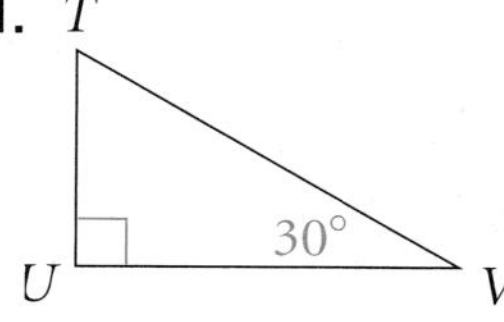

12.

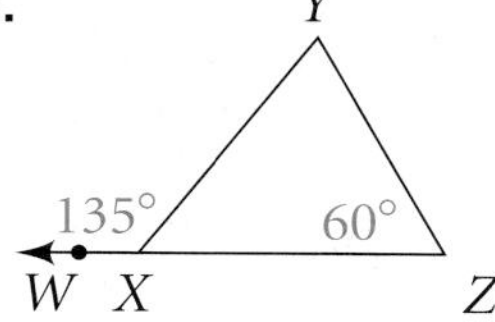

13. $\triangle ARK$, where $m\angle A = 90$, $m\angle R = 40$, and $m\angle K = 50$

14. $\triangle INK$, where $m\angle I = 20$, $m\angle N = 120$, and $m\angle K = 40$

List the angles of each triangle in order from smallest to largest.

15.

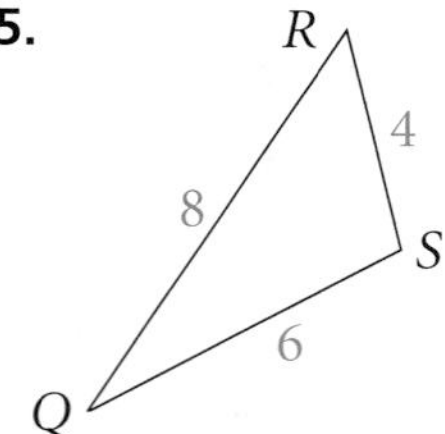

16.

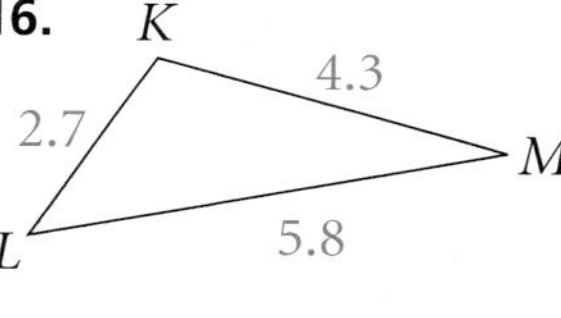

17.

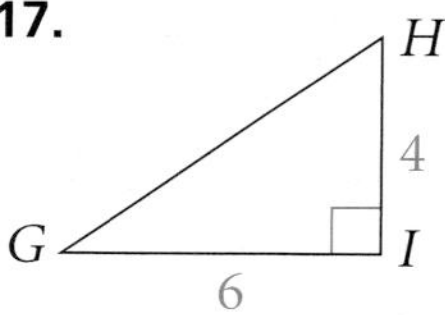

18.

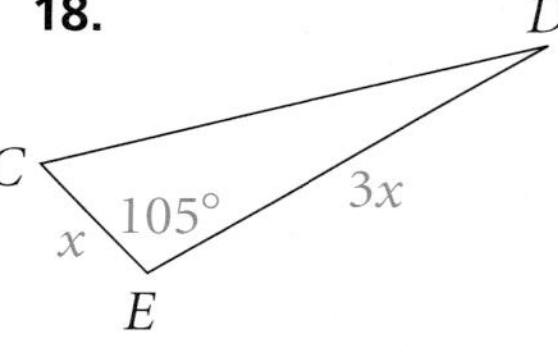

19. $\triangle ABC$, where $AB = 8$, $BC = 5$, and $AC = 7$

20. $\triangle DEF$, where $DE = 15$, $EF = 18$, and $DF = 5$

21. $\triangle XYZ$, where $XY = 2$, $YZ = 4$, and $XZ = 3$

22. **Geometry in 3 Dimensions** Refer to the pyramid shown. Explain why the altitude, $\overline{PT}$, must be shorter than edges $\overline{PA}$, $\overline{PB}$, $\overline{PC}$, and $\overline{PD}$.

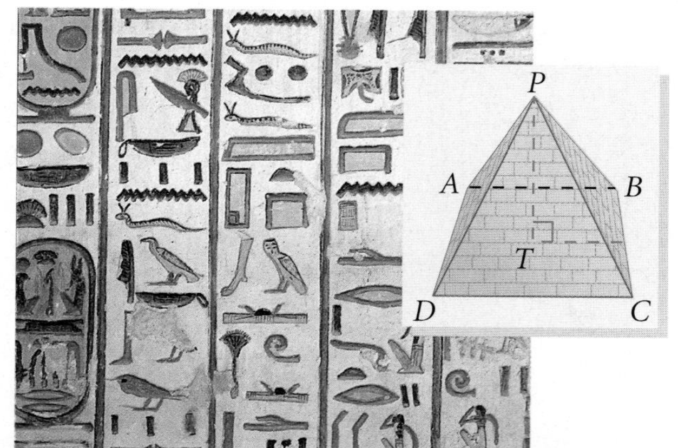

23. **Probability** A student picks two straws, one 6 cm long and the other 9 cm long. She picks another straw at random from a group of four straws whose lengths are 3 cm, 5 cm, 11 cm, and 15 cm. What is the probability that the straw she picks will allow her to form a triangle?

24. **Standardized Test Prep** Compare the quantities in Columns A and B. Select the best answer.

Column A	Column B
a	b

14, $b°$, $a°$, 16, 15

A. The quantity in Column A is greater.
B. The quantity in Column B is greater.
C. The quantities are equal.
D. The relationship cannot be determined from the information given.

25. **Technology** Darren used geometry software to draw $\triangle ACF$ and $\triangle DEH$ so that $\overline{AC} \cong \overline{DE}$ and $\overline{AF} \cong \overline{DH}$. He then manipulated point H to collect the data in the spreadsheet.

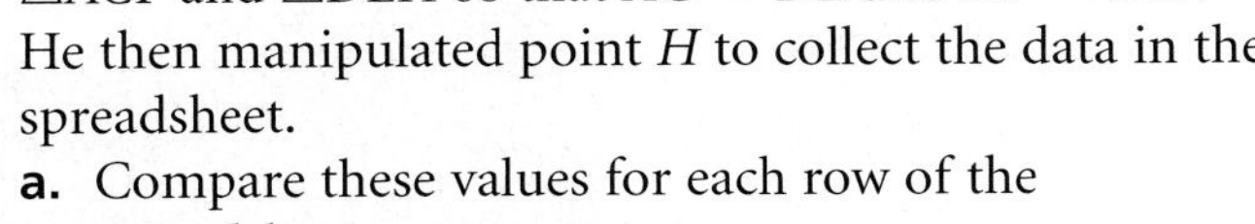

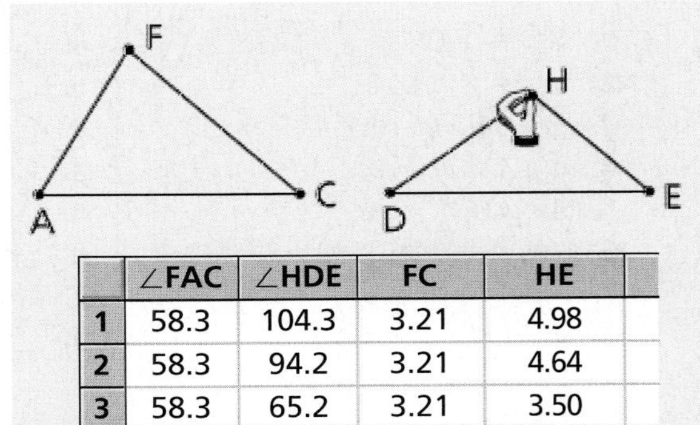

	∠FAC	∠HDE	FC	HE
1	58.3	104.3	3.21	4.98
2	58.3	94.2	3.21	4.64
3	58.3	65.2	3.21	3.50
4	58.3	50.7	3.21	2.88
5	58.3	34.7	3.21	2.18

a. Compare these values for each row of the spreadsheet.
$m\angle FAC$ __?__ $m\angle HDE$ FC __?__ HE

b. **Patterns** What pattern do you notice in part (a)?

c. The pattern that you noticed is stated as the Hinge Theorem. Complete the theorem:
Hinge Theorem *If two sides of one triangle are congruent to two sides of another triangle, and the included angle of the first triangle is greater than the included angle of the second triangle, then* __?__.

26. **Critical Thinking** Pliers, scissors, and many other tools are hinged. When the angle between the blades of a pair of scissors increases, what happens to the distance between the tips of the blades? Explain how this relates to the Hinge Theorem in Exercise 25.

27. **Critical Thinking** The Shau family is crossing Kansas on Highway 70. A sign reads "Topeka 110 miles, Wichita 90 miles." Avi says, "I didn't know that it was only 20 miles from Topeka to Wichita." Explain to Avi why the distance between the two cities doesn't have to be 20 miles.

Critical Thinking **Which segment is the shortest?**

28.

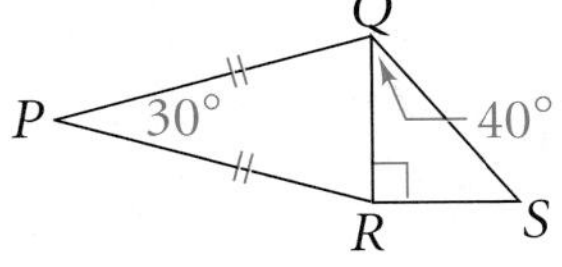

29.

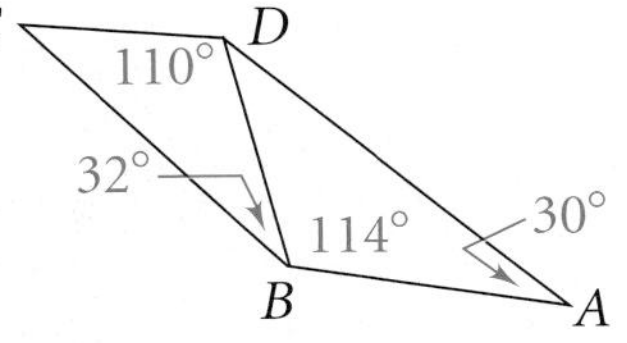

30.

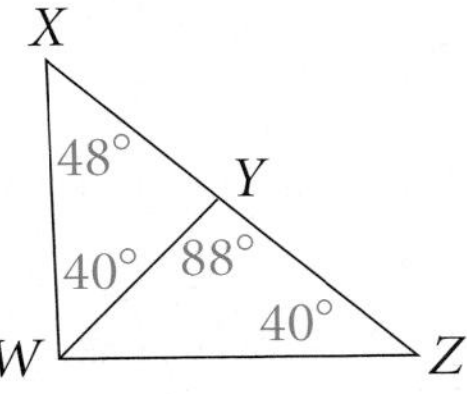

The lengths of two sides of a triangle are given. Write an inequality to represent the range of values for z, the length of the third side.

31. 8 ft, 12 ft

32. 5 in., 16 in.

33. 6 cm, 6 cm

34. x, y, where $x \geq y$

35. **Preparing for Proof** Theorem 4-10 states: If two sides of a triangle are not congruent, then the larger angle lies opposite the longer side. To prove this theorem, begin with $\triangle TOY$, with $OY > TY$. Find P on $\overline{OY}$ so that $\overline{TY} \cong \overline{PY}$. Draw $\overline{TP}$. Supply a reason for each statement.

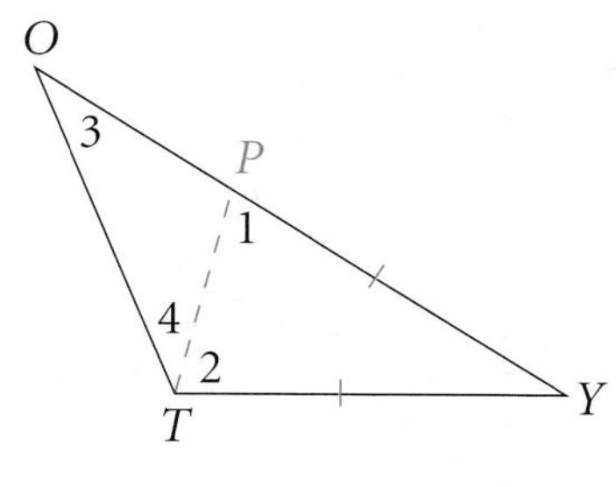

Given: $OY > TY$ and $\overline{TY} \cong \overline{PY}$

Prove: $m\angle OTY > m\angle 3$

Statements	Reasons
1. $\overline{YP} \cong \overline{YT}$	a. ?
2. $m\angle 1 = m\angle 2$	b. ?
3. $m\angle OTY = m\angle 4 + m\angle 2$	c. ?
4. $m\angle OTY > m\angle 2$	4. Comparison Prop. of Ineq. (p. 212)
5. $m\angle OTY > m\angle 1$	d. ?
6. $m\angle 1 = m\angle 3 + m\angle 4$	e. ?
7. $m\angle 1 > m\angle 3$	7. Comparison Prop. of Ineq.
8. $m\angle OTY > m\angle 3$	f. ?

36. **Logical Reasoning** A corollary to Theorem 4-11 states: The perpendicular segment from a point to a line is the shortest segment from the point to the line. Show that $PA > PT$, given that $\overline{PT} \perp \overline{TA}$.

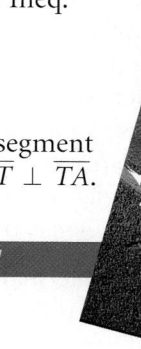

37. **Transformational Geometry** $\triangle SKY$ has vertices $S(-1, 0)$, $K(3, 8)$, and $Y(5, 4)$. A translation maps K to $K'(2, 1)$. Find the coordinates of the images of S and Y under this translation.

38. **Open-ended** Use a rhombus to create a tessellation.

39. Find the measure of an interior angle and an exterior angle of a regular 15-gon.

FOR YOUR JOURNAL

Write a summary of the key points of this lesson. Include diagrams with your summary where appropriate.

Getting Ready for Lesson 4-7

Describe the set of red points in terms of their distance from the set of blue points.

40.

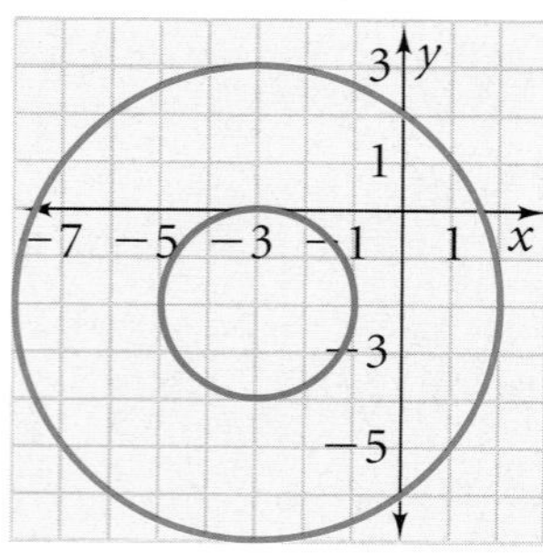

41.

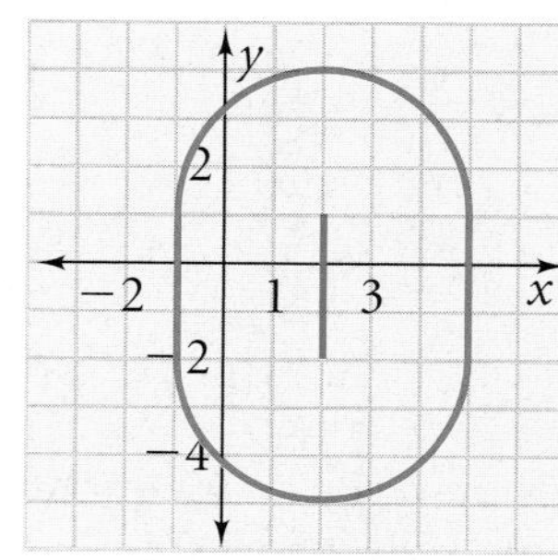

4-7 Bisectors and Locus

What You'll Learn

- Using properties of angle bisectors and perpendicular bisectors
- Solving locus problems

...And Why

To learn methods used by circuit designers and many other professionals who solve problems in which stated conditions must be met

What You'll Need

straightedge, compass, ruler, MIRA™

TECHNOLOGY HINT

The Work Together could be done using geometry software.

WORK TOGETHER

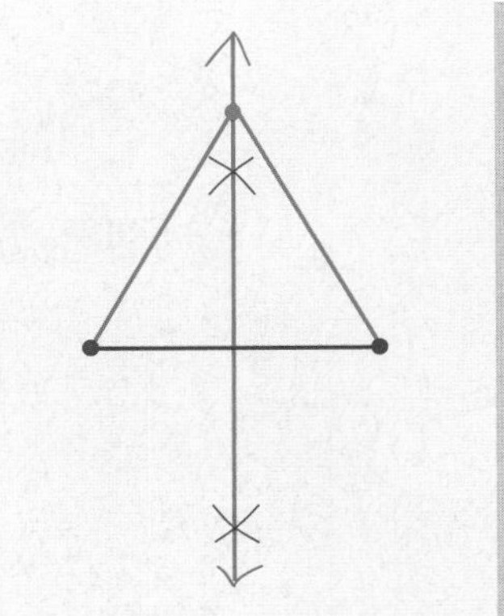

- Draw a segment and construct its perpendicular bisector by using a straightedge and a compass or a MIRA™.
- Draw a point on the perpendicular bisector and then draw segments connecting this point to the endpoints of the segment.

1. Compare the lengths of the segments. What do you notice?
2. Repeat this process with some other points. Does what you noticed still hold true?
3. Use what you discovered to complete this statement: If a point is on the perpendicular bisector of a segment, then _?_.
4. **a.** Write the converse of the statement you completed in Question 3.
   b. Explain how the converse is related to the method you use to construct a perpendicular bisector.

THINK AND DISCUSS

Perpendicular Bisectors and Locus

The properties you discovered in the Work Together are summarized in the following theorems.

Theorem 4-12
Perpendicular Bisector Theorem

If a point is on the perpendicular bisector of a segment, then it is equidistant from the endpoints of the segment.

Theorem 4-13
Converse of Perpendicular Bisector Theorem

If a point is equidistant from the endpoints of a segment, then it is on the perpendicular bisector of the segment.

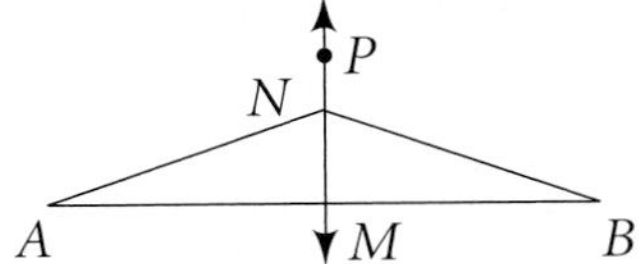

5. **a.** Given that $AN = BN$, what can you conclude about point N?
   b. Given that $\overline{MP}$ is the perpendicular bisector of $\overline{AB}$, what can you conclude about AN and BN? about $\triangle ABN$?
6. Rewrite the two theorems as a single biconditional statement.

7. Given isosceles triangle $\triangle URI$ with vertex angle $\angle R$, what does Theorem 4-13 tell you about point R?

Example 1 **Relating to the Real World** 

National Landmarks Find the set of points in Washington, D.C., that are equidistant from the Jefferson Memorial and the White House.

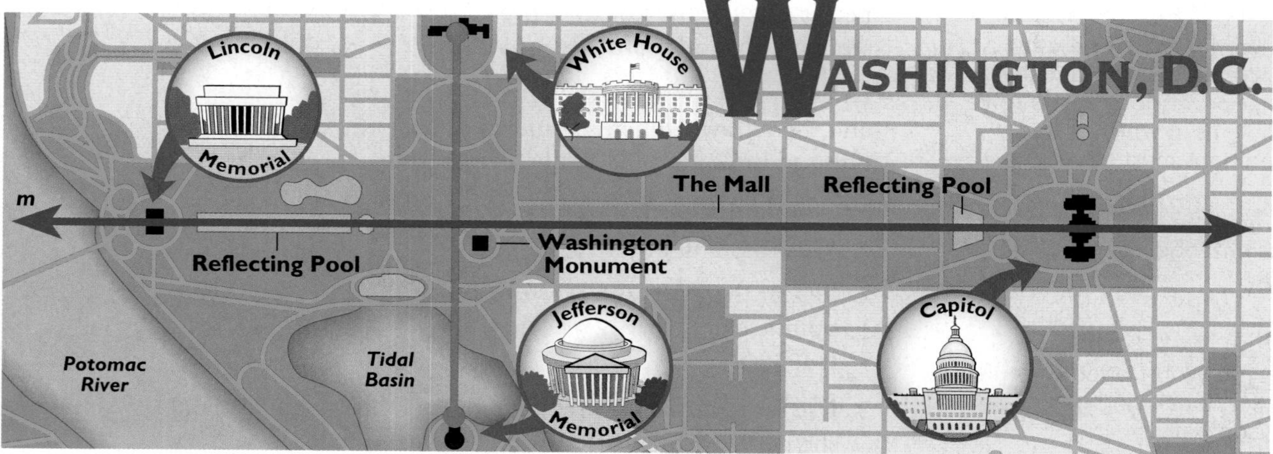

The red segment connects the Jefferson Memorial and the White House. All points on the perpendicular bisector m of this segment are equidistant from its endpoints. The perpendicular bisector passes through some of Washington's most famous landmarks.

Who? Benjamin Banneker (1731–1806) was an American astronomer, farmer, mathematician, and surveyor. In 1791, Banneker assisted in laying out the boundaries of Washington, D.C.

8. For which landmarks does line m appear to be a line of symmetry?

Example 1 involves the concept of locus. A **locus** is a set of points that meets a stated condition. In Example 1, the condition is "equidistant from the Jefferson Memorial and the White House." The locus is the perpendicular bisector of the segment connecting the two landmarks.

Example 2

Sketch the locus of points in a plane that are 1 cm from point C.

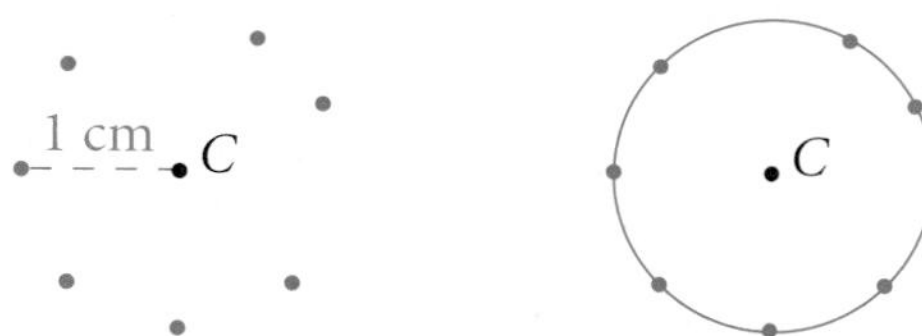

Locate several points 1 cm from C. Keep doing so until you see a pattern. The locus is a circle with center C and radius 1 cm.

9. **Try This** Sketch the locus of points in a plane that are 1 cm from a segment $\overline{VC}$.

10. What would the locus be in Example 2 if the words "in a plane" were replaced with "in space"?

As the answer to Question 10 implies, a locus of points in a plane and a locus of points in space can be quite different. For example, consider this condition: all points 3 cm from line ℓ.

The locus in a plane looks like this . . .

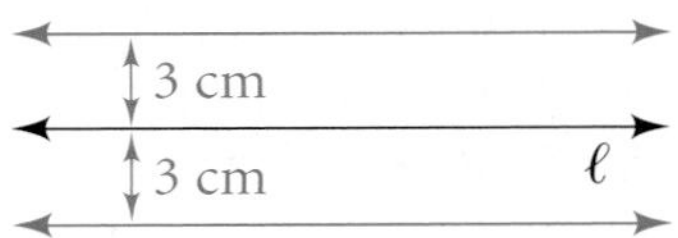

The locus is two parallel lines, each 3 cm from line ℓ.

The locus in space looks like this . . .

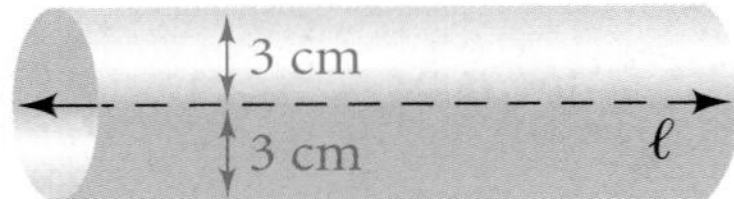

The locus is an endless cylinder with radius 3 cm and center-line ℓ.

Quick Review

To bisect an angle using paper folding, fold the paper so that the sides of the angle overlap.

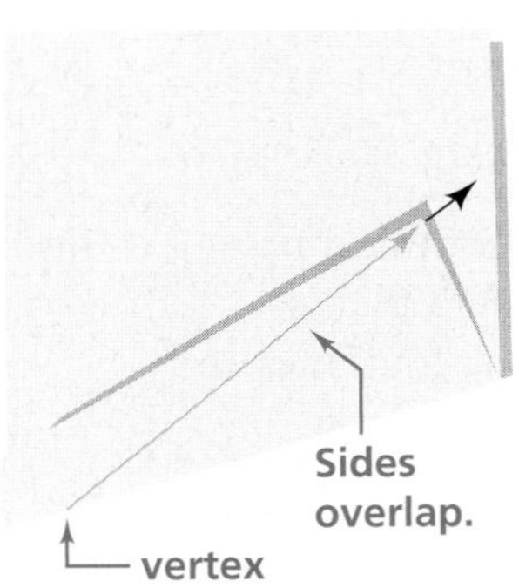

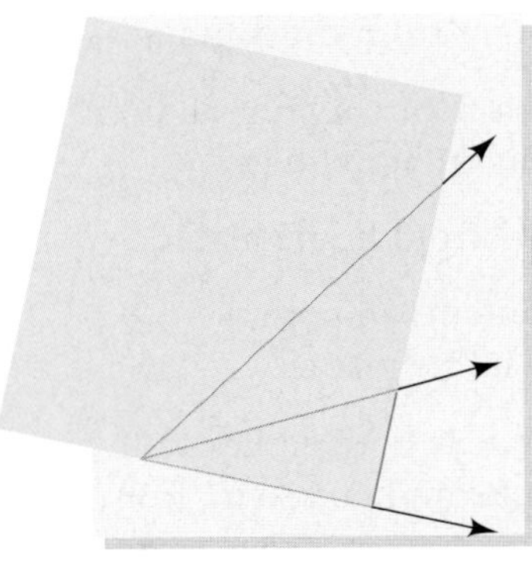

Angle Bisectors and Locus

The Work Together below involves the distance from a point to a line. The **distance from a point to a line** is the length of the perpendicular segment from the point to the line.

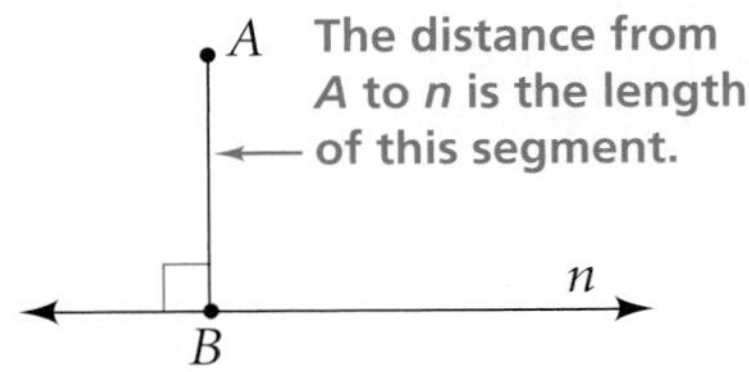

11. Let C be any point on line n other than B. Show that $AB < AC$.

WORK TOGETHER

- Draw an angle and use paper folding to create its bisector.
- Draw a point on the bisector. Use the corner of a piece of paper to create perpendicular segments from both sides of the angle to the point.

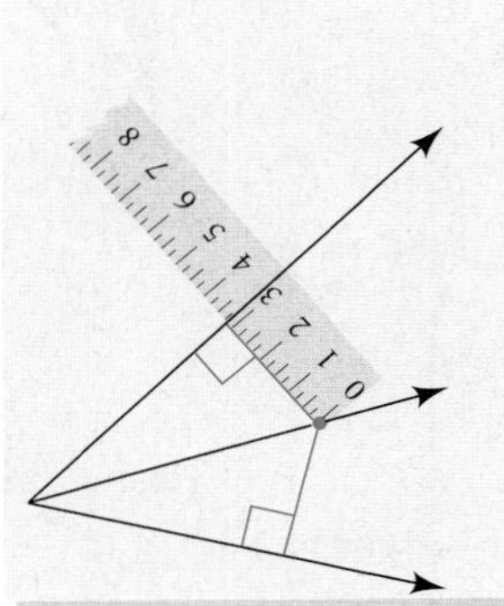

12. Measure the lengths of the two segments you drew. What do you notice?

13. Repeat with two other points. Does what you noticed still hold true?

14. Use what you discovered to complete the statement: If a point is on the bisector of an angle, then __?__.

THINK AND DISCUSS

The property that you discovered in the Work Together is stated below. Its converse, which also is true, follows it.

Theorem 4-14
Angle Bisector Theorem

If a point is on the bisector of an angle, then it is equidistant from the sides of the angle.

Theorem 4-15
Converse of Angle Bisector Theorem

If a point in the interior of an angle is equidistant from the sides of the angle, then it is on the angle bisector.

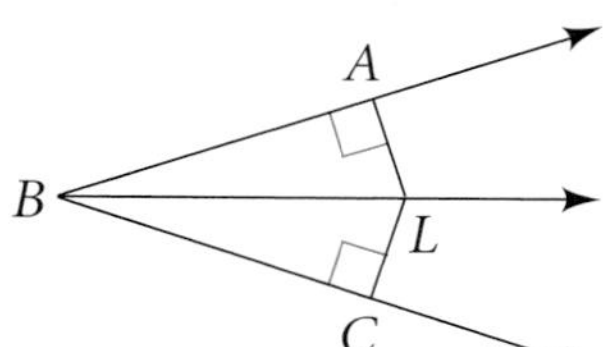

15. a. Given that $m\angle ABL = m\angle CBL$, what can you conclude about AL and CL?

b. Given that $AL = CL$, what can you conclude about $m\angle ABL$ and $m\angle CBL$?

16. What is the locus of all points in the interior of an angle that are equidistant from the sides of the angle?

Sometimes the condition in a locus problem has more than one part.

Example 3 **Relating to the Real World** 

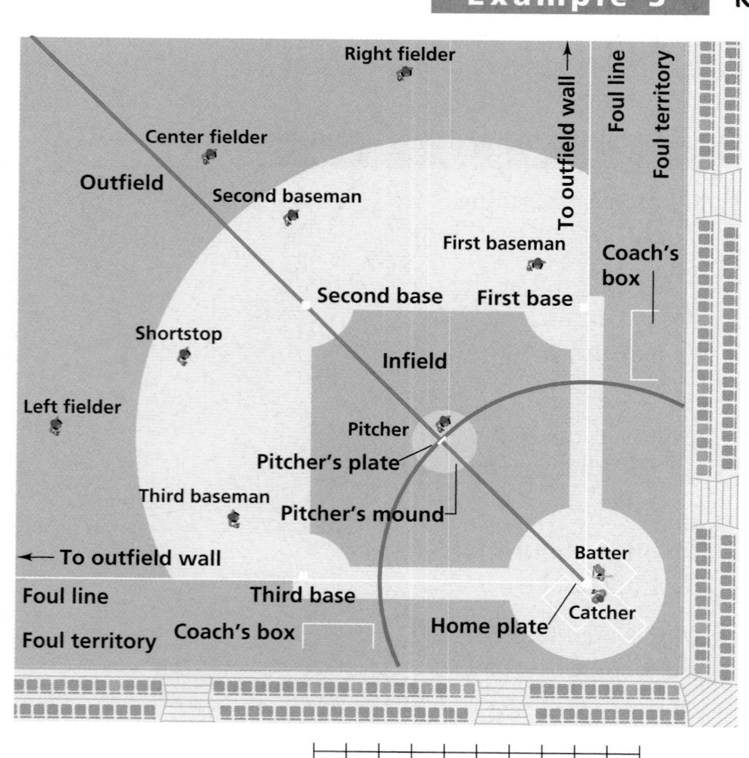

Sports What is a common name for the part of a baseball field that is equidistant from the foul lines and 60 ft 6 in. from home plate?

There are two parts to the condition stated in the problem.

Part 1: Equidistant from the foul lines

The red angle bisector contains all points equidistant from the foul lines.

Part 2: 60 ft 6 in. from home plate

The blue arc contains all points 60 ft 6 in. from home plate.

The pitcher's plate is both equidistant from the foul lines and 60 ft 6 in. from home plate.

Exercises ON YOUR OWN

Sketch and label each locus.

1. all points in a plane 4 cm from a point X

2. all points in a plane 1 in. from a line $\overleftrightarrow{UV}$

3. all points in a plane 1 in. from a segment $\overline{UV}$

4. all points in space 3 cm from a point F

5. all points in space a distance a from a line $\overleftrightarrow{DE}$

6. all points in a plane 1 in. from a circle with radius 0.5 in.

7. all points in a plane equidistant from two parallel lines

8. all points in a plane equidistant from the endpoints of $\overline{PQ}$

9. all points in space equidistant from two parallel lines

10. all points in a plane equidistant from $\overleftrightarrow{MN}$ and $\overleftrightarrow{OP}$ where $\overleftrightarrow{MN} \perp \overleftrightarrow{OP}$

11. all points in a plane 3 cm from $\overline{GH}$ and 5 cm from G, where $GH = 4.5$ cm

12. all points equidistant from two parallel planes

13. Find the locus of points equidistant from the sides of $\angle JKL$ and on $\odot C$.

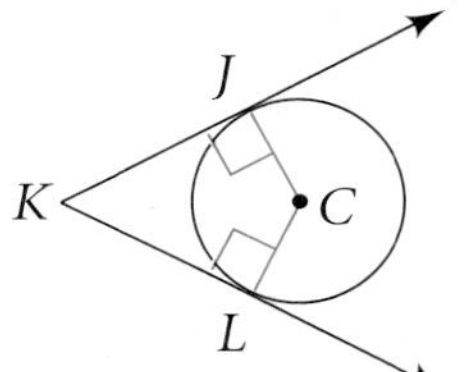

14. **Coordinate Geometry** Write an equation for the locus of points equidistant from $(2, -3)$ and $(6, 1)$.

15. **Sports** What is the common name for the part of a baseball field that is equidistant from first and third bases and 127 ft from home plate?

16. **Standardized Test Prep** The highlighted points are the locus of points on the coordinate plane that are
    - **A.** 2 units from the origin and 1 unit from the y-axis.
    - **B.** 1 unit from the origin and 2 units from the y-axis.
    - **C.** 2 units from the origin and 1 unit from the x-axis.
    - **D.** 1 unit from the origin and 2 units from the x-axis.
    - **E.** none of the above

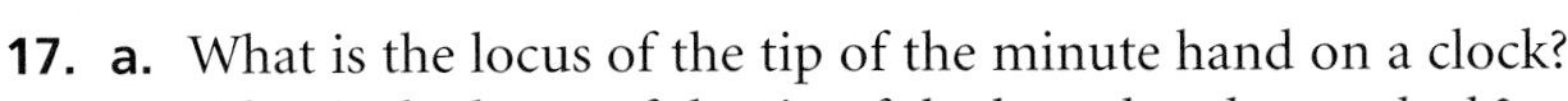

17. **a.** What is the locus of the tip of the minute hand on a clock?
    b. What is the locus of the tip of the hour hand on a clock?

18. **Open-ended** The smoke trails of the jets show the paths that they travel. Find a picture from a book or magazine or draw a sketch that shows an object and its path.

19. **Open-ended** Give two examples of locus from everyday life, one in a plane and one in space.

20. **Logical Reasoning** Rosie says that it is impossible to find a point equidistant from three collinear points. Is she correct? Explain your thinking.

21. Paul and Priscilla Wilson take new jobs in Shrevetown and need to find a place to live. Paul says "Let's try to move somewhere equidistant from both of our offices." Priscilla says, "Let's try to stay within three miles of downtown." Trace the map and suggest some locations for the Wilsons.

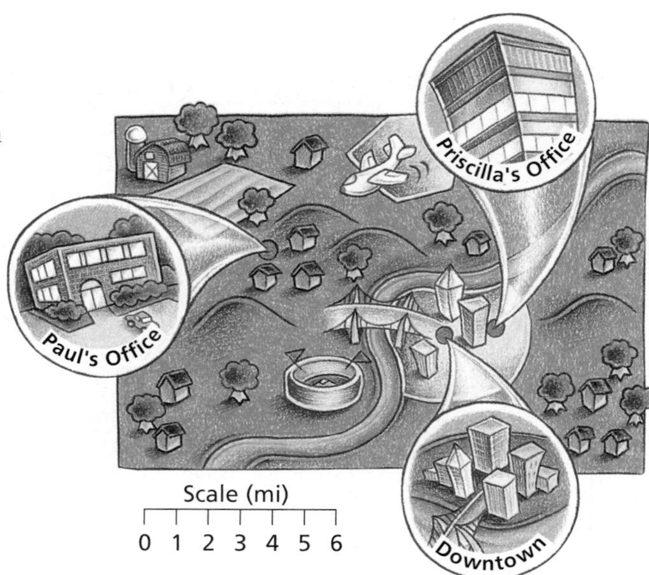

22. **Open-ended** Name a food with the shape described by each locus.
   a. all points in space no more than $1\frac{1}{2}$ in. from a point
   b. all points in space no more than $\frac{1}{2}$ in. from a circle with radius 2 in.

Coordinate Geometry **Sketch each locus on the coordinate plane.**

23. all points 3 units from the origin

24. all points 5 units from $x = 2$

25. all points equidistant from $A(0, 2)$ and $B(2, 0)$

26. all points equidistant from $P(1, 3)$ and $Q(5, 1)$

27. all points 4 units from the y-axis

28. all points equidistant from $y = 3$ and $y = -1$

Describe the locus that each blue figure represents.

29.
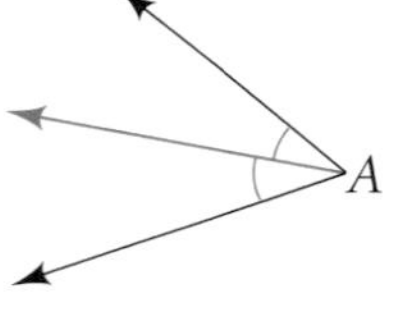

30.
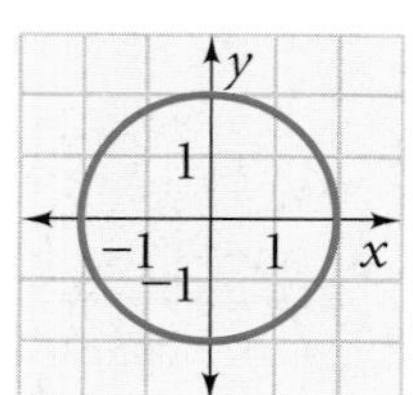

31.
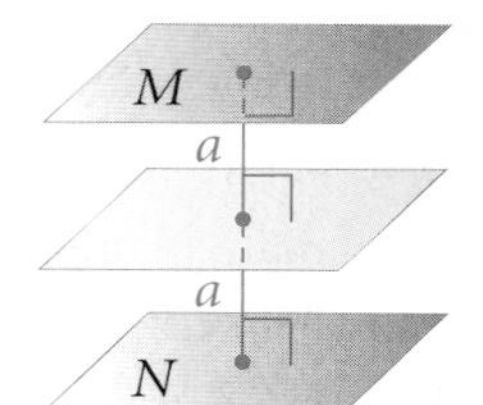

32.
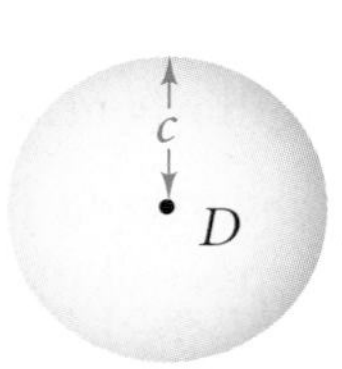

33. Think about the path of a child on a swing.
   a. Draw a side view of this path.
   b. Draw a top view of this path.
   c. Draw a front view of this path.

34. Alejandro draws a segment to use as the base of an isosceles triangle.
   a. Draw a segment to represent Alejandro's base. Locate three points that could be the vertex of the isosceles triangle.
   b. Describe the locus of points for the vertex of Alejandro's isosceles triangle.
   c. **Writing** Explain why the locus you described is the only possibility for the vertex of the triangle.

Sketch each path.

35. the swimmer's left foot

36. a doorknob as the door opens

37. a knot in the middle of a jump rope as the rope is being used

Chapter Project *Find Out by Writing*

Make up a logic puzzle in which the solver must use clues to match the people, places, or things you describe. Have a classmate solve your puzzle. If necessary, refine your puzzle based on input from your classmate.

Exercises MIXED REVIEW

Identify the following in ⊙*O*.

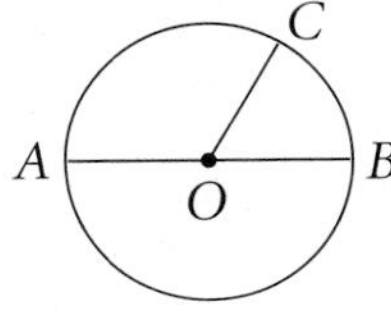

38. a central angle and its intercepted arc

39. two major arcs

40. a pair of adjacent arcs

Getting Ready for Lesson 4-8

Constructions **Draw a large triangle. Construct each figure.**

41. an angle bisector

42. a midpoint of a side

43. a perpendicular bisector of a side

Exercises CHECKPOINT

List the sides from shortest to longest.

1.

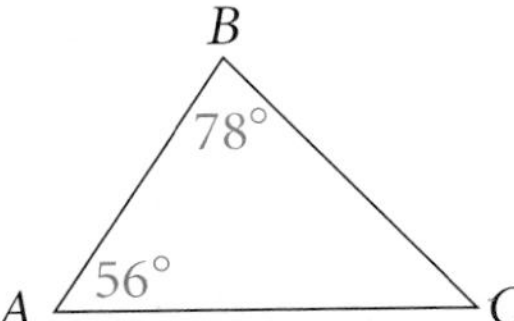

2.

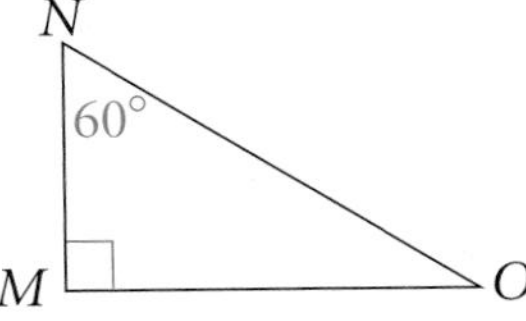

3.

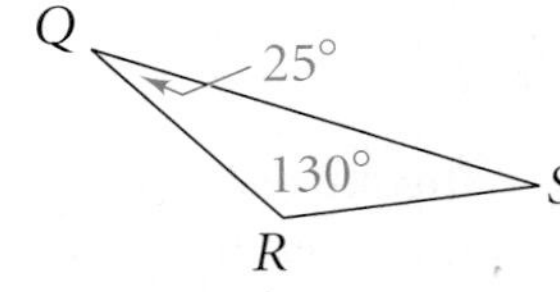

4. **Open-ended** Write a conditional that is true. Then write the first step of an indirect proof for your conditional.

Write the first step of an indirect proof of each statement.

5. February has fewer than 30 days.

6. A pentagon has at most three right angles.

Sketch and label the locus of points.

7. all points in a plane a distance *d* from a line $\overleftrightarrow{PR}$

8. all points in space 1 in. from a plane

Math ToolboX

Technology

Exploring Special Segments in Triangles

Before Lesson 4-8

Work in pairs or small groups.

Construct

Use geometry software.

1. Construct a triangle and the three perpendicular bisectors of its sides.
2. Construct a triangle and its three angle bisectors.
3. Construct a triangle. Construct a line through a vertex of the triangle that is perpendicular to the line containing the side opposite that vertex. Similarly, draw the perpendiculars from the other two vertices. Since an *altitude* of a triangle is the segment from a vertex to the line containing the opposite side, the three lines you have drawn contain the three altitudes of the triangle.

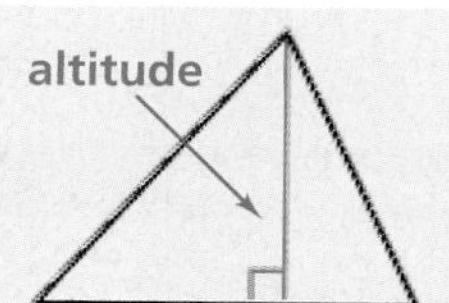

4. Construct a triangle. Construct the midpoint of a side of the triangle and draw the segment from the midpoint to the opposite vertex. This segment is called a *median* of the triangle. Construct the other two medians.

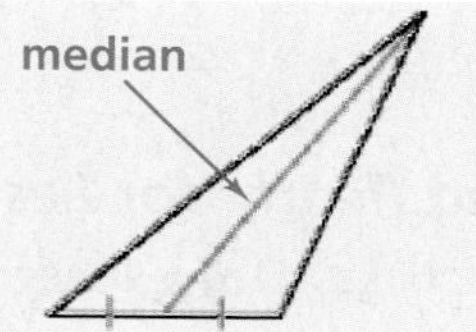

Investigate

- What do you notice about the lines, rays, or segments that you constructed in each triangle?
- Manipulate the triangles. Does the property still hold in the manipulated triangles?

Conjecture

List your **conjectures** about the angle bisectors, the perpendicular bisectors, the lines containing the altitudes, and the medians of a triangle.

Extend

- In what types of triangles do the perpendicular bisectors of the sides intersect inside the triangle? on the triangle? outside the triangle?
- Describe the triangles for which the lines containing the altitudes, the angle bisectors, or the medians intersect inside, on, or outside the triangles.

What You'll Learn

- Identifying properties of perpendicular bisectors, angle bisectors, altitudes, and medians of a triangle

...And Why

To understand the points of concurrency that are used in architecture, construction, and transportation

What You'll Need

- scissors

4-8 Concurrent Lines

WORK TOGETHER

Step 1: Each member of your group should draw and cut out five triangles: two acute, two right, and one obtuse. Make them big enough so that they are easy to fold.

Step 2: Use paper folding to create the angle bisectors of each angle of an acute triangle. What do you notice about the angle bisectors?

Step 3: Repeat Step 2 with a right and an obtuse triangle. Does what you discovered still hold true?

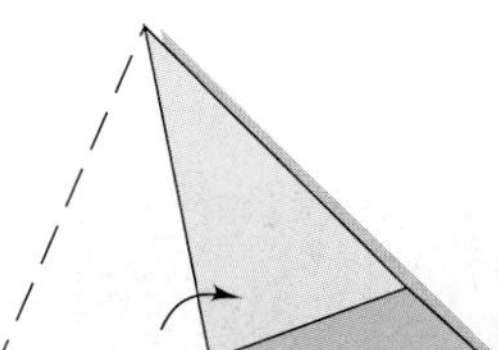

Folding an Angle Bisector

1. Make a **conjecture** about the bisectors of the angles of a triangle.

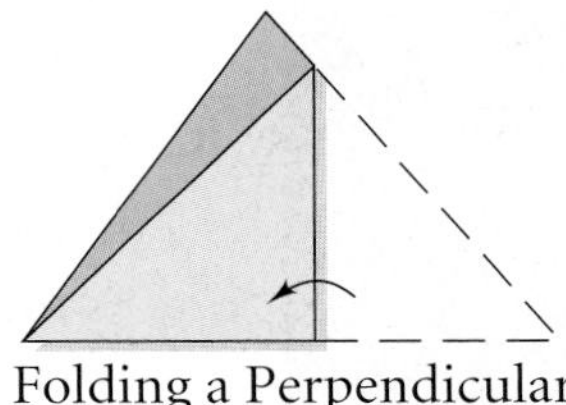

Folding a Perpendicular Bisector

Step 4: Use paper folding to create the perpendicular bisectors of each of the sides of an acute triangle. What do you notice?

Step 5: Repeat Step 4 with a right triangle. What do you notice?

Step 6: Draw an obtuse triangle in the middle of a piece of paper (do not cut it out!), then repeat Step 4 with this triangle. What do you notice?

2. Make a **conjecture** about the perpendicular bisectors of the sides of a triangle.

THINK AND DISCUSS

Perpendicular Bisectors and Angle Bisectors

When three or more lines intersect in one point, they are **concurrent.** The point at which they are concurrent is the **point of concurrency.** Your explorations in the Work Together lead to the following theorems.

Theorem 4-16 The perpendicular bisectors of the sides of a triangle are concurrent at a point equidistant from the vertices.

Theorem 4-17 The bisectors of the angles of a triangle are concurrent at a point equidistant from the sides.

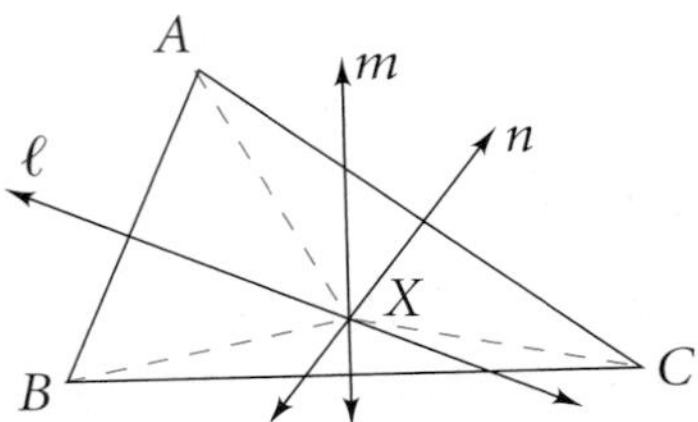

Paragraph Proof of Theorem 4-16

Given: Lines ℓ, m, and n are perpendicular bisectors of the sides of $\triangle ABC$. X is the intersection of lines ℓ and m.

Prove: Line n contains point X, and X is equidistant from A, B, and C.

Since m is the perpendicular bisector of $\overline{BC}$, $BX = CX$. Similarly, since ℓ is the perpendicular bisector of $\overline{AB}$, $AX = BX$. By substitution, $AX = CX$. So by the Converse of the Perpendicular Bisector Theorem, X is on line n. Since $AX = BX = CX$, X is equidistant from A, B, and C.

Example 1 *Relating to the Real World* 

Recreation The Jacksons want to install a circular pool in their backyard. They want the pool to be as large as possible. Where would the largest possible pool be located?

The point of concurrency of the angle bisectors is equidistant from the sides of the triangular yard (Theorem 4-17). If any other point were chosen as the center of the pool, it would be closer to at least one of the sides of the yard, and the pool would have to be smaller.

As Example 1 suggests, the points of concurrency in Theorems 4-16 and 4-17 have some interesting properties related to circles.

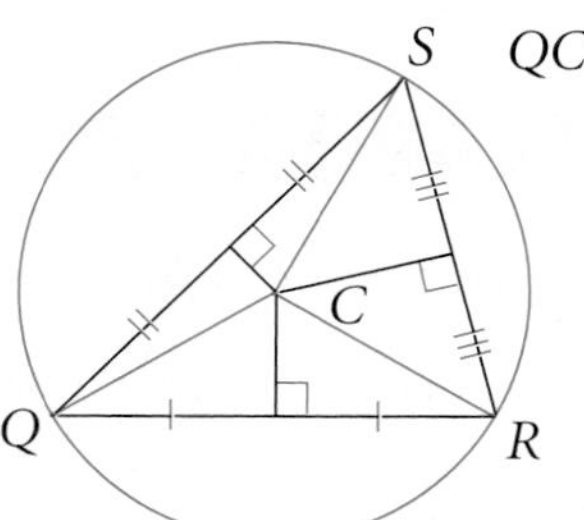

Point C, called the *circumcenter*, is equidistant from the vertices of $\triangle QRS$. The circle is *circumscribed* around the triangle.

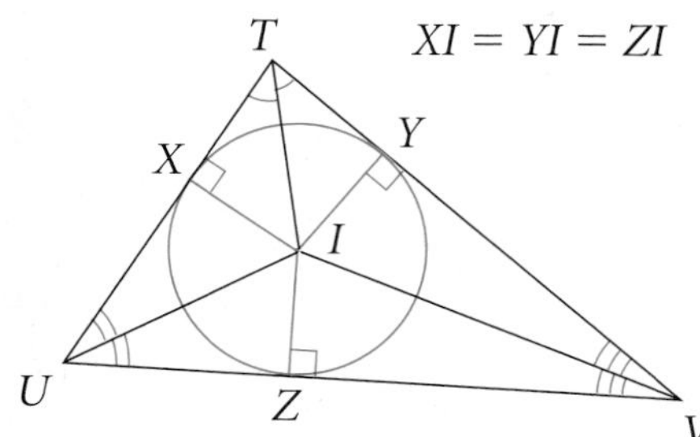

Point I, called the *incenter*, is equidistant from the sides of $\triangle TUV$. The circle is *inscribed* in the triangle.

Example 2

Coordinate Geometry Find the center of the circle that circumscribes $\triangle OPS$.

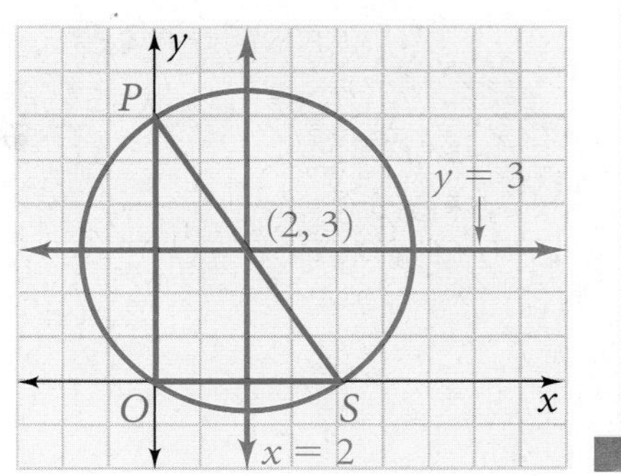

Two of the perpendicular bisectors of the sides of the triangle are $x = 2$ and $y = 3$. These lines intersect at (2, 3). This point is the center of the circle.

3. **Critical Thinking** Explain why it was not necessary to find the third perpendicular bisector in Example 2.
4. **Try This** Find the center of the circle that circumscribes the triangle with vertices (0, 0), (−8, 0), and (0, 6).

Medians and Altitudes

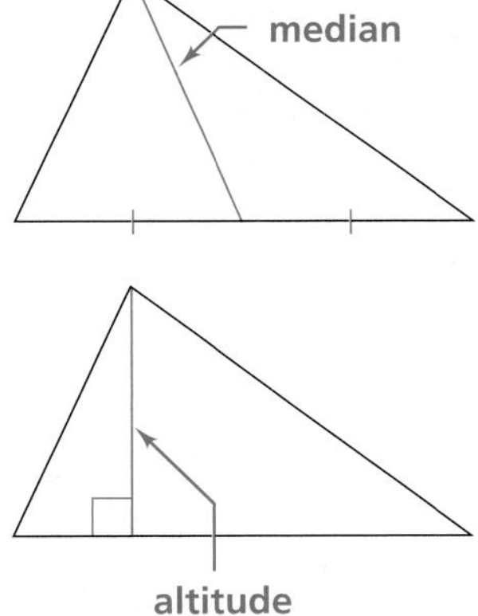

Two other special segments of a triangle are medians and altitudes. The **median of a triangle** is a segment whose endpoints are a vertex and the midpoint of the side opposite the vertex. The **altitude of a triangle** is a perpendicular segment from a vertex to the line containing the side opposite the vertex.

Unlike angle bisectors and medians, an altitude of a triangle may lie outside the triangle. Consider the following diagrams.

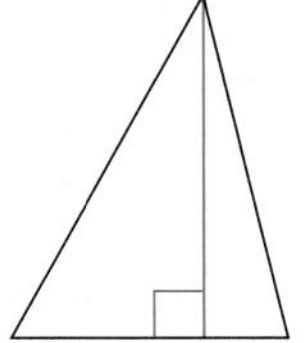

Acute Triangle: Altitude is inside.

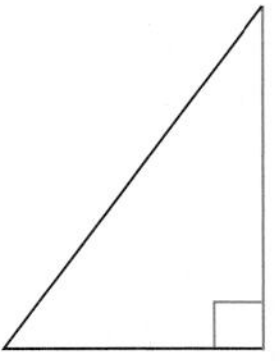

Right Triangle: Altitude is a side.

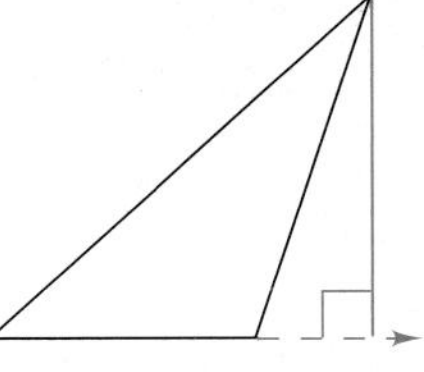

Obtuse Triangle: Altitude is outside.

You can use paper folding to find altitudes and medians.

To find an altitude . . .

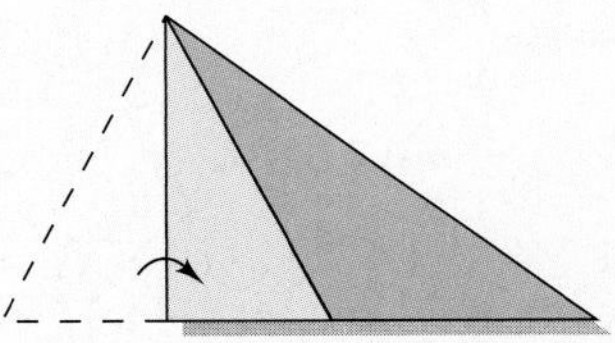

Fold so that a side overlaps itself and the fold contains a vertex.

To find a median . . .

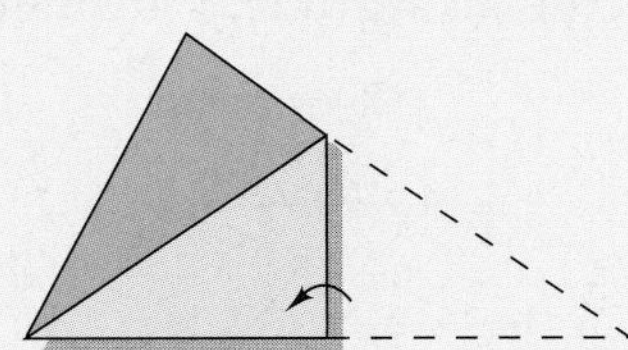

Fold one vertex to another to find the midpoint of a side,

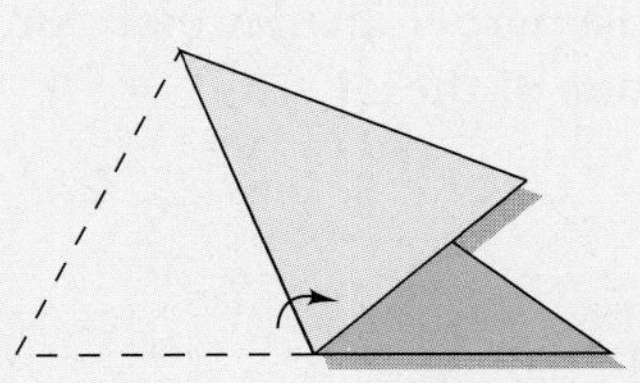

then fold from the midpoint to the opposite vertex.

Example 3

a. *Paper Folding* Use paper folding to create the altitudes from each of the three vertices of an acute triangle.

b. Use paper folding to create the three medians of an acute triangle.

The orange triangle shows the paper-folded medians.

The blue triangle shows the paper-folded altitudes.

Notice in Example 3 that the three altitudes and three medians are concurrent. This property holds true for any triangle.

Theorem 4-18 The lines that contain the altitudes of a triangle are concurrent.

Theorem 4-19 The medians of a triangle are concurrent.

5. *Critical Thinking* For what type of triangle is the point of concurrency of the altitudes outside the triangle?

Exercises ON YOUR OWN

Is $\overline{AB}$ a perpendicular bisector, an angle bisector, an altitude, a median, or none of these?

1.
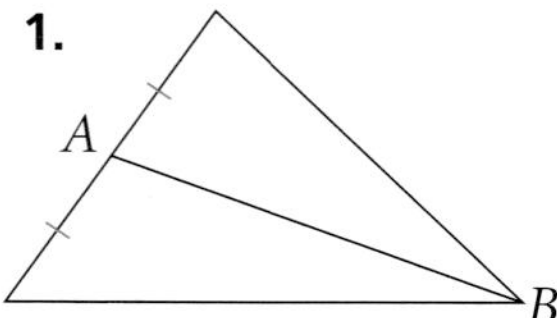

2.
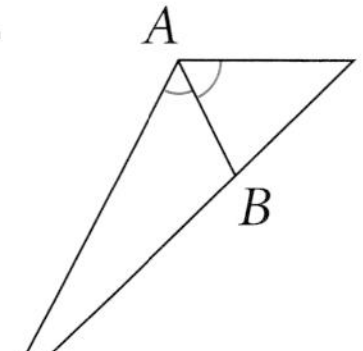

3.
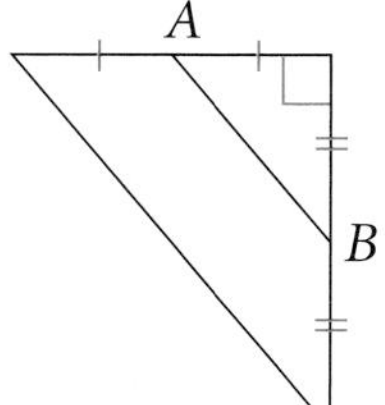

4.
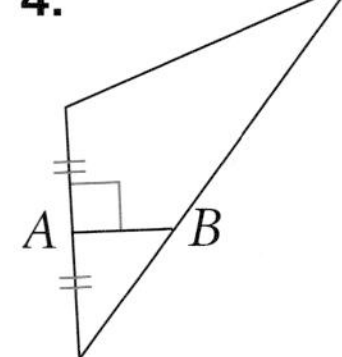

5.
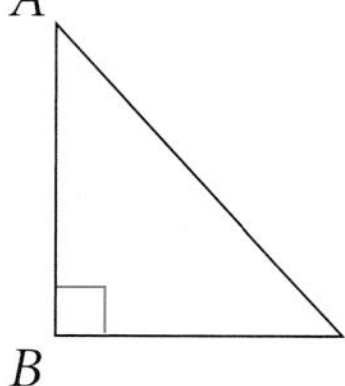

For each triangle, give the coordinates of the point of concurrency of (a) the perpendicular bisectors of the sides and (b) the altitudes.

6. 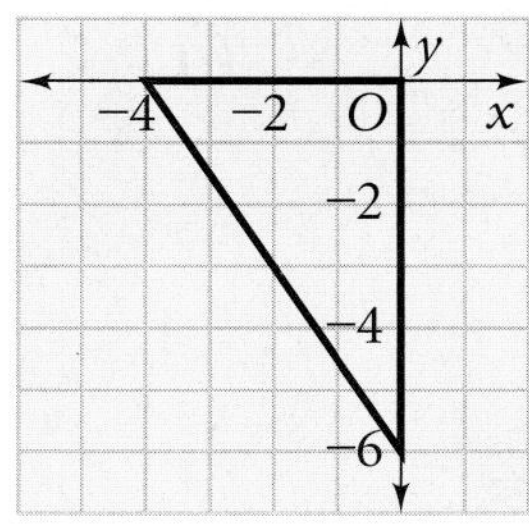

7. 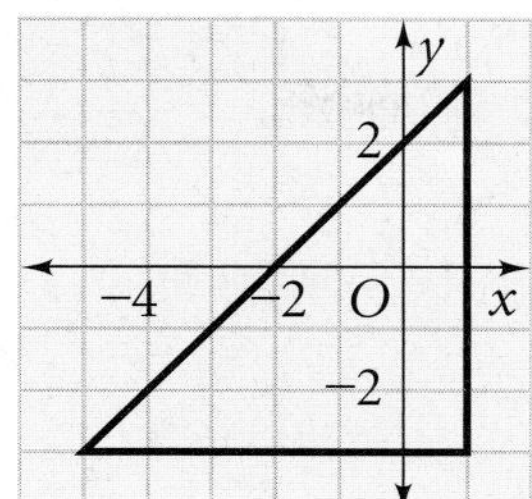

8. 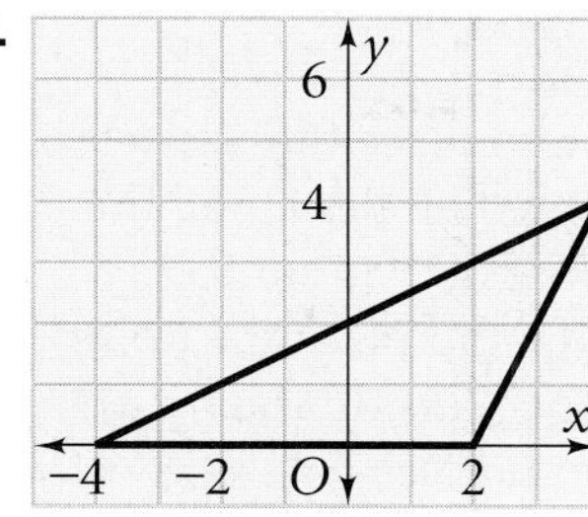

9. 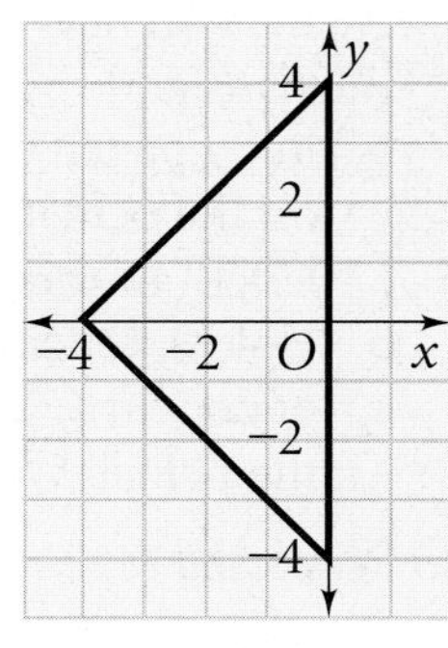

The points of concurrency for the lines and segments listed in I–IV have been drawn on the triangles. Match the points with the lines and segments.

I. perpendicular bisectors of sides

II. angle bisectors

III. medians

IV. altitudes

10. 
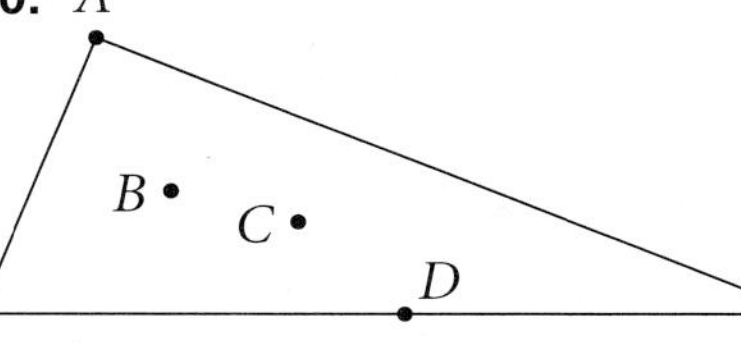

11. 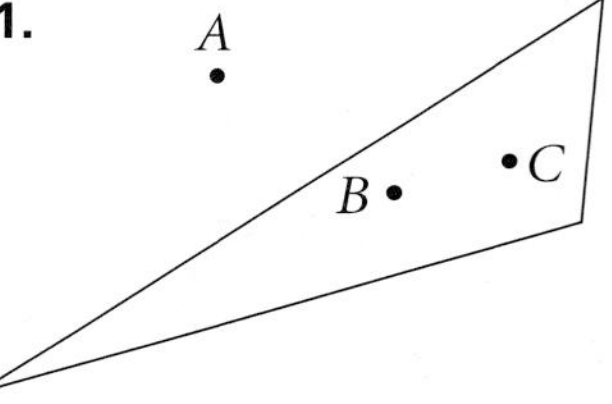

D

12. **History of Mathematics** Leonard Euler proved in 1765 that for any triangle, three of the four points of concurrency are collinear. The line that contains these three points is known as *Euler's Line.* Refer to Exercises 10 and 11 to determine which point of concurrency does *not* lie on Euler's Line.

13. **Park Design** Where should park officials place a drinking fountain in Altgeld Park so that it is equidistant from the tennis court, the playground, and the volleyball court?

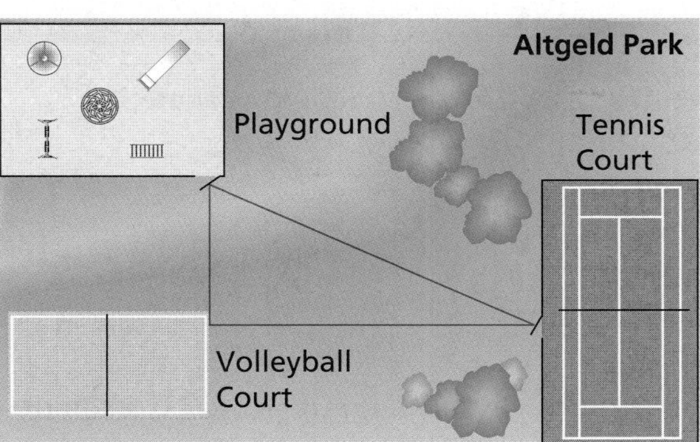

14. **Open-ended** Draw a triangle and construct the perpendicular bisectors of two of its sides. Then construct the circle that circumscribes the triangle.

15. **Coordinate Geometry** $\triangle DEF$ has vertices $D(0, 0)$, $E(12, 0)$, and $F(0, 12)$.

a. Find the equations of the lines that contain the three altitudes.

b. Find the equations of the three perpendicular bisectors of the sides.

c. **Writing** Are any of the lines in parts (a) and (b) the same? Explain.

16. **Locus** Three students are seated at uniform distances around a circular table. Copy the diagram and shade the points on the table that are closer to Moesha than to Jan or Chandra.

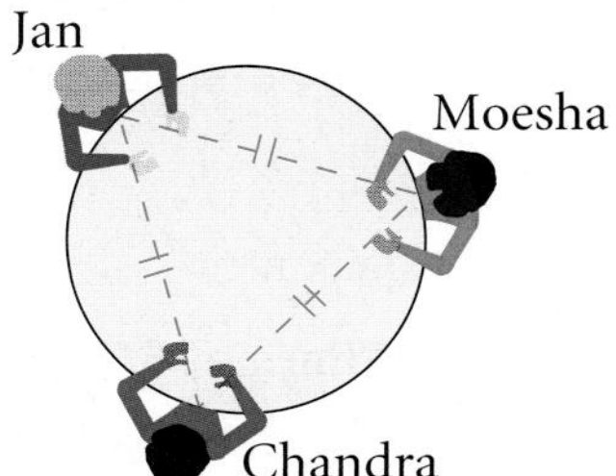

17. *Manipulatives* Medians of triangles have special physical properties related to balance. Draw a triangle on heavy cardboard, construct its medians and then cut it out.

a. Put a pencil on a table and place the triangle on the pencil so that a median lies along the length of the pencil. What do you notice?

b. Hold a pencil straight up and place the point of concurrency of the medians on the tip of the pencil. What do you notice?

18. *Preparing for Proof* Complete the proof of Theorem 4-17.

Given: Rays ℓ, m, and n are bisectors of the angles of $\triangle ABC$. X is the intersection of rays ℓ and m.

Prove: Ray n contains point X; $DX = EX = FX$

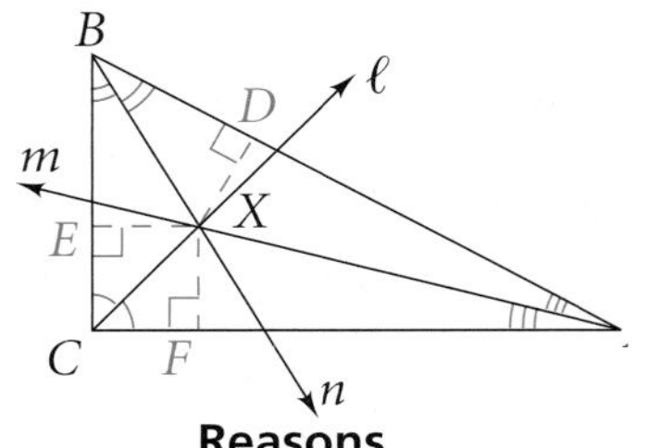

Statements	Reasons
1. Rays ℓ, m, and n are bisectors of the angles of $\triangle ABC$. X is the intersection of rays ℓ and m.	**a.** ___?___
2. $FX = EX$ and $DX = FX$	**b.** ___?___
3. $DX = EX$	**c.** ___?___
4. Ray n contains X.	**d.** ___?___
5. $DX = EX = FX$	**5.** Transitive Prop. of Equality

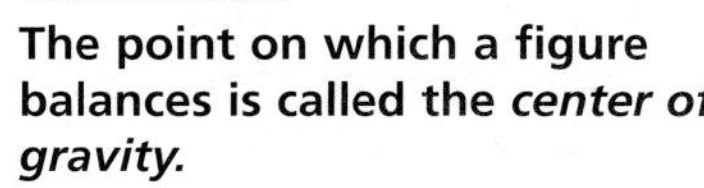

The point on which a figure balances is called the *center of gravity.*

Exercises MIXED REVIEW

Coordinate Geometry **Classify each triangle as acute, obtuse, or right.**

19. $M(-3, -4)$, $N(2, 5)$, $L(2, -4)$

20. $Q(-6, 1)$, $T(0, 0)$, $V(4, 3)$

21. $B(3, -4)$, $P(3, 5)$, $J(6, 5)$

Geometry in 3 Dimensions **In the diagram, *ABCD* is a square. Give an example of each figure or pair of figures.**

22. a plane and a point not on the plane

23. skew lines

24. intersecting planes

25. concurrent lines **26.** parallel lines

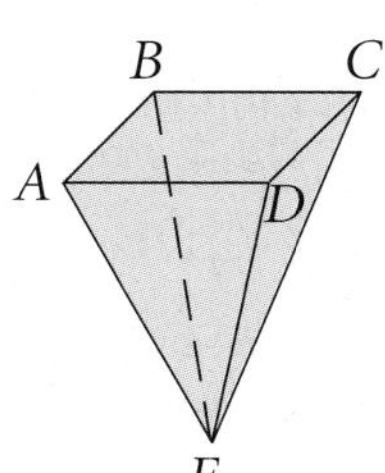

PORTFOLIO

For your portfolio, select one or two items from your work for this chapter. Here are some possibilities.

- corrected work
- work that you think best shows the things you learned or did in this chapter

Explain why you have included each selection.

CHAPTER PROJECT

Finishing the Chapter Project

PUZZLING PIECES

Find Out questions on pages 749, 760, 767, and 787 will help you complete your project. Prepare a display of logic puzzles. Include your own puzzles and solutions, those from the Find Out questions, or those found through research. Look at *Alice's Adventures in Wonderland* as well as the books listed below. Use puzzles and solutions to illustrate terms of logic, such as *conditional* and *conclusion*. Decide how best to organize your display.

Reflect and Revise

Review your display with a classmate. Together, check that your solutions are correct and that your diagrams and explanations are clear. Have you used logic terms correctly? Is the display attractive, organized, and comprehensive? Revise your work as needed. Consider doing more research.

Follow Up

A paradox is self-contradictory. Study these three paradoxes:

1. In a town, there is a librarian who reads to every person who does not read to himself or herself.
2. **A.** Statement (B) is false. **B.** Statement (A) is true.
3. This sentence contains two errers.

What can you conclude from each? Does the librarian read to himself? Is statement (A) true? How many errors does the sentence have? Study other paradoxes and create your own. Explain why each is a paradox.

For More Information

Gardner, Martin. *Aha! Gotcha: Paradoxes to Puzzle and Delight.* New York: W.H. Freeman and Company, 1982.

Shannon, George. *Stories to Solve: Folktales from Around the World.* New York: Greenwillow Books, 1985.

Smullyan, Raymond M. *Alice in Puzzle-Land: A Carrollian Tale for Children Under Eighty.* New York: William Morrow, 1982.

CHAPTER 4

Wrap Up

Key Terms

altitude of a triangle (p. 791)
base (p. 750)
base angle (p. 750)
biconditional (p. 745)
conclusion (p. 744)
concurrent (p. 789)
conditional (p. 744)
contrapositive (p. 746)
converse (p. 745)
distance from a point to a line (p. 783)
hypothesis (p. 744)
indirect reasoning (p. 769)
inverse (p. 746)
legs (p. 750)
locus (p. 782)
median of a triangle (p. 791)
midsegment (p. 763)
negation (p. 746)
point of concurrency (p. 789)
paragraph proof (p. 757)
truth value (p. 744)
two-column proof (p. 756)
vertex angle (p. 750)

How am I doing?

- State three ideas from this chapter that you think are important. Explain your choices.
- Describe the different styles of proof.

Using Logical Reasoning 4-1

An *if-then statement* is a **conditional.** The part following *if* is the **hypothesis,** and the part following *then* is the **conclusion.** You find its **truth value** when you determine if a conditional is true or false.

Statement	Form	Example
conditional	If ■, then ■.	If a polygon is a triangle, then it has three sides.
converse	If ■, then ■.	If a polygon has three sides, then it is a triangle.
inverse	If *not* ■, then *not* ■.	If a polygon is *not* a triangle, then it does *not* have three sides.
contrapositive	If *not* ■, then *not* ■.	If a polygon does *not* have three sides, then it is *not* a triangle.
biconditional	■ if and only if ■.	A polygon is a triangle if and only if it has three sides.

For Exercises 1–4: (a) Write the converse. (b) Determine the truth value of the conditional and its converse. (c) If both statements are true, write a biconditional.

1. If you are in Australia, then you are south of the equator.
2. If an angle is obtuse, then its measure is greater than 90 and less than 180.
3. If it is snowing, then it is cold outside.
4. If a figure is a square, then its sides are congruent.
5. **Open-ended** Write a conditional and then write its contrapositive.

Isosceles Triangles 4-2

If two sides of a triangle are congruent, then the angles opposite those sides are also congruent. The bisector of the vertex angle of an isosceles triangle is the perpendicular bisector of the base. If two angles of a triangle are congruent, then the sides opposite the angles are congruent.

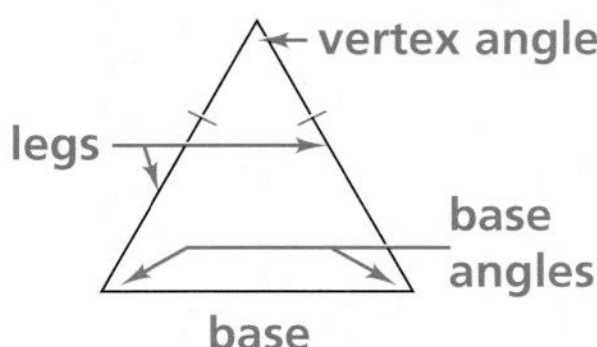

Find the values of x and y.

6. 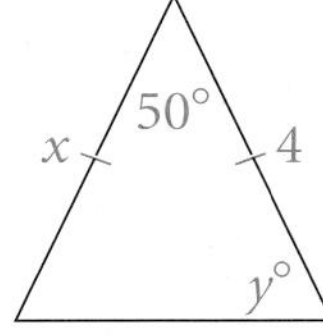

7. 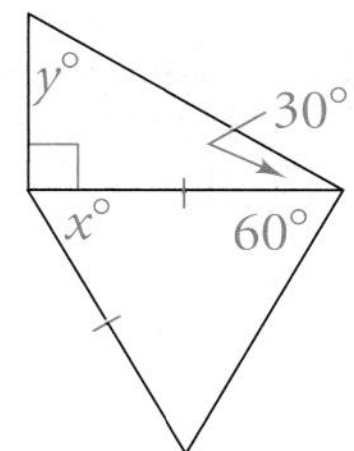

8. 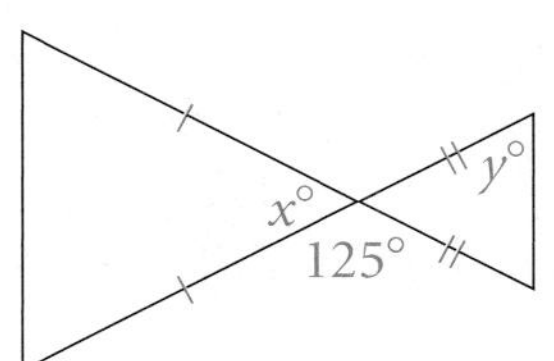

9. 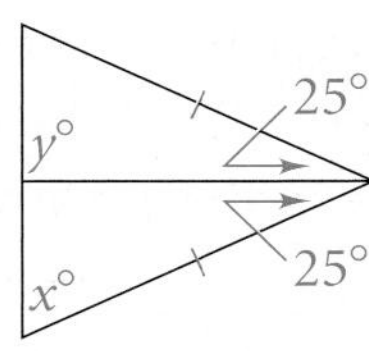

Midsegments of Triangles 4-3, 4-4

There are different types of proofs, including the **paragraph proof** and the **two-column proof.**

A **midsegment** of a triangle is a segment that connects the midpoints of its sides. The midsegment connecting two sides of a triangle is parallel to the third side and half its length.

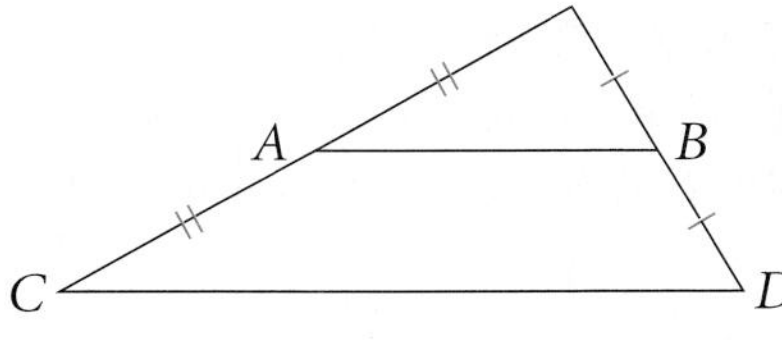

$\overline{AB} \parallel \overline{CD}$

$AB = \frac{1}{2}CD$

10. *Preparing for Proof* The reasons given in this proof are correct, but they are in the wrong order. List them in the correct order.

Given: $\triangle BCA \cong \triangle CDE$
$\triangle CDE \cong \triangle EGF$

Prove: $\overline{AF} \parallel \overline{BG}$

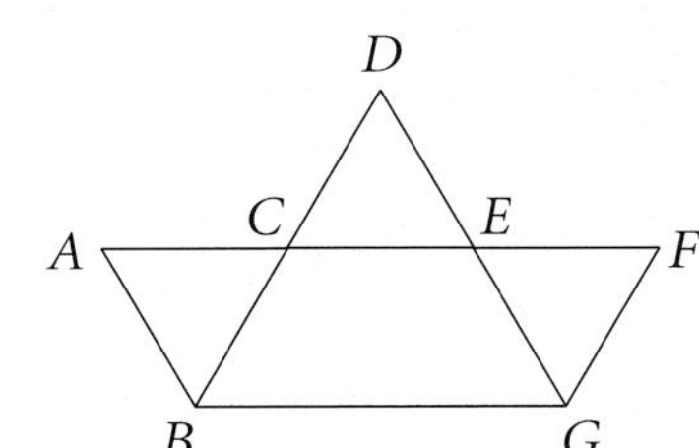

Statements	Reasons
1. $\triangle BCA \cong \triangle CDE$ $\triangle CDE \cong \triangle EGF$	a. Def. of midpoint
2. $\overline{BC} \cong \overline{CD}$, $\overline{DE} \cong \overline{EG}$	b. Triangle Midsegment Thm.
3. C is the midpoint of $\overline{BD}$. E is the midpoint of $\overline{DG}$.	c. Def. of congruent polygons
4. $\overline{AF} \parallel \overline{BG}$	d. Given

11. *Writing* Rewrite the proof above as a paragraph proof.

What can you conclude from each diagram? Justify your answers.

12. 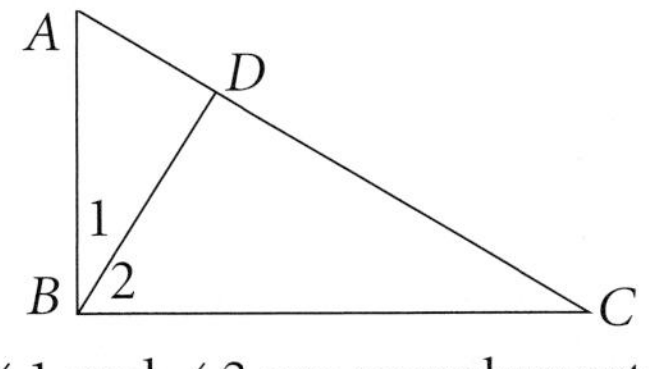

$\angle 1$ and $\angle 2$ are complementary.

13. 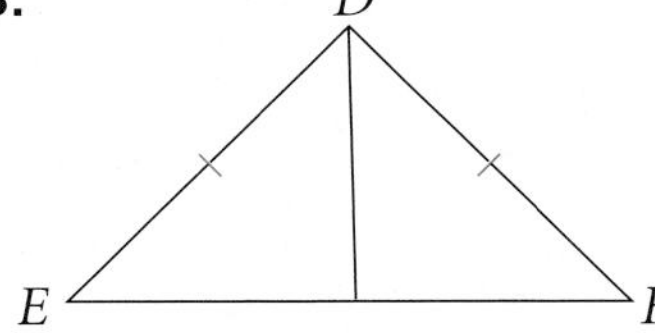

14. 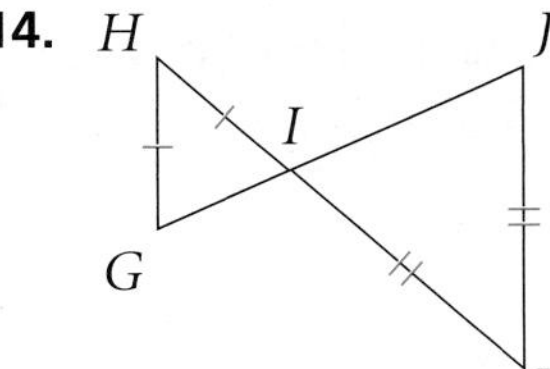

Algebra **Find the value of x.**

15.

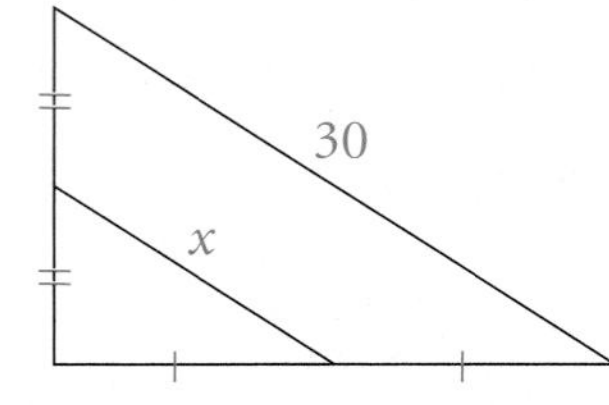

16.

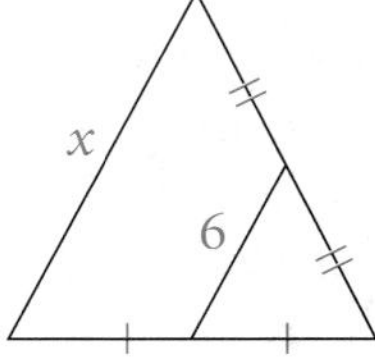

17.

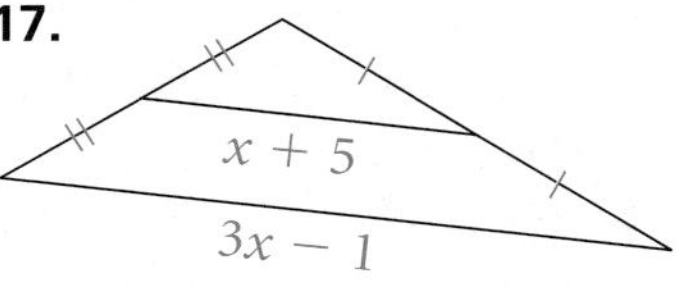

Using Indirect Reasoning 4-5

To use **indirect reasoning**, consider all possibilities and then prove all but one false. The remaining possibility must be true.

There are three steps in an indirect proof.

Step 1: Assume the opposite of what you want to prove is true.
Step 2: Use logical reasoning to reach a contradiction of an earlier statement, such as the given information or a theorem. Then state that the assumption you made was false.
Step 3: State that what you wanted to prove must be true.

Write a convincing argument that uses indirect reasoning.

18. Mary walks into a newly-painted room and finds 2 paint brushes rinsing in water. Show that the room was not painted with oil-based paint.

19. The product of two numbers is even. Show that at least one of the two numbers must be even.

20. Show that a triangle can have at most one obtuse angle.

21. Show that an equilateral triangle cannot have an obtuse angle.

Triangle Inequalities 4-6

The sum of the lengths of any two sides of a triangle is greater than the length of the third side. If two sides of a triangle are not congruent, the larger angle lies opposite the larger side.

List the angles and sides in order from smallest to largest.

22.

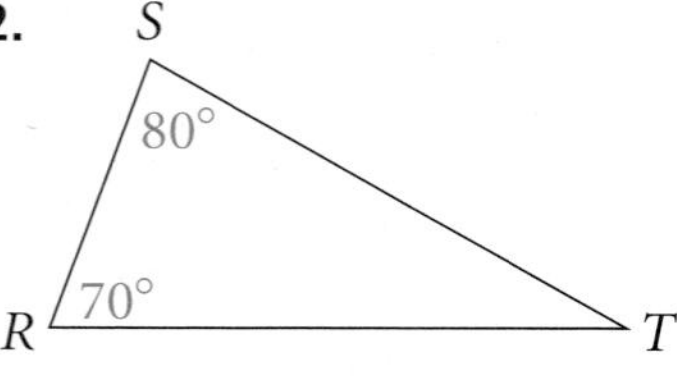

23.

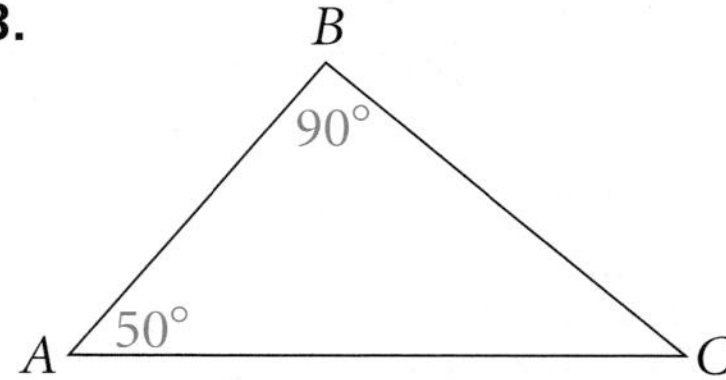

24.

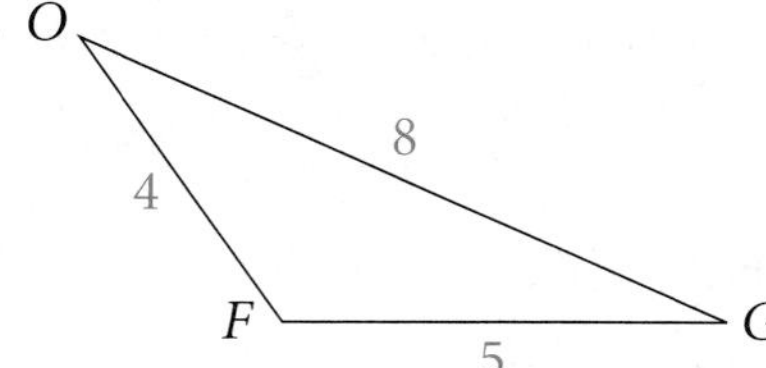

25. *Standardized Test Prep* Two sides of a triangle have lengths 4 and 7. Which could *not* be the length of the third side?

A. 5 **B.** 2 **C.** 7 **D.** 10 **E.** 8

Bisectors and Locus 4-7

A point is on the perpendicular bisector of a segment if and only if it is equidistant from the endpoints of the segment. A point is on the bisector of an angle if and only if it is equidistant from the sides of the angle. A set of points that meet a stated condition is a **locus**.

Sketch and label the locus of points.

26. all points in a plane 2 cm from a circle with radius 1 cm

27. all points in a plane equidistant from two points

28. all points in space a distance a from $\overline{DS}$

29. all points in space a distance b from a point P

Concurrent Lines 4-8

When three or more lines intersect in one point, they are **concurrent.**

The **median of a triangle** is a segment joining a vertex and the midpoint of the side opposite the vertex. The **altitude of a triangle** is a perpendicular segment from a vertex to the line containing the side opposite the vertex.

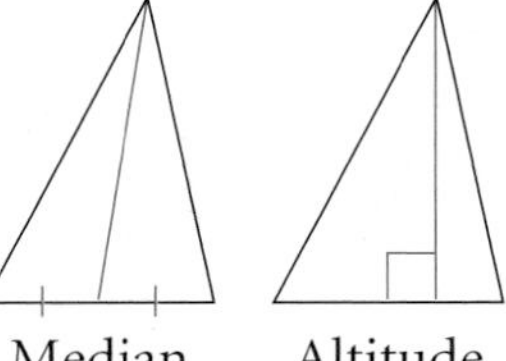

For any given triangle, each of the following are concurrent:

- The perpendicular bisectors of the sides
- The bisectors of the angles
- The medians
- The lines containing the altitudes

Coordinate Geometry **Graph $\triangle ABC$ with vertices $A(2, 3)$, $B(-4, -3)$, and $C(2, -3)$. Find the coordinates of each point of concurrency.**

30. perpendicular bisectors **31.** medians **32.** altitudes

Getting Ready for... CHAPTER 5

Find the perimeter and area of a rectangle with the given dimensions.

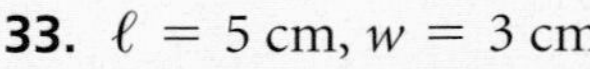

33. $\ell = 5$ cm, $w = 3$ cm **34.** $\ell = 6.2$ ft, $w = 9.0$ ft **35.** $\ell = 0.5$ m, $w = 1.5$ m

Find the value of $\sqrt{a^2 + b^2}$ for the given values of a and b.

36. $a = 4, b = 3$ **37.** $a = 5, b = 12$ **38.** $a = 9, b = 12$

CHAPTER 4

Assessment

For each statement, write (a) the converse, (b) the inverse, and (c) the contrapositive.

1. If a polygon has eight sides, then it is an octagon.
2. If it is a leap year, then it is an even-numbered year.
3. If it is snowing, then it is not summer.

Algebra **Find the values of *x* and *y*.**

4. 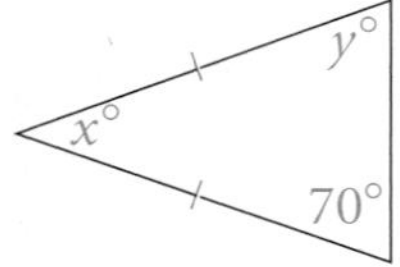

5. 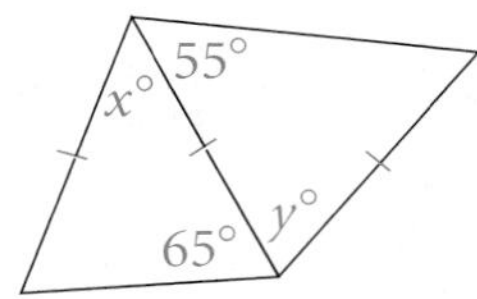

6. What can you conclude from the diagram? Justify your answer.

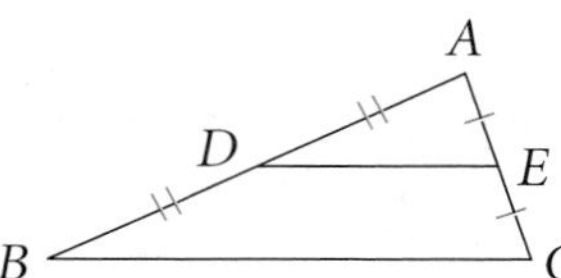

Identify the pair of statements that forms a contradiction.

7. **I.** $\triangle PQR$ is a right triangle.
   II. $\triangle PQR$ is an obtuse triangle.
   III. $\triangle PQR$ is scalene.
8. **I.** $\angle DAS \cong \angle CAT$
   II. $\angle DAS$ and $\angle CAT$ are vertical.
   III. $\angle DAS$ and $\angle CAT$ are adjacent.

List the angles of $\triangle ABC$ from smallest to largest.

9. $AB = 9, BC = 4, AC = 12$
10. $AB = 10, BC = 11, AC = 9$
11. $AB = 3, BC = 9, AC = 7$
12. **Open-ended** Write three lengths that cannot be the lengths of sides of a triangle. Explain your answer.

List the sides of each triangle in order from smallest to largest.

13. 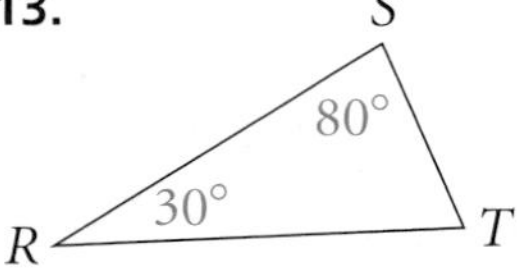

14. 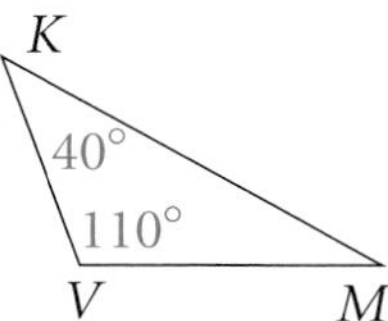

Find the value of *x*.

15. 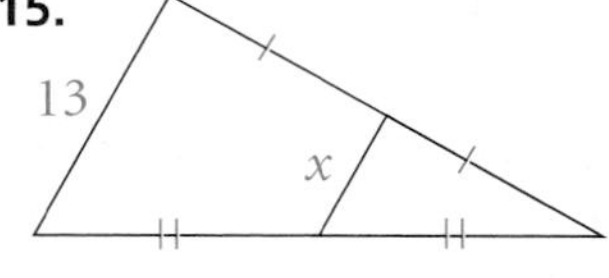

16. 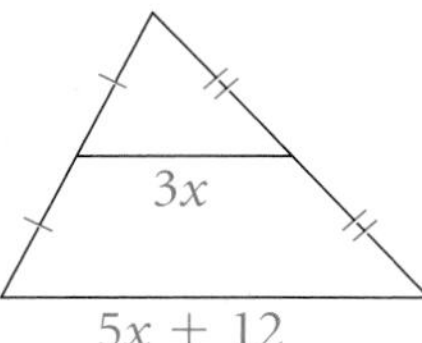

17. **Writing** Use indirect reasoning to explain why the following statement is true: If an isosceles triangle is obtuse, then the obtuse angle is the vertex angle.

Coordinate Geometry **Sketch each locus on a coordinate plane.**

18. all points 6 units from the origin
19. all points 3 units from the line $y = -2$
20. all points equidistant from points (2, 4) and (0, 0)
21. all points equidistant from the axes

Sketch each figure. Determine whether the point of concurrency is in the interior, exterior, or on the triangle.

22. acute triangle, perpendicular bisectors
23. obtuse triangle, medians
24. right triangle, altitudes
25. **Standardized Test Prep** $\triangle ABC$ has vertices $A(2, 5)$, $B(2, -3)$, and $C(10, -3)$. Which point of concurrency is at (6, 1)?
    A. angle bisectors **B.** altitudes
    C. perpendicular bisectors **D.** medians
    E. none of the above

CHAPTER 4

Preparing for the Math A Exam

Part I

1 What is the converse of the statement "If a strawberry is red, then it is ripe"?
(1) If a strawberry is not red, then it is not ripe.
(2) If a strawberry is ripe, then it is red.
(3) A strawberry is ripe if and only if it is red.
(4) If a strawberry is not ripe, then it is not red.

2 What is the value of x?
(1) 30°
(2) 140°
(3) 160°
(4) 70°

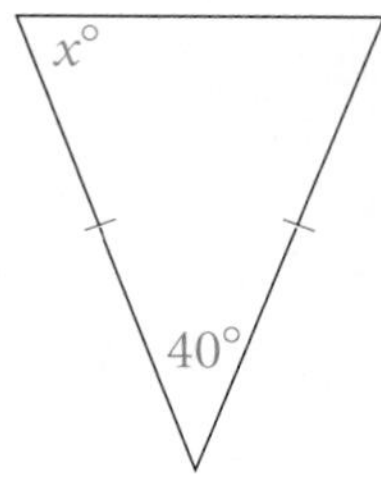

3 What is the length of a midsegment parallel to the side of a triangle 6 cm long?
(1) 3 cm (3) 12 cm
(2) 9 cm (4) 15 cm

4 Which of the following could *not* be the side lengths of a triangle?
(1) 4 in., 4 in., 4 in. (3) 6 cm, 5 cm, 9 cm
(2) 9 m, 17 m, 6 m (4) 15 ft, 4 ft, 15 ft

Part II

5 What is the value of x?

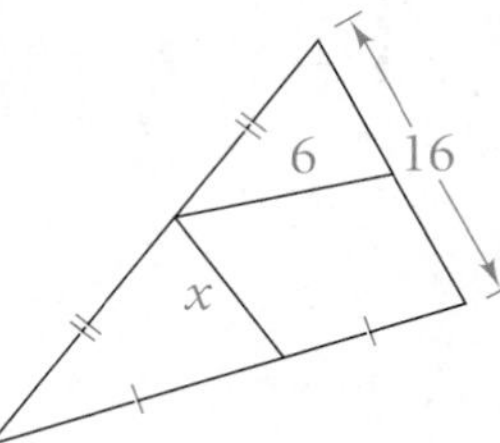

6 List the sides of the triangle in order from shortest to longest.

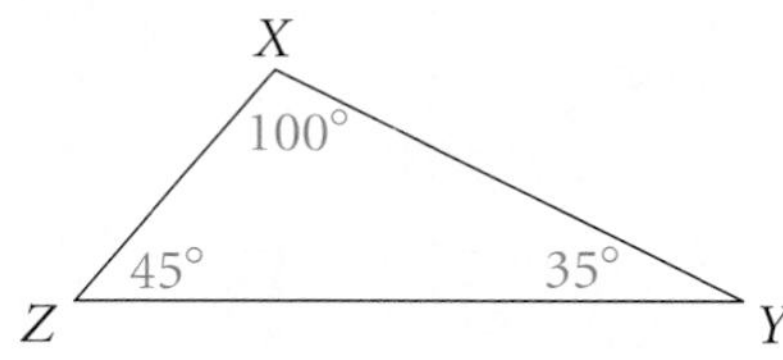

Part III

7 What are the values of x and y?

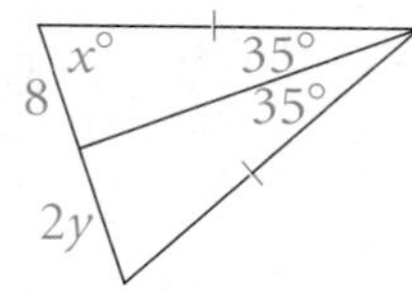

8 Write a convincing argument that uses indirect reasoning to show that a quadrilateral can have at most three obtuse angles.

9 Describe the locus of points in a plane equidistant from $y = x$ and $y = -x$.

10 Construct a right triangle. Then construct the angle bisector of each angle. Label the point of concurrency of the angle bisectors.

Part IV

11 James made the statement, "All rectangles are parallelograms."
a Rewrite this statement in if-then form, and find its truth value.
b Write the converse, inverse, contrapositive, and biconditional of the conditional statement you wrote in part (a). Find the truth value of each statement.

12 Every student in Mr. Hoover's homeroom studies a foreign language. The Venn diagram shows the number of students that study each language.

Foreign Language Study

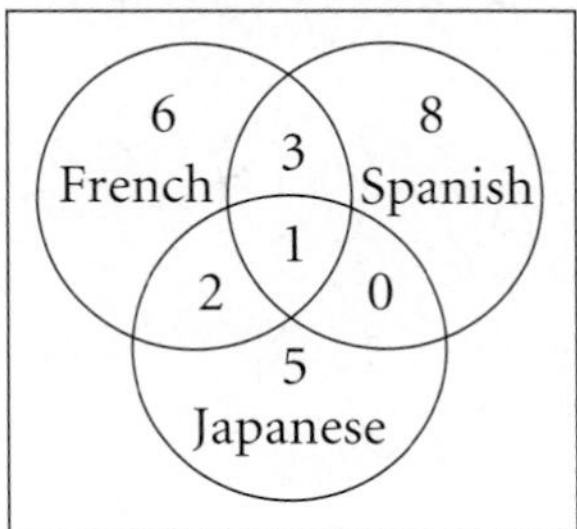

a How many students are in the group formed by the disjunction of *Japanese* and *Spanish*? Explain.
b A student from Mr. Hoover's homeroom is chosen at random. What is the probability that the student studies exactly two foreign languages?

CHAPTER 5

Measuring in the Plane

Relating to the Real World

From architects to race car designers, many careers make use of the concepts you will learn in this chapter. You will find the perimeters and areas of polygons and circles. You will also study one of the most famous theorems in geometry: the Pythagorean Theorem.

Lessons

- 5-1 *Understanding Perimeter and Area*
- 5-2 *Areas of Parallelograms and Triangles*
- 5-3 *The Pythagorean Theorem and Its Converse*
- 5-4 *Special Right Triangles*
- 5-5 *Areas of Trapezoids*

CHAPTER PROJECT

And SEW On

Throughout history people in all corners of the world have used patterns in their clothing, rugs, wall hangings, and blankets. Some of these articles were symbols of wealth and power. Today, textiles and fabrics still reflect social identity and cultural expression.

In your project for this chapter, you will explore patchwork techniques used by Native Americans and American pioneers. You will use these techniques to design your own quilt.

To help you complete the project:

- **p. 810** *Find Out by Modeling*
- **p. 816** *Find Out by Creating*
- **p. 835** *Find Out by Researching*
- **p. 852** *Find Out by Calculating*
- **p. 854** *Finishing the Project*

Areas of Regular Polygons — 5-6

Circles: Circumference and Arc Length — 5-7

Areas of Circles, Sectors, and Segments of Circles — 5-8

Connections Animal Science . . . and more

What You'll Learn

- Finding area and perimeter of squares and rectangles

...And Why

To find the perimeters of banners, animal pens, and gardens

To find the surface area to be covered by carpet or by tiles

What You'll Need

- centimeter grid paper

5-1 Understanding Perimeter and Area

WORK TOGETHER

In your group, draw each figure on centimeter grid paper.

- a rectangle with length 5 cm and width 3 cm
- a rectangle with base 8 cm and height 2 cm
- a rectangle with each side 4 cm

1. Record the perimeter of each rectangle.
2. Are the rectangles with equal perimeters congruent, similar, or neither?
3. To find the area of each rectangle, count the number of square centimeters in its interior. Record the area of each rectangle.
4. Are the rectangles with the same area congruent, similar, or neither?
5. Do the rectangles with equal perimeters have the same area?

THINK AND DISCUSS

Finding Perimeter

In the Work Together, you found the **perimeter of a polygon** by finding the sum of the lengths of the sides. In special cases such as squares and rectangles, you may use formulas for perimeter.

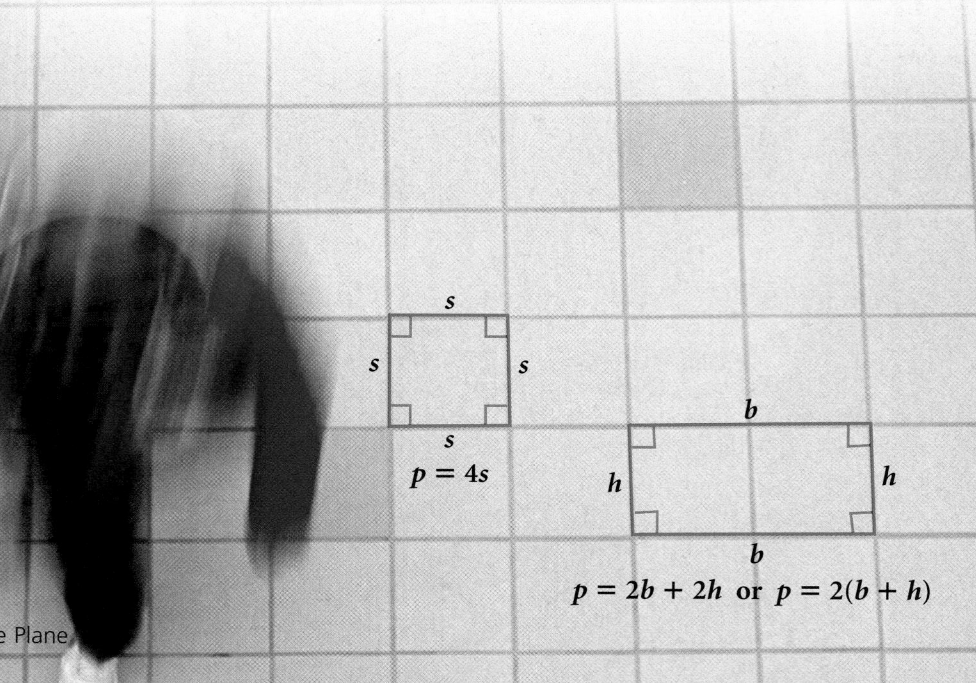

$p = 4s$

$p = 2b + 2h$ or $p = 2(b + h)$

6. Can you use the formula for the perimeter of a square to find the perimeter of any rectangle? Explain.

You can use the Distance Formula to find perimeter in the coordinate plane.

Example 1

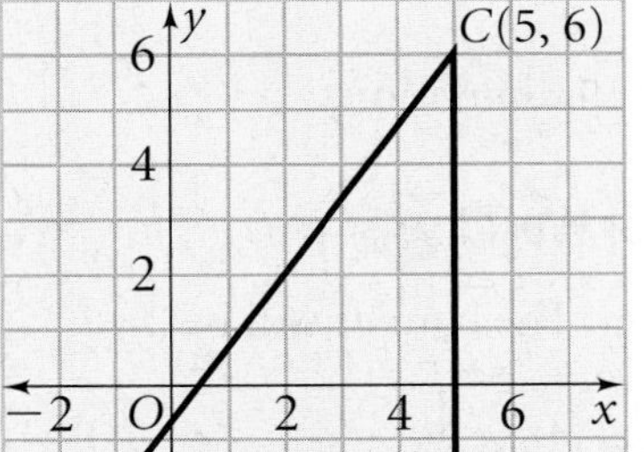

Coordinate Geometry Find the perimeter of $\triangle ABC$.

Find the length of each side. Add the lengths to find the perimeter.

$AB = 5 - (-1) = 6$

$BC = 6 - (-2) = 8$

$AC = \sqrt{(5-(-1))^2 + (6-(-2))^2}$ Use the Distance Formula.

$= \sqrt{6^2 + 8^2} = \sqrt{100} = 10$

$AB + BC + AC = 6 + 8 + 10 = 24$

The perimeter of $\triangle ABC$ is 24 units.

7. **Try This** Graph the quadrilateral with vertices $K(-3, -3)$, $L(1, -3)$, $M(1, 4)$, and $N(-3, 1)$. Find the perimeter of $KLMN$.

Finding Area

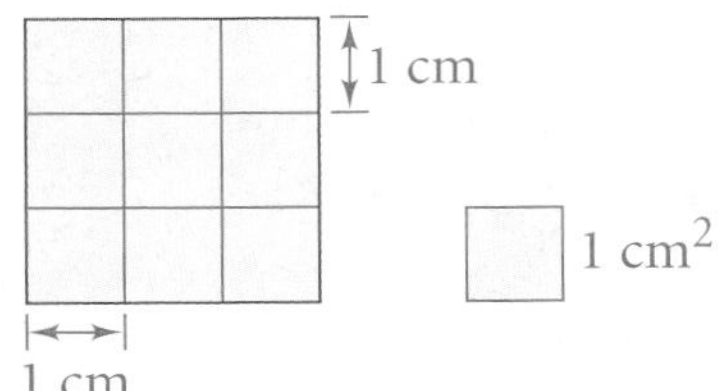

The **area of a polygon** is the number of square units enclosed by the polygon. The blue square at the left encloses nine smaller red squares. Each red square has sides 1 cm long and is called a square centimeter. By counting square centimeters, you see that the blue square has area 9 cm^2.

Postulate 5-1 The area of a square is the square of the length of a side.

$A = s^2$

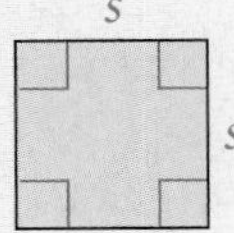

Postulate 5-2 If two figures are congruent, their areas are equal.

Postulate 5-3 The area of a region is the sum of the areas of its nonoverlapping parts.

8. a. **Try This** What is the area of a square whose sides are 12 in. long?
   b. What is the area of a square whose sides are 1 ft long?
   c. How many square inches are in a square foot?

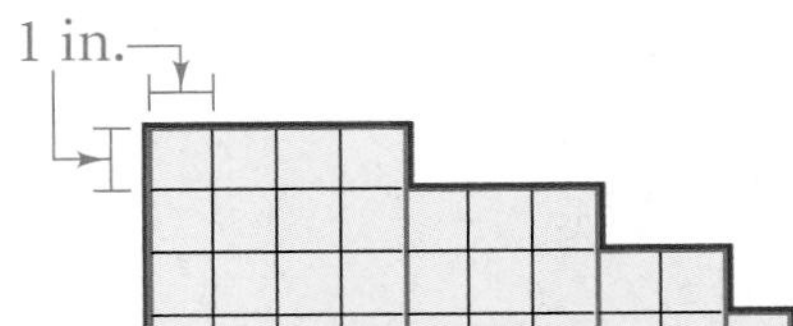

9. a. By counting squares, find the area of the polygon outlined in blue.
   b. Use Postulate 5-1 to find the area of each square outlined in red.
   c. How does the sum of your answers to part (b) compare to your answer to part (a)? Which postulate does this **verify?**

You can select any side of a rectangle to be the base. Because adjacent sides are perpendicular, the length of a side adjacent to the base is the height.

Theorem 5-1
Area of a Rectangle

The area of a rectangle is the product of its base and height.

$$A = bh$$

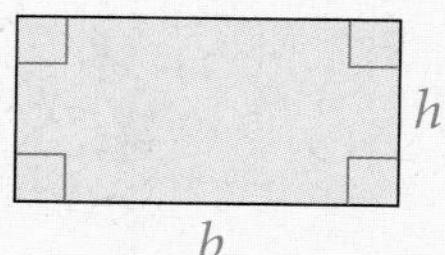

To find area, you must use the same units for all dimensions.

Example 2 **Relating to the Real World** 

Design You are designing a rectangular banner. The banner will be 2 yd long and 4 ft wide. How much material will you need?

2 yd = 6 ft	Change units using 1 yd = 3 ft.
$A = bh$	Use the formula for the area of a rectangle.
$= 6(4) = 24$	Substitute 6 for b and 4 for h.

The area of the banner is 24 ft^2. You will need at least 24 ft^2 of material.

PROBLEM SOLVING

Look Back Find the area of the banner in Example 2 by first changing all units to yards.

10. Try This Find the area of a rectangle with length 75 cm and width 2 m.

You can use a graphing calculator or spreadsheet technology to find maximum and minimum values for area and perimeter problems.

Example 3 **Relating to the Real World** 

Animal Science You have 32 yd of fencing. You want to make a rectangular pen for a calf you are raising for a 4-H project. What are the dimensions of the rectangle that will result in the maximum area? What is the maximum area?

Draw some possible rectangular pens and find their areas.

	A	B	C
1	b	h = 16 − b	A = bh
2	1	15	15
3	2	14	28
4	3	13	39
5	. . .	. . .	. . .

Create a spreadsheet to find area. Choose values for b from 0 to 15.

Make a graph of the spreadsheet values. Graph values of b on the horizontal axis and values of A on the vertical axis. Connect the points with a smooth curve.

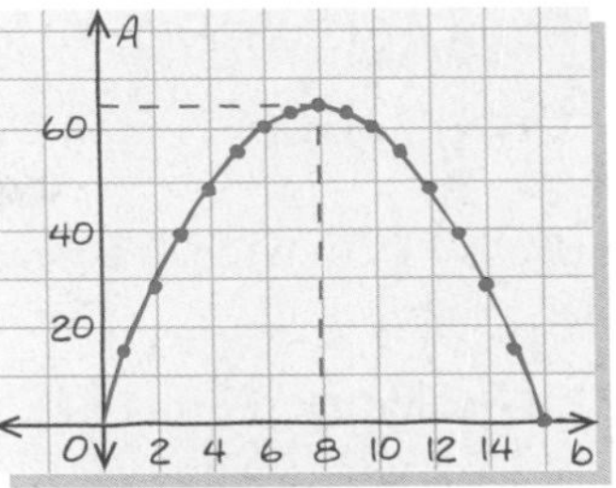

The maximum value occurs at $b = 8$. When $b = 8$, $h = 8$ and $A = 64$.

To have the maximum area for your calf, you should fence a square with sides 8 yd long. The maximum area is 64 yd^2.

11. **Critical Thinking** Show how the equation $h = 16 - b$ was derived from the formula $2b + 2h = 32$.

12. Use the answer to Example 3. Make a **conjecture** by completing this statement: If you have a fixed amount of fencing to enclose a rectangle, you can get the maximum area by enclosing a $\underline{\ ?\ }$.

Exercises ON YOUR OWN

Estimation **Estimate the perimeter of each item.**

1. the cover of this book

2. the cover of your notebook

3. a classroom bulletin board

Mental Math **Find the perimeter of each figure.**

4.

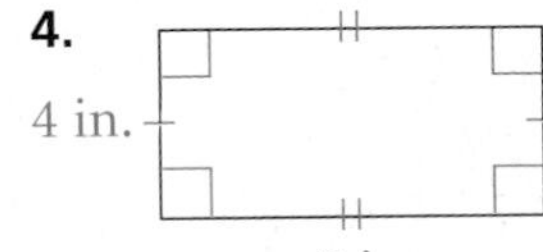

5.

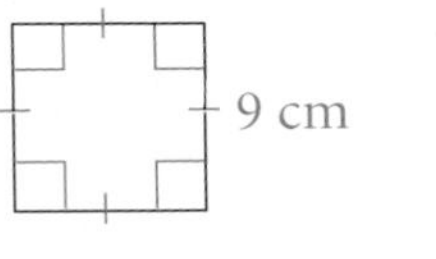

6.

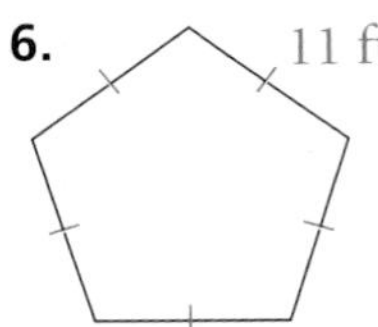

7.

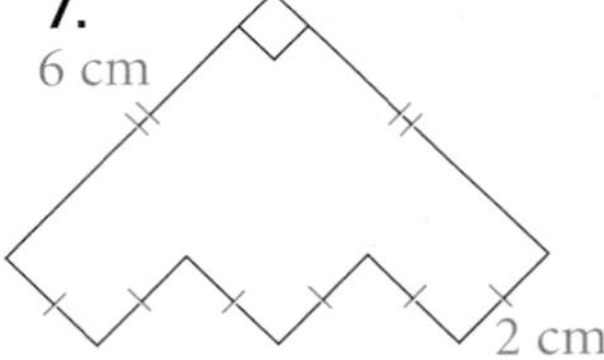

Find the perimeter of each rectangle with the given base and height.

8. 21 in., 7 in.

9. 16 cm, 23 cm

10. 24 m, 36 m

11. 14 ft, 23 ft

The figures below are drawn on centimeter graph paper. Find the area of the shaded portion of each figure.

12.

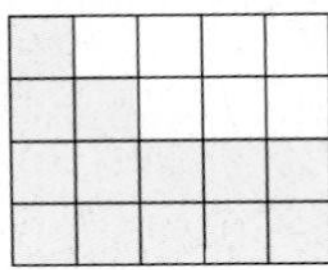

13.

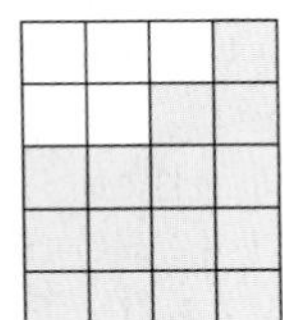

14.

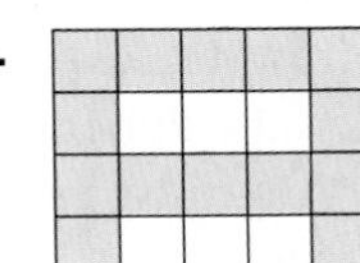

15.

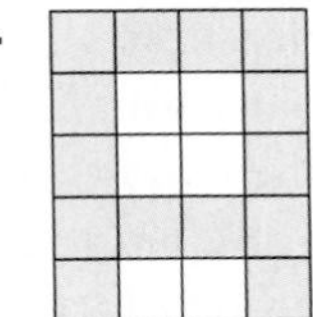

Coordinate Geometry **Graph each rectangle *ABCD* and find its area.**

16. $A(0, 0), B(0, 4), C(5, 4), D(5, 0)$

17. $A(1, 4), B(1, 7), C(5, 7), D(5, 4)$

18. $A(-3, 2), B(-2, 2), C(-2, -2), D(-3, -2)$

19. $A(-2, -6), B(-2, -3), C(3, -3), D(3, -6)$

20. A rectangle is 11 cm wide. Its area is 176 cm^2. What is the length of the rectangle?

21. **Coordinate Geometry** Points $A(1, 1)$, $B(10, 1)$, $C(10, 8)$, $D(7, 8)$, $E(7, 5)$, $F(4, 5)$, $G(4, 8)$, and $H(1, 8)$ are the coordinates of the vertices of polygon *ABCDEFGH*.
   a. Draw the polygon on graph paper.
   b. Find the perimeter of the polygon.
   c. Divide the polygon into rectangles.
   d. Find the area of the polygon.

22. The perimeter of a rectangle is 40 cm and the base is 12 cm. What is the area?

23. A square and a rectangle have equal areas. The rectangle is 64 cm by 81 cm. What is the perimeter of the square?

Find the area of each rectangle with the given base and height.

24. 4 ft 6 in., 4 in.

25. 1 yd 18 in., 4 yd

26. 2 ft 3 in., 6 in.

Building Safe Stairs

Since falls are a major cause of injury, it makes sense to be concerned about the safety of stairs. According to John Templer, the world's foremost authority on stairs, steps with a 7-in. riser and an 11-in. tread form the safest possible stairs.

Prior to his investigations, Francois Blondel's formula, dated 1675, had recommended that stair measurements conform to the formula 2(riser) + tread = 25.5 in.

Source: *Smithsonian*

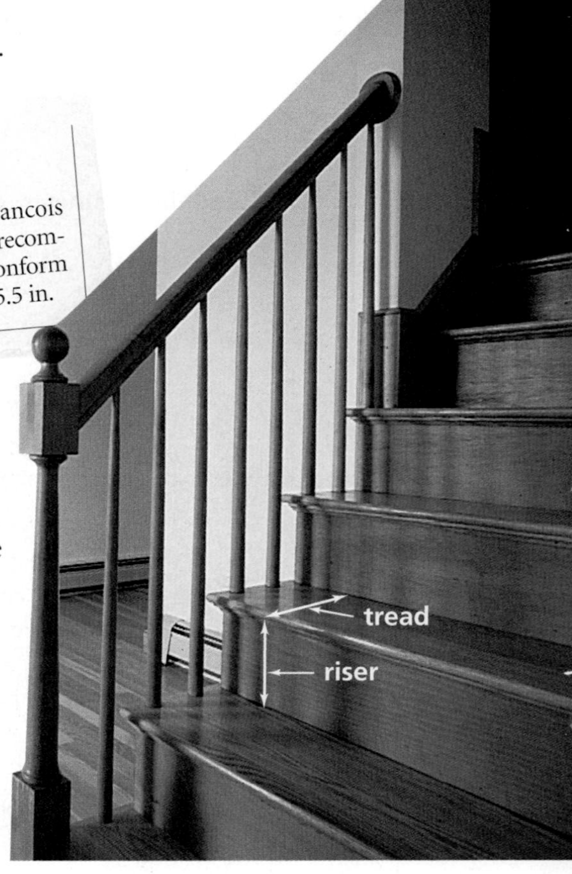

27. **Carpeting** You use John Templer's dimensions to build a stairway with six steps. You want to carpet the stairs with a 3-ft wide runner from the bottom of the first riser to the top of the sixth riser.
   a. Find the area of the runner.
   b. Since a roll of carpet is 12 ft across, a rectangle of carpet that measures 3 ft by 12 ft is cut from the roll to make the runner. How many square feet of the material will be wasted?
   c. The carpet costs \$17.95/yd^2. You must pay for the entire piece that is cut. Find the cost of the carpet.
   d. Binding for the edge of the runner costs \$1.75/yd. How much will the binding cost if the two long edges of the runner are bound?

Writing **Tell whether you need to know area or perimeter in order to determine how much of each item to buy. Explain your choice.**

28. edging for a garden

29. paint for a basement floor

30. wallpaper for a bedroom

31. weatherstripping for a door

32. **Tiling** The Art Club is tiling an 8 ft-by-16 ft wall at the entrance to the school. They are creating a design by using different colors of 4 in.-by-4 in. tiles. How many tiles do the students need?

33. **Gardening** You want to make a 900-ft^2 rectangular garden to grow corn. In order to keep raccoons out of your corn, you must fence the garden. You want to use the minimum amount of fencing so that your costs will be as low as possible.

a. List some possible dimensions for the rectangular garden. Find the perimeter of each rectangle.

b. **Technology** Create a spreadsheet listing integer values of b and the corresponding values of h and P. What dimensions will give you a garden with the minimum perimeter?

34. You want to build a rectangular corral by using one side of a barn and fencing the other three sides. You have enough material to build 100 ft of fence.

a. **Technology** Create a spreadsheet listing integer values of b and the corresponding values of h and A.

b. **Coordinate Geometry** Make a graph using your spreadsheet values. Graph b on the horizontal axis and A on the vertical axis.

c. Describe the dimensions of the corral with the greatest area.

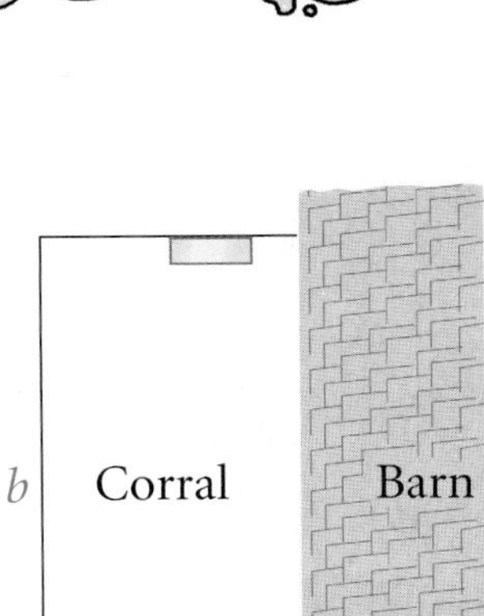

Find the area of the shaded portion of each figure. All angles in the figures are right angles.

35.

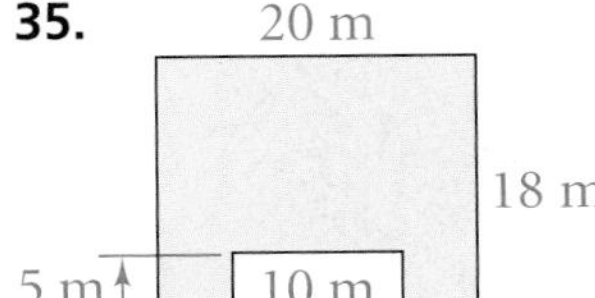

36.

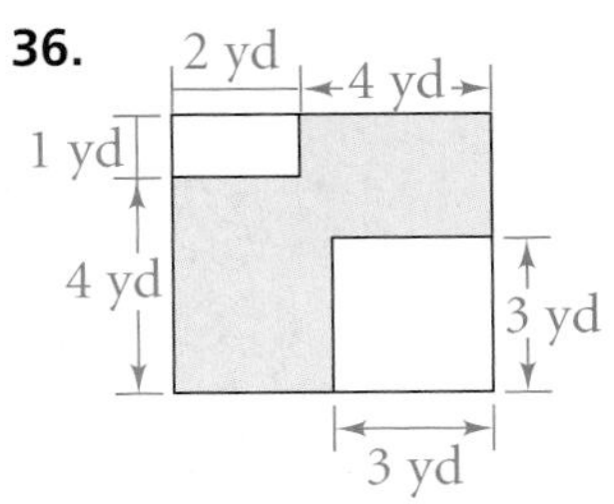

37.

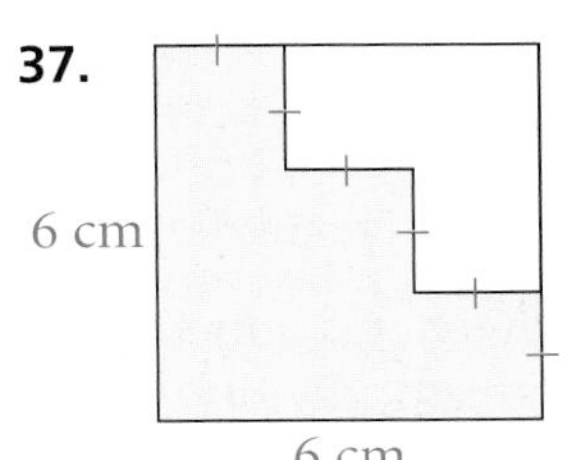

38.

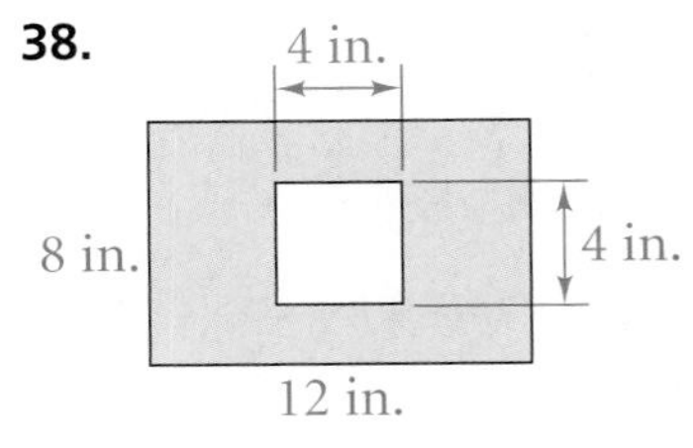

Coordinate Geometry **Graph each quadrilateral *ABCD*. Find its perimeter.**

39. $A(-2, 2), B(0, 2), C(4, -1), D(-2, -1)$

40. $A(-4, -1), B(4, 5), C(4, -2), D(-4, -2)$

41. $A(0, 1), B(3, 5), C(5, 5), D(5, 1)$

42. $A(-5, 3), B(7, -2), C(7, -6), D(-5, -6)$

43. **Open-ended** The area of a 5 in.-by-5 in. square is the same as the sum of the areas of a 3 in.-by-3 in. square and a 4 in.-by-4 in. square. Find two or more squares that have the same total area as an 11 in.-by-11 in. square.

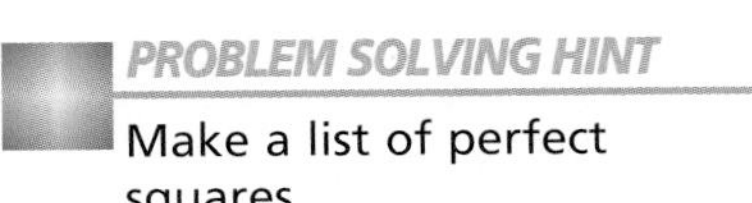

PROBLEM SOLVING HINT

Make a list of perfect squares.

44. *Standardized Test Prep* The length of a rectangle is increased by 50% and the width is decreased by 50%. How is the area affected?

A. increased by 25% **B.** decreased by 25% **C.** increased by 50%
D. decreased by 50% **E.** unchanged

Chapter Project — *Find Out by Modeling*

You can create a quilt by sewing together congruent squares to form blocks. To model a quilt block, cut four 3 in.-by-3 in. squares out of $\frac{1}{4}$-in. graph paper. Place one square on top of another and make a seam by stapling the two squares together $\frac{1}{4}$ in. from one of the edges. Unfold the squares and press the seam flat in the back.

Repeat this with the two other squares. Then place the two sections on top of each other. Staple a $\frac{1}{4}$-in. seam from one end to the other. Unfold and press the seams back.

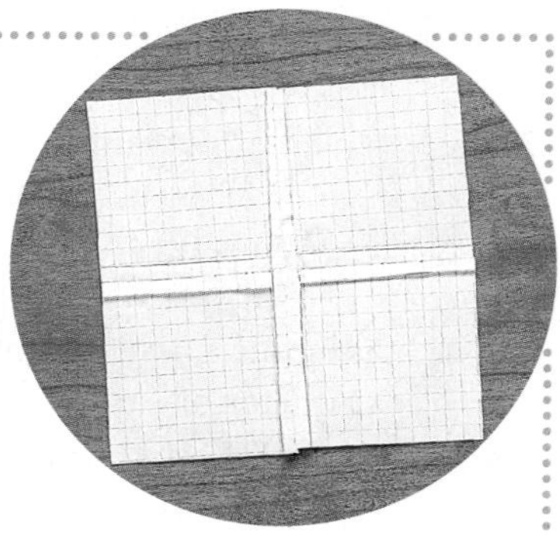

- What is the total area of the four paper squares that you started with?
- What is the area of your finished quilt block?

Exercises MIXED REVIEW

Coordinate Geometry **Find the coordinates of the midpoint of a segment with the given endpoints.**

45. $A(4, 1), B(7, 9)$

46. $G(0, 3), H(3, 8)$

47. $R(-2, 7), S(-6, -1)$

Write the converse of each conditional.

48. If you make a touchdown, then you score six points.

49. If it is Thanksgiving, then it is November.

50. If a figure is a square, then it is a rectangle.

51. A triangle has two sides with lengths 3 m and 5 m. What is the range of possible lengths for the third side?

SELF ASSESSMENT — FOR YOUR JOURNAL

Explain the difference between area and perimeter. Use examples to show how and when each type of measurement might be used.

Getting Ready for Lesson 5-2

Each rectangle is divided into two congruent triangles. Find the area of each triangle.

52. 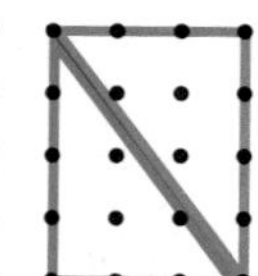

53. 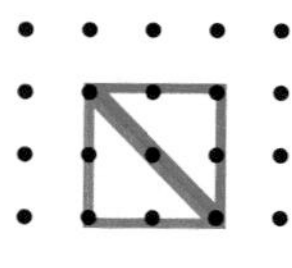

54. 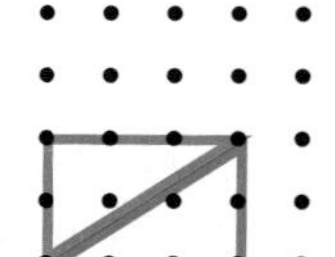

55. 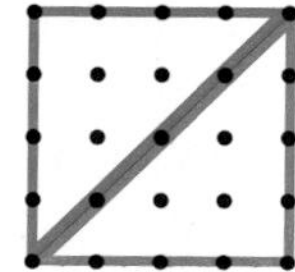

What You'll Learn

- Finding areas of parallelograms and triangles

...And Why

To solve design problems in architecture and landscaping

What You'll Need

- centimeter grid paper
- straightedge
- scissors
- tape

5-2 Areas of Parallelograms and Triangles

WORK TOGETHER

Have each member of your group cut out a different rectangle from centimeter grid paper.

- Record the base, height, and area of each rectangle.
- Cut out a triangle from one side of the rectangle as shown below. Tape it to the opposite side to form a parallelogram.

1. Compare each original rectangle with the parallelogram formed. With your group, list all the ways the rectangle and the parallelogram are the same and all the ways they are different.

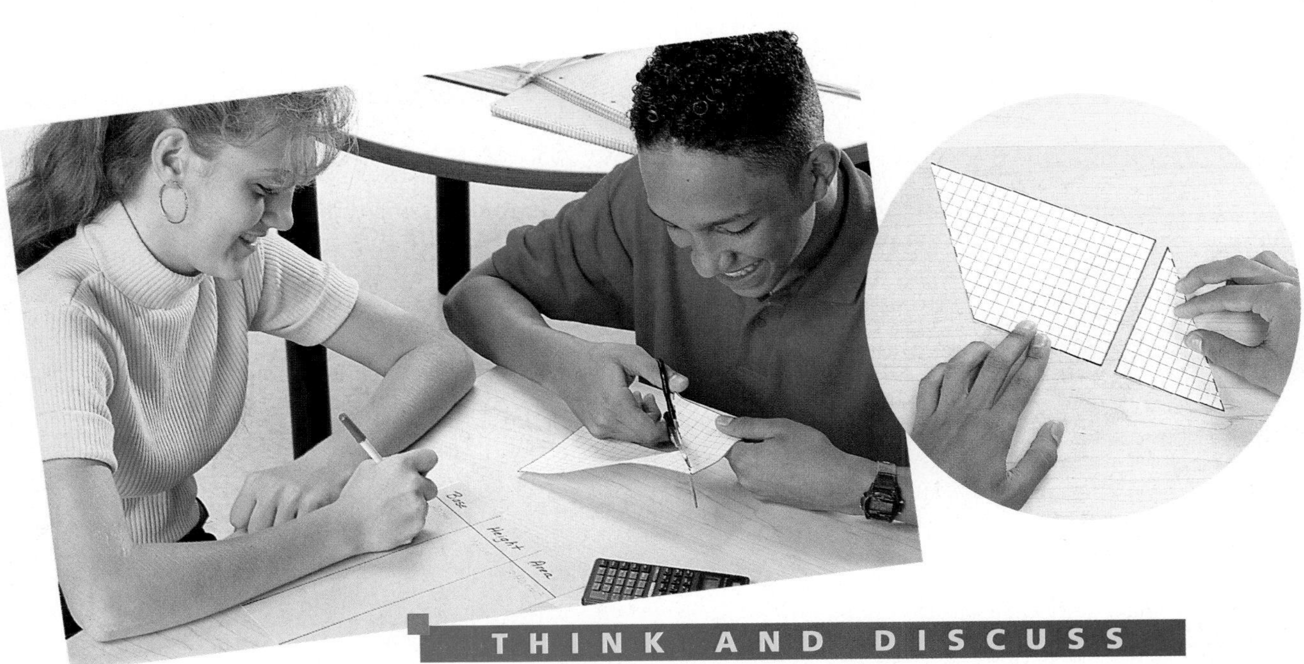

THINK AND DISCUSS

Areas of Parallelograms

In the Work Together, you cut a rectangle into two pieces and used the pieces to form another parallelogram. The area of the parallelogram was the same as the area of the rectangle. This suggests the following theorem.

Theorem 5-2
Area of a Parallelogram

The area of a parallelogram is the product of any base and the corresponding height.

$$A = bh$$

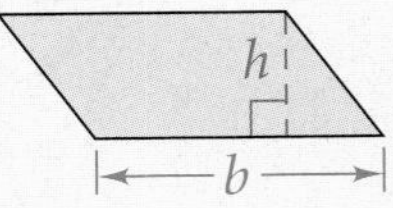

Math A Test Prep

1 What is the perimeter of a regular hexagon with sides of 9 in.?

(1) 81 in.^{2} (3) 54 in.
(2) 72 in. (4) $1\frac{1}{2}$ in.

2 Graph $\triangle WXY$ with vertices $W(8, 6)$, $X(1, 8)$, and $Y(1, 2)$ on a coordinate plane.

a What is the area of $\triangle WXY$?

b What is the perimeter of $\triangle WXY$ to the nearest tenth of a unit?

You can choose any side to be a **base** of a parallelogram. An **altitude** is any segment perpendicular to the line containing the base drawn from the side opposite the base. The **height** is the length of the altitude.

2. Draw any parallelogram and draw altitudes to two adjacent sides.

Example 1

Coordinate Geometry What is the area of $\square PQRS$ with vertices $P(1, 2)$, $Q(6, 2)$, $R(8, 5)$, and $S(3, 5)$?

Graph $\square PQRS$. If you choose $\overline{PQ}$ as the base, then the height is 3.

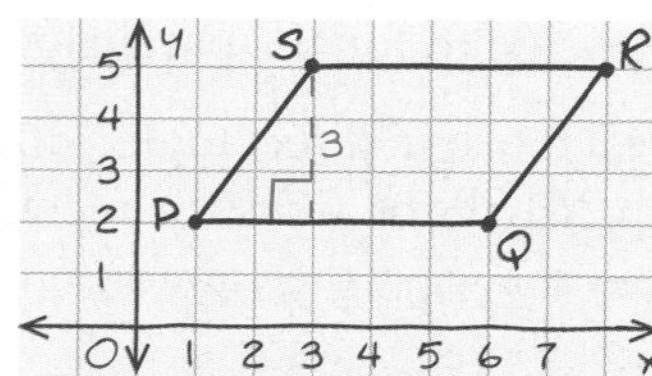

$b = PQ = 5$
$h = 3$
$A = bh = 5(3)$
$\quad = 15$

$\square PQRS$ has area 15 square units.

3. Try This What is the area of $\square EFGH$ with vertices $E(-4, 3)$, $F(0, 3)$, $G(1, -2)$, and $H(-3, -2)$?

You can use the area formula to find missing dimensions in a parallelogram.

Example 2

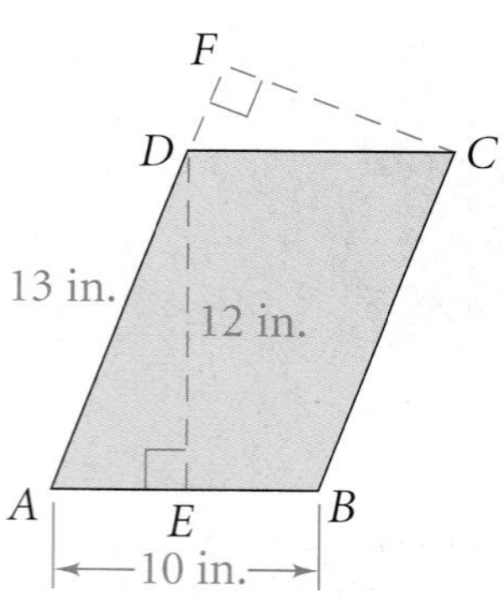

In $\square ABCD$, $\overline{DE}$ and $\overline{CF}$ are altitudes. Find CF to the nearest tenth.

Find the area of $\square ABCD$. Then use the area formula to find CF.

$A = bh$
$\quad = 10(12)$ — **Use base AB and height DE.**
$\quad = 120$

The area of $\square ABCD$ is 120 in.^{2}.

$A = bh$
$120 = 13(CF)$ — **Use base AD and height CF.**
$CF = \frac{120}{13}$ — **Divide each side by 13.**
$\quad \approx 9.2$

$\overline{CF}$ is about 9.2 in. long.

4. Try This A parallelogram has sides 15 cm and 18 cm. The altitude perpendicular to the line containing the 15 cm side is 9 cm long. Sketch the parallelogram. Then find the length of the altitude perpendicular to the line containing the 18-cm side.

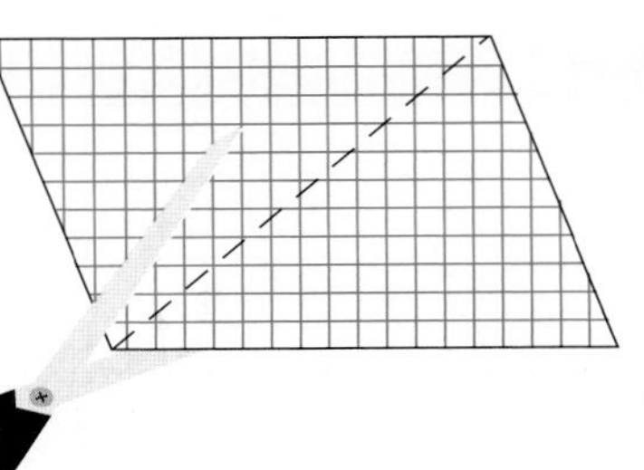

WORK TOGETHER

Work in groups. Have each member of your group cut out a different parallelogram from centimeter grid paper.

- Record the base, height, and area of each parallelogram.
- Cut each parallelogram along a diagonal as shown, forming two triangles.

5. How does the area of each triangle compare to the area of the parallelogram?

THINK AND DISCUSS

Areas of Triangles

In the Work Together, you cut a parallelogram into two congruent triangles of equal area. This suggests the following theorem.

Theorem 5-3
Area of a Triangle

The area of a triangle is half the product of any base and the corresponding height.

$$A = \frac{1}{2}bh$$

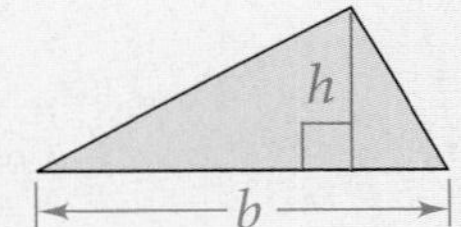

You can choose any side to be a **base** of a triangle. The corresponding **height** is the length of an altitude drawn to the line containing that base.

Example 3 **Relating to the Real World** 

Architecture When designing a building, an architect must be sure that the building can stand up to hurricane force winds, which have a velocity of 73 mi/h or more. The formula $F = 0.004Av^2$ gives the force F in pounds exerted by a wind blowing against a flat surface. A is the area of the surface in square feet, and v is the wind velocity in miles per hour. How much force is exerted by a 73 mi/h wind blowing directly against the side of this building?

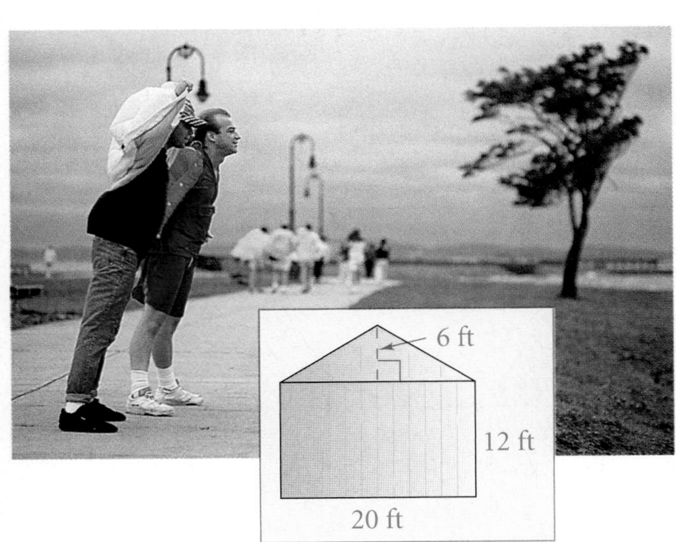

Find the area of the side of the building.

$$\text{triangle area} = \frac{1}{2}bh = \frac{1}{2}(20)6 = 60 \text{ ft}^2$$

$$\text{rectangle area} = bh = 20(12) = 240 \text{ ft}^2$$

$$\text{area of end of building} = 60 + 240 = 300 \text{ ft}^2$$

$F = 0.004Av^2$ — **Use the formula for force.**

$= 0.004(300)(73)^2$ — **Substitute 300 for A and 73 for v.**

$= 6394.8$

The force is about 6400 lb.

Exercises ON YOUR OWN

Find the area of each figure.

1. ▱$ABJF$
2. $\triangle BDJ$
3. $\triangle DKJ$
4. ▱$BDKJ$
5. ▱$ADKF$
6. $\triangle BCJ$

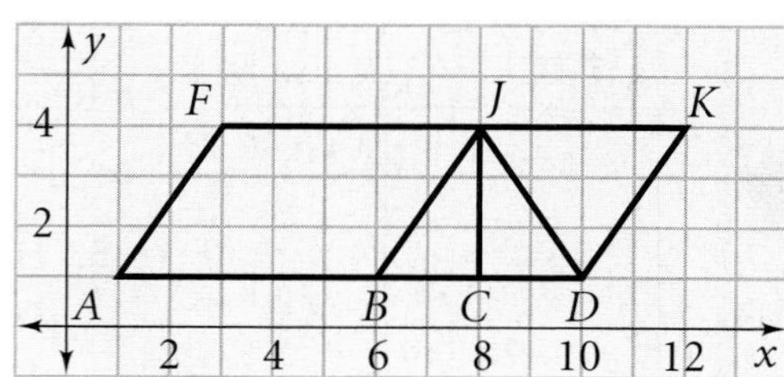

7. The area of a parallelogram is 24 in.^{2} and the height is 6 in. Find the length of the base.
8. An isosceles right triangle has area of 98 cm^2. Find the length of each leg.

Find the area of each shaded region.

9.

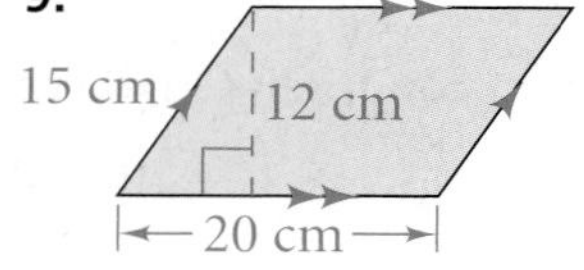

10.

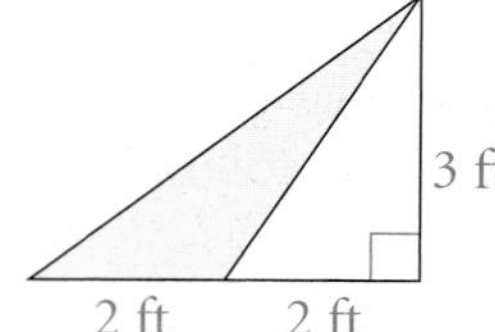

11.

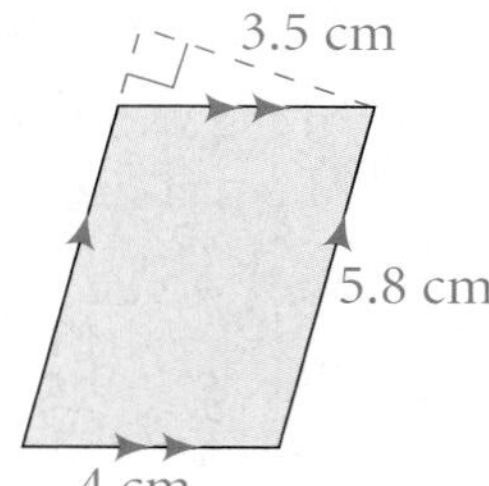

12.

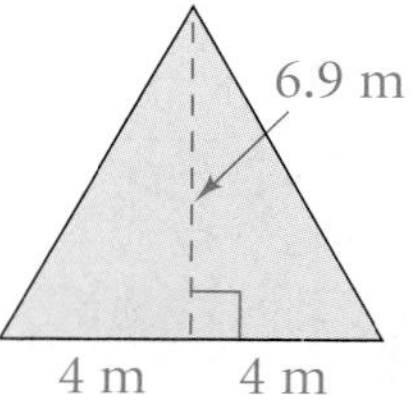

Coordinate Geometry **(a) Graph the lines. (b) Find the area of the triangle enclosed by the lines.**

13. $y = x, x = 0$, and $y = 7$
14. $y = x + 2, y = 2, x = 6$
15. $y = -\frac{1}{2}x + 3, y = 0, x = -2$

Find the value of h in each parallelogram.

16.

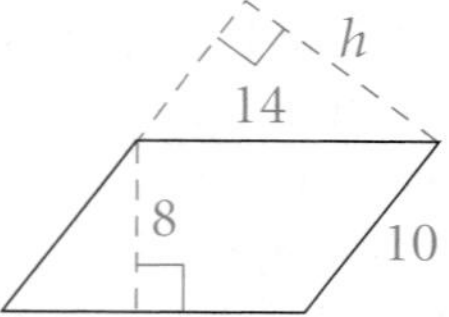

17.

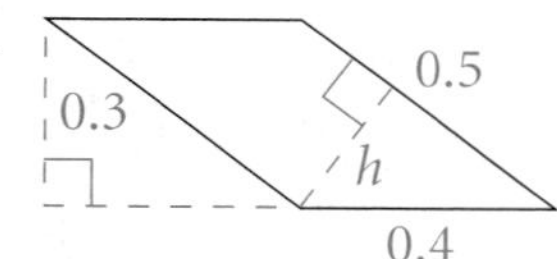

18.

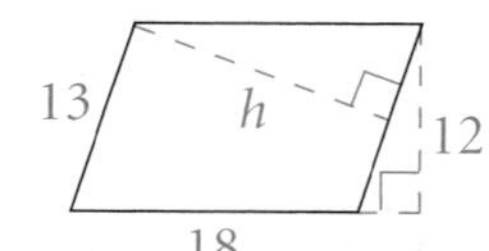

19. **Landscaping** Taisha's Bakery has a plan for a 50 ft-by-31 ft parking lot. The four parking spaces are congruent parallelograms, the driving area is a rectangle, and the two unpaved areas for flowers are congruent triangles.
    a. **Writing** Explain two different ways to find the area of the region that must be paved.
    b. **Verify** your answer to part (a) by using each method to find the area.

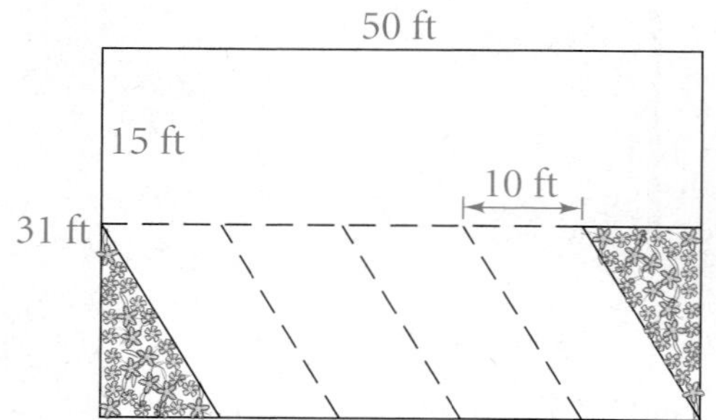

20. **Algebra** In a triangle, a base and the corresponding height are in the ratio 3 : 2. The area is 108 in.^{2}. Find the base and the corresponding height.

Find the area of each figure.

21. 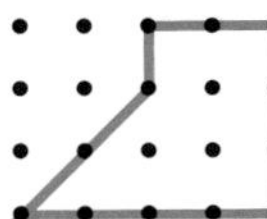

22. 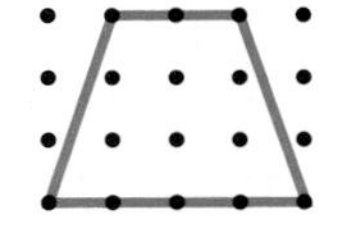

23. 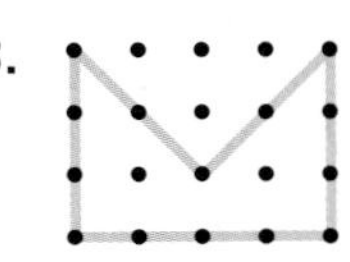

24. **Probability** Ann drew these three figures on a grid. A fly landed at random at a point on the grid.

a. Is the fly more likely to have landed on one of the figures or on the blank grid? Explain.

b. Suppose you know the fly landed on one of the figures. Is the fly more likely to have landed on one figure than on another? Explain.

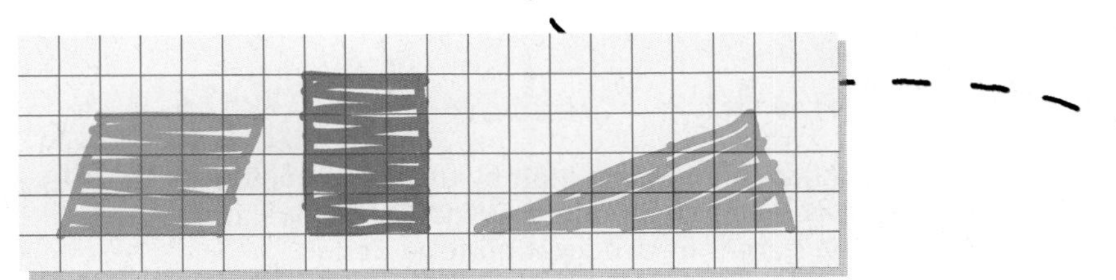

Find the area of each figure.

25. 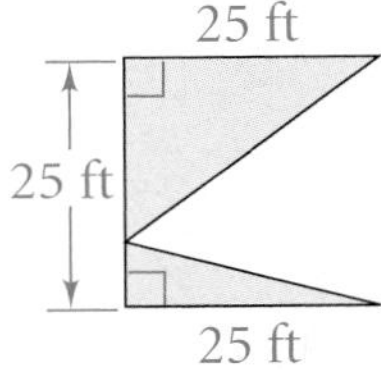

26. 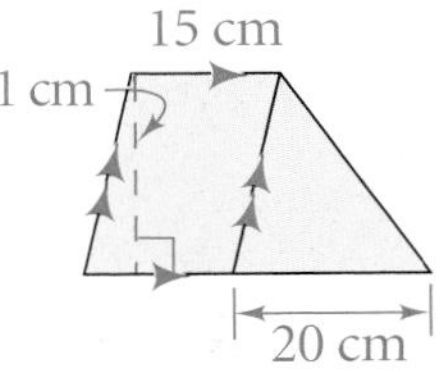

27. 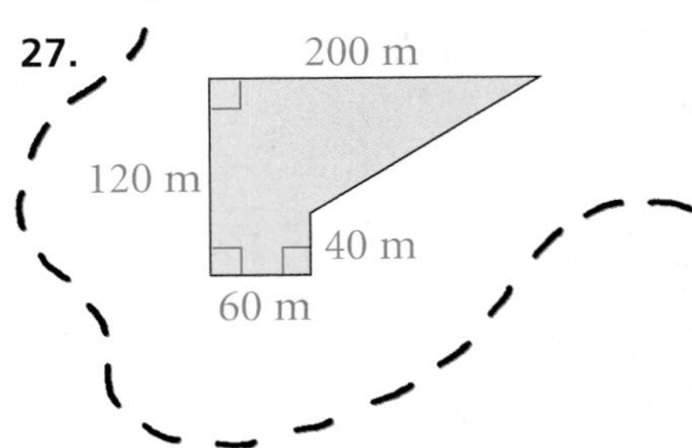

28. **Open-ended** Using graph paper, draw an acute triangle, an obtuse triangle, and a right triangle, each with area 12 units^2.

29. **Technology** Juanita used geometry software to create the figure at the right. She drew segment $\overline{AB}$, chose point C, and constructed line k parallel to $\overline{AB}$ through point C. Then Juanita chose point D on line k. Next she dragged point D along line k to form different triangles. How do the areas of the triangles compare? Explain.

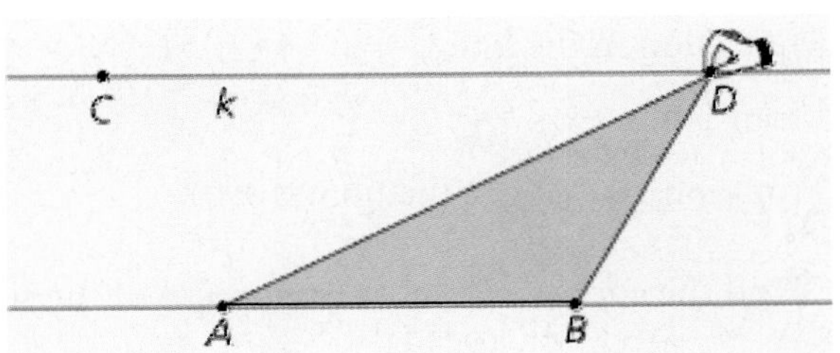

The ancient Greek mathematician Heron is most famous for his formula for the area of a triangle in terms of its sides a, b, and c.

$$A = \sqrt{s(s-a)(s-b)(s-c)}, \text{ where } s = \frac{1}{2}(a+b+c)$$

Use Heron's formula and a calculator to find the area of each triangle. Round your answer to the nearest whole number.

30. $a = 8$ in., $b = 9$ in., $c = 10$ in.

31. $a = 15$ m, $b = 17$ m, $c = 21$ m

32. **a.** Use Heron's formula to find the area of the triangle at the right.

b. **Verify** your answer to part (a) by using the formula $A = \frac{1}{2}bh$.

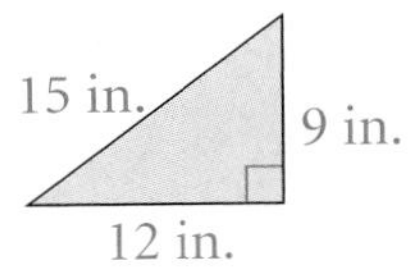

Coordinate Geometry **The vertices of a polygon are given. Graph each polygon and find its area.**

33. $A(3, 9), B(8, 9), C(2, -3), D(-3, -3)$

34. $E(1, 1), F(4, 5), G(11, 5), H(8, 1)$

35. $M(-2, -5), L(1, -5), N(2, -2)$

36. $R(1, 2), S(1, 6), T(4, 1)$

Chapter Project: *Find Out by Creating*

Your class can model a quilt by using the quilt blocks your classmates created in the *Find Out* activity on page 810. Here is one suggestion for a design.

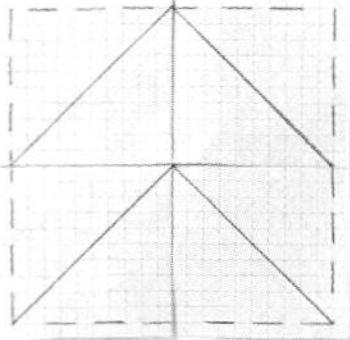

On each block, mark off a $\frac{1}{4}$-in. border for seams. Draw the four diagonals pictured.

Staple four blocks together in a row, keeping the orientation shown at the left throughout the row. Do this until you have four rows.

Staple the rows together, turning the second and fourth row upside down. Color the blocks to create a three-dimensional illusion.

Exercises MIXED REVIEW

Transformations **Find the coordinates of the images of *A, B, C,* and *D* after each transformation.**

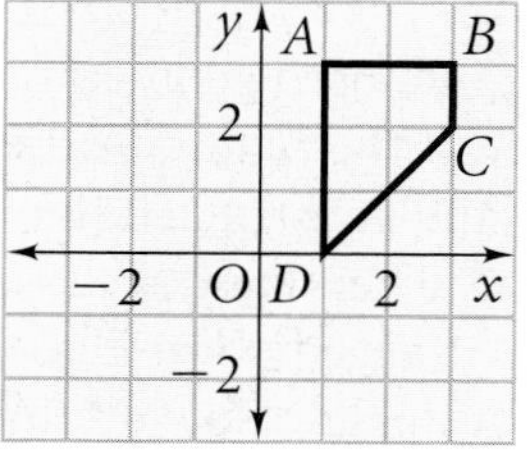

37. reflection in the line $x = 1$

38. translation $\langle -4, -7 \rangle$

39. rotation 180° about the point (0, 0)

40. Find the coordinates of the midpoint of the segment joining $P(-2, -3)$ and $Q(9, 12)$.

Getting Ready for Lesson 5-3

Square the lengths of the sides of each triangle. What do you notice?

41.

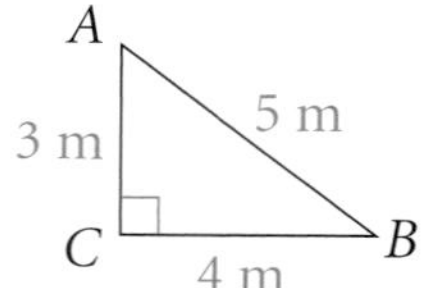

42.

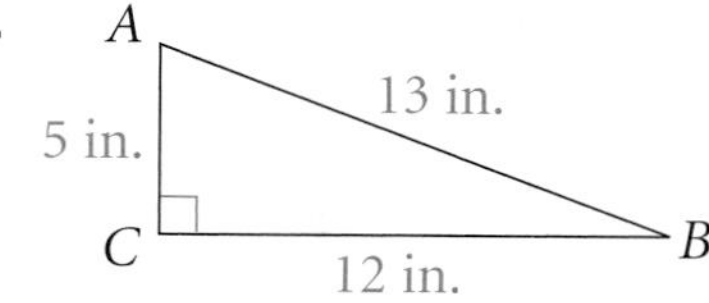

43.

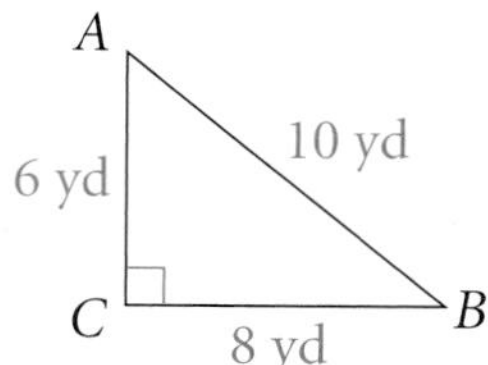

Math Toolbox — Algebra Review

Simplifying Radicals

Before Lesson 5-3

You can multiply and divide numbers that are under radical signs.

Example 1

Simplify the expressions $\sqrt{2} \cdot \sqrt{8}$ and $\sqrt{294} \div \sqrt{3}$.

$\sqrt{2} \cdot \sqrt{8} = \sqrt{2 \cdot 8}$	Write both numbers under one radical.
$= \sqrt{16}$	Simplify the expression under the radical.
$= 4$	Factor out perfect squares and simplify.

$$\sqrt{294} \div \sqrt{3} = \sqrt{\frac{294}{3}} = \sqrt{98} = \sqrt{49 \cdot 2} = 7\sqrt{2}$$

A radical expression is in simplest radical form when all the following are true.

- The number under the radical sign has no perfect square factors other than 1.
- The number under the radical sign does not contain a fraction.
- The denominator does not contain a radical expression.

Example 2

Write $\sqrt{\frac{4}{3}}$ in simplest form.

$\sqrt{\frac{4}{3}} = \frac{\sqrt{4}}{\sqrt{3}}$	Rewrite the single radical as the quotient of two radicals.
$= \frac{2}{\sqrt{3}}$	Simplify.
$= \frac{2}{\sqrt{3}} \cdot \frac{\sqrt{3}}{\sqrt{3}}$	Multiply by a form of 1 to rationalize the denominator.
$= \frac{2\sqrt{3}}{3}$	

Simplify each expression.

1. $\sqrt{5} \cdot \sqrt{10}$ **2.** $\sqrt{243}$ **3.** $\sqrt{128} \div \sqrt{2}$ **4.** $\sqrt{\frac{125}{4}}$

5. $\sqrt{6} \cdot \sqrt{8}$ **6.** $\frac{\sqrt{36}}{\sqrt{3}}$ **7.** $\frac{\sqrt{144}}{\sqrt{2}}$ **8.** $\sqrt{3} \cdot \sqrt{12}$

9. $\sqrt{72} \div \sqrt{2}$ **10.** $\sqrt{169}$ **11.** $24 \div \sqrt{8}$ **12.** $\sqrt{300} \div \sqrt{5}$

What You'll Learn

- Using the Pythagorean Theorem and its converse

...And Why

To solve problems involving boundaries, packaging, and satellites

What You'll Need

scissors, graph paper, colored paper, straightedge

5-3 The Pythagorean Theorem and Its Converse

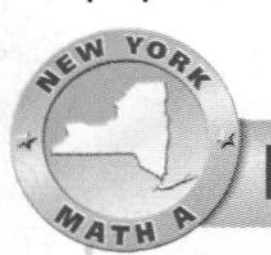

Math A Test Prep

1 One leg of an isosceles right triangle is 3 in. long. What is the length of the hypotenuse?
(1) 3 in. (3) $3\sqrt{3}$ in.
(2) $3\sqrt{2}$ in. (4) 6 in.

2 A 500-ft long sidewalk forms the diagonal of a square city park.
a To the nearest tenth of a foot, what is the perimeter of the park?
b To the nearest square yard, what is the area of the park?

WORK TOGETHER

Work in groups. Using graph paper, draw any rectangle. Label the sides a and b. Cut four rectangles with length a and width b from the graph paper. Then cut each rectangle on its diagonal, c, forming eight congruent triangles.

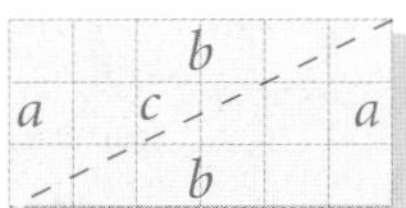

Cut three squares from the colored paper, one with sides of length a, one with sides of length b, and one with sides of length c.

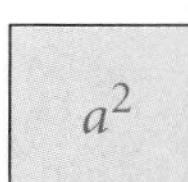

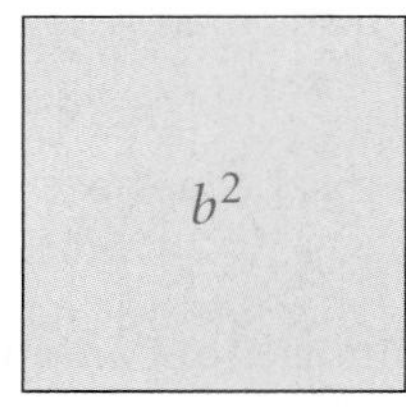

Separate the pieces into groups.

Group 1: four triangles and the two smaller squares

Group 2: four triangles and the largest square

Arrange the pieces of each group to form a square.

1. Write an algebraic expression for the area of each of the squares you formed. **$a^2 + b^2 + 2ab; c^2 + 2ab$**
2. How do the areas of the two squares you formed compare?
3. What can you conclude about the areas of the squares you cut from colored paper?
4. Express your conclusion as an algebraic equation.
   $c^2 = a^2 + b^2$

THINK AND DISCUSS

The Pythagorean Theorem

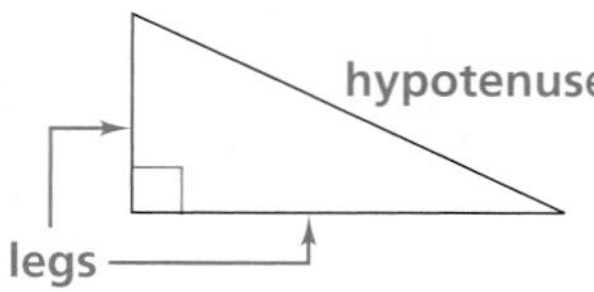

In a right triangle, the side opposite the right angle is the longest side. It is the **hypotenuse.** The other two sides are the **legs of a right triangle.**

The Work Together presents a justification of the well-known right triangle relationship called the Pythagorean Theorem.

Theorem 5-4
Pythagorean Theorem

In a right triangle, the sum of the squares of the lengths of the legs is equal to the square of the length of the hypotenuse.

$$a^2 + b^2 = c^2$$

c a b

5. a. A right triangle has sides of lengths 20, 29, and 21. What is the length of the hypotenuse?

b. Verify that the Pythagorean Theorem is true for the right triangle in part (a).

Example 1 **Relating to the Real World** 

Recreation A city park department rents paddle boats at docks near each entrance to the park. About how far is it to paddle from one dock to the other?

350 m
250 m

You can find the distance between the two docks by finding the hypotenuse of the right triangle.

$a^2 + b^2 = c^2$	**Use the Pythagorean Theorem.**
$250^2 + 350^2 = c^2$	**Substitute 250 for *a* and 350 for *b*.**
$62{,}500 + 122{,}500 = c^2$	**Simplify.**
$185{,}000 = c^2$	
$c = \sqrt{185{,}000}$	**Find the square root.**

185,000 [√] [=] 430.11626

It is about 430 m from one dock to the other.

6. Try This Find the length of the hypotenuse of a right triangle with legs of lengths 7 and 24.

QUICK REVIEW

A radical expression is in simplest radical form when all the following are true.

- The number under the radical sign has no perfect square factors other than 1.
- The number under the radical sign does not contain a fraction.
- The denominator does not contain a radical expression.

Sometimes you will leave your answer in simplest radical form.

Example 2

Find the value of x. Leave your answer in simplest radical form.

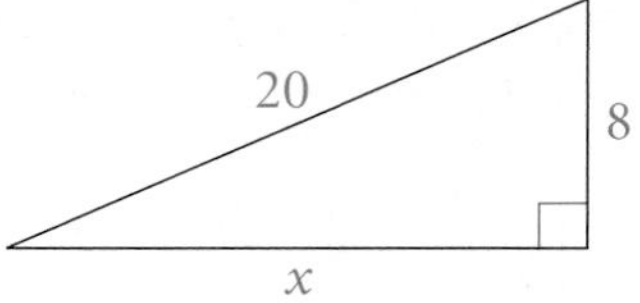

Use the Pythagorean Theorem.

$a^2 + b^2 = c^2$

$8^2 + x^2 = 20^2$ **Substitute.**

$64 + x^2 = 400$ **Simplify.**

$x^2 = 336$ **Subtract 64 from each side.**

$x = \sqrt{336}$ **Find the square root.**

$x = \sqrt{16(21)}$ **Simplify.**

$x = 4\sqrt{21}$

7. **Try This** The hypotenuse of a right triangle has length 12. One leg has length 6. Find the length of the other leg in simplest radical form.

When the lengths of the sides of a right triangle are integers, the integers form a **Pythagorean triple.** Here are some common Pythagorean triples.

3, 4, 5 5, 12, 13 8, 15, 17 7, 24, 25

8. **Open-ended** Choose an integer. Multiply each number of a Pythagorean triple by that integer. **Verify** that the result is a Pythagorean triple.

The Converse of the Pythagorean Theorem

You can use the Converse of the Pythagorean Theorem to determine whether a triangle is a right triangle.

Theorem 5-5 Converse of the Pythagorean Theorem

If the square of the length of one side of a triangle is equal to the sum of the squares of the lengths of the other two sides, then the triangle is a right triangle.

The Converse of the Pythagorean Theorem leads to the inequalities below. You can use them to determine whether a triangle is obtuse or acute.

In $\triangle ABC$ with longest side c,
if $c^2 > a^2 + b^2$, then the triangle is obtuse, and
if $c^2 < a^2 + b^2$, then the triangle is acute.

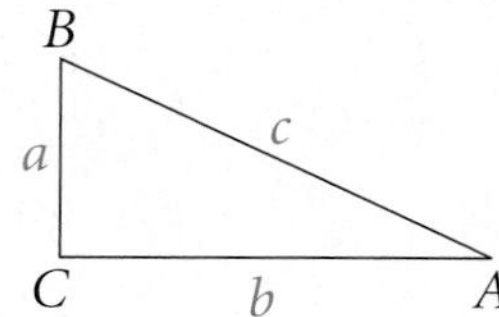

Who? Czech-American mathematician Olga Taussky-Todd (1906–1995) studied Pythagorean triangles. In 1970, she won the Ford Prize for her research.

The Pythagorean Theorem is named for Pythagoras, a Greek mathematician who lived in the sixth century B.C. We now know that the Babylonians, Egyptians, and Chinese were aware of this relationship before Pythagoras.

The diagram below illustrates an ancient Greek proof of the Pythagorean Theorem for an isosceles right triangle.

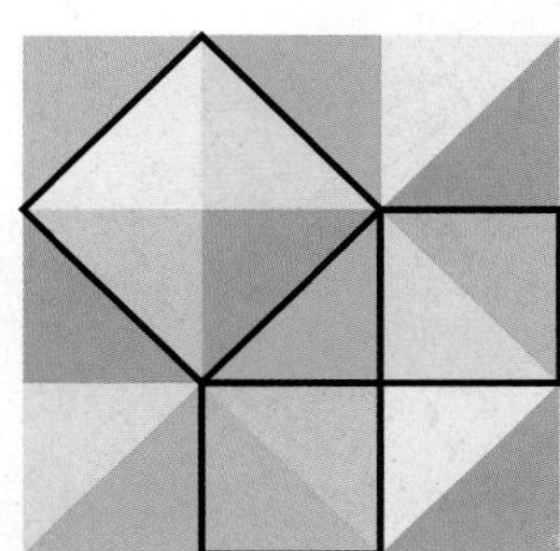

Example 3

The numbers represent the lengths of the sides of a triangle. Classify each triangle as acute, obtuse, or right.

a. 13, 84, 85

$85^2 \overset{?}{=} 13^2 + 84^2$ Compare c^2 to $a^2 + b^2$. Substitute the length

$7225 \overset{?}{=} 169 + 7056$ of the longest side for *c*.

$7225 = 7225$ $c^2 = a^2 + b^2$

The triangle is a right triangle.

b. 6, 11, 14

$14^2 \overset{?}{=} 6^2 + 11^2$ Compare c^2 to $a^2 + b^2$. Substitute the length

$196 \overset{?}{=} 36 + 121$ of the longest side for *c*.

$196 > 157$ $c^2 > a^2 + b^2$

The triangle is an obtuse triangle.

9. Try This A triangle has sides of lengths 7, 8, and 9. Classify the triangle as acute, obtuse, or right.

Exercises ON YOUR OWN

Algebra Find the value of *x*. Leave your answer in simplest radical form.

1.

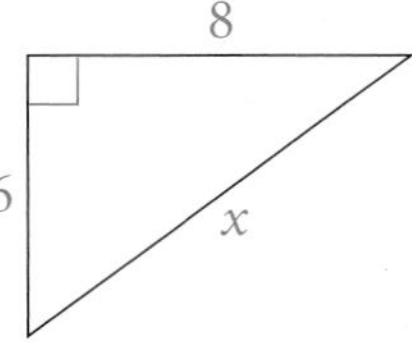

2.

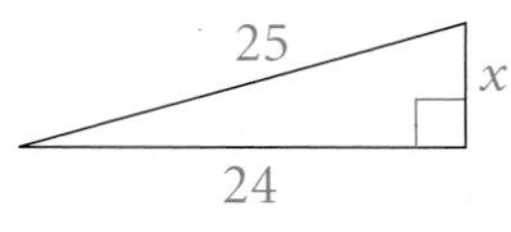

3.

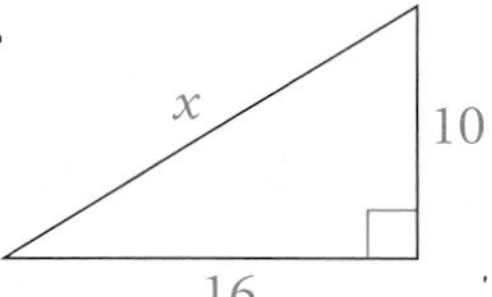

4.

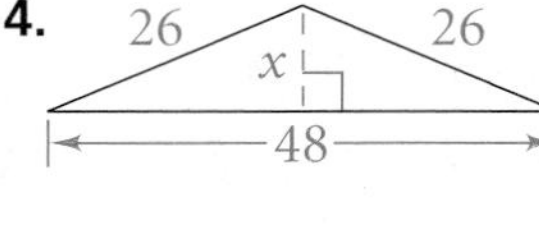

5.

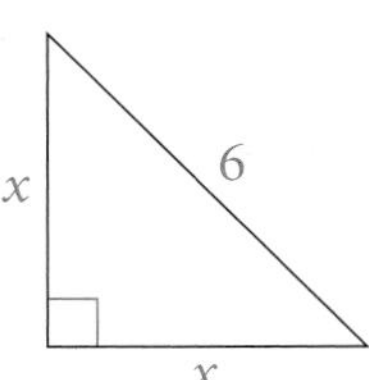

6.

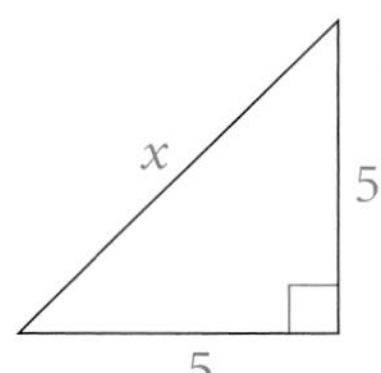

7.

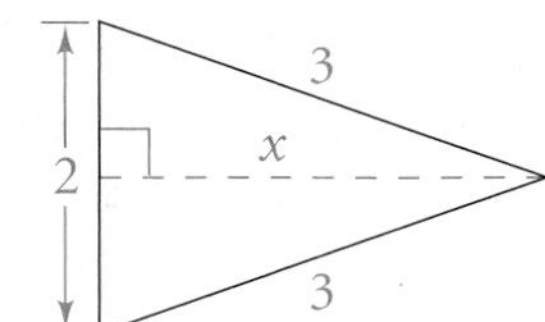

8.

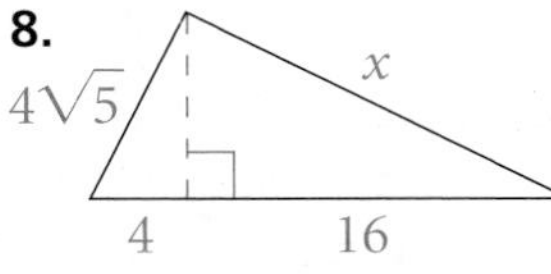

9. A 15-ft ladder is leaning against a building. The base of the ladder is 5 ft from the building. To the nearest foot, how high up the building does the ladder reach?

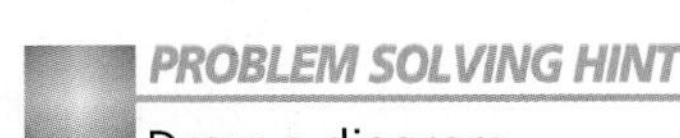

Draw a diagram.

10. A brick walkway forms the diagonal of a square playground. The walkway is 24 m long. To the nearest tenth of a meter, how long is a side of the playground?

Choose **Use mental math, paper and pencil, or a calculator. The lengths of the sides of a triangle are given. Classify each triangle as acute, right, or obtuse.**

11. 15, 8, 21 **12.** 12, 16, 20 **13.** 2, $2\frac{1}{2}$, 3 **14.** 30, 34, 16

15. 0.3, 0.4, 0.6 **16.** 11, 12, 15 **17.** $\sqrt{3}$, 2, 3 **18.** 1.8, 8, 8.2

19. 20, 21, 28 **20.** 31, 23, 12 **21.** 30, 40, 50 **22.** $\sqrt{11}$, $\sqrt{7}$, 4

23. **Ancient Egypt** Each year the Nile River overflowed its banks and deposited fertile silt on the valley farmlands. Although the flood was helpful to farmers, it often destroyed boundary markers. Egyptian surveyors used a rope with knots at 12 equal intervals to help reconstruct boundaries.

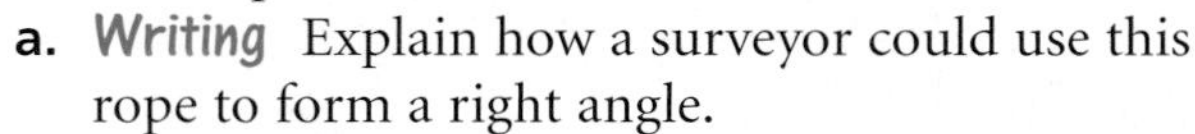

a. **Writing** Explain how a surveyor could use this rope to form a right angle.

b. **Research** Find out why the Nile no longer floods as it did in ancient Egypt.

24. **Open-ended** Draw a right triangle with three sides that are integers. Draw the altitude to the hypotenuse. Label the lengths of the three sides and the altitude.

Calculator **Use the triangle at the right. Find the missing length to the nearest tenth.**

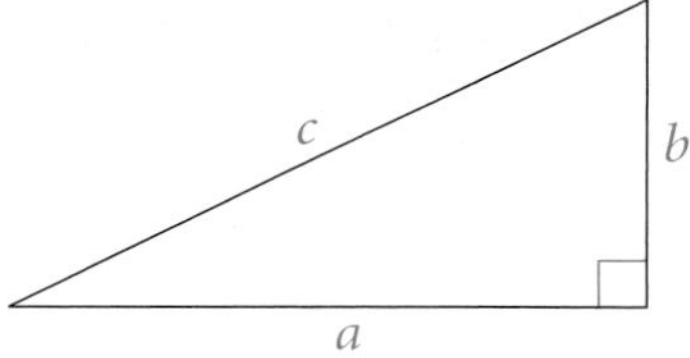

25. $a = 3, b = 7, c = ■$ **26.** $a = 1.2, b = ■, c = 3.5$

27. $a = ■, b = 23, c = 30$ **28.** $a = 0.7, b = ■, c = 0.8$

29. $a = 8, b = 8, c = ■$ **30.** $a = ■, b = 9, c = 18$

31. **Sewing** You want to embroider a square design. You have an embroidery hoop with a 6-in. diameter. Find the largest value of x such that the entire square will fit in the hoop. Round to the nearest tenth.

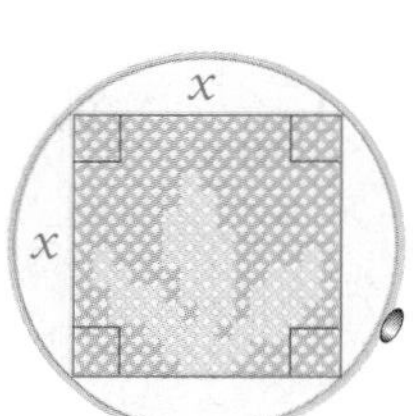

32. A rectangle has 10-in. diagonals and the lengths of its sides are whole numbers. Use the problem-solving strategy *Guess and Test* to find the perimeter of the rectangle.

Find the area of each figure. Leave your answer in simplest radical form.

33.

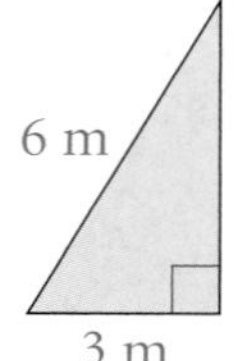

34.

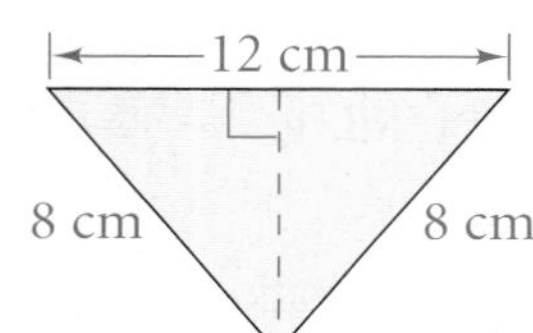

35.

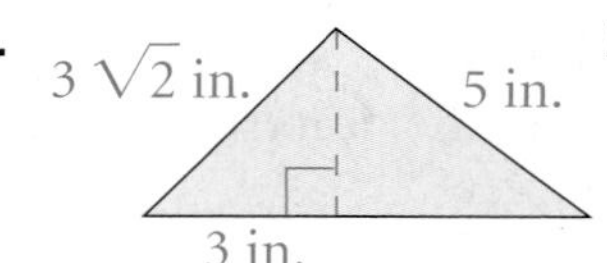

36.

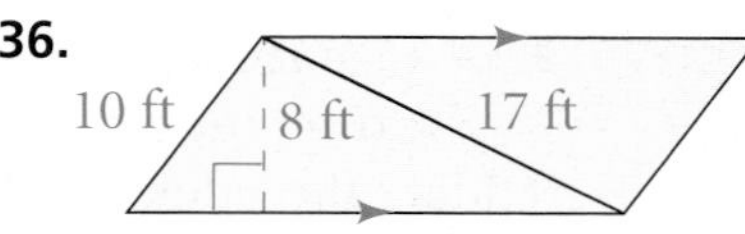

37. ***Coordinate Geometry*** You can use the Pythagorean Theorem to prove the Distance Formula. Let points $P(x_1, y_1)$ and $Q(x_2, y_2)$ be the endpoints of the hypotenuse of a right triangle.

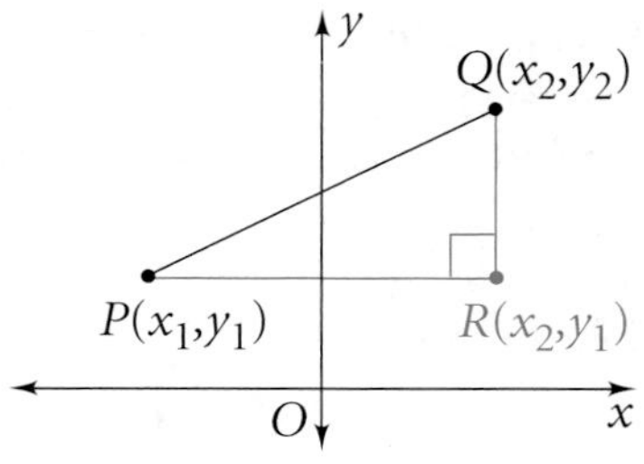

a. Write an algebraic expression to complete each of the following: $PR = ■$ and $QR = ■$.

b. By the Pythagorean Theorem, $PQ^2 = PR^2 + QR^2$. Rewrite this statement, substituting the algebraic expressions you found for PR and QR in part (a).

c. Complete the proof by finding the square root of each side of the equation that you wrote in part (b).

Find a third number so that the three numbers form a Pythagorean triple.

38. 9, 41 **39.** 14, 48 **40.** 60, 61 **41.** 8, 17

42. 20, 21 **43.** 13, 85 **44.** 12, 37 **45.** 63, 65

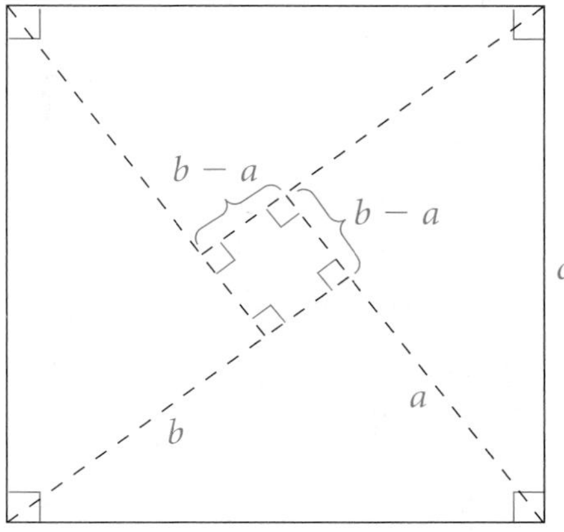

46. ***Logical Reasoning*** You can use the diagram at the right to prove the Pythagorean Theorem.

a. Find the area of the large square in terms of c.

b. Find the area of the large square in terms of a and b by finding the area of the four triangles and the small square.

c. Write an equation setting your answers to part (a) and part (b) equal to each other. Complete the proof by simplifying the equation.

Calculator **The figures below are drawn on centimeter graph paper. Find the perimeter of each shaded figure to the nearest tenth.**

47. 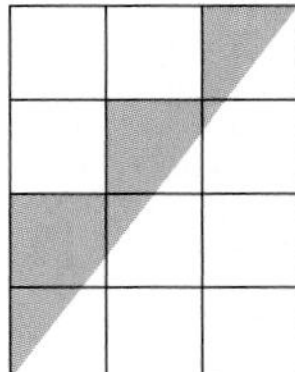

48. 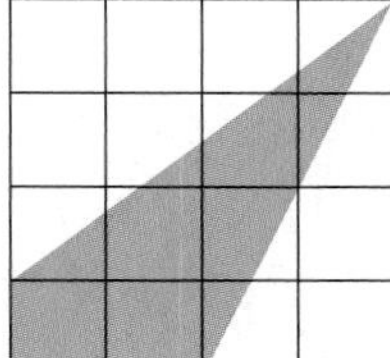

49. 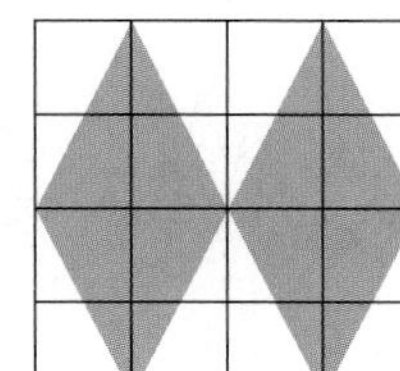

50. 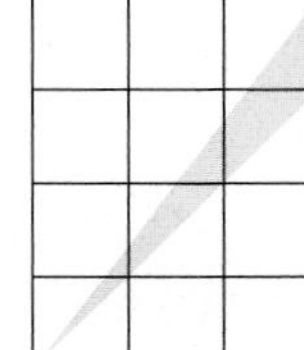

51. ***Geometry in 3 Dimensions*** The box at the right is a rectangular solid.

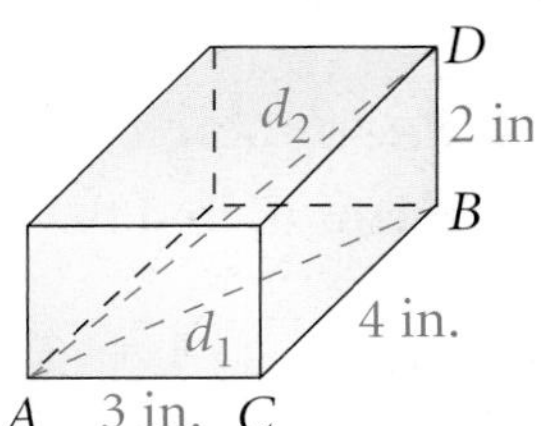

a. Use $\triangle ABC$ to find the length of the diagonal of the base, d_1.

b. Use $\triangle ABD$ to find the length of the diagonal of the box, d_2.

c. You can **generalize** steps in parts (a) and (b). Use the fact that $AC^2 + BC^2 = d_1{}^2$ and $d_1{}^2 + BD^2 = d_2{}^2$ to write a one-step formula to find d_2.

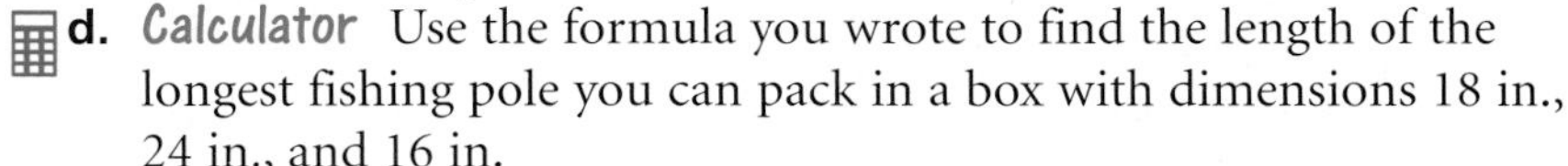

d. ***Calculator*** Use the formula you wrote to find the length of the longest fishing pole you can pack in a box with dimensions 18 in., 24 in., and 16 in.

Geometry in 3 Dimensions **Points $P(x_1, y_1, z_1)$ and $Q(x_2, y_2, z_2)$ are points in a three-dimensional coordinate system. Use the following formula to find PQ. Leave your answer in simplest radical form.**

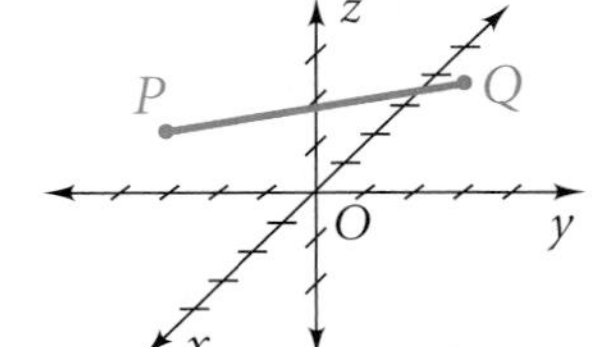

$$d = \sqrt{(x_2 - x_1)^2 + (y_2 - y_1)^2 + (z_2 - z_1)^2}$$

52. $P(0, 0, 0), Q(1, 2, 3)$

53. $P(0, 0, 0), Q(-3, 4, -6)$

54. $P(-1, 3, 5), Q(2, 1, 7)$

55. $P(3, -4, 8), Q(-1, 6, 2)$

56. **Space** The Hubble Space Telescope is orbiting Earth 600 km above Earth's surface. Earth's radius is about 6370 km. Use the Pythagorean Theorem to find the distance, x, from the telescope to Earth's horizon. Round your answer to the nearest ten kilometers.

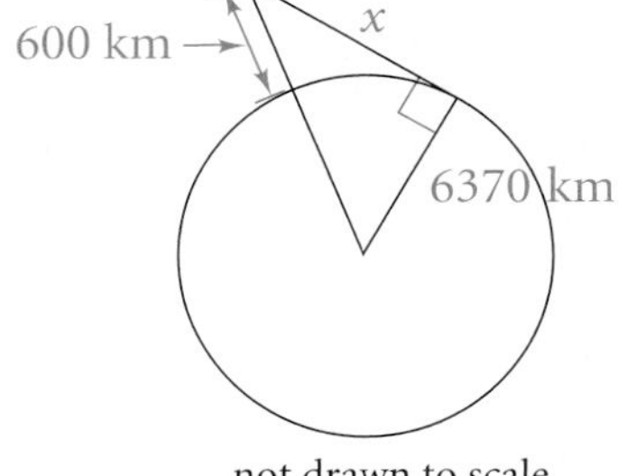

57. a. The ancient Greek philosopher Plato used the expressions $2n$, $n^2 - 1$, and $n^2 + 1$ to produce Pythagorean triples. Choose any integer greater than 1. Substitute for n and evaluate the three expressions.

b. **Verify** that your answers to part (a) form a Pythagorean triple.

58. **Standardized Test Prep** $\triangle ABC$ has perimeter 20 in. What is its area?

A. 12 in.^{2} **B.** 16 in.^{2} **C.** 24 in.^{2}

D. $8\sqrt{5}$ in.^{2} **E.** $16\sqrt{5}$ in.^{2}

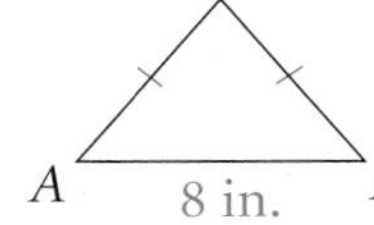

Exercises MIXED REVIEW

Sketch each figure after a counterclockwise rotation of 90° about C.

59.

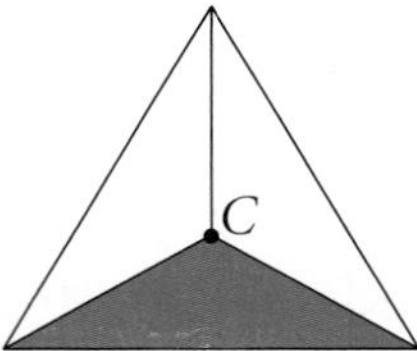

60.

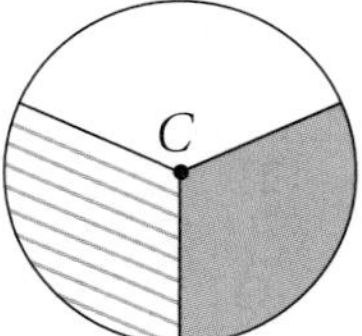

61.

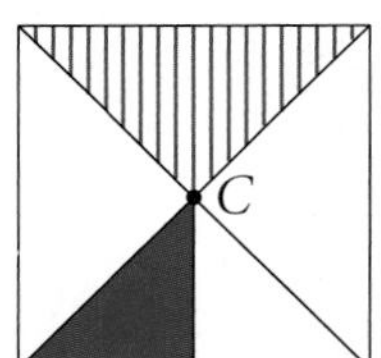

62. An angle is 87°. What is the measure of its complement?

Getting Ready for Lesson 5-4

Use a protractor to find the measures of the angles of each triangle.

63.

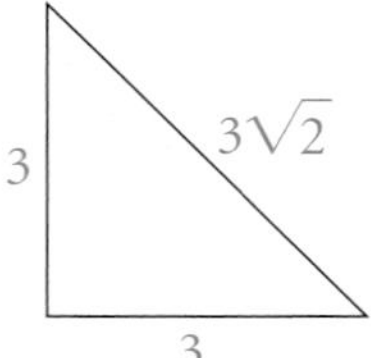

64.

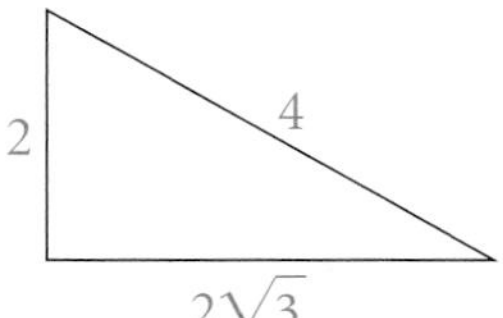

65.

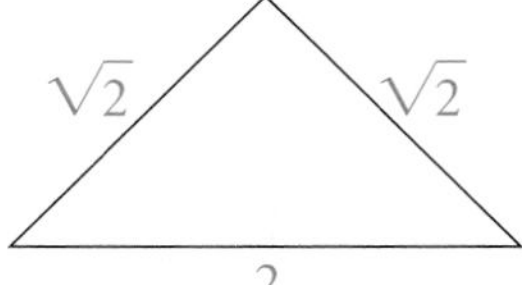

5-4 Special Right Triangles

What You'll Learn

- Using the properties of 45°-45°-90° and 30°-60°-90° triangles

...And Why

To study figures in real life, including baseball diamonds and helicopter blades, which use special right triangles

What You'll Need

- centimeter grid paper
- metric ruler
- calculator
- protractor

WORK TOGETHER

Work in a group. Have each person draw a different isosceles right triangle on centimeter grid paper. Choose integer values for the lengths of the legs.

- Record the length of each leg. Then use the Pythagorean Theorem to find the length of the hypotenuse. Leave your answers in simplest radical form.
- Organize your group's data in a table like the one below. Look for a pattern relating the side lengths of each triangle.

Triangle	Leg Length	Hypotenuse Length
Triangle 1	■	■
Triangle 2	■	■

- Make a **conjecture** about the relationship between the lengths of the legs and the length of the hypotenuse of an isosceles right triangle.

THINK AND DISCUSS

45°-45°-90° Triangles

1. What do you know about the measures of the acute angles of an isosceles right triangle?
2. If the measures of the angles of a triangle are 45, 45, and 90, why are the legs of the triangle congruent?

Another name for an isosceles right triangle is a 45°-45°-90° triangle.

3. a. Use the Pythagorean Theorem to solve for y in terms of x. Leave your answer in simplest radical form.
   b. Do the results of part (a) agree with the pattern you found in the Work Together?

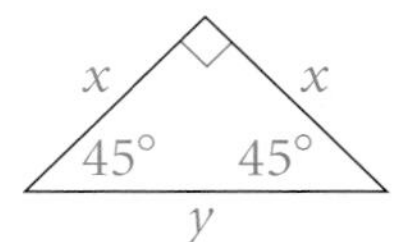

4. Find the value of each variable *without* using the Pythagorean Theorem.

a.
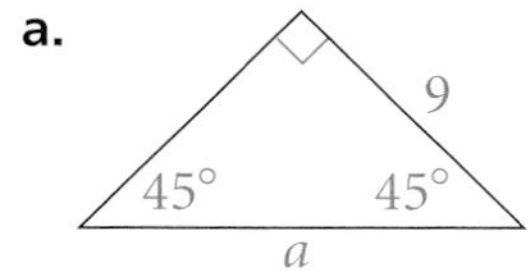

b.
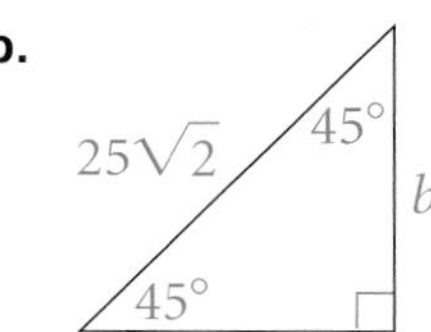

c.
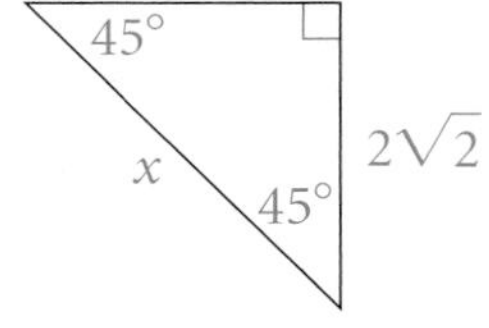

The pattern you observed in the Work Together (and generalized in Question 3) is the basis of the following theorem.

Theorem 5-6
45°-45°-90° Triangle Theorem

In a 45°-45°-90° triangle, both legs are congruent and the length of the hypotenuse is $\sqrt{2}$ times the length of a leg.

$$\text{hypotenuse} = \sqrt{2} \cdot \text{leg}$$

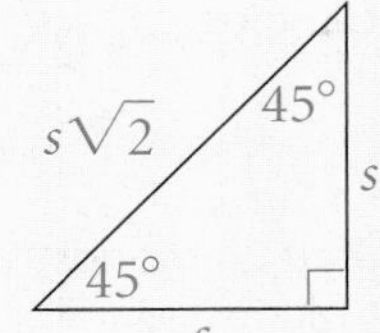

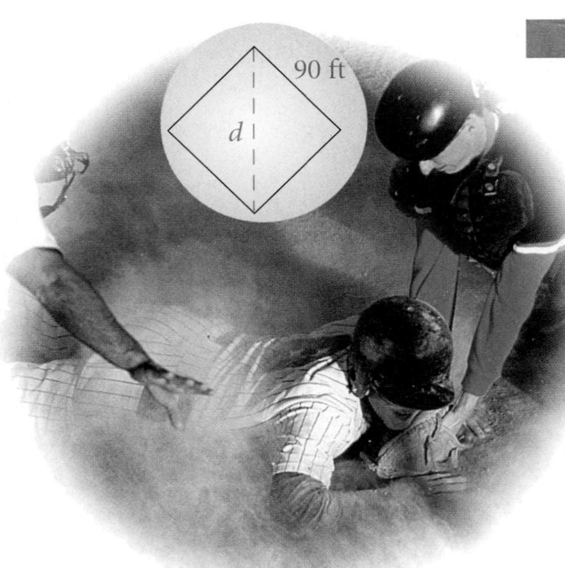

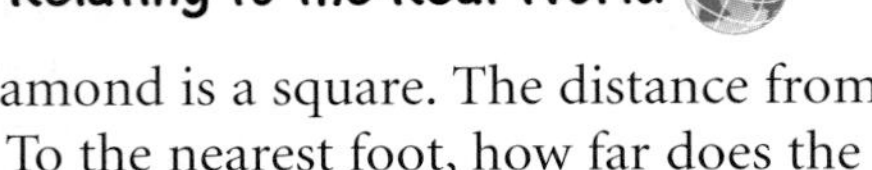

Example 1 *Relating to the Real World*

Sports A baseball diamond is a square. The distance from base to base is 90 ft. To the nearest foot, how far does the second baseman throw a ball to home plate?

The distance d from second base to home plate is the length of the hypotenuse of a 45°-45°-90° triangle.

$d = 90\sqrt{2}$ hypotenuse $= \sqrt{2} \cdot$ leg

90 ⊠ 2 [√] [=] 127.27922

The distance from second base to home plate is about 127 ft.

5. a. ***Calculator*** Find $\sqrt{2}$ to the nearest thousandth.
   b. ***Mental Math*** Use the answer to part (a) to estimate the length of a diagonal of a square with sides 100 ft long.

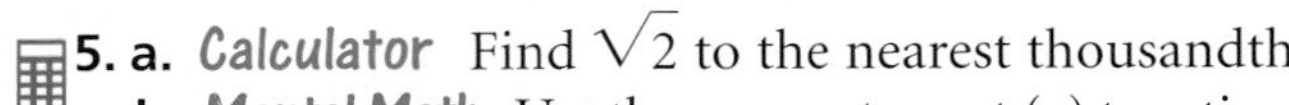

WORK TOGETHER

Work with a group.

- Draw an equilateral triangle with sides 6 cm long and cut it out. Label the vertices A, B, and C. Fold vertex A onto vertex C as shown at the left. Unfold the triangle and label the fold-line $\overline{BD}$.
- With your group, make a list of everything you know about $\triangle ABC$, $\triangle ABD$, and $\triangle CBD$, their angles and their sides.

6. Name a pair of congruent triangles.

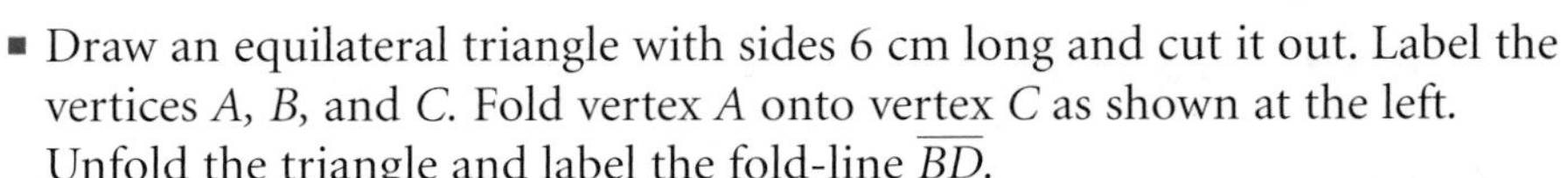

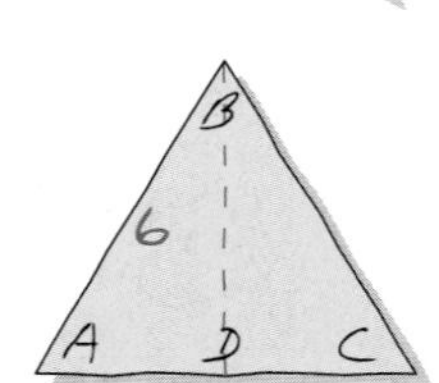

7. a. Find $m\angle A$, $m\angle ADB$, and $m\angle ABD$.
   b. Name $\triangle ABD$ using its angle measures.

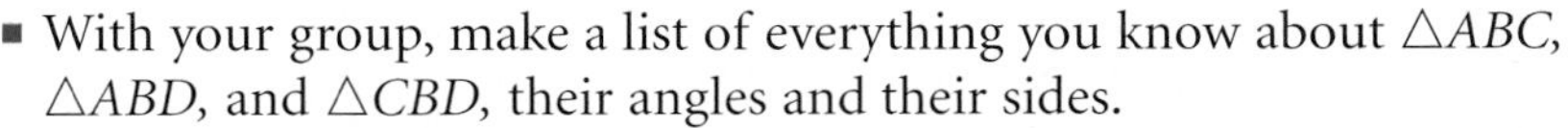

8. a. Complete: $\overline{DB}$ is the __?__ of $\overline{AC}$.
   b. If $AB = 6$, what is AD?
   c. Use the Pythagorean Theorem to find BD in simplest radical form.
   d. Find the ratios $\frac{AB}{AD}$ and $\frac{BD}{AD}$.

THINK AND DISCUSS

30°-60°-90° Triangles

The ratios you found in Question 8 part (d) suggest the following theorem about 30°-60°-90° triangles.

Theorem 5-7
30°-60°-90° Triangle Theorem

In a 30°-60°-90° triangle, the length of the hypotenuse is twice the length of the shorter leg. The length of the longer leg is $\sqrt{3}$ times the length of the shorter leg.

hypotenuse = 2 · shorter leg

longer leg = $\sqrt{3}$ · shorter leg

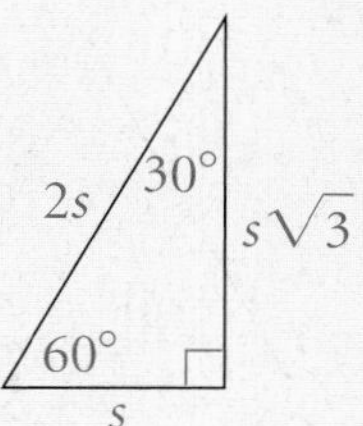

Justification:

Refer to $\triangle WXZ$ at the left. Since $\overline{WY}$ is the perpendicular bisector of $\overline{XZ}$, $XY = \frac{1}{2}XZ$. That means that if $XW = 2s$, then $XY = s$.

$XY^2 + YW^2 = XW^2$ — **Use the Pythagorean Theorem.**

$s^2 + YW^2 = (2s)^2$ — **Substitute s for XY and 2s for XW.**

$YW^2 = 4s^2 - s^2$ — **Subtract s^2 from each side.**

$YW^2 = 3s^2$

$YW = s\sqrt{3}$ — **Find the square root of each side.**

Example 2

Algebra Find the value of each variable.

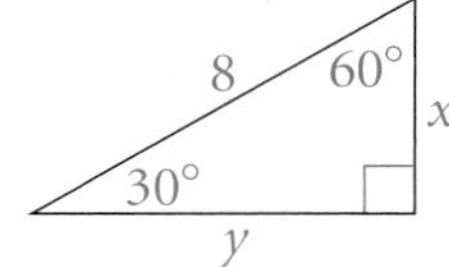

a. $8 = 2x$ — **hypotenuse = 2 · shorter leg**

$x = 4$

$y = x\sqrt{3}$ — **longer leg = $\sqrt{3}$ · shorter leg**

$y = 4\sqrt{3}$ — **Substitute 4 for x.**

b.

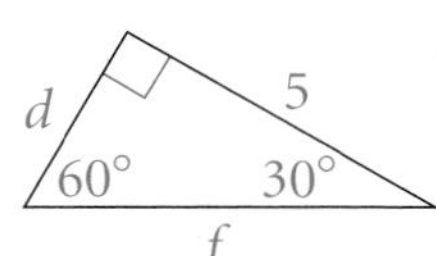

b. $5 = d\sqrt{3}$ — **longer leg = $\sqrt{3}$ · shorter leg**

$d = \frac{5}{\sqrt{3}} \cdot \frac{\sqrt{3}}{\sqrt{3}} = \frac{5\sqrt{3}}{3}$ — **Simplify.**

$f = 2d$ — **hypotenuse = 2 · shorter leg**

$f = 2 \cdot \frac{5\sqrt{3}}{3} = \frac{10\sqrt{3}}{3}$ — **Substitute $\frac{5\sqrt{3}}{3}$ for d.**

9. **Try This** The shorter leg of a 30°-60°-90° triangle has length $\sqrt{6}$. What are the lengths of the other two sides? Leave your answers in simplest radical form.

You can use the properties of 30°-60°-90° triangles to find the dimensions you need to calculate area.

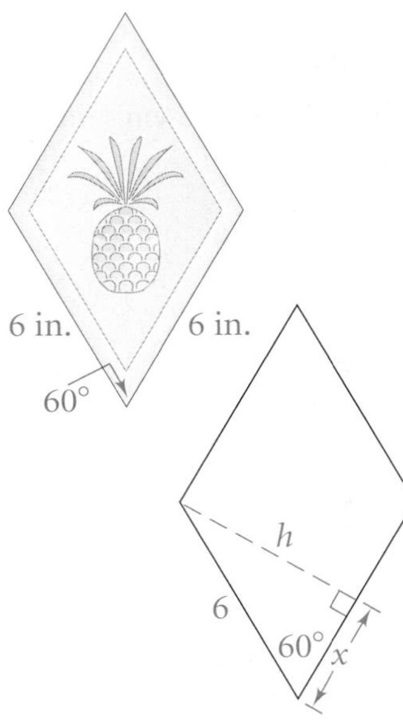

Example 3 *Relating to the Real World* 

Design The rhombus at the left is a glass panel for a door. How many square inches of colored glass will you need for the panel?

Draw an altitude of the rhombus. Label x and h as shown.

$6 = 2x$ — hypotenuse = 2 · shorter leg

$x = 3$

$h = 3\sqrt{3}$ — longer leg = $\sqrt{3}$ · shorter leg

Use the value of h to find the area.

$A = bh$ — Use the formula for area of a parallelogram.

$= 6(3\sqrt{3})$ — Substitute 6 for b and $3\sqrt{3}$ for h.

You will need about 31.2 in.^{2} of colored glass.

Exercises ON YOUR OWN

Find the value of each variable. Leave your answer in simplest radical form.

1. 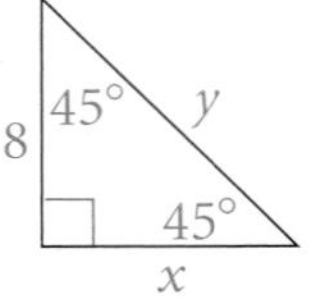

2. 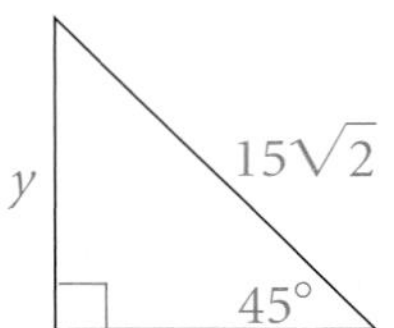

3. 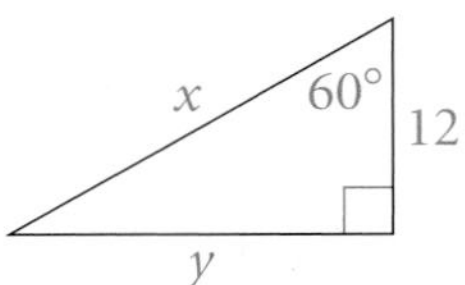

4. 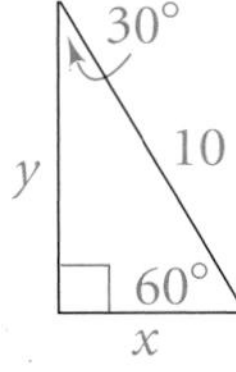

5. 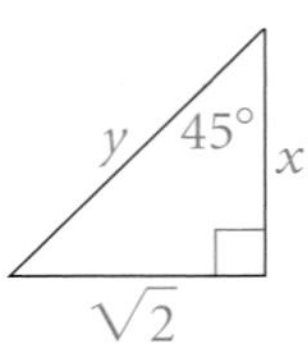

6. 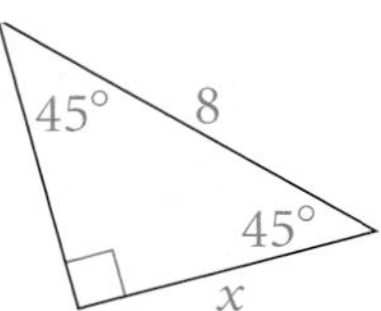

7. 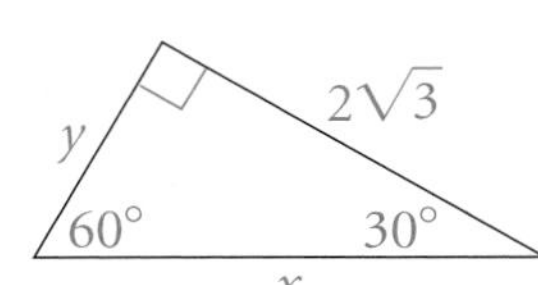

8. 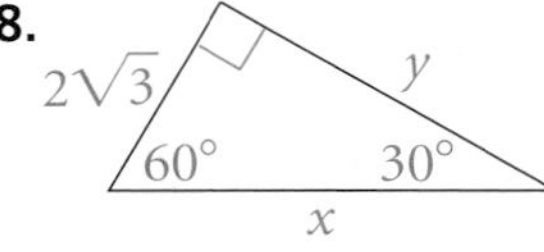

9. a. **Farming** A conveyor belt carries bales of hay from the ground to the loft of a barn 27.5 ft above ground. The belt makes a 30° angle with the ground. How far does a bale of hay travel on the conveyor belt?
   b. The conveyor belt moves at 100 ft/min. How long does it take for a bale of hay to go from the ground to the barn loft?

Find the value of each variable. Leave your answer in simplest radical form.

10.

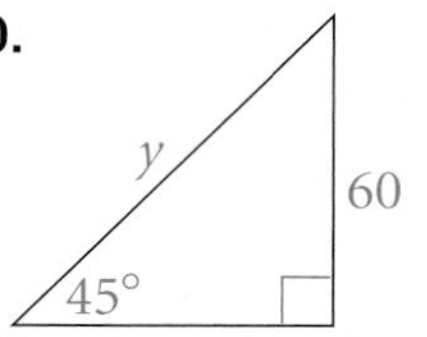

11.

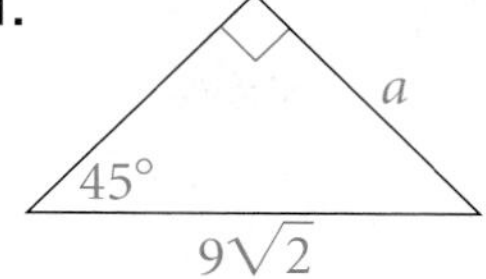

12.

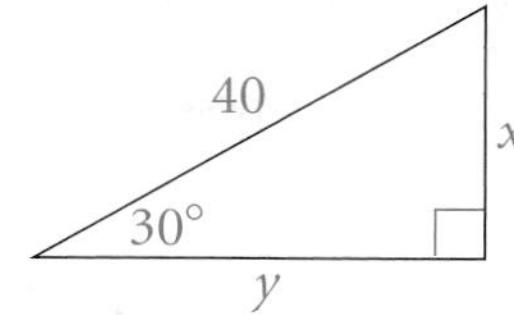

13.

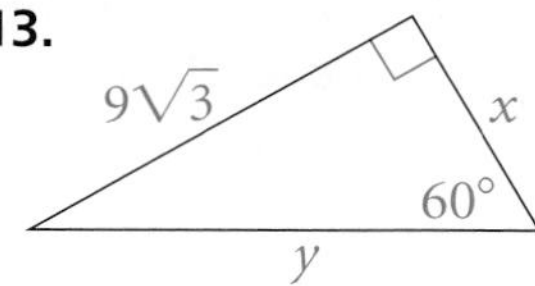

14.

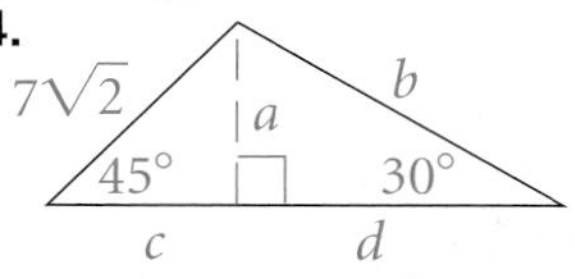

15.

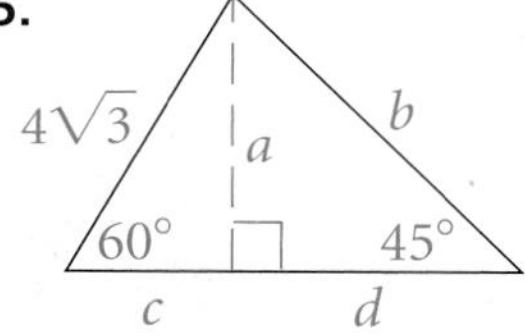

16.

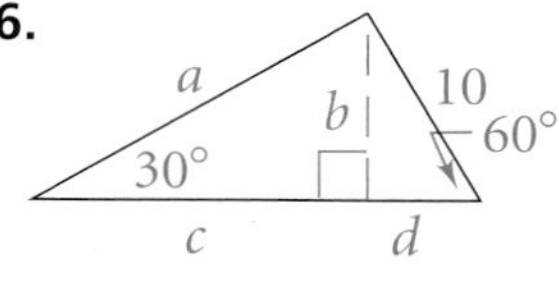

17.

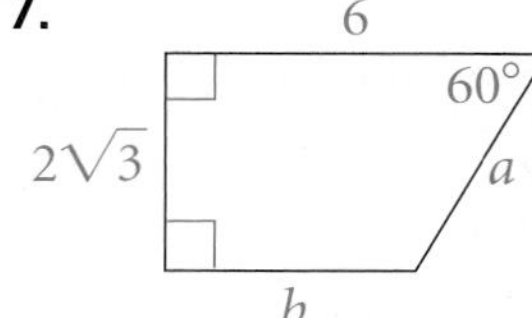

18. **Writing** Sandra drew this triangle. Rika said that the lengths couldn't be correct. With which student do you agree? Explain.

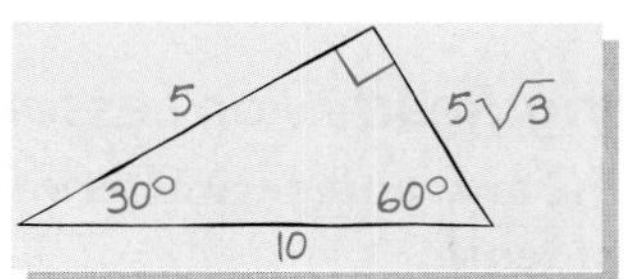

19. **Standardized Test Prep** Which of the following *cannot* be the lengths of sides of a 30°-60°-90° triangle?

A. $\frac{1}{2}, 1, \frac{\sqrt{3}}{2}$ **B.** $\sqrt{3}, 2\sqrt{3}, 3$ **C.** $1, \frac{1}{2}, \sqrt{3}$

D. $2\sqrt{2}, \sqrt{2}, \sqrt{6}$ **E.** $2, 4, 2\sqrt{3}$

Calculator **Find the area of each figure. When an answer is not a whole number, round to the nearest tenth.**

20.

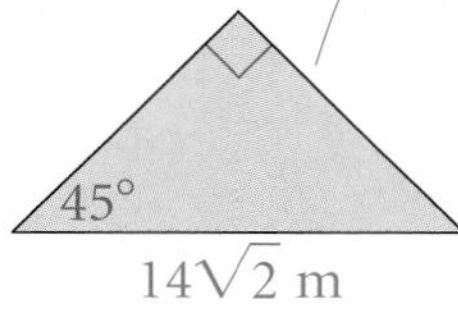

21.

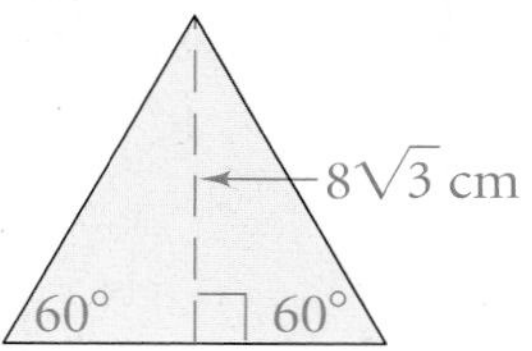

22.

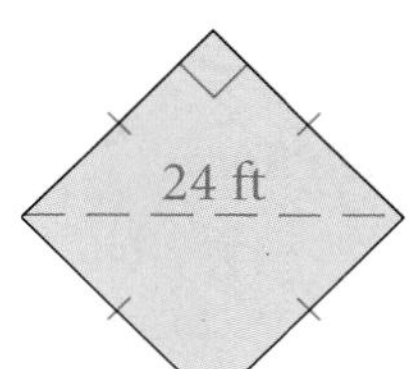

23.

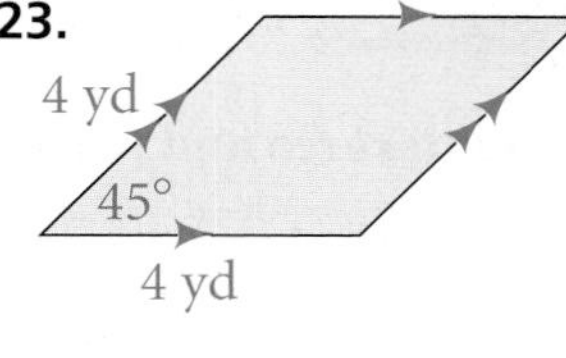

24. **Helicopters** The blades of a helicopter meet at right angles and are all the same length. The distance between the tips of two consecutive blades is 36 ft. How long is each blade? Round your answer to the nearest tenth.

25. **Open-ended** The hypotenuse of a 30°-60°-90° triangle is 12 ft long. Write a real-life problem that you can solve using this triangle. Show your solution.

26. A rhombus has a 60° angle and sides 5 cm long. What is its area? Round your answer to the nearest tenth.

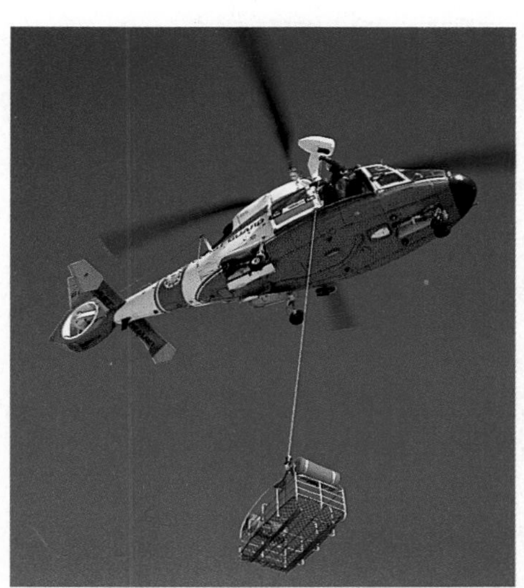

27. **a.** *Geometry in 3 Dimensions* Find the length d, in simplest radical form, of the diagonal of a cube with sides 1 unit long.

b. Find the length d of the diagonal of a cube with sides 2 units long.

c. *Generalize* Find the length d of the diagonal of a cube with sides s units long.

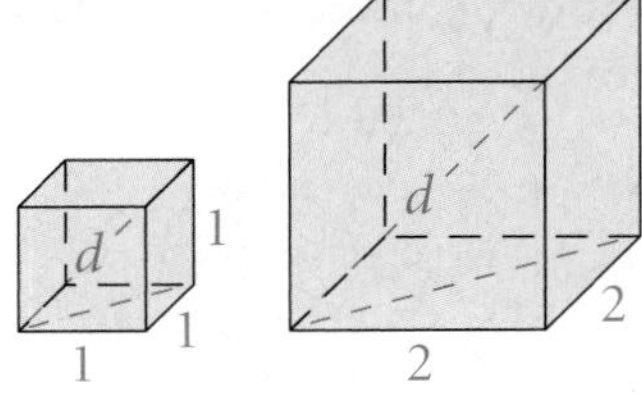

Exercises MIXED REVIEW

Find the slope of $\overline{AB}$.

28. $A(1, 0), B(-2, 3)$ **29.** $A(-5, 4), B(-1, 8)$

30. Find the equation of the line with slope $\frac{1}{2}$ containing the point $(-2, 5)$.

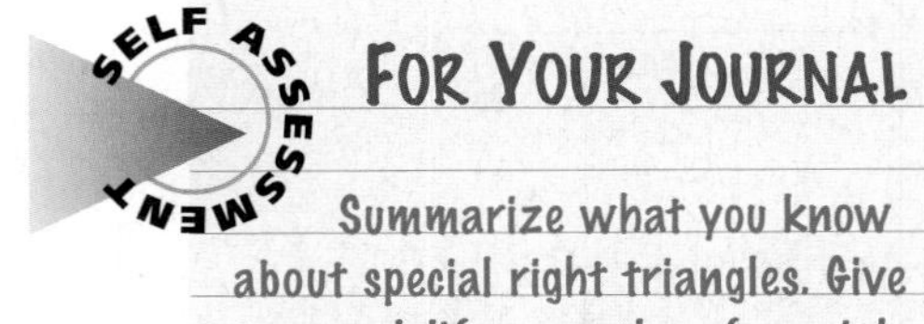

FOR YOUR JOURNAL

Summarize what you know about special right triangles. Give two real-life examples of special right triangles.

Getting Ready For Lesson 5-5

Find the area and perimeter of each trapezoid to the nearest tenth.

31. **32.**

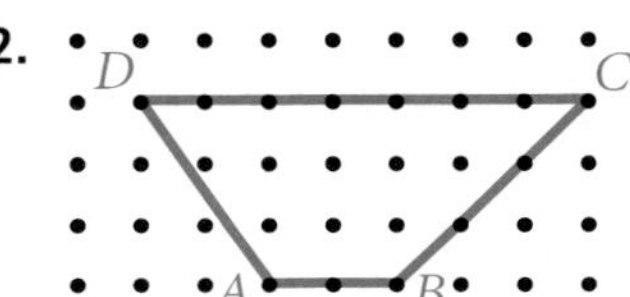

Exercises CHECKPOINT

Find the area and perimeter of each figure.

1.

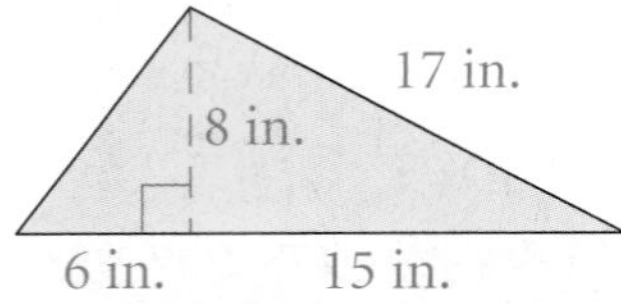

2.

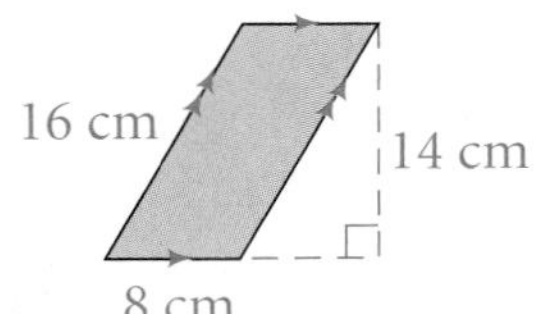

3.

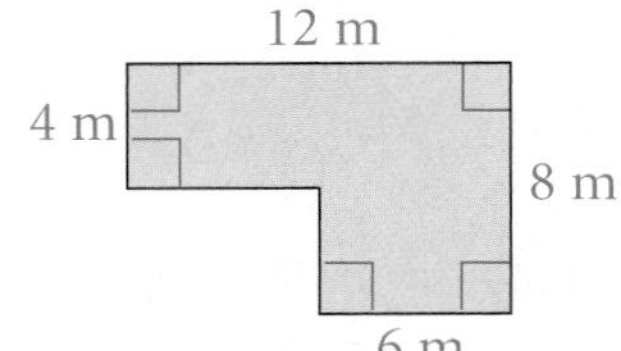

Algebra **Find the value of each variable. Leave your answer in simplest radical form.**

4.

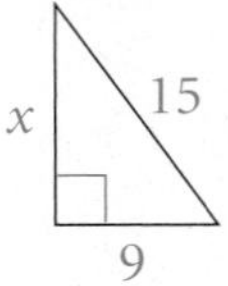

5.

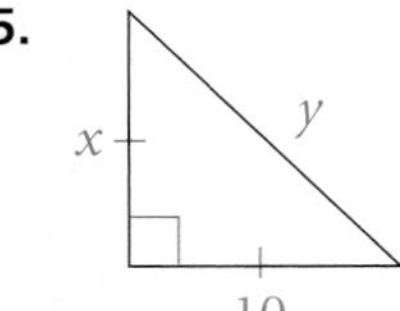

6.

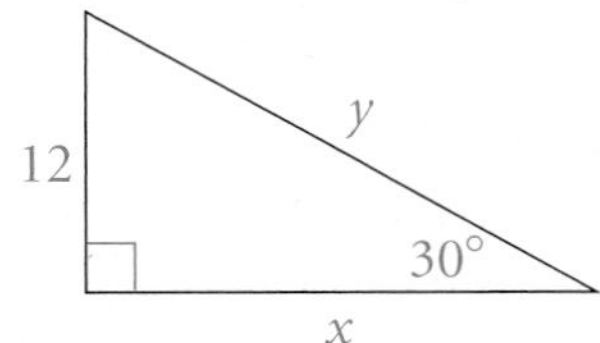

7. *Standardized Test Prep* Which numbers could represent the lengths of the sides of an acute triangle?

A. 3, 4, 5 **B.** 6, 8, 9 **C.** 14, 45, 50 **D.** 5, 12, 13 **E.** 5, 9, 13

8. *Open-ended* Sketch a rectangle and a triangle with the same perimeter. Label the lengths of the sides of the figures.

5-5 Areas of Trapezoids

What You'll Learn

- Finding the areas of trapezoids

...And Why

To approximate the areas of irregular figures

What You'll Need

- lined paper
- scissors

WORK TOGETHER

Work in groups. Fold a piece of lined paper in half along one of the lines. On two lines of the paper, draw parallel segments of different lengths. Connect the endpoints of the segments to form a trapezoid. Cut through both layers of the folded paper, so that you will have two congruent trapezoids. Label b_1, b_2, and h for each trapezoid.

- Arrange the congruent trapezoids to form a parallelogram as shown at the left below.

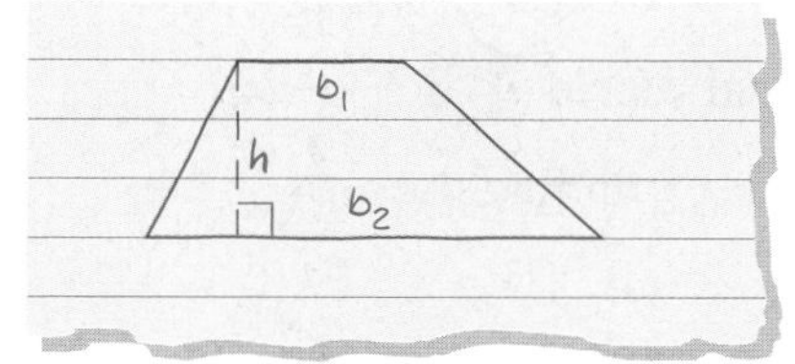

1. **a.** Write an expression for the length of the base of the parallelogram.
   b. Write an expression for the area of the parallelogram using b_1, b_2, and h.
2. How does the area of each trapezoid compare to the area of the parallelogram?
3. Use your answers to Questions 1 and 2 to write a formula for the area of each trapezoid.

THINK AND DISCUSS

In a trapezoid, the parallel sides are the **bases.** The nonparallel sides are the **legs.** The **height** h is the perpendicular distance between the two parallel bases.

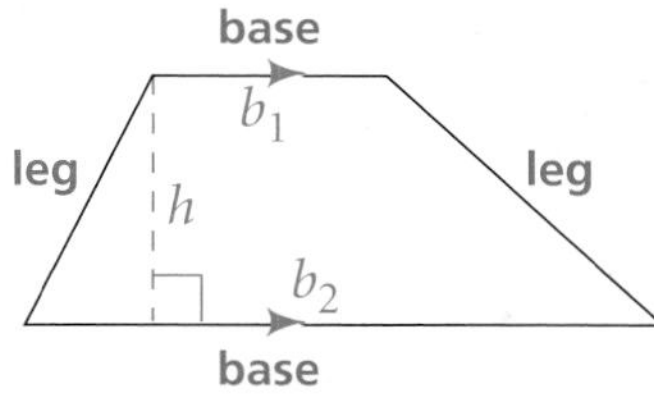

Your observations in the Work Together suggest the following theorem.

Theorem 5-8
Area of a Trapezoid

The area of a trapezoid is half the product of the height and the sum of the lengths of the bases.

$$A = \frac{1}{2}h(b_1 + b_2)$$

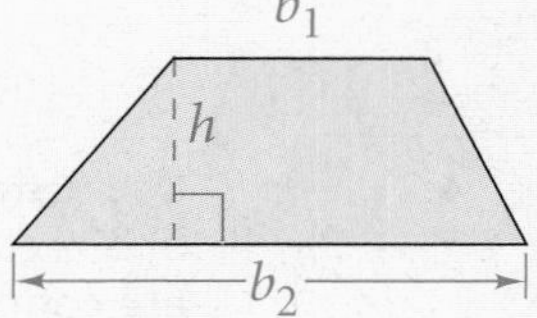

4. ***Critical Thinking*** When finding the area of a trapezoid, does it make a difference which base is labeled b_1 and which base is labeled b_2? Explain.

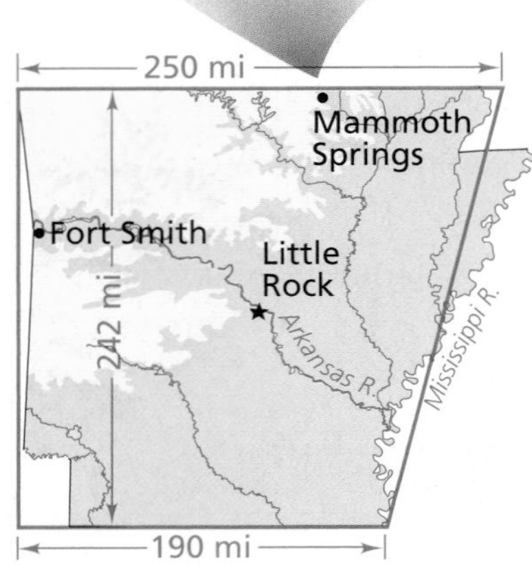

Example 1 Relating to the Real World 

Geography Approximate the area of Arkansas by finding the area of the trapezoid shown.

$A = \frac{1}{2}h(b_1 + b_2)$ **Use the area formula for a trapezoid.**

$= \frac{1}{2}(242)(190 + 250)$ **Substitute.**

$= 53{,}240$

The area of Arkansas is about 53,240 mi^2.

5. **Try This** Find the area of a trapezoid with height 7 cm and bases 12 cm and 15 cm.

Sometimes properties of special right triangles can help you find the area of a trapezoid.

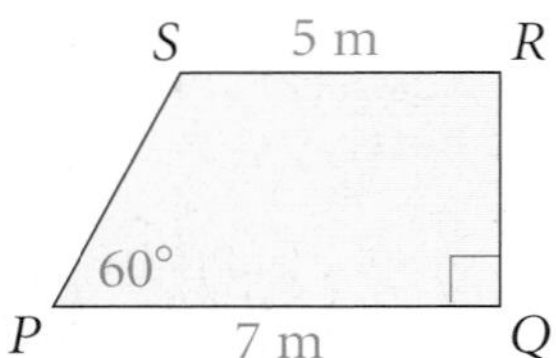

Example 2

Find the area of trapezoid *PQRS*. Leave your answer in simplest radical form.

You can draw an altitude that divides the trapezoid into a rectangle and a 30°-60°-90° triangle. Find h.

S 5 m R
h
60°
P 2 m 5 m Q
7 m − 5 m = 2 m
Opposite sides of a rectangle are congruent.

$h = 2\sqrt{3}$ **longer leg = shorter leg · $\sqrt{3}$**

$A = \frac{1}{2}h(b_1 + b_2)$ **Use the area formula for a trapezoid.**

$= \frac{1}{2}(2\sqrt{3})(5 + 7)$ **Substitute.**

$= 12\sqrt{3}$ **Simplify.**

The area of trapezoid *PQRS* is $12\sqrt{3}$ m^2.

6. Suppose $m\angle P = 45$. Find the area of trapezoid *PQRS*.

Exercises ON YOUR OWN

Find the area of each trapezoid.

1. 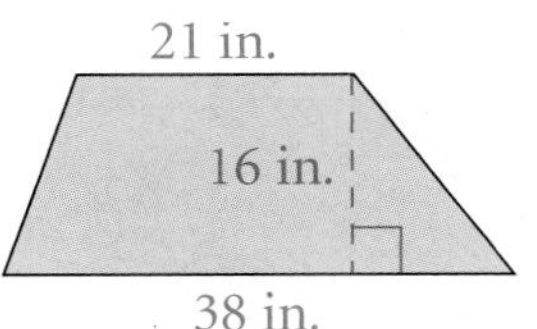

2. 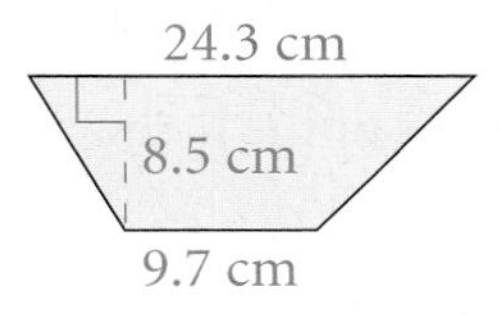

3. 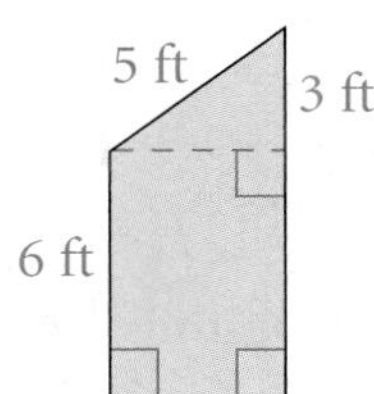

4. 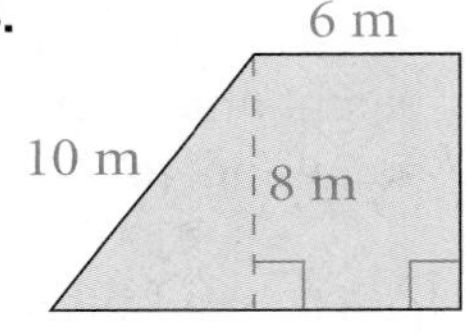

5. **Geography** Approximate the area of Nevada by finding the area of the trapezoid shown.

6. **Research** On a state map, select a town or county that is shaped like a trapezoid. Use the scale of the map to find values for b_1, b_2, and h. Then approximate the area.

7. The area of a trapezoid is 80 ft^2. Its bases have lengths 26 ft and 14 ft. Find its height.

8. **a.** A trapezoid has two right angles, bases of lengths 12 m and 18 m, and a height of 8 m. Sketch the trapezoid.
b. What is the perimeter?
c. What is the area?

Find the area of each trapezoid. Leave your answer in simplest radical form.

9. 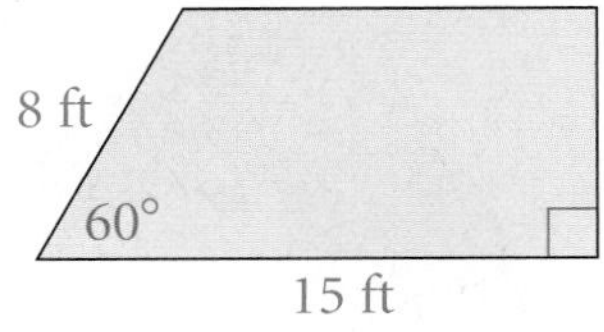

10. 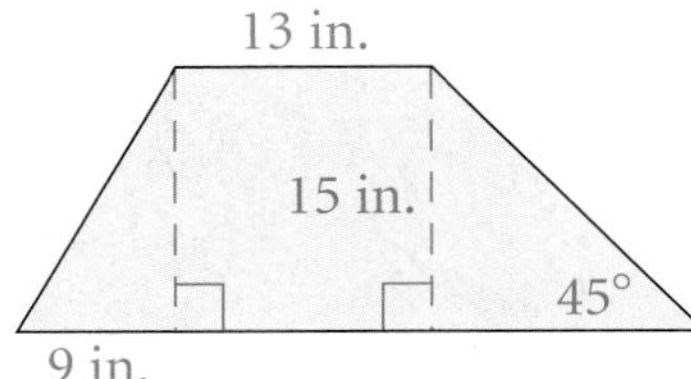

11. 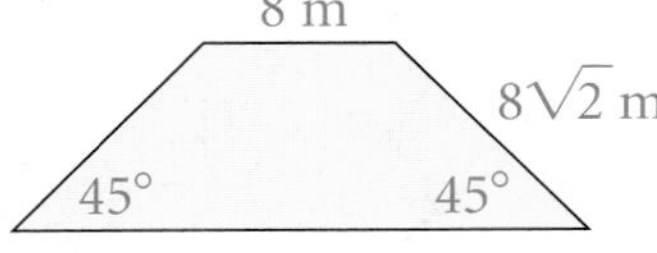

12. **Geometry in 3 Dimensions** A rain gutter has a trapezoidal cross section. The bottom is 4 in. wide, the top is 6 in. wide, and the gutter is 4 in. deep. What is the area of an end-piece?

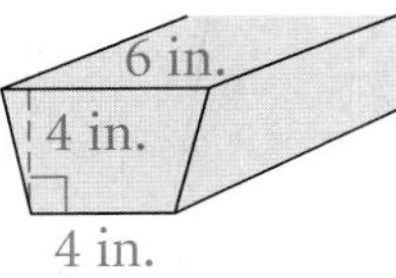

13. Draw a trapezoid. Label its bases and height b_1, b_2, and h. Then draw a diagonal of the trapezoid.
a. Write an expression for the area of each triangle determined by the diagonal.
b. **Writing** Explain how you can justify the trapezoid area formula using the areas of the two triangles.

14. **Open-ended** Draw a trapezoid. Measure its height and the lengths of its bases. Find its area.

15. **Crafts** You plan to lace together four isosceles trapezoids and a square to make the trash basket shown. How much material will you need?

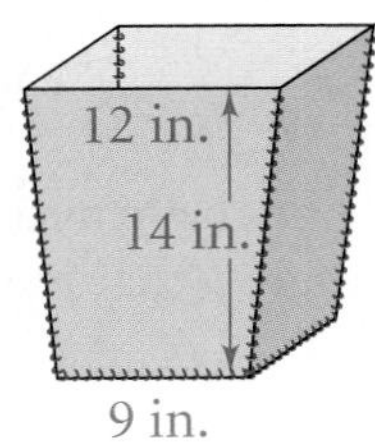

16. The area of an isosceles trapezoid is 160 cm^2. Its height is 8 cm and the length of its shorter base is 14 cm. Find the length of the longer base.

17. **Algebra** One base of a trapezoid is twice as long as the other. The height is the average of the two bases. The area is 324 cm^2. Find the height and the lengths of the bases. (*Hint:* Let the lengths of the bases be $2x$ and $4x$.)

Calculator **Find the area of each trapezoid to the nearest tenth.**

18.

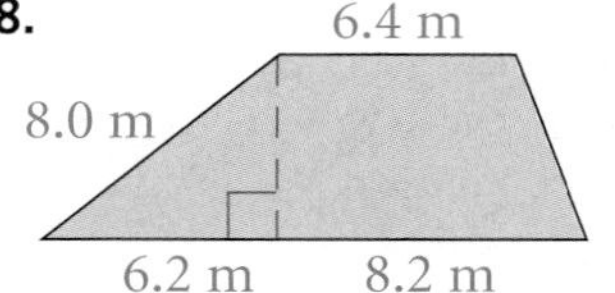

19.

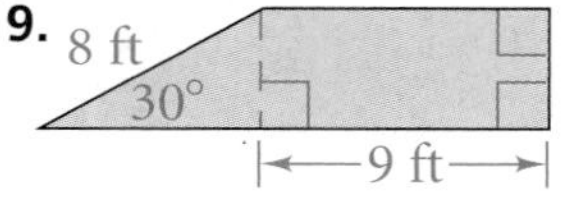

20.

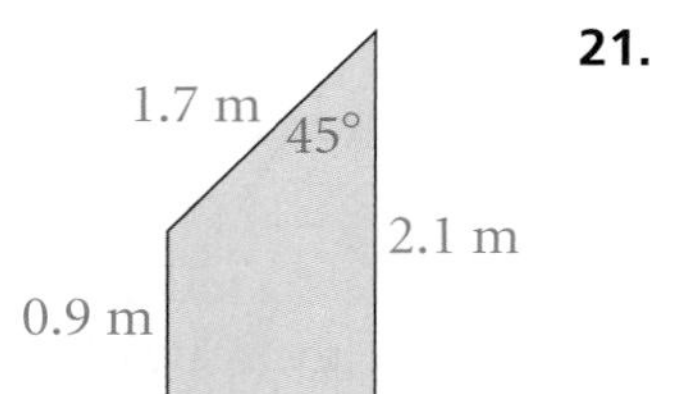

21.

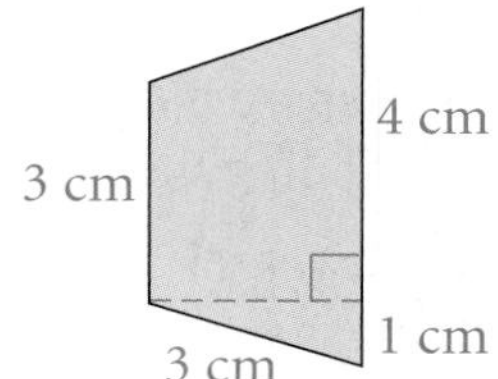

22. a. **Coordinate Geometry** Graph the lines $x = 0, x = 6, y = 0$, and $y = x + 4$.
 b. What quadrilateral do the lines form?
 c. Find the area of the quadrilateral.

23. **Recreation** A town youth center is building a skateboarding ramp. The ramp is 4 m wide, and the surface of the ramp is modeled by the equation $y = 0.25x^2$. You want to paint the front face of the ramp. Use the triangles and trapezoids shown to approximate the area of the face.

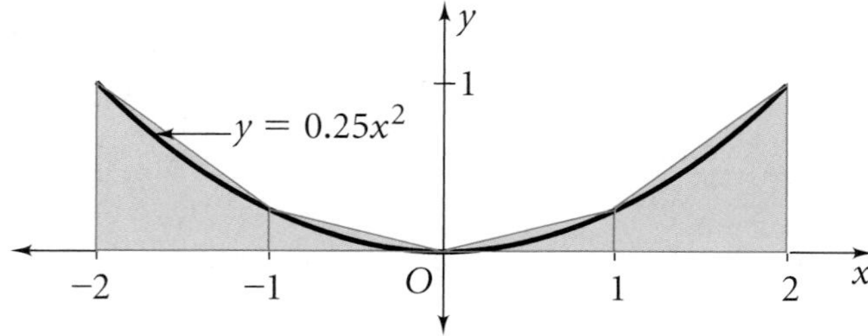

Exercises MIXED REVIEW

Open-ended **Find a possible length for the third side of a triangle that has two sides with the given lengths.**

24. 7 cm, 10 cm

25. 2 in., 8 in.

26. 13 mm, 6 mm

27. 4 ft, 9 ft

28. **Locus** Describe the locus of points in a plane equidistant from the sides of an angle. What is another name for this locus?

Getting Ready for Lesson 5-6

Find the area of each regular polygon. If your answer is not an integer, leave it in simplest radical form.

29. 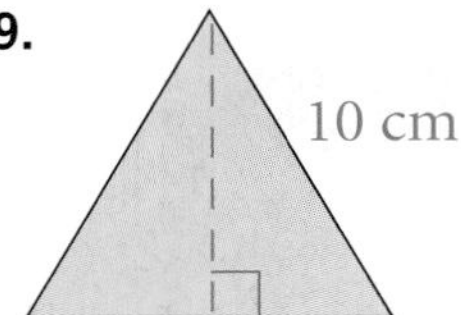

30. 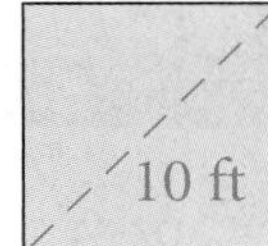

31. 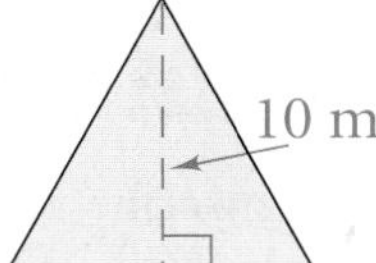

Chapter Project

Find Out by Researching

In the early 1900s, Seminoles of southern Florida developed a method of arranging strips of fabric to create geometric designs. These patchwork patterns sometimes serve to advertise the clan to which the wearer belongs.

- Research the patchwork techniques used by the Seminoles.
- Create your own Seminole patchwork design with colored paper, graphics software, or fabric.
- In the photo, notice the angled strips with trapezoids at each end. Explain, with diagrams or models, how this effect was created.

A Point in Time

1500 1600 1700 1800 1900 2000

Presidential Proof

Presidents are known more often for their foreign policy than for their mathematical creativity. James Garfield, the 20th President of the United States, was an exception. After serving as a general in the Civil War, in **1876** Garfield demonstrated this proof of the Pythagorean Theorem.

In the diagram, $\triangle NRM$ and $\triangle RPQ$ are congruent right triangles with sides of length a, b, and c. The legs of isosceles right triangle NRP have length c. The three triangles form trapezoid $MNPQ$. The sum of the areas of the three right triangles equals the area of trapezoid $MNPQ$.

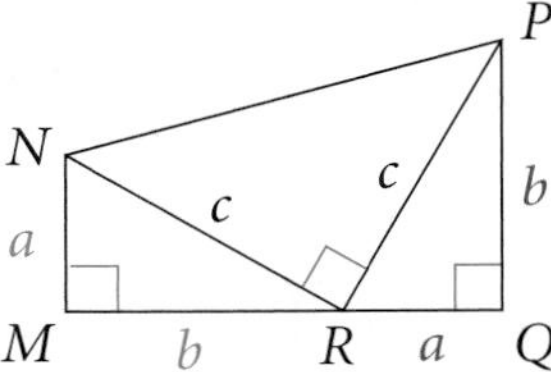

Areas of Triangles	=	Area of Trapezoid
$\frac{1}{2}ab + \frac{1}{2}ab + \frac{1}{2}c^2$	=	$\frac{1}{2}(a + b)(a + b)$
$ab + \frac{1}{2}c^2$	=	$\frac{1}{2}a^2 + ab + \frac{1}{2}b^2$
$\frac{1}{2}c^2$	=	$\frac{1}{2}a^2 + \frac{1}{2}b^2$
c^2	=	$a^2 + b^2$

What You'll Learn

- Finding areas of regular polygons

...And Why

To find amounts of materials used in manufacturing and in architecture

5-6 Areas of Regular Polygons

QUICK REVIEW

A regular polygon is any polygon that is both equilateral and equiangular.

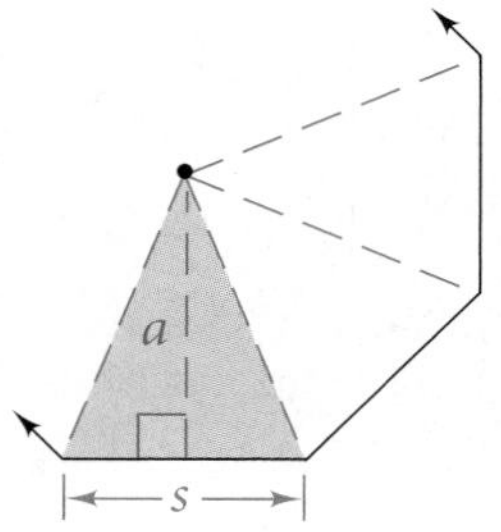

THINK AND DISCUSS

You can circumscribe a circle about any regular polygon. The **center** of a regular polygon is the center of the circumscribed circle. The **radius** of a regular polygon is the distance from the center to a vertex. The **apothem** of a regular polygon is the perpendicular distance from the center to a side.

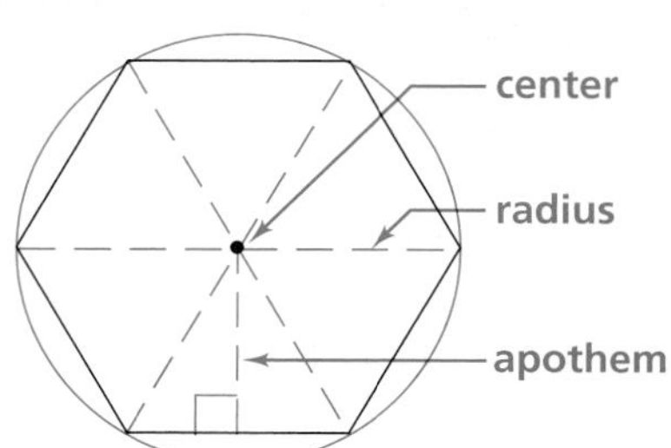

1. Suppose you have a regular n-gon with side s. The radii divide the figure into n congruent isosceles triangles.
   a. Write an expression for the area of each isosceles triangle in terms of the apothem a and the length of each side s.
   b. There are n congruent triangles. Use your answer to part (a) to write an expression for the area of the n-gon.
   c. The perimeter p of the n-gon is ns. Substitute p for ns in your answer to part (b) to find a formula for area in terms of a and p.

Your answers to Question 1 suggest the following theorem.

Theorem 5-9
Area of a Regular Polygon

The area of a regular polygon is half the product of the apothem and the perimeter.

$$A = \frac{1}{2}ap$$

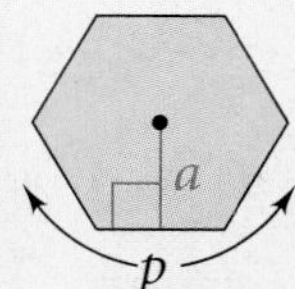

Example 1

Find the area of a regular decagon with a 12.3-in. apothem and 8-in. sides.

12.3 in.
8 in.

$p = ns$ — **Find the perimeter.**

$= 10(8) = 80$ — **A decagon has 10 sides; $n = 10$.**

$A = \frac{1}{2}ap$ — **Use the formula for the area of a regular polygon.**

$= \frac{1}{2}(12.3)(80) = 492$

The regular decagon has area 492 in.^{2}.

2. **Try This** Find the area of a regular pentagon with sides of length 11.6 cm and apothem 8 cm.

QUICK REVIEW

Regular polygons that tessellate are triangles, squares, and hexagons.

Engineers use regular polygons that tessellate because they fill the plane without wasting space. You can use special right triangles to find their areas.

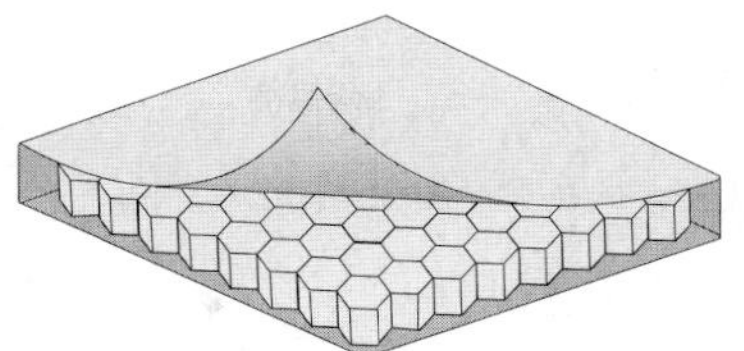

Example 2 **Relating to the Real World** 

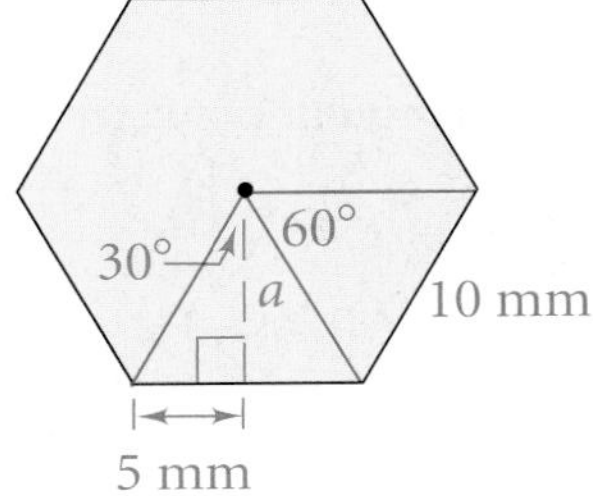

Racing Cars and boats used for racing need to be strong and durable, yet lightweight. One material that designers use to build body shells is a honeycomb of regular hexagonal prisms sandwiched between two layers of outer material. The honeycomb is plastic and provides strength and resilience without adding a lot of weight. The figure at the left is a cross section of one hexagonal cell.

The radii of a regular hexagon form six 60° angles at the center. So, you can use a 30°-60°-90° triangle to find the apothem *a*.

$a = 5\sqrt{3}$	longer leg = $\sqrt{3}$ · shorter leg
$p = ns$	Find the perimeter of the hexagon.
$= 6(10) = 60$	Substitute 6 for *n* and 10 for *s*.
$A = \frac{1}{2}ap$	Find the area.
$= \frac{1}{2}(5\sqrt{3})(60)$	Substitute.

0.5 [×] 5 [×] 3 [√] [×] 60 [=] 259.80762

The area is about 260 mm^2.

3. **Estimation** About how many hexagonal cells are in a 10 cm by 10 cm square panel?

4. **Try This** The apothem of a regular hexagon is 15 ft. Find the area of the hexagon.

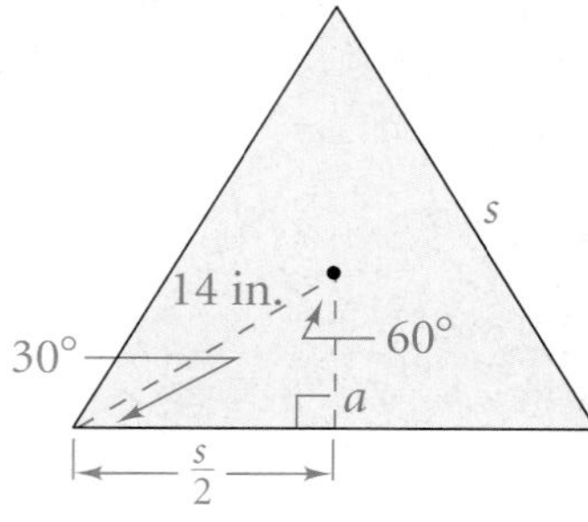

Example 3

Find the area of an equilateral triangle with radius 14 in. Leave your answer in simplest radical form.

You can use a 30°-60°-90° triangle to find the apothem a and the length of a side s.

$a = 7$	hypotenuse = 2 · shorter leg
$\frac{s}{2} = 7\sqrt{3}$	longer leg = $\sqrt{3}$ · shorter leg
$s = 14\sqrt{3}$	
$p = ns$	Find the perimeter.
$p = 3(14\sqrt{3})$	Substitute 3 for n and $14\sqrt{3}$ for s.
$= 42\sqrt{3}$	
$A = \frac{1}{2}ap$	Use the formula for area of a regular polygon.
$= \frac{1}{2}(7)(42\sqrt{3})$	Substitute 7 for a and $42\sqrt{3}$ for p.
$= 147\sqrt{3}$	

The area of the triangle is $147\sqrt{3}$ in.^{2}.

PROBLEM SOLVING

Look Back Check the solution to Example 3 by finding the area of the triangle using a different formula.

5. Try This Find the area of a square with radius 4 in.

Exercises ON YOUR OWN

Each regular polygon has radii and an apothem as shown. Find the measure of each numbered angle.

1.

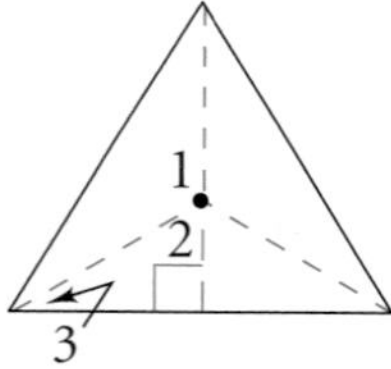

2.

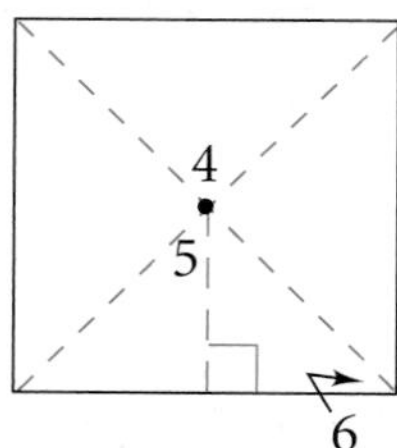

3.

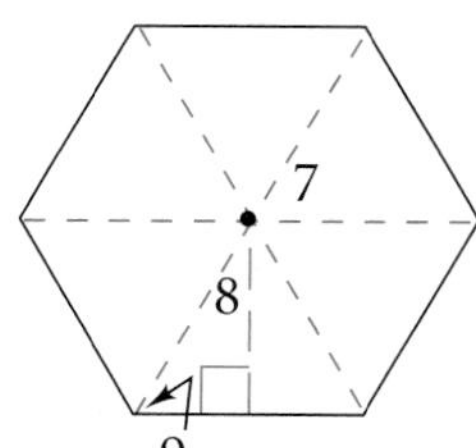

4. A regular pentagon has apothem 24.3 cm and side 35.4 cm. Find its area to the nearest tenth.

5. A regular octagon has apothem 60.5 in. and side 50 in. Find its area.

6. The apothem of a regular decagon is 19 m. Each side is 12.4 m. Find its area.

Calculator Find the area of each regular polygon to the nearest tenth.

7.

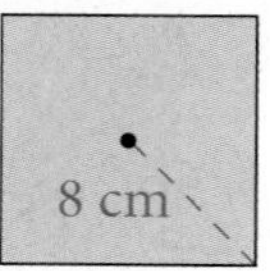

8.

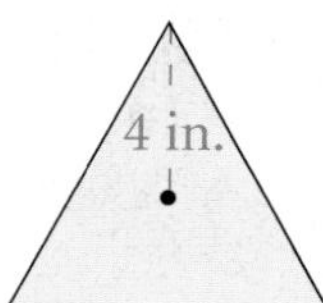

9.

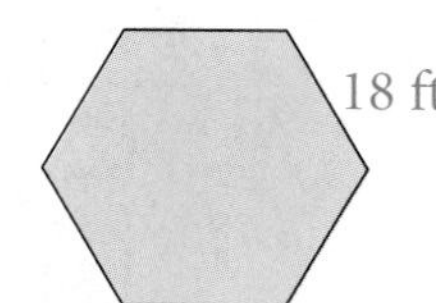

10.

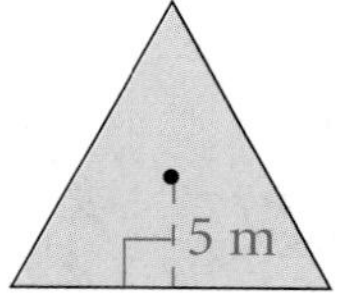

11. **Architecture** The floor of this gazebo is a regular octagon. Each side is 8 ft long, and its apothem is 9.7 ft. To the nearest tenth, find the area of the floor.

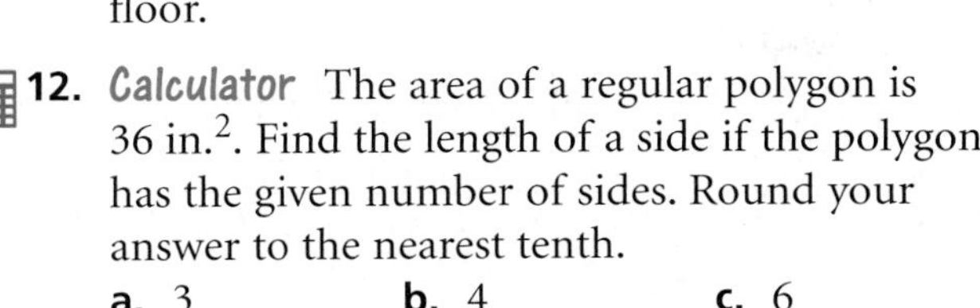

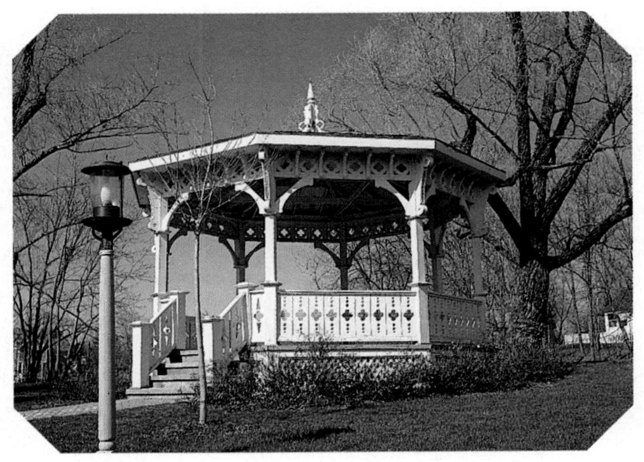

12. **Calculator** The area of a regular polygon is 36 in.^{2}. Find the length of a side if the polygon has the given number of sides. Round your answer to the nearest tenth.

 a. 3 b. 4 c. 6

 d. **Estimation** Suppose the polygon is a pentagon. What would you expect the length of its side to be? Explain.

13. **Writing** Explain why the radius of a regular polygon cannot be less than the apothem.

14. **Open-ended** Create a design using equilateral triangles and regular hexagons that have sides of the same length. Find the area of the completed design.

Find the area of each regular polygon with the given radius or apothem. Leave your answer in simplest radical form.

15. 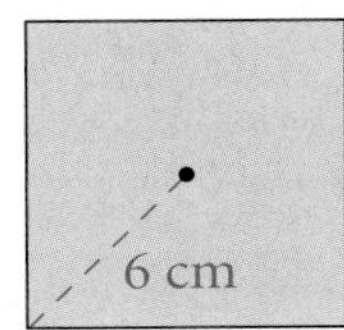

16. 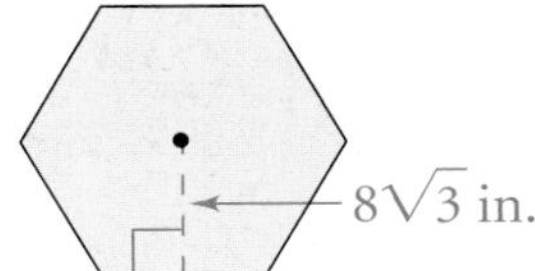

17. 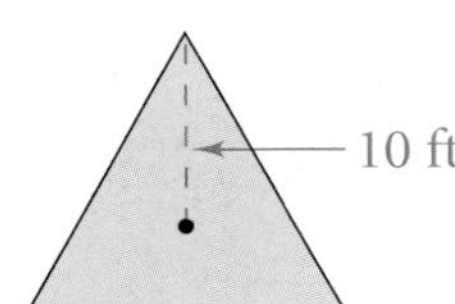

18. 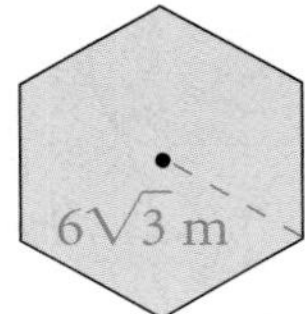

19. **Critical Thinking** To find the area of an equilateral triangle, you can use the formula $A = \frac{1}{2}bh$ or $A = \frac{1}{2}ap$. A third way to find the area of an equilateral triangle is to use the formula $A = \frac{1}{4}s^2\sqrt{3}$.

 a. **Verify** the formula $A = \frac{1}{4}s^2\sqrt{3}$ by finding the area of Figure 1 using the formula $A = \frac{1}{2}bh$.

 b. **Verify** the formula $A = \frac{1}{4}s^2\sqrt{3}$ by finding the area of Figure 2 using the formula $A = \frac{1}{2}ap$.

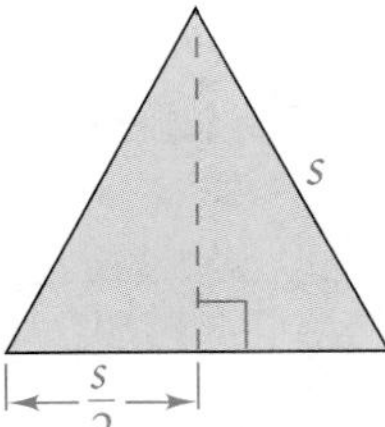

Figure 1

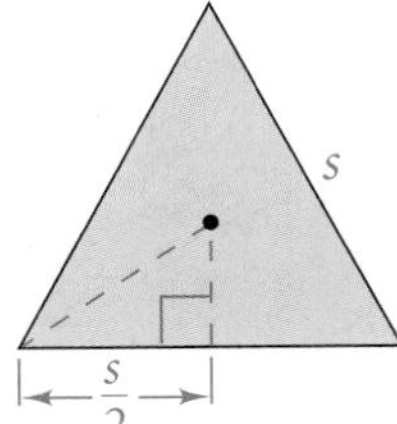

Figure 2

20. **Standardized Test Prep** A square and an equilateral triangle share a common side. What is the ratio of the area of the triangle to the area of the square?

 A. $1 : \sqrt{2}$ B. $\sqrt{2} : \sqrt{3}$ C. $\sqrt{3} : 4$ D. $\sqrt{2} : 1$ E. $\sqrt{3} : 1$

21. **Coordinate Geometry** A regular octagon with center at the origin and radius 4 is graphed in the coordinate plane.

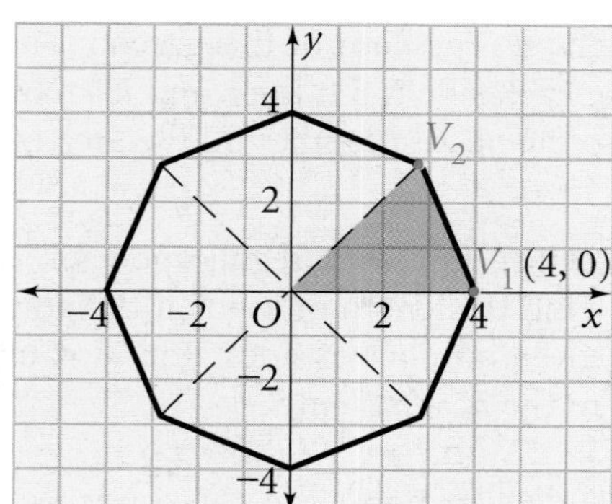

   a. Since V_2 lies on the line $y = x$, its x- and y-coordinates are equal. Use the Distance Formula to find the coordinates of V_2 to the nearest tenth.

   b. Use the coordinates of V_2 and the formula $A = \frac{1}{2}bh$ to find the area of $\triangle V_1OV_2$ to the nearest tenth.

   c. Use your answer to part (b) to find the area of the octagon to the nearest tenth.

22. **Satellites** One of the smallest satellites ever developed is in the shape of a pyramid. Each of the four faces of the pyramid is an equilateral triangle with sides about 13 cm long. What is the area of one equilateral triangular face of the satellite? Round your answer to the nearest tenth.

Find the area of each regular polygon. If your answer is not an integer, you may leave it in simplest radical form.

23.

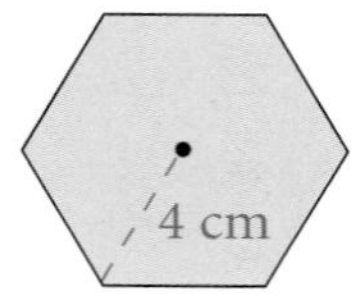

24.

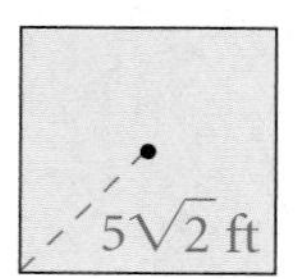

25.

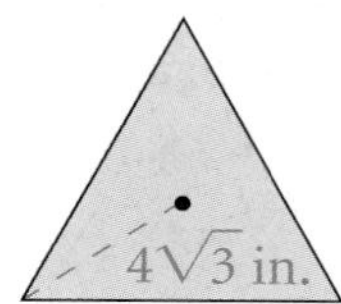

26.

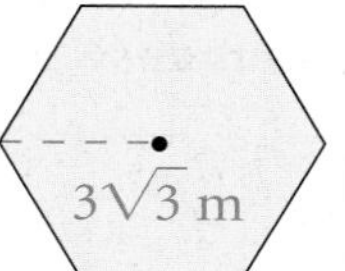

Exercises MIXED REVIEW

Create an isometric drawing for each foundation drawing.

27.

3	2
1	1

Right

Front

28.

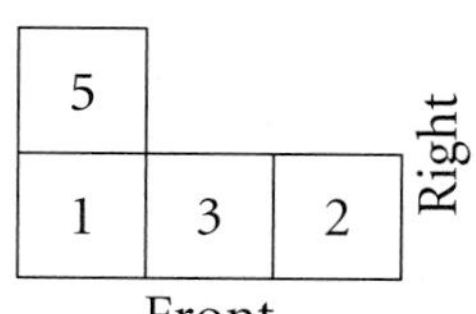

29.

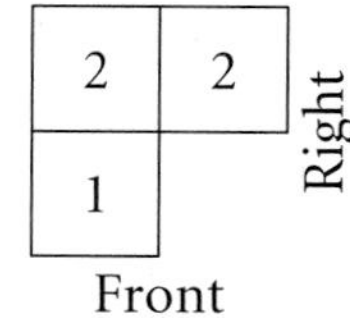

30. The measure of an angle is three more than twice the measure of its supplement. Find the measure of the angle.

Getting Ready for Lesson 5-7

Calculator **Evaluate each expression. Round your answer to the nearest hundredth.**

31. $2\pi r$ for $r = 4$

32. πd for $d = 7.3$

33. $2\pi r$ for $r = 5$

34. πd for $d = 11.8$

5-7 Circles: Circumference and Arc Length

What You'll Learn

- Finding the circumference of a circle and the length of an arc

...And Why

To solve problems involving auto safety, metalworking, and amusement park rides

What You'll Need

- circular objects
- string
- metric ruler
- calculator

WORK TOGETHER

Work in groups. Each member of your group should have one circular object such as a juice can or a jar lid.

- Measure the diameter of each circle to the nearest millimeter.
- Find the circumference of each circle by wrapping a string around each object. Straighten the string and measure its length to the nearest tenth of a centimeter.
- Organize your group's data in a table like the one below. Calculate the ratio $\frac{\text{circumference}}{\text{diameter}}$ to the nearest hundredth.

Name of Object	Circumference (C)	Diameter (d)	$\frac{C}{d}$
jelly-jar lid	19.6 cm	6.2 cm	3.16

1. Make a **conjecture** about the relationship between the circumference and the diameter of a circle.

THINK AND DISCUSS

Circumference

The ratios you found in the Work Together are estimates of the number **pi** (π), the ratio of the circumference of a circle to its diameter.

Theorem 5-10 Circumference of a Circle

The circumference of a circle is π times the diameter.

$C = \pi d$ or $C = 2\pi r$

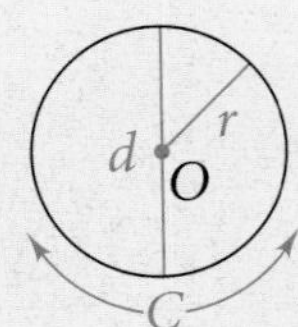

Example 1

Find the circumference of $\odot A$ and $\odot B$. Leave your answer in terms of π.

a.

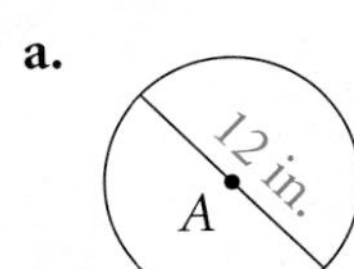

$C = \pi d$
$C = 12\pi$ in.

b.

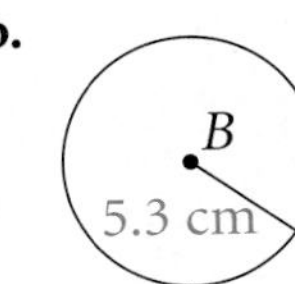

$C = 2\pi r$
$C = 2 \cdot \pi \cdot 5.3$
$C = 10.6\pi$ cm

2. **Try This** What is the radius of a circle with circumference 18π m?

Since the number π is irrational, you cannot write it as a decimal. You can use 3.14, $\frac{22}{7}$, or the $\boxed{\pi}$ key on your calculator as approximations for π.

Two circles that lie in the same plane and have the same center are **concentric circles.**

Example 2 Relating to the Real World 

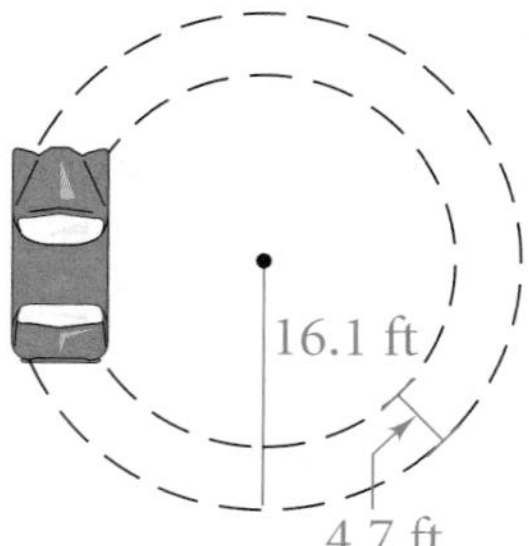

Automobiles A manufacturer advertises that a new car has a turning radius of only 16.1 ft. The distance between the two front tires is 4.7 ft. How much farther do the outside tires have to travel in making a complete circle than the tires on the inside?

The outside and inside tires travel on concentric circles. The radius of the outer circle is 16.1 ft. To find the radius of the inner circle, you must subtract 4.7 ft.

circumference of outer circle $= 2\pi(16.1) = 32.2\pi$

radius of the inner circle $= 16.1 - 4.7 = 11.4$ ft

circumference of inner circle $= 2\pi(11.4) = 22.8\pi$

The difference in the two distances is $32.2\pi - 22.8\pi = 9.4\pi$.

9.4 $\boxed{\times}$ $\boxed{\pi}$ $\boxed{=}$ 29.530971

The outside tires travel about 29.5 ft farther than the inside tires.

3. Try This The diameter of a bicycle wheel is 26 in. To the nearest whole number, how many revolutions does the wheel make when the bicycle travels 100 yd?

Arc Length

In Chapter 2 you found the measure of an arc in degrees. You can also find the **arc length,** which is a fraction of a circle's circumference.

An arc of 60° represents $\frac{60}{360}$ or $\frac{1}{6}$ of the circle. Its arc length is $\frac{1}{6}$ the circumference of the circle.

This observation suggests the following generalization.

Theorem 5-11
Arc Length

The length of an arc of a circle is the product of the ratio $\frac{\text{measure of the arc}}{360}$ and the circumference of the circle.

length of $\widehat{AB} = \frac{m\widehat{AB}}{360} \cdot 2\pi r$

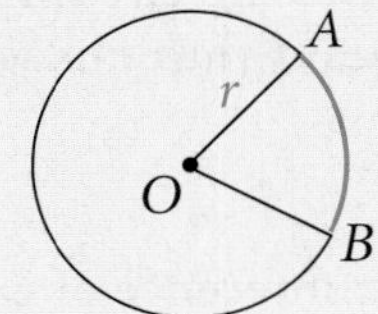

Math A Test Prep

1 What is the exact length of $\widehat{EFG}$?

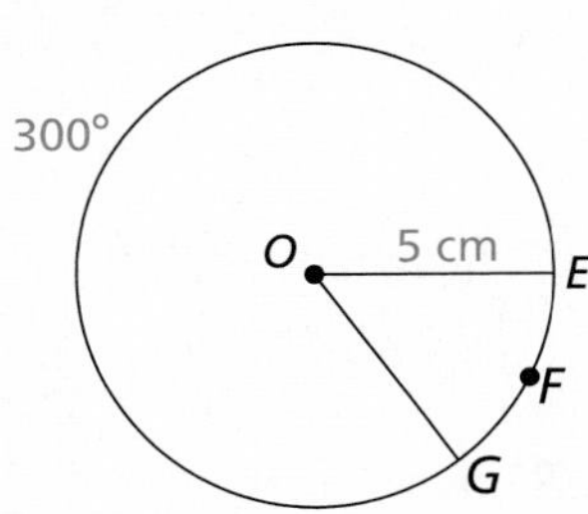

(1) $\frac{5}{3}\pi$ cm (3) $\frac{25}{3}\pi$ cm

(2) $\frac{5}{6}\pi$ cm (4) $\frac{5}{2}\pi$ cm

2 What is the area of the trapezoid?

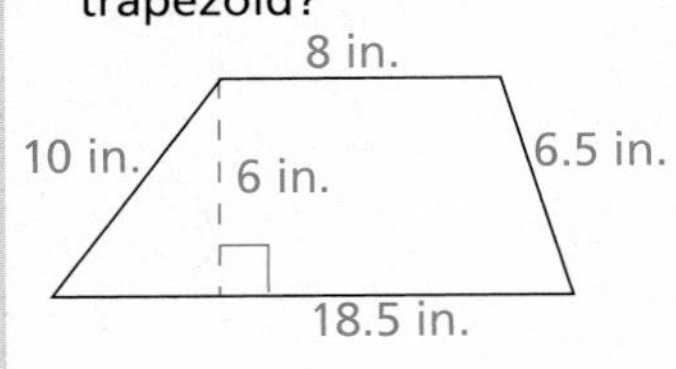

Example 3

Find the length of the arc shown in red on each circle. Leave your answer in terms of π.

a.

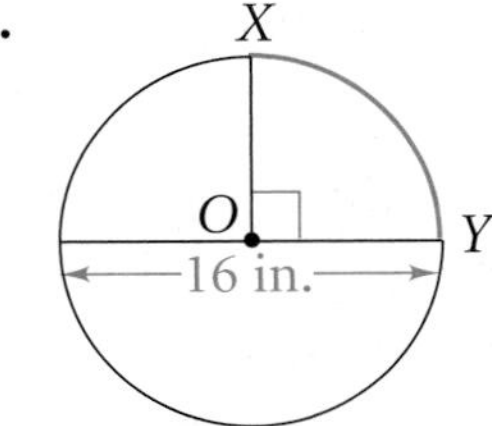

length of $\widehat{XY} = \frac{m\widehat{XY}}{360} \cdot \pi d$

length of $\widehat{XY} = \frac{90}{360} \cdot \pi(16)$

$= 4\pi$ in.

b.

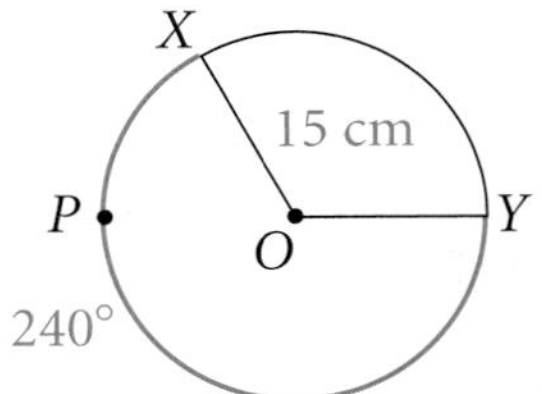

length of $\widehat{XPY} = \frac{m\widehat{XPY}}{360} \cdot 2\pi r$

length of $\widehat{XPY} = \frac{240}{360} \cdot 2\pi(15)$

$= 20\pi$ cm

4. **Try This** Find the length of a semicircle with radius 1.3 m. Leave your answer in terms of π.

5. **Critical Thinking** Is it possible for two arcs of different circles to have the same measure, but different lengths? Support your answer with an example.

6. **Critical Thinking** Is it possible for two arcs of different circles to have the same length but have different measures? Support your answer with an example.

Your answers to Questions 5 and 6 illustrate that for arcs to be congruent two things must be true. **Congruent arcs** are arcs that have the same measure and are in the same circle or in congruent circles.

Exercises ON YOUR OWN

Find the circumference of $\odot O$. Leave your answer in terms of π.

1\.
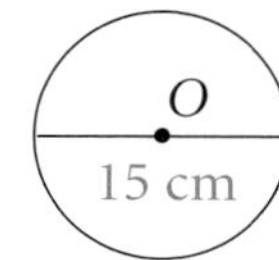

2\.
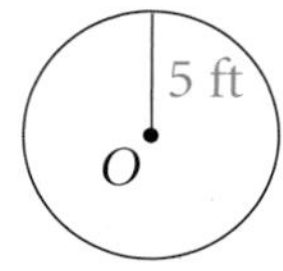

3\. (circle with center O and diameter 3.7 in.)

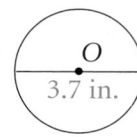

4\.
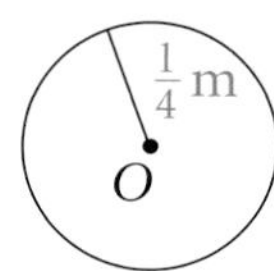

Calculator **Find the circumference of each circle with the given radius or diameter. Round your answer to the nearest hundredth.**

5\. $r = 9$ in.

6\. $d = 7.3$ m

7\. $d = \frac{1}{2}$ yd

8\. $r = 0.13$ cm

Find the circumference of each circle. Then find the length of the arc shown in red on each circle. Leave your answer in terms of π.

9\.
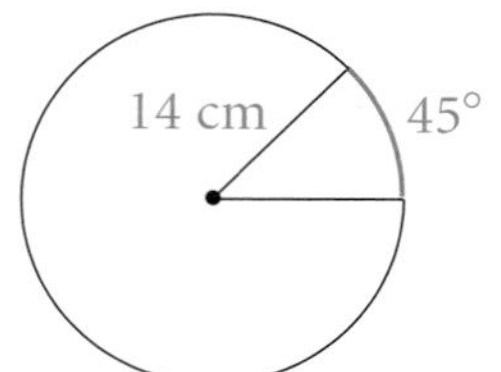

10\.
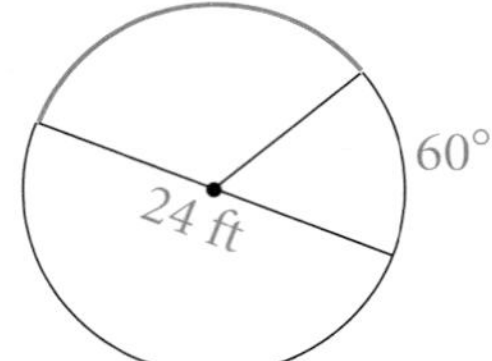

11\.
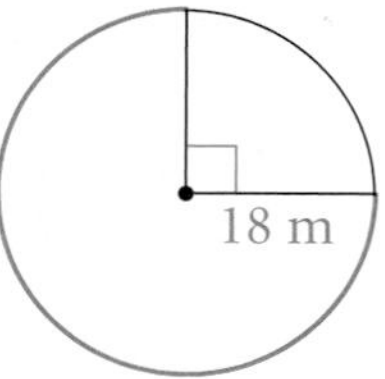

12\.
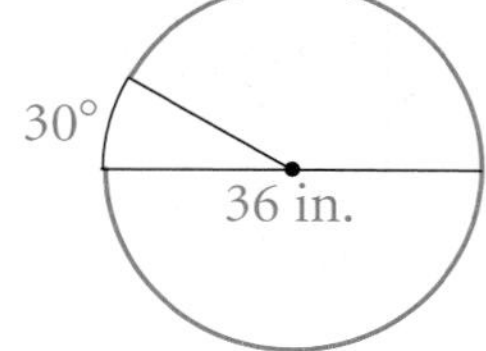

13\. The circumference of a circle is 100π in. Find each of the following.
   a. the diameter
   b. the radius
   c. the length of an arc of 120°

14\. **Coordinate Geometry** The endpoints of a diameter of a circle are $A(1, 3)$ and $B(4, 7)$. Find each of the following.
   a. the coordinates of the center
   b. the diameter
   c. the circumference

15\. **Metalworking** Miya constructed a wrought-iron arch to top the entrance to a mall. The 11 bars between the two concentric semicircles are each 3 ft long. Find the length of the wrought iron used to make this structure. Round your answer to the nearest foot.

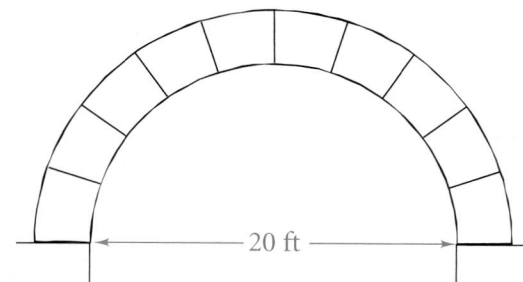

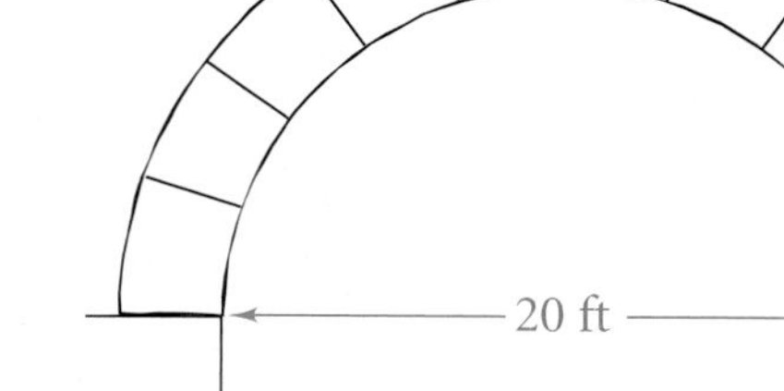

16\. A 60° arc of $\odot A$ has the same length as a 45° arc of $\odot B$. Find the ratio of the radius of $\odot A$ to the radius of $\odot B$.

17\. **Space Travel** The orbit of the space station *Mir* is 245 mi above Earth. How much greater is the circumference of *Mir's* orbit than the circumference of Earth? Earth's radius is about 3960 mi. Leave your answer in terms of π.

18\. **Open-ended** Use a compass and protractor to draw two noncongruent arcs with the same measure.

Calculator **Find the length of the arc shown in red on each circle. Round your answer to the nearest hundredth.**

19. 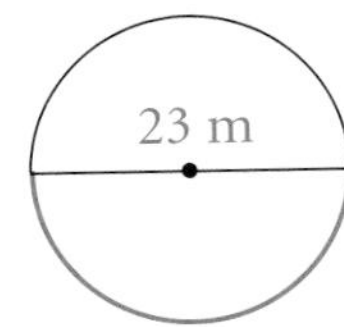

20. 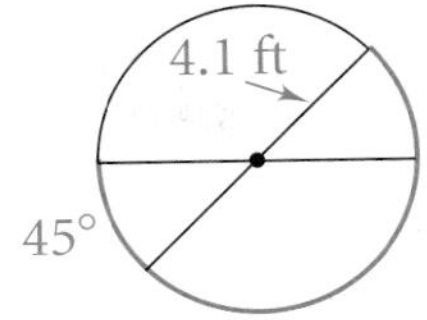

21. 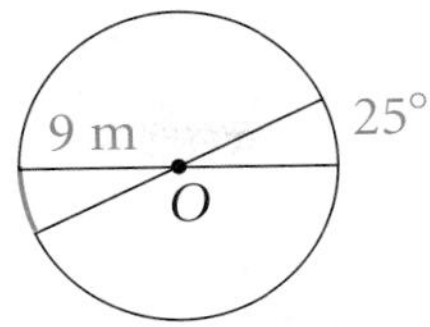

22. 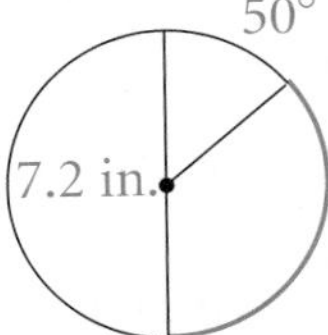

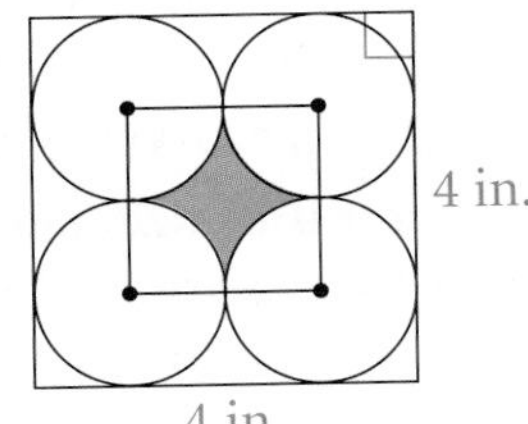

23. Find the perimeter of the shaded portion of the figure at the right. Leave your answer in terms of π.

24. **Standardized Test Prep** The length of $\widehat{AB}$ is 6π cm and $m\widehat{AB} = 120$. What is the diameter of the circle?

A. 2 cm **B.** 6 cm **C.** 9 cm
D. 18 cm **E.** 24 cm

25. **Coordinate Geometry** Find the length of a semicircle with endpoints (3, 7) and (3, −1). Round your answer to the nearest tenth.

CALVIN AND HOBBES by Bill Watterson

Cartoon **Use what you learned from Calvin's father to answer the following questions.**

26. In one revolution, how much farther does a point 10 cm from the center of the record travel than a point 3 cm from the center? Round your answer to the nearest hundredth.

27. **Writing** Kendra and her mother plan to ride the merry-go-round. Two horses on the merry-go-round are side by side. For a more exciting ride, should Kendra sit on the inside or the outside? Explain your reasoning.

Exercises MIXED REVIEW

Locus **Sketch and label each locus.**

28. all points in a plane equidistant from points A and B

29. all points in space equidistant from parallel lines m and n

30. **Transformations** A triangle has vertices $A(3, 2)$, $B(4, 1)$, and $C(4, 3)$. Find the coordinates of the image of the triangle under a glide reflection in $\langle 0, 1 \rangle$ and $x = 0$.

Getting Ready for Lesson 5-8

Estimation **A circle is drawn on three different grids. Use the scale of each grid to estimate the area of each circle in square inches.**

31.

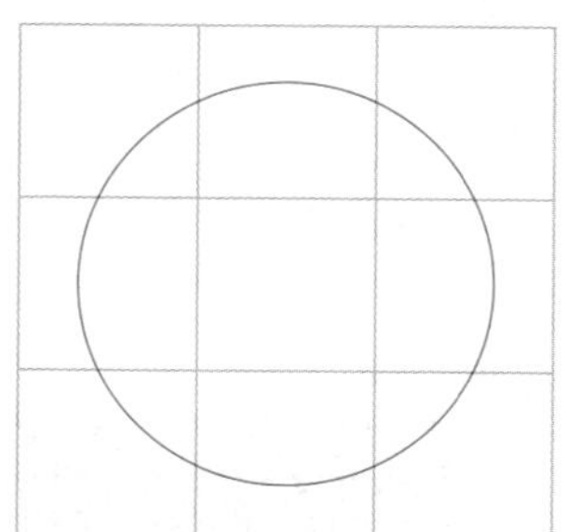

32.

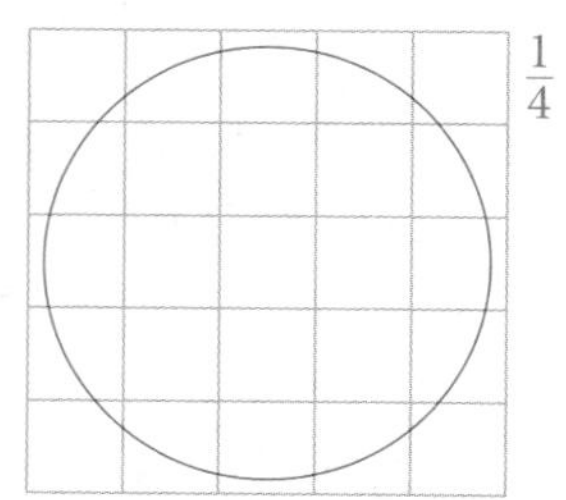

33.

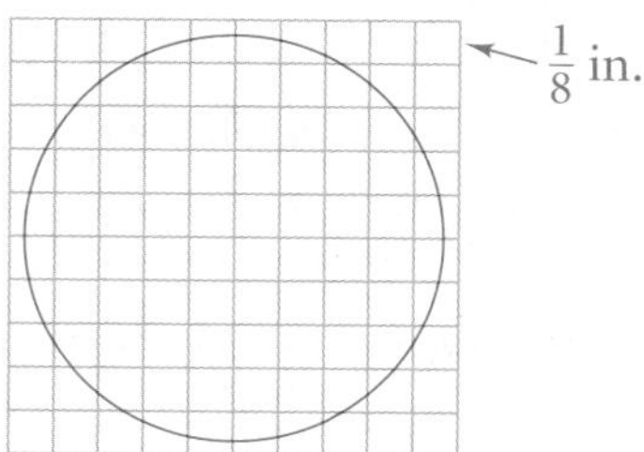

Exercises CHECKPOINT

Find the area of each trapezoid or regular polygon. Leave your answer in simplest radical form.

1.

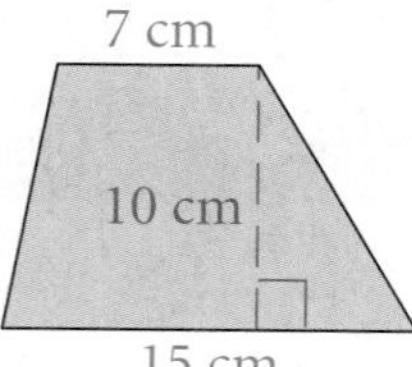

2.

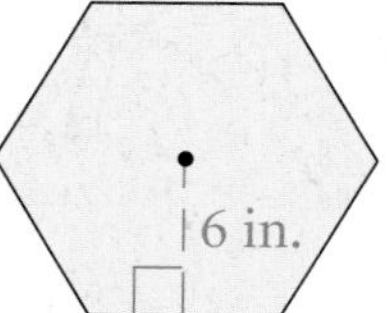

3.

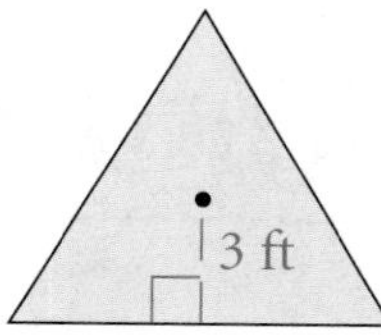

Calculator **Find the circumference of a circle with the given radius. Round your answer to the nearest hundredth.**

4. 8 in. **5.** 2 m **6.** 5 ft **7.** 1.4 km **8.** 9 mm

9. In a circle of radius 18 mm, $m\widehat{AB} = 45$. Find the length of $\widehat{AB}$. Leave your answer in terms of π.

10. **Writing** Explain at least two ways to find the area of an equilateral triangle. Use an example to illustrate your explanation.

5-8 Areas of Circles, Sectors, and Segments of Circles

What You'll Learn

- Computing the areas of circles, sectors, and segments of circles

...And Why

To solve real-world problems in food preparation, archaeology, and biology

What You'll Need

- compass
- scissors
- tape

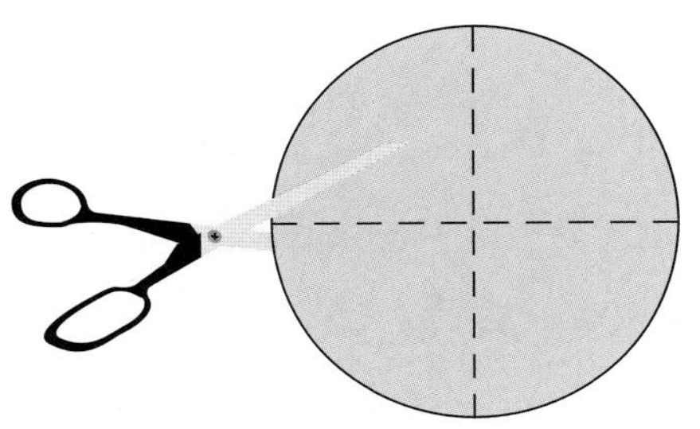

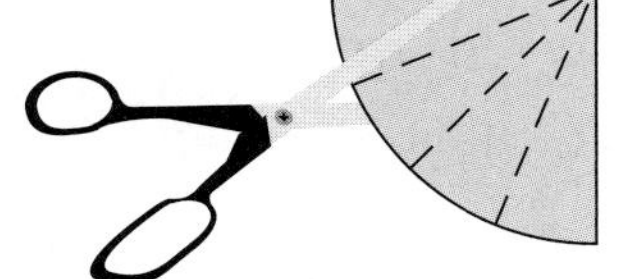

WORK TOGETHER

Work in groups. Have each member of your group use a compass to draw a large circle. Fold the circle in half horizontally and vertically. Cut the circle into four wedges on the fold lines. Then fold each wedge into quarters. Cut each wedge on the fold lines. You will have 16 wedges. Tape the wedges to a piece of paper to form the figure below.

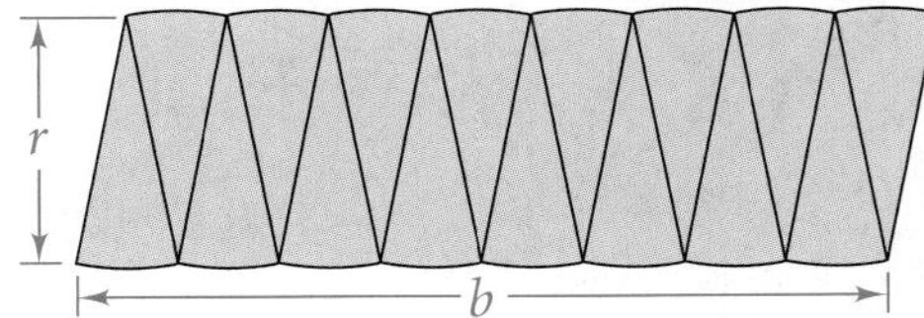

1. How does the area of the figure compare with the area of the circle?
2. The base of the figure is formed by arcs of the circle. Write an equation relating the length of the base b to the circumference C of the circle.
3. Write an equation for the length of the base b in terms of the radius r of the circle.
4. If you increase the number of wedges, the figure you create becomes more and more like a rectangle with base b and height r. Write an expression for the area of the rectangle in terms of r.

THINK AND DISCUSS

Areas of Circles

Your observations in the Work Together suggest the following theorem.

Theorem 5-12
Area of a Circle

The area of a circle is the product of π and the square of the radius.

$A = \pi r^2$

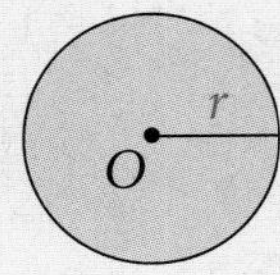

5. **Try This** What is the area of a circle with radius 15 cm? Leave your answer in terms of π.

Example 1 Relating to the Real World

Food The diameter of a small pizza is 10 in. How much more pizza do you get if you order a medium pizza with diameter 12 in.?

$$\text{radius of small pizza} = \frac{10}{2} = 5 \qquad r = \frac{d}{2}$$
$$\text{radius of medium pizza} = \frac{12}{2} = 6 \qquad r = \frac{d}{2}$$

Use the formula for the area of a circle.

$$\text{area of small pizza} = \pi(5)^2 = 25\pi \qquad A = \pi r^2$$
$$\text{area of medium pizza} = \pi(6)^2 = 36\pi \qquad A = \pi r^2$$
$$\text{difference in area} = 36\pi - 25\pi = 11\pi$$

11 [×] [π] [=] 34.557519

The medium pizza has about 35 in.^{2} more pizza than the small pizza.

6. Suppose the small pizza in Example 1 costs $5.00 and the medium pizza costs $6.00. Which pizza is a better buy? Explain your answer.

Sectors and Segments

A **sector of a circle** is the region bounded by two radii and their intercepted arc. A slice of pizza is an example of a sector of a circle. You name a sector using one endpoint of the arc, the center of the circle, and the other endpoint of the arc. Sector *XOY* is at the left.

The area of a sector is a fractional part of the area of a circle. The ratio of a sector's area to a circle's area is $\frac{\text{measure of the arc}}{360}$.

Theorem 5-13
Area of a Sector of a Circle

The area of a sector of a circle is the product of the ratio $\frac{\text{measure of the arc}}{360}$ and the area of the circle.

$$\text{Area of sector } AOB = \frac{m\overset{\frown}{AB}}{360} \cdot \pi r^2$$

Example 2

Find the area of sector ZOM. Leave your answer in terms of π.

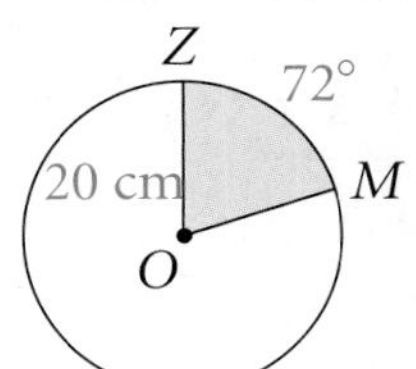

$$\text{area of sector } ZOM = \frac{m\widehat{ZM}}{360} \cdot \pi r^2$$
$$= \frac{72}{360} \cdot \pi(20)^2$$
$$= 80\pi$$

The area of sector ZOM is $80\pi \text{ cm}^2$.

7. **Calculator** A circle has diameter 8.2 m. What is the area of a sector with a 125° arc? Round your answer to the nearest tenth.

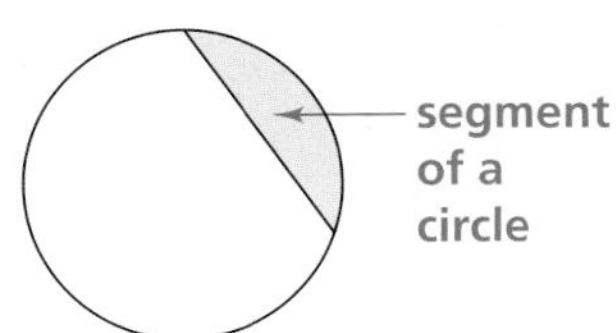

The part of a circle bounded by an arc and the segment joining its endpoints is a **segment of the circle.** To find the area of a segment, draw radii to form a sector. The area of the segment equals the area of the sector minus the area of the triangle formed.

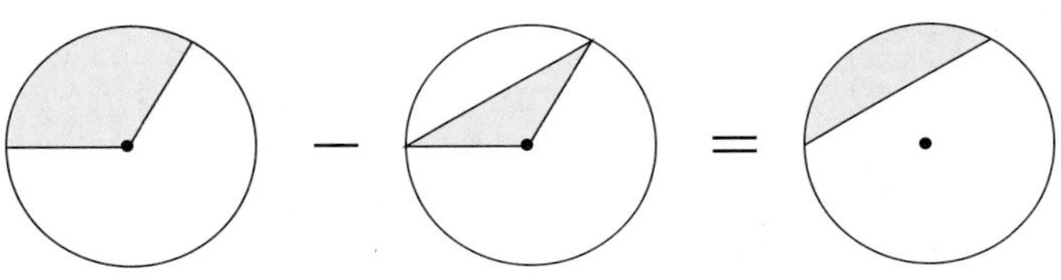

Area of sector　　Area of triangle　　Area of segment

Example 3

Find the area of the shaded segment.

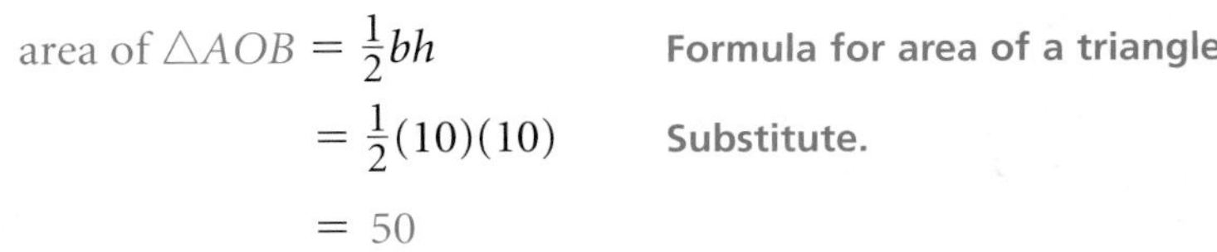

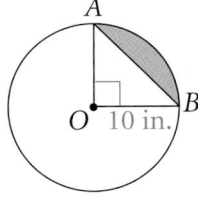

$$\text{area of sector } AOB = \frac{m\widehat{AB}}{360} \cdot \pi r^2 \qquad \textbf{Formula for area of a sector}$$
$$= \frac{90}{360} \cdot \pi(10)^2 \qquad \textbf{Substitute.}$$
$$= \frac{1}{4} \cdot 100\pi$$
$$= 25\pi$$

$$\text{area of } \triangle AOB = \frac{1}{2}bh \qquad \textbf{Formula for area of a triangle}$$
$$= \frac{1}{2}(10)(10) \qquad \textbf{Substitute.}$$
$$= 50$$

$$\text{area of segment} = 25\pi - 50$$

25 [×] [π] [−] 50 [=] 28.539816

The area of the segment is about 28.5 in.^{2}

8. **Try This** A circle has radius 12 cm. Find the area of a segment of the circle bounded by a 60° arc and the segment joining its endpoints. Round your answer to the nearest tenth.

Exercises ON YOUR OWN

Find the area of each circle. Leave your answers in terms of π.

1. 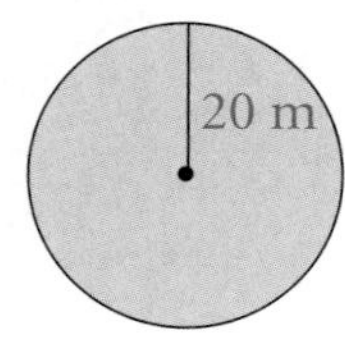

2. 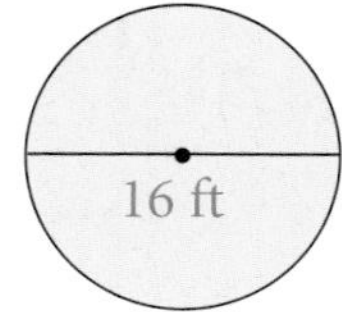

3. 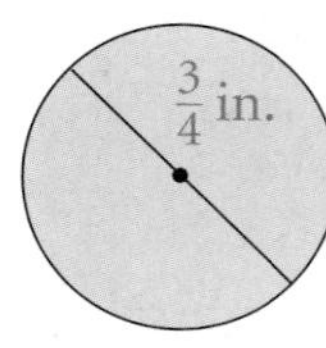

4. 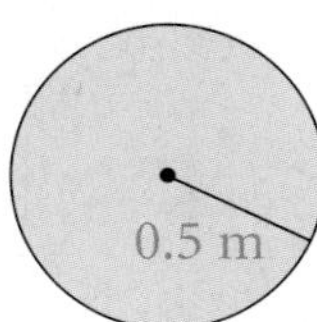

5. A circle has area 225π m^2. What is its diameter?

6. How many circles with radius 4 in. will have the same total area as a circle with radius 12 in.?

7. **Coordinate Geometry** The endpoints of a diameter of $\odot A$ are (2, 1) and (5, 5). Find the area of $\odot A$. Leave your answer in terms of π.

Calculator **Find the area of each circle. Round your answer to the nearest hundredth.**

8. $r = 7$ ft
9. $d = 8.3$ m
10. $d = 0.24$ cm

11. **Archaeology** Off the coast of Sweden, divers are working to bring up artifacts from a ship that sank several hundred years ago. The line to a diver is 100 ft long, and the diver is working at a depth of 80 ft. What is the area of the circle that the diver can cover? Round your answer to the nearest square foot.

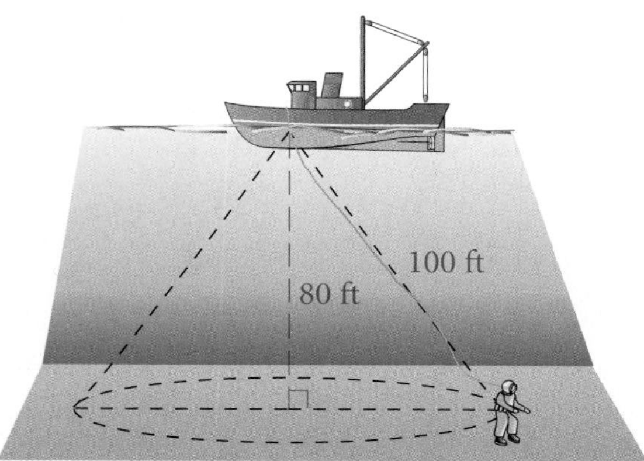

Find the area of each shaded sector of a circle. Leave your answer in terms of π.

12. 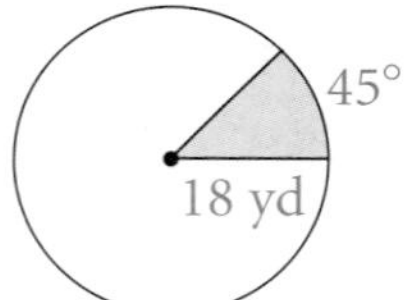

13. 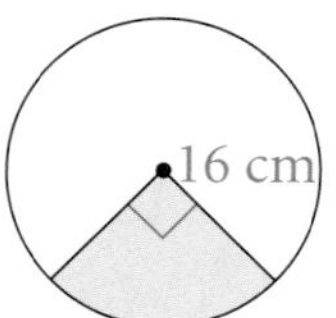

14. 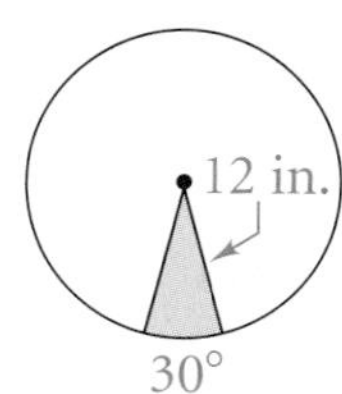

15. 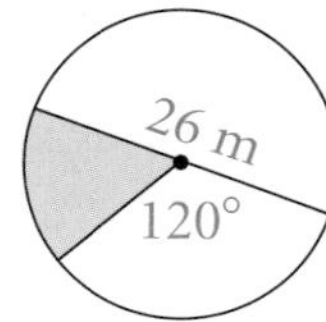

16. **Games** A dartboard has a diameter of 20 in. and is divided into 20 congruent sectors. Find the area of one sector. Round your answer to the nearest tenth.

17. **Animal Habitats** In the Pacific Northwest, a red fox has a circular home range with a radius of about 718 m. To the nearest thousand, about how many square meters are in a red fox's home range?

Calculator **Find the area of each shaded segment of a circle. Round your answer to the nearest hundredth.**

18. 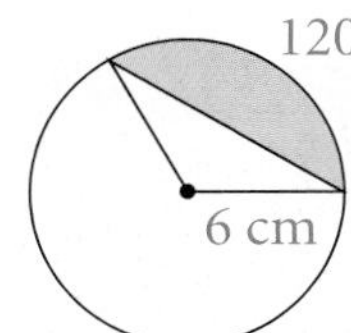

19. 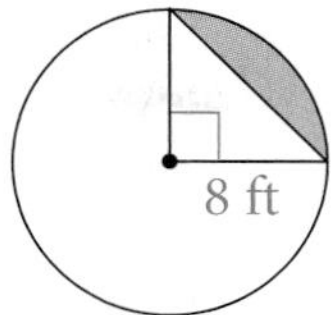

20. 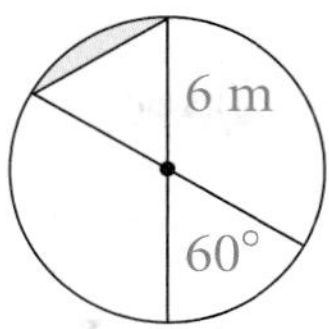

21. 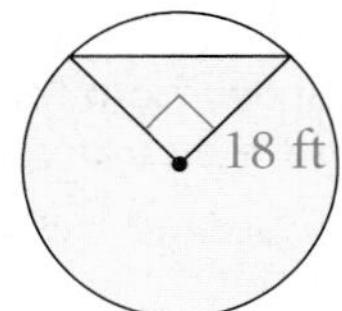

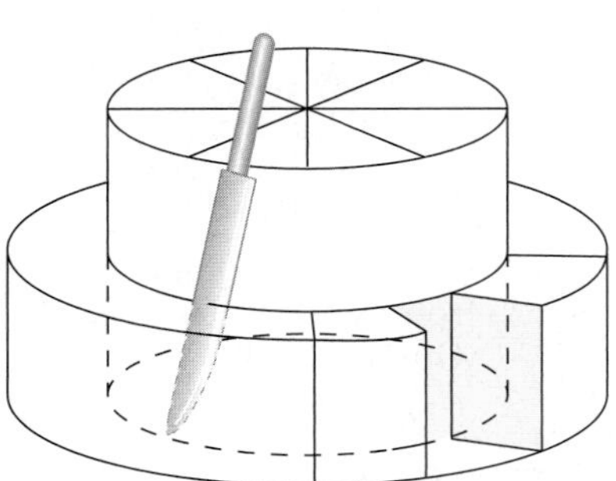

22. **Writing** The American Institute of Baking suggests a technique for cutting and serving a tiered cake. The tiers of a cake have the same height and have diameters 8 in. and 13 in. The top layer and the circle directly under it are cut into 8 pieces and the exterior ring of the 13-inch layer is cut into 12 pieces. Which piece would be biggest, a top, bottom-inside, or bottom-outside piece? Explain your answer.

23. A sector of a circle with a 90° arc has area 36π in.^{2}. What is the radius of the circle?

Find the area of the shaded figure. Leave your answer in terms of π.

24. 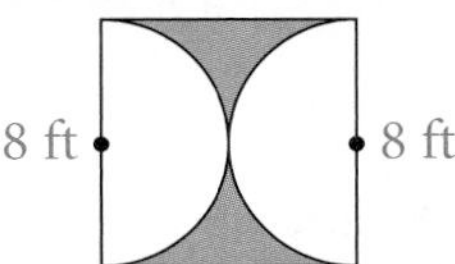

25. 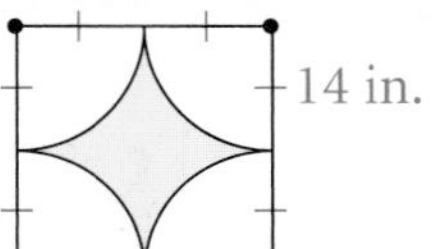

26. 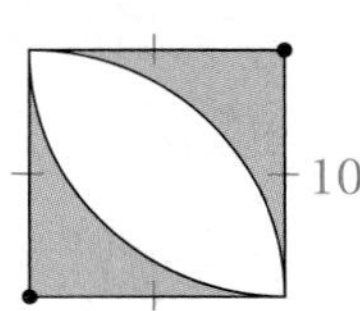

27. 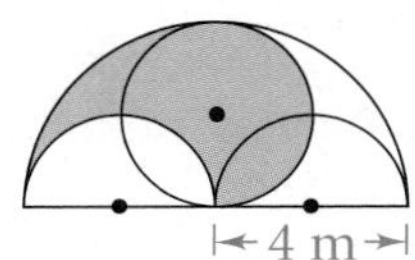

28. **Open-ended** Draw a diagram for a sector of a circle such that the sector has area 16π cm^2. Label the radius of the circle and the measure of the arc of the sector.

29. An 8 ft-by-10 ft floating dock is anchored in the middle of a pond. The bow of a canoe is tied to one corner of the dock with a 10-ft rope.

a. Sketch a diagram of the area in which the bow of the canoe can travel.

b. Write a plan for finding the area.

c. Find the area. Round your answer to the nearest square foot.

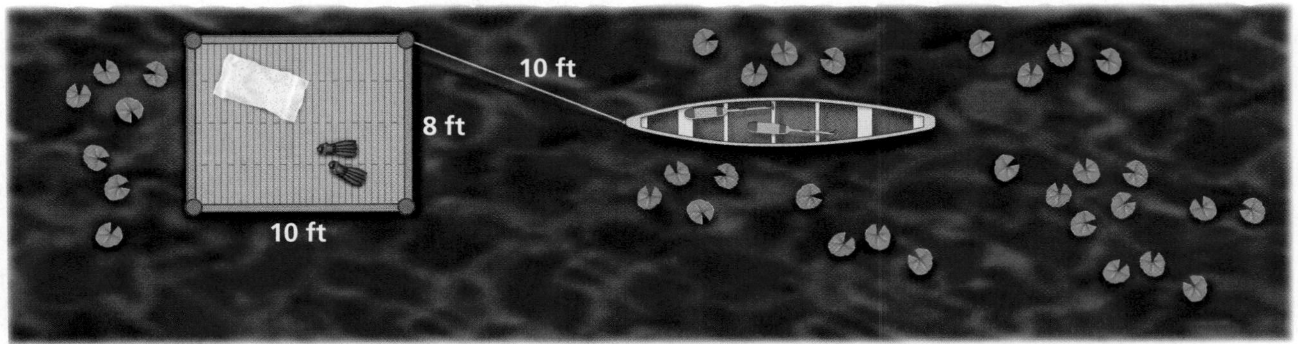

Chapter Project... Find Out by Calculating

The circles on this quilt were sewn onto the background cloth. Cutting circles from rectangles leaves some waste. Explore whether you can reduce waste by using smaller circles.

- Compare the percent of material wasted when the shaded circles are cut from squares A, B, and C below.

A. 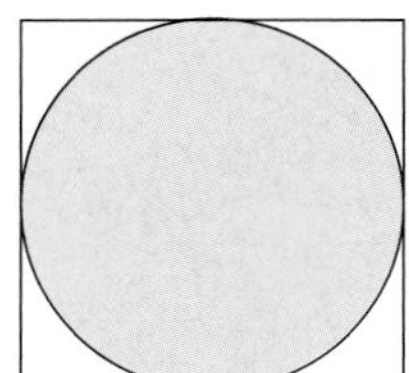 B. 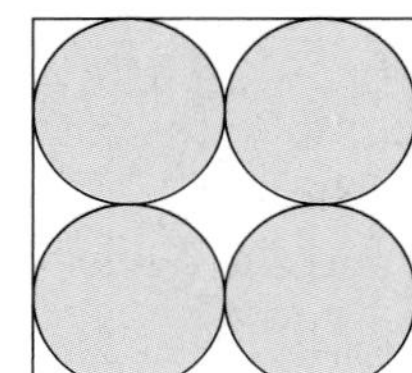 C. 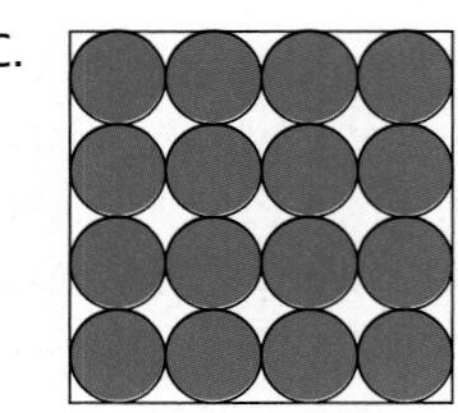

- Estimate how many times longer it would take to cut out the 16 circles from square C than the 1 circle from square A. Support your estimate with calculations.

Exercises MIXED REVIEW

Data Analysis **Use the line graph for Exercises 30–32.**

30. In 1990, how much did the average person spend on media such as printed material, videos, and recordings?

31. How much has spending increased from 1990 to 1994?

32. **Predict** how much the average person will spend on media in the year 2000.

Annual Dollars Spent per Person on Media

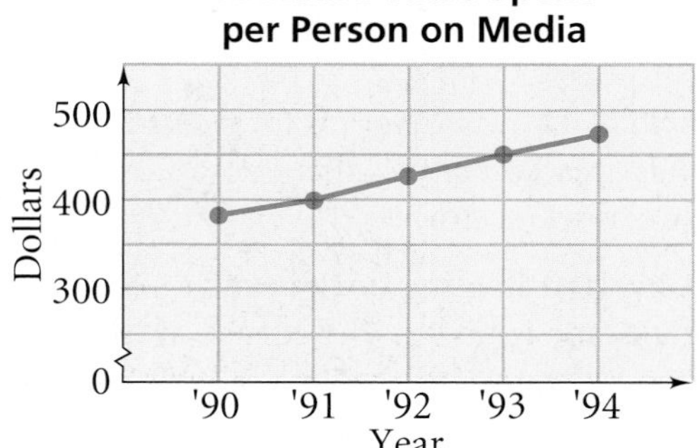

33. What is the area of a 30°-60°-90° triangle with hypotenuse 12 cm? Leave your answer in simplest radical form.

The measures of two angles of a triangle are given. Find the measure of the third angle. Then classify the triangle by its sides and angles.

34. 54°, 108° **35.** 72°, 36°

36. 36°, 54° **37.** 78°, 34°

38. 60°, 60° **39.** 90°, 45°

SELF ASSESSMENT

PORTFOLIO

For your portfolio, select one or two items from your work for this chapter. Here are some possibilities.
- corrected work
- a journal entry

Explain why you have included each selection.

Exploring Area and Circumference

After Lesson 5-8

A polygon that is *inscribed* in a circle has all its vertices on the circle. Work in pairs or small groups. Investigate the ratios of the perimeters and areas of inscribed regular polygons to the circumference and area of the circle in which they are inscribed. Begin by making a table like this.

Regular Polygon			Circle		Ratios	
Sides	Perimeter	Area	Circumference	Area	$\frac{\text{Perimeter}}{\text{Circumference}}$	$\frac{\text{Polygon Area}}{\text{Circle Area}}$
3						

Construct

Use geometry software to construct a circle. Find its circumference and area and record them in your table. Inscribe an equilateral triangle in the circle. Your software may be able to do this for you automatically, or you can construct three points on the circle and move them so they are approximately evenly spaced on the circle. Then draw the triangle.

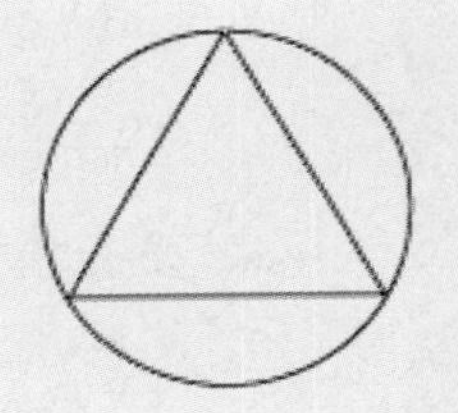

Investigate

Use your geometry software to measure the perimeter and area of the triangle and to calculate the ratios $\frac{\text{triangle perimeter}}{\text{circle circumference}}$ and $\frac{\text{triangle area}}{\text{circle area}}$. Record the results.

Manipulate the circle to change its size. Do the ratios you calculated stay the same or change?

Now inscribe a square in a circle and fill in your table for a polygon of four sides. Do the same for a regular pentagon.

Conjecture

What will happen to the ratios $\frac{\text{perimeter}}{\text{circumference}}$ and $\frac{\text{polygon area}}{\text{circle area}}$ as you increase the number of sides of the polygon?

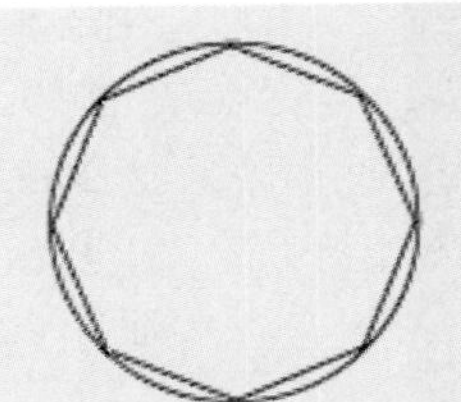

Extend

- Extend your table to include polygons of 12 sides. Does your conjecture still hold? Compare the two columns of ratios in your table. How do they differ?
- Estimate the perimeter and area of a polygon of 100 sides that is inscribed in a circle with a radius of 10 cm.

CHAPTER PROJECT

Finishing the Chapter Project

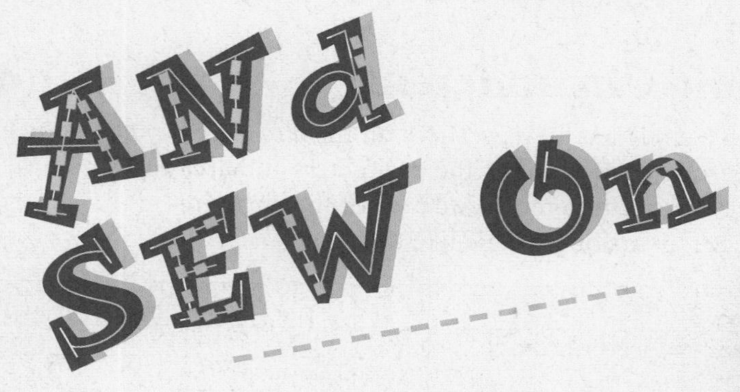

Find Out exercises on pages 810, 817, 835, and 852 should help you complete your project. Design a quilt for your bed. Use one of the techniques you learned. Include the dimensions of the quilt. List the size, shape, color, and number of each different piece. If available, use iron-on patches to color several small blocks that establish the design. Then iron the design on a T-shirt or a piece of fabric.

Reflect and Revise

Ask a classmate to review your project with you. Together, check that your quilt design is complete, your diagrams are clear, and your explanations and information are accurate. Is the display attractive, organized, and comprehensive? Consider doing more research (using some of the books listed below) on textiles of different cultures.

Follow Up

Go to a fabric store to find the different widths in which fabrics are sold. Determine the amount of each fabric you need, and estimate the cost.

For More Information

Bradkin, Cheryl G. *Basic Seminole Patchwork.* Mountain View, California: Leone Publications, 1990.

Fisher, Laura. *Quilts of Illusion.* Pittstown, New Jersey: The Main Street Press, 1988.

Kapoun, Robert W. *Language of the Robe: American Indian Trade Blankets.* Salt Lake City, Utah: Peregrine Smith Books, 1948.

Norden, Mary. *Ethnic Needlepoint Designs from Asia, Africa, and the Americas.* New York: Watson-Guptill Publications, 1993.

Schevill, Margot Blum. *Maya Textiles of Guatemala.* Austin, Texas: University of Texas Press, 1993.

CHAPTER 5

Wrap Up

How am I doing?

SELF ASSESSMENT

- State three ideas from this chapter that you think are important. Explain your choices.
- Explain how to find the area of different polygons.

Key Terms

altitude (p. 812)
apothem (p. 836)
arc length (p. 843)
area of a circle (p. 847)
area of a parallelogram (p. 811)
area of a polygon (p. 805)
area of a rectangle (p. 806)
area of a square (p. 805)
area of a trapezoid (p. 831)
area of a triangle (p. 813)
base (pp. 812, 813, 831)
center (p. 836)
circumference of a circle (p. 841)
concentric circles (p. 842)
congruent arcs (p. 843)
Converse of the Pythagorean Theorem (p. 820)
45°-45°-90° triangle (p. 826)
height (pp. 812, 813, 831)
hypotenuse (p. 818)
legs of a right triangle (p. 818)
legs of a trapezoid (p. 831)
perimeter of a polygon (p. 804)
pi (p. 841)
Pythagorean Theorem (p. 819)
Pythagorean triple (p. 820)
radius (p. 836)
sector of a circle (p. 848)
segment of a circle (p. 849)
30°-60°-90° triangle (p. 827)

Understanding Perimeter and Area 5-1

The **perimeter of a polygon** is the sum of the lengths of its sides.

The formula for the perimeter of a square is $P = 4s$. The formula for the perimeter of a rectangle is $P = 2b + 2h$.

The **area of a polygon** is the number of square units it encloses. The area of a region is the sum of the area of its nonoverlapping parts. If two figures are congruent, their areas are equal.

The formula for the **area of a square** is $A = s^2$. The formula for the **area of a rectangle** is $A = bh$.

s

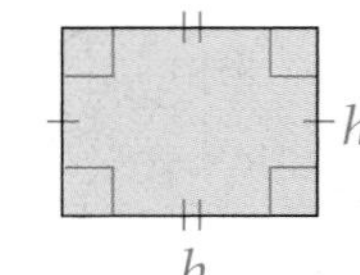

Find the perimeter and area of each figure.

1. 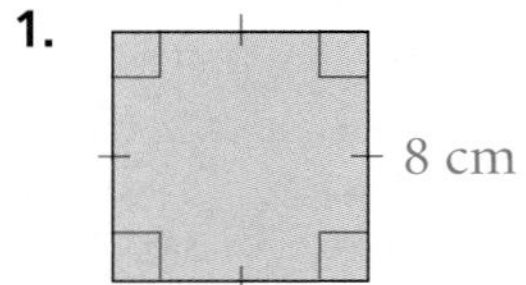

2. 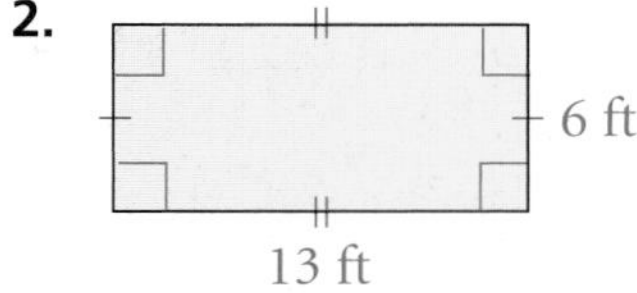

3. 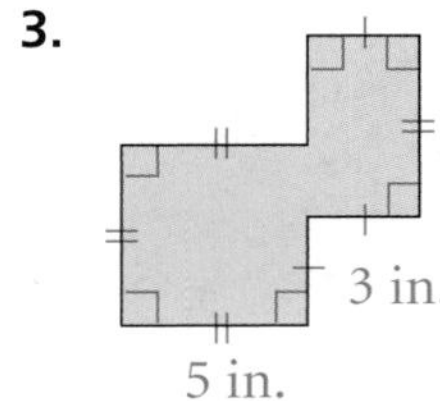

4. *Open-ended* Draw a polygon with perimeter 33 cm.

Areas of Parallelograms and Triangles 5-2

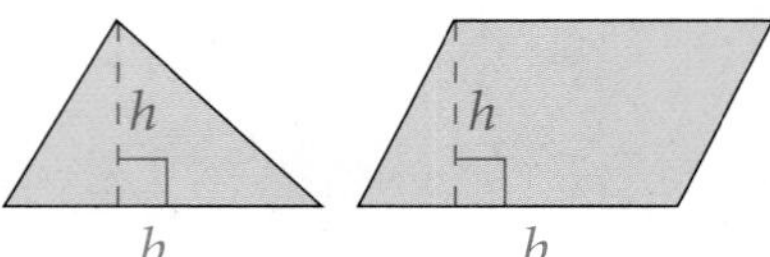

You can find the area of a parallelogram or a triangle if you know the **base** and **height**. The **area of a parallelogram** is $A = bh$. The **area of a triangle** is $A = \frac{1}{2}bh$.

Find the area of each figure.

5. 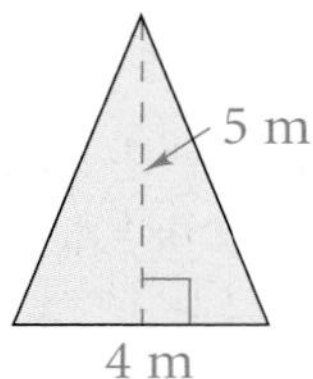

6. 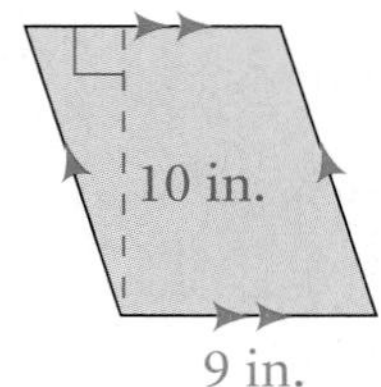

7. 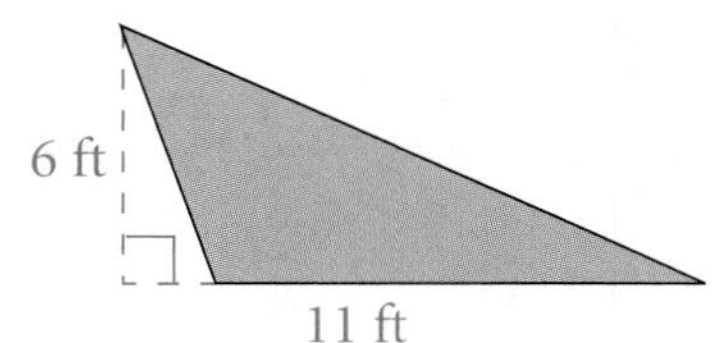

The Pythagorean Theorem and Its Converse 5-3

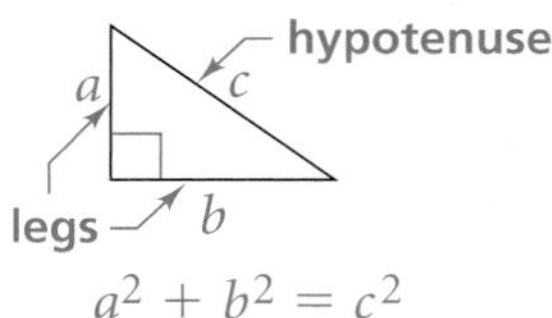

The **Pythagorean Theorem** states that in a right triangle the sum of the squares of the lengths of the legs equals the square of the length of the hypotenuse, or $a^2 + b^2 = c^2$.

Positive integers a, b, and c form a **Pythagorean triple** if $a^2 + b^2 = c^2$.

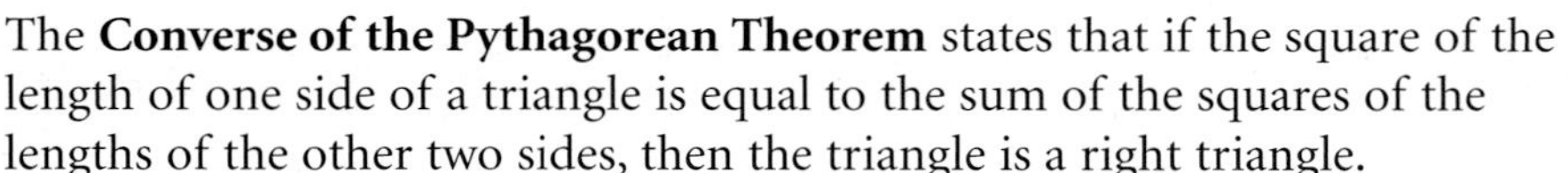

The **Converse of the Pythagorean Theorem** states that if the square of the length of one side of a triangle is equal to the sum of the squares of the lengths of the other two sides, then the triangle is a right triangle.

In a triangle with longest side c, if $c^2 > a^2 + b^2$, the triangle is obtuse, and if $c^2 < a^2 + b^2$, the triangle is acute.

Find each value of x. If your answer is not an integer, you may leave it in simplest radical form.

8. 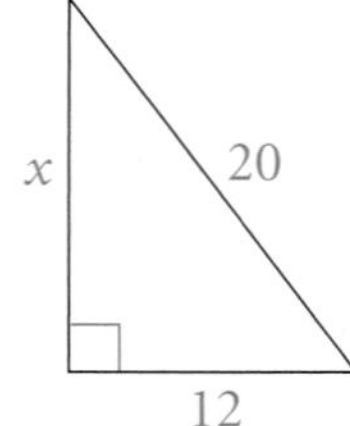

9. 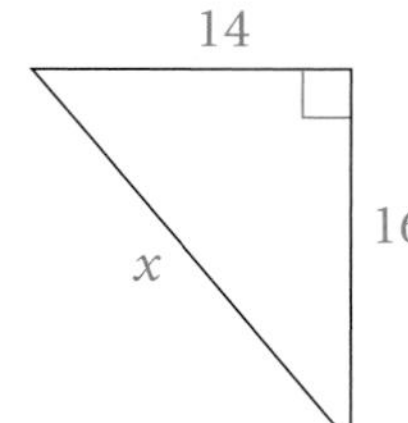

10. 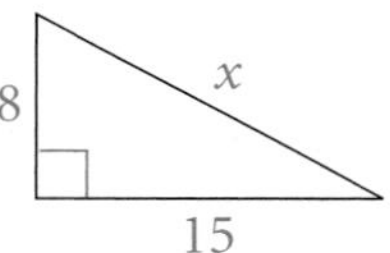

Special Right Triangles 5-4

In a **45°-45°-90° triangle,** both legs are congruent and the length of the hypotenuse is $\sqrt{2}$ times the length of a leg.

In a **30°-60°-90° triangle,** the length of the hypotenuse is twice the length of the shorter leg. The length of the longer leg is $\sqrt{3}$ times the length of the shorter leg.

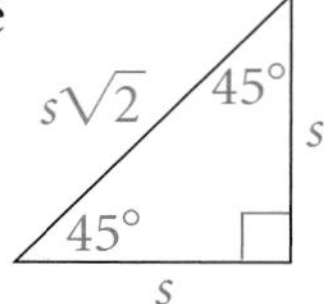

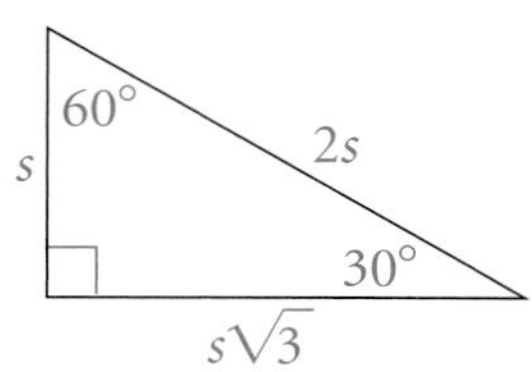

Find the value of each variable. If your answer is not an integer, you may leave it in simplest radical form.

11.

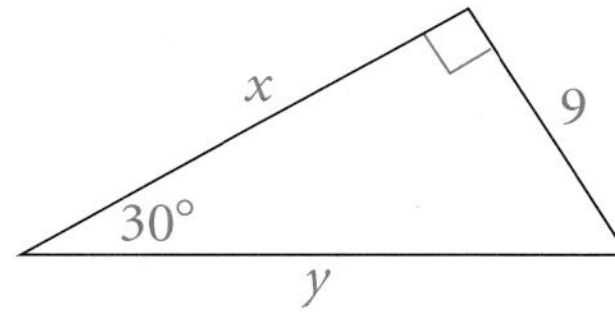

12.

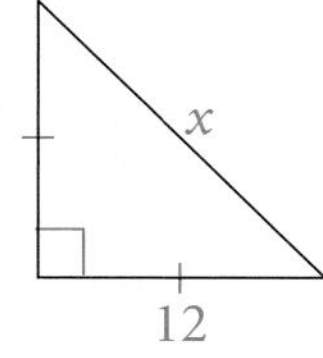

13.

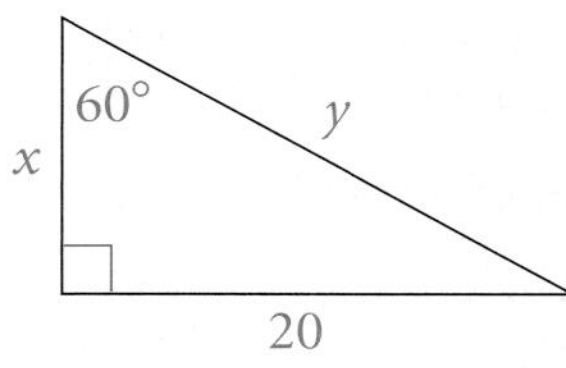

14. *Standardized Test Prep* A triangle has sides with lengths 4, 4, and $4\sqrt{2}$. What kind of triangle is it?

A. acute isosceles **B.** scalene right **C.** equilateral
D. obtuse right **E.** isosceles right

Areas of Trapezoids 5-5

The two parallel sides of a trapezoid are **bases.** The nonparallel sides are **legs.** The **height** is the perpendicular distance between the two bases. The **area of a trapezoid** is $A = \frac{1}{2}h(b_1 + b_2)$.

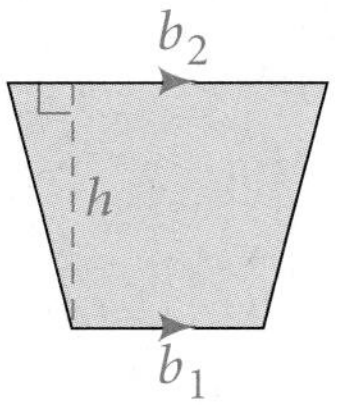

Find the area of each trapezoid. If your answer is not an integer, you may leave it in simplest radical form.

15.

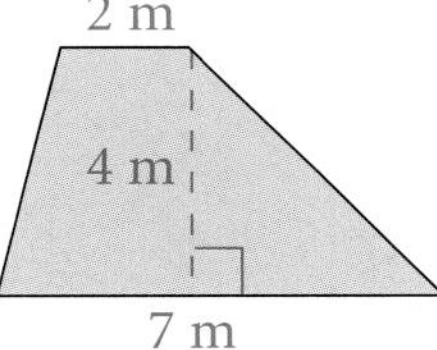

16.

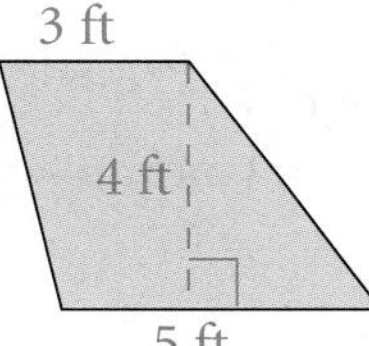

17.

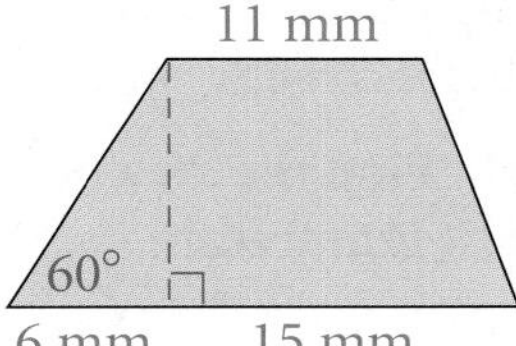

18. *Writing* Explain how the formula for the area of a trapezoid is related to the formula for the area of a triangle.

Areas of Regular Polygons 5-6

The **center** of a regular polygon is the center of its circumscribed circle. The **radius** is the distance from the center to a vertex. The **apothem** is the perpendicular distance from the center to a side. The area of a regular polygon with apothem a and perimeter p is $A = \frac{1}{2}ap$.

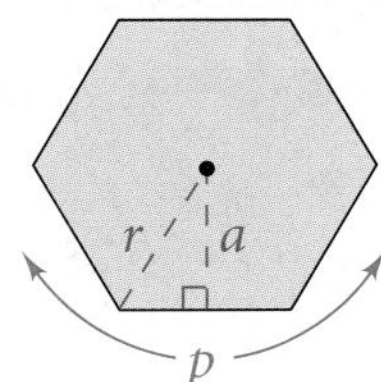

Calculator **Sketch each regular polygon with the given radius. Then find its area. Round your answer to the nearest tenth.**

19. triangle; radius 4 in.

20. square; radius 8 mm

21. hexagon; radius 7 cm

Circles: Circumference and Arc Length 5-7

The **circumference of a circle** is $C = \pi d$ or $C = 2\pi r$. The **length of an arc** is a fraction of a circle's circumference.

The length of $\widehat{AB} = \frac{m\widehat{AB}}{360} \cdot 2\pi r$.

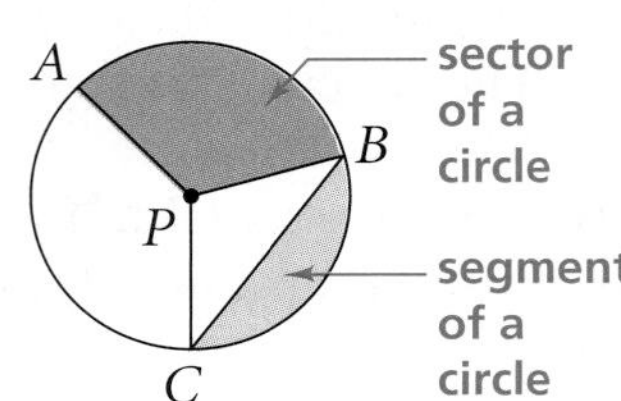

Find the circumference of each circle and the length of each arc shown in red. Leave your answer in terms of π.

22.

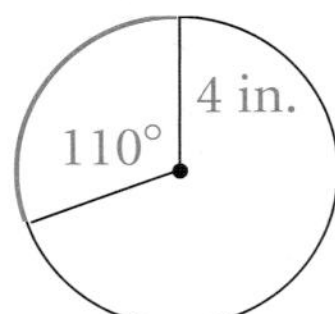

23.

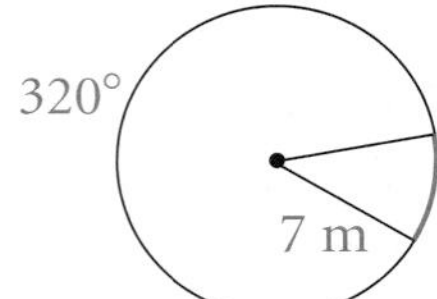

24.

Areas of Circles, Sectors, and Segments of Circles 5-8

The **area of a circle** is $A = \pi r^2$. The part of a circle bounded by two radii and their intercepted arc is a **sector of a circle.**

The area of sector $APB = \frac{m\widehat{AB}}{360} \cdot \pi r^2$.

The part of a circle bounded by an arc and the segment joining its endpoints is a **segment of a circle.** The area of a segment of a circle is the difference between the areas of the related sector and triangle.

A
B
P
C
sector of a circle
segment of a circle

Calculator **Find the area of each shaded region. Round your answer to the nearest hundredth.**

25.

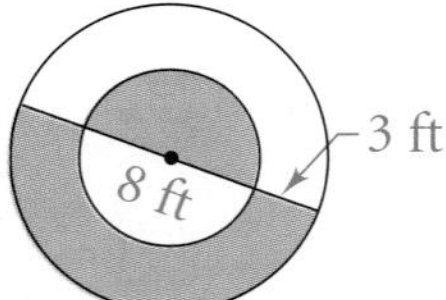

26.

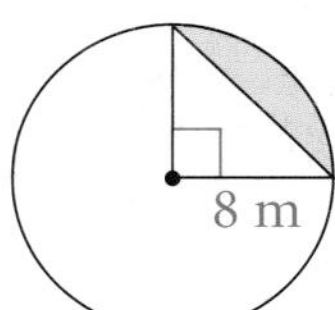

27.

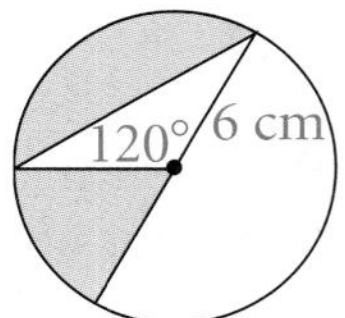

Getting Ready for CHAPTER 6

Find the area of each figure. If your answer is not an integer, round to the nearest tenth.

28.

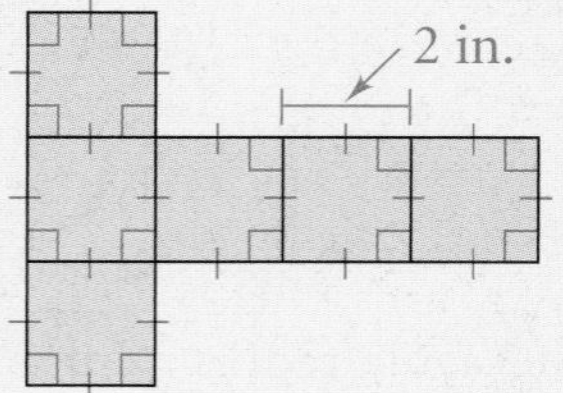

29.

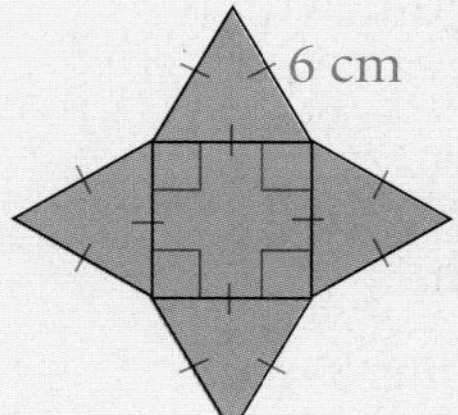

30.

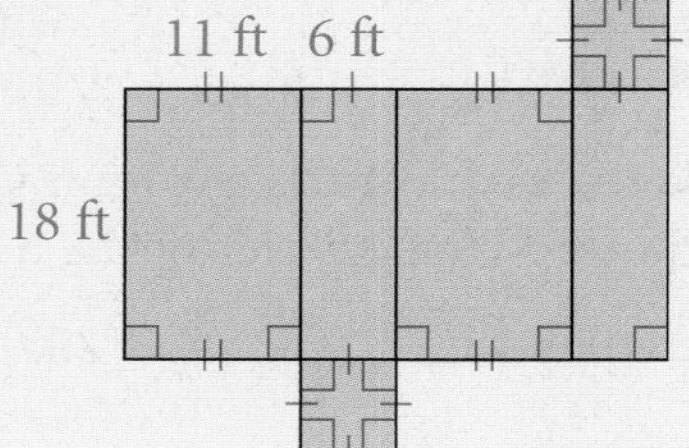

CHAPTER 5

Assessment

Find the perimeter of each figure.

1.

3 cm

7 cm

2.

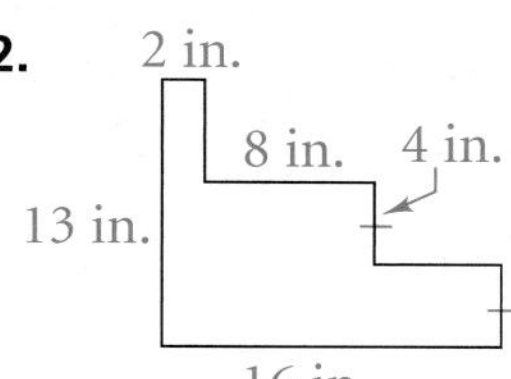

3. You have 64 ft of fencing. What are the dimensions of the rectangle of greatest area you could enclose?

Find the area of each figure. If your answer is not an integer, round to the nearest tenth.

4.

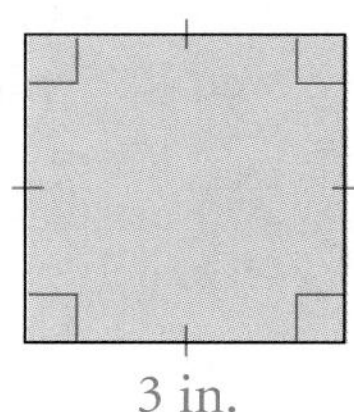

5.

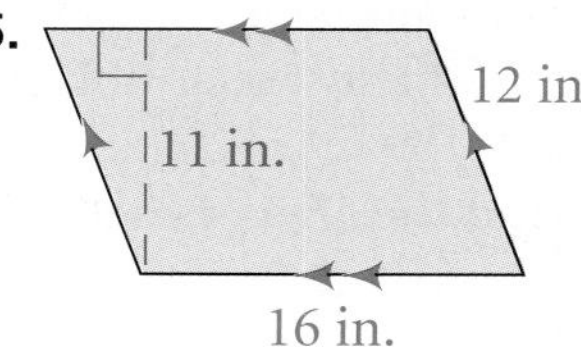

6.

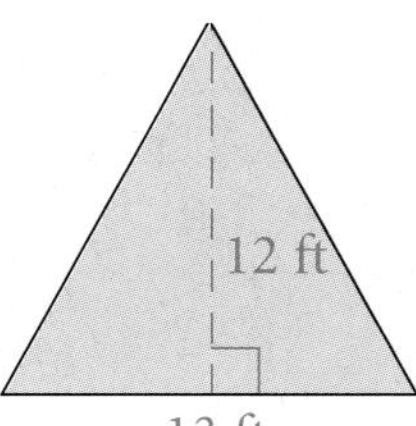

7.

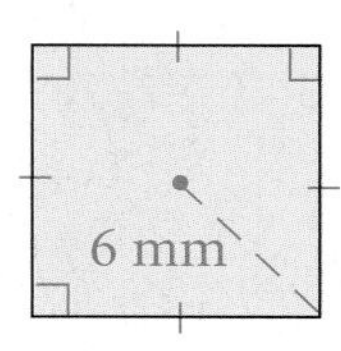

8.

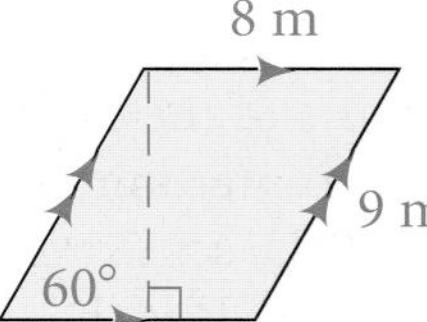

9.

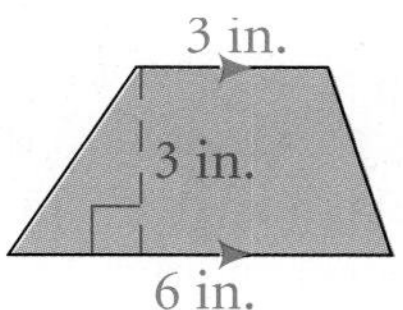

10. *Coordinate Geometry* A quadrilateral has vertices at $A(0, 7)$, $B(-2, 7)$, $C(-2, 0)$, and $D(0, 0)$. Find the area and perimeter of $ABCD$.

11. *Open-ended* An equilateral triangle, a square, and a regular pentagon all have the same perimeter. What can this perimeter be if all figures have sides that are integers?

Find the area of each regular polygon. Round to the nearest tenth.

12.

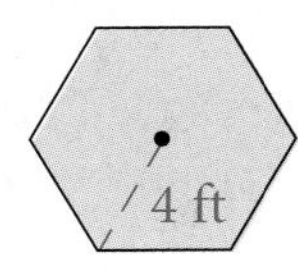

13.

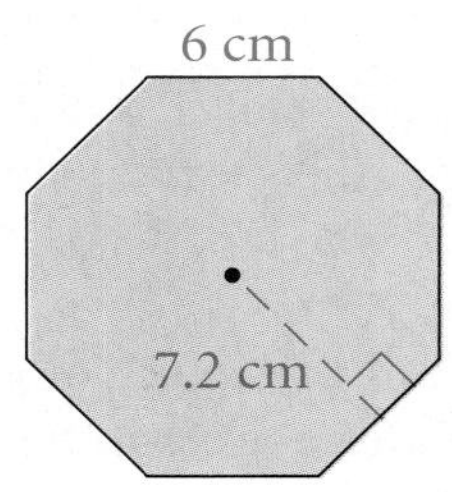

The lengths of two sides of a right triangle are given. Find the length of the third side. Leave your answers in simplest radical form.

14. one leg 9, other leg 6

15. one leg 12, hypotenuse 17

16. hypotenuse 20, leg 10

17. *Standardized Test Prep* Which integers form Pythagorean triples?

I. 15, 36, 39
II. 6, 8, 10
III. 16, 30, 34
IV. 10, 12, 14

A. I only **B.** IV only **C.** II and III
D. III and IV **E.** I, II, and III

Find the values of the variables. Leave your answers in simplest radical form.

18.

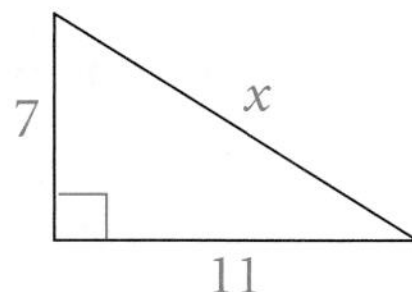

19.

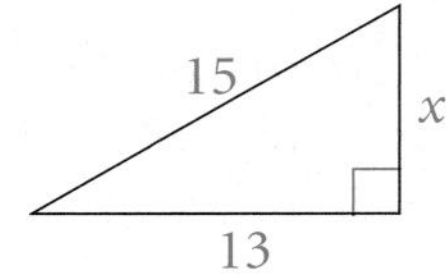

20.

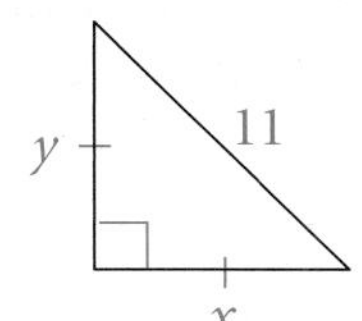

21.

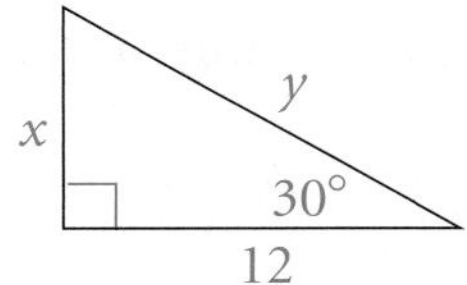

The lengths of three sides of a triangle are given. Describe each triangle as acute, right, or obtuse.

22. 9 cm, 10 cm, 12 cm

23. 8 m, 15 m, 17 m

24. 5 in., 6 in., 10 in.

25. *Writing* Explain how you can use the length of the shorter side of a 30°-60°-90° triangle to find the lengths of the other two sides.

Find the length of each arc shown in red. Leave your answers in terms of π.

26.

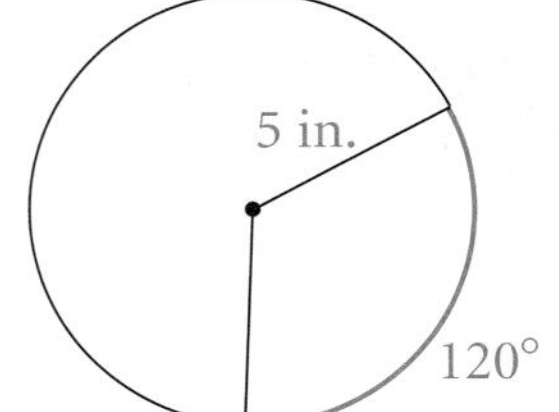

27.

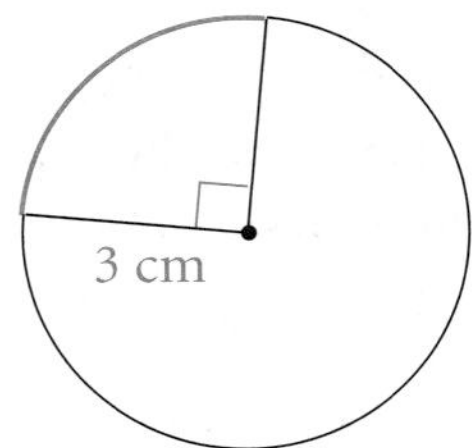

28.

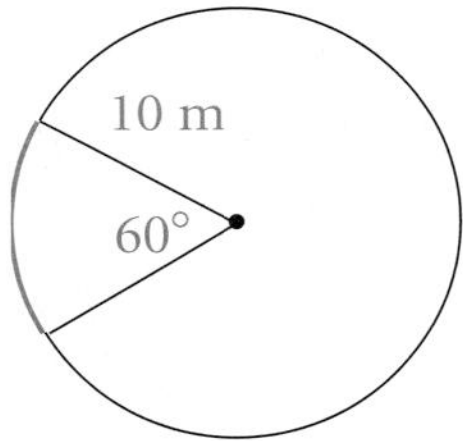

29.

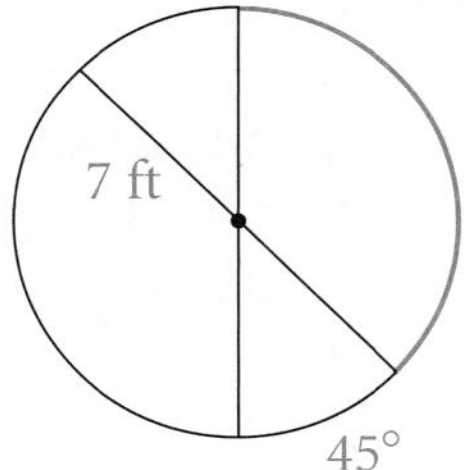

30. *Standardized Test Prep* Which length is greatest?

A. the diagonal of a 4-in. square
B. the diameter of a circle with 3-in. radius
C. the circumference of a circle with 2-in. radius
D. the length of a semicircle of a circle with diameter 6 in.
E. the perimeter of a 2 in.-by-3 in. rectangle

Find the area and circumference of a circle with the given radius or diameter. Leave your answers in terms of π.

31. $r = 4$ cm

32. $d = 10$ in.

33. $d = 7$ ft

34. $r = 12$ m

Calculator **Find the area of each shaded region. Round your answer to the nearest hundredth.**

35.

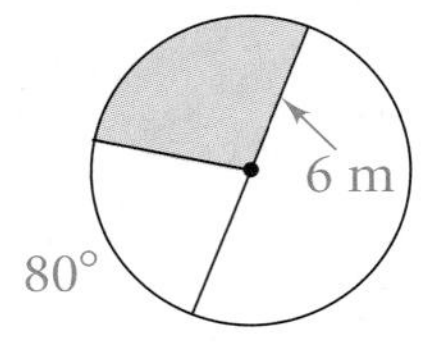

36.

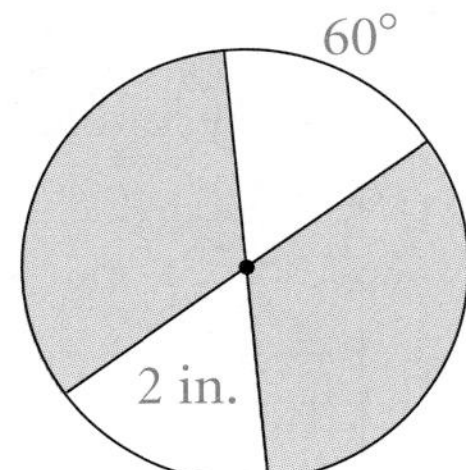

37.

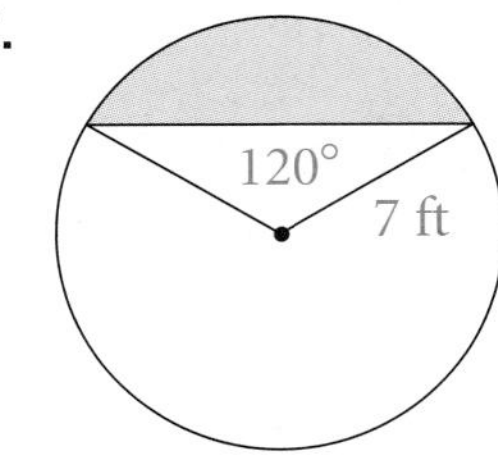

38.

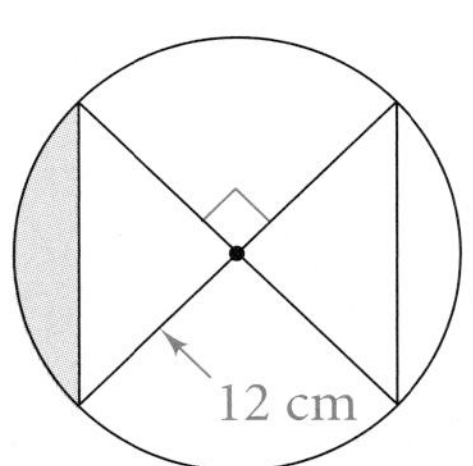

39. *Open-ended* Use a compass to draw a circle. Shade a sector of the circle and find its area.

Find the area of each figure. Leave your answer in terms of π.

40.

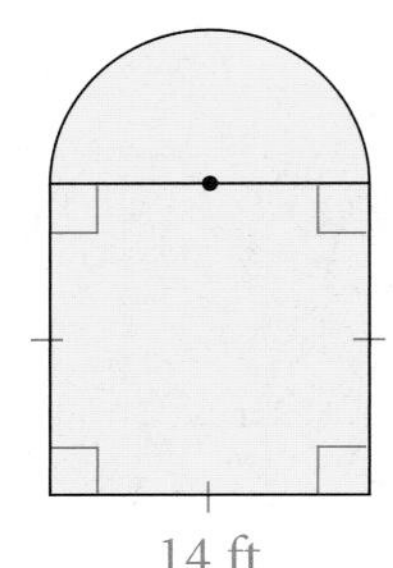

41.

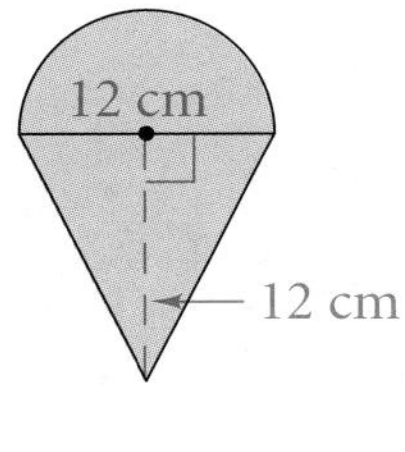

42. *Sports* Netball players in different positions are restricted to different parts of the court. A wing defense can play in the center third and in her own goal third, except in the semicircle around the net. How much area does she have to play in? Round your answer to the nearest tenth.

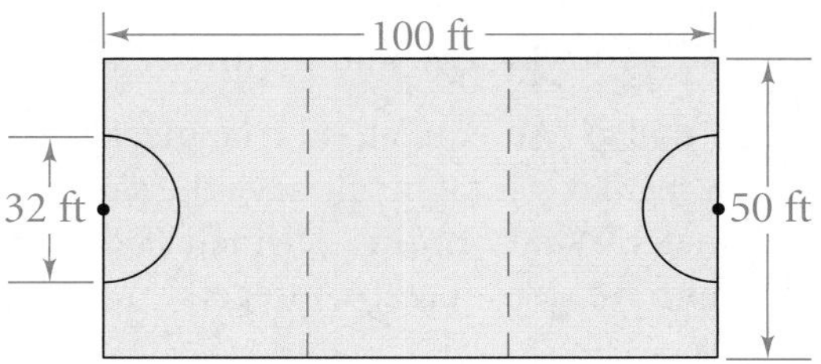

CHAPTER

5 Preparing for the Math A Exam

Part I

1 The perimeter of square $RSTV$ is $12x$. Which statement is false?

(1) The length of a side of $RSTV$ is $3x$.
(2) The lengths of $\overline{RS}$ and $\overline{TV}$ are equal.
(3) The lengths of $\overline{RS}$ and $\overline{RT}$ are equal.
(4) The length of $\overline{SV}$ is greater than $3x$.

2 Which figure has area 30 ft^2?

(1)
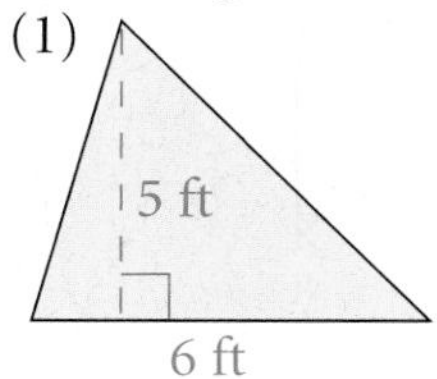

(3)
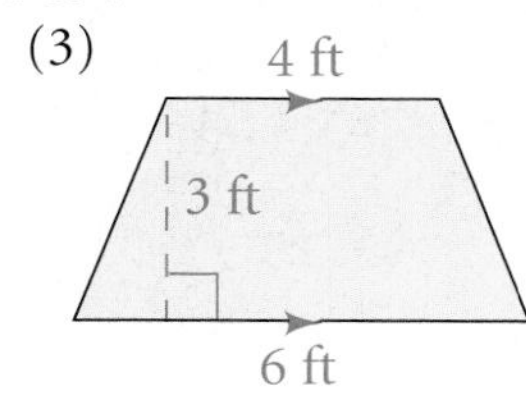

(2)
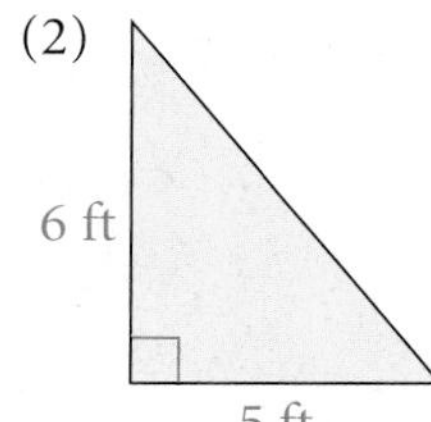

(4)
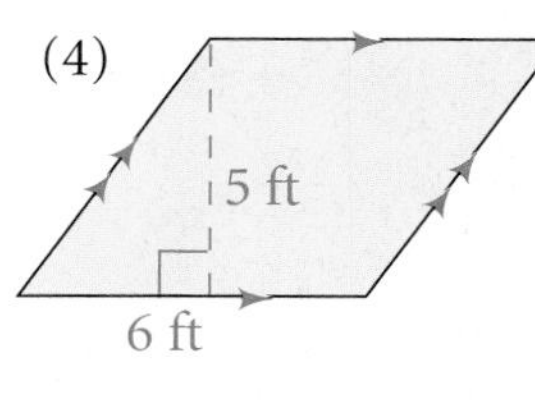

3 A triangle has sides with lengths 4 ft, 6 ft, and $2\sqrt{13}$ ft. What kind of triangle is it?

(1) isosceles right
(2) scalene right
(3) isosceles obtuse
(4) scalene acute

4 What is the circumference of a circle with radius 5 ft?

(1) 5π ft
(2) 25π ft
(3) 10π ft
(4) 125π ft

Part II

5 What is the area of the triangle?

12 cm, 7 cm

6 What are the values of e and f?

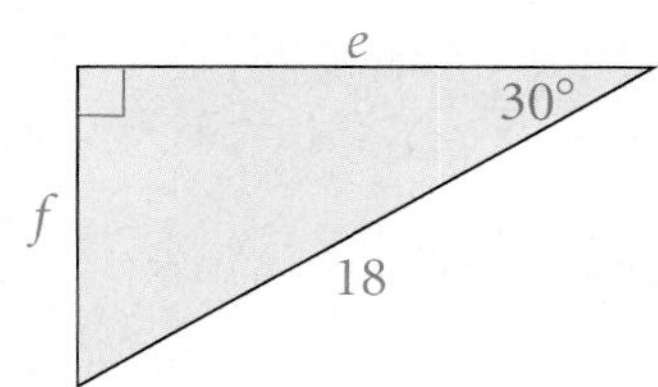

7 Find the area of the isosceles trapezoid.

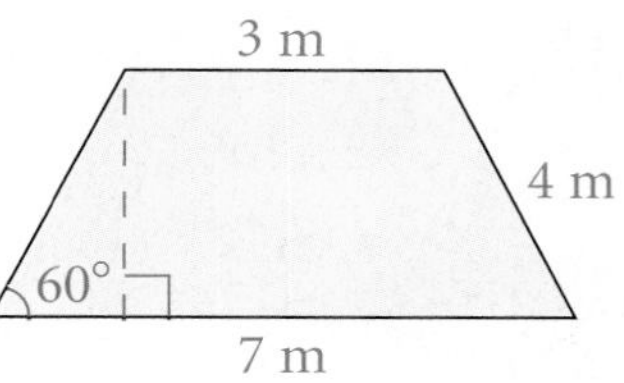

Part III

8 What is the area of a rectangle with vertices at $(-2, 5)$, $(3, 5)$, $(3, -1)$, and $(-2, -1)$?

9 The length of the hypotenuse of an isosceles right triangle is 8 in. Find the length of one leg.

10 Find the area of this regular hexagon. Round your answer to the nearest tenth.

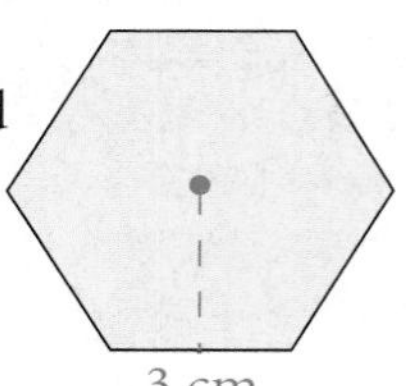

11 Find the length of $\widehat{JK}$.

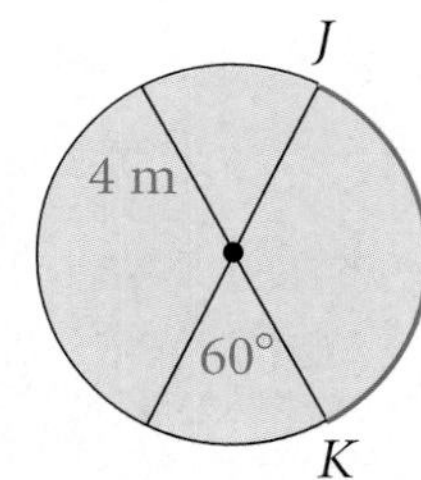

Part IV

12 What is the length of the slide starting from the top of the ladder?

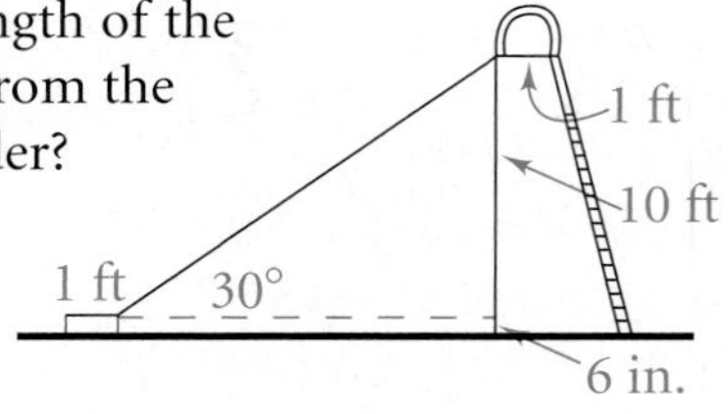

13 The radius of $\odot O$ is 12 cm.

a What is the area of sector ROS?

b What is the area of triangle ROS?

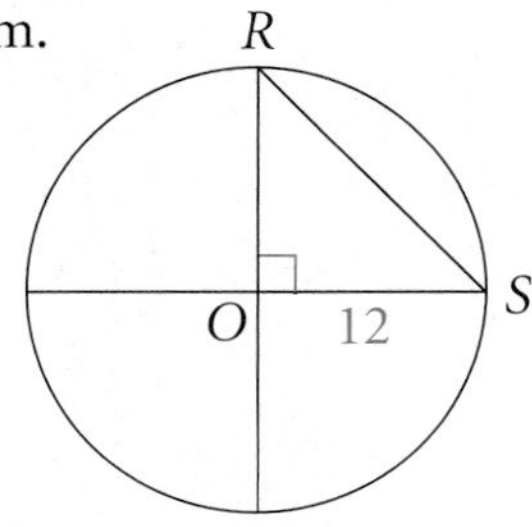

CHAPTER 6

Measuring in Space

Relating to the Real World

What types of space objects do you observe each day? As you ride down the street, you might pass by an office building, a water tower, or a house with a dormer window. At the grocery store, you see a variety of boxes, containers, cans, and bottles on the shelves. You can describe many space objects as prisms, cylinders, cones, pyramids, or combinations of these. In this chapter you will learn how to find the surface areas and volumes of space objects.

Lessons	6-1	6-2	6-3	6-4	6-5
	Space Figures and Nets	*Surface Areas of Prisms and Cylinders*	*Surface Areas of Pyramids and Cones*	*Volumes of Prisms and Cylinders*	*Volumes of Pyramids and Cones*

CHAPTER PROJECT

Walk into any supermarket and look at the shapes lining the shelves. Bottles of ketchup are tapered like cones. Boxes of cereal stand tall and wide but not too deep. Cylindrical cans of tuna are short and wide. Manufacturers consider dozens of factors before determining which shape will best suit the consumer and boost the company's profits.

In this chapter project, you will explore package design and uncover some of the reasons for the shapes that manufacturers have chosen. You will also design and construct your own package. You will see how spatial sense and business sense go hand in hand to determine the shapes of things you use every day.

To help you complete the project:

- **p. 868** *Find Out by Doing*
- **p. 876** *Find Out by Measuring*
- **p. 891** *Find Out by Analyzing*
- **p. 897** *Find Out by Investigating*
- **p. 915** *Finishing the Project*

Surface Areas and Volumes of Spheres 6-6

Composite Space Figures 6-7

Geometric Probability 6-8

6-1 Space Figures and Nets

What You'll Learn

- Recognizing nets of various space figures

...And Why

To help you visualize the faces of space figures that you encounter in everyday life

What You'll Need

straightedge, centimeter grid paper, scissors, tape

THINK AND DISCUSS

As you can see in the photo below, most buildings are polyhedrons. A **polyhedron** is a three-dimensional figure whose surfaces are polygons. The polygons are the **faces** of the polyhedron. An **edge** is a segment that is the intersection of two faces. A **vertex** is a point where edges intersect.

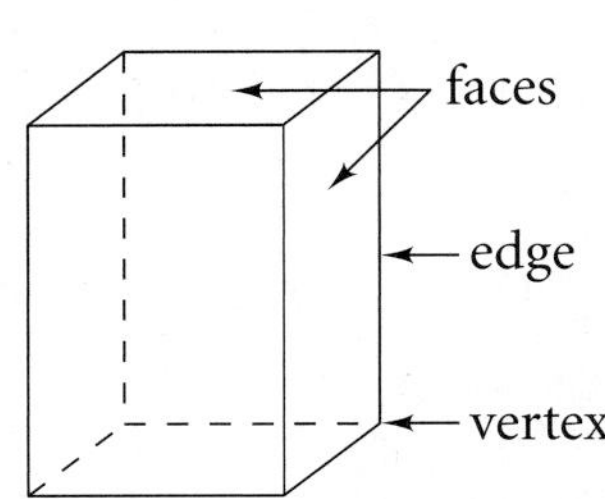

1. a. **Try This** How many faces does the polyhedron below have?
   b. How many edges does it have?
   c. How many vertices does it have?

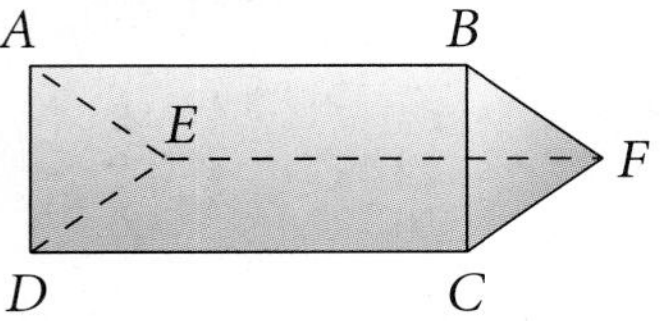

A **net** is a two-dimensional pattern that you can fold to form a three-dimensional figure. Packagers use nets to design boxes.

Who? Grace Chisholm Young (1868–1944) was the first woman to officially receive a doctorate in Germany. In her *First Book of Geometry,* she provides nets to cut out and fold to help students visualize theorems in solid geometry.

WORK TOGETHER

- Working in a group, draw a larger copy of this net on grid paper. Cut it out and fold it to make a cube.

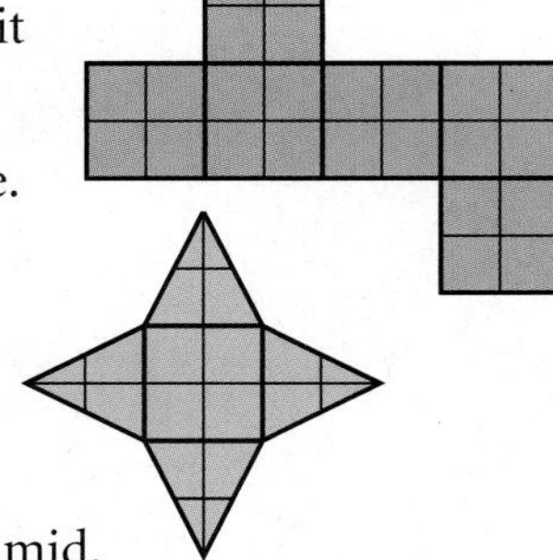

2. a. Describe the faces of the cube.
   b. Write a definition of cube.

- Draw a larger copy of this net on grid paper. Cut it out and fold it to make a pyramid.

3. a. Describe the faces of the pyramid.
   b. Describe the faces of other pyramids you have seen.
   c. Complete this definition: A pyramid is a polyhedron whose base is a polygon and whose other faces are __?__.

THINK AND DISCUSS

Example *Relating to the Real World* 

Packaging Draw a net for the graham cracker box. Label the net with the appropriate dimensions.

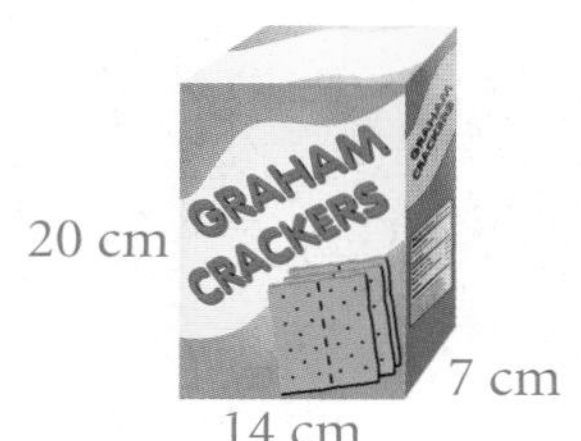

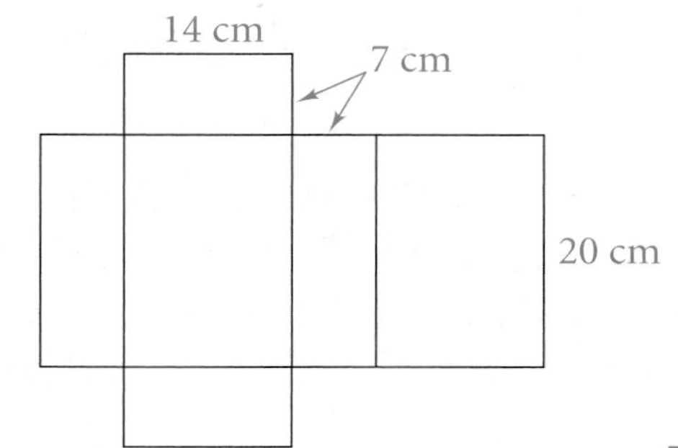

4. Draw a different net for this box. Include the dimensions.

WORK TOGETHER

Work in a group to draw larger copies of the nets below. Use the nets to make three-dimensional models.

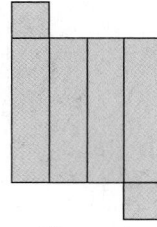

Figure 1

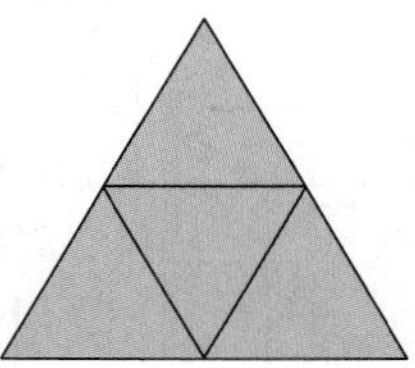

Figure 2

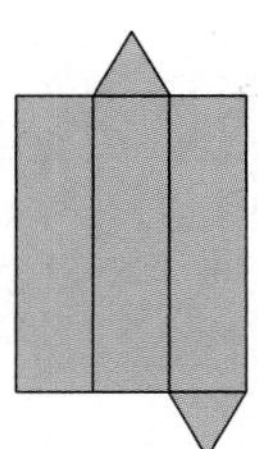

Figure 3

5. Complete the table below, using these three models and the cube and pyramid you made for the Work Together on page 864.

Polyhedron	Number of Faces (F)	Number of Vertices (V)	Number of Edges (E)
Cube	■	■	■
Pyramid	■	■	■
Figure 1	■	■	■
Figure 2	■	■	■
Figure 3	■	■	■

6. Look for a pattern in your table. Write a formula for E in terms of F and V. Then, compare your results with those of other groups. Euler discovered that this relationship is true for any polyhedron. This formula is known as Euler's Formula.

NEW YORK MATH A — Math A Test Prep

1 A polyhedron has 8 faces and 12 vertices. How many edges does it have?
(1) 20 (3) 6
(2) 22 (4) 18

2 Draw a net that will fold to make the box. Label the net with the appropriate dimensions.

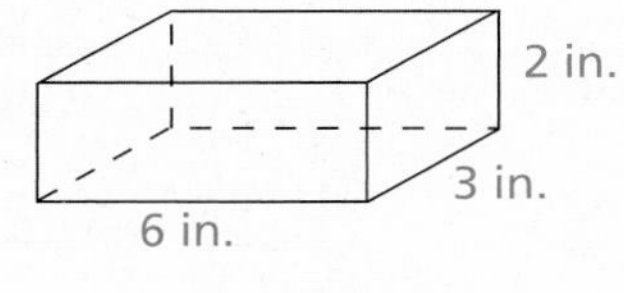

Exercises ON YOUR OWN

1. Which nets will fold to make a cube?

A. 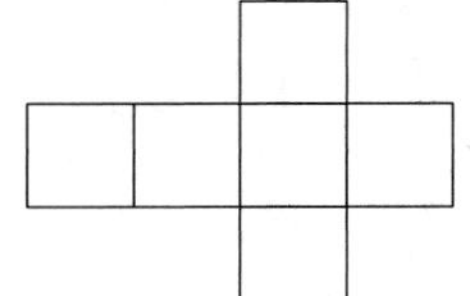
B. 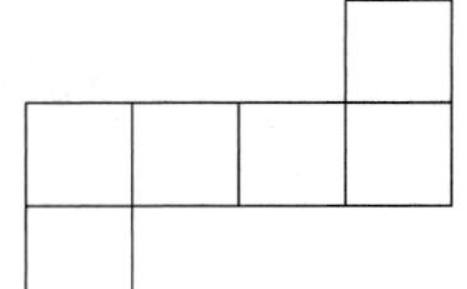
C. 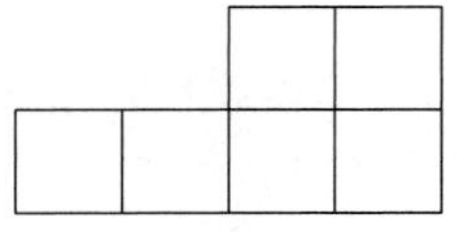
D. 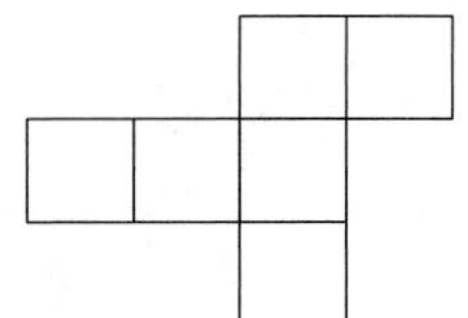

2. Which nets will fold to make a pyramid with a square base?

A. 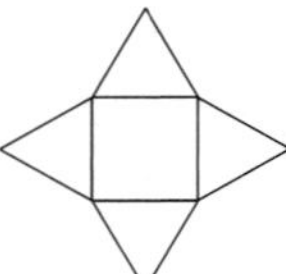
B. 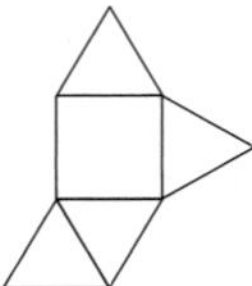
C. 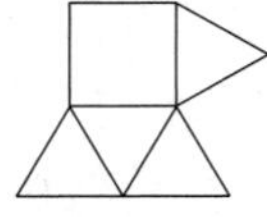
D. 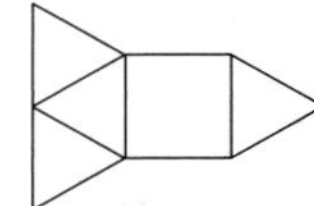

Match each three-dimensional figure with its net.

3. 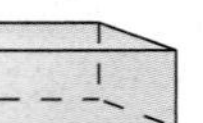
4. 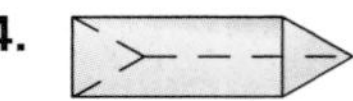
5. 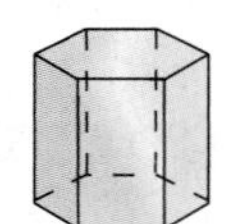
6. 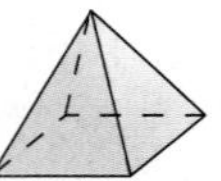
7. 

A. 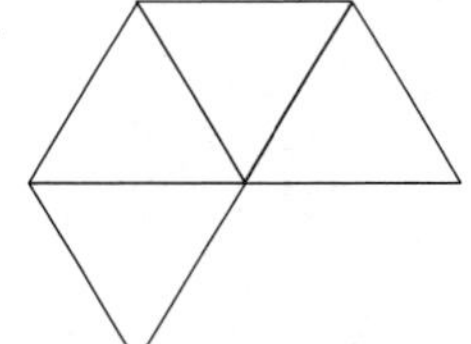
B. 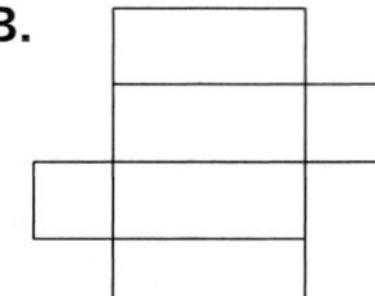
C. 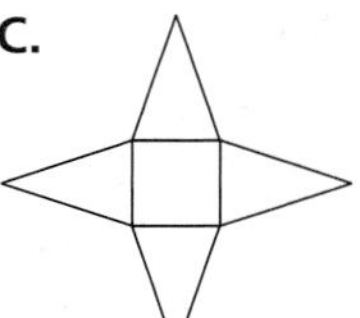
D. 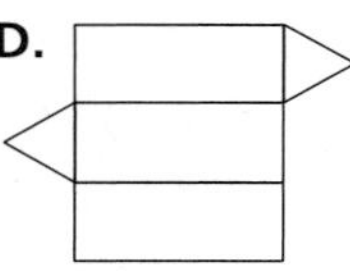
E. 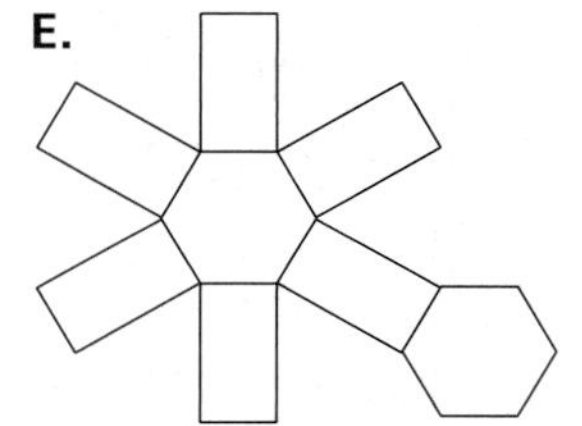

8. The fourth-century Andean textile at the right is now on display at the Museum of Fine Arts, Boston, Massachusetts.
   a. Which of the three outlined figures could be nets for the same polyhedron?
   b. Describe this polyhedron.

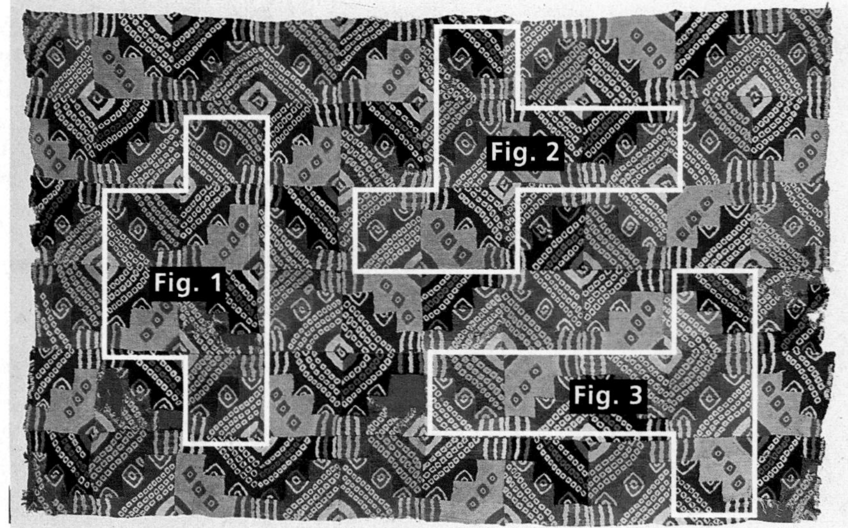

Spatial Visualization **Think about how each net can be folded to form a cube. What is the color of the face that will be opposite the red face?**

9. 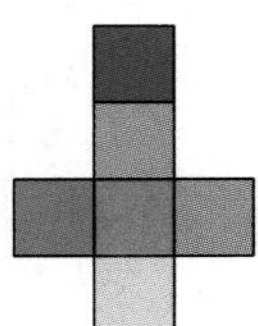

10. 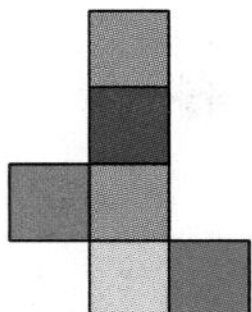

11. 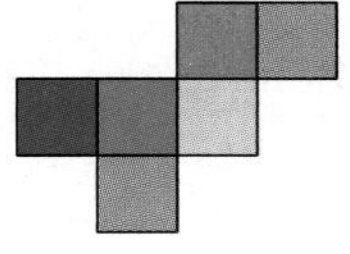

12. 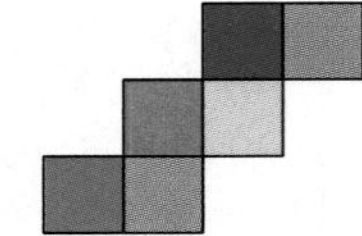

13. a. There are eleven different nets for a cube. Four of them are shown above. Draw as many of the other seven as you can.

b. *Writing* If you were going to make 100 cubes for a mobile, which of the eleven nets would you use? Explain why.

PROBLEM SOLVING HINT

Two nets are the same if one is a rotation or reflection of the other.

14. There are eight different nets for a pyramid with a square base. Draw as many of them as you can.

15. The total area of a net for a cube is 216 in.^{2}. What is the length of an edge of the cube?

16. a. *Open-ended* Draw a polyhedron whose faces are all rectangles. Label the lengths of its edges.

b. Use graph paper to draw two different nets for the polyhedron.

17. There are five regular polyhedrons. They are called *regular* because all their faces are congruent regular polygons, and the same number of faces meet at each vertex. They are also called Platonic Solids after the Greek philosopher Plato (427–347 B.C.)

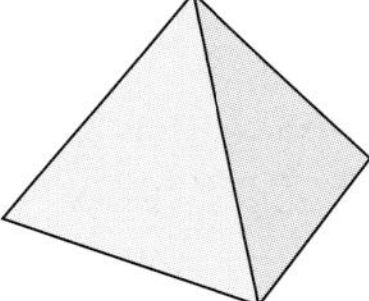

Tetrahedron

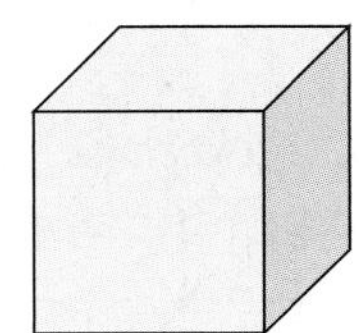

Hexahedron

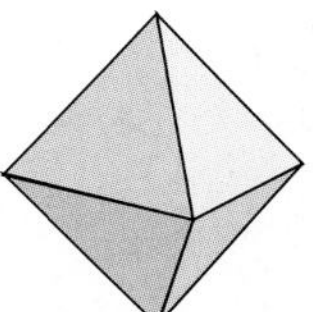

Octahedron

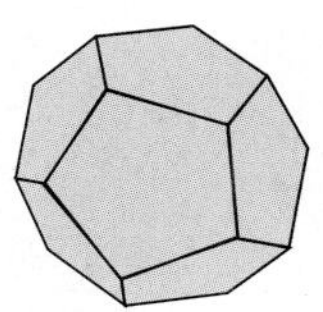

Dodecahedron

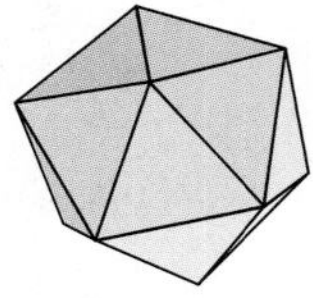

Icosahedron

a. Match each of the nets below with a Platonic Solid.

A. 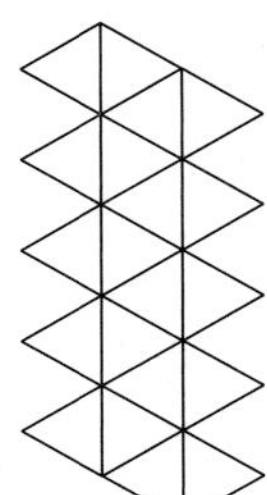

B. 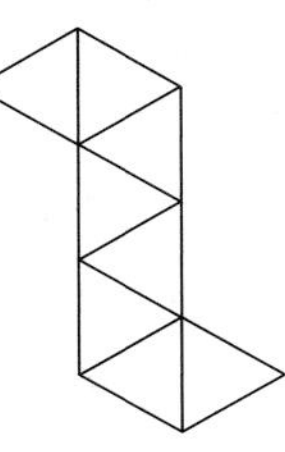

C. 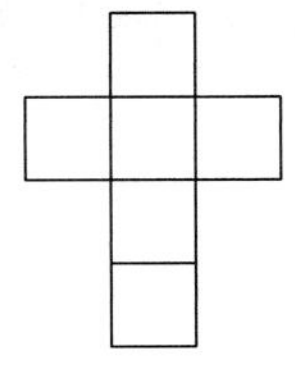

D. 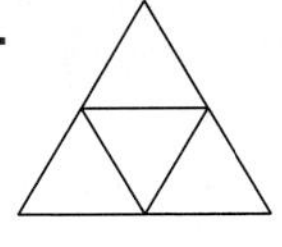

E. 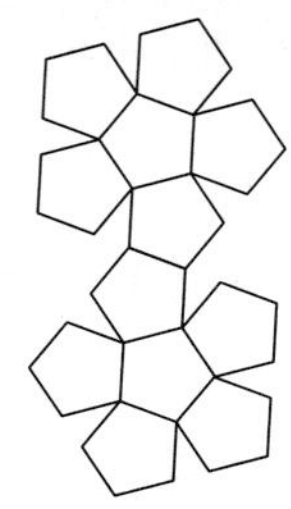

b. Which two Platonic Solids have common names? What are those names?

c. **Verify** that Euler's Formula, which you discovered in the Work Together on page 865, is true for an octahedron.

Chapter Project — Find Out by Doing

With one or two sheets of cardboard and a rubber band, you can make a pop-up version of one of the Platonic Solids.

- Draw and cut out two larger copies of this net. All of the faces are congruent regular pentagons.
- Fold along the dotted lines and then flatten again.
- Place one net on top of the other as shown. (The flaps of the top pattern should fold downward and the flaps of the bottom upward.) Hold the patterns flat and stretch a rubber band (shown in red) over and under the protruding vertices. Watch the flat patterns pop into a dodecahedron.

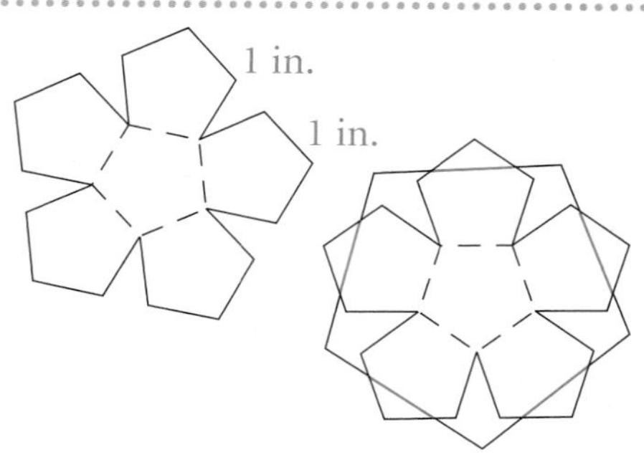

Exercises MIXED REVIEW

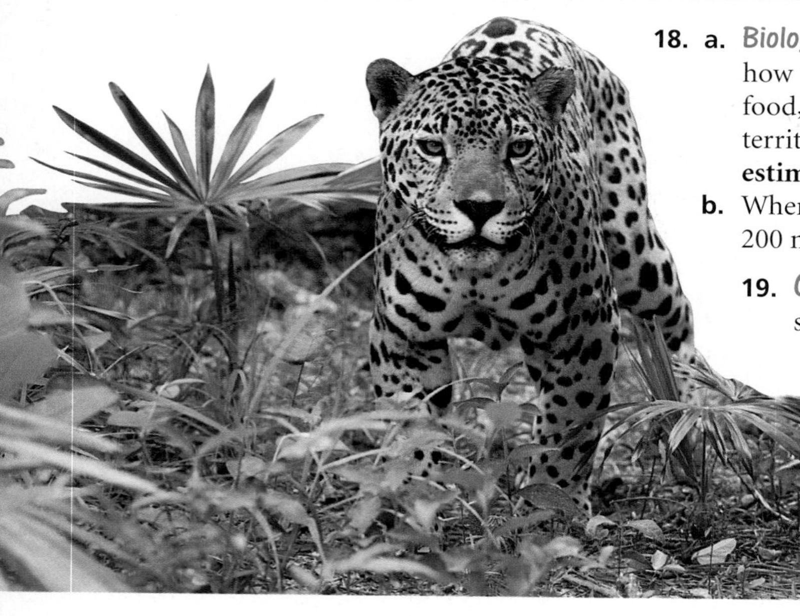

18. a. **Biology** The size of a jaguar's territory depends on how much food is available. Where there is a lot of food, such as in a forest, jaguars have circular territories about 3 mi in diameter. Use $\pi \approx 3$ to **estimate** the area of such a region.
    b. Where food is less available, a jaguar may need up to 200 mi^2. **Estimate** the radius of this circular territory.
19. **Open-ended** Draw a triangle that has no lines of symmetry.
20. **Constructions** Copy $\overline{TR}$. Construct its perpendicular bisector.

    T ————————— R

21. In $\triangle ABC$, $AC = 20$, $AB = 18$, and $BC = 13$. Which angle of the triangle has the greatest measure?

Getting Ready for Lesson 6-2

Find the area of each net.

22.

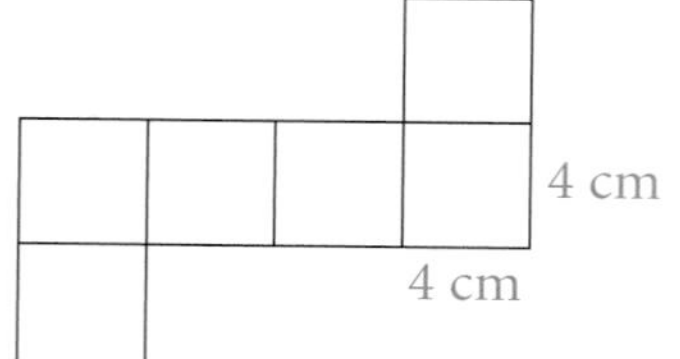

23.

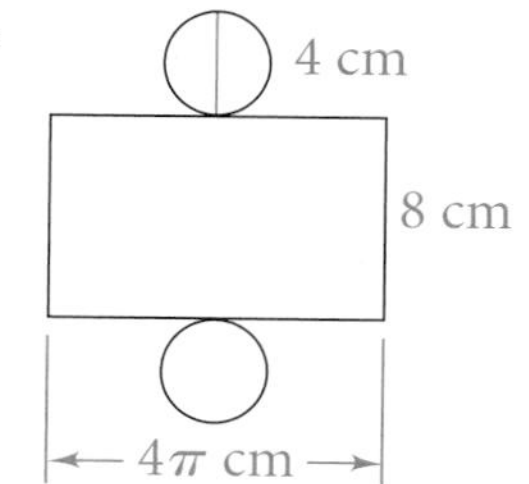

24.

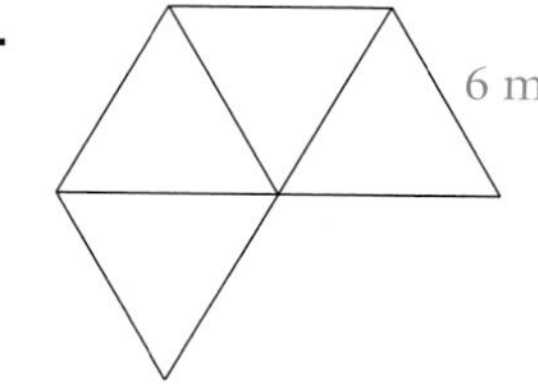

Algebra Review

Dimensional Analysis

Before Lesson 6-2

You can use conversion factors to change from one unit of measure to another. The process of analyzing units to decide which conversion factors to use is called **dimensional analysis.**

Since 60 min = 1 h, $\frac{60\text{ min}}{1\text{ h}}$ equals 1. You can use $\frac{60\text{ min}}{1\text{ h}}$ to convert hours to minutes.

$7\text{ h} \cdot \frac{60\text{ min}}{1\text{ h}} = 420\text{ min}$

The hour units cancel, and the result is minutes.

Sometimes you need to use a conversion factor more than once.

Example

The area of the top of a desk is 8 ft^2. Convert the area to square inches.

You need to convert feet to inches.

feet to inches | feet to inches

$$\begin{aligned} 8\text{ ft} \cdot \text{ft} \cdot \frac{12\text{ in.}}{1\text{ ft}} \cdot \frac{12\text{ in.}}{1\text{ ft}} &= 8\text{ ft} \cdot \text{ft} \cdot \frac{12\text{ in.}}{1\text{ ft}} \cdot \frac{12\text{ in.}}{1\text{ ft}} \\ &= 8 \cdot 12 \cdot 12\text{ in.}^2 \\ &= 1152\text{ in.}^2 \end{aligned}$$

← The feet units cancel. The result is square inches.

← Simplify.

The area of the desktop is 1152 in.^{2}.

Choose the correct conversion factor for changing the units.

1. centimeters to meters **A.** $\frac{100\text{ cm}}{1\text{ m}}$ **B.** $\frac{1\text{ m}}{100\text{ cm}}$
2. yards to feet **A.** $\frac{3\text{ ft}}{1\text{ yd}}$ **B.** $\frac{1\text{ yd}}{3\text{ ft}}$
3. inches to yards **A.** $\frac{36\text{ in.}}{1\text{ yd}}$ **B.** $\frac{1\text{ yd}}{36\text{ in.}}$

Write each quantity in the given unit.

4. 4 m = ■ cm
5. 360 in. = ■ yd
6. 9 mm = ■ cm
7. 17 yd = ■ ft
8. 2.5 ft = ■ in.
9. 35 m = ■ km
10. 2 yd = ■ in.
11. 23 cm = ■ mm
12. 2 ft^2 = ■ in.^{2}
13. 500 mm^2 = ■ cm^2
14. 840 in.^{2} = ■ ft^2
15. 3 km^2 = ■ cm^2
16. 7 m^2 = ■ km^2
17. 360 in.^{2} = ■ yd^2
18. 900 cm^3 = ■ m^3
19. 4 yd^3 = ■ ft^3

What You'll Learn

- Investigating the surface areas and lateral areas of prisms and cylinders

...And Why

To use surface areas of objects in daily life, from CD cases and videocassette boxes to buildings and storage tanks

What You'll Need

- straightedge
- $\frac{1}{4}$-in. graph paper

6-2 Surface Areas of Prisms and Cylinders

WORK TOGETHER

In 1993 the music recording industry changed the size of compact disc packaging. The change to smaller packaging was made in response to the concerns of major recording artists who were worried about the effects of wasted packaging on the environment. Nets for the two packages are shown.

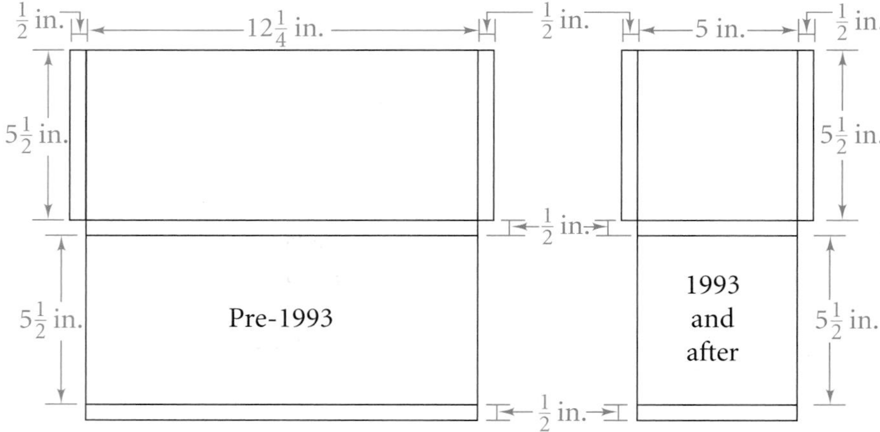

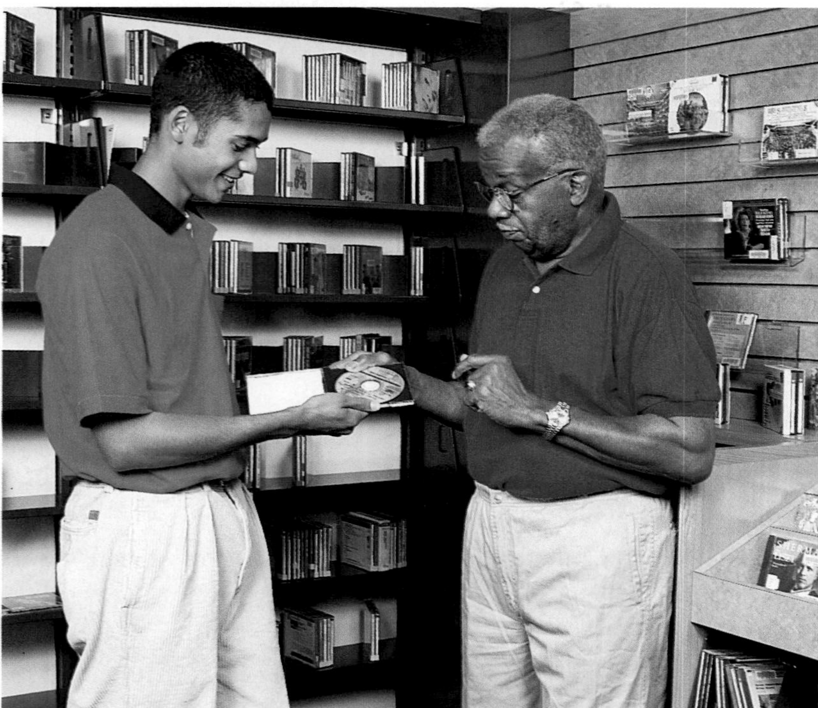

Work with a group. Draw nets on graph paper for each of the two packages.

1. a. What is the area of the net for the pre-1993 CD packaging?
   b. What is the area of the net for the new, smaller CD packaging?
   c. How many square inches of packaging are saved by using the smaller packaging?
2. How many pairs of congruent rectangles are in each net?
3. **Critical Thinking** Why do you think the earlier packaging was so large?

THINK AND DISCUSS

Lateral Areas and Surface Areas of Prisms

The CD packages in the Work Together are examples of rectangular prisms. A **prism** is a polyhedron with two congruent, parallel **bases.** The other faces are **lateral faces.** A prism is named for the shape of its bases.

Lateral edge

Bases

Lateral face

pentagonal prism

4. Match each prism with one of the following names: triangular prism, rectangular prism, hexagonal prism, octagonal prism.

a. 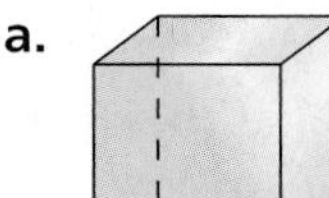

b. 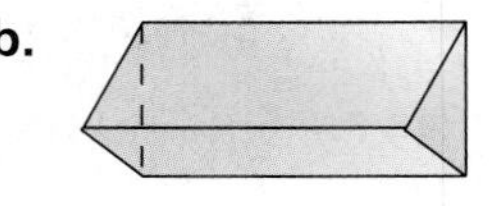

c. 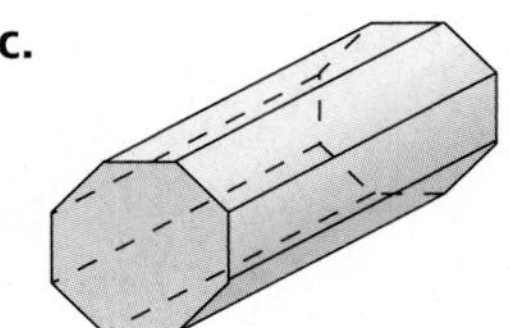

An **altitude** of a prism is a perpendicular segment that joins the planes of the bases. The **height** h of the prism is the length of an altitude. A prism may be either *right* or *oblique.* In a **right prism** the lateral faces are rectangles and a lateral edge is an altitude. In this book you may assume that a prism is a right prism unless you are told otherwise.

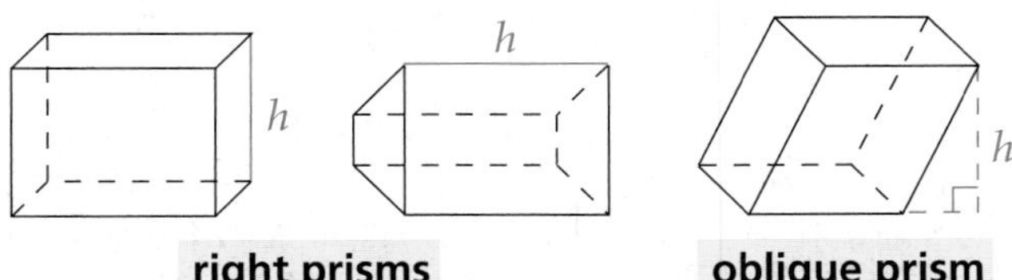

5. ***Open-ended*** Draw a right triangular prism and an oblique triangular prism. Draw and label an altitude in each figure.

The **lateral area** of a prism is the sum of the areas of the lateral faces. The **surface area** is the sum of areas of the lateral faces and the two bases. You can also find these areas by using formulas.

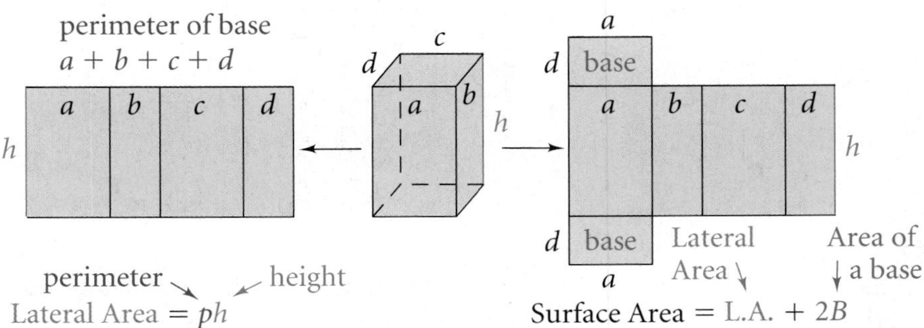

Math A Test Prep

1 What is the surface area of the cylinder?

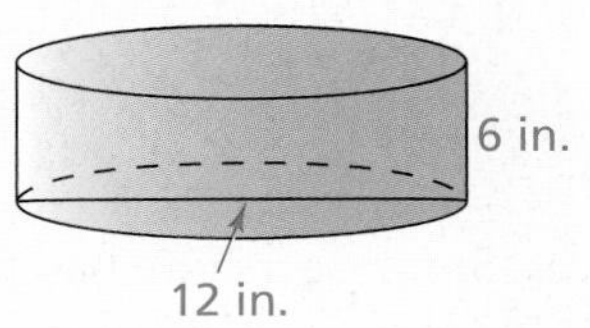

(1) 108π in.^{2}
(2) 144π in.^{2}
(3) 192π in.^{2}
(4) 216π in.^{2}

2 Carla observed that a polyhedron has two congruent, parallel bases, 12 edges, and 8 vertices. What kind of polyhedron is she looking at?

Theorem 6-1
Lateral and Surface Areas of a Right Prism

The lateral area of a right prism is the product of the perimeter of the base and the height.

$$\text{L.A.} = ph$$

The surface area of a right prism is the sum of the lateral area and the areas of the two bases.

$$\text{S.A.} = \text{L.A.} + 2B$$

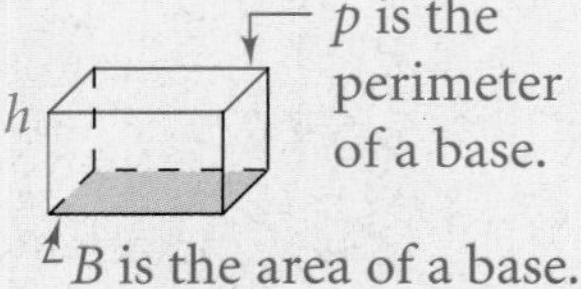

Example 1

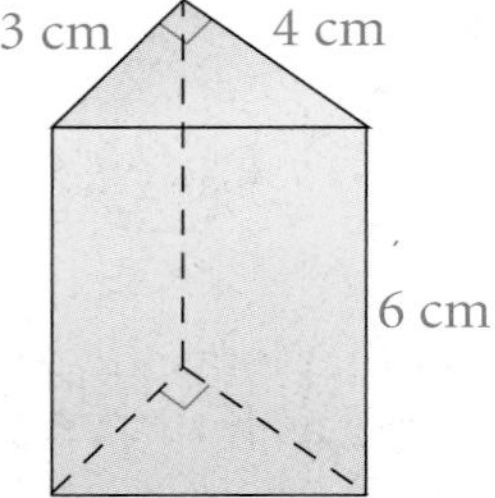

Find (a) the lateral area and (b) the surface area of the prism.

The hypotenuse of the triangular base is 5 cm, because the sides form a Pythagorean triple.

a. L.A. $= ph$ — **Use the formula for Lateral Area.**
$= 12 \cdot 6$ — $p = 3 + 4 + 5 = 12$ **cm**
$= 72$

The lateral area of the prism is 72 cm^2.

b. S.A. $= \text{L.A.} + 2B$ — **Use the formula for Surface Area.**
$= 72 + 2(6)$ — $B = \frac{1}{2}(3 \cdot 4) = 6 \text{ cm}^2$
$= 84$

The surface area of the prism is 84 cm^2.

6. Try This A **cube** is a prism with square faces. Suppose a cube has edges 5 in. long. What is its lateral area? its surface area?

Lateral Areas and Surface Areas of Cylinders

Like a prism, a **cylinder** has two congruent parallel bases. However, the bases of a cylinder are circles. An **altitude** of a cylinder is a perpendicular segment that joins the planes of the bases. The **height** h of a cylinder is the length of an altitude.

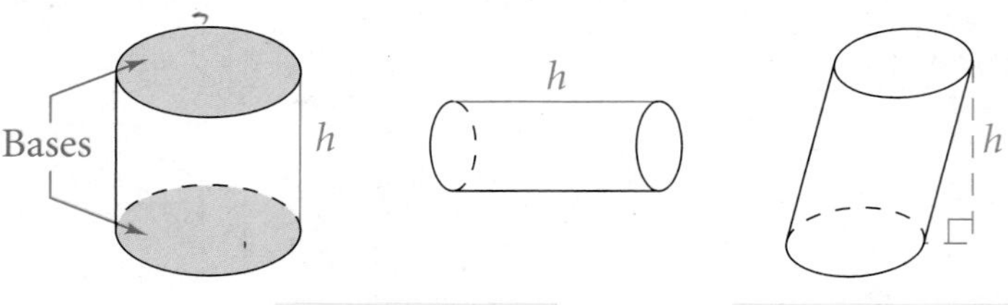

right cylinders **oblique cylinder**

In this book you may assume that a cylinder is a *right* cylinder, like the first two cylinders above, unless you are told otherwise.

To find the lateral area of a cylinder, visualize "unrolling" it. The area of the resulting rectangle is the **lateral area** of the cylinder. The **surface area** of a cylinder is the sum of the lateral area and the areas of the two circular bases. You can find formulas for these areas by looking at a net for a cylinder.

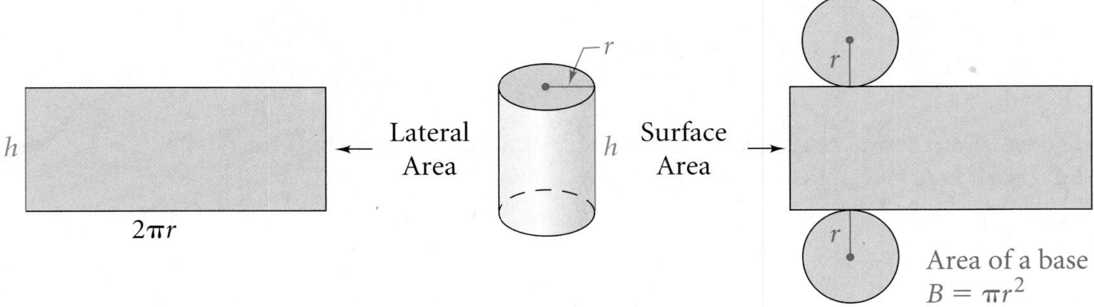

Theorem 6-2
Lateral and Surface Areas of a Right Cylinder

The lateral area of a right cylinder is the product of the circumference of the base and the height of the cylinder.

$$\text{L.A.} = 2\pi rh, \text{ or L.A.} = \pi dh$$

The surface area of a right cylinder is the sum of the lateral area and the areas of the two bases.

$$\text{S.A.} = \text{L.A.} + 2B$$

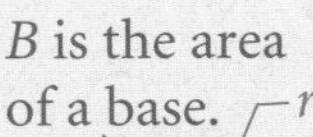

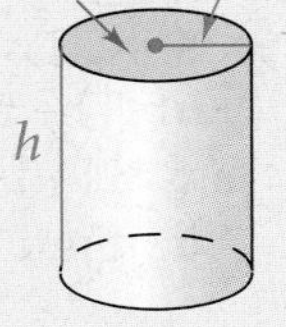

7. Try This The radius of the base of a cylinder is 4 in. and its height is 6 in.

a. Find the lateral area of the cylinder in terms of π.
b. Find the surface area of the cylinder in terms of π.

Example 2 ***Relating to the Real World***

Machinery The wheel of the steamroller at the left is a cylinder. How many square feet does a single revolution of the wheel cover? Round your answer to the nearest square foot.

The area covered is the lateral area of a cylinder that has a diameter of 5 ft and a height of 7.2 ft.

$\text{L.A.} = \pi dh$ — **Use the formula for Lateral Area of a cylinder.**
$= \pi(5)(7.2)$ — **Substitute.**
$= 36\pi$ — **Simplify.**

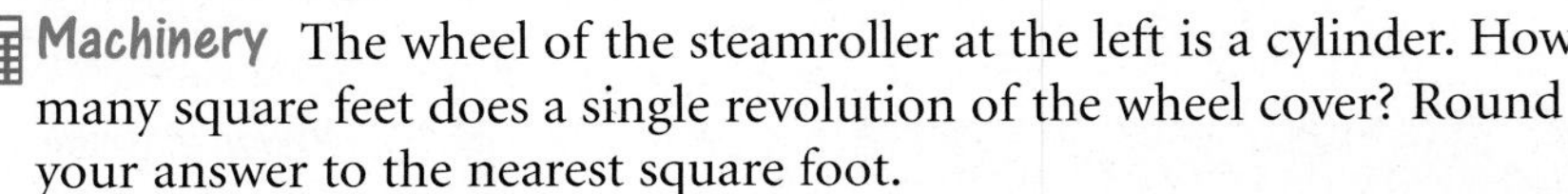

A single revolution of this steamroller wheel covers about 113 ft^2.

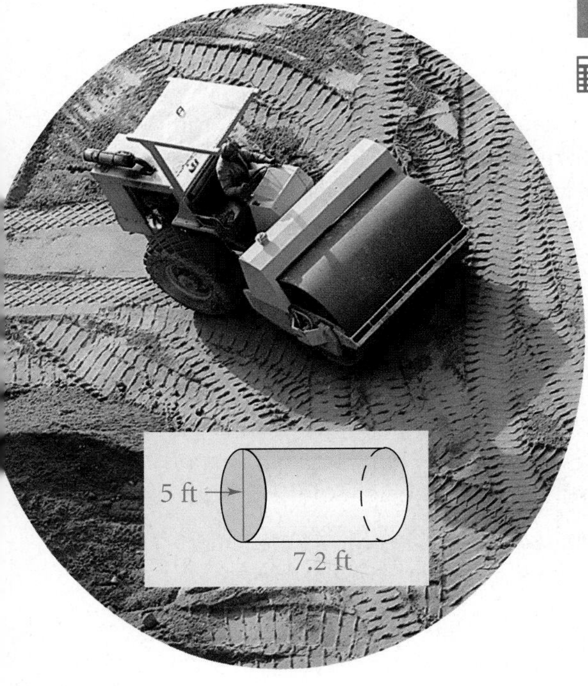

8. Estimation Use $\pi \approx 3$ to estimate the lateral area and surface area of a cylinder with height 10 cm and radius 10 cm.

Exercises ON YOUR OWN

Each structure is made of 12 unit cubes. What is the surface area of each figure?

1. 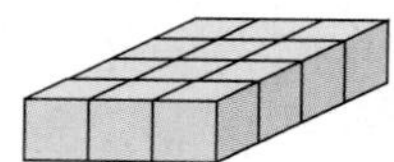

2. 

3. 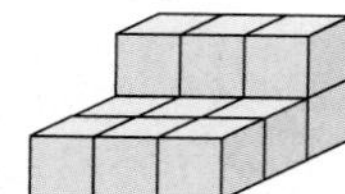

4. 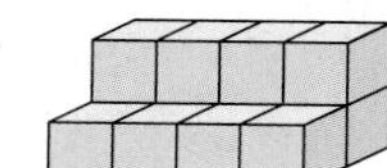

Choose **Use mental math, paper and pencil, or a calculator to find the lateral and surface areas of each figure.**

5. 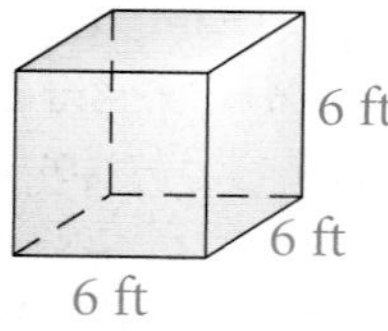

6. 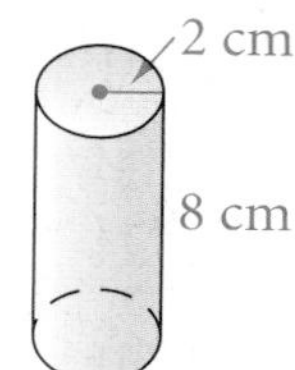

7. 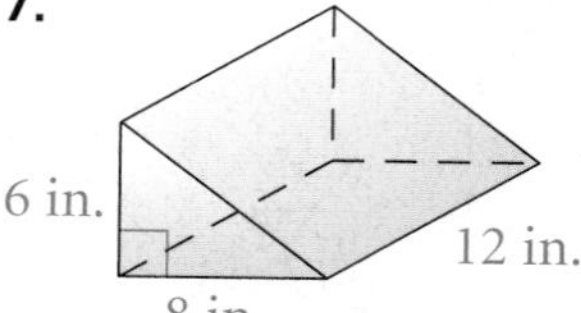

8. 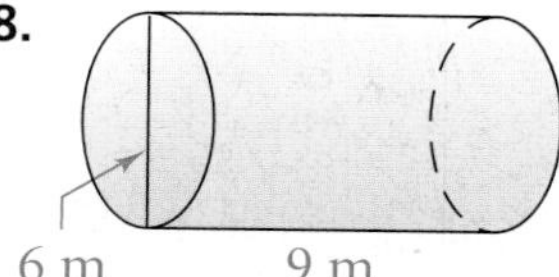

9. a. Classify the prism.

b. The bases are regular hexagons. Find the sum of their areas.

c. Find the lateral area of the prism.

d. Find the surface area of the prism.

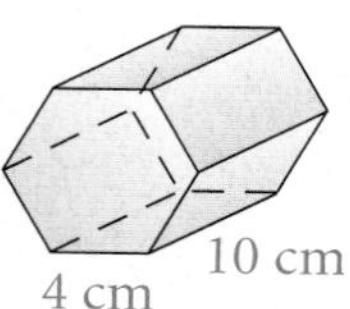

Calculator **Find the lateral area of each object. When an answer is not a whole number, round to the nearest tenth.**

10. 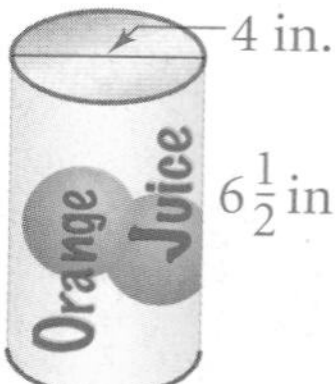

11. 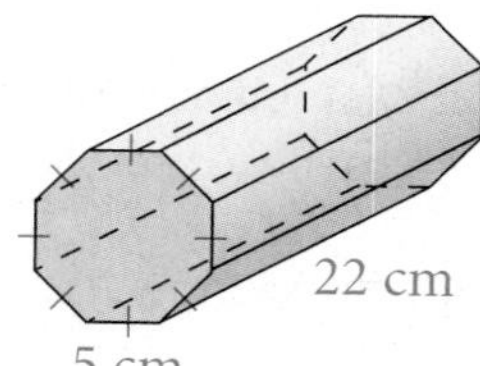

12. 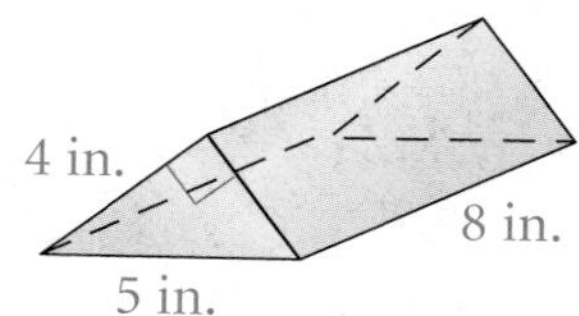

13. Manufacturing A standard drinking straw is 195 mm long and has a diameter of 6 mm. How many square centimeters of plastic are needed to make 1000 straws? Round your answer to the nearest hundred.

14. Packaging A typical video cassette tape box is open on one side. How many square inches of cardboard are in a typical video-cassette tape box?

15. Algebra A triangular prism has base edges 4 cm, 5 cm, and 6 cm long. Its lateral area is 300 cm^2. What is the height of the prism?

16. Open-ended Draw a net for a rectangular prism with a surface area of 220 cm^2.

17. a. *Geometry in 3 Dimensions* List the three coordinates (x, y, z) for vertices A, B, C, and D of the rectangular prism.
b. What is AB? c. What is BC? d. What is CD?
e. What is the surface area of the prism?

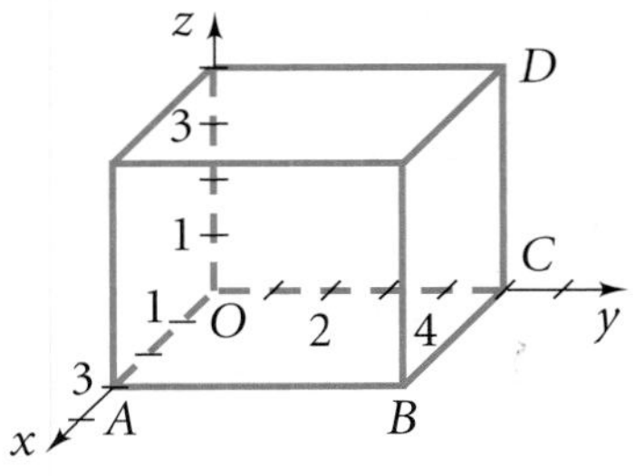

18. *Estimation* Estimate the surface area of a cube with edges 4.95 cm long.

19. *Writing* Explain how a cylinder and a prism are alike and how they are different.

Calculator **Find the surface area of each figure. When an answer is not a whole number, round to the nearest tenth.**

20. 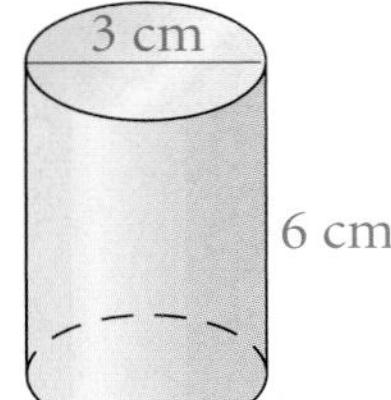

21. 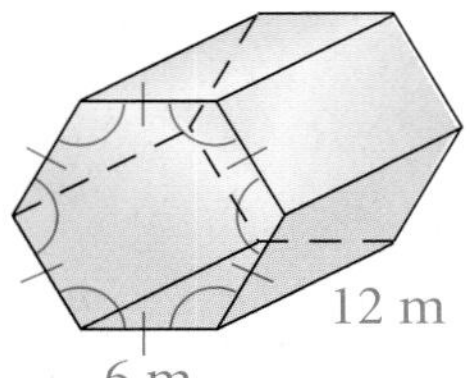

22. 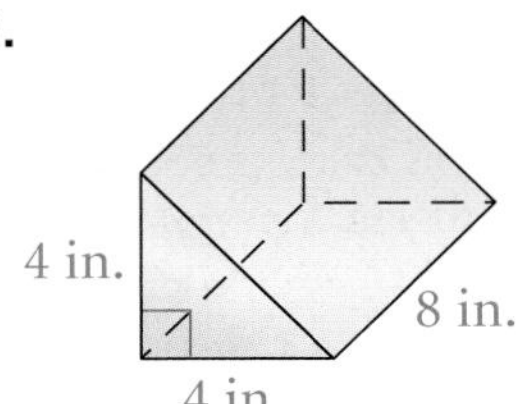

23. 

24. a. *Coordinate Geometry* Suppose the rectangle shown at the right is rotated 360° about the y-axis. What space figure will the rotating rectangle generate?
b. Find the surface area of this figure in terms of π.
c. What will be the surface area in terms of π if the rectangle is rotated 360° about the x-axis?

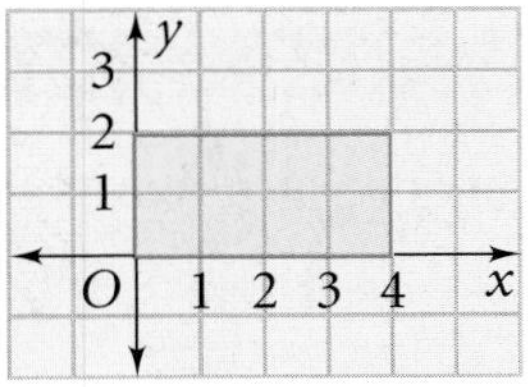

25. *Standardized Test Prep* If the radius and height of a cylinder are both doubled, then the surface area is ■.
A. the same B. doubled C. tripled D. quadrupled
E. not enough information given to determine the amount of change in the surface area

26. *Algebra* The sum of the height and radius of a cylinder is 9 m. The surface area of the cylinder is $54\pi\ m^2$. Find the height and radius.

27. *Frieze Patterns* From about 3500 B.C. to 2500 B.C., Sumerians etched cylindrical stones to form seals. They used the imprint from rotating the seal to make an official signature. These seals make interesting frieze patterns.
a. Two and one-quarter revolutions of a cylinder created the frieze pattern at the right. What are the dimensions of the cylinder? Round to the nearest tenth.
b. What type of transformation appears in the frieze pattern?

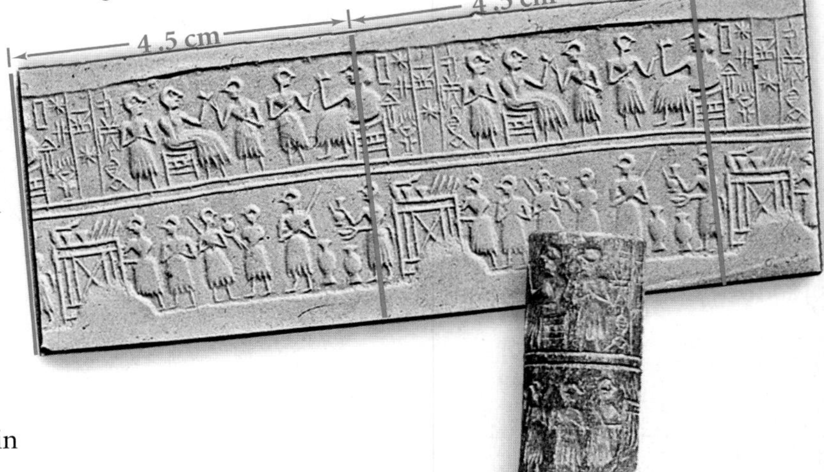

Chapter Project: Find Out by Measuring

Collect some empty cardboard containers shaped like prisms and cylinders.

- Measure each container and calculate its surface area.
- Flatten each container by carefully separating the places where it has been glued together. Find the total area of the packaging material used.
- For each container, find the percent by which the area of the packaging material exceeds the surface area of the container.

1. How does an unfolded and flattened prism-shaped package differ from a net for a prism?
2. Compare the percents you calculated. What did you find out about the amount of extra material needed for prism-shaped containers? for cylindrical containers?
3. Why would a manufacturer be concerned about the surface area of a package? about the amount of material used to make the package?

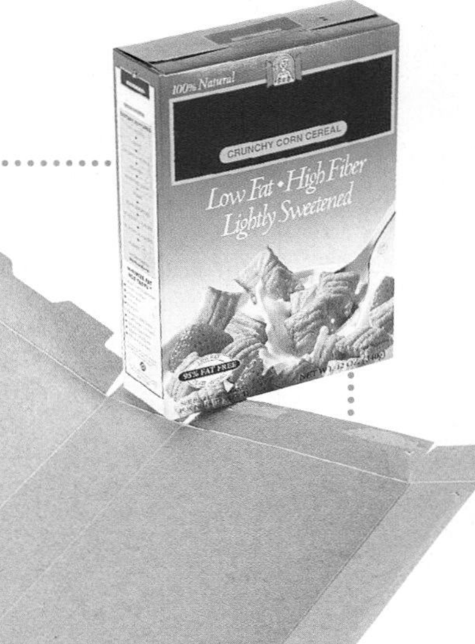

Exercises MIXED REVIEW

Find the area of each figure. You may leave answers in simplest radical form.

28.

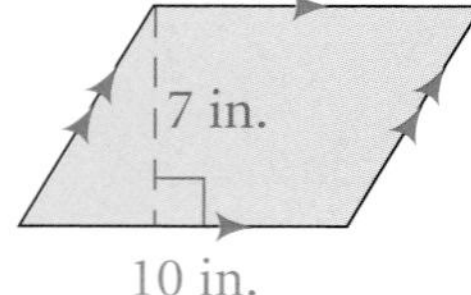

29.

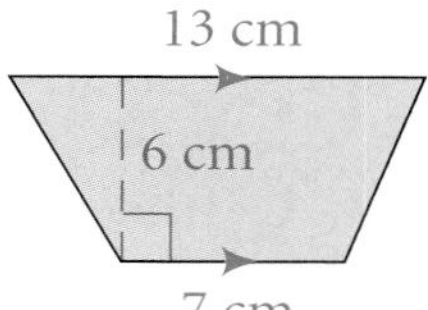

30.

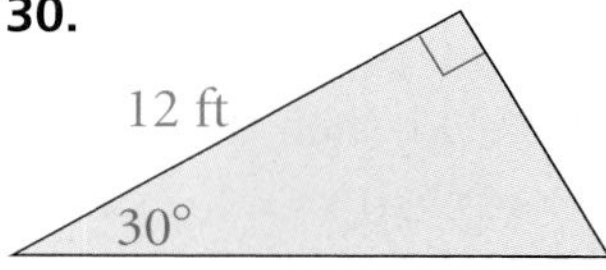

Transformations **Find the coordinates of the images of points $B(-4, 2)$, $I(0, -3)$, and $G(1, 0)$ under each reflection.**

31. in the y-axis **32.** in the x-axis **33.** in the line $x = 4$

34. Write a definition for a trapezoid. Write your definition as a biconditional.

Getting Ready for Lesson 6-3

Calculator **Use a calculator to find the length of each hypotenuse to the nearest tenth.**

35.

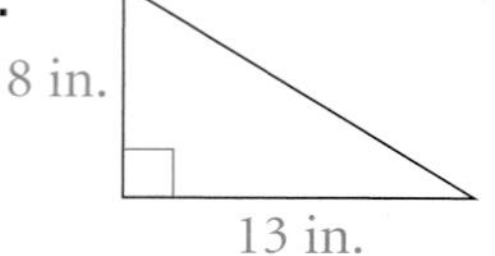

36.

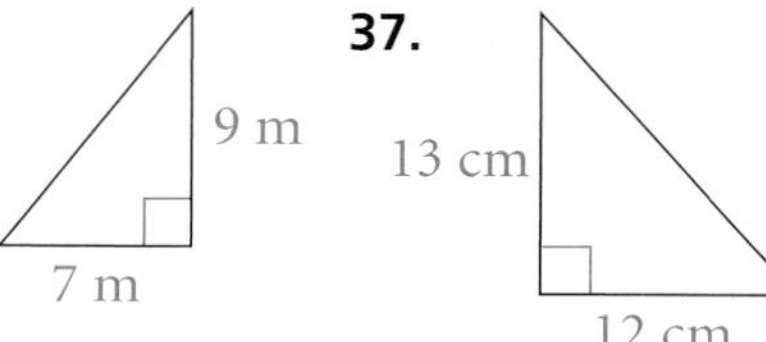

37. 13 cm, 12 cm

SELF ASSESSMENT

FOR YOUR JOURNAL

Give examples of products that are usually packaged in cylindrical containers. Then give examples of products that are usually packaged in boxes that are prisms. Explain why you think manufacturers choose particular container shapes.

Exploring Surface Area

After Lesson 6-2

Work in pairs or small groups.

Input

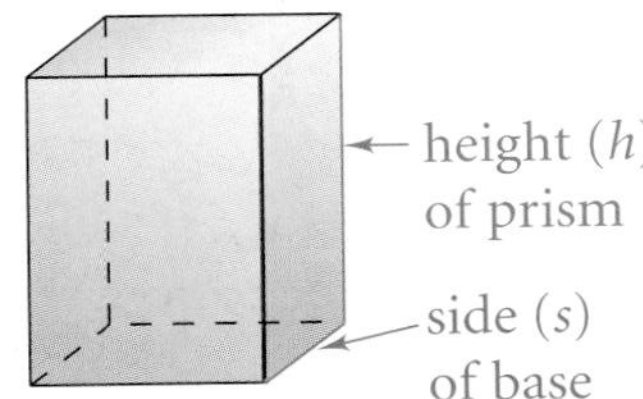

Use your spreadsheet program to investigate the surface areas of rectangular prisms with square bases. Consider square prisms with a volume of 100 cm^3 and see how the surface area (S.A.) changes as the length of the side (s) of a base changes.

The volume of a prism equals the area of a base times its height ($V = Bh$). Therefore, the height of the prism equals the volume divided by the area of the base ($h = \frac{V}{B} = \frac{V}{s^2}$). The surface area of a square prism equals two times the area of the base plus four times the area of a face (S.A. $= 2B + 4sh = 2s^2 + 4sh$). Set up your spreadsheet as follows.

	A	B	C
1	Square Prisms with a Volume of 100 cm^3		
2			
3	sides (s) of base	height (h) of prism	Surface Area (S.A.)
4		= 100/A4^2	= 2*A4^2+4*A4*B4

Investigate

Copy the formulas down several rows and enter different values for the length of the side of the base in Column A. How small can the surface area be? How large can it be?

Conjecture

Which dimensions give a very large surface area? Which dimensions give the smallest surface area? How do the side of the base and the height compare in the prism of smallest surface area? What is the shape of the square prism that has the smallest surface area?

Extend

- If a square prism has a volume of 1000 cm^3, what dimensions would give the smallest surface area?

Connections Social Studies . . . and more

What You'll Learn

- Finding the lateral areas and surface areas of pyramids and cones

...And Why

To find the lateral areas of pyramids, such as the Great Pyramid at Giza, and of conical tower roofs

What You'll Need

calculator, metric ruler, compass, protractor, scissors, tape

6-3 Surface Areas of Pyramids and Cones

THINK AND DISCUSS

Lateral Areas and Surface Areas of Pyramids

Many Egyptian pharaohs built pyramids as burial tombs. The Fourth Dynasty, 2615–2494 B.C., was the age of the great pyramids. The builders knew and understood the mathematical properties of a pyramid.

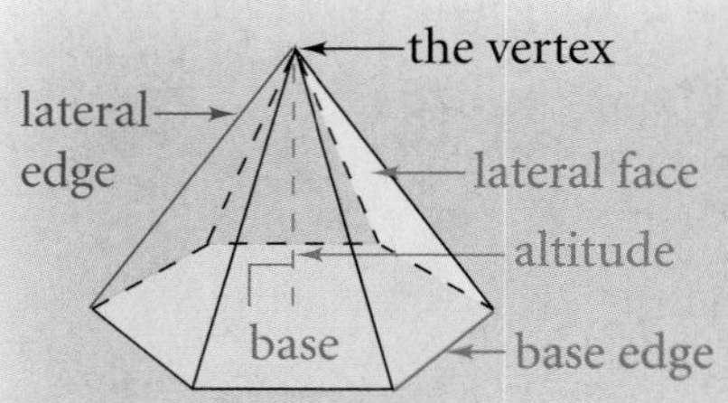

A **pyramid** is a polyhedron in which one face (the **base**) can be any polygon and the other faces (the **lateral faces**) are triangles that meet at a common vertex (called the **vertex** of the pyramid). You can name a pyramid by the shape of its base. The **altitude** of a pyramid is the perpendicular segment from the vertex to the plane of the base. The length of the altitude is the **height** h of the pyramid.

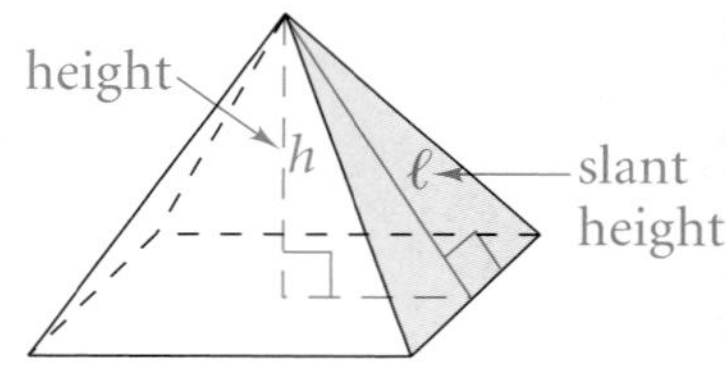

A **regular pyramid** is a pyramid whose base is a regular polygon. The lateral faces are congruent isosceles triangles. The **slant height** ℓ is the length of the altitude of a lateral face of the pyramid. In this book, you can assume a pyramid is regular unless you are told otherwise.

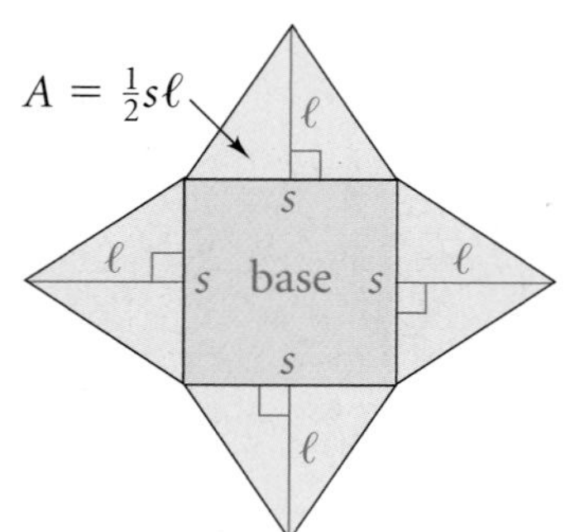

You can find a formula for the lateral area of a pyramid by looking at its net. The **lateral area** is the sum of the areas of the congruent lateral faces.

$\text{L.A.} = 4(\frac{1}{2}s\ell)$	The area of each lateral face is $\frac{1}{2}s\ell$.
$= \frac{1}{2}(4s)\ell$	Commutative Property of Multiplication
$= \frac{1}{2}p\ell$	The perimeter p of the base is $4s$.

To find the **surface area** of a pyramid, add the area of its base to its lateral area.

Theorem 6-3
Lateral and Surface Areas of a Regular Pyramid

The lateral area of a regular pyramid is half the product of the perimeter of the base and the slant height.

$$\text{L.A.} = \tfrac{1}{2}p\ell$$

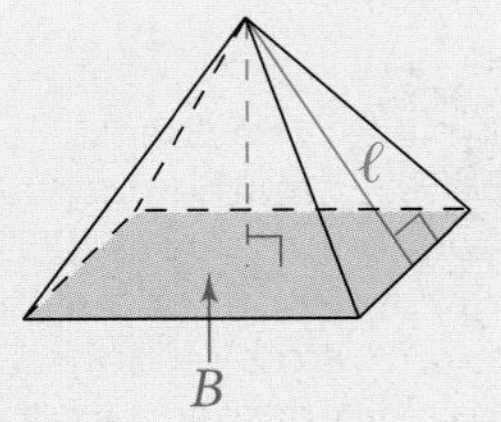

The surface area of a regular pyramid is the sum of the lateral area and the area of the base.

$$\text{S.A.} = \text{L.A.} + B$$

1. Try This A regular hexagonal pyramid has base edges 60 m long and slant height 35 m. Find the perimeter of its base and its lateral area.

Sometimes the slant height of a pyramid is not given. You must calculate it before you can find the lateral or surface area.

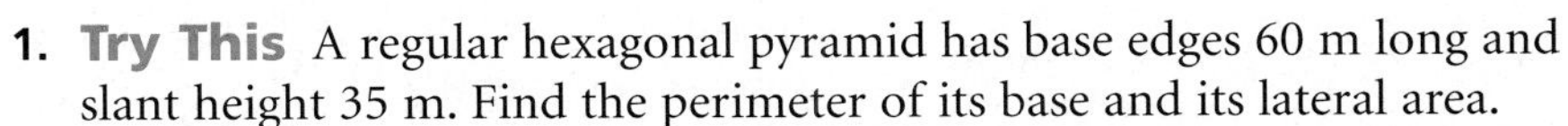

Social Studies The Great Pyramid at Giza, Egypt, was built about 2580 B.C. as a final resting place for Pharaoh Khufu. At the time it was built, its height was about 481 ft. Each edge of the square base was about 756 ft long. What was the lateral area of the pyramid?

- The legs of right $\triangle ABC$ are the height of the pyramid and the apothem of the base. The height of the pyramid is 481 ft. The apothem of the base is $\frac{756}{2}$, or 378 ft. You can use the Pythagorean Theorem to find the slant height ℓ.

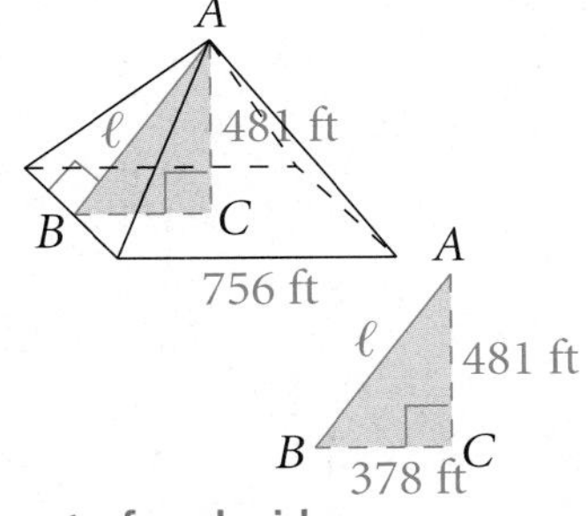

$$\ell^2 = AC^2 + BC^2$$
$$\ell^2 = 481^2 + 378^2$$
$$\ell = \sqrt{481^2 + 378^2} \qquad \textbf{Find the square root of each side.}$$

481 [x²] [+] 378 [x²] [=] [√] 611.75567

- Now use the formula for the lateral area of a pyramid. The perimeter of the base is approximately $4 \cdot 756$, or 3024 ft.

$$\text{L.A.} = \tfrac{1}{2}p\ell$$
$$= \tfrac{1}{2}(3024)(611.75567) \qquad \textbf{Substitute.}$$

0.5 [×] 3024 [×] 611.75567 [=] 924974.57

The lateral area of the Great Pyramid at Giza was about 925,000 ft^2.

2. Try This Find the surface area of the Great Pyramid at Giza.

Lateral Areas and Surface Areas of Cones

Who? The Greek mathematician Apollonius (about 225 B.C.) wrote a work about the cone and its cross sections. His *Conic Sections* earned him the title "The Great Geometer."

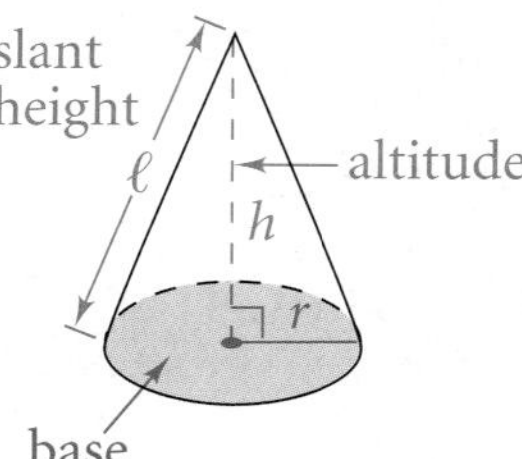

A **cone** is like a pyramid, but its base is a circle. In a **right cone** the **altitude** is a perpendicular segment from the vertex to the center of the base. The **height** h is the length of the altitude. The **slant height** ℓ is the distance from the vertex to a point on the edge of the base. In this book, all the cones discussed will be right cones.

The formulas for the lateral area and surface area of a cone are similar to those for a pyramid.

Theorem 6-4

Lateral and Surface Areas of a Right Cone

The lateral area of a right cone is half the product of the circumference of the base and the slant height.

$$\text{L.A.} = \frac{1}{2} \cdot 2\pi r \cdot \ell, \text{ or L.A.} = \pi r \ell$$

The surface area of a right cone is the sum of the lateral area and the area of a base.

$$\text{S.A.} = \text{L.A.} + B$$

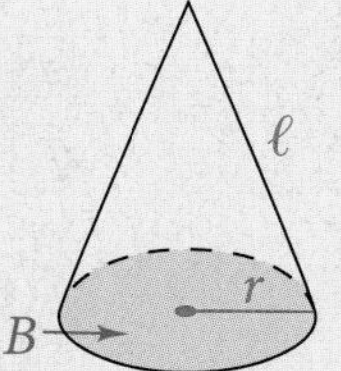

Example 2

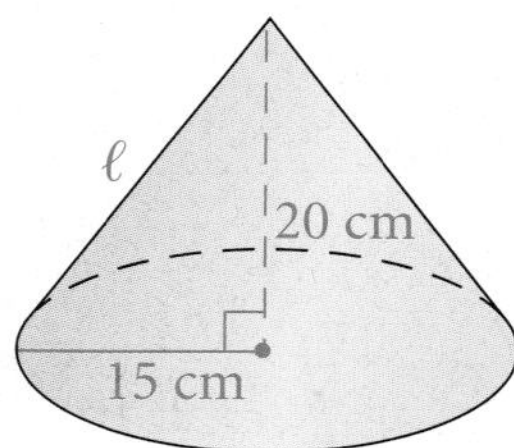

The radius of the base of a cone is 15 cm. Its height is 20 cm. Find its lateral area in terms of π.

- To determine the lateral area, you first must find the slant height ℓ.

$\ell^2 = 20^2 + 15^2$	Use the Pythagorean Theorem.
$= 400 + 225$	Simplify.
$= 625$	
$\ell = 25$	Find the square root of each side.

The slant height of the cone is 25 cm.

- Now you can use the formula for the lateral area of a cone.

$\text{L.A.} = \pi r \ell$	
$= \pi(15)25$	Substitute.
$= 375\pi$	Simplify.

The lateral area of the cone is 375π cm^2.

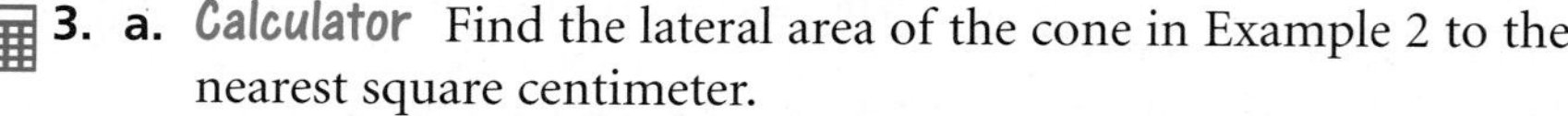

3. a. *Calculator* Find the lateral area of the cone in Example 2 to the nearest square centimeter.

b. Find the surface area of the cone to the nearest square centimeter.

WORK TOGETHER

- Work in a group. Use a compass to draw three congruent circles with radii 8 cm. Use a protractor to draw the shaded sectors shown below.

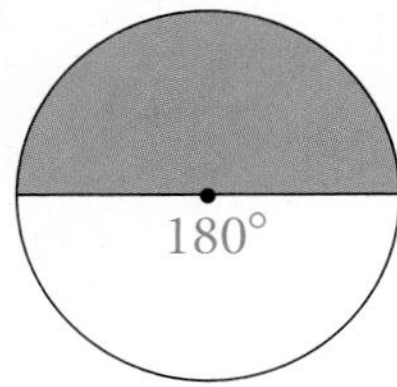

Figure 1

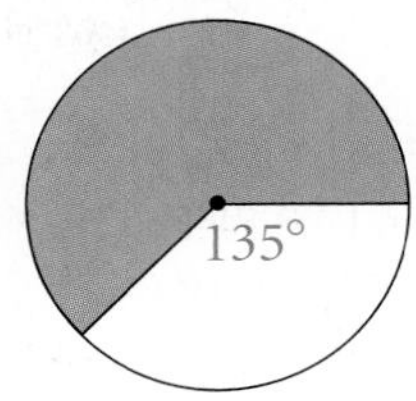

Figure 2

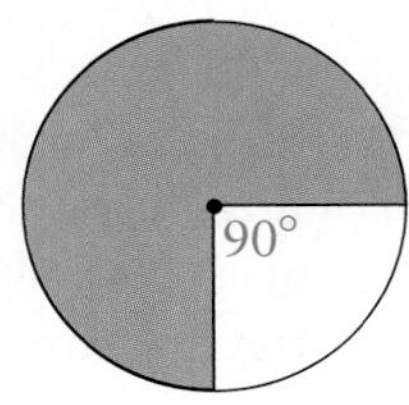

Figure 3

- Cut out the sectors. Tape the radii of each sector together, without overlapping, to form a cone without a base.

4. Find the slant height of each cone.

5. Find the circumference C and radius r of each cone. Then find the lateral area of each cone. Record your results in a table like the one shown at the left.

Cone	C	r	L.A.
1	■	■	■
2	■	■	■
3	■	■	■

Exercises ON YOUR OWN

Choose **Use mental math, pencil and paper, or a calculator to find the slant height of each figure.**

1. 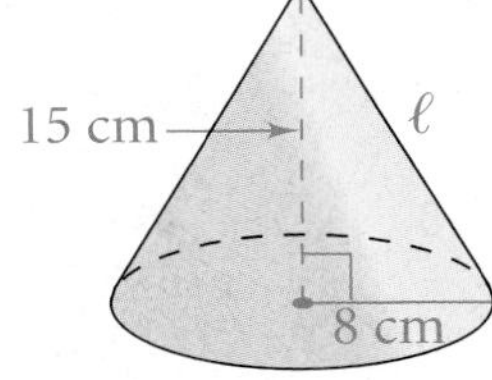

2. 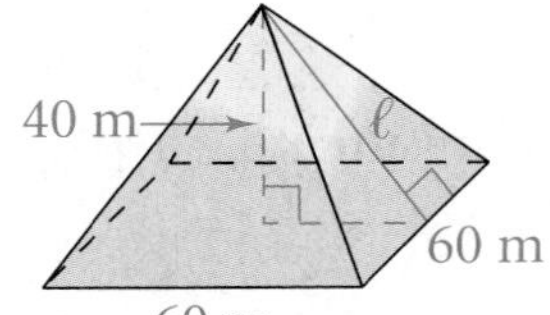

3. 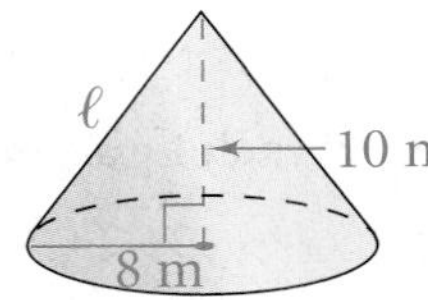

4. 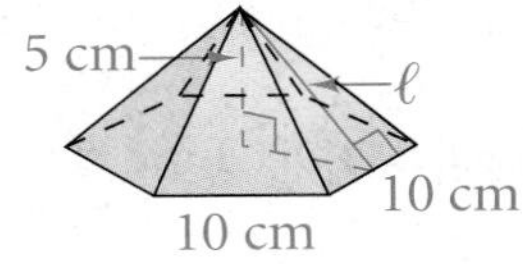

Find the lateral area of each figure. You may leave answers in terms of π.

5. 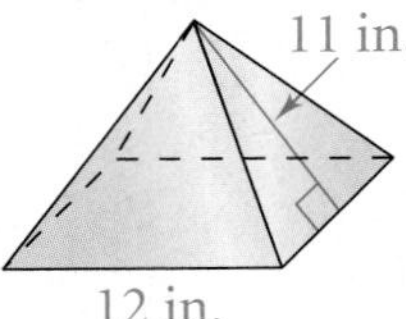

6. 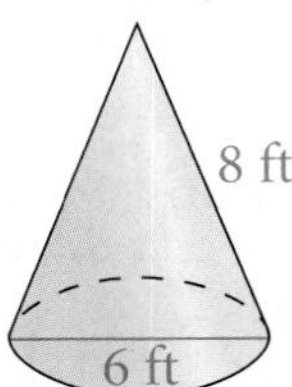

7. 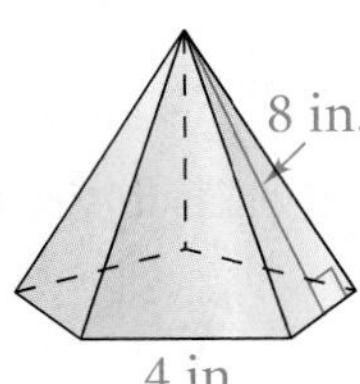

8. 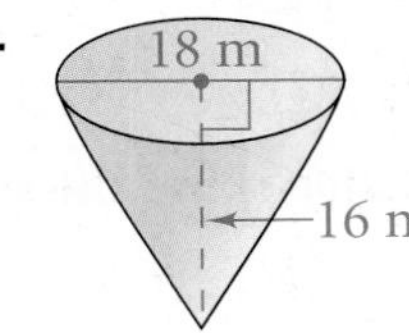

9. **Writing** How are a cone and a pyramid alike? How are they different?

10. **Architecture** The roof of the tower in a castle is shaped like a cone. The height of the roof is 30 ft and the radius of the base is 15 ft. What is the area of the roof? Round your answer to the nearest tenth.

11. **Critical Thinking** Anita says that when she uses her calculator to find the surface area of a cone she uses the formula S.A. $= (\ell + r)r\pi$. Explain why this formula works. Why do you think Anita uses this formula?

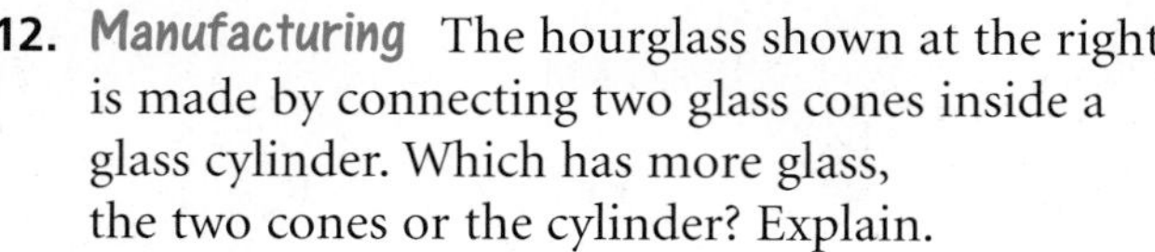

12. **Manufacturing** The hourglass shown at the right is made by connecting two glass cones inside a glass cylinder. Which has more glass, the two cones or the cylinder? Explain.

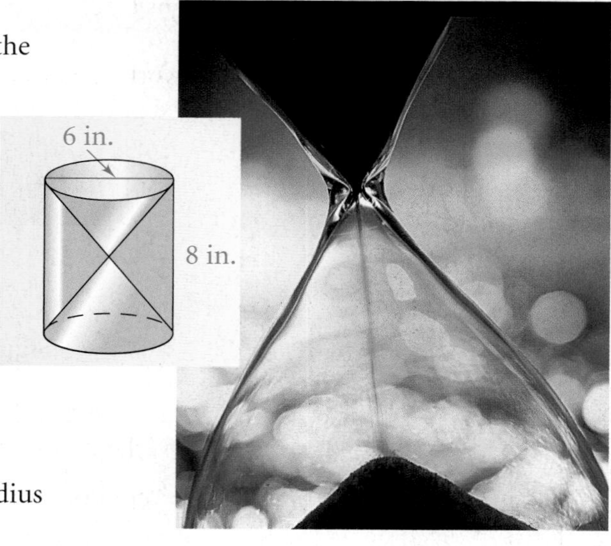

13. A regular square pyramid has base edges 10 in. long and height 4 in. Sketch the pyramid and find its surface area. Round your answer to the nearest tenth.

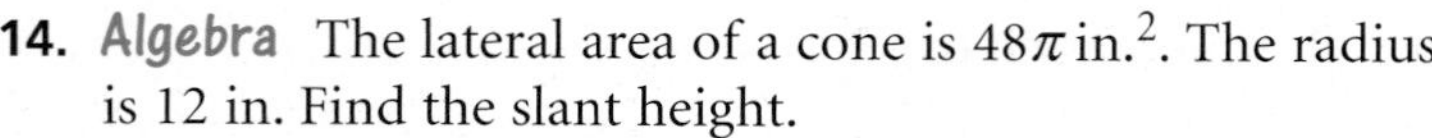

14. **Algebra** The lateral area of a cone is 48π in.^{2}. The radius is 12 in. Find the slant height.

15. **Open-ended** Draw a pyramid with a lateral area of 48 cm^2. Label its dimensions. Then find its surface area.

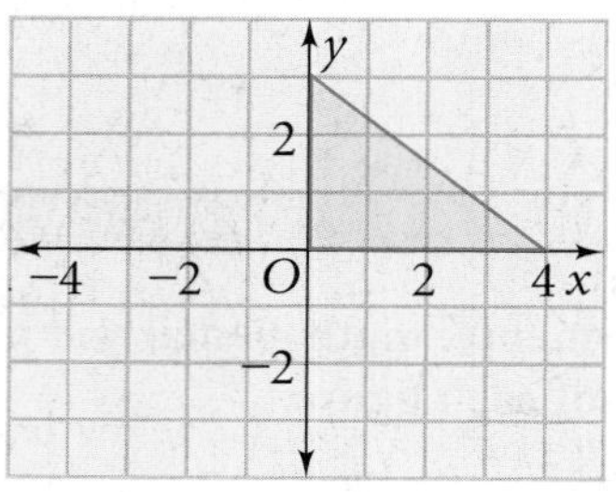

16. **a.** **Coordinate Geometry** Describe the figure that is formed when the right triangle at the right is rotated 360° about the x-axis. Find its lateral area. Leave your answer in terms of π.

b. What is the lateral area of the figure formed when the triangle is rotated 360° about the y-axis? Leave your answer in terms of π.

Calculator **Find the lateral area of each figure to the nearest tenth.**

17.

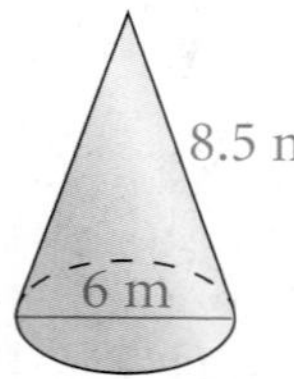

18.

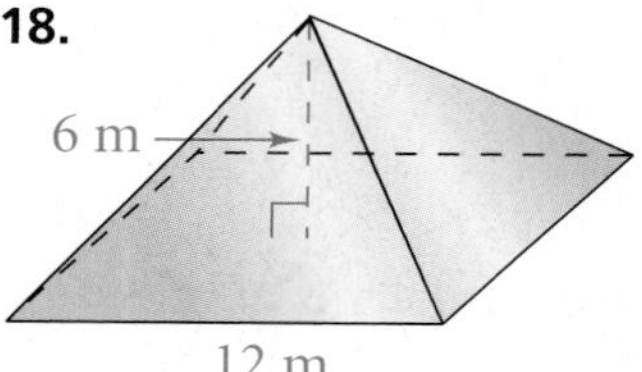

19.

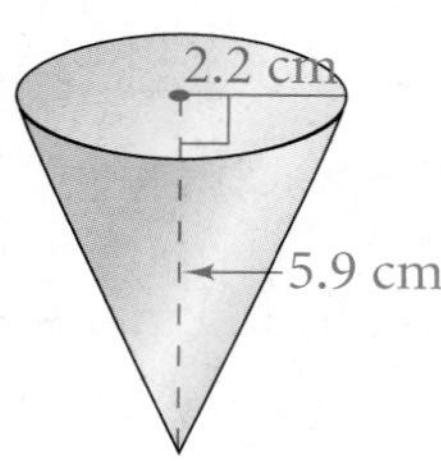

20.

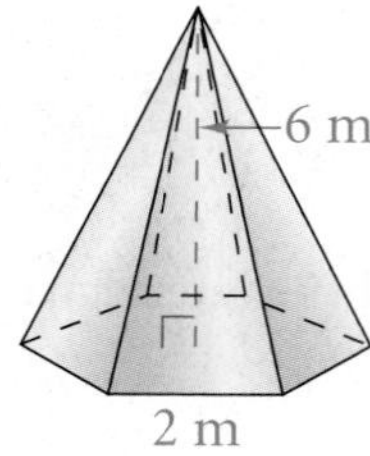

Calculator **Find the surface area of each figure to the nearest tenth.**

21.

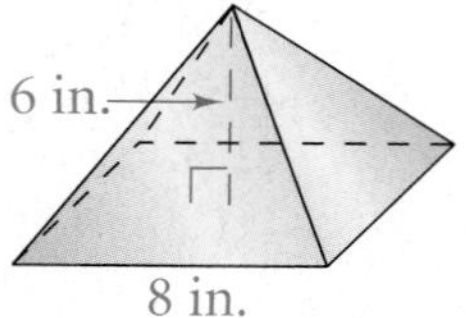

22.

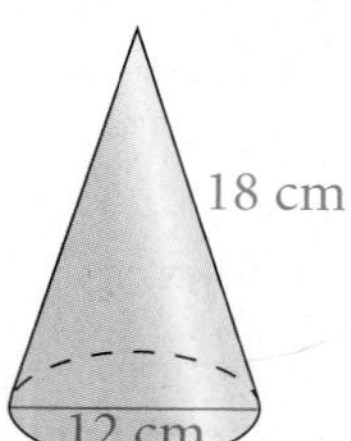

23.

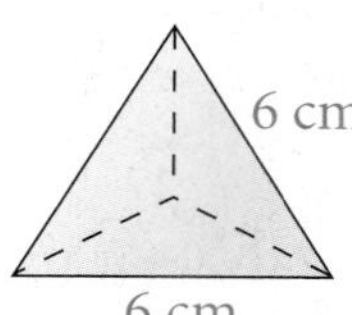

24.

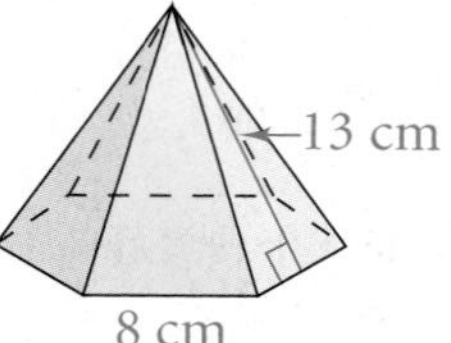

25. **Paper Folding** Follow the directions below to fold a dollar bill into a regular triangular pyramid, called a *tetrahedron.* Then find the surface area of your tetrahedron. How does this compare with the area of the dollar bill?

Step 1. Fold in half.

Step 2. Unfold and fold corners to foldline.

Step 3. Fold bottom left corner up.

Step 4. Fold top left corner down.

Step 5. Open and form this tetrahedon.

26. **Standardized Test Prep** The cylinder and cone have the same height 1 and the same radius $\sqrt{3}$. How does the lateral area x of the cylinder compare with the lateral area y of the cone?

A. $x = y$ **B.** $x = 2y$ **C.** $x > 2y$
D. $x < 2y$ **E.** cannot be determined

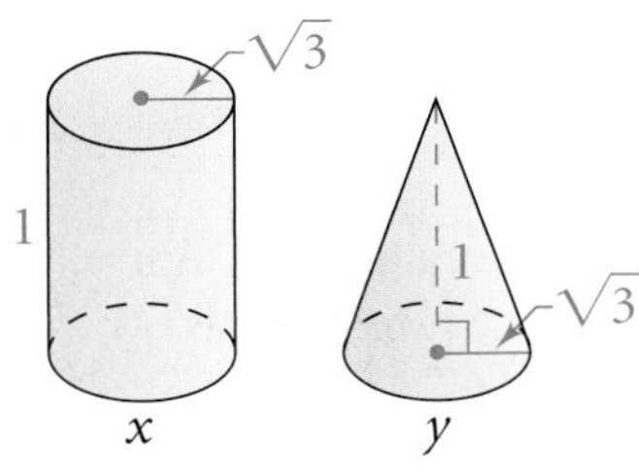

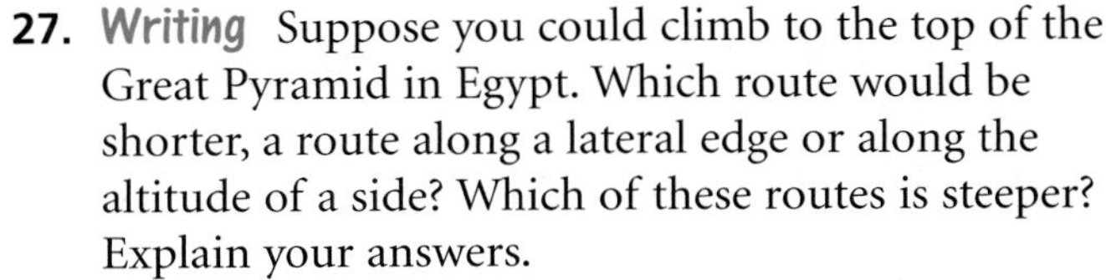

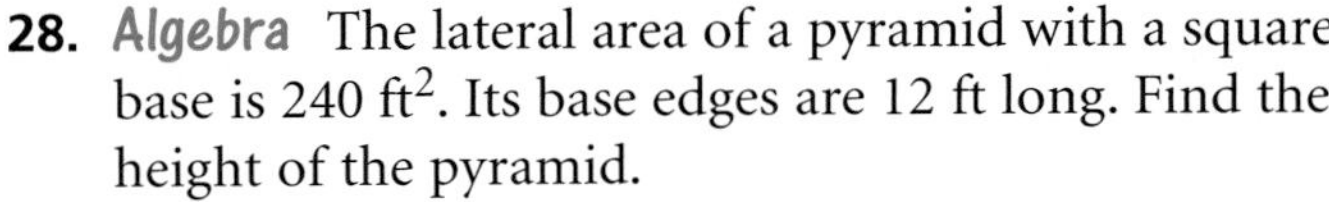

27. **Writing** Suppose you could climb to the top of the Great Pyramid in Egypt. Which route would be shorter, a route along a lateral edge or along the altitude of a side? Which of these routes is steeper? Explain your answers.

28. **Algebra** The lateral area of a pyramid with a square base is 240 ft^2. Its base edges are 12 ft long. Find the height of the pyramid.

29. **Algebra** The surface area of a cone is $24\pi\ cm^2$ and the lateral area is $15\pi\ cm^2$. Find the slant height and the height of the cone.

30. **Research** Find out about ancient Mexican and Egyptian pyramids. How are they alike? How are they different? **Summarize** your findings in a short report.

Pyramid of the Sun, Teotihuacán, Mexico

Exercises MIXED REVIEW

Coordinate Geometry **Find the lengths of the sides of triangles with the given vertices. Then classify each triangle by its sides.**

31. $A(0, 4), B(-3, 0), C(3, 0)$

32. $K(5, 0), L(1, 4), M(1, -1)$

33. $W(-2, 7), X(-3, -2), Y(0, 4)$

Write the converse of each statement. Determine whether the converse is true or false. If false, give a counterexample.

34. If two lines are skew, then they do not intersect.

35. If two angles are complementary, then the sum of their measures is 90.

36. **Transformations** Which letters of the alphabet can be rotated less than 360° and still look like the preimage? State each letter and the angle(s) of rotation.

Getting Ready for Lesson 6-4

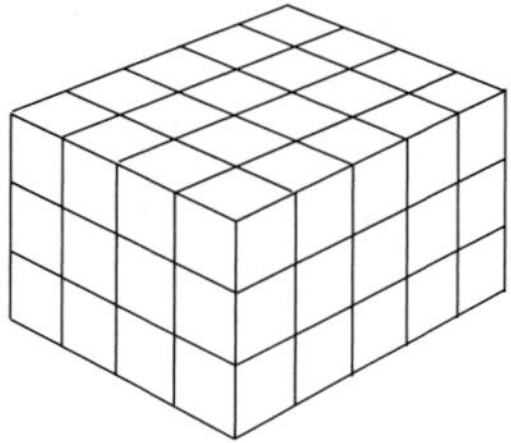

37. There are no hidden holes in the structure at the right. How many cubes make up this structure?

38. **Open-ended** Sketch a prism made with 24 unit cubes. Label its dimensions.

39. A cube is made of 27 unit cubes. What are its dimensions?

Exercises CHECKPOINT

Calculator **Find the surface area of each figure. When an answer is not a whole number, round to the nearest tenth.**

1.

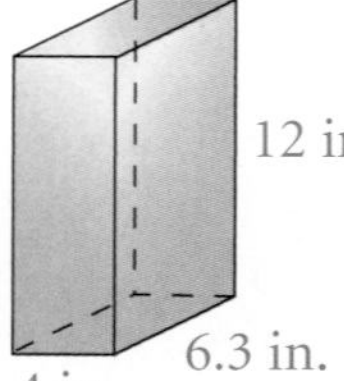

2.

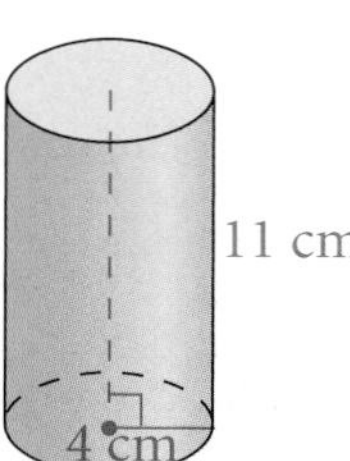

3.

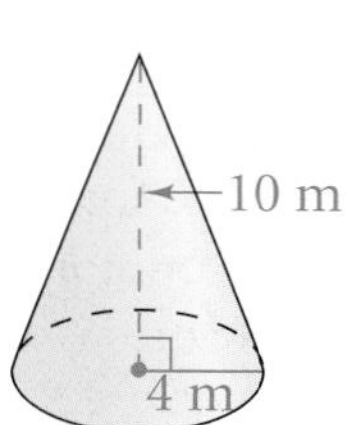

4.

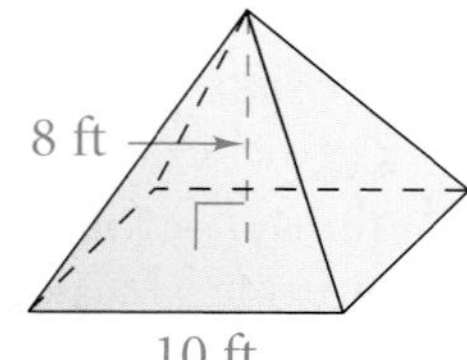

5. **Space Shuttle** The space shuttle *Atlantis* brought a docking module to the space station *Mir*. The module is a cylinder with an 8-ft diameter and a height of 15 ft. What is the surface area of the docking module? Round your answer to the nearest tenth.

6. **Open-ended** Draw a net for a regular triangular pyramid.

7. **Writing** Explain how the formulas for the lateral area of a prism and a cylinder are alike and how they are different.

6-4 Volumes of Prisms and Cylinders

What You'll Learn

- Finding the volumes of prisms and cylinders

...And Why

To find the space needed to store packages and the amount of water needed to fill an aquarium

What You'll Need

- unit cubes
- calculator

WORK TOGETHER

Work with a group. Explore the volume of a prism with unit cubes.

1. Make a single-layer rectangular prism that is 4 cubes long and 2 cubes wide. The prism will be 4 units by 2 units by 1 unit. How many cubes are in the prism?
2. Add a second layer to your prism to make a prism 4 units by 2 units by 2 units. How many cubes are in this prism?
3. Add a third layer to your prism to make a prism 4 units by 2 units by 3 units. How many cubes are in this prism?
4. How many cubes would be in the prism if you added two additional layers of cubes for a total of 5 layers?
5. How many cubes would be in the prism if there were 10 layers?
6. Compare a prism 2 cubes long by 3 cubes wide and 4 layers high with the prism in Question 3. What do you notice?
7. Compare a prism 3 cubes long by 4 cubes wide and 2 layers high with the prisms in Questions 3 and 6. What do you notice?

THINK AND DISCUSS

Volumes of Prisms

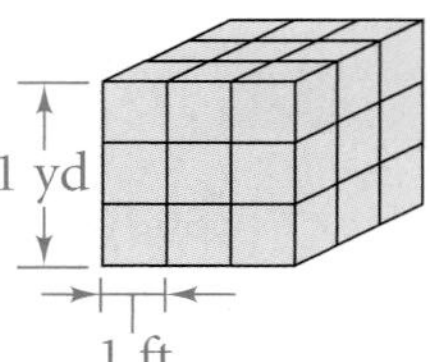

Volume is the space that a figure occupies. It is measured in cubic units such as cubic inches (in.^{3}), cubic feet (ft^3), or cubic centimeters (cm^3). The volume of a cube is the cube of the length of its edge, or $V = e^3$.

8. How many cubic feet are in a cubic yard?

9. How many cubic inches are in a cubic foot? in a cubic yard?

Each of the two stacks of paper at the left contains the same number of sheets. The first stack forms a right prism; the second forms an oblique prism. The stacks have the same height. The area of every cross section parallel to a base is the area of one sheet of paper. The stacks have the same volume. These stacks illustrate the following principle.

Theorem 6-5
Cavalieri's Principle

If two space figures have the same height and the same cross-sectional area at every level, then they have the same volume.

10. a. Try This What are the areas of the shaded cross sections of the space figures below?

b. Each of these figures has a height of 7 cm. What do you know about the volumes of these figures?

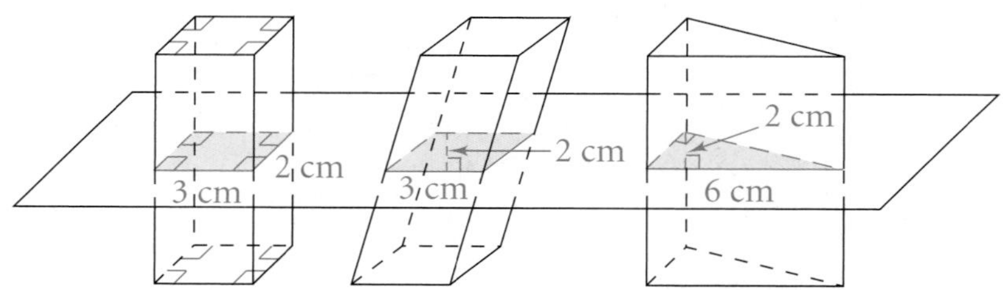

You can use what you discovered in the Work Together, along with Cavalieri's Principle, to find the volume of any prism.

Theorem 6-6
Volume of a Prism

The volume of a prism is the product of the area of a base and the height of the prism.

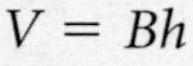

$$V = Bh$$

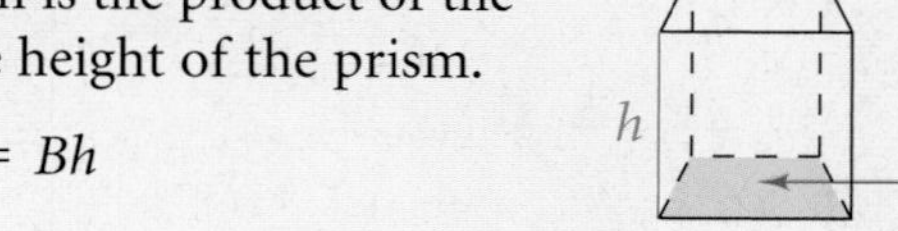

11. Try This Find the volume of each of the space figures in Question 10.

Example 1

Find the volume of each prism.

a.

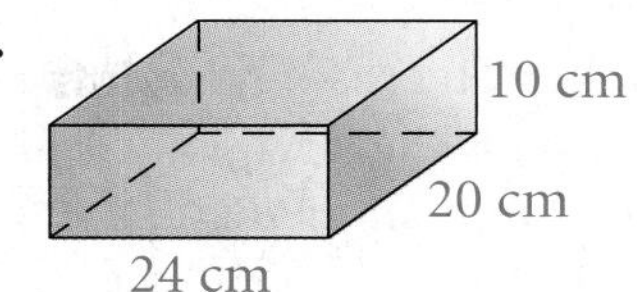

b.

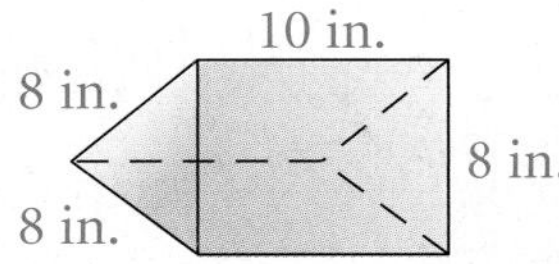

a. $V = Bh$ — **Use the formula for volume.**

$= 480 \cdot 10$ — $B = 24 \cdot 20 = 480 \text{ cm}^2$

$= 4800$ — **Simplify.**

The volume of the rectangular prism is 4800 cm^3.

b. The base of the triangular prism is an equilateral triangle. An altitude of the triangle divides it into two 30°-60°-90° triangles.

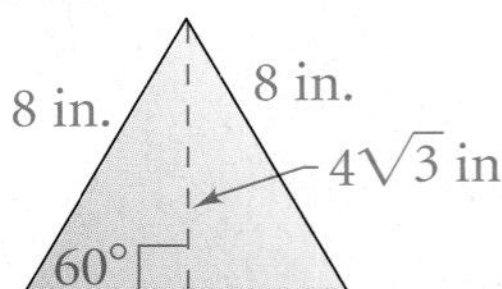

$V = Bh$ — **Use the formula for volume.**

$= 16\sqrt{3} \cdot 10$ — $B = \frac{1}{2} \cdot 8 \cdot 4\sqrt{3} = 16\sqrt{3} \text{ in.}^2$

$= 160\sqrt{3}$ — **Simplify.**

The volume of the triangular prism is $160\sqrt{3}$ in.^3.

12. Try This The volume of a triangular prism is 1860 cm^3. Its base is a right triangle with legs 24 cm and 10 cm long.

a. Draw and label a diagram.
b. Find the area of the base of the prism.
c. Find the height of the prism.

13. Try This Find the volume of this oblique prism with rectangular bases.

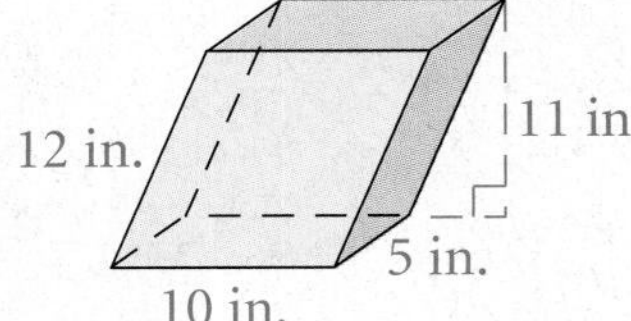

Volumes of Cylinders

The formula for the volume of a cylinder is similar to the formula for the volume of a prism.

Theorem 6-7
Volume of a Cylinder

The volume of a cylinder is the product of the area of a base and the height of the cylinder.

$$V = Bh, \text{ or } V = \pi r^2 h$$

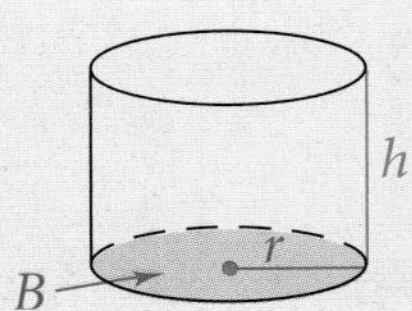

Sometimes you need to convert units of measure to solve a problem.

Example 2 Relating to the Real World 

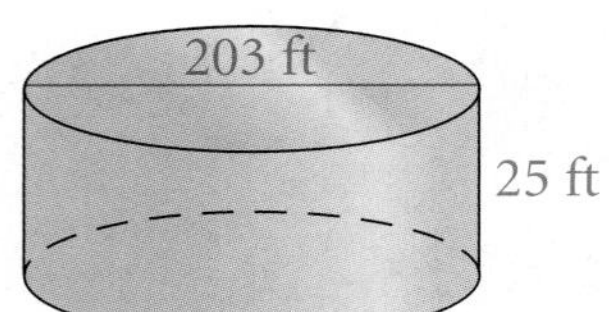

Aquarium Tanks The main tank at the Living Seas Aquarium at EPCOT Center in Florida is the largest enclosed tank in the world. It is a cylinder with diameter 203 ft and height 25 ft. About how many million gallons of water does this tank hold? (1 gal $\approx$ 231 in.^{3})

- Find the volume of the tank in cubic feet.

$r = \frac{203}{2} = 101.5$ **The radius equals half the diameter.**

$V = \pi r^2 h$ **Use the formula for the volume of a cylinder.**

$V = \pi(101.5)^2(25)$ **Substitute.**

 101.5  25 

- To convert cubic feet to cubic inches, multiply by 12^3.

809,136.8229 × 12  3 

- To find the number of gallons the tank can hold, divide by 231.

1,398,188,430 ÷ 231 = 6052763.766

The main tank can hold about 6 million gallons of water.

14. The main tank at the New England Aquarium in Boston, Massachusetts, has a diameter of 40 ft and is 23 ft deep.

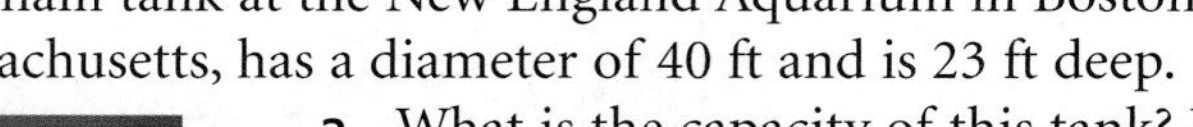

a. What is the capacity of this tank? Round your answer to the nearest thousand gallons.

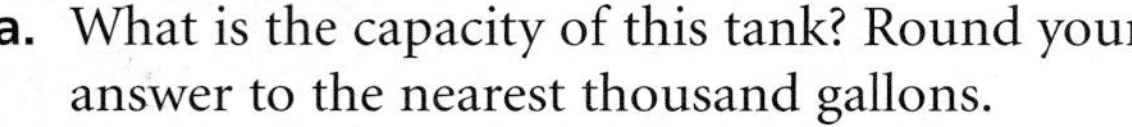

b. How does the size of this tank compare with the size of the one at the Living Seas Aquarium?

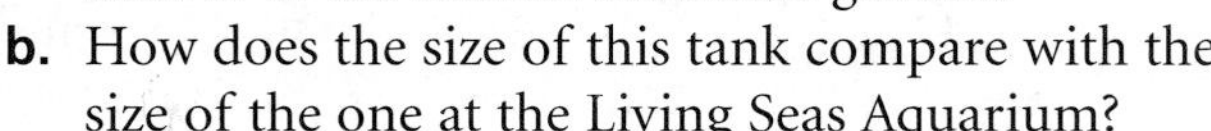

Exercises ON YOUR OWN

Choose **Use mental math, paper and pencil, or a calculator to find the volume of each figure. When an answer is not an integer, round to the nearest tenth.**

1. 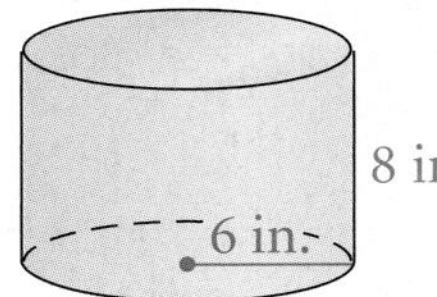

2. 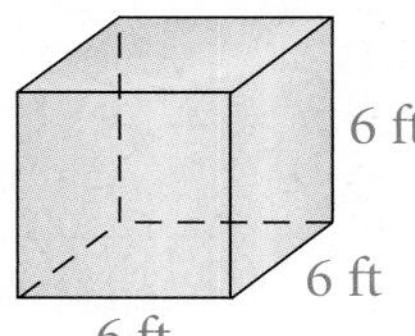

3. 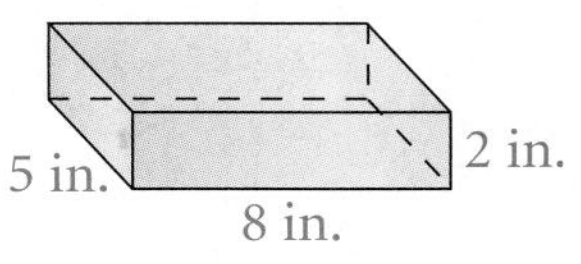

4. 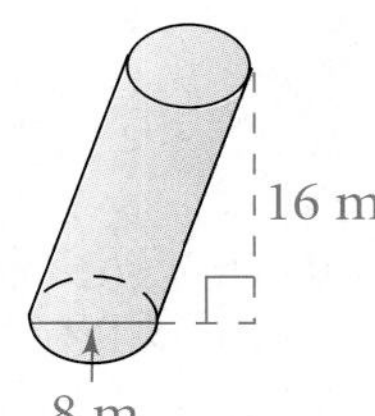

Calculator **Find the volume of each figure. When an answer is not a whole number, round to the nearest tenth.**

5. 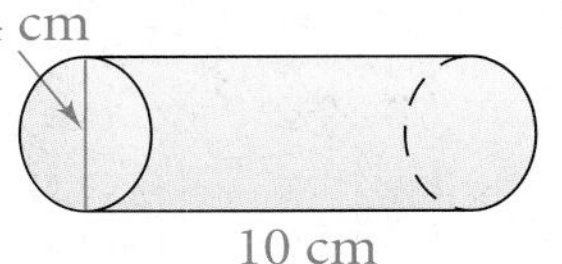

6. 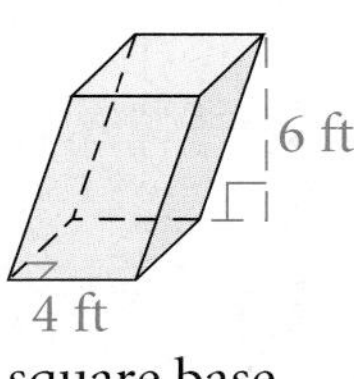

7. 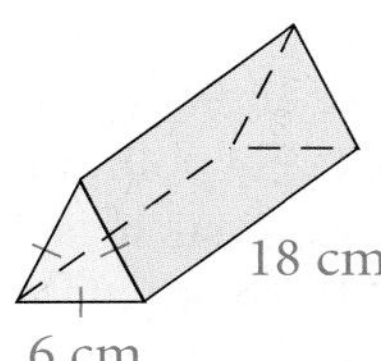

8. 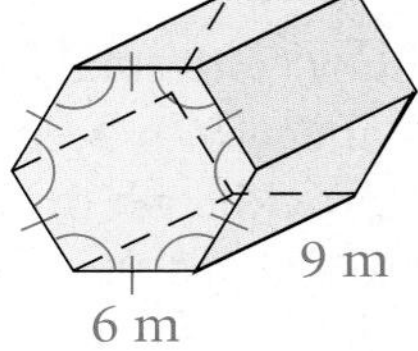

9. **a.** What is the volume of a 7 ft-by-4 ft-by-1 ft waterbed mattress?
   b. To the nearest pound, what is the weight of the water in a full mattress? (Water weighs 62.4 lb/ft^3.)

10. **Geometry in 3 Dimensions** Find the volume of the rectangular prism at the right.

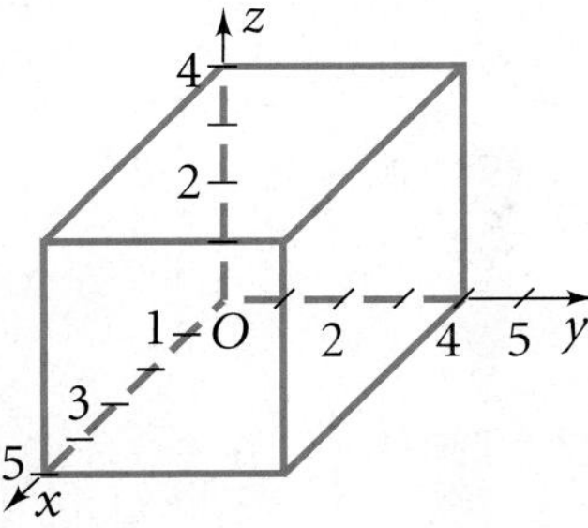

11. **Open-ended** Give the dimensions of two rectangular prisms that each have a volume of 80 cm^3 but have different surface areas.

12. **Landscaping** Zia is planning to landscape her backyard. The yard is a 70 ft-by-60 ft rectangle. She plans to put down a 4-in. layer of topsoil. She can buy bags of topsoil at $2.50 per 3-$ft^3$ bag, with free delivery. Or, she can buy bulk topsoil for $25.00 per yd^3, plus a $20 delivery fee. Which option is less expensive? Explain.

13. **Water Resources** One of the West Delaware water-supply tunnels is a 105-mi long cylinder with a diameter of 13.5 ft. To the nearest million cubic feet, how much earth was removed when the tunnel was built?

14. **Standardized Test Prep** The volume of a cube is 1000 cm^3. What is its surface area?
    A. 60 cm^2
    B. 600 cm^2
    C. 100 cm^2
    D. about 4630 cm^2
    E. cannot be determined

Find the height of each prism or cylinder with the given volume.

15.

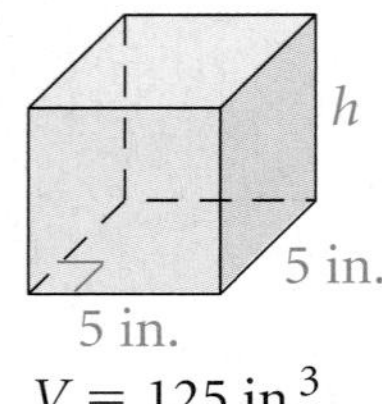

$V = 125$ in.^{3}

16.

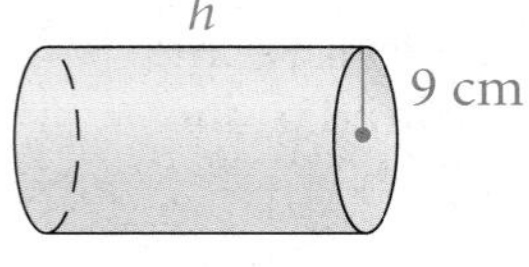

$V = 243\pi$ cm^3

17.

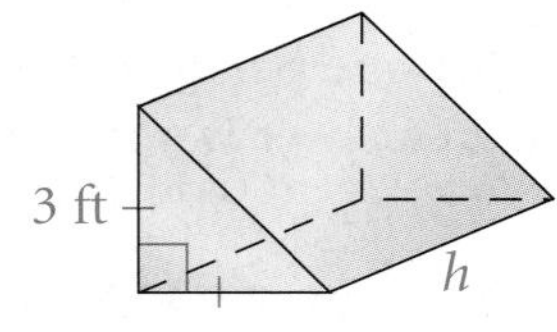

$V = 27$ ft^3

18.

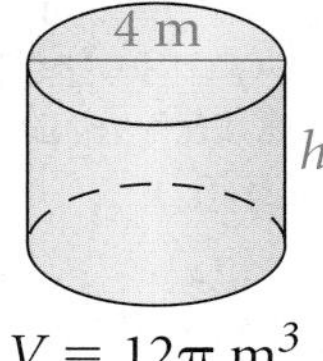

$V = 12\pi$ m^3

19. a. What is the volume of the "ordinary" cube in the cartoon if each edge is 18 in. long?

b. What is the volume of the "improved" cube if each edge is half as long as an edge of the "ordinary" cube?

c. **Writing** Do you agree with the cartoon statement that the "improved" cube is half the size of the "ordinary" cube? Explain.

GUINDON © News America Syndicate, 1985

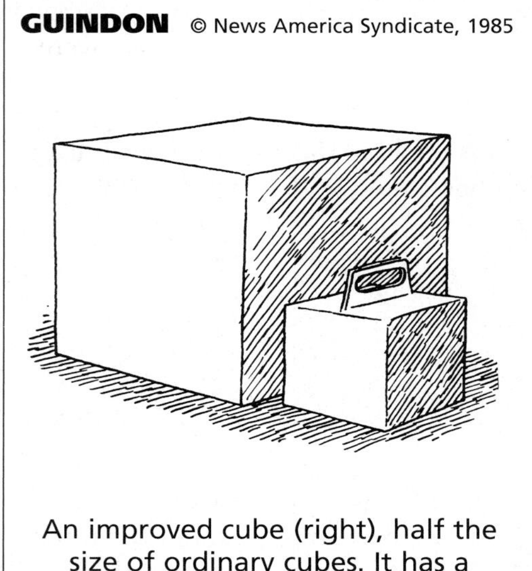

An improved cube (right), half the size of ordinary cubes. It has a convenient carrying handle.

20. **Environmental Engineering** A scientist has suggested that one way to keep indoor air relatively pollution free is to provide two or three pots of flowers such as daisies for every 100 ft^2 of floor space with an 8-ft ceiling. How many pots of daisies would a 35 ft-by-45 ft-by-8 ft classroom need?

21. a. The volume of a cylinder is 600π cm^3. The radius of a base of the cylinder is 5 cm. What is the height of the cylinder?

b. The volume of a cylinder is 135π cm^3. The height of the cylinder is 15 cm. What is the radius of a base of the cylinder?

A cylinder has been cut out of each figure. Find the volume of the remaining figure. Round your answer to the nearest tenth.

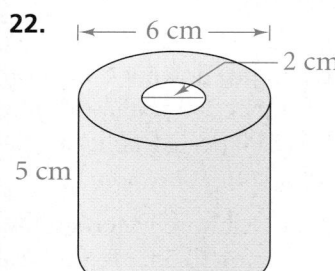

22.

23.

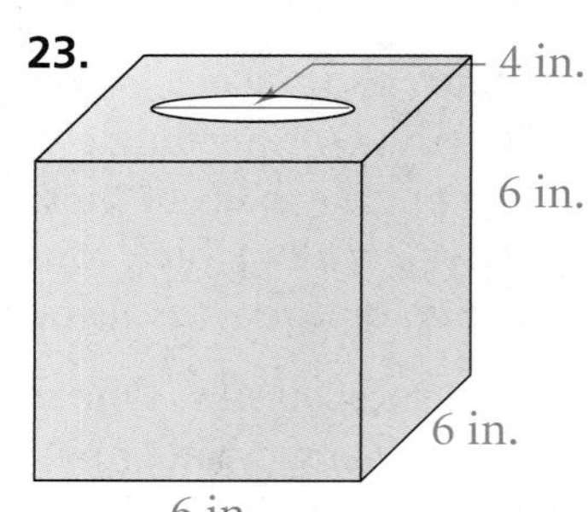

24. **Plumbing** The outside diameter of a pipe is 5 cm. The inside diameter is 4 cm. If the pipe is 4 m long, what is the volume of the metal used for this length of pipe? Round your answer to the nearest whole number.

25. a. **Geometry in 3 Dimensions** What is the volume, in terms of π, of the cylinder formed if the rectangle at the right is rotated 360° about the x-axis?

b. What is the volume, in terms of π, if the rectangle is rotated 360° about the y-axis?

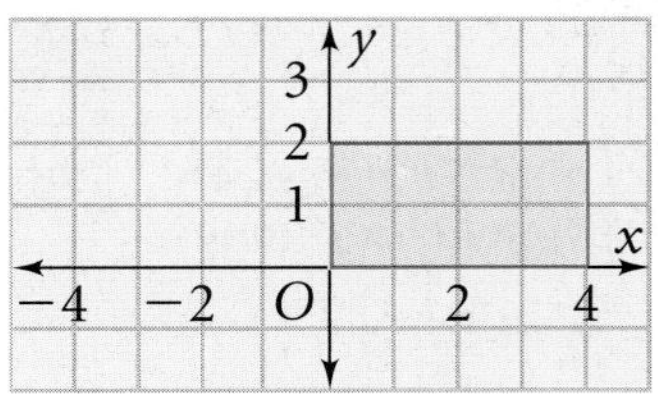

Chapter Project — Find Out by Analyzing

Copy and complete the table below for four *different* rectangular prisms that each have a volume of 216 cm^3.

Length (cm)	Width (cm)	Depth (cm)	Volume (V) (cm^3)	Surface Area (S.A.) (cm^2)	Ratio V : S.A.
6	6	■	216	■	■
■	■	■	216	■	■

1. Which of the prisms uses the container material most efficiently? least efficiently? Explain.
2. Why would a manufacturer be concerned with the ratio of volume to surface area?
3. Why do you think cereal boxes are not shaped to give the greatest ratio of volume to surface area?

Exercises MIXED REVIEW

Draw and label $\triangle ABC$. List the sides from shortest to longest.

26. $m\angle A = 67, m\angle B = 34, m\angle C = 79$

27. $m\angle A = 101, m\angle B = 13, m\angle C = 66$

28. $m\angle A = 98, m\angle B = 73, m\angle C = 9$

29. $m\angle A = 28, m\angle B = 81, m\angle C = 71$

30. **Critical Thinking** The area of a triangle is 24 cm^2. The longest side of the triangle is 13 cm long. The second longest side is 12 cm long. Is the triangle a right triangle? Explain.

Getting Ready for Lesson 6-5

Use the Pythagorean Theorem to find the height h of each space figure.

31.

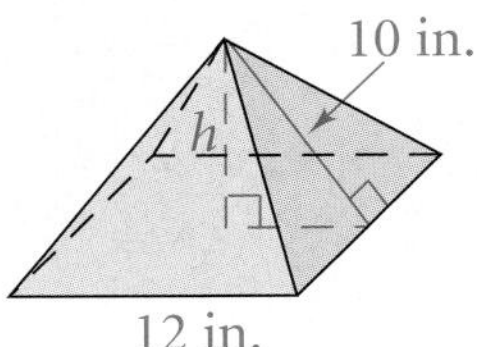

32.

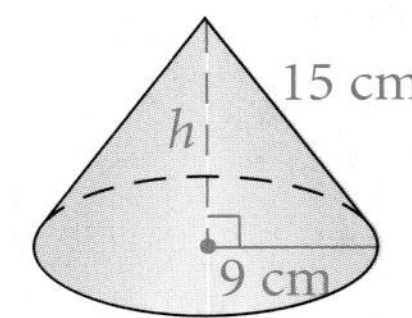

SELF ASSESSMENT — FOR YOUR JOURNAL

Describe some everyday situations in which you would want to know the volumes of prisms.

6-5 Volumes of Pyramids and Cones

What You'll Learn

- Finding volumes of pyramids and cones

...And Why

To solve problems concerning the amount of space in things such as a convention center or a popcorn box

What You'll Need

- cardboard
- ruler
- scissors
- tape
- rice
- calculator

WORK TOGETHER

You know how to find the volume of a prism. Work in a group to explore the volume of a pyramid.

- Draw the nets shown below on cardboard.
- Cut out the nets and tape them together to make a cube and a regular square pyramid. Each model will have one open face.

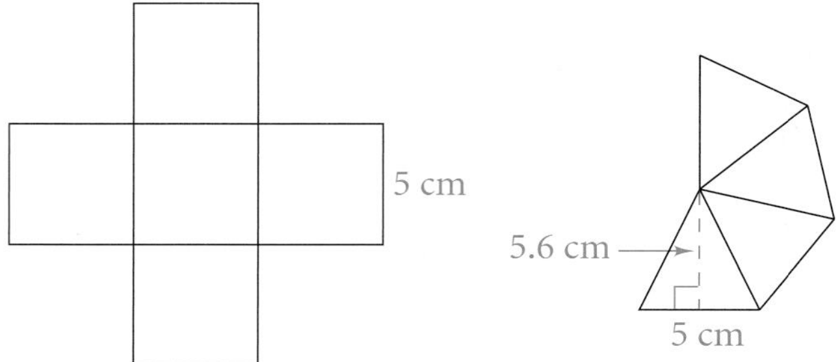

1. Compare the areas of the bases of the cube and the pyramid.
2. Compare the heights of the cube and the pyramid.
3. Fill the pyramid with rice. Then pour the rice from the pyramid into the cube. How many pyramids full of rice does the cube hold?
4. The volume of the pyramid is what fractional part of the volume of the cube?

THINK AND DISCUSS

Volumes of Pyramids

The Work Together demonstrates the following theorem.

Theorem 6-8
Volume of a Pyramid

The volume of a pyramid is one third the product of the area of the base and the height of the pyramid.

$$V = \frac{1}{3}Bh$$

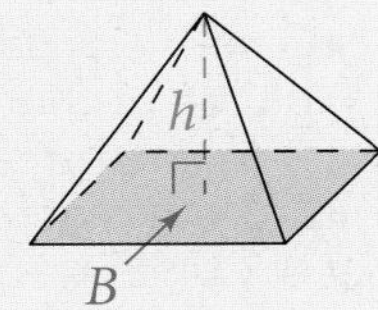

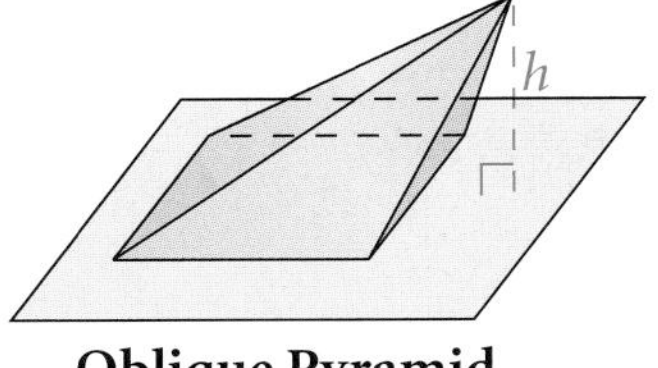

Oblique Pyramid

Because of Cavalieri's Principle, the volume formula is true for all pyramids, including *oblique* pyramids. The **height** h of an oblique pyramid is the length of the perpendicular segment from the vertex to the plane of the base.

Example 1 Relating to the Real World 

Architecture The Pyramid is an arena in Memphis, Tennessee. The area of the base of the Pyramid is about 300,000 ft^2. Its height is 321 ft. What is the volume of the Pyramid?

$V = \frac{1}{3}Bh$ **Use the formula for the volume of a pyramid.**

$= \frac{1}{3}(300,000)(321)$ **Substitute.**

$= 32,100,000$ **Simplify.**

The volume is about 32,100,000 ft^3.

5. **Try This** Find the volume of a regular square pyramid with base edges 12 in. long and height 8 in.

Math A Test Prep

1 A cylinder and a cone have the same radius. The cone is half as tall as the cylinder. How does the volume of the cylinder compare to the volume of the cone?
(1) 6 times greater
(2) 3 times greater
(3) 2 times greater
(4) $\frac{1}{2}$ as great

2 What is the surface area of this regular pyramid?

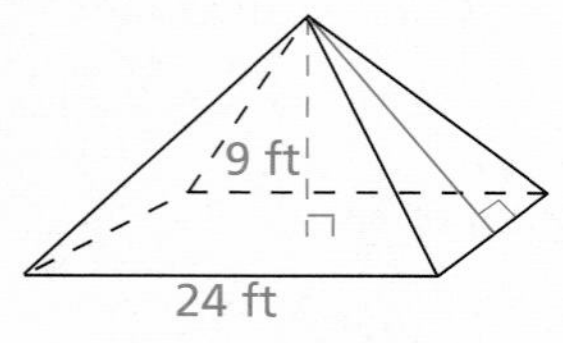

To find the volume of a pyramid you need to know its height.

Example 2

Find the volume of a regular square pyramid with base edges 40 ft long and slant height 25 ft.

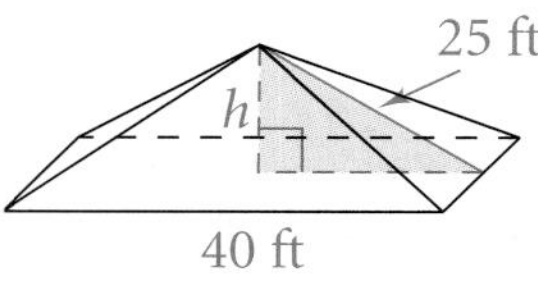

- Find the height of the pyramid.

$25^2 = h^2 + 20^2$	Use the Pythagorean Theorem.
$625 = h^2 + 400$	Simplify.
$h^2 = 225$	Subtract 400 from each side.
$h = 15$	Find the square root of each side.

- Find the volume of the pyramid.

$V = \frac{1}{3}Bh$	Use the formula for volume of a pyramid.
$= \frac{1}{3}(40 \cdot 40)15$	Substitute.
$= 8000$	Simplify.

The volume of the pyramid is 8000 ft^3.

6. **Try This** Find the volume of a regular square pyramid with base edges 24 m long and slant height 13 m.

Volumes of Cones

In the Work Together, you discovered that the volume of a pyramid is one third the volume of a prism with the same base and height. You can also find that the volume of a cone is one third the volume of a cylinder with the same base and height.

Theorem 6-9
Volume of a Cone

The volume of a cone is one third the product of the area of the base and the height.

$$V = \frac{1}{3}Bh, \text{ or } V = \frac{1}{3}\pi r^2 h$$

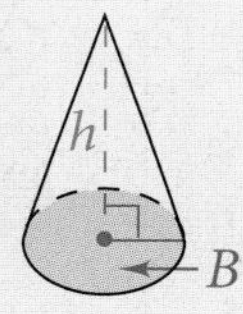

This volume formula applies to all cones, including *oblique* cones.

Example 3

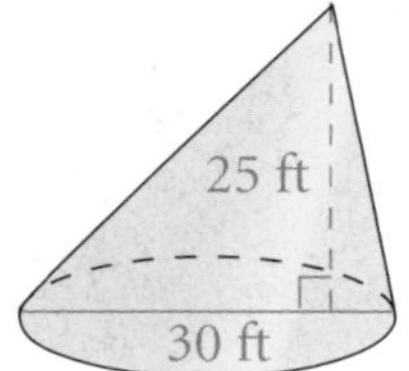

Find the volume of the oblique cone with diameter 30 ft and height 25 ft. Round to the nearest whole number.

$r = \frac{30}{2} = 15$ **The radius is half the diameter.**

$V = \frac{1}{3}\pi r^2 h$ **Use the formula for the volume of a cone.**

$= \frac{1}{3}\pi(15)^2 25$ **Substitute.**

1 ÷ 3 × π × 15 x^2 × 25 = 5890.4862

The volume of the cone is about 5890 ft^3.

7. **Try This** Find the volume of a cone with radius 3 in. and height 8 in. Round to the nearest tenth.

Exercises ON YOUR OWN

Calculator **Find the volume of each figure. When an answer is not a whole number, round to the nearest tenth.**

1. 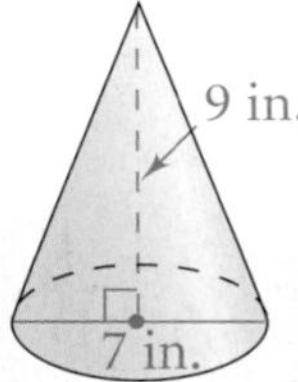

2. 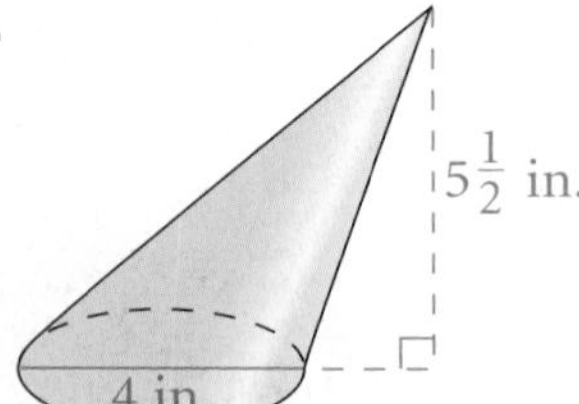

3. 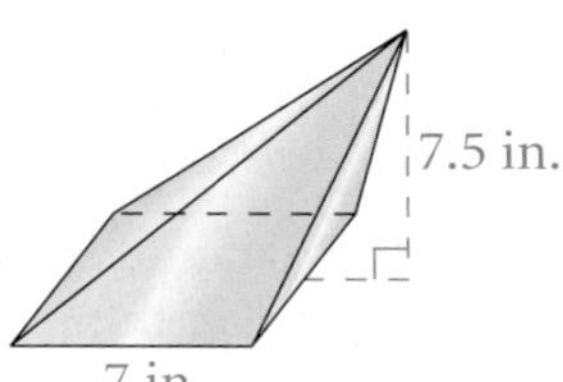

square base

4. 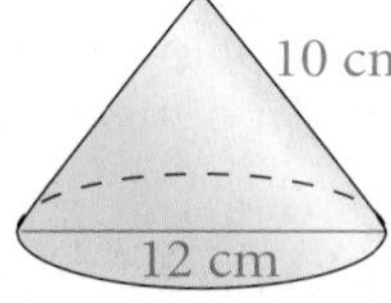

5. a. *Mental Math* A cone with radius 3 ft and height 10 ft has a volume of 30π ft^3. What is its volume when the radius is doubled?
   b. What is the volume when the height of the original cone is doubled?
   c. What is the volume when both the radius and the height of the original cone are doubled?

6. a. The largest tepee in the United States belongs to a member of the Crow (Native Americans of the Great Plains). It is 43 ft high and 42 ft in diameter. Find its volume to the nearest cubic foot.
   b. How does this compare with the volume of your classroom?

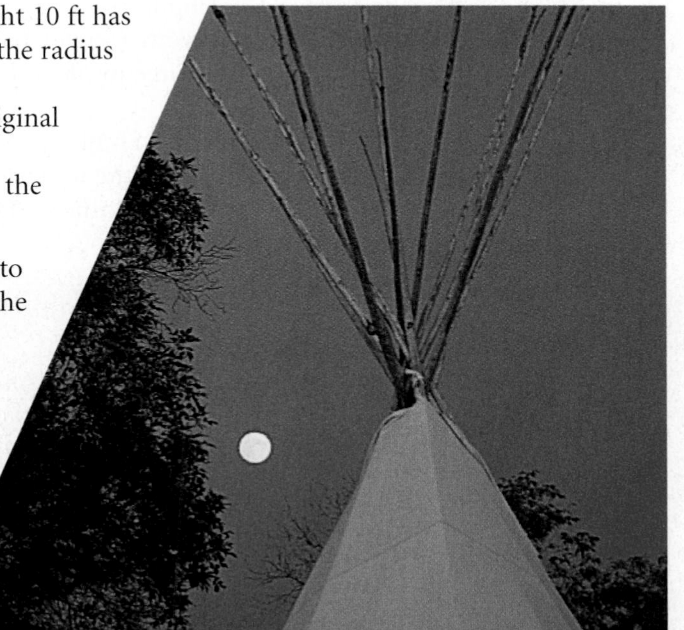

Find the volume of each figure. You may leave answers in terms of π or in simplest radical form.

7. 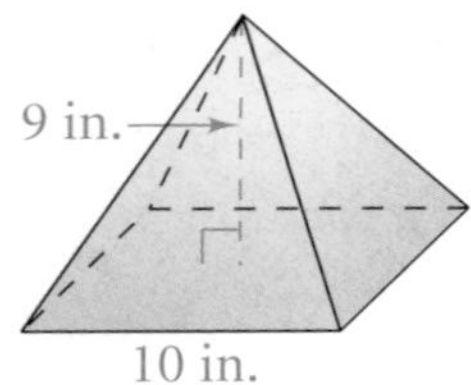

8. 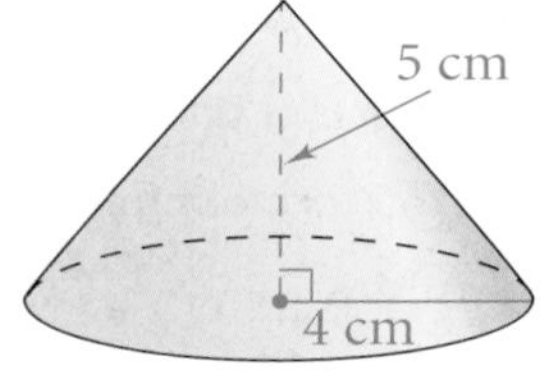

9. 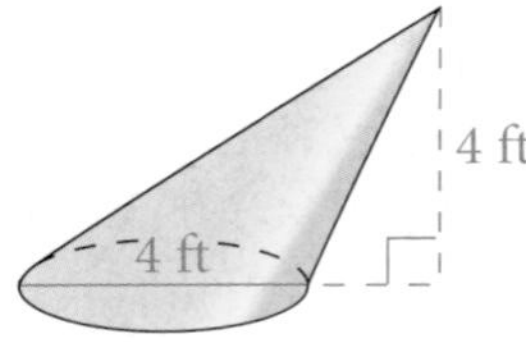

10. 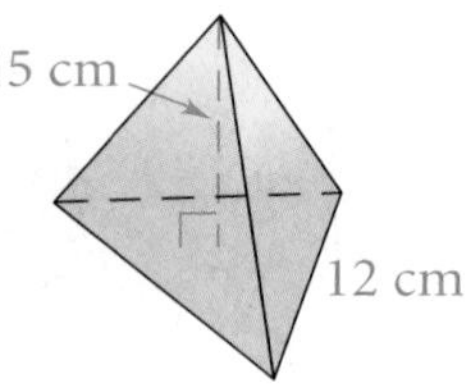

11. **Open-ended** A cone has a volume of 600π in.^{3}. Find two possible sets of dimensions for the height and radius of the cone.

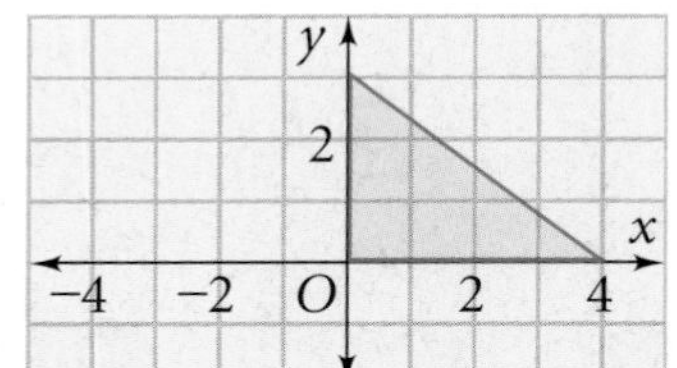

12. a. **Coordinate Geometry** Suppose you rotate the right triangle shown 360° about the x-axis. What is the volume of the resulting cone in terms of π?
    b. Suppose you rotate the triangle 360° about the y-axis. What is the volume in terms of π?

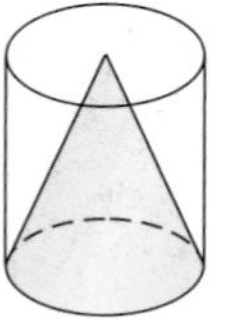
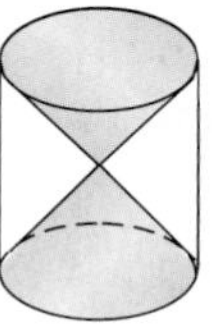

13. The two cylinders pictured at the right are congruent. How does the volume of the larger cone compare to the total volume of the two smaller cones? Explain.

14. The volume of a cone is 36π cm^3. If the radius is 6 cm, what is the height of the cone?

15. The volume of a regular square pyramid is 600 in.^{3}. The height is 8 in. What is the length of each base edge?

16. To the nearest tenth, find the volume of a regular hexagonal pyramid with base edges 12 cm long and height 15 cm.

17. a. **Architecture** The Transamerica Building in San Francisco is a pyramid 800 ft tall with a square base 149 ft on each side. What is its volume to the nearest thousand cubic feet?
    b. If the Transamerica Building had been built as a *prism* with the same square base, how tall to the nearest foot would it have to be to have the same volume as the existing building?

18. *Critical Thinking* A movie theater sells popcorn in cylindrical containers that are 4 in. in diameter and 10 in. high. As a special promotion, the theater plans to sell popcorn in a cone-shaped container for the same price. The diameter of the container will remain the same. The promotional cone will use the same amount of cardboard as the cylindrical container. Do you think this promotional cone is a good value? Why or why not?

19. Which container has the greatest volume?

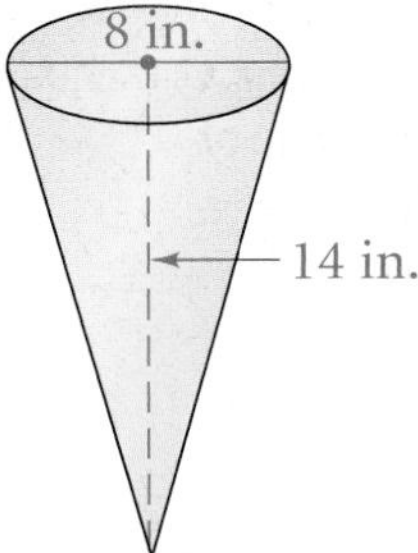

Figure 1

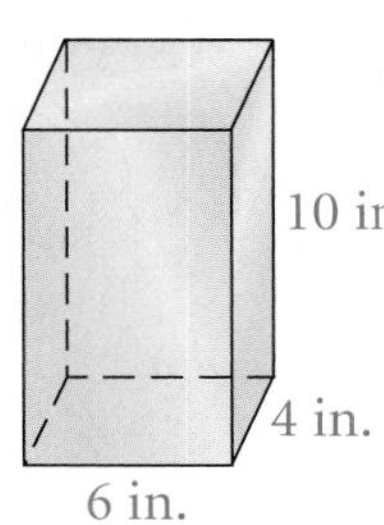

Figure 2

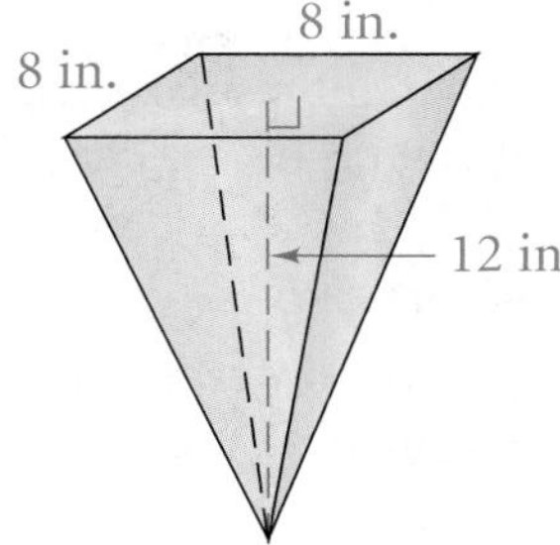

Figure 3

Algebra **Find the value of the variable in each figure. You may leave answers in simplest radical form.**

20.

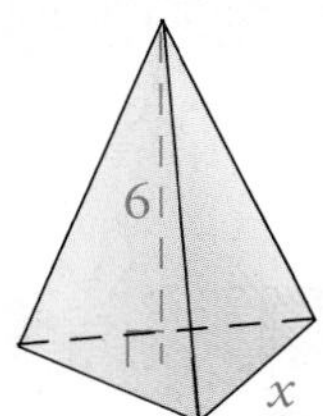

Volume $= 18\sqrt{3}$

21.

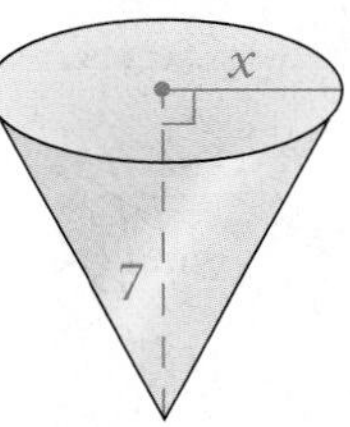

Volume $= 21\pi$

22.

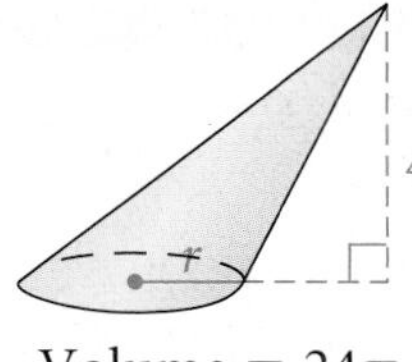

Volume $= 24\pi$

23.

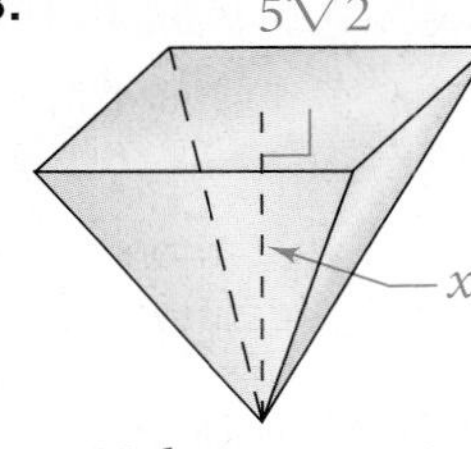

Volume $= 150$

24. *Writing* The figures at the right can be covered by an equal number of straws that are the same length. Describe how Cavalieri's Principle could be adapted to compare the areas of these figures.

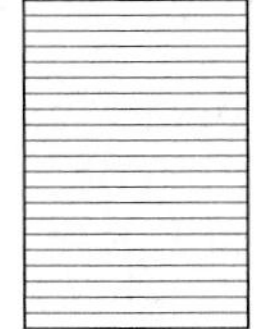

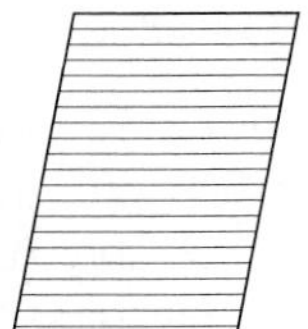

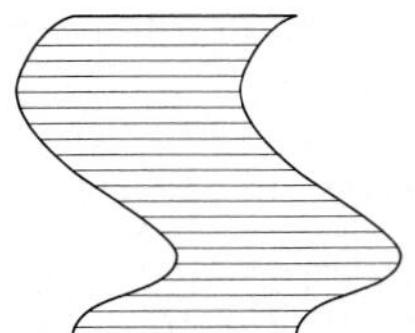

Chapter Project

Find Out by Investigating

Do some container shapes seem to give more product for the same money? Go to a supermarket and identify a variety of container shapes. Do some shapes make you think there's more in them than there actually is? What factors do you think a manufacturer considers in deciding the shape of a container? Write a report about your findings.

Exercises MIXED REVIEW

25. The vertices of quadrilateral $ABCD$ are $A(-4, -1)$, $B(-1, 3)$, $C(7, -3)$, and $D(4, -7)$.

a. Use the Distance Formula to find the length of each side.

b. Find the slope of each side.

c. Determine the most accurate name for quadrilateral $ABCD$.

26. *Movies* The largest permanent movie screen in the world is in Jakarta, Indonesia. It is 96 ft by 70.5 ft. What is its area?

SELF ASSESSMENT — FOR YOUR JOURNAL

Explain why finding the volume of a cylinder is like finding the volume of a prism. Then explain why finding the volume of a cone is like finding the volume of a pyramid.

Getting Ready for Lesson 6-6

Calculator **Find the area and circumference of a circle with the given radius. Round answers to the nearest tenth.**

27. 6 in. **28.** 5 cm **29.** 2.5 ft **30.** 1.2 m

Geometry at Work

Packaging Engineer

Each year, more than one trillion dollars in manufactured goods are packaged in some kind of a container. To create each new box, bag, or carton, packaging engineers must balance such factors as safety, environmental impact, and attractiveness against cost of production.

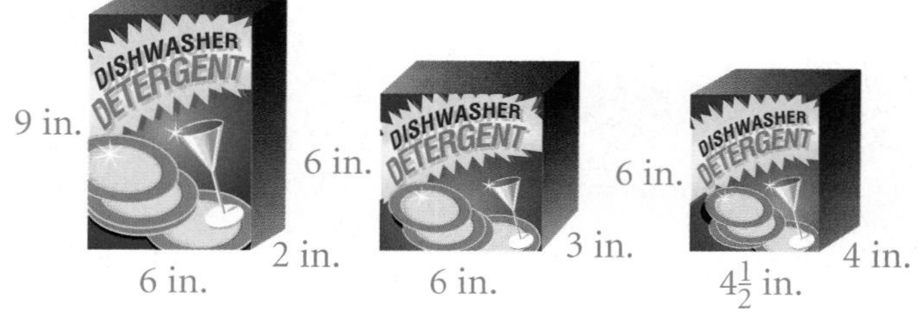

Consider the three boxes of dishwasher detergent. All three boxes have volumes of 108 in.^{3}, the volume of a standard box of automatic dishwasher detergent. The boxes have different shapes, however, and different surface areas. The box on the left has the greatest surface area and therefore costs the most to produce. Nevertheless, despite the higher cost, the box on the left has become standard. There are many reasons why a company might choose more expensive packaging. In this case, the least expensive package on the right is too difficult for a consumer to pick up and pour. To offset the extra cost, packaging engineers try to choose a package design that will attract enough additional buyers to outweigh the higher cost of production.

Mini Project: Choose a product that you enjoy using. Design and make a new package for the product. Calculate the surface area and volume of your package and describe advantages it has over the current package.

Connections Manufacturing . . . and more

6-6 Surface Areas and Volumes of Spheres

What You'll Learn

- Calculating the surface areas and volumes of spheres

...And Why

To solve real-world problems such as finding the surface area of a soccer ball and the volume of a scoop of ice cream

What You'll Need

- ruler
- scissors
- tacks
- foam balls (cut in half)
- string
- calculator

WORK TOGETHER

How do you compute the surface area of Earth or the amount of leather covering a baseball? Work in a group to explore the surface area of a sphere.

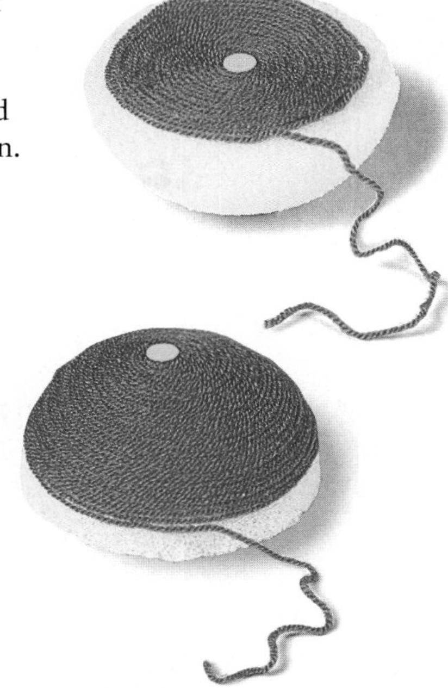

- The surface of half a foam ball consists of two parts—a plane circular region and a curved surface. Place a tack in the center of the circular region. Wind string around the tack covering the entire circular region.
- Once the circular region is covered, cut off any excess string. Measure the length x of string that covered the circular region.
- Place a tack in the center of the curved surface. Wind another string around the tack covering the entire curved surface.
- Once the curved surface is covered, cut off any excess string. Measure the length y of the string that covered the curved surface.

1. **a.** How do x and y compare?
   b. Express y as a multiple of x.
2. **a.** How much string would you need to cover the entire surface of an uncut foam ball? Express your answer as a multiple of y.
   b. Express your answer to part (a) as a multiple of x.
3. A string of length x covers an area of πr^2 where r is the radius of the foam ball. Substitute πr^2 for x in the expression you wrote for Question 2(b) to find a formula for the surface area of a sphere.

THINK AND DISCUSS

Finding the Surface Area of a Sphere

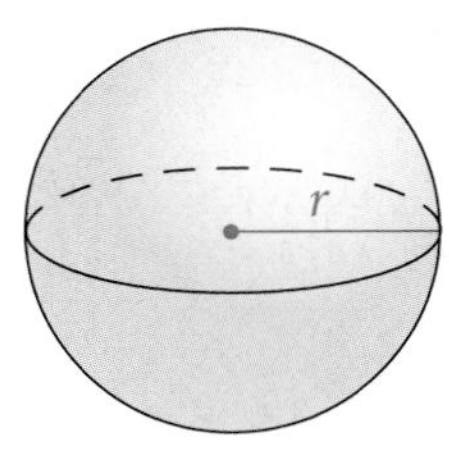

A **sphere** is the set of all points in space equidistant from a given point called the **center.**

4. How would you define a *radius* of a sphere?
5. How would you define a *diameter* of a sphere?

Your discovery in the Work Together leads to the following theorem.

Theorem 6-10
Surface Area of a Sphere

The surface area of a sphere is four times the product of π and the square of the radius of the sphere.

$$\text{S.A.} = 4\pi r^2$$

Example 1 *Relating to the Real World* 

Manufacturing Manufacturers make soccer balls with a radius of 11 cm by sewing together 20 regular hexagons and 12 regular pentagons. Templates for guiding the stitching are shown at the left. Approximate the surface area of a soccer ball to the nearest square centimeter using the following two methods.

4.5 cm
3.1 cm
4.5 cm

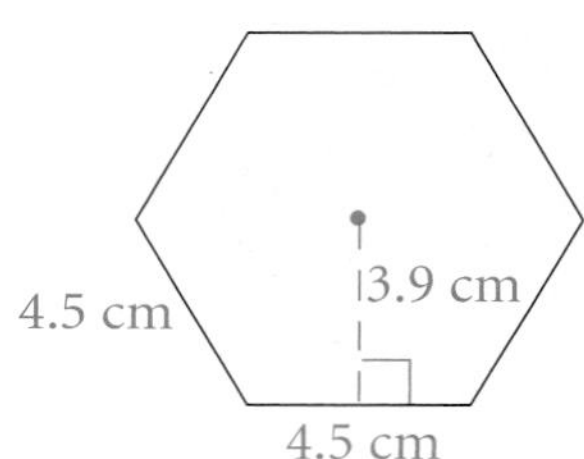

Method 1:
Find the sum of the areas of the pentagons and hexagons.

regular pentagon	regular hexagon
$A = \frac{1}{2}ap$	$A = \frac{1}{2}ap$
$= \frac{1}{2}(3.1)(5 \cdot 4.5)$	$= \frac{1}{2}(3.9)(6 \cdot 4.5)$
$= 34.875$	$= 52.65$

Area of the 12 regular pentagons $= (12)(34.875) = 418.5$

Area of the 20 regular hexagons $= (20)(52.65) = 1053$

The sum of the areas of the pentagons and the hexagons is about 1472 cm^2.

Method 2:
Use the formula for the surface area of a sphere.

$\text{S.A.} = 4\pi r^2$ **Use the formula for surface area.**
$= 4 \cdot \pi \cdot 11^2$ **Substitute.**

The surface area of the soccer ball is about 1521 cm^2.

6. Compare the answers for the two methods. Explain why they differ.

Finding the Volume of a Sphere

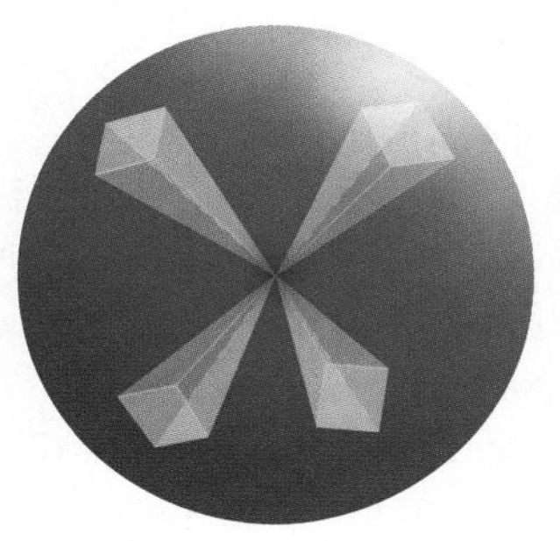

You can fill a sphere with a large number n of small pyramids. The vertex of each pyramid is the center of the sphere. The height of each pyramid is approximately the radius r of the sphere. The sum of the areas of all the bases approximates the surface area of the sphere. You can use this model to derive a formula for the volume of a sphere.

Volume of each pyramid $= \frac{1}{3}Bh$

Sum of the volumes of n pyramids $= n \cdot \frac{1}{3}Br$ **Substitute r for h.**

$= \frac{1}{3} \cdot (nB) \cdot r$

$= \frac{1}{3} \cdot (4\pi r^2) \cdot r$ **Replace nB with the surface area of a sphere.**

$= \frac{4}{3}\pi r^3$

The volume of a sphere is $\frac{4}{3}\pi r^3$.

Theorem 6-11
Volume of a Sphere

The volume of a sphere is four thirds the product of π and the cube of the radius of the sphere.

$$V = \frac{4}{3}\pi r^3$$

Example 2

The volume of a sphere is 4849.05 m^3. What is the surface area of the sphere? Round your answer to the nearest tenth.

- Find the radius r.

$V = \frac{4}{3}\pi r^3$ **Use the formula for the volume of a sphere.**

$4849.05 = \frac{4}{3}\pi r^3$ **Substitute.**

$4849.05(\frac{3}{4\pi}) = r^3$ **Multiply both sides by $\frac{3}{4\pi}$.**

$\sqrt[3]{4849.05(\frac{3}{4\pi})} = r$ **Find the cube root of each side.**

4849.05 [×] 3 [÷] 4 [÷] [π] [=] [$\sqrt[x]{y}$] 3 [=] 10.500001

The radius of the sphere is about 10.5 m.

- Find the surface area of the sphere.

S.A. $= 4\pi r^2$ **Use the formula for the surface area of a sphere.**

$= 4\pi(10.5)^2$ **Substitute.**

4 [×] [π] [×] 10.5 [x^2] [=] 1385.4424

The surface area of the sphere is about 1385.4 m^2.

QUICK REVIEW

The *cube root* of *x* is the number that when *cubed* is *x*.

7. **Try This** The volume of a sphere is 20,579 in.^{3}. What is the radius of the sphere to the nearest whole number?

8. **Try This** The radius of a sphere is 15 m. What is the volume to the nearest hundred?

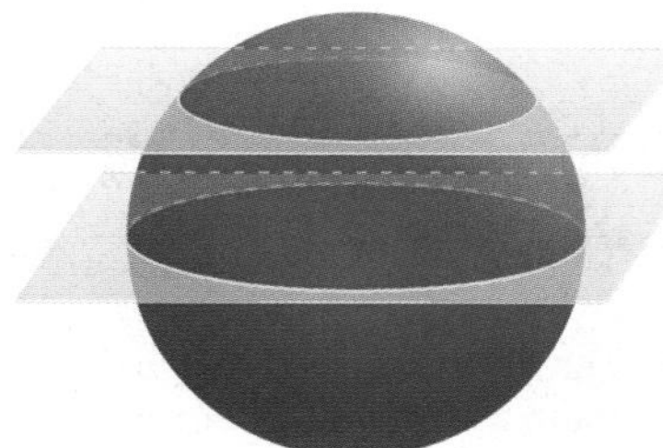

When a plane and a sphere intersect in more than one point, the intersection is a circle. If the center of the circle is also the center of the sphere, the circle is called a **great circle** of the sphere. The circumference of a great circle is the **circumference of the sphere.** A great circle divides a sphere into two **hemispheres.**

9. **Geography** What is the name of the best-known great circle on Earth?

10. **Geography** Describe the Northern Hemisphere of Earth.

Exercises ON YOUR OWN

Calculator **Find the surface area of each ball to the nearest tenth.**

1. 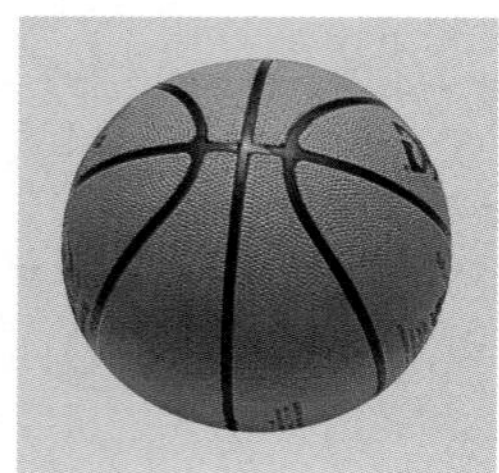

$d = 23.9$ cm

2. 

$d = 68$ mm

3. 

$d = 2\frac{3}{4}$ in.

4. 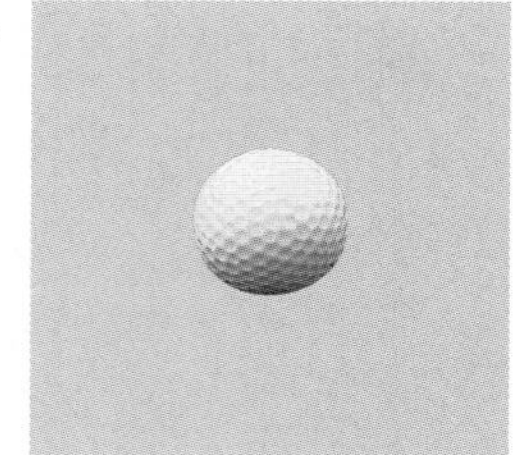

$d = 1.68$ in.

5. **Coordinate Geometry** Find the surface area and volume of the sphere formed by rotating the semicircle at the right 360° about the x-axis. Leave your answers in terms of π.

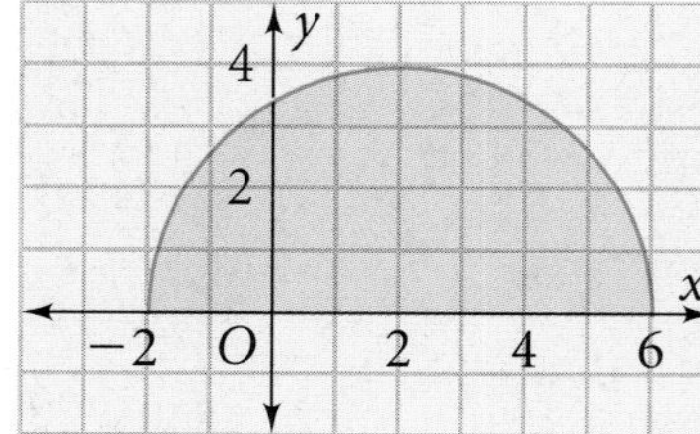

6. A balloon has a 14-in. diameter when it is fully inflated. Half the air is let out of the balloon. Assuming the balloon is a sphere, what is the new diameter? Round your answer to the nearest inch.

7. **Meteorology** On July 16, 1882, a massive thunderstorm over Dubuque, Iowa, produced huge hailstones. The diameter of some of the hailstones was 17 in. Ice weighs about 0.033 lb/in.^{3}. What was the approximate weight of these hailstones to the nearest pound?

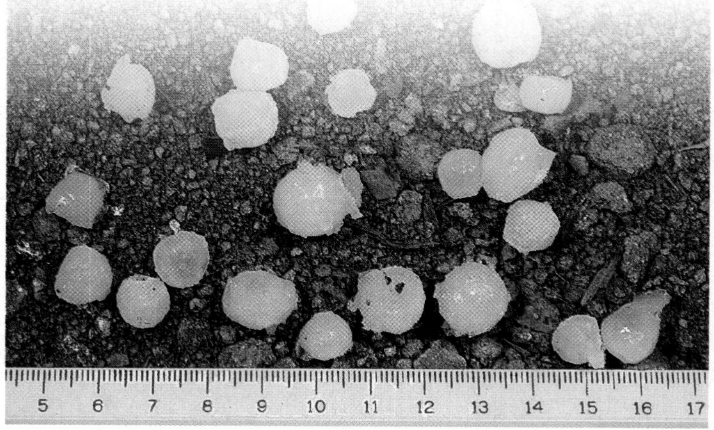

Find the volume of each sphere. Leave your answers in terms of π.

8. 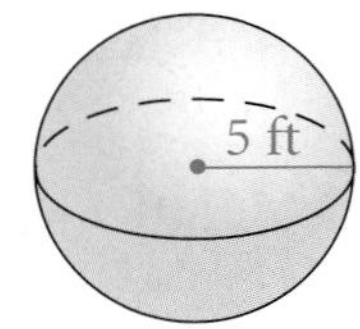

9. 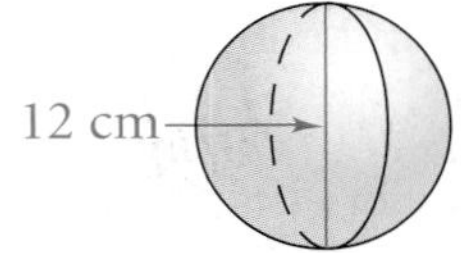

10. 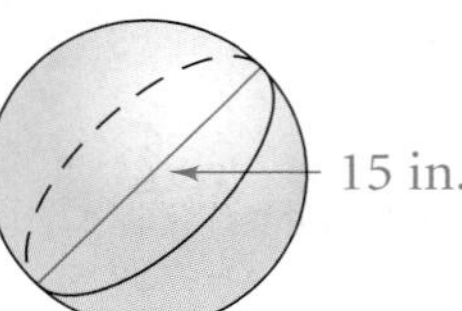

11. 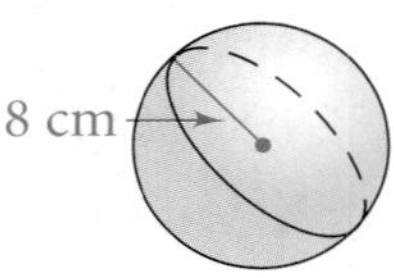

12. **Sports** The circumference of a bowling ball is about 27 in. Find its volume to the nearest tenth.

13. If the sphere of ice cream shown melts, is the cone large enough to hold the melted ice cream? Explain.

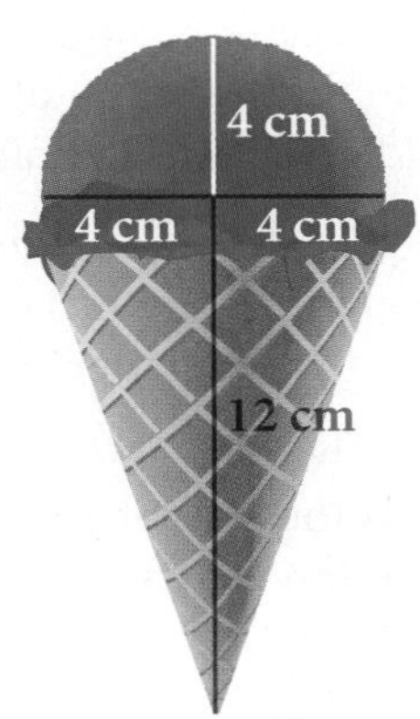

14. **Geometry in 3 Dimensions** The center of a sphere has coordinates $(0, 0, 0)$. The radius of the sphere is 5.

a. Name the coordinates of six points on the sphere.

b. Tell whether each of the following points is inside, outside, or on the sphere. (*Hint:* Use the formula from page 824.)
$A(0, -3, 4)$, $B(1, -1, -1)$, $C(4, -6, -10)$

Believe It Or Not

J.C. Payne, a Texas farmer, is the world champion string collector. The ball of string he wound over a three-year period has a circumference of 41.5 ft. It weighed 13,000 lb.

Listed in the Guinness Book of Records, the ball of string is now on display in a museum devoted to oddities. It took almost a dozen men with forklift trucks to load the ball onto a truck to move it to the museum.

15. **a.** What is the volume of the ball of string to the nearest cubic foot?

b. What is the weight of the string per cubic foot?

c. If the diameter of the string is 0.1 in., what is the approximate length of the string to the nearest mile? (*Hint:* Think of the unwound string as a long cylinder.)

CALCULATOR HINT

When answers will be used in later calculations, keep or store them in unrounded form so that rounding errors will not be introduced into the final answer.

16. The radius of Earth is approximately 3960 mi. The area of Australia is about 2,940,000 mi^2.

a. Find the surface area of the Southern Hemisphere.

b. **Probability** If a meteorite falls randomly in the Southern Hemisphere, what is the probability that it will fall in Australia?

17. The sphere just fits in a cube with edges 6 in. long.
   a. What is the radius of the sphere?
   b. What is the volume of the space between the sphere and cube to the nearest tenth?

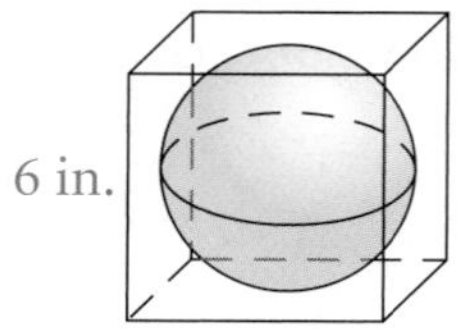

18. **Open-ended** Give the dimensions of a cylinder and a sphere that have the same volume.

19. The sphere just fits in the cylinder. Archimedes (about 287–212 B.C.) asked to have this figure engraved on his tombstone because he was the first to find the ratio of the volume of the sphere to the volume of the cylinder. What is the ratio that Archimedes discovered?

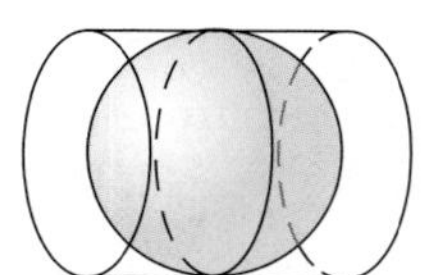

20. Which is greater, the total volume of three balls that each have diameter of 3 in. or the volume of one ball that has a diameter of 8 in.? Explain your answer.

21. A cube with edges 6 in. long just fits in the sphere. The diagonal of the cube is the diameter of the sphere.
   a. Find the length of the diagonal of the cube and the radius of the sphere. Leave your answers in simplest radical form.
   b. What is the volume of the space between the sphere and the cube to the nearest tenth?

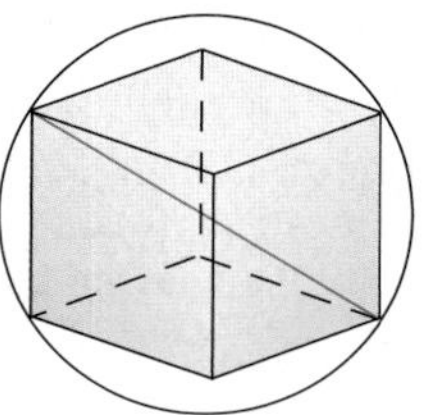

22. **Estimation** Use $\pi \approx 3$ to estimate the surface area and volume of a sphere with radius 30 cm.

23. **Standardized Test Prep** The cone and sphere just fit in cubes that are the same size. What is the ratio of the volume of the cone to the volume of the sphere?

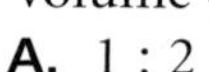

A. 1 : 2   B. 1 : 3   C. 1 : 4
D. 2 : 3   E. cannot be determined

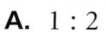

24. a. The number of square meters of surface area of a sphere equals the number of cubic meters of volume. What is the radius of the sphere?

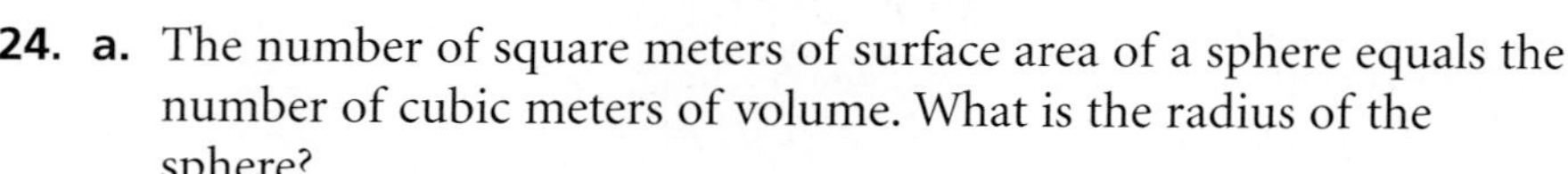

   b. **Algebra** The ratio of the surface area of a sphere in square meters to its volume in cubic meters is 1 : 5. What is the radius of the sphere?

25. **Science** The density of steel is about 0.28 lb/in.^{3}. Could you lift a steel ball with radius 4 in.? with radius 6 in.? Explain.

26. A plane that intersects a sphere is 8 cm from the center of the sphere. The radius of the sphere is 17 cm. What is the area of the cross section to the nearest whole number?

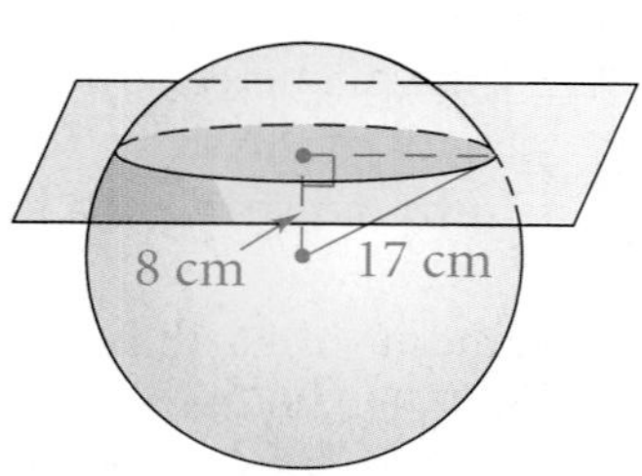

27. a. **Algebra** If a cube and a sphere have the same volume, which has the greater surface area? Explain.

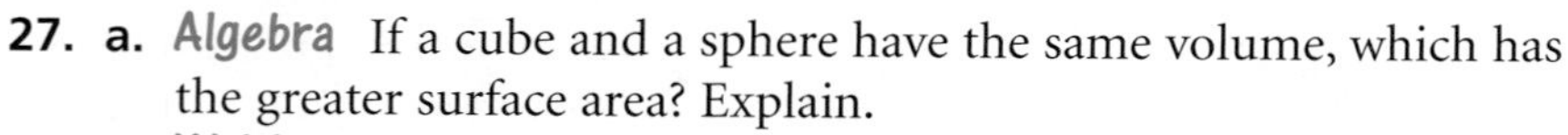

   b. **Writing** Explain why spheres are rarely used for packaging.

Exercises MIXED REVIEW

Make a sketch for each description.

28. a pair of supplementary angles

29. an obtuse triangle and one midsegment

30. a polygon with three lines of symmetry

31. a line segment and its perpendicular bisector

32. *Open-ended* Binary numbers are written with only the digits 0 and 1. These digits can be written so they have both vertical and horizontal lines of symmetry. Using such digits, write two binary numbers that do not have the same symmetries and describe the differences.

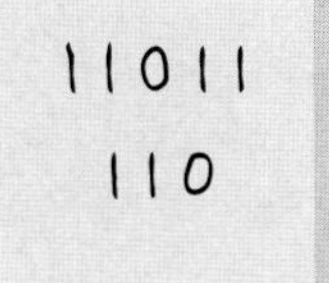

Getting Ready for Lesson 6-7

Calculator **Find the total volume of each pair of figures to the nearest tenth.**

33.

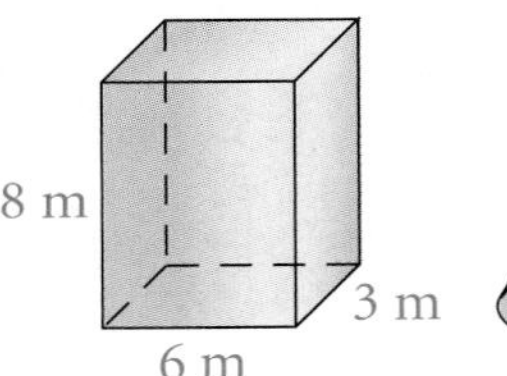

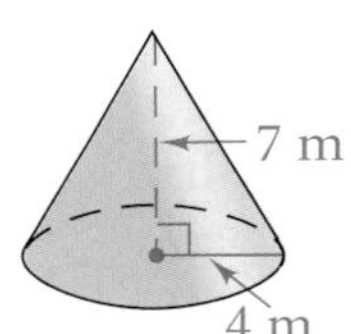

34.

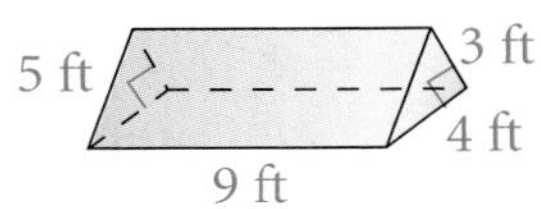

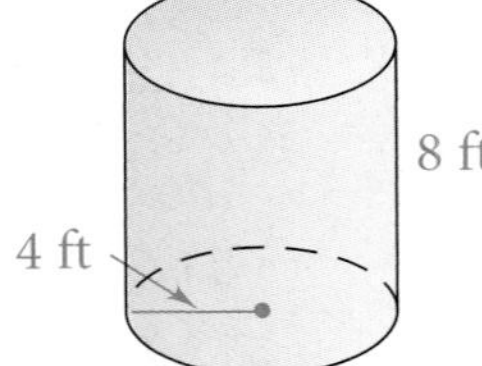

Exercises CHECKPOINT

Calculator **Find the surface area and the volume of each figure to the nearest tenth.**

1.

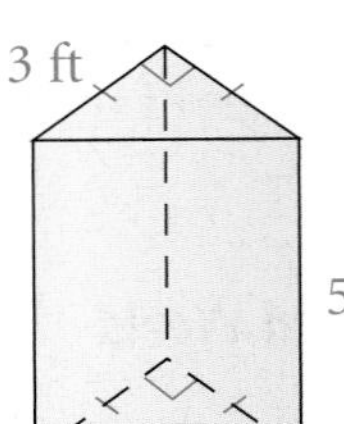

2.

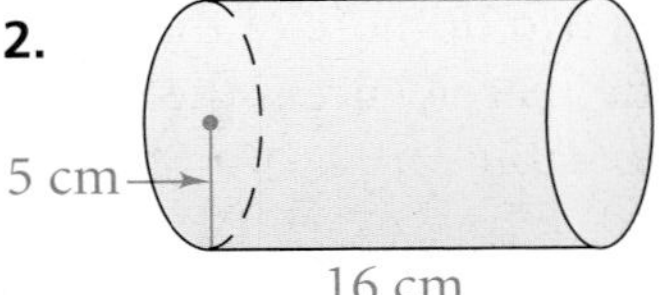

3.

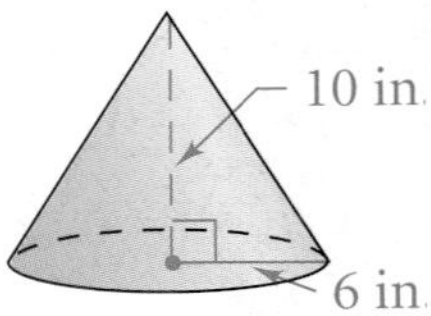

4.

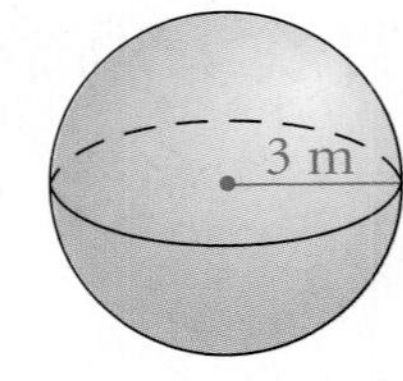

5. *Standardized Test Prep* What is the surface area of a sphere with radius 5 in.?

A. 5π in.^{2} **B.** 20π in.^{2} **C.** 100π in.^{2} **D.** 125π in.^{2} **E.** $166\frac{2}{3}\pi$ in.^{2}

6. *Critical Thinking* Tennis balls are packaged as shown at the right. Which is greater, the volume of a tennis ball or the space around the three balls? Explain.

What You'll Learn

- Recognizing composite space figures, which combine two or more simple figures

...And Why

To find the volumes and surface areas of composite space figures such as silos and backpacks

What You'll Need

- unit cubes

6-7 Composite Space Figures

WORK TOGETHER

1. Work in a group to build the prisms shown in Figures 1 and 2 using unit cubes. Find the surface area and volume of each prism.
2. What is the sum of the surface areas of the two prisms? What is the sum of their volumes?
3. Place one prism on top of the other as in Figure 3. Find the surface area and volume of the resulting space figure.
4. Compare your answers to Questions 2 and 3. How does the relationship of the volumes differ from that of the surface areas?

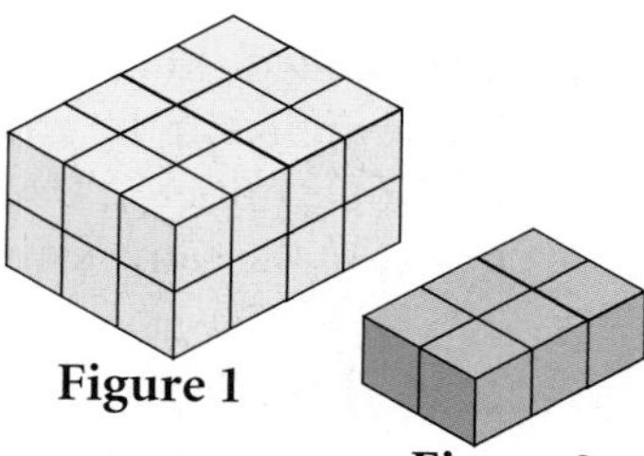

Figure 1

Figure 2

Figure 3

THINK AND DISCUSS

You can use what you know about the volumes of three-dimensional figures such as prisms, pyramids, cones, cylinders, and spheres to find the volume of a composite space figure. A **composite space figure** combines two or more of these figures. The volume of a composite space figure is the sum of the volumes of the figures that are combined.

Example 1 Relating to the Real World

Agriculture Find the volume of the grain silo at the left.

The silo combines a cylinder and a hemisphere.

- Volume of the cylinder $= \pi r^2 h = \pi(10)^2(40) = 4000\pi$
- Volume of the hemisphere $= \frac{1}{2}(\frac{4}{3}\pi r^3) = \frac{2}{3}\pi(10)^3 = \frac{2000\pi}{3}$
- Volume of the composite figure $= 4000\pi + \frac{2000\pi}{3}$

4000 [×] [π] [+] 2000 [×] [π] [÷] 3 [=] 14660.766

The volume of the silo is about 14,700 ft^3.

5. **Try This** Find the volume of each composite space figure to the nearest whole number.

a.

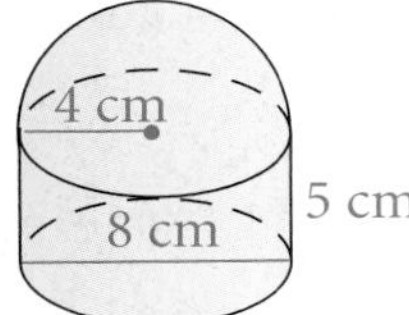

b.

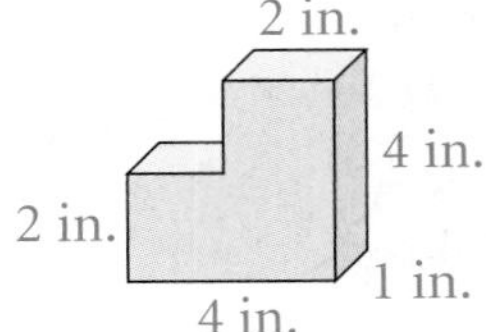

You can use geometric figures to approximate the shape of a real-world object. Then you can estimate the volume and surface area of the object.

Example 2 Relating to the Real World 

Estimation What space figures can you use to approximate the shape of the backpack? Use these space figures to estimate the volume of the backpack.

- You can use a prism and half of a cylinder to approximate the shape of the backpack.

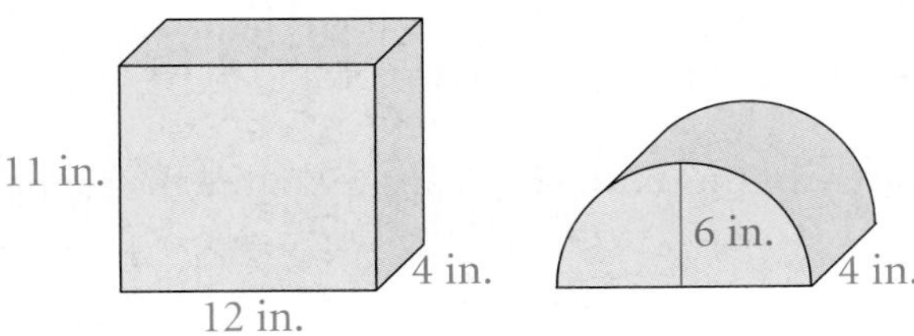

- Volume of the prism $= Bh = (12 \cdot 4)11 = 528$
- Volume of the half cylinder $= \frac{1}{2}(\pi r^2 h) = \frac{1}{2}\pi(6)^2(4)$
  $= \frac{1}{2}\pi(36)(4) \approx 226$
- Sum of the two volumes $= 528 + 226 = 754$

The approximate volume of the backpack is 754 in.^{3}.

6. What is the approximate surface area of this backpack?
7. **Try This** Describe the space figures that you can use to approximate the shape of each object.

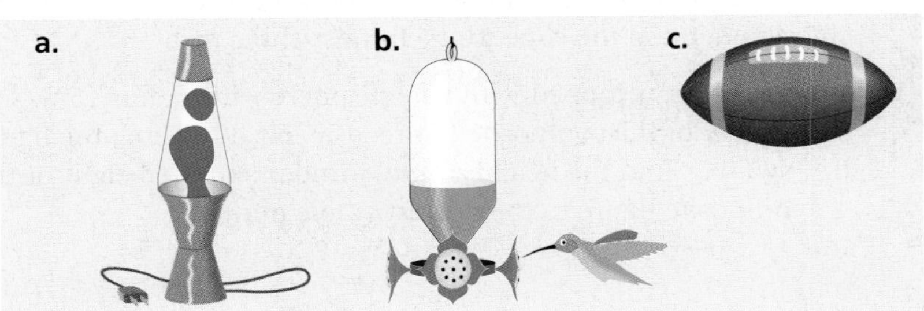

Exercises ON YOUR OWN

Find the volume of each composite space figure. You may leave answers in terms of π.

1. 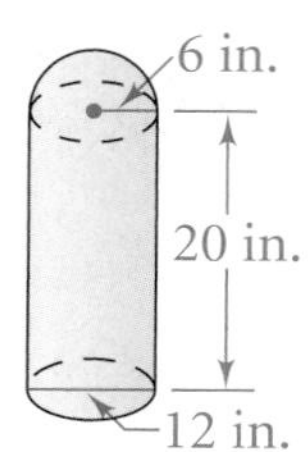

2. 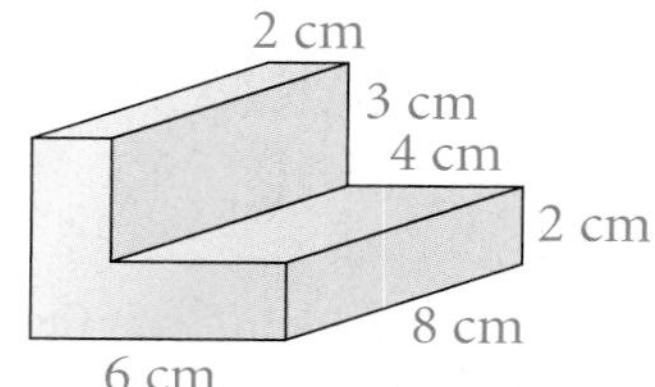

3. 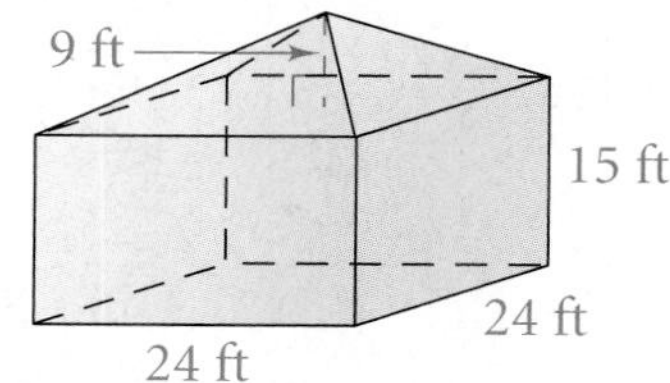

4. *Open-ended* Draw a composite three-dimensional figure, label its dimensions, and find either its surface area or its volume.

5. *Manufacturing* Find the volume of the lunch box shown at the right to the nearest cubic inch.

3 in.
6 in.
6 in.
10 in.

6. *Writing* Describe your home, school, or some other building that is a composite space figure. Explain why it is a composite space figure.

7. a. *Coordinate Geometry* Draw a sketch of the composite space figure formed by rotating this triangle 360° about the x-axis.

b. Find the volume of the figure in terms of π.

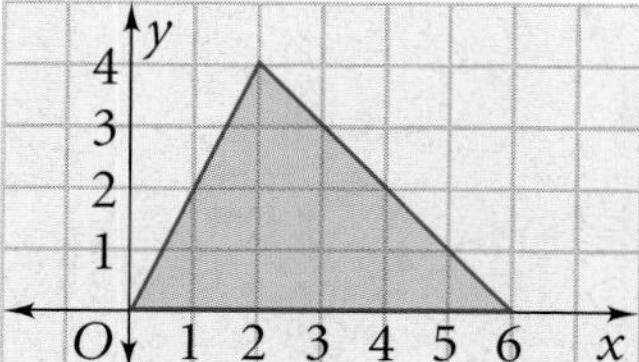

Describe space figures that you can use to approximate the shape of each object.

8. 

9. 

10. 

11. *Writing* Describe how you would find the volume of an octahedron if you know the length of an edge. (See the picture on page 867.)

12. In the diagram at the right, what is the volume of the space between the cylinder and the cone to the nearest cubic inch?

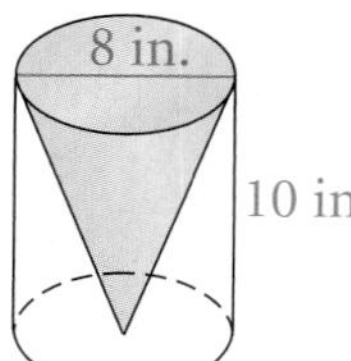

13. a. A cylinder is topped with a hemisphere with radius 15 ft. The total volume of the composite figure is 6525π ft^3. Sketch the figure.

b. *Algebra* Find the height of the cylinder and the height of the composite figure to the nearest whole number.

14. ***Coordinate Geometry*** Find the surface area of the figure formed by rotating the figure at the right 360° about the y-axis. Leave your answer in terms of π.

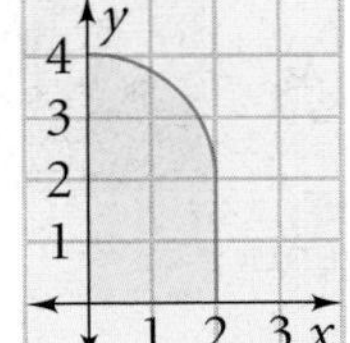

15. ***Carpentry*** Builders use a plumb bob to establish a vertical line. To the nearest cubic centimeter, find the volume of the plumb bob shown at the right. It combines a hexagonal prism with a pyramid.

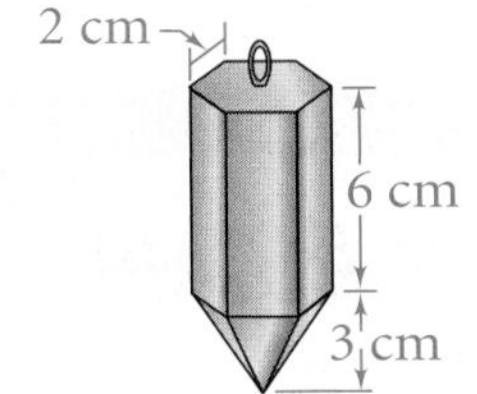

Engineering **Steelworkers use I-beams like the one shown to build bridges and overpasses.**

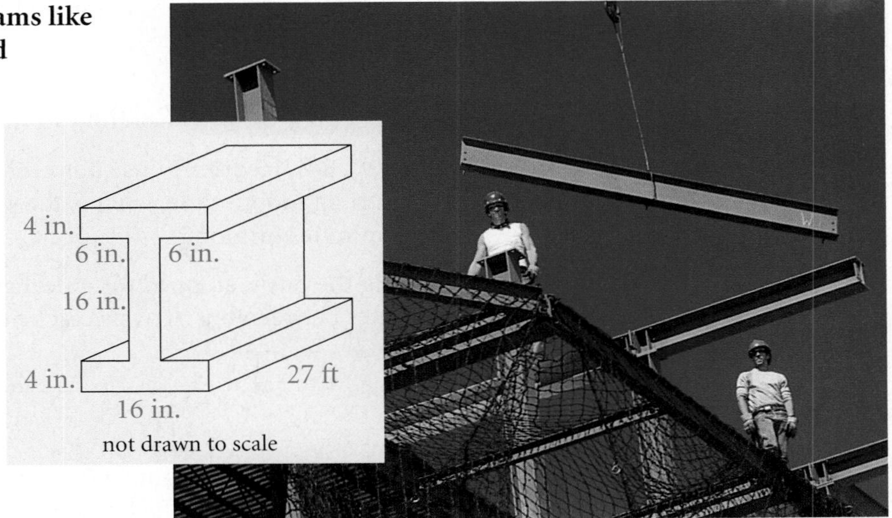

16. To the nearest cubic foot, find the volume of steel needed to make the beam.

17. a. To the nearest square foot, what is the surface area of the beam?

b. One gallon of paint covers about 450 square feet. How many 1-gallon cans of paint do you need to paint the beam?

Exercises MIXED REVIEW

Write an indirect proof for each statement.

18. If a triangle is isosceles, then a base angle is not a right angle.

19. In $\triangle MNP$, if $MP < MN$, then $\angle P \not\cong \angle N$.

20. ***Coordinate Geometry*** Find the circumference of a circle if the endpoints of a diameter are (3, 7) and (3, −1). Leave your answer in terms of π.

SELF ASSESSMENT

FOR YOUR JOURNAL

Describe an object in your classroom that is a composite space figure. Explain how you can approximate its volume.

Getting Ready for Lesson 6-8

You roll a number cube. Find each probability.

21. $P(4)$

22. P(odd number)

23. P(prime number)

24. P(2 or 5)

What You'll Learn

- Using geometric models to find the probability of events

...And Why

To solve probability problems about games, waiting times, and other random events

6-8 Geometric Probability

THINK AND DISCUSS

Using a Segment Model

Mathematicians use models to represent the real world. **Geometric probability** uses geometric figures to represent occurrences of events. Then the occurrences can be compared by comparing measurements of the figures.

QUICK REVIEW

The probability of an event is the ratio of the number of favorable outcomes to the number of possible outcomes.

$P(\text{event}) = \frac{\text{favorable outcomes}}{\text{possible outcomes}}$

Example 1 Relating to the Real World 

Commuting Mr. Hedrick's bus runs every 25 minutes. If he arrives at his bus stop at a random time, what is the probability that he will have to wait 10 minutes or more?

Assuming the bus is stopped for a negligible length of time, the 25 minutes between bus arrivals can be represented by $\overline{AB}$.

A ———— B
0 5 10 15 20 25

If Mr. Hedrick arrives 5 minutes after a bus has left (represented by point C on the segment below), he has to wait 20 minutes for a bus to arrive at time B. If he arrives 20 minutes after a bus has left (represented by point D), he has to wait only 5 minutes. If he arrives at any time represented by a point on $\overline{AR}$, he has to wait 10 minutes or more.

A C R D B
0 5 10 15 20 25

$$P(\text{waiting 10 min or more}) = \frac{\text{length of } \overline{AR}}{\text{length of } \overline{AB}} = \frac{15}{25} = \frac{3}{5}$$

The probability that Mr. Hedrick waits 10 minutes or more is $\frac{3}{5}$, or 60%.

1. **Try This** What is the probability that Mr. Hedrick has to wait 20 minutes or more?
2. **Critical Thinking** Suppose a bus arrives at Mr. Hedrick's bus stop every 25 minutes and waits 5 minutes before leaving. Draw a diagram and find the probability that Mr. Hedrick has to wait 10 minutes or more to get on the bus.

Using an Area Model

For some probability situations, you can use an area model.

Example 2 **Relating to the Real World** 

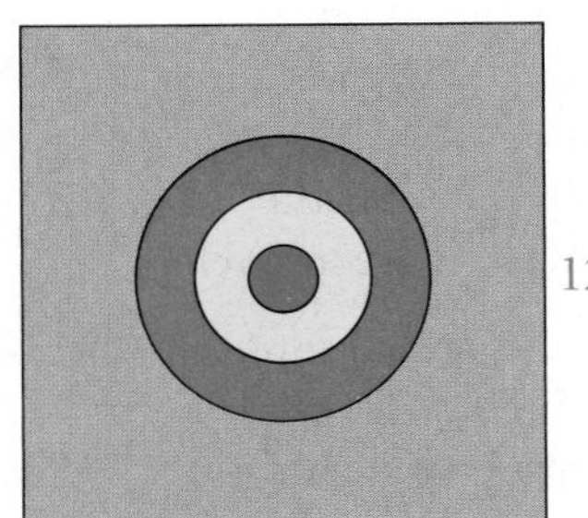

Dart Game At a carnival, you can win prizes if you throw a dart into the blue, yellow, or red regions of a 12 in.-by-12 in. dartboard. The radii of the concentric circles are 1, 2, and 3 inches. Assume that your dart lands on the board and that it is equally likely to land on any point. Find the probability of hitting each colored region.

$$P(\text{blue}) = \frac{\text{blue area}}{\text{area of square}} = \frac{\pi(1)^2}{12^2} = \frac{\pi}{144} \approx 2.2\%$$

Use a calculator.

$$P(\text{yellow}) = \frac{\text{yellow area}}{\text{area of square}} = \frac{\pi(2^2) - \pi(1^2)}{12^2} = \frac{3\pi}{144} \approx 6.5\%$$

$$P(\text{red}) = \frac{\text{red area}}{\text{area of square}} = \frac{\pi(3^2) - \pi(2^2)}{144} = \frac{5\pi}{144} \approx 10.9\%$$

The probability of hitting the blue region is about 2.2%, of hitting the yellow region is about 6.5%, and of hitting the red region is about 10.9%.

3. **Try This** What is the probability of winning some prize?
4. **Try This** What is the probability of winning no prize?
5. **Critical Thinking** If the radius of the blue circle were doubled, would the probability of hitting blue be doubled? Explain.

Some carnival games are more difficult than they appear. Consider the following coin toss game.

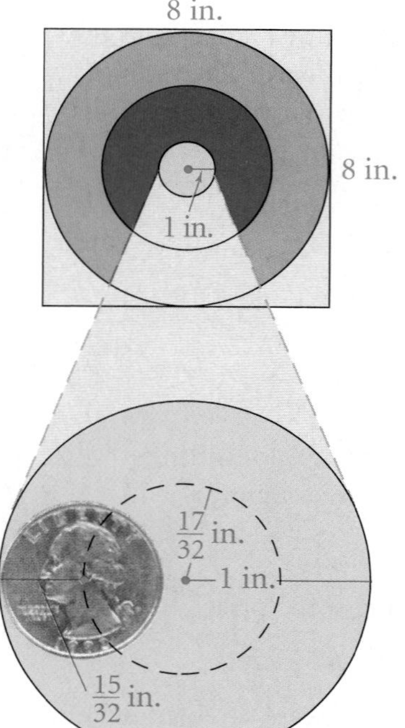

Example 3 *Relating to the Real World* 

Coin Toss To win a prize, you must toss a quarter so that it lands entirely within a green circle of radius 1 in. The radius of a quarter is $\frac{15}{32}$ in. Suppose that the center of a tossed quarter is equally likely to land at any point within the 8-in. square shown at the left. What is the probability that a quarter will land completely within the green circle?

When a quarter is within the green circle, its center must be more than $\frac{15}{32}$ in. from the edge of the circle. So, the center of the quarter must be less than $\frac{17}{32}$ in. from the center of the green circle. This means that the center of the quarter must be within the dashed circle of radius $\frac{17}{32}$ in. as shown in the diagram.

$$P(\text{quarter within green circle}) = \frac{\text{area of dashed circle}}{\text{area of square}}$$

$$= \frac{\pi\left(\frac{17}{32}\right)^2}{(8)^2} \approx 1.4\%$$

The probability of the quarter landing in the green circle is only about 1.4%.

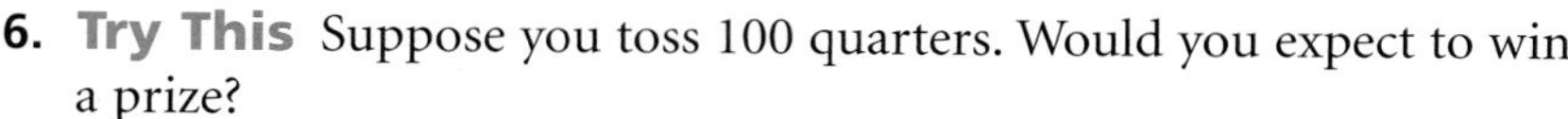

6. Try This Suppose you toss 100 quarters. Would you expect to win a prize?

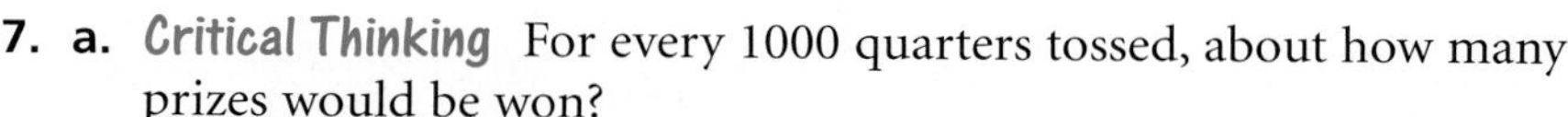

7. a. Critical Thinking For every 1000 quarters tossed, about how many prizes would be won?

b. Suppose the prize is \$10. About how much profit would the game operator expect for every 1000 quarters tossed?

Exercises ON YOUR OWN

Darts are thrown at random at each of the boards shown. If a dart hits the board, find the probability that it will land in the shaded area.

1.

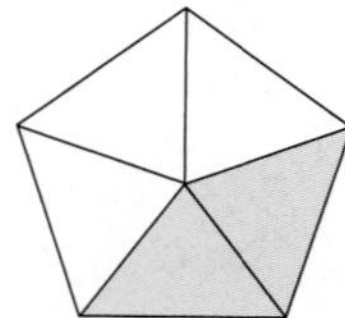

2.

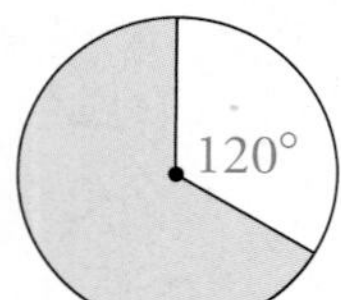

3.

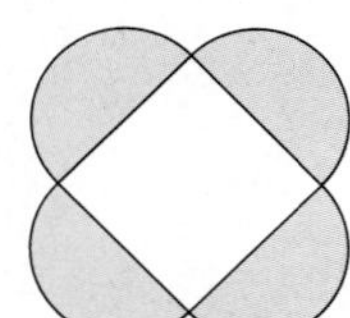

4.

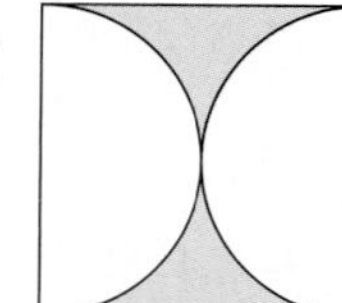

5. Transportation A rapid transit line runs trains every ten minutes. Draw a geometric model and find the probability that randomly arriving passengers will not have to wait more than four minutes.

Sketch a geometric model for each exercise and solve.

6. **Ducking Stool** At a fund raiser, volunteers sit above a tank of water hoping that they won't get wet. You can trip the ducking mechanism by throwing a baseball at a metal disk mounted in front of a 1-m square backboard. The volunteer gets wet even if only the edge of the baseball hits the disk. The radius of a baseball is 3.6 cm and the radius of the disk is 8 cm. What is the probability that a baseball that hits the backboard at a random point will hit the disk?

7. Amy made a tape recording of a choir rehearsal. The recording began 21 minutes into the 60-minute tape and lasted 8 minutes. Later she inadvertently erased a 15-minute segment somewhere on the tape.
   a. Make a drawing showing the possible starting times of the erasure. Explain how Amy knows that the erasure did not start after the 45-minute mark.
   b. Make a drawing showing the starting times of the erasure that would erase the entire choir rehearsal. Find the probability that the entire rehearsal was erased.

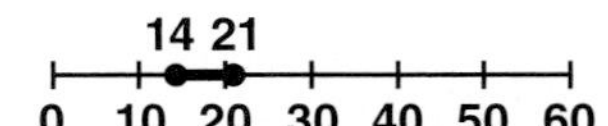

8. Kimi has a 4-in. straw and a 6-in. straw. She wants to cut the 6-in. straw into two pieces so that the three pieces form a triangle.
   a. If she cuts the straw to get two 3-in. pieces, can she form a triangle?
   b. If the two pieces are 1 in. and 5 in., can she form a triangle?
   c. If Kimi cuts the straw at a random point, what is the probability that she can form a triangle?

9. **Archery** An archery target with a radius of 61 cm has five scoring zones of equal widths. The colors of the zones are gold, red, blue, black, and white. The width of each colored zone is 12.2 cm and the radius of the gold circle is also 12.2 cm. If an arrow hits the target at a random point, what is the probability that it hits the gold region?

10. During the summer, the drawbridge over the Quisquam River is raised every half hour to allow boats to pass. It remains open for 5 min. What is the probability that a motorist arriving at the bridge will find it raised?

11. **Astronomy** Meteorites (mostly dust-particle size) are continually bombarding Earth. The radius of Earth is about 3960 mi. The area of the United States is about 3,679,245 mi^2. What is the probability that a meteorite landing on Earth will land in the United States?

12. a. ***Open-ended*** Design a dartboard game to be used at a charity fair. Specify the size and shape of the regions of the board.

b. ***Writing*** Describe the rules for using your dartboard and the prizes that winners receive. Explain how much money you would expect to raise if the game were played 100 times.

13. ***Sonar Sub Search*** A ship is trying to locate a disabled remote-controlled research submarine. The captain has determined that the submarine is within a 2000 m-by-2000 m square region. The depth of the ocean in this region is about 6000 m. The ship moves to a position in the center of the square region. Its sonar sends out a signal that covers a conical region. What is the probability that the ship will locate the submarine with the first pulse?

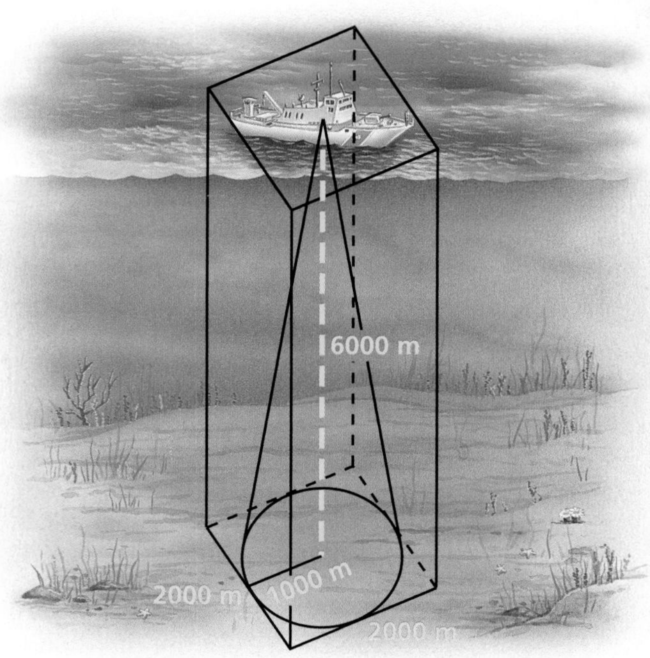

Exercises MIXED REVIEW

Data Analysis **Use the triple bar graph for Exercises 14–16.**

14. Which type of TV show is more popular with Latin American teens than with other teens?

15. In which region is stand-up comedy most popular?

16. ***Critical Thinking*** How can you tell that each teen who was polled was allowed to choose more than one type of TV show?

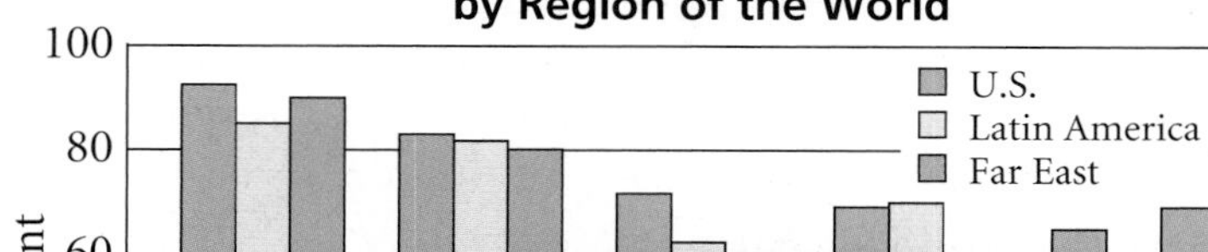

What Teens 15–18 Like to Watch on TV
by Region of the World

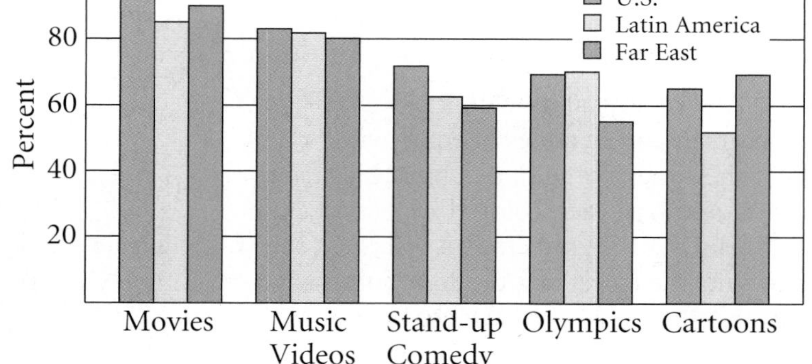

Find the perimeter of each figure.

17.

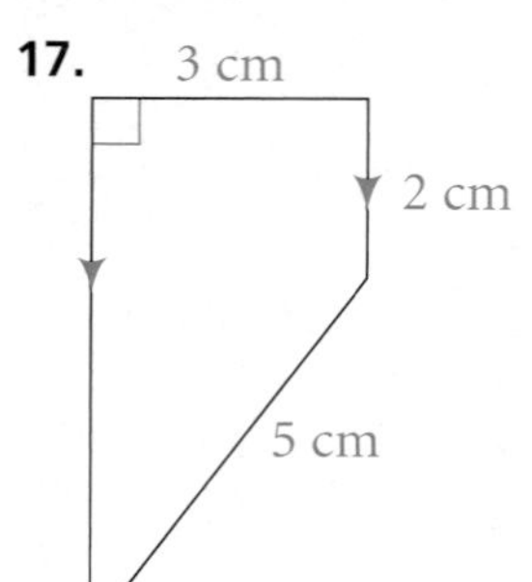

18.

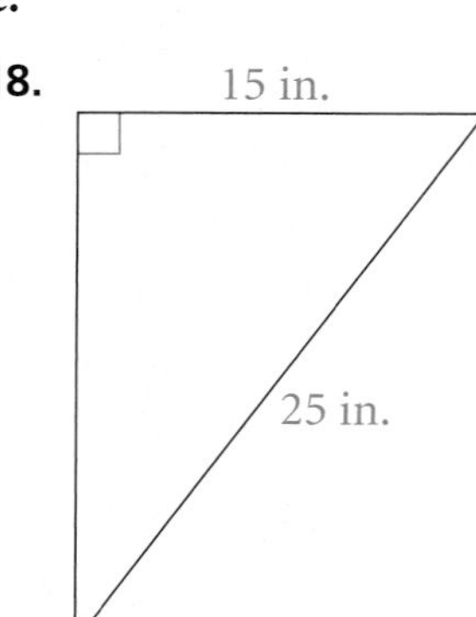

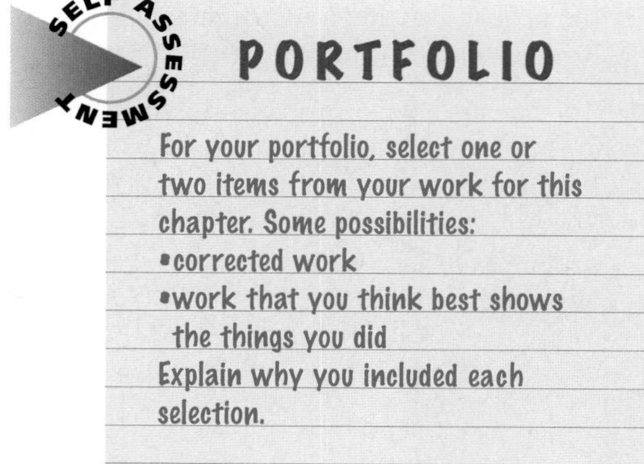

Finishing the Chapter Project

CHAPTER PROJECT

Find Out questions on pages 868, 876, 891, and 897 should help you complete your project. Design and construct your own package for a product. Specify the dimensions, surface area, amount and type of packaging material used, and volume of the package. Justify your design with mathematical and economic arguments.

Reflect and Revise

Ask a classmate to review your project with you. Together, check that your package design is complete, your diagrams and explanations clear, and your information accurate. Have you used geometric terms correctly? Have you considered other possible designs? Is the display attractive, organized, and comprehensive? Revise your work as needed.

Follow Up

Find pictures of packaged products in newspaper or magazine advertisements. Identify the shape of each package. Give possible reasons why the manufacturer chose each package design. Display your work on a poster.

For More Information

Botersman, Jack. *Paper Capers*. New York: Henry Holt and Company, 1986.

Davidson, Patricia, and Robert Willcutt. *Spatial Problem Solving with Paper Folding and Cutting.* New Rochelle, New York: Cuisenaire Company of America, 1984.

Pearce, Peter. *Structure in Nature Is a Strategy for Design*. Cambridge, Massachusetts: MIT Press, 1978.

Shell Centre for Mathematical Education. *Be a Paper Engineer*. Essex, England: Longman Group UK Limited, 1988.

CHAPTER 6

Wrap Up

Key Terms

altitude (pp. 871, 872, 878, 880)
bases (pp. 871, 878)
center (p. 899)
circumference of a sphere (p. 902)
composite space figure (p. 906)
cone (p. 880)
cube (p. 872)
cylinder (p. 872)
edge (p. 864)
faces (p. 864)
geometric probability (p. 910)
great circle (p. 902)
height (pp. 871, 872, 878, 880, 893)
hemisphere (p. 902)
lateral area (pp. 871, 873, 878)
lateral face (pp. 871, 878)
net (p. 864)
oblique cylinder (p. 872)
oblique prism (p. 871)
polyhedron (p. 864)
prism (p. 871)
pyramid (p. 878)
regular pyramid (p. 878)
right cone (p. 880)
right cylinder (p. 872)
right prism (p. 871)
slant height (pp. 878, 880)
sphere (p. 899)
surface area (pp. 871, 873, 878)
vertex (pp. 864, 878)
volume (p. 886)

How am I doing?

- State three ideas from this chapter that you think are important. Explain your choices.
- Describe how to find the volumes and surface areas of different space figures.

Space Figures and Nets 6-1

A **polyhedron** is a three-dimensional figure whose surfaces are polygons. The polygons are **faces** of the polyhedron. An **edge** is a segment that is the intersection of two faces. A **vertex** is a point where edges intersect. A **net** is a two-dimensional pattern that folds to form a three-dimensional figure.

1. *Open-ended* Draw a net for the space figure at the right.
2. *Standardized Test Prep* Which figure has the most edges?
   A. rectangular prism **B.** hexagonal prism
   C. pentagonal prism **D.** octagonal prism
   E. cannot be determined from the information given

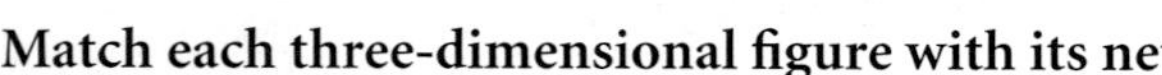

Match each three-dimensional figure with its net.

3. 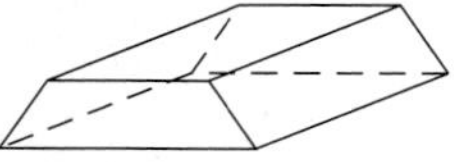
4. 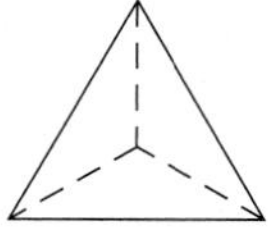
5. 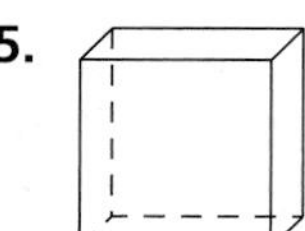

A. 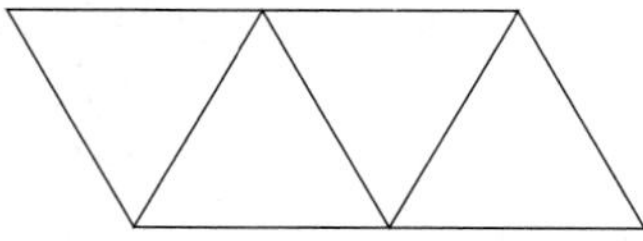
B. 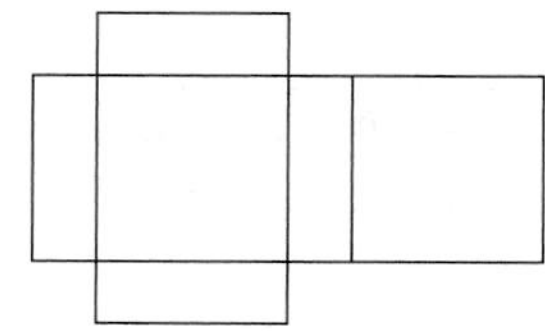
C. 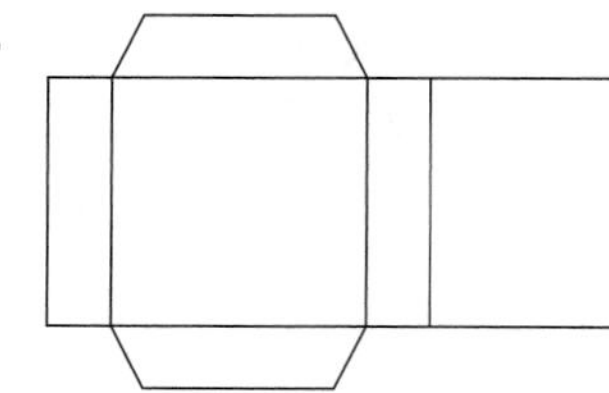

Surface Areas of Prisms and Cylinders 6-2

The **lateral area** of a **right prism** is the product of the perimeter of the base and the height. The **surface area** of a prism is the sum of the lateral area and the areas of the two bases.

$\text{L.A.} = ph$
$\text{S.A.} = \text{L.A.} + 2B$

p is the perimeter of a base.
h
B is the area of a base.

The **lateral area** of a **right cylinder** is the product of the circumference of the base and the height of the cylinder. The **surface area** is the sum of the lateral area and the areas of the two bases.

$\text{L.A.} = 2\pi rh$
or πdh
$\text{S.A.} = \text{L.A.} + 2B$

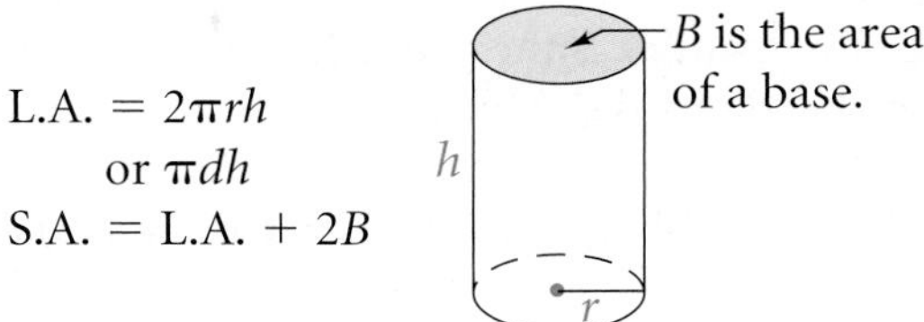

Find the surface area of each figure. You may leave answers in terms of π.

6.
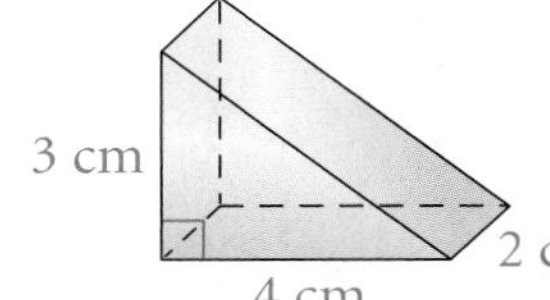

7.
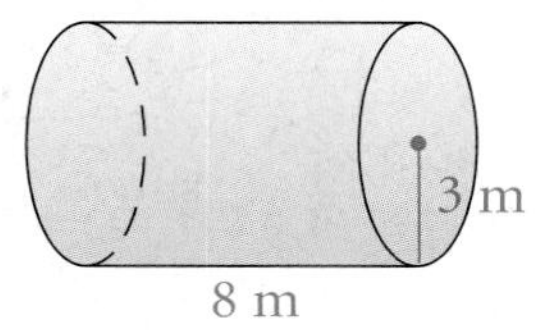

8.
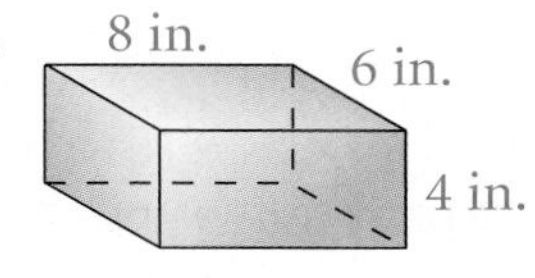

9.
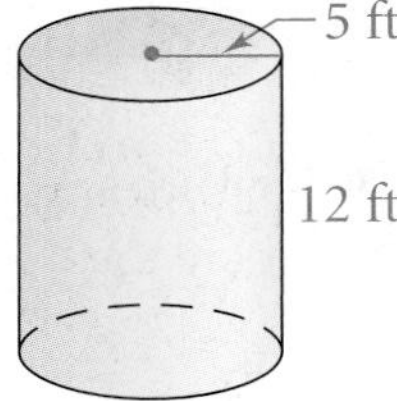

Surface Areas of Pyramids and Cones 6-3

The **lateral area** of a **regular pyramid** is half the product of the perimeter of the base and the slant height. The **surface area** is the sum of the lateral area and the area of the base.

$\text{L.A.} = \frac{1}{2}p\ell$
$\text{S.A.} = \text{L.A.} + B$

ℓ
B is the area of a base.

The **lateral area** of a **right cone** is half the product of the circumference of the base and the slant height. The **surface area** is the sum of the lateral area and the area of the base.

$\text{L.A.} = \pi r\ell$
$\text{S.A.} = \text{L.A.} + B$

ℓ
r
B is the area of a base.

Calculator **Find the lateral area and surface area of each figure. When an answer is not a whole number, round to the nearest tenth.**

10.
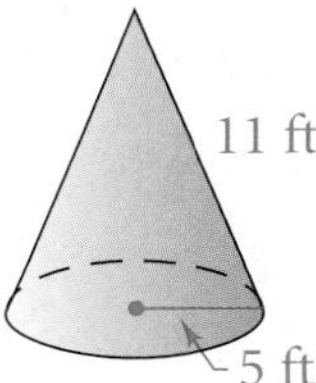

11.
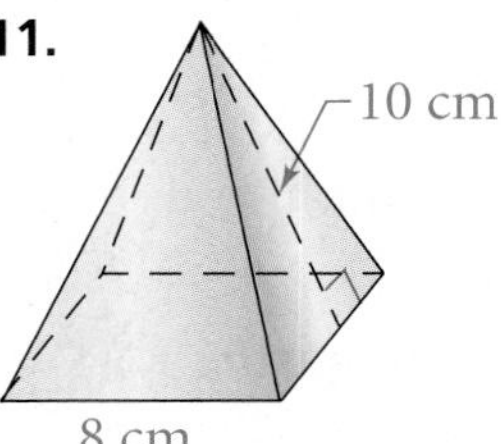

12.
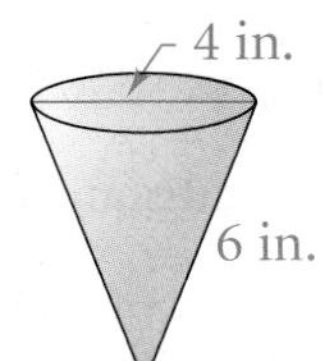

13.
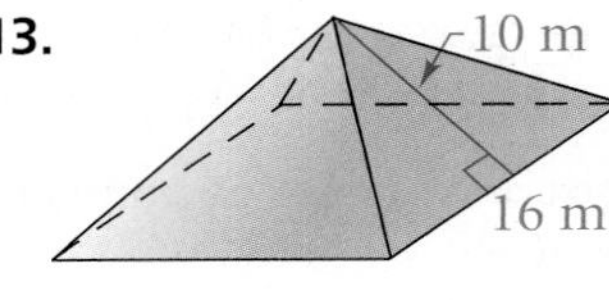

Volumes of Prisms and Cylinders 6-4

The **volume** of a space figure is the space that the figure occupies. Volume is measured in cubic units.

The **volume** of a **prism** is the product of the area of a base and the height of the prism.

The **volume** of a **cylinder** is the product of the area of a base and the height of the cylinder.

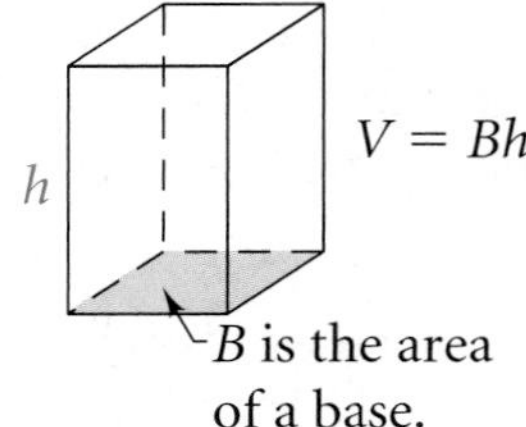

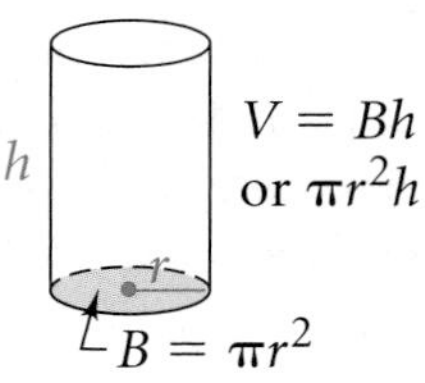

Find the volume of each figure. You may leave answers in terms of π.

14.

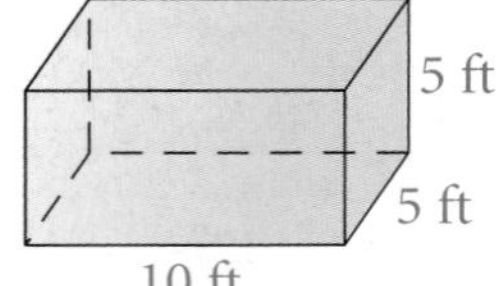

15.

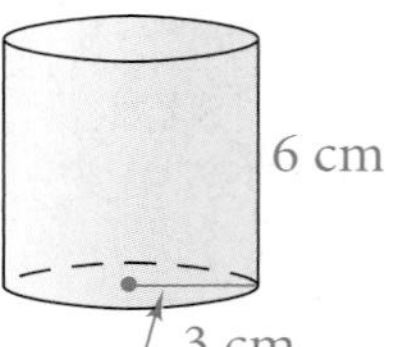

16.

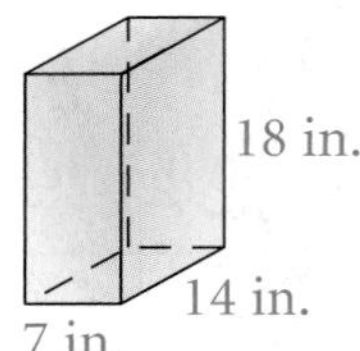

17.

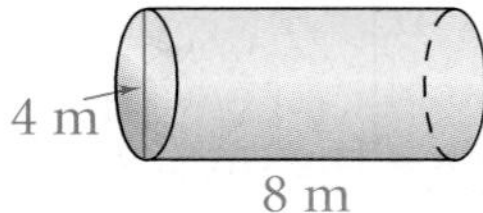

18. **Writing** Compare finding the volume and the surface area of a prism. What are the similarities and differences?

Volumes of Pyramids and Cones 6-5

The **volume** of a **pyramid** is one third the product of the area of the base and the height of the pyramid.

The **volume** of a **cone** is one third the product of the area of the base and the height of the cone.

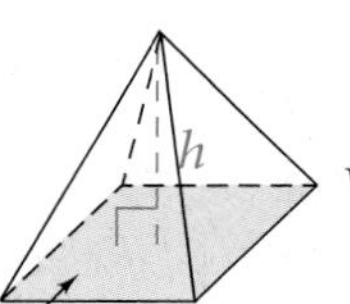

B is the area of the base.

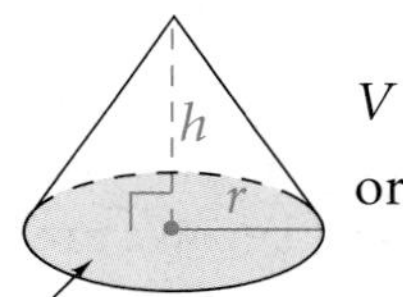

B is the area of the base.

Calculator **Find the volume of each figure. Round to the nearest tenth.**

19.

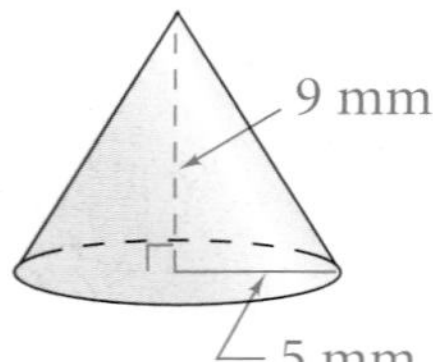

20.

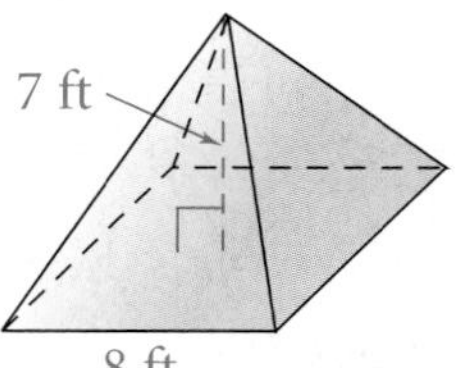

21.

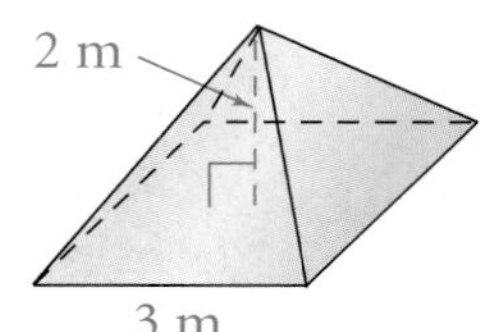

22.

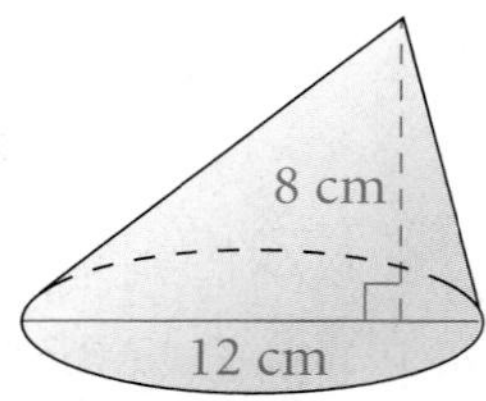

Surface Areas and Volumes of Spheres 6-6

A **sphere** is the set of points in space equidistant from a given point called the **center**.

The **surface area of a sphere** is four times the product of π and the square of the radius of the sphere. The **volume of a sphere** is $\frac{4}{3}$ the product of π and the cube of the radius of the sphere.

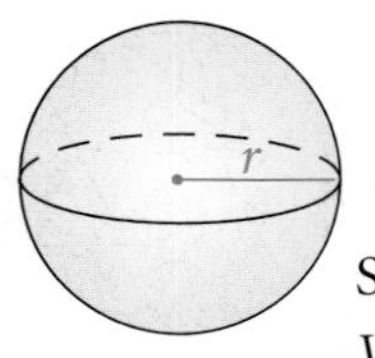

$\text{S.A.} = 4\pi r^2$
$V = \frac{4}{3}\pi r^3$

Calculator **Find the surface area and volume of a sphere with the given radius or diameter. Round answers to the nearest tenth.**

23. $r = 5$ in. **24.** $d = 7$ cm **25.** $d = 4$ ft **26.** $r = 0.8$ ft

27. *Sports* The circumference of a lacrosse ball is 8 in. Find its volume to the nearest tenth of a cubic inch.

Composite Space Figures 6-7

A **composite space figure** combines two or more space figures. The volume of a composite figure is the sum of the volumes of the combined figures.

Calculator **Find the volume of each figure. When an answer is not a whole number, round to the nearest tenth.**

28.

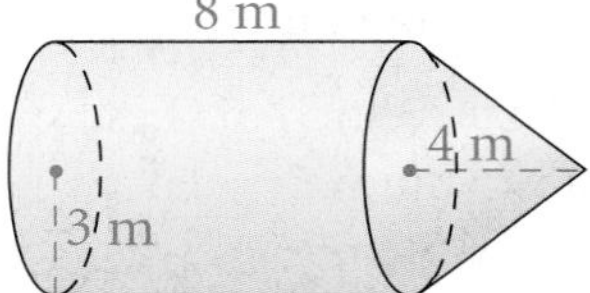

29.

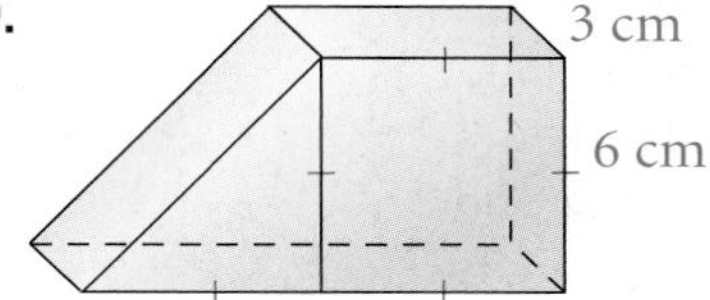

30.

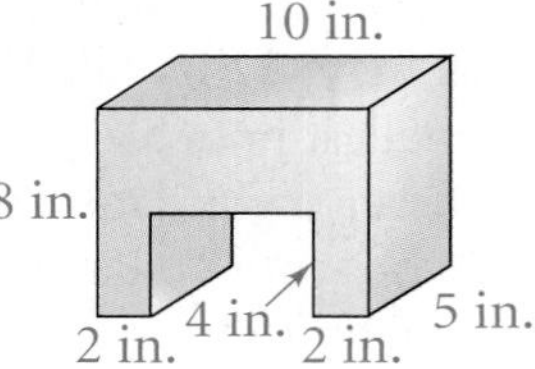

Geometric Probability 6-8

Geometric probability uses geometric figures to represent occurrences of events. You can use a segment model or an area model. Compare the part that represents favorable outcomes to the whole, which represents all outcomes.

Darts are thrown at random at each of the boards shown. If a dart hits the board, find the probability that it will land in the shaded area.

31.

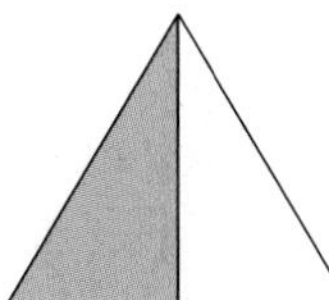

32.

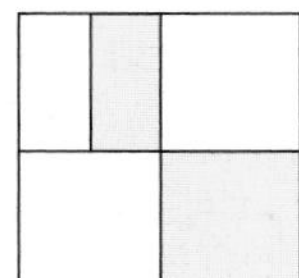

33.

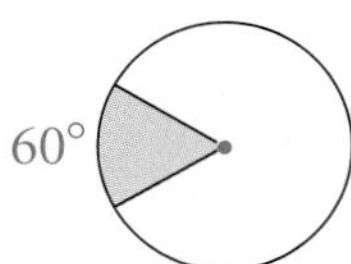

34. *Critical Thinking* If you are modeling probability with a segment, does the length of the segment matter? Explain.

CHAPTER 6

Assessment

Draw a net for each figure. Label the net with appropriate dimensions.

1. 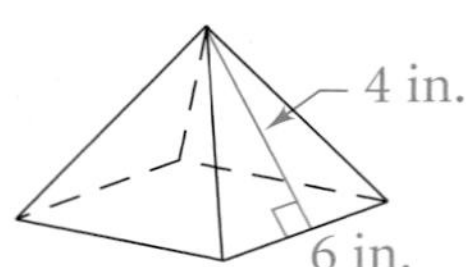

2. 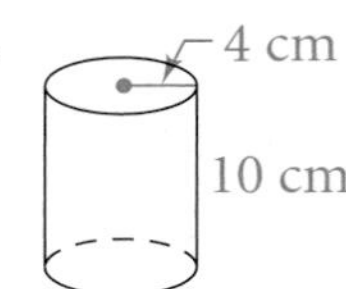

3. a. *Aviation* The "black box" information recorder on an airplane is a rectangular prism. The base is 15 in. by 8 in., and it is 15 in. to 22 in. tall. What are the largest and smallest possible volumes for the box?
   b. Newer flight data recorders are smaller and record more data. A new recorder is 8 in. by 8 in. by 13 in. What is its volume?

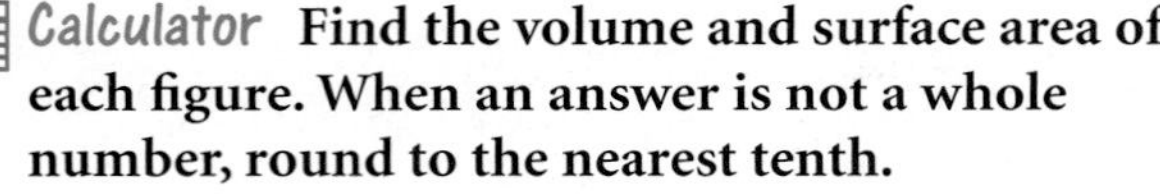

Calculator **Find the volume and surface area of each figure. When an answer is not a whole number, round to the nearest tenth.**

4. 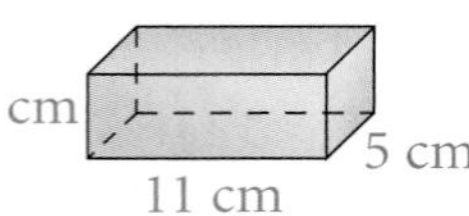

5. 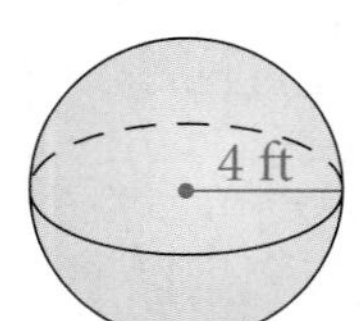

6. 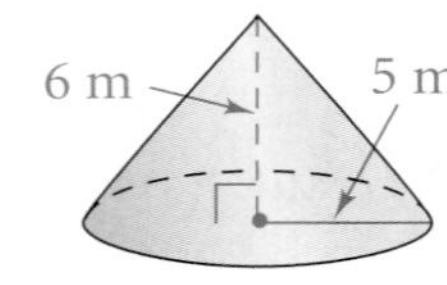

7. 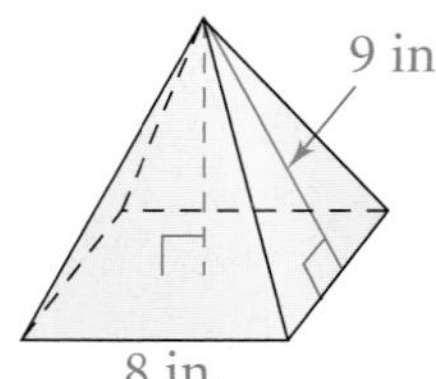

8. 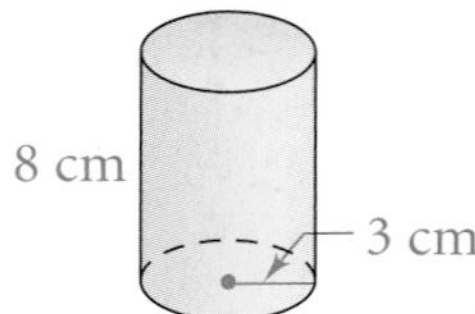

9. 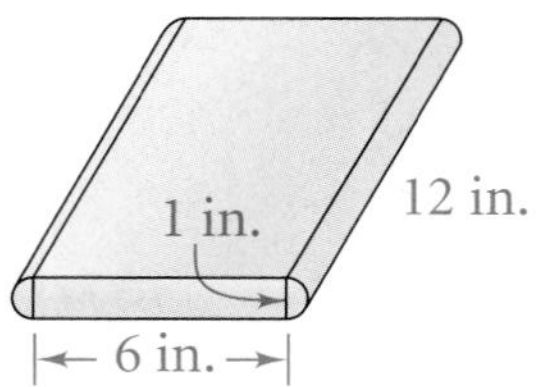

10. *Open-ended* Draw two different space figures that have a volume of 100 in.^{3}. Label the dimensions of each figure.

11. a. Describe the figure that is formed when the triangle is rotated 360° about the y-axis.
    b. What is its volume and lateral area in terms of π?

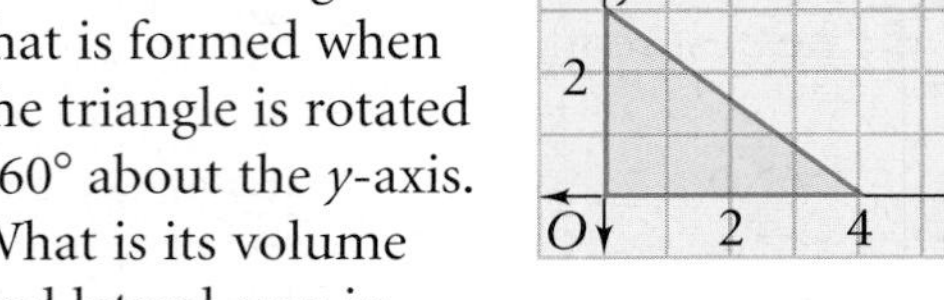

12. How many gallons of paint do you need to paint the walls of a bedroom? The floor is 12 ft by 15 ft and the walls are 7 ft high. One gallon of paint covers about 450 square feet.

13. *Standardized Test Prep* Which of these space figures has the greatest volume?
    A. cube with an edge of 5 cm
    B. cylinder with radius 4 cm and height 4 cm
    C. pyramid with a square base with sides of 6 cm and height 6 cm
    D. cone with radius 4 cm and height 9 cm
    E. rectangular prism with a 5 cm-by-5 cm base and height 6 cm

14. *Writing* Describe a real-world situation in which you would use the volume of an object. Then describe another situation in which you would use the lateral area of an object.

15. a. *Estimation* What space figures can you use to approximate the shape of the spring water bottle?
    b. Estimate the volume of the bottle.

16. *Probability* Every 20 minutes from 4:00 P.M. to 7:00 P.M., a commuter train crosses Main Street. For three minutes a gate stops cars from passing as the train goes by. What is the probability that a motorist driving by during this time will have to stop at the train crossing?

17. *Probability* What is the probability that a dart tossed randomly at this board will hit the shaded area?

CHAPTER 6

Preparing for the Math A Exam

Part I

1 Which figure has the most vertices?

(1) square pyramid (3) triangular prism
(2) triangular pyramid (4) cube

2 The length and width of a rectangular prism are doubled. The height remains the same. The lateral area of the prism

(1) is doubled. (3) is quadrupled.
(2) is tripled. (4) stays the same.

3 The volume of the cylinder is about ▇ the volume of the prism.

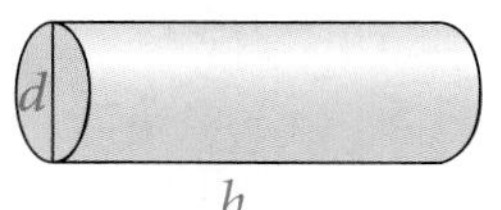

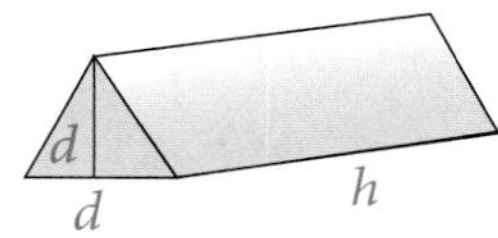

(1) the same as (3) $\frac{1}{2}$

(2) 2 times (4) $1\frac{1}{2}$ times

4 The volume of a regular square pyramid is 270m^3. The length of each base edge is 9 m. What is the height of the pyramid?

(1) 3.3 m (3) 30 m
(2) 10 m (4) 6.7 m

5 A commuter bus runs every 20 minutes. If a passenger arrives at a bus stop at a random time, what is the probability that he will have to wait 12 minutes or more?

(1) 60% (3) 40%
(2) 12% (4) 50%

Part II

6 Find the surface area of this cylinder. Round your answer to the nearest tenth.

6 cm
10 cm

7 Find the volume of this prism.

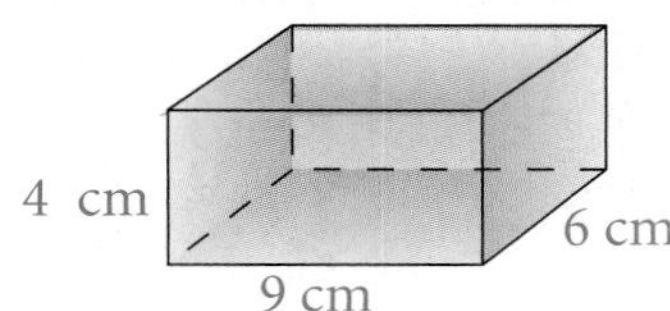

Part III

8 Find the volume of this cone. Round your answer to the nearest tenth.

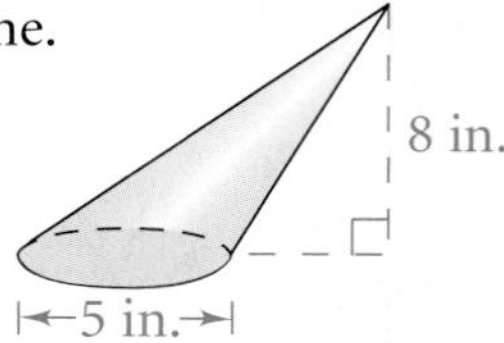

9 Draw a net for this space figure. Label the net with appropriate dimensions.

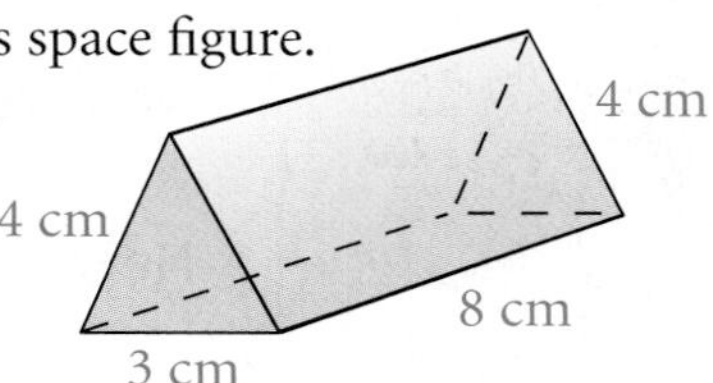

10 The marble paperweight on Ms. Miller's desk is a regular square pyramid with height 12 cm and base edges 10 cm long. Find the surface area.

11 The circumference of a ball is 20 in. Find to the nearest tenth:

a Volume
b Surface area

12 Find the volume of this figure to the nearest tenth.

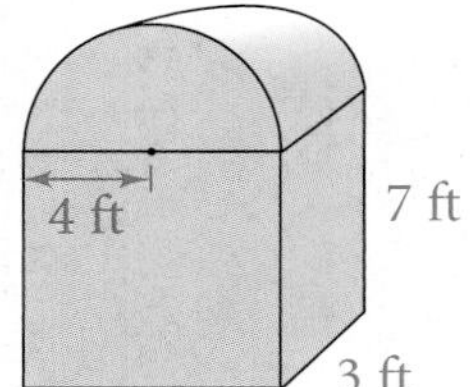

Part IV

13 The stand for a flag is a 20-cm cube of wood. A 7-cm round hole has been drilled all the way through its center. Find to the nearest tenth:

a the volume of the flag stand.
b the surface area of the flag stand.

14 The dartboard at a fair has four concentric circles set in a 24-in. wide square. The widths of the circles are 6 in., 12 in., 18 in., and 24 in. You win a prize if your dart hits any circular region.

a You win a stuffed toy if your dart hits the center circle. If you hit the board, what is the probability of winning a stuffed toy?
b What is the probability of hitting the dartboard but not winning a prize?

New York Lessons

Contents

This postcard shows the New York State Capitol in Albany. The building of the capitol began in 1867 and took more than thirty years to complete.

New York Lessons

New York 1

Connections Language . . . and more

Open and Closed Sentences

What You'll Learn

- Determining the truth value of mathematical sentences
- Finding the solution set of an open sentence

...And Why

To use the language of mathematics

THINK AND DISCUSS

Writing Mathematical Sentences

A view of the Hudson River Valley painted by Frederic Church

Language Is the caption under the picture a sentence? No, the caption is not a sentence, because it does not include a verb. (Insert the word *was* before *painted* and you'll have a sentence.)

PROBLEM SOLVING

Look Back What phrases indicate inequalities in word problems?

In the same way that sentences in English must have a verb, a mathematical sentence must also have a verb. Here are examples of how symbols are used as verbs in mathematical sentences. Notice that a slash through a symbol creates a **negation.**

Symbol	Meaning	Negation	Meaning
$=$	is equal to	$\neq$	is *not* equal to
$>$	is greater than	$\not>$	is *not* greater than
$\geq$	is greater than or equal to	$\not\geq$	is *not* greater than or equal to
$<$	is less than	$\not<$	is *not* less than
$\leq$	is less than or equal to	$\not\leq$	is *not* less than or equal to

The symbol $=$ is used to express an *equality.* Each of the other symbols is used to express an *inequality.*

A phrase such as $2xy - 3x$ is an *expression,* not a mathematical sentence, since it does not contain a symbol of equality or inequality.

Example 1 **Relating to the Real World** 

Jobs A student found that she could earn up to \$13 an hour working part-time for the local park district. State whether each of the following is an expression, an equation, or an inequality.

a. $13h$ The maximum amount earned for h hours of work

b. $e = 13h$ Amount earned e equals 13 times the number of hours h.

c. $e \leq 13h$ Amount earned e is less than or equal to 13 times the number of hours h.

a. $13h$ is an expression. It has no equal sign or inequality symbol.

b. $e = 13h$ is an equation, since it has an equal sign.

c. $e \leq 13h$ is an inequality, since it has an inequality symbol.

1. Try This State whether each of the following is an expression, an equation, or an inequality.

a. $5c \neq 20 + 1$ **b.** $4ab - 11$ **c.** $3 + 6x = 2$

Mathematical sentences can be true or false. To determine the **truth value** of an equation, check whether the value of one side of the equation equals the value of the other side. For inequalities, check whether the comparison or negation is correct.

$$14 \div 4 \neq 3$$
$$\frac{14}{4} \neq 3$$
$$3\tfrac{1}{2} \neq 3 \quad \textit{true}$$

$$17 \cdot (0.1) > 17$$
$$1.7 > 17 \quad \textit{false}$$

2. Mental Math State whether each mathematical sentence is true or false.

a. $-4 + 2 \ngtr 0$ **b.** $5 \cdot (0.5) = 1.5$ **c.** $10 < 27 \div 3$

Finding Solution Sets

Mathematical sentences can be *closed* or *open.* A **closed sentence** does not contain a variable. $6 + 2 > 1 - 4$ is an example of a closed sentence. An **open sentence** contains one or more variables. $8 + x = 7$ and $3a + b < 7 + 2$ are examples of open sentences.

QUICK REVIEW

An equation or inequality has a solution of all real numbers if it simplifies to a true statement. An equation or inequality has no solution if it simplifies to a false statement.

Most open sentences are neither true nor false until you replace each variable with a specific value. The set of values from which to choose is called the **replacement set.** If the replacement set is not specified, assume that it includes all real numbers.

A value that makes an open sentence true is a solution of that sentence. An open sentence has one solution, no solution, or many solutions.

The **solution set** for an open sentence is the set of all the values from the replacement set that makes the sentence true. The solution set can change depending on the replacement set used.

Example 2

Find the solution set of $c - 3 \geq 5$ for the replacement set {6, 7, 8, 9}.

c	$c - 3$	$c - 3 \geq 5$	Truth Value
6	3	$3 \geq 5$	false
7	4	$4 \geq 5$	false
8	5	$5 \geq 5$	true
9	6	$6 \geq 5$	true

The solution set is {8, 9}.

3. Try This What is the solution set for $3 + y < 6$ if the replacement set is {0, 1, 2, 3, 4, 5}?

Exercises ON YOUR OWN

State whether each is an expression, an equation, or an inequality.

1. $-14 + 2g$

2. $7 + w \neq 13$

3. $3(7 - 0.2)$

4. $5 \geq 2 - 8c$

5. $22 \div 2 < -3t$

6. $17 + 21 = 3 \cdot 14$

7. Copy and complete the table. Then write the solution set of $x + 2 < 7$ for the replacement set {1, 3, 5, 7}.

x	$x + 2$	$x + 2 < 7$	Truth Value
1	3	$3 < 7$	true
3	■	■	■
5	■	■	■
7	■	■	■

8. What is the solution set for $6x + 2 > 20$ if the replacement set is {0, 1, 2, 3, 4, 5}?

State the truth value of each sentence.

9. $14 + 2 > 3 \cdot 5$

10. $7(2 - 1) = 24 \div 4$

11. $6 \cdot 2 \not< 20 - 5$

12. $3 - 14 \leq -3 \cdot -5$

13. $6 + 29 = 5 \cdot 7$

14. $17 - 20 = -3 \cdot 0$

State whether each sentence is open or closed.

15. $5 + 3 = 8$

16. $x + 3 = 8$

17. $y - 4 > x + 2$

18. $37 - 9 > 3$

19. $7 < 8$

20. $y \geq 9$

21. $m + 17 \geq 25$

22. $137 \leq y + 14$

23. $37 + 8 + 3 \geq 29$

Write the negation of each sentence. Determine the truth value of the original sentence and its negation.

24. $18 - 3 = 10$

25. $14 \leq 4 \cdot 3$

26. $2 + 9 < 11$

State whether each sentence is true or false for the given value of the variable.

27. $18 - 3w > 15$ for $w = -1$

28. $8 - 2b = b + 5$ for $b = 1$

29. $2 + k \not< 5k$ for $k = 2$

30. $15 \div e = e + 2$ for $e = 3$

31. **Entertainment** A student has \$22.50 to buy three movie tickets. She wrote the inequality $3t \leq 22.50$ to show that the cost of three movie tickets has to be less than or equal to the money she has. If each ticket costs \$7, is her inequality true? Explain.

Find the solution set for each replacement set.

32. $8 - x > 2$ for $\{5, 6, 7, 8\}$

33. $3d = 14$ for {all whole numbers}

34. $2n \neq 12$ for {all real numbers}

35. $12 \leq f + 1$ for $\{10, 11, 12, 13, 14, 15\}$

State whether each open sentence is always true, sometimes true, or never true. Use the real numbers for the replacement set.

36. $2x = x + x$

37. $5 - n = 11$

38. $a + 0 = a \cdot 1$

39. $3g = 3(g - g)$

40. $3 + w = 2 + w$

41. $p + 1 = 5 - p$

State whether each mathematical sentence has one solution, more than one solution, or no solutions. Use the real numbers for the replacement set.

42. $2r \geq 10$

43. $5d + 2 = 12$

44. $8a = 6a$

45. $2y + 1 = 2 + 2y$

46. $3 - m < -2 + m$

47. $4(a + b) \neq 4a + 4b$

48. **Fitness** Refer to the photo.

a. Explain how the equation $C = 25m + 50$ represents the cost of club membership.

b. What is a reasonable replacement set for the variable m?

c. During a special promotion, Glennhill Fitness Club will waive the \$50 fee if you sign up for more than 10 months. Write a new equation to describe the cost of membership. Give a replacement set for the variable m.

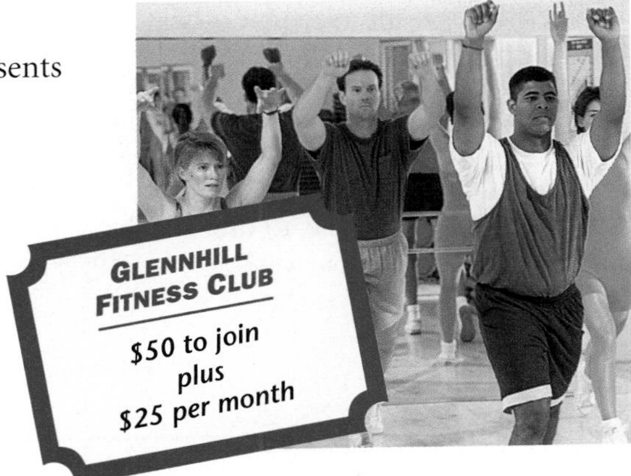

New York Lessons

Technology

Exploring Parallel Lines and Related Angles

Work in pairs or small groups.

Construct

Use geometry software to construct two parallel lines. Make sure that the lines remain parallel when you manipulate them. Construct a point on each line. Then construct the line through these two points. This line is called a *transversal.*

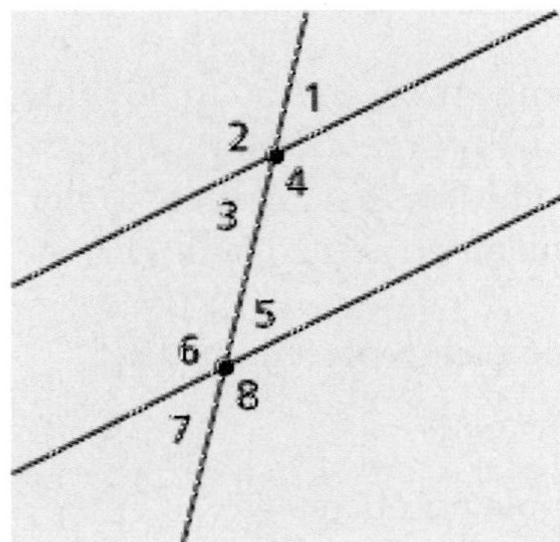

Investigate

Measure each of the eight angles formed by the parallel lines and the transversal and record the measurements. Manipulate the lines and record the new measurements. What relationships do you notice?

Conjecture

When two parallel lines are intersected by a transversal, what are the relationships among the angles formed? Make as many **conjectures** as possible.

Extend

- Use your software to construct three or more parallel lines. Construct a line that intersects one of the lines. Does it intersect the other lines also? If it does, what relationships exist among the angles formed? How many different measures are there?
- Construct two parallel lines and draw a transversal that is perpendicular to one of the parallel lines. What do you discover?

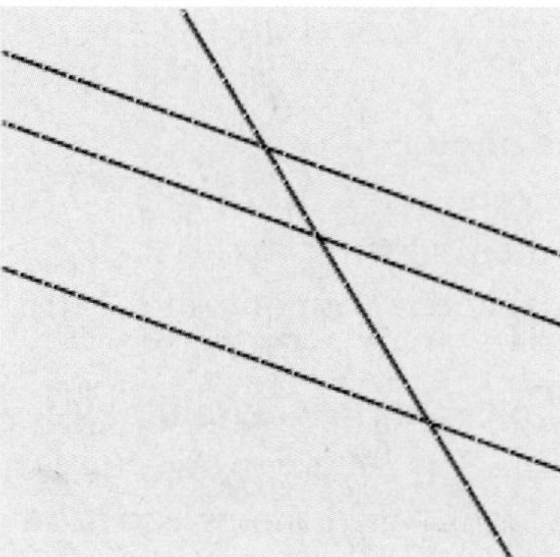

Parallel Lines and Related Angles

What You'll Learn

- Identifying pairs of angles formed by two lines and a transversal
- Relating the measures of angles formed by parallel lines and a transversal

...And Why

To understand how parallel lines are used in building, city planning, and construction

What You'll Need

- ruler
- protractor

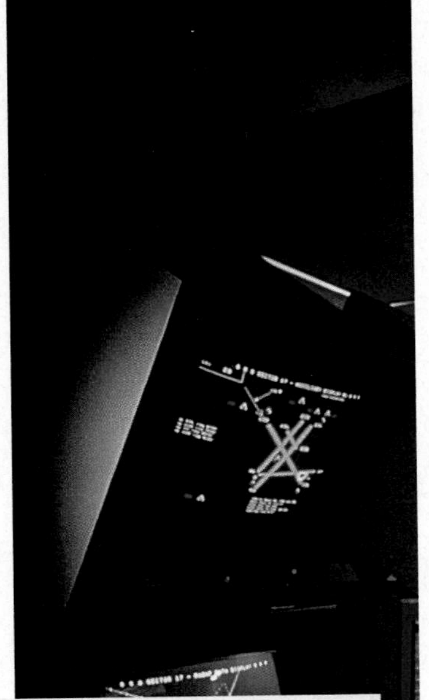

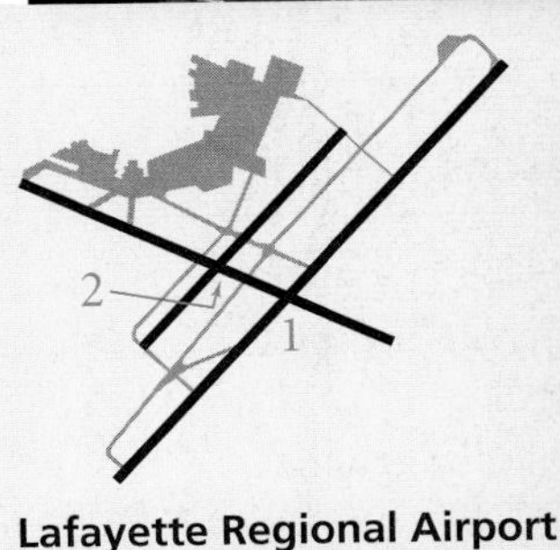

Lafayette Regional Airport
Lafayette, Louisiana

THINK AND DISCUSS

Angles Formed by Intersecting Lines

A **transversal** is a line that intersects two coplanar lines at two distinct points. The diagram shows the eight angles formed by the transversal and the two lines.

1. a. $\angle 3$ and $\angle 6$ are in the *interior* of ℓ and m. Name another pair of angles in the interior of ℓ and m.

b. Name a pair of angles in the *exterior* of ℓ and m.

2. a. $\angle 1$ and $\angle 4$ are on *alternate sides* of the transversal t. Name another pair of angles on alternate sides of t.

b. Name a pair of angles on the *same side* of t.

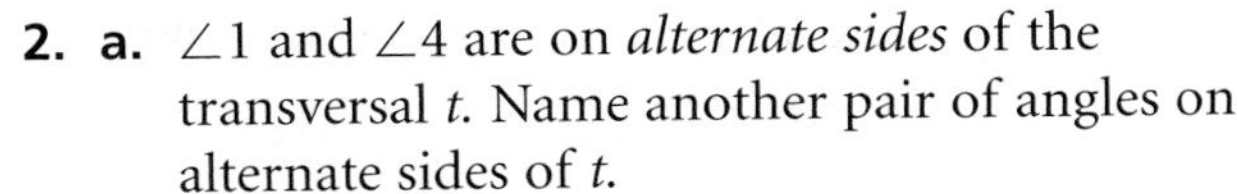

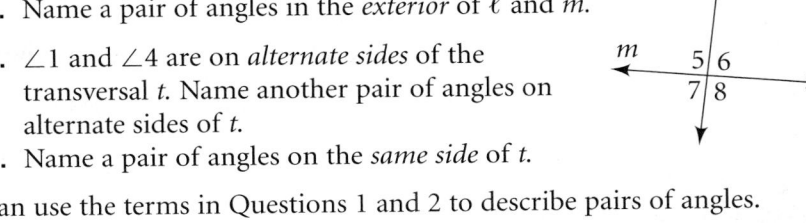

You can use the terms in Questions 1 and 2 to describe pairs of angles.

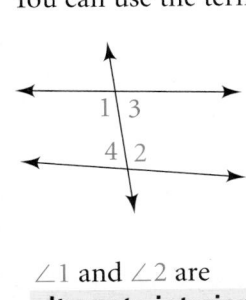

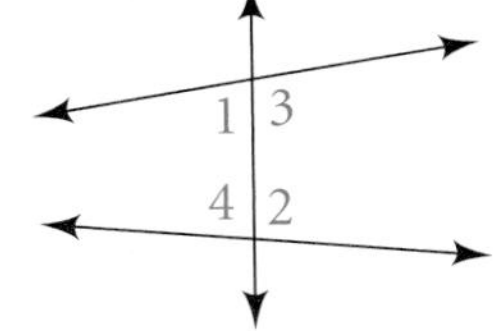

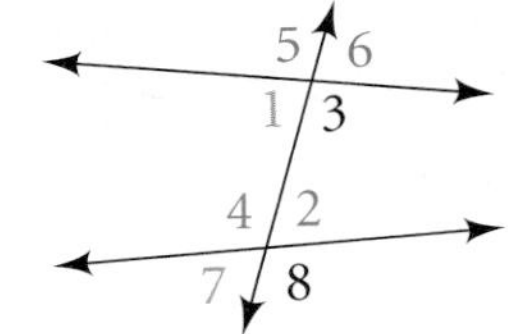

$\angle 1$ and $\angle 2$ are **alternate interior angles**, as are $\angle 3$ and $\angle 4$.

$\angle 1$ and $\angle 4$ are **same-side interior angles**, as are $\angle 2$ and $\angle 3$.

$\angle 5$ and $\angle 4$ are **corresponding angles**, as are $\angle 6$ and $\angle 2$, $\angle 1$ and $\angle 7$, and $\angle 3$ and $\angle 8$.

3. In the diagrams above, $\angle 1$ and $\angle 3$ are not alternate interior angles. What term decribes their positions in relation to each other?

Example 1

Relating to the Real World 

Aviation In the diagram of Lafayette Regional Airport, the black segments are runways and the grey areas are taxiways and terminal buildings. Classify $\angle 1$ and $\angle 2$ as alternate interior angles, same-side interior angles, or corresponding angles.

$\angle 1$ and $\angle 2$ are corresponding angles.

WORK TOGETHER

Work with a partner.

- Draw two parallel lines using lined paper or the two edges of a ruler. Then draw a transversal that intersects the two parallel lines.
- Use a protractor to measure each of the eight angles formed. Record the measures on your drawing.

4. Make **conjectures** about the measures of corresponding angles, alternate interior angles, and same-side interior angles. Compare your results with those of your classmates.

TECHNOLOGY HINT

The Work Together could be done with geometry software.

THINK AND DISCUSS

Angles Formed by Parallel Lines

The results of the Work Together lead to the following postulate and theorems.

Postulate 7-1
Corresponding Angles Postulate

If two parallel lines are cut by a transversal, then corresponding angles are congruent.

If $\ell \parallel m$, then $\angle 1 \cong \angle 5$, $\angle 2 \cong \angle 6$, $\angle 3 \cong \angle 7$, and $\angle 4 \cong \angle 8$.

Theorem 7-1
Alternate Interior Angles Theorem

If two parallel lines are cut by a transversal, then alternate interior angles are congruent.

If $\ell \parallel m$, then $\angle 3 \cong \angle 6$ and $\angle 4 \cong \angle 5$.

Theorem 7-2
Same-Side Interior Angles Theorem

If two parallel lines are cut by a transversal, then the pairs of same-side interior angles are supplementary.

If $\ell \parallel m$, then $\angle 3$ and $\angle 5$ are supplementary, and so are $\angle 4$ and $\angle 6$.

Proof of Theorem 7-1

Given: $a \parallel b$

Prove: $\angle 1 \cong \angle 3$

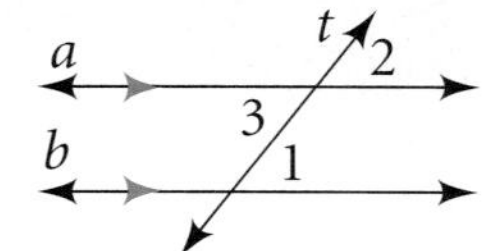

Statements	Reasons
1. $a \parallel b$	**1.** Given
2. $\angle 1 \cong \angle 2$	**2.** If $\parallel$ lines, then corresponding $\angle$s are $\cong$.
3. $\angle 2 \cong \angle 3$	**3.** Vertical angles are $\cong$.
4. $\angle 1 \cong \angle 3$	**4.** Transitive Prop. of Congruence

When writing a proof, it is often helpful to start by writing a plan. The plan should describe how you can reason from the given information to what you want to prove.

Example 2

Write a plan for the proof of Theorem 7-2.

Given: $a \parallel b$

Prove: $\angle 1$ and $\angle 2$ are supplementary.

Plan for Proof To show that $m\angle 1 + m\angle 2 = 180$, show that $m\angle 3 + m\angle 2 = 180$ and that $m\angle 1 = m\angle 3$. Then substitute $m\angle 1$ for $m\angle 3$.

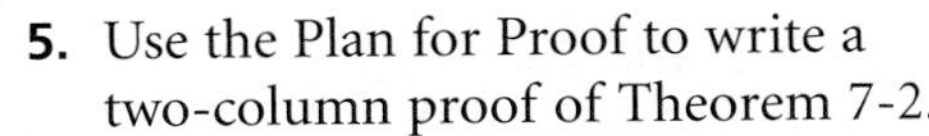

5. Use the Plan for Proof to write a two-column proof of Theorem 7-2.

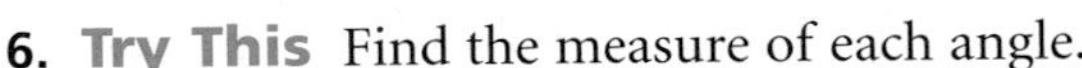

6. **Try This** Find the measure of each angle.

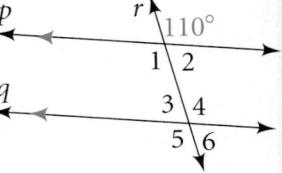

   a. $\angle 1$ b. $\angle 2$ c. $\angle 3$
   d. $\angle 4$ e. $\angle 5$ f. $\angle 6$

Example 3 Relating to the Real World 

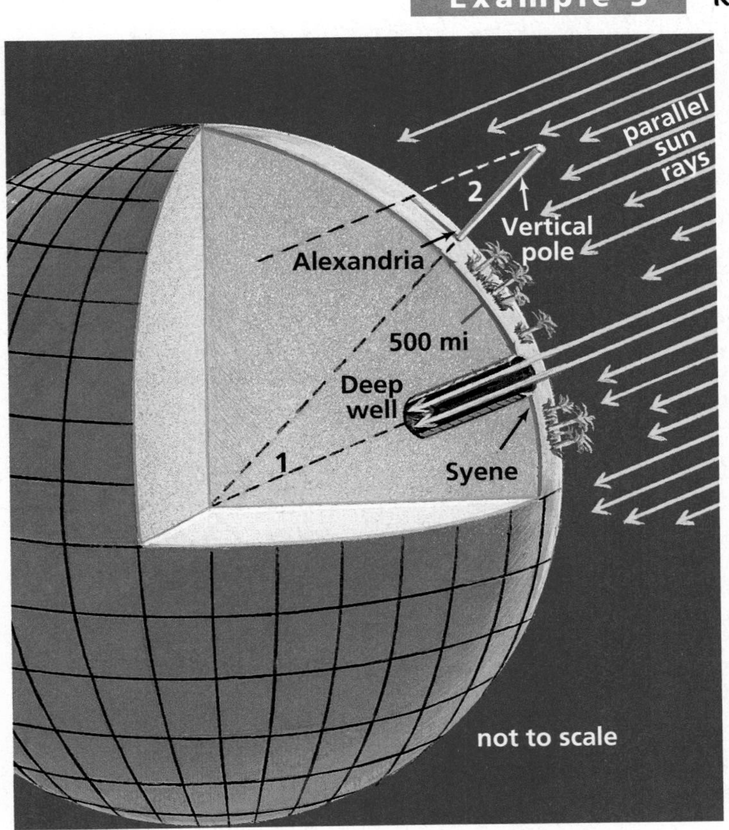

Measuring Earth About 220 B.C., Eratosthenes estimated the circumference of Earth. He achieved this remarkable feat by assuming that Earth is a sphere and that the sun's rays are parallel. He knew that the sun was directly over the town of Syene on the longest day of the year, because sunlight shone directly down a deep well. On that day, he measured the angle of the shadow of a vertical pole in Alexandria, which was 5000 stadia (about 500 miles) north of Syene. How did Eratosthenes know that $\angle 1 \cong \angle 2$? And how could he compute the circumference of Earth knowing $m\angle 1$?

Since $\angle 1$ and $\angle 2$ are alternate interior angles formed by the sun's parallel rays, the angles are congruent. The angle Eratosthenes measured was 7.2°. This is $\frac{1}{50}$ of 360°, so 500 mi is $\frac{1}{50}$ of the circumference of Earth. His estimate of 25,000 mi is very close to the actual value.

Exercises ON YOUR OWN

Classify each pair of angles labeled with the same color as alternate interior angles, same-side interior angles, or corresponding angles.

1.

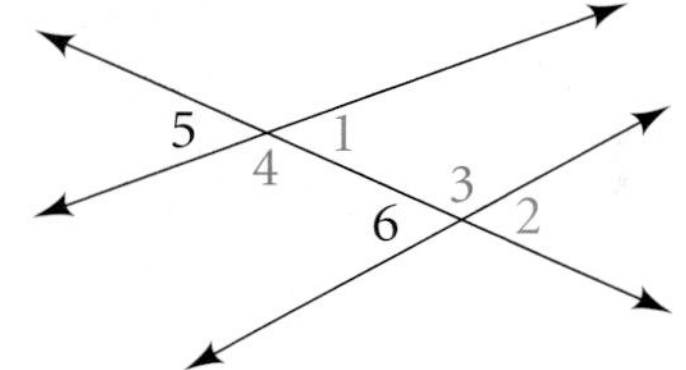

2.

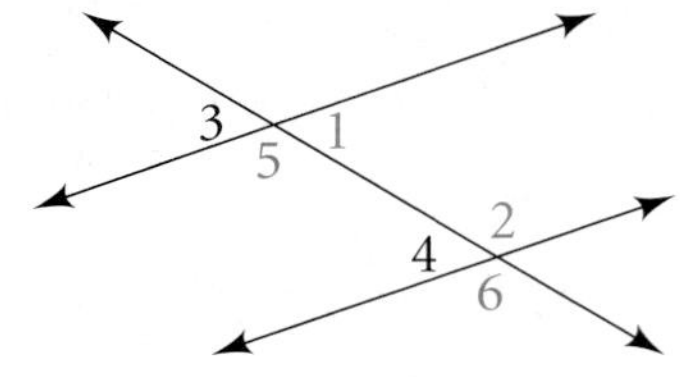

3.

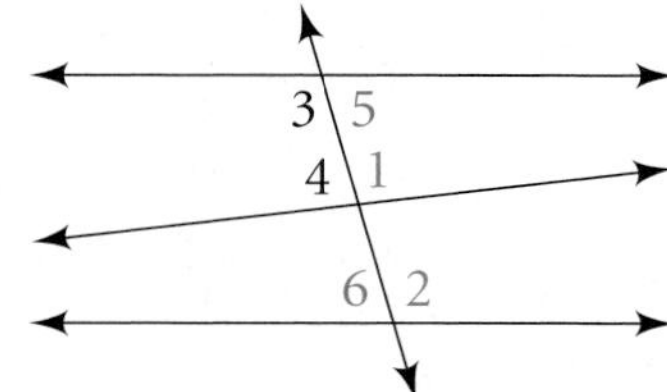

Find $m\angle 1$ and then $m\angle 2$. State the theorems or postulates that justify your answers.

4.

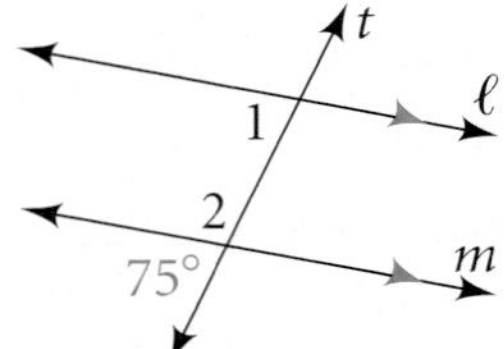

5.

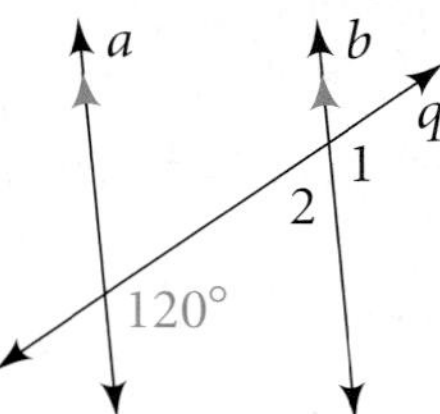

6.

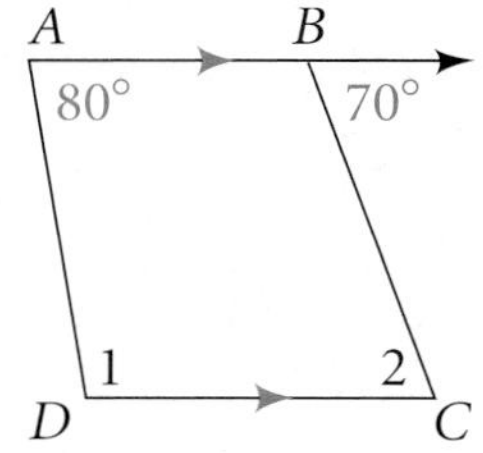

7.

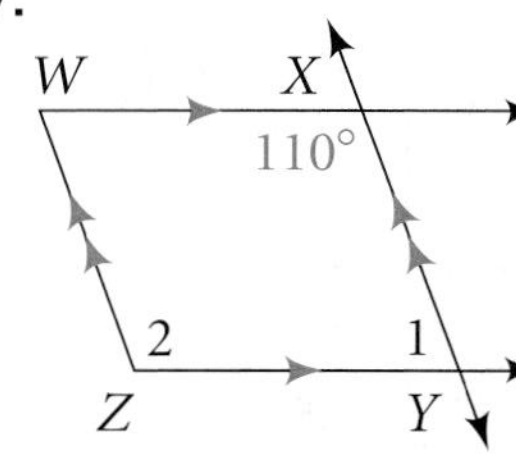

State the theorem or postulate that justifies each statement about the figure at the right.

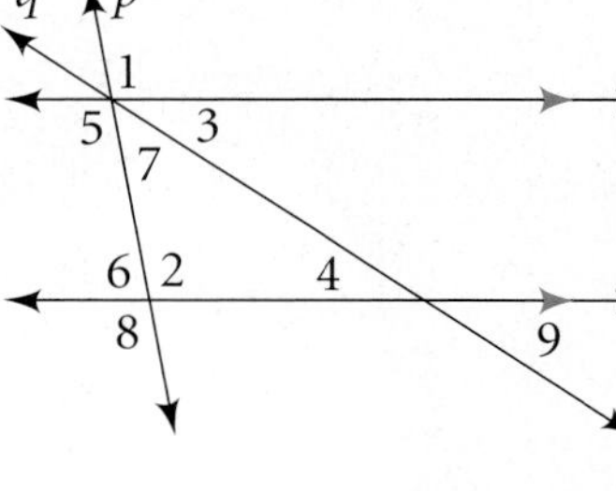

8. $\angle 1 \cong \angle 2$

9. $\angle 3 \cong \angle 4$

10. $m\angle 5 + m\angle 6 = 180$

11. $\angle 5 \cong \angle 2$

12. $\angle 5 \cong \angle 8$

13. $\angle 3 \cong \angle 9$

14. **Open-ended** The letter **Z** illustrates alternate interior angles. Find at least two other letters that illustrate the pairs of angles presented in this lesson. For each letter, show which types of angles are formed.

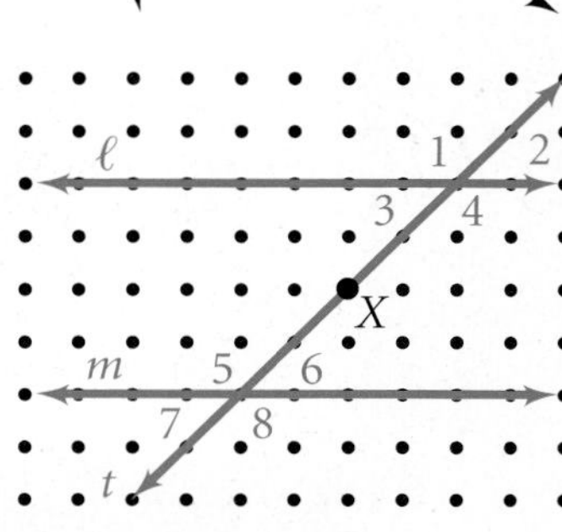

15. a. **Transformational Geometry** Lines ℓ and m are parallel, and line t is a transversal. Under the translation $\langle -4, -4 \rangle$, the image of each of the angles $\angle 1$, $\angle 2$, $\angle 3$, and $\angle 4$ is its __?__ angle.

b. Under a rotation of 180° in point X, the image of each of the angles $\angle 3$, $\angle 4$, $\angle 5$, and $\angle 6$ is its __?__ angle.

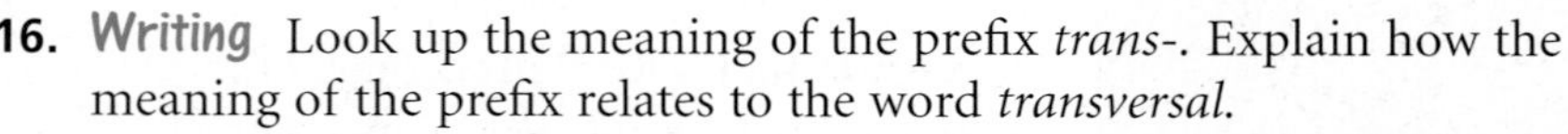

16. **Writing** Look up the meaning of the prefix *trans-*. Explain how the meaning of the prefix relates to the word *transversal.*

17. a. **Probability** Suppose that you pick one even-numbered angle and one odd-numbered angle from the diagram. Find the probability that the two angles are congruent.

b. **Open-ended** Write a probability problem of your own based on the diagram. Then solve it.

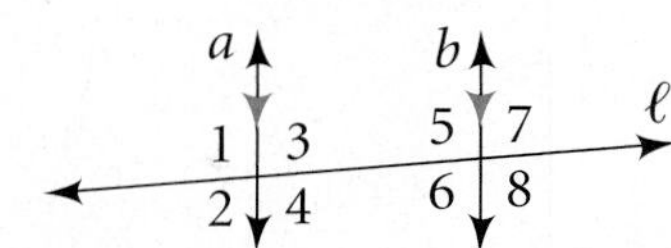

18. a. **Architecture** This photograph contains many examples of parallel lines cut by transversals. Given that $a \parallel b$ and $m\angle 1 = 68$, find $m\angle 2$.

b. Given that $c \parallel d$ and $m\angle 3 = 42$, find $m\angle 4$.

For Exercises 19–27, refer to the diagram below right.

19. Name all pairs of corresponding angles formed by the transversal p and lines ℓ and m.

20. Name all pairs of alternate interior angles formed by the transversal ℓ and lines p and q.

Name the relationship between $\angle 2$ and each of the given angles. In each case, state which line is the transversal.

21. $\angle 3$ 22. $\angle 10$ 23. $\angle 7$ 24. $\angle 4$

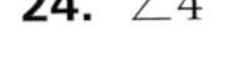

Find all angles that have the given relationship to $\angle 6$.

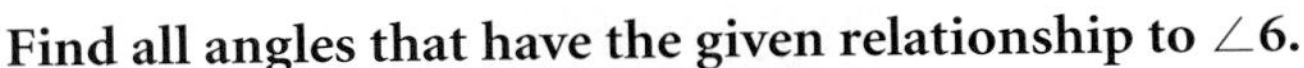

25. alternate interior 26. corresponding 27. same-side interior

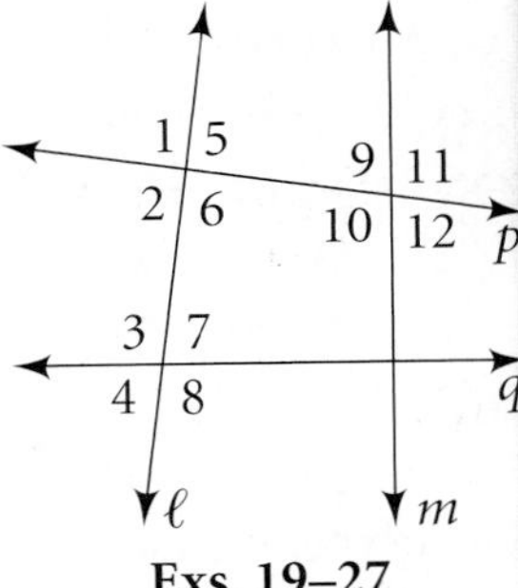

Exs. 19–27

28. **Preparing for Proof** Supply the reasons to complete this proof.

Given: B is the midpoint of $\overline{AC}$.
E is the midpoint of $\overline{AD}$.

Prove: $\angle 1 \cong \angle 2$

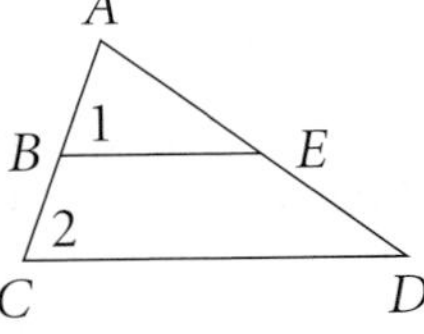

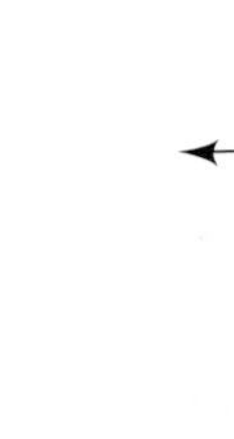

Statements	Reasons
1. B is the midpoint of $\overline{AC}$. E is the midpoint of $\overline{AD}$.	a. ?
2. $\overline{BE} \parallel \overline{CD}$	b. ?
3. $\angle 1 \cong \angle 2$	c. ?

29. **Preparing for Proof** Complete this paragraph proof.

Given: $BERT$ is a parallelogram.

Prove: $\angle 1 \cong \angle 2$

We are given that **a.** ? . By **b.** ? , $\overline{ER} \parallel \overline{BT}$. $\angle 1 \cong \angle 2$ because **c.** ? .

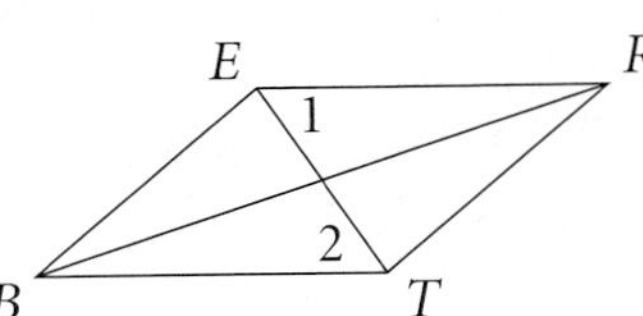

Algebra **Find the values of the variables.**

30.

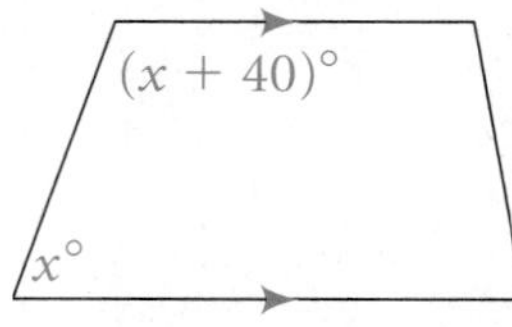

31.

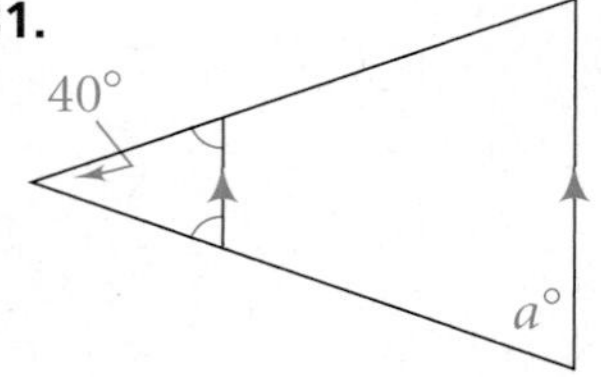

32.

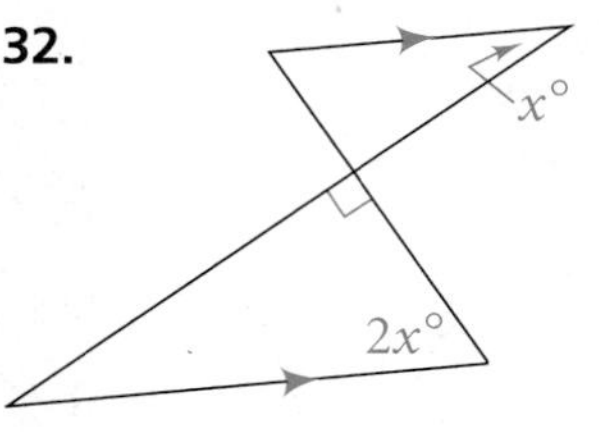

33.

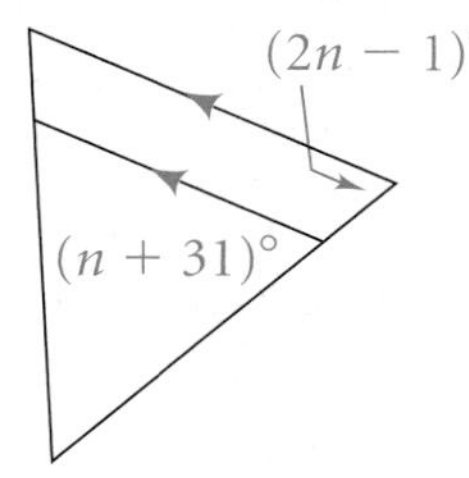

34.

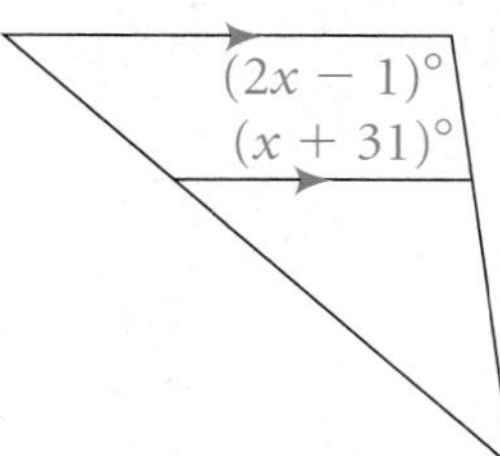

35.

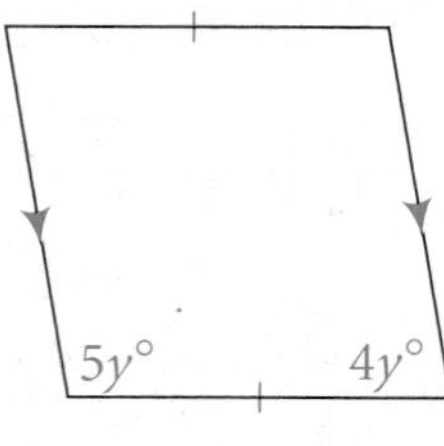

36.

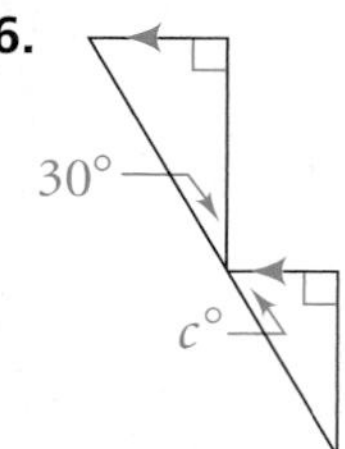

37.

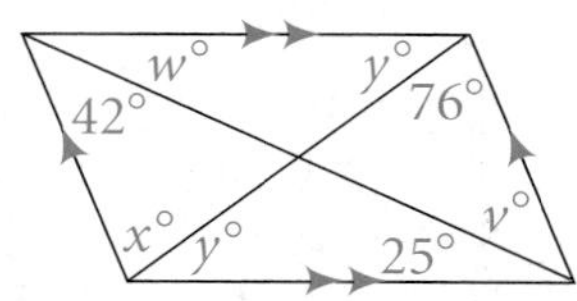

38. ∠1 and ∠3 are *alternate exterior angles*. Write a two-column proof of this statement: If two parallel lines are cut by a transversal, then alternate exterior angles are congruent.

Given: $a \parallel b$

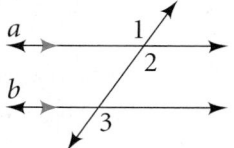

Prove: $\angle 1 \cong \angle 3$

Plan for Proof: Show that $\angle 1 \cong \angle 3$ by showing that both angles are congruent to ∠2.

39. **Critical Thinking** ∠4 and ∠5 are *same-side exterior angles*. Make a **conjecture** about the same-side exterior angles formed by two parallel lines and a transversal. Prove your conjecture.

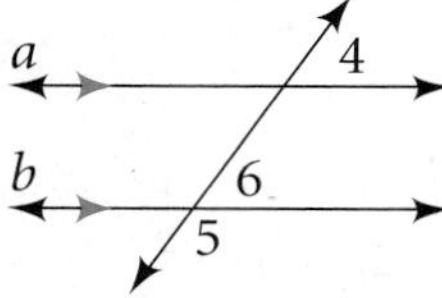

40. Use the diagram to write a paragraph proof of this statement: If a transversal is perpendicular to one of two parallel lines, then it is perpendicular to the other line.

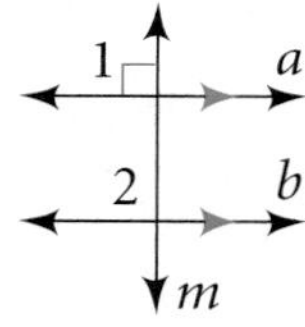

Given: $a \parallel b$, $m \perp a$

Prove: $m \perp b$

41. **Traffic Flow** You are designing the parking lot for a local shopping area, and are considering the two arrangements shown. Give the advantages and disadvantages of each.

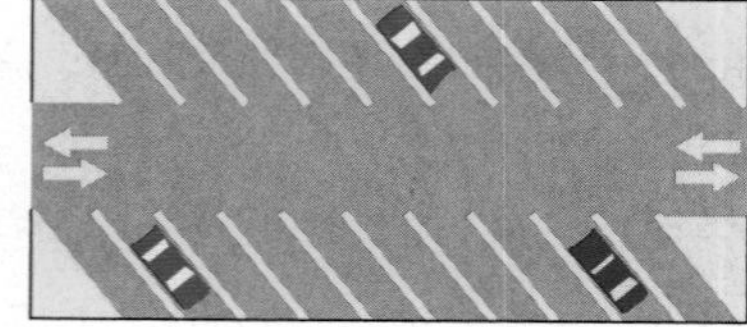

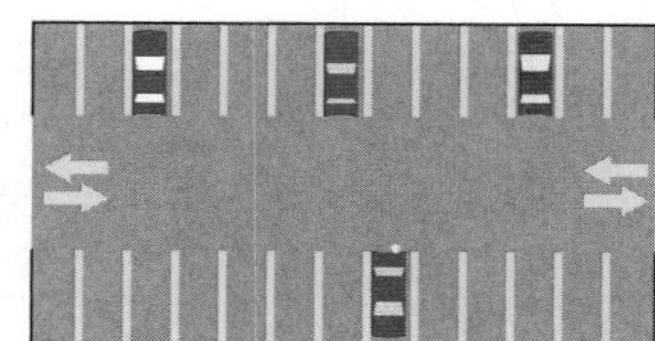

Chapter Project — Find Out by Investigating

Once a month a math coordinator starts at school *A*, drives to the 11 other schools labeled *B* through *L* on the map, and returns to *A*.

- Why must the coordinator backtrack on some of the roads?
- Sketch the shortest route that can be taken. How long is it?
- What additional roads could be built so that the trip could be made without backtracking? Minimize the total length of the new roads. Sketch the shortest route and find its length.

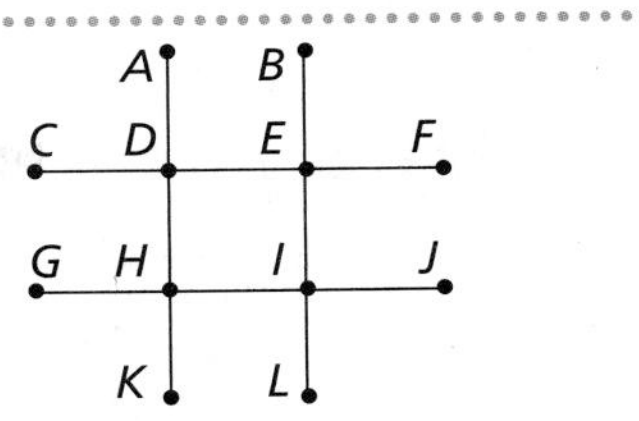

The distance from any school to an adjacent school is 10 mi.

Exercises — MIXED REVIEW

Coordinate Geometry **Find the coordinates of the midpoint of $\overline{AB}$.**

42. $A(0, 9), B(1, 5)$ **43.** $A(-3, 8), B(2, -1)$ **44.** $A(10, -1), B(-4, 7)$ **45.** $A(-5, -11), B(2, 6)$

Data Analysis **Use the double bar graph for Exercises 46–48.**

46. What percent of female players selected the piano as their favorite instrument?

47. Given 50 randomly selected male players, about how many are drummers?

48. Do males or females prefer guitar more?

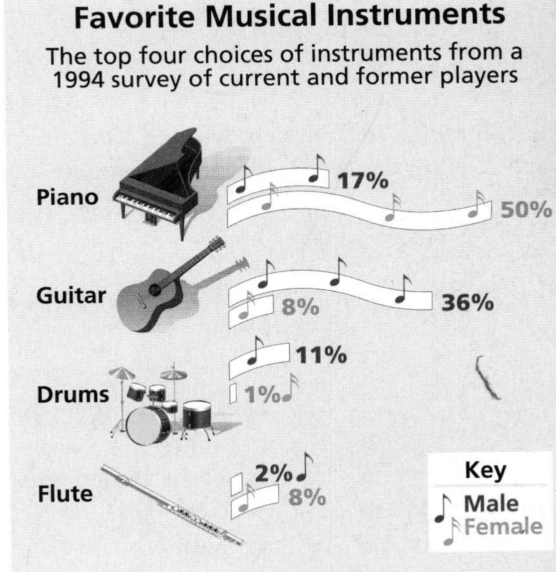

Source: *National Association of Music Merchants*

49. **Sports** The circumference of a regulation basketball is between 75 cm and 78 cm. What are the smallest and largest surface areas a basketball can have? Give your answers to the nearest whole unit.

50. a. **Photography** A regular-sized photo is 3 in. by 5 in. A larger-sized photo is 4 in. by 6 in. What percent more paper is used for a larger-sized photo than for a regular photo?

b. You are making a poster of photos from a class trip. What is the greatest number of regular-sized photos you can fit on a 2 ft-by-3 ft poster? What is the greatest number of larger-sized photos you can fit?

Getting Ready for the Next Lesson

Write the converse of each conditional statement.

51. If the sky is blue, then there are no clouds in the sky.

52. If ℓ and m are parallel, then corresponding angles $\angle 1$ and $\angle 2$ are congruent.

Math ToolboX

Algebra Review

Systems of Linear Equations

You can solve a system of equations in two variables by using substitution to create a one-variable equation.

Example 1

Solve the system: $y = 3x + 5$
$y = x + 1$

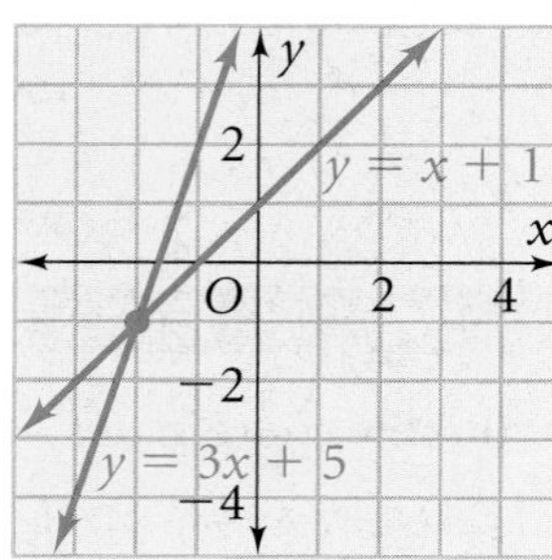

$y = x + 1$ ← Start with one equation.
$3x + 5 = x + 1$ ← Substitute $3x + 5$ for y.
$2x = -4$ ← Solve for x.
$x = -2$

Substitute -2 for x in either equation and solve for y.

$y = x + 1$
$= (-2) + 1 = -1$

Since $x = -2$ and $y = -1$, the solution is $(-2, -1)$.

The graph of a linear system with *no solution* is two parallel lines, and the graph of a linear system with *infinitely many solutions* is one line.

Example 2

Solve the system: $x + y = 3$
$4x + 4y = 8$

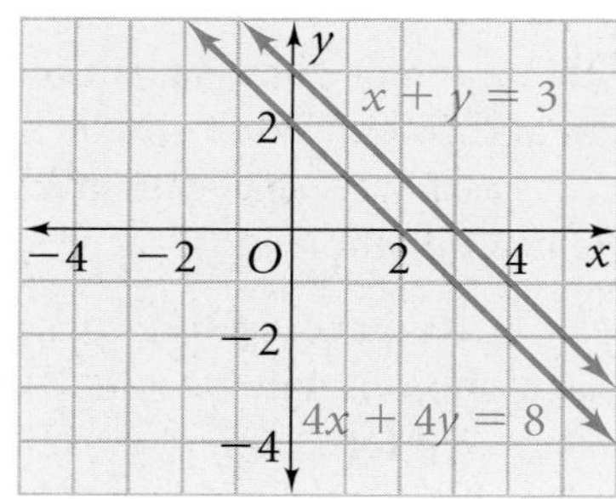

$x + y = 3$
$x = 3 - y$ ← Solve the first equation for x.
$4(3 - y) + 4y = 8$ ← Substitute $3 - y$ for x in the second equation.
$12 - 4y + 4y = 8$ ← Simplify.
$12 = 8$ ← False!

Since $12 = 8$ is a false statement, the system has no solution.

Solve each system of equations.

1. $y = x - 4$
$y = 3x + 2$

2. $2x - y = 8$
$x + 2y = 9$

3. $3x + y = 4$
$-6x - 2y = 12$

4. $y = -x + 2$
$2y = 4 - 2x$

5. $y = 2x + 1$
$y = 3x - 7$

6. $x - y = 4$
$3x - 3y = 6$

Constructing Parallel and Perpendicular Lines

What You'll Learn

- Constructing parallel and perpendicular lines

...And Why

To be able to use parallels and perpendiculars in arts and crafts

What You'll Need

straightedge, compass

THINK AND DISCUSS

Constructing Parallel Lines

You can use what you know about corresponding angles and parallel lines to construct parallel lines.

Construction 5
Parallel through a Point Not on a Line

Construct a line parallel to a given line and through a given point not on the line.

Given: Line ℓ and point N not on ℓ

Step 1
Label two points H and J on ℓ.
Draw $\overleftrightarrow{HN}$.

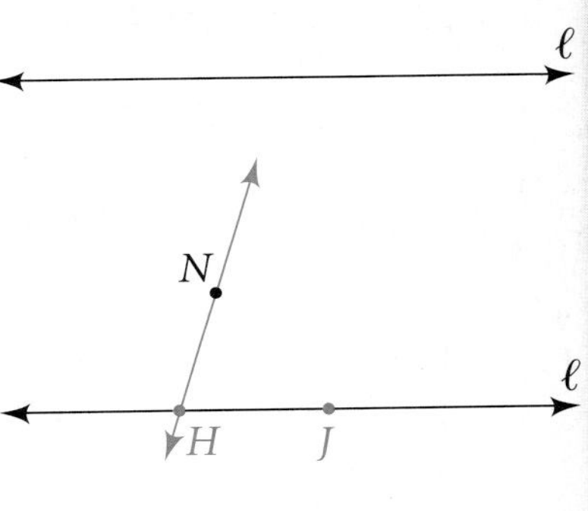

QUICK REVIEW
Instructions for constructing congruent angles are on page 602.

Step 2
Construct $\angle 1$ with vertex at N so that $\angle 1 \cong \angle JHN$ and the two angles are corresponding angles. Label the line you just constructed m.

$\ell \parallel m$

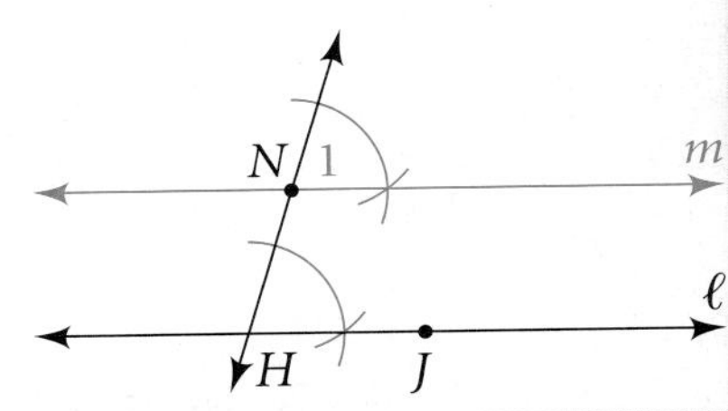

1. Explain why lines ℓ and m are parallel.

Example 1

Use the segments shown at the left to construct a trapezoid with bases of lengths a and b.

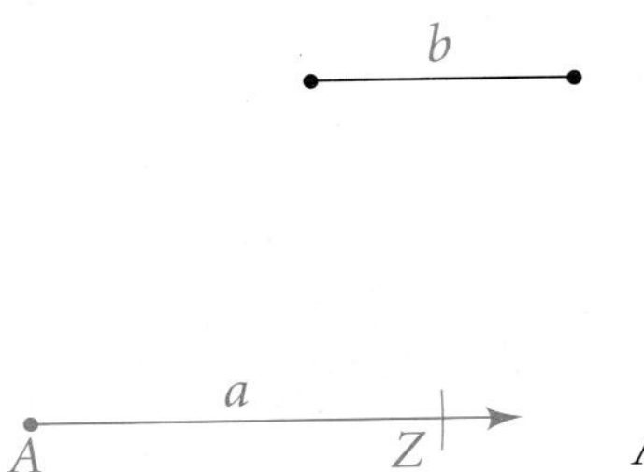

Step 1: Construct $\overline{AZ}$ with length a.

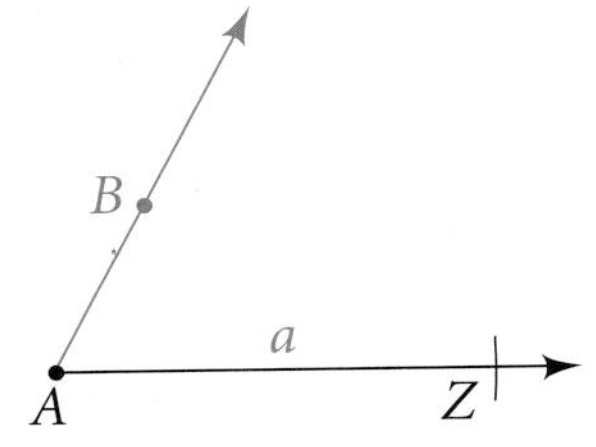

Step 2: Draw a point B not on $\overleftrightarrow{AZ}$. Then draw $\overrightarrow{AB}$.

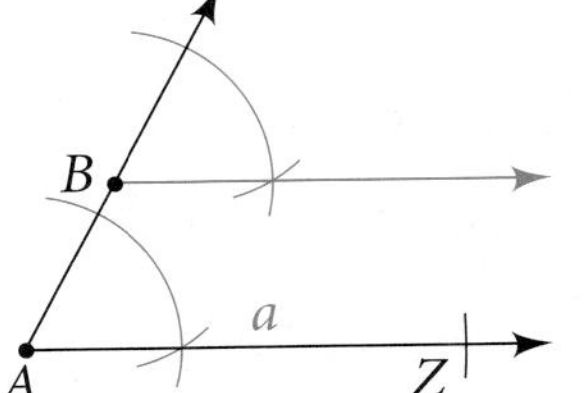

Step 3: Construct a line parallel to $\overleftrightarrow{AZ}$ through B.

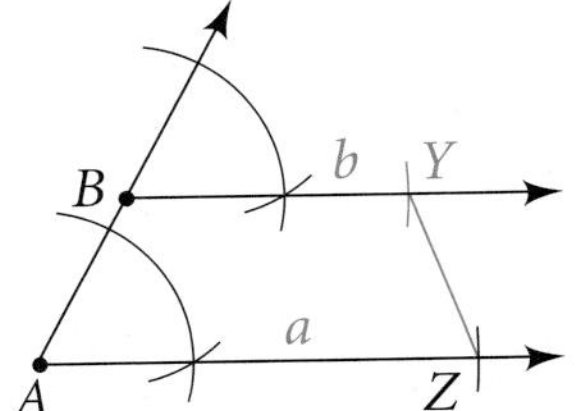

Step 4: Construct Y so that $BY = b$. Then draw $\overline{YZ}$. $ZABY$ is a trapezoid.

Constructing Perpendicular Lines

The two constructions that follow are based on Theorem 4-13: If a point is equidistant from the endpoints of a segment, then it is on the perpendicular bisector of the segment.

2. Explain why $\overleftrightarrow{AB}$ must be the perpendicular bisector of $\overline{CD}$.

3. **Critical Thinking** Turn to page 604 and study the method for constructing a perpendicular bisector of a segment. Explain why that construction works.

Construction 6
Perpendicular through a Point on a Line

Construct the perpendicular to a given line at a given point on the line.

Given: Point P on line ℓ

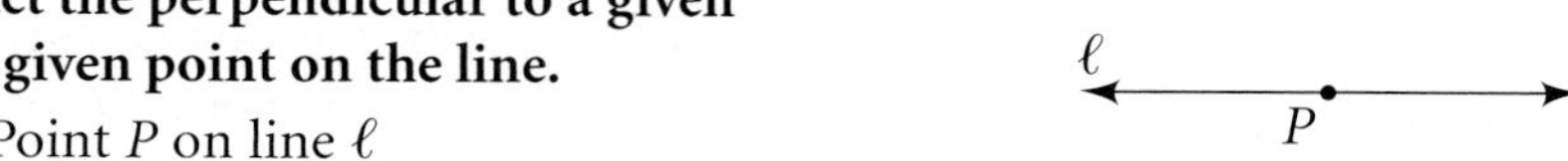

Step 1
Place the compass tip on P. Draw arcs intersecting ℓ in two points. Label the points A and B.

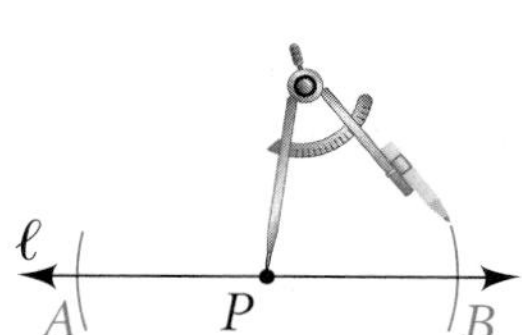

Step 2
Open the compass wider. With the compass tip on A, draw an arc above point P.

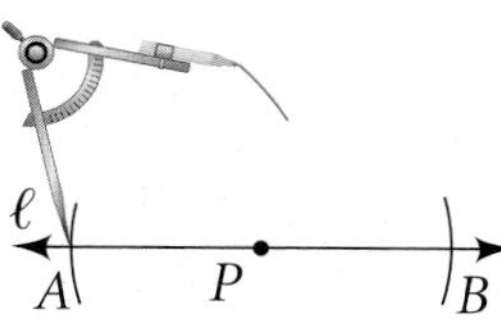

Step 3
Without changing the compass setting, place the compass tip on B. Draw an arc that intersects the arc from Step 2. Label the point of intersection C.

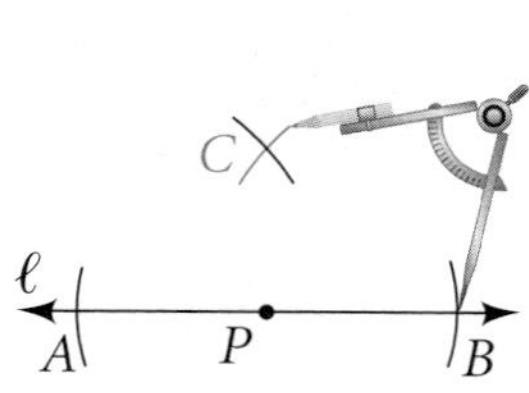

Step 4
Draw $\overleftrightarrow{CP}$.

$\overleftrightarrow{CP} \perp \ell$

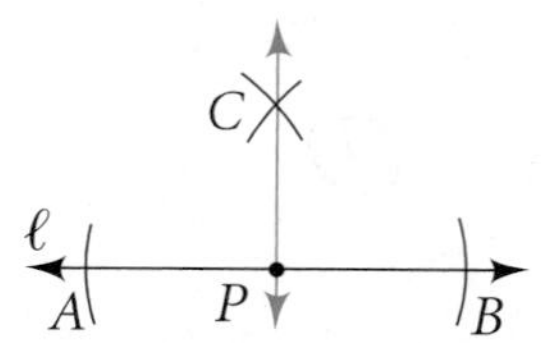

Justification of Construction 6

You constructed A and B so that $AP = BP$. You constructed C so that $AC = BC$. Because P and C are both equidistant from the endpoints of $\overline{AB}$, $\overleftrightarrow{CP}$ is the perpendicular bisector of $\overline{AB}$. So $\overleftrightarrow{CP} \perp \ell$.

4. **Try This** Draw a line $\overleftrightarrow{EF}$. Construct a line $\overleftrightarrow{FG}$ so that $\overleftrightarrow{EF} \perp \overleftrightarrow{FG}$.

American artist Sol LeWitt creates wall-sized drawings that contain geometric figures such as arcs and perpendicular lines. To create arcs, he uses simple, large-scale compasses like the one shown below. He often employs local students to assist in creating his artwork. The two works shown here were on display at the Addison Gallery in Andover, Massachusetts.

Construction 7
Perpendicular through a Point Not on a Line

Construct the perpendicular to a given line from a given point not on the line.

Given: line ℓ and point R not on ℓ

Step 1
Open your compass to a distance greater than the distance from R to ℓ. With the compass tip on R, draw an arc that intersects ℓ at two points. Label the points E and F.

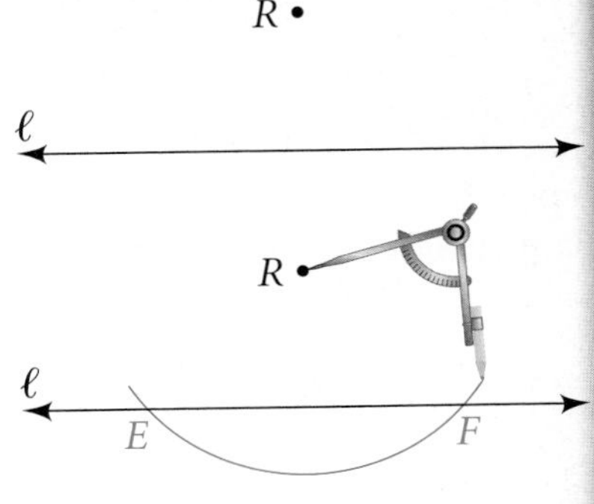

Step 2
Keep the same compass setting. Place the compass point on E and make an arc.

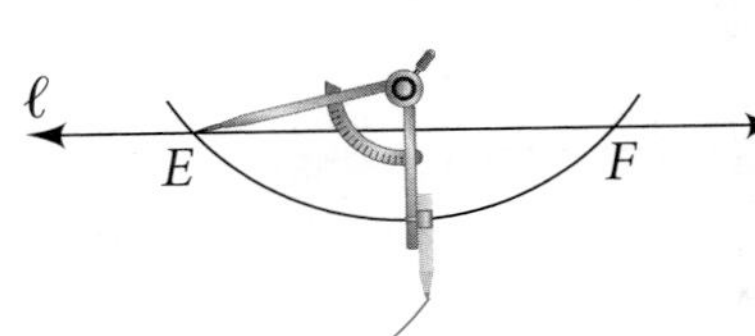

Step 3
Keep the same compass setting. With the compass tip on F, draw an arc that intersects the arc from Step 2. Label the point of intersection G.

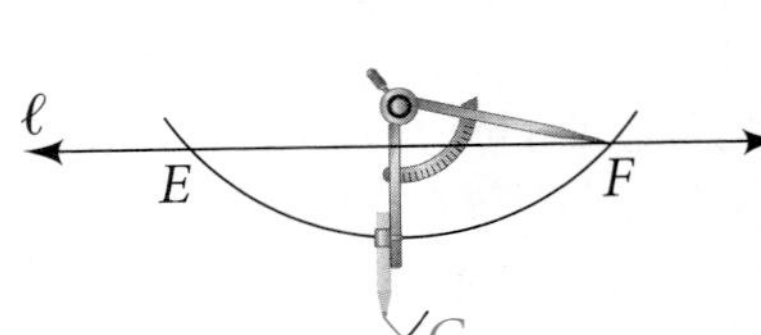

Step 4
Draw $\overleftrightarrow{GR}$.

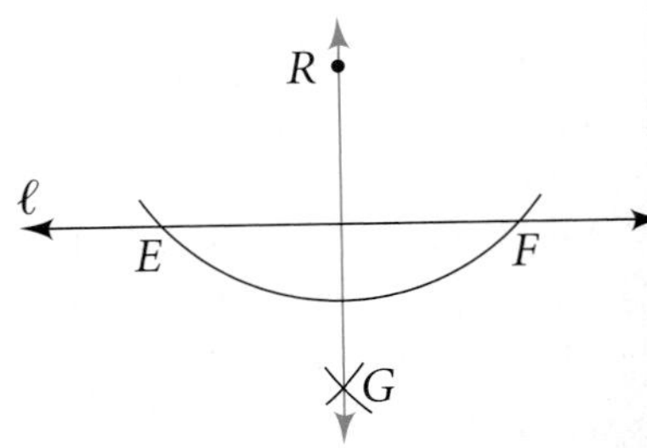

$\overleftrightarrow{GR} \perp \ell$

New York Lessons

5. **Try This** Draw a line $\overleftrightarrow{CX}$ and a point Z not on the line. Construct $\overleftrightarrow{ZB}$ so that $\overleftrightarrow{ZB} \perp \overleftrightarrow{CX}$.

6. **Critical Thinking** Explain why Construction 7 works.

Example 2

Technology Use geometry software to construct a right triangle in which one leg is twice as long as the other.

Step 1: Draw a segment of any length.

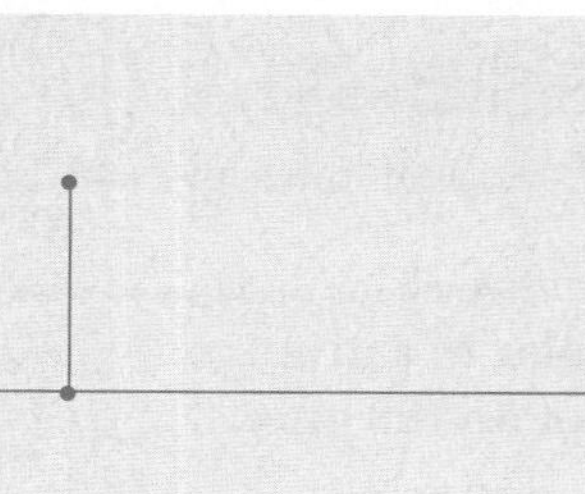

Step 2: Construct a line perpendicular to the segment through one of its endpoints.

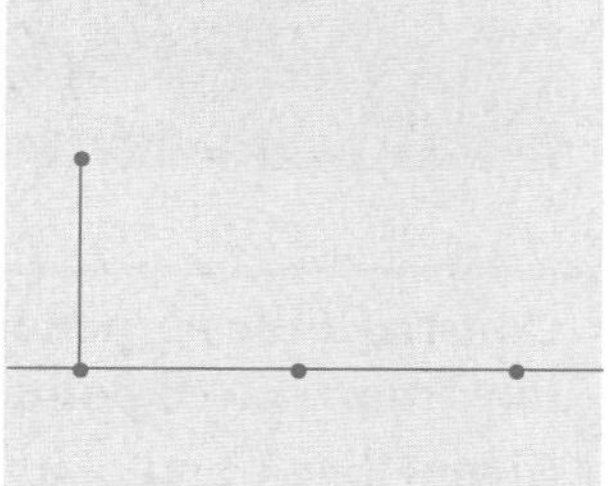

Step 3: On the line, construct two segments congruent to the original segment.

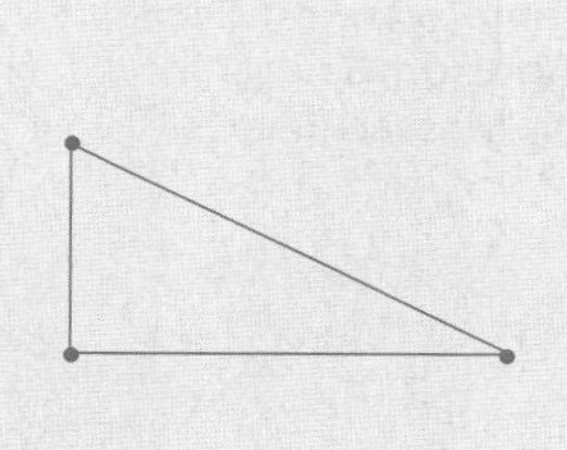

Step 4: Draw the hypotenuse of the triangle. Hide the construction points and lines.

Exercises ON YOUR OWN

1. Draw a line ℓ and a point S not on ℓ. Construct a line m through S so that $m \parallel \ell$.

2. **Transformations** Draw a line ℓ and a segment $\overline{PQ}$ as shown at the right. Construct the reflection image of $\overline{PQ}$ in line ℓ. (*Hint:* Construct a line perpendicular to ℓ through P. Construct P' on the perpendicular so that ℓ bisects $\overline{PP'}$.)

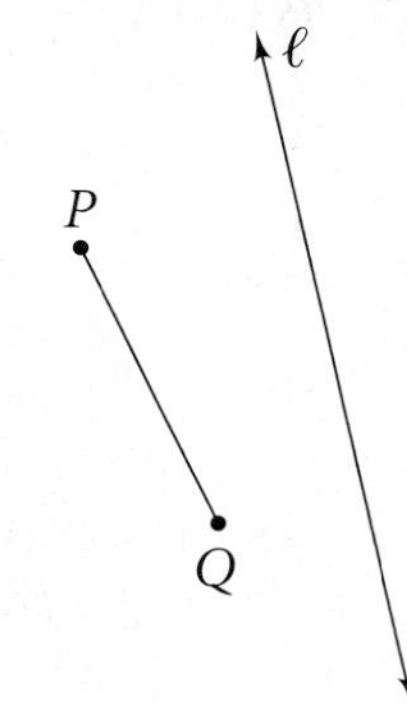

3. **a.** Draw an acute angle on your paper. Construct an angle congruent to the angle you drew so that the two angles are alternate interior angles. (*Hint:* The figure you end up with should look like a **Z**.)
   b. **Writing** Explain how to construct a line parallel to a given line through a point not on the line by using the Converse of the Alternate Interior Angles Theorem.

4. Line m was constructed perpendicular to ℓ through P by this method.
   - Draw two points on ℓ and label them R and S.
   - Construct a circle with center R and radius PR.
   - Construct a circle with center S and radius PS.
   - Draw line m through the intersections of the circles.

   a. **Critical Thinking** Why is line m perpendicular to line ℓ?
   b. Draw a line b and a point C not on b. Construct the perpendicular through C using this two-circle method.

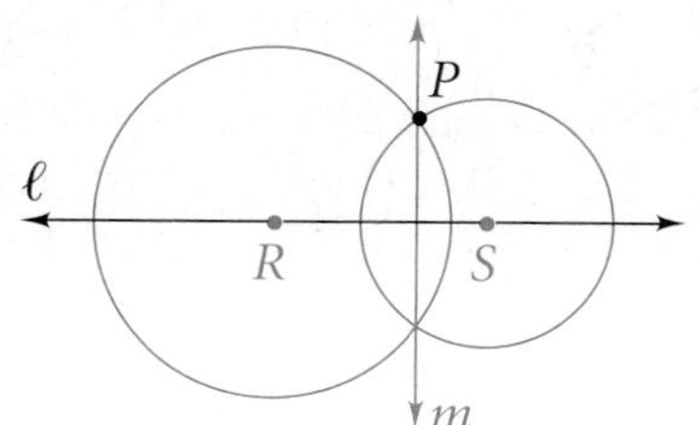

5. a. **Technology** In this computer drawing, R and Q are the intersections of $\odot P$ and line n, all three circles are congruent, and line m is determined by the intersection of $\odot Q$ and $\odot R$. Explain why line m must be perpendicular to line n.

   b. **Symmetry** Describe the symmetries of this drawing.

6. a. Draw a line t and a point P on t. Construct a line s through P so that $s \perp t$.

   b. Draw a point R that is neither on t nor s. Construct a line q through R so that $q \perp s$.

   c. **Critical Thinking** How are q and t related? Explain.

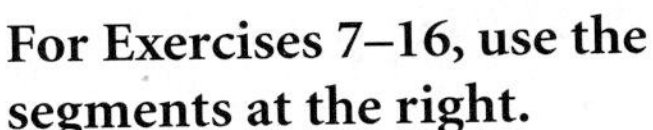

For Exercises 7–16, use the segments at the right.

7. Draw a line m. Construct a point C so that the distance from C to m is b. (*Hint:* Construct a perpendicular from a point on the line.)

8. Construct a trapezoid with bases of lengths a and b.

9. Construct an isosceles trapezoid with legs of length a.

10. a. Construct a quadrilateral with a pair of parallel sides of length c.

    b. What type of quadrilateral does the figure appear to be?

11. a. Construct a triangle with side lengths a, b, and c. Label the triangle $\triangle ABC$, where A is opposite the side of length a, and so on.

    b. Construct the altitude from C.

12. Construct a right triangle in which the length of a leg is a and the length of the hypotenuse is c.

13. Construct a right triangle with legs of lengths b and $\frac{1}{2}b$.

14. a. Construct an isosceles right triangle with legs of length b.

    b. What is the length of the hypotenuse of this triangle?

15. Construct a rectangle with base b and height c.

16. **Locus** Draw a segment of any length. Construct the locus of points in a plane a distance a from the segment.

17. **Paper Folding** You can use paper folding to create a perpendicular to a given line through a given point. Fold the paper so the line overlaps itself and so the fold line contains the point.

   a. Draw a line *m* and a point *W* not on the line. Use paper folding to create the perpendicular through *W*. Label the fold line *k*.

   b. Use paper folding to create a line perpendicular to *k* through *W*. Label this fold line *p*.

   c. What is true of *p* and *m*? **Justify** your answer.

18. **Critical Thinking** Jane was trying to construct a 45°-45°-90° triangle, but couldn't figure out how to construct a 45° angle. Lenesha told her that she didn't need to know how to construct a 45° angle in order to construct the triangle. What construction procedure do you think Lenesha had in mind?

19. Three methods for constructing a 30°-60°-90° triangle are shown. The numbers indicate the order in which the arcs should be drawn. Explain why each method works.

a.

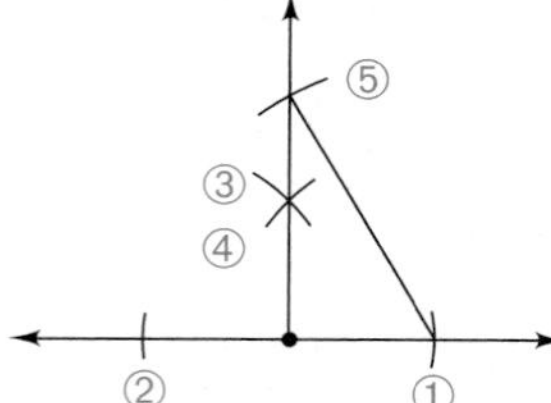

b.

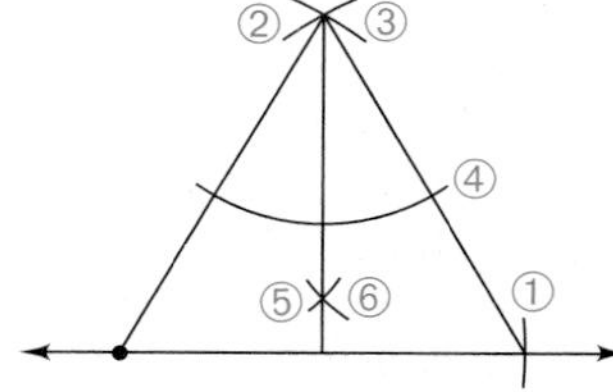

c.

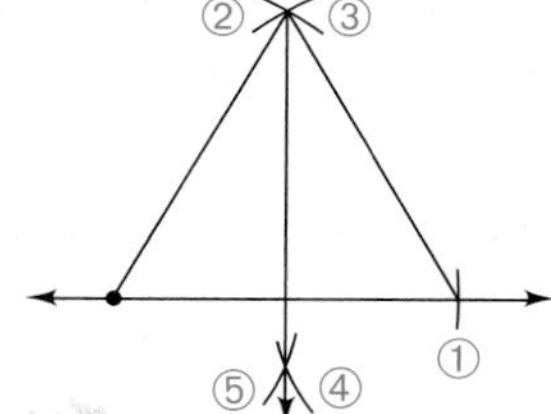

20. **a. Open-ended** Construct a rectangle whose length is twice its width.

   b. Construct a rectangle whose length is four times its width.

   c. Critical Thinking How could you construct a rectangle whose length is 1.5 times its width? (*Hint:* Use a ratio equivalent to 1.5 : 1.)

Chapter Project

Find Out by Designing

Design a network of fiber-optic cables to link the 12 schools labeled *A–L* in the diagram. Assume that a computer at each school can be programmed to route a signal from that school to any other school, even if the signal has to pass through other schools on the way. Assume also that a single cable can handle both incoming and outgoing signals—just as a two-lane road handles traffic in both directions. In your design, try to use the fewest miles of cable possible. The cables do not have to coincide with roads. When you've completed your design, compare it with those of your classmates. Describe the design that you recommend and explain your recommendation.

A B
C D E F
G H I J
K L

The distance from any school to an adjacent school is 10 mi.

Exercises MIXED REVIEW

If a triangle can be drawn with sides of the given lengths, will the triangle be acute, right, or obtuse? Explain.

21. 2, 3, 5

22. 3, 4, 6

23. 4, 5, 4

24. Coordinate Geometry Write the equation of a line through (5, −2) and (4, 3).

25. You may leave your answers to parts (a–c) in terms of π.

a. A circle has radius 8 cm. Two radii of the circle form a 120° angle. What is the arc length of the intercepted arc?

b. What is the area of the entire circle?

c. What is the area of the 120° sector?

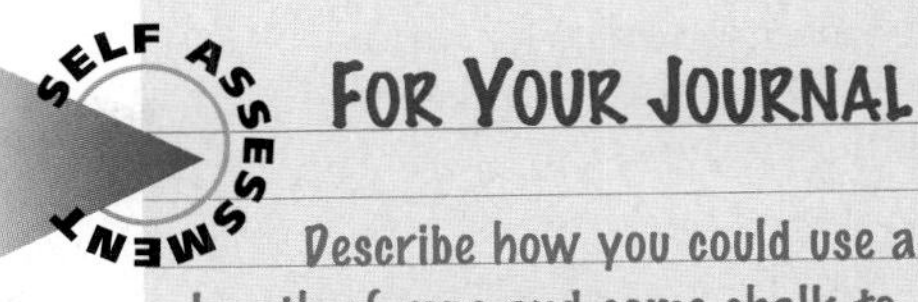

FOR YOUR JOURNAL

Describe how you could use a length of rope and some chalk to construct a right angle on a playground.

Getting Ready for the Next Lesson

Draw a prism with the given figure as a base.

26.

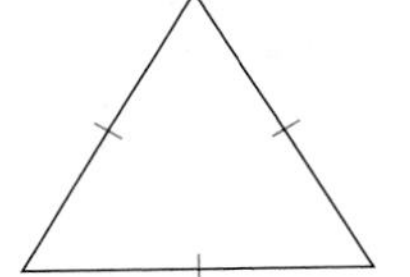

27.

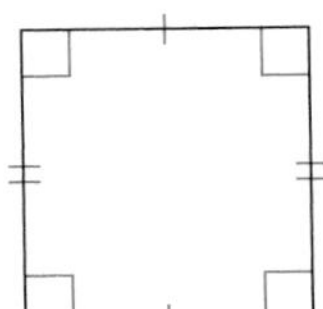

28.

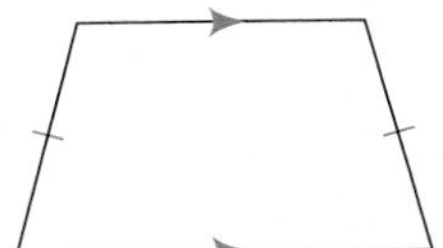

Exercises CHECKPOINT

State the theorem or postulate that justifies each statement.

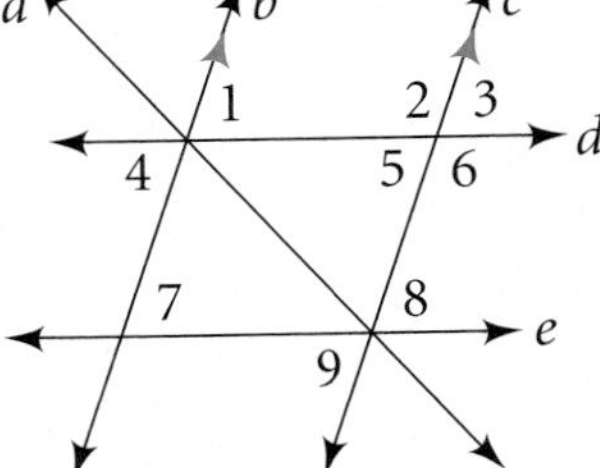

1. $\angle 1 \cong \angle 3$

2. If $\angle 5 \cong \angle 9$, then $d \parallel e$.

3. $m\angle 1 + m\angle 2 = 180$

4. If $\angle 4 \cong \angle 7$, then $d \parallel e$.

5. $\angle 1 \cong \angle 4$

6. $\angle 7 \cong \angle 9$

7. If $\angle 3 \cong \angle 8$, then $d \parallel e$.

8. $\angle 4 \cong \angle 5$

9. If $m\angle 8 + m\angle 6 = 180$, then $d \parallel e$.

10. Draw a line m and a point D on m. Then construct a line n through D so that $n \perp m$.

11. Open-ended Construct a trapezoid with a right angle and with one base twice the length of the other.

12. Standardized Test Prep Which of the following statements is *not* always true if two parallel lines m and n are cut by transversal t?

A. Corresponding angles are congruent.

B. Alternate interior angles are congruent.

C. Exterior angles are congruent.

D. Four of the eight angles formed are congruent.

E. Pairs of same-side interior angles are supplementary.

Connections Community Service . . . and more

Perimeters and Areas of Similar Figures

What You'll Learn

- Finding the relationships between the similarity ratio and the perimeters and areas of similar figures

...And Why

To determine the perimeter or area of a figure when you know the perimeter or area of a similar figure

What You'll Need

- graph paper
- calculator

WORK TOGETHER

Work with a partner to investigate perimeters and areas of similar rectangles.

In the corner of a sheet of graph paper, draw a 3 unit-by-4 unit rectangle as shown at the right.

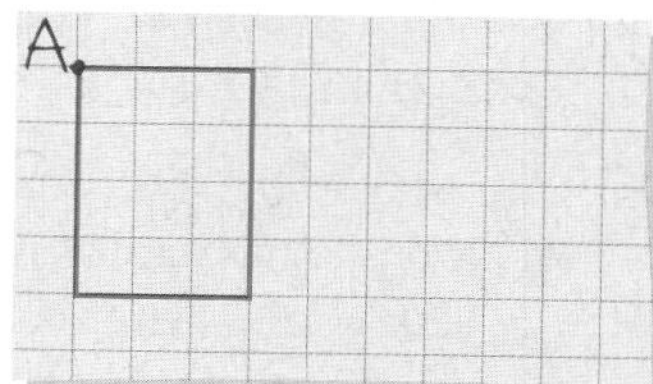

Choose three scale factors from the set {2, 3, 4, . . . , 10}. Using the three scale factors and point A as the center, draw three dilations of the rectangle. Label them Rectangles I, II, and III.

Rectangle	Scale Factor	Width	Length	Perimeter	Area
Original	—	3	4		
I					
II					
III					

1. Use your drawings to complete a chart like this.

Rectangles	Scale Factor	Ratio of Widths	Ratio of Lengths	Ratio of Perimeters	Ratio of Areas
I to Original	2	2:1	2:1		
II to Original					
III to Original					

2. Use the information in your first chart to complete a chart like this.

3. How do the ratios compare with the scale factor? Compare your results with the results of other groups.

Centimeter Grid Pap

THINK AND DISCUSS

Rectangle I is similar to Rectangle II with a similarity ratio of $1 : k$. You can use algebra to simplify the ratio of their perimeters and the ratio of their areas.

$$\frac{\text{Perimeter of Rect. I}}{\text{Perimeter of Rect. II}} = \frac{2l + 2w}{2(kl) + 2(kw)} = \frac{2l + 2w}{k(2l + 2w)} = \frac{1}{k}$$

$$\frac{\text{Area of Rect. I}}{\text{Area of Rect. II}} = \frac{lw}{(kl)(kw)} = \frac{lw}{(k^2)(lw)} = \frac{1}{k^2}$$

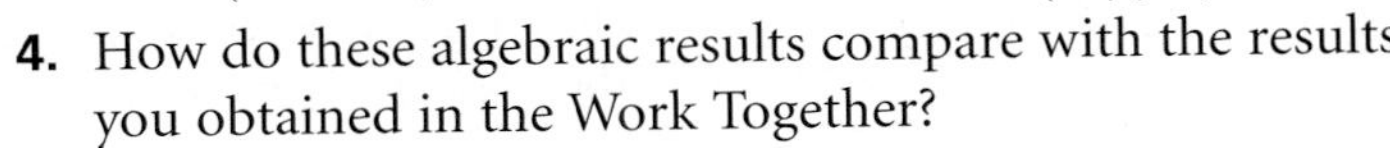

4. How do these algebraic results compare with the results you obtained in the Work Together?

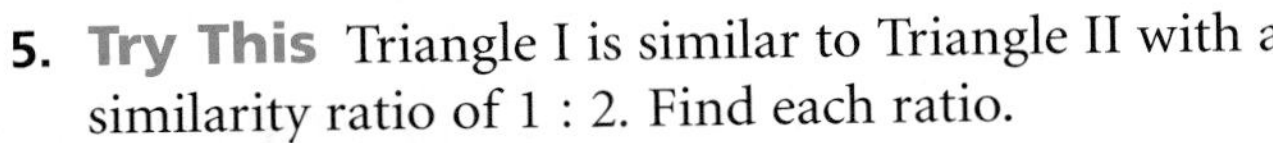

5. **Try This** Triangle I is similar to Triangle II with a similarity ratio of 1 : 2. Find each ratio.
   a. $\frac{\text{Perimeter of Triangle I}}{\text{Perimeter of Triangle II}}$ b. $\frac{\text{Area of Triangle I}}{\text{Area of Triangle II}}$

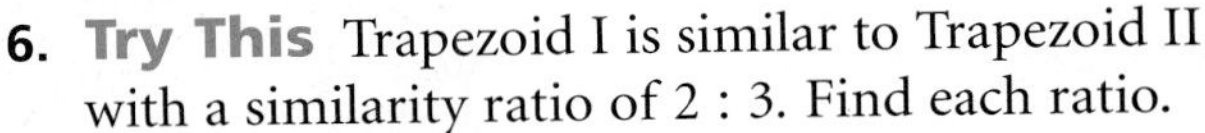

6. **Try This** Trapezoid I is similar to Trapezoid II with a similarity ratio of 2 : 3. Find each ratio.
   a. $\frac{\text{Perimeter of Trapezoid I}}{\text{Perimeter of Trapezoid II}}$ b. $\frac{\text{Area of Trapezoid I}}{\text{Area of Trapezoid II}}$

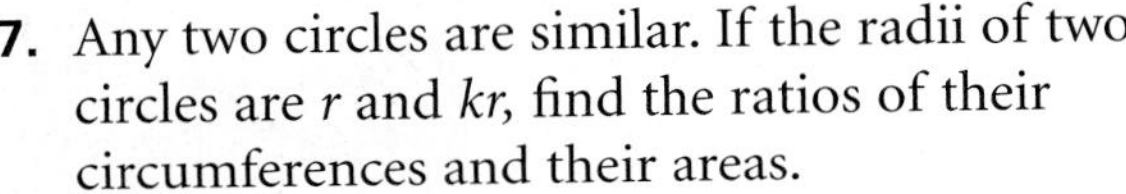

7. Any two circles are similar. If the radii of two circles are r and kr, find the ratios of their circumferences and their areas.

The results you obtained above for rectangles, triangles, trapezoids, and circles are generalized for all similar figures in the following theorem.

Theorem 10-6
Perimeters and Areas of Similar Figures

If the similarity ratio of two similar figures is $a : b$, then (1) the ratio of their perimeters is $a : b$, and (2) the ratio of their areas is $a^2 : b^2$.

Example 1

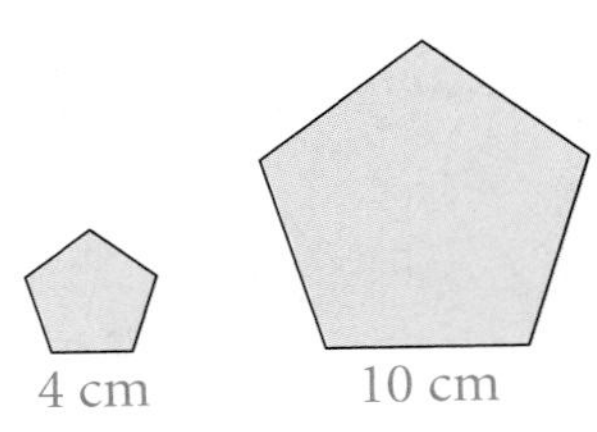

Calculator The area of the smaller regular pentagon is about 27.5 cm^2. Find the area A of the larger regular pentagon.

Any two regular pentagons are similar. The ratio of the lengths of the corresponding sides is $\frac{4}{10}$, or $\frac{2}{5}$. The ratio of the area is $\frac{2^2}{5^2}$, or $\frac{4}{25}$.

$$\frac{4}{25} = \frac{27.5}{A}$$

$A \approx 25$ ⊠ 27.5 ÷ 4 = 171.875

The area of the larger pentagon is about 172 cm^2.

8. **Try This** What is the area of a regular pentagon with sides 16 cm long? Round your answer to the nearest square centimeter.

New York Lessons

Example 2 **Relating to the Real World** 

Community Service During the summer, a group of high school students used a plot of town land to grow 13 bushels of vegetables, which they gave to shelters for the homeless. Their project was so successful that next summer the town will let them use a larger, similar plot of land where each dimension is two and a half times the dimension of the original plot. How much can they expect to grow?

The ratio of the dimensions is 2.5 : 1, so the ratio of the areas of the two plots is $(2.5)^2 : 1^2$, or 6.25 : 1. With 6.25 times as much land they can expect to raise 6.25 times as much, or about 81 bushels.

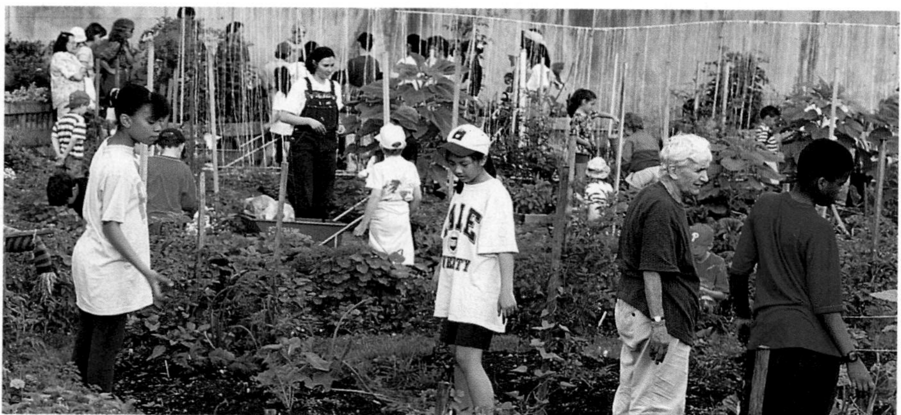

9. **Try This** The similarity ratio of the dimensions of two similar pieces of window glass is 3 : 5. If the smaller piece costs $2.50, what should be the cost of the larger piece?

When you know the ratio of the areas of two similar figures, you can work backward to find the ratio of their perimeters.

Example 3

The areas of two similar triangles are 50 cm^2 and 98 cm^2. What is the ratio of their perimeters?

First find the similarity ratio $a : b$.

$\frac{a^2}{b^2} = \frac{50}{98}$ The ratio of the areas is $a^2 : b^2$.

$\frac{a^2}{b^2} = \frac{25}{49}$ Simplify $\frac{50}{98}$.

$\frac{a}{b} = \frac{5}{7}$ Find the square root of each side.

The ratio of the perimeters equals the similarity ratio 5 : 7.

10. **Try This** The areas of two similar rectangles are 1875 ft^2 and 135 ft^2. Find the ratio of their perimeters.

Exercises ON YOUR OWN

For each pair of similar figures, give the ratio of the perimeters and the ratio of the areas of the first figure to the second one.

1.

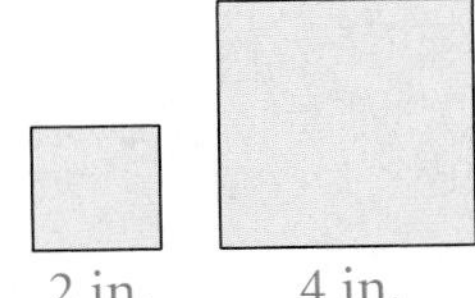

2.

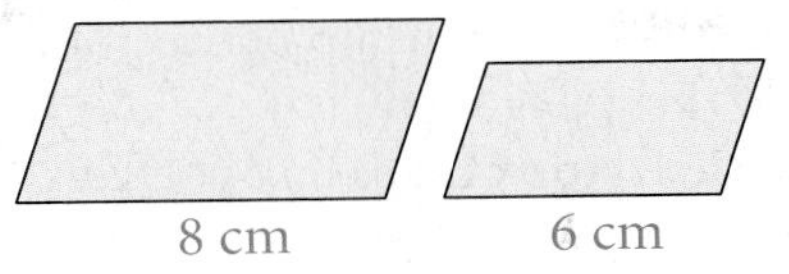

3.

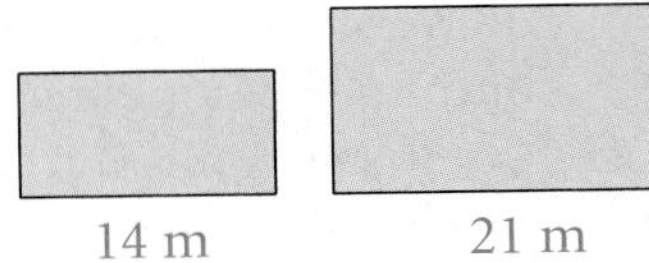

What is the similarity ratio of each pair of similar figures?

4. two circles with areas $2\pi \text{ cm}^2$ and $200\pi \text{ cm}^2$
5. two regular octagons with areas 4 ft^2 and 16 ft^2
6. two triangles with areas 80 m^2 and 20 m^2
7. two trapezoids with areas 49 cm^2 and 9 cm^2

8. a. **Data Analysis** A reporter used the pictograph at the right to show that the number of houses with more than two televisions has doubled in the past few years. Why is such a pictograph misleading?
   b. **Research** Find examples in magazines or newspapers in which areas of similar figures give misleading information.

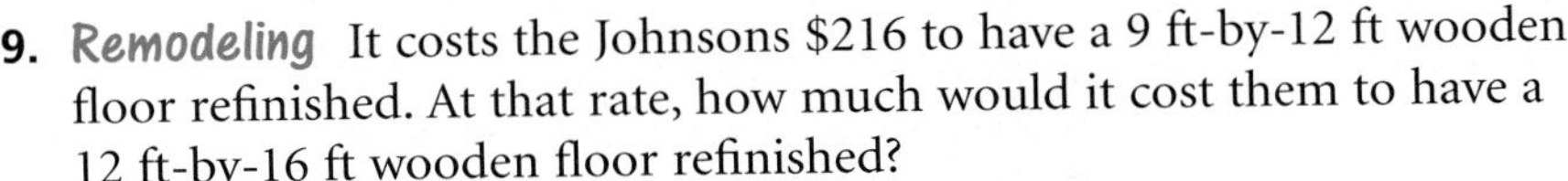
9. **Remodeling** It costs the Johnsons \$216 to have a 9 ft-by-12 ft wooden floor refinished. At that rate, how much would it cost them to have a 12 ft-by-16 ft wooden floor refinished?

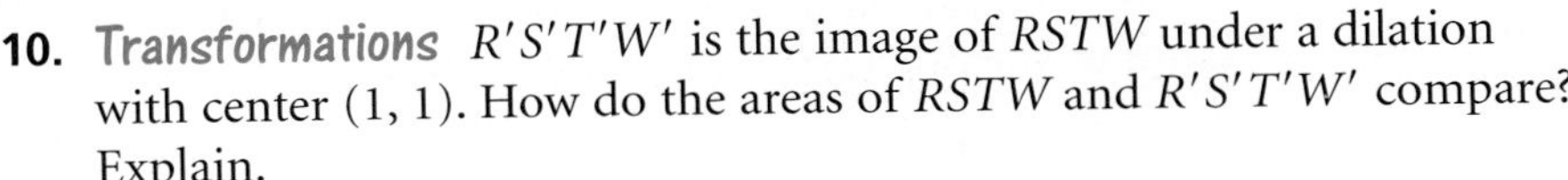
10. **Transformations** $R'S'T'W'$ is the image of $RSTW$ under a dilation with center (1, 1). How do the areas of $RSTW$ and $R'S'T'W'$ compare? Explain.

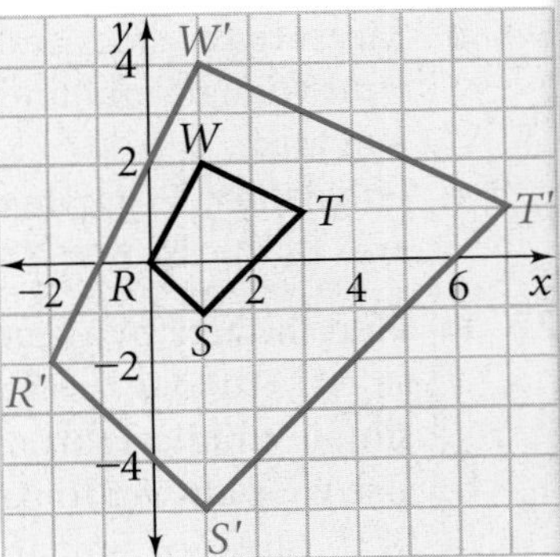

11. **Drawing** Draw a square with an area of 4 in.^{2}. Draw a second square with an area that is four times as large. What is the ratio of their perimeters?

12. The area of a regular decagon is 50 cm^2. What is the area of a regular decagon with sides four times the length of the smaller decagon?

13. In $\triangle RST$, $RS = 20$ m, $ST = 25$ m, and $RT = 40$ m.
    a. **Open-ended** Choose a convenient scale. Then use a compass and a metric ruler to draw $\triangle R'S'T' \sim \triangle RST$.
    b. **Constructions** Construct an altitude of $\triangle R'S'T'$ and measure its length. Find the area of $\triangle R'S'T'$.
    c. **Estimation** Estimate the area of $\triangle RST$.

14. The area of the smaller triangle shown at the right is 24 cm^2. Solve for x and y.

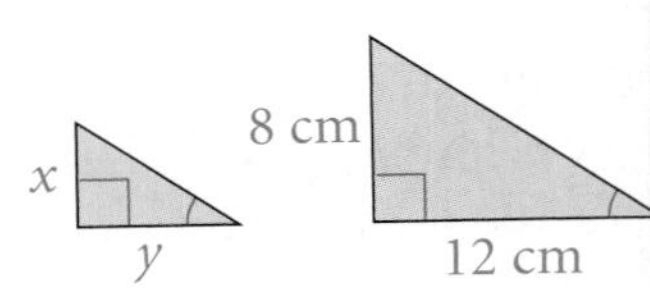

15. The areas of two similar rectangles are 27 in.^{2} and 48 in.^{2}. The longer side of the larger rectangle is 16 in. long. What is the length of the longer side of the smaller rectangle?

16. a. *Transformations* If a dilation with scale factor k maps a polygon onto a second polygon, what is the relationship between the lengths of the corresponding sides of the polygons?

b. Complete: A dilation with scale factor k maps any polygon to a similar polygon whose area is ▇ times as large.

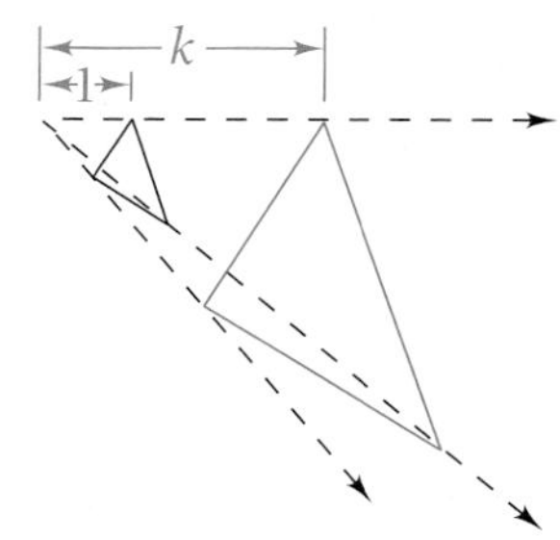

17. a. *Transformations* Graph $ABCD$ with vertices $A(4, 0)$, $B(-2, 4)$, $C(-4, 2)$, and $D(0, -2)$. Then graph its image $A'B'C'D'$ under the dilation with center $(0, 0)$ and scale factor $\frac{3}{2}$.

b. The area of $ABCD$ is 22 square units. What is the area of $A'B'C'D'$?

Find the ratio of the perimeters and the ratio of the areas of the blue figure to the red one.

18.

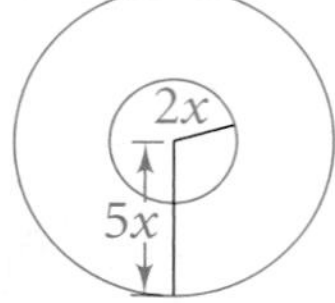

19.

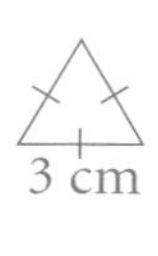

20.

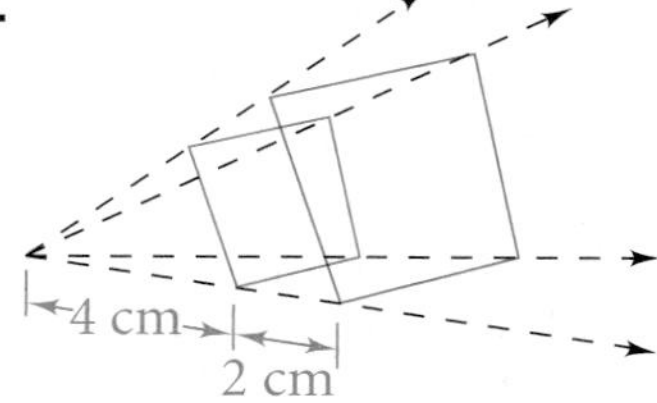

21. a. *Surveying* A surveyor measured one side and two angles of a field as shown in the diagram. Use a ruler and a protractor to draw a similar triangle.

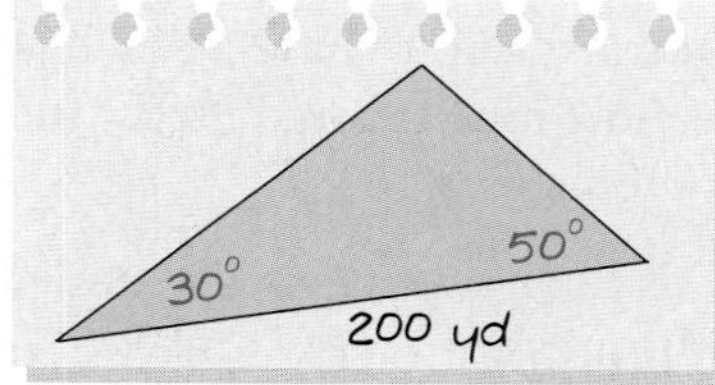

b. Measure the sides and an altitude of your triangle and find its perimeter and area.

c. *Estimation* Estimate the perimeter and area of the field.

22. a. Find the area of a regular hexagon with sides 2 cm long. Leave your answer in simplest radical form.

b. Use your answer to part (a) and the ratio of the areas of similar polygons to find the areas of these regular hexagons.

6 cm 3 cm 8 cm

23. *Writing* The enrollment at an elementary school is going to increase from 200 students to 395 students. The local parents' group is planning to increase the playground area from 100 ft by 200 ft to a larger area that is 200 ft by 400 ft. What would you tell the parents' group when they ask your opinion about whether the new playground area will be large enough?

Chapter Project — *Find Out by Thinking*

What is the area of the Koch snowflake? At each stage you increase the area by adding more and more equilateral triangles. Suppose the area of Stage 0 is 1 square unit. Copy the diagrams and explain why the area of the Koch snowflake will never be greater than 2 square units.

Stage 0
1 square unit of area

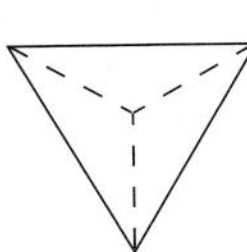

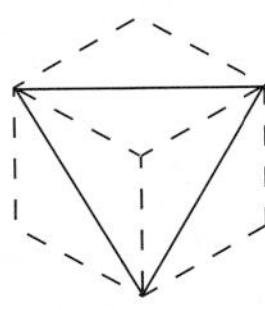

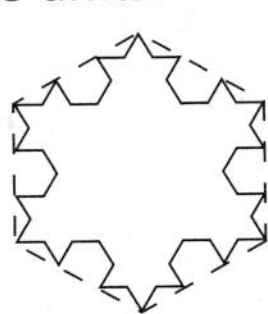

Exercises — MIXED REVIEW

Find the length of the hypotenuse of a right triangle with the given legs. Leave your answers in simplest radical form.

24. 8 cm, 9 cm **25.** 3 in., 5 in. **26.** 10 mm, 5mm

27. Drawing Use a protractor to draw a regular octagon.

Getting Ready for the Next Lesson

Find the volume and surface area of each space figure.

28. cube with a 3-in. side

29. 3 m-by-5 m-by-9 m rectangular prism

FOR YOUR JOURNAL

In your own words, explain the relationship among the similarity ratio of two similar polygons, the ratio of their perimeters, and the ratio of their areas. Include an example.

Exercises — CHECKPOINT

Algebra **Find the values of the variables.**

1.

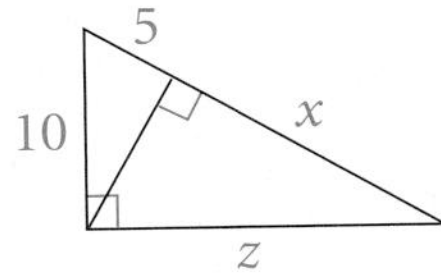

2.

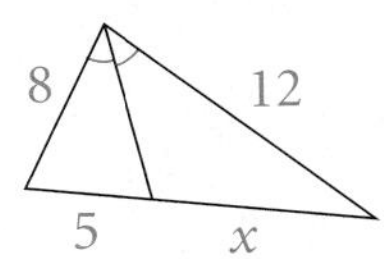

3.

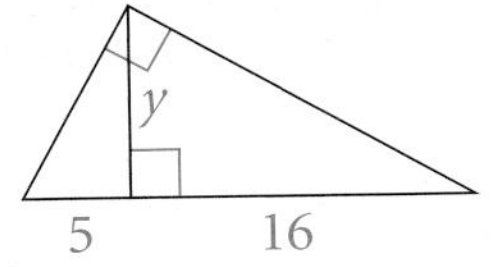

4.

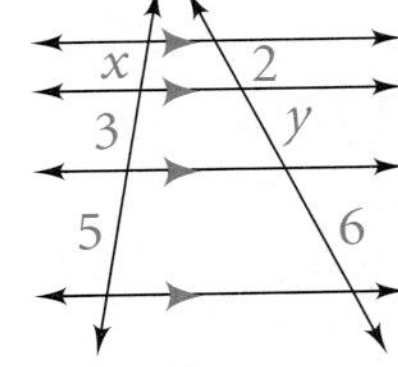

Find the ratios of the perimeters of these similar figures.

5. two triangles with areas 4 ft^2 and 16 ft^2

6. two kites with areas 100 cm^2 and 25 cm^2

7. two squares with areas 63 m^2 and 7 m^2

8. two hexagons with areas 18 $in.^2$ and 128 $in.^2$

9. Standardized Test Prep In $\triangle ABC$, $\overrightarrow{BD}$ bisects $\angle B$. Which of the following is true?

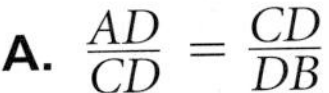

A. $\frac{AD}{CD} = \frac{CD}{DB}$ **B.** $\frac{AB}{CB} = \frac{CB}{DB}$ **C.** $\frac{AB}{AC} = \frac{AC}{AD}$

D. $\frac{AB}{BC} = \frac{AD}{DC}$ **E.** all of the above

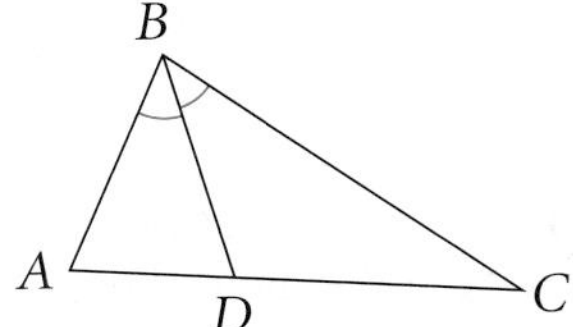

Math ToolboX

Technology

Exploring Similar Solids

Work in pairs or small groups.

Input

To explore surface areas and volumes of similar rectangular prisms, set up a spreadsheet like the one below. You choose numbers for the length, width, height, and similarity ratio. All other numbers will be calculated by formulas.

	A	B	C	D	E	F	G	H	I
1					Surface		Similarity		
2		Length	Width	Height	Area	Volume	Ratio (II : I)	Ratio of	Ratio of
3	Rectangular Prism I	6	4	23	508	552	2	Surface	Volumes
4								Areas (II : I)	(II : I)
5	Similar Prism II	12	8	46	2032	4416		4	8

In cell E3 enter the formula $= 2 * (B3 * C3 + B3 * D3 + C3 * D3)$, which will calculate the sum of the areas of the six faces of Prism I. In cell F3 enter the formula $= B3 * C3 * D3$, which will calculate the volume of Prism I.

In cells B5, C5, and D5 enter the formulas $= G3 * B3$, $= G3 * C3$, and $= G3 * D3$, respectively, which will calculate the dimensions of similar Prism II. Copy the formulas from E3 and F3 into E5 and F5 to calculate the surface area and volume of Prism II.

In cell H5 enter the formula $= E5/E3$ and in cell I5 enter the formula $= F5/F3$ to calculate the ratios of the surface areas and volumes.

Investigate

In row 3, enter numbers for the length, width, height, and similarity ratio. Change those numbers to investigate how the ratios of the surface areas and volumes are related to the similarity ratio.

Conjecture

Make conjectures about the relationships you have discovered.

Extend

- Set up a spreadsheet to investigate the ratios of the surface areas and volumes of similar right cylinders. Do the same for similar square pyramids.

Areas and Volumes of Similar Solids

What You'll Learn

- Finding the relationships between the similarity ratio and the ratios of the areas and volumes of similar solids

...And Why

To determine the area or volume of a solid when you know the area or volume of a similar solid

What You'll Need

- isometric dot paper
- calculator

WORK TOGETHER

Work with a group.

- Draw a 2-by-3-by-2 rectangular prism on isometric dot paper.
- Choose a value of k from the set {2, 3, 4, 5} and draw a $2k$-by-$3k$-by-$2k$ rectangular prism and call it Prism I. Choose two other values of k and draw Prisms II and III.
- Find the surface area and volume of each prism. Compare the original prism to each of the three prisms. Organize your data in a table like this.

	Value of k	Ratio of Corresponding Edges	Ratio of Surface Areas	Ratio of Volumes
Original to I	■	■ : ■	■ : ■	■ : ■
Original to II	■	■ : ■	■ : ■	■ : ■
Original to III	■	■ : ■	■ : ■	■ : ■

1. a. If the corresponding dimensions of two rectangular prisms are in the ratio $1 : k$, what will be the ratio of their surface areas?
   b. What will be the ratio of their volumes?
2. a. If the corresponding dimensions of two rectangular prisms are in the ratio $a : b$, what will be the ratio of their surface areas?
   b. What will be the ratio of their volumes?

THINK AND DISCUSS

These nested Russian dolls are similar solids. **Similar solids** have the same shape and all their corresponding dimensions are proportional.

3. **Critical Thinking** Which of the following *must* be similar solids?
   a. two spheres **b.** two cones **c.** two cubes

4. Can a right triangular prism be similar to an oblique triangular prism? Explain why or why not.

5. Can a triangular pyramid be similar to a square pyramid? Explain why or why not.

The ratio of corresponding dimensions of two similar solids is the **similarity ratio.** In the Work Together, you discovered that the ratio of the surface areas of similar solids equals the square of their similarity ratio, and the ratio of their volumes equals the cube of their similarity ratio. The ratios you have investigated for similar rectangular prisms apply to *all* similar solids.

Theorem 10-7
Areas and Volumes of Similar Solids

If the similarity ratio of two similar solids is $a : b$, then
(1) the ratio of their corresponding areas is $a^2 : b^2$, and
(2) the ratio of their volumes is $a^3 : b^3$.

Example 1

The lateral areas of two similar cylinders are 196π in.^{2} and 324π in.^{2}. The volume of the smaller cylinder is 686π in.^{3}. Find the volume of the larger cylinder.

First find the similarity ratio $a : b$.

$\frac{a^2}{b^2} = \frac{196\pi}{324\pi}$	The ratio of the surface areas is $a^2 : b^2$.
$\frac{a^2}{b^2} = \frac{49}{81}$	Divide the numerator and denominator by the common factor 4π.
$\frac{a}{b} = \frac{7}{9}$	Find the square root of each side.
$\frac{V_1}{V_2} = \frac{7^3}{9^3}$	The ratio of the volumes is $a^3 : b^3$.
$\frac{686\pi}{V_2} = \frac{343}{729}$	Substitute 686π for V_1.
$343V_2 = 686\pi \cdot 729$	Cross-Product Property
$V_2 = 1458\pi$	Divide both sides by 343.

The volume of the larger cylinder is 1458π in.^{3}.

6. **Try This** The surface areas of two similar solids are 160 m^2 and 250 m^2. The volume of the larger one is 250 m^3. What is the volume of the smaller one?

The weights of objects made of the same material are proportional to their volumes.

Example 2 **Relating to the Real World** 

Paperweights A marble paperweight shaped like a pyramid weighs 0.15 lb. How much does a similarly-shaped paperweight weigh if each dimension is three times as large?

The similarity ratio is 1 : 3, so the ratio of the volumes is $1^3 : 3^3$, or 1 : 27.

$\frac{1}{27} = \frac{0.15}{x}$ Let x = weight of the larger paperweight.

$x = 27\,(0.15)$ Cross-Product Property

$x = 4.05$

The larger marble paperweight weighs about 4 lb.

7. **Try This** There are 750 toothpicks in a regular-size box. If a jumbo box is made by doubling all the dimensions of the regular box, how many toothpicks will the jumbo box hold?

8. **Try This** A regular pentagonal prism with base edges 9 cm long is enlarged to a similar prism with base edges 36 cm long. By what factor is its volume increased?

New York Lessons

Exercises ON YOUR OWN

Are the solids similar? Explain.

1. 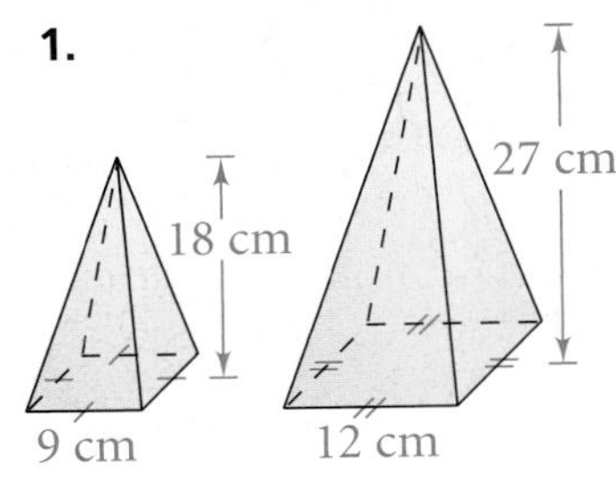

2. 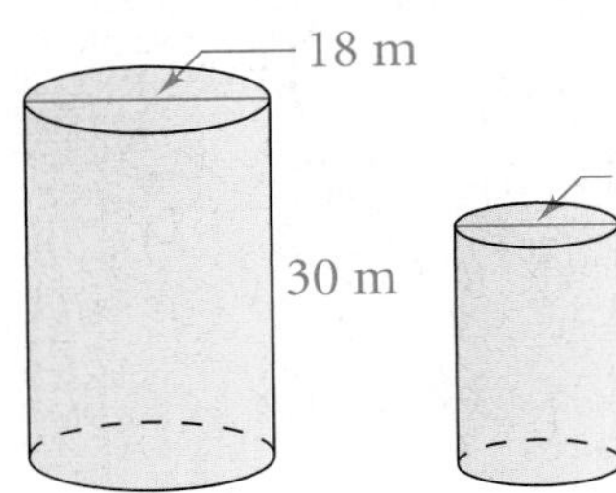

3. 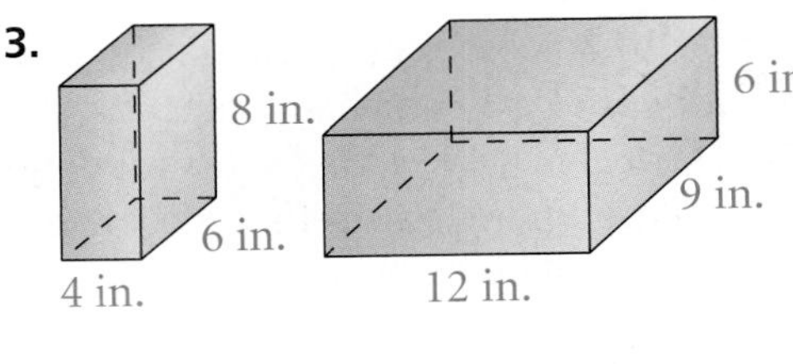

4. Two similar prisms have heights 4 cm and 10 cm.
   a. What is the similarity ratio?
   b. What is the ratio of the surface areas?
   c. What is the ratio of the volumes?

5. *Standardized Test Prep* The ratio of the surface areas of two similar solids is 16 : 49. What is the volume of the smaller one?

   A. 4 **B.** 7 **C.** 64 **D.** 343 **E.** cannot be determined

6. Is there a value of x for which the rectangular solids at the right are similar? Explain.

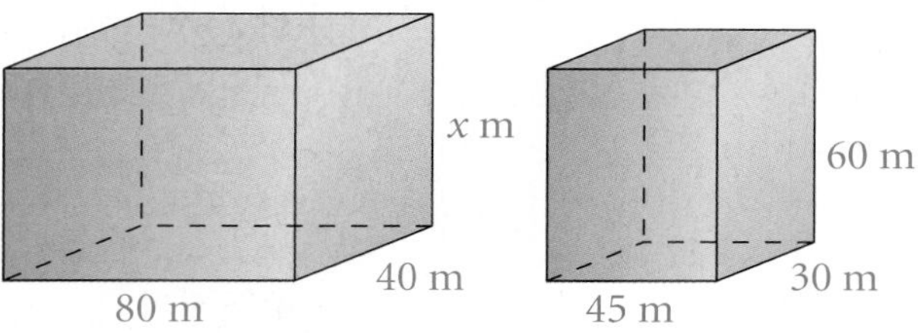

7. The volumes of two spheres are 729 in.^{3} and 81 in.^{3}. Find the ratio of their radii.

8. A carpenter is making a copy of an antique blanket chest that has the shape of a rectangular solid. The length, width, and height of the copy will be 4 in. greater than the original dimensions. Will the chests be similar? Explain.

9. **Estimation** The volume of a spherical balloon with radius 3.1 cm is about 125 cm^3. Estimate the volume of a similar balloon with radius 6 cm.

Copy and complete the table for two similar solids.

	Similarity Ratio	Ratio of Surface Areas	Ratio of Volumes
10.	1 : 2	■ : ■	■ : ■
11.	3 : 5	■ : ■	■ : ■
12.	■ : ■	49 : 81	■ : ■
13.	■ : ■	■ : ■	125 : 512

14. A clown's face on a balloon is 4 in. high when the balloon holds 108 in.^{3} of air. How much air must the balloon hold for the face to be 8 in. high?

15. **Critical Thinking** A company recently announced that it had developed the technology to reduce the size of *atomic clocks,* which are used in electronic devices that transmit data. The company claims that the smaller clock will be $\frac{1}{10}$ the size of existing atomic clocks and $\frac{1}{100}$ the weight. Do these ratios make sense? Explain.

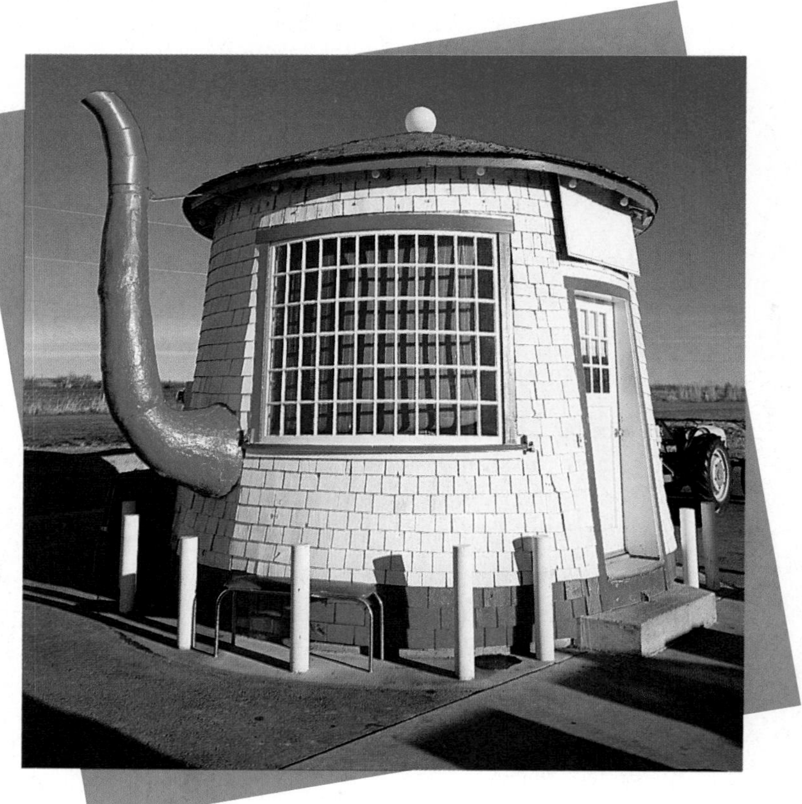

16. **Packaging** A cylinder 4 in. in diameter and 6 in. high holds 1 lb of oatmeal. To the nearest ounce, how much oatmeal will a similar 10-in. high cylinder hold?

17. **Estimation** A teapot 4 in. tall and 4 in. in diameter holds about 1 quart of tea. About how many quarts would this teapot-shaped building hold?

18. **Literature** In *Gulliver's Travels* by Jonathan Swift, Gulliver first traveled to Lilliput. The average height of a Lilliputian was one twelfth Gulliver's height.

a. How many Lilliputian coats could be made from the material in Gulliver's coat? (*Hint:* Use the ratio of surface areas.)

b. How many Lilliputian meals would be needed to make a meal for Gulliver? (*Hint:* Use the ratio of volumes.)

c. **Research** Visit your local library and read about Gulliver's voyage to Brobdingnag in *Gulliver's Travels.* Describe the size of the people and objects in this land. Use ratios of areas and volumes to describe Gulliver's life there.

19. Giants such as King Kong, Godzilla, and Paul Bunyan cannot exist because their bone structure could not support them. The legendary Paul Bunyan is ten times as tall as the average human.

a. The strength of bones is proportional to the area of their cross-section. How many times stronger than the average person's bones would Paul Bunyan's bones be?

b. Weights of objects made of the same material are proportional to their volumes. How many times the average person's weight would Paul Bunyan's weight be?

c. Human leg bones can support about 6 times the average person's weight. How many times the average person's weight could Paul Bunyan's legs support?

d. Use your answers to parts (b) and (c) to explain why Paul Bunyan's legs could not support his weight.

e. **Writing** Explain why massive animals such as elephants have such thick legs.

New York Lessons

Exercises MIXED REVIEW

Coordinate Geometry **Draw the image of each figure for the given transformation.**

20. 90° rotation clockwise about the origin

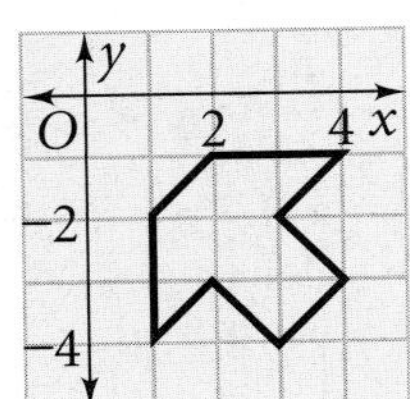

21. reflection in the line $y = x$

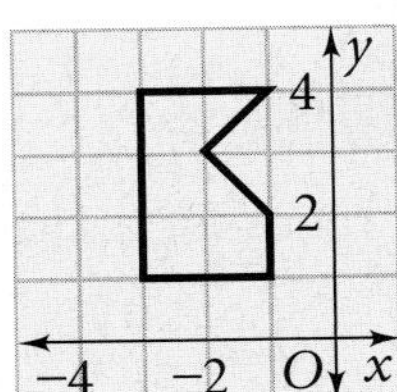

22. What is the area of a 30°-60°-90° triangle with a shorter leg that is 4 cm long? Leave your answer in simplest radical form.

SELF ASSESSMENT

PORTFOLIO

For your portfolio, select two or three items from your work for this chapter. Some possibilities:

- corrected work
- work that you think best shows what you learned or did in this chapter

Explain why you included each selection.

Connections Hiking . . . and more

The Tangent Ratio

What You'll Learn

- Calculating tangents of acute angles in right triangles
- Using tangents to determine side lengths in triangles

...And Why

To calculate distances that cannot be measured directly

What You'll Need

- protractor
- centimeter ruler
- calculator

WORK TOGETHER

- Work in small groups. Your teacher will assign each group a different angle measure from the set $\{10°, 20°, \ldots, 80°\}$.
- Have each member of your group draw a right triangle containing the assigned angle. Make the triangles different sizes. Label your triangle $\triangle PAW$, where $\angle P$ is the assigned angle.
- Use a ruler to measure and label the lengths of the legs of $\triangle PAW$ to the nearest millimeter.

1. *Calculator* Use a calculator to compute the ratio $\frac{\text{leg opposite } \angle P}{\text{leg adjacent to } \angle P}$. Round your answer to two decimal places.

2. Compare the results of Question 1 within your group. Make a **conjecture** based on your comparison.

3. Compare your results with those of other groups. What do you notice?

THINK AND DISCUSS

Using the Tangent Ratio

When? The word *trigonometry* was first used in a publication in 1595 by German clergyman and mathematician Bartholomaus Pitiscus (1561–1613).

The word *trigonometry* comes from the Greek words meaning "triangle measurement." In the Work Together, you made a discovery about a ratio of the lengths of sides of a right triangle. This ratio is called the tangent ratio.

tangent of $\angle A = \frac{\text{leg opposite } \angle A}{\text{leg adjacent to } \angle A}$

This equation can be abbreviated:

$$\tan A = \frac{\text{opposite}}{\text{adjacent}}$$

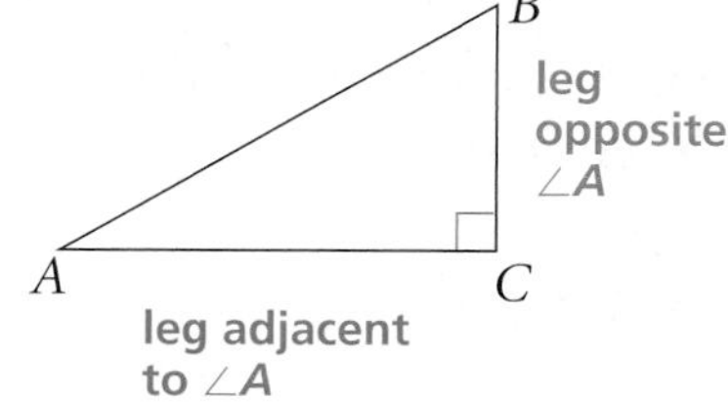

Example 1

Write the tangent ratios for $\angle U$ and $\angle T$.

$$\tan U = \frac{\text{opposite}}{\text{adjacent}} = \frac{TV}{UV} = \frac{4}{3}$$

$$\tan T = \frac{\text{opposite}}{\text{adjacent}} = \frac{UV}{TV} = \frac{3}{4}$$

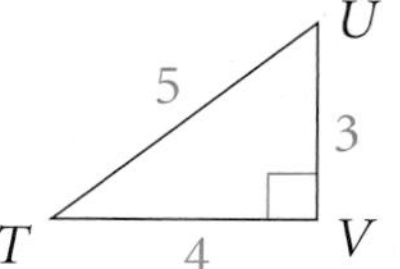

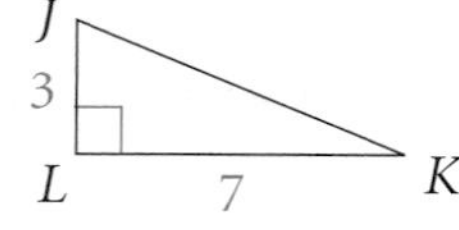

4. a. Try This Write the tangent ratios for $\angle K$ and $\angle J$.

b. How is $\tan K$ related to $\tan J$?

You discovered in the Work Together that the tangent ratio for a given acute angle does not depend on the size of the triangle. Why is this true? Consider the two right triangles shown below.

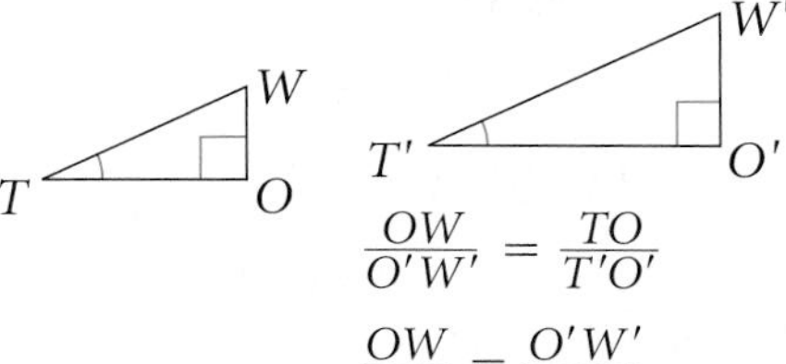

By the AA Similarity Postulate, the two triangles are similar.

$\frac{OW}{O'W'} = \frac{TO}{T'O'}$ Because the triangles are similar, these corresponding sides are in proportion.

$\frac{OW}{TO} = \frac{O'W'}{T'O'}$ Applying a property of proportions yields the tangent ratios for $\angle T$ and $\angle T'$.

You can use the tangent ratio to measure distances that would be difficult to measure directly.

Example 2 Relating to the Real World

Hiking You are hiking in the Rocky Mountains. You come to a canyon and follow these steps to estimate its width.

Step 1: Point your compass at an object on the opposite edge of the canyon and note the reading.

Step 2: Turn 90° and walk off a distance in a straight line along the edge of the canyon.

Step 3: Turn and point the compass at the object again, taking another reading.

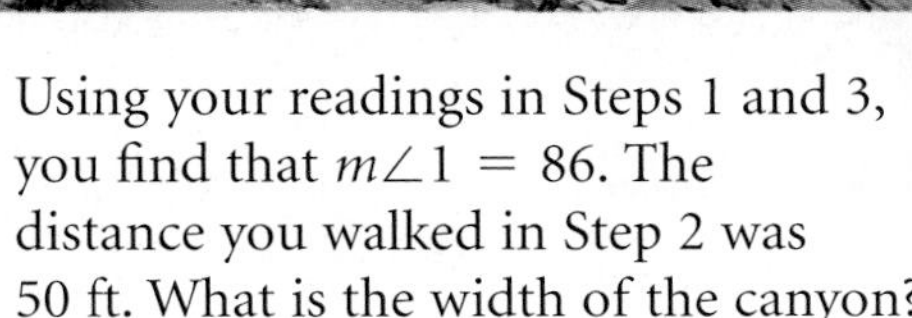

Using your readings in Steps 1 and 3, you find that $m\angle 1 = 86$. The distance you walked in Step 2 was 50 ft. What is the width of the canyon?

$\tan 86° = \frac{x}{50}$ Use the tangent ratio.

$x = 50(\tan 86°)$ Solve for x.

50 [×] 86 [TAN] [=] 715.03331

The canyon is about 700 ft wide.

GRAPHING CALCULATOR HINT

The keystrokes for a scientific calculator are shown at the right. On a graphing calculator, enter 50 [×] [TAN] 86 [ENTER].

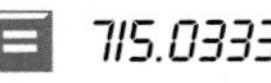

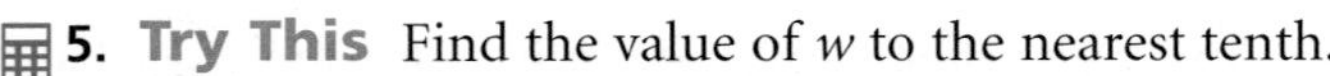

5. Try This Find the value of w to the nearest tenth.

a.

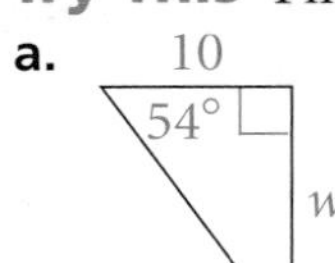

b.

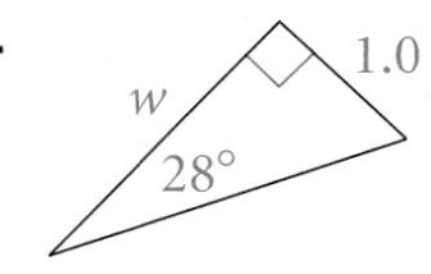

c.

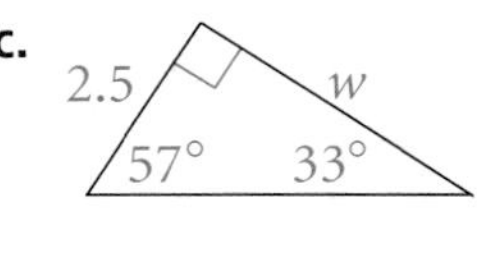

Using the Inverse Tangent Function

Consider $\triangle BHX$ at the left. Suppose you want to find $m\angle X$. You can use the tangent ratio to do so. You know that $\tan X = \frac{6}{8} = 0.75$. To find $m\angle X$, use the *inverse tangent* function on your calculator.

$\tan X = 0.75$

$m\angle X = \tan^{-1}(0.75)$ "$\tan^{-1}$" means "inverse tangent."

0.75 TAN⁻¹ 36.869898 Use the inverse tangent function on a calculator.

So $m\angle X \approx 37$.

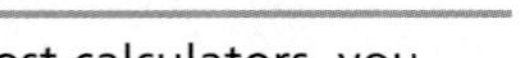

GRAPHING CALCULATOR HINT

On most calculators, you find the inverse tangent of 0.75 by entering .75 2nd TAN or .75 TAN⁻¹. On a graphing calculator, enter 2nd TAN .75 ENTER.

6. Find $m\angle J$ to the nearest degree.

a. $\tan J = 0.5$ **b.** $\tan J = 0.34$ **c.** $\tan J = 100$

7. Critical Thinking Given that $\tan C = 1$, explain how to find $m\angle C$ without using a calculator.

8. Find $m\angle Y$ to the nearest degree.

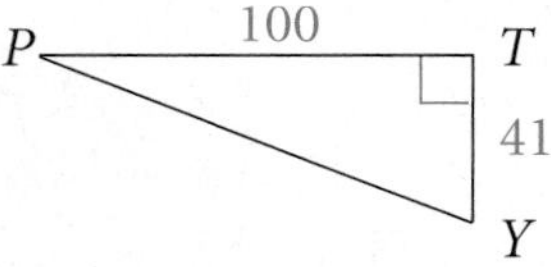

Example 3 shows how the tangent ratio is related to slope.

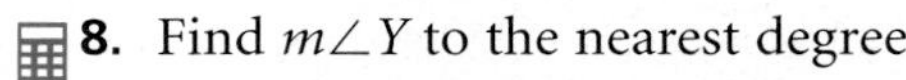

Example 3

Algebra Find the measure of the acute angle that the line $y = 3x + 2$ makes with a horizontal line.

The line $y = 3x + 2$ has a slope of 3. Notice that the ratio $\frac{\text{rise}}{\text{run}}$ is the same as $\frac{\text{leg opposite } \angle A}{\text{leg adjacent to } \angle A}$. So $\tan A = 3$, and $m\angle A = \tan^{-1}(3)$.

3 TAN⁻¹ 71.565051

$m\angle A \approx 71.6$

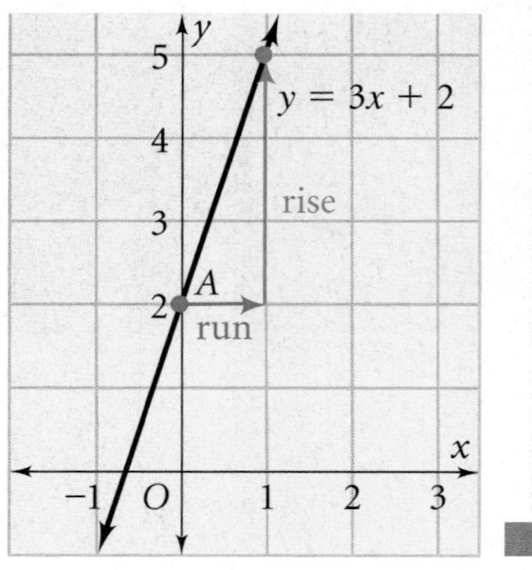

9. Try This Find the measure of the acute angle that each line makes with a horizontal line. Round your answer to the nearest tenth.

a. $y = \frac{1}{2}x + 6$ **b.** $y = 6x - 1$

Exercises ON YOUR OWN

Express tan A and tan B as ratios.

1. 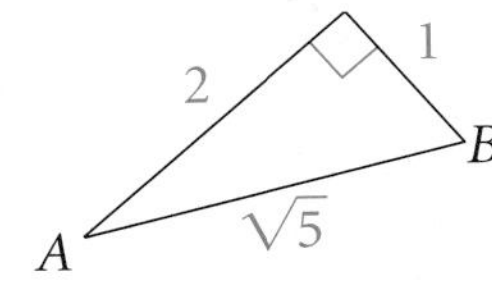

2. 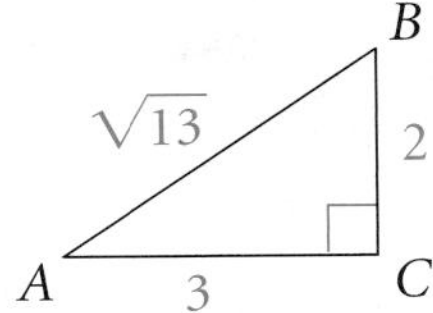

3. 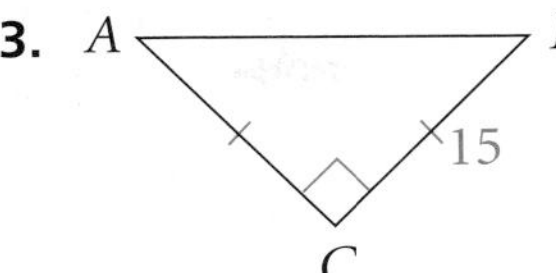

4. C 3 B 1 $\sqrt{10}$ A

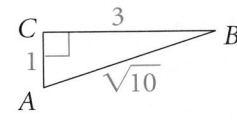

Find each missing value. Round your answer to the nearest tenth.

5. $\tan ■° = 3.5$ **6.** $\tan 34° = \frac{■}{20}$ **7.** $\tan 2° = \frac{4}{■}$ **8.** $\tan ■° = 90$

Find the value of x. Round lengths of segments to the nearest tenth and angle measures to the nearest degree.

9. 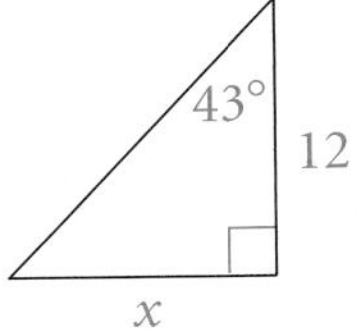

10. 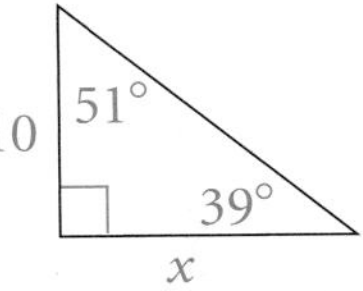

11. 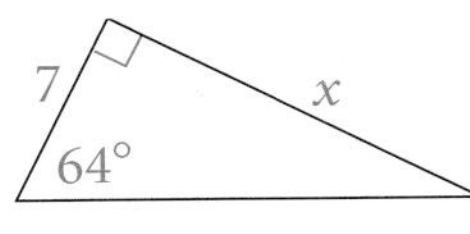

12. 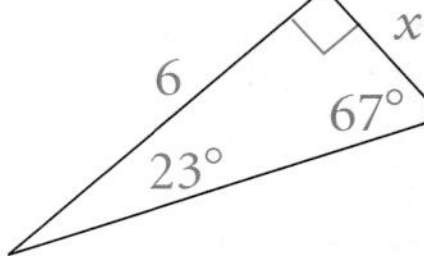

13. 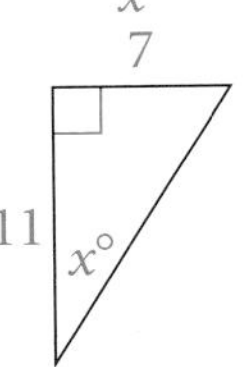

14. 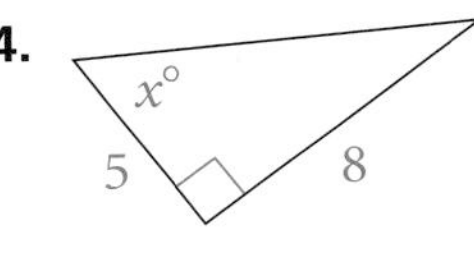

15. 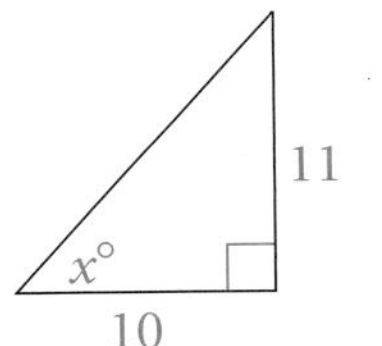

16. 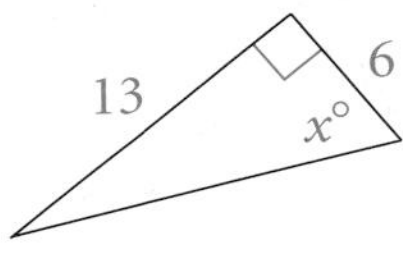

17. 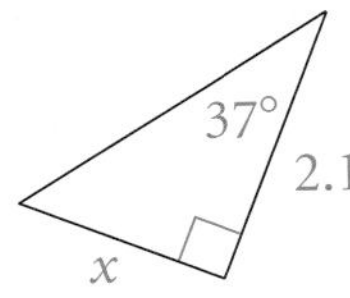

18. 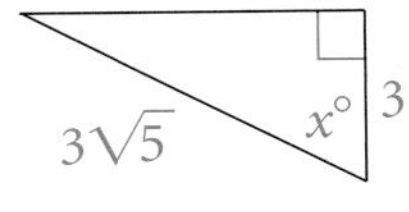

19. 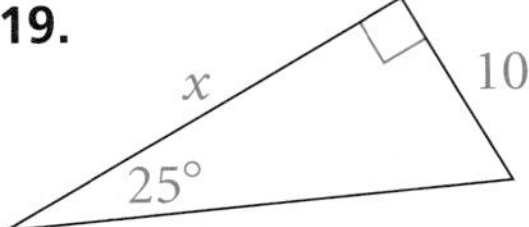

20. 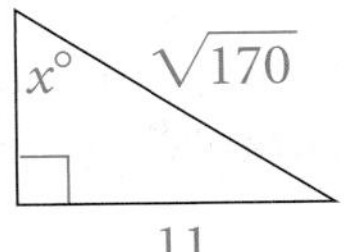

21. **Engineering** The *grade* of a road or railway is the ratio $\frac{\text{rise}}{\text{run}}$, usually expressed as a percent. For example, a railway with a grade of 5% rises 5 ft for every 100 ft of horizontal distance. The world's steepest railway is the Katoomba Scenic Railway in the Blue Mountains of Australia. It has a grade of 122%. At what angle does this railway go up?

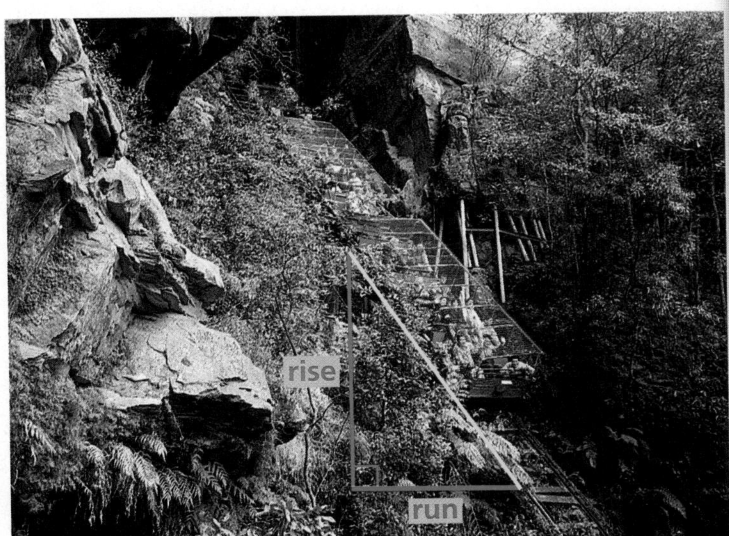

22. The lengths of the diagonals of a rhombus are 2 in. and 5 in. Find the measures of the angles of the rhombus to the nearest degree.

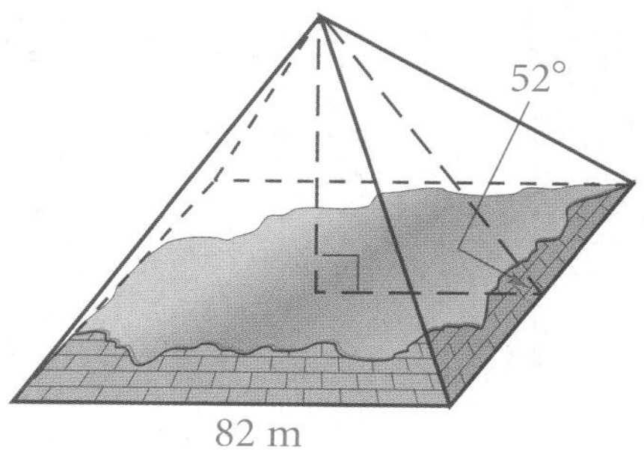

23. **Pyramids** All but two of the pyramids built by the ancient Egyptians have faces inclined at 52° angles. (The remaining two have faces inclined at $43\frac{1}{2}$°.) Suppose an archaeologist discovers the ruins of a pyramid. Most of the pyramid has eroded, but she is able to determine that the length of a side of the square base is 82 m. How tall was the pyramid, assuming its faces were inclined at 52°? Round your answer to the nearest meter.

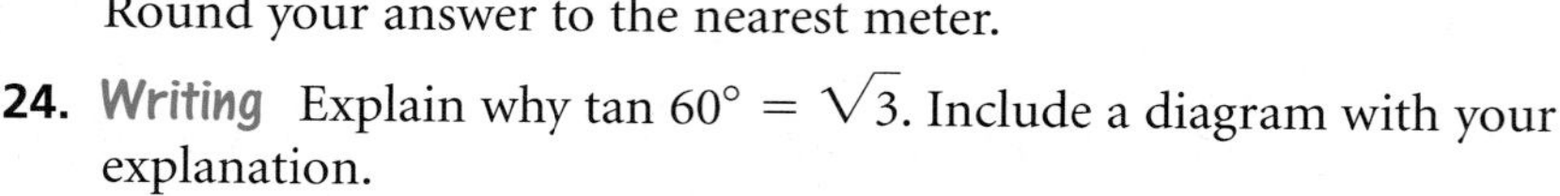

24. **Writing** Explain why $\tan 60° = \sqrt{3}$. Include a diagram with your explanation.

25. a. **Coordinate Geometry** Use a calculator to complete the table of values at the right. Give your answers to the nearest tenth.
    b. Plot the points $(x, \tan x°)$ on the coordinate plane. Connect them with a smooth curve.
    c. What happens to the tangent ratio as the measure of the angle approaches 0? as it approaches 90?
    d. Use the graph to estimate each value.
    $\tan$ ■° = 7 $\quad$ $\tan 68° =$ ■ $\quad$ $\tan$ ■° = 3.5

x	**tan x°**
5	■
10	■
⋮	⋮
85	■

Find w, then x. Round lengths of segments to the nearest tenth and angle measures to the nearest degree.

26.
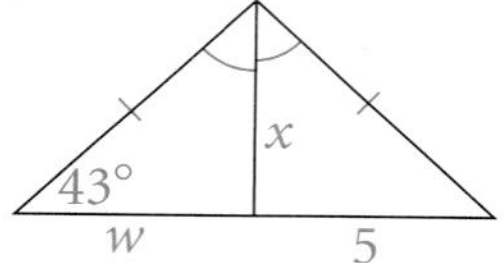

27.
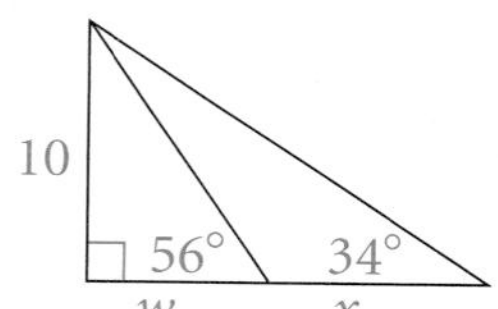

28.
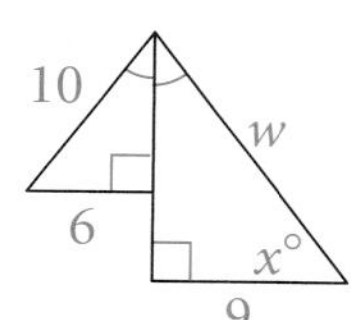

29.
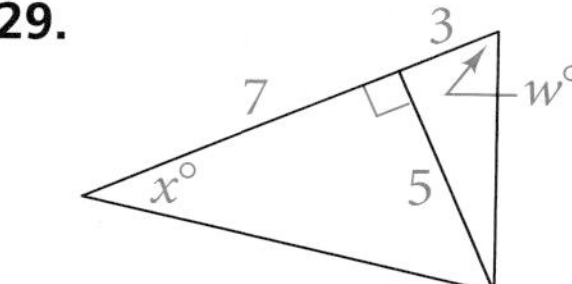

Algebra **Find the measure of the acute angle that each line makes with a horizontal line. Round your answer to the nearest tenth.**

30. $y = 5x - 7$

31. $y = \frac{4}{3}x - 1$

32. $3x - 4y = 8$

33. $-2x + 3y = 6$

34. **Construction** The roadway of a suspension bridge is supported by cables, as shown. The cables extend from the roadway to a point on the tower 50 ft above the roadway. The cables are set at 10-ft intervals along the roadway. Find the angles from the roadway to the top of the tower for the six cables nearest the tower. Round your answers to the nearest tenth.

35. **Open-ended** Select a Pythagorean triple other than a multiple of 3, 4, 5. Find the measures of the acute angles of the right triangle associated with your Pythagorean triple. Round each measure to the nearest tenth.

Chapter Project — Find Out by Building

Use the diagram at the right to build a *clinometer*, an angle-measuring device similar to instruments used by navigators for hundreds of years. You will need a protractor, string, tape, a piece of heavy cardboard, a small weight, and a straw.

To use the clinometer, look through the straw at the object you want to measure (the top of a building, for example). Have someone else read the angle marked by the hanging string.

- Why is the angle measure indicated by the string on the protractor the same as $m\angle 1$? (*Hint:* The string is always perpendicular to the horizon.)

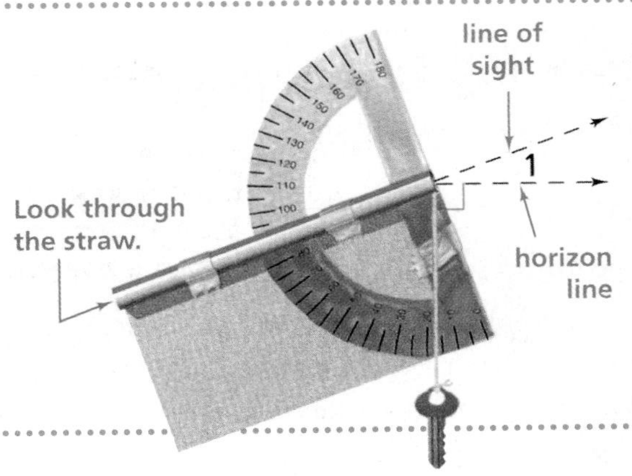

Exercises MIXED REVIEW

In Exercises 36–39: (a) Write the converse of each conditional. (b) Determine the truth value of the statement and its converse.

36. If a quadrilateral is a parallelogram, then the quadrilateral has congruent diagonals.

37. If a flag contains the colors red, white, and blue, then the flag is a United States flag.

38. If a quadrilateral is a rhombus, then its diagonals are perpendicular bisectors of one another.

39. If you live in Hawaii, then you live on an island.

SELF ASSESSMENT

FOR YOUR JOURNAL

Two different right triangles each have an angle that measures 60. Explain why tan 60° is the same for both of these triangles.

40. **Locus** Sketch the locus of points in a plane that are equidistant from the diagonals of a kite.

41. **a.** **Constructions** Draw a triangle. Then construct the perpendicular bisectors of two of its sides.

b. Draw the circle that circumscribes the triangle. (*Hint:* The intersection of the perpendicular bisectors is its center.)

Getting Ready for the Next Lesson

For each triangle, find the ratios $\frac{\text{leg opposite } \angle B}{\text{hypotenuse}}$ and $\frac{\text{leg adjacent to } \angle B}{\text{hypotenuse}}$.

42.

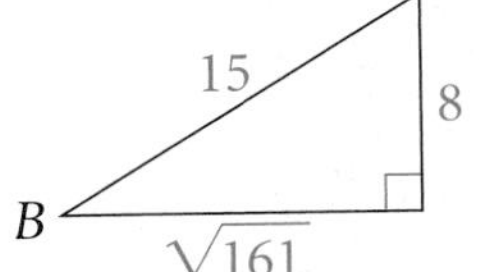

43.

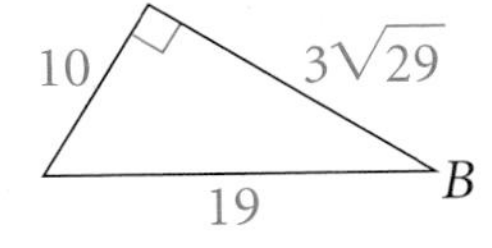

44.

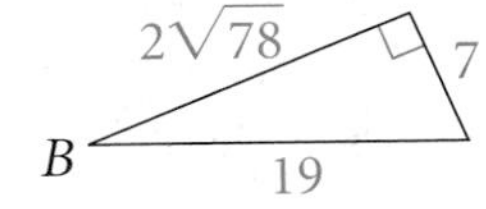

45.

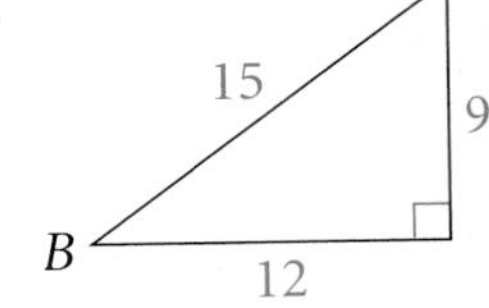

New York Lessons

Math ToolboX

Technology

Exploring Trigonometric Ratios

Work in pairs or small groups.

Construct

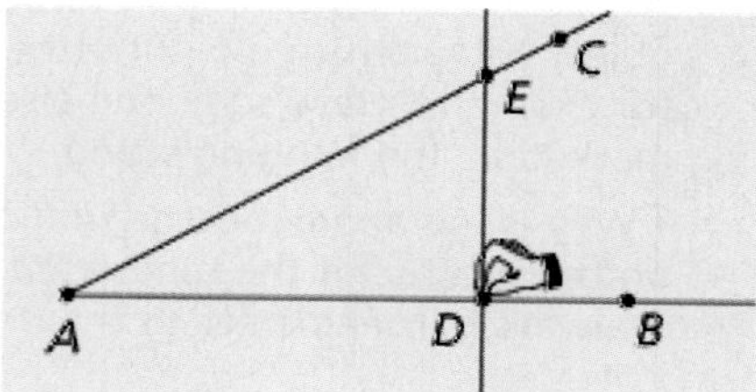

Use geometry software to construct $\overrightarrow{AB}$ and $\overrightarrow{AC}$ so that $\angle A$ is acute. Through a point D on $\overrightarrow{AB}$ construct a line perpendicular to $\overrightarrow{AB}$ that intersects $\overrightarrow{AC}$ in point E. Moving point D enlarges or reduces $\triangle ADE$. Moving point C changes the size of $\angle A$.

Investigate

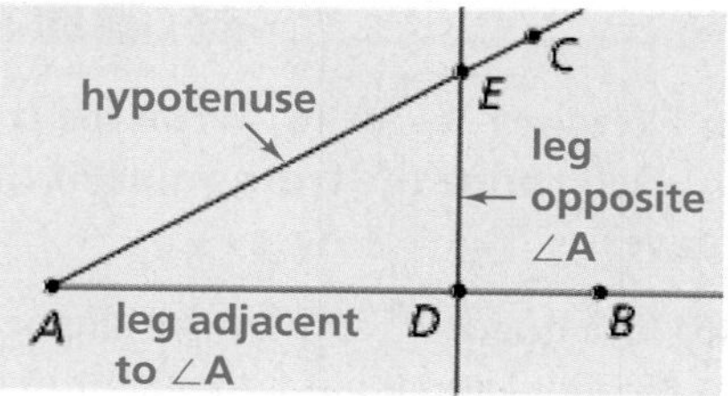

- Measure $\angle A$ and then find the lengths of the sides of the triangle. Calculate the ratio $\frac{\text{length of leg opposite } \angle A}{\text{length of hypotenuse}}$, which is $\frac{DE}{AE}$.
- Move point D to change the size of the right triangle without changing the size of $\angle A$. Does the ratio change as the size of the triangle changes?
- Move point C to change the size of $\angle A$. How does the ratio change as the size of $\angle A$ changes? What value does the ratio approach as $m\angle A$ approaches 0? as $m\angle A$ approaches 90?
- Make a table that shows $m\angle A$ and the ratio $\frac{\text{length of leg opposite } \angle A}{\text{length of hypotenuse}}$. In your table, include values of 10, 20, 30, . . . , 80 for $m\angle A$.

Conjecture

Compare your table with the table of trigonometric ratios on page 674. Do your values for $\frac{\text{length of leg opposite } \angle A}{\text{length of hypotenuse}}$ match the values in one of the columns of the table? What is the name of this ratio in the table?

Extend

- Repeat the investigation for the ratio $\frac{\text{length of leg adjacent to } \angle A}{\text{length of hypotenuse}}$, which is $\frac{DA}{EA}$.
- Repeat the investigation for the ratio $\frac{\text{length of leg opposite } \angle A}{\text{length of leg adjacent to } \angle A}$, which is $\frac{ED}{DA}$.

Connections Astronomy . . . and more

The Sine and Cosine Ratios

What You'll Learn

- Calculating sines and cosines of acute angles in right triangles
- Using sine and cosine to determine unknown measures in right triangles

...And Why

To understand how the ratios were used to calculate the sizes of orbits of planets

What You'll Need

- centimeter ruler
- graph paper
- calculator

THINK AND DISCUSS

The tangent ratio, as you've seen, involves both legs of a right triangle. The sine and cosine ratios involve one leg and the hypotenuse.

sine of $\angle A = \dfrac{\text{leg opposite } \angle A}{\text{hypotenuse}}$

cosine of $\angle A = \dfrac{\text{leg adjacent to } \angle A}{\text{hypotenuse}}$

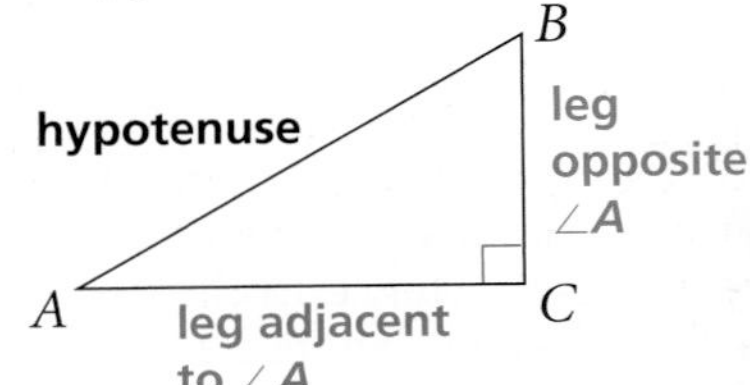

These equations can be abbreviated:

$$\sin A = \frac{\text{opposite}}{\text{hypotenuse}}$$

$$\cos A = \frac{\text{adjacent}}{\text{hypotenuse}}$$

Example 1

Refer to $\triangle GRT$ at the right. Find each ratio.

a. $\sin T$ **b.** $\cos T$
c. $\sin G$ **d.** $\cos G$

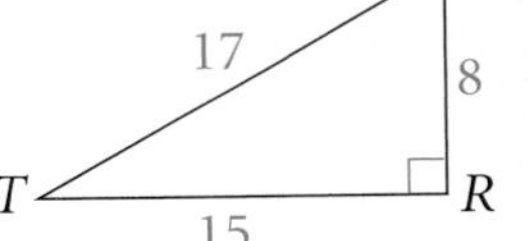

a. $\sin T = \dfrac{\text{opposite}}{\text{hypotenuse}} = \dfrac{8}{17}$ **b.** $\cos T = \dfrac{\text{adjacent}}{\text{hypotenuse}} = \dfrac{15}{17}$

c. $\sin G = \dfrac{\text{opposite}}{\text{hypotenuse}} = \dfrac{15}{17}$ **d.** $\cos G = \dfrac{\text{adjacent}}{\text{hypotenuse}} = \dfrac{8}{17}$

1. **a.** Explain why $\sin T = \cos G = \frac{8}{17}$.
   b. The word *cosine* is derived from the words *co*mplement's *sine.* Which angle in $\triangle GRT$ is the complement of $\angle T$? of $\angle G$?
   c. Explain why the derivation of the word *cosine* makes sense.

Another way of describing the pattern in Question 1 is to say that $\sin x^\circ = \cos (90 - x)^\circ$ for values of x between 0 and 90. This type of equation is called an **identity** because it is always true for the allowed values of the variable. You will discover other identities in the exercises.

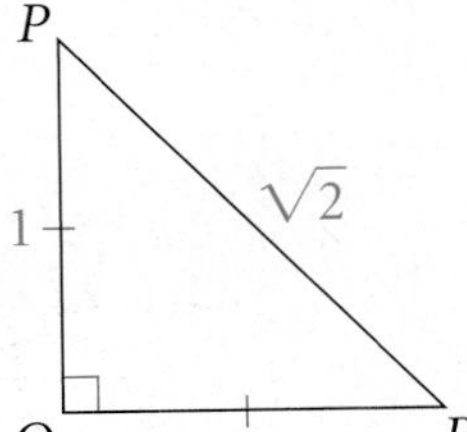

2. Refer to $\triangle PQR$ at the left. Find each ratio.
   a. $\sin P$ **b.** $\cos P$
   c. $\sin R$ **d.** $\cos R$
3. Refer to $\triangle TSN$ at the right. Find each ratio.
   a. $\sin S$ **b.** $\cos S$
   c. $\sin T$ **d.** $\cos T$

T, 2x, 30°, $x\sqrt{3}$, 60°, S, x, N

New York Lessons

Who? Vera Rubin (1928–) used techniques of indirect measurement to determine the speeds at which stars in far-off galaxies travel.

What? 1 AU (astronomical unit) is defined as the average distance from Earth to the sun (about 93 million miles).

GRAPHING CALCULATOR HINT

On a scientific calculator, enter 22.3 SIN. On a graphing calculator, enter SIN 22.3 ENTER.

The trigonometric ratios have been known for centuries. People in many cultures have used them to solve problems—especially problems involving distances that cannot be measured directly.

Example 2 **Relating to the Real World** 

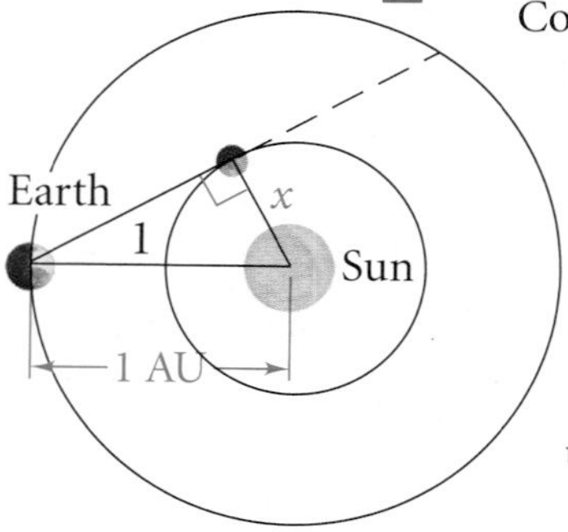

Astronomy The Polish astronomer Nicolaus Copernicus (1473–1543) developed a method for determining the size of the orbits of planets closer to the sun than Earth. The key to his method was determining when the planets were in the position shown in the diagram, and then measuring $\angle 1$. If $m\angle 1 = 22.3$ for Mercury, how far is Mercury from the sun in astronomical units (AU)?

$\sin 22.3° = \frac{x}{1}$ Use the sine ratio.

$0.38 \approx x$ Use a calculator to find sin 22.3°.

So Mercury is about 0.38 AU from the sun.

4. Try This If $m\angle 1 = 46.1$ for Venus, how far is Venus from the sun?

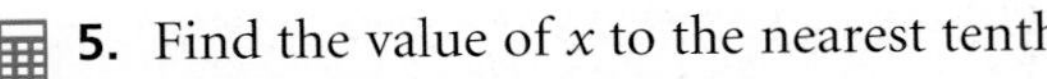

5. Find the value of x to the nearest tenth.

a.

b. 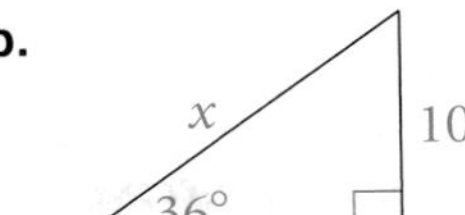

c. 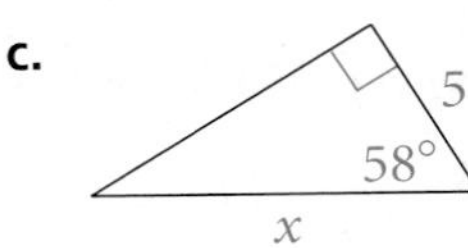

When you know the lengths of a leg and the hypotenuse of a right triangle, you can use inverse sine or inverse cosine functions on a calculator to find the measures of the acute angles.

Example 3

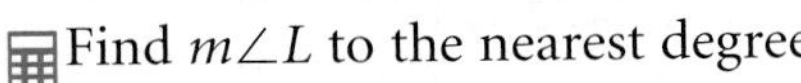

Find $m\angle L$ to the nearest degree.

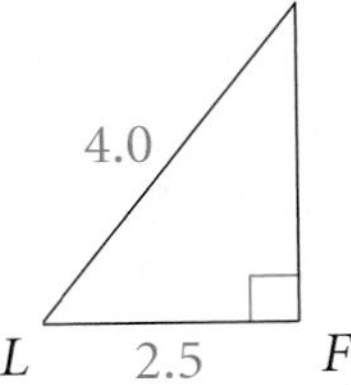

$\cos L = \frac{2.5}{4.0}$ **Use the cosine ratio.**

$= \frac{5}{8}$ **Simplify the right side.**

$m\angle L = \cos^{-1}\left(\frac{5}{8}\right)$ **Use inverse cosine.**

[( ] 5 [÷] 8 [ )] [COS⁻¹] 51.317813

So $m\angle L \approx 51$.

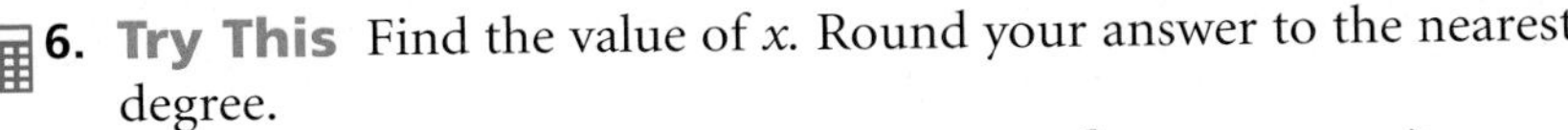

6. Try This Find the value of x. Round your answer to the nearest degree.

a. 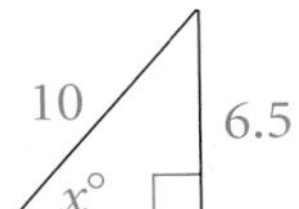

b. 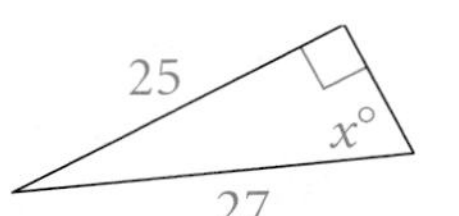

c. 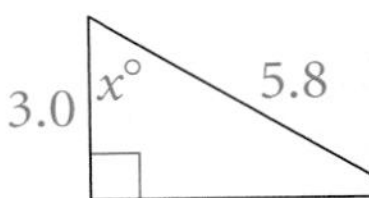

WORK TOGETHER

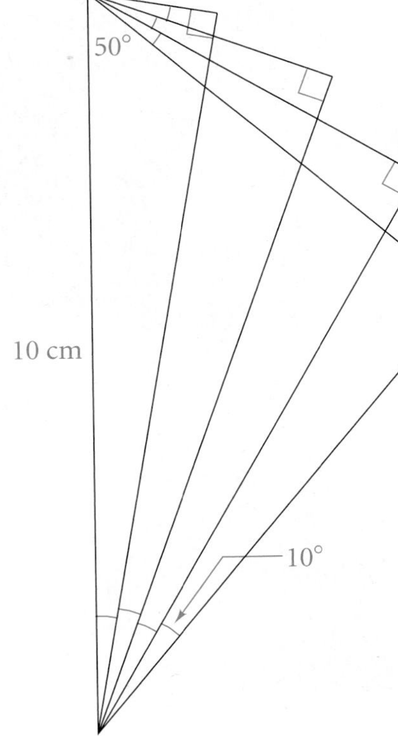

7. Copy the table at the right. Complete it by using a centimeter ruler to measure the triangles at the left to the nearest millimeter. Because the hypotenuse of each triangle is 10 cm, you shouldn't need a calculator to compute the ratios.

x	$\sin x°$	$\cos x°$
10	■	■
20	■	■
30	■	■
40	■	■
50	■	■
60	■	■
70	■	■
80	■	■

8. Algebra Graph the ordered pairs $(x, \sin x°)$ on the coordinate plane for values of x in the domain $0 < x < 90$. Connect the points with a smooth curve.

9. Algebra Graph the ordered pairs $(x, \cos x°)$ on the same coordinate plane. Again, connect the points with a smooth curve.

10. Transformations What transformation maps one of the curves onto the other?

Exercises ON YOUR OWN

Express sin *M* and cos *M* as ratios.

1.

2.

3.

4. **Escalators** The world's longest escalator is in the subway system of St. Petersburg, Russia. The escalator has a vertical rise of 195 ft 9.5 in. and rises at an angle of 10.4°. How long is the escalator? Round your answer to the nearest foot.

5. **Writing** Leona Halfmoon said that if she had a diagram that showed the measure of one acute angle and the length of one side of a right triangle, she could find the measure of the other acute angle and the lengths of the other sides. Is she right? Explain.

Find the value of *x*. Round lengths of segments to the nearest tenth and angle measures to the nearest degree.

6.

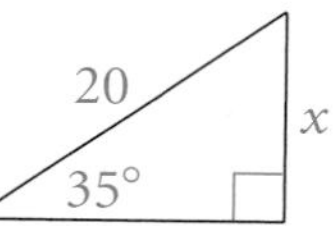

7.

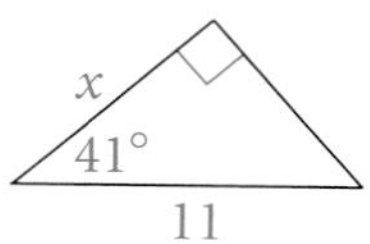

8.

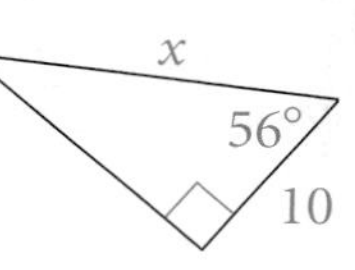

9.

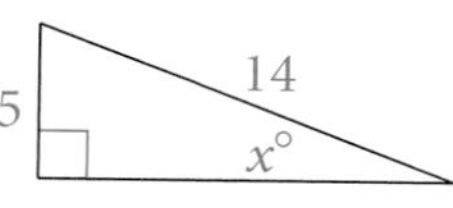

10.

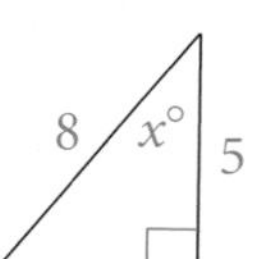

11.

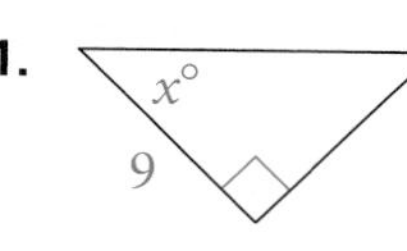

12.

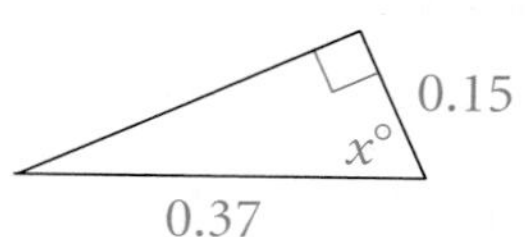

13.

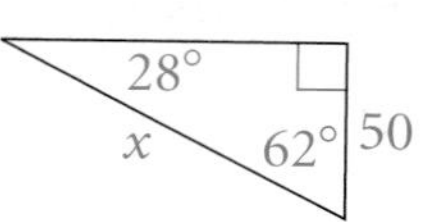

14.

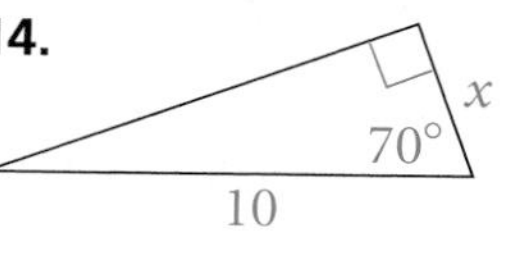

15. **Standardized Test Prep** In $\triangle ABC$, $m\angle B = 90$. Find sin *C*.

A. $\frac{BC}{AC}$ **B.** $\frac{BC}{AB}$ **C.** $\frac{AB}{BC}$ **D.** $\frac{AB}{AC}$ **E.** $\frac{AC}{AB}$

16. **Agriculture** Jane is planning to build a new grain silo with a radius of 15 ft. She reads that the recommended slope of the roof is 22°. She wants the roof to overhang the edge of the silo by 1 ft. What should the slant height of the roof be? Give your answer in feet and inches.

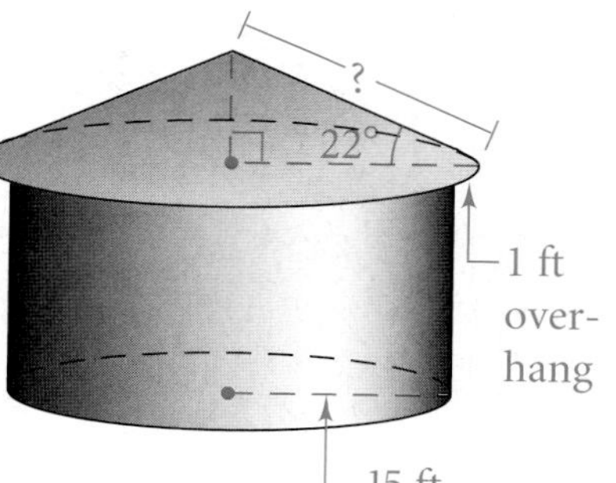

17. **Critical Thinking** Use what you know about trigonometric ratios to show that the following equations is an identity.

$$\tan A = \sin A \div \cos A$$

18. a. **Open-ended** Pick three values of x between 0 and 90. For each value, evaluate the expression $(\sin x^\circ)^2 + (\cos x^\circ)^2$.
b. **Patterns** Make a **conjecture** about the expression and prove it.

19. **Astronomy** Copernicus had to devise a method different from the one in Example 2 in order to find the size of the orbits of planets farther from the sun than Earth. His method involved noting the number of days between the times that the planets were in the positions labeled A and B in the diagram. Using this time and the number of days in each planet's year, he calculated the measures of the angles labeled 1 and 2.
a. For Mars, $m\angle 1 = 55.2$ and $m\angle 2 = 103.8$. How far is Mars from the sun in astronomical units (AU)?
b. For Jupiter, $m\angle 1 = 21.9$ and $m\angle 2 = 100.8$. How far is Jupiter from the sun in astronomical units (AU)?

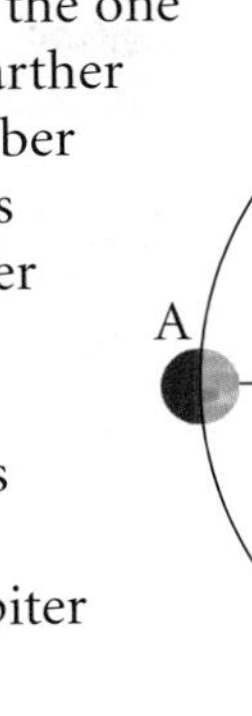
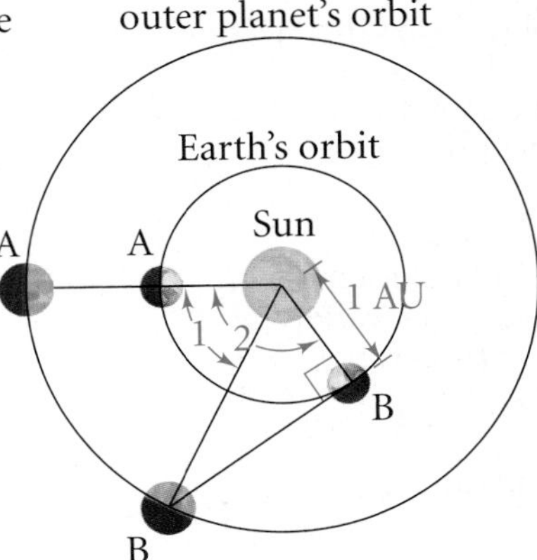

Find w and then x. Round lengths of segments to the nearest tenth and angle measures to the nearest degree.

20.
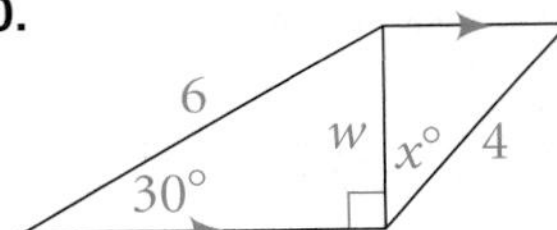

21.
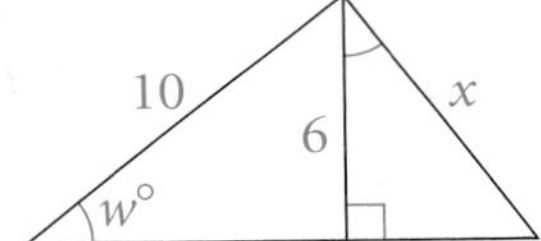

22.
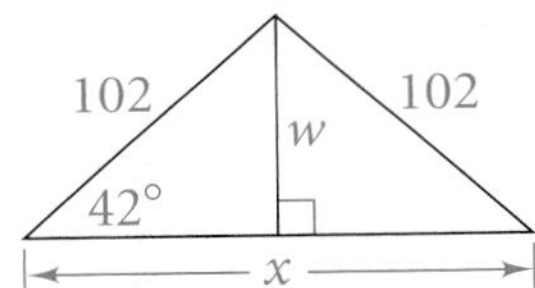

23.
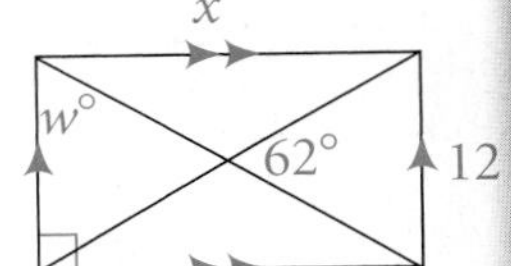

Exercises MIXED REVIEW

Find the value of each variable. When an answer is not a whole number, round to the nearest tenth.

24. ▱$ABCD$
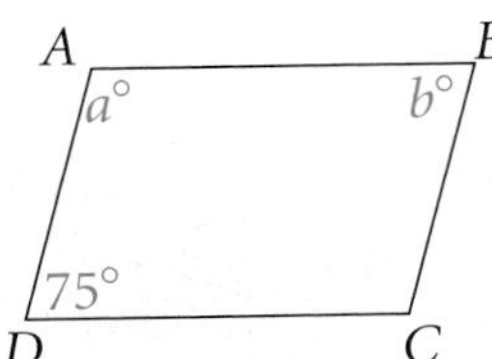

25. rhombus $QRST$
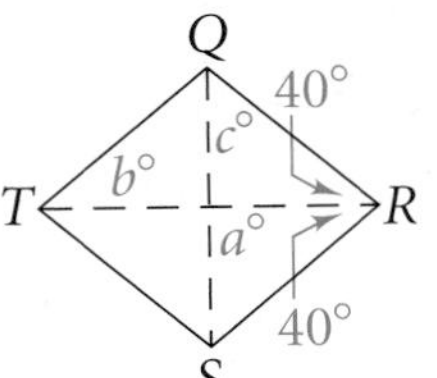

26. rectangle $JKLM$
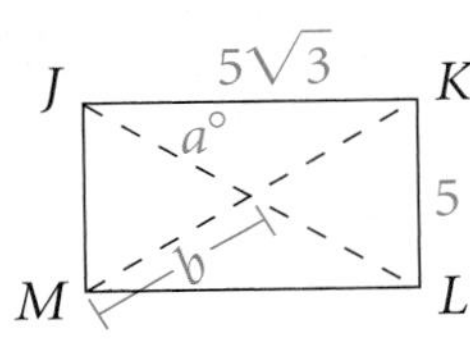

27. kite $WXYZ$
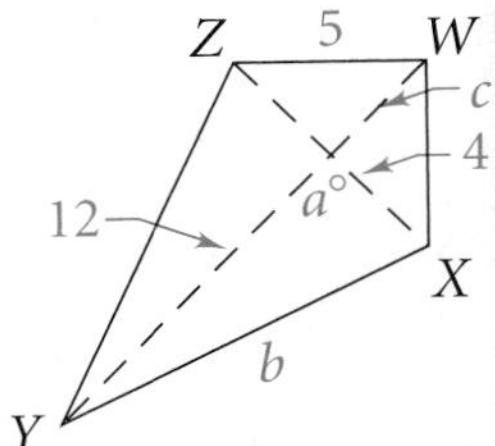

28. **Sports** The circumference of a softball is 12 in. The circumference of a field hockey ball is 9 in. How many times larger than the volume of the field hockey ball is the volume of the softball?

Getting Ready for the Next Lesson

Refer to rectangle $ABCD$ to complete the statements.

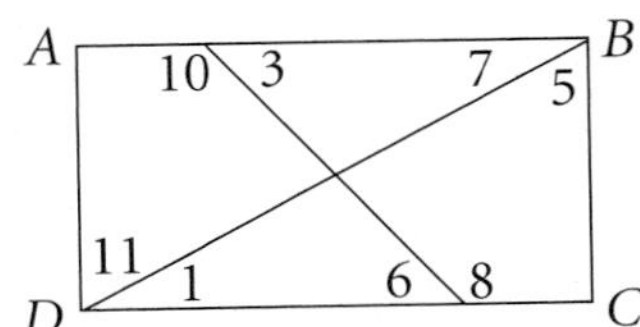

29. $\angle 1 \cong$ ■
30. $\angle 5 \cong$ ■
31. $\angle 3 \cong$ ■
32. $m\angle 1 + m\angle 5 =$ ■
33. $m\angle 10 + m\angle 3 =$ ■
34. $\angle 10 \cong$ ■

New York Lessons

Connections Surveying . . . and more

Angles of Elevation and Depression

What You'll Learn

- Identifying angles of elevation and depression
- Using angles of elevation and depression and trigonometric ratios to solve problems

...And Why

To calculate distances indirectly in a variety of real-world settings

What You'll Need

- calculator

THINK AND DISCUSS

Suppose a person in a hot-air balloon sees a person at an angle 38° *below* a horizontal line. This angle is an **angle of depression.** At the same time, the person on the ground sees the hot-air balloon at an angle 38° *above* a horizontal line. This angle is an **angle of elevation.**

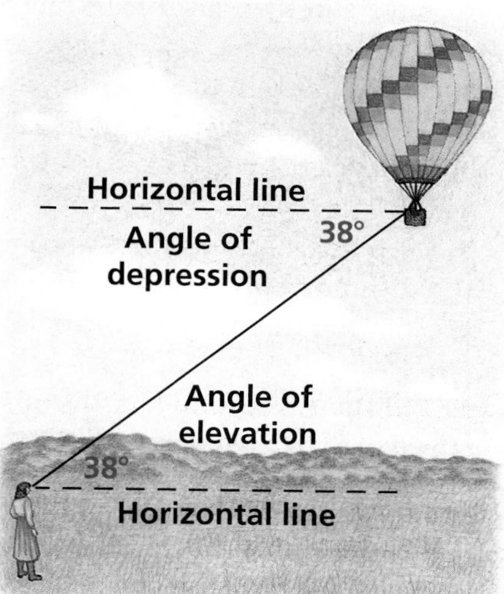

1. Refer to the diagram. What property of parallel lines ensures that the angle of elevation is congruent to the angle of depression?

Example 1

Describe each angle as it relates to the objects in the diagram.

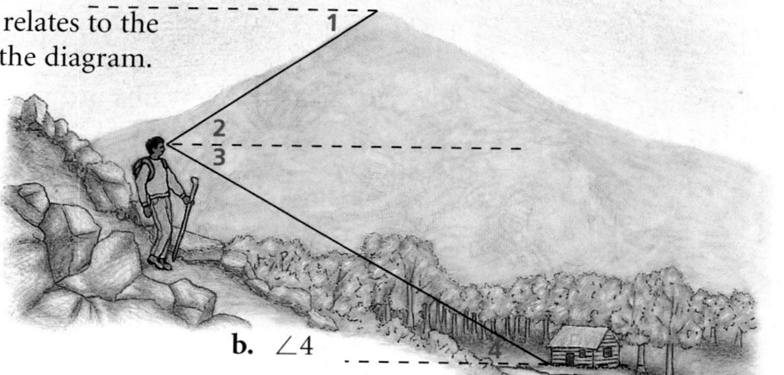

a. $\angle 1$ **b.** $\angle 4$

a. angle of depression from the peak to the hiker
b. angle of elevation from the hut to the hiker

2. **Try This** Describe each angle as it relates to the diagram in Example 1.
   a. $\angle 2$ **b.** $\angle 3$

Surveyors use two main instruments to measure angles of elevation and depression. They are the *transit* and the *theodolite.* On both instruments, the surveyor sets the horizon line perpendicular to the direction of gravity. Using gravity to find the horizon line ensures accurate measures even on sloping surfaces.

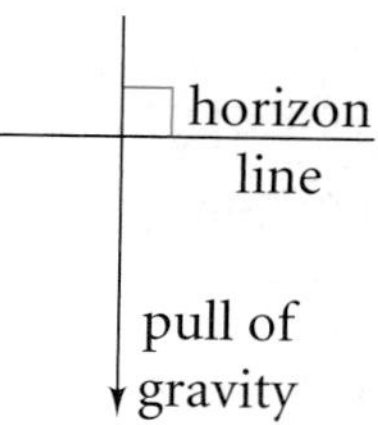

Example 2 Relating to the Real World

Surveying To find the height of Delicate Arch in Arches National Park in Utah, a surveyor places a theodolite at the same level as the bottom of the arch. From there, she measures the angle of elevation to the top of the arch. She then uses a steel tape to measure the distance from her location to the spot directly under the arch. The results of her survey are shown in the diagram. How tall is Delicate Arch?

$\tan 48^\circ = \frac{x}{36}$ Use the tangent ratio.

$x = 36(\tan 48^\circ)$ Solve for x.

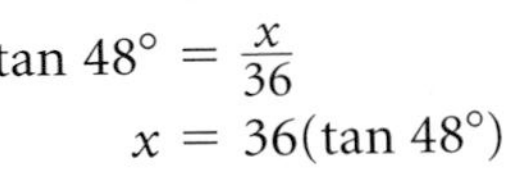

Use a calculator.

So $x \approx 40$. To find the height of the arch, add the height of the theodolite. $40 + 5 = 45$, so Delicate Arch is about 45 feet tall.

3. Try This A surveyor uses a theodolite to measure the angle of elevation to the top of a cliff. He then uses an electronic distance measurement device to measure the distance from the theodolite to the top of the cliff. His measurements are shown in the diagram. How tall is the cliff? Round your answer to the nearest foot.

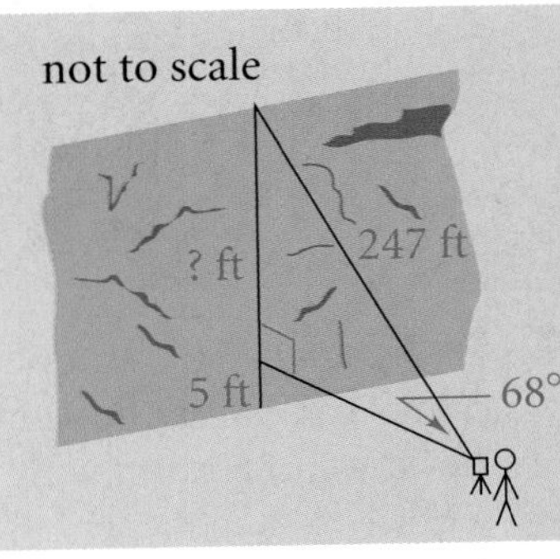

Example 3 Relating to the Real World 

Aviation If you live near an airport, you have probably noticed that airplanes follow certain paths as they prepare for landing. These paths are called *approaches.* The approach to runway 17 of the Ponca City Municipal Airport in Oklahoma calls for the pilot to begin a 3° descent starting from an altitude of 2714 ft. How many miles from the runway is an airplane at the beginning of this approach?

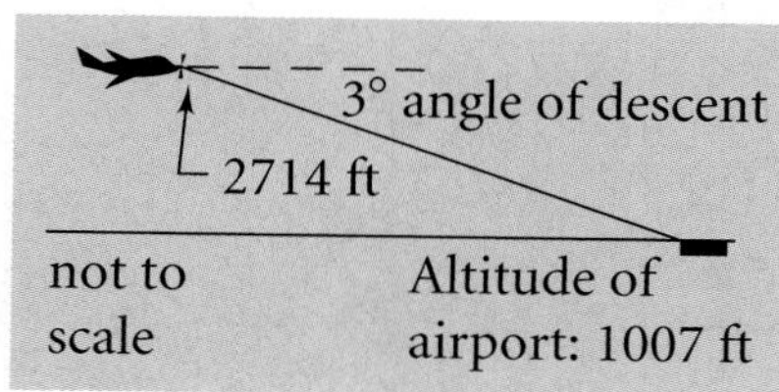

The airplane is 2714 − 1007, or 1707 ft above the level of the airport. Use trigonometry to find the desired distance.

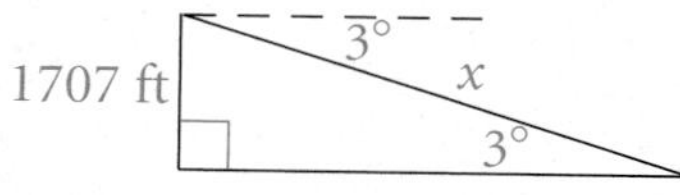

$\sin 3° = \frac{1707}{x}$ Use the sine ratio.

$x = \frac{1707}{\sin 3°}$ Solve for x.

1707 ÷ 3 SIN = 32616.2 Use a calculator to find x.

÷ 5280 = 6.1773105 Convert feet to miles by dividing by 5280.

An airplane is about 6.2 miles from the runway at the beginning of the approach to runway 17 at Ponca City.

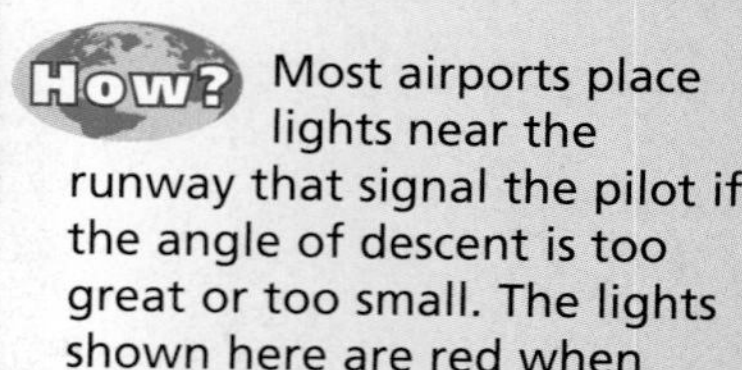

Most airports place lights near the runway that signal the pilot if the angle of descent is too great or too small. The lights shown here are red when viewed from above and white when viewed from below. Each of the four lights is tilted at a different angle.

Exercises ON YOUR OWN

Describe each angle as it relates to the objects in the diagram.

1. a. ∠1
   b. ∠2
   c. ∠3
   d. ∠4

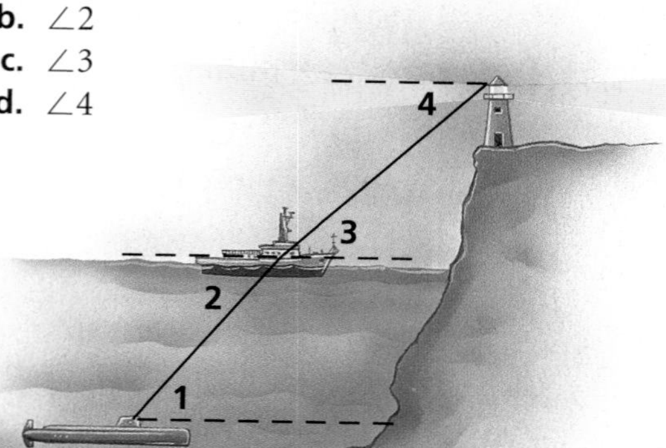

2. a. ∠1
   b. ∠2
   c. ∠3
   d. ∠4

3. **Engineering** The Americans with Disabilities Act states that wheelchair ramps can have a slope no greater than $\frac{1}{12}$. Find the maximum angle of elevation of a ramp with this slope. Round your answer to the nearest tenth.

Solve each problem. Round your answer to the nearest unit unless instructed otherwise.

4. Two office buildings are 51 m apart. The height of the taller building is 207 m. The angle of depression from the top of the taller building to the top of the shorter building is 15°. Find the height of the shorter building.

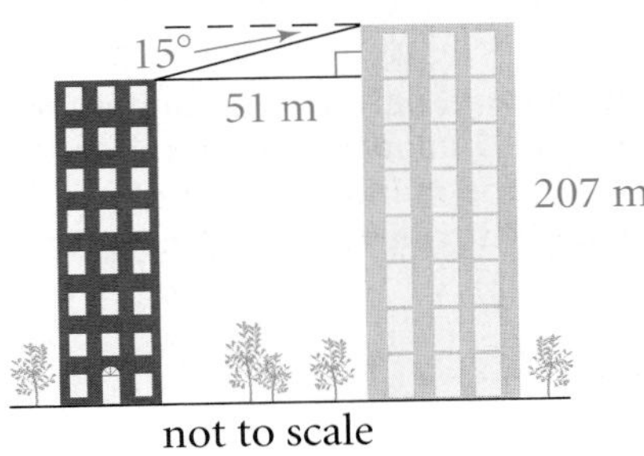

5. A surveyor is 980 ft from the base of the world's tallest fountain at Fountain Hills, Arizona. The angle of elevation to the top of the column of water is 29.7°. His angle measuring device is at the same level as the base of the fountain. Find the height of the column of water to the nearest 10 ft.

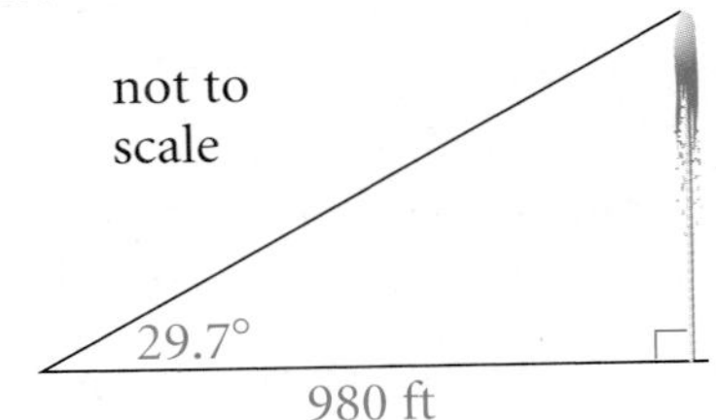

6. On the observation platform in the crown of the Statue of Liberty, Miguel is approximately 250 ft above ground. He sights a ship in New York harbor and measures the angle of depression as 18°. Find the distance from the ship to the base of the statue.

7. A meteorologist measures the angle of elevation of a weather balloon as 41°. A radio signal from the balloon indicates that it is 1503 m from her location. How high is the weather balloon above the ground?

8. The world's tallest unsupported flagpole is a 282-ft-tall steel pole in Surrey, British Columbia. The shortest shadow cast by the pole during the year is 137 ft long. What is the angle of elevation of the sun when the shortest shadow is cast?

PROBLEM SOLVING HINT

Draw a diagram using the given information. Then decide which trigonometric ratio you can use to solve the problem.

9. A blimp is flying to cover a football game. The pilot sights the stadium at a 7° angle of depression. The blimp is flying at an altitude of 400 m. How many kilometers is the blimp from the point 400 m above the stadium? Round your answer to the nearest tenth.

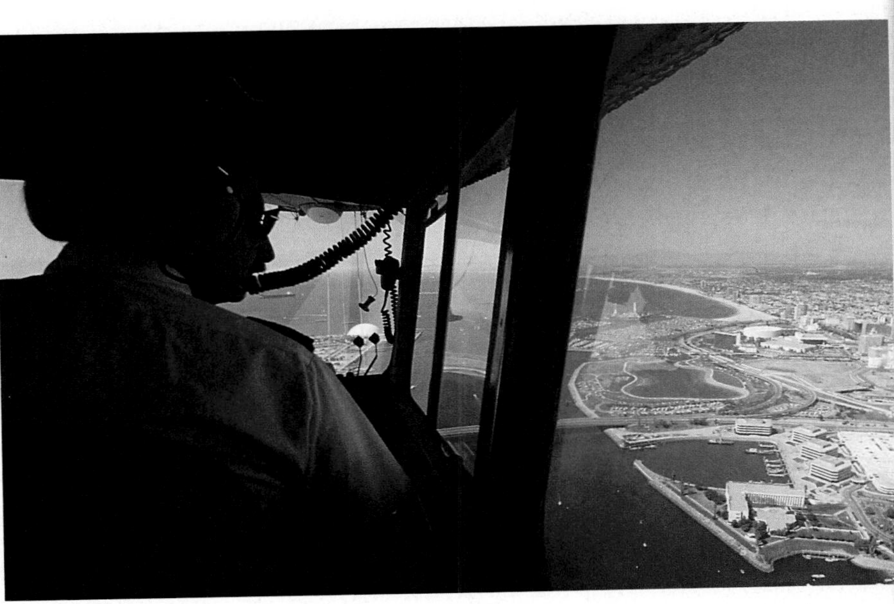

10. a. **Navigation** A simple method for finding a north-south line is shown in the diagram. How could you use this method to also find the angle of elevation of the sun at noon?

b. **Research** For locations in the continental United States, the relationship between the latitude ℓ and angle of elevation a of the sun at noon on the first day of summer is $a = 90° - \ell + 23\frac{1}{2}°$. Find the latitude of your town and determine the angle of elevation of the sun on the first day of summer.

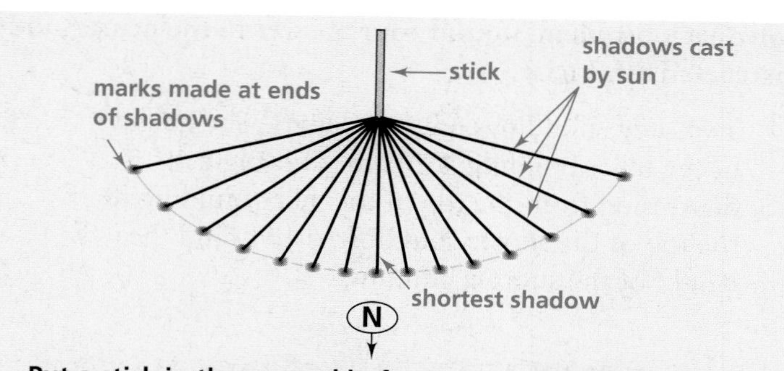

Put a stick in the ground before noon and mark the end of its shadow every 15 minutes. When the shadows begin to lengthen, stop marking the shadows. The mark closest to the stick is directly north of the stick.

11. **Critical Thinking** A television tower is located on a flat plot of land. The tower is supported by several guy wires. Explain how you could find the length of any of these wires. Assume that you are able to measure distances along the ground as well as angles formed by wires and the ground.

12. **Meteorology** One method that meteorologists use to find the height of a layer of clouds above the ground is to shine a bright spotlight directly up onto the cloud layer and measure the angle of elevation from a known distance away. Find the height of the cloud layer in the diagram to the nearest 10 m.

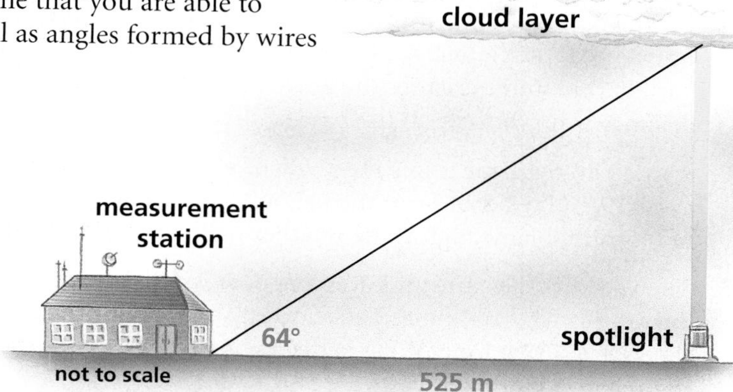

13. a. **Open-ended** Draw and label a diagram that shows a real-world example of an angle of elevation and an angle of depression.

b. **Writing** Write a word problem that uses the angle of depression from your diagram. Include a detailed solution to your problem.

14. **Standardized Test Prep** In the diagram, $m\angle Y > m\angle Z$. Which statement is *not* true?

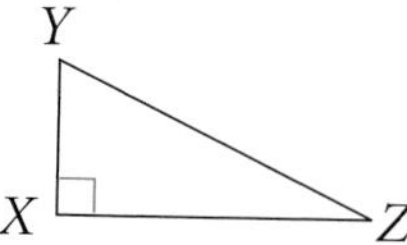

A. $\sin Y > \cos Y$
B. $\cos Y < \cos Z$
C. $\tan Y > \sin Y$
D. $\tan Z > \cos Y$
E. $\cos Z > \sin Y$

Chapter Project... Find Out by Measuring

Use your clinometer to measure the angle of elevation to an object such as the roof of your school or the top of a flagpole. Then determine how far away you are from the object that you measured. Use what you've learned about trigonometry to find the height of the object. Be sure to add your own height to the height you come up with!

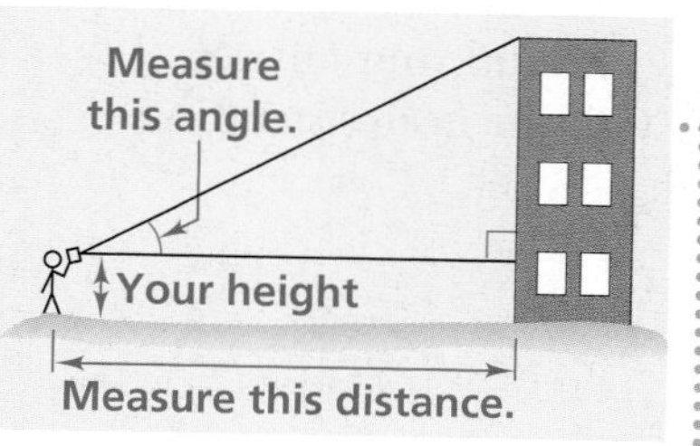

Exercises MIXED REVIEW

Data Analysis **Refer to the graph to answer the questions.**

15. What percent of adults are 18–24 years old?
16. What percent of bluegrass purchases did adults 18–24 make?
17. Which age group contains the least number of people?
18. Create two circle graphs using the data from the double bar graph.
19. a. Which age group buys more bluegrass: 35–44-year-olds or 55–64-year-olds?
    b. Which of these two age groups likes bluegrass more? Explain.
20. **Coordinate Geometry** Find the equation of the line that passes through (3, 7) and is parallel to the line $y = \frac{3}{2}x - 5$.

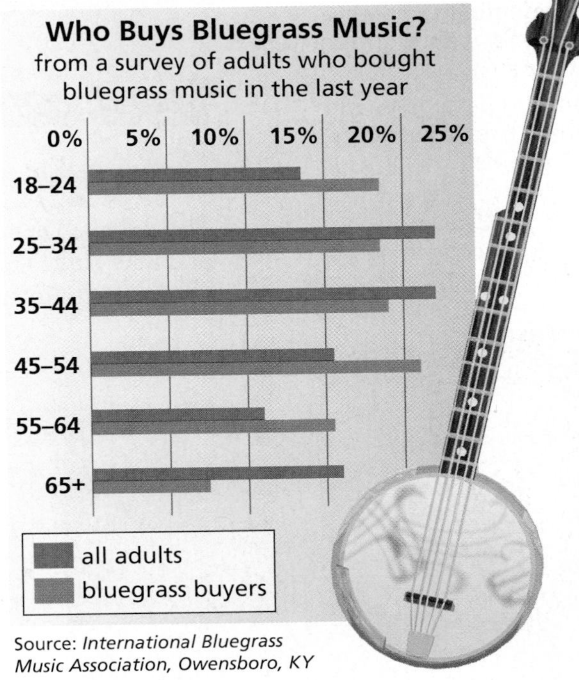

Source: *International Bluegrass Music Association, Owensboro, KY*

Getting Ready for the Next Lesson

Transformations **Find the image of each point under a translation with the given translation vector.**

21. $(2, 7); \langle 1, -9 \rangle$
22. $(-3, 0); \langle 6, -1 \rangle$
23. $(4, -7); \langle 5, 0 \rangle$
24. $(-5, 12); \langle -8, -11 \rangle$

Exercises CHECKPOINT

1. **Standardized Test Prep** Which value is greatest?
   A. $\sin 30^\circ$ B. $\cos 45^\circ$ C. $\tan 60^\circ$
   D. $\sin 10^\circ$ E. $\cos 70^\circ$
2. **Architecture** The Leaning Tower of Pisa leans about 5.5° from vertical. How far from the base of the tower will an object dropped from the tower land?
3. A captain of a sailboat sights the top of a lighthouse at a 17° angle of elevation. A navigation chart shows the height of the lighthouse to be 120 m. How far is the sailboat from the lighthouse?

5.5°

 **Find the value of x. Round lengths of segments to the nearest tenth and angle measures to the nearest degree.**

4. 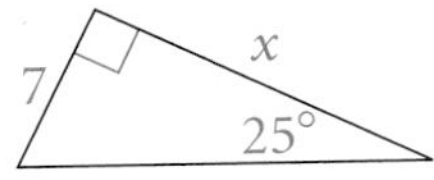

5. 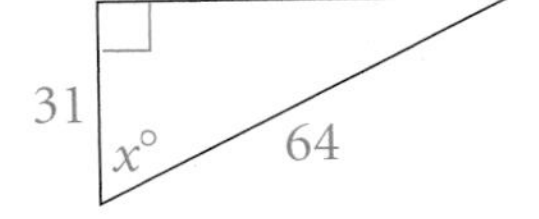

6. 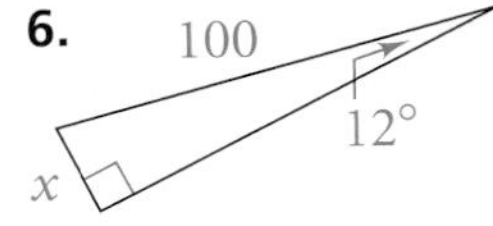

New York Lessons

Connections Recreation . . . and more

Cumulative Frequency and Percentiles

What You'll Learn

- Representing cumulative frequency with tables and histograms
- Showing percentiles with cumulative frequency histograms

...And Why

To analyze recreation data

THINK AND DISCUSS

Finding Cumulative Frequency

Recreation The frequency table shows the results of a survey of the users of a bike path. The users' ages have been rounded to the nearest year and grouped into intervals of 20 years.

Ages of Bike Path Users

Age Range	Frequency (Number of Users)
0–19	189
20–39	254
40–59	185
60–79	105
80–99	40

You might want to know how many people in the survey were under a certain age. You can add frequencies for the intervals to create a *cumulative frequency table*. The **cumulative frequency** for an interval is the sum of the interval's frequency and the frequencies of all previous intervals. For example, the cumulative frequency of all bike path users under the age of 40 is 189 + 254, or 443.

Example 1

Use the data above to create a cumulative frequency table.

Ages of Bike Path Users, Cumulative Frequency

Age Range	Frequency	Cumulative Frequency
0–19	189	**189**
20–39	254	**443**
40–59	185	**628**
60–79	105	**733**
80–99	40	**773**

← Add the first two frequencies to get 443.

← Add the next frequency to 443 to get 628, and so forth.

The cumulative frequency for an interval is the total number of all bike path users up through the given interval.

1. Explain how to find the cumulative frequency for the interval 60–79.

2. What does 773, the last entry in the third row, represent?

3. **Critical Thinking** Why is 189 the first entry in both the second and the third row?

A **cumulative frequency histogram** is a graph of the data in a cumulative frequency table.

QUICK REVIEW

Always use a regular interval when making a graph. Starting the scale at 0 helps in making accurate comparisons.

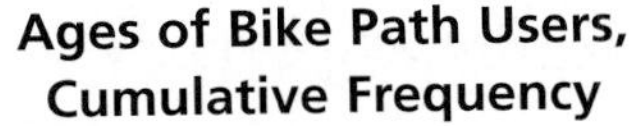

Draw a cumulative frequency histogram for the table in Example 1.

Since the largest number is 773, you can use a vertical scale numbered in intervals of 100.

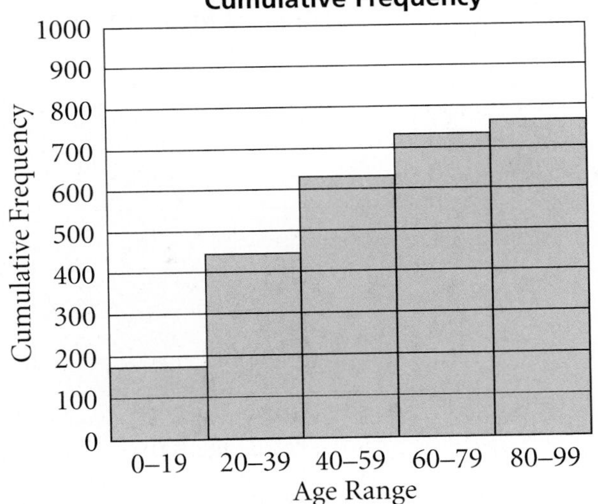

4. Which bar in the histogram shows the number of bike path users who are less than 60 years old?

5. Why do the bars get taller even though the number of users decreases after age 39?

6. How can you tell the number of people in the survey from this type of graph?

Finding Percentiles

The cumulative frequency histogram in Example 2 shows that more than half of the people in the survey are younger than age 40. Another way to show this is to use cumulative percents, or **percentiles.**

Example 3

Use the table in Example 1 to draw a cumulative frequency histogram with percentiles on the vertical scale.

Step 1 Compute the percentiles for each interval in the age data table. Since 773 people were surveyed, let 773 equal 100%. Find the percents for the other intervals by dividing the cumulative frequency by 773. Round to the nearest whole percent.

Ages of Bike Path Users, Percentiles

Ages	Cumulative Frequency	Percentile
0–19	189	24
20–39	443	57
40–59	628	81
60–79	733	95
80–99	773	100

Step 2 Draw a histogram. Use a vertical scale from 0% to 100% with intervals of 10%.

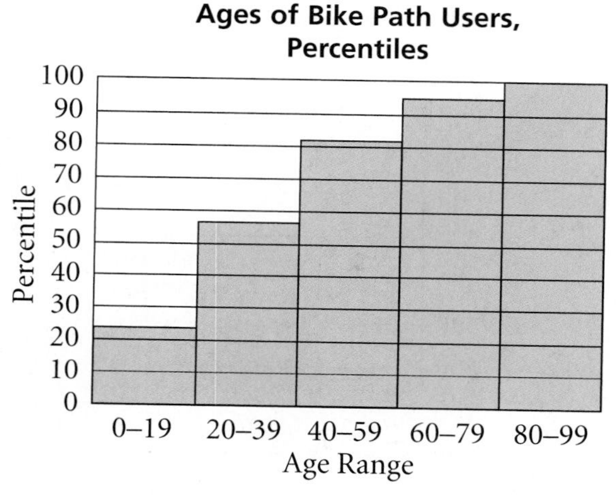

7. What age group would you be in if you were in the 60th percentile?

8. How old are the people in the bottom 10%?

Exercises ON YOUR OWN

Test Scores **A group of students took a test. There were 5 questions, each worth 5 points. The table at the right shows the test results. Use the table for Exercises 1–7.**

1. Make a cumulative frequency table for the data.
2. How many students took the test?
3. How many students scored 20 points or less?
4. Make a cumulative frequency histogram for the data.

Test Scores

Score	Frequency
0	2
5	5
10	8
15	15
20	15
25	17

5. What does the height of the final bar show?
6. Critical Thinking If a score of 20 or better allowed students to start the next chapter, how many students could start the next chapter?
7. If you were a student in the class that took this test and you got a score of 20, how many of your classmates got a lower score?

Tourism **A travel agency took a survey of visitors to New York City to find out how many historical sites they visited. The table shows the survey results. Use the table for Exercises 8–13.**

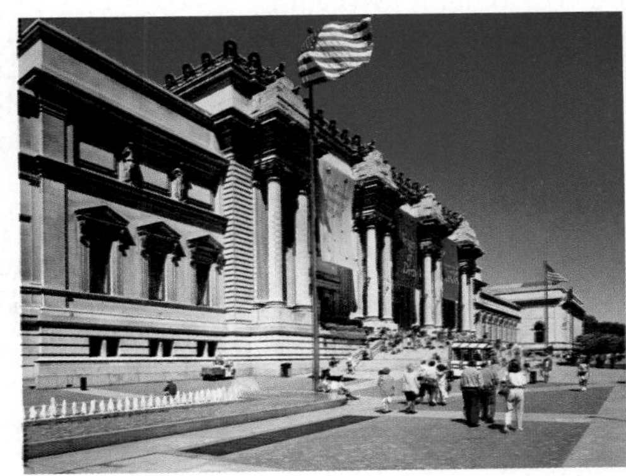

Number of Historical Sites Visited	Frequency
0	143
1	175
2	72
3	86
4 or more	24

8. How many people were surveyed?
9. Copy the table.
   a. Add a third column to show cumulative frequencies.
   b. Add a fourth column to show percentiles.
10. If you visited two historical sites, what percentile would you be in?
11. How many historical sites would you need to visit to be in the top 50%?
12. Critical Thinking Why is it easy to compute percentiles for this group of visitors?
13. Draw a histogram for the data that shows percentiles on the vertical scale.

Camping **The table below shows the ages of children who signed up for a summer camp. Use the ages for Exercises 14–17.**

Ages of Campers

10	12	12	12	14	14	13	12	12	10
11	11	13	10	12	13	11	12	14	10
10	10	11	12	13	12	11	10	11	14
10	10	13	13	12	12	11	12	14	10

14. Make a cumulative frequency table from the data in the table.
15. Make a cumulative frequency histogram.
16. Compute the percentiles for each age and then make a cumulative frequency histogram with percentiles on the vertical scale.
17. What percent of the children are 13 years old or younger?

Connections Decision Making . . . and more

Probability Distributions

What You'll Learn

- Representing probability distributions with tables and histograms

...And Why

To solve problems involving decision making and coin tosses

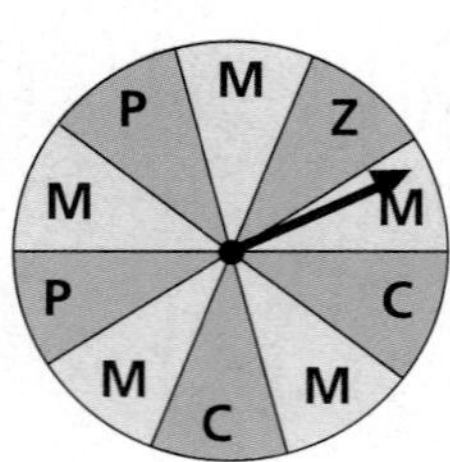

THINK AND DISCUSS

A group of 10 friends are trying to make plans for next Saturday. They can't decide whether to go to the zoo, take a canoe trip, visit the natural history museum, or have a picnic. Each person votes for one activity, with these results:

zoo: 1 canoe trip: 2 museum: 5 picnic: 2

The friends decide to let chance make the decision for them. They create a spinner with 10 sectors. They code the sectors to be proportional to the results of the vote.

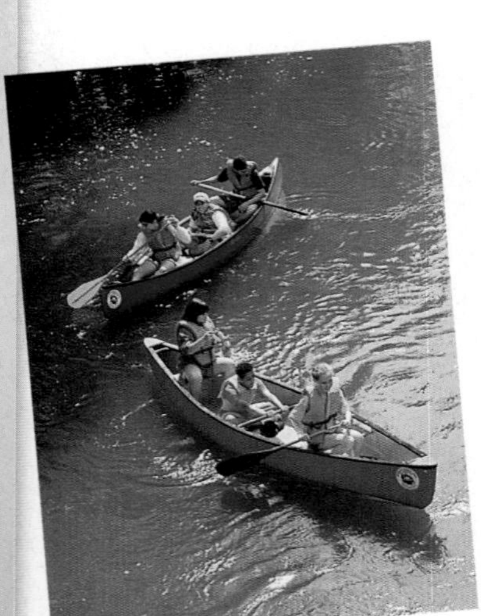

Example 1 Relating to the Real World 

Decision Making Find the probability of choosing each activity. Show the results in a table.

Use the probability formula to find the probability of each event.

$$P(\text{event}) = \frac{\text{number of favorable outcomes}}{\text{number of possible outcomes}}$$

Probabilities of Activities

Event	Probability
Zoo	$\frac{1}{10}$ or 0.1
Canoe Trip	$\frac{2}{10}$ or 0.2
Museum	$\frac{5}{10}$ or 0.5
Picnic	$\frac{2}{10}$ or 0.2

Since only one activity will be chosen, the activities are **mutually exclusive events.** The sum of the probabilities of mutually exclusive events is 1.

In Example 1,

$$\frac{1}{10} + \frac{2}{10} + \frac{5}{10} + \frac{2}{10} = \frac{10}{10} = 1$$

A table or a graph of the probabilities of mutually exclusive events shows the **probability distribution** of the events.

1. These letters are written on slips of paper: E N E O N R R N T T R R. One slip is drawn at random.
   a. Make a probability distribution table showing the probability of drawing each letter.
   b. Show that the sum of the probabilities equals 1.

2. ***Critical Thinking*** A probability distribution table shows six different events. The probability of one event equals 1. What are the probabilities of the other five events? Why?

Example 2 **Relating to the Real World** 

Coin Tossing Three coins are tossed. The table shows the probability distribution for tossing different numbers of heads. What is the probability of tossing two or more heads?

Tossing Three Coins

Event	Probability
0 heads	$\frac{1}{8}$ or 0.125
1 head	$\frac{3}{8}$ or 0.375
2 heads	$\frac{3}{8}$ or 0.375
3 heads	$\frac{1}{8}$ or 0.125

Add P(2 heads) and P(3 heads). The sum is $\frac{4}{8}$ or 0.5. The probability of getting 2 or more heads is 0.5.

3. List the possible outcomes for tossing two coins.

You can use a histogram to display a probability distribution.

Example 3 **Relating to the Real World** 

Decision Making Draw a histogram for the probability distribution in Example 1.

Use the vertical scale to show frequencies as probabilities.

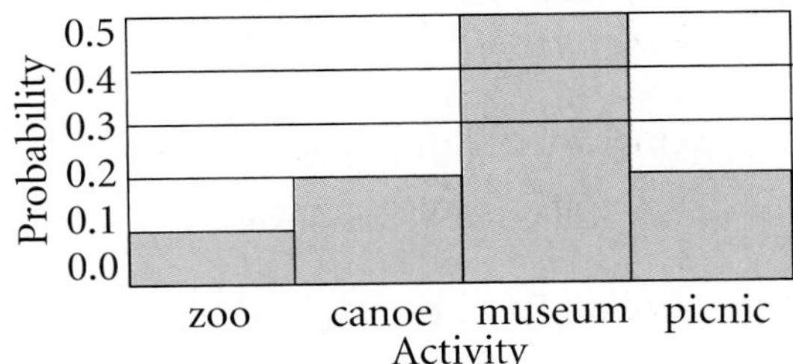

4. a. **Try This** Draw a histogram for the probability distribution shown in the table in Example 2.
   b. Draw a histogram that uses percentiles to show the cumulative probability of tossing heads in three coin tosses.

5. ***Critical Thinking*** What is the probability of tossing three coins and getting tails once? How can you find the answer using your histogram from Question 4(a)?

Exercises ON YOUR OWN

Contestants in a game spin the spinner shown at the right to win \$10, \$100, or \$1000.

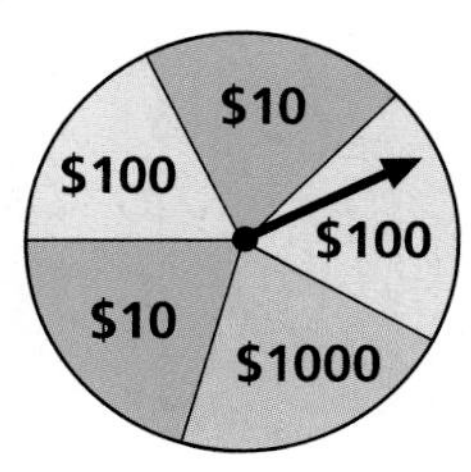

1. Draw a histogram showing the probability distribution of the prizes.
2. Is the chance of winning more than \$10 in one spin greater than 50%? Explain.
3. Eight people are planning a family reunion picnic. They can't decide on the main dish. Each person writes his or her choice on a slip of paper, and one slip is drawn. The table shows the number of votes for each dish. Draw a histogram showing the probability distribution of the main dishes.

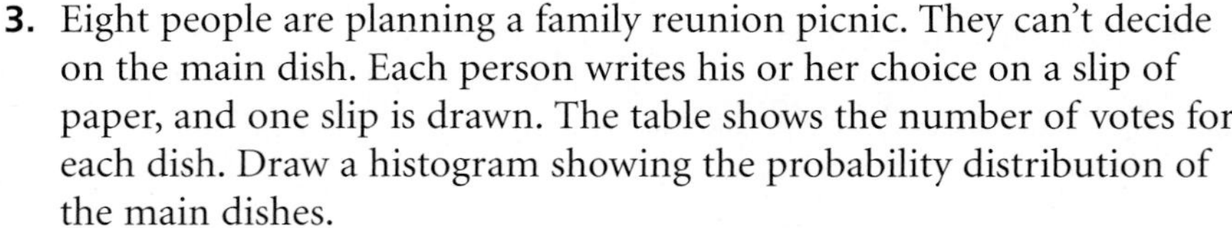

Main Dish	Hot Dogs	Fish	Chicken	Steak
Number of Votes	1	2	3	2

4. **Critical Thinking** Three people compete in a race. Helen is twice as likely to win as Josh. Josh is twice as likely to win as Vicki. Write and solve an equation to find each person's probability of winning.

Twenty people are taking a trip to a forest in New York State. Each person writes his or her favorite forest on a slip of paper. The histogram shows the probability of randomly drawing each of four forests. Use the histogram to answer Exercises 5 and 6.

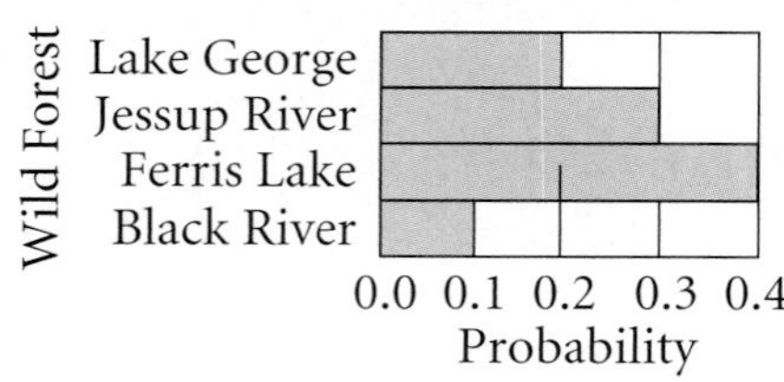

5. How many people wrote Black River on their slips of paper?
6. What is the probability that the group will go to Ferris Lake?

The histogram shows the probability distribution of the ages of spectators at a sporting event.

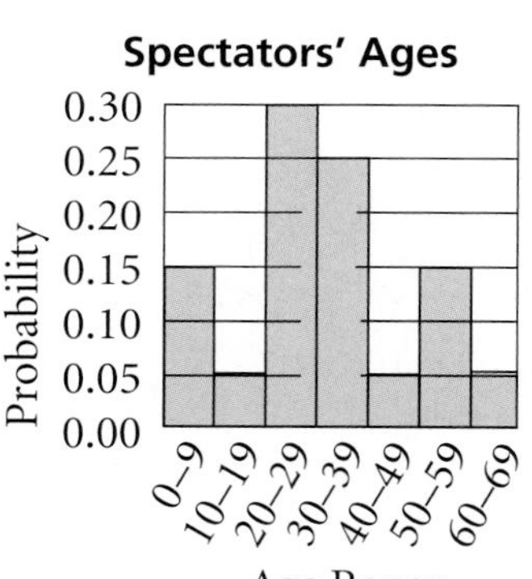

7. Show that the sum of the probabilities equals 1.
8. Draw a histogram that uses percentiles to show cumulative probability.
9. What is the probability that a person chosen at random is younger than 20?
10. **Critical Thinking** If you choose 30 people at the event at random, how many would you expect to be younger than 20? Explain.

Connections  Packaging Design . . . and more

Percent of Error

What You'll Learn

- Identifying the greatest possible error in measurements
- Expressing the error in measurements as percents

...And Why

To solve problems involving collectibles and packaging design

THINK AND DISCUSS

Finding Error in Measurement

Think about the last time you measured with a ruler. Perhaps you measured to the nearest inch, centimeter, or millimeter. Because no measurement is exact, you always measure to the nearest "something." The **greatest possible error** in a measurement is one half of the measuring unit.

Example 1 Relating to the Real World

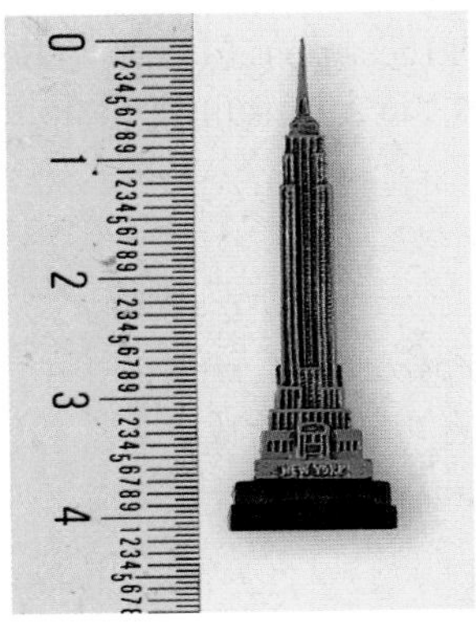

Collectibles What is the height of the magnet to the nearest millimeter? What is the greatest possible error of the measurement?

The height is about 41 mm. Since the measuring unit is 1 mm, the greatest possible error is one half of 1 mm, or 0.5 mm.

1. If you measure the magnet to the nearest centimeter, what is the greatest possible error?
2. **Try This** Find the greatest possible error for each measurement.
   a. 3 mL **b.** $1\frac{1}{2}$ in. **c.** 2.2 kg

Example 2 Relating to the Real World 

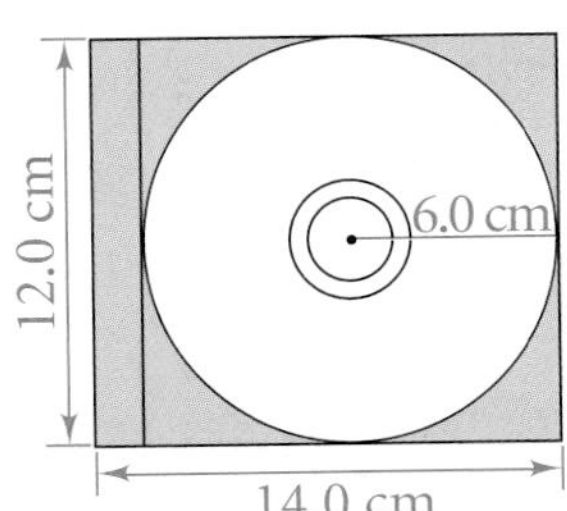

Packaging Design A packaging designer wants to know how much area is available on the inside face of a CD box, not including the area used by the CD. The diagram shows the designer's measurements. Find the minimum and maximum possible values of the shaded area.

Step 1 Find the minimum area. Since the measurements are to the nearest 0.1 cm, the greatest possible error for each is 0.05 cm.

$A = bh - \pi r^2$ ← Write an expression for the difference between the areas of the rectangle and the circle.

$= 13.95(11.95) - \pi(6.05)^2$ ← Substitute the appropriate values.

$= 51.7123549$ ← Use a calculator.

The minimum area is about 51.7 cm^2.

Step 2 Find the maximum area.

$A = bh - \pi r^2$

$= 14.05(12.05) - \pi(5.95)^2$ ← Substitute the appropriate values.

$= 58.08226608$ ← Use a calculator.

The maximum area is about 58.1 cm^2.

PROBLEM SOLVING HINT

To find the minimum area, subtract the largest possible inner area from the smallest possible outer area. To find the maximum area, subtract the smallest possible inner area from the largest possible outer area.

3. **Try This** Measure the dimensions of the figure below to the nearest tenth of a centimeter. Find the minimum and maximum possible values of the area of the shaded region. Round your answers to the nearest tenth.

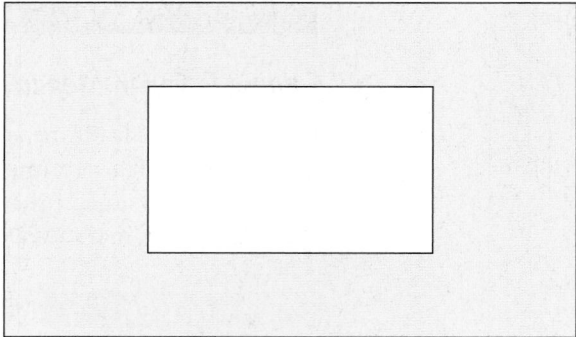

4. **Critical Thinking** Why do you subtract the largest possible inner area from the smallest possible outer area to find the minimum possible value of the shaded area?

Finding Percent of Error

You can represent error in measurements by the *percent of error*.

Percent of Error

percent of error $= \dfrac{\text{amount of error}}{\text{measurement}}$

Example 3

Find the percent of error in a measurement of 12.7 cm.

Since the measurement is to the nearest 0.1 cm, the greatest possible error is 0.05 cm.

percent of error $= \dfrac{\text{amount of error}}{\text{measurement}}$ ← Use the formula.

$= \dfrac{0.05}{12.7}$ ← Substitute.

$= 0.003937009$ ← Divide.

$\approx 0.4\%$ ← Round and write as a percent.

The percent of error is about 0.4%.

5. **Try This** Find the percent of error for each measurement.

   a. $2\frac{1}{2}$yd **b.** 10.0 L **c.** 2 kg

6. Suppose you measure the length of a book to the nearest inch and to the nearest centimeter. Which measurement involves a greater percent of error? Explain.

Errors in measurements will affect the results of computations using those measurements.

Example 4

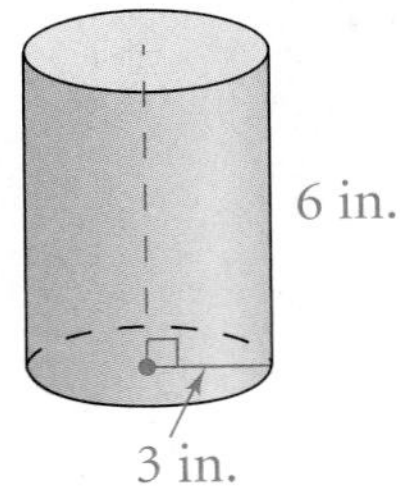

The diagram gives meaurements of the dimensions of a cylinder. Find the greatest possible percent of error in calculating the volume of the cylinder.

The measurements are to the nearest 1 in., so the greatest possible error is 0.5 in.

Volume without error:	Maximum volume:	Minimum volume:
$V = \pi r^2 h$	$V = \pi r^2 h$	$V = \pi r^2 h$
$= \pi \cdot 3^2 \cdot 6$	$= \pi \cdot 3.5^2 \cdot 6.5$	$= \pi \cdot 2.5^2 \cdot 5.5$
≈ 169.6	≈ 250.1	≈ 108.0
$V = 169.6$ in.^{3}	$V = 250.1$ in.^{3}	$V = 108.0$ in.^{3}

The greatest amount of error will result from the difference between the maximum volume and the volume without error.

$$\text{Percent of error} = \frac{\text{amount of error}}{\text{measurement}}$$
$$= \frac{250.1 - 169.6}{169.6}$$
$$= \frac{80.5}{169.6} \approx 47\%$$

The greatest possible percent of error is about 47%.

7. **Try This** Find the greatest possible percent of error in calculating the volume of a cube with edges measured as 3 cm. Round to the nearest whole percent.

Exercises ON YOUR OWN

Write the greatest possible error for each measurement.

1. 42 in.
2. 13.0 mg
3. 12,012 mi
4. $16\frac{1}{8}$ gal
5. 75.25 m
6. 43 mL

Using the given measurements for each polygon, find the greatest possible perimeter and area. Round each answer to the nearest tenth.

7. 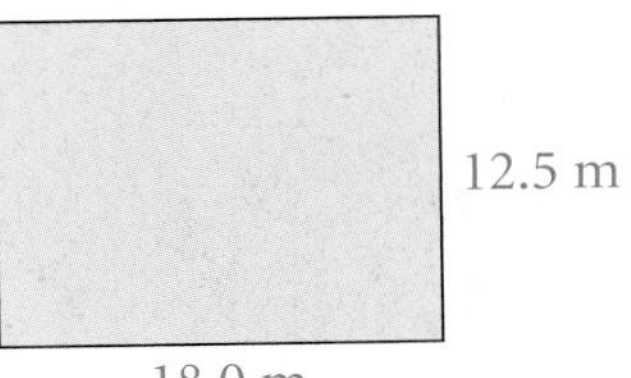

8. 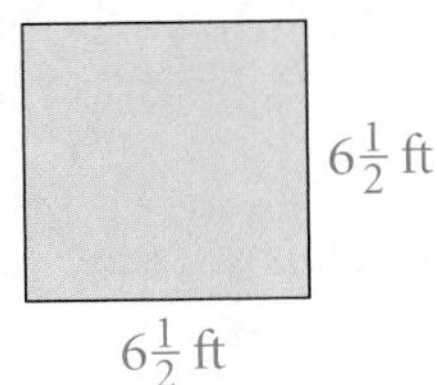

9. 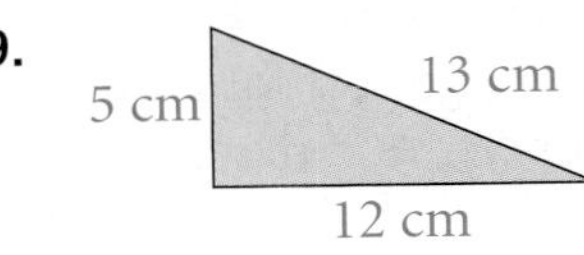

New York Lessons

Using the given measurements, find the greatest and least possible circumferences and areas for each circle. Use $\pi \approx 3.14$. Round answers to the nearest hundredth.

10.

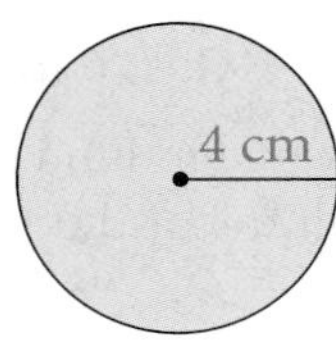

11.

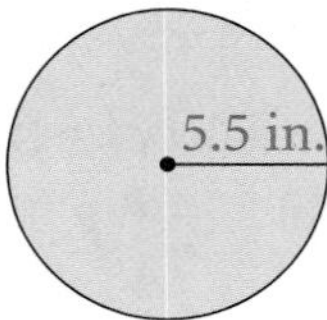

12.

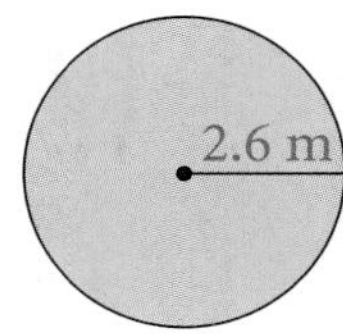

13. **Biology** A biologist measures frogs and tadpoles to the nearest tenth of a centimeter. What is the greatest possible error in millimeters?

14. **Graphic Arts** An artist measured a poster as $28\frac{1}{8}$ in. long. What is the greatest possible error in the artist's measurement?

15. **Landscape Architecture** An architect is creating a scale drawing for a garden. His measurements are accurate to the nearest tenth of a centimeter.

a. What is the greatest possible error in a calculation of the perimeter of a drawing of a rectangular flower bed?

b. If the scale of the drawing is 100 : 1, what is the greatest possible error in a calculation of the perimeter of the actual flower bed?

Write the greatest possible error for each measurement as a percent. Round to the nearest tenth of a percent.

16. $2\frac{1}{4}$ qt, measured to the nearest $\frac{1}{8}$ qt

17. 18 km, measured to the nearest 0.5 km

18. 0.6 g

19. $25\frac{1}{2}$ in.

20. 45 mL

Find the greatest possible percent of error to the nearest tenth of a percent.

21. Without error:
$P = 18$ cm
Greatest possible perimeter:
$P = 20$ cm
Least possible perimeter:
$P = 16$ cm

22. Without error:
$A = 24 \text{ ft}^2$
Greatest possible area:
$A = 29.75 \text{ ft}^2$
Least possible area:
$A = 18.75 \text{ ft}^2$

23. Without error:
$V = 30 \text{ in.}^3$
Greatest possible volume:
$V = 48.13 \text{ in.}^3$
Least possible volume:
$V = 16.88 \text{ in.}^3$

24. **Sports** After a fishing trip in the Catskills, a fisherman reported the length of a $6\frac{1}{2}$ in. salmon as 7 in. A second fisherman reported the length of a $36\frac{1}{2}$ in. salmon as 36 in. Compare the percents of error.

25. **Critical Thinking** For a given set of measurements, why is the percent of error greater for a calculation of area than for a calculation of perimeter or circumference?

26. Find the greatest possible percent of error to the nearest tenth of a percent for a calculation of the volume of the cone at the right. Use a calculator.

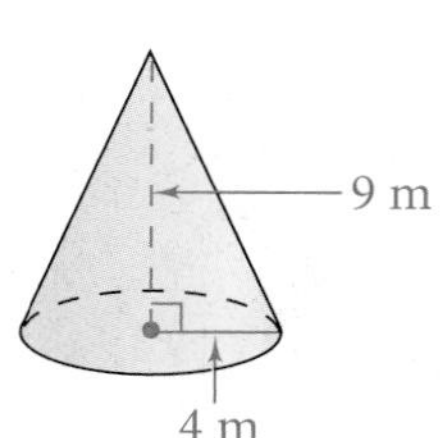

Properties of Real Numbers

What You'll Learn

- Using the Closure Property
- Using other properties in solving equations and simplifying expressions

...And Why

To solve problems involving purchase prices

THINK AND DISCUSS

Using the Closure Property

Nutrition Imagine you are creating new flavors of juice. When you mix two different juices together, you will always get juice. If you double the amount of this new juice, you will still have juice. You cannot create anything that is not juice when all you have is juice. This situation is like adding or multiplying real numbers. When you add or multiply two real numbers, the result is always a real number. This property is called *closure*.

Closure Properties of Addition and Multiplication

For all real numbers a and b:

The sum $a + b$ is a real number. The product $a \cdot b$ is a real number.

Closure is a property of a set of numbers such as integers and an operation, such as addition. To show that a set is *not* closed, find one example for which the operation results in a number outside of the given set of numbers.

Example 1

Is the set of positive odd integers closed under addition?

If you add $3 + 5$, you get 8. Since 8 is not a member of the set of positive integers, the positive odd integers are not closed under addition.

1. **Try This** Is the set of positive odd integers closed under multiplication?
2. **Critical Thinking** The real numbers are not closed under division unless you exclude one real number. What real number must be excluded?

Using Other Properties of Real Numbers

When you solve an equation or simplify an expression, you must be able to justify your steps with properties of real numbers. Closure is one property of real numbers. The table on the next page shows five additional important properties.

Commutative Properties of Addition and Multiplication

For all real numbers a and b:

$a + b = b + a$ $\qquad$ $a \cdot b = b \cdot a$

Associative Properties of Addition and Multiplication

For all real numbers a, b, and c:

$(a + b) + c = a + (b + c)$ $\qquad$ $(a \cdot b) \cdot c = a \cdot (b \cdot c)$

Identity Properties of Addition and Multiplication

$a + 0 = a$ and $0 + a = a$ $\qquad$ $a \cdot 1 = a$ and $1 \cdot a = a$

Inverse Properties of Addition and Multiplication

$a + (-a) = 0$ and $(-a) + a = 0$ $\qquad$ $a \cdot \frac{1}{a} = 1$ and $\frac{1}{a} \cdot a = 1$

Distributive Property

$a(b + c) = ab + ac$ $\qquad$ $a(b - c) = ab - ac$

$(b + c)a = ba + ca$ $\qquad$ $(b - c)a = ba - ca$

Example 2

Which property is shown by the equality $4x(x^2 - 3) = 4x^3 - 12x$?

The Distributive Property is used to multiply each of the two terms in $(x^2 - 3)$ by $4x$.

3. **Try This** Name the property shown by each equality.
   a. $(2 - a)b = b(2 - a)$ **b.** $5k + [-5k + 3] = [5k+(-5k)] + 3$

4. **Critical Thinking** How can the Inverse Property of Multiplication be used to solve the equation $5x = -8$?

Pete's News
Hudson, NY

Receipt	
Souvenirs	2.95
Sub-Total	2.95
Sales Tax 8.25%	.24
Sale Total	3.19
Cash	3.19
Change	.00

*** Thank You ***

Example 3 Connecting to the Real World

Purchase Price The expression $p + r \cdot p$ represents the total price of a purchase when sales tax at rate r is included. Simplify the expression for a sales tax rate of $8\frac{1}{4}\%$. Identify the properties you use.

$p + 0.0825p$ ← Change $8\frac{1}{4}\%$ to 0.0825 and substitute for r.

$(1)p + 0.0825p$ ← Identity Property of Multiplication

$p(1 + 0.0825)$ ← Distributive Property

$p(1.0825)$ ← Addition

$1.0825p$ ← Commutative Property of Multiplication

5. How much would you pay for a CD player marked $200 if the sales tax rate is $8\frac{1}{2}\%$?

Some properties do not hold for operations other than addition and multiplication. Furthermore, they may not hold for sets of numbers other than the real numbers.

Example 4

Show that subtraction of real numbers is not commutative.

$2 - 6 \stackrel{?}{=} 6 - 2$

$-4 \neq 4$

6. **Critical Thinking** Does the associative property hold for division of real numbers? Give an example or a counterexample.

Exercises ON YOUR OWN

Tell whether each set is closed under addition. If the set is not closed, give a counterexample.

1. positive integers
2. negative integers
3. odd integers
4. even integers
5. the square numbers {1, 4, 9, 16, 25, . . . }
6. the multiples of 5 {0, 5, 10, 15, 20, . . . }

Tell whether each set is closed under multiplication. If the set is not closed, give a counterexample.

7. positive integers
8. negative integers
9. odd integers
10. even integers
11. the square numbers {1, 4, 9, 16, 25, . . . }
12. the multiples of 5 {0, 5, 10, 15, 20, . . . }

Tell whether each set is closed under the operation of taking a principal square root.

13. positive integers
14. positive rational numbers
15. positive real numbers

The tables at the right show addition and multiplication for the set {0, 1}.

+	0	1
0	0	1
1	1	2

×	0	1
0	0	0
1	0	1

16. Is the set closed under addition? Why or why not?
17. Is the set closed under multiplication? Why or why not?
18. **Critical Thinking** The operation * is defined for the set of whole numbers as $a * b = \frac{ab}{2}$. Is * a closed operation over the set of whole numbers? If not, give a counterexample.
19. **Standardized Test Prep** Which set of numbers is closed under subtraction?
    A. positive integers **B.** negative integers **C.** even integers **D.** odd integers

New York Lessons

Name the property that justifies each statement.

20. $4(x + y) + 5(x + y) = (4 + 5)(x + y)$

21. $\frac{1}{2} \cdot (6 + 3) = (6 + 3) \cdot \frac{1}{2}$

22. $\frac{4}{3} \cdot \left(\frac{3}{4}\right) \cdot \left(-\frac{1}{4}\right) = 1 \cdot \left(-\frac{1}{4}\right)$

23. $7a + (2a + 3b) = (7a + 2a) + 3b$

24. If $k + 1 = 1$, then k must be equal to 0.

25. $4 \cdot 1 + (-4) = 4 + (-4)$

26. For any nonzero real number b, there must exist a real number d so that $bd = 1$.

One step in simplifying each expression is shown. Name the property used.

27. $-3 + (a)(-2) = -3 + (-2a)$

28. $-6 + 4m + 6 = -6 + 6 + 4m$

29. $-4 + 2(1 - x) = -4 + 2 - 2x$

30. $3a + [4a + (-7)] = (3a + 4a) + (-7)$

One step in solving each equation is shown. Name the property used.

31. $3x + 2 + (-2) = 11 + (-2)$
$3x + 0 = 11 + (-2)$

32. $6 = (1)(m)$
$6 = m$

33. $-5\left(-\frac{1}{5}y\right) = -5(12)$
$\left(-5 \cdot -\frac{1}{5}\right)y = -5(12)$

Simplify each expression. Identify the properties you use.

34. $5[x(-2)]$

35. $-4gk + 2k$

36. $-ab + 2ab + ab$

37. $-3[(-2x) + 1]$

Solve each equation. Identify the properties you use.

38. $0 = -m + (-2)$

39. $-[-3 + (-h)] = 0$

40. $\frac{1}{4}g = -2$

41. $1 = -\frac{2}{3}b + 5$

42. **Sports** A runner is training to run in the New York City Marathon. His goal is to run an average of 40 miles each week. If he ran 38 miles one week and 43 miles the next, how many miles must he run in the third week to reach his goal? Write and solve an equation. Name the properties you use.

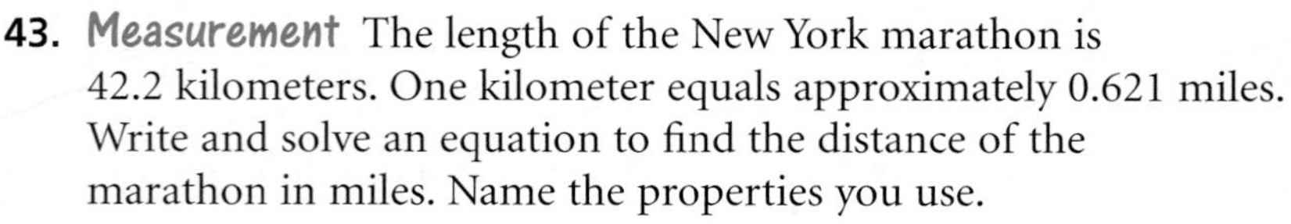

43. **Measurement** The length of the New York marathon is 42.2 kilometers. One kilometer equals approximately 0.621 miles. Write and solve an equation to find the distance of the marathon in miles. Name the properties you use.

44. Show that the Commutative Property does not apply to the division of real numbers.

45. Show that the Associative Property does not apply to the division of real numbers.

46. **Critical Thinking** The Distributive Property distributes multiplication over addition and subtraction.

a. Is addition distributive over multiplication? If so, state the property in algebraic terms. If not, give a counterexample.

b. Is subtraction distributive over multiplication? If so, state the property in algebraic terms. If not, give a counterexample.

Connections Travel . . . and more

Conjunctions and Disjunctions

What You'll Learn

- Using conjunctions and disjunctions

...And Why

To use logical reasoning to solve problems involving travel and geometry

THINK AND DISCUSS

Travel Here are four statements you might make after a visit to New York.

a: We toured the Statue of Liberty.
b: We saw the Capitol in Albany.
c: We rode a gondola at Gore Mountain.
d: We went on a guided boat ride at Niagara Falls.

Each of the statements has a truth value—you either visited the spot or you didn't. If you combine two or more simple statements, the result is a **compound statement.**

A compound statement joined by the word *and* is called a **conjunction.**

Example 1 **Relating to the Real World** 

Travel Use the four statements above about visiting New York. Assume that a and b are true and that c and d are false. Tell whether the following compound statement is true or false: *We toured the Statue of Liberty and we went on a guided boat ride at Niagara Falls.*

The compound statement is false, since the statement about Niagara Falls is false.

1. **Try This** Tell whether the following compound statement is true or false: *We saw the Capitol in Albany and we rode a gondola at Gore Mountain.*

A conjunction is true only if both statements are true. You can illustrate a conjunction with a truth table or a Venn diagram. Variables p and q are often used to represent the statements in a compound statement.

Truth Table for Conjunctions

p	q	p and q
T	T	T
T	F	F
F	T	F
F	F	F

The truth table shows the truth value of a conjunction in relation to the truth values of its statements.

Venn Diagram for a Conjunction

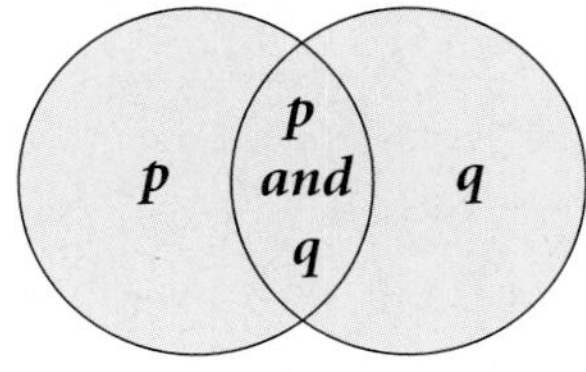

The Venn diagram shows a conjunction as the intersection of two statements.

New York Lessons

A compound statement joined by the word *or* is called a **disjunction.** A truth table or a Venn diagram can illustrate a disjunction.

Truth Table for Disjunctions

p	q	p *or* q
T	T	T
T	F	T
F	T	T
F	F	F

A disjunction is true if either or both of the statements are true.

Venn Diagram for a Disjunction

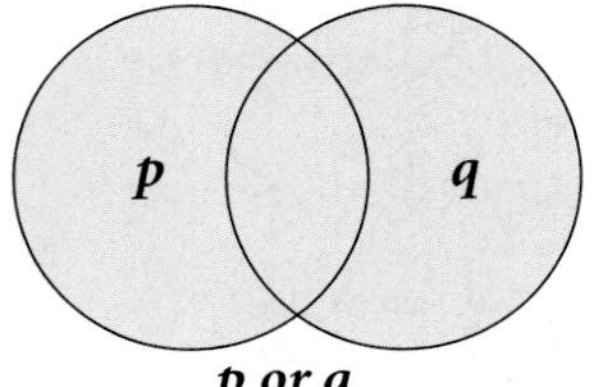

p *or* q

The Venn diagram shows a disjunction as the union of two statements.

Example 2

Geometry Use the following four statements. State the truth value for the compound statement *e or g*.

e: Perpendicular lines intersect in two points.
f: The formula for the circumference of a circle with radius r is $2\pi r$.
g: The area of a rectangle equals the product of its base and height.
h: Parallel lines intersect to form vertical angles.

The compound statement is true because at least one of its simple statements, statement *g*, is true.

2. Try This State the truth value for each compound statement.
a. *e or f* **b.** *e or h* **c.** *f or g* **d.** *g and h*

You can make truth tables for a compound statement made from three or more statements.

Example 3

Geometry Use statements *e* through *h* in Example 2 above. Find the truth value for *(e or f) and g*.

e	*f*	*g*	*e or f*	*(e or f) and g*
F	T	T	T	T

The compound statement *(e or f) and g* is true.

3. Copy and complete the truth table below.

e	*h*	*g*	*e or h*	*(e or h) and g*
F	■	T	■	■

4. Make a truth table to determine the truth value of *e and (f and g)*.

Exercises ON YOUR OWN

Geography **Use these four statements for Exercises 1–21.**

q: The Adirondack Mountains are east of Lake Ontario.
r: Niagara Falls is in Pennsylvania.
s: Washington, D.C., is north of New York City.
t: The Hudson River runs north and south through New York State.

What is the truth value of each statement?

1. q **2.** r **3.** s **4.** t

State the truth value for each compound statement.

5. *q and r* **6.** *q and s* **7.** *q and t* **8.** *r and s*

9. *r and t* **10.** *s and t* **11.** *q or r* **12.** *q or s*

13. *q or t* **14.** *r or s* **15.** *r or t* **16.** *s or t*

17. *q or r or s* **18.** *q and (s or r)* **19.** *q and (r or t)* **20.** *(q or t) and (r or s)*

21. Make a truth table to show the truth value of *(s and t) or q*.

Nutrition **The Venn diagram at the right shows the results of a survey that asked students what types of fresh fruit they had eaten in the previous week. State the truth value for each statement.**

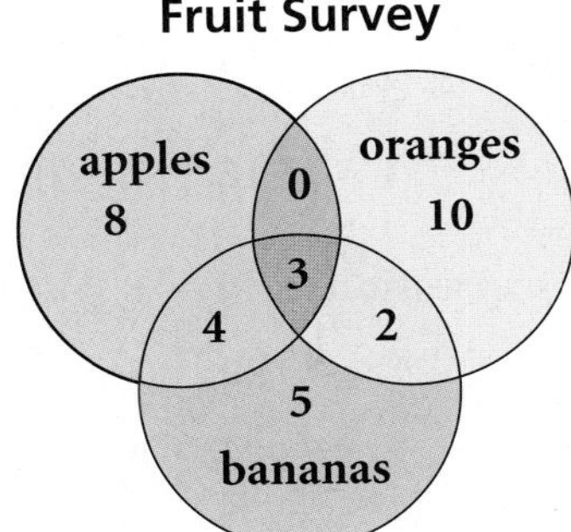

22. Fifteen students ate apples and nineteen students ate oranges.

23. Fourteen students ate bananas or oranges.

24. The same number of students ate apples as ate oranges.

25. The same numbers of students ate apples, bananas, and oranges.

26. The number of students who ate apples and bananas is the same as the number who ate oranges and bananas.

27. Three students ate apples, bananas, and oranges.

28. **Open-ended** Use the data in the Venn diagram.
a. Write two conjunctions.
b. Write two disjunctions.

29. **Writing** Explain the difference between a conjunction and a disjunction.

30. What is the truth value of the conjunction of two mutually exclusive events? Explain.

Extra Practice

Find the mean, median, and mode for each set of data. ■ **Lesson 1-1**

1. 36, 42, 35, 40, 35, 51, 41, 35
2. 1.2, 0.9, 0.7, 1.1, 0.8, 1.3, 0.6
3. 5, 8, 6, 8, 3, 5, 8, 6, 5, 9
4. A student surveyed the members of the drama club. She included a question about age. Her results are at the right.
   a. Make a line plot for the data.
   b. What is the median age of the drama club members?

Ages of Drama Club Members								
14	18	16	15	17	14	15	18	15
13	14	15	18	14	17	16	14	16

■ **Lesson 1-2**

5. Write an equation to model each situation.
   a. The length of three cars is 24 feet.
   b. The weight of two books equals 39 pens.
6. a. Write a sentence and an equation to describe the relationship between the number of notebooks and the price.
   b. If you have \$5, can you buy a notebook for each of your classes? Explain.

Notebooks	Price
1	\$.99
2	\$1.98
3	\$2.97

Simplify each expression. ■ **Lessons 1-3 to 1-6**

7. $4 + 3 \cdot 8$
8. $2 \cdot 3^2 - 7$
9. $6 \cdot (5 - 2) - 9$
10. $2 - 12 \div 3$
11. $\left(\frac{1}{3}\right)^2 + 8 \div 2$
12. $\frac{1}{2} \div \frac{4}{3}$
13. $-6 \cdot 4.2 - 5 \div 2$
14. $9 - (3 + 1)^2$
15. $\frac{1}{3} - \frac{5}{6}$
16. $-4 + 9 \div 3 - 2$
17. $(8 - 1.5) \cdot -4$
18. $\frac{3}{4} \cdot 6 - \frac{1}{2}$

Evaluate each expression for $a = 8$, $b = -3$, and $c = \frac{1}{2}$.

19. $a - b - c$
20. $c - a^2$
21. $8c + ab$
22. $c(a - 2c)$
23. $9b - 4a$
24. $\frac{1}{2}b - ac$
25. $(2b)^2 - 2b^2$
26. $\frac{1}{a} + \frac{1}{c}$

The results of rolling a number cube 54 times are at the right. Use the results to find each experimental probability. ■ **Lesson 1-7**

27. $P(3)$
28. $P(4)$
29. $P(\text{not } 5)$
30. $P(7)$
31. $P(\text{even number})$
32. $P(\text{not } 1)$

6	3	4	5	1	1	5	5	3	6	3	2	1	3	3	3	2	1
2	3	6	3	3	4	5	1	2	2	6	3	3	6	5	4	5	3
2	5	1	4	5	2	6	2	5	2	1	2	5	3	2	4	6	3

Find the sum or difference. ■ **Lesson 1-8**

33. $\begin{bmatrix} -3 & 0 \\ 11 & -5 \end{bmatrix} + \begin{bmatrix} -4 & 6 \\ -8 & 13 \end{bmatrix}$
34. $\begin{bmatrix} 6 & 12 \\ -9 & 7 \end{bmatrix} - \begin{bmatrix} 8 & -6 \\ 15 & 0 \end{bmatrix}$
35. $\begin{bmatrix} 4.2 & 0.6 \\ 1.7 & 9.5 \end{bmatrix} - \begin{bmatrix} 5.8 & -3.5 \\ 0.2 & 4.9 \end{bmatrix}$

■ **Lesson 1-9**

36. You can find the surface area of a cube using the formula $A = 6s^2$, where s is the length of a side.
   a. Write a spreadsheet formula for cell B2.
   b. Find the values for cells B2, C2, and D2.
   c. Write a spreadsheet formula to find the sum of the surface areas of the three cubes.

	A	B	C	D
1	Side Length	3	5.2	9
2	Surface Area	■	■	■

Extra Practice

Use the table for Exercise 1. ■ Lesson 2-1

Cover Price and Number of Pages of Some Magazines

Cover Price	\$2.25	\$2.50	\$3.75	\$3.00	\$4.95	\$1.95	\$2.95	\$2.50
Number of Pages	208	68	122	124	234	72	90	90

1. a. Draw a scatter plot of the data.
   b. Draw a trend line on the scatter plot. What is the relationship between the cover price and the number of pages in a magazine?
   c. How many pages would you expect a \$2.00 magazine to have? Explain.

Sketch a graph to describe each situation. Explain the activity in each section of the graph. ■ Lesson 2-2

2. the amount of milk in your bowl as you eat cereal
3. the energy you use in a 24-h period
4. your distance from home plate after your home run
5. the number of apples on a tree over one year

Graph the data. Then write a function rule for each table of values. ■ Lessons 2-3, 2-5, 2-6

6.

x	$f(x)$
–3	–1
–1	1
1	3
3	5

7.

x	$f(x)$
0	0
3	6
6	12
9	18

8.

x	$f(x)$
21	14
25	18
29	22
33	26

9.

x	$f(x)$
–8	–4
–6	–3
–4	–2
–2	–1

Find the range of each function when the domain is {–4, –1, 0, 3, 8}. Each equation belongs to what family of functions? ■ Lessons 2-4, 2-7

10. $y = 6x - 5$
11. $y = |x| - 2$
12. $y = x^2 + 3x + 1$
13. $y = \frac{1}{2}x + 8$
14. $y = -x^2 - x$
15. $y = \frac{2}{3}x$
16. $y = |x - 2|$
17. $y = 2x^2 - 5x$
18. $y = |4 - x|$
19. $y = x + 5$
20. $y = \frac{4}{9}x^2$
21. $y = |\frac{3}{5}x|$

Find each theoretical probability for one roll of a number cube. ■ Lesson 2-8

22. P(an odd number)
23. P(a negative number)
24. P(an integer)
25. P(a factor of 6)

At the Sock Hop, socks are sold in three sizes and six colors. The sizes are small, medium, and large. The color selection consists of white, gray, blue, red, black, and purple. Find the probability of choosing each kind of sock randomly.

26. P(large and gray)
27. P(blue or red)
28. P(small and purple)
29. P(medium)
30. Make a tree diagram to show all the kinds of socks.

Extra Practice

Solve each equation. ■ Lesson 3-1 to 3-5

1. $h - 4 = 10$
2. $8p - 3 = 13$
3. $8j - 5 + j = 67$
4. $6t = -42$
5. $-n + 8.5 = 14.2$
6. $6(t + 5) = -36$
7. $m + 9 = 11$
8. $\frac{1}{2}(s + 5) = 7.5$
9. $\frac{s}{3} = 8$
10. $7h + 2h - 3 = 15$
11. $\frac{7}{12}x = \frac{3}{14}$
12. $3r - 8 = -32$
13. $8g - 10g = 4$
14. $-3(5 - t) = 18$
15. $3(c - 4) = -9$
16. $\frac{3}{8}z = 9$
17. $0.1(h + 20) = 3$
18. $\frac{3m}{5} = 6$
19. $4 - y = 10$
20. $8q + 2q = -7.4$

Write an equation to solve each problem.

21. *School* Your test scores for the semester are 87, 84, and 85. Can you raise your test average to 90 with your next test?
22. You spend $\frac{1}{2}$ of your allowance each week on school lunches. Each lunch costs \$1.25. How much is your weekly allowance?

You pick two balls from a jar. The jar has five blue, three yellow, six green, and two purple balls. Find each probability. ■ Lesson 3-6

23. *P*(purple and blue), with replacement
24. *P*(yellow and purple), without replacement
25. *P*(green and yellow), with replacement
26. *P*(green and blue), without replacement
27. *P*(purple and green), without replacement
28. *P*(green and blue), with replacement
29. *P*(blue and yellow), without replacement
30. *P*(blue and purple), with replacement

Write and solve an equation to answer each question. ■ Lesson 3-7

31. What is 10% of 94?
32. What percent of 10 is 4?
33. 147 is 14% of what?
34. What percent of 1.2 is 6?
35. 13.2 is 55% of what?
36. What is 0.4% of 800?
37. What is 75% of 68?
38. 5 is 200% of what?
39. What percent of 54 is 28?
40. 114 is 95% of what?
41. What percent of 20 is 31?
42. What is 35% of 15?

Find each percent of change. Describe each as a percent of increase or decrease. Round to the nearest percent. ■ Lesson 3-8

43. \$4.50 to \$5.00
44. 56 in. to 57 in.
45. 18 oz to 12 oz
46. 1 s to 3 s
47. 8 lb to 5 lb
48. 6 km to 6.5 km
49. 39 h to 40 h
50. 7 ft to 2 ft
51. 0.2 mL to 0.45 mL
52. $\frac{1}{2}$ tsp to $\frac{1}{8}$ tsp
53. 18 kg to 20 kg
54. 55 min to 50 min
55. In 1988, the average resident of the United States ate about 2.4 lb of bagels per year. In 1993, bagel consumption had increased to about 3.5 lb annually. What percent increase is this?

Extra Practice

Solve each proportion. ■ Lesson 4-1

1. $\frac{3}{4} = \frac{-6}{m}$
2. $\frac{t}{7} = \frac{3}{21}$
3. $\frac{9}{j} = \frac{3}{16}$
4. $\frac{2}{5} = \frac{w}{65}$
5. $\frac{s}{15} = \frac{4}{45}$
6. $\frac{9}{4} = \frac{x}{10}$
7. $\frac{10}{q} = \frac{8}{62}$
8. $\frac{3}{2} = \frac{18}{y}$
9. $\frac{5}{9} = \frac{t}{3}$
10. $\frac{6}{m} = \frac{3}{5}$
11. $\frac{c}{8} = \frac{13.5}{36}$
12. $\frac{7}{9} = \frac{35}{x}$
13. **Architecture** A blueprint scale is 1 in. : 4 ft. On the plan, the garage is 2 in. by 3 in. What are the actual dimensions of the garage?

Solve and check. If the equation is an identity or if it has no solution, write *identity* or *no solution*. ■ Lessons 4-2, 4-3

14. $|t| = 6$
15. $5m + 3 = 9m - 1$
16. $8d = 4d - 18$
17. $4h + 5 = 9h$
18. $|k| - 4 = -7$
19. $7t = 80 + 9t$
20. $|w - 9| = 4$
21. $|m + 3| = 12$
22. $-b + 4b = 8b - b$
23. $8 - |p| = 3$
24. $|h + 17| = -8$
25. $6p + 1 = 3p$
26. $10z - 5 + 3z = 8 - z$
27. $3(g - 1) + 7 = 3g + 4$
28. $17 - 20q = -13 - 5q$
29. **Transportation** A bus traveling 40 mi/h and a car traveling 50 mi/h cover the same distance. The bus travels 1 h more than the car. How many hours did each travel?

Solve each equation for the given variable. ■ Lesson 4-4

30. $A = lw; w$
31. $c = \frac{w + t}{v}, t$
32. $h = \frac{r}{t}(p - m); r$
33. $P = 2l + 2w; l$
34. $v = \pi r^2 h; h$
35. $m = \frac{t}{b - a}; t$
36. $y = bt - c; b$
37. $g = 1.9\frac{m}{r^2}; m$

Solve each inequality and graph the solutions on a number line. ■ Lessons 4-5 to 4-8

38. $-8w < 24$
39. $9 + p \leq 17$
40. $\frac{r}{4} > -1$
41. $7y + 2 \leq -8$
42. $t - 5 \geq -13$
43. $9h > -108$
44. $|8w + 7| > 5$
45. $\frac{s}{6} \leq 3$
46. $\frac{6c}{5} \geq -12$
47. $-8l + 3.7 \leq 31.7$
48. $9 - t \leq 4$
49. $|m + 4| \geq 8$
50. $y + 3 < 16$
51. $|n - 6| \leq 8.5$
52. $12b - 5 > -29$
53. $4 - a > 15$
54. $6m - 15 \leq 9$ or $10m > 84$
55. $9j - 5j \geq 20$ and $8j > -36$
56. $37 < 3c + 7 < 43$
57. The booster club raised $102 in their car wash. They want to buy $18 soccer balls for the soccer team. How many can they buy?

Solve and graph each inequality. The replacement set is the positive integers. ■ Lesson 4-9

58. $t - 5 \leq -3$
59. $-6m + 2 > -19$
60. $|3c + 1| \geq 7$
61. $8 - w < 8$
62. $2b + 3 < 7$
63. $-c - 5 \leq 6$
64. $|n| + 4 \leq 5$
65. $\frac{3}{5}t > 6$
66. You are solving a problem involving weight. Find the replacement set.

Extra Practice

Find the slope of the line passing through each pair of points. Then write the equation of the line. ■ **Lessons 5-1, 5-5**

1. (2, 5) and (4, 8) **2.** (1, 6) and (7, 3) **3.** (–2, 4) and (3, 9) **4.** (1, 6) and (9, –4)

5. (–5, –7) and (–1, 3) **6.** (7, 0) and (3, –4) **7.** (0, 0) and (–7, 1) **8.** (10, –5) and (–2, 7)

Write an equation for a line through the given point with the given slope. Then graph the line.

9. (4, 6); $m = -5$ **10.** (3, –1); $m = 1$ **11.** (8, 5); $m = \frac{1}{2}$ **12.** (0, –6); $m = \frac{4}{3}$

13. (–2, 7); $m = 2$ **14.** (–5, –9); $m = -3.5$ **15.** (4, 0); $m = 7$ **16.** (6, –4); $m = -\frac{1}{5}$

Find the rate of change for each situation. ■ **Lesson 5-2**

17. growing from 1.4 m to 1.6 m in one year **18.** bicycling 3 mi in 15 min and 7 mi in 55 min

19. walking 3 blocks in 10 min and 12 blocks in 55 min **20.** reading 8 pages in 9 min and 22 pages in 30 min

Draw the graph of a direct variation that includes the given point. Write the equation of the line. ■ **Lesson 5-3**

21. (5, 4) **22.** (7, 7) **23.** (–3, –10) **24.** (4, –8) **25.** (–2, 9) **26.** (11, 1)

27. (8, –2) **28.** (–5, 9) **29.** (6, 8) **30.** (1, –4) **31.** (–3, 3) **32.** (1, 12)

Find the slope and *y*-intercept. Then graph each equation. ■ **Lessons 5-4, 5-7**

33. $y = 6x + 8$ **34.** $3x + 4y = -24$ **35.** $-2y = 5x - 12$ **36.** $6x + y = 12$

37. $y = \frac{-3}{4}x - 8$ **38.** $2y = 8$ **39.** $y = \frac{1}{2}x + 3$ **40.** $y = -7x$

41. a. Graph the ages and grade levels of some students in a school below. ■ **Lesson 5-6**

b. Draw a trend line.

c. Find the equation of the line of best fit.

(10, 6), (16, 10), (15, 10), (18,12), (17, 11), (17, 12), (19, 12), (16, 11), (11, 7), (15, 9), (13, 8)

Write an equation that satisfies the given conditions. ■ **Lesson 5-8**

42. parallel to $y = 4x + 1$, through (–3, 5) **43.** perpendicular to $y = -x - 3$, through (0, 0)

44. perpendicular to $3x + 4y = 12$, through (7, 1) **45.** parallel to $2x - y = 6$, through (–6, –9)

46. perpendicular to $y = -2x + 5$, through (4, –10) **47.** parallel to $2y = 5x + 12$, through (2, –1)

Solve each equation by graphing. ■ **Lesson 5-9**

48. $x + 5 = 3x - 7$ **49.** $-4x + 1 = 2x - 5$ **50.** $9x - 2 = 7x + 4$ **51.** $6x + 1 = 3x - 5$

52. $8x - 2 = 7x + 9$ **53.** $12x + 4 = x - 29$ **54.** $-x - 4 = x + 18$ **55.** $5x = 6x - 19$

Extra Practice

Choose your own method to solve each system. ■ Lessons 6-1 to 6-3

1. $x - y = 7$, $3x + 2y = 6$

2. $x + 4y = 1$, $3x - 2y = -25$

3. $4x - 5y = 9$, $-2x - y = -29$

4. $x - y = 13$, $y - x = -13$

5. $3x - y = 4$, $x + 5y = -4$

6. $x + y = 4$, $y = 7x + 4$

7. $x + y = 19$, $x - y = -7$

8. $-3x + 4y = 29$, $3x + 2y = -17$

9. $4x - 9y = 61$, $10x + 3y = 25$

10. $6x + y = 13$, $y - x = -8$

11. $3x + y = 3$, $-3x + 2y = -30$

12. $4x - y = 105$, $x + 7y = -10$

Write a system of equations to solve each problem. ■ Lesson 6-4

13. Suppose you have 12 coins that total \$.32. Some of the coins are nickels and the rest are pennies. How many of each coin do you have?

14. Your school drama club will put on a play you wrote. Royalties are \$50 plus \$.25 for each ticket sold. The cost for props and costumes is \$85. The tickets for the play will be \$2 each.
a. Write an equation for the expenses.
b. Write an equation for the income. What is the break-even point?
c. How much will the club earn if 200 tickets are sold?

Graph each linear inequality. ■ Lesson 6-5

15. $y \geq 4x - 3$

16. $y < x - 4$

17. $y > -6x + 5$

18. $y \leq 14 - x$

19. $x < -8$

20. $2x + 3y \leq 6$

21. $y \leq 12$

22. $y > -3x + 1$

Graph each system. ■ Lessons 6-6, 6-8

23. $y \leq 5x + 1$, $y > x - 3$

24. $y > 4x + 3$, $y \geq -2x - 1$

25. $y = |2x| - 3$, $y = x + 4$

26. $y < -2x + 1$, $y > -2x - 3$

27. $y = |6x| - 2$, $y = x^2 - 2$

28. $y = 4x^2 - 5$, $y = x$

29. $y \leq 8$, $y \geq |-x| + 1$

30. $y \leq 5x - 2$, $y > 3$

31. $y = -2x - 7$, $y = |x + 3|$

32. $y > -3x - 9$, $y < 5x + 7$

33. $y = x^2 + 2$, $y = |\frac{1}{2}x| + 4$

34. $y \geq x$, $y \leq x + 1$

Graph each system of restrictions. Find the coordinates of each vertex. Evaluate the equation to find the maximum and minimum values of *B*. ■ Lesson 6-7

35. $x \geq 0$, $y \geq 0$, $x \leq 5$, $y \leq 4$, $B = 2x + 5y$

36. $x \geq 2$, $x \leq 6$, $y \geq 1$, $y \leq 4$, $B = x + 3y$

37. $x \geq 2$, $y \geq 1$, $x + y \leq 10$, $B = 3x + 2y$

38. $x \geq 0$, $y \geq 0$, $y \leq -2x + 10$, $y \leq 4x + 2$, $B = x + y$

Extra Practice

Without graphing, describe how each graph differs from the graph of $y = x^2$. ■ Lessons 7-1 to 7-3

1. $y = 3x^2$
2. $y = -4x^2$
3. $y = -0.5x^2$
4. $y = 0.2x^2$
5. $y = x^2 - 4$
6. $y = x^2 + 1$
7. $y = 2x^2 + 5$
8. $y = -0.3x^2 - 7$

Graph each quadratic function. Label the axis of symmetry, the vertex, and the y-intercept.

9. $y = 3x^2$
10. $y = -2x^2 + 1$
11. $y = 0.5x^2 - 3$
12. $y = -x^2 + 2x + 1$
13. $y = 3x^2 + 5x$
14. $y = \frac{3}{4}x^2$
15. $y = 2x^2 - 9$
16. $y = -5x^2 + x + 4$
17. $y = x^2 - 7x$
18. $y = x^2 - 3x + 8$
19. $y = -x^2 + x + 12$
20. $y = -\frac{1}{2}x^2 + x - 3$

Graph each quadratic inequality.

21. $y > x^2 - 4$
22. $y \geq -x^2 + 3x + 10$
23. $y < 2x^2 + x$
24. $y \leq 2x^2 + 5$
25. $y > -\frac{1}{2}x^2 - 3x$
26. $y \leq x^2 + x - 2$

Find the square roots of each number. ■ Lesson 7-4

27. 25
28. $\frac{4}{9}$
29. 64
30. $\frac{25}{36}$
31. 0.81
32. 900
33. 2.25
34. 16
35. $\frac{1}{25}$
36. 169
37. $\frac{4}{36}$
38. 289

Solve each equation. Round solutions to the nearest hundredth when necessary. If the equation has no real solution, write *no real solution*. ■ Lessons 7-5, 7-6

39. $x^2 = 36$
40. $x^2 + x - 2 = 0$
41. $c^2 - 100 = 0$
42. $9d^2 = 25$
43. $(x - 4)^2 = 100$
44. $3x^2 = 27$
45. $2x^2 - 54 = 284$
46. $7n^2 = 63$
47. $h^2 + 4 = 0$
48. $x^2 + 6x - 2 = 0$
49. $x^2 - 5x = 7$
50. $x^2 - 10x + 3 = 0$
51. $2x^2 - 4x + 1 = 0$
52. $3x^2 + x + 5 = 0$
53. $\frac{1}{2}x^2 - 8 = 3x$
54. $x^2 + 8x - 5 = -9$
55. $2x^2 - 5x = x^2 - 3x + 6$
56. $-3x^2 + x - 2 = 5$

Evaluate the discriminant. Determine the number of real solutions of each equation. ■ Lesson 7-7

57. $x^2 - x + 5 = 0$
58. $3x^2 + 4x = -3 - 2x$
59. $-2x^2 - x + 7 = 0$
60. $3x^2 + 8x = 9$
61. $3x^2 + 5 = 6x$
62. $6x^2 + 11x - 4 = 0$
63. $-x^2 + x - 4 = 3$
64. $6x - x^2 = 4$
65. $x^2 = 5x - 1$

Extra Practice

■ Lessons 8-1 to 8-3

Graph each function. Label each graph as *exponential growth* or *exponential decay*.

1. $y = 3^x$ **2.** $y = \left(\frac{3}{4}\right)^x$ **3.** $y = 1.5^x$ **4.** $y = \frac{1}{2} \cdot 3^x$

5. $y = 3 \cdot 7^x$ **6.** $y = 4^x$ **7.** $y = 3 \cdot \left(\frac{1}{5}\right)^x$ **8.** $y = 2^x$

9. $y = 2 \cdot 3^x$ **10.** $y = (0.8)^x$ **11.** $y = 2.5^x$ **12.** $y = 4 \cdot (0.2)^x$

Identify the growth factor or decay factor for each exponential function.

13. $y = 8^x$ **14.** $y = \frac{3}{4} \cdot 2^x$ **15.** $y = 9 \cdot \left(\frac{1}{2}\right)^x$ **16.** $y = 4 \cdot 9^x$

17. $y = 0.65^x$ **18.** $y = 3 \cdot 1.5^x$ **19.** $y = \frac{2}{5} \cdot \left(\frac{1}{4}\right)^x$ **20.** $y = 0.1 \cdot 0.9^x$

Write an exponential function to model each situation. Find each amount after the specified time.

21. \$200 principal
4% compounded annually
5 years

22. \$1000 principal
3.6% compounded monthly
10 years

23. \$3000 investment
8% loss each year
3 years

■ Lessons 8-4, 8-6 to 8-8

Simplify each expression. Use only positive exponents.

24. $(2t)^{-6}$ **25.** $5m^5m^{-8}$ **26.** $(4.5)^4(4.5)^{-2}$ **27.** $(m^7t^{-5})^2$

28. $(x^2n^4)(n^{-8})$ **29.** $(w^{-2}j^{-4})^{-3}(j^7j^3)$ **30.** $(t^6)^3(m^2)$ **31.** $(3n^4)^2$

32. $\frac{r^5}{g^3}$ **33.** $\frac{1}{a^{-4}}$ **34.** $\frac{w^7}{w^{-6}}$ **35.** $\frac{6}{t^{-4}}$

36. $\frac{a^2b^{-7}c^4}{a^5b^3c^{-2}}$ **37.** $\frac{(2r^5)^3}{4t^8t^{-1}}$ **38.** $\left(\frac{a^6}{a^7}\right)^{-3}$ **39.** $\left(\frac{c^5c^{-3}}{c^{-4}}\right)^{-2}$

Evaluate each expression for $m = 2, t = -3, w = 4,$ and $z = 0$.

40. t^m **41.** t^{-m} **42.** $(w \cdot t)^m$ **43.** $w^m \cdot t^m$

44. $(w^z)^m$ **45.** w^mw^z **46.** $z^t(m^t)^z$ **47.** $w^{-t} \cdot t^t$

■ Lesson 8-5

Write each number in scientific notation.

48. 34,000,000 **49.** 0.000 63 **50.** 1500 **51.** 0.0002

52. 360,000 **53.** 6,200,000,000 **54.** 0.05 **55.** 0.000 000 000 891

56. 910,000,000,000 **57.** 0.38 **58.** 0.000 000 07 **59.** 5,070,000,000,000

Write each number in standard notation.

60. 8.05×10^6 **61.** 3.2×10^{-7} **62.** 9.0×10^8 **63.** 4.25×10^{-4}

Extra Practice

Could each set of three numbers represent the lengths of the sides of a right triangle? Explain your answers. ■ Lesson 9-1

1. 4, 5, 7 **2.** 6, 8, 10 **3.** 6, 9, 13 **4.** 10, 13, 17

5. 15, 36, 39 **6.** 3, 7, 10 **7.** 8, 15, 17 **8.** 9, 12, 15

Find the length of the diagonal of a rectangle with sides of the given lengths *a* and *b*. Round to the nearest tenth.

9. $a = 6, b = 8$ **10.** $a = 5, b = 9$ **11.** $a = 4, b = 10$ **12.** $a = 9, b = 1$

Find the distance between the endpoints of each segment. Round your answers to the nearest tenth. Then find the midpoint of each segment. ■ Lesson 9-2

13. $A(1, 3), B(2, 8)$ **14.** $R(6, -2), S(-7, -10)$ **15.** $G(4, 0), H(5, -1)$

16. $A(-4, 1), B(3, 5)$ **17.** $G(11, 7), H(-7, -11)$ **18.** $R(1, -6), S(4, -2)$

19. $R(-8, -4), S(5, 7)$ **20.** $A(0, 6), B(-2, 9)$ **21.** $G(5, 10), H(0, 0)$

Use $\triangle ABC$ to evaluate each expression. ■ Lesson 9-3

22. $\sin A$ **23.** $\cos A$ **24.** $\tan A$

25. $\sin B$ **26.** $\cos B$ **27.** $\tan B$

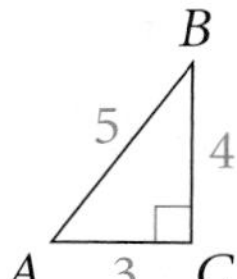

Simplify each radical expression. ■ Lessons 9-4, 9-5

28. $\frac{\sqrt{27}}{\sqrt{81}}$ **29.** $\sqrt{\frac{25}{4}}$ **30.** $\sqrt{\frac{50}{9}}$ **31.** $\frac{\sqrt{72}}{\sqrt{50}}$

32. $\sqrt{75} - 4\sqrt{75}$ **33.** $\sqrt{5}(\sqrt{20} - \sqrt{80})$ **34.** $\sqrt{25} \cdot \sqrt{4}$ **35.** $\sqrt{6}(\sqrt{6} - 3)$

36. $3\sqrt{300} + 2\sqrt{27}$ **37.** $5\sqrt{2} \cdot 3\sqrt{50}$ **38.** $\sqrt{8} - 4\sqrt{2}$ **39.** $\sqrt{27} \cdot \sqrt{3}$

Solve each radical equation. Check your solutions. ■ Lesson 9-6

40. $\sqrt{3x + 4} = 1$ **41.** $6 = \sqrt{8x - 4}$ **42.** $2x = \sqrt{14x - 6}$

43. $\sqrt{2x + 5} = \sqrt{3x + 1}$ **44.** $2x = \sqrt{6x + 4}$ **45.** $\sqrt{5x + 11} = \sqrt{7x - 1}$

Find the domain of each function. Then graph the function. ■ Lesson 9-7

46. $y = \sqrt{x + 5}$ **47.** $y = \sqrt{x} - 2$ **48.** $y = \sqrt{x + 1}$

49. $y = \sqrt{x} - 4$ **50.** $y = \sqrt{x - 3}$ **51.** $y = \sqrt{x} + 6$

Find the standard deviation of each set of data to the nearest tenth. ■ Lesson 9-8

52. 11, 14, 10, 13, 15 **53.** 2, 4, 3, 5, 3, 7 **54.** 21, 20, 26, 18, 30

55. 15, 13, 10, 20, 17 **56.** 32, 33, 30, 37 **57.** 7, 10, 4, 8, 2, 11

Extra Practice

Find each sum or difference. Write in standard form. ■ Lesson 10-1

1. $(5x^3 + 3x^2 - 7x + 10) - (3x^3 - x^2 + 4x - 1)$
2. $(x^2 + 3x - 2) + (4x^2 - 5x + 2)$
3. $(4m^3 + 7m - 4) + (2m^3 - 6m + 8)$
4. $(8t^2 + t + 10) - (9t^2 - 9t - 1)$
5. $(-7c^3 + c^2 - 8c - 11) - (3c^3 + 2c^2 + c - 4)$
6. $(6v + 3v^2 - 9v^3) + (7v - 4v^2 - 10v^3)$
7. $(s^4 - s^3 - 5s^2 + 3s) - (5s^4 + s^3 - 7s^2 - s)$
8. $(9w - 4w^2 + 10) + (8w^2 + 7 + 5w)$

Find each product. ■ Lessons 10-2, 10-3

9. $4b(b^2 + 3)$
10. $(5c + 3)(-c + 2)$
11. $(3t - 1)(2t + 1)$
12. $9c(c^2 - 3c + 5)$
13. $8m(4m - 5)$
14. $(w - 1)(w^2 + w + 1)$
15. $5k(k^2 + 8k)$
16. $(3t + 5)(t + 1)$
17. $(2n - 3)(2n + 4)$
18. $5r^2(r^2 + 4r - 2)$
19. $(b + 3)(b + 7)$
20. $2m^2(m^3 + m - 2)$

21. **Geometry** A rectangle has dimensions $3x - 1$ and $2x + 5$. Write an expression for its area as a product and in standard form.

Find the greatest common factor of each expression.

22. $t^6 + t^4 - t^5 + t^2$
23. $3m^2 - 6 + 9m$
24. $16c^2 - 4c^3 + 12c^5$
25. $8v^6 + 2v^5 - 10v^9$
26. $6n^2 - 3n^3 + 2n^4$
27. $5r + 20r^3 + 15r^2$
28. $9x^6 + 5x^5 + 4x^7$
29. $4d^8 - 2d^{10} + 7d^4$
30. $5t^2 + 3t - 8t^4$
31. $4m^2 + 16m - 20$
32. $7n + 14n^2 + 21n^3$
33. $5w - 8w^2 + 2w^3$

Factor each polynomial. ■ Lessons 10-4, 10-5

34. $x^2 + 6x + 9$
35. $x^2 - 25$
36. $4t^2 + t - 3$
37. $9c^2 - 169$
38. $2c^2 - 5c - 3$
39. $t^2 - 6t + 9$
40. $x^2 - 8x + 16$
41. $4d^2 - 12d + 9$
42. $4m^2 - 121$
43. $3v^2 + 10v - 8$
44. $4g^2 + 4g + 1$
45. $w^2 + 3w - 4$
46. $9t^2 + 12t + 4$
47. $12m^2 - 5m - 2$
48. $36s^2 - 1$
49. $c^2 - 10c + 25$

Solve each quadratic equation. Round answers to the nearest hundredth, if necessary. ■ Lessons 10-6, 10-7

50. $x^2 + 5x + 6 = 0$
51. $d^2 - 144 = 0$
52. $c^2 + 6 = 2 - 4c$
53. $x^2 + 4x = 2x^2 - x + 6$
54. $3x^2 + 2x - 12 = x^2$
55. $r^2 + 4r + 1 = r$
56. $d^2 + 2d + 10 = 2d + 100$
57. $3c^2 + c - 10 = c^2 - 5$
58. $t^2 - 3t - 10 = 0$
59. $4x^2 - 5x - 5 = 2x^2 + 4x$
60. $4m^2 + 6m + 1 = 6m + 82$
61. $d^2 - 5d = 3d^2 + 1$

62. **Agriculture** You are planting a rectangular vegetable garden. It is 5 feet longer than 3 times its width. The area of the garden is 250 ft^2. Find the dimensions of the garden.

Extra Practice

Find the constant of variation for each inverse variation. ■ Lesson 11-1

1. $y = 10$ when $x = 7$
2. $y = 8$ when $x = 12$
3. $y = 0.2$ when $x = 4$
4. $y = 4$ when $x = 5$
5. $y = 0.1$ when $x = 6$
6. $y = 3$ when $x = 7$

Each pair of points is from an inverse variation. Find the missing value.

7. $(5.4, 3)$ and $(2, y)$
8. $(x, 4)$ and $(5, 6)$
9. $(3, 6)$ and $(9, y)$
10. $(100, 2)$ and $(x, 25)$
11. $(6, 1)$ and $(x, 2)$
12. $(8, y)$ and $(2, 4)$
13. $(7, 35)$, and $(49, y)$
14. $(x, 32)$ and $(16, 1)$

Graph each function. Include a dashed line for each asymptote. ■ Lesson 11-2

15. $y = \frac{6}{x}$
16. $y = \frac{8}{x + 2}$
17. $y = \frac{4}{x} - 3$
18. $y = \frac{5}{x + 1} + 3$
19. $y = \frac{-1}{x}$
20. $y = \frac{5}{x} - 1$
21. $y = \frac{-2}{x - 3}$
22. $y = \frac{2}{x - 1}$
23. $y = \frac{3}{x} + 4$
24. $y = \frac{5}{x}$
25. $y = \frac{2}{x + 1} - 1$
26. $y = \frac{x - 3}{x + 3}$

Simplify each expression and state any values restricted from the domain. ■ Lessons 11-3, 11-4

27. $\frac{4t^2}{16t}$
28. $\frac{c - 5}{c^2 - 25}$
29. $\frac{4m - 12}{m - 3}$
30. $\frac{a^2 + 2a - 3}{a + 3}$
31. $\frac{4}{x} - \frac{3}{x}$
32. $\frac{6t}{5} + \frac{4t}{5}$
33. $\frac{6}{c} + \frac{4}{c^2}$
34. $\frac{6}{3d} - \frac{4}{3d}$
35. $\frac{5s^4}{10s^3}$
36. $\frac{4n^2}{7} \cdot \frac{14}{2n^3}$
37. $\frac{8b^2 - 4b}{3b} \div \frac{2b - 1}{9b^2}$
38. $\frac{v^5}{v^3} \cdot \frac{4v^{-1}}{v^2}$
39. $\frac{5}{t + 4} + \frac{3}{t - 4}$
40. $\frac{8}{m^2 + 6m + 5} + \frac{4}{m + 1}$
41. $\frac{3y}{4y - 8} \div \frac{9y}{2y^2 - 4y}$
42. $\frac{4}{d^2} - \frac{3}{d^3}$

Solve each equation. Check your answers. ■ Lesson 11-5

43. $\frac{1}{4} + \frac{1}{x} = \frac{3}{8}$
44. $\frac{4}{m} - 3 = \frac{2}{m}$
45. $\frac{1}{b - 3} = \frac{1}{4b}$
46. $\frac{4}{x - 1} = \frac{3}{x}$
47. $\frac{4}{n} + \frac{5}{9} = 1$
48. $\frac{x}{x + 2} = \frac{x - 3}{x + 1}$
49. $t - \frac{8}{t} = \frac{17}{t}$
50. $\frac{x + 2}{x + 5} = \frac{x - 4}{x + 4}$
51. $\frac{4}{c + 1} - \frac{2}{c - 1} = \frac{3c + 6}{c^2 - 1}$
52. $\frac{4}{m + 3} = \frac{6}{m - 3}$
53. $\frac{4}{t + 5} + 1 = \frac{15}{t^2 - 25}$

Evaluate. ■ Lessons 11-6, 11-7

54. ${}_6C_4$
55. ${}_7P_2$
56. ${}_{10}C_5$
57. ${}_8C_7$
58. ${}_{12}P_6$
59. ${}_9C_7$
60. ${}_6P_4$
61. ${}_9C_3$
62. ${}_5P_2$
63. ${}_{12}P_3$
64. ${}_8C_3$
65. ${}_7P_6$
66. You are choosing a personal identification number using the digits 1, 3, 5, and 6 exactly once each. How many different numbers can you choose from?
67. The 18 members of the debate team need to form a committee of five people. How many different five-person committees are possible?

Volume 2
A Focus on Geometry
Extra Practice

Extra Practice

Find the next two terms in each sequence. ■ Lesson 1-1

1. 12, 17, 22, 27, 32, . . . **2.** 1, 1.1, 1.11, 1.111, 1.1111, . . . **3.** 5000, 1000, 200, 40, . . .

4. 1, 12, 123, 1234, . . . **5.** 3, 0.3, 0.03, 0.003, . . . **6.** 1, 4, 9, 16, 25, . . .

Write *true* or *false*. ■ Lessons 1-2 and 1-3

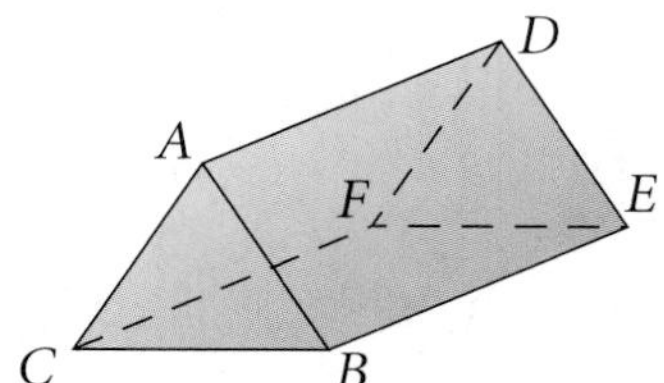

7. *A*, *D*, *F* are coplanar. **8.** $\overleftrightarrow{AC}$ and $\overleftrightarrow{FE}$ are coplanar.

9. *A*, *B*, *E* are collinear. **10.** *D*, *A*, *B*, *E* are coplanar.

11. $\overleftrightarrow{FC} \parallel \overleftrightarrow{EF}$ **12.** plane *ABC* $\parallel$ plane *FDE*

13. $\overleftrightarrow{BC}$ and $\overleftrightarrow{DF}$ are skew lines. **14.** $\overleftrightarrow{AD}$ and $\overleftrightarrow{EB}$ are skew lines.

Use the figure at the right for Exercises 15–19. ■ Lessons 1-4 and 1-5

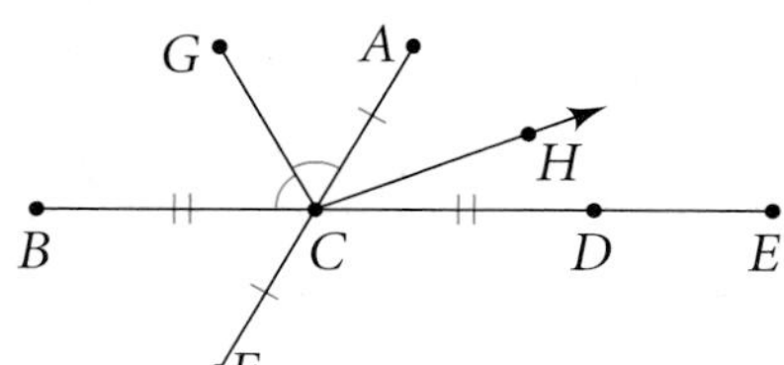

15. If $BC = 12$ and $CE = 15$, then $BE =$ ■.

16. ■ is the angle bisector of ■.

17. $BC = 3x + 2$ and $CD = 5x - 10$. Solve for *x*.

18. $m\angle BCG = 60$, $m\angle GCA =$ ■, $m\angle BCA =$ ■

19. $m\angle ACD = 60$ and $m\angle DCH = 20$. Find $m\angle HCA$.

Draw a diagram larger than the given one. Then do the construction. ■ Lesson 1-6

20. Construct the perpendicular bisector of $\overline{AB}$.

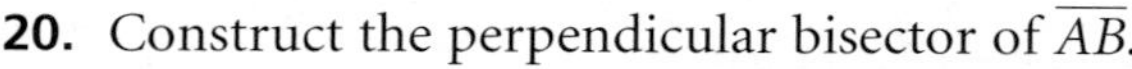

21. Construct $\angle A$ so that $m\angle A = m\angle 1 + m\angle 2$.

22. Construct the angle bisector of $\angle 1$.

23. Construct $\overline{FG}$ so that $FG = AB + CD$.

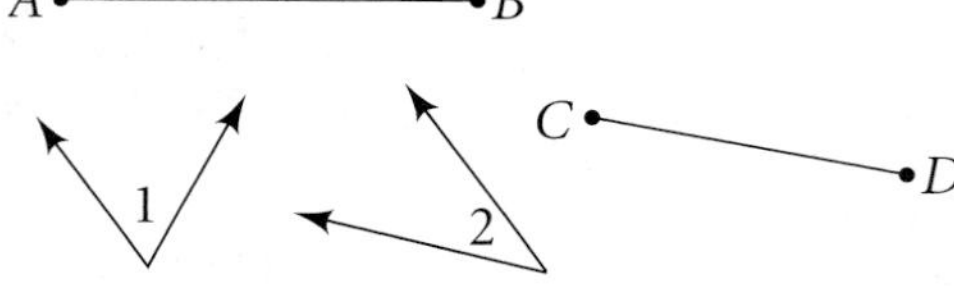

Algebra **Find the value of *x*.** ■ Lesson 1-7

24.

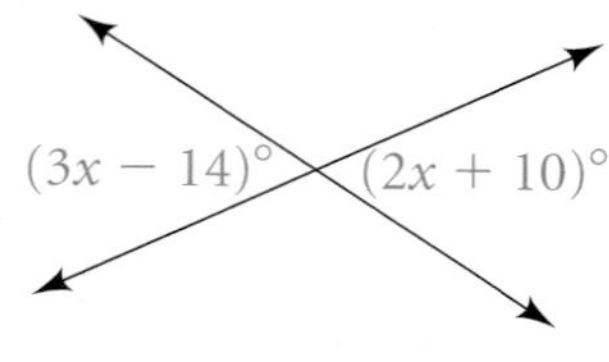

25.

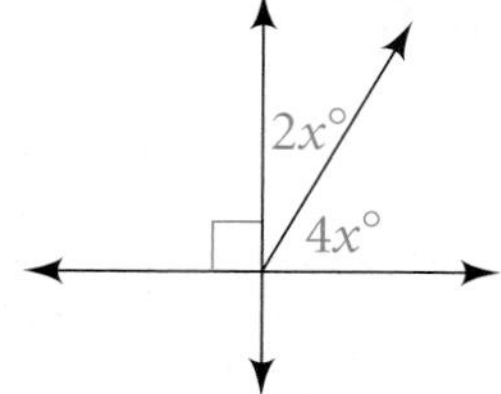

26.

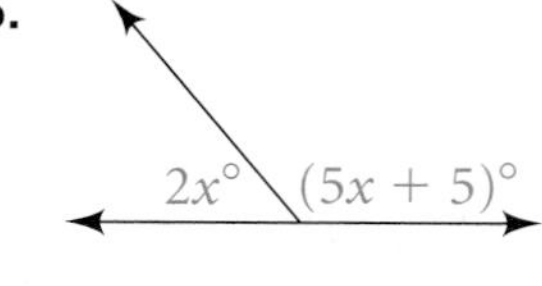

In Exercises 27–32: (a) Find the distance between the points to the nearest tenth. (b) Find the coordinates of the midpoint of the segment with the given endpoints. ■ Lesson 1-8

27. *A*(2, 1), *B*(3, 0) **28.** *R*(5, 2), *S*(−2, 4) **29.** *Q*(−7, −4), *T*(6, 10)

30. *C*(−8, −1), *D*(−5, −11) **31.** *J*(0, −5), *N*(3, 4) **32.** *Y*(−2, 8), *Z*(3, −5)

Extra Practice

Classify each triangle by its sides and angles. To do so, use a ruler to measure lengths of sides and a protractor to measure angles. ■ Lessons 2-1 and 2-2

1. 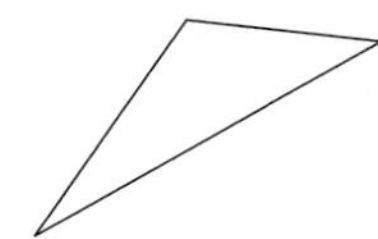

2. 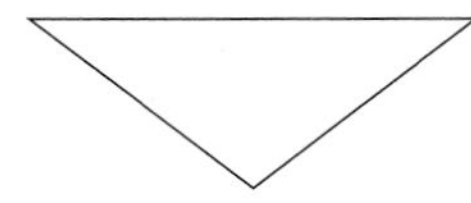

3. 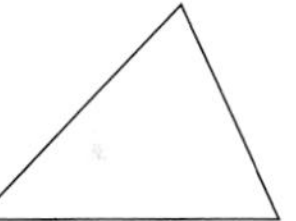

4. 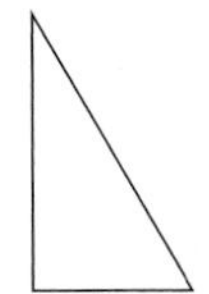

Algebra **Find the value of each variable.**

5. 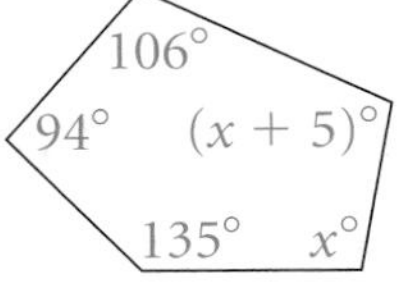

6. 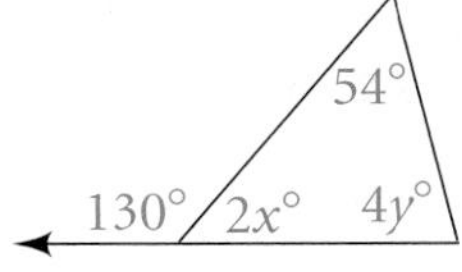

7. 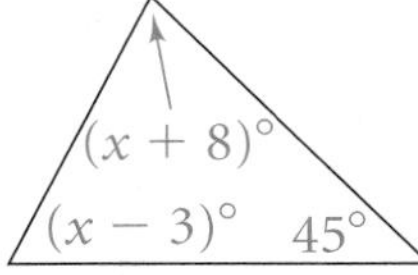

8. 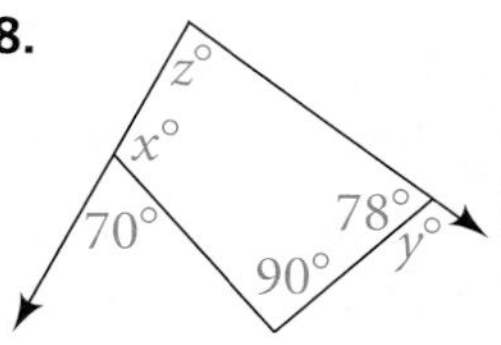

Graph the given points. Use the slope formula and/or the distance formula to determine the most precise name for quadrilateral $ABCD$. ■ Lessons 2-3 and 2-4

9. $A(3, 5), B(6, 5), C(2, 1), D(1, 3)$

10. $A(-1, 1), B(3, -1), C(-1, -3), D(-5, -1)$

11. $A(2, 1), B(5, -1), C(4, -4), D(1, -2)$

12. $A(-4, 5), B(-1, 3), C(-3, 0), D(-6, 2)$

Identify the following in $\odot P$.  ■ Lesson 2-5

13. three minor arcs

14. two major arcs

15. two adjacent arcs

16. two radii

17. an acute central angle

18. two diameters

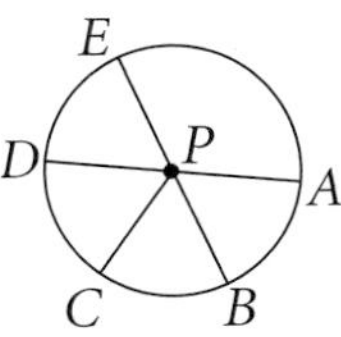

$\triangle SAT \cong \triangle GRE$. Complete the congruence statements. ■ Lesson 2-6

19. $\angle S \cong$ ■

20. $\overline{GR} \cong$ ■

21. $\angle E \cong$ ■

22. $\overline{AT} \cong$ ■

23. $\triangle ERG \cong$ ■

24. $\overline{EG} \cong$ ■

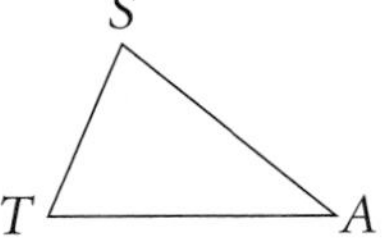

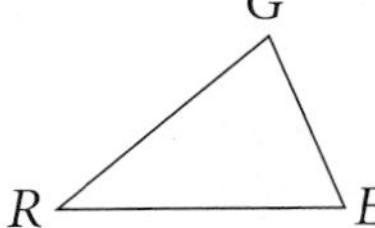

Create an isometric drawing and an orthographic drawing for each foundation plan. ■ Lesson 2-7

25. 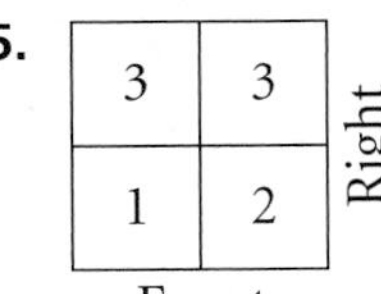

26. 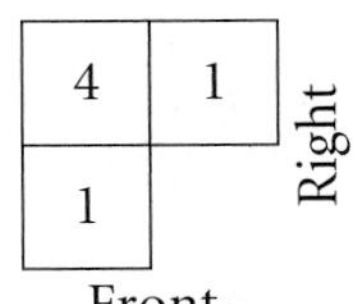

27. 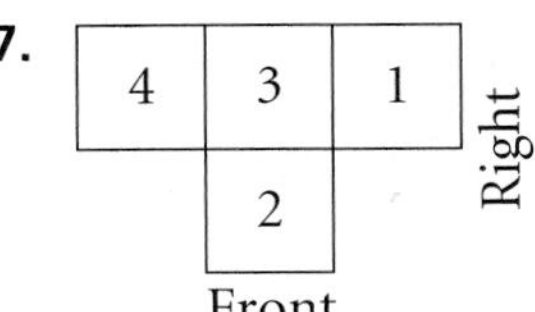

28. 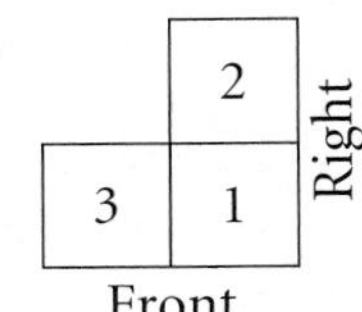

Extra Practice

Lesson 3-1

Coordinate Geometry **Given points $S(6, 1)$, $U(2, 5)$, and $B(-1, 2)$, draw $\triangle SUB$ and its reflection image in the given line.**

1. $y = 5$
2. $x = 7$
3. $y = -1$
4. the x-axis
5. $y = x$
6. $x = -1$
7. $y = 3$
8. the y-axis

Lesson 3-2

In Exercises 9–14, refer to the figure at the right.

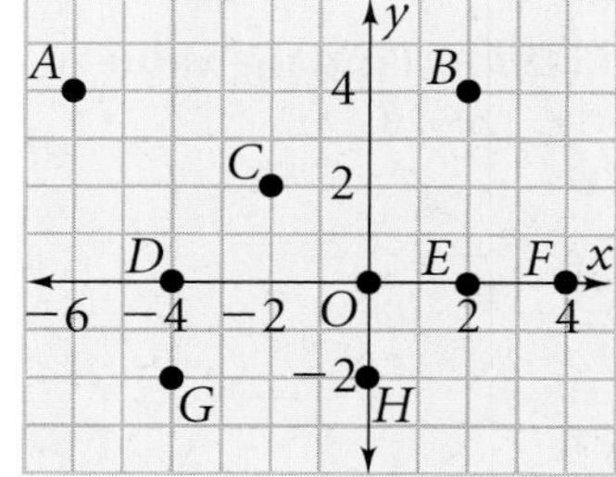

9. What is the image of C under the translation $\langle 4, -2\rangle$?
10. What vector describes the translation $F \longrightarrow B$?
11. What is the image of H under the translation $\langle -2, 4\rangle$?
12. What vector describes the translation $D \longrightarrow H$?
13. What is the image of C under the translation $\langle -2, -4\rangle$?
14. What vector describes the translation $B \longrightarrow A$?

Lesson 3-3

Copy each figure and point P. Rotate the figure the given number of degrees about P. Label the vertices of the image.

15. $60°$

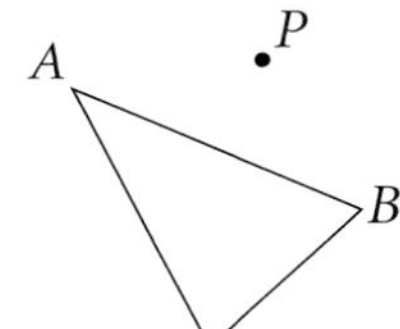

16. $90°$

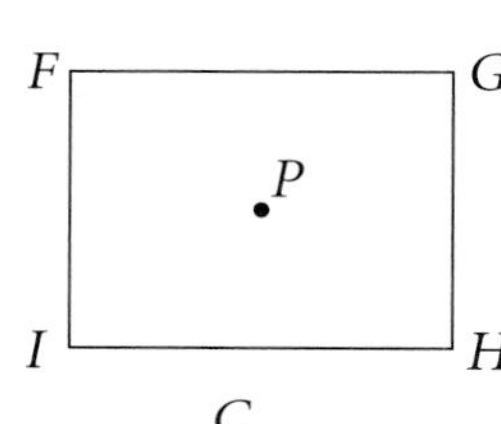

17. $180°$

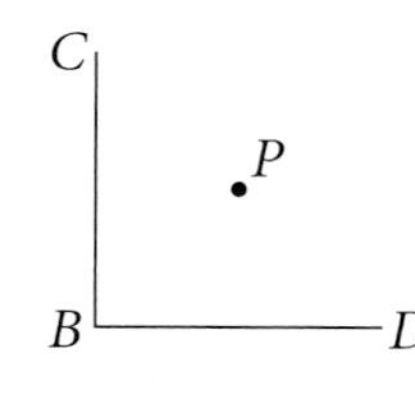

18. $45°$

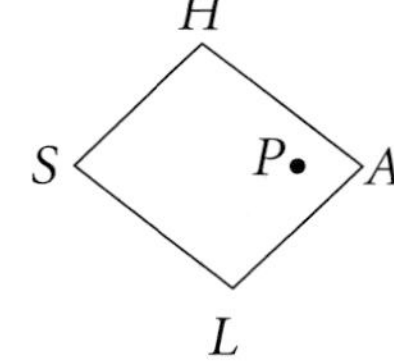

Lessons 3-4 and 3-7

The blue figure is the image of the black figure. State whether the mapping is a reflection, rotation, translation, glide reflection, or dilation.

19.

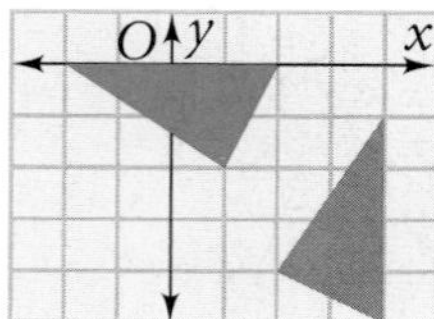

20.

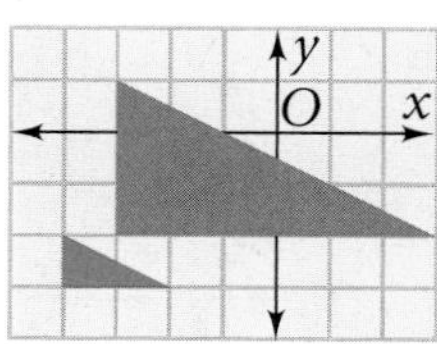

21.

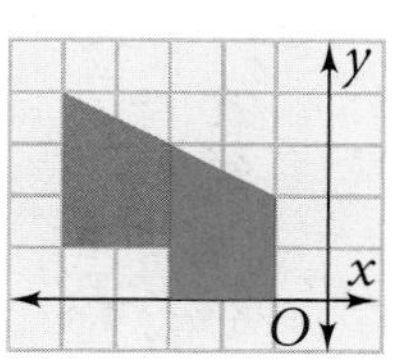

22.

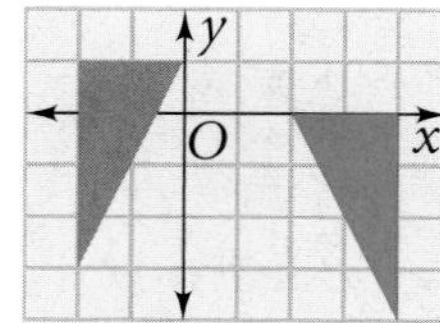

Lessons 3-5 and 3-6

In Exercises 23–26: (a) State what kind of symmetry each figure has. (b) State whether each figure tessellates.

23.

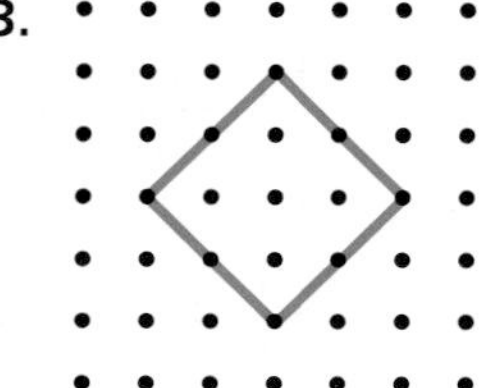

24.

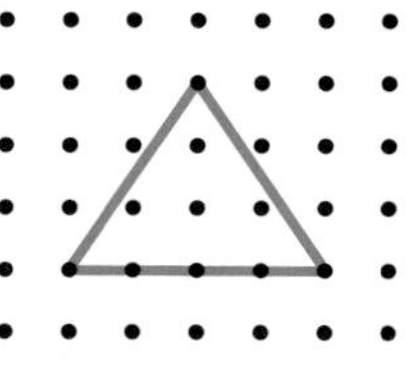

25.

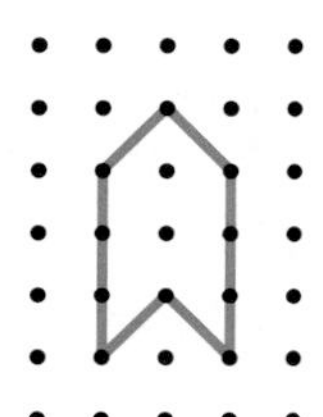

26.

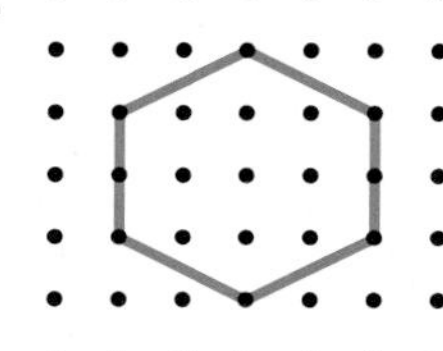

Extra Practice

For each statement, write the converse, the inverse, and the contrapositive. ■ Lesson 4-1

1. If two angles are vertical angles, then they are congruent.

2. If figures are similar, then their side lengths are proportional.

3. If a car is blue, then it has no doors.

Find the value of each variable. ■ Lessons 4-2 and 4-4

4.

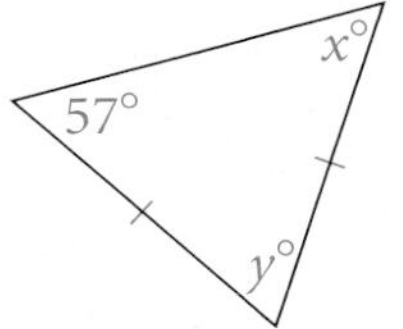

5.

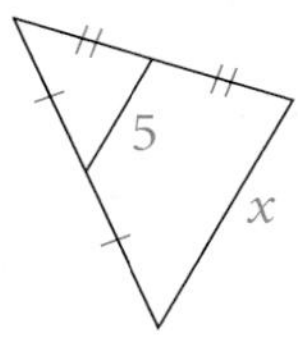

6.

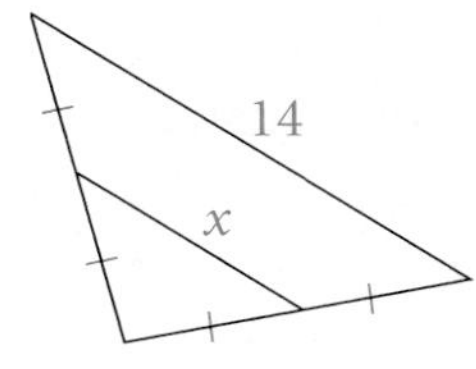

7.

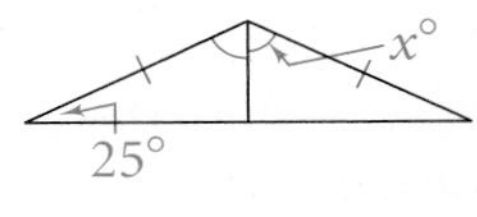

8. Rewrite this paragraph proof as a two-column proof. ■ Lesson 4-3

Given: $\square BGKM$, $m\angle B = m\angle G = m\angle K = m\angle M$

Prove: $\square BGKM$ is a rectangle.

By the Polygon Interior Angle-Sum Thm., $m\angle B + m\angle G + m\angle K + m\angle M = 360$. We are given that $m\angle B = m\angle G = m\angle K = m\angle M$, so by Substitution, $4(m\angle B) = 360$. Dividing each side by 4 yields $m\angle B = 90$. By Substitution, $m\angle G = m\angle K = m\angle M = 90$. So $\angle B$, $\angle G$, $\angle K$, and $\angle M$ are rt. angles. $\square BGKM$ is a rectangle by definition.

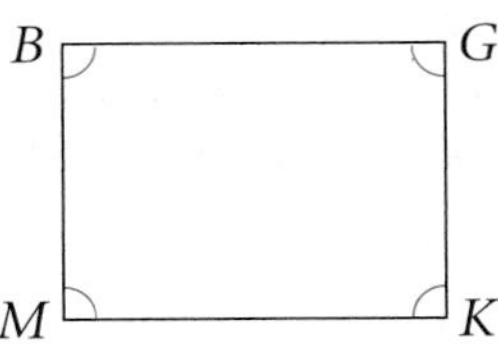

Write the first step of an indirect proof of each statement. ■ Lesson 4-5

9. $\triangle ABC$ is a right triangle.

10. Points J, K, and L are collinear.

11. Lines ℓ and m are parallel.

List the sides of each triangle in order from shortest to longest. ■ Lesson 4-6

12.

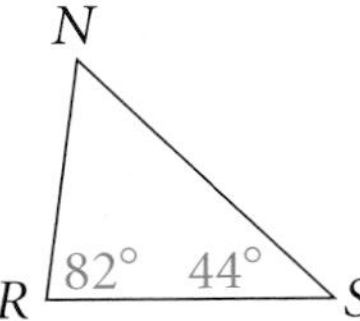

13.

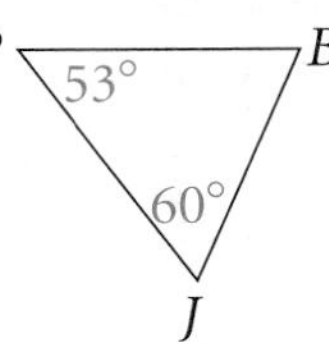

14.

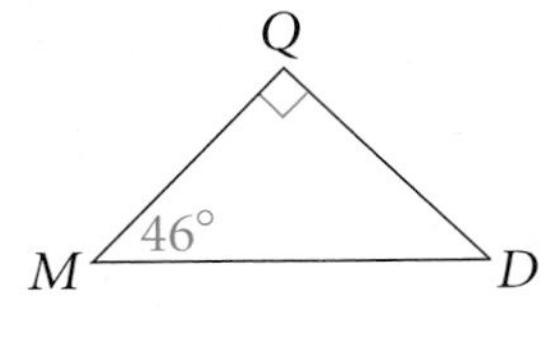

15.

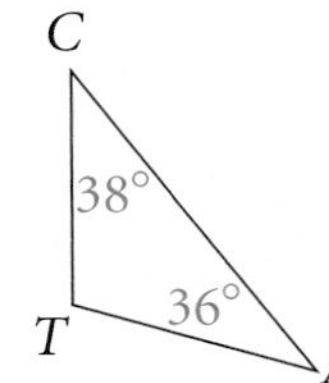

Sketch and label each locus. ■ Lesson 4-7

16. all points in a plane 2 cm from $\overrightarrow{AB}$

17. all points in space 1.5 in. from point Q

18. all points in a plane 3 cm from a circle with radius 2 cm

Is $\overline{AB}$ an angle bisector, altitude, median, or perpendicular bisector? ■ Lesson 4-8

19.

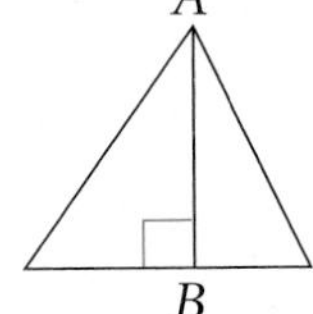

20.

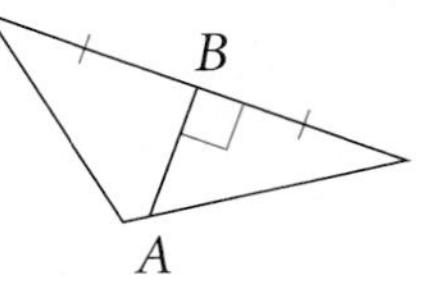

21.

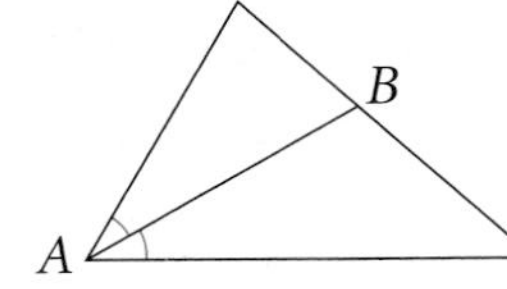

22.

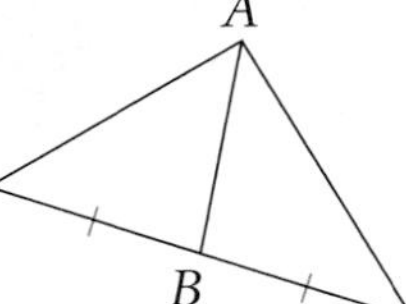

Extra Practice

Find the perimeter and area of each figure.

■ Lessons 5-1 and 5-2

1. 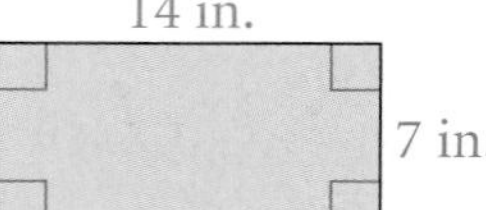

2. 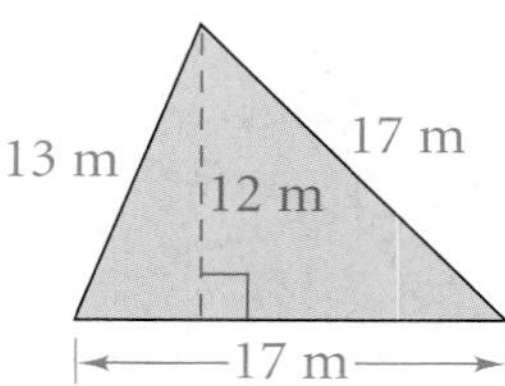

3. 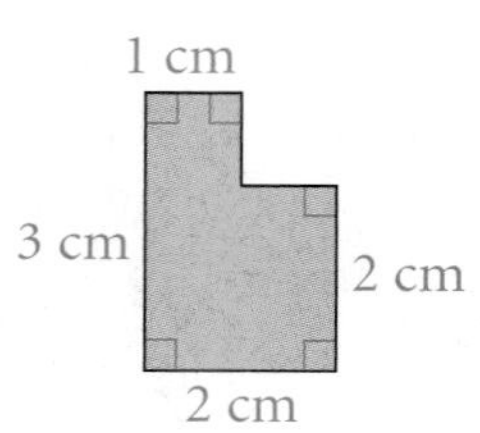

4. 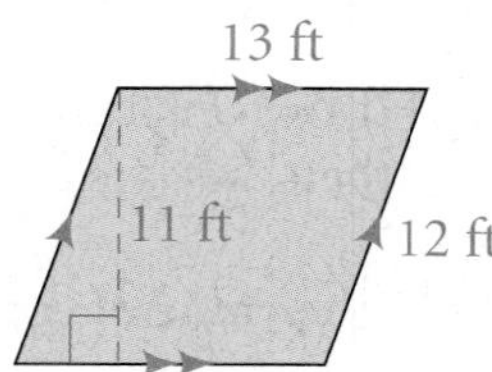

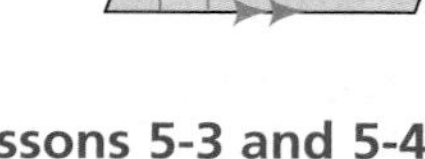

Algebra **Find the value of x. If your answer is not a whole number, leave it in simplest radical form.**

■ Lessons 5-3 and 5-4

5. 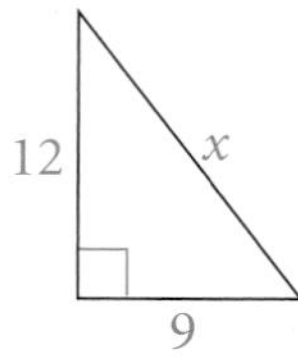

6. 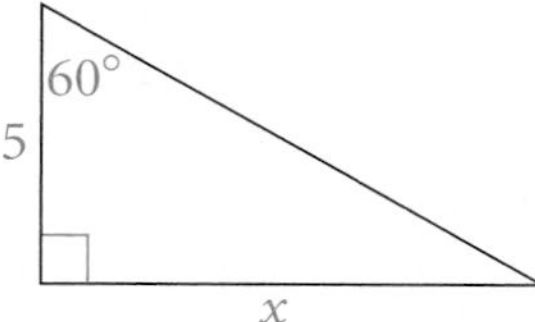

7. 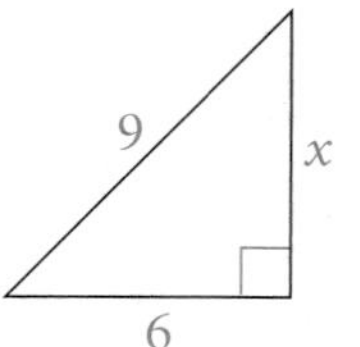

8. 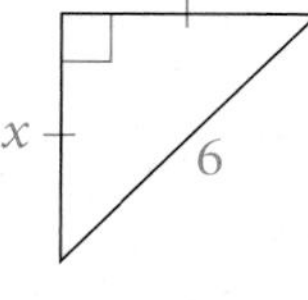

Find the area of each trapezoid or regular polygon. You may leave your answer in simplest radical form.

■ Lessons 5-5 and 5-6

9. 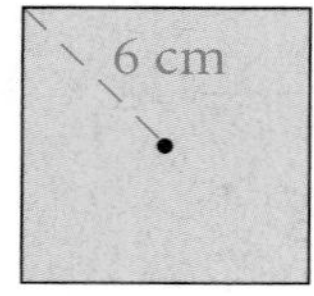

10. 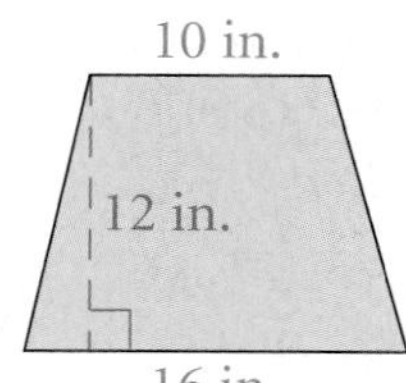

11. 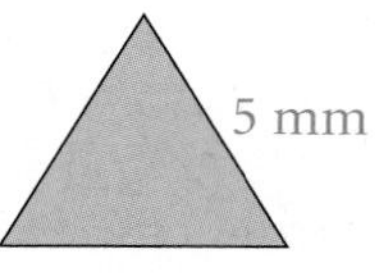

12. 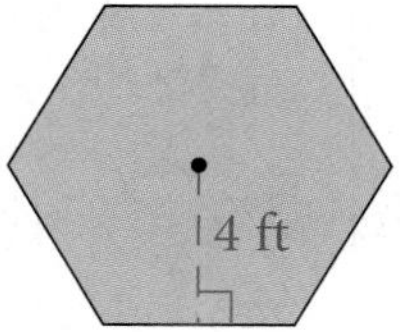

In Exercises 13–16: (a) Find the circumference of each circle. (b) Find the length of the arc shown in red. Leave your answers in terms of π.

■ Lesson 5-7

13. 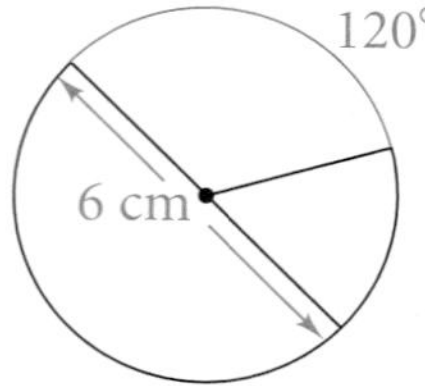

14. 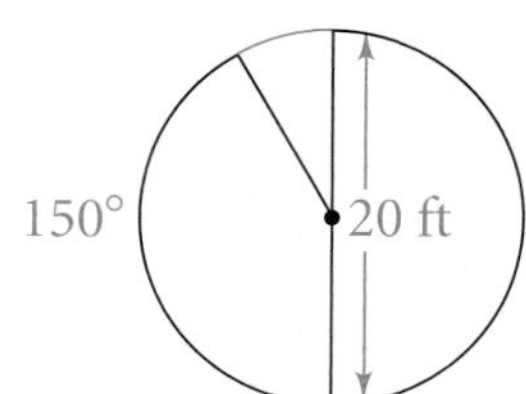

15. 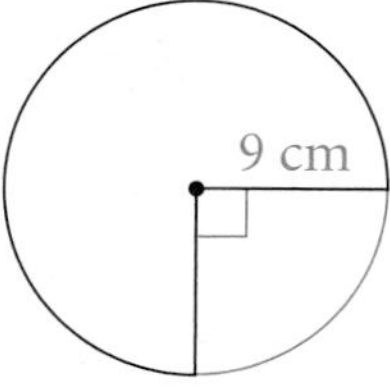

16. 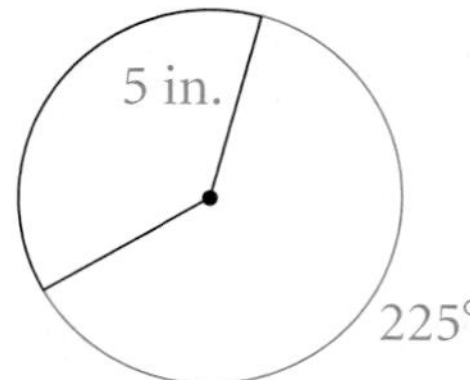

Find the area of each shaded sector or segment. Leave your answers in terms of π.

■ Lesson 5-8

17. 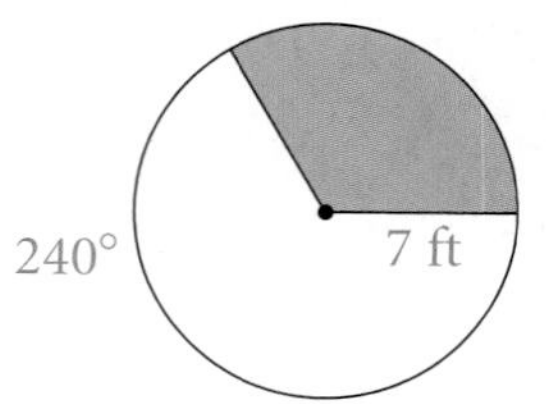

18. 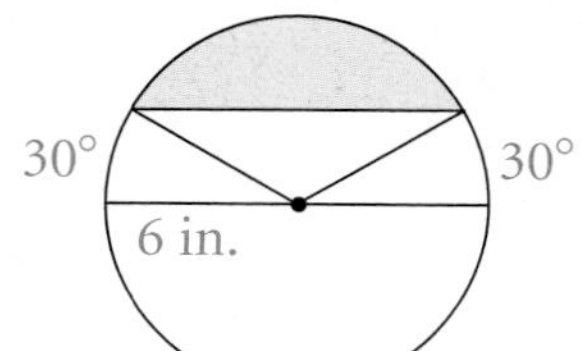

19. 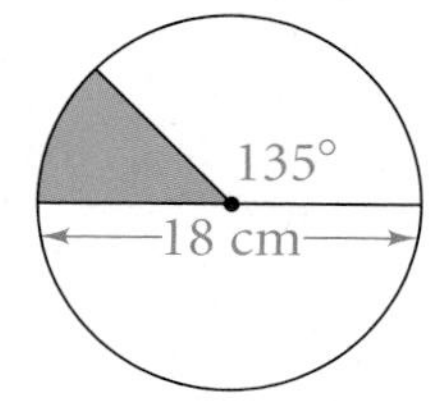

20. 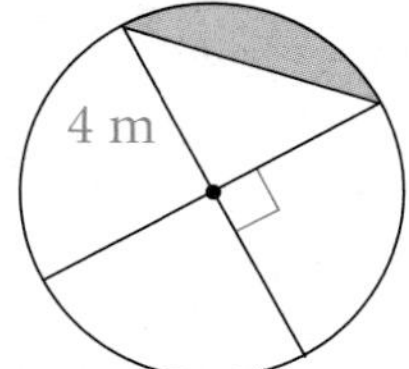

Extra Practice

Name the space figure that can be formed by folding each net. ■ Lesson 6-1

1. 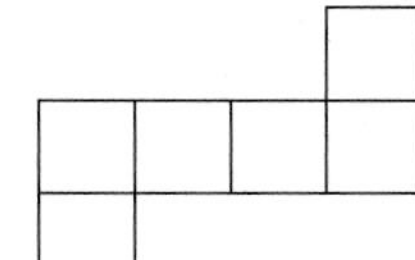

2. 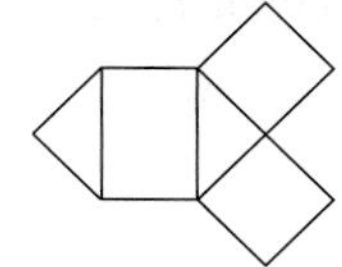

3. 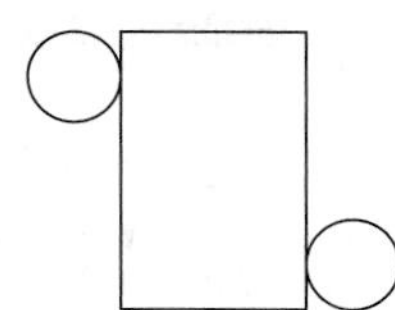

4. 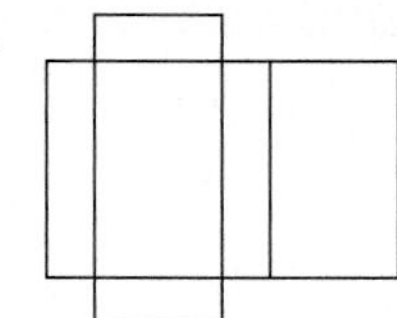

In Exercises 5–25, you may leave your answers in terms of π.

Find the lateral area and surface area of each figure. ■ Lessons 6-2 and 6-3

5. 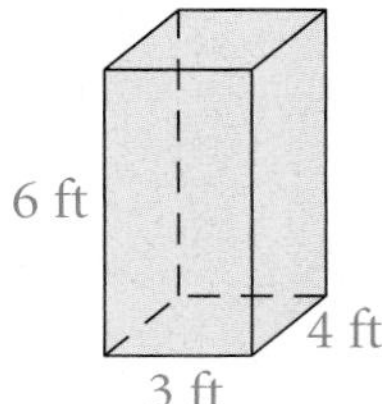

6. 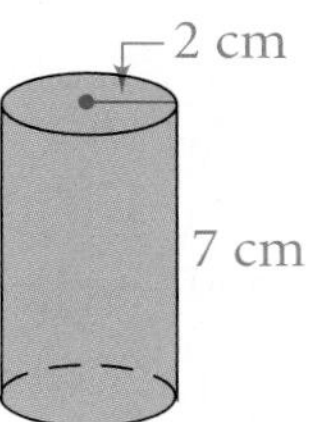

7. 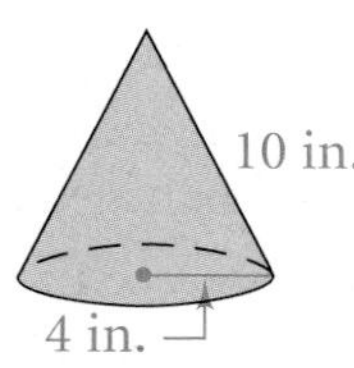

8. 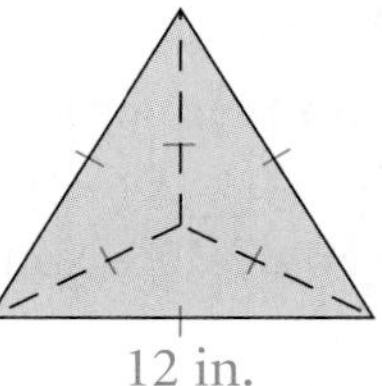

Find the volume of each figure. ■ Lessons 6-4 and 6-5

9. 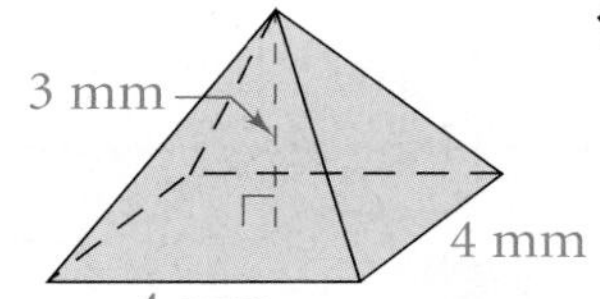

10. 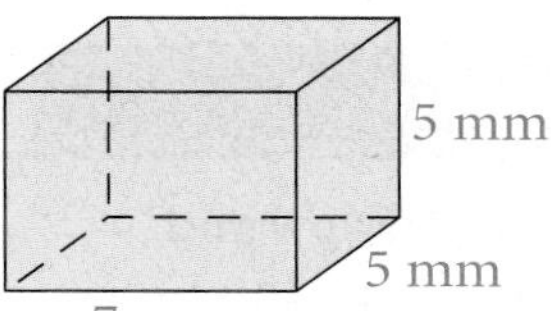

11. 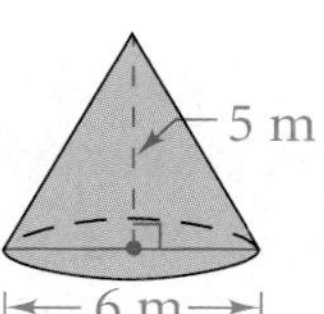

12. 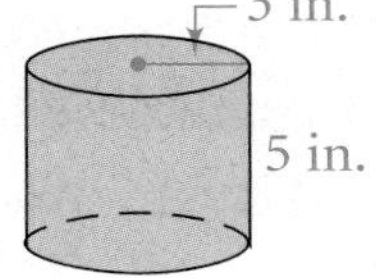

Find the volume and surface area of a sphere with the given radius or diameter. ■ Lesson 6-6

13. $r = 5$ cm **14.** $d = 8$ in. **15.** $d = 2$ ft **16.** $r = 0.5$ in. **17.** $d = 9$ m

Find the volume of each composite space figure. ■ Lesson 6-7

18. 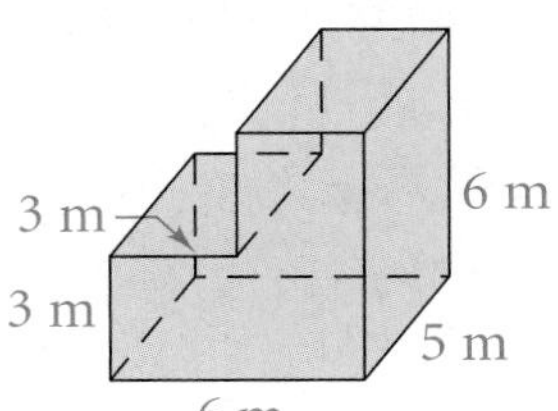

19. 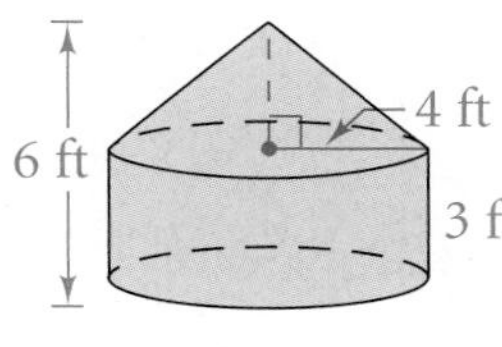

20. 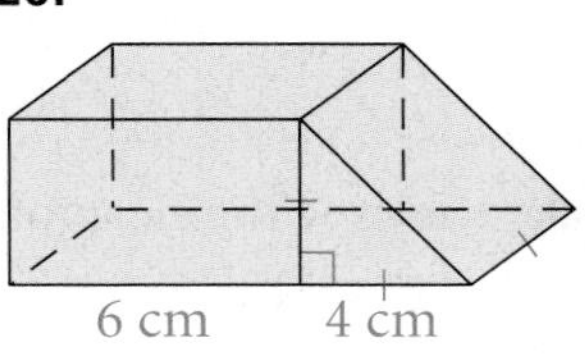

21. 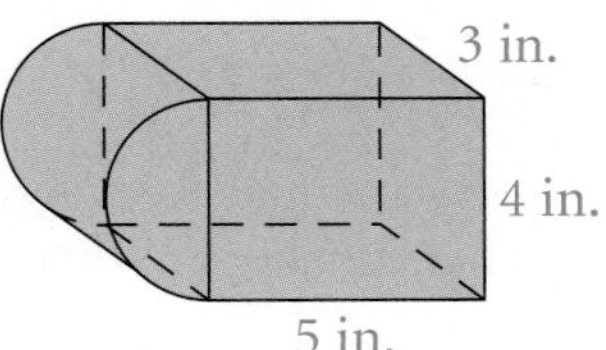

Darts are thrown at random at each of the boards shown. If a dart hits the board, find the probability that it will land in the shaded area. ■ Lesson 6-8

22. 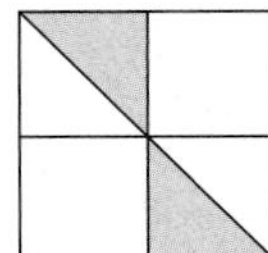

23. 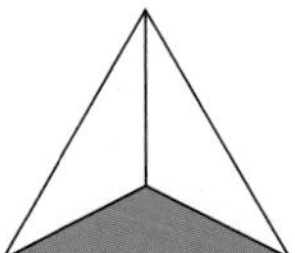

24. 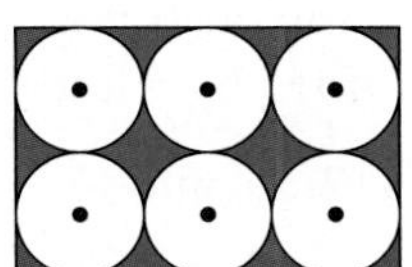

25. 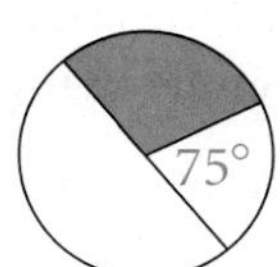

Problem Solving Strategies

You may find one or more of these strategies helpful in solving a word problem.

STRATEGY	WHEN TO USE IT
Draw a Diagram	You need help in visualizing the problem.
Guess and Test	Solving the problem directly is too complicated.
Look for a Pattern	The problem describes a relationship.
Make a Table	The problem has data that need organizing.
Solve a Simpler Problem	The problem is complex or has numbers that are too unmanageable to use at first.
Use Logical Reasoning	You need to reach a conclusion from some given information.
Work Backward	The answer can be arrived at by undoing various operations.

Problem Solving: Draw a Diagram

Example **Antoine is 1.91 m tall. He measures his shadow and finds that it is 2.34 m long. He then measures the length of the shadow of a flagpole and finds that it is 13.2 m long. How tall is the flagpole?**

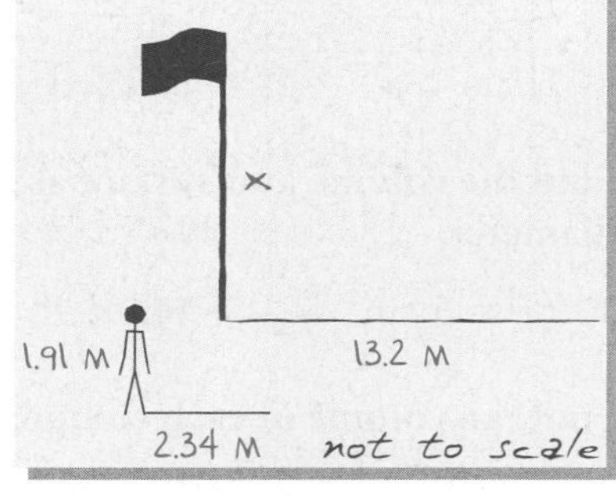

Start by drawing a diagram showing the given information. The diagram shows that the problem can be solved by using a proportion.

$\frac{1.91}{2.34} = \frac{x}{13.2}$ ← Write a proportion.

$x \approx 10.77$ ← Solve for *x*.

The flagpole is about 10.8 m tall.

EXERCISES

1. Five people meet and shake hands with one another. How many handshakes are there in all?
2. Three tennis balls fit snugly in a standard cylindrical container. Which is greater, the circumference of a ball or the height of the container?
3. Three lines that each intersect a circle can determine at most 7 regions within the circle, as shown in the diagram. What is the greatest number of regions that can be determined by 5 lines?

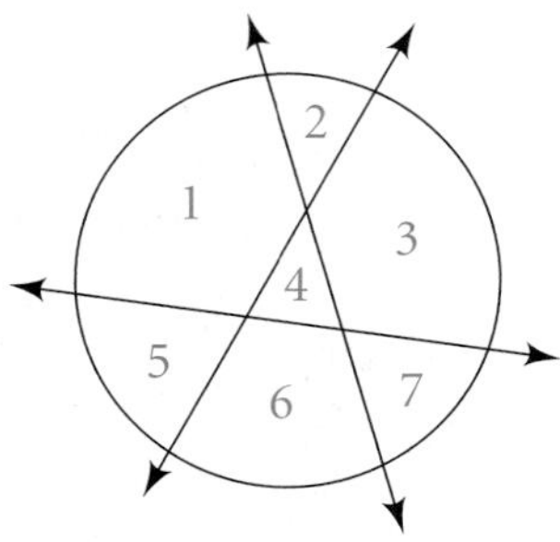

4. A triangle has vertices (1, 3), (2, 3), and (7, 5). Find its area.

Problem Solving: Guess and Test

Have you ever weighed yourself on a balance scale at a doctor's office? You start by guessing your weight, then you see if the scale balances. If it doesn't, you slide the weights back and forth until the scale does balance. This is an example of the *Guess and Test* strategy, a strategy that is helpful for solving many types of problems.

Example **You are offered two payment plans for a CD club. Plan 1 involves paying a \$20 membership fee and \$7 per CD. Plan 2 involves paying no membership fee and \$10 per CD. What is the least number of CDs you would have to buy to make Plan 1 the less expensive plan?**

	Plan 1	Plan 2	
Guess 4 CDs.	$20 + 7(4)$	$10(4)$	
	48	> 40	← Too low. Guess higher.
Guess 7 CDs.	$20 + 7(7)$	$10(7)$	
	69	< 70	← Plan 1 is less expensive!

You need to check 6 CDs, however, to be sure that 7 CDs is the *least* number you would have to buy to make Plan 1 less expensive.

$20 + 7(6)$	$10(6)$	
62	> 60	← Plan 1 is more expensive.

You need to buy at least 7 CDs to make Plan 1 the less expensive plan.

EXERCISES

1. Find three consecutive even integers whose product is 480.
2. The combined age of a father and his twin daughters is 54 years. The father was 24 years old when the twins were born. How old is each of the three people?
3. What numbers can x represent in the rectangle?

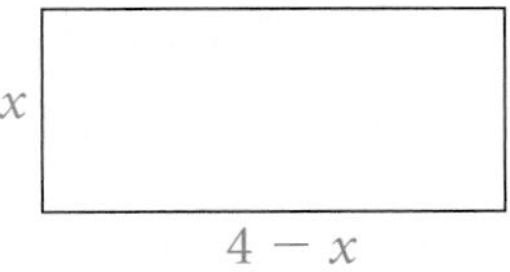

4. You are offered two payment plans for a video rental store. Plan 1 involves paying a \$30 membership fee and \$2 per rental. Plan 2 involves paying \$3.50 per rental. What is the least number of videos you would have to rent to make Plan 1 the less expensive plan?
5. Ruisa bought 7 rolls of film to take 192 pictures on a field trip. Some rolls had 36 exposures and the rest had 24 exposures. How many rolls of each type did Ruisa buy?
6. The sum of five consecutive integers is 5. Find the integers.
7. Paul buys a coupon for \$20 that allows him to see movies for half price at a local theater over the course of one year. The cost of seeing a movie is normally \$7.50. What is the least number of movies Paul would have to see to pay less than the normal price?

Problem Solving: Make a Table and Look for a Pattern

There are two important ways that making a table can help you solve a problem. First, a table is a handy method of organizing information. Second, once the information is in a table, it is easier to find patterns.

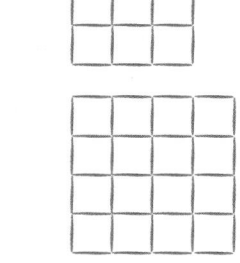

Example **The squares at the right are made of toothpicks. How many toothpicks are in the square with 7 toothpicks on a side?**

Make a table to organize the information.

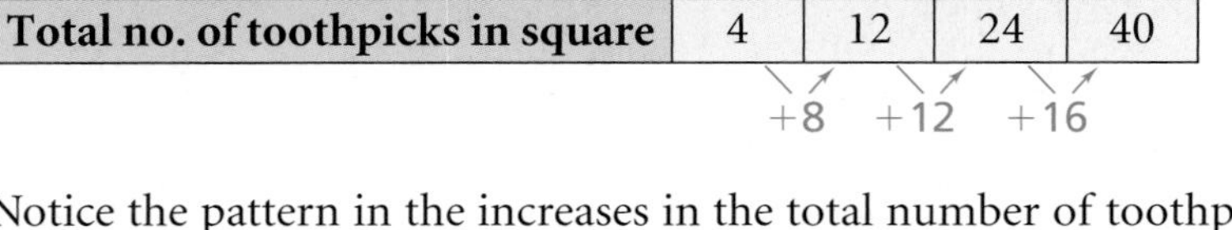

No. of toothpicks on a side	1	2	3	4
Total no. of toothpicks in square	4	12	24	40

+8 +12 +16

Notice the pattern in the increases in the total number of toothpicks in each figure. The total number in the 5th square is 40 + 20, or 60. The number in the 6th is 60 + 24, or 84, and the number in the 7th is 84 + 28, or 112.

EXERCISES

1. The triangles are made up of toothpicks. How many toothpicks are in Figure 10?

Figure 1

Figure 2

Figure 3

2. In each figure, the vertices of the smallest square are midpoints of the sides of the next larger square. Find the area of the ninth shaded square.

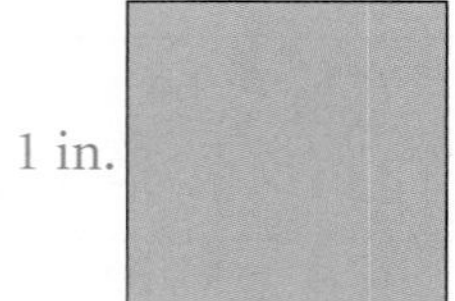

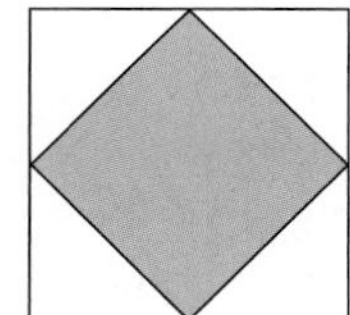

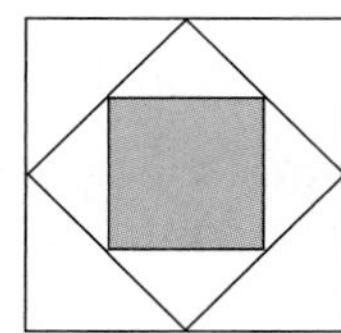

3. This pattern is known as the Sierpinski triangle. Find the total number of shaded triangles in Figure 8.

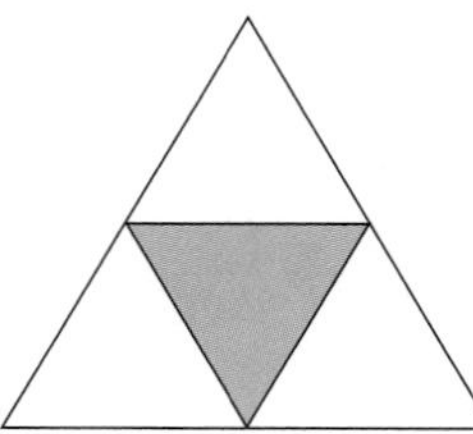

Figure 1

Figure 2

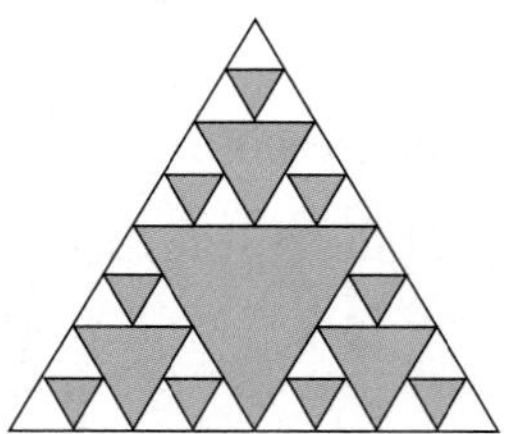

Figure 3

Problem Solving: Solve a Simpler Problem

Looking at a simpler version of a problem can be helpful in suggesting a problem-solving approach.

Example **A fence along the highway is 570 meters long. There is a fence post every 10 meters. How many fence posts are there?**

You may be tempted to divide 570 by 10, getting 57 as an answer, but looking at a simpler problem suggests that this answer isn't right. Suppose there are just 10 or 20 meters of fencing.

These easier problems suggest that there is always *one more* fence post than one tenth the length. So for a 570 meter fence, there are $\frac{570}{10} + 1$, or 58 fence posts.

EXERCISES

1. A farmer wishes to fence in a square lot with dimensions 70 yards by 70 yards. He will install a fence post every 10 yards. How many fence posts will he need?

2. Janette is planning to walk from her house to her friend Barbara's house. How many different paths can she take to get there? Assume that she walks only east and south.

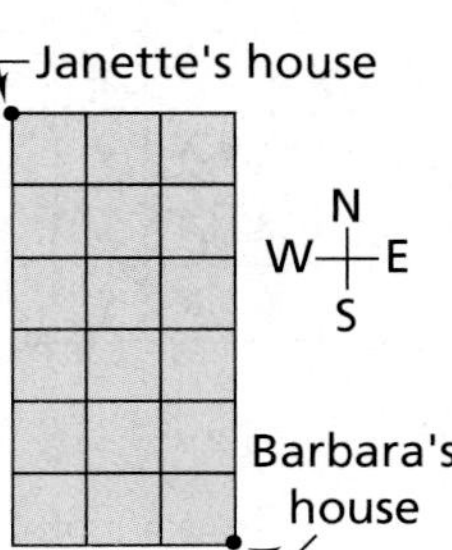

3. A square table can seat four people. For a banquet, a long rectangular table is formed by placing 14 such tables edge-to-edge in a straight line. How many people can sit at the long table?

4. Find the sum of the whole numbers from 1 to 999.

5. How many trapezoids are in the figure below? (*Hint:* Solve several simpler problems, then look for a pattern.)

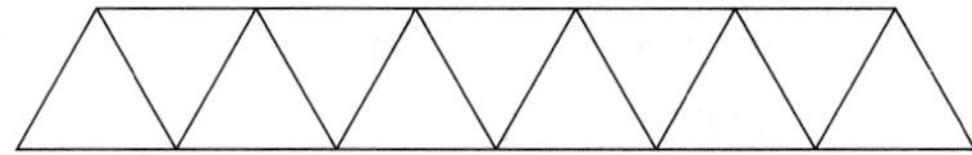

6. At a business luncheon, 424 handshakes took place. No two people shook hands with each other more than once. What is the least number of people in attendance at the luncheon?

7. On his fiftieth birthday, the President was honored with a 21-gun salute. The sound of each gunshot lasted 1 second, and 4 seconds elapsed between shots. How long did the salute last?

Problem Solving: Use Logical Reasoning

Some problems can be solved without the use of numbers. They can be solved by the use of logical reasoning, given some information.

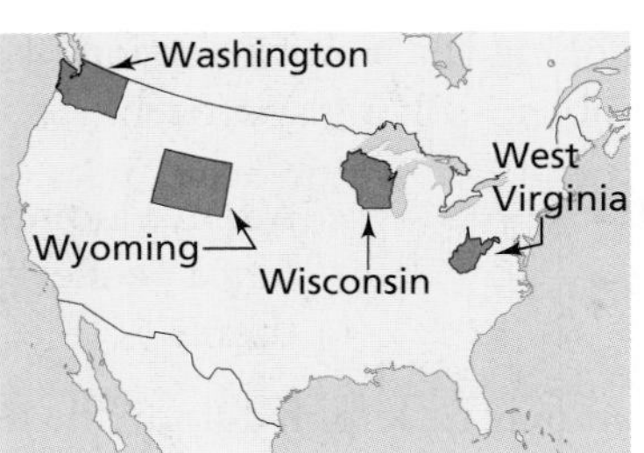

Example **Anna, Bill, Carla, and Doug are siblings. Each lives in a different state beginning with W. Use these clues to determine where each sibling lives:**
(1) Neither sister lives in a state containing two words.
(2) Bill lives west of his sisters.
(3) Anna doesn't cross the Mississippi River when she visits Doug.

Make a table to organize what you know. Use an initial for each name.

State	A	B	C	D
West Virginia	✗	✗	✗	
Wisconsin		✗		
Wyoming		✗		
Washington	✗	✓	✗	✗

← From Clue 1, you know that neither Anna nor Carla lives in West Virginia.

← Using Clues 1 and 2, you know that Bill must live in Washington if he lives west of his sisters.

Use logical reasoning to complete the table.

State	A	B	C	D
West Virginia	✗	✗	✗	✓
Wisconsin	✓	✗	✗	✗
Wyoming	✗	✗	✓	✗
Washington	✗	✓	✗	✗

← Doug lives in West Virginia because none of his siblings do.

← From Clue 3, you know that Anna must live in Wisconsin.

← Carla, therefore, lives in Wyoming.

EXERCISES

1. Harold has a dog, a canary, a goldfish, and a hamster. Their names are J.T., Izzy, Arf, and Blinky. Izzy has neither feathers nor fins. Arf can't bark. J.T. weighs less than the four-legged pets. Neither the goldfish nor the dog has the longest name. Arf and Blinky don't get along well with the canary. What is each pet's name?

2. At the state basketball championship tournament, 42 basketball games are played to determine the winner of the tournament. After each game, the loser is eliminated from the tournament. How many teams are in the tournament?

3. The sophomore class has 124 students. Of these students, 47 are involved in muscial activities: 25 in band and 36 in choir. How many students are involved in both band and choir?

4. Tina's height is between Kimiko's and Ignacio's. Ignacio's height is between Jerome's and Kimiko's. Tina is taller than Jerome. List the people in order from shortest to tallest.

Problem Solving: Work Backward

In some situations it is easier to start with the end result and work backward to find the solution. You work backward in order to solve linear equations. The equation $2x + 3 = 11$ means "double x and add 3 to get 11." To find x, you "undo" those steps in reverse order.

$2x + 3 = 11$

$2x = 8$ ← Subtract 3 from each side.

$x = 4$ ← Divide each side by 2.

Another time it is convenient to work backward is when you want to "reverse" a set of directions.

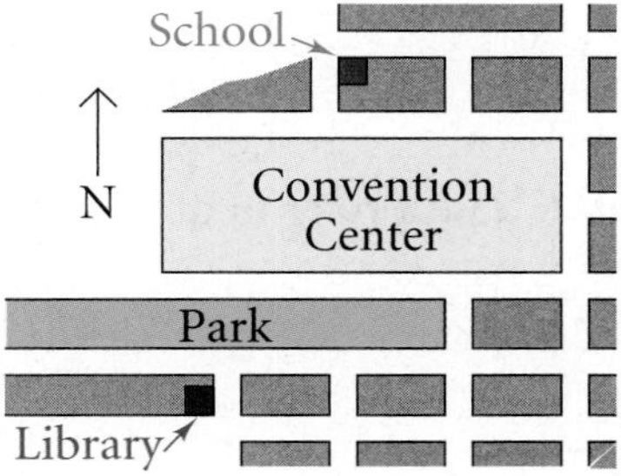

Example **To get from the library to the school, go 3 blocks east, then 5 blocks north, then 2 blocks west. How do you go from the school to the library?**

To reverse the directions, start at the school and work backward. Go 2 blocks east, 5 blocks south, and 3 blocks west.

EXERCISES

1. To go from Bedford to Worcester, take Route 4 south, then Route 128 south, then Route 90 west. How do you get from Worcester to Bedford?
2. Sandy spent $\frac{1}{10}$ of the money in her purse for lunch. She then spent \$23.50 for a gift for her brother, then half of what she had left on a new CD. If Sandy has \$13 left in her purse, how much money did she have in it before lunch?
3. Algae are growing on a pond's surface. The area covered doubles each day. It takes 24 days to cover the pond completely. After how many days will the pond be half covered with algae?
4. Don sold $\frac{1}{5}$ as many raffle tickets as Carlita. Carlita sold 3 times as many as Ranesha. Ranesha sold 7 fewer than Russell. If Russell sold 12 tickets, how many did Don sell?
5. At 6% interest compounded annually, the balance in a bank account will double about every 12 years. If such an account has a balance of \$16,000 now, how much was deposited when the account was opened 36 years ago?
6. Solve the puzzle that Yuan gave to Inez: I am thinking of a number. If I triple the number and then halve the result, I get 12. What number am I thinking of?
7. Carlos paid \$14.60 for a taxi fare from a hotel to the airport, including a \$2.00 tip. Green Cab Co. charges \$1.20 per passenger plus \$0.20 for each additional $\frac{1}{5}$ mile. How many miles is the hotel from the airport?

Using a Ruler and Protractor

Knowing how to use a ruler and protractor is crucial for success in Geometry.

Example **Draw a triangle that has sides of length 5.2 cm and 3.0 cm and a 68° angle between these two sides.**

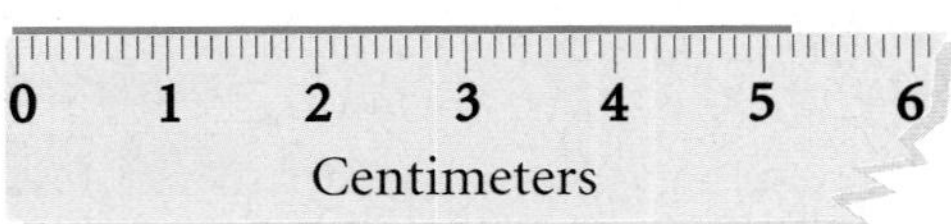

Step 1: Use a ruler to draw a segment 5.2 cm long.

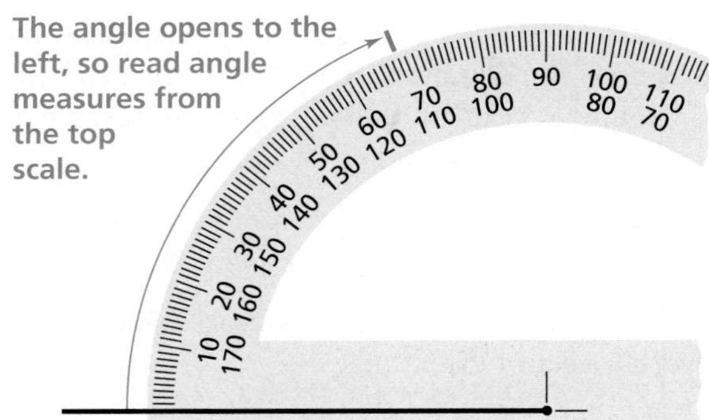

The angle opens to the left, so read angle measures from the top scale.

Step 2: Place the crosshairs of a protractor at one endpoint of the segment. Make a small mark at the 68° position along the protractor.

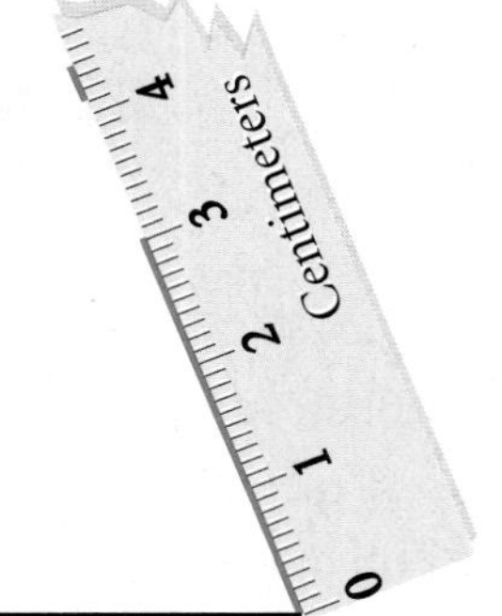

Step 3: Align the ruler along the small mark and the endpoint you used in Step 2. Place the zero point of the ruler at the endpoint. Draw a segment 3.0 cm long.

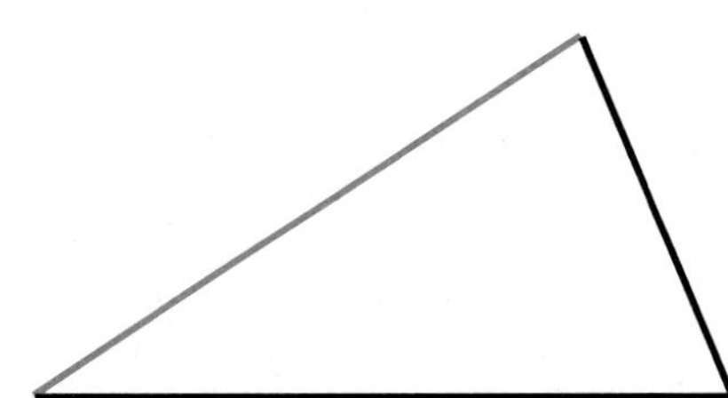

Step 4: Complete the triangle by connecting the endpoints of the first segment and the second.

EXERCISES

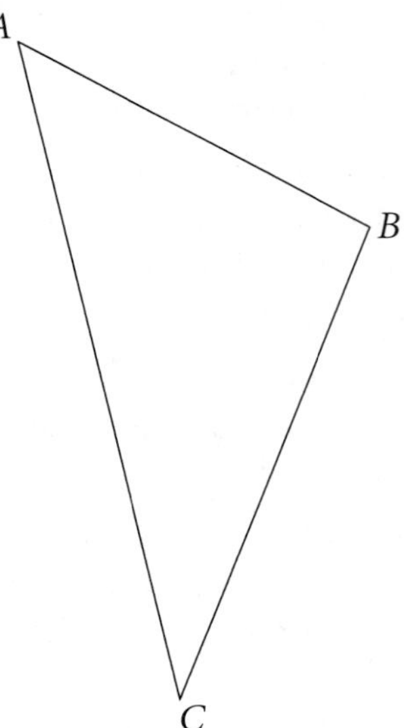

1. Measure sides $\overline{AB}$ and $\overline{BC}$ to the nearest millimeter.
2. Measure each angle of $\triangle ABC$ to the nearest degree.
3. Draw a triangle that has sides of length 4.8 cm and 3.7 cm and a 34° angle between these two sides.
4. Draw a triangle that has 43° and 102° angles and a side of length 5.4 cm between these two angles.
5. Draw a rhombus that has sides of length $2\frac{1}{4}$ in. and 68° and 112° angles.
6. Draw an isosceles trapezoid that has a pair of 48° base angles and a base of length 2 in. between these two base angles.
7. Draw an isosceles triangle that has two congruent sides $3\frac{1}{2}$ in. long and a 134° vertex angle.

Measurement Conversions

To convert from one unit of measure to another, you multiply by a conversion factor. A *conversion factor* is a fraction equal to 1 that has different units in the numerator and the denominator. An example of a conversion factor is $\frac{1\text{ ft}}{12\text{ in.}}$.

Example 1 **Complete.**

a. 88 in. = ■ ft **b. 5.3 m = ■ cm**

c. 3700 mm = ■ cm **d. 90 in. = ■ yd**

a. $88\,\cancel{\text{in.}} \cdot \frac{1\text{ ft}}{12\,\cancel{\text{in.}}} = \frac{88}{12}\text{ ft} = 7\frac{1}{3}\text{ ft}$

b. $5.3\,\cancel{\text{m}} \cdot \frac{100\text{ cm}}{1\,\cancel{\text{m}}} = 5.3(100)\text{ cm} = 530\text{ cm}$

c. $3700\,\cancel{\text{mm}} \cdot \frac{1\text{ cm}}{10\,\cancel{\text{mm}}} = 370\text{ cm}$

d. $90\,\cancel{\text{in.}} \cdot \frac{1\,\cancel{\text{ft}}}{12\,\cancel{\text{in.}}} \cdot \frac{1\text{ yd}}{3\,\cancel{\text{ft}}} = \frac{90}{36}\text{ yd} = 2\frac{1}{2}\text{ yd}$

Area is always in square units, and volume is always in cubic units.

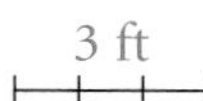

$1\text{ yd} = 3\text{ ft}$

3 ft

3 ft

$1\text{ yd}^2 = 9\text{ ft}^2$

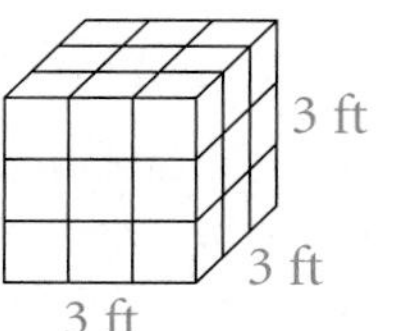

$1\text{ yd}^3 = 27\text{ ft}^3$

Example 2 **Complete.**

a. 300 in.^{2} = ■ ft^2 **b. 200,000 cm^3 = ■ m^3**

a. $1\text{ ft} = 12\text{ in.}$, so $1\text{ ft}^2 = (12\text{ in.})^2$ or 144 in.^2

$300\,\cancel{\text{in.}^2} \cdot \frac{1\text{ ft}^2}{144\,\cancel{\text{in.}^2}} = 2\frac{1}{12}\text{ ft}^2$

b. $1\text{ m} = 100\text{ cm}$, so $1\text{ m}^3 = (100\text{ cm})^3$ or $1{,}000{,}000\text{ cm}^3$

$200{,}000\,\cancel{\text{cm}^3} \cdot \frac{1\text{ m}^3}{1{,}000{,}000\,\cancel{\text{cm}^3}} = 0.2\text{ m}^3$

EXERCISES

Complete.

1. 40 cm = ■ m
2. 1.5 kg = ■ g
3. 60 cm = ■ mm
4. 200 in. = ■ ft
5. 28 yd = ■ in.
6. 1.5 mi = ■ ft
7. 42 fl oz = ■ qt
8. 430 mg = ■ g
9. 34 L = ■ mL
10. 1.2 m = ■ cm
11. 43 mm = ■ cm
12. 3600 s = ■ min
13. 15 g = ■ mg
14. 12 qt = ■ c
15. 0.03 kg = ■ mg
16. 14 gal = ■ qt
17. 4500 lb = ■ t
18. 234 min = ■ h
19. 12 mL = ■ L
20. 2 pt = ■ fl oz
21. 20 m/s = ■ km/h
22. 3 ft^2 = ■ in.^{2}
23. 108 m^2 = ■ cm^2
24. 2100 mm^2 = ■ cm^2
25. 1.4 yd^2 = ■ ft^2
26. 0.45 km^2 = ■ m^2
27. 1300 ft^2 = ■ yd^2
28. 1030 in.^{2} = ■ ft^2
29. 20,000,000 ft^2 = ■ mi^2
30. 1000 cm^3 = ■ m^3
31. 1.4 ft^3 = ■ in.^{3}
32. 3.56 cm^3 = ■ mm^3
33. 0.013 km^3 = ■ m^3

Factors and Multiples

A common factor is a number that is a factor of two or more numbers. The *greatest common factor* (GCF) is the greatest number that is a common factor of two or more numbers.

Example 1 **Find the GCF of 14 and 42.**

Factors of 24: 1, 2, 3, 4, 6, 8, 12, 24 — Find the common factors: 1, 2, 4, 8
Factors of 64: 1, 2, 4, 8, 16, 32, 64 ← The greatest common factor is 8.
GCF (24, 64) = 8

Another way to find the GCF is to first find the prime factors of the numbers.

$24 = 2 \cdot 2 \cdot 2 \cdot 3$ ← Multiply the common prime factors.
$64 = 2 \cdot 2 \cdot 2 \cdot 2 \cdot 2 \cdot 2$
$\text{GCF} = 2 \cdot 2 \cdot 2 = 8$ ← Use the factor the number of times it appears as a common factor.

A common multiple is a number that is a multiple of two or more numbers. The *least common multiple* (LCM) is the least number that is a common multiple of two or more numbers.

Example 2 **Find the LCM of 12 and 18.**

Multiples of 12: 12, 24, 36,. . . — List a number of multiples until you find the first common multiple.
Multiples of 18: 18, 36,. . .
LCM = (12, 18) = 36

Another way to find the LCM is to first find the prime factors of the numbers.
$12 = 2 \cdot 2 \cdot 3$
$18 = 2 \cdot 3 \cdot 3$
$\text{LCM} = 2 \cdot 2 \cdot 3 \cdot 3 = 36$ ← Use each prime factor the greatest number of times it appears in either number.

EXERCISES

Find the GCF of each set of numbers.

1. 12 and 22 **2.** 7 and 21 **3.** 24 and 48 **4.** 17 and 51
5. 9 and 12 **6.** 10 and 25 **7.** 21 and 49 **8.** 27 and 36
9. 14 and 42 **10.** 20 and 30 **11.** 27 and 15 **12.** 12 and 28
13. 10, 30, and 25 **14.** 56, 84, and 140 **15.** 42, 63, and 105 **16.** 20, 28, and 40

Find the LCM of each set of numbers.

17. 16 and 20 **18.** 14 and 21 **19.** 11 and 33 **20.** 8 and 9
21. 5 and 12 **22.** 54 and 84 **23.** 48 and 80 **24.** 25 and 36
25. 54 and 80 **26.** 75 and 175 **27.** 10 and 25 **28.** 24 and 28
29. 10, 15, and 25 **30.** 6, 7, and 12 **31.** 5, 8, and 20 **32.** 18, 21, and 36

Simplifying Fractions

A *fraction* can name a part of a group or region. This region is divided into 10 equal parts and 6 of the equal parts are shaded.

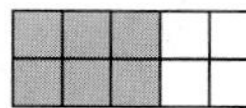

$\dfrac{6}{10}$ ← Numerator, ← Denominator   Read: *six tenths*

A fraction can have many names. Different names for the same fraction are called *equivalent fractions*. You can find an equivalent fraction for any given fraction by multiplying the numerator and denominator of the given fraction by the same number.

Example 1 **Write five equivalent fractions for $\frac{3}{5}$.**

$\frac{3}{5} = \frac{3 \cdot 2}{5 \cdot 2} = \frac{6}{10}$ $\quad$ $\frac{3}{5} = \frac{3 \cdot 3}{5 \cdot 3} = \frac{9}{15}$ $\quad$ $\frac{3}{5} = \frac{3 \cdot 4}{5 \cdot 4} = \frac{12}{16}$ $\quad$ $\frac{3}{5} = \frac{3 \cdot 5}{5 \cdot 5} = \frac{15}{25}$ $\quad$ $\frac{3}{5} = \frac{3 \cdot 6}{5 \cdot 6} = \frac{18}{30}$

The fraction $\frac{3}{5}$ is in *simplest form* because its numerator and denominator are *relatively prime*, that is, their only common factor is the number 1. To write a fraction in simplest form, divide its numerator and denominator by their greatest common factor (GCF).

Example 2 **Write $\frac{6}{24}$ in simplest form.**

First find the GCF of 6 and 24.

$6 = 2 \cdot 3$ ← Multiply the common prime factors.

$24 = 2 \cdot 2 \cdot 2 \cdot 3$ ← $\text{GCF} = 2 \cdot 3 = 6$

Then divide the numerator and denominator of $\frac{6}{24}$ by the GCF, 6.

$\frac{6}{24} = \frac{6 \div 6}{24 \div 6} = \frac{1}{4}$ ← simplest form

EXERCISES

Complete.

1. $\frac{3}{7} = \frac{\blacksquare}{21}$ **2.** $\frac{5}{8} = \frac{20}{\blacksquare}$ **3.** $\frac{11}{12} = \frac{44}{\blacksquare}$ **4.** $\frac{12}{16} = \frac{\blacksquare}{4}$ **5.** $\frac{50}{100} = \frac{1}{\blacksquare}$

6. $\frac{5}{9} = \frac{\blacksquare}{27}$ **7.** $\frac{3}{8} = \frac{\blacksquare}{24}$ **8.** $\frac{5}{6} = \frac{20}{\blacksquare}$ **9.** $\frac{12}{20} = \frac{\blacksquare}{5}$ **10.** $\frac{75}{150} = \frac{1}{\blacksquare}$

Which fractions are in simplest form?

11. $\frac{4}{12}$ **12.** $\frac{3}{16}$ **13.** $\frac{5}{30}$ **14.** $\frac{9}{72}$ **15.** $\frac{11}{22}$ **16.** $\frac{24}{25}$

Write in simplest form.

17. $\frac{8}{16}$ **18.** $\frac{7}{14}$ **19.** $\frac{6}{9}$ **20.** $\frac{20}{30}$ **21.** $\frac{8}{20}$ **22.** $\frac{12}{40}$

23. $\frac{15}{45}$ **24.** $\frac{14}{56}$ **25.** $\frac{10}{25}$ **26.** $\frac{9}{72}$ **27.** $\frac{45}{60}$ **28.** $\frac{20}{35}$

29. $\frac{27}{33}$ **30.** $\frac{18}{72}$ **31.** $\frac{45}{85}$ **32.** $\frac{63}{126}$ **33.** $\frac{125}{150}$ **34.** $\frac{256}{320}$

Fractions and Decimals

Fractions can be written as decimals.

Example 1 **Write $\frac{3}{5}$ as a decimal.**

$$5\overline{)3.0}\quad \text{quotient } 0.6,\ -3.0$$

Divide the numerator by the denominator.

The decimal for $\frac{3}{5}$ is 0.6.

Decimals can be written as fractions.

Example 2 **Write 0.38 as a fraction.**

$0.38 = 38$ hundredths $= \frac{38}{100} = \frac{19}{50}$

A fraction for 0.38 is $\frac{38}{100}$ or $\frac{19}{50}$.

Example 3 **Write $\frac{3}{11}$ as a decimal.**

Divide the numerator by the denominator. →

Notice that the remainders 8 and 3 keep repeating. Therefore 2 and 7 will keep repeating in the quotient. →

$$\frac{3}{11} = 11\overline{)3.0000\ldots}\quad \text{quotient } 0.2727;\ -22,\ 80,\ -77,\ 30,\ -22,\ 80,\ -77,\ 3$$

So, $\frac{3}{11} = 0.2727\ldots = 0.\overline{27}$

Example 4 **Write 0.363636 . . . as a fraction.**

Let $x = 0.363636\ldots$

Then $100x = 36.363636\ldots$ ← When 2 digits repeat, multiply by 100.

$99x = 36$ ← Subtract the first equation from the second.

$x = \frac{36}{99}$ or $\frac{4}{11}$ ← Divide each side by 99.

Example 5 **Write 0.42222 . . . as a fraction.**

Let $x = 0.42222\ldots$

Then $10x = 4.22222\ldots$ ← When 1 digit repeats, multiply by 10.

$9x = 3.8$ ← Subtract the first equation from the second.

$x = \frac{3.8}{9}$ or $\frac{38}{90}$ or $\frac{19}{45}$

EXERCISES

Write as a decimal.

1. $\frac{3}{10}$ **2.** $\frac{1}{5}$ **3.** $\frac{4}{20}$ **4.** $\frac{25}{75}$ **5.** $\frac{2}{3}$ **6.** $\frac{12}{6}$

7. $\frac{7}{100}$ **8.** $\frac{3}{2}$ **9.** $4\frac{3}{25}$ **10.** $\frac{13}{12}$ **11.** $\frac{3}{11}$ **12.** $\frac{5}{7}$

Write as a fraction in simplest form.

13. 0.3 **14.** 0.25 **15.** 2.37 **16.** 0.07 **17.** 0.875

18. 0.4545 . . . **19.** 6.333 . . . **20.** 7.2626 . . . **21.** 0.15151 . . . **22.** 0.123123 . . .

Adding and Subtracting Fractions

You can add and subtract fractions when they have the same denominator. Fractions with the same denominator are called *like fractions.*

Example 1 **Add $\frac{4}{5} + \frac{3}{5}$.**

$\frac{4}{5} + \frac{3}{5} = \frac{4+3}{5} = \frac{7}{5} = 1\frac{2}{5}$ ← Add the numerators and keep the same denominator.

Example 2 **Subtract $\frac{5}{9} - \frac{2}{9}$.**

$\frac{5}{9} - \frac{2}{9} = \frac{5-2}{9} = \frac{3}{9} = \frac{1}{3}$ ← Subtract the numerators and keep the same denominator.

Fractions with unlike denominators are called *unlike fractions.* To add or subtract fractions with unlike denominators, find the least common denominator (LCD) and write equivalent fractions with the same denominator. Then add or subtract the like fractions.

Example 3 **Add $\frac{3}{4} + \frac{5}{6}$.**

$\frac{3}{4} + \frac{5}{6} =$ ← Find the LCD. The LCD is the same as the least common multiple (LCM). The LCD(4, 6) is 12.

$\frac{9}{12} + \frac{10}{12} = \frac{9+10}{12} = \frac{19}{12}$ or $1\frac{7}{12}$ ← Write equivalent fractions with the same denominator.

Example 4 **Subtract $\frac{5}{12} - \frac{2}{9}$.**

$\frac{5}{12} - \frac{2}{9} =$ ← Find the LCD. The LCD (12, 9) is 36.

$\frac{15}{36} - \frac{8}{36} = \frac{15-8}{36} = \frac{7}{36}$ ← Write equivalent fractions with the same denominator.

To add or subtract mixed numbers, add or subtract the fractions. Then add or subtract the whole numbers. Sometimes when subtracting mixed numbers you may have to regroup.

Example 5 **Subtract $5\frac{1}{4} - 3\frac{2}{3}$.**

$5\frac{1}{4} - 3\frac{2}{3}$ ← Write equivalent fractions with the same denominator.

$5\frac{3}{12} - 3\frac{8}{12} =$ ← Write $5\frac{3}{12}$ as $4\frac{15}{12}$ so you can subtract the fractions.

$4\frac{15}{12} - 3\frac{8}{12} = 1\frac{7}{12}$ ← Subtract the fractions. Then subtract the whole numbers.

EXERCISES

Add. Write each answer in simplest terms.

1. $\frac{2}{7} + \frac{3}{7}$
2. $\frac{3}{8} + \frac{7}{8}$
3. $\frac{6}{5} + \frac{9}{5}$
4. $\frac{4}{9} + \frac{8}{9}$
5. $6\frac{2}{3} + 3\frac{4}{5}$
6. $1\frac{4}{7} + 2\frac{3}{14}$
7. $4\frac{5}{6} + 1\frac{7}{18}$
8. $2\frac{4}{5} + 3\frac{6}{7}$
9. $4\frac{2}{3} + 1\frac{6}{11}$
10. $3\frac{7}{9} + 5\frac{5}{27}$

Subtract. Write each answer in simplest terms.

11. $\frac{7}{8} - \frac{3}{8}$
12. $\frac{9}{10} - \frac{3}{10}$
13. $\frac{17}{5} - \frac{2}{5}$
14. $\frac{11}{7} - \frac{2}{7}$
15. $\frac{5}{11} - \frac{4}{11}$
16. $8\frac{5}{8} - 6\frac{1}{4}$
17. $3\frac{2}{3} - 1\frac{8}{9}$
18. $8\frac{5}{6} - 5\frac{1}{2}$
19. $12\frac{3}{4} - 4\frac{5}{6}$
20. $17\frac{2}{7} - 8\frac{2}{9}$

Multiplying and Dividing Fractions

To multiply two or more fractions, multiply the numerators, multiply the denominators, and simplify the product, if necessary.

Example 1 **Multiply $\frac{3}{7} \cdot \frac{5}{6}$.**

$$\frac{3}{7} \cdot \frac{5}{6} = \frac{3 \cdot 5}{7 \cdot 6} = \frac{15}{42} = \frac{15 \div 3}{42 \div 3} = \frac{5}{14}$$

Sometimes you can simplify before multiplying.

$$\frac{{}^{1}\not{3}}{7} \cdot \frac{5}{\not{6}_{2}} = \frac{5}{14}$$ ← Divide a numerator and a denominator by a common factor.

To multiply mixed numbers, change the mixed numbers to improper fractions and multiply the fractions. Write the product as a mixed number.

Example 2 **Multiply $2\frac{4}{5} \cdot 1\frac{2}{3}$.**

$$2\frac{4}{5} \cdot 1\frac{2}{3} = \frac{14}{{}_{1}\not{5}} \cdot \frac{\not{5}^{1}}{3} = \frac{14}{3} = 4\frac{2}{3}$$

To divide fractions, change the division problem to a multiplication problem. Remember that $8 \div \frac{1}{4}$ is the same as $8 \cdot 4$.

Example 3 **Divide $\frac{4}{5} \div \frac{3}{7}$.**

$$\frac{4}{5} \div \frac{3}{7} = \frac{4}{5} \cdot \frac{7}{3}$$ ← Multiply by the reciprocal of the divisor. Simplify the answer.

$$= \frac{4}{5} \cdot \frac{7}{3} = \frac{28}{15} = 1\frac{13}{15}$$

To divide mixed numbers, change the mixed numbers to improper fractions and divide the fractions.

Example 4 **Divide $4\frac{2}{3} \div 7\frac{3}{5}$.**

$$4\frac{2}{3} \div 7\frac{3}{5} = \frac{14}{3} \div \frac{38}{5} = \frac{14}{3} \cdot \frac{5}{38} = \frac{70}{114} = \frac{35}{57}$$

EXERCISES

Multiply. Write your answers in simplest form.

1. $\frac{2}{5} \cdot \frac{3}{4}$ **2.** $\frac{3}{7} \cdot \frac{4}{3}$ **3.** $\frac{5}{4} \cdot \frac{3}{8}$ **4.** $\frac{6}{7} \cdot \frac{9}{2}$ **5.** $\frac{7}{3} \cdot \frac{4}{7}$

6. $2\frac{3}{4} \cdot \frac{5}{8}$ **7.** $1\frac{1}{2} \cdot 5\frac{3}{4}$ **8.** $3\frac{4}{5} \cdot 10$ **9.** $12 \cdot 1\frac{2}{3}$ **10.** $5\frac{1}{4} \cdot \frac{2}{3}$

Divide. Write your answers in simplest form.

11. $\frac{3}{5} \div \frac{1}{2}$ **12.** $\frac{4}{5} \div \frac{9}{10}$ **13.** $\frac{4}{7} \div \frac{2}{3}$ **14.** $\frac{5}{8} \div \frac{7}{3}$ **15.** $\frac{4}{7} \div \frac{4}{3}$

16. $1\frac{4}{5} \div 2\frac{1}{2}$ **17.** $2\frac{1}{2} \div 3\frac{1}{2}$ **18.** $3\frac{1}{6} \div 1\frac{3}{4}$ **19.** $9\frac{1}{2} \div 4\frac{1}{4}$ **20.** $6\frac{3}{5} \div 2\frac{3}{5}$

Fractions, Decimals, and Percents

Percent means *per hundred.* 50% means 50 per hundred. $50\% = \frac{50}{100} = 0.50$

You can use a shortcut to write a decimal as a percent and a percent as a decimal.

Example 1 **Write each number as a percent.**

a. 0.47   b. 0.8   c. 2.475

Move the decimal point two places to the right and write a percent sign.

a. 0.47 = 47%   b. 0.80 = 80%   c. 2.475 = 247.5%

Example 2 **Write each number as a decimal.**

a. 25%   b. 3%   c. 360%

Move the decimal point two places to the left and drop the percent sign.

a. 25% = 0.25   b. 03% = 0.03   c. 360% = 3.6

You can write fractions as percents by writing the fraction as a decimal first. Then move the decimal point two places to the right and write a percent sign.

Example 3 **Write each number as a percent.** a. $\frac{3}{5}$ b. $\frac{7}{20}$ c. $\frac{2}{3}$

a. $\frac{3}{5} = 0.6 = 60\%$ b. $\frac{7}{20} = 0.35 = 35\%$ c. $\frac{2}{3} = 0.66\overline{6} = 66.\overline{6}\%$ or 66.7% (rounded to the nearest tenth of a percent)

You can write a percent as a fraction by writing the percent as a fraction with a denominator of 100 and simplifying if possible.

Example 4 **Write each number as a fraction or mixed number.**

a. $43\% = \frac{43}{100}$ b. $\frac{1}{2}\% = \frac{\frac{1}{2}}{100} = \frac{1}{2} \div 100 = \frac{1}{2} \cdot \frac{1}{100} = \frac{1}{200}$ c. $180\% = \frac{180}{100} = \frac{9}{5} = 1\frac{4}{5}$

EXERCISES

Write each number as a percent.

1. 0.56   **2.** 0.09   **3.** 6.02   **4.** 5.245   **5.** 8.2   **6.** 0.14

7. $\frac{1}{5}$ **8.** $\frac{9}{20}$ **9.** $\frac{1}{9}$ **10.** $\frac{5}{6}$ **11.** $\frac{3}{4}$ **12.** $\frac{7}{8}$

Write each number as a decimal.

13. 7%   **14.** 8.5%   **15.** 0.9%   **16.** 250%   **17.** 83%   **18.** 110%

Write each number as a fraction or mixed number in simplest form.

19. 19%   **20.** $\frac{3}{4}\%$ **21.** 450%   **22.** $\frac{4}{5}\%$ **23.** 64%   **24.** $\frac{2}{3}\%$

Exponents

You can express $2 \cdot 2 \cdot 2 \cdot 2 \cdot 2$ as 2^5. The raised number, 5, shows the number of times 2 is used as a factor. The number 2 is the *base*. The number 5 is the *exponent*.

2^5 ← exponent
↑ base

Factored Form		Exponential Form		Standard Form
$2 \cdot 2 \cdot 2 \cdot 2 \cdot 2$	=	2^5	=	32

A number with an exponent of 1 is the number itself: $8^1 = 8$.
Any number, except 0, with an exponent of 0 is 1: $5^0 = 1$.

Example 1 **Write using exponents.**

a. $8 \cdot 8 \cdot 8 \cdot 8 \cdot 8$ **b.** $2 \cdot 9 \cdot 9 \cdot 9 \cdot 9 \cdot 9 \cdot 9$ **c.** $6 \cdot 6 \cdot 10 \cdot 10 \cdot 10 \cdot 6 \cdot 6$

Count the number of times the number is used as a factor.

a. 8^5 **b.** $2 \cdot 9^6$ **c.** $6^4 \cdot 10^3$

Example 2 **Write each product.**

a. 2^3 **b.** $8^2 \cdot 3^4$ **c.** $10^3 \cdot 5^2$

Write in factored form and multiply.

a. $2 \cdot 2 \cdot 2 = 8$ **b.** $8 \cdot 8 \cdot 3 \cdot 3 \cdot 3 \cdot 3 = 5184$ **c.** $10 \cdot 10 \cdot 10 \cdot 5 \cdot 5 = 25{,}000$

In powers of 10, the exponent tells how many zeros are in the standard form.

$10^1 = 10$
$10^2 = 10 \cdot 10 = 100$
$10^3 = 10 \cdot 10 \cdot 10 = 1000$
$10^4 = 10 \cdot 10 \cdot 10 \cdot 10 = 10{,}000$
$10^5 = 10 \cdot 10 \cdot 10 \cdot 10 \cdot 10 = 100{,}000$

You can use exponents to write numbers in *expanded form*.

Example 3 **Write 739 in expanded form using exponents.**

$739 = 700 + 30 + 9 = (7 \cdot 100) + (3 \cdot 10) + (9 \cdot 1) = (7 \cdot 10^2) + (3 \cdot 10^1) + (9 \cdot 10^0)$

EXERCISES

Write using exponents.

1. $6 \cdot 6 \cdot 6 \cdot 6$ **2.** $7 \cdot 7 \cdot 7 \cdot 7 \cdot 7$ **3.** $5 \cdot 2 \cdot 2 \cdot 2 \cdot 2$ **4.** $3 \cdot 3 \cdot 3 \cdot 3 \cdot 3 \cdot 14 \cdot 14$

Write in standard form.

5. 4^3 **6.** 9^4 **7.** 12^2 **8.** $6^2 \cdot 7^1$ **9.** $11^2 \cdot 3^3$

Write in expanded form using exponents.

10. 658 **11.** 1254 **12.** 7125 **13.** 83,401 **14.** 294,863

Measures

United States Customary	Metric
Length	
12 inches (in.) = 1 foot (ft)	10 millimeters (mm) = 1 centimeter (cm)
36 in. = 1 yard (yd)	100 cm = 1 meter (m)
3 ft = 1 yard	1000 mm = 1 meter
5280 ft = 1 mile (mi)	1000 m = 1 kilometer (km)
1760 yd = 1 mile	
Area	
144 square inches (in.^{2}) = 1 square foot (ft^2)	100 square millimeters (mm^2) = 1 square centimeter (cm^2)
9 ft^2 = 1 square yard (yd^2)	10,000 cm^2 = 1 square meter (m^2)
43,560 ft^2 = 1 acre (a)	10,000 m^2 = 1 hectare (ha)
4840 yd^2 = 1 acre	
Volume	
1728 cubic inches (in.^{3}) = 1 cubic foot (ft^3)	1000 cubic millimeters (mm^3) = 1 cubic centimeter (cm^3)
27 ft^3 = 1 cubic yard (yd^3)	1,000,000 cm^3 = 1 cubic meter (m^3)
Liquid Capacity	
8 fluid ounces (fl oz) = 1 cup (c)	1000 milliliters (mL) = 1 liter (L)
2 c = 1 pint (pt)	1000 L = 1 kiloliter (kL)
2 pt = 1 quart (qt)	
4 qt = 1 gallon (gal)	
Mass	
16 ounces (oz) = 1 pound (lb)	1000 milligrams (mg) = 1 gram (g)
2000 pounds = 1 ton (t)	1000 g = 1 kilogram (kg)
	1000 kg = 1 metric ton (t)
Temperature	
32°F = freezing point of water	0°C = freezing point of water
98.6°F = normal body temperature	37°C = normal body temperature
212°F = boiling point of water	100°C = boiling point of water

Time

60 seconds (s) = 1 minute (min)	365 days = 1 year (yr)
60 minutes = 1 hour (h)	52 weeks (approx.) = 1 year
24 hours = 1 day (da)	12 months = 1 year
7 days = 1 week (wk)	10 years = 1 decade
4 weeks (approx.) = 1 month (mo)	100 years = 1 century

Symbols

Symbol	Meaning
$=$	equals
$\approx$	is approximately equal to
$\cdot$	multiplication sign, times ($\times$)
( )	parentheses for grouping
a^n	*n*th power of *a*
[ ]	brackets for grouping
. . .	and so on
$\|a\|$	absolute value of *a*
$-a$	opposite of *a*
$^\circ$	degree(s)
$<$	is less than
$>$	is greater than
π	pi, an irrational number, approximately equal to 3.14
$\frac{1}{a}$	reciprocal of *a*
$P(\text{event})$	probability of the event
$\begin{bmatrix} 1 & 2 \\ 3 & 4 \end{bmatrix}$	matrix
^	raised to a power (in a spreadsheet formula)
*	multiply (in a spreadsheet formula)
/	divide (in a spreadsheet formula)
(x, y)	ordered pair
$f(x)$	*f* of *x*; the function value at *x*
x_1, x_2, etc.	specific values of the variable *x*
y_1, y_2, etc.	specific values of the variable *y*
$\stackrel{?}{=}$	is the statement true?
$\angle A$	angle *A*
%	percent
$a : b$	ratio of *a* to *b*
$\neq$	is not equal to
$\triangle ABC$	triangle *ABC*
AB	length of $\overline{AB}$; distance between points *A* and *B*
$\leq$	is less than or equal to
$\geq$	is greater than or equal to
{ }	set braces
$\overleftrightarrow{AB}$	line through points *A* and *B*
m	slope of a linear function
b	*y*-intercept of a linear function
$\sqrt{x}$	nonnegative square root of *x*
$\pm$	plus or minus
a^{-n}	$\frac{1}{a^n}, a \neq 0$
$\overline{AB}$	segment with endpoints *A* and *B*
$\sin A$	sine of $\angle A$
$\cos A$	cosine of $\angle A$
$\tan A$	tangent of $\angle A$
$m\angle A$	measure of angle *A*
$\overline{x}$	mean of data values of *x*
$n!$	*n* factorial
${}_nP_r$	permutations of *n* things taken *r* at a time
${}_nC_r$	combinations of *n* things taken *r* at a time

Formulas from Geometry

You will use a number of geometric formulas as you work through your algebra book. Here are some perimeter, area, and volume formulas.

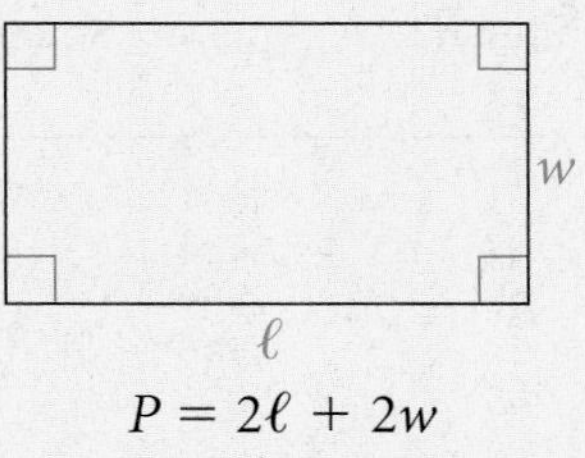

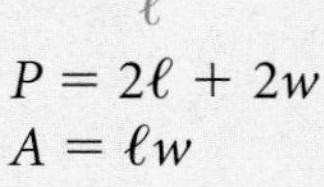

$P = 2\ell + 2w$
$A = \ell w$

Rectangle

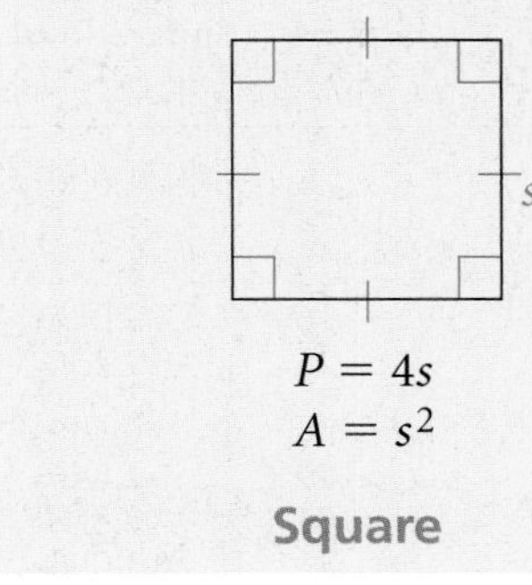

$P = 4s$
$A = s^2$

Square

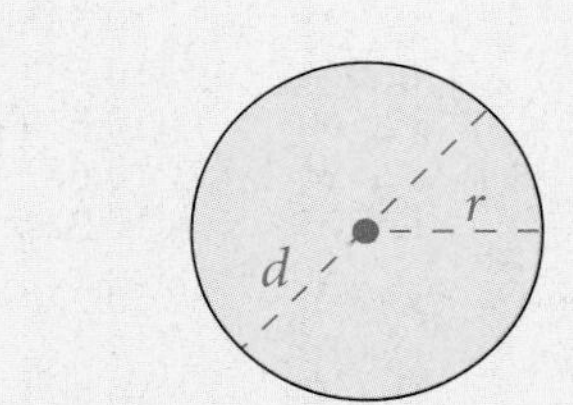

$C = 2\pi r$ or $C = \pi d$
$A = \pi r^2$

Circle

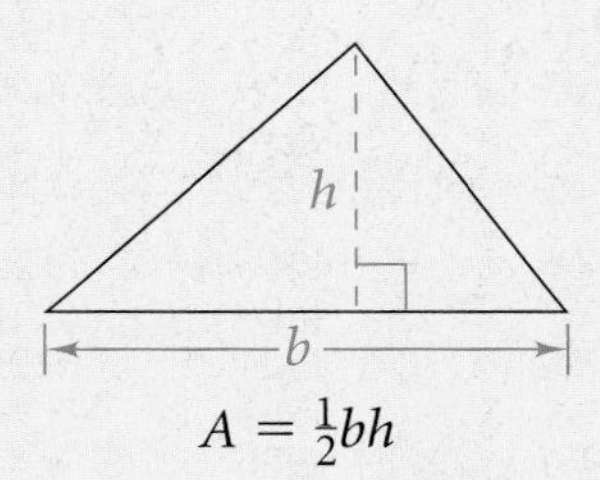

$A = \frac{1}{2}bh$

Triangle

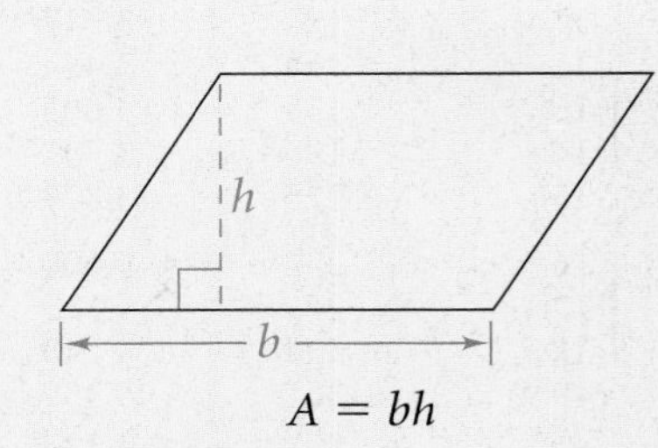

$A = bh$

Parallelogram

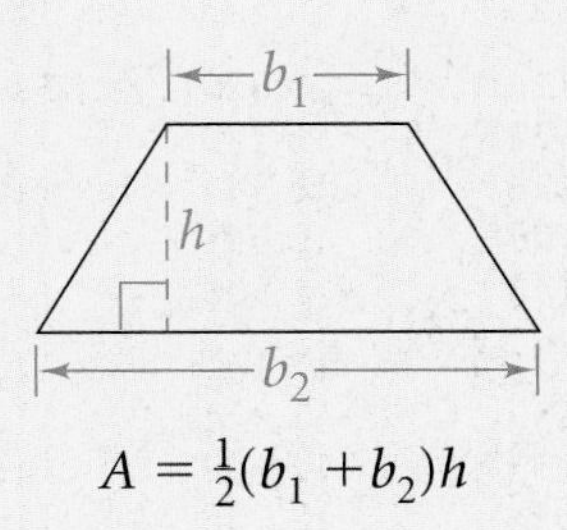

$A = \frac{1}{2}(b_1 + b_2)h$

Trapezoid

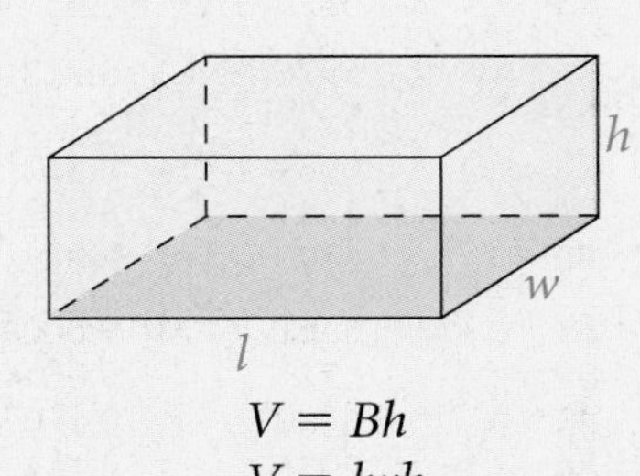

$V = Bh$
$V = lwh$

Rectangular Prism

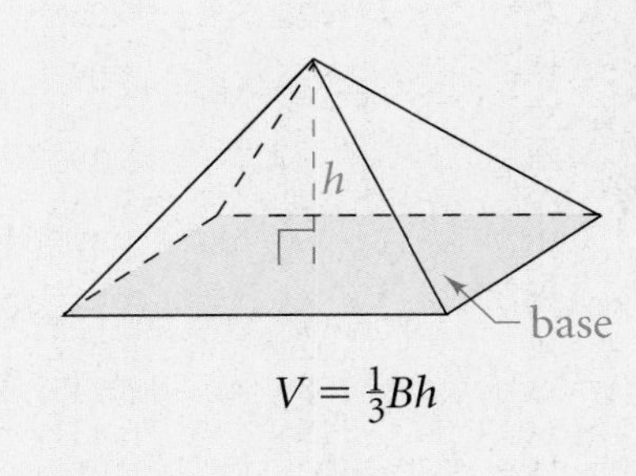

$V = \frac{1}{3}Bh$

Pyramid

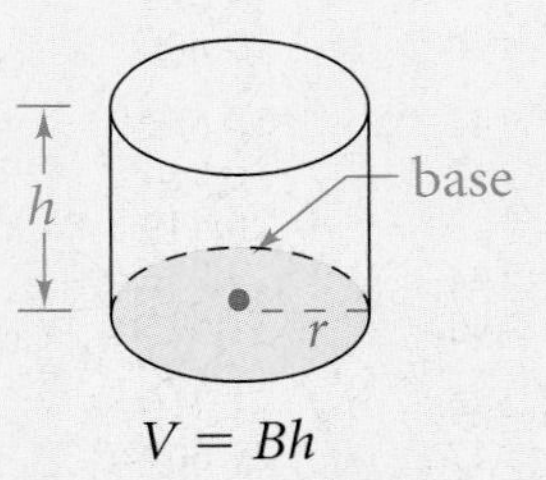

$V = Bh$
$V = \pi r^2 h$

Cylinder

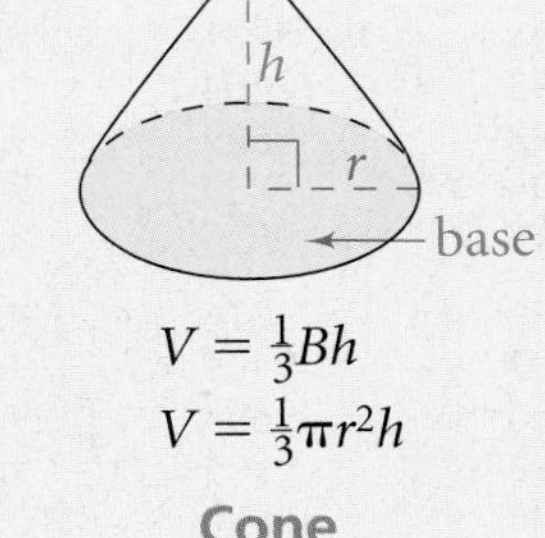

$V = \frac{1}{3}Bh$
$V = \frac{1}{3}\pi r^2 h$

Cone

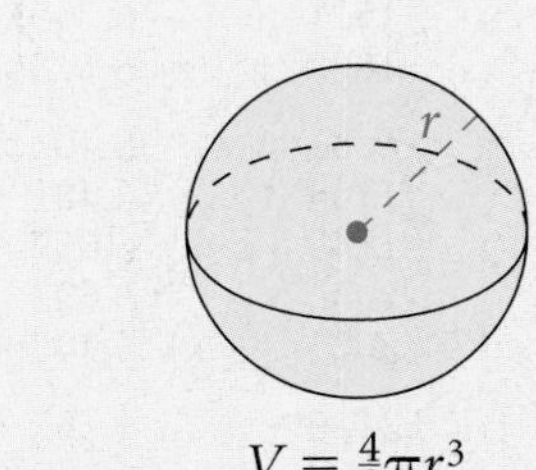

$V = \frac{4}{3}\pi r^3$

Sphere

Tables

Squares and Square Roots

Number n	Square n^2	Positive Square Root $\sqrt{n}$	Number n	Square n^2	Positive Square Root $\sqrt{n}$	Number n	Square n^2	Positive Square Root $\sqrt{n}$
1	1	1.000	**51**	2601	7.141	**101**	10,201	10.050
2	4	1.414	**52**	2704	7.211	**102**	10,404	10.100
3	9	1.732	**53**	2809	7.280	**103**	10,609	10.149
4	16	2.000	**54**	2916	7.348	**104**	10,816	10.198
5	25	2.236	**55**	3025	7.416	**105**	11,025	10.247
6	36	2.449	**56**	3136	7.483	**106**	11,236	10.296
7	49	2.646	**57**	3249	7.550	**107**	11,449	10.344
8	64	2.828	**58**	3364	7.616	**108**	11,664	10.392
9	81	3.000	**59**	3481	7.681	**109**	11,881	10.440
10	100	3.162	**60**	3600	7.746	**110**	12,100	10.488
11	121	3.317	**61**	3721	7.810	**111**	12,321	10.536
12	144	3.464	**62**	3844	7.874	**112**	12,544	10.583
13	169	3.606	**63**	3969	7.937	**113**	12,769	10.630
14	196	3.742	**64**	4096	8.000	**114**	12,996	10.677
15	225	3.873	**65**	4225	8.062	**115**	13,225	10.724
16	256	4.000	**66**	4356	8.124	**116**	13,456	10.770
17	289	4.123	**67**	4489	8.185	**117**	13,689	10.817
18	324	4.243	**68**	4624	8.246	**118**	13,924	10.863
19	361	4.359	**69**	4761	8.307	**119**	14,161	10.909
20	400	4.472	**70**	4900	8.367	**120**	14,400	10.954
21	441	4.583	**71**	5041	8.426	**121**	14,641	11.000
22	484	4.690	**72**	5184	8.485	**122**	14,884	11.045
23	529	4.796	**73**	5329	8.544	**123**	15,129	11.091
24	576	4.899	**74**	5476	8.602	**124**	15,376	11.136
25	625	5.000	**75**	5625	8.660	**125**	15,625	11.180
26	676	5.099	**76**	5776	8.718	**126**	15,876	11.225
27	729	5.196	**77**	5929	8.775	**127**	16,129	11.269
28	784	5.292	**78**	6084	8.832	**128**	16,384	11.314
29	841	5.385	**79**	6241	8.888	**129**	16,641	11.358
30	900	5.477	**80**	6400	8.944	**130**	16,900	11.402
31	961	5.568	**81**	6561	9.000	**131**	17,161	11.446
32	1024	5.657	**82**	6724	9.055	**132**	17,424	11.489
33	1089	5.745	**83**	6889	9.110	**133**	17,689	11.533
34	1156	5.831	**84**	7056	9.165	**134**	17,956	11.576
35	1225	5.916	**85**	7225	9.220	**135**	18,225	11.619
36	1296	6.000	**86**	7396	9.274	**136**	18,496	11.662
37	1369	6.083	**87**	7569	9.327	**137**	18,769	11.705
38	1444	6.164	**88**	7744	9.381	**138**	19,044	11.747
39	1521	6.245	**89**	7921	9.434	**139**	19,321	11.790
40	1600	6.325	**90**	8100	9.487	**140**	19,600	11.832
41	1681	6.403	**91**	8281	9.539	**141**	19,881	11.874
42	1764	6.481	**92**	8464	9.592	**142**	20,164	11.916
43	1849	6.557	**93**	8649	9.644	**143**	20,449	11.958
44	1936	6.633	**94**	8836	9.695	**144**	20,736	12.000
45	2025	6.708	**95**	9025	9.747	**145**	21,025	12.042
46	2116	6.782	**96**	9216	9.798	**146**	21,316	12.083
47	2209	6.856	**97**	9409	9.849	**147**	21,609	12.124
48	2304	6.928	**98**	9604	9.899	**148**	21,904	12.166
49	2401	7.000	**99**	9801	9.950	**149**	22,201	12.207
50	2500	7.071	**100**	10,000	10.000	**150**	22,500	12.247

Trigonometric Ratios

Angle	Sine	Cosine	Tangent	Angle	Sine	Cosine	Tangent
1°	0.0175	0.9998	0.0175	**46°**	0.7193	0.6947	1.0355
2°	0.0349	0.9994	0.0349	**47°**	0.7314	0.6820	1.0724
3°	0.0523	0.9986	0.0524	**48°**	0.7431	0.6691	1.1106
4°	0.0698	0.9976	0.0699	**49°**	0.7547	0.6561	1.1504
5°	0.0872	0.9962	0.0875	**50°**	0.7660	0.6428	1.1918
6°	0.1045	0.9945	0.1051	**51°**	0.7771	0.6293	1.2349
7°	0.1219	0.9925	0.1228	**52°**	0.7880	0.6157	1.2799
8°	0.1392	0.9903	0.1405	**53°**	0.7986	0.6018	1.3270
9°	0.1564	0.9877	0.1584	**54°**	0.8090	0.5878	1.3764
10°	0.1736	0.9848	0.1763	**55°**	0.8192	0.5736	1.4281
11°	0.1908	0.9816	0.1944	**56°**	0.8290	0.5592	1.4826
12°	0.2079	0.9781	0.2126	**57°**	0.8387	0.5446	1.5399
13°	0.2250	0.9744	0.2309	**58°**	0.8480	0.5299	1.6003
14°	0.2419	0.9703	0.2493	**59°**	0.8572	0.5150	1.6643
15°	0.2588	0.9659	0.2679	**60°**	0.8660	0.5000	1.7321
16°	0.2756	0.9613	0.2867	**61°**	0.8746	0.4848	1.8040
17°	0.2924	0.9563	0.3057	**62°**	0.8829	0.4695	1.8807
18°	0.3090	0.9511	0.3249	**63°**	0.8910	0.4540	1.9626
19°	0.3256	0.9455	0.3443	**64°**	0.8988	0.4384	2.0503
20°	0.3420	0.9397	0.3640	**65°**	0.9063	0.4226	2.1445
21°	0.3584	0.9336	0.3839	**66°**	0.9135	0.4067	2.2460
22°	0.3746	0.9272	0.4040	**67°**	0.9205	0.3907	2.3559
23°	0.3907	0.9205	0.4245	**68°**	0.9272	0.3746	2.4751
24°	0.4067	0.9135	0.4452	**69°**	0.9336	0.3584	2.6051
25°	0.4226	0.9063	0.4663	**70°**	0.9397	0.3420	2.7475
26°	0.4384	0.8988	0.4877	**71°**	0.9455	0.3256	2.9042
27°	0.4540	0.8910	0.5095	**72°**	0.9511	0.3090	3.0777
28°	0.4695	0.8829	0.5317	**73°**	0.9563	0.2924	3.2709
29°	0.4848	0.8746	0.5543	**74°**	0.9613	0.2756	3.4874
30°	0.5000	0.8660	0.5774	**75°**	0.9659	0.2588	3.7321
31°	0.5150	0.8572	0.6009	**76°**	0.9703	0.2419	4.0108
32°	0.5299	0.8480	0.6249	**77°**	0.9744	0.2250	4.3315
33°	0.5446	0.8387	0.6494	**78°**	0.9781	0.2079	4.7046
34°	0.5592	0.8290	0.6745	**79°**	0.9816	0.1908	5.1446
35°	0.5736	0.8192	0.7002	**80°**	0.9848	0.1736	5.6713
36°	0.5878	0.8090	0.7265	**81°**	0.9877	0.1564	6.3138
37°	0.6018	0.7986	0.7536	**82°**	0.9903	0.1392	7.1154
38°	0.6157	0.7880	0.7813	**83°**	0.9925	0.1219	8.1443
39°	0.6293	0.7771	0.8098	**84°**	0.9945	0.1045	9.5144
40°	0.6428	0.7660	0.8391	**85°**	0.9962	0.0872	11.4301
41°	0.6561	0.7547	0.8693	**86°**	0.9976	0.0698	14.3007
42°	0.6691	0.7431	0.9004	**87°**	0.9986	0.0523	19.0811
43°	0.6820	0.7314	0.9325	**88°**	0.9994	0.0349	28.6363
44°	0.6947	0.7193	0.9657	**89°**	0.9998	0.0175	57.2900
45°	0.7071	0.7071	1.0000	**90°**	1.0000	0.0000	

Tables

A

Examples

Absolute value (p. 20) The distance that a number is from zero on a number line.

-7 is 7 units from 0, so $|-7| = 7$.

Absolute value function (p. 92) Function whose graph forms a "V" that opens up or down.

$y = |x - 3|$

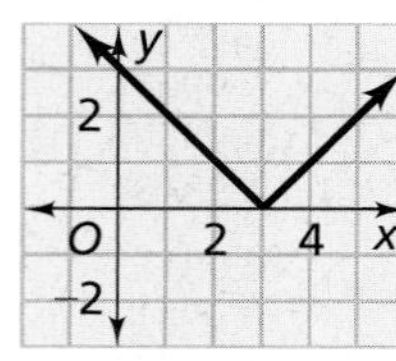

Addition Property of Inequality (p. 180) For all real numbers a, b, and c: if $a > b$, then $a + c > b + c$ and if $a < b$, then $a + c < b + c$.

$4 > -2$, so $4 + 3 > -2 + 3$.
$5 < 9$, so $5 + 2 < 9 + 2$.

Additive inverses (p. 20) A number and its opposite. Additive inverses have a sum of 0.

5 and -5 are additive inverses because $5 + -5 = 0$.

Angle of elevation (p. 426) Used to measure heights indirectly. An angle from the horizontal up to a line of sight.

Associative Properties of Addition and Multiplication (p. 35) Changing the grouping of the addends or factors does not change the sum or product.
$(a + b) + c = a + (b + c)$ and $(a \cdot b) \cdot c = a \cdot (b \cdot c)$

$(9 + 2) + 3 = 9 + (2 + 3)$.
$(5 \cdot 8) \cdot 2 = 5 \cdot (8 \cdot 2)$.

Asymptote (p. 516) A line the graph of a function gets closer and closer to, but does not cross.

Example: The y-axis is a vertical asymptote for $y = \frac{1}{x}$. The x-axis is a horizontal asymptote for $y = \frac{1}{x}$.

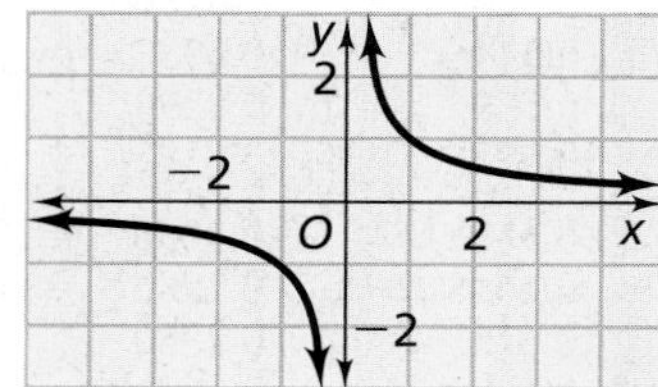

Axis of symmetry (p. 318) The line about which you can reflect a parabola onto itself.

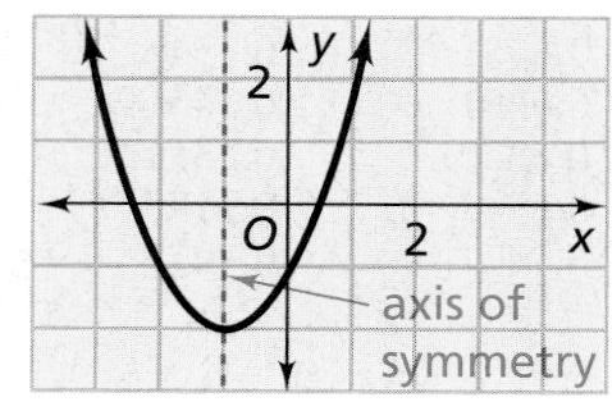

B

Examples

Bar graph (p. 6) A bar graph is used to compare amounts.

Example: The bar graph compares the number of students for grades 9, 10, and 11 over a three-year period.

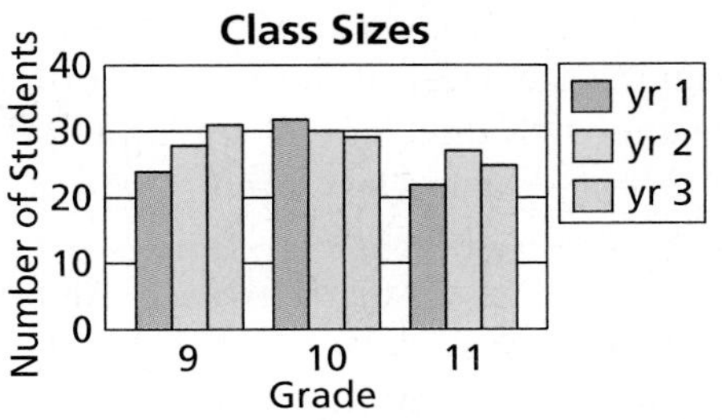

Base (p. 15) In an expression of the form x^n, x is the base.

$4^5 = 4 \cdot 4 \cdot 4 \cdot 4 \cdot 4$. The base 4 is used as a factor 5 times.

Binomial factors (p. 481) Some quadratic trinomials are the products of two binomial factors.

$(x + 2)(x + 1) = x^2 + 3x + 2$

↑ ↑ ↑

binomial factors quadratic trinomial

C

Cell (p. 45) A cell is a box where a row and a column meet in a spreadsheet.

	A	B	C	D	E
1	0.50	0.70	0.60	0.50	2.30
2	1.50	0.50	2.75	2.50	7.25

A2 is the cell where row 2 and column A meet. The entry 1.50 is in cell A2.

Certain event (p. 96) A certain event always happens, and has a probability of 1.

Rolling an integer less than 7 on a number cube is a certain event.

Coefficient (p. 119) The numerical factor when a term has a variable.

In the expression $2x + 3y + 16$, 2 and 3 are coefficients.

Combination (p. 543) An arrangement of some or all of a set of objects without regard to order. The number of combinations

$$= \frac{\text{total number of permutations}}{\text{number of times the objects in each group are repeated}}$$

You can use the notation ${}_nC_r$ to write the number of combinations of n objects chosen r at a time.

The number of combinations of 10 things taken 4 at a time is:

$${}_{10}C_4 = \frac{{}_{10}P_4}{{}_4P_4} = \frac{10 \cdot 9 \cdot 8 \cdot 7}{4 \cdot 3 \cdot 2 \cdot 1} = 210$$

Common factors (p. 471) Numbers, variables, and any products formed from the prime factors that appear in all the terms of an expression.

x, 2, and $2x$ are common factors of $2x^2 + 4x$.

	Examples
Commutative Properties of Addition and Multiplication (p. 35) Changing the order of the addends or factors does not change the sum or product. For all real numbers a and b: $a + b = b + a$ and $a \cdot b = b \cdot a$.	$5 + 7 = 7 + 5$ and $9 \cdot 3 = 3 \cdot 9$.
Complement of an event (p. 96) All possible outcomes that are not in the event. $P(\text{complement of event}) = 1 - P(\text{event})$	The complement of rolling a 1 or a 2 on a number cube is rolling a 3, 4, 5, or 6.
Compound inequality (p. 195) Two inequalities that are joined by *and* or *or*.	$5 < x$ and $x < 10$ $x < -14$ or $x \geq 3$
Constant of variation (p. 225) The constant k in a direct variation.	For the function $y = 24x$, 24 is the constant of variation.
Constant term (p. 119) A term that has no variable factor.	In the expression $4x + 13y + 17$, 17 is a constant term.
Continuous data (p. 65) Have measurements that change between data points, such as temperature, length, and weight.	The height of a tree changes between annual measurings.
Converse of the Pythagorean Theorem (p. 416) If a triangle has sides of lengths a, b, and c, and $a^2 + b^2 = c^2$, then the triangle is a right triangle with hypotenuse of length c.	
Conversion factors (p. 219) Used to change from one unit of measure to another.	Convert 2 h to minutes. Since 60 min $= 1$ h, $\frac{60 \text{ min}}{1 \text{ h}} = 1$. Use $\frac{60 \text{ min}}{1 \text{ h}}$ to convert 2 h to minutes. $\frac{2 \text{ h}}{1} \cdot \frac{60 \text{ min}}{1 \text{ h}} = 120$ min
Coordinate plane (p. 58) Formed when two number lines intersect at right angles. The x-axis is the horizontal axis and the y-axis is the vertical axis. The two axes meet at the origin, $O(0, 0)$.	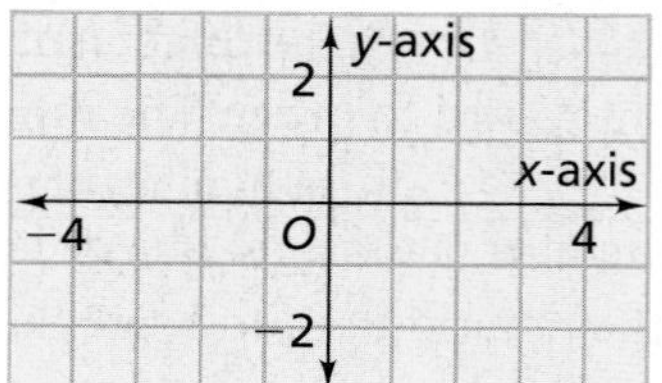
Correlation (p. 60) A trend between two sets of data. A trend shows positive, negative, or no correlation.	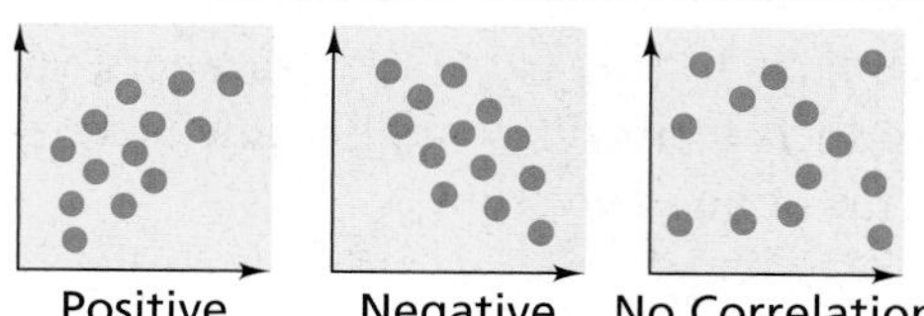

Examples

Correlation coefficient (p. 242) Tells how well the equation of best fit models the data. The value r of the correlation coefficient is in the range $-1 \leq r \leq 1$.

Example: The correlation coefficient for the data points (68, 0.5), (85, 0.89), (100, 0.9), (108, 1.1) is approximately 0.94.

```
LinReg
  y=ax+b
  a=.0134039132
  b=-.3622031627
  r=.9414498267
```

Cosine (p. 425) In $\triangle ABC$ with right $\angle C$,

$$\text{cosine of } \angle A = \frac{\text{length of side adjacent to } \angle A}{\text{length of hypotenuse}}, \text{ or } \cos A = \frac{b}{c}.$$

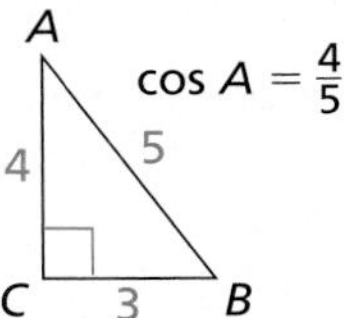

Cross products (p. 159) In a proportion, the product of the numerator of the first ratio and the denominator of the second ratio; also the product of the denominator of the first ratio and the numerator of the second ratio. These products are equal.

$\frac{3}{4} = \frac{6}{8}$
The cross products are $3 \cdot 8$ and $4 \cdot 6$.
$3 \cdot 8 = 24$ and $4 \cdot 6 = 24$

Cubic equation (p. 494) An equation in the form $ax^3 + bx^2 + cx + d = 0$, where a, b, c, and d are real numbers and $a \neq 0$.

$14x^3 + 2x^2 - 8x - 2 = 0$

D

Degree of a polynomial (p. 465) The highest degree of any of its terms.

The degree of $3x^2 + x - 9$ is 2.

Degree of a term (p. 465) For a term that has only one variable, the degree is the exponent of the variable. The degree of a constant is zero.

The degree of $3x^2$ is 2.

Dependent events (p. 135) When the outcome of one event affects the outcome of a second event, the events are dependent events.

If you pick a marble from a bag and pick another without replacing the first, the events are dependent events.

Dependent variable (p. 69) A variable is dependent if it relies on another variable.

In the equation $y = 3x$, the value of y depends upon the value of x.

Difference of two squares (p. 487) A quadratic binomial of the form $a^2 - b^2$.

$x^2 - 16$

Dimensional analysis (p. 219) The process of analyzing units to decide which conversion factors to use to solve a problem.

$0.5 \text{ mi} = \frac{0.5 \text{ mi}}{1} \cdot \frac{5280 \text{ ft}}{1 \text{ mi}} = 2640 \text{ ft}$

Examples

Direct variation (p. 225) A linear function that can be expressed in the form $y = kx$, where $k \neq 0$.

$y = 18x$ is a direct variation.

Discrete data (p. 65) Involves a count of data items, such as number of people or objects.

the number of books on a shelf in the library

Discriminant (p. 349) The quantity $b^2 - 4ac$ for a quadratic equation of the form $ax^2 + bx + c = 0$.

The discriminant of $2x^2 + 9x - 2 = 0$ is $9^2 - 4(2)(-2) = 97$.

Distance Formula (p. 420) The distance d between any two points (x_1, y_1) and (x_2, y_2) is $d = \sqrt{(x_2 - x_1)^2 + (y_2 - y_1)^2}$.

The distance between $(-2, 4)$ and $(4, 5)$ is

$$d = \sqrt{(4 - (-2))^2 + (5 - 4)^2}$$
$$= \sqrt{(6)^2 + (1)^2}$$
$$= \sqrt{37}$$

Distributive Property (p. 124) For all real numbers a, b, and c:

$a(b + c) = ab + ac$ $\quad (b + c)a = ba + ca$

$a(b - c) = ab - ac$ $\quad (b - c)a = ba - ca$

$3(19 + 4) = 3(19) + 3(4)$

$(19 + 4)3 = 19(3) + 4(3)$

$7(11 - 2) = 7(11) - 7(2)$

$(11 - 2)7 = 11(7) - 2(7)$

Division Property of Inequality (p. 187) For all real numbers a and b, and for

$c > 0$: If $a < b$, then $\frac{a}{c} < \frac{b}{c}$.

If $a > b$, then $\frac{a}{c} > \frac{b}{c}$.

$c < 0$: If $a < b$, then $\frac{a}{c} > \frac{b}{c}$.

If $a > b$, then $\frac{a}{c} < \frac{b}{c}$.

$2 < 8$, so $\frac{2}{4} < \frac{8}{4}$.

$5 > 1$, so $\frac{5}{2} > \frac{1}{2}$.

$-2 < 6$, so $\frac{-2}{-3} > \frac{6}{-3}$.

$-2 > -4$, so $\frac{-2}{-5} < \frac{-4}{-5}$.

Division Property of Square Roots (p. 431) For any numbers $a \geq 0$ and $b > 0$, $\sqrt{\frac{a}{b}} = \frac{\sqrt{a}}{\sqrt{b}}$.

$\sqrt{\frac{4}{9}} = \frac{\sqrt{4}}{\sqrt{9}} = \frac{2}{3}$

Domain (p. 74) The set of all possible input values.

In the function $f(x) = x + 22$, the domain is all real numbers.

E

Elimination (p. 280) A method for solving a system of linear equations. You add or subtract the equations to eliminate a variable.

$3x - y = 19$

$2x - y = 1$

$x + 0 = 18$ ← Subtract the second equation from the first.

$x = 18$ ← Solve for x.

$2(18) - y = 1$ ← Substitute 18 for x in the second equation.

$36 - y = 1$

$y = 35$ ← Solve for y.

The solution is (18, 35).

Examples

Entry (p. 40) An item in a matrix.	2 is an entry in the matrix $\begin{bmatrix} 9 & 2 \\ 5.3 & 1 \end{bmatrix}$.
Equation (p. 11) An equation shows that two expressions are equal.	$x + 5 = 3x - 7$
Equivalent equations (p. 109) Equations that have the same solution.	$a = 3$ and $3a = 9$ are equivalent equations.
Equivalent inequalities (p. 180) Equivalent inequalities have the same set of solutions.	$n < 2$ and $n + 3 < 5$ are equivalent inequalities.
Event (p. 36) In probability, any group of outcomes.	When rolling a number cube, there are six possible outcomes. Rolling an even number is an event with three possible outcomes: 2, 4, and 6.
Experimental probability (p. 36) The ratio of the number of times an event actually happens to the number of times the experiment is done. $P(\text{event}) = \frac{\text{number of times an event happens}}{\text{number of times the experiment is done}}$	A baseball player's batting average shows how likely it is that a player will get a hit based on previous times at bat.
Exponent (p. 15) In an expression of the form x^n, n is the exponent.	$3^4 = 3 \cdot 3 \cdot 3 \cdot 3$ The exponent 4 indicates that 3 is used as a factor four times.
Exponential decay (p. 373) For $a > 0$ and $0 < b < 1$, the function $y = ab^x$ models exponential decay. b is the decay factor.	$y = 5(0.1)^x$
Exponential function (p. 363) A function that repeatedly multiplies an initial amount by the same positive number. You can model all exponential functions using $y = ab^x$ where $b > 0$ and $b \neq 1$.	$y = 4.8(1.1)^x$
Exponential growth (p. 368) For $a > 0$ and $b > 1$, the function $y = ab^x$ models exponential growth. b is the growth factor.	$y = 100(2)^x$
Extraneous solution (p. 443) An apparent solution of an equation that does not satisfy the original equation.	$\frac{b}{b + 4} = 3 - \frac{4}{b + 4}$ Solving the equation by multiplying by $(b + 4)$ gives b as -4. Replacing b with -4 in the original equation makes the denominator 0, so -4 is an extraneous solution. The equation has no solution.

Glossary/Study Guide

F

Examples

Families of functions (p. 92) Similar functions can be grouped into families of functions. Some families of functions are linear functions, quadratic functions, and absolute value functions.

$y = 3x^2$, $y = -9x^2$, and $y = \frac{3}{4}x^2$ belong to the quadratic family of functions.

Favorable outcomes (p. 95) In a probability experiment, favorable outcomes are the possible results that you want to happen.

In a board game you advance more spaces if you roll an even number on a number cube. The favorable outcomes are 2, 4, and 6.

Function (p. 73) A relation that assigns exactly one value of the dependent variable to each value of the independent variable.

Earned income is a function of the number of hours worked. If you earn \$4.50/h, then your income is expressed by the function $f(n) = 4.5n$.

Function notation (p. 79) To write a rule in function notation, you use the symbol $f(x)$ in place of y.

$f(x) = 3x - 8$ is in function notation.

Function rule (p. 74) An equation that describes a function.

$y = 4x + 1$ is a function rule.

Histogram (p. 4) A bar graph that shows the frequency of data. The height of the bars shows the number of items in each interval.

The histogram shows the birth months of 27 students in one math class.

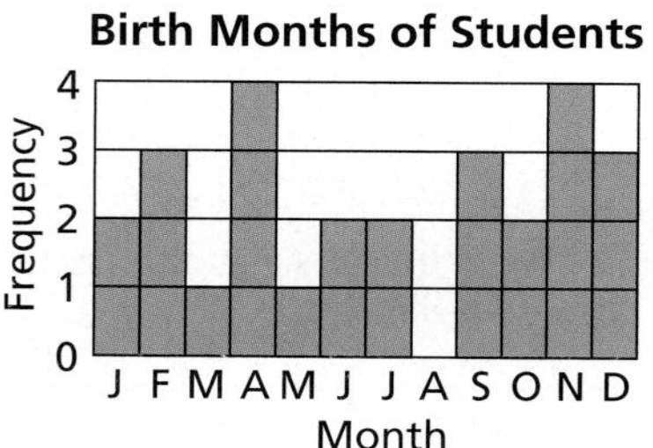

Hypotenuse (p. 414) In a right triangle, the side opposite the right angle. It is the longest side in the triangle.

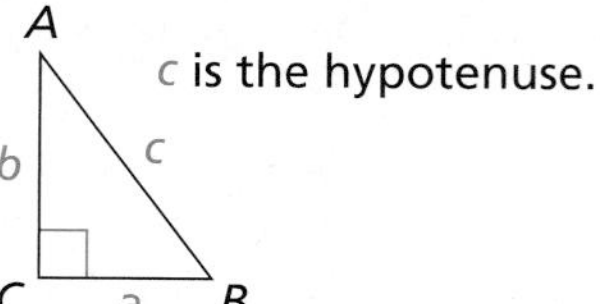

Identity (p. 166) An equation that is true for every value of the variable.

$5 - 14x = 5(1 - \frac{14}{5}x)$ is an identity because it is true for any value of x.

Examples

Identity Property of Addition (p. 35) The sum of any number and 0 is that number. For every real number a: $a + 0 = a$, $0 + a = a$.

$9 + 0 = 9, 0 + 9 = 9$

Identity Property of Multiplication (p. 35) The product of any number and 1 is that number. For every real number a: $a \cdot 1 = a, 1 \cdot a = a$.

$7 \cdot 1 = 7, 1 \cdot 7 = 7$

Impossible event (p. 96) An impossible event never happens, and has a probability of 0.

Getting a decimal when rolling a number cube is an impossible event.

Independent events (p. 134) Events are independent when the outcome of one does not affect the other.

Picking a colored marble from a bag, replacing it, and picking another are two independent events.

Independent variable (p. 69) A variable is independent if it does not depend on another variable.

In the function $y = -2x$, the value of x does not depend on the value of y.

Integers (p. 19) The whole numbers and their opposites.

$\ldots -3, -2, -1, 0, 1, 2, 3, \ldots$

Inverse operations (p. 108) Operations that undo one another are called inverse operations.

Addition and subtraction are inverse operations. Multiplication and division are inverse operations.

Inverse variation (p. 512) A function that can be written in the form $xy = k$ or $y = \frac{k}{x}$. The product of the quantities remains constant, so as one quantity increases, the other decreases.

The length x and the width y of a rectangle with a fixed area vary inversely. If the area is 40, $xy = 40$.

Irrational number (p. 30) A number that cannot be written as a ratio of two integers. Irrational numbers in decimal form are nonterminating and nonrepeating.

$\sqrt{11}$ and 3.141592653. . . are irrational numbers.

L

Legs of a right triangle (p. 414) The sides that form the right angle.

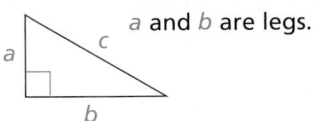

a and b are legs.

Like terms (p. 119) Terms with exactly the same variable factors in a variable expression.

$4y$ and $16y$ are like terms.

Examples

Line graph (p. 7) A graph that shows how a set of data changes over time.

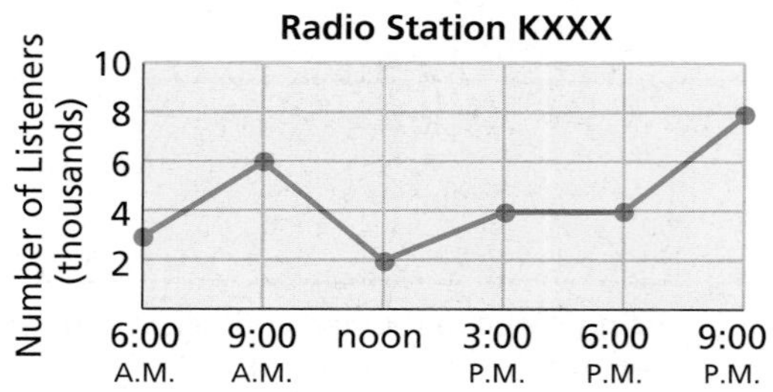

The line graph at the left shows the change in the number of listeners to station KXXX during the day.

Line of best fit (p. 242) The most accurate trend line showing the relationship between two sets of data. One way to find the line of best fit for two sets of data is to enter the data into a graphing calculator and then use the linear regression feature.

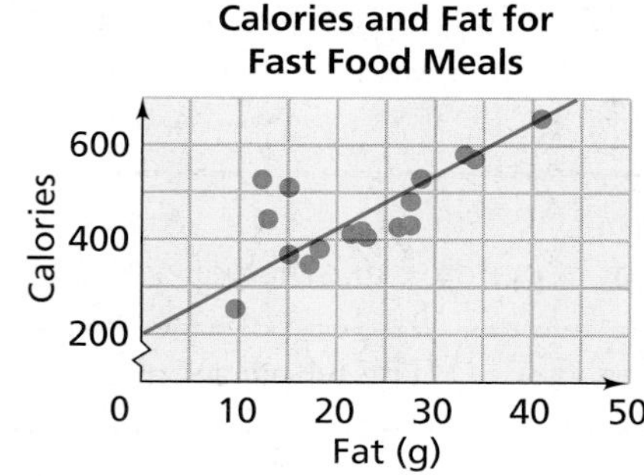

Line plot (p. 4) A graph that shows the number of times a data item appears.

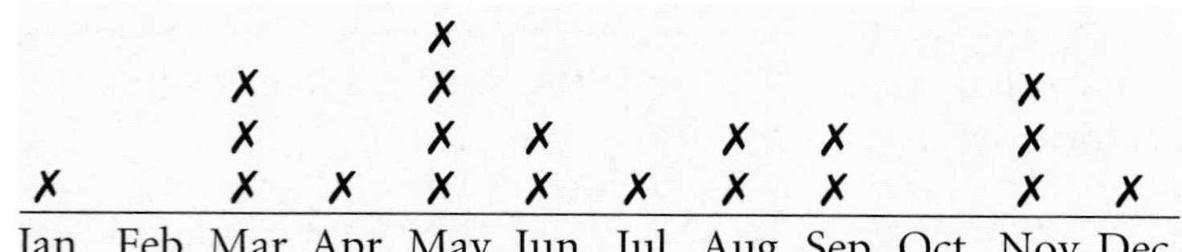

The line plot at the left shows the data collected on birth months for 20 people.

Linear function (pp. 92, 221) A function whose graph forms a straight line. Its rule is an equation that has 1 as the greatest power of x.

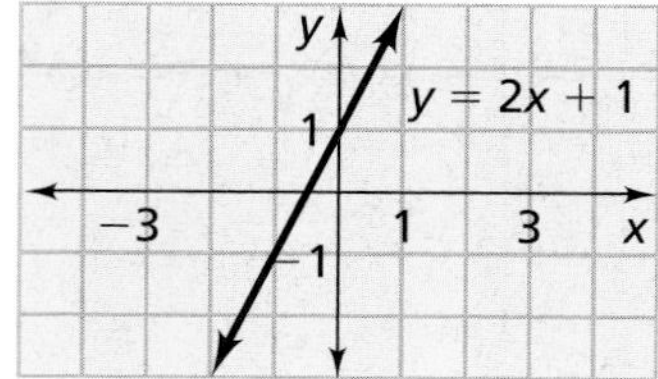

Linear inequality (p. 290) Describes a region of the coordinate plane that has a boundary line. Each point in the region is a solution of the inequality. A sign of $\leq$ or $\geq$ is represented by a solid boundary line. A sign of $<$ or $>$ is represented by a dashed boundary line.

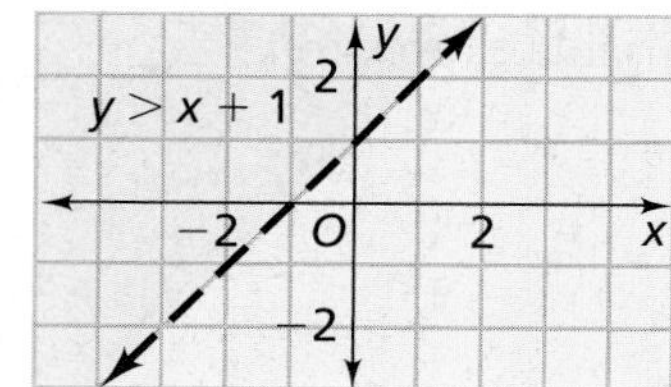

Examples

Linear programming (p. 300) A process that involves maximizing or minimizing a quantity. The quantity is expressed as the equation. Limits on the variables in the equation are called restrictions.

Example: Restrictions: $y \geq 1$, $x + y \leq 7$, and $y \leq x$
Equation: $B = 2x + 4y$
Graph the restrictions and find the coordinates of each vertex.
Evaluate $B = 2x + 4y$ at each vertex.
$B = 2(1) + 4(1) = 6$
$B = 2(3.5) + 4(3.5) = 21$
$B = 2(7) + 4(0) = 14$
The minimum value of B occurs at (1, 1).
The maximum value of B occurs at (3.5, 3.5).

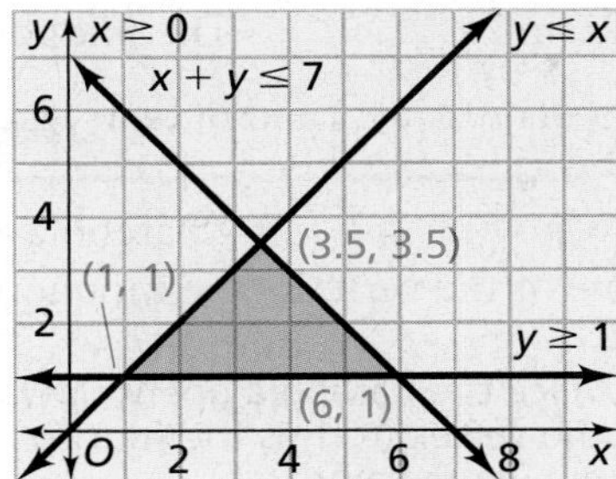

Literal equation (p. 176) An equation involving two or more variables.

$ax + b = c$ is a literal equation.

M

Matrix (p. 40) A rectangular arrangement of numbers. The number of rows and columns of a matrix determines its size. Each item in a matrix is an entry.

$\begin{bmatrix} 2 & 5 & 6.3 \\ -8 & 0 & -1 \end{bmatrix}$ is a 2×3 matrix.

Maximum value (p. 320) If a parabola opens downward, the y-coordinate of the vertex is the function's maximum value.

Example: Since the parabola opens downward, the y-coordinate of the vertex $(0, -2)$ is the function's maximum value. The maximum value is -2.

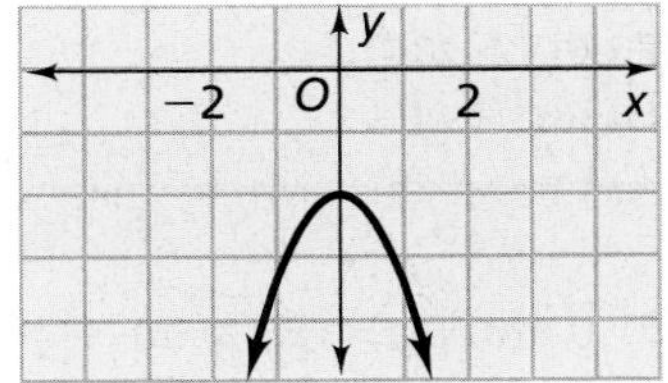

Mean (p. 5) To find the mean of a set of numbers, find the sum of the numbers and divide the sum by the number of items.

mean is $\frac{\text{sum of the data items}}{\text{number of data items}}$

In the set 12, 11, 12, 10, 13, 12, and 7, the mean is

$\frac{12 + 11 + 12 + 10 + 13 + 12 + 7}{7} = 11.$

Median (p. 5) The middle value in an ordered set of numbers.

In the set 7, 10, 11, 12, 15, 19, and 27, the median is 12.

Midpoint (p. 422) The point that divides a segment into two congruent segments.

M is the midpoint of $\overline{XY}$.

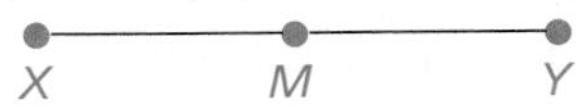

Examples

Midpoint Formula (p. 422) The midpoint M of a line segment with endpoints $A(x_1, y_1)$ and $B(x_2, y_2)$ is $\left(\frac{x_1 + x_2}{2}, \frac{y_1 + y_2}{2}\right)$.

The midpoint of a segment with endpoints $A(3, 5)$ and $B(7, 1)$ is $(5, 3)$.

Minimum value (p. 320) If a parabola opens upward, the y-coordinate of the vertex is the function's minimum value.

Example: Since the parabola opens upward, the y-coordinate of the vertex $(0, 1)$ is the function's minimum value. The minimum value is 1.

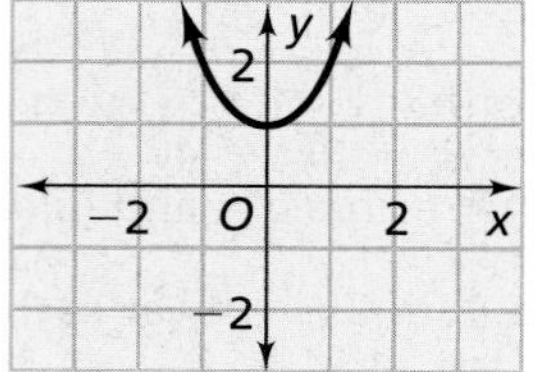

Mode (p. 4) The data item that occurs in a data set the greatest number of times. A data set may have no mode, one mode, or more than one mode.

In the data set 7, 7, 9, 10, 11, and 13, the mode is 7. The data set 5, 3, 2, 1.5, 9, 3, 6, 3, 2, 1, 4, 2 has two modes: 2 and 3.

Multiplicative inverse (p. 32) The multiplicative inverse, or reciprocal, of a nonzero number $\frac{a}{b}$ is $\frac{b}{a}$. The product of a nonzero number and its multiplicative inverse is 1.

$\frac{3}{4}$ is the multiplicative inverse of $\frac{4}{3}$ because $\frac{3}{4} \times \frac{4}{3} = 1$.

Multiplication Property of Inequality (p. 185) For all real numbers a and b, and for $c > 0$:
If $a > b$, then $ac > bc$.
If $a < b$, then $ac < bc$.
For all real numbers a and b, and for $c < 0$:
If $a > b$, then $ac < bc$.
If $a < b$, then $ac > bc$.

$5 > 1$, so $5(2) > 1(2)$.
$2 < 4$, so $2(3) < 4(3)$.
$-2 > -4$, so $-2(-5) < -4(-5)$.
$-2 < 6$, so $-2(-3) > 6(-3)$.

Multiplication Property of Square Roots (p. 430) For any numbers $a \geq 0$ and $b \geq 0$, $\sqrt{ab} = \sqrt{a} \cdot \sqrt{b}$.

$\sqrt{54} = \sqrt{9 \cdot 6} = \sqrt{9} \cdot \sqrt{6}$
$= 3 \cdot \sqrt{6} = 3\sqrt{6}$

N

Negative square root (p. 332) $-\sqrt{b}$ is the negative square root of b.

$-\sqrt{49} = -7$ is the negative square root of 49.

O

Opposites (p. 19) Two numbers are opposites, or additive inverses, if they are the same distance from zero on the number line. The sum of two opposites is 0.

-3 and 3 are opposites.
$-a$ is the opposite of a.

Examples

Order of operations (p. 15)
1. Perform any operation(s) inside grouping symbols.
2. Simplify any terms with exponents.
3. Multiply and divide in order from left to right.
4. Add and subtract in order from left to right.

$6 - (4^2 - [2 \cdot 5]) \div 3$
$= 6 - (4^2 - 10) \div 3$
$= 6 - (16 - 10) \div 3$
$= 6 - 6 \div 3$
$= 6 - 2$
$= 4$

Ordered pair (p. 58) An ordered pair of numbers identifies the location of a point on the coordinate plane.

The ordered pair $(4, -1)$ identifies the point 4 units to the right and 1 unit down from the origin.

Origin (p. 58) The axes of the coordinate plane intersect at the origin.

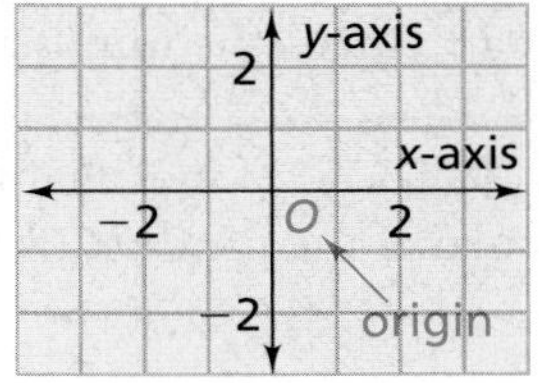

Outcomes (p. 95) The possible results of a probability experiment.

The outcomes of rolling a number cube are 1, 2, 3, 4, 5, and 6.

Parabola (p. 318) The graph of a quadratic function is a parabola.

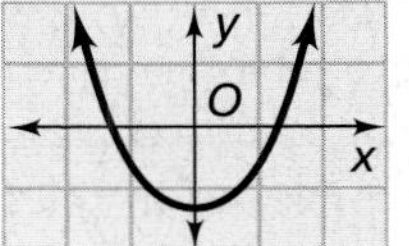

Parallel lines (p. 250) Two lines that are always the same distance apart. The lines do not intersect and have the same slope.

Example: Lines ℓ and m are parallel.

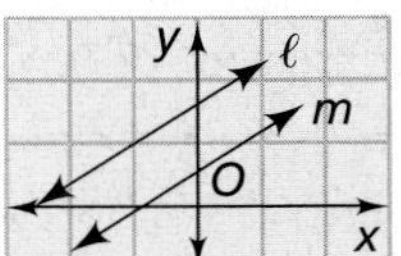

Percent of change (p. 146) The percent an amount changes from its original amount.
$\text{percent of change} = \frac{\text{amount of change}}{\text{original amount}}$

The price of a meal at a restaurant was \$7.95 last week; this week it is \$9.95.
$\text{percent of change} = \frac{9.95 - 7.95}{7.95} = \frac{2.00}{7.95}$
≈ 0.25 or 25%.

Percent of decrease (p. 147) When a value decreases from its original amount, you call the percent of change the percent of decrease.

The number of oranges in the bag decreased from 12 to 9.
$\text{percent of decrease} = \frac{3}{12} = 0.25$ or 25%

Percent of increase (p. 146) When a value increases from its original amount, you call the percent of change the percent of increase.

The average class size will increase from 30 to 33.
$\text{percent of increase} = \frac{3}{30} = 0.1$ or 10%

	Examples
Perfect square trinomial (p. 487) A trinomial whose factors are two identical binomials.	$x^2 + 6x + 9 = (x + 3)(x + 3)$ $= (x + 3)^2$
Perfect squares (p. 333) Numbers whose square roots are rational numbers.	The numbers 1, 4, 9, 16, 25, 36, . . . are perfect squares because they are the squares of integers.
Permutation (p. 539) An arrangement of some or all of a set of objects in a definite order. You can use the notation ${}_nP_r$ to express the number of permutations, where n equals the number of objects available and r equals the number of selections to make.	How many ways can 5 children be arranged three at a time? ${}_5P_3 = 5 \cdot 4 \cdot 3 = 60$ arrangements
Perpendicular lines (p. 251) Lines that form right angles. Two lines are perpendicular if the product of their slopes is -1.	Lines ℓ and m are perpendicular. 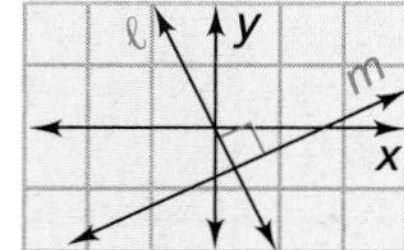
Point-slope form (p. 248) The point-slope form of a linear equation is $\frac{y - y_1}{x - x_1} = m$ where m is the slope and the point (x_1, y_1) is on the line.	
Polynomial (p. 465) A polynomial is one term or the sum or difference of two or more terms.	$2x^2$, $3x + 7$, 28, and $-7x^3 - 2x^2 + 9$ are all polynomials.
Power (p. 391) Any expression in the form a^n.	5^4
Principal square root (p. 332) For $b > 0$, the expression $\sqrt{b}$ is called the principal square root of b.	$\sqrt{25} = 5$ is the principal square root of 25.
Probability of two dependent events (p. 135) If A and B are dependent events, then $P(A \text{ and } B) = P(A) \cdot P(B \text{ after } A)$.	You have 4 red marbles and 3 white marbles. The probability that you select one red marble, and then, without replacing it, randomly select another red marble is $P(\text{red and red}) = \frac{4}{7} \cdot \frac{3}{6} = \frac{2}{7}$.
Probability of two independent events (p. 134) If A and B are independent events, you multiply the probabilities of the events to find the probability of both events occurring. $P(A \text{ and } B) = P(A) \cdot P(B)$	The probability of rolling a 1 on a number cube is $\frac{1}{6}$. The probability of rolling an even number on a number cube is $\frac{1}{2}$. The probability of rolling a 1 and then an even number is $P(1 \text{ and even number}) = \frac{1}{6} \cdot \frac{1}{2} = \frac{1}{12}$.

Examples

Properties of Equality (pp. 109, 110) For all real numbers a, b, and c:
Addition: If $a = b$, then $a + c = b + c$.
Subtraction: If $a = b$, then $a - c = b - c$.
Multiplication: If $a = b$, then $a \cdot c = b \cdot c$.
Division: If $a = b$, and $c \neq 0$, then $\frac{a}{c} = \frac{b}{c}$.

Since $\frac{2}{4} = \frac{1}{2}$, then $\frac{2}{4} + 5 = \frac{1}{2} + 5$.
Since $\frac{9}{3} = 3$, then $\frac{9}{3} - 6 = 3 - 6$.
Since $\frac{10}{5} = 2$, then $\frac{10}{5} \cdot 15 = 2 \cdot 15$.
Since $6 + 2 = 8$, then $\frac{6 + 2}{4} = \frac{8}{4}$.

Proportion (p. 158) A statement that two ratios are equal.

$\frac{2}{3} = \frac{10}{15}$ is a proportion.

Pythagorean theorem (p. 414) In a right triangle, the sum of the squares of the lengths of the legs is equal to the square of the length of the hypotenuse. $a^2 + b^2 = c^2$.

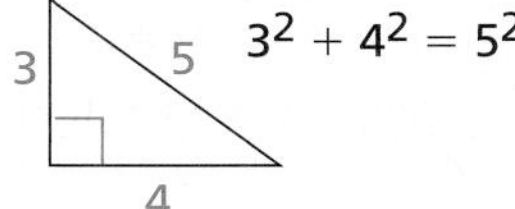

$3^2 + 4^2 = 5^2$

Quadrants (p. 58) The coordinate plane is divided by its axes into four quadrants.

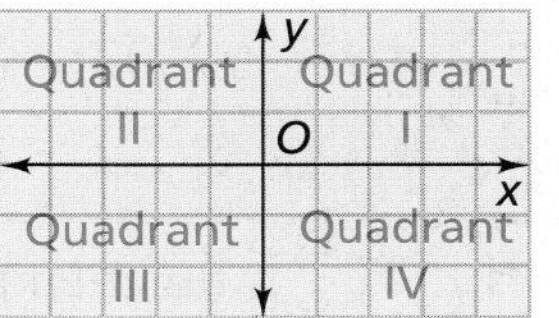

Quadratic equation (p. 337) An equation you can write in the form $ax^2 + bx + c = 0$, where a, b, and c are real numbers and $a \neq 0$.

$4x^2 + 9x - 5 = 0$

Quadratic Formula (p. 343) If $ax^2 + bx + c = 0$ and $a \neq 0$, then $x = \frac{-b \pm \sqrt{b^2 - 4ac}}{2a}$.

$2x^2 + 10x + 12 = 0$

$x = \frac{-b \pm \sqrt{b^2 - 4ac}}{2a}$

$x = \frac{-10 \pm \sqrt{10^2 - 4(2)(12)}}{2(2)}$

$x = \frac{-10 \pm \sqrt{4}}{4}$

$x = \frac{-10 + 2}{4}$ or $\frac{-10 - 2}{4}$

$x = -2$ or $x = -3$

Quadratic function (pp. 92, 319) A function with an equation of the form $y = ax^2 + bx + c$, where $a \neq 0$. The graph of a quadratic function is a parabola, which is a U-shaped curve that opens up or down.

$y = 5x^2 - 2x + 1$

Examples

R

Term	Examples
Radical equation (p. 440) An equation that has a variable under a radical.	$\sqrt{x} - 2 = 12$
Range (p. 74) The set of all possible output values of a function.	In the function $f(x) = \lvert x \rvert$, the range is the set of all positive numbers and 0.
Rate of change (p. 220) Allows you to see the relationship between two quantities that are changing. The rate of change is also called slope. Rate of change $= \frac{\text{change in dependent variable}}{\text{change in independent variable}}$	Video rental for 1 day is \$1.99. Video rental for 2 days is \$2.99. rate of change $= \frac{2.99 - 1.99}{2 - 1} = \frac{1.00}{1} = 1$
Ratio (p. 158) A comparison of two numbers by division.	$\frac{5}{7}$ and 7 : 3 are ratios.
Rational expression (p. 522) An expression that can be written in the form $\frac{\text{polynomial}}{\text{polynomial}}$. The value of the variable cannot make the denominator equal to 0.	$\frac{3}{x^2 - 4}$, $x \neq 2, -2$.
Rational function (p. 520) A function that can be written in the form $f(x) = \frac{\text{polynomial}}{\text{polynomial}}$. The value of the variable cannot make the denominator equal to 0.	$y = \frac{x}{x - 5}, x \neq 5$
Rational number (p. 30) A real number that can be written as a ratio of two integers. Rational numbers in decimal form are terminating or repeating.	$\frac{2}{3}$, 1.548, and 2.292929. . . are all rational numbers.
Rationalize the denominator (p. 432) Make the denominator of a fraction a rational number without changing the value of the expression.	$\frac{2}{\sqrt{5}} = \frac{2}{\sqrt{5}} \cdot \frac{\sqrt{5}}{\sqrt{5}} = \frac{2\sqrt{5}}{\sqrt{25}} = \frac{2\sqrt{5}}{5}$
Real number (p. 30) A number that is either rational or irrational.	5, –3, $\sqrt{5}$, 9.2, –0.666. . . , $5\frac{4}{11}$, 0, π, and $\frac{15}{2}$ are all real numbers.
Reciprocal (p. 32) The reciprocal, or multiplicative inverse, of a nonzero number $\frac{a}{b}$ is $\frac{b}{a}$. The product of a nonzero number and its reciprocal is 1. Zero does not have a reciprocal.	$\frac{2}{5}$ and $\frac{5}{2}$ are reciprocals because $\frac{2}{5} \times \frac{5}{2} = 1$.
Relation (p. 73) Any set of ordered pairs.	{(0, 0), (2, 3), (2, –7)} is a relation.
Replacement set (p. 202) The set of possible values for the variable in an inequality.	When the replacement set is all integers, the solution of the inequality $x > -2.5$ is {–2, –1, 0, 2, . . . }.

S

Examples

Sample space (p. 97) The set of all possible outcomes of an event.

When tossing two coins one at a time, the sample space is (H,H), (T,T), (H,T), (T,H).

Scatter plot (p. 59) A graph that relates data of two different sets. The two sets of data are displayed as ordered pairs.

Example: The scatter plot displays the amounts various companies spent on advertising versus product sales.

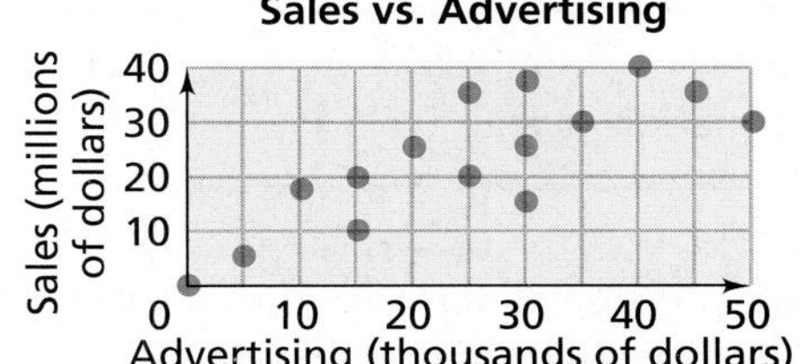

Scientific notation (p. 385) A number expressed in the form $a \times 10^n$, where n is an integer and $1 \leq a < 10$.

3.4×10^6

Similar figures (p. 159) Figures that have the same shape, but not necessarily the same size.

$\triangle DEF$ and $\triangle GHI$ are similar.

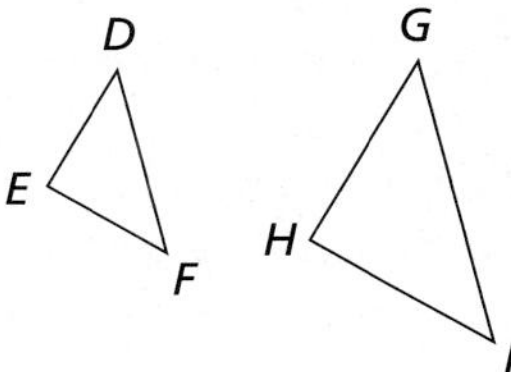

Simple interest (p. 141) Calculated using the formula $I = prt$, where p is the principal, r is the rate of interest per year, and t is the time in years.

The simple interest on \$200 with an annual rate of interest of 4% for 3 years is $I = prt = 200\ (0.04)\ (3) = 24$. The simple interest is \$24.

Simulation (p. 37) A simulation is a model of a real-life situation.

A random number table can be used to simulate many situations.

Sine (p. 425) In $\triangle ABC$ with right $\angle C$,

$$\text{sine of } \angle A = \frac{\text{length of side opposite } \angle A}{\text{length of hypotenuse}}, \text{ or } \sin A = \frac{a}{c}.$$

$\sin A = \frac{4}{5}$

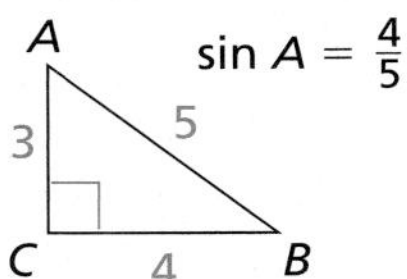

Slope (p. 220) The measure of the steepness of a line. The ratio of the vertical change to the horizontal change.

$$\text{Slope} = \frac{\text{vertical change}}{\text{horizontal change}} = \frac{y_2 - y_1}{x_2 - x_1}, \text{ where } x_2 - x_1 \neq 0$$

The slope of the line is $\frac{2 - 0}{4 - 0} = \frac{1}{2}$.

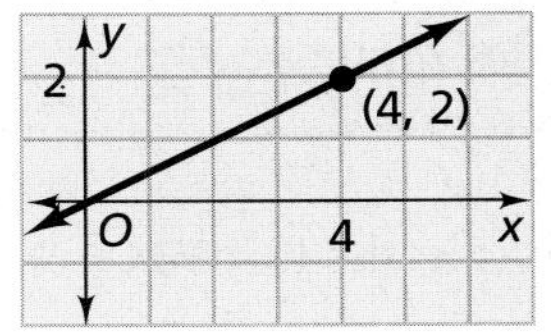

Examples

Slope-intercept form (p. 231) The slope-intercept form of a linear equation is $y = mx + b$ where m is the slope and b is the y-intercept.

$y = 8x + 2$

Solution of an equation (p. 108) Any value or values that make the equation true.

For the equation $y + 22 = 11$, the solution is -11.

Solution, no (pp. 165, 192, 271) (1) An equation has no solution if no value makes the statement true.

$2a + 3 = 2a + 5$

(2) An inequality has no solution if it is false for all values of the variable.

$4n + 1 > 4n + 7$

(3) A linear system has no solution if the graphs of the equations in the system are parallel.

$y = 3x + 9$ and $y = 3x + 28$

Solution of an inequality (p. 179) Any value or values of a variable in the inequality that makes an inequality true.

The solution of the inequality $x < 9$ is all numbers less than 9.

Solutions, infinitely many (p. 271) A linear system has infinitely many solutions when the equations are equivalent.

$2y = x + 7$ and $6y = 3x + 21$

Spreadsheet (p. 45) A table used in computer programs that contains numbers, text, or formulas in its cells.

In the spreadsheet, column C and row 2 meet at the shaded box, cell C2. The value in cell C2 is 2.75.

	A	B	C	D	E
1	0.50	0.70	0.60	0.50	2.30
2	1.50	0.50	2.75	2.50	7.25

Square root (p. 332) If $a^2 = b$, then a is a square root of b. $\sqrt{b}$ is the principal (positive) square root. $-\sqrt{b}$ is the negative square root.

-3 and 3 are square roots of 9. $\sqrt{9} = 3$; $-\sqrt{9} = -3$.

Standard deviation (p. 452) Shows how spread out a set of data is from the mean.

The standard deviation for the data set {2, 12, 6, 10, 9} is about 3.49.

Standard form of a polynomial (p. 465) When the degree of the terms in a polynomial decrease from left to right, it is in standard form, or descending order.

$15x^3 + x^2 + 3x - 9$

Standard form of a quadratic equation (p. 319) When a quadratic equation is in the form $ax^2 + bx + c = 0$.

$-x^2 + 2x + 9 = 0$

Examples

Stem-and-leaf plot (p. 10) A stem-and-leaf plot displays data items in order. A leaf is a data item's last digit on the right. A stem represents the digits to the left of the leaf.

This stem-and-leaf plot displays recorded times in a race. The stem records the whole number of seconds. The leaves represents tenths of a second. So, 27|7 represents 27.7 seconds.

stem	leaves
27	7
28	5 6 8
29	6 9
30	8

stem ⟶ 29 | 6 9 ⟵ leaves

Subtraction Property of Inequality (p. 181) For all real numbers a, b, and c, if $a > b$, then $a - c > b - c$ and if $a < b$, then $a - c < b - c$.

$5 > 2$, so $5 - 4 > 2 - 4$.
$9 < 13$, so $9 - 3 < 13 - 3$.

System of linear equations (p. 269) Two or more linear equations for which a common solution is sought.

$y = 5x + 7, y = \frac{1}{2}x - 3$

System of linear inequalities (p. 295) Two or more linear inequalities for which common solutions are sought.

$y \leq x + 11, y < 5x$

T

Tangent (p. 425) In $\triangle ABC$ with right $\angle C$,

$$\text{tangent of } \angle A = \frac{\text{length of side opposite } \angle A}{\text{length of side adjacent to } \angle A}, \text{ or } \tan A = \frac{a}{b}.$$

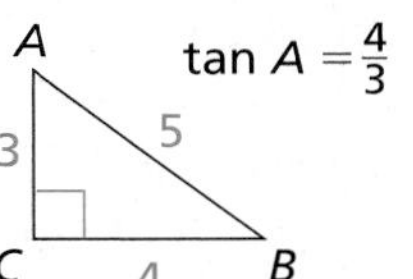

$\tan A = \frac{4}{3}$

Term (p. 11) A number, variable, or the product of numbers and variables.

The expression $5x + \frac{1}{2}y - 8$ has three terms: $5x$, $\frac{1}{2}y$, and -8.

Theoretical probability (p. 95) If each outcome has an equally likely chance of happening, you can find the theoretical probability of an event using the ratio of the number of favorable outcomes to the number of possible outcomes.

$$P(\text{event}) = \frac{\text{number of favorable outcomes}}{\text{number of possible outcomes}}$$

In tossing a coin the chance of getting heads or tails is equally likely. The probability of getting heads is $P(\text{heads}) = \frac{1}{2}$.

Examples

Tree diagram (p. 97) A diagram that shows all possible outcomes in a probability experiment.

Example: The tree diagram shows the 4 possible outcomes for tossing two coins one at a time: (H,H), (H,T), (T,H), (T,T).

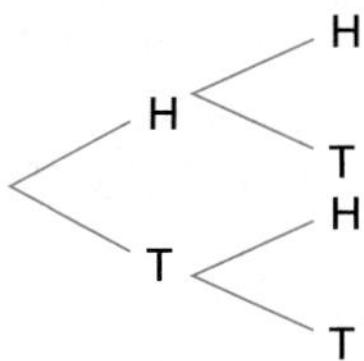

Trend line (p. 60) A line on a scatter plot that can be drawn near the points. It shows a correlation between two sets of data.

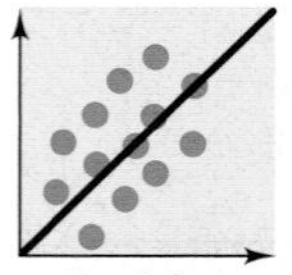
Positive

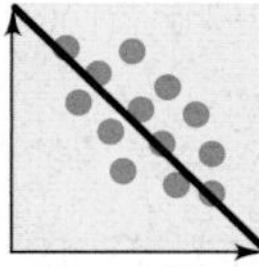
Negative

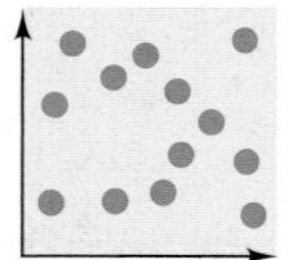
No Correlation

Trigonometric ratios (p. 425) See cosine, sine, and tangent.

Two-step equation (p. 114) An equation that has two operations.

$5x - 4 = 1$ is a two-step equation.

V

Variable (p. 11) A letter used to stand for one or more numbers.

x is a variable in the expression $9 - x$.

Variable expression (p. 11) A mathematical phrase that contains at least one variable.

$7 + x$ is a variable expression.

Vertex (p. 320) The highest point of a parabola that opens downward and the lowest point of a parabola that opens upward. The vertex is the point where the axis of symmetry intersects the parabola.

The vertex of the parabola is $(-1, -1)$.

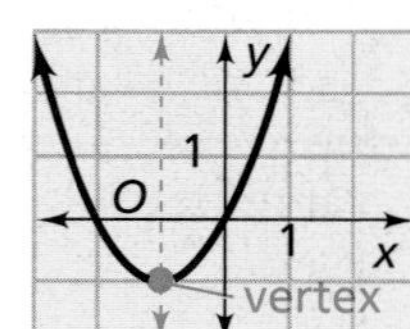

Vertical-line test (p. 75) A method used to determine if a relation is a function or not. If a vertical line passes through a graph more than once, the graph is not the graph of a function.

Vertical motion formula (p. 344) When an object is dropped or thrown straight up or down, you can use the vertical-motion formula to find the height of the object.

$h = -16t^2 + vt + s$, where h is the height of the object in feet, t is the time the object is in motion in seconds, v is the initial velocity in feet per second, and s is the starting height in feet.

An object is thrown straight up with a starting velocity of 36 ft/s. It is thrown from a height of 10 ft. The formula $h = -16t^2 + 36t + 10$ describes the height h of the object after t seconds.

W

Examples

Whole numbers (p. 19) Whole numbers are the nonnegative integers.

0, 1, 2, 3, . . .

X

x-axis (p. 58) The horizontal axis of the coordinate plane.

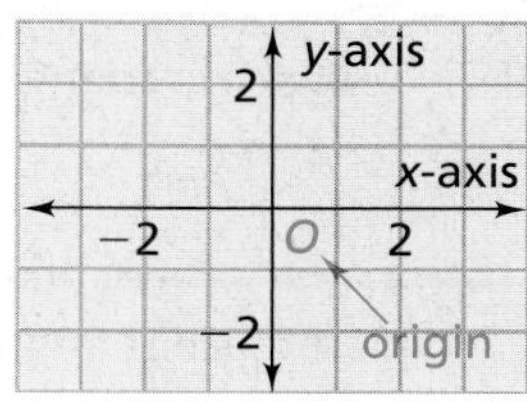

x-coordinate (p. 58) The first number of an ordered pair; indicates the distance left or right from the y-axis.

In the ordered pair $(4, -1)$, 4 is the x-coordinate.

x-intercept (p. 246) The x-coordinate of the point where a line crosses the x-axis.

The x-intercept of $3x + 4y = 12$ is 4.

Y

y-axis (p. 58) The vertical axis of the coordinate plane.

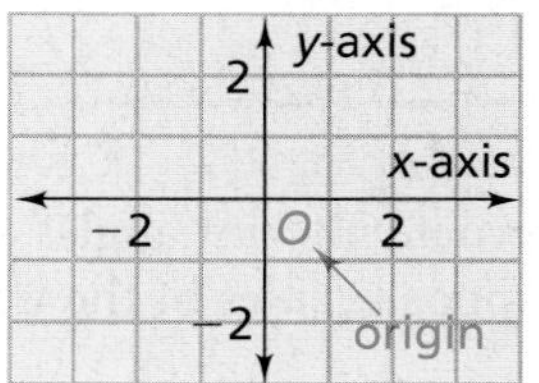

y-coordinate (p. 58) The second number of an ordered pair; indicates the distance above or below the x-axis.

In the ordered pair $(4, -1)$, -1 is the y-coordinate.

y-intercept (p. 230) The y-coordinate of the point where a line crosses the y-axis.

The y-intercept of $y = 5x + 2$ is 2.

Z

Zero pairs (p. 20) ▢■ is a zero pair.

Zero-product property (p. 491) For all real numbers a and b, if $ab = 0$, then $a = 0$ or $b = 0$.

$x(x + 3) = 0$
$x = 0$ or $x + 3 = 0$
$x = 0$ or $x = -3$

A

Examples

Acute angle (p. 589) An acute angle is an angle whose measure is between 0 and 90.

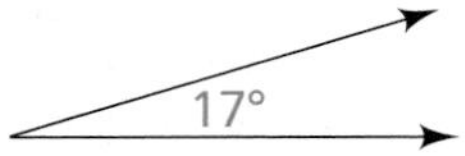

17°

Acute triangle (p. 633) An acute triangle has three acute angles.

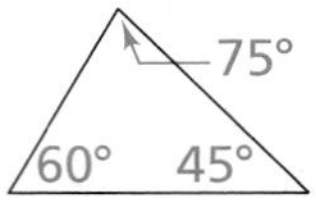

75° 60° 45°

Adjacent angles (p. 610) Adjacent angles are two coplanar angles that have a common side and a common vertex but no common interior points.

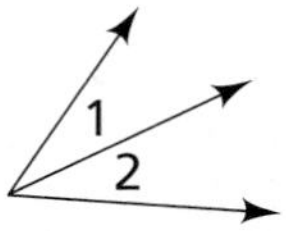

$\angle 1$ and $\angle 2$ are adjacent.

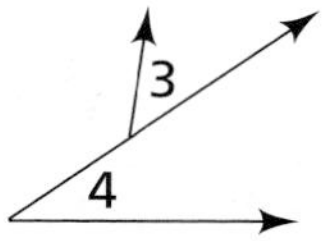

$\angle 3$ and $\angle 4$ are *not* adjacent.

Adjacent arcs (p. 660) Adjacent arcs are on the same circle and have exactly one point in common.

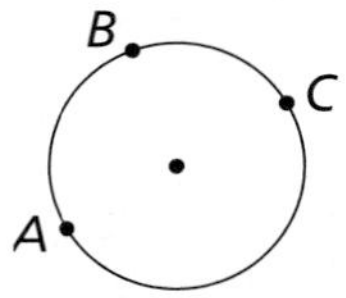

$\overset{\frown}{AB}$ and $\overset{\frown}{BC}$ are adjacent arcs.

Alternate interior angles (p. 929) Given two lines and a transversal, the alternate interior angles are nonadjacent interior angles that lie on opposite sides of the transversal.

Example: $\angle 1$ and $\angle 2$ are alternate interior angles, as are $\angle 3$ and $\angle 4$.

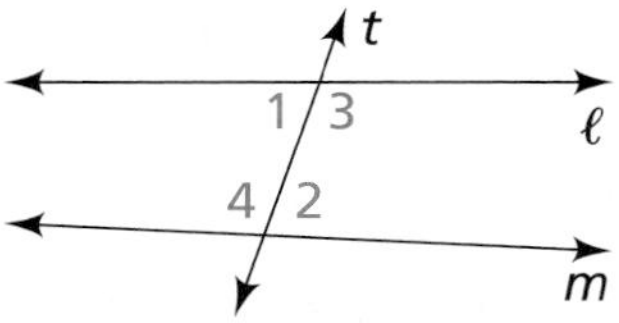

Altitude See *cone, cylinder, parallelogram, prism, pyramid,* and *trapezoid.*

Altitude of a triangle (p. 791) An altitude of a triangle is a perpendicular segment from a vertex to the line containing the side opposite that vertex.

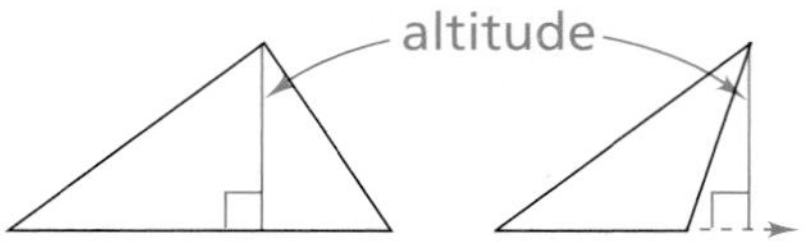

altitude

Angle (p. 588) An angle is formed by two rays with the same endpoint. The rays are the *sides* of the angle and the common endpoint is the *vertex* of the angle.

Example: This angle could be named $\angle A$, $\angle BAC$, or $\angle CAB$.

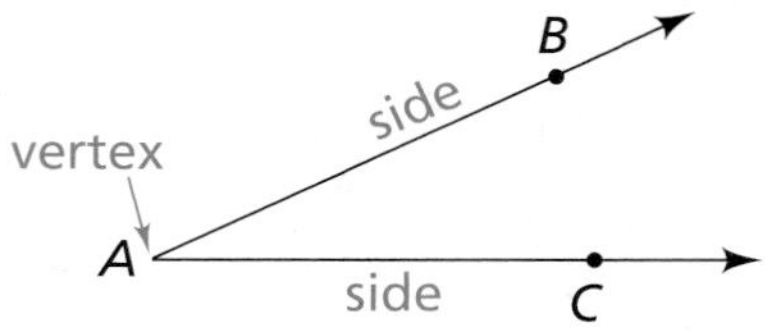

vertex A side B side C

Examples

Angle bisector (p. 596) An angle bisector is a ray that divides an angle into two congruent angles.

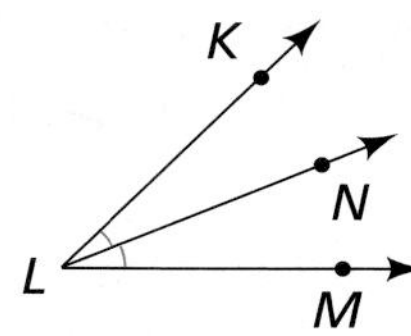

$\overrightarrow{LN}$ bisects $\angle KLM$.
$\angle KLN \cong \angle NLM$.

Angle of elevation or depression (p. 968) If B is above A, then the angle of elevation from A to B is the acute angle formed by $\overrightarrow{AB}$ and a horizontal line through A. The angle of depression from B to A is the acute angle formed by $\overrightarrow{BA}$ and a horizontal line through B.

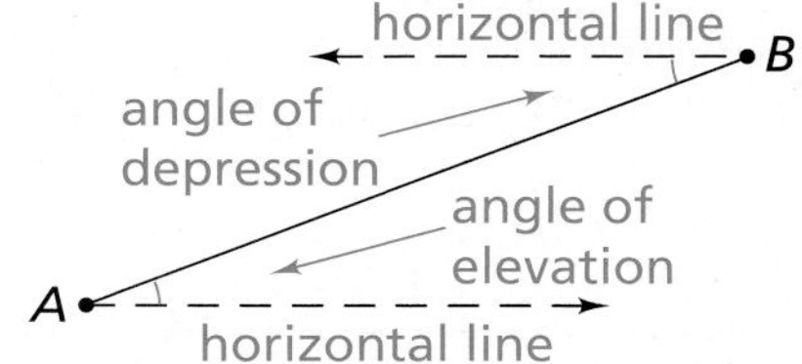

Apothem (p. 836) The apothem of a regular polygon is the distance from the center to a side.

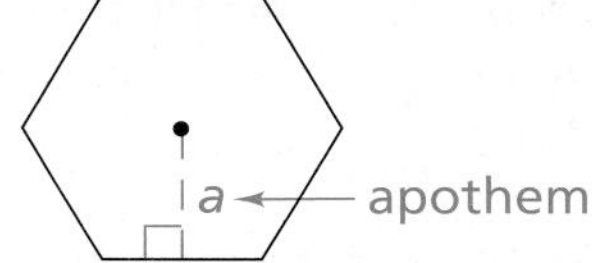

Arc (p. 660) An arc is part of a circle. See also *arc length, major arc, measure of an arc, minor arc,* and *semicircle.*

Arc length (p. 843) The length of an arc of a circle is the product of the ratio $\frac{\text{measure of the arc}}{360}$ and the circumference of the circle.

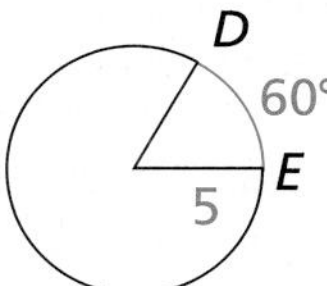

Example: length of $\widehat{DE} = \frac{60}{360} \cdot 2\pi(5) = \frac{5\pi}{3}$

Area (pp. 805–806, 811–813, 831, 847) The area of a plane figure is the number of square units enclosed by the figure.

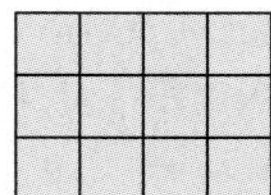

The area of the rectangle is 12 square units, or 12 unit^2.

Axes (p. 616) See *coordinate plane.*

B

Base(s) See *cone, cylinder, isosceles triangle, parallelogram, prism, pyramid, trapezoid,* and *triangle.*

Base angle See *isosceles trapezoid* and *isosceles triangle.*

Biconditional (p. 745) A conditional statement and its converse can be combined to form a biconditional statement. A biconditional contains the words "if and only if."

This biconditional statement is true: Two angles are congruent *if and only if* they have the same measure.

Examples

Bisector See *segment bisector* and *angle bisector.*

Center See *circle, dilation, regular polygon,* and *sphere.*

Central angle of a circle (p. 659) A central angle of a circle is an angle whose vertex is the center of the circle.

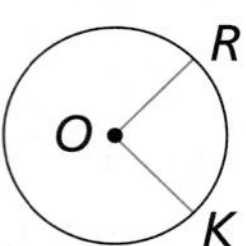

$\angle ROK$ is a central angle of $\odot O$.

Circle (p. 658) A circle is the set of all points in a plane that are a given distance, the *radius,* from a given point, the *center.* The standard form for an equation of a circle with center (h, k) and radius r is $(x - h)^2 + (y - k)^2 = r^2$.

Example: The equation of the circle whose center is (1, 3) and whose radius is 3 is $(x - 1)^2 + (y - 3)^2 = 9$.

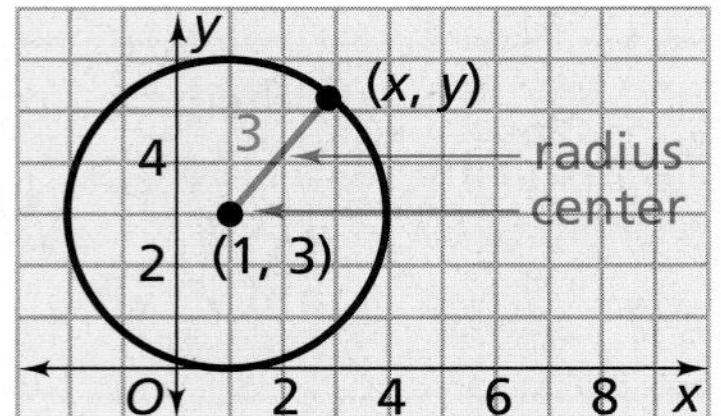

Circumference of a circle (p. 841) The circumference of a circle is the distance around the circle. Given the radius r of a circle, you can find its circumference C by using the formula $C = 2\pi r$.

$C = 2\pi r$
$= 2\pi(4)$
$= 8\pi$

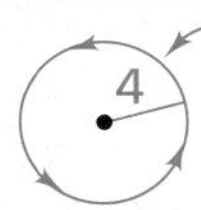

Circumference is distance around the circle.

Circumference of a sphere (p. 902) See *sphere.*

Circumscribe (p. 790) A circle is circumscribed about a polygon if the vertices of the polygon are on the circle.
A polygon is circumscribed about a circle if all the sides of the polygon are tangent to the circle.

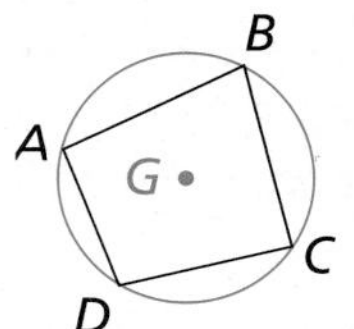

$\odot G$ is circumscribed about $ABCD$.

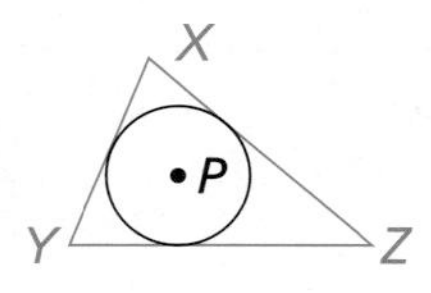

$\triangle XYZ$ is circumscribed about $\odot P$.

Collinear (p. 575) Collinear points lie on the same line.

Example: Points A, B, and C are collinear, but points A, B, and Z are noncollinear.

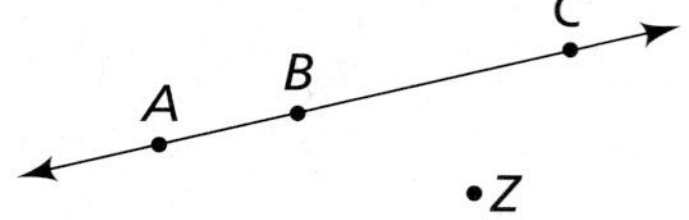

Examples

Complementary angles (p. 610) Two angles are complementary angles if the sum of their measures is 90.

Example: ∠*HKI* and ∠*IKJ* are complementary angles, as are ∠*HKI* and ∠*EFG*.

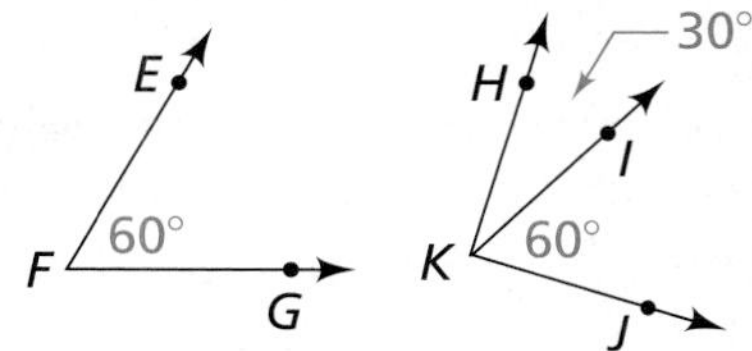

Composition of transformations (p. 697) A composition of two transformations is a transformation in which the second transformation is performed on the image of the first.

Example: If you reflect △*ABC* in line *m* to get △*A′B′C′* and then reflect △*A′B′C′* in line *n* to get △*A″B″C″*, you perform a composition of transformations.

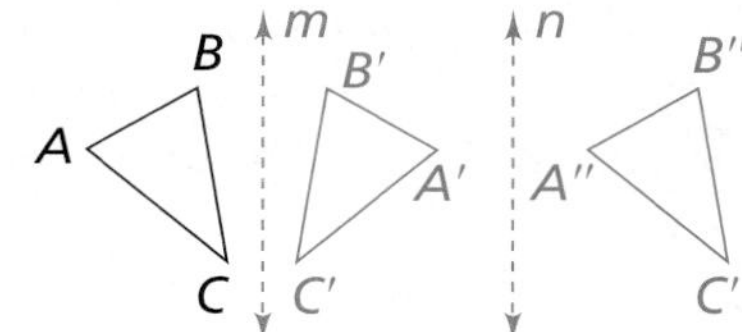

Concave polygon (p. 638) See *polygon.*

Concentric circles (p. 842) Concentric circles lie in the same plane and have the same center.

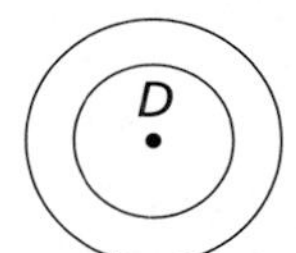

The two circles both have center *D* and are therefore concentric.

Conclusion (p. 744) In an *if-then statement* (conditional), the conclusion is the part that follows *then.*

In the statement, "If it rains, then I will go outside," the *conclusion* is "I will go outside."

Concurrent (p. 789) Concurrent lines are three or more lines that meet at one point. The point at which they meet is the *point of concurrency.*

Example: Point *E* is the point of concurrency of the bisectors of the angles of △*ABC*. The bisectors are concurrent.

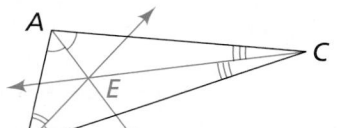

Conditional (p. 744) A conditional is an *if-then statement.*

If you act politely, *then* you will earn respect.

Cone (p. 880) A cone is a three-dimensional figure that has a circular *base,* a *vertex* not in the plane of the circle, and a curved lateral surface, as shown in the diagram. The *altitude* of a cone is the perpendicular segment from the vertex to the plane of the base. The *height* is the length of the altitude. A *right cone* is a cone in which the altitude contains the center of the base. The *slant height* of a right cone is the distance from the vertex to the edge of the base.

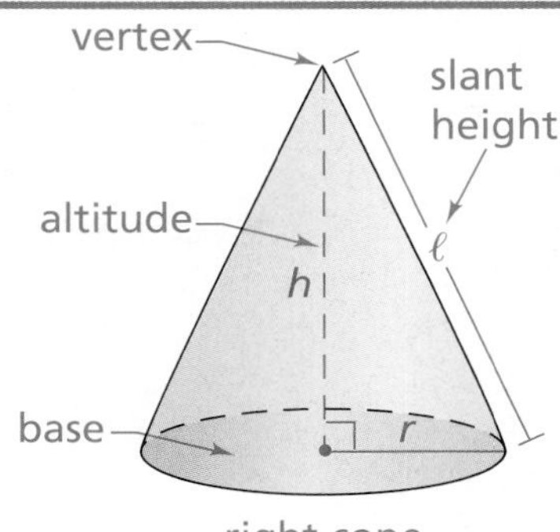

right cone

Examples

Congruence transformation (p. 686) See *isometry.*

Congruent angles (p. 590) Two angles are congruent if they have the same measure.

Example: $m\angle J = m\angle K$, so $\angle J \cong \angle K$.

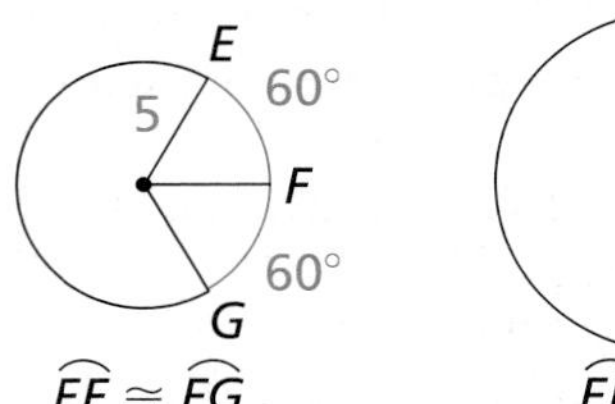

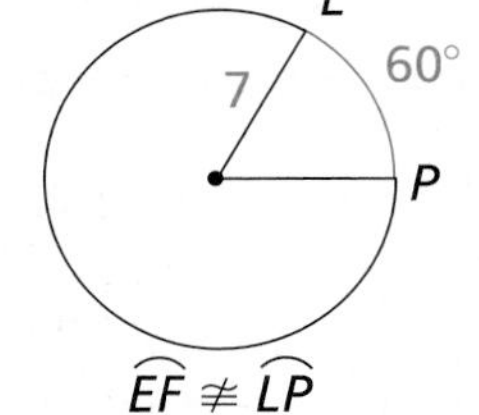

Congruent arcs (p. 843) Two arcs are congruent if they have the same measure and are in the same circle or congruent circles.

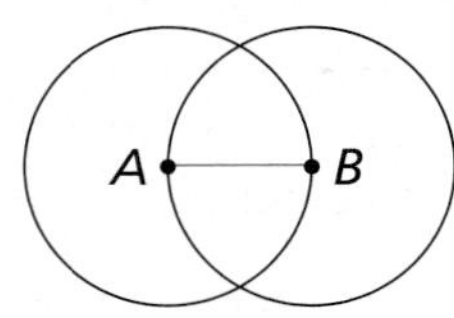

$\widehat{EF} \cong \widehat{FG}$

L

60°

7

P

$\widehat{EF} \ncong \widehat{LP}$

Congruent circles (p. 664) Two circles are congruent if their radii are congruent.

A B

$\odot A$ and $\odot B$ have the same radius, so $\odot A \cong \odot B$.

Congruent polygons (p. 664) Two polygons are congruent if their corresponding sides are congruent and their corresponding angles are congruent.

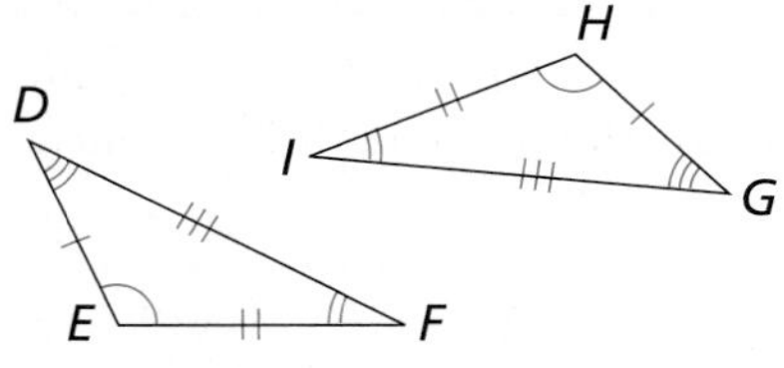

$\triangle DEF \cong \triangle GHI$

Congruent segments (p. 587) Two segments are congruent if they have the same length.

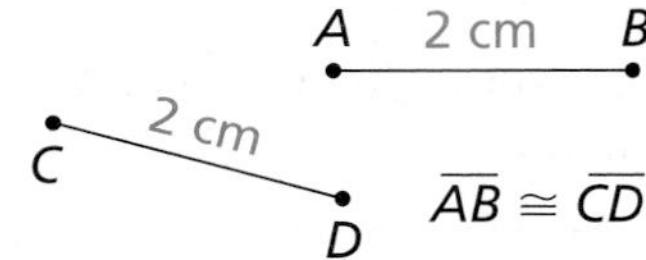

$\overline{AB} \cong \overline{CD}$

Conjecture (p. 567) A conjecture is a conclusion reached by using inductive reasoning.

As you walk down the street, you see many people holding unopened umbrellas. You make the conjecture that the forecast must call for rain.

Examples

Construction (p. 601) A construction involves using only a straightedge and compass to make geometric figures. A *straightedge* is a ruler with no markings on it. A *compass* is a tool used to draw circles and arcs.

Example: The diagram shows the construction of a line perpendicular to a line ℓ through a point P on ℓ.

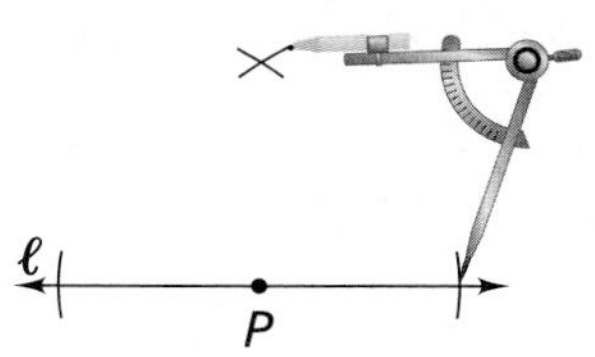

Contrapositive (p. 746) The contrapositive of the conditional "if p, then q" is the conditional "if not q, then not p." A conditional and its contrapositive always have the same truth value.

Conditional: If a figure is a triangle, then it is a polygon.

Contrapositive: If a figure is not a polygon, then it is not a triangle.

Converse (p. 745) The converse of the conditional "if p, then q" is the conditional "if q, then p."

Conditional: If you live in Cheyenne, then you live in Wyoming.

Converse: If you live in Wyoming, then you live in Cheyenne.

Convex polygon (p. 638) See *polygon.*

Coordinate(s) of a point (pp. 587, 616) The coordinate of a point on a number line is its distance and direction from the origin. The coordinates of a point on the coordinate plane are in the form (x, y), where x is the *x-coordinate* and y is the *y-coordinate.*

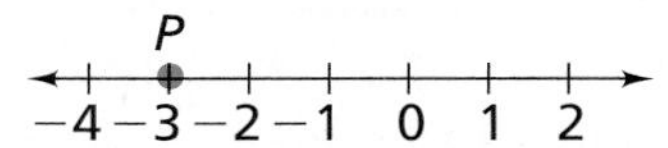

The coordinate of P is -3.

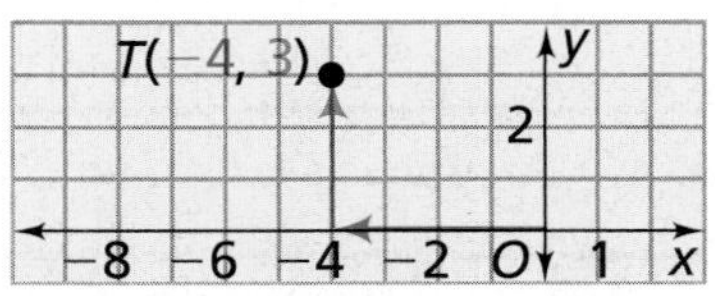

The coordinates of T are $(-4, 3)$.

Coordinate plane (p. 616) The coordinate plane is formed by two number lines, called the *axes,* intersecting at right angles. The *x-axis* is the horizontal axis, and the *y-axis* is the vertical axis. The two axes meet at the *origin,* $O(0, 0)$. The axes divide the plane into four *quadrants.*

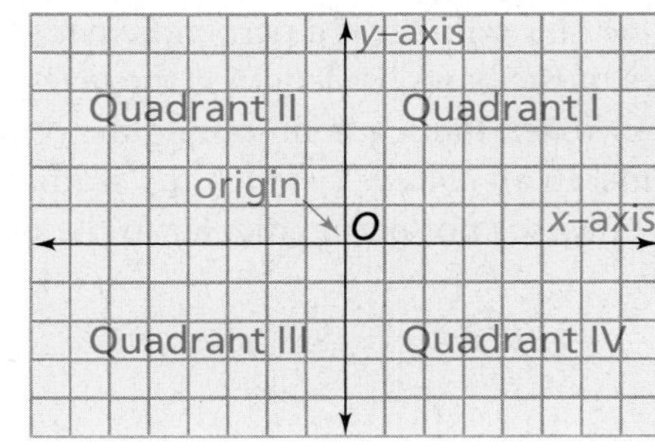

Examples

Coordinate proof (p. 763) See *proof.*

Coplanar (p. 575) Points and lines in the same plane are coplanar.

Example: Point *C* and $\overleftrightarrow{AB}$ are coplanar but points *A, B, C,* and *Q* are noncoplanar.

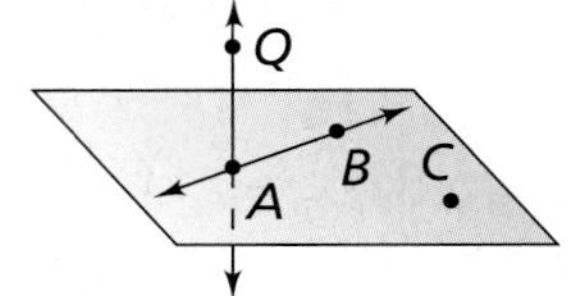

Corollary (p. 632) A corollary is a statement that follows directly from a theorem.

Theorem: If two sides of a triangle are congruent, then the angles opposite those sides are congruent.

Corollary: If a triangle is equilateral, then it is equiangular.

Corresponding angles (p. 929) Corresponding angles lie on the same side of the transversal *t* and in corresponding positions relative to ℓ and *m.*

Example: ∠1 and ∠2 are corresponding angles, as are ∠3 and ∠4, ∠5 and ∠6, and ∠7 and ∠8.

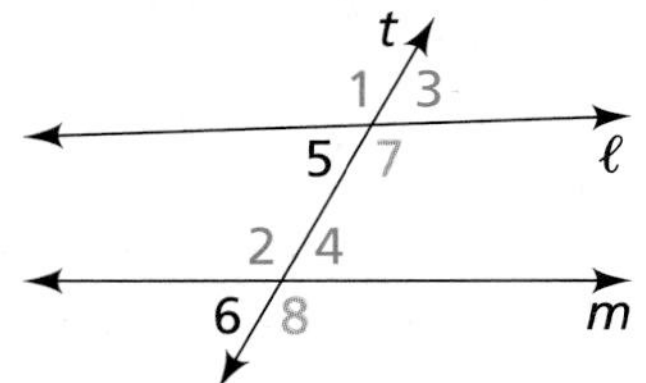

Counterexample (p. 744) A counterexample to a statement is a particular example or instance of the statement that is not true.

Statement: If you live in a state that begins with W, then you live in a state that does not border an ocean.

Counterexample: Washington

Cube (p. 872) A cube is a prism with all square faces.

Cylinder (p. 872) A cylinder is a three-dimensional figure with two congruent circular *bases* that lie in parallel planes. An *altitude* of a cylinder is a perpendicular segment that joins the planes of the bases. Its length is the *height* of the cylinder. In a *right cylinder,* the segment joining the centers of the bases is an altitude. In an *oblique cylinder,* the segment joining the centers of the bases is not perpendicular to the planes containing the bases.

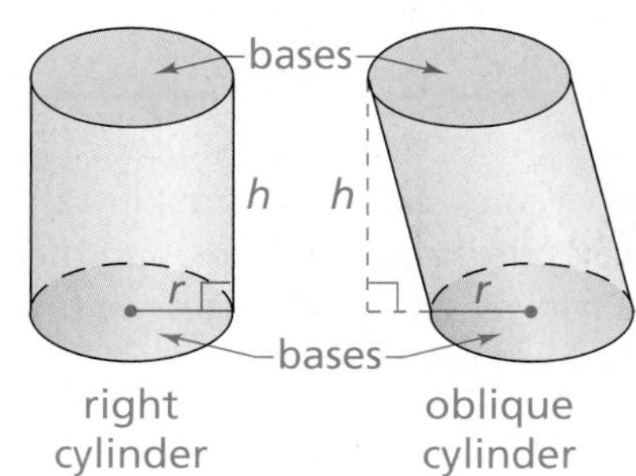

D

Examples

Decagon (p. 638) A decagon is a polygon with ten sides.

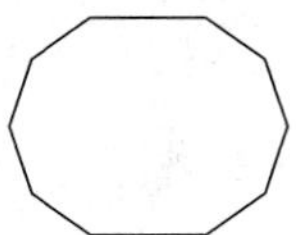

Deductive reasoning (p. 608) Deductive reasoning is a process of reasoning logically from given facts to a conclusion.

Based on the fact that the sum of any two even numbers is even, you can deduce that the product of an even number and any whole number is even.

Diagonal (p. 638) See *polygon.*

Diameter (p. 658) A diameter of a circle is a segment that contains the center of the circle and whose endpoints are on the circle. The term *diameter* can also mean the length of this segment.

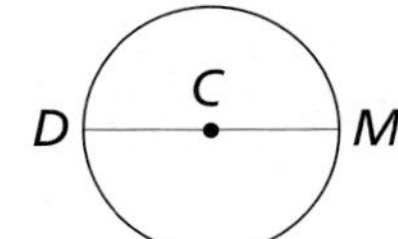

$\overline{DM}$ is a diameter of $\odot C$.

Dilation (p. 728) A dilation, or *similarity transformation,* with *center C* and *scale factor n,* where $n > 0$, maps a point R to R' in such a way that R' is on CR and $CR' = n \cdot CR$. The center of a dilation is its own image. If $n > 1$, the dilation is an *enlargement,* and if $0 < n < 1$, the dilation is a *reduction.*

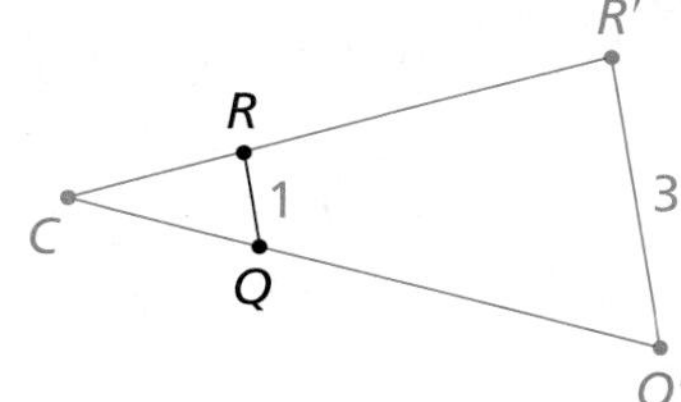

Example: $\overline{R'Q'}$ is the image of $\overline{RQ}$ under a dilation with center C and scale factor 3.

Distance from a point to a line (p. 783) The distance from a point to a line is the length of the perpendicular segment from the point to the line.

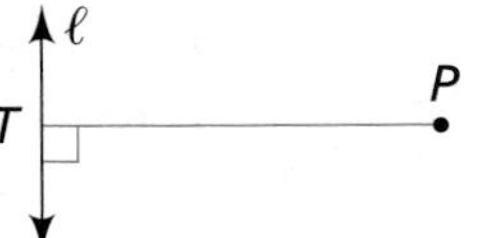

Example: The distance from point P to line ℓ is PT.

Dodecagon (p. 638) A dodecagon is a polygon with twelve sides.

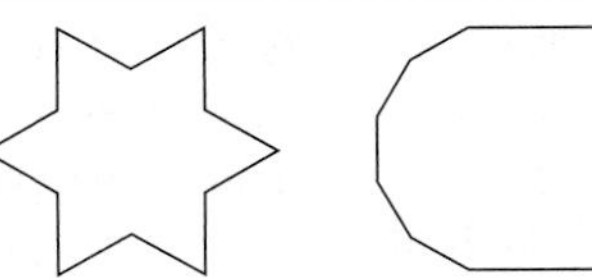

Glossary/Study Guide

E

Examples

Edge (p. 864) See *polyhedron.*

Endpoint (p. 580) See *ray* and *segment.*

Enlargement (p. 729) See *dilation.*

Equiangular triangle (polygon) (pp. 633, 640) An equiangular triangle (polygon) is a triangle (polygon) whose angles are all congruent.

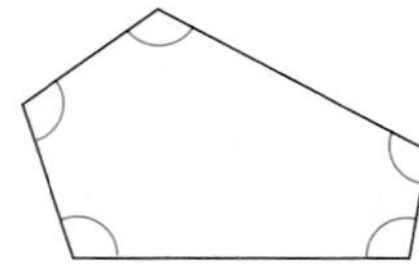

Each angle of the pentagon is a 108° angle.

Equilateral triangle (polygon) (pp. 633, 640) An equilateral triangle (polygon) is a triangle (polygon) whose sides are all congruent.

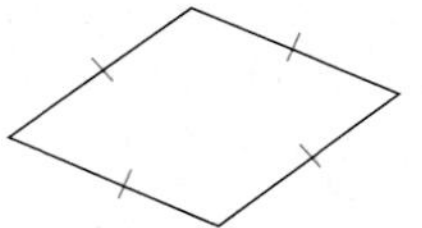

Each side of the quadrilateral is 1.5 cm long.

Exterior angle of a polygon (p. 631) An exterior angle of a polygon is an angle formed by a side and an extension of an adjacent side.

Example: $\angle KLM$ is an exterior angle of $\triangle JKL$.

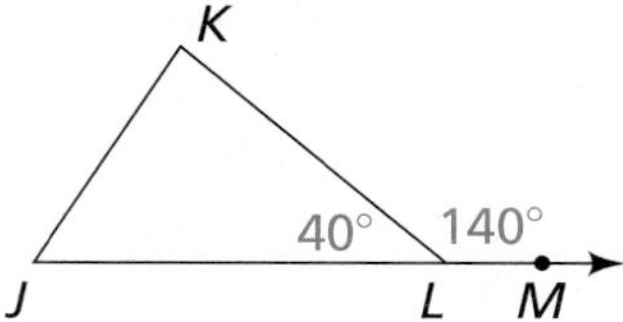

F

Face (p. 864) See *polyhedron.*

Foundation drawing (p. 672) A foundation drawing shows the base of a structure and the height of each part.

Example: The first drawing is a foundation drawing; the second is an isometric drawing based on the foundation drawing.

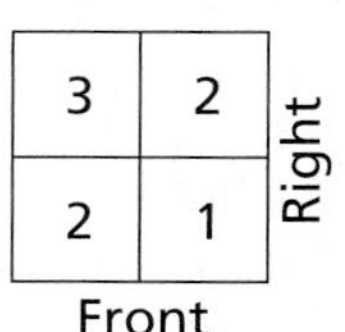

Frieze pattern (p. 699) A frieze pattern, also known as a *strip pattern,* repeats itself along a straight line. A frieze pattern can be mapped onto itself by a *translation.*

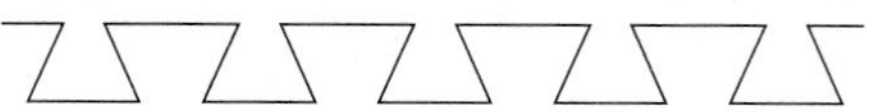

G

Examples

Glide reflection (p. 708) A glide reflection is a composition of three reflections in lines that intersect in more than one point. Equivalently, a glide reflection is a composition of a translation followed by a reflection in a line parallel to the translation vector.

Example: The blue G in the diagram is the glide reflection image of the black G.

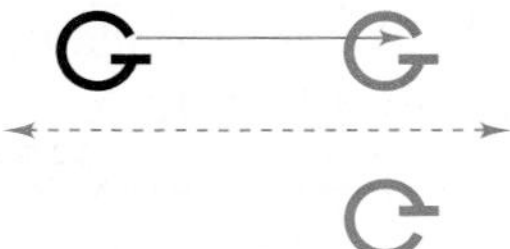

Glide reflectional symmetry (p. 723) A repeating pattern has glide reflectional symmetry if it can be mapped onto itself by a glide reflection.

Example: The tessellation shown can be mapped onto itself by a glide reflection in the given line and the given vector.

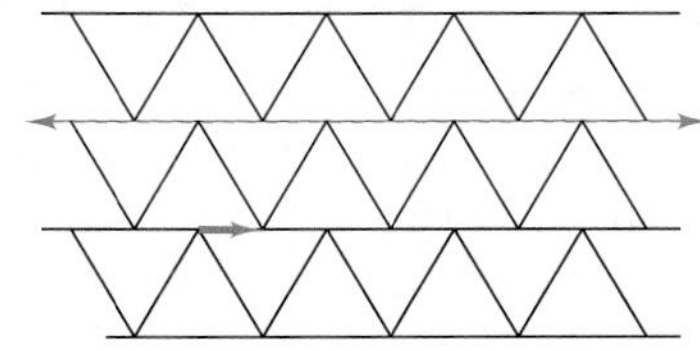

Great circle (p. 902) A great circle is the intersection of a sphere and a plane containing the center of the sphere. A great circle divides a sphere into two *hemispheres.*

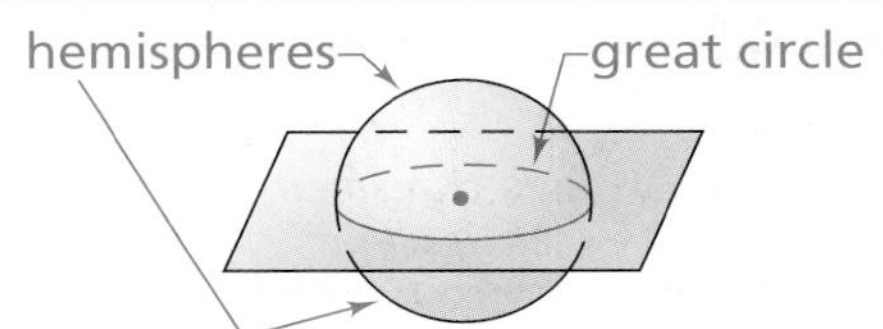

H

Half-turn (p. 716) A rotation of 180° is called a half-turn.

Example: The blue R in the diagram is the image of the black R under a half-turn about the given point.

Height See *cone, cylinder, parallelogram, prism, pyramid, trapezoid,* and *triangle.*

Hemisphere (p. 902) See *great circle.*

Heptagon (p. 638) A heptagon is a polygon with seven sides.

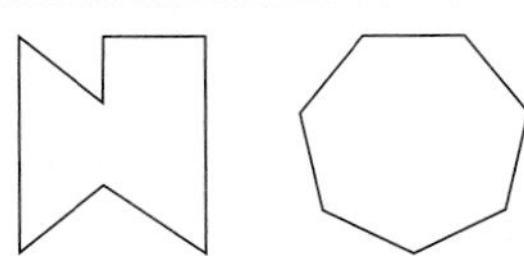

Glossary/Study Guide

Examples

Heron's formula (p. 815) A formula for finding the area of a triangle given the lengths of its sides.

$A = \sqrt{s(s - a)(s - b)(s - c)}$, where s is the semiperimeter of the triangle.

Hexagon (p. 638) A hexagon is a polygon with six sides.

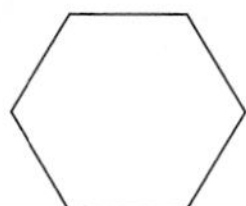

Hypotenuse (p. 818) See *right triangle.*

Hypothesis (p. 744) In an *if-then statement* (conditional), the hypothesis is the part that follows *if.*

In the statement "If she leaves, then I will go with her," the *hypothesis* is "she leaves."

I

Identity (p. 963) An identity is an equation that is true for all allowed values of the variable.

$\sin x° = \cos(90 - x)°$ for $0 < x < 90$

Image (p. 686) See *transformation.*

Indirect proof (p. 770) See *indirect reasoning* and *proof.*

Indirect reasoning (p. 769) In indirect reasoning, all possibilities are considered and then all but one are proved false. The remaining possibility must be true.

Eduardo spent more than \$60 on two books at a store. Prove that at least one book costs more than \$30.

Proof: Suppose neither costs more than \$30. Then he spent no more than \$60 at the store. Since this contradicts the given information, at least one book costs \$30 or more.

Inductive reasoning (p. 567) Inductive reasoning is a type of reasoning that reaches conclusions based on a pattern of specific examples or past events.

You see four people walk into a building. Each person emerges with a small bag containing hot food. You use inductive reasoning to conclude that this building contains a restaurant.

Initial point (p. 695) See *vector.*

Examples

Inscribe (p. 790) A circle is inscribed in a polygon if the sides of the polygon are tangent to the circle. A polygon is inscribed in a circle if the vertices of the polygon are on the circle.

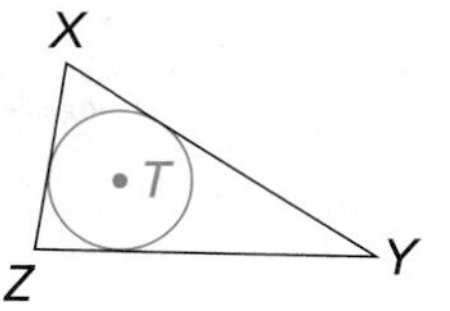

$\odot T$ is inscribed in $\triangle XYZ$.

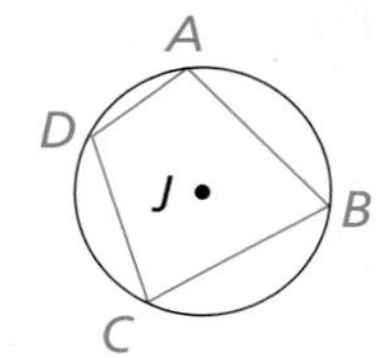

ABCD is inscribed in $\odot J$.

Inverse (p. 746) The inverse of the conditional "if p, then q" is the conditional "if not p, then not q."

Conditional: If a figure is a square, then it is a parallelogram.

Inverse: If a figure is not a square, then it is not a parallelogram.

Isometric drawing (p. 671) An isometric drawing of a three-dimensional object shows a corner view of the figure.

Isometry (p. 686) An isometry, also known as a *congruence transformation,* is a transformation in which the original figure and its image are congruent.

The four isometries are reflections, rotations, translations, and glide reflections.

Isosceles trapezoid (p. 653) An isosceles trapezoid is a trapezoid whose legs are congruent.

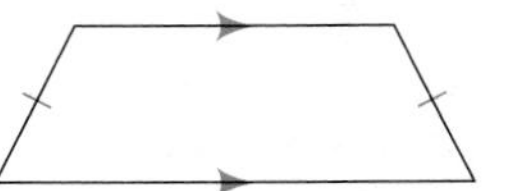

Isosceles triangle (pp. 633, 750) An isosceles triangle is a triangle that has at least two congruent sides. In an isosceles triangle that is not equilateral, the two congruent sides are called *legs* and the third side is called the *base.* The two angles with the base as a side are *base angles* and the third angle is the *vertex angle.*

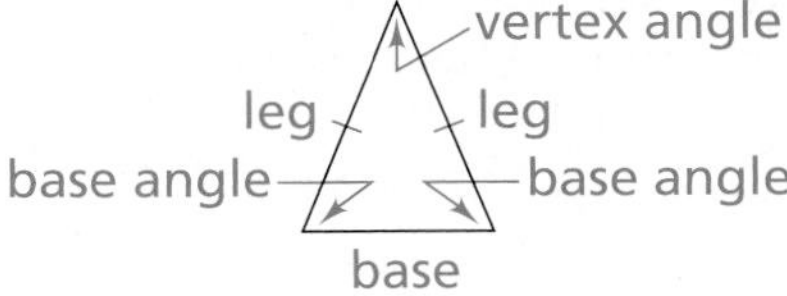

Examples

Kite (p. 653) A kite is a quadrilateral with two pairs of congruent adjacent sides and no opposite sides congruent.

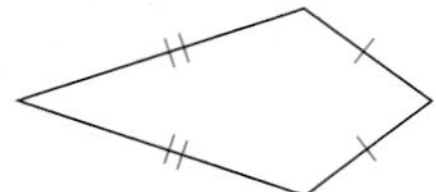

Lateral area (pp. 871, 873, 878, 880) The lateral area of a prism or pyramid is the sum of the areas of the lateral faces. The lateral area of a cylinder or cone is the area of the curved surface.

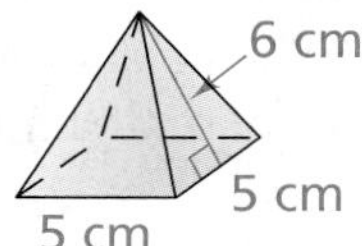

$$\text{L.A. of pyramid} = \tfrac{1}{2}p\ell = \tfrac{1}{2}(20)(6) = 60 \text{ cm}^2$$

Lateral face See *prism* and *pyramid.*

Leg See *isosceles triangle, right triangle,* and *trapezoid.*

Line (p. 575) In Euclidean geometry, you can think of a line as a series of points that extends in two opposite directions without end. In spherical geometry, you can think of a line as a great circle of a sphere.

Locus (p. 782) A locus is the set of points that meet a stated condition.

Example: The blue figure is the locus of points in a plane 1 cm from $\overline{DC}$.

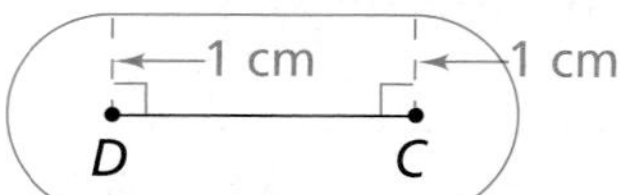

Major arc (p. 660) A major arc of a circle is any arc longer than a semicircle.

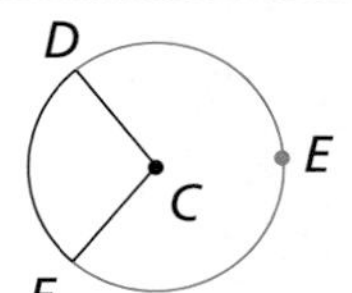

$\overset{\frown}{DEF}$ is a major arc of $\odot C$.

Examples

Map (p. 686) See *transformation.*

Matrix (p. 693) A matrix is a rectangular array of numbers. Each item in a matrix is called an *entry.*

The matrix $\begin{bmatrix} 1 & -2 \\ 0 & 13 \end{bmatrix}$ has dimensions 2×2. The number 1 is the entry in the first row and first column.

Measure of an angle (p. 588) Angles are measured in degrees. An angle can be measured with a *protractor.*

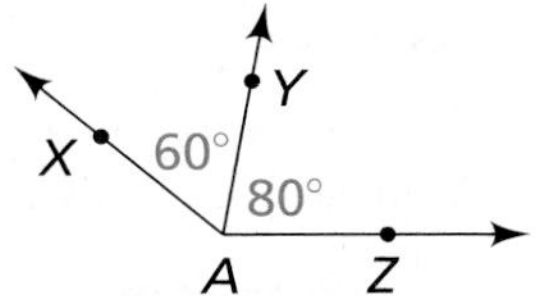

$m\angle ZAY = 80$, $m\angle YAX = 60$, and $m\angle ZAX = 140$.

Measure of an arc (p. 660) The measure of a minor arc is the measure of its central angle. The measure of a major arc is 360 minus the measure of its related minor arc.

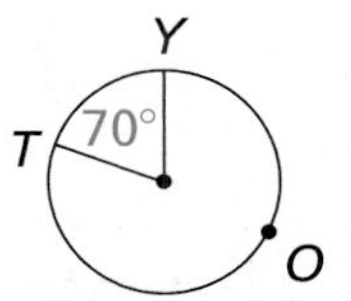

$m\overset{\frown}{TY} = 70$
$m\overset{\frown}{TOY} = 290$

Median of a triangle (p. 791) A median of a triangle is a segment that joins a vertex of the triangle and the midpoint of the side opposite that vertex.

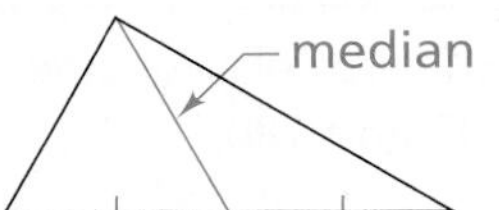

Midpoint of a segment (p. 595) A midpoint of a segment is the point that divides the segment into two congruent segments.

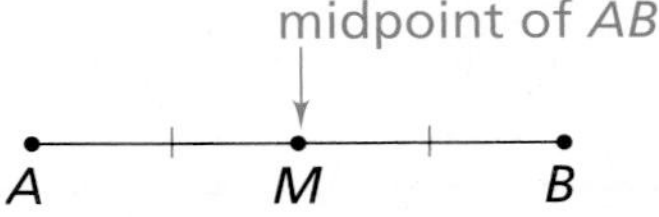

Midsegment of a triangle (pp. 763, 797) A midsegment of a triangle is a segment that joins the midpoints of two sides of the triangle.

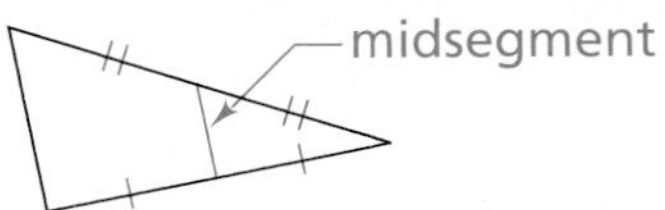

Minor arc (p. 660) A minor arc of a circle is any arc shorter than a semicircle.

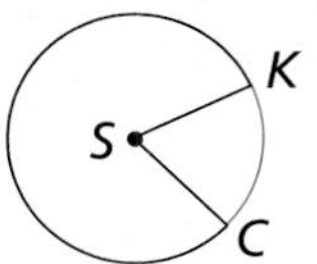

$\overset{\frown}{KC}$ is a minor arc of $\odot S$.

N

Examples

Negation (p. 746) A negation of a statement has the opposite meaning of the original statement.

Statement: The angle is obtuse.

Negation: The angle is not obtuse.

Net (p. 864) A net is a two-dimensional pattern that you can fold to form a three-dimensional figure.

Example: The net shown can be folded into a prism with pentagonal bases.

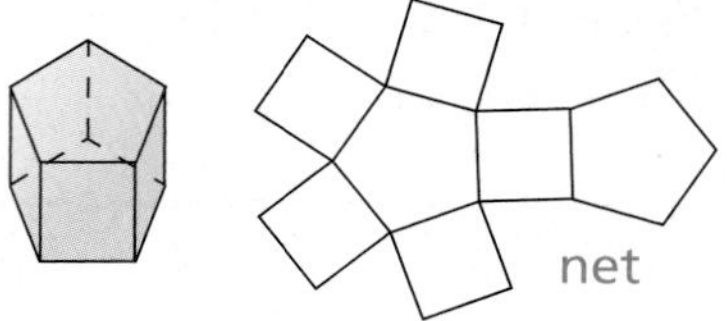

n-gon (p. 638) An n-gon is a polygon with n sides.

Nonagon (p. 638) A nonagon is a polygon with nine sides.

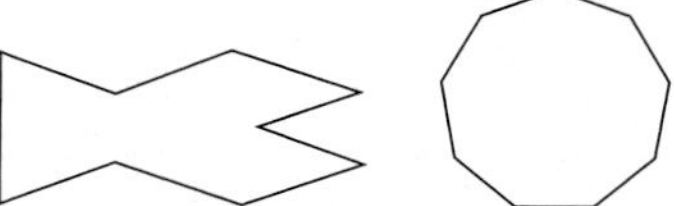

O

Oblique cylinder or prism See *cylinder* and *prism.*

Obtuse angle (p. 589) An obtuse angle is an angle whose measure is between 90 and 180.

147°

Obtuse triangle (p. 633) An obtuse triangle has one obtuse angle.

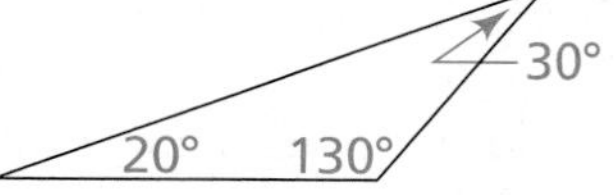

Octagon (p. 638) An octagon is a polygon with eight sides.

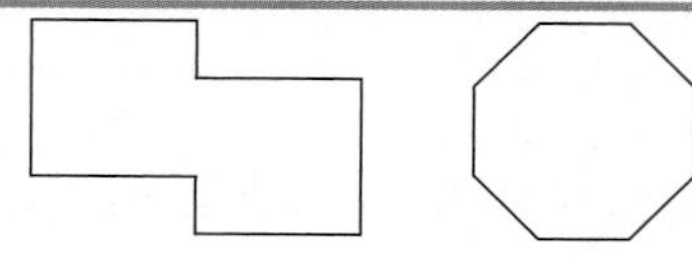

Opposite rays (p. 580) Opposite rays are collinear rays with the same endpoint. They form a line.

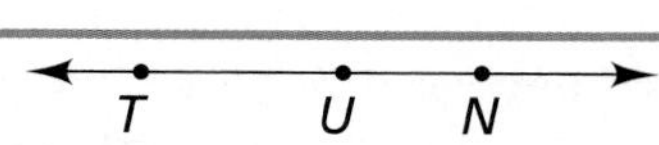

$\overrightarrow{UT}$ and $\overrightarrow{UN}$ are opposite rays.

Examples

Orientation (p. 688) Two figures have *opposite* orientation if a reflection is needed to map one onto the other. If a reflection is not needed to map one figure onto the other, the figures have the *same* orientation.

R Я The two R's have opposite orientation.

Origin (p. 616) See *coordinate plane.*

Orthographic drawing (p. 673) An orthographic drawing shows the top view, front view, and right-side view of a three-dimensional figure.

Example: The diagram shows an isometric drawing (upper right) and the three views that make up an orthographic drawing.

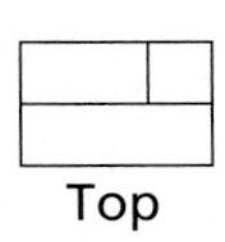
Top

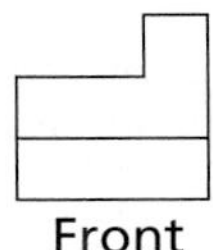
Front

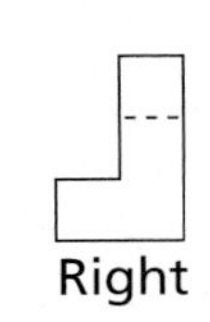
Right

P

Paragraph proof (p. 757) See *proof.*

Parallel lines (pp. 580, 929) Two lines are parallel if they lie in the same plane and do not intersect. The symbol || means "is parallel to."

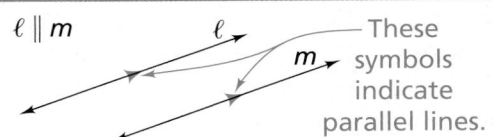

$\ell \parallel m$

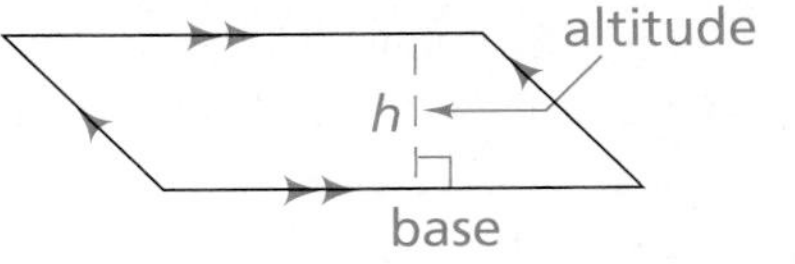

Parallelogram (pp. 653, 811–812) A parallelogram is a quadrilateral with two pairs of parallel sides. You can choose any side to be the *base.* An *altitude* is any segment perpendicular to the line containing the base drawn from the side opposite the base. The *height* is the length of an altitude.

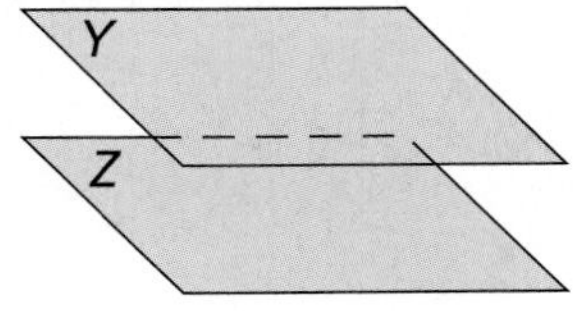

Parallel planes (p. 581) Parallel planes are planes that do not intersect.

Y Z Planes *Y* and *Z* are parallel.

Examples

Pentagon (p. 638) A pentagon is a polygon with five sides.

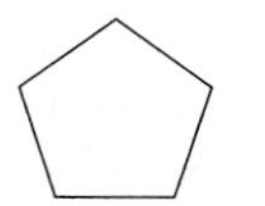
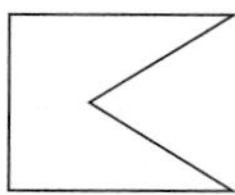

Perimeter of a polygon (p. 804) The perimeter of a polygon is the sum of the lengths of its sides.

$p = 4 + 4 + 5 + 3$
$= 16$ in.

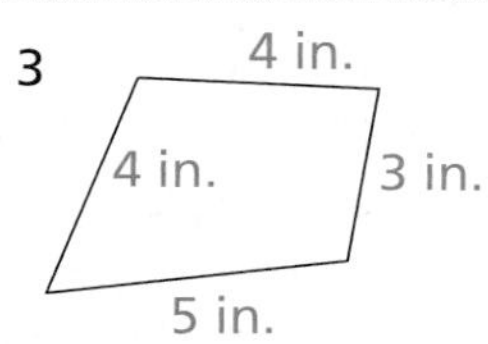

Perpendicular bisector (p. 596) The perpendicular bisector of a segment is a segment, ray, line, or plane that is perpendicular to the segment at its midpoint.

Example: $\overleftrightarrow{YZ}$ is the perpendicular bisector of $\overline{AB}$. It is perpendicular to $\overline{AB}$ and intersects it at its midpoint M.

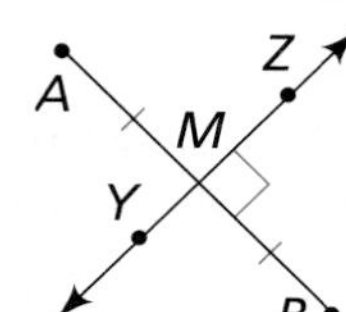

Perpendicular lines (p. 596) Two lines are perpendicular if they intersect and form right angles. The symbol $\perp$ means "is perpendicular to."

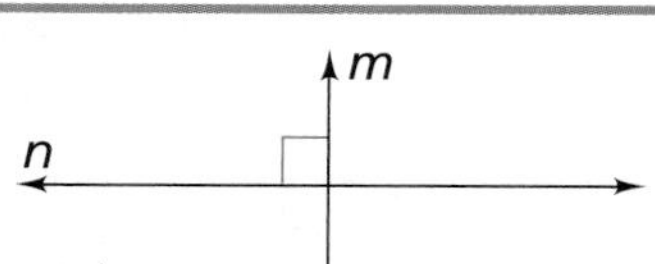

Pi (p. 841) Pi (π) is the ratio of the circumference of any circle to its diameter. The number π is irrational and can be approximated by $\pi \approx 3.14159$.

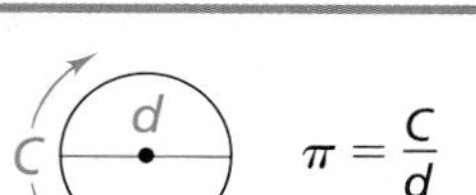

$\pi = \frac{C}{d}$

Plane (p. 575) In Euclidean geometry, you can think of a plane as a flat surface that extends in all directions without end. It has no thickness. In spherical geometry, you can think of a plane as the surface of a sphere.

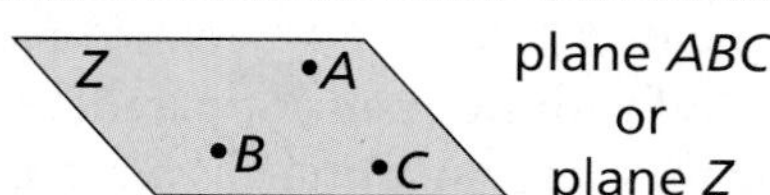

Point (p. 574) You can think of a point as a location. A point has no size.

• P

Examples

Point of concurrency (p. 789) See *concurrent.*

Point symmetry (p. 716) A figure with rotational symmetry of 180° has point symmetry.

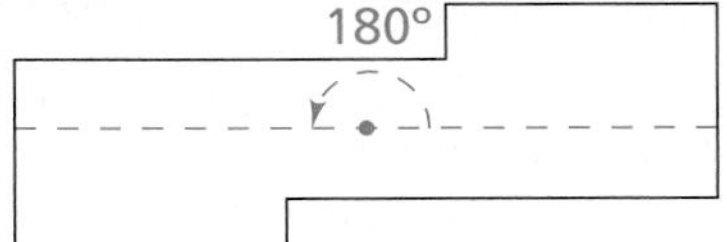

Polygon (p. 638) A polygon is a closed plane figure with at least three *sides*. The sides are segments and intersect only at their endpoints and no adjacent sides are collinear. The *vertices* of the polygon are the endpoints of the sides. A *diagonal* is a segment that connects two nonconsecutive vertices. A polygon is *convex* if no diagonal contains points outside the polygon. A polygon is *concave* if you can draw a diagonal that contains points outside the polygon.

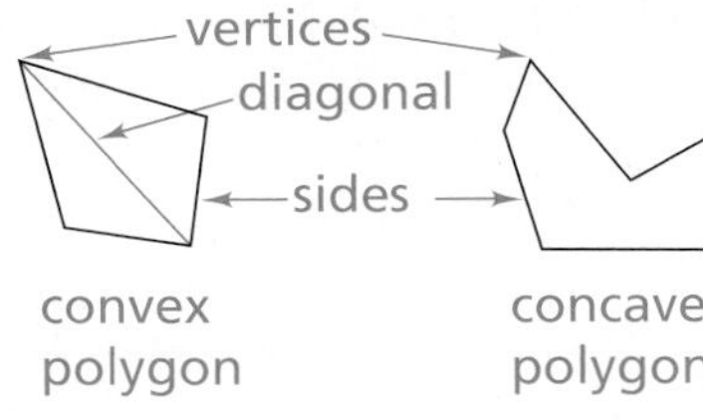

Polyhedron (p. 864) A polyhedron is a three-dimensional figure whose surfaces, or *faces*, are polygons. The vertices of the polygons are the *vertices* of the polyhedron. The intersections of the faces are the *edges* of the polyhedron.

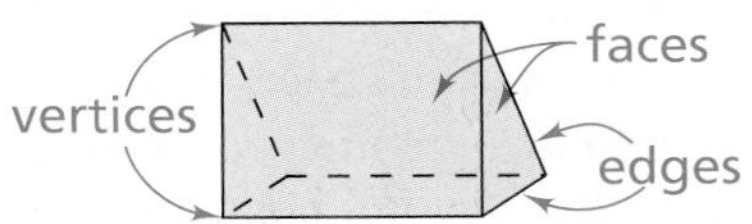

Postulate (p. 576) A postulate is an accepted statement of fact.

Postulate: Through any two points there is exactly one line.

Preimage (p. 686) See *transformation.*

Prime notation (p. 686) See *transformation.*

Prism (p. 871) A prism is a polyhedron with two congruent, parallel faces, called the *bases.* The other faces are parallelograms and are called the *lateral faces.* An *altitude* of a prism is a perpendicular segment that joins the planes of the bases. Its length is the *height* of the prism. In a *right prism,* the lateral faces are rectangular and a lateral edge is an altitude. In an *oblique prism,* some or all of the lateral faces are nonrectangular.

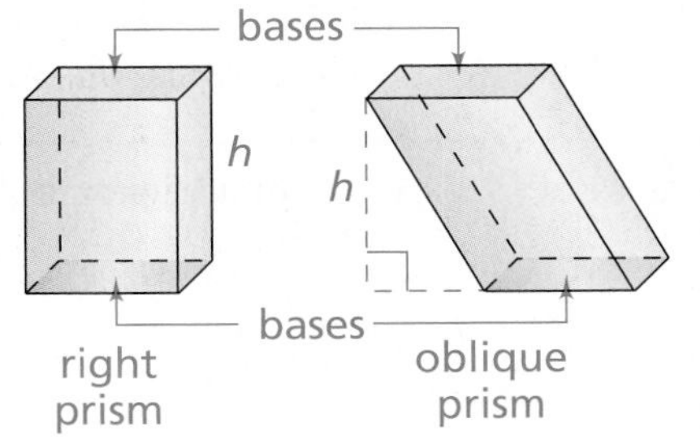

Glossary/Study Guide

Examples

Proof (pp. 611, 756, 770) A proof is a convincing argument that uses deductive reasoning. A proof can be written in many forms. In a *two-column proof,* the statements and reasons are aligned in columns. In a *paragraph proof,* the statements and reasons are connected in sentences. In a *flow proof,* arrows show the logical connections between the statements. In a *coordinate proof,* a figure is drawn on a coordinate plane and the formulas for slope, midpoint, and distance are used to prove properties of the figure. An *indirect proof* involves the use of indirect reasoning.

Given: $\triangle EFG$, with right angle $\angle F$
Prove: $\angle E$ and $\angle G$ are complementary.

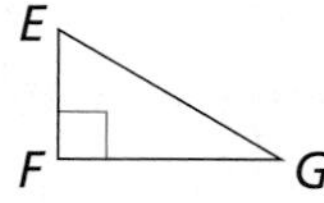

Paragraph Proof: Because $\angle F$ is a right angle, $m\angle F = 90$. By the Triangle Angle-Sum Thm., $m\angle E + m\angle F + m\angle G = 180$. By Substitution, $m\angle E + 90 + m\angle G = 180$. Subtracting 90 from each side yields $m\angle E + m\angle G = 90$. $\angle E$ and $\angle G$ are complementary by definition.

$\frac{x}{5} = \frac{3}{4}$ is a proportion.

Pyramid (p. 878) A pyramid is a polyhedron in which one face, the *base,* is a polygon and the other faces, the *lateral faces,* are triangles with a common vertex, called the *vertex* of the pyramid. An *altitude* of a pyramid is the perpendicular segment from the *vertex* to the plane of the base. Its length is the *height* of the pyramid. A *regular pyramid* is a pyramid whose base is a regular polygon and whose lateral faces are congruent isosceles triangles. The *slant height* of a regular pyramid is the length of an altitude of a lateral face.

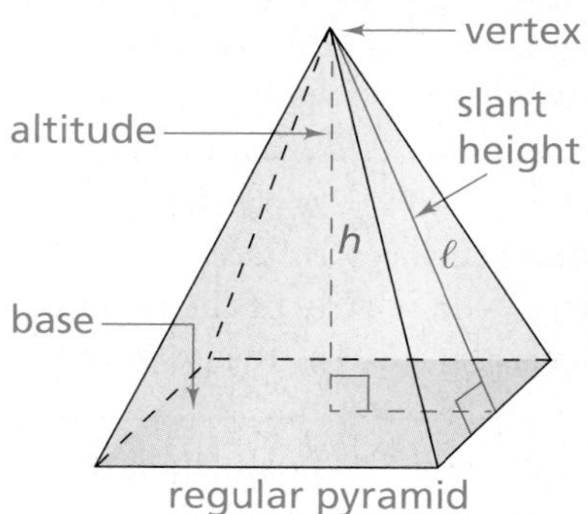

regular pyramid

Pythagorean triple (p. 820) A Pythagorean triple is a set of three positive integers that satisfy the Pythagorean Theorem.

The numbers 5, 12, and 13 form a Pythagorean triple because $5^2 + 12^2 = 13^2$.

Quadrant (p. 616) See *coordinate plane.*

Quadrilateral (p. 638) A quadrilateral is a polygon with four sides.

Radius of a circle (p. 658) A radius of a circle is any segment with one endpoint on the circle and the other endpoint at the center of the circle. *Radius* can also mean the length of this segment.

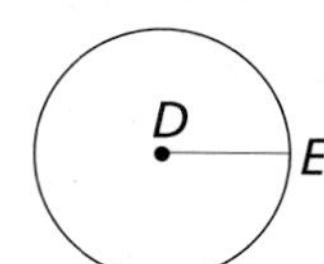

$\overline{DE}$ is a radius of $\odot D$.

Examples

Radius of a regular polygon (p. 836) The radius of a regular polygon is the distance from the center to a vertex.

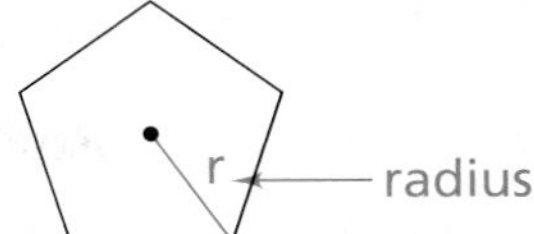

Ray (p. 580) A ray is a part of a line consisting of one *endpoint* and all the points of the line on one side of the endpoint.

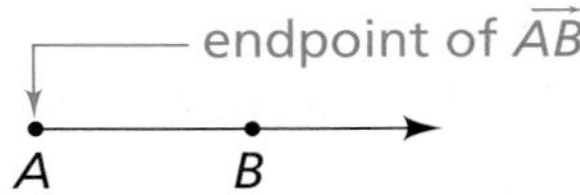

Rectangle (p. 653) A rectangle is a parallelogram with four right angles.

Reduction (p. 729) See *dilation.*

Reflection (p. 688) A reflection in line r is a transformation such that if a point A is on line r, then the image of A is itself, and if a point B is not on line r, then its image B' is the point such that r is the perpendicular bisector of $\overline{BB'}$.

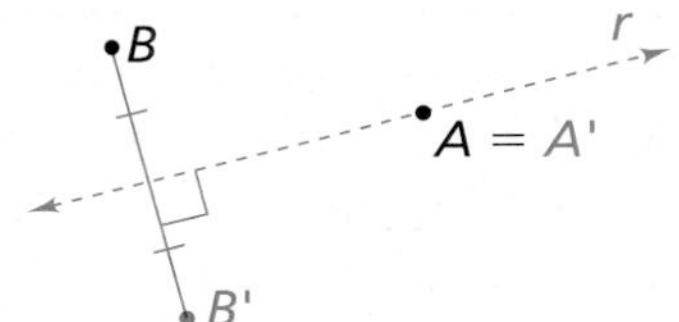

Reflectional symmetry (p. 714) A figure has reflectional symmetry, or *line symmetry,* if there is a reflection that maps the figure onto itself.

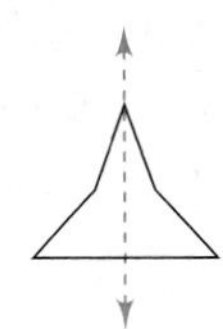

A reflection in the given line maps the figure onto itself.

Regular polygon (pp. 640, 836) A regular polygon is a polygon that is both equilateral and equiangular. Its *center* is the center of the circumscribed circle.

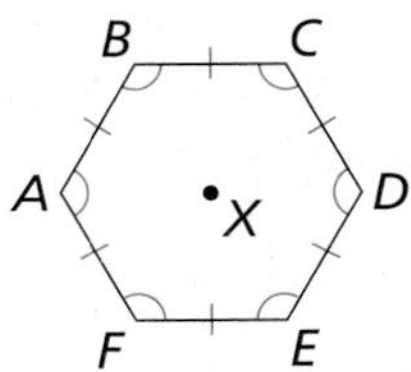

ABCDEF is a regular hexagon. Point *X* is its center.

Regular pyramid (p. 878) See *pyramid.*

Remote interior angles (p. 631) For each exterior angle of a triangle, the two nonadjacent interior angles are called its remote interior angles.

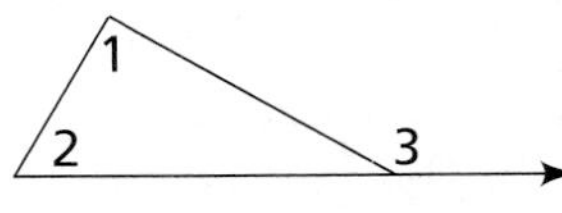

$\angle 1$ and $\angle 2$ are remote interior angles of $\angle 3$.

Rhombus (p. 653) A rhombus is a parallelogram with four congruent sides.

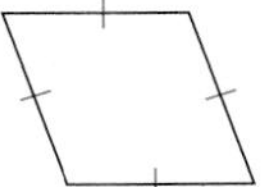

Glossary/Study Guide

Examples

Right angle (p. 589) A right angle is an angle whose measure is 90.

90°

This symbol indicates a right angle.

Right cone (p. 880) See *cone.*

Right cylinder (p. 872) See *cylinder.*

Right prism (p. 871) See *prism.*

Right triangle (pp. 633, 818) A right triangle contains one right angle. The side opposite the right angle is the *hypotenuse* and the other two sides are the *legs.*

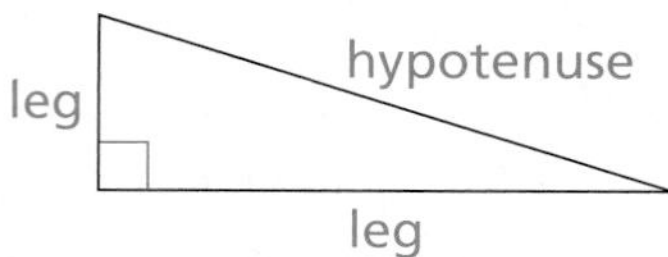

Rotation (p. 701) A rotation of $x°$ about a point R is a transformation such that for any point V, its image is the point V' where $RV = RV'$ and $m\angle VRV' = x$. The image of R is itself. All rotations in this text are *counterclockwise* rotations.

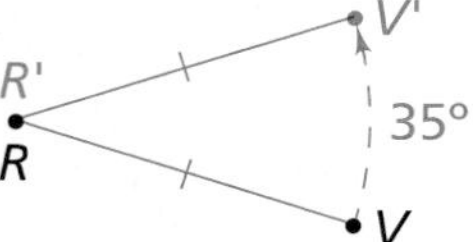

Rotational symmetry (p. 716) A figure has rotational symmetry if there is a rotation of 180° or less that maps the figure onto itself.

The figure has 120° rotational symmetry.

S

Same-side interior angles (p. 929) Same-side interior angles lie on the same side of the transversal t and between ℓ and m.

Example: ∠1 and ∠2 are same-side interior angles, as are ∠3 and ∠4.

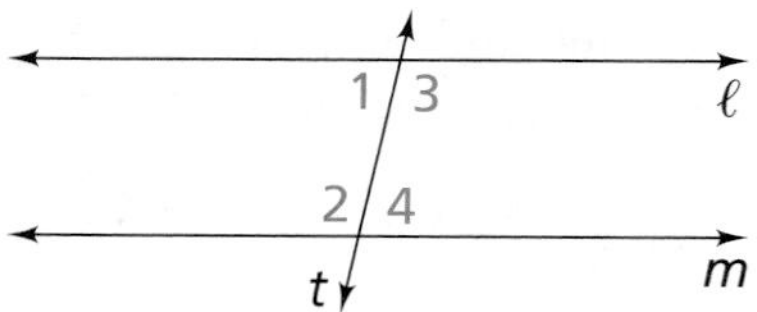

Scalar multiplication (p. 730) In scalar multiplication, each entry in a matrix is multiplied by the same number, the *scalar.*

$$2 \cdot \begin{bmatrix} 1 & 0 \\ -2 & 3 \end{bmatrix} = \begin{bmatrix} 2(1) & 2(0) \\ 2(-2) & 2(3) \end{bmatrix} = \begin{bmatrix} 2 & 0 \\ -4 & 6 \end{bmatrix}$$

Scale factor (p. 728) The scale factor of a dilation is the number that describes the size change from an original figure to its image. See also *dilation.*

Example: The scale factor of the dilation that maps $\triangle ABC$ to $\triangle A'B'C'$ is $\frac{1}{2}$.

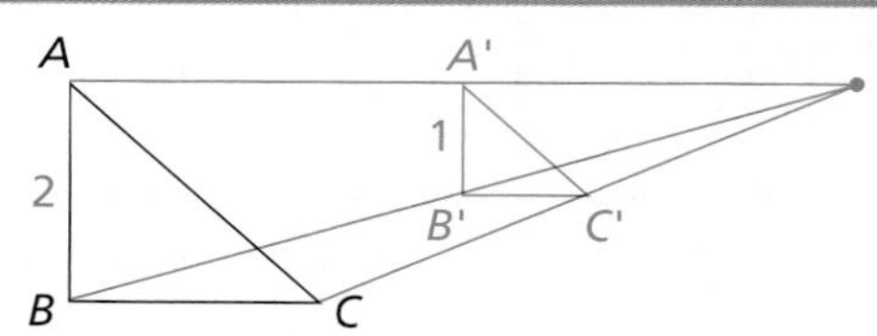

Examples

Scalene triangle (p. 633) A scalene triangle has no sides congruent.

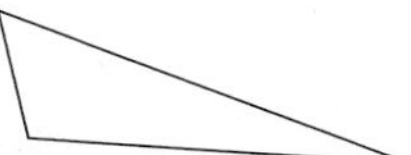

Sector of a circle (p. 848) A sector of a circle is the region bounded by two radii and their intercepted arc.

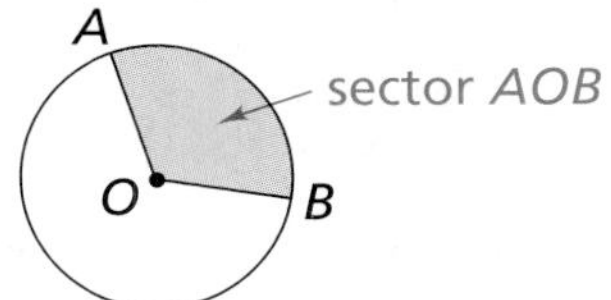

Segment (p. 580) A segment is a part of a line consisting of two points, called *endpoints*, and all points between them.

Segment bisector (p. 595) A segment bisector is a line, segment, ray, or plane that intersects a segment at its midpoint.

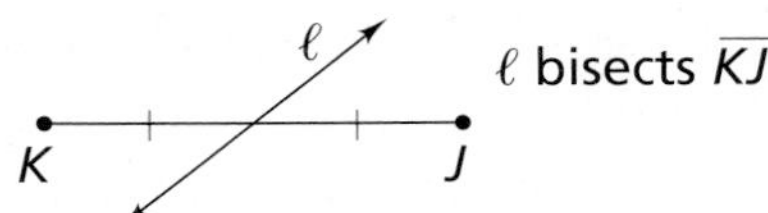

Segment of a circle (p. 849) The part of a circle bounded by an arc and the segment joining its endpoints is a segment of a circle.

Example: The portion of the interior of the circle bounded by $\angle ACB$ and outside $\triangle ACB$ is a segment of $\odot C$.

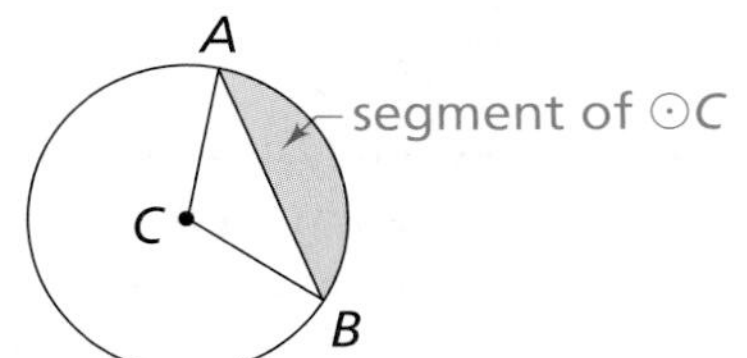

Semicircle (p. 660) A semicircle is half a circle.

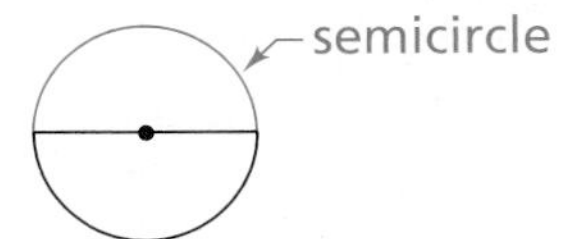

Side See *angle* and *polygon*.

Similarity ratio (p. 665) The ratio of the lengths of corresponding sides of similar polygons or solids is the similarity ratio.

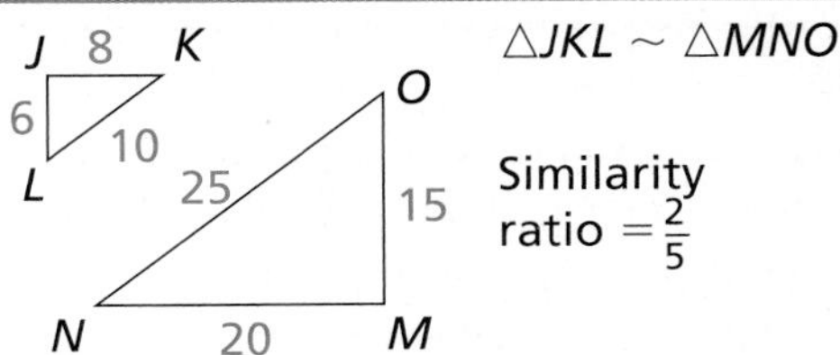

Examples

Similarity transformation (p. 729) See *dilation.*

Similar polygons (p. 665) Two polygons are similar if corresponding angles are congruent and corresponding sides are proportional. The symbol $\sim$ means "is similar to."

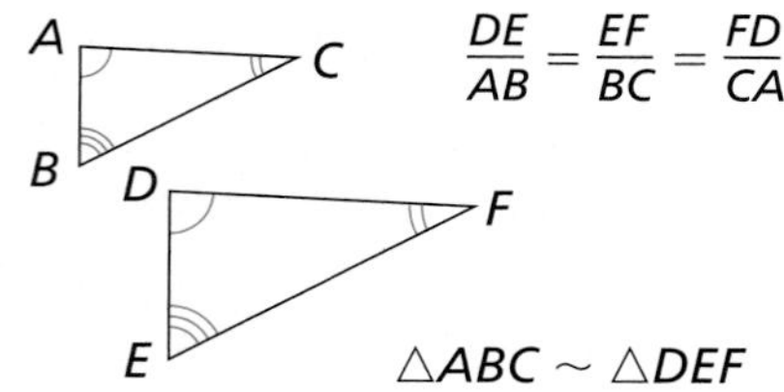

$\frac{DE}{AB} = \frac{EF}{BC} = \frac{FD}{CA}$

$\triangle ABC \sim \triangle DEF$

Similar solids (p. 951) Similar solids have the same shape and all their corresponding dimensions are proportional.

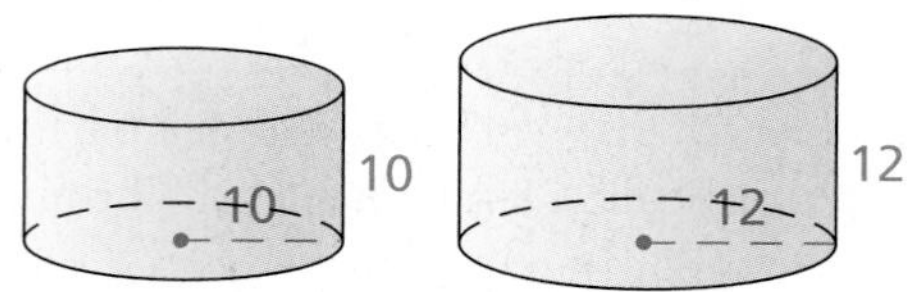

Sine ratio (p. 963) See *trigonometric ratios.*

Skew (p. 581) Two lines are skew if they do not lie in the same plane.

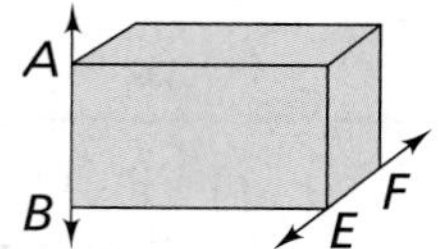

$\overleftrightarrow{AB}$ and $\overleftrightarrow{EF}$ are skew.

Slant height See *cone* and *pyramid.*

Slope of a line (p. 645) The slope of a line in the coordinate plane is the ratio of vertical change to the corresponding horizontal change. If (x_1, y_1) and (x_2, y_2) are points on a nonvertical line, then the slope is $\frac{y_2 - y_1}{x_2 - x_1}$. The slope of a horizontal line is 0, and the slope of a vertical line is undefined.

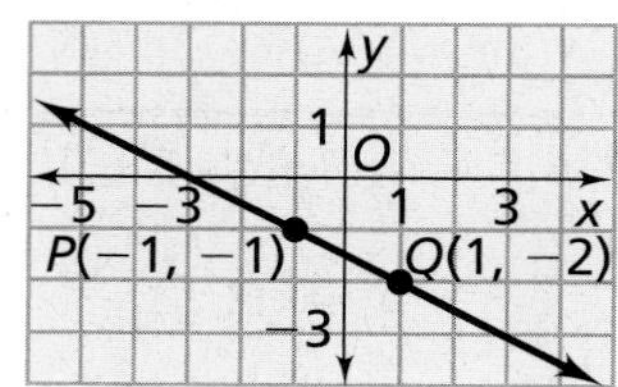

Example: The line containing $P(-1, -1)$ and $Q(1, -2)$ has slope $\frac{-2-(-1)}{1-(-1)} = \frac{-1}{2} = -\frac{1}{2}$.

Space (p. 574) Space is the set of all points.

Sphere (pp. 899, 902) A sphere is the set of all points in space a given distance *r*, the *radius*, from a given point *C*, the *center.* A *great circle* is the intersection of a sphere and a plane containing the center of the sphere. The *circumference* of a sphere is the circumference of any great circle of the sphere.

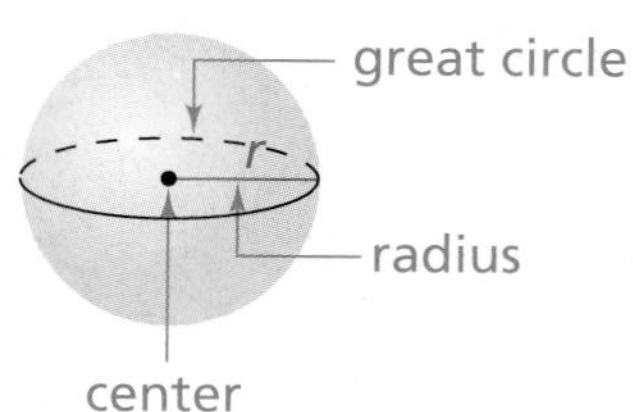

Examples

Square (p. 653) A square is a parallelogram with four congruent sides and four right angles.

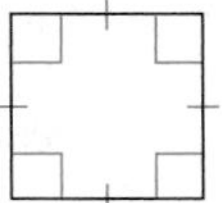

Straight angle (p. 589) A straight angle is an angle whose measure is 180.

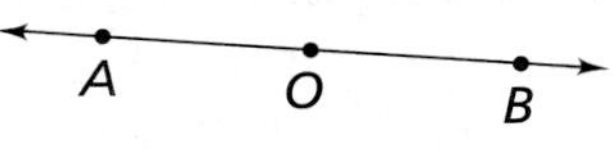

$m\angle AOB = 180$

Supplementary angles (p. 610) Two angles are supplementary if the sum of their measures is 180.

Example: $\angle MNP$ and $\angle ONP$ are supplementary, as are $\angle MNP$ and $\angle QRS$.

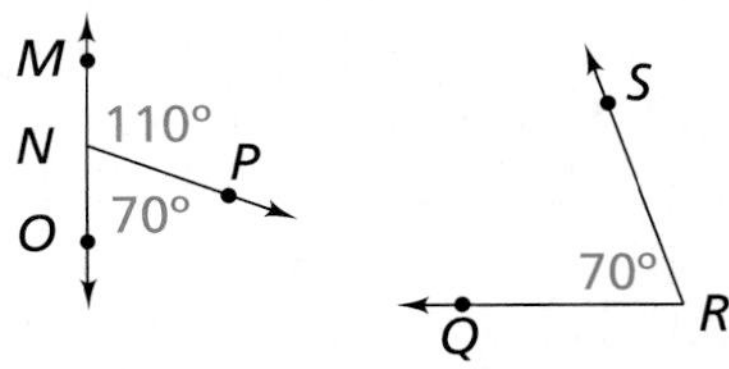

Surface area (pp. 871, 873, 878, 880, 900) The surface area of a prism, pyramid, cylinder, or cone is the sum of the lateral area and the areas of the bases.

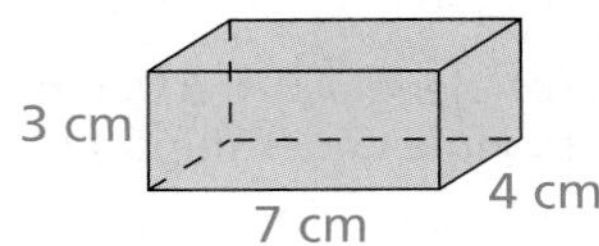

S.A. of prism = L.A. + $2B$
= 66 + 2(28)
= 122 cm^2

Symmetry (pp. 714–716) A figure has symmetry if there is an isometry that maps the figure onto itself. See *glide reflectional symmetry, point symmetry, reflectional symmetry, rotational symmetry,* and *translational symmetry.*

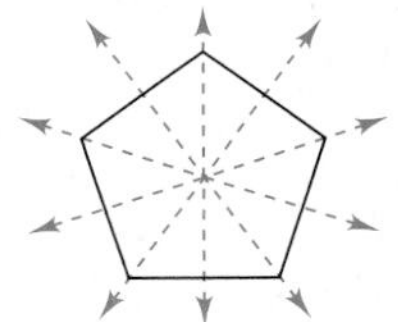

A regular pentagon has reflectional symmetry and 72° rotational symmetry.

Tangent ratio (p. 956) See *trigonometric ratios.*

Terminal point (p. 695) See *vector.*

Tessellation (pp. 721–722) A tessellation, or *tiling,* is a repeating pattern of figures that completely covers a plane without gaps or overlap. A *pure tessellation* is a tessellation that consists of congruent copies of one figure.

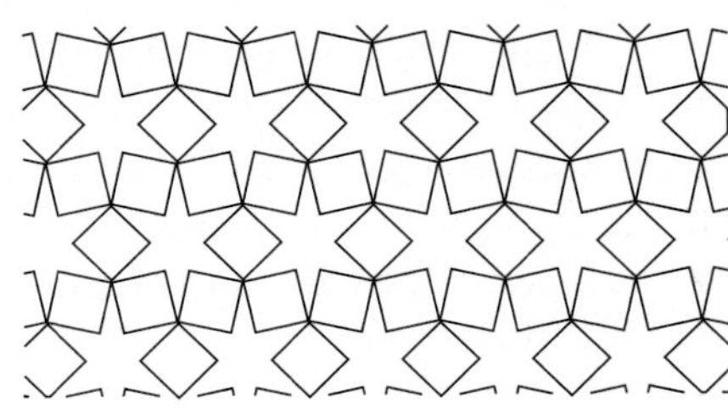

Examples

Theorem (p. 611) A conjecture that is proven is a theorem.

The theorem "Vertical angles are congruent" can be proven by using postulates, definitions, properties, and previously stated theorems.

Transformation (p. 686) A transformation is a change in the position, size, or shape of a figure. The given figure is called the *preimage* and the resulting figure is called the *image.* A transformation *maps* a figure onto its image. *Prime notation* is sometimes used to identify image points. In the diagram, X' (read "X prime") is the image of X.

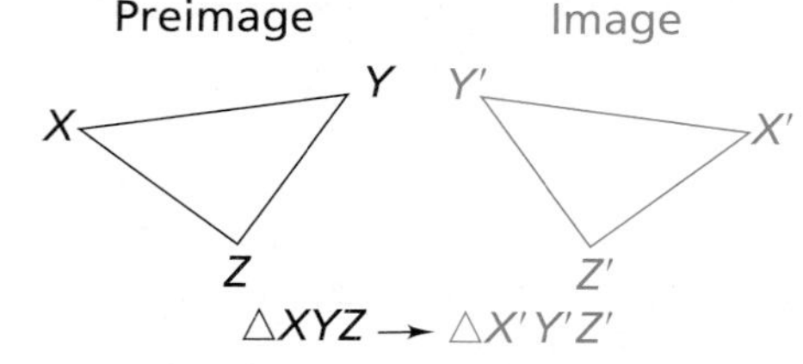

Translation (p. 694) A translation is a transformation that moves points the same distance and in the same direction. A transformation can be described by a vector.

Example: The blue triangle in the diagram is the image of the black triangle under the translation $\langle -5, -2 \rangle$.

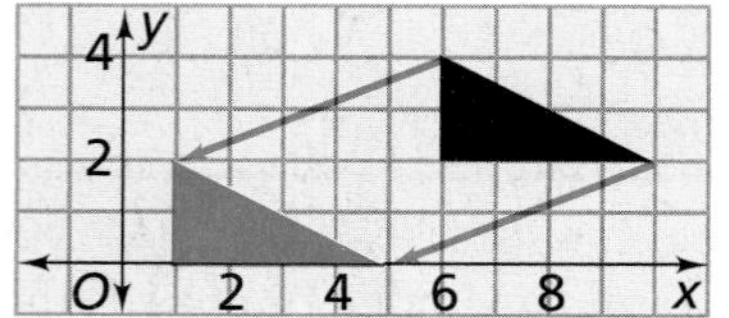

Translational symmetry (p. 723) A repeating pattern has translational symmetry if there is a translation that maps the pattern onto itself.

Example: The tessellation shown can be mapped onto itself by the given translation.

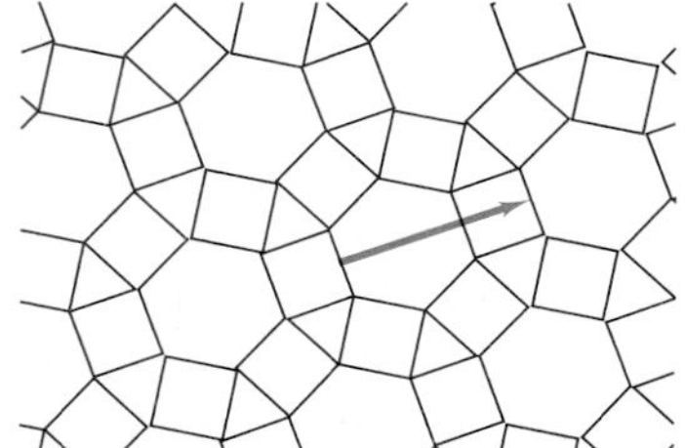

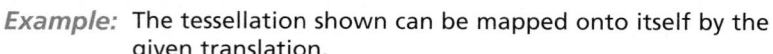

Transversal (p. 929) A transversal is a line that intersects two coplanar lines in two points.

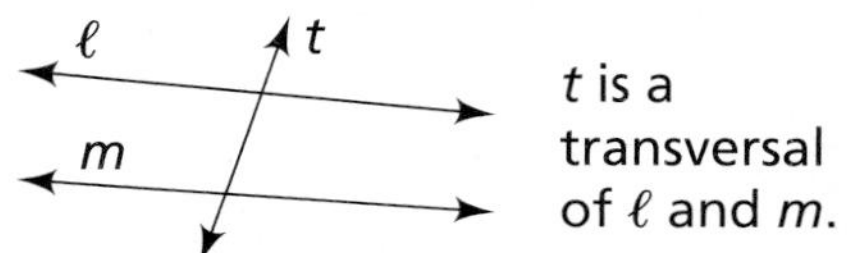

Trapezoid (pp. 653, 831) A trapezoid is a quadrilateral with exactly one pair of parallel sides, the *bases.* The nonparallel sides are called the *legs* of the trapezoid. Each pair of angles adjacent to a base are *base angles* of the trapezoid. An *altitude* of a trapezoid is a perpendicular segment from one base to the line containing the other base. Its length is called the *height* of the trapezoid.

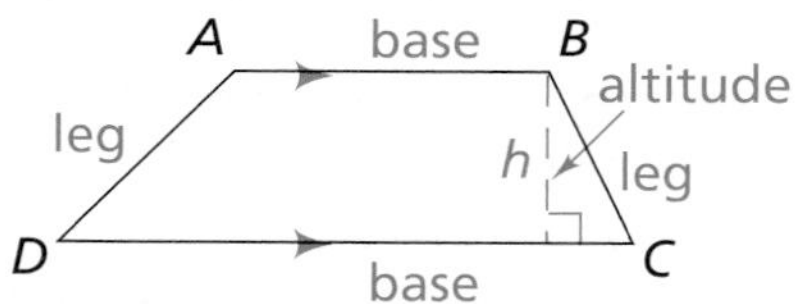

Triangle (pp. 633, 813) A triangle is a polygon with three sides. You can choose any side to be the *base.* Then the *height* is the length of the altitude drawn to the line containing that base.

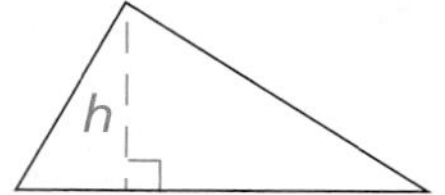

Examples

Truth value (p. 744) When you determine whether a conditional statement is true or false, you determine its truth value.

The truth value of the statement "If a figure is a triangle, then it has four sides." is **false.**

V

Vector (p. 695) A vector is any quantity that has magnitude (size) and direction. You can represent a vector as an arrow that starts at one point, the *initial point,* and goes to a second point, the *terminal point.* A vector can be described by *ordered pair notation* $\langle x, y \rangle$, where x represents horizontal change from the initial point to the terminal point, and y represents vertical change from the initial point to the terminal point.

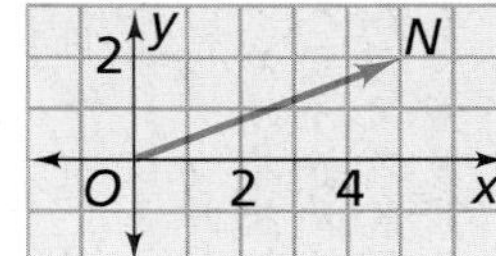

Vector $\overrightarrow{ON}$ has initial point O and terminal point N. The ordered pair notation for the vector is $\langle 5, 2 \rangle$.

Vertex See *angle, cone, polygon, polyhedron,* and *pyramid.* The plural form of vertex is *vertices.*

Vertex angle (p. 750) See *isosceles triangle.*

Vertical angles (p. 610) Two angles are vertical angles if their sides are opposite rays.

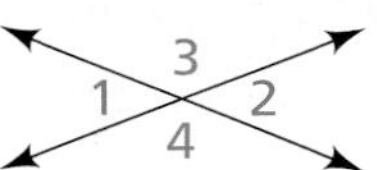

$\angle 1$ and $\angle 2$ are vertical angles, as are $\angle 3$ and $\angle 4$.

Volume (p. 886) Volume is a measure of the space a figure occupies. A list of volume formulas is on pages 670–671.

The volume of this prism is 24 cubic units, or 24 unit^3.

Selected Answers Volume 1

CHAPTER 1

Lesson 1-1 pages 4–9

ON YOUR OWN **1a.**

```
        X
      X X
      X X X
    X X X X
    X X X X
    X X X X X
    X X X X X   X
    -------------
    0 1 2 3 4 5 6
```

1b. 1.96; 2; 2 **3.** D **5.** 10; 10; 10 **7.** 25; 25; 25 **9.** 38.6; 37.9; 41.0 **11a.** 10 **13b.** English: 4.7; 4, 3; Spanish: 5.1, 5, 2

MIXED REVIEW **19.** 0.4; $\frac{2}{5}$ **21.** $\frac{1}{4}$; 0.25 **23.** 1.8; 180% **25.** 7, 9, 11 **27.** 108, 324, 972

Toolbox page 10

1. 27 students **3.** 8 students **5a.** 1.9, 2.0, 2.1, 2.2, 2.3, 2.4, 2.5 **5b.** Sample: 2.2 | 5 means $2.25

5c.

1.9	5 7 9
2.0	0 5 9
2.1	6
2.2	1 5 9
2.3	6
2.4	0 9
2.5	0 0 7

5d. $2.23; $2.50

Lesson 1-2 pages 11–14

ON YOUR OWN **1.** 3 **3.** 2 **7.** c = cost, n = number of cans; $c = 0.7n$ **9.** r = amount of rope, t = number of tents; $r = 60t$ **11.** $d = 50h$ **13.** $g = 0.165d$ **15.** $r = 13w$ **17.** $e = 0.4s$ **21a.** Sample: Statement (a) is better because it indicates that each lawn takes 2 h to mow. **21b.** 1 lawn: 2 hours; 2 lawns: 4 hours; 5 lawns should take 10 hours. **23.** s = height of second bounce; $s = \frac{1}{4}d$ **25a.** n = number of quarters, m = money in bag (in dollars); $m = 0.25n$ **25b.** $3.25

MIXED REVIEW **27.** Complete list: 23, 29, 31, 37, 41, 43, 47 **29.** 8 **31.** 7 **33.** 11

Lesson 1-3 pages 15–18

ON YOUR OWN **1.** 23 **3.** 1 **5.** 64 **7.** 50.43 **9.** 75 **11.** 14 **15.** 1 **17.** 12.8 **19.** 104.58 **21.** 26 **23.** 2.4 **25.** $14 - (2 + 5) - 3 = 4$ **29.** F; simplify the power before multiplying. **31.** F; simplify within parentheses first.

MIXED REVIEW **33.** $\frac{2}{3}$ **35.** $4\frac{1}{2}$ **37.** $\frac{4}{5}$ **39.** 2 units **41.** 3 units

Lesson 1-4 pages 19–24

ON YOUR OWN **1.** $-227 + 319$ is greater because the sum is positive and $227 + (-319)$ is negative. **3.** positive **5.** negative **7.** positive **9.** 15 **11.** 5 **13.** −35 **15.** 11 **17.** −28 **19.** 4 **21.** −43.9 **23.** 1.5 **25.** −26.9 **27.** 45.7 **29.** 0 **31.** Q; it is the farthest point from the midpoint between R and T. **33.** Yes; $3 - 4 = -1, 4 - 3 = 1; |-1| = |1|$. So $a - b$ and $b - a$ are opposites. Absolute values of opposites are equal. **37.** −11,331 ft **39.** 8 **41.** −9 **43.** −2 **45.** 1 **47.** −5 **49.** 14 **51.** 7 **53.** −1 **55.** B

MIXED REVIEW **57b.** A line graph shows change over time. **59.** 4 **61.** $\frac{1}{4}$ **63.** $\frac{1}{3}$ **65.** −3, −6, −9 **67.** 0, −2, −4

Lesson 1-5 pages 25–29

ON YOUR OWN **1.** −120 **3.** −81 **5.** −6 **7.** −4 **9.** −1 **11.** 30 **13.** 44 **15.** $5\frac{1}{2}$ **17a.** The product is positive when a and b have the same sign. **17b.** The product is negative when a and b have different signs. **19.** −12 **21.** −15 **23.** −8 **25.** −64 **27.** $-1\frac{1}{3}$ **29.** −27 **33.** positive; even number of factors **35.** negative; odd number of negative factors **37.** negative; $(-3)^2$ is positive. Its opposite is negative. **39.** negative; 5^{10} is positive. Its opposite is negative. **47a.** odd **47b.** even

MIXED REVIEW **49.** 5 people **51a.** 2.8; 2.5; 1 **51b.** Sample: The median is the most useful because it is not affected by extreme values. **53.** $\frac{1}{4}$ **55.** $\frac{1}{3}$

CHECKPOINT **1.** 20 **2.** 4 **3.** 6 **4.** 7 **5.** 7 **6.** 49 **7.** −3 **8.** 11 **9.** 11 **11.** −0.4; −3; −4 **12.** $t = 175b$

Lesson 1-6 pages 30–34

ON YOUR OWN **1.** > **3.** > **5.** > **7.** > **9.** $\frac{5}{3}$ **11.** $\frac{8}{7}$ **13.** −2 **15.** $\frac{2}{3}$ **17.** 1 **19.** $-6\frac{3}{4}$ **21.** $2\frac{1}{6}$ **23.** $-2\frac{1}{12}$ **25.** $-\frac{2}{3}, -\frac{1}{2}, \frac{1}{4}$ **27.** $-9\frac{3}{4}, -9.7, -9\frac{7}{12}$ **29a.** −44°F **29b.** −4°F **31.** $-\frac{9}{16}$ **33.** $-\frac{5}{48}$ **37.** $2\frac{3}{5}$ **39.** −4.5 **41.** $-\frac{1}{10}$ **43.** false; $-\frac{3}{4}$ **45.** true; since integers are real numbers, some real numbers are integers.

MIXED REVIEW **47.** c = change, p = purchase; $c = 10 - p$ **49.** $1,290,000

Toolbox page 35

1. identity prop. of mult. **3.** associative prop. of mult. **5.** commutative prop. of mult. **7.** 830 **9.** 7400 **11.** $9m + 15$ **13.** 13 **15.** $72pqr$

Lesson 1-7 pages 36–39

ON YOUR OWN **3.** $\frac{8}{15}$ **5.** $\frac{7}{15}$ **7.** 8.3% **9.** 62.5% **11.** P(test) ≈ 0.04%; P(control) ≈ 0.08%; control group children were about twice as likely to develop polio. **13.** $\frac{1}{9}$ **15.** $\frac{7}{18}$ **17.** $\frac{7}{9}$ **19.** 0.04, 4%

MIXED REVIEW **23.** −19 **25.** −49 **27.** 53.6

Lesson 1-8 pages 40–43

ON YOUR OWN **1.** 2 × 3 **3.** 3 × 2 **5.** 3 × 4

7. $\begin{bmatrix} 0 & 0 \\ 0 & 0 \end{bmatrix}$ **9.** –6; 5; 0

11. $\begin{bmatrix} 81 & -32 \\ 27 & 100 \end{bmatrix}$; $\begin{bmatrix} 3 & -40 \\ -47 & 8 \end{bmatrix}$ **13.** $\begin{bmatrix} 8.3 & -5.8 \\ -2.6 & 2.9 \\ 13.0 & -7.8 \end{bmatrix}$; $\begin{bmatrix} -1.5 & 10 \\ -10.2 & 8.5 \\ 4.6 & -10.8 \end{bmatrix}$ **15.** $\begin{bmatrix} 1\frac{1}{6} & 1\frac{1}{5} \\ \frac{7}{8} & 1\frac{1}{6} \end{bmatrix}$; $\begin{bmatrix} \frac{1}{6} & \frac{2}{5} \\ -\frac{5}{8} & -\frac{5}{6} \end{bmatrix}$

17. $\begin{bmatrix} 2.5 & 0.3 \\ -8.1 & 2.7 \end{bmatrix}$; $\begin{bmatrix} 4.5 & -0.7 \\ 8.1 & -16.7 \end{bmatrix}$ **21.** $\begin{bmatrix} 1\frac{1}{4} & -6\frac{1}{2} \\ 2\frac{1}{2} & 0 \end{bmatrix}$

23a. $\begin{bmatrix} 13 & 5 & 6 & 2 \\ 18 & 4 & 2 & 2 \\ 6 & 2 & 0 & 2 \end{bmatrix}$ **23b.** 4 employees

25. $\begin{bmatrix} -350 & -150 & 50 \\ -400 & -100 & 250 \end{bmatrix}$

MIXED REVIEW **27.** −7.9 **29.** 17.4 **31.** 24 in.^{2} **33.** 68.08 m^2

CHECKPOINT **1.** $\frac{5}{8}$ **2.** 12.1 **3.** $\frac{25}{32}$ **4.** $\begin{bmatrix} 3\frac{1}{2} & -1 \\ 4 & -9 \end{bmatrix}$

5. $\begin{bmatrix} 5.6 & -6.8 & 11.5 \\ -5.8 & 3.3 & -15.7 \end{bmatrix}$

Toolbox page 44

1. $\begin{bmatrix} 4.9 & 0.7 \\ 2.1 & 0.7 \\ -3.1 & 2.7 \end{bmatrix}$; $\begin{bmatrix} 2.7 & 3.5 \\ 0.9 & -2.3 \\ 0.3 & 1.1 \end{bmatrix}$

3. $\begin{bmatrix} 0 & 4 & 20 & -25 \\ 8 & 2 & -3 & 15 \\ -9 & -1 & -14 & 9 \end{bmatrix}$; $\begin{bmatrix} 10 & -12 & -6 & -1 \\ 0 & -20 & -17 & -5 \\ 21 & -13 & 2 & 15 \end{bmatrix}$

5a. $\begin{bmatrix} 4.9 & 0.7 \\ 2.1 & 0.7 \\ -3.1 & 2.7 \end{bmatrix}$; $\begin{bmatrix} -2.7 & -3.5 \\ -0.9 & 2.3 \\ -0.3 & -1.1 \end{bmatrix}$

Lesson 1-9 pages 45–49

ON YOUR OWN **3.** 4 * A2 ^ 2; 2 * A2 − 5; 3 * A2 + 7 **5.** 16, −9, 1 **7a.** −3 **7b.** −1.9 **9a.** A2 * B2 * C2 **9b.** D2: 1920; E2: 725.2; F2: 5334 **11a.** C2/B2 **11b.** D2: $18,569.23; D3: $24,259.50; D4: $27,702; D5: $30,861.03 **13a.** 1.766 or 1.76625 **13b.** 1562.665 **15a.** 52 **15b.** 118.72 **17a.** Jan.: $1136.65; Feb.: $1557.30; March: $1396.20 **17b.** Jan.: $279.40; Feb.: $382.80; March: $343.20 **19.** C

MIXED REVIEW **21.** −3 **23.** 2 **25.** 26 **27.** 3 **29.** −71

Wrap Up pages 51–53

1. 30.6; 27; 24 **2.** 84.3; 83; 80 and 87 **3.** 2.3; 2.3; 2.3 **4.** 4 recorders **5.** March **6.** 4.7 recorders; 8 recorders **7.** 8 **8.** 64 **9.** 4 **10.** 9 **12a.** $r = 140d$ **12b.** 2940 records; 4200 records **13.** −17 **14.** −12 **15.** 9.9 **16.** 24.9 **17.** −5 **18.** −12 **19.** 15 **20.** 13 **21.** 2 **22.** −1 **23.** 0

24. -18 **25.** -40 **26.** -8 **27.** 2 **28.** B
29. $2\frac{5}{6}$ **30.** $5\frac{1}{6}$ **31.** $-3\frac{1}{3}$ **32.** $-1\frac{1}{4}$ **33.** $1\frac{5}{18}$
34a. $\frac{3}{14}$ **34b.** $\frac{5}{14}$ **34c.** $\frac{3}{7}$ **34d.** $\frac{4}{7}$

35. $\begin{bmatrix} 7 & 7 \\ -2 & -10 \end{bmatrix}$; $\begin{bmatrix} -3 & -13 \\ 20 & 8 \end{bmatrix}$

36. $\begin{bmatrix} 4.3 & 0.6 \\ 1.0 & -0.3 \\ -1.7 & 1.2 \end{bmatrix}$; $\begin{bmatrix} -1.9 & -2.8 \\ 4.4 & 6.1 \\ -4.7 & -3.4 \end{bmatrix}$ **37.** $\begin{bmatrix} \frac{1}{8} \\ -\frac{7}{20} \end{bmatrix}$; $\begin{bmatrix} -1\frac{1}{8} \\ 1\frac{3}{20} \end{bmatrix}$

39. 5.6 **40.** -11 **41.** 80 **42.** 0; -4; 4; -8
43. 2; 0; 0; 0 **44.** 6; 8; 16; 64

Preparing for the Math A Exam page 55

1. 2 **3.** 3 **5.** 4 **7.** 4

CHAPTER 2

Toolbox page 58

1. H **3.** E **5.** $(4, 5)$ **7.** $(-5, 0)$ **13.** II **15.** IV

17a.

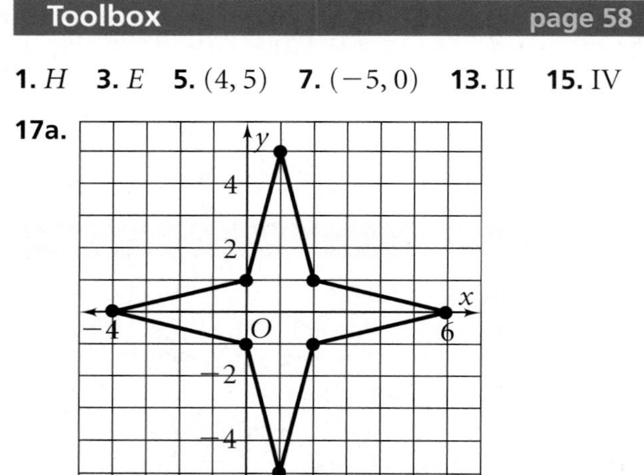

17b. It looks like a four-pointed star.

Lesson 2-1 pages 59–63

ON YOUR OWN **1.** Negative; with each class taken, you need to study more, so the amount of free time decreases. **3.** Positive; you expect to sell more shovels as the amount of snow increases.
5. Negative; as the temperature rises, people use less oil for heating. **7.** No correlation; shoes are not priced by size. **9a.** Negative correlation; everything else being equal, voters are more likely to stay home in bad weather. **9b.** Sample: Yes; a low voter turnout may favor the candidates whose supporters feel strongly about the issues in the campaign and the turnout may be low because of bad weather.

11a.

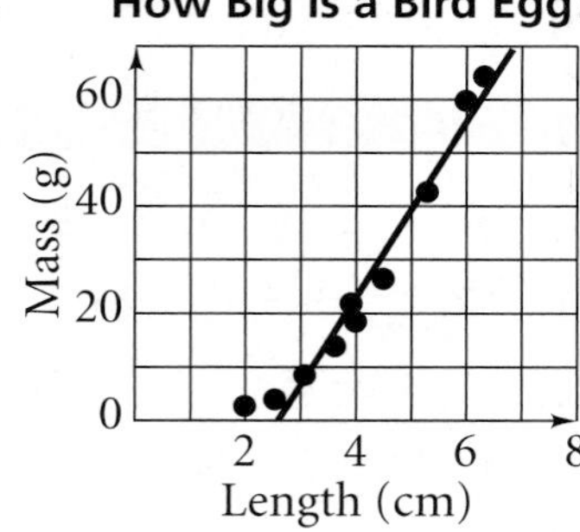

11b. There is a positive correlation between the length and the mass of a bird egg, because the larger eggs are heavier. **11c.** Sample: The egg is about 5.7 cm long. From the graph, its weight should be about 52 g. **13.** positive correlation
15. positive correlation

17a.

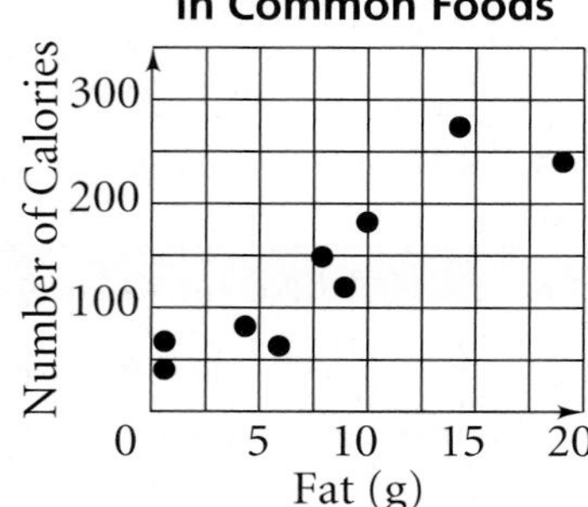

17b. positive correlation **19.** Each data point represents the total toll charged (y-coordinate) for a vehicle that traveled a specified number of miles (x-coordinate). **21a.** The corresponding points have the same y-coordinate.

MIXED REVIEW **23.** 0 **25.** -9 **27.** $\frac{3}{10}$ **29.** 33
31. Mode; the mean and the median need to be computed. You can read the mode off the plot.
33. 1981–1989 and 1991–1995

Lesson 2-2 pages 64–68

ON YOUR OWN
1. Sample:

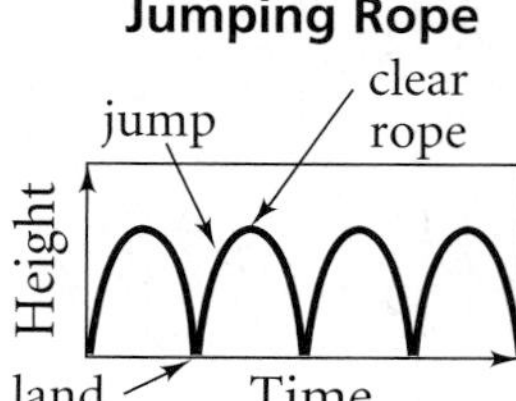

3. Sample:

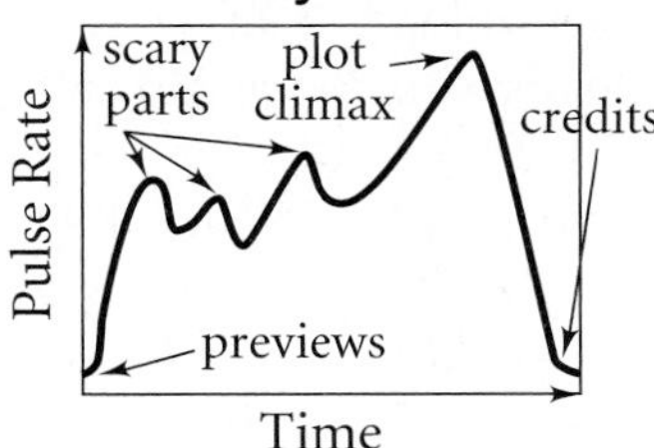

5. The graph is continuous but data are discrete. To fix the graph, you must remove all lines connecting data points. **7.** Sample: Continuous; between any two weights you measure, any value is possible.

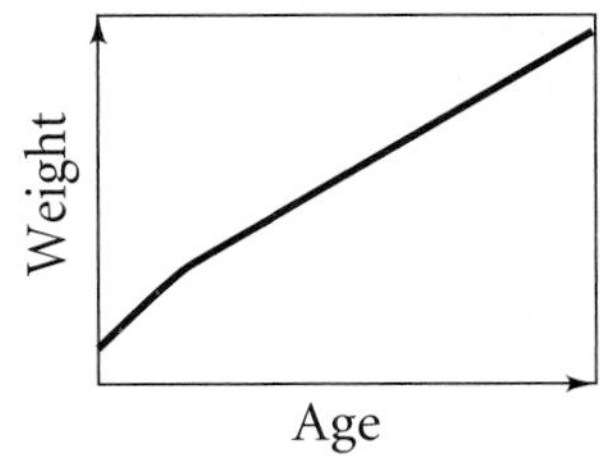

9. Sample: Discrete; there is only one time for each morning.

Getting-up Time

Time

M T W Th F Sa Su

Day

11. Sample: Discrete; you cannot have half a book.

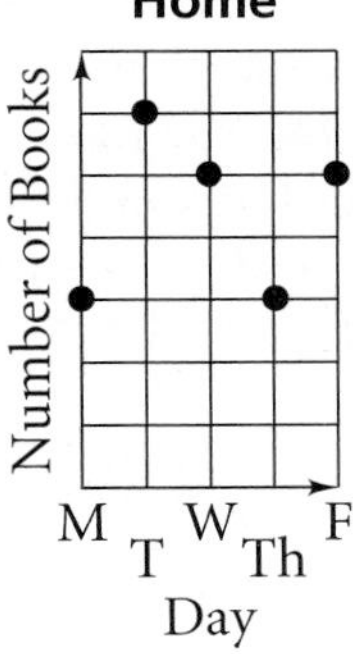

13. Sample: Continuous; walking speed can be measured at all times.

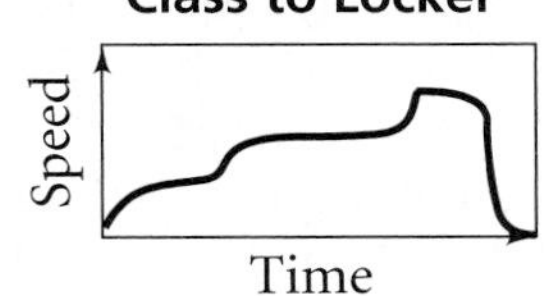

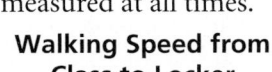

15a. blue; red **15b.** Growing at a steady rate, a puppy becomes heavier than a baby but stops growing soon after that. A baby's weight gain increases with time, so it outgrows the puppy. **17.** Graph II; graph I; at constant speed, distance increases with time.

MIXED REVIEW **21.** $\begin{bmatrix} -14 & 11 \\ -2 & -51 \end{bmatrix}$

23a. f = amount of fruit used per day; $f + 200$
23b. 15,400 lb

CHECKPOINT **1a–b.**

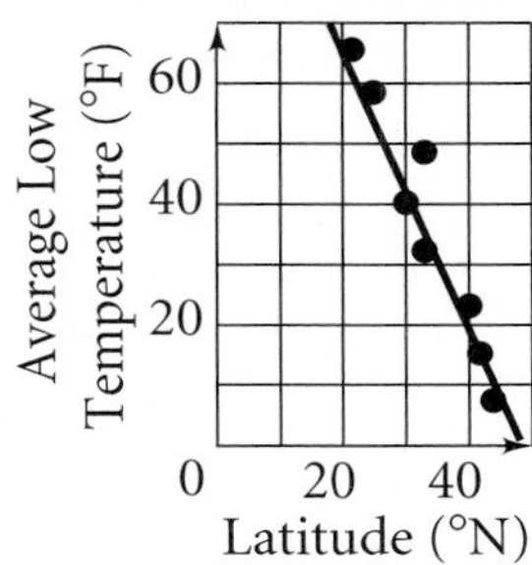

There is a negative correlation. **1c.** Sample: about 70°F **3.** C; this is the only graph where the distance from home drops back to 0, indicating that you came home.

Lesson 2-3 pages 69–72

ON YOUR OWN **1a.** Sample: Horizontal axis from 0 to 200 with a line of the graph every 25 lb; vertical axis 0 to 30 with a line of the graph every 5 lb.

1b.

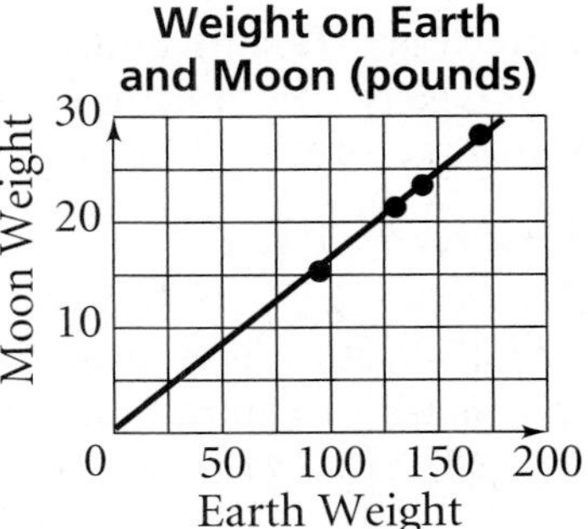

1c. Find the point on the graph that corresponds to your weight on Earth. Use this point to identify the coordinate for the moon. This is your weight on the moon. **3.** dependent; independent
5. independent; dependent **7.** B **9.** C

11a.

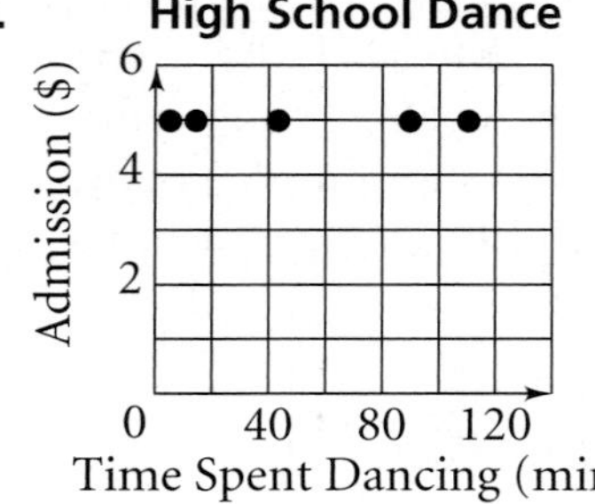

11b. Sample: The horizontal range is 0 to 120 with the scale marked every 20 min on the axis. The vertical range is 0 to 6 with the scale marked at every dollar on the axis.

MIXED REVIEW **15.** Sample:

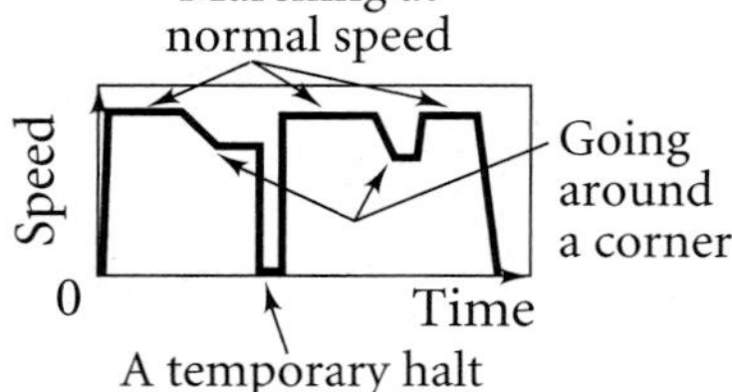

17a.

```
     ✗
     ✗         ✗
  ✗  ✗      ✗  ✗
 32 33 34 35 36
```

17b. 33 **19.** −1 **21.** 108 **23.** 3 **25.** 9

Lesson 2-4 pages 73–78

ON YOUR OWN **1.** 4 **3.** 9 **5.** 18 **7.** $-\frac{3}{4}$ **9.** No; graph fails the vertical-line test. **11.** Yes; graph passes the vertical-line test. **13.** function; amount of money, number of tickets **15.** function; monthly payment, number of years **17.** function; time, speed **19.** no **21.** yes **25.** {4, 5, 11} **27.** $\{-225\frac{1}{2}, -220, -187\}$ **29.** {−11, −7, 17} **31.** {6, 0, 216} **33.** {7, 6, −210} **35.** {2, 0, 30} **37a.** dependent variable **37b.** Input value is to output value as domain is to range. **39.** 2.13 **41.** −4.3 **43.** 0.04 **45.** 0.84 **47.** {0.25, 121} **49.** {25, 1, 0, 4, 100} **51.** The same *y*-value may correspond to any number of *x*-values. **53.** D

MIXED REVIEW **55.** 6 **57.** 80 **59.** $-\frac{1}{10}$ **61.** $s = \frac{1}{3}e$

Lesson 2-5 pages 79–83

ON YOUR OWN **1.** 16 **3.** 28 **5.** 2 **7.** 21 **9a.** amount of water; number of loads **9b.** $w(n) = 42n$ **9c.** 294 gal **9d.** 13 loads; you divide 546 gal by 42 gal/load. **13.** A **15a.** $T(a) = 10a + 1$ **15b.** $31 **19.** {18, 15, 13.8, 10} **21.** {−9, 0, −1.44, −25} **23.** {10, 1, 2.44, 26} **25.** {−22, −4, 3.2, 26} **27.** $y = 4x$ **29.** $f(x) = x^3$ **31.** $R(K) = 8 - K$; {0, 1, 2, 3, 4, 5, 6, 7, 8}; {8, 7, 6, 5, 4, 3, 2, 1, 0} **33.** $e(h) = 4.25h$

MIXED REVIEW **35.** 23 **37.** 10 **39.** −2.5

41.

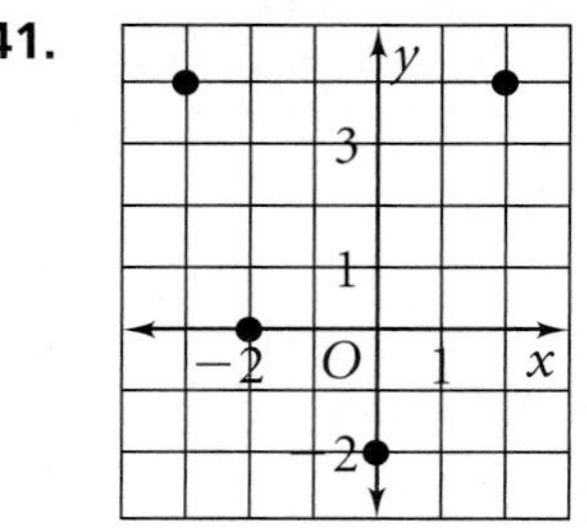

43.

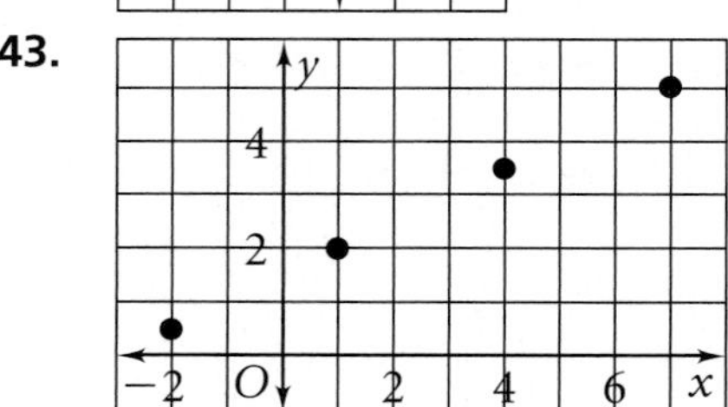

CHECKPOINT **1a.** number of minutes; number of words

1b.

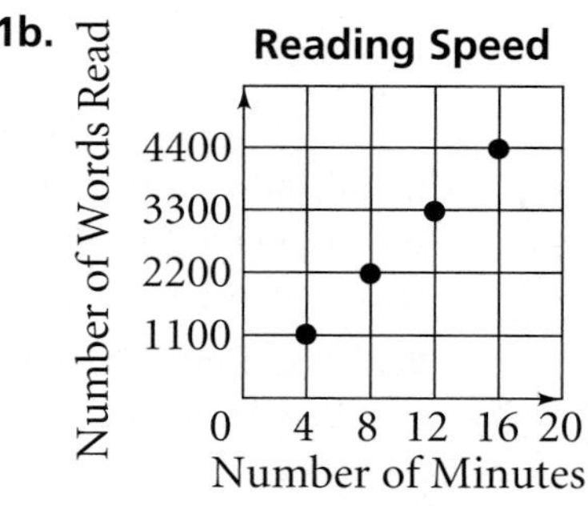

The *x*-value range is from 0 to 20. It is easiest to label every 4 minutes, to correspond to the given data. The *y*-value range is from 0 to 5500 with labels every 1100 words.

3. You multiply 3 by 4, then subtract 12 from the result. **4.** $p(r) = 0.3r$ **5.** $c(d) = 1.15d$ **6.** {−120, −36, −24, 0} **7.** {−40, 9, 8, 0} **8.** {−25.5, 2.5, 6.5, 14.5} **9.** {−3, 4, 5, 7}

Lesson 2-6 pages 84–88

ON YOUR OWN

1. Sample table:

x	y
−2	6
−1	3
0	0
1	−3
2	−6

3. Sample table:

x	$f(x)$
0	−7
1	−5
2	−3
3	−1
4	1

5. Sample table:

x	$f(x)$
−3	−1
−1	$-\frac{1}{3}$
0	0
1	$\frac{1}{3}$
3	1

7. Sample table:

x	$f(x)$
−2	2
−2	−1
0	−2
1	−1
2	2

9a. C **9b.** 9 **9c.**

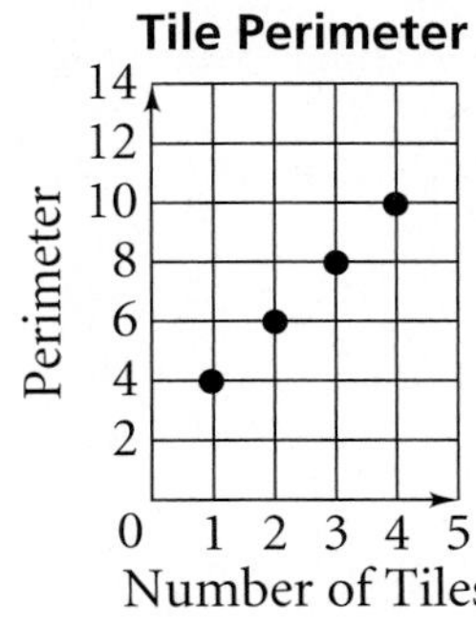

11a. $s(t) = 6t$ **11b.** $w(t) = 3t$ **11c.** 55.2 gal

11d.

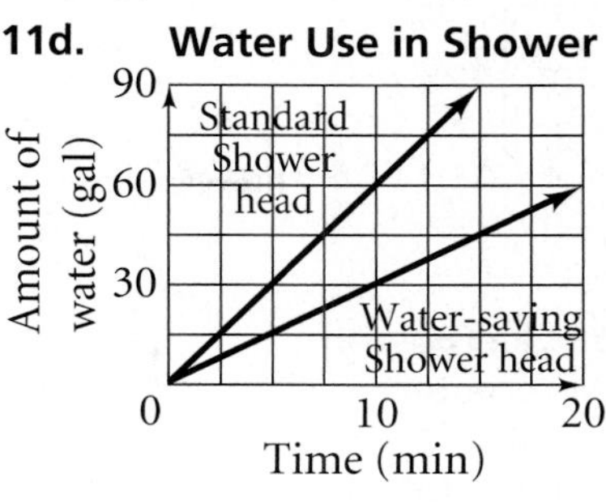

Sample: The graph shows that the difference in water use between the two shower heads grows quickly over time.

13.

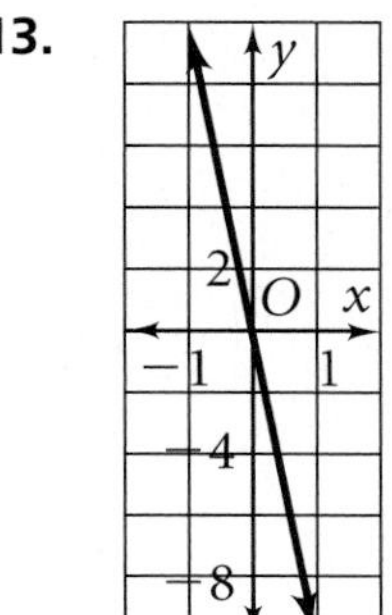

15.

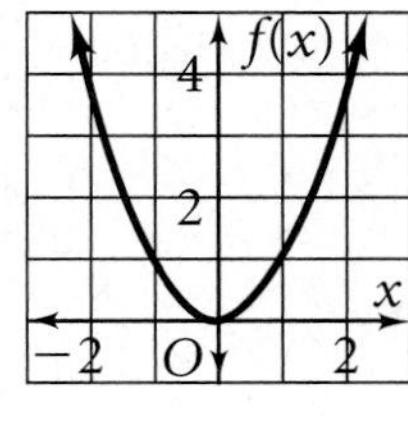

17.

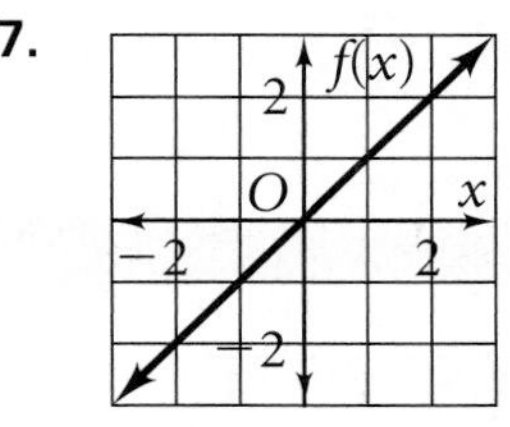

19.

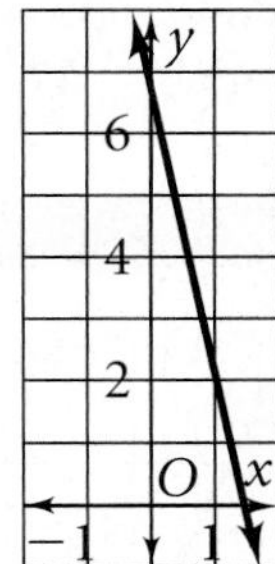

21.

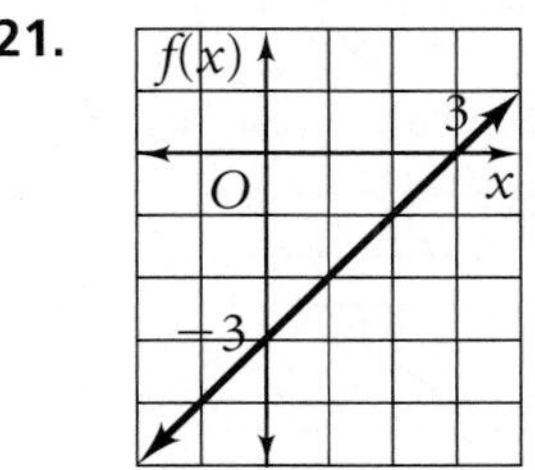

23.

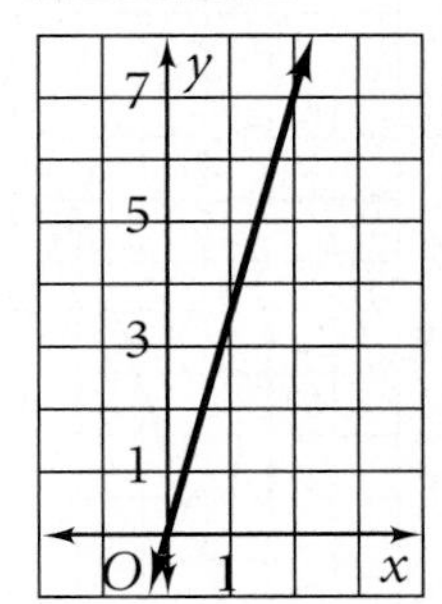

25.

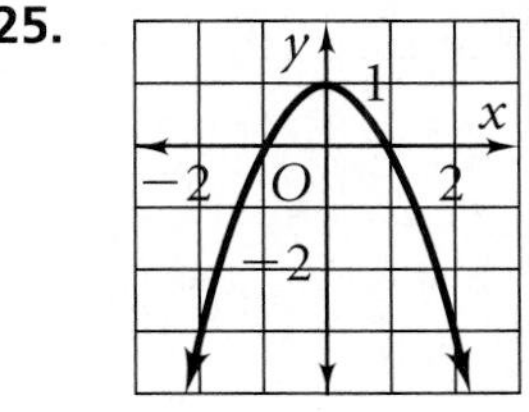

27.

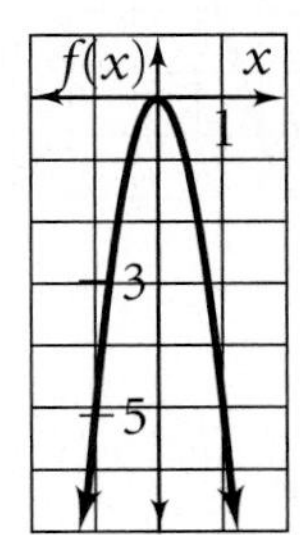

Selected Answers

29. Sample table:

x	y
−2	2
0	2
2	2
4	2

31a. $.71

31b. Sample table:

a	$C(a)$
0	$.27
1	$.38
2	$.49
3	$.60
4	$.71
5	$.82

Cost of Call (Boston to Worcester)

Cost ($): .20, .40, .60, .80

0 1 2 3 4 5
Additional Minutes

31c. at most 12 min **33.** B

MIXED REVIEW **39.** {3, 7, 9, 15} **41.** {4, 2, 1, −2} **43.** −20 **45.** 4 **47.** −1

Toolbox — page 89

1.

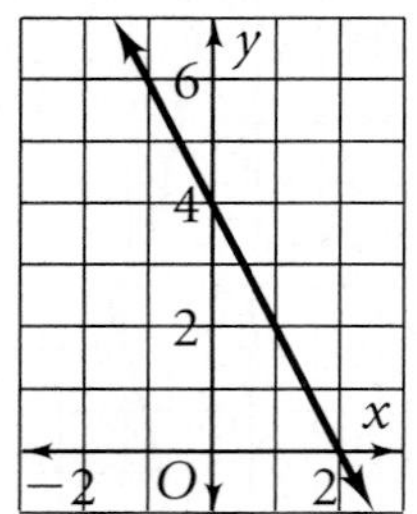

3.

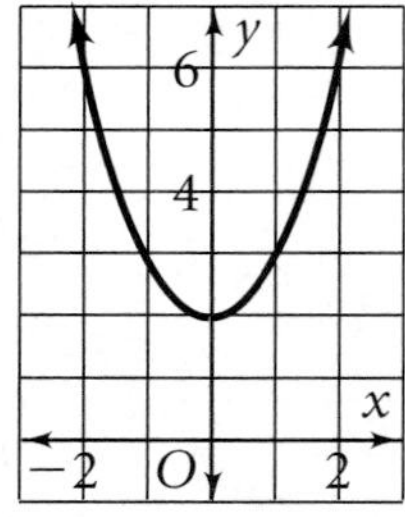

5.

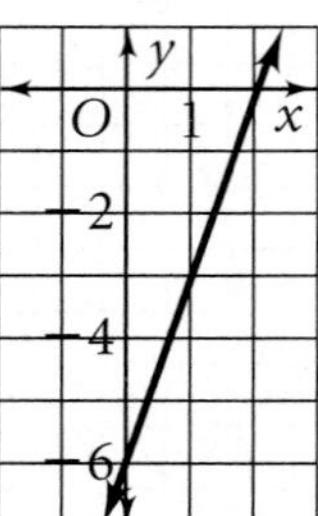

7.

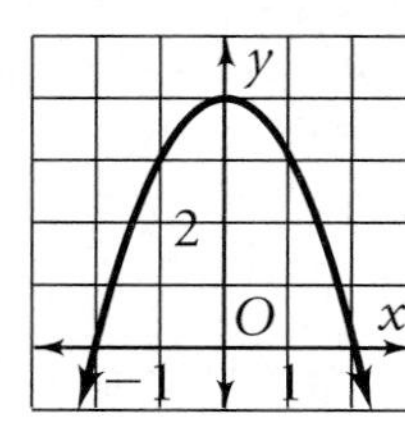

Lesson 2-7 — pages 90–94

ON YOUR OWN **1.** Linear function family; the highest power of the variable is 1. **3.** Absolute value family; there is a variable expression inside the absolute value symbol. **5.** Quadratic family; the highest power of the variable is 2. **7.** Quadratic family; the highest power of the variable is 2. **9.** Absolute value family; there is a variable expression inside the absolute value symbol. **11.** Absolute value; the graph forms a "V" that opens up or down. **13.** Quadratic; the highest power of the variable is 2. **15.** Sample: A family of functions is a collection of functions whose graphs and equations are alike. **17.** No; it fails the vertical line test so it is not a function. **19.** U-shaped curve **21.** V-shape **23.** linear

Income as a Function of Hours Worked

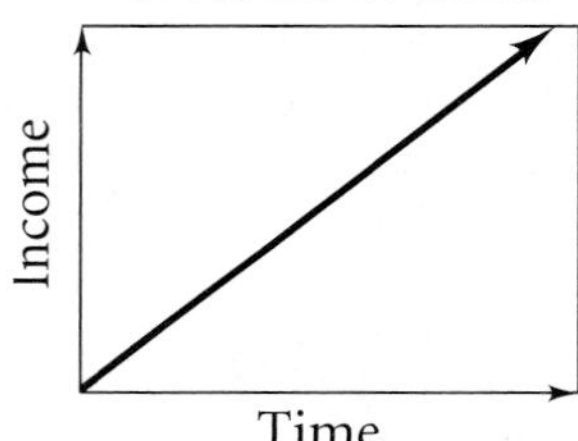

25. line; slants down from left to right

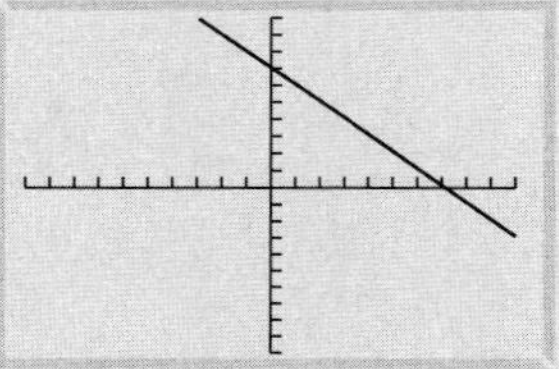

27. V-shaped; opens up

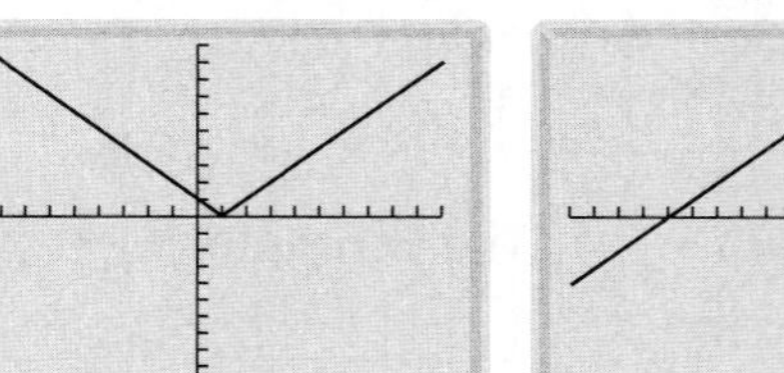

29. V-shaped; opens down

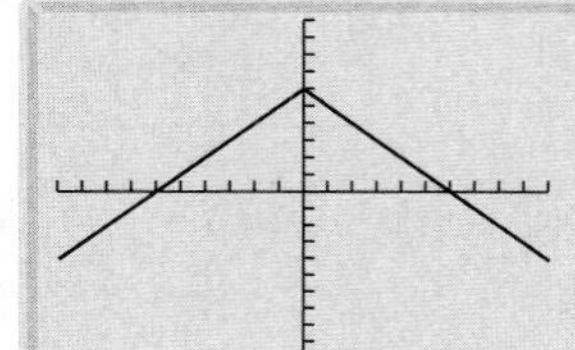

31. U-shaped; opens up **33.** V-shaped; opens up

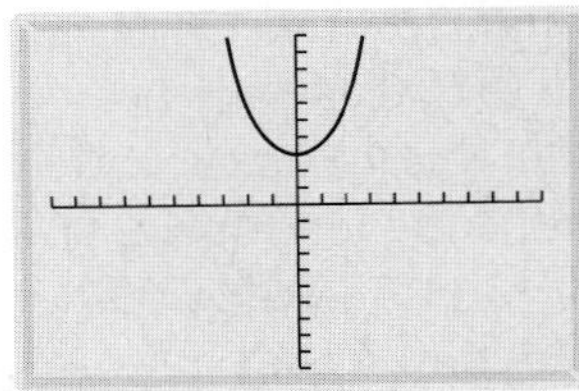

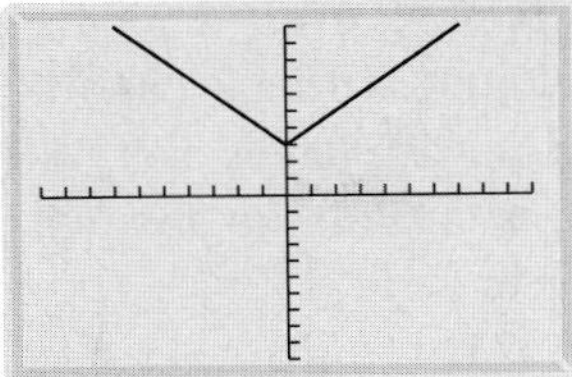

35. Quadratic family; the curve is U-shaped, opening down. **37.** Absolute value family; the path of the ball is V-shaped, opening up. **39a.** V-shaped; opens up

39b.

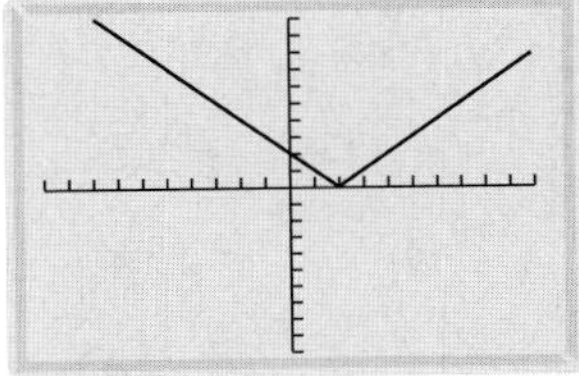

MIXED REVIEW

41.

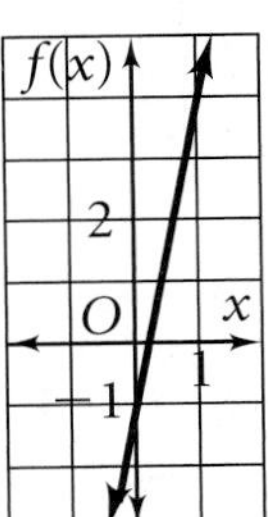

43.

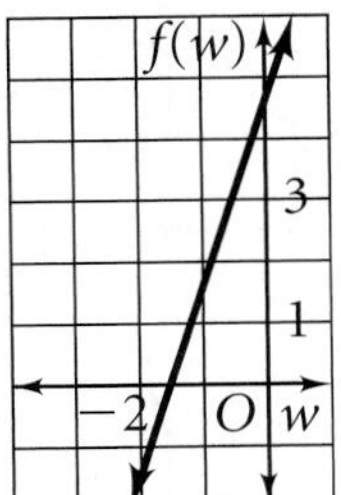

45.

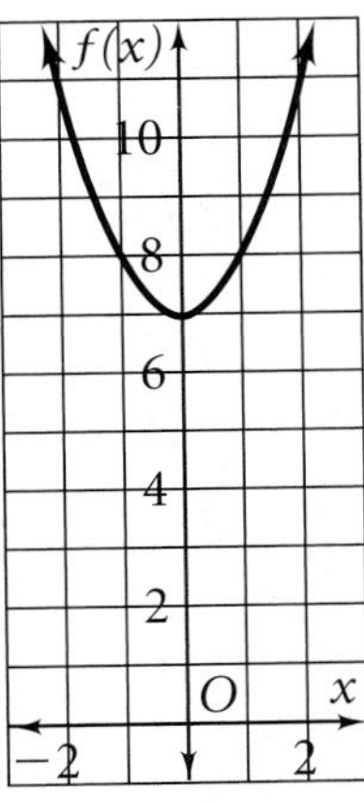

47.

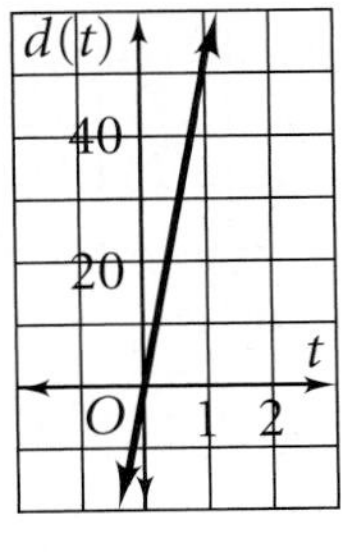

49a. −116 **49b.** Square −8; multiply by −2; add 12 to the result. **51.** $\frac{5}{16}$ **53.** $\frac{15}{16}$ **55.** $\frac{11}{16}$

Lesson 2-8 pages 95–99

ON YOUR OWN **1.** $\frac{1}{2}$ **3.** $\frac{1}{6}$ **5.** $\frac{2}{3}$ **7.** $\frac{1}{2}$ **9.** 0

11. Sample: For theoretical probability, you know all the possible outcomes and you want to find out how likely a specific event is to happen. For experimental probability, you know the results of an experiment and you want to find out how frequently a specific event has happened.

13b. $\frac{1}{12}$ **13c.** $\frac{1}{2}$ **13d.** $\frac{1}{4}$ **15.** $\frac{1}{2}$ **17.** 0 **19.** $\frac{4}{9}$
21b. $\frac{1}{12}$ **21c.** $\frac{1}{6}$ **23.** $\frac{1}{6}$ **25.** $\frac{17}{18}$ **27.** $\frac{1}{3}$ **29.** 0
31. $\frac{3}{8}$ **33.** $\frac{11}{16}$ **35.** $\frac{1}{4}$ **37.** 0 **39.** B **41.** $\frac{2}{6}$

MIXED REVIEW **45.** 5 **47.** 0.6 **49.** $-\frac{1}{9}$

Wrap-Up pages 101–103

1. Positive correlation; people drink more cold drinks in warm weather. **2.** Negative correlation; a better-trained swimmer takes less time to swim 100 m. **4.** Sample: A computer rental costs $2.50 per hour. If you start with a fixed amount of money, the longer you plan to work on the computer, the less money you will have left. **5.** Sample: A residential thermostat senses when the temperature in the room falls below the set level, turns the heater on until the temperature reaches 3°F above the set level, then turns the heater off. The graph shows the air temperature rising while the heater is working and then falling after the heater is turned off.
6. Sample: An elevator is on the second floor. Someone gets in, goes to the eleventh floor, and gets off.

7. Sample:

Height of a Sunflower Over a Summer

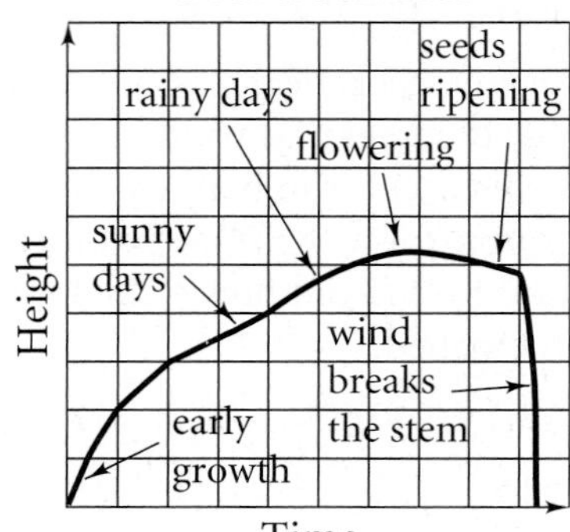

8. **Number of People in a Restaurant**

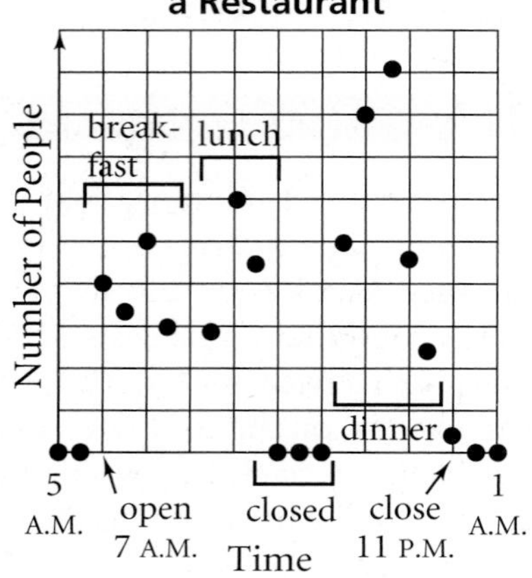

9a. year; price

9b. **Cost of a Median-Priced Home**

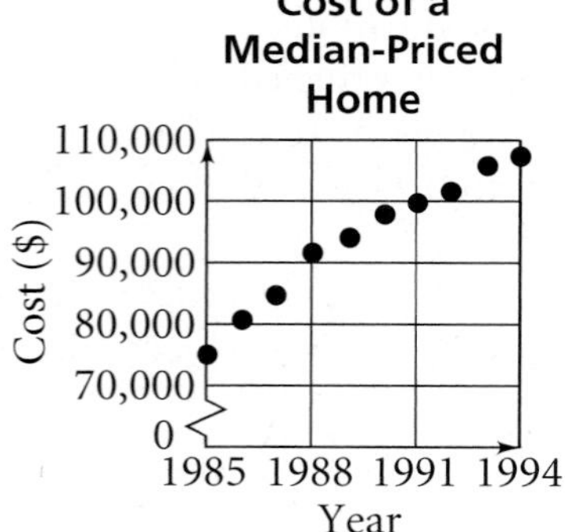

9c. Sample: Years from 1985 to 1994 on the x-axis with labels every 3 years; amounts from \$0 to \$110,000 with a break from \$0 to \$70,000 on the y-axis with labels every \$10,000; this graph accurately represents all the data without taking too much space. **10.** $\{-23, -7, -3, 13\}$ **11.** $\{1, 3, 3.5, 5.5\}$ **12.** $\{17, 1, 2, 26\}$ **13.** not a function **15.** $f(x) = x + 1$ **16.** $f(x) = -x$ **17.** $f(x) = x + 3.5$

18. Sample table:

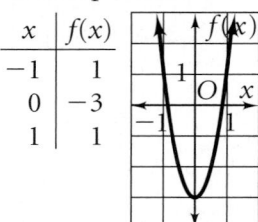

x	$f(x)$
-1	1
0	-3
1	1

19. Sample table:

x	$f(x)$
-6	1
-5	0
-2	3
0	5

20. Sample table:

x	$f(x)$
-2	-3
-1	-1
0	1
1	3

21. Sample table:

x	$f(x)$
-2	-5
-1	-6
0	-7
1	-6
2	-5

22. quadratic, highest power of x is 2; absolute value; linear, highest power of x is 1; absolute value
23. $\frac{1}{6}$ **24.** $\frac{5}{6}$ **25.** $\frac{1}{3}$ **26.** 0 **27a.** $\frac{1}{4}$ **27b.** P(not 3 heads) means the chances of getting 0, 1, 2, or 4 heads.
28. E **29.** 8 **30.** −3 **31.** 6 **32.** $\frac{1}{2}$ **33.** 5
34. −1.2 **35.** −1 **36.** 7 **37.** 4.5 **38.** $5\frac{1}{4}$

Preparing for the Math A Exam page 105

1. 3 **3.** 1 **5.** 3

CHAPTER 3

Lesson 3-1 pages 108–113

ON YOUR OWN **1.** Kendra's method is better; it needs only one operation and Ted's needs two. **3.** 6 **5.** 8 **7.** 14 **9.** 500 **11.** C **13.** $B + 109 = 180$; 71°
15. $38\frac{3}{4} + g = 41\frac{1}{2}$; $2\frac{3}{4}$ in. **17.** −1 **19.** −1.57
21. −196 **23.** −4.5 **25.** −20 **27.** $-5\frac{5}{6}$ **29.** $4\frac{1}{4}$
31. −245 **33.** subtraction property **39.** 31.5
41. −99 **43.** 13 **45.** $16\frac{1}{2}$ **47.** $-1\frac{1}{4}$ **49.** 11.5
51. $330 = 280 + x$; \$50 **53a.** $3L = 166.5$; \$55.50
53b. $1.5r = 55.5$; \$37 **55.** −18 **57.** −8 **59.** $-3\frac{3}{4}$
61. −262 **63.** −4.5 **65.** $-\frac{3}{8}$ **67.** 5.12 **69.** $-\frac{1}{24}$
71. $5s = 1.6$; 0.32 km

MIXED REVIEW **73.** 8 **75.** about 500,000 **77.** 42.3 **79.** 31 **81.** 28

Lesson 3-2 pages 114–118

ON YOUR OWN **1.** $3x + 2 = 5$ **3.** $3x + 1 = -2$
5. −1 **7.** −2 **9.** 1 **11.** −2 **13.** 21 **15.** 7
17. −6 **19.** 27 **21.** 0.382 **23.** −60 **25.** $18 + 2t = 60$; 21 min **27.** −6 **29.** 4.5 **31.** 16 **33.** 30
35. −6 **37.** 75 **39.** 0 **41.** −19 **43.** 2.2
45. 3.864 **47a.** Yes; with this estimate, the total bill is \$55, which is close to \$60. **47b.** 125 mi
49. 14 bulbs **51.** Multiplying by 100 changes all the numbers in the equation to integers and it might be easier to work with integers. **53.** $r = (2.8 - 1.34) \cdot 2$; 2.92 **55.** $n = (8 + 0.5) \div 0.05$; 170
57. $n = (7 - 5.3) \div (-0.8)$; −2.125
59. $t = (-7.06 - 3)(-2.5)$; 25.15

MIXED REVIEW **63.** 12 **65.** −9 **67.** 9 **69.** −20 **71.** 3

Lesson 3-3 pages 119–123

ON YOUR OWN

1.

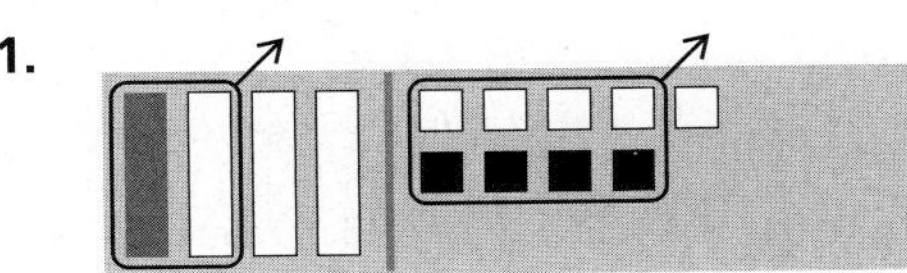

$2y + 1$; **3.** $-n$ **5.** $8b - 2$ **7.** $-4x + 8n$ **9.** $-6x + m + 8$ **11.** $2x - x = 4$; 4 **13.** $-x - 2 + 3x + 1 = 3$; −1 **15.** 8 **17.** 3 **19.** 7 **21.** 2 **23.** \$6.50
27. 6 **29.** −4 **31.** $5\frac{1}{2}$ **33.** $5\frac{4}{7}$ **35.** −0.48 **37.** 2.4
39. 7 **41.** $4\frac{1}{4}$ in. **43.** 1986, 1987, 1988 **45.** 60
47. 50 **49.** 50

MIXED REVIEW **51.** $y = -2x$
53. Sample:

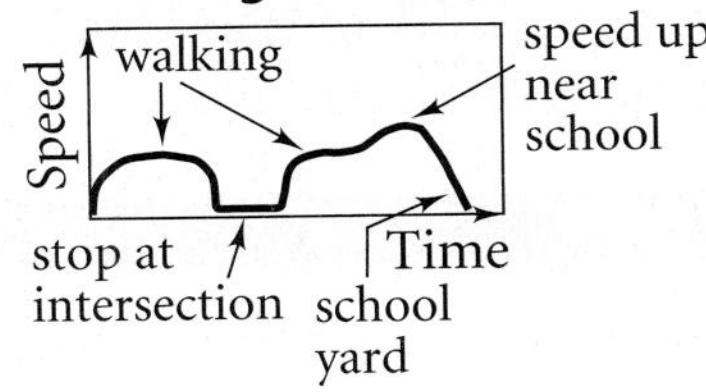

55. −9 **57.** −48

Lesson 3-4 pages 124–128

ON YOUR OWN **1.** $2(t - 2) = -6$; −1
3. $4(z + 1) = 4$; 0 **5.** No; $2a \cdot 2b = 4ab$. You cannot use the distributive property because ab is a product, not a sum. **7.** $-2n + 12$ **9.** $2b - \frac{8}{5}$ **11.** $4y + 6$
13. $18n - 42$ **15.** $-b$ **17.** $-11n$ **19.** 900° **21.** 3
23. 9 **25.** 1 **27.** −1 **29.** 8 **31.** −2 **33.** −1
35. 1 **37.** 380 mi; 280 mi **39.** 9 aluminum bats and 6 wooden bats **43.** \$3.96 **45.** \$29.55
47. \$98.97

MIXED REVIEW **49.** $-\frac{2}{3}$ **51.** −7 **53a.** B2/250
53b. 2.9; 0.9; 0.5 **53c.** \$504 million **55.** −17

Selected Answers

CHECKPOINT **1.** 1 **2.** 33 **3.** 20 **4.** $2\frac{1}{2}$ **5.** 120 **6.** -2 **7.** -2 **8.** 10 **9.** $18\frac{1}{3}$ **10.** -2.7 **11.** -16 **12.** 2 **13.** 63 in. by 83 in. **14.** B

Lesson 3-5 — pages 129–132

ON YOUR OWN **1.** 12 **3.** -10 **5.** -1 **7.** -48 **9.** In using the distributive property, the student did not multiply 1 by 8. **11.** A **13.** \$4/yd **15.** -45 **17.** -3 **19.** 15 **21.** -7 **23.** $-14\frac{1}{7}$ **25.** -10 **27.** 32 **29.** $\frac{6}{13}$ **31.** -60 **33.** 54 **35.** about 61.5 mi/h **37.** 33.7 h/wk **39.** -21 **41.** 5 **43.** -33 **45.** -1 **47.** $\frac{3}{5}$ **49.** -9 **51.** $1\frac{5}{6}$ **53.** $1\frac{1}{14}$ **55.** about \$141 million **57.** $2\frac{1}{2}$ h

MIXED REVIEW **59.** -7 **61.** $\frac{1}{2}$ **63.** 12 **65.** 1 **67.** $\frac{1}{5}$ **69.** $\frac{2}{5}$

Toolbox — page 133

1. Spain—gold; Poland—silver; Ghana—bronze
3. Coretta lives in New York; David lives in Houston; Nando lives in Dallas; Helen lives in Chicago.

Lesson 3-6 — pages 134–138

ON YOUR OWN **1.** independent **3.** dependent **5.** $\frac{1}{6}$ **7.** $\frac{1}{12}$ **9.** $\frac{5}{12}$ **11.** $\frac{3}{50}$ **13.** $\frac{3}{20}$ **15.** $\frac{1}{10}$ **17.** $\frac{1}{6}$ **19.** $\frac{1}{9}$ **21.** 0 **23.** D **27.** about 1.2% **29.** 0.0036 **31.** $\frac{1}{5}$ **33.** $\frac{3}{5}$ **35.** $\frac{4}{5}$ **37.** $\frac{3}{4}$ **39.** A

MIXED REVIEW **41.** -60 **43.** 10 **45.** 45% **47.** 32.8% **49.** 100%

Lesson 3-7 — pages 139–144

ON YOUR OWN **1.** $n = 0.04 \times 150$ **3.** $24 = 1.5 \times n$ **5.** $0.1 \times n = 8$; 80 **7.** $0.06 \times n = 36$; 600 **9.** $n \times 45 = 18$; 40% **11.** \$62.40 **15.** \$20 **17.** 50% **19.** 39.2 **21.** 4.5% **23.** 330 **25.** 60% **27.** \$84 **29.** \$320 **31.** about 12.6% **33.** 40%

35. The number of people 65 and over is projected to be 80 million, which is 20% of the total population, so the projected population is 400 million people. **37.** \$1250 **39.** 2 yr

MIXED REVIEW **41.** Sample table:

x	$f(x)$
0	-2
2	1
3	2.5
4	4

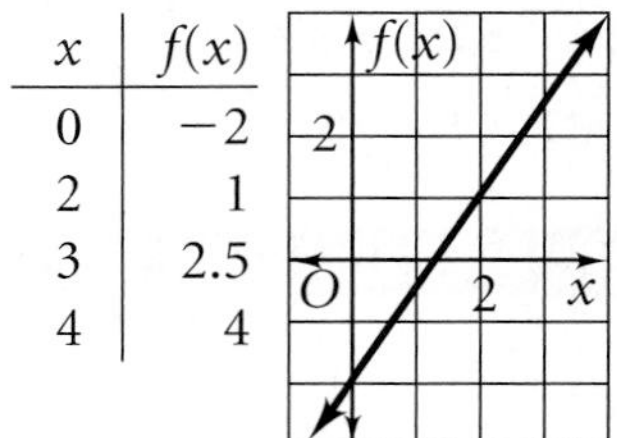

43. Sample table:

x	$f(x)$
-1	-3
0	1
1	5

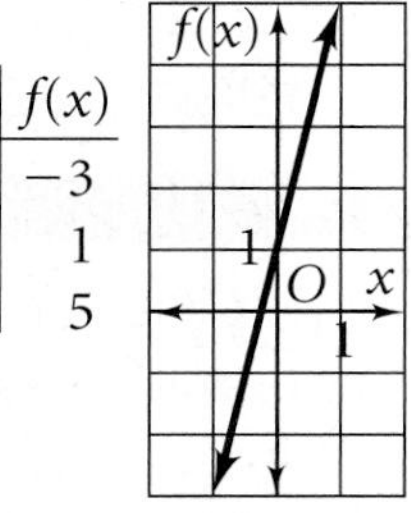

45. $\{-1, -2, -3\}$ **47.** 0.75 **49.** 0.88

CHECKPOINT **1.** $-\frac{14}{5}$ **2.** 9.6 **3.** $3\frac{11}{15}$ **4.** $-11\frac{1}{4}$ **5.** 3 **6.** $\frac{1}{9}$ **7.** $\frac{1}{24}$ **8.** $\frac{1}{27}$ **9.** $\frac{1}{36}$ **10.** The probability increases, because the first draw is the same, but for the second the number of marbles decreases and the number of favorable outcomes stays the same. **11.** 218 members

Toolbox — page 145

1.

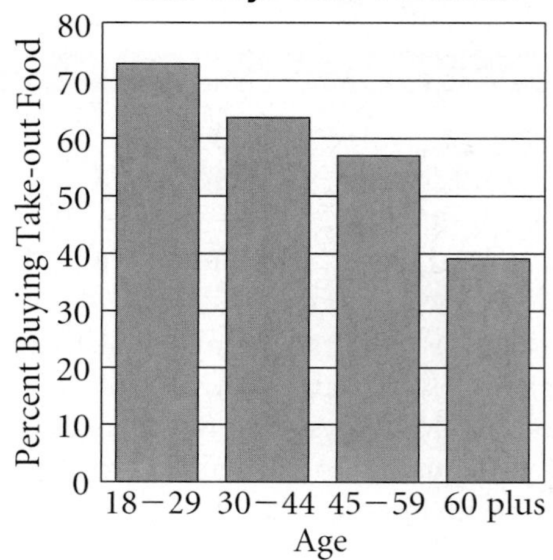

3.

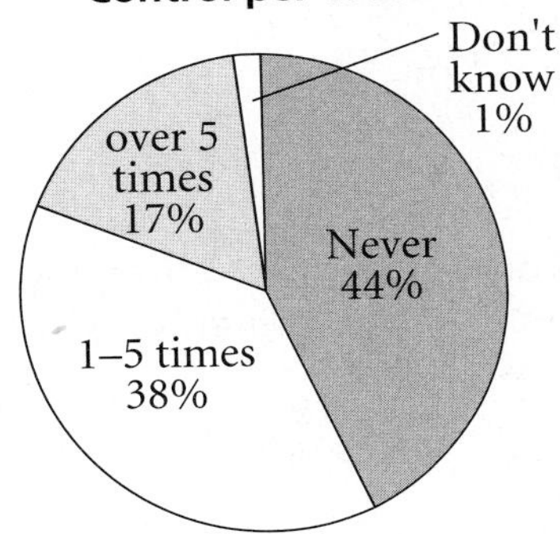

Lesson 3-8 pages 146–149

ON YOUR OWN **1.** 25% decrease **3.** 5% increase **5.** 3% decrease **7.** 29% decrease **9.** about 39% **11.** 100% **13.** 60% **15.** 33% **17.** 200% **21.** Less; the 20% you subtracted is 20% of an amount greater than the original amount, so it is greater than the 20% you added. **23.** 6% increase **25.** 22% decrease **27.** 4% increase **29.** 120% increase **31.** 22% increase **33.** 28% decrease **35a.** 100% **35b.** 100 **35c.** 50% **35d.** 50 **35e.** 100% **35f.** 100 **37.** C **39.** 60% **41.** about 14% **43.** about 50% **45a.** 25% **45b.** 20%

MIXED REVIEW **47.** 1.5 **49.** 13 **51.** 60%

Wrap-Up pages 151–153

1. 16 **2.** −36 **3.** 31 **4.** 24 **5.** 44 **6.** 4.25 **7.** 12 **8.** 2 **9.** $2x + 5 = 9$; 2 **10.** $3x - 2 = 7$; 3 **11.** $-4x + 2 = -6$; 2 **12.** $\frac{1}{2}$ **13.** 3 **14.** 3 **15.** 11 **16.** 18 **17.** 4 **18.** −2 **19.** −9 **21.** $4m + 3$ **22.** $b + 10$ **23.** $-5w + 20$ **24.** $36 - 27j$ **25.** −9 **26.** 4 **27.** −0.5 **28.** $1\frac{1}{2}$ **29.** −2 **30.** 1.5 **31.** 2 **32.** 1 **33.** $2[l + (l - 6)] = 72$; 15 cm × 21 cm **34.** C **35.** −45 **36.** 24 **37.** −11 **38.** −4 **39.** $40 **40.** dependent; $\frac{2}{45}$ **41.** independent; $\frac{1}{20}$ **43.** $n = 0.15 \times 86$; 12.9 **44.** $n \times 5 = 40$; 800% **45.** $1.8 = 0.72 \times n$; 2.5 **46.** 3.75% **47.** $220 **48.** about 13% increase **49.** 25% decrease **50.** about 33% decrease **51.** 27.2% **53.** −2 **54.** 1.4 **55.** 19 **56.** 7 **57.** 4.5 **58.** 18 **59.** $\frac{1}{4}$ **60.** $1\frac{1}{7}$ **61.** 3 **62.** $\frac{4}{9}$ **63.** −4 **64.** 5 **65.** 52 **66.** −3

Preparing for the Math A Exam page 155

1. 3 **3.** 4 **5.** 4 **7.** 4 **9.** 2

CHAPTER 4

Lesson 4-1 pages 158–162

ON YOUR OWN **1.** yes; $6 \cdot 20 = 8 \cdot 15$ **3.** yes; $-0.12 \cdot 0.5 = -0.4 \cdot 0.15$ **5.** no; $-3 \cdot 25 \neq -1 \cdot 100$ **7.** about 433 times **9.** $54 **11.** 20% **13.** 50 **15.** 27.6% **17.** 307.1 **19.** 15.6 **21.** 10 ft by 12 ft **23.** E **25.** 5 **27.** 12.5 **29.** 4 **31.** 5 **33.** 12.5 **35.** −0.864 **37a.** No; For an item that originally costs $12, $\frac{1}{3}$ off results in the price $8; 50% off results in the price $6. **39.** 9 **41.** 5.5 in. **43.** 7.1%

MIXED REVIEW **45.** $\begin{bmatrix} -1.2 & 14.6 \\ -1.4 & -5.7 \end{bmatrix}$ **47.** −11.5 **49.** 16 paperbacks **51.** −14.5

Lesson 4-2 pages 163–168

ON YOUR OWN **1.** $2x + 2 = x - 8$; −10 **3.** $2x + 3 = 3x - 7$; 10 **5.** 7 **7.** 3 **9.** no solution **11.** no solution **13.** identity **15.** You should add y, not subtract, on the third line; 5.3. **17.** 0 **19.** no solution **21.** 2 **23.** no solution **25.** −41 **27.** $-\frac{1}{2}$ **29.** identity **31.** $a = -\frac{1}{4}$; $w = -4$; $x = -1$; $y = 0$ **35.** 20 h **43.** $DF = 7$, $DE = 10$, $EF = 6$ **45.** 7 **47.** −3 **49.** −0.5 **51.** 10 **53.** C

MIXED REVIEW **55.** −28 **57.** 7.7 **59.** 15 **61.** 34 **63.** 11 **65.** −19 **67.** −2

Toolbox page 169

1a. $y = 2x - 1; y = x + 1$ **1b.** 2 **1c.** 2
3. 3 **5.** 30

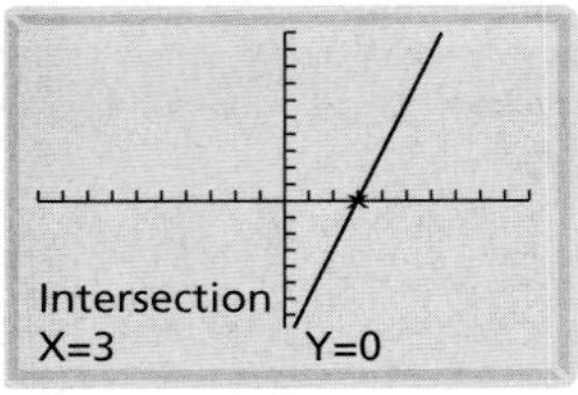

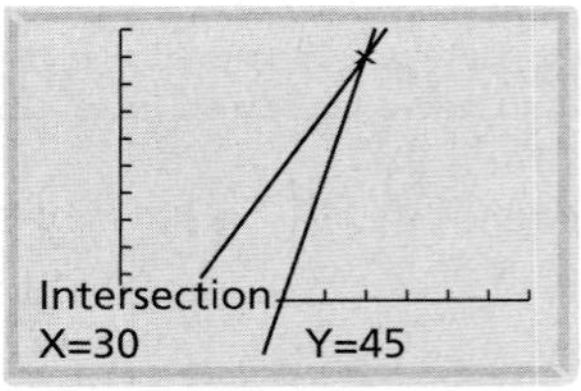

Xmin=–10 Ymin=–10
Xmax=50 Ymax=50
Xscl=5 Yscl=5

7. no; $-\frac{3}{4}$ **9.** no; $-\frac{2}{3}$

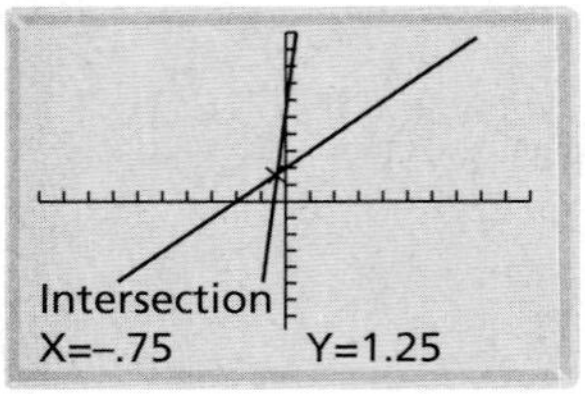

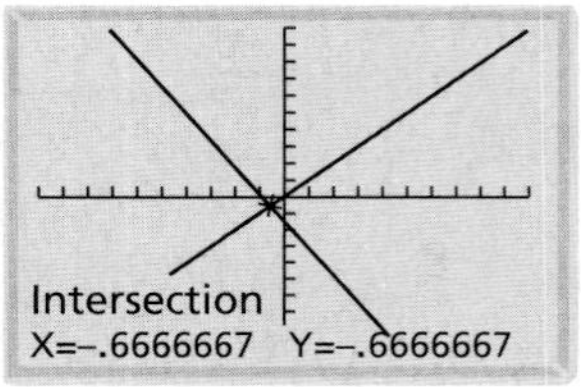

Lesson 4-3 pages 170–174

ON YOUR OWN **1.** 3 **3.** 2 **5.** 6 **7.** −4 **11.** −6, 6 **13.** −4, 3 **15.** 3, 13 **17.** −16, 2 **19.** −9, 5 **21.** −0.72, 0.72 **23.** $|x| = 3$ **25.** $|x| = 0$ **29.** True; absolute value cannot be negative. **31.** False; $z = 0$ or $z = -6$. **33.** −12, 12 **35.** −48 **37.** −10, 10 **39.** −9, 9 **41.** 39°F, 11°F **43a.** 7.265 oz; 7.235 oz **43b.** No; one coin may weigh much more than 0.18 oz, while another may weigh much less.

MIXED REVIEW **45.** −6 **47.** −0.5 **49.** −2.5 **51.** Ted earns $5.50 per hour; Elio earns $7.50 per hour. **53.** 24 ft

Lesson 4-4 pages 175–178

ON YOUR OWN **1.** $r = \frac{s-4}{3}$ **3.** $p = \frac{mq}{n}$ **5.** $r = \frac{C}{2\pi}$ **7.** $t = \frac{3m}{2} - 4$ **9a.** 5.85 **9b.** $b = 2m - a$ **9c.** 5.9 **11.** $n = 4m - 6$ **13.** $z = a + y$ **15.** $b = \frac{7a}{2}$ **17.** $b = \frac{2A}{h}$ **19.** $h = \frac{V}{lw}$ **21.** $p = \frac{b-r}{a}$ or $p = \frac{b+r}{a}$ **23a.** $A = \frac{s^2}{R}$ **23b.** 27 ft^2 **27a.** $y = -\frac{1}{2}x + 2$

27b.

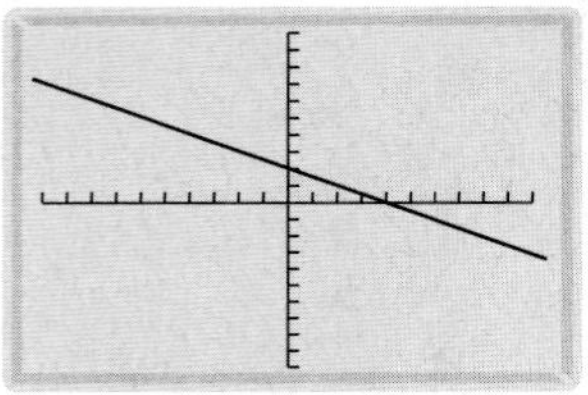

27c. $\frac{1}{2}$; 0; $-\frac{1}{2}$

MIXED REVIEW **29.** 560 **31a.** $69 **31b.** Sample: p = total pay; r = hourly rate; h = number of hours; $p = rh$ **33.** > **35.** >

CHECKPOINT **1.** $n = s + 90$ **2.** $b = y - mx$ **3.** $a = \frac{2b^2}{L}$ **4.** $f = \frac{W}{d}$ **5.** 16.8 **6.** no solution; $-4 \neq 4$ **7.** no solution; absolute value cannot be negative **8.** 0 **9.** −8, 8 **10.** $9\frac{2}{3}$ **11.** 5 **12.** 1.5, 7.5 **13.** $17\frac{1}{3}$ km **14.** C

Lesson 4-5 pages 179–184

ON YOUR OWN **1.** n = number of students; $n \leq 48$ **3.** a = age of applicant; $a \geq 16$ **5.** w = light bulb wattage; $w \leq 60$ **7a.** $6 < 9$ **7b.** $10 < 13$ **7c.** $-1 < 2$
7d.

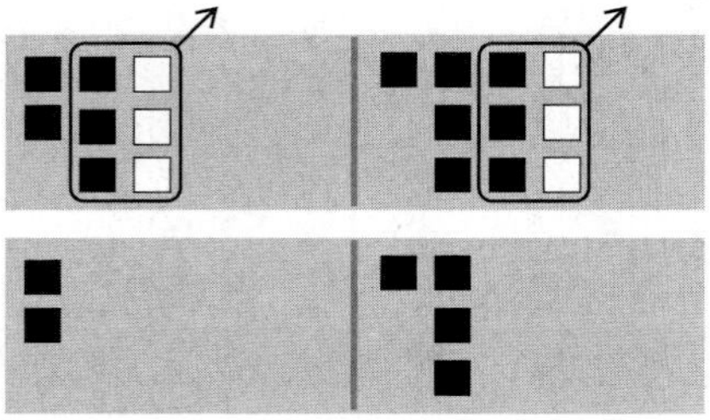

9. Sample: −20, −1, 0, 0.2 **11.** Sample: 1, 2, 3, 26 **13.** Add 4 to each side. **15.** Add $\frac{1}{2}$ to each side. **17.** b is greater than 0. **19.** m is at most −1. **21.** z is at least −4. **23.** 40 points

25. $x > 11$
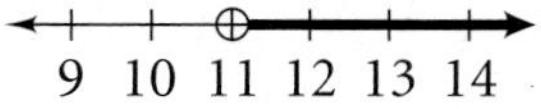

27. $h \geq -\frac{1}{4}$
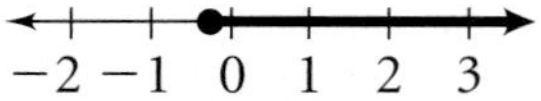

29. $x \geq -1.7$
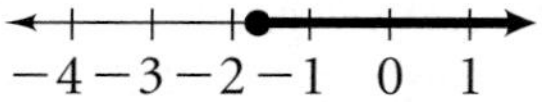

31. $m > 5.5$
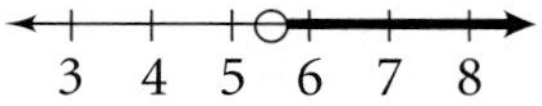

33. $y < 3.1$
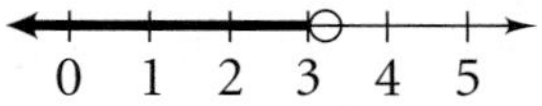

35. $t \geq 12.9$
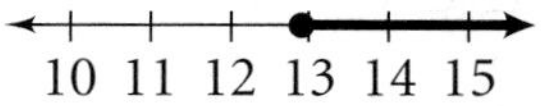

37. $n < -5\frac{4}{5}$

39. $x \neq -5.7$

41. $c \neq 2\frac{11}{14}$

43. $g \leq -1\frac{1}{6}$

45. $y < 5.5$

47. $m \leq 5$

51. E **53.** $s \leq 18{,}000$ **55.** about \$5000

MIXED REVIEW **59.** $\begin{bmatrix} -8 & 18 \\ -2 & 15 \end{bmatrix}$ **61.** $-11, -1$
63. $-12, 12$ **65.** Two quantities are equal. If you multiply (divide) both of them by a number, the products (quotients) are also equal. You cannot divide by 0. **67.** $-\frac{2}{3}$ **69.** 6.4

Lesson 4-6 pages 185–189

ON YOUR OWN **1a.** -1 **1b.** -1 **3.** Multiply by -1. **5.** Sample: $-5, -1, 0, 8$ **7.** Sample: $-4, -7, -10, -20$ **9.** Sample: $-12, -3, -1, 10$ **11.** -2
13. 4 **15.** -10

17. $x \geq 4$

19. $x > -6$

21. $d > 5\frac{1}{3}$

23. 18 h **25.** C **27.** $j > -6$ **29.** $s \leq -28$
31a. Kia should have divided each side by -15.
31b. 150 is a solution, but 151 is also a solution
31c. She could try any number less than -9; $(-15)(-10) \leq 135$ is false.

33. $u > 35$

35. $k \geq -30$

37. $t \leq -2.35$

39. $x < -8$

41. $b < 0$

43. $m \leq -47$

45a. 480 tiles **45b.** Sample: they may need to cut some tiles.
MIXED REVIEW **47.** $y = \frac{6 - 2x}{3}$ **49.** $y = \frac{15 - 4x}{-5}$
51a. 1750 tons **51b.** about 0.4 oz **53.** -4.4
55. -2.4 **57.** $-18\frac{6}{7}$

Lesson 4-7 pages 190–194

ON YOUR OWN **1.** Subtract 5 from each side. Then divide each side by 4. **3.** Subtract 8 from each side. **5.** Subtract y from each side. Then add 5 to each side. **7.** Add s to each side. Then subtract 6 from each side. **9.** Multiply or divide each side by -1. Reverse the order of the inequality. **11.** E **13.** A **15.** C

17. $h \geq -2$

19. $x > -2\frac{1}{2}$

21. $n \geq 2$

23. $m > -8$

25. $a < -3$

27a. 74 boxes **27b.** 5 trips **29.** $k > -\frac{1}{4}$
31. all numbers **33.** no solutions **35.** $k \leq -33$
37. $s \geq -\frac{22}{37}$ **41.** at least \$7000 **43.** $15n - (490 + 45 + 65) \geq 1200$

MIXED REVIEW **45.** $m > 1850$ **47.** Absolute value; variable expression is inside the absolute value symbol. **49.** Quadratic; highest power of x is 2.
51a. about 1.125 tons **51b.** about 10.7 million tons

53.

55.

Lesson 4-8 pages 195–200

ON YOUR OWN **1.** e = elevation anywhere in North America; $-282 \leq e \leq 20{,}320$ **3.** $-2 < x < 3$
5. $-4 \leq x \leq 3$ **7.** Sample: $x < 1$ or $x > 0$
9. $|x| < 3$ **11.** $|x - 6| > 2$
13. $-5 < j < 5$

15. $k < -5$ or $k > -1$

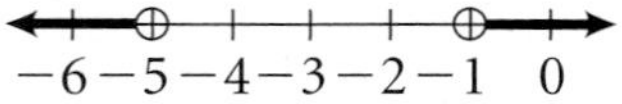

$-6\ -5\ -4\ -3\ -2\ -1\ \ 0$

17. $1 \leq r \leq 2$

$-1\ \ 0\ \ 1\ \ 2\ \ 3\ \ 4$

19. $-2 < r \leq -1.5$

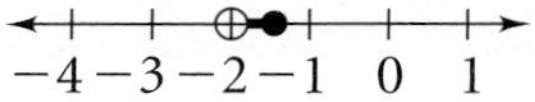

$-4\ -3\ -2\ -1\ \ 0\ \ 1$

21. $-1.5 < w < 3.5$

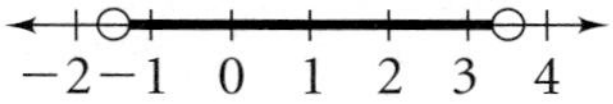

$-2\ -1\ \ 0\ \ 1\ \ 2\ \ 3\ \ 4$

23. $4 \leq t \leq 14$

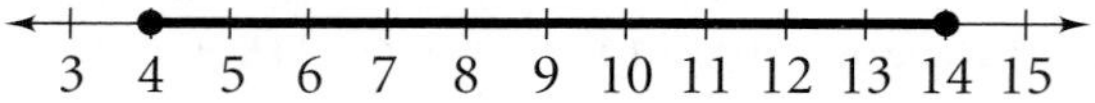

$3\ \ 4\ \ 5\ \ 6\ \ 7\ \ 8\ \ 9\ \ 10\ \ 11\ \ 12\ \ 13\ \ 14\ \ 15$

27. $7585 \text{ cm} \leq l \leq 7615 \text{ cm}$

29. $f < -2.5$ or $f > 2.5$

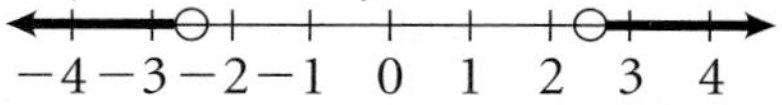

$-4\ -3\ -2\ -1\ \ 0\ \ 1\ \ 2\ \ 3\ \ 4$

31. $n \leq -13$ or $n \geq -3$

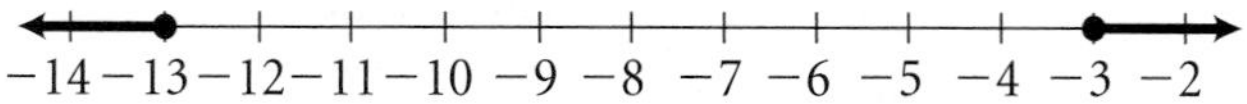

$-14\ -13\ -12\ -11\ -10\ -9\ -8\ -7\ -6\ -5\ -4\ -3\ -2$

33. $w < -2$ or $w > 2$

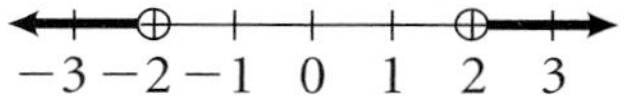

$-3\ -2\ -1\ \ 0\ \ 1\ \ 2\ \ 3$

35. $-6 < x < 6$

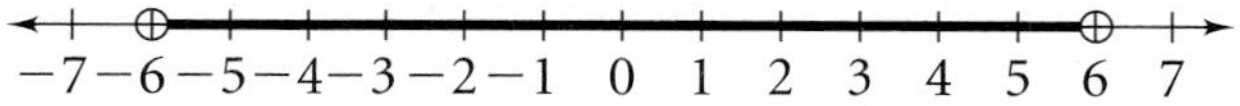

$-7\ -6\ -5\ -4\ -3\ -2\ -1\ \ 0\ \ 1\ \ 2\ \ 3\ \ 4\ \ 5\ \ 6\ \ 7$

37. $y \leq 1$ or $y \geq 3$

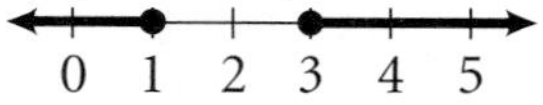

$0\ \ 1\ \ 2\ \ 3\ \ 4\ \ 5$

39. $t \leq -2.4$ or $t \geq 4$

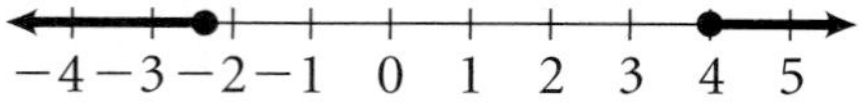

$-4\ -3\ -2\ -1\ \ 0\ \ 1\ \ 2\ \ 3\ \ 4\ \ 5$

41. $t < -3$ or $t > 2\frac{1}{3}$

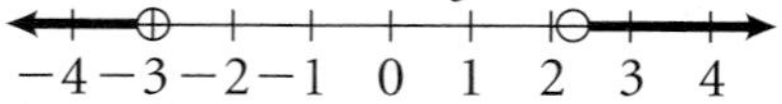

$-4\ -3\ -2\ -1\ \ 0\ \ 1\ \ 2\ \ 3\ \ 4$

43. all numbers

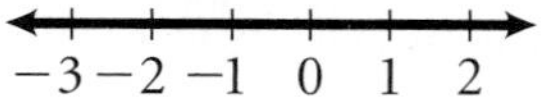

$-3\ -2\ -1\ \ 0\ \ 1\ \ 2$

45. $2.5 < x < 7.5$ **47.** $7 < x < 49$ **49.** $66 \leq C \leq 88$
51. Charlotte: $29 \leq C \leq 90$; Detroit $15 \leq D \leq 83$

MIXED REVIEW **53.** $-\frac{1}{8}$ **55.** -1 **57.** $-0.9, 0.9$
59. $-\frac{1}{4}, 1\frac{1}{4}$ **61.** $-3, -2, -1, 0, 1$ **63.** $-3, -2, -1, 0, 1, 2$

CHECKPOINT

1. $c > 6$

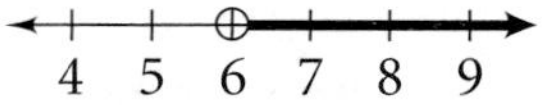

$4\ \ 5\ \ 6\ \ 7\ \ 8\ \ 9$

2. $x \leq -8$

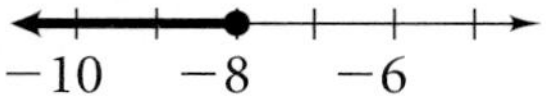

$-10\ \ -8\ \ -6$

3. $m \leq -4$

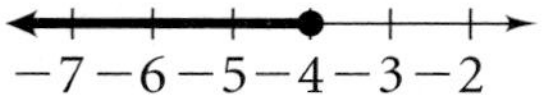

$-7\ -6\ -5\ -4\ -3\ -2$

4. $c \geq -5$

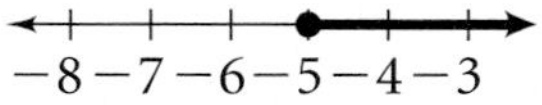

$-8\ -7\ -6\ -5\ -4\ -3$

5. $b > \frac{1}{3}$

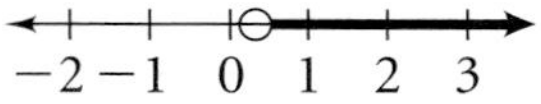

$-2\ -1\ \ 0\ \ 1\ \ 2\ \ 3$

6. $n \leq 3$

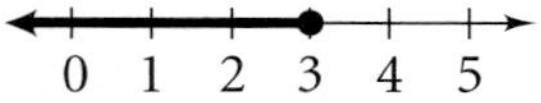

$0\ \ 1\ \ 2\ \ 3\ \ 4\ \ 5$

7. $r \leq 7$

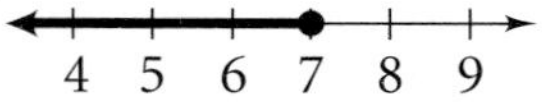

$4\ \ 5\ \ 6\ \ 7\ \ 8\ \ 9$

8. $w \leq -2$

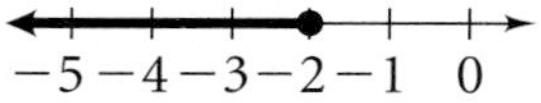

$-5\ -4\ -3\ -2\ -1\ \ 0$

9. $h \geq -4$

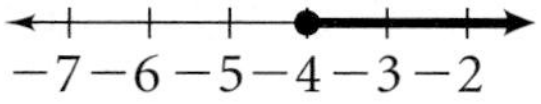

$-7\ -6\ -5\ -4\ -3\ -2$

10. $0 \geq t \geq -0.5$

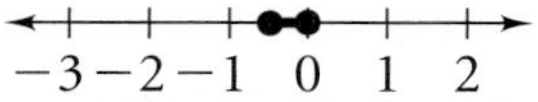

$-3\ -2\ -1\ \ 0\ \ 1\ \ 2$

11. $x < -27$ or $x > 4$

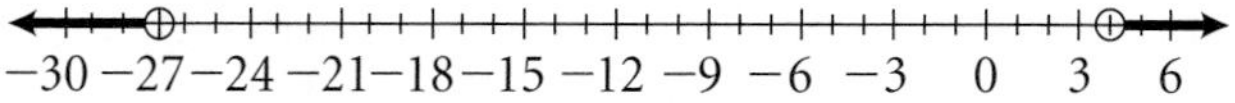

$-30\ -27\ -24\ -21\ -18\ -15\ -12\ -9\ -6\ -3\ \ 0\ \ 3\ \ 6$

12. $g < 1$ or $g > 5$

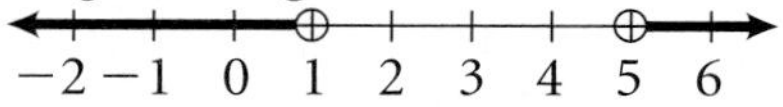

$-2\ -1\ \ 0\ \ 1\ \ 2\ \ 3\ \ 4\ \ 5\ \ 6$

13. $d \leq -3$ or $d \geq 3$

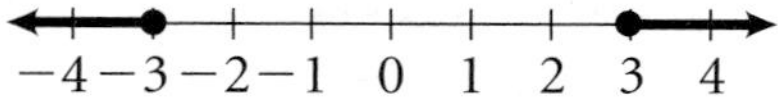

$-4\ -3\ -2\ -1\ \ 0\ \ 1\ \ 2\ \ 3\ \ 4$

14. $-10 < x < 4$

$-10\ \ -5\ \ 0\ \ 5$

15. $-1 < x < 4$

$-2\ -1\ \ 0\ \ 1\ \ 2\ \ 3\ \ 4\ \ 5$

16. $y \leq -4$ or $y \geq 5$

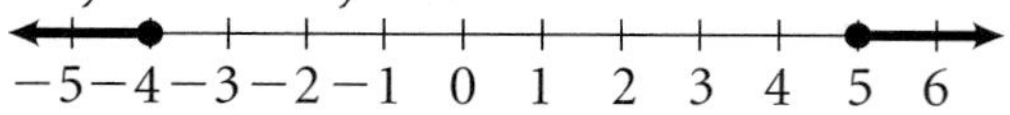

$-5\ -4\ -3\ -2\ -1\ \ 0\ \ 1\ \ 2\ \ 3\ \ 4\ \ 5\ \ 6$

17. $2\frac{2}{5} \leq x \leq 5\frac{3}{5}$

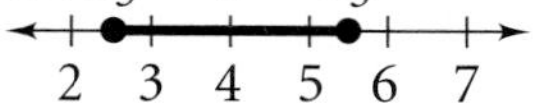

$2\ \ 3\ \ 4\ \ 5\ \ 6\ \ 7$

18. $36 < t < 37.2$

Toolbox page 201

1. 6

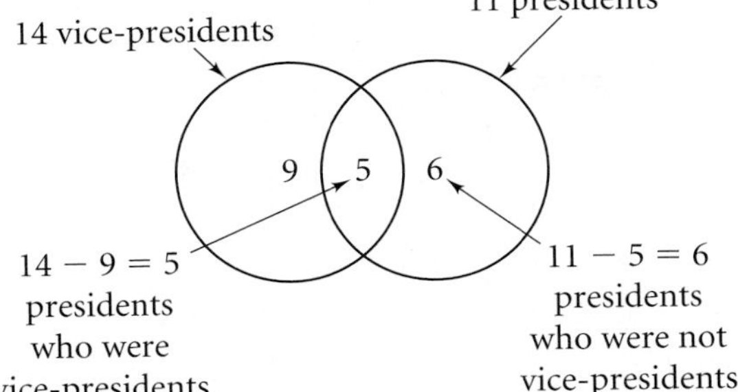

3a. 1 **3b.** 2 **3c.** 45

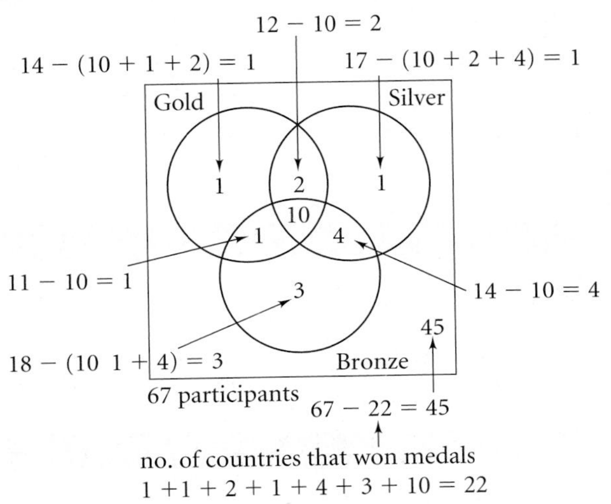

Lesson 4-9 pages 202–205

ON YOUR OWN

1. $p \leq 6$ (0 1 2 3 4 5 6 7)

3. no solutions **5.** no solutions

7. (−1 0 1 2 3 4 5 6)

9. (3 4 5 6 7 8 ...)

11. (0 1 2 3 4 5 ...)

13. (−5 −4 −3 −2 −1 0 1 2 3)

15. no solutions

17. $12 \leq a < 65$

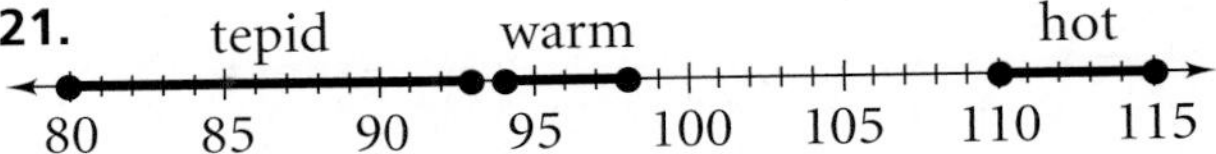

19. $23 < c < 23.5$ (21 22 23 24 25 26)

21. tepid warm hot (80 85 90 95 100 105 110 115)

23a. 6 h **23b.** Divide 175 by the hourly rate and subtract the hours worked so far. Round the result up to the next integer.

27. (−4 −3 −2 −1 0 1 2 3 4)

29. (−9 −8 −7 −6 −5 −4 −3 −2 −1 0 1 2 3)

MIXED REVIEW **31.** 5 **33.** 50% **35.** 150%

Wrap Up pages 207–209

1. 2 **2.** 2.3 **3.** −6 **4.** 10 **5.** −0.4 **6.** 1.5 **7.** 36 ft **8.** $2x - 6 = -3x + 4$; 2 **9.** $-x + 8 = -2x - 9$; −17 **10.** −11 **11.** identity **12.** 0 **13.** −2 **14.** −5, 5 **15.** −12.5, 6.5 **16.** No solution; absolute value cannot be negative. **17.** 8 **19.** $c = 3m - a - b$ **20.** $d = \frac{C}{\pi}$ **21.** $x = \frac{y - b}{m}$ **22.** $h = \frac{2A}{b}$ **23a.** $I = \frac{E}{R}$ **23b.** 40 amperes

24. $h > -1$ (−3 −2 −1 0 1 2)

25. $k \leq -\frac{1}{2}$ (−3 −2 −1 0 1 2)

26. $b < 40$ (37 38 39 40 41 42)

27. $y \leq -168$ (−170 −169 −168 −167 −166 −165)

28. $c \leq -2$ (−5 −4 −3 −2 −1 0)

29. $m < -6$ (−9 −8 −7 −6 −5 −4)

30. $t < -5$ (−8 −7 −6 −5 −4 −3)

31. $x \geq 9$ (7 8 9 10 11 12)

32. There is no solution because $\frac{3}{4} \leq \frac{1}{4}$ is false.

33. $n \leq -6$ or $n \geq 2$

34. $-2 \leq z < 7$

35. $t \leq -2$ or $t \geq 7$

36. $-1\frac{1}{2} \leq b < 0$

37. $2 \leq a < 4$

38. $-6\frac{1}{2} < d < 4$

39. $2 \leq a < 5$

40. all numbers

41. C

42. $h \leq -1.5$ or $h \geq 2$

43. $t \leq 3\frac{1}{3}$

44. no solution

45. $-3 \leq m < 0$

46. $q < 0$

47. $\frac{1}{4} \leq c \leq 4$

48. $l > 1000$

50.

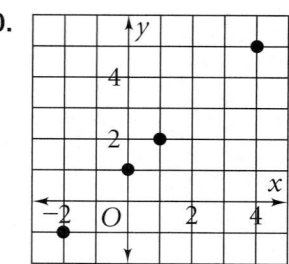

51.

52.

53. $f(x) = x - 5$ **54.** $f(x) = x + 9$ **55.** $f(x) = \frac{x}{2}$
56. $f(x) = 3x$

Preparing for the Math A Exam page 211

1. 3 **3.** 2 **5.** 3 **7.** 3

CHAPTER 5

Lesson 5-1 pages 214–218

ON YOUR OWN **1.** 1; -1 **3.** $\frac{5}{9}$ **5.** $-\frac{6}{5}$
7. undefined

9.

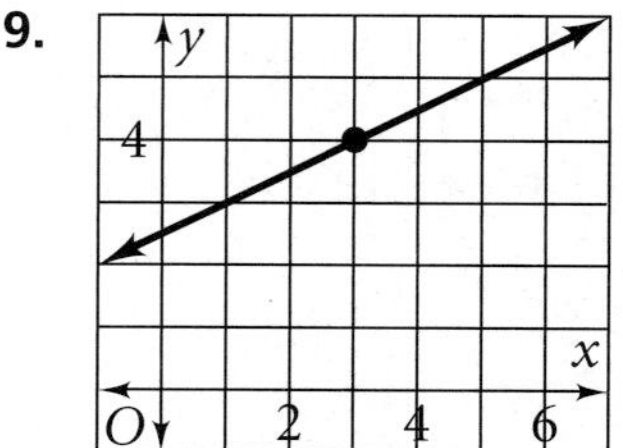

11.

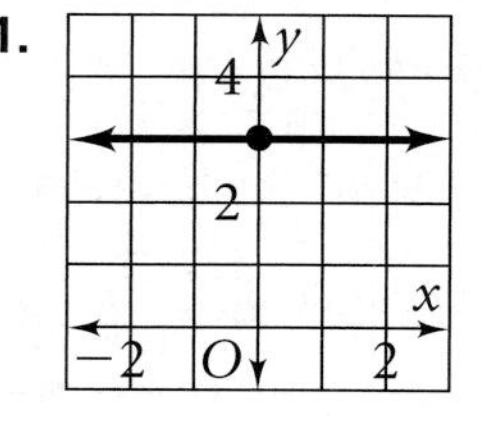

13.

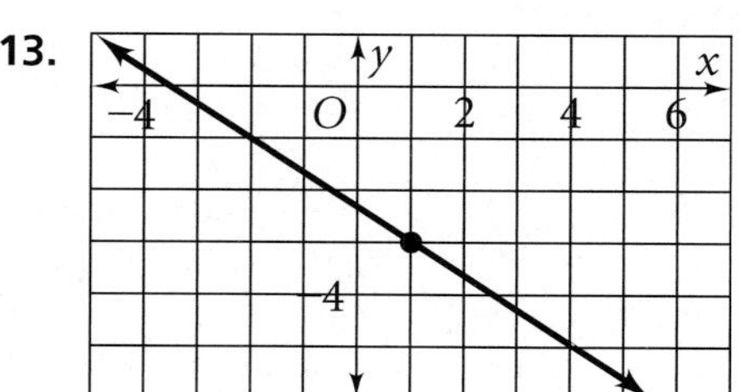

15.

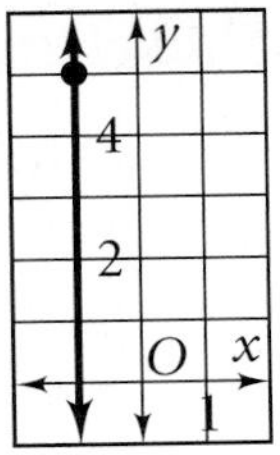

17. $y = 3, x = 4, y = 3, x = -1$ **19.** F; for example a line with slope 1 that passes through (0, 1) does not pass through the origin. **21.** F; a line through any point in Quadrant III can have positive, negative, zero, or undefined slope. **23.** increase **25.** $\overleftrightarrow{AB} : 0; \overleftrightarrow{BC} : \frac{5}{6}; \overleftrightarrow{AC} : \frac{5}{3}$ **27.** $\overleftrightarrow{JK} : -\frac{1}{2}; \overleftrightarrow{KL} : 2; \overleftrightarrow{LM} : -\frac{1}{2}; \overleftrightarrow{JM} : 2$ **29.** no **31a.** About 110; the rent is \$110 per hour. **31b.** 55 customers per hour **33.** E

MIXED REVIEW **35.** $\frac{1}{2}$ **37.** 1 **39.** 75%
41. independent: temperature; dependent: amount of fuel used

Toolbox — page 219

1. A **3.** B **5.** $3\frac{1}{3}$ **7.** 270 **9.** about 15.83 mi/h
11. 20,000 mi/h

Lesson 5-2 — pages 220–224

ON YOUR OWN **1.** 0.9 in./mo **3.** 30 mi/h **5.** $\frac{1}{4}$; \$1 buys 4 oz of oregano. **7a.** Yes; for every 6°F decline in temperature, the number of calories burned increases by 100. **7b.** Subtract 20°F. Multiply the difference by the rate of change. Then add the result to 3330 calories. The number of calories burned at 20°F is 3830. **9.** true **11.** F; the boiling temperature of water decreases as altitude increases. **13.** no **15.** no **17.** yes **19a.** *A*: fastest; *C*: slowest **19b.** *C*; you can record more if you use less tape per unit of time.

21a.

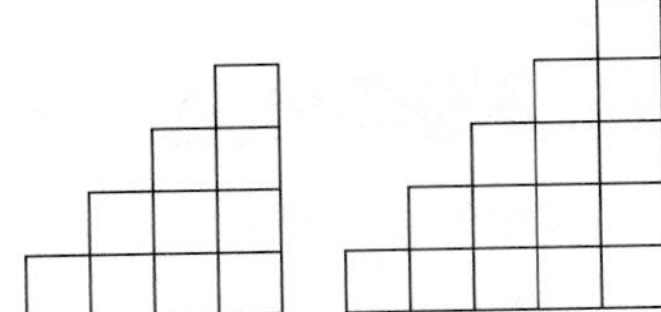

21b.

Number of Squares	Perimeter
1	4
2	8
3	12
4	16
5	20

21c. No; the number of squares increase by 1, 2, 3, etc.; but the perimeter increases 4 units with each figure.

MIXED REVIEW **25.** 4 **27.** 3 **29.** about 21%
31. Sample:

x	y
−3	−2.4
−1	−0.8
0	0
1	0.8

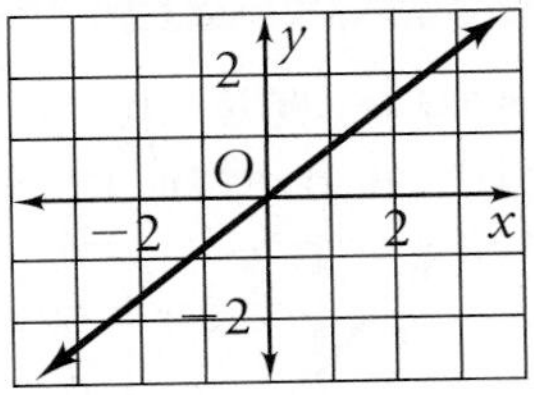

33. Sample:

x	y
−1	−7.2
−0.5	−3.6
0	0
0.5	3.6
1	7.2

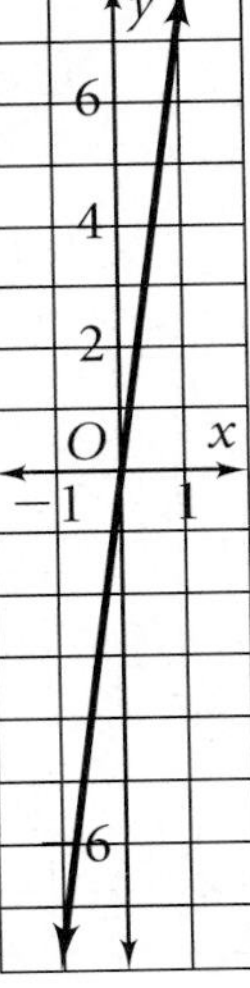

Lesson 5-3 — pages 225–229

ON YOUR OWN **1.** *A*; *B*; the graph of a direct variation must pass through the origin. **3.** no **5.** yes; $\frac{1}{4}$ **7.** no **9.** yes; $y = 1.8x$ **11.** yes; $y = -1.5x$ **13.** $y = \frac{5}{2}x$ **15.** $y = -\frac{5}{2}x$ **17.** 52 lb **19.** False; the graph must pass through (0, 0). **21.** False; a direct variation is a function. Vertical lines have more than one y-value for an x-value. **23a.** $\frac{1}{32}$; $b = \frac{1}{32}w$ **25.** 12 **27.** 8 **29.** 5 **31.** −2 **33a.** $d = 7p$ **33b.** 84 dog years

MIXED REVIEW **35.** $t > -1\frac{1}{3}$ **37.** B

39.

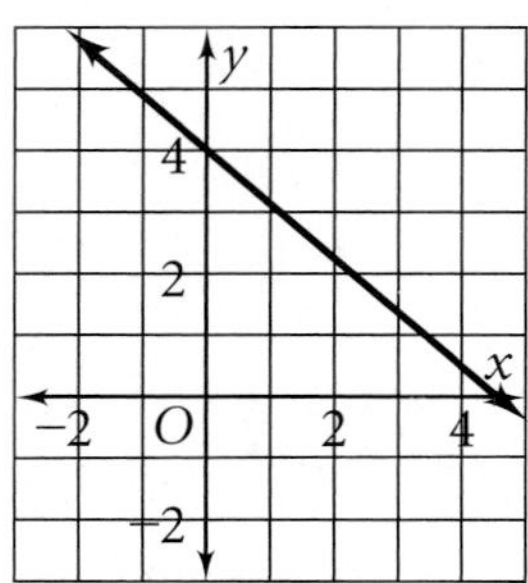

Lesson 5-4 pages 230–234

ON YOUR OWN **1.** $-\frac{3}{4}$; -5 **3.** 3; -9 **5.** 0; 3
7. III **9.** II **11a.** 12 in. **11b.** $h = -\frac{2}{15}t + 12$

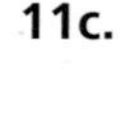

11c.

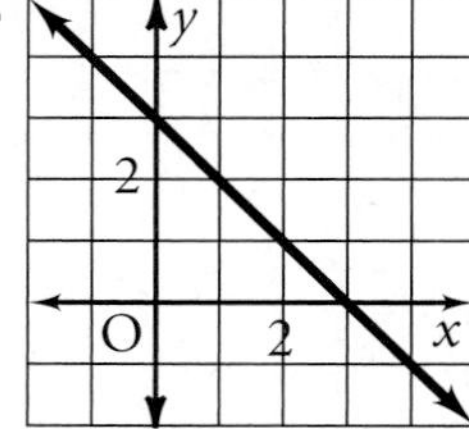

13.

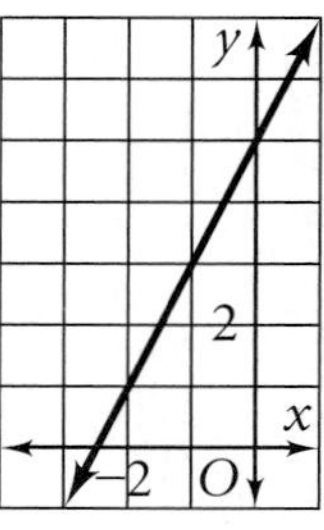

15.

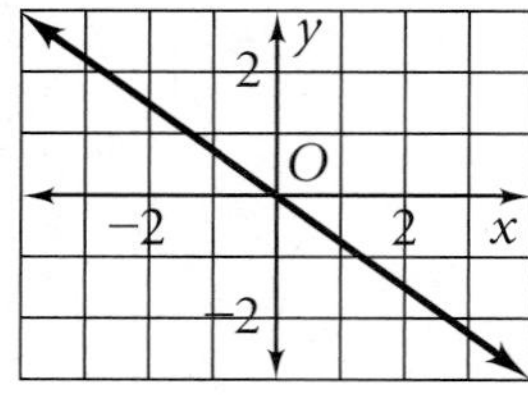

17.

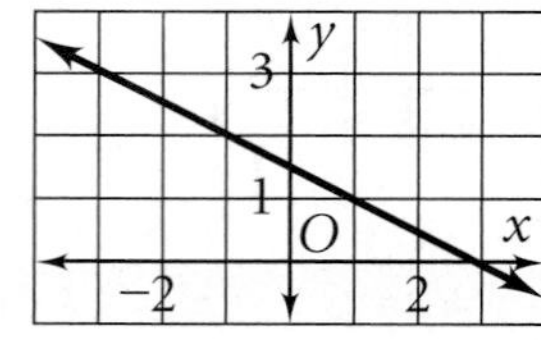

19. no; $4 \neq -2(-3) + 1$
21. $-\frac{2}{3}$; 2; $y = -\frac{2}{3}x + 2$ **23.** 0; 1; $y = 1$
27. $y = \frac{2}{9}x + 3$ **29.** $y = -\frac{5}{4}x$

MIXED REVIEW **31.** $-\frac{9}{7}$ **33.** $-\frac{1}{5}$ **35.** 2 **37.** 1

CHECKPOINT **1.** yes; $\frac{y}{x} = m$ **2.** no; $\frac{y}{x} \neq m$ **3.** No; a vertical line cannot be a direct variation. **4.** yes; $\frac{y}{x} = m$ **5.** $121.75 billion/yr

Toolbox page 235

1a. Divide Xmax and Ymax by the number of ticks between 0 and the edge; 5, 2 **1b.** $y = 2x + 5$

3.

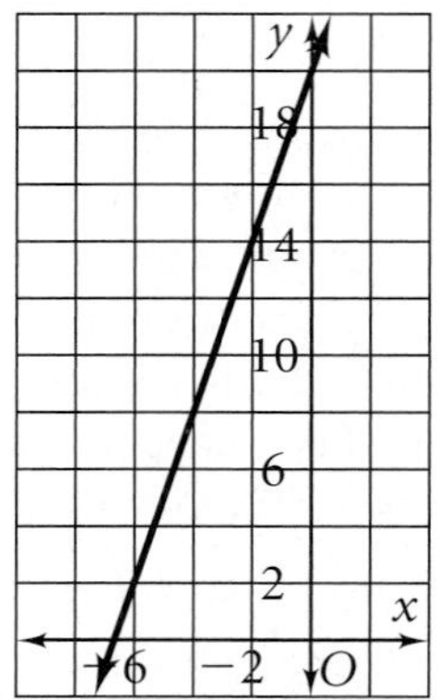

5.

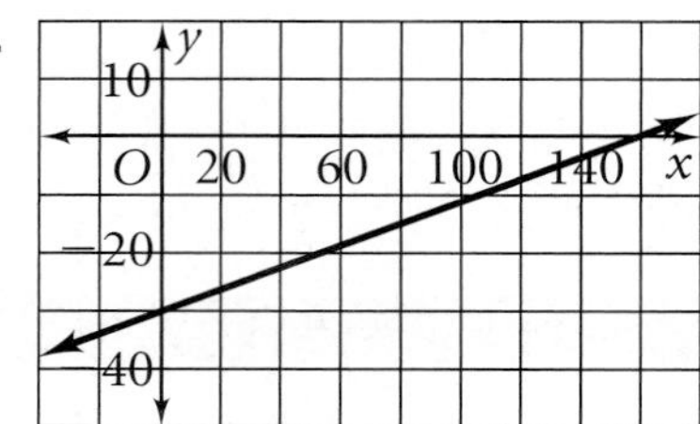

7.

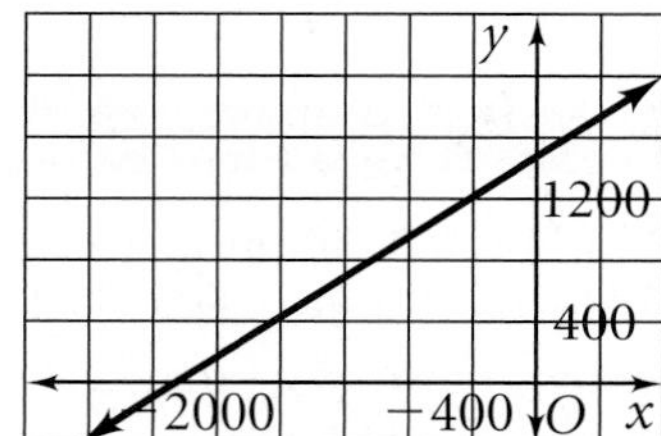

9.

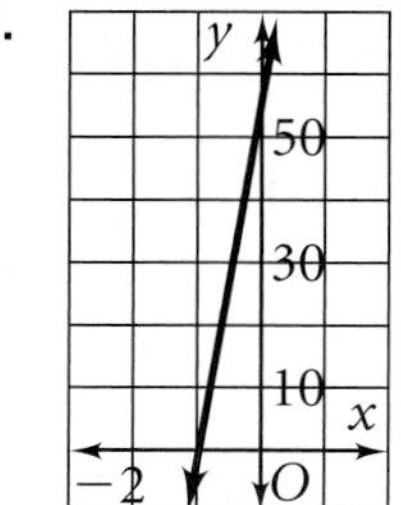

Lesson 5-5 pages 236–239

ON YOUR OWN **1.** $y = 2x - 11$ **3.** $y = \frac{4}{3}x + 3\frac{1}{3}$
5. $y = x + 3$ **7.** $y = 2$ **9.** $y = -\frac{1}{4}x + 3\frac{3}{4}$
11. $y = -\frac{3}{4}x - 3\frac{1}{2}$ **13a.** $L = 0.025M + 7.25$

13b. The y-intercept is the length of the spring when no mass is attached. **13c.** 9 cm **15.** $y = \frac{1}{5}x + 1\frac{3}{5}$ **17.** $y = \frac{1}{9}x + 2\frac{8}{9}$ **19.** $y = -2x + 150$ **21.** $y = -\frac{2}{5}x + 2\frac{4}{5}$ **23a.** For 86 corresponding to 1986, $r = 0.5t - 39.1$ **23b.** \$15.9 billion **25.** yes; $y = -2x + 1$ **27.** yes; $y = 3x + 25$ **29a.** $c = 2.5l + 2$ **29b.** slope: cost/mi; y-intercept: initial cost of ride

MIXED REVIEW **31.** $c < 8$ **33.** $m \leq -1\frac{3}{4}$ **35.** $-1\frac{4}{7}$ **37.** 928.6% increase **39.** positive **41.** positive

Toolbox page 240

1. positive

Lesson 5-6 pages 241–245

ON YOUR OWN **1.** Sample: yes; $y = 11.25x + 200$ **3.** Sample: yes; $y = 0.6x + 330$ **5.** no **9.** A **11b.** Sample: $y = 6.404761905x - 392.7261905$ **11c.** about 280 million TV sets **13b.** Sample: $y = 0.2278305085x - 11.71566102$ **13c.** about 12.2%

19a.

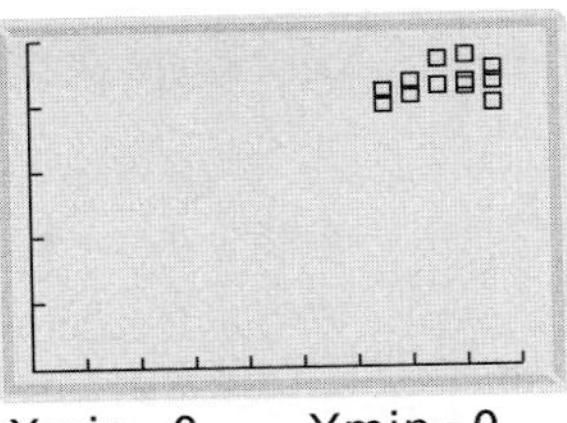

Xmin=0 Ymin=0
Xmax=18 Ymax=75
Xscl=2 Yscl=15

19b. $y = 1.206586826x + 45.71556886$ **19c.** No; $r \approx 0.448$, which is not close to 1.

MIXED REVIEW **21.** 23 **23.** -6 **25.** 3 **27.** $-\frac{8}{3}$ **29.** 20

Lesson 5-7 pages 246–249

ON YOUR OWN **1.** A **3.** C

5.

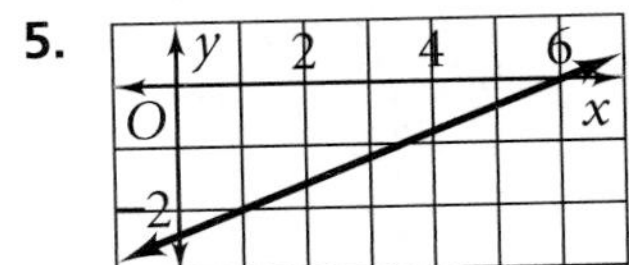

7.

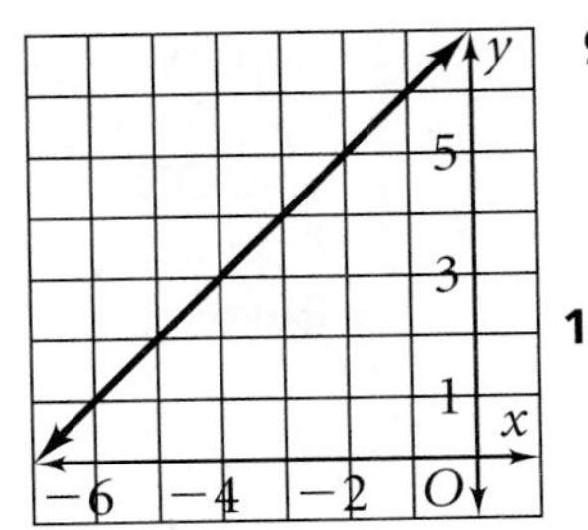

9.

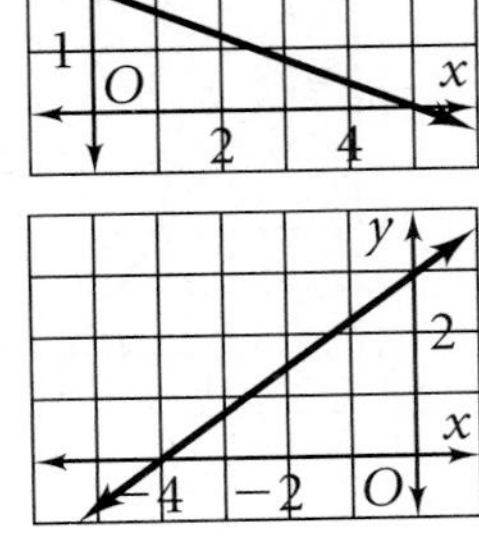

11.

15.

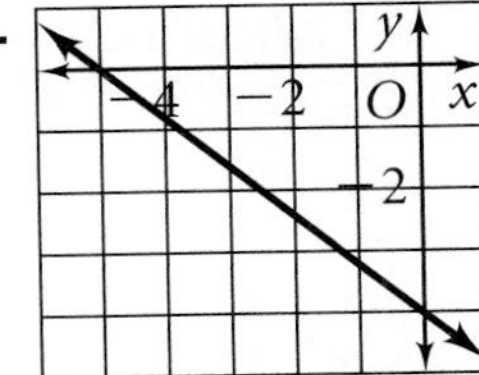

intercepts: $(0, -4)$ and $(-5, 0)$;

17.

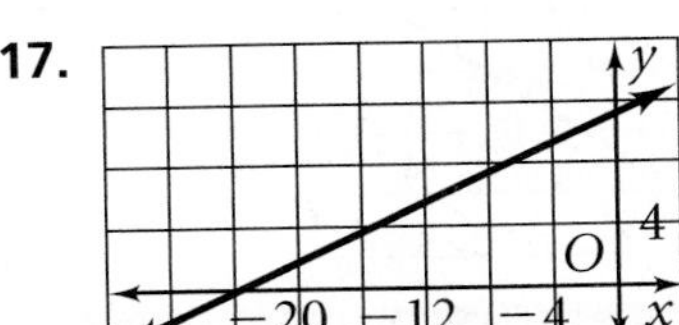

intercepts: $(0, 10\frac{10}{11})$ and $(-24, 0)$;

19.

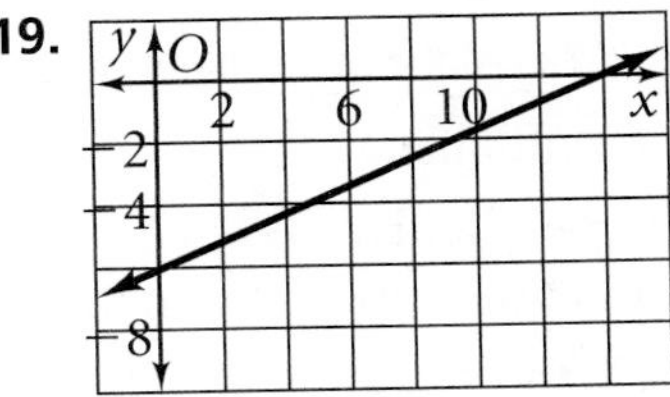

intercepts: $(0, -6)$ and $(14, 0)$;

Selected Answers

21. 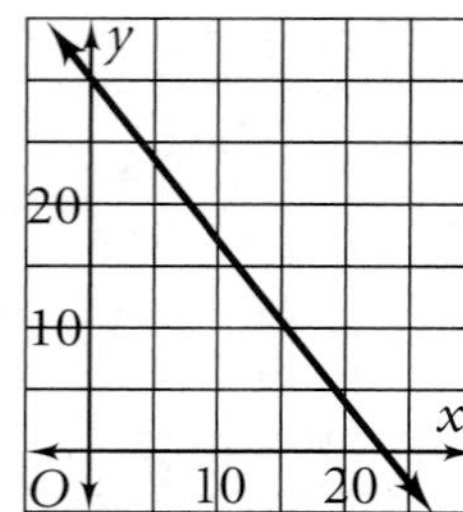

intercepts: (0, 30) and $(23\frac{1}{3}, 0)$;

23. $y = \frac{A}{B}x + \frac{C}{B}$ **25.** $x + 3y = 26$ **27.** $3x + 2y = -20$ **29.** $3x + y = 7$ **31.** $x + 5y = -39$

MIXED REVIEW **33.** $\frac{1}{36}$

35. 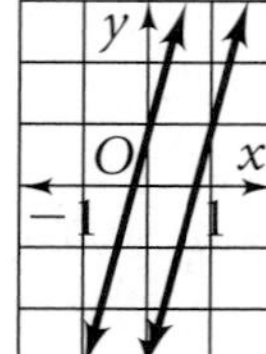

37. 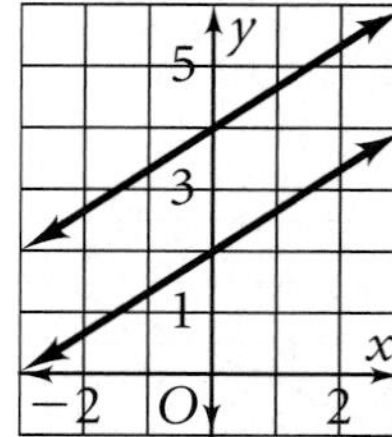

Lesson 5-8 pages 250–255

ON YOUR OWN **1.** $\frac{1}{2}$ **3.** $-\frac{3}{4}$ **5.** 0 **7.** 2 **9.** −3 **11.** $\frac{5}{4}$ **13.** $-\frac{1}{2}$ **15.** $-\frac{5}{7}$ **17.** $\frac{3}{2}$ **19.** undefined **21.** $-\frac{1}{2}$ **23.** $-\frac{2}{9}$ **25.** perpendicular **27.** perpendicular **29.** perpendicular **31.** The vertical and horizontal scales use units of different length. **33a.** Yes; they have the same slope, $-\frac{3}{5}$ **33b.** Since the coefficients of x and y are the same, the ratio for the slope will be the same. **35.** No; the slopes are $\frac{5}{6}$, −2, and $\frac{1}{8}$. No pair of slopes has product −1. **37.** The slope of $\overleftrightarrow{AD}$ and $\overleftrightarrow{BC}$ is undefined, so they are parallel. The slope of $\overleftrightarrow{AB}$ and $\overleftrightarrow{CD}$ is $\frac{1}{2}$, so they are parallel. The quadrilateral is a parallelogram. **39.** The slope of $\overleftrightarrow{PQ}$ and $\overleftrightarrow{RS}$ is $-\frac{1}{2}$. The slope of $\overleftrightarrow{QR}$ and $\overleftrightarrow{SP}$ is $-\frac{3}{2}$. The quadrilateral is a parallelogram. **41.** $y = 6x$ **43.** $y = -x + 10$ **45.** $y = -\frac{2}{3}x + \frac{1}{3}$ **47.** True; the definition of perpendicular lines says that horizontal and vertical lines are perpendicular. **49.** False; two positive numbers need not be equal. **51.** The slope of $\overleftrightarrow{AB}$ and $\overleftrightarrow{CD}$ is $\frac{2}{5}$. The slope of $\overleftrightarrow{BC}$ and $\overleftrightarrow{AD}$ is $-\frac{5}{2}$. The product is −1, so the quadrilateral is a rectangle. **53.** The slope of $\overleftrightarrow{PQ}$ and $\overleftrightarrow{RS}$ is $\frac{1}{2}$. The slope of $\overleftrightarrow{PS}$ and $\overleftrightarrow{QR}$ is −2. The product is −1, so the quadrilateral is a rectangle.

MIXED REVIEW **55.** $m < -2$ **57.** $y > 1$ **59.** $-\frac{8}{3}$ **61.** 20

CHECKPOINT **1.** $-2x + 3y = 6$ **2.** $-4x + y = -7$ **3.** $-\frac{1}{3}x + y = 5$ **4.** $-9x + 15y = -12$ **5.** $y = -\frac{1}{4}x + 4\frac{3}{4}$ **6.** $y = 18x - 3$ **7.** $y = \frac{5}{7}x$ **8.** $x = 5$ **9.** $y = 5.4x + 1.3$ **10.** $y = -6.1x + 62.7$ **15.** D

Lesson 5-9 pages 256–259

ON YOUR OWN **1.** $y = 3x - 8$ **3.** $y = -x - 4$ **5.** A **7.** $-\frac{3}{2}$ **9.** 3 **11.** $5\frac{2}{3}$ **13.** 25 **15.** 36 **17.** $7\frac{1}{4}$ **19a.** $15x = 100$ **19b.** $6\frac{2}{3}$ **19c.** \$50 **23.** −17.5 **25.** 3.75 **27.** False; a vertical line has no y-intercept. **29.** True; the x-intercept is the x-value for y-value 0.

MIXED REVIEW **31.** −11.6 **33.** 4.84

Wrap Up pages 261–263

1. Sample: (10, 0.5), (30, 1); $\frac{1}{40}$ **2.** Sample: (0, 150), (40, 150); 0 **3.** (1, 7.5) (3, 5); −1.25 **4.** $\frac{1}{2}$ page/min **5.** $\frac{1}{22}$ mi/min **6.** 3 goals/game **7.** 12 pages/min **8.** 6 **9.** 4 **10.** −4 **11.** $y = \frac{3}{4}x + 8$ **12.** $y = -7x + \frac{1}{2}$ **13.** $y = \frac{2}{5}x$ **14.** $y = -3$ **15.** $y = \frac{1}{3}x + 1\frac{2}{3}$ **16.** $y = -\frac{6}{5}x + 2$ **17.** $y = \frac{1}{2}x + \frac{1}{2}$ **18.** $y = \frac{3}{10}x + 6\frac{2}{5}$ **19.** $y = -\frac{1}{2}x - \frac{1}{2}$ **20.** $y = -3x$ **21.** $y = \frac{1}{4}x - 3$ **22a.** Sample: $y = 1.3x - 59$ **22b.** Using equation in (a): 77.5 lb/person **23.** 2; 5 **24.** 8; −13 **25.** 15; −5 **26.** 13; −104 **27.** $y = 5x - 11$ **28.** $y = \frac{1}{3}x + 4$ **29.** $y = 9x - 5$ **30.** $y = -\frac{1}{8}x + 10\frac{1}{2}$ **32a.** $30x = 175$ **32b.** $5\frac{5}{6}$ lawns, or 6 lawns to make a profit **33.** The break-even point is the amount you need to produce to make \$0 profit. **34.** C

35.

36.
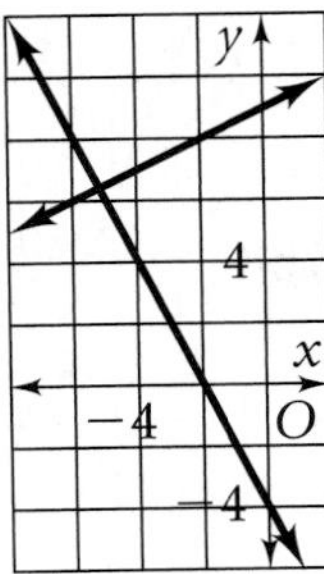

37.
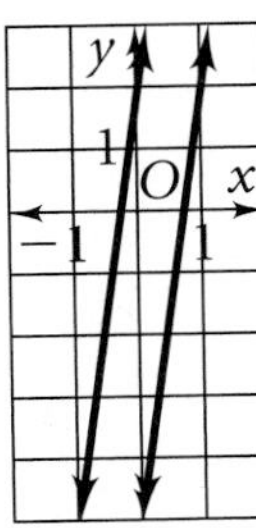

38.
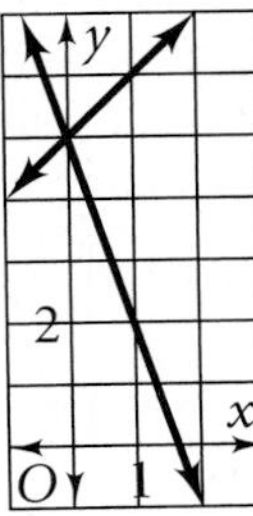

39.
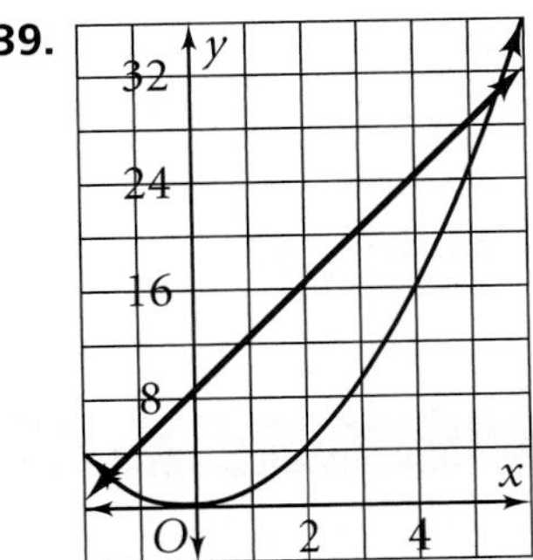

40.
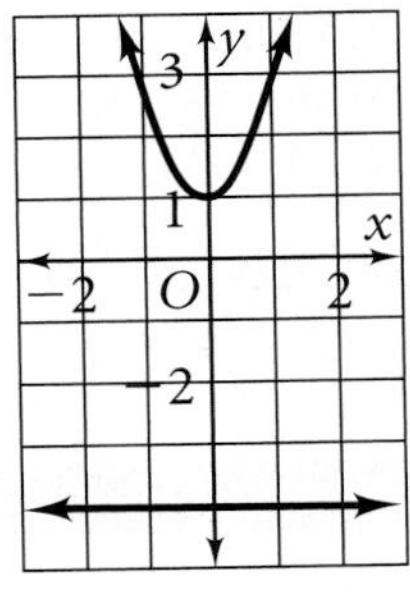

Preparing for the Math A Exam page 265

1. 2 **3.** 1 **5.** 4 **7.** 4

CHAPTER 6

Toolbox page 268

1. 4 and 8 **3a.** about 2:13 P.M. **3b.** about 13.5 mi

Lesson 6-1 pages 269–274

ON YOUR OWN

1. no solution;

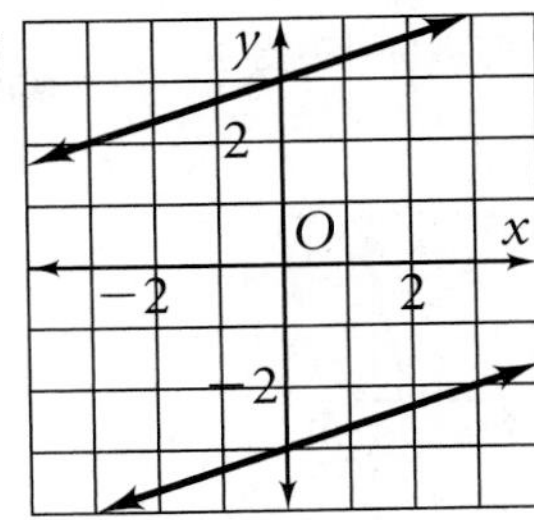

3. (1, 1);

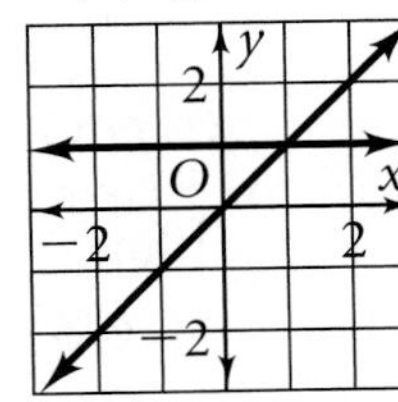

5. infinitely many solutions;

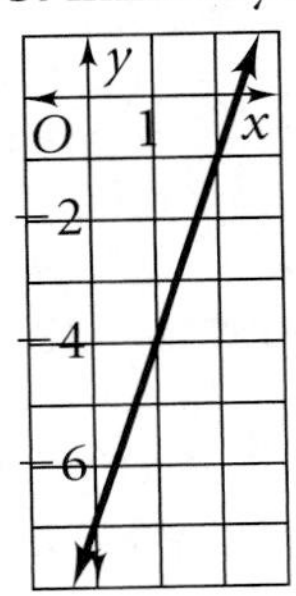

7. yes **9.** yes **11a.** No; the graphs are not straight lines. **11b.** The solution of the system is the point in time when the fear of commitment is equal to the fear of baldness. **11c.** The solution on Lily's chart shows the point in time when the level of hope of meeting Brad Pitt is equal to the level of fear of cellulite. **11d.** feelings; time

13. (1, 3);

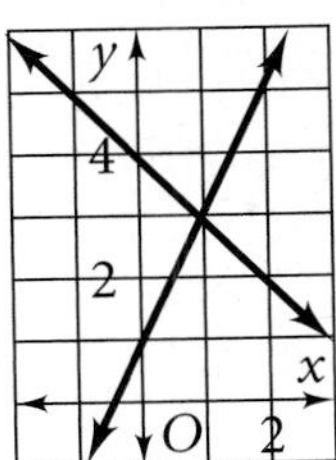

15. (0, 0);

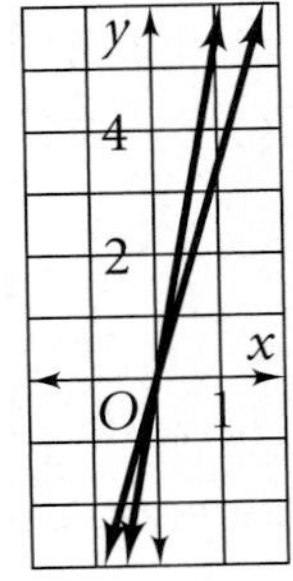

17. (3, −4);

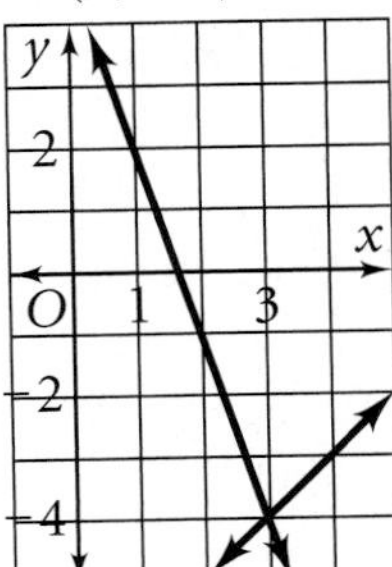

19. no solution;

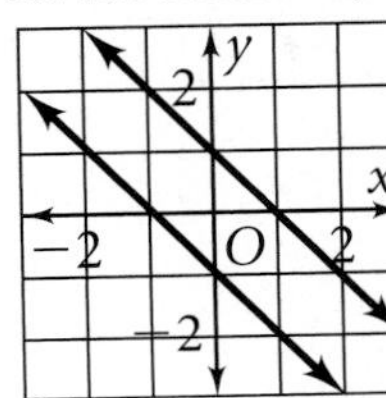

Selected Answers

21. $(0, -1)$;

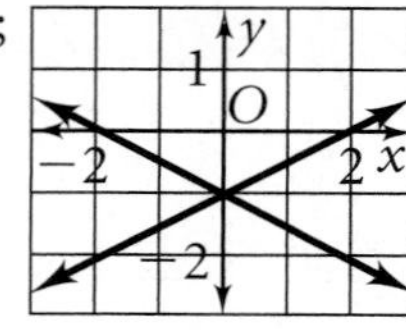

23. no solutions

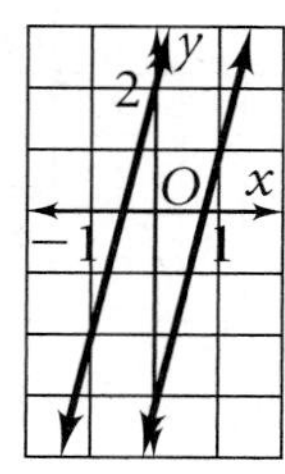

25. True; the graphs of lines can intersect once, not intersect, or be the same line. **27.** False; the system may have no solutions. **29.** parallel; no solutions **31.** intersect; one solution **33.** same line; infinitely many solutions **35.** intersect; one solution **41a.** $(2, 200)$ **41b.** Both studios charge $200 rent for 2 h. **43.** $(4.5, 6.5)$ **45.** $(4, -6)$

MIXED REVIEW **47.** $\frac{1}{36}$ **49.** 1 **51.** $b \leq 6$ **53a.** about 138.5 mi^2 **53b.** about 72 million **55.** $x = 8y$ **57.** $x = \frac{3}{2}y + \frac{5}{2}$

Lesson 6-2 pages 275–279

ON YOUR OWN **1.** one **3.** no solution **5.** infinitely many solutions **7.** one **9.** 12 cm by 3 cm **11.** $(2, 4)$ **13.** $(-\frac{1}{2}, -\frac{1}{2})$ **15.** $(2, \frac{1}{2})$ **17.** $(-\frac{1}{2}, 0)$ **19.** $(3, 5)$ **21.** infinitely many solutions

23. $(\frac{1}{2}, 1)$;

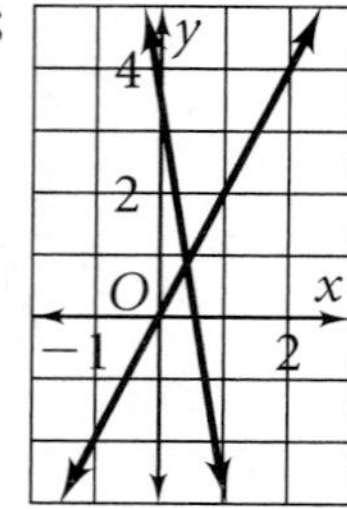

25. $(-1, 1)$;

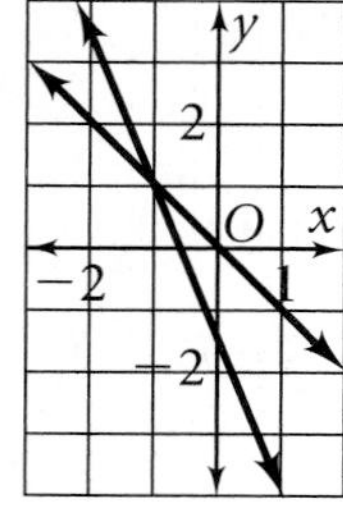

27. no solution;

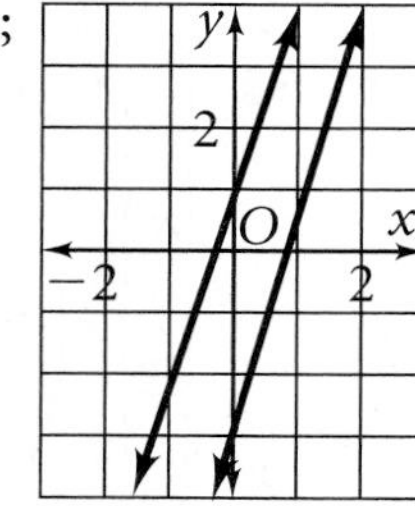

29. D **31.** C **33.** A **35.** infinitely many solutions **37.** no solution **39.** 160 acres of soybeans; 80 acres of corn **41.** $(3, -3)$ **43.** $(\frac{1}{4}, 0)$ **45.** $(12, -8)$ **47.** $(-2, -5)$

MIXED REVIEW **49.** 7; -4 **51.** 9; 0 **53.** $y = \frac{3}{2}x$ **55.** $-7x$ **57.** $15x$

Lesson 6-3 pages 280–284

ON YOUR OWN **1.** Add equations; $(5, -6)$ **3.** Multiply the first equation by 4; $(5, 4)$ **5.** Add equations; $(2, -3)$ **7.** Subtract first equation from second; $(4, 2)$ **9.** Brass parts cost $6; steel parts cost $3. **11.** $(5, 2)$ **13.** $(1, 3)$ **15.** $(-4.5, 8)$ **17.** $(14, 14)$ **19.** $(-\frac{2}{3}, 2)$ **21.** $(2, 0)$ **23.** infinitely many solutions **25.** $(2\frac{1}{2}, 3\frac{1}{2})$ **27.** 3 V, 1.5 V **29.** Agree; you do not need to solve an equation for y before substituting the values. **31.** infinitely many solutions **33.** $(18, 52)$ **35.** $(3, 4)$ **37.** $(1\frac{1}{2}, -\frac{1}{2})$ **39a.** $(81.25, 8.125)$ **39b.** Room for one night costs $81.25 per person; the average cost of one meal is about $8.13.

MIXED REVIEW **41.** $x = 0$ **43.** $x = 10$ **45.** $2s + d = 6.50$ **47.** $5p + 2n = 32$

CHECKPOINT **1.** $(-1\frac{2}{9}, 3\frac{1}{9})$ **2.** $(3, -4)$ **3.** $(9, 10)$ **4.** $(2, -5\frac{1}{3})$ **5.** Sample: $2x - y = 3$; $\frac{1}{2}x + \frac{1}{2}y = 6$ **6a.** $(p, c) = (20, 33)$

Lesson 6-4 pages 285–288

ON YOUR OWN **1.** 72.5° and 107.5° **3.** 7 dimes and 3 nickels **5.** $(\frac{1}{3}, 2\frac{1}{3})$ **7.** (5, 1) **9.** no solution **11.** (0, 0) **13a.** $m = 254 + 400 + 1.2n$ **13b.** $m = 4n + 150$ **13c.** 180 tickets **15.** 577 games **17.** C **19.** Sample: Substitution; at least one equation is solved for one of the variables. **21.** Sample: Elimination; coefficients match well for subtraction. **23.** Sample: Substitution; coefficients -1 and 1 make it easy to solve either equation for one of the variables. **25a.** $2s + t = 12$ **25b.** $s = 3t$ **25c.** $5\frac{1}{7}, 5\frac{1}{7}, 1\frac{5}{7}$

MIXED REVIEW **27.** -2 **29.** 25 or -17 **31.** \$130 billion

33.
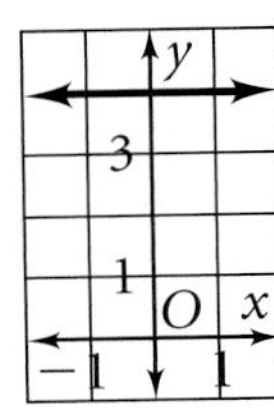

35.
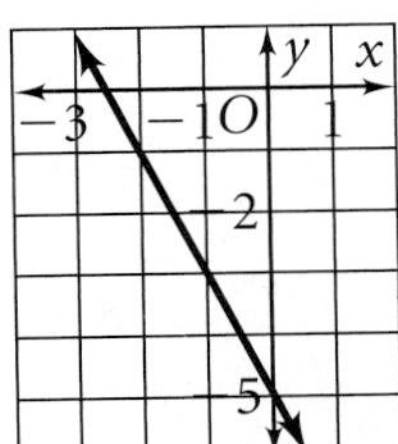

Lesson 6-5 pages 289–293

ON YOUR OWN **1.** A **3.** B **5.** 1 and 3

9.
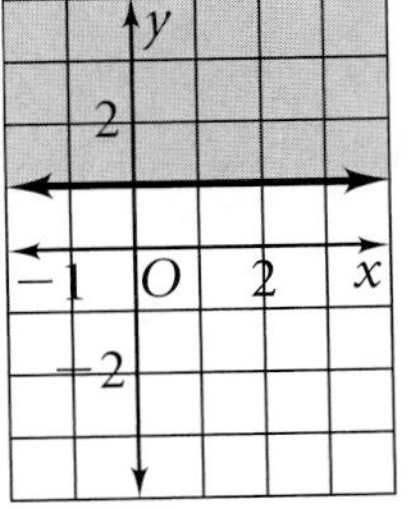

11.
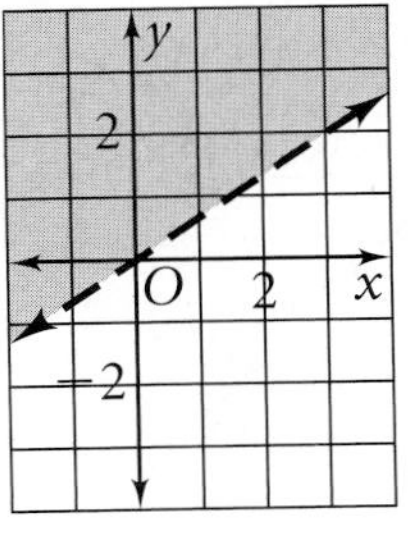

13.
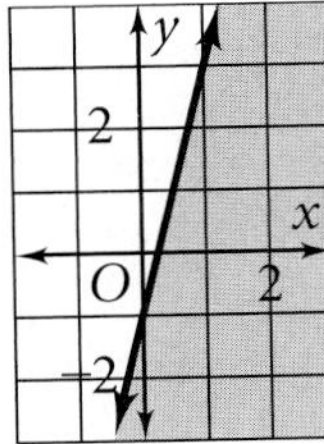

15.
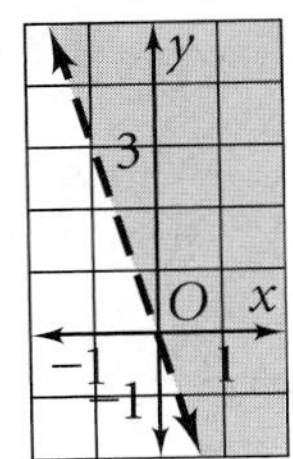

17.
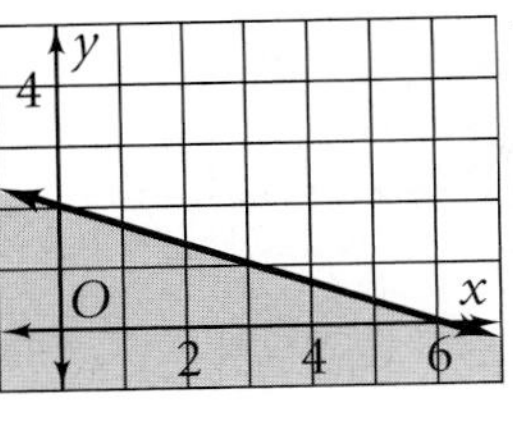

19.
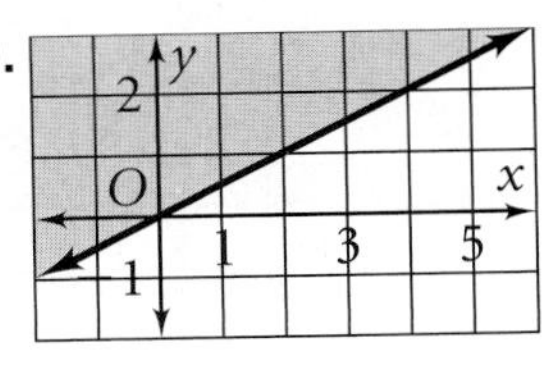

21.
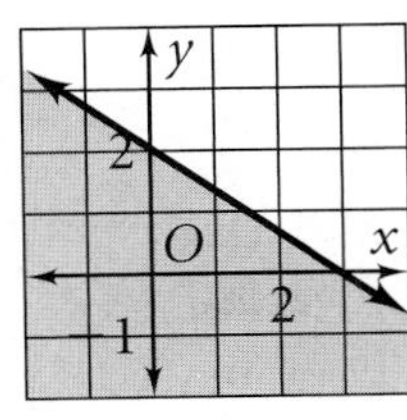

23.
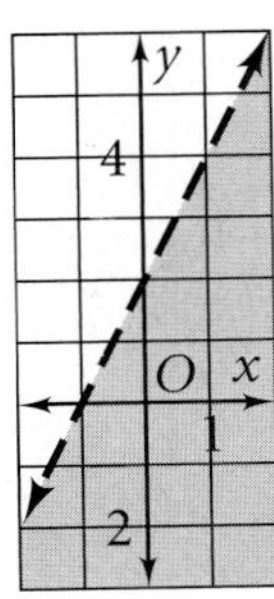

25. $y < x + 2$ **27.** $y > 2x + 1$ **29.** $y \leq \frac{1}{3}x - 2$

31. $x > 0$;
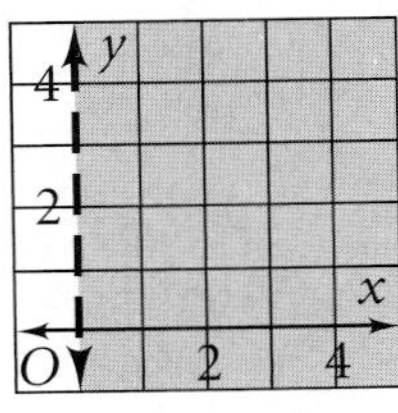

33. $y \geq 0$;
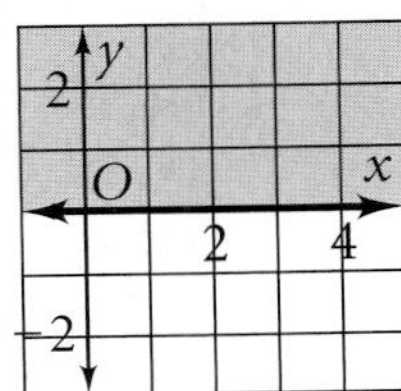

35a. $2x + 2y \leq 50$

35b.
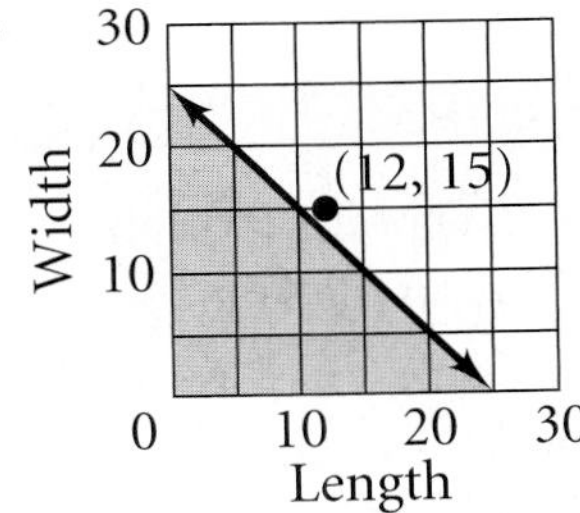

35d. No; $2(12) + 2(15) \leq 50$ is false. On the graph, (12, 15) is not in the shaded region. **37.** yes **39.** yes

MIXED REVIEW **41.** 5 **43.** $\frac{8}{3}$ **45.** 1.2 h **47.** (3, 5) **49.** $(4\frac{2}{3}, 37\frac{1}{3})$

Toolbox page 294

1.
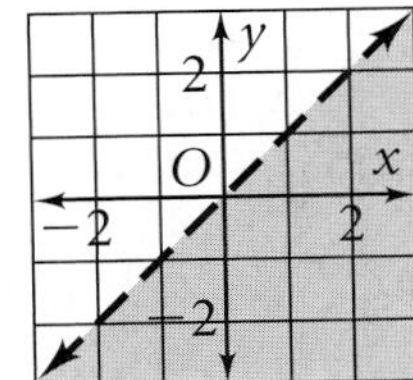

Selected Answers

3. 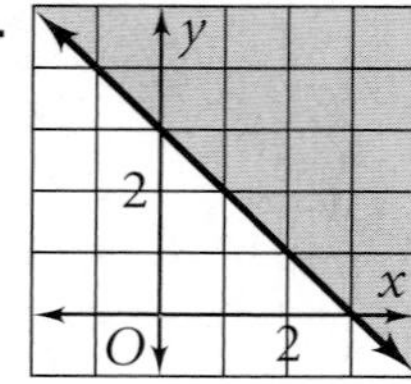

5. 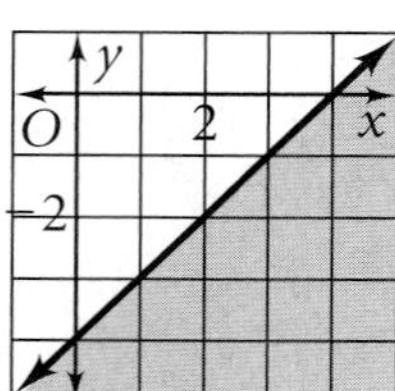

7. 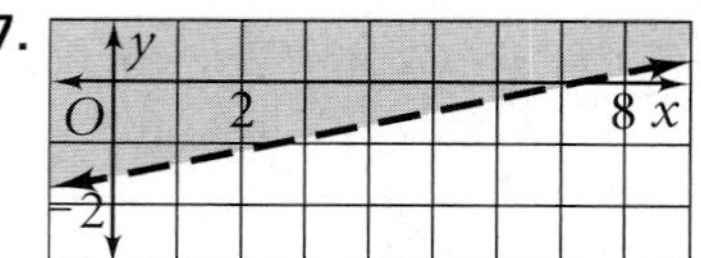

Lesson 6-6 pages 295–299

ON YOUR OWN **1.** C **3.** The point is on the boundary line of $2x + y > 2$, so it is not a solution of $2x + y > 2$.

5. 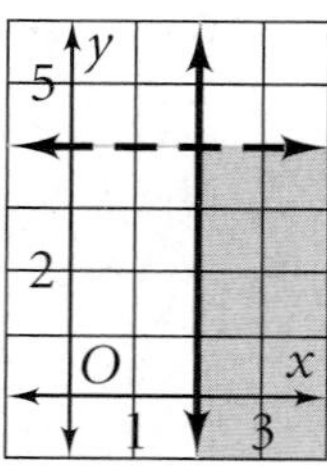

7. no solution;

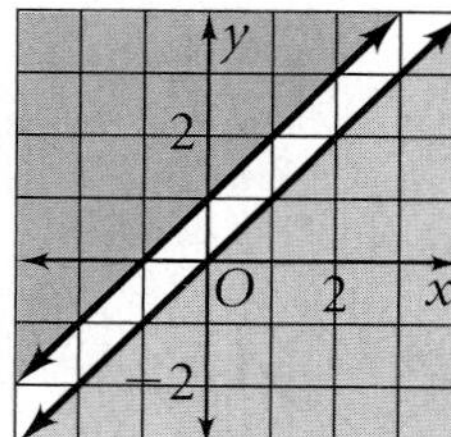

9. 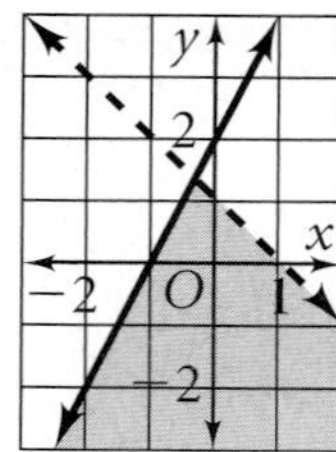

11. 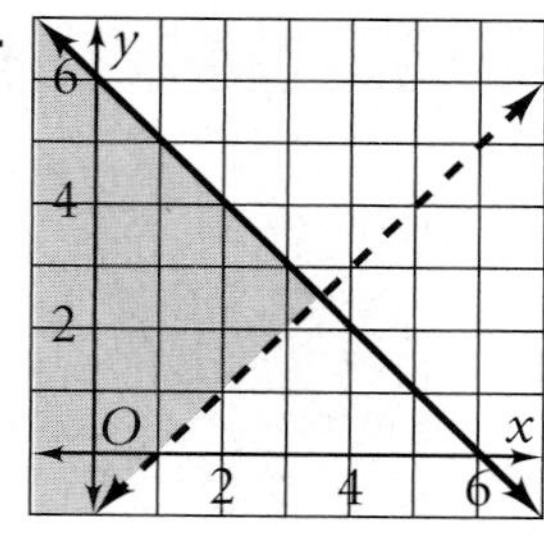

13. 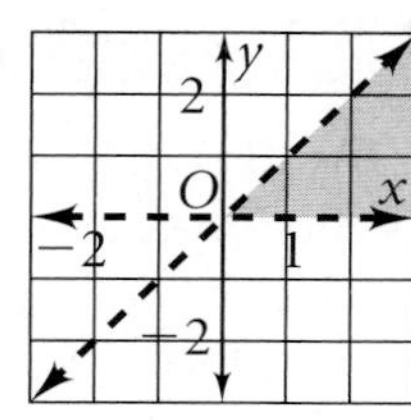

15. 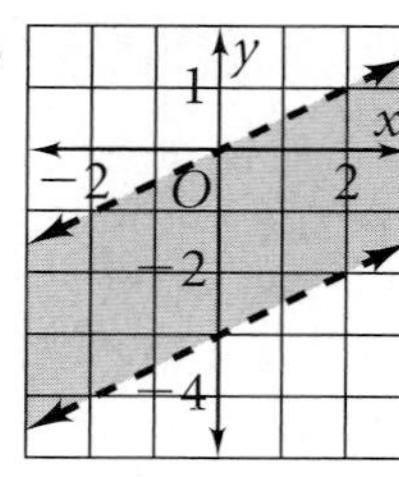

17a. $0.6f + 0.55c \leq 33; f \geq 9; c \geq 12$

17b. 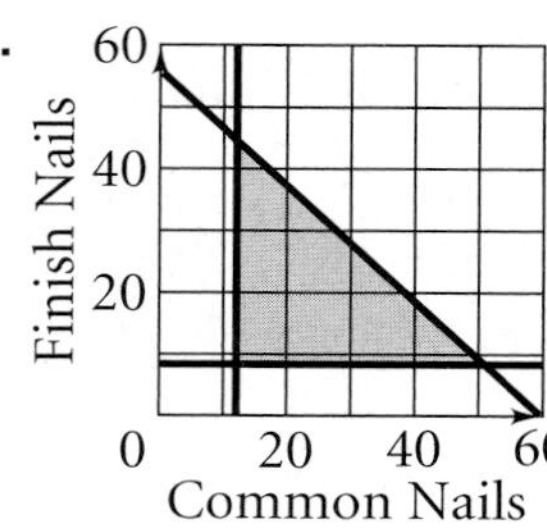

17c. Sample: (20, 20) **17d.** Sample: (40, 25)

23. 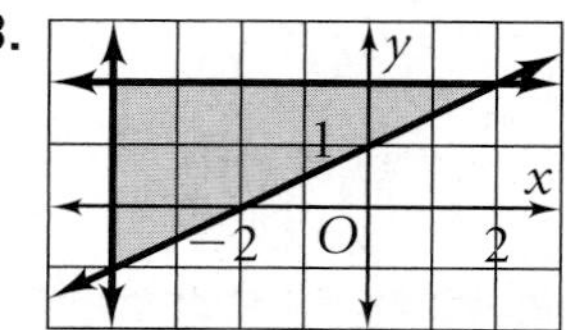

23a. triangle **23b.** $(-4, -1), (-4, 2), (2, 2)$
23c. 9 sq. units

25. 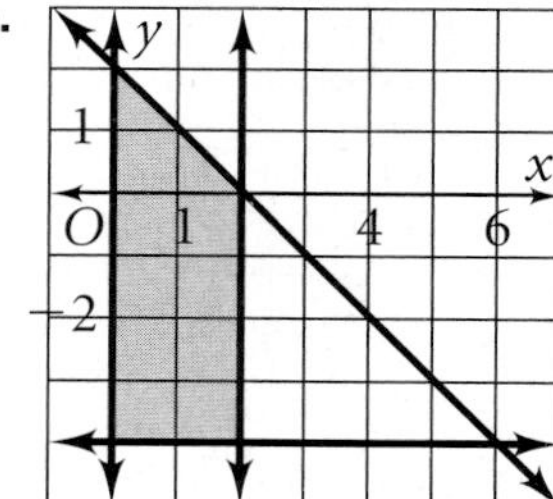

25a. trapezoid **25b.** $(0, -4)$ $(0, 2), (2, 0), (2, -4)$
25c. 10 sq. units **27a.** $5.99x + 9.99y \leq 50; x \geq 0; y \geq 1$

27b. 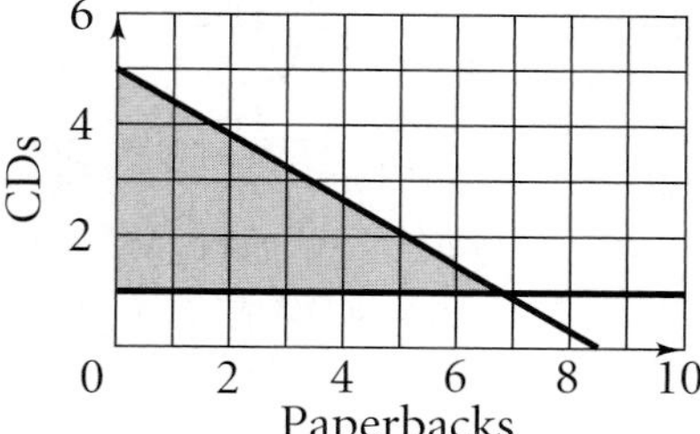

27c. 2 books and 6 CDs; (2, 6) is not a solution of the system because 2 books and 6 CDs cost $71.92.
27d. 5 CDs, no books **27e.** 8 books

MIXED REVIEW **29.** 1 **31.** 4 **33.** 4 **35.** 22 **37.** 62 **39.** 1350

CHECKPOINT

1. 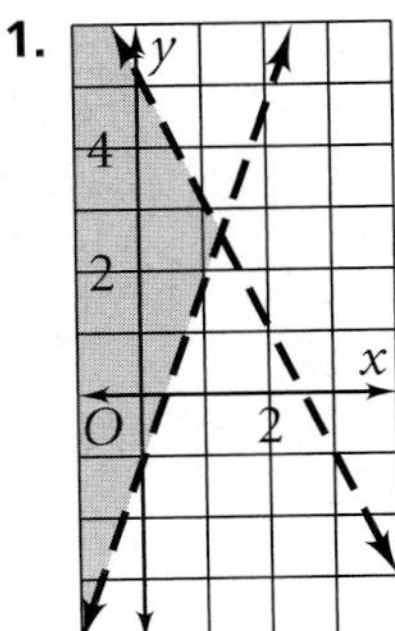

2. 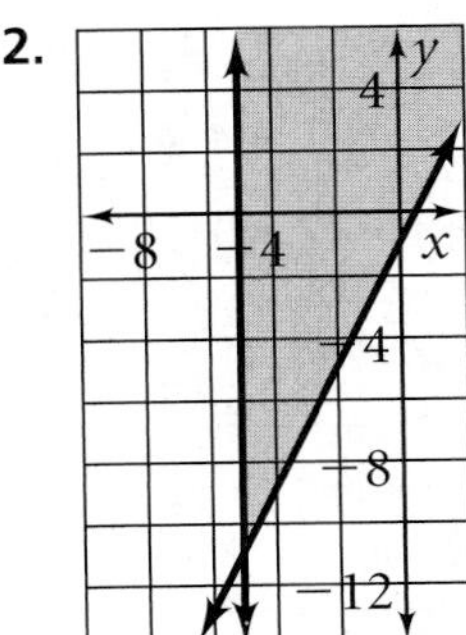

3. 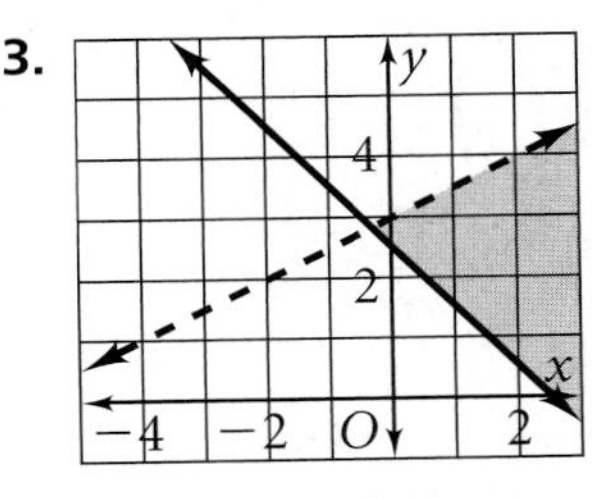

4. 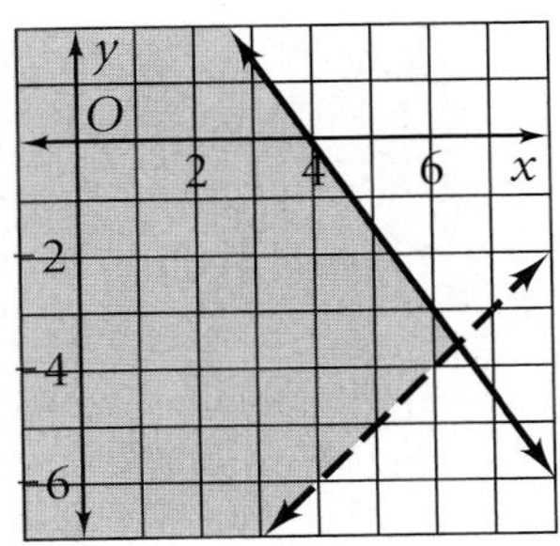

5. D **6a.** $p = 7 + 0.75t$; $p = 8 + 0.5t$ **6b.** (4, 10); a pizza with 4 toppings costs $10 in each restaurant.

Lesson 6-7 pages 300–304

ON YOUR OWN **1.** 24, 32, 34, 30; (3, 5), (8, 0) **3.** 0, 100, 400, 800; (20, 10), (0, 0) **5.** (6, 0) **7.** (4, 0) **9.** 0; 36 **11.** 1; 8 **13.** $c = 8d + 20t$
15b. $N = 30x + 40y$
15c. 400 ft^2 at Location A and 100 ft^2 at Location B

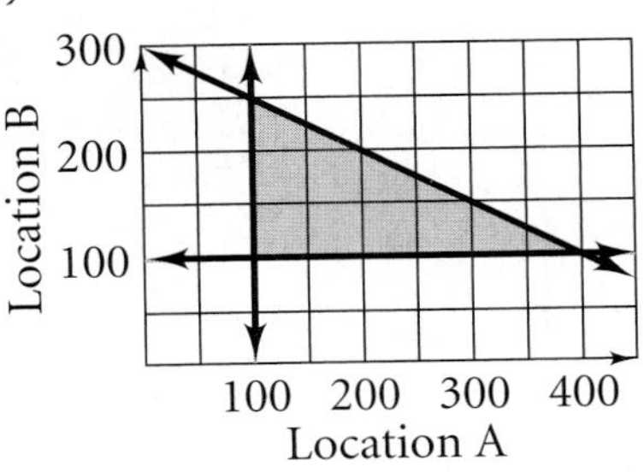

MIXED REVIEW **17.** $y = -\frac{1}{2}x + 2\frac{1}{2}$ **19.** $y = \frac{8}{3}x$
21. quadratic **23.** linear

Lesson 6-8 pages 305–309

ON YOUR OWN **1.** (0, 0), (2, 4) **3.** (0, 0) **5.** (−2, −2), (2, −2) **7.** (−2, 1), (2, 1)

9. (−1.94, 0.15), (1.94, 0.15)

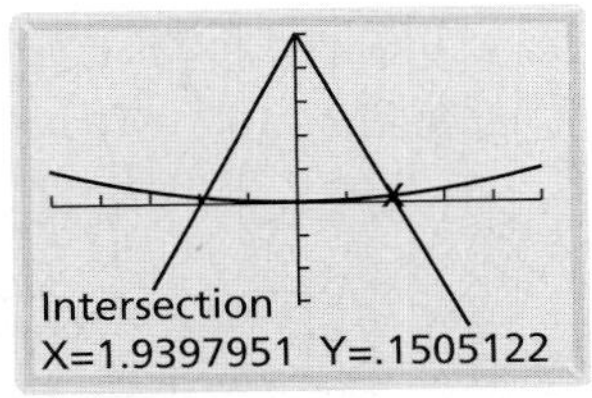

Xmin=−5 Ymin=−5
Xmax=5 Ymax=5
Xscl=1 Yscl=1

11. A; (−1, −2), (1, −2) **13.** C; no solution **15.** D

21. no solution;

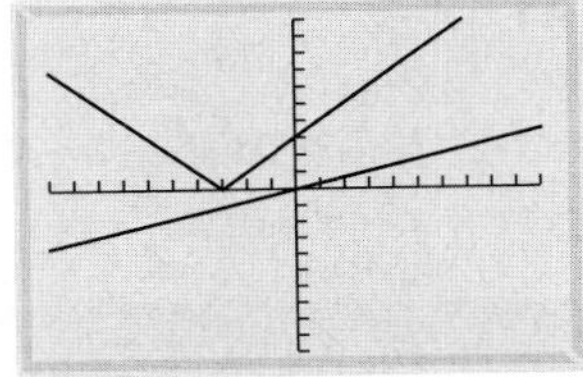

23. (−2, 3), (1, 0);

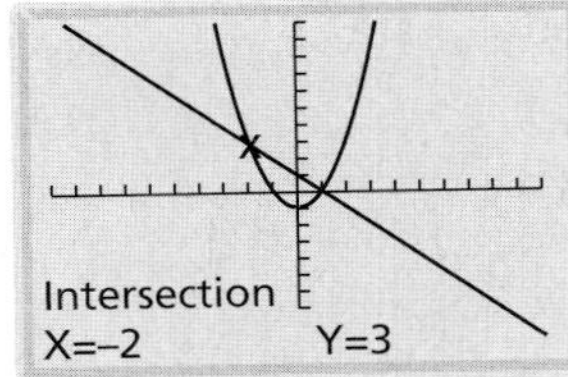

25. no solution;

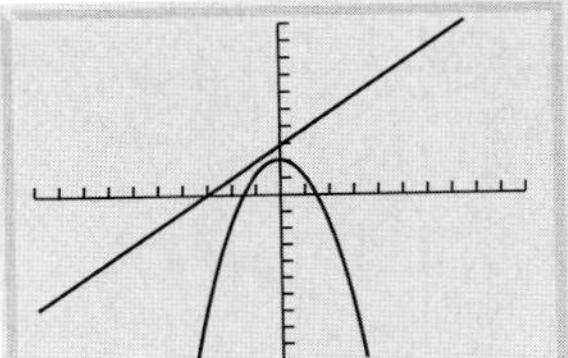

27. (−1, −2), (1, −2);

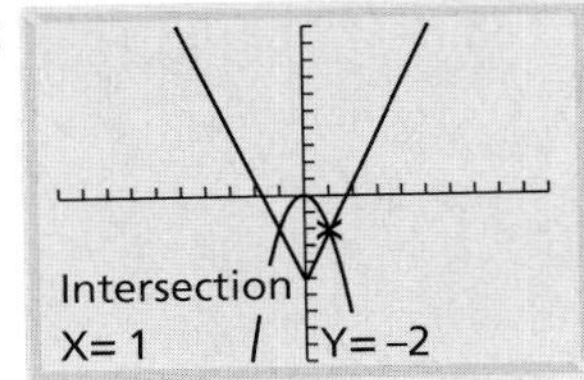

Selected Answers

29. no solution;

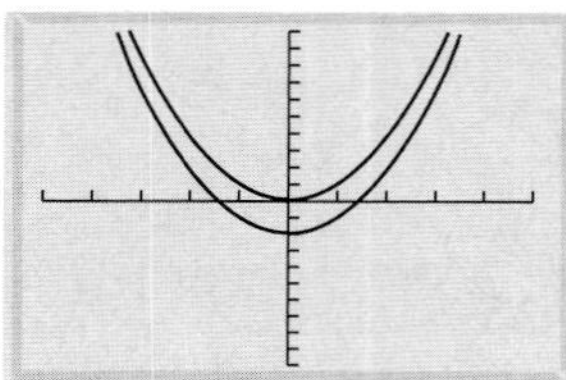

Xmin=–5 Ymin=–10
Xmax=5 Ymax=10
Xscl=1 Yscl=1

31. $(-2, 1), (4, 4)$;

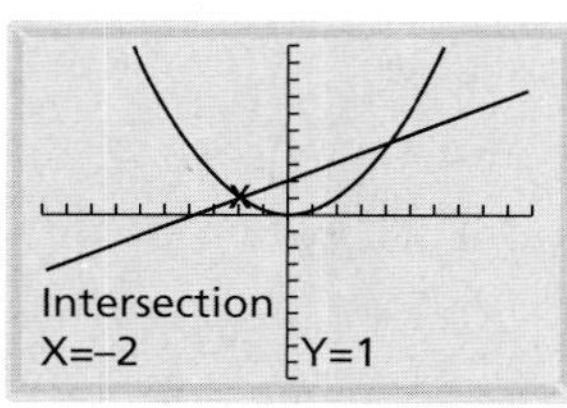

MIXED REVIEW **35.** 106.25% **37.** 6.5%

39. 91,800 **41.** $\begin{bmatrix} 7-x & x-5 \\ -3x & -y \\ 8z & 0 \end{bmatrix}$

43a. 1000000*B2/C2 **43b.** D2: 1576; D3: 2423

Wrap-Up pages 311–313

1. $x = 3, y = 1$; $(3, 1)$ **2.** $y = -\frac{3}{2}x - \frac{3}{2}, y = \frac{3}{2}x + \frac{3}{2}$; $(-1, 0)$ **3.** $y = x - 1, y = -x + 3$; $(2, 1)$
4. $x = -1, y = -x + 1$; $(-1, 2)$

5. $(1, 2)$;

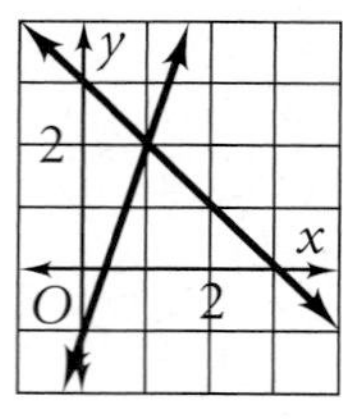

6. $(-1, 2)$;

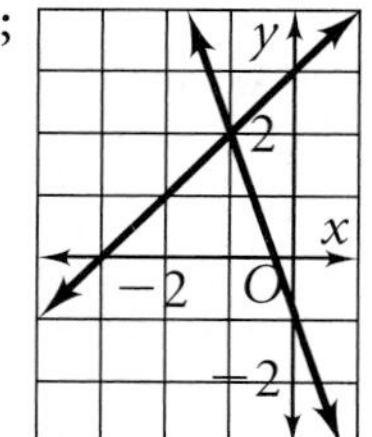

7. no solution;

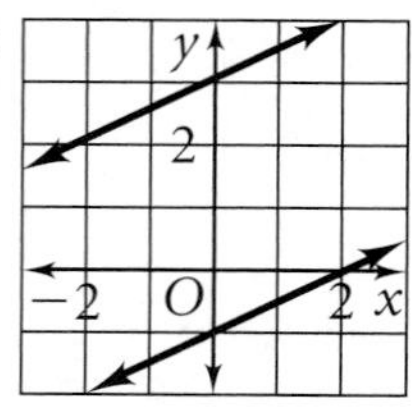

8. $(1, -1)$;

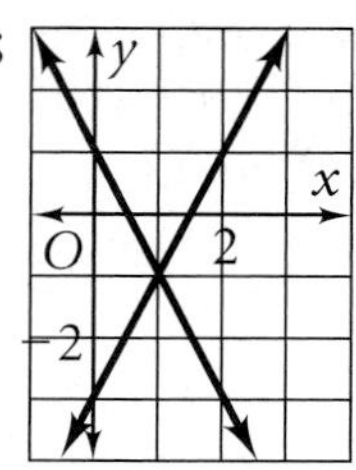

9. $(-2, 5)$ **10.** $(-4\frac{1}{2}, -6)$ **11.** $(2, 2)$
12. $(-1\frac{1}{9}, -\frac{5}{9})$ **14.** $(-6, 23)$ **15.** $(1, -1)$ **16.** $(6, 4)$
17. $(12, 6)$ **18.** $10\frac{2}{3}$ fl oz **19.** 63° and 27°

20.

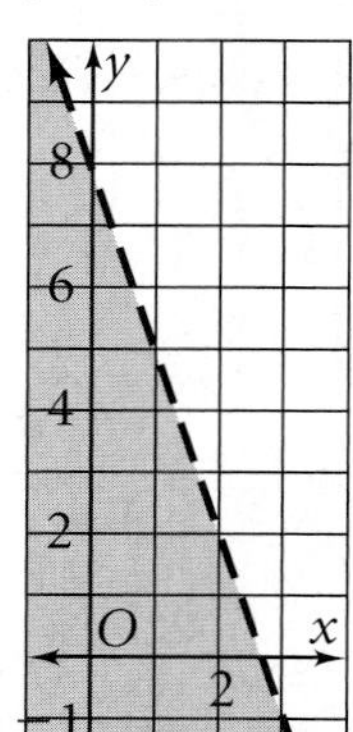

21.

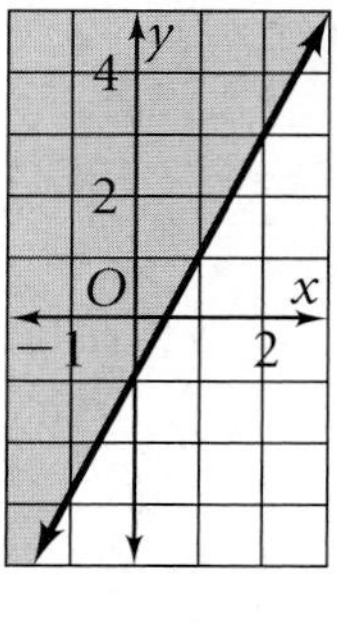

22.

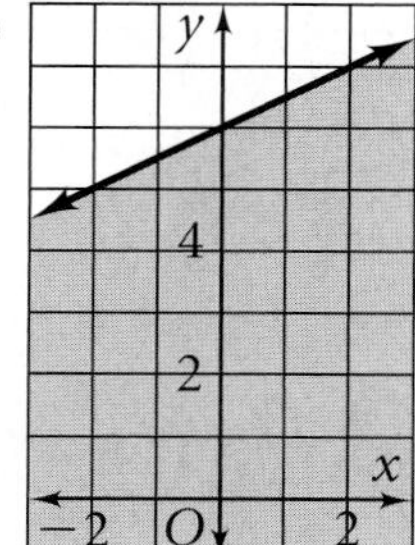

23.

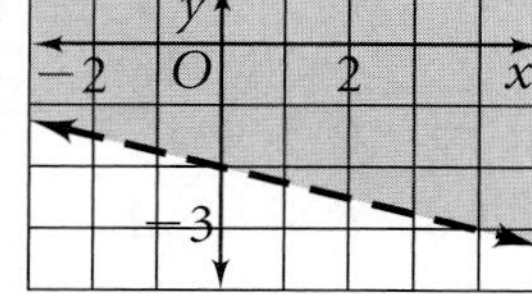

24.

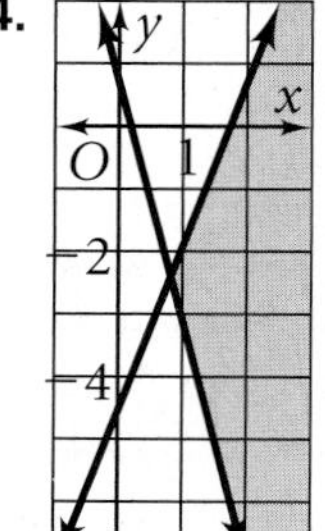

25.

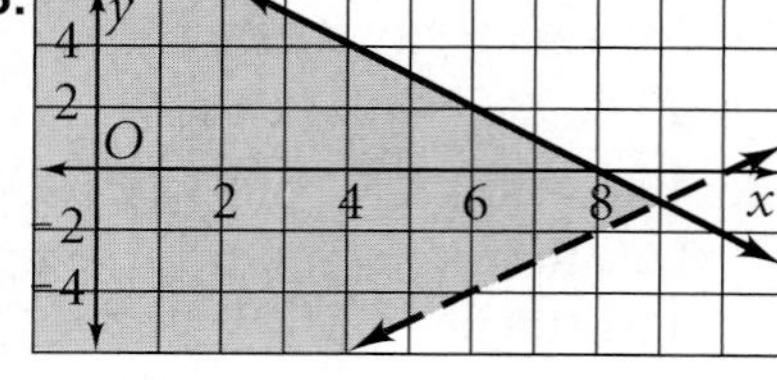

26. 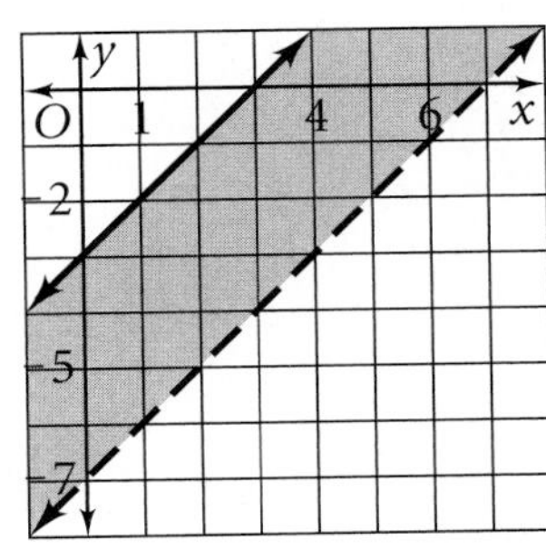

27. 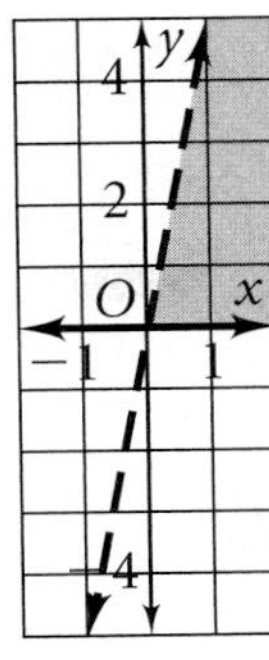

29. 0; 21; 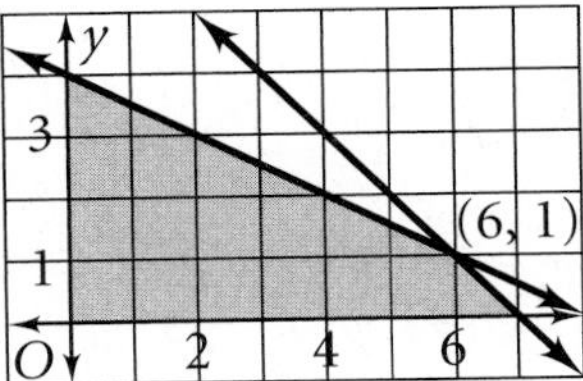

30. 3; 7.5; 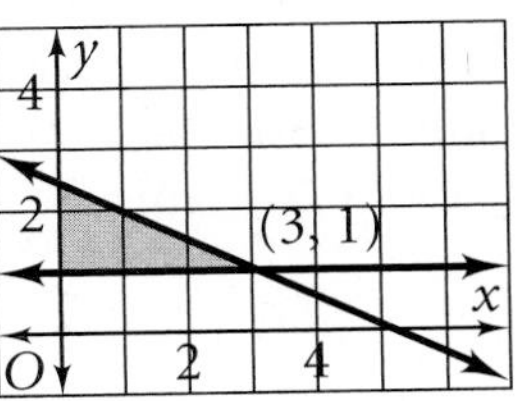

31. 0; 18; 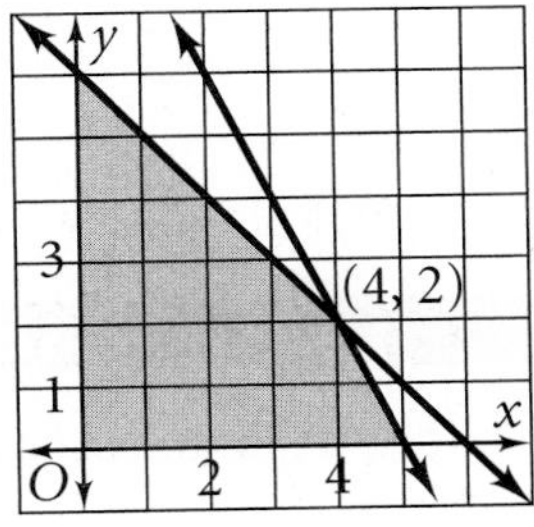

32. 7; 16; 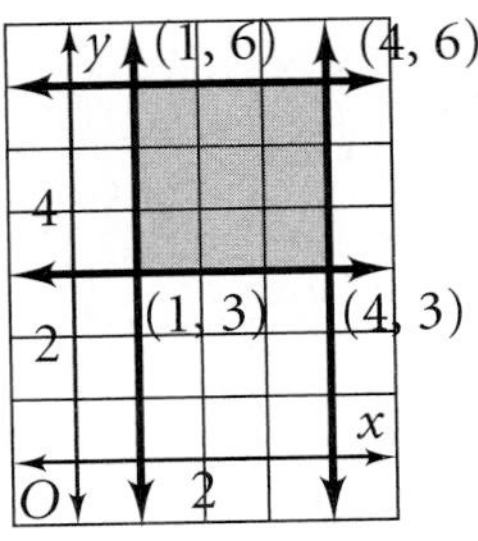

33. E

34. (2, 0), (−3, 5); 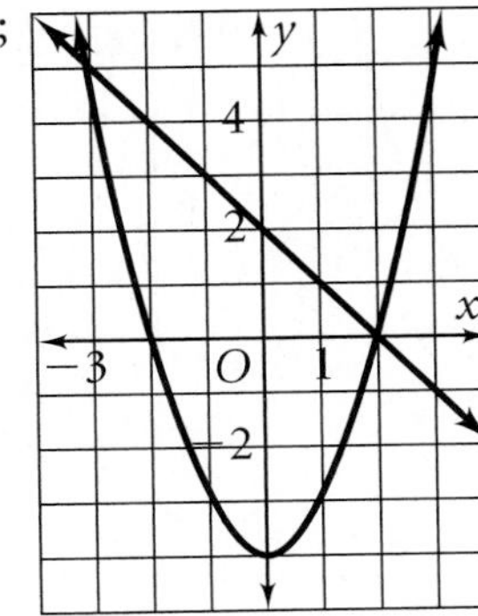

35. (2, 1), $(-\frac{2}{3}, -1\frac{2}{3})$; 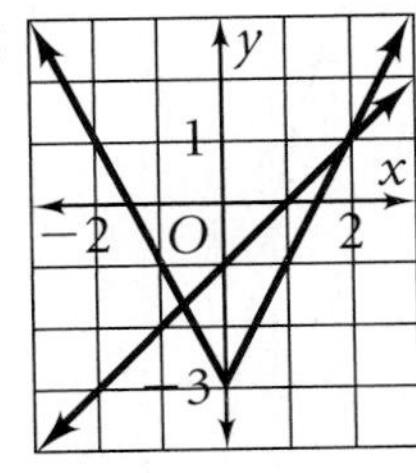

36. (0, 3), (2, 1); 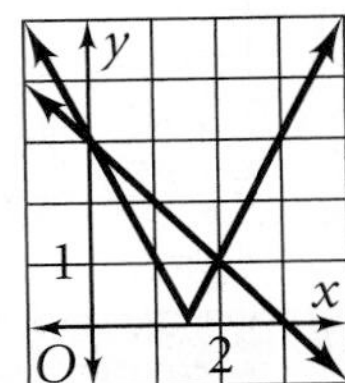

37. (−1, 4), (3, 12) 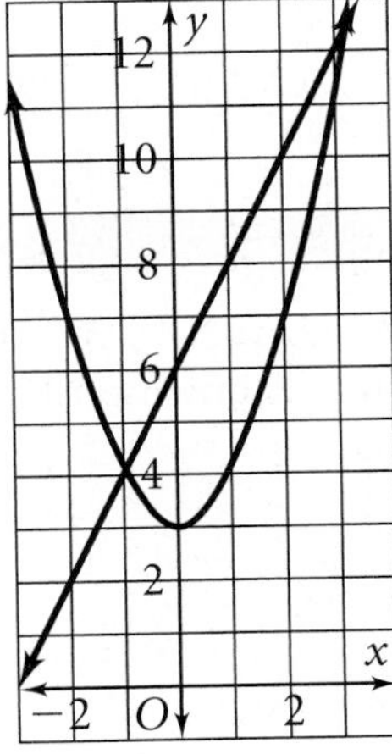

38. 0, 1, 2, 3, or 4; the number of solutions of a system with an absolute value equation and a quadratic equation correspond to the number of times the graphs of the equations intersect. It is possible for the graphs to intersect 0, 1, 2, 3, or 4 times. The graphs cannot intersect more than 4 times. **39.** 9 **40.** 49 **41.** 20.25 **42.** $\frac{1}{4}$ **43.** 121 **44.** 67.24

Selected Answers

45. 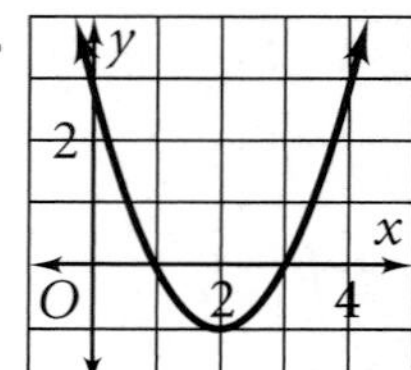

46. 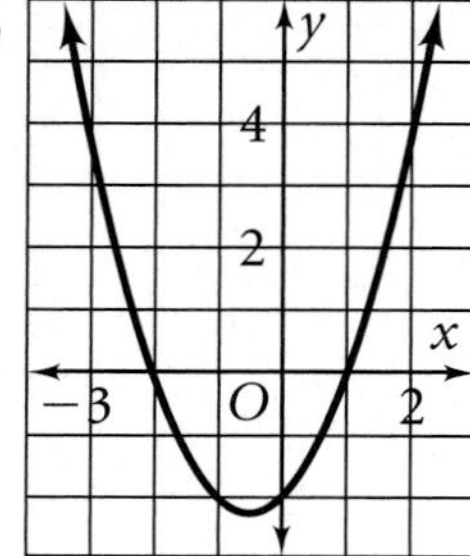

47. 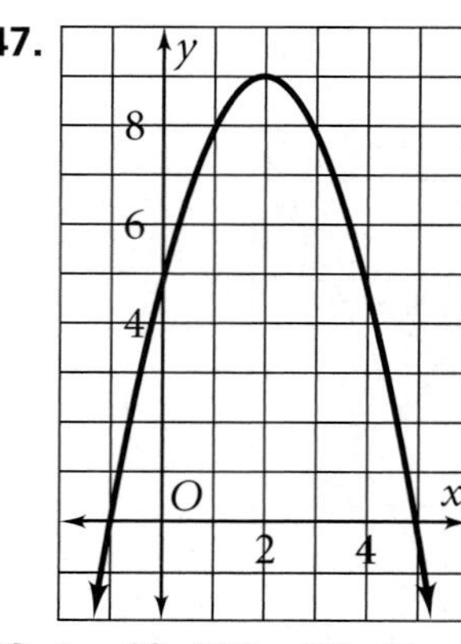

48. 1 **49.** 109 **50.** 64 **51.** 17 **52.** 11 **53.** 170.24

Preparing for the Math A Exam page 315

1. 1 **3.** 4 **5.** 2 **7.** 1

CHAPTER 7

Lesson 7-1 pages 318–322

ON YOUR OWN **1.** 1; 2; 4 **3.** −1, −3, −9
5. upward; min. **7.** downward; max.

9. 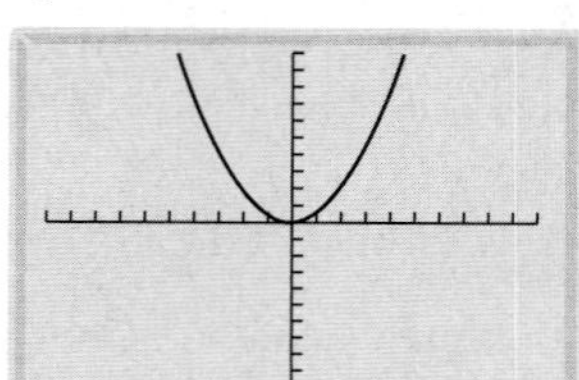

11. 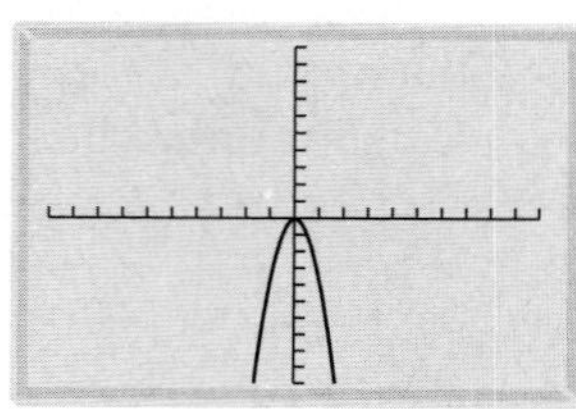

13. 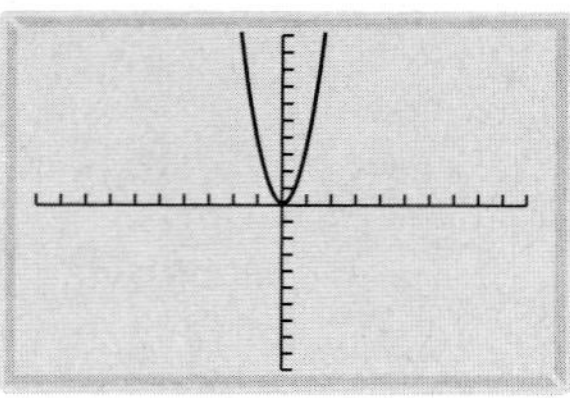

15. 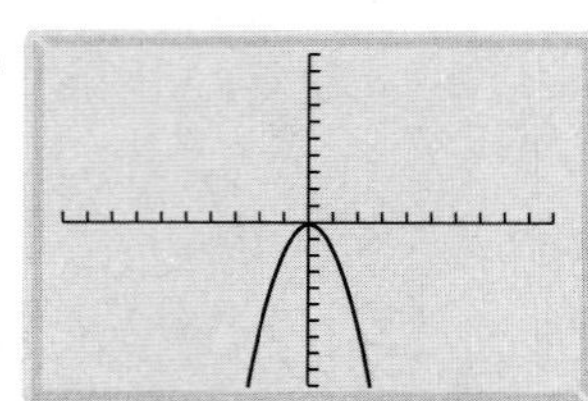

17. $y = x^2, y = 3x^2, y = 7x^2$ **19.** $y = -\frac{2}{3}x^2$, $y = -2x^2, y = -4x^2$ **21.** *K*; *L* **23.** *K*
29. narrower **31.** narrower **35.** E **37.** F **39.** C

MIXED REVIEW **41.** 40% increase
43a. 199,980,000 Slinkies **43b.** about 33 lb
43c. about 24,048 mi; about 7655 mi

45. 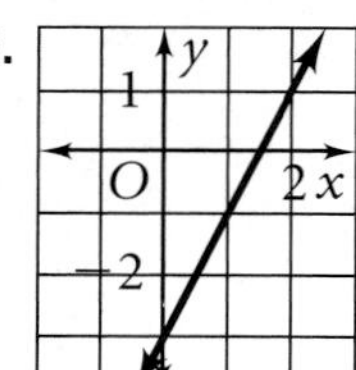

Lesson 7-2 pages 323–326

ON YOUR OWN **3.** maximum **5.** maximum

7. 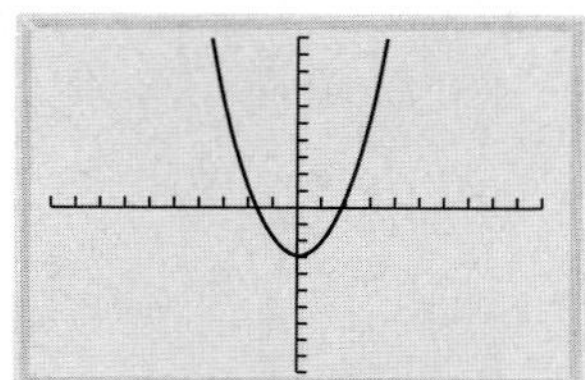

9. 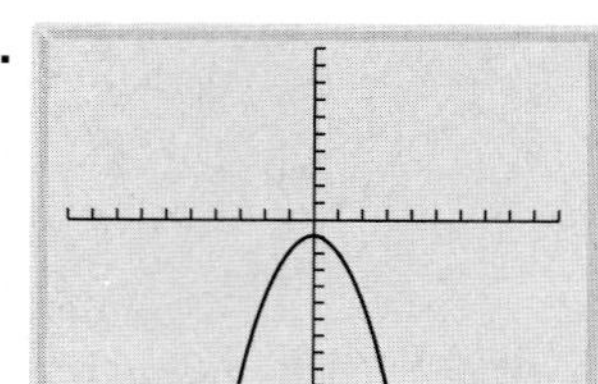

11.

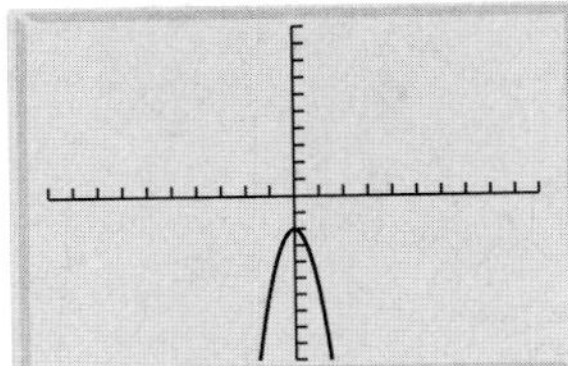

13.

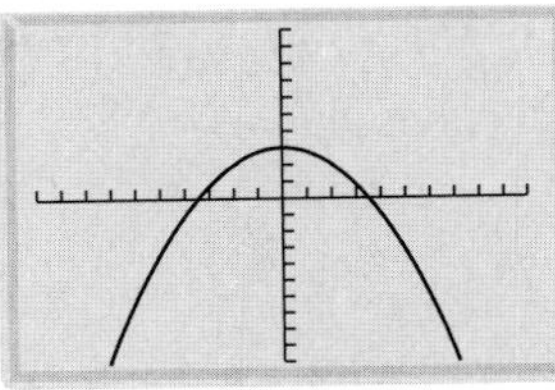

15.

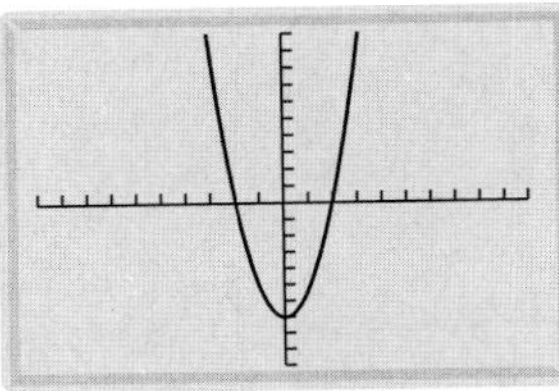

17.

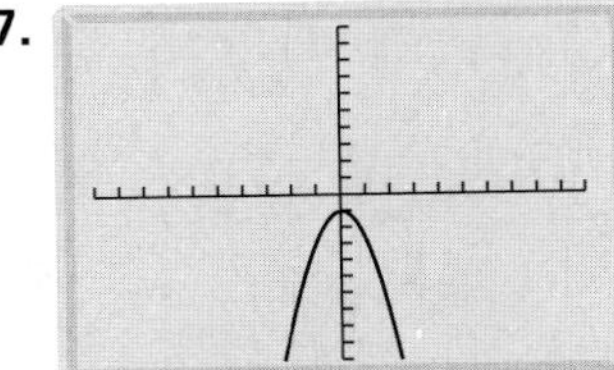

21. *E* **23.** *F* **25.** *C* **27.** *E* **29.** *E*, *F* **31.** *G*

33a.

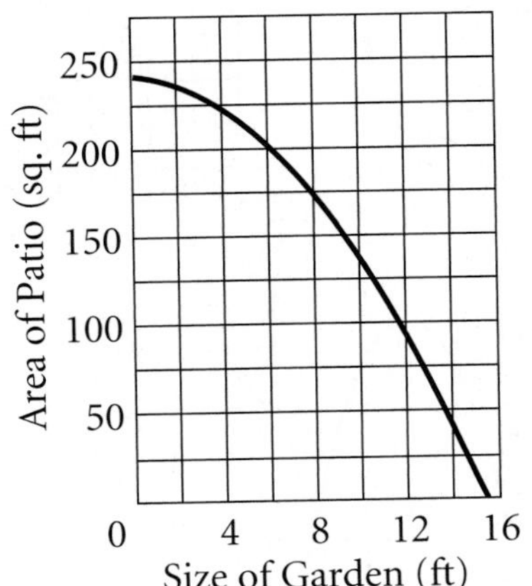

33b. $0 < x < 12$; the length of the side of the garden must be positive and shorter than 12 ft, the shorter side of the patio. **33c.** $96 < y < 240$; the larger the garden the smaller the area of the patio. As the length of the side of the garden changes from 0 to 12 ft, the value of the function changes from 240 to 96.

MIXED REVIEW **35.** $y = -\frac{1}{5}x + \frac{7}{5}$ **37.** $y = -2x - 18$ **39.** $y = -\frac{1}{4}x + 3$ **41.** about $129,067 **43.** $\frac{1}{16}$

Lesson 7-3 pages 327–331

ON YOUR OWN **1.** $x = 0$; $(0, 4)$ **3.** $x = -1$; $(-1, -7)$ **5.** $x = 0$; $(0, -3)$ **7.** $x = -2$; $(-2, -1)$ **9.** $x = 0$; $(0, 12)$ **11.** E **13.** F **15.** D

17.

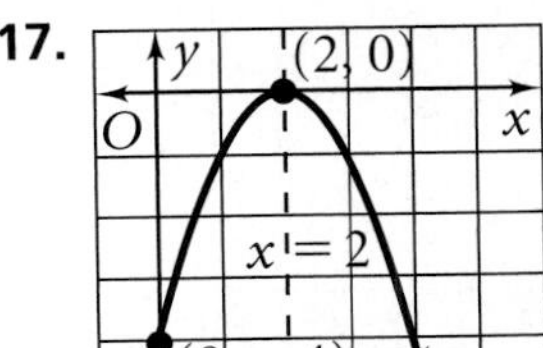

19.

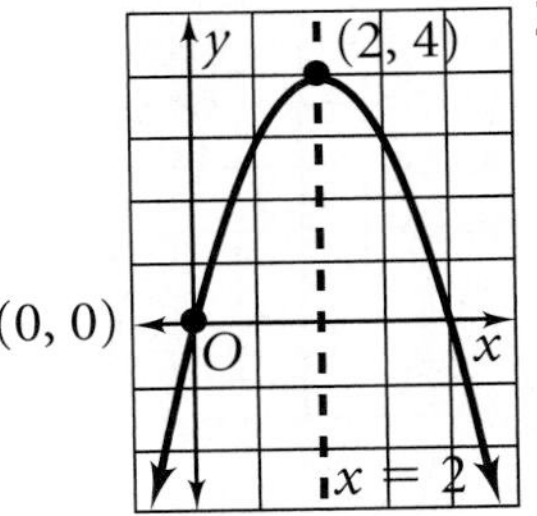

21.

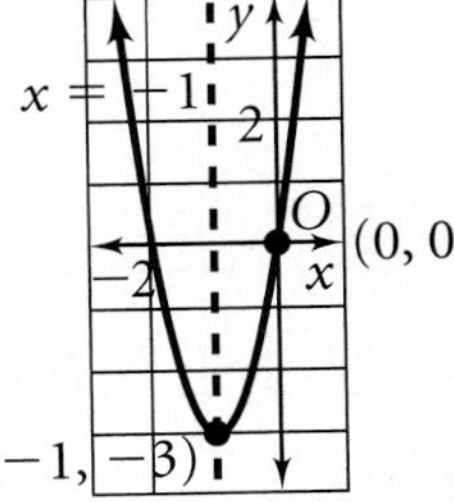

23.

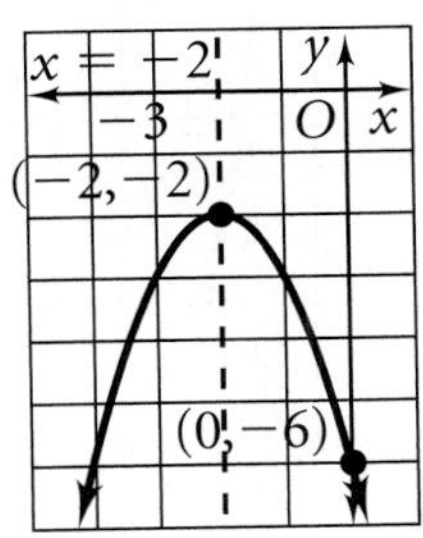

25.

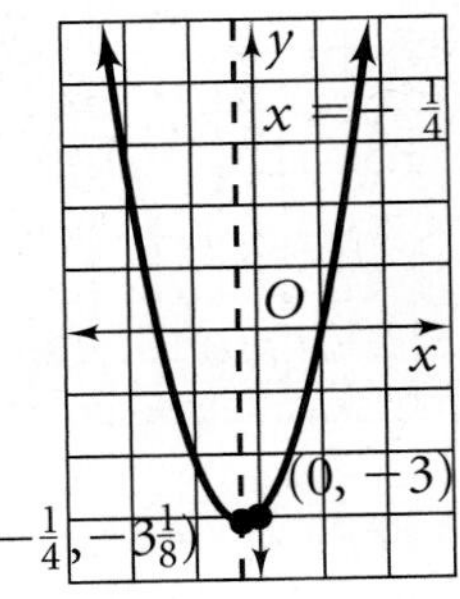

27.

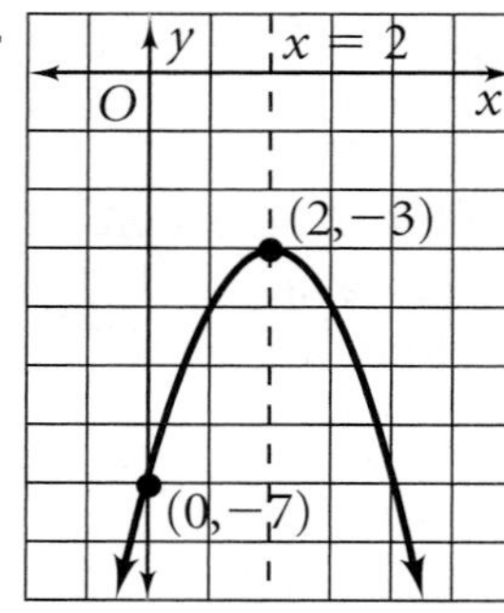

29. 20 ft; 400 ft^2 **31.**

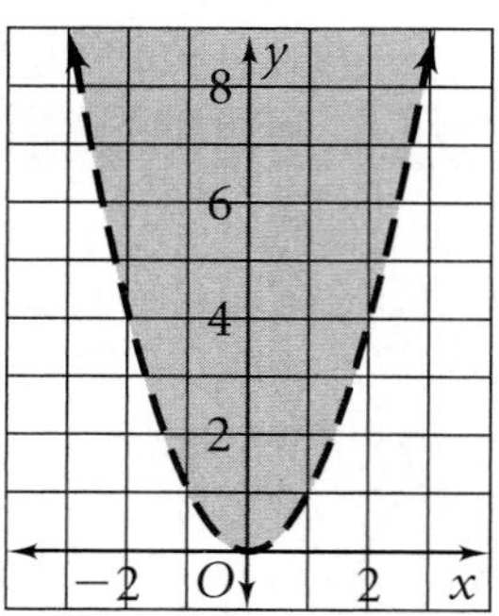

33.

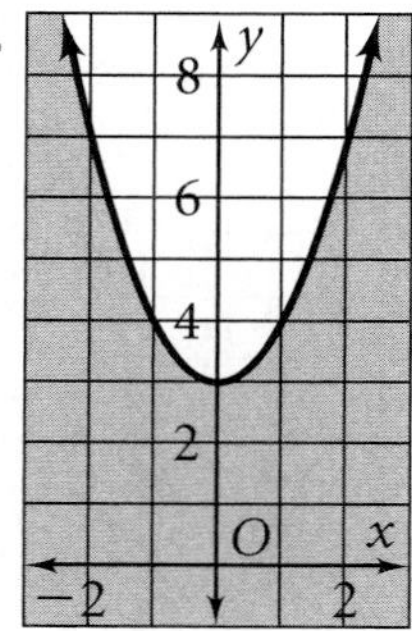

35.

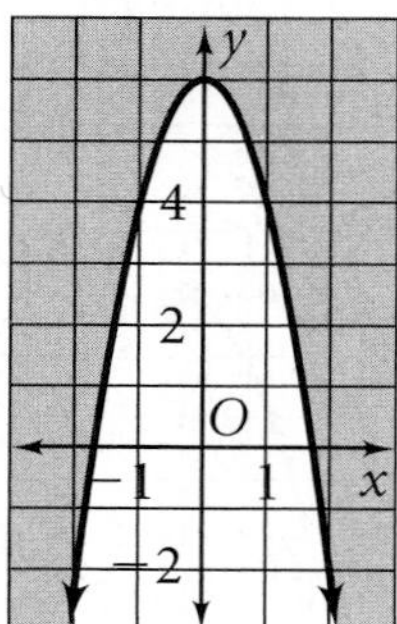

37.

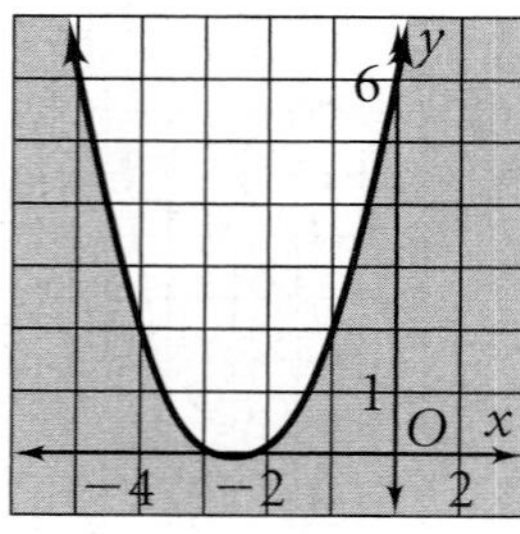

39.

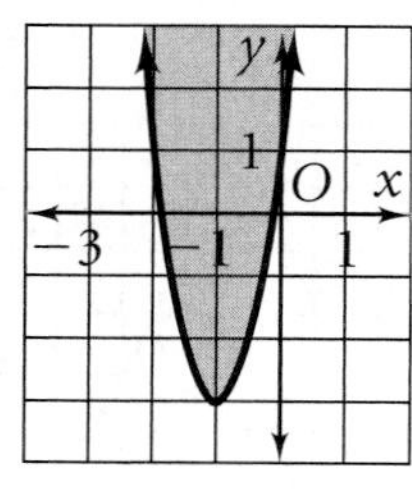

MIXED REVIEW **43.** $\frac{1}{4}$ **45.** $\frac{1}{4}$ **47a.** 10.1 mi/h **47b.** 569 strokes **49.** −1 **51.** −36

Lesson 7-4 pages 332–336

ON YOUR OWN **1.** ±13 **3.** $\pm\frac{1}{3}$ **5.** ±0.5 **7.** ±1.1 **9.** irrat. **11.** irrat. **13.** 5 and 6 **15.** −16 and −15

17. 3.46 **19.** 107.47 **21a.** about 0.93 **21b.** about 4.6 ft **23.** ±0.6 **25.** $\pm\frac{5}{4}$ **27.** ±20 **29.** ±25 **31.** $\pm\frac{1}{9}$ **33.** ±27 **35a.** about 8400 km **35b.** about 7700 km **37.** 4 **39.** $-\frac{2}{5}$ **41.** $\frac{1}{6}$ **43.** −12.53 **45.** −3.61 **47.** 33 **49.** 6.40 **53.** irrat. **55.** rat. **57.** irrat. **59.** undefined **61.** true **63.** false; $-5 < -\sqrt{17} < -4$ **65.** false; $-17 < -\sqrt{280} < -16$ **67.** false; $-37 < -\sqrt{1300} < -36$ **69.** true

MIXED REVIEW

71. $s < -2$; −5 −4 −3 −2 −1 0

73. $b < -6$; −9 −8 −7 −6 −5 −4

75. $c \leq \frac{1}{7}$; −2 −1 0 1 2 3

77. $t > 1\frac{2}{3}$; −1 0 1 2 3 4

79. $13\frac{2}{3}$ **81.** 0

CHECKPOINT

1. (0, 0);

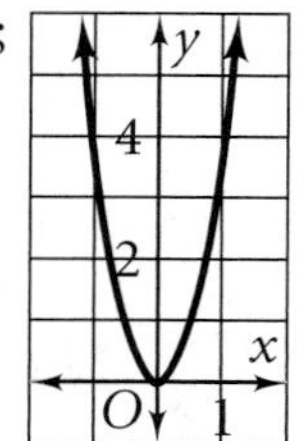

2. (0, 7);

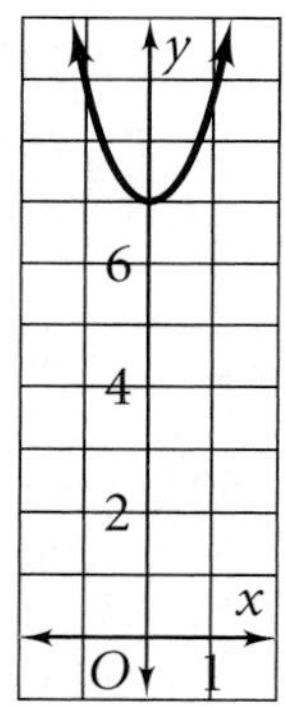

3. (−1, 11);

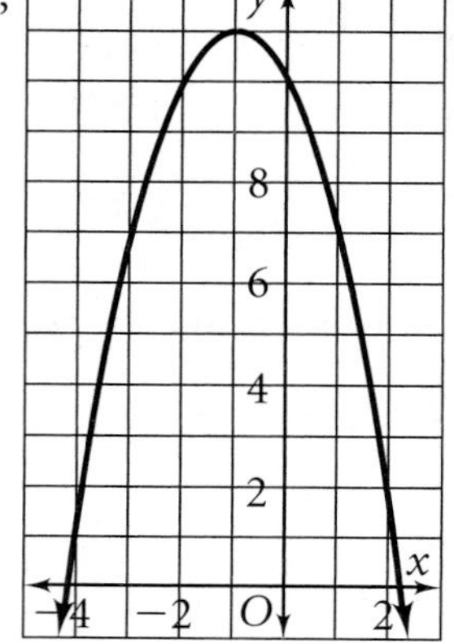

4. 2.65 **5.** −10 **6.** 4.80 **7.** 12 **8.** −12.25 **9.** $-\frac{1}{3}$

Lesson 7-5 pages 337–341

ON YOUR OWN **1.** $-2, 2$ **3.** no solution **5.** no solution **7.** $-\frac{3}{7}, \frac{3}{7}$ **9.** $-\frac{5}{2}, \frac{5}{2}$ **11.** 0 **13.** Sample: Michael used -5 and 5 as square roots of -25, which does not have a real number square root. **15.** $-2.8, 2.8$ **17.** $-1.4, 1.4$ **19.** $-4.6, 4.6$ **21.** 3.6 in. **23.** False; there are no solutions. **25.** False; there are two solutions **27.** true; $-8, 8$ **29.** true **31.** 11.2 ft **33.** 2.5 s **37.** $-2.5, 2.5$ **39.** $-2.4, 2.4$ **41.** $-2, 2$

MIXED REVIEW **43.** (2, 3) **45.** (15, -15) **47.** 3.16 **49.** 4.69

Toolbox page 342

1. about 10.78, 13.22 **3.** $-2, 1\frac{1}{2}$ **5.** about 0.28, 17.72 **7.** $-12, 6$

Lesson 7-6 pages 343–347

ON YOUR OWN **1.** $3x^2 + 13x - 10 = 0$ **3.** $x^2 - 5x - 7 = 0$ **5.** $12x^2 - 25x + 84 = 0$ **7.** $-1.67, 0.5$ **9.** $-4.65, 4.65$ **11.** $-2.2, 3$ **13.** 0, 0.56 **15.** $-1.78, 0.28$ **17.** $-1.5, -1$ **19b.** about 356.9 million **19c.** 2007 **21.** $-6, 6$ **23.** $-1.41, 1.41$ **25.** $-2, -3$ **27.** $-2, 3$ **29.** $-0.39, 1.72$ **31.** $-1.43, 2.23$ **35a.** 630 ft **35b.** 0 ft **35c.** about 6.3 s

MIXED REVIEW **37.** $\frac{1}{4}$ **39.** 0 **41.** 41 **43.** 24 **45.** 49

CHECKPOINT **1.** $-8.06, 8.06$ **2.** $-2, 2$ **3.** $-11, 11$ **4.** 1, 3 **5.** $-1, 0.4$ **6.** 0.23, 3.27 **7.** D

Toolbox page 348

1. $y = x^2 + 6x + 8$ **3.** $y = 2x^2 + 6x - 8$

Lesson 7-7 pages 349–353

ON YOUR OWN **1.** C **3.** A **5.** 1 **7.** 2 **9.** 2 **11.** 0 **13.** 1 **15.** 2 **17a.** no value of x **17b.** Yes; $266 = -x^2 + 3x + 270$ transforms to $-x^2 + 3x + 4 = 0$. The discriminant is positive. **19.** A **21.** Rational; the square root of the discriminant is a positive integer. **23.** 2 **25.** 2 **27.** 0 **29.** 0 **31.** B **33.** no **35.** yes; $(\frac{2}{3}, 0), (-1, 0)$ **37.** yes; $(-1, 0), (2\frac{1}{2}, 0)$ **39.** no **41a.** A2^2 − 4; A2^2 − 8 **41b.** for integer values ≤ -2 or ≥ 2 **41c.** integer values between -2 and 2

MIXED REVIEW **43.**

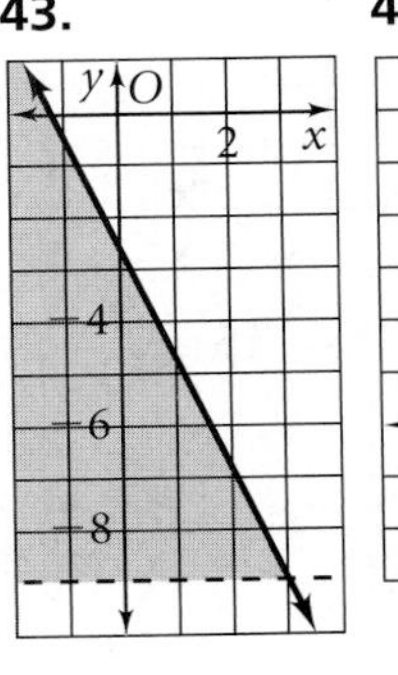

45.

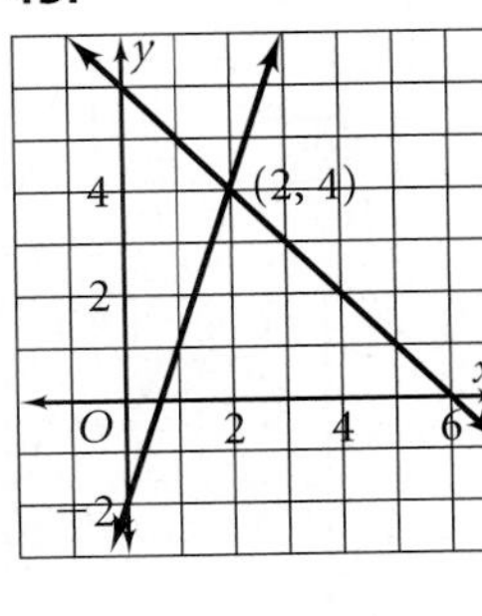

47. 3 **49.** -4

Wrap-Up pages 355–357

5.

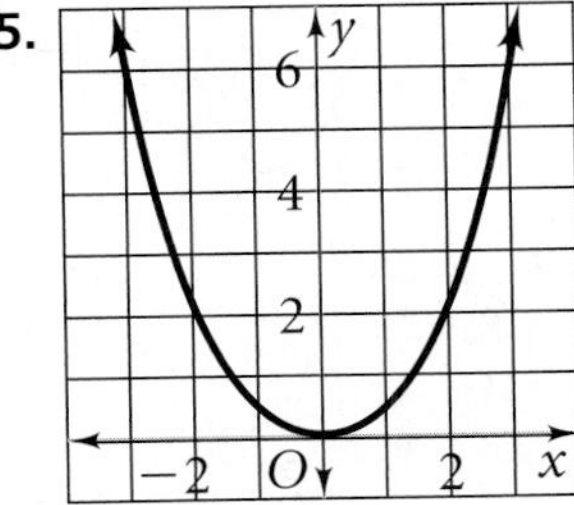

6.

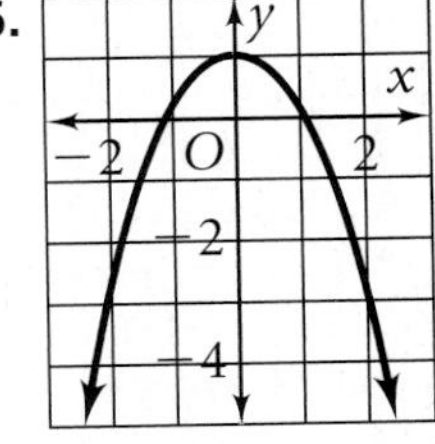

7.

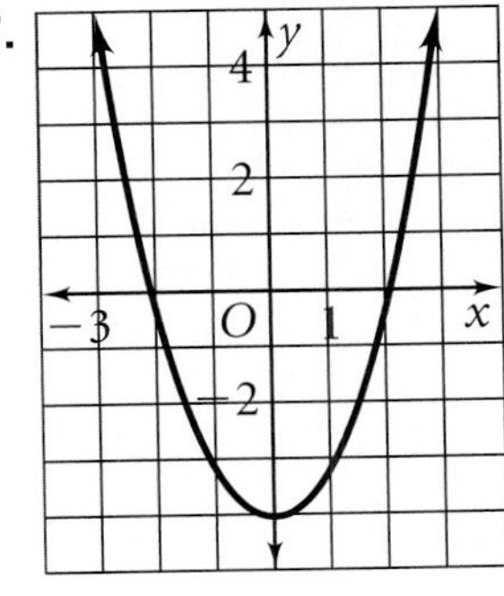

8.

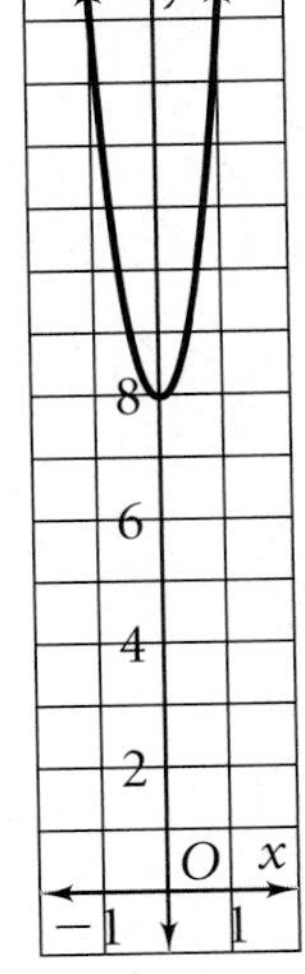

9. min. **10.** max. **11.** min. **12.** max.

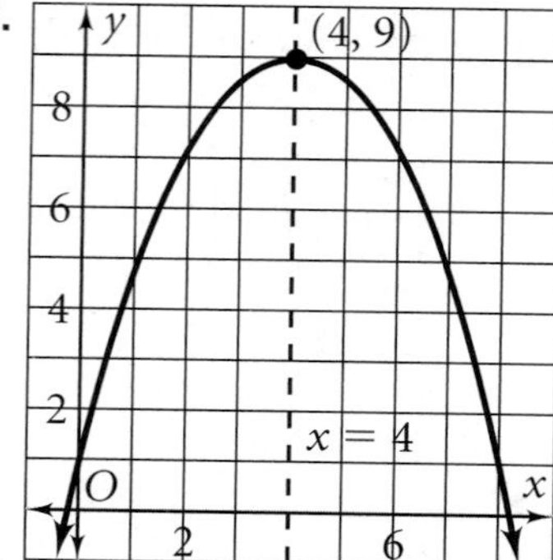

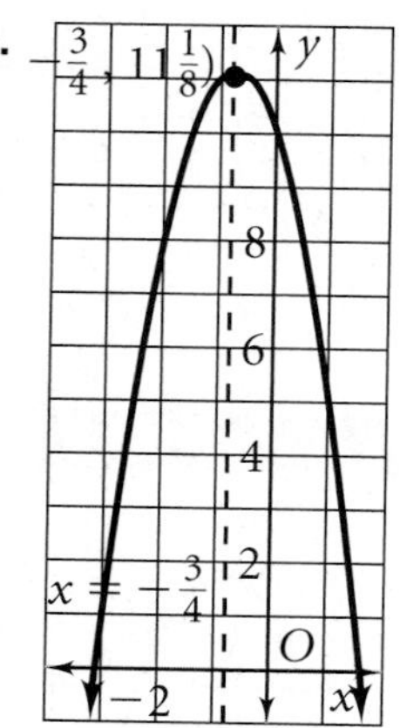

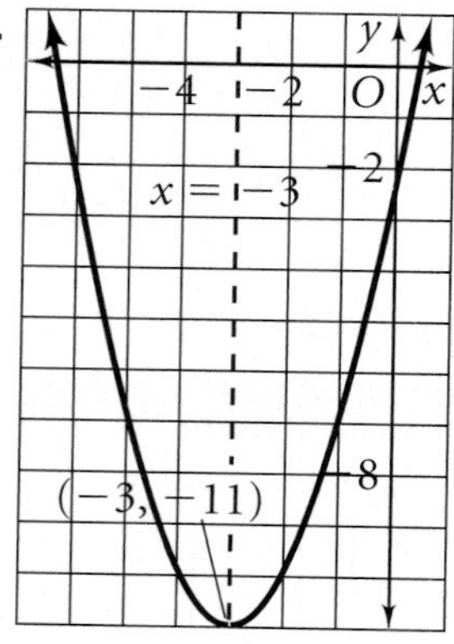

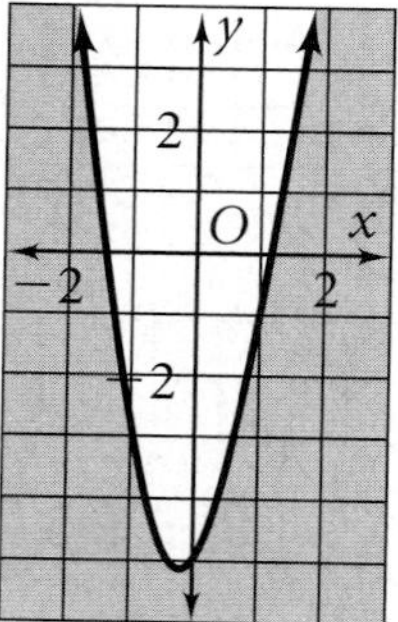

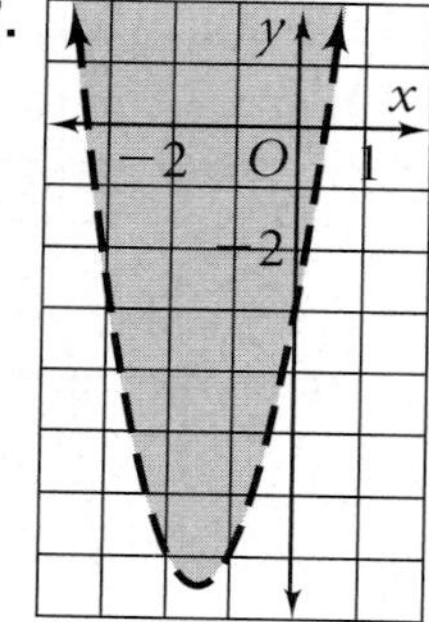

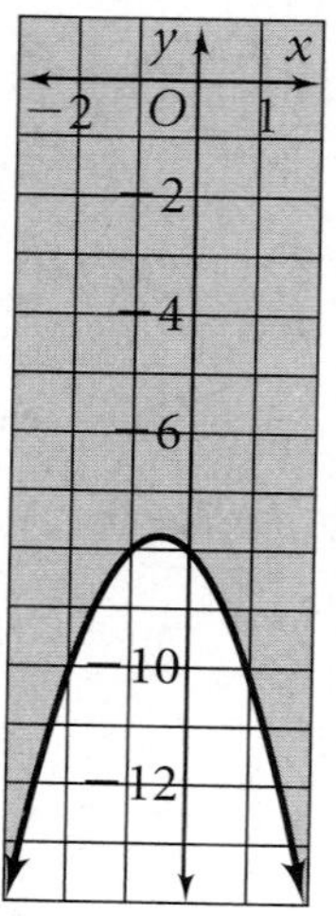

19. irrat. **20.** rat. **21.** irrat. **22.** rat. **23.** irrat. **24.** rat. **25.** 3 **26.** −6.86 **27.** 0.6 **28.** 11.83 **29.** −1 **30.** 14 **31.** B **32.** False; there are two solutions. **33.** true; −3, 3 **34.** −2, 2 **35.** −5, 5 **36.** 0 **37.** no solution **38.** 2.3 in. **39.** −1.84, 1.09 **40.** 0.5, 3 **41.** 0.13, 7.87 **42.** −5.48, 5.48 **43.** 1.5 s **44.** 49; 2 **45.** 112; 2 **46.** −39; 0 **48.** $3^2\ 5^3$ **49.** $8^3 x^4$ **50.** $h^5 w^2$ **51.** 5000 **52.** 0 **53.** 80,000 **54.** 9 **55.** −720 **56.** 0.7 **57.** 36 **58.** 12 **59.** $\frac{1}{3}$

Preparing for the Math A Exam page 359

1. 4 **3.** 1 **5.** 3 **7.** 2 **9.** 1

CHAPTER 8

Lesson 8-1 pages 362–366

ON YOUR OWN

1.

Time	Time Periods	Pattern	Number of Bacteria Cells
Initial	0	75	75
20 min	1	$75 \cdot 2$	$75 \cdot 2^1 = 150$
40 min	2	$75 \cdot 2 \cdot 2$	$75 \cdot 2^2 = 300$
60 min	3	$75 \cdot 2 \cdot 2 \cdot 2$	$75 \cdot 2^3 = 600$
80 min	4	$75 \cdot 2 \cdot 2 \cdot 2 \cdot 2$	$75 \cdot 2^4 = 1200$

There will be more than 30,000 bacteria cells after 3 h. **3.** equal **5.** $100x^2$ **7.** 4, 16, 64, 256, 1024; increasing **9.** 1, 1, 1, 1, 1; neither **11.** 0.5, 0.25, 0.125, 0.0625, 0.03125; decreasing **13.** 40, 400, 4000, 40,000, 400,000; increasing **15.** B **19.** 1.5625 **21.** 0.2 **23.** I: A; II: C; III. B

25a.

x	y
1	−2
2	4
3	−8
4	16
5	−32
6	64

25b. Sample: The positive and negative values alternate. The absolute values of the output are the same as the absolute values of the output of 2^x. **25c.** No; the shape of the graph cannot be similar to the shape of the graph of an exponential function.

27.

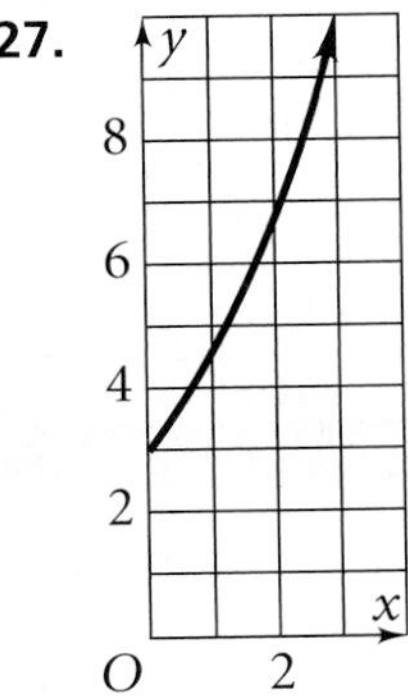

29.

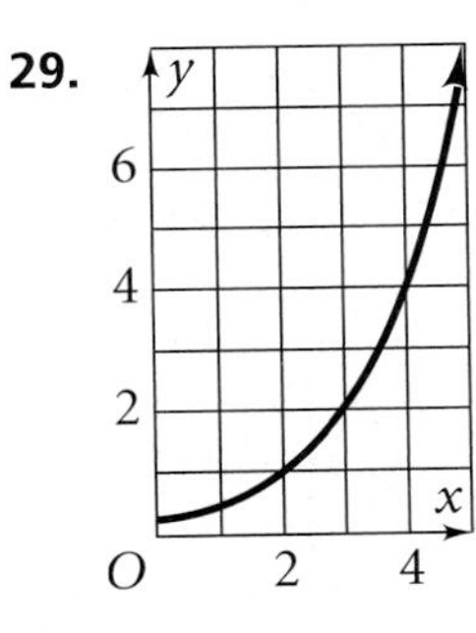

31.

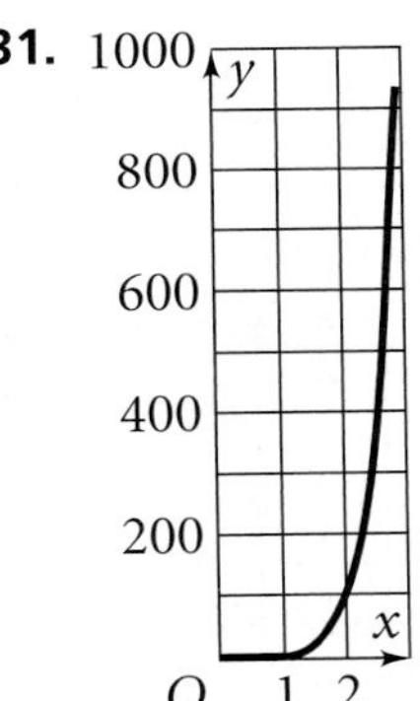

MIXED REVIEW **33.** 1, −4 **35.** 2, 3 **37.** {2, 4, 8, 16, 32} **39.** {1, 2, 4, 8, 16} **41.** {6, 12, 24, 48, 96}

Lesson 8-2 pages 367–372

ON YOUR OWN **1.** 20; 2 **3.** 10,000; 1.01 **5.** 50% **7.** 4% **9.** 1.04 **11.** 1.037 **13.** 1.005 **15.** x = number of years; y = population; $y = 130{,}000 \cdot 1.01^x$ **17.** x = number of months; y = deposit with interest; $y = 3000 \cdot \left(1 + \frac{0.05}{12}\right)^x$ **19a.** \$355 **19b.** 8% **19c.** about \$766 **21.** E

23. linear **25.** exponential

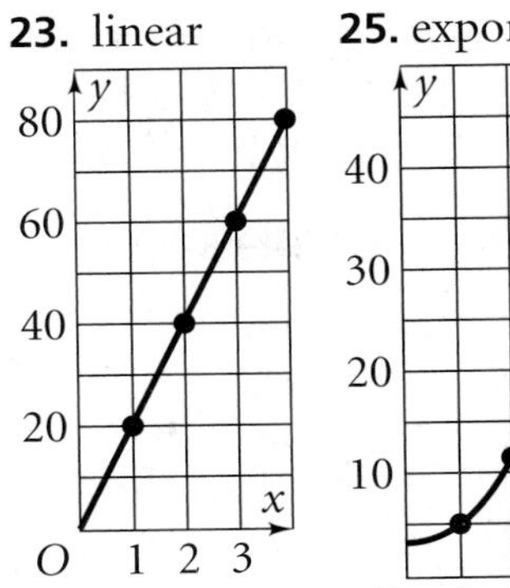

27. Linear; graph is a straight line. **29.** Exponential; graph curves upward. **31.** $y = 20{,}000 \cdot \left(1 + \frac{0.035}{4}\right)^{4x}$; \$28,338.18 **33.** $y = 2400 \cdot (1 + 0.07)^x$; \$4721.16

MIXED REVIEW **35.** $\left(-\frac{1}{3}, -8\frac{1}{3}\right)$; minimum **37.** (0, −11); minimum **39.** $\frac{1}{4}$ **41.** $\frac{3}{4}$ **43.** 0.9604

Lesson 8-3 pages 373–377

ON YOUR OWN **1.** exponential growth **3.** exponential growth **5.** 0.5 **7.** $\frac{2}{3}$ **9.** 10% **11.** 50% **13.** 4 da **15.** 2.5 yr

17. exponential decay

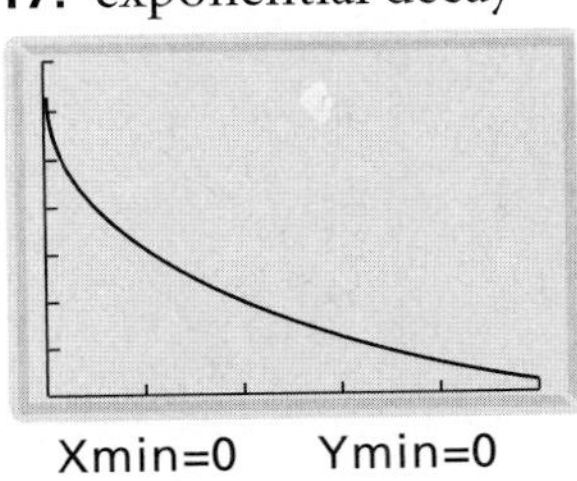

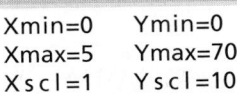

Xmin=0 Ymin=0
Xmax=5 Ymax=70
Xscl=1 Yscl=10

19. exponential decay

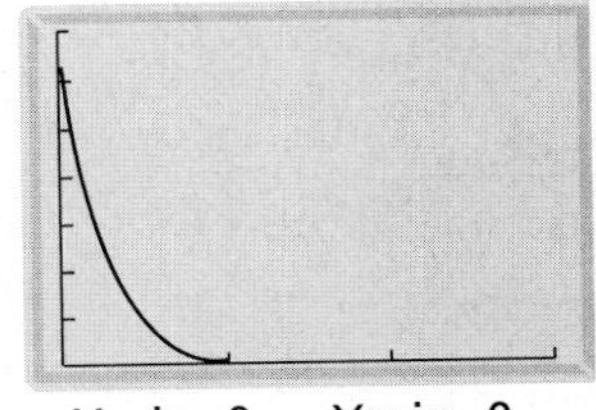

Xmin=0 Ymin=0
Xmax=3 Ymax=3.5
Xscl=1 Yscl=0.5

21. exponential decay

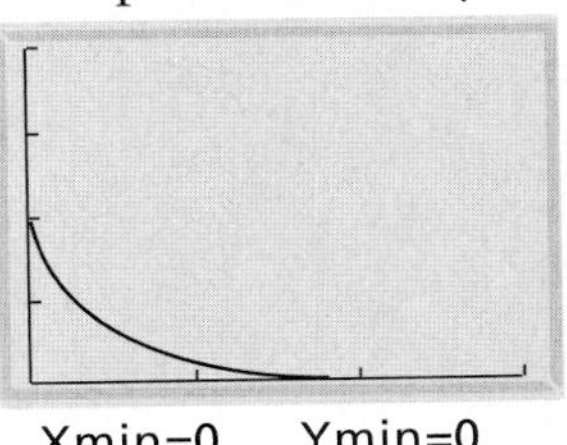

Xmin=0 Ymin=0
Xmax=3 Ymax=0.2
Xscl=1 Yscl=0.05

23. exponential decay

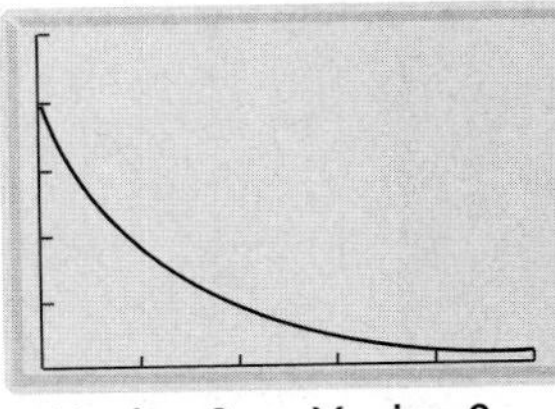

Xmin=0 Ymin=0
Xmax=5 Ymax=0.5
Xscl=1 Yscl=0.1

27. $y = 900 \cdot 0.8^x$; \$235.93 **29a.** $y = 161{,}000 \cdot 0.99^x$ **29b.** 145,606 **29c.** 119,092 **31.** 0.97 **33.** 0.974 **35.** 0.993 **37a.** about 4 h **37b.** about $\frac{1}{4}$

37c. $\frac{15 \cdot 0.84^8}{15} = 0.247875891 \approx \frac{1}{4}$ **39.** 4 half-lives

MIXED REVIEW **41.** $x < -3$ **43.** $-3, 3$ **45.** 4 **47.** 4; 16; $\frac{1}{4}$

CHECKPOINT **1.** $y = 65{,}000 \cdot 1.032^x$; \$104,257.86 **2.** $y = 200{,}000 \cdot 0.95^x$; 71,697 **3.** $y = 300 \cdot 2^x$; x = ten-year period; \$9600 **4.** B

5. exponential growth

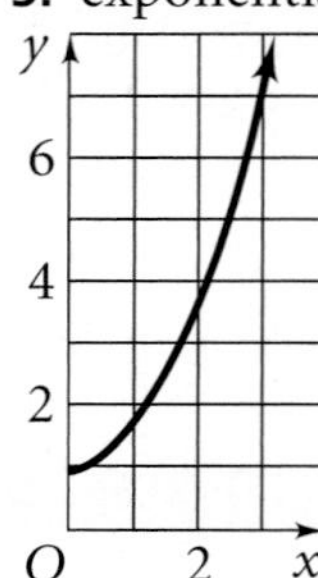

6. exponential decay

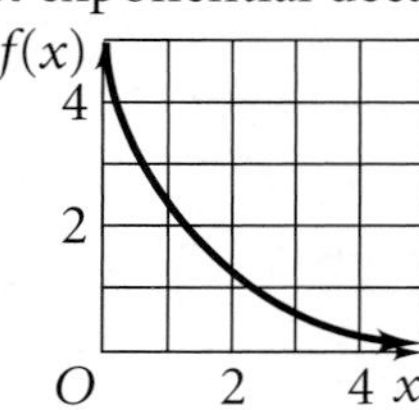

7. exponential growth

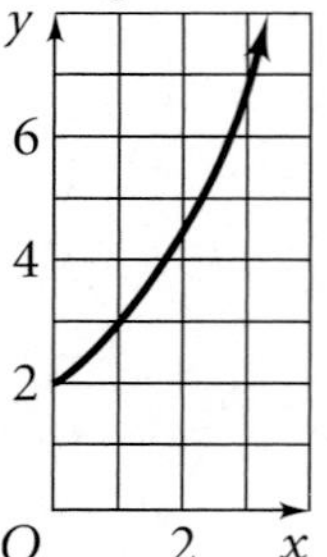

Toolbox page 378

1. $y = 13.65799901 \cdot 1.105628281^x$

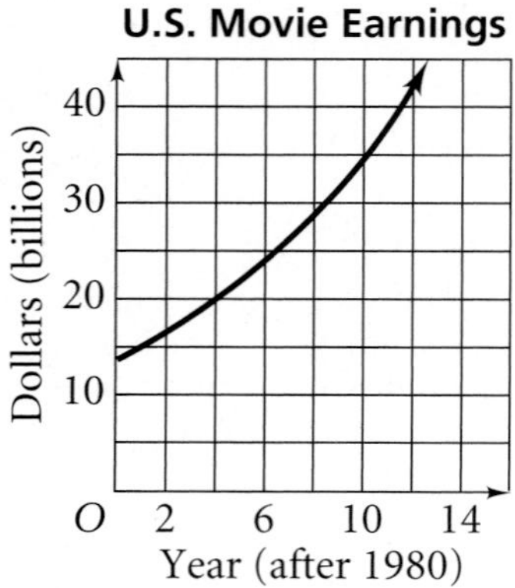

3a. Use $x = 0$ for 1970; $y = 1.040248033 \cdot 1.01999578^x$; 2.297 million

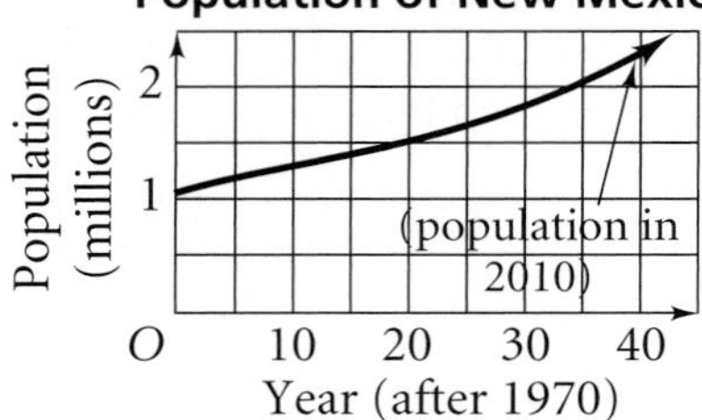

Lesson 8-4 pages 379–384

ON YOUR OWN **1.** -1 **3.** $-\frac{1}{5}$ **5.** 8 **7.** 9 **9.** $\frac{1}{64}$ **11.** 45 **13.** 6 **15.** $\frac{1}{20}$ **17.** $\frac{1}{4}$ **19a.** 5^{-2}; 5^{-1}; 5^0 or 1; 5^1; 5^2 **19b.** 5^4 **19c.** a^n **21.** x^7 **23.** $\frac{1}{625x^4}$ **25.** $\frac{1}{a^4}$ **27.** $\frac{12x}{y^3}$ **29.** $\frac{5a}{c^5}$ **31.** $\frac{8c^3}{a^5d^3}$ **33.** $\frac{7t^3}{5s^5}$ **35.** $\frac{a^3}{b^3}$ **37.** $\frac{mq^2}{n^4}$ **39.** $\frac{2}{9}$ **41.** $\frac{1}{16}$ **43.** -64

45.

47.

49. I

51.

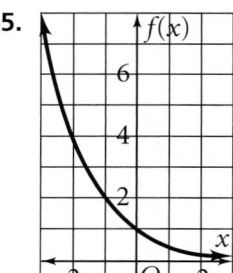

a	4	0.2	$\frac{1}{3}$	6	$\frac{7}{8}$	2
a^{-1}	$\frac{1}{4}$	5	3	$\frac{1}{6}$	$\frac{8}{7}$	0.5

53. positive **55.** negative **57.** positive **59.** -3 **61.** 0; -3 **63.** -3; -2 **65.** -2; -3 **67.** A, B, D **69a.** 10^{-15} m **69b.** 10^{-6} m **69c.** 10^{-10} m **71.** about 2 students; about 16 students; about 29 students

73. 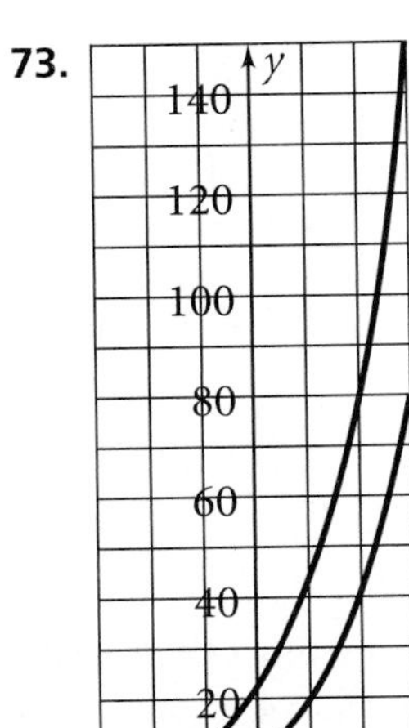

75a. $\frac{1}{2}, \frac{1}{4}, \frac{1}{8}, \frac{1}{16}$ **75b.** $2^{-1}, 2^{-2}, 2^{-3}, 2^{-4}$
75c. $r = 2^{-n}$ **75d.** 2^{-10} or $\frac{1}{2^{10}}$

MIXED REVIEW

77. 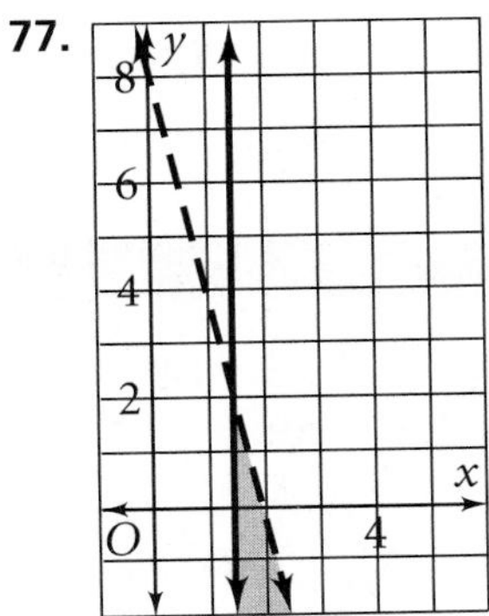

79a. $b = 31.17p$ **79b.** \$124.68 **81.** 0.07
83. 0.003 **85.** 3067.85

Lesson 8-5 pages 385–389

ON YOUR OWN **1.** $10^{-3}, 10^{-1}, 10^{0}, 10^{1}, 10^{5}$
3. $4.1 \times 10^4, 4 \times 10^5, 4.02 \times 10^5, 4.1 \times 10^5$
5. 2.3×10^8 **7.** 2.7×10^{-7} **9.** 2.579×10^{-4}
11. 9.04×10^9 **13.** 9.2×10^{-4} **15.** 3.7×10^{11}
17. 4.18×10^{10} **19.** 6.29×10^{16} **21.** 3.3×10^{-8}
23. 8.35×10^{-5} **25.** 4.18×10^5 **27.** 1.28×10^{-2}
29. 4×10^{-6} **33.** 0.000 004 69 **35.** 50,000,000,000
37. 5.6×10^{-2} **39.** 6×10^2 **41.** 2×10^{-8}
43. about 1.5×10^{-4} **45.** about 5×10^2 s
47. 7×10^{-3} **49.** 9×10^1 **51.** 5×10^7 **53.** about \$3426 per person

MIXED REVIEW **55.** $\begin{bmatrix} -3.2 & 2.4 \\ 4.1 & -1.2 \end{bmatrix}$ **57.** t^7
59. 5^3s^3

Toolbox page 390

1. 6 **3.** 3 **5.** 1.02×10^{-4} **7.** 2.53×10^5
9. 7.25×10^5

Lesson 8-6 pages 391–395

ON YOUR OWN **1.** $x^4 \cdot x^3 = x^7$ **3.** $x^{-2} \cdot x^{-5} = x^{-7}$ **5.** −4 **7.** 5 **9.** −4 **11.** 2; −3 **13.** 8×10^5
15. 6×10^9 **17.** 4×10^3 **21.** 1 **23.** $3r^5$ **25.** a^8b^3
27. $3x^4$ **29.** -0.99^3 **31.** b^3 **33.** −7 **35.** $-45a^4$
37. $\frac{b^2}{c^6}$ **39.** $12a^6c^8$ **41.** a^8b **43.** a^5 **45.** $6a^3 + 10a^2$
47. $-8x^5 + 36x^4$ **49a.** Jerome's work; Jeremy added exponents having different bases. **49b.** a^3b^6
51. $6x^3 + 2x^2$ **53.** $4y^5 + 8y^2$ **55.** $3(-2)x^{2+4} = -6x^6$ **57.** $x^{6+1+3} = x^{10}$ **59a.** about 10^{-7} m
59b. longer

MIXED REVIEW **61.** irrational **63.** rational; $\frac{1}{2}$
65. rational; $\frac{3}{4}$ **67.** 3^6 **69.** 5^{28}

CHECKPOINT **1.** 1 **2.** $\frac{1}{9}$ **3.** $-\frac{1}{8}$ **4.** 125 **5.** −16
6. $-\frac{1}{8}$ **7.** s^3 **8.** $21ab^2$ **9.** −1 **10.** $\frac{g^3}{h^4}$ **11.** $\frac{y^6}{x^5}$
12. 1.5×10^7 **13.** 8×10^{-8} **14.** 3×10^{11}
15. 2.4×10^4 **16a.** $3 \times 10^6; 9 \times 10^4$
16b. about 462

18. 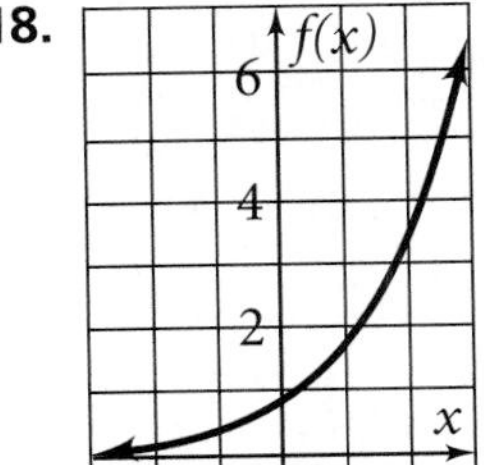

19. 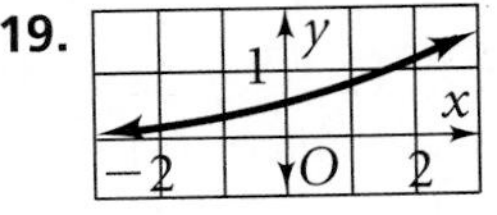

20. 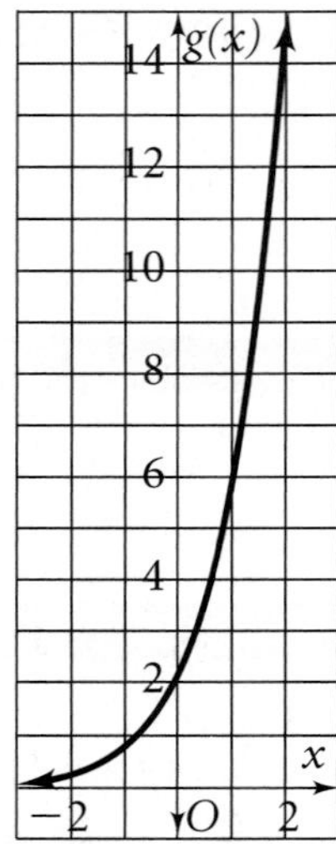

Lesson 8-7 pages 396–400

ON YOUR OWN **1.** x^9y^9 **3.** a^6b^{12} **5.** $\frac{1}{g^{40}}$ **7.** $x^{12}y^4$ **9.** 16 **11.** g^{10} **13.** s^{11} **15.** $\frac{m}{g^4}$ **17.** 1 **19.** $64a^9b^6$ **21.** 1 **23.** 10,000 **25.** b^{3n+2} **27.** 1 **29a.** about 5.15×10^{14} m^2 **29b.** about 3.6×10^{14} m^2 **29c.** about 1.37×10^{18} m^3 **31.** 8×10^{-9} **33.** 3.6×10^{25} **35.** 6.25×10^{-18} **41.** 3 **43.** 4 **45.** 0 **47.** 6 **49.** 3 **51.** 1.1×10^{18} insects **53.** $(ab)^5$ **55.** $(\frac{2}{xy})^2$

MIXED REVIEW **57.** −1 **59.** $\frac{1}{x}$ **61.** $\frac{1}{t^5}$

Lesson 8-8 pages 401–405

ON YOUR OWN **1.** $\frac{1}{4}$ **3.** $\frac{9}{16}$ **5.** $\frac{1}{9}$ **7.** y **9.** a^6 **11.** $-\frac{27}{8}$ **13.** $5^3 = 125$ **15.** $(2c)^4 = 16c^4$ **17.** $x^0 = 1$ **19.** 5×10^7 **21.** 9×10^2 **23.** about 1.52×10^{-6} **25a.** about 1642 h **25b.** about 4.5 h/da **27.** 4 **29.** 729 **31.** $2c^6$ **33.** $\frac{a^5}{b^3}$ **35.** $\frac{d^8}{c^5}$ **37.** $\frac{1}{25}$ **39.** $\frac{1}{c^{12}}$ **41.** $\frac{9}{25}$ **43.** $\frac{125n^3}{m^6}$ **45.** $\left(\frac{3}{5}\right)^5$ **47.** d^3 **49.** $\left(\frac{3x}{2y}\right)^3$ **51a.** about \$4013 **51b.** about \$17,846 **51c.** about 345% **53.** division and negative exponent properties; $\frac{1}{2^3}$ **55.** multiplication property; $\frac{1}{2^3}$

57a.

Mercury	≈ 1.52
Venus	≈ 1.01
Earth	≈ 1.03
Mars	≈ 1.21
Jupiter	≈ 1.10
Saturn	≈ 1.12
Uranus	≈ 1.10
Neptune	≈ 1.02
Pluto	≈ 1.67

57b. Pluto; its circularity is farthest from 1; Venus; its circularity is closest to 1.

MIXED REVIEW **59.** 0.6, −0.6 **61.** −6

63. 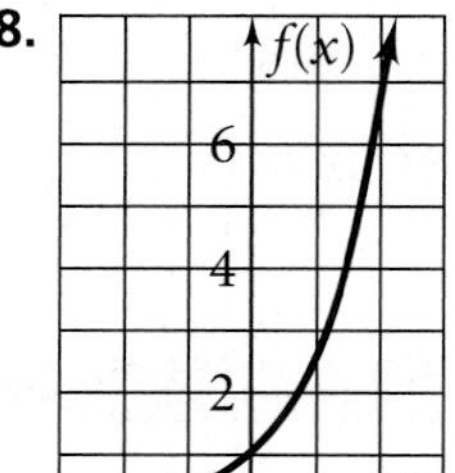

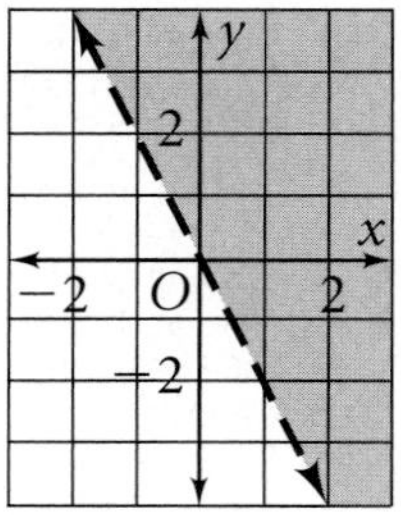

65. 3.26×10^{11} gal

Wrap-Up pages 407–409

1. 6, 12, 24, 48 **2.** 7.5, 5.625, 4.21875 **3a.** 2430 bacteria **3b.** about 178 min **4.** growth; 3 **5.** growth; $\frac{3}{2}$ **6.** decay; 0.32 **7.** decay; $\frac{1}{4}$

8. 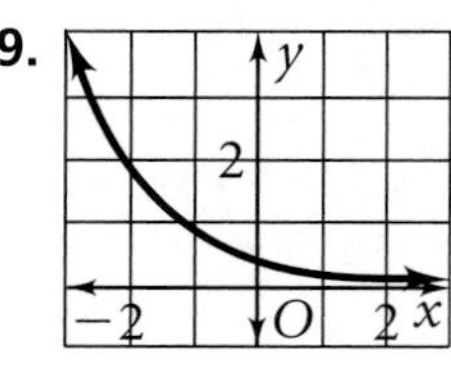

9.

10. 11.

12. 2.5% inc. **13.** 25% dec. **14.** 100% inc. **15.** 10% dec. **16a.** $y = 100{,}000 \cdot 1.07^x$ **16a.** $y = 100{,}000 \cdot 1.07^x$ **16b.** 542,743 **17a.** \$1250.18; \$1267.37 **17b.** 6%; it pays more interest. **18.** 2.5 mCi **19.** $\frac{d^6}{b^4}$ **20.** $\frac{y^8}{x^2}$ **21.** $\frac{7h^3}{k^8}$ **22.** $\frac{q^4}{p^2}$ **23.** $\frac{3^4}{2^4}$ or $\frac{81}{16}$ **24.** Yes, if $b = 0$; no if $b \neq 0$. **25.** C **26.** 9.5×10^7 **27.** 7.235×10^9 **28.** yes **29.** 8.4×10^{-4} **30.** 2.6×10^{-4} **31.** 2.793×10^6 **32.** 1.89×10^8 **33.** 1.606×10^8 **34.** 4.6×10^{-9} **35.** 1.4168×10^7 **36.** 1×10^{-12} **37.** $2d^5$ **38.** $q^{12}r^4$ **39.** $-20c^4m^2$ **40.** 1.7956 **41.** $\frac{243}{64}x^2y^{14}$ **42.** Sample: about 7.8×10^3 pores **44.** $\frac{1}{w^3}$ **45.** $\frac{1}{64}$ **46.** yes **47.** $\frac{n^{35}}{v^{21}}$ **48.** $\frac{c^3}{e^{11}}$ **49.** $s^{15}x^{45}$ **50.** 2×10^{-3} **51.** 2.5×10^1 **52.** 5×10^{-5} **53.** 3×10^3 **55.** 2 **56.** 11 **57.** 6 **58.** $77r + 28rx$ **59.** $24m - 16mt$ **60.** $8b + 2b^2$ **61.** $5p + 6d$ **62.** n **63.** 61 **64.** 65 **65.** $13t^2$ **66.** $4y^2$ **67.** \$19; about \$48.86 **68.** 5 kg; 4.5 kg **69.** 0.4 min; 1.24 min

Preparing for the Math A Exam page 411

1. 2 **3.** 3 **5.** 4 **7.** 3 **9.** 2

CHAPTER 9

Lesson 9-1 pages 414–418

ON YOUR OWN **1.** 10 **3.** 2.2 **5.** 7.1 **7.** 5.7 **9.** 20 **11.** 66.1 **13a.** $6^2 + 8^2 = 100$ and $10^2 = 100$

13b.

a	b	c
3	4	5
5	12	13
7	24	25
9	40	41

13c. Sample: 8, 15, 17 **15.** 9.7 **17.** 559.9 **19b.** 6 in., $\sqrt{10^2 - 8^2}$; about 12.8 in., $\sqrt{10^2 + 8^2}$ **21.** yes; $9^2 + 12^2 = 15^2$ **23.** no; $2^2 + 4^2 \neq 5^2$ **25.** no; $4^2 + 4^2 \neq 8^2$ **27.** yes; $1.25^2 + 3^2 = 3.25^2$ **29.** yes; $14^2 + 48^2 = 50^2$ **31.** no; $1^2 + 1.5^2 \neq 2^2$ **33.** no; $4^2 + 5^2 \neq 6^2$ **35.** yes; $18^2 + 80^2 = 82^2$ **37a.** about 3610 ft **37b.** about 180 ft/min; about 2 mi/h **39.** 4.3 cm

MIXED REVIEW **41.** $\frac{1}{2}, \frac{1}{2}$ **43.** 5 **45.** 8.5

Toolbox page 419

1. yes **3.** yes **5.** yes **7.** yes **9.** no **11.** yes **13.** yes **15.** yes

Lesson 9-2 pages 420–424

ON YOUR OWN **1.** 10.6 **3.** 8.2 **5.** 11.3 **7.** 2.2 **9.** 11.2 **11.** 8.2 **13.** 14 **15.** 1.4

17a.

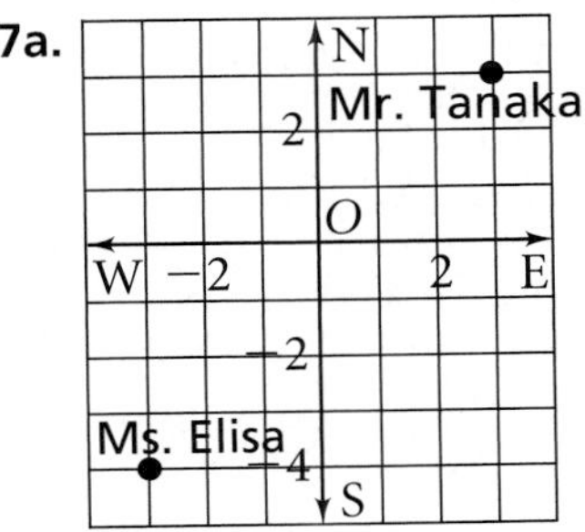

17b. $(0, -0.5)$ **17c.** The meeting point is 0.5 mi south of the substation. **19.** $(1\frac{1}{2}, 7\frac{1}{2})$ **21.** $(-2\frac{1}{2}, 3)$ **23.** $(-4, 4)$ **25.** $(8\frac{1}{2}, -9)$ **27.** $(7, 7)$ **29.** $(0, 0)$ **31.** 16 **33.** 21.6 **35.** x-coordinates are opposites; y-coordinates are opposites.

Selected Answers

MIXED REVIEW **37.** $2 - \frac{7}{2}y$ **39.** $\frac{V}{\pi r^2}$ **41.** \$720 **43.** $\frac{5}{13}, \frac{12}{13}, \frac{12}{5}$ **45.** 6.8 **47.** 7.28

Lesson 9-3 pages 425–429

ON YOUR OWN **1.** Sample: Kentucky and Virginia are adjacent states. **3.** $\frac{4}{5}$ **5.** $\frac{4}{5}$ **7.** $\frac{4}{3}$ **9.** 0.7660 **11.** 0.9962 **13.** $\frac{21}{29}, \frac{20}{29}, \frac{21}{20}$ **15.** $\frac{12}{13}, \frac{5}{13}, \frac{12}{5}$ **17.** 10.4 **19.** about 250 ft **21.** about 10,000 ft **23.** 78.4 **25.** 514.3

MIXED REVIEW

29.

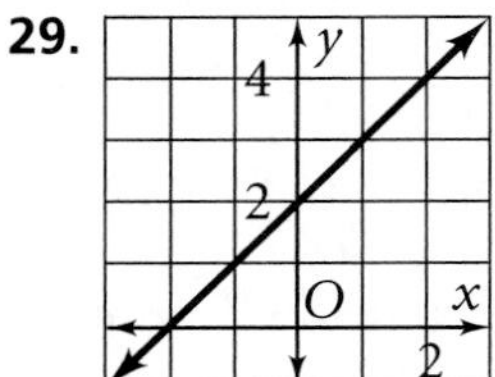

31.

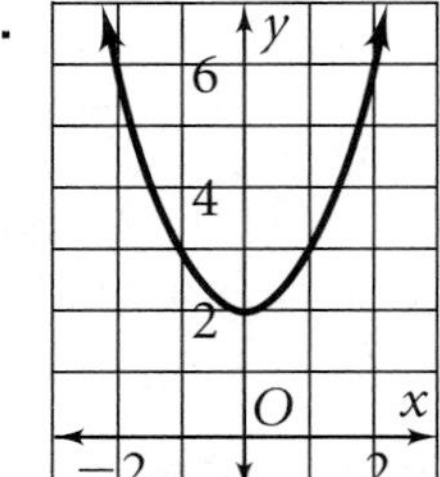

33. 250 mi **35.** 13 **37.** −6

CHECKPOINT **1.** $c \approx 4.5$ **2.** $c \approx 5.8$ **3.** $c \approx 7.1$ **4.** $c = 5$ **5.** $b = 24$ **6.** $a \approx 8.5$ **7.** $b \approx 8.9$ **8.** $a = 15$ **10.** about 270 ft **11.** 3.2 **12.** 6.7 **13.** 9.8 **14.** 3.2 **16.** about 2.7 **17.** about 4.5

Lesson 9-4 pages 430–434

ON YOUR OWN **1.** no **3.** no **5.** no **7.** 16 **9.** 20 **11.** $10\sqrt{2}$ **13.** $875\sqrt{7}$ **15.** 72 **17.** $3\sqrt{17}$ **19.** $4\sqrt{6}$ **21.** 10 **23.** $5\sqrt{10}$ **25.** $\frac{3}{2}$ **27.** $\frac{5}{2}$ **29.** $\frac{2\sqrt{30}}{11}$ **31.** $\frac{3\sqrt{2}}{4}$ **33.** $\frac{13}{12}$ **35.** 1.2 m **37a.** $\sqrt{18} \cdot \sqrt{10} = \sqrt{180} = \sqrt{36 \cdot 5} = 6\sqrt{5}$ **39.** D **41.** $\frac{2\sqrt{a}}{a^2}$ **43.** $ab^2c\sqrt{abc}$ **45.** $2y^2$ **47.** $\frac{\sqrt{2x}}{3}$ **49.** $2\sqrt{3}$ **51.** $\frac{9\sqrt{2}}{4}$ **53.** $5\sqrt{5}$ **55.** $\frac{8\sqrt{6}}{3}$

MIXED REVIEW **57.** 3; 2 **59.** −5; 3 **61.** For c = crab and t = turkey, $5c + 3t \leq 30$. **63.** −1 **65.** 10

Lesson 9-5 pages 435–439

ON YOUR OWN **1.** 42 **3.** $3\sqrt{2} + \sqrt{3}$ **5.** $6 - 2\sqrt{3}$ **7.** $3\sqrt{3} - 3\sqrt{2}$ **9.** $\sqrt{7}$ **11.** $3\sqrt{5} + 2\sqrt{3}$ **13.** $2\sqrt{3} + 2\sqrt{6} - 6$ **15.** $4 - 4\sqrt{2}$ **17.** 3.1 **19.** 15.8 **21.** 6.0 **23.** 8.5 **25.** −1.0 **27.** $2\sqrt{3} + 4\sqrt{2}$ **29.** −24 **31.** $6\sqrt{2} + 6\sqrt{3}$ **33.** $2\sqrt{17} + 17$ **37a.** $2\sqrt{6} + 4\sqrt{3}$ **37b.** Bill simplified $\sqrt{48}$ as $2\sqrt{24}$ instead of $2\sqrt{12}$ or $4\sqrt{3}$. **39.** $8\sqrt{2}$ **41.** $6\sqrt{10}$ **43.** E

MIXED REVIEW **45.** −3; 5; rational **47.** 1 **49.** 0

Lesson 9-6 pages 440–444

ON YOUR OWN **1.** 3 **3.** 27 **5.** 625 **7a.** 25 **7b.** $11\frac{1}{4}$ **9.** no solution **11.** $-\frac{1}{4}$ **13.** 0, 12 **15.** 7 **17.** 3 **19.** about 98.2 in.^{3} **21.** 2 **23.** 3, 6 **25.** no solution **27.** 4 **29.** 1, 6 **31a.** $V = 10x^2$ **31b.** $x = \frac{\sqrt{10V}}{10}$ **33.** −4 **35.** $-\frac{1}{2}$ **37.** none

MIXED REVIEW **39.** $\frac{1}{a^5b^5}$ **41.** $\frac{2}{xy^2}$ **43.** 0 **45.** 2

Lesson 9-7 pages 445–449

ON YOUR OWN **1.** $x \geq 2$ **3.** $x \geq 0$ **5.** $x \geq -7$ **7.** $x \geq -3$ **9.** $x \geq 5$ **11.** B **13.** A

15.

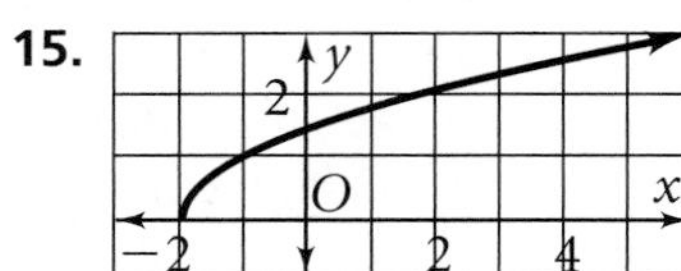

17.

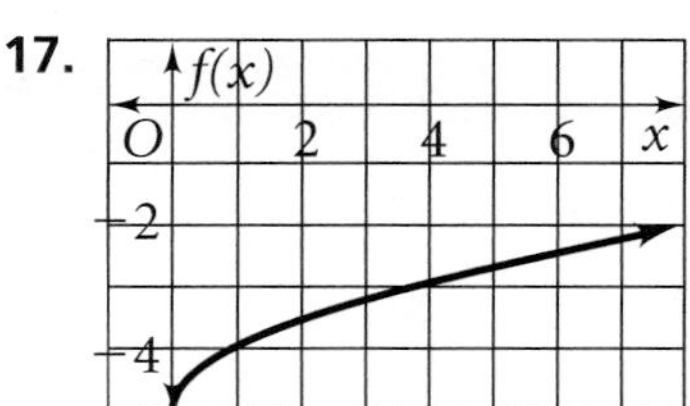

19.

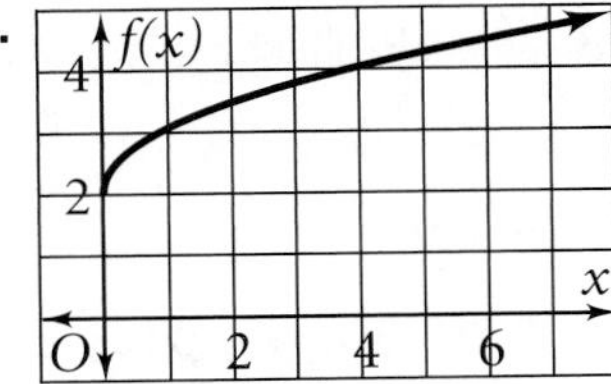

21.

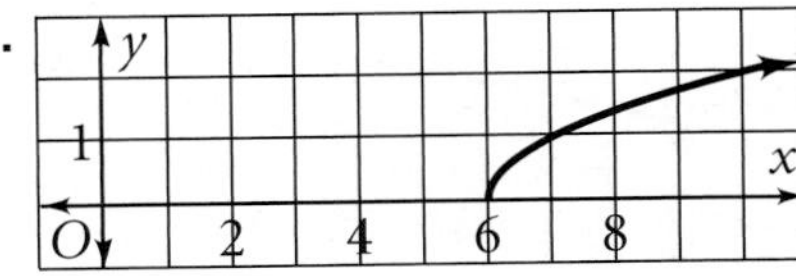

23.

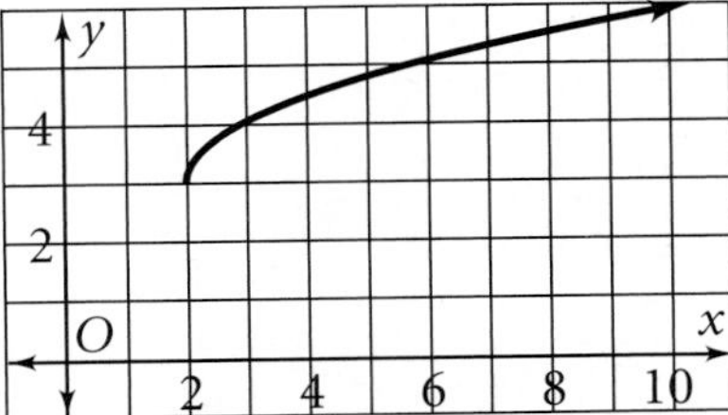

25.

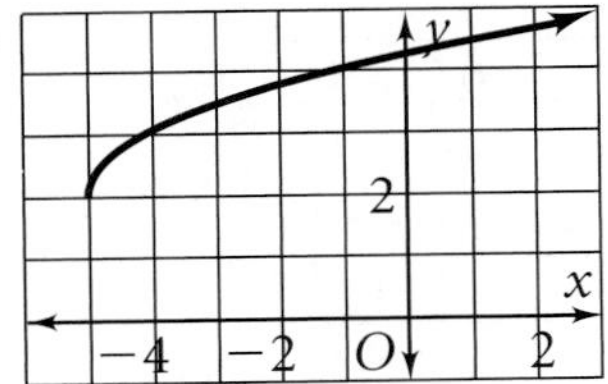

27. shift left 8 **29.** shift up 12

MIXED REVIEW

33.

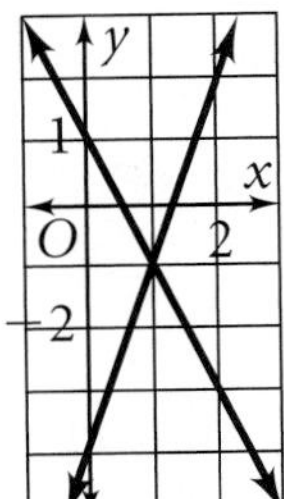

$(1, -1)$ **35.** 7.8 **37.** -1.8

CHECKPOINT **1.** 9 **2.** 14 **3.** $8b^2\sqrt{b}$ **4.** $\sqrt{2}$ **5.** $3 + 4\sqrt{3}$ **6.** $2\sqrt{2}$ **7.** $\frac{x\sqrt{x}}{2}$ **8.** $2\sqrt{3}$ **9.** 68 **10.** 6 **11.** 8 **12.** 18

13.

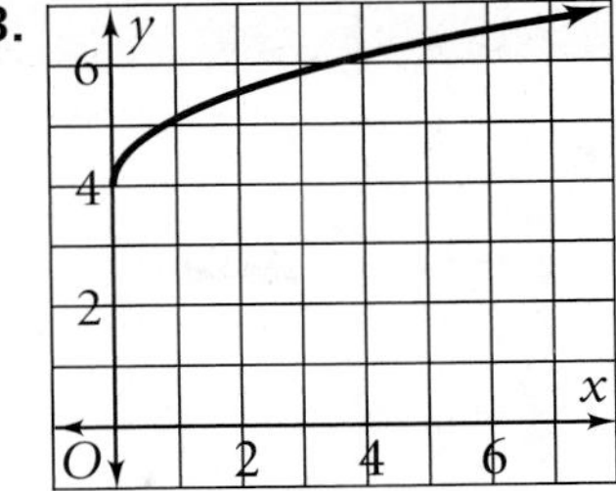

14.

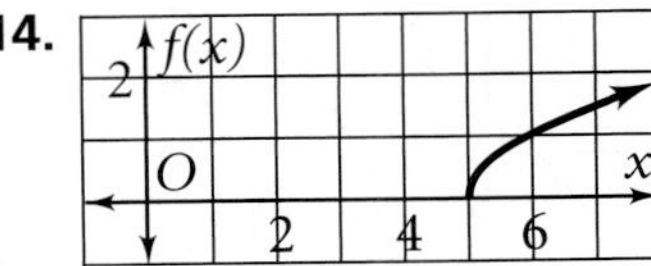

15.

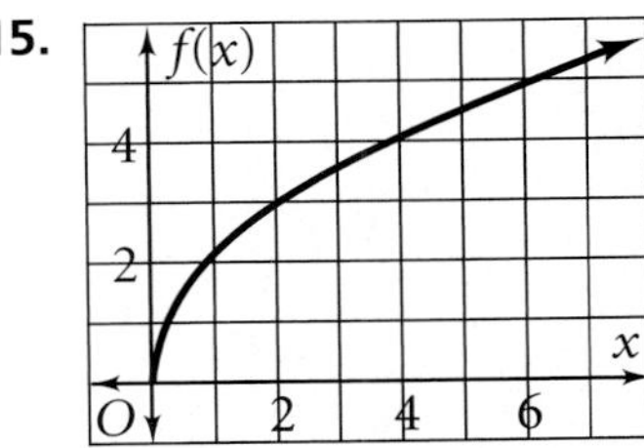

16.

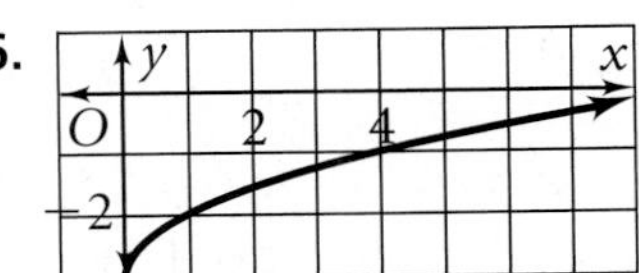

18. D

Toolbox page 450

1.

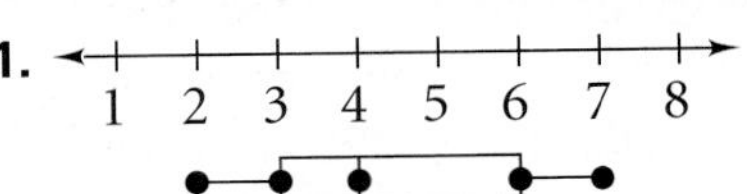

3. 0 2 4 6 8 10 12 14

5. 26 28 30 32 34 36 38 40 42 44

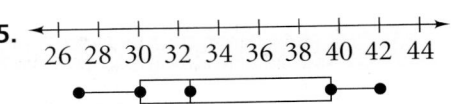

7. 0 1 2 3 4 5 6 7 8

9b. 2; 33; 33 **9c.** 21 h; 23 h; both are much less than the typical 29-h week.

Lesson 9-8 pages 451–455

ON YOUR OWN

1.

x	$\bar{x}$	$x - \bar{x}$	$(x - \bar{x})^2$
5	5	0	0
3	5	−2	4
2	5	−3	9
5	5	0	0
10	5	5	25
		Sum:	38

standard deviation: about 2.8

3.

x	$\bar{x}$	$x - \bar{x}$	$(x - \bar{x})^2$
3.5	4	−0.5	0.25
4.5	4	0.5	0.25
6.0	4	2	4
4.0	4	0	0
2.5	4	−1.5	2.25
2.5	4	−1.5	2.25
5.0	4	1	1
		Sum:	10

standard deviation: about 1.2

5a. The data are spread far apart **5b.** Most data are near 25. **9a.** Sample: Lyman should have asked about the range and the standard deviation or the median salary and the mode. The range and the standard deviation would have told him that the salaries are widely distributed. The mode and the median, both \$265, would have told him that the mean does not represent the data well. **9b.** \$1165 **9c.** Large; all the data are far from the mean. **9d.** about 321.36 **11.** about 0.98 **13.** about 25.47 **15a.** \$20 **15b.** about 5.83 **15c.** 6; 39

MIXED REVIEW **17.** 3.47×10^{-3} **19.** 8.25×10^{-4} **21.** (1, 2) **23.** (5, 2) **25.** $x \geq 5$ **27.** \$14,961.04

Wrap-Up pages 457–459

1. 5.83 **2.** 17.80 **3.** 14.76 **4.** 9.85 **6.** (0.5, 5.5) **7.** (5.5, 6) **8.** (8.5, 3.5) **9.** (2.5, 13) **11.** $BC \approx 6.71$; $AC \approx 9.95$ **12.** $AC \approx 27.7$; $AB \approx 29.12$ **13.** $BC \approx 6.25$; $AB \approx 10.15$ **14.** C **15.** $48\sqrt{2}$ **16.** $\frac{2\sqrt{21}}{11}$ **17.** $20\sqrt{6}$ **18.** $\frac{10}{13}$ **19.** $10\sqrt{2}$ cm by $70\sqrt{2}$ cm **20.** $2\sqrt{7}$ **21.** $30\sqrt{5}$ **22.** $\sqrt{6}$ **23.** $2\sqrt{5}$ **24.** $10 - 10\sqrt{2}$ **25.** $25\sqrt{10}$ **26.** $18\sqrt{2}$ **27.** $17\sqrt{7}$ **28.** $\sqrt{29}$ in. **29.** 2 **30.** 16 **31.** 8 **32.** 81 **33.** 2.93 in.

34. $x \geq 0$;

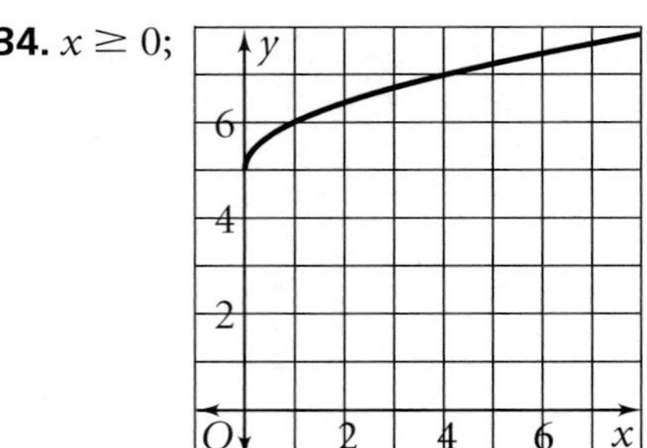

35. $x \geq 2$;

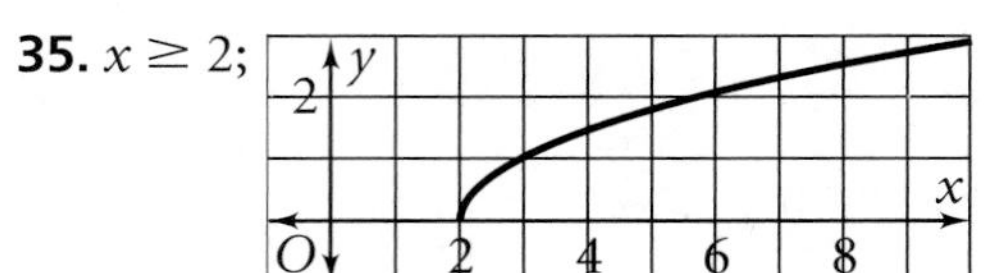

36. $x \geq -1$;

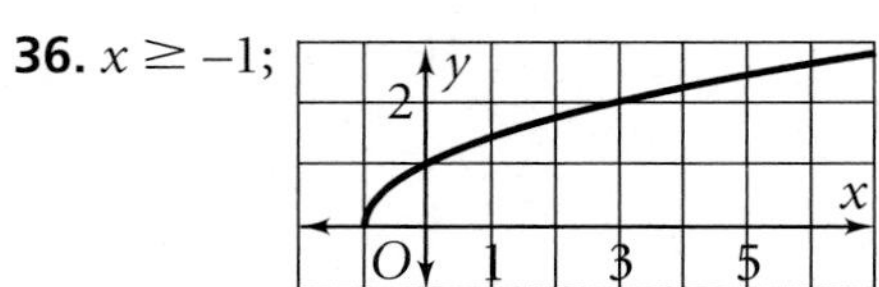

37. $x \geq 0$;

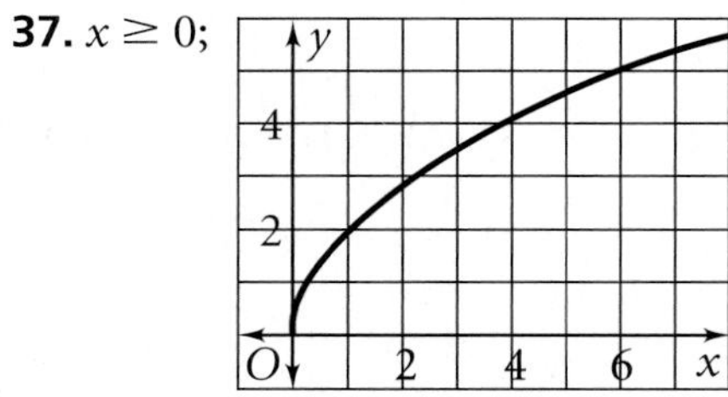

38. about 5.44 **39.** about 4.69 **40.** about 6.15 **41.** about 7.44 **42.** 0.64, −3.14 **43.** 1.90, −1.23 **44.** 4.70, −1.70 **45.** no solution **46.** 2, −1.2 **47.** 1.47, −1.75

Preparing for the Math A Exam page 461

1. 2 **3.** 3 **5.** 4 **7.** 1

CHAPTER 10

Lesson 10-1 pages 464–469

ON YOUR OWN **1.** C **3.** E **5.** A **7.** $4x + 9$; linear binomial **9.** $-11z^3 + 9z^2 + 5z - 5$; cubic with four terms **11.** $c^2 + 4c - 2$; quadratic trinomial **13.** $4q^4 + 3q^2 - 8q - 10$; fourth degree polynomial with four terms **15.** $x^2 - 1$ **17.** $-6x^3 + 3x^2 - x - 4$ **19.** $7a^3 + 11a^2 - 4a - 2$ **21.** $6x^2 - 12$ **25.** $8y$ **27.** $28c - 16$ **31.** $5x + 18$ **33.** $6y + 2$ **35.** $-2x^2 - 7x - 11$ **37.** $2r^2 - r - 7$ **39.** $9b^4 - 3b^2 + 7b - 6$

MIXED REVIEW **41.** 4^4 **43.** $\left(\frac{2}{3}\right)^4$ **45.** 5.0 **47.** 1.9 **49.** $2x - 6$ **51.** $15a - 21$

Lesson 10-2 pages 470–474

ON YOUR OWN **1.** $3x + 12$ **3.** $4x^2 + 2x$ **5.** $8x^2 + 12x$

7. $(x + 2)(3x) = 3x^2 + 6x$

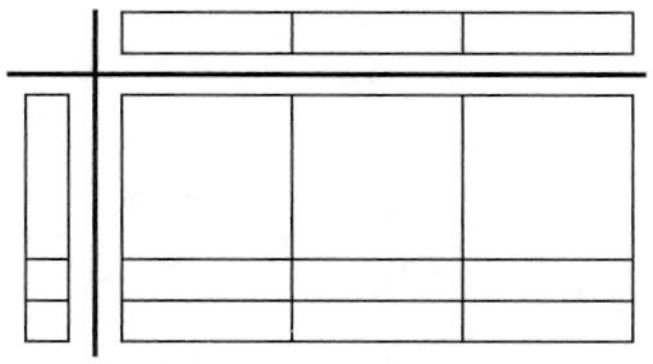

9. $8x + 28$ **11.** $-54x^4 + 36x^2 - 48x$ **13.** $-12a^3 + 15a^2 - 27a$ **15.** $6p^5 - 15p^3$ **17.** $-4x^2 + 13x$ **19.** $x^2 + x$ **21.** 3 **23.** 12 **25.** 5 **27.** $3x$ **29.** $5s$ **31.** $8x^2$ **35a.** $V = 64s^3$ **35b.** $V = 48\pi s^2$ **35c.** $V = 64s^3 - 48\pi s^2$ **35d.** $V = 16s^2(4s - 3\pi)$ **35e.** about 182,071 in.^{3} **37.** $s(s^3 + 4s^2 - 2)$ **39.** $2x^2(1 - 2x^2)$ **41.** $7k(k^2 - 5k + 10)$ **43.** $3x(3 + 4x)$ **45.** $6m^2(m^4 - 4m^2 + 1)$ **47.** $m^2(5m - 7)$ **49.** $(x^2 - 7)(2x + 1)$ **51a.** 7; 4 **51b.** $n - 3$ **51c.** $\frac{1}{2}n^2 - \frac{3}{2}n$

MIXED REVIEW **53.** $\frac{4}{5}$ **55.** $\frac{3}{5}$ **57.** $\frac{3}{4}$ **59.** $28x^3 - 48x^2 + 128x$

Lesson 10-3 pages 475–479

ON YOUR OWN **1.** $x - 4$; $-x + 2$; $-x^2 + 6x - 8$ **3.** $x - 3$; $-x + 3$; $-x^2 + 6x - 9$ **5.** $x^2 - x - 20$ **7.** 30 **9.** 7 **11.** $x^2 + x - 42$ **13.** $2y^2 - y - 15$ **15.** $5y^2 + 12y - 32$ **17.** $a^3 - 6a^2 + 9a - 4$ **19.** $4t^3 - 22t^2 + 36t - 15$ **23.** $x^2 + 8x + 15$ **25.** $a^2 - 8a + 7$ **27.** $5a^2 + 13a - 6$ **29.** $-6y^2 + 20y - 14$ **33.** 1; rational **35.** $26 + 10\sqrt{5}$; irrational

MIXED REVIEW **37.** 2, −2 **39.** 2, −1 **41.** $(2x + 4)(3x + 5)$ **43.** $(-3x + 5)(4x + 1)$

CHECKPOINT **1.** $3x^2 + 5x - 4$ **2.** $2a^3 + a^2 - 7$ **3.** $-2m^2 - 5m + 8$ **4.** $9x^2 - x - 8$ **5.** $-w^2 + 9$ **6.** $-6t^3 - 4t^2 + 12t$ **7.** $m^2 + m - 12$ **8.** $b^2 - 9b + 18$ **9.** $-3c(c^2 - 5c + 1)$ **10.** $5a(2a^2 + a + 1)$ **11.** $4p(2p^2 - 5p - 6)$ **12.** $x(x^2 + 4x + 7)$

Toolbox page 480

1. $x^4 - x^3 + x^2$

3. $3x^2 + 2x - 1$

5. $x - 4 + \frac{7}{x + 4}$

7. $m^2 + 5m + 4$

Lesson 10-4 pages 481–485

ON YOUR OWN **1.** $x + 3$, $x + 2$; $x^2 + 5x + 6$ **3.** $x + 2$, $x + 2$; $x^2 + 4x + 4$ **5.** No; no two numbers with product 8 can have sum 5. **7.** Yes; $(x + 8)(x + 1) = x^2 + 9x + 8$

9. 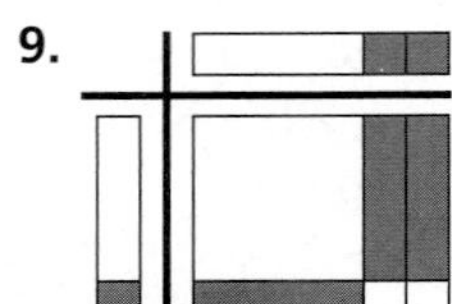

$(x - 2)(x - 1)$

11. 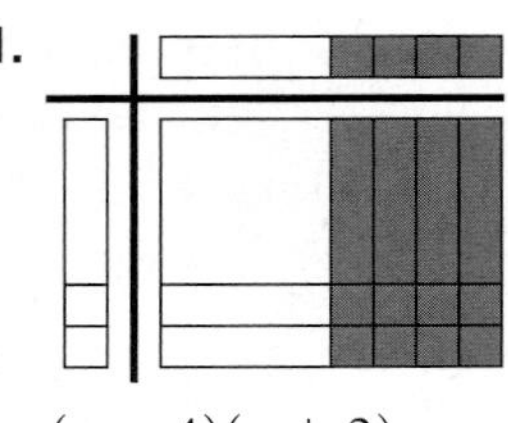

$(x - 4)(x + 2)$

13. 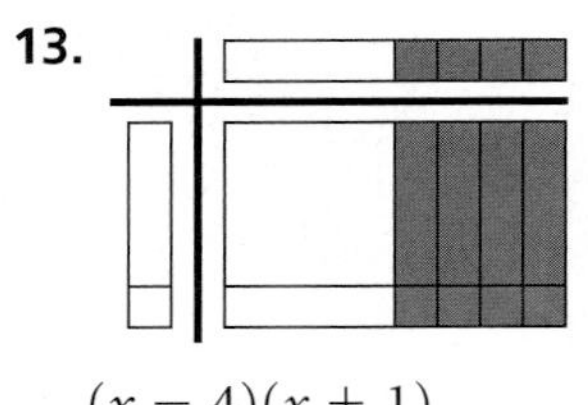

$(x - 4)(x + 1)$

15. 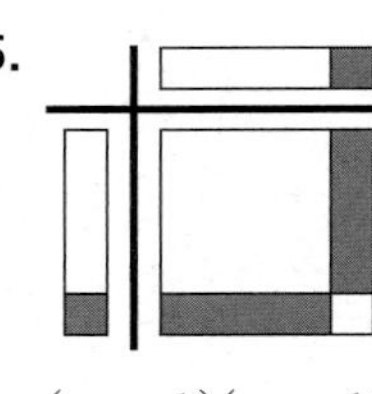

$(x - 1)(x - 1)$

17. 2 **19.** -1 **21.** -3 **23a.** $x^2 + 15x + 56$ **23b.** $(x + 7)(x + 8)$ **25.** $(a - 2)(a - 3)$ **27.** $(k + 1)(k + 8)$ **29.** $(r - 11)(r + 1)$ **31.** $(x + 5)(x - 3)$ **33.** $(x + 5)(x + 7)$ **35.** $(a - 7)(a - 2)$ **37.** $(y + 16)(y - 3)$ **39.** $(w - 6)(w + 4)$ **43.** $(2x - 1)(x - 7)$ **45.** $(2x - 3)(x + 1)$ **47.** $(2x + 3)(x - 7)$ **49.** $(2x - 1)(x - 3)$ **51.** $(7x + 1)(x - 3)$ **53.** $(3x + 5)(x + 4)$

MIXED REVIEW **55.** 5 **57.** about 8.1

59. 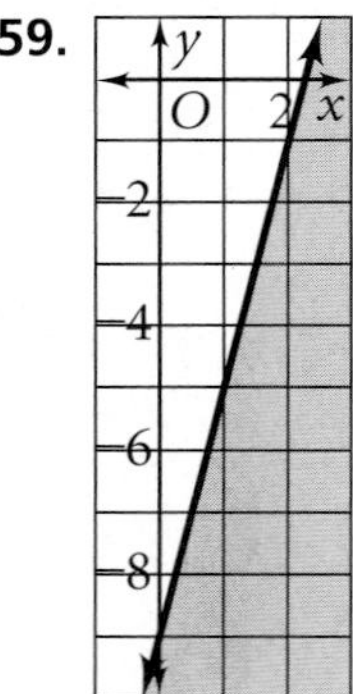

61. 84 **63.** $4x^2 + 12x + 9$ **65.** $x^2 - 64$ **67.** $4x^2 - 49$ **69.** $4x^2 - 4x + 1$

Lesson 10-5 pages 486–490

ON YOUR OWN **1.** $x^2 + 10x + 25$; $x + 5, x + 5$ **3.** $9x^2 + 6x + 1$; $3x + 1, 3x + 1$ **5.** $(x + 1)^2$ **7.** $(x - 9)^2$ **9.** $3(x - 1)^2$ **11.** $6(x + 5)(x - 5)$ **13.** $(x + 7)(x - 7)$ **15.** $(2x - 1)^2$ **17.** $(3x + 1)^2$ **19.** $(x + 20)(x - 20)$ **23a.** $3.14n^2 - 3.14m^2$; $3.14(n + m)(n - m)$ **23b.** 285.74 in.^{2} **25.** 891 **27.** 1591 **29.** 384 **31.** 396 **33.** $\left(\frac{1}{2}m + \frac{1}{3}\right)\left(\frac{1}{2}m - \frac{1}{3}\right)$ **35.** $\left(\frac{1}{3}n + \frac{1}{5}\right)\left(\frac{1}{3}n - \frac{1}{5}\right)$ **37a.** $t - 3$; 4 **37b.** $(t + 1)(t - 7)$

MIXED REVIEW **39.** $5 + 6\sqrt{2}$ **41.** $\sqrt{41}$ **43.** 30% **45.** $-\frac{4}{3}$ **47.** $\frac{5}{3}$

Lesson 10-6 pages 491–495

ON YOUR OWN **1.** 3, 7 **3.** $-\frac{2}{7}, -\frac{4}{5}$ **5.** $-2, 7$ **7.** 5, 11 **9.** $-4, 3$ **11.** 0, 10 **13.** $-4, \frac{2}{5}$ **15.** $-1, 10$ **17.** 5 cm **19.** $x^2 - 10x + 24 = 0$; 4, 6 **21.** $2q^2 + 22q + 60 = 0$; $-6, -5$ **23.** $6n^2 - 5n - 4 = 0$; $-\frac{1}{2}, \frac{4}{3}$ **25.** $20p^2 - 80 = 0$; $-2, 2$ **27.** $4n^2 - 100 = 0$; $5, -5$ **29.** $9c^2 - 36 = 0$; $2, -2$ **31.** 5 in. **33a.** 10 ft base; 22 ft height **33b.** about 24.2 ft **35.** 0, 4, 6 **37.** 0, 3 **39.** 0, 1, 9 **41.** 3, 4, 5 **43.** $0, -1$ **45.** 8 in. × 10 in.

MIXED REVIEW **47.** $\frac{1}{3y^3}$ **49.** 1 **51.** $\frac{25}{3}$ **53.** 60 students **55.** $\frac{1}{5}, -\frac{3}{2}$

CHECKPOINT **1.** $(x - 3)(x - 2)$ **2.** $(n - 3)^2$ **3.** $(g - 10)(g + 2)$ **4.** $(3x + 7)(3x - 7)$ **5.** $-3, \frac{2}{3}$ **6.** $6, -\frac{3}{2}$ **7.** $-7, -2$ **8.** $2, -2$ **9.** $-\frac{4}{3}$ **10.** $\frac{3}{2}, -\frac{2}{5}$ **11.** A

Toolbox page 496

1. 4 **3.** 49 **5.** Sample: Divide the coefficient of the first degree term in half and square the result. **7.** $-6, -2$ **9.** $-8, 2$ **11.** $-6, 2$ **13.** $9, -5$ **15.** $-5 \pm \sqrt{35}$ **17.** $-4 \pm \sqrt{13}$

Lesson 10-7 pages 497–501

ON YOUR OWN **1.** $-0.08, -13$ **3.** $1.25, -1.33$ **5.** no real solutions **7.** $3, -3$ **9.** $2, -2$ **11a.** $-\frac{1}{2}, 3$ **11b.** $-\frac{1}{2}, 3$ **11c.** $(2x + 1)(x - 3) = 0$, so $x = -\frac{1}{2}$ or $x = 3$. **13.** $-4, 2$ **15.** no real solutions **17.** no real solutions **19.** 4 **21.** $0, \frac{4}{5}$ **23.** $-1.85, 4.85$ **25.** 1.75 **27.** $\frac{13}{7}, -\frac{13}{7}$ **29.** B **31.** about 167.7 ft

MIXED REVIEW **35.** 13; 28 **37.** the parabola $y = x^2$ shifted 2 units right, 1 unit down; $x = 2$; 3; 1 and 3.

Wrap-Up pages 503–505

1. $7x^3 + 8x^2 - 3x + 12$ **2.** $8g^4 - 5g^2 + 11g + 5$ **3.** $-b^5 + 2b^3 + 6$ **4.** $t^3 - 5t^2 + 12t - 8$ **6.** $-40x^2 + 16x$ **7.** $35g^3 + 15g^2 - 45g$ **8.** $-40t^4 + 24t^3 - 32t^2$ **9.** $5m^3 + 15m^2$ **10.** $-6w^4 - 8w^3 + 20w^2$ **11.** $-3b^3 + 5b^2 + 10b$ **12.** $3x$; $3x(3x^3 + 4x^2 + 2)$ **13.** $4t^2$; $4t^2(t^3 - 3t + 2)$ **14.** $10n^3$; $10n^3(4n^2 + 7n - 3)$ **15.** $x^2 + 8x + 15$ **16.** $15x^2 - 29x - 14$ **17.** $6x^2 + 11x - 10$ **18.** $-x^2 + 5x - 4$ **19.** $x^3 + 3x^2 + 3x + 2$ **20.** $4x^2 - 21x + 5$ **21.** $x^3 - 9x^2 + 18x + 8$ **22.** $3x^2 + 10x + 8$ **23.** $(2x + 1)(x + 4)$; $2x^2 + 9x + 4$ **24.** $(x + 2)(x + 1)$ **25.** $(y - 7)(y - 2)$ **26.** $(x - 5)(x + 3)$ **27.** $(2w - 3)(w + 1)$ **28.** $(-b + 4)(b - 3)$ **29.** $(2t - 1)(t + 2)$ **30.** $(x - 1)(x + 6)$ **31.** $2(3x + 2)(x + 1)$ **32.** A **33.** $(q + 1)^2$ **34.** $(b - 4)(b + 4)$ **35.** $(x - 2)^2$ **36.** $(2t + 11)(2t - 11)$ **37.** $(2d - 5)^2$ **38.** $(3c + 1)^2$ **39.** $(3k + 5)(3k - 5)$ **40.** $(x + 3)^2$ **41.** The factors are equal. **42.** -3, -4 **43.** 0, 2 **44.** 4, 5 **45.** $-3, \frac{1}{2}$ **46.** $-\frac{2}{3}, 1\frac{1}{2}$ **47.** 1, 4 **48.** 10 ft by 17 ft **49.** $-5, 5$ **50.** $-4.12, 0.78$ **51.** 0.18, 2.82 **52.** 324 ft^2 **53.** $\frac{57}{10}$ **54.** $-\frac{33}{4}$ **55.** $\frac{157}{100}$ **56.** $\frac{52}{5}$ **57.** $-\frac{1849}{1000}$ **58.** $\frac{767}{100}$ **59.** $\frac{1}{3}$ **60.** $-1\frac{1}{2}$ **61.** $-\frac{3}{7}$ **62.** $\frac{10}{13}$ **63.** $7\frac{1}{2}$ **64.** $2\frac{1}{3}$ **65.** $9\frac{1}{6}$ **66.** 26

Preparing for the Math A Exam page 507

1. 1 **3.** 1 **5.** 2 **7.** 4 **9.** 2

CHAPTER 11

Lesson 11-1 pages 510–514

ON YOUR OWN **1a.** 16 h; 10 h; 8 h; 4 h **1b.** hourly wage and time worked **1c.** $xy = 80$ **3.** 8 **5.** 7 **7.** 96 **9.** $\frac{1}{6}$ **11.** 20 **13.** 130 **15.** D **17.** 1.1 **19.** 2.5 **21.** 375 **23a.** 120; distance from your house to the lake **23b.** 3 h **25.** 2.4 da **27.** $y = 70x$ **29.** $xy = 48$ **31.** Direct; as s increases, P increases. **33.** Inverse; as r increases, t decreases.

MIXED REVIEW **37.** $(x + 5)^2$ **39.** $(x - 3)^2$ **41.** $\frac{1}{5}$ **43.** $\frac{3}{8}$ **45.** -1

Toolbox page 515

1.

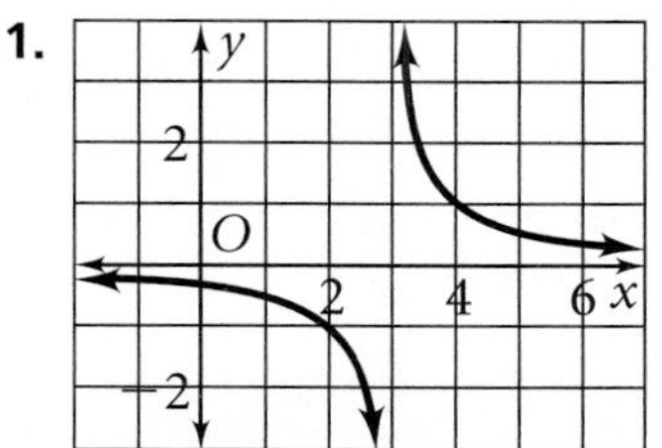

3.

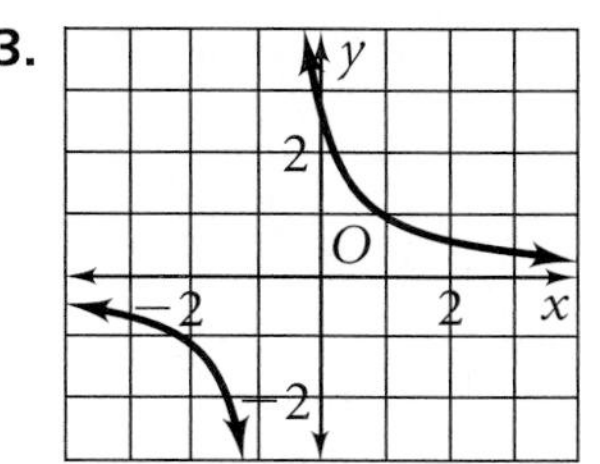

5.

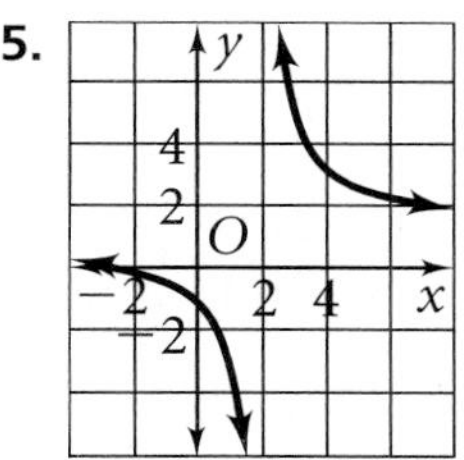

7.

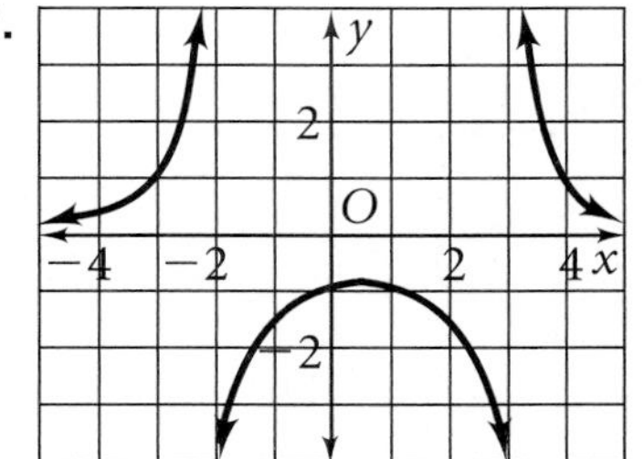

9.

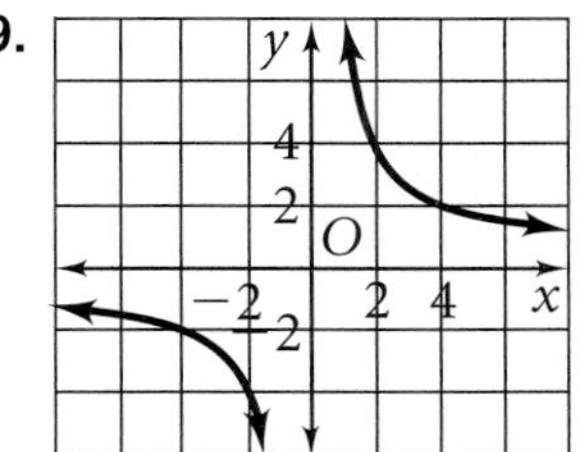

Selected Answers

11.

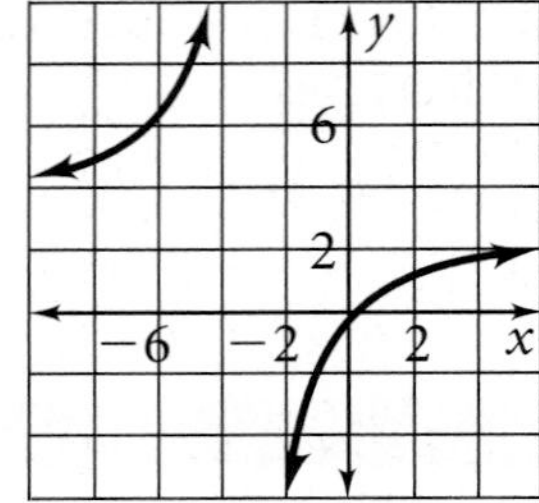

13a. The shapes of the graphs are the same, but they are in different positions along the x-axis. **13b.** The shapes of the graphs are the same, but they are in different positions along the y-axis.

Lesson 11-2 pages 516–521

ON YOUR OWN **1.** 3; 0; $\frac{1}{2}$ **3.** $\frac{1}{2}$; -4; 8 **5.** 0 **7.** -2 **9.** $x = 2, y = 0$ **11.** $x = 1, y = -1$

13.

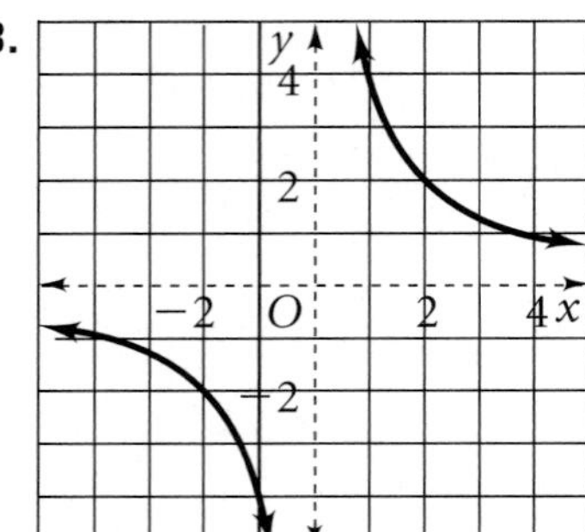

15.

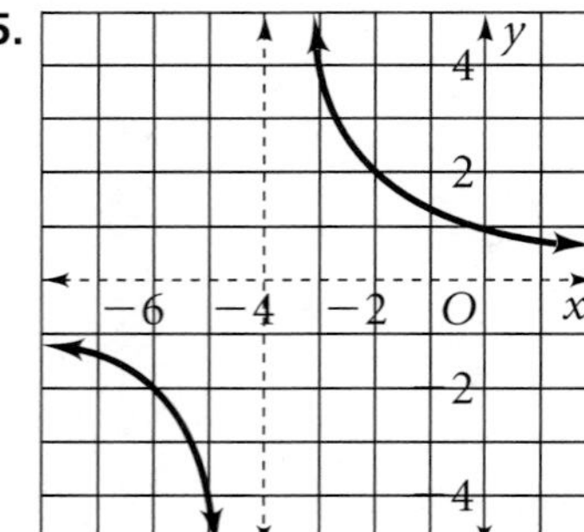

17.

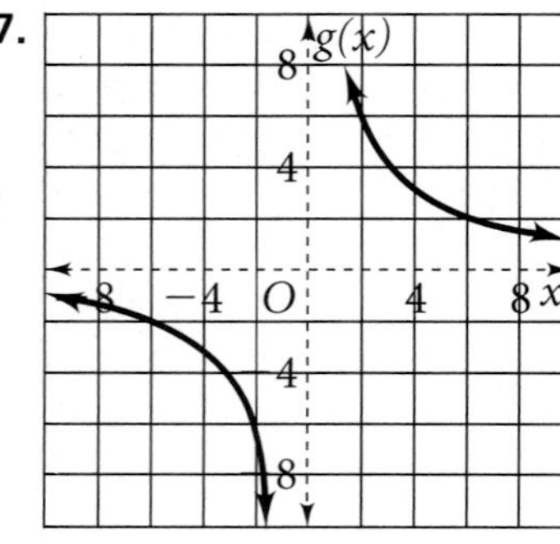

19.

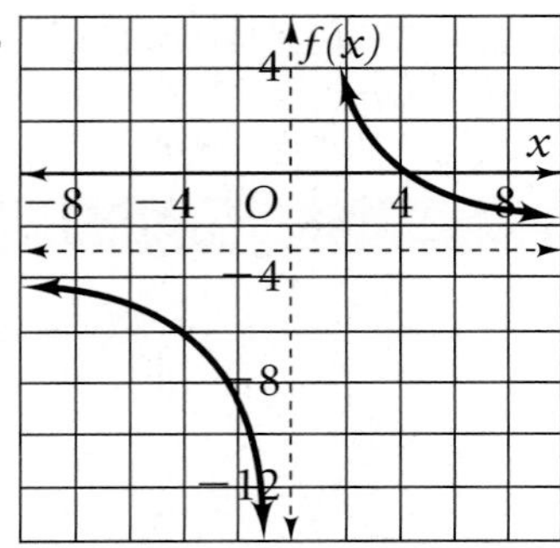

21.

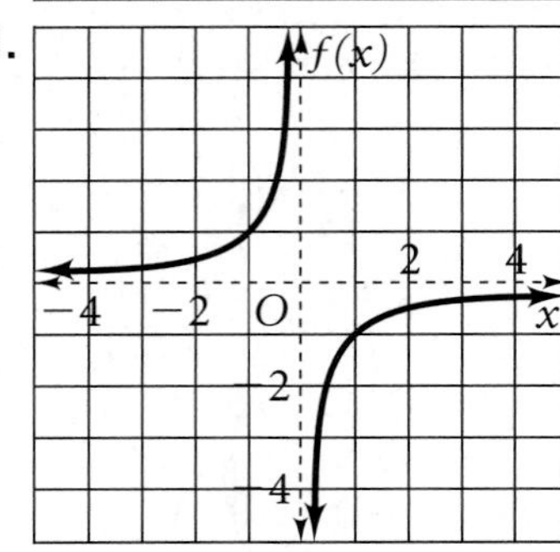

23.

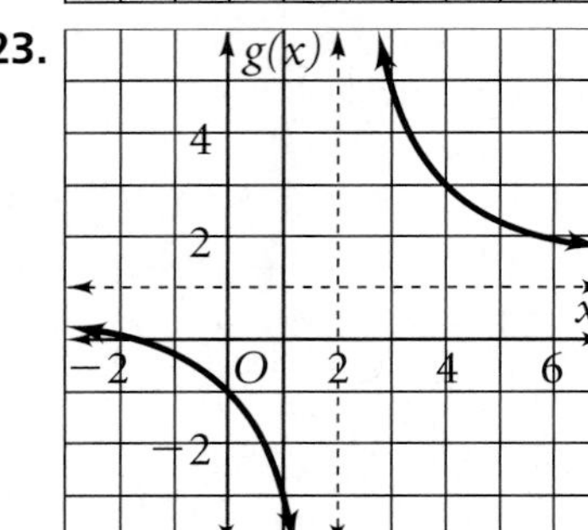

25a.

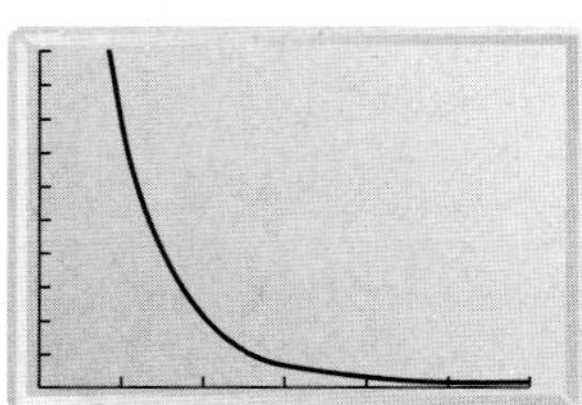

Xmin=0 Ymin=0
Xmax=6 Ymax=2000
Xscl=1 Yscl=200

; $d \geq 40$ **25b.** 16; 1600; 160,000

29.

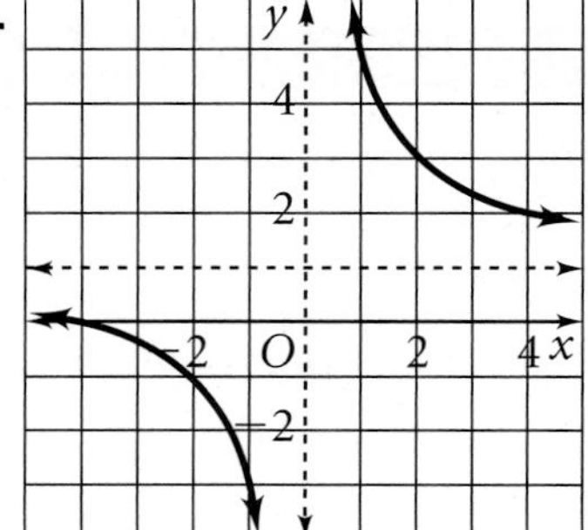

31.

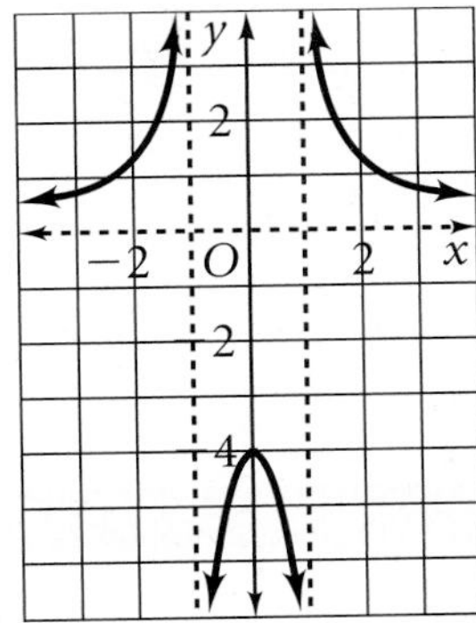

33.

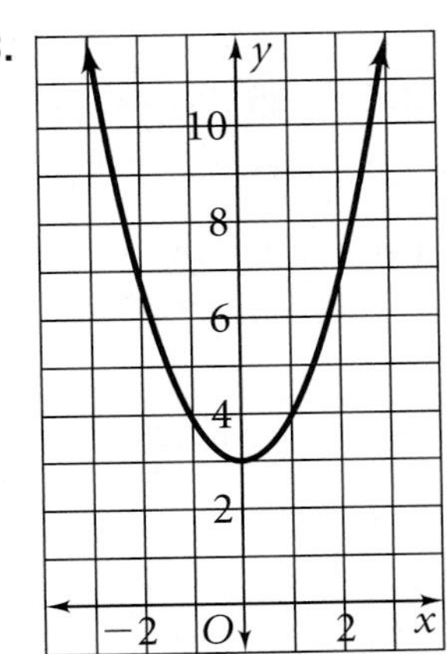

35.

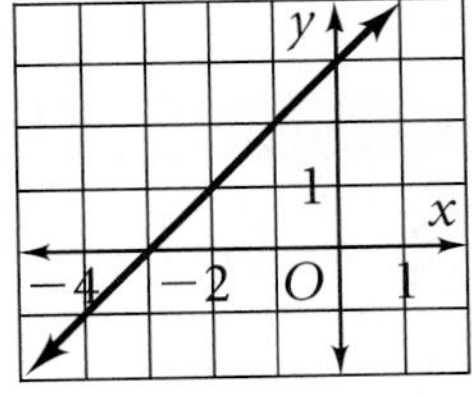

37.

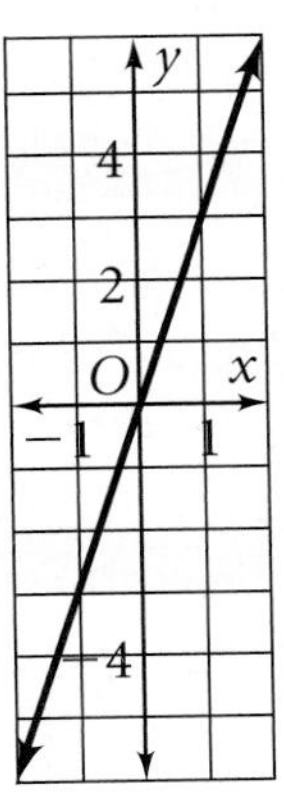

39.

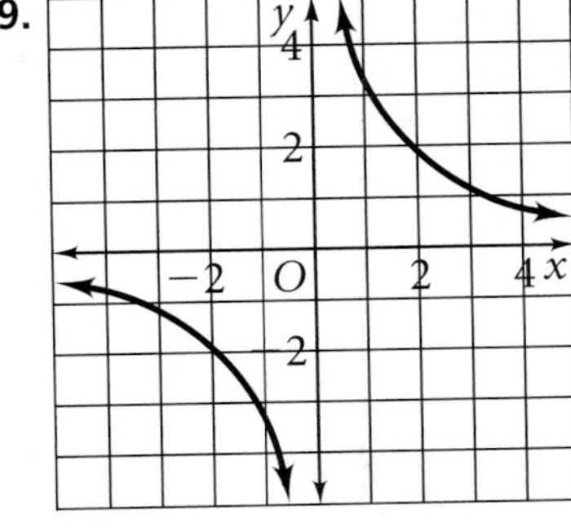

41.

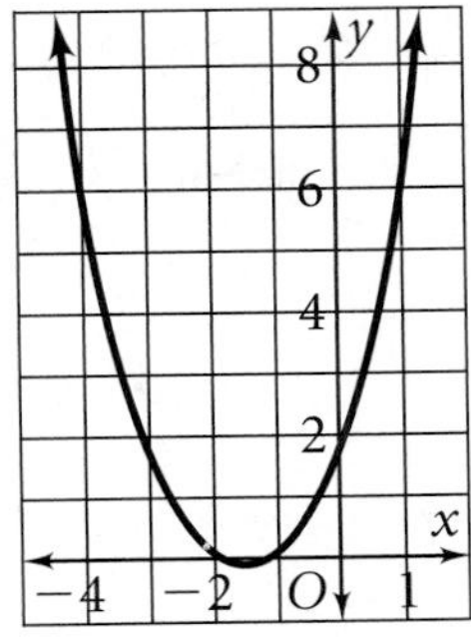

43.

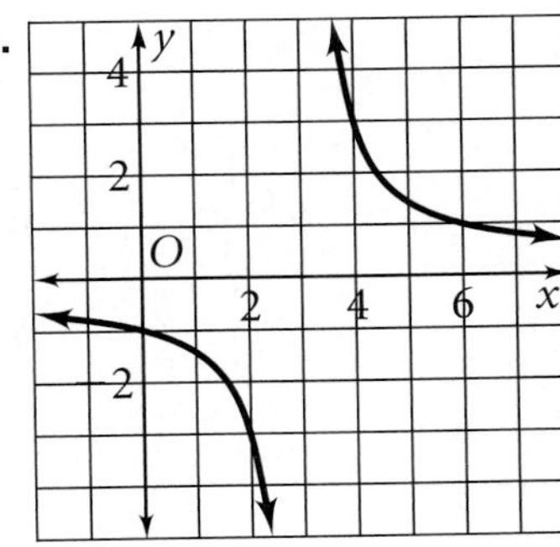

MIXED REVIEW **45.** $(g - 7)(g - 5)$ **47.** $(a + 7)(a - 1)$ **49.** $10 **51.** 0, 3 **53.** −4, 4

CHECKPOINT **1.** 3 **2.** 2 **3.** 4

4.

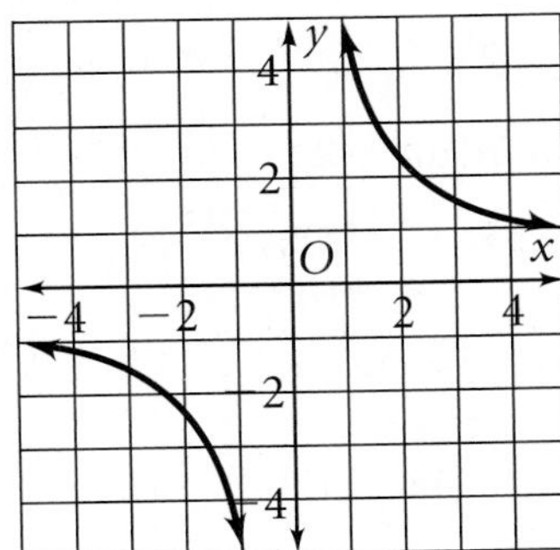

5.

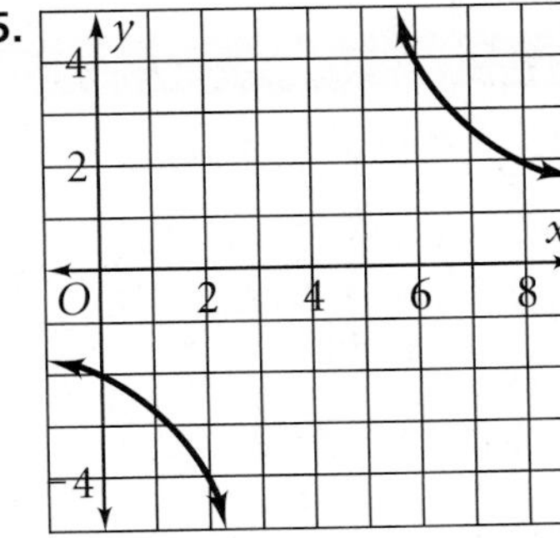

Selected Answers

6. 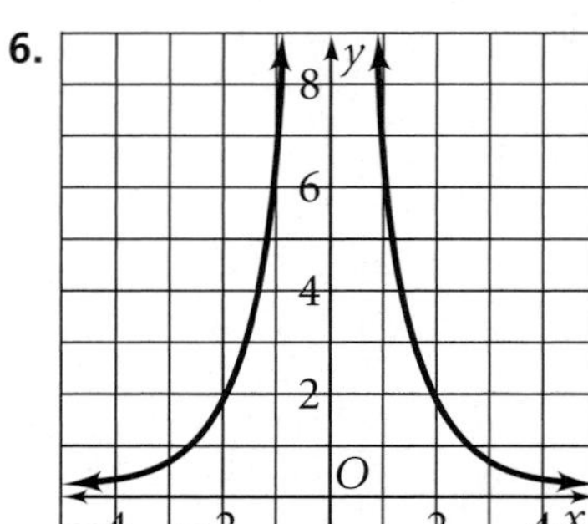

7. 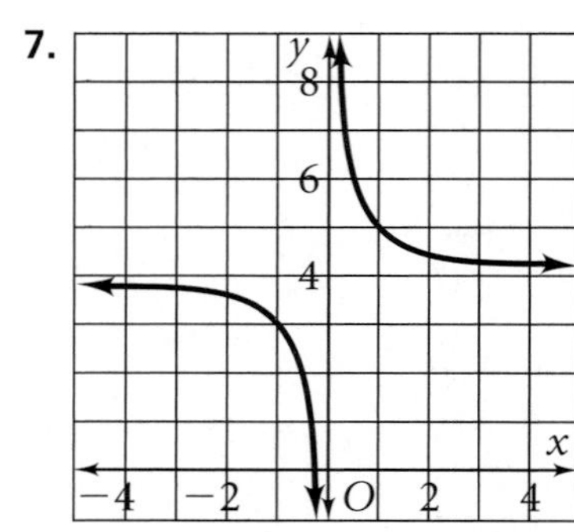

9. 91 lb

Lesson 11-3 pages 522–526

ON YOUR OWN **1.** $\frac{a}{4}$; $a \neq 0$ **3.** $\frac{x-2}{x+2}$; $x \neq -2$ **5.** $\frac{2a+3}{4}$ **7.** $\frac{1}{7x}$; $x \neq 0$ **9.** $\frac{1}{2}$; $p \neq 12$ **11.** $\frac{2}{3}$; $x \neq 0$, -1 **13.** $3x$; $x \neq 3$ **15.** $\frac{w}{w-7}$; $w \neq -7, 7$ **17.** $\frac{x^2-9}{x+3}$ does not have -3 in its domain. **21.** $-\frac{125}{16}$ **23.** $\frac{12}{x}$ **25.** $2x$ **27.** $\frac{3x^4}{2}$ **29.** 6 **31.** $-\frac{1}{2}$ **33.** $\frac{11}{7k-15}$ **35.** $\frac{\frac{4}{3}\pi r^3}{\pi r^2} = \frac{r}{3}$ **37.** $\frac{5w}{5w+6}$ **39.** $\frac{3y}{4(y+4)}$

MIXED REVIEW **41.** 3^{x+5} **43.** $-12m^4 - 18m$ **45.** $\frac{2}{3}$ **47.** $\frac{3}{5}$

Lesson 11-4 pages 527–531

ON YOUR OWN **1.** $\frac{7}{5}$ **3.** $-\frac{2}{b}$ **5.** $\frac{4}{11g}$ **7.** $\frac{2}{d}$ **9.** $\frac{5n}{7}$ **11.** $\frac{26r}{5}$ **13.** $4x^2$ **15.** $2m^2$ **17.** $6t^5$ **19.** $46d^4$ **21.** $5a$ **23.** $35b^3$ **25.** $\frac{35a^3+6}{15a^4}$ **27.** $\frac{18+20x^2}{15x^8}$ **29.** $\frac{b^3-4}{2b^4}$ **31.** $\frac{9+2m}{24m^3}$ **33.** $-\frac{77}{36k}$ **35.** $\frac{45+36x^2}{20x^2}$ **37a.** $\frac{17}{7r}$ **37b.** about 0.81 h, or 49 min **39.** $\frac{10}{m+1}$ **41.** $\frac{m+2}{m+3}$ **43.** $\frac{2}{t^2+1}$ **45.** $\frac{s^2+1}{2s^2+1}$ **47.** $\frac{1}{m+1}$ **49.** $\frac{5y-11}{(y+2)(y-3)}$

MIXED REVIEW **53.** about 12.2 **55.** about 10.8 **57.** 4 **59.** 6

Lesson 11-5 pages 532–536

ON YOUR OWN **1a.** 32 **1c.** no **3.** 12 **5.** -1 **7.** 2 **9.** no solution **11.** $-3\frac{1}{9}$ **13.** $-\frac{1}{3}$ **15.** $22\frac{1}{2}$ min **17.** 2 **19.** $\frac{1}{2}$ **21.** $-2, 4$ **23.** $5\frac{1}{3}$ **25.** 6 **27.** 5 **29.** A **31.** $a = 4$; $b = \frac{7}{27}$; $c = 11$; $d = -\frac{1}{3}$

MIXED REVIEW **33.** $-2, 2$ **35.** -5.5 **37.** 1, 2, 3, 4, 5, 6 **39.** H1, H2, H3, H4, H5, H6, T1, T2, T3, T4, T5, T6

CHECKPOINT **1.** $\frac{4}{m}$; $m \neq 0$ **2.** $6(x-2)$; $x \neq -2$ **3.** $\frac{c+3}{c-3}$; $c \neq 3$ **4.** $\frac{3z+12}{z^3}$; $z \neq 0$ **6.** $\frac{6}{7}$ **7.** -9 **8.** $\frac{5}{2}$ **9.** $-0.74, 10.74$ **10.** $\frac{9}{c}$ **11.** $\frac{5}{x-3}$ **12.** $\frac{2(7m-6)}{(m+2)(m-3)}$ **13.** $\frac{6t+3}{t^2}$ **14.** B

Toolbox page 537

1. symmetric **3.** reflexive **5a.** division property of equality **5b.** distributive property **5c.** subtraction property of equality

Lesson 11-6 pages 538–542

ON YOUR OWN **1.** 10 choices **3.** 30 ways **5a.** 24 different numbers **5b.** 6 even numbers **5d.** $\frac{1}{4}$ **7.** 210 **9.** 60 **11.** 6 **13.** 5040 **15.** 840 **17.** 7 **21.** 40,320 orders **23.** ${}_9P_7$ **25.** C **27a.** 2520 **27b.** $\frac{1}{2520}$

MIXED REVIEW

29.

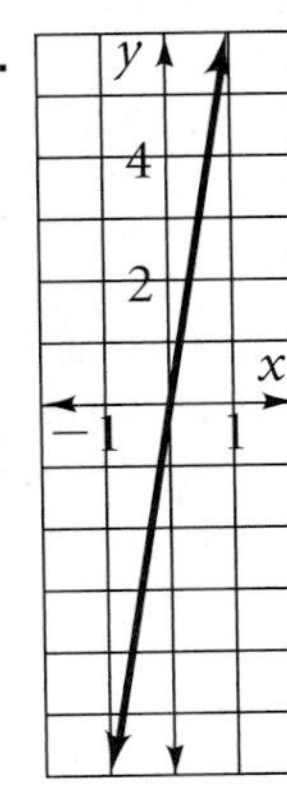

31.

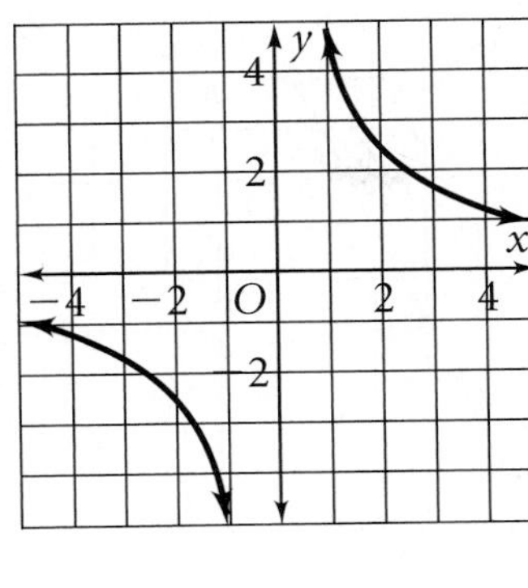

33. campsite \$20; family trail pass \$5 **35.** $\frac{5}{72}$

Lesson 11-7 pages 543–547

ON YOUR OWN **1a.** 14,886,690 different arrangements **1b.** about 1.94×10^{17} combinations **5.** 6 **7.** 20 **9.** 6 **11.** 1365 **13.** 56

15. 35 **17a.** **17b–c.** 6 segments

17d. 45 segments **19.** 126 different combinations **21.** Permutation; the order of videos is important. **23.** Combination; the order of committee members is not important. **25.** 10 **27.** 35 **31a.** 792 different choices **31b.** 36 ways **31c.** $\frac{1}{22}$ **33a.** 45 possible combinations **33b.** 3 combinations **33c.** $\frac{1}{15}$ **33d.** $\frac{2}{15}$

MIXED REVIEW **35.** 12 **37.** 5040 **39.** 9 **41.** $\frac{4x^2 + 5}{3x}$ **43.** $\frac{13x - 8}{(x + 2)(x - 2)}$ **45.** $-\frac{27}{20n}$ **47a.** about 1143 times **47b.** 6 t

Wrap-Up pages 549–551

1. 6 **2.** 9 **3.** 4.4 **4.** no **5.** yes; $xy = 10.6$

6.

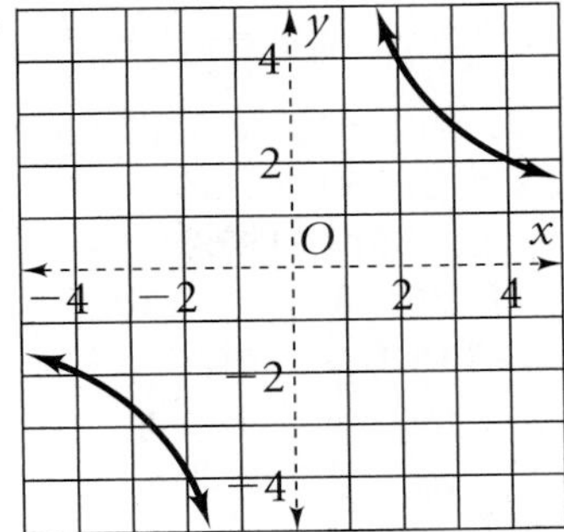

7.

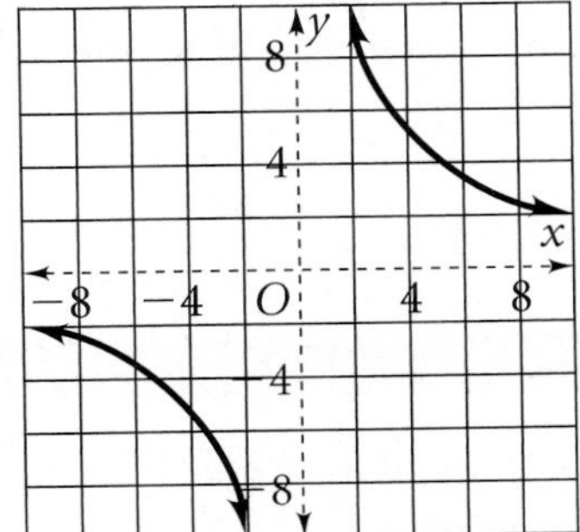

8.

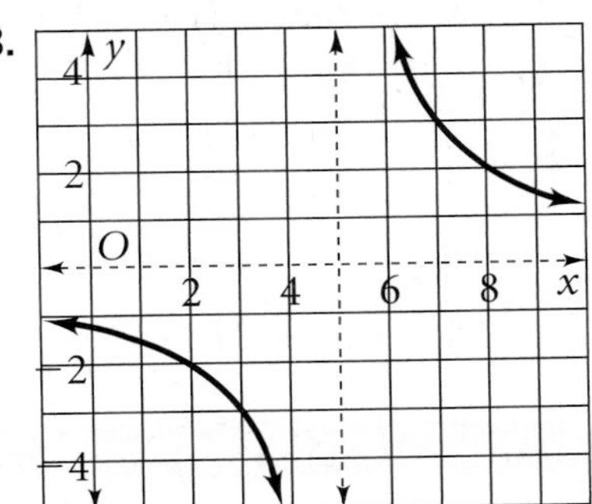

9.

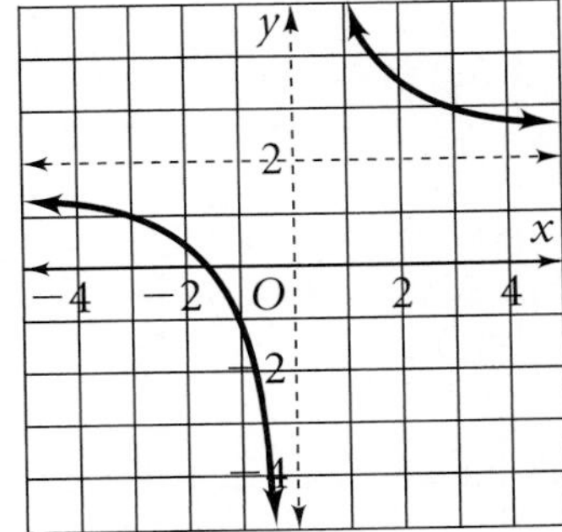

12. $x - 2; x \neq -2$ **13.** $\frac{x}{4x + 3}; x \neq -\frac{3}{4}$ **14.** $\frac{-3}{t(t - 1)}$; $t \neq 0, 1$ **15.** $\frac{1}{2z - 3}; z \neq -2, 1\frac{1}{2}$ **16.** $\frac{24m}{(m - 3)(m + 1)}$ **17.** $\frac{1}{2(2e + 1)}$ **18.** $\frac{5c + 3}{2c(c - 1)}$ **19.** $3(n + 2)$ **20.** $\frac{8}{k}$

21. $\frac{4(2x-1)}{x-7}$ **22.** $\frac{15x^2+13x+27}{(3x-1)(2x+3)}$ **23.** $\frac{-3m+10}{(m-1)(m+1)}$

24. C **25.** 24 **26.** 9 **27.** −14 **28.** 6 min **29.** 60 **30.** 1680 **31.** 360 **32.** 20 **33.** 3024 **34.** 42 **35a.** 160 possible area codes **35b.** 640 new area codes **36.** 6 **37.** 210 **38.** 36 **39.** 165 **40.** 5 **41.** 15 **42.** 4 different combinations **43.** 45 ways **44.** $\frac{3}{28}$

Preparing for the Math A Exam page 553

1. 2 **3.** 1 **5.** 1 **7.** 1 **9.** 3 **11.** 3 **13.** 1 **15.** 4 **17.** 1 **19.** 1 **21.** 4 **23.** 3

EXTRA PRACTICE

Chapter 1 page 992

1. 39.375; 38; 35 **3.** 6.3; 6; 5 and 8 **5a.** c = length of a car; $3c = 24$ **5b.** b = weight of a book, p = weight of a pen; $2b = 39p$ **7.** 28 **9.** 9 **11.** $4\frac{1}{9}$ **13.** −27.7 **15.** $-\frac{1}{2}$ **17.** −26 **19.** $10\frac{1}{2}$ **21.** −20 **23.** −59 **25.** 18 **27.** $\frac{7}{27}$ **29.** $\frac{22}{27}$ **31.** $\frac{23}{54}$ **33.** $\begin{bmatrix} -7 & 6 \\ 3 & 8 \end{bmatrix}$ **35.** $\begin{bmatrix} -1.6 & 4.1 \\ 1.5 & 4.6 \end{bmatrix}$

Chapter 2 page 993

1a.

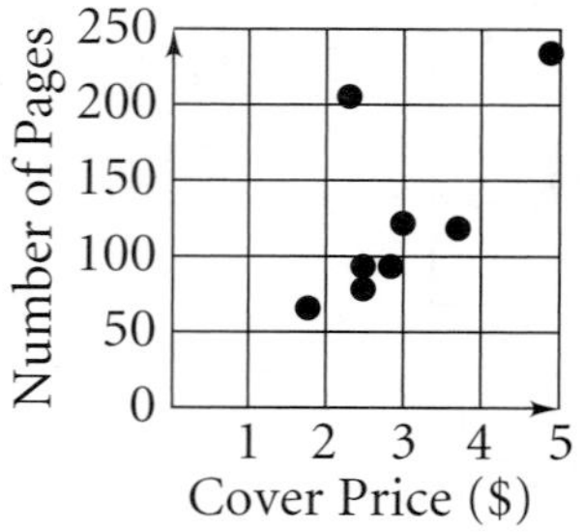

1b. The number of pages increases as the price increases. **1c.** About 75 pages; you can find the y-coordinate of the point on the line with x-coordinate 2.00.

7. $f(x) = 2x$

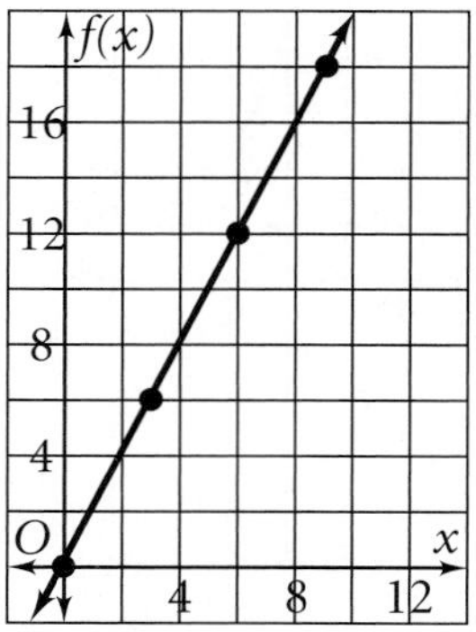

9. $f(x) = \frac{1}{2}x$

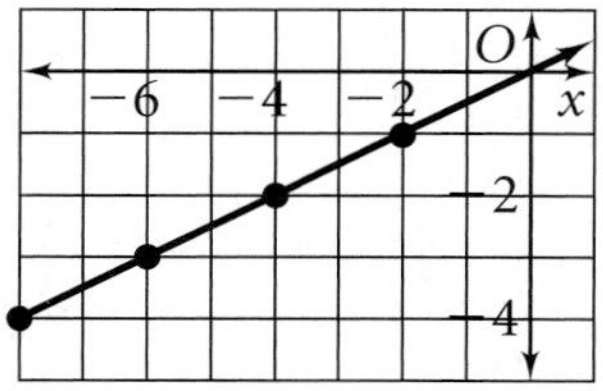

11. $\{-2, -1, 1, 2, 6\}$; absolute value **13.** $\{6, 7\frac{1}{2}, 8, 9\frac{1}{2}, 12\}$; linear **15.** $\{-\frac{8}{3}, -\frac{2}{3}, 0, 2, \frac{16}{3}\}$; linear **17.** $\{0, 3, 7, 52, 88\}$; quadratic **19.** $\{1, 4, 5, 8, 13\}$; linear **21.** $\left\{0, \frac{3}{5}, \frac{9}{5}, \frac{12}{5}, \frac{24}{5}\right\}$; absolute value **23.** 0 **25.** $\frac{2}{3}$ **27.** $\frac{1}{3}$ **29.** $\frac{1}{3}$

Chapter 3 page 994

1. 14 **3.** 8 **5.** −5.7 **7.** 2 **9.** 24 **11.** $\frac{18}{49}$ **13.** −2 **15.** 1 **17.** 10 **19.** −6 **21.** n = next test score; $\frac{87+84+85+n}{4} = 90$; no **23.** $\frac{5}{128}$ **25.** $\frac{9}{128}$ **27.** $\frac{1}{20}$ **29.** $\frac{1}{16}$ **31.** $n = 0.1 \times 94$; 9.4 **33.** $147 = 0.14 \times n$; 1050 **35.** $13.2 = 0.55 \times n$; 24 **37.** $n = 0.75 \times 68$; 51 **39.** $n \times 54 = 28$; 52% **41.** $n \times 20 = 31$; 155% **43.** about 11% increase **45.** about 33% decrease **47.** 38% decrease **49.** about 3% increase **51.** 125% increase **53.** about 11% increase **55.** about 46%

Chapter 4 page 995

1. −8 **3.** 48 **5.** $\frac{4}{3}$ **7.** $\frac{155}{2}$ **9.** $\frac{5}{3}$ **11.** 3 **13.** 8 ft × 12 ft **15.** 1 **17.** 1 **19.** −40 **21.** 9, −15 **23.** 5, −5 **25.** $-\frac{1}{3}$ **27.** identity **29.** The bus traveled 5 h; the car traveled 4 h. **31.** $cv - w$ **33.** $\frac{P-2w}{2}$ **35.** $m(b-a)$ **37.** $\frac{gr^2}{1.9}$

39. $p \leq 8$;

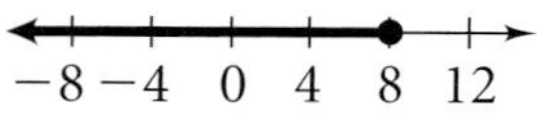

41. $y \leq -1\frac{3}{7}$;

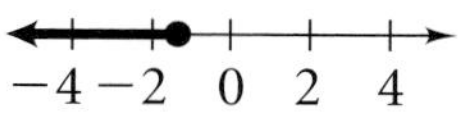

43. $h > -12$; 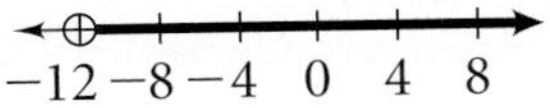

45. $s \leq 18$; 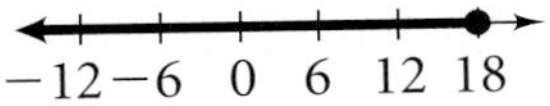

47. $l \geq -3.5$; 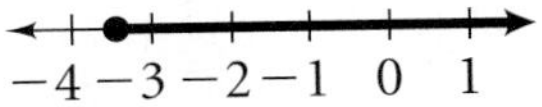

49. $m \leq -12$ or $m \geq 4$;

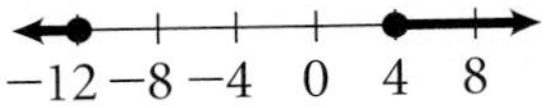

51. $-2.5 \leq n \leq 14.5$;

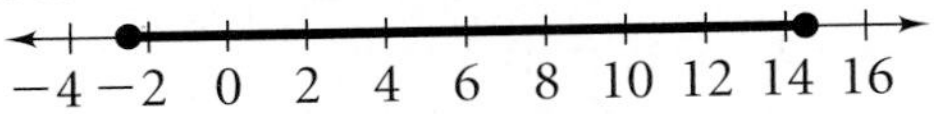

53. $a < -11$ 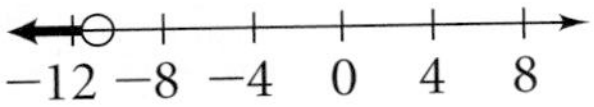

55. $j \geq 5$; 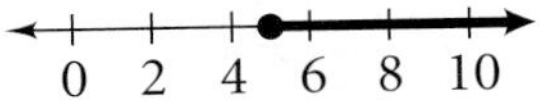

57. no more than five balls

59. $\{1, 2, 3\}$; 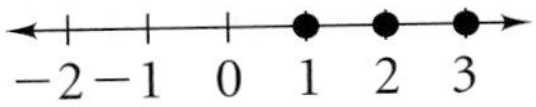

61. integers > 0; 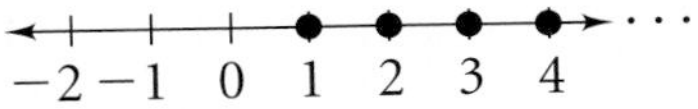

63. integers ≥ 1; 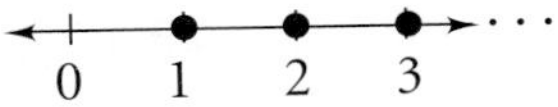

65. integers > 10;

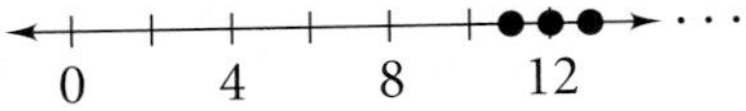

Chapter 5 page 996

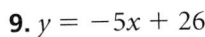

1. $\frac{3}{2}$; $y = \frac{3}{2}x + 2$ **3.** 1; $y = x + 6$ **5.** $\frac{5}{2}$; $y = \frac{5}{2}x + 5\frac{1}{2}$ **7.** $-\frac{1}{7}$; $y = -\frac{1}{7}x$ **17.** 0.2 m/yr **19.** 0.2 blocks/min

9. $y = -5x + 26$

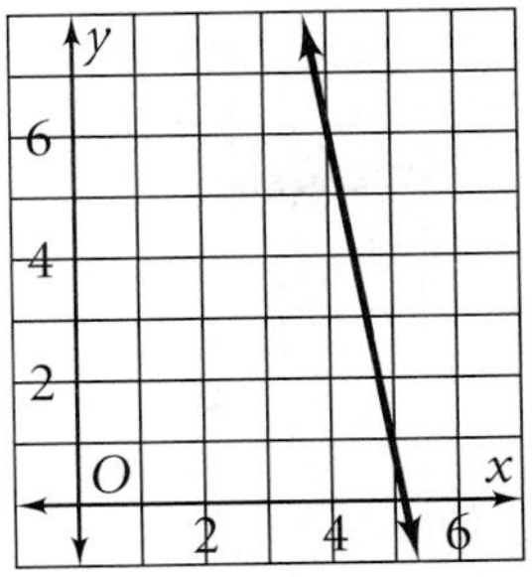

11. $y = \frac{1}{2}x + 1$

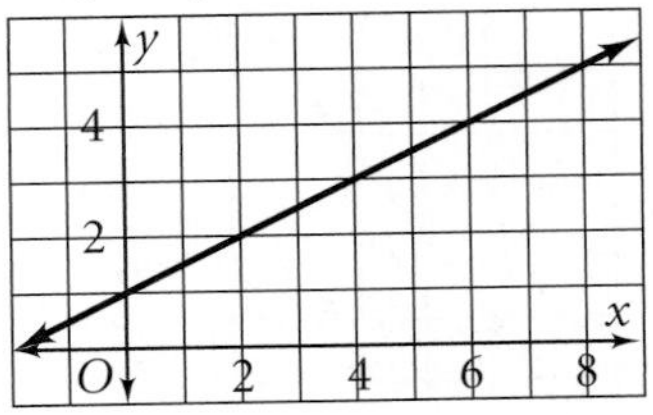

13. $y = 2x + 11$

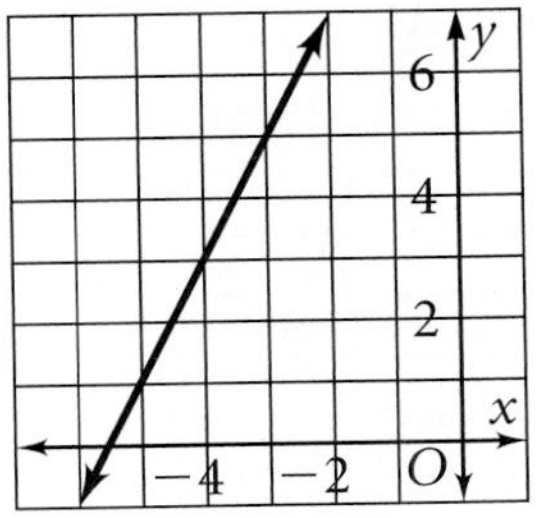

15. $y = 7x - 28$

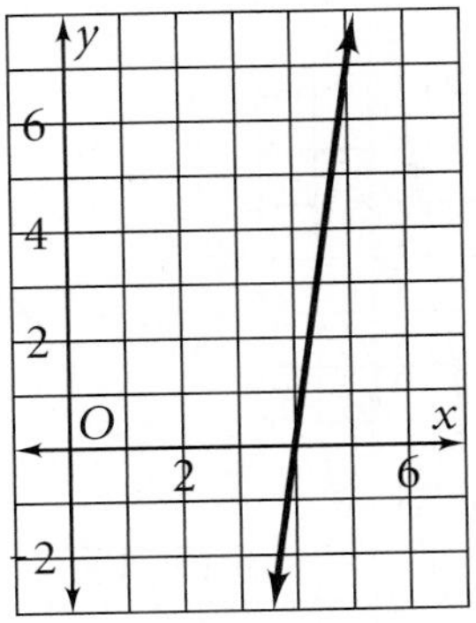

21. $y = \frac{4}{5}x$

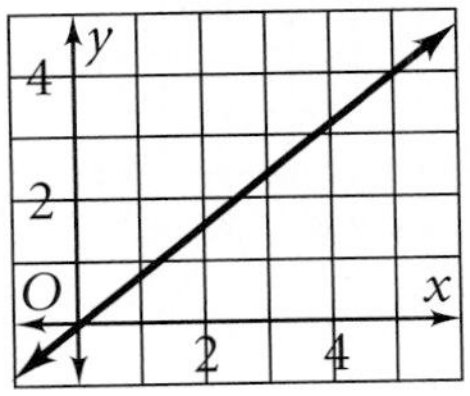

23. $y = \frac{10}{3}x$

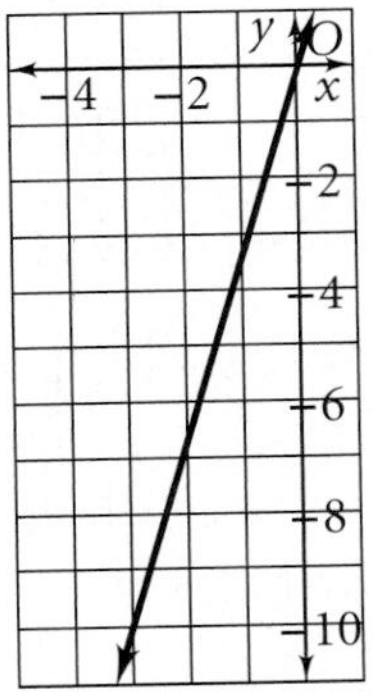

25. $y = -\frac{9}{2}x$

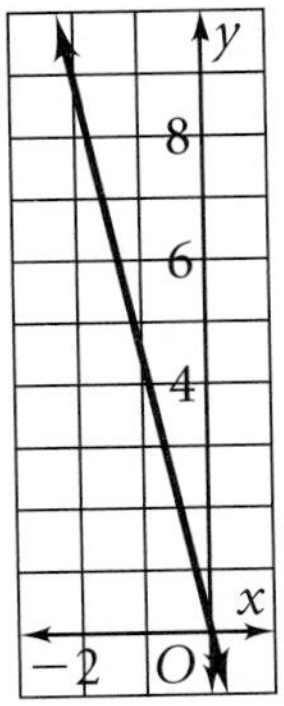

27. $y = -\frac{1}{4}x$

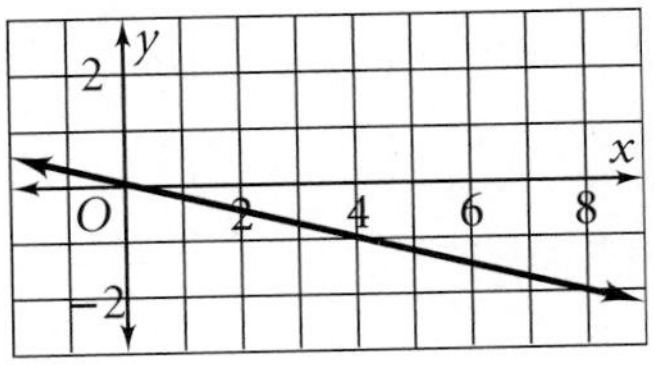

Selected Answers

29. $y = \frac{4}{3}x$

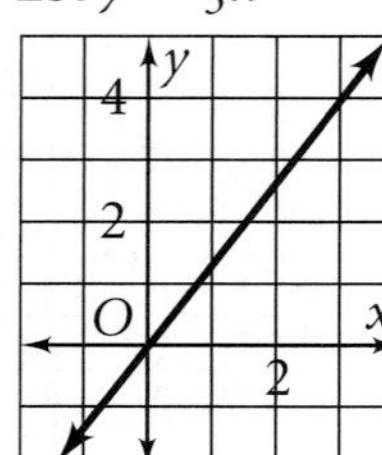

31. $y = -x$

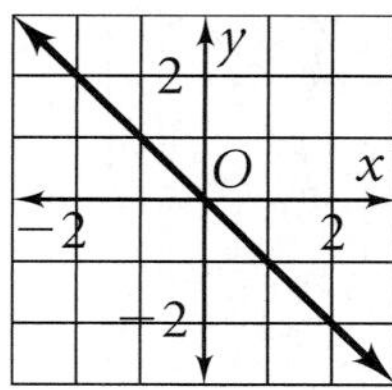

33. 6; 8;

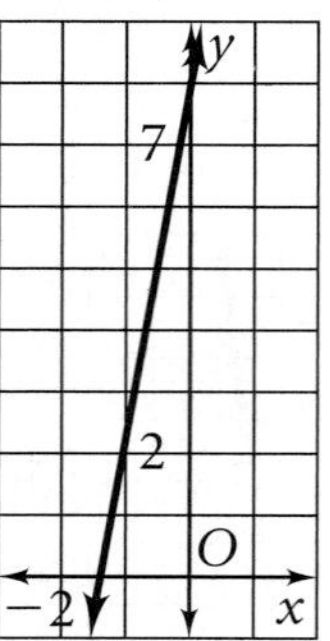

35. $-\frac{5}{2}$; 6;

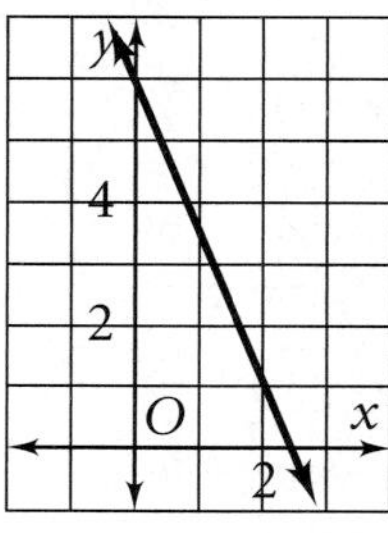

37. $-\frac{3}{4}$; −8;

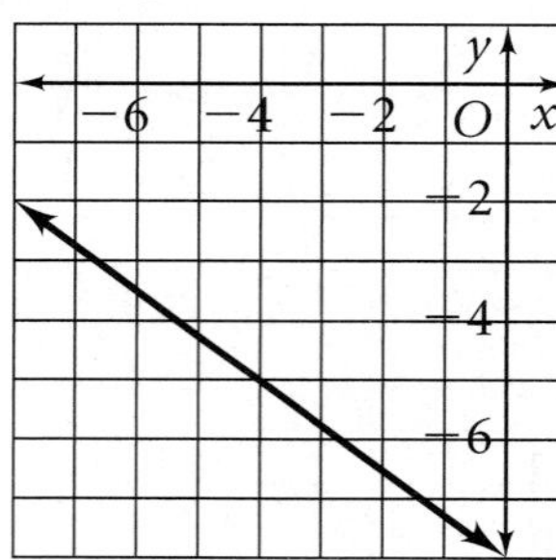

39. $\frac{1}{2}$; 3;

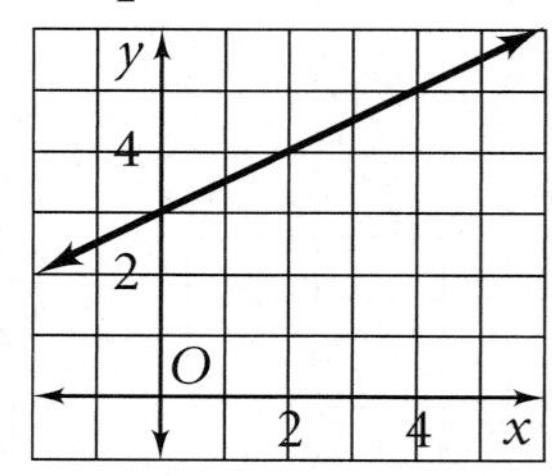

41a–b.

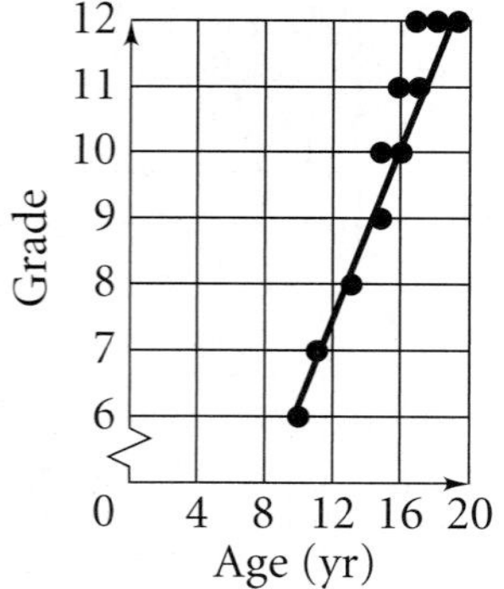

41c. $y = 0.7203196347x - 1.117579909$

43. $y = x$ **45.** $y = 2x + 3$ **47.** $y = \frac{5}{2}x - 6$

49. 1 **51.** − 2 **53.** − 3 **55.** 19

Chapter 6 page 997

1. (4, −3) **3.** (11, 7) **5.** (1, −1) **7.** (6, 13) **9.** (4, −5) **11.** (4, −9) **13.** $n + p = 12$, $5n + p = 32$

15.

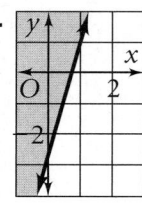

17.

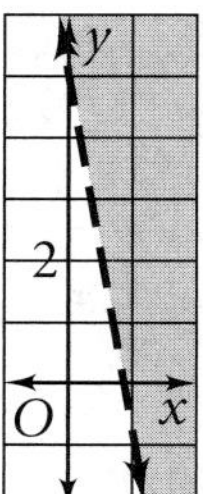

19.

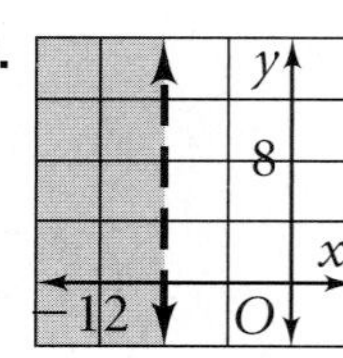

21.

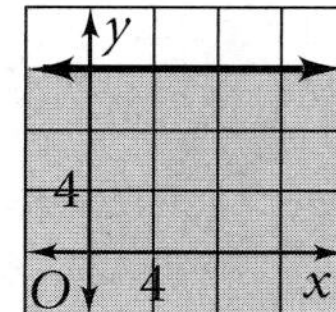

23.

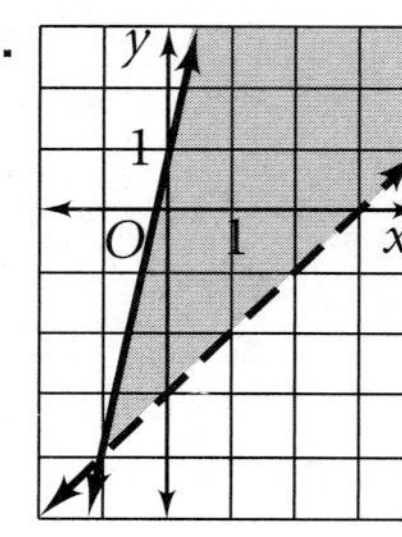

25.

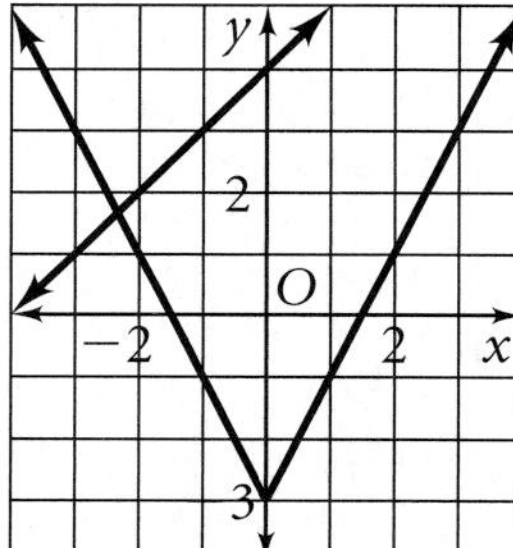

27.

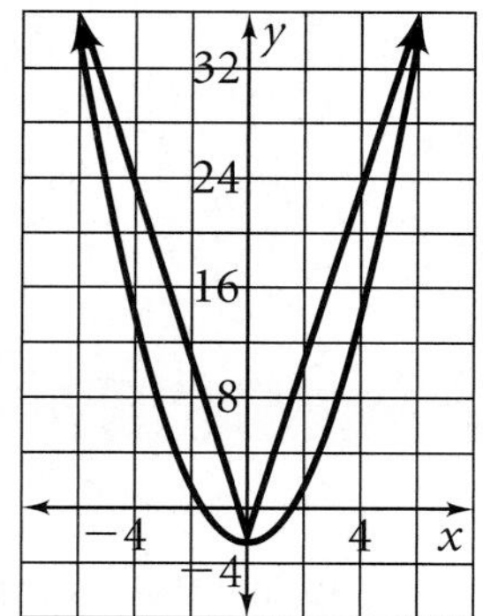

29.

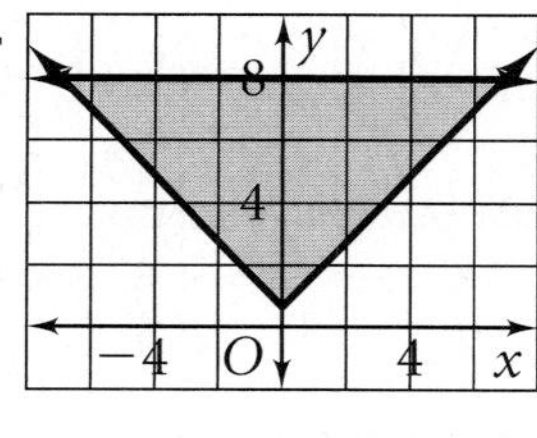

31.

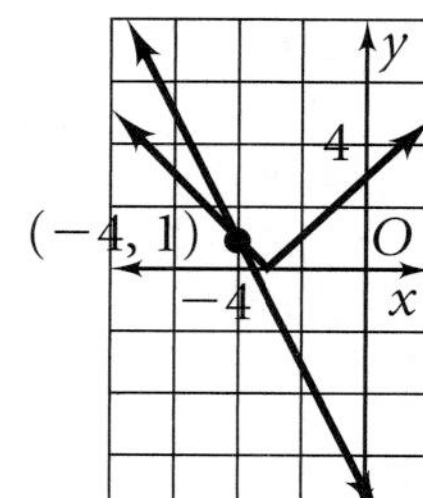

33.

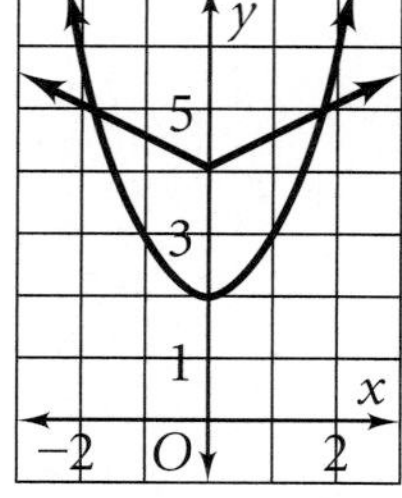

35. 30; 0

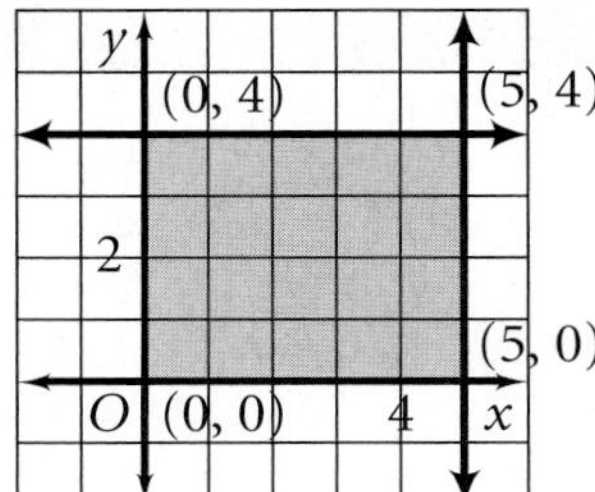

37. 29; 8

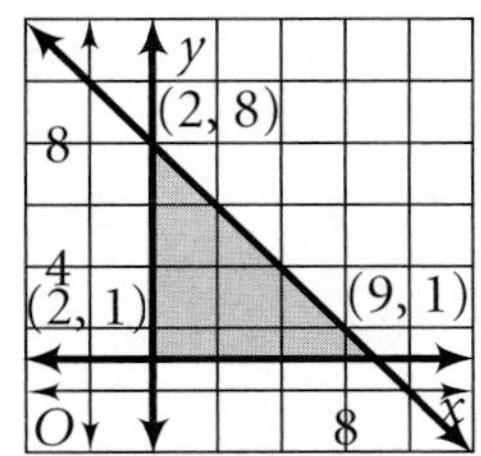

Chapter 7 page 998

1. narrower **3.** opens down, wider **5.** down 4
7. narrower, up 5

9.

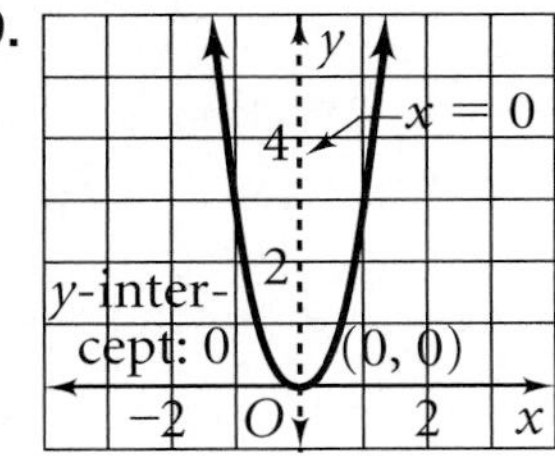

11.

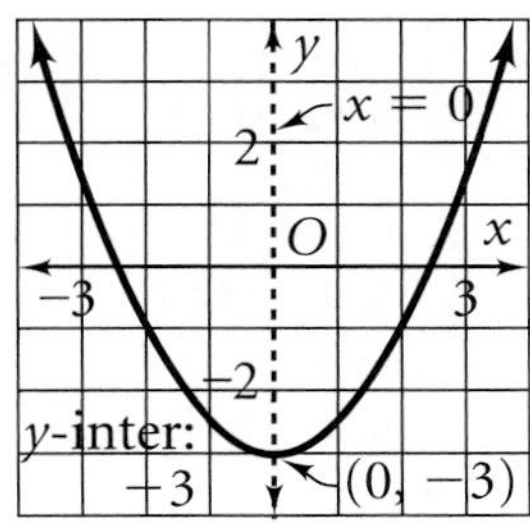

13.

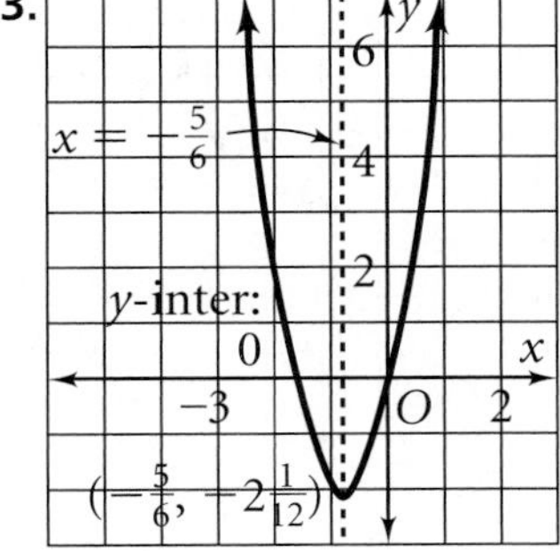

15.

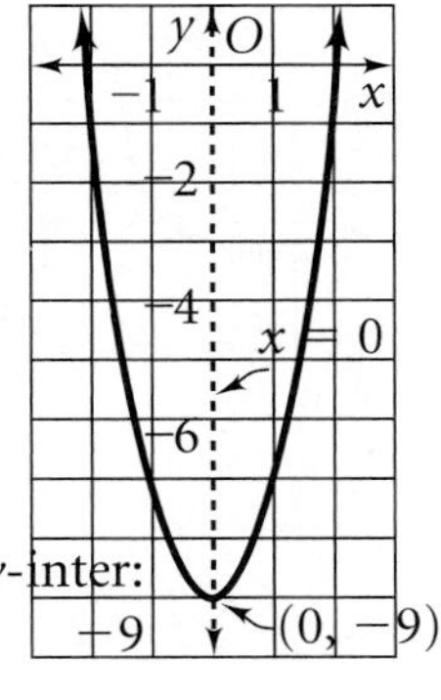

17.

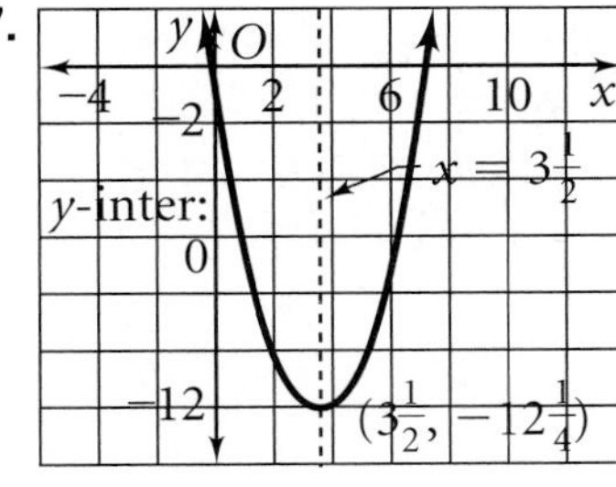

21.

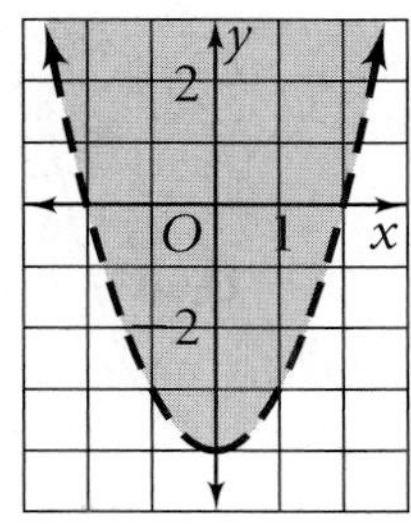

23.

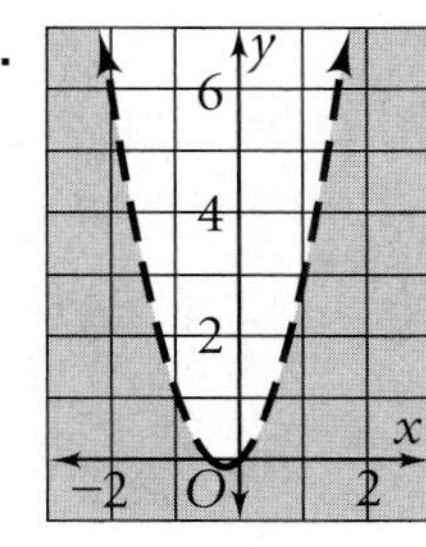

25.

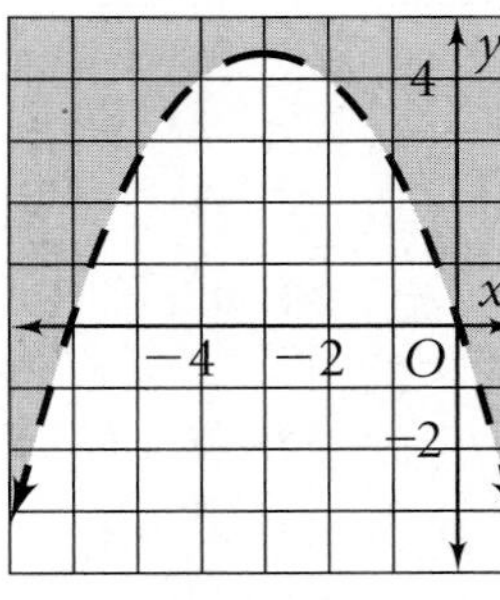

27. 5, −5 **29.** 8, −8 **31.** 0.9, −0.9 **33.** 1.5, −1.5
35. $\frac{1}{5}, -\frac{1}{5}$ **37.** $\frac{1}{3}, -\frac{1}{3}$ **39.** 6, −6 **41.** 10, −10
43. 14, −6 **45.** 13, −13 **47.** no real solution
49. 6.14, −1.14 **51.** 1.71, 0.29 **53.** 8, −2
55. 3.65, −1.65 **57.** −19; 0 **59.** 57; 2 **61.** −24; 0
63. −27; 0 **65.** 21; 2

Chapter 8 page 999

1. exponential growth

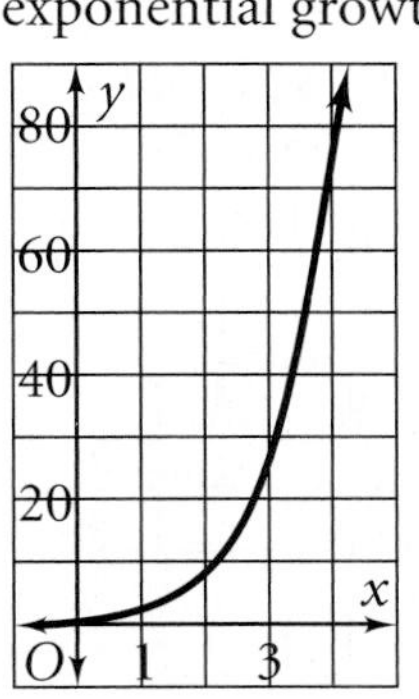

3. exponential growth

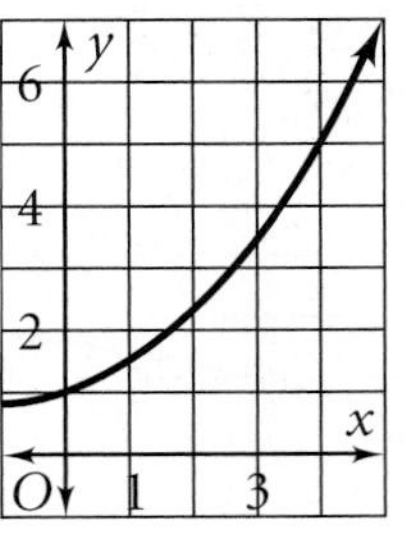

5. exponential growth

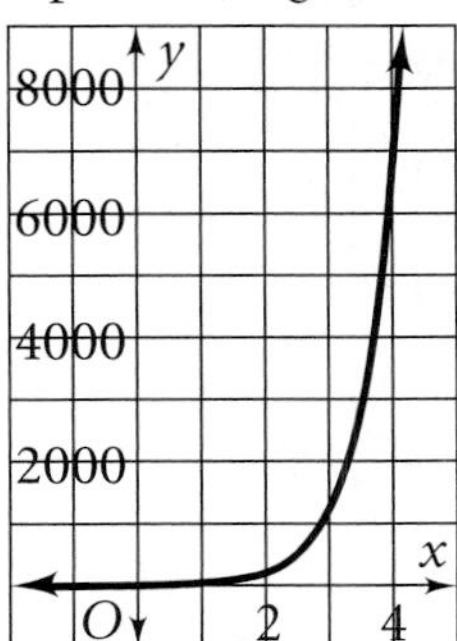

7. exponential decay

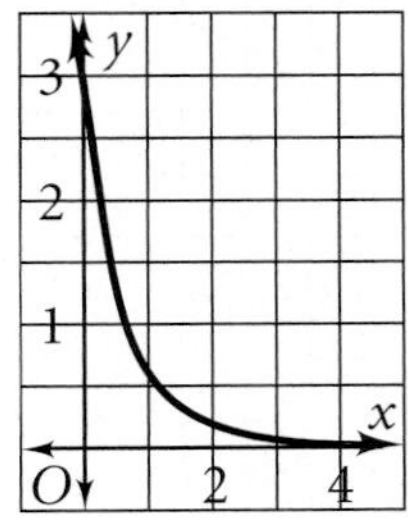

Selected Answers

9. exponential growth

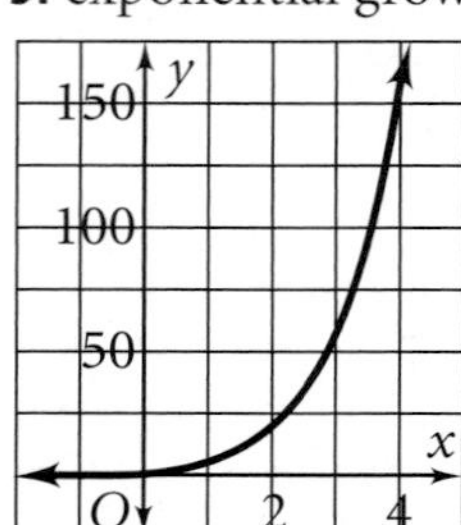

11. exponential growth

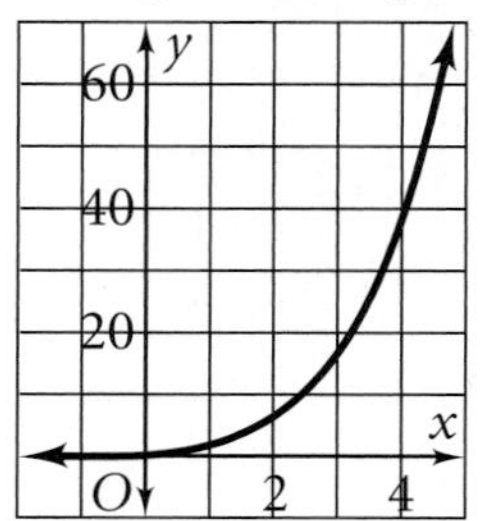

13. 8 **15.** $\frac{1}{2}$ **17.** 0.65 **19.** $\frac{1}{4}$ **21.** $y = 200 \cdot 1.04^x$; \$243.33 **23.** $y = 3000 \cdot 0.92^x$; \$2336.06 **25.** $\frac{5}{m^3}$ **27.** $\frac{m^{14}}{i^{10}}$ **29.** $w^6 j^{22}$ **31.** $9n^8$ **33.** a^4 **35.** $6t^4$ **37.** $\frac{2r^{15}}{t^7}$ **39.** $\frac{1}{c^{12}}$ **41.** $\frac{1}{9}$ **43.** 144 **45.** 16 **47.** $-\frac{64}{27}$ **49.** 6.3×10^{-4} **51.** 2×10^{-4} **53.** 6.2×10^9 **55.** 8.91×10^{-10} **57.** 3.8×10^{-1} **59.** 5.07×10^{12} **61.** 0.000 000 32 **63.** 0.000 425

Chapter 9 page 1000

1. no; $4^2 + 5^2 \neq 7^2$ **3.** no; $6^2 + 9^2 \neq 13^2$ **5.** yes; $15^2 + 36^2 = 39^2$ **7.** yes; $8^2 + 15^2 = 17^2$ **9.** 10 **11.** 10.8 **13.** 5.1; (1.5, 5.5) **15.** 1.4; (4.5, −0.5) **17.** 25.5; (2, −2) **19.** 17.0; (−1.5, 1.5) **21.** 11.2; (2.5, 5) **23.** $\frac{3}{5}$ **25.** $\frac{3}{5}$ **27.** $\frac{3}{4}$ **29.** $\frac{5}{2}$ **31.** $\frac{6}{5}$ **33.** −10 **35.** $6 - 3\sqrt{6}$ **37.** 150 **39.** 9 **41.** 5 **43.** 4 **45.** 6

47. $x \geq 0$;

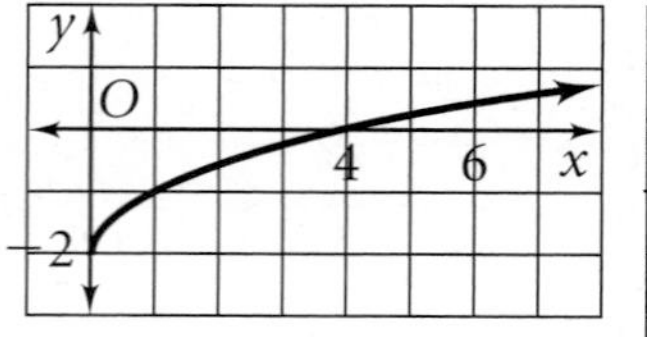

49. $x \geq 0$;

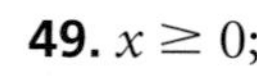

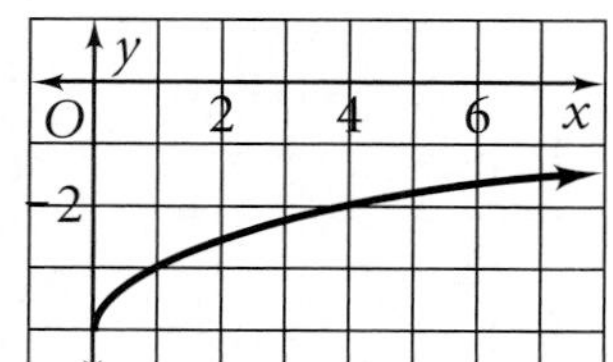

51. $x \geq 0$;

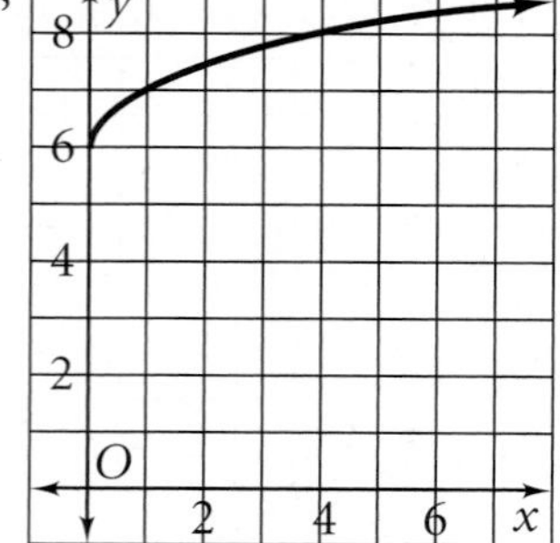

53. 1.6 **55.** 3.4 **57.** 3.2

Chapter 10 page 1001

1. $2x^3 + 4x^2 - 11x + 11$ **3.** $6m^3 + m + 4$ **5.** $-10c^3 - c^2 - 9c - 7$ **7.** $-4s^4 - 2s^3 + 2s^2 + 4s$ **9.** $4b^3 + 12b$ **11.** $6t^2 + t - 1$ **13.** $32m^2 - 40m$ **15.** $5k^3 + 40k^2$ **17.** $4n^2 + 2n - 12$ **19.** $b^2 + 10b + 21$ **21.** $(3x - 1)(2x + 5)$, $6x^2 + 13x - 5$ **23.** 3 **25.** $2v^5$ **27.** $5r$ **29.** d^4 **31.** 4 **33.** w **35.** $(x + 5)(x - 5)$ **37.** $(3c + 13)(3c - 13)$ **39.** $(t - 3)^2$ **41.** $(2d - 3)^2$ **43.** $(3v - 2)(v + 4)$ **45.** $(-w + 1)(w - 4)$ or $(-w + 4)(w - 1)$ **47.** $(4m + 1)(3m - 2)$ **49.** $(c - 5)^2$ **51.** 12, −12 **53.** 2, 3 **55.** −0.38, −2.62 **57.** 1.35, −1.85 **59.** 5, $-\frac{1}{2}$ **61.** −0.22, −2.28

Chapter 11 page 1002

1. 70 **3.** 0.8 **5.** 0.6 **7.** 8.1 **9.** 2 **11.** 3 **13.** 5

15.

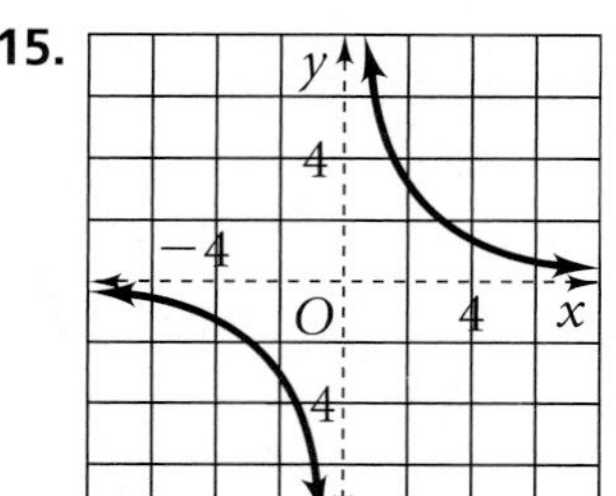

17.

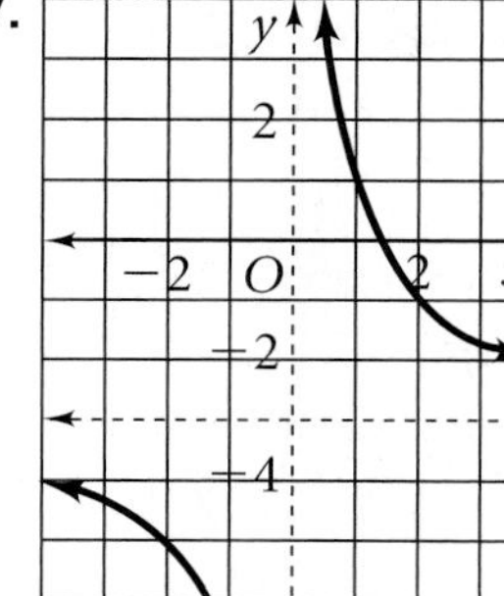

19.

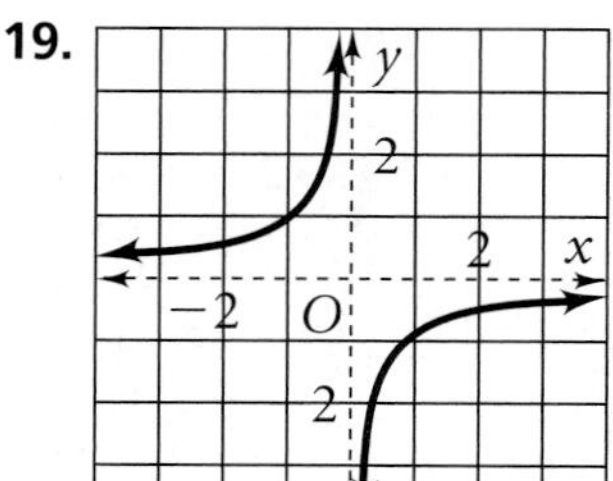

21.

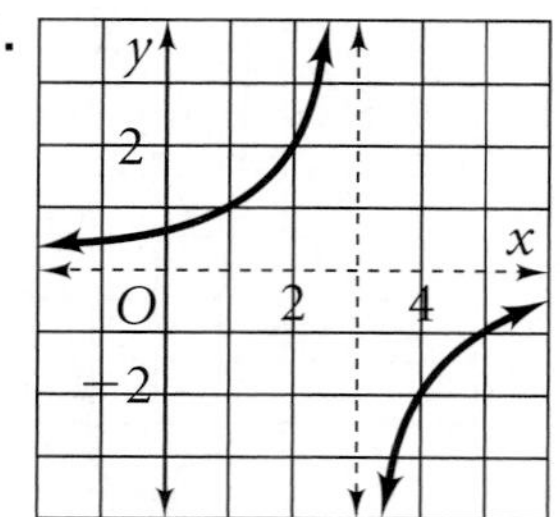

27. $\frac{t}{4}$; 0 **29.** 4; 3 **31.** $\frac{1}{x}$; 0 **33.** $\frac{6c + 4}{2}$; 0 **35.** $\frac{s}{2}$; 0 **37.** $12b^2$; 0, $\frac{1}{2}$ **39.** $\frac{8(t - 1)}{(t - 4)(t + 4)}$; 4, −4 **41.** $\frac{y}{6}$; 0, 2 **43.** 8 **45.** −1 **47.** 9 **49.** 5, −5 **51.** −12 **53.** 6, −10 **55.** 42 **57.** 8 **59.** 36 **61.** 84 **63.** 1320 **65.** 5040 **67.** 8568 committees

CHAPTER 1

Lesson 1-1 pages 569–572

ON YOUR OWN **1.** 80, 160 **3.** −3, 4 **5.** 3, 0 **7.** N, T **9.** 720, 5040 **11.** $\frac{1}{36}, \frac{1}{49}$ **15.** The trip takes about 25 min.

17. 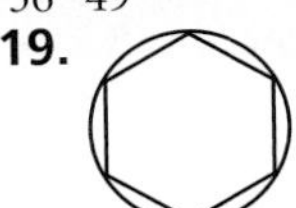 **19.** 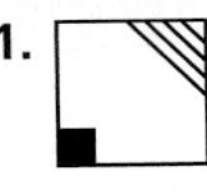 **21.**

23. a line parallel to the first two and midway between them **25.** It's possible but not likely. As he grows older, his growth will slow down and eventually stop.

27a. 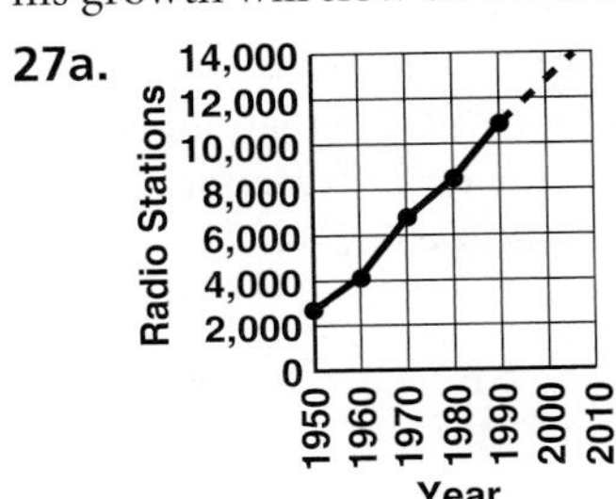

There will be about 15,000 radio stations. **29.** 123454321 **31.** 75° **33a.**

33b. 20^2, or 400; the sequence is the squares of successive counting numbers. **33c.** n^2 **35a.** Women may soon outrun men in running competitions. **35b.** The conclusion was based on continuing the trend shown in past records. **35c.** The conclusions are based on fairly recent records for women, and those rates of improvement may not continue. The conclusion about the marathon is most suspect because records date only from 1955. **37a.** Answers may vary. Sample: Leap years are divisible by 4. **37b.** Answers may vary. Sample: 2020, 2100, 2400 **37c.** Leap years are divisible by 4 except years ending in 00, which are leap years only if they are divisible by 400. **39.** 2

MIXED REVIEW **53a.** *B* and *W* **53b.** *N* and *T*

Toolbox page 573

1. $\frac{3}{10}$ **5.** $\frac{9}{10}$ **9.** $\frac{1}{10}$ **13.** $\frac{1}{3}$ **15.** $\frac{2}{3}$ **17.** $\frac{2}{3}$

Lesson 1-2 pages 577–579

ON YOUR OWN **1.** no **3.** no **5.** no **7.** no **9.** yes **11.** *C* **13.** yes **15.** no **17.** yes **19.** yes **21.** no **23.** *U* **25.** Answers may vary. Sample: plane *XWST* and plane *UVST* **29.** An infinite number; infinitely many planes can intersect in one line. **31.** C **33.** 1; points *A*, *B*, and *C* are points on the 2 lines and these 3 points are noncollinear, so exactly 1 plane contains them. **35.** never **37.** always **39.** never **41a.** $\frac{1}{4}$ **41b.** 1 **43.** collinear **45.** noncollinear

MIXED REVIEW **49.** 34 **51.** 20 **53.** 3 **55.** yes **57.** no

Lesson 1-3 pages 582–584

ON YOUR OWN **1.** $\overline{DF}$ **3.** $\overline{CF}, \overline{BE}$ **5.** plane *ABC* and plane *DEF* **7.** $\overline{RS}, \overline{RT}, \overline{RW}, \overline{ST}, \overline{SW}, \overline{TW}$

9. 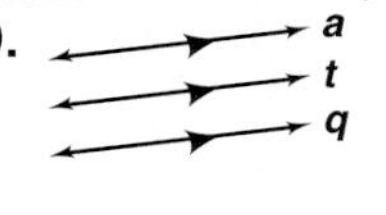

11. 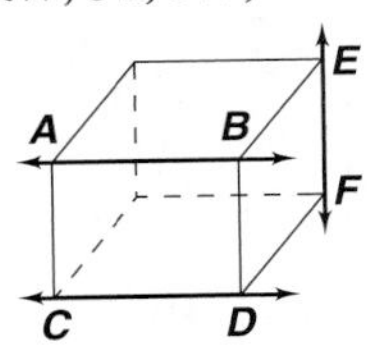

13. false **15.** true **17.** true **19.** true **21.** never **23.** always **25.** always **27.** always **29.** always **35.** The lines of intersection are parallel. Answers will vary. Sample: the ceiling and floor intersect a wall in two parallel lines. **39.** E

MIXED REVIEW **41.** −22, −29 **43.** by 2 points on the line or with a single lower-case letter **45.** with the word *plane* followed either by a single capital letter or the names of at least 3 noncollinear points in the plane **47.** 6 **49.** 3 **51.** 3 **53.** 9 **55.** 9 **57.** 7 9 11

61. −4 −2 0

Toolbox page 585

1. −9 **5.** 16 **9.** 6 **13.** $-\frac{7}{3}$ **17.** 4

Lesson 1-4 pages 590–593

ON YOUR OWN **1.** 9 **3.** 11 **5.** false **7.** false **9.** $\overline{AB} \cong \overline{CD}, \overline{AC} \cong \overline{BD}$ **11.** 24 **13.** 13; 40; 24 **15.** 125 **17.** Answers may vary. Samples: **17a.** $\angle QVM$, $\angle PVN$ **17b.** $\angle QVP$, $\angle MVN$ **17c.** $\angle MQV$, $\angle QNP$ **21–23.** Estimates may vary slightly. **21.** 60; acute **23.** 135; obtuse **27.** 15 **33.** 8 **35.** 7

MIXED REVIEW **37.** 25 **39.** 30 **41.** coplanar **43.** collinear **45.** C D **47.** A B

CHECKPOINT **1.** 29, 31.5 **2.** 3.45678, 3.456789 **3.** −162, 486 **5.** yes **6.** no **7.** yes **8.** yes **9.** yes **10.** *H* **11.** $\overline{DC}, \overline{EF}, \overline{AB}$ **12.** Sample: $\overleftrightarrow{AB}, \overleftrightarrow{EH}$ **13.** Sample: plane *ABFE* ∥ plane *DCGH* or plane *HEFG* ∥ plane *ABCD* **14.** Sample: $\angle EAB$; $\angle AEF$; $\angle EHG$ **15.** 17

Lesson 1-5 pages 597–600

ON YOUR OWN **1.** b **3.** 6 **5.** 5 **7.** *CM* (or *DM*) **9.** 20; 40 **11.** *AOC* **13.** $\overrightarrow{OB}$; $\angle AOC$ **15.** true **17.** true **19.** false **21.** false

23.

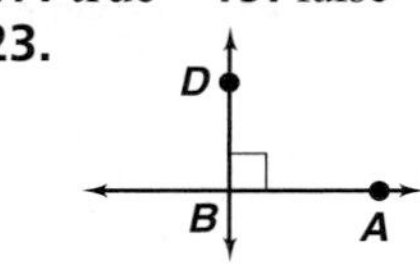

25.

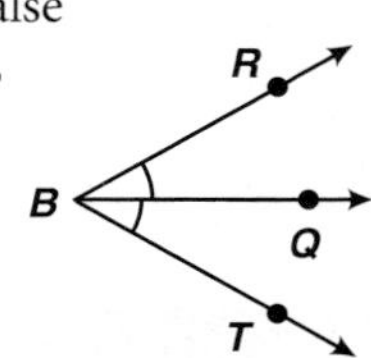

27.

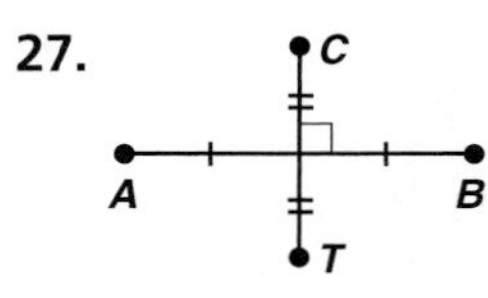

29. *Q* **31.** −4 **33.** 12 **35.** 4 **37.** 6 **39.** 20 **41a.** one; infinitely many **41b.** one **41c.** infinitely many **47.** b **49.** 15 **51.** 48 **53.** D **55.** perpendicular; it intersects

MIXED REVIEW **57.** Answers may vary. Sample: $\angle AOD$ **59.** $\angle BOE$ **61.** 3 **63.** $\angle APT \cong \angle TPR$

Lesson 1-6 pages 605–606

ON YOUR OWN **1.**

3.

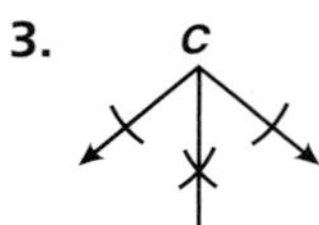

5.

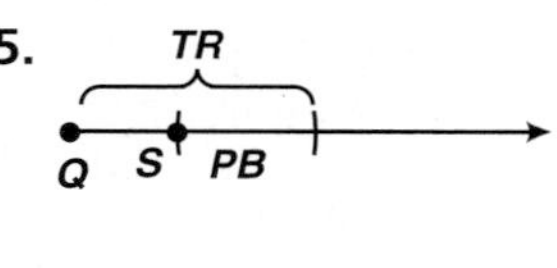

7.

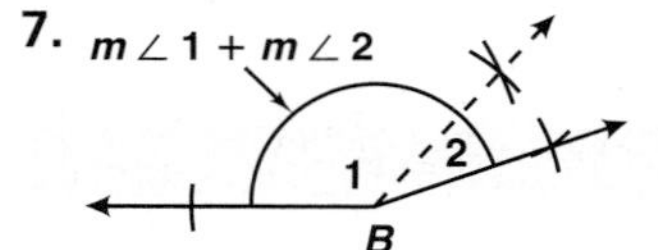

9.

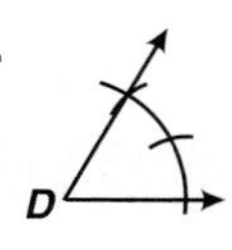

11.

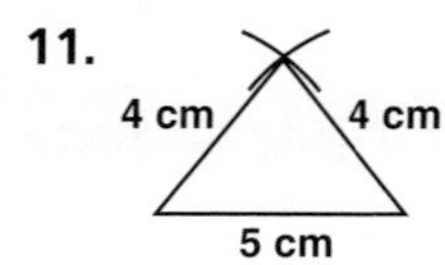

15. The angle bisectors of the 3 angles of any triangle intersect in a single point.

17a. Sample:

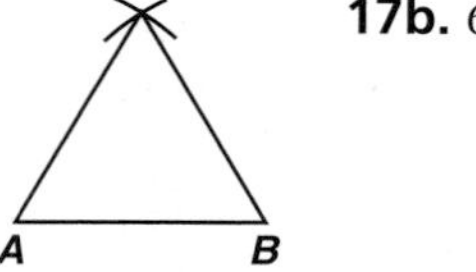

17b. 60

19a–b. Answers may vary. Sample: **19c.** Point *O* is the center of the circle.

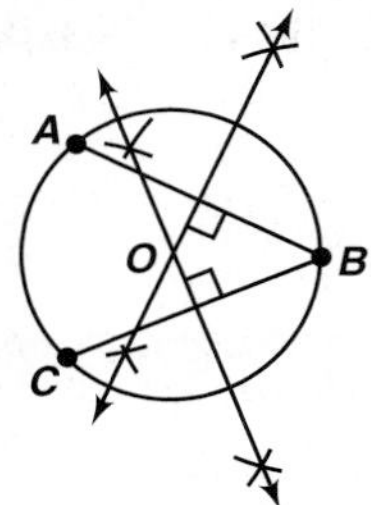

MIXED REVIEW **21.** 16 **23.** 8 **25.** 50 **27.** 45

Toolbox page 607

INVESTIGATE yes; $\overleftrightarrow{HG}$ intersects $\overline{EF}$, but it is not the $\perp$ bisector of $\overline{EF}$.

SUMMARIZE A figure created by *draw* has no constraints. A figure created by *construct* is dependent upon an existing object.
Since $\overleftrightarrow{DC}$ was constructed as the $\perp$ bisector of $\overline{AB}$, it remains the $\perp$ bisector through any manipulation. Since point *G* was constructed on $\overline{EF}$, the only restriction on $\overleftrightarrow{HG}$ during any manipulation is that it must contain point *G* which has to be on $\overline{EF}$.

EXTEND $\overrightarrow{KM}$ is always the angle bisector of $\angle JKL$. $\overrightarrow{OQ}$ is not always the bisector of $\angle NOP$.

Lesson 1-7 pages 612–614

ON YOUR OWN **1.** Reflexive Prop. of $\cong$ **3.** Symmetric Prop. of $\cong$ **5.** Substitution Prop. **7.** Mult. Prop. of = **9.** Trans. Prop. of $\cong$ **13.** 9 **15.** 18 **17.** 10 **19a.** *B* can be any point on the positive *y*-axis, for example, (0, 5). **21.** $x = 14$; $y = 15$ **23a.** 90 **23b.** 45 **23c.** Not possible; all vert. angles are $\cong$. **25.** 30 and 60 **27.** $\angle EIG$ and $\angle FIH$ are right angles by the markings. $\angle EIF \cong \angle GIH$ because they are complements of the same angle. **29.** Add. Prop. of =; Div. Prop. of = **31.** Mult. Prop. of =; Distr. Prop.; Add. Prop. of = **33.** Because $\angle 1$ and $\angle 2$ are supplementary, $m\angle 1 + m\angle 2 = 180$. Because $\angle 3$ and $\angle 4$ are supplementary, $m\angle 3 + m\angle 4 = 180$. So, $m\angle 1 + m\angle 2 = m\angle 3 + m\angle 4$. Because $\angle 2 \cong \angle 4$, $m\angle 2 = m\angle 4$. Thus, by Subtraction Prop. of =, $m\angle 1 = m\angle 3$ and $\angle 1 \cong \angle 3$. **35.** No; guys with beards may not park on Mon. **37.** No; parking is not allowed from 6:49 A.M. to 9:11 A.M. on Tues.

MIXED REVIEW **39.** A B C

41.

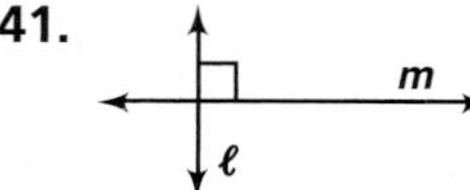

43. 5 **45.** 11.1 **47.** 9.8

CHECKPOINT **1.** A good definition states precisely what a term is, using commonly understood or previously defined terms. **2a.**

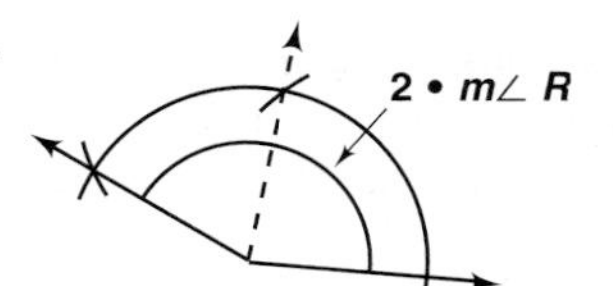

2b. **2c.**

3. $m\angle 1 + m\angle 2 = 90$

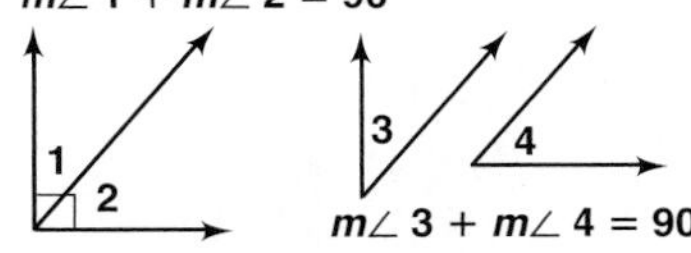

4. C

Lesson 1-8 pages 618–619

ON YOUR OWN **7.** 6 **9.** 8 **11.** 23.3 **13.** 25 **15.** 12.0 **17.** (3, 1) **19.** (6, 1) **21.** $\left(3\frac{7}{8}, -3\right)$ **23.** (8, 18) **25.** No; $AD = AB \approx 4.2$, $DC = CB \approx 3.2$. **29a.** 19.2 **29b.** (−1.5, 0) **31a.** 5.4 **31b.** (−1, 0.5) **33a.** $A(0, 0, 0)$, $B(3, 0, 0)$, $C(3, -3, 0)$, $D(0, -3, 0)$ $E(0, 0, 5)$, $F(3, 0, 5)$, $G(0, -3, 5)$
33b.

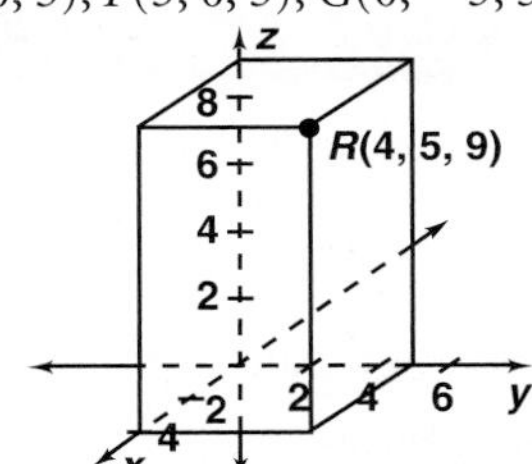

MIXED REVIEW **35.** 72; 162 **37.** 66.5; 156.5 **39.** 12; 102

Wrap Up pages 621–624

1. 17, 21; add 4 to the previous term to get the next term. **2.** 63, 127; add consecutively increasing powers of 2 to the previous term to get the next term. **3.** $\frac{5}{6}, \frac{6}{7}$; add 1 to the numerator and denominator of the preceding term to get the next term. **4.** 5, −6; write the sequence of whole numbers and then change the signs of the even whole numbers.
5. **6a.** 76 **6b.** The last two digits will always be 76. **7.** If the points were collinear, an infinite number of planes would pass through them. **8–13.** Answers may vary. Samples are given. **8.** $\overleftrightarrow{QR}$ and $\overleftrightarrow{RS}$ **9.** $\overleftrightarrow{QR}$ and $\overleftrightarrow{SC}$ **10.** Q, R, and S **11.** Q, R, S, C **12.** plane $QRST$ and plane $ABCD$ **13.** $\overleftrightarrow{AD}$, $\overleftrightarrow{CD}$, $\overleftrightarrow{TD}$ **14.** always **15.** sometimes **16.** never **17.** always **18.** always **19.** never **21.** 3 or −7 **22.** 18 **23.** 31 **24.** 20 **25.** $m\angle KJD + m\angle DJH = m\angle KJH$ by the Angle Add. Post.; $m\angle KJD = m\angle DJH$ by the markings; $\overrightarrow{JD}$ bisects $\angle KJH$ by the definition of angle bisector. **26.** $AB = CD$ by the markings; $AC = BD$ by the Seg. Add. Post. **27.** $\angle 1 \cong \angle 4$ by the markings; $\angle 1 \cong \angle 2$ and $\angle 3 \cong \angle 4$ because vert. angles are $\cong$; $\angle 2 \cong \angle 3$ by the Trans. Prop. of $\cong$. **29.** No; $\overleftrightarrow{BK}$ may not bisect $\overline{LJ}$. **30.** 3 **31.** 1 **32.** D **33.**

34a–b.

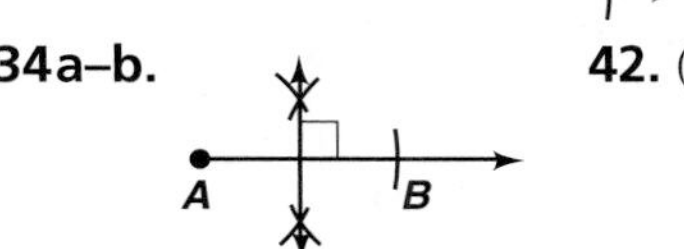

42. (0, 0) **43.** 3.2

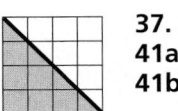

44a. **44b.** $AB = 3$, $AC = 5$, $BC \approx 5.8$ **44c.** $\overline{BC}$, $\overline{AC}$, $\overline{AB}$

Preparing for the Math A Exam page 627

1. 2 **3.** 1 **5.** 3

CHAPTER 2

Lesson 2-1 pages 633–636

ON YOUR OWN **1.** acute isosceles **3.** right scalene **9a.** 60; the sum of measures is 180 and the 3 measures are =. **9b.** 90; the sum of measures is 180 and the measure of the 3rd angle is 90. **11.** 115.5 **13.** $t = 60$; $w = 60$ **15.** 83.1 **17.** $a = 67$; $b = 58$; $c = 125$; $d = 23$; $e = 90$ **19.** 103 **21.** C **25.** 33° **27.** 37, 78, 65; acute **29.** $>$ 180; measures of both angles at the equator = 90 and the angle at the pole has pos. measure. **31a.** $\frac{1}{3}$ **31b.** $\frac{1}{7}$ **33a.** 900; 30, 60, 90 **33b.** right

MIXED REVIEW **35.** **37.** 10.0 **39.** 7 **41a.** 60, 120, 60, 120 **41b.** 360

Toolbox page 637

INVESTIGATE 360

CONJECTURE The sum of measures of the exterior angles of a polygon is always 360.

EXTEND When the polygon "disappears," the angles become adjacent. The sum of their measures is 360.

Lesson 2-2 pages 641–643

ON YOUR OWN **1.** convex dodecagon **3.** convex octagon **5.** **7.**

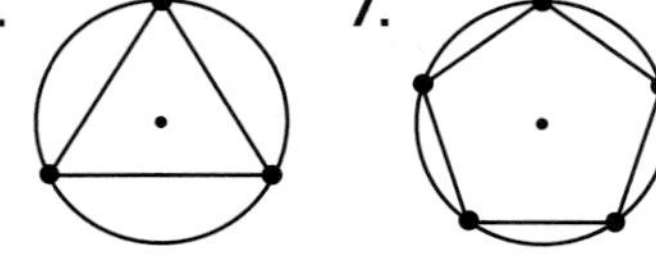

9. octagon; $m\angle 1 = 135$; $m\angle 2 = 45$ **11.** 140; 40
13. $\frac{180y - 360}{y}$; $\frac{360}{y}$ **15.** 10 **17.** $\frac{360}{x}$ **19.** 102
21. $y = 103$; $z = 70$ **23.** $x = 69$; $w = 111$ **25.** 113
27a. (20, 162), (40, 171), (60, 174), (80, 175.5), (100, 176.4), (120, 177), (140, 177.4), (160, 177.8), (180, 178), (200, 178.2)
27b.

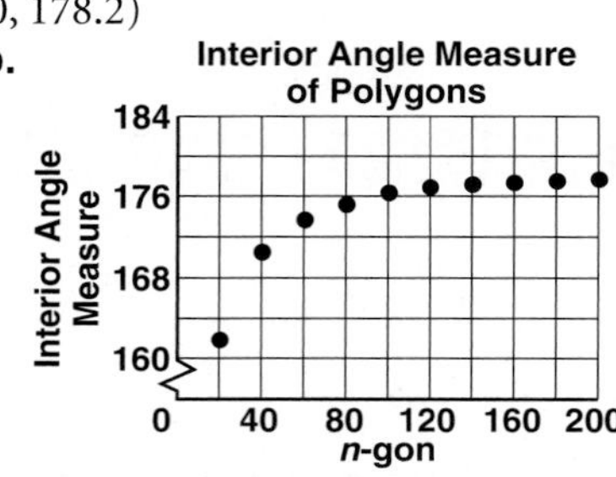

27c. very close to 180 **27d.** No; a regular polygon with all straight angles would have all its vertices on a straight line.

MIXED REVIEW **31.** $\overrightarrow{RT}$ and $\overrightarrow{RK}$ **33.** Answers may vary. Sample: $\angle BRT$ and $\angle BRK$ **35.** 40.25 **37.** $x = 104$; $y = 35$ **39.** 72 and 18 **41.** -1 **43.** 0

Toolbox page 644

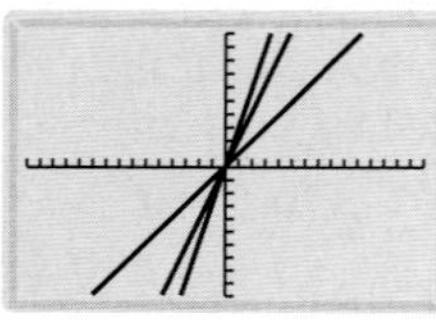

INVESTIGATE The value of m affects the steepness of the line.

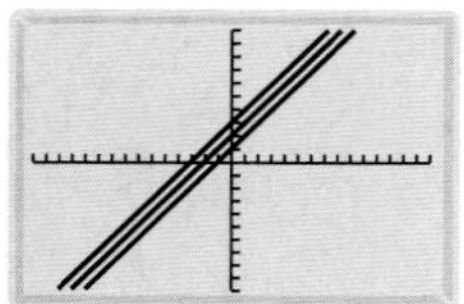

Changing the value of b shifts the line vertically.

CONJECTURE Answers may vary. Samples: A line with pos. value of m goes from the lower left to the upper right. The greater the abs. value of m the steeper the line. For neg. values of b, the line shifts down by the number of units = to the abs. value of b. The line passes through the origin if $b = 0$.

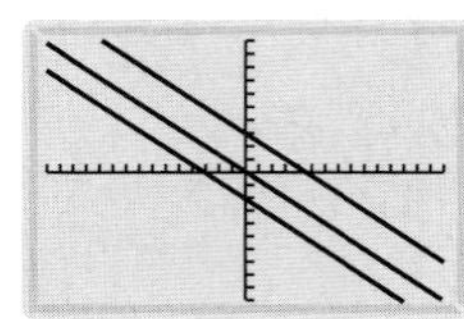

EXTEND The lines are $\parallel$; the values of m are =; lines with equations that have = values of m are $\parallel$.

a.

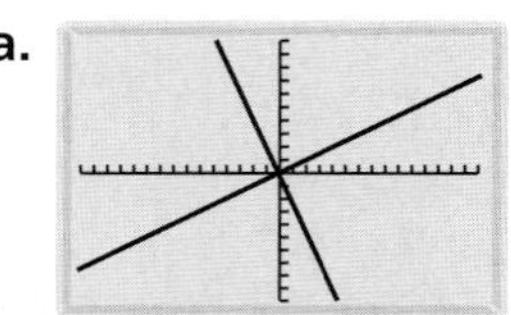

b.

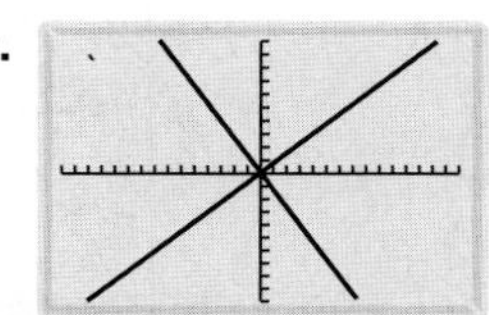

c.

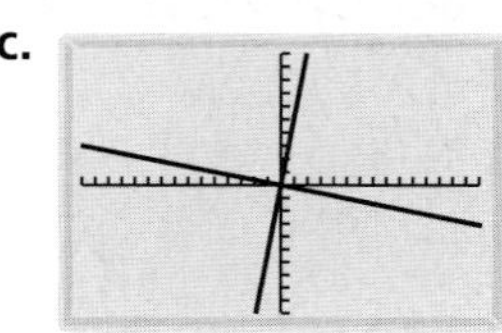

The lines are $\perp$; the product of the values of m is -1; 2 lines with equations in which the product of values of m is -1 are $\perp$.

Lesson 2-3 pages 648–650

ON YOUR OWN **1.** k: pos.; ℓ: neg.; s: 0; t: undef.
3. No; lines with no slope are vert. Lines with slope 0 are horizontal. **5.** undef.; 0; perpendicular **7.** $-\frac{1}{8}$; 8; perpendicular **9.** 0; 0; parallel **11.** No; the slopes of the sides are $\frac{3}{5}$, $-\frac{5}{8}$, and $-\frac{8}{3}$. No 2 sides are $\perp$.

13.

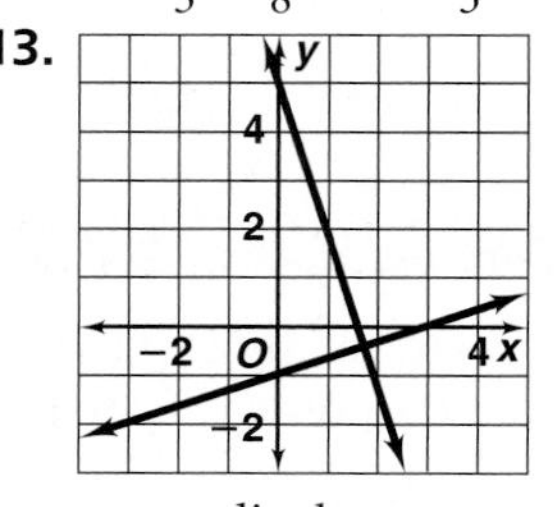

perpendicular

15.

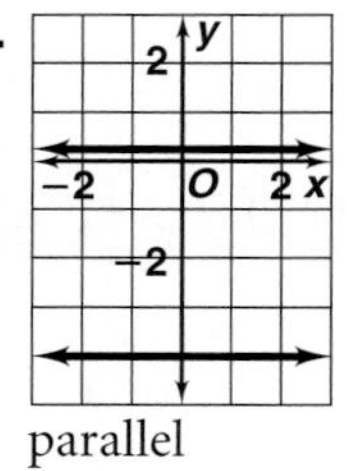

parallel

17.

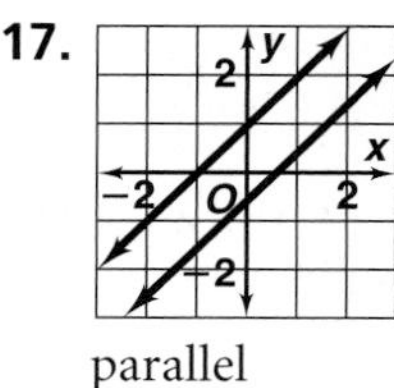

parallel

19.

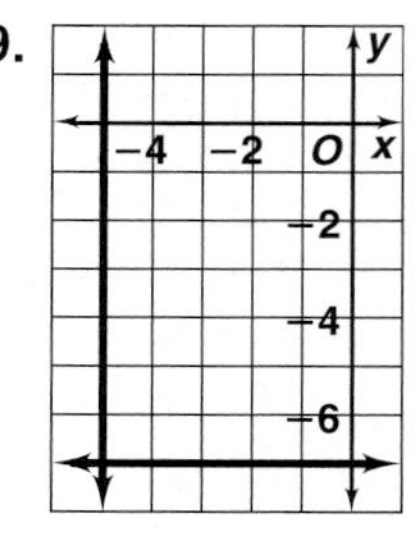

perpendicular

21a.

21b. $x = -5$ **21d.** $y = 2$ **21e.** The lines are $\perp$; a horizontal line is always $\perp$ to a vert. line. **23.** yes

25.

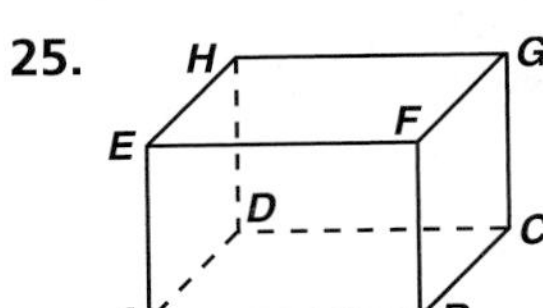

25a. $\overleftrightarrow{AB} \perp \overleftrightarrow{FB}$, $\overleftrightarrow{BC} \perp \overleftrightarrow{FB}$, $\overleftrightarrow{AB} \perp \overleftrightarrow{BC}$
25b. $\overleftrightarrow{AB} \perp \overleftrightarrow{BC}$, $\overleftrightarrow{BC} \perp \overleftrightarrow{CG}$, $\overleftrightarrow{AB}$ and $\overleftrightarrow{CG}$ are skew lines. **27.** Answers may vary. Sample: No; the "lines" intersect twice. **29a.** (1, 10), (2, 20), (3, 30), (4, 40), (5, 50), (6, 60), (7, 70), (8, 80), (9, 90), (10, 100)

29b.

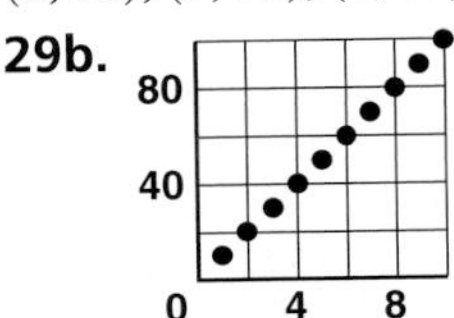

29c. The slope is 1000. **29d.** Sample: Yes; you can make the slope as steep as you want, but it will never be vertical.

MIXED REVIEW **31.** 25.5 **33.** 22.5 and 67.5 **35.** $\overline{FG}$ and $\overline{EH}$, $\overline{EF}$ and $\overline{GH}$

CHECKPOINT **1.**

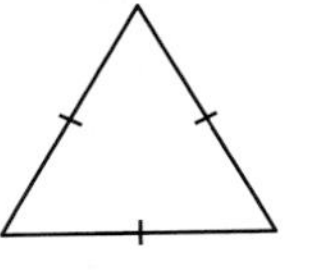

2.

3.

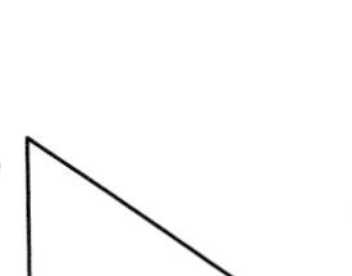

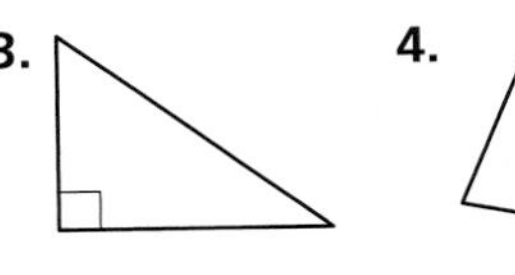

4.

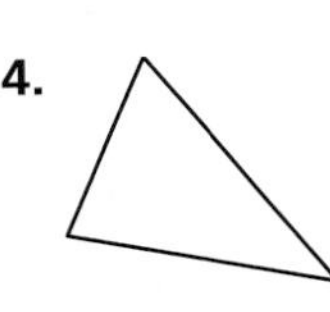

5.

6.

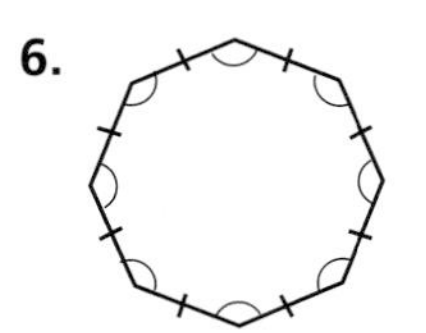

7.

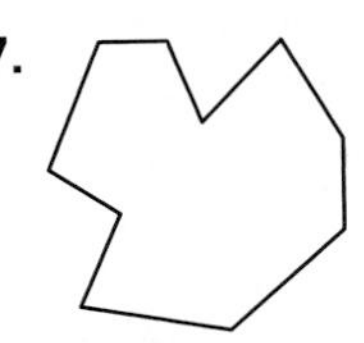

8.

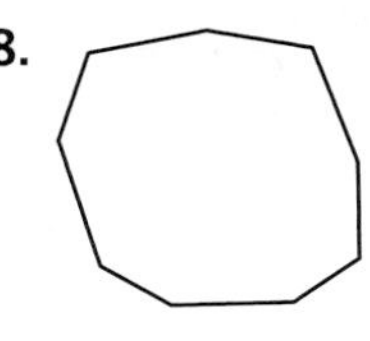

9. (1) Divide 360 by n to find the exterior angle measure. Subtract the result from 180.
(2) Multiply 180 by $n - 2$ and divide the result by n.
10. $-\frac{2}{5}$; $\frac{5}{2}$; perpendicular **11.** 1; -1; perpendicular
12. $-\frac{5}{4}$; $\frac{4}{5}$ perpendicular **13.** $\frac{2}{9}$; $\frac{2}{9}$; parallel

Toolbox page 651

1. $y = 3x + 5$ **5.** $y = -\frac{5}{4}x + 8$ **9.** $y = -x + 7$

13. $y = 5x - 10$

Lesson 2-4 pages 655–657

ON YOUR OWN **1.** parallelogram, rhombus, rectangle, square **3.** trapezoid **5.** true **7.** false **9.** false

17.

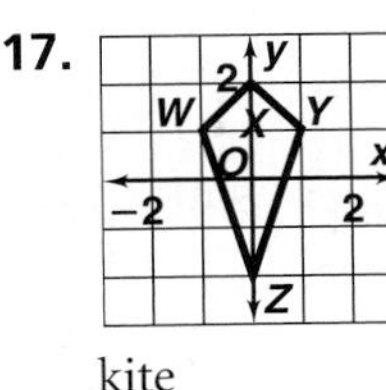

kite

19.

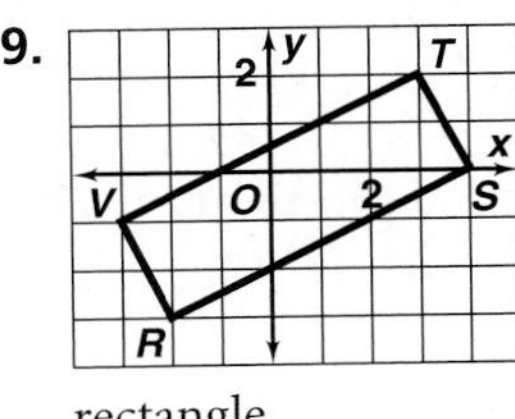

rectangle

21. some isosceles trapezoids some trapezoids

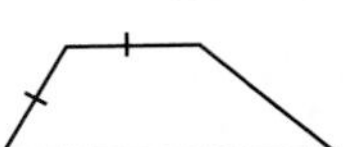

23. rectangle square

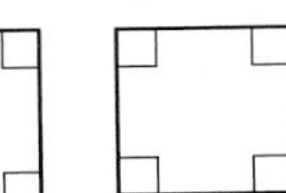

25. $x = 11$; $y = 21$; 13, 13, 15, 15 **27.** $b = 9$; $r = 5$; 6, 6, 6, 6 **29.** parallelogram, kite, rhombus, trapezoid, isos. trapezoid **31.** parallelogram, rectangle, square, kite, trapezoid

MIXED REVIEW **33.** 8.2
35a. **35b.** **37.** 33% **39.** 75%

Lesson 2-5 pages 661–663

ON YOUR OWN **1, 3, 7.** Answers may vary. **1.** Sample: $\widehat{BC}$, $\widehat{CD}$ **3.** Sample: $\widehat{BCE}$, $\widehat{BFE}$ **5.** $\overline{BE}$, $\overline{CF}$ **7.** Sample: $\angle BOC$ **9.** $\angle BOC$, $\angle EOF$ **11.** 10 cm **13.** $12\sqrt{2}$ in. **15.** 6.5 cm **17.** $\frac{5\sqrt{3}}{2}$ in. **19.** $\frac{d}{2}$ km **23.** $(-2, 5)$; $\sqrt{5}$ **25.** $(-1, 4)$; $\sqrt{10}$ **27.** $(3, -4.5)$; 8.5 **29.** 180 **31.** 52 **33.** 180 **35.** 90 **39a.** 6°; 30°; 120° **39b.** 2.5°; 5°; 10° **39c.** 102.5 **41a.** 90 **41b.** 30 **41c.** 145 **41d.** 125 **41e.** 235 **41f.** 215 **43a.** 80 **43b.** 100 **43c.** 150 **43d.** 210 **43e.** 280 **45.** 160 **47.** Stay in the circle for a 220° arc before exiting.

MIXED REVIEW **51.** 95 **53.** $t = 120$; $y = 60$ **55.** 37

Lesson 2-6 pages 667–670

ON YOUR OWN **1.** A and H, B and G, C and E, F and D **3.** $\overline{CM}$ **5.** $\angle B$ **7.** $\angle J$ **9.** $\triangle CLM$ **11.** HY **13.** HY **15.** $\angle R$ **17.** $\frac{2}{3}$ **19.** 50 **21.** 70 **23.** 7.5 cm **25.** $\angle P \cong \angle S$; $\angle O \cong \angle I$; $\angle L \cong \angle D$; $\angle Y \cong \angle E$ **27a.** *IDES* **27b.** *LYPO* **31.** Yes; the ratios of radii, diameters, and circumferences of 2 circles are =. **33.** $\triangle BEC \cong \triangle AED$ **35.** $t = 2$ in.; $x = 15$ **37.** 2.3 cm **39a.** 7.2 cm; 9.6 cm; 12 cm **39b.** 53; 90; 37 **39c.** 9 cm; 12 cm; 15 cm **41.** $\frac{3}{4}$ **43a.** yes; $\frac{8}{16} = \frac{10}{20}$ **43b.** no; $\frac{4}{5} \neq \frac{5}{7}$

MIXED REVIEW

47.

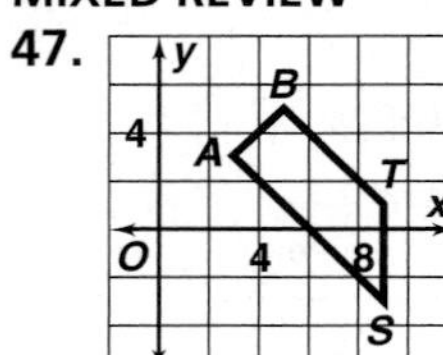

Trapezoid; slope of $\overline{BT}$ = slope of $\overline{AS}$.
Trapezoid; slope of $\overline{AB} \neq$ slope of $\overline{ST}$.
49. 160 **51.** a rectangle

CHECKPOINT **1.** (5.5, 3); 2.5 **2.** (1.5, 7); $\frac{\sqrt{13}}{2}$ **3.** (0.5, 3.5); $\frac{\sqrt{170}}{2}$ **4.** (−5, −0.5); $\frac{\sqrt{117}}{2}$ **5.** 65 **6.** 90 **7.** 25 **8.** 245 **9.** 115 **10.** 90 **11.** 25 **12.** 180 **13.** 180

14.

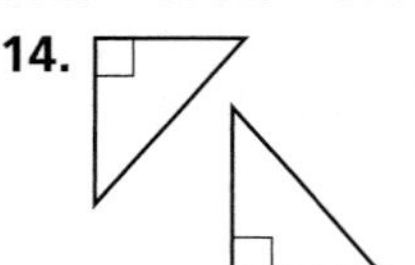

15.

16.

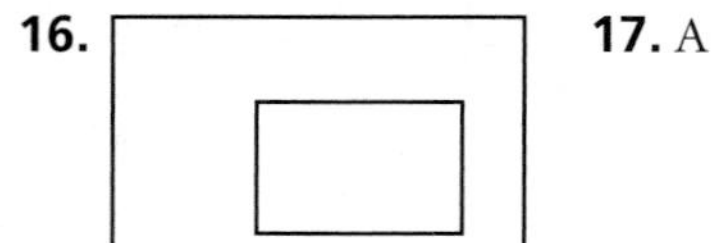

17. A

Lesson 2-7 pages 674–677

ON YOUR OWN

1a.

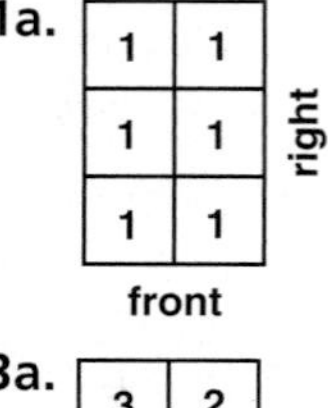

1b.

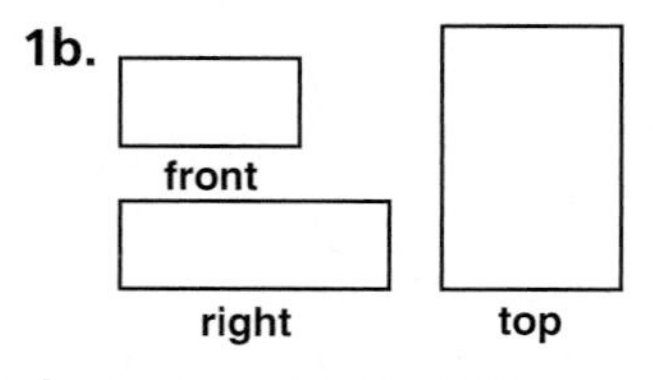

3a.

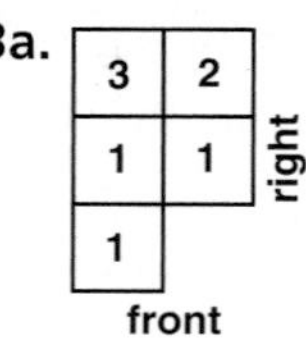

3b.

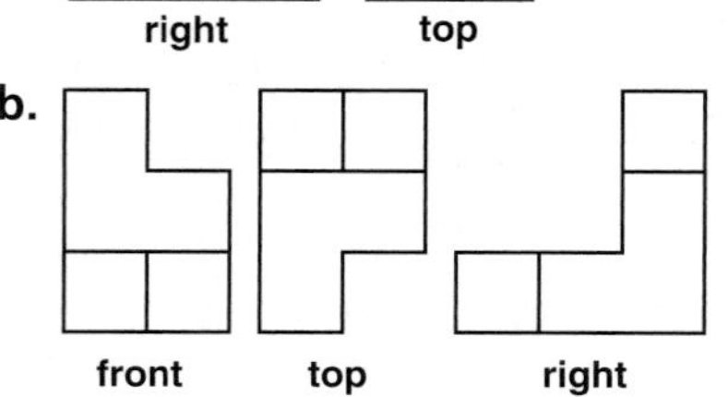

5a.

5b.

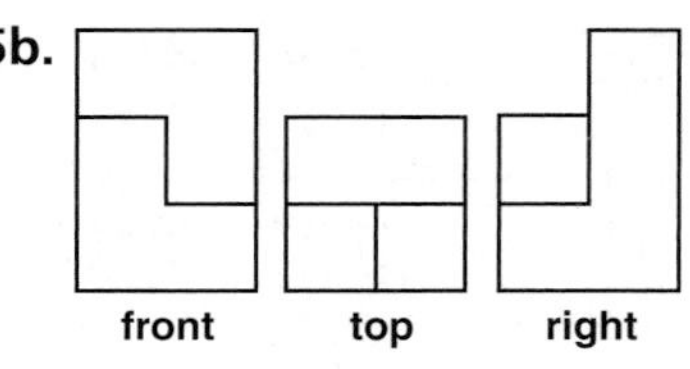

7a.

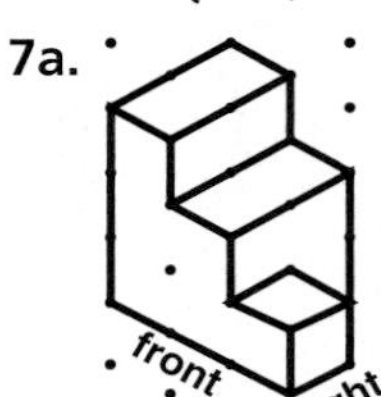

7b.

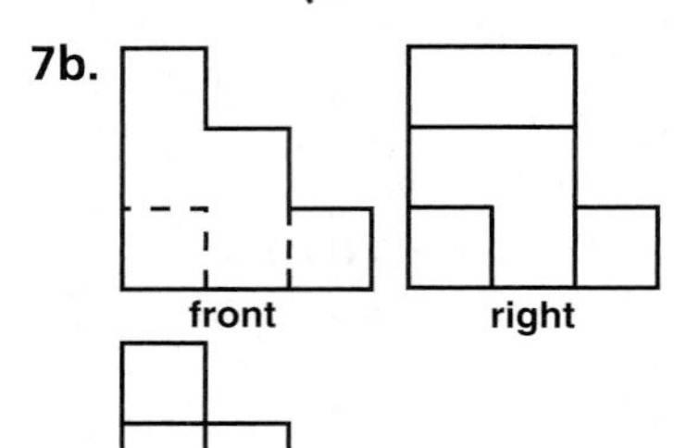

13. triangle
15. isosceles triangle
17. B **19.** D

21. **23.**

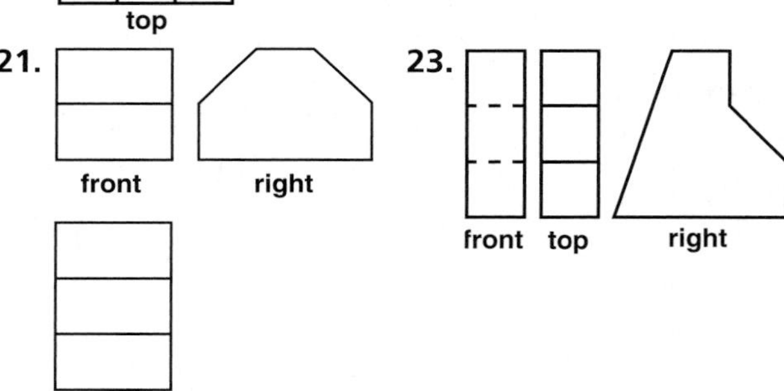

25.

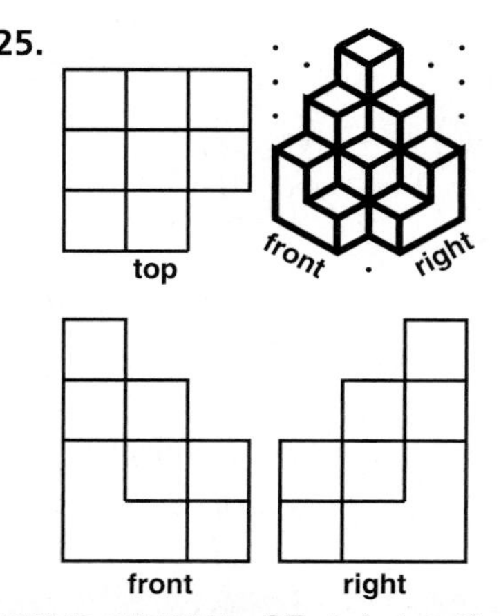

MIXED REVIEW **27.** 5; (−1, 0.5)

Wrap Up pages 679–681

1. 61; scalene acute **2.** 35; isosceles obtuse **3.** $x = 60$; $y = 60$; equilateral; equiangular **4.** $x = 45$; $y = 45$; isosceles; right **5.** D **6.** 120; 60 **7.** 135; 45 **8.** 144; 36 **9.** 165; 15 **10.** 8; 14, 9, 7, 9 **11.** $m = 4$; $t = 5$; 7, 14, 14, 7 **12.** $a = 1$; $b = 2$; 6, 6, 6, 6 **13.** 5; 3; neither **14.** 4; 4; parallel **15.** $-\frac{1}{3}$; 3; perpendicular **16.** 1; 1; parallel **17.** (4, 3); 3 **18.** (1, −1); $\sqrt{5}$ **19.** (−1, −3); $\sqrt{13}$ **20.** (5.5, 5); $\frac{3\sqrt{5}}{2}$ **21.** 30 **22.** 120 **23.** 330 **24.** 120 **25.** $\overline{ML}$ **26.** $\angle U$ **27.** $\overline{ST}$ **28.** *ONMLK*

30a. **30b.**

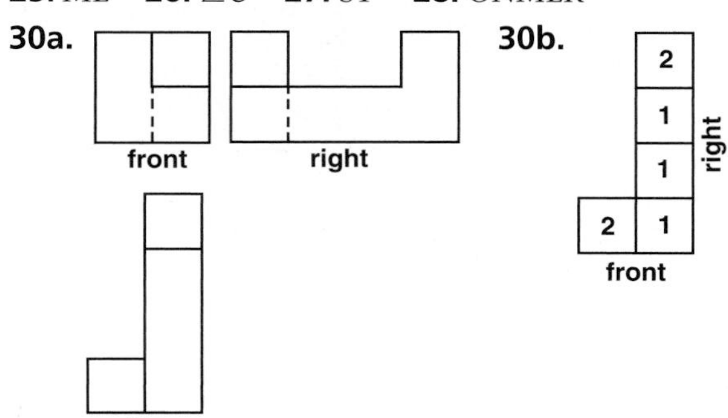

32. **33.**

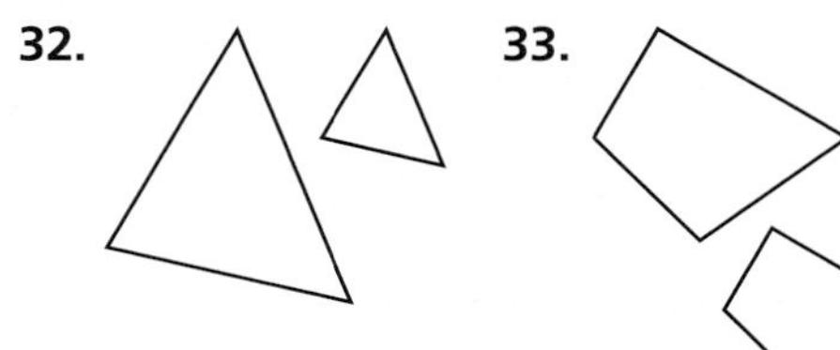

34. **35.**

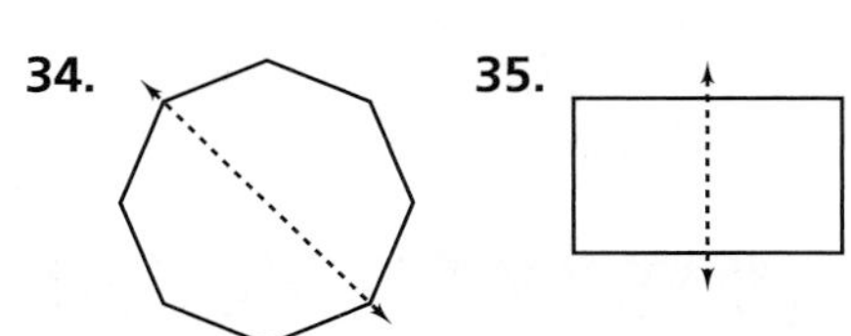

36. **37.**

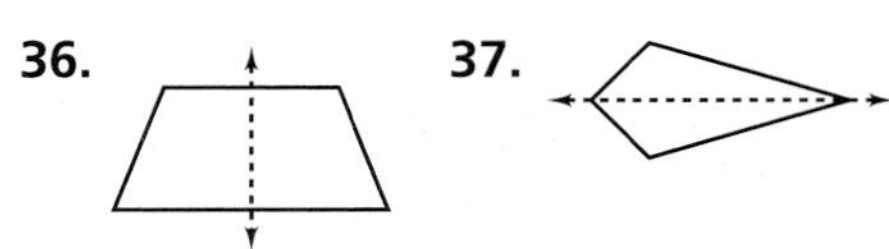

Preparing for the Math A Exam page 683

1. 1 **3.** 2 **5.** 3

CHAPTER 3

Lesson 3-1 pages 690–692

ON YOUR OWN

1. **3.** BOX

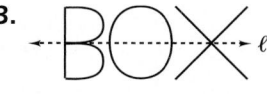

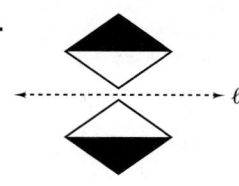

5a. $\overline{PQ}$ and $\overline{P'Q'}$, $\overline{QR}$ and $\overline{Q'R'}$, $\overline{RS}$ and $\overline{R'S'}$, $\overline{SP}$ and $\overline{S'P'}$ **5b.** isometry **5c.** opposite **7a.** $\overline{AR}$ and $\overline{A'R'}$, $\overline{RT}$ and $\overline{R'T'}$, $\overline{TA}$ and $\overline{T'A'}$ **7b.** not isometry **7c.** opposite **9a.** $\overline{RI}$ and $\overline{R'I'}$, $\overline{IT}$ and $\overline{I'T'}$, $\overline{TR}$ and $\overline{T'R'}$ **9b.** not isometry **9c.** opposite

11. **15.**

17.

21a. Answers may vary. Sample: The writing hand would not cover what was already written.

21b. Write the mirror image of this sentence. **23.**

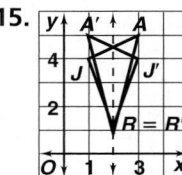

25a. S-Isomer
25b. Samples: gloves, shoes, scissors **27.** First and third panels; the figures in the second panel are not ≅, and the fourth panel shows a slide. **29.** No; the points farthest from the line of reflection move the farthest.

MIXED REVIEW **31.** rectangle **33a.** (−1, −1) **33b.** 2 **33c.** $-\frac{1}{2}$ **33d.** $y = -\frac{1}{2}x - \frac{3}{2}$

Toolbox page 693

1. $\begin{bmatrix} 11 & 10 \\ 1 & 12 \end{bmatrix}$ **5.** $\begin{bmatrix} 8 & 11.3 \\ 15 & 11.1 \end{bmatrix}$ **9.** $\begin{bmatrix} 447 & 18 & 20 \\ 546 & 23 & 10 \\ 450 & 22 & 18 \\ 396 & 30 & 22 \end{bmatrix}$

Selected Answers

Lesson 3-2 pages 697–699

ON YOUR OWN **1.** $\langle 1, -3\rangle$ **3.** $\langle 1, -1\rangle$ **5.** $\langle 4, -2\rangle$ **7.** C **9.** I **11.** H **13.**

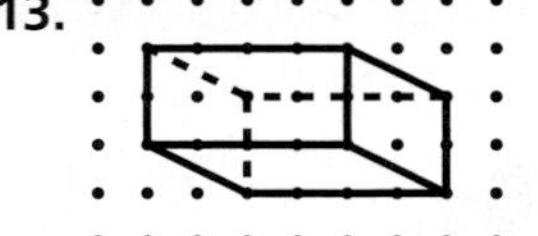

15.

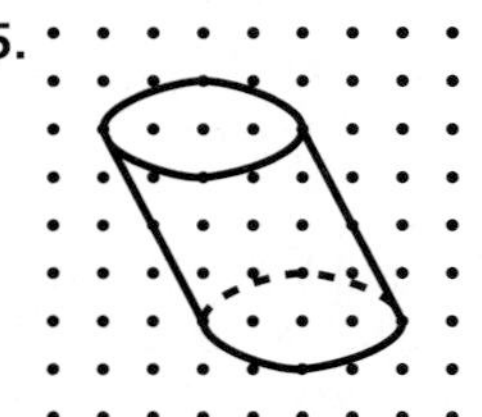

17. $\begin{matrix} A' & C' & E' \end{matrix}$ $\begin{bmatrix} -2 & -17 & -9 \\ 6 & 9 & -2 \end{bmatrix}$

19. $\begin{matrix} N' & I' & L' & E' \end{matrix}$ $\begin{bmatrix} -1 & -1 & -6 & -6 \\ -9 & -2 & 0 & -7 \end{bmatrix}$

21. $U'(1, 16)$; $G'(2, 12)$ **25.** $\langle 0, 0\rangle$ **27a.** $\langle -4, -2\rangle$

27b.

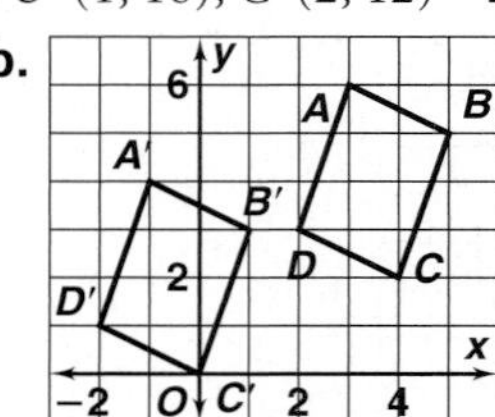

MIXED REVIEW **29.** bisector **31a.**

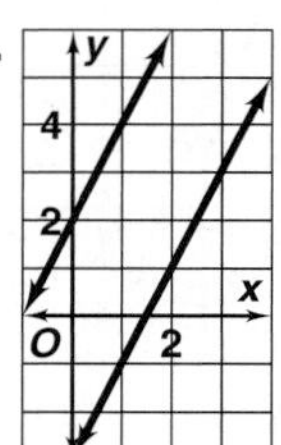

31b. 2, −3; 2, 2
31c. The lines are ∥.
33. 300°
35. 450°

Lesson 3-3 pages 703–705

1.

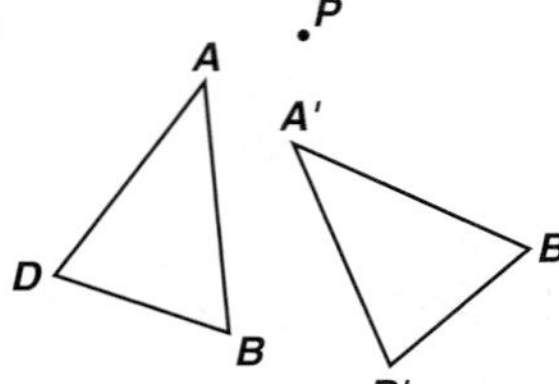

3.

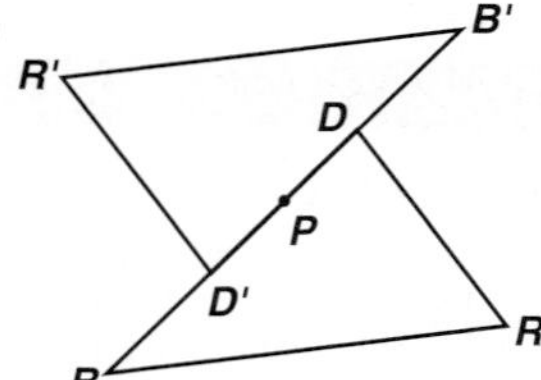

5. K P P' T' T K'

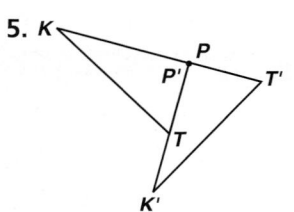

7. 110 **9.** 180 **11.** M **13.** $\overline{BC}$ **15.** I **17.** J
21. $\overline{MN} \cong \overline{M'N'}$, $\overline{ME} \cong \overline{M'E}$, $\overline{EN} \cong \overline{EN'}$, $\angle MEN \cong \angle M'EN'$, $\angle MNE \cong \angle M'N'E$, $\angle EMN \cong \angle EM'N'$, $\angle MEM' \cong \angle NEN'$

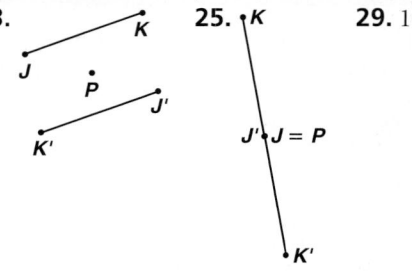

23. K J P J' K' **25.** K J' J = P K' **29.** 108

MIXED REVIEW **31.** Sample:

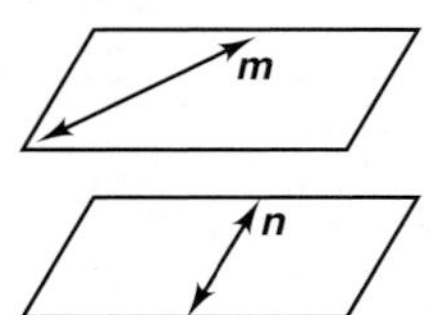

35. Sample:

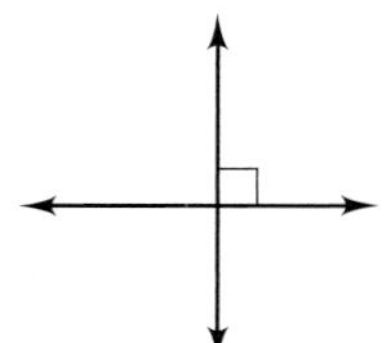

CHECKPOINT **1.** (3, −4) **2.** (−4, 3) **3.** (1, 11) **4.** (4, −3) **5.** (4, −1) **6.** (4, 3) **7.** Images and preimages under translations, reflections, and rotations are congruent to each other. Translations and rotations do not affect orientation. Reflection reverses orientation. **8a.** $\overline{AD}$ and $\overline{A'D'}$, $\overline{AF}$ and $\overline{A'F'}$, $\overline{DF}$ and $\overline{D'F'}$ **8b.** No; the image is not ≅ to the preimage.

Lesson 3-4 pages 709–712

ON YOUR OWN **1.** 60° **3.** 30° **5a.** III **5b.** IV **5c.** II **5d.** I

7.

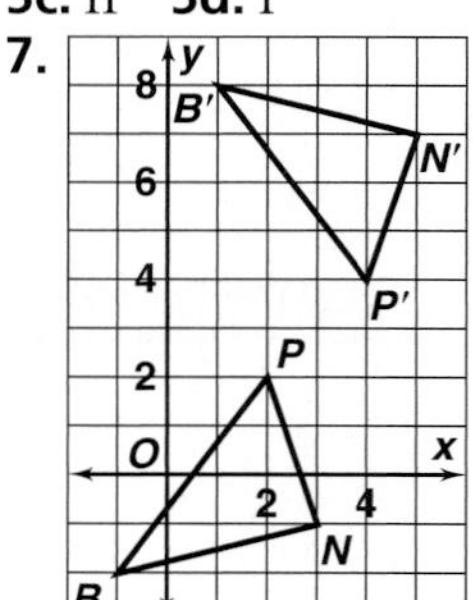

11. y N' 4 P' P B' O x 2 4 N B

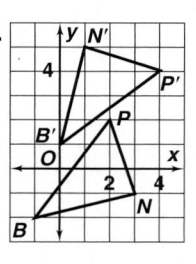

13. translation **15.** rotation **17.** glide reflection **19.** glide reflection **21.** rotation **23.** translation **25.** reflection **27.** rotation **31.** Rotations and glide reflections are equally likely to occur. They are more likely

to occur than translations and reflections.

MIXED REVIEW **33.** 79, 130 and 151 **35a.** true **35b.** false **35c.** true **37.** Each figure maps onto itself.

Toolbox page 713

INVESTIGATE All 6 polygons change in the same way; yes.

Lesson 3-5 pages 717–720

ON YOUR OWN

1. 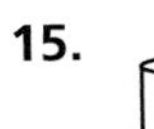

3. rotational: 90°, point **5.** point **7.** no symmetry **9.** reflectional **11.** rotational **13.** any isosceles but not equilateral △

15. 

17.

19. reflectional, rotational **21.** point **23.** reflectional, rotational **25.** reflectional, rotational **27.** reflectional, point

31.

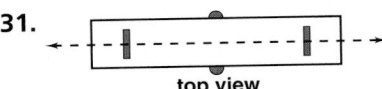

top view

33a.

Language	Horizontal Line	Vertical Line	Point
English	B, C, D, E, H, I, K, O, X	A, H, I, M, O, T, U, V, W, X, Y	H, I, N, O, S, X, Z
Greek	B, E, H, Θ, I, K, Ξ, O, Σ, Φ, X	A, Δ, H, Θ, I, Λ, M, Ξ, O, Π, T, Y, Φ, X, Ψ, Ω	Z, H, Θ, I, N, Ξ, O, Φ, X

35. reflectional in y-axis

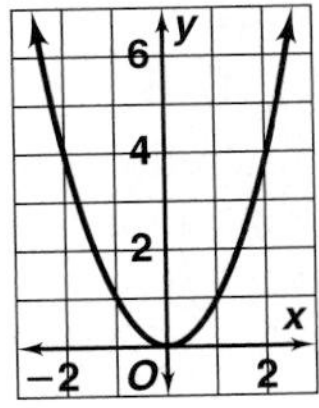

37. point

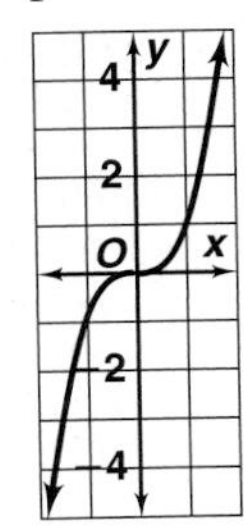

45. (3, −4)

MIXED REVIEW **47.** 1 **49.** $\frac{7}{3}$ **51.** 0; 3

CHECKPOINT **1.** rotational **2.** point **3.** reflectional, point **4.** $C'(-4, 3), A'(-1, 6), L'(-3, 2)$

Lesson 3-6 pages 725–727

ON YOUR OWN

1. 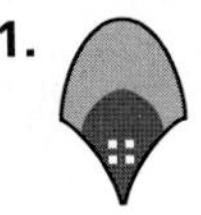

3. 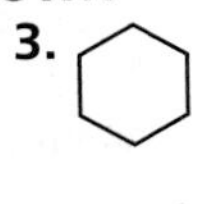

5. 

rotational, point, reflectional, glide reflectional, and translational

9. 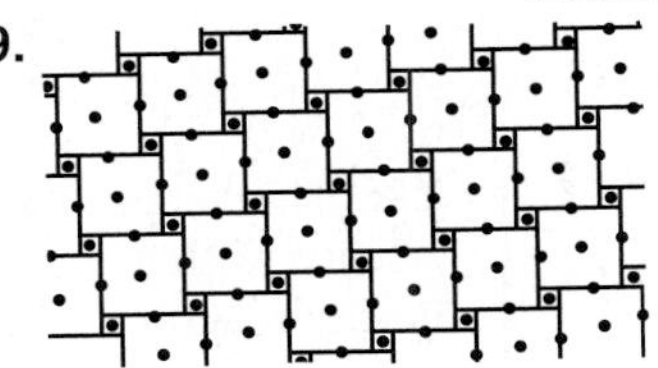

rotational, point, and translational

13. **15.**

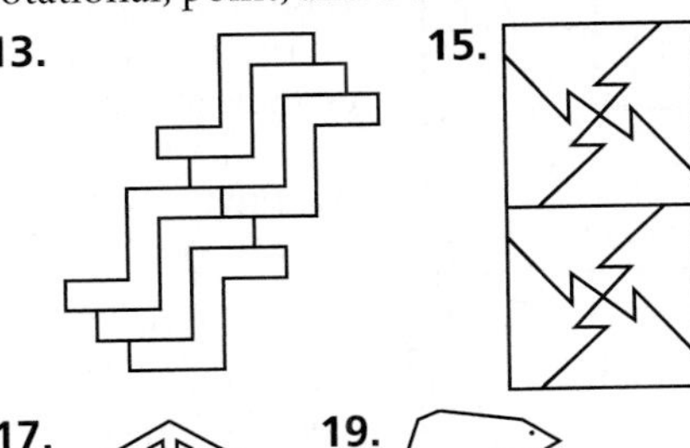

17. 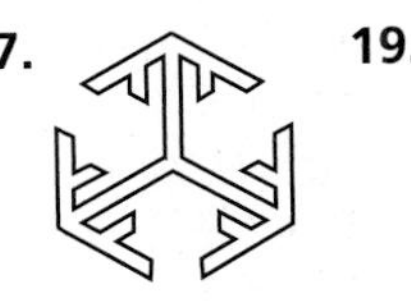

19. 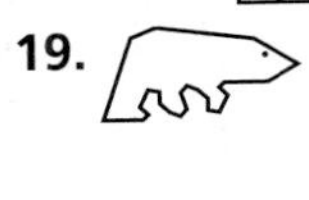

MIXED REVIEW **21.** equilateral, equiangular **23.** scalene, right **25a.** $\overline{BD}$ **25b.** Sample: $\widehat{BCE}$ **25c.** Sample: $\widehat{ED}$ **25d.** Sample: $\overline{AE}$ **25e.** Sample: $\angle BAE$ **25f.** Sample: $\widehat{BE}$ and $\widehat{ED}$ **27a.** 3; 10 **27b.** 2

Lesson 3-7 pages 730–734

ON YOUR OWN

1. 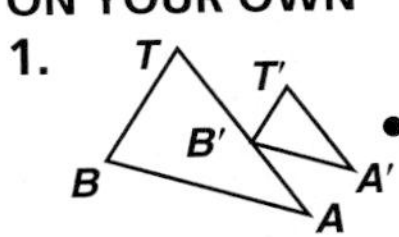

3. $T' = T$

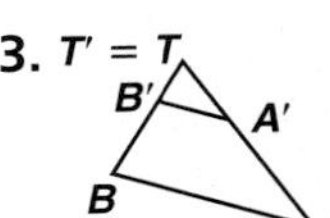

5a. reduction **5b.** $\frac{1}{3}$ **7a.** enlargement **7b.** 3 **9a.** enlargement **9b.** $\frac{3}{2}$ **11a.** reduction **11b.** $\frac{2}{5}$

13. $\begin{matrix} A' & B' & C' \end{matrix}$ $\begin{bmatrix} 3 & 9 & 15 \\ 0 & 6 & 3 \end{bmatrix}$ **15.** $\begin{matrix} A' & B' & C' \end{matrix}$ $\begin{bmatrix} -4 & -8 & -6 \\ 0 & -6 & 0 \end{bmatrix}$ **17.** about 343

19.

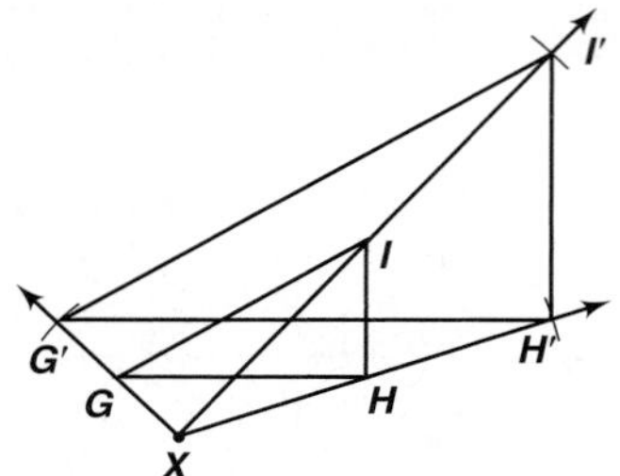

21. M = M' y N x −2 N' 4 6 Q' P' Q P

23a. $\begin{matrix} A' & B' & C' & D' \end{matrix}$

$$\begin{bmatrix} -6 & 6 & 6 & -6 \\ -6 & -6 & 6 & 6 \end{bmatrix}$$

23b.

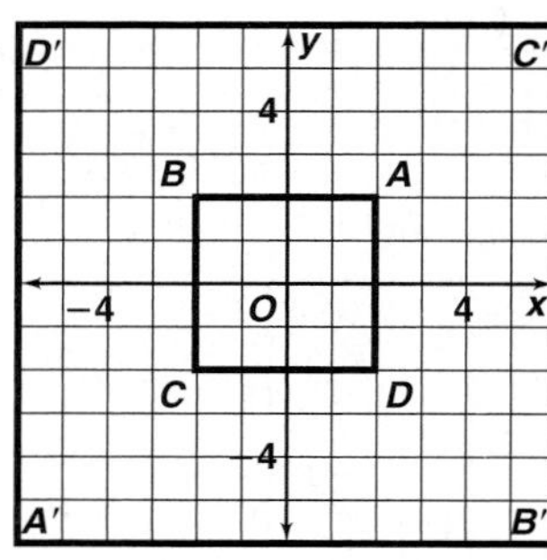

23c. The image of a dilation with a negative factor is the image of a dilation with a positive factor with the same absolute value, rotated 180° about the origin.

25. $\begin{matrix} Q' & R' & T' & W' \end{matrix}$

$$\begin{bmatrix} -9 & -6 & 9 & 9 \\ 12 & -3 & 3 & 15 \end{bmatrix}$$

27. $\begin{matrix} Q' & R' & T' & W' \end{matrix}$

$$\begin{bmatrix} -6 & -4 & 6 & 6 \\ 8 & -2 & 2 & 10 \end{bmatrix}$$

29a. vertex of V **29b.** $\frac{1}{2}$ **33.** 10; 12 **35.** 32; 7.5
37. True; the image and the preimage are similar.
39. False; a dilation does not change orientation.

MIXED REVIEW **41.** $x = 105; y = 75; z = 35$
43. $x = 85; y = 125$ **45.** trapezoid

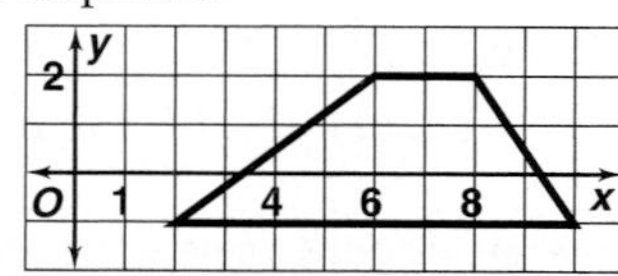

47.

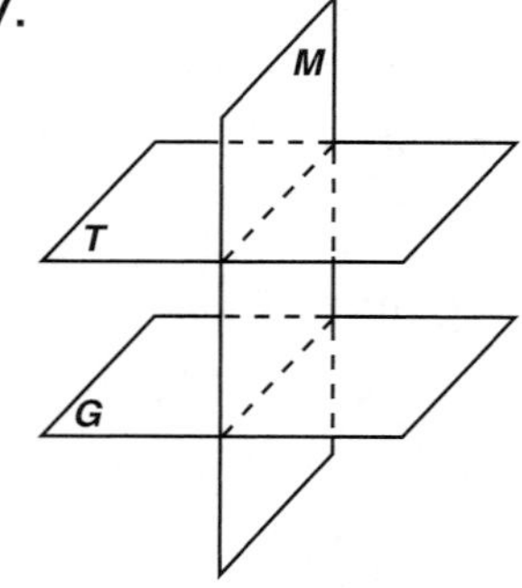

Wrap Up pages 736–739

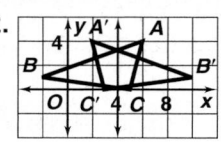

1.

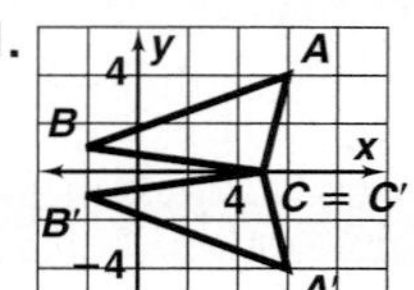

2. y A' A 4 B B' O C' 4 C 8 x

6. j

8.

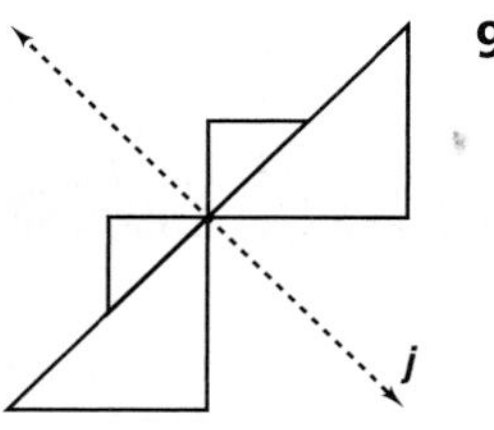

9. E

11. $A'(7, 12), B'(6, 6), C'(3, 5)$ **12.** $R'(-4, 3), S'(-6, 6), T'(-10, 8)$ **13.** $\langle 2, 8 \rangle$ **14.** $\langle -2, -1 \rangle$ **15.** $\langle 11, -4 \rangle$

16.

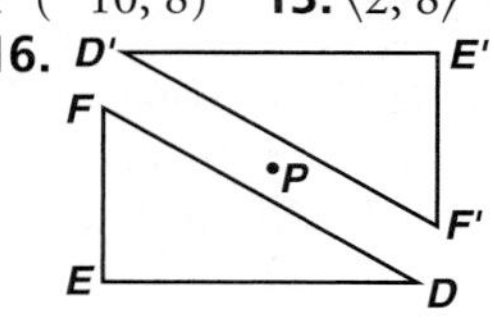

17.

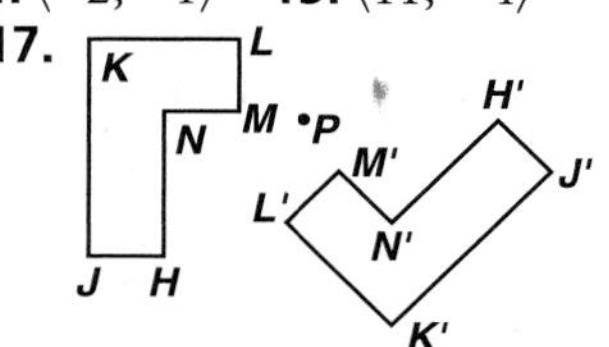

18.

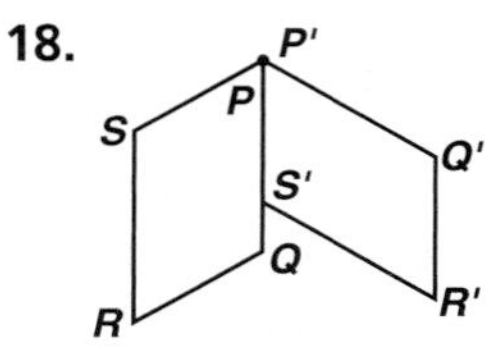

19.

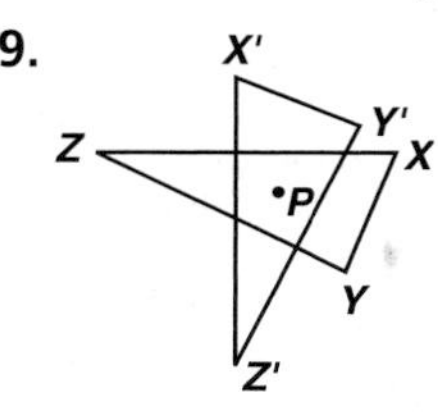

20. $(-2, 5)$ **21.** $(-3, 0)$ **22.** $(-1, -4)$ **23.** $(0, 7)$
24. $(8, -2)$ **25.** $(0, 0)$ **26a.** II **26b.** I **26c.** III
26d. IV **27a.** III **27b.** IV **27c.** II **27d.** I
28. $T'(-4, -9), A'(0, -5), M'(-1, -10)$ **29.** reflectional
30. 72° rotational **31.** 90° rotational, point
32a. **32b.** rotational, point, reflectional, translational, glide reflectional
33a. and **33b.** point, reflectional, translational, glide reflectional
34a. and **34b.** rotational, point, reflectional, translational, glide reflectional

35. $\begin{matrix} M' & A' & T' & H' \end{matrix}$

$$\begin{bmatrix} -15 & -30 & 0 & 15 \\ 20 & -5 & 0 & 10 \end{bmatrix}$$

36. $\begin{matrix} A' & N' & D' \end{matrix}$

$$\begin{bmatrix} 14 & -8 & 0 \\ -2 & -6 & 4 \end{bmatrix}$$

37. $\begin{matrix} W' & I' & T' & H' \end{matrix}$

$$\begin{bmatrix} 12 & 6 & 9 & 0 \\ 15 & 18 & 24 & 21 \end{bmatrix}$$

38. $\begin{matrix} F' & U' & N' \end{matrix}$

$$\begin{bmatrix} -2 & 2\frac{1}{2} & -1 \\ 0 & 0 & -2\frac{1}{2} \end{bmatrix}$$

39. Rotations, dilations and translations preserve orientation. Reflections and glide reflections reverse orientation. **40.** $(2, 8)$ **41.** $(1, 7)$ **42.** $(5, 4)$
43. isosceles, acute **44.** scalene, right **45.** isosceles,

obtuse **46.** scalene, acute

Preparing for the Math A Exam page 741

1. 4 **3.** 1 **5.** 1

CHAPTER 4

Lesson 4-1 pages 747–749

ON YOUR OWN **1.** You send in a proof-of-purchase label; they send you a get-well card. **3.** If $\underline{3x - 7 = 14}$, then $\underline{3x = 21}$. **5.** If a triangle is isosceles, then it has two congruent sides. **7.** 1 and 9 are not prime. **9.** Softball and cricket are sports played with a ball and a bat. **11a.** If you grow, then you will eat all of your vegetables. **11b.** If you do not eat all of your vegetables, then you will not grow. **11c.** If you do not grow, then you will not eat all of your vegetables. **15a.** If 2 segments have the same length, then they are ≅. **15b.** If 2 segments are not ≅, then they have different lengths. **15c.** If 2 segments have different lengths, then they are not ≅. **19a.** If you have a passport, then you travel from the U.S. to Kenya. **19b.** true; false **23a.** If the slopes of 2 nonvertical lines are =, then they are ∥. **23b.** true; true **23c.** 2 nonvertical lines are ∥ if and only if their slopes are =. **29.** If the sum of the digits of a number is divisible by 3, then the number is divisible by 3; if a number is divisible by 3, then the sum of the digits of the number is divisible by 3. **33a.** If a polygon is regular, then all its sides are ≅. **33b.** If not all the sides of a polygon are ≅, the polygon is not regular. **35a.** If a transformation is a rotation, then it is an isometry. **35b.** If a transformation is not an isometry, it is not a rotation.

MIXED REVIEW
37.

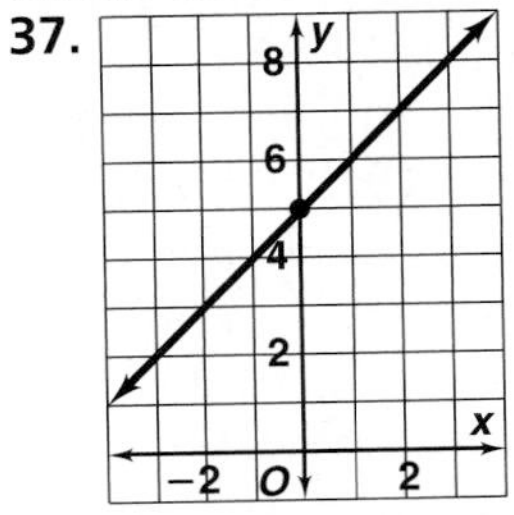

39.

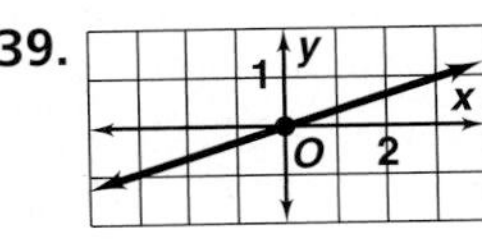

41. $A'(0, -3), B'(4, 6), C'(-6, -1)$ **43.** 35

Lesson 4-2 pages 753–755

ON YOUR OWN **1.** $x = 80; y = 40$ **3.** $x = 4.5; y = 60$ **5.** $x = 92; y = 7$ **7.** $x = 64; y = 71$ **9.** The measure of each base angle is 70. **11.** The 3rd vertex must be on the ⊥ bisector of the base, the line $x = 3$. **13.** False; a rectangle need not have 4 ≅ sides. **15.** true **17.** (0, 5), (5, 0), (0, 10), (10, 0), (−5, 5), (5, −5) **19a.** 25 **19b.** 40, 40, 100 **19c.** Isosceles; the △ has 2 ≅ angles. **21a.** isosceles **21b.** 900 ft; 1100 ft **21c.** Answers may vary. Sample: The tower is the ⊥ bisector of the base. **23.** 2.5 **25.** 35 **27.** 60 **29.** 50 **31.** 120 **33.** 70 **35.** No; the base is the side opposite the vertex angle. **37.** $m = 20; n = 45$ **39.** $m = 36; n = 27$

MIXED REVIEW **41.** $(1, 5); \sqrt{13}$ **43.** $(0.5, 6.5); \frac{1}{2}\sqrt{26}$ **45.** 24 sides **47.** $\overline{DF} \parallel \overline{EG}$ because in a plane, 2 lines ⊥ to a 3rd line are ∥.

Lesson 4-3 pages 758–761

ON YOUR OWN **1.** Answers may vary. Samples: $m\angle V = 45$ because acute angles of a rt. △ are complementary; $UT = TV$ because if 2 ∠s of a △ are ≅, the sides opposite them are ≅. **3.** $ABCD$ is a rectangle; sum of the measures of angles of a quadrilateral = 360 so each angle is 90°. **5.** Answers may vary. Sample: $MP = MN$ and $NO = PO$ because if 2 ∠s of a △ are ≅, the sides opposite them are ≅. **7.** C **9.** E; assume (A) is T. Then (B–F) are all T. But (B) is F if (C–F) are T. So the assumption that (A) is T must be F and (A) is F. Assume (B) is T. Then (C–F) are F. But (C) is T if (B) is T, so the assumption that (B) is T must be F and (B) is F. Since (A) and (B) are F, (C) is F. Since (A–C) are F, (D) is F. Since (A–D) are F, (E) is T. Since (E) is T, (F) is F. **11a.** $\angle ONK$ **11b.** $\angle MNO$ **11c.** $\angle MON$ **13.** d, f, b, a, c, e **15.** By Substitution, $m\angle 1 + m\angle 2 = m\angle 2 + m\angle 3$. Subtracting = quantities from each side yields $m\angle 1 = m\angle 3$. **17.** Given; Isosceles Triangle Thm.; Isosceles Triangle Thm.; Transitive Prop. of ≅

MIXED REVIEW **19.** 147.6, 144, 54, 14.4
21a.

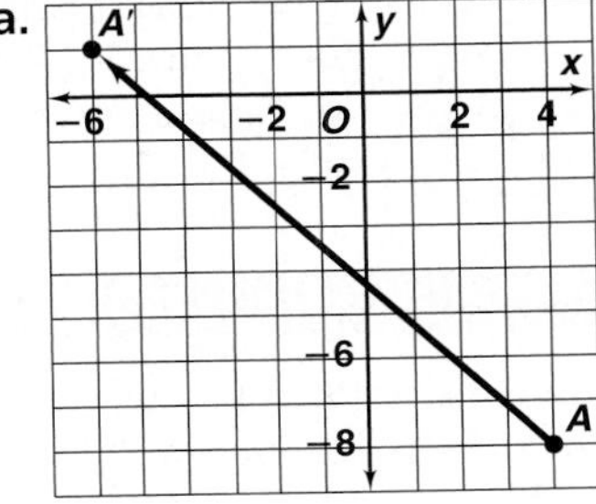

21b. shift left 10 and up 9; ⟨−10, 9⟩

Toolbox page 762

CONJECTURE The midsegment is ∥ to a side of the △ and is half its length.

EXTEND Opp. angles of the orig. △ and the midsegment △ have = measures; corr. angles in the 4 smaller △s have = measures.

The sides of the midsegment △ are each $\frac{1}{2}$ of the corr. side of the original △; the 4 △s are ≅; the 4 △s are ~ to the original △. The area of each smaller △ is $\frac{1}{4}$ the area of the original △; the perimeter of each smaller △ is $\frac{1}{2}$ the perimeter of the orig. △.

Lesson 4-4 pages 765–768

ON YOUR OWN **1.** 9 **3.** 31 **5a.** $H(2, 0)$; $J(4, 2)$ **5b.** slope of $\overline{HJ} = 1$, slope of $\overline{EF} = 1$ ✔ **5c.** $HJ = 2\sqrt{2}$, $EF = 4\sqrt{2}$, $HJ = \frac{1}{2}EF$ **7a.** Answers may vary. Sample:

F, T′, S′, T, S

7b. Dilation with center F and scale factor $\frac{1}{2}$ **7c.** The triangles are ~. **9.** 60 **11.** 10 **13.** 45 **15.** 154 cm **17.** 2 cm; the length of a side of the largest square = the length of the diagonal of the middle square. The length of the diagonal of that square is twice the length of the sides of the smallest square.

MIXED REVIEW **19.** 5 **21.** (−2, 6) **23.** Lines m and n do not intersect. **25.** △ABC is isosceles. **27.** 180; it must be a straight angle.

CHECKPOINT **1a.** If the measure of at least one of the angles of a triangle is 60, then the triangle is equilateral. **1b.** true; false **2a.** If all the angles of a polygon are ≅, then the polygon is regular. **2b.** true; false **3.** A converse reverses the hypothesis and the conclusion. The truth value of a converse does not depend on the truth value of the original statement. A contrapositive reverses and negates the hypothesis and the conclusion of the original statement. The truth values of a statement and its contrapositive are the same. **4.** C **5a.** 9 **5b.** 54, 54, 72 **5c.** Isosceles; the △ has 2 ≅ angles. **6.** False; a △ with angles 30°, 30°, 120° is an obtuse isosceles △. **7.** 36

Lesson 4-5 pages 771–773

ON YOUR OWN **1.** Assume it is not raining outside. **3.** Assume △PEN is scalene. **5.** Assume $\overline{XY} \ncong \overline{AB}$. **7.** I and II **9.** I and III **11.** This bridge is a bascule. **13.** Sumiko is not an air traffic controller. **15.** Assume ∠A ≅ ∠B. Then △ABC is isosceles with $BC = AC$. This contradicts the assumption. Therefore, ∠A ≇ ∠B. **17.** E **19.** Assume that the driver had not applied the brakes. Then the wheels would not have locked and there would be no skid marks. There are skid marks. Therefore, the assumption is false. The driver had applied the brakes. **21.** Assume the polygon is a hexagon. Then the sum of measures of its interior angles is 720. But the sum of measures of the polygon's interior angles is 900, not 720. Therefore, the assumption is false. The polygon is not a hexagon. **23.** Assume $m\angle P = 90$. By def., $m\angle Q > 90$. The sum of the angle measures of △PQR is > 180. By the Triangle Angle-Sum Thm., the sum of the angle measures of a △ is 180. Therefore, the assumption is false, and an obtuse △ cannot contain a rt. angle. **25.** Mr. Pitt was in Maine on April 8 and stayed there at least until 12:05 A.M. Assume Mr. Pitt is the robber. Then he took < 55 min to travel from Maine to Charlotte. It is not possible to travel from Maine to Charlotte in 55 min or less. Therefore, Mr. Pitt is not the robber. **27.** The hole in the roof; of 5 possibilities, 4 have been eliminated.

MIXED REVIEW **29.** Answers may vary. Sample: $ABCD$ and $BCFG$ **31.** Answers may vary. Sample: A, B, C, and D **33.** B **35.**

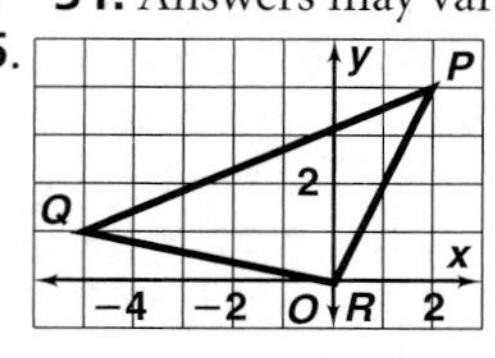

$\overline{PR}$, $\overline{QR}$, $\overline{PQ}$

Toolbox page 774

1. $x \leq -1$ **5.** $a \leq 18$ **9.** $n \leq -3\frac{1}{2}$ **13.** $n \geq -119$ **17.** $b \geq 8$ **21.** $x < -5$ **25.** $a \geq -1$

Lesson 4-6 pages 778–780

ON YOUR OWN **1.** no; $2 + 3 \not> 6$ **3.** Yes; the length of each segment is < the sum of the lengths of the other 2. **5.** Yes; the length of each segment is < the sum of the lengths of the other 2. **7.** Yes; the length of each segment is < the sum of the lengths of the other 2. **9.** $\overline{MN}$, $\overline{ON}$, $\overline{OM}$ **11.** $\overline{TU}$, $\overline{UV}$, $\overline{TV}$ **13.** $\overline{AK}$, $\overline{AR}$, $\overline{KR}$ **15.** ∠Q, ∠R, ∠S **17.** ∠G, ∠H, ∠I **19.** ∠A, ∠B, ∠C **21.** ∠Z, ∠Y, ∠X **23.** $\frac{1}{2}$ **25b.** The directions of each pair of inequalities match. **25c.** The 3rd side of the 1st triangle is longer than the 3rd side of the 2nd triangle. **27.** The 2 cities may not be both straight ahead. For instance, Topeka might be 110 mi east, and Wichita might be 90 mi south. **29.** $\overline{CD}$ **31.** $4 < z < 20$ **33.** $0 < z < 12$ **35a.** Given **35b.** Isosceles Triangle Thm. **35c.** Angle Addition Post. **35d.** Substitution **35e.** Exterior Angle Thm. **35f.** Transitive Prop. of Inequality

MIXED REVIEW **37.** $S'(-2, -7)$, $Y'(4, -3)$ **39.** 156; 24 **41.** The set of red pts. is 3 units from the set of blue pts.

Lesson 4-7 pages 785–787

ON YOUR OWN

1.

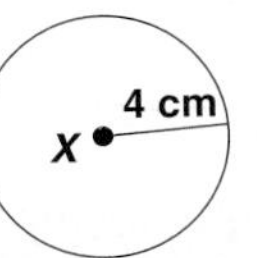

3.

1 in.
U V
1 in.

5.

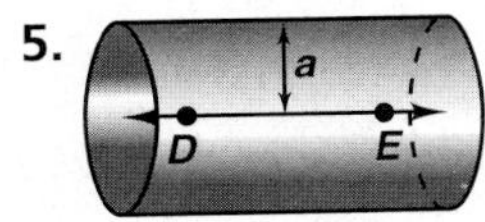

9.

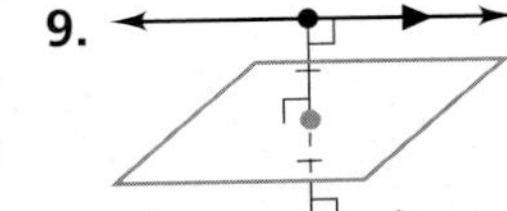

11.

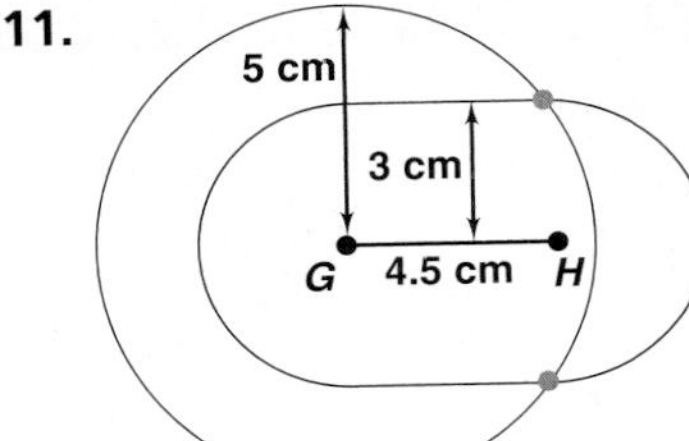

13. The locus is the two points at which the bisector of $\angle JKL$ intersects $\odot C$. **15.** second base **17a.** a circle **17b.** a (smaller) circle

21. The locations that meet Paul's requirement are on the $\perp$ bisector of the segment connecting their offices. The locations that meet Priscilla's requirement are within a circle centered at the downtown with radius 3 mi. The locations that meet both requirements lie along the portion of the $\perp$ bisector that is within the circle.

23.

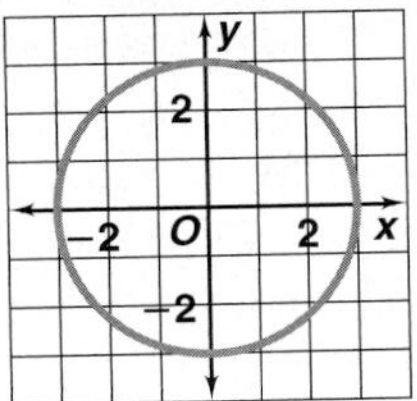

27.

y
−2
O
2
x
−2

29. pts. equidistant from the sides of $\angle A$

31. pts. equidistant from two parallel planes

33a.

33b.

33c.

35.

side view

37.

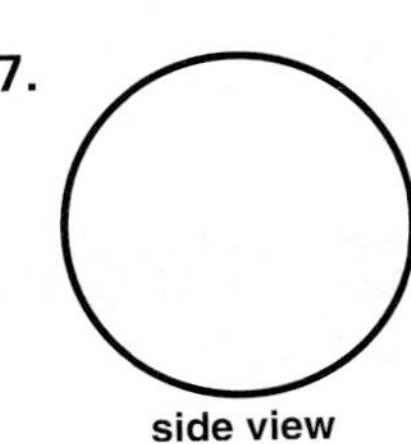

side view

MIXED REVIEW **39.** $\overset{\frown}{CBA}$, $\overset{\frown}{CAB}$

41.

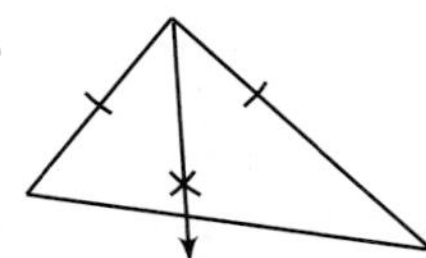

CHECKPOINT **1.** $\overline{AB}$, $\overline{BC}$, $\overline{AC}$ **2.** $\overline{MN}$, $\overline{MO}$, $\overline{NO}$ **3.** $\overline{QR} \cong \overline{RS}$, $\overline{QS}$ **4.** Sample: If $x = |x|$, then $x \geq 0$; assume $x < 0$. **5.** Assume February has at least 30 days. **6.** Assume pentagon has at least 4 rt. angles.

7.

d
d

8.

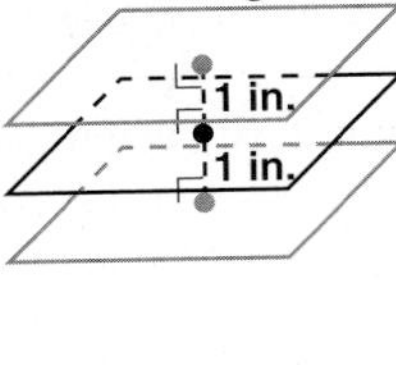

Toolbox page 788

CONJECTURE Each set of lines intersects at a single pt.

EXTEND acute $\triangle$; right $\triangle$; obtuse $\triangle$; The medians and angle bisectors always intersect inside the $\triangle$. Altitudes intersect inside the $\triangle$ for acute $\triangle$s, at a vertex for rt. $\triangle$s, and outside the $\triangle$ for obtuse $\triangle$s.

Lesson 4-8 pages 792–794

ON YOUR OWN **1.** median **3.** none of these **5.** altitude **7a.** $(-2, 0)$ **7b.** $(1, -3)$ **9a.** $(0, 0)$ **9b.** $(-4, 0)$ **11.** IA, IIC, IIIB, IVD **13.** the pt. of concurrency of the $\perp$ bisectors of segments connecting the 3 areas **15a.** $x = 0, y = 0, y = x$ **15b.** $x = 6, y = 6, y = x$ **15c.** The line $y = x$; since the altitude from D bisects the base of isosceles $\triangle DEF$, the altitude is also the $\perp$ bisector of the base. **17a.** The triangle balances. **17b.** The triangle balances.

MIXED REVIEW **19.** right **21.** right **23.** Sample: $\overleftrightarrow{AB}$ and $\overleftrightarrow{DE}$ **25.** Sample: $\overleftrightarrow{AB}$, $\overleftrightarrow{BC}$, $\overleftrightarrow{BE}$

Wrap Up pages 796–799

1a. If you are south of the equator, then you are in Australia. **1b.** true; false **2a.** If the measure of an angle is > 90 and < 180, then the angle is obtuse. **2b.** true; true **2c.** An angle is obtuse if and only if its measure is > 90 and < 180. **3a.** If it is cold outside, then it is snowing. **3b.** true; false **4a.** If the sides of a figure are $\cong$, then it is a square. **4b.** true; false **6.** $x = 4$; $y = 65$ **7.** $x = 60$; $y = 60$ **8.** $x = 55$; $y = 62.5$ **9.** $x = 65$; $y = 90$ **10.** d, c, a, b **12.** Answers may vary.

Sample: $\angle ABC$ is a rt. angle by def. of complementary angles and the Angle Addition Post. $\angle A$ and $\angle C$ are complementary because acute angles of a rt. $\triangle$ are complementary. **13.** $\angle E \cong \angle F$ because base $\angle$s of an isosceles $\triangle$ are $\cong$. **14.** Answers may vary. Samples: $\angle HIG \cong \angle JIK$ because they are vert. angles. $\angle HIG \cong \angle G$ and $\angle JIK \cong \angle J$ because base $\angle$s of an isosceles $\triangle$ are $\cong$. **15.** 15 **16.** 12 **17.** 11
18. Assume that the room had been painted with oil-based paint. Then the brushes would be soaking in paint thinner, but they are not. So the assumption is false. The room must not have been painted with oil-based paint.
19. Assume that both numbers are odd. The product of 2 odd numbers is always odd, which contradicts the fact that their product is even. So the assumption that both numbers are odd is false, and at least 1 must be even.
20. Assume that a triangle has 2 or more obtuse angles. By def., the measure of each of these angles is > 90. Then the sum of angle measures of the $\triangle$ is > 180. By the Triangle Angle-Sum Thm., the sum of angle measures of a $\triangle$ is 180. Therefore the assumption was false, and a $\triangle$ has no more than 1 obtuse angle. **21.** Assume 1 angle of an equilateral $\triangle$ is obtuse. Then its measure is > 90 and < 180. By the Isosceles Triangle Thm., the remaining angles are each $\cong$ to the 1st angle. By def. of $\cong$ angles and the Transitive Prop. of $=$, the measures of the 3 angles are $=$, and all the angles are obtuse. Then the sum of the measures of the angles is > 270. But the sum of the measures of angles of a $\triangle$ is 180. Therefore, the assumption is false. An equilateral $\triangle$ cannot have an obtuse angle. **22.** $\angle T, \angle R, \angle S; \overline{SR}, \overline{TS}, \overline{TR}$
23. $\angle C, \angle A, \angle B; \overline{AB}, \overline{BC}, \overline{AC}$
24. $\angle G, \angle O, \angle F; \overline{OF}, \overline{FG}, \overline{OG}$ **25.** B

27. **28.**

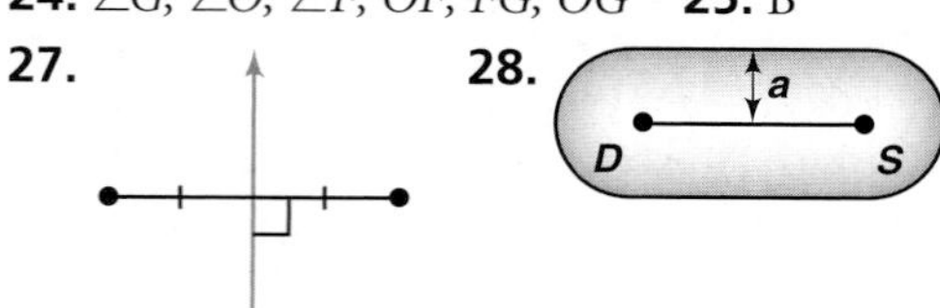

30. $(-1, 0)$

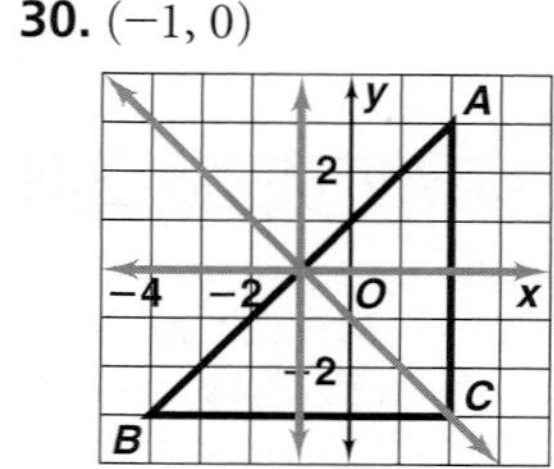

31. $(0, -1)$

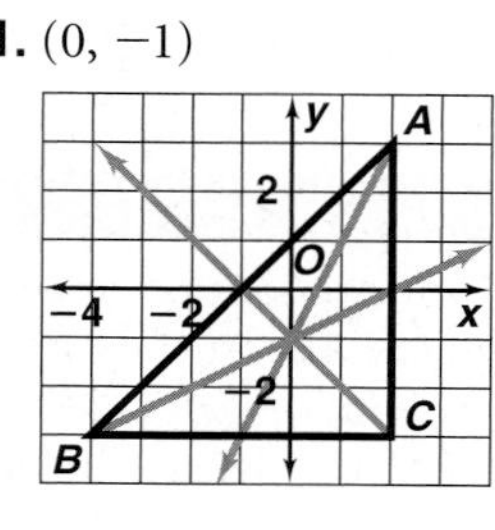

32. $(2, -3)$

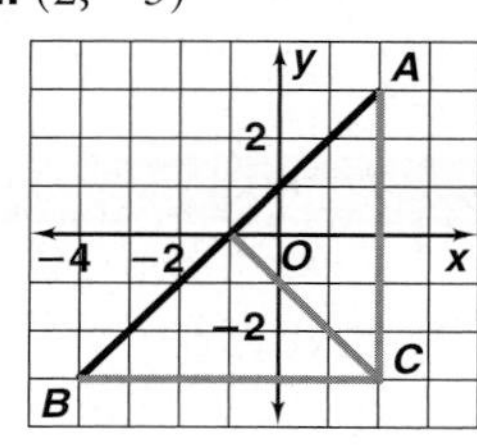

33. 16 cm; 15 cm^2
34. 30.4 ft; 55.8 ft^2
35. 4 m; 0.75 m^2
36. 5 **37.** 13 **38.** 15

Preparing for the Math A Exam page 801

1. 2 **3.** 1

CHAPTER 5

Lesson 5-1 pages 807–810

ON YOUR OWN **1.** about 40 in. **3.** about 20 ft **5.** 36 cm **7.** 24 cm **9.** 78 cm **11.** 74 ft **13.** 15 cm^2 **15.** 14 cm^2 **17.** 12 units^2 **19.** 15 units^2 **21b.** 38 units **21d.** 54 units^2 **23.** 288 cm **25.** 6 yd^2 **27a.** 3492 in.^{2} or $24\frac{1}{4}$ ft^2 **27b.** $11\frac{3}{4}$ ft^2 **27c.** \$71.80 **27d.** \$9.43 **33a.** Samples: 10 ft by 90 ft, 200 ft; 15 ft by 60 ft, 150 ft **33b.** 30 ft by 30 ft. **35.** 310 cm^2 **37.** 24 cm^2 **39.** 16 **41.** 16

MIXED REVIEW **45.** $(5.5, 5)$ **47.** $(-4, 3)$ **49.** If it is November, then it is Thanksgiving. **51.** between 2 m and 8 m **53.** 2 units^2 **55.** 8 units^2

Lesson 5-2 pages 814–816

ON YOUR OWN **1.** 15 units^2 **3.** 6 units^2 **5.** 27 units^2 **7.** 4 in. **9.** 240 cm^2 **11.** 20.3 cm^2 **13b.** 24.5 units^2 **15b.** 16 units^2 **17.** 0.24 **21.** 8 units^2 **23.** 8 units^2 **25.** 312.5 ft^2 **27.** 12,800 m^2 **29.** The areas of the $\triangle$s are $=$; they have the same bases and $=$ heights. **31.** 126 m^2 **33.** 60 units^2 **35.** 4.5 units^2

MIXED REVIEW
37. $A'(1, 3), B'(-1, 3), C'(-1, 2)\ D'(1, 0)$
39. $A'(-1, -3), B'(-3, -3), C'(-3, -2)\ D'(-1, 0)$
41. $9 + 16 = 25$ **43.** $36 + 64 = 100$

Toolbox page 817

1. $5\sqrt{2}$ **3.** 8 **5.** $4\sqrt{3}$ **7.** $6\sqrt{2}$ **9.** 6 **11.** $6\sqrt{2}$

Lesson 5-3 pages 821–824

ON YOUR OWN **1.** 10 **3.** $2\sqrt{89}$ **5.** $3\sqrt{2}$ **7.** $2\sqrt{2}$ **9.** 14 ft **11.** obtuse **13.** acute **15.** obtuse **17.** obtuse

19. acute **21.** right **25.** 7.6 **27.** 19.3 **29.** 11.3
31. 4.2 in. **33.** $\frac{9\sqrt{3}}{2}$ m^2 **35.** 10.5 $in.^2$
37a. $|x_2 - x_1|$; $|y_2 - y_1|$
37b. $PQ^2 = (x_2 - x_1)^2 + (y_2 - y_1)^2$
37c. $PQ = \sqrt{(x_2 - x_1)^2 + (y_2 - y_1)^2}$ **39.** 50 **41.** 15
43. 84 **45.** 16 **47.** 12 cm **49.** 17.9 cm **51a.** 5 in.
51b. $\sqrt{29}$ in. or about 5.4 in.
51c. $d_2 = \sqrt{AC^2 + BC^2 + BD^2}$ **51d.** 34 in.
53. $\sqrt{61}$ **55.** $2\sqrt{38}$

MIXED REVIEW
59.

61.

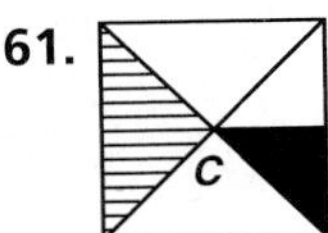

Lesson 5-4 pages 828–830

ON YOUR OWN **1.** $x = 8; y = 8\sqrt{2}$ **3.** $x = 24;$ $y = 12\sqrt{3}$ **5.** $x = \sqrt{2}; y = 2$ **7.** $x = 4; y = 2$ **9a.** 55 ft **9b.** 0.55 min or 33 sec **11.** 9 **13.** $x = 9;$ $y = 18$ **15.** $a = 6; b = 6\sqrt{2}; c = 2\sqrt{3}; d = 6$ **17.** $a = 4; b = 4$ **19.** C **21.** 110.9 cm^2 **23.** 11.3 yd^2 **27a.** $\sqrt{3}$ units **27b.** $2\sqrt{3}$ units **27c.** $s\sqrt{3}$ units

MIXED REVIEW **29.** 1 **31.** 7 $units^2$; 12.1 units

CHECKPOINT **1.** 84 $in.^2$; 48 in. **2.** 112 cm^2; 48 cm **3.** 72 m^2; 40 m **4.** 12 **5.** $x = 10; y = 10\sqrt{2}$ **6.** $x = 12\sqrt{3}; y = 24$ **7.** B **8.** Sample:

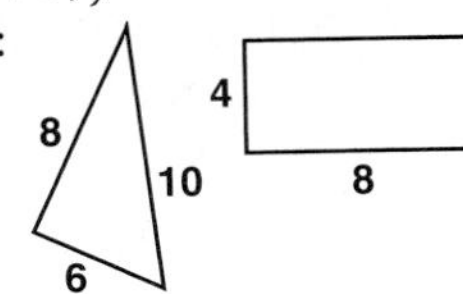

Lesson 5-5 pages 833–835

ON YOUR OWN **1.** 472 $in.^2$ **3.** 30 ft^2 **5.** 108,990 mi^2 **7.** 4 ft **9.** $52\sqrt{3}$ ft^3 **11.** 128 m^2 **13a.** $\frac{1}{2}hb_1; \frac{1}{2}hb_2$ **15.** 669 $in.^2$ **17.** 18 cm; 12 cm, 24 cm **19.** 49.9 ft^2 **21.** 11.3 cm^2 **23.** 1.5 m^2

MIXED REVIEW **29.** $25\sqrt{3}$ cm^2 **31.** $\frac{100\sqrt{3}}{3}$ m^2

Lesson 5-6 pages 838–840

ON YOUR OWN **1.** 120; 60; 30 **3.** 60; 30; 60 **5.** 12,100 $in.^2$ **7.** 128 cm^2 **9.** 841.8 ft^2 **11.** 310.4 ft^2 **15.** 72 cm^2 **17.** $75\sqrt{3}$ ft^2 **21a.** (2.8, 2.8) **21b.** 5.6 $units^2$ **21c.** 44.8 $units^2$ **23.** $24\sqrt{3}$ cm^2 **25.** $36\sqrt{3}$ $in.^2$

MIXED REVIEW
27.

29.

31. 25.13 **33.** 31.42

Lesson 5-7 pages 844–846

ON YOUR OWN **1.** 15π cm **3.** 3.7π in. **5.** 56.55 in. **7.** 1.57 yd **9.** 28π cm; 3.5π cm **11.** 36π m; 27π m **13a.** 100 in. **13b.** 50 in. **13c.** $\frac{100}{3}\pi$ in. **15.** 105 ft **17.** 490π mi **19.** 36.13 m **21.** 3.93 m **23.** 2π in. **25.** 12.6

MIXED REVIEW
29.

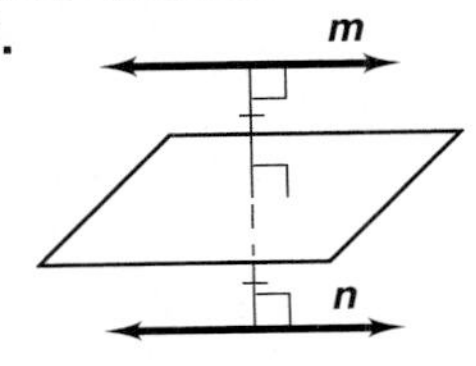

31. about 1 $in.^2$
33. about 1 $in.^2$

CHECKPOINT **1.** 110 cm^2 **2.** $72\sqrt{3}$ $in.^2$ **3.** $27\sqrt{3}$ ft^2 **4.** 50.27 in. **5.** 12.57 m **6.** 31.42 ft **7.** 8.80 km **8.** 56.55 mm **9.** 4.5π mm

Lesson 5-8 pages 850–852

ON YOUR OWN **1.** 400π m^2 **3.** $\frac{9}{64}\pi$ $in.^2$ **5.** 30 m **7.** 6.25π $units^2$ **9.** 54.11 m^2 **11.** 11,310 ft^2 **13.** 64π cm^2 **15.** $\frac{169}{6}\pi^2$ m^2 **17.** 1,620,000 m^2 **19.** 18.27 ft^2 **21.** 925.41 ft^2 **23.** 12 in. **25.** $(784 - 196\pi)$ $in.^2$ **27.** 4π m^2

29a.

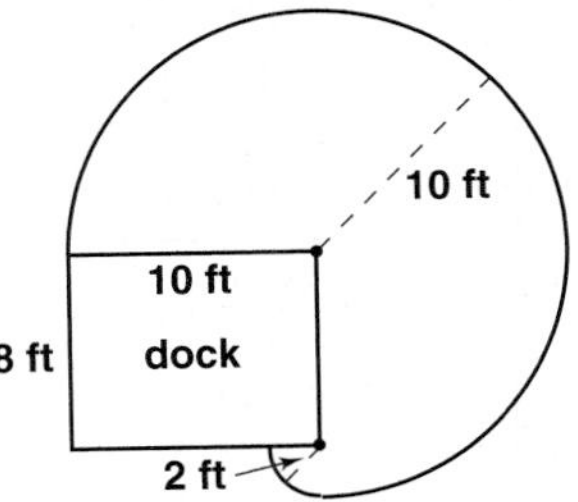

29b. the area of $\frac{3}{4}$ circle with radius 10 ft and $\frac{1}{4}$ circle with radius 2 ft
29c. about 239 ft^2

MIXED REVIEW **31.** \$90 **33.** $18\sqrt{3}$ cm^2 **35.** 72; isosceles, acute **37.** 68; scalene, acute **39.** 45; isosceles, right

Toolbox page 853

INVESTIGATE The ratios do not change with size.

CONJECTURE As the number of sides increases, each ratio comes closer to 1.

EXTEND Yes; the ratio of the perimeter to the circumference gets closer to 1 faster than the ratio of the areas.

about 63 cm; about 314 cm^2

Wrap Up pages 855–858

1. 32 cm; 64 cm^2 **2.** 38 ft; 78 ft^2 **3.** 32 in.; 40 in^2 **5.** 10 m^2 **6.** 90 in.^{2} **7.** 33 ft^2 **8.** 16 **9.** $2\sqrt{113}$ **10.** 17 **11.** $x = 9\sqrt{3}; y = 18$ **12.** $x = 12\sqrt{2}$ **13.** $x = \frac{20\sqrt{3}}{3}; y = \frac{40\sqrt{3}}{3}$ **14.** E **15.** 18 m^2 **16.** 16 ft^2 **17.** $96\sqrt{3}$ mm^2

19.

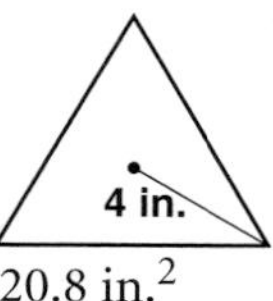

20.8 in.^{2}

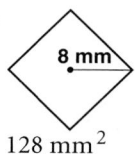

20.

8 mm

128 mm^2

21.

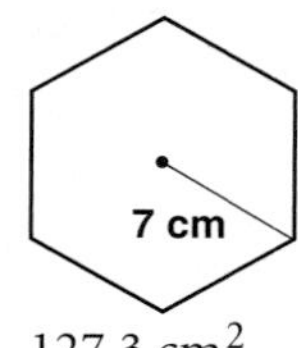

127.3 cm^2

22. 8π in.; $\frac{22}{9}\pi$ in. **23.** 14π m; $\frac{14}{9}\pi$ m

24. 6π mm; π mm **25.** 76.97 ft^2 **26.** 18.27 m^2 **27.** 40.96 cm^2 **28.** 24 in.^{2} **29.** 98.4 cm^2 **30.** 684 ft^2

Preparing for the Math A Exam page 861

1. 3 **3.** 2

CHAPTER 6

Lesson 6-1 pages 866–868

ON YOUR OWN **1.** A, B, D **3.** B **5.** E **7.** A **9.** blue **11.** brown **13a.**

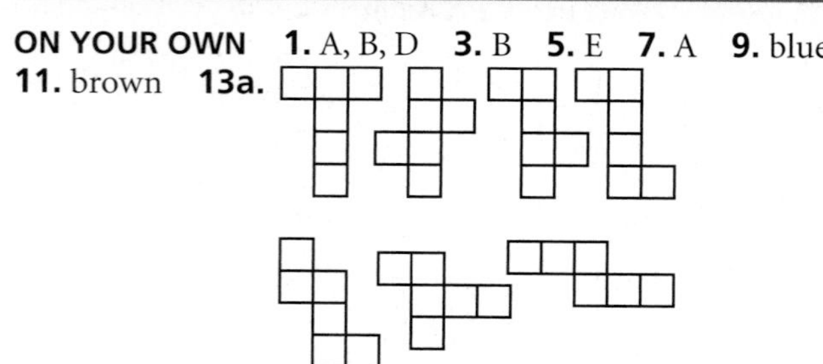

15. 6 in. **17a.** A: icosahedron; B: octahedron; C: hexahedron; D: tetrahedron; E: dodecahedron **17b.** tetrahedron, hexahedron; triangular pyramid, cube **17c.** $12 = 8 + 6 - 2$

MIXED REVIEW **21.** $\angle B$ **23.** 40π cm^2

Toolbox page 869

1. B **3.** B **5.** 10 **7.** 51 **9.** 0.035 **11.** 230 **13.** 5 **15.** 30,000,000,000 **17.** $\frac{5}{18}$ **19.** 108

Lesson 6-2 pages 874–876

ON YOUR OWN **1.** 38 units^2 **3.** 38 units^2 **5.** 144 ft^2; 216 ft^2 **7.** 288 in.^{2}; 336 in.^{2} **9a.** right hexagonal prism **9b.** $48\sqrt{3}$ cm^2 **9c.** 240 cm^2 **9d.** $(240 + 48\sqrt{3})$ cm^2 **11.** 880 cm^2 **13.** 36,800 cm^2 **15.** 20 cm
17a. $A(3, 0, 0), B(3, 5, 0), C(0, 5, 0), D(0, 5, 4)$ **17b.** 5 **17c.** 3 **17d.** 4 **17e.** 94 units^2 **21.** 619.1 m^2 **23.** 1726 cm^2 **25.** D **27a.** $r = 0.7$ cm, $h = 4$ cm **27b.** a translation

MIXED REVIEW **29.** 60 cm^2 **31.** $B'(4, 2), I'(0, -3), G'(-1, 0)$ **33.** $B'(12, 2), I'(8, -3), G'(7, 0)$ **35.** 15.3 in. **37.** 17.7 cm

Toolbox page 877

INVESTIGATE about 130 cm^2; arbitrarily large

CONJECTURE either a large side length or a large height; $s = h \approx 4.6$ cm; length of side of base = height; cube

EXTEND 10 cm-by-10 cm-by-10 cm

Lesson 6-3 pages 881–884

ON YOUR OWN **1.** 17 cm **3.** 12.8 m **5.** 264 in.^{2} **7.** 80 in.^{2} **13.** 228.1 in.^{2} **17.** 80.1 m^2 **19.** 43.5 cm^2 **21.** 179.4 in.^{2} **23.** 62.4 cm^2 **25.** They are =. **29.** 5 cm; 4 cm

MIXED REVIEW **31.** $AB = 5, BC = 6, AC = 5$; isosceles **33.** $WX = \sqrt{82}, XY = 3\sqrt{5}, YW = \sqrt{13}$; scalene **35.** If the sum of measures of 2 angles is 90, then they are complementary; true. **37.** 60 cubes **39.** 3 by 3 by 3

CHECKPOINT **1.** 297.6 in.^{2} **2.** 377.0 cm^2 **3.** 185.6 m^2 **4.** 288.7 ft^2 **5.** 477.5 ft^2

Lesson 6-4 pages 889–891

ON YOUR OWN **1.** 904.8 in.^{3} **3.** 80 in.^{3} **5.** 125.7 cm^3 **7.** 280.6 cm^3 **9a.** 28 ft^3 **9b.** 1747 lb **13.** 79 million ft^3 **15.** 5 in. **17.** 6 ft **19a.** 5832 in.^{3} **19b.** 729 in.^{3} **21a.** 24 cm **21b.** 3 cm **23.** 140.6 in.^{3} **25a.** 16π units^3 **25b.** 32π units^3

MIXED REVIEW **27.** $\overline{AC}, \overline{AB}, \overline{BC}$ **29.** $\overline{BC}, \overline{AB}, \overline{AC}$ **31.** 8 in.

Lesson 6-5 pages 895–898

ON YOUR OWN **1.** 115.5 $in.^3$ **3.** 122.5 $in.^3$ **5a.** $120\pi\ ft^3$ **5b.** $60\pi\ ft^3$ **5c.** $240\pi\ ft^3$ **7.** 300 $in.^3$ **9.** $\frac{16}{3}\pi\ ft^3$ **13.** The volumes are =; the volume of the large cone is $\frac{1}{3}$ of the volume of the cylinder; the volume of each small cone is $\frac{1}{3}$ of the volume of half the cylinder. **15.** 15 in. **17a.** 5,920,000 ft^3 **17b.** 267 ft **19.** pyramid **21.** 3 **23.** 9

MIXED REVIEW
25a. $AB = 5, BC = 10, CD = 5, AD = 10$
25b. $AB = \frac{4}{3}, BC = -\frac{3}{4}, CD = \frac{4}{3}, AD = -\frac{3}{4}$
25c. rectangle **27.** 113.1 $in.^2$; 37.7 in.
29. 19.6 ft^2; 15.7 ft

Lesson 6-6 pages 902–905

ON YOUR OWN **1.** 1794.5 cm^2 **3.** 23.8 $in.^2$ **5.** 64π $units^2$; $\frac{256}{3}\pi$ $units^3$ **7.** 85 lb **9.** $288\pi\ cm^3$ **11.** $\frac{2048}{3}\pi\ cm^3$ **13.** No; the volume of the ice cream is $\frac{4}{3}$ times the volume of the cone. **15a.** 1207 ft^3 **15b.** 10.8 $\frac{lb}{ft^3}$ **15c.** 4191 mi **17a.** 3 in. **17b.** 102.9 $in.^3$ **19.** 2 : 3 **21a.** $6\sqrt{3}$ in.; $3\sqrt{3}$ in. **21b.** 371.7 $in.^3$ **23.** A **25.** The balls weigh 75 lb and 253 lb, respectively.
27a. Cube; the edge of the cube is about 1.61 times as long as the radius r of the sphere. The surface area of the cube, about $15.59r^2$, is > surface area of the sphere, about $12.57r^2$.

MIXED REVIEW **33.** 261.3 m^3

CHECKPOINT **1.** 60.2 ft^2; 22.5 ft^3 **2.** 659.7 cm^2; 1256.6 cm^3 **3.** 332.9 $in.^2$; 377.0 $in.^3$ **4.** 113.1 m^2; 113.1 m^3 **5.** C **6.** The remaining volume is $2\pi r^3$, which is > $\frac{4}{3}\pi r^3$ (volume of one ball).

Lesson 6-7 pages 908–909

ON YOUR OWN **1.** $864\pi\ in.^3$ **3.** 10,368 ft^3 **5.** 501 $in.^3$
7a.

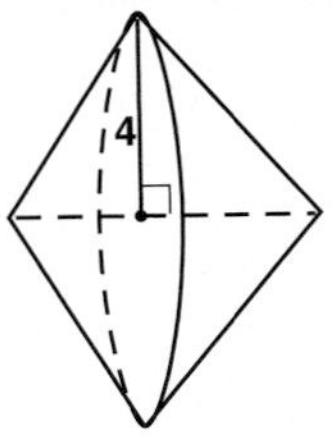

7b. 32π $units^3$ **9.** cone, hemisphere
13a.

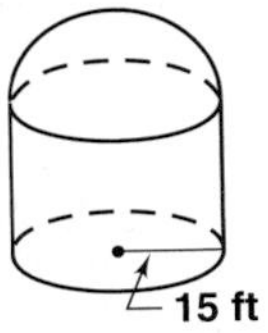

13b. 19 ft; 34 ft **15.** 73 cm^3
17a. 237 ft^2 **17b.** 1 can

MIXED REVIEW **19.** Assume $\angle P \cong \angle N$. By the Converse of the Isos. Triangle Thm., $\overline{MN} \cong \overline{MP}$, which contradicts the hypothesis. Therefore, $\angle P \not\cong \angle N$.
21. $\frac{1}{6}$ **23.** $\frac{1}{2}$

Lesson 6-8 pages 912–914

ON YOUR OWN **1.** $\frac{2}{5}$ or 40% **3.** about 61%
5.

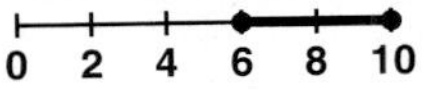

40% **7a.** The erasure must start at least 15 min before the end of the tape.

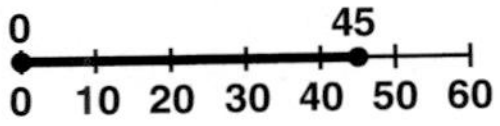

7b.

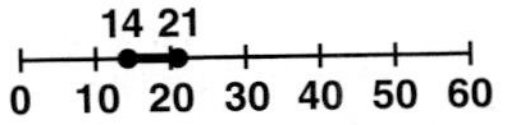

$\frac{7}{45}$ **9.** 4% **11.** about 1.9% **13.** about 26%

MIXED REVIEW **15.** U.S. **17.** 16 cm

Wrap Up pages 916–919

1.

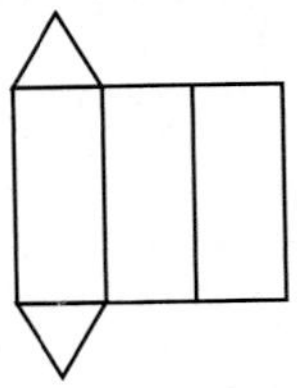

2. D **3.** C **4.** A **5.** B **6.** 36 cm^2 **7.** $66\pi\ m^2$ **8.** 208 $in.^2$ **9.** $170\pi\ ft^2$ **10.** 172.8 ft^2; 251.3 ft^2 **11.** 160 cm^2; 224 cm^2 **12.** 37.7 $in.^2$; 50.3 $in.^2$ **13.** 320 m^2; 576 m^2 **14.** 250 ft^3 **15.** $54\pi\ cm^3$ **16.** 1764 $in.^3$ **17.** $32\pi\ m^3$ **19.** 235.6 mm^3 **20.** 149.3 ft^3 **21.** 6 m^3 **22.** 301.6 cm^3 **23.** 314.2 $in.^2$; 523.6 $in.^3$ **24.** 153.9 cm^2; 179.6 cm^3 **25.** 50.3 ft^2; 33.5 ft^3 **26.** 8.0 ft^2; 2.1 ft^3 **27.** 8.6 $in.^3$ **28.** 263.9 m^3 **29.** 162 cm^3 **30.** 280 $in.^3$ **31.** $\frac{1}{2}$ or 50% **32.** $\frac{3}{8}$ or 37.5% **33.** $\frac{1}{6}$ or about 16.7% **34.** No; you model probability by ratio of lengths of segments. **35.** Sample: $\overline{AB}, \overline{EF}, \overline{CD}$ **36.** Sample: $\overline{AB}, \overline{BC}, \overline{BF}$

Preparing for the Math A Exam page 921

1. 4 **3.** 4 **5.** 3

Index

Index

Acknowledgments

VOLUME 1 — Focus on Algebra

Cover Design Sweetlight Creative Partners; Kerry Loftus Design; Suzanne Schineller

Book Design Linda Johnson, Eve Melnechuk, Stuart Wallace, Alan Lee Associates

Technical Illustration ANCO/Outlook

Illustration

Leo Abbett: 67

ANCO/Outlook: 16, 18, 26, 82, 87, 95, 193, 227, 230, 249, 253, 270, 274, 279, 289, 326, 399, 439

David Frazier: 116, 117, 143, 167, 170

Kathleen Dempsey: 273, 298

Dave Garbot: 161

Barbara Goodchild: 12

Fran Jarvis: Technical Illustration Manager

Keith Kasnot: 392

Ellen Korey-Lie: 3, 57, 61, 107, 157, 213, 267, 317, 361, 413, 463, 509

Seymour Levy: 107, 150, 291, 346, 371, 455, 464, 489, 490, 513, 539

Andrea G. Maginnis: 147, 221, 241, 286, 287, 292, 298, 299, 302, 369, 429, 464, 468, 529, 546

Gary Phillips: 129

Matthew Pippin: 122, 124

Pond Productions: 9

Gary Torrisi: 276-277, 306

Feature Design Alan Lee Associates

Photography

Photo Research Toni Michaels

Abbreviations: KO = Ken O'Donoghue; MT = Mark Thayer; JC = Jon Chomitz; TSW = Tony Stone Images; SM = Stock Market; FPG = Freelance Photographer's Guild; SB = Stock Boston; PH = Prentice Hall File Photo

Cover: Joseph Sohm; ChromoSohm Media/Corbis

Front matter: Page vii, ©Markus Amon/TSW; **viii,** KO; **ix,** MT; **x,** ©Mark Burnett/SB; **xi,** ©Paramount Studios/The Kobal Collection; **xii,** ©David Young Wolff/TSW; **xiii,** Johnny Johnson/Animals Animals; **xiv,** ©Nigel Cattlin/Photo Researchers; **xv,** ©John Gilmoure/The Stock Market; **xvi,** MT; **xvii,** ©Charles West/SM; **xix,** FPG; **xxi,** JC; **xxii,** ©John Madere/SM; **xxv,** ©Andy Sacks/TSW.

Chapter 1: Pages 2-3, O. Louis Mazzatenta/National Geographic Image Collection; **3 inset,** JC; 4, ©David Noble/FPG; **5 t,** ©Tony Freeman/PhotoEdit; **5 b,** ©Marcel Ehrhard; **6, 8 t, 8 b,** ©Andy Sacks, Lonnie Duka, Darrell Gulin all TSW; **9,** Superstock, **12 l,** ©Markus Amon/TSW; **12 r,** KO; **14,** PH; **15,** NASA; **16,** ©Toni Michaels; **17,** KO; **19 l,** Karl Kreutz; **19 r,** ©Bruce Coleman; **20,** ©Uniphoto/Alan Lardman; **21,** ©Fotoconcept/Bertsch/Bruce Coleman; **23,** FRANK & ERNEST reprinted by permission of Newspaper Enterprise Association, Inc.; **23 t,** ©Janice Rubin/Black Star; **25,** NASA; **28,** Courtesy, Cedar Point/Photo by Dan Feicht; **30 all,** KO; **33,** ©Nicholas Devore III/Bruce Coleman; **34,** ©Michael Holford; **37,** ©Bob Daemmrich/The Image Works; **38,** ©Toni Michaels; **41,** ©Paul Souders/TSW; **42,** PH; **46,** KO; **48,** ©Gary Geer/TSW.

Chapter 2: Pages 56-7, ©Larry Lawfer; **57 inset, 59,** JC; **61,** PH; **62,** ©Leonard Lees Rue III/Bruce Coleman; **64,** ©Richard Wood/The Picture Cube; **66,** Courtesy, Professor Bernie Phinney, University of California; **69,** Martha Cooper/Peter Arnold; **71,** NASA; **72,** PH; **74-5,** Steve Greenberg; **77,** ©JC; **80,** The Computer Museum, Boston; **82,** JC; **84,** KO; **88 t,** PH; **88 b,** UPI/Bettmann; **90-1,** JC; **93 tl, br,** ©David McGlynn, Ralph Cowan both FPG; **95,** ©Winter/The Image Works; **98,** JC.

Chapter 3: Pages 106-7, JC; **108,** MT; **112,** ©Baloo/Rothco; **114, 115 all,** KO; **117,** PH; **120,** MT; **124,** ©Kevin Morris/Allstock; **126,** Schomburg Center for Research in Black Culture, New York Public Library; **130,** ©Michael Newman/Photo Edit; **135, 137,** MT; **140,** ©M. Siluk/The Image Works; **143,** ©David Young-Wolff/TSW; **144,** ©Jose L. Pelawz/SM; **146,** Courtesy, Dr. Graciela S. Alarcon; **147,** ©Arthur C. Smith III/Grant Heilman Photography; **148,** ©Charles Krebs/SM.

Chapter 4: Pages 156-57, ©Telegraph/FPG; **157 inset,** PH; **158 t,** ©Superstock; **158 b,** ©Bonnie Kamin/PhotoEdit; **160 l,** ©Fred Whitehead/Animals Animals; **160 r,** ©Mark Burnett/SB; **163, 164 all,** KO; **167,** ©Michelle Bridwell/PhotoEdit; **170 t,** ©Bob Daemmrich; **170 b,** ©Anthony Edgeworth/SM; **171,** MT; **173,** JC; **174,** ©Bob Daemmrich; **175,** ©Bill Luster/NCAA Photos; **176 all,** The Granger Collection; **177,** ©Guido Alberto Rossi/Photo Researchers; **179 br,** JC; **179 TR,** ©David Frazier/Photo Researchers; **179 l,** JC; **182,** PH; **184,** ©George Disarid/SM; **187,** JC; **189,** ©Stephen Dalton/Animals Animals; **190,** JC; **193,** TSW; **195,** ©Melinda Berge/Bruce Coleman; **196,** ©Bob Daemmrich/SB; **199,** ©Lawrence Migdale/Photo Researchers; **203,** ©John Madere/SM; **204,** Custom Medical Stock Photo.

Chapter 5: Pages 212-13, Larry Lawfer; **213 inset,** PH; **214 l,** ©Dean Siracusa/FPG; **214 r,** ©Chris Cheadle/TSW; **215 t,** ©Valder Tormey/Picture Perfect; **215 inset,** ©John McGrail/FPG; **219,** ©E&P Bauer/Bruce Coleman; **220,** ©Gary Bigham/International Stock; **222,** ©Paul Silverman/Fundamental Photographs; **223,** ©Bruce Hands/ TSW; **225,** JC; **226,** ©Telegraph/FPG; **229 tr,** ©David Madison/Bruce Coleman; **229 b,** Reprinted by permission: Tribune Media Services; **230 both,** ©Jean-Pierre/Sygma; **232,** MT; **234,** ©Peter Vanderworker/SB; **236,** ©LOL/FPG; **237,** PH; **239,** ©C. C. Lockwood/Bruce Coleman; **241,** ©Paramount Studios/The Kobal Collection; **244,** ©Chris Jones/SM; **247,** ©Nathan Bilow/Allsport; **248 l,** ©Lynn Karlin/FPG; **248 br,** Jeff Spielman/ Stockphotos/The Image Bank; **250,** ©Tony Freeman/ PhotoEdit; **257,** MT; **258,** ©The Granger Collection; **259,** NASA.

Chapter 6: Pages 266-67, ©David Austen/SB; **269,** ©Mary Kate Denny/TSW; **270,** ©Jose L. Pelaez/SM; **272,** Kim Barnes; **274,**©Robert Caputo/SB; **278,** ©David Young Wolff/TSW; **279,** Courtesy, Rubber Stamps of America; **281,** JC; **283,** PH; **284,** ©Will & Deni McIntyre/ TSW; **285,** ©Bob Daemmrich/The Image Works; **286 tl,** JC; 286 br, ©Mark Burnett/SB; **286 tr,** ©David Young Wolff/PhotoEdit; **288,** ©Don Johnson/SM; **291 r,** Spencer Grant/The Picture Cube; **292,** ©D. Well/The Image Works; **296,** ©Stephen Kline/Bruce Coleman; **298 both,** PH; **300-301,** JC; **300 l,** ©Lawrence Migdale/Photo Researchers; **301 tr,** ©Bob Daemmrich; **301 b, 302,** ©John Eastcott, Frank Pedrick/The Image Works; **304,** ©Brian Smith/SB; **308,** From American Indian Design & Decoration by LeRoy H. Appleton, Dover Books; **309,** ©Charles Mercer Photography.

Chapter 7: Pages 316-17, Larry Lawfer; **317 inset,** Courtesy, Indiana Department of Motor Vehicles; **318,** ©Richard Megna/Fundamental Photographs; **321,** PH; **324,** ©Johnny Johnson/Animals Animals; **326,** ©Granitsas/The Image Works; **327 all,** JC; **328,** ©Mark Burnett/SB; **329,** ©Joe Szkodzinski/The Image Bank; **330,** ©Richard Pasley/SB; **333,** ©David Austen/TSW; **334,** NASA; **335,** Reprinted by permission: Tribune Media Services; **338,** ©Gene Peach/The Picture Cube; **340,** ©Nebraska State Historical Society; **341,** ©John Lund/TSW; **344 l, r** ©Chuck Savage, Jon Feingersh both SM; **346,** ©Hank del Espinasse/The Image Bank; **350 b,** ©Yellow Dog Productions/The Image Bank; **350 t,** ©Tony Page/TSW; **353 inset,** The Granger Collection; **353,** UPI/Corbis/Bettmann.

Chapter 8: Pages 360-61, ©Bob Daemmrich/SB; **361 inset,** ©Sidney Moulds/Science Photo Library/Photo Researchers; **363,** ©Andrew Henley/Auscape; **364,** PH; **365,** ©Chris Rogers/SM; **367,** ©Mark Burnett/SB; **371 l,** ©Alan McFee/FPG; **371 r,** ©Chip Henderson/TSW; **372,** ©Miro Vintoniv/SB; **373,** ©Corbis/Bettmann; **374** ©Grant Heilman Photography; **380 both,** ©Nigel Cattlin/Photo Researchers; **383,** ©Jack Stein Grove/Tom Stack and Assoc.; **385,** ©Bob Daemmrich/TSW; **386,** ©Telegraph/FPG; **387,** Martucci Studio; **388 tl,** Ray Ng; **388 br,** ©Paul S. Howell/Gamma Liaison; **389,** FOXTROT ©1991 Bill Amend. Reprinted with permission of UNIVERSAL PRESS SYNDICATE. All rights reserved; **390,** ©Dan McCoy/Rainbow; **392,** ©Nathan Benn/SB; **394,** ©Dr. Jeremy Burgess/Science Photo Library/Photo Researchers; **398,** The Granger Collection; **400,** Courtesy Dr. Jewel Plummer Cobb; **402 all,** MT.

Chapter 9: Pages 412-13, ©Paul Chesley/TSW; **415,** ©Spencer Jones/FPG; **417,** ©Jose Fuste Raga/SM; **418,** ©Mark Antman/The Image Works; **421,** ©Bob Daemmrich; **423,** ©Torleif Sënsson/SM; **424,** Cindy Loo/The Picture Cube; **426,** ©Joe McDonald/Bruce Coleman; **427,** T. Kevin Smyth/SM; **428,** D&J Heaton/SB; **431,** ©Dave Watters/TSW; **433,** ©Bob Daemmrich/The Image Works; **434,** PH; **436,** ©ABC/Mondrian Estate/ Holtzman Trust/Haags Gemeentemuseum; **438,** Reprinted by permission: Tribune Media Services; **439 t,** ©Porterfield-Chickering/Photo Researchers; **439 b,** ©Ron Sherman/ Stock Boston; **441,** ©Jim Tuten/FPG; **443,** ©Chris Jones/SM; **445,** ©John Gilmore/SM; **448,** KO; **451 tr,** ©James Shaffer/PhotoEdit; **451 bl,** ©Bob Daemmrich/SB; **453,** ©Anton Want/Allsport; **453 inset,** PH; **454,** ©Kindra Clineff/The Picture Cube; **455,** ©Jonathan Rawle/Stock Boston.

Chapter 10: Pages 462-63, ©Bob Daemmrich/TSW; **463 inset,** ©Don Mason/SM; **464 all,** MT; **472,** ©Patrick Ingrand/TSW; **476,** ©Bob Daemmrich; **479,** Courtesy, Southern Forest Products Association; **481,** ©Stacy Pick/SB; **484,** ©Kevin R. Morris/TSW; **485,** ©Tom & Pat Leeson/Photo Researchers; **486 both,** MT; **489,** ©Frank Gordon/FPG; **490,** ©Michael Newman/PhotoEdit; **492,** ©Robert Essel/SM; **493,** ©Henryk T. Kaiser/The Picture Cube; **494,** ©Michael Keller/FPG; **498,** Joachim Messerschmidt/FPG; **500,** CLOSE TO HOME copyright John McPherson. Reprinted with permission of UNIVERSAL PRESS SYNDICATE. All rights reserved; **501 t,** ©Mike Surowiak/TSW; **501 b,** ©Needham Research Institute.

Chapter 11: Pages 508-09, ©Jean-Claude Lejeune/SB; **509 inset,** ©Leonard Lessin/Peter Arnold; **510,** ©Ron Sherman/TSW; **513,** CLOSE TO HOME copyright John McPherson. Reprinted with permission of UNIVERSAL PRESS SYNDICATE. All rights reserved.; **514 r,** ©Lawrence Migdale/SB; **514 l,** ©Richard Laird/FPG; **516,** ©Michael Keller/SM; **518,** ©Michael Grecco/SB; **523,** ©Charles West/SM; **525 all,** KO; **530,** ©Bill Bachmann/PhotoEdit; **531 b,** ©Gerald Gscheidle/Peter Arnold; **531 t,** ©Greg Mancuso/Stock Boston; **533 c, l,** ©Spencer Jones/FPG; **533 r,** Lee Snider/The Image Works; **535,** Courtesy, Yield House; **540,** ©Steve Dunwell/The Image Bank; **541,** ©Christian Michaels/FPG; **544;** Ron Chapple/FPG.

VOLUME 2 — Focus on Geometry

Technical Illustration Fran Jarvis, Technical Illustration Manager; ANCO/Outlook

Illustration

Leo Abbett: 659 ml
Kim Barnes: 586, 761
Tom Barrett: 748, 903 b(inset)
Judith Pinkham-Cataldo: 864 inset
Jim DeLapine: 790, 851 b, 901, 902
Peggy Dressel: 729 b
Howard S. Friedman: 931
Function Thru Form Inc.: 615, 696, 782 t, 865 all, 874 b, 875 t, 898, 903 t, 907 all, 908 all
Dave Garbot: 809 t, 815 t
GeoSystems Global Corporation: 689 b
Dale Glasgow & Associates: 935
Kelley Hersey: 659
Linda Johnson: 718 m, 719 b
Seymour Levy: 691 m, 712 m, 748 inset, 808, 903 b
Andrea G. Maginnis: 579 t, 592 b, 652, 699 t
Ortelius Design Inc.: 575 t, 586 inset, 832 b, 833
Gary Phillips: 592 m
Lois Leonard Stock: 724 b, 726 b, 968 all
Gary Torrisi: 767 t, 832 t, 914 t, 970 all, 972 m
Gregg Valley: 786 t
Joe Veno: 566, 594

Photography

Photo Research Sue McDermott

Abbreviations: JC = Jon Chomitz; FPG = Freelance Photographer's Guild; KO = Ken O'Donoghue; PR = Photo Researchers, Inc.; PH = Prentice Hall File Photo; SB = Stock Boston; SM = The Stock Market; MT = Mark Thayer; TSI = Tony Stone Images

Front matter: Page 558, David Young-Wolff/PhotoEdit; **559,** Jerry Jacka; **560,** Photofest; **561,** Superstock; **562,** Tony Freeman/PhotoEdit; **563.**

Chapter 1: Pages 564-565, Anselm Spring/The Image Bank; **564 & 565 insets,** Used with permission of Sterling Publishing Co., Inc., 387 Park Ave. Sl, NY, NY 10016 from BEST EVER PAPER AIRPLANES by Norman Schmidt. ©1994 by Norman Schmidt. A Sterling/Tamos Book; **564 & 565 insets,** JC; **567,** David Young-Wolff/PhotoEdit; **570,** Tom Pantages; **571,** JC; **574,** Jack Newton/Masterfile; **578,** Johnny Johnson/DRK Photo; **580,** Superstock; **581,** John Gerlach/DRK Photo; **582,** JC; **583,** Will Ryan/SM; **584,** KO; **588,** Mark Bolster/International Stock Photo; **589,** JC; **591 t,** Glyn Kirk/TSI; **591 b,** Ralph Cowan/FPG; **595,** Michael Hart/FPG; **596,** JC; **598,** KO; **600,** Dan McCoy/SM; **601,** JC; **603,** JC; **606,** KO; **608,** Larry Grant/FPG; **610,** Telegraph Colour Library/FPG; **617,** Mike Agliolo/International Stock Photo; **618,** Paul Chesley/TSI; **619,** Tom Pantages.

Chapter 2: Pages 628-629, Jason Hawkes/TSI; **629 inset,** Russ Lappa; **630,** KO; **632,** Sunstar/The Picture Cube; **634,** John Coletti/The Picture Cube; **635 t,** Tom Van Sant/Geosphere Project, Santa Monica/PR; **635 bl & br,** Jerry Jacka; **638,** John Elk/SB; **640,** Richard Pasley/SB; **641 t,** KO; **641 bl,** Superstock; **641 bml,** Nawrocki Stock Photo/Picture Perfect; **641 bmr,** Jerry Jacka; **642,** Barbara Adams/FPG; **645,** Gary Brettnacher/TSI; **647,** Photo courtesy of Jacob Albert; **649 t,** B. Busco/The Image Bank; **649 b,** Frank Rossotto/SM; **652,** KO; **655,** Michael Nelson; **656,** Photograph copyright ©1996: WHITNEY MUSEUM OF AMERICAN ART, NEW YORK. Photography by Sheldan C. Collins; **658,** Courtesy of Paramount's Carowinds; **660,** Dale O'Dell/SM; **662,** David Weintraub/SB; **663,** David Weintraub/SB; **664,** NASA; **666,** Rosanne Olson/TSI; **667,** Cathlyn Melloan/TSI; **668,** Rod Planck/Tom Stack & Associates; **670,** MT; **671,** ©1996, Microsoft Corporation. Image created with SOFTIMAGE (R/3D); **672,** Barry Durand/Odyssey/Chicago; **674,** MT; **675,** Reprinted by Permission: Tribune Media Services; **677 t,** MT; **677 b,** Rick Altman/SM.

Chapter 3: Pages 684-685, MT; **685,** Bob Daemmrich/SB; **686,** KO; **688,** Frances M. Roberts; **691,** Biblioteca Ambrosiana, Milan/The Bridgeman Art Library; **692,** MAURICE HORN, THE WORLD ENCYCLOPEDIA OF COMICS (PAGE 41), reprinted with permission of Chelsea House Publishers; **694,** Photri, Inc.; **698,** Chris Michaels/FPG; **702,** NASA; **704,** Jerry Jacka; **707 l,** JC; **707 r,** Alfred Pasieka/SPL/PR; **709 bl,** Viviane Moos/SM; **709 bm,** Paul Jablonka/International Stock Photo; **709 br,** Adam Peirport/SM; **711,** KO; **714 t,** Keystone/Sygma; **714 b,** JC; **715,** PH; **716,** Frank Fornier/Contact Press Images; **717 tl,** John Kaprielian/PR; **717 tr,** Floyd Dean/FPG; **717 bl,** Michael Simpson/FPG; **717 br,** Dave Gleiter/FPG; **718,** PH; **721 t,** Tom Pantages; **722,** KO; **723,** KO; **725 l,** Russ Lappa; **725 tr,** M.A. Chappell/Animals Animals; **726 tm,** Guido Alberto Rossi/The Image Bank; **726 tr,** Courtesy of Francois Brisse; **727,** Robert Frerck/Odyssey/Chicago; **729,** Charles Gupton/TSI; **731,** Photofest; **734,** Stephen Frisch/SB; **738 l,** Patti Murray/Animals Animals; **738 m,** Russ Lappa; **740 l,** Don & Pat Valenti/DRK Photo; **740 r,** Jeff Foott/DRK Photo.

Chapter 4: Pages 742-743, Richard T. Nowitz/PR; **743,** Peter Menzel/SB; **744,** Framed. ©William Wegman 1995. 20 x 24 inches. Unique Polacolor ER photograph. Courtesy PaceWildenstein MacGill Gallery. New York; **745,** JC; **747,** ©1977 NEA, Inc.; **750,** Visuals Unlimited; **753,** Fernando Serna/Department of the Air Force; **755,** Russ Lappa, **756,** JC; **760,** John M. Roberts/SM; **761,** Corbis-Bettmann; **766,** Superstock; **769,** MT;

771 t, Mike Penney/David Frazier Photolibrary; **771 m,** Peter Menzel/SB; **771 b,** Lynn McLaren/The Picture Cube; **773 t,** Photofest; **773 b,** PH; **775,** JC; **778,** George Holton/PR; **779,** PH; **780,** Larry Lefever/Grant Heilman Photography; **781,** JC; **782,** The Granger Collection; **785,** Mike Shirley/Picture Perfect; **786,** Martin Rogers/TSI; **787,** Globus Brothers/SM; **792,** KO; **794,** KO.

Chapter 5: Pages 802-803, John Madere/SB; **803,** Wolfgang Kaehler/Liason International; **804,** Superstock; **806,** Tony Freeman/PhotoEdit; **808,** Bill Gallery/SB; **811,** MT; **813,** Bill Horsman/SB; **816,** MT; **819,** Tom Dietrich/TSI; **822,** Robert Caputo/SB; **825,** Superstock; **826,** Nathan Bilow/Allsport; **829,** Joe Towers/SM; **832,** Terry Donnelly/TSI; **834,** William R. Sallaz/Duomo; **835 t,** Doll by Mary Tiger. Photo courtesy of the U.S. Department of the Interior, Indian Arts and Crafts Board; **835 b,** The Granger Collection; **837,** Photo courtesy of Nida-Core; **839,** G. Ross/FPG; **841,** Russ Lappa; **842,** Tony Freeman/PhotoEdit; **845 t,** CALVIN AND HOBBES ©Watterson. Dist. by UNIVERSAL PRESS SYNDICATE. Reprinted with permission. All rights reserved; **845 b,** Superstock; **848,** Gerald French/FPG; **849,** Jerry Tobias/Sharpshooters; **850,** Joe McDonald/DRK Photo; **852,** America Hurrah Archive, NYC.

Chapter 6: Pages 862-863, MT; **863,** Russ Lappa; **864,** Leigh/Stock Imagery; **866,** Sleeveless Tunic (?) with Stepped Triangles, Middle Horizon, 500-800 AD., Textile Income Purchase Fund and General Funds, Courtesy of Museum of Fine Arts, Boston; **868,** Tom & Pat Leeson/DRK Photo; **870,** KO; **873,** Greig Cranna/SB; **874,** David Young-Wolff/PhotoEdit; **875,** Scala/Art Resource; **876,** KO; **878-879,** David Sutherland/TSI; **882,** Richard Clintsman/TSI; **883 t,** KO; **883 b,** Uniphoto; **885,** KO; **888 t,** David Harp/Folio, Inc.; **888 b,** L. Kolvoord/The Image Works; **890,** Mark C. Burnett/PR; **892,** KO; **893,** Uniphoto; **896,** Uniphoto; **899,** KO; **900 l,** Mark C. Burnett/PR; **902 tl,** Mark C. Burnett/PR; **902 tml,** Richard Hutchings/PR; **902 tmr,** Tony Freeman/PhotoEdit; **902 tr,** David Young-Wolff/PhotoEdit; **902 b,** Breck Kent/Earth Scenes; **905,** KO; **906,** Don Spiro/TSI; **907,** Tom Stewart/SM; **909,** Robert Brenner/PhotoEdit; **911,** Jim Corwin/SB; **913,** Frank Fournier/SM.

New York Lessons

922, Lake County Museum/Corbis; **923,** Kunio Owaki/The Stock Market; **924,** *Twilight in the Wilderness* by Frederick Edwin Church. Cleveland Museum of Art, OH, USA/Bridgeman Art Library; **927,** John Henley/The Stock Market; **929,** Charles Feil/SB; **933,** Richard Bryant/ARCAID; **934,** David Frazier/TSI; **939 t,** Photo by Richard Cheek; **939 b,** Jock Reynolds, Installation view from Sol Lewitt: Twenty-five Years of Wall Drawings, 1968-1993, ©1993, Addison Gallery of American Art, Phillips Academy, Andover, MA; **941,** JC; **942 t,** JC; **942 b,** Andrew Brookes/TSI; **944,** JC; **946,** Alan and Linda Detrick/PR; **948,** Bob Daemmrich/The Image Works; **951,** B. Swersey/Gamma Liason; **954,** Kevin Schafer/TSI; **955,** The Granger Collection; **957,** Richard Steedman/SM; **959,** Courtesy of Katoomba Scenic Railway; **960,** Kaluzny/Thatcher/TSI; **964,** AGE Fotostock/First Light; **966,** Toyohiro Yamada/FPG; **969 tl,** Paul Berger/TSI; **969 tr,** Tom Carroll; **969 bl,** Bob Daemmrich/SB; **973,** Hideo Kurihara/TSI; **974,** Jonathan Nourok/PhotoEdit; **977,** Rafael Macia/Photo Researchers, Inc.; **978,** Richard Hutchings/PhotoEdit; **981,** Susan Gentry McWhinney; **988,** Index Stock Photography; **989,** Lake County Museum/Corbis.